THE ENCYCLOPEDIA OF OCEANOGRAPHY

VAN NOSTRAND REINHOLD
ONE-VOLUME ENCYCLOPEDIAS

The

ENCYCLOPEDIA

of

OCEANOGRAPHY

ENCYCLOPEDIA OF EARTH SCIENCES SERIES, VOLUME I

EDITED BY

Rhodes W. Fairbridge

Professor of Geology
Columbia University
New York

 VAN NOSTRAND REINHOLD COMPANY
New York Cincinnati Toronto London Melbourne

VAN NOSTRAND REINHOLD COMPANY Regional Offices:
New York   Cincinnati   Chicago   Millbrae   Dallas

VAN NOSTRAND REINHOLD COMPANY International Offices:
London   Toronto   Melbourne

Copyright © 1966 by LITTON EDUCATIONAL PUBLISHING, INC.

Library of Congress Catalog Card Number: 66-26059

ISBN: 0-442-15070-9

Manufactured in the United States of America

Published by VAN NOSTRAND REINHOLD COMPANY
450 West 33rd Street, New York, N.Y. 10001

15   14   13   12   11   10   9   8   7   6   5   4

CONTRIBUTORS

C. D. AHLQUIST, Oceanografiska Institutionen, Göteborgs Universitet, Göteborg, Sweden. *Transparency.*

PENTTI ALHONEN, Department of Geology and Paleontology, University of Helsinki, Helsinki, Finland. *Baltic Sea.*

ERNEST E. ANGINO, State Geological Survey, University of Kansas, Lawrence, Kansas. *Antarctic Pelagic Sediments: Geochemistry; Ross Sea.*

ALLAN BÉ, Lamont Geological Observatory, Columbia University, Palisades, New York. *Deep Scattering Layers.*

JOHN BERRY, Lamont Geological Observatory, Columbia University, Palisades, New York. *North Sea.*

ROBERT BIERI, Antioch College, Yellow Springs, Ohio. *Pelagic Distribution.*

JACOB BJERKNES, Department of Meteorology, University of California, Los Angeles, California. *Ocean-Atmosphere Interaction (Macroprocesses).*

J. BLANCHARD, Institute of Oceanography, Dalhousie University, Halifax, Nova Scotia. *Grand Banks and the East Seaboard of Canada; Gulf of St. Lawrence.*

J. CLAUD DE BREMAECKER, Department of Geology, Rice University, Houston, Texas. *Microseisms.*

C. L. BRETSCHNEIDER, National Engineering Science Company, Washington, D.C. *Storm Surges.*

MARGARETHA BRONGERSMA-SANDERS, Rijksmuseum v. Natuurlijke Historie, Leiden, Netherlands. *Mass Mortality in the Sea.*

EDWIN C. BUFFINGTON, United States Navy Electronics Laboratory, San Diego, California. *Sounding.*

R. W. BURLING, Institute of Oceanography, University of British Columbia, Vancouver, British Columbia, Canada. *Ocean-Atmosphere-Interaction (Microprocesses).*

WAYNE V. BURT, Department of Oceanography, Oregon State University, Corvallis, Oregon. *Oceanography.*

KARL W. BUTZER, Department of Anthropology and Geography, University of Chicago, Chicago, Illinois. *Mediterranean Area: Quaternary History.*

BORIS CHOUBERT, Office de la Recherche Scientifique et Technique d'Outre-Mer (C.N.R.S.) Paris, France. *Sunspots and Sedimentation.*

A. E. COLLIN, Bedford Institute of Oceanography, Dartmouth, Nova Scotia, Canada. *Canadian Arctic Archipelago and Baffin Bay; Hudson Bay and Approaches.*

L. H. N. COOPER, Marine Biological Association of United Kingdom, Plymouth, Devon, England. *English Channel; Irish Sea and Celtic Sea.*

HENRY L. COX, JR., Westinghouse Electric Corporation, Baltimore, Maryland. *Underwater Television.*

JOSEPH R. CURRAY, Scripps Institution of Oceanography, La Jolla, California. *Continental Terrace.*

M. DARBYSHIRE, "Eigionfa," Menai Bridge, Wales, Great Britain. *Agulhas Current; Benguela Current.*

G. E. R. DEACON, National Institute of Oceanography, Surrey, England. *Convergence, Antarctic; Subtropical Convergence.*

RAYMOND DELAND, Geophysics Science Laboratory, New York University, New York. *Advection.*

ROBERT F. DILL, Sea Floor Studies, United States Navy Electronics Laboratory, San Diego, California. *Sand Flows and Sand Falls.*

D. T. DONOVAN, Department of Geology, University, Hull, England. *English Channel; Irish Sea and Celtic Sea.*

PATRICIA DUDLEY, Department of Zoology, Barnard College, New York. *Nekton, Marine.*

TERENCE EDGAR, Lamont Geological Observatory, Columbia University, Palisades,

New York. *Abyssal Sediment (Thickness); Caribbean Sea—Sediments and Crust; Seismic Reflection Profiling at Sea.*

RICHARD S. EDWARDS, Woods Hole Oceanographic Institution, Woods Hole, Massachusetts. *Oceanographic Ships—Past and Present.*

SAYED Z. EL-SAYED, Department of Oceanography, Texas A & M University, College Station, Texas. *Amundsen Sea; Bellingshausen Sea; Scotia Sea and Drake Passage; Weddell Sea.*

SAYED A. EL WARDANI, Lockheed Marine Laboratory, San Diego, California. *Pelagic Biogeochemistry.*

K. GÖSTA ERIKSSON, Geological Department, Chalmers Tekniska Högskola, Göteborg, Sweden. *Mediterranean Sea—A Late Pleistocene Sedimentary Core.*

HANS EUGSTER, Department of Geology, Johns Hopkins University, Baltimore, Maryland. *Seawater—Its History.*

GRAHAM EVANS, Geology Department, Imperial College of Science and Technology, London, England. *Persian Gulf.*

JOHN I. EWING, Lamont Geological Observatory, Columbia University, Palisades, New York. *Abyssal Sediment (Thickness); Caribbean Sea—Sediments and Crust; Seismic Reflection Profiling at Sea.*

RHODES W. FAIRBRIDGE, Department of Geology, Columbia University, New York. *Abyssal Hills; Amphidromic Point, Region; Archipelagic Aprons; Aseismic Ridges; Atlantic Ocean; Austausch, Exchange Coefficient; Bali Sea; Bathyal Zone; Bismarck Sea; Brazil Current; Calcium Carbonate Compensation Depth; Canaries Current; Capillarity; Caribbean Current; Ceram Sea; Conduction; Continental Rise; Continental Slope; Convergence and Divergence; Coral Sea; East China Sea; Fetch; Flux Density; Fracture Zones; Greenland Sea; Hodograph; Indian Ocean; Irminger Sea; Kara Sea; Laminar Flow, Boundary Layer; Marine Sediments; Mean Sea Level Changes, Long Term; Mediterranean Sea; Natural Regions in Oceans; neritic Zone (and Sedimentation Facies);*

North Sea; Norwegian Sea; Ocean Bottom Features; Terminology, Nomenclature; Oceanic Rise; Pacific Ocean; Rossby Number; Sahul Shelf; Savu Sea; Sea Ice— Transportation; Solomon Sea; Storm, Storminess; Streamlines and Streamline Analysis; Submarine Cones or Fans; Submarine "Plateaus"; Sunda Shelf; Tasman Sea; Trenches and Related Deep Sea Troughs; Troposphere and Stratosphere in the Ocean; Underwater Photography; Volcanic Ridges; Waves as Energy Sources; West Greenland Current.

FELIX FAVORITE, Bureau of Commercial Fisheries, United States Department of the Interior, Seattle, Washington. *Bering Sea.*

H. FLOHN, Meteorologisches Institut der Universität Bonn, Bonn, Germany. *Energy Budget of Earth's Surface.*

PAUL J. FOX, Lamont Geological Observatory, Columbia University, Palisades, New York. *Mid-oceanic Ridge.*

ROBERT D. GERARD, Lamont Geological Observatory, Columbia University, Palisades, New York. *Oceanographic Surveys; Salinity in Ocean.*

ARNOLD GORDON, Lamont Geological Observatory, Columbia University, Palisades, New York. *Atlantic Ocean; Caribbean Sea—Oceanography; Sargasso Sea; Water Masses and the Core Method.*

DONN S. GORSLINE, Department of Geology, University of Southern California, Los Angeles, California. *Continental Borderland.*

JAMES L. HARDING, Oceanonics, Inc., Morgan City, Louisiana. *Gulf of Mexico.*

JOEL W. HEDGPETH, Marine Science Laboratory, Newport, Oregon. *Marine Ecology.*

BRUCE C. HEEZEN, Lamont Geological Observatory, Columbia University, Palisades, New York. *Abyssal Plains; Bathymetry; Indian Ocean; Mid-oceanic Ridge; Ocean Bottom Currents.*

H. F. P. HERDMAN, National Institute of Oceanography, Surrey, England. *Southern Ocean.*

KOJI HIDAKA, Ocean Research Institute,

University of Tokyo, Tokyo, Japan. *Japan Sea; Kuroshio Current.*

TROY L. HOLCOMBE, Lamont Geological Observatory, Columbia University, Palisades, New York. *Precision Depth Recorders.*

CHARLES HOLLISTER, Lamont Geological Observatory, Columbia University, Palisades, New York. *Ocean Bottom Currents.*

DONALD W. HOOD, Institute of Marine Science, University of Alaska, College, Alaska. *Seawater: Chemistry.*

KEN HUNKINS, Lamont Geological Observatory, Columbia University, Palisades, New York. *Chukchi Sea; Drifting Ice Stations.*

TAKASHI ICHIYE, Lamont Geological Observatory, Columbia University, Palisades, New York. *Aleutian Current; Austausch, Exchange Coefficient; Bernoulli's Theorem; Brazil Current; Density; Diffusion in the Ocean; Dynamics of Ocean Currents; Ekman Spiral; Fetch; Greenland Sea; Gulf of Thailand; Indian Ocean; Irminger Current; Labrador Sea; North Sea; Oyashio Current; Slicks, Ripples and Windrows; Somali Current; Turbulence in the Ocean; Vector Analysis; West Australian Current; West Greenland Current.*

A. S. IONIN, Institute of Oceanology, Moscow, Union of Soviet Socialist Republics. *East Siberian Sea; Laptev Sea.*

LELA JEFFREY, The University of Nottingham, University Park, Nottingham, England. *Nutrients in the Sea.*

N. G. JERLOV, Oceanografiska Institutionen, Göteborg, Sweden. *Optical Oceanography.*

G. LEONARD JOHNSON, United States Naval Oceanographic Office, Washington, D. C. *Bathymetry.*

J. W. JOHNSON, Department of Civil Engineering, University of California, Berkeley, California. *Ocean Currents, Introduction.*

RALPH G. JOHNSON, Department of Geophysical Sciences, University of Chicago, Chicago, Illinois, *Benthos, Marine.*

GLENN H. JUNG, Department of Meteorology and Oceanography, United States Naval Postgraduate School, Monterey, California. *Heat Transport by Ocean Currents.*

JOHN KANWISHER, Woods Hole Oceanographic Institution, Woods Hole, Massachusetts. *Carbon Cycle in the Oceans.*

P. A. KAPLIN, Institute of Oceanography, Moscow, Union of Soviet Socialist Republics. *Chukchi Sea.*

CHARLOTTE KEEN and M. J. KEEN, Institute of Oceanography, Dalhousie University, Halifax, Nova Scotia, Canada. *Grand Banks and the Eastern Seaboard of Canada; Gulf of St. Lawrence.*

CUCHLAINE A. M. KING, Department of Geography, University of Nottingham, Nottingham, England. *Ocean Waves; Oceanography (Nearshore).*

M. V. KLENOVA, Institute of Oceanography, Academy of Sciences USSR, Moscow, Union of Soviet Socialist Republics. *Barents Sea and White Sea.*

JOHN A. KNAUSS, Department of Oceanography, University of Rhode Island, Kingston, Rhode Island. *Equatorial Currents.*

F. F. KOCZY, Institute of Marine Science, University of Miami, Miami, Florida. *Radionuclides in Oceans and Sediments; Radionuclides: Their Applications in Oceanography.*

F. A. KOHOUT, United States Geological Survey, Water Resources Division, Miami, Florida. *Submarine Springs.*

PH. H. KUENEN, Geologisch Instituut, Rijks Universiteit, Groningen, The Netherlands. *Turbidity Currents.*

G. KULLENBERG, Oceanografiska Institutionen, Göteborgs Universitet, Göteborg, Sweden. *Transparency.*

S. A. KULM, Oregon State University, Department of Oceanography, Corvallis, Oregon. *Oceanography.*

E. C. LAFOND, United States Navy Electronics Laboratory, San Diego, California. *Bay of Bengal; Fixed Platforms; Internal Waves; South China Sea; Temperature Structure in the Sea; Upwelling.*

L. K. LEPLEY, Department of Oceanography, Texas A & M University, College Station, Texas. *Ross Sea.*

Y. H. LI, Lamont Geological Observatory, Palisades, New York. *Alkalinity of Sea Water.*

LOUIS LIDZ, Institute of Marine Sciences, University of Miami, Miami, Florida. *Littoral Zone (and Sedimentation Facies).*

D. A. LIVINGSTONE, Zoology Department, Duke University, Durham, North Carolina. *Sediment Coring—Unconsolidated Materials.*

F. JENSENIUS MADSEN, Universitetets Zoologiske Museum, Copenhagen, Denmark. *Abyssal Zone.*

J. MAUCHLINE, The Marine Station, Millport, Isle of Cumbrae, Scotland. *Radioactive Waste in Ocean.*

DAVID A. MCGILL, Woods Hole Oceanographic Institution, Woods Hole, Massachusetts. *Fertility of the Ocean.*

WILLIAM T. MCGUINESS, Alpine Geophysical Associates, Norwood, New Jersey. *Acoustics (Underwater).*

JOHN L. MERO, Ocean Resources, Inc., La Jolla, California. *Manganese Nodules (Deep Sea), Mineral Potential of the Ocean.*

ALTON MOODY, Long Distance Navigation Bureau, Federal Aviation Agency, Washington, D. C. *Navigation.*

WILLARD S. MOORE, Lamont Geological Observatory, Columbia University, Palisades, New York. *Alkalinity; Isotope Fractionation.*

CONRAD NEUMANN, Marine Laboratory, University of Miami, Miami, Florida. *Red Sea.*

WORTH D. NOWLIN, JR., Dept. of Oceanography and Meteorology, Texas A & M Univ., College Station, Texas. *Gulf of Mexico.*

ERIC OLAUSSON, Göteborgs Universitet, Oceanografiska Institutionen, Göteborg, Sweden. *Atlantic Ocean; Mediterranean Sea; Pacific Ocean.*

CARL H. OPPENHEIMER, Institute of Marine Sciences, University of Miami, Miami, Florida. *Marine Microbiology; pH and Eh of Marine Sediments.*

N. A. OSTENSO, Department of Geology, University of Wisconsin, Madison, Wisconsin. *Arctic Ocean; Beaufort Sea.*

HAROLD D. PALMER, Department of Geology, University of Southern California, Los Angeles, California. *Seamounts.*

EUGENE K. PARKER, Westinghouse Electric Corporation, Underseas Division, Baltimore, Maryland. *Scuba as a Scientific Tool; Underwater Photography.*

JUNE G. PATTULLO, Department of Oceanography, Oregon State University, Corvallis, Oregon. *Mean Sea Level (Short Range); Tides.*

BERNARD R. PELLETIER, Bedford Institute of Oceanography, Department of Mines and Technical Surveys, Dartmouth, Nova Scotia, Canada. *Canadian Arctic Archipelago and Baffin Bay; Hudson Bay and Approaches.*

J. M. PERES, Station Marine d'Endoume, University de Marseille, Marseille, France. *Benthonic Zonation.*

B. P. PETELIN, Institute of Oceanology, Academy of Sciences USSR, Moscow, Union of Soviet Socialist Republics. *Okhotsk Sea.*

GEORGE PETER, United States Coast and Geodetic Survey, Washington, D. C. *Andaman Sea, Geophysics of.*

MELVIN N. A. PETERSON, Scripps Institution of Oceanography, La Jolla, California. *Pacific Ocean.*

CHARLES PHIPPS, Department of Geology, University of Sydney, Sydney, Australia. *Gulf of Carpentaria.*

NOEL PLUTCHAK, Lamont Geological Observatory, Columbia University, Palisades, New York. *Guiana Current; Guinea Current; Labrador Current; Thermocline.*

JOSEPH M. PROSPERO, Institute of Marine Science, University of Miami, Miami, Florida. *Radionuclides in Oceans and Sediments; Radionuclides: Their Application in Oceanography.*

JOSEPH REID, JR., Scripps Institution of Oceanography, La Jolla, California. *California Current; Pacific Ocean.*

FRANCIS A. RICHARDS, Department of Oceanography, University of Washington, Seattle, Washington. *Chemical Oceanography, General.*

M. K. ROBINSON, Scripps Institution of Oceanography, La Jolla, California. *Arabian Sea.*

KEVIN S. RODOLFO, Department of Geology, University of Southern California, Los Angeles, California. *Andaman Sea.*

RICHARD J. ROMMER, Department of Meteorology, City College of New York, New York. *Gravity and Geopotential; Vorticity.*

WILLIAM RYAN, Lamont Geological Observatory, Columbia University, Palisades, New York. *Mediterranean Sea.*

IRVING SCHELL, Ocean-Atmosphere Research Institution, Cambridge, Massachusetts. *Icebergs.*

R. S. SCHELTEMA, Woods Hole Oceanographic Institution, Woods Hole, Massachusetts. *Pelagic Life; Zooplankton.*

ERIC D. SCHNEIDER, Lamont Geological Observatory, Columbia University, Palisades, New York. *Abyssal Plains.*

DAVID W. SCHOLL, United States Naval Ordinance Test Station, China Lake, California. *Florida Bay—A Modern Site of Limestone Formation.*

JOHN J. SCHULE, JR., United States Naval Oceanographic Office, Washington, D. C. *Sea State.*

MAURICE L. SCHWARTZ, Department of Geology, Columbia University, New York. *Subaqueous Sand Dunes.*

F. B. SHEPARD, Scripps Institution of Oceanography, La Jolla, California. *Continental Shelf Classification; Submarine Canyons and Other Sea Valleys.*

ROBERT SHERIDAN, Lamont Geological Observatory, Columbia University, Palisades, New York. *Submarine Plateaus.*

GEORGE SHOR, Scripps Institution of Oceanography, La Jolla, California. *Bering Sea.*

R. SILVESTER, School of Engineering, University of Western Australia, Nedlands, Western Australia. *Wave Refraction.*

RICHARD SKALAK, Department of Civil Engineering and Engineering Mechanics, Columbia University, New York. *Fluid Mechanics.*

THEODORE J. SMAYDA, Narragansett Marine Laboratory, University of Rhode Island, Kingston, Rhode Island. *Phytoplankton.*

R. W. STEWART, Institute of Oceanography, University of British Columbia, Vancouver, British Columbia, Canada. *Ocean-Atmosphere Interaction (Microprocesses).*

DONALD J. P. SWIFT, Department of Geology, Dalhousie University, Halifax, Nova Scotia, Canada. *Bay of Fundy.*

TARO TAKAHASHI, University of Rochester, College of Arts and Science, Rochester, New York. *Carbon Dioxide Cycle—In the Sea and Atmosphere.*

MARIE THARP, Lamont Geological Observatory, Columbia University, Palisades, New York. *Indian Ocean.*

HONG DJIN TJIA, Department of Geology, Institute of Technology, Bandung, Java, Indonesia. *Arafura Sea; Banda Sea; Flores Sea; Halmahera Sea and Kau Bay; Java Sea; Molucca Sea; Sulawesi (Celebes) Sea; Sulu Sea; Timor Sea.*

J. STEWART TURNER, Dept. of Applied Mathematics and Theoretical Physics, University of Cambridge, Cambridge, England. *Turbulence.*

M. UDA, Tokyo University of Fisheries, Minato-ku, Tokyo, Japan. *Philippine Sea and the Waters South of Japan; Yellow Sea.*

NORBERT UNTERSTEINER, Department of Atmospheric Sciences, University of Washington, Seattle, Washington. *Sea Ice.*

T. H. VAN ANDEL, Scripps Institution of Oceanography, La Jolla, California. *Gulf of California; Timor Sea.*

WILLEM J. M. VAN DER LINDEN, New Zealand Oceanographic Institute, Wellington, New Zealand. *Coral Sea; Southwest Pacific Ocean; Tasman Sea.*

WILLIAM G. VAN DORN, Scripps Institution of Oceanography, La Jolla, California. *Tsunami.*

VICE-ADMIRAL ALFREDO VIGLIERI, International Hydrographic Bureau, Monaco, France. *Oceans: Limits, Definitions, Dimensions.*

BRUCE WARREN, Woods Hole Oceanographic Institution, Woods Hole, Massachusetts. *Coriolis Force; Gulf Stream;*

CONTRIBUTORS

Oceanic Circulation Patterns; Physical Oceanography.

H. WEIDEMANN, Deutsches Hydrographic Institut, Hamburg, West Germany. *Oceanic Current and Wave Recording—Instrumentation.*

ROBERT L. WIEGEL, University of California, College of Engineering, Berkeley, California. *Wave Theory.*

BASIL WILSON, Science Engineering Associates, Kaman Aircraft Corporation, San Marino, California. *Seiche.*

TORBEN WOLFF, Universitetets Zoologiske Museum, Copenhagen, Denmark. *Hadal Zone.*

WARREN WOOSTER, Scripps Institution of Oceanography, La Jolla, California. *Peru (Humboldt) Current.*

FREDERICK WRIGHT, Department of Geology, University of Southern California, Los Angeles, California. *Marine Geology Techniques and Tools.*

KLAUS WYRTKI, Department of Oceanography, University of Hawaii, Honolulu, Hawaii. *East Australian Current.*

C. S. YENTSCH, Woods Hole Oceanographic Institution, Woods Hole, Massachusetts. *Planktonic Photosynthesis; Primary Production.*

V. P. ZENKOVITCH, Institute of Oceanology, Academy of Sciences USSR, Moscow, Union of Soviet Socialist Republics. *Black Sea.*

PREFACE

The idea of an Encyclopedia of Earth Sciences series arose from Reinhold Publishing Corporation's successful introduction of the autonomous, single-volume encyclopedia for specialist subjects, such as spectroscopy, microscopy, X rays and gamma rays, patent law, and for general science disciplines: chemistry, physics, biological sciences and electronics. For the earth sciences, which comprehend the entire environment of the planet earth, its oceans, air, land surface and planetary interior, it has been found that a subject approach is better than a disciplinary one. This was an inevitable decision, inherent in the subject. Thus, oceanography, for example, is the description and study of the oceans by *all* the classical disciplines rolled into one—physics, chemistry, geology, biology; in addition there are certain applied arts specifically appropriate to the subject such as *navigation, oceanographic ships*.

The Earth Sciences

A distinction is commonly made between the physical sciences (physics & chemistry) and the natural sciences. While the former are concerned largely with the formulation of fundamental and universal laws, the latter involve the natural universe —its description and explanation in terms of the former. Furthermore it is observed that the intense study of the natural sciences, which basically consist of the life sciences and the earth sciences, brings about a recognition of laws of their own, and in realms at present closed to the experimental physicist; for example, the interior of the planet or the stars. They may in return offer study models that permit the formulation of new laws of fundamental meaning. To the ancient Greeks and Romans, "natural philosophy" was the only science, but gradually a dichotomy took place, a segregation of the "pure" and the "descriptive." However, the two are not exclusive or distinct. History has shown that there has been a constant feeding of new material from the latter to the former.

By definition, therefore, the descriptive sciences of the natural universe are the explorative, pioneer disciplines. In this encyclopedia, as a phenomenon in one of those fields, we have the very first attempt ever made at a comprehensive alphabetic treatment of this subject. In many of the articles one will find the author cautiously saying "at the time of writing . . . ," or "at the present limited state of knowledge . . . ," or "as a tentative conclusion . . .". Such remarks are necessarily "hedging," and many personal opinions have to be given, because this is a new field, in a state of vigorous exploration and almost explosive development.

A few years ago a distinguished scientist wrote that the floor of the ocean was less well mapped than is the surface of the moon, and with improved methods for lunar exploration emerging every day, this condition is likely to continue for some time. There are formidable difficulties in the way of exploring territory underneath a blanket of water several miles thick, to say nothing of the problems of studying the dynamics of the water layer itself. Someone has described the problem of sampling the deep-ocean floor as attempting to obtain representative samples of a modern city while flying over it in a thick fog in a helicopter equipped with nothing but radar and a fishing line.

Intended Use

The "Encyclopedia of Oceanography" is intended for the use of all scientists, young and old. There is much here that the mature specialists will find new and useful. Many of the articles are written in such a style that the modern secondary school student can plunge into them without a qualm. We have tried to plan general articles that span the field for the newcomer. Then we have tried, by many cross-references, to lead into the highly technical areas, which may call for a fairly rigorous background in mathematics and the classical sciences. With comprehensive literature references, we have tried to lead the researcher to the publications in the library. Within the scope of a thousand pages, we have been limited, but to go further would ruin the intent of a single autonomous volume that contains from A-Z the nuclei of human knowledge about this vast field. Let it be constantly stressed that we are still exploring and experimenting—a vast and fascinating field lies open to the would-be traveler. The experiments can be made as well by an individual with a modest laboratory aquarium, as by a group of high school student explorers in a rowboat on a lagoon or by a deep-sea exploration group with a multimillion dollar investment in electronics and ocean-going ships.

Mechanics of Production

The mechanics of encyclopedia production are difficult enough. Few publishers have the courage to attempt it. In physics and chemistry, the field is relatively stable, the laws are established and the problem is one of best presentation. In natural sciences, one is on shifting sand: the subject matter is in constant flux and it is often difficult to find a specialist in the field, ready and available. The contributors are, for the most part, the leaders in their various fields. They were selected from all over the world; in this series we have authors ranging from Albania to Ethiopia, from the U.S.S.R. to Sierra Leone. Editorially we have "polished up" the English, but we have tried not to alter any author's own style or accent. Many of our writers were interrupted in their labors by long expeditions to the farthest oceans. We received some wonderful excuses for delayed manuscripts; our best was a crumpled and water-stained missive from somewhere in east Africa ". . . you see, it was like this, we were crossing Lake Tanganyika in a rubber canoe and were attacked by a very large crocodile; its jaw opening exceeded three feet. Well, the canoe was bitten in two and we had to swim for all our lives. Your manuscript, alas . . .".

The contributors have been the academic people, professors of oceanography, the explorers themselves and the industrial experts. We are intensely grateful to all of them. Their labors were donated freely for the good of our science. Many specialists have graciously helped out by technical review of articles; we have tried to get a critical review from an "outsider" on almost every article written. The major portion of the editing costs were underwritten to the tune of several thousand dollars by the editor and his wife. So it has been a labor of love. It is frankly difficult not to be carried away by enthusiasm for one's field when the game itself is so exciting. In their state of constant dynamism, the earth sciences attract the young in spirit, the adventurous and the courageous. These people today are analogous to the greats of yesteryear—Leif Erikson, Magellan, Vasco da Gama, Sir Francis Drake, Captain James Cook, Shackleton, Scott and Amundsen.

To our stalwart helpers a word of appreciation: our patient and skilled draftsman Ernest Adelberg; our enthusiastic editorial assistants Mary-Lou Lindquist, "Sandy" Feldman and "Dotty" Spiro; our proofreaders and indexers, notably Ted Kipping; our photographer, Herbert Dreiwitz; our ever-friendly and never-failing librarians at Columbia University; our devoted and careful compositors (Willmer Bros., Birkenhead, England); and lastly, but not by any means least, our gracious publishers and their staff, notably G. G. Hawley (the father of the "one autonomous volume" idea), Charles Hutchinson (with his background in geology and excellent capacity for taking pains in getting the scientific world channeled into the publishing mold), and Alberta Gordon and Florence Poillon (copy editors of supreme efficiency). The entire final proof was critically read and corrected by our esteemed friend, the oceanographer, Dr. Takashi Ichiye. To these good people, the readers of the Earth Science Encyclopedias must be grateful. Our imperfections are many, but it is better to publish today when the book is needed than to delay and deprive people of what is wanted now.

Authors have been invited to contribute to the field in their specialties or on general topics; the editor has endeavored to indicate areas to be covered but has tried to remain unbiased, even when opinions diametrically opposed to his own are stated (sometimes with great emphasis!). This permissive approach results inevitably in some overlaps, but such dual treatment can in itself be very helpful inasmuch as a second or even third viewpoint may bring further illumination. And it must be freely confessed that some of our concepts are slightly befogged.

Abbreviations and References

In the body of the text, there are two standard abbreviations:

q.v. (Latin: *quod vide*), meaning see another article of that title;

see pr Vol. . . . , see proposed volume (planned for future production).

Throughout this volume numerous literature references are given. We could not always be consistent about the style, but we have tried to be as complete as possible, without spending precious time on long library hunts. The system of citations and abbreviations is one widely used in the sciences and may be found summarized in the *Chemical Abstracts* instructions.

Future Volumes

For the purpose of cross-referencing between volumes, numbers have been assigned to the volumes in the order of their publication. The first three volumes will be:

The Encyclopedia of Oceanography
The Encyclopedia of Atmospheric
    Sciences and Astrogeology
The Encyclopedia of Geomorphology

Future volumes will deal with hydrology, pedology, geochemistry, mineralogy, geophysics, petrology, petrography, structural geology, sedimentation, stratigraphy, paleontology, world regional geology and geological biographies.

RHODES W. FAIRBRIDGE

THE ENCYCLOPEDIA OF OCEANOGRAPHY

A

ABSORPTIVITY—See Vol. II

ABYSSAL CONES, FANS—*See* **SUBMARINE CONES; SUBMARINE CANYONS**

ABYSSAL FAUNA—*See* **ABYSSAL ZONE**

ABYSSAL HILLS

A term for certain submarine geomorphic features found only in the deep-sea (3000–6000 meters), this is also applied as a province term for large parts of this realm. According to Heezen *et al.* (1959, pp. 61–62):

"An abyssal hill is a small hill that rises from the ocean-basin floor and is from a few fathoms to a few hundred fathoms in height and from a few hundred feet to a few miles in width. The term *abyssal hills province* is applied to those areas of the ocean-basin floor in which nearly the entire area is occupied by hills —that is, the province lies at approximately the depth of the adjacent abyssal plain but lacks a smooth floor. (Figs. 1 and 2). Isolated abyssal hills and groups of abyssal hills also occur in the abyssal plains.

"Abyssal hills are found along the seaward margin of most abyssal plains and probably occur in profusion in basins isolated from adjacent land areas by ridges, rises, or trenches. In the North Atlantic the abyssal hills form two strips parallel to the Mid-Atlantic Ridge for virtually its entire length . . . ."

Seismic reflection recording, particularly by Maurice and John Ewing and their colleagues, has subsequently demonstrated that the abyssal hills topography covers much of the deep-ocean floor, being partly or wholly covered by an unconsolidated sedimentary blanket. Prominent abyssal hills often project through that blanket of sediments (see *Abyssal Sediment Thickness*). It should be stressed that the sediment covering may be one of several types:

(a) A relatively thin *pelagic veneer* (0–400 meters) in the open ocean and marked by a gently undulating topography ("swales" in Heezen's terminology). The veneer is described by geophysicists as "seismically transparent" in contrast to the "opaque" hill material. As shown by Menard (1964), there

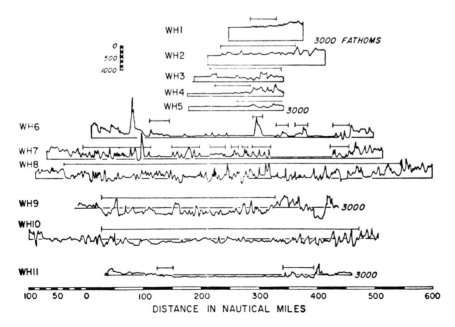

Fig. 1. Eleven profiles, Western Atlantic Abyssal Hills Province. 40:1 vertical exaggeration; profile series from north to south (Heezen *et al.*, 1959).

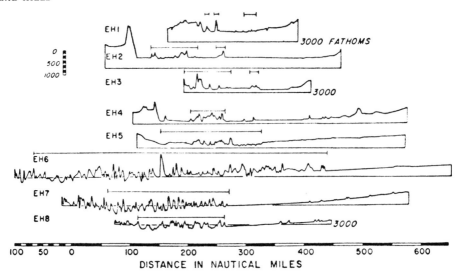

Fig. 2. Eight profiles, Eastern Atlantic Abyssal Hills Province. Vertical exaggeration 40:1 profile series from north to south (Heezen *et al.,* 1959).

is generally a thin layer of Quaternary sediments in the lower parts and only Tertiary or even Cretaceous outcropping on the higher parts. These undulations of the abyssal hills provinces are not like a sine wave, but in low arches, "like inverted catenaries," with kinks between. The pelagic veneer is notably thicker in zones of high pelagic organic productivity, e.g., at the equator and at the subtropical and antarctic convergences.

(b) An *abyssal plain* (q.v.), a generally thicker filling of depressions often adjacent to, but not necessarily near, continents (0–5000 meters), that has accumulated largely by turbidite transportation and is marked by an extremely flat, smooth surface, but often with a distinct though very gentle slope (less than 1:1000), away from the principal source area; in scattered mid-oceanic areas, at the foot of rises or low elevations there are small abyssal plains consisting equally of slumps and turbidites of essentially local (non-terrigenous) origin.

(c) A *submarine cone or fan* (q.v.), a large-scale analog of alluvial cones or fans in semiarid landscapes. At least in part such cones overlap the continental rises, which in places merge with abyssal hill topography.

Origin of Abyssal Hills Topography

"The topography of the abyssal hills is considered to represent the original surface buried beneath the abyssal plains and perhaps beneath the continental rise. . . . We have no rock samples from these provinces. Individual hills cannot be studied with present seismic-refraction techniques. . . . At present we have only topography as a basis of speculation of their origin. As far as we know, individual abyssal hills are not discernibly different from the smaller hills of the steps of the Mid-Atlantic Ridge or much of the topo-

graphy of the oceanic rises, and thus there is no reason to assume that the abyssal hills have a different origin."

Krause and Menard (1965) have shown that hill frequency is roughly related to heights, and rather closely to widths. Classification can be made on the basis of height to width (Fig. 3 and 4). Individual hills are usually 100–2000 meters in height (higher examples, see *Seamounts*), and 7–15 km across, but their length is unknown and a statement on this question must await new precision navigational aids (as with satellites). Tolstoy (1951) suggested that they might be long and sinuous, rather than conical as suggested on the physiographic maps of Heezen and Tharp. Possibly they are in discontinuous rows of more or less conical units. If this were so, it might be that they are reflected by the long sinuous belts of high and low magnetism such as those mapped in the northeastern Pacific by Mason, Vacquier and others of the Scripps Institution of Oceanography. Certainly it is to be noted that areas of high magnetic anomaly seem to correspond to regions of more pronounced topography. In regions of quasicratonic history, there seem to be very prominent hills (really mountains) in wild profusion (see Fig. 3).

It seems certain now that the hills originate in the "Second Layer" of the seismologists. That layer has long been difficult to interpret, since its velocities correspond to either dense sediment or variegated volcanics (velocities over broad range of 4–6 km/sec). The writer rejects the sediment interpretation (favored by Hamilton) because this layer is separated by a very sharp seismic discontinuity from the overlying Mesozoic-Tertiary sediments. No sedimentary process in diagenesis is known that would cause such a discontinuity

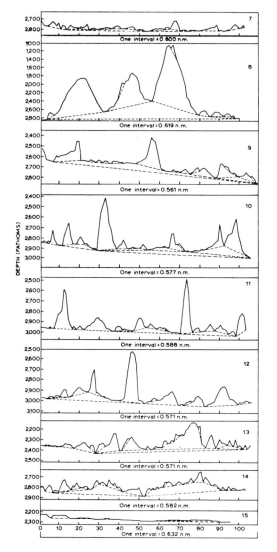

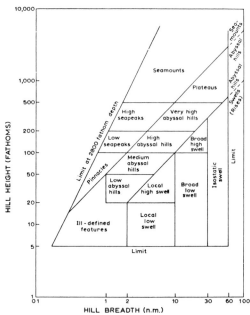

Fig. 4. Classification of positive bathymetric features (Krause and Manard, 1965).

Fig. 3. Bathymetric profiles divided into abyssal hills. Units in 3 minute intervals along profile (total length = 60 n mi). Selected profiles between San Francisco and Hawaii (Krause and Menard, 1965).

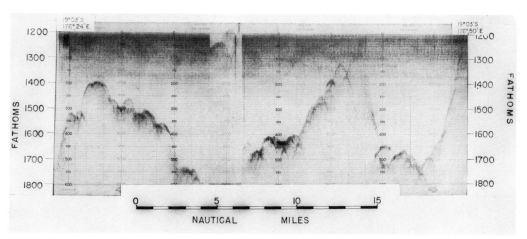

Fig. 5. Abyssal hills of 100–1500 m relief in the Pandora or North Fiji Basin, Southwest Pacific.

except exposure to subaerial processes or to metamorphism; both of these concepts call for catastrophic explanations. This leaves only the conclusion that the abyssal hills consist of submarine volcanic and/or intrusive igneous material (see discussion by Menard, 1964, p. 39). Their age is unknown, but according to various theories of oceanic expansion or stretching, it would appear to be most probably that the ages of the hills correspond to a progressive evolution of the oceanic crust.

RHODES W. FAIRBRIDGE

References

Heezen, B. C., Tharp, M., and Ewing, M., 1959, "The floors of the oceans," *Geol. Soc. Am. Spec. Papers,* **65**, No. 1, 122pp.

Krause, D. C., and Menard, H. W., 1965, "Depth distribution and bathymetric classification of some sea-floor profiles," *Marine Geology,* **3**, No. 3, 169–193.

Menard, H. W., 1964, "Marine Geology of the Pacific," New York, McGraw-Hill Book Co., 271pp.

Tolstoy, I., 1951, "Submarine topography in the North Atlantic," *Bull. Geol. Soc. Am.,* **62**, 441–450.

Cross-references: *Abyssal Plain; Abyssal Sediment Thickness; Abyssal Zone; Seismic Reflection Profiling at Sea.*

ABYSSAL PLAINS

Abyssal plains are flat areas of the ocean basin floor which slope less than 1 part in 1000. These geomorphic features were not discovered until 1947 when oceanographic expeditions began to record continuous depth profiles. Continuous precision depth soundings have shown abyssal plains to have slopes ranging from 1:1000 to as little as 1:10,000. All long sediment cores taken from abyssal plains contain sands and silts apparently derived from shallow continental areas, while cores from adjacent submarine rises and hills are devoid of such sediment.

Origin

Studies of the topography and sediments of the abyssal plains suggest that the abyssal plains were formed by turbidity currents which covered the preexisting topography (see *Abyssal Sediment (Thickness)* and *Turbidity Currents).* This hypothesis is supported by (1) the existence of graded silt and sand beds found on the abyssal plains; (2) the fact that the seismic reflection studies of abyssal plains show that they cover preexisting rough basement with a succession of horizontal layers; and (3) the fact that abyssal plains are always found in topographic localities favorable for receiving continentally derived turbidity current or slump induced sediment.

Various other theories have been suggested as to the origin of abyssal plains, i.e., atectonic areas, lava plains and subaerial erosion, and have later been rejected.

Most abyssal plains lie at the base of the continental rise and extend to the abyssal hills seaward of the abyssal plain. The boundary between the continental rise and the abyssal plain is often marked by a distinct break, but in other cases, it is a transitional boundary. The seaward boundary of abyssal plains is abrupt where the abyssal plain abuts against the abyssal hills. Abyssal plains appear to be fed by submarine canyons which act as conduits for turbidity currents descending from

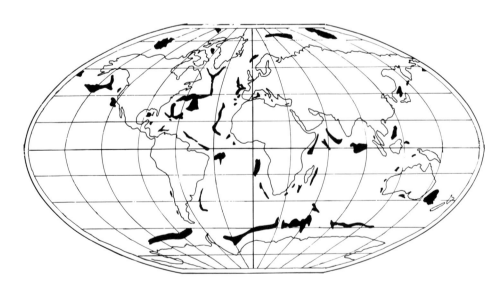

Fig. 1. Distribution of major abyssal plains of the world. The abyssal plains are adjacent to land masses and are often fed by submarine canyons or canyon systems.

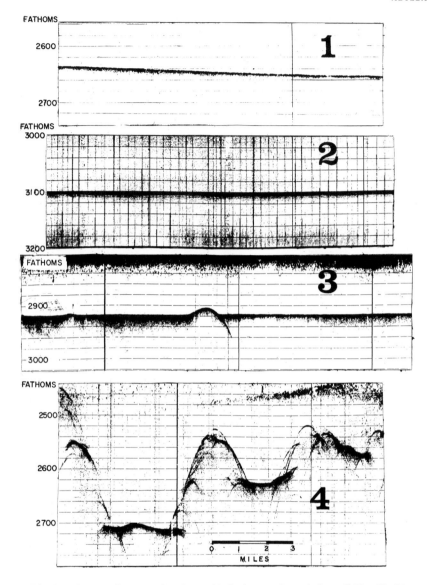

Fig. 2. Echo-sounding records: (1) gently sloping continental rise (off New York); (2) abyssal plain with numerous sub-bottom echoes which sediment cores show to be coarser silt beds or turbidites (Nares Abyssal Plain); (3) abyssal plain with protruding sea knolls showing partial covering of preexisting topography (Southern Sohm Abyssal Plain); (4) rugged hills and small ponded valleys of the abyssal hills province (Southeast of Bermuda).

the continental margins. Once a turbidity current reaches the abyssal plain, it flows toward the lowest level of the plain, depositing material as it travels.

Trench abyssal plains are abyssal plains lying in the bottom of deep-sea trenches. The Puerto Rico Trench, the Middle America Trench and the Peru-Chile Trench are examples of oceanic trenches with flat-floored trench abyssal plains. Sediment slumps and/or turbidity currents flow into these closed basins and sediment ponds to form flat horizontal layers. Seaward of oceanic trenches, abyssal plains are not found because the trenches trap the continentally derived turbidity current sediment. Much of the Pacific Ocean floor lacks large open ocean abyssal plains because the surrounding continents are rimmed by a nearly continuous line of deep-sea trenches.

Sediments

The composition of clastic sediments of the abyssal plains varies in accordance with source area. Silts, sands and gravels comprise from 2–90% of the cored (upper 15 meters) sediments in the plains, with the remaining sediments being clay-sized material derived from turbidity currents and from normal pelagic sedimentation in the area. Oceanic turbidites generally consist of quartz silts and sand, but sands and gravels consisting of foraminifera, pelecypods, volcanic glass, manganese nodules, rock fragments and leaves and twigs have been found in abyssal plains.

Abyssal Gaps

Abyssal gaps are passages connecting two abyssal plains lying at different levels in the vicinity of the gap. Clastic sediment transport is apparently channeled through these passages.

Archipelagic Plains

Archipelagic plains are extremely smooth portions of the archipelagic aprons which lie at the base of the pedestal of an island or an island group. Cores from archipelagic plains contain graded silts and sands. These plains appear to have a similar origin to abyssal plains, namely, burial of the former relief by turbidity current deposition, although a lava plain hypothesis is favored by several investigators.

B. C. HEEZEN
E. D. SCHNEIDER

References

Heezen, B. C., and Ewing, M., 1952, "Turbidity currents and submarine slumps and the Grand Banks earthquake," *Am. J. Sci.*, **250**, 849–873.

Heezen, B. C., Tharp, M., and Ewing, M., 1959, "The floors of the oceans. I: The North Atlantic," *Geol. Soc. Am. Spec. Papers*, **65**, 129pp.

Hill, M. N., 1963, "The Sea, Ideas and Observations on Progress in the Study of the Seas," Vol. 3, Chs. 12, 14, 17, 20, 27, New York, Interscience Publishers, 963pp.

Menard, H. W., 1955, "Deep-sea channels topography and sedimentation," *Bull. Am. Assoc. Petrol. Geologists*, **39**, 236–255.

Menard, H. W., 1956, "Archipelagic aprons," *Bull. Am. Assoc. Petrol. Geologists*, **40**, 2195–2210.

ABYSSAL SEDIMENT (THICKNESS)

Sedimentation Rates and Periods of Accumulation. Until the first refraction measurements were made in the oceans, there was no factual information available on the oceanic sediment thicknesses. Estimates based on the rates of continental erosion and carbonate productivity multiplied by the geologic age of the continents indicated that the average thickness of the sediments in the oceans should be of the order of several kilometers. The use of seismic refraction and reflection methods has revealed a sediment cover thinner than that calculated from these assumptions. The average sediment thickness over the mid-ocean ridges and in many deep basin areas of the Pacific and Indian Oceans was found to be of the order of 100–200 meters, and abyssal plain thicknesses average about 1 km. Only in the continental rise regions very close to large land masses have sediment thicknesses as great as 3–4 km been measured. (In this discussion, we consider as sediments that material lying above the layer whose seismic wave velocity is 4.5–5.5 km/sec and has generally been called basement or layer 2).

A more recent method of determining carbonate sediment accumulation rates, based on radiocarbon dating of core samples yields values that average 2–4 cm/1000 yr for the last 30,000 years (Broecker *et al.*, 1958). Red clay, which cannot be dated by radiocarbon, has been dated by the ionium/thorium method and was found to accumulate at about 1 mm/1000 yr over the last 400,000 years (Goldberg and Koide, 1962). If the minimum accumulation rate of red clay is considered constant through time then, based on the average measured pelagic sediment thickness, the oldest sediments correspond to Cretaceous age. Therefore, either or both of the following conditions must prevail: (a) the average rate of sedimentation must have been very much lower than the present rate, or (b) the observed accumulation does not represent deposition through all of geologic time.

In view of these conditions, several hypotheses have been proposed to account for the anomaly.

(1) The continents and the ocean basins are permanent features and the sediments, thin as they are, represent the total accumulation of billions of years. This concept presupposes that the rate of sedimentation was very much less throughout most of the earth's history than it is today.

(2) The earth's earlier deposits (pre-Cretaceous) have been buried or altered by extensive lava flows. The basement would be considered a mixture of igneous and sedimentary rocks. Even accepting this hypothesis, the combined thickness of the basement and the abyssal sediments barely accounts for the discrepancy under a constant minimum accumulation figure of 1 mm/1000 yr. Therefore condition (a) must also prevail, or we must allow that the main ocean crustal layer (6.7 km/sec velocity) is also partially composed of sedimentary material.

(3) The continents were once all one land mass and have since separated, presumably burying or absorbing the Paleozoic and early Mesozoic sediments by some process of crustal renewal. Three proposals have been offered to explain the mechanics of continental displacement.

(i) The continents moved or floated through the mantle (Wegener, 1912), implying that the central

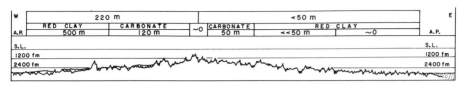

Fig. 1. Tracing of a reflection profile in the North Atlantic Ocean between Dakar and Halifax showing sediment distribution on the Mid-Atlantic Ridge. Grid lines represent 1 second of reflection time (approximately 400 fathoms or 730 meters in water—10–30% more in sediment). The profile is 1560 nautical miles (2886 km) long.

part of the oceans (or the ridges) is the oldest and should contain the thickest sediments. However, seismic profiler records show that this is not the case and in fact the crests of the ridges in many places are notably barren of sediment. It has been suggested that strong currents acting on the steep slopes of the ridge crests have kept them free of sediments.

(ii) The sea floor, which is involved in great convection systems, is spreading from the mid-ocean ridges and passing under the continents, contributing the sedimentary material to the continental crust (Dietz, 1961). In this system, the ridges would be the youngest part of the ocean and the crests would have the least amount of sediment.

(iii) An expanding earth split the continents, and new material reaches the earth's surface along the fractures or mid-ocean ridges (Heezen, 1959). In this case, too, the ridges would be the youngest and expected to have a thin sediment cover.

Processes affecting Abyssal Sediment Accumulation. Sediment distribution in the oceans is considerably more complex than was originally considered. Ocean basin accumulation is apparently controlled by numerous factors of which proximity to land source, depth, climate, bottom topography and currents are considered of major importance (see *Marine Sedimentation*).

Based on the study of some 300,000 miles of continuous reflection profiler traverses, the following general statements can be made about the accumulation of sediments in the oceans.

(1) *Mid-ocean Ridges.* Figure 1 shows a tracing of a reflection profile across the ridges in the North Atlantic. The average thickness of the sediments and the sediment type are represented above the profile. Of the pelagic sediments, carbonates accumulate the fastest, but are dissolved at depths greater than 2500 fathoms. The residual material is the common abyssal lutite and is considerably thinner than the carbonate. Much of the sediment has accumulated in the depressions or pockets which indicates that sediment has flowed off the peaks and slopes. Note the anomalously thick sediments that have accumulated immediately adjacent to the abyssal plain on the west side of the Mid-Atlantic Ridge. These are apparently

ocean basin lutites that were deposited and deformed prior to the deposition of the abyssal plain turbidites which are probably mostly of Pleistocene Age.

The ridge in the South Atlantic has a similar overall pattern except that the sediments are not largely collected in pockets but instead are draped over the basement, probably because the slopes are not sufficiently steep to initiate movement of the sediment. The western Mid-Indian Ridge contains pelagic sediments, probably mainly carbonates, that are draped over all but the steepest peaks. The eastern Mid-Indian Ridge and the Pacific-Antarctic Ridge have essentially no sediments on the crests and thin pelagic deposits of approximately uniform thickness on the flanks.

(2) *The Ocean Basins.* The abyssal plains are flat, almost level areas of the ocean basins and usually lie at the base of the continental rise. Figure 2 shows a reflection profile in the Hatteras abyssal plain of the Atlantic Ocean. The upper laminated layers are thought to be Pleistocene turbidite sediments which mask the topography of the bottom on which they were originally deposited. In contrast, underlying the turbidites are homogeneous, acoustically transparent sediments which form the uppermost layers on the Bermuda Rise (right side of profile). Sediments of the transparent type cover many oceanic rises and underlie most of the modern abyssal plain turbidite layers.

The abyssal plain sediments are normally lutites with interbedded sands or silts. The exact manner in which sediments are transported to the ocean basins is still debated. The sands and coarse silts found in the abyssal plains are considered by most to be carried from the continental margins by large, high-velocity turbidity currents, whereas others consider the transport to be a slow trickling, perhaps aided by bottom currents. The deposition of the lutite layers also appears to be a flow process. The pattern of stratification in these sediments, judged to be clays on the basis of homogeneity and high degree of acoustic transparency, does not generally indicate particle-by-particle deposition uniformly over the sea floor. Although there are broad areas where a thin layer of homogeneous transparent sediments uniformly covers the sea floor, the thickest bodies of these sediments,

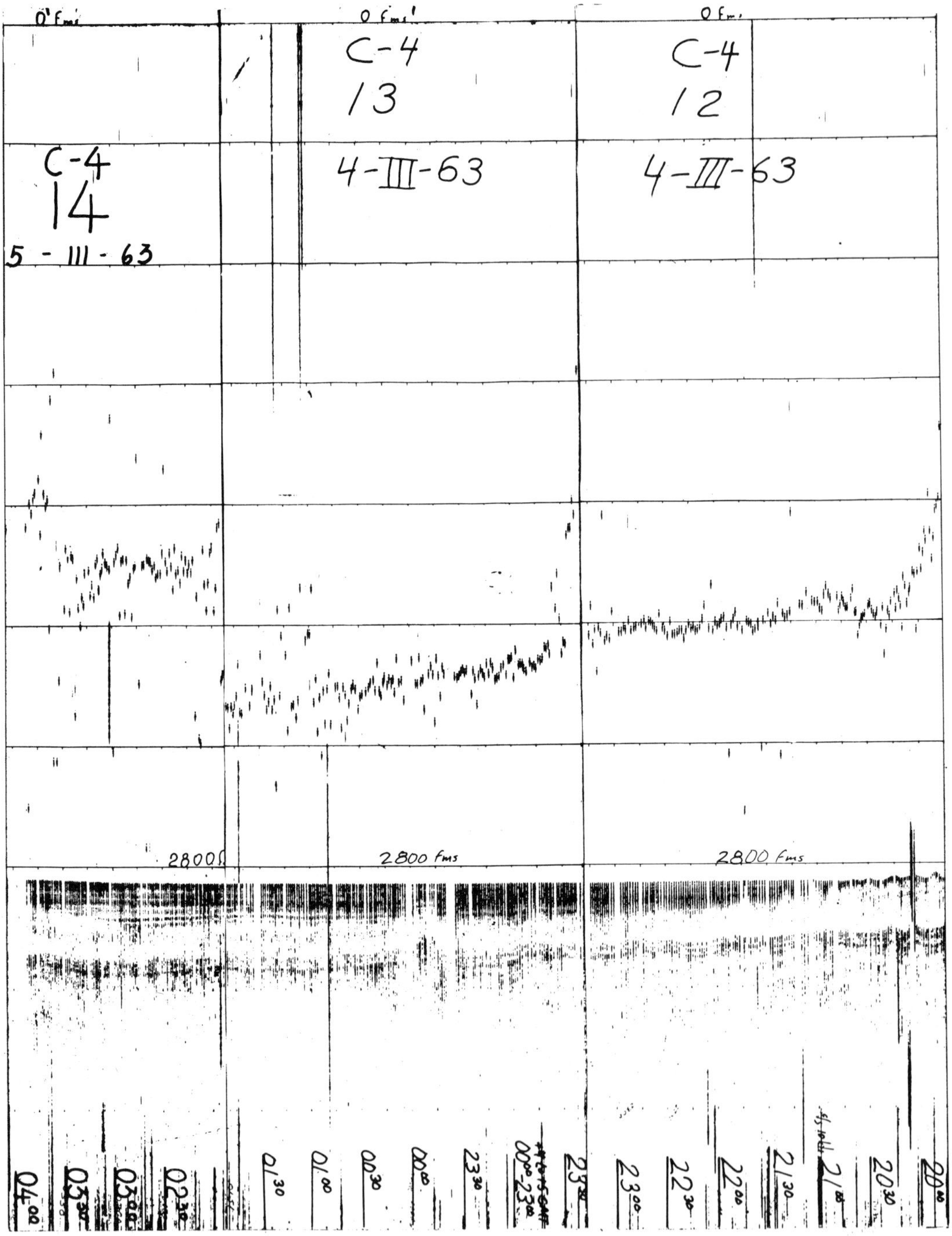

Fig. 2. Reflection profile in the Hatteras abyssal plain of the North Atlantic showing relationship of turbidities to underlying transparent clay deposits. The profile extends onto the edge of Bermuda Rise on the right. Grid lines represent 1 second of reflection time (approximately 400 fathoms or 730 meters in water—10–30% more in sediment). The profile is 80 nautical miles (148 km) long.

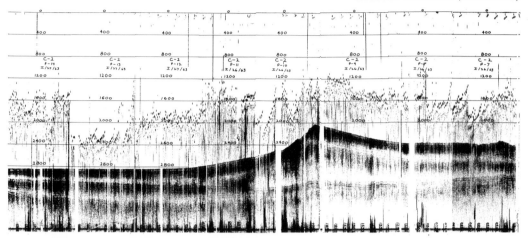

Fig. 3. Reflection profile of the Blake-Bahama outer ridge showing a thick accumulation of sediments on a relatively flat base. Grid lines represent 1 second of reflection time (approximately 400 fathoms or 730 meters—10–30% more in sediment). The profile is 300 nautical miles (555 km) long

usually occupying the deeper parts of the basins, appear to have flowed from a continental source to the greatest accessible depth. There are examples, notably the Blake-Bahama outer ridge east of Florida, where deposition of the sediment has apparently been controlled by a substantial deep current and has resulted in the formation of a prominent topographic feature, i.e., a ridge of sediment several hundred miles long, several tens of miles in width and as much as a mile in thickness (Fig. 3). In other areas, strong evidence of erosion on the deep sea floor is indicative of the important role of currents or turbidity flows on the distribution of oceanic sediments.

It has been observed that deep cold water rich in nutrients rises to the surface at the equator supporting a zone of high organic productivity. The remains of these organisms contribute a great amount of biogenous sediment to the ocean floor, resulting in an increased sediment thickness coincident with the equatorial belt (Arrhenius, 1963). This effect has been clearly demonstrated by profiler traverses in the Pacific. A similar thickening has been found at the Antarctic Convergence.

(3) *Trenches.* Sediment thickness in the trenches is a function of proximity to land source and age of the trench and, therefore, varies considerably, even within the same deep. In some places, seismic refraction measurements have revealed a substantially greater thickness of low-velocity material, particularly on the landward side of the trench axis, than is indicated by the reflection profiler. This apparently means that some of this sediment is acoustically very opaque or that processes, probably connected with trench-forming tectonics, have distorted the reflecting surfaces so badly that no reflections are observed with the profiler.

Areal Distribution. The greatest accumulations of basin sediments have been found in the Atlantic, Arctic and North Indian Oceans and the shallower mediterranean seas. The average thickness in the Atlantic basins is 1 km, with exceptionally thick deposits in the Argentine and Guiana basins. In the Indian Ocean, the Somali and Arabian basins and the area southeast of Ceylon, the sediments are in many places too thick to be completely penetrated with reconnaissance reflection techniques. Where basement was recorded, deposits are generally well in excess of 1 km thick.

Very little information is available on the sediment thickness in the Arctic Ocean. From the limited seismic work that has been done, it is evident that turbidite deposition has played a major role and the deposits are believed to cover extensive areas of the bottom. In many areas, basement was not recorded, but more than 1.5 km of sediment has been indicated by reflection methods (Kutschale, 1963). Gravity and geomagnetic measurements suggest that local thicknesses may be considerably greater.

In most of the Pacific Ocean, turbidite deposits are restricted by the island arc and the marginal trench barrier to a relatively narrow belt adjacent to the continents. Abyssal plains are found in the Gulf of Alaska and off the west coast of Canada and the northern United States, where turbidites have apparently filled the trenches and flowed over them into the basins.

With the exception of the equatorial belt, where thicknesses of the order of 0.6 km have been measured, the southern and central Pacific basins contain very little sediment (less than 100 meters average thickness). In the northern Pacific, the sediment thickness gradually increases from a low value (0.1 km) near the Hawaiian Islands to more than 0.5 km near the Aleutians and the Kuriles. In the Gulf of Alaska, Shor (1962) reported values of over 0.4 to 1.2 km from refraction measurements. Refraction surveys in other widely scattered parts of the Pacific Ocean (Raitt, 1956) indicate an average thickness of 0.3 km.

In the mediterranean areas such as the Gulf of Mexico, the Caribbean Sea, the South China Sea, the Bering Sea and the Mediterranean Sea, sediment thicknesses average well over 1 km and in places are of the order of 4–5 km.

The sediment thickness in the Puerto Rico trench has been well established at about 1.7 km, and other trenches in which thick sediments have been measured include the Aleutians (.5–2 km) and the Japanese trench (.5–2 km). Other trenches, such as the Tonga-Kermadec, the Marianas and the South Sandwich trenches appear to contain very little sediment.

The investigations described here were supported by the United States Office of Naval Research and Bureau of Ships.

JOHN EWING
TERENCE EDGAR

References

Arrhenius, G., 1963, "Pelagic Sediments," in (Hill, M. N., editor) "The Sea," Vol. 3, pp. 655–727, New York, Interscience.

*Broecker, W. S., Turekian, K. K., and Heezen, B. C., 1958, "The relation of deep sea sedimentation rates to variation in climate," *Am. J. Sci.*, **258**, 429–448.

Dietz, R. S., 1961, "Continent and oceanic basin evolution by spreading of the sea floor," *Nature*, **190**, 185–201.

*Ewing, M., Ewing, J. I., and Talwani, M., 1964, "Sediment distribution in the oceans: Mid-Atlantic Ridge," *Geol. Soc. Am. Bull.*, **75**, 17–36.

Ewing, M., Ludwig, W. J., and Ewing, J. I., 1964, "Sediment distribution in the oceans: the Argentine Basin," *J. Geophys. Res.*, **69**, 2003–2032.

Goldberg, E. D., and Koide, M., 1962, "Geochemical studies of deep sea sediments by the ionium/thorium method," *Geochim. Cosmochim. Act*, **26**, 417–450.

Heezen, B. C., 1959, "Paleomagnetism, continental displacements, and the origin of submarine topography," in (Sears, M., editor) *International Oceanographic Congress Preprints*, American Association for the Advancement of Science, Washington, D.C., p. 26.

Kutschale, H., 1963, "Seismic profiler measurements in the Siberian basin: Arctic Ocean (abstract)," *Am. Geophys. Union*, **44**, 63.

Raitt, R. W., 1956, "Seismic-refraction studies of the Pacific Ocean basin, Part 1: Crustal thickness of the central equatorial Pacific," *Geol. Soc. Am. Bull.*, **67**, 1623–1640.

Shor, G., 1962, "Seismic refraction studies off the coast of Alaska; 1956–1957," *Seismological Soc. Am. Bull.*, **52**, No. 1, 37–57.

Wegener, A., 1912, "Die Enstehung der Kontinente," *Petermanns Mitt.*, **58**, 185–195, 253–256, and 305–309.

ABYSSAL ZONE

(1) Introduction

Definition. The term abyssal originally defined the entire depth area beyond the reach of fishermen. But after the 1860's when explorations of the deep sea began, culminating with the cruise of the *Challenger* (1872–76), it became evident that two main faunistic regions were to be distinguished: (1) a lower region with a uniform fauna and a low temperature (to which the term abyssal became restricted) and (2) an upper region, now called the bathyal (or archibenthal) zone, with a more varied and richer fauna and relatively high temperatures. The upper boundary of the abyssal zone toward the bathyal lies about 2000 m, varying in different areas from 1000–3000 m, in accordance with the different position of the 4°C isotherm which roughly delimits the distribution of the endemic elements. The distinction between an abyssal and a bathyal fauna is thus obscured in the polar regions. The recent deep-sea investigations have further led to the conception that the trenches and deeps with depths exceeding 6000–7000 m constitute a special faunistic region, the hadal (q.v.).

Area. The abyssal is the world's largest ecological unit, occupying more than three-quarters of the total area of the oceans and adjacent seas and slightly more than half of the total area of the globe (see Table 1).

TABLE 1. AREAS OF ABYSSAL ZONE

	Area (million km^2)
Total area of the globe	510
The oceans and adjacent seas	361
Depths exceeding 2000 m	305
Depths exceeding 3000 m	278
Depths exceeding 6000 m	5
Calcareous oozes	128
Abyssal clay	102
Siliceous oozes	38

(2) Life Conditions

Environmental factors. Life conditions are very uniform, except for food. The temperature over the greater part of the oceanic deep sea is between 0 and 2°C, constant within the geographical areas and with no seasonal variation. The low temperature is conditioned by the cold water masses sinking down in the polar regions and from here streaming over the bottom towards the equator. Enclosed deep-sea basins such as the Mediterranean, the Japan Sea, and the Sulu Sea without direct communication with the oceanic abyssal have higher bottom temperatures and do not possess a true abyssal fauna.

The salinity is $34.8 \pm 0.2\permil$. The concentrations of phosphate, carbon dioxide, and silicate, and the alkalinity, also vary only slightly. The oxygen content is entirely dependent on the continuous supply

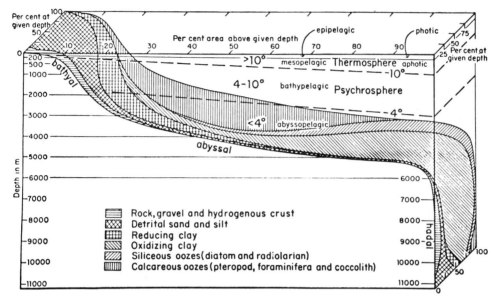

Fig. 1. Ecologic zonation of the deep sea (from *Galathea* Report, Vol. 1, Fig. 6, 1959).

of oxygenated water masses, as oxygen can only be added in the upper water layers, by the photosynthesis of the pelagic plants and by absorption of air at the surface. Generally, however, the bottom water contains sufficient oxygen for the support of animal life, i.e., on an average 5–6 cc/liter in the Atlantic and 3.5–4 cc/liter in the Pacific. Close to the bottom there may be a decrease in oxygen content which is evidently connected with the biological processes. The pressure in the abyssal ranges from 200–700 atm. How far it directly affects the abyssal animals has not yet been discovered.

Substratum. The abyssal is normally a calm milieu where very small particles may settle. The bottom, apart from the mountain ranges and sea mounts, is also mainly covered by a soft clayey ooze of very considerable thickness, perhaps hundreds of meters thick. Near land, the bottom sediments are derived to a varying degree from terrigenous mineral and organic material, as well as from planktonic organisms. Farther from land, the deposits are almost exclusively of pelagic origin, and at the greatest distance from land, the sedimentation becomes very slow, only a fraction of a centimeter per 1000 years. The change from primarily terrigenous to pelagic deposits generally takes place at an approximate depth of 2000 m, thus coinciding with the upper limit of the abyssal fauna. Down to depths around 4000 m (in mid and low latitudes), the sediment is primarily a greyish calcareous ooze, largely consisting of the sunken shells of pelagic foraminifera (e.g., *Globigerina*), and skeletons of pelagic flagellates, especially Coccolithidae. Globigerina ooze occupies most of the ocean floor of the Atlantic and the Indian

Ocean, and parts of the Southern Pacific. Pteropod shells are dominant in the calcareous ooze in certain areas. In depths exceeding 4000 m, i.e.,

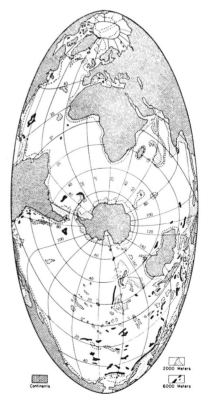

Fig. 2. Abyssal region of the earth, showing 2000 meter contour and depths greater than 6000 meters (Hammer-Aitoff projection; from Bruun, 1957).

11

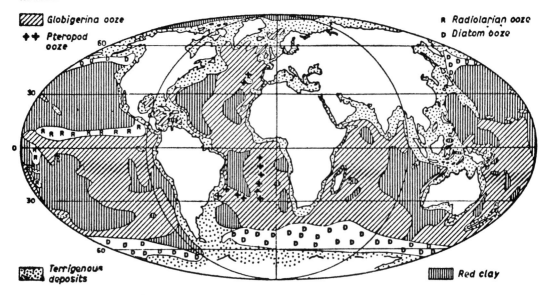

Fig. 3. Distribution of abyssal sediments (from Guilcher, 1954).

most of the Pacific, the calcareous deposits have largely been dissolved (see *Calcium Carbonate Compensation Depths*), and the sediment is the brownish abyssal clay (red clay) composed mainly of aluminium silicate. In the deeper areas of the Pacific and Indian Oceans, the siliceous shells of radiolarians are the main constituent of the sediment. In the Antarctic and northernmost Pacific, the sediment is mainly a siliceous ooze formed by the accumulated shells of diatoms living in the cold surface waters. Slow currents occur along the bottom, varying in velocity to around 5 cm/sec, and deep-sea photographs showing ripple marks indicate that at least to depths about 3000 m and around sea mounts, the currents may occasionally increase to 16 cm/sec.

Food Supply. Ultimately, the food supply for deep-sea life is totally dependent upon the supply of organic matter from land and from the upper water layers where it is basically produced by the photoautotrophic phytoplankton, the first link in the oceanic food chain. When the epipelagic organisms sink, they are utilized by the bathypelagic fauna. However, the remains of plants, animals and excrements which sink below a depth of 2000 m will reach the bottom having been little influenced by the depths as the abyssopelagic life is very poor. The common assertion that the greater the depth, the less is the supply of food, is, therefore, true only in connection with distance from land or from areas with a high productivity at the surface. Abyssal heterotrophic bacteria assimilate the organic matter and are considered to constitute the main source of food, either directly or as the second link in a new food chain. Terrigenous deposits which support a much richer animal life

than the eupelagic deposits may be transported far into the ocean by turbidity currents. Plant debris are very abundant on the abyssal bottom in certain tropical areas and cause a concentration of life. The sunken dead bodies of large animals, e.g., whales, form temporary local food supplies and are mentioned as being one explanation of the patchy distribution of many abyssal species.

(3) The Fauna

Morphological Characteristics. The environmental conditions are, apart from the pressure, no different from any that can be found in shallower regions, and the abyssal fauna shows no fundamental differences from the fauna of these regions. Characteristics shown by the abyssal animals are correlated with their life in darkness, in a calm milieu with a soft bottom. They are uniformly colored, often greyish or black, and often very delicately built. The mobile animals have long slender legs, and the sessile ones are often stalked (which may in part be an adaptation for raising them above the oxygen-poor water layer close to the bottom). Many fishes and crustaceans are blind, and in some fishes the pelvic fins are developed as tactile organs.

Composition. Life in the abyssal region is concentrated on or close to the bottom. All the major groups of marine invertebrates are represented, in addition to several benthic kinds of fish. Examples are:

PORIFERA: Tetractinellida, Hexactinellida (Euplectellidae, Hyalonematidae).

COELENTERATA: Hydrozoa (*Branchiocerianthus*); Scyphozoa (Coronatae: *Stephanoscyphus*); Anthozoa (Gorgonaria: Clavularidae; Pennatularia:

12

Umbellulidae); Actiniaria; Madreporaria (solitary forms); Antipatharia (*Bathypathes*).

POLYCHAETA: Aphroditidae, Eunicidae, Maldanidae, Terebellidae.

Echiuridae; Sipunculoidea; Priapuloidea; Nematoda; Nemertini; Bryozoa; Brachiopoda; Pogonophora; Enteropneusta; Pycnogonida.

CRUSTACEA: Cirripedia (*Scalpellum*); Cumacea; Tanaidacea; Isopoda (*Haploniscus, Storthyngura, Arcturus*); Amphipoda; Decapoda (Eryonidea, Paguridae, Galatheidea, Brachyura).

ECHINODERMA: Crinoidea (stalked forms); Asteroidea (Brisingidae, Pterasteridae, Porcellanasteridae); Ophiuroidea; Echinoidea (Echinothuridae, Spatangoidea); Holothurioidea (Elasipoda: *Elpidia, Peniagone, Psychropotes, Benthodytes*).

MOLLUSCA: Monoplacophora (*Neopilina*); Bivalvia (Nuculidae, Limopsidae, Cuspidariidae, Xylophaginidae); Gastropoda (Pleurotomella); Cephalopoda.

TUNICATA: Ascidiacea (*Culeolus, Styela, Octacnemus*).

VERTEBRATA: Selachii; Holocephali; Teleostei (Bathypteroidae, Synaphobranchidae, Macrouridae, Brotulidae, Liparidae, Ceratiidae).

Infauna and Epifauna. The abyssal fauna, like the cold-water faunas and infaunas of the shallower depths, is to a large extent composed of comparatively few widespread species with a relative abundance of individuals. In addition there are many species, especially the epifauna, which show patchy distributions. The epifauna will also be concentrated on and around the sea mounts where increased currents may expose a firm surface or a coarser grade of bottom. Deep-sea photographs have shown, for example, that crinoids may dominate on one sea mount and poriferans on another.

Feeding Types. With increasing depth, the number of suspension feeders (feeding from the suspended detritus) and deposit feeders (feeding on the deposited organic matter), increase in relation to that of carnivores and scavengers. The Porcellanasteridae, a family of mud eaters within the otherwise carnivorous sea stars, are unknown from depths less than 1000 m. They constitute a fourth of the species of sea stars recorded from 4000 m, and half of those from 6000 m. The mud-eating holothurians, the Elasipoda, are the all-dominant animals in the abyssal, and some of the abyssal fishes are also deposit feeders.

Density of Life. The density of life is very low compared to that of the moderate depths. Expressed in biomass (i.e., quantity of substance in live organisms in grams per square meter), it is even in the richer abyssal regions (the Antarctic and northern Boreal) no more than 1% of that in the richer sublittoral, and some eupelagic deposits may be almost barren. The productivity may further be extremely poor.

Reproduction. The rate of reproduction seems slow, and a considerable longevity is also postulated for abyssal animals in general. It is yet unknown whether they show seasonal life rhythms, but there are indications that for the true abyssal species this is not the case and that reproduction may take place at any time of the year, with only a small number of eggs ripening simultaneously. A non-pelagic development seems to be usual for the true abyssal benthic species and for the majority of those extending into the zone, though some may be expected to have free-swimming larval stages of some duration. Some species possess pelagic larvae,

Fig. 4. An abyssal holothurian, *Psychropotes* (from Bruun, 1957).

Fig. 5. An abyssal angler fish, *Galatheathauma* and crustacean. Note depressible teeth, and light organ inside mouth (from Bruun, 1957).

and some of the benthic-abyssopelagic fishes, the Synaphobranchidae and Ceratiidae, have larvae living in the upper pelagial.

(4) Subdivisions of the Abyssal Zone

Vertical subdivision. The abyssal zone may be divided into an upper and a lower zone at a depth of about 4500 m where a change in the composition of the species occurs. A number of the worldwide distributed species belong exclusively to the lower abyssal. At about 4500 m, the water becomes undersaturated with calcite, and this in part may account for the faunal change.

Regional Distribution and Subdivisions. The uniform life conditions and the absence of definite topographical barriers account for the wide distribution of many of the endemic forms in the abyssal. An almost cosmopolitan distribution

TABLE 2. FIGURES FOR BIOMASS IN NORTHWESTERN PACIFIC IN GRAM PER SQUARE METER (BIRSTEIN AND BELYAEV, 1955, BIRSTEIN 1959)

Coastal zone	1000–5000
50–200 m	200
ca. 4000 m	ca. 5
Kuril-Kamchatka Trench ca. 6000 m	1.2
ca. 8500 m	0.3
Central part of the ocean floor	0.01
Tonga Trench 10,500 m	0.001

seems to be a general rule for species of benthic fishes, anthozoa, echinoderms and tunicates, whereas crustaceans and mollusks show restricted distributions. The greatest difference in the composition of the abyssal fauna is found between the faunas on either side of the American continent (this area also constitutes the most marked barrier in the abyssal region). With respect to the echinoderms, another barrier for the distribution would seem to be the mid-Pacific deep sea with its very sparse food resources. The extremely cold water ($< 0°C$) of the Antarctic deep sea probably accounts for the special composition of the abyssal fauna there. Three main zoogeographical subdivisions of the abyssal region thus may be distinguished: (1) the Atlantic and Indian Ocean inclusive of the Southwestern Pacific, (2) the East Pacific and (3) the Antarctic deep sea. A more detailed zoogeographical subdivision will, for the greater part, reflect the zoogeography of the bathyal region.

Secondary Abyssal Species. Numerous species extend from the bathyal into the neighboring abyssal and constitute a very considerable part of the actual abyssal fauna. Such species have been called secondary abyssal species or guests, since they, though able to live in the abyssal habitat, may be unable to produce a constant series of generations there. It is probable also that many species may be prevented from spreading into the distant oceanic deep sea because of the decreasing food supply.

(5) Origin of the Fauna

Endemic Forms. Only few groups of higher taxonomic categories are peculiar to the deep sea. A family of sea anemones is as yet known solely from hadal depths (q.v.). The sea stars, Porcellanasteridae, are almost exclusively abyssal (1000–7600 m). Two-thirds of the species of the holothurian order, the Elasipoda, are abyssal, and one-third bathyal. The mollusks of the class Monoplacophora (*Neopilina*) are exclusively bathyal-abyssal and represent the only abyssal group with a paleozoic fossil record (see pr Vol. VI). The most dominant abyssal groups, such as the Elasipoda, are without fossil records, and only few of the other families represented can be traced as far back as Mesozoic.

Non-endemic Forms. It is believed (see Emiliani's oxygen isotope studies, pr Vol. VI) that the low temperature in the recent abyssal deep sea is a character only acquired in rather recent geological time and that during Late Mesozoic and Early Tertiary the abyssal temperature were about 10°C. The gradual Late Tertiary cooling, culminating during the Quaternary glaciations, may have had a very selective influence on the fauna. Stenothermic abyssal forms adapted to a temperature of about 10°C would become extinct, although they might possibly persist in the bathyal region. Taxonomic evaluations of different genera and species of echinoderms, polychaetes and crustaceans occurring at various levels of depths have led to the conviction that they become more advanced with increasing depth, and thus indicate a progressive distribution into the abyssal zone. The region may since Late Mesozoic or Early Tertiary have been repopulated gradually from the bathyal depths. The endemic deep-sea genera and families, e.g., the hexactinellids, the recent crinoids, the cidaroids and elasipods, probably constitute the oldest element. *Neopilina* also may not have invaded the abyssal until Early Tertiary. Other groups, gorgonarians, astropectinids and the macrourids, with shallow-water relatives in the tropical sublittoral, may have extended their range into the abyssal during Early Tertiary, before the fall in temperature had begun to tell. A Late Tertiary invasion may be assumed for the groups which are extensively distributed in the abyssal and have their shallow-water relatives in the colder regions. A Late Quaternary (postglacial) invasion must have taken place, and is still going on, with regard to those species which have their main occurrence in the polar regions and only a restricted distribution in the neighboring deep sea.

F. Jensenius Madsen

References

*Bruun, A. F., 1957, "Deep sea and abyssal depths," *Tr. Mar. Ecol. Paleocol. I., Geol. Soc. Am. Mem.*, **67**.
Ekman, S., 1953, "Zoogeography of the Sea," London, Sidgwick and Jackson.
*Madsen, F. Jensenius, 1961, "On the zoogeography and origin of the abyssal fauna," *Galathea Report*, **4**.
Marshall, N. B., 1954, "Aspects on Deep-Sea Biology," Philosophical Library.
Murray, J., 1895, "A summary of the scientific results," *Challenger Report, Summary* 2.
*Zenkevitch, L., 1963, "Biology of the Seas of the U.S.S.R.," London, Allen & Unwin.

ACOUSTICS (UNDERWATER)

Acoustics, as herein described, is concerned with the production, transmission, reception and utilization of underwater sound. Sound is a form of mechanical energy and can be described as a periodic variation in pressure, particle velocity or displacement in an elastic medium. Since light and radio waves are highly absorbed by the oceans and sound waves are not, sound is used to probe the ocean's depth, locate objects in the ocean, investigate the nature of sediments, and communicate. Sound is essential in most underwater operations.

The earliest application of underwater sound was the installation of submerged bells under lightships and buoys. During periods of poor visibility, the underwater sound from the bells could be detected at considerable distances by use of a stethoscope or microphone mounted on a ship's hull.

In 1912, Reginald Aubrey Fessenden developed an electromagnetic sound source that made ship-to-ship communication possible by Morse code underwater signaling. The first large-scale research and development efforts in underwater sound were initiated by the British Admiralty during World War I. The development of the echo sounder is another early application of underwater sound. The echo sounder measures the depth of water under a ship's hull by timing the echoes of short sound pulses from the ocean's bottom. The military aspects of underwater sound, submarine detection, echo ranging, etc., have been the prime concern of underwater sound research. Today, underwater sound is both an area for applied research and an important scientific tool. The refraction and reflection of sound is used by geophysicists and marine geologists to explore the sub-bottom structures of the ocean bottom (seismic profiling) and to map the topography of the ocean floor (echo sounding). Marine biologists study the sound scattering effects as well as the sounds emitted by various forms of marine life.

Velocity of Sound

The velocity of sound equals the square root of the ratio of elasticity to density and in the ocean is dependent in an empirical manner on the temperature, salinity, and pressure (depth). The primary dependence is upon temperature. The velocity of sound in seawater varies from about 1450–1570 m/sec; it increases with temperature at a variable rate of about 4.5 m/sec/°C; it increases with salinity at 1.3 m/sec per one thousandth part increase in salinity; and it increases with depth at 1.70 m/sec/ 100 m. In general, the sound velocity profile for a

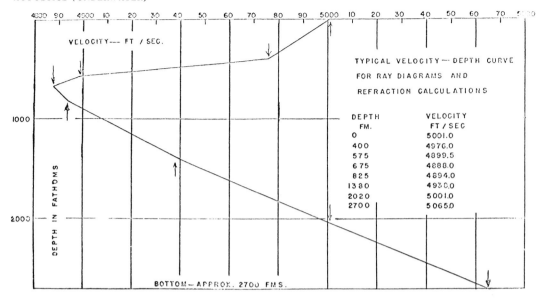

Fig. 1. Sound velocity profile [after Ewing, Worzel, and Pekeris, "Propagation of Sound in the Ocean," *Geol. Soc. Am., Mem.* 27 (1948)]. (Note: 1 fathom = 1.8288 meters; 1 ft/sec = 0.30480 m/sec; thus at 5000 meters, the velocity is approximately 1520 m/sec.)

particular part of the ocean is determined from the temperature and salinity versus depth measurements through a set of empirical tables or graphs such as Wilson's Tables.

The velocity of sound for seawater as a function of temperature, salinity and depth may be expressed by the following empirical formula:

$$C = 1449 + 4.6t - 0.055t^2 + 0.0003t^3 + \\ (1.39 - 0.012t)(s - 35) + 0.017d$$

where C is the velocity in meters per second, t is the temperature in degrees centigrade, s is the salinity in parts per thousand, and d is the depth below the surface in meters. Figure 1 is a typical sound velocity profile of the oceans.

Standard instruments and procedures available for computing the sound velocity profile in the oceans include computations made with data from Nansen bottles and reversing thermometer casts; temperature versus depth profiles from bathythermographs; and direct sound velocity measurements by velocimeters. A sound velocimeter is lowered on a conducting cable to the ocean bottom and, as it is lowered, measures the sound velocity of the seawater at the instrument, by precise timing of a reflected sound pulse over a known path length. A pressure gauge mounted on the instrument measures the depth. With the use of appropriate recording equipment, an X-Y plot of sound velocity versus depth can be traced automatically aboard a survey ship.

The vertical variation of the sound velocity in the deep oceans has three main parts: (1) a variable layer about 120 m below the surface, (2) a strong negative gradient to about 1500 m where the velocity decreases with depth (thermocline), (3) a layer to ocean's bottom where the velocity increases (positive gradient) with the depth. It is this vertical variation of sound velocity which largely determines the propagational path of sound in the oceans. A velocity of 1500 m/sec (4921.26 ft/sec) is commonly used as a standard velocity for making simple calculations rather than the more precise formula given above or those given in Wilson's Tables.

The Decibel Scale (db)

In acoustics the logarithmic scale is commonly used to compare variables. In comparing two intensity levels I_0 and I_1 the ratio (N) in decibels is defined as:

$$N = 10 \log_{10} \frac{I_1}{I_0} \text{ decibels}$$

where I_0 is the reference intensity. For pressure levels this becomes:

$$N = 20 \log_{10} \frac{P_1}{P_0} \text{ (decibels)}$$

Acoustic Energy and Sound Intensity

The vibration of the particles of a fluid involves both kinetic and potential energy. The kinetic energy of motion is given by

$$\text{K.E.} = \frac{1}{2} \rho_0 v_0 \mu^2$$

where ρ_0 is the density and v_0 is the volume element at equilibrium and μ is the particle velocity. The potential energy possessed by the volume element v is the work done during the volume change from the equilibrium to the compressed state. The potential energy per unit volume can be given by:

$$\text{P.E.} = v_0 x \int_0^\sigma \sigma \, d\sigma = \frac{1}{2} v_0 x \sigma^2, \text{ or } \frac{v_0 P^2}{2x}$$

where x is the bulk modulus and σ is the dilatation, the volume change per unit volume. The energy density (W) is the total energy per unit volume, the sum of the kinetic and potential energy.

$$(W) = \frac{1}{2} \rho_0 v_0 \mu^2 + \frac{v_0 P^2}{2x}$$

For progressive plane waves the kinetic and potential energies possessed by a small volume element at any time are equal. Therefore, $(W) = P^2/\rho C^2$ where P is the rms sound pressure at the point. The sound intensity (I) is defined as the rate of energy flow per unit time across a unit area normal to the direction of propagation. Since the energy travels at the same rate as the sound pulse, the intensity at a point will be equal to the energy density times the sound velocity at that point.

$$I = \frac{P^2}{\rho C}$$

The sound pressure level is normally measured in dynes per centimeter square, the intensity in ergs per second per centimeter square, the density in grams per cubic centimeter, the velocity of sound in centimeters per second. If the intensity (I) is measured in watts the above equation becomes

$$I = \frac{10^{-7} P^2}{\rho C}$$

The quantity ρC is referred to as the acoustic impedance of a medium.

For sound sources small compared to the wavelengths of sound produced, the acoustic energy propagates in a homogeneous medium as a spherically spreading wave. If the source level (L) is known, $L = 20 \log P$ (decibels) then the sound level (L_1) at any range (r) from the source is determined by the inverse square law:

$$L_1 = L - 20 \log r$$

Where L and L_1 are in decibels usually (L) is referred to 1 yard from the sound source. The conditions in the ocean, however, are far from ideal, and the problem of sound transmission is very complex varying from place to place and from time to time at any given place.

As sound energy is propagated through the oceans, a portion of the energy is absorbed by the water and converted to heat (absorption). The vertical change in sound velocity causes refraction of sound and development of sound channels. Large numbers of discontinuents, such as gas bubbles, particles of plant and animal life act as scatters to the sound.

The decrease in sound energy per unit length of ray path is not entirely due to geometric spherical spreading. A portion of the sound energy is absorbed and turned into heat by the medium as the result of viscosity and dissolved salts. In a viscous medium, the sound pressure amplitude delays exponentially with distance by a factor, e^{-ar} where r is the distance and a is a positive real number. If absorption were due entirely to viscosity, then a would be equal to $8\pi\eta f^2/3\rho C^2$ where η = viscosity, f = frequency, ρ = density and C = sound velocity. In actual practice viscosity does not account for all the absorption. The absorption coefficient has been determined by empirical means and is given in terms of decibels per meter:

$$a = \frac{0.036 f^2}{3600 + f^2} + 3.2 \times 10^{-7} f^2$$

where f is the frequency in kilocycles. The second term represents the absorption due to viscosity. This equation holds for about 5°C. The absorption decreases by a small amount as the temperature increases. At 5°C,

$$a = 0.0001 \text{ db/m at 1 kc/sec,}$$
$$a = 0.001 \text{ db/m at 10 kc/sec, and}$$
$$a = 0.015 \text{ db/m at 50 kc/sec.}$$

The transmission loss due to geometrical spherical spreading and absorption is given by

$$H = 20 \log r + ar$$

The discrepancy between the measured intensity and that predicted by the above equation is referred to as the transmission anomaly.

Deviation of sound rays from a straight line path is called refraction and it is caused by variations in the velocity of sound along the ray path. Refraction accounts for the development of shadow zones, sound channels, and focusing and defocusing effects in underwater sound.

The path of any sound ray may be traced by applying Snells' Law, which is expressed mathematically as $V_n/\cos \theta_n$ to the special case where the velocity V is only a function of depth (y). $V = V(y)$. Snells' Law states that $V(y)/\cos \theta$ is a constant along the ray path, where θ is the angle between the ray and the horizontal direction, and y is taken positive downward. Consider a ray emitted by a

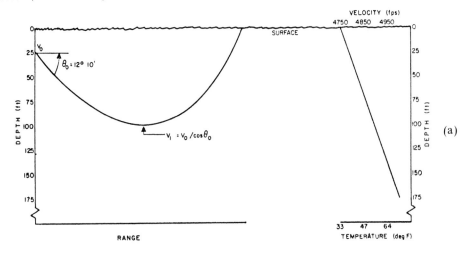

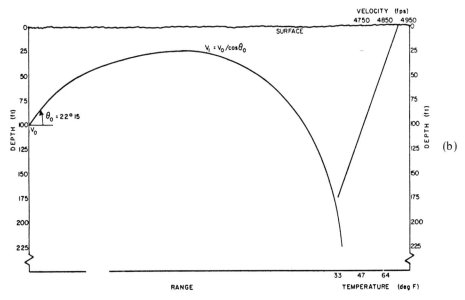

Fig. 2. (a) Refraction in positive temperature gradient; (b) refraction in negative temperature gradient (from Albers, 1960).

source where the velocity is V_0 and initial inclination θ_0. At some other point on the ray where the velocity is V_1, the inclination with the horizontal will be θ_1.

The curvature of the ray path $d\theta/ds$ at any given point (the angle through which the tangent turns as one travels along the curve for unit distance S) is given by

$$\frac{d\theta}{ds} = \frac{dV}{dy} \frac{\cos \theta_0}{V_0}$$

If the velocity increases as a function of depth, dV/dy is positive, the curvature is negative and the ray is bent upward with respect to the horizontal.

A ray can never reach a depth greater than that corresponding to the velocity $V_0/\cos \theta_0$ (Fig. 2). When the velocity gradient dV/dy is negative, the curvature is positive. The rays are bent downward. In a layer with $dV/dy = 0$, the rays are propagated without refraction. In cases where dV/dy is constant (linear gradient), the curvature of the ray is constant and the ray is an arc of a circle of radius

$$r = \frac{V_0}{\dfrac{dV}{dy} \cos \theta_0}$$

The centers of the circles which form the rays lie on a line at depth

18

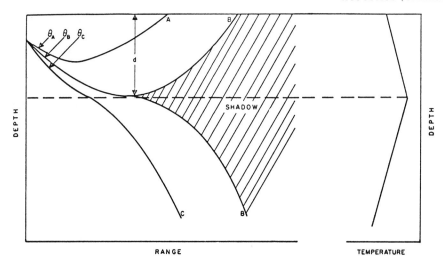

Fig. 3. Shadow zone formation. Ray diagram for the condition in which a positive temperature gradient lies above a negative temperature gradient and the sound projector is mounted in the positive gradient (from Albers, 1960).

$$y = \frac{V_0}{\frac{dV}{dy}}$$

Ray paths (ray diagrams) may be traced by digital computers by treating the more complex velocity V_s depth profile as being composed of a series of layers having linear gradients. Machines are also available which plot mechanically the ray path for a given horizontal range and velocity profile.

Shadow Zones

Refraction of sound leads to the development of shadow zones and sound channels. A shadow zone (Fig. 3) is produced when a positive velocity gradient lies above a negative velocity gradient and the sound source is in the positive gradient. The positive gradient may be due to an isothermal layer with the velocity of sound increasing with depth because of increasing pressure. In this case the sound rays will bend upward in the upper layer and downward in the lower layer. The shadow zone is defined by the limiting ray B (Fig. 3) which diverges at depth d corresponding to an abrupt change in the sound velocity profile.

According to ray theory, no sound energy enters the shadow zone. In actuality, the shadow zone is insonified at a greatly reduced intensity. The intensity decreases away from the limiting ray boundary as an expotential function of range.

Sound Channels

Two important sound channels exist in the oceans. The surface sound channel and the SOFAR channel. Sound channels are caused by velocity minima in the velocity profile. Along the axis of the sound velocity, minimum rays are refracted upward and downward and are trapped. The sound is focused in the channels (nodes), and attenuation in the channel is less than that predicted by the inverse square law. Small charges exploded in the SOFAR channel (1500 meters depth) may be detected by hydrophones placed in the channel many thousands of miles distant from the source.

Ambient Noise

Ambient noise is the background noise level present at any specific location in the ocean outside of the measuring platform or equipment itself. Ambient noise may be man-made such as ships' noise, biological noise caused by snapping shrimp or other organisms, rain noise, surf noise, or sea surface noise associated with waves. In the deep open ocean, the sea surface noises usually predominate. The frequency of the sea surface noise is from about 100 cycles/sec to 50 kc/sec. The noise level increases with sea state as is approximated by Knudsen Curves (Fig. 4). The variation of noise level with sea state indicates that the noise is generated at the surface. Ambient noise, therefore, does not decrease appreciably with depth because the surface behaves as a semi-infinite plane source. The ambient noise levels produced by sources other than the sea surface conditions have a wide range of variability. The noise from a rain storm at 10 kc for instance may be as much as 20 or 25 decibels above the level of the ambient noise measured before the storm. Work at sea using underwater sound is often hampered because of the increase in ambient noise at any specific location.

Reflection

Sound may be reflected from the surface, bottom, or from submerged objects in the ocean. The

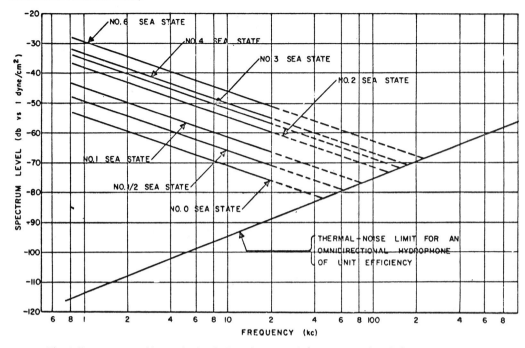

Fig. 4. Deep-water ambient noise levels (Knudsen curves) for sea states 0 to 6 (from Albers, 1960).

amount of sound energy reflected at a boundary is quantitatively related to the specific acoustic impedance ρC between the two media at the boundary. The simplest and most basic theoretical description of reflection is given by the Rayleigh reflection coefficient, R, for plane waves reflecting on a flat boundary between two fluid layers.

$$R = \frac{\dfrac{\rho_2}{\rho_1} - \dfrac{\sqrt{C_1^2/C_2^2 - \sin^2 \theta_1}}{\sqrt{1 - \sin^2 \theta_1}}}{\dfrac{\rho_2}{\rho_1} + \dfrac{\sqrt{C_1^2/C_2^2 - \sin^2 \theta_1}}{\sqrt{1 - \sin^2 \theta_1}}}$$

where R is the ratio of amplitude of the reflected wave to the amplitude of the incident wave, ρ_1 is the density in upper medium, C_1 is the sound velocity in the upper medium, ρ_2 is the density in lower medium, C_2 is the sound velocity in the lower medium, and θ = angle of incidence = angle of reflection.

Surface reflection is nearly perfect at all angles of incidence because of the marked contrast in acoustic impedance between the water and the air above. However, sea surface roughness causes scattering of the sound at the water-air interface so that reflection from surface is far from ideal. When a sound source is located close to the surface, reflection gives rise to surface-image interference, called Lloyd mirror effect. Figure 5 shows the geometrical arrangement that causes the image interference effect. S is the location of the source, I

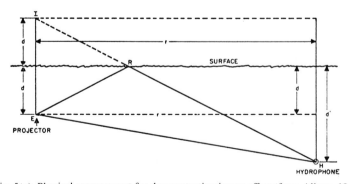

Fig. 5(a). Physical arrangement for demonstrating image effect (from Albers, 1960).

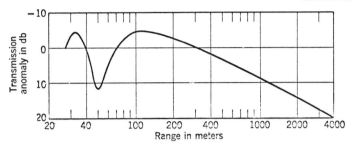

Fig. 5 (b). Example of the transmission anomaly produced by the surface image effect (from Kinsler and Frey, 1962).

is the image, d is the depth of source below surface, and D is the depth of receivers below surface. The direct wave travels the path from S to R; the reflected sound appears as though it came from a source at I, the image of S. Sound received at R is the resultant of two signals one from S and one from I. Depending upon the phase between the two sounds, the resultant amplitude will be greater or less than the source level from S. At the surface the sound undergoes a 180° phase shift due to the release of sound pressure at the free surface.

If the resultant sound intensity at R is plotted as a function of range, a series of maxima and minima will result. The transmission anomaly as a result is given by

$$A = 20 \log 2 \sin \frac{2\pi d_1 d_2}{D\lambda}$$

where D is the distance between S and R and λ is the wavelength of sound. The sound intensity becomes zero when $Zd_1d_2/D\lambda = 1$, where d_1 and d_2 are depth of source and receiver, respectively. The image-interference effect limits the effectiveness of sound transmission at short ranges and is most pronounced when the sea is calm and at low frequencies.

Bottom Reflection

Bottom reflection over the oceans displays great variability due to composition of the bottom sediments, bottom roughness, topography and sub-bottom structures. In general, reflections are good over hard, sandy bottoms and very poor over muddy bottoms. The reflectivity of the bottom can be approximately described by application of the Rayleigh reflection coefficient. One of the more important dependences of this equation is the ratio of the two velocities C_1/C_2. If C_2 is greater than C_1, the reflectivity will increase as a function of grazing angle, and at some angle θ_c known as the critical angle, where $\sin \theta_c = \dfrac{C_1}{C_2}$, the reflectivity will become unity and remain unity out to grazing incidence. No sound energy enters the bottom at angles less than θ_c. If C_2 is less than C_1 and $\rho_2 C_2$ is greater than $\rho_1 C_1$, the reflectivity will decrease

with increasing angle, become zero at an angle defined by

$$\sin \theta = \sqrt{\frac{\dfrac{\rho_2^{\,2}}{\rho_1^{\,2}} - \dfrac{C_1^{\,2}}{C_2^{\,2}}}{\dfrac{\rho_2^{\,2}}{\rho_1^{\,1}} - 1}}$$

and then increase toward unity at grazing incidence.

If, as a limiting condition, C_2 is equal to C_1, the reflectivity will be independent of the incident angle and will be given by $\dfrac{\rho_2 - \rho_1}{\rho_2 + \rho_1}$ which describes the contrast in the densities.

The sound reflected from the bottom as a function of grazing angles often shows a multiplicity of maximum and minimum points from normal incidence out to grazing incidence. The peaks and troughs in the reflectivity can be attributed to interference effects from sound reflected from sub-bottom layering. At low frequencies, the effective reflector is often a subsurface layer rather than the water sediment interface. Bottom reflection losses in the oceans vary from about 5 decibels for low grazing angles to over 20 decibels at normal incidence.

Scattering of Sound

Sound is scattered from objects or surfaces which have dimensions smaller than a wavelength λ of the impinging sound. The scatters for instance may be air bubbles, marine organisms or other particles in the water or microrelief on the surface of the bottom. The phenomena of the deep scattering layer (DSL) seen on echo sounding records is due to the sound scattering properties of marine organisms. Often, it is not possible to make a distinction between scattered and reflected sound.

A theoretical study of sound scattering can be made for small spherical objects. When sound strikes a rigid sphere, it is scattered symmetrically about the direction of the incident wave. The intensity I_s of the sound scattered at a distance r from the sphere is

$$I_s = \frac{I_i \sigma_s}{4\pi r^2}$$

where I_i is the intensity of the incident sound wave, σ is the target strength or cross-sectional area of the sphere and $4\pi r^2$ is the area insonified by the scattered sound at distance r. When the diameter of the scattering sphere is much less than λ, the effective cross-sectional area is no longer $\pi d^2/4$, but is less by approximately $(\pi d/\lambda)^4$. This is known as the Rayleigh Law of Scattering. For air bubbles, the theoretical description is quite complex due to the introduction of compressibility and the effects of resonance. In general, small air bubbles are very effective sound scatterers and often limit the effectiveness of hull mounted transducers.

Reverberation

Sound scattered toward the source from either the surface, the bottom or small scatters along the transmission path is reverberation. Theoretically, no reverberation exists in an unbounded, homogeneous, uniform fluid. The oceans are far from ideal and reverberation is often a limiting factor in SONAR or echo ranging operations. Reverberations, which are unwanted signals, often determine the minimum level a target echo can be detected.

The whole subject matter of reverberation is not well understood but certain facts are known: (1) Reverberation levels are proportional to source level. If reverberation masks the return echo, no improvement can be made by increasing the source level. (2) Reverberation levels increase with pulse duration. The use of short-pulse echo sounders helps to overcome the reverberation effect. (3) Reverberation effects increase with range. Thus, if the reverberation effects mask an echo at range r, the effect at longer ranges will be even greater. (4) Reverberation levels increase as the number of scatterers increase or as their average cross section increases.

In deep water, volume reverberation levels predominate, while in shallow water, surface and bottom reverberations are predominant.

Sound Sources and Receivers

A number of different types of sound sources are in current use. For echo sounding, SONAR, etc., the most commonly used projectors and transducers are those which convert electrical energy into mechanical energy making use of the piezoelectric or magnetostrictive effects. Certain crystals, such as quartz ammonium dihydrogen phosphate, Rochelle salt and ceramic barium titanate exhibit the piezoelectric effect. When an electrical potential is applied across a slab of these crystals, the crystal vibrates mechanically. Sound is produced by direct coupling of the mechanical vibration to the water. Magnetostrictive materials such as nickel and some of its alloys will expand and contract when placed in a varying magnetic field. A magnetostrictive sound projector consists of a bar of magnetostrictive material surrounded by a coil carrying an electric current. Piezoelectric and magnetostrictive transducers or projectors are essentially high-frequency sources because of the practical limit imposed by physical dimensions. To achieve the higher energies and low frequencies needed in sub-bottom profiling or for other special purposes, a variety of different sources are being used. These include: explosives such as TNT, high-energy electrical discharges (Sparker), mixtures of explosive gases such as oxygen and propane, release of highly compressed air and hydraulic-mechanical resonators. Most of these devices are capable of producing sound energy down to 50–100 cycles/sec. These low frequencies are needed to achieve deep penetration into the ocean sub-bottom.

Most hydrophones which receive the sound energy and convert it into electrical energy operate on either the piezoelectric or magnetostrictive principle. There are a class of hydrophones which are pressure-sensitive moving-coil types and operate on the same principle as a geophone. For geophysical purposes, arrays are constructed out of a number of hydrophones and arranged in such a manner (linear array) as to enhance and amplify the desired signal while canceling out by the correct spacing undesired noise. For high-speed sub-bottom profiling in the oceans, the use of a multi-element hydrophone array is essential.

WILLIAM T. MCGUINNESS

References

Albers, V. M., 1960, "Underwater Acoustics Handbook," The Pennsylvania State University Press.
Horton, J. W., 1959, "Fundamentals of Sonar," U.S. Naval Institute.
Kinsler, L. E., and Frey, A. R., 1962, "Fundamentals of Acoustics," second ed., New York, John Wiley & Sons, Inc.
Officer, C. B., 1958, "Introduction to the Theory of Sound Transmission," New York, McGraw-Hill Book Co.

ADIABATIC PHENOMENA—*See* Vol. II

ADVECTION

The rate of change of a property of a moving parcel of air can be expressed as the sum of the "local change" (the change occurring at a fixed point) plus an "advective change" (the change occurring because the parcel is moving into a region of different value of the property). In vector form, this division of the rate of change can be written as

$$\frac{d\Psi}{dt} = \frac{\partial\Psi}{\partial t} + \mathbb{V} \cdot \nabla\Psi$$

where the first term on the right is the local change and the second is the advective change, or "advection."

The above equation can be rewritten as

$$\frac{\partial \Psi}{\partial t} = \frac{d\Psi}{dt} - \mathbb{V} \cdot \nabla \Psi$$

i.e., the local change at a given place can be expressed as the sum of two effects, the real change of the property for the moving parcels of air, absorption of heat for instance, plus a change "due to advection," $- \mathbb{V} \cdot \nabla \Psi$, for instance due to warmer air being brought to the place. This analysis is common in meteorology, and the use of the term "advection" for the expression $(- \mathbb{V} \cdot \nabla \Psi)$ is probably more common than for $\mathbb{V} \cdot \nabla \Psi$ as given above.

It is common to separate the advection into two parts, the horizontal advection $(\pm) \left(u\frac{\partial \Psi}{\partial x} + v\frac{\partial \Psi}{\partial y} \right)$ and the vertical advection $(\pm) \left(w\frac{\partial \Psi}{\partial z} \right)$, mainly because the horizontal wind components u and v can be measured directly while the vertical velocity component w must usually be inferred from other information.

The distinction between convection and vertical advection is commonly a matter of scale. Convectional transport is that due to small-scale (the definition depends on the context), thermally induced currents ("convection currents") which are considered as random and are treated statistically. Vertical advection is that due to steady or mean vertical currents. In fact, even the largest-scale motions of the atmosphere have been handled statistically and referred to as "convection" processes.

RAYMOND DELAND

References

Byers, H. R., 1959, "General Meteorology," Third ed., New York, McGraw-Hill Book Co., 540pp.

Charney, J. G., 1951, "Dynamic Forecasting by Numerical Process," in "Compendium of Meteorology," pp. 470–482, Boston, American Meteorological Society.

Petterssen, S., 1956, "Weather Analysis and Forecasting," Second ed., Vol. 2, New York, McGraw-Hill Book Co.

Cross-references: *Atmosphere; Baroclinity; Circulation of Atmosphere; Stability and Lapse Rate.*

AGULHAS CURRENT [and Mozambique Current]

(1) General Description

Ocean currents are very largely wind-driven, not necessarily by the winds prevailing over the area of current flow, but often indirectly by wind systems operating many miles away. The direction of such flow is modified both by the effect of the earth's rotation and by the configuration of the ocean basins and boundaries. The Agulhas Current forms part of the large scale circulation ot the southern Indian Ocean. It flows off the east coast of southern Africa between the latitudes 25 and 40°S, in a generally southwesterly direction with a return flow further out to sea. The whole system is usually concentrated within 300 miles of the coast.

In the southern hemisphere a wind current is deflected to the left of the prevailing wind direction due to the rotation of the earth, the angle being about 45° at the surface. The southeast trade winds blowing toward the equatorial regions set up a current flowing from east to west which is known as the South Equatorial Current. When this nears the coast of Africa it is deflected to the left by the earth's rotation and flows along the coast, its direction being determined largely by the shape of the coastline and the continental shelf. Part of this current flows between Madagascar and the African continent to form the Mozambique Current, and part flows to the east of Madagascar. Either or both of these streams feed into the Agulhas Current. A little of the Agulhas stream may find its way round the Cape of Good Hope into the Atlantic Ocean, but it seems that most of it doubles back to form a return flow, the southern part of which mingles with the West Wind Drift which is associated with the westerly winds blowing over the Southern Ocean. The circulation of the southern Indian Ocean has an anticyclonic or counterclockwise current pattern similar to that of the South Atlantic and South Pacific Oceans. A generalized picture of the currents near the coasts of southern Africa, compiled from various sources, is given in Fig. 1. This tries to present an average of conditions existing at different times of year, but although there is little seasonal variation in the direction of the Agulhas Current, differences in temperature structure and current speed have been found.

The Agulhas area has been studied intensively as part of the International Indian Ocean Expedition. The data has been published in a report by Shipley and Zoutendyk (1964), and an analysis has been made by J. Darbyshire (1964). The Mozambique Current has been studied by Menache (1963) and the area off the Cape of Good Hope by M. Darbyshire (1963). Sections covering the Indian Ocean circulation are to be found in the oceanographic text books by Sverdrup *et al.* and Defant.

(2) The Temperature Structure

In order to study the characteristics of the Agulhas Current it is necessary first to look at the temperature structure of the water. The current is a warm one, since water is transported from low to higher latitudes. Temperature measurements have been made at a number of depths at stations along lines roughly at right angles to the coast, and the surface temperatures for January and July are

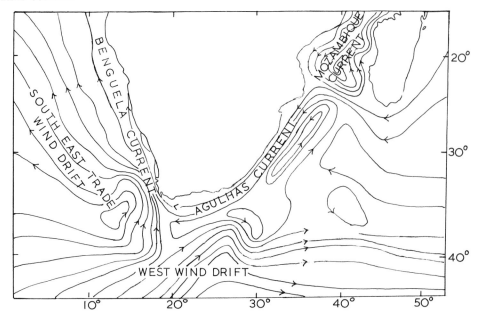

Fig. 1. The currents near the coast of southern Africa.

shown in Fig. 2. At all seasons, a tongue of warm water, above 20°C is found at the surface. It is very near the shore in the north of the area but the distance widens as one moves down the coast. In January, the southern summer, the warm water extends to about 40°S and some miles west of Cape Agulhas and the core of the tongue has a temperature of 26°C. In July, however, the tongue has retreated northwards, the maximum temperature is only 22°C, and coastal temperatures range from 14°C at Cape Agulhas to 18°C further north.

A typical vertical temperature section is given in Fig. 3. The measurements on which this section is based were made in April 1962 along a line southeastward from Port Elizabeth. The vertical scale is logarithmic since this allows the surface layers to be shown in greater detail. The tongue of warm water may be clearly seen. This is usually found above 150-meter depth and has been termed Warm Agulhas Water. An outer tongue, 17 to 20°C, is usually found above 400-meter depth and this is known as Cool Agulhas Water. In these surface layers there is a very marked temperature gradient on both sides of the warm tongue. The temperature decreases more slowly at depths greater than 400 meters, and the isotherms tend to become more horizontal. On the continental shelf the bottom temperature may be fairly high, but in the deep ocean temperatures of nearly 0°C are found in some places.

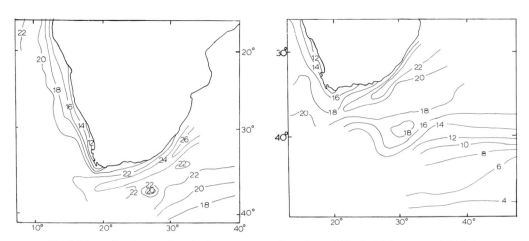

Fig. 2. The surface temperatures in the oceans around southern Africa in (a) January and (b) July.

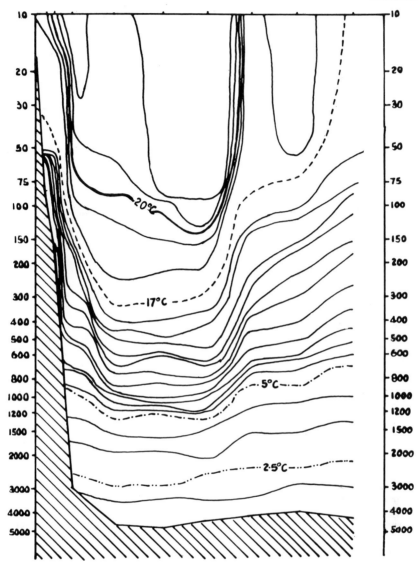

Fig. 3. The temperature distribution along a line of stations southwest of Port Elizabeth (after J. Darbyshire). Depths in meters. Total horizontal distance 500 miles (from "A hydrological investigation of the Agulhas Current area," *Deep Sea Res.*, **11**, Fig. 8c).

(3) The Water Masses

The salinity of seawater is another important variable, and temperature and salinity observations are usually carried out simultaneously. If temperature is plotted against salinity as in Fig. 4, the resulting distribution is known as the T-S curve. The data shown here are for four lines of stations across the Agulhas Current, including line C, shown in Fig. 3, and they vary only slightly from T-S curves obtained from widely spaced stations in the South Atlantic and South Indian Oceans.

If the T-S curve is studied in conjunction with the vertical temperature section, we can build up a picture of the type of water to be found at various depths. From about 1000 meters down to the sea bed, the temperature is less than 6°C, and a salinity maximum and minimum can both be readily identified. The maximum at 2.5°C, 34.8‰ represents the North Atlantic Deep Water which is found at about 3000 meters, while below this is the colder but slightly less saline Antarctic Bottom Water. The salinity minimum at 5°C, 34.4‰ represents the Antarctic Intermediate Water usually found in this area at about 1200 meters. The Antarctic waters have flowed outwards from the Polar regions and have been identified at different depths in various parts of the ocean—for instance the Antarctic Intermediate Water occurs at the

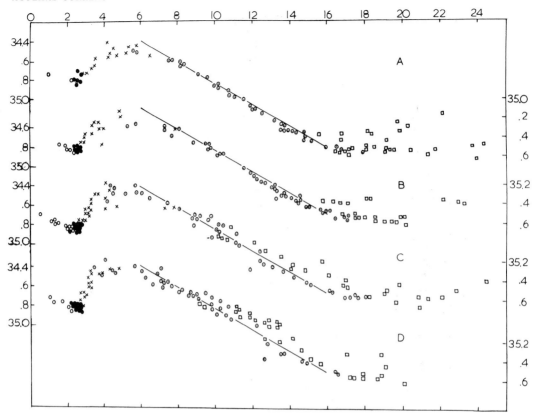

Fig. 4. The T-S curves for four lines of stations across the main stream of the Agulhas Current. Depth classes O > 3000 m, 3000 m > ● > 2000 m, 2000 m > × > 1000 m, 1000 m > ⊙ > 200 m, 200 m > □ > 50 m (after J. Darbyshire; from "A hydrological investigation of the Agulhas Current area," *Deep Sea Res.*, **11**, Fig. 1).

surface between 45 and 50°S—while the North Atlantic Deep Water has moved from the North Atlantic, across the South Atlantic and into the Indian Ocean forming a very deep ocean current.

At medium depths and sometimes appearing at the surface, there exists a water mass which is represented on the T-S curve by a straight line joining the points 6°C, 34.4‰ and 16°C, 35.5‰. This is known as Central Water and is very probably a mixture of Subtropical and Intermediate Waters. However since similar water has been identified in other parts of the Indian Ocean and in the South Atlantic, it is convenient to treat it as a separate water mass.

Above 17°C we have the Cool and Warm Agulhas Waters mentioned earlier. These have similar temperature and salinity to the subtropical and tropical waters found nearer the Equator. They are of low density and have moved along the surface in the form of southerly moving currents. There is some evidence of a salinity maxima at 20°C, 35.6‰ which may be regarded as the boundary between the cool and warm type of Agulhas water.

(4) Density Distribution

From the temperature and salinity observations it is possible to calculate the water density. σ_t is a term very widely used in oceanography. It represents the density of water of given salinity and temperature at surface pressure, and by definition

$$\sigma_t = 10^3(\rho_{s,t,0} - 1)$$

where $\rho_{s,t,0}$ is the density of water of given salinity and temperature at surface pressure.

In Fig. 5, σ_t is plotted against depth for the same line of stations off Port Elizabeth mentioned earlier. Density increases downward as one would expect so that the tongue of Agulhas Water remains at the surface on top of the denser Central Water and more dense intermediate and bottom waters. The North Atlantic Deep Water is sandwiched between the two waters of Antarctic origin because the densities decrease in magnitude in that order.

Planes of equal σ_t value are known as σ_t surfaces and movement of water tends to take place along these planes. Some indication of current motion can thus be obtained from a study of σ_t surfaces.

SEA MILES

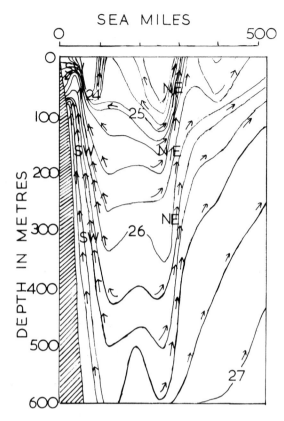

Since all sections at right angles to the coast are similar to that shown here, there will be strong currents parallel to the shore where the contours are most closely spaced, that is, on each side of the warm tongue. Since the σ_t surfaces are deeper in the middle, the flow will be anticyclonic. σ_t decreases very slowly in the deeper layers and the surfaces become almost horizontal.

(5) Current Velocity

Very few direct current measurements have been made in this area so far, and we have to rely on computed values derived from temperature and salinity readings. By plotting the depths of the various σ_t surfaces, it is possible to get an estimate of the water movements at those levels. A more sophisticated method is due to Helland-Hansen. His formula gives a way of calculating differences in horizontal currents at different levels from the

Fig. 5. The σ_t distribution along a line of stations southwest of Port Elizabeth. SW and NE show the direction of the current normal to the plane of the section, the arrows show upward movement.

Fig. 6. The dynamic topology with reference to the 1000-decibar surface. April 1962 (after J. Darbyshire: from "A hydrological investigation of the Agulhas current area," *Deep Sea Res.*, 11, Fig. 4a).

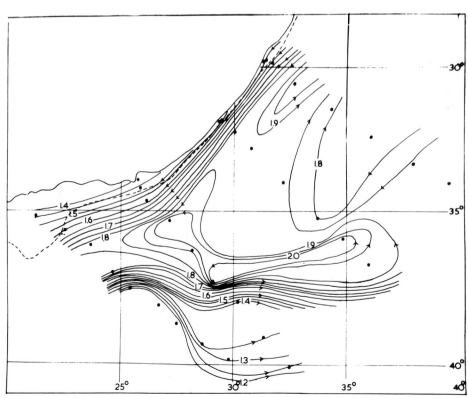

densities. It involves the use of the geopotential change or the so-called dynamic height difference between two levels. A deep level of no motion must be assumed. The dynamic height anomalies at the required level, usually the surface, are plotted on a chart, and from the contour spacing the horizontal current can be calculated. The current direction is along the line of the contours with the higher levels to the left.

A number of charts of dynamic topology have been prepared for the Agulhas Current area, assuming a level of no motion at 1000 decibars (approximately the 1000-meter level). The chart for April 1962 is shown in Fig. 6. Other charts vary in detail, but some general conclusions may be made. The main southwesterly stream is constant in direction but varies at different seasons of the year from 20 cm/sec to 60 cm/sec. An eddy system between 25 and 32°S is fairly constant in position with velocities of about 10 cm/sec. Other eddies, further south, are more variable. The return flow is also rather variable in velocity and direction, sometimes flowing northeastward parallel to the main stream and sometimes merging with the West Wind Drift.

The Mozambique Current often forms an anti-cyclonic system as shown in Fig. 1, but on some occasions there is a direct flow into the Agulhas Current.

The seasonal variation of the Agulhas Current depends on the variations of the South Equatorial Current and the West Wind Drift. There is no correlation with the local wind systems. The southwest stream is much stronger in summer than in winter. The South Equatorial Current extends north of the Equator during the southern winter and some of it is deflected into the southwest monsoon system. The West Wind belt moves north and the warm water associated with the Agulhas Current retreats northward also. In the southern summer, however, the South Equatorial Current flows much further south and is reinforced by the northeast monsoon north of the Equator. The southwest stream of the Agulhas Current reaches its maximum velocity and the warm tongue of water moves south and west, often round the Cape into the South Atlantic Ocean.

MOLLIE DARBYSHIRE

References

Darbyshire, J., 1964, "A hydrological investigation of the Agulhas Current area," *Deep-Sea Res.*, **11**, 781–815.
Darbyshire, M., 1963, "Computed currents off the Cape of Good Hope," *Deep-Sea Res.*, **10**, 623–632.
*Defant, A., 1961, "Physical Oceanography," Vol. 1, pp. 566–568.
Menache, M., 1963, "Premiere campagne oceano-graphique du 'Commandant Robert Giraud' dans le canal de Mozambique 11 octobre–28 novembre 1957," *Cahier Oceanographique*, **15**, No. 4.
Shipley, A. M., and Zoutendyk, 1964, "Hydrographic and Plankton Data Collected in the South West Indian Ocean during the S.C.O.R. International Indian Ocean Expedition 1962–1963," University of Cape Town, Data Report, No. 2.
*Sverdrup, Johnson and Fleming, 1942, "The Oceans," pp. 690–697

ALBEDO—*See* Vol. II

ALEUTIAN CURRENT

Also known as the *Subarctic Current*, the Aleutian Current flows eastward parallel to the Aleutian Islands and to the north of the North Pacific Current. The water mass of this current is a mixture of Kuroshio and Oyashio water, but the temperature and salinity in the upper layer are reduced by cooling and by excessive precipitation, respectively. This water mass called the "Subarctic Water" shows a marked distinction from the water of the North Pacific Current which is an extension of the Kuroshio. The eastward transport of the Aleutian Current between the Aleutian Islands and latitude 42°N amounts to about 15 million m^3/sec above a depth of 2000 meters.

One branch of the Aleutian Current turns north and enters the Bering Sea. It flows along the northern side of the Aleutian Islands but splits again in several branches moving northward. The remaining part of the Aleutian Current divides in two branches before reaching the American coast. One branch moves northeast into the Gulf of Alaska and forms a part of the counterclockwise gyre there (*Alaska Current*). The water of this branch is warmer than the original water of the gulf though it consists of the Subarctic Water. A westward countercurrent flows out from the gyre in the Gulf of Alaska along the south coast of the Alaska Peninsula and continues west close to the southern side of the Aleutian Islands. The major branch of the Aleutian Current turns to the south along the west coast of the United States and becomes the California Current.

TAKASHI ICHIYE

References

Barnes, C. A., and Thompson, T. G., 1938, "Physical and chemical investigation in Bering Sea and portions of the North Pacific Ocean," *University of Washington, Pub. in Oceanography*, **3**(2), 35–79, and Appendix 1–169.
Favorite, F., and Pedersen G., 1959, "North Pacific and Bering Sea oceanography 1957 and 1958," *U.S. Fish Wildlife Serv. Spec. Sci. Rept.*, **292** (1957), 1–106; **312** (1958), 1–230.
Fleming, R. H., 1955, "Review of the oceanography of the Northern Pacific," *Bulletin International North Pacific Fisheries Commission* (*Vancouver, Canada*), No. 2, 1–43.
Sverdrup, H. U., Johnson, M. W., and Fleming, R. H., 1942, "The Oceans," pp. 1087, Englewood Cliffs, N.J., Prentice-Hall.

ALKALINITY [OF SEAWATER]

The International Association of Physical Oceanography in 1939 defined the term alkalinity as the number of milliequivalents of hydrogen ion neutralized by 1 liter of seawater at 20°C. The major influence is from bicarbonate ion although ions of carbonate, borate, silicate, phosphate, and arsenite play a minor role. Alkalinity had previously been referred to as buffer capacity, titratable base, excess base, or titration alkalinity.

Alkalinity is not only a measure of the quantity of weak acids in a water sample but also of the cations that are balanced against these weak acids. We may write

$$\text{Alkalinity} = [HCO_3^-] + 2[CO_3^{2-}] + [H_2BO_3^-] +$$
$$[OH^-] - [H^+] + [\text{negl. } H_2PO_4^-,$$
$$HSiO_3^-, H_2AsO_4^-]$$

$$= [K^+] + [Na^+] + 2[Ca^{2+}] + 2[Mg^{2+}]$$
$$- [Cl^-] - 2[SO_4^{2-}]$$

where the brackets indicate molar concentrations. Early measurements were made by direct titration with strong acid (HCl) in the presence of CO_2. It was found that above a pH of 4.5 all of the strong acid was used to free the anions of weak acids that had been bound to basic cations. Therefore, the number of milliequivalents of acid used in the titration to lower the pH of the 1 liter of sea water to 4.5 was taken as the alkalinity.

Another early titrimetric method used an excess of HCl which was then back titrated with NaOH colorimetrically after the CO_2 had been driven off.

Recently electrometric methods have been employed. A standard HCl solution is added to the sample in selected increments and the conductivity or the pH is measured after each addition by the inductive conductivity meter or by the glass electrode pH meter, respectively. At a sharply defined end point or equivalence point, the conductivity and the pH change rapidly with the addition of more acid. This equivalence point is the point at which the anions of the weak acids have been set free and it thus defines the alkalinity of the sample.

The term carbonate alkalinity is used if alkalinity contributions from weak acids other than bicarbonate and carbonate are not considered. Thus we may write

$$\text{Carbonate Alkalinity } [A] = [HCO_3^-] + 2[CO_3^{2-}]$$
$$[A] = [HCO_3^-] + 2[CO_3^{2-}]$$

Alkalinity and so-called carbonate alkalinity are important measurable factors in the total CO_2 system of seawater. By solving the following four equations

$$[A] = [HCO_3^-] + 2[CO_3^{2-}]$$

$$[\Sigma CO_2] = [HCO_3^-] + [CO_3^{2-}] + [H_2CO_3]$$

$$K_1 = \frac{[H^+] \times [HCO_3^-]}{[H_2CO_3]}$$

$$K_2 = \frac{[H^+] \times [CO_3^{2-}]}{[HCO_3^-]}$$

where $[A]$, $[\Sigma CO_2]$, and $[H^+]$ are measurable, all components of the CO_2 system in sea water may be determined (K_1, K_2, $[CO_3^{2-}]$, $[HCO_3^-]$, and $[H_2CO_3]$).

There is generally a linear relation between alkalinity and the total salt content of ocean water. Thus

$$\frac{\text{Alkalinity} \times 10^3}{\text{Chlorinity (‰)}} = 0.123$$

This ratio of alkalinity to chlorinity is defined as specific alkalinity; so if we know the chlorinity we can roughly calculate the alkalinity.

In seawater there is an increase in the calcium/chloride ratio with depth. The change in this ratio is equivalent to a rise in the specific alkalinity with depth. This indicates that changes in the alkalinity and $[Ca^{2+}]$ are of common origin, i.e., the precipitation or solution of $CaCO_3$. The alkalinity and calcium content of seawater may be related by the following equation

$$[Ca] \text{ (mg-atoms/liter)} = \tfrac{1}{2} \text{Alkalinity} + 0.465 \times \text{Chlorosity}$$

Y. H. Li

W. S. Moore

References

Anderson, D. H., and Robinson, R. J., 1946, "Rapid electrometric determination of the alkalinity of sea water," *Ind. Eng. Chem., Anal. Ed.*, **18**, 767–769.

Park, Kilho, Oliphant, M., and Freund, H., 1963, "Conductometric determination of the alkalinity of sea water," *Anal. Chem.*, **35**, 1549–1550.

*Sverdrup, H. U., Johnson, W. M., and Fleming, R. H., 1942, "The Chemistry of Sea Water," in "The Oceans, Their Physics, Chemistry, and General Biology," pp. 192–210, Eaglewood Cliffs, N.J., Prentice-Hall.

AMPHIDROMIC POINT, REGION

In oceanic tides a point about which the cotidal lines radiate is known as an *amphidromic point*. The area affected by any such radiating system is identified as the *amphidromic region*.

Cotidal lines are those joining the points of simultaneous tidal waves. The amphidromic point is really the spot where the tide vanishes to zero. For example, there is an amphidromic point a short distance southeast of Puerto Rico; at Ponce on the south coast of Puerto Rico the tidal range is only 1 cm.

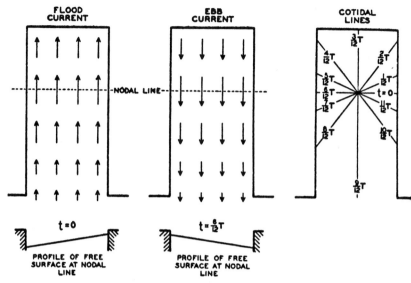

Fig. 1. Schematic representation of transverse oscillations in a bay in the northern hemisphere leading to the development of an amphidromic point.

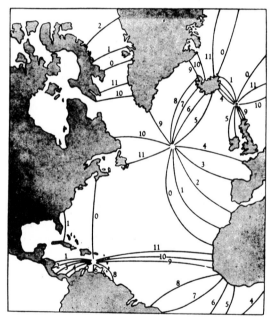

Fig. 2. Co-tidal lines of the Atlantic Ocean according to Sterneck (1920).

When the cotidal lines rotate around the amphidromic point, counterclockwise in the northern hemisphere and clockwise in the southern, it is evident that it is related to the rotation of the earth. An ideal example (Fig. 1) shows transverse oscillations set up by the Coriolis effect, accumulating the water to the right of the current in a northern hemisphere case. The North Atlantic responds rather like a gigantic bay of the same sort (Fig. 2).

Most of the marginal seas in the northern hemisphere (including the North Sea and the Baltic) have counterclockwise amphidromic points. This fact suggests that the Coriolis effect is present even in seas of the dimensions of the North Sea and the Baltic.

The interference of two tidal waves can also lead to the development of such a null point; such interference points, of course, are not related to earth rotation and may not have the characteristic sense of rotation in each hemisphere.

RHODES W. FAIRBRIDGE

References

Defant, A., 1958, "Ebb and Flow," Ann Arbor, Mich., University of Michigan Press, 121pp.

Defant, A., 1961, "Physical Oceanography," Vol. 2, New York, Pergamon Press.

Dietrich, G., 1963, "General Oceanography," New York, Interscience Publishers, 588pp. (translated by F. Ostapoff).

Proudman, J., 1953, "Dynamical Oceanography," London.

Sverdrup, H. U., Johnson, M. W., and Fleming, R. H., 1942, "The Oceans: Their Physics, Chemistry and General Biology," New York, Prentice-Hall, 1087pp.

Cross-reference: *Tides.*

AMUNDSEN SEA

Geography

The Amundsen Sea is an Antarctic body of water located between the Bellingshausen Sea and the Ross Sea. It lies between Thurston Island (formerly believed to be a peninsula) on the east

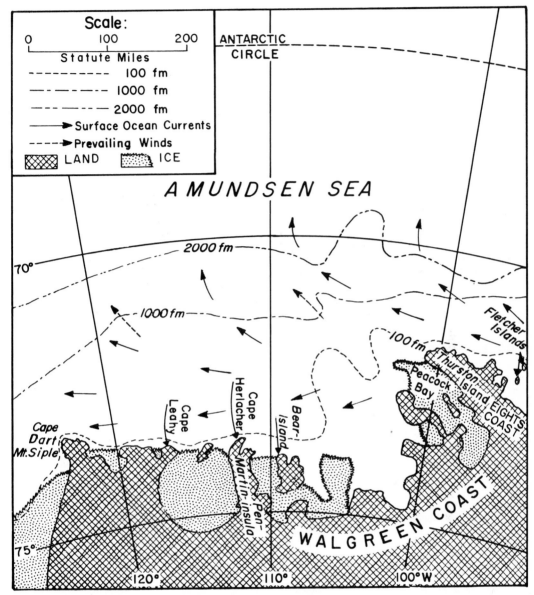

Fig. 1. Bathymetric sketch map of Amundsen Sea.

and Mount Siple 400 miles to the west (approximately 100–120°W, and northward to about the Antarctic Circle).

The Amundsen Sea was named after Roald Amundsen, the Norwegian explorer, who was a mate aboard the *Belgica*, which was the first ship to winter in the Antarctic in 1879. Continuous pack ice always covers about the first 100 miles from the coast. The edge of the continental shelf is unusually depressed and offshore depths to over 4000 m are known.

Oceanography

The Amundsen Sea is one of the least known

bodies of water in the Antarctic. Prior to *Operation Deep Freeze 61* (U.S. Navy Hydrographic office, TR-105) very little has been published on the Amundsen Sea.

Temperature profiles show a thin layer of Antarctic Surface Water with Winter Water immediately beneath, this is followed by a rapid transition due to the Antarctic Circumpolar Water.

Maximum temperatures are between 1.50 and 2.0°C except in the southern Amundsen Sea where temperatures slightly colder than 1.50°C are encountered. Surface temperatures vary widely ranging from 0.23 to −1.77°C. Between 100 and 200 m, a rapid temperature increase (the transition zone into Circumpolar Water) is indicated by the heavy concentration of isotherms. Farther south, this transition zone is found at greater depths. Below the temperature maximum, a gradual decrease to bottom temperatures of around 0.4°C is observed.

The range of surface salinities is from 32.38–34.00‰. In the upper 200 m, salinities increase rapidly to 34.50‰, with 34.00–34.25‰ appearing in the area of minimum temperatures. Salinities continue to increase with depth to a maximum of about 34.74‰ at approximately 800 m and decrease to a minimum of 34.68‰ near the bottom.

Dissolved oxygen content in the surface water of this area is usually greater than 7.00 ml/liter. Below the surface, oxygen values decrease rapidly to about 400 m, where minimum values of about 4.00 ml/liter are observed. Below this minimum layer, oxygen content increases to the bottom with values approaching 5.00 ml/liter.

South of the Amundsen Sea, the cold air of the continent encounters southward-blowing winds, creating cyclones. These whirl eastward gathering strength and finally break up over the Antarctic Peninsula.

Submarine Geology

The sediments in the Amundsen Sea are glacial marine. This is composed mainly of material which has been transported from land or shallow water by ice rafting, and has been dropped to the bottom when the ice melted. To the north follows a belt of diatom ooze, also with sporadic glacial boulders.

SAYED Z. EL-SAYED

References

Bruns, E., 1958, "Ozeanologie," Vol. 1, Berlin, V.E.B. Deutsch. Verl. Wiss.
Korotkevitch, Y. S., and Ledenev, V. G., 1962, "Proposal to distinguish five seas at the coast Antarctic," *Soviet Antarctic Exped. Inf. Bull.* **4**(35), 3pp.
U.S. Hydrographic Office, 1960, "Sailing Directions—Antarctica," Second ed., Washington D.C.

Cross-references: *Antarctic Meteorology; Bellingshausen Sea; Ross Sea; Southern Ocean.*

ANDAMAN SEA

Location and Gross Configuration

The Andaman Sea is contained by a physiographic basin which covers 798,000 km² (Fig. 1). From the Irrawaddy Delta in Burma, the Andaman Basin's length extends 1200 km southward to northern Sumatra and the contiguous Malacca Straits. It measures 650 km in an east–west direction from the Malay Peninsula to the Andaman-Nicobar Ridge.

Waters of the Andaman Sea and the Bay of Bengal communicate through several channels.

TABLE 1. STATISTICAL SUMMARY OF ANDAMAN SEA
(MAINLY AFTER KOSSINNA, 1921)

Location: Latitudes 5–17°N; longitudes 92–98°E

	English	Metric
Length	746 miles	1200 km
Width	404 miles	650 km
Area	308,000 square miles	798,000 km²
Average depth	2856 ft	870 m
Greatest depth	13,700 ft	4180 m
Volume	24,509,000 ft³	694,000 km³

From north to south these are (1) Preparis Channel, over 200 m deep, divided by the island of the same name; (2) Ten Degree Channel, between the Andaman and Nicobar islands, approximately 800 m deep; and (3) Great Channel, between Great Nicobar Island and Sumatra 1800 m deep.

The northern and eastern third of the Andaman Basin is comprised of the submarine Irrawaddy-Salween Delta and Mergui Platform, respectively 200 and 170 km broad from the coast to the 200-m depth contour. From these shallow shelves, the sea bottom drops off rapidly into a large central basin and two smaller basins to the north and south. Each of these depressions is deeper than 2000 m. The greatest known depth, 4180 m, is located at the south end of the central basin, 150 km east of Car Nicobar Island. Overall average depth of the Sea is 870 m. A north–south arc of volcanic arcs and seamounts, including Barren and Narcondam islands, separates the basins. Other seamounts stud the sea floor to the east of the volcanic arc.

Investigators

Scientific exploration of the Andam Sea has proceeded intermittently since the visit of the Austrian Frigate *Novara* in 1857–59 and the work of H.M.S. *Investigator* during the 1920s. Little has been added to our knowledge of the Sea since Sewell (1925–38) summarized all existing oceanographic data. Numerous ships worked here during the International Indian Ocean Expedition of 1960–65. Investigations by the U.S. Navy Oceanographic Office Ship *Serrano* and the U.S. Coast and Geodetic Ship *Pioneer* have added significant data.

Physiographic Features and Geologic History

Mergui Platform. The Malay Peninsula, forming the eastern border, has stood above the sea as far back as 150 million years ago during the Jurassic Period, and may have emerged for a time during the Devonian Period, 400 million years ago. The Mergui Platform is an extension of the Sunda Shelf, peneplaned during the late Tertiary Period and inundated by the last Pleistocene rise in sea level. Most of the Mergui Islands are monadnocks of early Mesozoic granites which have resisted erosion more than the early Paleozoic sedimentary rocks associated with the Mergui granites along the Burmese coast of the Malay Peninsula.

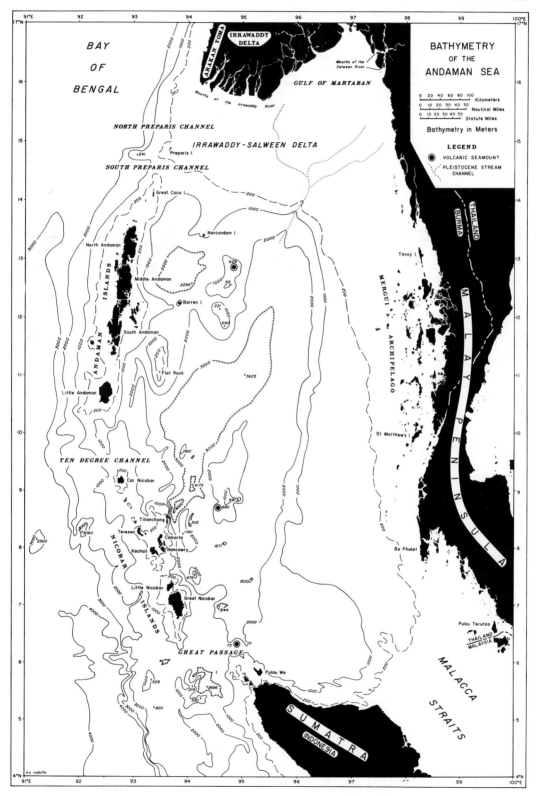

Fig. 1.

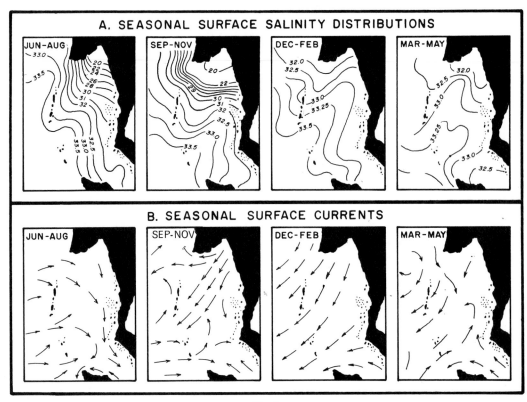

A. SEASONAL SURFACE SALINITY DISTRIBUTIONS

JUN-AUG   SEP-NOV   DEC-FEB   MAR-MAY

B. SEASONAL SURFACE CURRENTS

JUN-AUG   SEP-NOV   DEC-FEB   MAR-MAY

Fig. 2.

Modern sediments of the Mergui Platform are a thin, discontinuous, shifting cover of coarse-to-fine sand derived from the Mergui granites, overlying a stiff clay. The yearly monsoonal gales prevent the permanent deposition of sediments on the Platform.

Andaman-Nicobar Ridge. The Andaman Sea is thought to have first formed as a separate physiographic feature with the initial uplift of the Andaman-Nicobar Ridge during the Cretaceous Period, more than 60 million years ago. Cretaceous serpentines and associated deep-water radiolarian cherts are the oldest rocks found on the Andaman and Nicobar islands and are the rock assemblage which characteristically forms during the initiation of island arcs. A continuous sequence of Lower Tertiary marine rocks overlying the serpentines and charts suggest that the Ridge first emerged above sea level some 20 million years ago. The rocks which overlie the Lower Tertiary sequence are probably little more than a million years old and are coral limestones and shelly sands which were deposited in shallow water, indicating at least one submergence and emergence during the Pleistocene. At present corals are building reefs around the islands.

Volcanic Arc. The volcanic islands Barren and Narcondam belong to an inner arc of active volcanism which continues southward as seamounts

from which volcanic rocks were recently dredged by the *Pioneer* (Fig. 1), and which ultimately connect with the line of Sumatra volcanoes. To the north, the volcanic trend continues under the Irrawaddy Delta, where geophysical data from the *Pioneer* indicates its burial under 250 m of delta sediment; thence to late Tertiary volcanic sites in central Burma. Barren Island last erupted in 1852 and still emits fumes and occasional lavas.

Irrawaddy-Salween Delta. Two of the world's greatest rivers, the Irrawaddy and the Salween, deposit enormous quantities of sediment into the Andaman Sea. The annual sediment discharge of the Irrawaddy River has been estimated at 250 million tons; lesser amounts are discharged by the Salween River. The Irrawaddy Delta is building seaward at a rate of 5 km every hundred years, and the seaward advance of the Gulf of Martaban at its 40-m depth contour is estimated at 55 km every hundred years.

Some evidence suggests that the Irrawaddy River has emptied into the Sea for much longer than has the Salween River, which may have debouched formerly into the Gulf of Thailand through the present-day Meping River until it was rerouted by movements associated with the close of the Himalayan Orogeny, less than a million years ago.

A dendritic channel on the floor of the Gulf of Martaban may have formed when the area stood above water during a lower sea stand. Such features are common elsewhere on the Sunda Shelf. It is surprising that the tremendous sediment loads discharged into the Gulf have not covered up the channel system. Possibly the channels today serve the function of funneling Salween River sediment as turbidity currents down to the central Andaman Basin floor.

Modern sediments of the Delta are brown silts and clays with patches and streaks of sand. Geophysical data gathered by the *Pioneer* indicate a delta thickness well in excess of 1000 m.

Deep Basins. The central deeps are at present accumulating fine olive-green clays and turbidity-current sands and silts. The Andaman Sea is an interesting example of an actively forming geosymeline that is filling from one end, and only a little from the sides. Besides the Gulf of Martaban's subsea channel system, other canyons incised into the slope of the Mergui Platform and the east slopes of the Andaman-Nicobar Ridge may bring coarse sediment to the basin floors. Layers of volcanic ash have been found in sediment cores taken between Narcondam and Barren islands.

Waters

Temperatures. The surface water temperatures of the Sea fluctuate very little, as may be expected of the tropical location. From a maximum monthly average of about 30°C in the summer, the temperature falls to a winter minimum monthly average of about 27.5°C. Temperatures drop off rapidly with depth, to about 5°C at 2000 m. Deeper waters have an interesting areal variation. In the vicinity of the volcanic arc, bottom water temperatures average about 5.25°C; in abyssal areas remote from the volcanic arc, temperatures average 4.95°C. Heat-flow investigations of the U.S. Coast and Geodetic Survey have studied the possible relationships between volcanicity and the thermal anomaly.

Salinity. Surface salinities of the Andaman Sea exhibit strong seasonal variations (Fig. 2). The tremendous influx of fresh water from the Irrawaddy and Salween rivers during the southwest monsoon dilutes the waters at the north end of the Sea to a salinity of only about 20‰ from June to November. During this period, salinity at the southwest end of the sea is about 33.5‰.

The comparatively dry winter and spring are reflected in more normal salinity distributions, from about 32‰ at the northern delta area to about 33.5‰ in Great Channel. In the central deeps, salinity increases with depth to a maximum of about 35‰ at about 1500 m.

Currents. The tropical monsoonal regime is the primary current-controlling factor. Throughout most of the year, northwestward currents of 1/3–2 knots flow into the southern Andaman Sea from the Malacca Straits; elsewhere in the Sea currents shift with the monsoons (Fig. 2). From June to August, the southwest monsoon drives Bay of Bengal waters into the Sea through the various channels, and the Malacca Straits current is at its weakest and hugs the Sumatran coast as Andaman Sea waters are forced into the Straits. When the southwest monsoon starts to die down in September, the high water-density gradient still exists at the north end of the Sea, causing southwestward currents to form. By November, the northeast monsoon begins to blow over the Sea, maintaining the southwestward currents through December, January, and February. The greatest current changes occur from March to May, as the monsoons start to shift again and when the northern salinity-induced density gradient is at its lowest. By June, the southwest monsoon again dominates.

Current data are scarce. Normal currents in the Andaman Sea flow at rates of 1/3–2 knots.

KELVIN S. RODOLFO

References

Chibber, H. L., 1934, "The Geology of Burma," London, Macmilland and Co. Ltd., 530pp.
Krishnan, M. S., 1953, "The structural and tectonic history of India," *Mem. Geol. Soc. India*, **81**, 137pp.
Sewell, R. B. S., 1925–1938, "Geographic and oceanographic research in Indian waters," *Mem. Asiat. Soc. Bengal*, **9**, No. 1–9, 539pp.

ANDAMAN SEA: GEOPHYSICS OF

The geophysical anomaly trends in the Andaman Sea are related to the general morphology of the area. The dominant trends follow the "Indonesian Arc" which is part of the system of young primary arcs of southeastern Asia. Other pronounced trends are parallel to the west Malaysian shelf, which in turn is parallel to the Triassic-Jurassic fold-mountain system of Thailand and Malaysia.

The free-air gravity anomalies (Fig. 1) reflect the basic bathymetric and tectonic patterns. The extension of the Java-Sumatra trench and the Andaman-Nicobar islands lie in a broad belt of negative free-air anomalies. Within this belt, there is a narrow zone where positive free-air anomalies occur. These are associated with Nias and Simalur Islands, southwest of Sumatra, and the western margin of the Nicobar and Andaman Islands. The axis of the minimum of the negative anomaly belt is on the eastern side of the sedimentary island platform; it passes through the Nicobar Islands, but shifts to the inner (eastern) side of the Andaman Islands.

The volcanic arc is indicated by generally high positive free-air anomalies, specifically prominent at the northern tip of Sumatra, at the Invisible Bank, and the Barren and Narcondam Islands. In other areas of the volcanic arc, especially in the

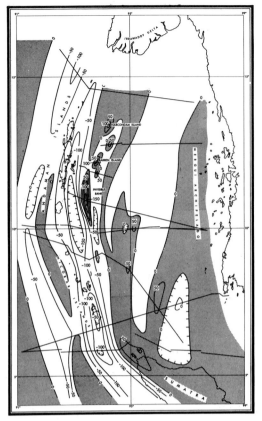

Fig. 1. Gravity free air anomaly contours in the Andaman Sea (after Peter *et al.*, 1966).

Fig. 2. Magnetic anomaly trends and sea-floor heat flux (10^{-6} cal cm^{-2} sec^{-1}) (after Peter *et al.*, 1966).

middle of the Andaman Sea, the local free-air anomaly highs are subdued by the larger negative anomalies which are associated with the sedimentary arc.

There is a major north-northeast trending belt of magnetic (Fig. 2) and gravity anomaly highs along the edge of the continental shelf of the Thai-Malay Peninsula in the northern half of the Andaman Sea. The trend continues into the southern half also, but here it is located in deeper water (> 1000 m). A change in the character of the magnetic field at the 200 m shelf break, and bathymetric indications of faulting in the same area, however, suggest that the west Malaysian shelf is down-faulted in the southern part of the Andaman Sea. Therefore, the magnetic and gravity anomaly trends, represent the edge of the Sunda shelf in this deep-water area as well.

The magnetic and gravity anomalies, together with the occurrence of high heat flow (Fig. 2), clearly mark the extension of the volcanic inner arc from the Barrisan Range of Sumatra north to the Burma Range. The central graben of the Barrisan Range extends into the Andaman Sea and forms a continuous valley up to 10°N latitude.

The general trend (north-northeast) of two other volcanic seamount groups are also indicated in

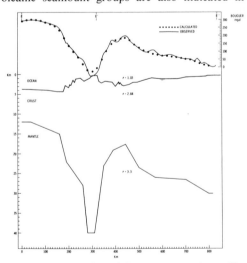

Fig. 3. Bathymetric and Bouguer anomaly profiles and calculated crustal section along the trackline immediately south of Great Nicobar Island (after Peter *et al.*, 1966).

Fig. 2. These join the seamounts of the inner volcanic arc east of the Invisible Bank and the Great Nicobar Island.

A crustal section calculated on the basis of Bouguer anomalies (topographic corrections are applied to the free-air anomalies) is shown in Fig. 3. The accuracy of the depth of the crust-mantle interface is estimated to be 10% for this type of calculation.

The Airy-Heiskanen isostatic anomalies closely resemble the free-air anomalies and suggest that further elevation of the Andaman-Nicobar island platform can be expected.

GEORGE PETER

References

Peter, G., Weeks, L. A., and Burns, R. E., 1966, "A Reconnaissance Geophysical Survey in the Andaman Sea and across the Andaman–Nicobar Island Arc," *J. Geophys. Res.*, vol. 71, No. 2.

ANGULAR MOMENTUM, ANGULAR VELOCITY

An important physical concept appropriate to a rotating globe such as a planet, angular momentum is defined as the moment of the linear momentum of a particle about a point, thus:

$$M = \vec{r} \times m\vec{V}$$

where M is the angular momentum about a point 0, $\vec{r}$ the position vector from 0 to the particle, m the mass of the particle and $\vec{V}$ the velocity.

Angular momentum plays an important role in both the earth's rotation and the coupling of the solid earth to the atmosphere. The speed of rotation (angular velocity) of the earth varies only by small amounts, and these may be related in part to angular momentum lost to or received from the atmosphere. The atmospheric circulation patterns are modified by these energy transfers. The earth's *angular velocity* is the speed of its rotation about the geographic pole, thus its pole of instantaneous rotation, and not with reference to a point in space. The angular velocity is approximately $2\pi/S$, or sidereal day of 86,164.09 seconds, roughly 24 hours, or 15.04106863 seconds of arc per second of time.

As C. G. Rossby (1941) explained it, the earth's angular momentum can easily be visualized by taking a marble on the end of a string and rotating it on a smooth table. If the string is shortened the rate increases; if lengthened it slows. The speed is inversely proportional to radius, the product of the two remaining constant. This product, the angular momentum per unit mass, is a constant unless energy is added or subtracted (Newton's *Law of Conservation of Momentum*, his "first law of motion").

If part of the atmospheric envelope, rotating with the earth at the equator at a speed of 465 m/sec, moves poleward it will tend to speed up. At latitude 60°, the radius (distance from axis of rotation) being reduced to half that at the equator, would indicate that the *linear velocity* of the earth's surface would be reduced to 232 m/sec. However, a frictionless atmosphere here (of the same mass, but halved radius) should be accelerated to double its original velocity, thus 930 m/sec, but the *relative* speed would be higher, the earth's surface linear velocity here being reduced by 232 m/sec, the resultant relative ground speed of the atmosphere being 698 m/sec /1560 mph); the direction would be easterly, since the earth's sense of rotation is from west to east. The velocity would also be reduced owing to friction, etc. In the upper atmosphere (see *Mesosphere* and *Stratosphere*) high-velocity easterlies are often observed, but they are far from universal, being replaced by westerlies under the influence of frictional and differential heating, thermodynamic phenomena (see *Atmospheric Circulation*).

The easterlies have the effect of removing angular momentum from the earth. If they were the only planetary winds, they would cause a gradual deceleration of the earth. The westerlies, however, compensate, and traveling faster than the earth, impart angular momentum to it (through friction). The westerlies thus lose angular momentum to the earth, and they would die out if they had no powerful source of energy. From one or possibly both sides of the westerly belts, the easterlies introduce large eddies such as cyclones and anticyclones set up by

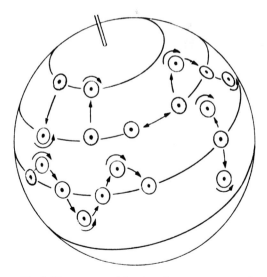

Fig. 1. Planetary vorticity: angular momentum tends to be conserved in columns of constant height as they change latitude along different trajectories (Von Arx, 1962). (By permission of Addison-Wesley, Reading, Mass.)

the shears of the westerlies and in lesser degree by thermodynamic processes that bring in the necessary momentum to keep the westerlies in motion.

An additional important principle, illustrated in Fig. 1, is the conservation of angular momentum in any parcel of air (or water) as it changes latitude.

RHODES W. FAIRBRIDGE

References

Clough, H. W., 1920, "The principle of angular momentum as applied to atmospheric motion," *Monthly Weather Rev.,* **45**(8), 463.

Von Arx, W. S., 1962, "An Introduction to Physical Oceanography," Reading, Mass., Addison-Wesley, 432pp.

Widger, W. K., 1949, "A study of the flow of angular momentum in the atmosphere," *J. Meteorol.,* **6**, 291.

Cross-references: *Atmospheric Circulation; Jet Stream; Oceanic Circulation; Vorticity; Zonal Index.*

ANTARCTIC CONVERGENCE—*See* CONVERGENCE, ANTARCTIC

ANTARCTIC PELAGIC SEDIMENTS: GEOCHEMISTRY

(1) Introduction

Detailed information on the geochemistry of recent Antarctic sediments, and the distribution patterns related thereto, is extremely limited. To understand the chemistry of these sediments, even in an imperfect way, it is necessary to bear in mind that the conditions of sedimentation prevalent in Antarctica are unique.

Recent sedimentation in the Southern Ocean (q.v.) around Antarctica is characterized by complicated and peculiarly local conditions (Lisitzen, 1962) which strongly influence the geochemistry of the sediments. Among these conditions are:

(1) Lack of runoff or river drainage from the continent—the snow line is at sea level.

(2) Lack of large-scale chemical weathering—water on the continent is dominantly in the solid state.

(3) Little chemical precipitation of sediments owing to the low temperature of the Antarctic water which precludes the precipitation of $CaCO_3$.

(4) Luxurious growth of phytoplankton near the edge of the pack ice.

(5) Recent volcanism, especially in the Ross Sea area.

(6) Large-scale glacial erosion and discharge—subsequently the chief means of transporting the sediments from land.

Unlike other sedimentary areas, much of the sedimentary material deposited in the region south of the Antarctic circle accumulates away from the Antarctic Coast in the region of maximum deposition by melting icebergs.

In general, Antarctica is surrounded by three types of sediments, each with its own geochemical characteristics. Immediately encircling the continent is a 200–400 mile wide ring of glacial marine sediment roughly correlative in position with the northern extent of the pack ice. Next to the north is a band of distinctive sedimentary material of variable width commonly referred to as diatom ooze (dominantly siliceous in character) which extends to the general area of the Antarctic Convergence. This in turn is followed by the zone of globigerina ooze (dominantly calcareous) characteristic of wide areas of the southern oceans.

(2) Chemistry of Sediments

(2.1) Major Element Chemistry of Sediments. Glacial marine sediments are essentially devoid of carbonates (0–10% $CaCO_3$, rarely higher, and 0–3% $MgCO_3$); the content of amorphous silica normally is variable between 1–20%, the chief sources of the silica being diatom fistrules and

TABLE 1. CHEMICAL COMPOSITION OF ANTARCTIC PELAGIC SEDIMENTS

Component (%)	Glacial Marine Sediment	Sediments Dominantly Planktonic in Origin	
		Diatom Ooze	Foraminiferal Ooze
$CaCO_3$	0–25	10–50	70–95
$MgCO_3$	0–3	0.4–2	0.3–3
SiO_2 (amorphous)	1–20	30–75	1–10
C (organic)	0.03–2.0	0.09–0.4	0–0.4
P	0.05–0.07	0–0.06	0.02–0.03
N	0.001–0.116	—	—
Fe	2–10	0.1–1	1–6
Mn	0.02–0.45	0.1–1	0.06–0.09
Ti	0–3	0.03–0.6	0.06–0.3
Rate of sedimentation, cm/1000 yr	0.3–30	0.5–2	0.3–2.6

sponge spicules. In the band of siliceous sediments (diatom ooze), the SiO_2 content can reach 75% and clearly is the dominant component—Antarctica is the area of classical diatom sedimentation. Farther north in the zone of globigerina ooze, carbonate is the principal constituent—in places attaining values of 95–98% of the total sediment material. Much of this data is summarized in Table 1.

No distinctive and consistent geographical distribution other than latitudinal is evident. The difference in the major and, on a limited basis, trace element composition in the sediment bands encircling Antarctica is clearly shown in Table 1. Trace element studies *per se* have been restricted primarily to sediment material of the glacial marine type.

(3) Trace Element Chemistry of Sediments

The paucity of data on the trace element content of Antarctic pelagic sediments is striking. Mention of only a few elements is possible; however, that information which is available—primarily from the Ross, Amundson, and Bellingshausen Seas—allows some of the general features to be distinguished. For the three sediment types mentioned earlier, these data are summarized in Table 1, compiled chiefly from the work of Lisitzen (1962) and Angino (1964).

(3.1) Trace Element Content in Glacial Marine Sediments. The trace element composition of Antarctic glacial marine sediments varies con-

siderably, both in absolute concentration and from one area to another. Of the trace element data reported, molybdenum was always less than 20 ppm (0.002%); lead, less than 50 ppm (0.005%); zinc and tungsten, less than 200 ppm (0.02%). Table 2 lists the elements for which information is available (Angino, 1964). It can be seen that for glacial marine sediments as a type, the elements Cr, Ni, Ti, Fe, and Al are deficient when compared to the figures for crustal abundances; Cr and Ni are considerably deficient. This is true even on a geographical basis as is evident from Table 3. Conversely, the elements Cu, V, and Mn are considerably more abundant when compared to the crustal figures, especially the first two. The reasons for these variations are not clear. Reference to Table 3 indicates clearly the differences in trace element content existent between the Ross, Bellingshausen, and Amundsen Seas. Such data likely reflects differences in source rock, but again proof is lacking.

Studies of long cores taken from the different areas show that down the core repeated changes in sediment type and trace element content can be delimited. Such changes strongly suggest that considerable climatic changes have taken place during late Quaternary time as a result of which the boundaries of the main sediment bands have shifted northward or southward accordingly. Those strata with a marked increase in manganese concentration (frequently found in these pelagic sediments) probably correspond to periods with a lower depositional rate, resulting in decreased dilution by terrigenous silicates of the oxide minerals formed in place. In terms of the other elements noted, considerable vertical variations in trace element content down a core are reported, again suggesting changes in sedimentation rate during Quaternary time.

Aluminosilicates constitute a major part of the inorganic mineral content of the sediment. Owing to this, absolute concentration figures for aluminum are useful indicators of the per cent insoluble portion of the sediment. In one core (78° 08'S, 162° 51'E) from the western Ross Sea, the Cu/Al ratio remained essentially constant (13×10^{-4} to

TABLE 2. TRACE ELEMENT CONTENT IN GLACIAL MARINE SEDIMENT (PPM UNLESS OTHERWISE INDICATED)

Element	Range	Average	Crustal Abundance
Cr.	40–130	90	200
Ni	20–70	40	80
Co	10–40	30	23
V	80–560	200	110
Cu	40–480	140	45
Mn	400–4400	1400	1000
Ti	2400–6000	3600	4400
Fe, %	2.0–5.5	3.7	5.0
Al, %	4.1–11.3	7.3	8.1

TABLE 3. GEOGRAPHICAL DISTRIBUTION OF TRACE ELEMENTS IN GLACIAL MARINE SEDIMENT (PPM UNLESS OTHERWISE INDICATED)

	Cr	Ni	Mn	% Fe	% Al	Ti	Co	V	Cu
Ross Sea	95	40	1240	3.40	6.8	3470	30	160	90
Amundsen Sea	90	40	1730	4.10	7.5	3960	30	240	185
Bellinghausen Sea	70	30	960	3.5	7.6	3040	20	185	120
Crustal abundance	200	80	1000	5.0	8.1	4400	23	110	45

18×10^{-4}) down the length of the core (Angino, 1964), indicating that copper is being transported into the basin of deposition. No data on other elemental ratios with Al have been reported from this region.

ERNEST E. ANGINO

References

Angino, E. E., 1964, "Trace elements in Antarctic bottom sediments," *Bull. U.S. Antarctic Project Officer*, **5**, No. 10, 164–166.

Lisitzen, A. P., 1962, "Bottom sediments of the Antarctic," in (Wexler, H., Rubin, M. J., and Caskey, J. E., Jr., editors) "Antarctic research," *Geophysical Monograph, No.* 7, NAS-NRC, No. 1036, 81–88.

AQUALUNGS—*See* SCUBA

ARABIAN SEA

The geographic boundaries of the Arabian Sea, according to the International Hydrographic Bureau (Sp. Publ. 23, 1953), are established in the southwest by a line from Ras Hafun (Somalia) to Addu Atoll, thence up the western edge of the Maldives and Laccadives to Sadashivgad Light on the west coast of India (14°48′N 74°07′E). The *Gulf of Aden* is marked off by the meridian of Cape Guadafui (Ras Asir, 51°15′E) and the *Gulf of Oman* by a line from Ras Limah (25°57′N) in Oman to Ras al Kuh (25°48′N) in Iran.

From an oceanographic point of view, Schott (1935) bounded the Arabian Sea as follows: the southern boundary runs from the Indian coast near Goa, along the west side of the Laccadive Islands to the equator; thence, it trends slightly to the south to a point on the East African coast near Mombasa at approximately 5°S latitude. Exclusive of the Gulfs of Aden and Oman, this covers an area of 7,456,000 km² (2,880,000 square miles statute). It includes 95% of the Arabian Basin but only the northern two-thirds and the deepest part of the Somali Basin. The area between the Laccadive Islands and Ceylon (recognized as the Laccadive Sea by I.H.B.) is excluded from the Arabian Sea on the basis of water mass considerations.

Although the Arabian Sea has been crossed by many famous expeditions (*Dana, Albatross,* etc.), its first systematic study was by the John Murray Expedition (*Mahabis*).

During the International Indian Ocean Expedition, 1960–65, United States, British, Russian and German ships collected oceanographic and geologic data in the Arabian Sea. These investigations covered detailed studies of its currents, water masses, bottom topography and sediments. The following description, however, is based primarily on earlier data.

Bottom Topography and Sediments

The Arabian Sea is divided into two major basins by the northwest-southeast trending *Carlsberg Ridge,* the northwesterly extension of the Mid-Indian Ridge. These basins in turn are bordered by two semicontinental submarine plateaus; one, in the southwest extends from approximately 15°S, 65°E as the *Seychelles Mauritius Ridge,* reaching northwest to the Seychelles and the Amirantes, while the eastern plateau follows approximately the meridian 73°E from the Chagos Islands and runs up through the Maldives and Laccadives, connecting with the southwest Indian shelf. The top of this plateau shows depths of less than 1800 m (1000 fathoms) over most of its length. In contrast, the mean depth of the Carlsberg Ridge is between 1800 m (1000 fathoms) and 3600 m (2000 fathoms). Depths greater than 3600 m (2000 fathoms) have been observed in the median rift valley in the center of the mid-ocean ridge (Heezen and Ewing, 1963). The rift turns west, north of Socotra, joining the East African rifts southwest of the Gulf of Aden. The Arabian Sea is thus separated into two basins whose depths exceed 3600 m (2000 fathoms), the *Arabian Basin* in the northeast and the *Somali Basin* in the southwest. The Somali Basin also connects with the Mascarenes and Madagascar Basins to the south, with sill depths greater than 3600 m (2000 fathoms). The deepest portion of the Somali Basin exceeds 4600 m (2500 fathoms), with deepest soundings up to 5300 m (2900 fathoms). The sill depth between the Arabian and Somali Basins is approximately 3000 m (1700 fathoms).

Off the southern tip of India, the continental shelf is approximately 120 km (60 nautical miles) wide, with depths up to 220 m (120 fathoms). To the north, the shelf narrows to 56 km (30 nautical miles) at 11°N but widens to 352 km (190 nautical miles) off the Gulf of Cambay, with depths of 90 m (50 fathoms). The outer shelf is largely sand covered, but mud occurs in places along the coast. The shelf remains 185 km (100 nautical miles) or more in width as far north as Karachi; in this region, the shelf is primarily mud covered with some sand on the outer edge. The shelf is cut by a submarine canyon off the Indus River. West of Karachi, the shelf narrows abruptly, and off Baluchistan and southern Iran (the Makran coast), the shelf averages 37 km (20 nautical miles) with a gradual decrease in width to the west. The edge of the shelf is much shallower along this Makran coast with depths averaging 37 m (20 fathoms). The shelf here is primarily mud covered.

The Gulf of Oman has a broad mud-covered shelf at its head, but depths greater than 1800 m (1000 fathoms) are found in the Oman Basin, which extends from Oman to form a trough parallel to the Makran Coast, separated by a narrow ridge from the Arabian Basin proper. This ridge, the Murray Ridge, also extends southwest to meet the Carlsberg

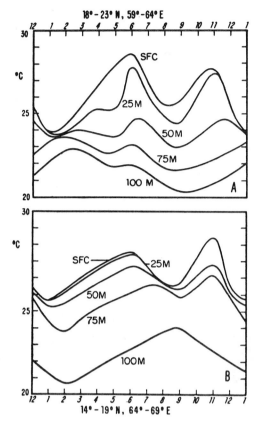

18° – 23° N, 59° – 64° E

14° – 19° N, 64° – 69° E

Fig. 1. Annual temperature variation in the Arabian Sea from bathythermograph observations.

Ridge. The shelf is narrow all along the Arabian coast. The bottom is sand covered, primarily of terrigenous or eolian derivation. The shelf is approximately 37 km (20 nautical miles) across in the Gulf of Aden at the entrance to the Red Sea, where it is cut by a channel with depths greater than 183 m (100 fathoms). From Cape Guardafui to Mombassa along the Somali coast, the extremely narrow shelf is suggestive of a fault coast.

Sediments of terrigenous origin cover the Arabian Sea continental slope down to approximately 2750 m (1500 fathoms). Red clay deposits cover a large part of the basins below 4000 m. The balance is covered by calcareous (globigerina) ooze (Stubbings, 1939). Wiseman and Bennett (1939) analyzed the organic carbon and nitrogen in the sediments. Neprochnov (1961) prepared a chart of sediment thickness in the Arabian Basin based on 23 seismic refraction stations. The sediment thickness decreases from 2.5 km in the northern portion to 0.5 km in the southern part of the Arabian Basin. Seismic refraction work by the Scripps *Zephyrus* Expedition revealed a sediment thickness of 0.87 km at 8°19′N–70°32′E in agreement with Neprochnov's chart. At 9°5′N–73°E on the western slope of the Maldive-Laccadive Ridge, a sediment thickness of

1.87 km was found. Neprochnov's data also indicated a thickening of the sediments west of the Nine Degree Channel between the Maldive and Laccadive Islands.

The five deep cores collected in the Somali Basin during the Swedish Deep-Sea Expedition, 1947–48, are described in detail by Kolbe (1960) and Olausson (1960). Preliminary findings from the 104 cores collected in 1960 during the 33rd voyage of the Russian research vessel *Vityaz* are discussed by Bezrukov (1961).

The origin and geological history of the Arabian Sea ridge and basin topography are still a matter of hypothesis, involving the theories of continental drift, land bridges and permanency of ocean basins and continents (Termier and Termier, 1952; Ahmad, 1961; see also *Gondwanaland*, pr Vol. V). Geologists, however, are rather generally agreed that the Arabian Sea evolved during the Mesozoic-Cenozoic eras and important segments were only established during the Pliocene.

Surface Currents

The monsoon winds (q.v.) are the dominating factor in the surface currents. The northeast monsoon prevails from November until March; the winds are light to moderate and it is the mild season here. There is little precipitation since the winds blow from the land. The weak northeast monsoon drift current flows south along the Indian coast; then, at about 10°N it turns west; one branch flows into the Gulf of Aden and the other south along the Somali coast. There is a convergence line between the Arabian Sea water and the North Equatorial Current which comes from the east, south of Ceylon, because of the contrast in surface salinity between these waters of different origin.

The atmospheric pressure and the wind distribution north of the equator change drastically during April with the introduction of the stronger, moisture-laden southwest monsoon winds; these continue until November. The sea surface currents react almost immediately to the wind change. A branch of the South Equatorial Current now turns north between 5°S and the equator, and flows along the coast into the Arabian Sea as the strong *Somali Current* (q.v.), with speeds up to 7 knots.*Beyond Socotra, the Somali Current becomes part of an anticyclonic circulation which continues to the northeast along the coast of Arabia, thence, south along the coast of India to 10°N. At this point, it joins the southwest monsoon drift current, flowing east between 5 and 10°N; then both continue east, south of Ceylon. Pronounced upwelling occurs along the African and Arabian coasts during this period.

* Maximum speeds of more than 6 knots were observed at 8°N in August 1964 (Stommel and Wooster. 1965).

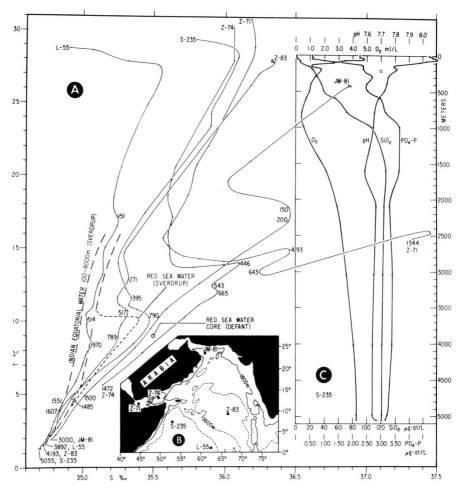

Fig. 2. (A) Typical T–S curves: J.M.–81 John Murray Expedition, December 1933. S–235 Swedish Deep-Sea Expedition, April 1948. L–55 Scripps Lusiad Expedition, August 1962. Z–71, Z–74, Z–83 Scripps Zephyrus Expedition, September 1962.

(B) Bottom topography of the Arabian Sea and station locations (after Shepard, 1963). (By permission of Harper's Pub. Co., New York, N.Y.)

(C) O_2, pH, Si, PO_4–P distributions for Station S–235.

Seasonal variation in the Upper Layers of the Arabian Sea

Considerable seasonal variation in temperature occurs between the surface and 100 m in the central Arabian Sea (see Fig. 1) (Robinson, 1960). Minimum temperatures (24–25°C) at the surface occur in January and February, and there are two maxima greater than 28°C—one in June, the other in November—and a secondary minimum (26°C) in August. At 100 m, in the area 18–23°N, 59–64°E, the maximum temperature (22°C) is in February, the minimum (20°C) at 100 m in September. In contrast, in the area 14–19°N, 64–69°E, the minimum temperature (20°C) at 100 m is in February and the maximum (24°C) in September. The

September minimum in the first area is related to upwelling along the Arabian coast.

During the rainy season (northwest monsoon) salinities of less than 35‰ have been observed in the upper 50 m; during the northeast monsoon, on the other hand, salinities greater than 36‰ are found at the surface over the entire Arabian Sea north of 5°N with the exception of the Somali coast, where values less than 35.5‰ are found. The source of this lower-salinity water is the less saline South Equatorial Current, which is further diluted by upwelling.

Water Masses between 200 and 4000 m

Sverdrup *et al.* (1946) described an Indian Ocean Equatorial Water mass between 200 and 4000 m and indicated an intrusion of high-salinity Red Sea water with a core at approximately 750 m, with temperatures of 10°C and salinities of 35.4‰. Defant (1961) identified the core of the Red Sea water with temperatures of 9°C and salinities of 35.5‰. There appears to be also a spread of Persian Gulf water, according to Schott (1935), associated with a secondary salinity maximum between 200 and 400 m.

In Fig. 2, the T-S curves for six hydrographic stations (Bruneau *et al.* 1954; Sewell, 1935–36; University of California, MSS) demonstrate the spread of both Persian Gulf and Red Sea water and the extent to which they differ from Sverdrup's and Defant's preliminary definitions. All stations with the exception of J.M.–81 were taken during the southwest monsoon. Stations L–55 and S–235 in the Somali Basin showed minimum salinities at the surface associated with precipitation during the southwest monsoon period. Station Z–71 and Z–74 in the Gulf of Aden, and Z–83 in the Arabian Basin do not reflect an excess of precipitation over evaporation at the surface. At stations J.M.–81, at the mouth of the Gulf of Oman, maximum salinities of 36.89‰ occurred at the surface during the period of the northeast monsoon. Beneath the surface, the salinities decrease at all stations until the influence of Persian Gulf and Red Sea water is encountered. This occurs at different levels on each of the stations.

Below 1500 m all station curves converge and take on the character of Indian Ocean Deep and Bottom Waters with temperatures between 1.3 and 2.0°C and salinities of 34.69–34.77‰. The source of these waters is in the Antarctic.

Sill depths between the Somali and Arabian Basins have been deduced from the minimum temperatures observed in the two areas. Temperatures of 1.30°C occur in the Somali Basin, while in the central Arabian Sea minimum temperatures of 1.66°C were found. These values indicate that the sill between the Somali and Arabian Basins is at a depth of approximately 3000 m.

A second insert in Fig. 2 presents curves of O_2, pH, PO_4–P and SiO_2 for station S–235. Oxygen values show a maximum of 4.74 ml/liter at 70 m, a rapid decrease to a secondary minimum of 1.1 ml/liter at 109 m and a minimum of 0.45 ml/liter at 790 m (the core of the Red Sea water). Below this level, the oxygen increases, reaching values greater than 3.0 ml/liter below 2088 m where Antarctic source water can first be recognized. Oxygen continues to increase with depth, reaching 4.27 ml/liter at a depth of 5055 m.

The pH distribution is similar to that of oxygen with the exception that the minimum pH value (7.59) occurs at a depth of 1607 m. Below 2100 m, the pH is relatively constant (7.64) to a depth of 5000 m. There is an increase in pH at the bottom to 7.67 indicating the solution of carbonate from the bottom sediments (Mohamed, 1940).

The SiO_2 and PO_4–P distributions are somewhat similar, with very low values in the surface layer above the thermocline and relatively constant high values beneath 2100 m. The increase of the properties between 100 and 2100 m is somewhat different, indicating different rates of utilization of these properties by organisms.

Recent observations of the *Vityaz* (Bezrukov, 1961) confirm the observations of the John Murray Expedition (Sewell, 1935–36) of the existence of hydrogen sulfide on the continental slope between depths of 40 and 1000 m in the northern part of the Arabian Sea (Oman Basin). The hydrogen sulfide is found at depths coinciding with the minimum oxygen layers.

Margaret K. Robinson

References

Ahmad, F., 1961, "Palaeography of the Gondwana period in Gondwanaland . . .," *India,* **90**, 142pp.

Baker, B. H., and Miller, J. A., 1963, "Geology and geochronology of the Seychelles Islands and the structure of the floor of the Arabian Sea," *Nature,* **199**, 346–348.

Bezrukov, P. L., 1961, "Research on the Indian Ocean during the 33rd voyage of the research vessel *Vityaz* in 'Oceanology'," *Acad. Sci. USSR,* No. 4, 745–753.

Bruneau, L., Jerlov, N. G., and Koczy, F. F., 1954, "Physical and chemical methods," No. 4, *Rep. Swedish Deep-Sea Expedition 1947–48,* **3**, 101–112.

Defant, Albert, 1961, "Physical Oceanography," Vol. I, London, Pergamon Press, 707pp.

Heezen, Bruce C., and Ewing, Maurice, 1963, "The Mid-Oceanic Ridge," in (Hill, M. N., editor) "The Sea," Vol. 3, pp. 388–408, New York, Interscience Publishers.

Koble, R. W., 1960, "Sediment cores from the Indian Ocean," No. 1, *Rept. Swedish Deep-Sea Expedition 1947–48,* **9**, 50pp.

Mohamed, A. F., 1940, "The distribution of hydrogen-ion concentration in the North-Western Indian Ocean and adjacent waters," No. 5, *The John Murray Expedition 1933–34,* **2**, 122–202.

Neprochnov, IU. P., 1961, "Sedimentary thickness in the Arabian Sea Basin," *Dokl. Akad. Nauk SSR,* **139**, No. 1, 177–179.

Olausson, Eric, 1969, "Sediment cores from the Indian Ocean," No. 2, *Rep. Swedish Deep-Sea Expedition 1947–48,* **9**, 88pp.

Robinson, Margaret K., 1960, "Indian Ocean vertical temperature sections," *Deep-Sea Res.,* **6**, 249–258.

Schott, G., 1935, "Geographie des Indischen und Stillen Ozeans," Hamburg, Verlag Boysen, 413pp.

Sewell, R. B. S., 1935–36, "Introduction and list of stations," *The John Murray Expedition 1933–34,* **1**, 1–15.

Shepard, F. P., 1963, "Submarine Geology," New York, Harper's, 557pp.

Stubbings, H. G., 1939, "The marine deposits of the Arabian Sea," No. 2, *The John Murray Expedition 1933–34,* **3**, 31–158.

Sverdrup, H. U., Johnson, M. W., and Fleming, R. H., 1946, "The Oceans," Englewood Cliffs, N.J., Prentice-Hall, 1087pp.

Termier, H., and Termier, G., 1952, "Histoire Géologique de la biosphere," Masson, Paris, 721pp.

Thompson, E. F., 1939, "The Exchange of Water Between the Red Sea and the Gulf of Aden Over the 'Sill',"

University of California, Scripps Institution of Oceanography: Zephyrus and Lusiad Expeditions, 1962, Temperature, Salinity and Seismic Data (unpublished).

Wiseman, John D. H., and Bennet, H., 1939, "The distribution of organic carbon and nitrogen in sediments from the Arabian Sea," No. 4, *The John Murray Expedition 1933–34*, **3**, 194–221.

ARAFURA SEA

(1) Limits and Oceanography

(a) Limits and Dimensions. Bordered by the Outer Banda Arc, West Irian (former Dutch New Guinea), Torres Strait, the Gulf of Carpentaria, and 130°E longitude, the Arafura Sea covers an area of 650,000 km² (center: 10°S, 137°E). Its northern limit is located arbitrarily east of Ceram, where the Arafura Sea merges with the Ceram Sea (Fig. 1). The Arafura Sea largely covers a vast shallow bank (named *Arafura Shelf* by Krummel in 1897) belonging to the eastern part of the large Northern Australian or Sahul Shelf (*sensu lato*), first recognized by Earl in 1845; only its central part is now called "Sahul Shelf" (q.v.). The Arafura Shelf is separated from the Outer Banda Arc by the deep Aru Trough (−3650 meters). In plan, this trough is elongate and convex toward the shelf, closely following the outline of the Banda Arcs. The Aru depression is part of a long zone of troughs extending from the Ceram Sea, through the Aru and Timor troughs into the Java Trench in the Indian Ocean (see *Trench*). Steep sides, a flat floor, and abrupt termination against Irian are other characteristics of the Aru Trough. Toward the southwest, it continues as a narrow, shallow depression (about 1600 meters deep and 40 km wide) till about 130°E longitude where it broadens and deepens into the Timor Trough. The Aru Trough below the 3000-meter isobath has an area of 11,000 km². Its deepest entrances are located at the extremities leading into the Ceram and the Timor seas where the separating sills are both 1480 meters deep.

Depths on the Arafura Shelf generally range between 50 and 80 meters. Deeper parts are located near the edge where corals rise steeply from depths of 600 meters. The Aru islands form the most extensive land area on the shelf. The five larger islands of this group are mutually separated by narrow, river-like straits ("sungeis") with depths greater than the surrounding shelf bottom (Fairbridge, 1953). From the Aru islands, an inconspicuous rise (Merauke Ridge) extends southeastward along the south coast of Irian toward the York Peninsula in Australia forming the Oriomo Axis or Merauke zone (Van Bemmelen, 1949, p. 721).

Fig. 1. The Arafura Sea, eastern Indonesia. Map shows bathymetry, flow of bottom water (arrows) and bottom sediments.

T: terrigenous mud; G: Globigerina ooze. Striped area in the Aru Trough is below the 3000 meters isobath. Data from the Snellius Expedition 1929–1930.

TABLE 1. DEEP-WATER PROPERTIES WITHIN THE ARU TROUGH AND OUTSIDE ITS TWO SILLS AT THE INDICATED SNELLIUS STATIONS AND OBSERVATION DEPTHS (BOTH SILLS ARE 1480 METERS DEEP)

	Outside in Timor Sea, Station 109, 1473 meters	Within trough Station 104, 3265 meters	Outside in Ceram Sea, Station 95, 1500 meters
Temperature, °C	3.38	3.945	3.935
Salinity, ‰	34.64	34.63	34.63
Oxygen, cc/liter	2.49	2.25	2.32
Density	1027.585	1027.52	1027.52

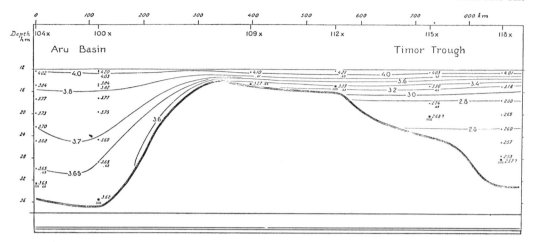

Fig. 2. Section between Timor Trough and Aru Trough showing potential temperature and salinity. After Van Riel, Snellius Expedition (Van Riel, 1934).

(b) Deep-water Properties and Flow of Bottom Water. Based on the bathymetric data and properties of the water within the Aru depression such as salinity, oxygen content and temperature, collected by the Dutch oceanographic Snellius Expedition in 1929/1930, Van Riel (1950) concluded that the Aru Trough receives new bottom water from the Indian Ocean through the Timor Trough and also from the Pacific Ocean through the Molucca and Ceram seas (Fig. 1).

Figure 2 shows the distribution of potential temperatures (corrected temperatures after the elimination of the influence of compression) and salinities near the entrance between the Aru and Timor troughs.

(c) Surface Properties and Meteorology. Surface salinities in the Arafura Sea are shown as averages in Table 2.

TABLE 2. AVERAGE SURFACE SALINITIES IN ‰

Periods	North Aru Trough	South Aru Trough	Arafura Shelf
December–February	33.6	34.2	34.2
March–May	—	34.6	—
June–August	33.9	34.4	35.0
September–November	34.8	34.3	—

The sea surface temperatures attain their maximum values in December–February (28.4°C) and their lowest in June–August (26.1°C). In the southern summer, winds blow from west northwest (Northwest monsoon) in the area of the Arafura Sea between 4 and 10°S with strengths of 1.5–4.4 (Beaufort scale). Off the coast of Australia, the wind direction is north northwest (1.5–2.4). During the southern winter, the southeast monsoon winds blow with equal strengths of 1.5–2.4 across the whole Arafura Sea. For the same periods, the air pressures are respectively 756.5–756 mm (from north to south) and 757.5–759 mm (from north to south).

(d) Currents and Tides. Surface currents in the Arafura Sea north of the 8°S latitude have irregular directions and are generally unsteady. South of this latitude the currents are predominantly westward running at 10–20 nautical miles per day (n mi/day) during the southern winter. In the southern summer the currents have no general directions; in the southwest and southeast parts of the sea, the currents are directed outward, respectively into the Indian Ocean and the Coral Sea. A third system revolves counterclockwise around 10°S, 136°E. Speeds do not exceed 10 n mi/day.

Tidal ranges in the Arafura Sea reach 4.5 meters at springs on the coast of Irian (average of 4 gauging stations) and 2.5 meters at Dobo in the Aru islands. At one locality on the Irian coast, Muli Strait, the maximum tidal current recorded is 4.6 n mi/day toward the north northeast. Off the Australian coast, tidal currents of 5–10 n mi/day occur.

The Snellius Expedition made current measurements in October 1930 at station 364a; this was in the strait between the Tanimbar and Kai island groups, connecting the Arafura with the Banda seas (Fig. 3).

TABLE 3. CURRENT MEASUREMENTS AT SNELLIUS STATION 364a

Depth:			
0 meters	46 cm/sec	N 75° W	
100 meters	22 cm/sec	N 20° E	
400 meters	13 cm/sec	S 60° W	
3000 meters	4 cm/sec	N 20° E	

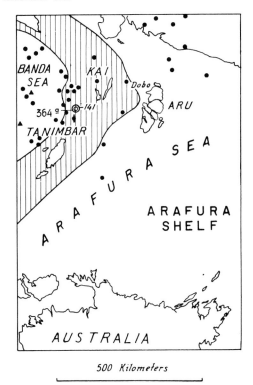

Fig. 3. The Arafura Sea, eastern Indonesia. Gravimetry (shading indicates the belt of negative anomalies), active volcanoes (triangles) and earthquake foci (dots: less than 100 km depth; with one stripe: 100–199 kilometers; with two stripes: 200–299 km).

(2) Bottom Sediments

(a) Aru Trough. Terrigenous muds with quartz grains (probably turbidities) cover the deeper parts of the Aru Trough. Slopes of the trough about 200–2000 meters are covered by Globigerina ooze (30% or more calcium carbonate).

The deposition of the terrigenous mud takes place at a slow rate, which is also shown by the high glauconite content in the bottom samples from this trough. Another evidence of little sedimentation in the area expresses itself in the clear water around the Aru islands favoring extensive coral growth. Up to several kilometers inland, corals are growing in the tidal channels ("Sungeis").

(b) Arafura Shelf. Terrigenous deposition is also slow on the Arafura Shelf. The bottom sediments are best classified as glauconitic sand and calcareous mud (Fairbridge, 1953). Near the Australian coast, extensive expanses of hard bottom point to nondeposition for lack of sufficient material, because the tidal currents are only moderate (0.5 to 1.0 n mi/day). Also coral debris washed from drowned reefs and located in places along the shelf edge suggest fossil coastlines of a Pleistocene glaciation, after which little deposition has occurred.

(3) Geophysics and Geological Structure

The Aru Trough is marked by gravity anomalies ranging between -11 to $+25$ mgal. Over the Arafura Shelf, only small positive gravity anomalies have been observed.

Weak to moderate earthquakes of shallow type occur in the Aru Trough and are irregularly distributed along the shelf edge. Toward the South Banda Basin, increasingly deeper foci have been recorded (at 600–700 km depths). Berlage, Vening Meinesz, Gutenberg and Benioff have discussed the geological implications of such a distribution of hypocenters.

Kuenen has classified the Aru Trough into his fourth group of deep-sea depressions; i.e., it is thought to have formed predominantly by downwarping but with local faulting. The morphology of the trough has been advanced as evidence for this assumption; this includes its parallelism with the outer Banda geanticline, its elongate plan, and its cross section resembling that of a syncline. Faulting or flexuring is indicated by the abrupt termination in the north against Irian and a more U-shaped section in that region. The Aru Trough may also be classified into the class of marginal deeps (see Kuenen, 1950). It appears to be part of an extensive series of eugeosynclines *in statu nascendi*, according to Fairbridge (see *Geosynclines*, pr Vol. V).

Raised terraces of Recent corals on the neighboring islands suggest a young origin for the Aru Trough. Its parallelism with the Banda arcs suggests a common origin. The latter were largely formed in the Plio-Pleistocene (Van Bemmelen, 1949).

A thin veneer of young Neogene and Quaternary sediments nonconformably overlie the pre-Tertiary basement of the Arafura Shelf. They outcrop on the Aru islands and in southern New Guinea. Nearer to Australia, there occur submarine shelf valleys and narrow canyons (see Fig. 4) evidently submerged arid land forms (Fairbridge, 1953). Contemporary Australian and New Guinea fauna and flora are represented in the Aru islands. Such evidences imply that during the larger part of the Tertiary the Arafura Shelf area was developing into a peneplain, which was submerged in the Upper Neogene and part of the Quaternary. Eustatic emergence during the maximum Pleistocene glaciation partially exhumed the old peneplain. At this time, faunal migrations occurred freely over the shelf area. The postglacial submergence of the Arafura Shelf was by the eustatic rise of sea level for the most part of the shelf, but was accompanied by active subsidence of the margins as indicated by the coral reefs standing in 400–600 meters depths. The Aru islands indicate positive uplift along the Merauke Ridge (see Van Bemmelen, 1949).

H. D. TJIA

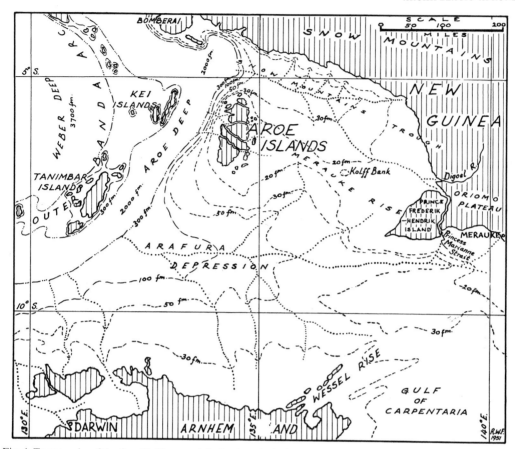

Fig. 4. Topography of Arafura Shelf exposed during last glaciation, showing fluvial pattern (after Fairbridge, 1953).

References

*Fairbridge, R. W., 1953, "The Sahul Shelf, Northern Australia: Its structure and geological relationships," *J. Roy. Soc. W. Australia*, **37**, 1–33.

*Kuenen, Ph. H., 1950, "Marine Geology," Ch. 3, pp. 175–209, New York, John Wiley & Sons.

*Van Bemmelen, R. W., 1949, "The Geology of Indonesia. General Geology," Vol. IA, pp. 257–297, 721–722, The Hague, Martinus Nijhoff.

*Van Riel, P. M., Hamaker, H. C., and Van Eyck, L., 1950, "The Snellius Expedition. Tables. Serial and Bottom Observations. Temperature, Salinity and Density," Vol. 2, Part 6, pp. 1–44, Leiden, Brill.

ARCHIPELAGIC APRONS

Isolated seamounts rising from the deep ocean floor possess a volcanic foundation in the form of a cone, with dips diminishing with increasing depth up to diameters of 20–500 km. Rows of seamounts and/or emergent islands often cluster or overlap to form volcanic ridges or archipelagoes. The broad cone or fan-like slopes were named "archipelagic aprons" by Menard (1956). Generally they are smooth, but in certain instances they are hilly or even mountainous. These are most common in the central and south Pacific. In composition they appear to be underlain by lava flows, in part succeeded by, or alternating with, layers of turbidite transported pelagic material with minor *in situ* pelagic material and small areas of ash. Since submarine landslides from insular volcanic slopes are very common (Fairbridge, 1950), the unconsolidated ash and pelagic muds are liable to slump and develop turbidity current flows that carry the sediment far out beyond the usual limit of lava flows. Menard observed that the largely volcanic nucleus of the aprons is probably of the same material as the "second layer" (seismic velocity 4–5 km/sec) that underlies deep oceanic sediments (probably the pre-sedimentary volcanic crust; see *Abyssal Hills*).

Most aprons, according to Menard, form a smooth curve grading up into the insular slopes. These two geomorphic types are thus superficially analogous, respectively, to continental rises and continental slopes; the aprons, in contrast to continental rises, are more characterized by volcanic intercalations. The upper parts of the aprons are inclined at 1–2°, but at 70–90 km from the island, the inclination is reduced to 1 in 2000, flattening very gradually in the manner of abyssal plains (q.v.). Much of the area between the volcanic ridges is covered by *archipelagic plains*. The upper slopes may have deep-sea channels (turbidity current raceways). The microtopography of the lower aprons and archipelagic plains is remarkably smooth, but distally the tops of abyssal hills project through them, and in the open parts of the oceans (away from belts of heavy sediments), the outer limits pass into the "endless fields of abyssal hills of the Pacific Basin" (Menard, 1964, p. 83).

Some aprons are dotted with parasitic volcanic cones, e.g., east of Tahiti. Menard believes the Hawaiian archipelagic apron has been structurally deformed. Around the Hawaiian ridge, there is a broad saucer-like depression or "moat," but the sedimentary apron crosses this smoothly to reach the encircling "arch." Thus the new apron slopes up away from the islands, suggesting that the moat developed by subsidence after most of the apron was formed; Oahu has subsided 500 meters since the Miocene, and if this lowering were removed, the moat would disappear and the apron would have its usual shape.

Seismic refraction work over aprons in the western Pacific (Gaskell, Raitt, Shor, reported by Menard, 1964) shows that the average thickness of sediment in them is 400 meters, while the probably volcanic "second layer" under them is 2.4 km. In contrast, the sediment is about 200 meters thick in the abyssal hill provinces nearby, and the "second layer" is only 1.1 km thick beneath them. Thus the volcanic crust is greatly thickened under the volcanic ridges. Menard suggests that the lavas were initially of the very fluid type, such as form plateaus

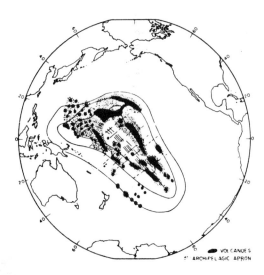

Fig. 2. Distribution of archipelagic aprons around volcanic belts and seamounts in the central Pacific (Menard, 1964). The three contours represent the mean degree of submergence (from the inside = 1500 meters 1000 meters, 500 meters), since the guyot tops were drowned, thus terminating most seamount erosion and principal apron building. (By permission of McGraw-Hill Book Co., N.Y.)

(mainly tholeiites) while the steep-sided cones represent the more viscous types. Some fissure-type liquid flows could be expected on the lower flanks in subsequent effusions, especially if deep-seated fracturing accompanied moat-type subsidence. Most of the smaller guyots and atolls lack moats. In some cases, e.g., the Emperor Seamounts and the Line Islands, moats of 0.5–1.5 km depth are known.

According to Menard (1964, p. 95) in the entire Pacific Basin, assuming an average thickness of 2 km for archipelagic aprons (sediment plus volcanics), the total volume would be 20×10^6 km^3 compared with about 4×10^6 km^3 for all volcanic islands, seamounts and ridges put together. No calculation of archipelagic aprons in the other oceans has yet been made, but they appear to be present around a number of the volcanic features as well as "aseismic ridges."

RHODES W. FAIRBRIDGE

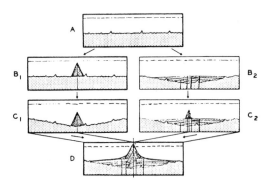

Fig. 1. Possible sequences of development of archipelagic aprons. In A, B_1, C_1, D sequence, a line of submarine volcanoes (seen in cross section) develops on a rough sea floor, the load depresses the crust, and lava and sediment fill in the depression. All stages in this sequence have been found on sea floor. In other sequence, a lava plain covers irregular sea floor, a line of volcanoes grows on plain, and apron develops. Stages B_2 and C_2 have not been observed (Menard, 1956).

References

Fairbridge, R. W., 1950, "Landslide patterns on oceanic volcanoes and atolls," *Geograph. J.*, **115**, 84–88.

Heezen, B. C., Ewing, M., and Tharp, M., 1959, "The floors of the oceans: I. The North Atlantic," *Geol. Soc. Am. Spec. Papers*, **65**, 113pp.

Menard, H. W., 1956, "Archipelagic aprons," *Bull. Am. Assoc. Petrol. Geologists*, **40**, 2195–2210.

Menard, H. W., 1964, "Marine Geology of the Pacific," New York, McGraw-Hill Book Co., 271pp.

ARCTIC OCEAN

The Arctic Ocean is the smallest of the earth's oceans, having an area of 14,000,000 km², and is unique in several significant respects: (1) it is nearly land-locked; (2) it is divided by three submarine ridges, the Alpha Ridge, the Lomonosov Ridge and a trans-Arctic Ocean extension of the mid-Atlantic ridge; (3) one third of its floor is continental shelf; and (4) it hosts a perennial surface cover of pack ice.

Because of its isolation from centers of population, inclement weather and perpetual ice cover, the Arctic Ocean is the most poorly studied of the earth's oceans. By the late nineteenth century, most of its coast-line had been fairly well charted, although the greater part of the ocean itself was still unexplored. The northward extent of Greenland and the island groups to the west were unknown. The opinions of geographers were divided concerning the distribution of land and sea. Many joined the German geographer Petermann in believing that Greenland extended across the North Pole to Wrangel Land, now Wrangel Island; others believed that the unknown central polar region consisted of numerous islands separated by shallow waters. The ill-fated drift of the *Jeannette* (1879–81) demonstrated that Wrangel Island was not contiguous with Greenland. During the years 1893–96 Nansen's ship *Fram* drifted, with the ice pack, across the Arctic Basin from the New Siberian Islands to Spitsbergen and obtained eleven soundings which showed water depths ranging from 3400 to 4000 meters and establishing for the first time that a deep basin underlies at least part of the North Polar Sea. These soundings may properly be regarded as the true discovery of the Arctic "Ocean." As late as 1949 the Arctic Ocean was still believed to be comprised of a single, presumably homogeneous, deep basin.

Physiography and Geology

In discussing the topography of the Arctic Ocean Basin, one is confronted by a bewildering absence of standardization in nomenclature. An attempt will be made in the following discussion to arrive

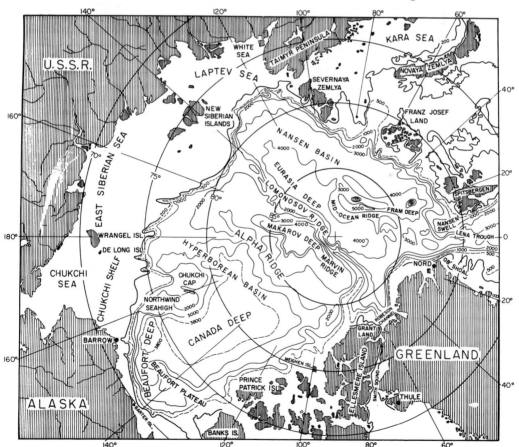

Fig. 1. Physiography of the Arctic Ocean Basin. Recommendations have been made that Alpha Ridge be designated *A. Cordillera* and Mid-Ocean Ridge *Nansen Cordillera*. Further, Canada and Makarov Deeps become *Basins*, Hyperborean Basin the *Amerasia Basin*, Eurasia Deep the *E. Basin* and Nansen Basin becomes *Fram Basin*.

49

at logical compromises in selecting geographic names, priority being given to names dating from discovery and to those most commonly used.

By virtue of its classic usage, the term "Arctic Basin" or "Arctic Ocean Basin" will be used to refer to the entire complex of basins, shelves and ridges underlying the waters of the Arctic Ocean. In view of the confusing overuse of the term "basin" in the literature, the deep-water sub-basins will be called "deeps." The Lomonosov Ridge is the earliest discovered and major dividing feature of the Arctic Basin. For the convenience of having a single term to apply to each of the physiographically complex regions on either side of the Lomonosov Ridge, the names Hyperborean Basin and Nansen Basin have been suggested by Ostenso (1962) to apply to the North American and Eurasian sides of the Ridge respectively.

Continental Margin. The continental shelf bordering the Arctic Ocean is not of uniform extent, being several times wider off the Eurasian coast than off the North American coast. North of Alaska and Greenland the shelf is 100–200 km wide, which can be considered a normal shelf width, whereas the Siberian and Chukchi shelves range from 500–1700 km in width. Soviet investigators believe that continental glaciation probably covered the entire shelf region east of the Taimyr Peninsula, accounting for much of the microrelief recently reported on the Beaufort Sea shelf and the Chukchi Cap.

The continental slope begins at the usual depth of 200 meters, excepting off Greenland where the break occurs at approximately 300 meters. This 300-meter depth probably reflects isostatic depression by the Greenland ice sheet. North of Alaska the gradient of the continental slope is similar to that of other oceans, ranging from $1\frac{1}{2}$–4°. However, slopes as steep as 23° have been reported. Several submarine valleys dissecting the continental margin have been charted. The largest of these, the St. Anna Trough, lying east of Franz Josef Land, is 180 km wide and 500 km long.

In cooperation with the IGY oceanographic programs, the Soviet vessels *Ob'* and *Lena* completed a detailed sounding survey of the northern Greenland Sea. This survey disproved the existence of Nansen's Sill which was believed to connect Greenland and Spitsbergen and to impede water exchange between the Arctic and Atlantic Oceans. Rather, Nansen's Sill was shown to be pierced by a trench (Lena Trough),* whose depth is in excess of 3000 meters. Hope (1959) and Heezen and Ewing (1961) consider the discovery of this channel as evidence supporting the continuation of the mid-Atlantic ridge system into the Arctic Ocean,

the trough being the medial rift valley. This argument is attractive because an earthquake epicenter belt is superimposed upon the trough in a similar relationship to that observed along the mid-Atlantic rift.

The name Nansen Swell is now applied to the eastern shoulder of "Nansen's Sill" and Ob' Shoal** to the smaller western shoulder. The continental shelf adjoining the northeast coast of Greenland is dissected by numerous channels which appear to be glacially scoured valleys from past glacial advances.

Chukchi Cap. Projecting northward from the Chukchi Shelf is a semidetached piece of continental shelf called the Chukchi Cap. This feature is approximately 200 km in diameter, rises abruptly from the floor of the ocean deep, and has a truncated and dissected top, suggesting surf or glacial planation.

Canada Deep. The Canada Deep† extends for approximately 1100 km from the Beaufort Shelf to the Alpha Ridge. The floor of the deep lies at an elevation of −3940 meters and appears to be strikingly smooth, interrupted in some regions by sea knolls. Heezen and Ewing (1961) suggest that, as the submarine canyons dissecting the Beaufort and Chukchi Shelves are probably similar in origin to submarine canyons in general, abyssal plains should be found spreading out from the edge of the continental margin. Further, abyssal cones analogous to those of the Mississippi, Hudson and Ganges Rivers, may occur on the floor of the ocean deeps off the mouths of the major arctic rivers. Evidence for such cones has been suggested by recent geophysical studies from ice island *Arlis-II*.

A smaller deep, the Beaufort Deep, underlies the Beaufort Sea and is separated from the main Canada Deep by a broad unnamed sill, rising 350 meters above the abyssal plain. Because of the low relief of this sill and because it is still uncertain that the Canada and Beaufort Deeps are completely separated, it is suggested that the name Canada Deep apply to both. A peninsula-like segment of continental shelf projects from the vicinity of Banks Island westward into the Beaufort Deep, and is called the Beaufort Plateau.

Soviet geologists have postulated the existence of a Precambrian shield (Hyperborean platform), underlying the Canada Deep and having an eastward extension joining the Canadian shield. However, recent aeromagnetic evidence restricts such a

** Gordienko and Laktionov (1960) call these features the Yermak Plateau and Ob' Shelf respectively.

† Canada Basin (Dietz and Shumway, 1961), North Canada Basin (Heezen and Ewing, 1961), Beaufort Deep (Gordienko and Laktionov, 1960; Treshnikov, 1960; Fisher, Carsola and Shumway, 1958). The term Canada Basin and North Canada Basin commonly appears on U.S.C. & G.S. and U.S. Oceanographic Office charts.

* Heezen and Ewing (1961) call this feature Nansen's Strait. Preference is given to the Soviet nomenclature by virtue of discovery.

platform to the region west of the Deep and suggests that the Beaufort and Canada Deeps are underlain by a great volume of sediments with the crystalline basement sloping downward to the east.

Alpha Ridge. The Alpha Ridge* lies on the North American side of, and subparallel to, the Lomonosov Ridge. It ascends to a minimum depth of about 1400 meters and is approximately 900 km long, varying considerably in width. The ridge is joined to the continental shelf at either end by broad triangular plateaus and is divided by a broad shallow trough, the Alpha Gap, which extends to a depth just below —2000 meters. Seismic dip information and bathymetric profiles across the crest of the ridge show rugged topography which led Hunkins *et al.* (1962) to suggest that this is an area of fault blocks.

On either side of the Alpha Ridge the sea floor drops off gradually to the abyssal plains but does not merge smoothly into the deep ocean floor. Instead, the flanks of the ridge are terminated abruptly by escarpments about 600 meters high which presumably mark major faults. The flanks contain relatively large undulations with relief of as much as 1000 meters. There is no evidence of seismic activity or volcanism associated with the Alpha Ridge. Gravity and aeromagnetic surveys support the thesis that the Ridge is possibly a horst structure.

Lomonosov Ridge. The Lomonosov Ridge extends 1800 km from the continental shelf north of Ellesmere Island to the continental shelf off the New Siberian Islands. The depth of the ridge summit appears to be fairly uniform, generally varying between 950 and 1650 meters. The average relief of the ridge is about 3000 meters above the adjacent basin floors, and it ranges in width from 60–200 km. A crossing of the ridge by the *U.S.S. Nautilus* showed its flanks to be slightly convex upward. The south flank slopes, at the point of traverse, at an angle of 13°; the north flank is less steep, the region shallower than 3850 meters being steeper than the deeper portion. The summit was observed to be 26 km wide and remarkably flat, with suggestions of truncation to a depth of 1400

meters below the present sea level.

Between the Lomonosov and Alpha Ridges another low ridge, the Marvin Ridge, extends into the Makarov Deep. These three ridges are aseismic and join in the vicinity of 88°N, 90°W where they form a broad shelf.

Soviet geologists have hypothesized that the Lomonosov Ridge is structurally the connecting link between the Mesozoic Verkhoyan folded mountain range of Siberia and the Franklin fold belt of northern Ellesmere Island and the group of smaller islands to the southwest. Recent aeromagnetic data show that, in contrast to the Alpha Ridge, the magnetic field is little disturbed on trans-Lomonosov Ridge profiles. Such evidence would add support to the theory of Soviet investigators.

Makarov Deep. The Makarov Deep** is enclosed by the Lomonosov, Alpha, and Marvin Ridges. Echograms from the *Nautilus* show its floor to be featureless and flat at an elevation of —4030 meters, 120 meters deeper than the Canada Deep. The extreme flatness of its floor and its abrupt contact with the adjoining ridges suggest that the deep has been a catch-basin for a considerable thickness of sediments.

Eurasia Deep. Soviet investigators contoured the basin on the European side of the Lomonosov Ridge as a single deep which they called the Nansen Deep.† However, Heezen and Ewing (1961), based upon the distribution of earthquake epicenters and the recent discovery of the Lena Trough, argue for the division of this deep by a trans-Arctic Ocean extension of the mid-Atlantic ridge system. They name the deep adjacent to the Lomonosov Ridge, the Eurasia Basin, and the deep adjoining the Barents and Kara Shelves, the Fram Basin. Soundings from the *Nautilus* (Dietz and Shumway, 1961) and aeromagnetic data (Ostenso, 1962) support the Heezen-Ewing hypothesis.

The water depth over the Eurasia Deep is 4290 meters and the North Pole is located close to its contact with the Lomonosov Ridge. The sounding profile from the *Nautilus* shows the floor of the Eurasia Deep to be, like other abyssal plains, flat and featureless. However, the Deep floor appears to slope gently southward, being 410 meters deeper at the mid-oceanic ridge than along its contact with the Lomonosov Ridge. Dietz and Shumway (1961) suggest that this depression of the floor may be the result of crustal flexure in response to the loading effect of the mid-oceanic ridge, similar to that observed with the Hawaiian Ridge.

---

* Alpha Ridge (Heezen and Ewing, 1961), Central Arctic Rise (Dietz and Shumway, 1961), Mendeleyev Ridge (Gordienko and Laktionov, 1960; Treshnikov, 1961). Although lettering a feature of this magnitude seems singularly unimaginative, the term Alpha (Hunkins, 1960) is given preference by virtue of discovery. The feature was named Alpha Rise after drifting station Alpha. However, to be consistent with internationally accepted nomenclature conventions, this feature should properly be called Alpha Ridge. Rise is defined as, "A long and broad elevation of the deep-sea floor which rises gently and smoothly." Such a definition is hardly applicable to the Alpha Ridge. A ridge is defined as, "A long elevation of the deep-sea floor having steeper sides and less regular topography than a rise."

** Central Arctic Basin (Dietz and Shumway, 1961), Siberia Basin (Heezen and Ewing, 1961). Preference is given to the name Makarov Deep (Gordienko and Laktionov, 1960; Treshnikov, 1961) by virtue of prior usage.

† European Basin (Hope, 1959).

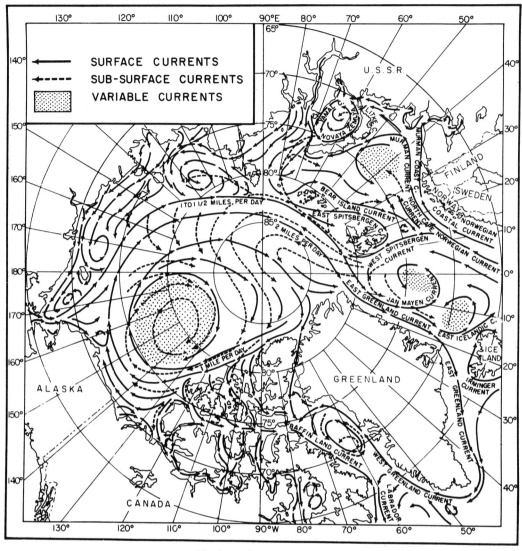

Fig. 2. Arctic Ocean currents.

Mid-ocean Ridge. Lacking adequate data, it must be assumed that the mid-ocean ridge† is similar in physiography to the mid-Atlantic ridge, of which it is presumably an extension. The most salient feature of the mid-Atlantic ridge is the rift valley which forms a deep cleft along the axis of the ridge. Rift mountains rise to an elevation of 900–2700 meters above the valley floor. The Atlantic rift mountains, in turn, are flanked by high fractured plateaus. The rift valley and mountain system in the Atlantic is generally less than 200 km in width, the valley itself varying in width from 40–150 km.

Both the *U.S.S. Skate* and *U.S.S. Nautilus* traversed the mid-oceanic ridge province. Their echograms show the region to be one of jagged topography, containing continuous strings of peaks

of various sizes and having a maximum relief of about 1000 meters. From the sounding profiles one cannot tell if the peaks are conical seamounts or cross sections of ridge. Dietz and Shumway (1961) refer to this physiographic province as the "Region of Seamounts" and point out the similarity of the echo profile in this region to those obtained when passing over the mid-Atlantic ridge.

Fram Deep. The Fram Deep* is the smallest of the four deeps, being 950 km in length and 350 km wide. With a floor elevation of −5180 meters it is also the deepest of the abyssal basins. Adjacent to the deepest part of the depression, a suboceanic

† Nansen Ridge or "Cordillera."

* Fram Basin (Heezen and Ewing, 1961).

TABLE 1. WATER, SALT AND HEAT BALANCE OF THE ARCTIC OCEAN (AFTER MOSBY, 1963)

	Volume ($10^6 m^3$/sec)	Salinity (‰)	Temperature (°C)	Heat Gain (10^9 kcal/sec)	Heat Loss (10^9 kcal/sec)
Inflow					
Bering Strait	1.20	32.0	2.10	2.52	
Norwegian Sea (Atlantic water)	1.40	35.10	3.25	4.55	
Norwegian Sea (bottom water)	0.60	34.92	−0.90		0.54
Precipitation	0.03	0.00	0.00	0.00	
Runoff	0.12	0.00	5.00	0.60	
Outflow					
East Greenland Current	−2.00	34.00	−1.80	3.60	
Canadian Archipelago	−1.10	34.00	−1.80	1.98	
Ice	−0.04	5.00	−10.00	0.40	
Melting water	−0.10	0.00	0.30		0.03
Atlantic water to Barents Sea	−0.05	34.92	2.70		0.14
Evaporation					
Fresh water loss	−0.02	0.00			
Heat loss, vaporization					0.80
Heat loss, "sensible" heat				6.80	1.35
Radiation, net gain				6.80	
Conduction through ice					20.90
Conduction through bottom				0.10	
Freezing of ice				3.20	
Glacier ice					0.03

mountain rises to within 730 meters of the surface. In a distance of only 80 km, there is a 4450-meter change in bottom elevation. Another seamount, 400 km north of Spitsbergen, rises over 3000 meters above the 4000-meter deep abyssal floor. Little is known about the Fram deep. The scant information available suggests that its character may be complex.

Waters of the Arctic Ocean

Scant and widely scattered data obtained over many decades and during all seasons indicate a remarkable regularity in the vertical distribution of temperature and salinity throughout the year. The surface water shows a marked seasonal variation in temperature and salinity in response to melting and freezing of the ice pack. However, because the fresh melt water is less dense than the underlying sea water, this fluctuation is not transmitted to any great depth. In the cold Arctic waters, temperature influences density less than salinity, and the vertical distribution of salinity and density are nearly parallel.

The hydrosphere of the Arctic Basin is recognized as possessing four major components:

Arctic Surface Water. The surface water layer is the most variable of the water masses. The temperature varies seasonally from −1.4°C at the end of summer to −1.7°C at the end of winter. Concomitantly, salinity varies from 28–32‰. With the summer melt, warm water of low salinity will often form an irregular layer less than 1 meter thick beneath the ice pack. This melt water mixes down-

ward with agitation of the ice pack and eventually re-freezes in winter. Below about 50 meters, salinity increases sharply with depth. At about 100 meters in the Nansen Basin and 150 meters in the Hyperborean Basin temperature also rises.

Pacific Water. In the Hyperborean Basin only a thin interlayer of Pacific water underlies the surface layer. This water, entering through the Bering Strait, is warm (−0.7°C) and carries typical Pacific plankton assemblages which die as the water mixes with the colder underlying water in the anticyclonic eddy of the Hyperborean Basin.

Atlantic Water. Atlantic water lies immediately below the surface layer and extends to a depth of 900 meters. It is the warmest water mass, with temperatures above 0°C and occasionally as high as +1°C. Its salinity is quite uniform at approximately 34.92‰.

Bottom Water. Below the Atlantic water and extending down to the ocean floor is a water mass with almost uniform salinity (34.93 to 34.99‰) and temperature. The bottom water in the Nansen Basin, however, is 0.4°C colder (−0.70 to −0.80°C), than in the Hyperborean Basin (−0.30 to −0.40°C). This temperature differential started the first speculation concerning the division of the Arctic Basin by a submarine mountain ridge which would because of speculation mentioned above impede the interchange of deep water masses.

Inflow, Outflow and Thermal Budget

The water budget of the Arctic Ocean is balanced by inflow through the Bering Strait and

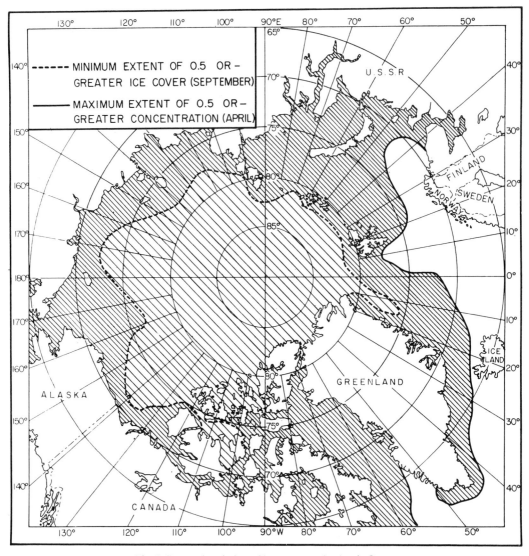

Fig. 3. Seasonal variation of ice cover on the Arctic Ocean.

Norwegian Sea, by water received as precipitation plus runoff from land and by outflow to the Barents and Greenland Sea and through the Canadian Archipelago in addition to losses by evaporation. It is estimated that nearly twice as much water enters the Arctic Ocean Basin through the Norwegian Sea as through the Bering Strait which, in turn, is ten times the amount contributed by runoff from adjoining lands. The contribution of precipitation is minor, being but 0.01% of the total. The East Greenland Current accounts for nearly two-thirds of the water outflow from the Basin.

Additional factors involved 'in considering thermal budget are heat lost by evaporation (including heat of vaporization), by conduction, and by

glacial discharge into the Arctic Ocean and heat gained by insolation, by geothermal conduction, and by latent heat of freezing. Recognizing the hazards of quantitative estimations based upon the sketchy data available, Mosby (1963) prepared the balance sheet on water, salt and heat shown in Table 1.

The seasonal variation in ice cover is shown in Fig. 3. The ice pack ranges in overall thickness up to 3 meters, although it will get considerably thicker locally in response to pressure buckling. The pack is in a constant state of motion in response to surface currents and shifting winds. The relationships between wind and current in generating pack motion are complex but may often be successfully approximated by Nansen's empirical law that the ice drifts at about 1/50 of the wind-speed with a 28° right deviation.

NED A. OSTENSO

References

Boosman, J. W., 1964, "Seismic crustal studies in the Arctic Ocean Basin," *U.S. Naval Res. Rev.*, **17** (2), 7–12.

Dietz, R. S., and Shumway, G., 1961, "Arctic Basin geomorphology," *Bulls Geol. Soc. Am.*, **72**, 1319–1330.

Fisher, R. L., Carsola, A. J., and Shumway, G., 1958, "Deep-sea bathymetry north of Point Barrow," *Deep-sea Res.*, **5**, 1–6.

Gordienko, P. A., and Laktionov, A. F., 1960, "Principal results of the latest oceanographic research in the Arctic Basin," *Izv. Akad. Nauk SSSR, Geograph. Ser.*, **5**, 22–23 (DRB trans T35OR, by Hope, Feb. 1961).

Heezen, B. C., and Ewing, M., 1961, "The Mid-oceanic Ridge and to Extension through the Arctic Basin," in "Geology in the Arctic," Vol. 1, pp. 622–642, University of Toronto Press.

Hope, E. R., 1959, "Geotectonics of the Arctic Ocean on the Great Arctic Magnetic Anomaly," *J. Geophys. Res.*, **64**, 407–427.

Hunkins, Kenneth, 1960, "Seismic Studies of the Arctic Ocean Floor," Air Force Cambridge Res. Lab., AF 19 (604) 2030, pp. 15.

Hunkins, Kenneth, Herron, T., Kutschale, H., and Peter, G., 1962, "Geophysical studies of the Chukchi Cap, Arctic Ocean," *J. Geophys. Res.*, **67**, No. 1, 235–247.

Mosby, Hakon, 1963, "Water, salt and heat balance in the North Polar Sea," *Proc. Arctic Basin Symposium, Arctic Inst. North America*, pp. 69–83.

Ostenso, N. A., 1962, "Geophysical Investigations of the Arctic Ocean Basin, University of Wisconsin Geophys. and Polar Res. Center Report 62–4, pp. 124.

Treshnikov, A. F., 1960, "The Arctic discloses its secrets: New data on the bottom topography and the meters of the Arctic Basin," *Priroda*, **2**, 25–32 (DRB translation T357R, by Hope, Aug. 1961).

ARCTIC REGIONS—*See* Vol. III

ASEISMIC RIDGES

The term "aseismic ridge" was devised to distinguish certain submarine ridges from the Mid-Ocean Ridge (q.v.) with its strikingly seismic median rift. Ridges of this inactive sort were noted by Ewing and Heezen (1956), quoting as examples the Walvis Ridge, Rio Grande Plateau, Kerguelen Plateau (a connection to a Gaussberg Ridge has been disproved), Mascarene Plateau (or Seychelles Ridge), and Lomonosov Ridge. A world map of aseismic ridges was given by Heezen (1962; reproduced in *Mid-Ocean Ridge*).

The most "classical" aseismic ridge is certainly the Walvis Ridge in the southeast Atlantic, extend-ing 3000 km diagonally from the foot of the Mid-Atlantic Ridge between Tristan da Cunha and Gough Island in a northeasterly direction to the vicinity of Walvis (Walfish) Bay in Southwest Africa. It has been suggested by some geologists (Krenkel, H. Cloos and others) that the ridge continues inland in the Damara Axis to Zambia, but the "match" is not very satisfactory. Structurally the ridge seems to be built of oceanic crustal rocks and lacks any indication of deep continental "roots." Bathymetrically it is strongly asymmetric, narrow and with a steep scarp on the south side. For some distance there is a lower step with a similar southeast-facing scarp some 80 km southeast of the main scarp, which in many places is over 2000 meters high. The ridge surface is remarkably smooth and largely devoid of abyssal hills or seamounts. This suggests long stability and pelagic sedimentation. A core from the scarp showed a condensed section of Tertiary pelagic sediments, reaching a globigerina ooze of Upper Cretaceous age (Ericson, as noted by Heezen and Menard, 1963). This would suggest a relief established at least by Cretaceous times, a slope kept steep but relatively sediment-free by periodic slumping.

Other examples of major ridges in the Atlantic suggested by the mapping of Stocks and Wüst (1935) based on the *Meteor* (1925–28) surveys have not all been confirmed by later surveys, notably by the *Vema*, but several (e.g., Guinea Rise, Rio Grande Ridge) may also be aseismic ridges of the Walvis type. The Guinea Rise seems to continue very convincingly into the northeast–southeast trend of the Cameroons.

In the Arctic Ocean, the *Lomonosov Ridge* seems to be of this type; it seems to run, approximately parallel to an extension of the Mid-Ocean Ridge, from Greenland toward eastern Siberia.

In the Indian Ocean, the longest rectilinear geotectonic structure in the world, the *Ninetyeast Ridge* of Heezen and Tharp (1965) seems to be equally an aseismic ridge. It is marked by several enormous escarpments and has a rectilinear extension, almost north–south in trend, of 2400 km (1320 nautical miles). Its northern end disappears under the submarine cone of sediments spread out by the Ganges; a portion of the ridge here was long ago recognized by Seymour Sewell and so marked in Bartholemew's *Times Atlas* (sheet 26 of Vol. 2, 1959) as *Carpenter Ridge*. Heezen and Tharp have also loosely referred to certain submarine plateaus of obviously continental origin under the heading of "aseismic ridges" (Madagascar Ridge, Mascarene Plateau, etc.), but these are best classified under their new term "microcontinents" (see *Submarine Plateaus*).

In the Pacific, Menard has suggested that the ridges paralleling the great *fracture zones* (q.v.) are also to be classified as aseismic ridges. Thus the Mendocino Ridge is a characteristic example.

Dredgings show that basic volcanic rocks outcrop at least in places, but the ridge is in no way comparable with the *volcanic ridges* (q.v.) which consist of progressively evolved series of volcanic cones.

RHODES W. FAIRBRIDGE

References

Cloos, H., 1937, "Zur Grosstektonik Hochafrikas und seiner Umgebung," *Geol. Rundschau*, **28**, 333–348.

Ewing, M., and Heezen, B. C., 1956, "Some problems of Antarctic submarine geology," in "Antarctica in the International Geophysical Year," *Am. Geophys. Union Publ.* No. 462, 75–81.

Heezen, B. C., 1962, "The Deep-sea Floor," in (Runcorn, editor) "Continental Drift," pp. 235–288, New York, Academic Press.

Heezen, B. C., and Menard, H. W., 1963, "Topography of the Deep-Sea Floor," in "The Sea," Vol. 3, pp. 233–280, New York, Interscience Publishers.

Heezen, B. C., and Tharp, M., 1965a, "Descriptive sheet to accompany physiographic diagram of the Indian Ocean," *Geol. Soc. Am.*

Heezen, B. C., and Tharp, M., 1965b, "Tectonic fabric of the Atlantic and Indian Oceans, and Continental drift," *Phil. Trans. Roy. Soc. London Ser. A* (1088), **258**, 90–106.

Menard, H. W., 1964, "Marine Geology of the Pacific," New York, McGraw-Hill Book Co., 271pp.

Stocks, T., and Wüst, G., 1935, "Die Tiefenverhältnisse des offenen Atlantischen Ozeans," *Wiss. Ergebn. Deut. Atlant. Exped. "Meteor," 1925–1927*, **3**, No. 1, 1, 31.

Cross-references: *Atlantic Ocean; Fracture Zones; Indian Ocean; Mid-Ocean Ridge; Pacific Ocean; Submarine Plateaus.*

ATLANTIC OCEAN

The Atlantic is the second largest of the world's oceans, was the first to be explored, and for long has been the best known. The first deep soundings were made by Sir James Ross, and the first good bathymetric chart was completed by Matthew Maury over a century ago. Geotectonically, it now seems that the Atlantic is possibly the youngest ocean. There is little trace of any north–south waterway in this part of the world before the late Mesozoic, say, about 100 million years ago, and indicates of a marine connection between the South Atlantic and the Indian Ocean emerging from the fossil evidence first appear in Upper Cretaceous formations.

The symmetric S-shape of the North and South Atlantic, equidistantly arranged on either side of the Mid-Atlantic Ridge, has attracted scientific attention for over a century and has been the cornerstone of theories involving continental drift and the more modern concept of crustal spreading (mantle expansion). It was only after the very detailed systematic east–west traverses of both North and South basins by the German *Meteor* Expedition in 1925–27 (Merz, Wüst, Correns, Wattenburg, and others) that structural theories began to emerge, with some foundation of bathymetric data. Kober (1928) was the first to propose the existence of a world-encircling ridge system; while he regarded it as an embryonic orogenic belt (in contrast to Heezen's taphrogenic hypothesis), this illustrates how quickly the new data could be noticed and incorporated into contemporary thinking.

Following the commonly quoted figures of Kossinna (1921), the area of the Atlantic, in its limited sense, is about 8.2×10^7 km^2 (or 31,814,600 square miles), or including its marginal seas (Caribbean, Mediterranean, etc.) it amounts to about 10.6×10^7 km^2 (41,081,000 square miles). The mean depth according to the first category is 3926 m and in the second 3332 m. It is thus similar to, but somewhat shallower than, the Pacific and Indian Oceans, which points up the extensive continental shelves in the far north and the large amounts of sedimentary filling.

According to Sir John Murray (1888), the total area draining the Atlantic (s.s.) is about 3.5×10^7 km^2 (13,431,600 square miles). or including the Arctic about 5.0×10^7 km^2 (19,691,000 square miles) which is four times the area draining into the Indian Ocean and nearly four times that draining into the Pacific. This is a particularly important fact when considering its oceanography at the close of the last ice stage (Würm or Wisconsin); the melt-waters of the latter poured into the Atlantic largely by way of the Mississippi, Hudson and St. Laurence, Elbe and Rhine. This occurred from about 16,000–6,000 years B.P. (before present), a 10,000-year period when about 40 million km^3 of fresh water was added to the ocean. Relatively little of this amount reached the Indian or Pacific Oceans, because the great rivers there do not have drainage regions of intense glaciation and the Antarctic ice-continent is believed to have melted very little at this time. It is evident from the above that even today the world's hydrologic balance can only be maintained if there is a constant flow from the Atlantic to the other oceans.

The Atlantic differs in many other ways from the Indo-Pacific realm. It lacks the wonderful displays of coral atolls and has numerically few seamounts or guyots. Long sectors of the coasts are quite devoid of fringing reefs, even though temperatures, salinities, and nutrient supplies are favorable. Nevertheless certain cold-water coral banks are known (Teichert, 1958). The biological history of extreme Pleistocene cooling, and its isolation from east–west currents since the blocking of the Panama and Middle East gateways by earth movements in the late and middle Tertiary, have combined to provide the Atlantic with a rather impoverished and "isolated" benthonic marine fauna (Clark, 1913), which contrasts notably with its "universal" character in the early Tertiary and Cretaceous.

Not counting Greenland, the Canadian Arctic

Archipelago, Spitzbergen, the British Isles, the Falklands and the Scotia Arc (continental type islands), the Atlantic contains only a few oceanic islands, in all covering 5.0×10^5 km² (193,000 square miles), including Iceland (1.05×10^5 km²; 40,540 square miles, Jan Mayen, Bermuda, Azores, Madeira, the Canaries, Cape Verde Islands, Fernando de Noronha, Ascension, St. Helena, Tristan da Cunha, Gough, Bouvet, etc. These are mostly volcanic (see details below) but partly with limestone veneers.

Boundaries of the Atlantic Ocean

The Atlantic Ocean is essentially a meriodional canal when compared to the other oceans. It is an S-shaped ocean stretching between the polar latitudes of both hemispheres and intersecting every climatic zone. Its lateral boundaries are for the most part well defined, i.e., the Americas on the west and Eurafrica (Europe and Africa) to the east. The North Atlantic has many marginal seas, some of which have an important influence on the circulation of the entire ocean. The two largest are the Mediterranean Sea and the Caribbean–Gulf of Mexico system (waters originating in each affect large areas of the Atlantic Ocean). Through these seas, the Atlantic Ocean is connected to the Indian and Pacific Oceans, but only by man-made canals. Other important marginal seas of the North Atlantic are the *North Sea, Baltic Sea, English Channel, Irish and Celtic Seas, Norwegian Sea, Greenland Sea, Irminger Sea, Labrador Sea,* and *Hudson* and *Baffin Bays* (q.v. for each, except the last, included in the *Canadian Arctic Archipelago*). The South Atlantic, in contrast, has only one marginal sea, the *Weddell Sea* (q.v.), though the International Hydrographic Bureau (Sp. Publ. 23, 1953) recognizes also the Gulf of Guinea.

The northern and southern boundaries of the Atlantic Ocean are not well defined. By convention, the polar oceans (Arctic Ocean and Southern Ocean) are not always recognized as distinct bodies of water (the "three ocean concept" of de Fleurieu, 1798; Krümmel, 1897, etc.). Therefore, the Atlantic Ocean in the broadest sense extends from the shores of the Antarctic continent to the Bering Straits. The Atlantic is then separated from the Pacific Ocean by the Bering Straits, and in the south along the shortest distance from South America to the Antarctic Peninsula (Palmer Land and Graham Land). The I.H.B. draws the line of the latter from Cape Horn (68°04′W) along the *meridian* to the Antarctic Peninsula. Some (e.g., Wüst, 1936; Schott, 1942) prefer to consider this latter boundary to be along the line of shallowest depth, the South Sandwich arc, thus including the Scotia Sea with the Pacific Ocean. The separation with the Indian Ocean is almost always considered to be along the 20°E meridian.

The world ocean can also be divided on the basis of broad physical oceanographical regions, making *five oceans;* this procedure was recommended by a Committee of the Royal Geographical Society (under the chairmanship of Sir Roderick I. Murchison) which was formed in 1845, though its findings were not issued generally until 1893. It was favoured by Sir John Murray and many oceanographers. If this is accepted, then two polar oceans or regions are recognized, and the Atlantic Ocean can be considered to stretch from the latitude of 55°S (alternately listed by different authors as 60°S, 40°S, 35°S, etc.) to the latitude of northern Spitsbergen. This would include the Greenland and Norwegian Sea, but would exclude the Arctic Ocean. The Southern Ocean boundary separates the Atlantic from the well-developed circumpolar current system, which is common to all three major oceans. The I.H.B. recognizes the Arctic Ocean as a separate major ocean, and while it formerly admitted the Southern Ocean (see Sp. Publ. 23, Second ed., 1937), after its Third Edition (1953) the latter was dropped, so that at present four major oceans are accepted by this body.

Bathymetry

The Atlantic possesses a basically simple bathymetric plan, symmetrically distributed on either side of the Mid-Atlantic Ridge. Two gigantic troughs are thus separated by the median ridge, sometimes called the Western Atlantic Trough and Eastern Atlantic Trough, but these terms are not adopted into the usual hierarchy of bathymetric divisions. Each of these depressions is subdivided into more or less distinctive basins (some quite imperfect), and locally interrupted by rises or transverse ridges. Outside of these basic features, there are the so-called marginal or mediterranean seas: the actual *Mediterranean* (q.v.), the *Black Sea* (q.v.), the *Caribbean* (q.v.), *Gulf of Mexico* (q.v.), *Scotia Sea* (q.v.), the "arctic mediterranean," *Norwegian* and *Greenland Seas* (q.v.) and the *Arctic Sea* (q.v.), usually treated as a separate ocean.

Basins

The basins (and intermediate highs) of the main Atlantic are as follows:

(A) Western Atlantic. *(1) Labrador Basin* of Groll, 1915: Situated between Labrador, Greenland and Newfoundland, this basin extends considerably further than the Labrador Sea (q.v.) and includes most of the area of the Irminger Sea (q.v.). According to Heezen *et al.* (1959), its floor collects sediment-laden flows that pass down the "Mid-Ocean Canyon" to the Sohm Abyssal Plain.

(2) Newfoundland Basin (of Wüst, 1936): Lying between Newfoundland and the Azores, the Newfoundland basin is imperfectly separated from adjacent basins, but it is broadly limited by the Southeast Newfoundland Ridge in the south and the Flemish Cap in the north where an imaginary

line to the northeast can be drawn to join a westerly swing of the Mid-Atlantic Ridge about 55°N. Its floor from north to south is transected by the Mid-Ocean Canyon, which joins the Labrador Basin with the Sohm Abyssal Plain.

(3) North America Basin (of Supan, 1899): This is a very large depression, not by any means a true basin, centered around the *Bermuda Rise* with several abyssal plains: the *Sohm Abyssal Plain* to the northeast (the "Suhm Deep" of Sir John Murray, 1895; the spelling "Sohm" is apparently a widely copied slip) the *Hatteras Abyssal Plain* to the west, and the *Nares Abyssal Plain* covering 900,000 km² or 350,000 square miles, to the southeast (formerly "Nares Deep" of Murray). An "abyssal gap" (deep-sea channel), the *Vema Gap*, separates the last two at 24°N 68°W. The *Blake-Bahama Outer Ridge* (an extended sedimentary tongue) separates the Hatteras Plain from the narrow *Blake-Bahama Basin* (Ericson *et al.,* 1952) and abyssal plains. It includes one of the two true "island arc" type trenches of the Atlantic, the *Puerto Rico Trench* (of Supan, 1899); its deepest area was sometimes called "Brownson Deep," and a maximum depth was named *Milwaukee Deep* (after the ship that first sounded it), but greater depths were later discovered. (Features within the Caribbean and Gulf of Mexico areas are treated separately under those headings.)

(4) Guinea Basin (of Wüst, 1936; "Makaroff Deep" of Murray): This is situated off the Venezuela, Guiana and Amazon coast of Brazil. There are two subdivisions within this basin, on the west the *Demerara A.P.* (335,000 km² or 130,000 square miles) which is fed by the Orinoco and the rivers of the Guianas and part of the Amazon flow; while on the east comes the *Ceara A.P.,* which is separated from the former by the enormous bulge of the Amazon abyssal cone, which is also its principal feeder.

(5) Brazil Basin (of Supan, 1899; "Tizard Deep" of Murray): Situated off the eastern coast of Brazil, this is bounded on the north by the *Para Rise* (Para is now Belém) which extends out with a partly volcanic ridge, and is marked by the islets of Fernando Noronha and Atoll de Rocas. At its northern end is the broad depression of the *Pernambuco A.P.* (Pernambuco is now known as Recife). To the south of the *Trinidad-Martin Vaz Volcanic rise,* however, the abyssal plain areas are "surprisingly small and intermittent" (Heezen and Laughton, 1963).

(6) Argentine Basin (of Supan, 1899): Southwest of the *Rio Grande Rise* is the long narrow *Argentine A.P.* (200,000 km² or 80,000 square miles), but east of it is the broad low *Argentine Rise,* an area of inconspicuous abyssal hills.

(7) Atlantic-Antarctic Basin (or "Atlantic South Polar Basin" of Wüst, 1936): Extending all across the South Atlantic from the Weddell Sea into the Indian Ocean, it includes a long depression, the *Weddell A.P.* A separate depression between the South Sandwich Island and Bouvet Island (Bouvetøya in Norwegian) is the *Sandwich A.P.*

Also found here is the second island-arc type trench of the Atlantic, the *South Sandwich Trench* (or simply Sandwich Trench), deepest sounding 8264 m. It is separated by some distinctive ridges from the Atlantic-Antarctic Basin. Numerous little closed basins, not distinctively named, occur within the *Scotia Sea* (q.v.).

(B) Eastern Atlantic. *(1) West Europe Basin* (of Wüst, 1936; also called "Northeastern Atlantic Basin"): The principal deeps recognized here are the *Porcupine A.P.* west of Britain, which connects to the *Biscay A.P.* (80,000 km² or 30,000 square miles) and this in turn in the south is connected by an abyssal gap, *Theta Gap,* at 43°N 12°W with the Iberia A.P. (see below). These west Europe abyssal plains have been described by Laughton (1960), as part of a step-like system dropping progressively to the south through a series of narrow gaps and channels.

(2) Iberia Basin (of Wüst, 1936) or *Spanish Basin* (of Supan, 1899): This is situated west of Spain. (The term "Iberia Basin" is sometimes used for one in the western Mediterranean Basin, *east* of Spain; this is unfortunate, and the term Balearic Basin is appropriate for the latter.) As indicated above, this is fed through an abyssal gap from the Biscay A.P. (see above). A smaller depression is the *Tagus A.P.* (15,000 km² or 6000 square miles), fed by a submarine canyon from the Tagus (Portugal). South again, west of Gibraltar and the Guadiana and Guadalquivir sediment sources, is the *Horseshoe A.P.* (14,000 km² or 5400 square miles).

(3) Canaries Basin (of Wüst, 1936; "Monaco Deep" of Murray): Lying south of the *Azores Rise,* a belt of seamounts extending east–southeast, this basin is largely occupied by the *Madeira A.P.* (Heezen and Laughton, 1963) and is now found to include a sector formerly labeled *Canaries A.P.* (Heezen, 1959). Separate from it and apparently fed by it is a smaller depression, the *Seine A.P.* (39,000 km² or 65,000 square miles), lying east of Seine Bank. Wüst recognized a "North Canaries Basin" and a "South Canaries Basin," but this distinction is not very clear. Much of the Canaries Basin consists of the broad continental rise of Morocco and the volcanic plateaus of the Canaries and Madeira.

(4) Cape Verde Basin (of Wüst, 1936; "North African Trough" of Supan, 1899; "Chun Deep" and "Moseley Deep" of Murray): Ill-separated from the Madeira A.P., the *Cape Verde A.P.* (together 530,000 km² or 200,000 square miles), the boundary being a belt of abyssal hills, continues the extensive belt about 1000 km following the outer limits of West Africa, to swing around to the west and southwest of the Cape Verde Islands. South of these islands is the *Gambia A.P.*

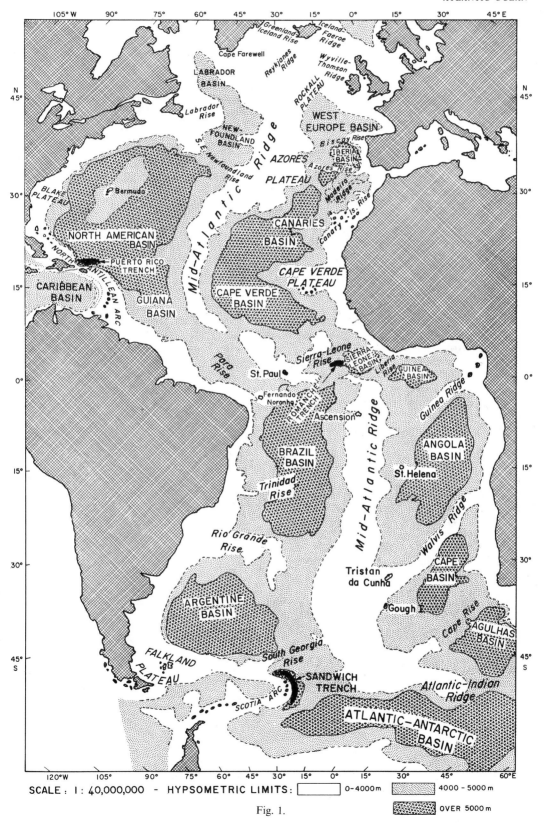

Fig. 1.

SCALE : 1 : 40,000,000 - HYPSOMETRIC LIMITS: ☐ 0-4000m ▨ 4000 - 5000 m ▩ OVER 5000 m

(5) Sierra Leone Basin (of Wüst, 1936): The above-mentioned belt swings around the West Africa coast, separated by the aseismic rise and abyssal hills of the *Sierra Leone Rise*. The latter is separated from the continental rise by the *Sierra Leone A.P.* At the same time, the width of the continental rise shrinks to about 500 km.

(6) Guinea Basin (of Wüst, 1936; West African Trough" of Deutsche-Seewarte Atlas, 1902): This continues the same belt into the *Gulf of Guinea*, but contains a longer depression, the *Guinea A.P.*, largely fed by the largest river of West Africa, the Niger, and the Niger abyssal cone, at its eastern end.

(7) Angola Basin (of Wüst, 1936; "Buchanan Deep" of Murray): South of the volcanic *Guinea Ridge* (with Fernando Po, etc.) there follows, in sequence, the large depression of the *Angola A.P.* (140,000 km²) fed from the north end by the Congo and the Congo abyssal cone through the *Congo Canyon*, the biggest submarine canyon in the eastern Atlantic.

(8) Cape Basin (of Supan, 1899; also called "Walvis Basin"): After the northeast–southwest trending Walvis (Walfish) Ridge which parallels the Guinea Ridge, but in contrast is non-volcanic and aseismic today, there comes the *Cape A.P.*, which is fed by the Orange River.

(9) Agulhas Basin (of Wüst, 1936): In a complex area of continental borderlands (Agulhas Bank) and down-faulted quasicratonic crust, the principal depression is the *Agulhas A.P.* (east of latitude 20° belongs within the Indian Ocean).

Rises and Ridges

As indicated above, the Mid-Atlantic Ridge (or Rise) is the dominant positive topographic feature of the Atlantic floor, dividing the main ocean into what amounts to two parallel troughs of very large dimensions. Secondary ridges or rises partly segment these troughs into basins; however, the ridges are rarely continuous, so that bottom waters from the Antarctic are able to migrate northward, up the west side of the Atlantic into the North American Basin and a branch swings eastward and then southward into the eastern trough through the Romanche Trench (or "Romanche Gap") that corresponds to a major east–west fracture zone (q.v.). Another important fracture zone to the north of the latter is known as the Guinea Fracture Zone. Yet another zone of important fracture occurs about latitude 50–53°N, a region named because of the cable layers as the Telegraph Plateau.

The transverse ridges were mainly identified and named by the *Meteor* Expedition (Stocks and Wüst, 1935). From north to south, starting on the west side, they are:

(A) Western Atlantic. *(1 Greenland-Iceland Rise*: Corresponding to Denmark Strait, a well-marked sill of less than 1000 m, this separates the Greenland Sea (q.v.) from the Irminger Sea (q.v.).

(2) Labrador Rise This is an ill-defined extension from Flemish Cap, directed northeastward. It has no continuity and is cut by the Mid-Ocean Canyon (of Heezen). Beyond the cap, no continental rocks are believed to occur here.

(3) Southeast Newfoundland Rise: This is a southeastward extension from the Grand Banks. Like the above, it is poorly defined and is cut across by the Mid-Ocean Canyon.

(4) Antillean or Caribbean Arc (Ridge): This is a typical double island arc, but only Barbados represents the outer non-volcanic ridge, while the numerous Windward Islands represent the volcanic line.

(5) Para Rise: This extends between the northeastern part of Brazil and the Mid-Atlantic Ridge; it is in no sense a barrier to deep currents. It is partly the sedimentary "fill" from the Amazon and adjacent submarine fans; the city of Para (now called Belém) is just south of the Amazon delta. The rise proper is a deep offshore feature (about 3000 m) that Heezen has classified as an aseismic ridge. Of minor importance to the southeast is a small volcanic ridge with the mature, deeply dissected volcanic piles of Fernando de Naronha and Atoll de Rocas, reaching some 300 km northeast of Cape Sao Roque.

(6) Trinidad Rise: This is a well-marked volcanic ridge extending due east 1200 km from the Espiritu Santo province of Brazil, culminating in the Trinidad islet and Vas reefs. It forms a partial boundary between the North and South Brazil Basins, but to the east of Trinidad there is no barrier at all.

(7) Rio Grande Rise (sometimes called "Bromley Plateau"): This is a massive aseismic ridge extending 1500 km due east from the Rio Grande do Sul province of Brazil. It almost but not quite reaches the edge of the Mid-Atlantic Ridge. On the landward side, it is offset somewhat from a broad plateau, a continental borderland, situated southeast of Sao Paulo and almost certainly consisting of continental rocks, cut off by block-faulting from the main shelf.

(8) Falkland Plateau: This is what Stille calls a structural spur of borderland, consisting of typical continental rocks (Devonian, etc., outcropping in the Falklands) extending 1800 km east of the Argentina Shelf. It is somewhat split up by faulting, which leads to the Malvinas Trough south of the Falklands.

(9) South Georgia Rise: Extending northeastward of South Georgia is the short South Georgia Rise.

(10) Scotia Arc or Ridge (or South Antillean Arc or South Sandwich Ridge): This is a typical island arc with non-volcanic components, seen in South Georgia and South Orkneys, and an active volcanic sector, about the angle of maximum curvature, in

the South Shetlands. Major east–west strike-slip faults are suspected both along the northern and southern borders of the arc, as in the Caribbean (see *Fracture Zones*). These two arcs are thus almost identical in structure.

(B) Eastern Atlantic. In the eastern half of the Atlantic, the ridges and rises are as follows:

(1) Iceland-Faeroe Ridge: This is an aseismic ridge that forms a massive barrier in the North Atlantic. The Faeroe Islands consist of a mature volcanic accumulation, long ago inactive.

(2) Wyville Thomson Ridge (also Scotland-Faeroe Ridge): A similar aseismic barrier which overlaps the Iceland-Faeroe Ridge on the south, but joins it west of the Faeroes, this is separated in the south by the faulted trough of the Faeroe Channel.

(3) Rockall Bank (or Plateau): This extends southwest from the Wyville Thomson Ridge and is crowned by an isolated igneous stock, Rockall (see section on Rocks, below). It is likewise an aseismic ridge in Heezen's classification.

(4) Porcupine Bank: Situated off the continental shelf southwest of Ireland, this is a fragment of continental borderland.

(5) Biscay Rise: This extends due west from the Galician province of Spain and essentially connects with the eastern borders of the Mid-Atlantic Ridge, except that it is crossed by a series of connected deep-sea channels which carry turbidity currents toward the south.

(6) Azores Rise: This extends eastward from the *Azores Plateau* which is an unusual dome-like area of the Mid-Atlantic Ridge, rather like an immature Icelandic Plateau. The rise is a volcanic ridge marked discontinuously by seamounts which continue to the Seine Bank and almost to Gibraltar.

(7) Madeira Ridge: This is a short volcanic ridge southwest of Portugal.

(8) Canary Islands Rise: This is a broad volcanic plateau, of unknown basement characteristics. It parallels the North African coast rather like a continental borderland.

(9) Cape Verde Plateau: A similar but larger plateau or rise, indicated as an aseismic ridge by Heezen, this extends about 800 km west of the African coast of Senegal. It is marked by mature volcanics, but there are also Tertiary rocks, and it would seem to be, in part at least, a continental borderland.

(10) Sierra Leone Rise: This is a poorly developed rise of abyssal hills extending southwest of Freetown to reach the Mid-Atlantic Ridge, northeast of St. Pauls Rocks. It is cut through by several important east–west fracture zones, notably the Guinea Fracture Zone. Heezen classified it as an aseismic ridge; it seems to be completely isolated from the continental border zone.

(11) Liberia Rise: This is a minor but unusual eastnortheast–westsouthwest wedge of mid-ocean character, apparently cut off north and south by east–west faults partly separating the Sierra Leone Basin from the Guinea Basin.

(12) Guinea Ridge: This is an important northeast–southwest volcanic ridge that extends the similar-trending volcanic belt of the Cameroons through Fernando Po and other volcanic islands in the Gulf of Guinea in a ridge to meet the northeastern part of the Mid-Atlantic Ridge just below the equator.

(13) Walvis (Walfish) Ridge: The most important transverse ridge in the South Atlantic, also trending northeast–southwest, this connects Southwest Africa with the Mid-Atlantic Ridge, with over 1000 m scarps, but at its southwest end drops away to an almost insignificant trace, in the direction of Tristan da Cunha and Gough Island.

(14) Cape Rise: The most southerly transverse feature, a partly volcanic ridge, extending from the Cape of Good Hope to the southwest, in the direction of Bouvet Island, it has little topographic significance, with scattered seamounts.

Oceanography

The Atlantic Ocean has the greatest oceanographic data coverage of the world oceans. This is due primarily to the work of the R/V *Meteor*, the IGY and EQUALANT work and the many Gulf Stream studies. Therefore, the geographic distribution of the more commonly measured parameters such as temperature and salinity can be mapped with confidence, and maps of the various chemical and biological parameters can be plotted more completely than for the other oceans. The data also permits calculations of the water and heat budget terms, as evaporation and the exchange of sensible heat between the ocean and the atmosphere.

Temperatures and Salinities

The Atlantic Ocean is the warmest, saltiest of the world oceans. (It receives by far the largest-fraction of the world's river water.) The average potential temperature and salinity are 3.73°C and 34.90‰, respectively. The range of surface temperature (average 16.9°C between 90°N and 80°S) is primarily a function of latitude and the current systems. The surface salinity (average 34.87‰ between 90°N and 80°S) is controlled by the precipitation minus evaporation value, the land freshwater runoff and the currents. Below the surface, advection and eddy diffusion are the controlling factors of both parameters. Figures 2 and 3 show the average annual surface temperature and salinity of the Atlantic Ocean. Figures 4 and 5 are graphs of the vertical distributions. There are seasonal variations of the surface values which extend down to approximately 200 m. These variations are strongest near coasts which have continental-type climates.

The annual range of surface temperatures in the open ocean is greatest between 40–50°N and 30–40°S,

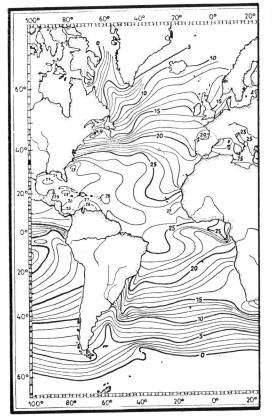

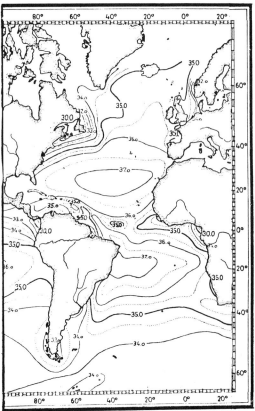

Fig. 2. Mean surface water temperature of Atlantic Ocean during northern hemisphere (August), adapted from Sverdrup (1942).

Fig. 3. Mean surface salinity of Atlantic Ocean. adapted from Sverdrup (1942).

having a maximum value of 7°C. (This is a zonal average; the fluctuations in northwestern Atlantic Ocean can be as high as 15°C.) The variation in the equatorial and polar regions is less than 2°C. In coastal areas, the surface temperature can vary by amounts of 25°C during the year. The annual variation of surface salinity is affected by factors which are of only secondary importance to the temperature, and so the salinity variations may differ from the annual fluctuations of temperature. Melting and freezing of sea ice (polar regions) and seasonal variations in the rate of evaporation and precipitation (Caribbean Sea) cause significant salinity variations in the surface layer. Coastal areas which are subject to high spring runoff, as off the northeast coast of the United States, can have fluctuations of 3‰; however, in the open ocean the surface salinity varies by a much smaller amount rarely changing by more than 1‰.

Water and Heat Budget

The rate of evaporation of seawater can be calculated from a knowledge of the surface temperature and atmospheric conditions. This has

been done in a general approach for the Atlantic Ocean. The precipitation can be approximated from coastal and island weather records. Empirical equations have been formulated relating the surface salinity to the values of precipitation and evaporation which are of much greater importance than land freshwater runoff expect in localized coastal areas. Figure 6 shows the average zonal values of surface salinity and the difference between the two terms of the water budget. The atmosphere over the Atlantic Ocean gains water vapor over the "horse latitudes" (q.v.) and transports it to the more northern latitudes and towards the equator. Thus, the arid mid-latitudes act as a major source for water vapor, and demonstrate the importance of the sea-air interface in the transfer of material between the atmosphere and the hydrosphere.

Not only does evaporation represent the most important water sink for the oceans, but it accounts for the largest heat loss; some 51% of the incoming energy is lost as latent heat of evaporation. The heat or energy exchange between the air and water has significant effects on the climate of an area. For example, the northeastern Atlantic Ocean loses

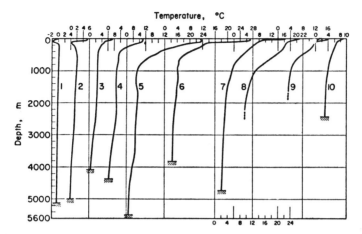

Fig. 4. Vertical temperature distribution at a series of stations along a meridian in the Atlantic Ocean (Defant, 1961):

1.	"Will. Scoresby" 554	63° 20′ S.	17° 23′ W.	5143 m	5. ii. 1931
2.	"Meteor" 58	48° 30′ S.	30° 0′ W.	4989 m	7/8. x. 1925
3.	"Meteor" 83	32° 9′ S.	25° 4′ W.	4506 m	29. xi. 1925
4.	"Meteor" 170	22° 39′ S.	27° 55′ W.	5454 m	9. vii. 1926
5.	"Meteor" 191	9° 7′ S.	2° 2′ W.	4533 m	9/10. ix. 1926
6.	"Meteor" 212	0° 36′ N.	29° 12′ W.	3773 m	19. x. 1926
7.	"Meteor" 283	17° 53′ N.	39° 19′ W.	5748 m	22/23. iii. 1927
8.	"Dana" 1376	33° 42′ N.	36° 16′ W.		10. vi. 1922
9.	"Armauer Hansen" 17	58° 0′ N.	11° 0′ W.	1860 m	29. vii. 1913
10.	"Fram" 29	78° 1′ N.	9° 10′ E.	1075 m	22. vii. 1910

(By permission of Pergamon Press, N.Y.)

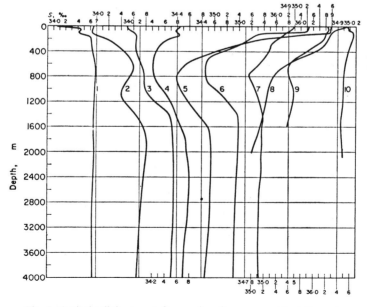

Fig. 5. Vertical salinity curves for a series of oceanographic stations along a meridional section through the Atlantic (corresponding vertical temperature curves are shown in Fig. 4 (Defant, 1961). (By permission of Pergamon Press, N.Y.)

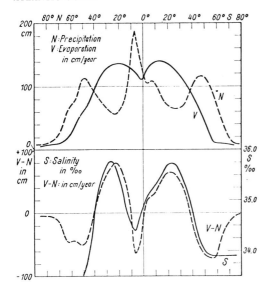

Fig. 6. Zonal distribution, in the annual mean, of precipitation N, evaporation V, V-N, and salinity at the ocean surface, including the marginal seas (according to G. Wüst, 1954).

large amounts of heat to the atmosphere (4200 cal cm^{-2} yr^{-1} in the Norwegian Sea) which has the effect of warming the atmosphere of Great Britain and northern Europe; likewise the cold water surface off northwestern Africa causes heavy fog and strong atmospheric stratification. The oceans act as a climatic flywheel in that, due to their high heat capacity, they damp out variations of air temperature. Figure 7 shows the average annual heat exchange across the sea-air interface for the North Atlantic. Heat transport by ocean currents must compensate their values to maintain the steady-state conditions. In the western Atlantic Ocean, there are very large seasonal variations in

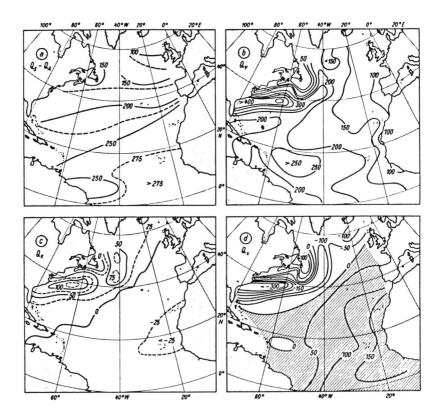

Fig. 7. Average annual heat exchange at the sea surface of the North Atlantic Ocean, expressed in calories per square centimeters per day. (a) Heat gain by radiation exchange $Q_s - Q_A$ (according to H. U. Sverdrup, 1943); (b) heat loss Q_v owing to evaporation of water (according to W. C. Jacobs, 1951); (c) heat loss Q_K as result of direct conduction of heat to the air (according to W. C. Jacobs, 1951); (d) total heat exchange $Q_\Sigma = (Q_s - Q_A) - Q_V - Q_K$ (areas with positive Q_Σ are cross hatched; from Dietrich, 1963). (By permission of Interscience Publishers, N.Y.)

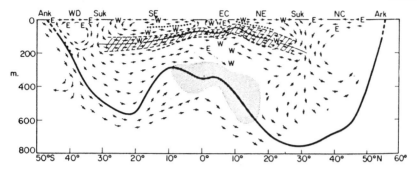

Fig. 8. Structure and circulation in the warm water sphere along the central axis of the Atlantic Ocean (according to A. Defant, 1936; from Dietrich, 1963, who gives the following description, slightly "edited").

▬▬▬	Boundary between warm and cold water sphere.
⌒	Position of largest density gradient (thickness of line proportional to density gradient).
/////↗	Lower boundary of homogeneous top layer.
	Tropical-subtropical discontinuity layer.
↘	Lower boundary of discontinuity layer.
⣿	Very low oxygen content, $O_2 < 1.5$ cc. per 1.
······ ·	Position of tropical-subtropical salinity maximum.
------	Oxygen discontinuity layer.
··············	Oxygen minimum within top layer (axes of meridional circulation eddies).
▬ ▬	Vertical and meridional components of motion of the warm water sphere.
W, E	Zonal components of motion (W towards the west, E towards the east).

Ank, Suk, Ark: Antarctic, Subtropic, and Arctic Convergence.
Zonal components of motion (W towards the west, E towards the east).
SE, NE, EC: South Equatorial Current, North Equatorial Current, and Equatorial Counter Current.
WD, NC: Westwind Drift, North Atlantic Current.

the heat budget terms, especially between 30 and 40°N. These are no doubt due to the continental influence on the climate.

General Circulation of the Atlantic Ocean

Before the work of the *Meteor* Expedition (1925–27) the average meridional circulation of the Atlantic was assumed to be symmetrical about the equator. Since then, various indirect (geostrophic, isentropic) and direct (Eulerian and Lagrangian) methods have revealed that this is not the case. The circulation pattern can be divided into two parts: the warm and the cold water sphere. The boundary between these two parts is taken to be the 9°C isothermal surface, although in the tropical latitudes an absolute oxygen minimum can be used. The schematic meridional cross section of the warm water sphere along the central axis of the Atlantic Ocean is shown in Fig. 8. In this layer, the flow is primarily produced by the wind, although strong thermohaline alterations at the sea surface do occur at the "horse latitudes" (q.v.). These alterations, resulting from the relative desert conditions in these latitudes, cause a zone of convergence. This subtropical Convergence is the source region of the highly saline water which spreads at a depth of the main thermocline. The cold water

sphere is in contact with the atmosphere poleward of the two polar fronts, where the deep water masses are formed. The deep flow is primarily due to a deep baroclinic field of mass and lateral eddy diffusion. Figure 9 is a schematic representation of the circulation in the "Cold Water Sphere" (so-called Stratosphere). Table 1 lists the mean temperatures and salinities of a water column passing through the warm and cold water spheres.

Warm Water Sphere. The warm water sphere can be divided into two parts: an active circulation above a strong thermocline and a much more sluggish flow below. The topography of the thermocline is shown in Fig. 10. The thermocline is depressed below the zones of convergence and elevated at the zones of divergence. Figure 11 shows the positions of the major singular lines of the Atlantic Ocean. All of these are caused by the wind action, with some thermohaline effect in the Subtropical Convergence (mentioned above) and the Antarctic Convergence. Since the warm water floats in nearly hydrostatic equilibrium, the highest sea level would occur above the deepest penetration of the warm water body. The absolute sea surface topography is shown in Fig. 12. The topographic high at 65°W and 30°N is the Sargasso Sea (q.v.). A similar mound occurs in the southern hemisphere.

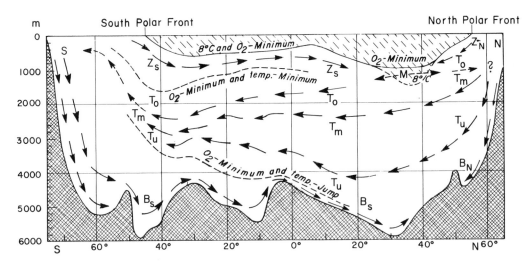

Fig. 9. Diagram of the meridional advection of the cold water control masses in the Atlantic Ocean (from Wüst). Broken lines indicate thermoclines.

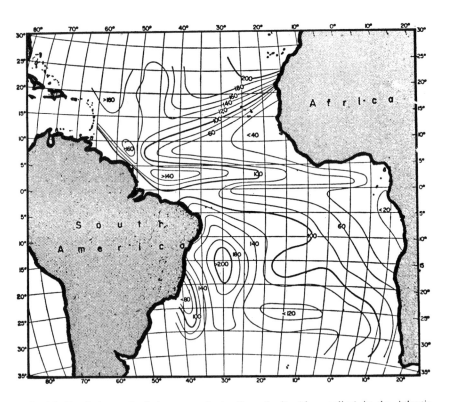

Fig. 10. Depth (meters) of the tropospheric discontinuity (thermocline) in the Atlantic Ocean between 25°N and 25°S (Defant, 1961). (By permission of Pergamon Press, N.Y.)

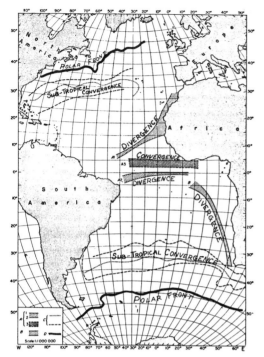

Fig. 11. Singular lines in the current field of the sea surface in the Atlantic Ocean. (A) in the system of the tropospheric circulation: (1) the divergence region in the area of the Cape Verde Islands (7–15°N); (2) the equatorial divergence region; (3) the convergence region in the Equatorial Counter Current. In the region of the tropical thermocline these singular lines correspond to inverse ones. (B) the divergence region of the Benguela Current. (C) ...., subtropical convergence; ----, polar and equatorial limits of the subtropical convergence regions. (D) ----, the oceanic polar front (Arctic and Antarctic convergence; from Defant, 1961). (By permission of Pergamon Press, N.Y.)

The steepest gradient is found along the east coast of the United States where the Gulf Stream occurs.

The surface circulation of the Atlantic Ocean is shown in Fig. 13. The flow on the equatorial side of the polar fronts is included in the warm water sphere. They reach depths at least to the main thermocline and usually deeper, though their velocities are much decreased. The thermocline acts as a barrier to vertical transport of material and momentum. This results in sluggish flow and low oxygen content of the water below this layer. The North Atlantic Ocean is dominated by a clockwise gyre. It is not symmetric, but is compressed against North America. Its most prominent feature is the intense *Gulf Stream* (q.v.), which develops from water passing through the Florida Straits and that entering north of the Bahamas. It transports between 75 and 115 million m^3/sec of seawater northward. It extends down to the sea floor in most regions, but there are indications that a narrower

and/or fluctuating countercurrent (representing the North Atlantic Deep Water of the Cold Water Sphere) may be present. The thermocline dips steeply to the east under the Gulf Stream. North of Cape Hatteras, the Gulf Stream turns away from the coast and breaks into a series of loops or meanders, whose dynamics are not yet fully understood. The northern edge of the Gulf Stream forms a weak polar front, to the north of which is the cold water sphere (see *Labrador Current*). When the Gulf Stream passes the Grand Banks it becomes more diffuse and is known as the *North Atlantic Current*. Here the flow is divided into branches. The term *North Atlantic Drift* can also be used for the weaker circulation in this region. Velocities as high as 4–5 knots have been found in the main axis of the Gulf Stream. The circulation between the Stream and the coast is variable, though more often a southward flowing pattern (joined by some part of the *Labrador Current*, (q.v.)) occurs along the coast from Newfoundland to north of Cape Hatteras.

The North Atlantic Current, which forms the northern section of the central gyre, is thus a continuation of the main Gulf Stream. The branches of eastward flowing currents are often separated by countercurrents or eddies. The weak polar front to the north of the Gulf Stream and north of the western section of the North Atlantic Current, loses its identity in the northeastern Atlantic. In crossing the Mid-Atlantic Ridge, there is indication that the current system undergoes a cyclonic loop. This is consistent with the present dynamical understanding of the effect of bottom topography on ocean flow. To the east of the Mid-Atlantic Ridge, the current divides into two parts: one arm flows towards the north and northeast (it is diluted slightly by water from the north), and the other arm flows to the east and eventually southward to form the eastern side of the central gyre. The northward flowing segment itself divides into two parts: one part crosses the Wyville Thomson Ridge to the east of Iceland, and the other part turns toward the west, moving south of Iceland becoming the *Irminger Current* (q.v.). Some of the Irminger water moves up the west coast of Iceland, but the larger portion mixes with the colder water forming the *East Greenland Current* (q.v.) The flow in the Greenland and Norwegian Seas is described below. The branch of the North Atlantic Current which flows eastward (along 45°N) turns to the south and continues as an irregular flow between the Azores and Spain (see *Canaries Current*). Most of this water continues to flow southward and eventually joins the North Equatorial Current. Both main branches of the North Atlantic Current have an important warming influence on the climates of Norway, Iceland and Great Britain.

The surface circulation pattern in the Greenland and Norwegian Seas (q.v.) should be considered part of the cold water sphere if the 9°C isotherm

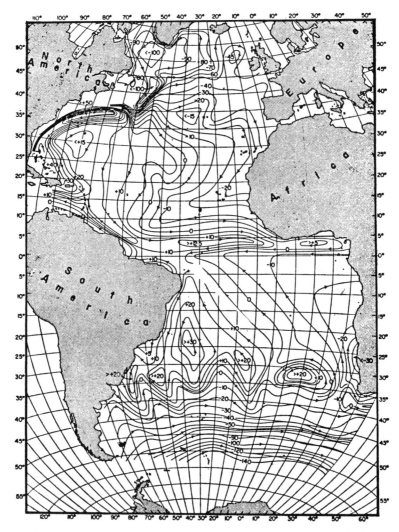

Fig. 12. Absolute topography of the physical sea surface (dynamic isobaths drawn from 5 to 5 dyn cm, 10 to 10 respectively) (Defant, 1961). (By permission of Pergamon Press, N.Y.)

taken as the boundary. However, in the northeastern Atlantic there is no polar front as is found to the west. Instead there is a gradual cooling of the northward flowing current. This area is a major heat sink of the world ocean. The northward flow is concentrated in the Norwegian Sea, while a return flow of much colder water occupies the western region. Between these two currents are cyclonic eddies at which there is active cooling and sinking. The very cold water which sinks becomes the bottom and deep water of the basins, some of which escapes into the Atlantic Ocean forming the lower strata of the North Atlantic Deep Water (see below). The warm water flow along the coast of Norway turns eastward between Spitsbergen and Norway entering the Barents Sea, where further cooling takes place.

The *North Equatorial Current* (q.v.) makes up the southern edge of the North Atlantic gyre, the center of which is the calm *Sargasso Sea* (q.v.). The North Equatorial Currents receives its water from the southward flowing branch of the North Atlantic Drift, called the Portugal Current and/or the Canary Current (q.v.). In addition to this, a large contribution comes from the zone of divergence (upwelling) along the coast of northwest Africa. The North

Fig. 13. Principal currents of the Atlantic Ocean (after Schott, 1943; from Dietrich, 1963). The longer the arrows, the greater the stability. Velocity is indicated by thickness of arrow: finest 0–36, thickest over 108 nautical miles per day. (By permission of Interscience Publishers, N.Y.)

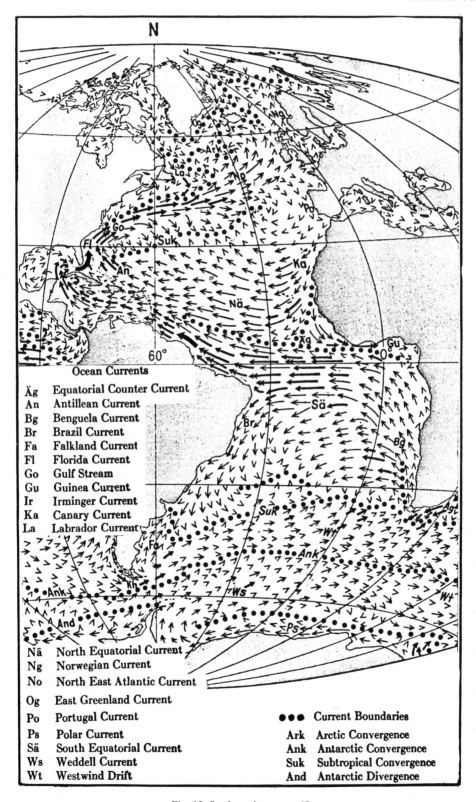

N

60°

Ocean Currents

Äg	Equatorial Counter Current
An	Antillean Current
Bg	Benguela Current
Br	Brazil Current
Fa	Falkland Current
Fl	Florida Current
Go	Gulf Stream
Gu	Guinea Current
Ir	Irminger Current
Ka	Canary Current
La	Labrador Current
Nä	North Equatorial Current
Ng	Norwegian Current
No	North East Atlantic Current
Og	East Greenland Current
Po	Portugal Current
Ps	Polar Current
Sä	South Equatorial Current
Ws	Weddell Current
Wt	Westwind Drift

●●● Current Boundaries

Ark	Arctic Convergence
Ank	Antarctic Convergence
Suk	Subtropical Convergence
And	Antarctic Divergence

Fig. 13. See legend on page 68.

Equatorial Current flows directly west and then west–northwest as the *Guiana Current* (q.v.), turning to a more northerly direction after crossing the 60°W meridian. It then is called the *Antillean Current*, with the Gulf Stream system completing the loop. Some of the North Equatorial Water enters the northern Caribbean Sea where it becomes part of the *Caribbean Current* (q.v.). This current leaves the Sea through the Yucatan Straits and with little penetration into the Gulf of Mexico flows through the Straits of Florida.

The North Equatorial Current is situated north of 10°N. Immediately to its south in the eastern and central Atlantic is a countercurrent. From 5°N southward is the South Equatorial Current which forms the northern edge of the South Atlantic gyre. Thus, the Equatorial Current System (q.v.) is not perfectly symmetrical to the equator, except for the recently discovered undercurrent. This eastward flow undercurrent has a well-defined core of high-velocity water, centered at approximately 100 m but reaching to within 25 m of the surface (occasionally breaking the surface) and extending to depths of 200 m. The center of the Equatorial Undercurrent is situated on the equator flowing directly under the South Equatorial Current.

A large percentage of the South Equatorial Current is diverted to the north by the coast of South America. Most of its water enters the Caribbean Sea and eventually flows through the Straits of Florida. Since the major source of water for the South Equatorial Current is the *Benguela Current* (q.v.), this system represents a major inter-hemispherical water transport. The return flow occurs in the North Atlantic Deep Waters (which also balances the northward flowing Antarctic components of the cold water circulation).

The South Atlantic gyre is cyclonic. It is bounded on the east by the Benguela Current, on the north by the South Equatorial Current, on the west by the *Brazil Current* (q.v.), and on the south by the Westward Drift. There is no real counterpart of the powerful Gulf Stream in the South Atlantic. A zone of upwelling is found along the coast of South-western Africa, but it is not as extensive as that found to the north. The Brazil Current is composed of that South Equatorial Water which turns southward along the coast of South America. It meets the cold northward flowing *Falkland Current* (Malvinas Current) at approximately 35°S.

Cold Water Sphere. Below the 9° isothermal surface lie three extensive cold water layers: the intermediate, deep and bottom water masses (see Fig. 9). All have their origins in the polar regions where the cold water sphere reaches the sea surface. This first layer, directly below the warm water sphere is formed along a narrow band to the poleward side of the polar fronts. The Subantarctic Intermediate Water is of far greater importance in the Atlantic Ocean than the Arctic or Subarctic

Intermediate Water, which is formed in only local regions of the Northwestern Atlantic. The same is true of the bottom water masses, i.e., that of Antarctic origin is more extensive than the Arctic Bottom Water. This results from the series of submarine ridges separating the northern basins (Greenland-Scotland ridge) from the open Atlantic Ocean. These ridges prohibit the extremely cold deep and bottom water of the Greenland and Norwegian Seas from flowing southward. There is no such hindrance to the Antarctic Bottom water in the western Atlantic Ocean which is the main corridor of the northward penetration of Antarctic Bottom Water. In the eastern Atlantic Ocean there are blocking ridges, such as the Walfish Ridge, which prevent an active bottom circulation. The thick layer of water between the two Antarctic components called the North Atlantic Deep Water flows southward and is formed for the most part in the subarctic areas near Greenland, though a portion of it is formed in the Mediterranean Sea.

Subantarctic Intermediate Water. This water mass is formed at the Antarctic Polar Fronts with a salinity of 33.8‰ and a temperature of 2.2°C. The origin of the Intermediate Water is not fully understood; it is probably a mixture of meltwater from the polar ice and Subantarctic Water in the vicinity of the Polar Front where precipitation greatly exceeds evaporation. The core of Subantarctic Intermediate Water (see *Water Masses and the Core Method*) sinks to 800 m north of the Polar Front and reaches its maximum depth of 900–1000 m between 30 and 37°S (see Fig. 9). A core map and the geostrophic velocities (q.v.) are shown in Fig. 14. Notice the preference for spreading along the western Atlantic. The reason for this is believed to be the deflecting effect of the earth's rotation (Coriolis Force, q.v.). The Subantarctic Intermediate Water can be traced by the core method to approximately 20°N. North of this latitude, no salinity minimum is found until the subarctic latitudes are reached. Here there is some minor influence of a Subarctic Intermediate Water, but as can be seen from Fig. 14, it is not as widespread as the intermediate water of the south. The total northward geostrophic volume transport of the Subantarctic Intermediate Water has been calculated to be 7 million m^3/sec.

North Atlantic Deep Water. This water mass is made up of three subdivisions: the upper (from the Mediterranean Sea), the middle (from the areas near southern Greenland), and the lower (from overflow of the Arctic Bottom Water across the ridges separating the Greenland and Norwegian Basins from the Atlantic). All three components (which occupy the depths from 1400–4000 m) flow southward and so compensate for the northward flowing Antarctic water masses and the inter-hemispheric transport of the South Equatorial Current in the warm water sphere. The North

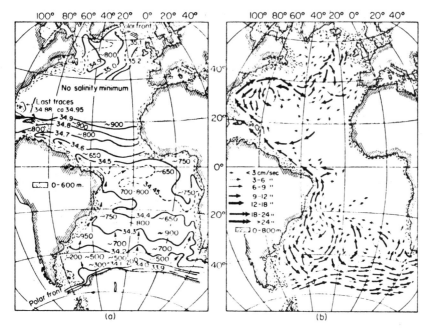

Fig. 14. Spreading of core water masses of Subantarctic and Subarctic Intermediate Water in the Atlantic Ocean. (a) Represents the distribution of salinity in the layer of salinity minimum (at approximately 500–900 m). Added figures: Depth distribution of this layer (according to G. Wüst, 1936). (b) Represents the current field at an 800 m depth (according to A. Defant, 1941; from Dietrich, 1963). (By permission of Interscience Publishers, N.Y.)

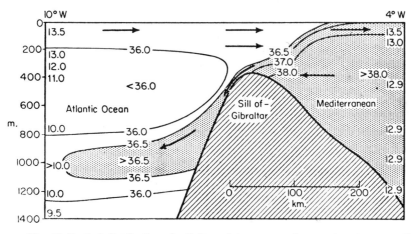

Fig. 15. Vertical distribution of salinity and temperature in a west–east cross section through the Strait of Gibraltar at 36°N. Arrows: main direction of spreading of the water. Exaggeration of vertical scale: 200-fold (according to G. Schott, 1942).

Atlantic Deep Water is most active under strong northward flowing currents, i.e., the western Atlantic. Figure 9 of the article on "Water Masses and the Core Method" is a core map (oxygen is used as the parameter) and the geostrophic flow of the Middle North Atlantic Deep Water. This layer is the largest and has considerable influence on the deep flow in the Indian and Pacific Oceans. The entire

Deep Water is identified with a secondary salinity maximum, which reaches its greatest magnitude with the upper layers entering the Atlantic Ocean through the Straits of Gibralter (Fig. 15). The oxygen values of this upper layer are low, in contrast to fairly high oxygen concentrations in the lower two layers (which is used for identification for the middle water). The depths, temperatures,

TABLE 1. MEAN STRATIFICATION AND MAIN WATER MASSES (G. WÜST, PERSONAL NOTES)

(45°N—45°S)

Depth (m)	T (°C)	S(‰)	Water Masses	Sphere
0	21.3°	35.42	Surface waters	
100	18.3	.32		Warm water
200	14.0	.18	Subtropical	sphere
400	10.0	24.86	Underwater	$t > 9°C, S > 34.8‰$
			Boundary layer	(Intermediate) (O_2—minimum)
600	7.4	.65	Subpolar	
800	5.9	.59$^+$	Intermediate	
1000	4.9	.61	Water	Cold water
1200	4.2	.65		sphere
1600	3.3	.72	Deep	
2000	2.8	.76	Water	$t < 9°C, S < 34.8‰$
3000	2.1	.75		
4000	1.6$^+$	.73$^+$	Polar Bottom Water	

salinities and velocities can be found in Fig. 9 and Table 1 of this article and Fig. 2 of the *Water Masses and the Core Method* article. The geostrophic volume transport of the entire North Atlantic Deep Water is about 27×10^6 m^3/sec toward the south (Figs. 16 and 17).

The worldwide importance of the North Atlantic Deep Water is demonstrated in the schematic view of the deep circulation (Fig. 16). The two major hydrodynamical sinks of the world oceans are both located in the Atlantic. Secondary Deep Water sources exist in the northwestern Indian Ocean (*Red Sea; Arabian Sea,* q.v.), but these contribute only a small percentage of the total volume of the world's Deep Water. The Pacific Ocean strikingly lacks source regions of Deep Water. The corridor connecting the North Atlantic Deep Water to the rest of the oceans is the Circum-Polar Current of the *Southern Ocean* (q.v.). Figure 17 is a schematic representation of the interaction of the shallow and deep circulations of the Atlantic Ocean; this ocean has the most active vertical convection of the world circulation. Due to this overturning the deep Atlantic has a high oxygen concentration, in sharp contrast to the nearly anaerobic conditions of the deep Pacific Ocean.

Antarctic Bottom Water. Due to freezing in the Sea (q.v.) dense water is formed (with a temperature of $-1.9°C$ and a salinity of 34.63‰). This water mixes with some of the warmer North Atlantic Deep Water in the circumpolar current system and sinks to the bottom with a bottom

potential temperature of $-1.0°C$ and a salinity of 34.65‰. Here it is channeled by the South Sandwich Trench into the western Atlantic Ocean where it can be traced by its cold bottom potential temperature to 40°N. Figure 18 shows the spreading of the Antarctic Bottom Water in the Atlantic Ocean. The bottom water velocities in the western Atlantic averages 7.2 cm/sec. The main axis of flow does not occupy the deepest channel but rides up on the continental slope of South America due to the Coriolis force. The Walfish Ridge blocks northward penetration in the eastern Atlantic Ocean, and Antarctic Bottom Water enters the eastern Atlantic through a gap in the Mid-Atlantic Ridge in the vicinity of the equator. The isotherms show that only in the western trough is there a real Antarctic Bottom Current with measurable velocities and that in the eastern trough there is only lateral diffusion.

Interaction between the Warm and Cold Water Spheres

Due to the stratification there is little transfer of horizontal momentum between the warm and cold water sphere (see *Troposphere and Stratosphere in the Ocean*). The former is almost entirely wind driven while the latter flows in response to a deep baroclinic field of mass produced by thermohaline alterations in the polar regions. There is some interaction which must take place; this is a slight amount of upwelling of the cold water to compensate the downward flux of heat due to solar heating. This condition must exist for a steady-state con-

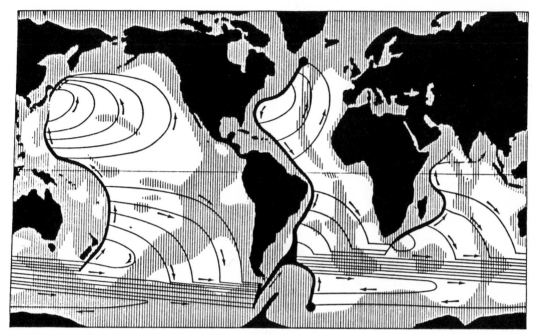

Fig. 16. World "deepwater" circulation, showing polar "sinks," and predominant Atlantic control (Stommel, 1958). Vertical hachures indicate ocean floor less than 4000 m.

dition to be reached, which is apparently the case. It has been estimated that the average vertical velocity needed to sustain the steady-state condition is 3×10^{-5} cm/sec. With the exception of this possible upwelling and some vertical exchange of material, the two water spheres are dynamically isolated from each other.

Tides in the Atlantic Ocean

Almost all of our current knowledge of tides at sea comes from tidal records along the coast and the application of the tidal theory (Villain, 1953). There are very few measurements of tides in the

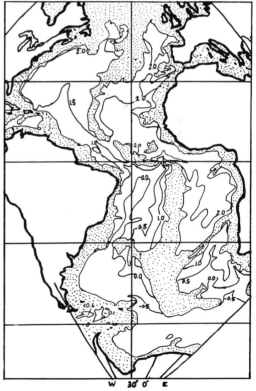

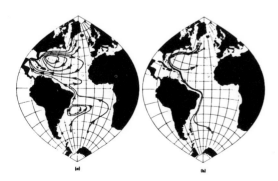

Fig. 17. Relationship of the surface (a) and deep (b) circulations of the Atlantic Ocean. Little circles mark upwellings and sinks (H. Stommel, 1957).

Fig. 18. Bottom potential temperature distribution (in degrees C) below 4000 m in the Atlantic Ocean (from Wüst, 1938).

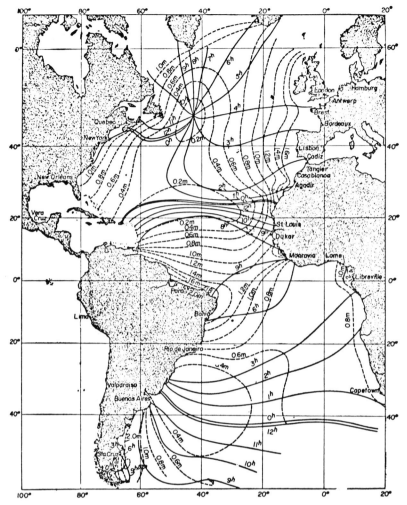

Fig. 19. Cotidal and co-range lines of the M_2 Atlantic tide (after W. Hansen; from Defant, 1958). The times of high water refer to the moon's transit through the Greenwich meridian, the co-range lines are in meters. (By permission of Pergamon Press, N.Y.)

open sea. Only recently have attempts been made to measure both surface tides and internal tidal waves in the open ocean.

The tides of the Atlantic Ocean are predominantly of lunar semidiurnal form, M_2, which is contrary to the other oceans where the diurnal form is not so small, $K_1 + O_1$ (the soli-lunar constituent and main lunar diurnal constituent). In fact, the ratio F, characteristic number of the tide, which is $(K_1 + O_1)/(M_2 + S_2)$ (S_2 is the main solar semidiurnal constituent) is very small for the Atlantic Ocean. Values range mostly from 0.10–0.25 (though values as low as 0.05 and as high as 0.70, occur). The ratios for the Indian Ocean and Pacific Ocean average above 0.50.

Figure 19 shows the cotidal and co-range lines of the M_2 Atlantic tide, and Table 2 lists some tidal constants of the coastal Atlantic and island stations; notice the great predominance of the M_2 compo-

nent. In the southern Atlantic Ocean, the M_2 wave travels northward. There are no clearly defined amphidromic points in the South Atlantic Ocean (with the possible exception of one located near 55°S, 15°E) though there may be two nodal lines. In the North Atlantic Ocean, there is one well-defined amphidromic point with counter-clockwise circulation about it. There are others in the marginal seas, one in the North Sea and one in the Caribbean Sea just south of Puerto Rico. (The tides in Ponce, P. R. are only 1 cm in amplitude.) The diurnal tide maps (K) are simpler with two amphidromic points, one in each hemisphere. In short, the tides of the Atlantic Ocean are a progressive wave from south to north of semidiurnal character, with some reflection in the north Atlantic Ocean causing superposed waves that are not in phase. There is little east–west component except in the latitudes above 40°N.

TABLE 2. SOME TIDAL CONSTANTS IN THE ATLANTIC (DEFANT, 1958)
(By permission of University of Michigan Press, Ann Arbor, Michigan)

Place	Latitude	Longitude	Amplitude (cm)				Phase (degrees)				Form Number
			M_2	S_2	K_1	O	M_2	S_2	K_1	O	%
St. John's (Newfoundland)	47°34'N	52°51'W	35.7	14.6	7.6	7.0	210	254	108	77	29
New York (Sandy Hook)	40°28'	74°01'	65.4	13.8	9.7	5.2	218	245	101	99	19
St. George (Bermuda)	32°22'	64°42'	35.5	8.2	6.4	5.2	231	257	124	128	27
Port of Spain (Trinidad)	10°39'	61°31'	25.2	8.0	8.8	6.7	119	139	187	178	47
Pernambuco (Recife, Brazil)	8°04'S	34°53'	76.3	27.8	3.1	5.1	125	148	64	142	8
Rio de Janeiro	22°54'	43°10'	32.6	17.2	6.4	11.1	87	97	148	87	35
Buenos Aires	34°36'	58°22'	30.5	5.2	9.2	15.4	168	248	14	202	70
Moltke Harbor (S. Georgia)	54°31'	36°0'	22.6	11.7	5.2	10.2	213	236	52	18	45
Capetown	33°54'S	15°25'	48.6	20.5	5.4	1.6	45	88	126	243	10
Freetown	8°30'N	13°14'	97.7	32.5	9.8	2.5	201	234	334	249	9
Puerto Lux (Las Palmas)	28°9'	25°25'	76.0	28.0	7.0	5.0	356	19	21	264	12
Ponta Delgada (Azores)	37°44'	25°40'	49.1	17.9	4.4	2.5	12	32	41	292	10
Lisbon	33°42'	9°8'	118.3	40.9	7.4	6.5	60	88	51	310	9
Brest	48°23'	4°29'	296.1	75.3	6.3	6.8	99	139	69	324	5
Londonderry	55°0'N	7°19'W	78.6	30.1	8.2	7.8	218	244	181	38	15

Sediments of the Atlantic Ocean

The marine deposits of the Atlantic consist of (a) *terrigenous material* (relatively unaltered grains: detrital and volcanic; ultimate products of the chemical weathering of rocks on land: clay minerals, hydroxides, etc.); (b) *biogenous material*, pelagic organic debris (skeletal and soft remains of organisms); (c) *authigenic material* formed in place on the sea bottom (manganese and other nodules, sulfides, zeolites, glauconite, etc.); (d) *cosmic material* (dust and spherules from extraterrestrial sources) (Fig. 20).

The proportion between the groups varies in both time and space. They are intimately mixed in their occurrence. The amount of cosmic dust is small compared with other groups and probably rather constant in time. Authigenic substances are most frequent in areas of slow sedimentation (in red clay) or occur in current-winnowed deposits. The supply of terrigenous matter increases, broadly speaking, toward the coast, especially where large rivers debouch or deserts deliver dust. The sedimentation of biogenous matter is a function of the productivity. It is highest in convergence belts, in upwelling regions and lowest within the anticyclonic eddies (horse latitudes).

Classification

The marine sediments can be subdivided as follows:

(I) *Pelagic deposits*: white, yellow red or brown in color and with $< 25\%$ consisting of detrital or volcanic matter larger than the clay fraction. Characteristic of the deep-sea floor.

(A) Calcareous oozes: $CaCO_3 > 30\%$.

(B) Siliceous oozes: $CaCO_3 < 30\%$ and siliceous organic material $> 30\%$.

(C) Red clay: $CaCO_3 < 30\%$ and siliceous organic material $< 30\%$.

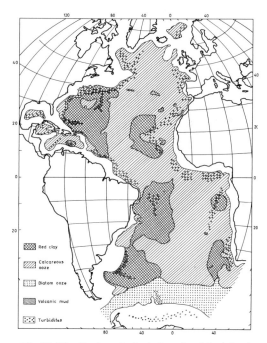

Fig. 20. Distribution of pelagic deposits of the Atlantic. The rest of the Atlantic floor is covered by hemipelagic and terrigenous deposits (mainly after Schott). Abyssal plain areas have been added, where turbidites contribute appreciably (10–25%) to the sum total (from Heezen and Laughton). (By permission of Interscience Publishers, N.Y.)

(II) *Hemipelagic and terrigenous deposits:* sediments, gray, green, blue or black in color or/and with $> 25\%$ consisting of detrital or volcanic matter larger than the clay fraction. They occur from the coasts down to the abyssal plains.

(A) Organic (calcareous and siliceous) muds: $CaCO_3$ or siliceous organic material $> 30\%$.

(B) Inorganic muds (sandy muds, silty muds, etc., depending on their texture).

The distribution of the different sediment types is shown on Fig. 20.

Composition and Stratigraphy

Calcareous Oozes. Among the most important organisms secreting calcium carbonate there are the foraminifera, coccolithophorids and pteropods. Both foraminifera and coccolithophorids have calcitic tests or plates while pteropods have aragonite shells. Because aragonite dissolves faster than calcite, pteropod ooze accumulates only in comparatively shallow areas in warmer water. Foraminifera are predominately planktonic animals, but larger benthonic foraminifera are always present in the calcareous oozes, constituting up to 10% of the carbonate fraction. In certain horizons in deep-sea cores they may be much more frequent than in others; such beds consist of redeposited beds (slumped or turbidite) where many planktonic foraminifera have been crushed during the transport. The coccolithophorids, unicellular algae with minute circular, elliptical or angular plates (coccoliths, rhabdoliths, pentaliths, etc.), constitute an appreciable portion of the calcareous matter especially in oligotrophic regions.

The calcareous oozes can be subdivided on the basis of the carbonate content into marly ooze ($CaCO_3 = 30-60\%$) and chalky ooze ($CaCO_3 > 60\%$), and named according to the type of planktonik remains that are dominant, e.g., foraminiferal chalky ooze, pteropod chalky ooze, coccolith marly ooze.

Most of the calcareous skeletons produced in the sea dissolve on their way down to or at the bottom. Calcareous matter which comes to rest at shallow depths is only attacked by solution to a lesser extent. Lower down, below about 4000 m, the carbonate content in sediments decreases rapidly with increasing depth, and below 5000 m the rate of solution exceeds the rate of supply. This "calcium carbonate compensation depth" (q.v.) seems to depend chiefly on this matter of relative rates. In the South Atlantic (and Weddell Sea) and in a restricted region of the North Atlantic, extremely cold polar surface water sinks down to the bottom and migrates equatorward, constituting the bottom water. Because the solubility of carbon dioxide (as well as carbonate minerals) increases with decreasing temperature, the deep water has a high content of carbon dioxide and thus a strong capacity for dissolving carbonates at the sea floor. In areas which are largely protected against such bottom water, e.g., the Congo Basin, the carbonate content at equal depth is much higher than in the Brazil Basin which is flushed by Antarctic bottom water.

When in equilibrium, the amount of calcium carbonate buried in marine sediments can be supposed to be equal to the amount of carbonates from weathering on land discharged to the sea by rivers. The present rate of calcium from weathering should result in a deposition to 0.34 g/cm^2 per thousand years for an area equal to the whole ocean floor. Probably two-thirds or more of these carbonates are discharged into the North Atlantic. The area of the Pacific is, however, nearly 70% larger than the Atlantic and if no calcium carbonate were transported from the Atlantic to the Pacific the accumulation of carbonates in the Atlantic would be very high but in the Pacific very low. However, the deep water from the North Atlantic dissolves carbonates on its way to the Pacific, thus acting as a transport route.

In the North Atlantic and the Central Pacific cores, a carbonate minimum in one region is isochronous with a maximum in the other. Judging from the distribution of carbonate with depth in cores (Fig. 21), there has been a changing rate in the transport (and solution) of carbonate from the Atlantic to the Pacific which is explained by an assumption of a varying rate in the convective sinking in the northernmost Atlantic. The carbonate content or other parameters showing changes in the dissolving capacity of the water can therefore be supposed to mirror changes in the climate on a worldwide basis.

The living species of pelagic foraminifera number about 25, of which 15 are common. Their distribution in the seawater is dependent on temperature (and other factors). Some species are abundant in

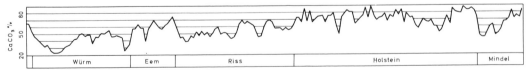

Fig. 21. The distribution of calcium carbonate in a North Atlantic core (the Swedish core 280; 34° 57′ N and 44° 16′ W). The correlation with the continental stratigraphy is tentative. Approximate ages: Riss (Illinoian) 210,000–100,000 years, Eem (Sangamon) 100,000–*c.* 70,000, Würm (Wisconsin) 70,000–10,000, and Holocene 10,000 to present.

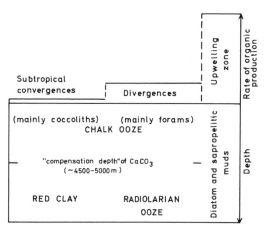

Fig. 22. The distribution of deep-sea deposits in relation to the depth and the rate of organic production. The supply of detrital matter larger than the clay fraction is presumed to be small.

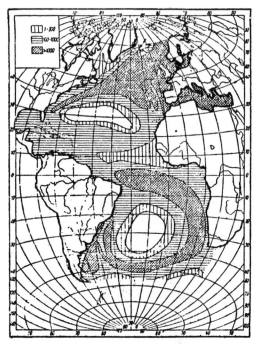

Fig. 23. Quantitative distribution of coccolithophoridae *Pontosphaera* Huxley in the Atlantic Ocean (after Lohmann).

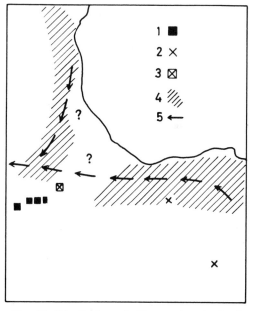

Fig. 24. Distribution of siliceous deposits in the Central Atlantic. Key: (1) diatom ooze (Würm), (2) radiolarian ooze (Riss), (3) siliceous ooze (Riss), (4) area of numerous siliceous fossils, and (5) current streams during northern winter. The radiolarian ooze occurs at depth over 5000 m. Diatom mud is also found in Walvis Bay. This Figure is based on core analyses from various expeditions (Olausson). (By permission of Pergamon Press, N.Y.)

low latitudes, other at higher latitudes. Alternations between dominance by low-latitude species and dominance by high-latitude species in core sequences may be assumed to indicate climatic changes. However, the species composition of the thanatocoenoses of deep-sea sediments are strongly influenced by differential solution (Fig. 22).

The O^{18}/O^{16} ratio in tests of pelagic foraminifera is in equilibrium with the isotopic ratio of the near-surface water where the calcite was formed. The isotopic composition of the water changes not only because of temperature factors (evaporation) but also because of the waxing and waning of ice sheets. It has been shown that the average isotopic composition of seawater has varied so much that the measured isotopic changes in the foraminiferal tests are due mainly or even totally to the glacial storage effect, which would cause a small rise in the general salinity of the ocean.

Some foraminifera have both dextral and sinistral tests. Variation in coiling direction from time to time is observed to occur and coincides with major climatic changes.

Among the *phytoplankton*, the coccolithophorids in oligotrophic regions as well as in the anticyclonal eddies, but the relative number here is low (Fig. 23). In the more fertile areas, foraminifera outweigh coccolithophorids. Attempts have been made to establish a relationship between certain species and paleotemperatures. Discoasters, stellate or rosette-shaped calcareous plates, presumably derived from plankton organisms related to the coccolithophorids, are common in Tertiary deposits but are apparently absent in the Pleistocene. The level where discoasters disappear has been suggested as a boundary for the Pliocene/Pleistocene.

Calcareous oozes are generally white or pinkish white. Calcareous deep-sea deposits which are gray, blue, etc., are classified as hemipelagic deposits.

Siliceous Oozes. Siliceous deposits accumulate in belts where the solution of carbonates exceeds its production and where the supply of terrigenous matter is comparatively low compared with the accumulation rate of siliceous organic remains.

Diatoms are frequent where the concentration of nutrients is high, as in upwelling zones, or where other organisms are inhibited, as off large rivers, by the lower salinity which does not discourage production of diatoms. They are common in both cool and warm water. Most of the diatom frustules dissolve on their way down to the bottom and only larger ones are conspicuous in the sediments. The distribution of siliceous deposits in lower latitudes may be seen in Fig. 24.

The amount of nutrients transported to the euphotic zone in the Northern Atlantic by turbulence, seasonal convection, and rivers is smaller than the supply from below in the upwelling zone in the Antarctic region, south of the Antarctic convergence. The production of organisms, e.g., diatoms, is therefore larger in the South Atlantic than in the northern part of the Ocean. Further, the floating ice from the Antarctic has smaller loads of sediments than that from northern ice sheets and there is, in addition, a large supply of terrigenous matter by rivers to the northernmost Atlantic. These factors may explain the widespread accumulation of diatomaceous deposits in the southernmost Atlantic in contrast to the low amounts in the higher latitudes of the North Atlantic.

Toward the poles, the production and the accumulation of calcareous organisms fall and diatoms predominate in the plankton. The line separating the predominantly diatom and carbonate oozes closely follows the zone of the Antarctic Convergence.

Radiolaria are planktonic animals which have complex and ornate siliceous skeletons (those rare ones with strontium sulfate, celestite, skeletons are not found in sediments owing to their higher solubility). The radiolaria, like diatoms, are most frequent at lower latitudes. In the surface fauna, however, they are greatly outnumbered by the foraminifera. Nevertheless, where the calcium carbonate is dissolved and where the production of diatoms is not excessive, as in moderate productive areas, radiolarian ooze is accumulated. These requirements are only exceptionally fulfilled in the Atlantic. In the Pacific, the "compensation depth" is reached in the fertile regions and radiolarian ooze is common there.

Diatom ooze is yellowish, straw or cream colored, and radiolarian ooze is generally yellowish brown. Radiolaria and diatoms can only be used for the relative dating of a deposit. This procedure is based on the presence and/or absence of species known to occur during a certain epoch.

Red Clay. Red clay occurs in oligotrophic regions where calcium carbonate is chiefly or totally dissolved and where the supply of siliceous organisms is low. The red clay may be of extremely fine grade but contains also larger remnants of calcareous and siliceous organic remains, sharks teeth, ear bones of whales ("otoliths"), etc. The color is brownish red or chocolate brown but grades into blue, gray or green near shore (hemipelagic deposits). The red-brown color is due to the presence of ferric hydroxide or oxide, and a small amount of manganese oxide minerals. The chief components consist of clay minerals which are primarily of detrital origin. Their distribution is strongly correlated with regional continental sources of weathered material modified by the ocean circulation. Off lands covered by lateritic soils (notably Brazil and southeastern United States), kaolinite and gibbsite are frequent (Figs. 25 and 26). In volcanic areas, montmorillonite and the zeolite phillipsite are common. They may be the products of altered volcanic ash and pumice. Illite is characteristic of cool, temperate soils, and chlorite is derived mainly from metamorphic sources.

Manganese nodules (q.v.) are most frequent in red clay although they also occur in organic oozes. They cover an important part of the pelagic area,

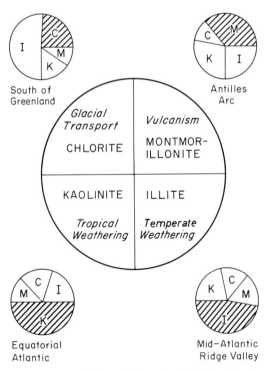

Fig. 25. Distribution of clay minerals in the Atlantic (modified after Goldberg).

Note = illite was first labeled "arid" weathering, but is more characteristic of temperate weathering.

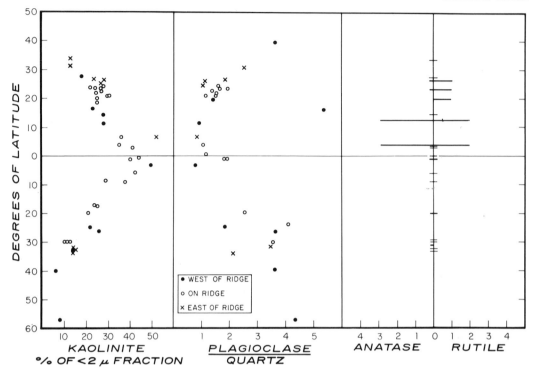

Fig. 26. Relation of clays to latitude in the Atlantic Ocean (Goldberg).

perhaps 10% as average. The nodules range in size from a few microns, suspended in the sediments or coating other minerals, to rounded balls and intergrowths forming large slabs. The nodules display a zoned growth structure with alternating goethite and manganese oxide minerals. The average concentrations of Mn and Fe are 16 and 17.5%, respectively. The accretion occurs at the sediment surface only, and the growth is very slow (10^{-5}–10^{-6} cm/yr). Therefore, nodules can be formed only where the rate of deposition is of that order or lower, or perhaps there may exist some sort of mechanism which helps them to stay at the sediment-water interface. They do not seem to occur down in the cores much below the surface.

The rate of red clay accumulation may be of the order of 10^{-3}–10^{-4} cm/yr and probably higher during glacial ages. The stratigraphic value of red clay is limited because of the scarcity of fossils and other datable materials and because of the difficulty in interpreting the record offered by clay mineralogy.

Terrigenous and Hemipelagic Deposits. *(a) Deep-Sea Sediments.* On the continental rises, on the abyssal plains and in deep-sea trenches, sand layers may alternate with mud. The deep-sea sands, usually fine to very fine sand, often contain mixed shallow and deep-water foraminifera indicating displacement. The sands are thus transported from the shallower water, moved down the slopes along the axes of submarine valleys. Most authors explain almost all deep-water sands as turbidity current deposits (Fig. 27).

Around the Antarctic continent and in the north polar seas, ice-borne deposits are widespread. Rock floor (silt fraction), produced by the land ice, constitutes the main portion of the sediment, and angular, unweathered rock fragments (sand, gravel and boulder fractions) are scattered through the fine-grained sediment. Diatoms occur while carbonates are often absent. During glacials, the limits of drifting ice were shifted equatorward some 1000 km (to about 35 or 40°N and S), which is seen from deep-sea cores and dredging.

Large amounts of eolian dust from the Sahara are transported into the Cape Verde Basin. The windblown matter increases in size toward the coast; its mean diameter is in the silt fraction. Quartz grains, coated with hematite, are recognized in the offshore deposits. They are considered as desert grains. The sediments of this region and other volcanic areas (Cape Verde Islands Canaries, Azores, Iceland, Antilles, Scotia Arc, etc.) are rich in volcanic materials.

Hemipelagic deposits are typical pelagic deposits where colors are gray, blue, green, or black. The rate of accumulation is probably higher and in places the renewal of the bottom water is slower than in areas of true pelagic deposition. Both phenomena would lead to higher organic entrapment, bacterial activity and reducing reactions within the sediments.

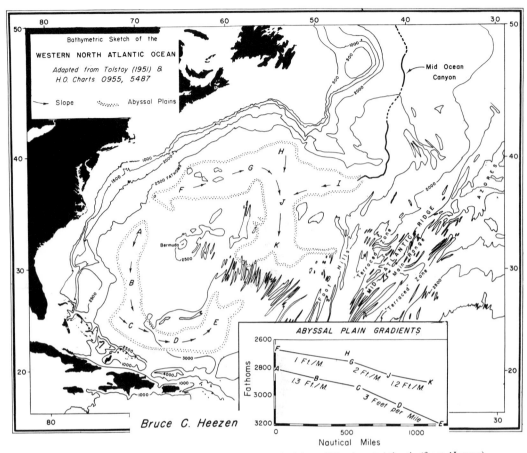

Fig. 27. Distribution of turbidites within the abyssal plains of Northwest Atlantic (from Heezen).

The hemipelagic deposits are most frequent in regions with higher supply of soft organic remains and/or clayey material. In cores, oxidized and reduced horizons may alternate.

Mud is the most abundant sediment on the continental slopes and rises, covering about 60% of the area; 25% is covered by sand, whereas rock, gravel, and shells comprise the rest. The mud is often green in color, containing glauconite; such is particularly the case off arid coasts where there is very little other sediment which would mask or inhibit the slow development of such authigenic minerals.

(b) Shallow Water Sediments. The nearshore sedimentation pattern is very complex. This is because of the normally complex relief and the many variables involved.

Sand is the most common type of deposit on shelves. The sand can be terrigenous or biogenic in origin, i.e., it may consist of quartz, shells, coral debris, etc. Authigenic sands (oolites, glauconite, etc.) are less frequent. Sand is, according to Shepard, generally found on open shelves (representing former Pleistocene beaches), off long sand beaches

and sandy points, outside narrow bay entrances, and on banks off former or present glaciated areas (often mixed with gravel and boulders).

Muds are the second most abundant type of deposits on the shelves and are prominent off large rivers, in sheltered bays and gulfs, and in depressions of the open shelf.

Solid rocks ("hard-grounds") outcrop over the continental shelf in bay entrances, straits or between islands, along coasts having sea cliffs cut in rock, on rises or ridges, and wherever strong currents sweep the bottom (except off glaciated areas).

If the sea level were to remain constant for a long time and if waves were the only important factor in sedimentation, a progressive decrease in average grain size with increasing distance from shore would be expected. However, the succession outward from the coast is often terrigenous sand, mud, sand, and mud which continues on the continental slope. The coarser deposits on the outer shelf are relict sediments of periods of lower sea level and often include long belts of boulder deposits left by melting of stranded icebergs.

Terrigenous sediments of lower latitudes are largely composed of calcareous remains of benthonic organisms (including coral reefs) in contrast to those of higher latitudes which chiefly consist of mineral fragments.

Sapropel mud is formed in certain hypotrophic areas as in the Walvis Bay of Southwest Africa.

Rocks of the Atlantic Ocean

The nature of the oceanic crust beneath the Atlantic can be partly appraised by geophysical methods, mainly earthquake seismology and refraction surveys (see pr Vol. V), but its petrographic characteristics may be partly deduced from studies of oceanic island rocks. Care should be taken not to confuse dredged erratics with *in situ* rocks; erratics from the glacial maxima range equatorward as far as 35°N and 35°S.

The volcanic rocks are distributed in the following categories:

(a) Orogenic Volcanoes: Island Arcs: Marked by "Pacific Suite" calc-alkaline rocks, in the West Indies (Caribbean), the inner arc of the Lesser Antilles. A newly recognized indicator of island arc volcanics is the 2–3% TiO_2 in their composition in contrast to the less than 1% in oceanic types. The outer arc is represented only in Barbadoes with its abyssal-type sediments (analogous to Timor in the East Indies), and joins the more continental type sequences in Trinidad and in the Greater Antilles. In the South Atlantic, a very similar island loop is represented by the Scotia Arc or Southern Antilles (South Georgia, South Sandwich Islands, and South Orkneys).

(b) Lava Plateaus: Marked by "Atlantic Suite" alkaline rocks, in Iceland ("Thulean Province"), the Faeroes, Rockall, the Azores, Madeira, the Canary Islands, and the Cape Verde Islands.

(c) Volcanic Ridges or Seamounts: Represented by Bermuda, St. Helena, Fernando Po, Principe, Sao Thome, Annobon, Fernando Noronha, Trinidad and Martin Vaz. Several of these are only represented by coral or eolianite rocks at the surface; a deep boring at Bermuda disclosed its volcanic basement.

(d) Mid-Atlantic Ridge Volcanoes: represented by Jan Mayen, Iceland (in part), Azores (in part), St. Paul's Rocks (sometimes called St. Peter's and St. Paul's Rocks), Ascension, Tristan da Cunha, Gough Island, Bouvet Island (Bouvetøya, in Norwegian).

Most of the mid-oceanic rocks are basalts ranging from the strictly alkaline to the tholeiitic, and seem to be derived directly from an upper mantle source.

The basalts situated farthest away from the Mid-Atlantic Ridge (Madeira, Canaries, Cape Verde Islands) are "distinctly more alkaline" than those of the ridge (Muir, 1965). The mature islands give highly differentiated rocks, but those dredged from near the ridge are extremely fresh, mostly spilites in the form of pillow lavas (many bottom photographs show this characteristic form). Inclusions in the lavas (noted in the Azores, Madeira, the Canaries, Ascension, Tristan da Cunha and Gough) include tholeiitic and alkali gabbros, dunite and peridotite, with mineral characteristics that suggest source regions at over 50 km depth, in the upper mantle (Le Maitre, 1965). Of special interest are St. Paul's Rocks, which coincide with one of the great east–west fracture zones and expose intensely mylonitized mantle rocks of several unique types (Wiseman, 1965).

It has recently emerged that a differentiate from these alkaline to tholeiitic types of basaltic magma can produce certain acid rocks, including special types of granite. At Rockall, for example, an isolated peak 320 km west–northwest of the Outer Hebrides rises from a submarine plateau of under 1000 m (measuring 640 × 160 km); it is an aegirine granite with a darker variety called rockallite. Its radiogenic age is 60 ± 10 million years (pyroxene), according to Sabine (1965), which places it along with the "North Atlantic Tertiary Province," including the Lundy granite (off North Devon) of 52 ± 2 million years, varied rocks from Rhum, Skye, Arran, Ardnamurchan and Mull, including quartz gabbro, granophyre and granite, acid rocks from Iceland which include vast areas of rhyolitic tuffs (Walker, 1965). On Ascension, ejected plutonic blocks include monzonite, peralkaline granite and syenite (Cann, 1965). At Jan Mayen, 560 km north–northeast of Iceland, there is a transition from basaltic to trachytic and rhyolitic flows, resembling Ascension and St. Helena. Bouvet is a trachytic dome.

Structural History of Atlantic Ocean

Theories of the structural history of the Atlantic depression go back at least to Plato and the "Atlantis" saga. Interpretations of the latter differ, but essentially suggest that Atlantis was a large archipelago situated to the west of Gibraltar, whose inhabitants began to invade adjacent Mediterranean lands about 9600 BC, their homeland eventually being entirely engulfed by the waves. This date, especially if converted to geological time scale as 11,500 B.P., is a singularly seductive one, since it marks the Alleröd Stage of the postglacial transgression, a time when coastal and insular tribes would be forced by the rising eustatic sea level to seek other territory. This naturalistic explanation of the saga can be applied equally well to the broad continental shelf areas around northwestern Europe and northeastern United States, both of which are known to archeologists to have furnished avenues for the movements of late Paleolithic/Mesolithic man, thanks to dredged artifacts, traces of submerged middens, and so on. The present sea level was reached about 6000 B.P.

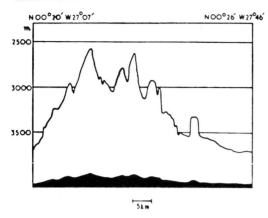

Fig. 28. A part of the Mid-Atlantic Ridge near the equator (Koczy, 1954).

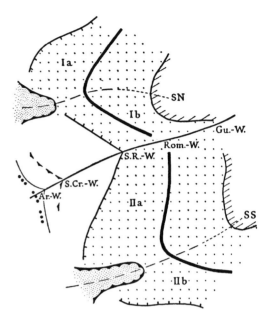

Fig. 29. The Atlantic transverse relations and transverse symmetries. The definitions are as follows: SR.-W. = San Roque Angle ("Winkel"); R.W. = Romanche Angle; Gu.W. = Guinea Angle; Ar.-W. = Arica Angle; S. Cr.-W. = Santa Cruz Angle. The Arica-Guinea line is a line of symmetry between the Northern Structure (I) and the Southern Structure (II). SN = North Atlantic axial line, as line of symmetry between the areas Ia and Ib of the North Antillean–Mid-Atlantic Structure. SS = South Atlantic axial line, as line of symmetry between the areas IIa and IIb of the South Antillean-South Atlantic Structure (Stille, 1939).

so that Neolithic man and subsequent inhabitants have been restricted to basically "modern" physical geography.

Explanations of shelf areas aside, the rest of the Atlantic depression requires special structural studies, but it is important to stress that the fundamentally different crustal categories each call for individual treatment and analysis: *Mid-Atlantic Ridge* (a *Mid-Ocean Ridge*, q.v.) (Fig. 28), *Aseismic Ridges* (q.v.), *Continental Borderlands* (q.v.) and/or *Submarine Plateaus* (q.v.), *Abyssal Plains* (q.v.) and *Abyssal Hills* (q.v.), and deep oceanic *Trenches* (q.v.). Each of these geomorphic and geotectonic province types has representations in the world oceans and is therefore treated separately in this Encyclopedia.

General consideration of the Atlantic depression calls for brevity (the best summary, with verbatim quotations, of all the early theories is to be found in Hume, 1948). The nature of oceanic depressions in general has attracted geological speculation and study for at least one and a half centuries. The Atlantic is really the simplest ocean and has called for the principal focus of attention. Four categories of explanations have been offered:

(1) Permanence Theories. This "conservative" approach is based on the belief that suboceanic crust is fundamentally different from continental crust, and that once established in the earliest history of the globe, oceanic depressions were more or less immutable (except perhaps marginally, through geosynclinal evolution). An argument for permanence is the mathematical symmetry of many world lineament patterns, as discussed by J. D. Dana, Lowthian Green, George Darwin, Vening Meinesz, Cloos, Brock and others (Figs. 29 and 30).

(2) Collapse Theories. It is recognized that many mountain ranges end "blind" and are cut off abruptly by the ocean, e.g., in Newfoundland, western Europe, Greenland, Morocco, the Cape

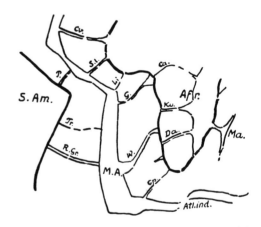

Fig. 30. Geometric blocks or "felder" proposed by Cloos, by analogy with the Precambrian basement of Africa. Abbreviations correspond to principal ridges: P. = Para; Tr. = Trinidad; R.Gr. = Rio Grande; CV. = Cape Verde; S.L. = Sierra Leone; Li. = Liberia; G. = Guinea; W. = Walvis; Cp. = Cape; Ca. = Cameroons; Ku. = Kuanza; Da. = Damara; Ma. = Madagascar, (Cloos, 1937).

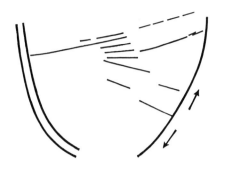

FRACTURE PATTERN OF NORTH ATLANTIC
SIMPLIFIED BY OMISSION OF TRANSCURRENT MOVEMENT

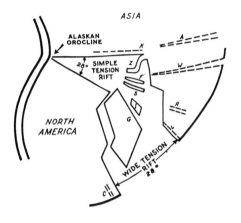

Fig. 31. Diagram illustrating the fracture pattern of the North Atlantic, radiating with a 28° opening from the Alaskan "Orocline" (Carey, 1958)

Ranges, etc. Furthermore, sedimentational paleogeographic data seem to call for the former presence of "borderlands" or "lost continents," e.g., Appalachia, off the eastern side of North America. Proposals to substitute such land masses with sunken "island arcs" are inadequate, since island arc lithologies are inappropriate. Besides they have left no geophysical traces. The fragmentation and collapse theories were formalized by Edward Suess and carried on by Hans Stille, who devised the idea of the "Ur-ozean" (a primary ocean basin sector, like parts of the deep Atlantic) and "Neu-ozean" (secondary collapse areas, like marginal seas on the Caribbean, Mediterranean, and continental borderlands). These, Stille called *quasicratonic*, and modern geophysical work brings considerable support to this viewpoint.

(3) Drift Theories. The postulated tidal resonance theory of George Darwin, whereby the moon separated from the earth (leaving the Pacific Ocean as a scar), would leave a shortage of continental crust that would cause tension over the rest of the globe, and continental drifting would result; the Atlantic would thus be an extensional effect and the ocean floor would be an exposed scar of basaltic crust away from which the continents had drifted. The matching coasts, especially of the South Atlantic, have been a strong argument for "drifters" —from Richard Owen in 1857, through Snider, Pickering, Taylor, Baker and Wegener up to J. Tuzo Wilson. From its most eloquent exponent, the drift concept is usually known as the Wegenerian Hypothesis.

(4) Spreading Theories. Stimulated by the recognition of the youthfulness and mantle-type rocks of the mid-ocean ridge, several explanations invoke the

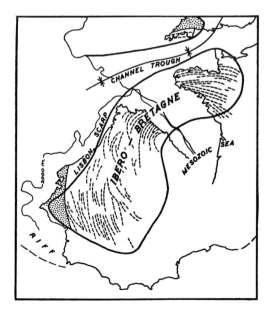

Fig. 32. Reconstruction of the Ibero-Bretagne fold belt (of Hercynian or late Paleozoic age), prior to its postulated hingelike opening during Mesozoic times, following Carey's suggestion. Recent British geomagnetic measurements have traced the Hercynian trends of the continental shelf in the same pattern (Carey, 1958).

concept of oceanic growth, an expansion of the area of ocean floor, spreading the continents apart, a growth of new sub-ocean crust, but not drifting of continents across a preexisting basaltic layer (Figs, 32, 32 and 33). There are two mechanisms (not mutually exclusive) proposed:

(a) Convection Currents in the Mantle. Either the mid-ocean ridge is a region of compression and crumpling, a submarine orogenic belt, due to convergent currents (which rise up and separate under the radioactively warmed continents), *or* it is a region of tension and volcanic effusion (high heat flow), the site of divergent currents that sink under the continental borders. Neither theory is satisfactory when seen in three dimensiions: the mid-ocean ridge passes *into* continents near the Lena delta, in the Gulf of Aden and in the Gulf of California—in each place convection streams would be expected to rise and sink in the same spot, a very serious difficulty.

(b) Expansion in the Mantle. The earth's history of magmatic differentiation, to a denser iron-nickel core below and lighter basaltic and granitic crusts above, calls for progressively lower-density minerals toward the surface with progressive upward phase changes. The paleogeographic history of the continents suggests that the cover of epicontinental seas has (with oscillations) been progressively reduced. An assumption of differentiation would make an accelerating rate of expansion predictable (the area increases in comparison to radius by $4\pi r^2$). Several different methods give mean rates of radius increase of about 1 mm/yr over the last 0.5×10^9 years; the earlier rate of growth would be much less, but recent rates may well be higher. Calculations have been offered variously by Egyed, Carey, Heezen, Creer, and Runcorn.

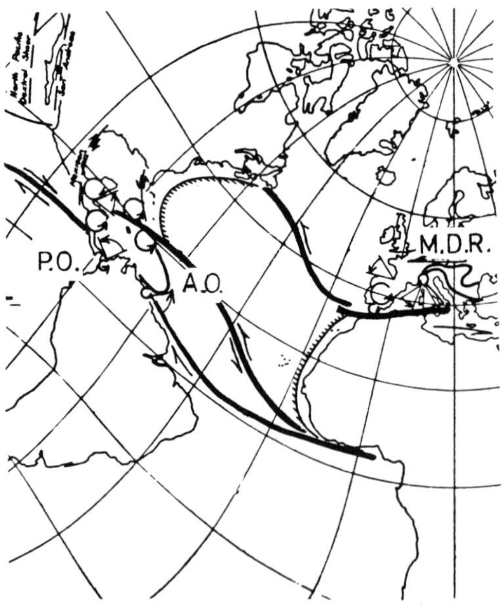

RHODES W. FAIRBRIDGE
ARNOLD GORDON
ERIC OLAUSSEN

References

Ampferer, O., 1941, "Gedanken über das Bewegungsbild des atlantischen Raumes," *Sitzber. Akad. Wiss. Wien, Math.-Nat. Kl.,* Abt. I, **150,** 19–35.

Browne, B. C., and Cooper, R. I. B., 1950, "The British submarine gravity surveys of 1938 and 1946," *Phil. Trans. Roy. Soc. London Ser. A,* **242,** 243–310.

Bruns, E., 1958, "Ozeanologie," Berlin, Deutscher Verlag d. Wiss., 2 vols.

Cann, J. R., 1965, "Preliminary investigations on the acid ejected blocks of Ascension Island," *Proc. Geol. Soc. London,* No. 1621, 62–63.

Clark, A. H., 1913, "The Atlantic Ocean biologically an inland sea," *Intern. Rev. Hydrob. Hydrog.,* **6.**

Clay, C. S., and Rona, P. A., 1965, "Studies of seismic reflections from thin layers on the ocean bottom in the western North Atlantic," *J. Geophys. Res.,* **70,** 855–871.

Cloos, H., 1939, "Hebung-Spaltung-Vulkanismas," *Geol. Rundschau,* Sp. No. 4A, **30,** 405–527.

Correns, C. W., 1937, "Die Sedimente des Aquatorialen Atlantischen Ozeans," *Wiss. Ergeb. Deutsch Atlantisch Exped. Meteor 1925–27,* **3,** Pt. 3, 298pp.

Correns, C. W., 1939, "Pelagic Sediments of the North Atlantic Ocean," in (Trask) "Recent Marine Sediments," pp. 373–395, Tulsa, Okla. American Association of Petroleum Geologists.

Defant, A., 1958, "Ebb and Flow," Ann Arbor, University of Michigan Press, (translated by A. J. Pomerans) 121pp.

Defant, A., 1961, "Physical Oceanography," Vols. I and II, New York, Pergamon Press.

de Fleurieu, C. F. C., 1798–1800, "Observations sur la Division Hydrographique du Globe, et Changements Purposes dans la Nomenclature Generale et Particuliere de l'Hydrographie," *Voyage autour du Monde* par E. Marchand, **4,** 1–74.

Dietrich, G., 1963, "General Oceanography," New York, Interscience Publishers.

Dietrich, G., 1964, "Oceanic Polar Front Survey in the North Atlantic," in (Odishaw; Hugh, editor) "Research in Geophysics," Vol. 2, pp. 291–309, Cambridge, Mass., The M.I.T. Press.

Emiliani, C., 1956, "Oligocene and Miocene temperatures of the equatorial and subtropical Atlantic Ocean," *J. Geol.,* **64,** No. 3.

Ericson, D. B., Ewing, M., and Heezen, B. C., 1952, "Turbidity currents and sediments in the North Atlantic," *Bull. Am. Assoc. Petrol. Geologists,* **36,** 489–512.

Ericson, D. B., Ewing, M., Heezen, B. C., and Wollin, G., 1955, "Sediment deposition in deep Atlantic," *Geol. Soc. Am. Spec. Papers,* **62,** 205–220.

Fig. 33. Careys' postulated fracture zones in his "Tethyan Shear", a left-lateral shift between the two hemispheres, producing eddy motions in the Caribbean and Mediterranean (Carey, 1958). P.O. = Panama Orocline; A.O. = Antillean Oroclinotath; M.D.R. = Mediterranean Drag Region.

Ericson, D. B. *et al.*, 1961, "Atlantic deep-sea sediment cores," *Bull. Gol. Soc. Am.*, **72**, 193–286.

Gagel, C., 1910, "Die Mittelatlantischen Vulkaninseln," *Hanb. Regional Geol.*, **7**, No. 10.

Goldberg, E. D., and Griffin, J. J., 1964, "Sedimentation rates and mineralogy in the South Atlantic," *J. Geophys. Res.*, **69**, 4293–4311.

Gregory, J. W., 1929, "Geological history of the Atlantic Ocean," *Presid. Address, Quart. J. Geol. Soc.*, **85**, Pt. 2, 93–96.

Groot, J. J., and Groot, C. B., 1964, "Quaternary stratigraphy of sediments of the Argentine Basin—A palynological investigation," *Trans. N.Y. Acad. Sci.*, Ser. 2, **26**, 881–886.

Heezen, B. C., and Laughton, A. S., 1963, "Abyssal Plains," in "The Sea," Vol. 3, pp. 312–364, New York, Interscience Publishers.

Heezen, B. C., and Tharp, M., 1961, "Physiographic diagram of the South Atlantic Ocean, the Caribbean Sea, the Scotia Sea, and the eastern margin of the South Pacific Ocean," *Geol. Soc. Am. Spec. Publ.*

Heezen, B. C., Tharp, M., Ewing, M., 1959, "The floors of the oceans. I. The North Atlantic," *Geol. Soc. Am. Spec. Papers*, **65**.

Hill, M. N. (editor), 1963, "The Sea," Vols. 1, 2 and 3, New York, Interscience Publishers.

Hull, E., 1912, "Monograph on the Suboceanic Physiography of the North Atlantic Ocean," London.

Kossinna, E., 1921, "Die Tiefen des Weltmeerěs," *Veroeffentl. Inst. Meeresk. Berlin, N.F. Ser. A*, No. 9, 70pp.

Krümmel, O., 1897, "Handbuch der Ozeanographie," Stuttgart, Engelhorn's Nachf., 2 vols.

Laughton, A. S., 1960, "An interplain deep-sea channel system," *Deep-Sea Res.*, **7**, 75–88.

Le Maitre, R. W., 1965, "Basic inclusions from some Atlantic volcanoes," *Proc. Geol. Soc. London*, No. 1626, 143.

Muir, I. D., 1965, "Basalt types from the floor of the atlantic Ocean," *Proc. Geol. Soc. London*, No. 1626, 141–142.

Murchison, R. I., 1893, "Nomenclature of the oceans," *Geograph. J.*, **1**, 535–536.

Murray, J., 1888, "On the height of the land and the depth of the ocean," *Scott. Geogr. Mag.*, **4**, 1.

Murray, J., 1895, "Summary of Results," in "*Challenger* Expedition," London, chart IA.

Murray, Sir J., and Hjort, J., 1912, "The Depths of the Ocean," London, Macmillan and Co., 821pp.

Neumann van Padang, M., 1938, "Über die Unterseevulkane der Erde," *De Ingenieur in Ned-Indie*, **5**, 69–83, 85–103.

Nicholls, G. D., Nalwalk, A. J., and Hays, E. E., 1964, "The Nature and composition of rock samples dredged from the Mid-Atlantic Ridge between 22°N and 52°N," *Marine Geology*, **1**, 333–343.

Olausson, E., 1964, "On Evidences of Climatic Changes in North Atlantic Cores," in "Progress in Oceanography," Vol. 3, Oxford, Pergamon Press.

Rothe, J. P., 1951, "The structure of the bed of the Atlantic Ocean," *Trans. Am. Geophys. Union*, **32**, 457–461.

Sabine, P. A., 1965, "Rockall: An unusual occurrence of Tertiary granite," *Proc. Geol. Soc. London*, No. 1621, 51.

Sachs, P. L., 1963, "A visit to St. Peter and St. Paul Rocks," *Oceanus*, **9**, 2–5.

Schott, G., 1942, "Geographie des Atlantischen Ozens," Third ed., Hamburg, Boysen, 438pp.

Stille, H., 1948, "Ur- und Neuozeane," Berlin, *Abhandl. Deut. Akad. Wiss.*, No. 6, 68pp.

Stocks, T., and Wüst, G., 1935, "Die Tiefenverhältnisse des Offenen Atlantischen Ozeans," (Begleitworte zur Übersichtskarte 1:20 million) *Wiss, Ergebn. "Meteor" Exped.*, **3**, Pt. 1.

Stommel, H., 1957, "A survey of ocean current theory," *Deep-Sea Res.*, **4**, 149–184 (also 1958, *ibid.*, **5**, 80–82).

Supan, A., 1899, "Bodenformen des Weltmeeres," *Peterm. Mitt.*, a77f.

Swedish Deep-Sea Expedition, 1947–1948, Rept. **VII**.

Teichert, C., 1958, "Cold- and deep-water coral banks," *Bull. Am. Assoc. Petrol. Geologists*, **42**, 1064–1082.

Turekian, K. K., and Stuiver, M., 1964, "Clay- and carbonate-accumulation rates in three South Atlantic deep-sea cores," *Science*, **146**, 55–56.

U.S. Navy, 1955, "Marine Climatic Atlas of the World," Vol. 1: "North Atlantic Ocean," (Navaer 50-1V-528),. Washington, D.C.

Villain, C. M., 1953, "Carte des Lignes Cotidales dans les Oceans," Paris, *Annales Hydrographiques, Ser. 4*, **3** (for 1952), 269–388.

Walker, G. P. L., 1965, "Acid rocks of Iceland," *Proc. Geol. Soc. London*, No. 1621, 61–62.

Wiseman, J. D. H., 1965, "Petrography, mineralogy, chemisty, and mode of origin of St. Paul Rocks," *Proc. Geol. Soc. London*, No. 1626, 146–147.

Wüst, G., 1933, "Das Bodenwasser und die Gliederung der Atlantischen Tiefsee," *Wiss. Ergebn. Deutsch. Atlantisch. Exped. "Meteor" 1925–27*, **6**, Pt. 1.

Wüst, G., 1936, "Die Gliederung des Weltmeeres," *Petermanns Mitt*, No. 2, 33–38 (also translation *Hydrographic Rev.*, **13**, No. 2, 46–55).

Wüst, G., 1936, "Deep circulation in the expanse of the North Atlantic Ocean," *Naturwissenschaften* **24**(9) (English translation) in *Int. Hydr. Rev.*, **13**(26), 23–31.

Wüst, G., and Defant, A., 1936, "Schichtung und Zirkulation des Atlantischen Ozeans," *Wiss. Ergebn. Deutsch. Atlantisch. Exped. "Meteor" 1925–27*, **6** (Atlas).

ATMOSPHERIC OCEAN INTERACTIONS— *See* OCEAN, ATMOSPHERE INTERACTIONS

AUSTAUSCH, EXCHANGE COEFFICIENT

"Austausch" is a brief term to cover eddy friction, eddy conduction and eddy diffusion. It is simply the German word for "exchange" or *turbulent exchange coefficient,* but since the German schools of meteorology and oceanography have been pioneers in these fields, with respect to thermodynamic exchange, the original name has been widely adopted; the basic reference is to W. Schmidt (1917). The terms *exchange* and *exchange coefficient* also have wide currency; "eddy coefficient," "eddy diffusivity" and "mixing coefficient" are also used.

In any turbulent flow (atmosphere, oceans, rivers, etc.) momentum, heat, water vapor, chemical components and dispersed materials are transported not only by a mean flow but also by the turbulent components. A time- or space-averaged

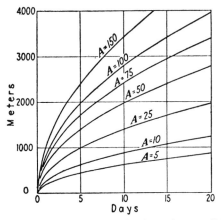

Fig. 1. Height of mean heating for various coefficients of turbulent mass exchange on Austausch (A in cgs units) in the atmosphere (from Haurwitz, 1941). (By permission of McGraw-Hill, N.Y.)

fluid and increases with its energy $(u')^2$. Therefore, the austausch is generally a function of time and space.

Turbulent motions in the atmosphere and in the oceans are more vigorous in the horizontal than in the vertical direction except close to the upper and lower boundaries because a horizontal dimension is much larger than a vertical one. Therefore, in the open oceans and free atmosphere, horizontal austausch is 10^5–10^7 times vertical austausch. Particularly, vertical austausch decreases at the pycnoclines (ocean) or at the inversions (atmosphere) because turbulent motions in these layers are drastically diminished owing to the strong vertical stability.

TAKASHI ICHIYE
RHODES W. FAIRBRIDGE

flux by the latter is called *eddy flux* and is expressed by $\overline{u'S'}$ where u' and S' are fluctuating parts of a velocity component in any direction and a quantity S, respectively, and the bar indicates the mean value. Although $\overline{u'} = \overline{S'} = 0$, by definition, the quantity S is transported by the eddy flux in the direction opposite to the mean gradient of S. Therefore, the eddy flux is finite and is proportional to $-\partial S/\partial n$, where n is the direction of the velocity component u. This proportion coefficient is defined as *austausch*. It is dependent on the turbulent motion of the

References

Defant, A., 1961, "Physical Oceanography," Vol. I, Oxford, Pergamon Press, 729pp.
Hauriwitz, B., 1941, "Dynamic Meteorology," New York, McGraw-Hill Book Co., 365pp.
Priestley, G. H. B., 1959, "Turbulent Transfer in the Lower Atmosphere," Chicago, Ill., University of Chicago Press, 130pp.
Sverdrup, H. U., Johnson, M. W., and Fleming, R. H., 1942, "The Oceans," Englewood Cliffs, N.J., Prentice-Hall, 1087pp.

Cross-references: *Diffusion in the Ocean; Turbulence.*

B

BAFFIN BAY—See CANADIAN ARCTIC
ARCHIPELAGO

BALI SEA

Defined as that part of the East Indian (Indonesian) Archipelago that lies east of Java, and
extends east to the edge of the *Flores Sea* (q.v.),
the Bali Sea is bounded on the south (from the
Indian Ocean) by a line from Cape (Tanjong)
Bantenan through the southern points of Bali,
Lombok to Sumbawa; from Tg. Saroka (8°22'S
117°10'E) it extends to the western Paternoster
Island and thence to Kangean Islands and Tg.
Sedano on Java. It covers an area of about 45,000
km².

The above definition, recommended by the
International Hydrographic Bureau (*Sp. Publ.* 23,
1953), is one used mainly by mariners, but from the
oceanographic point of view this body of water is
normally classified along with the *Flores Sea* (q.v.).

Bathymetrically, the Bali Sea is largely represented
as a small trough extending to the west of the Flores
Trough, being hemmed in by the edge of the Sunda
Shelf in the north and west, and by relatively
shallow sills of Bali Strait (less than 200 m) and
Lombok Strait (220 m) to the south. Below 1000 m
the Bali Trough is almost completely cut off.
Greatest depth is 1590 m. There is a narrow passage
of about 600 m connecting it to Makassar Strait.

Oceanographically its surface waters are in complete continuity with the Flores Sea to the east and
the Java Sea to the west. Considerable surface
transport occurs southward through Bali and
Lombok Straits into the Indian Ocean. However,
the eastern Indonesian deep water that comes from
the Pacific, through the Banda and Flores Seas,
becomes progressively more impoverished in oxygen,
dropping from 2.8 cc/liter off Halmahera to less
than 2.0 cc/liter in the western Bali Sea, which is
essentially a *cul-de-sac*.

Structurally the Bali Trough is classified by
Kuenen (1935) into one of his "category C"
features (steep sides and flat bottom), which
correspond closely to Kay's group of "zeugogeo-
synclines." Vertical crustal subsidence along major
faults is suggested by the bathymetry. To the south
lies the east–west row of giant volcanoes that extend
through East Java (Mt. Smeru, Mt. Ruang, etc.),
Bali (Mt. Batur—last eruption 1926; Mt. Agung—
last violent eruption 1964), Lombok (Mt. Rinjani),
and Sumbawa (Mt. Tambora—last major eruption
1815). To the north is a belt of non-volcanic geosynclinal rocks uplifted in Madura and the Kangean
Islands.

Sediments are mainly terrigenous, dominantly
tuffs on the south side. Some 60–80% of the
tuffaceous material came from Tambora ash, blown
westward during the southeast monsoon (radius
about 500 km; maximum limit of ash 1000 km). The
Paternoster Islands in the east and the Kangean
Islands etc., to the north, being largely limestone
rocks, furnish little sediment apart from coral
sands and muds, but nowhere are pelagic sediments
dominant.

Of great paleogeographic and zoogeographic
interest is *Wallace's Line* which passes between
Bali and Lombok. As Wallace recognized almost a
century ago, major mammals and numerous smaller
organisms characteristic of southeast Asia occur
west of this line, while to the east the faunas show
increasingly distinctive Australian characteristics.
The implication is that a fundamental geotectonic
boundary of intercontinental significance runs
north–south through the Bali Sea.

RHODES W. FAIRBRIDGE

References

Kuenen, P. H., 1935, "Geological Interpretation of the
Bathymetrical Results," in "Snellius Expedition,"
Vol. 5, Pt. 1, Utrecht, Kemink en Zoon, 124pp.
Kuenen, P. H., and Neeb, G. A., 1943, "Geological
Results; Bottom Samples," in "Snellius Expedition,
1929–1930," Vol. V, Pt. 3, Leiden, E. J. Brill, 268pp.
Wyrtki, K., 1961, "Physical oceanography of the
southeastern Asian waters," *Rept. Naga Exped.*, **2**,
Scripps Institute of Oceanography.

Cross-references: *Flores Sea; Java Sea.* pr Vol. VI:
Wallace's Line.

BALTIC SEA

(1) Introduction

The Baltic Sea is an intracontinental Sea of
384,700 km² (154,000 square miles) lying between
North and Central Europe. It is connected with
the North Sea by the Danish Sounds, i.e., Little
Belt, Great Belt and the Sound (Öresund). The

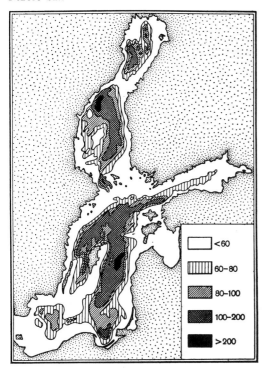

Fig. 1. Depths of the Baltic Sea (Ekman). Bathymetry in meters.

Gulf of Bothnia, which extends northwards, is separated from the Central Baltic by the Aaland Sea, whereas the Gulf of Finland, which extends eastwards, is directly connected with the Central Baltic.

(2) Depth

The mean depth is about 65 meters. The greatest depth, off Landsort about 100 km north of the island of Gotland, is 459 meters. Immediately east of Gotland is another deep area reaching 249 meters. South of Gotland there is the Hoburg Shallow which in places is only 12 meters deep, and further southwest the Öland Shallow with a minimum depth of 9 meters. There are also shallows off the Pommeranian coast and between the islands of Bornholm and Rügen. The Gulf of Riga reaches a depth of 50 meters and the Gulf of Finland over 100 meters. The greatest depth of the Aaland Sea is 301 meters and of the Gulf of Bothnia 254 meters.

(3) Hydrography

(3a) Circulation, Salinity and Temperature. The catchment area is about four times that of the total area of the Baltic Sea. The yearly inflow of water is about 1/40 of the total volume of water in the Baltic. The brackish surface water flows into the North Sea through the Danish Sounds, and salt water flows into the Baltic Sea at a greater depth.

The salinity in the Baltic therefore remains the same. At the surface, the speed of flow is 10–60 cm/sec, but is less for the salt water at greater depths. As a result of the rotation of the earth, the water circulates counterclockwise, for instance northwards along the west coast of Finland in the Gulf of Bothnia and southwards along the east coast of Sweden towards the Danish Sounds. In the Gulf of Finland, there is a current which flows eastwards along the Estonian coast and westwards along the Finnish coast. Strong winds may influence the currents of the surface waters and cause irregularities in the general pattern as described above. In addition, the winds cause changes in the height of the water level. The seasonal variation is about $\frac{1}{2}$ meter, and MSL is highest in August and September and lowest in April and May. The tidal range is very small in the Baltic Sea. It is greatest in the inner part of the Gulf of Finland, where the difference between high and low tide is 20 cm.

The salinity is highest in the Danish Sounds, where it is about 10‰ at the surface and about 15‰ near the bottom. The salinity markedly decreases towards the north and the east. The surface water in the middle of the Central Baltic has, for instance, a salinity of 7 to 7.5‰, the water at greater depths 9–10‰. The corresponding figures are 5.5–6 and 7–8‰ off Helsinki, 0–1 and 2–4‰ in the inner part of the Gulf of Finland, 5–6 and 7–8‰ in the Aaland Sea, 4–5 and 5–6‰ in the southern part of the Gulf of Bothnia and 2.5–3 and 3.5–4‰ in the northern part.

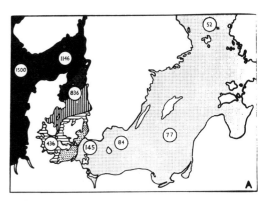

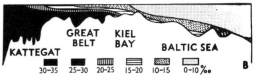

Fig. 2. Alteration of salinity from the North Sea into the Baltic. (A) Surface salinity in February; (B) Change of salinity along the vertical cross section in August (Remane and Wattenberg). Numbers of animal species are encircled in A (from Zenkevitch, 1963).

The temperature of the water in the deeper parts is 4–5°C. At 40–90 meter depth, there is a temperature minimum. Above this depth, the summer temperature rises steeply towards the surface.

(3b) Ice Conditions. The Baltic usually begins to freeze over at the end of October in the northern part of the Gulf of Bothnia and at the end of November in the eastern part of the Gulf of Finland. In March the sea ice is most extensive. Towards the end of January, the sea ice usually connects the Aaland Islands with the Finnish coast. The ice cover normally extends to the outer islands along the coast of the Gulf of Bothnia and along the Finnish coast of the Gulf of Finland. The open water first has drifting ice which later forms a continuous ice cover. The average thickness of the ice is about 65 cm. Sea ice melts more quickly than it forms. Most of the ice has melted by early April, but in the northern parts of the Gulf of Bothnia, drifting ice often occurs as late as June.

(3c) Depth of Visibility and Color. The clearest water in the Baltic Sea is found in the central parts of the Gulf of Finland and the Gulf of Bothnia, where the depth of visibility is about 12 meters. In the Central Baltic the water is clear blue or bluish green. Closer to the coasts the water usually has a yellow, or in some areas, a brownish tinge.

(4) Stages in the Development of the Baltic

The extent and connection with the ocean have varied in the Baltic Sea after the last Quaternary glaciation of Fennoscandia. The Baltic Sea was influenced by the withdrawal of the continental ice sheet, the uplift of land and the eustatic changes of sea level. The first stage, the Baltic Ice Lake, was dammed by the ice margin (see Fig. 4), and the lake drained, at least at one time, towards the east into the White Sea. The final stage corresponds to the formation of the Fennoscandian moraines. When the ice withdrew from Central Sweden, the Baltic Ice Lake was drained and the water level dropped. The drainage took place in 8305 BC. During the subsequent Yoldia Sea stage (from *Yoldia arctica*) the ice withdrew to the Scandinavian mountains. There was first a transgression of the water level and later a regression as a result of the rapid uplift of land. The connection with the ocean through Central Sweden eventually closed because of the uplift and the Baltic became a lake, the Ancylus Lake (from *Ancylus fluviatilis*), about 7000 BC. The diatom flora of this stage is a fresh water flora, but in some of the deeper areas there was brackish water at this time.

The Ancylus Lake stage was followed by the Litorina Sea stage (from *Litorina littorea* and *L. rudis*), from which the present Baltic Sea developed.

The Litorina Sea was connected with the ocean through the Danish Sounds. The Litorina sediments are rich in mollusks, which indicate that the

Fig. 3. Retreat (morainal) stages of the Fennoscandian ice. The Brandenburg moraines mark the limit of the latest Pleistocene advance (somewhat less than 20,000 years ago). The Poznan moraine formed about 18,000 years ago; the Pomeranian, about 16,000. The Daniglacial (Scanian) lasted until about 13,000; the Gothiglacial until about 11,000, and the Finiglacial (Scandinavian) moraines until 11,000–10,000 years ago. The evolution of the Baltic proper may be traced from Daniglacial times.

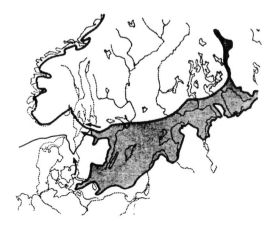

Fig. 4. Baltic Ice Lake which was in existence from about 11,000–10,000 years ago. It was eventually drained to the west and southwest.

Fig. 5. Ancylus Lake about 8200 years ago; the Danish sounds were closed but some connections occurred through the Svea-alv (central Sweden).

salinity in the Baltic was higher when these sediments were formed than it is at present. The diatoms also reflect the same difference in salinity. During the Litorina stage, the mollusks were bigger (as shown by *Mytilus edulis*) than at present, as well as being more numerous. The beginning of the Litorina Sea stage starts with Clypeus sediments (named after the brackish water diatom *Campylodiscus clypeus* often found in Litorina sediments). Some investigators have separated a transitional brackish water stage, called the Mastogloia Sea stage, between the Ancylus and Litorina stages. As a result of eustatic changes of sea level and a relatively slow uplift of land, there were several transgressions during the Litorina Sea stage in the southern part of the Baltic Sea. The first Litorina transgression occurred about 5000 BC, and at least two more followed.

(5) Ecology

The Baltic Sea is the largest brackish water body in the world. Great variations in productivity occur in different sections of the Baltic. The productivity is greater in the Gulf of Finland than in the Gulf of Bothnia, where there are fewer plankton. The Central Baltic has a comparatively high productivity. The flora and fauna are poor in species compared with the ocean. The number of species decreases with decreasing salinity from the Danish Sounds. The seals, *Phoca hispida* and

Halichoerus grypus, occur throughout the Baltic Sea. Ocean forms which have spread as far as the Gulf of Finland are *Zostera, Fucus* and *Mytilus edulis*, but many species do not reach the same size in the Baltic as they do in the ocean. Many species spread from the White Sea after the ice age and now occur as relics. The diatom flora of the Baltic is very poor in species. The most common diatoms are *Thalassiosira baltica, Actinocyclus ehrenbergii, Achnanthes taeniata, Chaetoceros borealis* and *Cocconeis scutellum*. The most important fish in the Baltic Sea are Baltic herring (*Clupea harengus*), sprat (*Clupea sprattus*), cod (*Gadus morrhua*), salmon (*Salmo salar*), flounder (*Pleuronectes flesus*), northern pike (*Esox lucius*), perch (*Perca fluviatilis*), bream (*Abramis brama*), whitefish (*Coregonus lavaretus* coll.) and trout (*Salmo trutta*).

(6) Sediments

In most parts of the Baltic Sea, the bottom sediments consist of green, brown or black clay-mud. Underlying this is gray or red varved clay, which was deposited on top of till. Occasionally the mud is missing and, on steep slopes, the clay as well. The till forms the bottom. Sands are common in the coastal areas. During the ice retreat, the yearly sedimentation (as shown by the thickness of varves) was 5–200 mm, whereas the yearly sedimentation in the postglacial period decreased to 0.2–2 mm.

PENTTI ALHONEN

Fig. 6. Litorina Sea, which reached its maximum about 5000 years ago, with warmer than present climate (after Sauramo, 1938).

References

Florin, Sten, 1944, "Havstrandens förskjutningar och bebyggelseutvecklingen i östra Mellansverige under senkvartär tid," *Geol. Fören. i Stockholm Förh.*, **66** (3), 551–634.

Fromm, Erik, 1963, "Absolute chronology of the late-Quaternary Baltic. A Review of Swedish investigations," *Baltica*, **1**, 46–59.

Ignatius, Heikki, 1958, "On the rate of sedimentation in the Baltic Sea," *Bull. Comm. géol. Finlande*, **180**, 135–144.

Kalle, Kurt, 1948, "Zur Frage der Produktionsleistung des Meeres," *Deut. Hydrograph. Z.*, **1**, No. 1, 1–15.

Sauramo, Matti, 1958, "Die Geschichte der Ostsee," *Ann. Acad. Sci. Fennicae, Ser. A*, **111**, 1–522.

BANDA SEA

(1) Limits and Oceanography

(a) Limits and dimensions. The Banda Sea (center: 126°E, 5°S) covers an area of 470,000 km^2 and is limited by the Sula Islands, Buru-Ceram-Outer Banda Arc islands (Kei, Tanimbar, Timor) to Alor Island, then a line from Komba Island to the Tukangbesi Islands, and the southeastern arm of Sulawesi (Celebes). This boundary differs in the west from the convention of the International Hydrographic Bureau (Sp. Publ. 23, 1953), which extends the western limit to the eastern tip of Flores and a line through Salayar I. to the southwestern arm of Sulawesi. The Banda Sea consists of several basins and troughs, interconnected by sills having for the larger part abyssal environments of 3000 meters and deeper.

Tables 1 and 2 come from the work of the Snellius Expedition in 1929–30. The latest report of the expedition by Van Riel *et al.* (1950) lists all of its publications.

The *North Banda Basin* has an irregular but comparatively low bottom relief with an average depth of 4700 meters, marked by steep sides. This basin is separated from the South Banda Basin by a broad submarine rise of complicated relief striking between the Tukangbesi islands and Buru-Banda islands. The barrier is designated as the Luymes Ridge and Siboga Ridge. Clusters of coral islands occupy their culminations.

The *South Banda Basin* has also an average depth of 4700 meters with a relatively flat bottom and steep sides. Only the volcano Gunungapi forms an important elevation by rising directly from 4500 meters deep to 280 meters above sea level.

The *Weber Trough* is characterized by steep sides and a flat bottom in cross section, evidently an abyssal plain. This floor is not quite horizontal as is shown by the varying depths along the trough line. The greatest depth in the East Indonesian Archipelago is located in the Weber Trough (7440 meters).

TABLE 1. DEEP-SEA DEPRESSIONS OF THE BANDA SEA

Depression	Limiting Isobath	Area (km²)	Sill Depth (m)	Maximum Depth (m)
North Banda Basin	4000	80,000	3130	5800
South Banda Basin	4000	120,000	3130	5400
Weber Trough	4000	50,000	3130	7440
Manipa Basin	3000	2,800	3100	4360
Ambalau Basin	4000	7,000	3130	5330
Butung Trough	4000	1,200	3130	4180

TABLE 2. PROPERTIES OF DEEP WATER IN THE DEPRESSIONS AND OUTSIDE THEIR RESPECTIVE SILLS OF THE BANDA SEA

Snellius Stations and Observation Depths are as Indicated	Temperature (°C)	Salinity (‰)	Oxygen (cc/liter)	Density
Sill at No. 221, 3000	3.06	34.59	±2.50	1027.575
North Banda Basin at No. 218, 4371	3.16	34.60	2.39	1025.575
Sill at No. 249, 2990	3.095	34.61	±2.50	1027.59
South Banda Basin at No. 246, 4331	3.19	34.60	2.40?	1027.57
Sill at No. 321, 2990	3.07	34.61	2.33	1027.59
Weber Trough at No. 362, 7293	3.635	34.63	2.38	1027.55
Sill at No. 255, 3185	3.105	34.605	2.50	1027.585
Manipa Basin at No. 253, 3991	3.235	34.605	2.42	1027.57
Sill at No. 209, 2980	3.04	34.63	±2.50	1027.61
Ambalau Basin at No. 251, 5045	3.25	34.605	2.39	1027.57
Butung Trough at No. 201, 2936	3.05	34.605	2.45	1027.59

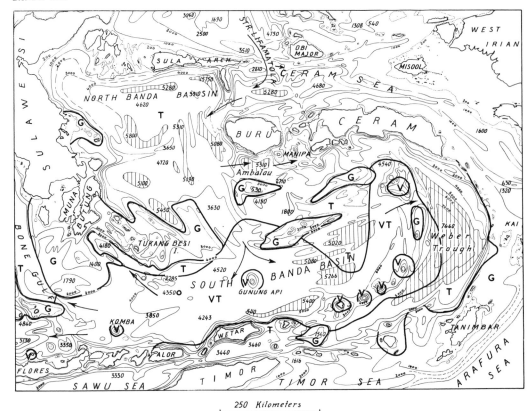

Fig. 1. The Banda Sea, eastern Indonesia. Map shows bathymetry, flow of bottom water (arrows) and bottom sediments. T: terrigenous mud; G: globigerina ooze; VT: volcanic mud (data from the Snellius Expedition, 1929–1930).

A triangular outline, steep sides and a rather flat bottom mark the *Manipa Basin*. Steep sides and a flat bottom are also found in the *Ambalau Basin*. The *Butung Trough* has gentle slopes except the scarp off Butung Island; its cross section is synclinal.

(b) Deep-water Properties and Flow of Bottom Water. The bathymetric data on the various depressions of the Banda Sea, combined with the deep-water properties within and outside the entrances of the sea, indicate that the depressions receive water from the Pacific Ocean through the Molucca Sea (Fig. 2).

(c) Surface Properties and Meteorology. The meteorology of the Banda Sea is entirely governed by the monsoons. Table 3 shows the variations of salinity, surface temperature, wind and air pressure throughout the year in the Banda Sea.

(d) Currents and Tides. Table 4 shows the surface currents in the Banda Sea in nautical miles per day towards the directions as indicated.

In Tjapalulu Strait (Sula islands), the maximum tidal currents are 7.9 and 9.3 knots, respectively, toward south and north. The tidal range in the South Banda Sea is 2.0 meters (Ambon).

The Snellius Expedition made current measurements in October 1930 at its station No. 364a, which is located between the Kai and Tanimbar islands, as follows:

0 meters 46 cm/sec toward N 75° W
100 meters 22 cm/sec toward N 20° E
400 meters 13 cm/sec toward S 60° W
3000 meters 4 cm/sec toward N 20° E.

(2) Bottom Sediments

According to Neeb (1943), the distribution of the bottom sediments in the Banda Sea are as follows (see also Fig. 1):

North Banda Basin: Terrigenous mud principally derived from silicious igneous rocks.

South Banda Basin: Volcanic and terrigenous mud with concentrations of volcanic mud around the volcanic islands. Globigerina ooze (at least 30% calcium carbonate) covers those submarine parts above the 3000 meters isobath.

Weber Trough: Terrigenous mud, partially derived from crystalline schists.

Manipa Basin: Terrigenous mud and locally hard bottom.

TABLE 3. (ACCORDING TO VAN DER STOK, 1922)
Average salinity, ‰

	Dec–Feb	Mar–May	Jun–Aug	Sep–Nov
North Banda Basin	34.0	33.5	34.2	34.5
South Banda Basin	34.3	33.5	34.3	34.5
Weber Trough	34.3	33.3	34.3	34.6
Manipa Basin	33.8	33.7	34.4	34.6
Ambalau Basin	33.9	33.6	34.4	34.5
Butung Trough	33.5	33.1	34.2	34.3

Average sea surface temperatures, °C

	Maximum	Minimum
North Banda Basin	28.9 November	25.6 August
South Banda Basin	28.8 November	25.9 August
Weber Trough	28.8 November	25.9 August
Manipa Basin	28.9 November	25.8 August
Ambalau Basin	28.9 November	25.8 August
Butung Trough	28.8 November	25.9 July

Wind in Beaufort scale (from quadrant indicated)
Average air pressure, cm

North Banda Basin	Dec–Feb	Mar–May	Jun–Aug	Sep–Nov
North Banda Basin	N 0.5–1.4 755.4	N 0.5–1.4 756.6	SSE 2.5–3.4 755.3	SSE 1.5–2.4 758.5
South Banda Basin Ambalau Basin	NW 1.5–5.4 756.9	irregular 757.5	SE 3.5–4.4 758.0	SE 0.5–4.4 758.4
Weber Trough	NNW 1.5–2.4 757.7	WSW 1.5–2.4 757.5	SE 2.5–3.4 758.0	SSE 1.5–2.4 759.2
Manipa Basin	NNW 1.5–2.4 755.8	N 1.5–2.4 756.5	SSE 2.5–3.4 757.8	S 1.5–2.4 758.0
Butung Trough	NW 1.5–2.4 755.7	W 1.5–2.4 757.5	ESE 2.5–3.4 758.4	SE 1.5–2.4 757.7

TABLE 4. CURRENTS IN NAUTICAL MILES PER DAY
(ACCORDING TO VAN DER STOK, 1922)

	Dec–Feb	Mar–May	Jun–Aug	Sep–Nov
North Banda Sea	E 1–5	WSW 15–20	W 15–20	WNW 5–10
South Banda Sea	E 10–25	ENE 5–25	W 5–20	W 5–10

Ambalau Basin: Terrigenous mud principally derived from crystalline schists.

Butung Trough: Probably terrigenous mud.

Luymes and Siboga ridges: Elevations shallower than −2500 meters are covered by globigerina ooze, while the deeper parts are composed of terrigenous mud. Around the coral islands, coralline mud and sand accumulate.

Hard grounds are generally encountered on the submarine entrances of the various depressions, implying strong bottom currents.

By using the distinct ash of the Tambora eruption of 1815 as a marker bed, Neeb (1943) has determined the sedimentation rate of the non-volcanic terrigenous deposits to be 75 cm in 1000 years which is at least 40 times higher than in the

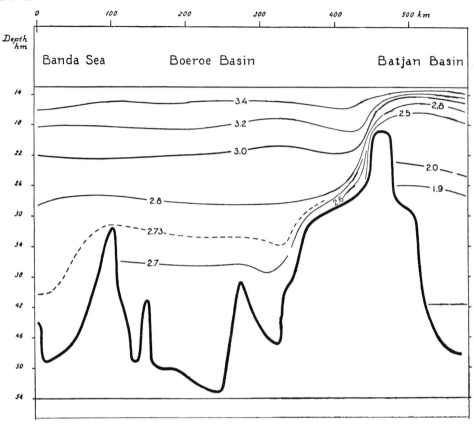

Fig. 2. Section from Molucca Sea (Batjan Basin) to Banda Sea, showing potential temperature (after Van Riel, 1934, Snellius Expedition). Note: "Boeroe Basin" (Dutch orthography) is now preferably given as "Buru Basin" (English style, preferred in Indonesia today); it is situated in the Ceram Sea (q.v.) and connects with the Molucca Sea (q.v.).

equatorial Atlantic Ocean (see the discussion in *Flores Sea*).

It is still problematical why bottom samples of even 2 meters length of the East Indonesian deep-sea basins do not show diastems or stratification (see Kuenen, 1950, pp. 368–374).

(3) Geophysics and Geological Structure

The North and South Banda basins are characterized by positive gravity anomalies with maxima in their central parts, respectively 154 mgal and 91 mgal. The eastern limits of the Banda Sea consisting of Timor, the Outer Banda Arc, Ceram and Buru mark an important belt of negative gravity anomaly with an extreme departure of − 150 mgal. The Manipa and Ambalau basins occupy the northernmost end of the above mentioned gravity belt and have anomalies in the order of − 50 mgal. The Butung Trough (− 50 mgal) lies at the southern end of another belt of negative gravity anomalies. The latter zone continues across the southeast and east arms of Sulawesi into the central ridge of the Molucca Sea.

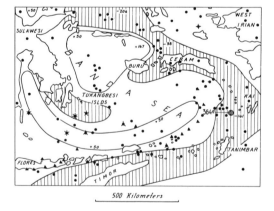

Fig. 3. The Banda Sea, eastern Indonesia. Gravimetry (shading indicates the belt of negative anomalies; positive anomalies of 50 mgal and more are also delineated), active volcanoes (triangles) and earthquake foci (dots: less than 100 km depth; with one hachure: 100–199 km; with two hachures: 200–299 km; etc.). Double circles indicate current recording station 364a of the Snellius Expedition.

The Luymes and Siboga ridges are underlain by positive gravity anomalies of 50 mgal or less.

The distribution of earthquake epicenters in the Banda Sea area is depicted in Fig. 3. From west to east, the foci decrease in depth in a systematic way. The geological interpretations of such distributions of foci in Indonesia have been propounded by Vening Meinesz, Berlage and others (see Van Bemmelen, 1949).

The volcanoes in the Banda Sea area are of the orogenic type with an explosivity index of 99.

On account of their respective morphology, the depressions of the Banda Sea are ascribed to faulting (i.e., North and South Banda basins, Manipa and Ambalau basins) while the Weber and Butung troughs are ascribed to folding combined with faulting. The very irregular relief on the Luymes and Siboga ridges may also be ascribed to folding accompanied by faulting. Both Banda basins may be classified as nuclear basins, whereas the Weber Trough belongs to the intramontane depression class (Kuenen, 1950). These are, respectively, potential zeugo- and eugeosynclines (see pr Vol. V, *Geosynclines*).

Several geological features in the Banda Sea area point to a late Tertiary or even younger age for the relief phenomena. The more important indications are: (1) the high frequency of earthquakes and volcanic eruptions of the orogenic type in modern times; (2) the isostatic inequilibrium of parts of the rim; (3) transections of Miocene folds by present coastlines; (4) elevated Plio-Pleistocene coral reef terraces, which attain heights of 1283 meters in Timor; (5) the presence of thick series of Tertiary, nonvolcanic, clastic sediments on islands surrounded by deep sea; (6) atolls rising steeply from depths too deep for coral growth. Continued vertical movements, both positive and negative, of the order of 1 to 10 mm/yr are in progress.

H. D. TJIA

References

*Kuenen, Ph. H., 1950, "Marine Geology," Ch. 3, pp. 175–209, 368–374, New York, John Wiley & Sons.

*Neeb, G. A., 1943, The Snellius Expedition: Bottom Samples; the Composition and Distribution of the Samples, Vol. 5, Part 3, Section 2, pp. 55–268, Leiden, Brill.

*Van Bemmelen, R. W., 1949, "The Geology of Indonesia; General Geology," Vol. 1A, pp. 257–297, The Hague, Martinus Nijhoff.

*Van Der Stok, J. P., 1922, "De zeeën van Nederlandsch Oost-Indië; maritieme meteorologie en getijden," pp. 182–212, Leiden, Brill.

*Van Riel, P. M., Hamaker, H. C., and Van Eyck, L., 1950, "The Snellius Expedition: Tables. Serial and Bottom Observations. Temperature, Salinity and Density," Vol. 2, Part 6, pp. 1–44, Leiden, Brill.

BARENTS SEA AND WHITE SEA

Barents Sea

Dimensions and Boundaries. Barents Sea is in the most western part of the Eurasian shelf. Its area is 1,300,000 km:. According to the International Hydrographic Bureau (*Sp. Paper* 23, 1953), it is separated from the Arctic basin by the Spitsbergen Archipelago, White Island, Victoria Island, and Franz Joseph Land (Zemlya Fridtjof Nansen). On the east, its boundary with the Kara Sea runs between Graham-Bell Island and Cape Jelanya (Zhelaniya) and in the straits Matochkin Shar (Nova Zemlya Island) Kaza Gate and Iugor Shar (between Novaya Zemlya Island, Vaigatch Island and mainland). In the south, the Barents Sea is bounded by the Norwegian coast, and the Kola and Kanin Peninsulas. East of here lies the large Cheshskaya Bay. West of the Kanin Peninsula is the strait Gorlo (Gorge) of the White Sea. In the southeast of the Barents Sea, the coast is backed by the Petchora Depression and by the northern termination of the Pay-Khoy range (a branch of the northern Urals). The Barents Sea is largely open to the Norwegian Sea in the west and thereby with the Atlantic Ocean (Fig. 1).

Historical. The Barents Sea was first explored by Scandinavian and Russian sailors, fishermen and sealers. Since the thirteenth century, the Russians have sailed to Spitzbergen (Groumant), to Novaya Zemlya and farther east. In 1553, the British merchant sailors, Willoughby and Chancellor sailed up the Barents Sea, in 1594–97, the Sea was crossed several times by the Dutchman Willem Barents. Scientifically, it was first explored by the Norwegian F. Nansen, the Russians Knipovitch, Breitfuss and Derjuguin, and the Germans Schulz and Wulff. In 1922–40, the Russian research ship *Persey* made 84 oceanographic cruises. The scientific results (I. I. Mesyatzev, L. A. Zenkevitch, V. A. Jashnov and others) were published in a series of transactions and some monographs.

In the Barents Sea is a very abundant and varied organic life (Fig. 2) and an extremely important shelf fishery. There is a Polar Marine Fishery and Oceanographic Institute at Murmansk.

Hydrographic Features. The position of the Barents Sea between the Atlantic and Arctic oceans is the main cause of its many interesting hydrographic features. There is a large stream of Atlantic waters, a branch of the Gulf Stream called the North Cape Current, which flows in from the west between Bear Island and North Cape. This current gives rise to many branches, and the circulation following the bottom relief as it moves to the east.

The Atlantic waters have temperatures of 4–12°C and salinity about 35‰. On their passage to the north and east, they cool and mix with the local waters. The surface salinity falls to 32–33‰ and

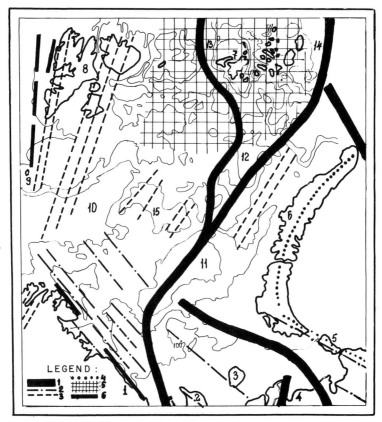

Fig. 1. Structure of Barents sea bottom: (1) Depression axis; (2) Proterozoic folding; (3) Caledonian folding; (4) Hercynian folding; (5) Tertiary movements; (6) Fractures.

Geographic names: (1) Kola Peninsula (Murman Coast); (2) Kanin Peninsula; (3) Kolgev Island; (4) Petchora Mouth; (5) Vaigatch Island; (6) Novaya Semlya Island; (7) Franz Joseph Land; (8) Spitsbergen; (9) Bear Island; (10) West (Bear Island) Basin; (11) Central Basin; (12) Northeastern Basin; (13) Franz Josef–Victoria Trench; (14) Polar Basin Bay; (15) Central Rise.

bottom temperature to −1.9 to −2.0°C. Small tongues of the Atlantic water enter the Barents Sea from the Arctic basin at depths of 150–200 m through the deep straits between the islands. The surface cold waters from the Arctic basin bring the polar ice. The cold current together with the local Barents Sea waters leaves the region near Bear Island south of it.

Ice Conditions. The good isolation from the pack ice of the Arctic basin and of the Kara Sea is of special importance in the hydrographic picture of the Berents Sea. Its southern part does not freeze except for isolated fiords along the Murman coast. The floe-ice boundary lies at 400–500 km from the shore and marks the edge of the Berents Sea to the east of the Kola Peninsula. In summer, floating ice mostly thaws and it lasts only in the coldest years in the middle and northern part of the sea and near Novaya Zemlya.

The Chemical Conditions of the Barents Sea Waters. As a consequence of the intensive vertical temperature mixing, the Barents Sea waters are well aerated. In summer, the surface water is oversaturated by the oxygen owing to the abundance of phytoplankton. The oxygen saturation is not less than 70–78% even in winter in the most stagnant regions on the bottom.

Owing to the low temperature, the deep layers are enriched by carbon dioxide. The alkali coefficient is 663×10^{-1}.

The Barents Sea is noted for the phenomenon of the "polar front" at the boundary of cold Arctic and warm Atlantic waters. This is accompanied by a rise of the biogenic elements (P, N, etc.) and is the reason for the luxurious flora of phytoplankton and of the general abundance of organic life.

Tides. Maximum tides are noted at the North Cape (up to 4 m), at the Strait Gorlo of the White Sea (up to 7 m) and in the Murman fiords; further to the northeast, the range of the tides diminishes to 1.5 m at Spitsbergen and to 0.8 around Novaya Zemlya.

Climate and Wave Action. The climate of the

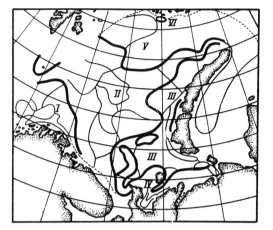

Fig. 2. Benthonic biocoenoses in Barents Sea (from Zenkevitch, 1963):
(I) *Southwestern* with prevalence of Spongia, some spots Brachiopoda; (II) *Central* with Lamellibranchiata, Echinodermata, Polychaeta etc.; (III) *Eastern Shallows* with predominance of Lamellibranchiata and Echinodermata; (IV) *Eastern coastal* with Lamellibranchiata, Crustacea, Gastropoda, Coelenterata etc.; (V) *Northern (deep)* with Echninodermata, Lamellibranchiata, Polychaeta; (VI) *Northern Shallows* with strong predominance of Brachiopoda, partly of Spongia.

Barents Sea is very unstable. This Sea is one of the most stormy in the world. Through the Barents Sea pass warm cyclones from the North Atlantic and cold anticyclones from the Arctic. That is the reason for somewhat higher air temperatures compared to other Arctic seas, temperate winters and abundant atmospheric precipitation. The active wind regime and the large area of open water provide conditions for a maximum of the storm waves on the southern coast up to 3.5–3.7 m.

Bottom Relief and Geological Structure (Fig. 1). The bottom of the Barents Sea is slightly inclined from east to west. The depths vary for the most part from 100–350 m and only drop near the boundary of the Norwegian Sea to 600 m. Bottom relief is complicated. Many gentle submarine rises and depressions lead to conditions resulting in a complicated distribution of the water masses and of the sedimentation. As in other marine basins, the bottom relief of the Barents Sea is determined by the geological structure, which is related to the structure of the nearby land areas.

The Kola peninsula (Murman coast) is a part of the Precambrian Fennoscandian crystalline shield and is composed of metamorphic rocks, mostly Archean granite-gneisses. A folded zone of Proterozoic composed of dolomites, sandstones, slates and tillites extends along the northeast border of the shield. The remnants of this folded zone are preserved on the Varanger and Rybachy peninsulas, on Kildin Island, and in a series of

submarine banks along the coast. Proterozoic folds are known farther to the east on the Kanin Peninsula and in the Timan Range. The submarine rises of the southern part of the sea, Pay-Khoy Range, the north end of the Urals and the southern part of the fold system of Novaya Zemlya follow in the same northwest direction (Fig. 1).

The broad Petchora depression between the Timan and Paykhoy ranges is filled by a thick series of deposits ranging up to the Quaternary; its extension to the north is the even floor of the southeast part of the Barents Sea (Petchora Sea).

The low Kolguev Island to the northeast from Kanin Peninsula is composed of horizontally bedded Quaternary deposits.

In the west at the North Cape region, the Proterozoic complex is cut off by the Caledonian folds of Norway. These folds proceed north northeast along the western border of the Fennoscandian shield. The Caledonides of the same submeridional direction form the western part of Spitsbergen. The Bear Island–Spitsbergen shallow, Central rise, as well as the fold system of Novaya Zemlya with the nearby banks, follows the same strike.

Novaya Zemlya is formed of folded Paleozoic rocks: slates, shales, limestones, sandstones. Traces of Caledonian movements are found along its west coast, and we can presume that Caledonian structures are partly buried by recent sediments here and disappear under the sea floor. The Vaygatch–Novaya Zemlya fold system of Hercynian age is an S-shaped curve and probably follows around massif of older rocks or of Precambrian crystalline basement. The series of basins: Central Basin, Northeastern Basin, Franz-Victoria Trench on the west side of Franz Joseph Land and the Embayment of the Polar basin to the east of it— all have the same submeridional trend with an S-shaped curve. The deep straits of the Franz Joseph Land and submarine valleys on its prolongations sloping north into the Polar basin and south in the northern plateau of the Barents Sea also have this trend.

The islands in the northern part of the Barents Sea have a general platform structure and are formed mostly of the sedimentary rocks that are gently dipping or horizontally bedded; they are Upper Paleozoic and Trias on Bear Island, Jurassic and Cretaceous on Franz Joseph Land, Mesozoic and Tertiary on the eastern part of the West Spitsbergen. All these rocks are clastic, sometimes slightly carbonaceous; in the upper Mesozoic, they are interbedded with basalts.

The development of the Barents Sea tectonic framework is mainly due to the faults and fractures at meeting points of the submeridional North Atlantic system and of the sublatitudinal one of the southern border of Arctic basin. The Tertiary movements and submergence, which originated as early as Jurassic, are accompanied by fractures and by basalt effusions and continued into the Quaternary, even probably up till today.

Young faults border the Barents Sea platform on the sides of Kola Peninsula, Finnmarken, Franz Joseph Land and Spitsbergen. On the whole, the Barents Sea in its geological structure corresponds to the Russian platform. On the sea floor may be seen also the alternation of submeridional and more or less east-west movements through its geologic history.

Submarine Terraces. The structural relief of the Barents Sea is marked by two distinct terrace levels at about 200 and 70 m. They correspond to two stages of the Quaternary and are connected with the two glaciations most developed in Russia. The submerged shore line at about 200 m (180 m east and 220 m west) forms a terrace escarpment. Abundant rocks, boulders and other rock fragments of local origin are dredged here. Outcrops of the underlying older clay sediments are frequent. The rock fragments at depths of more than 200 m are very altered and covered by thick Fe-Mn oxide crusts. This testifies to their long exposure on the sea floor. The submarine slopes above 200 m are very dissected, possibly because of their long subaerial erosion. The younger level (70 m) has milder expression in the relief, the sea floor at less than 70 m is very flat, and among clastics there are many well rolled fresh pebbles.

The position of the submerged shore line is somewhat distorted by the differential movements. The maximum uplift occurs on Novaya Zemlya with parallel subsidence in the nearby Novaya Zemlya Trough and in the Petchora Depression. Synchronous raised shore lines are found on Kolguev Island at 70 m, on Pay-Khoy and in the Polar Urals at 20 m. The uplift of Novaya Zemlya attains 240 m. The West and Norwegian trenches and the northern part of the Sea are regions of subsidence.

Sources of Sediments. The fractures and step subsidence dividing the Barents Sea platform from the Russian platform cause a very limited supply of river waters. The relation of the sea area to the drainage area is nearly the oceanic type. Only the Petchora River (disregarding small streams) flows directly into the sea. The rivers of the Kola Peninsula are small and flow into fiords, as do the rivers of Novaya Zemlya, which in any case freeze right through in winter. Permafrost contributes to the small quantity of the river silts. Permafrost is found locally on the Kola and Kanin Peninsulas, but farther to the east it is continuous.

The glaciation on northern island of Novaya Zemlya, Franz Joseph Land and Northeast Land of Spitsbergen is of a relict character. Ice caps on the small islands (Victoria, White, Evalive) mostly break off near the shore. Glaciers on northern Novaya Zemlya and Franz Joseph Land only locally form ice streams. They give small icebergs

no more than 12–15 m long, which for the most part decay near the shore. The glacier flows are unloaded in the bays.

The eolian drift and the sand carried away from the beach by flotation of marine foam also play only a small part. The Barents Sea water is very clear and transparent.

Organic remains in the sediments are not abundant. There are patches of the coarse shell sand only on the shallows. The sand and silt fractions are enriched locally near the Murman coast and on the slopes of Bear Island–Spitsbergen bank by siliceous sponge spicules. Remains of diatoms are noted almost in all samples, but they are sparse and then only as fragments of species having solid tests. Foraminifera are more frequent and chiefly agglutinate forms. They comprise the bulk of the sand particles in the deeper sediments in the west.

On the whole, the Barents Sea sediments belong to the terrigenous clastic facies. The chief process of sedimentation is the mechanical differentiation under hydrodynamic influences.

Sediment Distribution. At depths of less than 100 m, the sea floor is covered by sand, often enriched by boulders, pebbles, shingle, gravel, shell, shell sand. Sand is replaced by muddy sand in zones of sluggish water movements in the shallows, but sand also moves down the steep slopes, for instance, along Bear Island–Spitsbergen bank under active hydrodynamic conditions into greater depths.

Note: We use the classification of sediments based on the quantity of particles less than 0.01 mm. *Sand* has less than 5% of this grade; *muddy sand*, 5–10%; *sandy mud*, 10–30%; *mud*, 30–50%; and *clayey mud*—more than 50% of particles less than 0.01 mm.

Sand is replaced also by muddy sand and sometimes by sandy mud even at shallow depths on the large flat areas. In the basins, the floor is covered by mud at depths of more than 300 m in the southern and middle part of the sea and at more than 200 m in the northern part. Some patches of the clayey mud occur in the sluggish waters in halistatic zones in the northern part of the Sea.

Sandy mud predominates on the Barents Sea floor. The mechanical composition of the sediments clearly reflects in detail the hydrodynamics.

The color of the sediments changes from greenish-gray in the south, to yellow-gray in the southeast, to brownish-gray in the central part at intermediate depths, and to brown and dark brown on the greater depths and northward 76°N at all depths.

Dynamics of the Sediments (Fig. 3). The differential tectonic movements are reflected by the composition of the bottom deposits. The large-grained material such as boulders, pebbles, shingle, etc., accumulates at all submarine rises (elevations). Each bank or rise has an indigenous assemblage of

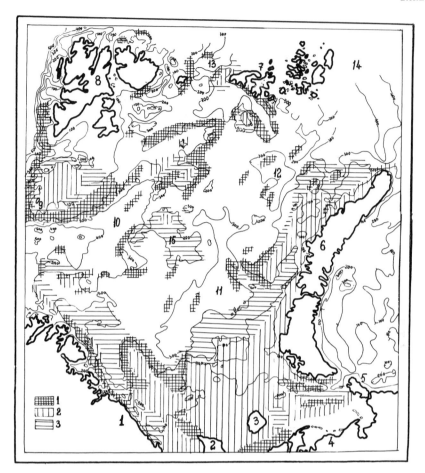

Fig. 3. Sediment dynamics of the Barents Sea. The areas of slow and "negative" sedimentation: (1) active erosion affecting the mechanical composition of the sediments (bimodal histograms); (2) residual cover; (3) alternation of erosion and accumulation of sediments.

rocks fragments, which indicates their local and residual origin. A thin (10–20 cm) layer of Holocene sediments is underlain by a late Pleistocene layer of different composition. The latter is frequently a gray or pink-gray clay of glacial origin, sometimes the product of weathering ("head") of the bedrock. The small thickness of Holocene sediments on the surface of rises and flanks coincides with poor sorting. This is reflected also by the mechanical composition (bimodal histograms) and indicates active hydrodynamic action. For this reason, there is an enriching of the sediments by sand particles accompanied by an increase of heavy minerals (density over 2.71), which is characteristic for places of high current activity and of slow sedimentation.

The thickness of the upper sediment (Holocene) layer increases in the basins. The sediments have here traces of climatic rhythms in the form of fine sand sprinklings at definite horizons in the cores, which can be correlated very well across broad areas.

Mineral and Chemical Composition of Barents Sea Sediments. The quantity of heavy minerals in the surface layer is 1–2%, on the slopes it reaches 3%, near the shores and on the shallow banks with active hydrodynamics, 5%, but rarely more. The heavy minerals are usually amphiboles, pyroxenes, garnet, ilmenite, magnetite, etc. The light minerals, quartz, feldspars, and in the fine-grained sediments also clay minerals (chiefly hydromicas of illite type), form the main part of sediments.

The SiO_2 ranges from 85% for the sands to 58% for mud and clayey mud; R_2O_3, from 8–25%; this shows that the chemical composition depends directly on the mechanical one. Consequently, the part soluble in HCl increases in the most fine sediments. The carbonate content ranges from 0–2% near the shore but only in those composed of limestone rocks.

Active chemical processes on the floor of the Barents Sea are associated with the migration of Fe-Mn oxides in interaction with the organic matter and other components originating in the seawater. The sesquioxides leached out from the podzol soils of the northern forest zone are transported by rivers to the shelf seas of the Arctic Ocean and precipitate there.

The manganese content of the sediments range from 0.01–0.02% in the sand of the southern part to 0.56% in the mud and clayey mud in the north (mean values). The increase of Mn coincides with some freshening of the surface water and with the weakening of vertical circulation. This leads to conditions that are poor for organic life and to a low accumulation of organic matter.

The organic content in Barents Sea sediments is from 0.15–3.12% for carbon, 0.02–0.42% for nitrogen, both increasing in proportion to the pelite (clay-size) grade. Organic carbon rises in the sediments of the same mechanical composition corresponding to the oxidation stage of the sesquioxides, i.e., to the color. The organic carbon content in the greenish-gray sediments is always higher than in the brown ones. The maximum carbon is found at the foot of the banks, on the flanks and surface of which rich organic life develops, especially in the regions of the "Polar front." In the sediments rich in organic matter it oxidizes and reduces the ferric oxides to the ferrous ones, and in consequence, the sediments have a greenish-gray color as in the southern part of the sea.

The slow sedimentation in the northern part and in places of active hydrodynamics leads to a relatively high accumulation of sesquioxides. In such areas, there is submarine weathering (halmyrolysis), as well as Fe-Mn concretions, crusts and coatings on the stones. The rock fragments are here replaced by sesquioxides partly or completely.

The relative enrichment by manganese is noted in the places where there is a meeting of normal marine waters with fresher waters containing organomineral components.

The quantity of phosphorus in the Barents Sea sediments ranges from "traces" to 0.05% in the southern part and 0.32% in the northern. The precipitation of P takes place in regions of Atlantic water inflow and in areas where there is a meeting with the waters rich on sesquioxides. In this case, iron plays the role of the reagent leading to the precipitation of the phosphorus. The quantity of P increases everywhere in sediments with the maximum thickness of the oxidized surface layer.

Conclusion. The basement under the Barents Sea sediments is composed of the old bedrock and products of their weathering and Quaternary deposits formed by such weathering. Such material provided for outwash and redeposition in the not too distant past. The sedimentation on the Barents Sea floor is very slow: not more than 1–3 cm/1000 yr. There is no accumulation in many places. As in other seas, the geologoical structure of the Barents Sea bottom controls the conditions for

morphology, hydrographic features, and sedimentation.

White Sea

Position, Dimensions and Shapes. The White Sea occupies a long gulf southeast of the Kola Peninsula and is joined to the Barents Sea by the Strait Gorlo (Gorge) as far north as Cape Kanin. Its area is about 95,000 km^2. The sea has four large bays—Mezen, Dvina, Onega and Kandalaksha—and numerous islands chiefly in the western part. Many rivers debouch into it: the Dvina, the Mezen, the Onega and others.

Climate and Hydrologic Features. The climate is more continental than that of the Barents Sea. The surface water is considerably fresher (S = 24–26‰), differing from the bottom water with higher salinity (30–30.5‰). The variation of surface water temperature is 20°C; the bottom waters have a constant negative temperature down to −1.5°C. The bays of the White Sea are frozen in winter, and the central part is covered by floating ice. The tide flows in from the Barents Sea and has, in some bays, the height of 7 m.

The overflow of fresh water goes out into the Barents Sea. A circulation is developed in the central part of the White Sea under the wind action.

The maximum depth is 340 m, predominately 100–200 m. The central part of the White Sea is a closed basin isolated from the Barents Sea by a shallow sill which prevents exchange of bottom waters. The vertical circulation and the aeration of bottom waters depend on winter cooling of surface waters. Therefore, the chemical conditions on the White Sea bottom are oxidizing. The oxygen deficit is very small.

Coastal Geology. The White Sea coasts are of tectonic origin in the Kandalaksha bay and on the west part of the Onega Bay. They have numerous comparatively open and shallow bays and inlets like the fiards of Sweden. The coast of the Kola Peninsula is bordered in many places by the faults. The eastern coast of the White Sea is flat, and geologically it is a submerged part of the Russian platform. Islands and shores of the west part are formed by the metamorphic rocks, chiefly by Archean granites and gneisses. The southern coast consists of Quaternary deposits.

Sediments. The sediments are pebbles, gravel and sand in the regions of heavy currents in Strait Gorlo (Gorge) and on the shallows. They are replaced by muddy sand, sandy mud and mud on the slopes. The central part of the sea is covered by a very fine-grained, distinctly brown clayey mud.

The Fe-Mn concretions are found in the Sea and in its strait. The sediments are formed largely of river silts mostly from the Dvina River which drains the forest-covered areas and leaches out the sesquioxides of podzol soils. The mean Mn content in the White Sea deposits is 0.81%, and phosphorus is 0.3%. The sediments are limeless. The shell deposits occur only in some places on the shallow banks. The organic carbon content does not exceed 1.8%.

The thickness of recent sediments ranges from zero in the areas of strong water movements and 22 cm in the central basin, to 100–150 cm near shores and more than 3 m off the river mouths. Rate of sedimentation is 2 cm/1000 yr in the central part and more than 30 cm/1000 yr near shores. The Holocene sediments are underlain by Late-glacial clays. Varve clays are found in some places on the bottom, which indicate the former ice-lake stage of the White Sea (analogous to the Baltic). The White Sea ice lake developed at the close of late (Würm) glaciation, i.e., not more than 12,000 years ago.

M. V. KLENOVA

References

Anon., 1950, "Bolishaja Sovetskaja Enciklopedija," Vol. 4, pp. 240, 456, Moscow.

Avilov, I. K., 1956, "Moshchnost' sovremennyx osadkov i poslelednikovaja istorija Belogo mor'a," *Tr. Gos. Okeanogr. Inst.*, **31/43**, 5–57.

Bruns, Erich, 1958, "Ozeanologie," Vol. 1, pp. 329–336, Berlin.

Klenova, M. V., 1960, "Geologija Barencova mor'a," *Izv. Akad. Nauk. SSSR*, 1–365 (with bibliography).

Klenova, M. V., 1961, "Sovremennoje osadkoobrazovanije v Barencovom more v knige 'Sovremennyje osadki morej i okeanov'," *Izv. Akad. Nauk SSSR*, 419–436.

Knipovitch, N., 1905, "Hydrologie des europäischen Eismeeres," *Ann. Hydrogr.*

Nansen, F., 1902/07, "The Norwegian North Polar Expedition," *Scientific Results*, **3** and **4**.

Schulz, B., and Wulff, A., 1928, "Hydrographische und planktonologische Forschungen in der Barents See," *Deut. Komm. Meeresforschung*, **4**.

Schulz, B., and Wulff A. Hydrographische und planktologische Ergebnisse der Fahrt des Fischereischutzbootes "Zieten" in das Barents Meer im August-September 1926.
    Berichte der deutschen Wissenschaftlichen Kommission für Meeresforschung, N.F. (B.III), H.3, Berlin, 1927.

Schulz, B., and Wulff A. Hydrographie und Oberflächenplankton des Westlichen Barentsmeeres im Sommer 1927.
    Berichte d. Deutsch. Wissenschaftlichen Kommission für Meeresforschung. N.F. (B. IV), Heft 5, Berlin, 1929.

Zenkevitch, Lev, 1963, "Biology of the Seas of the U.S.S.R.," New York, Interscience Publishers, 955pp.

BATHYAL ZONE

The marine ecologic zone that occupies a deeper position than the continental shelf but is shallower than the deep-ocean floor is known as the *bathyal zone* (Greek *bathos*, deep). Like other ecologic zones its characteristics are not defined wholly in terms of depth, but relate to light penetration, which is mainly latitude dependent, and to other biogeographic factors. The bathyal zone is aphotic, and light penetration depends on the angle of the sun and transparency due to local factors such as salinity, sediment in suspension and plankton. In terms of depth, the range is often given as 100–1000 *meters,* but some other authors give 100–1000 *fathoms,* so that the cynic might wonder if the round number is not the crucial factor and the unit of measurement is merely a matter of taste. A sober statement would more accurately express the range as from 100–300 m down to 1000–4000 m, varying according to the local depth of shelf break, latitudinal control of light penetration, and local conditions of currents, salinity, transparency, etc. In terms of bottom topography, the bathyal zone in the major ocean corresponds to the depths of the continental slope and continental rise. In the upper part of the latter, it merges with the abyssal zone. In narrow, closed basins the whole sea floor may fall into the bathyal depth range. For organisms such as plankton and nekton, the term *mesopelagic* applies to about 200–1000 m and *bathypelagic* is an appropriate ecologic term for 100–4000m. For the bottom dwellers, the term proposed by Alexander Agassiz, *archibenthos* (or archibenthic zone), is sometimes used, but the Mediterranean Commission (Pérès) prefers "epibathyal" and "mesobathyal" benthos. Almost everyone today refers to it as "bathyal benthos."

Some of these biogeographic controls are related to the distance from the shore, or better, the relative influence of land-generated factors: supply of fresh water, sediment in suspension, etc. Accordingly, a second descriptor is often applied: *hemipelagic facies,* implying a realm not wholly characteristic of the open sea, yet free from most of the characteristics of the shelf, the *neritic facies.* As Kuenen (1950, 0. 315) has stressed, a mid-oceanic bank, e.g., a guyot (strictly within the normal bathyal depth range) usually carries a wholly pelagic ("eupelagic") sediment such as foraminiferal, pteropod or coccolith ooze. The same is true even for the borders of some wide continental shelves, characterized by arid hinterlands and offshore winds (as off northwestern Australia: Fairbridge, 1954). In contrast, some inner basins of Indonesia, surveyed by Kuenen, show hemipelagic, nearshore sediments, extending down to 7000 m and more.

It should be stressed that terms like "bathyal zone" and "hemipelagic facies" are used by both marine biologists and marine geologists, but when defined by specialists of either discipline there is often a regrettable tendency to forget the other.

Such terms refer equally to *biofacies* and *lithofacies:* both to the bionomy and ecology of the organisms and to the physical substrate, the sediments or rock floor, and furthermore to the physicochemical environment (the seawater, its chemistry, temperature, pressure, circulation, etc.).

There is also a further professional group that uses these terms and often, regrettably, lacks a close liaison with the first two mentioned; this group consists of paleoecologists, stratigraphers and paleontologists, who are constantly involved in the problem of reconstructing a picture of a past environment, an exercise in paleogeography or paleobiogeography, using *indicators* of various sorts: ecologic habit, tracks and trails, sedimentary mineral characteristics, penecontemporaneous structures (ripple mark, cross-bedding, slumps, flow features, etc.). Failure of some very distinguished geologists, e.g., Lucien Cayeux (1941), to appreciate the importance of local conditions and their causes (notably distance from shore, sediment source, prevailing currents) has led them to deduce that violent oscillatory vertical movements of the earth's crust must be postulated in order to explain the rhythmic sequence of neritic and pelagic facies (see discussion by Woolnough, 1942, and Rutten, 1949). Such a sequence may better be viewed in the light of such potential factors as (a) turbidity currents, (b) cyclic shifts of the boundaries of regional wind systems, (c) cyclic variations in the rainfall of the hinterland, (d) eustatic and geodetic oscillations of sea level. Since the bathyal-benthic zone is the *boundary zone* between eupelagic and neritic facies, it is an area particularly sensitive to relatively modest changes in the physical environment. In the writer's opinion, many of the rhythmic stratigraphic sequences of the geological past call for no crustal changes but for minor paleoclimatic controls such as are predictable from the Milankovitch calculations of planetary motions, precession and so on.

Characteristics of the Bathyal Zone

(1) **Light.** The bathyal zone is almost entirely aphotic, though in the tropics under favorable conditions some feeble light is recorded to over 600 m; in high latitudes, this penetration drops to less than 50 m, and beyond the polar circles a winter season of continuous darkness causes the biomass to drop by some orders of magnitude (Moore, 1958). In tropical and some temperate seas, proximity to large mud-laden rivers causes a serious drop in transparency, even for distances of 100 km and more from the river mouth. Deepest light penetration in bathyal zones is recorded off the arid lands in the high-pressure climatic belts (around the Tropics of Cancer and Capricorn). Essentially there are no seasons in the bathyal zone (though the lower light boundary varies and some currents vary seasonally). A transitional "disphotic" light zone recognizes a twilight, permitting a certain visibility but not enough for photosynthesis.

(2) **Temperature.** Close study of the water masses and general oceanic circulation is essential. In general terms, in the low and middle latitudes, it may be said that bathyal temperatures will range from 15–5°C. For organisms, the range is not critical as a rule, and appropriate for *stenothermal* forms. East coasts of continents in these latitudes will normally be warmer than west coasts, receiving currents from equatorial regions. West coasts mainly receive boreal currents and, in addition, are particularly susceptible to upwelling of cold bottom water. In higher latitudes the bathyal temperatures usually range from about 3 to −1°C.

(3) **Salinity.** This may range in the bathyal zone from 34–36‰ and will depend mainly on the water mass involved: salinity is high in high evaporation areas (high-pressure zones and partially closed basins like the Mediterranean Sea, Red Sea and Persian Gulf), as well as areas of sea-ice formation, and water masses derived therefrom; low salinity marks water masses in areas of high precipitation, high cloud cover, and areas of melting ice. The salinity range in the bathyal zone is not high, however, by ecologic standards, and the organisms are described as *stenohaline* (i.e. of narrow tolerance).

(4) **Oceanic Circulation.** Current movement will be extremely slow in this zone and is essentially geostrophic except where modified by bottom friction. In many areas of the low and mid-latitudes, the basal waters of the warm water sphere (so-called subtroposphere of Defant) are almost stagnant at about 1000 m. Oxygen concentration falls off and the biota drops far below the level of the eupelagic population. In the higher latitudes along the continental slopes, the so-called countercurrents assume considerable importance in bathyal depths. In some restricted basins of the marginal seas (e.g., Black Sea, Kaoe Bay, Cariaco Trench) and some deep fiords with shallow sills, stagnant conditions develop, O_2 drops to zero, and lethal quantities of H_2S accumulate.

(5) **Fauna.** Eupelagic plankton, e.g., small foraminifera, are essentially universal (although scarce in polar waters), so that foraminiferal tests are constantly falling into the bathyal province. In the middle to high latitudes, countercurrents and upwelling favor vigorous bathyal biologic activity, and considerable nektonic development makes these depths favorable for deep fishing grounds. The work of the *Challenger Expedition* showed that in benthic populations both the number of varieties and the total numbers dropped sharply with depth, the mean for the bathyal zone being about 50% of that for the neritic. Bathybenthos depends in large measure on the substrate, provided there is adequate circulation. Cold water bathyal coral patches and banks (not true "reefs") are known in the eastern Atlantic from the latitude of northern Norway to the equator (Teichert, 1958). Hermatypic corals

which form the great mid-oceanic atolls cannot adjust to the aphotic condition and, only growing close to the littoral zone, prove a slow submergence of their foundations.

(6) Flora. In low latitudes, coccolithophoridae join the eupelagic foraminifera in contributing to the rain of organic sediment into the bathyal zone. In higher latitudes, these are replaced largely by diatoms; off some of the major northern rivers, the supply of fresh water is so great that some fresh-water and brackish diatom species are found quite far from land. Benthonic flora in bathyal depths is largely restricted to bacteria, but certain algae, including the lime-secreting encrusting or nodular form, *Lithothamnion*, are reported from considerable depths and very cold waters; its metabolic conditions are somthing of a mystery.

(7) Sediments. These are of three basic types, among which there is every stage of mixing.

(a) Pelagic "Rain," shells of pelagic forms (foraminifera, pteropoda, coccolithophoridae, etc.) sink down from upper waters and in favorable circumstances form a usually white or pinkish organogenic *"ooze"*; those conditions required include an absence of other sediment types that would dilute the numbers of tests and thus mask their presence, an absence of cool upwelling currents, high in CO_2, that might locally reduce the calcium carbonate compensation depth (q.v.) and thus destroy the shells by solution.

(b) Authigenic Sediments, being products of the interaction of seawater with existing grains ("halmyrolysis"), e.g., the modification of clay minerals, the formation of glauconite from feldspars and micas, of phillipsite (a zeolite) and palagonite from volcanic ash; the resultant sediment is often a *"green mud,"* green from chlorite or glauconite. The formation of new minerals also occurs directly from solution ("halmeic," according to Arrhenius), sometimes around an organic nucleus (which leads to a microenvironment of low pH), e.g., barite, phosphorite, ferromanganese nodules, concretions of silica, calcite, gypsum, etc. (in part already syn-diagenetic).

(c) Terrigenous Sediments, particularly the clays and silts, commonly a *"blue mud,"* reducing in character because of organic debris and bacterial production of ferrous iron sulfide (hydrotroilite). The surface layer of a few centimeters often oxidizes to a reddish brown. Special types of terrigenous sediment include glacial material ("marine till") which may be distributed over several million km^2, also volcanic ash and pumice, which may be heavily concentrated for about 100 km around a particular source, and coral muds and sands which are equally restricted to a specific source point. Being too fine to rest long on the continental shelf, the terrigenous muds are carried down the continental slope by gravity and *along it* by geostrophic currents. Since almost every longitudinal current affecting the

continental slope (and rise) has its "countercurrent," a zone of slack water must exist where suspended sediment will tend to accumulate. Since there are seasonal and long-term variations in current energy (and width), the locus of this belt will shift up and down the bathyal slope to distribute such sediments over a broad zone. This is probably the *most important source of geosynclinal sedimentation* (Bruce Heezen, personal communication). Studies of ancient geosynclinal sediments, e.g., in the Carpathian Flysch, by Dzulynski, Kşiazkiewicz and Kuenen (1959) and by others in other geosynclinal zones, have shown that the principal current directions are *parallel* to the structural axis, but that indications of gravity displacement (slumps, etc.) are *normal* to the axis; the structures created by the latter (see Fairbridge, 1946) are entirely distinct from those associated with general geostrophic currents.

A second source of transportation of terrigenous sediments is by *turbidity currents*. These develop along specific channels, generally fed directly by fluvial sources or longshore littoral drift, and include a heterogeneous mixture of grain sizes from the finest grades even up to boulders. Such currents are discontinuous, seasonal or cyclic phenomena, large ones occurring perhaps on a decade or century basis. The resultant turbidites are often marked by graded bedding and may interfinger the normal bathyal deposition. Turbidites find two types of resting place (*i*) in *submarine cones or fans* (q.v.) as seen off northwestern North America, off the Congo, Ganges, etc., or (*ii*) in *abyssal plains* (q.v.) as occur here and there around all major continents; where such plains occupy deep-sea basins, especially as in the North Atlantic, the environment is strictly in the abyssal zone (q.v.), but where there are smaller basins, "ponding" at intermediate, bathyal depths is observed, e.g., in some marginal seas. The paleoecologist must constantly be on guard against confusing transported thanatocoenotic assemblages, i.e., those swept down by turbidity currents from shallow depths into bathyal resting places (Ager, 1963). Detailed foraminiferal analyses made in the continental borderland basins, first shown by Natland off southern California, demonstrate clearly the transportation of shallow biofacies to deeper environments (Emery, 1960). An interesting controversy has arisen over the interpretation of certain flysch structures in the Pyrenees (see Kuenen, 1964; De Raaf, 1964); it has been claimed that the flysch is not a bathyal facies at all, as evidenced by the discovery of birds' footprints and salt pseudomorphs. There seems to be no reason why, along a steep orogenic coast, certain littoral facies should not pass directly into bathyal facies. Even so, the "salt pseudomorphs" do not really resemble modern evaporite crystal mats, but the surrounding matrix shows flow structures and the "cubes" are probably intraformational breccias (which sometimes develop a cubic fracture pattern). The controversy reminds one of the extraordinary and totally imaginary "Precambrian arthropods" reconstructed from angular intraformational breccia fragments in South Australia by David and Tillyard (1936).

RHODES W. FAIRBRIDGE

References

Ager, D. V., 1963, "Principles of Paleoecology," New York, McGraw-Hill Book Co., 371pp.

Cayeux, L., 1941, "Causes anciennes et causes actuelles en gèologie," Paris, Masson, 82pp.

David, Sir T. W. W., and Tillyard, R. J., 1936, "Memoir on Fossils of the Late Pre-Cambrian (Newer Proterozoic)," Sydney, Angus & Robertson, 122pp.

De Raaf, J. F. M., 1964, "The Occurrence of Flute Casts and Pseudomorphs After Salt Crystals in the Oligogene 'grès à ripple-marks, of the southern Pyrenees," in (Bouma and Brouwer, editors) "Turbidites," pp. 192–198, Amsterdam, Elsevier Publishing Co.

Dzulynski, S., Kşiazkiewicz, M., and Kuenen, P. H., 1959, "Turbidites in flysch of the Polish Carpathian Mountains," *Bull. Geol. Soc. Am.*, **70**, 1089–1118.

Emery, K. O., 1960, "The Sea off Southern California," New York, John Wiley & Sons, 366pp.

Fairbridge, R. W., 1946, "Submarine slumping and location of oil bodies," *Bull. Am. Assoc. Petrol. Geologists*, **30**, 84–92.

Fairbridge, R. W., 1953, "The Sahul Shelf, northern Australia; its structure and geological relationships," *J. Roy. Soc. W. Australia*, **37**, 1–33.

Hedgpeth, J. W. (editor), 1957, "Treatise on marine ecology and paleoecology," Vol. 1: "Ecology," *Geol. Soc. Am. Mem.*, **67**, 1296pp.

Heezen, B. C., 1962, "The Deep-Sea Floor," in "Continental Drift," Vol. 3, pp. 235–288, New York, Academic Press.

Kuenen, P. H., 1950, "Marine Geology," New York, John Wiley & Sons, 568pp.

Kuenen, P. H., 1964, "Deep-Sea Sands and Ancient Turbidites," in (Bouma and Brouwer, editors) "Turbidites," pp. 3–33, Amsterdam, Elsevier Publishing Co.,

Moore, H. B., 1958, "Marine Ecology," New York, John Wiley & Sons, 493pp.

Potter, P. E., and Pettijohn, F. J., 1963, "Paleocurrents and Basin Analysis," New York, Academic Press, 296pp.

Rutten, M. G., 1949, "Actualism in Epeirogenetic Oceans," *Geol. Mijnbouw*, N.S. **11**, 222–226.

Teichert, C., 1958, "Cold- and deep-water coral banks," *Bull. Am. Assoc. Petrol. Geologists*, **42**, 1064–1082.

Woolnough, W. G., 1942, "Geological extrapolation and pseudabyssal sediments," *Bull. Am. Assoc. Petrol. Geologists*, **26**, 765–792.

Zenkevitch, L. A., 1963, "Biology of the Seas of the U.S.S.R." New York, Interscience Publishers, 955pp. (translated by S. Botcharskaya).

Cross-references: *Abyssal Zone; Benthonic Zonation; Continental Rise; Marine Ecology; Neritic Zone; Pelagic Life; Troposphere and Stratosphere in the Ocean; Turbidity Currents.*

BATHYMETRY

Bathymetry concerns the measurement and charting of ocean depths. Bathymetric information on nautical charts allows the navigator to avoid dangerous shoals and provides information which helps him to determine his position. It is for this reason that each maritime nation has established governmental offices to construct and issue nautical charts. Although most maritime nations conduct surveys of their own shores and continental shelves, the larger maritime nations have also undertaken the task of mapping the shores of underdeveloped countries. Sounding in ocean depths greater than 100 fathoms has until very recently been considered purely an academic pursuit (except in limited areas where submarine cable routes were involved). In 1903, Prince Albert I of Monaco brought out the first General Bathymetric Chart of the Oceans at a scale of 1:10 million. Soundings from all sources were compiled, and generalized bathymetric contours were drawn by a group of experienced marine scientists who served on Prince Albert's scientific cabinet.

In recent decades, both oceanographic and military studies have resulted in a great increase in the number of soundings (q.v.) in the deep sea, but since there is little direct commercial need for such information, the majority of bathymetric charts still concern only the shelves, bays and nearshore areas. The techniques and procedures of shallow-water hydrographic surveying are discussed at length in hydrographic manuals (Adams, 1942) and have varied little since fundamental principles were laid down in the early nineteenth century except that more modern techniques of navigation control and better methods of sounding have evolved in the past century and a half. This article will be concerned with the bathymetry of the deep sea.

Sounding Surveys

Deep-sea soundings are largely collected by oceanographic vessels, by naval survey vessels running from one nearshore survey to another, by cable ships, and by naval vessels employed in military or other tasks. However, occasionally ships are employed in more detailed special surveys. In reconnaissance surveys, the pattern employed depends upon the feature. A canyon is surveyed after original discovery by a series of zig-zag crossings by which the feature is traced up or down slope. Seamounts are investigated by radial search patterns generally aimed at discovering successively shallower points. Island slopes are sometimes investigated by circular tracks if the investigator is interested in detecting canyons or other small detail, or by radial patterns if only the gross morphology is to be investigated. The pattern used is, to a great extent, determined by the navigational

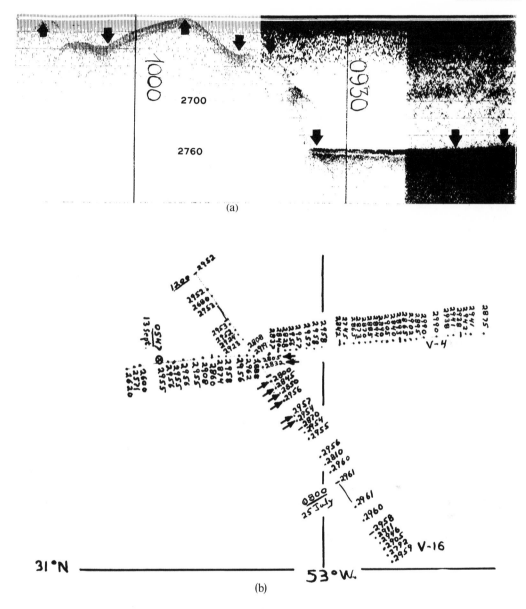

Fig. 1. Echogram plot on a chart: (a) Section of a typical precision depth recorder record. Arrows denote the depths read and plotted on (b). (b) Illustrates a typical navigational plot. The soundings marked with arrows are those read from (a).

control available. Thus, where precision navigational control is not available, surveyors tend to avoid recrossing areas surveyed earlier to diminish the number of readjustments at track intersections.

Where high-precision navigation is available, frequent recrossing of previous lines is desirable to verify the precision of navigation and to define greater detail.

The pattern of sounding lines to be used in precision surveys depends to some extent on the nature of the feature or features to be surveyed. Radial patterns are sometimes used on circular features such as seamounts. A series of parallel lines, all in one direction, is a frequently used pattern but has the obvious disadvantage that topographic trends paralleling the grid are usually undetected or are at least poorly delineated. A rectangular grid with equal line spacing in either direction is the best plan, particularly if accurate navigation control is available. Many surveyors, however, do not use this system because of the tedious work of readjusting line crossings to bring them into agreement.

In normal practice, echo soundings are read from the continuous record at each summit, trough and significant change in slope. In deep-sea areas, one or two soundings are recorded per mile. Although soundings are recorded in an appalling number of units (over 20), most organizations use a unit based on 1/400 second travel time which is variously referred to as the "standard unit" or "nominal fathom." When true depth rather than echo time is required for special studies, these units can be converted to meters or fathoms by correcting for variations in sound velocity. In detailed surveys, corrections can be made for the slope of the bottom in order to obtain vertical depths.

Soundings are plotted as a series of closely spaced numbers along the ship's track. Standard Mercator position plotting sheets at 4 or 8 inches to the degree of longitude (at a scale of about 1:1,000,000 or 1:500,000) are utilized.

In Fig. 1 a section of a Precision Depth Recorder (q.v.) record has been reproduced. The arrows denote the actual depth read and plotted on the chart [Fig. 1(B)]. For routine work it is necessary to filter out the important depths, since at standard plotting sheet scale, it is difficult to plot depths with a greater density than one per mile.

Bathymetric Charts

Contours were first used in the construction of bathymetric charts and only later adapted to the representation of subaerial topography. However, since the terrestrial surveyor can see the land, subaerial contours have become an extremely precise, nonsubjective manner of relief representation. Bathymetric contours are isobaths drawn from a collection of spot soundings, sounding lines and sounding profiles ([Fig. 2(a) and (b)]. The contourer has to imagine what the relief must be and then portray this abstraction on paper. There is a

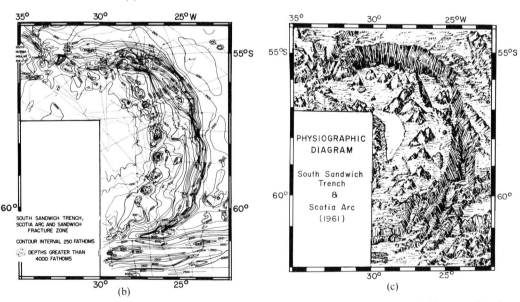

Fig. 2. Contour and physiographic charts: (a) Contour chart of South Sandwich Trench. Chart was based on relatively few soundings. Contours in meters. (b) Contour chart of some area based on several surveys subsequent to 1960. Note the greater detail and reflection of the structural trends in the contours (Heezen and Johnson, 1965). (c) Physiographic diagram of the South Sandwich Trench (Heezen and Tharp, 1961).

greater range in the quality of isobaths shown on published bathymetric charts than there is in sub-aerial topographic maps. Since the drawing of contours is essentially subjective, the quality is in part related to the time, care and thought devoted to the subject by the contourer. It is also a function of his experience and the correctness of his hypothesis. After careful examination, some depths will be eliminated as being unreliable. A familiarity with echo sounders is necessary to be able to recognize scale and timing errors. A knowledge of geology and sedimentology is highly desirable so that the contours will not violate any natural processes. A glaring example of this would be apparent crevices or hollows in an abyssal plain caused by timing errors in the echo sounder. A practical acquaintance with navigation is necessary for the various difficulties encountered in overcast regions,

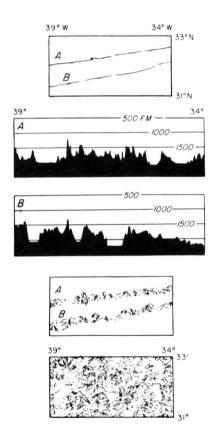

Fig. 3. Method of preparation of physiographic diagram: (a) Positions of sounding lines (A, B) are plotted on chart. (b) Soundings are plotted as profiled (A, B) at 40:1 vertical exaggeration. (c) Features shown on profiles (A, B) are sketched on chart along tracks. (d) After all available soundings profiles are sketched the remaining unsounded areas are filled in by extrapolating and interpolating trends observed in a succession of profiles (Heezen et al., 1959).

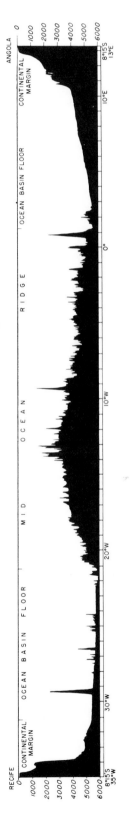

Fig. 4. Typical transatlantic profile. This profile across the South Atlantic was obtained by R. V. Crawford in 1957 (Heezen et al., 1961). (For a 100:1 exaggeration the profiled are plotted at a scale of 200 fathoms to an inch and horizontally 20 nautical miles equal an inch. In a typical area, approximately 50 soundings are plotted for sixty miles of profiles. The points are connected and then qualitatively checked against the original echograms.)

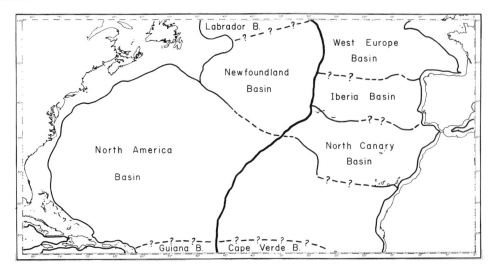

Fig. 5. Major basins of the North Atlantic, after Wüst (1940). Heavy solid lines indicate boundary formed by axis of Mid-Atlantic Ridge. Light solid lines indicate boundary formed by shelf breaks and submarine ridges. Dashed lines indicate arbitrary boundaries.

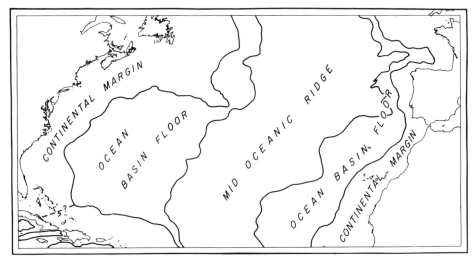

Fig. 6. Major morphologic divisions: North Atlantic Ocean (after Heezen, 1959).

in high latitudes, and in areas of strong currents. The ocean floor may at first appear chaotic, but an order is generally found in nature.

It is not possible to evaluate or to make detailed use of contour charts unless locations of the sounding lines used in construction are shown. (The actual soundings are usually not shown on published charts.)

Physiographic Diagrams. Marine physiographic diagrams [Figs. 2(c) and 3] have been constructed for several marine areas (Heezen *et al.*, 1959). Unlike their terrestrial counterparts, the author is required to postulate the structural features and

patterns on the basis of echo-sounding profiles. Topographic profiles are the primary data utilized in the drawing of a physiographic diagram (Figs. 3 and 4). The features shown on the profiles are sketched in along the track. Adjacent tracks are examined for trends and regional characteristics. When all the tracks in an area are sketched, the major trends are estimated and the intervening areas are completed by both interpolation and extrapolation.

Topographic Profiles. Profiles are generally constructed at a 100:1 vertical exaggeration to emphasize the topographic form of the bottom

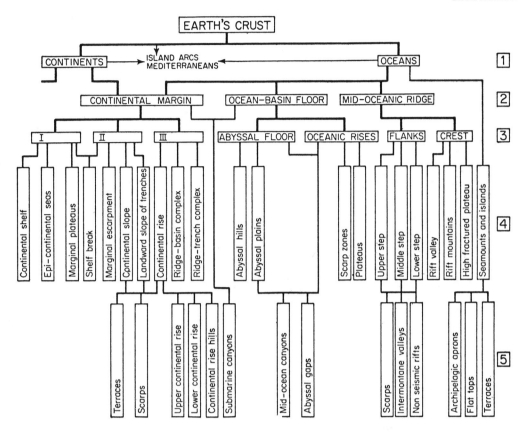

Fig. 7. Outline of submarine topography. Line 1, first-order features of the crust; line 2, major topographic features of the ocean; line 3, categories of provinces and superprovinces; line 4, provinces; line 5, subprovinces and other important features (Heezen, *et al.,* 1959).

(Fig. 4). Features less than two or three miles in width are best studied by examination of the original echograms. A precision depth recorder is ideal for this purpose. A careful study of the echogram by an experienced observer can reveal microfeatures such as sand waves and slumps, and certain inferences can be made concerning the composition of the bottom.

Physiographic Regions. The oceans are divided by the physical oceanographers into broad basins (Fig. 5). These basins are generally defined by the contours shown on the bathymetric charts published by the International Hydrographic Bureau. The basins are bounded by land masses and major oceanic ridges. This system is adequate when studying water masses; however, it is not suited for studies of submarine physiography. The generalized isobaths upon which this system is based will cut across the physiographic boundaries as revealed by precision echo sounding.

Marine physiographic regions are defined according to a system similar to that used in land physiography (Lobeck, 1939). The oceans are basically

divided into three morphologic units: the continental margin, ocean-basin floor and mid-oceanic ridge (Figs. 6 and 7).

Continental Margin. The continental margins are characterized by three categories of provinces. The relatively flat portions of the submerged continental platform form the continental shelf. The continental shelf is generally less than 100 fathoms in depth with a width ranging from a few miles to over two hundred miles.

Seaward of the continental shelf is the steeper *continental slope.* The continental slope commences abruptly at the edge of the continental shelf usually within a depth range of 40–100 fathoms. The declivity of the slope generally is from 3–6°.

The *continental rise,* marginal *trenches* and outer ridge lie at the base of the continental slope. The continental rise is a relatively smooth wedge of sediments with a usual gradient of 1:100 to 1:700. Its width ranges from a few miles to several hundred miles. A marginal trench is a narrow depression which extends at least 1000 fathoms below the level of the adjacent ocean floor.

109

The typical continental margin is composed of continental shelf, continental slope and continental rise. In some instances, such as Puerto Rico or the Blake Plateau, the upper continental rise is replaced by a marginal trench or basin and the lower continental rise is replaced by an outer ridge.

Ocean Basin Floor. The abyssal floor includes *abyssal plains* (q.v.) and *abyssal hills*. Abyssal plains are those areas with a gradient of less than 1:1000. This extremely low slope may be due to deposition of terrigenous sediments carried to and across the abyssal plains by various forms of gravity flow. An oceanic rise is a broad relatively smooth elevation measured in hundreds of square miles which is not connected to the continental margin or mid-oceanic ridge system. The Bermude Rise and the Sierra Leone Rise are typical examples. Seamounts, isolated or related groups of volcanic edifices, are scattered throughout the oceans but the majority lie on the ocean basin floor.

Mid-oceanic Ridge. The Mid-oceanic Ridge is a continuous median ridge which runs the length of the North Atlantic, South Atlantic, Indian and South Pacific oceans for more than 40,000 miles. It is essentially a broad fractured swell which rises some 500–1500 fathoms above the ocean basin floor (Fig. 4). The ridge is generally characterized by a median rift valley which is the locus of the earthquake epicenters.

B. C. HEEZEN
C. L. JOHNSON

References

Adams, K. T., 1942, "Hydrographic Manual," Special Publication No. 143, Supt. of Documents, U.S. Govt. Printing Office, Washington, D.C. 940pp.

*Heezen, B. C., Tharp, M., and Ewing, M., 1959, "The floors of the oceans, I. The North Atlantic," *Geol. Soc. Am. Spec. Paper*, **65**, 122pp.

Heezen, B. C., and Tharp, M., 1961, "The Physiographic Diagram of the South Atlantic, the Caribbean, the Scotia Sea, and the Eastern Margin of the South Pacific Ocean," The Geological Society of America, New York.

Heezen, B. C., and Tharp, M., 1964, "The Physiographic Diagram of the Indian Ocean, the Red Sea, the South China Sea, the Sulu Sea, and the Celebes Sea," The Geological Society of America, New York.

*Heezen, B. C., and Menard, H. W., 1963, "Topography of the Deep-sea Floor," in (Hill, M. N., editor) "The Sea," pp. 233–280, New York, John Wiley & Sons.

Heezen, B. C., and Johnson, G. L., 1965, "The South Sandwich Trench," *Deep-sea Res.* (in press).

Lobeck, A. K., 1939, "Geomorphology," New York, McGraw-Hill Book Co., 731pp.

*Shepard, F. P., 1963, "Submarine Geology," Second ed., New York, Harper & Row, 555pp.

Wüst, G., 1940, "Zur Nomenklatur der Grossformen der Ozeanboden," *Assoc. Oceanog. Union Geod. Geophys. Internat.*, *Publ. Sci.*, No. 8, 12–124.

BAY OF BENGAL

The Bay of Bengal, which takes its name from that of the old Mogul state of India, is the northeastern arm of the Indian Ocean lying between peninsular India and Burma. The bay occupies about 2.2×10^6 km². It is bordered on the north by the deltaic regions of the Ganges and Brahmaputra Rivers. On the east is the Burmese Peninsula and its extension to the south, the Andaman and Nicobar Ridges, which are submerged continuations of the Arakan Yoma ranges. Following the International Hydrographic Bureau (Sp. Publ. 23, 1953), the southern boundary extends from Dondra Head at the south end of Ceylon to the north tip of Sumatra and is open to the central Indian Ocean (Fig. 1).

Oceanography

The northern Indian Ocean, which includes the Bay of Bengal, is characterized by periodic monsoon winds. A seasonal, low-pressure area developing over the Persian Gulf during the summer causes these wind systems to blow persistently from the southwest during this period. In winter, the monsoons, issuing from a high-pressure source forming over the Tibetan Plateau, come from the northeast. The northern Indian Ocean wind system, coupled with the Himalaya Mountains, thus creates the world's highest rainfall. The heaviest rains, which occur during autumn when the wind direction is unstable and reversing, drain into the Bay of Bengal and dominate the oceanographic conditions of the northern Indian Ocean.

Physical Properties. The annual reversal of wind causes a corresponding change in the flow of surface water in the bay. During the spring there is a clockwise circulation of this water, which combines in the south with the eastward moving North Equatorial Current. The swiftest flow is close to the central Indian Continental shelf, where the speed reaches 3 to 5 knots. In autumn the surface circulation is reversed and forms an anticlockwise gyral, with lesser speeds in the central and eastern parts (Fig. 1).

The wind system, in accordance with Coriolis force, develops peripheral vertical circulations around the Bay of Bengal. After the spring southwest winds begin, the surface water is displaced from the east Indian Coast. This causes the deeper water to upwell, and tilts the isopicnals upward toward shore. In autumn, when the surface water piles up on the west side of the bay (Fig. 2), the isopicnal surface tilts downward toward the coast.

The influence of water density and wind changes is shown by the average sea level, which at Visakhapatnam, on the east coast of India, has an annual cycle of about 1.5 feet. A yearly seasonal change of 4 feet, the largest on record in the world, occurs on the northeast shore at Chittagong, in southeast Pakistan.

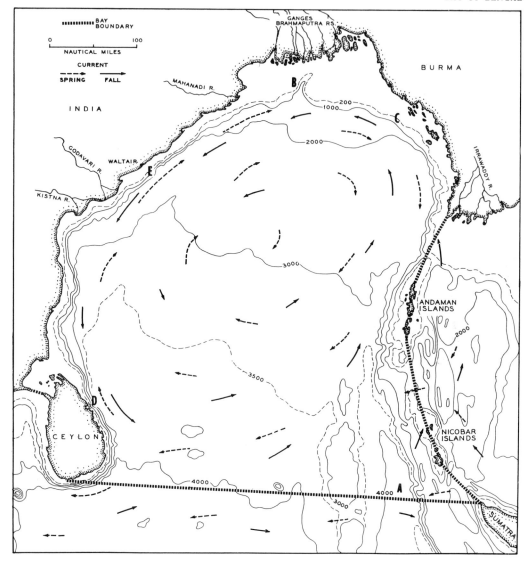

Fig. 1. Bathymetry of Bay of Bengal (contours in meters): (A) Indonesian trench, (B) swatch of no ground, (C) Burma Canyon, (D) Triconomi Canyon, (E) Andhra, Mahadevan, and Krishna Canyons (Andhra Shelf).

The funnel shape of the sides of the Bay of Bengal, and the shoaling of its bottom, cause high tides, seiches, and internal waves of varying period of heights. The tidal ranges, which displace large masses of water, make the tidal periods of water properties conspicuous. Internal waves of shorter period are also prominent because they occur between the shallow, low-density surface layer and the denser water below. Vertical oscillations, or internal waves, by convergence and divergence, appear as long bands of alternately smooth and rough water. Since these waves, 20–30 feet high, refract when crossing the continental shelf, the bands tend to parallel the coast as they move slowly shoreward.

Chemistry. The high river discharge into the northern Bay of Bengal during autumn is due to the extremely heavy rainfall of the general area. The rivers Krishna, Godavari, Mahanadi, Ganges, Brahmaputra, and Irrawaddy influence, in differing degree, the water properties near their confluences. The southerly flow of diluted seawater down the west side of the bay during autumn reduces the surface salinity at latitude 17°N from the normal 33–34‰ to as low as 18‰, and the low salinity is confined mainly to the nearshore areas. The dry season is characterized by a northerly flow and upwelled high-salinity water, around 34‰. Although surface salinity varies, the bay as a whole is noted for having a lower salinity than other oceanic areas. The head of the bay is lowest and becomes progressively higher at the other extremity.

The composition of chemical nutrients in the Bay of Bengal is related to the water changes in surface salinity. During the upwelling period over the continental shelf, the phosphate content increases from 6–10 μg atoms/liter and silicate rises from 8 to 20 μg atoms/liter. Oxygen decreases when deeper water is brought up by upwelling. In the center of the bay, a marked oxygen minimum at around 300 meters occurs, where the oxygen is less than 0.1 ml/liter. The nearshore upwelling zone not only has a high yield of nutrients, but also is a high primary production area for phytoplankton and related zooplankton. This occurs in the northeast part during the northeast winds and on the west side during southwest winds. Organic production, including fish, is higher in late winter off the Burma Coast, Hooghly Delta, and Andaman Islands than off other shores.

Geology

Topography. The sea floor topography of the Bay of Bengal shows a broad, U-shaped basin open to the south (Fig. 1), the central part of which slopes almost uniformly from around 2000–4000 meters at a rate of about 2 m/mile. This shape shows that the sea bottom has been tectonically stable for long periods. The initially large tectonic features of the plain have been masked by a high rate of sedimentation. This plain ends in a rise up to the broad delta at the head of the bay. The rounded edge of the continental shelf occurs between 130 and 180 meters on the west side, where the steepest part is about 4-$\frac{1}{2}$ degrees. To the south, off Ceylon, the continental slope, over 45 degrees, is the sharpest known.

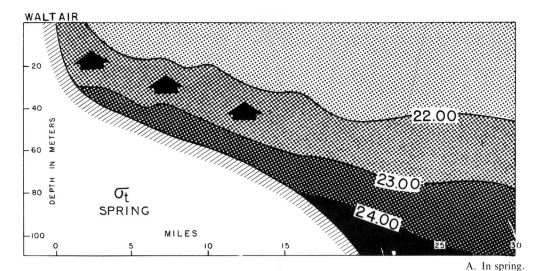

A. In spring.

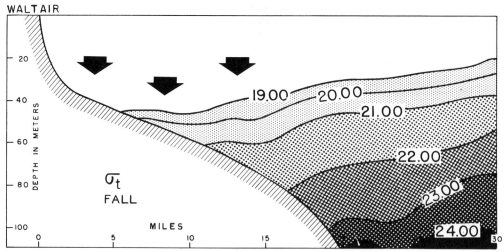

B. In fall.

Fig. 2. Vertical Density Structure off Andhra Coast.

Submarine Canyons. One of the submarine features is the north-south Indonesian Trench, near the Nicobar-Sumatra mainland, which extends into the bay at a maximum depth of over 4500 meters. Another noted geological conformation is the Ganges Canyon, or "Swatch of No Ground," which begins in shallow water off the Ganges delta and indents into the continental shelf in a northeast-southwest direction. Its width is 8 miles at a depth of 700 fathoms, and it gouges into the surrounding plain as much as 300–400 fathoms. According to Harris Stewart, it appears to be partly faulted and partly scoured. The sides of the Ganges Canyon are steep, about 1:1.5, but the bottom is nearly level.

In 1963, the Andhra, Mahadevan, and Krishna Canyons were discovered off the Andhra coast of India. Their profiles at 700 fathoms showed them to be V-shaped, with sides having slopes of 1:5 (Fig. 3). Several of these and other canyons, as yet neither named nor adequately surveyed, are instrumental in funneling the sediment discharged by the rivers. Numerous turbidity channels, similar to the braided channels on land, meander, split and rejoin, and run the length of the bay with subsurface tributary channels from either side. Small, trough-shaped depressions in the extreme south end, with leveed sides, may also be the result of sediment flows from the head of the bay.

Continental Shelf. Detailed profiles of the continental shelf at the head of the Bay of Bengal, and off the Andhra coast of India, reveal it to be as much as 100 miles wide, but narrowing to the south. The Andhra shelf has an average width of about 24 miles, an average slope of $0° 15'$, and an average depth at the outer edge of around 100 fathoms (Fig. 4). The shelf can be divided into five zones, each having characteristic slopes and sediments. The average widths and slopes of these zones are given in Table 1.

All zones are relatively smooth, with the exception of zones C-D, lying between 35 and 58 fathoms, where bottom irregularities measure as much as 2–3 fathoms. From the appearance of the slope and the breaks in the different zones, it is believed that the sea-floor deposition and erosion are caused by currents and water masses oriented parallel to the coast. Farther north, a terrace occurs at depths varying from 104–150 fathoms. At the base of the continental slope are turbidity canyons running parallel with the slope.

Sea-floor Sediments. *Deep-water Sediments.* The sediments in the Bay of Bengal are characterized by their content of globigerina ooze, which is present mainly in the central and deeper parts of the bay. Terrigenous deposits are found in the northern and shallower portions and are dispersed throughout by turbidity currents. No measurement of the amount of sediment discharged by the Ganges, Brahmaputra, Mahanadi, and other rivers has been made; however, one estimate holds that the seaward edge of the continental shelf is moving

TABLE 1. CHARACTERISTICS OF THE ANDHRA (WALTAIR)
CONTINENTAL SHELF

Zone	(miles)	Slope (degrees)	Depth (fathoms)	Sediment Zones*
Shore A–B	2	0° 26′	0	S
			15	S
B–C	11	0° 04′	15	S, Cl
			30	Sh, Cl
			35	S, Sh, R?, Co?
C–D	6	0° 11′	35	S, Sh, R?, Co?
			40	S, Sh, C, R?, Co?
			58	S, Sh, C, R?, Co?
D–E	2	0° 35′	58	S, Sh, C, R?, Co?
			70	S, Sh, C
E–F	2	1° 09′	70	S, Sh, C
			100	Sh, M, C
			112	M
Beyond F	5	4° 38′	112	M
			500	M

* Predominate sediments in zones. (S=sand, Cl=clay, Sh=shell, Co=coral, R=rock, C=concretions, M=mud).

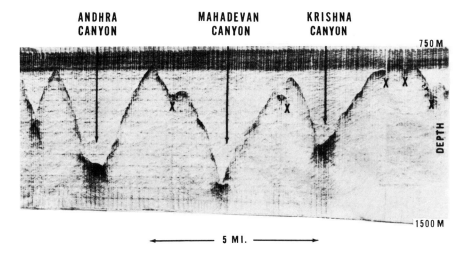

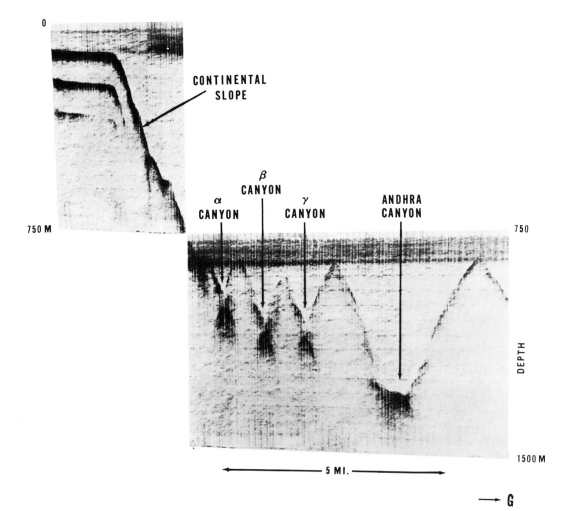

Fig. 3. Echogram of section across Andhra, Mahadevan and Krishna Canyons (see Fig. 1 for location).

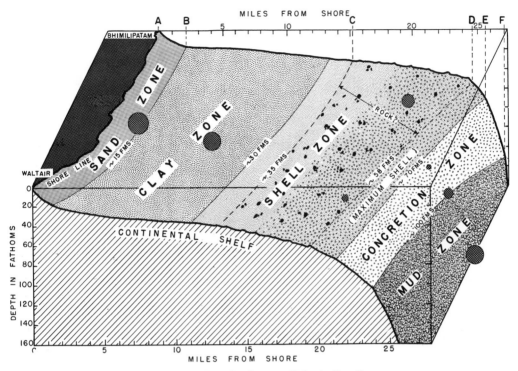

Fig. 4. Distribution of sediments off the Andhra Coast.

southward at the rate of one mile every 40 years. Another estimate is that a 1% sediment count in the discharge during flood season would amount to 4×10^9 cubic meters, or enough to cover the bay bottom to a depth of 2 mm every year. These speculations provide a general idea of the vast sedimentation that exists and its influence on the topography and geological processes.

Shelf Sediments. The Bay of Bengal shelf sediments, which closely correspond with the slopes of the shelf (Fig. 4), can be divided into sedimentary zones, and although overlapping exists, the zones are distinct enough for delineation. In the first zone, up to 2 miles from shore and 15 fathoms deep, the sediment is composed of sand, which is graded and sorted, the fineness of the grains increasing with distance from shore.

The second zone, extending from about 2–13 miles offshore, and ranging from 15–30 fathoms, is of clay, and the sediment consists of clay minerals and fine grains of sand.

The third zone is partly composed of shell. It lies between about 13 and 21 miles offshore, and it ranges from 30–70 fathoms in depth. This zone is characterized by fragments of shell and higher concentrations of sand. The maximum shell content is found at a depth from 58–70 fathoms. This shell zone is composed of a central, hard zone, around 35–58 fathoms. Although no rock or coral has been dredged or sampled, the evidence points strongly to its presence. A dredging did expose

bryozoan, sponge, hydroid, and pecten, organisms which are associated with hard sediments. Echo sounder traces give multiple echoes in this zone but not adjacently, and indicate the presence of rock or old coral.

The fourth, or concretion zone, overlaps the shell region and extends from 40 fathoms to the continental slope. Its outer part, often called the oolite area, extends beyond the shell zone and lies between 70 and 100 fathoms, roughly 21–23 miles off the Waltair coast. A unique feature of this zone is that much of its material, although composed of clay, fine sand, and shell fragments, is cemented together into oval-shaped concretions or oolites about 1 mm in diameter.

Continental slope sediments are plastic and soft in consistency and are colored dark gray with a blue tinge. They are composed of clay minerals, glauconite, fine mineral grains, and microorganisms such as foraminifera, radiolaria, etc.

Delta Sediments. Sediments in the Bay of Bengal from the Ganges, Mahanadi, Godavari, Krishna, and Pennar deltas, are finer, consist mostly of silts and clays, and are generally darker than the coastal samples. Since a deltaic environment does not produce coral or numerous molluscan organisms, the calcium carbonate content off the deltas is low.

Radioactive Sediments. On the continental shelf in the Waltain area of the Bay of Bengal, the relative radium content (β-activity) of the sediments follows zonal patterns similar to those of the bottom slopes and sediments. In Fig. 4 the dark circles indicate a zone of relatively high intensity (11–14 $\times$ 10^{-6} gram of U per gram of sediment) extending 12 miles from shore and to a depth of 30 fathoms. This high value is due to the presence in the sediment of monazite and zircon, minerals commonly found on the beach.

A second radioactive area, composed of sediments with low values of radioactivity (3–7 $\times$ 10^{-6} gram of U per gram of sediment), is located between 12 and 23 miles offshore at a depth of 30–100 fathoms.

The third outer radioactive zone has a relatively high concentration (13–15 $\times$ 10^{-6} gram of U per gram of sediment).

Beach Erosion. Sandy beaches, which extend along the east coast of India in the Bay of Bengal, drive their sand from the small rivers in the south and from the erosion of the shore line.

Sand Sorting. When sediment is first deposited at the confluences of rivers, natural processes impel a sorting of sand content according to size and density. Monozite, garnet, ilmenite, and magnetite, which are heavier minerals, settle near the confluences; quartz, feldspar, and mica, all lighter minerals, are carried farther north by the predominant littoral drift along the beach. Commercial mining of such minerals is conducted in southern India.

A principal reason for the concentration of black sand is beach regressions, which occurs when man-made structures, such as the Madras Harbor or the Visakhapatnam breakwater, are erected. Sand from the south is trapped by such an obstruction, while the beach to the north continues to erode. The heavy sand deposition at Godavari Point, which has developed over the past century, has resulted in a beach regression of the Uppada beach to the north and the creation of a mineral deposition of considerable commercial value.

Annual Sand Level Cycles. The sand level at Waltair Beach on the Bay of Bengal is influenced by waves, currents, tides, winds, and rains.

The changes in sand level are shown in Fig. 5, together with the cycles of wind, waves, and current for the central east coast. During the period of maximum waves and northerly currents, the beach is eroded and the sand is deposited offshore. When the milder weather period and weaker southerly currents prevail, the sand returns shoreward and rebuilds the beach. This fluctuation in sand level on the Waltair Beach amounts to as much as 10 feet.

Bimonthly Sand Level Cycles. The profile of Waltair beach, which varies between spring and neap tides, also reflects a small bimonthly cycle of change in the sand level. An example of this change during spring and neap tides is given in Fig. 6. The tide level, wave wash levels, and sand level are all shown in the same vertical scale.

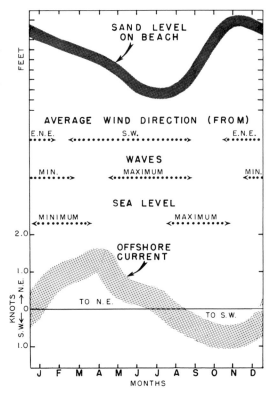

Fig. 5. Seasonal variation of sand level, sand deposition, and the environmental factors affecting beach erosion.

The sand level oscillates about a nodal point approximately 1 foot below mean tide level. The environmental flux involves a transition in water height, the ensuing difference in wave character, and the duration of tidal action on the beach. During spring tides, an average wave produces two zones of long-duration wash (B); neap tides produce one (B'). The wave energy at low tides is dissipated over a longer, shallow offshore area. At high tide, it is expended high on the foreshore.

Littoral Drift of Sand. The littoral drift of sand on the east coast of India is toward the northeast or head of the Bay of Bengal. Some reversals are evident, but the environmental conditions which cause the maximum drift exert their forces prevailingly toward the northeasterly direction. Figure 5 shows that the current flows northeasterly for 7 of the 12 months, and its speed is greater than when flowing in the southwesterly direction. Also, the waves, which come from a southerly direction, are higher during the northerly flowing current. This so facilitates the suspension of sand that it is easily transported by the shore currents. The littoral drift of sand in a northerly direction is shown by the presence of sand bars which lay partially across the small river mouths. These bars

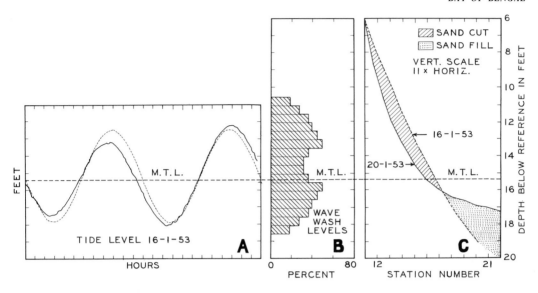

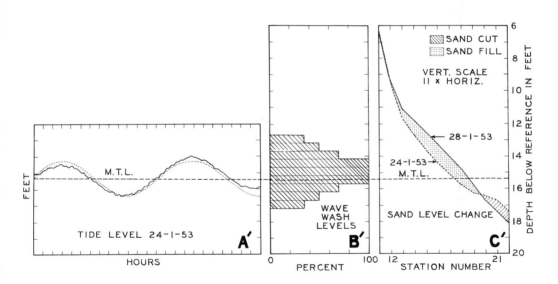

Fig. 6. Comparison (to same vertical scale) of observed tide level in Visakhapatnam Harbor during neap tide (A′) and spring tide (A), calculated per cent of time each beach level is washed by waves during neap tides (B′) and spring tides (B), and the change in sand level during neap tides (C′) and spring tides (C).

invariably extend from the south bank and indicate a sand flow from that direction.

The broad beach south of the Madras Harbour breakwater is a result of sand accumulated from the south. The Visakhapatnam breakwater ingeniously traps sand from the south before it fills the channel. The building up of Godavari Point was also caused by a northerly drift and deposition of sand. Godavari Point was originally indis-

tinguishable from other sand bars at the mouth of the Godavari River, but floods and deforestation of the Godavari delta caused more of the river to discharge in the open sea than into Kakinada Bay. Increased sedimentation thus began to flow up the coast and deposit at Godavari Point, which has grown for the past century from south to north at the rate of about 8 miles in 100 years. At this rate Kakinada Bay will be a lake in about 50 years.

The deposition at Madras, Visakhapatnam, and Godavari Point proceeds at the rate of one million tons per year, or about 400,000 cubic yards at each place.

E. C. La Fond

References

Dietz, R. S., 1953, "Possible deep-sea turbidity-current channels in the Indian Ocean," *Bull. Geol. Soc. Am.*, **64**, 375–76.

Ganapati, P. N., LaFond, E. C., and Bhavanarayana, P. V., 1956, "On the vertical distribution of chemical constituents in the shelf waters off Waltair," *Proc. Indian Acad. Sci.*, **44**, No. 2, 68–72.

LaFond, E. C., 1957, "Oceanographic studies in the Bay of Bengal," *Proc. Indian Acad. Sci., Sect. B*, **46**, 1–47.

LaFond, E. C., 1964, "Andhra, Mahadevan, and Krishna Submarine Canyons and other features of the continental slopes off the east coast of India," *J. Indian Geol. Union*, **1**, No. 1.

LaFond, E. C., and Rao, R. Prasada, 1956, "On the erosion of the beach at Uppada," *Port Engineer*, **5**, No. 2, 2–9.

LaFond, E. C., and Rao, R. Prasada, 1956, "Beach erosion cycles near Waltair on the Bay of Bengal," *Andhra Univ. Mem. Oceanog.*, **1**, 63–77

Mahadevan, C., and Aswathanarayana, U., 1954, "Radioactivity of sea floor sediments off the east coast of India," *Andhra Univ. Mem. Oceanog.*, **1**, 36–50.

Mahadevan, C., and Rao, M. Poornachandra, 1954, "Study of ocean floor sediments off the east coast of India," *Andhra Univ. Mem. Oceanog.*, **1**, 1–35.

BAY OF FUNDY

Introduction

The Bay of Fundy is a funnel-shaped body of water between Nova Scotia and the Canadian mainland (Fig. 1). Fundy proper is 144 km long, 100 km wide at the base, and averages 75 meters deep. The northeast end bifurcates into northeast-trending Chignecto Bay and the east-trending Minas Basin. The bay has been incised into the friable red sediments and tholeiitic basalts of a Triassic half-graben.

Tides

Fundy has long been famous for its enormous tides; the highest tides in the world have been recorded off Burncoat Head in the Minas Basin, where the perigean spring tide may exceed 17 meters (Goldthwait, 1924).

The anomalous range is in part due to the concentration of energy in the entering tidal prism as its cross-sectional area is reduced towards the bay's head. More important is the wall-like standing wave generated by the entering tide. The dimensions of the bay are such that its natural period of oscillation is nearly that of the tide's semidiurnal component, hence the latter is greatly reinforced by resonance.

Because of the Coriolis effect, the entering tidal stream is deflected to the south shore of the bay, and the withdrawing stream to the north shore. Consequently the south shore experiences a greater tidal range, and there is a counterclockwise system of residual tidal currents.

Tidal streams attain 2 knots in the lower bay, and 4 knots in the narrower upper basins. A turbulent hydraulic current in the narrow strait between the Minas Channel and the Minas Basin reaches 11 knots (Cameron, 1961). Tidal currents are the dominant agent of sedimentation.

Sediments

The sediments of Fundy's floor and margin (Fig. 1) reflects the bay's Quaternary history. Till and outwash were deposited subaerially during the Pleistocene, and these materials are presently moving towards equilibrium with Holocene marine processes.

The most extensive facies is the discontinuous gravel veneer on the rocky bay floor (Burbank, 1929; Forgeron, 1962: Swift, in press). The composition and angularity of the fragments show that this is a lag deposit, winnowed from till.

A second facies consists of large, tide-maintained bodies of texturally mature sand, whose upper surfaces, where intertidal, are molded into complex assemblages of megarippled bars. Localization of these bodies is in part a matter of sand supply; rapidly retreating cliffs of Triassic sandstone or masses of outwash are in many cases close at hand. Localization is also effected by the pattern of tidal circulation. Sand bodies studied in the Minas Basin occur where basin currents are out of phase with the rectilinear regimes of nearby estuaries; the estuaries are still ebbing while the basin has begun to flood. Here interdigitating ebb and flood channels are separated by elongated sand bars.

A silt facies occurs between Grand Manan Island and the New Brunswick mainland. This area is partially protected from wave attack, is the site of a tidal eddy, and is close to several river mouths.

The most complex facies is a narrow band of marginal sediments. The following marginal subfacies have been noted by Klein (1963). The wave-cut rock terraces of the open coast are veneered with poorly sorted sediment of local origin. The heads of coves and sides of estuaries have developed thick tidal marshes and tidal flats of silt and clay. Tidal flats in the lee of bedrock islands resemble those of the Dutch Wadden Sea. Marginal sediments in several places are separated from Triassic bedrock by a till sheet, whose upper surface exhibits a podzolic soil profile, and a "drowned forest" of scattered tree stumps. Radiocarbon dating of these stumps by Harrison and Lyon (1963)

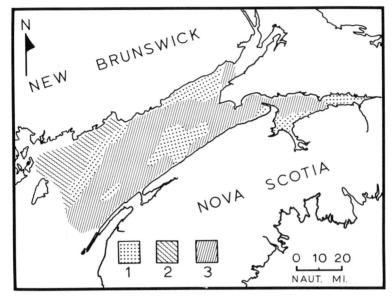

Fig. 1. Facies of the Bay of Fundy, modified from the reconnaissance studies of Forgeron (1962) and Swift (in press): (1) Sand, (2) Silt, (3) Gravel. Marginal facies not shown.

suggests that in addition to the eustatic rise, Nova Scotia has undergone tectonic sealevel fluctuations (mainly negative) during the Holocene.

D. J. P. SWIFT

References

Burbank, W. S., 1929, "Petrology of the sediment of the Gulf of Maine and Bay of Fundy," *U.S. Geol. Surv. Open File Rept*, **524**, 74pp.

Cameron, H. L., 1961, "Mapping tidal currents in the Bay of Fundy by high altitude photography," *Nova Scotia Research Foundation Memorandum*, 12pp.

Forgeron, F. D., 1962, "Bay of Fundy Bottom Sediments," Unpublished Master's Thesis, Carleton University, Ottawa, Canada, 117pp.

Goldthwait, J. W., 1924, "Physiography of Nova Scotia," *Geol. Surv. Can. Mem.*, **140**, 179pp.

Harrison, W., and Lyon, C. J., "Sealevel and crustal movements along the New England–Acadian shoreline, 4,500–3,000 B.P.," *J. Geol.*, **71**, 96–108.

Klein, G. deV., 1963, "Bay of Fundy intertidal zone sediments," *J. Sediment Petrol.*, **33**, 844–854.

Swift, D. J. P., in press, "Sedimentary reconnaissance of the Minas Basin, Nova Scotia," *Trans. Nova Scotia Acad. Sci.*

BEACHES, BEACH ROCK—*See* Vol. III

BEAUFORT SEA

Beaufort Sea is the name traditionally applied to the waters off the northern coast of Alaska and Canada, bounded on the east by Banks Island of the Canadian Arctic Archipelago and on the west by the Chukchi Sea. It is, however, an integral part of the Arctic Ocean and there is no physiographic or oceanographic justification for separate identity.

However, the term is firmly established in geographic nomenclature. The International Hydrographic Bureau (Sp. Pap. 23, 1953) takes its northern boundary as a line joining Pt. Barrow and Cape Lands End (Pr. Patrick I).

Bathymetry

The continental shelf along the Beaufort Sea coastline is the narrowest found anywhere on the periphery of the Arctic Ocean, seldom exceeding 150 km in width. Beyond the continental margin the ocean bottom drops rapidly to the −3940 m floor of the Beaufort Deep (see *Arctic Ocean*). Nearshore, the shelf is studded with gravel islands whose surface relief rarely exceeds a few meters and whose shapes are continually being modified by the action of strong offshore currents and ice pressure. The largest of these are Barter and Hirschal Islands which are 14 and 19 km² in area respectively. Much of the microrelief observed on the Beaufort Shelf and the Chukchi Cap could be explained by ice scouring, and consequently, Soviet investigators have suggested erosion by Quaternary glaciation.

Three submarine valleys are known to dissect the continental shelf; the largest, off Point Barrow, Alaska, is 45 km wide.

The Colville, MacKenzie and Anderson Rivers, in addition to numerous smaller streams, empty into the Beaufort Sea to deposit their sedimentary loads and influence the oceanographic environment. Aeromagnetic and geologic evidence suggests that the Beaufort Deep is underlain by an exceedingly thick sedimentary section with the

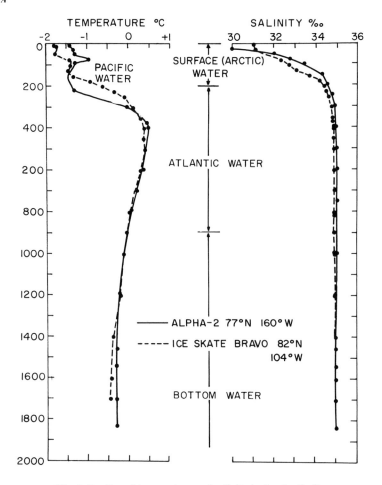

Fig. 1. Profiles of temperature and salinity in the Arctic Ocean.

crystalline basement sloping downward to the east, possibly being depressed by sedimentary loading.

Physical Oceanography

The circulation pattern in the Beaufort Sea is dominated by the clockwise Pacific Gyral which covers the entire Canada and Beaufort Deeps (see *Arctic Ocean*). Offshore, these currents flow at a rate of 2–4 km/day. Along the coast, however, currents depend largely on local winds, are highly variable, and may even reverse directions. The clockwise currents of the Pacific Gyral pile up pack ice along the Canadian and Alaskan coast, limiting dependable navigation to mid-August through September, and thus accounting to some degree for the paucity of observational data in this region.

The Beaufort Sea is comprised of four water masses. The surface layer of Arctic water is the only one which undergoes marked seasonable changes in temperature and salinity in response to the freeze and thaw of the pack ice. Beneath the surface water there is a remarkable regularity in temperature and salinity distribution throughout the year. The surface Arctic water is about 100 m thick and is the coldest of the water masses. Its temperature varies seasonally from −1.4°C at the end of summer to −1.7°C at the end of winter; its salinity ranges from 28–32‰.

Near the base of the surface layer is a warmer interlayer of Pacific water which enters through the Bering Strait. Underlying the near-surface waters is the Atlantic water mass which begins at a depth of about 200 m and has a thickness of about 700 m. The Atlantic water is the warmest of the water masses with temperature above 0°C and occasionally as high as +1°C. Its salinity is nearly uniform with depth, varying between 34.9–35.0‰. Maximum temperature lies between 300 and 500 m, below which there is a gradual decrease to 0°C at the contact with the bottom water mass. The bottom water mass begins at a depth of 900 m and exhibits extremely uniform salinities between 0 and 34.93‰. Temperature decreases slowly with depth to −0.40°C.

The Beaufort Sea was named after Admiral Sir

Francis Beaufort. It is largely covered by floating ice, though each summer the Alaskan and Canadian coasts become ice free and open for navigation. Its ice-covered areas have been traversed by D. Macmillan (1914) and S. Storkersen (1918) and examined by aerial reconnaissance by Amundsen and Nobile (1926) and by Wilkins (1927–28).

NED A. OSTENSO

References

Hand, C., and Kan, B. K., "Medusae of the Chukchi and Beaufort Seas," *Arctic. Inst. N. Am., Tech. Paper*, **6**.

Johnson, M. W., "The Plankton of the Beaufort and Chukchi sea areas of the Arctic and its relation to the Hydrography," *Arctic Inst. N. Am., Tech. Paper*, **1**.

Stefansson, V., 1925, "The Friendly Arctic," New York, The Macmillan Co.

BEAUFORT WIND SCALE—*See* WIND

BELLINGSHAUSEN SEA

Geography

The Bellingshausen Sea is an Antarctic body of water located between Thurston Island on the west and the Antarctic Peninsula on the east (approximately 70–100°W, and northward to the Antarctic Circle). It was named after the Russian admiral, Fabian Gottlieb von Bellingshausen, who discovered it in 1819. This large sea includes Ronne Bay, Marguerite Bay, as well as Peter I Island, Charcot Island, and Alexander I Island (see Fig. 1).

Exploration

In 1814 a Russian expedition was sent out under the command of Bellingshausen on the *Vostok* with M. P. Lazarev on the *Mirny*. The object was to circumnavigate the Antarctic Continent (1819–21). As he was completing his journey, Bellingshausen sighted the first land ever seen within the Antarctic Circle, the extensive Alexander I Land, later proved to be an island.

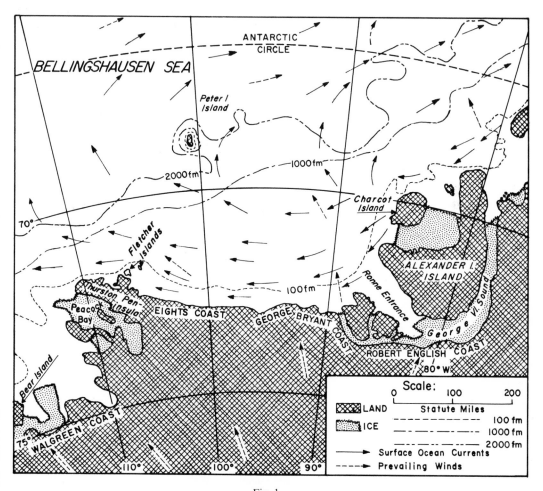

Fig. 1.

The Belgian explorer Adrian de Gerlache aboard the *Belgica* reached the position 71° 31′S, 85° 16′W in March, 1898 in the Bellingshausen Sea. When his ship froze in, the expedition became the first to winter in the Antarctic. The *Belgica* drifted from 71° 30′S, 85° 15′W to 70° 50′S, 102° 15′W between February 1898 and March 1899, a total of 1706 miles.

In more recent times the U.S. Navy ice-breakers *Glacier* and *Staten Island* have penetrated farther into the Bellingshausen Sea than any previous ships and explored the Eights Coast in February 1961. Aerial reconnaissance confirmed that previously charted Thurston "Peninsula" is really an island.

Oceanography

Very little information is available about the Bellingshausen Sea. The *Discovery* traversed the eastern part (80°W) as reported by Deacon (1937). Oceanographic studies recently made in the Bellingshausen Sea during "Operation Deep Freeze 61" (U.S. Navy Hydrographic Office, TR-105) have contributed further to our knowledge of this little-known Antarctic region.

Temperature and salinity profiles at the stations occupied in the Bellingshausen Sea showed two distinct water masses: an Antarctic upper water above 200 m and an Antarctic deep water which extends to the bottom. Separating these two water masses is a transition layer identified by steep positive salinity and density gradients.

The most rapid increase in salinity occurred in the upper 75 m in the area of transition from the thin layer of surface water to the subsurface layer which is characterized by minimum temperature

(colder than −1.5°C). Below this minimum layer, temperatures increased with depth to the bottom where maximum temperatures were observed.

Salinity on the other hand increased with depth; at a station located in the southern part of the Bellingshausen Sea, salinity increased from 33.76‰ at the surface to 34.69‰ at 525 m.

Dissolved oxygen content decreased with depth; from 9.0 m/liter at the surface to 4.5 ml/liter near the bottom at one of the deepest stations.

Very little information on water movements in the Bellingshausen Sea has been obtained by actual current observation. The *Pourquoi Pas?* experienced a southerly set near Adelaide Island and Alexander I Island, but a northward movement was observed in Matha Bay and Marguerite Bay. The *Pourquoi Pas?* in 1908–10 and the *William Scoresby* and *Discovery II* in 1930–31 each found more numerous icebergs south of the Palmer Archipelago than in the neighborhood of the South Shetland Islands. This concentration may be partly caused by the northeasterly current from the Bellingshausen Sea turning towards the coast and back to the southwest.

The sea between Adelaide Island and Charcot Island has generally been found closely packed with ice, and this may be an indication that the surface water is piled up toward the coast, as it would be on the left flank of a current toward the southwest. The density distribution in the surface water also points to this conclusion.

Submarine Geology

The sediments in the eastern Bellingshausen Sea are glacial marine in character. This is composed mainly of material which has been transported from

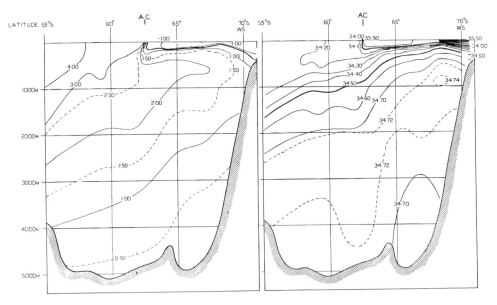

Fig. 2. The distribution of temperature, (left) and salinity, (right) along section from 55°20′S to 70°31′S in 80°W October 1932, March 1934, and February 1930 (Deacon, 1937).

land or shallow water by ice-rafting and has been dropped to the bottom when the ice melted.

Biological Productivity

Data collected in the Bellingshausen Sea by the author (February 1965) on the phytoplankton standing crop (in terms of plant pigment, chlorophyll *a* and the photosynthetic activity of the phytoplankton (in terms of C^{14} uptake) showed higher productivity values to the east of the Bellingshausen Sea (e.g., Marguerite Bay and north of Adelaide Island) than any other region. Average values of chlorophyll *a* and C^{14} uptake in the Bellingshausen Sea were: 1.33 mg/m^3 and 1.46 mgC/m^3/h, respectively. Compared to other Antarctic bodies of water, the density of phytoplankton in the Bellingshausen Sea is greater than in the Drake Passage, Weddell Sea and the Bransfield Strait.

SAYED Z. EL-SAYED

References

Butler, R. A., 1958, "The Bellingshausen Sea, Antarctica," Wash. D.C., U.S. Antarctic Project's Officer, 1957, 20pp.

Deacon, G. E. R., 1937, "Hydrology of the Southern Ocean," *Discovery Rept.*, **15**, 1–124.

Hart, T. J., 1934, "On the phytoplankton of the Southwest Atlantic and Bellingshausen Sea 1929–1931," *Discovery Rept.*, **8**, 1–268.

Neaverson, E., 1940, "General character of sea-floor deposits from the Bellingshausen Sea and the western coast of South America," *Proc. Pacific Sci. Congr. Pacific Sci. Assoc. 6th, 1939,* **2**, 779–781.

Valdez, A. J., and Nawratil, R., 1962, "Glaciological phenomenon in the Bellingshausen Sea during the 1959–60 Antarctic Campaign," *Amer. Geophys. Union Geophys. Mono.,* No. 7, 171 (National Research Council, Washington, D.C., No. 1036).

U.S. Hydrographic Office, 1960, "Sailing Directions—Antarctica, Second ed., Washington, D.C.

BENGAL, BAY OF—See BAY OF BENGAL

BENGUELA CURRENT

(1) General Description

The Benguela Current flows northward along the west coast of southern Africa between about 15 and 35°S. It is distinguished by an area of cool upwelling water within 100 miles of the coast, and apart from a small area near the Cape of Good Hope, the coastal strip is desert or semi-desert.

The currents of the South Atlantic Ocean form an anticyclonic gyral similar to those in the South Pacific and South Indian Oceans. This is a wind-driven system, modified by the effects of the earth's rotation. In the southern hemisphere a wind current is deflected to the left of the wind direction by an angle of about 45° at the surface. The two major wind systems operating are the southeast trades and the westerlies. The trade winds blowing toward the equator set up a current flowing from east to west just south of the equator which is known as the South Equatorial Current. On meeting the coast of South America, this is deflected to the left and flows southward as the Brazil current. In the latitude of the westerlies it is again deflected to the left and merges with the West Wind Drift. South of the African continent, part of the current turns northward to flow up the eastern side of the ocean, reinforced perhaps by some flow from the Indian Ocean.

It is with this east limb of the South Atlantic gyral that we are concerned here, but the Benguela Current forms only a small part, since this name is reserved for the cold water near the coast. The remainder of the north flowing current, associated with the warmer subtropical water to the west and north, may be termed the South East Trade Wind Drift. (For a general picture of these currents see Fig. 1 of *Agulhas Current*, this volume.)

The earliest extensive oceanographic measurements in this area were made by the German expedition "Meteor." From this data, Defant has studied the mechanism of the current. Sections on the currents of the South Atlantic and on upwelling may be found in his book (Defant, 1961). An account of the Benguela current has also been given by Sverdrup *et al.* A very detailed description, dealing with both the physical and biological aspects, has been given by Hart and Currie (1960) using data obtained by them on the "*William Scoresby*." A good deal of work in this area has also been carried out by the South African Division of Fisheries and some of their data has been used by M. Darbyshire (1963) in an account of the currents near the Cape of Good Hope.

(2) The Temperature Structure

The surface temperatures near the coast in the Benguela Current area are generally about 8° lower than the average for these latitudes, and the current is thus relatively a cold one. The surface temperature distributions for March and September are shown in Fig. 1 (see also Fig. 2 of *Agulhas Current* for January and July temperatures and comparison with other areas). The isotherms usually run parallel to the coast, and the coldest water is found inshore. The temperature gradient normal to the shore is greatest in summer when the highest temperatures are found offshore. Near the coast there is little seasonal variation except in the extreme south where it is colder in summer than winter.

The vertical temperature structure along three east-west lines of stations in latitudes 17, 27 and 34°S is shown in Fig. 2. This data is taken from the South African Division of Fisheries survey in January 1959. The vertical scale is logarithmic in order to show more detail in the surface layers. In all three sections, the isotherms slope upwards

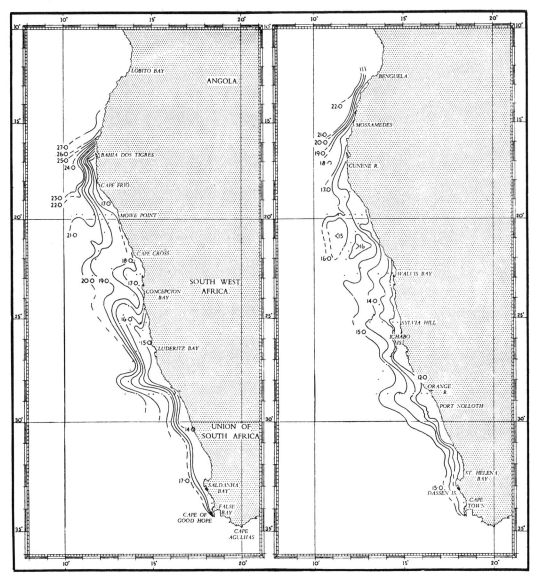

Fig. 1. The distribution of surface temperature for (a) March 1950 and (b) September–October 1950 (after Hart and Currie).

towards the shore in the upper water layers which may be evidence of upwelling of the subsurface waters. Below about 400 meters the isotherms become almost horizontal and the temperature decreases slowly downwards becoming about 3°C at 2000 meters.

(3) The Water Masses

If temperature is plotted against salinity for all measured depths, the points are found to lie very close to a smooth curve which has particular characteristics for a given area. This is known as the *T-S* curve. In Fig. 3, the full line is the *T-S* curve for an offshore station in latitude 34°S in January, 1959, the small figures giving the depth

at each point. If this is compared with the curves shown in Fig. 4 of *Agulhas Current* (page 00), they are seen to be very similar. The salinity minimum at about 4°C, 34.3‰, again represents the Antarctic Intermediate Water, but whereas this layer was found at about 1200 meters in the Agulhas Current, at this station it is at 800 meters, and further north it rises to 500 meters. This is water of Antarctic origin and it occurs at the surface in higher latitudes. Below this is the North Atlantic Deep Water, of lower temperature but higher salinity, which has flowed southwards at very deep levels from the North Atlantic Ocean. The measurements here do not go deep enough to show the salinity maximum usually associated with this water mass

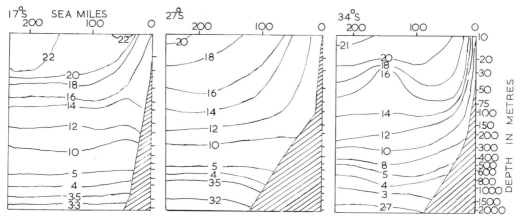

Fig. 2. The vertical temperature distribution along three east–west lines of stations, January 1959. Isotherms in degrees centigrade.

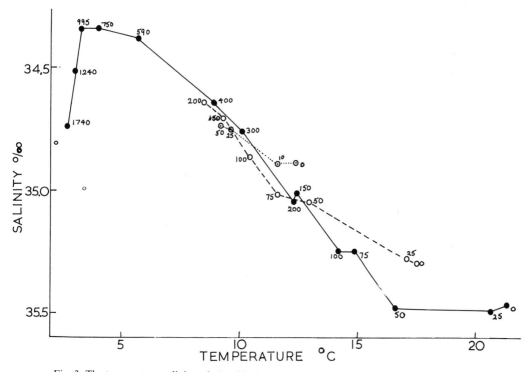

Fig. 3. The temperature-salinity relationship for three stations in latitude 34°S, January 1959.

and which can be seen in the Agulhas diagram. Above the Antarctic Intermediate Water is the South Atlantic Central Water represented by a straight line joining the points 6°C, 34.4‰ and 16°C, 35.5‰. This has the same characteristics as the Indian Ocean Central Water and has probably been formed by mixing of the subtropical surface water with the Antarctic Intermediate Water. This subtropical water of high salinity and temperatures above 16°C is found above 100 meters depth.

(4) The Prevailing Winds

The wind systems in this area are largely controlled by the subtropical high-pressure system over the South Atlantic Ocean. Very near the coast, however, the continental high-pressure system exerts some influence. In the oceanic area the Trade Winds blow from the southeast for 80% of the time in summer. In winter, the pressure belts move north so that the northern part of the area is still within the trade wind belt while the southern part, south of 30°S, is affected by the westerlies which bring depressions and winter rainfall to the Cape. In the inshore area there is a diurnal variation in wind due to the alternate heating and cooling of the land. Winds tend to blow onshore during the afternoon and evening and offshore in the night and morning. Over much of the coast, winds are mainly south or southeast in the morning, veering to the south or southwest later in the day, with the exception of the Cape in winter where the winds blow mainly from the western sector.

The land bordering the coast is very dry north of 30°S. This is due to the presence of cold water near the shore which cools the air above it and causes condensation of moisture from winds blowing off the warmer ocean. The coastal strip is thus in a rain shadow area similar to that in the lee of a mountain range. The offshore winds are very dry, having traveled over many miles of land, and so bring no rain to this area.

(5) The Density Distribution

Water density can be calculated from its temperature and salinity. The function used most often in oceanographic work is σ_t which is equal to 10^3 (density at surface pressure -1). The vertical σ_t sections for several lines of stations, again in January 1959, are drawn in Fig. 4. σ_t increases downward so that the most dense water is found at the sea bottom and the least dense subtropical water remains on the surface. The $27.2\ \sigma_t$ isopycnal in latitude 17 and 27°S gives the depth of the Antarctic Intermediate minimum at between 500 and 600 meters. At 34°S it is slightly deeper and does not appear in the diagram.

Water tends to move along σ_t surfaces so that the arrows in the diagram indicate possible water movement upward toward the coast. As well as

this, the σ_t surfaces sloping upward will give a downward gradient of sealevel consistent with a north flowing current parallel to the shore. In latitude 17°S there is some evidence of a downward movement and a southerly current between 100 and 300 meters.

(6) Upwelling

The phenomenon of upwelling is fairly well known and occurs on the west coast of the other continents in latitudes similar to that of the Benguela upwelling. The mechanism of the flow is less well understood, but it seems to be due to wind action in some way. The water coming from the subsurface layers reaches the surface without much mixing en route so that it retains recognizable characteristics. In Fig. 3, the broken line gives the *T-S* relationship for an inshore station in latitude 34°, the depths again being marked. The curves are almost coincident for depths 400–150 meters at the offshore station and 200–50 meters at the inshore station. This illustrates very well the upward movement of the Central Water without change of temperature and salinity. Above these depths, the agreement is not quite so good because the upwelled water on reaching the surface is warmed by heat from the sun and increases in temperature by one or two degrees. The *T-S* curve for a shallow station, closer inshore still, is shown by a small dotted line. Except for the surface reading, this is also almost coincident with the curve for the offshore station, and it shows an upwelling of about 300 meters with water of 12°C at the surface.

The prevailing southerly winds in the inshore area would cause a current of 45° to the left of this direction, i.e., northwest, and a water transport 90° to the left, toward the west and away from the

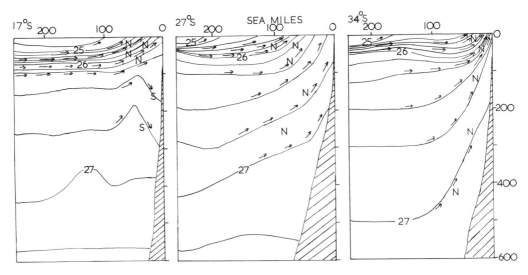

Fig 4. The vertical distribution of σ_t for three east–west lines of stations, January 1959.

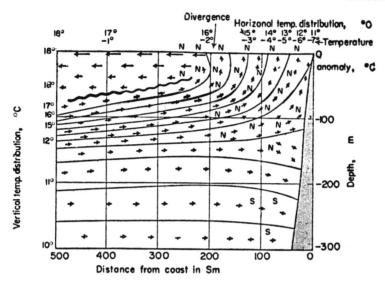

Fig. 5. A schematic cross section normal to the coast in the area of the Benguela Current (after Defant). (By permission of Pergamon Press.)

shore. If this water being carried away from the shore at the surface is replaced by upwelling, then a kind of convection cell is established. Defant illustrates this idea in a diagram (Defant, 1961, p. 647) reproduced here in Fig. 5. He also suggests a southerly current beneath the main stream but much weaker in magnitude.

The pattern of isotherms and σ_t surfaces sloping upward do not by themselves prove the existence of active upwelling. The same effect would be created by the presence of oceanic water close to the shore pressing the coastal water inward and upward. In the oceanic area to the west, the winds are southeasterly, causing a westerly current and a transport toward the southwest. There is, therefore, no tendency for oceanic water to move close inshore, and the theory of pure wind upwelling seems most plausible. The cold upwelled water at the surface is always separated from the surface water of similar temperature found in higher latitudes, and there is no question of a direct surface current flow from the south.

(7) Current Velocity

Since very few direct current measurements have been made in the Benguela Current, most information has been gained from the temperature and salinity readings. The dynamic height anomalies at the surface with respect to an assumed level of no-motion have been computed from these and plotted on a chart. The dynamic topology for January 1959 is shown in Fig. 6. The current is rather weak, not more than 25 cm/sec, and there are a number of irregularities and little eddies but the general set is clearly from north to south.

(8) The Southern Boundary of the Benguela Current

The area off the Cape of Good Hope forms a transition between the Agulhas and Benguela Current systems. In winter, the southern limits of both systems move northward with the trade wind belt, and temperatures near the Cape are fairly uniform over both inshore and offshore areas. In summer, the cold upwelling on the west coast extends right to the Cape and eastward to Cape Agulhas, while at the same time the tongue of warm Agulhas water spreads westward into the Atlantic. The current systems off the Cape are very complicated. There are strong anticyclonic eddies with velocities of 70 cm/sec or more which vary in intensity and position. There is very little evidence of a continuous flow from the Agulhas Current into the Benguela except very near the coast, but the extension westward of the warm Agulhas tongue in summer suggests that some of this water finds its way round the Cape and then perhaps flows northward. The eddy systems seem more closely connected with the West Wind Drift.

The Agulhas is much stronger than the Benguela Current and is composed of a main stream and a return flow. The tongue of warm water at the surface displaces the normal surface water, and the density surfaces slope sharply upward on both sides of it suggesting that upwelling might be taking place. Central Water very rarely occurs at the surface east of Cape Agulhas, but it is found within 100 meters of the surface near the shore and on the seaward side of the current. This is not wind upwelling as in the Benguela Current but merely the response of the water to a redistribution of density. The sharp density gradient on both

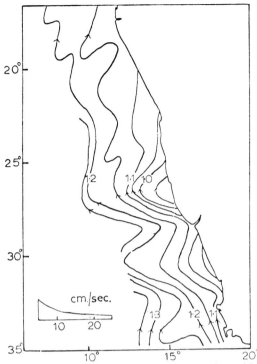

Fig. 6. The dynamic topology at the surface with respect to the 1000 decibar surface. Contours in dynamic meters.

sides of a wedge of low-density water is not favorable to the establishment of a convection cell.

(9) The Significance of the Benguela Current

This current, though rather limited in extent and weak in velocity, plays an important part in the oceanography of the South Atlantic Ocean by virtue of the upwelling associated with it. The highly nutrient Central Water obtains extra light at the surface so that it provides an excellent habitat for plankton and other marine life, giving rise to fertile fishing grounds. If for any reason the normal circulation is interrupted, as for example in time of calm conditions or of northerly winds in summer in the northerly part of the region, the supply of oxygen to the shallow water over the continental shelf may be temporarily decreased and bacterial action in the bottom sediment may flourish. Large quantities of hydrogen sulfide have been produced by these sulfate reducing bacteria in the bottom sediments and heavy sulfurous fumes have penetrated as far as 40 miles inland. This H_2S has occasionally led to mass mortalities (q.v.) of fish, notably in the Walvis Bay region. The large quantities of poisonous gas, together with the oxygen deficiency, cause the death not only of fish but also of other marine life. A similar mass mortality in this region associated with a phenomenon known as the "Red Tide" is quite different in origin. It is related to an overproduc-

tion of plankton and has occurred as far south as False Bay near Cape Town. The sulfurous eruptions have only occurred in the northern part of the Benguela area north of 25°S where the hydrogen sulfide producing sediments are found.

The Benguela Current is thus seen to be extremely interesting in many respects. The mechanism of the current and the chemical constituents of the water and the biological life are all well worth detailed study.

M. DARBYSHIRE

References

Darbyshire, M., 1963, "Computed currents off the Cape of Good Hope," *Deep-Sea Res.*, **10**, 623–632.
*Defant, A., 1961, "Physical Oceanography," Vol. 1, pp. 558–566 and 642–656, Oxford, Pergamon Press.
*Hart, J. J., and Currie, R. I., 1960, "The Benguela Current," *Discovery Reports*, **31**, 123–298.
*Sverdrup, Johnson, and Fleming, 1942, "The Oceans," p. 625.
Union of South Africa, Department of Commerce and Industries, Division of Fisheries, 1960, Annual Report.

BENTHONIC ZONATION

(1) General Remarks

The term benthos includes all animal (zoobenthos) and plant (phytobenthos) organisms which comprise the totality of organisms living on (epifauna) or in (endofauna) marine substrata; it also includes animals swimming in the close proximity of the bottom without ever really leaving it. The minimum size limit of 2 mm separates the macrobenthos from the microbenthos. These benthonic animals can be either fixed to the substratum or completely free.

Animal and vegetal benthonic organisms are grouped into various units. The composition of these units is conditioned by the needs of each species with regard to different environmental factors (temperature, salinity, nature of the substratum, hydrodynamic movements, etc.) and the relationship existing among the species which comprise the animal unit. The comparison of the lists of species, taken in a certain number of samplings, demonstrates which species are characteristic of a determined animal stocking. Such an animal stocking, which is endowed with a lasting qualitative stability and which corresponds to the indicated environmental conditions, is called a "biocoenose." A biocoenose presents a "facies" when a local predominance of certain ecological factors provokes the superabundance of one or a small number of species (whether or not these species are characteristic of the biocoenose) which do not, however, alter the qualitative composition of the biocoenose. The definition of "community" is derived from the study of the predominant species as to the number and weight of the specimens. "Biomass" is defined as the weight of living matter, either wet or dryed, per unit area of the surface of a substratum.

Vertical Zonation

Generally speaking, species that are found in depths of a few meters are not found in depths of of several thousand meters. Thus, it is necessary to establish a system of vertical zonation in order to classify the different animal stockings.

The vertical zonation of the existing species depends upon three fundamental factors: light, moisture and pressure.

Light, which conditions plant life (photosynthesis), has its origin from the sun. As one penetrates progressively into the depths, the absorption of solar radiation is characterized by a diminution of the amount of light as well as a modification of its spectral composition. The red and yellow of the spectrum are absorbed first, while the blue radiations in offshore waters and the green radiations in coastal waters penetrate the deepest. The marine substratums which receive a sufficient amount of light for plant life constitute the Phytal System, sometimes called the Littoral System. This zone extends to a maximum depth of 150 to 160 meters in the most transparent seas, which receive the brightest rays of the sun. The lowest limit of the zone where plant life most able to tolerate feeble lighting lives is the beginning of the Aphytal System (Deep System).

The amount of moisture becomes a factor in zonation only for animals living in the zone where the water level varies according to tidal action or varying meteorological conditions. The degree of moisture can vary from a light spray to complete immersion due to a rise in the water level.

The hydrodynamic pressure in the sea increases 1 kg/cm^2 with every 10 meters of depth. This pressure is certainly important to animal life, but its exact influence is not yet known.

Considering these three factors, it is possible to divide benthonic animals into seven zones:

$$\left.\begin{array}{l}\text{Supralittoral}\\\text{Mediolittoral}\\\text{Infralittoral}\\\text{Circalittoral}\end{array}\right\}\text{Phytal System}$$

$$\left.\begin{array}{l}\text{Bathyal}\\\text{Abyssal}\\\text{Hadal}\end{array}\right\}\text{Aphytal System}$$

Main Zones

(*a*) *Supralittoral*. The animals living in this zone either can tolerate or require continued or almost continued emersion. In seas where the tidal amplitude is great, the marine animals are immersed only during the high tides of the equinox. The supralittoral animals living on hard substratums are remarkably homogeneous on a world wide scale. There are practically always: unicellular *Cyanophyceae* and *Chlorophyceae*, a lichen, small gasteropods of the genus *Littorina*, and small crustacean isopods (*Ligiidae*).

On the beaches, the animal population is constituted of highly mobile amphipods, plus various crabs in tropical regions which are more or less well adapted to an aerial life.

(*b*) *Mediolittoral*. The mediolittoral zone is the level which is more or less regularly emerged and submerged. In seas having a large tidal amplitude, this zone is represented by the middle part of the intertidal zone. Mediolittoral species are adapted to resist prolonged emersion and generally are incapable of living if continually immerged.

On mobile substratums (sand or mud), the mediolittoral biocoenoses are difficult to delimit since they are not often very scattered out. When the level of the sea drops, the animals burrow into the mud which holds a certain quantity of water by imbibition. In this manner, the animals are protected from the harmful influences of emersion. On the beaches, the mediolittoral fauna consists of several annelid polychaetes (*Ophelia* and *Nerine*), and crustacean isopods and amphipods. In addition, on tropical coasts, there are several crabs of the genus *Uca* and the "false crabs" of the family *Hippidae*.

In the upper level of the mediolittoral zone on rocky coasts, one generally finds a biocoenose constituted primarily by thoracic cirripeds which are very tolerant to the effects of emersion (*Chthamalus*). In the lower level is found a rich stocking of calcareous algae (except in the higher latitudes), often mixed with other Cirripeds (*Balanus* and *Tetraclita*) and mussels (see *Trottoir*). There is a rich accompanying fauna of gasteropods with a cone-shaped shell from the group *Patellidae*. On tropical coasts, mussels are often replaced by oysters. In seas having a large tidal amplitude, especially in the middle latitudes, groups of brown algae which grow parallel to the shoreline (for this reason they are called belts) can superpose and eventually more or less supersede the preceeding animal stocking.

(*c*) *Infralittoral*. The infralittoral zone is defined as the vertical space of the benthonic domain which is compatible to life of marine phanerogams or photophilous algae which have the same needs for light as the phanerogams. The upper fringe of this zone is occasionally emerged, but prolonged emersion kills the infralittoral plants and animals.

On rocky substratums, in the infralittoral zone, one can distinguish two types of animal stockings.

One is comprised basically of photophilous algae, especially of brown algae, in the higher latitudes, while red algae are dominant in the middle latitudes, and green algae in the intertropical regions.

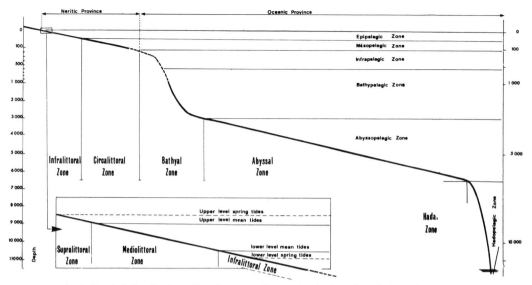

Fig. 1. Vertical distribution of benthos according to the depth and equivalents for pelagos.

The associated fauna is variable, but the biomass is generally lower than that of the plant fraction. In certain facies, various invertebrates (gasteropods *Vermetidae* and polychaetes of the family *Serpulidae*) can be of great quantitative importance (see *Trottoir*).

The other type of animal stocking is represented by coral reefs in tropical seas. In appearance, the animals seem much more numerous than the plants, but in reality this is not true. The presence of symbiotic algae with coral constructors and various other invertebrates causes the plant biomass to be about three times more important than that of the animal biomass. The accompanying fauna is one of the richest and most varied in the world.

An example of an infralittoral biocoenose of great interest from a practical point of view is the stocking of animals with several seaweeds which covers the hulls of ships and piers in ports where the water is polluted (fouling).

On mobile substrata in the infralittoral zone, one can distinguish two types of animal stockings, the existence of which is conditioned by the presence or absence of multicellular plants (metaphytes). When there is no metaphytic vegetation, the animal stocking is often constituted of species living in the sediment, of which bivalve mollusks and annelid polychaetes are generally predominant. The predators of these groups are represented by echinoderms (which are generally absent in the most superficial levels) or by prosobanch gasteropods (especially numerous in tropical seas).

The mobile, infralittoral substrata with a metaphytic vegetation are very varied. In warm seas, the vegetative covering of the substratum is often assured by green algae which are commonly of the genus *Caulerpa*, and sometimes by species of the genus *Halimeda* having their thalluses impregnated with limestone. In temperate or temperate-to-cold seas, the substrata covered by coarse sand or scattered blocks are often occupied by fields of brown algae belonging to the laminarian group, which exist also on hard substrata. But the main characteristic of the mobile infralittoral substrata is their capacity to accommodate stockings of marine phanerogams, which are taken as the reference base of this zone. These plants with flowers, belonging to the group of the monocotyledons, require a true soil from which they extract certain mineral nutrients (in exactly the same way as terestrial plants), while benthonic algae use the substratum simply as anchorage, extracting the mineral foods from seawater. These marine phanerogams, which often form real submarine meadows, are especially numerous and varied in tropical seas. They also cover large areas of the infralittoral bottoms in temperate seas (*Zostera* in the northern Atlantic, *Posidonia* and *Cymodocea* in the Mediterranean). When these phanerogams are very dense, they can greatly reduce the endofauna of the animal stocking. The fauna which attaches itself on the leaves of the phanerogams, or on the parts of the rhizomes which stick out of the sediment, contributes to the richness of the global animal stocking. These phanerogams also create a shelter for numerous mobile species in the forest of their leaves.

(*d*) *Circalittoral.* The lower limit of the .circalittoral zone, which is the last zone of the Phytal System, corresponds to the maximum depth compatible with the life of the algae which can still live in the most feeble rays of light.

On rocky substrata, one finds a stocking where

the animal biomass is generally greater than the plant biomass and where there is a dominance of fixed forms: sponges, alcyonarians, gorgonians, madreporarians (non-constructors of reefs), and notably bryozoans, which form erect or ramified calcified colonies. The algae are represented chiefly by red algae which have their thalluses impregnated with limestone.

The stockings on soft substrata depend largely on the nature of the sediment. On coarse sediments (gravel and coarse sands mixed with broken shells), large stocks of calcareous algae belonging to the group *Lithothamniae* sometimes develop freely on the bottom. Certain other algae equally calcified (*Melobesiae* or *Squamariacea*) are capable of transforming a mobile bottom to a hard substratum by solidifying different elements. This transition is reversible if the ambient conditions become more favorable to the algae and animals which destroy limestone.

In general, the substrata of the circalittoral zone are composed primarily of mud and muddy sand. On these bottoms, algae are few or completely absent, since the substratum is not suitable to their fixation. The varied invertebrate fauna serves, according to the nature of the substratum, as an alimentary support to more or less rich animal stocks of fish. The circalittoral zone which occupies the lower part of the continental shelf is the essential center of action for trawl fishing.

(e) *Bathyal.* The bathyal zone, which is devoid of autotrophic vegetation, as is the rest of the Aphytal System, corresponds approximately to the animal stockings which are located either on the continental slope or at the immediate foot of the slope at a depth of from 2500–3000 meters. The lower limit of this zone is marked by a radical renewal of the benthonic fauna—chiefly for mollusks and echinoderms. This boundary is also marked by the lower limit of extension of certain animal species of the Phytal System which are capable of descending from the continental shelf. These littoral species which are apt to extend into greater depths (eurybathic species) only exceptionally pass the bathyal zone. On rocky substratums which become rarer as one goes progressively deeper, the most remarkable biocoenose is that of the "deep corals," constituted of large masses of madreporarians (especially of the genus *Lophelia* and *Madrepora*), which are devoid of symbiotic algae since there is a lack of light. These deep corals constitute oases of marine life accompanied by a rich and varied fauna in depths which are generally poorly populated.

The soft substrata are represented by muddy bottoms having rather uniform animal stockings in the ensemble of the zone, but the facies are remarkable. The most common ones in the Atlantic are the facies of large alcyonarians which stick out of the sediment (*Funiculina*, for example),

the facies of gorgonians (*Isidella* accompanied by the large shrimps *Aristeidae* which are of commercial interest), and the facies of the Hexactinellides sponges which seem to exist principally in regions of decantation of debris (especially plant fragments) coming from the continental shelf.

(f) *Abyssal.* The abyssal zone extends from the foot of the continental shelf to the breaking off of the slope which precedes the deep trenches: i.e., at a depth of from 3000 meters to 6500–7000 meters. This zone is populated almost exclusively by characteristic biocoenosis of muddy bottoms. The rare solid substrata (recent volcanic rocks, nodules of ferrous and manganese oxides) generally present a very sparse fauna. The animal stockings of abyssal muds are varied, but, in general, the biomass is low average: 1 g/m^2 (wet weight); practically all the groups of invertebrates present in the fauna of the continental shelf are also present in the abyssal zone, but the percentage of archaic forms (like living fossils) is higher in relation to the ensemble of the fauna in the bathyal and abyssal zones. Fish are still present in the abyssal depths, but the number of animal species undergoes a marked diminution.

(g) *Hadal.* The hadal zone corresponds to the great trenches and in depths ranging from 6500–7000 meters to more than 11,000 meters in the Pacific Ocean.

The substrata are composed primarily of ooze and mud, and the biomass, which is very small, drops to several milligrams (wet weight) per square meter. The animal stocking is characterized by the total absence of a certain number of phyla, classes or orders, and notably those which are predators for food—crustacean decapods, asteroids, and fish—certain groups, particulariy holothurian elasipods, echiurids, isopods and polychaetes, predominate. In addition, the sediments of the hadal zone contain bacteria adapted to life under great pressure (barophilous) which are very abundant (several million germs by gram of wet sediment). These microorganisms are an essential element of the food for detritus-feeders.

(2) The Marine Benthos of Different Zones in the General Economy of the Oceans

It is interesting to try to find out if man correctly exploits the animal stockings (mainly fish) for his food and if there are ways to ameliorate the yield of benthic species. The biomass of the animal stockings diminishes as the depth increases. In the infralittoral zone, certain stockings of animals on rocky bottoms attain a wet weight of several kilograms per square meter (sometimes attaining 80 kg), while the animal stockings of mobile substrata represent a weight of a few hundred grams (rarely more than 1 kg/m^2). In the circalittoral zone, the biomass may be several hundred grams per square meter.

As one goes deeper, the biomass diminishes. This diminution is slower when the great depths are in the immediate proximity of emerged land. However, the biomass considered alone is not sufficient to express the richness of the bottom of the sea. If one considers two communities, A and B, having the same biomass of 100 g/m², if A is constituted by species that live an average of five years while B is constituted by species living only one year, it is clear that community A needs five years to produce 100 grams of living matter, while community B needs only one year to produce the same amount. Thus, the production of B is five times greater than that of A.

The comparison of respective production offers a better appreciation of the real richness, but it seems that the best indications of richness are furnished by the relation Production/Biomass or P/B. This relation, P/B, is much less favorable in the benthonic domain than in the pelagic one; it is also greater in tropical seas than in the cold waters of the high latitudes or in the bathyal zone.

In order to rationally exploit the benthonic species, it is necessary to study the production in order to avoid the "overfishing" which now characterizes the continental shelf of the North Sea and the North Atlantic in general. "Overfishing," a result of the improved techniques, threatens the upper part of the bathyal zone (200–600 meters), where trawlers have tried to transfer their activity when the continental shelf showed signs of becoming impoverished. The bottoms of the bathyal zone, which have a rather small biomass, have, in addition, an even smaller production due to the greater average longevity of the species populating these bottoms.

When the waters which cover the sea bottom have a rich plankton population and when the depth is not too great, the descent of cadavers or debris from plankton can noticeably enrich the bottom population by supplying a form of food. The artificial enrichment of sea bottoms is easy to conceive but more difficult to bring about if it is to be advantageous. The idea of raising or cultivating marine benthonic species is not excluded, but it would be difficult to do in the near future. The experiment of placing in the middle of a biocoenose either individuals of a species of which the natural population is exhausted by "overfishing" or species that are foreign to the biocoenose has been tried. These species which have a rapid growth or a good yield in transforming food are utilizable directly as food for man or as food for commercial species. In the present state of our knowledge, this method seems the most likely to better, within reasonable economic conditions, the profit that humanity can acquire for its subsistence from the resources of the marine benthos.

J. M. PÉRÈS

References

*Hedgpeth, J. W., *et al.*, 1957, "Treatise on marine ecology and paleoecology," *Geol. Soc. Am. Mem.*, **67**, 1296.

*Moore, H. B., 1958, "Marine Ecology," 493pp., New York, John Wiley & Sons.

*Peres, J. M., 1961, "Oceanographie Biologique et Biologie Marine," T.I., "La Vie Benthique," 541pp., Paris, Presses Universitaires, France.

BENTHOS, MARINE

The benthos is that assemblage of organisms that live on or in the bottom of oceans, lakes, and streams. In habitat and mode of life the benthos is distinguished from the plankton, which comprise floating organisms, and the nekton, the active swimmers. Most benthic animals have planktonic larvae, and some members of the nekton are closely associated with the benthic environment. The term, demersal, has also been used to denote organisms found on or near the bottom.

The marine benthos is an important ecological group because it occurs over most of the earth's surface and is of consequence in the economy of the sea. Benthic animals modify the physical and chemical properties of sediments. In addition, most of the fossil record consists of the remains of benthic organisms. The benthos of fresh waters is similarly important to aquatic ecosystems (Reid, 1961).

It is convenient to divide benthic animals into epifauna and infauna. The epifauna consists of all those animals that live upon the sea floor or upon plants, rocks, and other objects extending above the bottom. The infauna consists of those animals that live within the sediment of the sea bottom. While most benthic species are associated with either the epifauna or infauna, a few occur in both habitats.

(1) Composition. All marine phyla are well represented in the benthos except the Ctenophora and Chaetognatha. Characteristic groups represented in the macrobenthos, organisms larger than 1 mm, are the polychaetes, pelecypods, anthozoans, echinoderms, sponges, ascidians and crustacea. Most faunal surveys of the sea floor have dealt only with the macrobenthos. The meiobenthos, consisting of organisms about 0.1–1 mm in size, commonly includes small polychaetes and pelecypods, harpacticoid copepods, ostracodes, cumaceans, nematodes, turbellarians, and foraminifera. The interstitial fauna of sands in shallow water constitutes a unique meiobenthos (Swedmark, 1964). Organisms smaller than 0.1 mm comprise the microbenthos. This group includes bacteria, benthic diatoms, ciliates, amoebas, and flagellates. Although bacteria contribute very little to the total weight or biomass of a benthic community, they are of great importance in the food web of the sea. Benthic bacteria release plant nutrients back into the system and convert detritus and dissolved organic matter into a particulate form that can be utilized by larger organisms.

The variety and abundance of species of the benthos vary with latitude and depth as well as with local environmental conditions. The number of macrobenthic species may exceed a hundred per square meter in shallow water. The number of individuals range from a few to thousands per square meter. The microbenthos has been scarcely studied, but 10^5–10^9 individuals per square meter have been reported. The biomass of the benthos may range from several kilograms to tenths of a gram per square meter. Diversity and abundance decrease with depth, the lower values being obtained in the deep sea. This depth-abundance relationship is a feature on the scale of the ocean basins and is less evident within major habitats. Under stringent environmental conditions, such as are encountered in parts of polar seas and estuaries, the fauna may consist of a few species represented by huge populations.

(2) Environment. The benthic environments are commonly classified into divisions that approximate physiographic provinces: supralittoral, littoral, sublittora bathyal, abyssal, and hadal (see *Ecology, Marine*). The depths associated with each of these major habitats vary with latitude, geological structure, and various environmental factors. The fauna of the sea floor at depths exceeding 2000 meters is commonly referred to as the deep-sea or abyssal benthos. The chemical and physical properties of the benthic environment are gradational so that sharp boundaries cannot be drawn around major habitats.

The most important physical features of the benthic environment appear to be the nature of the sediment, the temperature, and the salinity. These factors vary rapidly in time and space in shallow water. In the deep sea the constancy of the environment over wide areas is associated with faunal homogeneity. In very shallow waters, exposure to drying, light, and water movement are quite important factors. Predation, parasitism, commensalism, and competition for food and space are among the biotic environmental features influencing the distribution and abundance of species. Most of the macrobenthos is exposed to predation by fishes and other nektonic animals. Biotic factors are probably of less importance in shallow water benthic communities than physical ones. The infaunal environment is subject to less rapid fluctuation in its physical and chemical properties than the epifaunal environment.

(3) Food Cycles. The primary sources of food for the benthos are the plankton, terrigeneous organic detritus, and, in shallow water, the larger algae and flowering plants. Where light penetrates to the bottom, benthic diatoms can contribute significant amounts of food. In most areas, the plankton is the chief source, and high benthic productivity is usually associated with high planktonic productivity in overlying or upcurrent water masses. Terrestrially derived detritus can be transported great distances from shore as float or introduced into the deep sea by turbidity currents. Bacteria may also be important food sources for the deep-sea benthos.

Detritus feeders are the most characteristic feeding type of the benthos. Suspension feeders, such as sponges, many pelecypods, crinoids, and brachiopods, obtain detritus from overlying waters. Deposit feeders ingest the sediment to derive nourishment from its digestible organic detritus. The polychaetes are the most important of the deposit feeders. Their activity tends to destroy sedimentary structures and modify the textural and chemical properties of the sediment. Deposit feeders are common in muds and muddy sands. Suspension feeders dominate the epifauna of hard substrates and the infauna of coarse sands and gravels. Suspension feeders on or in fine sediments often possess special adaptations to avoid clogging the filtering apparatus. These forms may be killed or their growth may be retarded by increased sedimentation.

Fishes, starfish, ophiuroids, nereid polychaetes, some snails, cephalopods, and the larger crustacea are among the important predators and scavengers. Herbivorous animals are found in shallow water where the larger plants and encrusting algae occur. Many species are capable of changing their method of feeding as circumstances permit. Thus some pelecypods that are normally suspension feeders may feed directly on surface deposits at times. Active polychaetes may function both as deposit feeders and carnivores.

(4) Reproduction. The mode of reproduction of the benthos is one of its most singular features. Most benthic species possess pelagic larvae. Larvae may spend from a few hours to several months in the overlying water mass. A benthic species represents two kinds of animals inhabiting grossly different kinds of environments and possessing separate sets of adaptations. The continuity of any species in an area is dependent on the survival of larvae so that offsite conditions of current, temperature, or predation may affect the permanency of a benthic population. Direct development within the benthos is more common in deep and polar seas than elsewhere.

The larvae of many benthic species are capable of actively selecting a suitable environment. Metamorphosis may be delayed until a suitable place is encountered. The nature of the substrate appears to be the key factor in inducing larval settlement in many species and particularly among detritus feeders. Settlement may be associated with particle size, particle shape, organic content, surface roughness, or some chemical property of the substrate.

In some instances, as among oysters and barnacles, the larvae are attracted to sites occupied by adults.

(5) Benthic Communities. The recurrence of particular suites of species has led to the recognition of benthic communities. The association of a particular community with a particular type of substrate is so common that benthic communities are designated by characteristic species and substrate. The substrate-community association is related to the fact that most benthic species are detritus feeders. The nature of the substrate reflects other important environmental factors such as water movement and distance from shore. Faunal differences indicate that the more important subdivisions of the substrate are muds, muddy sands, coarse sand and gravel, and rock surfaces. The coral reef is a special community type which is ecologically related to communities developed upon rocky bottoms and shores (see *Coral Reefs*).

Benthic communities occur everywhere in the sea except in a few special circumstances such as in those parts of the Black Sea where the hydrogen sulfide concentration in the water is extremely high. The abundance and diversity of epifaunas decrease markedly in higher latitudes while the infauna remains nearly constant. In addition, the infaunas of similar sediments at comparable depths are also similar in taxonomic composition throughout the world. These distributional features are believed to reflect the fact that, except for temperature, the infaunal environment is less variable than that of the epifauna. The greatest contrast in abundance and diversity is between shallow and deep-sea benthos.

A characteristic of shallow water benthic communities is the marked dominance of one or a few species. One to a dozen species may account for 95% of the individuals and biomass of the community. The composition of many benthic communities changes over relatively short periods of time. Seasonal fluctuations appear to be more pronounced in shallow waters. Almost all of the fluctuations in animal numbers that have been studied were associated with changes in the physical rather than the biological environment. In shallow water, abnormal weather often destroys large numbers of benthic organisms. The reproductive capacities of marine invertebrates are so enormous that areas may be rapidly repopulated by a very small number of survivors.

(6) Geological Significance. The benthos modifies sediments in several important ways. The movement of infaunal organisms destroys fine scale sedimentary structures such as bedding. Detritus feeders may change the texture of the sediment by the production of fecal pellets, and in many places in shallow water pellets are a major constituent of the sediment. The chemical composition of ingested sediment may also be altered in passage. The benthos contributes significant amounts of durable remains to the sediment. Shelly sands and gravels composed almost entirely of benthic remains are common today and are widely represented as bioclastic carbonate rocks in the fossil record. Almost all marine sediments are changed to some degree by benthic organisms.

Most of the fossil record in the crust of continents consists of the remains of benthic animals. Although we possess direct evidence of only those animals that had durable hard parts, Paleozoic benthic communities resemble modern ones in several important ways. The recurrence of particular species and lithologies resemble substrate relations observable today. The modes of life represented indicate structural similarities to modern benthic communities developed in like substrates. Detritus feeders were as dominant then as now. Most Paleozoic fossil assemblages largely consist of the remains of epifaunal organisms, but this feature may be due to factors of preservation. By late Mesozoic times the benthos had attained its present taxonomic character.

The ecological similarities between ancient and modern benthic communities provide a means of reconstructing past environments and studying evolution in the context of communities of organisms. More elements of benthic communities are preserved than in all other animal communities. A high proportion of the members of benthic communities possess durable skeletons, and the benthos inhabits a major environment of deposition. The nature of the substrate, a key environmental factor, is preserved. In order to utilize the record of benthic communities, the paleontologist must be able to differentiate between the remains of animals that lived at the site of deposition and those swept in by currents from elsewhere. The state of preservation, the ecological aspect of the fossil assemblage, and the physical properties of the sediment are valuable criteria in reconstructing the mode of formation of a fossil assemblage.

R. G. JOHNSON

References

*Hedgpeth, J. W. (editor), 1957, "Treatise on marine ecology and paleoecology," in "Ecology," Vol. 1, *Geol. Soc. Am.*, Mem. 67, **1**, 296 pp.

*Raymont, J. E. G., 1963, "Plankton and Productivity in the Oceans," New York, Macmillan Co., 620pp.

*Reid, G. K., 1961, "Ecology of Inland Waters and Estuaries," New York, Reinhold Publishing Corp., 375pp.

*Swedmark, B., 1964, "The Interstitial Fauna of Marine Sand," *Biol. Rev. Cambridge Phil. Soc.*, **39** (1), 1–42.

*Zenkevitch, L., 1963, "Biology of the Seas of the U.S.S.R.," New York, Interscience Publishers, 955pp.

BERING SEA

The Bering Sea, which lies between latitudes 51°N and 66°N, and longitudes 157°W and 163°E, is usually considered an extension of the North Pacific Ocean. Having an area of 2.3×10^6 km², a volume of 3.7×10^6 km³ and an average depth of 1636 meters, it is the second largest of the relatively confined seas; the Mediterranean Sea being the largest. Its configuration at sea level approximates that of a sector with a radius of 1500 km bounded on the west and east by the land masses of Siberia and Alaska, respectively, and on the south by the Alaska peninsula and Aleutian island arc. Bering Strait is situated near the vertex (Fig. 1). The Sea and Strait are named after Vitus Bering who commanded an extensive Russian expedition during the years 1725 to 1743 which explored the coasts of Kamchatka Peninsula and Alaska.

Bathymetry

The bathymetry is unusual because the neritic (0 to 200 meters) and abyssal (below 1000 meters) zones are about equal in size and constitute almost 90% of the total area. The vast continental shelf extending over 400 miles offshore in the northeastern part of the sea is one of the largest in the world. Continuing northward through the narrow, shallow Bering Strait into the Chukchi Sea, the shelf restricts exchange of all but near-surface water between the Arctic basin and Bering Sea and is sometimes referred to as the Bering-Chukchi platform.

Although the platform is submerged at the present time, geological and paleontological evidence indicates that Siberia and Alaska represent segments of a single continental mass separated by a land connection which has been interrupted by temporary submergence several times during the last 50 or 60 million years. The last submergence is believed to have occurred near the end of the Pliocene or beginning of the Pleistocene epoch, about a million years ago. The continental shelf along the Aleutian island arc and Siberian shore is very narrow. Around the entire Sea, at the edge of the shelf, an abrupt submarine escarpment descends to the floor of the basin. Slopes of 4–5° occur except in the southeastern corner where *Bering Canyon*, perhaps the largest in the world, has a slope of $\frac{1}{2}°$. Two submarine ridges penetrate the basin: *Olyutorski Ridge*, which extends southward from Kamchatka along longitude 170°E almost to the Aleutian island arc and separates the western from the central Aleutian basin, and *North Rat Island Ridge*, which extends northward from the island arc in a counterclockwise direction. The *Alaska peninsula* and *Aleutian island arc*, which restrict the exchange of water between the Bering

Sea and North Pacific Ocean, are of late Cenozoic volcanic origin. The island arc, northernmost of a series of arcs in the Pacific, consists of six island groups: Komandorski, Near, Rat, Andreanof, Four Mountains and Fox which rise from depths of approximately 7600 meters in the Aleutian trench and 4000 meters in the Bering Sea basin.

The deepest passage, 4420 meters, occurs at the extreme western end between Kamchatka and the westernmost Komandorski Island. This is also the deepest verified sounding in the Bering Sea. North of this strait a sill at 3589 meters provides the true closure of the basin. Within the deep basin is a vast plain lying at a depth of 3800–3900 meters; a few gently sloping hollows have depths to 4151 meters. Occasional plotted soundings at greater depths are suspect and require verification.

Except for a very narrow passage at longitude 180°, the sill depth eastward of longitude 171°E is considerably less than 1000 meters, and the total cross section permitting exchange of water through the southern boundary is only 731 km².

Sediments

Bottom sediments follow a general bathymetric pattern. The continental shelf is covered with sand, near the continental slope the sand changes to silt sizes ("aleurites" of the Russian workers), and the deep basins are covered with clayey diatomaceous oozes. Sediment cores over 30 meters in length obtained from the basins show well preserved shells of contemporary foraminifera and numerous individual lenses of fine and coarse silt and ash material imbedded between layers of ooze. Foraminifera analyses have permitted identification of four horizons which indicate that volcanic activity increased sharply during periods of glaciation, and at the present time the bottom of the Bering Sea has reached its greatest depth since the second half of the Quaternary period.

Climate

The climate of the Bering Sea is not well known because there are no established weatherships or steamship routes that provide periodic observations; practically all climatological data comes from shore stations. Mean air temperatures during winter range from −25°C in Bering Strait to 2°C near the Aleutian Islands, and during summer, the mean temperatures are 6 to 10°C. Precipitation occurs about 35% of the time and snow is common from September to June. Mean sea level pressure varies from 1000 millibars in winter when the Aleutian low is predominant and centered in the southern central part of the sea, to 1011 millibars during summer when the influence of the eastern Pacific high is felt. Although short periods of good weather occur, the sky is usually overcast and fog is frequent.

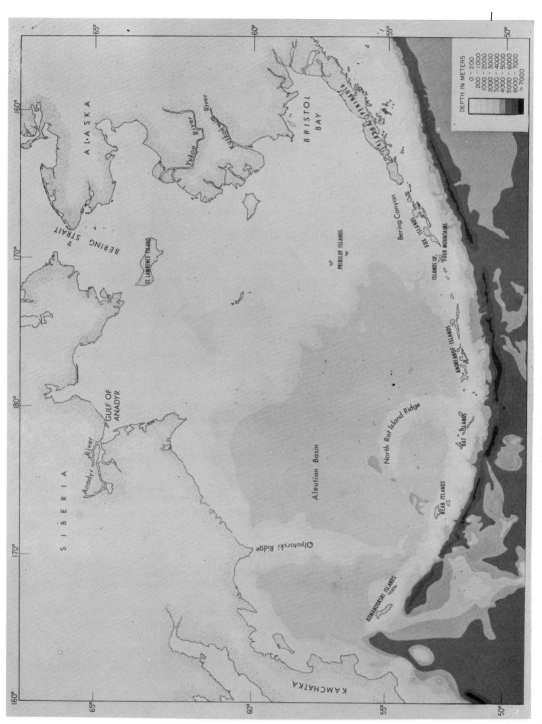

Fig. 1. Bathymetric map of Bering Sea.

Along the continental coastlines from Kamchatka to Bristol Bay, ice begins to form on the rivers in October and by the beginning of November, fast ice is present in most bays and harbors, and sea ice occurs south of Bering Strait. By January, the sea ice has reached its maximum coverage and extends as far offshore as the 200-meter depth contour. There are two exceptions: off the Kamchatka coast where very cold air moving off the continent permits formation of sea ice

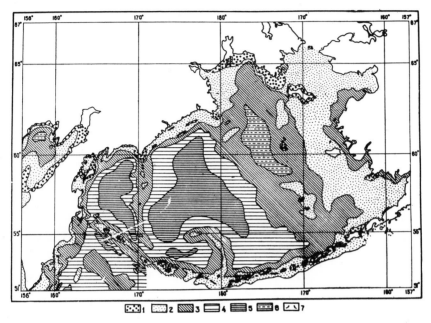

Fig. 2. Sediments of Bering Sea (Lisitzin). 1 Boulders-shingle-gravel; 2 Sands.

well seaward of the 200-meter contour, and along the Aleutian Islands and the western end of the Alaska Peninsula where relatively warm water flowing westward south of the islands inhibits the formation of sea ice anywhere in this area. The sea ice usually covers 80 to 90% of the sea surface indicated, but at no time, even in Bering Strait, is the Bering Sea one solid sheet of ice. Ice flows are usually up to 2 meters thick, and rafting and hummocking, particularly inshore, can result in thicknesses of 5 to 10 meters, but no icebergs are present. The position of the ice field is relatively constant until April, at which time a rapid disintegration and an apparent, northward movement occurs. Ice in the inshore areas, melted by spring runoff, disappears first, and usually by the end of July there is no ice in Bering Sea.

Tides and Currents

Tides along the Siberian coast in the southwestern part of the Sea are diurnal and become mixed at about latitude 60°N; northward of latitude 62°N only semidiurnal tides occur. Along the Alaskan coast from Bering Strait to the Alaska Peninsula mixed tides occur, and diurnal tides are found along the central and western Aleutian Islands. Mean semimonthly tidal ranges are small, 0.5 to 1.5 meters, except in the Gulf of Anadyr and Bristol Bay where they are 2.5 and 5.0 meters, respectively. Tidal currents in some of the Aleutian Island passes have velocities of 150 to 400 cm/sec. Early investigations indicated the Alaskan Stream, which flows westward south of the Aleutian Islands

had an appreciable northward component through all island passes, but recent work indicates that the flow in the passes is chiefly tidal with equally strong ebb and flood components. Flow into the Bering Sea which is of basic significance to the water balance occurs at longitude 170°E where the Stream converges with water moving northward in the Western Subarctic Gyre resulting in the formation of a cyclonic eddy over the western Aleutian basin and an anticyclonic eddy in the vicinity of the North Rat Island Ridge (Fig. 3). The main flow continues northward around the Ridge and turns eastward establishing the general cyclonic circulation over the deep basin. In the eastern part of the Sea, cyclonic and anticyclonic eddies are created as the current turns northward adjacent to the continental shelf; and, in the northern part, the current diverges sending one branch northward toward Bering Strait, and the other southwestward along the shores of Kamchatka where it eventually becomes the East Kamchatka Current and discharges back into the North Pacific Ocean. Currents over the continental shelf off the Alaskan coast are chiefly tidal, except adjacent to the coastline where runoff from the Alaskan coast flows northward and is discharged through Bering Strait. Speeds up to 300 cm/sec have been observed near the eastern side of the Strait. The flow is approximately 3 to 4 times greater during August and September than in February and March when ice is present. The principal characteristics of this current, which supplies about 20% of the inflow into the Arctic

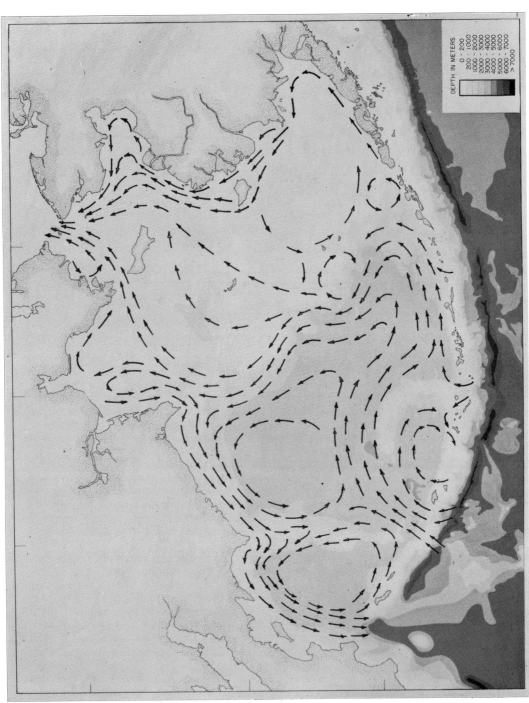

Fig. 3. Surface circulation during summer.

basin, can generally be explained in terms of the prevailing winds above the Arctic basin, and Bering and Greenland Seas. In the extreme western part of the Strait, a southward flowing counter current, or "Polar" current, is occasionally observed. Currents at depth are not well known.

Although the temperature of the water over the northern shelf is very low during winter, the salinity values are not high enough to permit the formation of deep water. Deep water enters through the passage between Kamchatka and the Komandorski Islands, and is dissipated by a slow, vertical movement through the weak halocline which exists over the entire basin.

Water Masses

There are three distinct water masses in the Bering Sea. Water over the shallow, broad continental shelf is cooled during winter from the surface to bottom by convection currents under the ice, diluted in spring by runoff from large rivers, such as the Kuskokwim, Yukon and Anadyr, and warmed during summer at the surface. These conditions result in temperatures from −1.6 to 10°C, and surface salinities from 22.0 to 32.8‰ (bottom salinities are slightly higher). Although some low dissolved oxygen values have been reported under the ice, usually near-saturated values are found from the surface to bottom throughout the year. Water in the surface layer (0 to 150 meters) overlying the deep basins originates south of the Aleutian Islands, but is modified by seasonal cooling and heating. Oxygen values are at or near saturation, but, because ice rarely occurs except in the western part, temperatures range from 1 to 9°C and surface salinities are high, 32.9 to 33.2‰. Water below 200 meters in the

central basins originates from depths greater than 600 meters in the Pacific Ocean and brings cold, oxygen-depleted water to within 200 meters of the surface (Fig. 4). Separation of water in the surface layer and the water below 200 meters is clearly marked by a temperature-minimum stratum, and a sharp gradient in dissolved oxygen between 100 and 200 meters (Table 1). Temperature and salinity values at the bottom, between 3500 and 4000 meters, are $1.51 \pm .02°C$ and $34.68 \pm .02‰$.

TABLE 1. OCEANOGRAPHIC STATION DATA—SUMMER 1962
(LATITUDE 56° 52′ N, LONGITUDE 166° 37′ E)

Depth (m)	Temperature (°C)	Salinity (‰)	O_2 (mg atm/L)
0	10.51	32.94	.620
50	3.02	33.10	.696
100	1.33	33.22	.639
200	3.71	33.88	.104
300	3.60	34.03	.046
500	3.34	34.18	.034
1000	2.63	34.40	.040
2000	1.84	34.59	.120
3000	1.57	34.65	.197
3500	1.53	34.66	.245

Plankton

Although extensive sampling has occurred, the variability in method and period of observation permit only general conclusions concerning the biomass. Of the 163 phytoplankton species reported, 104 are Diatomaceae and 55 Peridinea. The maximum phytoplankton biomass occurs during spring in surface waters over the continental shelf—0.150 to 350 g/m² compared to approximately 1.5 g/m² in surface waters overlying the deep basin. The biomass decreases in summer, but has a secondary peak in autumn that is about an order of magnitude less than the spring bloom. Vertical distribution studies indicate that the maximum diatom population is not always at the surface and is sometimes found as deep as 30 meters. In late spring and early summer, the number of diatoms vary from 0.3×10^5 to 5×10^8 cells/m³; the most common forms are *Nitzschia seriata* and *Rhizosolenia hebetata*. Zooplankton, captured in small mesh nets, can be separated into two main groups—oceanic and neritic. In the upper 150 meters of the water column overlying the deep basin, Copepoda represent over 50% of the zooplankton biomass present, the dominant ones being *Eucalanus bungii*, *Oithona similis*, *Calanus plumchrus* and *C. cristatus*; Euphausiacea, chiefly *Thysanoessa longipes* constitute about 25%; Chaetognatha 20%; and Amphipoda, and Pteropoda the remainder. The neritic forms are chiefly Copepoda—*Calanus finmarchicus* and *Acartia*

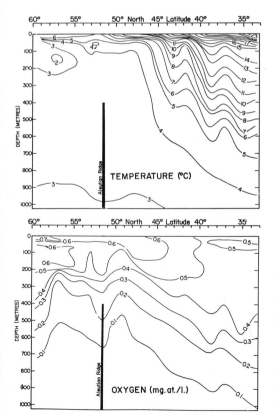

Fig. 4. Vertical sections of salinity, temperature and dissolved oxygen along longitude 180°.

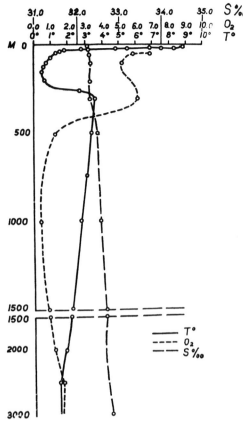

Fig. 5. Vertical distribution of temperature (continuous line), oxygen (short dashes), and salinity.

longiremis. Very little is known about the vertical migration of zooplankton in this area.

Fish and Mammals

Approximately 315 species of fish are found, of which 25 are of commercial value. The herring, salmon, cod, halibut, ocean perch and flatfish are the most important of the commercial species. King crab and shrimp are commercially important crustacea. Sea otter, sea lion and walrus are found, and the Pribilof and Komandorski islands are nursery grounds for fur seals. Whales such as the killer, sperm, bowhead, humpback, right, finback, sei, beaked and beluga are numerous.

F. FAVORITE

Structure

The deep basin of the Bering Sea is part of a typical "island arc" sequence as propounded by Gutenberg. The Aleutian Islands form a nearly perfect arc of a circle, centered near Bering Strait. The Aleutian Ridge, on which they lie, is of volcanic origin and is underlain by a thickened section of oceanic crustal material. The deep basin of the Bering Sea is underlain by at least 2 km and possibly as much as 4 km of layered sediments; beneath this sedimentary load is normal oceanic crust with the mantle depressed to a depth of 15 km below sea level in adjustment to the superimposed sediments. Apparently the Aleutian Ridge has cut off a corner of the Pacific basin and has acted as a dam behind which an exceedingly rapid accumulation of sediments (probably mostly turbidites) has occurred. The basin has filled almost to the level of the sill north of Kamchatka Strait and should

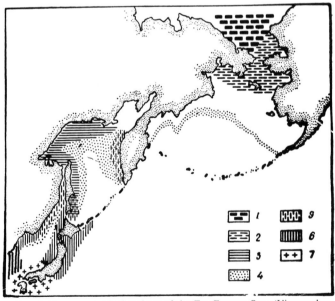

Fig. 6. Zoogeographical regions of the Far Eastern Seas (Vinogradov, 1948). 1 High Arctic; 2 Low Arctic; 3 Glacial; 4 Sub-Arctic; 5 North-boreal; 6 South-boreal; 7 Sub-tropical regions.

soon start to overflow into the north end of the Kurile Trench.

Measurements of geothermal gradients in the deep-water sediments of the Bering Sea show, surprisingly, that the basin itself has a heat flow of only 1.1 μcal/cm^2 sec, actually less than the mean value for the Pacific basin as a whole. Clearly, the vulcanism is concentrated along the Aleutian arc and does not penetrate into the interior of the basin.

The eastern and northeastern shelves are apparently normal portions of the continental mass, with a granitic basement and mantle depth of 29 km. Large accumulations of sedimentary rocks have been reported from Bristol Bay where there have been recent oil exploration efforts. The area of Bering Strait has little or no sedimentary deposit, with granite outcrops reported from the sea floor in the Strait itself.   G. G. SHOR, JR.

References

Bezrukov, P. L. (editor), 1959, "Geographical description of the Bering Sea bottom relief and sediments," *Trans. Akad. Nauk. SSSR Institut. Okeanol.,* **29**, 187pp. (translation 1964, SFCSI Comm., 192pp.; see O.T.S., H.C.).

Dodimead, A. J., Favorite, F., and Hirano, T., 1963, "Review of Oceanography of the Subarctic Pacific Region," *Int. N. Pac. Fish. Comm. Bull.,* **13**, 195pp.

Hopkins, D. M., 1959, "Cenozoic history of the Bering land bridge, 1959," *Science,* **129** (3362), 1519–1527.

Karohji, Kohei, 1959, "Report from the *Oshoro Maru* on oceanographic and biological investigations in the Bering Sea and northern North Pacific in the summer of 1955. IV. Diatom standing crops and the major constituents of the populations as observed by net sampling, 1959," *Bull. Fac. Fisheries, Hokkaido Univ.,* **8** (4), 243–252.

Leonov, A. K., 1960, "Currents of the Bering Sea," pp. 103–123, Leningrad, Regional 'naya Okeanografiya, (translation either O.T.S. or E.T.S.).

Nicols, H., Perry, R. B., and Kofoed, J. W., 1964, "Bathymetry of Bower's Bank, Bering," *Surveying and Mapping,* **24** (Sept.), 443–48.

Saidova, Kh. M., and Lisitsyn, A. P., 1961, "Sedimentary stratigraphy and paleogeography of the Bering Sea during the Quaternary period," *Dokl. Akad. Nauk SSSR,* **139** (5), 1221–1224. In Russian. [Translation in *Translated Doklady Oceanography Sections,* **136–141**, 59–63 issued Am. Geophys. Union (1963).]

Schmidt, R. A. M., 1963, "Pleistocene marine microfauna in the Bootlegger Cove clay, Anchorage, Alaska," *Science,* **141**, 350–351.

Shor, G. G., Jr., 1964, "Structure of the Bering Sea and the Alentian Ridge," *Marine Geol.,* **1**, 213–19.

Shor, G. G., Jr., 1964, "Structure of the Bering Sea and the Gulf of Alaska," *Marine Geol.,* **1**, 213–19.

U.S. Weather Bureau and Hydrographic Office, 1961, "Climatological and Oceanographic Atlas for Mariners. Volume II—North Pacific Ocean," U.S. Govt. Print. Office, Washington D.C., 159pp.

Zenkevitch, L., 1963, "Biology of the Seas of the U.S.S.R.," New York, Interscience Publishers, 955pp.

BERNARD CELL—*See* Vol. II

BERNOULLI'S THEOREM

In the case of steady flow of an isentropic fluid under conservative forces, the total energy of the fluid particle is constant along each streamline. This is called Bernoulli's theorem. Steady motion means that the velocity is constant in time at any point in this fluid. In an isentropic fluid, isopicnals are parallel to isobars and the density is a function of pressure only. Conservative forces mean forces which have a potential. Gravity is one of them. Bernoulli's theorem is written as

$$\tfrac{1}{2}v^2 + a\,dp + \varphi = \text{constant} \tag{1}$$

where v is the velocity, a and p are specific volume and pressure, respectively, and φ is the potential for the forces. The constant may take different values along different streamlines. The first, second or third term on the left-hand side of this equation indicates respectively the kinetic energy, enthalpy or potential energy (per unit mass). When density is constant and the force is gravity only, the above equation becomes

$$\tfrac{1}{2}\rho v^2 + p + \rho gh = \text{constant} \tag{2}$$

where ρ is density and h is the height of a point on the streamline from some standard level. This is original form of Bernoulli's equation.

Daniel Bernoulli (1700–82) was one of the members of the Bernoulli family in Basel and his father (Johann), uncle (Jacob) and brother (Nikolaus) were also famous mathematicians. In his 1738 treatise on hydrodynamics, he described the principle of what is now called the Bernoulli theorem by use of examples of flow in pipes and reservoirs. The mathematical formula similar to Eq. (2) was actually derived by Euler in his 1755 treatise.

Equation (2) and its generalized forms including effects of friction are widely used in hydraulics. In engineering terms of open channel flows which are applicable to rivers, Eq. (2) is divided by ρg or the specific weight of the fluid. Then each term is energy per unit weight and has a dimension of length: It is called *velocity head, pressure head* and *elevation*, respectively, and the sum is called *total head*. The sum of pressure head and elevation is also called *potential head*. In an open channel, the velocity is approximately constant on a section. Therefore, the potential head is considered to be constant on the section and equal to the depth h plus the height h_o of the bottom from a datum. The total head E_w equals $v^2/2g + y + h_o$. The quantity $H = E_w - h_o$ represents the elevation of the total head above the bottom and is called the specific energy. When a channel is wide, the rate of discharge q per unit width of section approximately equals yv. Thus, we have

$$H = q^2/2gy^2 + y \tag{3}$$

If q is constant, there will be two possible depths y

for every value of H. However, the specific energy cannot decrease below the minimum value which is determined from the relation $dH/dy = 0$. The depth and specific energy corresponding to this minimum value are called critical values and denoted by the subscript c. Then

$$y_c = (2/3)H_c = (q^2/g)^{1/3} \qquad (4)$$

At some value of H above H_c the current velocity v is smaller for $y > y_c$ than for $y < y_c$ corresponding to the same discharge q. Therefore, the former is called tranquil flow and the latter rapid flow. The curve of y/y_c against H/y_c is shown in Fig. 1. This

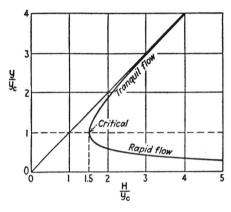

Fig. 1. Dimensionless specific energy diagram for two-dimensional flow (Rouse, 1938). (By permission of Dover Publications, New York.)

curve indicates that y increases with increasing H for a tranquil flow and vice versa for a rapid flow. This can be applied to a channel or river, where the total head is constant but H decreases due to the rise of the bottom by Δh_o (Fig. 2). When the initial flow is tranquil ($y > y_c$), the water surface drops in the second portion of the channel. When the initial flow is rapid ($y_1 < y_c$), the surface rises. Rossby (1950) applied a generalized form of this principle to explain the downstream intensification of the velocity of the Gulf Stream which has depths above the critical value (tranquil flow) upstream. Accord-

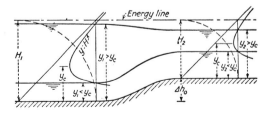

Fig. 2. Application of the energy diagram to a change in channel elevation (Rouse, 1938). (By permission of Dover Publications, New York.)

ing to him, in the Gulf Stream the decrease of the specific energy H is caused by frictional loss rather rather than by the change of the lower boundary. Ichiye (1960) generalized Rossby's idea to include the effect of change of lateral width of the Gulf Stream.

In meteorology, Bernoulli's theorem has been applied to air flow over a hill or mountain. In such a flow, the wind increases at the hill top resulting in pressure drop which may amount to a few millibars. Therefore, barometric observations from such a station may not be representative of the atmospheric pressure of the area.

TAKASHI ICHIYE

References

Hess, S. L., 1959, "Introduction to Theoretical Meteorology," New York, Henry Holt and Company, 362pp.
Ichiye, T., 1960, "On critical regimes and horizontal concentration of momentum in ocean currents with two-layered system," *Tellus,* **12,** 149–158.
Lamb, H., 1945, "Hydrodynamics," pp. 20–22, New York, Dover Publications.
Rossby, C. G., 1951, "On the vertical and horizontal concentration of momentum in air and ocean currents," *Tellus,* 3(1), 15–27.
Rouse, H., 1938, "Fluid Mechanics for Hydraulic Engineers," New York, Dover Publications (reprint), 422pp.
Rouse, H., and Ince, S., 1957, "History of Hydraulics, New York, Dover Publications, 269pp.

Cross-references: *Density; Dynamics of Ocean Currents; Gulf Stream (Vol. II); Entropy and Isentropic Flow; Pressure; Vector Analysis.*

BIOCHEMICAL PRODUCTIVITY—*See* **PRIMARY PRODUCTION**

BIOMASS—*See* **FERTILITY OF THE OCEAN**

BISMARCK SEA

The Bismarck Sea is part of the southwest Pacific Ocean, surrounded by the Bismarck Archipelago, situated north of New Guinea, within a line from Bandissin Pt. (142° 02′E) to Wuvulu Island, Aua, Manu (Ninigo Gp.) to Hermit Island, to the Admiralty Island, thence to New Ireland, New Britain, connecting through Umboi Island to Teliata Pt. (5° 55′S 147° 24′E), following the definition of the International Hydrographic Bureau (*Sp. Publ.* 23, 1953). The sea extends from $142\frac{1}{2}$°E to 153°E and from the Equator to 6°S, covering about 40,000 km² with a volume of about 60×10^{12} m³.

The islands of the Bismarck Archipelago are politically under Australian mandate (along with the Mandated Territory of New Guinea). They

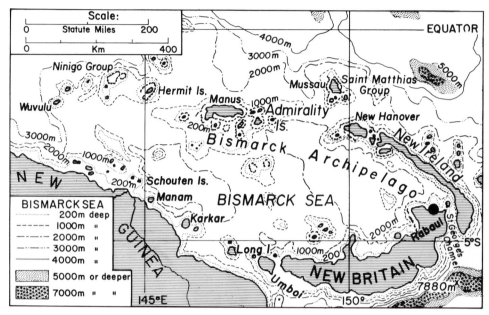

Fig. 1. Bismarck Sea.

were occupied before World War I by Germany (1885–1914), and the major islands are referred to in the early literature as follows: New Britain (Neupommern), New Ireland (Neumecklenburg), New Hanover or Lavongai (Neuhannover). The first scientific visit to this region was by HMS *Challenger* in 1875. German naval vessels carried out systematic charting in the pre-World War I period (see references in *Solomon Sea*). Later work was done by HMS *Cook* and the Russian ship *Vitiaz*. A 1961 crossing was made by the cable survey ship *Recorder* (Krause, 1965).

Bathymetrically, the area is an ovoid region bounded on the southwest by New Guinea and surrounded on the east and north by an almost continuous ridge, the *Bismarck Ridge*, of mean depth about 1000 m, but studded with islands and reefs; the interior depression is largely over 2000 m and is bisected by a rise (500–1000 m), isolating the *New Ireland* Basin on the east and the *New Guinea* Basin on the west. Depths do not seem to exceed 2500 m. Numerous seamounts and small volcanic islands mark the southern margin of the Sea.

Oceanography and Climate

Mean annual isotherms at the sea surface are close to 83°F (28°C) with little annual variation. Rainfall exceeds 2000 mm (75 inches). The area has two wet seasons corresponding to the passage of the tropical frontal zone of disturbances at about the equinoxes. The region is cloud-covered six-tenths of the time and the average seawater salinity is somewhat reduced (34.5‰).

Northerly winds (Northeast Trades) blow mainly in the January–March season, Southeast Trades in July to September, with doldrums or frontal conditions about the equinoxes. The South Equatorial Current sets westward through the area much of the year with rates of less than $\frac{1}{2}$ knot as a rule, but the northerly winds of the southern summer lead to eddy motions to south and southeast.

The tides are predominantly only once per day with a rather small spring range, 30–50 cm (Dietrich, 1944).

Sediments

Most of the basin floors and rises are covered with globigerina ooze, to be replaced around the largely coral-veneered Admiralty Islands and adjacent islets by carbonate reef deposits. Emerged reefs, described by Christiansen (1964), with familiar low-level platforms and notches, suggest eustatic levels and thus at least Holocene stability.

Along the southwestern border of the Bismarck Sea and in the southeast, the New Guinea and New Britain coasts, there are numerous youthful, active volcanic cones (basaltic), which are feeding ash and tuffaceous material as well as submarine lava flows into the basin. Active island centers, from WNW–ESE, are Bam, Manam (Schouten Island),* an unnamed submarine volcano, Karkar, Long Island and Talo (on Umboi), according to Fisher (1956). Blupblup, west of Bam, is extinct. Volcanic cones in the Vuvulu group are inactive. In the straits, Krause (1965) reported volcanic sands mixed with small shells, Foraminifera and fecal pellets.

---

* Not to be confused with another group of this name north of West Irian.

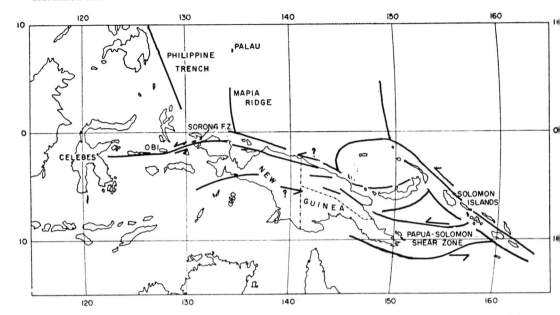

Fig. 2. Suggested continuity of left-lateral shear zones between the Sorong Fault Zone and the Papua–Soloman Shear Zone. Horizontal displacement occurs on many other fault zones in the area (after Krause, 1965; with additions).

Structure

The Bismarck Sea is one of the quasi-cratonic basins of the western Pacific, which appears to have been a region of crustal stretching and subsidence during the last 1–10 million years or so, leading to block faulting, central downwarping and marginal uplift. Thus elevated coral reefs are known along the Finsch coast to heights of over 1000 m (see literature review by Davis, 1928, p. 392). Off Madang, Krause (1965) reported a 45° slope with reefs down to 280 m, evidently tectonically depressed, while farther seaward, a 320 m scarp of 38° was observed below 650 m. The North Coast Ranges of New Guinea were evidently eugeosynclinal for a long time (since Cretaceous), and in the main range sediments of miogeosynclinal type can be traced back to Cambrian. However, the main orogeny in the Northern Ranges probably reached its climax in Pleistocene times. Major vertical faults of tremendous throw (5000 m and more) parallel the present coast.

It is probable that a major sinistral strike-slip fault, which may be called the *New Guinea Fault*, extends approximately 3000 km, from the east arm of Halmahera, south of Obi, crossing the northern Vogelkop, north of Japan, between the Unake-Serre Mts. and the Bewani-Toricelli Mts. to cross the southern part of the Bismarck Sea in an important submarine scarp east of Blupblup (1000 m scarp), directed eventually toward the major volcanic center of Rabaul. A branch to the southeast seems to be indicated by the row of volcanoes Blupblup–Bam–Manam–Karkar–Long Island–

Vitiaz Strait, possibly to join the Papua–Solomon Shear Zone (of Krause, 1965). No indication of the strike-slip displacement can be offered at present. The line is one of high seismicity with numerous shallow shocks (up to class a, Gutenberg and Richter, 1949–54). Intermediate focus shocks occur at distances up to 100 km to the south of this line.

Rhodes W. Fairbridge

References

Christiansen, S., 1964, "Morphology of some coral-cliffs, Bismarck Archipelago," *Collected Papers, Geogr. Inst., Univ. Copenhagen, Denmark*, 1–21.

David, T. W. E., 1950, "The Geology of the Commonwealth of Australia," Vol. 1, pp. 662–685, London, Edward Arnold.

Davis, W. M., 1928, "The Coral Reef Problem," *Am. Geograph. Soc., Spec. Publ. 9*.

Dietrich, G., 1944, "Die Schwingungssysteme der halb und eintägigen Tiden in den Ozeanen," *Veroeff. Inst. Meeresk. Berlin*, N.F.R.A., **41**.

Fisher, N. H., 1956, "Catalogue of the active volcanoes and solfatara fields of Melanesia," *Intern. Vol. Assoc.*, Rome, 5–15.

Gutenberg, B., and Richter, C. F., 1949, "Seismicity of the Earth and Associated Phenomena," Princeton, N.J., *Princeton University Press*, 273pp. (second ed., 1954).

Krause, D. C., 1965, "Submarine geology north of New Guinea," *Geol. Soc. Am. Bull.*, **76**, 27–42.

Schott, G., 1935, "Geographie des Indischen und Stillen Ozeans," Hamburg, Boysen, 413pp.

Udintsev, G. B., 1960, "On the bottom relief of the western region of the Pacific Ocean," *Akad. Nauk SSSR, Oceanological Researches*, No. 2, 5–32.

Udintsev, G. B., *et al.*, 1963, "The new bathymetric map of the Pacific," *Akad. Nauk SSSR, Oceanological Researches*, No. 9, 60–101.

Visser, W. A., and Hermes, J. J., 1962, "Geological results of the exploration for oil in Netherlands New Guinea," *Verhandel. Koninkl. Ned. Geol. Mijnb. Genoot., Geol. Ser.*, **20**, 265pp.

Cross-references: *Pacific Ocean; Solomon Sea. pr* Vol. VI: *New Guinea.*

BLACK-BODY RADIATION—*See* RADIATION LAWS, VOL. II

BLACK SEA

The oval basin of the Black Sea lies in an east-west intermontaine depression between two Alpine fold belts and separates eastern Europe from Asia Minor. The area of the Black Sea proper amounts to 423,000 km^2 and, together with the Sea of Azov (38,000 km^2) which is essentially a large gulf or lagoon, the Black Sea (*sensu lato*) reaches 461,000 km^2. Its mean depth is 1197 m. The volume of the Black Sea proper amounts to 537,000 km^3, and the Sea of Azov 300 km^3. The narrow Bosporus Strait (maximum depth of 27.5 m) connects the Black Sea with the Sea of Marmara and further with the Dàrdanelles and the Mediterranean Sea. The narrow Kerch Strait (only 5 m deep) links the Black Sea with the Sea of Azov.

The wide geosynclinal part of the Black Sea is a depression with a flat floor (maximum depth 2245 m) bordered by a very steep continental slope (up to 20° in some places). In the eastern part of the Black Sea, the slope is dissected by numerous submarine canyons. The northwestern part of the Black Sea and the Sea of Azov are within the platform area and are shallow. The maximum depth of the Sea of Azov is only 13.5 m.

Bathymetry

The western part of the Black Sea is a wide shelf which gradually narrows to the south and reaches the Bosporus Strait. The shelf break to the continental slope occurs at a depth of 100–150 m. Around the other Black Sea shores, there is either no shelf at all since the shelf has been replaced by a narrow abrasion terrace, or the width of the shelf does not exceed 10–15 km.

Geologic History

The Black Sea basin was initially formed in early Tertiary time as a median mass ("Zwischengebirge"), a zeugogeosyncline which subsided between the mountain ranges of the Caucasus and the Crimea on the one hand, and the Pontus mountains in Anatolia on the other. In Cretaceous times, this block was a mountainous area, supplying sediment to the north and to the south. The tectonic movements which shaped the depression went on throughout the Tertiary and Quaternary periods and have continued to the present day. Geophysical exploration shows that the earth's crust under the floor of the central basin is of oceanic type. There is no granite layer. The Black Sea is therefore a classic case of "oceanization" of former continental crust. However, in distinction to the oceans, the layer of sedimentary rock is up to 10–15 km thick (Y. P. Neprochnov). Benches of fault origin have been found on the continental slope to a depth of some 1500 m, on which are found shallow-water sediments of quite recent origin. The zone of the continental slope, especially along the Crimean and Anatolian shores, is highly seismic. Arkhangelsky (1938) has suggested therefore that the slope is of a fault origin and that the movements along the step faults continue to this day.

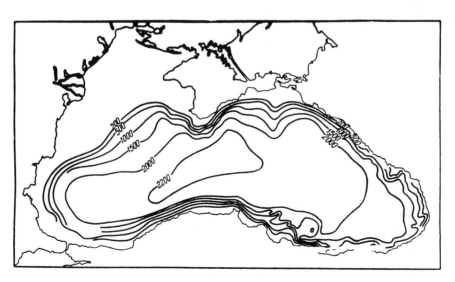

Fig. 1. Bottom topography of Black Sea (Archangelsky and Strahov).

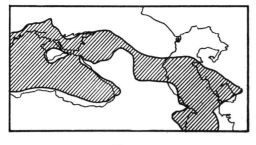

Fig. 2a.

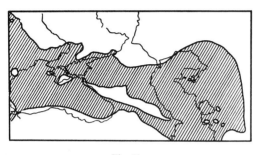

Fig. 2b.

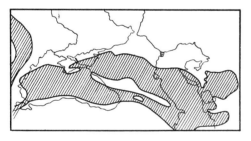

Fig. 2c.

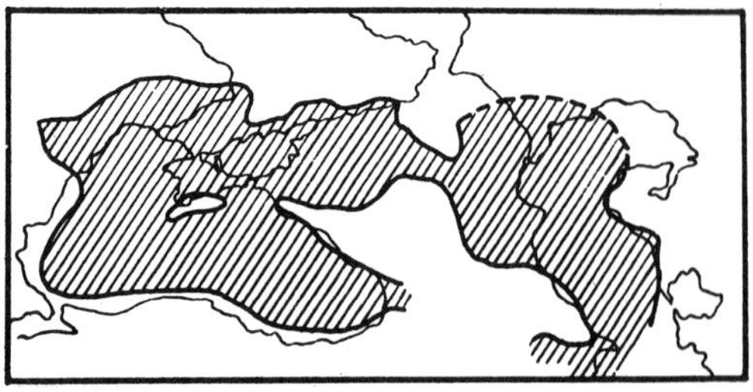

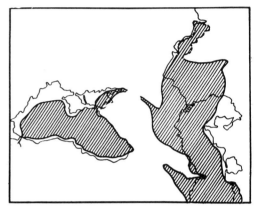

Fig. 2d.

Fig. 2e.

Fig. 2. Geologic evolution of Black Sea and Caspian Sea (assembled by Zenkevitch, 1963). (a) Middle Miocene Depression (Zhizhenko, 1940); marine. (b) Sarmatian Basin (Kolesnikov); brackish. (c) Maeotic Basin (Kolesnikov); euxinic. (d) Pontic Lake (Andrussov); nearly fresh. (e) Chaudin Basin (evolved from Cimmerian and Kuyalnits basins) and Apsheron Basin (evolved from Akchagyl Basin) (Archangelsky and Kolesnikov); fresh.

During the Quaternary there was also considerable uplift of the mountain belts on either side of the Black Sea, as indicated by the variable heights of the Quaternary marine terraces in different sectors.

During the Neogene (Late Tertiary), the configuration, area and salinity of the Black Sea changed repeatedly. At some stage it became connected with the Caspian Sea and turned into a closed lake basin of vast dimensions. The Pliocene history and evolution of the Black Sea fauna was first worked out in a general way by Andrusov (1918).

The Quaternary was also characterized by multiple changes in the level of the Black Sea, related to the general course of eustatic change of the world ocean, which in turn was closely involved in the sequence of glacial epochs. Whenever the sea-level dropped below that of the Bosporus sill depth, the Black Sea would turn into an open lake and its water was freshened. On the other hand, at higher sea-level stands, the water exchange with the Mediterranean Sea became more active and the Black Sea area was invaded by organisms which required a relatively greater salinity. Variation in the specific composition of mollusks makes it possible to date very accurately the sediments representing the various phases of the Quaternary history of the Black Sea and its shores.

An adequate study has been made of the "New Euxine" freshwater phase of the Black Sea, which coincided with the latest glacial (Würm) period. These sediments are found in many places, both in shallow water and deep water, but they are rarely, if ever, encountered on land. The fauna of that period consisted of species which could withstand considerable dilution. The level of the Black Sea was considerably lower than that of the Bosporus sill (within -40 to -60 m). This was followed by a relatively rapid transgression and salinization of

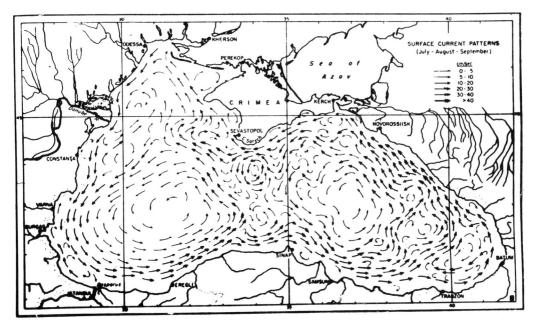

Fig. 3. Black Sea circulation patterns.

the Sea, and a level close to the present one was reached approximately 5000 years ago.

Terraces

Most pronounced on land are the two Karangat terraces. Their shore lines are found elevated at 12–14 m in the Caucasus and 22–25 m in Bulgaria. This was a phase of more complete connection with the Sea of Marmara; from here many large stenohaline forms (e.g., the *Cardium tuberculatum* mollusks, sea urchins, etc.) penetrated into the Black Sea. Many researchers compare this phase with the Monastirian one of the Mediterranean Sea.

Early Euxine (55–60 m) and Usunlar (35–40 m) terraces occur in the same areas. They correspond to the Tyrrhenian terraces. The Early Euxine basin was freshened, and Caspian relicts and endemic forms prevailed.

At the turn of the Pliocene Quaternary, the Chaudian terrace was formed. In the Crimea, its sediments occur at elevation of 30 m. In the Caucasus, they are substantially higher (95–100 m), but here they are deformed owing to the crustal movement.

In recent years, the material on terraces has been revised by Fyodorov (1963). In his opinion, the Black Sea has likewise witnessed a high-level phase, corresponding to the Flandrian terrace in Western Europe.

In the Sea of Azov, the terraces are poorly preserved since it is a region of intensive recent downwarping. During low-level periods of the Black Sea, the Sea of Azov turned into a swampy alluvial plain.

Hydrology

The Black Sea represents the standard example of a land-locked "euxinic" sea which leaves a striking imprint on its hydrologic condition. In 1882, S. O. Makarov for the first time investigated the currents of the Bosporus Strait. It was found that in the lower layers of the salt water (36‰) of the Sea of Marmara penetrates into the Black Sea, and in surface layers the fresh water of the Black Sea flows into the Sea of Marmara. According to the latest investigations, the lower current carries 202 km³ yearly, and the upper one, 348 km³. Over 400 km³ of water flow into the Black Sea from the numerous rivers. All these figures are subject to slight yearly fluctuations.

The average salinity of the surface water in the central part of the Black Sea amounts to 16–18‰. At a depth greater than 150–200 m, salinity increases to 21–22.5‰. The surface water gets warmer in summer to 25°C (up to 28°C at the shores). In winter in the open sea, it cools down to 6–8°C. The Sea of Azov and the northwestern part of the Black Sea are covered with ice in winter. Deep water has a temperature of 8–9°C all the year round.

As the surface and deep water differ in density, there is very little intermixing. Only the upper 50 m of water are saturated with oxygen. At a lower level its oxygen content diminishes, and at a depth of 150–200 hydrogen sulfide appears. The amount of the latter in bottom layers is as great as 6 cm³/liter. The origin of hydrogen sulfide is accounted for through the activity of both anaerobic bacteria (notably *Desulfovibrio aestuarii*), which decompose the protein matter, and desulfurizing bacteria.

Analysis of the balance of fresh and salt water of the Black Sea indicates that despite the difficulty in exchange between the upper and lower layers, such exhange still exists. Every year up to 3000 km³ of deep salt water rises to the surface. The mechanism of this phenomenon is not quite clear at this time.

The inland position of the Black Sea, the abundant river discharge and the hydrologic conditions resulted in some modification of the chemical composition of the water: namely, it exhibits a somewhat lower content of sulfates and a sharp increase in the content of carbonates.

Movement of surface water is controlled by both winds and river discharge. In general, the surface water of the Black Sea circulates along the shores counter-clockwise. Against the background of the general circulation two gyrals exist: the eastern and the western. At the boundaries between them, water moves either to the south or to the north. Velocities of these currents range from 0.1–0.3 m/sec. Drift currents develop in coastal areas at velocities of up to 0.5 cm/sec.

The water level of the Black Sea is subject to seasonal fluctuations averaging about 20 cm. In coastal areas, especially in the northwest, wind effects attain a considerable amplitude. Tidal oscillations to 8–9 cm are quite unnoticeable when compared with wind effects in the east, where waves up to 7 m high are formed.

Fauna and Flora

The bottom vegetation of the Black Sea consists of 285 species of brown, red and green algae.

It is essentially an impoverished Mediterranean flora. Worth noting is the abundant Cystoseira along the rocky shores as well as enormous beds of Phyllophora in the northwestern part of the sea. The latter are used in industry.

Phytoplankton include 350 Mediterranean species. They are widespread in the open sea to a depth of 100–125 m. Near the shores, they go down to a depth of 200 m. The phytoplankton biomass averages 0.1 g/m³ in the open sea, increasing sharply at the shores. Diatoms contribute to 79% of the plankton. In spring their numbers reach up to 20 million/liter. In summer the dinoflagellates may rise to 48,000/liter.

Zooplankton includes over 70 species; their biomass in the open sea amounts to an average of 0.3 g/m³.

The benthos and nekton organisms belong to three categories. Most abundant are the immigrants from the Mediterranean Sea which withstand fresh water. The bays and the northwestern part of the Sea are inhabited by relicts of the Pontian (Pliocene) and are similar to the Caspian forms There, too, are encountered river forms which adapted themselves to the brackish water.

Because of the low salinity, the fauna and flora of the Black Sea and, particularly, of the Sea of Azov are qualitatively very poor as compared with those of the Mediterranean Sea. Whereas the latter total some 7000 various plants and animals, the Black Sea contains about 1200 of them, and the Sea of Azov about 100. Many groups of animals are nonexistent in the Black Sea (coral hydranths,

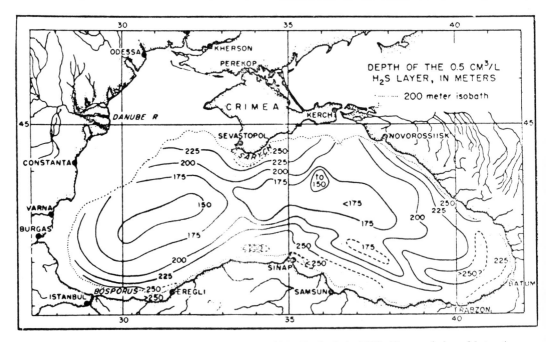

Fig. 4. Depth of the 0.5 cm³/liter layer of hydrogen sulfide (Zenkevitch, 1963). (By permission of Interscience Publishers, N.Y.).

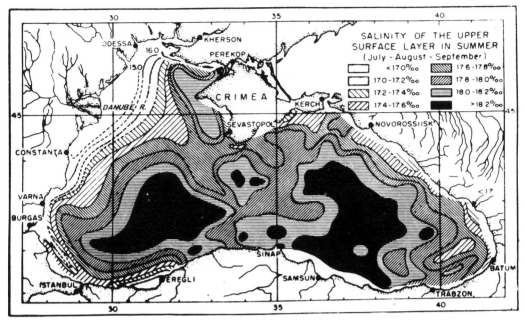

Fig. 5. Distribution of surface salinity in the Black Sea in summer (Neumann, 1943).

calamaries and pteropods). Of echinoderms, only small forms of some holothurians and brittle stars are encountered. All representatives of the benthos fauna are of small dimensions as compared with those of the Mediterranean Sea.

The Black Sea benthos biomass is relatively rich at the shores, but both biomass and number of species gradually decrease downward beginning with a depth of 50–70 m. Below 50 m the most common benthos is provided by the pelecypod *Modiolus phaseolina*. There is no benthos whatsoever (except bacteria) at depths of more than 130–180 m.

The fauna of the Sea of Azov is still poorer qualitatively but a tremendous development of three species of mollusks is recorded there, which contribute great quantities of biomass (up to 400 g/m²).

About 180 species of fish are known in the Black Sea-Azov basin. Many of them migrate from the Black Sea to the Sea of Azov and back. Fishing is highly developed, especially in the Sea of Azov. The Black Sea abounds in dolphins and seals.

Sediments

Of considerable interest are the bottom sediments of the Black Sea which were studied for the first time in detail by Arkhangelsky and Strakhov. As far back as 1927, they obtained material collected with core samplers 4 m long. In recent years cores up to 30 m long have been received from the ship *Vityaz*. Shell deposits are common on the broad shelf as well as along the shores of the northwestern part of the Black Sea and south of the Kerch

Strait. The shells also form beaches and large beach ridges. Terrigenous mud occurs along the mountainous shores of the Black Sea beginning at a depth of about 20 m.

Very large sections on the continental slope are devoid of recent sediments. Core samplers bring up old sediments (New Euxine or Karangat) or impact against exposed bedrock. Extensive belts near the shelf break have been swept clear by gravitational sliding on a giant scale. Lower down, mixed-up sediments of subaqueous slumps have been found in many places (Arkhangelsky, 1927).

A thick layer of argillo-calcareous mud of varying composition and structure occurs in the deep-sea depression. Almost pure lime mud ($> 50\%$ $CaCO_3$) has been deposited in two "chalistatic" sites of the eastern and western part of the basin (in the centers of water gyrals). A band of quite pure argillaceous mud ($< 20\%$ $CaCO_3$) stretches from the north to the south in the central part of the Black Sea. The rest of the bottom is occupied by so-called transition mud. Its typical indication consists of an exceptionally distinct microlamination of annual nature. A varve-like parting of organic matter reflects the dying off of plankton in summer and autumn. A fine-grained layer of calcite is deposited in winter, and a thin layer of clay in spring. The thickness of the layers amounts to hundredths or tenths of a millimeter in different areas. The microlamination has made it possible to calculate the rate of mud depositing. Within 5000 years, there is an average accumulation of 1 m of clay mud but only 10–20 cm of lime mud. All the types of deep-sea mud contain a great deal

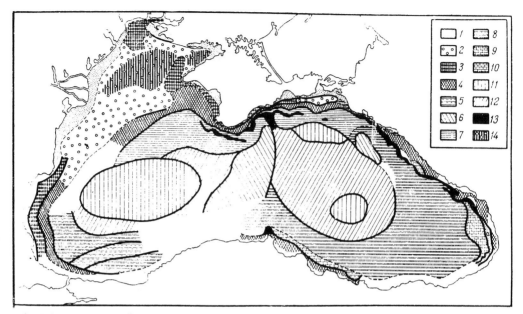

Fig. 6. Contemporary sediments (Archangelsky and Strahov, 1938, with additions by Zenkevitch, 1963): (1) sand, (2) shell gravel, (3) mussel grounds, (4) *Phaseolina* mud, (5) gray deep-sea clay, (6) gray clay with calcareous layers, (7) transitional muds, (8) same with gray mud layers, (9) same with mud and sand, (10) same with multiple gray mud layers, (11) calcareous mud, (12) calcareous mud with gray layers, (13) slump areas (no contemporary sediments), (14) *Pyllophora* beds. (By permission of Interscience Publishers, N.Y.).

of diagenetic ferrous sulfide (pyrite, hydrotroilite), reflecting the strongly reducing environment.

By changes in the lithologic composition at the bottom of the deep-sea depression, it has been possible to distinguish deposits of several phases in the development of the Black Sea up to the New Euxine deposits. The connate water that permeates them has retained an extremely low salinity: 4‰ in the layer of mud at a depth of 6 m below the bottom surface (Bruyevich, 1953).

Layers and lenses of sand which appear to represent the results of turbidity currents have been found in the deep-sea mud along the periphery of the depression.

The Black Sea shores almost everywhere have a simple outline. The only exception is western Crimea where long spits have been developed. Large islands are not present. The "Limans" (or lagoons) of the western part of the Black Sea are of a peculiar kind. They represent flooded river estuaries shut off from the sea by bay-mouth bars. There is considerable movement of sand and pebbles along the straight coasts of the western Black Sea and the Caucasian shores.

In the Sea of Azov, the rate of abrasion of the clayey shores is very high, attaining 12 m/yr. On its northern shore a series of spits has been formed under the waves action from the northeast, extending from the shore at an angle of about 45°.

Descriptions of the Black Sea and of its shores date back to ancient time since it was an area of

Greek and Roman colonization. Remnants of many settlements have been preserved both along the shore and underwater. By skin diving, archaeologists have obtained a considerable amount of material from the bottom.

Historical Notes

The first descriptions of the Black Sea were furnished by Russian seamen in the eighteenth century. They also compiled the first maps and sailing directions. Oceanographic research was conducted for the first time by the Russian expedition of 1890–1891, led by I. B. Shpindler. Important oceanographic data were collected in 1923–27 by Y. Shokalsky; simultaneously, scientific and fishing investigations were carried out by the Knipovich expedition. Since 1871, hydrobiological research has been conducted by the Sevastopol hydrobiological station. An important pioneer monograph was written in 1913 by Zernov, from the material collected.

A large number of Soviet research institutes are now engaged in an important integrated series of oceanographic investigations on the Black Sea.

V. P. ZENKOVITCH

References

Andrusov, N. I., 1918, "Relationships between the Euxine and Caspian basins in the Neogene," *Izv. Ross. Akad. Nauk* (in Russian).

Arkhangelsky, A. D., and Strakhov, N. M., 1938, "Geology and history of development of the Black Sea," *Akad. Nauk SSSR* (in Russian).

Bruyevich, S. V., 1953, "The chemistry and biological productivity of the Black Sea," *Tr. Inst. Okeanol. Adad. Nauk SSSR,* **7,** (in Russian).

Caspers, H., 1957, "Black Sea and the Sea of Azov," in "Treatise on Marine Ecology I," *Geol. Soc. Am. Mem.,* **67,** 803–889.

Chilingar, G., 1956, "Review," *Bull. Am. Assoc. Petrol. Geol.,* **40**(11), 2765–2769.

Chilingar, G., 1959, "Review," *Intern. Geol. Rev.,* **1**(3), 74–81.

Federov, P. V., and Skiba, L. A., 1960, "The fluctuations in the sea level of the Black and Caspian Seas in the Holecene," *Izv. Akad. Nauk SSSR,* **4,** 24–34 (in Russian).

Fyodorov, P. V., 1963, "Stratification of Quaternary deposits of the Crimean-Caucasian coast and some questions of the geological history of the Black Sea," *Tr. Geol. Inst. Akad. Nauk SSSR,* **88** (in Russian).

Knipovich, N. M., 1932, "Hydrological research in the Black and Azov seas," *Tr. Azovo-Chernomorskoy Nauchno-Promyslovoy Ekspeditsii* (in Russian).

Neumann, G., 1942, "Die absolute Topographie des Physikalischen Meeresniveaus und die Oberflächen-strömungen des Schwarzen Meeres," *Ann. Hydr. Marit. Meteorol.,* **70,** No. 9, 265–282.

Neumann, G., 1943, "Uber den Aufbau und die Frage der Tiefenzirkulation des Schwarzen Meeres," *Ann. Hydr. Marit. Meteorol.,* **71,** No. 1, 1–20.

Nevessky, Y. N., 1964, "Postglacial transgressions of the Black Sea," *Dokl. Akad. Nauk SSSR,* **137**(3), 667–670 (in Russian).

Smirnow, L. P., 1958, "Black Sea Basin," in "Habitat of Oil," pp. 982–994, Tulsa, A.A.P.G.

Sorokin, J. I., 1964, "On the primary production and bacterial activities in the Black Sea," *J. Cons. Int. Exp. Mer.,* **29** (1), 41–60.

Zenkevitch, L. A., 1963, "Biology of the Seas of the USSR," New York, Interscience Publishers, 955pp.

Zenkovitch, V. P., 1958, "The Shores of the Black and Azov Seas," Moscow, Izdatelstvo Geographycheskoi Literatury (in Russian).

Zernov, S. A., 1913, "To the problem of studying the life in the Black Sea," *Rossiiskaya Akad. Nauk* (in Russian).

Cross-references: *Mediterranean.* Vol. III: *Caspian Sea.*

BRAZIL CURRENT

The South Equatorial Current on reaching the South American coast swings southward to become the warm Brazil Current, marked also by its high salinity. It is deflected offshore farther south and does not reach the Argentine coast, in the same way as the Gulf Stream is forced away from the northeast coast of North America. At about 35–40°S, it meets the cold *Falkland Current* and the two swing eastward to form the *South Atlantic Current* (or "Southern Ocean Current").

The Brazil Current is weak (1–2 knots in the surface) and shallow (100–200 m) compared with the Gulf Stream. Below depths of 100–200 m a greater part of the South Equatorial Current turns northeast off Recife (to join the Gulf Stream system; see *Guinea Current*), while the deeper current along the Brazilian coast is much weaker. The difference between the Brazil Current and the Gulf Stream has been explained by the different function of the thermohaline western boundary current in the North and South Atlantic; while the wind-driven western boundary current is similar in both oceans, northerly off North America and southerly off Brazil, the thermohaline circulation off Brazil is easterly and weakens the southerly flow. In the Gulf Stream, the thermohaline circulation reinforces the northerly wind-driven western boundary current. The maximum salinity layer of the Brazil Current off Recife is at about 100–200 m depth and its value is 37‰. The high-salinity water flows to the east from near Recife, while its salinity decreases to 36‰ at about 10°W on the equator. This water is the core of the Equatorial Undercurrent in the Atlantic Ocean.

RHODES W. FAIRBRIDGE

TAKASHI ICHIYE

References

Bjerknes, J., 1964, "Atlantic air-sea interaction," in *Advan. Geophys.,* **10,** 1–82.

Defant, A., 1936, "Die Troposphäre," *Deutche Atlantische Exped. METEOR, 1925–1927, Wiss. Erg.,* **6,** Tpl. 1, Sect. 3, 289–411.

Metcalf, W. G., Voorhis, A. D., and Stalcup, M. C., 1962, "The Atlantic Equatorial Undercurrent," *J. Geophys. Res.,* **67**(6), 2499–2508.

Schott, G., 1942, "Geographie des Atlantischen Ozeans," Hamburg, Boysen, 438pp.

Stommel, H., 1958, "The Gulf Stream," University of Calif. Press, 200pp.

Sverdrup, H. U., Johnson, M. W., and Fleming, R. H., 1942, "The Oceans: Their Physics, Chemistry and General Biology," New York, Prentice-Hall, 1087pp.

BROWNIAN MOTION, MOVEMENT— *See* Vol. II

BURMA SEA—*See* ANDAMAN SEA

BURU SEA—*See* CERAM SEA

C

CALCIUM CARBONATE COMPENSATION DEPTH

In oceanography, it has been well known, since the days of the *Challenger Expedition* (1872–1876) that pelagic plankton of calcium carbonate composition were not to be found in the very deep ocean floor, although the organisms were present in the overlying surface waters. The geographic limits of globigerina ooze, for example, were largely dictated by a critical depth, apart from subpolar regions which are too cool for the organisms themselves.

This critical depth, defined as the level below which the rate of $CaCO_3$ solution exceeds the rate of $CaCO_3$ deposition, is called the "*calcium carbonate compensation depth.*" It lies about 4000–5000 m in the Pacific Ocean and is somewhat deeper in the Atlantic and Indian Oceans (Fig. 1). It is abnormally shallow in regions of upwelling and polar mixing (either colder waters or rapid burial affects). It is a function of total pressure, temperature and pCO_2 of the bottom waters. The solubility of $CaCO_3$ (unlike most compounds) rises as the water temperature drops; in tropical oceans, the temperature drops from about 20°C near the surface to about 2–4°C at the bottom.

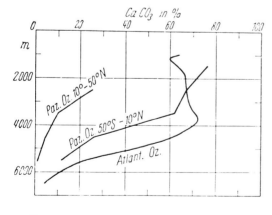

Fig. 1. Average C_aCO_3 content of deep-sea sediments as a function of depth in the Atlantic Ocean (Pia, 1933) compared with the North and South Pacific (Revelle, 1944) (from Dietrich, 1957).

Furthermore, the solubility of $CaCO_3$ is related to the pCO_2, which rises with increasing depth (increasing pressure accompanied by decreasing temperature). This question is partly related to the genesis of the bottom water, which under the normal ocean circulations system is generally coming from a cool, polar source where it has been in equilibrium with the higher atmospheric pCO_2 prevalent at high latitudes. The world distribution of deep-sea red clays (essentially carbonate free) shows a close correlation with the pattern of subpolar bottom water currents, as recognized by Wüst (1938), largely stemming from the Antarctic (see Fig. 2). These bottom currents, of course, also reflect the deepest areas.

The effect of the increase of hydrostatic pressure with depth is particularly important in equatorial latitudes (in polar regions it is less important than temperature). Increasing pressure increases the dissociation of $CaCO_3$ and CO_2 in seawater. It also varies the alkalinity, which would raise the pH, but it also raises the total CO_2 per unit volume, which would depress the pH. It is actually observed that the pH in the tropical ocean may drop from about 8.2 at the surface to 7.6 in 5000 m. The fact that the alkalinity-chlorinity ratio rises with depth is evidence that the carbonate here does indeed go into solution. A calculation that the ratio of the calcite solubility product would rise from 1.0 at the surface to 6.5 at 10,000 m at a theoretical 25°C still requires experimental demonstration at observed temperatures and pressures (Revelle and Fairbridge, 1957).

The ion activity product (IAP) for $CaCO_3$ in seawater of normal characteristics has been studied theoretically by Berner (1965). Tropical, surface seawater at 25°C and one atmosphere pressure would show an IAP $= 12.5 \times 10^{-9}$. The carbonate solubility products are: $K_{calcite} = 4.5 \times 10^{-9}$, $K_{aragonite} = 7.1 \times 10^{-9}$. Thus, as already indicated by Wattenberg and others, tropical surface seawater is supersaturated with respect to both carbonates. With increasing pressure and decreasing temperature, they rapidly become undersaturated (see Table 1), and at all depths below a few hundred meters, calcium carbonate (especially aragonite) is likely to pass into solution (Fig. 3). If, however, the rate of accumulation exceeds the rate of solution, carbonate deposits will form.

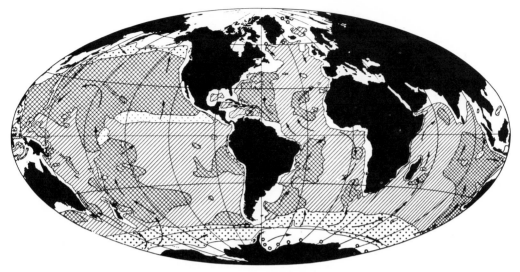

Fig. 2. Present-day world distribution of deep-sea sediments in relationship to deep bottom currents (mainly from the Antarctic). Note the correlation between carbonate-free red clay and the CO_2-rich cold currents (following Wüst, 1938; Dietrich, 1957).

Cross hatched = Red clay	Light dots = Radiolaria ooze
NE/SW diagonals = Globigerina ooze	White = Littoral and hemipelagic ooze
NW/SE diagonals = Volcanic ooze	Arrows = Bottom currents
Heavy dots = Diatom ooze	Circles = Source areas of cold currents

Tertiary Compensation Depth

The present oceanic bottom temperatures are considered abnormally low for the general geological past, the present being merely a relatively brief warm oscillation during the Quaternary Ice Age sequence. The O^{18}/O^{16} paleotemperature isotope analyses of deep tropical globigerina ooze samples by Emiliani (1954, 1961) suggest that the Tertiary bottom water temperatures became progressively cooler; for example in the Eocene there was a mean bottom temperature of 12°C, at least 8° warmer than now. Deep-sea cores show Eocene carbonates at high latitudes, also suggesting higher temperatures (Fairbridge, 1964).

Accordingly, Revelle (in Bramlette, 1958) calculated that, upon available evidence of $CaCO_3$ solubility in the deep Pacific, the Tertiary com-

pensation depth should have been about 6700 m. However, deep-sea coring in the Pacific, largely by Scripps Institution of Oceanography, has shown that the distribution of globigerina ooze at the various horizons of the Tertiary is not as different from the present as might have been expected (Riedel and Funnell, 1964). It is true that the northern edge of the high productivity belt due to the Equatorial Current lay about 5° (550 km) farther north, as indicated already by Arrhenius 1952, 1963); on the other hand, this can possibly be interpreted as being related to a broader spread of Tertiary productivity (or to polar shift). The number of undisturbed Tertiary cores available to Riedel was not very great (85 in all), however, in comparison with the expanse of the Pacific Ocean. Only one showed what seemed to be an appre-

TABLE 1. DISTRIBUTION OF VARIOUS PROPERTIES WITH DEPTH FOR AN AVERAGE[a] OCEAN MODEL

Depth (m)	Pressure (atm)	Temperature (°C)	K calcite $\times 10^9$	pH	IAP $\times 10^9$
0	0	20	4.9	8.2	12.8
500	50	13	6.2	7.8	5.5
1000	100	6	7.4	7.6	3.2
2000	200	5	9.7	7.6	3.7
3000	300	4	12.8	7.6	4.2
5000	500	3	21.2	7.6	5.3

[a]$Cl^- = 19.0‰$, $A = 2.3 \times 10^{-3}$ m, m $Ca^{++} = 0.0103$.

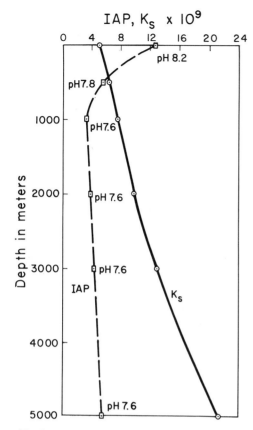

Fig. 3. Saturation product for calcite (K_s) indicated for depth in a typical oceanic profile (North Pacific) where the pH drops from 8.2 to 7.6. Note that the calculated ion activity product, allowing for decreasing temperature and rising pressure, is well below the saturation level everywhere below 400 meters (after Berner, 1965).

ciably lower compensation depth, an undisturbed Oligocene carbonate deposit at 5100 m.

The explanation of this situation is not clear at present, because latitudinal shifts of near-surface temperatures from cool to warm periods and vice versa, e.g., from glacial to interglacial, were of the order of 2000–3000 km. It seems probable that the role of hydrostatic pressure and pCO_2 is less important than simply the total supply of $CaCO_3$ to the oceans. The compensation depth would then represent an equilibrium level (a ratio between rate of supply and rate of solution).

RHODES W. FAIRBRIDGE

References

Arrhenius, G., 1952, "Sediment cores from the East Pacific," *Rept. Swedish Deep-Sea Exped.*, **5**.
Arrhenius, F., 1963, "Pelagic Sediments," in (Hill, M. N., editor) "The Sea," Vol. 3, pp. 655–727, New York, Interscience Publishers.

Berner, R. A., 1965, "Activity coefficients of bicarbonate, carbonate and calcium ions in sea water," *Geochim. Cosmochim. Acta* **30**, 947–965.
Bramlette, M. N., 1958, "Significance of coccolithophorids in calcium-carbonate deposition," *Bull. Geol. Soc. Am.*, **69**, 121–126.
Dietrich, G., 1963, "General Oceanography," New York, Interscience Publishers (translation of 1957 German ed.), 588pp.
Emiliani, C., 1954, "Temperatures of Pacific Bottom Waters and Polar Superficial Waters during the Tertiary," *Science*, **119**, 853–855.
Emiliani, C., 1961, "The temperature decrease of surface sea-water in high latitudes and of abyssalhadal water in open ocean basins during the past 75 million years," *Deep-Sea Res.*, **8**, 144–147.
Fairbridge, R. W., 1964, "The Importance of Limestone and its Ca/Mg Content to Palaeoclimatology," in "Problems of Palaeoclimatology," pp. 431–530, New York, Interscience Publishers.
Riedel, W. R., and Funnell, B. M., 1964, "Tertiary sediment cores and microfossils from the Pacific Ocean floor," *Quart. Geol. Soc. London*, **120**, 305–368.
Revelle, R., and Fairbridge, R., 1957, "Carbonates and carbon dioxide," in "Treatise on marine ecology," *Geol. Soc. Am. Mem.* 67, **1**, 239–296.
Wüst, G., 1938, "Bodentemperatur und Bodenstrom in der Atlantischen, Indischen und Pazifischen Tiefsee, *Gerlands Beitr. Geophys.*, **54**, 1–8.

CALIFORNIA CURRENT

This name has been given to the eastern limb of the wind-driven subtropical anticyclone of the North Pacific Ocean: it applies to the southeastward flow carrying water from the West Wind Drift to join the North Equatorial Current. Its eastern boundary is the coast of North America: it has no well-marked western boundary, but it has been common to define one arbitrarily at a distance 1000 km from shore.

(1) Current

(a) Surface Current. The surface currents near the coast vary with season: those waters within about 150 km of the coast flow northwestward along most of the coast in the winter months (November-February) and southeastward in summer. Within the channel islands off southern California, flow is to the northwest throughout the year and a nearly permanent Southern California Eddy obtains. The inshore countercurrent at the surface appears in winter all along the coast except off northern Baja California, just south of the Southern California Eddy.

The speed of surface flow is usually less than 25 cm/sec, though speeds as high as 100 cm/sec have been observed occasionally in the shoal water of the interisland passages. Drift bottles released near the coast off central California in winter have sometimes been recovered more than 1000 km northward at time intervals indicating average speeds of at least 25 cm/sec.

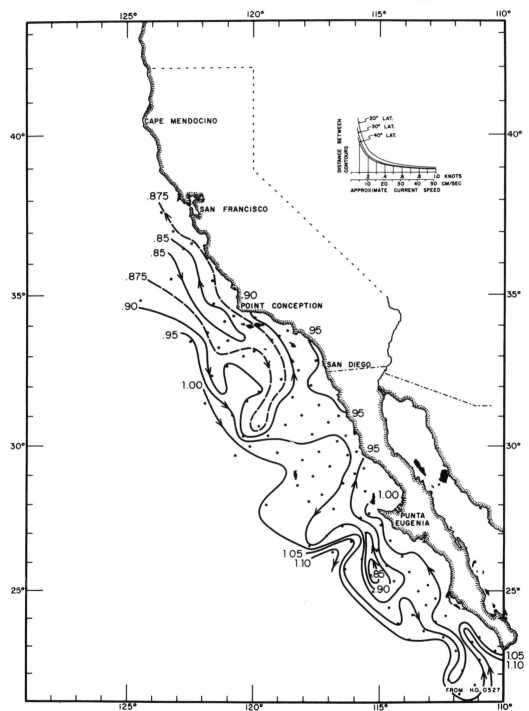

Fig. 1. Surface geostrophic flow (topography of the sea-surface relative to the 500-decibar surface, in dynamic meters) in January 1958.

(b) Subsurface Current. Near the coast (within about 100 km), the waters below about 150-meter depth flow northwestward throughout the year at speeds of 25 cm/sec or less. As a result, the inshore deep waters have more of the characteristics of lower-latitude waters than do those offshore.

(c) Transport. Within 1000 km of the coast, the net transport (calculated from the geostrophic

155

current with respect to the 1000-decibar surface) is to the south at a rate of about 11×10^6 m³/sec. The inshore countercurrent transport is harder to calculate (since the bottom is shallower and irregular), but it may approach 3×10^6 m³/sec.

(2) Upwelling

The prevailing winds are from the northwest throughout the year except in the northern area. The longshore component of the wind stress combined with the effect of the earth's rotation drives some of the surface waters offshore: they are replaced by rising deeper waters near the coast. This process is known as upwelling (q.v.) and it is extremely important to the heat, salt and nutrient distributions in the California Current. It varies seasonally with the wind: these vary in such a way that it is most marked north of 35°N in midsummer but occurs earlier (March–May) off Baja California. Estimates of the offshore transport indicate extreme values as high as 10 kg/cm/sec. This may correspond to an upward speed of a few meters per month in the inshore areas. In the northern area downwelling is indicated in winter when the winds are from the southwest.

(3) Temperature and Salinity

(a) At the Surface. Since the southward-flowing waters come from the higher-latitude West Wind Drift, they are relatively low in temperature and salinity compared to the water of the central North Pacific Ocean and the California Current is known as a cool current. Surface temperatures vary from less than 9°C in the north in the colder months to more than 26°C in the south in the warmer months. Salinity in the open ocean varies from about 32.5‰ in the north to more than 34.5‰ in the south. Near the mouth of the Columbia River the surface salinity may be less than 30‰ but these low values are confined within the upper 10 meters and do not extend far offshore.

(b) At Depth. Temperature decreases monotonically with depth with a few minor exceptions. Beneath the thermocline and offshore there is a well marked salinity minimum that is probably a consequence of the surface waters having mixed laterally with the higher-salinity waters to the west. There is another salinity minimum at about 350-meter depth that indicates the presence of North Pacific Intermediate Water, whose characteristics are acquired in the extreme North Pacific and are transmitted southward by mixing and flow.

(c) Seasonal Variations. Temperature and salinity vary as a result of seasonal differences in insolation, upwelling and flow. The normal period of minimum ocean temperature in the northern ocean is February–May and this overlaps the period of upwelling of colder water off southern Baja California. Therefore, the range of variation there is about 6°, more than twice that of the central

Pacific at that latitude. North of 35°N, the period of maximum of upwelling occurs in midsummer, and the range is correspondingly reduced (to about 3°C, while the central ocean values at that latitude may reach 8 or 10°C).

Since salinity increases with depth near the coast (especially in the north), upwelling brings up more saline water and a marked seasonal variation occurs, with the highest values found in July–September. In the south, the seasonal variation of salinity is dominated by the winter countercurrent that brings high salinity water northward so that the maximum value occurs in December–January. In the central area of the current, these two effects nearly cancel each other and the range is small.

(4) Oxygen

In the mixed layer, the water is very nearly saturated with oxygen, and the range is from more than 7 ml/liter in the north to about 4.5 in the south. Seasonal variations are about 1 ml/liter except off southern Baja California where the range is higher.

Beneath the mixed layer, the oxygen concentration decreases to a minimum value. This value is less than 0.25 unit at 300-meter depth in the southeast; in the northwestern area, the minimum is only a little below 0.5 unit and is found somewhat deeper. The extremely low value in the southeast is found in the Intermediate Water that is moving northwestward along the coast from the tropical regions.

(5) Nutrients

Measurements of nutrients have consisted mostly of determinations of inorganic phosphate-phosphorus. This nutrient is more heavily concentrated in the Pacific Ocean than in the Atlantic. Consumption in the mixed layer keeps the concentration lower than at greater depths, but in the California Current upwelling of the deeper water is very effective in maintaining the surface concentrations at high levels. Central-ocean values in the Pacific are typically less than 0.25 μg atoms/liter, but in the richer coastal regions of the California Current, the values are rarely less than 0.5 and on occasion may reach as high as 1 and 2 over large sections of the coast.

(6) Zooplankton

An index of the great biomass maintained in the California Current may be obtained from the measurements of zooplankton volume in the upper 140 meters of the water column. Open-ocean values are typically less than 25 parts per billion by volume, but the average concentration in the inshore 200 km of the Current is more than 300 parts per billion. Greatest volumes are found in summer, and there are large year-to-year variations.

J. L. REID, Jr.

References

The early studies of this area were carried out by Thorade, McEwen, Skogsberg, Sverdrup, and Fleming; these are cited in Sverdrup, *et al.* (1942).

Reid, J. L., Jr., Roden, G. I., and Wyllie, J. G., 1958, "Studies of the California Current system," *Progr. Rep. Calif. Coop. Ocean. Fish. Invest.*, 1 July 1956 to 1 Jan. 1958, 28–56.

Reid, J. L., Jr., 1962, "On the circulation, phosphate-phosphorus content and zooplankton volumes in the upper part of the Pacific Ocean," *Limnol. Oceanog.*, 7, 287–306.

Sverdrup, H. U., Johnson, M. W., and Fleming, R. H., 1942, "The Oceans; Their Physics, Chemistry, and General Biology," New York, Prentice Hall, 1087pp., 7 charts.

Wooster, W. S., and Reid, J. L., Jr., 1963, "Eastern Boundary Currents," in "The Sea: Ideas and Observations on Progress in the Study of the Sea," Vol. 2, pp. 253–280.

CANADIAN ARCTIC ARCHIPELAGO AND BAFFIN BAY

Part A. Introduction and Oceanography

The Canadian Arctic Archipelago forms a network of shallow channels connecting the Arctic Ocean with Baffin Bay and Hudson Strait. The Archipelago contains some 16 major passages that range in width from 10 to 120 km and in depth from a few meters to over 700 meters. Oceanographic observations in these waters have been carried out in recent years by the Fisheries Research Board of Canada and by the Marine Sciences Branch of the Canadian Department of Mines and Technical Surveys. Much of this work has been directed toward fisheries research and has been concentrated in the eastern Arctic. Since severe winter ice conditions make navigation hazardous and impractical, almost all oceanographic observations within the Archipelago have been obtained during the summer months of July and August. A detailed review of the published material has recently been prepared by Collin and Dunbar (1964).

Bathymetry. There is considerable variation in the depth and extent of the continental shelf surrounding the Archipelago. Along the west shore of Baffin Bay, to the north of Hudson Strait, the width of the shelf seldom exceeds 55 km and the depth is about 200 meters. Little is known about the bathymetry on the Arctic Ocean coast. To the northwest of Ellef Ringnes Island, where measurements have been made, the break in slope of the continental shelf occurs at a depth of 550 meters, 170 km offshore. In this area the continental shelf appears to be remarkably uniform and there is little indication of gulleys or canyons indenting the slope.

According to the International Hydrographic Bureau (*Sp Publ.* 23, 1953), the Canadian Arctic Archipelago (or "North West Passages") has its western limit along a line from Cape Bathurst to Banks I., thence through Pr. Patrick I., Brock I., Borden I., Cape Isachsen, Meighen I. and Cape Colgate (Ellesmere I.); then in the northeast from Cape Sheridan to Cape Bryant (Greenland); to the south, the area between the Archipelago and Greenland, to 70°N, is occupied by Baffin Bay.

The greatest depths in the Archipelago occur in the troughs that have been discovered in Parry Channel and the Prince Gustaf Adolf Sea. Pelletier (1962) suggests that these channels, which may reach a depth of over 700 meters, are likely the result of glacial over-deepening of the valley floor during Pleistocene glacial maxima.

The threshold depth of the Archipelago is no more than 150 meters, in Barrow Strait near Lowther Island; in Smith Sound, between Ellesmere Island and Greenland, the limiting depth is 200 meters.

Sea Ice. The waters of the Archipelago are covered by a mantle of sea ice for at least seven months of the year. Initial freeze-up occurs in all the coastal waters by mid-September, and the general breakup and discharge of the ice in the eastern Arctic does not take place before early July.

Moira Dunbar (1954) has shown that the severity of ice conditions increases from east to west rather than from south to north. All the areas of unconsolidated pack ice and almost all the open water regions are in the east. Throughout the winter, at the present time, open water occurs in the Baffin Bay–Davis Strait area and considerable open water may exist in Lancaster Sound and Smith Sound. Hudson Bay is perhaps exceptional because of its southern latitude and inland sea characteristics. It freezes over completely and is filled with pack ice by February or March; nevertheless, significant leads and cracks persist in the bay ice throughout the winter.

In the western channels of the Archipelago, the ice cover is complete and there is virtually no movement of ice during the winter. In summer the drift is irregular. Detailed summer ice reconnaissance has shown that the movement is generally eastward, following the easterly water circulation through the Archipelago into Parry Channel.

The General Circulation. The circulation through the shallow channels of the Archipelago is weak and influenced by the circulatory system of the Arctic Ocean and Baffin Bay.

There are few oceanographic measurements taken along the northwestern coast of the Archipelago. Observations recorded on the ice island T-3 when it was in the vicinity of the western islands show that along this coast, the surface water movement is to the southwest at a rate of about 2 km/day in summer and slightly over 1 km/day in winter.

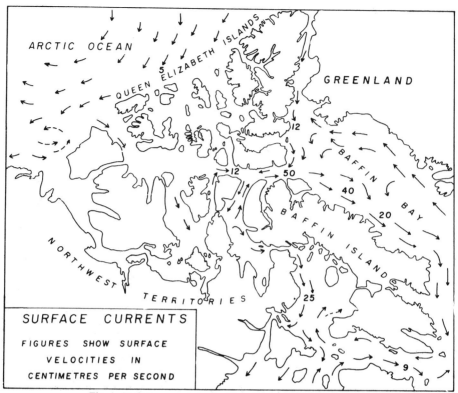

Fig. 1. Surface currents in the Canadian Arctic Archipelago.

To the east, the Archipelago is bordered by Baffin Bay and Nares Strait, the series of channels that connects northern Baffin Bay to the Arctic Ocean. The circulation pattern in Baffin Bay is composed of the West Greenland Current that passes northward through the eastern section of Davis Strait and the Baffin Current which moves southward along the coast of Baffin Island. The West Greenland Current is relatively temperate as it carries with it waters from the East Greenland Current which continues westward around Cape Farwell and from the comparatively warm Irminger Current which impinges on the southeast coast of Greenland.

The Baffin Current is formed of the outflow of cold Arctic Ocean water from the channels of the Archipelago and the northern, cooled remnant of the West Greenland Current. Kiilerich (1939) determined that this current moves in a southerly direction along the east Ellesmere coast at a rate of 17 km/day. Small branches from this current enter Jones Sound and Lancaster Sound.

The predominant flow through the Archipelago is in a south and easterly direction through the main passages of Parry Channel, Prince Regent Inlet, and Jones Sound. This flow is disturbed by a permanent eddy circulation in the eastern end of Lancaster Sound and a consistent, westward current that is confined to the northern side of Lancaster Sound. This westward current appears to be a constant feature of the circulation and is continuous from Baffin Bay to Barrow Strait. Recently calculated summer velocities in Lancaster Sound indicate a westward current along the northern side of the passage of 19 km/day and an eastward flow of 17 km/day along the south coast of the channel. These figures are slightly higher than those presented by Bailey (1957) but are in fair agreement with Kiilerich's results.

In Prince Regent Inlet and Wellington Channel, the predominant current is to the south; however, in both passages, a comparatively weak northerly drift has been observed along the eastern coast.

Characteristics of the Water Masses. The Parry Channel system including M'Clure Strait, Viscount Melville Sound, Barrow Strait, and Lancaster Sound forms a zone of transition between the waters to the west, characteristic of the Polar Basin, and those to the east in Baffin Bay. Along the western continental shelf, oceanographic conditions are identical to those of the Arctic Ocean. In general, the western channels of the Archipelago contain three water masses. The surface layer has varying characteristics but is generally cold (near the freezing point) and is relatively dilute at the surface. Below 50 meters, salinity increases rapidly

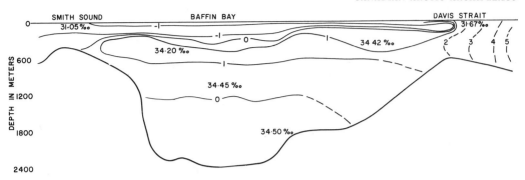

Fig. 2. The vertical distribution of temperature (°C) and salinity (parts per thousand) in Smith Sound, Baffin Bay and Davis Strait, September–October, 1964.

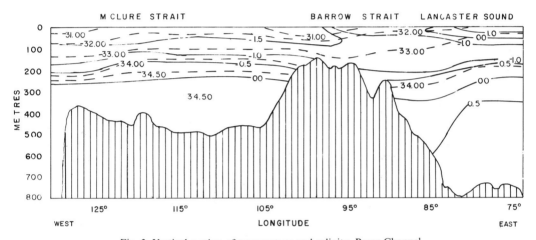

Fig. 3. Vertical section of temperature and salinity, Parry Channel.

through the cold water layer, identified by a range in temperature of −1.2 to −1.4°C and salinity of 32.2–33.5‰ between 70 and 140 meters.

Evidence of the shallow temperature maximum, or Pacific interlayer, at 75 meters described by Worthington (1953) does not appear to any extent in the inshore waters of the western continental shelf; Coachman and Barnes (1961) have shown that this feature is weakest in the region along the western coast of the Canadian Archipelago. Between 150 and 250 meters, there is a uniform increase in temperature and salinity. Below this depth lies the Polar Atlantic water first described by Nansen in 1902. This water mass is defined by a distinct temperature maximum between 400 and 600 meters and is of Atlantic origin. The polar Atlantic water occurs on the western continental shelf between 250 and 1000 meters and may be identified by a temperature maximum of 0.43°C and salinity of 34.9‰ at 500 meters.

In Baffin Bay, on the eastern side of the Archipelago, four water layers can be recognized. In summer, surface water has variable temperatures from −1.0 to 5.0°C and salinity of 30.0–33.5‰.

The surface layer owes its range of characteristics to the local effects of summer heating, winter chilling, and changing ice concentration. Below the surface layer, a distinct cold water mass with temperatures to −1.6°C and salinity less than 33.8‰ occupies the depth interval 50–200 meters. The higher salinity at this depth as compared to water at the same level in the Archipelago or Arctic Ocean indicates that this water does not enter Baffin Bay from the north but must be the result of local weather conditions and the general circulation pattern.

Below 200-meters depth, a warm intermediate layer is defined by temperatures greater than −0.5°C and salinity 34.2–34.5‰. Off Lancaster Sound this layer extends from 200–1000 meters and may have a maximum temperature of 1.0°C at 500 meters. At depths greater than 1000 meters, the temperature decreases to less than −0.5°C, and salinity is practically constant at 34.45‰. This deep Baffin Bay water was thought, at one time, to be formed by freezing at the surface and consequent sinking. However, it is likely that the deep water is of Arctic Ocean origin and enters Baffin

159

Bay as an irregular discharge through Smith Sound. The low oxygen content of the deep Baffin Bay water, 3.6 ml/liter at 2000 meters, indicates that this water does not contribute to the general circulation in the bay and that the renewal of the deep water takes place only at infrequent intervals.

Figure 3 represents a longitudinal section through Parry Channel, the main east-west passage through the Archipelago, illustrating the topographic features of the passage and the vertical distribution of temperature and salinity recorded during the summer months of August and September.

Within the surface layer, Baffin Bay water of temperature greater than $-1.0°C$ and salinity less than $33.5‰$ forms a conspicuous intrusion that extends from Baffin Bay through Lancaster Sound to Barrow Strait. To the west of Barrow Strait cold, less saline water typical of the Arctic Ocean forms the surface layer. At 150-meter depth, temperature and salinity are relatively uniform throughout the channel, while at greater depths, temperature and salinity increase to $0.0°C$ and $34.7‰$ in M'Clure Strait and $0.5°C$ and $34.5‰$ in Lancaster Sound.

An estimate of the net volume transport through the major eastern channels of the Archipelago was made by Kiilerich (1939) in 1928 and by Bailey (1957) in 1954. Additional calculations of the summer flow through Lancaster Sound and Jones Sound based on observations recorded in Lancaster Sound in 1956 and 1957, in Eureka Sound and Parry Channel in 1960 and 1961, and Smith Sound in 1963 were computed and are presented with the previous data in Table 1.

TABLE 1. CALCULATED VOLUME TRANSPORT THROUGH CHANNELS LEADING INTO NORTHERN BAFFIN BAY FOR 1928, 1954, AND DERIVED FROM RECENT DATA (MILLIONS CUBIC METERS PER SECOND)

Section	1928	1954	Recent Data
Lancaster Sound	0.64	1.48	1.00 (1956, 1957)
Jones Sound	0.29	−0.39*	0.27 (1960, 1961)
Smith Sound	0.47	−0.42*	0.28 (1963)
	1.40	0.67	1.55

* The negative sign indicates water movement out of Baffin Bay.

The eastward transport through Jones Sound of 0.27 million m^3/sec was determined from dynamic calculations of the southern transport through Peary Channel and estimates of the southward flow through Eureka Sound based on winter current observations.

Oceanographic observations made in Smith Sound in September 1963 indicate that the movement of water through this channel is not constant but may vary to such an extent that the net

transport is not always in a southerly direction. Results of these observations are presented in Table 2.

TABLE 2. CALCULATED VOLUME TRANSPORT THROUGH SMITH SOUND (MILLION CUBIC METRES PER SECOND)

Date	Volume Transport
Sept. 22, 1963	0.28 southward
Sept. 22, 1963	0.21 southward
Sept. 20, 1963	0.13 northward

These observations indicate that the volume transport from the Arctic Ocean through the Archipelago and Smith Sound may be reasonably estimated at 0.67–1.55 million m^3/sec in the summer months of August and September.

A. E. COLLIN

References

Bailey, W. B., 1957, "Oceanographic features of the Canadian Archipelago," *J. Fisheries Res. Board Canada*, **14**, 731–769.

Coachman, L. K., and Barnes, C. A., 1961, "The contribution of Bering Sea water to the Arctic Ocean," *Arctic*, 14, 147–161.

*Collin, A. E., and Dunbar, M. J., 1964, "Physical oceanography in Arctic Canada," *Oceanogr. Mar. Biol. Ann. Rev.*, **2**, 45–75.

Dunbar, Moira, 1954, "The pattern of ice distribution in Canadian arctic seas," *Trans. Roy. Soc. Canada*, Sect. III, **48**, 9–18.

Kiilerich, A. B., 1939, "A theoretical treatment of the hydrographical observational material," The Godthaab Expedition, 1928, *Medd. Grønland*, 78 (5), 149pp.

Pelletier, B. R., 1962, "Submarine geology program, Polar Continental Shelf Project, Isachsen, District of Franklin," *Geol. Surv.*, Canada, Paper 61–21, 10pp.

Worthington, L. V., 1953, "Oceanographic results of Project Ski Jump I and Ski Jump II in the polar sea, 1951–1952," *Trans. Am. Geophys. Union*, **34**, 543–551.

Part B. Bathymetry and Geology

Bathymetry. The depth of water over the Arctic Continental Shelf is generally deeper than that over the Atlantic Shelf. In the Arctic, the continental shelf consists of two marked physiographic provinces: (1) an inner portion made up mostly of submerged headlands and low-flying coastal and fluvial features and (2) an outer portion consisting of a broad featureless area with local relief varying up to 25 meters (Figs. 1 and 2). The sea floor of the inner portion commences at the seaward tips of the islands and falls gently to a depth of 425 meters approximately where it is terminated by a series of topographic nick points at distances 20–50

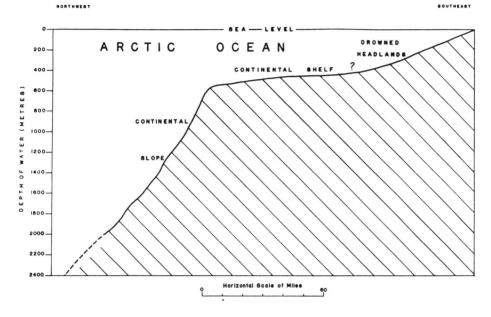

Submarine topographic profile northwesterly from Ellef Ringes Island across the continental shelf.

(Polar Continental Shelf Project.)

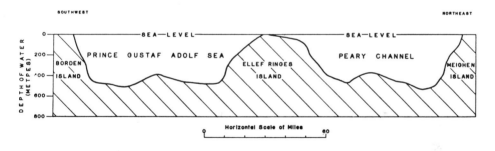

Submarine topographic profile along base-line between Borden and Meighen Islands.

(Polar Continental Shelf Project.)

Fig. 1. Physiographic profiles of the Arctic Continental Shelf and adjacent channels. In the upper figure, a limit of drowned headlands is shown at a depth of about 425 meters. In the lower figure, U-shaped valleys and median ridges of the two main interisland troughs are evident. (For "Ellef Ringes Island", read "Ellef Ringnes Island".)

miles offshore. The sea floor of the outer continental shelf falls away more gradually to the northwest, to a point 100–115 miles offshore where the water is 650 meters deep. Here, the true continental slope begins, marked by a major break in the bathymetric profile.

Depths of water in adjacent western channels of the Arctic Islands are deep (450–550 meters) close to shore, and at the approaches of the Arctic Ocean. Toward the central part of the Archipelago, the channels are shallow and reach a threshold depth of less than 100 meters. Nansen Sound, Sverdrup Channel, Peary Channel, Prince Gustaf Adolf Sea and M'Clure Strait are examples of such bathymetry. Depths of water range from 450–750 meters in the western part, but may shallow to 100 meters near the center of the Arctic Islands. In some cases, submerged longitudinal ridges divide the channels. These ridges rise toward the center of the archipelago where they terminate as islands. Ballantyne and Wilkins Straits are exceptions to this rule in that they have an oceanic and insular portion separated by a submerged transverse ridge, or watershed, at depths which may be less than 50 meters. Along the axes of the channels, small basins occur and, in

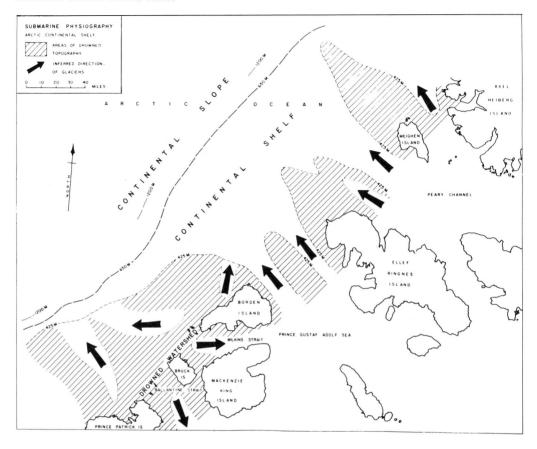

Fig. 2. Interpretation of Arctic physiographic events. Deep troughs separated by median ridges in main channels are evident; also the drowned water shed and the wide area of deep submergence. The general limit of the Continental Slope is consistently 80–110 miles off shore, the outer Continental Shelf varies in width because of the submergence of drowned headlands and other topographic features.

transverse profile, the channels are broadly U-shaped and may be joined by other submerged U-shaped valleys which hang 200 meters above the main floor.

In the eastern part of the Archipelago, water depths and shallow sills occur similar to those in the west. Nares Strait (Fig. 3 a and b) appears to be a long submerged trough characterized by a sill at 100 meters in Kane Basin. From this sill, the sea floor falls away northward to depths of 550 meters at the entrance to the Lincoln Sea on the Arctic Ocean, and southward to 650 meters at the northern entrance to Baffin Bay. The submerged walls of Nares Strait are broken by several submerged U-shaped valleys which hang 200 meters or more above the main floor of the Strait. The main floor is characterized by small elongate basins which resemble a system of paternoster lakes that are common to glaciated valleys.

Jones Sound is about 550 meters in depth, broadly U-shaped in transverse profile, and is characterized by a shoal of less than 100 meters at the western end. Submerged U-shaped valleys adjoin the main valley, where they hang 200–300 meters above its floor. As in several other areas of the Arctic, these submerged valleys can be traced landward to glacial valleys headed by ice caps or barren cirques.

Lancaster Sound is another example of a deep U-shaped trough associated with submerged U-shaped valleys leading into it. Such tributary valleys hang 200–300 meters above the main floor and are traceable to glacial valleys on land which are commonly occupied by glaciers. The north side of Lancaster Sound has undergone some faulting, but such tectonic activity does not appear to have been the major cause of the origin of the Sound.

The origin of the channels of the Arctic Archipelago has been explained by Fortier and Morley (1956). These workers deduced that the channels are a submerged fluvial system that once drained a continuous land mass during pre-Pleistocene times.

Pelletier (1961, 1962, 1963, 1964), Horn (1963), and Marlowe and Vilks (1963) developed this idea further, and showed that this submergence was preceded by glacial action and that modification of the trunk system resulted. This evidence is summed as follows: U-shaped transverse profiles of the interisland channels; hanging U-shaped valley; hummocky terrain in the troughs; possibility that the longitudinal basin in the troughs may be paternoster lakes; cirque-like features in the upland portion of the troughs and tributaries, some of which are submerged; the presence of ice caps at the headward portion of some of the tributaries; the longitudinal profiles of the main floors in which they exhibit a "toeing-up" in the seaward direction together with the possibility of terminal morraines on the floor of the Arctic Ocean at the seaward end of these main channels; submerged faceted spurs occurring between mouths of tributaries; and sills at the mouths of these tributaries.

In Baffin Bay, the bottom slopes from depths of 200–400 meters below sea level in the northern part, where the sea floor is continuous with that of Smith Sound, to depths greater than 2300 meters in the central part of the basin. In the northern area, which extends south from Greenland, the submarine topography is somewhat hilly and resembles a submerged headland previously exposed to subaerial weathering. This submerged headland drops to a regular sloping surface about 140 miles from shore and at depths of 600 meters. Here it merges into a wide terrace which appears to be a true continental shelf.

On the eastern side of Baffin Bay, the continental shelf is dissected by deep sinuous valleys which extend from valleys existing along the western coast of Greenland. Similarly, drowned headlands or interfluvial areas occur between these valleys and are contiguous with similar features on land. A profile drawn along a headland westerly from Greenland (latitude 72°N) shows a hilly topography extending about 70 miles offshore which resembles a drowned headland and which occurs at depths of more than 300 meters. From this point seaward, the topography drops regularly to 400 and 500 meters at a point 140 miles offshore, and then drops rapidly to 2300 meters in the central part of the basin. In the area between the steep slope and the shore, the sinuous valleys occur at depths of 600 meters. The mouths of these valleys merge onto the continental shelf in the vicinity of the upper part of the steep, continental slope.

On the west side of Baffin Bay, the physical situation is similar except that the continental shelf is narrower and contains more morphologically irregular features. These features are traced with some difficulty, by means of bathymetric contours, toward headlands and valleys on the adjacent coast. This area of drowned headlands and valleys extends 5–70 miles offshore, but is generally 20 miles in width on the average. As in the case of the east side these submerged features, which can be traced across the full width of the slope to the headlands and valleys on shore, are truncated at the seaward edge of the shelf by the steep, planar face of the continental slope.

The submarine valleys on both sides of Baffin Bay are U-shaped in profile, have U-shaped hanging tributaries leading in to them, and extend in to valleys on land occupied by glaciers at the valley head. Thus a development of pre-Pleistocene fluvial erosion was followed by valley glaciation which subsequently modified the river valleys into their present forms. Submergence and post-Pleistocene emergence appear to have been the final stages in the physiographic history of these shallow-water areas.

The central area, or basin, of Baffin Bay is approximately 5–10 times the average depth of all the previously discussed channels of the Arctic. Beneath the central part of Baffin Bay, the sea floor is featureless and abyssal in aspect, and bears marked resemblance to a true oceanic basin. This sea floor does not appear to have undergone extensive subaerial erosion. It is bounded on the east and west by steep slopes which, in turn, show no evidence of terrestrial erosion or of the physiographic modifications which are present on the adjacent continental shelves. In fact, these slopes exhibit no evidence of a continuation of the submerged valleys and ridges which occur on the adjacent shelves.

The origin of the central part of Baffin Bay is unknown. However, on the basis of a marked contrast in submarine physiography and bathymetry, it is felt that Baffin Bay has a different origin from the areas underlying the island channels. This origin may be due to some form of rifting, faulting or down-flexuring of the earth's crust. The parallelism of the opposite sites has been discussed by Wegener, Carey, and others. Such tectonic activity may have taken place before the Pleistocene epoch as the basin floor shows no evidence of glacial or terrestrial erosion, and the continental slope shows no extension of the physiographic lineation which occurs on the adjacent continental shelves.

Evidence of vertical crustal movement, exclusive of submergence which has been deduced on physiographic evidence to be about 1200 feet (Pelletier, 1962, 1964), is the presence of raised beaches reported by Craig and Fyles (1960). One of these beaches is dated at 8700 years ± 400 years, B.P.; they occur at elevations up to 800 feet. These facts, together with decrease in elevation of younger beaches in a seaward direction, indicate that the Arctic Islands have been rising continually since about the close of the Pleistocene, i.e., over the last 10,000 years.

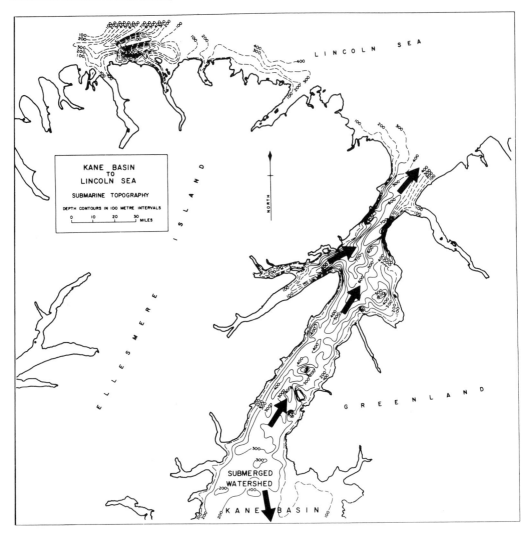

Fig. 3 (a). Submarine topography of upper Nares Strait. Arrows indicate direction of flow of valley glaciers from presumed watershed in Kane Basin. Sea floor drops away to north. Hanging tributaries occur about 200–300 meters above main sea floor. Sills are common at mouths of submerged valleys, and a chain of basins presumed to be former paternoster lakes, occurs down the length of the channel.

Further suggestion of uplift is in the cores obtained from the western channels of the islands. These cores show a coarsening in texture from bottom to top which indicates the general change from quiescence to a hydrological environment of increasing energy. This change may be partly related to the climatic change and partly induced by uplift which in turn produced shoaling conditions in the areas formerly thought to be sites of quieter, deeper-water sedimentation.

Other evidence from the cores, which indicates uplift, is the occurrence of a fauna in the lower part, that formerly existed in areas overlain by fairly deep water; the upper part contains a fauna that presently exists in shallower water. Such diverse faunas are generally zoned a few hundred meters apart vertically although the geographic limits may be of the order of tens of miles.

Sediments. On the Arctic Continental Shelf, sediments consist predominantly of mud and silt, but sand may be present in various areas in amounts up to 100%. This is particularly the case in areas that are underlain by Late Mesozoic and Tertiary sandstones. Generally in areas situated over topographic highs and drowned headlands, the sand content is consistently high. Off the headlands at distances up to 40 miles sand makes up half the sample, and sorting is fair to good. In

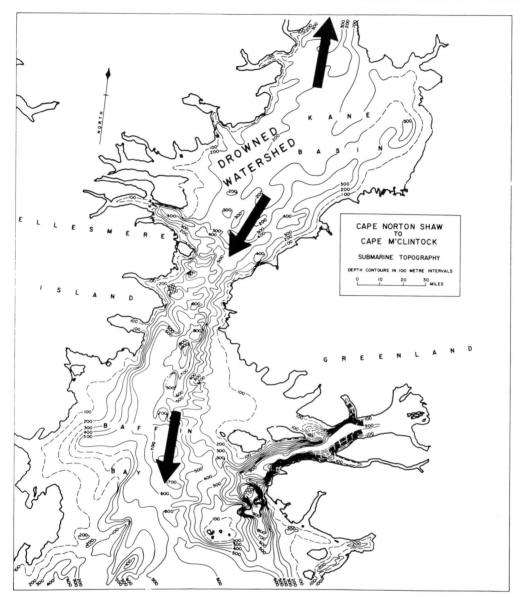

Fig. 3 (b). Submarine topography of lower Nares Strait and northern Baffin Bay. Arrows indicate direction of flow of valley glaciers from presumed watershed in Kane Basin. Note decrease in depth of topography south of watershed, and the hanging tributaries occurring above 200 meters above main submarine floor of Nares Strait.

areas of topographic lows, fine materials have settled and accumulated, and sorting is poor. Over the entire area of the continental shelf, coarse material was deposited from ice and this process is continuing.

Within the western islands, the sediments are generally fine and poorly sorted, except in mid-channel areas and shoals where currents are active and sorting is fair to good. This is described by

Pelletier (1962), Marlowe and Vilks (1963), Horn (1963), Vilks (1964), and Marlowe (1964). Note-worthy is the occurrence of two contrasting sedi-mentary environments: (1) a deltaic type occurring off river mouths, and (2) a non-deltaic type occur-ring in all areas of the island channels within a few miles of shore, and in areas not associated with fluvial deposition. Generally, the deltaic sediments are coarser nearshore and decrease in diameter seaward. They are fairly well sorted and may contain an admixture of windblown sediment. Mostly the sediments are deposited directly from the associated river and may consist chiefly of sand, although fine-grained in an area less than a few hundred feet from shore. About one mile from shore, the sand content is less than 5%. The lithofacies trends of such deposits are generally arcuate about the river mouths, particularly in the area of protected bays. Non-deltaic sediments are generally very fine-grained, poorly sorted, and brought to the area of deposition by longshore currents, ice-rafting, and wind. Very little contribution is received directly from rivers.

In Nares Strait, the mid-channel areas are underlain chiefly by Precambrian granites, gneisses, schists, sandstones and lower Paleozoic carbonates. Here, the sea floor may be barren of sand and finer material due to strong currents. Pebbles of granite were recovered by means of a bottom grabber, and it was generally felt that bedrock was exposed in these areas. In eastern Kane Basin, a layer of morainal material, deposited from the Humboldt Glacier to the east, occurs as a deposit of fairly uniform thickness. It is about 50 feet thick, according to sub-bottom profiles obtained by means of electrical sonic devices. On both sides of the main channels of Nares Strait, sand and silt deposits intermingled with gravel are common.

In the southeastern part of the Arctic Archipelago, the underlying geology consists of metamorphic rocks, granites, and early Paleozoic carbonates. Perry (1961) reports that in this area most of the sea floor is covered with a poorly sorted olive gray material which is generally fine-grained. In the shoals and over sills where currents are stronger than in the deep areas, sand content is higher. Boulders and coarse pebbles are common everywhere, but mostly in nearshore areas, and this is thought to be due to ice rafting. Buckley (1963, 1964) noted the same in Lancaster Sound and showed that, generally, fine sediments accumulated in the central part of the channel.

In Baffin Bay, Trask (1932) found that the texture of the sediments varied with the nature of the submarine topography. Over shoals and steep slopes, the sediments are coarse but in the deep they are fine and consist mostly of mud and silt. Ice-rafted material is also common in this area. Kranck (1964) made the same observation from material collected in Exeter Bay, on the southeast coast of Baffin Island. Here two dominant sedimentary facies persist: (1) an inner-shelf type with heavy mineral assemblages typical of the accessories from the Precambrian metamorphic and igneous rocks on shore, and presumably derived there and (2) an outer-shelf assemblage of carbonate pebbles mainly, which appear to be ice rafted from islands to the north which contain limestone and dolomite. Although ice rafting is dominant,

many authors report the occurrence of frosted grains which are thought to be aeolian in origin.

Foraminifera. Bottom samples taken at various depths over the Arctic Continental Shelf have been examined for foraminiferal content. Wagner (1962, 1964) has made a comparison of such fauna with that from other parts of the Arctic Ocean obtained by other workers such as MacGinitie (1955), Loeblich and Tappan (1953), Green (1959) and Vilks (see Marlowe and Vilks, 1963). The foraminifera assemblages on the Arctic Continental Shelf of Canada are more closely related to those of the Point Barrow area, secondarily with the continental slope and Arctic basin west of the Arctic Islands, and thirdly with the Beaufort–Chukchi Seas. *Trochammina nama* is the only species common to all four areas. Ten species common to the Arctic Shelf have been identified by Vilks in the Prince Gustaf Adolf Sea. Both Wagner and Vilks note that numerically, the arenaceous forms are much more abundant in the inshore waters. Offshore the situation is reversed with only 7 of 86 species being arenaceous. Temperature may be a controlling factor with regard to the marked difference between the faunas of the two areas. Carsola (1952) offers the explanation that low temperature combined with low salinity and high carbon dioxide content may increase the solubility of calcium carbonate, hence the paucity of calcareous forams in the colder nearshore waters.

Wagner has also studied the ecology from the point of view of bathymetry. Relationships of foraminifera are given by Wagner, and it is clear that certain species are common only in areas overlain by deep water. The naming key is as follows:

Species A   *Cribrostomoides crassimargo* (Norman)
      B   *Cribrustomoides jeffreysi* (Williamson)
      C   *Astrononion stellatum* Cushman & Edwards
      D   *Buccella frigida* (Cushman)
      E   *Cassidulina islandica* Norvang
      F   *Cassidulina laevigata* d'Orbigny
      G   *Cassidulina norcrossi* Cushman
      H   *Cassidulina teretis* Tappan
      I   *Cibicides lobatulus* (Walker & Jacob)
      J   *Elphidiella arctica* (Parker & Jones)
      K   *Elphidium bartletti* Cushman
      L   *Elphidium clavatum* Cushman
      M   *Elphidium frigidum* Cushman
      N   *Guttulina* sp.
      O   *Nonion labradoricum* (Dawson)
      P   *Nonionella auricula* Heron-Allen & Earland
      Q   *Oolina costata* (Williamson)
      R   *Protelphidium orbiculare* (Brady)
      S   *Pyrgo williamsoni* (Silvestri)
      T   *Quinqueloculina seminulum* (Linné)
      U   *Cibicides wuellerstorfi* (Schwager)
      V   *Eponides tenera* (Brady)

W *Planispirinoides bucculentus*

X *Quinqueloculina arctica* Cushman

Y *Quinqueloculina* sp. (?=*Q.* sp. of Green, 1959)

Z *Valvulineria horvathi* Green

This key also refers to the discussion of foraminifera in the Hudson Bay approaches (q.v.).

A somewhat finer zonation based on percentage occurrence of the foraminifera is apparent, and is shown in Table 1 where shelf stations (depths less than 604 meters for this study only) are compared with slope stations (depths greater than 604 meters).

TABLE 1

Species	Shelf Stations* (average of 27 stations) (%)	Slope Stations (average of 2 stations) (%)
Cibicides lobatulus	15.3	00.0
?Biloculinella sp.	5.2	1.0
Cassidulina teretis	17.6	4.0
Quinqueloculina sp. A	23.8	13.5
Miliolinella chukchiensis	6.5	00.0
Planispirinoides bucculentus	6.4	00.0
Eponides tenera	8.4	23.5
Globigerina pachyderma	48.9	91.6
Cibicides wuellerstorfi	00.0	1.0

Wagner has also indicated a more detailed zonation for stations on the continental shelf (see Table 2).

TABLE 2

Species	200 meter Depth (2 stations) (%)	200–540 meter Depth (18 stations) (%)	540–694 meter Depth (7 stations) (%)
Cibicides lobatulus	60.4	12.8	8.5
?Biloculinella sp	19.4	1.9	9.6
Cassidulina teretis	4.6	23.9	5.0
Planispirinoides bucculentus	5.2	8.9	0.3
Miliolinella chukchiensis	2.7	7.3	5.3
Quinqueloculina sp. A.	0.0	18.8	43.5

With regard to all stations below a depth of 200 meters, Wagner concludes that type of bottom apparently does not influence the composition of the assemblages, nor does topography, i.e., headland, channel, or level bottom.

Vilks (1963, 1964) has reported on shallow water, nearshore benthos in Prince Gustaf Adolf Sea. With regard to the foraminifera, he notes that the number of individuals per gram of sample

TABLE 3

Zone (m)	Tests/100 g of Sample	Species/Sample
0–30	4620	8
30–60	3740	14
60–90	1400	8
90–120	1820	17
120–150	2680	12
150–180	1810	13
180–210	2310	18
210–240	3570	12
240–300	1100	17

Vilks has also reported his complete faunal list.

increases toward shore, as the number of species per sample decreases. This lack of variation is offset by a larger number of individuals per species, and suggests that the nearshore environment provides more severe conditions. Species that are well adapted to such conditions have a tendency to dominate over other forms. The large number of individuals in the nearshore zone may also show that the area is richer in food, as a result of more intensive photosynthesis taking place in the open shore leads during the summer months. The general trend of abundance shows higher numbers of tests in the shallow zones (see Table 3).

B. R. PELLETIER

References

Buckley, D. E., 1963, "Bottom Sediments of Lancaster Sound, District of Franklin," University of Western Ontario, London, Ontario, M.Sc. Thesis.

Buckley, D. E., 1964, "Mechanical Analysis of Macrascopic Dispersal System of Means of a Settling Tube," Bedford Institute of Oceanography, Dartmouth, N.S., Report B.I.O. 64–2.

Carsola, A. J., 1952. "Marine Geology of the Arctic Ocean and Adjacent Seas off Alaska and Northwestern Canada," University of California, Los Angeles, Doctoral Thesis.

Craig, B. G., and Fyles, J. G., 1960, "Pleistocene geology of Arctic Canada," *Geol. Surv. Canada, Paper 60–10.*

Fortier, Y. O., and Morley, L. W., 1959. "Geological unity of the Arctic Islands," *Trans. Roy. Soc. Can.*, **1**, Ser. 3, Canadian Committee on Oceanography.

Green, K. E., 1959, "Ecology of some Arctic foraminifera," in Scientific Studies at Fletcher's Ice Island, T-3 (1952–1955), U.S.A.F., Cambridge Research Centre, Bedford, Mass., *Geophys. Res. Paper No.* **63**, **1**, 59–81.

Horn, D. R., 1963, "Marine Geology, Peary Channel, District of Franklin, Polar Continental Shelf Project," *Geol. Surv. Can., Paper 63–11.*

Kranck, K. M., 1964, "Sediments of Exeter Bay, District of Franklin," Bedford Institute of Oceanography, Dartmouth, N.S., Report B.I.O. 64–15.

Loebloch, A. R., Jr., and Tappan, Helen, 1953, "Studies of Arctic Foraminifera," *Smithsonian Inst. Misc. Collections*, **121**, No. 7, 1–150, Pls. 1–24.

MacGinitie, G. E., 1955, "Distribution and ecology of the marine invertebrates of Point Barrow, Alaska," *Smithsonian Inst. Misc. Collections*, **128**, No. 9, 1–201.

Marlowe, J. I., 1964, "Marine Geology, Western Part of Prince Gustaf Adolf Sea, District of Franklin (Polar Continental Shelf Project)," Bedford Institute of Oceanography, Dartmouth, N.S., Report B.I.O. 64–9.

Marlowe, J. I., and Vilks, G., 1963, "Marine geology, eastern part of Prince Gustaf Adolf Sea, District of Franklin (Polar Continental Shelf Project)," *Geol. Surv. Can., Paper 62–22.*

Pelletier, B. R., 1961, "Progress report of the Submarine Geology Group, Polar Continental Shelf Project," *Geol. Surv. Can., Topical Report No. 47.*

Pelletier, B. R., 1962, "Submarine Geology Program, Polar Continental Shelf Project, Isachsen, District of Franklin," *Geol. Surv. Can., Paper 61–21.*

Pelletier, B. R., 1963, "Contributions of the Marine Geology Unit of the Geological Survey of Canada to the Polar Continental Shelf Project, District of Franklin, 1962," *Geol. Surv. Can., Topical Report No. 69.*

Pelletier, B. R., 1964, "Development of Submarine Physiography in the Canadian Arctic and its Relation to Crustal Movements," Bedford Institute of Oceanography, Dartmouth, N. S., Report B.I.O. 64–16.

Perry, R. B., 1961, "A Study of the marine sediments of the Canadian Eastern Arctic Archipelago," *Fisheries Res. Bd. Canada, MS Report No. 89*, 89pp.

Trask, P. D., 1932, "Origin and Environment of Source Sediments of Petroleum," Houston, Texas, Gulf Pub. Company, 323pp.

Vilks, G., 1964, "Foraminiferal Study of East Bay, MacKenzie King Island, District of Franklin (Polar Continental Shelf Project)," Bedford Institute of Oceanography, Dartmouth, N.S., Report B.I.O. 64–4.

Wagner, F. J. E., 1962, "Faunal Report, Submarine Geology Program, Polar Continental Shelf Project, Isachsen, District of Franklin," *Geol. Surv. Can., Paper 61–27.*

Wagner, F. J. E., 1964, "Faunal Report—II, Marine Geology Program, Polar Continental Shelf Project, Isachsen, District, of Franklin," Bedford Institute of Oceanography, Dartmouth, N.S., Report B.I.O. 64–1.

CANARIES CURRENT

The Canaries Current is a cool current which represents a southerly branch of the North Atlantic Current, swinging south off the continental shelf of northwestern Europe, leading to frequent sea fogs off northwestern Spain and the coast of Portugal (especially when offshore winds lead to upwelling), and then on past the Canary Islands and Northwest Africa. It helps to cool the Canaries which consequently enjoy a "mediterranean" climate in the latitude of the Sahara. It eventually joins the North Equatorial Current. According to Sverdrup (1942), the water transport of the Canaries Current is about 16 million m³/sec.

The surface current usually has speeds less than 10 cm/sec, but the speeds and directions are variable due to changes in winds. Below 1000 m the current shows a well-defined pattern with speeds of 3–6 cm/sec north of Madeira and flows southward and then southwestward south of the Canaries. A great part of the deep water does not join the North Equatorial Current but flows southerly off the African Coast. Measurements with neutrally buoyant floats at 1900 m north of the Canaries have shown that the current is divergent and a part of the current flows northeast.

RHODES W. FAIRBRIDGE
TAKASHI ICHIYE

References

Defant, A., 1936, "Schichtung and Zirkulation des Atlantischen Ozeans. Die Troposphäre," *Wiss. Erg. Deutsch. Atlant. Exp. "Meteor" 1925–27*, **6**(1), 289–411.

Defant, A., 1941, "Quantitative Untersuchungen zur Statik und Dynamik des Atlantischen Ozeans," Part 5, "Die absolute Topographie des physikalischen Meeresniveaus und der Druckflächen, sowie die Wasserbewegungen im Atlantischen Ozean," 260pp.

Schott, G., 1942, "Geographie des Atlantischen Ozeans," Third ed., Hamburg, Boysen, 438pp.

Sverdrup, H. U., Johnson, M. W., and Fleming, R. H., 1942, "The Oceans: Their Physics, Chemistry and General Biology," New York, Prentice-Hall, Inc., 1087pp.

Swallow, J. C., 1957, "Some further deep current measurements using neutrally-buoyant floats," *Deep-Sea Res.*, **4**, 99–104.

Trewartha, G. T., 1961, "The Earth's Problem Climates," Madison, University of Wisconsin Press, 334pp.

Cross-references: *Atlantic Ocean; Oceanic Circulation.*

CAPILLARITY, CAPILLARY WAVE

Capillary force is commonly known as *surface tension*. It is often observed in liquids in narrow tubes and is responsible for the meniscus on the liquid; the meniscus is convex up against dry walls, but convex down for wet walls. Capillarity (capillary fringe) is particularly important in soil science (see pr. Vol. IV).

A *capillary wave* or *ripple* is one of such short wavelength that its restoring force is surface tension. On a free surface, the phase speed C of such waves decreases with increasing wavelength:

$$C = \sqrt{2\pi \, T/\rho L}$$

where the surface is T, the density ρ and wavelength L. In the case of a water-air surface, the wave of period 1 m/sec has a wavelength of 0.04 cm. Since the period of gravity waves increases with wavelength, a wave subject to both gravity and surface tension has a minimum period (phase speed) of 23.2 cm/sec.

RHODES W. FAIRBRIDGE

References

Baver, L. D., 1956, "Soil Physics," Third ed., New York, John Wiley & Sons, 489pp.

Deacon, E. L., and Webb, E. K., 1962, "Small-scale Interactions," in (Hill, M. N., editor) "The Sea," pp. 43–87, New York, Interscience Publishers.

Dietrich, G., 1963, "General Oceanography," New York, Interscience Publishers, 588pp. (translated by F. Ostapoff).

Huschke, R. E., 1959, "Glossary of Meteorology," Boston, American Meteorological Society, 638pp.

Kazmann, R. G., 1965, "Modern Hydrology," New York, Harper and Row, 301pp.

CARBON CYCLE (ORGANIC) IN THE OCEANS

The cycle of organic carbon in the sea begins with photosynthetic production in the surface layers (upper 2%) where there is appreciable light. Only about 1/1000 part of the sunlight striking the sea is effectively used. This low efficiency is due to much of the light being absorbed by the water rather than the phytoplankton. Also growth is frequently prevented by lack of other nutrients, principally nitrogen and phosphorous. Thus only about one-tenth of the 22 mg/liter of inorganic carbon can be converted to living material. This is in sharp contrast to the land where the concentration of nutrients in the soil is more than 10^4 times greater.

In the average marine situation, most of the current photosynthetic product is rapidly oxidized biologically back to inorganic carbon. This includes respiration of the plant itself, of some animal higher in the food chain, or of bacteria decomposing either of them. A fraction of the organic carbon leaks from organisms and becomes part of the sizable pool of dissolved organic carbon. A smaller fraction becomes relatively undigestible particulate detritus which floats about for many

years before being deposited in the sediments. A resistant fraction of this escapes bacterial oxidation and, during subsequent diagenesis, forms at least part of the starting material of petroleum. This is more important in shallow seas where productivity is high and therefore the amount of falling detritus is greater. The more rapid sedimentation here also buries it before it can be oxidized.

In no case is there more than a sketchy insight into the interlocking prey-predator relationships, nutrient dependence, and other factors pertinent to an understanding of life in the sea. For instance, it is not surprising that most life is concentrated near the sea surface where all of the primary production is. But the diurnal difference is large since many animals migrate down hundreds of meters away from the light during the day. We have no satisfactory explanation for even this major feature of life in the sea.

Since production occurs entirely in the lighted surface layer, it is not surprising that the concentration of living organic matter is greater there. Even in this upper hundred meters it is rarely more than 1–10 ppm of the seawater.

Below this (depths of 100–1000 m) live populations of animals which either feed on the material falling from above or rise to the surface nightly to feed (scattering layers). The density of these animals is down by 1–2 orders of magnitude over the surface. They may constitute only 10–100 ppb of the water.

In the great mass of water below this (which makes up 80–90% of the oceans), the occurrence of living things is reduced again by a similar amount (.1–1 ppb). Here animals become really rare, and evolution has had to face, in addition to problems of high pressure and food scarcity, the difficulty of male and female finding each other for mating.

Population density figures from the deep sea are difficult to obtain because nets can only be towed slowly at great depth. It takes a long time to sieve

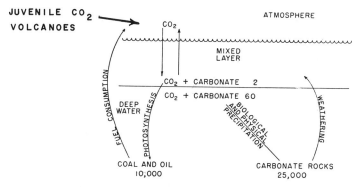

Fig. 1. Diagram abstracted from Redfield to show that large amounts of CO_2 have moved through the ocean-atmosphere system in geological time. The quantities are expressed on the basis of atmospheric CO_2 equals 1.

enough of the rare animals, and many of the faster species may escape the net.

The oxygen content of the deep water provides a rough check on these low population estimates. We find that $\frac{1}{3}-\frac{2}{3}$ of this gas is consumed by the respiration of organisms while it is at depth. Thus the 5–7 ml/liter of oxygen must be more than enough to support the meager deep population for the 500–1000 years that we know has been its residence time. We can assume an average picture (from plankton tows) of a 1-gram crustacean occupying a volume of 10^3 m^3. With a reasonable respiratory rate it would consume this amount of oxygen in about 1000 years. There clearly can not be a 10 times high population density since all of the deep water would have become anaerobic before it returned again to the surface.

Along with the living organisms is a fine particulate organic fraction already mentioned. It is highly decay resistant since the total amount in the water column is more than can be accounted for, even if all of the surface productivity was channeled into this form for many years. In all but the surface layer, this particulate fraction contains about 10% of the organic carbon that is in a truly dissolved form.

The amount of this dissolved organic carbon has been shown to have surprisingly little concentration variation in all but the rich surface layers. It occurs at a level of about 1 ppm even in the deep oceans. Thus the average water column contains some 5 kg of reduced carbon per square meter. This huge reservoir represents 25–100 years of total surface productivity so its turnover time must be much longer than this (hundreds of years). Carbon dating may clarify this. It is tempting to speculate that this material is important ecologically as a source of heterotrophic nutrition. Some of the flocculent material may be formed from surface active components in the dissolved organic pool. through the action of bubbles at the surface.

The rate of deposition plus the amount of organic material in the sediment gives the rate at which carbon is being removed from the water above. This amounts to 0.1% of surface productivity or 1 part in 10^6 of the sun's energy reaching the sea. Knowledge of petroleum reserves, however, shows that most of the deposited organic carbon is digested. Only 1 part in 10^4 of it appears to be going into eventual petroleum. We are now extracting oil some 10^5 times faster than it is being deposited. The total deposits of oil, however, contain 10^4 times the carbon now present as CO_2 in air. It appears that some source of juvenile carbon is continually entering the geochemical system to be ultimately removed as oil (plus coal) and carbonates). Man's increasingly rapid use of fossil fuels has temporarily reversed the process.

JOHN KANWISHER

References

*Basse, K., 1964, "On the vertical distribution of zooplankton in the sea," in "Progress in Oceanography," Vol. II, New York, Pergamon Press.

Brancazio, P. J., and Cameron, A. G. W., 1964, "The Origin and Evolution of Atmospheres and Oceans," New York, John Wiley & Sons, 326pp.

Emery, K. O., 1963, "Oceanographic factors in the accumulation of petroleum," *Proc. World Petrol. Congr. Proc. 6th*, 1–7.

Kanwisher, J. W., 1963, "Effect of wind on CO_2 exchange across the sea surface," *J. Geophys. Res.*, **68**, 3921–3927.

Menzel, D. W., 1964, "The distribution of dissolved organic carbon in the western Indian Ocean," *Deep Sea Res.*, **11**, 757–765.

Ryther, J. H., 1963, "Geophysical Variations in Productivity," in (Hill, M. N. editor) "The Sea," Ch. 17, New York, Interscience Publishers.

Cross-references: *Chemical Oceanography*, Vol. II; *Greenhouse Effect*.

CARBON DIOXIDE CYCLE IN THE SEA AND ATMOSPHERE

In the natural cycle of carbon, carbon dioxide is the most important compound because of its stability and distribution among gaseous, aqueous and solid phases of the earth. Carbon dioxide gas from the atmosphere is continuously transferred into the biosphere by photosynthesis but is, at the same time, replenished by the oxidation of organic debris and by the respiration of animals. Atmospheric carbon dioxide is in direct communication with the dissolved carbon dioxide in the hydrosphere via molecular exchange through the interfaces between those reservoirs. The dissolved carbon dioxide in the hydrosphere may have been transferred from the atmosphere, having been produced from the oxidation of organic carbon by biogenic and non-biogenic processes, or having originated from the dissolving of carbonates. In short, carbon dioxide is a medium for the transportation and exchange of carbon in its dynamic natural cycle. That carbon dioxide plays such a significant role may be understood by considering (a) its wide range of thermodynamic stabilities in nature, particularly in the highly oxidizing atmosphere, (b) its participation in photosynthesis, (c) its high solubility in seawater and its mobility with the ocean currents, and (d) its rapid diffusion in the atmosphere. No other carbon compound abundant in nature possesses such chemical and physical characteristics. The estimated mass of each carbon reservoir in nature is summarized in Table 1. It is seen that the lithosphere is the largest reservoir of all and has 660 times the mass of CO_2 in the hydrosphere, 3200 times that in the biosphere, and 3800 times that in the atmosphere. Therefore, the CO_2 content in the atmosphere, the smallest of all the carbon reservoirs, may be strongly influenced

TABLE 1. CARBON RESERVOIRS IN NATURE

Reservoirs	Mass as CO_2 (10^{18} g)	References
Atmosphere (CO_2 gas)	2.41	Takahashi (1961)
Hydrosphere		
Total inorganic in ocean ($CO_3^=$, HCO_3^-, $MgHCO_3^+$, etc.)	130	Sverdrup *et al.* (1942)
Dissolved organic matter in ocean	10	Goldschmidt (1954)
Lithosphere		
Carbonate rocks ($CaCO_3$ etc.)	67,000	Rubey (1951)
Organic carbon in rocks (bitumen, coal, oil, etc.)	25,000	Rubey (1951)
Biosphere		
Terrestrial living organisms	0.3	Revelle and Suess (1957)
Terrestrial organic debris	2.6	Rubey (1951)
Marine organisms	0.03	Revelle and Suess (1957)
Marine organic sediments	3.5	Trask (1939)

by slight changes in the dynamic balance between the reservoirs.

Since the end of World War II, the study of the carbon cycle in nature has attracted increasingly more attention due to its significances in meteorological, geological, biological, and oceanographic problems. A change in the CO_2 concentration in the atmosphere could appreciably affect the thermal budget of the surface of the earth, and might cause a long-term change in the weather and climate due to the "greenhouse effect" (q.v.). A change in the atmospheric CO_2 concentration could not only have a far-reaching effect on the climate, but also on biological productivity, on various geological phenomena such as rate of erosion, and on the chemical properties of ocean water. A study of the dynamic carbon cycle requires an extensive knowledge of the mechanisms and rates of carbon exchange between the reservoirs, their capacities and the distribution of carbon within them. However, not all of those factors are known on a worldwide scale with desirable certainty. In the succeeding pages, the present status of our knowledge and current research approaches will be discussed.

Distribution of CO_2 in the Atmosphere

Since the 1800's the CO_2 concentrations in the atmosphere have been investigated by many workers using a variety of analytical means. A majority of the data falls between 270 and 350 ppm by volume (1 ppm$=10^{-4}\%$, therefore 270 ppm$=0.027\%$). Local variations ranging between 250 and 600 ppm or higher have been reported. Most of those samples collected before 1958 were from the ground level on the European continent not far from various sources of human activities or from active photosynthesis, and may not be representative samples for the air over the whole

earth. In addition, the lack of interlaboratory calibrations for the analyses caused a serious difficulty in utilizing those data for the estimation of the mean atmospheric CO_2 concentration and its variation through time.

The International Geophysical Year, 1957–1958, provided an excellent opportunity for initiating a well-coordinated worldwide survey of the atmospheric CO_2 concentration. Supported by funds from the National Science Foundation and the U.S. Weather Bureau, four fixed stations equipped with precision infrared gas analyzers (accuracy = ± 0.3 ppm CO_2) were established under the supervision of C. D. Keeling at widely separated locations and altitudes along the 160°W longitude in both the northern and southern hemispheres. Those are at Point Barrow (elevation$=2$ meters), Alaska; Mauna Loa (elevation$=3500$ meters), Hawaii; Little America (elevation$=10$ meters), Antarctica; and the South Pole (elevation$= 3000$ meters), all of which are far from major industrial activities and free from local contaminations. To supplement those fixed stations, worldwide air sampling was conducted from oceanographic vessels and weather observation aircrafts.

Based upon the data thus obtained, Bolin and Keeling (1963) reported that the worldwide average of the atmospheric CO_2 concentrations was 314.5 ppm as of January, 1960, and increasing with a rate of 0.72 ppm annually. It has also been found that a geographical variation does not exceed 6 ppm, the maximum being in the northern high latitudes and the minimum being in the southern high latitudes.

The annual rate of CO_2 production by combustion of fossil fuel was approximately 0.01×10^{18} grams for 1960. This would cause an annual increase of 1.3 ppm in the atmospheric CO_2 concentration if all the fossil fuel CO_2 remained

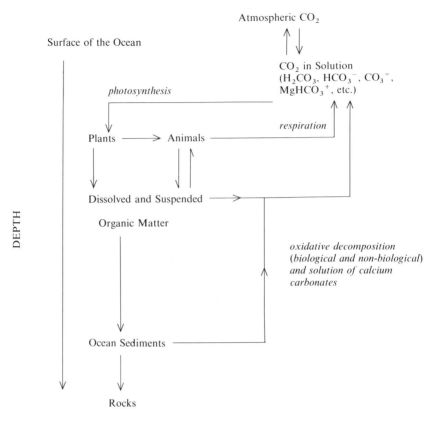

Fig. 1. The CO_2 cycle in the oceanic system.

in the atmosphere. The observed annual increment is only about half of this value, and it, therefore, implies that a portion of the fossil fuel CO_2 is being absorbed by other carbon reservoirs. Riley (1953) has estimated the rate of CO_2 consumption by photosynthesis is $0.08 \pm 0.02 \times 10^{18}$ g CO_2/yr on land and $0.43 \pm 0.30 \times 10^{18}$ g CO_2/yr in the sea. Since both the rate of photosynthesis and storage of carbon in the form of humus are being reduced because of the clearing of forests and cultivation of farm land, it is unlikely that the land vegetation and its debris can be capable of accommodating the fossil fuel CO_2 being added to the atmosphere at an ever increasing rate. However, the observed rate of increase in the atmospheric CO_2 may be accounted for by the large storage capacity of the ocean.

CO_2 Cycle in the Sea

Being a melting pot of large-scale biochemical and inorganic processes, the ocean encompasses a multitude of complexities in its dynamic regulation of CO_2. Near the surface of the ocean, photosynthesis by marine plants and the formation of calcium carbonate by plants and animals remove the dissolved CO_2 from the seawater (Fig. 1). To compensate for this loss, atmospheric CO_2 diffuses

through the atmosphere-ocean interface into the surface water of the ocean at a rate comparable to the photosynthetic consumption. The quantity of CO_2 supplied by river water to the ocean is probably on the order of 1/500 of the photosynthetic consumptions by marine plants and may be neglected for the following discussions.

At greater depths of the ocean where photosynthesis diminishes due to the limited penetration of the solar radiation, CO_2 can be produced from the decomposition of suspended organic matter by bacterial activities utilizing dissolved oxygen in the water. This view is substantiated by the observed increase in CO_2 content and decrease in O_2 content with depth, and also by the scarcity of organic carbon in the deep ocean sediments. An increase in CO_2 in the deep water would, in turn, increase the solubility of $CaCO_3$ in the seawater, and consequently the skeletons of calcareous organisms formed in the surface water would be partially or entirely dissolved during their descent to the bottom of the sea Since biological productivity depends largely on the availability of nutrients such as phosphates which are supplied by deep water swelling upward to the surface, the biological consumption of CO_2 from the seawater depends strongly on the circulation rate and pattern of the ocean water. The solubility of CO_2 in seawater is also a sensitive function of temperature and pressure, both of which vary widely with depth and geographical locations. Since those factors critical for the consumption and retention of CO_2 in the oceanic system are controlled by the lateral and vertical circulation of the ocean water, the atmospheric CO_2 contents are eminently affected by the circulation rate of the ocean water, particularly the turnover time of the deep water which contains a large quantity of dissolved CO_2.

Chemistry of CO_2 in the Seawater and Exchange of CO_2 between the Atmosphere and the Sea

When CO_2 gas is equilibrated with a given quantity of aqueous solution, it reacts with water and forms carbonic acid. The solution would exert a finite equilibrium partial pressure of CO_2, which is, in turn, in balance with the ionic species such as HCO_3^- and $CO_3^=$ as specified by the thermodynamic constants. The reactions may be written in simplified form as:

$$CO_2 \text{ (gas)} + H_2O \text{ (liquid)} \overset{K_1}{\rightleftharpoons} H^+ + HCO_3^-$$

$$HCO_3^- \overset{K_2}{\rightleftharpoons} H^+ + CO_3^=$$

and with a presence of calcium ions, as:

$$Ca^{++} + CO_3^= \overset{K_3}{\rightleftharpoons} CaCO_3 \text{ (calcite or aragonite)}$$

The equilibrium constants at standard conditions, 1 atm and 25°C, are: $K_1 = 1.10 \times 10^{-7}$, $K_2 = 4.84 \times 10^{-11}$, K_3 (aragonite) $= 1.45 \times 10^8$ and K_3 (calcite) $= 2.12 \times 10^8$. These reactions would be shifted to the left when (1) the H^+ concentrations are increased, (2) the temperature of solution is increased, (3) the CO_2 is extracted from the solution, and the CO_2 partial pressure is reduced. In other words, the solubility of CO_2 in solution would be increased with decreasing temperature, increasing pressure and/or increasing alkalinity.

Although such simplified chemical equations could provide qualitative explanations, they fail to yield quantitative information on the chemical behavior of CO_2 in seawater. Average seawater, which contains 3.5 weight % of electrolytes, equivalent of an ionic strength of 0.7, may not be treated as a simple ideal solution, since it may contain appreciable quantities of various complex ions in addition to the simple ionic species described above. Garrels and Thompson (1962) have made a detailed experimental study of the carbonate chemistry in nonideal solutions similar to seawater and discovered that the cations ordi-

narily present in seawater, particularly Mg ions, form stable carbonate and bicarbonate ion complexes such as $MgHCO_3^+$ and $MgCO_3^0$. Because of the formation of such complex ions, 81% of $CO_3^=$ and 31% of HCO_3^- in solution exist as complex ions under standard condition, and therefore, the unusually large solubilities of $CaCO_3$ and CO_2 in seawater can be quantitatively explained.

When a portion of the CO_2 dissolved in seawater is consumed by photosynthesis, the CO_2 partial pressure over the water would be reduced below the atmospheric values, and therefore, the atmospheric CO_2 would be absorbed by the seawater to restore the equilibrium. Seawater would also absorb the atmospheric CO_2 as its CO_2 partial pressure is lowered by cooling, which would cause a reduction of 12×10^{-6} atm/°C in average seawater having 2.0 millimoles CO_2/liter and 8.0 pH at 25°C. Buch (1939), the father in the field of CO_2 chemistry of seawater, found from the direct measurements at sea that the average CO_2 partial pressure in the North Atlantic surface water was some 5% lower than that in the atmosphere, indicating the absorption of the atmospheric CO_2 by the seawater. The CO_2 partial pressures in the Atlantic surface water were measured by Takahashi (1961) on an extensive traverse from Greenland to the Antarctica during the International Geophysical Year. It was found that waters north of the equator and south of 35°S had lower CO_2 partial pressures than those of the atmosphere, indicating that those areas of the Atlantic were absorbing CO_2 from the atmosphere.

The rate of the CO_2 exchange between the atmosphere and ocean has been investigated by using the natural carbon isotopes, C^{12}, C^{13} and C^{14}, as well as the C^{14} produced by the thermonuclear explosions. Craig (1957) assumed a steady state in the distribution of radioactive C^{14} in the carbon reservoirs and estimated the average annual exchange flux of CO_2 into the sea to be 0.32×10^{18} grams CO_2, which is consistent with the estimated rate for CO_2 consumption by marine photosynthesis. Broecker et al. (1960) made an extensive survey of the distribution of carbon isotopes in the Atlantic Ocean and the atmosphere and discussed the rate of large scale ocean circulations and the fluctuation of the atmospheric CO_2 concentrations in the past 2000 years due to a non-steady state circulation of seawater. If the turnover rate of ocean water had changed in the last 2000 years, the concentration of the atmospheric CO_2, and consequently the isotopic composition of the atmospheric CO_2, should be altered because of the differences in the carbon isotope ratios of the CO_2 in the atmosphere and the ocean. Assuming that the C^{14}/C^{12} ratios in the annual growth rings of trees represent those of the atmospheric CO_2, the ratios in each tree ring indicate isotopic variation in the atmosphere through time. The observed constancy in the C^{14}/C^{12} ratios in tree rings throughout the past 2000 years suggests that the ocean circulation has been in a steady state since then, with a mean residence time of 650 years for the Atlantic deep water and 800 years for the Pacific deep water. The annual CO_2 flux into the ocean from the atmosphere has been estimated to be $0.49 \pm 0.14 \times 10^{18}$ grams, a value consistent with the photosynthetic consumption of CO_2 in seawater.

The CO_2 Theory of the Origin of Ice Ages

The effect of atmospheric CO_2 on the heat balance of the earth's atmosphere has been discussed as early as 1861 by Tyndall (1861) and many others. Considering such an effect, Chamberlin (1899) was the first one to suggest that the fluctuation of the atmospheric CO_2 content might cause ice ages. Based upon an experimental study on the absorption spectrum of CO_2 in the infrared region, Plass (1956a) calculated that, if the atmospheric CO_2 was reduced to half of the present value, the surface temperature of the earth would fall by $3.8°C$. Plass (1956b) further considered that if a large quantity of CO_2 was rapidly removed from the atmosphere by photosynthesis and locked into ground as peat or coal, the atmospheric CO_2 concentration might be reduced considerably thus causing a much colder climate. Large ice caps could form and cover large areas on the high latitudes of the both northern and southern hemispheres, and thus an ice age could be started. The formation of the ice caps would reduce the volume of the ocean water which, with growth of the ice caps, would eventually become supersaturated with CO_2. The excess oceanic CO_2 would then be released to the atmosphere in the process of restoring the chemical equilibrium. Consequently, the atmospheric CO_2 concentration should rise, resulting in warmer climate, i.e., the interglacial period. Because of this warmup, the ice caps covering a large area of the continents would gradually disappear, and the water from the melting ice would increase the volume of the ocean. The ocean would thus be diluted with fresh water from the ice, become undersaturated with respect to CO_2, and start absorbing CO_2 from the atmosphere, restoring the cold trend and starting another ice age. The four successive ice ages during the Pleistocene time may be explained by assuming an appropriate rate of ocean water turnover.

Plass' theory is attractive because (1) it assumes as a triggering mechanism the removal of the atmospheric CO_2 by the chemical erosion of a newly formed mountain range and/or the burials of a large quantity of plant materials, both of which are geologically plausible and (2) it explains the interglacial periods and successive ice ages by the dynamic balance of CO_2 between the atmo-

sphere and ocean water. It also predicts that there would be no possible stable state for the climate when the total CO_2 in the atmosphere–ocean system is reduced below a critical value. However, a seawater supersaturated with respect to CO_2 is impossible because of the $CaCO_3$ buffer (Revelle and Fairbridge, 1957). Furthermore, a recent work by Möller (1963) suggests that the effect of CO_2 on the earth's climate is less than half of the Plass' estimate, and a slight change in cloudiness would completely mask the effect of CO_2. Eriksson (1963) has calculated the effect of temperature and volume of the ocean water on the total content of CO_2 in ocean, and concluded that neither factor within its possible range of variation could affect the atmospheric CO_2 content to the extent of climatic importance. Nevertheless, our knowledge of the turnover rate of deep ocean water and of the chemistry and concentrations of CO_2 in deep water is rather limited at present, and further research is needed in order to discuss the CO_2 in deep ocean water more confidently.

Taro Takahashi

References

Bolin, B., and Keeling, C. D., 1963, "Large-scale atmospheric mixing as deduced from the seasonal and meridional variation of carbon dioxide," *J. Geophys. Res.*, **68**, 3899–3920.

Broecker, W. S., Gerard, R., Ewing, M., and Heezen, B. C., 1960, "Natural radiocarbon in the Atlantic Ocean," *J. Geophys. Res.*, **65**, 2903–2932.

Buch, K., 1939, "Kohlensäure im Atmosphäre und Meer an der Grenze zum Arktikum," *Acta Acad. Aboensis, Math. Phys.*, **11**, No. 12.

Chamberlin, T. C., 1899, "An attempt to frame a working hypothesis of the cause of glacial periods on an atmospheric asis," *J. Geol.*, **7**, 545–584, 667–685, 751–787.

Craig, H., 1957, "The natural distribution of radiocarbon and the exchange time of carbon dioxide between atmosphere and sea," *Tellus*, **9**, 1–17.

Eriksson, Erik, 1963, "Possible fluctuations in atmospheric carbon dioxide due to changes in the properties of the sea," *J. Geophys. Res.*, **68**, 3871–3876.

Garrels, R. M., and Thompson, M. E., 1962, "A chemical model for sea water at 25°C and one atmosphere total pressure," *Am. J. Sci.*, **260**, 55–66.

Goldschmidt, V. M., 1954, "Geochemistry," pp. 1–730, London, Oxford University Press.

Harvey, H. W., 1957, "The Chemistry and Fertility of Sea Waters," pp. 1–234, Cambridge, The University Press.

Hutchinson, G. E., 1954, "The biochemistry of the terrestrial atmosphere," in (Kuiper, editor) "The Earth as a Planet," pp. 371–433.

Möller, F., 1963, "On the influence of changes in the CO_2 concentration in air on the radiation balance of the Earth's surface and on the climate," *J. Geophys. Res.*, **68**, 3877–3886.

Plass, G. N., 1956a, "The influence of the 15μ carbon dioxide band on the atmospheric infra-red cooling rate," *Quart. J. Roy. Meteorol. Soc.*, **82**, 310–324.

Plass, G. N., 1956b, "Carbon dioxide and the climate," *Am. Scientist*, **44**, 302–316.

Revelle, R., and Fairbridge, R., 1957, "Carbonates and carbon dioxide: Treatise on marine ecology and paleoecology," Vol. 1, *Geol. Soc. Am. Mem.* 67, 239–295.

Revelle, R., and Suess, H. E., 1957, "Carbon dioxide exchange between atmosphere and ocean and the question of an increase in atmospheric CO_2 during the past decades," *Tellus*, **9**, 18–27.

Rubey, W. W., 1951, "Geologic history of sea water," *Bull. Geol. Soc. Am.*, **62**, 1111–1148.

Sverdrup, H. U., Johnson, M. W., and Fleming, R. H., 1942, "The Oceans," pp. 1–1087, Eaglewood Cliffs, N.J., Prentice-Hall.

Takahashi, T., 1961, "Carbon dioxide in the atmosphere and in Atlantic Ocean water," *J. Geophys. Res.*, **66**, 477–494.

Trask, P. D., 1939, "Recent Marine Sediments," pp. 1–428, Tulsa.

Tyndall, J., 1861, "On the absorption and radiation of heat by gases and vapours, and on the physical connection of radiation, absorption and conduction," *Phil. Mag.*, **22**, Ser. 4, 169–194, 273–285.

CARIBBEAN CURRENT

The Caribbean Current is a powerful warm current setting westward through the Caribbean Sea, formed from the junction of the North Equatorial Current and the *Guiana Current* (q.v.). With increasing velocity it passes through the Caribbean and the Yucatan Channel to form the Florida Current and thus contributes importantly to the Gulf Stream (see also *Caribbean Sea*).

The maximum flow is about 200–300 km north of the Venezuelan coast, most of it entering the Caribbean in the straits north and south of St. Lucia. Its main stream crosses the Jamaica Ridge southwest of Jamaica, turns west in the Cayman Basin and then north again to pass through the Yucatan Strait, thus following generally the line of maximum depths. Mean velocities are of the order of 0.7–0.8 knot (38–43 cm/sec), with peak flows up to 2.7 knots. Flow decreases with depth, being only 5 cm/sec at over 1500 m in the deep basins. The transport is about 30 million m^3/sec (for further details, see *Caribbean Sea*).

RHODES W. FAIRBRIDGE

References

Dietrich, G., 1939, "Das Amerikanische Mittelmeer: Ein Meereskundlicher Uberlick," *Z. Ges. Erdkunde Berlin*, 3/4, 108–130.

Wüst, G., 1963, "On the stratification and the circulation in the cold water sphere of the Antillean-Caribbean basins," *Deep-Sea Res.* **10**, No. 3, 165–187.

Wüst, G., 1964, "Stratification and Circulation in the Antillean-Caribbean Basins," Pt. 1, VEMA Series II, pp. 1–201, New York, Columbia University Press.

CARIBBEAN SEA—OCEANOGRAPHY

The Caribbean, or Central American Sea, is one of the many marginal seas of the world which has an island arc structure as a section of its boundary —in this case, the Antillean chain, which is divided in two parts, the Greater and Lesser Antilles. The Greater Antilles is made up of three large islands which form the northern boundary of the Caribbean, Cuba, Hispaniola and Puerto Rico, and a fourth, Jamaica, which lies south of Cuba. To the east of Puerto Rico are the Virgin Islands and the Anegada or Jungfern Passage, which separates the Greater from the Lesser Antilles. The latter are made up of many small islands which follow an arc running southeast from the Anegada Passage turning south, to join the continental shelf of South America, and form the eastern boundary of the Caribbean Sea. The major islands of this chain are Guadeloupe, Martinique, St. Lucia and Barbados. The principal arc is volcanic, but an outer arc in the southeast runs through Barbados and Tobago to join up with Trinidad and the east-west chains of Venezuela. According to the International Hydrographic Bureau (*Sp. Publ.* 28, 1953), the Caribbean may be taken to include the Lesser Antilles completely, and is limited on the north by a line joining the Greater Antilles and Yucatan.

The southern boundary of the Caribbean Sea is the northern coast of the South American countries of Venezuela and Colombia. The Isthmus of Panama forms the rest of the southern boundary. The east coast of Central America follows a zigzag boundary, Honduras forming the first step and Yucatan the second. The 220-km Yucatan Strait, separating Cuba from the northeastern tip of Yucatan, forms the boundary between the Caribbean Sea and the Gulf of Mexico.

The upper 2000 m of the Caribbean Sea have access to the waters of the Atlantic Ocean through numerous passages. The total area is 2,640,000 km^2. The greatest depth is slightly over 7100 m in the Cayman Trench. The major basins are from east to west: Grenada (>3000 m), Venezuela (>5000 m), Colombia (>4000 m), Cayman (>6000 m) and the Yucatan (>5000 m). There are minor basins such as the Virgin Islands Basin, the Dominican Trench and the anaerobic Cariaco Trench (Richards and Vaccaro, 1956). The average depth of the basin floors is approximately 4400 m. The major ridges from east to west are: Aves Ridge, Beata Rise, Jamaica Ridge and the Cayman Ridge (see Fig. 1).

The Caribbean Sea is situated in the northern trade wind belt and, therefore, has very steady winds from the east and east-northeast. The rainfall is heavier during the summer months when more tropical weather prevails. The highest rainfall is to the east of the Central American isthmus

Fig. 1. Basins and ridges of the Caribbean–Antillean Region.

where orographic lifting of moist air causes more than 200 cm of rain to fall in the 6-month period from June to November. While few hurricanes form in the Caribbean Sea, many enter by way of the Lesser Antilles during late summer and early fall.

Exploration

The first European to explore the Caribbean area was Christopher Columbus. After his landing in the Bahamas on October 12, 1492, he turned south to discover Cuba, or Colba as the natives called it. Columbus, to the day he died, believed that Cuba was a promontory from India or China. He sailed eastward across the Windward Passage to discover Hispaniola. He interpreted the destruction of the *Santa Maria* there as a sign from God to start a colony in Haiti, which he called Navidad. On Columbus' second voyage, he discovered Puerto Rico and Jamaica. On his third voyage, which embarked May 30, 1498, from San Laca de Barremeda, he took six ships and discovered Trinidad. His last voyage brought him to the Caribbean coast of Honduras and Costa Rica. The voyages of Columbus encompassed the whole boundary of the Caribbean Sea, which he explored for gold and a new route to Asia. It was many years later that the Spanish began exploiting the natives for gold and destroying the complex indigenous culture.

The oceanographic history begins with the traverse of the *Challenger* in 1873 which took a total of eight stations in the area. The first major American oceanographic undertaking in the Caribbean Sea was by the U.S. Coast and Geodetic Survey during the period 1877–89 aboard the *U.S.S. Blake*. This voyage resulted in a great addition of direct current information, which is still considered as excellent data today; in addition, information was gathered on bottom sediments and in the temperature field. The first monograph on the Caribbean Sea and adjacent areas was written in 1888 by A. Agassiz.

Modern oceanographic work began in the period 1913–1928 when the Danish expeditions with *Margrethe* and *Dana I* and *II* took many exact serial measurements. During the 1930's, *R/V Atlantis* carried on a systematic survey of the Caribbean under the direction of A. E. Parr, which led to many scientific papers (Parr, Seiwell, Dietrich). Data have been accumulating since then, with a great concentration during the IGY. For Wüst's recent study of the Caribbean, there was a total of 1725 hydrographic stations from 30 research vessels.

Circulation

Most of the passages between the Caribbean and the Atlantic Ocean are shallow and do not permit much interaction of the two water bodies. However, some are deeper than 1000 m, and these play a primary part in the Caribbean circulation.

The depth of such passages, or sill depths, can be determined either by sonar, or by inspection of the oceanic parameters. The most commonly used parameter is the temperature (or more accurately the potential temperature, which is the temperature of the water at atmospheric pressure). The coldest

PASSAGES		SILL DEPTHS IN TRUE M	
N A M E	WIDTH at 1500m	BY BATHOGRAM	BY tp-AND O₂-SECTIONS [3]
WINDWARD PASSAGE	12 MILES	$\underline{1650}$ [1]	$\underline{1600-1625}$
VIRGIN ISLANDS PASSAGE	8 MILES	1960 [2]	1725 – 1775
ANEGADA PASSAGE	8 MILES	2208 [2]	NORTH ~ 1950 SOUTH ~ 2300
DOMINICA PASSAGE		1372 [2]	~1400
JAMAICA PASSAGE	20 MILES (AT 1000 m)	$\underline{1500}$ [1]	1450 – 1500
SOUTH AVES PASSAGE			~2200

1) After Heezen - Johnson - Allen 1961
2) After Frassetto - Northrop 1957
3) After Wüst - Gordon 1962
The most probable values are underlined

Fig. 2. Sill depths between the basins of the Caribbean–Antillean Region.

temperature at the bottom of the "leeward" basin should correspond to the temperature of the sill depth on the "windward" side of the passage. Figure 2 gives the sill depths of the most important passages of the Caribbean Sea's eastern and northern boundaries. The Yucatan Strait is the major outlet of Caribbean water and has a sill depth of approximately 2000 m.

The general water flow in the Caribbean Sea is from east to west in the upper 1500 m, with very sluggish and variable motion below this depth at which the Caribbean waters are isolated from the surrounding ocean. The source of the waters entering the Caribbean Sea is from the wind-driven Guiana Current which flows northwest along the South American Coast before reaching the Lesser Antillean island chain. Most of the Guiana Current's water is forced through the central section of this island chain, principally in the passages north and south of St. Lucia Island. The remaining waters join the North Equatorial current and flow around the Caribbean's eastern and northern boundaries and toward the Bahamas. The waters which enter the Caribbean are streaky due to the grating action of the islands, but they form a well-developed zonal Caribbean current with a maximum flow 200–300 km north of the South American coast, after crossing the Grenada Basin and Aves Ridge. The axis of the Caribbean Current continues westward through the Aruba Gap and Colombia Basin. It turns northward in the western section of the basin, crosses the Jamaica Ridge, and then flows along the Cayman Basin to longitude 85–86°W before again turning northward and leaving the Caribbean Sea in the Yucatan Strait. The axis of the Caribbean Current generally flows over the deepest path from the Lesser Antilles 'to the Yucatan Strait.

The flow north and south of the axis is essentially parallel. Its direction varies little with depth, though the magnitude of the flow decreases continuously with increasing depth from the surface or near-surface value until it becomes less than 5 cm/sec at depths greater than 1500 m in the Venezuela and Colombia Basins; in the Cayman and Yucatan Basins, the deep flow is better developed, but it can still be considered sluggish by oceanic standards.

The magnitude of the surface flow is dependent on season and is in phase with the seasonal variations of the strength of the trade winds. The Caribbean Current has its highest surface velocity in late winter and again in early summer (Fuglister, 1951), the early summer value being slightly higher (0.80 knot vs 0.76 knot for the late winter peak). The average surface velocity for the year is 0.70 knot or 38 cm/sec. These are average values; higher velocities have to be observed from ship drift records with maximum surface velocities of 2.7 knots in the main axis of the Caribbean Current.

Calculations of the expected velocities from the measured density field can be made. This is the geostrophic flow and represents the balance of the Coriolis' force with the pressure gradient. Using this method, the subsurface flow can be calculated. The results show that the main axis of flow remains the maximum for all depths in the upper 300–400 m, its value decreasing rapidly from 40–60 cm/sec at the surface to 10 cm/sec at 300 m. Below this depth, there is a slow decrease to about zero velocity at 1000–1500 m; at deeper depths, the flow is not strong enough to be measured by the geostrophic method. There are countercurrents (toward the east) along some coastal segments of South America, Cuba and Haiti. In the western regions

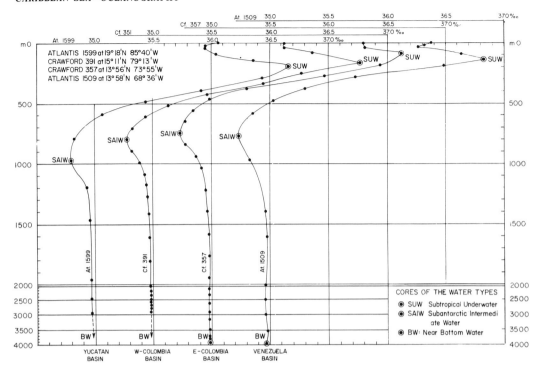

Fig. 3. Vertical distribution of salinity.

of the Colombia Basin and the Cayman–Yucatan Basins, countercurrents are found to exist at mid-sea positions, and the zonal flow is upset by more meriodional motion. This is due to the western land boundary which disturbs the zonal water flow and the wind field.

The volume transport through north-south profiles can be calculated from the geostrophic velocities. The average value is 30,000,000 m³/sec toward the west. The water passages in the Greater Antilles do not affect the total transport to a significant degree. The transport across the meridian of 64°W is essentially the same as that across the 84°W meridian. The total volume transport of the Gulf Stream is about 75–90 million m³/sec; therefore, the Caribbean Current contributes about 30% of this, the rest coming from the Antillean current which enters the Gulf Stream just north of the Bahamas.

An interesting feature of the water circulation in the Caribbean Sea is upwelling along the coast of Venezuela and Columbia. This vertical motion, like other upwelling areas of the world, is essentially a wind feature. Surface water is drawn away from the coast and is replaced by deeper water. The upwelling does not extend to great depths, usually becoming unimportant below 250 m. It leads to high productivity and good fishing areas.

Related sinking occurs in the Venezuela and Colombia Basins along 17°N latitude.

Salinity

The salinity field of the Caribbean Sea is controlled by four layers or "cores" (Wüst). Two of these, the *surface waters,* and *Subtropical Underwater* (50–200 m), are associated with the warm water sphere of the ocean and are separated from the lower cold water sphere by a layer of low oxygen (below 3.0 ml/liter) at 400–600 m; the other two cores are cold water layers which are the *Subantarctic Intermediate Water* (700–850 m) and the *North Atlantic Deep Water* (1800–2500 m). The waters between the core layers are made up of mixtures of core water due to the normal vertical *austausch* (mixing by turbulence) process (see Fig. 3).

The surface salinity values are dependent upon evaporation, precipitation, runoff from the land and horizontal advection by currents. The winter values are higher along the South American Coast (>36‰), and this is due in part to the upwelling of deeper water which brings the high salinity of the Subtropical Water to the surface. The surface salinity decreases in the north and becomes less than 35.5‰ in the northern half of the Sea. In the Cayman–Yucatan Basins, the salinity is highest

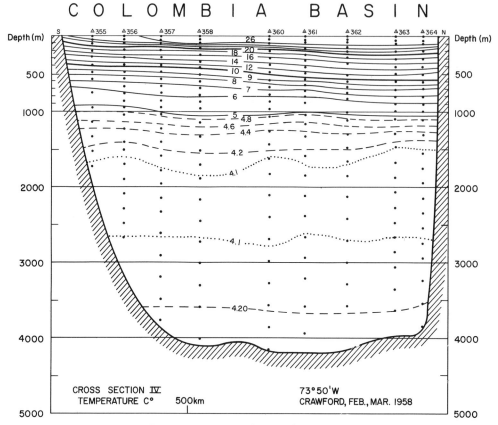

Fig. 4 (a). Temperature in the Colombia Basin.

south of Cuba, >36‰, and decreases toward the southwest to values <35.5‰ at the Honduras Coast. In the summer, the higher precipitation and the greater land runoff make the surface salinity about 0.5‰ lower in the south and up to 1.0‰ lower in the north. Lack of data in the western Caribbean makes the salinity field obscure.

The Subtropical Underwater is an absolute salinity maximum in the water column. It is a sheetlike core (which demonstrates the greater amount of horizontal mixing over vertical mixing in this stable layer) which slopes down from the south (50–100 m) to the north (200 m). Its main axis of spreading follows the axis of flow of the Caribbean Current. The salinity value in this core layer is >37‰ in the eastern points of the Venezuela Basin and decreases (by mixing) to 36.7‰ at the Yucatan Straits.

The Subantarctic Water which originates at the south polar front is an absolute salinity minimum which also slopes down toward the north but at a slightly smaller gradient than the salinity maximum core—600–700 m in the south to 800–850 m in the north. This core is thicker in the southern part of the Sea. At longitudes west of 65°W, its northern part thins and disappears before reaching the

northern land boundary. Its salinity values are slightly less than 34.7‰ in the east and increase so that the core cannot be detected at the Yucatan straits. It, too, has its main axis of spreading along the main axis of flow.

Below this core layer, the water is North Atlantic Deep Water which enters the Caribbean basins by "cascading" over the sills of the many passages in the Antillean Islands. The water is fairly homogeneous having a value just under 35‰. This deep water is renewed only when the water at the sill depths is dense enough to replace the water already in the basins. This may not have happened for hundreds of years (Worthington, Richards), though Wüst shows by oxygen sections across the passages that a certain amount of renewal occurs, and Dietrich (1939) believes that the deep water is continuously flowing over the sills.

Temperature

The temperature field of the Caribbean is of tropical character, i.e., warm surface values and a well-developed thermocline at 100–200 m which hinders vertical mixing and keeps the surface heat from reaching the deeper water. Below 1500 m, the waters are about 4°C and vary little from basin to

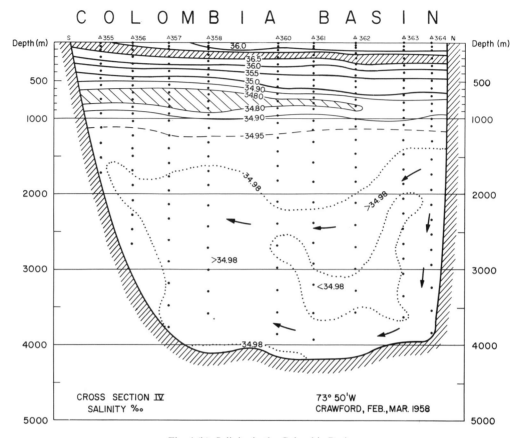

Fig. 4 (b). Salinity in the Colombia Basin.

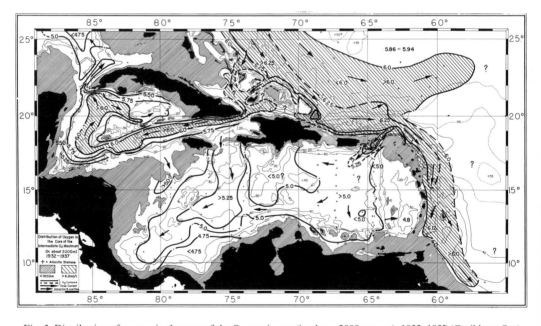

Fig. 5. Distribution of oxygen in the core of the O_2 maximum (in about 2000 meters), 1932–1937 (Caribbean Sea).

basin; they increase by a few tenths of a degree at the great depths (below 3000 m) due to the adiabatic effect of the increased pressure. The surface temperatures are such as to make the thermal equator pass through the northern third of the Caribbean Sea. In late summer, the temperature of the sea surface is 28.3°C in the south and 28.9°C in the north. The western sections of the sea have the warmest month in August, while in the east the warmest month is September. The winter surface temperatures are about 3°C lower.

The surface temperatures have small gradients and little seasonal variation in the Caribbean. There is no seasonal variation at all below 150 m. The central regions of the Caribbean Sea absorb, on an annual average, 6.26×10^{18} cal/day from the atmosphere (Colón), and the variation from this average is only 0.5×10^{18} cal/day which explains the small seasonal surface temperature variations. Figure 4 (a) and (b) shows the salinity and temperature structure of a north-south profile along 73° 50′W.

Oxygen Distribution

The vertical column shows an oxygen distribution of 4.2 ml/liter at the surface and a minimum at 500 m of below 3.0 ml/liter. Below this depth, the value increases to a maximum of over 5.5 ml/liter and over 6.0 ml/liter near the passages. Wüst shows that the oxygen entering the Caribbean varies for different years with a great amount of influx during the period 1932–37 (see Fig. 5).

ARNOLD GORDON

References

Colón, F. A., 1963, "Seasonal variations in heat flux from the sea surface to the atmosphere over the Caribbean Sea," *J. Geophys. Res.*, **68** (5), 1421–30.

Dietrich, G., 1939, "Das Amerikanische Mittelmeer: Ein Meereskundlicher Uberblick," *Z. Ges. Erdkunde Berlin*, **1939** (3/4), 108–30.

Parr, A. E., 1937, "A contribution to the hydrography of the Caribbean and Cayman Seas," *Bulletin of the Bingham Oceanographic Collection*, **5**, Art. 4, 1–110.

*Wüst, G., 1964, "Stratification and Circulation in the Antillean-Caribbean Basins. Part One: Spreading and Mixing of the Water Types," pp. 1–201, VEMA Series II, New York, Columbia University Press.

CARIBBEAN SEA—SEDIMENTS AND CRUST*

For this discussion, "sediments" include all layers in which the speed of the compressional waves is less than about 4 km/sec. Our knowledge of the sediments is derived from the interpretation of data received from direct sampling (core and

* The investigations described here were supported by the United States Navy Office of Naval Research and Bureau of Ships.

dredge) and geophysical methods (reflection, refraction and gravity). The crust in the Caribbean has been examined only by refraction, gravity and geomagnetic methods. Figure 1 is a map of the Caribbean and shows the traverses along which these measurements have been made.

Sediments

(A) Cores. Core samples from the Caribbean Sea indicate that carbonates form a major part of the recent sediments. Most of the carbonates are tan to brown muds containing variable percentages of coarse organic and inorganic fragments. Foraminifera and pteropods are commonly the dominant organisms. Turbidity currents (see *Turbidity Currents*, pr Vol. VI) are considered the depositional mechanism for much of the sediment in the Caribbean. Cores recovered from the abyssal plains (see *Abyssal Plains*) contain typical turbidite deposits which are responsible for the very flat topography in the Yucatan, Colombian and southern Venezuelan Basins (Heezen, 1956).

The Cariaco Trench has maintained oxygen depleted water below 200 fathoms since the end of the Pleistocene (Heezen *et al.*, 1958). As a result the upper few meters of sediment have a high hydrogen sulfide concentration and lack benthonic fauna.

(B) Reflections. Figure 2 shows a sample reflection profile-tracing with two strong sub-bottom reflectors which appear to be characteristic of the Venezuelan Basin. The two horizons may be present in the Colombian and Yucatan Basins, but they are masked by thick turbidity current deposits. They are strong reflectors and may mask deeper horizons that might otherwise be recorded. Hard, light gray calcilutite (consolidated carbonate mud) chips of Eocene age have been recovered from about the depth of the first strong sub-bottom reflection by coring at the base of a fault on the northeastern side of the Beata Ridge. The flat-lying sediments in the bottom of the trough immediately adjacent to the slope of the Curaçao Ridge are considered Pleistocene turbidity deposits.

(C) Refraction. Refraction measurements at present offer the only means of determining total sediment thicknesses in some parts of the Caribbean. The North Venezuelan Trough extends along the continental slope off Colombia and Venezuela and contains up to 12 km of sediment and sedimentary rock under the Curaçao Ridge, the thickest deposit recorded in the Caribbean.

Figure 3 compares the average seismic sections in the three basins with the Atlantic Ocean structure, indicating much thicker sediments in the Caribbean. Figure 1 shows the location of two refraction sections (Figs. 4 and 5) which indicate the sediment distribution in each of the basins.

The 4.8–5.1 km/sec layer controls the topography on the Cayman Ridge, but in the absence

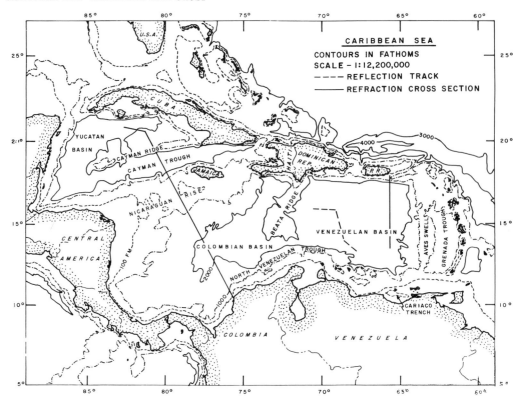

Fig. 1. Map of Caribbean showing physiographic provinces and location of reflection track and refraction cross sections.

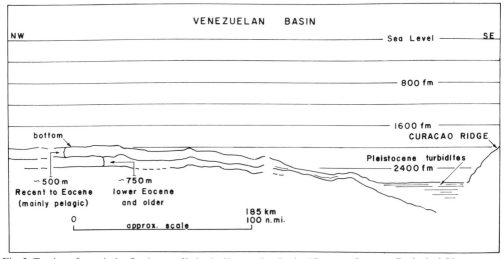

Fig. 2. Tracing of a typical reflection profile in the Venezuelan Basin. (Courtesy Lamont Geological Observatory)

of short-period magnetic anomalies, it is doubtful that basic intrusive or volcanic material is involved.

Crust

The velocity of the crustal layer in the Caribbean varies from 5.8–7.5 km/sec. The lower velocities are recorded in the upper part and the higher velocities in the lower part, indicating an increase in density of the crustal rocks with depth.

The average thickness of the crust in the Caribbean basins is greater than that of the oceanic basins, but it is considerably thinner than the crust of the continents (Fig. 3).

It should be noted in Fig. 4 that generally where the bottom topography is high, the crust is thick. The crust in the Colombian basin is thicker than in the Venezuelan or Yucatan Basins, and the water depth is about 1 km less. It thins southward to a minimum of 6 km under the North Venezuelan Trough, then thickens rapidly under the South American Continent. The crust thickens slightly under the Beata Ridge and becomes so thick under the Nicaraguan Rise and Cayman Ridge that the mantle has not been recorded by standard seismic refraction profiles. It has been thought that the thickness may be comparable to that of a continental crust. It thins to 4 km in the Cayman Trough, and the mantle is found only 11 km below sea level, the shallowest depth recorded in the Caribbean.

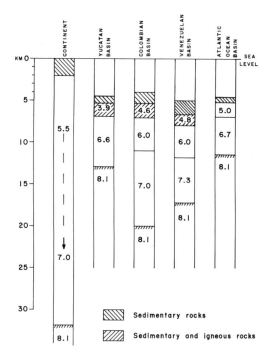

Fig. 3. Average seismic sections for the continents, Atlantic Ocean and Caribbean basins.

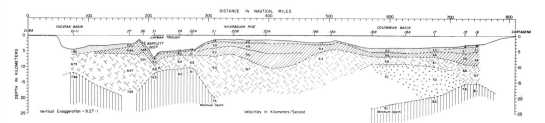

Fig. 4. Structure section across the Colombian and Yucatan Basins (from Ewing, Antoine and Ewing, 1960).

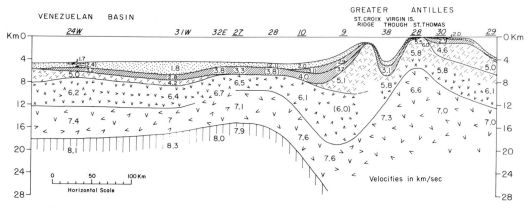

Fig. 5. Structure section across the Venezuelan Basin (from Officer *et al.*, 1957). (By permission of Pergamon Press, N.Y.)

Figure 5 is a cross section through the Venezuelan Basin and clearly shows two crustal layers, the total thickness of which varies between 8 and 10 km. The 5.1–5.8 km/sec layer recorded in the island arc is appropriate for intrusive igneous rocks, metamorphic rocks, or limestones. Short-period magnetic anomalies indicate the presence of intrusive igneous rocks. Outcrops of volcanic and intrusive rocks are chiefly andesites and diorites and to a lesser degree basalts, which are generally associated with oceanic structures. The Aves Swell (Ewing *et al.*, 1957) and the Bonaire Ridge (Butterlin, 1956) are both considered to be of volcanic origin.

Many hypotheses have been proposed concerning the origin of the Caribbean structure (Hess, 1938; Eardley, 1954; and others), most of which have been reviewed by Butterlin (1956). Some geologists feel the Caribbean is a permanent ocean basin, and others believe that it is a drowned continent. It appears that the structure is neither continental nor oceanic but is more closely related to the oceanic (Officer *et al.*, 1957) (Fig. 3). Hypotheses suggesting that the Caribbean area is a drowned continent must contend with this evidence. Consideration has been given to the theory that the Caribbean represents an embryonic continent eventually to be accreted to the Americas.

JOHN EWING
TERENCE EDGAR

References

Butterlin, J., 1956, "La constitution geologique et la structure des Antilles," Centre National de la Recherche Scientifique.

Eardley, A. J., 1954, "Tectonic relations of North and South America," *Bull. Am. Assoc. Petrol. Geologists*, **38**, 707–773.

Ewing, J. I., Antoine, J., and Ewing, M., 1960, "Geophysical measurements in the western Caribbean Sea and in the Gulf of Mexico," *J. Geophys. Res.*, **65**, 4087–4126.

Ewing, J. I., Officer, C. B., Johnson, H. R., and Edwards, R. S., 1957, "Geophysical investigations in the eastern Caribbean; Trinidad Shelf, Tobago Trough, Barbados Ridge, Atlantic Ocean," *Geol. Soc. Am. Bull.*, **68**, 897–912.

Heezen, B. C., 1956, "Corrientes de turbidez del Rio Magdalena, Colombia," *Biol. Soc. Geog. Colombia*, Nos. 51 and 52, 135–143.

Heezen, B. C., Ewing, M., Menzies, R. J., and Broecker, W. S., 1958, "Date of stagnation of the Cariaco Trench," *Geol. Soc. Am. Bull.*, **69**, 1579.

Hess, H. H., 1938, "Gravity anomalies and island arc structures with particular reference to the West Indies," *Proc. Am. Philos. Soc.*, **79**, 71–96.

*Officer, C. B., Ewing, J. I., Hennion, J. F., Harkrider, D. G., and Miller, D. E., 1959, "Geophysical Investigation in the Eastern Caribbean; Summary of 1955 and 1956 Cruises," in "Physics and Chemistry of the Earth," Vol. 3, pp. 17–109, New York, Pergamon Press.

CARPENTARIA, GULF OF—*See* GULF OF CARPENTARIA

CASPIAN SEA—*See* Vol. III

CELEBES SEA—*See* SULAWESI SEA

CERAM SEA

This is situated in the Moluccan region of the East Indies (Indonesia) between the "tail" of the outer Banda arc, the islands of Buru (Boeroe in Dutch orthography), Ceram and Kai Islands, and the Bird's Head (Vogelkop) of New Guinea or West Irian. The northern boundary, according to the International Hydrographic Bureau (*Sp. Publ.*, 1953), may then be traced from Tanjong Sele (1° 26′S, 130° 55′E) the west tip of New Guinea, through Kofiau, Boo Islands, Pisang, Obi Major, to Mangoli in the Sula (Soela) Islands, thence south through Sanana Island to Buru. The area covered is about 160,000 km². The *Snellius* Expedition recognized a *Buru Sea* in the western part of the Ceram Sea.

Structurally, the Ceram Sea is situated on the boundary of the young Tertiary orogenic belt of the Banda Arc, Buru-Ceram-Kai being in the nonvolcanic outer series. In contrast, the Bird's Head, Obi Major, and Sula are part of the structural foreland, an extension referred by Hans Stille as the "Sula Spur." Youthful uplift is evidenced by numerous terraces on Buru-Ceram, while numerous coral reefs with deep foundations demonstrate downwarping, e.g. Gorong Islands and Watubela (Strait of Ceram), around Misool (on the western edge of the Bird's Head Shelf) in the Boo Islands and elsewhere along the Sula Spur.

There is a deep trough between Buru-Ceram and the Sula with some 16,000 km² over 3000 m known as the *Buru Basin* (Van Riel, 1934). It may be compared with a modern exogeosyncline, at present filling from sediments mainly supplied from the Buru-Ceram arc. The maximum depth sounded here by the *Snellius* Expedition was 4680 m. The bottom is very complicated with several east-west rifts and intermediate ridges. Deep water from the Pacific moves from the Molucca Sea (Batjan) Basin into the Buru Basin through the Lifamatola Strait over a sill of 1880 m. This sill is much deeper than that leading from the Halmahera Sea (east of Obi Major, about 800 m). It is in this way that Pacific bottom water reaches into almost the whole eastern Indonesian Archipelago (Figs. 2 and 3). The sill depth to the south, the Manipa Straits between Buru and Ceram, is over 1000 m, but to the west between Sanana and Buru it is over 3000 m.

As shown by Van Riel (1934, p. 34), the Buru Basin is warmer than the Moluccan Sea at depth

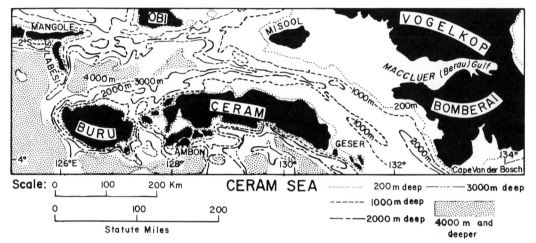

Fig. 1. Bathymetric map of Ceram (Seram) Sea, showing elongate trough (exogeosyncline).

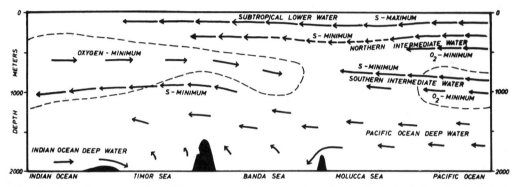

Fig. 2. Schematic representation of the core layers in a section from the Pacific to the Indian Ocean. Note the intermediate position of the Ceram Sea between the Molucca Sea and Banda Sea (from Wyrtki, 1961).

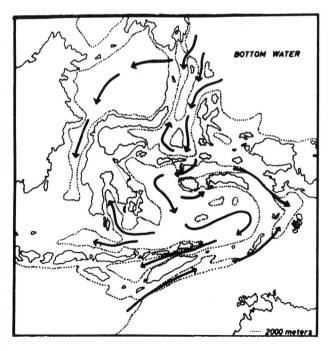

Fig. 3. Map of bottom water motions through the Ceram Sea, showing its important position in permitting Pacific deep water to reach almost all the eastern archipelago. (Wyrtki, 1961)

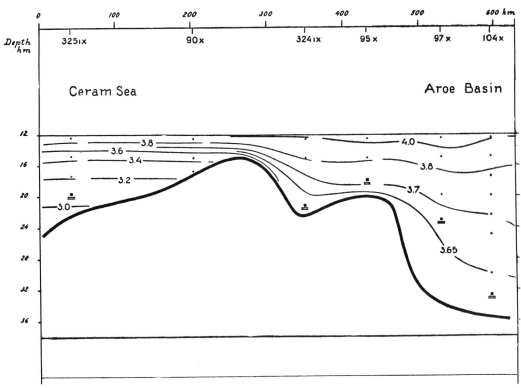

Fig. 4. Section between Ceram Sea and Aroe (Aru) Basin of Arafura Sea (q.v.). Potential temperature (Van Riel, 1934). For a similar profile through the western part of the Ceram Sea (Buru or Boeroe Basin) into the Banda Sea, see article *Banda Sea*. The flow of cold Pacific bottom water from north to south (left to right in figure) is quite evident. Depths in 100's of meters (hm).

(Batjan Basin), with a minimum bottom potential temperature measured at 2.66°C (Fig. 4). It is also marked by a drop in oxygen, to 2.56 cc/liter at the bottom (Van Riel, 1943, p. 51), with a pH of 7.77.

RHODES W. FAIRBRIDGE

References

Kuenen, P. H., 1935, "The Snellius Expedition. Geological Interpretation of the Bathymetrical Results," Vol. 5, Pt. 1, Utrecht, Kemink en Zoon.

Kuenen, P. H., and Neeb, G. A., 1943, "The Snellius Expedition. Bottom Samples," Vol. 5, Pt. 3, Leiden, E. J. Brill.

Stille, H., 1945, "Die tektonische Entwicklung der hinterindischen Festlands und Inselgebiet," *Geotektonische Forschungen, Berlin*, No. 78, 34–153.

Van Riel, P. M., 1934, "The Snellius Expedition. The bottom configuration," Vol. 2, Pt. 2, Ch. 2, Utrecht, Kemink en Zoon.

Van Riel, P. M., 1943, "The Snellius Expedition. Introductory Remarks and Oxygen Content," Vol. 2, Pt. 5, Ch. 1, Leiden, E. J. Brill.

Van Riel, P. M., Hamaker, H. C., and Van Eyck, L., 1950, "The Snellius Expedition. Tables. Serial and Bottom Observations. Temperature, Salinity and Density," Vol. 2, Pt. 6, pp. 1–44, Leiden, E. J. Brill.

Wyrtki, K., 1961, "Physical oceanography of the southeastern Asian water," *Repts. Naga Exped.*, 2, La Jolla, Calif., Scripps Institute of Oceanography.

CHEMICAL OCEANOGRAPHY, GENERAL*

Introduction

(1) Definition and Role of Chemical Oceanography. (*a*) *General.* Oceanography can be defined as the scientific study of the seas, and chemical oceanography is the application of chemical techniques, laws and principles to oceanography. It is devoted to the accurate description of the chemical nature of the seas, to the elucidation of the processes that produce and alter the distribution of chemical species in the oceans (in both time and space), and to the consequences of the chemical nature of seawater on biological, geological, and physical processes in the marine environment. The

* Contribution No. 351 from the Department of Oceanography, University of Washington.

chemical nature of seawater may control, limit, or help define these processes, which in turn may alter the chemical makeup of the environment.

In many respects, chemical oceanography serves to elucidate biological, physical, and geological processes in the ocean more than it serves to elucidate chemical processes, and it tends to be analytical and diagnostic. In general, knowledge of the chemistry of seawater is of more application to biological, geological, and physical problems than it is to problems of chemistry *per se*.

(*b*) *Marine Chemical Engineering*. The recovery of chemical products of value from seawater and the corrosive effects of seawater on man-made objects are primarily chemical problems, but they have little to do with the study of the oceans themselves, and therefore are of more interest to chemical engineers than to chemical oceanographers. In general, such problems require a knowledge of the composition of seawater and its variability, but their solution is concerned only to a limited degree with the processes by which the properties of seawater were acquired or are altered.

(*c*) *The Chemical Environment*. Chemical oceanography is primarily an environmental science and is concerned with describing, explaining, and predicting the environment in which biological, geological, and physical events take place or have taken place, and the ways in which the environment may control or limit such events. The process of describing this environment is an analytical one, so the analysis of seawater and the development of adequate analytical methods have taken up a large fraction of the efforts of chemical oceanographers. Many effects of the chemical environment on the marine biological system have been reviewed by Harvey (1957).

Historical

(1) **The Beginnings of Chemical Oceanography.** Man's early interests in the chemical nature of seawater were no doubt highly practical ones, primarily concerned with the recovery of table salt. Robert Boyle (1627–1691), however, turned his attention to matters of scientific chemical oceanography as defined above. Boyle was interested in many aspects of oceanography, and T. G. Thompson has referred to him as the father of modern chemical oceanography. He devised the silver nitrate test for seawater and observed that, when silver nitrate was added to seawater, a heavy precipitate was formed but only a cloudiness formed with river or lake water, and he concluded that the sea got its saltiness from the leaching of the land.

(2) **Early Analyses of Seawater.** Goldberg (1961) has credited Torbern Bergman (1735–1784) and Antoine Lavoisier (1743–1794) with the first quantitative analyses of seawater, but these investigations

shed little light on the chemical nature of the oceans as a whole. Lavoisier's interest in seawater was primarily because of its use as a medicinal.

(3) **The Concept of Uniform Composition of Seawater.** The general chemical nature of seawater began to be understood as a result of analyses made by Forchhammer and published in 1865. Even though major solutes were omitted from these analyses, they led Forchhammer to conclude that the composition of sea salts was always much the same, regardless of the source of the seawater. The uniformity of the composition of seawater was emphasized by M. F. Maury in his book "Physical Geography of the Sea," published in 1855, where he pointed out that the total salt content of seawater did not depart widely from 3.5% except in regions of excessive evaporation, such as the Red Sea, or excessive river runoff, such as the outfall of the Amazon River. He appears also to have realized that the composition of the sea salts was similarly uniform, and he concluded that the reason for the uniformity was that the oceans were well mixed—"well shaken together," in his words. The work of Dittmar, published in 1884, placed the concept of the uniformity of the ratios of the major constituents of seawater (see *Chemistry of Seawater*) on a firm footing that has received substantial confirmation by many subsequent analyses. Real and significant variations in the ratios of the major constituents of seawater to each other do exist, especially in seawaters highly influenced by land runoff, such as the Baltic Sea, and probably in waters highly influenced by the freezing and thawing of sea ice, but the variations are generally small.

(4) **Dissolved Gases.** Attempts were made to determine the dissolved oxygen content of seawater as early as 1869, and these attempts were continued during the scientific cruise of the *Challenger* (1873–1876), but the analytical methods were inadequate until the Winkler titrimetric method, described in 1888, was introduced to oceanography in the first decade of the twentieth century. Since that time, a large body of data on the distribution of dissolved oxygen has been acquired, and dissolved oxygen has been more widely observed than any other constituent of seawater except the chlorinity. The subject of oxygen in the ocean was reviewed by Richards (1957a).

(5) **Solubility of Dissolved Gases.** C. J. J. Fox made careful determinations of the solubilities, published in 1909, of oxygen, carbon dioxide, and nitrogen (including the other inert gases, principally argon) in seawater equilibrated with air under varying conditions of chlorinity and temperature. The validity of Fox' data came into question in 1955, but more recent work suggests that his data were generally highly accurate, so far as O_2 solubility is concerned, although the values of these constants await definitive determination.

(6) Concept of Limiting Nutrients. Near the end of the nineteenth century, K. Brandt suggested that depletion of phosphorus and nitrogen compounds might limit plant production in the sea, but analytical difficulties prevented the satisfactory investigation of this idea until sensitive colorimetric methods were applied to the analysis of seawater in the early 1920's, primarily by W. R. G. Atkins of the Laboratory of the Marine Biological Association, Plymouth, England. These methods have permitted extensive studies of the nutrient distributions to be carried out in the intervening years and have led to our understanding of some of the biochemical circulations in the sea referred to below.

H. Wattenberg, chemist aboard the German research vessel *Meteor*, developed the concept of a modern shipboard chemical laboratory, and his observations of dissolved oxygen, nutrients, pH, and alkalinity during the investigations of the South Atlantic Ocean in 1925–1927 greatly extended the concepts of the biochemical circulation of nutrients and their importance in limiting primary production by phytoplankton organisms.

(7) Recent Advances in Radiochemistry and Isotope Distributions. Since World War II, there have been marked advances in the development of methods for the analysis of seawater and in the fields of radiochemistry and isotope distributions in the ocean. Although the radioactivity of seawater was first reported by R. J. Strutt in 1906, its exact determination was difficult and its distribution essentially unknown until the introduction of modern methods of radiochemistry. Y. Miyake successfully followed the distribution of artificially introduced radionuclides by United States bomb tests in the Pacific Ocean and used his observations to estimate rates of oceanic circulation. Artificial radioactivity provides the first tracer that man has been able to introduce into the ocean in sufficient quantity to permit its being followed over vast expanses. The natural fractionation and distribution of stable isotopes of several of the elements, particularly of dissolved oxygen and of hydrogen and oxygen combined as water, have been observed in recent years.

Processes Leading to and Altering the Distribution of Chemical Variables in the Oceans

(1) General. Solutes, solids, and gases enter and leave the oceans across its boundaries between solid earth and the atmosphere. The composition of solutes introduced by rivers and streams differs markedly from those in seawater, being generally dominated by the alkaline earth metal cations and the anions of carbonic acid, while seawater is dominated by the ions of sodium chloride. Other solutes can be introduced directly with rainfall on the oceans; some nitric acid, formed during lightning discharges, is supposed to enter by this source. Volcanism, both submarine and subaerial, introduces other solutes. Dust, the particulate burdens of rivers and streams, volcanism and meteorites provide solid matter to the oceans. Bottom materials may be redissolved or resuspended through the agencies of wave action, biological activity, or changing physicochemical conditions.

(2) Gas Exchanges. The surface waters of the oceans are nearly in equilibrium with the atmosphere, i.e., they are saturated, or nearly so, with the air gases. There are net exchanges of dissolved gases across the sea surface in response to changes in temperature and changes in dissolved gas contents resulting from biological activity. The circulation of the oceans may bring waters into the surface layers that are oversaturated or undersaturated with respect to the atmosphere. Seawater saturated with air gases at high latitudes and low temperatures will give up some of its gas content to the air if brought into contact with the atmosphere at lower latitudes and higher temperatures, but subsurface waters introduced into the surface layers will generally be undersaturated with oxygen, because of its consumption during respiration and decomposition of organic matter.

(3) Changes in Chemical Species and Physical State. Within the body of the ocean, chemical species will be altered by inorganic and by biological-biochemical reactions. These reactions include the life processes, by which relatively simple inorganic substances are transformed into complicated living forms, but most of the inorganic materials are eventually returned to solution through the processes of excretion, respiration, and decomposition, although some of the materials combined into the bodies of plants and animals will fall to the ocean floor and be incorporated in the sediments.

(4) Aggregates and Precipitates. Inorganic and organic aggregates and precipitates can be formed from soluble or more finely divided materials. The formation of organic aggregates from soluble organic compounds at the surfaces of bubbles and other interfaces has recently been demonstrated. The formation of pelagic sediments is not well understood, but they apparently represent solids that were introduced to the sea as inorganic matter or by life processes and were subsequently altered by physicochemical exchanges with seawater solutes. The direct inorganic precipitation of insoluble salts is relatively rare in the ocean, but $CaCO_3$ is known to precipitate under conditions of high temperature and low carbon dioxide concentrations, for example on the Bahama Banks. The formation of insoluble sulfides in anoxic, sulfide-bearing waters may take place—it appears that copper is precipitated under these conditions, and the Black Sea is probably saturated with ferrous sulfide. The ocean may be supersaturated with other inorganic salts, notably calcium carbonate.

(5) Body or *in situ* Processes. In the body of the oceans, chemical species can be altered by chemical or biochemical processes, and atoms and molecules can pass into and out of the liquid, solid, and gaseous (under limited circumstances near the surface) states. The distribution of solutes will be determined by the hydrodynamics of the system, but matter in the particulate form, which can be living or not, will also be subject to the swimming of organisms and to sinking (or rising, in the case of bubbles) under the influence of gravity. Colloid-sized particles will behave more like true solutes, but they may be gathered into aggregates or sorbates and precipitated.

(6) Conservative and Non-conservative Solutes. There can be considered to be two major classes of solutes in the oceans, and their distributions accordingly differ widely. The first class, the conservative solutes, are those which are present in such abundance or are so chemically and biochemically inert that only minute fractions of their total amounts enter the particulate state. These elements make up over 99.9% of the solutes and are distributed as (and make up) the solutes measured as the *salinity* (see *Chemistry of Seawater*). Except at the boundaries of the ocean, changes in the concentration of these solutes in a unit volume are brought about by mixing or diffusion with adjacent units of water and by advection of water into the unit. The magnitude of the concentration changes will depend on the amount of mixing or diffusion and advection, and the concentration gradients. Dynamic or molecular diffusion is generally too slow to bring about major changes in the distribution of chemical variables, so eddy diffusion assumes the major role. Molecular diffusion coefficients for solutes have values of about 2×10^{-5} g/cm^2, depending somewhat on the nature of the solute. Eddy diffusion coefficients can be expected to be several orders of magnitude larger and to vary widely.

Most of the major constituents of seawater (Na^+, Mg^{++}, Ca^{++}, K^+, Sr^{++}, Cl^-, $SO_4^=$, Br^-, F^-, and H_3BO_3) are generally considered to be conservative solutes, although biological activity may make significant changes in the ratios of the alkaline earth metal ions to the chloride ion, and about 20% of the HCO_3^- ions can be involved in biological cycles. The ratios of boric acid and fluoride ions to the other major constituents may also vary considerably, and appreciable fractions of the sulfate ions may be reduced to sulfides under anoxic conditions such as occur in the Black Sea and other stagnant basins and fjords. Of the dissolved gases, nitrogen, argon, and the other rare gases are conservative, or nearly so, although there is some evidence that nitrogen fixation may occur fairly extensively in the surface layers of the

tropics. Nitrogen has been shown to be produced in oxygen-free marine environments, but this process is quantitatively of little importance in considerations of the entire oceans.

The non-conservative solutes are generally present in low concentrations, and *major fractions* of their total amounts enter and leave the particulate phase, where they are redistributed by swimming motions and under the influence of gravity in a way different from the more abundant, conservative major solutes. Although these constituents form a small fraction of the total matter dissolved in seawater, they include many that are essential to life processes (e.g., phosphorus, nitrogen, and manganese), others that are useful as tracers of water masses (dissolved oxygen and silicates are examples), and others that are of particular geochemical interest. The deposition of sediments may remove large fractions of some of these materials from the sea, but it is generally assumed that equal amounts are being added from extraoceanic sources so that an overall steady state exists.

(7) Biochemical Circulation. Large fractions of the non-conservative constituents are involved in biological cycles in the sea (see articles on carbon dioxide cycle, organic; iron cycle; phosphate cycle; nitrogen cycle; nutrients, etc.). The biological aspects (see Redfield, Ketchum, and Richards, 1963, for details) of this redistribution involve the incorporation of inorganic ions into the bodies of plants and animals, ultimately by means of photosynthesis and therefore primarily in the upper levels that visible light penetrates. While in the particulate form, there will tend to be a net downward transport of large fractions of these materials which may later be either returned to solution by decomposition (remineralization) or incorporated into the sediments. Thus, there are large reservoirs of the nutrients, for example nitrogen and phosphorus compounds, at depths below the photosynthetic zone, and they can be returned to the photosynthetic zone only by the physical circulation of the water. This return is accomplished on a worldwide scale by the general circulation of the oceans, in regions of upwelling along certain coastal regions and along the equator, and by annual vertical mixing in the temperate zone and high latitudes. Thus, the biochemical circulation produces a net downward flux of non-conservative constituents in the particulate form that is essentially balanced, in the long run, by a net upward flux of these constituents in solution, as a result of water motions.

(8) Geochemical Circulations. Some constituents are introduced to the oceans from outside sources, such as the leaching of the land, volcanism, meteoritic bombardment, and the radioactive decay of elements in the atmosphere and lithosphere. Such materials can accumulate in the oceans, be removed to the atmosphere, or be incorporated in the sediments. The latter eventually may be incorporated in sedimentary rock which may, in geologic time, be returned to the land and again cycled through the weathering process. Geochemical estimates of the residence times of many of the elements in the sea have been made. These are based on the assumption that the sea is in a steady state, that is, that the rate at which a given element is being introduced to the oceans is balanced by the rate at which it is being deposited in the sediments or otherwise lost (such as by volatilization or as sea spray). Goldberg (1963) has listed a set of such residence times for most of the elements whose abundance in seawater has been estimated. They range from 100 years for aluminum to 2.6×10^8 years for sodium. The long residence times for sodium, Li $(2.0 \times 10^7$ years), Mg (4.5×10^7), K (1.1×10^7), Ca (8.0×10^6), and Sr (1.9×10^7) in comparison with estimates of the age of the oceans $(10^9$ years) is associated with the lack of reactivity of these elements in the marine environment. Conversely, it is evident that such elements as aluminum and silicon (residence time 8.0×10^3 years) enter the oceans and are then deposited in the sediments relatively rapidly.

The Methods and Materials of Chemical Oceanography

(1) **Seawater Analyses.** The description of the distribution of chemical variables in the oceans depends on the accumulation of accurate analyses of seawater samples taken within appropriate networks in time and in horizontal and vertical space. The most frequent analyses have been made of (1) the salinity, estimated from the chlorinity, the electrical conductivity, or some other physicochemical property of the water, (2) the dissolved oxygen content of the water, (3) the nutrient ions in the water, principally phosphate, nitrite, nitrate, and silicate, and (4) the pH and alkalinity of the water. Other chemical properties of seawater have been observed less frequently or rarely, and the observations have often been confined to surface waters or carried out using methods of dubious reliability (see Goldberg, 1961 and article on *Chemistry of Seawater*).

In 1932, Thompson and Robinson reviewed the then extant knowledge on the occurrence of the various elements in the sea and discussed the physical-chemical properties of seawater and their precise determination. This review also contains information on analytical methods. There are more recent reviews by Sverdrup, Johnson, and Fleming (1942), Richards (1957b), and Hood (1963), that contain many references to the distributions of various constituents of seawater, the oceanographic processes that contribute to the chemical environment, and the reaction chemistry of seawater.

(2) **Discrete Sampling Programs.** Oceanographic

observations are usually designed to give a synopsis of the distribution of a variable within a definite area of the ocean, or to show the changes of a variable in a limited area as a function of time. In the former case, attempts have been made to describe the variable in horizontal or vertical space, requiring observations at various depths at a network of oceanographic stations. Changes in time have been described by making repeated observations (sometimes at a selection of depths) at a station or series of stations. Some of these time-dependent series have been carried out over many years, such as the long series of nutrient observations that have been made at specific locations near the laboratory of the Marine Biological Association at Plymouth, England. The Woods Hole Oceanographic Institution has made repetitive observations of chemical, physical, and biological variables along a section between Cape Cod, Massachusetts and Bermuda. These series and similar ones permit the examination of temporal changes in the chemical properties of the waters and facilitate attempts to relate these changes to the factors causing them and to evaluate their effects on biological and other oceanographic events in the region. Other programs have been carried out in attempts to detect longer-term secular changes. One of the objectives of the oceanographic program of the International Geophysical Year (1957–1958) was to detect and evaluate secular changes in the properties of the South Atlantic Ocean by comparing the distribution of these properties observed during the IGY with those observed during the *Meteor* expedition in 1925–1927. However, uncertainties in the validity and comparability of the respective analyses are major problems in such comparative studies. This has proved particularly true of dissolved oxygen analyses, and it is difficult to judge whether apparent changes are due to real differences or to variations in the analytical methods used by the various observers.

(3) **Continuous Sensing Devices.** As chemical observations in the oceans have become closer, both in time and space, more and more detailed structure has been revealed in the chemical distributions. It has been possible to make continuously sensing devices to record chemical variations as a function of depth at one point in the ocean, or as a function of distance from a continuously moving vessel, or as a function of time at a fixed point. So far, these devices have been successfully used to record the temperature, electrical conductivity, and the dissolved oxygen content. In all cases, they have revealed details of the variations in these properties that would have been missed by more conventional spot sampling at discrete depths at an array of stations arranged in horizontal space.

(4) **Analytical Problems.** In most cases, chemical observations at sea still require the collection of

water samples and their subsequent analysis either aboard ship or at a land-based laboratory. For many of the more usual chemical constituents, this is a relatively routine matter, but the observation of some of the more transitory or very dilute constituents becomes difficult and uncertain. Some of the constituents may be rapidly and radically altered by increased biological activity in the water after the sample is taken, requiring either immediate analysis under frequently difficult shipboard conditions or the careful preservation of the samples by methods that have proved to be effective. Many of the procedures for the analysis of seawater constituents are given by Barnes (1959). The observation of highly dilute constituents, such as many trace metals and organic compounds, requires rigid precautions to prevent contamination of the samples. An example is copper, for which no valid subsurface observations were made until sampling devices that prevented any contact of the sample with metal were devised. Only surface samples, taken directly in glass or other non-metallic samplers, could be considered to be valid.

(5) **Analytical Advances.** Advances in analytical and radiochemistry have made possible the detection and determination of a variety of chemical constituents of seawater that could not readily be observed formerly. Many of the older methods of analysis, particularly for the trace metals, required the separation and concentration of the element from very large volumes, and these pretreatments frequently resulted in losses or contamination or both. Modern methods, depending on activation analysis, spectrometric methods, various forms of polarography, probes for the direct *in situ* observation of radionuclides, etc., avoid many of the former difficulties and should result in a more rapid increase in our knowledge of the distributions of some of these elements than was previously possible. It should be emphasized that investigations of the processes significant in controlling these distributions and the specific effects of these distributions has to await the accurate description of the variations in time and space.

FRANCIS A. RICHARDS

References

Barnes, H., 1959, "Apparatus and Methods of Oceanography," Part One: Chemical, London, George Allen and Unwin Ltd., 341pp.

Goldberg, E. D., 1961, "Chemistry in the Oceans," in (Sears, Mary, editor) "Oceanography," pp. 583–597, American Association for the Advancement of Science, Washington, D.C., 654pp.

Goldberg, E. D., 1963, "The Oceans as a Chemical System," in (Hill, M. N., editor) "The Sea—Ideas and Observations on Progress in the Study of the Seas," Vol. 2, pp. 3–25, New York and London, Interscience Publishers, 3 vols.

Harvey, H. W., 1957, "The Chemistry and Fertility of

Sea Waters," Second ed., Cambridge, Cambridge University Press, 240pp.

Hood, D. W., 1963, "Chemical oceanography," in (Barnes, H., editor) *Oceanogr. Marine Biol. Ann. Rev.*, **1**, 129–155.

Redfield, A. C., Ketchum, B. H., and Richards, F. A., 1963, "The influence of Organisms on the Composition of sea-water," in (Hill, M. N., editor) "The Sea—Ideas and Observations on Progress in the Study of the Seas," Vol. 2, pp. 26–77, New York and London, Interscience Publishers, 3 vols.

Richards, F. A., 1957a, "Oxygen in the ocean," in (Hedgpeth, J. W., editor) "Treatise on marine ecology and paleoecology," Vol. 1, pp. 185–238, *Geol. Soc. Am. Mem.* 67, **1**, 1269pp.

Richards, F. A., 1957b, "Some Current Aspects of Chemical Oceanography," in (Ahrens, L. H., Press, F., Rankama, K., and Runcorn, S. K., editors) "Physics and Chemistry of the Earth," Vol. 2, Ch. 4, pp. 77–128, London, Pergamon Press.

Sverdrup, H. U., Johnson, M. W., and Fleming, R. H., 1942, "The Oceans," New York, Prentice Hall, 1087pp.

Thompson, T. G., 1932, "The physical properties of sea water," in "Physics of the earth," *Bulletin of the National Research Council, No. 85*, **5**, Ch. 5, 63–94.

Thompson, T. G., and Robinson, R. J., 1932, "Chemistry of the sea," in "Physics of the earth," *Bulletin of the National Research Council, No. 85*, **5**, Ch. 5, 95–203.

CHUKCHI SEA

(1) Introduction

The Chukchi Sea is the easternmost of the shallow seas lying north of the Eurasian continent. Its area is 582,000 km². It extends from Wrangel Island in the west to Pt. Barrow in the east. On the north, it is bounded by the edge of the continental shelf which trends northwest from 72°N near Pt. Barrow to 75°N in the longitude of Wrangel Island. The International Hydrographic Bureau has defined the Arctic Circle as the southern limit, but the narrow part of Bering Strait is the more natural and preferable boundary. The Chukchi shelf forms a part of the large Bering–Chukchi platform (Fig. 1). This platform is of interest to geology and ecology since it served as a land bridge between the Old and New Worlds in previous times. The Chukchi Sea has a special interest for physical oceanography and marine biology since it is the connection between the Arctic and Pacific Oceans.

The name, Chukchi Sea, was proposed by H. U. Sverdrup after the native people who inhabit its Siberian coasts. In Russian papers, it is given as Chukotsk Sea (Zenkovitch, 1963); the easternmost part of Siberia is called the Chukotskij Peninsula. The shores of this sea have been inhabited for centuries by the Chukchi tribes and by the Alaskan Eskimos. The first recorded voyage in the Chukchi Sea was led by the Siberian Cossack, Simon Dezhnev, who sailed from the Kolyma River

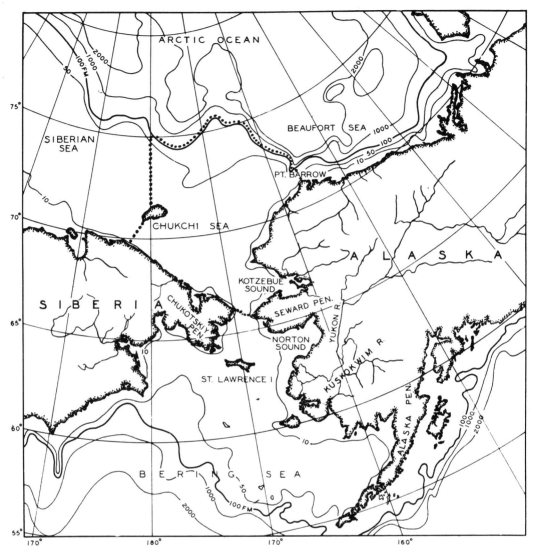

Fig. 1. Location map showing the Bering-Chukchi platform (from Moore, 1964). Boundary of Chukchi Sea shown dotted. (By permission of the Macmillan Co., New York City). The "Siberian Sea" is better referred to as "East Siberian Sea" (q.v.).

around East Cape (Mys Dezhneva) to the mouth of the Anadyr River in 1648. In 1847, Herald Island was discovered by the British expedition with the *Herald* and *Plover* under Captain Kellett. Wrangel Island was discovered in 1867 by Thomas Long, commander of an American whaling vessel. The relatively small extent of Wrangel Island was discovered in 1879 by DeLong during the ill-fated American expedition with the *Jeannette*. Extensive scientific research was conducted in the Chukchi Sea by the Norwegian North Polar Expedition with the *Maud*, 1918–1925. Since the Second World War, both the United States and the USSR have sponsored a number of oceanographic research expeditions to the Chukchi Sea.

The climate of the Chukchi Sea is Arctic. The coldest month is February, air temperature being from $-21°C$ on the south to $-27°C$ on the north. Minimum air temperatures may be as low as -42 to $-46°C$. Mean air temperatures of July range from $+2°C$ on the north to $+6°C$ on the south. Most of the year, the sea is covered with ice. In the years of great ice development when the packed ice-edge is close to the shores of the continent, surface water temperature off the coast does not exceed -0.5 to $0.9°C$, and that in the central part will range from $2–4°C$. In the periods of minor ice development, the water temperature of the surface layer at the coast may rise to $6°C$, and in the central part of the sea to $4–6°C$. The highest surface water temperature is observed in the southeastern part where the temperature regime is influenced by a warm current from the Bering Sea and by continental runoff from Kotzebue Sound.

(2) Currents

Throughout most of the year a current sets northward through Bering Strait carrying warm waters (4–12°C) of low salinity (<30‰) into the Chukchi Sea (Fig. 2). The low salinity is due to the Yukon River discharge south of Bering Strait. The flow is swiftest on the eastern side of the strait where speeds of up to 4 knots have been recorded. The northward flow is strongest during the summer months. The average annual transport through Bering Strait is 1.2×10^6 m³/sec (Bloom, 1964). After entering the Chukchi Sea, this current flows northward along the Alaskan Coast. In the vicinity of the Lisburne Peninsula this current divides, part of it flowing westward toward Wrangel Island and part continuing along the Alaskan coast to Pt. Barrow. North of Pt. Barrow, the current turns westward with the prevailing Arctic Ocean currents. From the East Siberian Sea, a colder current (4–6°C) with low salinity enters the Chukchi Sea through DeLong Strait south of Wrangel Island. Fresh water introduced from the Siberian rivers produces the low salinity. This current flows southeast along the Siberian coast mixing with the warmer shelf waters as it travels. On exceptional occasions, this current may continue southward through Bering Strait on the western side, but generally the current turns north again before the strait is reached. Along the northern part of the Chukchi Sea, the currents set to the west with the general Arctic Ocean flow. These current patterns are best developed during the summer. They represent average conditions and at any given time the circulation may be quite different from this due to wind influences.

During the summer a shallow thermocline develops in the northern Chukchi Sea at depths of 10–20 m due to surface heating. A subsurface temperature maximum may occur due to advection of warmer waters. Details of the temperature and salinity distribution depend on the pack ice limits.

Storm surges, which are an extreme example of local wind effects, are observed along the coasts. For example, a storm surge on October 3, 1963, caused considerable damage at Pt. Barrow when water levels rose 3 m above normal. While Fletcher's Ice Island was grounded in the eastern Chukchi Sea 130 km from shore, storm surge heights of 40 cm were recorded although the tide heights were only 12 cm. Cyclones originating in Siberia or the Aleutians and traveling northward across the Chukchi Sea are the usual cause of these storm surges.

(3) Tides and Waves

The tidal range in the Chukchi Sea is small. The mean spring tide range at Pt. Barrow, for example, is only 15 cm. The tides of the Chukchi Sea originate principally in the Atlantic Ocean. The narrow opening at Bering Strait prevents any significant influence from the Pacific Ocean. The tidal wave enters the Arctic Ocean between Spitsbergen and Greenland. It crosses the Arctic Ocean to the Chukchi Sea in about 12 hours and travels southward across it. The tidal currents have a rotary character.

Wave conditions of the Chukchi Sea are directly dependent on atmospheric circulation in the eastern sector of the Arctic. In winter, i.e., from October to May, a wedge of the Siberian anticyclone is located above the Chukotka (Chukchi) Peninsula. A weak saddle stretches from the Aleutian Low to this wedge. In summer a high-pressure area is formed over the Chukchi Sea (Alisov, 1956). As a result of this distribution of pressure centers around the Chukchi Sea, north and northwesterly winds prevail (mean velocity above the sea is 5–6 m/sec). They set up waves of the same direction at almost all the seasons of the year, although in summer the influence of the Pacific monsoons is also apparent. That is why sometimes in summer or autumn northwesterly winds are interrupted by southeasterly and south winds carried by cyclones from the Bering Sea. Wave pattern changes considerably depending on ice conditions. The highest waves are in autumn, up to 7 m. With increase of ice formation at the end of October wave action grows weak. However, in the southern part of the sea where new ice appears late (in the years of little ice development), considerable wave action may continue up to the beginning of November. In summer the waves in the central part of the sea are not higher than 5 m. In general, storms in the Chukchi Sea very seldom

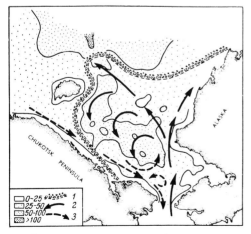

Fig. 2. The Chukchi Sea showing depths, direction of the warm (2) and cold (3) currents and the summer boundary of the ice (1) (from Zenkevich, 1963).

occur in summer, averaging 1–4 stormy days per month; in November, there is an average of 7–9 stormy days and in isolated years there may be about 20–24 stormy days per month.

(4) Ice

Ice conditions in the Chukchi Sea are not only dependent on the season but also show year-to-year variations. Ice covers the Chukchi Sea for most of the year. Only during two or three summer months do the southern parts become completely free of ice. The warm current along the Alaskan coast generally opens that region earliest and prevents its freezing until last. The colder current along the Siberian coast generally carries ice down into the Chukchi Sea from the East Siberian Sea and that coast is rarely free of ice.

In the northern Chukchi Sea, polar pack ice similar to that in the central Arctic Ocean usually prevails. The ice in the southern Chukchi Sea is usually winter ice, one year in age.

(5) Submarine Topography

Depths vary between 40 and 60 m over the greater part of the Chukchi Sea. Off the Siberian coast, depths of 40 m are generally reached in a few kilometers. Off the Alaskan coast, 40 m depths are generally encountered 50–100 km from shore. Two large shallow bays, Kolyuchin Bay and Kotzebue Sound, flank the southern Chukchi Sea. They are less than 20 m deep.

Several irregular bottom features occur in the northern Chukchi Sea. Two submarine canyons cross the shelf. Herald Canyon heads at about 70°N and extends northward along 175°W longitude to the continental margin. A depth of 90 m is found east of Herald Island, but the depth decreases to 70 m before the continental margin is reached. Barrow Canyon heads on the shelf about 150 km west of Pt. Barrow. It trends northeast, parallel to the Alaskan coast, and crosses into the Beaufort Sea north of Pt. Barrow. The part of Barrow Canyon in the Chukchi Sea is 6–10 km wide with depths of 50–100 m. Barrow Canyon was used by SSN *Nautilus* for gaining entrance beneath the ice to the Arctic Basin in 1957. Herald Shoal, with a depth of 13 m, lies almost due north of Bering Strait at 70° 30′N.

Microrelief of various types is also present. A small channel south of Pt. Hope and other features near the Alaskan coast have been interpreted as part of a drowned Pleistocene drainage system. Grounded ice near the Pt. Barrow coast produces a characteristic roughness of the bottom on a small scale.

(6) Sediments and Geologic Structure

The floor of the Chukchi Sea is covered with a thin veneer of unconsolidated muds, sands, and gravels over most of its area. The sorting is

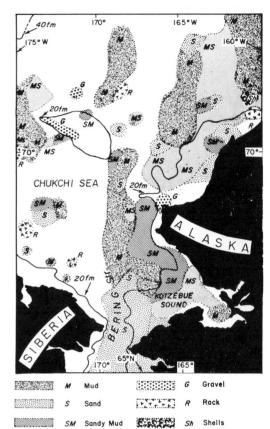

	M	Mud		G	Gravel
	S	Sand		R	Rock
	SM	Sandy Mud		Sh	Shells
	MS	Muddy Sand			20 fm Line
					40 fm Line

Fig. 3. Sediment chart of the Chukchi shelf (modified after Dietz *et al.*, 1964).

generally poor due to the mixing of ice-rafted debris with normal shelf deposits. The distribution of sediment types as found from American expeditions is shown in Fig. 3.

An acoustic-reflection survey in the eastern Chukchi Sea has shown that these unconsolidated recent sediments form only a thin covering (0–12 m) over the bedrock (Moore, 1964). The thickest accumulation was in the Kotzebue Sound area where evidences of buried Pleistocene drainage patterns were also noted. The accumulation in the Kotzebue area is apparently from the river sediment load discharged there. Bering Strait, swept clean by the swift currents, is devoid of unconsolidated sediment. Other areas are locally devoid of unconsolidated sediments which often occur as fill in slight topographic depressions. The acoustic-reflection records over the eastern Chukchi Sea often have a patchy appearance which is attributed to irregular deposits of ice-rafted sands and gravels. Thicker sediments were found further north by seismic methods at Fletcher's Ice Island when it was grounded on the shelf (Hunkins and

Kutschale, 1963). At 72°N 160°W the unconsolidated sediment was 30 m thick. Along a 164 km profile northwest of that location, the thickness averaged 200 m. The average water depth along this profile was 230 m since it extended into deeper waters near the continental margin.

The Bering–Chukchi platform joins the Asian and North American continents. The crustal structure is continental rather than oceanic in character and the geologic structures of the adjacent Siberian and Alaskan land masses undoubtedly continue seaward beneath the Chukchi Sea. In particular, a structural continuity between Wrangel Island and the Lisburne Peninsula is evident on the basis of stratigraphic and tectonic trends. The two areas represent exposures of a continuous Paleozoic and Mesozoic structure across the Chukchi shelf (Hopkins, 1959). The Alaskan coastal plain north of the Brooks Range contains the greatest area of Cretaceous rocks in Alaska and these rocks must also continue seaward northwest of Alaska. Direct evidence for the extension of these structures beneath the Chukchi shelf has come from acoustic-reflection surveys. Truncated folds and monoclinal sequences are evident in the bedrock of the eastern Chukchi Sea.

The Chukchi continental shelf is part of the Chukchi (Chukotskaya) geosyncline zone which began to develop at the end of the Paleozoic period (Baranova and Biské, 1964). During the Mesozoic era this area underwent repeated changes of marine and continental conditions which indicates intensive tectonic activity and gradual transformation of the Chukchi geosyncline zone into a fold belt. Folded structures of the continental shelf were finally shaped in the Late Cretaceous and the beginning of the Paleogene period. In the Paleogene and Neogene a considerable part of the Chukchi shelf was developed as a lake and river valley area; only as far back as the Pliocene did the sea begin to invade the land, and by the beginning of the Quaternary period, its coastal terraces extended up to the level of + 100 m. Middle and Late Quaternary (Wisconsin, Würm) glaciations in northeast Asia coincided in time with major regressions (Petrov, 1960). There was already land in place of the Bering Strait in the early stages of Wisconsin glaciation. The coast bears no traces of glaciation. Strata of lacustrine, alluvial and fluvioglacial sediments from mountainous regions accumulated in the area. The postglacial period was characterized by rising of sea level and this continues at the present time (Kaplin, 1957; Ionin, 1959).

The shore line of the Chukchi Sea is straight and has neither capes protruding far into the sea nor deep bays. Kolyuchinskaya Guba (inlet) on the west and Kotzebue Sound on the east are two exceptions. Coastal topography may be divided into two types: either there is hilly lowland or else there are spurs of coastal mountain masses that come down to the sea. In many places in the lowland areas the rise of sea level has produced estuaries along river valleys and has led to the origin of coastal lagoons. The lagoons stretch along the entire Asian shore, and they are also widespread on the Alaskan side.

(7) Marine Geophysics

Earthquake surface wave measurements show the Chukchi shelf to be continental in type, in agreement with other lines of evidence.

Gravity anomalies, both free air and Bouguer, are slightly positive over the shelf indicating that the area is approximately in isostatic equilibrium.

A magnetically disturbed zone with amplitudes of up to 750 gammas crosses the Chukchi shelf parallel to the Alaskan coast. It extends across the continental margin northwest of Pt. Barrow. It covers an area about 100×600 km in extent. Magnetic anomalies are difficult to interpret geologically and the origin of this one is not yet known.

Lying immediately to the north of the Chukchi Sea in the Arctic Ocean basin are traces of a subsided continental structure in the Chukchi Cap and west of it is the Chukchi Abyssal Plain (Shaver and Hunkins, 1964).

(8) Biology

In comparison with other polar seas, the Chukchi Sea is richer in fauna and flora both qualitatively and quantitatively. Warm waters penetrating to the sea through the Bering Strait carry in a boreal fauna (Zenkevitch, 1963). The sea is inhabited by walruses, seals, sea hares, polar bears, and whales (in summer), in quantities of commercial value. Arctic char and polar cod are the most common fish. In summer, both over the coast and over the sea, there are abundant ducks, geese, eiders, seagulls, auks and murres.

KENNETH HUNKINS
P. A. KAPLIN

References

Baranova, Yu. P., and Biske, S. Ph., 1964, "The Northeast of the USSR," Moscow, "Nauka" Publishing House.

Bloom, G., 1964, "Water transport and temperature measurements in the eastern Bering Strait, 1953–1958," *J. Geophys. Res.*, **69**, 3335–3354.

Dietz, R., Carsola, A., Buffington, E., and Shipek, C., 1964, "Sediments and Topography of the Alaskan Shelves," in "Papers in Marine Geology—Shepard Comm. Vol.," pp. 241–256, New York, The Macmillan Co.

Hopkins, D., 1959, "Cenozoic history of the Bering land bridge," *Science*, **129**, 1519–1528.

Hunkins, K., and Kutschale, H., 1963, "Shallow-water propagation in the Arctic Ocean," *J. Acoust. Soc. Am.*, **35**, 542–551.

Ionin, A. S., 1959, "Investigations on the dynamics and morphology of the Soviet shores of the Chukotskoye and Bering seas," *Proc. Oceanographic Comm. Acad. Sci. USSR*, **4**.

Kaplin, P. A., 1957, "On some peculiarities of lagoons in the north-eastern coast of the USSR," *Proc. Oceanographic Comm. Acad. Sci. USSR*, **2**.

Moore, D., 1964, "Acoustic-reflection reconnaissance of continental shelves: eastern Bering and Chukchi Seas," in "Papers in Marine Geology—Shepard Comm. Vol.," pp. 319–362, New York, The Macmillan Co.

Petrov, O. M., 1960, "On the history of development of topography of coastal valleys of the Chukotka Peninsula," *Materials of 2nd All-Union Geomorphological Meeting, Moscow*.

Shaver, R., and Hunkins, K., 1964, "Arctic Ocean geophysical studies: Chukchi Cap and Chukchi Abyssal Plain," *Deep-Sea Res.*, **11**, 905–917.

Sverdrup, H. U. (editor), 1936, "Scientific Results of the Norwegian North Polar Expedition with the *Maud*, 1918–1925," Bergen, Norway.

U.S. Navy Oceanographic Office, 1958, "Oceanographic Atlas of the Polar Seas, Part II, Arctic," H.O. Publ. No. 705.

Zenkevich, L., 1963, "Biology of the Seas of the USSR," English edition, New York, Interscience Publishers.

Cross-references: *Arctic Ocean; Beaufort Sea; Bering Sea; East Siberian Sea.*

CIRCULATION—*See* OCEAN CURRENTS

COASTAL CURRENTS—*See* OCEAN CURRENTS

COLD WATER SPHERE—*See* TROPOSPHERE, AND STRATOSPHERE IN THE OCEAN

CONDUCTION

Conduction is a transfer of energy by means of some sort of conductor, that permits transfer of molecular or particle activity without overall motion. It is contrasted against other forms of energy transfer such as heat convection and any form of radiation. In both oceanography and meteorology, conduction involves heat, electricity and sound (the last is *transmitted*). *Conductivity* is the unit or conduction potential of a medium.

(a) Thermal Conductivity

In the conduction of heat, the kinetic energy of random motion of molecules is passed along from molecule to molecule by simple exchange of momentum, as by collision. In the case of air, which is a poor conductor, conduction of heat is important over distances of only a few centimeters in the atmosphere. Except very near a solid or liquid surface, *convection* (q.v.) and *eddy heat conduction* are much more effective means of heat transfer in the atmosphere than conduction (see *Turbulence*).

In the oceans also, thermal conductivity is only important near boundary surfaces, transfer by

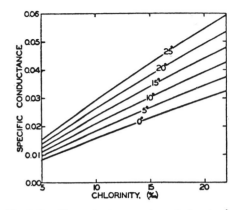

Fig. 1. Specific conductance, reciprocal ohms/cm³, of seawater as a function of temperature and chlorinity (Sverdrup, 1942). (By permission of Prentice, Hall, Englewood Cliffs, N.J.)

means of currents and turbulence being predominant in general.

The coefficient of thermal conductivity is defined through Fourier's equation of heat transfer: $H = -k\dfrac{\partial T}{\partial n}$, where H is the heat conduction rate (per unit area, per unit time), $-\dfrac{\partial T}{\partial n}$ is the temperature gradient normal to the surface across which heat is being conducted, and k is the conductivity of the material. For air at 0°C, $k = 5.66 \times 10^{-5}$ cal/(cm sec °C). For pure water at 15°C, the coefficient is equal to 1.39×10^{-3}. It is smaller for seawater and increases with increasing temperature and pressure.

(b) Electrical Conductivity

This is the flow of electricity in the form of transfer of electric charge through a material, usually by movement of ions. In the most common form, conduction by a metal, the ions are free electrons, and in an electrolyte they are both positive and negative ions resulting from the dissociation of the solute. In certain semiconductors, conduction is due to the migration of "holes," or "missing electrons." In general, the rate of transfer of charge is proportional to the electric field intensity, as expressed in Ohm's law: $J = \sigma E$, where J is the flow, σ the conductivity (mhos) and E the intensity of the electric field in the direction of J.

The lower atmosphere is a good *dielectric*, i.e., a poor conductor, though there are enough ions from radioactive processes to conduct a very small current (4×10^{-16} ampere/cm² downward on the average) in the ever-present vertical field of approximately 100 V/m. The conductivity rises to high values in the upper atmosphere (see *Ionosphere* and *Magnetosphere*).

Resistivity, the reciprocal of conductivity, is an intrinsic property of materials and is temperature dependent; the former is measured in *mhos*, the latter in *ohms*, each for a 1-cm cube. *Conductance* is the measure of the volumetric conductivity and depends on the dimensions of the conductor; its reciprocal is *resistance*.

Seawater, due to the presence of dissolved and dissociated salts, is a good electrical conductor. Seawater with a salinity of 35‰ at 0°C has a conductivity of about 0.03 mhos/cm, compared to a value for distilled water of about 1×10^{-6} and for copper, about 5×10^5 mhos/cm. Due to the constancy of the relative proportions of the salts dissolved in seawater, its electrical conductivity is very highly correlated with salinity. The relatively simple measurement of conductivity is therefore widely used as a method of determining the salinity and thus the density of seawater.

Conductivity of the seawater increases with increasing temperature and salinity, almost linearly. Its specific values (per cm^3) are shown in Fig. 1. The thermal effect is related to the mobility of the ions, being subject to internal friction in water. As temperature rises, friction decreases. Since conductivity of true seawater can be measured with accuracy up to 10^{-6} mhos/cm ^{3} with bridge methods, the salinity can be determined up to 10^{-3}‰ by measuring conductivity. Therefore, the conductivity measurement method is generally replacing the titration method to determine salinity.

A further use of conductivity is found in determining redox potential in sediments, since it varies with the oxygen content (see *pH–Eh of Marine Sediments*).

RHODES W. FAIRBRIDGE

References

Byers, H. R., 1959, "General Meteorology," Third ed., New York, McGraw-Hill Book Co.; 540pp.

Cox, R. A., 1963, "The Salinity Problem," in (Sears, M., editor) "Progress in Oceanography," Vol. I, pp. 243–261, New York, Pergamon Press.

LaFond, E. C., 1951, "Processing Oceanographic Data," pp. 103–104, U.S. Navy Hydrographic Office.

Sutton, O. G., 1953, "Micrometeorology," New York, McGraw-Hill Book Co., 333pp.

Sverdrup, H. U., *et al.*, 1942, "The Oceans," pp. 71–72, Englewood Cliffs, N.J., Prentice-Hall.

Cross-references: *Convection; Diffusion in the Oceans; pH–Eh of marine sediments; Salinity; Turbulence.*

CONFLUENCE AND DIFFLUENCE—*See* Vol. II

CONTINENTAL BORDERLAND

An examination of the topographic profiles of the submerged shelves of the continents reveals that a few recurring forms typify the great bulk of these marginal zones. Most typical is a simple terrace with a gently sloping upper surface containing many smaller subsidiary terrace sets which terminates at its seaward edge in depths ranging from about 50 meters to over 200 meters. The bottom then deepens at steeper gradients to the depths of the oceanic floor.

In a few localities, the profile is strikingly different and includes numerous depressions and rises. Such areas occur off southern California, the South China Sea, the Coral Sea, several belts in the northwest Indian Ocean, the northern shelf of Venezuela and the broad zone off the Atlantic coast of Canada and adjacent New England, the Bahamas and the Blake Plateau. Some of the depressions approach bathyal depths, and some of the banks and shoals rise above the water surface to form islands. The feature is normally bounded on its seaward side by the main continental slope as in other continental margin profiles. This particular feature has been termed the *Continental Borderland* by Shepard and Emery (1941), and the broad borderland off southern California has been chosen as the type area (Fig. 1).

In this southern Californian borderland, the surface is a checkerboard of basins, banks and islands with a regional physiographic trend similar to that of the adjoining land area. The individual basins are oriented with their long axes in a northwest-southeast direction and are truncated at their ends by east-west lineaments. The area has long been thought to be a region of block-faulted highs and lows, but recent work with continuous seismic profiling equipment shows that numerous large fold structures are present as well. Thus the structure as well as the topography is closely related to the dominant patterns of the adjacent land. Observations of the depths of the tops of banks and knolls in the borderland and the depth of the shelf break lead to the conclusion that the area has been downwarped to the south and west and is, therefore, simply a drowned portion of the continental province of basins and ranges which includes much of the southwestern United States and western Mexico.

The southern half of the southern Californian borderland, lying off the northern portion of the Baja California peninsula, is less well known but apparently is generally similar to the northern half and also shows the effect of downwarping, but more to the north and west. The area, therefore, has roughly the shape of a giant bowl tipped toward the sea. At the northern and southern extremities, the continental slope has been broken by fractures and gaps which may be indicative of major structural features. At the northern end, near Point Conception, the slope is broken and offset. This feature appears to be a zone in which the Transverse Range structures and the deep-sea Murray Fracture Zone meet. At the southern end off Baja California, the slope is broken into a series of great embayments or gaps which terminate in the reentrant in the coast at Sebastian Viscaino Bay. Several large structures are associated with

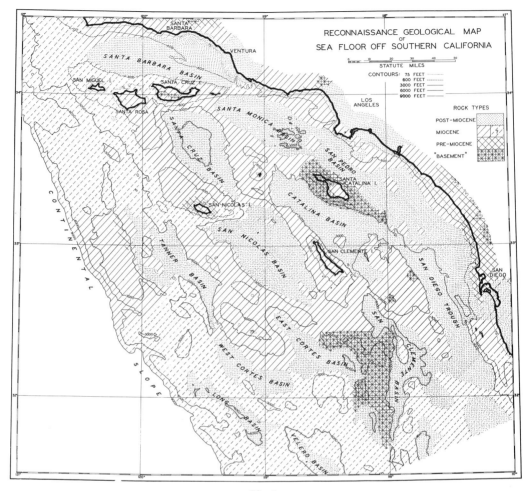

Fig. 1.

this southern embayment including the Baja California Syncline axis.

Sedimentologically, the borderlands form sediment traps for the materials slumping or flowing off the continental margins, and for this reason, the depressions all possess flat depositional floors. The banks, ridges and islands are only thinly veneered by sediments or are bare rock surfaces. In southern California, these rocks are mainly older sediments and sedimentary rocks of Tertiary and Late Mesozoic age with associated volcanics and intrusives similar in general pattern and lithologies to the rocks that form the coastal and interior mountains of the adjacent land. Again, the similarity suggests that the borderland is simply a downwarped and flooded part of a formerly larger geological province, i.e., continental cratonic crust.

Off southern California, the sedimentary deposits are thickest in the inner basins and probably total several thousand meters of sediments. The fill becomes thinner in each successively more distant row of basins because of the effectiveness of the inner basins as sediment traps. The outer series of basins receive principally pelagic and suspended load with minor turbidite or slump contribution. Typically, the coastal slopes are bounded by aprons of probable slump origin, in contrast to the thinly veneered slopes of the islands and banks which terminate abruptly at the flat basin floors. Submarine canyons commonly are found along the coastal slopes, while only a few features of this type are in evidence in the bank and island slopes. If canyon formation is dependent on large volumes of longshore drifted material, then this is an expectable association.

Sediments in the southern Californian basins are mainly silts and sands with minor clay content. The clay content increases seaward as does the carbonate fraction, which is dominantly composed of the tests of foraminifera. Organic content is highest in the central and inner basin sediments where relatively large supplies and moderate transport lead to a net accumulation. The slower rates of deposition and the greater depth to the bottom and opportunity for destruction produce much smaller net accumulations in the outer deep basins. Several of the basins have sills at or close to the depth of the oxygen minimum in the water column, and this also contributes to the relative preservation and accumulation of organic debris by inhibiting the work of benthonic scavengers.

The general sediment minerology shows a similar provenance, but a few broadly drawn mineral provinces can be defined. In the northern area, including the northern channel islands and extending south along the outer margins of the borderland, epidote and opaque minerals predominate. In the central zone, the opaques increase; in the inner and southern zone, amphiboles become an important constituent. The southernmost area off northern Baja California has the above suites plus increasing amounts of pyroxenes. However, the heavy mineral suites are remarkably similar. Clays are also apparently well-mixed suites of the three principal families, but the very general and relatively old work on these mineral distributions does not define any important differences beyond a gross seaward increase in illitic species and a matching decrease in the kaolinite fraction. Much remains to be done in this regard using modern techniques.

Typically, the bank tops and distant ridges in the southern Californian borderland are rock surfaces with coatings and nodules of phosphatic rock, and some glauconite is also present. Evidence indicates active deposition in Late Miocene through Late Pliocene time. The shelf edge sediments are typically the main sites of glauconite accumulation.

The shelf sediments along the California mainland platform and surrounding the islands are complexes of relict sediments representing several discrete episodes of changes in sea level associated with the Pleistocene Ice Ages. These interfinger with contemporary depositional lenses and, in turn, have been reworked to produce residual deposits on areas of relief.

Submarine fans at the mouths of the several active canyons incising the mainland slope contain numerous sand and gravel lenses in alternation with gray-green clay silts. The coarser layers show flow bedding, cross lamination, graded bedding and other structures typically associated with turbidites. The green clay silts of the basins, slopes and aprons appear to be massive and structureless as the result of the churning and mixing action of benthic burrowing organisms. Only in the Santa Barbara Basin where the low oxygen content of the bottom water inhibits burrowing forms are the finely laminated primary structures of these sediments preserved, illustrating an annual cycle of suspended load sedimentation. The annual nature is evidenced by the close agreement of the ages of cores in this basin as determined by laminae counts and by radiocrabon dates.

History of the Southern California Borderland

The continental borderland off California was probably initiated in later Miocene time, and the various trends have been emphasized by late Tertiary and Pleistocene orogenic activity. The history of the borderland is similar to that of the adjacent land as noted earlier, and the episodes of folding and faulting preserved in the land record probably apply to the borderland as well. After the area was originated, sedimentation commenced to fill the rows of basins in turn, beginning with the now filled Ventura, Los Angeles, San Fernando and Santa Maria Basins. After these had filled to overflowing, shallow shelf and coastal sedimentation regimes rapidly prograded the surfaces to form the present coastal plains. At present, the next row of basins is being filled, and the San Diego Trough is presently filled to its sill over which material is beginning to spill into the next seaward line of basins. If no major structural change intervenes, the borderland will ultimately be prograded and filled by an encroaching lens of continental sediment which will produce a more typically mature continental terrace profile. Thus the California Borderland represents a youthful stage in the development of a continental margin.

Economics

Economic exploitation of the borderland is presently centered on the oil reserves to be found in the various offshore structures of the mainland shelf, banks and shoals. The phosphatic deposits will possibly be of commercial value in the future. Heavy-mineral deposits in the shelf and shallow bank top areas may conceivably also prove amenable to economic recovery.

Other Continental Borderlands

Each of the other continental borderlands seems to have a similar history of fairly recent subsidence and breakup into quasi-cratonic crust, and each differs from the last, although some common features are apparent. Most are similar in that the depressions are sites of sedimentation; the highs are exposed rock or are loci for the deposition of authigenic mineral nodules and coatings. All are probably structurally youthful margins. It is possible that the borderland form is represented in fossil form in the broad terrace bordering the southern Atlantic coastal region of the United States (Blake Plateau and Bahamas). Geophysical studies show that this terrace is composed of older filled and structurally deformed basins and ridges. Future studies of other older margins may reveal similar structures. It is possible that this topographic form represents one initial type of continental margin, while others may begin as a scarp and marginal trench profile which appears to be the typical initial stage off many coasts of youthful origin such as the Pacific margins of South

America and the island arcs of the eastern Pacific. (See also article: *Submarine Plateaus.*)

Oceanography

Oceanographically, the California Borderland is especially interesting because of the complex interaction of sill depth with the water of the open ocean. These provide the main control for the character of subsill water characteristics. For example, as noted earlier, the sill of the Santa Barbara Basin is located near the oxygen minimum in the open ocean water column. Thus the water that fills the subsill portion of this basin has a constant temperature and salinity similar to that found at the sill depth in the open ocean column and has low-to-vanishing oxygen contents. The pattern of basin water mass characteristics indicates that the motion of water into the various basins is from south to north following the downwarped trend of the borderland. The surface circulation is dominated by the south-flowing California Current which passes along the seaward edge of the northern borderland and then turns in over the margin to form a large gyral. The north central zone of the region has been termed an area of regional upwelling and has been attributed to the action of the prevailing northwest winds. This pattern may also be generated by entrainment of surface water in the California Current and a subsequent rising of deeper water to replace this loss. In either instance, the central zone is typically one of colder surface water temperature and high productivity.

Local surface circulation takes on the pattern of the local wind drift patterns. Where these winds are the product of the land-sea breeze mechanism, fogs are sometimes generated in morning and evening during spring and summer. The northwest prevailing wind works over the water surface downwind of coastal promontories and produces local pockets of strong shallow upwelling on the southern sides of points and bluffs. The great gyral motion of the California Current and the entrainment of deeper waters and adjacent surface waters produces a mixed water type of a transitional nature. The area is a meeting ground for subtropic and boreal water masses, and this is reflected in the variety of intermixed and transitional faunal communities.

Borderlands are of great scientific interest since they provide numerous models of oceanic conditions. Each basin can be considered as a model ocean with deep floors, slopes, bordering islands and canyons. The great variety of water conditions and topographic and sedimentologic environments provides numerous niches for study by the marine biologist. Studies of sediment accumulation budgets are possible in the closed basins. Circulation studies can be made in individual basins to illustrate mechanisms of multilayer flow. Although

short-lived geologically, this form is an important initial phase of continental margin development.

D. S. GORSLINE

References

Emery, K. O., 1960, "Sea off Southern California," New York, J. Wiley & Sons, Inc., 366pp.
Gorsline, D. S., and Emery, K. O., 1959, "Turbidity current deposits in San Pedro and Santa Monica Basins off So. Calif.," *Bull. Geol. Soc. Am.*, **70**, 279–290.
Hersey, J. B., Bunce, E. T., Wyrick, R. F., and Dietz, F. T., 1959, "Geophysical investigation of the Continental Margin between Cape Henry, Va., and Jacksonville, Fla.," *Bull. Geol. Soc. Am.*, **70**, 437–466.
Shepard, F. P., 1963, "Submarine Geology," Second ed., New York, Harper & Brothers, 557pp.
Shepard, F. P., and Emery, K. O., 1941, "Submarine topography off the California Coast," *Geol. Soc. Am. Spec. Papers*, **31**, 171pp.
Uchupi, E., and Emery, K. O., 1964, "The Continental Slope between San Francisco, Calif., and Cadros Island, Mexico," *Deep-Sea Res.*, **10**, 397–448.

CONTINENTAL RISE

A geomorphic feature of the lower continental margin (see *Continental Terrace*) where the gradient ranges from 1:40 to 1:2000 (name first proposed by Heezen *et al.*, 1959, 1965). Its width varies from 0–600 km. Its position always comes between the continental slope (q.v.) and the abyssal plain or abyssal hills. The upper boundary is gradational, but the lower boundary is more often abrupt. The depth range is 1400–5100 meters (750–2800 fathoms). Local relief is moderate to low (20–40 meters), except where dissected at submarine canyons (rather frequent) or punctuated by seamounts (rather infrequent). In some places, as off the eastern United States, the rise is divided into two steps, the "upper" (3000 meters; 1600 fathoms) and the "lower" (4200 meters; 2300 fathoms) continental rise. South of Cape Hatteras these two broad platforms break up into "a series of broad steps that resemble a giant staircase . . . (which then) merge with the benches of the Blake Plateau" (Heezen *et al.*, 1965 p. 29). In some regions the rise is extremely narrow, even nonexistent, and in others very broad.

The rise appears to consist, at least superficially, of fans or aprons of sediment that have been derived largely from the finer terrigenous silts and clays of the (neritic) continental shelf, but carried by bottom currents and gravitational creep down to the bathyal environment below the continental slope.

The structural nature of the continental rise is a sedimentary prism, as demonstrated by seismic refraction and reflection. Its origin may be in one or a combination of two ways:

(a) It is faulted along both margins and has

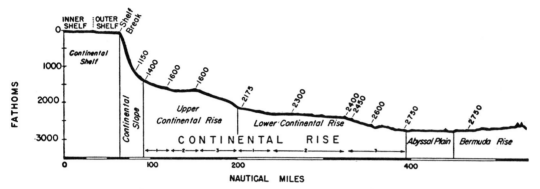

Fig. 1. Continental margin provinces: type profile off northeastern United States. Profile plotted from PDR records. This profile is representative of the sector from Georges Bank to Cape Hatteras (Heezen *et al.*, 1959).

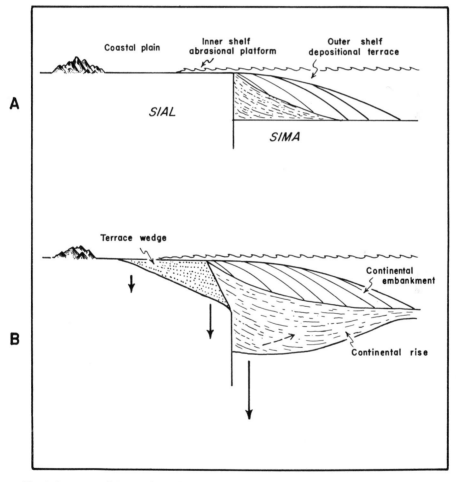

Fig. 2. Isostasy and the continental embankment. Simplified diagram to show the buildup of a continental rise uplapping the continental slope. This is followed by the prograding of a continental embankment. Without the effect of isostasy an inner abrasion platform and an outer terrace of accumulation would form (A), but because isostasy does come into play, a terrace wedge develops instead of an abrasion platform (B). Because of the continent-ocean floor topographic contrast, the rise thickness attains great dimensions before reaching isostatic equilibrium. According to Lawson (1942), such thickness in the Mississippi delta region would be 40,000 feet. As shown by the dashed arrow, the sedimentation axis moves seaward with time (from Dietz, 1963).

subsided as segment of the continental margin formerly at or above sea level; in short, it is a continental borderland which has subsided to the abyssal depths, or

(b) It is a former extension of the continental terrace sedimentary wedge that is down-faulted at about the former continental slope margin and downwarped at the seaward edge. An illustration of the second model is offered by Dietz (1964) see Fig. 2. Recognition of such a feature along the Atlantic slope of the northeastern United States was identified by Drake, Ewing and Sutton (1959) as a contemporary evolving geosyncline. According to Hsu (1965) the floor of this feature is the site, now subsided, of the hypothetical Paleozoic "continent" of *Appalachia*.

RHODES W. FAIRBRIDGE

References

Dietz, R. S., 1964, "Origin of Continental Slopes." *Am. Scientist*, **52**, No. 1, 50–69.

Drake, C. L., Ewing, M., and Sutton, G. H., 1959, "Continental Margins and Geosynclines: The East coast of North America North of Cape Hatteras," in "Physics and Chemistry of the Earth," Vol. 3, pp. 110–198, New York, Pergamon Press.

Heezen, B. C., Ewing, M., and Tharp, M., 1959, "The floors of the oceans. I. The North Atlantic," *Geol. Soc. Am. Spec. Paper*, **65**, 113pp.

Heezen, B. C., and Tharp, M., 1965, "Descriptive sheet to accompany physiographic diagram of the Indian Ocean," *Geol. Soc. Am. Spec. Paper*.

Hsu, K. J., 1965, "Isostasy, crustal thinning, mantle changes, and the disappearance of ancient land masses," *Am. J. Sci.*, **263**, 97–109.

Cross-references: *Bathymetry; Continental Borderland; Continental Terrace.*

CONTINENTAL SHELF, CLASSIFICATION

The continental shelves are usually defined as the gently sloping shallow-water platforms that extend from the coasts out to the shelf "break," to a point where there begins a relatively steep descent to the deep ocean floor. The average width of the shelves of the world is 44 miles. The average depth at which the shelf terminates is approximately 450 feet, although there is a great variation depending in part on the type of continental shelf. There are some very distinct varieties of shelves that are well shown on the coastal charts of the world. These include shelves off glaciated areas, shelves with parallel ridges and troughs, smooth shelves off some high-latitude areas, shelves along which there are strong currents, shelves in clear tropical seas, shelves with rocky banks along the outer rim, and shelves bordering large deltas (Fig. 1). Each of these will be described briefly.

Shelves off Glaciated Land Masses. In those areas where the continents were covered with ice during the glacial period, the ice margin almost always appears to have continued out from the coast and across the continental shelves. The result of this coverage of ice has been the production of a shelf type that contrasts with all others in being very irregular. There are many deep basins and troughs, particularly on the inside of the shelves. Some of the troughs extend all the way across, e.g., outside the Gulf of St. Lawrence (Fig. 2), the Juan de Fuca Straits, and beyond some of the fiords of Norway and British Columbia. Depths in these basins are commonly as great as 1000 feet and exceptionally as much as 3000–5000 feet. In almost all cases, the depths decrease in crossing the shelf, in contrast to those of submarine canyons.

Along the outer portions of the shelves off glaciated areas there are many banks, most of them being covered by shallow water but locally coming to the surface, as in the case of Sable Island off Nova Scotia. These banks include some of the best fishing areas in the world, for example Georges Bank off New England and the Grand Bank of

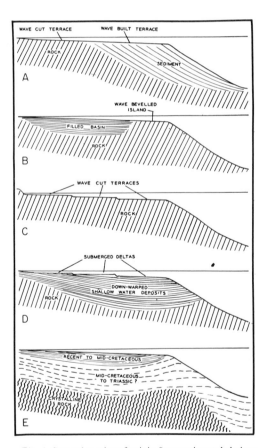

Fig. 1. Several modes of origin for continental shelves. (From "Submarine Geology," 2nd Ed., Shepard.)

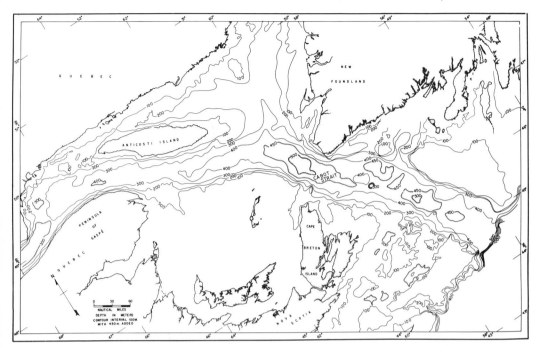

Fig. 2. The deep trough which extends across the continental shelf beyond the equally deep Gulf of St. Lawrence.

Newfoundland. Strong tidal currents swirl over these shoaler banks and produce submarine sand bars and mega-ripples that are elongate in the direction of the currents. Apparently the topography of these shelves is mainly the result of former glaciation, with excavation forming the troughs and inner basins, and morainal deposition forming the outer banks.

Shelves with Parallel Ridges and Troughs. Among the relatively smooth shelves off unglaciated areas, a type which is quite common is found to have low ridges and troughs that extend roughly parallel to the coast and to the edge of the shelf (Fig. 3). These longitudinal features have low relief, ordinarily not more than about 20 or 30 feet. The ridges are usually sand covered, and muddy sediments are found in the troughs. Shells found on some of the ridges are of a type indicating that the sea was lower during deposition. It seems likely that these features represent drowned barrier islands formed during a lower stand of sea level. Examples are found off the east central United States.

Smooth Shelves in High Latitudes. Some of the flattest continental shelves in the world are found in the Bering Sea and off Northern Alaska and Siberia. In these places, the lands have not been glaciated except on the mountain ranges. It would appear that the shore ice prevented any development of barrier islands along these Arctic coasts during the lower sea levels of the glacial stages.

Constant movement of floating ice would have a planing action on the shelf floor. The smaller hills in these areas are probably related to grounded ice.

Shelves with Strong Currents. A great contrast in shelf width is seen between southeast and west Florida. The shelf is extremely narrow south of Miami but wide off the west side of the peninsula. The zone of narrow shelf is one along which the Gulf Stream flows with a velocity of 3 knots or more. A similar situation is found along the east side of Yucatan. In these places, shelves have either been cut away by the currents, or the currents have prevented sediment accumulation on the shelves such as has occurred in other areas. Elsewhere, ripple marks in sand and even mega-ripples indicate that the effect of the strong surface currents extends to the bottom, although in some areas there is a countercurrent that may flow in the opposite direction.

Shelves in Clear Tropical Seas. Some of the shelves in tropical areas have extensive shallow banks, covered partly with corals and other calcareous types of plants and animals. The widest of these reefs is found off the Queensland coast of Australia (see *Great Barrier Reefs*). Here, a relatively open ship channel can be followed for some 1200 miles inside the reefs. Some other wide shelves in clear tropical seas are, anomalously, rather poor in corals (see *Sahul Shelf*). Such shelves commonly show terraces and other traces of Quaternary shore lines and are patterned by traces of old ice-age

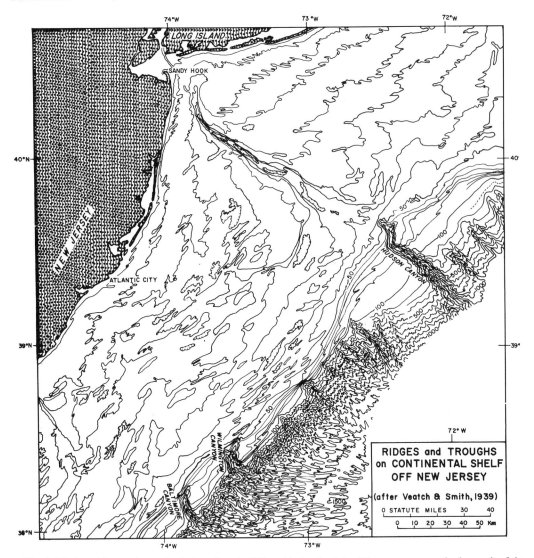

Fig. 3. The low ridges and troughs that are found off the midatlantic states. These are apparently the result of the drowning of barrier islands and bars by the rising sea level after the last glacial episode (after Veatch and Smith 1935).

river valley systems (e.g., "Molengraaff River" on Sunda Shelf; see *Java Sea*).

Shelves with Rocky Banks along the Outside. Many narrow shelves are bordered on the outside by rocky banks. Some of them rise as islands above the surface. These are particularly common along the west coast of the United States, with the Farallon Islands off San Francisco as a prototype (Fig. 4). Recent geophysical surveys show that this variety of shelf has resulted from a combination of block faulting and partial erosion of former islands, that existed as a ridge along the outside, and of deposition of sediment in troughs that occurred nearer the shore. The outer slope is also marked by faulting and large-scale slumping.

Shelves bordering Large Deltas. Most of the large deltas of the world are encroaching onto the adjacent continental shelves, so one might expect these shelves to be narrow. Off the Mississippi passes, the shelf is virtually eliminated, but the average shelf width off large deltas is more than twice that off other areas. These wide shelves are apparently due to a recent submergence of old deltas, partly the result of the sea level rise across the broad flat deltaic surface at the end of the last glacial stage, and partly a result of the independent subsidence that characterizes deltas in general. Broad shallow terraces found outside the deltas commonly have a broad mud zone near-shore and a narrower sandy area near the edge of the continental shelf.

FRANCIS P. SHEPARD

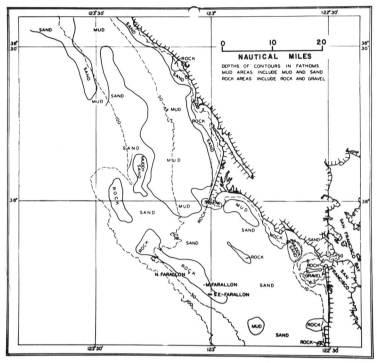

Fig. 4. The rock islands and banks found along the outer shelf off San Francisco Bay. The nature of bottom type on the shelf is indicated.

References

Carrigy, M. A., and Fairbridge, R. W., 1964, "Recent sedimentation, physiography and structure of the continental shelves of Western Australia," *J. Roy. Soc. W. Australia*, **38**, 65–95.

Curray, J. R., 1960, "Sediments and History of Holocene Transgression, Continental Shelf, Northwest Gulf of Mexico," in "Recent Sediments, NW Gulf of Mexico" (A.A.P.G.), pp. 221–266.

Guilcher, André, 1958, "Coastal and Submarine morphology," London, Methuen, 274pp. (includes long bibliography).

Guilcher, A., 1963, "Continental Shelf and Slope," in (Hill, M. N., editor) "The Sea," pp. 281–311, New York, Interscience Publishers.

Holtedahl, H., 1958, "Some remarks on the geomorphology of continental shelves off Norway, Labrador and S.E. Alaska," *J. Geol.*, **66**, 461–471.

Shepard, F. P., 1963, "Submarine Geology," Second ed., New York, Harper & Row, 557pp.

Stetson, H. C., 1949, "The Sediments and Stratigraphy of the East Coast Continental Margin: Georges Bank to Norfolk Canyon," M. I. T. Woods Hole Oceanographic Inst., 66pp.

Sverdrup, H. U., Johnson, M. W., and Fleming, R. H., 1942, "The Oceans—Their Physics, Chemistry, and General Biology," New York, Prentice-Hall, 1087pp.

Trask, P. D. (editor), 1939, "Recent Marine Sediments: A Symposium," Tulsa, 736pp.

Umbgrove, J. H. F., 1947, "The Pulse of the Earth," Second ed., The Hague, M. Nijhoff, 358pp.

CONTINENTAL SLOPE

The term "continental slope" was proposed near the turn of the present century by Hermann Wagner (1900) for the entire slope from the shelf break to the abyssal sea floor. A more restricted use was recommended by Heezen *et al.* (1959, p. 18) for "that relatively steep (3–6°) portion of the sea floor which lies at the seaward border of the continental shelf." Its average slope is 1:75 (4°), and its lower boundary is arbitrarily established at the point where the gradient gently flattens to 1:40. Its width is generally 20–100 km, and its depth range is 100–200 meters (50–100 fathoms) to 1400–3200 meters (750–1750 fathoms). However, along trenches the steep slope may continue down into abyssal depths. The slope may be smooth, or terraced, as first noted by Buchanan (1887) off West Africa (see also *Continental Rise*).

Continental slopes are a worldwide phenomenon and generally pass downward into continental rises. Off oceanic islands there are analogous *insular slopes*, although coral islands sometimes display steps with remarkably steep declivities (1:1 or 45°) down to considerable depths. Volcanic island slopes may also be rather steep in places, e.g., submarine landslip scarps, but normally are more like the normal continental slope, showing slopes of primary accumulation, modified by furrows and ravines.

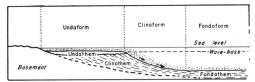

Fig. 1. Basic environments of deposition showing the development of the continental shelf and slope according to Rich (1951). His concept follows closely the classical view and he shows the continental terrace to be like a submerged delta with deposition being controlled by wave base.

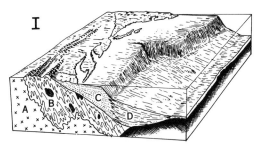

Fig. 2. Continental slopes as the seaward flank of an orogen. A continental slope may form by the collapse of a prism of sediments on the continental rise to form a eugeosynclinal orogen which is accreted to the continent. Dietz considers this the primary origin for continental slopes. *Stage I:* The geologic situation along the mid-Atlantic coast is shown as it presumably exists today (vertical scale greatly exaggerated). The basement consists of a Paleozoic eugeosynclinal orogen (*B*) with intruded plutons (*A*). This basement is overlapped by a more recent wedge of Mesozoic and of Cenozoic sediments (*C*) and its couplet, a prism of sediments resulting from deposition from turbidity currents on the continental rise (*D*) (Dietz, 1964).

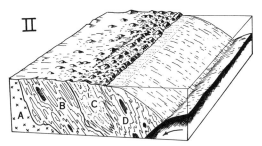

Fig. 3. *Stage II:* At some future date, it is presumed that underthrusting by the sea floor will collapse the terrace wedge and the continental rise into an orogen. The seaward flank of the new orogen will constitute a new continental slope of structural origin (Dietz, 1964).

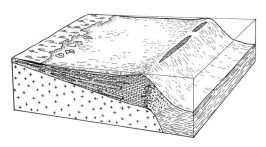

Fig. 4. Secondary (sedimentational) continental slope and rise construction by buildup carbonate sediments. Atoll-like carbonate buildup may account for at least the upper parts of some continental slopes. Reef limestones would tend to impound detritus shed from the island. Such reef buildup is capable of producing a very steep slope. In the more common case, carbonate and clastic buildup would be intermixed. A preexisting continental slope of structural origin is required before this carbonate modification can begin (Dietz, 1964).

TABLE 1. CLASSIFICATION OF CONTINENTAL SLOPES

		Example	*Declivity*
(I)	*Primary* (Structural)		
	Flank of an accretionary folded belt or *orogen* (usually a collapsed continental rise prism)	California (Mesozoic); West coast of South America	Steep
(II)	*Secondary* (Structural)		
	Continental Rift Scar (the slope left after the rifting apart of a continental block)	Atlantic coast of Africa, Gulf of California	Steep
(III)	*Secondary* (Modified by Sedimentation)		
Type	(1) Face of prograded shore zone or *paralic* beds	Atlantic coast of U.S.A.	Moderate
Type	(2) Up-lapped Continental Rise	Parts of Antarctica	Gentle
Type	(3) Continental Embankment (up-lapped continental rise in turn covered by prodelta beds)	Gulf Coast of U.S.A. Texas and Louisiana	Very gentle
Type	(4) Carbonate up-building (atoll-like)	Florida (west coast); Yucatan	Very steep

In cases where there is a continental borderland (q.v.) or marginal plateau seaward of the continental shelf, the continental slope is liable to be divided into two sectors, one at the inner edge and the other at the outer edge of the borderland. The latter has been termed the *marginal escarpment* by Heezen *et al.* (1959).

The continental slope, from the sedimentary point of view may be either:

(a) A site of nondeposition, over which there is flow or slumping of sediments (Fairbridge, 1947) destined to come to rest on the continental rise or to be swept by turbidity currents out onto the abyssal plain. In this case, coring and dredging may reveal traces of continental rocks (e.g., massive rocks like granite, as off southern California, or horizontally bedded Mesozoic-Cenozoic rocks, as in parts of the Atlantic coast), or

(b) A site of slope deposition with foreset beds, where the finer terrigenous neritic materials carried across the shelf come to rest. Such sites are to be found off major deltas or on gentler continental slopes, e.g., off parts of the U.S. Atlantic coast, as shown by subbottom sounding. This is the environment that Rich (1951) recognized in stratigraphy as the *clinothem* facies, as contrasted with the *undathem* facies of the neritic shelf surface and the *fondothem* facies (turbidite environment of the abyssal plain); the terminology, however, has only historical interest, not having been widely adopted.

Thus, structurally, either the continental slope is a constructional feature (sedimentary, biohermal or volcanic) or it may be faulted or folded. Dietz (1964) has offered the following classification of continental slopes (Table 1).

RHODES W. FAIRBRIDGE

References

Buchanan, J. Y., 1887, "On the land slopes separating continents and ocean basins, especially those on the West Coast of Africa," *Scot. Geogr. Mag.,* **3**, 217–238.

Cotton, C. A., 1918, "Conditions of deposition on the continental shelf and slope," *J. Geol.,* **26**, 135–160.

Curray, J. R., 1965, "Structure of the continental margin off central California," *Trans. N.Y. Acad. Sci., Ser. 2,* **27**, 794–801.

Dietz, R. S., 1964, "Origin of continental slopes," *Am. Scientist,* **52**, No. 1, 50–69.

Emery, K. O., 1965, "Characteristics of continental shelves and slopes," *Bull. Am. Assoc. Petrol. Geologists,* **49**, 1379–1384.

Fairbridge, R. W., 1947, "Coarse sediments on the edge of the continental shelf," *Am. J. Sci.,* **245**, 146–153.

Heezen, B. C., Ewing, M., and Tharp, M., 1959, "The floors of the oceans: I. The North Atlantic," *Geol. Soc. Am. Spec. Papers,* **65**, 113pp.

Holtedahl, O., 1950, "Supposed marginal fault lines in the shelf area off some high northern lands," *Bull. Geol. Soc. Am.,* **61**, 493–500.

Korotkevich, Y. S., 1963, "The Intra-shelf Trench in East Antarctica," *Soviet Antarctic Exped. Inf. Bull.,* **4**, No. 41, 4pp.

Rich, J. L., 1951, "Three critical environments of deposition, and criteria for recognition of rocks deposited in each of them," *Bull. Geol. Soc. Am.,* **62**, No. 1, 1–19.

Wagner, H., 1900, "Lehrbuch der Geographie," Hanover, Hahn.

Cross-references: *Continental Rise; Continental Terrace; Submarine Plateaus.*

CONTINENTAL TERRACE*

Introduction

The *continental terrace* (Fig. 1) is defined as the sediment and rock mass underlying the coastal plain, the continental shelf, and the continental slope. The *continental shelf* is the shallow submerged platform bordering the continents. It slopes gently seaward to the *shelf break,* an increase in slope at an average depth of about 130 m. There is considerable variation in depth of the shelf break, from a few tens of meters to several hundred meters, but use of the term "shelf" is reserved for those features which terminate at a depth of less than 550 m (300 fathoms) (Shepard, 1963, p. 206). The steeper surface below the shelf break is the *continental slope.* It is a topographic feature of first order on the face of the earth, with a total length of over 300,000 km and a height of almost 4 km. The continental slope marks the structural edge of the continent and overlies the change from thick continental crust to thin oceanic crust. The base of the continental slope may terminate in a continental rise, or fan of sediments shed off the continent (Fig. 1); it may drop off into a bordering deep-sea trench or depression; or it may stop abruptly at the deep-sea floor.

A diagrammatic profile across one kind of continental margin is shown in Fig. 1, with a coastal plain, shelf, slope, and continental rise. Averages and ranges of widths, depths, and slopes are indicated. This article will deal with the surface sediments and shallow structure of the shelf and slope portions of the continental terrace only. For an excellent survey of the morphology and surface sediments of continental shelves and slopes of the world, the reader is referred to Shepard (1963, pp. 216–310).

The Continental Shelf

Numerous studies on morphology, surface sediment characteristics, and attempts at evaluation of the "principles" of transportation and deposition on continental shelves have been published (see *Neritic Sedimentation;* also see van Andel and Curray, 1960; Emery, 1961; Curray, 1960, 1965a).

* Contribution from the Scripps Institution of Oceanography, University of California, La Jolla, Calif. Financial support furnished by National Science Foundation and Office of Naval Research.

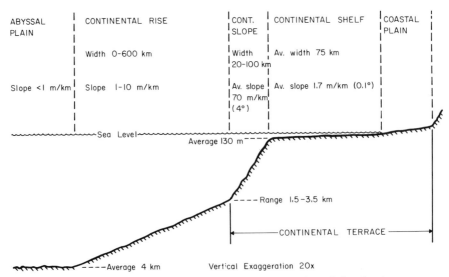

Fig. 1. Diagrammatic profile of one type of continental terrace with continental rise, showing average or range of depth, width, and slope of component parts.

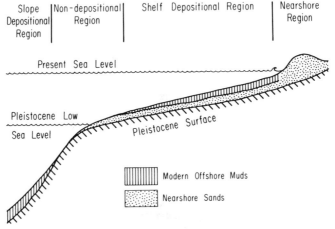

Fig. 2. Idealized model of deposition of sediment on the continental terrace, showing effects of rise of sea level after the end of the Pleistocene on the distribution of surface sediments, with a wide continental shelf and moderate to high rate of supply of sediments.

The rate of supply of sediments, the width of shelves, the intensity and direction of current systems and other oceanographic agents of distribution, and the nature of the preexisting shelf surface vary widely throughout the world. Evaluation of these variables is necessary to understand local conditions and processes of distribution and deposition of shelf surface sediments.

Eustatic Influences. Large areas of modern continental shelves are nondepositional and are covered with relict sediments from conditions of lowered Pleistocene sea level (see *Eustasy* and *Mean Sea Level*). The most recent (i.e., Last Glacial/Wisconsin) maximum lowering of sea level, accompanying the advances of glaciers over high-latitude portions of the continents, subaerially exposed most of the surface of these continental shelves approximately 18,000 years ago. As continental glaciers retreated, the meltwater returned to the oceans and sea level rose from a low stand of about —125 m to its present level. The rise of sea level caused the shore line to migrate across the shelf surface (marine transgression). This was probably a complex sequence of events and climatic changes, manifested in brief periods of falling sea level (marine regression) and changes in wind and current directions (i.e., cooler episodes) interrupting this general period of warming. These reversals and changes of wind and current directions have left their marks in the

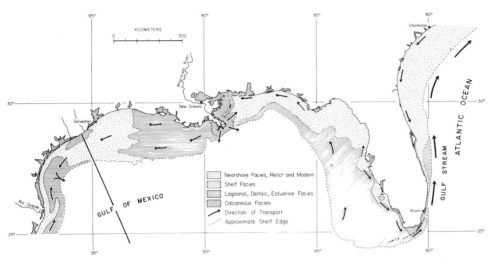

Fig. 3. Generalized distribution of surface sediments on the continental shelf of southeastern United States. Data from Shepard (1932), Gorsline (1963), Uchupi (1963), Emery (in press), Gould and Stewart (1955), Ginsburg (1956), Tanner (1960, 1961), Goodell and Gorsline (1961), Kofoed and Gorsline (1963), Scholl (1963), Tanner *et al.* (1963), Ludwick and Walton (1957), Ludwick (1964), Shepard (1956), Fisk and McFarlan (1955), and Curray (1960). Section line off Galveston indicates location of section of Fig. 4.

sedimentary and bathymetric records on both shelves and subaerial environments, but have thus far been recognized only locally (see for example, Curray, 1960; Fairbridge, 1961, 1964).

An idealized model of distribution of modern and transgressive terrigenous sediment over a continental shelf is illustrated in Fig. 2. Approximately 18,000 years ago the shore line lay near the edge of the shelf. As sea level rose, the shore line migrated across the shelf surface and in most regions deposited a basal shore line, or nearshore sand of the marine transgression, covering over the Pleistocene land surface. In some places this Pleistocene surface was a soil horizon on alluvial, deltaic or other coastal plain deposits, but elsewhere it is a bedrock surface eroded during the rise and fall of the sea. In high-latitude glaciated regions, the pre-transgressive surface is glacial drift (till).

The basal sands of the transgression generally grade continuously into the nearshore sands of the present stand of sea level. These present-day shoreline developments in most regions started to form within the last 5000–7000 years when the "Flandrian" transgression was completed and the sea came to approximately its present level. During the rapid rise of the sea, muddy sediments (silt and clay) were dispersed over the surface of the shelf, but generally were deposited for too short a time in any one place to really cover the basal sands. As the transgression slowed, deposition of silts and clays started to cover over the sands on the inner shelf.

At the present time, muds of shelf facies are being deposited generally only on the inner shelf (the inner 30–40 km of wide shelves) where rivers are supplying sediments at a great enough rate and where turbulence of the ocean is not excessive. The outer portions of these same wide shelves are nondepositional partly because of distance from shore and sources of sediment and partly because of increased turbulence of wave action, tidal currents, and semipermanent currents over the shelf edge. This increased turbulence may prevent deposition, keep the sediment in suspension, and contribute to bypassing of the suspended sediment over the shelf edge to the upper slope.

One consequence of fluctuations of sea level throughout the Quaternary is seen in the morphology of the shelf. The configuration of the shelf as it exists today is most certainly an inherited product of migrations of the zones of deposition and erosion back and forth across this surface many times during the Quaternary. During periods of relatively high sea level (as today), the deposition was concentrated on the inner shelf, in the estuaries of rivers drowned by the rise of sea level, or in deltas. During periods of relatively low sea level, deposition was transferred to the outer shelf or upper slope, and in some regions is known to have prograded the edge of the shelf seaward. During the rapid swings back and forth, the zones of erosion and deposition migrated accordingly. The result is some uniformity of the shelf break throughout the world. Pre-Quaternary shelves must have lacked this uniformity, although the stratigraphic record of some regions shows undeniable evidence of features which resemble our modern shelves.

Gulf Coast Shelf. The surface sediments of southeastern United States have been accorded

209

very thorough studies, notably on the northern shelf of the Gulf of Mexico, which is dominated by the influence of the Mississippi Delta. This particular shelf has been studied in great detail, and the sediment distribution is summarized and generalized in Fig. 3. In response to the semipermanent current system, much of the sediment has been distributed toward the west and has blanketed the shelf during the period of rising sea level as well as more recently. Farther to the west is a large area of relict sandy sediments, the basal sands of the transgression, which have not yet been covered with modern shelf muds. A small tongue of modern muds lies off Galveston, Texas, supplied by the Colorado and Brazos rivers; farther southwest, a current convergence has distributed sediment across the wide shelf and over the shelf edge.

East of the Mississippi Delta, modern terrigenous deposition has been confined to the very nearshore area and bays, and the nondepositional shelf surface is largely covered with relict sands. A calcareous sediment band on the outer shelf includes small bioherm banks which probably developed during Pleistocene lowered sea level but are deeply drowned today. This calcareous band widens to the southeast off Florida and includes bathymetric zonation of clastic carbonate particle types relict from deposition during lowered sea level. Active carbonate deposition and reef growth is occurring nearshore. To the north along the Atlantic coast, north of Miami, the facies changes from primarily carbonate to primarily terrigenous. This nondepositional shelf is influenced by the Gulf Stream and the sands contain abundant authigenic mineral species.

The Gulf of Mexico example illustrates only one type of continental terrace: a wide shelf with terrigenous sediments which grade toward the south into more tropical waters with clastic carbonate sediments. Many other variations are found throughout the world.

Shelf Types. This article is not intended as an exhaustive treatment of shelves of the world, but some of the more important types are classified and described briefly as follows:

(I) Cold-water, High-latitude shelves. (A) Shelves Adjacent to Glaciated Areas. The bathymetry of these shelves frequently shows deep troughs or clefts both perpendicular and parallel to the shore line. Those trending more or less normal to the coastline were probably eroded by glaciers during lowered sea level (Shepard, 1963). Those parallel to shore are thought to mark the positions of major fracture zones along which late-Cenozoic uplift has occurred (Holtedahl, 1958). Surface sediments of these shelves frequently contain muds, sands, and gravels, suggesting relict glacial contributions. Examples are the shelves of Canada, Norway (Holtedahl, 1958), and Antarctica (Lepley, 1965). Some of these shelves are extremely wide

and deep. The Barents Sea, north of Norway and part of the Soviet Union, is over 1100 km wide and approaches 500 m deep. The Antarctic shelf is also very deep, about 500 m or more, probably due to subsidence from glacial loading.

(B) Shelves Adjacent to Non-glaciated Areas. These shelves, such as off Siberia and Alaska in the Arctic Ocean, are generally very smooth and broad, but are not unusually deep. Surface sediments are frequently muddy, with much loose gravel and boulders in part carried out by ice rafting. Modern deposition may be occurring on these broad shelves many kilometers from shore (Creager, 1963).

(II) Temperate-latitude Shelves. (A) Wide-to-intermediate Width Shelves with High Rate of Supply of Sediment. The Louisiana shelf west of the Mississippi River is an example (Fig. 3). Most of the shelf is blanketed with Recent (Holocene) muddy sediments. Elsewhere, as farther west off central Texas, Recent muds may cover only the inner part of the shelf. This is a rather common sediment distribution pattern typical of many of the shelves of the world.

(B) Wide Shelves with Low Rate of Supply of Sediment. Typical of this type is the east coast of the United States (partly shown in Fig. 3). Shelf surface is generally covered with relict shallow water basal transgressive sands, and the present supply of river muds is either trapped in the estuaries of drowned river valleys or kept in suspension by turbulence until it bypasses the shelf to deeper water on the continental slope. Other examples are discussed in Shepard (1963).

(C) Narrow Shelves. Three general classes of narrow shelves exist. First are the portions of wide shelves across which the shore line has prograded by deposition. Examples are deltas (Mississippi, Niger, etc.) and cuspate forelands (Cape Hatteras, etc.) (Shepard, 1963, p. 257). This type is considered only as deviation from other classes discussed. The second type is characterized by the narrow shelves which commonly occur along coastlines of young mountain ranges. These shelves are commonly shoaler than the average and have occasional bedrock outcrops protruding through the sediment cover. Where there is a supply of sediment, the entire shelf may be blanketed with Recent sediment many tens of meters thick (Moore, 1960), which grade from sandy nearshore to muddy offshore. Examples are the west coast of South America and southern California. A third type of narrow shelf is that marked by youthful faulting, such as those off Portugal, and in the Mediterranean, not parallel to, but truncating, older tectonic patterns.

(III) Warm-water, Tropical, Low-latitude Shelves. (A) Humid Tropics, High Rate of Sediment Supply. Many of the world's larger rivers occur in the humid tropics and contribute large volumes of

sediment to the continental shelf. Mangrove growth speeds progradation of the coastline, but despite this deltaic progradation, the shelves may be rather wide. Subsidence by loading tends to deepen them while deposition tends to counteract this and cause shoaling. The sediments are generally Recent muds, but current action may prevent distribution of these muds all the way across the shelf to cover relict sands. Examples are the northeast coast of South America, the Niger, Congo, Indus, Ganges, Irrawaddy, Mekong, etc.

(B) Clear Water, Low Rate of Sediment Supply. These are the well-known carbonate shelves, with reef growth, clastic carbonates, and lime muds mixed with varying proportions of terrigenous sediment. Off Florida (Fig. 3) terrigenous deposition is largely confined to the lagoons, marshes and inner shelf, while on others such as the Great Barrier Reef coast of Australia, much of the back reef facies on the shelf is probably Recent muds supplied by rivers.

The Continental Slope

Much less is known about either the sediments or the bathymetry of the continental slope than the continental shelf. The gross features of bathymetry of the slope are known for most of the slopes of the world, but the details are known for only a few. Similarly, most slope sediments are known to be muddy, but relatively little is known of details, variability, and modern rates of deposition.

The average gradient for the upper 2000 m of the continental slope is about 4.25° (Shepard, 1963, p. 298), but with considerable regional variation. Most continental slopes do not terminate directly at the deep-sea floor. About half of them terminate in bordering deep-sea trenches or shallower bordering depressions, while most of the remainder terminate in fans of sediment or continental rises (Fig. 1). According to Shepard (1963, p. 298), slopes off major deltas average about 1.3° for the upper 2000 m; those off "fault coasts" with insignificant shelves average 5.6°; those off young mountain range coasts average 4.6°; and those off stable coasts lacking major rivers average about 3°. All of these vary rather widely, however. In general, Pacific slopes are steeper than Atlantic slopes, which are in turn steeper than Indian Ocean slopes.

The trends of continental slopes are remarkably straight or gently curving, in contrast to the more irregular nature of the shore line. The thinning from continental crust to oceanic crust usually occurs beneath the slope. Thus the true nature of the shelf as a submerged portion of the edge of the continent is revealed. The shore line is ephemeral at the whims of eustatic sea level (see *Eustasy* and *Mean Sea Level*) and regional and local tectonics, while the true margin of the continent is a much more slowly changing, more nearly stable feature.

In many cases, e.g., the southern California continental borderland (q.v.) or the Blake Plateau off southeastern United States, the continental slope is separated from the continental shelf by a marginal plateau of intermediate depth. The Blake Plateau has a relatively smooth surface while the southern California borderland consists of banks and islands with intervening deep basins. These marginal plateaus are a "quasi-cratonic" part of the continental block; the edge of the continental block underlies the continental slope which drops to the deep sea.

Muds are the predominant sediments of continental slopes, with lesser amounts of sandy or gravelly sediments, apparently consisting of material carried off the edge of the shelf. Again, some of these sediments may be relict from times when deposition was directly on the upper slope during Pleistocene lowered sea level. Rock outcrops are common on some slopes, generally the steeper slopes off mountainous coastlines and narrow shelves. The following section on structure will further discuss the outcropping of rock on the slope and summarize the present state of knowledge. The nature of submarine canyons which cut into the continental shelf and slope is discussed in another article of this volume.

Internal Structure of the Continental Terrace

Study of the internal structure of the continental terrace is developing rapidly. Instrumental techniques suitable for determination of details of shallow internal structure have existed only during the last few years, although determination of the gross features has been possible for a somewhat longer time by gravity and seismic refraction. The new methods are continuous acoustic reflection profiling, in which a low-frequency, high-intensity sound pulse is produced every few seconds or minutes while the survey ship proceeds underway. Reflections resulting from acoustical discontinuities within the sediment and rock section are received by towed hydrophone arrays and are recorded on a continuous strip chart resembling a geological cross section. Figure 5 is a tracing of the major reflecting layers of such a profile. Various sound sources are now in use, such as small explosive charges, electric spark discharge in seawater, explosion of a combustible gas mixture, or a brief high-pressure pulse of compressed air. The technology was summarized by Hersey (1963).

Internal structure of portions of two continental terraces are shown in Figs. 4 and 5. Figure 4 is a section in the Gulf of Mexico along the line shown in Fig. 1 south of Galveston. The upper kilometer or so of sediment is traced from continuous reflection records (Moore and Curray, 1963), and the remainder is based on refraction work (Ewing *et al.*, 1960). The lowest layer, with a velocity of 8.3 km/sec represents the mantle, deepening under the

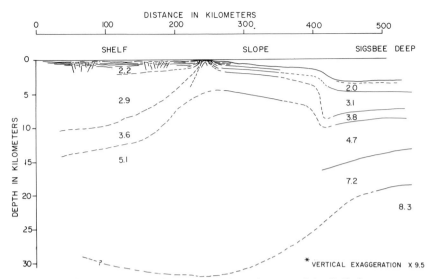

Fig. 4. Structure section across continental terrace of the Gulf of Mexico from Galveston, Texas, along section line indicated in Fig. 3. Data modified from Ewing *et al.* (1960) and Moore and Curray (1963). Numbers indicate interval velocities in kilometers per second.

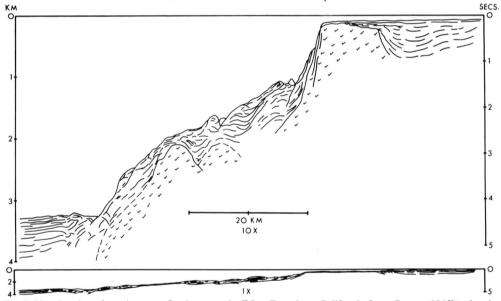

Fig. 5. Line drawing of continuous reflection record off San Francisco, California from Curray (1965b), showing distribution of granitic and sedimentary rocks.

slope and outer shelf. The layers of velocity 3.6–3.8 km/sec and less are probably consolidated-to-unconsolidated sediments, while the deeper, higher-velocity layers may represent evaporites, volcanics, or other "intermediate" rocks (Ewing *et al.*, 1962). The rise of the 3.6–3.8 km/sec layer under the outer shelf may represent a salt dome intruding the younger sediments from depth. The figure represents a composite, and the reflection records (Moore and Curray, 1963) which revealed a near surface salt dome were actually run several

kilometers away. Such intrusions are, however, quite common, and the different types of information from slightly different areas have been combined for sake of illustration. The sediment column over the salt dome is thinned and faulted. Other, more deeply buried domes are probably indicated by the fault patterns underlying the shelf.

The steeper portion near the base of the slope is the Sigsbee Scarp. The deeper structure of the 3.6–3.8 km/sec layer suggests faulting which has been subsequently mantled with younger sediment.

Gross structure of the continental terrace is dominated by deposition of a thick column of sediment underlying the continental shelf and continental slope. This is the so-called Gulf Coast Geosyncline (see *Geosynclines* and *Geosynclines, Modern Equivalents*).

A portion of the continental terrace off San Francisco, California, is shown in Fig. 5. This is a tracing from continuous reflection records (Curray, 1965b), extending from the middle of the continental shelf, between the Farallon Islands located on the shelf edge, down the continental slope, to the upper part of the continental rise. The same section is shown in the lower part of the Figure without vertical exaggeration. The Farallon Islands consist of quartz diorite of Cretaceous age. This rock can be traced in the reflection records a short distance landward, and intermittently seaward to near the base of the slope. A thicker section of Tertiary and Quaternary sediment lies behind the basement rock under the continental shelf. The veneer of sediment overlying the basement rock on the slope has been contorted by sliding and slumping down the slope. Another thicker section of sediment of probable Quaternary and Tertiary age underlies the continental rise. This same basic structure is found continuously along the central California continental terrace. Here the gross structure is dominated by the presence of this ridge of basement rock. The structure known for the terrace off the east coast of the United States is basically the same as this (Drake *et al.*, 1959), except that the basement ridge is more deeply buried and the filled sediment basins under the continental rise and under the shelf contain much more sediment.

Considerable variation can be seen to exist in the basic structure of different portions of the continental margin. Only two have been illustrated here. Another type which may be regionally important shows outcropping of gently seaward dipping shelf strata on the continental slope, indicating that the slope in this region may be an erosional rather than a depositional regime. This has been proposed as the structure of parts of the terrace off eastern United States by Heezen *et al.* (1959), but the worldwide importance of this type of structure has not yet been established. Many other structural types probably exist throughout the world, as well as variations of the types illustrated.

Structure of the continental terrace depends upon many factors, most important of which are probably the tectonic background or past history, the rate of supply and deposition of sediments, and the secondary modifying influences during the deposition of these sediments. These will be discussed individually:

(1) Tectonic background or past history determines an arbitrary starting point in the evolution of a continental terrace. This gives a preexisting surface on which sediments are deposited, and establishes an initial drainage and supply system of the adjacent land area to furnish sediments.

(2) The primary process in the evolution of the terrace is deposition of sediments. Initially the rate and locus of deposition will depend largely upon the preexisting surface, width, steepness, etc. Ultimately, sufficient deposition can blanket and subdue the preexisting surface and, in some cases, establish a depositional profile underlain by coastal plain, shelf, slope, and continental rise deposits.

(3) During the depositional process, the development of the terrace is sensitive to further modifying processes, such as subsidence or uplift, other tectonic disturbance, eustatic sea-level fluctuations, intrusion by igneous rock or salt domes, and many others. With sufficient time, deposition of sediment, subsidence due to loading, and minimal secondary disturbance, the ultimate product may resemble the "old age" or "mature" continental terrace of Dietz (1952).

JOSEPH R. CURRAY

References

Creager, J. S., 1963, "Sedimentation in a high energy, embayed, continental shelf environment," *J. Sediment. Petrol.*, **33**, 815–830.

Curray, Joseph R., 1960, "Sediments and History of Holocene Trangression, Continental Shelf, Northwest Gulf of Mexico," in "Recent Sediments, Northwest Gulf of Mexico, 1951–1958," p. 221–266, Tulsa, Oklahoma, Am. Assoc. Petrol. Geologists.

Curray, Joseph R., 1965a, "Late Quaternary history, continental shelves of the United States," in (Wright, H. E., and Frey, D. E., editors) "The Quaternary of the United States," Princeton, N.J., Princeton University Press, p. 723–735.

Curray, Joseph R., 1965b, "Structure of the continental margin off Central California," *Trans. N.Y. Acad. Sci.*, Ser. II, v. 27, p. 794–801.

Dietz, R. S., 1952, Geomorphic evolution of the continental terrace (continental shelf plus slope)," *Bull. Assoc. Petrol. Geologists,* **36**, 1802–1820.

Drake, C. L., Ewing, M., and Sutton, G. H., 1959, "Continental Margins and Geosynclines: The East Coast of North America North of Cape Hatteras," in "Physics and Chemistry of the Earth," Vol. 3, pp. 110–198, New York, Pergamon Press.

Emery, K. O., 1961, "Submerged marine terraces and their sediments," *Ann. Geomorphol. N.S. Suppl.*, **3**, 2–29.

Emery, K. O., in press, "The Continental Shelf off the Atlantic Coast of the United States," U.S. Geological Survey.

Ewing, J., Antoine, J., and Ewing, M., 1960, "Geophysical measurements in the western Caribbean Sea and in the Gulf of Mexico," *J. Geophys. Res.*, **65**, No. 12, 4087–4126.

Ewing, John I., Worzel, J. L., and Ewing, Maurice, 1962, "Sediments and Oceanic Structural History of the Gulf of Mexico," *J. Geophys. Res.*, **67**, No. 6, 2509–2527.

Fairbridge, Rhodes W., 1961, "Eustatic Changes in

Sea Level," in "Physics and Chemistry of the Earth," Vol. 4, pp. 99–185, London, Pergamon.

Fairbridge, Rhodes W., 1964, "African Ice-Age Aridity," in "Problems in Palaeoclimatology," pp. 356–363, London, Interscience.

Fisk, H. N., and McFarlan, E., Jr., 1955, "Late Quaternary deltaic deposits of the Mississippi River," in "Crust of the earth," *Geol. Soc. Am. Spec. Paper* 62, 279–302.

Ginsburg, R. N., 1956, "Environmental relationships of grain size and constituent particles in some south Florida carbonate sediments," *Bull. Am. Assoc. Petrol. Geologists*, **40**, No. 10, 2384–2427.

Goodell, H. G., and Gorsline, D. S., 1961, "A sedimentologic study of Tampa Bay, Florida," *Rept. Intern. Geol. Congr.*, **21**, Pt. 23, 75–88.

Gorsline, Donn S., 1963, "Bottom sediments of the Atlantic Shelf and Slope off the Southern United States," *J. Geol.*, **71**, No. 4, 422–440.

Gould, H. R., and Stewart, R. H., 1955, "Continental terrace sediments in the Northeastern Gulf of Mexico," in "Finding ancient shorelines," *Soc. Econ. Paleon. Min. Spec. Publ.*, No. 3, 2–20.

Heezen, Bruce C., Tharp, Marie, and Ewing, Maurice, 1959, "The floors of the oceans: I. The North Atlantic," *Geol. Soc. Am. Spec. Paper* 65, 113pp.

Hersey, J. B., 1964, "Continuous reflection profiling," in "The Sea," Vol. 3, pp. 47–52, New York, Interscience Publishers.

Holtedahl, Hans, 1950, "Some remarks on geomorphology of continental shelves off Norway, Labrador, and Southeast Alaska," *J. Geol.*, **66**, 461–471.

Lepley, L. K., 1965, "Submarine geomorphology of eastern Ross Sea and Sulzberger Bay, Antarctica," *Marine Geol.*

Ludwick, John C., 1964, "Sediments in Northeastern Gulf of Mexico," in "Papers in Marine Geology," New York, The Macmillan Co., 522pp.

Ludwick, John C., and Walton, W. R., 1957, "Shelf-edge, calcareous prominences in Northeastern Gulf of Mexico," *Bull. Am. Assoc. Petrol. Geologists*, **41**, No. 9, 2054–2101.

Moore, D. G., and Curray, J. R., 1963, "Structural framework of the continental terrace, Northwest Gulf of Mexico," *J. Geophys. Res.*, **68**, No. 6, 1725–1747.

Shepard, Francis P., 1932, "Sediments of the continental shelves," *Bull. Geol. Soc. Am.*, **43**, 1017–1040.

Shepard, Francis P., 1956, "Marginal sediments of Mississippi Delta," *Bull. Am. Assoc. Petrol. Geologists*, **40**, No. 11, 2537–2623.

Shepard, Francis P., 1963, "Submarine Geology," Second ed., New York, Harper & Row, 557pp.

Shepard, Francis P., 1961, "Offshore shoals in area of energy deficit," *J. Sediment. Petrol.*, **31**, No. 1, 87–95.

Tanner, W. F., Evens, R. G., and Holmes, C. W., 1963, "Low-energy coast near Cape Romano, Florida," *J. Sediment. Petrol.*, **33**, No. 3, 713–722.

Uchupi, Elazar, 1963, "Sediments on the continental margin off eastern United States," *U.S. Geol. Surv. Profess. Papers*, **475-C**, No. 94, C132–C137.

Van Andel, Tj. H., and Curray, J. R., 1960, "Regional aspects of modern sedimentation in northern Gulf of Mexico and similar basins, and Paleogeographic significance," in "Recent Sediments, Northwest Gulf of Mexico, 1951–1958," pp. 345–364, Am. Assoc. Petrol. Geologists, Tulsa, Oklahoma.

CONTINENTS AND OCEANS—STATISTICS OF AREA, VOLUME AND RELIEF—*See* Vol. III

CONVERGENCE AND DIVERGENCE

Convergence is the contraction of a vector field and is, mathematically, simply negative divergence. In the atmosphere, it refers to the velocity vector and thus to an increase of mass within a given volume, so that if convergence occurs near the ground there must be rising air along either side of a *convergence line* (see *Fronts and Frontogenesis*), this feature often forming beneath convective clouds. Typically, cyclones or low-pressure areas are regions of convergence at lower levels in the atmosphere.

In contrast, *divergence* is the spreading or expansion of a vector field. A high is generally a region of divergence at the ground. In the upper atmosphere these situations are likely to be reversed (above a "level of non-divergence," often about 600 millibars).

The continuity equation requires that the upper convergence is balanced by the lower divergence and *vice versa*. Therefore, if a disturbance or other

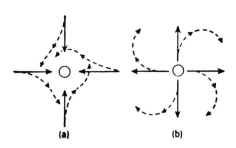

Fig. 1. (a) Creation of cyclonic circulation by horizontal convergence. As the air flows toward the center, it is deflected to the right (in the northern hemisphere), by the Coriolis force. (b) Creation of anticyclonic circulation by horizontal divergence (Taylor, 1954).

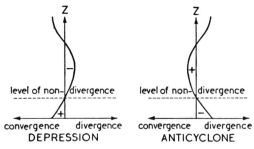

Fig. 2. Typical convergence and divergence profiles over deepening depression and developing anticyclone (Gordon, 1962). (By permission of Van Nostrand Co., New Jersey.)

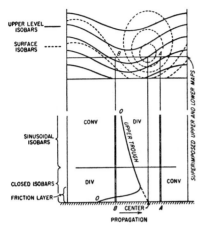

Fig. 3. Distribution of convergence and divergence in a zonal section through a cyclone (after Bjerknes and Holmboe, 1944). In the upper part of the diagram are indicated the superimposed surface and upper level pressure distributions for the cyclone indicated in the lower part (from Petterssen, 1956). (By permission of McGraw-Hill Book Co., N.Y.)

circulation system originates above, it will be followed by one below and *vice versa*. Since the two circulations are related by the mean temperature field between them, the advection caused by one circulation system will affect the mean temperature field. The resultant wind shear will transmit the initial circulation to other levels with which it is coupled (see *Thermal Wind*).

Within a given volume the mean divergence F equals the net outflow of the vectors F through the surface bounding the volume. Divergence of a quantity is a mathematical concept in vector analysis (q.v.), expressed by the scalar product of the del operator and the quantity q, thus $\nabla \cdot q$.

In Cartesian coordinates if F has components F_x, F_y, F_z, the divergence is

$$\frac{\partial F_x}{\partial x} + \frac{\partial F_y}{\partial y} + \frac{\partial F_z}{\partial z}$$

For an incompressible fluid (or air of constant density), according to the Law of Conservation of Mass (Equation of Continuity), the divergence of the velocity is zero, thus:

$$\frac{\partial y}{\partial x} + \frac{\partial v}{\partial y} + \frac{\partial w}{\partial z} = 0$$

In meteorology the concept of two-dimensional horizontal divergence of the velocity field is generally employed, thus:

$$\frac{\partial u}{\partial x} + \frac{\partial v}{\partial y}$$

when u and v are the x and y components of velocity. Horizontal convergence in an upper layer is accom-

panied by subsiding air and divergence with rising air. The ideal geostrophic wind has no divergence, but upper air winds (approaching the geostrophic) generally have a divergence of about 10^{-6} sec^{-1}, cyclonic winds 10^{-5} sec^{-1}, while gravity waves, frontal waves, cumulus convection, etc., have about 10^{-4} or 10^{-3} sec^{-1} divergence.

RHODES W. FAIRBRIDGE

References

Bjerknes, J., and Holmboe, J., 1944, "On the theory of cyclones," *J. Meteorol.,* **1**, 1–22.
Gordon, A. H., 1962, "Elements of Dynamic Meteorology," Princeton, N.J., D. Van Nostrand Co., 217pp.
Huschke, R. E. (editor), 1959, "Glossary of Meteorology," Boston, American Meteorological Society, 638pp.
Petterssen, S., 1956, "Weather Analysis and Forecasting," Second ed., New York, McGraw-Hill Book Co., 2 vols. (first ed., 1940).

Cross-reference: *Confluence and Diffluence; Fronts and Frontogenesis; Lapse Rate; Thermal Wind.* (All in Vol. II.)

CONVERGENCE, ANTARCTIC

The decrease in surface temperature from north to south across the Antarctic Ocean is not as uniform as is suggested by the climatological charts which meteorologists have based on ships' observations averaged over relatively large areas and, for the same season of the year, over many years. Instead of being almost uniformly spaced circles around the Antarctic continent, the isotherms of surface temperature are somewhat crowded together near 40°S where warm water typical of warm temperate or subtropical conditions converges with water which can be considered typical of cold temperate or subantarctic conditions. There is another sharpening of the meridional temperature gradient in 50–60°S, where cold Antarctic surface water spreading northward from the Antarctic sinks below the warmer subantarctic water. These natural boundaries are generally referred to as the Subtropical and Antarctic Convergences.

The main flow of water in the Antarctic Ocean is from west to east under the influence of the prevailing west wind, but the eastward flow has a significant northward component in the surface and bottom layers, and a southward component in the intervening deep layer. The northward movement at the surface is partly due to the effect of the earth's rotation combined with that of the wind stress and to the relatively high density of the Antarctic water compared with the warmer surface waters farther north. This tends to make it sink downward to the north above the more saline deep and bottom waters but below the warmer surface waters of the subantarctic region.

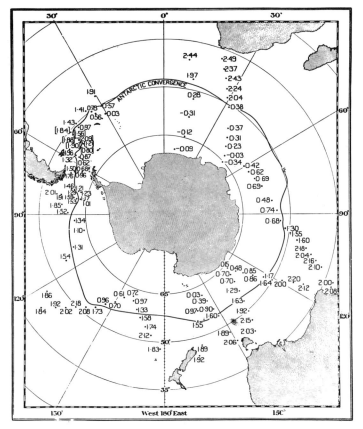

Fig. 1. Position of the Antarctic Convergence following *Discovery* observations (Deacon). Temperatures (in degrees Celsius) are indicated for 2500 meters depth, except for those in brackets (2000 meters).

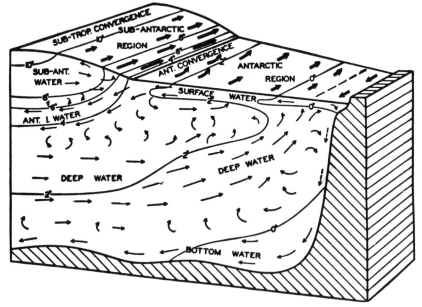

Fig. 2. Schematic representation of Antarctic currents and water masses, in relation to temperature, showing position of Antarctic Convergence and also the Subtropical Convergence (from Sverdrup).

Professor W. Meinardus, who studied the meteorological results of the German South Pacific Expedition of 1901–1902, seems to have been the first to note that the decrease in surface temperature toward the south became noticeably slower south of 50°S, and he showed that the contrast between the meridional surface temperature gradients north and south of this latitude was sufficient to divide the west wind drift into a cold zone to the south and a warm zone to the north. He recognized the boundary as a line along which the cold Antarctic water sinks below the warmer subantarctic water, with a consequent rise in surface temperature from south to north of about 2°C. Combining the observations of other expeditions with his own, he was able to plot the latitude of the boundary from the West Pacific sector, across the Atlantic Ocean into the eastern part of the Indian Ocean. By 1933, the *Discovery* observations had shown that it was continuous all around the continent. Figure 1 shows its approximate position.

Furthermore, the *Discovery* observations showed that the sharp increase of temperature from south to north at the surface occurred where the warm water, spreading southward at a depth of 2000–3000 m, climbed relatively steeply above cold Antarctic bottom water that spread northward. The water circulation in a vertical section along any meridian through the Antarctic Ocean is shown schematically in Fig. 2. The Antarctic surface layer is shallowest in about 65°S in the boundary between the east and west winds, and then it deepens slightly as far as 50°S. North of this, water as dense as the Antarctic surface water lies at a much deeper level in the ocean and the Antarctic water sinks to this deep level on its way northward. There is, in fact, a frontal region, with warm water to the north and cold water to the south, extending from the surface to the bottom of the ocean, which resembles the more familiar frontal conditions between warm and cold air masses. The sharp increase of temperature from south to north occurs at much the same latitude at all depths.

The surface boundary was first called the Meinardus line and later the oceanic polar front. This would seem to be a very reasonable name for it, but later, to prevent confusion with the atmosphere, it became known as the Antarctic Convergence. One of its most remarkable features is that its position changes very little from time to time, the north-south variation being probably less than ±60 miles, and there is no evidence of any regular seasonal fluctuation. The data are of course relatively scarce, and since few of the ships which go to the Antarctic have continuous recording thermographs or equipment for taking subsurface samples which leave no doubt as to whether the surface layer is Antarctic or subantarctic, there are some questionable identifications. The great weight of evidence seems, however, to give a clear indication that the position of the deep frontal region and of the surface convergence varies very little about a very stable mean position. The convergence cannot really be a straight line because the water movements north and south of it are influenced by the day-to-day changes in wind and weather. The presence of the temperature discontinuity is unmistakable evidence of the meeting of two different water masses, but the mixing processes between them must be something like the eddying motions that appear as cyclonic and anticyclonic disturbances traveling along an atmospheric front. The diagram drawn by Berggren, Bolin and Rossby (in Rossby, 1959) to illustrate such processes in the atmosphere may prove to be equally useful for the sea surface, though the eddies in the water will be typically some 50 miles across. A ship steaming almost due south or north will generally find a recognizable sharpening of the temperature gradient like that which first called attention to the Meinardus line, but if she is on a slanting course, she is more likely to pass through alternate bands of warm and cold water as though she were cutting through a zigzag boundary. The stationary character of the mean position of both front and convergence is difficult to explain if the existence and the latitude of the convergence are determined directly by meridional gradients in wind strength, since, as far as we can see, surface currents produced by the wind would converge farther north and the position of the convergence would, like the winds themselves, be more variable.

Another significant feature of the convergence is that it is about 15° farther north in the East Atlantic Ocean than in the East Pacific Ocean. There is a ready qualitative explanation of this difference if the point at which the Antarctic surface water sinks is determined by the latitude in which more saline deep water rises to the south above the Antarctic bottom water, and thus by some kind of dynamic balance between the northward flow of the bottom water and southward flow of the deep water, since the cold bottom water is formed very largely in the Atlantic sector. The salinity of the surface water in the Antarctic coastal current rises very sharply with the approach of winter when the drainage from the land ceases, ice separates out, snow lies unmelted above the sea ice, and mixing with the more saline deep water is intensified. These processes are very much intensified on the broad continental shelf far south in the Weddell Sea, and in this region particularly, cold surface water mixes with the more saline deep water and sinks to the bottom of the ocean. The bottom temperatures are colder in the Weddell Sea than anywhere else round the continent and they increase continuously toward the east so that those on the west side of the Antarctic Peninsula (Graham

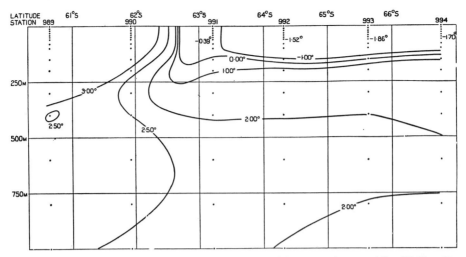

Fig. 3. Distribution of temperature in depth of 1000 meters over a N-S traverse about meridian 80° West (Deacon).

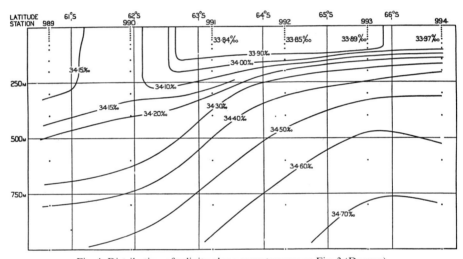

Fig. 4. Distribution of salinity along same traverse as Fig. 3 (Deacon).

Land) are 1°C warmer than those on the Weddell Sea side. There is also a continuous increase in salinity and decrease in oxygen content all around the continent, and all the evidence suggests a lessening of the volume and weakening of the northward thrust of the bottom water, and a change of balance in favor of the southward flow of deep water, toward the eastern part of the Pacific Oean.

Several authors have maintained that the position of the surface boundary is determined by the wind pattern, and the fact that the west winds are strongest near the convergence or a little to the north of it; but it seems just as reasonable to argue that the latitude of the strongest winds is determined by that of the strongest meridional temperature gradient, and thus by the frontal conditions

between the deep and bottom water masses. The southward trend of the convergence from the Atlantic Ocean to the Pacific is by no means uniform: it tends to advance to the north over submarine ridges and to the south over deep basins. This is in keeping with the hypothesis that its position is determined by bottom and deep currents as well as by events at the surface, since the bottom current will be deflected to the north as it approaches a ridge. The overall mechanism must be very complex: bottom water flowing to the north must be deflected to the west by the effect of the earth's rotation if it is not turned to the east by the frictional forces and pressure gradients due to the wind and the effect of the wind on the surface and deep currents, and the warm highly saline deep water which moves southward between the Antarctic surface and bottom currents must be accelerated to the east. The formation of the frontal region and the surface convergence must be linked to such considerations and are clearly ocean-wide phenomena whose study will repay further work. To make direct measurement of the zonal and meridional transports of the currents involved seems the most profitable thing to try, although extremely difficult. The formation of the frontal zone is also a very promising field for theoretical study. Recent closely spaced series of temperature observations with bathythermographs have emphasized the complexity of the surface water movements near the convergence, but in the absence of salinity determinations and of some knowledge of the temperature and salinity structure at deeper levels, they have tended to obscure the main features which seem to be the continuous sinking of the Antarctic surface water to the north and the rise of the underlying warm highly saline water to the south.

Just north of the Antarctic Convergence there is a mixed water region in which the vertical temperature and salinity gradients are very small. This is particularly true in winter and spring. Figures 3 and 4 show the vertical distribution of temperature and salinity in a section through the first 1000 m of water between 60 and 67°S along the meridian 80°W. The observations were made in October. The convergence is in about 62½°S, and the minimum salinity and temperature which mark the nucleus of the sinking Antarctic water are found at depths of 300 to 400 m. At Station 989, the temperature decreased only 0.13°C and the salinity only 0.01‰ between the surface and 300 m. It is difficult to guess at the water movements in this region. The main movement must be to the east and there must be some southward trend in the body of the water to maintain the contrast at the convergence. Farther north, there is clear evidence of a southward movement in the subsurface layer as shown in Fig. 1. The surface water flows north as well as east under the influence of the west wind, but between it and the sinking Antarctic there is a layer of higher salinity which must be fed from the north.

Many of the zoologists who have examined the *Discovery* collections from the Antarctic Ocean have remarked on the significance of the convergence as a biological boundary. Among the floating and drifting plants and animals, there are many species which are typical of either Antarctic or subantarctic water and sufficiently rare on the other side of the convergence to be exceptional. Others are common to both sides. The fish too, and many of the birds, can be characteristically divided into Antarctic and subantarctic species. The northward flow of water does not stop at the convergence; icebergs and plankton drift across it, but the sinking of the Antarctic water and the

different layering on each side produce contrasting conditions on the two sides. It may not be the actual differences of temperature and salinity that decide why some animals live on one side and some on the other; the different types of water circulation on the two sides may produce some measure of isolation and some tendency for concentration of animals with particular breeding, feeding and migratory habits on the two sides. On the south side, the surface water is derived predominantly from the Antarctic, and although it spreads slowly northward, a plankton species which migrates vertically and spends part of the day or part of its life in the deep water might tend to maintain its position or, by processes of evolution, might even have become typical of what can be regarded as an oceanic territory:

There is a marked change of climate across the convergence. The snow line of South Georgia, which is surrounded by Antarctic water, is lower than the tree line on Staten Island in the same latitude but surrounded by subantarctic water.

G. E. R. DEACON

References

Rossby, C. T., 1959, "The Atmosphere and Sea in Motion," Rossby Memorial Volume, p. 27, New York, Rockefeller Institute Press.

Deacon, G. E. R., 1937, "The hydrology of the Southern Ocean," *Discovery Rept.*, **15**, 1–124.

Deacon, G. E. R., 1963, "The Southern Ocean," in "The Sea," Vol. 2, pp. 281–296, New York, Interscience Publishers.

Kort, V. C., 1964, "Antarctic Oceanography," in "Research in Geophysics," Vol. 2, pp. 309–333, Cambrig, Mass., M.I.T. Press.

Cross-reference: *Oceanic Circulation; Southern Ocean; Subtropical Convergence.*

CORAL SEA

According to the International Hydrographic Bureau (*Sp. Publ. 23*, 1953) the Coral Sea has been formally defined as follows: western side, the coast of Queensland (Australia) to include the Torres Straits, the western limit being a line from the northwest point of Cape York Peninsula (11°05′S 142°03′E) to the Bensbak River mouth in New Guinea (141°01′E). Then the north side follows the coast of Papua to Gado-Gadoa Island (10°38′S 150°34′E), thence along the 100-fathom line skirting the Tagula–Papua barrier reef, through Uluma (Suckling) Reef, to Lawik Reef (11°43′S 153°56′E) off Tagula Island, thence to the south point of Rennell Island, the south point of San Cristobal Island (Solomons), to Nupani (Santa Cruz Islands, 10°4′S 16°40′E) and Duff or Wilson Group (9°48′S 167°06′E). From here, the border runs south to Mera Lava, New Hebrides (14°25′S 168°03′E) and down the east side of these islands to Aneityum

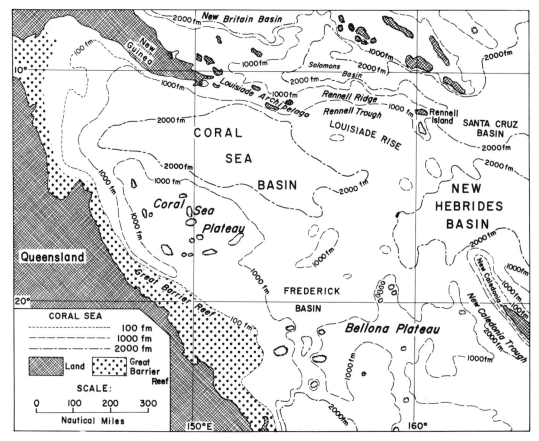

Fig. 1. Bathymetry of the Coral Sea. (The deep channel between the Bellona Plateau and the southeastern Coral Sea Plateau has been named Cato Trough.)

(20°11'S 169°51 E). From here, the line runs south-west to Nakanhui Island (22°46'S 167°34'E) off New Caledonia, thence to Middleton Reef, Eliza-beth Reef and the 30°S parallel and westward to the coast of Australia.

There is a narrow and shallow connection in the west through the Torres Straits to the Arafura Sea, Timor Sea and *Indian Ocean* (q.v.). In the north, there are connections to the *Solomon Sea* (q.v.); in the east, to the *Fiji Sea* (treated with *Southwest Pacific Ocean*, q.v.); in the south, with the *Tasman Sea* (q.v.).

Bathymetry

The Coral Sea is largely bounded by distinct structural borders, the continent of Australia or the island arc ridges of New Guinea, Rennell Ridge, Santa Cruz Plateau, New Hebrides, New Caledonia, etc. In the southwest and south, respectively, there are two enormous submarine plateaus, the *Coral Sea Plateau* (sometimes called "Queensland Pla-teau:" Carte Internationale, sheet A'III), and the *Bellona Plateau*, each exceeding 250,000 km² but with extensive shoals and shallows under 200 m; there are also extensive intermediate depths (down

to 1000 m), and the surfaces are punctuated by enormous atolls and coral platform reefs. (The above names were applied by Fairbridge after ex-tensive studies of the Australian reefs, including the preparation of a new contoured map of the region after the Scripps Expedition *Capricorn* in 1951; recommended names for the southwest Pacific were provided for the J. Bartholemew Mid-Century Edi-tion of the *Times Atlas* (1958, Plate 10); a historical review of all oceanographic names in the area was published in 1962, and a detailed analysis is in press.)

The three largest barrier reefs of the world lie in the area: the *Great Barrier Reefs of Queensland* on the northeast Australian continental shelf; the *Tagula Barrier Reef* of southeastern Papua and the Louisiade Archipelago; and the *New Caledonia Barrier Reef* surrounding that island and extending to the northwest as far as the D'Entrecasteaux Reefs (not to be confused with the "Islands" east of Papua) and in the southeast to the Ile des Pins.

There are three broad rises in the Coral Sea: *Mellish Rise* near the center punctuated by Mellish Reef and largely outlined by the 3000-m contour; *Louisiade Rise* connecting the Louisiades with New

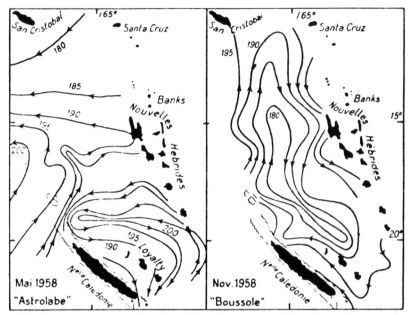

Fig. 2. Dynamic topography of the 1000-decibar surface (giving the surface currents) for the northeastern Coral Sea of two seasons (surveys by *Astrolabe* and *Boussole*, according to Rotchi, in Guilcher, 1965).

Caledonia; and the *Indispensable Rise* joining Rennell Island and the Indispensable Reefs with northern New Hebrides.

There are three major basins: the *Coral Sea Basin* (after Supan, 1899; including *Carpenter Deep*, 4899 m, named by Petermann in 1877; *New Hebrides Basin* (modified from Supan, 1899); the *Santa Cruz Basin* (Fairbridge, in Bartholemew's Atlas). There are several minor troughs and imperfect basins: *Queensland Trough* (called "trench" by Fairbridge, 1950) separating the Coral Sea Plateau from the Great Barrier Reefs shelf; the *Frederick Basin* (Fairbridge ms.) separating these two from Bellona Plateau, but probably connected by a shallow channel in the south to the Tasman Basin (q.v.); the *New Caledonia Trough* (Fairbridge ms.), separating New Caledonia from Bellona Plateau in the manner of a "foredeep," but connected by deep sills to the Norfolk Island Trough in the south and to the New Hebrides Basin in the north; the *Loyalty Trough* separating New Caledonia from the Loyalty Islands.

Finally, there are three of the world's great trenches near the eastern margin of the Coral Sea: *San Cristobal Trench* (Fairbridge, in Bartholemew's Atlas), 5658 m, forming an arc around the south end of the Solomons Ridge; *Torres Trench* (Fairbridge, in Bartholemew's Atlas) joined to the San Cristobal Trench with a "dog-leg" and trending north–south on the west side of the Santa Cruz Plateau; *New Hebrides Trench* of similar trend along the west side of the New Hebrides, curling around the south end in a manner suggesting a diagonal symmetry with the north end of the Tonga Trench.

Its maximum depth is 7661 m, the deepest sounding in the whole Coral Sea region. It is an interesting example of a bathymetric feature that was discovered as a result of a definite search; its presence was expected from the evidence of the New Hebrides seismic zone, but it was first sought on the east side of the New Hebrides and, only after failing to find it there, was it discovered by the German naval vessel S.M.S. *Planet* on the west side (in 1910).

The area of the Coral Sea (I.H.B. limits) is 4,791,000 km², and with a mean depth of 2394 m, its volume is 11,470,000 km³.

Physical Oceanography

Tides. The tidal oscillation of the Coral Sea is predominantly lunar semidiurnal in character, and appears to be due to a wave from the Pacific Ocean which enters the Coral Sea between the Solomon Islands and New Caledonia. This wave progresses southward through the Tasman Sea between Australia and New Zealand to link with the east-going tidal oscillation of the Southern Ocean. Cotidal and equirange patterns for this area have been collated by Dietrich (1963) and by Bogdhunov (1962).

There is an amphidromic point in the M_2 tide in the Solomons, and the mean spring range of the semidiurnal tide $2(M_2 + S_2)$ is as follows: Guadalcanal 12 cm, Cairns 476 cm, Sydney 83 cm, Melbourne 92 cm, Hobart 39 cm, Wellington 104 cm, Noumea 118 cm.

Surface Circulation. The South Equatorial Current enters the Coral Sea between the Solomon Islands and the New Hebrides from January to

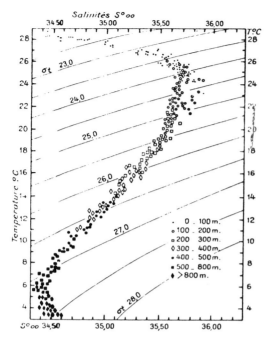

Fig. 3. Temperature-salinity curve obtained in the northeastern Coral Sea by the Boussole, November 1958 (from Rotchi, in Guilcher, 1965).

March under monsoon influence. During the remainder of the year, the Trade Wind Drift flows into this area. Both these movements feed the East Australian Current which flows southward over the East Australian Continental slope from about 20°S.

Water Masses. Water masses are formed originally under the influence of various climatic regimes and spread out across the oceans at various depths appropriate to their characteristic densities. The spreading and intermixing of these water masses may be followed by an examination of the variation of salinity at depth.

In the Coral Sea, water properties at the surface are derived mainly from the circulation of the East Australian Current system. This, in turn, is composed of warm, moderately saline equatorial water and of cooler, more saline subtropical water. Over much of the Coral Sea, a layer of high-salinity water is found at a depth of 100–200 m below the surface. This *Subtropical Lower Water* can be traced back to its origin at the surface in the southern subtropical anticyclone in the vicinity of Easter Island, one branch of which flows into the Coral Sea between the New Hebrides and the Solomon Islands.

Below the salinity maximum (about 35.9‰) at the core of the Subtropical Lower Water, salinity decreases steadily to reach a minimum (about 34.5‰) at a depth of some 1000 m below the surface where the temperature is around 5°C. This minimum locates the core of the *Antarctic Intermediate Water*. This can be traced back to the surface of the

Southern Ocean in the vicinity of the Antarctic Convergence. This water flows into the Coral Sea from the South Pacific Ocean between New Zealand and the Fiji Islands, around 25°S (Fig. 3).

The bottom of the Coral Sea Basin is filled with Deep Water (whose origin is in North Atlantic Deep Water; see *Atlantic Ocean*). The core of the Deep Water mass is marked by a weak salinity maximum at about 34.73‰ at a temperature of about 1.7°C.

Chemical Oceanography

The P/O ratio in the water mass below the euphotic zone and above the deeper waters, above which the influence of intermediate Antarctic waters is dominant, is very close to the ratio in other oceans.

In contrast, the deeper waters, where the consumption is apparently less than at the surface, are richer in oxygen, while the surface waters have a higher P content.

This confirms the Antarctic origin of the intermediate water mass whereas the P in the surface waters shows a closer relation to Pacific rather than to Atlantic waters.

Sediments

The Coral Sea Basin is covered mainly by pelagic red clay and globigerina ooze. Under the red clay in the abyssal plain of Papua at a depth of a few inches, Krause has found turbidites consisting of olive-colored silts with carbonized wood fragments. It is suggested that these have been derived by turbidity currents from the Fly River area of New Guinea by way of a deep channel that leads into the basin somewhat south of Port Moresby. The large plateau areas are largely covered by coral sands and carbonate muds, but the lagoons of the various great barrier reefs are largely filled by terrigenous deposits, coral-derived material being found only in patches. Around the New Hebrides there are extensive volcanic sediments.

Structural History

The tectonic units of the Coral Sea (after the I.H.B. definition) fall into seven principal types: *continental shelves and borderlands* (Queensland and Great Barrier Reef—Torres Straits—Papua shelf zone; Mesozoic–Cenozoic *orogenic belts* (Papua—Rennell Ridge—New Caledonia); Cenozoic *volcanic belts* (Solomons—Santa Cruz—New Hebrides); *submarine plateaus* (Coral Sea Plateau, Bellona Plateau); *oceanic rises and ridges* (Mellish Rise, etc.); *ocean basins* (Coral Sea Basin, New Hebrides Basin, etc.); deep-sea *trenches* and troughs (San Cristobal, Torres, New Hebrides, New Caledonia).

According to modern interpretations, the basins are underlain by oceanic crust (thickness about 5 km), the submarine plateaus by thinned quasi-cratonic, formerly continental crust (thickness 10–20 km), the orogenic belts by sialic roots (15–25 km), and the older continental borders by regular continental crust (30 km or more).

The structural pattern of eastern Queensland includes a Precambrian basement that comes out to the shelf edge in the northeast and continues under Torres Straits and outcrops or occurs at shallow depth under southern Papua; farther south there are successive belts of early Paleozoic and late Paleozoic orogenic belts. Triassic and younger sediments occur in small taphrogenic basins, mainly of continental facies. The eastern border of Queensland does not appear to have been exposed to oceanic waters until the great block faulting of the Kosciusko Epoch (Plio-Pleistocene).

The orogenic belt of New Guinea–New Caledonia contains eugeosynclinal facies mainly of Paleozoic and Mesozoic age with ultrabasic intrusions and considerable thicknesses of submarine lavas. Orogenic events have continued up till Tertiary times, but Pleistocene events have been milder and largely restricted to local faulting, and the great New Caledonia barrier reefs appear to be mainly due to eustatic control. Nevertheless the parallel Loyalty Ridge to the northeast shows both strong emergence and submergence during the late Quaternary and here the orogeny seems to be still active. The New Caledonia orogen continues southward through the Norfolk Ridge into New Zealand and shows many closely related lithologic and paleontologic correlations. In contrast, there is a total lack of similarity with eastern Queensland.

The volcanic belt of the Solomons, Santa Cruz and New Hebrides appears to be a juvenile eugeosyncline, with complex volcanic accumulations with related marine tuffs and limestones dating back no further than mid-Tertiary, while many of the islands are strictly Quaternary volcanoes, some still active. The zone is marked by high seismicity at both shallow and medium depth.

The trenches appear to be open tension gashes, mainly conditioned by dilation and strike-slip motion along great crustal lineaments (transcurrent faults). The basins, with thin oceanic crustal floors pose a yet unsolved problem in geophysics. Whether they represent new crust, formed by stretching apart of the borders, or some form of drift, or are relics of a primary ocean, is not yet clear. The submarine plateaus, on the other hand, are unequivocal: they were formerly shallow shelf areas that have subsided while extensive reef patches, which can only be initiated in water of 20-m depth or less, have grown up into some of the greatest atoll reefs of the world. This aspect is of very great interest for geotectonicists, because coral grows relatively slowly, and would be "drowned" by any sudden tectonic collapse of the plateau. Therefore we know positively that these plateaus (which completely lack volcanic cones) have subsided slowly from the level of continental crust to depths of 1000–2000 m and possibly more. The Coral Sea Plateau seems to be cut off from the Queensland continental shelf by a precipitous fault gash, and to have tilted downward to the north as it subsided. An explanation that involves continental stretching and thinning seems appropriate. Stille (1958) calls the region *quasi-cratonic* and relates the stretching to the earth's rotation, as does Fairbridge (1964).

Paleogeographically, the region east of Australia has long been recognized as a region of continental fracturing (Schuchert, 1916) and has often been referred to as "Tasmantis" (an analog of "Atlantis"), following Süssmilch and David (1919). The existence of such a land is most probable in view of the quartz and feldspars in the eastern Australian Triassic and younger sediments, bedding structures of which indicate provenance from the east. In New Caledonia, Avias (1953, 1955) has written of a Paleozoic–Mesozoic *Austro-Melanesian Geosyncline*, connecting to the Maorian Geosyncline of New Zealand, which seems to require a land area to its west. Such deductions must not be taken to imply that the entire Coral Sea area from New Guinea–New Caledonia to Australia must have been a former continent, but they would suggest that considerable parts of it were so.

RHODES W. FAIRBRIDGE
W. J. M. VAN DER LINDEN

References

Bogdhunov, K. T., 1962, "Tides of the Pacific Ocean," *Proc. Inst. Oceanol. (Moscow)*, **60**.

Brodie, J. W., 1952, "Features of the sea floor west of New Zealand," *New Zealand J. Sci. Techol. B*, **33**, 373–384.

Fairbridge, R. W., 1950, "Recent and Pleistocene coral reefs of Australia," *J. Geol.*, **58**, 330–401.

Fairbridge, R. W., 1961, "The Melanesian Border Plateau, a zone of crustal shearing in the S.W. Pacific," *Publ. Bur. Cent. Seism. Internat.*, Ser. *A*, No. 22, 137–149.

Fairbridge, R. W., 1962, "Basis for submarine nomenclature in the southwest Pacific Ocean," *Deut. Hydrograph. Z.*, **15**(1), 1–15.

Fairbridge, R. W., 1964, "Thoughts About an Expanding Globe," in (Subramanian, A. P., editor) "Advancing Frontiers in Geology and Geophysics," pp. 59–88, Indian Geophys. Union.

Fairbridge, R. W., 1966, "Bathymetric features of the Melanesian Region," *Deut. Hydrograph.* (in press).

Guilcher, A., 1965, "Précis d'Hydrologie Marine et Continentale," Paris, Masson & Cie, 389pp.

Krause, P. C., 1966, "Bathymetry and geologic structure of the Northwestern Tasman Sea—Coral Sea—South Solomon Sea," *New Zealand Oceanogr. Inst. Mem.*

Krebs, B. N., 1964, "A bibliography of the oceanography of the Tasman and Coral Seas, 1860–1960," *New Zealand Oceanogr. Inst. Mem.* 24.

Rochford, D. J., 1958, "The seasonal circulation of the surface water masses of the Tasman and Coral Seas," *C.S.I.R.O. Aust. Div. Fish. Oceanogr.*, Rep. 16.

Rotschi, H., 1959, "Remarques sur la circulation océanique entre la Nouvelle-Calédonie et l'ile Norfolk," *Cahiers Oceanogr.*, Paris, **11**, 416–424.

Rotschi, H., 1959, "Hydrologie et dynamique du NE de la Mer de Corail." *Cahiers Oceanogr.*, Paris, **11**, 627–750.

Rotschi, H., 1960, "Récents progrès des recherches océanographiques entreprises dans le Pacifique SW," *Cahiers Oceanogr.*, Paris, **12**, 248–267.

Rotschi, H., 1961, "Contribution française en 1960 à la connaissance de la Mer de Corail," *Cahiers Oceanogr.*, Paris, **13**, 434–455.

Schuchert, C., 1916, "The problem of continental fracturing and diastrophism in Oceania," *Am. J. Sci.*, Ser. 4, **42**.

Stille, H., 1958, "Einiges über die Weltozeane und ihre Umrahmungsräume," *Geologie*, **7**, 237–306.

Wyrtki, K., 1960, "The surface circulation in the Coral and Tasman Seas," *C.S.I.R.O. Aust. Div. Fish. Oceanogr. Tech. Pap.* 8.

Wyrtki, K., 1961, "The flow of water into the deep basins of the Western South Pacific Ocean," *Australian J. Marine Freshwater Res.*, **13**.

Wyrtki, K., 1962, "Geopotential topographies and associated circulation in the Western South Pacific Ocean," *ibid.*, **13**.

Wyrtki, K., 1962, "The subsurface water masses in the Western South Pacific Ocean," *ibid.*, **13**.

Cross-reference: *East Australian Current; Solomon Sea; Southwest Pacific Ocean; Tasman Sea.*

CORIOLIS FORCE

The Coriolis force is a concept used in the analysis of motions which are measured with respect to rotating coordinate systems. Measurements of acceleration in such reference frames differ from the corresponding measurements made from unaccelerated (inertial) systems. Hence they are not described directly by Newton's Second Law of Motion, which is formulated for inertial systems, but they must be supplemented by certain other terms in order to represent values of acceleration as would be observed from the inertial frame. These terms are usually grouped with the forces affecting the motions and, for convenience of nomenclature, are styled "forces" themselves.

One such term corresponds to the centripetal acceleration of a particle at rest in the rotating coordinates. In discussions of motions relative to the earth, this term is generally absorbed into what one calls "gravity" (as distinguished from gravitation) and does not appear explicitly in the equations of motion.

The other term is the *Coriolis force per unit mass,* named in honor of G. G. Coriolis, an early investigator of fluid motions on the rotating earth. It is measured as $-2\Omega \times \mathbf{V}$ where Ω is the angular velocity vector of the rotating coordinate frame and $\mathbf{V}$ is the vector velocity of the motion relative to the rotating system. With regard to fluid motions, it is often convenient to speak of the *Coriolis force per unit volume,* $-2\Omega \times \rho\mathbf{V}$ where ρ is the fluid density. Since the force is perpendicular to the velocity, it plays no role in the energetics of the motion—as must be the case, because its existence reflects only the observer's reference frame, not the configuration of the physical system. By introducing this force to Newton's Second Law, however, it becomes possible to discuss in a fairly convenient way motions measured in rotating coordinates as if they were observed instead from an inertial frame of reference.

The earth itself constitutes a rotating coordinate system, and, in principle, all motions observed from it are subject to a Coriolis force due to its rotation. In many phenomena, however, such as the propagation of sound waves or production of high-energy charged particles, this Coriolis force is completely insignificant in comparison with other forces present. On the other hand, an important correction must be applied to missile trajectories for its effect, and the large-scale motions of the ocean and atmosphere are dominated by it.

In studies of the latter motions, it is usually possible to employ a simplified representation of the Coriolis force. The balance of vertical forces in the ocean and atmosphere is almost always overwhelmingly dominated by gravity and the vertical pressure gradient (hydrostatic balance) and is completely unaffected by the vertical component of Coriolis force. Although the horizontal component of Coriolis force is of the same order of magnitude as the vertical one, it cannot be neglected, because the remaining horizontal forces are several orders smaller than gravity and are in fact comparable with the Coriolis force. Except on the equator, however, this component receives no significant contribution from the vertical velocity, since that component of the large-scale oceanic and atmospheric motions is much smaller than the horizontal one. Accordingly, it becomes practical in discussing these motions to substitute for the full Coriolis force an approximate version of the local horizontal component: its magnitude (per unit volume) is $2\Omega\rho v \sin\varphi$, where v is the magnitude of the horizontal velocity, Ω is the earth's angular rotation rate, and φ is the geographic latitude of observation; its direction is perpendicular to the horizontal velocity vector, to the right in the northern hemisphere (positive φ), to the left in the southern (negative φ). The factor $2\Omega \sin\varphi$ is called the *Coriolis parameter,* and is often abbreviated as f (see *Geostrophic Motion*).

BRUCE WARREN

References

Hess, Seymour L., 1959, "Introduction to Theoretical Meteorology," Ch. 11, New York, Henry Holt and Co.

McDonald, J. E., 1952, "The Coriolis effect," *Sci. An.* (May, 1952).

Cross-reference: *Ferrell's Law and Buys Ballot's Law; Geostrophic Motion.*

COSMIC DUST

In 1923, Oliver C. Farrington commented that "...(meteorites) are our only *tangible* source of knowledge of the universe beyond the earth." There is strong evidence from recent artificial satellite data, however, that dust is falling on the earth in addition to meteorites, and this dust is a possible second tangible source of knowledge about the universe around us. Reasons for studying extraterrestrial (cosmic) dust, therefore, are equally as strong as reasons for studying meteorites.

At present, much less is known about cosmic dust than about meteorites. Also, judging by the intense current debate over the origin of meteorites, it should not be hoped that the study of cosmic dust would be a simple one with clear-cut conclusions. It is a study, however, that is being undertaken by greater numbers of scientists every succeeding year.

Cosmic dust undoubtedly exists between the planets, the stars, and the galaxies. It has a variety of postulated origins and sources, such as primordial condensation or sublimation products, debris from comets, debris from collisions between meteorites or asteroids, and collisions of meteorites, asteroids, and comets with the moon and earth. Suspected cosmic dust particles have been collected on the ocean floor, in sediments as ancient as the Ordovician, from ancient Arctic and Antarctic ices, from rainwater, and from the atmosphere. Impacts, presumably due to cosmic dust particles, have been recorded by satellite-borne instruments.

Hypotheses for the origin of the elements differ, but most postulate initial conditions of extremely high temperature and pressure such as might obtain today inside certain stars. After formation, the elements were dispersed from one or a number of centers at one time or at a number of different times. Aggregations of elements then occurred to form galaxies, stars, planets, and smaller bodies. The impalpable residues from these gigantic operations were primordial dust particles that had condensed from vapor as liquid droplets and frozen and/or solidified directly from the vapor state as a smoky sublimate. Primordial dust existing today is presumably part of a decreasing supply, at least in our part of the universe, because it is constantly subject to capture and incorporation into larger bodies. Even though we know it must exist, primordial dust has never been identified as such.

In addition to the primordial dust that must be present, other processes are constantly producing secondary dust within the solar system. Mass-wasting or disruption of comets that pass too close to the sun, and perhaps to Jupiter, and collisions between comets, meteorites, and asteroids seem to be the main such processes. The dust so produced, along with primordial dust, tends to fall onto larger bodies such as the moon and planets or, much more probably, into the sun (see *Poynting-Robertson Effect**). Extremely tiny particles, however, are repelled from the sun by the pressure of light and move out of the solar system unless captured by a planet on the way (see *Radiation Pressure**).

In addition to satellite data, astronomical evidence can be cited for the existence of dust in the solar system. The zodiacal light is a faint band of light oriented along the ecliptic and increasing in intensity toward the sun. It is caused by the scattering of sunlight by small particles in orbit between the earth and the sun. The color of the scattered light suggests the particles are around 10μ (0.0004 inch) in diameter.

Accounts of dust falling on the earth have been found in records dating back to the year 472. Dust is often reported as coming down with rain or hail. There is no reason to disbelieve these reports, but it should be pointed out that modern-day collections are not reliable in this respect because of the tremendous quantities of fine dust of artificial origin that are presently being added to the atmosphere by industrial smoke. Occurrences reported before the industrial revolution could have resulted from distant dust storms and been of terrestrial origin.

Murray found microscopic magnetic spherules on the ocean floor in 1884 and suggested they were of extraterrestrial origin. Such spherules are also found in ancient ice, salt, and terrestrial sediments and are now believed to be either cosmic dust particles or droplets swept off the molten surfaces of falling meteorites. Magnetic spherules have also been found in great numbers around some meteorite craters and presumably were produced at the instant of impact by melting of part of the meteorite or vaporization of part of the meteorite and recondensation as droplets. Some workers have also reported finding highly siliceous nonmagnetic spherules in ancient deposits but in smaller quantities than magnetic spherules.

"Cosmic spherules" range in size from $200-300\mu$ in diameter ($300\mu = 0.3$ mm $= 0.012$ inch) down at least to $1-5\mu$. Compositional analysis is difficult because of their small size. Methods that have proved helpful are optical metallography, X-ray crystallography, neutron-activation analysis, and electron microprobe analysis. The predominant element found in the magnetic spherules is iron, presumably present as oxides, with accessory concentrations (less than 1%) of Mn and, in some cases, several per cent silicon. Nickel is present in some spherules and not in others.

Estimates of the accumulation rate of cosmic dust on the earth range between 35,000 and 1,000,000 tons/yr. There is no known way to prove that a microscopic particle collected on the earth is of extraterrestrial origin. It must also be remembered that spherules, if they are extraterrestrial, may be only one type of extraterrestrial dust falling

*See Vol. II.

on the earth; other types may have escaped notice so far (see also Vol. II, *Meteor* and *Micrometeorite*).

WILLIAM A. CASSIDY

References

Brandt, John C., and Hodge, Paul W., 1964, "Solar System Astrophysics," New York, McGraw-Hill Book Co., 457pp.

Cassidy, William A., (editor), 1964, "Cosmic dust," *Ann. N.Y. Acad. Sci.*, **119** (1), 368pp.

CURRENTS—*See* **OCEANIC CIRCULATION PATTERNS; OCEAN BOTTOM CURRENTS.**

D

DATING—*See* **RADIONUCLIDES: THEIR APPLICATION IN OCEANOGRAPHY**

DAVIS STRAIT—*See* **CANADIAN ARCTIC ARCHIPELAGO**

DEEP SCATTERING LAYERS

Deep scattering layers (DSL's) are sound-reflecting layers that commonly appear on echograms of precision depth recorders (Figs. 1 and 2). The outgoing sound signals from the transducer, operating at a frequency of 12 kc/sec (or higher), are partially scattered, and the reverberations are recorded as one or more diffuse layers at depths most commonly between 200 and 600 m in the daytime. The traces are at times so distinct that they represent "false bottoms."

Because the layers generally rise to the surface at dusk and descend to their daytime depths at sunrise, this widely observed phenomenon has been attributed to diurnal vertical migration of marine animals. In addition to the latter, there are shallower, nonmigratory scattering layers in the upper 100 m that are also commonly recorded throughout the day and night. The common belief is that the migratory organisms of the scattering layers hide from predators in the darkness of deep waters during the day and swim upward to feed themselves in the plankton-rich surface waters at night. The nature of the DSL's and related phenomena have been reviewed by Boden (1962) and Hersey and Backus (1962).

Light

The negatively phototropic behavior of the DSL's is controlled by the amount of light penetrating into ocean waters and the length of day, both of which exert an influence on the DSL's maximum daytime depth and the timing of the evening rise and morning descent. Kampa and Boden (1954) noted that the DSL's upward movements at sunset followed closely the movements of certain isolumes, although Clarke and Backus (1956) found that they migrated more rapidly than a given value of isolumes.

Distribution

DSL's are observed in all the oceans of the

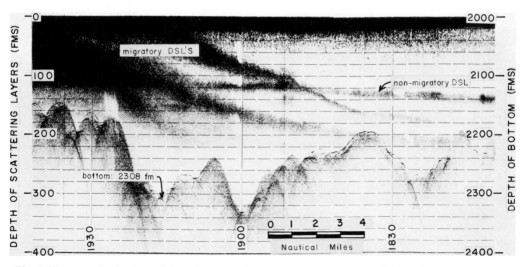

Fig. 1. The upward migration of three deep scattering layers at sunset are recorded in this echogram obtained by Lamont Geological Observatory's R/V *Conrad* in the southeastern Pacific Ocean (21° 02′S, 95° 28.5′W) at 1830, February 18, 1965. One non-migratory DSL is shown between 120 and 140 fathoms depth. (*Courtesy M. Ewing, B. C. Heezen, and A. Lonardi*)

227

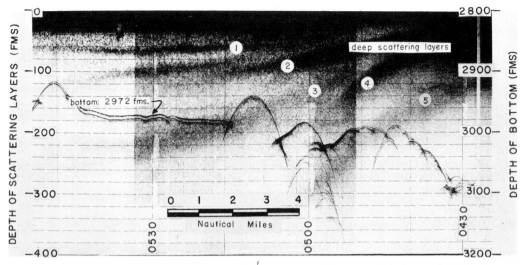

Fig. 2. Five deep scattering layers are shown migrating downward at different speeds during sunrise. This echogram was recorded by R/V *Conrad* on April 2, 1965, in the southwestern Pacific Ocean (27° 32'S. 165° 36'W at 0430). (*Courtesy M. Ewing, B. C. Heezen, and A. Lonardi*)

world, being more distinct in fertile oceanic regions such as the waters off Peru and California. In low and middle latitudes, the alternation of day and night is followed by correspondingly regular, diurnal movements of the scattering layers. As the length of day increases toward summer in polar latitudes, the periodicity of the diurnal rhythm is altered toward prolonged submergence at daytime depths and only brief periods in surface waters. The DSL's were considered to be lacking or occurring sporadically in the Arctic and Antarctic Oceans, but Hunkins (1965) has recently observed their presence below Arctic pack ice at depths of 50–200 m for 3–5 month periods during the summer and fall, while during the rest of the year, discrete echoes were observed near the surface. Arctic scattering layers thus have an annual rather than a diurnal cycle.

Faunal Composition and Biological Properties

In considering the animals that make up the DSL's, Marshall (1951) noted that they must possess certain attributes. The organisms must have an ocean-wide distribution. They must be shown to occur abundantly at the appropriate depth(s), between 250 and 800 m, during the daytime. They must be able to swim rapidly to accomplish diurnal vertical migration. They must be able to reflect sound.

Attempts at capturing or photographing the animals of a DSL have met with mixed success, because either the rapid swimmers escape capture by a slow-moving net, resulting in a highly selective catch, or they are too sparsely distributed to be photographed *en masse*. The present consensus is that DSL's are composed of heterogeneous taxo-

nomic groups, which may also vary with region, depth, and season.

Organisms that reflect discrete echoes must have cross sections between 0.1 and 10 cm^2 (Raitt, 1948). This size range could include fish, squid, and larger, fast-swimming crustaceans such as euphausids and sergestids. However, it would exclude the smaller zooplankters, less than 2 cm in length, that compose the microplankton usually caught with plankton nets.

Small air bubbles are excellent sound scatterers, because their density and compressibility are greatly different from those of seawater. Thus, gas-filled chambers only several millimeters in diameter belonging to certain animals may be highly resonant for 12-kc sound (Dietz, 1948). Two groups that possess such structures and occur abundantly and extensively at depths between 250 and 800 m are the bathypelagic fish (families Gonostomatidae, Sternoptychidae, and Myctophidae) and siphonophores (Marshall, 1951; Barham, 1963). Both groups, as well as squid and larger crustaceans, are known to migrate diurnally and can swim at a rate of 5–15 m/min, which falls within the range of travel times of the deep scattering layers.

ALLAN W. H. BÉ

References

Barham, E. G., 1963, "Siphonophores and the deep scattering layer," *Science*, **140**, 826–828.
Boden, B. P., 1962, "Plankton and sonic scattering," *Cons. Intern. Explor. Mer*, **153**, 171–177.
Clarke, G. L., Backus, R. H., 1956, "Measurements of light penetration in relation to vertical migration and

records of luminescence of deep-sea animals," *Deep-sea Res.*, **4**, 1–14.

Dietz, R. S., 1948, "Deep scattering layer in the Pacific and Antarctic Oceans," *J. Marine Res.*, **7**, 430–442.

Hersey, J. B., and Backus, R. H., 1962, "Sound Scattering by Marine Organisms," in (Hill, M. N., editor) "The Sea," Vol. 1, pp. 498–539, New York, Interscience Publishers.

Hunkins, K., 1965, "The seasonal variation in the sound scattering layer observed at T-3 with a 12 kcps sounder," *Deep-Sea Res.*, **12**, 879–881.

Kampa, E. M., and Boden, B. P., 1954, "Submarine illumination and the twilight movements of a sonic scattering layer," *Nature*, **174**, 869–871.

Marshall, N. B., 1951, "Bathypelagic fishes as sound scatterers in the ocean," *J. Marine Res.*, **10**, 1–17.

Raitt, R. W., 1948, "Sound scatterers in the sea," *J. Marine Res.*, **7**, 393–409.

DEEP-SEA CURRENTS—*See* BOTTOM OCEAN CURRENTS

DEEP-SEA FAN—*See* SUBMARINE CONES OR FANS

DEEP-SEA FAUNA—*See* ABYSSAL ZONE; BATHYAL ZONE

DELTA—*See* Vol. III

DENSITY

The density of any substance is defined as the mass per unit volume. The density of seawater which is usually stated in grams per cubic centimeter ranges from nearly 1 for fresh water to about 1.07 for the water at a great depth of the ocean. In oceanography, in order to save space, density is expressed with its sigma value defined by (density -1) $\times$ 1000. The sigma value at atmospheric pressure is particularly written σ_t. The density of seawater at the place where it collected and at the sea surface to which it is brought up adiabatically is called *density in situ* and *potential density,* respectively. The sigma value of potential density is approximately equal to σ_t.

The density of seawater depends on three variables: temperature, salinity and pressure. In ordinary seawater, density decreases with increasing pressure at a rate of about 45×10^{-4} (g/cm^3) per 1000 decibars which correspond to an increase of depth by about 1000 meters. The rate of increase of density with increasing salinity is about 8×10^{-4} (g/cm^3) per 1‰. The rate of change of density with temperature is a complicated function of the three variables. For example, for seawater of salinity 35‰, the rate of decrease of density with increasing temperature at atmospheric pressure ranges from 5×10^{-5} per 1°C at 0°C, to 34×10^{-5} per 1°C at 30°C while this rate for pure water ranges from -7×10^{-5} per 1°C at 0°C to 30×10^{-5} per 1° at 30°C with zero at 4°C corresponding to the maximum density at this temperature.

The potential density of a water parcel does not change when the parcel moves adiabatically. In the stationary large-scale oceanic circulation, density distributions do not change with time. Therefore, the water movements in such circulation are considered to occur along surfaces of equal potential density. Thus these surfaces indicate the level of large-scale water movements. When potential density increases downward as usually encountered in oceans, the water stratification is stable and vice versa. Therefore, vertical distributions of potential density indicates vertical stability of the water layer. In oceanography σ_t is more frequently used than potential density, since the former is easier to

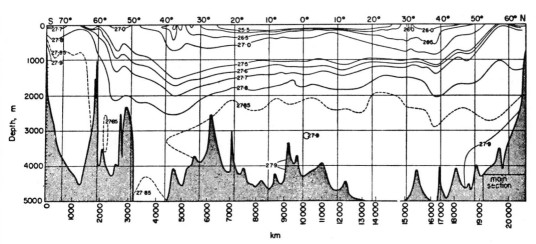

Fig. 1. Longitudinal density section along the Western Trough of the Atlantic (Defant, 1961). (By permission of Pergamon Press, N.Y.)

calculate than the latter. In Fig. 1 the vertical section of σ_t along the Western Trough of the Atlantic is shown (Defant, 1961). At the surface there is a gradual increase of density from the equator toward high latitudes. Between 100 and 2000 meters, horizontal density gradient is opposite to the surface gradient from the equator to the two subtropical regions because in the equatorial zone the heavier water of deeper layers extends up to just below the surface. Also Fig. 1 shows that the deep waters are formed in high latitudes and that particularly the bottom water below 2000 meters spreads to the north from the Antarctic Ocean. In Fig. 2, vertical distributions of σ_t at four oceanographic stations in the Atlantic are shown. The density *in situ* may be obtained by adding the values due to the pressure effect. In the equatorial and subtropical regions, the upper layer above 100 meters has homogeneous density. The σ_t increases from this layer down to 1000–2000 meters and forms

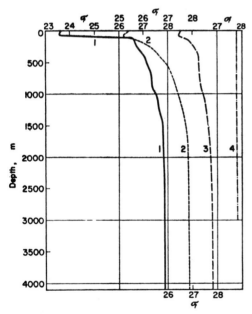

Fig. 2. Vertical distribution of the density σ_t at some oceanographic stations in the Atlantic (Defant, 1961):
    (1) "Meteor" 254   2° 27′ S   34° 57′ W
    (2) "Meteor" 170 22° 39′ S   27° 55′ W
    (3) "Meteor"   8 41° 39′ S   30° 06′ W
    (4) "Meteor"
        Greenland 122 55° 03′ N 44° 46′ W
(By permission of Pergamon Press, N.Y.)

picnocline. The vertical gradient of σ_t below the homogeneous layer is strongest in the equatorial regions. In the subpolar regions the σ_t is almost uniform vertically, indicating that the water stratification is less stable than in lower latitudes.

TAKASHI ICHIYE

References

Defant, A., 1961, "Physical Oceanography," Vol. 1, New York, Pergamon Press, 729pp.
Dietrich, G., 1963, "General Oceanography," New York, Interscience Publishers, 588pp.
Sverdrup, H. U., Johnson, M. W., and Fleming, R. H., 1942, "The Oceans," 1087pp, Englewood Cliffs, N.J., Prentice-Hall.

DIFFUSION IN THE OCEAN

(1) Molecular Diffusion and Eddy Diffusion

Mass of a dissolved substance is transferred from a region of higher concentration to that of lower concentration by irregular motions of molecules of a fluid. This is called molecular diffusion. The transport of thermal energy from warmer to colder regions due to molecular action is (molecular) thermal conductivity. The amount of the substance which diffuses per unit time through a surface of unit area is proportional to the gradient of concentration normal to that surface. The coefficient of proportionality is called molecular diffusivity; for water it is equal to about 2×10^{-5} in cgs units, but it depends on the character of the solute. The proportionality coefficient for the transport of heat is called (molecular) thermal conductivity and is about 10^{-3} in cgs units for seawater (Sverdrup et al., 1942).

However, in the ocean turbulent motion prevails (see *Turbulence in the Ocean*), and transfer of mass and heat by turbulent motion is larger by several orders of magnitude than molecular diffusivity and thermal conductivity. From an analogy with molecular processes, the rate of transfer of mass is assumed to be proportional to the gradient of the average concentration. The proportionality coefficient is called eddy diffusivity, which, like eddy viscosity, is not a physical constant but depends on the nature of the turbulent motion. Also, the values of eddy diffusivity determined empirically in the ocean are of the same orders of magnitude as those of kinetic eddy viscosity (eddy viscosity per unit mass).

(2) Empirical Methods of Determining Eddy Diffusivity

Eddy diffusivity in the ocean is empirically determined (1) from the mean distributions of passive quantities like temperature and salinity, (2) from measurements of fluctuations of these quantities continuously at fixed places, and (3) from determination of dispersion of tracers such as effluent from rivers and dye or isotopes artificially released. The first and second methods yield eddy diffusivity in the fixed coordinate system or Eulerian reference frame, while the third method yields eddy diffusivity in the coordinate system moving with the flow or Lagrangian reference frame.

The first method has been widely used since 1900

in the various parts of the ocean under different conditions. Eddy diffusivity is much larger in the vertical than in horizontal directions as is kinetic eddy viscosity. Also, vertical eddy diffusivity decreases with increasing stability as does vertical eddy viscosity. In order to determine eddy diffusivity from the transport equation or Fickian equation, it is usually assumed that two or three terms in the equation are retained among terms representing time-change rate, advection and vertical and horizontal diffusion, according to different situations (Proudman, 1953). The ranges of eddy diffusivity (per unit mass) thus determined are about $0.1–10^2$ cm^2/sec in the vertical and about $10^6–10^8$ cm^2/sec in the horizontal direction (Sverdrup et al., 1942).

The second method is to determine a flux of a physical quantity from cross-correlations of fluctuations of the quantity and the velocity component. The eddy diffusivity is defined as the ratio of the flux to the gradient of the mean concentration. Russian workers have used this method to determine vertical eddy diffusivity in various parts of the oceans. They have measured fluctuations of temperature, salinity and horizontal and vertical velocities at two depths with intervals ranging from 0.5–2 meters. They found that the vertical eddy diffusivity is almost inversely proportional to the Richardson number or the ratio of stability to square of vertical shear (Ichiye, 1963).

The third method is usually utilized to determine horizontal eddy diffusivity in the ocean. There are three approaches in this method. The first is to study movements of a single object, such as a drogue, floating in the current and to determine (Lagrangian) eddy diffusivity from correlations of velocities of the object at different times. The second approach is to measure the mean distance of pairs of objects. In this approach, neighbor diffusivity is obtained by the rate of change of the mean distance. Richardson, Stommel, Ozmidov, Olson and Ichiye determined the neighbor diffusivity in the various parts of the ocean with turnips, papers, drogues and drift bottles, and obtained values ranging from $10–10^9$ cm^2/sec (Bowden, 1962). The third approach is to release many particles or a marked fluid, such as a dye, at one point and to determine eddy diffusivity from the rate of change of the mean distance of particles or marked fluid about its center of gravity. In recent years, dye has been widely used in the ocean to study turbulent diffusion.

(3) Statistical Theories of Turbulent Diffusion

Eddies producing mixing and diffusion have different sizes and energies. The energy distribution among eddies, or the energy spectrum, is determined statistically from hydrodynamic equations of motion with assumptions about randomness of the motion. Diffusion processes due to turbulent flow can be predicted from the energy spectrum of eddies (see *Turbulence in the Ocean*). There are two approaches to studying the statistical nature of diffusion processes: Eulerian and Lagrangian approaches.

Kolmogoroff derived the energy spectrum of eddies of an intermediate size range, in which energy is transferred from larger to smaller eddies. Eckart and Russian workers applied Kolmogoroff's theory to mixing processes in the ocean, and the latter deduced that the eddy diffusivity is proportional to the 4/3 power of the mean diameter of eddies contributing to diffusion. These studies were made from an Eulerian approach (Ichiye, 1963).

A Lagrangian approach for one-particle diffusion problem was initiated by Taylor, who determined the correlations between velocities of a particle at different times. His theory is also applied to the change with time of the mean distance of many particles from their center. The theory indicates that a diffusion process approaches a constant eddy diffusivity only a long time after release of a cluster of particles (Batchelor and Townsend, 1956; Bowden, 1962).

Richardson proposed a Lagrangian approach of the variation with time of the mean distance separating two particles. He introduced the concept of neighbor concentration to represent percentage of pairs of particles having a certain mean distance (neighbor separation), where the change of the neighbor concentration is governed by a neighbor diffusivity instead of ordinary diffusivity. He deduced from data in atmospheric diffusion that the neighbor diffusivity is proportional to the 4/3 power of the neighbor separation. Later, Ichiye and Olson confirmed this relation by use of the data in the ocean and also deduced it from the Kolmogoroff's energy spectrum (Bowden, 1962).

Approximate treatments of a Lagrangian theory of many-particle diffusion in two dimensions were made by Joseph and Sendner and by Schönfeld. Their theories, based on a hypothesis of random motion of particles, lead to diffusion equations similar to the Fickian equation with variable eddy diffusivity. The results were applied to prediction of diffusion of dye patches or radioactive substances released in the ocean (Bowden, 1962; Ichiye, 1963).

TAKASHI ICHIYE

References

Batchelor, G. K., and Townsend, A. A., 1956, "Turbulent Diffusion," in (Batchelor, G. K., and Davis, R. M., editors) "Surveys in Mechanics," pp. 352–399, Cambridge, Cambridge University Press.

Bowden, K. F., 1962, "Turbulence," in (Hill, M. N., editor) "The Sea," Vol. 1, Sect. VI, pp. 802–825, New York, Interscience Publishers.

Ichiye, T., 1963, "Oceanic Turbulence" (Review), p. 200, Technical Report No. 2 of Oceanographic Institute, Florida State University to the Office of Naval Research.

Proudman, J., 1953, "Dynamical Oceanography," pp. 409, New York, Dover Publications.

Sverdrup, H. U., Johnson, M. W., and Fleming, R. H., 1942, "The Oceans," pp. 1060, Englewood Cliffs, N.J., Prentice-Hall Inc.

DRAKE PASSAGE—*See* SCOTIA SEA

DRIFTING ICE STATIONS

Scientific research stations mounted on floating ice in the Arctic Ocean are generally known as "drifting ice stations." The drifting ice provides a stable platform for oceanographical, meteorological, and other geophysical studies. Since the central Arctic Ocean is inaccessible to surface ships, drifting ice stations serve as research vessels for this ice-covered ocean.

The predecessors of modern drifting stations were the strengthened ships of earlier explorers which were frozen into the pack ice and allowed to drift with it. Notable expeditions of this type were the Norwegian North Polar Expeditions with the *Fram* (1893–1896) led by Fridtjof Nansen and with the *Maud* (1918–1925) led by Roald Amundsen. These expeditions produced important contributions in the fields of oceanography and meteorology, and they showed the value of drifting stations. The improvements in air transportation and radio communication during the first third of the twentieth century made it possible to eliminate the ship and establish a camp upon the ice itself.

Two types of ice are available as floating platforms for stations in the Arctic Ocean. Ice floes of frozen seawater are the normal ice type and have been the bases for most camps. The Arctic pack is composed of great numbers of ice floes in close contact. Ice floes suitable for camps are usually about 3 meters thick and several square kilometers in area. Ice islands are the second type of platform. They are thick ice masses which have broken from the land-fast ice shelves of Ellesmere and other northern Canadian islands. Ice islands range from about 15–50 meters in thickness and from a few to several hundred square kilometers in area. They have the advantage over ice floes of a longer life before breakup. For example, the U.S. station *Fletcher's Ice Island (T-3)* has been in use as a research station from 1952 to the present, while most ice floe stations last only a year or two. However, floes are preferable as a base for certain researches, such as heat budget studies, which require ice conditions typical of the entire Arctic Ocean.

The first drifting ice station was established by the U.S.S.R. in May 1937 by aircraft landings on the ice near the North Pole. A party of four led by Ivan Papanin carried out a program of scientific observations for nine months. During this time, they drifted a total of 2050 km. The station was finally evacuated in February 1938 by icebreaker off Scoresbysund, Greenland. Some anxious moments occurred toward the end of the drift as the ice floe began to disintegrate. The pioneering example of this station, *North Pole*-1, showed the feasibility of aircraft-supported ice stations for the detailed exploration of the Arctic Ocean.

Polar investigations lapsed during the war years. A second drifting station, *North Pole*-2, was established by the U.S.S.R. in 1950. Since 1950, many stations have been established by both the Russians and the Americans. Two drifting stations are maintained continuously in the Arctic Ocean by the U.S.S.R. at present. When poor ice conditions force the evacuation of a station, a new one is almost immediately set up in a new location.

The U.S. drift program began with the camp for scientific research on *Fletcher's Ice Island (T-3)* in 1952. During the International Geophysical Year (1957–1958), *Station Alpha* as well as the camp on *T-3*, was operated. *Station Charlie* was a U.S. contribution to the International Geophysical Cooperation of 1959. More recent U.S. stations have been *Arlis I* (1960–1961) and *Arlis II* which was established in 1961 and is still in operation at the present. *Arlis I* is the only station to have been supplied initially by icebreaker rather than aircraft. Both *T-3* and *Arlis II* are located on ice islands. Apparently the only Soviet ice island station during IGY was *North Pole*-6; their other stations were on pack-ice.

The ice drifts under the influence of winds and ocean currents. The drift is generally about 1/50 of the wind speed, and is directed about 30° to the right of the direction toward which the wind is blowing due to the effect of the earth's rotation. This empirical rule was first noted by Nansen. The ice in the Canadian side of the Arctic Ocean describes a clockwise movement. This gyre is driven by the winds associated with the high-pressure area often found over this part of the ocean. About 10 years are required to complete an orbit around this gyre. *Fletcher's Ice Island (T-3)* has been followed through two orbits (Fig. 1). On the Eurasian side of the Arctic Ocean, ice drift is predominantly toward the exit between Greenland and Spitzbergen, although eddies do occur on the broad shelf areas. The most rapid ice drifts in the Arctic Ocean take place in the East Greenland Current, and in this area, permanent ocean currents probably play a larger part in the drift.

Investigations conducted from ice stations have included marine geology and geophysics, marine biology, underwater acoustics, physical oceanography, ice structure and properties, synoptic meteorology, heat budget, and ionospherics. For such studies as marine geology and geophysics, ice movement is important for geographical coverage.

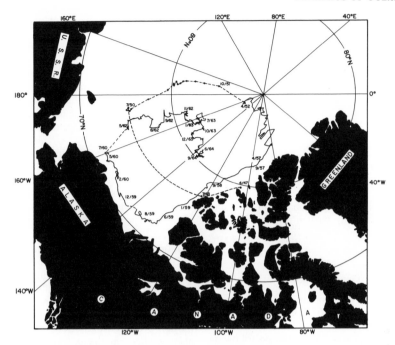

Fig. 1. Drift track of Fletcher's Ice Island (T-3) from 1947–64. T-3 was occupied as a drifting ice station along solid portions of the track. T-3 was unoccupied along dotted portions but was spotted from aircraft.

For other studies such as heat budget and ionospherics, the movement may have little importance.

Drifting stations, together with submarines and aircraft, are the only vehicles for carrying scientists into the Arctic Ocean. Drifting stations are particularly valuable for long and detailed observations which are not easily carried out from submarines or aircraft. Many of the special Arctic phenomena, such as auroras, magnetic effects, and the role of the polar region as a heat sink for the atmospheric and oceanic heat engines, will probably continue to be studied from drifting stations in the future.

KENNETH L. HUNKINS

References

*Crary, A. P., 1956, "Arctic ice island research," in (Landsberg, H. E., editor) *Advan. Geophys.*, **3**, 1–41. 1958, "Arctic sea ice," *Natl. Acad. Sci.—Natl. Res. Council, Publ.* **598**, 271pp. 1963, "Proceedings of the Arctic Basin Symposium, Oct. 1962," Arctic Institute of North America, Wash., D.C., 313pp.

DYNAMICS OF OCEAN CURRENTS

Dynamical oceanography is a branch of physical oceanography, and it treats various kinds of movement of the ocean water. Among motions in the oceans, gravity waves and tides are discussed elsewhere. Therefore, only the motion of a stationary or of a slowly changing nature is discussed here. This motion is generally called circulation. Emphasis will be placed particularly on large-scale circulation in which effects of earth's rotation and stratification play an important role. Classical hydrodynamics treats a homogeneous fluid in a nonrotating system. The meanings of stationary, slow change, and large-scale will be explained in the course of discussion.

Movement of the ocean water is governed by Newton's law of dynamics. When this law is applied to a fluid, three sets of equations of motion are derived from the conservation of three components of momentum. There are two ways to represent motion of a fluid: the Lagrangian and the Eulerian methods (Lamb, 1945). The former is to describe the motion of a marked particle of the fluid, like tracking a trajectory of a buoy or balloon, while the latter is to describe the motion at a fixed point in the fluid, like watching a river flow from a bridge. In dynamical oceanography, the Eulerian method is used almost exclusively. Besides conservation of momentum, the fluid motion must observe the law of conservation of mass. Further, density of seawater depends on temperature and salinity; thus, the relationships between density and such quantities as temperature and salinity (equation of state) and laws of conservation of temperature and salinity must be satisfied.

The equations of motion representing conservation of momentum also indicate balance of different forces. The balance of forces acting on a fluid particle on the earth is expressed by an equation

Inertial Force + Coriolis' Force = − Pressure
Gradient Force + Gravity Force +
Frictional Force   (A)

Mathematical forms of equation of motion (A) and other laws of conservation can be written concisely by use of vectors or tensors (Defant, 1961; Fofonoff, 1962). Equations of motion and conservation of mass are written in vectorial form as

$$D\mathbf{u}/Dt + 2\,\mathbf{\Omega} \times \mathbf{u} = -\rho^{-1}\nabla p - \nabla G + \mathbf{F} \quad (1)$$

$$\partial\rho/\partial t + \nabla \cdot \rho\mathbf{u} = 0 \quad (2)$$

where $\mathbf{u}$, $\mathbf{\Omega}$ and $\mathbf{F}$ are vectors of velocity, angular velocity of the earth and frictional force respectively; p is pressure, G is gravitational potential, ρ is density, D/Dt indicates differentiation following the fluid motion, being equal to $\partial/\partial t + \mathbf{u}\cdot\nabla$ and ∇ is gradient.

For an ordinary range of temperature and salinity encountered in the ocean, the equation of state is approximately given by

$$\rho = 1 - aT + bS \quad (3)$$

in which T and S are temperature and salinity, respectively, and a and b are numerical constants to be determined from Knudsen's empirical formula for the range of temperature and salinity considered. Also, equations of conservation of temperature and salinity are given by

$$\partial\,(\rho q)\,\partial t + \nabla \cdot \rho q\mathbf{u} = -\nabla\mathbf{Q} \quad (4)$$

in which q represents temperature or salinity and $\mathbf{Q}$ is the flux of q due to internal forces such as heat conduction or diffusion (Fofonoff, 1963). Equations (1)–(4) are a complete set of basic equations of dynamic oceanography. The unknown functions are three components of $\mathbf{u}$, pressure p, density ρ, temperature T and salinity S. Since there are seven equations for seven unknowns, the system of equations is complete.

Relative importance of each term in eq. (A) has been expressed in ratios of these terms which define several dimensionless numbers. These numbers expressed with characteristic quantities are:

Froude number (Fr) = Inertial Force/Gravitational Force = V^2/Lg

Rossby number (Ro) = Inertial Force/Coriolis' Force = V/fL

Reynolds number (Re) = Inertial Force/Frictional Force = VL/v

Ekman number (Ek) = Coriolis' Force/Frictional Force = $L\sqrt{f/v}$

Euler number = Inertial Force/Pressure Gradient Force = $\rho V^2/\nabla p$

where L is a characteristic length, V is a characteristic velocity, g is gravity, f is the Coriolis' parameter ($= 2\,\mathbf{\Omega}_z \cos\varphi$ where $\mathbf{\Omega}_z$ is the vertical component of the earth's angular velocity and φ is the latitude) and v is the molecular kinematic viscosity.

One feature of oceanic circulation which makes mathematical treatment simple is that the effect of gravity force is so predominant in the vertical component of equations of motion that hydrostatic pressure is always valid. This is represented by an extremely small value of the Froude number $(Fr \ll 1)$. The molecular viscosity of water is about 0.01 cm^2/sec and $Re > 10^8$ if we consider the motion with scales larger than 1 km for the velocity of 10 cm/sec. This indicates that oceanic circulation is always turbulent according to a criterion determined in experimental fluid mechanics. (In this estimation, another feature of oceanic circulation is used. It is predominance of horizontal motion over vertical motion, and in many cases, it also makes mathematical treatment simple.) Another implication of an extremely large Reynolds' number is that the terms with molecular viscosity can be neglected in the equations of motion.

The Rossby number may vary from near unity to extremely small values for oceanic circulation. For instance, R_0 equals 1 or 0.002 corresponding to circulation in estuaries and bays $(L = 10$ km$)$ or in world oceans $(L = 5000$ km$)$ for $U = 100$ cm/sec and $f = 10^{-4}$ sec^{-1}. A large-scale circulation means that the Rossby number corresponding to the circulation is much less than unity. When a characteristic time scale T is used, a ratio of the Coriolis' term to the time-varying inertia term is expressed by $(fT)^{-1}$, which has a meaning similar to the Rossby number. For a motion with a time scale of more than six days $(T \geqslant 5 \times 10^5$ seconds$)$, this ratio becomes less than 0.02. A slowly changing motion means that this ratio is much less than unity.

The circulation in the oceans can be separated into averaged (steady) and instantaneous (time-dependent) motion for an averaging time chosen by considering what type of motion is to be studied. Velocity components are expressed by the sum of averaged values (for instance, $\bar{u}_i$) and instaneous values (u_i'), whose average with time vanishes. When equations of motion are averaged with time and two components $\bar{u}_i$, and u_i are substituted, additional terms are created from inertia terms of the original equations. These terms in tensorial form are given by $-\partial \overline{u_i' u_j'}/\partial x_i$ where the bar indicates average with time and x_i represents the coordinates expressed in tensorial form. These additional terms represent the effect of time-dependent motion on steady-state motion owing to the noncorrelated movement among three components of instantaneous velocity. The term $u_i' u_j'$ is called Reynolds' stresses and plays an important role in turbulence theory and applied hydrodynamics. In dynamical oceanography, these terms become important because we have to treat the circulation only in an averaged state over a certain time or area.

In many studies of ocean circulation, the Reynolds' stresses have been expressed in a similar way to molecular viscosity stresses, using eddy viscosity instead of molecular viscosity (see Bowden, 1962). This is not satisfactory but tolerable in many cases in which the Reynolds' stresses have a minor role compared with other terms and in which they work only as a dissipative force of the major circulation system. However, since the Reynolds' stresses also express energy exchange between the averaged motion and instantaneous motion, there are some cases in which instantaneous motion supplies energy to the average motion. In such cases, the expression using eddy viscosity is inadequate. In order to evaluate these stresses properly, we have to measure not only the averaged currents but also their fluctuations with sufficient accuracy and durability. In other words, we must know dynamical structures of prevalent eddies in the ocean. Recent developments in current measurement techniques promise for such information.

There are three approaches to apply principles of dynamical oceanography to the study of oceanic circulation. One is to use laboratory models of oceans of various types. The other is mathematical treatment of the system of basic equations [Eqs., (1) through (4)]. The third is analysis of hydrographic data.

Model studies are based on a similarity principle that a model with the same numerical value of one or more dimensionless parameters (Froude number, etc.) behaves in a similar manner to the prototype, as far as the characteristic features represented by such parameters are concerned. There are two kinds of models simulating ocean circulation. One is called hydraulic model, in which a rather small-scale circulation with Rossby number of larger than unity is simulated. In such models, the earth's rotation is completely neglected and, instead, similarity of Froude number is achieved. Many civil engineering problems relating to circulation in estuaries and bays are studied by such models. For a larger-scale oceanic circulation, the Rossby number is much less than one and the effect of Coriolis' force cannot be neglected. In such cases, a model must be rotated. In 1951 Von Arx started experiments on the wind-driven circulation in the world ocean whose scale model was built in a rotating basin of about four feet in diameter. He succeeded in obtaining the major features of

oceanic circulation, such as the Gulf Stream and the West Wind Drifts (Von Arx, 1957). There are other examples of utilizing a rotating basin of a simple geometrical configuration in order to test a theory of ocean circulation, e.g., effects of sink and source on generation of a western boundary current.

Mathematical treatment of ocean circulation problems was started at the beginning of the century by Ekman who developed a theory on the currents caused by wind stresses. He considered a model of an ocean of homogeneous water driven by winds on a rotating disk, where he neglected inertial terms and retained vertical eddy viscosity term. The hodograph of the currents varying with depth for a case of steady-state motion in an infinite ocean is called the Ekman spiral (Fig. 1), whose main features are that the surface current is deviated to the right of leeward direction by 45° (in the northern hemisphere) and that the speed

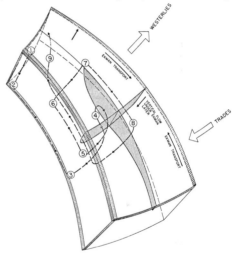

Fig. 1. Diagram showing circulation pattern in an idealized ocean. A cooled water parcel (1) sinks to the bottom (2) and flows southwards along a western boundary current and in a few weeks reaches a lower latitude (3), where it enters the geostrophic interior, flowing northeasterly and gradually ascending over a period of perhaps 200 to 600 years until it presses against the warm water being forced down from above by the Ekman layer at (4). As it becomes warmed it starts to flow southward at a higher rate of flow and in perhaps 1 to 3 years enters the western boundary current again at a higher level (5), this time flowing northward until it reaches a point (6) where it leaves the boundary current and ascends to the surface into a divergent Ekman layer. Once in the Ekman layer it is quickly (a month or two) passed southward until it reaches the region (8) of convergent Ekman layers, where it sinks into the geostrophic region, to meet the water ascending from (4), and is then passed through the western boundary current to the north (9) again—this cycle occurring 10 or more times until it returns to point (1) and the cycle repeats. (Stommel, H. M., 1966, "The large-scale oceanic circulation," M.I.T. Press, p. 183).

decreases rapidly with depth, falling to $\frac{1}{23}$ of the surface value at a depth given by $\pi(2K_z/f)^{\frac{1}{2}}$ (frictional depth), where K_z is the vertical eddy viscosity (Defant, 1961). This depth is about 50 meters for the reasonable value of K_z equaling to 100 cm²/sec. This theory was successfully applied to explanation of wind-driven motion of floating ice in the Arctic Ocean, where famous polar explorer Fritjof Nansen observed that ice floes always moved to the right of the leeward of the wind.

The first attempt to explain the reason why strong currents, such as the Gulf Stream and the Kuroshio, exist near the western coast of the North Atlantic and Pacific Ocean was made by Stommel in 1948 and by Munk in 1950. They considered the volume transport or vertically integrated velocity instead of velocity field itself. The vertically integrated vorticity equation which eliminates pressure from equations of motion [Eq. (1)] is given by

$$\beta V = \text{Curl} (\tau + \mathbf{F}) \qquad (5)$$

where β is latitudinal change of Coriolis' coefficient f, V is the poleward volume transport, τ is the wind stress vector, and $\mathbf{F}$ is the frictional force. The left-hand side of Eq. (6) is called planetary vorticity, whose important role to the generation of strong western boundary currents was first discovered by Stommel. This is simply explained as follows: The wind stress curl is almost uniform over the ocean, while the frictional force is domin-

ant only near the coast, thus causing a strong curl there. The westerly wind in the northern half and the easterly wind in the southern half of the ocean (in the northern hemisphere) cause the counterclockwise circulation in the ocean, thus generating northward and southward currents along western and eastern coasts, respectively. The curl of the frictional force near these coasts is approximately given by $\partial F_y/\partial x$ where F_y is the northward component of the frictional force and x is the eastward coordinate. Since the force is reverse to the flow in the direction and is approximately proportional to the velocity in the magnitude, the value of $\partial F_y/\partial x$ is always positive near the western or eastern boundary (see Fig. 2), while the planetary vorticity is positive along the west coast but negative along the east coast owing to northward or southward flow. Therefore, Eq. (5) indicates that the strong southward current along the east coast is impossible, while the strong and narrow current should transport the water along the west coast in order to maintain the counterclockwise circulation. (All over the interior part of the ocean, the volume transport is southward from Eq. (5) owing to the negative value of curl of the wind stresses.) Charney in 1955 and Morgan in 1958 discussed the mathematical model of wind-driven ocean circulation by taking into account the effect of inertia terms which are neglected in Eq. (5) but become dominant near the coastal boundaries (Defant, 1961). This effect also causes a narrow and strong current on the western coast. Their model of ocean circulation is called the inertia boundary layer model, as compared with the frictional boundary layer model of Stommel and Munk.

Although the wind stresses on the surface of the ocean are major driving forces of the ocean currents, density gradients due to differential heating at the surface also generate a large-scale circulation or thermohaline circulation. In fact, the wind-driven circulation theories discussed above predict only the distribution of volume transports which can be comparable with observed values. In order to determine vertical structures of ocean currents, the effect of density structures must be taken into account. The major difficulty in mathematical treatment of this problem is nonlinearity of equations of conservation of mass and of temperature or salinity [Eqs. (2) and (4)] which play an important role in this model. Lineikin in 1955 started mathematical discussion of thermohaline circulation by introducing linearized forms to Eqs. (2) and (4), the latter of which becomes, for example,

$$aw = A\partial^2 T/\partial z^2 \qquad (6)$$

in which a is the averaged vertical gradient of temperature and A is the vertical eddy conductivity. Later Robinson and Stommel in 1959 and Welander in 1959 elaborated on this kind of analysis and determined density stratification in a model ocean

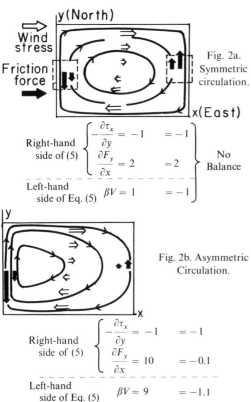

Fig. 2a. Symmetric circulation.

Right-hand side of (5)
$$-\frac{\partial \tau_x}{\partial y} = -1 \qquad = -1$$
$$\frac{\partial F_y}{\partial x} = 2 \qquad = 2$$
No Balance

Left-hand side of Eq. (5) $\beta V = 1 \qquad = -1$

Fig. 2b. Asymmetric Circulation.

Right-hand side of (5)
$$-\frac{\partial \tau_x}{\partial y} = -1 \qquad = -1$$
$$\frac{\partial F_y}{\partial x} = 10 \qquad = -0.1$$

Left-hand side of Eq. (5) $\beta V = 9 \qquad = -1.1$

as well as vertical structure of the ocean circulation by prescribing density distribution at the surface similar to the observed values (Fofonoff, 1962).

Mathematical treatment of time-dependent motion of ocean currents is less complete than the steady-state motion discussed above. It is also more difficult to compare the results with observed data, since the data are so scanty. Periodic change of circulation of an enclosed, vertically uniform ocean due to annual change of wind systems was treated by Ichiye in 1951 and by Veronis and Morgan in 1955. These studies indicate the maximum amplitude of fluctuations in mass transports near the western boundary and this was confirmed in an ocean consisting of two layers by Ichiye in 1958 (Fofonoff, 1962).

In meteorology, hydrodynamic principles are quite often applied to synoptic isobaric charts in order to predict the change of pressure systems. In oceanography, lack of synoptic observations hinder development of the similar technique in analysis of ocean currents, except dynamic calculation of geostrophic flow (Defant, 1961). A few attempts were made to apply the conservation of absolute vorticity (Coriolis' coefficient plus ordinary or relative vorticity) to determine the course of a narrow current like the Kuroshio or the Gulf Stream. Ichiye in 1955 applied to the Kuroshio the constant vorticity trajectory method, originally developed by Rossby for forecasting trajectories of atmospheric jet streams, and obtained the result that the amplitudes and wavelengths of meander of the Kuroshio after leaving the Japanese coast are dependent on its transport and direction at the latitude of separation from the coastline, in agreement with Rossby's principle. Warren in 1962 incorporated the effect of depth of the ocean along the continental slope off the United States to the law of conservation of the absolute vorticity and mass, and he showed that the separation of the Gulf Stream from the continent is due to the effect of bottom topography.

It is also rather rare, compared with examples for dynamical meteorology, for hydrographic data to be employed to determine quantities useful for dynamic oceanography. One such use is estimation of energy exchange between the mean ocean current and its surroundings through irregular fluctuations or large-scale horizontal turbulence. When the mean flow is written as $\bar{u}$ and the longitudinal and lateral components to the mean flow of fluctuating currents are written as u' and v', respectively, the energy transport from the fluctuating currents to the mean flow is given by $\overline{u'v'}\,(\partial u/\partial y)$, where the y-axis is lateral to the mean flow and the bar indicates the averaged value. This quantity was determined from the surface current data obtained with GEK by Ichiye in 1957 for the Kuroshio and by Webster in 1961 for the Gulf Stream (Bowden, 1962). The former used the continuous recordings

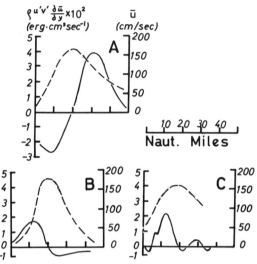

Fig. 3. Mean velocity (broken lines in cm/sec) and kinetic energy transfer (solid lines in erg cm³/sec) across the Kuroshio: (A) west of 141°E, (B) east of 141°E and the Gulf Stream, (C) off Onslow Bay.

at various longitudinal transections of the Kuroshio, while the latter used the 120 transversal crossings of the Gulf Stream off Onslow Bay. The average current and the energy exchange (the plus values indicate that the energy is transferred from the fluctuations to the mean flow) for these two currents are shown in Fig. 3. The data in the Kuroshio indicate a remarkable difference between the regions west and east of 141°E; to the west, the Kuroshio flowed closely to the coastline, while to the east, it left the continent. Webster's result is similar to the atmospheric westerlies in which the energy is, in most cases, transferred from the disturbances to the mean current. This kind of approach will become more feasible as underway current meters are developed and will yield valuable information on mechanism of the strong current like the Gulf Stream and the Kuroshio.

TAKASHI ICHIYE

References
Bowden, K. F., 1962, "Turbulence," in (Hill, M. N., editor) "The Sea," Vol. 1, Ch. 6, pp. 802–825, New York and London, Interscience Publishers.

Defant, A., 1961, "Physical Oceanography," Vol. 1, pp. 729, New York, Oxford, London, Paris, Pergamon Press.

Fofonoff, N. P., 1962, "Dynamics of Ocean Currents," in (Hill, M. N., editor) "The Sea," Vol. 1, Ch. 3, pp. 323–395, New York and London, Interscience Publishers.

Lamb, H., 1945, "Hydrodynamics," Sixth ed., pp. 738, New York, Dover Publications.

Von Arx, W. S., 1957, "An Experimental Approach to Problems in Physical Oceanography," in "Progress in Physics and Chemistry of the Earth," Vol. 2, pp. 1–29, New York, Oxford, London, Paris, Pergamon Press.

E

EAST AUSTRALIAN CURRENT

Along the east coast of Australia, a strong and narrow current flows south and forms the western part of the anticyclonic circulation in the South Pacific Ocean. The current is formed at about 20°S between the Great Barrier Reef and the Chesterfield Reef, which is approximately between 153 and 158°E. From January to March, it is supplied with equatorial water masses driven westsouthwest by the monsoon winds and entering the Coral Sea from the north and northeast. From April to December, subtropical water masses entering the Coral Sea from the east supply its water. Between 20 and 25°S, the current becomes narrower, deeper, and is strengthened by the integration of more subtropical water from the east.

The East Australian Current is strongest off Cape Byron (28.5°S), where its average speed is about 50 cm/sec (24 nautical miles/day) from December to April, but remains always above 30 cm/sec during the remainder of the year. In the center of the current, the speed often exceeds 75 cm/sec. Between 25 and 32°S, the current is between 100 and 200 km wide and reaches with decreasing velocities to depths of more than 1000 meters. During winter, in June and July when southerly winds are frequently very strong, a countercurrent flowing north is developed farther offshore.

South of 32°S, the East Australian Current becomes broader, weaker, and disintegrates into an eddy system. These anticyclonic eddies, having a southerly flow along the coast and a northerly flow farther offshore, drift south along the Australian coast as far as Tasmania. In this part of the East Australian Current, most of its water turns northeast, flows across the Tasman Sea, and leaves it north of New Zealand. Most of the water of the East Australian Current remains to the north of the Subtropical Convergence, which stretches from Tasmania towards the northeast.

At the surface, the East Australian Current carries subtropical water to the south. The salinity of this water is in excess of 35‰, and the temperature decreases from more than 25°C in its northern part to about 15°C in its southern part. From January to March, the current receives an admixture of tropical surface water which slightly reduces its salinity. In about 100–200-meter depth, a salinity maximum is found with salinities of more than 35.8‰, which is of subtropical origin, and its water is carried south by the current. Below this depth temperature and salinity decrease.

The East Australian Current carries approximately 30 million m³/sec to the south, but transports as high as 45 million m³/sec have been observed. Dynamically, the East Australian Current is considered as a western boundary current and as such has been compared with the Gulf Stream (q.v.) and the Kuroshio (q.v.). However, it lacks the most important of the main features of these two large northern hemisphere current systems; namely, it does not form a huge current system which extends eastward over the whole ocean, but it disappears rapidly when departing from the coast. This phenomenon is conditioned by the fact that the Australian continent ends at 44°S and that south of the continent there is the large Circumpolar Current which is completely self-contained. Due to this, there is no necessity for the East Australian Current to form and supply a large eastward-flowing current system. The Gulf Stream and the Kuroshio maintain the balance between the high sea level in lower latitudes and the water masses required for the formation of east-going currents in higher latitudes, while the East Australian Current lacks the second stimulus. This explains its comparative weakness. There is also no "cold wall" formed on its poleward side, which leads to the immense intensification of the two other current systems. Hence, the conditions in the northern part of the East Australian Current are similar to those of the two big northern hemisphere current systems, but those in its southern part are entirely different. The current system itself is affected to a high degree by local weather conditions and, especially in its southern part, is variable.

KLAUS WYRTKI

Reference

Wyrtki, Klaus, 1960, "The surface circulation in the Coral and Tasman Seas," *Div. of Fish. and Oceanogr. Tech. Paper No. 8*, C.S.e.R.O., Australia, 44pp.

EAST CHINA SEA

The East China Sea, or Tung Hai, is situated to the east of the middle sector of the China coast with Shanghai and the mouth of the Yangtze Kiang. Its

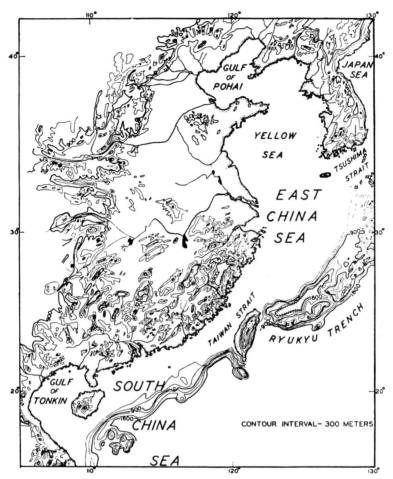

Fig. 1. General topography of region. Same contour interval is used for sea floor and land. Contours of sea floor are based on soundings given on charts of Japan Hydrographic Office supplemented by data from sample sites; drawn only to maximum depth of 1800 m, part way down the slope of Ryukyu Trench. Contours on land have been taken from U.S. Coast and Geodetic Survey's World Aeronautical Charts; no reliable information exists for blank areas along western margin (Niino and Emery, 1961).

northern border, according to the convention of the International Hydrographic Bureau (Sp. Publ. 23, 1953), extends from the mainland coast along parallel 33°17′N to Saisyu To (Quelpart Island), through its south point Hunan Kan to Ose Saki (Cape Goto) to the south point of Hukae Sima (Goto Retto) and to Nomo Saki (32°35′N) on Kyushu in Japan. From its south point, Hi Saki (31°17′N) the line goes through Tanega Sima (30°30′N) to the east point of Kikai Sima (28°20′N) and so on through the Ryukyu Retto or Nansei Shoto chain: Ada-Ko Sima (Sidmouth Island), Okinawa, Miyako to Haderuma Sima (24°03′N, 123°47′E), and Yonakuni to Formosa (Taiwan) at Santyo Point. From Fuki Kaku, the north point of Formosa the southern boundary runs to Kiushan Tao (Turnabout Island) on Haitan Tao (25°25′N)

and thence westward on parallel 25°24′N to the China mainland coast of Fukien.

The area of the East China Sea takes in 752,000 km^2; the mean depth is 349 m and the volume is calculated at 263,000 km^3. The most important strait is the Formosa Strait (Fukien or Taiwan Strait), 115 miles wide and 150 miles long, with average depths of about 60 m, but with scattered coral reefs.

Bathymetry

The East China Sea floor is divided into two contrasting provinces: the continental shelf with shelfbreak at 150–166 m and a broad trough extending from Formosa to Kyushu along the inner side of the Ryukyu island arc. For easy identification we suggest it be referred to as the

239

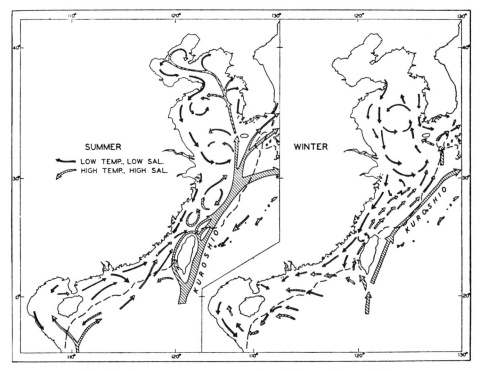

Fig. 2. Surface currents, summer and winter (Niino and Emery, 1961).

Okinawa Trough, to distinguish it from the trench along the outer edge of the Ryukyus (Nansei Shoto), the *Ryukyu* or *Nansei Shoto Trench* (which belongs in the *Philippine Sea,* q.v.). The Okinawa Trough has a large area over 1000 m and a maximum depth of 2717 m. The shelf is part of one of the largest shelves in the world, extending from the Gulf of Pohai and the *Yellow Sea* (q.v.), and south through the Formosa Strait to the South China Sea shelf and the Gulf of Tonkin. There are some scattered islets near its outer edge, the Senkaku Gunto. The mainland coast is low with large offshore sand shoals and mudbanks north of Hangchow and Shanghai. To the south it is a rocky coast with classical rias (q.v., Vol. III).

Sediments

The East China Sea shelf is mainly cloaked in terrigenous sediments brought down by the Yangtze Kiang and to a minor extent by the Min Kiang (debouching at Foochow). The Yangtze discharges 400 million tons of sediment annually, compared with 500 million by the Mississippi. There is a 75-mile-wide belt of mud close to the shore paralleled by an even broader zone of residual sediments, mainly sand and mud, reflecting low Pleistocene shore lines, almost entirely calcareous or siliceous sand in the outer part. Shell banks and authigenic sediments (glauconite and phosphorite) also occur in this belt, a line from Formosa to Korea. There are

scattered areas of rock bottom, especially in the middle of Formosa Strait which is scoured clean.

In the Okinawa Trough, terrigenous muds are reported with pelagic carbonate oozes (exceeding 40% in foraminifera).

Oceanography

The main stream of the *Kuroshio* (q.v.) or "Black Current" passes east of Formosa with a secondary branch swinging round the western side, together setting northwest along the axis of the Okinawa Trough, the main current turning to the east south of Kyushu and minor streams reaching up into the Yellow Sea and through Tsushima Strait to the Japan Sea. This is a high-temperature, high-salinity stream, derived from the Pacific North Equatorial Current. It is greatly strengthened by the monsoon winds in summer, but still important in winter. It is up to 100 miles wide between Formosa and Miyako, with velocities of 18–42 nautical miles per day. Over the Okinawa Trough it is 18–30 nautical miles per day.

During the southwest monsoon, beginning in April, a coastwise current sets northeast from Hong Kong and Amoy to pass through the Formosa Straits at 3–4 knots, to join the Kuroshio. In the northwest monsoon, beginning in September, a southwesterly setting coastal current develops south of Shanghai and continues to beyond Hong Kong thus completely reversing the southwest monsoon

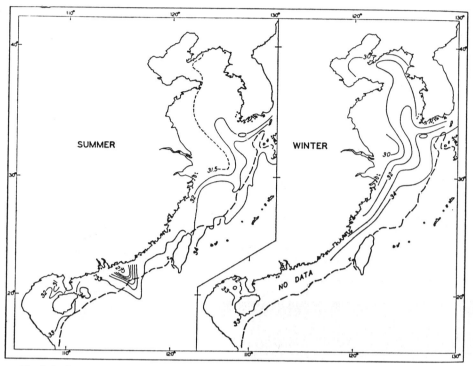

Fig. 3. Surface-water salinity, summer and winter (parts per thousand) (Niino and Emery, 1961).

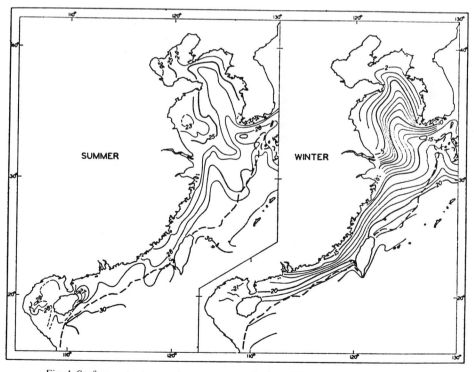

Fig. 4. Surface-water temperature, summer and winter (°C) (Niino and Emery, 1961).

stream. North of Shanghai the Yellow Sea surface water, of low temperature (8–12°C) and low salinity (31.2–33.5‰) flows southeastward and extends to about 200 nautical miles south of Sai Syuto. Large eddies are set up in the middle East China Sea, from the interactions with the Kuroshio. There is a striking contrast between the dark-blue Kuroshio and the pale-blue to greenish coastal currents of low salinity and low temperature to the west.

Considerable quantities of fresh water enter the East China Sea from the mainland. The Kuroshio is up to 30°C in summer and is 6–10°C warmer than the coastal waters of the Chinese mainland between 28 and 33°N latitude, as an annual average. An undercurrent of reversed direction is recognized.

Wind waves in the East China Sea are reported by Hansen (in Bruns, 1958) up to 79 m length and 6.9-second period. Paris (1872; see Bruns, 1958) reported waves up to 6.5 m high with lengths of 39–102 m and periods of 4.2–10.0 seconds with wind force of up to 14.6 m/sec.

Tides

The tidal systems emanate from the Pacific, encountering first the east coast of Taiwan and Ryukyus, which divide them into many local variations. In the Ryukyus the spring ranges are 1.24–1.90 m. In Taiwan these rise to 5–6 m, and in some bays reach greater amplitudes, e.g., 7 m in Sansa Bay, and on the mainland coast at Hangchow Bay, southwest of Shanghai, they reach 11 m. The tides are semidiurnal but may be dominated either by a lunar or solar cycle. Highest spring ranges occur in summer and winter and smallest neap ranges in spring and autumn.

Structural History

Most of the shelf area belongs to the stable Cathaysian Platform of Paleozoic or older consolidation. The orogenic belt that runs through Formosa and the Ryukyus is mainly Mesozoic in age with Tertiary revival. This belt is called "Nansei Shoto Geanticline" by Hess (1948). The Okinawa Trough appears to be a thalassocratonic area of late Tertiary and Quaternary subsidence. It would seem to be a zeugogeosyncline in an early stage of development. The Ryukyus are a typical *double island arc,* with a volcanic string as the inner (continent) side, with several still active or recently active volcanoes, and an outer row of non-volcanic islands, mostly Tertiary limestones, terrigenous and volcanogenic deposits. There is an inactive volcano at the northern tip of Formosa and two submarine volcanoes offshore. Active vulcanicity increases from southwest to northeast along the Ryukyus towards Kyushu.

Deep focus earthquakes are distributed to the northwest of the Ryukyu chain, corresponding to

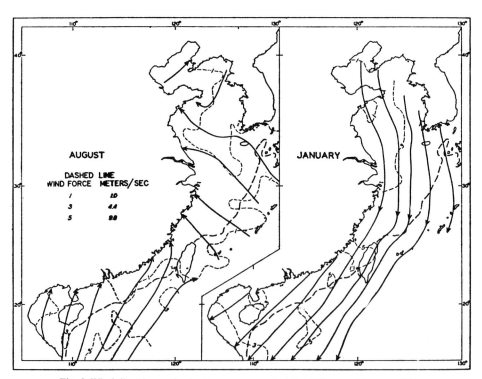

Fig. 5. Wind direction and velocity, summer and winter (Niino and Emery, 1961).

the axis of the Okinawa Trough. Shallow earth-quakes are common in Formosa and the outer island arc.

RHODES W. FAIRBRIDGE

References

Bruns, E., 1958, "Ozeanologie," Berlin, Deutscher Verlag d. Wiss., 2 vols.
Gutenberg, B., and Richter, C. F., 1949, "Seismicity of the Earth and Associated Phenomena," Princeton, Princeton University Press, 273pp. (second ed., 1954).
Hess, H. H., 1948, "Major structural features of the Western North Pacific: An interpretation of H. O. 5485 Bathymetric Chart, Korea to New Guinea," *Bull. Geol. Soc. Am.*, **59**, 417–446.
Koizumi, M., 1962, "Seasonal variation of surface temperature of the East China Sea," *J. of Oceanog. Soc. Japan, 20th Anniversary Volume*, 321–329.
Niino, H., and Emery, K. O., 1961, "Sediments of shallow portions of East China Sea and South China Sea," *Bull. Geol. Soc. Am.*, **72**, 731–762.
Shepard, F. P., Emery, K. O., and Gould, H. R., 1949, "Distribution of sediments on East Asiatic continental shelf," *Allan Hancock Foundation, Occasional Paper 9*, 64pp.

EAST SIBERIAN SEA

The *East Siberian Sea* is a continental shelf sea off the northern coast of Asia between Kotelny (New Siberian Islands) and Wrangel islands. The straits of Dimitriy Laptev, Eteriken and Sannikov connect the East Siberian Sea with the Laptev Sea on the west, and De Long Strait connects it with the Chukchi (Chukotskoye) Sea on the east. The northern boundary of the sea coincides with the 200-m isobath which is located in about latitude 79°N in the northwest (the meridian of 139°E) and in latitude 76°N in the east (the meridian of 180°E). This is the convention adopted in 1936 (see Anon., 1936). The area of the sea within these boundaries is 660,000 km² or 255,200 square miles. The prevailing depths in the western and central parts of the sea are 10–20 m, while those in the eastern part are 30–40 m.

The first chart of the East Siberian Sea was published by the Russian explorer, Wrangel, who investigated the sea and adjacent coasts in 1820–24.

The East Siberian Sea was traversed (near the coast) from west to east by Nordenskjöld in the *Vega* in 1878 and later by Amundson. The ill-fated *Jeanette* (under George Washington De Long) drifted westward in the ice pack close to the shelf edge from 1879–81 until it was lost off Kotelny Island, June 14, 1881.

Structure

Much of the floor of the East Siberian Sea consists of a thin sedimentary platform, complicated by fractures and faults. As far back as the late Tertiary and the beginning of the Quaternary period this basement was a nearly peneplaned area drained by the ancient river systems of the paleo-Indigirka and the paleo-Kolyma, the traces of which on the sea floor can be recognized even now (Gakkel, 1962; Lazukov, 1964). Most of the archipelagos and isolated islands encountered in the shelf area are composed of this basement rock (Medvezhii and Rautan islands, Shalaurov Island, part of Aion Island, etc.). In the vicinity of De Long Islands and in the northern part of the East Siberian Sea there is the so-called Hyperboreal Shield (of N. S. Shatskiy). Aeromagnetic surveys confirm the existence here of a rigid part of the earth's crust overlapped and bordered by Mesozoic rocks, locally with folded structures.

Sediments

The sediments of the shelf area are mainly sandy silt material containing fractured boulders and pebbles, some of which rock debris comes from Wrangel or other islands. The latter sediments are ice-transported deposits.

The coast eastward of the Kolyma River mouth is mountainous: spurs of the Anyuisky Khrebet (ridge) and Chukotskoye Nagorye (upland) come very close to the shore. The coastal land westward of the mouth of the Kolyma River is low and at the surface is composed of permafrost-affected Quaternary strata including ice-lenses. Thermo-abrasion and abrasion-solifluction types of shore line characterized by extremely shallow water are typical for this area (Ionin, Kaplin, Medvedev, 1961). Suspended sediment carried out by rivers causes shoaling of the nearshore areas and the formation of estuarine bars. The Indigirka River carries out 16.7 and the Kolyma River 8.3 million tons of suspended sediment per year. The discharge of the Kolyma River has been calculated as 132×10^3 m³/yr (Belov and Lapina, 1961).

The warming action of the river waters in the adjoining coastal areas results in intensive erosion of estuarine shores. According to V. S. Lomachenkov's data (1959) the rate of erosion here is from 1–5 m/yr to 10–15 m/yr.

In all the places where the shores are composed of rock (the area of Cape Baranov and Cape Shelagskiy, the western coast of Wrangel Island, etc.), denudation types of shore line are usually developed, formed almost exclusively by non-wave factors, namely physical weathering, etc. Accumulative shores, on the other hand, with extensive sandy-pebble bars separate chains of lagoons on the southern coast of De Long Strait.

Climate

The East Siberian Sea has a typically Arctic climate (q.v.). The mean temperature of the coldest months (January and February) is −26 to −33°C

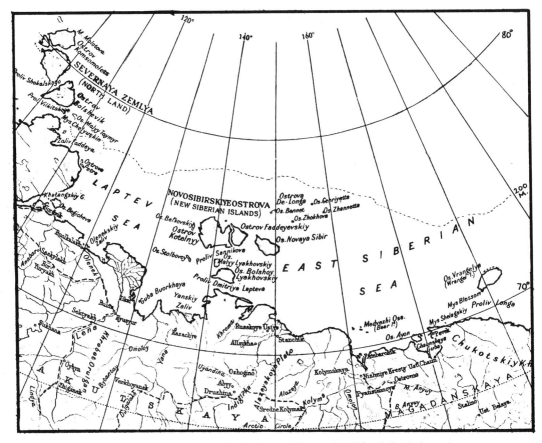

Fig. 1. Location map, East Siberian Sea and Laptev Sea (from J. Bartholemew).

and the absolute minimum temperature is −48 to −50°C. The mean air temperature of July in the southern part of the sea is 3–7°C, while that in the northern part is from 0–2°C.

Most of the year the East Siberian Sea is ice covered. In the eastern part of the sea, floating ice often remains off the coast even in summer. Observations carried out at high-latitude stations of the Soviet Union have shown that ice drift direction depends on the distribution of atmospheric pressure. In winters, when polar high pressure is greatly developed, the anticyclonic (clockwise) water circulation increases which causes northwestward ice drift (see *Arctic Meteorology*). Average daily speed of ice drift is between 3 and 8 km (Gordienko, 1962; Sokolov, 1962).

When the polar anticyclone weakens, the area of cyclonic water circulation widens which hinders the outflow of ice from the East Siberian Sea and, on the contrary, favors the inflow of pack ice to the sea from high latitudes and ice blocking of the De Long Strait.

Temperature and salinity of the surface waters depend on ice conditions and river runoff. The eastern part of the sea is usually characterized by greater salinity and lower water temperature as compared with the western part. The highest water temperature (6–7°C) is observed in August near the mouths of big rivers when south winds are blowing. Water salinity here ranges from 10–15‰, increasing to 30‰ near the ice edge. Water temperature near the ice edge sinks to 1–2°C. When north winds are blowing, the water temperature even off the coast does not exceed 2°C.

Tide fluctuations of the sea level are not great but piling up and removal of water under wind stress may cause 1–2 m changes of the sea level in the littoral zone.

In July and August easterly and northeasterly winds predominate while in autumn westerly and southwesterly winds blow near the coast. North-westerlies and northeasterlies often have speeds of 20–25 m/sec and generate 4–5 m high waves. Westerly winds favor the formation of a warm current flowing eastward from the Kolymsky Zaliv (bay). It is this warm current that clears the De Long Strait of ice (Speicher, 1963). Off the coast, gales often occur with speeds of 40–45 m/sec, they are accompanied by foehn phenomena (air heating, etc., see *Winds—Local*).

Fauna and Flora

Marine flora and fauna are poor qualitatively as compared with the adjacent seas, due mainly to severe ice conditions. However, in the vicinity of river mouths there are found rather large shoals of whitefish (coregonidae), besides omul, cisco, grayling. There are also many other species of fish which include Arctic smelt, navaga, polar cod, pole flounder and salmonid fishes, such as Arctic char and nelma. The mammals are represented by walrus, seal and polar bear. Coastal colonies of birds abound in murres, guillemots, sea gulls and cormorants (Zenkevitch, 1963).

A. S. IONIN

References

Anon., 1936, "Limits of oceans and seas—U.S.S.R.," *Int. Hydr. Rev.*, **13**(25), 160–163 (translation in English of Decision of Central Executive Committee of USSR), with map.
Belov, N. A., and Lapina, N. N., 1961, "Bottom Deposits of the Arctic Basin," "Morskoy Transport" Publishing House.
Gakkel, YA. YA., 1962, "Morphotectonic Features of the Arctic Basin. Problems of the Arctic and the Antarctic," Issue II "Morskoy Transport" Publishing House.
Gordienko, P. A., 1962, "Scientific Observations and Conditions of Drift of the "North Pole" Stations. Problems of the Arctic and the Antarctic," Issue II, "Morskoy Transport" Publishing House.
Ionin, A. S., Kaplin, P. A., and Medvendev, V. S., 1961, "Classification of the world sea shores," *Proceedings of the Oceanographic Commission of the Academy of Sciences of the USSR*, **12**.
Lazukov, G. I., 1964, "Level fluctuations of the Polar basin in the Quaternary period," *Okeanologiya*, **4**, Issue I.
Lomachenkov, V. S., 1959, "Experience in mapping of shore morphology and dynamics of low river terraces in the permanently frozen area," *Proceedings of the Institute of the Arctic Geology*, **65**.
Sokolov, A. L., 1962, "Ice Drift in the Arctic Basin and Changes of Ice Conditions along the Northern Sea Route. Problems of the Arctic and the Antarctic," Issue II, "Morskoy Transport" Publishing House.
Speicher, A. O., 1963, "The role of the Kolyma river runoff in the formation of hydrological conditions of the East Siberian Sea in summer," *Proceedings of the Arctic and Antarctic Research Institute*, **264**.
Zenkevitch, L. A., 1963, "Biology of the Seas of the USSR," Second ed. (Russian), "UCHPEDGIZ" Publishing House (English edition, New York, Interscience Publishers, translated by S. Botscharskaya, 955pp.

(All references in Russian unless otherwise stated.)

Cross-references: *Arctic Ocean; Chukchi Sea; Laptev Sea.*

EDDY FLUX—*See* **AUSTAUCH,** Vol. II

EDDY VISCOSITY—*See* **TURBULENCE**

EKMAN SPIRAL

In the lower layer of the atmosphere or in the upper layer of the ocean, the pressure gradient or wind stress which may generate motion of air or water, respectively, is balanced by the Coriolis force and friction. These layers are called planetary boundary layers. The friction is mostly due to turbulence caused by a rough underlying surface (for atmosphere) or by wind stirring (for ocean). Ekman (1905) assumed that the friction is represented by the vertical eddy viscosity term $A d^2 \vec{U}/dz^2$, where A is the vertical eddy viscosity, $\vec{U}$ is a vector of horizontal velocity and z is the vertical coordinate.

In the open ocean with an infinite depth a pure drift current is generated by the wind stress acting on the surface of the sea when there is no pressure gradient in the water. In such cases, a body force balancing with the friction is the Coriolis force only. When u and v are horizontal velocity components of the pure drift current caused by the wind stress in the direction of v, the vertical distributions of u and v are expressed by

$$u = V_0 \exp(-\pi z/D) \cos(45° - \pi z/D)$$
$$v = V_0 \exp(-\pi z/D) \sin(45° - \pi z/D)$$
(1)

where z is positive downward from the sea surface ($z = 0$), V_0 is the speed at the sea surface and D is defined by

$$D = \pi\sqrt{2A/f}$$
(2)

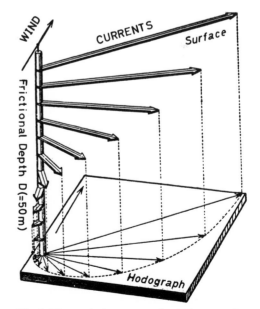

Fig. 1. The vertical structure of a drift current from Ekman's theory (Defant, 1961 P. 401). (By permission Pergamon Press, N.Y.)

In Eq. (2) f is a Coriolis coefficient. The quantity D has a dimension of length and is called friction depth. Figure 1 shows the distributions defined by Eq. (1). The double arrows projecting from the central column represent the current vector at levels of an equal distance of $0.1D$ from the surface. The arrow at the top shows the wind direction. The projections (*hodograph*, q.v.) of the arrow heads on a horizontal plane lie on a logarithmic spiral which is called an *Ekman spiral*.

In the atmospheric planetary boundary layer, the geostrophic wind which is caused by the pressure gradient and the Coriolis force in the upper layer is modified by the friction at the ground. The velocity profiles corresponding to Eq. (1) are expressed by

$$u = -v_g \exp(-\pi z/D) \sin(\pi z/D)$$
$$v = v_g [1 - \exp(-\pi z/D) \cos(\pi z/D)]$$

(3)

where v_g is the geostrophic wind speed and z is positive upward from the ground ($z = 0$). In this example it is assumed that the wind vanishes at the ground and that the geostrophic wind is in the direction of v. If a finite surface wind is assumed in agreement with actual situations, the arguments of sine and cosine in Eq. (3) have an additional constant. The hodographs of the wind vector are shown in Fig. 2. In this Figure the hodograph corresponding to Eq. (3) (zero surface wind) is represented with a dotted curve while the one for a finite surface wind which has the same direction with the vertical wind shear at the surface is shown with a full curve. The number at the end points of the vector indicates the height of the wind in meters. The eddy viscosity is chosen as the same in both cases.

When there is a pressure gradient in the ocean besides wind stresses at the surface, the Ekman spiral is produced near the bottom (Fig. 3) as in the ground layer of the atmosphere. In such cases, both the layer near the surface and the layer near the bottom are influenced by friction and are called the upper

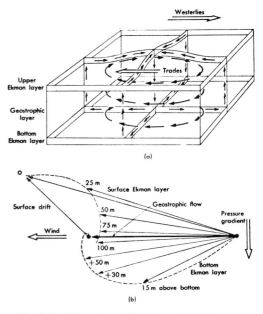

Fig. 3. (a) Ekman's model of the wind-driven ocean circulation; (b) motions in the upper and lower Ekman layers (Von Arx, 1962). (By permission of Addison-Wesley Pub. Co., Mass.)

and lower Ekman layers, respectively. The flow between the upper and lower Ekman layers is geostrophic.

A net transport of the water in the upper Ekman layer of the pure drift current is called *Ekman transport*. When equations of motion of the pure drift current $-fv = \partial(T_{uz})/\partial z$ and $fu = \partial(T_{vz})/\partial z$ (T_{uz} and T_{vz} are components of the stress) are integrated with depth from the surface to a great depth, the components of the Ekman transport are equal to T_v/f and $-T_u/f$, respectively, where T_u and T_v are wind stress components in the u and v directions, respectively. Therefore, the Ekman transport is directed at right angles to the wind direction, on the

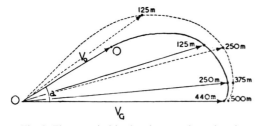

Fig. 2. Ekman spiral in the planetary boundary layer of the atmosphere. The Ekman spiral shows the variation with height of the inclination of the surface wind to the isobars. The wind velocity is represented by the radius vector from O. The dotted curve indicates the spiral for zero surface wind. The full curve for the finite wind (from Gordon, 1962).

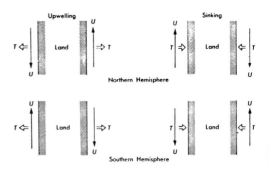

Fig. 4. Ekman upwelling and sinking along coastlines (Von Arx, 1962). (By permission of Addison-Wesley Pub. Co., Mass.)

246

right in the northern hemisphere and on the left in the southern hemisphere. A component of winds parallel to a coastline produces the Ekman transport either toward or away from the coast. When the Ekman transport is seaward, the deeper water must move shoreward and upwelling will occur along the coast. When the Ekman transport is shoreward, sinking will occur. Eight cases of up-welling and sinking due to winds parallel to the coast in both hemispheres are shown in Fig. 4, where U is the surface wind and T is the Ekman transport.

The most outstanding examples of upwelling due to the seaward Ekman transport are found along the coasts of Morocco, Southwest Africa, California and Peru. In these areas off the eastern coasts of the Atlantic and the Pacific Oceans there is no strong current such as the Gulf Stream and the Kuroshio near the western sides. Therefore, the wind force has a direct influence on the circulation near the eastern coast and the Ekman transport produces vertical motion without being affected by the ocean current in the area. Upwelling off California and Peru has been studied intensively. When winds blow equatorward on these coasts, upwelling occurs and it lowers the water temperature in upper layers. Off California, upwelling is conspicuous only in spring and early summer when the prevailing winds have a predominant southerly component. On the other hand, off Peru the prevailing winds have a northerly component throughout the year and, thus, upwelling is consistent except during February and March. Particularly during these months of certain exceptional years, the winds with a strong southerly component produce coastal sinking which induces warm equatorial water flowing southward almost to 15°S along the coast. This water is mixed with the ordinary cold coastal waters causing destruction of coastal marine life, from plankton to fish, and severe rainfalls. This phenomenon is called El Niño.

TAKASHI ICHIYE

References

Defant, A., 1961, "Physical Oceanography," Vol. 1, Oxford, Pergamon Press, 729pp.
Ekman, F. W., 1905, "On the influence of the earth's rotation on ocean currents," *Arkiv Mat., Astr. o Fysik,* **2**(11), 53pp.
Godske, C. L., et al., 1957, "Dynamic Meteorology and Weather Forecasting," Boston, American Meteorological Society, 800pp.
Sverdrup, H. U., Johnson, M. W., and Fleming, R. H., 1942, "The Oceans," Englewood Cliffs, N.J., Prentice-Hall.
Von Arx, W. S., 1962, "An Introduction to Physical Oceanography," Reading, Mass., Addison-Wesley Publication Company, 422pp.

Cross-references: *California Current; Coriolis Force; Dynamics of Ocean Currents; El Nino; Geostrophic Wind; Hodograph; Turbulence in the Ocean; Upwelling.*

EL NIÑO EFFECT

The coastal desert of Peru is one of the driest littorals in the world, with a somewhat more extensive latitudinal distribution even than that of South Africa, and considerably longer extension than those of Northwest Africa or Western Australia.

The normal coastal current is the *Peru or Humboldt Current* (q.v.), which sets northward with very cold waters from Antarctic latitudes. Normally the offshore winds, combined with the Coriolis effect, tend to deflect this current somewhat away from the shore, resulting in considerable *upwelling*

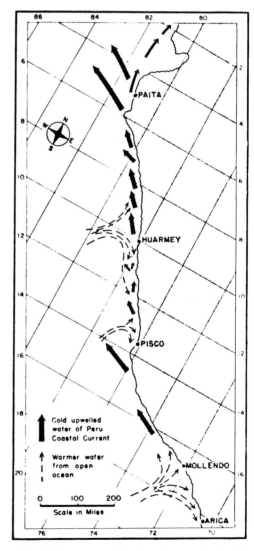

Fig. 1. The pattern of the coastal currents along the coast of Peru (after Schweigger; from Trewartha, 1961). (By permission of University of Wisconsin Press, Madison, Wis.)

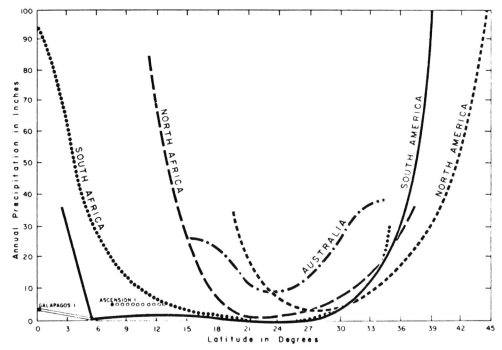

Fig. 2. The annual precipitation curves plotted against latitude for five coastal deserts in tropical—subtropical latitudes. Note that the desert of Chile–Peru exhibits the highest intensity of aridity, maintained throughout the largest span of latitude (after Lydolph).

(q.v.), rising from depths of 50–300 m, and resulting in even colder waters inshore, 2–3°C cooler than the main current. This cooler water mass is sometimes differentiated as the "Peru Coastal Current," in contrast to the main "Peru Oceanic Current." Upwelling does not occur everywhere, but usually about 7–8°S, 15–16°S, and to a lesser extent about 22–23°S and 30°S. Alternating between these latitudes are stretches where warmer water comes in, sometimes strengthened by onshore winds. The diurnal alternation of very strong land and sea breezes may block or amplify these effects.

In the north of Peru, north of about 6°S, a tongue of the equatorial countercurrent sets southward from the Gulf of Guayaquil; its temperature is 6–7°C warmer and it has a much lower salinity. It is a regular phenomenon in the north, occurring every year in February and March and is called El Niño, because "The Child" (Christ Child) is symbolic of the Christmas season. Periodically this current is greatly strengthened so that it reaches much farther south (to 12° or more), displacing the cold Peru current and causing catastrophic destruction of plankton and fish life. Dead fish accumulating on the beaches rot and lead to the formation of H_2S and, combined with sea fog, may even blacken the paint on ships, which has led to the name "*Callao Painter*." Sea birds die of starvation, and the annual guano "crop" fails, leading to impoverishment of agriculture. This is the *El Niño Effect*.

Some confusion is caused by the term "Callao Painter," because this comes every year with a warmer swirl of the equatorial counter-current and reaches offshore to about latitude 9–12°S to cause mass fish mortality and H_2S poisoning (locally called *Aguaje*), but not on the catastrophic scale of El Niño.

Meteorologically the El Niño Effect seems to be related to an extraordinary change in the weather regime, related to a weakening of the trade winds, extraordinary because it does not occur every year but in cycles of approximately 7 years (with some variations at 6 or 8 year intervals). Normally the coast is one of complete aridity, but in the summers of the El Niño years (January-February) there may be torrential rainfalls, especially in the north, and decreasing southward. The usual southeast (trade) wind pattern is temporarily replaced by a northwesterly tropical air flow. Heavy rains cause flooding and severe crop damage, adding to the catastrophes and misfortunes on the coast.

The ultimate meteorological cause of the El Niño Effect is not yet satisfactorily established. It seems that the ITC (intertropical convergence) is displaced considerably to the south in the El Niño years. This displacement is related to global circulation anomalies, in turn steered by solar radiation (UV ozone control). Berlage (1961) has shown that sea-surface temperature at Puerto Chicama (7°47 S, 79°28′W) rises and falls in con-

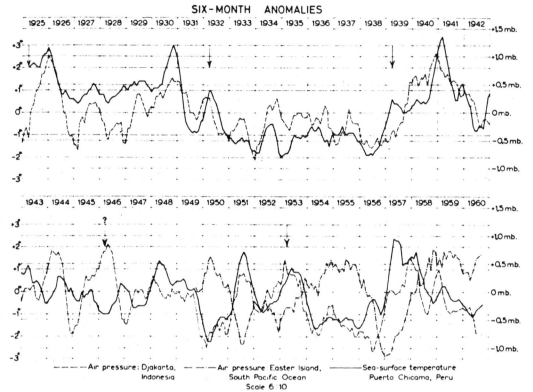

Fig. 3. Djakarta and Easter Island running six-monthly anomalies of air pressure, and Puerto Chicama running six-monthly anomalies of sea-surface temperature. Peaks of sea temperature on the Peru coast reflect El Niño activity (from Berlage, 1961).

sonance with the air pressure at Djakarta (also on the equator, but nearly 180° away). The two-year minor cycle is the "Southern Oscillation" (see *Meteorologic Cycles and Oscillation*; note that on Fig. 3, Easter I. air pressure anomalies are exactly out of phase. Arrows indicate a 7-year cycle, but it is not too closely followed by the El Niño years— 1925, 1930, 1941, 1951, 1953 (mild), 1957/8. Interaction between the Southern Oscillation and the sunspot cycle has been followed by Berlage, since 1807. He observed empirically that when the sunspot number drops below 13 an El Niño occurs, followed by a series of 7-year recurrences, but when another below 13-year comes just before or after an El Niño, another 7-year sequence begins. Even so, there is an occasional anomaly.

RHODES W. FAIRBRIDGE

References

Berlage, H. P., 1957, "Is the Southern Oscillation in meteorology becoming the classical example of a terrestrial cycle steered by the solar cycle?," *Verh. Kon. Ned. Geol. Mijn. Gen., Geol. Serv.,* **18**, 13–21.

Berlage, H. P., 1961, "Variations in the general atmospheric and hydrospheric circulation of a few years period, affected by variations of solar activity," *Ann. N.Y. Acad. Sci.,* **95**(1), 354–367.

Bjerknes, J., 1961, "*El Niño:* study based on analysis of ocean surface temperatures, 1935–1957," *Bull. Inter-Amer. Trop. Tuna Comm.,* **5**, 217–303.

Gunther, E. R., 1936, "Variations in behaviour of the Peru Coastal Current—with an historical introduction," *Geograph. J.,* **88**, 37–65.

Lydolph, P. E., 1957, "A comparative analysis of the dry western littorals," *Ann. Assoc. Am. Geographers,* **47**, 213–230.

Malkus, J. S., 1962, "Large-scale Interactions," in (Hill, M. N., editor) "The Sea," Vol. 1, pp. 88–294, New York, Interscience Publishers.

Rudolph, W. E., 1953, "Weather cycles on the South American West Coast," *Geograph. Rev.,* **43**, 565–566.

Schell, I. I., 1965, "The origin and possible prediction of the fluctuations in the Peru Current and Upwelling." *Jour. Geophys. Res.,* **70** (22), 5529–5540.

Schott, G., 1932, "The Humboldt current in relation to land and sea conditions on the Peruvian coast." *Geography,* **17**, 87–98.

Schweigger, E., 1949, "Der Perustrom nach Zwölfjährigen Beobachtungen," *Erdkunde,* **3**, 121–132, 229–241.

Schweigger, E., 1959, "Die Westküste Südamerikas im Bereich des Peru-Stroms," pp. 56–174, Heidelberg-Munich.

Trewartha, G. T., 1961, "The Earth's Problem Climates," Madison, University of Wisconsin Press, 334pp.

Cross-references: *Meteorological Cycles; Oscillation; Peru Current.*

ENERGY BUDGET OF THE EARTH'S SURFACE

(1) Solar Radiation

The total energy used and converted in the earth's atmosphere is primarily of solar origin. Radiation from the sun is produced (and has been for at least 5×10^9 years) by nuclear reactions in the interior of the sun. The extraterrestrial radiation of the sun at the top of the atmosphere, on a surface perpendicular to the solar beam (the "Solar Constant"), is now accepted to be 2.00 ± 0.04 gcal cm^{-2} min^{-1} or Langley (Ly) min^{-1}, equivalent to 1395 watts/m^2. This value of the solar constant S_0 is based on a reduction to the average radius of a circular orbit of the earth; it varies very little with time. However, there are strong variations in the short-wavelength, ultraviolet end of the spectrum.

The Roentgen (X-ray) and microwave part of the spectrum yields only about 10^{-5} of the total energy. The largest portion of the energy is provided in the wavelengths between 0.2 and about 3μ, i.e., in the visible part of the spectrum and in the near infrared, with a maximum near 0.45μ. The variations due to the ellipticity of the earth's orbit are $\pm 3.34\%$, with a maximum at the beginning of January (perihelion), and a minimum at the beginning of July (aphelion). Since the cross section of the earth, as seen from the sun, is only πr^2 ($r =$ radius of the earth), as compared to the total área of the surface of the globe ($4\pi r^2$), the annual global average of the *incoming solar radiation* received on a horizontal plane at the top of the atmosphere is 720 Ly/day or about 0.35 kW/m^2.

From this quantity, about 35% is reflected or scattered back into space, mostly (24%) by reflection from clouds (planetary albedo a_p). The seasonal and latitudinal variations of the incoming radiation at the top of the atmosphere (Milankovitch, 1930) are given in Fig. 1.

(2) Outgoing Radiation

Since the system earth + atmosphere ought to be very nearly in a radiational equilibrium, the same amount of energy must be radiated back into space. If we denote the effective radiation temperature of the system earth + atmosphere with T_E and the constant of Stefan-Boltzmann's law with σ, we obtain a balanced equation between the incoming solar radiation and the *outgoing terrestrial radiation*:

$$S_0(1 - a_p)\pi r^2 = 4\pi r^2 \sigma T_E^4$$

From this equation, we obtain $T_E = 250°$K or $-23°$C, which is equivalent to the atmospheric temperature at an altitude of about 6 km. Thus the cold source of the atmospheric heat engine is situated much higher and at a lower pressure (about 450 millibars) than the heat source at the earth's surface (with an average global temperature of slightly more than $+15°$C). Therefore, we understand that in accordance with Carnot's law and the second law of thermodynamics, the atmosphere can act as a work-producing heat engine, and that all atmospheric motions and transports including the hydrological cycle are driven by radiational processes. We should also remember that the whole energy produced by fossil fuels (coal and oil) is nothing but a minute fraction of

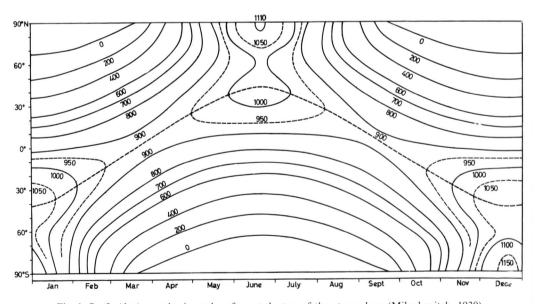

Fig. 1. S_0 (Ly/day) on a horizontal surface at the top of the atmosphere (Milankovitch, 1930).

Radiation Budget (N-Hemisphere, Year) after J. London (1957)

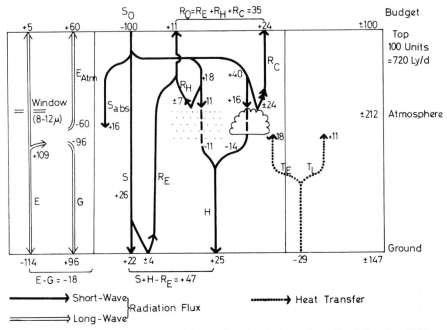

Fig. 2. Radiation and heat budget of the northern hemisphere (data after J. London, 1957).

the solar energy consumed by biological processes and stored within the earth's crust during the last 500 million years.

(3) Incoming Radiation

From the energy of the *incoming solar radiation* S_0 at the top of the atmosphere, about 16% is absorbed within the atmosphere, mainly by the rotation bands of water vapor, carbon dioxide, ozone and molecular oxygen. The most efficient absorber is water vapor (main bands in the near infrared between 0.8 and 7μ); ozone absorbs strongly in the ultraviolet part of the spectrum. About 24% of S_0 is reflected by the cloud cover with its average global coverage of 52% and its large reflectivity (R_C); the albedo, i.e., that part of the incoming radiation energy which is reflected, of clouds varies between about 0.15 for thin cirrus sheets and 0.80 for thick cumulonimbus or nimbo-stratus layers. About 7% of S_0 is radiated back into space (R_H) by back-scattering from molecules of the atmospheric gases and from dust particles, water droplets, etc., suspended in the atmosphere (aerosols). Only about 51% of S_0 reaches the earth's surface, nearly half of it as direct solar radiation S, the other half as scattered radiation H from the sky and the clouds; we are used to taking both components together $(S + H)$ under the term "global radiation" on a horizontal surface. When the sun's elevation above the horizon is greater than $20°$, the spectral distribution of the global radiation is nearly independent of the elevation angle. Near the horizon, we observe a shift

of the distribution toward the red end of the visible spectrum, which is responsible for the beautiful colors at sunset and dawn.

A not inconsiderable part of $S + H$ (global radiation) is reflected from the earth's surface, this reflected shortwave radiation R_E yields only slightly more than 4% of S_0. The albedo $a_{sf} = [R_E/S + H]$ of typical surfaces varies widely, e.g., between 0.04 (dark forest) and about 0.28 (bright sand dunes). The albedo of the ocean is, at high elevations of the sun, only 0.05–0.06. In contrast to these low values, the albedo of fresh snow is 0.80–0.90, and similar values are observed for Antarctica for the entire year.

Taking these considerations into account, we come to the conclusion that only about 47% of the extraterrestrial solar radiation S_0 is absorbed at the earth's surface and can be converted into other energy forms. We may use the term "*effective incoming* (shortwave) *radiation*" for the quantity $S + H - R_E$ or $(S + H)(1 - a_{sf})$. One of the most careful estimates of this quantity has been given by J. London (1957) for the northern hemisphere to be 341 Ly/day; from his data, Fig. 2 is derived, representing all essential terms of the global radiation budget.

(4) Longwave Radiation

The second essential part of the radiation processes at the earth's surface and in the atmosphere deals with the longwave (infrared) or thermal radiation, the bulk of which is situated in the wavelengths $4–100\mu$. The earth's surface itself radiates, according to Stefan-Boltzmann's law, an energy $E = \sigma T_{Sf}^4$ as a function of the radiation temperature T_{Sf} of the earth's surface. A reliable estimate of E annually averaged over the northern hemisphere is 824 Ly/day, i.e., much greater than the effective incoming radiation. Fortunately, the atmosphere acts as a greenhouse in absorbing and emitting all long-wave radiation, mainly due to the existence of H_2O and CO_2 (with a slight addition from ozone). In fact, nearly all long-wave radiation is absorbed by these constituents, with exception of a few atmospheric "windows," especially between 8 and 12μ, where only 39 Ly/day can escape to space. The absorbed energy is reradiated according to Kirchhoff's law; the greater part of these long-wave radiation fluxes is directed toward the earth as atmospheric counter-radiation G, which yields, at the earth's surface, about 695 Ly/day, i.e., nearly the same value as the solar constant and much more than the effective incoming radiation. In the long-wave spectrum, it is very difficult to separate the reflected part of the radiation, which is included in E. Now we can sum up the net effect of the long-wave radiation processes and use the term "*effective outgoing* (terrestrial) *radiation*" for the quantity $E - G$ with a hemispheric annual value of 129 Ly/day.

(5) Net Radiation

From the point of view of the energy processes at the earth's surface, we have to consider the balance of all these radiation processes, i.e., the *net radiation*

$$Q = (S + H - R_E) - (E - G)$$

Using London's data, we obtain as a realistic estimate (annually and hemispherically averaged) for $Q = 341 - 129 = 212$ Ly/day, i.e., slightly less than 30% of the energy of the extraterrestrial solar radiation S_0. Figure 3 demonstrates the latitudinal variations of the net radiation Q and of both its effective constituents in the shortwave and longwave part of the spectrum, together with the extraterrestrial solar radiation S_0; one of the most striking results is the small latitudinal variation of $E - G$. Thus Q is to a large extent determined by the global radiation $S + H$ (Fig. 4). Unfortunately, the determination of Q (and its individual terms) in its horizontal and time variation depends nearly completely on theoretical considerations and semi-empirical formulas; direct measurements of Q, even if free from instrumental errors, are rarely representative for a large area. Thus all data given here can only be considered as carefully evaluated estimates. An independent estimate has been recently published in an excellent atlas by M. J. Budyko (revised edition, 1963), with slightly different results.

This net radiation energy Q is now available for a number of highly efficient processes at the earth's

surface, which will be dealt with in the following paragraphs. Compared with Q, all other energy sources at the earth's surface are negligibly small. This is not only true for the back radiation from moon and planets and the energy of other stars, but also for the *heat flow* (q.v. in Vol. V) within the earth's crust, from the interior, which yields in the average about 0.13 Ly/day or less than 0.1% of Q. Even in regions of active volcanism, where geothermal energy is directly utilized, as at Larderello (Italy) or Wairakei (New Zealand), this heat flow can locally only rise by a factor of about 10–50. On the other hand, the energy received from the sun is equal to only about 0.5×10^{-9} of the total energy emission of the sun, which amounts to 5.2×10^{27} g cal/min; each square centimeter of the sun's surface emits 6.125 kW equivalent to 127×10^6 Ly/day.

(6) Heat Balance

Having thus discussed the radiation processes in the atmosphere, which finally result in a net radiation Q at the earth's surface, we have to consider the conversion of this radiation energy into other forms in the soil and in the oceans, in the atmosphere and in the biosphere. These transfer processes (T) may be summarized in the following *equation of heat balance*:

$$Q = T_S + T_A + T_E + T_{Biol}$$

Here T_S means the heat transfer into the soil or into the sea (cf. Section 8); for brevity we may include here two atmospheric processes, namely the amount of energy needed for melting of snow and ice, which in polar areas can be considerable, and the small amount of heat needed for the warming of fallen precipitation. The largest quantities are the direct warming of the air or, more precisely, the transfer of sensible heat T_A from the surface into the air, and, even more important, the transfer of latent heat of vaporization T_E released by evaporation from the surface into the air (cf. Section 7). Both processes maintain the heat source of all atmospheric motions including the hydrologic cycle (q.v.) in pr Vol. VI.

A small portion of the net radiation energy is used for biological processes, such as production of plant (and animal) tissues. In turn, rotting of plants and respiration of warmblooded animals adds an unknown, but little, amount to the available heat energy at the earth's surface, and some remnants of the tissues may be fossilized (in peat bogs or at the bottom of the sea), and after a large time-lag, they can be utilized as an energy source. Unfortunately no reliable estimate of these processes is available, but it seems almost certain that the term T_{Biol} does not reach 1% of Q.

(7) Vertical Heat Transport

Generally—but with noteworthy exceptions—

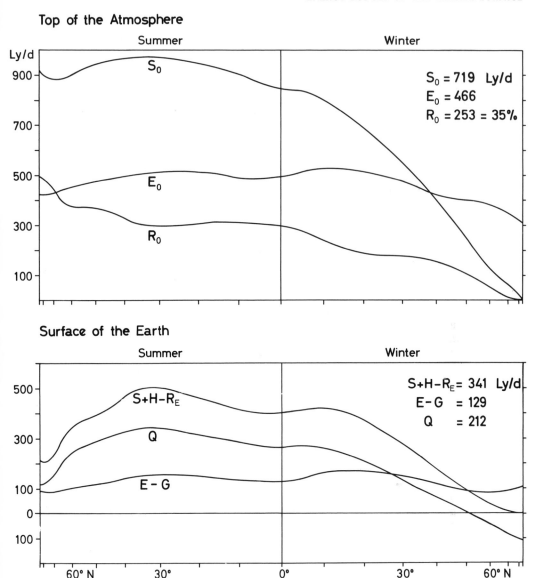

Fig. 3. Latitudinal variations of the extraterrestrial radiation S_0, the net radiation at the earth's surface Q, the effective incoming radiation $S + H - R_E$ and the effective outgoing radiation $E - G$ (London, 1957).

tropospheric air temperature decreases with height between 0 and 10°C per km; in this case, vertical exchange processes (turbulent mixing of the air) transport *sensible heat* from the ground *into the air*. This transport can be reversed during nighttime (in polar regions even in daytime), where air temperature increases with height (surface inversion), but, due to thermal stability and low wind velocities, the downward transport of sensible heat is comparatively small. This vertical transfer of sensible heat T_A depends mainly on the intensity of the turbulent mixing, as described by the "eddy diffusivity" or an "Austausch" coefficient; this

parameter increases rapidly with diminishing thermal stability, i.e., with heating of the air from below. As a hemispheric annual average, T_A reaches about 78 Ly/day, with highest values in the subtropical continents. Exactly the same turbulent mixing processes are responsible for the vertical transfer T_E of latent heat of water vapor, evaporated at the earth's surface.

The *evaporation* at the earth's surface is, in principle, produced by the net radiation Q. At many places, however, horizontal advection processes contribute substantially both to evaporation and to direct heating of the air, but this horizontal

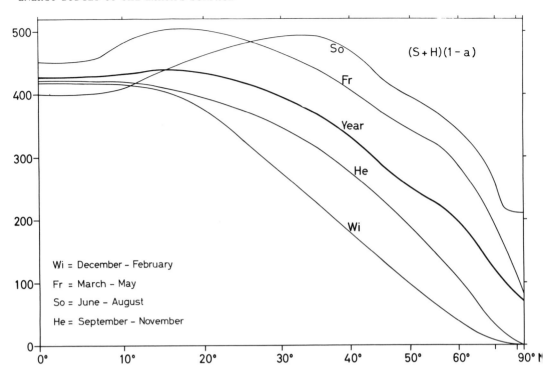

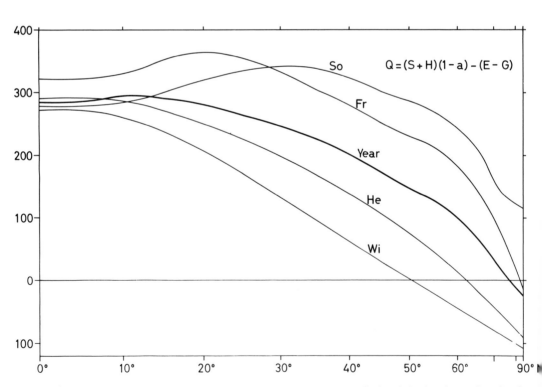

Fig. 4. Seasonal variation of effective incoming radiation (above) and net radiation (below) at the northern hemisphere (Ly/day).

advection is driven by differential heating of the surface and therefore leads only to a redistribution of the available energy Q on a local (or regional) scale. The global average of T_E is equal to 134 Ly/day, thus using about 63% of the net radiation Q or 18.6% of the solar constant S_0. This is equivalent to an annual hemispheric evaporation of 82 cm. Most reliable estimates of the global rainfall (Möller, 1951) yield 83 cm, with 82 cm for the northern hemisphere alone. (Because of the intrinsic difficulties in measuring either precipitation or evaporation over the oceans, i.e., over 71% of the earth's surface, we can rely, at present, only on such carefully weighed estimates, to which the terms of the heat balance contribute essentially.) Thus the hydrologic cycle uses the largest part of the radiation budget at the earth's surface.

(8) Heat Transfer with Soil and Ocean

Compared with the two processes concerning T_A and T_E, all other constituents of the heat budget are small, when averaged over the whole globe and periods on the order of several years. This is generally assumed for the ensemble of all biological processes (T_{Biol}) and also for the heat transfer into the soil T_S on the continents. Only for melting processes of snow and ice, a large quantity of Q is needed, frequently supported by horizontal advection of relatively warm air. Seasonal and diurnal variations in the soil temperature are certainly caused by T_S, but the vertical extension of these periodic variations is usually small; they disappear practically (with values of a few $0.01°C$) at the depth of 30–50 cm for the diurnal cycle and at about 5 meters for the annual cycle.

Much larger quantities are converted in the *heat transfer* T_S between *ocean* and *atmosphere*, but because of its large regional and seasonal variations, they disappear in hemispherical averages. They can contribute very substantially to the regional heat balance, especially in such areas where, during winter, extremely cold continental air is transported over warm oceanic currents of tropical origin (northeastern United States, eastern coasts of Siberia and Manchuria). Here the transfer of both sensible and latent heat from the warm water surface (with temperatures near $10–15°C$) into the continental arctic air (originally with temperatures below $-30°C$) can reach values above 1000 Ly/day, i.e., more than the solar constant. Under such circumstances, the largest energy conversions at the earth's surface are observed, together with impressive steaming fogs, known as "arctic sea-smoke." In general, the role of cold and warm ocean currents for regional climates can hardly be overestimated; they effectively redistribute the net radiation energy Q received at their surface. The physical reason for this large role of T_S in the local heat budget above

the oceans is found in the turbulent mixing of water; the heat transfer produced by this process is 10^3–10^4 times more powerful than that of pure heat conduction in the soil. One of the consequences of this fact is the small diurnal variation of temperature above the oceans (on the order of $0.3°C$), together with other characteristics of maritime climates.

(9) Heat Storage

Certainly, the generally assumed hypothesis of an exact balance of the incoming and outgoing radiation and heat fluxes is only a first-order approximation. There are *storage* processes in the atmospheric budget; water-vapor and latent heat remain in the atmosphere, on the average, for about 11 days, but in water in the oceans for up to 5000 years. Snow is stored seasonally on the polar continents and in arctic sea ice; ice has been stored on the icecaps of Greenland and Antarctica for periods of 10^4 to at least some 10^5 years, while during the largest portion of the earth's geological history no evidence of polar ice is known. Since about 1880, the temperatures of air, sea and soil have increased by about $0.01°C/yr$, averaged over the whole globe; only after 1945 has this *global warming* trend stopped or, in some regions, been reversed. Such a global trend cannot be produced by regional redistribution of energy, correlated with time variations in the large-scale atmospheric circulation patterns. In fact, we must envisage that there exist some storage terms in the global heat and radiation budget, which are, however, certainly small when compared with the uncertainties in the determination of the individual terms.

One of the most challenging explanations of the recent global warming was the CO_2-hypothesis of G. N. Plass (1956). He attributed the general warming to the observed increase of the CO_2 content of the atmosphere (from about 290 ppm in the 1870's to 332 ppm in 1960), which should be responsible for an increase of the powerful atmospheric counter-radiation G. But the coincidence of the absorption bands of CO_2 with those of H_2O has been neglected in the hypothesis, and certainly the recent reversal of the warming trend is inconsistent with it. The increase of CO_2 is at least partly produced by the burning of fossil fuel, such as coal and oil, and probably also partly by the destruction of natural vegetation by man. Recent investigations of the C^{14} content of living wood, etc., have shed some light on the highly differentiated CO_2 budget of the earth's atmosphere. In any case CO_2 variations are so well buffered by oceanic bicarbonate that they can play only a slight role.

Another contribution of man to the global heat budget is the efficient release of aerosol particles with diameters near or below 1μ, which remain some 3–6 days in the lower layers, 20–30 days in the upper and middle troposphere. Together with the industrial output of smoke and haze, the burning of the natural vegetation above most of the tropical semihumid and semiarid continental areas is the source of an unknown, but certainly large part of the atmospheric dust; its role in the atmospheric radiation budget is shown in Fig. 2.

(10) Energy Conversion

On a global scale, the work produced by the atmosphere is balanced by a variety of *energy conversion* processes. Work against surface friction is estimated to 1–2 watts/m^2; this quantity is converted into heat equivalent to 2–4 Ly/day. The energy necessary to elevate the evaporated water vapor to the average condensation level (at about 730 millibars or 2700 meters) is negligible, since the density of water vapor is smaller (only 60%) than that of dry air. The most effective energy conversions are those between the kinetic energy of winds and the potential energy of the pressure field, mainly within the higher troposphere (6–12 km), which are completely balanced on a global scale.

H. Flohn

References

Budyko, M. J., 1963, "Atlas Teplowogo Balansa Zemnogo Schara," Moscow.
London, J., 1957, "A Study of the Atmospheric Heat Balance," Final Report Contract No. AF 19 (122)—165, Department of Meteorology, New York, University, 99pp.
Möller, F., 1957, "Strahlung in der unteren Atmosphäre," in (Flügge, S., editor) "Encyclopedia of Physics," Vol. 48, pp. 155–253.

ENGLISH CHANNEL

Relief. The floor slopes steeply down from the coast to a depth of between 15 and 30 fathoms. Off southwest England, this slope is formed of Palezoic rocks and is terraced by submerged wave-cut platforms separated by cliffs. The most prominent cliff has its foot at a depth of 25 fathoms. Below this coastal zone, the floor is generally flat and slopes very gently down to the maximum depth which increases from about 20 fathoms at the eastern end to about 60 fathoms at the Channel mouth. This flat floor is broken by three kinds of features: (1) shoals or islands which occur west of 2°W and consist of igneous or metamorphic rocks; (2) superficial accumulations—sandbanks, in the easternmost Channel, and sand waves, near its western mouth; (3) depressions below the general level of the floor. The largest depressions extend from northwest of Cherbourg to Ushant: the Hurd Deep (49° 55′N, 2° 00′W, to 49° 20′N, 4° 00′W) the Fosse de l'île Vierge (49° 2′N, 4° 40′W) and the Fosse d'Ouessant (48° 30′N, 5° 15′W). They have several features in common:

all are narrow, parallel-sided trenches, with the northern side usually the steeper, and all show abrupt displacements of their contours. They occur in areas of Mesozoic rocks. Their origin is unknown: a tectonic cause is suggested by Hinschberger (1963). Small depressions near the English coast have been explained by tidal scour of soft rocks (Donovan and Stride 1961a).

Geology. The western part of the Channel is flanked by Paleozoic rocks, the eastern by Mesozoic and Cenozoic. The Channel itself is floored almost entirely by Cretaceous and later rocks. Paleozoic formations occur only close to the coasts in the western part, and Jurassic outcrops are very limited in area. The eastern end of the Channel crosses obliquely the Wealden anticline and its continuation in the Boulonnais. The continuity of the northern limb across the Strait of Dover has been proved by detailed surveys for the proposed Channel Tunnel. The rest of the Channel is dominantly synclinal, preserving Upper Cretaceous and Tertiary rocks. The distribution of outcrops is shown in Figs. 1 and 2. The map of the eastern part is generalized, being based on evidence assembled from various sources by King. The large area of Tertiary north of 50°N and east of 0° is postulated from three dredged samples which yielded *Nummulites laevigatus*, also found in the Eocene (Lutetian) of the Paris Basin and southern England. The large area of Jurassic between 49 and 50°N, and 0 and 2°W, is likewise assumed on the basis of a few dredged samples of Lower and Middle Jurassic rocks. If it exists, it is the largest Jurassic outcrop in the Channel. Two areas, outlined in Fig. 1, are known in detail. Area A has been described by Curry (1962): an elongated inlier of Kimmeridge Clay (Jurassic) is separated by a fault or steep monocline from an outlier of Eocene to the south. Area B was described by Donovan and Stride (1961) who mapped an elongated dome, exposing Corallian Beds (Jurassic) in the center, overstepped on its southern limb by unconformable Upper Cretaceous. South of the Channel Islands (around 49°N, 2½°W), dredging by Dangeard indicates an area of Eocene (Lutetian) limestones resting unconformably on crystalline rocks.

The map of the western Channel and its approaches by Whittard is the result of systematic sampling at intervals of 10 miles or less. The structure is synclinal with minor folds superimposed on it. The geological succession is very incomplete: there are unconformities at the base of the New Red Sandstone, Upper Cretaceous, Paleogene, Pliocene and Recent (superficial) deposits.

Up to the present, sampling has been carried out to 7½°W, and an increasing area of superficial sediments is being met with. On the continental slope and southwest of the Channel, Tertiary rocks

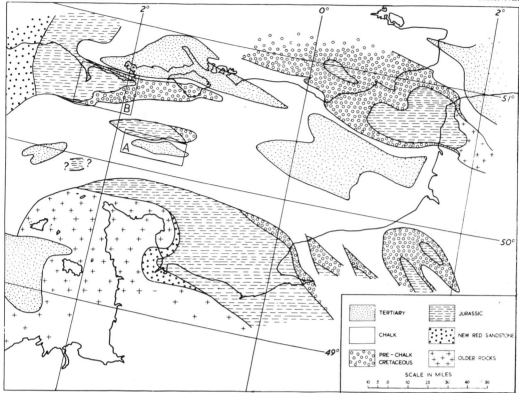

Fig. 1. Geological map of the eastern part of the English Channel, after King (1954, Pl. 4), slightly modified. Land outcrops are projected onto a plane 100 feet below sea level. (*Courtesy Council of the Geological Society of London*)

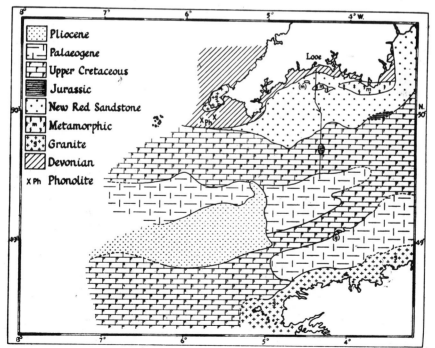

Fig. 2. Geological map of the western part of the English Channel and its western approaches, after Whittard (1962, Fig. 35). (*Courtesy Council of the Royal Society of London and W. F. Whittard*)

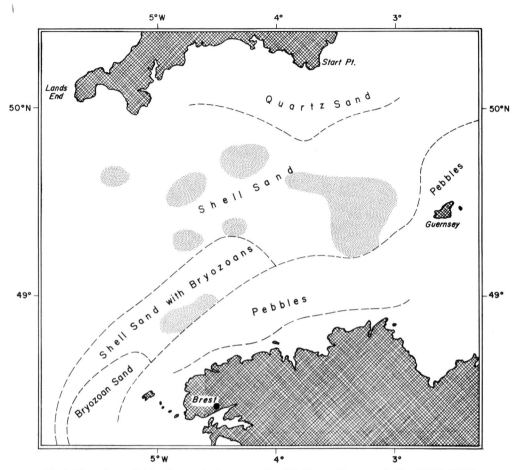

Fig. 3. Map of superficial sediments in the western English Channel based on Boillot (1961). Pebbles are present in the sandy areas and in the parts shaded, they formed between 10 and 50% of samples.

of various ages have been dredged between 500 and 1400 fathoms and are believed to outcrop in place (Curry *et al.*, 1962). The Tertiary must become both thicker and less incomplete between the area shown in Fig. 2 and the continental slope.

The site of the western Channel was occupied by a trough in which sediments were accumulating during the Trias, but apart from this there is no evidence that the Channel existed before the Tertiary. It appears to have been formed by folding and downwarping, probably post-Eocene, accompanied by erosion of the existing Tertiary rocks and, to a lesser extent, of older rocks.

Superficial Sediments. These are shown in British Admiralty Oceanographical Information Sheet H.D. 487 (based largely on work by Pratje, who established the dependence of the grade of the deposits upon tidal currents) and, for the western Channel, by Boillot (1961, Fig. 4). These two sources use different classifications of the bottom and direct comparison is not possible. Transport of sediment in the Channel is reviewed by Stride (1963).

In many parts of the Channel, bedrock may be sampled with a gravity corer, showing that superficial deposits are not more than a few inches thick. This lack of permanent accumulation is due to the strength of the tidal currents, which throughout the Channel reach $1\frac{1}{2}$ knots, and locally exceed 3 knots, at spring tides. The deposits which do occur fall into two categories: first, pebbles too large to be moved by existing currents, and second, finer grained sediments which are undergoing transport. The pebbles are characteristic of a zone off the French coast between Ushant and Cap de la Hague (Fig. 3), but they have also been found at numerous other places. Their origin seems to be twofold. Some are flints which are residual from erosion of the Upper Cretaceous. Others are of Paleozoic rocks, derived from the land. They are often well rounded and presumably reached their present positions as a result of wave action during low sea levels of the Pleistocene. Quartz sand occurs in a belt south of the Devon and Cornwall coast and is probably derived from submarine out-

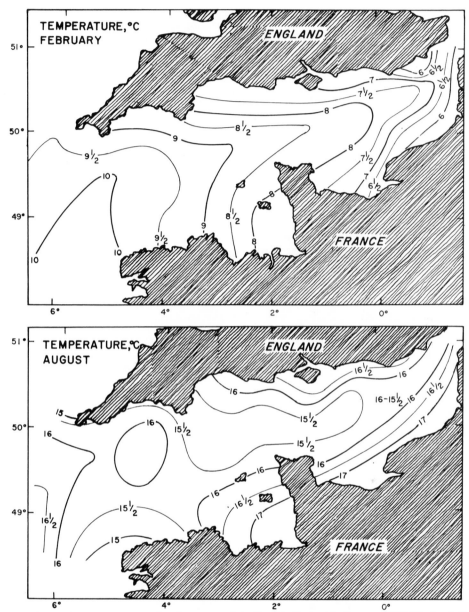

Fig. 4. Mean temperatures of surface water of the English Channel in the years 1903–27 after J. R. Lumby (1935), February and August. (*Courtesy Her Majesty's Stationery Office*)

crops of New Red Sandstone. Elsewhere sand-grade material is largely of organic origin, consisting of broken shells and bryozoans. Mud occurs only in a few small areas near the coast.

Stride (1963, p. 188) has inferred that sediment transport is dominantly toward the east in the eastern Channel, and toward the west in the western Channel, the dividing line being about 2°W. About 600 cubic meters of sand passes through the Straits of Dover into the North Sea each year. The westerly traveling sand is believed to continue toward the edge of the continental shelf. Sand waves are absent east of about 3°W; west of this line they are present with a westerly direction of movement. Sandbanks are absent from the Channel except for a few at the extreme eastern end.

Superficial deposits of the Western Approaches are little known. Charts indicate sand and shells, but gravel is also recorded especially on the outer part of the shelf. Sand waves are also known to occur.

D. T. DONOVAN

259

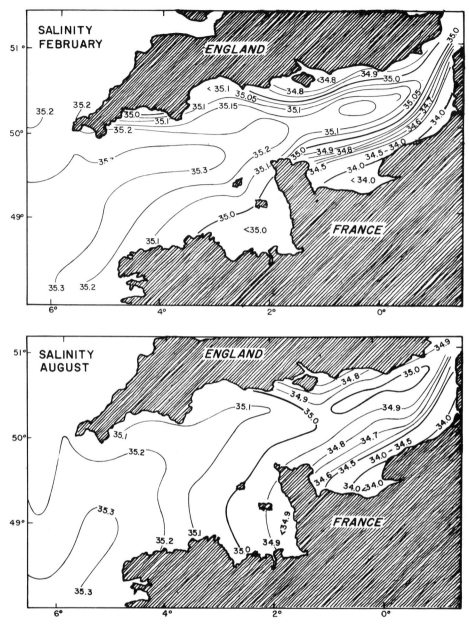

Fig. 5. Mean salinity of surface water of the English Channel in the years 1903–27 after J. R. Lumby (1935), February and August. (*Courtesy Her Majesty's Stationery Office*)

Physical Oceanography. The climate is windy, cloudy, rainy and, for the latitude (50°N), temperate (Meteorological Office, 1940). For the Channel as a whole, Matthews' reports (1907, 1909, 1911) still provide the best picture of the oceanography. Armstrong and Butler (1962), repeatedly working a very close network of stations in the area within 50 miles of the coast of Devon and Cornwall, have shown that the properties of the water are so variable from place to place, and the changes in them are so rapid, that it is difficult to accept results from single stations or from a widely spaced network as representative. It can be said, however, that in winter there is an eastward movement of water, whereas in summer it would seem that there may be an offshore movement at the surface and an onshore movement of the deeper water. Irregular water movements may occur at any time of year. Much local information is to be found in the Channel Pilot (Admiralty, 1947).

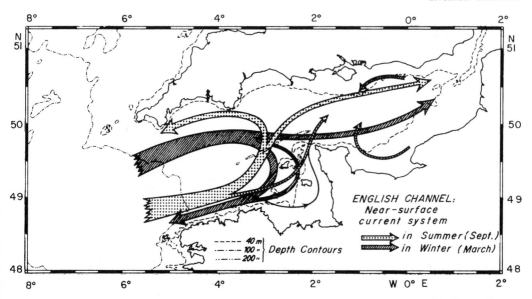

Fig. 6. Circulation in late winter and late summer in the English Channel according to Dietrich (1950). (*Courtesy Deutsches Hydrographisches Institut*).

For the whole area, Lumby (1935) evaluated mean sea temperatures and salinities for the years 1903–27; his charts for February and August are presented as Figs. 4 and 5. Sea temperatures have since warmed up by about half a degree C. Surface salinity reaches a maximum, and temperature a minimum, in late winter (35.3‰, 9–10°C at the western and 35.0‰ and 6–6.5°C at the eastern end). In summer, salinity falls by 0.1–0.5‰ and surface temperatures reach 15–17°C. From year to year, there are considerable variations. East of the meridian (2°W), due to strong tidal mixing, the water remains vertically isohaline and isothermal throughout the year, whereas west of the meridian (3°W), a strong thermocline builds up so that bottom temperatures do not exceed 10–11°C. In some years, summer gales destroy the thermocline. Due to technical difficulties, the important region of the Channel Islands has been little studied.

Tides, which are generally strong, have received much attention (Doodson and Warburg, 1941; Admiralty, 1942; Hansen, 1950). At springs the flood tide reaches 9.7 knots in the Alderney Race and carries toward the eastern English Channel much water which is biochemically conditioned in the turbulent waters among the Channel Islands. Many tables of tidal currents are printed on Admiralty charts.

Water flows from the Atlantic through the Channel and Straits of Dover into the North Sea (Carruthers, 1935), though this flow may be reversed by winds blowing from the North Sea. In autumn, winter and spring, new water enters mostly from the west or northwest, but in summer it is recruited from water lying at thermocline level

to the southwest (Cooper, 1960a). Much water seems to be exchanged with neighboring sea areas by narrow currents around the Ushant and Land's End promontories (Cooper, 1960b), but the process has been studied very little. Dietrich (1950) drew attention to the anomalous heat budget of the English Channel and deduced a pattern of currents (Fig. 6) agreeing broadly with opinion at the Plymouth Laboratory. There are large variations about the mean state.

A long series of papers by Poole and Atkins (Poole, 1959) described the penetration of light in the Channel.

Chemical Oceanography. For 40 years, with short breaks, one station E1 (50° 04′N, 4° 22′W) has been visited monthly. Much is known about it, and many textbooks illustrate work done there, particularly studies of seasonal cycles of compounds of phosphorus, nitrogen, silicon, iron and metals of biological importance. The broad pictures are sound, with winter maxima, withdrawal of nutrients in spring by plants, followed by summer minima. For many years it had been thought that the station represented an extensive, reasonably uniform water mass occupying the western English Channel so that small displacements had no effect on legitimate deductions. Since around the position of the station E1 a number of markedly different water masses are now known to occur, tidal currents and wind drift may pass them through the station in quick succession. Many of the earlier, finer deductions based on the single station are therefore now under revision, making it unwise to summarize them here. Readers are referred to the many papers by Atkins, Harvey, Cooper and

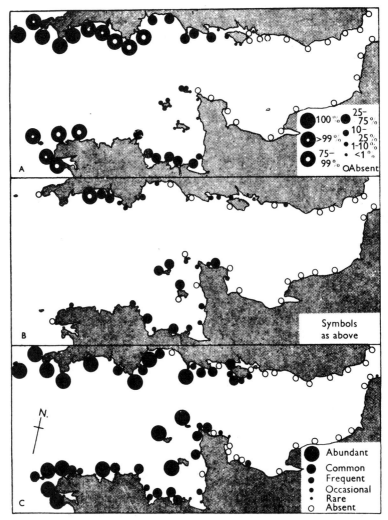

Fig. 7. Distribution of some representative species in the Channel. (A) confined exclusively to the western part; Chthamalus stellatus, shown as percentage of population of Chthamalus and Balanus balanoides: (B) common in the west and rare in the east; Hemioniscus balani, shown as percentage infection of Balanus balanoides; (C) present in the eastern basin on the French side only; Littorina neritoides (after D. J. Crisp and A. J. Southward, 1958). (*Courtesy Council of Marine Biological Association*)

Armstrong in the *Journal of the Marine Biological Association* and in publications of the International Council for the Exploration of the Sea, and to the reviews by Harvey (1957 and earlier books), Armstrong and Butler (1962), and Raymont (1963). The experience of the Plymouth Laboratory is likely to be repeated elsewhere.

The English Channel is not rich, due to an adverse partition of nutrients during recruitment of new water. During the 1920's, the winter maximum of phosphate lay around 0.7 μg atom/liter but about 1931 this fell to about 0.45–0.5 μg atom/liter and has ever since remained at the lower level. This chemical change was accompanied by a profound change in the nature of the biological population and in the output of the fisheries. The changes are believed to be due to fluctuations in Arctic climate, causing variable overspill of cold Arctic water over the Iceland Faeroe Ridge into the Atlantic, where consequent variations in upward displacement of nutrients in the Eastern North Atlantic affect the water to be recruited to the Channel (Cooper, 1955a and b).

Biological Oceanography. The fauna of the waters and sea bed of the western English Channel has been described in the Plymouth Marine Fauna (Marine Biological Association, 1957) and the flora in a check list by Parke and Dixon (1964).

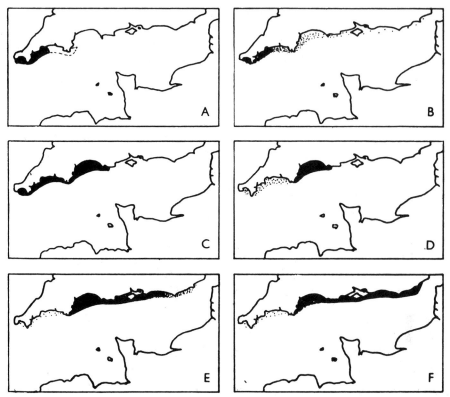

Fig. 8. Distribution patterns on the English side of the Channel. (A) Western species. The pecked line shows the maximum penetration into the Channel at any time as shown by dead shell records, the black area the present distribution. (B) Cornubian species. (C) West Channel species. (D) West Channel species mainly confined to Great West Bay (possibly a combination of distributions shown in C and E). (E) Sarnian species. (F) Northern species. Occurrences outside the area covered by the survey are not shown (after N. A. Holme, 1961). (*Courtesy Council of Marine Biological Association*)

The distribution of intertidal organisms (Fig. 7) (Crisp and Southward, 1958) and of bottom fauna (Fig. 8) (Holme, 1961) shows strong zonation, different communities inhabiting different areas of the Channel. In part, control is maintained by temperature, but there seems little doubt that it is also in part biochemical, depending on the previous history of the several water masses. This conclusion was also drawn by Russell (1936, *inter alia*; also Southward, 1963) for zooplankton some of which gave indications of water movements confirmed in quite a remarkable way by later physical and chemical studies.

L. H. N. COOPER

References

Admiralty, Hydrographic Dept., 1942, "English Channel, Pocket Tidal Stream Atlas."

Admiralty, Hydrographic Dept., 1947, "The Channel Pilot," Parts I and II.

Armstrong, F. A. J., and Butler, E. I., 1962, "Hydrographic surveys off Plymouth in 1959 and 1960," *J. Marine Biol. Assoc. U.K.*, **42**, 445–463.

Boillot, G., 1961, "La répartition des fonds sous-marins dans la Manche occidentale," *Cahiers Biol. Marine*, **2**, 187–208.

Boillot, G., 1963, "Sur un nouvelle fosse de la Manche occidentale, la fosse du Pluteus," *Comps. Rend. Acad. Sci., Paris*, **257** (22), 3448–3451.

Boillot, G., 1963, "Sur la fosse de la Hague (Manche centrale), *Compt. Rend. Acad. Sci., Paris*, **257** (25), 3963–3966.

Carruthers, J. N., 1935, "The flow of water through the Straits of Dover," *Fish. Invest., Lond., Ser. II*, **14**, No. 4, 1–67.

Cooper, L. H. N., 1955a, "Deep water movements in the North Atlantic as a link between climatic changes around Iceland and biological productivity of the English Channel and Irish Sea," *J. Marine Res.*, **14**, 347–362.

Cooper, L. H. N., 1955b, "Hypotheses connecting fluctuations in Arctic climate with biological productivity of the English Channel," *Papers Marine Biol. Oceanogr., Suppl. to Deep-Sea Res.*, **3**, 212–223.

Cooper, L. H. N., 1960a, "The water flow into the English Channel from the south-west," *J. Marine Biol. Assoc. U.K.*, **39**, 173–208.

Cooper, L. H. N., 1960b, "Exchanges of Water between the English and Bristol Channel around Land's End," *J. Marine Biol. Assoc. U.K.*, **39**, 637–658.

Crisp, D. J., and Southward, A. J., 1958, "The distribution of intertidal organisms along the coasts of the English Channel," *J. Marine Biol. Assoc. U.K.*, **37**, 157–208.

Curry, D., 1962, "A Lower Tertiary outlier in the central English Channel, with notes on the beds surrounding it," *Quart. J. Geol. Soc. Lond.*, **118**, 177–205.
report," *Proc. Roy. Soc. London, Ser. A*, **265**, 395–406.

Curry, D., Martini, E., Smith, A. J., and Whittard, W. F., 1962, "The geology of the Western Approaches of the English Channel. I. Chalky rocks from the upper reaches of the continental slope," *Phil. Trans. Roy. Soc. London, Ser. B*, **245**, 267–290.

Dietrich, G., 1950, "Die anomale Jahresschwankung des Wärmeinhalts im Englischen Kanal, ihre Ursachen und Auswirkungen," *Deut. Hydrograph. Z.*, **3**, 184–201.

Donovan, D. T., and Stride, A. H., 1961, "An acoustic survey of the sea floor south of Dorset and its geological interpretation," *Phil. Trans. Roy. Soc. London, Ser. B*, **244**, 299–330.

Donovan, D. T., and Stride, A. H., 1961a, "Erosion of a rock floor by tidal sand streams," *Geol. Mag.*, **98**, 393–398.

Doodson, A. T., and Warburg, H. D., 1941, "Admiralty Manual of Tides," pp. xii and 270, London.

Hansen, W., 1950, "Gezeitenströme im Englischen Kanal," *Deut. Hydrograph. Z.*, **3**, 169–183.

Harvey, H. W., 1957, "The Chemistry and Fertility of Sea Waters," Second ed., pp. viii and 234, Cambridge.

Hinschberger, F., 1963, "Un problème de morphologie sous-marine: la Fosse d'Ouessant," *Norois*, **39** (Jul. Sept. 1963), 217–233.

Holme, N. A., 1961, "The bottom fauna of the English Channel," *J. Marine Biol. Assoc. U.K.*, **41**, 397–461.

King, W. B. R., 1954, "The geological history of the English Channel," *Quart. J. Geol. Soc. London*, **110**, 77–101.

Lumby, J. R., 1935, "Salinity and temperature of the English Channel, Atlas of Charts," *Fish. Invest.*, London, Ser. II, **14**, No. 3, Atlas.

Marine Biological Association of the U.K., 1957, "Plymouth Marine Fauna," Third ed., pp. xliii and 1–457.

Matthews, D. J., 1907, 1909, 1911, "Reports on the physical conditions in the English Channel and adjacent waters, 1903–06," *Internat. Fish. Investigations. Marine Biol. Assoc. Reports II*, Parts 1 and 2 and *III*. (Cd. 3837, 4641 and 5546).

Meteorological Office, 1940, "Weather in Home Waters and the North-eastern Atlantic," Vol. II, Pt. 3, "The English Channel."

Parke, Mary, and Dixon, P. S., 1964, "Revised check list of British marine algae," *J. Marine Biol. Assoc. U.K.*, **44**, No. 2 (in press).

Poole, H. H., 1959, "William Ringrose Gelston Atkins," *Biographical Memoirs of Fellows of the Royal Society*, 1959, **5**, 1–22.

Pratje, O., 1950, "Die Bodenbedeckung des Englischen Kanals und die maximalen Gezeitenstromgeschwindigkeiten," *Deut. Hydrograph. Z.*, **3**, 201–205.

Raymont, J. E. G., 1963, "Plankton and Productivity in the Oceans," pp. viii and 1–660, Oxford, Pergamon Press.

Russell, F. S., 1936, "The importance of certain plankton animals as indicators of water movements in the western end of the English Channel," *Rapp. Procès-verbaux Reunions, Conseil Perm. Intern. Explor. Mer*, **100**, III, 7–10.

Southward, A. J., 1963, "The distribution of some plankton animals in the English Channel and approaches. III. Theories about long-term biological changes, including fish," *J. Marine Biol. Assoc. U.K.*, **43**, 1–29.

Stride, A. H., 1963, "Current-swept sea floors near the southern half of Great Britain," *Quart. J. Geol. Soc. London*, **119**, 175–199.

Whittard, W. F., 1962, "Geology of the western approaches of the English Channel: a progress report," *Proc. Roy. Soc. London, Ser. A*, 395–406.

ENTROPY, ISENTROPIC FLOW—*See* Vol. II

EPHEMERIS—*See* Vol. II

EQUATION OF MOTION—*See* FLUID MECHANICS

EQUATORIAL CURRENTS

The equatorial currents flow in an east-west direction. In many respects they are analogous to the trade winds, and their position and strength are apparently controlled by the overlying wind system. Sverdrup was able to derive the existing current structure for the Pacific Ocean by consideration of the known wind stress.

Although there has been some recent work to suggest otherwise, it has generally been believed that the equatorial currents are confined to the upper 500 meters of the water column. All evidence to-date indicates that the highest velocities are confined to the region in or above the thermocline which is usually shallower than 200 meters in tropical latitudes. Characteristic speeds of these major currents are from 0.5–2 knots (25–100 cm/sec).

The classic picture of the equatorial current system is one of two comparatively broad (1000–1500 km) westward flowing currents, separated by a comparatively narrow (500 km) eastward flowing countercurrent. The two westward currents, the north and south equatorial currents, are analogous to the northeast and southeast trades, and the equatorial countercurrent is related to the region of low winds between these two trade wind belts. Since the intertropical convergence (q.v.) which separates the northeast from the southeast trades is 200–500 miles north of the equator in most of the Atlantic and Pacific, the equatorial countercurrent also lies north of the equator. This pattern exists in both the Atlantic and the Pacific oceans. In the Indian Ocean, there is a seasonal reversal in the currents north of the equator which is related to the reversal in the monsoon winds. Recently, Reid has presented evidence for an equatorial counter-

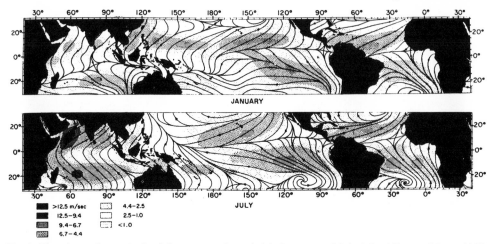

Fig. 1. Direction and magnitude of the mean surface wind in January and July (after Mintz and Dean, 1952).

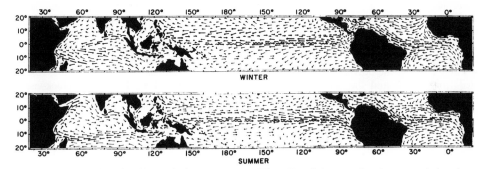

Fig. 2. Current chart for the tropical ocean areas. "Winter" and "summer" refer to northern winter and summer respectively. The chart is derived mainly from that of Schott (1943). The only major changes are those of the equatorial undercurrents in the Atlantic and Pacific (wiggly lines) and the Pacific South Equatorial Countercurrent (after Knauss, 1963). (By permission of Interscience Publishers, Inc., N.Y.C.)

current south of the equator in both the Pacific and the Atlantic oceans. The speeds are of the order of 0.2 to 0.3 knot. The relationship of this current to the known wind field is not immediately clear.

Perhaps the most interesting currents in the equatorial regions are the equatorial undercurrents. These flow from west to east and are centered on the equator. They are about 300 meters thick and up to 400 km wide. They are subsurface currents, the highest speeds (up to 3 knots) are centered in the thermocline at depths of from 50–150 meters. The equatorial undercurrents are imbedded in the westward-flowing south equatorial currents. When the south equatorial current is weak, the equatorial undercurrent apparently breaks the surface on occasion.

Although it now appears that this flow was first described in the Atlantic in 1886, the evidence was neglected and the undercurrents were rediscovered in the Pacific in 1952. Extensive observational work has been conducted since 1958, and the currents have been well described now in all three oceans. The equatorial undercurrent appears to be a regular feature in the Atlantic and Pacific and is present intermittently in the Indian Ocean. The question of what drives and maintains these equatorial undercurrents is one of the most interesting unsolved problems in dynamical oceanography.

J. A. KNAUSS

Reference

Knauss, J. A., 1963, "Equatorial Current Systems," in (Krauss, J. A., editor) "The Sea," Vol. II, Ch. 10, New York, Interscience Publishers.

ESTUARY—*See* Vol. III

EUSTASY—*See* Vol. III

EXCHANGE COEFFICIENT—*See* **AUSTAUSCH**

EXPLOSION CRATERS—*See* Vol. II

F

FALKLAND CURRENT — *See* **BRAZIL CURRENT**

FERREL'S LAW AND BUYS BALLOT'S LAW

William Ferrel was an American meteorologist who first recognized the effect of the rotation of the earth (Coriolis force, q.v.) on the wind systems. It was published obscurely in 1856, and quite independently of a related (and resultant) principle which was published (in November, 1857) by C. H. D. Buys Ballot, Chief of the Dutch Meteorological Service from 1854–89. The dynamic concept that winds in the northern hemisphere are deflected to the right and those in the southern hemisphere are deflected to the left is known as *Ferrel's law.*

Ferrel's law is due to the Coriolis force (acceleration) on any moving particle, say of air or water, on a rotating globe. The result of this apparent force is a *deflection* nearly balanced by the pressure gradient (q.v.), but not quite balanced due to friction. Where there is no friction, the result of this balance is the geostrophic wind (q.v.), the conditions for which are stated qualitatively by Buys Ballot's Law (see below).

This deflection of winds was first drawn on a sketch of planetary circulation by Ferrel in 1856 (see Fig. 1, in *Ferrel Cell*). In consequence of it, in the northern hemisphere the northerly setting winds of the mid-latitudes were indicated as *veering winds* (turning to the right), so that they become westerlies; in the southern hemisphere similar winds were indicated as *backing winds* (turning to the left). Excellent simple explanations of the Coriolis force, pressure gradient, etc., may be found in Taylor (1954) and Donn (1965). (Note: The terms *veer* and *back* are given above in their international usage. Certain U.S. meteorologists use "veering" in the sense of "in the direction of the Coriolis force"; this will be the same thing, i.e., clockwise in the northern hemisphere, but counterclockwise in the southern hemisphere. The international usage is strongly urged.)

It is important to recognize that Ferrel's law of deflection applies equally well to winds blowing from any direction, e.g., in northern mid-latitudes the southerlies become southwesterlies and westerlies, and correspondingly in the trade-wind belts the northerly, equator-directed winds are deflected to become northeasterlies and easterlies.

Ferrel's law and Buys Ballot's law (see below) are applicable in the ocean, too, where the pressure gradient is balanced only by the Coriolis force, in

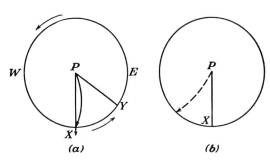

Fig. 1. North polar projection of the earth; (a) a moving body from P to X will appear to curve to its right, but is not actually curving because the solid earth underneath it is progressively moving to the east. Point X will move to Y. From the observer's viewpoint (fixed with respect to the earth), as indicated in (b) the moving body *appears* to swing from the direction of X to the right (from Donn, 1965). (By permission of McGraw-Hill Book Co., N.Y.)

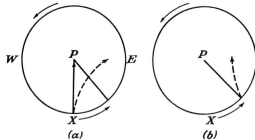

Fig. 2. Conversely to Fig. 1, (a) a moving body directed *toward* the pole will also be deflected to the right, because of the law of inertia; since at X it is traveling eastward on the commencement of its trajectory toward P, it will complete its course a similar distance east of P as the point X has moved (disregarding other factors). From the observer's point of view (b) it still *appears* to have been deflected to the right (from Donn, 1965). (By permission of McGraw-Hill Book Co., N.Y.)

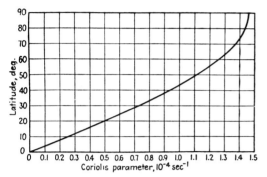

Fig. 3. Curve of values of Coriolis parameter, showing zero value at the equator.

Vortices and the Equator

Fig. 4. Neptune observes (with acknowledgment to "Timothy" and the *Sunday Times*, London, April 29, 1962).

most cases of circulation with horizontal scales of more than 100 km (large scale only because of the relatively sluggish motion). In the ocean the pressure gradients are manifested as slopes of the sea surface with respect to the level surface. Thus the Gulf Stream, where it passes between Miami and the Bahamas, is found at times to be almost 1 meter higher on the right-hand side; owing to seasonal variation in its velocity, there is a semiannual variation in this tilt.

On a rotating sphere like the earth, any object or body moving over its surface tends thus to be deflected by the Coriolis force (q.v.), which modifies Newtonian mechanics to the earth's frame of reference. It changes the direction but not the speed of the moving body. Without its effect, idealized atmospheric pressure cells would lead to surface winds blowing directly toward or away from one another (see *Geostrophic Motion*). The Coriolis effect may be expressed as fv, where v is the velocity and f is $2\Omega \sin \varphi$ (Ω being the angular velocity of the earth and φ the latitude). The force is zero at the equator because it varies with the sine of the latitude, and increases to a maximum at the pole.

Moving bodies of inland water are likewise affected. It is suspected that in the higher latitudes, river meanders undercut their banks more rapidly on the right-hand loops; note, for example, the great westerly loops of the Danube in its course between successive rock barriers.

Some years ago an interesting controversy arose about the vorticity of bath water running down the waste pipe in each hemisphere. Did it respond to the Coriolis force? In a letter to the London *Sunday Times* (April 29, 1962), one correspondent claimed that he experimented with the bath water while his ship was actually crossing the equator; precisely at the moment of crossing, the left-handed swirl stopped and changed to a right-handed one. Considering that the Coriolis effect is zero at the equator, this was quite a remarkable experience. Accordingly Father Neptune (see Fig. 4) on observing such swirls may be understandably puzzled (us too!). Many such effects have been claimed from

time to time, but most of them may rather be explained by inequalities in the current or the duct and, once established, by the conservation of angular momentum.

Buys Ballot's law (also called the "law of storms" or "basic wind law") states that an observer in the northern hemisphere, standing with his back to the wind, will have the low pressure to his left and the high pressure to his right; conversely in the southern hemisphere. Thus in the northern hemisphere winds blow counterclockwise into a low, clockwise out of a high; and conversely in the southern hemisphere. This law has been particularly handy for mariners who had to navigate near cyclones and hurricanes. Essentially it is one *result* of Ferrel's law and defines the *geostrophic wind* (q.v.), recognized later by Sir Napier Shaw, which is the concept of a wind that, independently of friction, etc., blows under the action only of the Coriolis force and the pressure gradient force. In 1876, the Norwegian meteorologists Guldberg and Mohn (q.v.) developed a mathematical theory on Buys Ballot's law.

Since the frictional deviation of any wind near the earth's surface is usually no more than 30° over land (and 20° over the ocean), Buys Ballot's law almost always applies; because of the reduced friction over the ocean, it is particularly useful there.

RHODES W. FAIRBRIDGE
RICHARD J. ROMMER

References

Bergeron, T., 1959, "Weather Forecasting," in (Bolin, B., editor) "The Atmosphere and the Sea in Motion," pp. 440–474, New York, Rockefeller Institute Press and Oxford University Press.
Buys Ballot, C. H. D., 1860, "Eenige regelen voor anstaande weersveranderingen in Nederland," Utrecht.
Donn, W. L., 1965, "Meteorology," Third ed., New York, McGraw-Hill Book Co., 484pp.
Ferrel, W., 1856, "The winds and currents of the ocean," *Nashville J. Medic. and Surgery.*

Guldberg, C. M., and Mohn, H., 1876, "Etudes sur les mouvements de l'atmosphère," Christiania, Pt. I (revision 1883) (translated by Abbe, "Mechanics of the Earth's Atmosphere," Smithsonian Institution, Washington, 1910).

Shaw, Sir. N., 1933, "Manual of Meteorology," London, Cambridge University Press, 3 vols.

Taylor, G. F., 1954, "Elementary Meteorology," New York, Prentice-Hall, 364pp.

Cross-references: *Coriolis Force; Gulf Stream; Pressure Gradient.* In Vol. II: *Cyclogenesis; Geostrophic Wind; Gradient Wind; Guldberg and Mohn's Rule; Hadley Cell; Tropical Cyclones.*

FERTILITY OF THE OCEANS

Fertility is a broad concept for organic synthesis potential. Although ensconced in the popular vocabulary, it is inadequate to express fully this ecological concept. A term is required which measures the ability of an area to support biological populations and to sustain a level of growth and reproduction. Such expressions as *standing crop* and *productivity* are distinctive and contribute to this need and are widely used in oceanic ecology.

Standing Crop Measurement

The standing crop is, simply, the abundance of organisms existing in the area at the time of observations. It may be expressed as number of individuals, as *biomass*, as *energy content*, or in some other suitable terms. These are not altogether simple parameters to measure. In oceanography, standing crop data are commonly reported as milligrams of carbon per unit volume. The range is commonly 10–1000 $mg/C/m^3$. Values are usually derived from measurement of phytoplankton pigments, especially chlorophyll *a*. Strickland (1960) has intensively reviewed the problems in such analysis. Table 1 gives some selected values for Atlantic and Pacific areas.

The standing crop is an instantaneous measure of the oceanic system, but it provides no information on extended conditions. It gauges an equilibrium at any one moment between production and destruction. The growth of phytoplankton is largely dependent on the supply of nutrient materials and energy. The general conditions in offshore temperate waters are represented by Fig. 1, which indicates the complex interaction of physical and chemical conditions that support the biological system. Mixing of the water column in winter provides regenerated nutrients which supply a spring bloom of phytoplankton that is shortly followed by an increase in zooplankton as well. This growth causes a decline in the nutrient level, which the stratification and the stability of the

TABLE 1. Oceanic Standing Crop Measurements, Compiled from Original References as Listed in Strickland (1960) (All Values Derived from Chlorophyll Determinations)

Region	Time of Year	Standing Crop (mg C/m³)
Atlantic Ocean Areas		
Southeast North Sea, yearly minimum range	March	600–700
Kiel Bay, North Germany, average for euphotic zone	January (min)	80
	April (max)	250
North Sea, 10–20 m	May (max)	100
English Channel, 20 miles off Plymouth, surface values	January (min)	10
	July (max)	150
	August (min)	20
	November (max)	40
Northwest Atlantic, Long Island Sound, USA, average for euphotic zone	March (max)	300–600
	Winter	100
Off New England coast, USA, average for euphotic zone	March	100
Inshore waters off Florida	Summer	400
	September (max)	650
Pacific Ocean Areas		
California coast, USA, inshore surface waters	August	50
Northeast Pacific		
Near end of Aleutian islands	November	200
Oceanic area, 55°N, 155°W	August–September	20
Off Alaska Panhandle, 55°N, 135°W	August–September	60
Off Kodiak Island, 57°N, 153°W	August–September	50
Equatorial Pacific		
Near coast of Ecuador	November	35
East of 160°W, near surface		
Range (min–max)	November	5–150
Average value	November	20

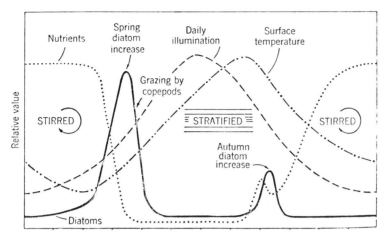

Fig. 1. Generalized diagram of seasonal cycle of diatom abundance and certain controlling factors in the temperate ocean (Clarke, 1954). (By permission of John Wiley and Sons, Ltd., New York City.)

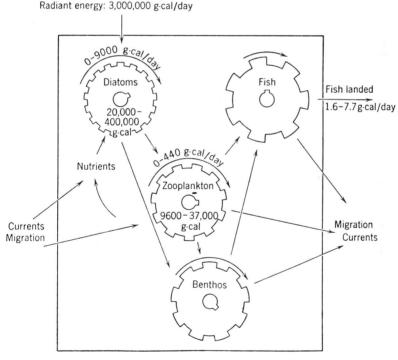

Fig. 2. Principal components and processes involved in production on Georges Bank, off Massachusetts. Values are average for the whole bank per square meter of sea surface. Maximum and minimum values within the cog wheels are for the standing crop; those over the wheels are for net production rate. Average yield during 1923–45 is indicated at right (Clarke, 1946).

water column in the summer then maintain, and growth levels decline. Some regeneration of nutrients may cause a slight autumn bloom. The main restoration of nutrient levels occurs with the winter period of turbulence. At this period, however, the surface illumination is low and it is not until spring that all conditions are again in phase for a large growth. This cycle is reflected in standing crop measurements in Table 1 for the English Channel, Kiel Bay or Long Island Sound.

The standing crop in marine environments tends to be larger in absolute values in high latitudes than in regions near the equator, but the reasons for this are complex. Under tropical conditions, growth is faster and regeneration of dead material is more rapid. However, stratification of the water column is pronounced and only limited recycling of nutrients takes place. The greater rate of supply of nutrients to the surface in temperate and polar regions is a result of the nature of vertical circulation in the ocean. This is coupled with reduced metabolic demands at lower temperatures to make possible support of a large crop. In regions with exceptionally great upwelling (q.v.), an enormous standing crop exists as seen off the Peruvian coast in the Pacific (see *Peru Current*), near southwest

TABLE 2. OCEANIC PRODUCTIVITY MEASUREMENTS, BASED ON C^{14} FIXATION
[ORIGINAL SOURCES COMPILED IN STRICKLAND (1960), RYTHER (1963), EXCEPT EQUATORIAL ATLANTIC FROM IGY CRUISE DATA]

Region	Time of Year	Primary Productivity (mg C/m²/day)
Atlantic Ocean Areas		
Arctic		
Ice Island T3	Midsummer	0–24
Station Alpha	Late summer	0–6
Western Barents Sea, near Bear Island		
Arctic water	May	1300
Atlantic water	May	275
Norwegian Sea, near Spitzbergen		
North Atlantic water	June	2400
Arctic water	June	400–600
Northern North Atlantic		
Faroe-Iceland Ridge	Summer	650–2700
Near Iceland	Summer	530–1300
South of Greenland	Summer	550
Irminger Sea	Summer	150–250
North Sea		
Annual range	Yearly	100–1500
Northeast coast of England	May	220
	October	110
	February	5
Danish coastal waters	March bloom	300
	August (max)	700
	December (min)	10
Eastern North Atlantic		
15 miles off Oporto	September	100
200 miles off Oporto	September	150
Mediterranean Sea		
2 miles off French coast	Midsummer	30–40
Western North Atlantic		
Continental shelf and inshore		
Spring flowering	Spring	1930
Mean rate		560
Weighted annual mean		330
Sargasso Sea	April bloom	890
	Summer	100–200
Caribbean Sea (10–20°N)		100–200
Equatorial Atlantic		
West basin		
Near 20°N	February	60–160
At 8° 15′N	April–May	230–300
At 8° 15′S	March	70–280
At 15° 45′S	April	20–130
East Basin		
Near 20°N	February	190–780
At 8° 15′N	April–May	180–1480
At 8° 15′S	March	100–370
At 15° 45′S	April	90–420
Southwest Atlantic		
Walvis Bay and Benguela Current	December	500–4000

TABLE 2 *continued*

Region	Time of year	Primary Productivity (mg C/m²/day)
Pacific Ocean Areas		
Equatorial Pacific		
Near coast of Ecuador	Autumn	500–1000
9°N, 90°W (Costa Rica dome)	November	410–800
11°N, 115°W	Autumn	10
Range, 30°N–30°S	March	100–250
Northwest Pacific		
Sea of Japan		
Kuroshio current	Summer	50–100
Oyashio system	Summer	250–500
Sea of Okhotsk, North of Japan		
Range of values	May	6–5100
Mean value	May	2000
Indian Ocean Areas		
Equatorial Indian Ocean		200–250

Africa in the region of the Benguela current (q.v.), and in the Gulf of Aden and Arabian Coast. In the relatively shallow waters of marine banks, the abundance of nutrients is high since they may be recovered and recycled, and this leads to a high standing crop that can be maintained over a long period. Such areas provide good fisheries due to this heavy production.

Productivity Measurements

Knowledge of the standing crop of an area does not give a complete picture of fertility or productivity. In addition, the rates at which the different constructive and destructive processes are going forward within the area must be considered. Energy from sunlight is used by green plants to form carbohydrate which represents gross plant production. Consideration of the amount of this material lost in the accompanying respiration and excretion of the autotrophs results in the net plant production, which is often referred to as the primary productivity. This net rate of autosynthesis of the organic constituents of plant material in seawater is measured on the basis of organic carbon assimilated per unit volume or beneath unit area of sea surface and is expressed as mg C/m^3/day or mg C/m^2/day. The definition of day generally refers to the hours of daylight during which net photosynthesis occurs in the sea surface water. The definition refers to assimilation mainly from inorganic sources of carbon and does not include the rate of loss of primary material by death or predation. At higher levels, herbivorous and carnivorous zooplankton in turn will subsist on this net production, but with additional losses in efficiency due to metabolic requirements. The total system has been described diagrammatically by Clarke (1946) in Fig. 2, indicating the interrelationships and efficiencies at the various levels.

The oceanographic literature reports primary productivity of the phytoplankton, usually based on measurements of C^{14} fixation on a sample maintained under circumstances which reproduce actual oceanic conditions. A compilation of regional measurements given in Table 2 shows the range of values found. Broadly speaking, the range is 5–5000 mgC/m^3/day. As with standing crop measurements, variation seasonally and by oceanic region occurs, and factors of nutrient supply and available illumination help to explain the wide variation in values. Since there is always adequate CO_2, the limiting factors are usually nitrogen, phosphorus and radiant energy. Geographical variation in productivity measurements is given detailed consideration by Ryther (1963). On the basis of the productivity measurements, the tropical seas do not show a marked reduction over other areas. Although, as noted previously, the standing crop may be less than the summer standing crop in higher latitudes, the depth of the photic zone is greater in the tropics and the total crop in the entire vertical water column is thereby increased. The entire oceanic productivity has been variously estimated at $1.6–15.5 \times 10^{10}$ tons C/yr, as compared with 1.9×10^{10} tons for the land areas.

Efficiency of Marine Production

Estimates of the photosynthetic activity of the world ocean attribute over half of the total world annual production of carbon to the seas. The efficiency of production is, however, quite low. This efficiency is the ratio of the energy fixed in chemical compounds to the incident light energy.

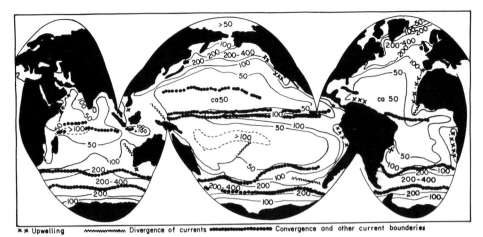

Fig. 3. Estimated amounts of basic organic production in the oceans as grams of carbon per square meter of sea surface (g C/m²/year) (after Hela and Laevastu, 1962).

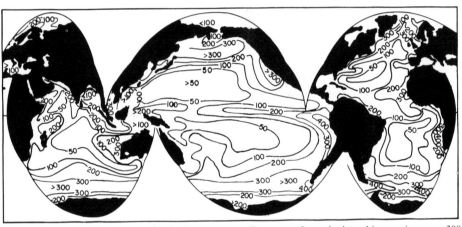

Fig. 4. Estimates of amounts of animal average standing crop of zooplankton biomass in upper 300 meters (in milligrams per cubic meter). Compare this with Fig. 3 (after Hela and Laevastu, 1962).

Part of the incident light is reflected and part is absorbed by the water and by particles other than plant cells, so that the overall efficiency is always less than the photosynthetic efficiency. Efficiencies of plant production have been computed as 0.3% in Long Island Sound and Georges Bank. If the production of animal material is also considered, a further decrease in efficiency is observed. Thus, Clarke estimates that the herbivorous zooplankton utilize about 0.015% of the incident light energy and that the efficiency of fish production is only 0.00005–0.00025%. At best, then, less than one one-thousandth of the total plant production in the sea is converted into commercial fish harvest. Only 0.1% of the production over an intensively fished area such as Georges Bank is available as food for man, and the production of vast areas of the sea is not utilized at all.

DAVID A. McGILL

References

Clarke, G. L., 1946, "Dynamics of production in a marine area," *Ecol. Monographs*, **16**, 321–335.
Clarke, G. L., 1954, "Elements of Ecology," New York, John Wiley and Sons, Inc., 534pp.
*Ryther, J. H., 1963, "Geographic Variations in Productivity," in (Hill, M. N., editor) "The Sea," Vol. 2, pp. 347–380, New York, Pergamon Press.
*Strickland, J. D. H., 1960, "Measuring the production of marine phytoplankton," *Bull. Fisheries Res. Board, Can.*, **122**, 1–172.
Cross-reference: *Planktonic Photosynthesis; Primary Production.*

FETCH

Fetch is defined either as the length of a sea surface over which a more or less constant wind direction is maintained and thus generates a wave system, or as the generating area of a given wave system. The boundaries of an area of fetch may be defined by coastlines, by frontal systems or by curvature of isobars.

The height and period of wave depend only in part on fetch, naturally, being also dependent on wind velocity and duration, i.e., the length of time over which the wind has acted.

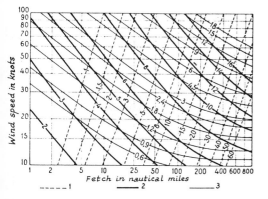

Fig. 1. Diagram for prediction of deep water wave characteristics (simplified after Bretschneider). (1) Minimum duration of wind (hours). (2) Wave period (seconds). (3) Wave height (meters). Significant height is the *maximum* height; significant period is the *mean* period.

When both duration and fetch are quite large, the wind waves in a generating area reach a fully developed stage, in which the wave heights are expressed as a definite function (amplitude spectrum of the wave) of wave periods (or wavelengths) for different wind speeds. The form of the spectrum of the fully developed wave is different according to various authors, but generally it has a maximum at a certain wave period. Both the maximum and the period of its occurrence increase with the wind speed. When either fetch or duration is limited, the waves generated consist of waves of shorter wave periods than the period of the maximum spectrum. These waves have a chaotic appearance because they have no predominant period.

After both fetch and duration exceed certain limits, the waves reach almost the equilibrium state of fully developed waves. These waves have predominant periods corresponding to the maximum spectrum. Statistical studies of wind-waves indicate that this state is reached for fetch above 300 nautical miles and for duration above 24 hours with constant wind of about 30 knots. When the wind speed is 20 or 34 knots, these limiting values become 75 nautical miles and 10 hours or 4500 nautical miles and 32 hours, respectively.

RHODES W. FAIRBRIDGE

TAKASHI ICHIYE

References

Bascom, W., 1964, "Waves and Beaches," New York, Anchor Books, Doubleday & Co., 267pp.

Bretschneider, C. L., 1952, "The generation and decay of wind waves in deep water," *Trans. Am. Geophys. Union*, **33**, 381–389.

Darbyshire, J., 1957, "Attenuation of swell in the North Atlantic Ocean," *Quart. J. Roy. Meteorol. Soc., 83*, 351–359.

Dietrich, G., 1963, "General Oceanography," New York, Interscience Publishers.

King, C. A. M., 1959, "Beaches and Coasts," London, E. Arnold Ltd., 403pp.

Kinsman, B., 1965, "Wind Waves," Englewood Cliffs, N.J., Prentice-Hall, 676pp.

Neumann, G., 1953, "An ocean wave Spectra and a new method of forecasting wind generated Sea," *Techn. Memor., No. 43, Beach Erosion Board.*

Pierson, W. J., Newman, G., and James. R. W., 1955, "Oberving and forecasting ocean waves," *H. O. Publ. No. 603 U.S. Hydrographic Office*, 284pp.

Sverdrup, H. U., and Munk, W. H., 1947, "Wind, sea and swell: Theory of relations for forecasting," *H. O. Publ. No. 601, Hydrographic Office.*

Cross-reference: *Waves.*

FIJI SEA—*See* **SOUTHWEST PACIFIC**

FIXED PLATFORMS

In contrast to cruising research vessels that travel the oceans, other vehicles for oceanographic and related research are designed to remain in a fixed position through anchoring or, in shallow water, through rigid attachment to the sea floor. These are called *fixed platforms*, and their locations, together with Weather Ship stations and geographic positions where measurements are repeatedly made, are termed *fixed oceanographic stations*. A network of such stations, comprised of unmanned anchored buoys with suspended sensing instruments, provides a synoptic coverage of oceanographic variables at less expense than ships.

Anchored buoys of varying geometric form have been used in recent years for the deployment of oceanographic instruments, mainly current meters and temperature-measuring devices. Several types are designed for meteorological observations.

The instruments operating from the buoy systems will acquire data in the following fields:

Oceanographic	Meteorological
Sea temperatures	Air temperature
Current speed	Wind speed
Current direction	Wind direction
Ambient sound	Incident radiation
Surface waves	Reflected radiation
Light intensity	Radioactivity
Turbulence	Turbulence
Water transparency	
Salinity, Tide	

Anchored Buoy Systems

Two basic systems involving the buoys and their moorings are used. The selection of either arrangement, used separately or in combination with the other, depends on the requirements of the oceanographer or meteorologist.

The first is the *slack wire* system, which consists of a float at the sea surface connected by a line to an anchor on the sea floor. Sufficient slack is left in the line (1) to avoid having the float submerge with changing tide and current and (2) to allow sufficient scope to avoid dragging of the anchor. One arrangement includes a self-contained sensor on the bottom for currents and tide. Here the sensor and the housing act as an anchor, and the buoy is merely a marker. However, the most common is a surface float that contains the power supply and recorders. Sensors may be suspended along the anchor line, either self-contained or connected with the power supply and recorders in the surface buoy (Fig. 1A). An extensive slack wire string of Savonius rotor-type meters at various depths was used in a series of buoys in the Gulf Stream.

The second is the *taut wire* mooring system in which a submerged or partially submerged float keeps the vertical line to the anchor taut and nearly vertical. This reduces the horizontal and vertical motion, and is thus advantageous for current meters and sensors in which constant depth and extraneous motions are critical. Another desirable feature is that it permits the submergence of a power supply and recorders, which may or may not be connected to a surface floating marker buoy (Fig. 1B).

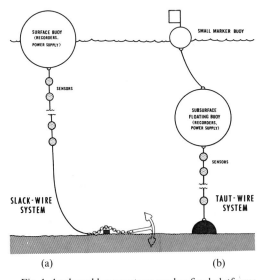

SLACK-WIRE SYSTEM

TAUT-WIRE SYSTEM

(a)   (b)

Fig. 1. Anchored buoy systems used as fixed platforms in oceanographic and meteorological work: (A) slack-wire system, (B) taut-wire system.

This system makes it less likely for the valuable instrument package float to be run down by ships or stolen; however, the float is difficult either to find or to maintain at a near-surface depth when in deep water, and the transmission of data by radio is hampered.

Germans and Russians have operated paddle-wheel-type current meters by a taut wire system with the meter buoyed up near the surface. Other combinations of slack and taut wire anchor arrangements use multiple anchors with the instrument buoy between. This allows sensors to be suspended free of the anchor lines. One disposition involves multiple buoys, which furnish stable support for a framework of instruments. The slack wire systems, easier to install, are more suitable for meteorological measurements and radio links.

Anchor Lines: In addition to wire rope, nylon and polypropylene lines are widely used for anchoring since both are very light in water and noncorrosive. Nylon is about $1\frac{1}{2}$ times stronger than polypropylene, but tends to stretch more, and both must be protected from abrasion at their connections and on the sea floor. Numerous swivels in all arrangements are needed although in some nylon lines, to reduce twisting, half of the strands are laid in one direction and half in the opposite. Chains are normally used at both ends to withstand the wear since there is a high mortality in anchored buoys through anchor line failures. A variation used by Germans in the shallow Baltic Sea consists of long connecting sections of aluminum tubing and represents a combination slack and taut wire system. The tubes are coupled by universal joints. A number of pendulum-type current meters, suspended along the tubes, record data on self-contained strip charts. There is, however, a growing utilization of electrical conductor cables, which are needed for the more sophisticated systems.

Buoys: The uses of the buoy or floats vary widely. One role of the buoys is to serve as a marker float for navigational purposes or to fix a position for repeated observation at the same location. The trend is, however, toward the storing of data in the surface buoy from all underwater sensors and their transmission by radio to a mother ship, shore base, or an earth satellite. Anchored buoys or floats are manufactured in varied sizes and shapes, including spheres, spars or cylinders, large flat "pancakes," boat hulls, etc. One toroidal or "doughnut" configuration, with a small, aluminum tripod on top serving as a frame for warning lights and meteorological instruments, has proved very successful.

Buoys which form a navigational hazard to ships and incur damage themselves when struck by ocean traffic, require flashing lights and are painted in a bright color to aid in retrieval or avoid collision. The Maritime Safety Committee has specified the required lights and markings on oceanographic buoys for identification and navigational safety, which represents recognition of their necessity. Although data are now stored within sealed containers on the buoy, and periodically gathered when batteries are recharged, the oceanographic instrument buoys of the future will telemeter data from the site. Radio frequencies, which are in use by various agencies, have not as yet been assigned specifically for use by oceanographers. This feature requires more study and planning as to the exact number and proposed location of buoys, the data to transmit, and the receiving stations. Development programs are in progress on buoy systems, but only a few anchored buoys have been successful.

Floating Instrument Platform: A sophisticated, stable, manned floating platform for oceanographic measurements is called FLIP (Floating Instrument Platform). This new vehicle is essentially a larger spar buoy 355 feet long (in its working position it has a draft of 300 feet and a laboratory 30 feet above the surface) with a circular beam of about 20 feet at the stern and a weight of about 600 tons. The buoy is narrower at the waterline ($12\frac{1}{2}$ feet) when in a vertical or working position. In the vertical position, the research laboratories, living quarters, and engine room are located on four levels above water in a cabin with roughly rectangular cross section of 14 by 25 feet. The lower deck contains, for power supply, two 60-kW diesel-driven generators mounted in trunnions to permit operation in both horizontal and vertical positions. Above this are quarters in which up to six people can live without outside support for about two weeks. The research laboratory is still higher and houses all the electronic equipment. Outside the research laboratory, approximately 30 feet above water, is an open grill control platform manned by at least two people during the flipping operations. Above this electronics space is still another laboratory, also with an outside open grill platform, in which are located two air compressors. FLIP is towed in horizontal position to the observation site where it is ballasted into a vertical position. In its working position it is remarkably stable, the vertical oscillation being less than 10% of the surface waves. This makes the vehicle suitable for a variety of hydroacoustical studies.

The French have constructed a floating platform quite similar to, though smaller than, FLIP which is also towed to the selected site where it is to be anchored. Four persons, two scientists and two crew members, can be accommodated. Observations can be conducted by descending through the main tubular body of the buoy and using the portholes situated at various depths. Fuel, fresh water, and food are supplied on a bimonthly basis by a supporting vessel. Biological, chemical, and physical studies have been conducted from this vehicle in the Mediterranean sea between Corsica and the south coast of France.

Meteorological Buoys: A variety of fixed platform buoys, usually containing vertical masts, have been designed to make meteorological observations at several levels above the sea. Some buoys have been operated close to shore with connected signal cables, others are tethered from a nearby mother ship.

The most successful type of moored buoy is the NOMAD (Navy Oceanographic Meteorological Automatic Device). See Fig. 2. This is a deep-water, slack wire system anchored with heavy lines, including chain, wire rope, nylon and polypropylene line, and a number of swivels and anchor. The float is essentially a 10-by-20-foot boat-shaped buoy containing meteorological sensors and power supply, and radio telemeters its observations. The generator is nuclear powered and designed to produce electric power for 10 years, the fuel being strontium 90. This eliminates reliance upon electrical power produced by short-life batteries. One NOMAD, started in August 1962 at a location in the Gulf of Mexico (25° 00′N, 90° 00′W), has successfully withstood two hurricanes and provided meteorological data on both storms in

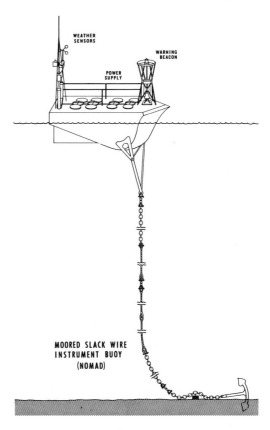

Fig. 2. Example of fixed platform for marine meteorology (Navy Oceanographic Meteorological Automatic Device).

advance of their crossing the coast. The device contains sensors for measuring the air temperature, air pressure, wind speed and direction, and surface water temperature. Data are transmitted to shore automatically at six-hour intervals, and when the wind speed reaches 33 knots, the transmission rate automatically increases to hourly intervals. The buoy is capable of running unattended for about two years. Development work is in progress with the NOMAD to add measurements of the speed and direction of the surface current and of the incoming solar radiation. Another device of this type has operated in the Bay of Bengal and several more are planned for the Atlantic and the Pacific Oceans at distances up to 1000 miles from shore.

Oceanographic Towers

The most successful fixed platforms are those attached to the sea floor. Some oil derricks, radar towers, navigational towers, and piers, though not originally designed for oceanographic research, have served as fixed platforms for the measurement of oceanographic and meteorological variables. Only a few platforms have been designed specifically for oceanographic research. A manned oceanographic tower with an adequate power supply can make possible a sophisticated variety of observations and compare favorably with oceanographic vessels. The advantages of an oceanographic tower over a ship or buoy anchored in the same location lie in the tower's stability, continuous measurements, economy, and convenience.

Stability: An important benefit from a bottom-mounted tower is stability. A ship is constantly vibrated by wind, current, wave action, or its own power plant. By contrast, a tower provides instruments such as television and motion-picture cameras with the stability in depth and orientation that is necessary for their successful application to many underwater experiments. Stability is essential for most acoustic studies and, in addition, the photographing of sea-surface and sea-floor changes by time-lapse movies. Microscopes for the study of live organisms can also function more efficiently from a fixed tower.

Long-period Measurement: An oceanographic research tower permits long-period, uninterrupted measurements to be made readily and economically. Tower instruments may be suspended in the water, mounted on the structure or sea floor, and allowed to record continuously in the instrument house. This makes possible the recording of oceanographic variables for periods of weeks or months. The tower can operate efficiently during a high sea when a research ship would find it difficult to anchor safely.

Economy: A preeminent advantage of a tower over a ship for oceanographic studies is in the economy of operation.

Convenience: Since the tower is at a permanently fixed position, and available 24 hours per day, it is possible to go "to sea" in a matter of minutes.

The most important oceanographic research tower was designed and built by the U.S. Navy Electronics Laboratory and located in the open sea about a mile off Mission Beach, California (Fig. 3). The NEL tower has a truncated pyramid shape, and its 90-foot structure is fastened to the sea floor by steel pins driven 63 feet into the ocean bottom through each of its four hollow pipe legs. The mean depth of water at the tower site is 60 feet, and the main deck is 27 feet above sea level. The upper deck, which is the strong, flat roof of the instrument house, supports meteorological instruments, a mast, and booms. The main deck, a slab of concrete 22 by 38 feet, supports the 13-by-31-foot instrument house. Below its main deck is a catwalk around all four sides to permit handling of equipment and mounting of winches. Within the instrument house are recorders, instrument racks, space heaters, a fresh-water supply, and sleeping quarters.

Electric power is supplied by underwater cable from shore. Vertical railway tracks, located on three sides of the pipe structure, are used for cars carrying various sensing instruments. A first railway track car contains two cameras, one for taking underwater motion pictures and the other for televising the water motion and biological population throughout a water column. The monitoring screen is in the instrument house.

A hydrophotometer is emplaced on a second track car for the study of light scattering and absorption. The intake of an underwater pump is mounted alongside the hydrophotometer to permit the acquisition of water samples for analysis of plankton in studies of the light properties of water. The third track car carries an acoustic transducer and hydrophone for use in sound transmission investigations, and all sensors are easily exchanged for others as required.

Three 50-foot booms from the tower support isotherm followers that automatically record the depth of isotherms. The tower boom system makes

Fig. 3. U.S. Navy Electronic Laboratory's Oceanographic Research Tower with its arrangement of instrument sensors: (1) motion picture camera, (2) anemometer, (3) 180° reflecting mirror and camera, (4) isotherm follower, (5) sound velocity sensor, (6) radioactivity sensor, (7) underwater television, movie camera and reference grid, (8) water sampling bottle, (9) underwater sampling pump and water intake, (10) bottom mounted acoustic transducer, (11) long-period wave sensor, (12) ambient light sensor, (13) remote temperature sensors, (14) tower mounted temperature sensors, (15) acoustic transducer, (16) narrow-beam vertical transducer, (17) transparency sensor, (18) surface wave sensor.

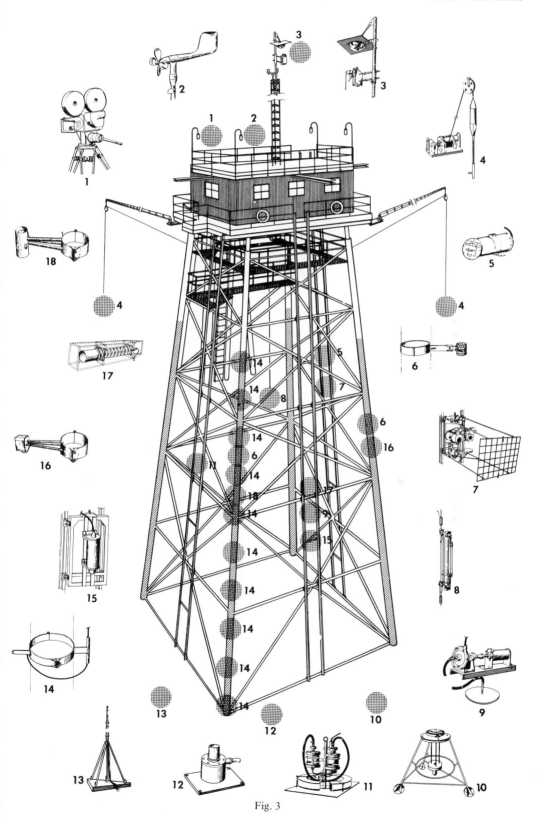

Fig. 3

possible a detailed study of internal wave speed and direction.

A unique oceanographic device on the NEL tower is a 40-foot vertical mast, which supports a convex mirror. By directing a camera into this mirror, oceanographers can photograph the surrounding ocean for an investigation of surface waves and the nature of sea surface slicks.

An oceanographic research tower of the NEL type, with stably mounted equipment either installed on the tower or on subsurface mountings a short distance away, permits a wide variety of studies. The investigations already made include radioactivity, heat conduction through the bottom, water motions, tide, fouling, corrosion, gravity waves, seiches, water chemistry, and sea floor properties. Some of the tower instruments are depicted in Fig. 3. This type of fixed platform is expected to be used widely in the future for shallow-water research.

E. C. LaFond

References

Fisher, F. H., and Spiess, 1963, "FLIP—Floating Instrument Platform," *J. Acoust. Soc. Am.*, **35**, No. 10, 1633–1644.

International Buoy Technology Symposium, Washington, 1964, "Buoy Technology," pp. 1–503.

LaFond, E. C., 1960, "Oceanographic tower," *Bur. Ships J.*, **9**, No. 4, 21–22.

UNESCO, 1964, "Fixed Oceanographic Stations of the World, 1963," pp. 1–76, Intergovernmental Oceanographic Commission.

FLOATING ICE PLATFORMS—*See* DRIFTING ICE STATIONS

FLORES SEA

(1) Limits and Oceanography

(a) **Limits and Dimensions.** The boundaries of the Flores Sea (Center: 121°E, 8°S) are formed by the southern entrance of Makassar Strait, South Sulawesi (Celebes) peninsula, Bone Gulf, a line from southeast Sulawesi to the eastern tip of Flores island across Komba volcanic island, the volcanic Lesser Sunda islands (Flores and Sumbawa), and finally by the Paternoster islands and the eastern edge of the Sunda Shelf. According to the International Hydrographic Bureau (*Sp. Publ.* 23, 1953), a more restricted, artificial limit is drawn; the western part is placed in the Java Sea and Bali Sea (the latter not a distinct oceanographic entity), and the northeastern part is taken into the Banda Sea.

The Flores Sea (*sensu lato*) occupies an area of approximately 240,000 km² (but 121,000 km² according to the International Hydrographic Bureau limits). The mean depth is about 1800 m,

with a volume of 432,000 km³ (only 222,000 km³ according to the International Hydrographic Bureau definition). It covers four regions with different bottom configurations (Fig. 1). Most western is a broad bank, a submerged plateau with depths less than 1000 m and generally being around − 500 m. Atolls are common on its submarine elevations, like the Paternoster and Postiljon islands. This bank has two deep channels, one near the Sunda Shelf boundary in the southwest and the other off the coast of South Sulawesi. These channels connect the deeper parts of the Flores Trough with Makassar Strait.

The second subdivision comprises the deep, central Flores Trough, which is elongate, below the 3000 m isobath, with irregular bottom relief and gently sloping sides, and attaining a maximum depth of 5140 m.

The third region consists of two parallel ridges with an intervening depression striking from South Sulawesi southward till they reach the Flores Trough, whence they bend eastward. Of the two ridges the westernmost one bears Salajar Island and other islands including Bonerate. The second ridge starts with a barrier reef off the east coast of South Sulawesi and runs through the Tijger coral island group, beyond which it joins the coral-crowned elevations in the east end of the Flores Trough. Both ridges have moderate steep sides, but they show a particular steep slope off the east coast of Salajar Island where the Salajar Trough is located (− 3370 m).

The easternmost portion of the Flores Sea covers the area south of the Bone Gulf and it merges into the Banda Sea north of Komba Island. The Flores Sea is separated from the Bone Gulf by two broad-topped submarine elevations bearing several coral islands.

Most of the data in the following tables have been compiled from reports of the *Snellius* oceanographic Expedition of 1929–1930 (Van Riel *et al.*, 1950 and others).

(b) **Deep Water Properties and Flow of Bottom Water.** From an analysis of the deep water properties combined with the bathymetrical data of the Flores Sea, the *Snellius* Expedition found that the Flores Trough is replenished by the deeper water from the Pacific Ocean along a route through the Molucca, North Banda and South Banda depressions (Figs. 2 and 3). In the various depressions along the path of this flow of bottom water, the oxygen content characteristically diminishes (see Table 2).

(c) **Surface Properties and Meteorology.** Surface salinities in the Flores Sea range between 34.0 and 34.6‰ from June through November. Lower values have been recorded for December through May: 32.0‰ in the northwest and 33.8‰ in the southeast (Fig. 4).

Sea surface temperatures are lowest in August

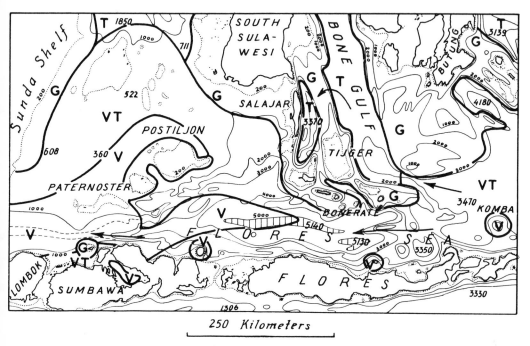

Fig. 1. The Flores Sea, eastern Indonesia. Map shows bathymetry (shading indicates depths lower than 5000 m), flow of bottom water (arrows) and bottom sediments. (T) terrigenous mud; (G) globigerina ooze; (VT) volcanic and terrigenous mud; (V) volcanic mud (data from the *Snellius* Expedition, 1929–30).

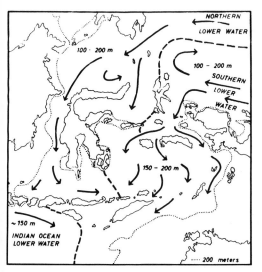

Fig. 2. Movement patterns of 100–200 m waters in the East Indian Archipelago, showing mixing in the eastern Flores Sea (prepared by Wyrtki, 1961).

Fig. 3. Movement patterns of deep 1000–1500 m waters into the Flores Sea (Wyrtki, 1961).

and September (25.9°C) and highest in November (28.8°C) (Fig. 5).

In the southern winter, the wind blows from the southeast at 2.5–4.4 (Beaufort scale), whereas during the southern summer, the wind is weaker (1.5–2.4) and comes from the west. For the same

periods, the air pressures are 757 and 758–758.5 mm, respectively.

(d) **Currents and Tides.** Surface currents during the southern winter are toward south of west at 10–15 knots. During the southern summer, the direction is reversed at rates of 5–10 knots in the western half of the Flores Sea and 10–15 knots in its eastern part. At Bima (Sumbawa) the tidal range is 1.6 m.

At the *Snellius* station No. 317a in the eastern part of the Flores Sea (see position on Fig. 6), current measurements at depth were carried out on August 21 through 24, 1930 (Table 4).

(2) Bottom Sediments

The broad, almost featureless bank in the western part of the Flores Sea appears from *Snellius* Expedition data to be covered by volcanic and terrigenous muds except for three zones. Two of these zones correspond to the deeper passages

TABLE 1

Depression	Limiting Isobath (m)	Area (km²)	Sill Depth (m)	Maximum Depth (m)
Salajar Trough	2000	4000	1350	3370
Flores Trough	3000	30,000	2450	5140

TABLE 2

	Oxygen Content (cc/liter)
Morotai Basin ⎫	3.06
Ternate Trough ⎬ Molucca Sea	3.04
Batjan Basin ⎭	2.63
Buru Basin—Ceram Sea	2.52
North Banda Basin ⎱ Banda Sea	2.50
South Banda Basin ⎰	2.45
Flores Trough—Flores Sea	2.28

between the Flores Trough and Makassar Strait and are marked by globigerina ooze (more than 30% calcium carbonate). The third zone extends from the central Bali Basin northward along the west side of the Paternoster and Postiljon islands and consists of volcanic mud. Volcanic mud also forms the bottom of the west end of the Flores Trough. Terrigenous mud covers the Bone Basin and the Salajar Trough, while the adjacent elevations above the 2000 m isobath have globigerina ooze. Coralline mud and sand are confined to the surroundings of coral islands. The remainder of the Flores Sea bottom consists of volcanic and terrigenous muds. Volcanic mud predominates near the volcanoes. The ash of the Tambora eruption of 1815 forms an excellent key bed in the cores.

The absence of red deep-sea clay in the deeper parts of the Flores Trough has been ascribed to the insufficient amount of oxygen for the oxidation of the terrigenous mud. The low oxygen content is due to the presence of sills between the Flores Sea and the open oceans, which prevent deep oxygenated ocean waters from entering the Flores Trough.

Neeb (1943) found 20–150 mm of blue mud over the Tambora ash, which is marked by six-sided, brown biotite crystals in the samples collected in 1930. The average rate of sedimentation is 75 cm/1000 yr for the terrigenous mud in the Flores Sea, which is about 40 times higher than the rate recorded in the equatorial Atlantic Ocean (0.9–3.3 cm/1000 yr). The sedimentation rate of globigerina ooze, however, is 1 cm/1000 yr which is similar to the rate in the Atlantic Ocean (0.5–2 cm/1000 yr).

TABLE 3. DEEP WATER PROPERTIES OF THE FLORES SEA AND THOSE OF THE WATER OUTSIDE THE SILL OF THE FLORES TROUGH

Properties measured at the indicated *Snellius* Stations and depths	Temperature (C)	Salinity (‰)	Oxygen (cc/liter)	Density
Sill at No. 194, 2658 m	3.08	34.62	2.33	1027.595
Flores Trough at No. 197, 5100 m	3.505	34.60	2.28	1027.54
Salajar Trough at No. 196, 2183 m	3.22	34.60	2.31	1027.57

TABLE 4. CURRENT MEASUREMENTS AT SNELLIUS STATION No. 317a

Observation Depth (m)	Strength (cm/sec)	Direction
0	15	N 23° E
25–75	22	N 30° E
125–300	38	N 88° E
600	11	S 40° E
1000	2	N 85° W
1500	5	S 84° E
2000	3	S 27° W

The heavy rate of terrigenous deposition in the Flores Trough, as well as in other East Indonesian deep-sea depressions, has been ascribed to the contemporary orogenic activity in this part of the world, accentuating the relief. Moreover, submarine slumping on oversteepened slopes has accelerated the sedimentation from time to time.

(3) Geophysics and Geological Structure

The deepest earthquake foci in Indonesia are located below the Flores Sea. The maximum depth recorded is 720 km (see Fig. 6). Traverses southward across the Lesser Sunda islands and eastward across the Aru Trough indicate that the epicenters decrease in depth. Several theories have been advanced to explain this phenomenon, e.g., by Berlage and Vening Meinesz (see Van Bemmelen, 1949).

The Flores Sea is marked by positive anomalies of gravity amounting to 50 mgal. Higher values are found in a wide belt extending from the Bone Gulf across the east end of the Flores Trough into the

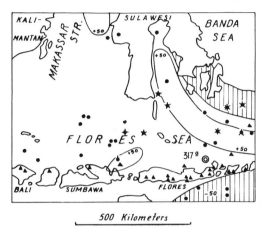

Fig. 6. The Flores Sea, eastern Indonesia. Gravimetry (shading indicates the belt of negative anomalies; positive anomalies of 50 mgal and more are also delineated), active volcanoes (triangles) and earthquake foci (dots: less than 100-km depth; with one hachure: 100–199 km; with two hachures: 200–299 km, etc.). Double circles indicate current recording station 317a of the *Snellius* Expedition.

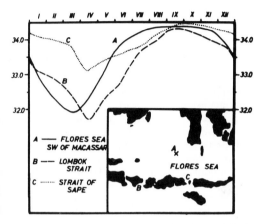

Fig. 4. Average annual variation of surface salinity in the Flores Sea (Wyrtki, 1961).

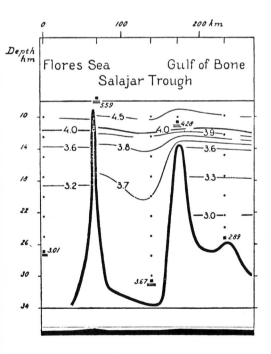

Fig. 5. Section from Gulf of Bone to Flores Sea along Salajar trough showing potential temperature and salinity. Lower profile indicates true scale (after Van Riel, *Snellius* Expedition).

central part of the South Banda Basin. The volcanoes of the Lesser Sunda islands forming the southern border of the sea are of the orogenic ("Pacific" or andesitic) type with an explosivity index of 99.

On account of its morphology and its parallelism to the Lesser Sunda geanticline, the Flores Trough has been interpreted to represent downwarping. The scarp-like margins of the Salajar Trough, its straight outlines, and the presence of essentially flat lying, elevated coral reefs on the adjacent Salajar Island are evidence for block-faulting.

Geological evidence indicates a late Tertiary or younger origin for the Flores and Salajar troughs, by downfaulting and subsidence of the quasi-cratonic (former continental) crust. The facts may be summarized as follows: (1) cutting off of Miocene folds by the coastline on Butung Island; (2) parallelism of the Flores Trough with the Tertiary folds in the Lesser Sunda islands; the Flores Trough appears to be a young revived miogeosyncline; (3) high frequency of seismicity and volcanism in the Lesser Sunda belt; (4) elevated Plio-Pleistocene coral reef terraces on the adjacent islands (up to heights of 550 m in East Flores); (5) atolls rising steeply from submerged plateaus, from depths which are clearly too deep for coral growth, e.g., Tijger Atoll in the Flores Sea stands on a submarine ridge more than 2000 m deep; (6) the thick series of Tertiary non-volcanic, clastic sediments on islands surrounded by deep sea which require diastrophic movements for their formation (Kuenen, 1950).

H. D. TJIA

References

*Kuenen, Ph. H., 1950, "Marine Geology," Ch. 3, pp. 175–209, New York, John Wiley & Sons.

*Neeb, G. A., 1943, "The *Snellius* Expedition: Bottom Samples; the Composition and Distribution of the Samples," Vol. 5, Part 3, Section 2, pp. 55–268, Leiden, Brill.

*Van Bemmelen, R. W., 1949, "The Geology of Indonesia; General Geology," Vol. 1A, pp. 257–297, The Hague, Martinus Nijhoff.

*Van Riel, P. M., Hamaker, H. C., and Van Eyck, L., 1950, "The *Snellius* Expedition; Tables. Serial and Bottom Observations. Temperature, Salinity and Density," Vol. 2, Part 6, pp. 1–44, Leiden, Brill.

Wyrtki, K., 1961, "Physical oceanography of the southeast Asian waters," *Scripps Inst. Oceanogr., Repts. Naga Exped.*, **2**.

FLORIDA BAY: A MODERN SITE OF LIME-STONE FORMATION

Introduction

Florida Bay, located at the southern tip of Florida, has been of special interest to the geological scientist since the late nineteenth century when it became generally known that "limy" sediments were forming in this shallow-water tropical embayment. Interest arose because detailed studies of the neritic calcareous deposits (otherwise rather

rare today) would afford a better understanding of the depositional environment of their lithified counterpart, limestone. Limestone is substantially composed of calcium carbonate in the form of the mineral calcite and is a much-studied fossiliferous rock type, of particular interest to oil geologists, that probably forms slightly more than 20% of the sedimentary rocks (a volume amounting to about 30×10^7 km^3 or 7×10^7 cubic miles) of the lithosphere.

Important papers on the calcareous sediments of Florida Bay have been written by Thorp (1936, 1939), Ginsburg (1956, 1957), Stehli and Hower (1961), Fleece (1962), Gorsline (1963), and Taft and Harbaugh (1964).

Physical Setting

Florida Bay is a triangular-shaped embayment lying immediately south of the Florida peninsula (Fig. 1). A curved archipelago of elongate islands, the Florida Keys, on which are exposed Late Pleistocene (last interglacial) coral reefs of the Key Largo Limestone, forms the eastern and southeastern boundaries of the bay. To the west, the bay is open and faces the Gulf of Mexico; this side is conveniently limited by longitude 81° 05′W. The average depth over the central part is between 4 and 5 feet; the bay as defined above occupies an area of about 841 square miles (Table 1).

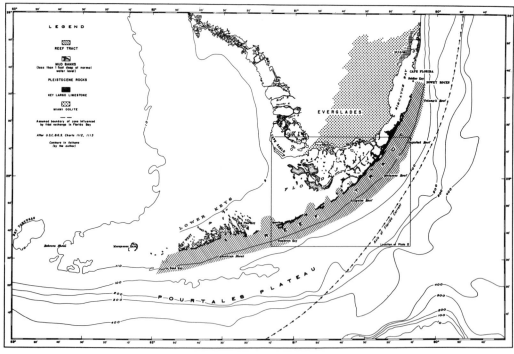

Fig. 1. Index map of southern Florida and Florida Bay (after Ginsburg, 1956). Cross-hatched region designated "reef tract" is an area of modern coral reef formation lying seaward of the Florida Keys, an archipelago of exposed Late Pleistocene coral reef (Key Largo Limestone) forming the southeastern margin of Florida Bay.

TABLE 1. MAJOR PHYSIOGRAPHIC ELEMENTS OF FLORIDA BAY

	Area		% of Total Area	Number in Bay
	(sq miles)	(sq km)		
Key (islands)	26	67	3	approx. 105
Mud banks (including keys)[a]	192	496	23	
Intra-bay lakes[b]	406	1050	48	approx. 17
Florida Bay[c]	598	1546	74	
Florida Bay[d]	841	2179	100	

[a] Areas of bay having depth less than 2 ft.
[b] Areas of bay 2–7 ft deep and essentially surrounded by mud banks.
[c] Area if western boundary is taken along outer edge of westernmost banks.
[d] Area if western boundary of bay is taken at longitude 81° 05′W.

The most characteristic feature of Florida Bay is an anastomosing array of shallow mud banks composed of shelly calcareous silts that cordon the bay into a lacework of interconnected shallow basins referred to as "lakes" (Fig. 2). The lakes are typically 5–6 feet deep, 3–4 miles long, and 2–3 miles wide, and except for a thin veneer of sandy calcareous sediment, they overlie a nearly flat limestone surface composed of the Miami Oolite of Late Pleistocene age. The tops of the banks are partially exposed at times of low water; however, portions of many of them rise about 0.5 foot above the average bay level to form mangrove-crested or fringed keys (islands). The inner or eastern banks are sinuous and chain-like; they are narrow, about 0.5 mile across, and more keys rise from them than from the much broader (1–3 miles) amoeba-shaped banks along the western or open side of the bay.

Based on radiocarbon dates, calcareous sediments began to accumulate over 4000 years ago when the Flandrian transgression (rise in sea level

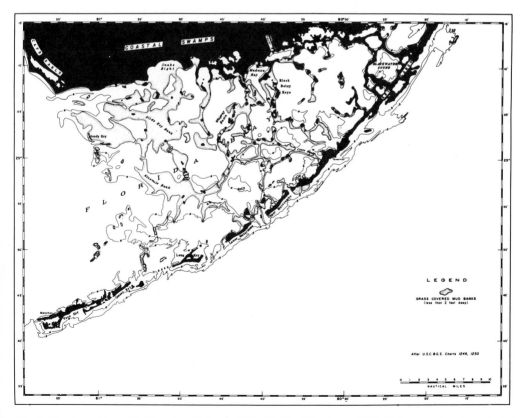

Fig. 2. Physiographic and bathymetric features of Florida Bay (Ginsburg, 1956). Bottom contours read in feet below mean low water.

TABLE 2. ENVIRONMENTAL PARAMETERS OF FLORIDA BAY

	Yearly Average	Range
Rainfall[a]	41 in.	21–83 in.
Evaporation (estimated)[a]	60–70 in.	
Air temperature[a]	75°F; 24°C	34–94°F; 1–34°C
Water temperature[b]		59–104°F; 15–40°C
Water salinity		
Northwest corner of bay[a]	39‰	20–70‰
Bay in general[b,c]		10–70‰
Current velocities[b,c]		
In passes between Florida Keys		3–4 knots setting NW or SE
Within intra-bay lakes	Few hundredths of a knot, counterclockwise rotation	
Turbidity (after two days of 10–20 knot winds)[b]		
Surface water		11.0–17.1 mg/liter
1.5 ft above bottom (depth about 4 ft)		9.4–17.6 mg/liter
Tidal range [b,d]		
Vicinity of Cape Sable		2.9 ft
Along inner (bayside) margin of Florida Keys		0.3 ft
Interior sub-environment of bay		< 0.2 ft

[a]Tabb, Durbrow, and Manning, 1962.
[b]Ginsburg, 1956.
[c]Gorsline, 1963.
[d]U.S. Coast and Geodetic tide tables.

that accompanied the melting of the last continental ice sheets) flooded the area of Florida Bay. Bank formation probably began early in the history of the bay, presumably in areas where slack water was produced by converging currents. As the bay evolved, the banks grew upward and outward to their present configuration; colonization of the banks by marine grasses and mangroves must also have contributed to their stability. The keys that crown the banks may not have developed in their present form until about 3000 years ago when the rate of filling decreased considerably. The keys are evidently built up above the average level of the bay during storm surges, when the water in the bay may deepen by 3–4 feet.

Since the bay was formed, approximately 1.5×10^9 cubic meters of calcareous sediment have accumulated. Over the banks and their slopes, the average sedimentation rate has been about 6 $g/cm^2/100$ yr. Because most of the banks are about 6 feet thick, the average maximum sedimentation rate over them can also be expressed as 0.15 ft/100 yr (.04 mm/yr), if a slight amount of compaction is neglected.

Environmental Factors

Florida Bay can be divided into two sub-environments, the interior and the marginal (Ginsburg, 1956). The interior sub-environment is characterized by a low tidal range, less than 0.2 foot, weak currents and a large seasonal variation in water salinity and temperature. The surrounding marginal sub-environment is one of more uniform water characteristics and stronger water motion because of good tidal exchange with the Gulf of Mexico and the Atlantic Ocean. A dashed line on Fig. 1 approximately delineates the two sub-environments.

A tropical wet-and-dry climate prevails over southern Florida and Florida Bay. This climate is characterized by a long dry season, lasting from mid-fall to late spring, and by an intense rainy period during the summer and early fall months. Precipitation is approximately 40 in./yr with about 70% of this falling during the rainy season. Evaporation probably exceeds rainfall by a factor of 1.5 (Table 2).

During the rainy season, water salinity in the interior sub-environment may fall as low as 10–15‰ (parts per thousand, i.e., weight of dissolved salts in grams per kilogram of bay water) owing primarily to the influx of runoff from the extensive fresh-water swamps (the Everglades) which overlie southern Florida. Water salinity during the dry season is typically 35–40‰; however, over the shallowly submerged mud banks, excessive evaporation during spring months may raise salinity values to 70‰, twice that of typical seawater for this region (Table 2). During years of normal rainfall, water salinity throughout the outer parts of the marginal sub-environment stays near 35–36‰ owing to good tidal exchange with adjacent oceanic and gulf water masses.

Water temperature within the interior sub-environment changes markedly with the seasons and ranges from 15–40°C. Sudden temperature changes accompany strong winds that thoroughly mix and muddy the water of the shallow intra-bay lakes (Table 2).

Owing to the baffling effect of the mud banks, water circulation in Florida Bay is very complex. Tidal and wind-stress currents are weak owing to this baffling and also to the shallowness of the bay, which appreciably dampens the height of the tidal wave as it sweeps northwestwardly across the bay. Based on hydrographic data, Gorsline (1963) computed a weak counterclockwise rotation (Table 2) for the water mass within several of the lakes. Strong tidal currents of several knots, however, carry water into the bay from the Atlantic through between-island passes separating the Florida Keys.

Fauna and Flora

The bottom fauna in Florida Bay is dominated by mollusks (at least 100 genera are known) and to a far lesser extent by Foraminifera, especially large tropical forms (Table 3). The flora is predominantly turtle grass, *Thalassia testudium*, a true marine phanerogam or seed producing plant. Turtle grass thrives on the shallow mud banks, and its root system may be instrumental in their stabilization. Calcified or partially calcified green algae, principally species of *Halimeda* and *Penicillus*, are common in current-swept areas near the Florida Keys. Small corals also thrive in these areas.

Unconsolidated Calcareous Sediments

Texture. Unconsolidated sediments in Florida Bay are typically more than 90% composed of calcium carbonate; the remainder primarily comprises quartz, opal (as tests of Radiolaria and as sponge spicules), and disseminated and fibrous organic matter. The grain size of the calcareous matter ranges from large mollusk or coral fragments, measuring several centimeters or more in length, to ultrafine particles less than 1 μ in greatest dimension. The mud banks are approximately 30% (by weight) composed of sand-size (larger than 0.062 mm) carbonate particles, 48% silt- and clay-size constituents (0.062–0.001 mm) and 22% subclay-size particles (less than 0.001 mm or 1μ). The average median grain size is close

to 0.028 mm, which means the average bank sediment is a medium silt (Table 4). In lithified form (as limestone), these sediments would be classified as fossiliferous calcilutites or as biomicrites.

Ginsburg (1956) determined that for particles larger than 0.125 mm, 76% are derived from mollusks and 11% from Foraminifera. Under the microscope, virtually all of the calcareous matter down to a size of 0.020 mm can also be recognized as skeletal in origin, i.e., derived from calcified parts of plants and animals (Taft and Harbaugh, 1964). Fragmentation of coarse skeletal parts to particles as small as 20μ may to some extent be accomplished by physical abrasion, but doubtless sediment-ingesting and sediment-burrowing organisms account for much of the comminution (Ginsburg, 1957). Interestingly, some sediment-ingesting organisms also increase the grain size of the calcareous muds by aggregating fine-grained matter, during the digestive process, into firm ellipsoidal fecal pellets. The pellets are up to several millimeters in length and may constitute as much as 50% of the sediment. The origin of calcareous grains smaller than 0.020 mm is much debated; this problem is largely centered around the precipitation of minute needles of aragonite, which form a substantial proportion of particles less than 0.010 mm in length.

Mineralogy. Four minerals form the calcareous fraction of silty muds in Florida Bay: aragonite, high-magnesian calcite, low-magnesian calcite, and dolomite, listed here in their order of abundance (Table 4).

Aragonite is composed of calcium carbonate and crystallizes in the orthorhombic system; this mineral is an unstable polymorph of calcium carbonate and converts to calcite (perhaps even dolomite) during some phase of limestone formation. In Florida Bay, aragonite forms about 65% of the sediment and is primarily contributed by mollusks (Tables 3 and 4). Most of the aragonite

TABLE 3. IMPORTANT ANIMAL AND PLANT GENERA THAT CONTRIBUTE CALCIUM CARBONATE TO SEDIMENTS IN FLORIDA BAY[a]

Animals			Plants
Mollusks	Corals[b]	Foraminifera	Green Algae[b]
Anomalocardia	Porites	Archaias	Halimeda
Bulla	Siderastrea	Peneroplis	Penicillus
Brachidontes		Quinqueloculina	Udotea
Cerithium			
Chione			
Modulus			
Pinctada			
Tellina			

[a]Data are from Thorp (1936 and 1939) and Ginsburg (1956).
[b]Common only in vicinity of Florida Keys and in tidal channels.

TABLE 4. PHYSICAL, MINERALOGICAL AND CHEMICAL CHARACTERISTICS OF
SEDIMENTS IN FLORIDA BAY

	Western Florida Bay		Eastern Florida Bay	
Mass properties	Average[a]		Average[b]	
Water content (dry weight basis), %	71.5			
Porosity, %	65.9			
Grain density, g/cc	2.71			
Bulk density, g/cc	1.58			
Grain size distribution				
Median diameter, mm	0.028		0.025	
Trask sorting coefficient	6.81			
	Average[c]	Range[c]	Average[d]	Range[d]
Wt % > 0.125 mm (sand)			51	15–90
Wt % > 0.062 mm (sand)	30	1–52		
Wt % < 0.062–0.001 mm (silt-clay)	48	9–70		
Wt % < 0.001 mm (subclay)	22	5–50		
Carbonate mineralogy	Subsurface and surface sediments[c]		Surface sediment[c]	
	Average	Range	Average	Range
% aragonite	59	35–77	46	20–78
% high-Mg calcite	27	3–54	37	0–51
% low-Mg calcite	14	1–29	17	4–80
	Surface sediment[c]		Surface sediment[e]	
	Average	Range	Average	Range
% aragonite	59	41–70	67	40–100
% high-Mg calcite	26	10–47	19	0–39
% low-Mg calcite	15	10–20	16	0–44
General sediment chemistry	Average[c]	Range[c]	Average[e]	Range[e]
Ca/Mg	25	6–41		
$Sr/Ca \times 10^3$	8.7	6.3–11.7		
% Sr			0.42	0.20–0.64
% Mg			1.4	0.06–4.1
% Mn			0.006	0.0005–0.04
% Ba			0.002	0.001–0.004
	Average[a]	Range[a]	Average[b]	
% calcareous minerals	87	81–90		
% non calcareous minerals	9	8–13		
% organic matter	4	2–6	6.2	
% organic carbon	2.1	1.3–3.7	3.5	
% organic nitrogen	0.15	0.29–0.09	0.1	
Organic carbon/organic nitrogen	17	13–26	27.5	

[a] Previously unpublished data (from author's files) based on entire thickness, up to 5 ft, of bank sediments.
[b] Fleece (1962).
[c] Taft and Harbaugh (1964).
[d] Ginsburgh (1956).
[e] Stehli and Hower (1961).

occurs as aggregates of light-brown crystals, but a small amount consists of acicular needles generally less than 0.010 mm in length (Taft and Harbaugh, 1964). Aragonite needles are found in the sediments of other shallow tropical seas as well, especially in those of the neighboring Bahaman platform. Initially, denitrifying bacteria living in the bottom mud were thought to bring about precipitation of the needles. Subsequently it was thought that loss of carbon dioxide, either through high photosynthetic activity of marine plants or by evasion of the gas produced by evaporation or solar heating, prompts precipitation of aragonite from supersaturated water. Most recently aragonitic skeletal rods found in partially calcified green algae, especially species of *Penicillus*, have been considered the source of the aragonite needles. A thorough discussion of these ideas and of the physical chemistry involved in precipitating calcium carbonate in the metastable aragonite form is given by Cloud (1962).

High-magnesian calcite is calcite with more than

4%, and up to about 19%, randomly substituted $MgCO_3$ in the lattice of this hexagonal mineral. High-magnesian calcite constitutes 20–30% of the mud banks and occurs as microcrystalline aggregates of light-brown crystals similar to the aragonite aggregates (Taft and Harbaugh, 1964). Like aragonite, high-magnesian calcite is metastable and during some phase of limestone formation converts to low-magnesian calcite or dolomite. Calcite containing large amounts of magnesium is undoubtedly derived mostly from Foraminifera, especially the species *Peneroplis proteus* and *Archais angulatus*. Other organisms, both plant and animal, supply secondary amounts of high-magnesian calcite to the sediments of Florida Bay.

Only about 15% of the deposits of Florida Bay is composed of low-magnesian calcite (essentially common calcite), the stable hexagonal polymorph of calcium carbonate. The bulk of this mineral is derived from mollusks. However, some of the low-magnesian calcite occurs as colorless transparent hexagonal prisms less than 0.062 mm in length; the source of these prisms is not fully known. Prisms of low-magnesian calcite are typically pitted and etched, and the impression is gained that they are undergoing solution (Taft and Harbaugh, 1964). Crystals of aragonite and high-magnesian calcite do not show this effect. This is paradoxical because at ambient earth temperature and pressures, thermodynamic calculations predict and experiments show that low-magnesian calcite is the least soluble of the three.

Dolomite is a stable double-carbonate mineral bearing equal atomic amounts of calcium and magnesium; this mineral crystallizes in the hexagonal system typically as unit rhombohedrons. Dolomite accounts for a maximum of about 5% of most sediments in Florida Bay. This mineral, a subject of intense research, was not found in the bay until 1961 (Taft and Harbaugh, 1964). Within the bay, dolomite occurs as vitreous rhomboid crystals measuring less than 0.062 mm across; they commonly have a dark central area.

Implicit in the foregoing discussion is the fact that the calcareous silts of Florida Bay are 80–85% composed of metastable carbonate minerals (aragonite and high-magnesian calcite) that will convert to calcite or dolomite during some phase of limestone formation. The obvious question to ask, therefore, is how soon and under what conditions will the transformation take place? Stehli and Hower (1961) have shown that exposures of the young (about 100,000 year-old) Miami Oolite and Key Largo Formations, which immediately underlie the sediments of the bay, contain little to no high-magnesian calcite and moderate to low concentrations of aragonite (typically less than 17%). Because both limestone units contain fossils that were originally substantially composed of these minerals, it is obvious that relatively early

post-depositional (diagenetic) changes have induced conversion of these minerals to low-magnesian calcite. Two studies of unconsolidated bank sediments in Florida Bay have shown that little if any diagenetic mineral transformation has occurred since calcareous sediments began to accumulate in the bay approximately 4000 years ago (Ginsburg, 1957; Taft and Harbaugh, 1964). However, Fleece (1962) believes he has detected a significant loss of high-magnesian calcite and some aragonite in sediments about 4000 years old which immediately overlie bedrock at the base of mud banks in eastern Florida Bay. The general consensus, nonetheless, is that Recent aragonite and high-magnesian calcite are "stable" within the environmental framework of Florida Bay. Conversion of these minerals to low-magnesian calcite and/or dolomite must probably await a pronounced change in this environment—for example, the marked change in interstitial water chemistry that would accompany subaerial exposure of the sediments of Florida Bay.

Value of Shallow-water Carbonate Studies

The results of sedimentological research on calcareous deposits in Florida Bay and over the nearby Bahaman platform have in many ways enhanced our ability to reconstruct the amalgam of physical, chemical and biological processes that created limestones in the past. A number of papers incorporating some of these results are collected in a publication edited by Bass and Sharps (1963). Considering the number of symposia on carbonate sediments that have been held within the last several years, there is little doubt that scientific interest in limestone formation and diagenesis will continue in the future. Florida Bay will continue to be a focal point of this interest because it is one of our most readily accessible natural laboratories for the investigation of shallow-water carbonate sedimentation and carbonate mineralization.

DAVID W. SCHOLL

References

Bass, R. O., and Sharps, S. L., 1963 (editors), Symposium on Shelf Carbonates of the Paradox Basin, Four Corners Geological Society, Denver, Colo., 273pp.

*Cloud, P. E., 1962, "Environment of calcium carbonate deposition west of Andros Island, Bahamas, *U.S. Geol. Survey Profess. Papers*, **350**, 138pp.

*Fleece, J. B., 1962, "The Carbonate Geochemistry and Sedimentology of the Keys of Florida Bay, Florida," Unpublished M. S. Thesis in Geology, Florida State University, Tallahassee, Florida, 112pp. (available as report to U.S. Office of Naval Research, Sedimentological Res. Lab., Dept. Geol.).

*Ginsburg, R. N., 1956, "Environmental relationships of grain size and constituent particles in some south Florida carbonate sediments," *Bull. Am. Assoc. Petrol. Geologists*, **40**, 2384–2427.

Ginsburg, R. N., 1957, "Early diagenesis and lithification of shallow-water carbonate sediments in south
Florida," in (Le Blanc, R. J., and Breeding, J. G.,
editors) "Regional aspects of carbonate deposition,"
Soc. Econ. Paleontologists Mineralogists Spec. Publ.,
5, 80–100.

Gorsline, D. S., 1963, "Environments of Carbonate
Deposition Florida Bay and the Florida Straits," in
(Bass, R. O., and Sharps, S. L., editors) Symposium
on Shelf Carbonates of the Pardox Basin, pp. 130–
143, Four Corners Geological Society, Denver, Colo.,
273pp.

Stehli, F. G., and Hower, J., 1961, "Mineralogy and
early diagenesis of carbonate sediments," *J. Sediment.
Petrol.*, **31**, 358–371.

Tabb, D. C., Dubrow, D. L., and Manning, R. B.,
1962, "The ecology of northern Florida Bay and
adjacent estuaries," *State of Florida Board of Conservation Technical Series*, **39**, 81pp. (Tallahassee,
Florida).

*Taft, W. H., and Harbaugh, J. W., 1964, "Modern
carbonate sediments of southern Florida, Bahamas
and Espiritu Santo Island, Baja, California; a comparison of their mineralogy and chemistry," *Stanford
Univ. Publ. Univ. Ser. Geol. Sci.*, **8**, No. 2.

*Thorp, E. M., 1936, "Calcareous shallow-water
marine deposits of Florida and the Bahamas,"
Carnegie Inst. Wash. Publ., **452**, *Papers Tortugas
Lab.*, **29**, 37–119.

*Thorp, E. M., 1937, "Florida and Bahama Marine
Calcareous Deposits," in (Trask, P. D., editor)
"Recent Marine Sediments," pp. 283–297, Amer.
Assoc. Petroleum Geologists, Tulsa, Oklahoma,
736pp.

FLOW—*See* FLUID MECHANICS

FLUID MECHANICS

(1) Scope of Fluid Mechanics

Fluid mechanics is the science dealing with the
behavior of liquids, gases and vapors at rest and in
motion. Branches of fluid mechanics include:

(a) *Hydraulics* which deals with liquids, usually
water, and includes applications to water supply,
water power, irrigation, flood control, and hydraulic
machinery.

(b) *Hydrodynamics* which refers to the mathematical theory of the motion of ideal, inviscid
fluids. It is useful in the theories of wave motion,
wind theory, and groundwater flow, for example.

(c) *Aerodynamics* which deals with compressible
fluids (gases) and considers such applications as
aircraft, missiles, jet engines, atmospheric motions,
and shock waves.

Other phenomena included in fluid mechanics are
acoustics, turbulence, lift, drag, lubrication, flow in
rivers and canals, ocean currents, jets, boundary
layer theory, cavitation and magnetohydrodynamics
(see Streeter, 1961, for references). All of these subdivisions are based on the same principles of fluid
mechanics, but the particular phenomena and
vocabulary involved plus the necessary admixture
of empirical information often obscure the underlying unity.

(2) Classification of Fluids

(a) A *fluid* is a substance which deforms continuously as long as any shearing stress is exerted
on it.

(b) *Liquid* and *vapor:* If a fluid can exist in two
different density states at a given temperature and
pressure, the more dense state is called the *liquid*
and the less dense state is called the *vapor*.

(c) *Gas:* A fluid is said to be a *gas* at a given
temperature if the density varies continuously with
pressure at this temperature.

Gases and vapors are usually much more compressible than liquids. In most applications, the
variation of density of a liquid is negligible but may
be important as in acoustics and thermal convection
currents. Gases and vapors also may be treated as
compressible or incompressible depending on the
variation of density involved.

(3) Properties of Fluids

Fluid mechanics usually ignores microscopic or
molecular structure and deals in terms of bulk or
macroscopic properties. Definitions and units (English and cgs) of properties of interest are:

(a) *Density*, ρ. The mass per unit volume, slug/ft^3,
g/cm^3.

(b) *Specific weight*, γ. The gravitational force per
unit volume of fluid, lb/ft^3, dyne/cm^3. Note $\gamma = \rho g$
where g is the gravitational acceleration, ft/sec^2,
cm/sec^2.

(c) *Viscosity*, μ. Also called *absolute or dynamic
viscosity*. The ratio of shear stress to the rate of
shearing strain it produces, lb sec/ft^2, dyne sec/cm^2.
Other units of viscosity are the *poise* defined equal
to 1 dyne sec/cm^2 and the *centipoise* equal to 0.01
poise.

If μ is constant so that the relation of shear stress
to shearing strain rate is linear, the fluid is called
Newtonian; if this relation is nonlinear, the fluid is
called *non-Newtonian* (see Wilkinson, 1960). Most
fluids may be regarded as Newtonian for practical
purposes.

In general, the viscosity is defined in tensor equations (see Aris, 1962). The viscosity μ is associated
with deformational motions, but there may also be
a second coefficient of viscosity which is associated
with expansion or compression. By the so-called
Stokes assumption, this second coefficient is usually
taken to be zero which is satisfactory in most
applications.

(d) *Surface tension*, σ. The apparent tension in the
surface of a liquid, lb/ft, dyne/cm. The surface tension
of a liquid is due to molecular attractions and produces a pressure difference across the surface equal
to $\sigma(1/R_1 + 1/R_2)$ where R_1 and R_2 are the two
principal radii of curvature of the surface.

(f) *Bulk modulus, E_b*. The eleastic modulus of a
liquid in hydrostatic compression, lb/ft^2, dyne/cm^2.

(g) *Equation of state.* A relation between pressure,
density and temperature characteristic of a gas or

liquid. For most cases, the equation of state of an *ideal gas* is satisfactory: $p = \rho RT$, where p is pressure, T the absolute temperature, and R is a gas constant.

(h) *Specific heats,* C_v, C_p. The specific heat C_v is the heat required to raise a unit mass of fluid one degree of temperature at constant volume; C_p is the heat required for the same temperature rise at constant pressure, ft-lb/slug °R, dyne cm/g °K, where °R = degree Rankine and °K = degree Kelvin. The ratio $C_p/C_v = k$ is an important parameter in gas dynamics. For a perfect gas, C_v and C_p are constant and $k = 1 + R/C_v$.

(i) *Internal energy, e.* The energy per unit mass of a fluid due to the thermal motion of its molecules, ft-lb/slug, dyne cm/g. For the perfect gas, $e = C_v T$.

(j) *Enthalpy, h.* The sum of internal energy and p/ρ, i.e., $h = e + p/\rho$, ft-lb/slug, dyne cm/g. For a perfect gas $h = C_p T$.

(k) *Entropy, S.* The change in entropy between any two states is defined as the integral $\int dQ/T$ where dQ is the heat added per unit mass by any reversible process between the two states, ft-lb/slug °R, dyne cm/g °K. Entropy is a measure of the unavailability of energy for mechanical work. For a perfect gas the change in entropy between states 1 and 2 is: $S_2 - S_1 = C_p \ln (T_2/T_1) - R \ln (p_2/p_1)$.

(l) *Thermal conductivity,* $\bar{k}$. The ratio of heat transmitted per unit area per unit time to the gradient of temperature causing the heat flow, lb/sec °R, dyne/sec °K.

Numerical values of the properties of many fluids may be found in references such as Streeter (1961) and International Critical Tables (1933). The quantities used above are defined mechanical terms for convenience in the equations below. Thermal units may be converted to mechanical units using the factors: 1 Btu (British thermal unit) = 778.3 ft-lb and 1 calorie = 4.1858 × 10⁷ dyne cm.

(4) Basic Equations

There are three fundamental laws which govern all of fluid mechanics: the conservation of mass, the equations of motion, and the conservation of energy. In any particular case, the nature and properties of the fluid must also be specified and sometimes the second law of thermodynamics must be invoked. The latter requires that the entropy of an isolated system must remain fixed or increase.

(a) **Conservation of Mass.** In terms of velocity components u, v, w in the x, y, z directions, respectively (Fig. 1), and the density ρ, the principle of conservation of mass is expressed by the equation (called the equation of continuity):

$$\frac{\partial \rho}{\partial t} + \frac{\partial \rho u}{\partial x} + \frac{\partial \rho v}{\partial y} + \frac{\partial \rho w}{\partial z} = 0 \qquad (1)$$

where t is the time. In general, u, v and w are functions of x, y, z and t; such functions constitute a spatial (also called Eulerian) description of the

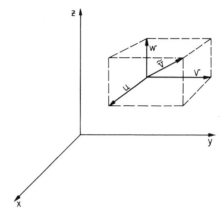

Fig. 1. Definition of velocity components, u, v, w.

motion. An alternate description is the material (or Lagrangian) description which is less often used and not discussed here (see Aris, 1961).

(b) **Equations of Motion.** The differential equations of motion for a Newtonian fluid are called the *Navier-Stokes equations.* These equations are an expression of Newton's second law of motion in which the appropriate relation of viscous stress to strain rate has been incorporated. For a compressible fluid with a single, constant coefficient of viscosity, the Navier-Stokes equations are:

$$\rho \left(\frac{\partial u}{\partial t} + u \frac{\partial u}{\partial x} + v \frac{\partial u}{\partial y} + w \frac{\partial u}{\partial z} \right) =$$
$$-\frac{\partial p}{\partial x} + \frac{1}{3}\mu \frac{\partial \theta}{\partial x} + \mu \nabla^2 u + \rho f_x \qquad (2)$$

$$\rho \left(\frac{\partial v}{\partial t} + u \frac{\partial v}{\partial x} + v \frac{\partial v}{\partial y} + w \frac{\partial v}{\partial z} \right) =$$
$$-\frac{\partial p}{\partial y} + \frac{1}{3}\mu \frac{\partial \theta}{\partial y} + \mu \nabla^2 v + \rho f_y \qquad (3)$$

$$\rho \left(\frac{\partial w}{\partial t} + u \frac{\partial w}{\partial x} + v \frac{\partial w}{\partial y} + w \frac{\partial w}{\partial z} \right) =$$
$$-\frac{\partial p}{\partial z} + \frac{1}{3}\mu \frac{\partial \theta}{\partial z} + \mu \nabla^2 w + \rho f_z \qquad (4)$$

where θ is the rate of dilatation defined by

$$\theta = \frac{\partial u}{\partial x} + \frac{\partial v}{\partial y} + \frac{\partial w}{\partial z} \qquad (5)$$

and ∇^2 is the Laplacian operator $\dfrac{\partial^2}{\partial x^2} + \dfrac{\partial^2}{\partial y^2} + \dfrac{\partial^2}{\partial z^2}$; f_x, f_y and f_z are components of the body force per unit mass.

In the case of the usual earth's gravity, $g = 32.2$ ft/sec², with the z axis vertical, $f_x = f_y = 0$ and $f_z = -g$.

The bracket on the left-hand side of Eq. (2) represents the acceleration of the fluid in the x direction; the right-hand side represents forces per unit volume. The terms involving μ represent the effect of viscous stresses.

For an incompressible fluid, the equation of continuity, Eq. (1), becomes $\theta = 0$ which simplifies Eqs. (2), (3) and (4) somewhat.

(c) Conservation of Energy. The differential equation of conservation of energy may be written in the form

$$\rho\left(\frac{\partial e}{\partial t} + u\frac{\partial e}{\partial x} + v\frac{\partial e}{\partial y} + w\frac{\partial e}{\partial z}\right) = -p\theta + \Phi + \bar{k}\nabla^2 T \quad (6)$$

where Φ is the dissipation function and the other symbols are as previously defined. For a Newtonian fluid with constant coefficient of viscosity, the dissipation function is:

$$\Phi = -\frac{2}{3}\mu\theta^2 + 2\mu I \quad (7)$$

where

$$I = \left(\frac{\partial u}{\partial x}\right)^2 + \left(\frac{\partial v}{\partial y}\right)^2 + \left(\frac{\partial w}{\partial z}\right)^2 + \frac{1}{2}\left[\left(\frac{\partial w}{\partial y} + \frac{\partial v}{\partial z}\right)^2 + \left(\frac{\partial u}{\partial z} + \frac{\partial w}{\partial x}\right)^2 + \left(\frac{\partial v}{\partial x} + \frac{\partial u}{\partial y}\right)^2\right] \quad (8)$$

The dissipation function Φ represents the rate at which mechanical energy is dissipated into heat by the action of viscosity. The left-hand side of Eq. (6) represents the rate of increase of internal energy of the fluid. The right-hand terms represent the rate of work done by pressure, the dissipation, and the effect of heat conduction, respectively.

The general Eqs. (1–8) govern a wide variety of flow phenomena and applications, but in most cases purely analytical solutions of some approximation to the general equations are combined with experimental information to obtain practical results.

(5) Regimes of Flow

Depending on certain dimensionless parameters, the type and general characteristics of fluid flow vary widely.

(a) *Laminar flow* occurs at low velocities, small sizes and highly viscous fluids. In this type of motion, neighboring layers of fluid move smoothly, without mixing, one over the other. The controlling parameter which determines whether laminar or turbulent flow will occur is the Reynolds number. For flow in a circular pipe, for example, the Reynolds number is $R = \rho V d/\mu$, where V is the mean velocity of flow and d is the diameter of the pipe. For Reynolds' numbers below about 2000, pipe flow is laminar. Low Reynolds number flows are dominated by viscous forces (see Happel and Brenner, 1965).

(b) *Turbulent flow* occurs at high Reynolds numbers. It is characterized by a random, fluctuating motion superimposed on an average motion which is usually more regular. Turbulence results in mixing of adjacent fluid layers. Most flows of practical interest involving dimensions of more than 1 or 2 cm are turbulent. Pipe flow is turbulent for Reynolds' numbers over about 2000 (see *Turbulence*).

(c) *Subsonic flow*. In a compressible fluid, the ratio of the velocity of flow V to the speed of sound c in the fluid is called the Mach number, $M = V/c$. Subsonic flow is defined as one in which $M < 1$ throughout. For low subsonic flow ($M < 0.3$), the effects of compressibility are small and incompressible flow theory will yield a good approximation.

(d) *Transonic flow* is one in which the Mach number is near unity. The flow pattern may shift rapidly and violently in this region and drag may be very large.

(e) *Supersonic flow* is defined by the Mach number range $M > 1$. In supersonic flow, phenomena not otherwise possible are observed, such as the formation of shock waves and the fact that sound from a body moving at supersonic speed cannot be heard until the body has passed the observer (see Shapiro, 1954).

(f) *Hypersonic flow* is very high Mach number flow, $M > 3$, approximately. Effects of aerodynamic heating and ionization become important in this range.

(g) *Subcritical flow*. In open channel flow, the counterpart of the Mach number is the Froude number F, defined as the ratio of the flow velocity V to an elementary gravity wave velocity, $c = \sqrt{gd}$, where d is the depth of flow. For Froude number $F = V/\sqrt{gd}$ less than unity, the flow is called subcritical and is in many ways analogous to subsonic flow.

(h) *Supercritical flow* is defined as open channel with Froude number $F > 1$. It is analogous to supersonic flow (see Chow, 1956). Flow in a tranquil river is usually subcritical, but rapids are supercritical.

(6) Hydraulics

The principal types of flow of interest in hydraulics are pipe flow and open channel flow. Both cases are treated as one-dimensional, i.e., approximate equations in terms of the mean velocity of flow are used rather than the full equations given above. In most cases, the flow is turbulent and the effect of viscosity is expressed in empirical friction coefficients.

(a) Pipe Flow. The equations of motion lead to the following approximate equation for a length of pipe L, Fig. 2:

$$\left(\frac{V_1^2}{2g} + \frac{p_1}{\gamma} + z_1\right) - \left(\frac{V_2^2}{2g} + \frac{p_2}{\gamma} + z_2\right)$$
$$= \Sigma h_f + \frac{1}{g}\frac{\partial V}{\partial t} \quad (9)$$

where V is the mean velocity and Z is the elevation of

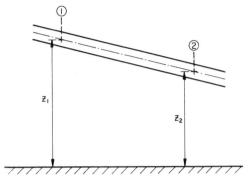

Fig. 2. Pipe flow terminology. The direction of flow is assumed to be from point 1 to point 2.

the pipe. The equation of continuity becomes $Q_1 = V_1 A_1 = V_2 A_2 = Q_2$ where Q is the discharge (ft³/sec, cm³/sec) and A is the cross-sectional area of the pipe. The two brackets on the left-hand side of Eq. (9) are called the totals heads, H_1 and H_2, at sections 1 and 2 respectively. The term Σh_f is the sum of frictional head losses due to viscosity. The term $\dfrac{L}{g}\dfrac{\partial V}{\partial t}$ represents the effect of the acceleration, $\dfrac{\partial V}{\partial t}$, due to changing flow rates. In a steady flow, neglecting

viscous effects, the right-hand side of Eq. (9) is zero and the equation becomes $H_1 = H_2$ which is called Bernoulli's equation (q.v.).

The head loss due to pipe friction may be computed by the Darcy-Weisbach formula:

$$h_f = f \frac{L}{d}\frac{V^2}{2g} \tag{10}$$

where d is the diameter of the pipe and f is a friction factor which depends on the roughness of the pipe and the Reynolds number of the flow as shown in Fig. 3. The term Σh_f in Eq. (10) includes losses due to bend, valves, junctions and other irregularities (see Davis, 1952).

(b) Open Channel Flow. Various empirical formulas are used to compute the velocity of flow in open channels. One widely used formula for steady, uniform flow is the Manning formula:

$$V = \frac{1.49}{n} R^{0.67} S^{0.50} \tag{11}$$

where S is the slope of the channel, n is a roughness factor and R is the hydraulic radius which is equal to the area of the cross section of flow divided by the length of its perimeter excluding the free surface. Typical values of n vary from 0.013 for concrete to

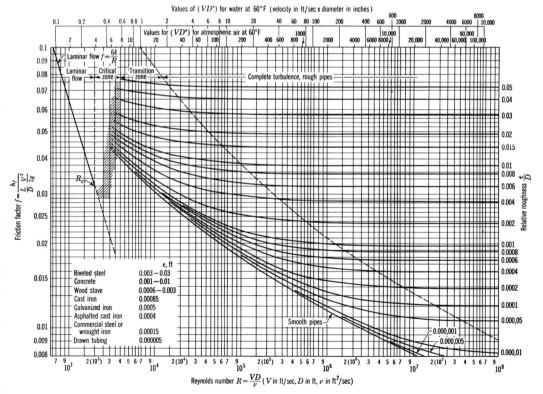

Fig. 3. Moody diagram for friction factors of pipe flow (from Streeter, V. L., "Fluid Mechanics," Third ed., New York, McGraw-Hill Book Co., 1962).

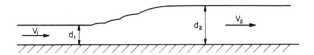

Fig. 4. The hydraulic jump.

0.025 for an earthen canal or stream bed (see Chow, 1959).

If the slope and the cross section of a canal or river are not uniform, the velocity and depth of flow will vary and a variety of surface profiles or backwater curves may result; for computational procedures, see Chow (1959).

(c) **Hydraulic Jump.** A supercritical flow can be decelerated into a subcritical flow by a hydraulic jump which is a highly turbulent wave front (Fig. 4). The depths d_1 and d_2 upstream and downstream of the jump are related by

$$d_2 = \tfrac{1}{2}d_1[(1 + 8V_1^2/gd_1)^{\frac{1}{2}} + 1] \tag{12}$$

Bores in rivers or estuaries are moving hydraulic jumps; the velocities V_1 and V_2 are then measured relative to the moving wave front.

(7) Lift and Drag

The force, F_0 (Fig. 5), exerted on a body by a fluid in a relative motion past a body, may be resolved into components called lift, F_L, and drag, F_D, perpendicular and parallel to the fluid velocity, respectively.

(a) **Lift.** The lift force on a wing or other body may be expressed in terms of the formula

$$F_L = \tfrac{1}{2}C_L A\rho V^2 \tag{13}$$

where A is the area of the wing in plan and C_L is a lift coefficient which depends on the shape of the body and the Reynolds number of the flow. For a typical wing shape C_L is of the order $0.11a$, where a is the angle of attack (Fig. 5) in degrees. The

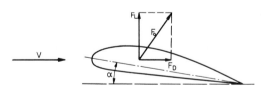

Fig. 5. Definition of lift and drag forces.

origin of the lift force at subsonic speeds may be explained by Bernoulli's equation: the velocity is greater and hence the pressure is less on the upper side of a lifting surface. At supersonic speeds, the flow pattern and the lift are affected by the presence of shock waves (see Shapiro, 1954).

(b) **Drag.** The drag force on a body is, in general, due in part to pressure differences and in part to viscous shear stresses. For a blunt body such as a sphere, the pressure effect predominates except at low Reynolds numbers; for a thin object like a flat plate held parallel to the stream, the viscous drag or skin friction predominates. The drag force is generally expressed by

$$F_D = \tfrac{1}{2}C_D A\rho V^2 \tag{14}$$

where A is the area of projection either perpendicular to the fluid flow for blunt bodies or perpendicular to the flow for a thin body like a wing. Typical values of C_D are shown in Fig. 6.

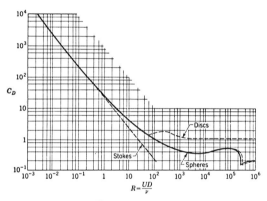

Fig. 6. Drag coefficients for spheres and disks (from Streeter, V. L., "Fluid Mechanics," Third ed., New York, McGraw-Hill Book Co., 1962)

At low Reynolds numbers, the flow past any body is entirely laminar in which case the drag coefficient varies inversely as the Reynolds number, e.g., in the case of a sphere, Stokes formula gives $C_D = 24/R$ where $R = Vd/v$. Other cases of viscous drag are discussed by Happell and Brenner (1965).

At high Reynolds numbers, the skin friction is developed close to the surface of the body in a thin layer called the *boundary layer*. Outside the boundary layer, the flow behaves as an inviscid fluid and hydrodynamic theory of ideal flow is applicable. The boundary layer also affects the drag due to pressure because it controls the so-called point of separation which is the point at which the main stream leaves the surface of the body to form the turbulent wake typically found behind a body in motion. Details of boundary layer computations may be found in Schlichting (1955).

In supersonic flow, the drag is strongly influenced by the presence of shock waves (see Shapiro, 1954).

(8) Hydrodynamics

Hydrodynamics is concerned with the analytical study of the motion of ideal, nonviscous fluids. The equations of motion, Eqs. (2)–(4), become mathematically much more tractable in this case ($\mu = 0$) and many solutions are available. Many flows of real fluids approximate inviscid fluid flow when the viscosity is small and dimensions are large.

The largest and most useful group of solutions is that of *irrotational* flow which is defined as one in which the average rotation or vorticity is zero. The vorticity is a vector whose x, y and z components are ξ, η and ζ defined by

$$\xi = \frac{\partial w}{\partial y} - \frac{\partial v}{\partial z}, \quad \eta = \frac{\partial u}{\partial z} - \frac{\partial w}{\partial x}, \quad \zeta = \frac{\partial v}{\partial x} - \frac{\partial u}{\partial y} \quad (15)$$

The mathematical simplification inherent in irrotational flow lies in the fact that $\xi = \eta = \zeta = 0$ is the necessary and sufficient condition for the existence of a *velocity potential* φ which is a function of x, y, z and t such that

$$u = \frac{\partial \varphi}{\partial x}, \quad v = \frac{\partial \varphi}{\partial y}, \quad w = \frac{\partial \varphi}{\partial z} \quad (16)$$

This means that instead of the three unknowns u, v, w, only one unknown, φ, need be found.

In the case of incompressible fluid, the equation of continuity reduces to $\nabla^2 \varphi = 0$ which is sufficient to find φ when the velocity on the boundary of the fluid or other appropriate boundary conditions are given. Further, the equations of motion can be integrated to find the pressure. The resultant pressure equation is

$$\frac{\partial \varphi}{\partial t} + \tfrac{1}{2}(u^2 + v^2 + w^2) + gz + \frac{p}{\rho} = 0 \quad (17)$$

If the motion is restricted to two dimensions ($w = 0$ and u and v being functions of x, y and t only), the analytical tools of the theory of functions of a complex variable can be applied. In the two dimensional case, a *stream function* exists such that

$$u = \frac{\partial \psi}{\partial y} \qquad v = -\frac{\partial \psi}{\partial x} \quad (18)$$

The curves on which ψ is constant are streamlines. The grid of lines $\varphi = $ constant, and $\psi = $ constant form a *flow net* which is composed of approximately square meshes. The complex potential $f = \varphi + i\psi$ (where i is the unit imaginary $= \sqrt{-1}$) is an analytic function of the complex variable $z = x + iy$. This fact allows the use of analytic function theory (see Milne-Thomson, 1960).

Applications of hydrodynamics include surface wave theory (see *Ocean Waves*), lift, and groundwater flow. In the case of groundwater flow the motion is, in fact, a viscous flow, but a velocity potential exists by virtue of Darcy's law and much of the vocabulary and solutions of hydrodynamics apply (see Streeter, 1961).

(9) Aerodynamics

In a general compressible flow, the heating effect of viscous dissipation and the tendency of the fluid to expand on heating interact so that the equations of continuity, the Navier-Stokes equations and the energy equation must be all considered simultaneously. Even the comparatively simple case of one-dimensional pipe flow with or without heating is relatively complex.

If heat conduction and viscous dissipation are neglected, the flow is isentropic and usually irrotational. In this case, a velocity potential exists but satisfies a more complicated and less tractable equation than for incompressible flow (see Shapiro, 1954).

In the subsonic range up to a Mach number of 0.3, compressible flow may be treated as incompressible with good approximation. The speed of sound in a gas is $c = (kp/\rho)^{1/2}$ or about 1100 ft/sec at sea level. Hence for velocities up to about 300 mph the effects of compressibility are small at sea level.

In the range of Mach numbers up to 0.7, approximate corrections may be used such as the Prandtl-Glauert rule:

$$C'_L = C_L (1 - M^2)^{-\frac{1}{2}} \quad (19)$$

where C_L is the lift coefficient for incompressible flow and C'_L is the lift coefficient for the same body in compressible flow.

In the transonic range from Mach number 0.7–1.2, both subsonic and supersonic flow may exist at the same time in different regions of a flow past a body. The drag coefficient in this range may be several times its value at lower or higher speeds.

In the supersonic range, shock phenomena become important. For a stationary *shock wave* normal to the fluid velocity, the equations of continuity, motion and energy lead to the *Rankine-Hugoniot equation* relating properties ahead of and behind the shock:

$$\rho_2/\rho_1 = \frac{1 + \beta\, p_2/p_1}{\beta + p_2/p_1} = V_1/V_2 \quad (20)$$

where

$$\beta = \frac{k+1}{k-1} \quad (21)$$

and k is the ratio of specific heats C_p/C_v. The fluid flowing toward the shock (subscript 1, Fig. 7) must be supersonic and the fluid behind the shock (subscript 2) will be subsonic. When a shock wave moves through a fluid at rest, the velocity V_1 above becomes the shock velocity, and $(V_1 - V_2)$ becomes the fluid velocity behind the shock.

Oblique shocks at an angle to the approaching flow can also occur, for example, at the nose of a

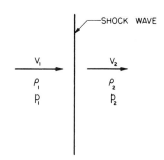

Fig. 7. Shock wave terminology.

supersonic airplane or rocket. Such shock waves are similar to normal shock waves in effect, but they deflect the incoming flow as well as decelerating it (see Shapiro, 1954).

RICHARD SKALAK

References

Aris, R., 1962, "Vectors, Tensors and the Basic Equations of Fluid Mechanics," Englewood Cliffs, N.J., Prentice-Hall.
*Chow, V. T., 1959, "Open-channel Hydraulics," New York, McGraw-Hill Book Co.
*Davis, C. V., 1952, "Handbook of Applied Hydraulics," Second ed., New York, McGraw-Hill Book Co.
*Happel, J., and Brenner, H., 1965, "Low Reynolds Number Hydrodynamics," Englewood Cliffs, N.J., Prentice-Hall.
International Critical Tables, 1933, National Research Council, U.S.A., New York, McGraw-Hill Book Co.
Milne-Thomson, L. M., 1960, "Theoretical Hydrodynamics," Fourth ed., New York, The Macmillan Co.
*Schlichting, H., 1955, "Boundary Layer Theory," New York, McGraw-Hill Book Co.
*Shapiro, A. H., 1954, "The Dynamics and Thermodynamics of Compressible Fluid Flow," New York, Ronald Press.
*Streeter, V. L., 1961, "Handbook of Fluid Dynamics," New York, McGraw-Hill Book Co.
Wilkinson, W. L., 1960, "Non-Newtonian Fluids," London, Pergamon Press.

FLUX DENSITY

Flux is a rate of flow, usually of energy, through a unit area, as for example, heat flow, or transfer. Radiation flux density (electromagnetic radiation) is somewhat different from heat flux in that it involves a volumetric density, rather than a flow across a surface. Thus in a consideration of scattering, electromagnetic flux density would usually be measured in watts per square meter. The Van Allen Belts (q.v.) represent essentially flux patterns of this radiation (see Vol. II).

At any given reference level in the atmosphere, there should be an ideal steady-state condition of flux transfer. Following Kirchhoff's laws, the flux emitted must be equal to the flux absorbed. The flux measured above that reference plane must therefore be equivalent to all forms of flux below it (Johnson, 1954).

In flux of heat or water vapor, it is necessary to consider *austausch* (exchange) and eddy coefficients. Particularly the upward heat flux H in the atmosphere is an important quantity in energy transfer of the atmosphere and in the air-sea interaction. This flux is given by $-\rho C_p K_H (\partial \overline{T}/\partial z + \alpha)$ where C_p is specific heat at constant pressure, $\partial \overline{T}/\partial z$ is the mean vertical gradient of air temperature, α is the adiabatic lapse rate, and K_H is eddy conductivity of heat. Since eddy conductivity is not constant but depends on turbulence structure in the atmosphere, the above expression does not give values of actual heat flux. In order to measure H directly, the relation $H = C_p \overline{(\rho w)' \, T'}$ is used, where the prime denotes instantaneous departures from the mean, the bar denotes the average over a period of time and w is vertical velocity. Simultaneous measurements of temperature and vertical wind fluctuations give the value of H directly.

RHODES W. FAIRBRIDGE
TAKASHI ICHIYE

References

Byers, H. R., 1959, "General Meteorology," Third ed., New York, McGraw-Hill Book Co., 540pp.
Huschke, R. E. (editor), 1959, "Glossary of Meteorology," Boston, American Meteorological Society, 638pp.
Johnson, J. C., 1954, "Physical Meteorology," Tech. Press of M.I.T. and John Wiley & Sons, 393pp.
Sutton, O. G., 1953, "Micrometeorology," New York, McGraw-Hill Book Co., 333pp.

FOREL SCALE—*See* **TRANSPARENCY**

FRACTURE ZONES

From the orientation of long rows of oceanic volcanoes, e.g., Hawaii, Society Islands, etc., across the Pacific, and from the rectilinearity of many fault zones on the continents, e.g., the East African taphrogenic system, as well as dominant coastal and orographic trends, it has long been postulated that the earth's crust has been fractured into systematic patterns. Oceanographic expeditions during the last two decades or so have disclosed vast numbers of fracture zones on the deep-sea floor. These features, when traceable for hundreds or even thousands of kilometers are termed *lineaments*. They often correspond to great circle patterns (Boutakoff, 1952).

Vening Meinesz (1947) proposed that a shift of the earth's axis of rotation with respect to the crust would change the coordinates of the geoid and lead to a fundamental lineament fracture pattern, which would result from the vertical readjustments to the new levels. It is now believed from paleomagnetic measurements that aperiodic shifts of the relative axis position have in fact taken place; accordingly, old lineaments should be revived from time to time and new ones should develop (see experiments by Knetch, 1964).

A special terminology has grown up around these concepts: the major lineaments are called *geofractures* and *geosutures* (Hans Cloos, 1939); the geometry is called *lineament tectonics* (Sonder, 1938); the fracturing process is called *taphrogeny* (Krenkel); the worldwide trend development is called *rhegmagenesis* (Sonder, 1956); the polygonal shaped mosaic of blocks of the earth's crust that result are called "*felder*" (in German, by Cloos), or *tesserae* (by Brock), or by the delightful term lineamenttektonische Bruchschollenstruktur (Sonder, 1938). Cloos believed that there was an optimum size for such blocks, 1100 km in diameter, from his African studies, but Brock believed that several classes are recognizable but as fractions of the first-order blocks. (This important problem is discussed in several entries in pr Vol. V of this Encyclopedia.)

Sonder has pointed out the parallelism of the mid-oceanic ridge to the continental lineaments, and in a detailed analysis of Iceland showed that its position falls logically at the intersection of the Mid-Atlantic Ridge and the diagonally trending Scottish–Greenland ridge system. Impressive photographs by Heezen (1962) in the central graben of Iceland show clearly that dilatation is currently quite active. Cloos has analyzed the Azores Plateau in rather similar terms, and constantly revived vulcanism is also in evidence.

Stille (1939, 1944, 1945) has emphasized the triangular shapes of continental blocks and the symmetrical patterns of many geotectonic units. He pointed out that for every major reentrant angle of a continental border, there seems to be a matching open angle on an opposing coast; complex arcuate (orogenic) sectors are always matched by a projecting "spur" or wedge of continental origin, e.g., *Bahama Spur* and *Falkland Spur* in the Atlantic, *Sula Spur* in the Pacific and so on (see discussion in Hume, 1948). Each is marked off by gigantic fracture zones.

Oceanic Fracture Systems

The Mid-Pacific fracture zones were first discussed in terms of strike-slip faulting by Betz and Hess (1942). Precision depth recording by oceanographic vessels has brought much light to this question and disclosed many more fracture zones, often but not necessarily marked by volcanoes or seamounts. Menard and Dietz (1952) first identified one of these submarine fracture zones in the north-

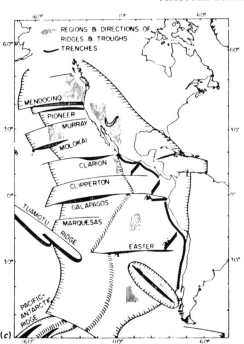

Fig. 1. Principal fracture zones in the eastern Pacific (Menard, 1964); note displacements of mid-ocean ridge. Tuamotu Ridge and the South Chile Ridge (farther southeast) appear to be preexisting features. (By permission of McGraw-Hill Book Co., N.Y.)

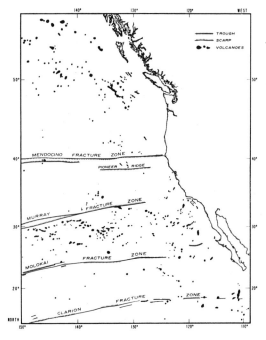

Fig. 2. The influence of fracture zones on the grouping of volcanoes in the northeastern Pacific (Menard, 1964). (By permission of McGraw-Hill Book Co., N.Y.)

east Pacific and since then a series of remarkable straight and parallel, east–west trending fractures have been recognized all down the eastern part of the Pacific, from north to south: *Mendocino F. Z., Pioneer F. Z., Molokai F. Z., Clarion F. Z., Clipperton F. Z., Galapagos F. Z., Marquesas F. Z., Easter Island F. Z.*, and another about 50°S. Now, in the Atlantic and Indian Oceans sheafs of great fracture zones have been discovered, so that they have indeed proved to be worldwide (as proposed by Carey, 1958, 1963).

Bathymetrically, the submarine fracture zones are described by Heezen and Menard (1963, p. 260) as: "long thin bands that are conspicuously more mountainous than the sea floor in general and ordinarily separate regions with different depths. . . . Each (of the E. Pacific ones) is about 100 km wide and more than 2000 km long. Within the zones are asymmetrical ridges and narrow troughs parallel to the general trend. Large volcanic seamounts are common. . . . The total relief (of one ridge) is about 1600 m, and most of the changes in depth are abrupt." In one and the same fracture zone, the facing of the scarps may alternate. There is likely to be a regional change in depth of the sea floor on opposite sides of up to 500 m. In the case of Erben Seamount on the Murray Fracture Zone, the local relief is 7450 m; it is actually a guyot, flat-topped with fossil evidence of exposure twenty million years ago.

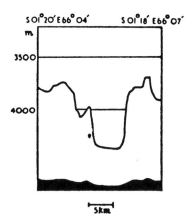

Fig. 4. A fracture zone in the Carlsberg Ridge in the Indian Ocean. Below (in black) = true scale profile (Koczy, 1954).

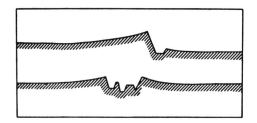

Fig. 3. Profiles of idealized types of topography of fracture zones in the northeastern Pacific (Menard, 1964). (By permission of McGraw-Hill Book Co., N.Y.)

In the Atlantic Ocean, the bulk of the fracture zones cross and displace the central rift of the mid-oceanic ridge, whereas those in the northeastern Pacific cross a virtually flat-floored province of low abyssal hills. Those of the southeastern Pacific, however, cross the ridge in that sector, while those in the Indian Ocean are in part displacing the ridge and in part in the open sea floor. An intriguing contrast however is immediately apparent; while the ridge-displacing fracture zones in all three oceans run essentially east–west, the major fracture pattern in the Indian Ocean is north–south or north northeast–south southwest.

Trenches in Fracture Zones

A number of fracture zones have open rifts, so that deep-sea *trenches* are formed. In the Atlantic, the best known example is the *Romanche Trench* and in the Indian Ocean there is the *Diamantina Trench* (in the southeast) and the *Vema Trench* (in the northwest). An unfortunate confusion is apparent over the last-named; there is a previously named *Vema Fracture Zone* in the mid-Atlantic (Heezen *et al.*, 1964) and there is a *Vema Trench* (situated on a fracture zone) in the Indian Ocean (Heezen and Nafe, 1964).

Close to land a number of transitional fracture zones exist: in both the northern and the southern Caribbean there are giant east–west fractures (Bucher, 1947); likewise in the Scotia Arc. Around the Pacific margin there are subparallel faults in Chile, in the San Andreas Line, in Alaska, Japan, the Philippines and so on. In the southwest Pacific, the trend of the Great Alpine Fault of New Zealand appears to continue in the Tonga-Kermadec Trench. A series of great fractures can be followed from northwestern New Guinea along the north coast and into the Solomons Sea. Along the northern border of Melanesia, a major trench (the *Vitiaz Trench*) passes from the outer oceanic side of the Andesite Line into the shallow borderland area. Series of smaller fractures, with horsts or grabens between, appear to lie *en échelon* along the borderland margin (Fairbridge, 1961), and there is evidence of crustal subsidence in numbers of "drowned" atolls or other coral banks (Fairbridge and Stewart, 1960).

Strike-slip Motion

There is some disagreement as to the meaning of deep-sea fracture zones. In structural geology it is geometrically impossible to produce a long rectilinear fracture by any process other than *strike-slip motion*. It is customary to apply Geikie's priority term *transcurrent fault* to those that transect continents or whole orogenic belts; evidently their hade is close to vertical and the fracture extends at least to the base of the crust. For similar fractures *within* orogenic zones that only reach down to a shallow discontinuity, such as the Triassic salt horizon in the Jura or the Paleozoic shales and evaporites in the Appalachians, the name *wrench fault* is recommended. It is unwise to use these two terms indiscriminately for both categories of strike-slip structure.

In the case of transitional fractures that intersect the continental borders, it is sometimes possible to demonstrate strike-slip displacement (usually in terms of tens or hundreds of kilometers). In the case of those transecting the mid-oceanic ridge, there is evident displacement of the median rift. In the case of the northeast Pacific fractures, such obvious displacement is not so apparent, but Menard (1964) believes a definite relationship is proved by related structures (Fig. 5), and further-more, systematic, closely spaced geomagnetic sur-veys have disclosed what appear to be major offsets (Mason, Raff, Vacquier and others: see summary by Menard, 1964). Vacquier proposed a 1175-km (730-mile) left lateral offset for the Mendocino Line. This interpretation has been doubted by some workers, but close scrutiny of the geology suggests that there are in fact continental transitions, which confirm strike-slip motion; the

Mendocino physically offsets the continental shelf break; the Murray seems to continue into the east–west Transverse Ranges of Southern California; the Clarion seems to continue in the great east–west volcanic belt of southern Mexico.

A partial solution to the disagreement has been offered by J. Tuzo Wilson (1965), who proposed

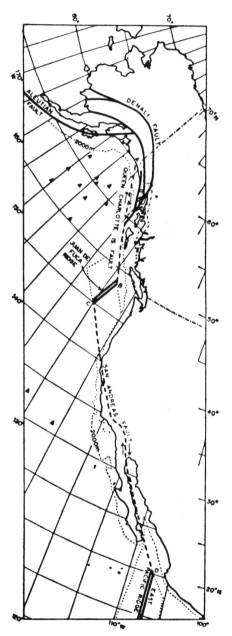

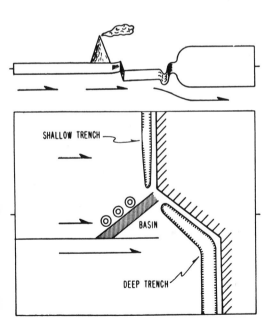

Fig. 5. Diagrammatic plan and profile, to suggest the relationship of major Pacific (east–west) fractures, the trenches, and diagonal volcanic ridges, such as the Nasca, Cocos and Tehuantepec ridges (Menard, 1964). (By permission of McGraw-Hill Book Co., N.Y.)

Fig. 6. Sketch map showing the location of some of the principal faults off the west coast of North America. The black triangles are guyot areas. "Transform faults" are postulated in Juan de Fuca Ridge, between the strike-slip pair A–B, C–D (Wilson, 1965).

that for the special category of transcurrent faults that displace recently formed crust (Heezen, 1962), the term *transform fault* should be applied (Fig. 6). Obviously if new crust is forming between faulted and separating crustal segments there will be no strike-slip motion, though the latter may pass into preexisting areas with measurable displacement.

Other Lineations and Fractures

There seems to be little doubt that the vast numbers of steep escarpments throughout the entire length of the mid-oceanic ridge are almost certainly faulted. The borders of aseismic ridges (q.v.) are frequently abrupt and probably faulted. In the open ocean floor, far removed from sediment sources that might otherwise block them, there appear innumerable small open gashes that show up on echo-sounding traces as V-shaped notches; owing to side echoes they are difficult to appraise, but one might visualize large-scale features analogous to those illustrated by Heezen (1962) from central Iceland. In dimensions they seem to range from 10–200 km in length, 1–10 km in width and 100–500 m in depth. Recently active fractures of this sort are believed by Holtedahl to ring the glaciated lands: Norway, Labrador, Antarctica, etc. Russian surveys have shown those around Antarctica to reach considerable dimensions (1000–1500 m deep). Other lineations are marked by rows of knolls, seamounts, atolls or islands (see *Volcanic Ridges*).

RHODES W. FAIRBRIDGE

References

Anon., 1964, "Oceanographical observations in the Indian Ocean in 1962; H.M.A.S. Diamantina Cruise," *Oceanographic Cruise Report 14, Australia, Commonwealth Sci. Ind. Res. Organ., Div. Fisheries Oceanog.,* 128pp.

Betz, F., and Hess, H. H., 1942, "The floor of the North Pacific Ocean," *Geograph. Rev.,* **32,** 99–116.

Boutakoff, N., 1952, "The great circle stress pattern of the earth," *Australian J. Sci.,* **14,** 108–111.

Bucher, W., 1947, "Problems of earth deformation illustrated by the Caribbean Sea Basin," *Trans. N.Y. Acad. Sci., Ser. 2,* **9,** No. 3, 98–116.

Carey, S. W., 1958, "A tectonic approach to continental drift," *Continental Drift* (Symposium: Univ. Tasmania), 177–355.

Carey, S. W., 1963, "Asymmetry of the earth," *Australian J. Sci.,* **25,** 369–384.

Cloos, H., 1939, "Hebung, Spaltung, Vulkanismus," *Geol. Rundschau,* **30,** 403–527.

Cloos, H., 1948, "Grundschollen und Erdnähte; Entwurf eines konservativen Erdbildes," *Geol. Rundschau,* **35,** 133–154.

Fairbridge, R. W., 1961, "The Melanesian Border Plateau, a zone of crustal shearing in the S. W. Pacific," *Publ. Bur. Cent. Seism., ser. A.,* **22** (Helsinki, 1960), 137–149.

Fairbridge, R. W., and Stewart, H. B., Jr., 1960, "Alexa Bank, a drowned atoll on the Melanesian Border Plateau," *Deep-Sea Res.,* **7,** 100–116.

Heezen, B. C., 1962, "The Deep-Sea Floor," in (Runcorn, S. K., editor) "Continental Drift," pp. 235–288, New York, Academic Press.

Heezen, B. C., Gerard, R. D., and Tharp, M., 1964, "The Vema Fracture Zone in the equatorial Atlantic," *J. Geophys. Res.,* **69**(4), 733–739.

Heezen, B. C., and Menard, H. W., 1963, "Topography of the Deep-Sea Floor," in "The Sea," Vol. 3, pp. 233–280, New York, Interscience Publishers.

Heezen, B. C., and Nafe, J. E., 1964, "Vema Trench: Western Indian Ocean," *Deep-Sea Res.,* **11,** 79–84.

Hume, W. F., 1948, "Terrestrial Theories," *Geol. Sur., Cairo,* 522pp. + 160pp. index.

Knetch, G., 1964, Uber ein Struktur-experiment an einer Kugel und Beziehungen zwischen Gross-lineamenten und Pol-lagen in der Erdgeschichte. Geol. Rundschau, **54,** 523–548.

Koczy, F. F., 1954, "A survey on deep-sea features taken during the Swedish Deep-Sea Expedition," *Deep-Sea Res.,* **1,** 176–184.

Krause, D. C., 1964, "Guinea Fracture Zone in the equatorial Atlantic," *Science,* **146,** 57–59.

Menard, H. W., 1964, "Marine Geology of the Pacific," New York, McGraw-Hill Book Co., 271pp.

Menard, H. W., and Dietz, R. S., 1952, "Mendocino submarine escarpment," *J. Geol.,* **60,** 266–278.

Sonder, R. A., 1938, "Die Lineamenttektonik und ihre Probleme," *Eclogae Geol. Helv.,* **31,** 199–238.

Sonder, R. A., 1956, "Mechanik der Erde, Elemente und Studien zur tektonischen Erdgeschichte," Stuttgart, Schweizerbart, 291pp.

Stille, H., 1939, "Kordillerisch-atlantische Wechselbeziehungen," *Geol. Rundschau,* **30,** 315–342.

Stille, H., 1944, "Geotektonische Probleme des Pazifischen Erdraumes," *Abh. Preuss. Akad. Wiss. Math.-naturw. Kl., Berlin,* No. 11, 77pp.

Stille, H., 1945, "Die Zirkumpazifische Faltungen in Raum und Zeit," *Geotekton. Forschungen,* (7/8), 261–323.

Vening Meinesz, F. A., 1947, "Shear patterns of the earth's crust," *Trans. Am. Geophys. Union,* **28,** 1–61.

Wilson, J. T., 1965, "Transform faults, oceanic ridges, and magnetic anomalies southwest of Vancouver Island," *Science,* **150,** 482–485.

Cross-references: *Mid-ocean Ridge; Seamounts; Trenches; Volcanic Ridges.* pr Vol. V: *Structural and Geophysical entries.*

FREE OSCILLATIONS—*See* SEICHE

FUNDY, BAY OF—*See* BAY OF FUNDY

G

GRAND BANKS AND THE EASTERN SEABOARD OF CANADA

Geographical Setting

The eastern seaboard of North America runs uninterrupted by any major change in direction from Florida in the south to Nova Scotia in the north, but at the latitude of the Gulf of St. Lawrence it juts abruptly eastward into the North Atlantic Ocean (Fig. 1). Similarly, the Appalachian Mountain System, bounded to the south on its eastern side by the cover of the sediments of the

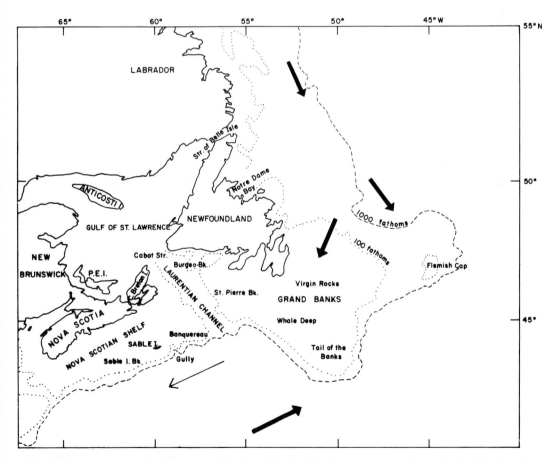

Fig. 1. The eastern seaboard of Canada and the Grand Banks. The heavy arrows on the north side of the Grand Banks indicate the Labrador Current. The heavy arrow south of the Tail indicates the Gulf Stream. The light arrow indicates Slope Water.

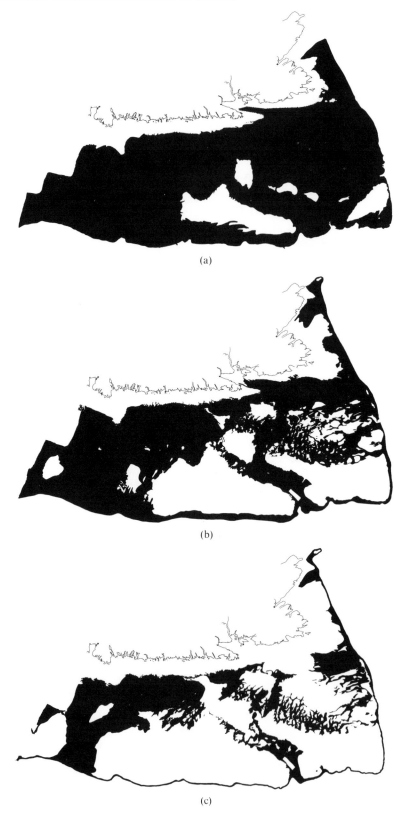

(a)

(b)

(c)

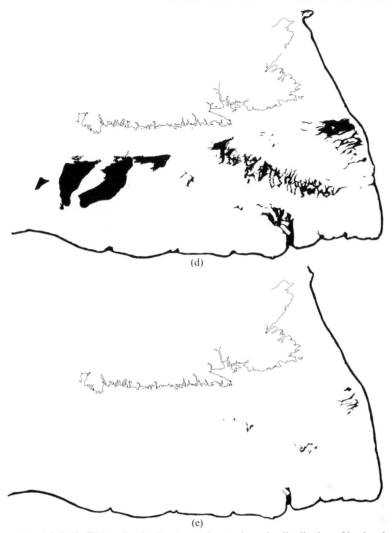

(d)

(e)

Fig. 2. The continental shelf off Nova Scotia. A presentation to show the distribution of land and sea as it would appear if sea level were reduced successively. The land is white, the sea black (but note that the area beyond the outer black margin is wholly sea, being the Laurentian Channel on the right, the continental slope at the bottom). The complexity of the eastern part of the shelf is shown clearly in (b) and (c), and the pattern in the right central part of (d) has been interpreted as a dendritic drainage pattern. Note in (d) that the troughs trending toward the Laurentian Channel do not in fact merge with the Channel. (a) Sea level at the present 30-fathom line, (b) 50, (c) 70, (d) 100, (e) 150 (from surveys by the Canadian Hydrographic Service, contoured and prepared by A. E. Cok).

Atlantic coastal plain, and which also runs along the eastern seaboard, is bent in the same direction at the Gulf, and eventually disappears northeast of Newfoundland.

The continental shelf off Nova Scotia (Figs. 1 and 2) is about 190 km wide and water depths range from 40 m on the outer banks, such as Sable Island Bank and Banquereau, to 300 m and deeper in the holes of the inner parts of the shelf. This shelf is bounded on its northeast side by the Laurentian Channel, about 110 km wide and 400 m deep, which separates it from the Grand Banks of Newfoundland. This Channel, trough-like in form with gentle smooth sides, runs southeast from

the Gulf of St. Lawrence through the Cabot Strait to the edge of the shelf. To the southwest, a series of elongate deeps run perpendicular to the channel across the Nova Scotian shelf. But they do not intersect it, being barred by banks at the edge of the channel; this side indeed appears as it would if a giant bulldozer had scooped the channel out. Not so the northeast side which merges smoothly with the shelf south of Newfoundland. This side is interrupted only by a trough smaller in size than the Laurentian Channel, which runs southwest from the south coast of Newfoundland. Although the banks south of Newfoundland are shallow, the water depths being in the general range of 40–100

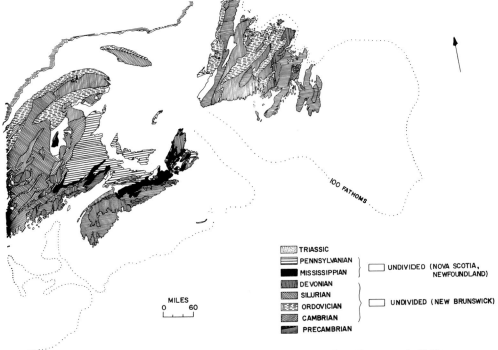

Fig. 3. A simplified geological map of eastern Canada (from Barret *et al.*, 1964).

m, northeast of Newfoundland the general level is deeper, at about 400 m, and the inlets of the northeastern coast (such as Notre Dame Bay) are often very deep—750 m in some cases. The Banks extend finger-like into the Atlantic Ocean to the Tail of the Banks; to the northeast is a curious feature—Flemish Cap, itself shallow, but separated from the continental shelf proper by a trough 1300 m deep. In this respect it resembles Galicia Bank off Cape Finisterre, Portugal.

Physical Oceanography

Circulation on the Grand Banks and the eastern seaboard of Canada is dominated by the Gulf Stream and the Labrador Current. The Labrador Current has its source in the Labrador Sea and moves southeast along the coast of Labrador. It is split where it encounters the northern edge of the Grand Banks so that part flows over the Banks and part continues southeast along the continental slope. These waters supply the Gulf of St. Lawrence through the Cabot Strait and the Strait of Belle Isle. The Gulf Stream is a major circulatory system of the North Atlantic Ocean which has its beginning in the equatorial regions. It forms a band of high-salinity, high-temperature water off the Nova Scotian continental shelf and comes into direct contact with the Labrador Current on the Tail of the Banks.

Proceeding outward from the coast of Nova Scotia, four bands of water can be distinguished:

coastal water, slope water, Gulf Stream water and Atlantic water (see Fig. 1). Only the first two of these are relevant to this discussion of the Canadian Atlantic Seaboard.

The relatively fresh coastal waters extend approximately from the coast of Nova Scotia to the edge of the continental shelf. Distinct stratification exists, especially in the summer months, and three layers can be identified. The surface layer, greater than 73 m thick, has temperatures of 5°C or more and salinities less than 32‰. A cold intermediate layer characterized by temperature less than 4°C and salinities between 32 and 33.5‰ is due in part to the incursion of Labrador Current water. Its thickness varies from 31–146 m. The bottom layer is warm, with temperatures greater than 5°C and salinities greater than 33.5‰.

The slope waters occupy the area between the edge of the continental shelf and the Gulf Stream. Coastal, Labrador Current and Gulf Stream waters combine to produce this water mass which has salinities and temperatures intermediate between those found in coastal and Gulf Stream waters. The width of this band, approximately 315 km, varies with changes in the northern edge of the Gulf Stream.

The Grand Banks are occupied by the cold waters of the Labrador Current. Surface temperatures are about 3°C and salinities vary from 30–34.8‰. However, on the southern and western slopes of the Grand Banks, the waters of the

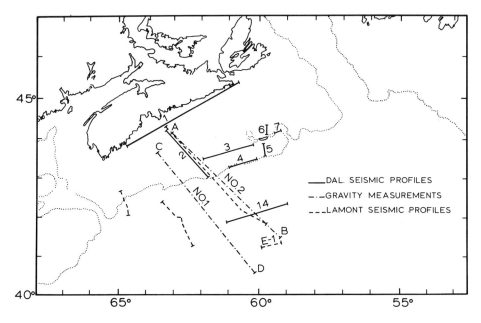

Fig. 4. (a) Seismic lines and ship's tracks along which gravity measurements have been made.

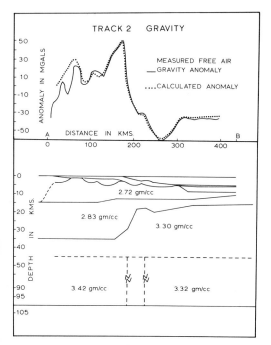

Fig. 4. (b) The structure of the crust and upper mantle beneath the continental margin off Nova Scotia (after Keen and Loncarevic, 1965).

Labrador Current mix with the warm waters of the Gulf Stream producing surface temperature as high as 10°C. The current strengths vary widely in this area, from about 9–44 km/day. The characteristics of the deep waters on the Banks are controlled by the relative strengths and boundaries of the two contributing systems, the Labrador Current and the Gulf Stream.

Geological and Geophysical Studies

The structure of the Grand Banks and of the eastern seaboard of Canada is dominated by the Appalachian Mountain System, the presence of the Atlantic Coastal Plain to the southwest of the area, and the Pleistocene glaciation. The Appalachian system runs from southwest to northeast, changing strike at the latitude of the Gulf of St. Lawrence, and its erosion before and during the Pleistocene has led to the characteristic shore line of Newfoundland and the Atlantic coast of Nova Scotia. However, both off Nova Scotia and south of Newfoundland, the rocks of the Appalachian System are overlain by gently folded sedimentary rocks, responsible for the morphology of the major part of the shelves (see Fig. 3).

The thickness of unconsolidated sediment on the shelves and banks is variable; on the banks south of Newfoundland, it appears as a veneer some tens of meters thick at most, and quite distinct from the underlying bedded rock. In some of the holes of the Nova Scotian Shelf, the veneer of soft sediment is less clearly distinguishable from the underlying rocks, and the reasons for these differences, if they are of a general nature, are not known. The shelves and banks at the edge of the Nova Scotian Shelf, on which little fine-grained sediment is now found, must have acted as a supply of sediment to the Sohm abyssal plain at the foot of the continental slope; Heezen, Drake and Ewing have put forward convincing evidence that the 1929 earthquake beneath the continental slope off the Laurentian Channel led to slumping and to the generation of turbidity currents.

The thickness of the sedimentary rocks underlying these unconsolidated sediments is at least 5 km in some areas, e.g., beneath Sable Island at the edge of the Nova Scotian Shelf. In part, they must be Carboniferous in age—off Cape Breton, for example, but evidence has been obtained by J. I. Marlowe that rocks dredged from the Gully, a submarine canyon off Sable Island, may be in part Tertiary rocks, suggesting that a system equivalent to the Atlantic Coastal Plain is present off Nova Scotia, beneath the Grand Banks and northeast of Newfoundland.

The crustal structure to the northeast of Newfoundland and on the Nova Scotian shelf appears to be controlled by the Appalachian System (see Fig. 5). The crust is about 35 km thick beneath the shelf off Nova Scotia, but thins to about 15 km at the foot of the continental slope, where the sediment thickness is still approximately as great as

beneath Sable Island. Evidence from seismic studies and gravity observations suggest that the mantle beneath the continent differs from that beneath the ocean basin—beneath the continent it is likely to become more dense at depths of the order of 45 km (see Fig. 4). Corresponding perhaps to this, the crust beneath the central mobile belt of the Appalachian system is thicker than the crust beneath the Atlantic coast of Nova Scotia. Also, it may be that the velocity of compressional waves in the upper mantle is higher beneath the central belt, 8.50 km/sec, than beneath the regions near the margins of the Appalachian System, 8.1 km/sec.

The Appalachian system disappears northeast of Newfoundland, and it is likely that it is covered in part by sediments equivalent to those beneath the shelf in other parts of the region. It is also likely, from evidence of magnetic field measurements that the system stops abruptly, as though it were brutally ruptured northeast of Newfoundland at some time past. The crustal structure beneath the Grand Banks is not well known. The seismic refraction profiles of Bentley and Worzel indicate that the compressional wave velocities of the subcrustal material, possibly the upper mantle, beneath the continental slope near the Grand Banks are anomalously low, between 7.2 and 7.6

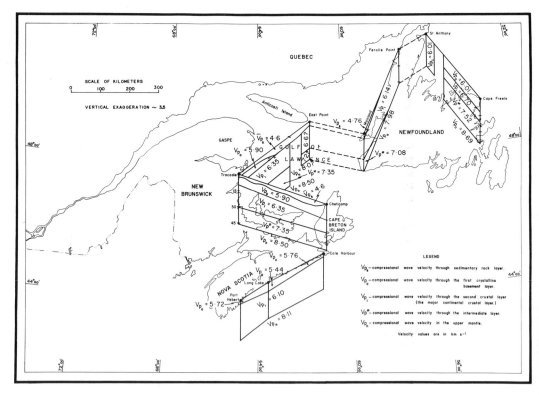

Fig. 5. Cross sections through the Appalachian System (from G. N. Ewing *et al.*, 1965).

km/sec, but these may represent a layer of the crust above the Mohorovičič discontinuity, as is found in the Gulf of St. Lawrence.

Charlotte Keen
J. E. Blanchard
M. J. Keen

References

Barrett, D. L., Berry, M., Blanchard, J. E., Keen, M. J., and McAllister, R. E., 1964, "Seismic studies on the eastern seaboard of Canada: the Atlantic Coast of Nova Scotia," *Can. J. Earth Sci.*, **1**, 10–22.

Bentley, C. R., and Worzel, J. L., 1956, "Geophysical investigations in the emerged and submerged Atlantic coastal plain: Part X, Continental shelf, slope and rise south of the Grand Banks," *Bull. Geol. Soc. Am.*, **67**, 1–18.

Ewing, G. N., Dainty, A. M., Blanchard, J. E., and Keen, M. J., 1966, "Seismic studies on the eastern seaboard of Canada: the Appalachian System I," *Can. J. Earth Sci.*, **3**, 89–109.

Hachey, H. B., 1961, "Oceanography and Canadian Atlantic waters," *Bull. Fisheries Res. Board Can.*, **134**.

Heezen, B. C., and Drake, C. L., 1964, "Grand Banks slump," *Bull. Am. Assoc. Petrol. Geologists*, **48**, 221–233.

Keen, Charlotte, Blanchard, J. E., and Keen, M. J., 1966, "Gulf of St. Lawrence" (this volume).

Keen, Charlotte, and Loncarevic, B. D., 1966, "Crustal structure on the eastern seaboard of Canada: studies on the continental margin," *Can. J. Earth Sci.* **3**, 65–75.

Lilly, H. D., 1965, "Submarine examination of the Virgin Rocks area, Grand Banks, Newfoundland: Preliminary note," *Bull. Geol. Soc. Am.*, **76**, 131–32.

Officer, C. B., and Ewing, M., 1954, "Geophysical investigations in the emerged and submerged Atlantic coastal plain: Pt. VII, Continental shelf, continental slope and continental rise south of Nova Scotia," *Bull. Geol. Soc. Am.*, **65**, 653–670.

GRASSHOF—*See* THERMAL INSTABILITY, Vol. II

GRAVITY AND GEOPOTENTIAL

Gravity is generally taken to be the force of attraction of the earth for a separate body or another part of the earth. In fact, all masses are attracted to each other according to Newton's *Law of Universal Gravitation*. The force of attraction is gravitation. It is given by

$$F = G\,\frac{Mm}{r^2}$$

where F is the force of gravitation, M and m are the two masses, r is the distance between them. G is the universal gravitational constant. The distance is measured from the "center of gravity" of one mass to the corresponding center of gravity of the other. This center is the point at which all mass of such a body can be said to be concentrated.

True gravity is not directly measurable in the earth, but the combined effect of gravity and centrifugal force, known as *apparent gravity*, is. Because of the rotation of the earth on its axis, there is a centrifugal force directed outward on each mass with respect to the earth. This force is combined with true gravity, the result being "apparent gravity." In dealing with the earth, the term is generally simplified to "*gravity*" ("little g"), while *gravitation* is recognized as a universal constant ("big G"). The standard acceleration of gravity, at sea level at 45° latitude, is $g_\phi = 980.665\ \text{cm/sec}^2$.

Apparent gravity decreases with altitude above the earth; the rate is approximately $-0.0003086\ \text{cm/sec}$ per meter of elevation. Toward the interior of the earth, gravity rises to a maximum at 2900 km depth and then diminishes to zero at the center. It is also less at the equator than at the poles, increasing steadily poleward. The latter is due to two factors. Since the earth is an oblate spheroid, the polar diameter is 22 km less than the equatorial diameter, thereby increasing the gravity. Furthermore, the centrifugal force is directed outward from the earth's axis perpendicular to it. Thus this component increases from pole to equator, being zero at the axis of instantaneous rotation (see Figs. 2 and 3, different representations of the same principles).

Since, according to Newton's *Second Law of Motion*, $F = ma$ and in meteorology unit mass is

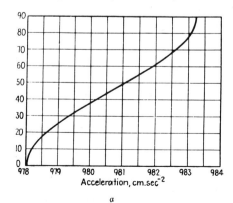

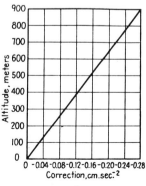

a *b*

Fig. 1. Variation of acceleration due to gravity (a) with latitude and (b) with altitude (Byers, 1944).

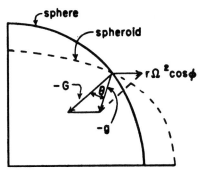

Fig. 2. Gravitational and centrifugal forces on an equilibrium oblate spheroid (Hess).

In this case $-G$ = Earth's geocentric gravity, $r\Omega^2 \cos\varphi$ = the centrifugal force, $-g$ is the resultant acceleration of apparent gravity, and θ is the angular difference.

assumed, the force of gravity is also known as the acceleration of gravity. It is given by

$$g = g_\phi - (3.085462 \times 10^{-4} + 2.27 \times 10^{-7} \cos 2\varphi)z \\ + (7.254 \times 10^{-11} + 1.0 \times 10^{-13} \cos 2\varphi)z^2 \\ - (1.517 \times 10^{-17} + 6 \times 10^{-20} \cos 2\varphi)z^3 \ (cm/sec^2)$$

where φ is latitude, z is geometric height (in meters) above MSL in free air, and $g_\phi = 980.6160 \ (1 - 0.0026373 \cos 2\varphi + 0.0000059 \cos^2 2\varphi$. In rough calculations, 980 cm/sec² is used.

In meteorology, the concept of *geopotential* is often used. This is the potential energy of unit mass at a point, given by

$$\Phi = \int g\,dz$$

where Φ is geopotential, z is height, g is gravity. Height

TABLE 1. ATMOSPHERE WITH THE SAME PROPERTIES AS THE NACA STANDARD, EXCEPT HEIGHT IS IN GEOPOTENTIAL FEET (AND GpM) AND THE LAPSE RATE OF TEMPERATURE IS CONSTANT AT 6.5°C PER GEOPOTENTIAL KILOMETER (after Saucier, 1955)

Pressure (millibars)	Temperature (°C)	Altitude	
		(Gpft)	(Gpm)
1013.25	15.0	0	0
1000	14.3	370	113
850	5.5	4780	1457
700	− 4.6	9880	3011
600	− 12.4	13800	4206
500	− 21.2	18290	5577
400	− 31.7	23580	7187
300	− 44.6	30070	9163
250	− 52.4	34000	10363
200	− 61.5	38630	11776
150	− 72.8	44320	13511
125	− 79.6	47770	14554
100	− 87.7	51830	15792

in this system is given in *dynamic meters* according to the formula

$$\Phi = \frac{gz}{10}\left(1 - \frac{z}{E}\right)$$

where E is the radius of the earth in meters. Since the factor in parenthesis is almost zero, the geopotential is for most practical purposes 0.98z. In cgs units, the unit of the geopotential is 1 gram × 1 cm × 1 sec^{-2}, but the dynamic meter is 10⁵ times as great and more convenient to use, though sometimes the geopoten-

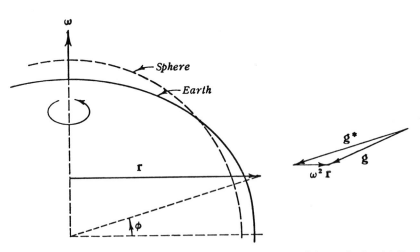

Fig. 3. Cross section through the earth showing the vector sum of the gravitational (q*) and centrifugal (ω²r) forces acting on unit mass fixed with respect to the rotating earth and the resulting distortion of the earth's figure. Latitude is represented by φ and the earth's angular frequency by ω (Fleagle and Businger, 1963).

tial foot is used (see Table 1). The geopotential (in dynamic meters), a unit of energy, is about 2% less than the actual geometric height (in meters), a unit of distance.

RICHARD J. ROMMER

References

Fleagle, R. G., and Businger, J. A., 1963, "An Introduction to Atmospheric Physics," New York, Academic Press, 346pp.

Hess, S. L., 1959, "Introduction to Theoretical Meteorology," New York, Holt and Co., 362pp.

Hewson, E. W., and Longley, R. W., 1944, "Meteorology Theoretical and Applied," New York, John Wiley & Sons, 468pp.

Huschke, R. E. (editor), 1959, "Glossary of Meteorology," Boston, American Meteorological Society, 638pp.

Cross-reference: *Centrifugal Force.*

GREENLAND SEA

One of the so-called Arctic Mediterranean seas (Kossinna, 1933, p. 871) situated between Greenland, Iceland and Spitsbergen, the Greenland Sea is defined by the International Hydrographic Bureau (*Sp. Publ.* 23, 1953) as bounded on the south by a line joining Straumness (northwest point of Iceland) to Cape Nansen (68°15′N 29°30′W) in Greenland; its northern boundary is a line joining the northern limits of Greenland and Spitsbergen (Svalbard); its eastern side is a line from the southernmost point of West Spitsbergen to Jan Mayen Island, and the eastern limit of Gerpir in Iceland. The area of the Greenland Sea is 1,205,000 km², and with a mean depth of 1444 m, its volume is 2,408,000 km³.

The Greenland Sea was studied in the early part of this century by Nansen and by Helland-Hansen, since when it has been explored by many investigators. Nevertheless, the western, often ice-covered areas are still poorly known.

Bathymetry

The Greenland Sea is divided into two large basins by the *West Jan Mayen Ridge* or *Rise* (1000–1500 m). The southerly of these is the *Iceland Basin* with a maximum depth of 2793 m, while the northerly and larger one is called the *Greenland Basin,* maximum depth 4846 m. A smaller trough, the Jan Mayen Basin is separated from the latter by the *North Jan Mayen Ridge.* The eastern border of these depressions is a zigzag extension of the mid-oceanic ridge (q.v.) from northeast of Iceland to Jan Mayen (the *Iceland–Jan Mayen Ridge*) and from there to the northeast and north to pass just west of Spitsbergen (*East Jan Mayen Ridge,* also called Mohns Ridge). Between Spitsbergen and the Belgica Bank (broad continental shelf east of northeast Greenland), there are two small oblique

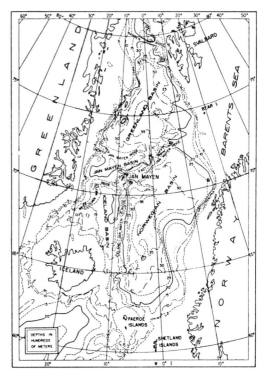

Fig. 1. Bathymetry of the Greenland Sea (after Stocks, 1950; from Metcalf, 1960).

transverse ridges, the *Barentsberg Ridge* in the south and the *Spitsbergen Ridge* (*Nansen Sill*) in the north which enclose the South Spitsbergen Basin, while the North Spitsbergen Basin (*Lena Trough*) lies north of the Spitsbergen Ridge; maximum depths are, respectively, 3750 m and 4000 m (according to Stocks, 1950), while sill depths are of the order of 1500 m. Hope (1959) believes the Lena Trough is part of the mid-ocean rift system.

Sediments

Greenland, the world's largest island, is structurally part of the North American continent and under its 2–3 km thick ice sheet it has a foundation of Precambrian crystalline rocks, with a belt of older Paleozoic (Caledonian) geosynclinal rocks along the northeastern margin, locally penetrated by swarms of Tertiary basaltic and doleritic dikes in the famous Skaergaard intrusion (studies especially by Wager and Deer). These rocks are deeply dissected by enormous partly glacier-filled fiords along the coast, and ice-borne erratic blocks and finer debris are carried all over the Greenland Sea and beyond.

Along the East Greenland Shelf there are morainic deposits alternating with areas of hard-ground (rocky floor) stripped bare by grounding ice and currents. Most of the basins are filled with terrige-

307

neous material, ice-rifted or turbidity-current transported, but with some pelagic components: small minor amounts of globigerina ooze (southwest of Jan Mayen) and diatom ooze. Around the Jan Mayen and north of Iceland, the active volcanoes furnish ash deposits.

Structure

The Greenland Sea is widely considered as a quasi-cratonic basin, produced by the spreading apart of Greenland and Scandinavia during the late Mesozoic and Cenozoic. The Paleozoic fold belts of East Greenland, Norway and Spitsbergen seem to match in a very remarkable way, as if split down the center. The mid-ocean rift from Iceland through Jan Mayen and passing northward seems to be a belt of active crustal growth today, and is extremely seismic (Sykes, 1965). There is probably some east–west shearing through Jan Mayen.

Meteorology

The air mass in the northern part of the Greenland Sea is Arctic, while that over the southern part is usually Polar Maritime. In winter the Atlantic Arctic Front runs over the Greenland Sea past Iceland to Novaya Zemlya and storms frequently sweep along this front. Monthly mean surface air temperature shows a minimum of 14–27°F (-10 to -3°C) in February and a maximum of 34–46°F (1–8°C) in August at Jan Mayen (at 72°N latitude), but it has a larger range (-35 to -16°F or -37 to -26.5°C) in March and 33–48°F or 0.5–9°C in July) on the northern Greenland coast. Monthly precipitation frequency reaches a maximum (43%) in December and a minimum (15%) in July at Jan Mayen, and it is lower by about 30% on the northern Greenland coast.

The predominant surface wind is north to east with average forces of 5–6 (Beaufort scale) at Jan Mayen and south to southwest (at Nord) or west to northwest (at Danmarkshaven) with average forces of 3–4 on the northern Greenland coast. In winter, the mean sea level pressure over the area is low owing to intensification of Icelandic Low over the Irminger Sea; this pressure is 1000 millibars along the north coast of Iceland and 1005 millibars from Scoresby Sund to the southern tip of Spitsbergen. In summer, the mean sea level pressure increases by 10–12 millibars over the Denmark Straits and by 5–8 millibars in the northern part due to the pressure of an Arctic High over the Polar Sea.

Oceanography

The water masses of the Greenland Sea consist of four types. The "Polar Water" has low temperature of about -1.85°C and low salinity below 34.50‰. This water is present over the East Greenland Shelf and flows southward, forming a part of the Greenland Current. As it flows along the Greenland coast, land drainage and melting ice

are added and the salinity decreases to less than 30.0‰ in August.

The "Intermediate Water" comes from the West Spitsbergen Current which is a continuation of the Norwegian Current of the North Atlantic Water. A part of the former current flows counterclockwise around Spitsbergen. Another part turns to the south and forms the Greenland Current together with the Polar Water. This water has temperature of 5°C and salinity of 34.90–35.0‰ west of Spitsbergen. Through mixing with the Polar Water, the temperature decreases to below 2°C and the salinity becomes 34.95‰ between Jan Mayen and Scoresby Sund. As this water flows south, it sinks below the Polar Water which spreads in the upper layer east off the Greenland Shelf. The Intermediate Water is present between 200 and 500 m to the north of the Denmark Straits.

The third water mass is the "Norwegian Deep Water" which is formed north of Jan Mayen. This water is present below the Intermediate Water. It has a temperature of -0.5 to 0°C and a salinity of about 34.92‰, and is colder and less aline than the Intermediate Water. Although this water exists below the sill depth of the Greenland–Iceland Ridge, it flows across the ridge forming a narrow southerly current near the bottom. The North Atlantic water which appears above in the Denmark Straits comes from the Irminger Current (q.v.). This water is warm (higher than 8°C) but saline (more than 35‰); thus it is heavier than the Polar Water but lighter than other two water masses. This water is present near the Iceland Shelf in the Denmark Straits and above the Intermediate Water and the Deep Water.

The (East) Greenland Current is a continuation of the slow drift of surface water across the Polar Sea. As the flow becomes concentrated off Greenland, its speed increases and reaches about 25 cm/sec in the surface layer. The northeasterly winds also intensify the surface current. To the north of the Denmark Straits, the strong southward current of 10–20 cm/sec is obtained by dynamic calculations in deep layers of 200–600 m on the slope off the Greenland Shelf. Also, a northward current of almost the same speed is determined in the deeper layers just to the east of the southerly current. Both currents are about 20–30 nautical miles wide and thus rather narrow. There is a cyclonic gyral north of Jan Mayen between the Greenland current and a branch of the Norwegian current flowing west of Spitsbergen. This gyral occupies almost the entire Greenland Basin. It is called the Greenland gyral and is distinguished from the southern Norwegian gyral.

The surface current in the southern section of the Greenland Sea was measured by Krauss (1958) and Stefansson (1962). A current of 15–20 cm/sec flows southwestwards on the Greenland Shelf. This current branches at about 68°N. One branch flows

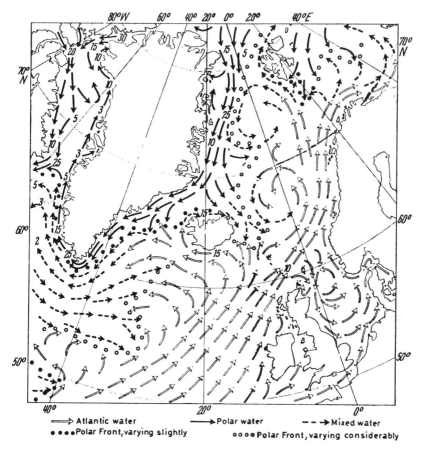

Fig. 2. Surface currents in the Northeast Atlantic Ocean (after B. Helland-Hansen and F. Nansen, 1909; J. B. Tait, 1934; A. B. Kiilerich, 1939, 1945; F. Hermann, H. Thomsen, 1946; G. Dietrich, 1956; from Dietrich, 1963).

south and the other branch flows southwest along the coast. To the east of these currents a weak (less than 5 cm/sec) and broad current flows south. A branch of the Irminger Current with speeds of 5–10 cm/sec flows northeastward in the Denmark Straits and turns east to the north of Iceland. It forms the "polar front" with the southerly current. In summer the front runs northeast from about 66°N and 28°W and turns east at about 68°N and 22°W, encircling Iceland. The branch of the North Irminger Current for the most part returns to the south off the east coast of Iceland.

Off East Greenland a belt of sea ice is present for the whole year. The ice coverage reaches maximum in April covering the entire sea, and the ice may be sighted along the north coast of Iceland. In September the ice coverage becomes minimum and the coast south of 70–72°N becomes navigable for specially built ships. Systematic changes in the mean ice front have been recorded for over 1000 years (see *Sea Ice—Climatic Cycles*).

The tidal range is about 1.9 m on the East Green-

land coast and 2.0–5.0 m at Spitsbergen, with two tides daily. The tide waves from the North Atlantic Ocean pass the Greenland Sea and enter into the Polar Sea between Greenland and Spitsbergen. Transverse oscillations between the Norwegian coast and East Greenland are produced due to the effect of rotation of the earth. Superposition of progressive waves and transverse oscillations causes a positive amphidromic point near Spitsbergen both for semidiurnal and diurnal tides.

RHODES W. FAIRBRIDGE
TAKASHI ICHIYE

References

Dorsey, H. G., 1951, "Arctic Meteorology," in "Compendium of Meteorology," pp. 942–964, Boston, American Meteorological Society.

Hope, E. R., 1959, "Geotectonics of the Arctic Ocean—on the Great Arctic Magnetic Anomaly," *J. Geophys. Res.*, **64**, 407–427.

Jakhelln, A., 1936, "Oceanographic investigations in east Greenland waters in the summers of 1930–1932," *Skrifter om Svalbard og Ishavet,* **67**, 79pp.

Kiilerich, A., 1945, "On the hydrography of the Greenland Sea," *Medd. Grønland,* **144**, Appendix No. 2.

Kossinna, E., 1933, "Die Erdoberfläche," *Handb. Geophys. Berlin,* **2**, 867–954.

Krauss, W., 1958, "Die hydrographischen Untersuchungen mit 'Anton Dohrn' auf dem ost-und Westgrönlandischen Schelf im September-Oktober 1955," *Ber. Dtsch. Wiss. Komm. Meeresforsch.,* **15**(2), 77–104.

Metcalf, W. G., 1960, "A note on water movement in the Greenland–Norwegian Sea," *Deep-Sea Res.,* **7**, 190–200.

Stefansson, U., 1962, "North Icelandic Waters," Reykjavik, University Research Institute, 269pp.

Stocks, T., 1950, "Die tiefenverhältnisse des Europäischen Nordmeers," *Deut. Hydrograph. Z.,* **3**(1/2), 93–100.

Sverdrup, H. V., Johnson, M. W., and Fleming, R. H., 1942, "The Oceans," Englewood Cliffs, N.J., Prentice-Hall, 1087pp.

Sykes, L. R., 1965, "The seismicity of the Arctic," *Bull. Seism. Soc. Amer.,* **55**, 519–536.

U.S. Navy, Chief of Naval Operations, 1963, "Marine Climatic Atlas of the World Ocean, VI. Arctic Ocean," NAVWEPS 50-1C-533, U.S. Government Printing Office.

GUIANA CURRENT

The name Guiana Current has been used by some investigators to label the movement of water along the northern coast of South America. Its origin is in the neighborhood of Cape San Roque where the South Equatorial Current divides—with part turning to the south to form the *Brazil Current* (q.v.) and the rest turning northward across the equator to join with some of the components of the North Equatorial Current and a component of the river drainage. This three-component current then moves northwesterly along the South American coast with its axis almost always over the continental shelf. Its identity terminates as it passes through the passages of the Lesser Antilles (sill depth less than

1000 m) to add its share to the *Caribbean Current* (q.v.).

Its physical characteristics include a surface temperature that varies from 26–27°C in the months of February and March, to 27°C in May through August, and as high as 28°C by November. Its surface salinity falls within the range of 35.0–36.5‰. The less saline waters from the Amazon and Orinoco rivers contribute to the lower values. The oxygen saturation values show a minimum of 3.0 cc/liter. The main stream retains its physical character for its entire length. It does, however, show variability in its speed. The records of the *Challenger* Expedition note that on the morning of August 25, 1874 near St. Paul's Rocks a surface current of 2 knots was running west, while in the afternoon in the same area they measured only 1 knot in the same direction. The current being very shallow in nature, its speed decreases rapidly with depth; at 27 m, it is about $\frac{3}{4}$ of a knot; at 90 m, $\frac{1}{2}$ knot; at 137 m, not detectable.

The originator of the name is obscure, though the source of inspiration is evident in the name of the three countries whose coast it parallels—British Guiana, French Guiana, and Surinam (or Dutch Guiana). Some of the earliest work done in the area was by the *Albatross* Expedition (1887–88) and the *Dana* Expedition (1921–22), while the *Meteor* Expedition (1925–27) produced a comprehensive survey.

NOEL B. PLUTCHAK

References

Defant, Albert, 1961, "Physical Oceanography," New York, Pergamon Press, 2 vols. (see esp. Vol. I, p. 606).

Krummel, Otto, 1911, "Handbuch der Ozeanographie," Second ed., Stuttgart, 2 vols.

Schott, G., 1942, "Geographie des Atlantischen Ozeans," Third ed., Hamburg, Boysen, 438pp.

Seiwell, H. R., 1937, "The minimum oxygen concentration in the western basin of the North Atlantic,"

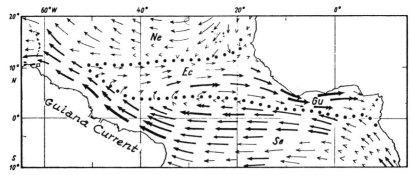

Fig. 1. Currents at the sea surface in the equatorial region of the Atlantic Ocean in the northern summer showing the course of the Guiana Current (modified after G. Schott, 1943). (Heaviest arrow indicates over 108 nautical miles per day; finest 0–36 nautical miles per day. Dots indicate convergence.) Note: Gu = Guinea Current (q.v.).

Papers in Physical Oceanography and Meteorology, Cambridge, Mass., **5**(3).

Expedition Reports:

Albatross (U.S.), 1887–88.
National (German), 1889.
Dana (Danish), 1921–22.
Meteor (German), 1925–27.
Atlantis (U.S.), 1932.

GUINEA CURRENT

The Guinea Current is an eastward extension of the Equatorial Counter-current. It has as its chief source the water of the South Equatorial Current as it curves back to the east along its northern edge.

The Guinea Current always runs north of the equator; its position changes with the season. During the winter months, its axis moves south so that its northern and southern limits are at about 7°N and 3°N latitude, respectively at 20°W longitude, and it extends west only to 25°W longitude. During the summer months of July through September, it broadens and shifts north so that its limit is 15–3°N latitude and it extends to the west to 40°W longitude. The illustration depicts these changes. It moves in along the Coast of Africa from about Cape Roxo at the Bay of Bifa and continues to move south into the Gulf of Guinea. Here its warm, deep-blue water of relatively high salinity moves into the Gulf to meet the fresh waters of the Gulf and encounters the cold green water of the Benguela Current moving up from the south.

The first notice of the existence of the current seems to have been made on an English chart dated October 4, 1850, drawn by Findlay. About the same time, Heinrich Berghaus, a geographer, was impressing the fact upon the merchant fleet of the day, that travel time could be shortened by staying outside of the current while heading west and sailing within the current while moving east. Later it was found that retardation of 40–50 nautical miles/day was possible for the sailing vessels of the day.

Although intensive studies of the current have not been made, work done thus far shows the current to move at speeds of 13 nautical miles/day to a maximum of 22 nautical miles/day. The speeds vary from the edges to the center of the current, and from season to season, being at maximum from June through September. The temperature of the surface water is generally about 27–28°C, but around September it may get as low as 25°C. The salinity is rather high, varying from 34.5–36.3‰ as a representative summer value, to 35.0–37.0‰ as a representative winter value. The oxygen saturation is relatively poor with its maximum 4.5 cc/liter at the surface. The current is shallow, being very weak at 120–150 meters and disappearing at 180–200 meters. It has been suggested by several investigations that the great variability of the current is attributable to the wind and its variations. A very recent study of currents in the Gulf of Guinea gives some evidence of the existence of a Guinea undercurrent. Measurements by Gerard and Sexton (1965) detected a current speed of 13.5 nautical miles/day at a depth of 60 meters while on

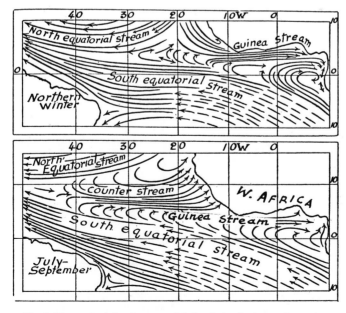

Fig. 1. *Upper*: the Atlantic equatorial circulation in the northern winter; *lower*: the same during July and September (from J. Johnstone, 1928).

station at 3°N latitude, 8°W longitude south of Cape Palmas.

The major investigations of the Guinea Current have been made by the *Meteor* expedition (1925–1927), *Discovery* (1925–1927, 1929–1931), the *Dana* cruise (1928), the *Carnegie* (1928), and the *Möwe* (1911). In more recent times, the combined efforts of many countries in the equatorial expeditions (see especially *Equalant II*) have added more data, but the results are not yet analyzed.

Descriptions of the currents of the equatorial region have been made by Krümmel (1902, 1911). Defant (1936) made another analysis of the system utilizing the data from virtually all the expeditions to that time. In 1938, Montgomery used a different technique of isentropic analysis to determine the structure of the equatorial current system in the upper layers on potential density surfaces.

NOEL B. PLUTCHAK

References

Gerard, R., Sexton, R., and Mageike, P., 1965, "Parachute drogue measurements in the eastern tropical Atlantic in September 1964,"*J. Geophys. Res.,* **70,** 5696.

Krümmel, Otto, 1902, "Der Ozean," Vienna, O Freytag, G.M.B.H.

Krümmel, Otto, 1911, "Handbuch der Ozeanographie," Band II, Stuttgart, J. Engelhorns Nachf.

Montgomery, R. B., 1938, "Circulation in upper layers of Southern North Atlantic deduced with use of isentropic analysis," *Papers in Physical Oceanography and Meteorology.* V **6**, No. 2, 55 (Massachusetts Institute of Technology, Mass.).

Rauch, J., 1948, "Traité d'Oceanographie Physique; les mouvements de la mer," Paris, Payot.

Reports

Carnegie Cruise, 1928–1929.

Data Report *Equalant II,* 1964, Pub. G-5 of NODC Series, U.S. Government Printing Office, Washington, D.C.

Deutsche Atlantisch Expedition, Georg Wüst, 1932.

Discovery Report—1:3—140, 1929; 4:3—230, 1932.

Meteor, 1925–1927, Band VI—Band III.

The Danish *Dana* Expedition, 1920–1922, In the North Atlantic and the Gulf of Panama, No. 1.

Möwe, Gerhard Schott and Bruce Schuly, 1914, Die Forschungsreise S.M.S. *Möwe* in Jahre 1911.

GULF OF CALIFORNIA

Discovery and Scientific Exploration

The Gulf of California was first seen by Europeans in 1532 by Nuñez de Guzmán. In 1539, Francesco de Ulloa circumnavigated the Gulf, which he named *Mar Bermejo* (Vermilion Sea) owing to the red color of the plankton blooms (analogous to the Red Sea). He established the peninsular nature of Lower California, a fact which did not find its way into European maps until the eighteenth century. The Gulf of Cali-

fornia is a naturalist's paradise, but it was only infrequently visited by scientific investigators until the middle 1950's (see van Andel and Shor, 1964, for references).

Morphology

The Gulf is an elongate, northwest-southeast-trending trough, some 1200 km long and, on the average, 150 km wide. It is bordered on the west by the mountainous peninsula of Lower California,

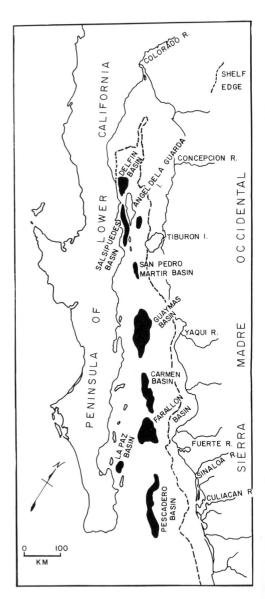

Fig. 1. Submarine morphology of the Gulf of California. Black areas are basins separated by sills, and deepening from 980 m in the northwest (Delfin Basin) to 3700 m (Pescadero Basin) in the southeast. Dotted line is shelf edge at 200 m.

a westward-tilted plateau with a precipitous eastern side. On the east, the Gulf is fringed by a broad coastal plain consisting in the north of late-Cenozoic desert plains and minor ranges, and in the central and southern parts of modern deltas, lagoons, and strand plains. Landward from this coastal plain rises the high range of the Sierra Madre Occidental. At the northwestern end of the Gulf, the Colorado has built a large delta with extensive flanking tidal flats.

The Gulf proper can be divided into two morphologic provinces, separated by a constriction and several large islands (Fig. 1). The northern area is generally shallow, with little relief and depths of less than 200 m. Exceptions are the deep basins on both sides of Angel de la Guarda Island, with maximum depths of 1500 and 550 m. The southern and central Gulf consists of a series of basins, deepening from 980 m in the northwest to 3700 m in the extreme southeast. These basins are separated by sills which also deepen southeastward from 880–3300 m. The continental shelf varies in width from 5–50 km along the eastern side, and it is approximately 110 m deep at the edge. The eastern slope to the basin floors is gentle, smooth, and obviously depositional. No shelf occurs along the western side, which is only locally bordered by a narrow, rock-cut platform with a depth of 100 m and a steep, sometimes precipitous, rocky slope.

Submarine canyons cut the slope around the southern tip of the peninsula and along the eastern side off some major deltas.

Structure and Origin

The Gulf usually has been considered a graben, a sunken block of the continent. Recent gravity studies, however, have shown that the area is in isostatic equilibrium and that there is no large mass of light crustal material beneath. Seismic surveys have indicated that the boundary between the crust and the mantle, the Mohorovičić discontinuity, lies at a depth of 10–11 km, a normal figure for the oceans. Under the peninsula and the Mexican mainland, the depth to the discontinuity is greater (25–35 km). Hence, the Gulf is structurally a part of the Pacific Ocean, and most prob-

ably not a foundered portion of the North American continent.

The Gulf is located where a broad elevation of the Pacific Ocean floor, the East Pacific Rise, meets the continent. The rise is considered by some geologists to be the result of uplift of the earth's crust by rising convection currents in the earth's interior. The Gulf topography indicates the presence of several large northwest-southeast-trending faults, and the most important group of faults in California, the San Andreas family (mainly dextral strike-slips), probably forms the northward extension of the Gulf. Moreover, shallow earthquakes are common in the Gulf. This evidence has induced G. A. Rusnak and R. L. Fisher (see van Andel and Shor, 1964) to postulate that a large system of fractures has formed where the East Pacific Rise disappears under the continent, and that the Gulf was produced by northwestward sliding of the peninsula and all of California, west of the San Andreas fault, down the slope of the rise (see *Expansion Theory*, pr. Vol. V).

Climate and Oceanography

Most of the Gulf and the adjacent lands are arid. Mean annual temperatures range from 22–25°C. The peninsula has an annual rainfall of approximately 10–20 cm, and no permanent streams enter the Gulf from this side. Along the eastern margin, rainfall increases from less than 10 cm in the northwest to more than 85 cm in the southeast, near Mazatlan. In the northeast, all streams are seasonal, but south of Guaymas, permanent rivers occur, although with large seasonal variations in discharge. Several of these rivers have extensive drainage basins and carry large amounts of water and sediment. The Colorado River, once the major source of fresh water and sediment, has become an insignificant source since the completion of Hoover Dam in 1935 (Table 1).

In the northern Gulf, the annual range of surface water temperatures is considerable (summer: 29–30°C; winter: 16–19°C). In winter, the water is almost isothermal from surface to bottom,

TABLE 1. DISCHARGE AND SEDIMENT LOAD OF GULF OF CALIFORNIA RIVERS

River	Average Annual Flow (millions m³)	Annual Sediment Load (tons)
Colorado 1911–1935	17,985	161,000,000
1935–1951	8,077	15,000,000
Concepcion	742	7,422,894
Yaqui	2,666	26,670,397
Fuerte	4,707	47,088,357
Sinaloa	1,659	16,596,470
Culican	3,833	33,843,194
San Lorenzo	4,728	47,298,439

owing to convective mixing; in summer, evaporation produces a marked stratification in the water with a warm, slightly more saline surface layer. In the deep basins of this area, strong tidal mixing results in an almost totally homogeneous water mass. In the central and southern Gulf, the water below the thermocline is identical in salinity and temperature to equatorial Pacific water. As in the equatorial Pacific, a pronounced oxygen minimum (0.01–0.02 ml/liter) is present between 400 and 800 m. Above the thermocline, the water is modified slightly by evaporation, and in the southern Gulf, by surface inflow of equatorial Pacific water

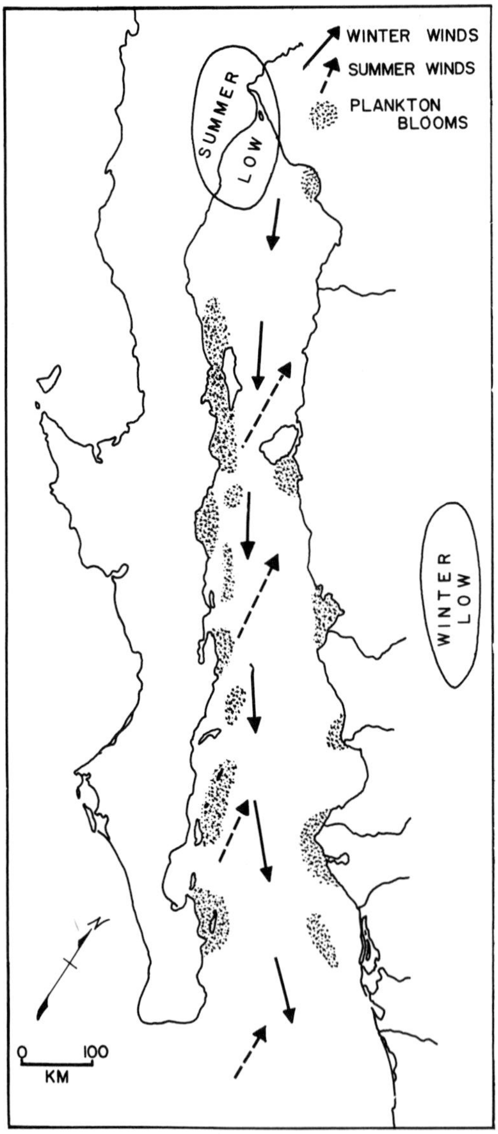

Fig. 2. Wind distribution, position of winter and summer low atmospheric pressure areas, and occurrence of plankton blooms in the Gulf of California.

and water from the California Current flowing southeastward around the peninsula.

The surface circulation pattern is controlled by the dominant seasonal winds (Fig. 2). In winter, a low-pressure system east of the Gulf produces strong northerly winds which blow the surface water out of the Gulf and cause a compensating subsurface inflow of Pacific water. As a result, cool, nutrient-rich water upwells from shallow depths in the lee of capes, islands, and submarine scarps, mainly along the eastern side. In summer, the low-pressure system is located over the northern peninsula. Winds blow from the south, driving surface Pacific water into the Gulf; upwelling occurs primarily along the peninsular coast.

The widespread upwelling results in an extremely high plankton productivity. Plankton blooms, mainly of diatoms and dinoflagellates, are abundant in all seasons, particularly in the central Gulf; in turn, they support a large zooplankton and fish population.

The mean tidal range in the Gulf increases progressively from 1 m in the south to 7 m near the mouth of the Colorado, where it exceeds 10 m at spring tides. The tidal wave behaves as a progressive, northward-traveling wave, and tidal-current velocities are high in the northern Gulf and between the large islands of Tiburón and Angel de la Guarda.

Sediments

Three main components form the sediments of the Gulf: land-derived (terrigenous) sands, silts, and clays; calcareous skeletal debris from planktonic Foraminifera and from bottom-dwelling organisms; and biogenous silica from diatoms and radiolarians (Fig. 3).

In the northern Gulf, an extensive area is occupied by Colorado sediments, but elsewhere, material derived from the eastern margin is dominant, and sediment transportation is mainly across the Gulf. The arid western side supplies very little sediment, and rock bottoms are common. On the eastern side, however, the depositional coastal plain, sedimentary shelf, and depositional slope indicate a high rate of sediment supply.

At shallow depths, most of the sediments are relicts of beach and nearshore deposits submerged by the rise of sea level following the last glacial low. These sediments, not yet covered by more recent deposits, are characterized by mixed shallow- and moderately deep-water faunal assemblages and by the mineral glauconite, an indicator of very slow deposition.

The distribution of modern shallow-water sediments in the Gulf is governed by the location of sediment sources, the rate of sediment supply, the surface currents, and the efficiency with which waves sort it into sand, silt, and clay. On the southeastern shelf, where the Pacific swell is felt

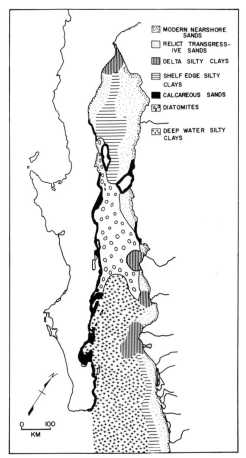

MODERN NEARSHORE SANDS

RELICT TRANSGRESSIVE SANDS

DELTA SILTY CLAYS

SHELF EDGE SILTY CLAYS

CALCAREOUS SANDS

DIATOMITES

DEEP WATER SILTY CLAYS

0   100
KM

Fig. 3. Distribution of sediment types in the Gulf of California. For explanation, see text.

and where there are many small sediment sources, the supply is completely sorted into sand, silt, and clay. The sands form a littoral zone, while the silts and clays are deposited in deeper, quieter water along the shelf edge. Farther north, wave action decreases in the lee of the peninsula, and larger rivers supply sediment at a rapid rate. Here, sorting is diminished, large deltas rapidly prograde seaward, and fine-grained sediments cover the entire shelf. Even farther north, sediment supply is again small and seasonal, and although wave action is only moderate, there is much time for sorting. The shelf sediments are again sandy, and all fine-grained material is removed to deep water. Along the western side, the terrigenous sediment supply is so low that calcareous skeletal debris forms from 25–50% of the platform sediments and a significant proportion of the slope deposits.

The deep-water sediments are fine-grained. An exception of minor importance is represented by thin sands (a few centimeters thick) which are locally found below the mouths of submarine canyons and beyond the major deltas. These sands

probably have been deposited by dense turbidity currents flowing down the canyons.

In the deep basins of the southern Gulf, the sediments consist mainly of terrigenous silty clays with small amounts of Foraminifera and radiolarians. On high, isolated hills and seamounts, Foraminifera may form the bulk of deposits. Sedimentation rates in these basins are low (0.01–0.10 g/cm^2/yr), and the deposits are similar to open-ocean sediments near the continents. In the central Gulf, on the other hand, the deposits are highly diatomaceous, containing 10–50% biogenous silica, some biogenous carbonate, and terrigenous clay and silt. These unusual sediments, which have been studied in detail by S. E. Calvert (see van Andel and Shor, 1964), reflect the great importance of the plankton blooms in the central Gulf. They accumulate at a rate of 0.05–0.15 gram silica and 0.09–0.3 gram terrigenous material per square centimeter per year. The silica is derived from the inflowing and upwelling Pacific Ocean water, and during plankton blooms, the surface waters may become entirely depleted of this nutrient. Thus, the Gulf forms a trap for oceanic silica and annually accommodates as much as 1% of the total silica supply to all oceans.

Throughout the year, the plankton blooms provide a continuous rain of biogenous silica to the basin floors. On the other hand, silt and clay are most abundantly supplied in the late summer and fall when thunderstorms cause the streams to rise. Hence the sediments are deposited as thin alternating layers of rather pure diatomite, representing the winter to early summer deposit, and of slightly diatomaceous silty clay, representing the late summer to fall deposit. Each pair, averaging 2.5 mm thick, represents one year's deposit, and thickness variations reflect climatic changes. On the slopes of the basins between 400 and 800 m, little oxygen is present in bottom waters. Hence, few bottom-dwelling organisms can live, and the laminations are preserved. Below the oxygen minimum zone, on the other hand, burrowing animals have homogenized the sediments.

Similar biogenous siliceous deposits are common in many ancient sedimentary basins. The Gulf of California illustrates the genesis of modern counterparts of these sediments and the relationships to their environments. It also demonstrates that, given the correct circumstances, the ocean provides an adequate supply of silica, contrary to a commonly held belief that to be supplied in sufficient quantities, silica must be of volcanic origin.

TJEERD H. VAN ANDEL

References

Munk, W. H., 1941, Internal Waves in the Gulf of California, *Jour. Mar. Res.*, **4**, (1).

Van Andel, Tj. H., and Shor, G. G., Jr., (editors), "Marine geology of the Gulf of California," *Am. Assoc. Petrol. Geologists, Mem.*, **3**, 409pp.

GULF OF CARPENTARIA (NORTHERN AUSTRALIA)

The Gulf of Carpentaria is defined as the large rectangular embayment of some 120,000 square miles bounded by Cape York on the east and Arnhem Land on the west. In this article the area has been extended north of the Gulf, as strictly defined, to New Guinea and is bounded on the west by the Wessel Rise (Fig. 1). According to the International Hydrographic Bureau (Sp. Publ., 1953), the whole area is included in the *Arafura Sea* (extending eastward to a line joining Bensbak River to the northwest point of the Cape York Peninsula).

There is a difference of opinion about the oceanic affinities of the Gulf; the C.S.I.R.O. Fisheries Department regards it rather more as Pacific in character, and this follows the recommendation of the Murchison Committee of the Royal Geographical Society (London) of 1845 (published in 1893). The writer prefers the more modern recommendation of Schott (1935) which placed the eastern limit of the Indian Ocean at the Torres Strait; oceanographically, there is no definite eastern boundary to the Indian Ocean water in the Timor or Arafura Sea.

History of the Gulf

The eastern side of the Gulf of Carpentaria was first explored by the Dutch between 1605 and 1628, and many of the names of coastal features originate from these early voyages. The southern and western coasts were discovered by Abel Tasman in 1644. The Gulf was named after one of the early Dutch explorers, Pieter Carpenter, who visited the area in 1628. The first chart was prepared by Matthew Flinders in 1802. This was supplemented by Captain J. L. Stokes in H.M.S. *Beagle* in 1841 and has remained essentially unchanged to the present day.

There has been recent activity in the area, connected with the development of bauxite deposits at Weipa on Cape York (Loughnan and Baylis, 1961), the manganese deposits on Groote Eylandt, the exploration for petroleum in the Mesozoic and Tertiary (?) sediments, and the research by C.S.I.R.O. Division of Fisheries and Oceanography into the prawn resources in the southeastern corner of the Gulf.

Tectonic Pattern

The rectangular character of the present outline of the Gulf of Carpentaria suggests faulted margins. Magnetometer surveys (Fig. 2) by oil exploration companies and bottom and sub-bottom information collected by the writer confirm this view. The Gulf depression can be defined as a graben with the down-faulted block hinged and partially faulted along the southern margin.

The eastern fault zone has been most accurately defined from bottom profiles south from the latitude 11° 20′S to latitude 15° 30′S. These records indicate an increase in vertical displacement toward the north. At latitude 11° 50′S the displacement indicated by geophysical survey is 2500 feet.

The western fault zone has been defined by aerial magnetometer survey and bathymetry. This fault results in steep margins to the Gulf in the vicinity of Groote Island and northward. It is probable that this fault continues southward along the eastern side of the Groote-Pellew Rise (Fig. 2) to the eastern side of Vanderlin Island in the Sir Edward Pellew Group where faulting is reported by Smith (1962). A second fault may occur further west between Groote Island and Arnhem Land and southwest to the Roper River, marking the western boundary of a small basin in the southwest corner of the Gulf.

From evidence obtained by the writer, the age of formation of the major Gulf graben is mid-Pleistocene, since late Pleistocene sediments in the center of the Gulf lie directly on an erosion surface of Mesozoic or Tertiary (?) rocks, suggesting that no earlier Pleistocene sedimentation occurred.

Besides these major faults, a number of minor faults have been located by both airborne work and sub-bottom profiles. Since both surveys are reconnaissance in character, the significance or the extent of these secondary fractures is unknown.

Hills (1945) considered the Gulf of Carpentaria the location of one of a series of early Precambrian continental nucleii (*Carpentaria Nucleus*). Trend lines of mid-Precambrian rocks (Fig. 1) suggest early Precambrian rocks in the center of the area, but no direct evidence has been found to date to indicate the character of the basement in the central portion. Sedimentation in the area since the Precambrian appears to have been restricted to post-Triassic times. Warping of the basement during Mesozoic subsidence or basement topography features have produced three sub-basins of Mesozoic deposition (Fig. 2):

(i) A northwest trending trough extending from latitude 13°S—longitude 138°E toward the Arafura Sea. Sedimentation increases in thickness toward the northwest to approximately 12,500 feet at the northwest limit of available data.

(ii) A northerly trending basin adjacent to the eastern fault zone with a marked depression centered about latitude 13°S—longitude 140°E. An east-west basement ridge partially cuts off the northern end of this basin. A southeasterly extension of this depression has been the location of Tertiary sedimentation in the southeastern corner of the Gulf in the Gilbert River area (latitude 17°S—longitude 141° 30′E).

(iii) A small deep basin in the southwestern corner of the Gulf centered about latitude 15°S—longitude 136°E. This basin is limited to the south

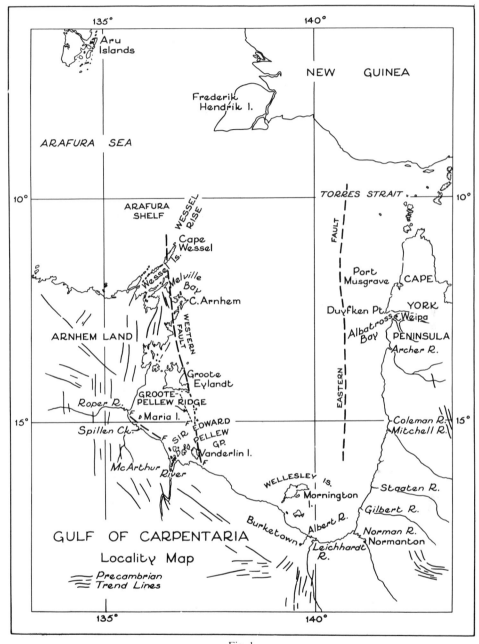

Fig. 1.

and possibly the west by faults; it is separated from the remainder of the Gulf by a basement ridge extending from the Sir Edward Pellew Islands (latitude 15° 40′S—longitude 137°E) to Groote Island (latitude 14°S—longitude 136° 40′E). This basin contains an estimated 10,000 feet of Mesozoic (?) sediment.

The basement ridge dividing basins 1 and 2 rises north causing a marked thinning of the Mesozoic-Tertiary (?) cover around latitude 11°S—

longitude 139°E. The thickness then increases again in the southern New Guinea area (Fig. 2). Fairbridge (personal communication) regards the Gulf (from Mesozoic to Recent) as a classical autogeosyncline.

Bathymetry. The whole area of the Gulf is shallow, not exceeding 38 fathoms, and generally between 25 and 35 fathoms (Fig. 3). The bathymetry for the most part is governed by the structure of the Gulf. Between the eastern fault and the present shore is a flat platform with occasional "hills" of coarse grained Mesozoic sandstone. To the south, the bottom rises gradually to extensive shallow areas along the south coast—mud banks exist at low tide along much of the southern shore. The western margin fault (mentioned above) produces a steep slope to portions of the western side, for example, the eastern coast of Groote Island (Fig. 3).

The Pellew Island–Groote Island basement rise is reflected in a number of bottom "hills," presumably of Precambrian Masterdon formation quartzites similar to the Pellew Islands. These extend some miles north of the Pellew Islands. The deepest portion of the Gulf is a depression adjacent to the eastern fault and is very similar in extent to the basement depression No. (ii) mentioned above (Fig. 2).

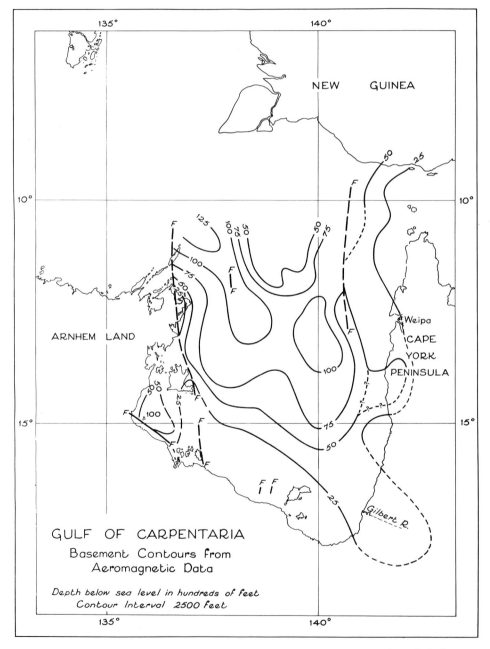

Fig. 2. Courtesy Delhi Australian Petroleum Ltd. and Marathon Petroleum Australia Ltd.

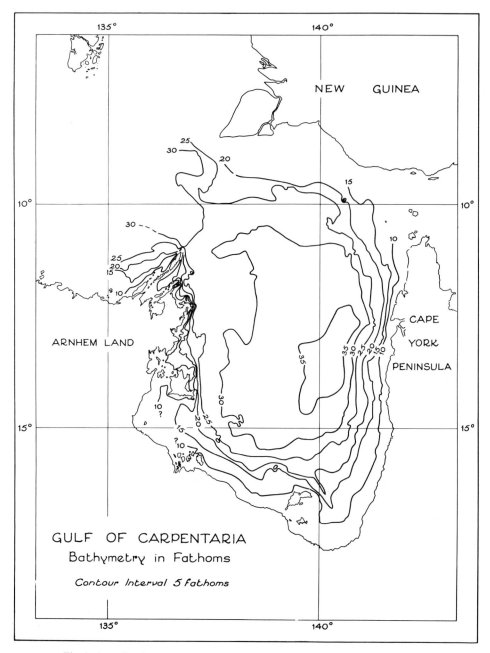

135° 140°

NEW GUINEA

25
30
20

15

10°   10°

30

25
20
15

10

30

ARNHEM LAND

CAPE

YORK

PENINSULA

35
30
25
20
15

35

10
?

30

15°   15°

20
25
15
30

?
10

GULF OF CARPENTARIA
Bathymetry in Fathoms

Contour Interval 5 Fathoms

135° 140°

Fig. 3. Compiled from soundings provided by Royal Aust. Navy Hydrographic Office.

The Wessell Rise (Fairbridge, 1952) is indicated by a broad ridge extending south from Frederick Hendrick Island towards Cape Wessell. A prominent narrow channel has been scoured along the eastern margin of the Wellesley Islands by tidal currents which are very evident in this area.

Stratigraphy of the Gulf Area

Precambrian. From approximately longitude 138°E westward, the rocks of the shore areas are Precambrian belonging to the Masterdon Group. These are quartzites and lavas which are very little disturbed in some areas. The basement encountered in the Mornington and Karumba bores suggest that these rocks continue eastward, at least to the southeast corner of the Gulf.

Paleozoic. It is doubtful whether any Paleozoic sedimentation occurred except in the northern

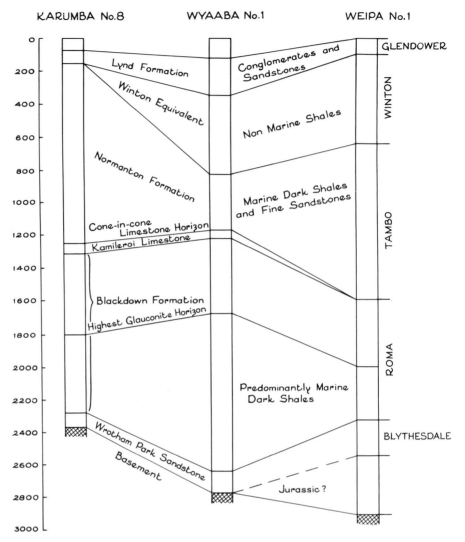

Fig. 4. Gulf of Carpentaria. Lithological correlation chart for oil bores. (*Courtesy Bureau Mineral Resources*)

Cape York–Torres Strait area. Hill and Denmead (1960) describe ignimbrites from Torres Strait as possible Permian.

Mesozoic. During late Jurassic and the Cretaceous, the area of the Gulf of Carpentaria was one of the principal connections between the open sea and the extensive epeiric sea which covered much of the eastern half of Australia at that time. The stratigraphy of the Mesozoic is known mainly from oil drilling operations (Fig. 4). The locations of wells drilled to date are given in Table 1. Details of the Mesozoic stratigraphy through central Queensland are given in Hill and Denmead (1960).

Tertiary. The extension of the eastern basin area to the southeast in early (?) Tertiary has given rise to a small area of Tertiary in the Gilbert River area of the southern east coast. Apart from this,

Tertiary rocks consist of laterites along the east and northwestern coasts. This lateritization has produced the extensive bauxite deposits of the Weipa area on Cape York and the Gove Peninsular in Arnhem Land. Rock from bottom cores in the northern central part of the Gulf suggests Tertiary sedimentation in that area, and probably represents an extension of the southern New Guinea shelf province (see *New Guinea,* pr Vol. VI).

Pleistocene and Recent. Pleistocene sedimentation on the mainland and islands of the southern Gulf consist principally of raised benches along the coast of the Wellesley Island, Sir Edward Pellew Islands and the Arnhem Land coast.

Overlying the Tertiary laterites are strongly cross-bedded calcarenites—the Vanderlin Limestone (Smith, 1962). These have been examined by

TABLE 1. DRILLING LOCATIONS, DEPTHS AND DEPTH TO BASEMENT IN THE VICINITY OF THE GULF OF CARPENTARIA

	Latitude	Longitude	Depth (ft)	Elevation above Sea Level
Normanton (municipal water bore)	17° 40′ 15″S	141° 04′ 44″E	2330	22
Burketown (municipal water bore)	17° 44′ 04″S	139° 32′ 55″E	2304	14
Margoura (station water bore)	17° 55′ 20″S	140° 56′ 20″E	2084	121
Inverleigh (station water bore)	17° 55′ 00″S	140° 05′ 10″E	2451 (basement 2442 ft)	100
Moorehead No. 1 (oil exploration by APC = IEC)	8° 15′ 5″S	141° 31′ 5″E	8087	25
Aram No. 1 (oil exploration by APC = IEC)	8° 15′ 5″S 7° 50′ 5″S	141° 31′ 5″E 142° 19′ 5″E	8087 6628 (granite 6524 ft)	25 25
Mornington No. 1 (oil exploration by Delhi–Santos)	16° 32′ 14″S	139° 15′ 27″E	2764 (granite 2743 ft)	57
Mornington No. 2 (oil exploration by Delhi–Santos)	16° 29′ 13″S	139° 31′ 11″E	3000 (quartzite basement 2991 ft)	34
Weipa No. 1* (oil exploration by Zinc Corp)	12° 43′ 00″S	141° 55′ 50″E	3243 (basement 2906 ft)	51
Wyaaba No. 1* (oil exploration by Frome–Broken Hill)	16° 29′ 30″S	141° 37′ 22″	2822 (basement 2763 ft)	40
Karumba No. 8* (oil exploration by AAO)	17° 24′ 36″S	140° 52′ 22″E	2364 (quartzite basement 2360 ft)	20

* See Fig. 4 for Stratigraphy.

the author in the Wellesley and Sir Edward Pellew islands where they extend to 105 feet above sea level and may represent the result of a higher sea level stand.

Recent Sedimentation in the Gulf. Recent coring and sub-bottom profiles by the University of Sydney have shown the nature of post-Tertiary sedimentation. These cores have not been examined to date, so only the generalized character of these sediments can be given. Three distinct sedimentary horizons occur on top of a weathered basement of Mesozoic or Tertiary rocks.

	Maximum Thickness Encountered (ft)
(a) Green marine mud	6
(b) Dark grey to chocolate clay or fine silt	4
(c) At the base a white clay	4
	14

The basal unit occurs only in the western area from Cape Wessell to latitude 14°S, approximately. The other two horizons are almost universal, though varying greatly in thickness.

Unit (b) has been shown to be estuarine (?) clay with an impoverished fauna in the center of the Gulf, and fine silt with no marine fauna at a latitude of 15°S. This unit was deposited after the down-faulting of the Gulf as it lenses out against the fault on the eastern side and does not occur on the shore platform east of the fault.

The surface green muds and silts (a) contain abundant marine fauna remains. This sediment has a sharp, nongradational contact with the underlying horizon indicating a sudden change from an estuarine or fresh-water to marine conditions. This is attributed by the author to the rise in sea level at the end of the Pleistocene and the consequent covering of a barrier, probably the Wessell Rise,

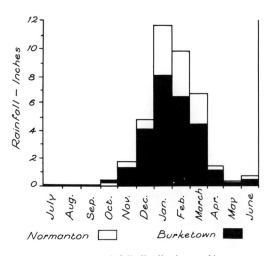

Fig. 5. Average rainfall distribution at Normanton and Burketown. (Data from Commonwealth Meteorological Office.)

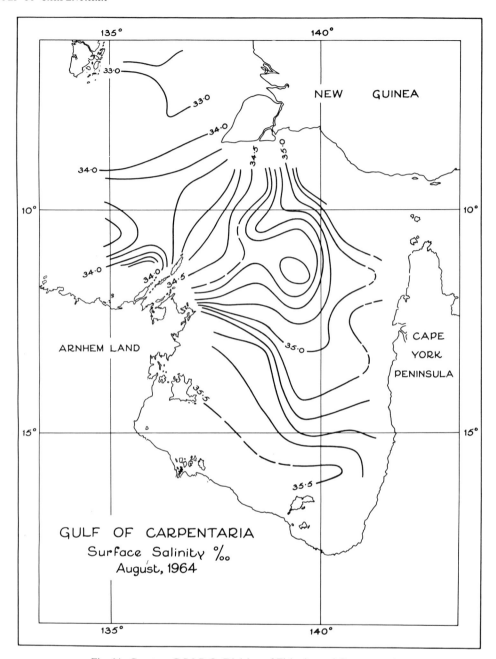

Fig. 6A. Courtesy C.S.I.R.O. Division of Fisheries and Oceanography.

which had divided lagoonal conditions in the Gulf from the Arafura Sea.

The absence of coral reefs south of latitude 12°S might seem to be anomalous, particularly considering the abundance of coral reefs in Torres Strait.

Seasonal low salinity inshore is the critical factor (Fairbridge).

Salinity and Water Movement

The climate of the area is monsoonal with the majority of the rain falling in the months December to March (Fig. 5). Rivers entering the Gulf affect the waters of the Gulf significantly only during the wet season. At this time, a great amount of water enters the Gulf from the south and east coastal rivers. How this affects the salinity and current pattern is not known, but presumably the high salinity in the south measured at the end of the dry season [Figs. 6(a) and 6(b)] would be considerably reduced.

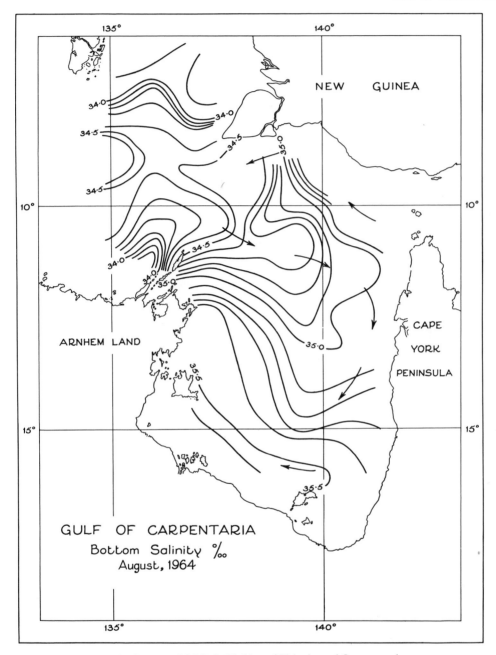

Fig. 6B. Courtesy C.S.I.R.O. Division of Fisheries and Oceanography.

Salinity distribution for the surface and bottom Gulf water [Figs. 6(a) and 6(b)] were determined by C.S.I.R.O. Division of Fisheries and Oceanography, in August 1964, and this probably defines the situation during the latter part of the dry season. This work indicates a static high-salinity situation in the south and a slow clockwise current originating from a nutrient-rich upwelling in the eastern Arafura Sea, in the main portion of the area.

Superimposed on this current are tidal effects. The tides at Karumba, at the entrance to the Norman River, rise to 12 feet in the spring and, as is characteristic of the Gulf, are diurnal during the spring tides and semidiurnal during the neap tides. (The Australian Pilot, 1959). Tidal currents of 2–3 knots are common around the Wellesley and Sir Edward Pellew Islands. Significant scouring has been observed as a result of tidal currents on the east side of the Wellesley Islands, Fig. 3. Details of currents within the body of the Gulf are unknown, but on a recent cruise, variations in the ship's speed of the order of one knot were noted on north-south traverses due to currents.

CHARLES V. G. PHIPPS

References

Admiralty, 1959, "The Australian Pilot," Vol. 5, Fifth ed. Hydrographic Department, London.

Fairbridge, R. W., 1952, "The Sahul Shelf—northern Australia—its structural and geological relationships," *J. Roy. Soc. W. Australia*, **38**, 1–33.

Hill, D., and Denmead, A. K., 1960, "The Geology of Queensland," *J. Geol. Soc. Australia*, **7**.

Hills, E. S., 1945, "Some aspects of the tectonics of Australia," *Roy. Soc. N.S.W.*, **79**, 67–91.

Loughnan, F. C., and Baylis, P., 1961, "The minerals of the bauxite deposits near Weipa, Queensland," *Am. Mineral.*, **46**, 209–217.

Smith, J. W., 1962, "Explanatory Notes on the Pellew Group—1:250,000 Geological Sheet," Bureau of Min. Resources report.

GULF OF MARACAIBO—*See* **LAKE MARA-CAIBO,** Vol. VI

GULF OF MEXICO

(1) General Description

The Gulf of Mexico is a relatively shallow, oceanic-type basin located at the southeastern boundary of North America. The greatest depth recorded therein is somewhat greater than 2000 fathoms. Its horizontal area is approximately 0.619 million square statute miles (1.602 million km²). Together with the Caribbean Sea it forms the "American Mediterranean" (comprised of five major basins), and in this context the Gulf is frequently referred to as the *Mexican Basin*. By comparison with the other basins of the American Mediterranean, the Mexican Basin is a simple, regular feature containing no large submarine trenches or ridges. Figure 1 shows the bottom topography of the Gulf of Mexico as constructed on the basis of U.S.C.G.S. Chart 1007 and unpublished soundings collected by the Department of Oceanography, Texas A & M University.

(2) Geological Structure

The structural evolution of the Gulf of Mexico is, to a large extent, unknown. Aside from the extreme northern and southwestern continental shelves, under which vast petroleum reserves lie, few systematic geophysical surveys have been made in the Gulf. Most such work accomplished to date has been restricted to measurements (employing seismic, magnetic, gravimetric and sonic techniques) of large-scale geological structures and gross parameters.

Early ideas concerning the Gulf of Mexico were variations of a postulation of Suess (1885), who maintained that the central portion of the Gulf was originally an extension of the coastal plain of the United States and that the present basin resulted from the collapse of this extension sometime during the Cenozoic era. Eardley (1951) estimated the time of origin for the Gulf of Mexico as being in the Late Paleozoic.

However, recent geophysical information (Ewing *et al.*, 1955; Ewing *et al.*, 1962; Antoine and Ewing, 1963) suggests that at least the central portion of the Gulf of Mexico is underlain by a typically oceanic crust; some observers would take this as implying that it has always been a basin, but others regard such areas of quasi-cratonic nature as the sites of crustal collapse, extension and the development of new oceanic floor (Fairbridge, personal communication). An outstanding structural feature of the Gulf is a sedimentary trough filled with 50,000 feet of sediments and located off the coasts of Texas and Louisiana. The axis of this trough trends approximately east–west, paralleling the northern margin of the Gulf. This *Gulf Coast Geosyncline* is filled with arenaceous-argillaceous sediments, which are chiefly of Tertiary age in the western and central portions where the trough has its maximum development, and carbonates of Tertiary and Late Mesozoic age in the eastern part. The exact location of its eastern boundaries is poorly defined. This is due in part to a scarcity of information and in part to the lithology of the sediments changing from sands and shales to carbonates. Carbonate sediments accumulate slower than do clastics. Therefore, 10,000 feet of limestones and dolomites adjacent to the coast of Florida would be time-equivalents to perhaps two or three times that thickness of sands and shales off the coast of Louisiana.

It is thought that the geosyncline began to develop when sediments, eroded from uplifts associated with the Laramide orogeny at the end of the Cretaceous, began to find their way down to the coast. Most of these sediments were deposited in river deltas which, like the present Mississippi Delta, built outward over the existing continental shelf. As the shelf received more and more deposits, the underlying strata became depressed in the area of maximum deposition, or depocenter, thereby allowing more sediments to be filled in on top. Thus, the trough, or geosyncline, may have begun. Some downward displacement of the coastal margins was necessary in order to allow room for additional sediments.

Earth scientists are still debating the exact mechanism of formation of the geosyncline (q.v.; pr Vol. V). The extent to which it is depressed by active subsidence under load and passive compaction of the strata beneath fresh deposits, and the extent that is due to tectonism are not yet resolved. The type of geosyncline represented by the Gulf Coast trough

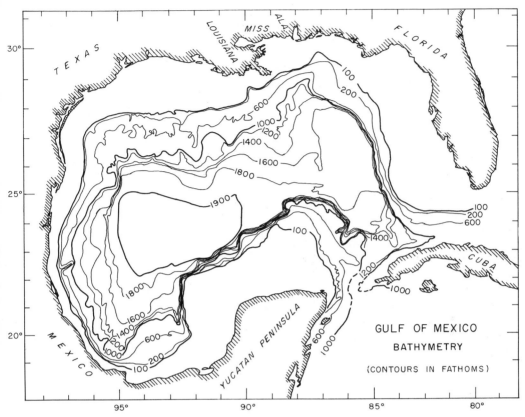

Fig. 1. Bathymetry of the Gulf of Mexico.

is probably the "paraliageosyncline" of the Kay classification.

Studies concerning the geology of the Gulf of Mexico have recently received impetus by investigations into the nature of a series of submarine hills called the *Sigsbee Knolls*, which rise as much as 200 fathoms above the Sigsbee Abyssal Plain in the central Gulf Basin. For the location of the plain and knolls, see Fig. 2, which gives the major physiographic provinces of the Gulf of Mexico. Ewing *et al.,* (1962) contend that these knolls are surface expressions of underlying salt domes. Salt domes are numerous along the Texas and Louisiana coastlines and in the interior of these states. Salt structures are also known to exist adjacent to the Isthmus of Tehuantepec, in the extreme southern portion of the Gulf of Mexico. No salt has been collected from the knolls, and although they superficially resemble volcanic structures, magnetic and gravimetric measurements do not support this possibility. Salt, therefore, remains a logical mechanism for their formation. On the other hand, diapirs filled with plastic clay offer an alternative.

It is possible that the domes of the central Gulf Coast and its adjacent shelf, the Sigsbee Knolls, and the domes of the Tehuantepec Embayment are derived from the same salt layer, the Louann Salt (of Jurassic to Permian age) which is thought to be the "mother-salt" for the Gulf Coast domes. This can only be confirmed by additional geological investigations.

(3) Sediments and Topography of the Gulf of Mexico

(a) Continental Shelves. The Campeche or Yucatan Shelf and the continental shelf off the western coast of Florida form the southern and northeastern boundaries of the Gulf basin, respectively. These carbonate platforms, together with the shelf off the Texas coast are the widest portions. The shelf is interrupted only by the Florida Straits (between the Florida Keys and Cuba), by the Yucatan Channel (between Mexico and Cuba), and by the vast deltaic deposits of the Mississippi River, which have built out over the shelf to reach nearly to the continental slope.

The continental shelf of the Gulf of Mexico is related to the mainland both geologically and geomorphologically. Off the coast of western Florida, where the shelf is merely an extension of the limestone karst surface of the Florida peninsula, the sediments consist of a thin, unconsolidated veneer of carbonate detritus. Part of this detritus is relic

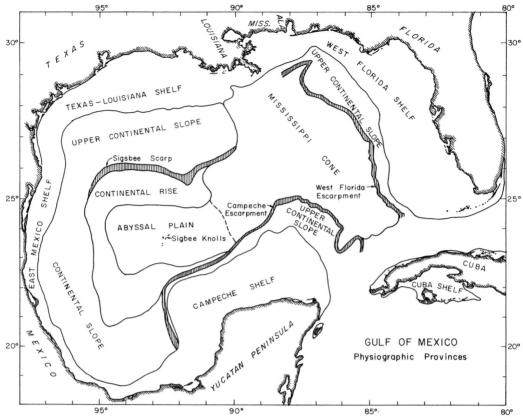

Fig. 2. Physiographic subdivisions of the Gulf of Mexico (after Ewing *et al.*, 1958, p. 998).

from the Pleistocene, but part is Holocene, for the oceanographic conditions there have remained favorable for the deposition of carbonate. This shelf is relatively smooth but terraced. The only interruptions in the surface are small mounds and ridges near the 30-fathom isobath. These were interpreted by Gould and Stewart (1955) to be reefs formed during the Pleistocene, when sea level was lower than at present.

Jordan and Stewart (1959) noted four distinct physiographic types on the upper slope and outer shelf west of central Florida. They include zones of small-scale ridge and trough topography, reef patches and pinnacles, dome-like rises and spur-shaped ridges. Their profiles show a broad terrace at about 115 fathoms in the same area and later (1961) they describe a terrace of comparable depth south of the outer Florida Keys. The latter is characterized by a Karst-like topography (discussed also by Jordan, Malloy and Kefoed, 1964).

Off the northwestern coast of Florida and the narrow shelf off Alabama, the neritic sediments become clastic, with quartz being the dominant component of the sands. Quartz sands extend westward to coastal Mississippi, where they become mixed with a silt and mud facies delivered by

rivers that flow into Mobile Bay. Near the western end of the Mississippi Barrier Islands, the influence of the Mississippi River system on the sediments is first noticed. Although the deltaic mudflats overlap the sediments of the shelf zone in this area, sands and silts exist in places beneath and incorporated in the deltaic deposits. These sandless terraces extend westward to the central coast of Louisiana, where some sands and silts begin to appear once again on the sediment surface.

According to Van Andel (1960) and Shepard *et al.* (1960) sediments are contributed to the northern Gulf of Mexico primarily by two large rivers, the Mississippi and the Rio Grande, with the former being more important. Sediments from the Mississippi River are swept westward by littoral drift and seasonal currents, resulting in a wide dispersion pattern. Between these two major river systems are smaller rivers, such as the Sabine, Trinity, Colorado, Brazos, etc. Some of these smaller streams, however, flow into bays, so that the major part of their loads never reaches the open shelf.

On the northern and northwestern shelves, non-calcareous sands and clays are dominant. The sands are found in bands paralleling the coast and reflect former sea-level stands; the finer fractions are found farther offshore on the outer shelf margins.

The submarine topography of the northern and northwestern continental shelf is less uniform than that of the west Florida Platform, as it contains knolls, mounds, ridges and domes. Most of the knolls and mounds are capped by algal reefs which formed during a low stage of sea level during the Pleistocene. Moreover, some of the domes, and perhaps some of the sub-reef mounds, are caused by the upward movement of salt masses. Offshore oil well structures are located near many of these latter domes.

The shelf off the eastern coast of Mexico is the narrowest portion of the Gulf of Mexico shelf. Although almost no information exists as to the nature of its sedimentary cover, sands are known to extend offshore in the vicinity of Tampico, having been brought Gulfward by the Panuco River which drains that section of eastern Mexico. Farther to the south, near Vera Cruz, coral patch reefs and mixed carbonate-clastic sediments constitute the sediment veneer. These mixed environments extend around the southern margin of the Gulf of Mexico to the Bay of Campeche, adjacent to the Isthmus of Tehuantepec. There, local rivers, draining nearby mountainous terrain, deliver a dominantly clastic suite of sediments to the shelf. This sedimentary environment ends at about 92°W longitude, where the Yucatan Shelf begins. The Yucatan Platform, like the shelf off western Florida, is an extensive carbonate plateau and, like Florida, is an extension of the karst surface of the mainland. The shelf sediments are similarly unconsolidated carbonates.

The Yucatan Shelf, although remarkably smooth, is broken by terraces associated with former stands of sea level (Logan, 1962). These terraces take the form of breaks in the gentle seaward slope of the shelf at the intervals between the 16–20, 28–35 and 50–75 fathom bathymetric contours. Also, an arcuate line of coral reefs and non-reef-supporting mounds is present on this shelf. The reefs are located parallel to the 30-fathom isobath, in the same relative position as those on the western Florida Shelf.

(b) Continental Slopes. The continental slopes of the Gulf of Mexico are, as in the case of the shelves, continuous around the margins of the basin. That off the western Florida carbonate platform is the steepest. The shelf-slope contact here occurs at the 35-fathom contour (Gould and Stewart, 1955). Between the 35- and 100-fathom isobaths, the slope of the bottom is about 10 ft/mile, but it increases to 300 ft/mile between the 400- and 500-fathom contours. Seaward, it forms one of the steepest submarine slopes known, possessing a declivity of of about 39°. The relative steepness of this slope has led to the suggestion that it is a fault scarp, although positive proof of faulting is lacking.

The slope is broken in many places by ridges and knobs. In the northwestern section it is interrupted by the DeSoto Canyon, a trough which heads near the 240-fathom contour and terminates near the 500-fathom contour, with a maximum relief of about 100 fathoms (Jordan, 1951).

The slope is less steep off the northern shelf and is characterized in the northwestern Gulf of Mexico by an extremely hummocky topography. The relief of the surface is due to the intrusive nature of underlying salt deposits, erosion associated with lower stands of Pleistocene sea level and probably submarine slumping.

Less is known concerning the slope off the eastern coast of Mexico, though bathymetric data indicate that it is quite narrow and very steep.

The slope in the extreme southern portion of the Gulf of Mexico is also steep and is broken between the Isthmus of Tehuantepec in the Bay of Campeche and the Yucatan Shelf by the Campeche Canyon (Creager, 1958). The slope adjacent to the Yucatan Shelf is steep and continuous down to the abyssal plain. The sediment cover consists of foraminiferal lutites with some coarser material which has slumped from the carbonate shelf above.

(c) Basin Topography and Sediments. The floor of the Gulf of Mexico is dominated by a sedimentary feature called the Mississippi Cone (Ewing et al., 1958). This is a cone-like accumulation of sedimentary detritus, the apex of which is a few hundred feet below present sea level at the place thought to have been the mouth of the Pleistocene Mississippi River (Ewing et al., 1958). It spreads out in an ever-broadening, convexly shaped fan down the slope and out over the floor of the basin.

Cores from this mass have been found to be similar in composition to the sediments on the floor of the abyssal plain of the Sigsbee Deep. The upper portion of each core consists of reddish-brown foraminiferal lutite, which overlies beds of grey silty clay. According to Ewing et al. (1958), this latter material, on the basis of carbon-14 and paleontological dating techniques, is Pleistocene in age. The overlying lutite is thought to represent the Holocene (Recent) accumulations.

The origin of the Mississippi Cone must be the result of the vast quantity of silty sediments which came out of the Mississippi River system throughout the Pleistocene and which spread out over the floor of the basin by turbidity transport. Evidence for such an origin is that the sediment cover of the Sigsbee Knolls, which rise above the flat abyssal plain, does not contain the grey silts associated with the cone sediments. This suggests that the latter spread out around the knolls, but not on top of them as the knolls rose above the level of sediment dispersal. The sediments on the knolls, at least those which have been cored, consist entirely of foraminiferal oozes and represent the deposition from ages of planktonic rain.

Nowlin *et al.* (1965) reported several additional knolls some 150 km southwest of those indicated in Fig. 2.

The abyssal plain of the Gulf of Mexico is partially covered by sediments associated with the Mississippi Cone, although the nature of the sediments in the extreme western portion of the plain is unknown.

This abyssal plain is remarkably flat; in fact, Ewing *et al.* (1962) state that it may well be one of the flattest portions of any sea floor, having gradients of only 1 : 8000.

As oceanographic and marine geophysical techniques continue to improve, and more and better measurements are taken, the deeper portions of the Gulf of Mexico will become as well known as are the shallow shelves today. For two excellent reviews on the general nature of the Gulf of Mexico, the reader is referred to Lynch (1954) and Murray (1962).

(4) Regional Oceanography

(a) **The Water Masses.** The principal inflow of water to the Gulf of Mexico is through the Yucatan Channel, which has a sill depth of between 1500 and 1900 m (McLellan and Nowlin, 1963). This sill depth determines the greatest depth from which water in the Yucatan Basin of the Caribbean Sea is allowed to enter the Gulf of Mexico. Most of the outflowing water passes directly into the North Atlantic through the Florida Straits, which is the only other natural passage connecting the Gulf with

the open ocean. This passage has a sill depth of some 800 m. Since the sill depths of the Anegada, Jungfern and Windward Passages, which connect the Caribbean with the North Atlantic, are all greater than the sill depth of the Florida Straits, open ocean waters may flow unobstructed through the American Mediterranean in the upper 800 m.

The water mass entering the Gulf through the Yucatan Channel at these upper levels results from an admixture of South Atlantic Water, transported northwestward by the Guiana and Equatorial Current systems, with North Atlantic Water, from the West Sargasso Sea. The ratio of South Atlantic to North Atlantic water in the Yucatan Channel has been estimated to be between 1 : 4 and 1 : 2.

The isohalines that delineate the core of the subtropical salinity maximum (Fig. 3) give some indication of the general spatial distribution of the currents flowing through the eastern Gulf of Mexico at 100–200 m depth. Although the water of the subtropical salinity maximum greatly influences the characteristics of the upper layers of water in the Gulf, its identity is little changed in passing through this region and it is not as well mixed laterally in the Gulf as in the Caribbean.

The thickness of the well-mixed surface layer, as defined by the depth range over which temperature remains uniform, may vary from a small fraction of a meter to over 125 m, depending upon the location, time of year and local influences. Over the central Gulf the mean depth of this layer is of the order of

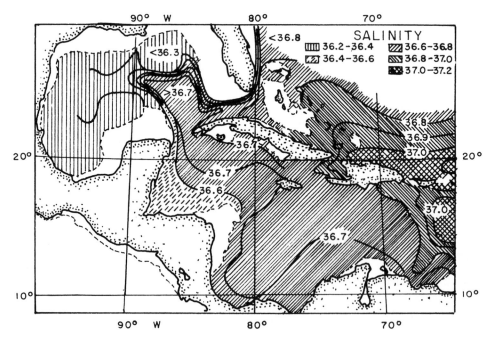

Fig. 3. Salinity distribution in the core of the subtropical salinity maximum in the Gulf of Mexico region (according to Dietrich; after Defant, 1961, p. 606). (By permission of Pergamon Press, N.Y.)

90 m during the months of January and February. These months are generally the coolest for the Gulf of Mexico.

Studies of average sea surface temperatures for February show the principal variation to be meridional, with temperatures of approximately 18 and 24°C off the northern Gulf coast and the Yucatan coast, respectively. There is, however, a northward shift of the isotherms in the region north of the Yucatan Channel, marking the influence of the northward flowing Yucatan Current. The diurnal, annual and regional variations of surface temperature are not well established, although considerable variations of each type are known to occur.

References to compilations of average sea surface temperatures, as well as other specific information regarding the surface layers, is included in a summary of the physical oceanography of the Gulf of Mexico by Leipper (1954).

Over the central Gulf basin the salinity of the surface waters is greater than 36.0‰, and generally within the range 36.0–36.3‰. However, surface values as great as 36.6‰ have been observed in the west central Gulf more than 100 miles north of the 100-fathom isobath at the edge of the Yucatan Shelf. The salinity of the nearshore surface water is greatly influenced by local runoff and river discharge, evaporation, intrusion of water from the Caribbean (in the case of the Yucatan Shelf area) and, possibly, by upwelling. The Mississippi River provides the most extensive influence; its waters have been reported to depths of 50 m and to distances of over 150 km from the coast, as determined by water of salinity less than 35.5‰ extending to the bottom or superimposed upon higher-salinity water. Of course, as the river mouth is approached the surface salinity decreases greatly; salinities less than 25‰ have been reported several miles offshore. In many other nearshore areas considerable salinity variation also occurs; however, due partially to the paucity of data, it is difficult to assign to specific regions definitive values of temporal variations.

In Fig. 4 is shown the temperature-salinity relationship which characterizes the waters in the Gulf of Mexico beneath the surface layer and the core of the subtropical salinity maximum. Of course, there is some variation in the depth at which a given temperature and salinity as related by this curve are to be found. However, 200 m can be taken as the approximate average depth of the 16°C isothermal surface in the Gulf.

The waters of minimum salinity which occur near the bottom of the main thermocline in the Gulf of Mexico can be identified as the last remnants of the northward flowing Antarctic Intermediate Water, which originates in the South Atlantic at approximately 45–50°S latitude, in the region of the Antarctic Polar Front. The depth of its core across the Yucatan Channel ranges between 850 and 1000

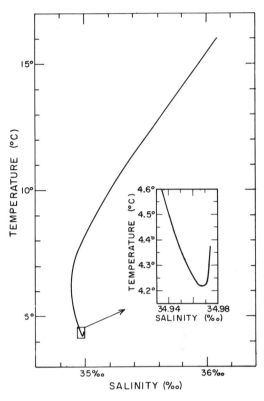

Fig. 4. Characteristic temperature-salinity relation for the waters beneath the 16°C isothermal surface in the Gulf of Mexico.

m. At this location it is characterized by a salinity of 34.86‰ and a temperature of approximately 6.2°C. This water is identifiable throughout the Gulf, although within the core the salinity is 0.02‰ greater and the temperature is about 0.1°C less in the western than in the eastern Gulf. The core depth, which is determined by the dynamics of the current regimes and consequently is nonuniform, is generally less within the Gulf proper than in the channel, having been observed as shallow as 550 m. The last vestiges of this water's original identity seem destroyed in passing out of the Gulf through the Florida Straits, for this water is not identified in the North Atlantic to the north of that position.

At 1500 m the approximate mean temperature and salinity are 4.22°C and 34.97‰, respectively. Below this level, especially from 2000 m to the bottom, the temperature and salinity show no significant horizontal variations. The characteristics of these deep waters are consistent with the idea that the basin was filled by Caribbean waters flooding over the sill in the Yucatan Channel. Below 2000 m, very small increases in mean temperature (less than or equal to 0.1°C per thousand meters) and in mean salinity (approximately 0.002‰ per thousand meters) continue to the bottom and produce near neutral (slightly positive) stability (McLellan and Nowlin, 1963).

The oxygen distribution within the Gulf, based on only a few cruises, has been discussed by several workers, e.g., Seiwell (1938; see Sverdrup *et al.*, 1942, p. 759) and McLellan and Nowlin (1963). However, a summary based on all existent oxygen data has not been published to date. The available data representing the concentrations of other sea-water constituents, e.g., phosphate-phosphorus or nitrate-nitrogen, are not sufficient to warrant conclusions as to the general distributions of these variables in the Gulf of Mexico.

Further information regarding the water masses of the Gulf may be found in the works of Dietrich, Iselin, Parr, Sverdrup and Wüst. References to these and other papers may be found in Sverdrup *et al.* (1942, Ch. 15) or in Defant (1961), which also serve as references to other topics concerned with the oceanography of the Gulf of Mexico.

(b) Currents. Certainly the most prominent feature of the surface circulation of the Gulf of Mexico is the large clockwise current in the eastern Gulf. The general shape of this feature is that of a loop. The western portion of this loop is formed by the Yucatan Current, which extends from north of Honduras in the Caribbean, through the Yucatan Channel and along the eastern edge of the Yucatan Shelf, into the central eastern Gulf. From this area the loop turns eastward, southeastward and again veers eastward to issue into the Atlantic via the Florida Straits as the Florida Current.

The Yucatan Current has been studied by Cochrane (1963), whose measurements show maximum surface velocities within the core of from 50 to over 200 cm/sec. The surface current attains a maximum in early summer, at which time its narrow core is situated approximately over the 100-fathom isobath on the western side of the Yucatan Channel. The velocities appear to decrease much more rapidly to the west of the core than to the east, the overall current width being some 60–80 miles. The surface velocity drops sharply during mid-fall to a minimum in October or November, at which time the core is broader and situated in water of somewhat greater depth. On the right-hand side of the current, several eddies seem to exist as semipermanent features. There is also some evidence that, at least seasonally, a surface countercurrent flows south–southwestward along the Cuban coast and into the Caribbean.

The Yucatan Current appears to be in approximate geostrophic balance (Cochrane, 1963). Its location, and that of the remainder of the loop current, can be readily discerned by marked slopes of the isothermal surfaces in a direction normal to the surface velocities, the warmer water being found on the right-hand side of the current.

The northern portion of the loop current has received only scant attention, although the dynamic coupling of this current with the northern Gulf waters may prove to be quite important in explaining the circulation of the northeastern Gulf.

The Florida current, having an estimated transport of 25 million m³/sec, is properly a portion of the Gulf Stream system, and will not be discussed here. For references, see Defant (1961).

In contrast to the previously mentioned currents of the eastern Gulf, which appear at least semi-permanent in nature, the weaker currents of the western Gulf are not well defined, but appear to vary temporally in location and intensity. However, based on the available data and geostrophic assumptions, there appears to be a large, elongated gyre (a high) approximately over the abyssal plain in the central West Gulf. Its major axis runs northeast–southwest, so that the current on the southeastern side of the gyre flows toward the southwest and the currents on the northwest flow toward the northeast. Velocities in the core of the northeastward flowing current have been computed to be some 50 cm/sec. This feature does not appear to be stationary and its study is difficult.

The nearshore currents of the Gulf show wide seasonal fluctuations, in direction as well as intensity at some localities. The studies which have been conducted have not been summarized and the information is often difficult to obtain.

(c) Tides and Waves. The average tidal range in the Gulf of Mexico is small, being only 1 or 2 feet at most coastal stations. Generally the type of tide in the Gulf is diurnal, i.e., at a given location only one high water and one low water occur during a lunar day. However, in the coastal region of the Florida Straits, semidiurnal and mixed tides are observed and the average tidal range seems slightly greater than that along the coasts of the Gulf proper. The reader is referred to Marmer (1954) for a summary of the tides and recently recorded sea-level changes in the Gulf of Mexico.

Wind waves generated within the Gulf are not large; the maximum waves encountered in this region rarely attain heights over 5 m. For specific information, the atlases and publications of the United States Navy Oceanographic (formerly Hydrographic) Office or the references contained in *Beach Erosion Board Technical Memo 98* (1957) may be consulted. As regards waves, the principal potential danger to the inhabitants of low-lying coastal areas surrounding the Gulf is from inundation due to storm surges. Such surges, usually caused by hurricanes in the Gulf of Mexico, sometimes reach heights of 5 m. Since hurricanes entering the Gulf generally pass through the Yucatan Channel and thereafter maintain northerly courses, storm surges occur more frequently along the northern than along the southern or western Gulf coasts.

JAMES L. HARDING

WORTH D. NOWLIN, JR.

References

Antoine, John, and Ewing, J. I., 1963, "Seismic re-fractions measurements on the margins of the Gulf of Mexico," *J. Geophys. Res.,* **68**, 1975–1996.

Cochrane, J. D., 1963, "Yucatan Current," in Unpubl. report of the Department of Oceanography and Meteorology, The A & M. College of Texas, Reference 63–18A.

Creager, J. S., 1958, "Marine Geology of the Bay of Campeche," Unpubl. Ph.D., A. & M. College Texas.

Defant, Albert, 1961, "Physical Oceanography," Vol. 1, New York, Pergamon Press.

Eardley, A. J., 1951, "Structural Geology of North America," New York, Harper Bros.

Ewing, J. I., Worzel J. L., and Ewing, M., 1962, "Sedi-ments and oceanic structural history of the Gulf of Mexico," *J. Geophys. Res.,* **67**, No. 6, 2509–2527.

Ewing, M., Ericson, D. B., and Heezen, B. C., 1958, "Sediments and topography of the Gulf of Mexico," (Weeks, L. G., editor), *Habitat Oil, American Associa-tion of Petroleum Geologists,* Tulsa.

Ewing, M., Worzel, J. L., Ericson, D. B., and Heezen, B. C., 1955, "Geophysical and geological investiga-tions in the Gulf of Mexico," *Geophysics,* **20**, 1–18.

Gould, H. R., and Stewart, R. H., 1955, "Continental terrace sediments in the northeast Gulf of Mexico," in "Finding ancient shorelines," *Soc. Econ. Paleon-tologists Mineralogists, Spec. Publ.,* **3**.

Ichiye, T., 1962, "Circulation and water mass distribu-tion in the Gulf of Mexico, *Geofis. Intern.* [Mexico] 2, (3), 47–76.

Jordan, G. F., 1951, "Continental slope off Apalachicola River, Florida," *A.A.P.G.,* **35**, 1978–1993.

Jordan, G. F., Malloy, R. J., and Kefoed, J. W., 1964, "Bathymetry and geology of Pourtales Terrace, Florida," *Marine Geology,* **1**, 259–287.

Jordan, G. F., and Stewart, H. B., 1959, "Continental slope off southwest Florida," *Bull. Am. Assoc. Petrol. Geologists,* **43**, 974–991.

Jordan, G. F., and Stewart, H. B., 1961, "Submarine topography of the western straits of Florida," *Geol. Soc. Am. Bull.,* **72**, 1051–1058.

Leipper, D. F., 1954, "Physical oceanography of the Gulf of Mexico," in "Gulf of Mexico, its origin, waters and marine life," *U.S. Fish Wildlife Serv. Fishery Bull. 89,* **55**, 119–137.

Logan, Brian W., 1962, "Submarine Topography of the Yucatan Platform," in "Guide Book, Field Trip to Yucatan," New Orleans Geological Society.

Lynch, S., 1954, "Geology of the Gulf of Mexico," in "Gulf of Mexico, its origin, waters and marine life," *U.S. Fish Wildlife Serv., Fishery Bull. 89,* **55**, 67–86.

Marmer, H. A., 1954, "Tides and sea level in the Gulf of Mexico," in "Gulf of Mexico, its origin, waters and marine life," *U.S. Fish Wildlife Serv., Fishery Bull. 89,* **55**, 101–118.

McLellan, H. J., and Nowlin, W. D., 1963, "Some features of the deep water in the Gulf of Mexico," *J, Marine Res.,* **21**, 233–245.

Murray, G. E., 1961, "Geology of the Atlantic and Gulf Coastal Province of North America," New York, Harper Bros.

Nowlin, W. D., Jr., Harding, J. L., and Amstutz, D. E., 1965, "A reconnaissance study of the Sigsbee Knolls of the Gulf of Mexico," *J. Geophys. Res.,* **70**, 1339.

Shepard, F. P. (editor), 1960, "Recent sediments, North-west Gulf of Mexico," A symposium, American Association of Petroleum Geologists, Tulsa.

Staub, N., 1965, "Entstehung und Alter des Golfstromes, Florida-Strom," *Zeitsch f. Geomorph.,* **9**, 237–246.

Suess, E., 1885, (English translation 1904–1924), "The Face of the Earth," Oxford, Clarendon Press, 5 vols.

Sverdrup, H. U., Johnson, M. W., and Fleming, R. H., 1942, "The Oceans; Their Physics, Chemistry and General Biology," Englewood Cliffs, N.J., Prentice-Hall.

Van Andel, T. H., 1960, "Source and dispersion of Holocene sediments. Northern Gulf of Mexico," in (Shepard, F. P., editor), "Recent Sediments, North-west Gulf of Mexico," American Association of Petroleum Geologists, Tulsa.

Cross-references: *Caribbean Sea; Gulf Stream; Storm Surge.*

GULF OF ST. LAWRENCE

Geographical Setting

The Gulf of St. Lawrence is an epicontinental marginal sea which lies at the mouth of the River St. Lawrence in eastern Canada. It is somewhat triangular in shape, but with a semicircular southern part; it covers an area of approximately 150,000 km^2, receiving the drainage of an area of about 1,300,000 km^2. The two outlets to the North Atlantic Ocean are the Strait of Belle Isle between Newfoundland and Labrador and the Cabot Strait between Newfoundland and Nova Scotia (see Fig. 1; see also *Continental Shelf, Classification,* Fig. 2). It is bounded by the hilly and mountainous countryside of west Newfoundland, Labrador, Quebec and Cape Breton Island to the north, west and east, but to the south is the low lying and flat terrain of Prince Edward Island and New Bruns-wick. The water depths in the Gulf are rather variable; the southern portion is for the most part fairly flat and shallow, with water depths of the order of 60–80 m, but this is separated from the northern part, in which the depths are more variable, by the Laurentian Channel, in which the depth is 400–500 m. This channel runs as a con-tinuous entity from Quebec City in an arc to the edge of the continental shelf southeast of the Cabot Strait, and is joined by a northern and shallower branch which runs northeast toward the Strait of Belle Isle.

Oceanography

The main circulatory pattern in the Gulf of St. Lawrence is counterclockwise. Cold waters of the Labrador Current flow in through the Strait of Belle Isle. The Gaspé Current, produced by water from the St. Lawrence River, flows into the Gulf between the Gaspé Peninsula and Anticosti Island. The major efflux of water, called the Cabot stream in which the salinity is 28‰, takes place through the Cabot Strait onto the Scotian Shelf. Deep currents through the Cabot Strait, consisting

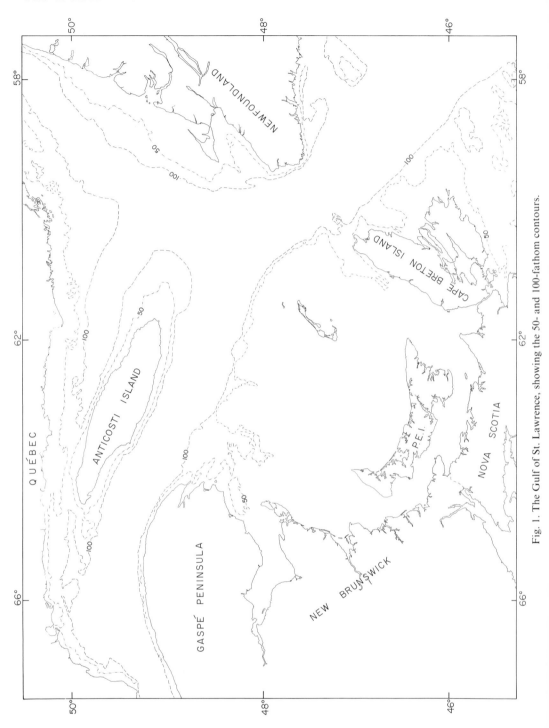

Fig. 1. The Gulf of St. Lawrence, showing the 50- and 100-fathom contours.

of a mixture of Labrador Current water and slope water from the Scotian Shelf, flow into the Gulf. Net transport via the Cabot Strait is 1.5×10^{13} m³/yr.

Three distinct layers of water can be distinguished in the Gulf. The most striking of these is the surface layer which, in any one location, is almost homogeneous with respect to temperature and salinity. The water temperatures in this layer range from −1.8 to 20°C and salinities vary between 26.0 and

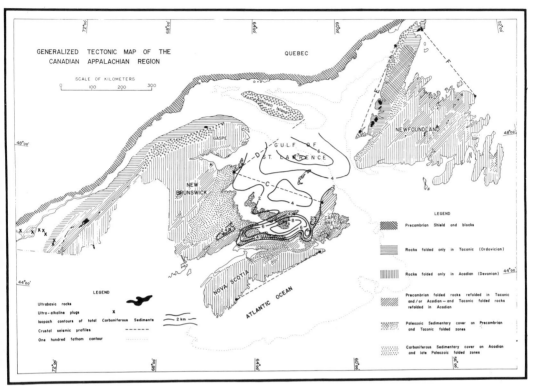

Fig. 2. A simplified tectonic map of the Appalachian system in Canada (from G. N. Ewing *et al.*, 1965; drawn from a tectonic map prepared by Poole *et al.*).

32.0‰. The surface layer exhibits seasonal variations. In the summer months it is very thin—18.3 m or less and has then the lowest values of salinity. In the spring and autumn its lower boundary may be as deep as 54 m. A cold intermediate layer with temperatures less than 0°C and salinities between 32 and 34‰ also shows seasonal variations in thickness, thinning in the summer months to about 27 m. Its maximum thickness is 54 m approximately. Slope water and Labrador Current water flowing into the Gulf of St. Lawrence through the Cabot Strait form a warm deep layer in the Gulf. The temperatures of the seawaters may be as high as 5.6°C and salinities are greater than 34‰.

Geology

The Gulf is bounded on its northern shores by the Grenville Province, part of the Precambrian Canadian Shield. The Appalachian Mountain System forms the boundary to the south, and runs from southwest to northeast from New Brunswick to Newfoundland (see Fig. 2). This consists of Lower Paleozoic deformed rocks into which are intruded Devonian granites, and on which are superimposed less deformed Carboniferous, Permian and Triassic sediments and volcanic rocks. The Appalachian System is bent at the Gulf of St. Lawrence, the change in strike following approxi-

mately the curve of the Gaspé Peninsula. In the upper reaches of the River St. Lawrence, the main deformed belt of the system is separated from the northern foreland by a fault system—"Logan's Line" (see Fig. 3). It has been suggested that this fault system is responsible for the trough of the Laurentian Channel, but there is no good evidence for this or for the existence of "Logan's Line" in west Newfoundland.

Geophysical studies show that the southern part of the Gulf is underlain by Carboniferous sedi-

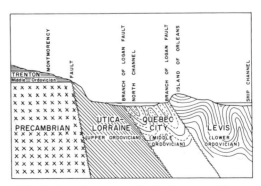

Fig. 3. A section across the St. Lawrence River at Québec City (drawn after Alcock).

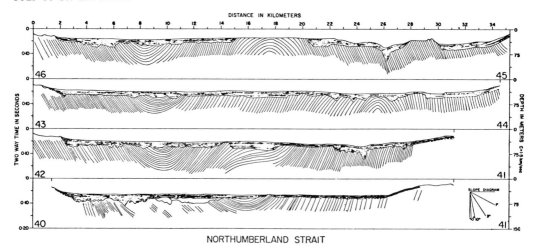

Fig. 4. Seismic reflection studies in the Northumberland Strait, showing folding in Carboniferous sedimentary rocks (reproduced from a report by K. S. Manchester).

ments, similar to those of the surrounding mainland, and detailed surveys in the Northumberland Strait have established continuity of structures from Prince Edward Island to Nova Scotia, for example (see Fig. 4). This sedimentary basin reaches its maximum thickness of about 6 km near the Magdalen Islands (see Fig. 2). North of the Laurentian Channel, the Gulf is underlain by a lesser thickness of rock which is probably sedimentary, but whether this is Carboniferous (as in southwest Newfoundland) or is a part of the undeformed Lower Paleozoic cover on the Shield (as on Anticosti Island) is not known.

The present morphology of the Gulf is thought by Nota and Loring to be due to Pleistocene and Recent modifications of a pre-Pleistocene landscape, controlled in part by structural features. The topography of the bottom of the Laurentian Channel appears to support the view that the channel owes its present shape to glacial action, and to modifications in the Pleistocene, by the

deposition of debris from ice and subsequent reworking and redistribution by ice-rafting. (The larger part of the Gulf is covered by ice from January to April each year). Similarly, the petrological characteristics of the superficial sediments have their origin in the subarctic climatic conditions of the present time and in the glacial regime of the Pleistocene. The sediments are mineralogically immature, and the principal sources are the rocks which surround the Gulf and border the River St. Lawrence. In these respects the Gulf is very different from environments such as those of the Gulf of Mexico or the Orinoco delta.

Geophysical Studies

Seismic experiments in the Gulf of St. Lawrence show that the crust of the earth here differs from the crust in the surrounding regions (see Fig. 5 of *Grand Banks* and Table 1). The crust beneath the less deformed part of the Appalachian System, and beneath that part where there are thick granitic

TABLE 1. A COMPARISON OF THE CRUST BENEATH THE ATLANTIC COAST OF NOVA SCOTIA AND BENEATH THE GULF OF ST. LAWRENCE[a]

	Thickness (km)	Gulf Compressional Wave Velocity (km/sec)	Thickness (km)	Atlantic Coast Compressional Wave Velocity (km/sec)
Sedimentary rocks	1.8	4.6	Nil	—
"Basement"	8.4	5.9	2.1	5.3
Main crustal layer	21.2	6.3	30.5	6.1
"Intermediate" layer	14.9	7.2	Nil?	—
Mantle	—	8.5[b]	—	8.1
Crustal thickness	46.3	—	32.6	—

[a]Note that these values are particular values, not average ones, but are representative of the regions, so far as we know.
[b]See text.

intrusions, is about 35 km thick and rather simple —essentially a single layer in which the compressional wave velocity is about 6.2 km/sec—overlying the mantle in which the comparable velocity is 8.1 km/sec. Beneath the Gulf, however, the crust is of the order of 45 km thick and can be thought of as being composed of a number of layers in which the compressional wave velocities are in the range 4.5–7.5 km/sec. These velocities reflect the presence of the Carboniferous sediments at the surface, and rocks of greater than normal density at depth, probably associated with the central part of the Appalachian System. This is comparable with those structures found in other areas of the world in which there is evidence of extreme tectonic activity in the past. Specifically, ultrabasic rocks in which are found high compressional wave velocities outcrop in the Gaspé Peninsular and these have been traced by gravity surveys part way across the Gulf of St. Lawrence. Beneath the crust of the Gulf the upper mantle may be anomalous—with an apparently high compressional wave velocity, about 8.5 km/sec, due either to material of high density or to a dipping crust-mantle interface. Because the Appalachian System bends at the Gulf, resolution between these two possibilities is not easy.

The circular form of the southern part of the Gulf has led some to suggest that the Gulf is a meteorite crater. This view is naïve.

CHARLOTTE KEEN
J. E. BLANCHARD
M. J. KEEN

References

Ewing, G. N., Dainty, A. M., Blanchard, J. E., and Keen, M. J., 1966, "Seismic studies on the eastern seaboard of Canada: the Gulf of St. Lawrence," *Can. J. Earth Sci.*, **3**, 89–109.

Hachey, H. B., 1961, "Oceanography and Canadian Atlantic waters," *Fisheries Res. Board Can. Bull.*, **134**.

Keen, Charlotte, Blanchard, J. E., and Keen, M. J., 1966, "Grand Banks and the Eastern Seaboard of Canada" (this volume).

Nota, D. J. G., and Loring, D. H., 1964, "Recent depositional conditions in the St. Lawrence River and Gulf—a reconnaissance survey," *Marine Geology*, **2**, 198–235.

GULF STREAM

This is a narrow, intense ocean current—or part of a system of such currents—generated in equatorial latitudes, moving off the Atlantic coast of North America. It forms the boundary zone between the relatively warm, saline water of the Sargasso Sea and the colder, fresher waters near the continent. Its name reflects the early misconception that the source of the Stream was the Gulf of Mexico; it is retained as established usage even though the contribution of Gulf water to the Stream is now recognized as insignificant.

The nomenclature pertaining to the Stream is both arbitrary and uncertain; considering present ignorance of the motion and its known complexity, there does not seem much point in demanding precise definitions. Downstream from the Yucatan Channel, the term *Florida Current* is applied to the flow emerging from the Caribbean Sea; some oceanographers limit this name only to the current within the Straits of Florida, but others have applied it as far north as Cape Hatteras. The term *Gulf Stream* is then given in a restricted sense to the flow between the Florida Current and roughly the Grand Banks of Newfoundland. Eastward and northward moving currents are well known beyond the Grand Banks, but their relation to the flow west of the Banks is unclear; consequently they are all included rather vaguely under the heading *North Atlantic Current*. East of Cape Hatteras, it is especially difficult to set precise lateral boundaries for the Stream: the flow is characterized by multiple currents, countercurrents, discrete zones of swiftly moving water, meanders, eddies and lateral influxes and offshoots. This entire segment of the North Atlantic circulation, from the Yucatan Channel to well east of the Grand Banks (sometimes as far as northern Europe), is occasionally called the Gulf Stream in a loose sense, but more frequently, the *Gulf Stream System*.

The currents separate the Sargasso Sea from the colder, fresher water to the west and north, and are therefore characterized by sharp horizontal gradients of temperature and salinity (and also of most other water properties). This demarcation is often especially pronounced at the sea surface, where temperature differences of 10°C may be encountered over a ship's length, and changes in water color and sea state may be so abrupt as to be clearly visible. Figure 1 shows temperature and salinity profiles made across the current near latitude 30°N (150 miles beyond the mouth of the Straits of Florida). The water moves along the inshore edge of the Blake Plateau, and the depth of the current is limited to about 800 m. The zone of abrupt slope in isopleths—roughly coincident with the intense flow—is pressed tightly against the continental slope, so that the only substantial body of water inshore of the strong current is the band of rather fresh coastal water lying on the continental shelf.

Near Cape Hatteras, the Gulf Stream departs from the continental slope, and its character changes drastically. Figure 2 shows a temperature profile made across the Stream along longitude 66° 30′W. The current is no longer limited by the Blake Plateau, but it flows along the continental rise, at depths of 4000–5000 m. The horizontal gradients associated with the Stream again extend all the way to the bottom, but through a consider-

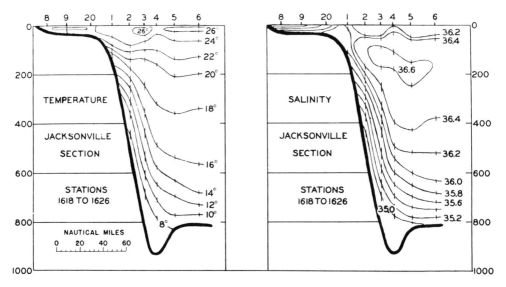

Fig. 1. Profiles of temperature (°C) and salinity (‰) across the Florida Current approximately along latitude 20° 30′N; based on *Atlantis* stations 1618–1626, occupied 12–13 May 1933. Depth in meters. (*Courtesy of C. O'D. Iselin*).

able column of water both colder and fresher than the bottom water on the Blake Plateau. All the way from Hatteras to the Grand Banks, the gradient zone now separates the Sargasso Sea from an extensive inshore water mass, the slope water; it is characterized by a temperature-salinity relation nearly identical to that of the Sargasso Sea at temperatures less than 10°C, but particular water types are found at appreciably shallower depths. North of the major gradient zone, there is another sharp transition, this one constituting the boundary between the slope and coastal water.

In the near-surface water of the Stream are usually found a warm core, most pronounced very close to the sea surface, and a high-salinity core centered at 100–200 m, underlying surface water fresher than that adjacent in the Sargasso Sea. Both features can be traced from the Florida Straits to the vicinity of the Grand Banks; they occur through advection by the swift surface current of water generic to lower latitudes. Thus the popular conception of the Gulf Stream as a warm current passing through colder flanking waters applies only to near-surface conditions, and even at the sea surface itself the temperature of the warm core exceeds that in the Sargasso Sea by only a few degrees.

The magnitudes of Gulf Stream velocities and their scales of time and space variation are such that the motion must be quasi-geostrophic (see *Geostrophic Motion*): the flow is directed approximately along isobars, its speed is proportional to the cross-stream pressure gradient, and the sharp cross-stream density gradient implied by the profiles of temperature and salinity above is associated

with pronounced vertical shear of horizontal velocity. Thus while deep motions appear quite small (a few tenths of a knot), the surface current may attain speeds of 4–5 knots. Figure 3 is a typical profile of geostrophic velocity in the Stream; it was obtained by integrating vertically the measured horizontal density gradient and assuming the speed of flow at 2000 m as zero. Although more recent observations suggest speeds of 10–20 cm/sec (1 knot = 51.5 cm/sec) as more appropriate to that level, the discrepancy does not much distort either the surface velocities or the general pattern of the distribution, nor does it affect at all the vertical shear. The Gulf Stream jet is accordingly about 50 miles wide, rather uneven in structure, and with high velocities concentrated in the upper few hundred meters.

Within the Florida Straits, the current transports water at the rate of 25–30 million m^3/sec (almost a thousand times the transport of the Mississippi), though apparently with variations about the mean of the order 10×10^6 m^3/sec. North of the Straits on the Blake Plateau, the transport is probably a little greater. In this general region, the current adheres very closely to the continental slope—its lateral fluctuations in position have amplitudes of only about 10 miles, with dominant periods of a few days to a week.

As the Gulf Stream passes Cape Hatteras and flows onto the continental rise, it becomes a truly deep current, probably reaching to the ocean bottom without much variation in direction. In so doing, its volume transport increases severalfold through inflow from the Sargasso Sea and, perhaps, the slope water. Thus if the bottom velocity

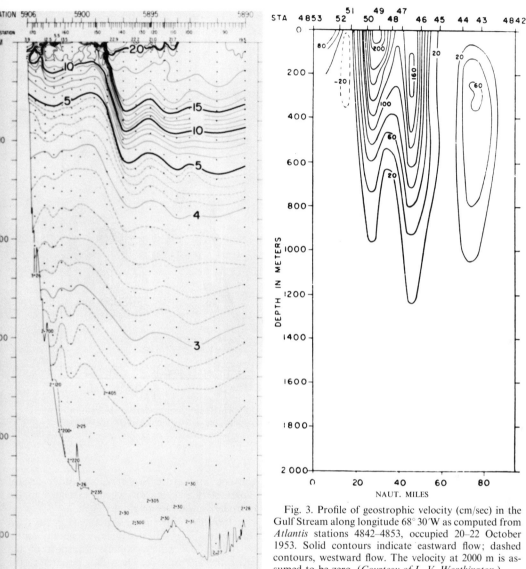

Fig. 2. Profile of temperature (°C) across the Gulf Stream along longitude 66° 30'W as determined by *Atlantis* stations 5890–5906, occupied 14–19 April 1960. Depth in meters. Dots indicate observation positions and serve as decimal points for bottom temperatures. (*Courtesy of F. C. Fuglister.*)

Fig. 3. Profile of geostrophic velocity (cm/sec) in the Gulf Stream along longitude 68° 30'W as computed from *Atlantis* stations 4842–4853, occupied 20–22 October 1953. Solid contours indicate eastward flow; dashed contours, westward flow. The velocity at 2000 m is assumed to be zero. (*Courtesy of L. V. Worthington.*)

were zero on the section shown in Fig. 2, the volume transport (into the section) between latitudes 37° and 39°N would be 106×10^6 m³/sec; with the more likely estimate of 10 cm/sec for the bottom velocity, the transport would be nearly

50% larger. The path of the Stream seems largely determined by the topography of the continental rise; the current tends to meander as a whole about bottom contours, with meander amplitudes of roughly 40 miles and wavelengths of 200 miles. These large-scale meanders move and change shape relatively slowly, having periods of the order of a month. Near longitude 64°W, the Stream flows off the rise over the abyssal plain, and its meander amplitudes tend to increase by a factor of two or more. The amplification is due in part to loss of the constraint of sloping topography—with subsequent behavior of the Stream as a Rossby wave (q.v.)—and possibly also to some perturbing effect of the many high seamounts in the area. On a few occasions, meanders have been observed to detach

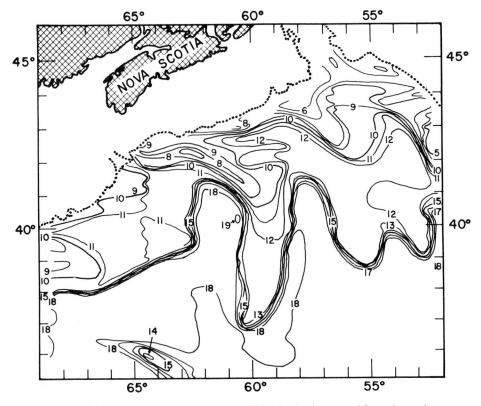

Fig. 4. Distribution of temperature (°C) at the 200-m level as interpreted from observations made during April 1960. The dotted contour is the 200-m isobath. (*Courtesy of F. C. Fuglister*)

from the Stream in the vicinity of these seamounts and become isolated eddies of slope water in the Sargasso Sea. It is quite possible, however, that some instability of the flow pattern is responsible instead for the formation of eddies.

Near-surface conditions especially are complicated by a multiplicity of currents between Cape Hatteras and the Grand Banks. The abrupt transition between slope and coastal water north of the Stream corresponds to a second eastward-flowing current, the Slope Water Current. How deep it extends is not known; if it extends to 2000 m, its volume transport is of the order 10×10^6 m³/sec. Between this current and the Gulf Stream itself lies a countercurrent, associated with the reverse slope of thermocline isotherms in Fig. 2; it draws water away from the Gulf Stream and feeds it into the Slope Water Current. Weak, superficial countercurrents are occasionally observed on the right-hand side of the Stream, although none are apparent in Fig. 3. Figure 4, a chart of the temperature at 200 m as observed during April 1960, illustrates this complex flow pattern. The sharp gradients identify the elaborately meandering path of the Gulf Stream, the position of the Slope Water

Current, and at 36°N, 64°W, an eddy—one of those referred to above—which is related to the meander lying along longitude 60°W.

A few direct current measurements in the deep slope water have indicated a slow, generally southwestward flow with a volume transport of the order 50×10^6 m³/sec. Deep flow counter to the Gulf Stream has also been observed directly beneath the surface Stream near Cape Hatteras, and farther south, on the eastern side of the Stream at about latitude 33°N. The estimated volume transport at the latter location, however, was only 7×10^6 m³/sec. These scattered observations thus suggest a deep countercurrent in the vicinity of the Stream, but its permanence, extent, and sources, and its relation to the Gulf Stream itself, are virtually unknown.

As the Stream approaches the Grand Banks of Newfoundland, its volume transport diminishes by roughly 20–30% through efflux of water into the Sargasso Sea and Slope Water Current. Its subsequent course is an unsettled question. It has been traditionally supposed that the Stream turns north around the Banks, then east again, and continues as a rather diffuse, possibly branching flow toward

Europe. It is difficult, however, to reconcile the distribution of dissolved oxygen to such a flow scheme; these data suggest that both the Stream and the Slope Water Current may instead turn south near the Grand Banks and be confined almost entirely to the western North Atlantic. The currents observed north of the Banks would then form part of a secondary gyre, tied only weakly to the Gulf Stream gyre. More detailed surveys are obviously required to resolve this dilemma.

The North Atlantic circulation, of which the Gulf Stream is the most striking aspect, is presumably driven both by the stress imposed on the sea surface by the trade winds and westerlies, and through the combination of polar cooling and equatorial heating. Considerable attention has been given to theories of wind-driven circulations in idealized ocean models. These have deduced asymmetric quasi-geostrophic gyres having narrow, intense flow near the western boundaries of the models, and relatively weak, diffuse flow in the eastern regions. The westward intensification is due to the meridional variation of the Coriolis parameter, for in a current whose cross-stream pressure gradient balances the Coriolis force acting upon it, mass conservation requires that northward flow be accompanied by a downstream increase in pressure gradient to compensate for the increase in the Coriolis parameter; similarly, a decrease in pressure gradient must accompany southward motion. Such effects can be achieved by drawing isobars out of the meridional boundaries into the adjacent flow, but with the necessary consequence of small components of pressure-gradient force parallel to the flow. Regardless of whether the circulation is cyclonic (clockwise in the southern hemisphere, counterclockwise in the northern) or anticyclonic, the component in the west acts in the direction of motion, but that in the east, counter to it.

The manner by which other forces balance these components drastically affects the circulation pattern. Thus, in an anticyclonic circulation driven by a zonal wind system where eastward motion increases toward the poles, e.g., the low-latitude easterlies and mid-latitude westerlies of the atmosphere, the associated pressure field can be distorted so as to balance the pressure force *opposing* the motion by the zonal wind stress; the horizontal scale of this flow would therefore be large, corresponding to that of the wind field. The force component in the *direction* of motion, however, can only be balanced by acceleration of the current, i.e., intensification and concentration of the flow, or by frictional (turbulent) retardation. With reasonable estimates of friction parameters, it turns out that the latter balance can occur only in a relatively narrow, high-velocity flow. Hence, both forms of balance require an intense current along the western boundary of the ocean, while broad, slow motion prevails in the east. (The same asym-

metry would characterize a cyclonic circulation driven by a wind system of opposite meridional shear.)

Although such circulation patterns are qualitatively similar to those observed, and the mechanisms involved are surely related to the nature of the Gulf Stream, theories have not yet been developed to treat realistic ocean models or to deduce current systems of realistic complexity.

Surface heating and cooling as a cause of oceanic circulation has not been given such extensive consideration as the wind stress. One such theory, however, requires a deep current to lie along the North American continent and flow counter to the Gulf Stream. While it was this prediction which stimulated the first observations of deep counterflow near the Stream, it is by no means clear whether the "observed" countercurrent is in fact the one predicted (see *Geostrophic Motion, Ocean Currents, Physical Oceanography*).

BRUCE WARREN

References

Fuglister, F. C., 1963, "Gulf Stream '60," in (Sears, editor) "Progress in Oceanography," Vol. 1, London, New York, Pergamon Press.

Stommel, Henry, 1965, "The Gulf Stream," Berkeley, Univ. of California Press.

GULF OF THAILAND

(1) Geography

The Gulf of Thailand (Siam) is a shallow arm of the South China Sea with a mean depth of 45.5 m. Its extent is approximately 300 by 450 nautical miles (Fig. 1). The eastern side is generally shallower and flatter than the rocky steep slopes of the western coast. The central depression reaches 12°N and its maximum depth is 83 m. The mouth of the Gulf opening to the South China Sea is about 200 miles wide at the surface, but below 50 m there is only a 30-mile wide channel connecting with the inner deep basin of the South China Sea with a sill depth of 58 m. This channel cuts between a 30-m ridge on the north extending southwest from Cape Ca Mau and a 50-m ridge extending northeast from Kota Bharu (6.3°N, 103.2°E). Four large rivers, the largest of which is the MeNam, empty into the head of the Gulf, as do many smaller ones along both shores.

(2) Hydrography

The Gulf may be considered as a two-layered shallow water estuary. Low-salinity water which has been diluted by heavy precipitation and river runoff flows out of the Gulf at the surface. Average surface salinity is 30.5–32.5‰ in winter and 31.0–32‰ in summer. There is an inflow of water from the South China Sea (q.v.) into the Gulf over the 58-m sill in the entrance channel. This water has

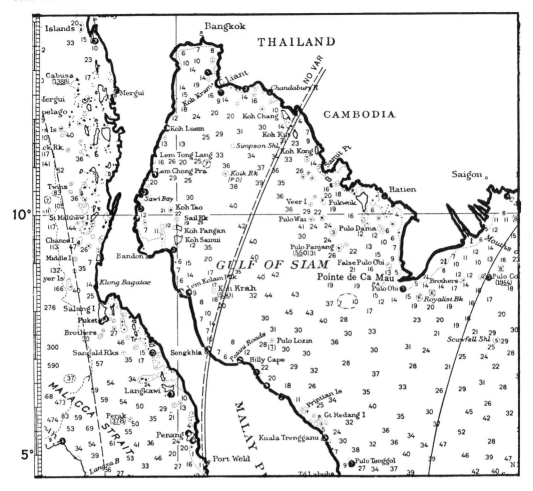

Fig. 1. Chart of Gulf of Siam (Thailand) (from the Chart H. O. 5590, U.S. Navy Oceangraphic office, Revised Edition, July 4, 1960). Soundings in fathoms.

high salinity above 34.0‰ and relatively low temperature below 27.0°C, and it fills the deep central depression below a depth of approximately 50 m (Figs. 2 and 3).

Wind-driven currents are generally less than half a knot, north to northeast at entrance, counterclockwise inside during the summer, but southerly at the entrance and clockwise inside during fall and winter. However, neither the northeast nor the southwest monsoon during winter and summer, respectively, is constant in direction or velocity over the Gulf as a whole.

The combined effects of the variable winds, tidal currents, freshwater runoff and excessive precipitation produce localized areas of divergence and convergence. In divergence areas, water of low temperature, high salinity and low oxygen content is upwelling from deep layers, and in convergence areas, water of high temperature, low salinity and high oxygen content is sinking from the upper layer.

The hydrographic data from 1959–61 showed that strongest upwelling occurred along the western coast in August and on the northeastern coast in October and January, while slight upwelling was detected on five cruises carried out in all seasons in a localized area south of 12°N and 101°W. Convergence and sinking occurred in all cruises in the central part of the Gulf but were only occasionally observed along both the east and the west coasts. Surface water temperatures are highest in April with more than 31°C on the eastern side and 30–31°C in the inner and western portions; they are lowest in January. Salinities of the inner Gulf are highest in August and lowest in October.

Productivity of the Gulf is higher than in the eastern side of the South China Sea and in the Philippine waters and the Celebes Sea. The surface productivity in the Gulf is 1–2 in the central part and 6 g C/m^2 per day at the head while it is less than 0.5 g C/m^2 per day in the latter areas. The rich

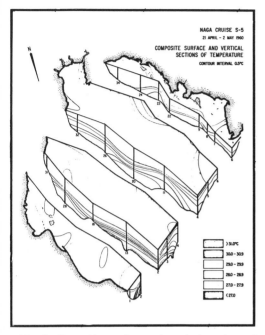

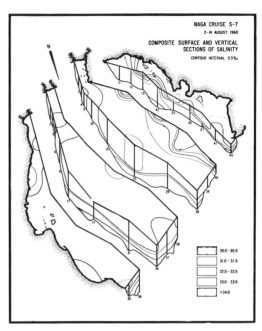

Fig. 2. Composite surface and vertical sections of temperature (from NAGA Cruise S-5 of 21 April to 2 May 1960).

Fig. 3. Composite surface and vertical sections of salinity (from NAGA Cruise S-7 of 14-2, August 1960).

productivity of the Gulf is attributed to vertical mixing and upwelling which bring the nutrients from the bottom.

(3) Tide and Tidal Currents

The wave of the semidiurnal tide progresses southwestward in the South China Sea and takes about eight hours between the edge of the Sunda Shelf and the coast of Malaya. One branch of the wave enters the Gulf of Thailand and the other moves south, entering the Riau Archipelago. The branch entering the Gulf rotates clockwise around an amphidromic point at the island Palau Panjang at 9° 18′N and 103° 28′E. The amplitudes are less than 80 cm in the amphidromic region which covers the southern three-quarters of the Gulf. In the northern part a wave separated from the amphidromic region moves to the north. It generates large tides at the northern coast of the Gulf where the amplitudes reach 82 cm at the mouth of the MeNam.

The wave of the diurnal tide moves southwestward in the South China Sea much faster than that of the semidiurnal tide. It takes only about two to three hours from the Sunda Shelf to the coast of Malaya. The wave splits into two branches off Malaya as the semidiurnal wave. The branch moving into the Gulf rotates counterclockwise around an amphidromic point at 8°N and 102°E, west of the one of the semidiurnal tide. The amplitudes are less than 40 cm in the amphidromic region covering the southern two-thirds of the bay, and they reach

the highest value of 113 cm at the mouth of the MeNam.

Tidal types are classified according to the ratio of the predominant diurnal and semidiurnal tides, $(K_1 + O_1)/(M_2 + S_2)$. In the largest part of the Gulf, this quotient is 1.5–3.0, indicating the mixed tide with prevailing diurnal tides. In the north-western sector between 9° and 12°N, the quotient is more than 3, and the tide is predominantly diurnal.

Tidal currents in the Gulf are relatively strong and exceed 1 knot in many locations.

(4) Climatology

The climate of the coast of the Gulf is different in the northern part and in the southern part. At Bangkok in the northern part, the total annual precipitation is 1307 mm. The rainy season is from May to October with maximum precipitation of 300 mm in September, and the dry season is the rest of the year with minimum precipitation of 3 mm in January. Humidity has a minimum of 70% in January and a maximum of 85% in September. Air temperature is minimum in January with 26°C and maximum in April with 30°C. At Kuala-Trengganu (5.3°N, 103.2°E) on the Malayan Coast, the total annual precipitation is 2826 mm with maximum monthly precipitation of 760 mm in November and with a minimum of 110 mm in April. The rainy season is from October to January, contrary to Bangkok. Humidity is slightly higher than in

Bangkok and shows a maximum of 88% in November and a minimum of 82% in June. Air temperature has smaller annual range than in Bangkok and shows a maximum of 27°C in May and a minimum of 25°C in February.

The southwest monsoon from May to September over the South China Sea has wind forces less than 3 Beaufort scale over the Gulf. In October when the northeast monsoon begins over the South China Sea, the wind over the Gulf is south to southeast and brings humid air into the coast of the Gulf. In January and February the wind over the northern Gulf is from the east and brings dry air while the wind over the southern Gulf is northeast and still brings humid air. In April, the surface wind over the southern Gulf shows divergent patterns and, thus, the precipitation there is low compared with other seasons.

TAKASHI ICHIYE

References

Robinson, M. K., 1963, "Physical Oceanography of the Gulf of Thailand," Section II of "Ecology of the Gulf of Thailand and the South China Sea" (Report of the NAGA Expedition, 1959–1961), SIO Ref. 63–6, 34–50.

Steemann-Nielsen, E., and Jensen, E. A., 1957, "Primary oceanic production," *Galathea Report* 1, 49–125.

U.S.S.R. Akademia Nauk, 1964, "Fiziko-geograficheskii atlas mira" (Physical-Geographical Atlas of the World), Akademia Nauk, USSR, Moskow, 298pp.

Wyrtki, K., 1957, "Die Zirkulation an der Oberfläche der südostasiatischen Gewässer," *Deut. Hydrograph. Z.*, **10**(1), 1–13.

Wyrtki, K., 1961, "Physical Oceanography of the Southeast Asian Waters," *NAGA Report*, **2**, Scripps Inst. Oceanog., 195pp.

GUYOT—*See* **SEAMOUNT**

H

HADAL—*See* **ABYSSAL PLAIN**

HADAL ZONE

(1) Introduction

(a) Definition. The development of self-recording, high-precision echo sounders and improvements in trawling techniques in the early 1950's led to the investigation of the deepest parts of the oceans, resulting in the discovery of a special fauna which inhabits the greatest depths exceeding 6–7000 m. This faunal zone was found to be comparable to the three previously recognized zones: the *littoral*, the *bathyal* and the *abyssal*. It was named *hadal* by

Bruun (1956) and so called by subsequent authors (*hadal* corresponds to the term *ultra-abyssal*, suggested by Zenkevitch (1956) and used by subsequent Russian authors). The zone is located in narrow trenches, the only places where such great depths are to be found.

(b) Exploration. Apart from a single haul in 1948 at 7600–7900 m depth by the Swedish Deep-Sea Expedition, the Danish *Galathea* Expedition 1950–52 was the first to trawl at the greatest depths (down to 10,200 m in the Philippine Trench), sampling successfully in five trenches. Since 1953, the Soviet research vessel *Vityaz* has been very active in similar work, first in the Kuril-Kamchatka

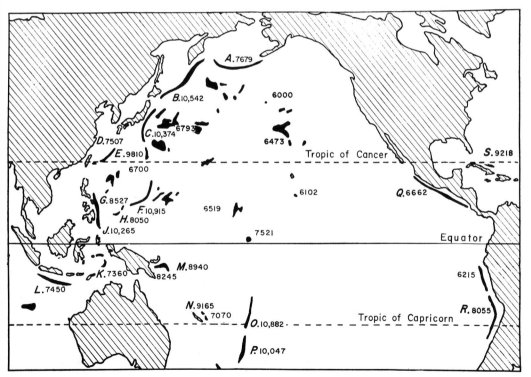

Fig. 1. Location and depth of the trenches and major troughs of the oceans. Not included are the South Sandwich Trench (8264 m), the Argentine Basin and the Romanche Deep in the Atlantic. A, Aleutian Trench; B, Kuril-Kamchatka; C, Japan; D, Ryuku (Nansei Shoto); E, Idzu-Bonin; F, Marianas; G, Yap; H, Palau; J, Philippine; K, Banda; L, Java; M, New Britain, North Solomons (Bougainville), and South Solomons; N, North and South New Hebrides; O, Tonga; P, Kermadec; Q, Middle America; R, Peru-Chile; S, Puerto Rico (partly after Dajoz, and Fisher and Hess, 1963).

Trench, later in at least 10 more trenches. The pioneering investigation by the *Vityaz* in the Japan Trench was later carried on by Japanese scientists. In 1962, the American "Proa" Expedition obtained bottom photographs and sediment samples from five trenches in the Southwest Pacific. In 1960, a single diving operation with the bathyscaph *Trieste* was made to the bottom of the Marianas Trench (10,915 m), and in 1964, several descents were carried out in the Puerto Rico Trench by French and American scientists.

(c) Extent. Although depths exceeding 6000 m are distributed throughout the oceans, the total area amounts to only 1.2% of the total ocean area and is very insignificant compared to areas with depths between 3000 and 6000 m, occupying 76% of the ocean area.

(d) Depth. So far, a total of 22 trenches with depths exceeding 7000 m has been recognized (Fig. 1). About another 20 isolated troughs are between 6000 and 7000 m deep. Six (the Marianas, Tonga, Kuril-Kamchatka, Japan, Philippine and Kermadec Trenches) exceed 10,000 m.

(e) Location. All trenches (except the Peru-Chile Trench) are located along the larger, but usually the smaller, oceanic islands, often forming characteristic arcs. The greatest number are found in the Western Pacific, exceptions being two in the Eastern Pacific and four (the Java, Vema, Puerto Rico and South Sandwich Trenches) outside the Pacific area.

(2) Environmental Factors

(a) Substratum. The sediments mainly consist of the same soft oozes as those occurring in the abyssal zone (see p. 10). In addition, the presence of volcanic rock, "drowned" pumice and large and small jagged stones of littoral origin indicates eruptions of submarine volcanoes, earthquakes and turbidity currents, which may at intervals cause extensive disturbances but may also supply oxygen (and food ?) as well as substrata for sessile animals.

(b) Oxygen. Oxygen has been found in sufficient quantities to support animal life in all areas measured, e.g., 4.5 ml/liter in the Kermadec and Tonga Trenches.

(c) Salinity and Temperature. Salinity and temperature are also as in the abyssal zone (see p. 10), although with a slight increase toward the bottom, due to adiabatic heating (Fig. 2). The recorded temperatures vary between 1.2°C (6200 m in the Kermadec Trench) and 3.6°C (7300 m in the Banda Trench).

(d) Pressure. The only physical factor which really differs from that of abyssal depths is the hydrostatic pressure, which, at 10,000 m, amounts to 1000 atm or more than 6 tons/in². Pressure is a limiting factor, as indicated by experiments on the effect of increased pressure on various marine

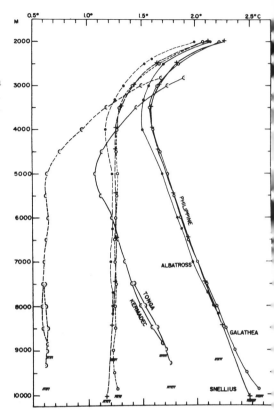

Fig. 2. Temperature of the Philippine, Tonga, and Kermadec Trenches. Full drawn line indicates temperatures *in situ*, broken line potential temperature (after Bruun and Kiilerich).

animals and the total absence of important groups (particularly the decapod crustaceans) in the hadal zone. The demonstration of barophilic bacteria in the trenches also suggests the presence of special physiological adaptations which determine the upper limit of occurrence of hadal organisms.

(e) Food Supply. The source of food is the same as in the abyssal zone (see p. 10). In spite of greater depth, almost the same quantity of food reaches the bottom in the hadal zone as in the abyssal zone because the hadopelagic fauna is extremely poor. The presence in some trenches of great numbers of Pogonophora (which probably require high concentration of food), the gigantism found in certain hadal crustaceans, and the extraordinary wealth of animals shown on recent trench photographs, suggest that in many trenches the amount of food available may be even greater than at abyssal depths.

(3) The Bottom Fauna

(a) Number of Species. According to available records (Wolff, 1960 and later papers), the total number of species from depths exceeding 6000 m

TABLE 1. NUMBER OF IDENTIFIED AND NON-IDENTIFIED SPECIES OF MAJOR HADAL GROUPS AND OF THE MOST SIGNIFICANT SUBGROUPS (IN PARENTHESIS)

	Identified	Non-identified		Identified	Non-identified
Porifera	3	8–9	Pycnogonida	2	0
Hydrozoa	(3)	(1)	Gastropoda Prosobr.	(6)	(13–18)
Anthozoa	(6)	(8–11)	Bivalvia	(10)	(24–27)
Coelenterata	10	17–21	Mollusca	17	43–51
Nemertini	0	1	Asteroidea	(5)	(8–9)
Nematoda	0	2–3	Ophiuroidea	(3)	(4–5)
Polychaeta	22	42–64	Holothurioidea	(15)	(11–18)
Echiuroidea	5	5–7	Echinoderma	25	27–36
Sipunculoidea	3	1–2	Pogonophora	8	1
Priapuloidea	1	0	Enteropneusta	0	1
Amphipoda	(20)	(16–21)	Tunicata	1	3
Isopoda	(41)	(8)	Pisces	3	1
Tanaidacea	(7)	(3–4)			
Crustacea	71	33–40	Total	171	185–240

is at least 356, 171 of which have been worked up, i.e., described as new species or referred to previously known forms (Table 1). The greater number of the 118 different species collected by the *Galathea* have now been worked up, while 72 species from the rich *Vityaz* collections and 13 species from other sources have been similarly treated.

(b) Dominant Groups. The dominant animal groups (Table 1) are coelenterates (actinians), polychaetes, crustaceans (isopods and amphipods), mollusks (gastropods and bivalves), and echinoderms (holothurians or sea cucumbers).

If the number of species occurring deeper than 6000 m is considered as a function of the total number of species in each major group, the following four groups are the most important: Pogonophora (Fig. 3), echiurid worms, holothurians, and isopods. The percentage of hadal species in these groups is 11.5, 9, 1.7, and 1.4, respectively.

Some major groups which play an important role in littoral, bathyal and even abyssal depths, are totally absent or occur in insignificant numbers. Decapod crustaceans have never been recorded from depths exceeding 5020 m and i.a. bryozoans, brachiopods and turbellarian worms also seem to be absent. Sponges, barnacles (stalked), sea stars, brittle stars, sea urchins, tunicates and fishes (Fig. 4) are rare.

(c) Endemism. Although it is premature to draw definite conclusions, it appears that the true hadal animals are only very occasionally found at depths of less than 6800–7000 m. At present, a total of 83 such species is known to be restricted to depths between 6800 and 10,700 m, constituting 82% of the 101 identified species (and subspecies) of metazoa from that depth interval. If, however, the upper limit of the zone is set at 6000 m, there are 109 such endemic species (64% of the 171 species so far found deeper than 6000 m). Among the more

important groups of hadal animals, the most pronounced endemism occurs among actinians (100%), amphipods (83%), isopods (77%), and Pogonophora (75%). The polychaetes have only 36% endemic species.

Seventeen genera are restricted to the hadal zone, and four more are mainly hadal. However, the number of species amounts to three in only one of the genera (the polychaete genus *Macellicephaloides*). Only one endemic family is known, the

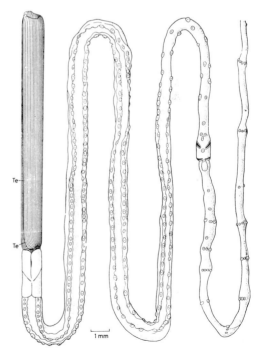

Fig. 3. *Spirobrachia beklemischevi*, an endemic hadal pogonophor (Kuril-Kamchatka Trench, 9000 meters) (after Ivanov, 1957).

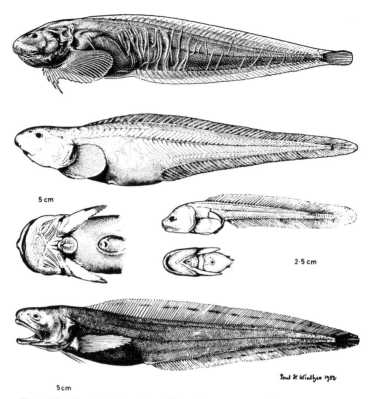

Fig. 4. The three hadal species of fish: *Careproctus amblystomopsis* (N.W. Pacific, 6150–7590 m), *C. kermadecensis,* adult and young (Kermadec Trench, 6660–6770 m), and *Bassogigas profundissimus* (Atlantic Ocean and Java Trench, 5610–7160 meters) (after Andriashev, 1955, and Nielsen, 1964).

Galatheanthemidae (a group of aberrant sea anemones), with two described species and at least another four (Fig. 5). The species are recorded from more than 15 localities in 6 different trenches.

(d) **Vertical Distribution.** There is less of a decrease in the number of species within the hadal zone than might be expected. The average number of species per trawling is as follows (number of trawlings of which the contents have so far been recorded in detail, in parenthesis):

Depth (m)	No. of Species
6000–7000 m (9):	22
7000–8000 m (7):	26
8000–9000 m (4):	17
9000–10,000 m (6):	10
10,000–10,700 m (4):	8

The decrease seems to be greater in the Kuril-Kamchatka Trench than in the other fairly well-investigated trenches. On the whole, the decrease is rather uniform within the different groups, slight in the case of mollusks and greatest in the case of

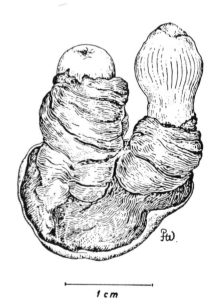

Fig. 5. Two contracted individuals of the sea-anemone *Galatheanthemum hadale* (Philippine Trench, 10,200 meters).

TABLE 2. MAXIMUM DEPTH OF OCCURRENCE OF DIFFERENT GROUPS OF BOTTOM ANIMALS (AFTER VINOGRADOVA, SOMEWHAT MODIFIED BY T. WOLFF)

Group	Trawling Depth (m)	Locality Trench	Expedition	
Foraminifera	10415–10687	Tonga	Vityaz	1957
Spongia	8610–8660	Kuril-Kamchatka	,,	1953
Hydrozoa	8210–8300	Kermadec	Galathea	1952
Octocorallia	8610–8660	Kuril-Kamchatka	Vityaz	1953
Hexacorallia	10630–10710	Marianas	,,	1958
Nematoda	10415–10687	Tonga	,,	1957
Nemertini	7210–7230	Kuril-Kamchatka	,,	1953
Priapuloidea	7565–7587	Japan	,,	1957
Sipunculoidea	8210–8300	Kermadec	Galathea	1952
Echiuroidea	10190	Philippine	,,	1951
Polychaeta	10630–10710	Marianas	Vityaz	1958
Copepoda Harpacticoida	9995–10002	Kermadec	,,	1958
Ostracoda	6920–7657	Bougainville	,,	1957
Cirripedia	6960–7000	Kermadec	Galathea	1952
Amphipoda	10415–10687	Tonga	Vityaz	1957
Isopoda	10630–10710	Marianas	,,	1958
Tanaidacea	8928–9174	Kermadec	,,	1958
Cumacea	7974–8006	Bougainville	,,	1957
Mysidacea	7210–7230	Kuril-Kamchatka	,,	1953
Decapoda (Paguridea)	5020	Western Indian Ocean	Galathea	1951
Pycnogonida	6860	Kuril-Kamchatka	Vityaz	1953
Amphineura	6680–6830	New Hebrides	,,	1958
Solenogastres	6935–7060	Java	,,	1959
Loricata	6920–7657	Bougainville	,,	1957
Scaphopoda	6930–7000	Java	Galathea	1951
Gastropoda Opistobranchia	6820–6850	Java	Vityaz	1959
Gastropoda Prosobranchia	10415–10687	Tonga	,,	1957
Bivalvia	10415–10687	Tonga	,,	1957
Cephalopoda Octopoda	8100	Kuril-Kamchatka	,,	1949
Bryozoa	5850	Kermadec	Galathea	1952
Brachiopoda	5430–5458	Floor of the Pacific Ocean	Vityaz	1957
Asteroidea	7584–7614	Marianas	,,	1955
Ophiuroidea	7974–8006	Bougainville	,,	1957
Echinoidea	7250–7290	Banda	Galathea	1951
Holothurioidea	10630–10710	Marianas	Vityaz	1958
Crinoidea	9715–9735	Idzu-Bonin	,,	1955
Pogonophora	9700–9950	Kuril-Kamchatka	,,	1953
Enteropneusta	8100	Kuril-Kamchatka	,,	1949
Tunicata	7210–7230	Kuril-Kamchatka	,,	1953
Pisces	7565–7579	Japan	,,	1957

echinoderms (thus indicating the non-hadal status of all echinoderms except the holothurians).

The maximal recorded depths of the various marine groups are given in Table 2.

(e) **Regional Distribution.** While the greater number of the exclusively hadal species seems to be restricted to one trench only, there are 15 species which occur in more than one trench. Most of these are found in neighboring trenches, connected by depths of almost 6000 m (Aleutian, Kuril-Kamchatka, Japan and Idzu-Bonin Trenches), but others (e.g., Philippine and Kermadec Trenches) are widely separated.

Many of the non-endemic species are recorded from shallower depths in the close vicinity of their hadal occurrence, but several have a worldwide distribution—especially within the polychaetes and holothurians.

(f) **The Hadal Community.** So far, very little is known about the quantitative composition. It varies considerably with increasing depth (cf. p. 346) and from trench to trench. The richest bottom samples taken by the *Galathea* are from the Banda Trench; they contained, within an area of 0.2 m², 8 species, 12 specimens, total weight 2.2 grams (6580 m) and 3 species, 5 specimens, total weight 0.25 gram (7270 m). Similarly, the *Vityaz* obtained (with a 0.25 m² sampler) one echiurid worm weighing 10.1 grams and other invertebrates weighing 0.1 gram.

An attempt to outline the animal community of the various trenches was made by Wolff (1960,

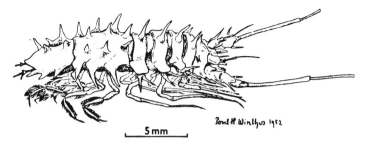

Fig. 6. A species of *Storthyngura* (*S. benti*, Kermadec Trench, 7000 meters);
the largest hadal isopods belong to this genus which has nine species in the
hadal zone (after Wolff, 1956).

Appendix 3). The number of species obtained at each station varies considerably. The number is largest in the Kuril-Kamchatka Trench (up to 46), and the Kermadec Trench (up to 32), including almost all groups with hadal occurrence and being in keeping with the high production of plankton at the surface. By far the greatest total number of species has also been recorded from these two trenches (101–127 and 81–83, respectively), followed by the Japan and Bougainville and Banda Trenches (40, 38–69, and 27 species).

The number of specimens also varies greatly. Most species are known from a single or a few specimens, but holothurians and Pogonophora in particular must be very abundant in places. For example, regarding the former, 3000 specimens of one species were obtained in a single haul at 7160 m in the Sunda Trench, 1800 specimens of another species from 8100 m in the Kermadec Trench, and 2000 Pogonophora (2 species) from 9000 m in the Kuril-Kamchatka Trench.

(g) Special Peculiarities. Morphologically, the hadal animals show the same adaptations to life in eternal darkness and on soft sediments as many abyssal and even bathyal (and cave-dwelling) species, e.g., greyish and whitish colors, probably always complete blindness, and, in many crustaceans, extreme long-leggedness.

A peculiar overgrowth or gigantism has been noted for many crustaceans. There are 37 hadal species of asellote isopods belonging to 12 different genera (with more than one species). Only five of these 37 species are smaller than the average size of the total number of species in the genus to which they belong, and some are real giants: *Storthyngura herculea* is 45 mm (average length of the 30 species of the genus is 18.3 mm), and *Eurycope magna* is 40 mm (average length of 40 species: 6.6 mm). By far the largest tanaid is one of the three hadal species; most of the amphipods and the only known hadal mysid shrimp also reach an extraordinary size. It seems most probable that this overgrowth is a result of the hydrostatic pressure, which has been shown experimentally to cause growth acceleration of trench bacteria. It may in some way affect the metabolic rate, retard the sexual maturity, or increase the longevity of the animals in question.

(h) Origin. The relatively sudden onset of the Ice Ages must have produced fundamental temperature changes of some 10°C to below 4°C at abyssal and hadal depths. Thus, the hadal fauna may have two origins. (1) It may be derived from the group in the original preglacial fauna which was hardy enough to survive the fall in temperature. (2) It may originate from a new invasion of pressure-adaptable (eurybathic) animals from the abyssal or perhaps even bathyal zones. It is likely that this invasion is still going on. Other changes in the composition of the hadal fauna probably stem from the volcanic activity and tectonic movements which alter the configuration of the ocean floor and cause extensive mud slides and turbidity currents down the slopes of the trenches.

(4) The Hadopelagic Fauna

Up to the present, only Russian scientists have worked with closing nets in the hadal zone, and little has yet been published. A remarkably rich fauna consisting of 20 species of copepods, 4 species of ostracods and 5 species of amphipods was recorded from a haul between 8500 and 6000 m in the Kuril-Kamchatka Trench. The hadopelagic animals are consistently unpigmented, compared to the usual dark red color of plankton from the abyssal zone.

T. WOLFF

References

Birstein, J. A., 1963, "Deep-sea isopods of the northwestern Pacific," *Akad. Nauk S.S.S.R., Moscow*, 1–214 (in Russian).

Fisher, R. L., and Hess, H. H., 1963, "Trenches," in "The Sea," Vol. 3, 411–436, New York.

Galathea Report, Copenhagen, especially **1, 2, 5, 7**, and **8.**

Tr. Inst. Okeanol. Akad. Nauk S.S.S.R., especially **12, 27,** and **41** (in Russian).

Wolff, T., 1960, "The hadal community, an introduction," *Deep-Sea Res.*, **6**, 95–124.

HALMAHERA SEA AND KAU BAY

(1) Limits and Oceanography

(a) **Limits and Dimensions.** The Halmahera Sea (center: 0°, 129°E) occupies the area between Halmahera Island and the Bird's Head or Vogelkop of West Irian (West New Guinea) and is bordered less distinctly in the north by the Pacific Ocean and by the Ceram Sea in the south; it covers about 95,000 km². A number of separate basins and ridges form the submarine topography of this sea. The main depression is the Halmahera Basin (Fig. 1) which reaches a depth of 2039 m with a generally flat bottom except for one elevation. Part of the ridge forming the northern boundary of this basin is narrow and straight, while the southern margin consists of a broad ridge with highly irregular topography. The broad bank connecting Halmahera Island with Waigeo incorporates two more basins 1260 and 1105 m deep. This bank also carries several atolls and almost-atolls. Its northern slope down to the 2500 m isobath is studded by a number of secondary ridges giving a highly irregular topography.

Kau (Kaoe) Bay is partly separated from the Halmahera Sea proper by the northeastern arm of Halmahera Island and oceanographically is directly connected with the Pacific Ocean. According to the International Hydrographic Bureau (*Sp. Publ.*

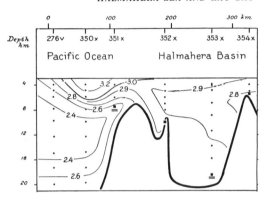

Fig. 2. Oxygen distribution in the Halmahera Sea. Note enrichment of Ceram waters (right) by Pacific surface waters (left) (from Van Riel, 1943). Scale of depth in hundreds of meters (*Snellius* station numbers).

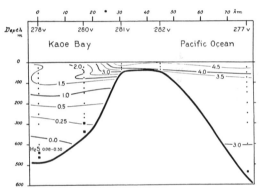

Fig. 3. Section showing the quantities of oxygen and hydrogen sulfide in Kau Bay as compared to those outside the basin in the Pacific Ocean (according to Van Riel, 1943, with *Snellius* station numbers).

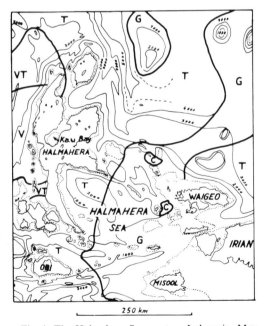

Fig. 1. The Halmahera Sea, eastern Indonesia. Map shows bathymetry, flow of bottom water, and the distribution of bottom sediments. T: terrigenous mud; G: globigerina ooze; VT: volcanic and terrigenous mud; V: volcanic mud; C: coralline debris (data from the *Snellius* Expedition, 1929–30).

28, 1953) the eastern limit of Halmahera Sea runs from the north point of Morotai to the western limit of Waigeo, so that Kau Bay is included. The bay is composed of an inner basin (−502 m) which is separated by a shallow sill (40–50 m) from the outer depression. The latter slopes down northeastward into the south end of the deep Mindanao Trough east of Morotai.

(b) **Replenishment of the Basins and Water Properties.** The Dutch *Snellius* oceanographic expedition of 1929–1930 found, through analysis of the distribution of the potential temperature and the salinity, that the Halmahera Basin is renewed by water from the Pacific Ocean passing from north to south successively an outer threshold at 700 m and an inner one at 940 m depths. Oxygen-rich surface water from the Pacific mixes with O_2-poor Ceram water and, as a result, the Halmahera Basin is relatively well oxygenated compared with other East Indian basins (Fig. 2).

The shallowness of the sill barring the inner Kau Bay from the open sea is clearly reflected by the diminishing quantity of oxygen with depth until below —400 m it completely disappears (Fig. 3), while hydrogen sulfide becomes important (up to 0.3 cc/liter). The pH only drops from 8.4 at the surface to 8.01 at the bottom.

The water properties of the Halmahera Basin and Kau Bay have been derived from reports by the *Snellius* Expedition (among others by Van Riel, 1943) and are presented below.

parts of the Halmahera Sea north and south of the equator.

(d) Surface Currents. The strengths of the surface currents in knots per day and the directions in which they flow are indicated in Table 3.

(2) Bottom Sediments

The bottom sediments of the Halmahera Sea consist of globigerina ooze (30% or more calcium carbonate), terrigenous mud, and coralline debris in a few localities along its eastern boundary.

TABLE 1. DEEP WATER PROPERTIES WITHIN THE HALMAHERA AND INNER KAU BASINS AND OUTSIDE THEIR RESPECTIVE THRESHOLDS AT THE INDICATED *Snellius* STATIONS AND OBSERVATION DEPTHS

	Halmahera Basin	
	Within Basin at Station 353, 1839 m	Outside Basin at Station 351, 755 m
Temperature, °C	7.545	5.53
Salinity, ‰	34.60	34.55
Oxygen, cc/liter	2.92	2.58
Density [sigma *t*]	27.01	27.27

	Inner Kau Basin	
	Within Basin at Station 278, 441 m	Outside Basin at Station 282, 35 m
Temperature, °C	28.21	—
Salinity, ‰	34.48	34.27
Oxygen, cc/liter	0.00	—
Hydrogen sulfide, cc/liter	0.30	—
pH	8.01	—
Density	21.915	—

(c) Surface Properties and Meteorology. The surface salinities range between 34‰ (March through May) and 34.6‰ (September through November). The sea surface temperature is highest in May (28.6°C) and is lowest in August (25.7°C). The air pressures vary from 755.4 to 758.7 mm.

Table 2 shows the direction and the strength of the wind according to the Beaufort scale for those

Figure 1 depicts the distribution of the above-mentioned sediments. Hard bottom was sounded on the central ridge and on the sill barring the Halmahera Sea from the Ceram Sea in the south.

Kau Bay proper consists of terrigenous mud containing mafic to intermediate volcanic particles and much serpentine. The quantities of hydrogen sulfide as well as organic matter (just over 3%) are too low to produce a black mud in this closed-off basin. The Recent marine sediments are thicker than 168 cm, as proved by a core collected by the *Snellius* Expedition. Kuenen (1950) believed that during the glacial, low sea-level stages, freshwater conditions should have prevailed in the Kau depression. The core of Recent marine sediments

TABLE 2

	June–August	December–February
North part	From SSW 2.5–3.4	From N 0.5–1.4
South part	From S 2.5–3.4	From NNW 0.5–1.4

TABLE 3

	June–August	September–November	December–February	March–May
North part	NW 20–24.9	ESE 1–4.9	SW 1–4.9	SW 1–4.9
South part	SW 15–19.9	SW 5–9.9	SE 5–9.9	ESE 1–4.9

and other considerations led Kuenen to suggest that postglacial sedimentation in this particular depression and also in other Moluccan basins is rapid and amounts to a few dozen meters.

(3) Geophysics and Geological Structure

For the most part, the Halmahera Sea is characterized by slight, positive gravity anomalies. Anomalies higher than 50–100 mgal are found in the Halmahera Basin and Kau Bay.

By virtue of their rather flat bottoms and a few scarp-like boundaries, the Halmahera Basin and those basins enclosed within the central ridge of the Halmahera Sea have been interpreted as the results of flexuring or faulting.

The age of the submarine relief is most probably post Plio-Pleistocene, for uplifted coral reefs of that age are present in several of the neighboring islands.

H. D. TJIA

References

*Kuenen, Ph. H., 1950, "Marine Geology," Fig. 94 and pp. 371–372, New York, John Wiley & Sons.

Van Riel, P. M., 1943, "The *Snellius* Expedition. Oceanographic Results. The Bottom Water, Introductory Remarks and Oxygen Content," Vol. 2, part 5, Ch. 1, Leiden, Brill.

HEAT TRANSPORT BY OCEAN CURRENTS

Energy Transport Required in Planet System

The earth, together with its atmosphere and oceans, makes up a planet system which exchanges radiation with the sun. The tropical latitudes of the system are oriented to receive much solar radiation while the polar latitudes receive relatively little. The resulting distribution of incoming radiant energy, considered together with the fairly uniform radiation emitted to space, determines the net accumulation or loss of radiant energy within portions of the planet system. There remains a net surplus of radiation in tropical latitudes on an annual average basis and a net deficit within the polar latitudes.

If this radiation imbalance were uncompensated, the meriodional temperature gradient of the planet system would continually increase. This is not observed, however; instead, the temperature gradient remains unchanged over long periods of time, and annual average temperatures remain essentially constant for given locations. The net radiation imbalance apparently is compensated by flow of energy within components of the planet system. Since the solid earth is a very poor conductor of energy, the required energy transport must take place within the atmosphere and the oceans. These can transfer energy easily in various ways, since both are fluids. Although the relative importance of atmosphere and oceans in effecting such energy transport has been debated for many years, it is now firmly established that the atmosphere provides a major portion of the required transport. However, the contribution by the oceans cannot be neglected, especially in certain latitudes. The general picture of ocean energy transport involves poleward flow of energy outside the subtropical regions.

Evaluation Techniques

Either direct or indirect means can be used to evaluate the amount of energy transported by ocean currents. The indirect method involves calculating components of the heat budget for a particular ocean region from empirical equations, using observations made at the ocean surface or in the atmosphere. No appreciable trend in temperature change is evident in any ocean region. To maintain this energy balance which apparently exists, an amount of energy (which can be computed as the difference between components of the heat budget) must be advected into or out of the region by ocean currents.

For the direct evaluation method, the observed temperature distribution can be used along with evaluations of the ocean current velocities to obtain the energy transported across a vertical section by the currents. The following paragraphs illustrate how this direct evaluation is accomplished. Later, studies using the indirect method will be described.

(A) Direct Methods. Two sets of studies have been made using this approach within the past decade. Both authors (Jung, 1952, 1956; Bryan, 1962) have shown, in different degrees of generality, that energy transported by ocean currents is evaluated essentially by

$$\int_o^L \int_{-H}^0 c_p \, \rho v \theta \, dz \, dx \qquad (1)$$

where θ is potential temperature, c_p is the specific heat of seawater, v is the current velocity, and dx and dz are incremental distances in the horizontal and vertical directions; integration is performed vertically from the ocean bottom ($z = -H$) to the ocean surface ($z = 0$), and horizontally from the origin (O) on one side of the ocean to its maximum value (L) on the other side. Since the net flow of energy is directed poleward, it is customary to study a vertical ocean section erected along a latitude circle, which thus is perpendicular to the net flow direction; x then is taken as positive toward the east.

Direct observations of temperatures within the oceans are relatively plentiful, with no particular problem involved in obtaining a reasonable (although not always an optimum) amount of data for direct energy transport calculations. However, there are too few direct observations of ocean current velocities to permit use of directly observed current data. Rather, relations between density fields and associated ocean currents must be used in evaluating current velocities. Density, a quantity which cannot be measured easily by direct observation techniques, can be evaluated by use of empirical relations and observations of the variables on which it depends: temperature, salinity and pressure. The vertical change of current velocity associated with the density distribution is described through the well-known geostrophic relationship. The temperature distribution thus enters into energy transport evaluation in two ways: in evaluation of the current velocities (v) and in evaluation of the potential temperature (θ) used in Eq. (1). Computations from the geostrophic equation are dependent on determining the depth of a reference level where the velocity is zero (Jung, 1952, 1955); to bypass this critical step, complex procedures must be employed which use additional surface data and assumptions (Bryan, 1962).

(1) Earlier Calculations (Jung, 1955, 1956).
(1.1) DATA AND METHOD: *Meteor* Expedition Atlases, based on complete data for the North Atlantic Ocean prior to 1927, were used as primary temperature and salinity data sources; data from 56 deep oceanographic soundings from the U.S. Naval Oceanographic Office files were used as well in the upper North Atlantic Ocean regions. Vertical cross sections were plotted for the equator and thereafter at intervals of 9° of latitude, with the final section at 63°N latitude. From analyzed contours on the vertical sections, readings were made for the study computations. For all sections except that at the equator, the geostrophic current velocity distribution perpendicular to the section was calculated.

The necessary reference level was established so that continuity of total mass and of salt content

was maintained across a given latitude section. Continuity was required also for water mass boundaries from section to section, and with all previous regional studies of mass flow in particular areas. Detailed pictures of the circulation of mass and of salt were obtained for the North Atlantic Ocean at all levels. Mass transport estimates across the equator were adopted from studies by Riley.

The product of the mass flow and the potential temperature for each incremental area was integrated across the section to provide the calculated total energy transport. During this study, the author had access to independent estimates made by Sverdrup (1954, 1957) for energy transport across latitude sections of both the Atlantic Ocean and the northern hemisphere oceans. From Sverdrup's estimates, factors were obtained and used to extrapolate Jung's values of energy transport for the North Atlantic Ocean to values for the northern hemisphere oceans in the latitudes studied. Values shown in Table 2 are obtained by interpolation at each 10° of latitude.

Jung's values agree well with those of Sverdrup, although the computation methods are completely different. The role the ocean plays in transferring surplus energy from the tropical to the polar regions is considerably larger in some latitudes (especially in the subtropics) than had been indicated in earlier studies. The reference level used is considerably shallower than that for previous studies of the North Atlantic Ocean, although it is consistent with mass and salt continuity requirements.*

(1.2) IMPLIED OCEAN CIRCULATION: The mass circulation in the Atlantic Ocean which appears to effect this heat flow is described in this study and consists of a horizontal as well as a vertical gyre. The simplest concept of ocean mass flow to transfer energy effectively involves poleward flow of water in the surface layers with high temperatures and equatorward flow of water in the deep ocean layer with cold temperatures (Jung, 1952). A modification of this simple picture appears to exist within the North Atlantic Ocean, where the surface layers move essentially in horizontal circulation patterns (i.e., the Gulf Stream system and its associated southward flow on the eastern side of the Atlantic Ocean); the net flow from this circulation is directed toward the poles and is compensated by the Deep Water flow equatorward.

This circulation pattern applies generally to the upper regions of all the major oceans; however, the heat transfer in other oceans is not as large as in the Atlantic, the only ocean possessing the distinct Deep Water motion described. In the Pacific and Indian Oceans, the upper water circula-

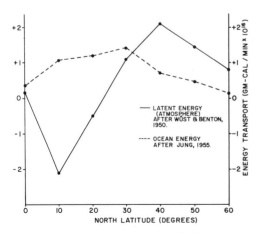

Fig. 1. Annual average values of latent energy (atmosphere) and sensible energy (ocean) transports (adapted from Jung, 1956).

* This level is not uniquely determined, and is only one of a number of configurations which meet specified requirements.

tions are shallower in the northern hemisphere and do not have a net poleward circulation. There appears to be a sluggish motion poleward in all southern hemisphere oceans, but few data are available there applying to heat transport study (Jung, 1956).

(2) Recent Study (Bryan, 1962). (2.1) PROCEDURE SUMMARY: Geostrophic calculations from hydrographic observations are made, measuring the integral of the covariance of the meridional velocity and temperature over an entire vertical section across an ocean basin. A method is used which divides the heat transport into two parts; one part can be calculated from hydrographic data alone and is independent of the reference level (unlike the direct calculations just previously described); the other part of the integral is calculated from the field of surface windstress.

(2.2) METHOD AND DATA: After defining

$$\overline{F(z)} = \frac{1}{H} \int_{-H}^{o} F(z)\,dz$$

to represent the vertically averaged value of $F(z)$, both ρv and θ can be expressed as

$$\rho v = \overline{\rho v} + (\rho v)', \qquad \theta = \bar{\theta} + \theta'$$

Further, assume that the velocity vector

$$v = v_g + v_\tau + v_i$$

where v_g is the geostrophic component, v_τ is the component arising from the stress in the x–z plane, and v_i represents the contributions of accelerations and stresses in the other planes. For this study, v_i is neglected as small compared with v_g and v_τ; v_τ is assumed important only in the layer just below the surface, where it balances the divergence of momentum transferred by turbulence in the mixed layer, and it is neglected elsewhere. Bryan rewrites Eq. (1) as:

$$\int_o^L \int_{-H}^o c_p \rho v\,\theta\,dz\,dx = \int_o^L \int_{-H}^o c_p\,\overline{\rho v}\,\bar{\theta}\,dz\,dx$$
$$\text{(a)}$$

$$+ \int_o^L \int_{-H}^o c_p(\rho v_g)'\,\theta'\,dz\,dx$$
$$\text{(b)}$$

$$+ \int_o^L \int_{-H}^o c_p(\rho v_\tau)'\,\theta'\,dz\,dx \quad (2)$$
$$\text{(c)}$$

Sverdrup's 1947 formula is used in term (a) to calculate $\overline{\rho v}$; the transport is expressed as a function of surface windstress:

$$\overline{\rho v} = \frac{1}{\beta H}\left[\frac{\partial}{\partial x}\tau_{ys} - \frac{\partial}{\partial y}\tau_{xs}\right] \quad (3)$$

This formula neglects advection of relative vorticity and bottom torque, which cannot be omitted in boundary currents such as the Gulf Stream. An estimate of the boundary current transport (T_{BC})

can be obtained from Eq. (3) however, since it must "match" interior flow from continuity considerations; thus, for interior flow,

$$\int_{-H}^o \rho v\,dz = H\overline{\rho v} = \frac{1}{\beta}\left[\frac{\partial}{\partial x}\tau_{ys} - \frac{\partial}{\partial y}\tau_{xs}\right]$$

$$T_{BC} \cong -H\overline{\rho v}.$$

The total average transport becomes

$$\frac{1}{\beta}\left[\frac{\partial}{\partial x}\tau_{ys} - \frac{\delta}{\partial y}\tau_{xs}\right] + T_{BC}$$

and term (a) of Eq. (2) is expressed as

$$\frac{c_p}{\beta}\int_o^L \left[\frac{\partial}{\partial x}\tau_{ys} - \frac{\delta}{\partial y}\tau_{xs}\right]\bar{\theta}\,dx + c_p T_{BC}\theta_{BC} \quad (4)$$

Only when $\bar{\theta}$ differs appreciably between the boundary and interior flow does this term contribute significantly to the total heat transport.

To evaluate term (b),

$$(\rho v_g)' = \rho v_g - \overline{\rho v_g}$$

$$\rho v_g = -g/f\,\frac{\partial}{\partial x}\int_{-z}^o \rho\,dz + c_1$$

$$\overline{\rho v_g} = -\frac{1}{H}\frac{g}{f}\frac{\partial}{\partial x}\left[\int_{-H}^o \int_{-z}^o \rho\,dz'\,dz + c_1\right]$$

Term (b) becomes

$$\int_o^L \int_{-H}^o c_p(\rho v_g)'\,dz\,dx$$

$$= -\int_o^L \int_{-H}^o \frac{c_p g}{f}\left[\frac{\partial}{\partial x}\int_{-z}^o \rho\,dz + c_1\right]$$

$$+ \int_o^L \int_{-H}^o \frac{c_p g}{fH}\left[\frac{\partial}{\partial x}\int_{-H}^o \int_{-z}^o \rho\,dz'\,dz + c_1\right] \quad (5)$$

This can be computed directly from the field of density based on hydrographic station data and is independent of the value of c_i.

In considering term (c) of Eq. (2), v_τ cannot be determined as a function of z; however, the integral of v_τ through the friction layer can be expressed in terms of surface windstress

$$\int_{-z_r}^o \rho v_\tau\,dz = -\tau_{xs}/f$$

where τ_{xr} is surface stress and z_s is the depth of the main thermocline.

$$\rho v_\tau' = \rho v_\tau - \overline{\rho v_\tau}$$

and $$\int_{-z_r}^o \rho v_\tau\,dz = \int_{-z_r}^o (\rho v_\tau - \overline{\rho v_\tau})\,dz$$

$$= -(1 - z_r/H)\frac{\tau_{xs}}{f}$$

353

Term (c) thus becomes

$$- \int_o^L c_p(1 - z_r/H) \frac{\tau_{xs}}{f} \theta'_s \, dx \qquad (6)$$

θ'_s is an average θ' in the mixed layer.

Bryan expresses Eq. (2) then as the sum of Eqs. (4), (5) and (6):

$$\int_o^L \int_{-H}^0 c_p \rho v \, \theta \, dz \, dx$$

$$= \underbrace{\frac{\bar{c}_p}{\beta} \int_o^L \left[\frac{\partial}{\partial x} \tau_{ys} - \frac{\partial}{\partial y} \tau_{xs} \right] \theta \, dx + c_p T_{BC} \bar{\theta}_{BC}}_{I_2} \qquad (7)$$

$$\underbrace{+ \int_o^L \int_{-H}^0 c_p (\rho v'_g) \theta' \, dz \, dx - \int_o^L c_p(1 - z_r/H) \frac{\tau_{xs}}{f} \theta'_s \, dx}_{\underbrace{}_{I_1}}$$

$$\text{(b)}$$

Bryan used data for the various sections shown in Table 2 to evaluate the terms in Eq. (7); hydrographic data were taken during the IGY, the *Norpac* expedition, and from the *Meteor* Atlases. Wind stress data were calculated from climatological summaries.

(2.3) OCEAN CIRCULATIONS EFFECTING ENERGY TRANSPORT: It was seen that the term I_1 in Eq. (7) predominates, and that term (b) in I_1 is the principal contributing term toward heat transport by ocean currents. Term (b) represents the correlation between deviations from the vertical average of potential temperature and similar deviations of the geostrophic transport. Term (b) was broken down into two subintegrals which represent contributions of correlations in the vertical and the horizontal planes.

The energy transport was seen to depend largely on the integral which is independent of the reference level, for calculations based on sections where there is no pronounced correlation between temperature anomaly and meridional velocity (i.e., sections are excluded where powerful currents flow in shallow water with associated warm temperatures). Quantitative information was obtained as well on the relative importance of circulations in the vertical plane (connected with the thermohaline circulation) as compared with horizontal circulations primarily driven by the wind. Although weak in terms of volume transport, the vertical circulations dominate the heat transport.

(B) Heat Balance Methods. For an incremental volume of ocean lying beneath the ocean surface, one can evaluate energy income and losses. These energy exchanges occur primarily through the processes of radiation or conduction, or they are associated with changes of state. Over an interval of time which extends beyond short-term and seasonal variations, it is possible to calculate an energy budget for that ocean volume. Since the temperature of the volume is not observed to change over such a time interval, the amount of energy can be calculated which must be advected into or from the volume in order to maintain its energy balance. Several investigators have used this method to establish requirements for energy transport by ocean currents (Sverdrup, 1954; Budyko, 1956; Privett, 1960).

(1) Evaporation Differences (Sverdrup, 1954, 1957). From the energy equation and knowledge of the Bowen ratio (between energy amounts used for conduction and those used as latent heat of

TABLE 1. OCEAN TRANSPORTS OUT OF LATITUDE BANDS

All values $\times 10^{16}$ g-cal/min

Latitude Band	Sverdrup, 1954	*Sverdrup, 1957	Jung,* 1955 (Sv54)	Jung,* 1955 (Sv55)	Budyko, 1956
°N					
60–50	−0.42	−0.3	−0.48	−0.33	−0.37
50–40	−0.32	−0.2	−0.35	−0.24	−0.34
40–30	−0.85	−0.9	−0.64	−0.72	−0.28
30–20	+0.16	+0.2	+0.18	+0.23	+0.38
20–10	+0.41	+0.3	+0.17	+0.12	+0.96
10–0	+0.95	+0.8	+0.93	+0.75	+1.69
°S					
0–10					+1.22
10–20					+0.06
20–30					−0.18
30–40					−0.98
40–50					−0.52
50–60					−0.87

* Values are inferred from transport calculations across latitude walls. (−) values indicate transport into the region.

vaporization), Sverdrup (1954) computed the evaporation between parallels of latitude, assuming that no energy is transported by ocean currents. The evaporation was also computed in a second way which depends on knowing the character of eddy diffusivity of the air and its relation to the wind velocity; the evaporation thus can be computed from the product of vapor pressure gradient immediately above the sea surface and the wind velocity at a low elevation. A coefficient which multiplies the product is adjusted so that for all oceans the average evaporation as computed in this way agrees with that computed by the heat budget method. Finally, the evaporation can be directly observed from pans on board ships; these values must be corrected in elaborate and somewhat uncertain methods to obtain estimates of evaporation from the sea surface.

Comparing evaporation estimates obtained from these three methods, Sverdrup notes that reasonable agreement occurs between the direct measurements and those values derived from wind and vapor pressure observations. However, these meteorologically derived values differ systematically from values calculated by the heat budget method. The latter values are lower from the equator to 30°N, and they are higher beyond 30°N, and the comparison suggests that considerable amounts of energy are carried poleward by the ocean currents. These values are calculated and shown in Table 1, along with values recalculated in a later study (Sverdrup, 1957). Sverdrup notes no such systematic difference in evaporation values for the southern hemisphere.

(1.1) TRANSPORT CHARTS: In his later paper (1957), Sverdrup also calculates the transport of heat by ocean currents from charts of loss or surplus of energy and from water transport values for the upper ocean layers. Where these values differ from the values calculated from the heat budget, they are entered in Table 2 in parentheses; otherwise, the two estimates agree. A northward transport of energy is assumed to occur across the equator in these results, based on oceanographic observations in the Atlantic Ocean which show that warm surface water is carried northward across the equator while cold deeper water flows south. Sverdrup notes that a corresponding northward transport does not take place in the Pacific Ocean. Later, both Budyko (1956) and Bryan

TABLE 2. OCEAN HEAT TRANSPORTS NORTHWARD ACROSS LATITUDE CIRCLES*

All values in units of 10^{16} g-cal/min

Latitude	Sverdrup 1957	Jung (Sv 1954)	Jung (Sv 1955)	Jung 1955 (Raw values Atlantic Ocean)	Privett 1960	Bryan 1962
°N						
60	+0.3	0.14	0.14	(63°) 0.05		
50	+0.6	0.62	0.47	(54°) 0.37		
40	+0.8	0.97	0.71	(45°) 0.57		Atl.　　 0.0
30	+1.7	1.61	1.43	(36°) 0.81		Atl. 36°　1.08
				(27°) 1.13		Pac. 32° −0.90
20	+1.5 (1.7)	1.43	1.20			
10	+1.2 (1.5)	1.26	1.08	(18°) 0.80		
0	+0.4	0.33	0.33	(9°) 0.71 (0°) 0.33		
°S						
10						(Atl. 16°) +1.62 IGY (Atl. 16°) +0.94 Meteor
20						(Atl. 24°) +0.48 IGY
30	( ) values from charts of energy carried by currents.					
40					−4.9	

* (−) values indicate transport to the south.

(1962) provide some evidence that heat transport takes place toward the *south* across the equator in the Pacific Ocean.

(2) Heat Balance Atlas (Budyko, 1956). Calculations on the world maps of heat balance constituting the *Atlas of the Heat Balance* (edited by Budyko in 1955) were used to compute mean latitudinal heat balance components for land surfaces, oceans, and for the whole earth's surface. From these values for the oceans is derived a term which represents the mean latitudinal redistribution of heat by sea currents. These values were converted to the units of Table 1, where they are shown to correspond to the other studies for only the latitudes from 40–60°N; the values are considerably smaller in the 30–40°N belt and are considerably larger in remainder of the northern hemisphere.

Values are included by Budyko for the southern hemisphere as well; only the Atlantic transport values estimated by Bryan (1962) and by Privett (1960) are available at the present for comparison. Bryan's estimates appear to be the same order of magnitude as those of Budyko while Privett's estimate is one order larger.

(3) Southern Hemisphere Energy Surplus (Privett, 1960). This estimated transport across 40°S latitude involved taking the calculated heat energy surplus between the equator and 40°S in all the southern oceans, subtracting an amount estimated as the northward transport in the Atlantic Ocean, and adding the surplus heat energy of the North Indian Ocean, assumed to be transported southward across the equator (no equatorial transport is assumed for the Pacific Ocean). The net value is shown in Table 2.

Discussion

Tables 1 and 2 compare the transport of energy by ocean currents as evaluated by the methods discussed above. General agreement occurs on the order of magnitude and sign of the terms across the various latitudes of the northern hemisphere. It should be noted, however, that the Pacific Ocean is relatively unstudied compared with the North Atlantic; Budyko's results for the Pacific Ocean indicate that circulation may be far different from that of the Atlantic (contrary to the assumption made by Jung, 1955). The southern hemisphere has been studied relatively little to date; Bryan has worked with two of the latitude sections taken during the IGY, and Privett has provided one estimate based on heat studies of the southern hemisphere oceans. The author is working now with the sections of the IGY for the South Atlantic Ocean in extending these heat transport estimates.

The magnitude of the ocean energy transports lies well below that of the atmosphere, although it attains about the same importance as the transfer of energy within the atmosphere in the form of latent energy; the maximum transfer of energy by the ocean currents is displaced relative to the maximum transfer by the atmosphere for latent energy (see Fig. 1 adapted from Jung, 1956). The ocean transport, shown here as total values across latitude sections, appears to be localized in narrow regions on the western ocean regions in the northern hemisphere. Thus the Gulf Stream, with its strong poleward velocity component that is well correlated with a high temperature, appears to contribute a major portion of the net energy transported poleward by ocean currents of the Atlantic Ocean (data not shown). It is expected, although not yet clearly demonstrated, that the same phenomenon occurs in the Kuroshio of the North Pacific Ocean. Budyko's results raise the question of whether or not this "extrapolation" is valid in going from the Atlantic Ocean data to the Pacific Ocean.

GLENN H. JUNG

References

Bryan, Kirk, 1962, "Measurements of meridional heat transport by ocean currents," *J. Geophys. Res.*, **67**, No. 9, 3403–3414.

Budyko, M. I., 1956, "The heat balance of the earth's surface, Leningrad." Translated by Nina A. Stepanova, Office of Climatology, United States Weather Bureau, Washington, D.C., 1958, 259pp.

Jung, Glenn H., 1952, "Note on the meridional transport of energy by the oceans," *J. Marine Res.*, **11**, No. 2, 139–146.

Jung, Glenn H., 1955, "Heat Transport in the North Atlantic Ocean," Technical Report 55–34T, Texas A & M Research Foundation (also doctoral dissertation, Department of Oceanography and Meteorology, Texas A & M College, 1955), 41pp.

*Jung, Glenn H., 1956, "Energy Transport by Air and Sea," Part XIV, The Dynamic North, Vol. I, Technical Asst. to CNO for Polar projects, 19pp.

Privett, D. W., 1960, "The exchange of energy between the atmosphere and the oceans of the southern hemisphere," *Geophys. Mem. No. 104*, **13**, No. 4, Meteorological Office of Great Britain, London, 61pp.

Sverdrup, H. U., 1954, "Oceanography," Vol. II, Ch. 5, Chicago, University of Chicago Press, pp. 215–257.

Sverdrup, H. U., 1957, "Oceanography," in "Encyclopedia of Physics," Vol. 48, No. 28, Berlin, Springer Verlag, pp. 608–670 (available in manuscript form in 1955, and referred to as "Sverdrup, 1955").

HODOGRAPH

A hodograph is a graphical representation of time and distance traveled. The mathematical concepts of the hodograph (and its name) are due to Sir William Rowan Hamilton (1846), though independently worked out by Möbius. The motion of the mean tidal current cycle may be plotted on nautical charts, the *tidal hodograph*, which can be very helpful to mariners (Smith, 1867). In seismology (pr. Vol. V), travel time is plotted as a function of distance from the earthquake epicenter to the point of observation measured along the surface of the earth. In oceanography, a special application is in the celebrated "Ekman Spiral" which indicates the progressive departure of an ocean current (q.v., Vol. I) from the initial bearing, with time, distance and depth under the Coriolis Effect (q.v., Vol I); the end points of the vectors for each depth when projected onto a horizontal plane are found to lie on a logarithmic spiral.

RHODES W. FAIRBRIDGE

References

Dietrich, G., 1963, "General Oceanography," New York, Interscience Publishers, 588pp. (translated from German by F. Ostapoff).

Hamilton, W. R., 1846–47, "On a theory of hodographic isochronism," *Proc. Roy. Irish Acad.*, **3**, 417–8, 465–470.

Schou, A., 1952, "Direction determining influence of the wind on shoreline simplification and coastal dunes," *Proc. Intern. Geogr. Congr., Washington*, 370–373.

Smith, A., 1867, *Proc. Roy. Soc., London*, **15**.

Cross-references: *Coriolis Force; Ocean Currents.*

HUDSON BAY AND APPROACHES

Part A. Introduction and Oceanography

Hudson Bay is a shallow, subarctic, inland sea situated in the middle of the Canadian Shield. It is 520,000 km² in area, has an average depth of about 100 meters, and a maximum depth of about 250 meters. To the north, the shallow depression of Foxe Basin forms a connecting passage leading to the Canadian Archipelago and the Arctic Ocean, while Hudson Strait joins Hudson Bay and Foxe Basin with the Atlantic Ocean. The International Hydrographic Bureau (*Sp. Publ.* 23, 1953) defines Hudson Bay as extending as far northeast as a line from Nuvuk Pt. (62° 21′N, 78° 06′W) to Leyson Pt. on Southampton Island, and in the north from a line joining Southampton Island and Beach Pt.

The hydrologic system may be considered to be an enormous estuarine basin into which is periodically poured the drainage water from 5,832,000 km² of the continent. For this reason, there is a marked seasonal change in the oceanography of Hudson Bay which is apparent in the pronounced and changing stratification of the Bay waters.

Considerable attention has been directed to Hudson Bay from the navigational point of view during the last quarter century, and in this respect its waters are relatively well known. However, it is only recently that serious study has been given to the many and varied oceanographic problems of the area. The first detailed examination of the Bay was made by Hachey (1931) while he was officer in charge of the Hudson Bay Fisheries Expedition

in 1930. Limited but detailed oceanographic observations which contributed insight into the Atlantic influence in the circulation in the Bay were made from the destroyer *Haida* in 1948.

In 1947 the Fisheries Research Board of Canada initiated a research program in the eastern arctic, and in 1948 the 50-foot research vessel *Calanus* was built and sailed into Ungava Bay. Since 1949 a series of exploratory marine biological investigations, covering a large area of the eastern Canadian arctic, including Hudson Bay, has been undertaken aboard this vessel. A collection of the published reports of these investigations is contained in the "Calanus" Series of the Fisheries Research Board of Canada.

In addition to the biological investigations, there has recently been a renewal of geophysical activity to investigate the physical characteristics of Hudson Bay and the adjacent waters. This work has been stimulated by the prospect of economic minerals in the region and the possibility of extending the shipping season into the port of Churchill. Some 50 grain ships now use the Hudson Bay route each summer. Research cruises have been conducted in Hudson Bay aboard the icebreaker *Labrador* in 1955, 1956, 1957 and 1959, and a more detailed geophysical reconnaissance survey of the Bay was undertaken in 1961. A comprehensive review of the published material dealing with marine research in arctic Canada has recently been prepared by Collin and Dunbar (1964).

Ice Conditions

Little was known of the winter ice conditions of Hudson Bay before Hare and Montgomery (1944) published the results of their research showing that Hudson Bay froze over completely for several months of the year. Ice conditions in Hudson Strait and Foxe Basin are reported to be heavy, but aerial reconnaissance has shown that the Strait never freezes over completely, presumably as a result of the wind distribution and strong currents which keep the ice in motion. Foxe Basin is covered with severely hummocked ice in winter, but in late summer (August and September) the ice generally disappears either by melting or by discharge into Hudson Bay and Hudson Strait. Foxe Basin is unique in that much of the ice formed in the area has a surface covering of mud and fine silt which produces a distinct brown color on the ice. The entrapment of the sediment by the ice is believed to be caused by the vigorous tidal mixing which occurs in the Basin and the rapid freezing of the surface water containing the suspended material.

Traditionally, ice begins to clear from southern James Bay about mid-June, but Hudson Bay is not clear of ice until the first week in August at the earliest. In Hudson Strait, the summer breakup is complicated by the discharge of ice from Foxe

Basin and the inflow of ice from Baffin Bay. This ice may also be accompanied by icebergs which originated in Greenland and pass across Baffin Bay to enter the Strait along the south coast of Baffin Island.

The General Circulation. There are no published accounts of the water movements in Hudson Bay as derived from dynamic computations or analyses of the density distribution; the best account of the surface circulation has been presented by Hachey (1935) who used the evidence from 500 drift bottles released in 1930 to establish the general circulation pattern in the Bay.

In general, the circulation is anticlockwise with a southward flow on the west side and a northward flow on the east side. In James Bay, the predominant movement of the surface water is northward in the eastern part of the bay. There is no information on the rate of this circulation.

There is interesting evidence which suggests that the general circulation in Hudson Bay is triggered in some way by the spring discharge off the drainage basin. A stationary configuration of the sea ice which is observed during breakup is an indication of a "calm" period of the circulation cycle in spring. In October, the density distribution in the northern section of the Bay indicates that a northerly flow of water extends almost across the entire breadth of the Bay during the peak "discharge" period.

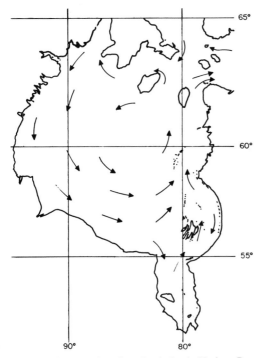

Fig. 1. The general surface circulation in Hudson Bay (after Hachey, 1935; Campbell, 1958).

Knowledge of oceanographic conditions in Foxe Basin is derived from observations recorded by research cruises in 1955, 1956, and 1957, as well as a complete set of marine observations for the entire year collected by Grainger (1959) in 1955–56 in northern Foxe Basin. Knowledge of the current pattern has been gained largely from dynamic calculations of the station data and from radar photographs of ice drift. These observations indicate that the dominant movement of the surface water is southerly along the western side of the Basin at a rate of 1–1.5 knots. A countercurrent moves to the north through the eastern sector of Foxe Channel and continues for a considerable distance into Foxe Basin. An easterly surface movement in the eastern part of the Basin is associated with this northern drift.

The dominant feature of the circulation through Hudson Strait is the easterly current along the south coast which persists as an outgoing stream from Hudson Bay to Ungava Bay despite seasonal changes. The currents on the northern side of the Strait are much weaker and appear to be influenced by the topography and fluctuations in the volume discharge.

Midway through the Strait the residual current at a depth of 30 meters, as determined by direct reading current meters, moves westward along the north shore at a rate of 1 knot and eastward at 0.7 knot along the south shore. The residual current at this depth, in the middle of the Strait, moves to the south at about 0.2 knot.

Tidal action displays an important influence on the oceanographic situation in the Hudson Bay system owing to the extreme tidal range which occurs in Ungava Bay. In Hudson Bay, the rise of the tide is from 0.5–0.8 meter at Port Harrison on the east coast, and from 3.5–4.6 meters at Churchill. In the western end of Hudson Strait, the mean tidal range is 2.4–3.5 meters and a rise of tide of 6.1–9.1 meters has been reported in southern Foxe Basin. At the head of Ungava Bay, the tidal range is from 9.6–12.5 meters. It is believed that recent observations in this area have recorded the highest tides in the world. These large and violent tidal fluctuations apparently give rise to density inversions (Dunbar, 1958).

Characteristics of the Water Masses

Hudson Bay may be considered a large estuary, since in summer an intense salinity stratification in the upper 25 meters is a characteristic feature of the water column. Surface salinities in the open Bay, in summer, may be as low as 23‰, and salinities at 25 meters, lower than 31‰ with the intensity of the stratification decreasing from James Bay to Hudson Strait. This marked summer salinity stratification of the surface layer is wholly contained within the upper 50 meters. A well-defined temperature stratification is most pronounced in

September and is mainly confined to the upper 25 meters. Offshore surface temperatures may be as high as 9.5°C; at 25 meters depth, temperatures may vary from −1.8–1.5°C in August and from 0.6–7.8°C in September.

In Hudson Bay, the deeper water, at depths greater than 50 meters, is identified by temperatures ranging between −1.0 and −1.8°C and salinities of 32–33.5‰. It is improbable that this water is involved in the seasonal overturn within the Bay owing to the intense salinity stratification observed within the upper 50 meters in late summer. Such reasoning implies that replenishment of this deep water takes place only in the winter in adjoining areas where surface salinity is high enough to result in the formation of such high-density water. Possibly surface chilling in Hudson Strait or Foxe Basin produces such extreme conditions.

The waters flowing eastward through Hudson Strait originate in Hudson Bay and Foxe Basin. As these waters proceed toward the east, they tend to be confined to a thinner surface layer and finally lose their identity as they reach the open ocean. The vertical distribution of salinity through the Strait is estuarine in character as indicated by the marked increase in salinity from west to east and the distinct penetration of the less saline Bay water over the denser water to the east. The distribution of temperature through Hudson Strait shows a corresponding gradient from west to east from about 4°C at the surface in Hudson Bay to 1°C at the surface in the eastern end of the Strait.

In northern Foxe Basin, water temperatures at all depths decrease from September until November while from November until May there is only slight variation throughout the water column. In this shallow area, the coldest water (−1.75°C) is found at 50 meters during April. Summer warming at the surface commences in mid-June and has been recorded at a depth of 50 meters in mid-July. An increase of salinity occurs in September and November producing a winter maximum of 32.6‰ in early May. Coincident with the spring melting, salinity at the surface decreases rapidly to a minimum of less than 2‰ in early July and rises slowly through August. Oxygen determinations indicate the development of a summer maximum of 9.5 ml/liter at 10 meters, and the dissolved inorganic phosphate content reaches a maximum of 1.5 μg-atm PO_4-P per liter at the surface in mid-June.

Remarkably low temperatures, −1.8 to −1.9°C, and relatively high salinities, 33.75–34.07‰, were recorded in Foxe Basin and Foxe Channel in the summer of 1955. These observations represent a significant deviation from the normal character of the water found in eastern arctic Canada. An investigation of the possible source areas and mechanism of formation of this water suggests that it attains its peculiar characteristics locally, i.e., in

Foxe Basin, as a result of freezing on the tidal flats. By this means, both the temperature and the salinity are altered as brackish water is separated out in the freezing process. The increase in density and redistribution of the water brings it into the deep areas of Foxe Channel where it remains relatively undisturbed. The fact that these conditions have not been observed on subsequent surveys may be due to the extremely limited distribution of this water but more likely is the result of a weakening of the formation processes owing to recent mild winters.

The transport of water through Hudson Strait is related to the influx of Atlantic water, the discharge of water through Fury and Hecla Strait, and the rainfall over the drainage basin. The net volume transport through the Strait must therefore closely approximate the excess of water originating from the land drainage into the Hudson Bay system and the eastward transport of water through Fury and Hecla Strait.

Campbell (1958) has calculated that the influx of water from Fury and Hecla Strait is of the order of .05–0.1 × 10^6 m³/sec and that the overall eastward volume transport through Hudson Strait reaches a summer maximum of 0.3 × 10^6 m³/sec and a winter maximum of 0.1 × 10^6 m³/sec.

A. E. Collin

References

Campbell, N. J., 1958, "The oceanography of Hudson Strait," *Fisheries Res. Board Can., Mans. Repot.,* No. 12, 82pp.

*Collin, A. E., and Dunbar, M. J., 1964, "Physical oceanography in Arctic Canada," *Oceanogr. Mar. Biol. Ann. Rev.,* **2**, 45–75.

Dunbar, M. J., 1958, "Physical oceanographic results of the *Calanus* expeditions in Ungava Bay, Frobisher Bay, Cumberland Sound, Hudson Strait and Northern Hudson Bay, 1949–1955," *J. Fisheries Res. Board Can.,* **15**, 155–201.

Grainger, E. H., 1959, "The annual oceanographic cycle at Igloolik in the Canadian Arctic. 1. The zooplankton and physical and chemical observations," *J. Fisheries Res. Board Can.,* **16**, 454–501.

Hachey, H. B., 1931, "The general hydrography and hydrodynamics of the waters of the Hudson Bay region," *Contrib. Can. Biol. Fisher.,* **7** (9), 93–118.

Hachey, H. B., 1935, "The circulation of Hudson Bay water as indicated by drift bottles," *Science,* **82** (2125): 275–6.

Hare, F. K., and Montgomery, M. R., 1949, "Ice, open water, and winter climate in the Eastern Arctic of North America. 11, The problem of winter ice," *Arctic,* **2** (3), 149–64.

Part B. Bathymetry and Geology

Bathymetry. Hudson Bay is dish-shaped, and depths are generally less than 200 meters (Fig. 2). Bell (1881) remarked on the featureless aspect of the submarine topography, but later soundings

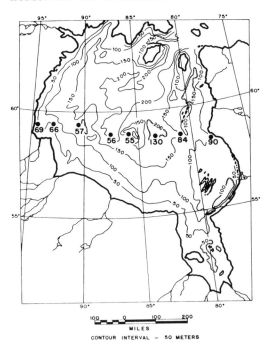

Fig. 2. Bathymetric chart of Hudson Bay showing station locations. Note the concentric saucer shape appearance of the sea floor in general and the major topographic depths in the central and eastern side of Hudson Bay.

show that several interesting features are present throughout the Bay. In the central and northern parts of the Bay, an irregularly shaped basin occurs with depths exceeding 200 meters and with a trough extending from it toward Hudson Strait. The trough is thought to be the main channel of a submerged drainage system that once drained the area now covered by the Bay. From the echo-sounding records, Leslie and Pelletier observed that several V-shaped valleys about 60–80 feet deep occurred about 80–100 miles offshore from the western side of the Bay, and leading away from the Severn, Nelson, and Churchill Rivers. As gravels and coarse sands were found in cores obtained from these areas, these workers thought that formerly shallows or terrestrial areas existed there. Varved sediments and till-like material present in cores from the central area further suggested that a terrestrial environment occurred earlier in the area now occupied by Hudson Bay.

Another topographic feature (Campbell, 1958; Leslie, 1963) is the deep hole or trough located just off the northern shore of Digges Island, in the western end of Hudson Strait. The maximum depth of the trough is about 540 meters which is much deeper than any part of Hudson Bay. Glacial ice moving out of the Bay presumably scoured and deepened the trough. In the center of

the Bay is a prominent shoal of less than 50-meter depth that is surrounded on all sides by depths greater than 150 meters. This feature could be due to resistant rock-capping occurring as a remnant from a previous interval of terrestrial erosion or to the occurrence of a structural high in the bedrock. A combination of both possibilities may also be responsible for this feature.

Geology is a controlling factor of the topography in much of Hudson Bay. On the southwest side, the water is extremely shallow, islands are absent, and the bottom is smooth and is underlain by flat-lying Paleozoic sedimentary rocks. In the eastern portion of the Bay, the water deepens rapidly offshore, the bottom is very irregular, and there are many islands. This area is underlain by folded Proterozoic metasedimentary rocks and Archeozoic crystalline rocks.

Sediments. Leslie (1964) reports the general occurrence of fine sediments in Hudson Bay well offshore, and coarse material mostly inshore. However, the regional trends show sediments to be coarser on the west side of the Bay than on the east side, but the main part of the central region consists of mud and silt (Fig. 3). Ice-rafted material accumulates to a greater extent in the peripheral areas of the Bay than in the central part due to the pattern of water circulation and the presence of

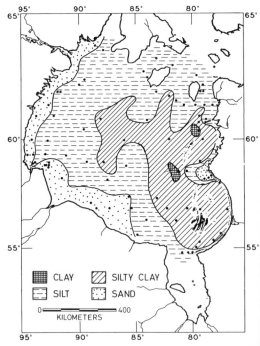

Fig. 3. Distribution of bottom sediment finer than 200 mm in diameter, or the predominantly water deposited material. Generally the coarser material is on the west side of the bay with the finer material on the east.

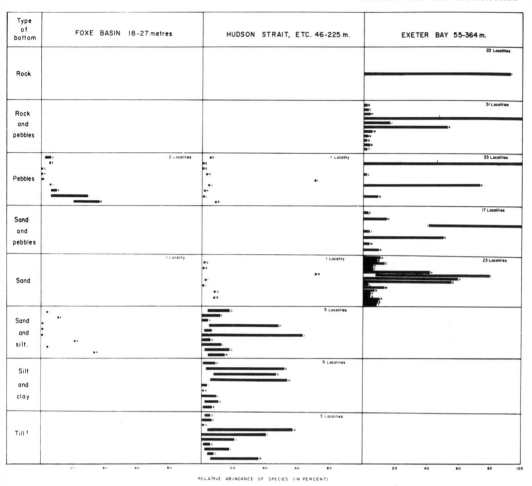

Fig. 4. The relationship of foraminifera to sea bottom according to frequency of occurrences of certain species. Note the depth is relatively uniform across the three areas (after F. J. E. Wagner).

Circles indicate species obtained from a single locality. The length of bars indicate range in frequencies of species obtained from more than one locality.

stronger currents in the former areas. Leslie determined that the higher content of calcium carbonate occurred in sediments associated with areas underlain by Paleozoic limestones. He also determined that sediments high in content of organic carbon coincided with the occurrence of silt and clays. Both the organic material and fine detritus settle slowly, and the former is preserved. Also ice-rafting is minimal in this area and hence masking of organic material by such detritus is not excessive.

Hood (1964) conducted a sparker survey in the southern part of Hudson Bay, and together with Leslie and Pelletier made an examination of the sub-bottom profiles. The graphic record showed that the steeply undulating rocks of Precambrian age could be traced westward from the Belcher Islands a distance of 30–40 miles. Further to the west, the sub-bottom profile was gently undulating,

and this structure extended to Churchill where the strongly undulating profile of the Precambrian was again obtained. At Churchill, the contact between the steeply dipping Precambrian metasediments and the flat-lying lower Paleozoic carbonates was observed, thus confirming the inference on the geological nature of Hudson Bay. These sub-bottom profiles also showed that about 60–80 feet of sediment occurred in the steeply dipping troughs of the Precambrian and that an even layer of sediments about 10 feet in thickness occurred over most of the Bay underlain by the presumed Lower Paleozoic rocks.

Foraminifera. A study of the relationship of Foraminifera to type of bottom in the Hudson Bay approaches was made by F. J. E. Wagner of the Geological Survey of Canada, Ottawa. This study includes examination of material from Exeter Bay and all areas are illustrated in Fig. 4. The

361

depths are somewhat uniform in the three areas, but the substrate is different. From this, it is seen that most species are common to all substrates, but a few prefer coarse material to fine.

A summary of research on the Foraminifera of Hudson Bay and Approaches as well as the Arctic waters of eastern Canada and Greenland is given by Leslie (1963). It includes the work of Cushman

STATION NUMBER	69	66	57	56	55	13?	84	90
DEPTH IN METERS	33	65	115	201	100	228	194	52
PLANKTONIC POPULATION								
GLOBIGERINA PACHYDERMA		100			100		100	
BENTHONIC POPULATION								
ADERCOTRYMA GLOMERATA			7	10	3	20	13	
ALVEOLOPHRAGMIUM CRASSIMARGO	X		1	10		5		
ANGULOGERINA ANGULOSA	1	2	1		4	1	X	
ASTRONONION GALLOWAYI	15	18	2		16	1	13	2
BOLIVINA PACIFICA	9	2	X		2			
BUCCELLA TENERRIMA		3	8	2	9	2	4	3
BULIMINA EXILIS			2	2	23	5	19	X
CASSIDULINA ISLANDICA	7	41	1		3	1	15	1
CASSIDULINA LATICAMERATA		1	X		7		1	
CASSIDULINA NORCROSSI	1	X	4	8	16	2	4	
CIBICIDES LOBATULUS	X	X			X			
DENTALINA BAGGI					X			
DENTALINA FROBISHERENSIS					X			
DENTALINA ITTAI		1			X			X
DENTALINA PAUPERATA					X			
EGGERELLA ADVENA	46	3	5		1	5	1	52
ELPHIDIELLA ARCTICA	X	2			X			
ELPHIDIUM BARTLETTI	4	1	X		X			X
ELPHIDIUM INCERTUM	1	4	X		1		X	4
ELPHIDIUM ORBICULARE	2	5	X		X			X
FISSURINA MARGINATA		3						
FISSURINA SERRATA			X		X			X
GLANDULINA LAEVIGATA	X							
GUTTULINA GLACIALIS	1		X					
HAPLOPHRAGMOIDES MAJOR			4		X			X
HIPPOCREPINA INDIVISA	X							
HYPERAMMINA ELONGATA			X	5	X	X		
LAGENA APIOPLEURA					X			
LAGENA GRACILLIMA					X			
LAGENA LAEVIS	1	X			X		1	
LAGENA MERIDIONALIS				1				
LAGENA MOLLIS		X	X		1			
LAGENA PARRI	X							
LAGENA SEMILINEATA	X							
LAGENA STRIATOPUNCTATA	X							
NONION ZAANDAMAE			X	14	1	1		
NONIONELLA ATLANTICA	X							X
NONIONELLA LABRADORICA			X		2			X
OOLINA COSTATA	X	2	X					
OOLINA LINEATA	X	X			X			
OOLINA LINEATOPUNCTATA					X			
OOLINA MELO	X	X						
PATELLINA CORRUGATA		2						
POLYMORPHINA SP.	X							
PYRGO WILLIAMSONI	X							
QUINQUELOCULINA AGGLUTINATA	1	X						
QUINQUELOCULINA ARCTICA	1				2			
QUINQUELOCULINA STALKERI	2	2					X	
QUINQUELOCULINA SUBROTUNDA	1							X
REOPHAX ARCTICA	X	1	4		2	6		5
REOPHAX CURTUS	1		X	25				2
SACCAMMINA DIFFLUGIFORMIS	1	X	4	6	1	9	4	1
SIGMOMORPHINA SP.	X							
SPIRILLINA VIVIPARA					1		X	
SPIROPLECTAMMINA BIFORMIS		X	9	1	1	1	4	10
TEXTULARIA TORQUATA	2	4	45	8	3	30	18	6
TRILOCULINA TRIGONULA					X			
TROCHAMMINA QUADRILOBA					6		2	X
TROCHAMMINA ROTALIFORMIS			X				6	6
TROCHAMMINA SQUAMATA	1	1			X		2	6
TROCHAMMINELLA ATLANTICA							1	1
FORAMINIFERAL NUMBER	35	316	28	12	303	12	23?	113
PERCENTAGE LIVING FORAMINIFERA	32	4	17	6	6	6	14	17
PERCENTAGE HYALINE TESTS	43	88	19	27	88	13	58	11
PERCENTAGE PORCELANEOUS TESTS	5	2			3		1	
PERCENTAGE ARENACEOUS TESTS	52	10	81	70	12	87	41	89
NUMBER OF GENERA	23	21	23	14	26	16	16	17
NUMBER OF SPECIES	35	29	28	14	37	19	18	23
PERCENTAGE PLANKTONIC FORAMINIFERA		0.8			0.5		4.0	
OSTRACOD NUMBER	0.4	0.5						

Fig. 5. Foraminiferal list and percentage occurrences (after R. J. Leslie).

(1948), Bé (1960), Loeblich and Tappan (1953). The faunal assemblage in Hudson Bay is generally similar to that in Hudson Strait, as identified by Wagner. This list of the Hudson Bay Foraminifera according to Leslie is shown in Fig. 5. Leslie has also drawn foraminiferal trends based on samples obtained along an east-west line across central Hudson Bay (Figs. 2, 6, 7). These trends illustrate some of the following conclusions:

(1) There are three distinctive Foraminifera faunas in an east-west cross section of Hudson Bay: (a) nearshore; (b) central basins, and (c) central shoal.

(2) *Eggerella advena* is dominant at stations on either end of the section, in depths from 33–52 meters. Abundance of *E. advena* at this depth range is typical throughout the Arctic, and it is an important member of Anderson's (1961) Inner Shelf Fauna.

(3) Planktonic Foraminifera are represented by the lone species *Globigerina pachyderma*, which is present at only three stations and in numbers less than 1%. The tests represent all stages of growth and are thin shelled, which agrees with Bé's (1960) report that thick, crystalline tests in *G. pachyderma* indicate a living depth greater than 200 meters.

(4) The fauna from the deep stations in the section is characterized by high percentages of *Textularia torquata*. The findings in Hudson Bay agree with the work of Phleger (1952) who reported

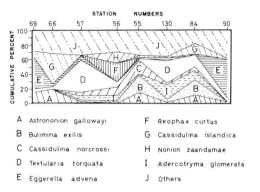

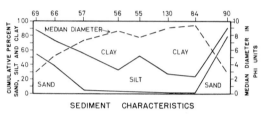

A Astrononion gallowayi	F Reophax curtus
B Bulimina exilis	G Cassidulina islandica
C Cassidulina norcrossi	H Nonion zaandamae
D Textularia torquata	I Adercotryma glomerata
E Eggerella advena	J Others

Fig. 7. Hudson Bay foraminifera and sediment distribution (after R. J. Leslie).

only one occurrence of this species at depths less than 100 meters around the Arctic Archipelago.

(5) The central shoal in Hudson Bay has a distinctive fauna including high percentages of *Cassidulina norcrossi*, *Bulimina exilis*, and *Astrononion gallowayi*. The fauna is composed of 88% hyaline tests as compared to 27 and 13% at adjacent stations to the east and west.

(6) Ice rafting has had little effect upon foraminiferal distribution. Evidence from sediment studies indicates that only the two stations farthest west have been influenced. The current pattern and large size of the Bay tend to reduce faunal masking by ice rafting.

(7) Sediment size is closely related to bottom topography and current direction in the Bay. Since the grain size and bottom topography are related, the foraminiferal population varies with both.

(8) Ostracods occur at station 69 and 66 at the western end of the section. Influx of food from the western rivers may affect their distribution.

(9) Centric and pennate diatoms are present in all the samples, but they are abundant only at station 69 on the western side of Hudson Bay. Heavy runoff and current concentration probably increase nutrient content in the water of this region, which enables the support of a large diatom population.

(10) Radiolarians were not found in any of the samples, and if they are living in Hudson Bay, it is probably near the entrance to Hudson Strait where more normal marine conditions exist.

B. R. PELLETIER

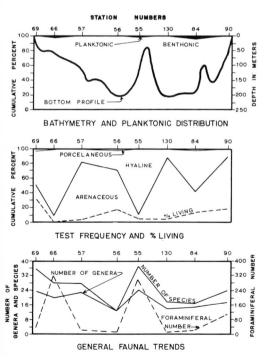

Fig. 6. Hudson Bay foraminiferal trends (after R. J. Leslie).

363

References

Anderson, Gordon J., 1961, "Distribution patterns of recent Foraminifera of the Arctic and Bering Seas," Unpublished Master's Thesis, University of Southern California, 90pp.

Be, Allen W. H., 1960, "Some observations on Arctic planktonic Foraminifera," *Contr. Cush. Found. Foram. Research,* **11**, Pt. 2, 64–68.

Bell, Robert, 1881, "Report on Hudson Bay and some of the lakes and rivers lying to the west of it," *Geol. Surv. Canada, Rept. Prog.* 1879–80, 1c–56c.

Campbell, N. J., and Collin, A. E., 1956, "A preliminary report on some of the oceanographic features of Foxe Basin," *Fisheries Res. Bd., Canada,* MS Rept., Biol. Sta. No. 613, 42pp. (unpublished).

Cushman, Joseph A., 1948, "Arctic Foraminifera," *Cush. Lab. Foram. Research,* Sp. Pub. No. 23, 95pp.

Hood, Peter, 1964, "Sea Magnetometer Reconnaissance of Hudson Bay," *Geophysics,* **39**, No. 6, 916–921.

Leslie, R. J., 1963, "Foraminiferal study of a cross-section of Hudson Bay, Banada," *Geol. Surv. Canada,* Paper 63–16, 28pp.

Leslie, R. J., 1964, "Sedimentology of Hudson Bay, District of Keewatin," *Geol. Surv., Canada,* Paper 63–48, 31pp.

Loeblich, A. R., Jr., and Tappan, Helen, 1953, "Studies of Arctic Foraminifera," *Smithsonian Inst. Misc. Collections,* **121**, No. 7, 150pp.

Phleger, Fred B., 1952, "Foraminifera distribution in some sediment samples from the Canadian and Greenland Arctic," *Contr. Cush. Found. Foram. Research,* **3**, Pt. 2, 80–89.

HUMBOLDT CURRENT-*See* **PERU CURRENT**

HYDRAULICS-*See* **FLUID MECHANICS**

HYDROCLIMATE-*See* Vol. II

HYDRODYNAMICS-*See* **FLUID MECHANICS**

HYPSOGRAPHIC CURVE

Definition

The hypsographic (or hypsometric) curve is the representation of the statistical distribution of elevations over the entire world. In the areas which are covered with water (lakes, seas, oceans), the relief is mostly below sea level and the figures are consequently negative (generally): they are bathymetric values, determined nowadays by acoustic sounding. The curve was first prepared by Krümmel (1897) but the modern curve is based on the statistics of Kossinna (1921, 1933).

Let us call dS the total of the areas whose elevation (positive or negative) is included between the values z and $z + dz$, and let us call S the total area of the world. The hypsographic curve represents dS/S as function of z (Fig. 1, devised by Wegener, 1924).

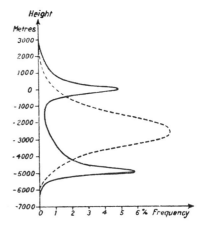

FIG. 1. The two frequency maxima of elevation (after Wegener).

Instead of such a "curve of frequencies," we may consider the "curve of cumulative frequencies," i.e., the representation of the integral of dS/S (Fig. 2).

We may also use a schematic table, such as Table 1.

TABLE 1

z between	dS/S (%)
Zero and $+1000$ m	21.3
$+1000$ and $+2000$ m	4.7
$+2000$ and $+3000$ m	2.0
$+3000$ and higher	1.2
Zero and -200 m	5.5
-200 and -1000 m	2.9
-1000 and -2000 m	3.5
-2000 and -3000 m	7.1
-3000 and -4000 m	15.5
-4000 and -5000 m	22.0
-5000 and -6000 m	13.2
-6000 and deeper	1.1

Peculiarities

The peculiarities of this curve are:

(1) The existence of two maxima of frequencies, i.e., bimodal; they appear in Fig. 1 and are located at the elevations $+100$ and -4700 meters. In the same Figure, the broken line represents a gaussian (stochastic) distribution.

(2) The existence of two zones of elevations in which the cumulative frequency changes quickly with an increasing magnitude (this peculiarity is not independent from the first one).

(3) The existence of an intermediate zone (continental slope) where the integral curve (Fig. 2) is characterized by a sharp curvature (beginning at the shelf edge).

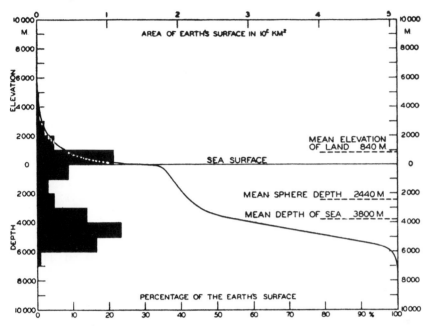

FIG. 2. Hypsographic curve showing the area of the earth's solid surface above any given level of elevation or depth. At the left in the figure is the frequency distribution of elevations and depths for 1000-meter intervals (from Sverdrup, Johnson, Fleming, 1942).

(4) The hypsographic curve is such that the so-called mean "eustatic level" of the oceans, controlled by isostatic equilibrium, does not depend from the volume of continental ice.

Explanations

The existence of two frequency maxima reveal two plainly different parts of the earth's crust (independent of the presence of water in the oceans). Such a duality, confirmed by the seismologic and gravimetric studies, conforms to the isostatic hypothesis of Airy, as modified by Gutenberg; it played an important part in the Wegener's theory of continental drift, which has both numerous supporters and numerous opponents. Wegener pointed out that if there was a uniform crust as argued by some of his critics, the hypsographic frequency curve would have to be controlled by the gaussian law of errors. Goguel (1950), for example, urged an originally random distribution of the earth's crust, modified only by erosion/sedimentation and isostasy.

The rapid variation of frequency in the two domains (modes) of elevation correlates with the existence of two frequency maxima. But the fact that one of these domains includes the zero level must be explained: We are in the presence, on the one hand, of epeirogenic processes (the theories of which have yet to be proved) and, on the other hand, of the processes of erosion and sedimentation. The principal consequence of these opposed actions is that the continental areas only gently emerge from oceans; they are smoothed down to near the zero level in proportion to the degree of their epeirogenic uplift.

This is the reason why the first frequency maximum is of low altitude ($+100$ meters).

The intermediate zone (with steep curve) corresponds to the transition between the continental and oceanic domains; here, the following peculiarity must be noted: The sudden change of frequency near the zero level does not stop at that zero level itself, but at about the isobath of 200 meters; at that negative level, the transition or intermediate zone begins. The continental shelf statistically extends to that level and must be considered as an integral part of the continental domain. The continental slope, with its steep declivity constitutes the intermediate zone.

If an isostatic readjustment takes place, following a major variation of the volume of the continental ice, we must presume that the vertical motion of the oceanic floor (subsidence after a melting of the ice, uplift after a glacial accumulation) will be limited to the deepest zones, whereas the intermediate zone constitutes a more or less plastic junction between oceans and continents.

Lastly, the form of the hypsographic curve is such that the so-called eustatic level of the oceans, controlled by isostatic equilibrium, does not depend on the volume of the continental ice. That statement has the following implication: Let us

365

imagine a general melting of the continental ice (Greenland, Antarctica and so on), in a short time (on the geological scale). The volume of the oceans increases, and a transgression takes place; but such a displacement of mass from the continental ice to the ocean, disturbs the isostatic equilibrium. The mass displacement is consequently followed by a compensating displacement of mass beneath the earth's crust, somewhere in the mantle; this is an isostatic readjustment. For the oceans the effects of this will be a subsidence; for the continental zones initially with ice caps, this means uplift; for the continental areas without initial ice, there will be only a moderate uplift.

The variation of the mean elevation of the continents (considered before the melting and after the readjustment, assuming in both cases a perfect isostatic equilibrium) is proportional to the value of the expression $a - 1 + \varepsilon/\delta$, in which a is the total continental area (the unit being the area of the whole earth), $1 + \varepsilon$ is the density of the oceans, and δ is the density of the mantle (Airy's model). With the values $1 + \varepsilon = 1.05$ and $\delta = 3.27$, the expression $a - 1 + \varepsilon/\delta$ is zero for $a = 0.32$.

The value 1.05 takes into account the mean depth of the oceans; the value of δ is not quite certain. The value of a represents approximately the true continental area, including the continental shelf. Consequently, although the mean elevation of the continents may show small variations, corres-ponding to temporary disturbances in the equilibrium, the readjustments tend to bring it back to a constant value, independent of the volume of the continental ice (after allowing time for adjustment). We could get a different result with another hypsographic curve; if a was greater, then a glaciation would cause an increase of the mean elevation and melting would cause a decrease; if a was smaller, then those consequences would be reversed. One does not know if this peculiarity is fortuitous or not.

J. LAGRULA

References

Francis-Boeuf, C., 1942, "Les Océans," Paris, Presses Universitaires de France.
Goguel, J., 1950, "Sur l'interprétation de la courbe hypsographique," *Acad. Sci. Paris, C.R.*, **230**, 219–221.
Lagrula, J., 1950, "Sur la courbe hypsographique," *Acad. Sci. Paris, C.R.*, **230**, 1413–1415.
Lagrula, J., 1959, "Nouvelles études gravimétriques," *Bull. Serv. Carte. Géol. Algerie,* No. 25.
Kossinna, E., 1921, "Die Tiefen des Weltmeeres," *Veroeffentl. Inst. Meereskunde, Berlin,* **9**.
Kossinna, E., 1933, "Die Erdoberfläche," in (B. Gutenberg, ed.) "Handbuch der Geophysik," Vol. 2, pp. 869–954, Berlin, Borntraeger.
Krummel, O., 1897, "Handbuch der Ozeanographie," Stuttgart, Engelhorn's Nacht., 2 vols.
Wegener, A., 1924, "The origin of continents and oceans," London, Methuen, 212pp. (translated by J. G. A. Skerl).

I

ICE—*See* **SEA ICE**

ICE, STRUCTURE AND PROPERTIES—*See* Vol. III

ICE TRANSPORTATION—*See* **SEA-ICE TRANSPORTATION**

ICEBERGS

(a) Birth, Distribution, Drift, Destruction

When the terminus of a glacier moves into the sea either as a vertical wall or an inclined plane, it experiences, because of its smaller density, an upward force which fluctuates with the periodic and aperiodic variations in sea level. The force increases as the glacier extends farther into the sea and finally causes the protruding end of the glacier to break off in pieces of different size, or to calve icebergs.

At present, a little over a quarter of the ice from the world's glaciers is lost through melting and sublimation, and the other three-quarters is lost through calving of the icebergs which melt as they drift to warmer waters. The icebergs calved in the Antarctic make up $1.63 \pm 0.10 \times 10^{18}$ g/yr which is 6.5 times the mass (2.5×10^{17} g/yr) of the icebergs calved in the Arctic. The total mass of icebergs in the world is 7.65×10^{18} grams, approximately, of which 93% is in the southern hemisphere.

The icebergs regularly carried equatorward are spread over an area of 63×10^6 km², approximately, or 18.7% of the world's ocean, of which 56×10^6 km² is in the southern hemisphere. The icebergs are carried much farther out toward the equator than sea ice; in the southern hemisphere at the present time, they are carried to between 44 and 57°S, on the average. Pleistocene ice-rafted boulders occur in profusion to latitude 35°S off South Africa and Australia. In the northern hemisphere, the icebergs brought down by the Labrador Current (see below) reach at times to the low latitude of 36°N and, as small pieces of ice, even further south on occasion. Elsewhere in the northern oceans, icebergs are met only in the high latitudes. Pleistocene ice-rafted boulders are found in the eastern North Atlantic to the latitude of North Africa (35°N).

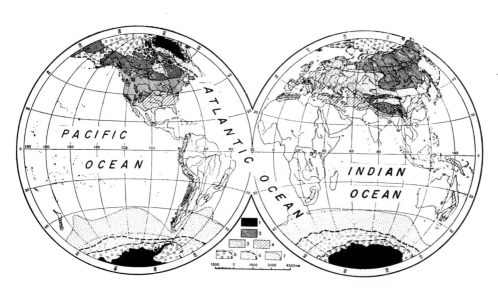

Fig. 1. Extent of ice on the globe: (1) glaciers; (2) underground ice (permafrost). Seasonal snow and ice on land; (3) yearly; (4) individual years. Sea-ice and icebergs; (5) entire year; (6) seasonal; (7) icebergs.

The average life of an iceberg is about four years—those in the Antarctic lasting a little longer than those in the Arctic. An Antarctic iceberg as large as the state of Connecticut has been observed. Some icebergs have a much longer life, e.g., when they find themselves in the closed circulation of the Canadian sector of the Arctic Ocean, when they are grounded in the shoal waters, and when they attach themselves to the large ice shelves in the Antarctic.

By far the most productive glaciers in the northern hemisphere are those on the west coast of Greenland due to their relatively rapid movement. The speed of some of the West Greenland glaciers is 20–25 m/day as compared with 1 m/day for the fastest of Alpine glaciers. Thus, the Jacobshavn glacier, which keeps moving even in winter, produces over 1000 bergs/yr, filling the fjord with thousands of icebergs which move out irregularly, on the average of once a month, at first very slowly then more rapidly at 10–15 km/hr, the movement being accompanied by an intense noise that can be heard several miles away. The icebergs produced by this glacier are of many, often fantastic, shapes; a large number of them attain a height of 200 feet above the water, and one measured at 500 feet. They are easily surpassed in size by the icebergs in the Antarctic waters, however, most of which are tabular in shape, one measuring 80 miles in length and 300 feet in height, and others even bigger.

In the very high latitudes of the northern hemisphere and also in the Antarctic where it is extremely cold and where heavy pack ice extends outward from the coast for many miles, the termini of the glaciers push out into the frozen sea for many miles and break off infrequently.

After the glacier has calved, the bergs under the influence of wind and current move into the open ocean, unless they drift into shallow water where they very slowly disintegrate. During their journey, and especially as they reach lower latitudes, the icebergs lose their sharp features under the action of the sun and warm winds and sometimes even rain, the melted ice forming rivers on the berg's surface that run into the sea.

Because of the slowness with which the iceberg forms while still part of a glacier, it contains many air bubbles, the aeration amounting to as much as 15% of its volume. Thus, the degree of submergence of an iceberg is, in addition to the density of the water, dependent also on its air content, and it is further greatly dependent on the iceberg's shape or form. If the lower part of a berg is wide, while its upper part tapers up sharply, the narrow part will stick out considerably above the water. According to the late Rear Admiral Smith, who, as a Commander of the International Ice Patrol and leader of special cruises in Baffin Bay, Davis Strait, and the Labrador Sea, was able to observe many bergs, the ratios of the height of an iceberg above the surface to the submerged portion are for a rect-

angular or tubular berg, 1:7; a rounded berg, 1:4; pyramidal type, 1:3; pinnacled berg, 1:2; and winged or horned berg, usually in the last stages of its disintegration, 1:1.

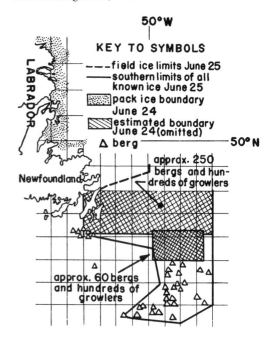

Fig. 2. Iceberg distribution as of 25 June 1957, showing heavy concentration of icebergs southeast of Newfoundland. (Weekly Ice Chartlets, U.S. Navy, Hydrographic Office).

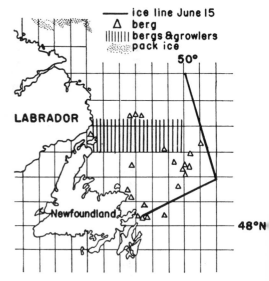

Fig. 3. Iceberg distribution as of 17 June 1958, showing no bergs southeast of Newfoundland. (Weekly Ice Chartlets, U.S. Navy, Hydrographic Office).

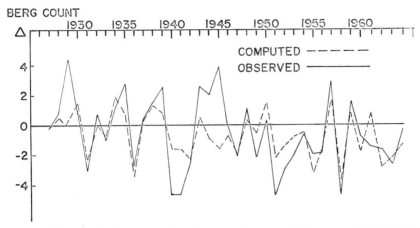

Fig. 4. Computed and observed deviations from the average iceberg count (1880–1926) on scale 0 to 10 during 1927–64, 1961 (after Schell, 1962); 1962–64 (after Schell, unpublished).

In the beginning, when the iceberg is still in cold waters, it melts very slowly below the surface and more rapidly above, but as it reaches warmer waters the rates of melting are reversed. Also, the smaller the berg is, the more rapidly will it melt since then it does not extend into the deeper, colder water. Many attempts have been made to destroy icebergs by shooting at them with cannons, bombing them from airplanes, placing thermite bombs into holes dug in the iceberg that will cause an explosion and a shattering of the berg, and also spreading lampblack to absorb the sun's radiation and cause it to melt. All these attempts, however, have met with no appreciable success.

(b) Icebergs off Newfoundland

Of special interest are the icebergs off Newfoundland, which drift southward from Baffin Bay along the Labrador and Newfoundland coasts and which pose great danger to shipping, necessitating a southward shift of the transatlantic shipping lanes in some years to avoid a repetition of the disaster that occurred on April 14, 1912, with the sinking of the *Titanic*. (A more recent sinking was that of the *Hans Hedtoft* that went down off Cape Farewell, the southern tip of Greenland, on January 30, 1959, with the loss of all aboard.)

On the average, about 400 icebergs are counted each year, crossing 48°N off Newfoundland on their way southward, mostly during the months of April, May and June, when approximately 80% of the yearly total drifts by that latitude. The yearly number of bergs varies from as few as a dozen or less in 1924, 1940, 1941, 1951, 1958 to as many as 1000 or more in 1909, 1912, 1929 and 1945 (the last count is doubtful because of war conditions). Examples of severe and light iceberg conditions off Newfoundland are shown in Figs. 2 and 3.

The causes of the large variations in the yearly count of icebergs have also been investigated.

Following the pioneering efforts by the late E. H. Smith, it has been possible to develop a base for predicting at the end of March the rough count each season from a consideration of the strength of the winds and severity of the cold along the Labrador and Newfoundland coasts during the preceding December–March months. Figure 4 shows computed and observed deviations in the berg count on scale 0–10 for the period 1927–1964.*

The icebergs off Newfoundland are carefully watched by the International Ice Patrol which, by agreement with other nations, is operated by the U.S. Coast Guard, using both planes and ships. Information on the size, location, and movement of the bergs is frequently broadcast.

I. I. SCHELL

References

Lebedev, V. L., 1961, "Classification of Antarctic icebergs," (Problems of the North; translation of "Problemy Severa," *Akademiia Nauk S.S.S.R.*, No. 2 (1958); translation published 1961, pp. 77–88.

Schell, I. I., 1962, "On the iceberg severity off Newfoundland and its prediction," *J. Glaciol.*, **4**, 161–172.

Shumskii, P. A., and Krenke, A. N., 1965, "The present glaciation of the earth and its changes," *Geophys. Bull.*, No. 14, 128–158 (Soviet Geophysical Committee of the Academy of Sciences, U.S.S.R.).

Smith, E. H., 1931, "The Marion Expedition to Davis Strait and Baffin Bay, 1928," *U.S. Coast Guard Bull.* No. 19, Part 3, 1–221.

Zubov, N. N., 1945, "Arctic Ice," U.S. Navy Electronics Laboratory, San Diego, California, (translated from the Russian).

* The agreement between the computed and actual deviations in 1942, 1943, 1944 and 1945 would be closer if allowance was made for the apparent over-counting in the war years by less-experienced personnel.

INDIAN OCEAN

Introduction*

The Indian Ocean is the smallest of the three "great" oceans and geologically much of it is also rather youthful, although as with the early history of the other oceans, many aspects are still totally unknown.

Following the International Hydrographic Bureau (*Sp. Publ. 23, 1953*), its boundaries are as follows: *Western limits*: The meridian of Cape Agulhas (20°E) to Antarctica (Queen Maud Land, the boundary of the Princess Ragnhild Coast on the east and Princess Astrid Coast on the west). *Eastern limits, south of Australia*: The western boundary of Bass Strait from Cape Otway to King Island, thence to Cape Grim (Northwestern Tasmania); and from the Southeast Cape of Tasmania, along meridian 147°E, to the Antarctic continent near Fisher Bay, George V Coast. *Eastern limits, north of Australia*: Much controversy has occurred about this boundary. Most geologists prefer the narrowest sea crossing in Torres Straits; I.H.B. gives the western limit of the Straits, from Cape York (11°05′S, 142°03′E) to Bensback River, New Guinea (141°01′E) as the eastern limit of the *Arafura Sea* (q.v.), but some workers would place the latter within the Pacific and some even place the *Timor Sea* (q.v.) in the Pacific, though with what logic it is hard to tell, since the Timor Sea is in complete hydrologic continuity with the Indian Ocean, and the geological foundations (*Sahul Shelf*, q.v.) are clearly part of the northwestern Australian shield, a unit of the old Gondwana land mass with its evident Indian Ocean alignment (see discussion of boundary in *Pacific Ocean*). The northeastern boundary runs from island to island through the Lesser Sunda Islands, to Java and Sumatra, and thence to Singapore.

Marginal seas that belong unequivocally to the Indian Ocean are situated along the northern parts of the ocean and are mostly dealt with in more detail elsewhere in this Encyclopedia, thus *Red Sea* (q.v.), *Gulf of Aden, Persian Gulf* (q.v.), *Gulf of Oman, Arabian Sea* (q.v.), *Laccadive Sea, Bay of Bengal* (q.v.), *Andaman Sea* (q.v.), *Malacca Straits and Singapore Straits* (the last sometimes included in the Pacific); two additional marginal areas are the *Mozambique Channel* and the *Great Australian Bight*, not treated separately here.

The southern sector of the Indian Ocean is sometimes taken as that part south of a line from Cape Agulhas to Cape Leeuwin (Western Australia), recommended by the I.H.B. in 1928, but withdrawn in their recent editions. Other definitions of the *Southern Ocean* (q.v.) are dealt with under that heading; in general that sea may be taken as a special subdivision of each of the three oceans. ·

The area covered by the Indian Ocean (using the I.H.B. limits, but excluding the Arafura Sea) is 74,917,000 km² (28,920,000 miles²); with a mean depth of 3897 m, the volume is 291,945,000 km³. With the Arafura Sea, the area is 75,940,000 km². The maximum depth recorded is 7437 m (24,444 feet).

History*

The early navigators of the Indian Ocean were probably ancient Egyptians and later the Arabs and Chinese. About 600 B.C., Necho, King of Egypt, sent out an expedition that succeeded in circumnavigating the African continent. Phoenecian trading settlements are known on the Persian Gulf, and Marco Polo returned from China by well-used trading routes via the Malacca Straits. Nevertheless it was with considerable surprise and some chagrin that the Moslem seafarers noted the arrival of Vasco da Gama and the Portuguese in 1497, who had rounded the Cape of Good Hope and thus opened a new era of eastern trade. This was first shared with Arabs and Chinese by the Portuguese, but later the Dutch came in with the United East India Company, and then the British, leading eventually to the occupation of India and Malaya, and finally the French, who also established small trading posts.

The central part of the Indian Ocean was crossed by Del Cano in the *Victoria* (A.D. 1521), following Magellan's death in the Philippines. Sir Francis Drake followed in 1580, and in the seventeenth century, the Dutch were the principal voyagers here. Apparently they were aware of the basic principles of the planetary winds (probably a closely guarded company secret), usually sailing eastward at about latitude 40°S to catch the westerlies, and then turning north to benefit from the Southeast Trade Wind to bring them up to Java. It was in this way that they discovered Australia, in the most disagreeable manner, numbers of ships being wrecked along the west coast. Important encounters were recorded in 1616 by A. Hartog, in 1619 by B. Houtman, in 1627 by C. Nuyts and in 1629 by D. Pelsart.

Abel Tasman, circumnavigating Australia in 1642, gave the entire west and south coasts a wide berth, to discover Tasmania (first dutifully called Van Diemen's Land after his sponsor). The best early descriptions of the west Australian coast come from that remarkable scientist-pirate, William Dampier (in 1679 and 1699).

The southernmost waters of the Indian Ocean were first crossed by Captain James Cook on two voyages (1772, 1776), accomplishing a first encounter with the Antarctic ice pack. He was followed by the Russian expedition under Fabian von Bellingshausen in 1820 and by Charles Wilkes (with geologist C. D. Dana on board) with U.S. Navy Exploration Expedition, when definite land was sighted in East Antarctica, now recognized as

---

* Rhodes W. Fairbridge.

* Rhodes W. Fairbridge.

Wilkes Land. Other early voyagers in Indian-Antarctic waters included Dumont d'Urville, Sir James Ross (in *Erebus* and *Terror*) and Commandant Charcot.

Great oceanographic expeditions in the Indian Ocean included those of the *Challenger* (1872–76,

with Sir George Nares, Sir Wyville Thomson and John Murray), followed by the Austrian *Novara* voyage, several German expeditions, *Valdivia* (1898–99) and *Gauss* (1901–03, von Drygalski), the Dutch expeditions to the East Indies, which also took in Indian Ocean waters (*Siboga*, 1899–1900, Weber;

Fig. 1. Physiographic provinces of Indian Ocean.

Snellius, 1929–30, v. Riel, Kuenen), various British Navy hydrographic surveys with H.M.S. *Investigator* and others, the John Murray Expedition on the Egyptian vessel *Mahabis* (Wiseman and others, 1933–34), the Danish voyages of the *Dana* (1928–30) and *Galathea* (1950–52), the Swedish Deep-Sea Expedition of the *Albatross* (1950–52, Pettersson and Kullenberg), which brings us to the time of the *International Indian Ocean Expedition* of the period 1960–65, with numerous ships of many nations, notably the *Vema, Conrad, Argo, Horizon, Serrano, Pioneer, Chain, Te Vega, Anton Bruun, Discovery,*

Fig. 2. Bathymetric sketch of Indian Ocean.

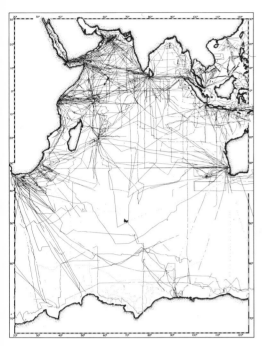

Fig. 3. Track chart of Indian Ocean showing control used in preparation of Figs. 1 and 2.

Challenger II, Commandant Charcot, Lomonosov, Ob, and *Vityaz.*

An important event which occurred in the scientific study of the Indian Ocean and its marginal lands was the establishment of the PIOSA, the *Pan-Indian Ocean Science Association*, following a proposal by this writer to the West Australian Branch of the Australian National Research Council. Following the lines of the Pacific Science Association, this group meets every few years in various Indian Ocean countries. It was at the request of the first committee that this writer prepared a review of all the definitions and limits proposed at various times for the Indian Ocean boundaries (Fairbridge, 1954).

Bathymetry and Bottom Characteristics*

There are five major divisions of the Indian Ocean bed (Figs. 1, 2, 3).

Continental Margin. The continental shelves of the Indian Ocean are somewhat narrower on the average than those of the Atlantic, ranging in width from a few hundred meters around some oceanic islands to more than 200 km off Bombay. The shelf break which forms the outer edge of the continental shelf of Asia, Africa, and Australia (Fig. 4) averages 140 m in the Indian Ocean.

The continental slope, the marginal escarpments, and the landward slopes of trenches mark the boundary of the continental blocks (Fig. 4). Numerous

* Bruce C. Heezen and Marie Tharp.

submarine canyons indent the continental slope. Particularly prominent submarine canyons spread out from the Ganges and Indus Rivers.

The continental rise lies at the base of the continental slope. Regional gradients range from 1:40 at the base of the slope to 1:1000 at the boundaries with the abyssal plains. The low local relief consists of occasional seamounts, knolls and canyons. Submarine canyons extending across the continental rise are generally small in cross section and impossible to detect without the aid of modern precision sounders; thus few are adequately surveyed. Large sediment accumulations known as abyssal cones are associated with both the Ganges and the Indus rivers (Fig. 5).

The arcuate *Java Trench* bordering the Indonesian arc forms the northwestern boundary of the Indian Ocean between Burma and Australia (Fig. 6). A gentle outer ridge lies seaward of the trench.

Ocean-basin Floor. The most conspicuous provinces of the ocean-basin floor are the abyssal plains which stand out sharply (Fig. 1). These are the flattest surfaces on the face of the earth. Regional gradients range from 1:1000 to 1:7000. Except for isolated peaks of buried hills and mid-ocean canyons, local relief does not exceed 1–2 m. Abyssal plains, although well-developed in the northern and southern parts of the Indian Ocean, are relatively poorly developed off Australia (Fig. 4).

Abyssal hills characteristically lie along the seaward margins of the abyssal plains (Fig. 1). In a few areas, it has been determined that the relief of this province is characterized by low linear ridges.

Microcontinents. Some of the most notable features of the Indian Ocean are the generally north-south trending microcontinents. From west to east, the following north-south trending linear aseismic microcontinents can be recognized in the northern part of the Indian Ocean: *Mozambique Ridge, Madagascar Ridge, Mascarene Plateau, Chagos-Laccadive Plateau, Ninetyeast Ridge* (Fig. 7). In the south, the *Kerguelen Plateau* has a strong meridional linearity (Fig. 8). *Broken Ridge*, a large east-west asymmetrical feature, lies east of the Ninetyeast Ridge near 30°S (Fig. 1). Easily distinguished on morphological grounds from the mid-oceanic ridge, the microcontinents are generally higher, blockier features with lower local relief (Fig. 7).

Madagascar is clearly a microcontinent, and the granitic Seychelles suggest that at least the northern portion of the Mascarene Plateau is a continent. The Chagos are coral islands which rise from a long, broad, slightly curved plateau. The Ninetyeast Ridge is perhaps the longest and straightest ridge so far discovered in any ocean. Completely unknown until discovered by the International Indian Ocean Expedition, this ridge has been traced from 10°N to 32°S (Figs. 1 and 7).

Probably the most striking difference between the Indian Ocean and the South Atlantic is the presence of so many microcontinents. In addition to the dominantly north-south ridges discussed heretofore, the prominent east-west Diamantina Fracture Zone extends 1500 miles westward from the southwest tip of Australia. Broken Ridge, which forms the nor-

thern boundary of the fracture zone, merges at 30°S with the Ninetyeast Ridge which marks a north-south fracture at right angles to the Diamantina Fracture Zone.

The Mid-oceanic Ridge. The most conspicuous

Fig. 4. The Eastern Indian Ocean; portion of the Physiographic Diagram of the Indian Ocean, published by the Geological Society of America (copyright 1964 by Bruce C. Heezen and Marie Tharp; reproduced by permission).

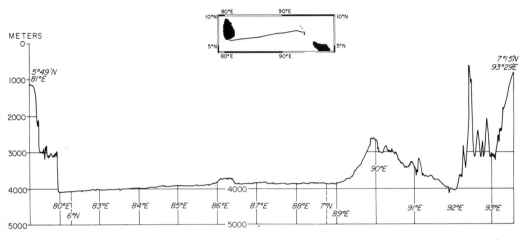

Fig. 5. Topographic profile of Ganges Cone and Ninetyeast Ridge between Ceylon and Andaman Islands.

feature of the Indian Ocean is the Mid-Indian Ocean Ridge, that section of the world-encircling mid-oceanic ridge which lies as an inverted "Y" in the center of the Indian Ocean. Along the axis of the mid-oceanic ridge, a seismically active depression or rift is characteristically found. The entire ridge is

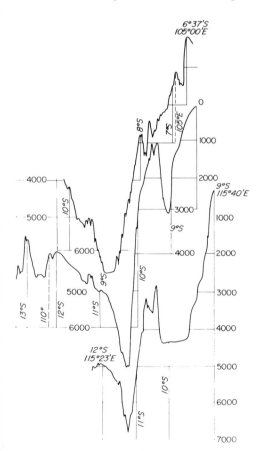

Fig. 6. Topographic profiles of Java Trench.

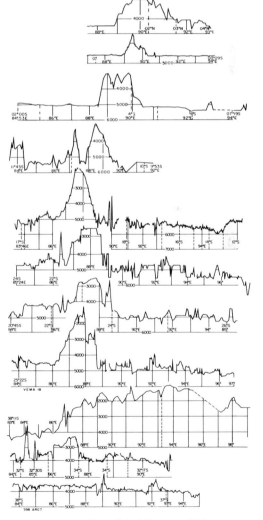

Fig. 7. Profiles of the Ninetyeast Ridge.

375

mountainous, with linear trends paralleling the axis of the ridge (Fig. 9).

Fracture Zones. The Indian Ocean is cut by several prominent fracture zones which offset the axis of the mid-oceanic ridge. The *Owen Fracture Zone* lies east of Arabia and the Gulf of Aden, offsetting the axis of the mid-oceanic ridge by approximately 200 miles to the right. Recent displacement on this fracture zone is indicated by the *Wheatley Trench*, a sharp depression which drops more than 1000 m below the India Abyssal Plain. Several small right-lateral fracture zones offset the Carlsberg Ridge. In the Gulf of Aden, the mid-oceanic ridge is offset by several left-lateral fracture zones that lie roughly parallel to the Owen Fracture Zone. In the southwest Indian Ocean, the mid-oceanic ridge is offset by a series of

Fig. 8. The Southcentral Indian Ocean; portion of the Physiographic Diagram of the Indian Ocean, published by the Geological Society of America (copyright 1964 by Bruce C. Heezen and Marie Tharp; reproduced by permission).

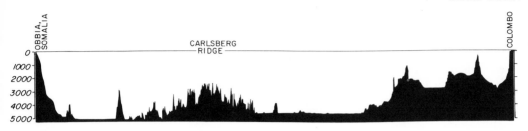

Fig. 9. Topographic profile of the mid-oceanic ridge and Ninetyeast Ridge between Somalia and Ceylon.

left-lateral fracture zones which have roughly the same orientation as the Owen Fracture Zone (Fig. 10). The *Malagasy Fracture Zone*, which lies to the east of the Madagascar Ridge, appears to be a southern extension of the Owen Fracture Zone (Fig. 1). The *Amsterdam Fracture Zones* offset the axis of the mid-oceanic ridge in the region of St. Paul and Amsterdam islands. These fracture zones appear sub-parallel to the Ninetyeast Ridge and have roughly the same north-south orientation as the fracture zones of the western Indian Ocean. Although the nearly north-south lineations are most prominent in the Indian Ocean, the *Diamantina Fracture Zone* and the *Rodriguez Fracture Zone* add a significant roughly east-west trend.

The rugged tectonic relief of the mid-oceanic ridge normally contrasts markedly with the very smooth depositional topography of the continental rise and the almost perfect flatness of the abyssal plains. In the Indian Ocean, there are areas of smooth-rolling or swale topography, apparently produced by the blanketing effect of thicker pelagic sediments (Fig. 8). The flanks of the mid-oceanic ridge south of the Polar Front are markedly smoother than the northern flanks north of the Polar Front. This may be the result of a higher rate of pelagic deposition resulting from the higher organic productivity of the Southern Ocean.

The *Crozet Rise* is extremely smooth. In this area the narrow crest zone of the mid-oceanic ridge exhibits the usual rugged topography; elsewhere in the area the bottom is extremely smooth.

General Distribution of Sediments*

The Indian Ocean floor is covered by sediments which may be divided into six broad categories. Their boundaries are not precise but merge into one another (Murray and Renard, 1891; Murray and Philippi, 1908; Schott, 1939).

Pelagic Types. These sediments are distributed over most of the Indian Ocean basin:

(i) *Red clay* dominates about 25% of the total area, especially between latitudes 10°N and 40°S, in the eastern half of the ocean and away from islands and continents. Owing to the semi-arid nature and

lack of perennial rivers around much of Western Australia, the red clay facies is found right up to the edge of the continental rise in many places. Toward the tropics, the red clay merges locally with *radiolarian ooze*. Riedel reports widespread occurrence of Tertiary and Cretaceous radiolaria.

(ii) *Calcareous ooze*, especially the *globigerina* type, covers some 54% of the ocean floor, mainly where the depth is not excessive (on account of solution) and in areas of warmth and very high organic productivity, thus the equatorial belt from 20°N to 40°S. Pteropod ooze occupies small patches, notably off northwestern Australia. Frequent reports of Tertiary and Cretaceous foraminifera match those of the radiolaria, but nothing older.

(iii) *Diatom ooze*, the siliceous ooze covers about 20% of the total area in the sub-polar areas, beyond 50°S latitude.

Terrigenous Types. These sediments are distributed close to continents (tropical and polar) and island belts (less so, off subtropical arid lands). Areas more than 1000 km from land receive relatively little terrigenous material, and then it is mainly wind-borne. In the tropical latitudes, kaolinite is the most common clay, but it decreases rapidly toward the south (Gorbunova, 1962).

(i) *Geosynclinal trenches, troughs, and basins* of several different classifications are located around the northern periphery of the Indian Ocean basin (notably the Oman and Makran Troughs in the northwest, the Andaman Basin, and Java-Bali-Timor trenches and troughs of the northeast. Transport of sediment is mainly by turbidity currents, but partly by volcanic action, submarine slumping, etc.

(ii) *Mid-ocean volcanic areas* lie mainly in the western half; they are marked by lava and ash accumulations, passing peripherally to fine tuffs and pelagic oozes, in places forming an archipelagic apron (q.v.). An ash alteration product, the zeolite mineral philippsite, is characteristic in these marginal volcanic zones. On relatively few volcanic foundations, there is a crown of coral limestone in the form of an atoll (e.g., Cocos-Keeling Islands).

(iii) *Circum-Polar belts* are marginal to the Antarctic glaciated regions; fine and coarse terrigenous marine tillite material is provided by the melting of ice floes and icebergs. Glacio-terrigenous material is

* Rhodes W. Fairbridge

dominant up to 500 km north of Antarctica, but scattered deposits sometimes reach 3000 km from that shore.

(iv) *Coral reefs and biohermal facies* are widespread in the western parts of the Indian Ocean from 15°N to 20°S, but in the Red Sea with an extension

to 30°N. Classical areas for study of compound or complex atolls and faros are found in the Laccadives and Maldives (Agassiz, 1903; Biewald, 1964; Gardiner, 1903–06; Sewell, 1936) and in the Chagos group, with the great Diego Garcia atoll (Bourne, 1888; Gardiner, 1936). These are the reefs *not* asso-

Fig. 10. The Southwest Indian Ocean; portion of the Physiographic Diagram of the Indian Ocean; published by the Geological Society of America (copyright 1964 by Bruce C. Heezen and Marie Tharp; reproduced by permission).

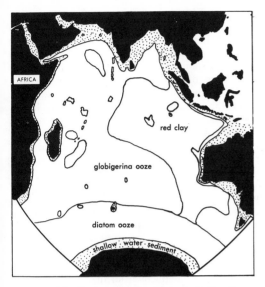

Fig. 11. Distribution of sediments in the Indian Ocean (after Wolfgang Schott, 1955; redrawn by E. W. Spencer).

ciated with submerged volcanic cones, but with "microcontinent" type mid-oceanic submarine plateaus (q.v.).

Numbers of interesting reefs of various types are found on the various submarine plateaus and volcanic areas between Chagos and Madagascar. Extensive visits to these reefs were made by Voeltzkow (1903–06), as well as to the fringing reefs of Zanzibar, Pemba and the Comores Islands. Voeltzkow (1901) also made the interesting discovery of extensive coccolith and rhabdolith ooze in the lagoon of Aldabra, an island described further by Fryer (1911). Gardiner and Cooper (1907) carried out an expedition for the Percy Sladen Trust which took in Chagos, Amirantes, Cardagos, Farquahar, Coetivy and others. In recent years, the French workers under Guilcher have been active studying the reefs and reef sediments of northern Madagascar and the Comores Islands.

In the eastern part of the Indian Ocean, there are very limited occurrences along the West Australian shelf (reaching as far south as the Houtman's Abrolhos Islands and in a little patch on Rottnest Island, 32°S. Elsewhere there are no islands or shallow plateaus suitable for reef growth, except for two isolated spots, the Cocos-Keeling atolls (made famous by Charles Darwin; later described in detail by Wood-Jones, 1910) and the elevated phosphatized reef of Christmas Island (Andrews, 1900).

Climatology*

Air Temperature. In January (Fig. 12), the thermal equator over the Indian Ocean is slightly south of the geographic equator; and the area with

* Takashi Ichiye.

air temperature above 27°C lies between 10°N and 20°S. In the northern hemisphere, the 20°C isotherm which divides the tropical zone from the temperate zone runs from south of the Gulf of Suez and Arabia, via the Persian Gulf to north of the Gulf of Bengal almost parallel to the Tropic of Cancer. The 10°C isotherm in the southern hemisphere which divides the temperate zone from the subpolar zone runs nearly parallel to the latitude circle of 45°S. In the middle latitudes of the southern hemisphere between 10° and 30°S, the isotherms of 27–21°C over the ocean run from west-southwest off South Africa to east-northeast west of Australia, indicating that the western section is warmer by 1–3°C than the eastern section at the same latitudes. These isotherms turn sharply to the south off the west coast of Australia due to the effect of strong heating of the continent.

In May, the highest temperature (above 30°C) is found in the inland areas of southern Arabia, northeast Africa, Burma and India. In India, it reaches above 35°C. The thermal equator over the ocean lies at about 10°N. In the southern hemisphere between 30 and 45°S, the isotherms of 20–10°C run from east-southeast to west-northwest and indicate that the western section is warmer than the eastern section. In July, the highest temperature zone on land shifts north of the Tropic of Cancer. The temperature over the Arabian Sea and the Gulf of Bengal shows a decrease from May, and also it is colder in the former than in the latter. Particularly off the Somali coast, temperature is below 25°C owing to upwelling of cold water; thus, the temperature there is lowest in August. In the southern hemisphere, the west side off South Africa is slightly warmer than the central part at the same latitudes. Also, temperature off the west coast of Australia is much higher than inland.

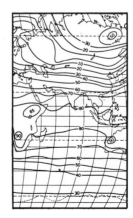 

Fig. 12. Surface air temperatures over the Indian Ocean and surroundings: (a) mean isotherms for January; (b) mean isotherms for July, in degrees Fahrenheit (80°F = 27°C, 70°F = 21°C, 60°F = 15°C).

In November, the thermal equator with a small area of temperature above 27.5°C is nearly on the equator. Also, the oceanic area north of 20°S has rather uniform temperature between 25 and 27.5°C, except for a small area in the central part of the ocean. The annual range of air temperature shows less than 2.5°C in the central portion between 10°N and 12°S, with an area of the range below 1° between 4°N and 7°S. The area which has annual ranges above 5°C covers the coastal regions of the Bay of Bengal and the Arabian Sea and the area between 10° and 40°S west of 100°W.

Pressure Field and Surface Winds. In January (Fig. 13), the meteorological equator which is characterized by the lowest pressure, between 1009 and 1012 mb, and by calms and variable winds is located at about 10°S (like the thermal equator) and divides the northern and southern hemispheres into distinct meteorological provinces. The prevailing wind to the north of the meteorological equator is a Northeast Trade Wind or actually a Northeast Monsoon, which becomes a north wind at the equator and a northwest wind in the southern hemisphere. This northwest wind from west of Sumatra to the Malayan Archipelago is called the Northwest Monsoon. To the south of the meteorological equator, the pressure minimum areas (with less than 1009 mb' lie over the Australian and African continents and Madagascar due to continental heating during the southern summer. The high-pressure zone of the southern horse latitudes is located around 35°S, and the maximum pressure above 1020 mb is observed in the central portion or near St. Paul–New Amsterdam Islands. The northward bulging of the isobars of 1014 mb in the central portion is due to effects of lower air and sea surface temperature there and is in contrast with the South Pacific where such bulging occurs in the eastern sector of off South America (see *Pacific Ocean*). To the south of the high-pressure zone, the pressure decreases uniformly to the subpolar trough with the pressure below 990 mb at about 64.5°S. This pressure system generates two kinds of wind systems to the south of the meteorological equator (Fig. 15). In the northern part, the Southeast Trade Wind covers the entire ocean except off Australia where it becomes south to southwest winds. To the south of the trade wind, the Westerlies blow from the Cape of Good Hope to Cape Horn between 50 and 40°S, which is called the "roaring forties." The essential difference between the Westerlies and the Trade Wind is not only that the former has much higher wind speeds than the latter but also that the day-to-day fluctuations in wind directions and speeds are much greater in the former than in the latter.

In July (Fig. 14), the wind to the north of 10°S is completely reversed to the January pattern. The equatorial trough with pressure below 1005 mb lies in the Asiatic continent from the Arabian Sea to the east-northeast. To the south of this trough, the pressure increases steadily from 20°N to 30°S, the southern horse latitudes. In the northern hemisphere the Southern Trade Winds cross over the equator and become the Southwest Monsoon, which is stormy and strongest off the Somali coast in the Arabian Sea. This area is a good example of the complete shift of winds with an annual cycle in the northern trade zone which is dominated by the strong effect of heating and cooling of the Asiatic continent (Fig. 15). In the middle and high latitudes of the southern hemisphere, the moderating effect of the ocean makes the pressure and wind fields in June not very different from January. However, the Westerlies in the high latitudes become much stronger, and also their fluctuations in directions and speeds are greater.

The frequency distributions of the storm winds with forces above 7 Beaufort scale show that in the northern winter the greater part of the Indian Ocean north of 15°S is virtually free of stormy winds with a frequency of less than 1%. *Tropical cyclones* (q.v.) are generated occasionally from November to April around the area 10°S and 85–95°E, or northwest of Australia, and then move southeast and southwest, respectively, in the western or eastern sides of the ocean.

To the south of 40°S, the storm frequency is more than 10% even in the southern summer (see *Storms and Storminess* in another volume). In the northern summer, the Southwest Monsoon in the western Arabian Sea off the Somali coast always blows so strongly from June to August that 10–20% of wind observations are above 7 on the Beaufort scale. In this season, the calm zone with less than 1% of stormy winds shrinks to the area between 1°S and 7°N and west of 78°E. In latitudes of 35–40°S, the storm wind frequency increases 15–20% in all months of the year.

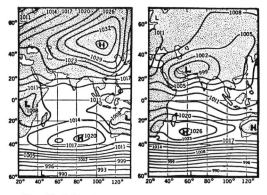

Fig. 13 (left). January mean sea level pressure, in millibars (after Mintz and Dean).

Fig. 14 (right). July mean sea level pressure, in millibars (after Mintz and Dean).

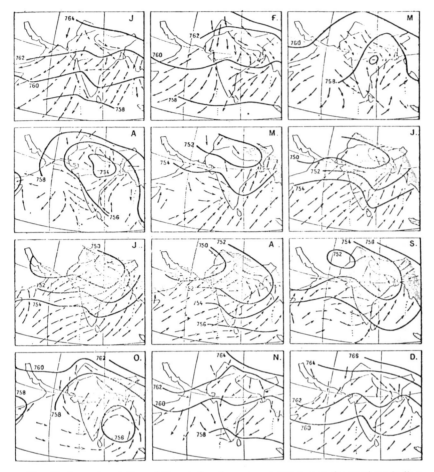

Fig. 15. Annual evolution of the wind and pressure systems over the northern Indian Ocean from January to December. Rainfall areas are shaded (from de Martonne, 1950). (750 mm = 1000 mb; 760 mm = 1013 mb)

Cloud Cover and Precipitation

In the northern hemisphere, the cloud cover changes greatly by seasons. During the period of Northeast Monsoons (December to March), the average cloud cover over the Arabian Sea and the Bay of Bengal is less than 2. However, the Southwest Monsoon in summer brings the rainy season to Malaya and Burma causing the average cloud cover of 6–7. The area south of the equator to the Southeast Trade Wind zone is more overcast the whole year and is covered by clouds of 5–6 in the southern summer and 6–7 in the southern winter. Even the southeast trade zone has a relatively large cloud cover and lacks the cloudless zone characteristic of the central Pacific. The cloud cover west of Australia is above 6 and greater than the western half. However, near the coast of Western Australia the weather is relatively fair.

Sea fog is frequently observed (20–40%), and visibility is poor during the summer off the Somali coast and south of Arabia. The water temperature,

lower by 1–2°C than the air temperature over this area, causes condensation which is stimulated by dusts coming from the inland deserts. The area south of 40°S is also frequented by sea fog all throughout the year.

The total annual precipitation (Fig. 16) is high, over 3000 mm in the central equatorial belt and above 1000 mm in the westerly zone of the southern hemisphere. The area between 35 and 20°S is the dry zone of the trade winds, and it is particularly dry off the west coast of Australia with precipitation below 500 mm. The northern boundary of this dry zone is 12–15°S and does not reach the equator as in the South Pacific. The region of the Northwest Monsoon is, in general, the boundary area between the northern and southern wind systems, which leads to an equatorial wet zone between the equator and 10°S from the Sunda Sea to the Seychelles. Also, the eastern part of the Bay of Bengal, particularly off Malaya, is quite rainy. The west side of the Arabian Sea is very dry, and the precipitation of the Gulf of

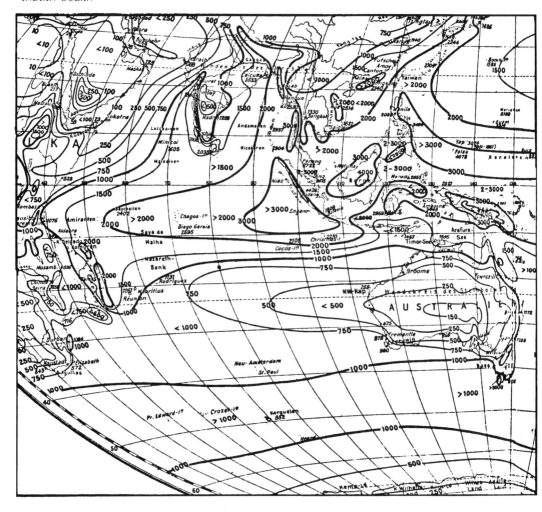

Fig. 16. Total annual precipitation (in millimeters) over the Indian Ocean (Schott, 1935).

Aden and the Red Sea is less than 100 mm. The annual cycle of the precipitation shows that the maximum rainfall of the wet areas occurs during December to February between 10 and 25°S and March to April between 5°N and 10°S on the western side. These are maxima during the northern summer on the Bay of Bengal, and there is heavy rain almost all the months in the wettest area between 5°N and 10°S east and west of Sumatra.

Oceanography*

Temperature, Salinity and Density of the Surface Water. In February the northern part shows a typical winter condition of the sea. The Persian Gulf and the Red Sea show low temperatures of 15 and 17.5°C, respectively, in their inner parts, although the Gulf of Aden in the latter has a surface tempera-

* Takashi Ichiye.

ture of 25°C. The isotherms of 23–25°C run from southwest to northeast, and thus the western half is much warmer than the eastern half in the same latitudes, just as with the air temperature. Such a difference is due to the ocean circulation and is observed in all seasons. In the southern hemisphere which is in summer, the belt of the highest temperature above 28°C runs east-northeast from the East African Coast to the west of Sumatra and continues to south of Java and north of Australia where the water temperature sometimes exceeds 29°C. Isotherms of 25–27°C run from west-southwest to east-northeast between 15 and 30°S from the African Coast to about 90–100°E; they then turn southeast in the same way as the warm belt, in contrast to the South Pacific where the isotherms run to east-northeast near the South American coast. The area between 40 and 50°S is a transition zone from the middle-latitude water to the polar water and shows

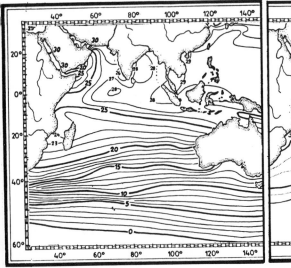

Fig. 17. Sea surface temperatures over the Indian Ocean in August.

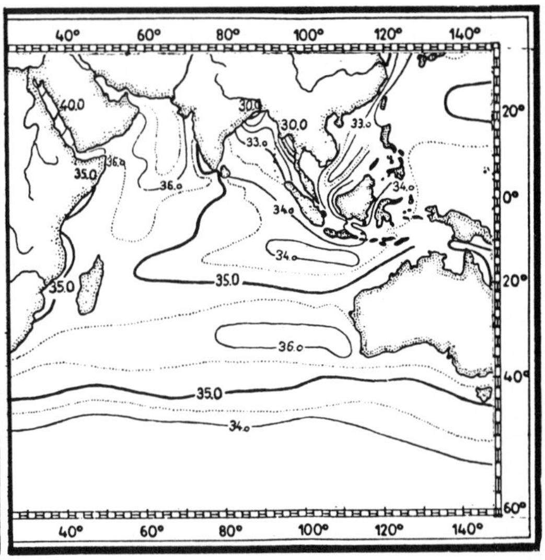

Fig. 18. Sea surface salinity in the Indian Ocean in August (after Schott, 1935).

crowded isotherms with about 12°C difference between 40 and 50°S along the middle section.

In May the northern part receives maximum heating and shows temperatures above 29°C in most parts while the Northeast Monsoon is shifting to the Southwest Monsoon, although the rainfall and upwelling accompanying the latter do not occur quite so early.

In August (Fig. 17), only the Red Sea and the Persian Gulf reach an annual maximum temperature above 30°C, and most of the northern part, including the Gulf of Aden, the Arabian Sea and most of the Bay of Bengal, except the western sections, show lower temperatures than in May. The low-temperature area below 25°C extends from the Somali Coast to the southeast coast of Arabia owing to intense upwelling caused by the Southwest Monsoon. To the south of 30°S, three characteristics of temperate distribution in February are also recognized: the WSW-ENE trend of the isotherms of 20–25°C in the eastern and central portion, the crowded isotherms between 40 and 48°S, and the southward turning of the isotherms west of Australia.

In November, the surface temperature is generally near the annual mean. The cold area off the Somali-Arabian coast below 25°C and the warm area in the western side of the Bay of Bengal almost disappear. The vast area north of 10°S is between 27 and 27.7°C.

The surface salinity (Fig. 18) in the southern hemisphere has the same features as in the South Pacific and has the oval area of maximum value above 36.0‰ west of Australia. The equatorial low-salinity area corresponding to the transition zone

between Southeast Trade Winds and Monsoon extends to 10°S but is conspicuous only in an eastern half with the minimum zone south of Sumatra and Java. Surface salinity in the northern part is variable not only locally but also seasonally (Fig. 19). However, the salinity in the northern summer has a characteristic feature in that it is extremely low in the Bay of Bengal but rather high in the Arabian Sea and is extremely high with values above 40‰ in the Persian Gulf and the Red Sea.

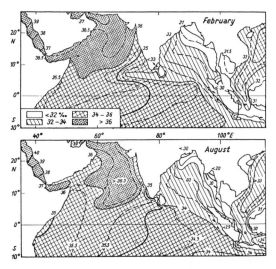

Fig. 19. Sea surface salinity (in per thousand in February and August in the northern Indian Ocean and the waters of Indochina (according to G. Schott, 1935; P. Ch. Veen, 1951; from Dietrich, 1963).

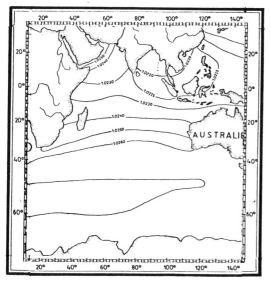

Fig. 20. Mean surface water density of the Indian Ocean.

The density of the surface water (Fig. 20) in the southern hemisphere increases regularly to the north from about 27.0 (all densities are expressed in sigma-t) at the latitude of 53 ~ 54°S to 23.0 at 17°S in the southern summer, and the isopicnals are almost parallel to the isotherms. In the equatorial zone between 20°S and 0°, there is a vast area of low density below 23.0, and a zone below 21.5 lies off Sumatra and Java, corresponding to the salinity minimum there. In the northern hemisphere, the local change of density is influenced by salinity. In the summer, it decreases from 22.0 of the southern part to below 19.0 of the northwestern side in the Bay of Bengal, while it is above 24.0 in most of the Arabian Sea and it reaches above 28.0 and 25.0 near Suez and in the Persian Gulf, respectively. Also, the seasonal change of the surface density is mostly due to the change in temperature; thus the northern part shows an increase of 1.0–2.0 from summer to winter.

Currents. The major current systems of the Indian Ocean are named according to the patterns of the surface currents as in other oceans. Particularly, the currents in the northern part are strongly influenced by the monsoons and change with seasons. Therefore, they are called the Southwest and Northeast Monsoon Drift in summer and winter, respectively. In the southern hemisphere, there are the South Equatorial Current and the Westwind Drift. Besides these currents closely related to the wind system, there are currents of a local nature, due mainly to the density structure of the water, such as the Mozambique Current, the Agulhas Current (q.v.), the Equatorial Countercurrent, the Somali Current (q.v.) and the West Australian Current (q.v.; Fig. 21).

In the southern hemisphere, a large anticyclonic gyre of the circulation is similar to gyres in the South Pacific and Atlantic Oceans, but it is subject to greater annual variations. The southernmost leg of the gyre is the Westwind Drift between about 38 and 50°S, with a width of 200–240 nautical miles, increasing eastward. This current is bounded by the Subtropical Convergence (q.v.) and by the Subpolar (Antarctic) Convergence. The velocity is dependent on the wind and is variable seasonally and regionally, but the mean speed reaches a maximum with 20–30 nautical miles/day near the Kerguelen Islands. In the southern summer, the current turns north before reaching Australia and is joined by a current flowing south of Australia from the Pacific. In winter, the current is joined by the southward flow along the west coast of Australia and continues toward the Pacific off the Australian south coast.

The eastern leg of the gyre is the West Australian Current which flows northward steadily only in the southern summer, reaching 10–15 nautical miles/day north of 30°S. The current becomes southerly and weak in winter. The northern leg of the gyre is the South Equatorial Current which continues from the West Australian Current at the Tropic of Capricorn due to the effect of the Southeast Trades. The eastern part of the current reaches its greatest velocity (above 1 knot) during the southern winter when the westward flow north of Australia from the Pacific Ocean reinforces it. In the southern summer, when the flow becomes eastward, the northern boundary of the South Equatorial Current is at about 9°S between 100 and 80°E, and it is shifted slightly to the south east of 80°E; the southern boundary lies at about 22°S in the eastern section. In the southern winter, the northern boundary moves to the north by 5–6°, following the northward shift of the Southeast Trade Wind. The current splits in several branches before Madagascar. One

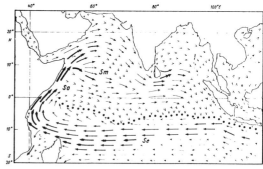

Fig. 21. Currents at the sea surface in the Indian Ocean in northern summer. So: Somali Current; Sm: Southwest Monsoon Current; Se: South Equatorial Current (according to G. Schott, 1943). Strength and persistence of the current is indicated by the thickness and length (respectively) of the arrow.

branch flows northward around the Island, reaching 50–60 nautical miles/day, and turns westward. It splits again in two branches off Cape Delgado. One branch turns north and the other turns south, flowing through Mozambique Channel as the Mozambique Current. The velocity of the current fluctuates from almost zero to 3–4 knots in the Northeast Monsoon.

The Agulhas Current is formed with continuation of the Mozambique Current and the southern branch of the South Equatorial Current south of Mauritius. This current which is well defined and narrow extends to a distance from the coast of less than 100 km. As expected in a southerly flow in the southern hemisphere, the coldest water is found inshore and the sea surface rises towards the offshore by about 29 cm in a distance of 110 km off Port Elizabeth. Between Durban and the meridian of 25°E, the speed reaches 3–4.5 knots at the edge of Agulhas Bank. To the south of South Africa, a greater part of the current bends sharply to the south and then to the east, thus joining the Westwind Drift, but a smaller portion continues into the Atlantic Ocean. Owing to reversal of directions and branching of the current, numerous eddies which are variable with time develop off South Africa.

To the north of latitude 10°S, the surface currents vary greatly from winter to summer. During the Northeast Monsoon season from November to March, the North Equatorial Current or the North-east Monsoon Drift is well developed flowing to the west and southwest. The southern boundary changes from 3–4°N in November to 2–3°S in February and turns to the north again in March, disappearing as the Southwest Monsoon Drift begins. During the Northeast Monsoon, the Equatorial Countercurrent sets in from November and is formed by confluence of the current flowing southwest off the Somali coast and the East African coastal current flowing northward north of Cape Delgado. The countercurrent is narrow and almost reaches Sumatra. The northern boundary runs north of the equator in November and shifts to the southernmost latitudes of 2–3°S in February. Later it moves again to the north and disappears. The southern boundary lies between 7 and 8°S. The speed reaches 40 nautical miles/day between 60–70°E and decreases further east.

During the Southwest Monsoon from April to October, the North Equatorial Current (the North-east Monsoon Drift) disappears and is replaced by the Southwest Monsoon Drift which flows eastward south of India. The speed south of Ceylon is 1–2 knots and occasionally up to 3 knots. Its branches flow clockwise in the Arabian Sea and the Bay of Bengal, following the coastlines. The velocity of the southeast flow off the west coast of India reaches 10–42 nautical miles/day. During this season, the Somali Current along the Somali coast is directed north from latitude 10°S. Water of the S. Equatorial

Current crosses the equator, and strong upwelling takes place off the Somali coast, causing the vast area of low surface temperature.

Subsurface currents in the Indian Ocean north of 10°S were measured directly in the *Vityaz* Cruise 31 (January–April, 1960) at 15, 50, 100, 200, 300, 500 and 700 m at about 140 deep stations (Ovchinnikov, 1961). At a depth of 15 m, the current is almost similar to the climatological surface current chart (Fig. 21) for the northern winter, except that the Equatorial Countercurrent starts from 60°E and is located between 0° and 3°S, much narrower than in the climatological chart. At 200 m the currents south of 5°N are reverse to 15 m, and they are eastward below the North and South Equatorial Currents and westward below the Countercurrent east of 70°E longitude. At 500 m the currents between 5°N and 10°S are generally eastward with a small clockwise gyre around a center at 5°S, 60°E. Also, direct current measurements and dynamic topography obtained from November to December in 1960 on the *Vityaz* Cruise 33 indicate that the current system did not correspond yet to that for the winter monsoon in spite of the fact that the winds were already northwesterly (Bezruna, 1961).

Zaklinskii (1963) made dynamic topographies at 1500, 2000, 3000 and 4000 m, based on data collected by the *Vityaz* in 1960 and the *Ob* in 1956–57, as well as *Discovery II*. At the 1500-m level (Fig. 22), a broad current of 2.5–4.5 cm/sec flows eastward south of 18°S. At about 80°E this current merges with a southerly current with speeds of 4.5–5.5 cm/sec and increases its speed rapidly. At about 95°E it turns sharply north, then to the west and forms an anticyclonic gyre, whose northern and southern legs have speeds of 15–18 cm/sec and 54 cm/sec, respectively. A branch flowing southward at about 70–80°E and 20–25°S has speed less than 3.5 cm/sec. At the 2000-m level, the same eastward current flows between 15 and 23°S with speeds less than 4 cm/sec.

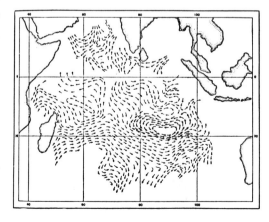

Fig. 22. Currents at the 1500-m level based on the dynamic topography (Zahlinskii, 1963).

385

A branch is separated at about 68°E, flowing northward with a speed of 5 cm/sec. The anticyclonic gyre between 80 and 100°E at the 1500-m level covers a greater area extending between 70 and 100°E. The speeds of each segment are almost the same at both levels. A current coming down from the Bay of Bengal meets another coming from the east at the equator and turns north and then northwest toward the Red Sea. At the 3000-m level, the eastward current flows between 20 and 23°S with speeds of 9 cm/sec in some places. The cyclonic gyre at 25–35°S and 58–75°E becomes conspicuous with speeds up to 5 cm/sec. The anticyclonic gyre between 80 and 100°E in the 1500-m level degenerates into smaller eddies.

Direct current measurements in four meridional sections across the equator with stations at 1° intervals from 2°N to 2°S were made by the Scripps Institution of Oceanography from July to September 1962, during the Southwest Monsoon, and from February to May 1963, during the transition from Northeast to Southwest Monsoon (Knauss, 1964). The three sections at 79°E (September), 89°E (September) and 90°E (April) showed the eastward flow in the middle of the thermocline similar to the Pacific Equatorial Undercurrent. The 92°E section showed eastward flows from 40–300 m, the maximum being 80 cm/sec at about 100 m on the equator, and westward flow near the surface. The 79 and 89°E sections showed the maximum eastward speeds at the equator of 60 cm/sec and 50 cm/sec, respectively, and the eastward surface current. The 61°E (March) section showed the maximum eastward flow of 38 cm/sec, but not at the equator. However, the measurements three weeks after at the same section showed the maximum eastward flow of 57 cm/sec at the equator, indicating that the undercurrent was present but weakly developed. On the three sections previously discussed, measurements were also repeated 1–3 weeks later. In all cases, the maximum eastward flow at the equator was measured at almost the same depth with differences in speed ranging from 6–30 cm/sec, indicating that the undercurrent was steady at least for several weeks.

Four sections, i.e., 53°E in May and August, 62°E in August, and 85°E in February, lacked the undercurrent. The 85°E showed the eastward flow, but its speed was 5 cm/sec. The 53 and 62°E sections showed small westward flows and stronger meridional flows. On the sections of 79 and 92°E where the undercurrent was well developed, the thermocline thickness indicated by the distance of the 15 and 25°C isotherms was maximum at the equator, and there were cores of high salinity and low oxygen near the core of maximum eastward flow. A slope of the sea surface in July and in March–April determined by dynamic calculation showed a rise to the east with magnitudes of 5×10^{-8} and 2.5×10^{-8}, respectively, which was comparable to the Pacific and Atlantic but of opposite sign. However, the slope of about 100 decibars became negative (rising westward), and

thus the undercurrent seemed to be associated with the eastward pressure gradient even though the pressure gradient at the surface is westward.

Water Masses. The composite T-S diagrams characterizing different water masses, their regions of formation and their distribution in the Indian Ocean are shown in *Ocean Circulation* and *Water Masses* [also Figs. 23(a) and (b)]. There are three major water masses proper to the Indian Ocean besides the Subantarctic Water: the Indian Ocean Central Water and the Indian Ocean Equatorial Water extend to moderate depths, and the Indian

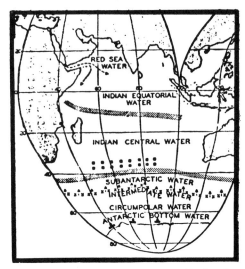

Fig. 23 (a) Approximate boundaries of Indian Ocean water masses (Sverdrup *et al.*, 1942). (By permission of Prentice-Hall, N.J.)

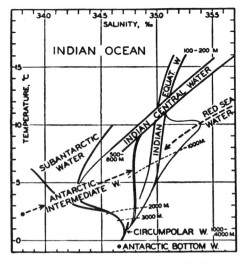

Fig. 23 (b). Temperature and salinity of Indian Ocean water masses (Sverdrup *et al.*, 1942). (By permission of Prentice-Hall, N.J.)

Ocean Deep Water is present below a depth of about 1000 m. There are transition types, too. Two minor types of water, the Antarctic Intermediate Water and the Red Sea Water, spread out at mid-depths.

The Central Water mass is present between the Subtropical Convergence (q.v.) of about 35–40°S and the southern boundary of the South Equatorial Current of about 15–20°S. The latter limit was discovered by observations made during the IGY cruises and the IIOE (International Indian Ocean Expedition). The temperature-salinity relations of this water fall on a straight line between the points $T = 8°C$, $S = 34.60‰$ and $T = 15°C$, $S = 35.50‰$, with scattering of salinities of ± 0.07 and $\pm 0.08‰$ respectively at each end point. The horizontal T-S relations in the region of the Subtropical Convergence agree very well with the vertical T-S relations between depths of 100 and 800 m of the Central Water, indicating that this water is formed by sinking at the convergence.

The Equatorial Water is not so well defined as the Central Water, but at most of the stations north of the equator the temperatures and salinities fall nearly on a straight line between the points $T = 4°C$, $S = 34.90‰$ and $T = 18°C$, $S = 32.25‰$. The salinity ranges corresponding to fixed temperatures are much larger than in the Central Water, owing to admixture of high-salinity water of the Red Sea and low-salinity water of coastal origin. The T-S relations south of the equator are intermediate between the Equatorial Water and the Central Water.

The Subantarctic Water occurs between the Central Water and the Antarctic Convergence and has nearly the same character all around the earth. It has low salinity, and is formed by mixing and vertical circulation between the Subtropical and the Antarctic Convergences. It is distinctly different in character from the Antarctic Intermediate Water.

The Antarctic Intermediate Water originates with a salinity of $33.80‰$ and a temperature of $2.2°C$, sinking along a well-defined belt around the Antarctic Continent. After sinking, the water spreads to the north between $\sigma = 27.2$ and 27.4. It mixes with the over- and underlying waters, forming a water mass characterized by a salinity minimum which becomes less conspicuous with increasing distance from the originating area. The water has a low salinity of $34.20–34.50‰$, a relatively low temperature of $3.4–4.0°C$, and high oxygen content of $6.5–4.5$ ml/liter in the depths of 200–700 m between the Antarctic and Subtropical Convergences. It sinks to the depth of 800–1500 m north of the Subtropical Convergence and again rises to the depths of 500–900 m near 10°S where the water loses its identity with salinity increasing to $34.75‰$ (Ivanenkov and Gubin, 1960). West of Australia, the water spreads to the north along two main paths: the eastern one between 100 and 110°E terminates at 15°S at the depth of 600 m, and the western one between 90 and 100°E terminates at 12°S at a depth

of 500 ~ 600 m. Such separation seems to be due to the submarine ridge around 90–100°E and 32°S. Also, northwest of Australia, the Banda Intermediate Water with low salinities of $34.60–34.70‰$ for temperatures 4–5°C originating in the Banda Sea (q.v.) spreads westward south of Indonesia and southwestward off Australia in a depth of 1000–1400 m below the Antarctic Intermediate Water. The Northwest Indian Intermediate water with high salinities of $34.70–34.90‰$ for 7–8°C spreads eastward between 10 and 20°S in the depth of 700–1000 m above the Banda Intermediate Water and mixes with the northern ends of the two branches of the Antarctic Intermediate Water (Rochford, 1961, 1963).

The high-salinity subsurface water in the northern part was considered as spreading from the Red Sea only. However, Rochford (1964) determined five different origins of high-salinity waters in the upper 1000 m by use of recent data including those of the *Vityaz* in 1960 and the *Ob* in 1958. The method used is to determine salinity maxima of a T-S curve at each station and to plot each maximal value separately for the corresponding sigma-t value. The Red Sea water spreads between $\sigma = 27.3$ and 27.1 in depths of 600–900 m, and the salinity ranges from $36.3–34.9‰$. The Persian Gulf water spreads between $\sigma = 26.4$ and 26.8 in depths of 300–400 m and has a salinity range from $36.1–35.00‰$. The third water designated by C has its source region in the northern Arabian Sea and spreads in a limited extent between $\sigma = 24.9$ and 26.0 in depths of 100–200 m. The salinities of this water range from $36.5‰$ for low density ($\sigma = 24.9$) to 35.0 for high density ($\sigma = 26.0$). The fourth water (the Arabian Sea water) which has its origin at the surface of the central Arabian Sea is so shallow (above 100 m) that it is subject to seasonal changes in its distribution, particularly influenced by the Northeast Monsoon. The salinities of the water range from 36.6 for $\sigma = 23.8$ to 35.2 for $\sigma = 25.0$. The fifth water designated by E is found throughout in the equatorial region of the Indian Ocean from 10°S to 10°N only. The depths of the water are 0–110 m, and the salinities range from 35.8 for $\sigma = 23.0$ to 35.2 for $\sigma = 23.5$. The major paths of the five high-salinity waters with corresponding depths are shown in Fig. 24.

The water masses in the deep layers are classified as deep waters and bottom waters according to their depths. In the Indian Ocean, there are five water masses in the deep layers. Two water masses, the Circumpolar Deep Water mass and the Antarctic Bottom Water mass, are common to other oceans while the North and South Indian Deep Water mass and the North Indian Bottom Water mass are proper to the Indian Ocean. The Circumpolar Deep Water from the South Atlantic Ocean continues into the Indian Ocean and is particularly conspicuous in the western part where maximum salinities of

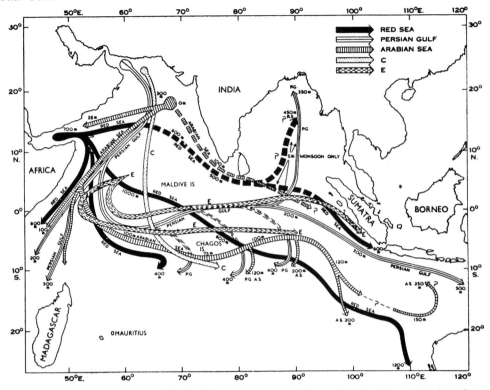

Fig. 24. The major flow paths of high-salinity water masses of the north Indian Ocean. Numbers along these paths show the depth at that point (Rochford, 1964).

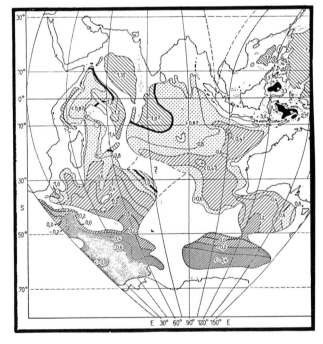

Fig. 25. Bottom-water temperatures of the Indian Ocean (Defant, 1961). (By permission of Pergamon Press, N.Y., London.)

34.80‰ have been observed. This water flows mainly eastward between 65 and 35°S and is relatively warm. It is diluted by admixtures of intermediate and bottom waters. To the south of the Subtropical Convergence, the upper boundary of this water is easily determined from the maximum gradient of temperature, salinity and stability. It is located at depths of 300–800 m to 400–200 m in the southern summer and from 400–600 m to 300–150 m in winter from north to south, respectively. The lower boundary is rather vague but coincides approximately with the 27.87–27.88 isopycnal to the south of 60°S. The salinity maximum is located in the depths of 1900–2500 m, with 34.86–34.72‰ in the western part and 34.75–34.70‰ in the southeastern part. This maximum is partly due to admixture of the North Atlantic Deep Water which spreads south across the equator. Ivanenkov and Gubin (1960) considered that the North Atlantic Deep Water with temperatures 1.0–2.5°C, salinities 34.86–34.72‰ and oxygen contents 3.8–4.4 ml/liter is distinguished from the Circumpolar Deep Water. According to them, the former water enters the Indian Ocean at depths below 2000 m south of 35°S at 20°E longitude and reaches as far north as 28–22°S between 30 and 45°E longitude. The northern end at about 35°S latitude of the Circumpolar Deep Water (and the North Atlantic Deep Water below it) contacts with the South Indian Deep Water which moves southward compensating northward movements of the intermediate and bottom waters. This deep water forms in the region between 10 and 16°S in depths of 1500–3500 m from three water masses: North Indian Deep, Subantarctic Intermediate and a small portion of the Antarctic Bottom Water. The water is entrained into the Circumpolar Deep Water south

of 35°S latitude, and it predominates in the latter east of 115°E. The North Indian Deep Water forms in the Arabian Sea from the Red Sea water and the water of the Gulf of Oman, the latter playing only a minor role. The Red Sea water has temperatures of 8–4°C and salinities of 35.9–35.0‰ in the layers 1000–1500 m at Cape Guardafui, and it moves to the east and southeast with temperatures decreasing considerably but salinities changing slightly. Thus the water sinks to depths of 2000–2500 m even in the north of the equator. South of 10°S this water has characteristic high salinities (35.5–34.8‰), high temperatures (10–2.5°C) and low oxygen contents (0.40–3.5 ml/liter). In the region between 10 and 16°S, this water mixes with the Subantarctic Intermediate Water and with the Antarctic Bottom Water and is transformed into the South Indian Deep Water.

The Antarctic Bottom Water forms near the Antarctic Continental slope mostly through mixing in winter of the Antarctic Surface Water with salinities of 34.58–34.62‰ and the Circumpolar Deep Water with salinities of 34.76–34.70‰, both of which have a freezing temperature. The major generating areas of this water are five regions including the Weddell Sea and the Antarctic coastal area between 20 and 145°E south of the Indian Ocean. The western half of the Indian Ocean is dominated by the bottom water formed in the Weddell Sea, while the eastern half is dominated by that formed east of 90°E. The shelf water can form the bottom water when its density exceeds 27.87 or when it has temperatures of −1.8 to 1.9°C and salinities above 34.58‰. This condition is satisfied during formation of ice with a thickness of more than 1.5–2.5 m. The bottom water in its originating region has low temperatures

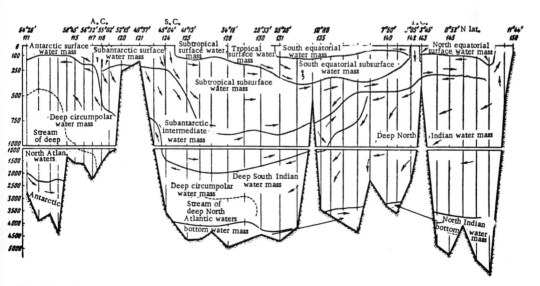

Fig. 26. Vertical distribution of water masses along the Davis Sea–Cape Guardafui profile (*Ob*, May 12–June 8, 1956; Ivanenkov and Gubin, 1960).

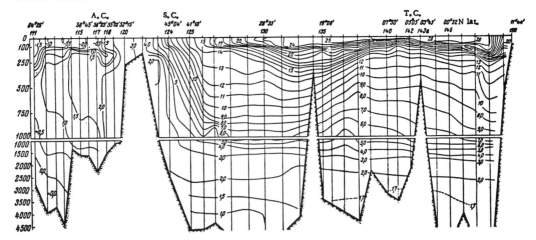

Fig. 27. Water temperature distribution along the Davis Sea–Cape Guardafui profile (*Ob*, May 12–June 8, 1956; Ivanenkov and Gubin, 1960).

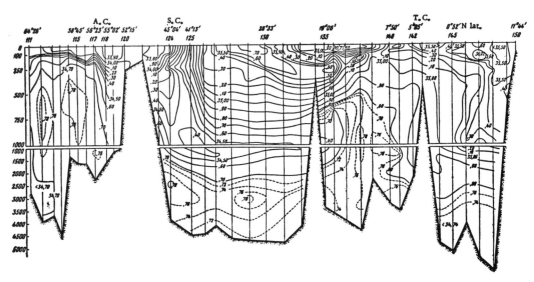

Fig. 28. Salinity distribution (in parts per thousand) along the Davis Sea–Cape Guardafui profile (*Ob* c., May 12–June 8, 1956; Ivanenkov and Gubin, 1960).

(−0.9 to 0.0°C), low salinities (34.66–34.69‰) high densities (27.87–27.95) and high oxygen contents (6.8–5.3 ml/liter). In winter, the upper boundary of this water is located at depths of 500–800 m at distances of 60–80 nautical miles from the edge of the shelf and sinks to 3000–3500 m in the northern part of the Antarctic zone. In summer it is deeper than in winter and is 1200 m deep on the continental shelf. The water becomes the North Indian Bottom Water by mixing with the North Indian Deep Water in the region between 16 and 10°S (Fig. 25). The transition is recognized by a sharp increase in temperature and salinity from below 1.0°C to 1.5–1.7°C and from below 34.72‰ to 34.74–34.76‰, and

decrease in oxygen contents from 4.6–4.8 ml/liter to 4.1–4.5 ml/liter.

The vertical distributions of water masses, temperatures and salinities are shown in Figs. 26, 27 and 28 which were made from the data of the *Ob* on May 12–June 8, 1956 from the Davis Sea (Queen Mary Coast) (66°S, 92°E) to Cape Guardafui (12°N, 52°E).

Pollak (1958) studied frequency (or volume) distributions of the water of the entire Indian Ocean divided by intervals of 0.5°C and 0.1‰ of potential temperature (θ) and salinity (S), respectively. He used about 67 hydrographic stations taken in the course of twenty years at nearly uniform horizontal

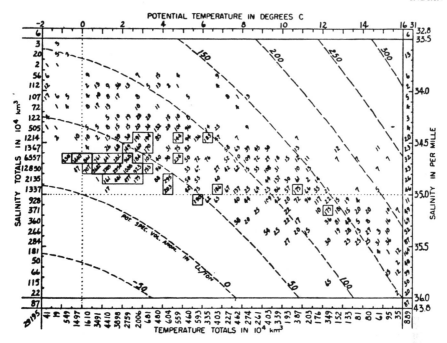

Fig. 29. Frequency distribution, in terms of 104 km³, of Indian Ocean potential temperatures and salinities by classes of 0.5°C × 0.1 per mile. Heavy class boundaries include 50% and light class boundaries 75% of the total volume. High-temperature classes, compressed in the marginal band, comprise 3% of the volume (Pollak, 1958).

spacings. The total volume of the Indian Ocean is 29,195 × 10⁴ km³. In Fig. 29 is shown the result for the whole Indian Ocean in which slant figures indicate the volume (in terms of 10⁴ km³) of the water classified by the intervals of θ and S. Also, the 50 and 75% boundaries are established by the cumulative addition of frequencies in descending order of magnitude. The three largest classes within the ranges 0.5–2.0°C and 34.7–34.8‰ include nearly one-third of the total volume and comprise the core of the deep water which may originate in the circumpolar regions. The average values of θ and S of the entire ocean are 3.72°C and 34.76‰, respectively. The frequency distributions based on intervals of 2.5°C by 0.5‰ is shown in Fig. 30. This Figure indicates the isolation of high-salinity waters of the Red Sea and Arabian Gulf. Also, it shows the wide temperature and salinity ranges of the surface water (above 200 m) in the equatorial and subtropical regions.

Chemical Oceanography. The distributions of hydrochemical components all over the Indian Ocean have not yet been studied. Sverdrup et al. (1942) discussed the oxygen distributions based on the observations of *Discovery* and *Dana*. Ivanenkov and Gubin (1960) treated distributions of the chemical components mostly based on the *Ob* cruise of

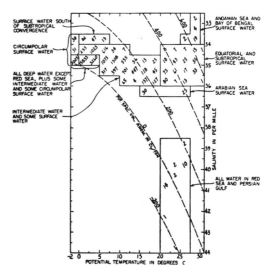

Fig. 30. Frequency distribution, in terms of 104 km³, of all Indian Ocean potential temperatures and salinities by classes of 2.5°C × 0.5 per mile. Boundaries demarcate the various types of water found. Surface, intermediate, and deep water are here defined, respectively, as the water between the sea surface and 200 m, between 200 and 1500 m, and below 1,500 m (Pollak, 1958).

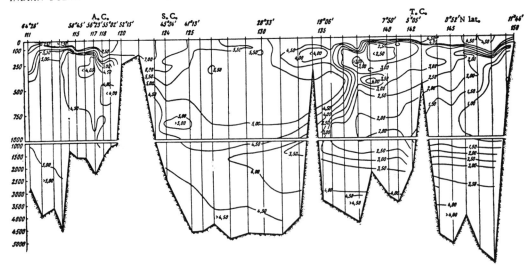

Fig. 31. Oxygen distribution (in milliliters per liter) along the Davis Sea–Cape Guardafui profile (*Ob*, May 12–June 8, 1956; Ivanenkov and Gubin, 1960).

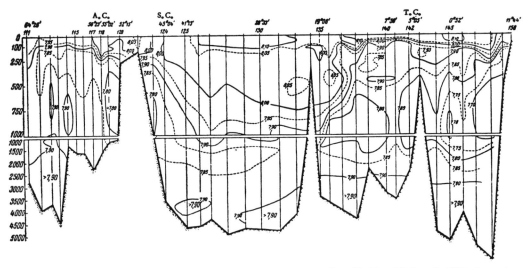

Fig. 32. pH^B distribution along the Davis Sea–Cape Guardafui profile (*Ob*, May 12–June 8, 1956; Ivanentov and Gubin, 1960).

1956. The oxygen section between the Davis Sea and Cape Guardafui based on this observation is shown in Fig. 31. Comparison of this Figure with the water mass distribution on the same section in Fig. 26 indicates close relation between the two distributions. Generally, oxygen contents are large at the surface where they increase as the surface temperature decreases. Thus, the upper layer of the Antarctic region has richest oxygen above 7.5 ml/liter. This supply of oxygen is carried to the north by the Subtropical Subsurface Water, the Antarctic Intermediate Water and the Antarctic Bottom Water, the largest values of oxygen in each water mass being above 5.5, 5.0 and 4.5 ml/liter, respective-

ly. On the other hand, in the South Equatorial Current the layer of 100–300 m is poor in oxygen, with less than 2.5 ml/liter, because the large stability at the sea surface prevents oxygen from being supplied from the air. Also, the North Indian Deep Water is poor in oxygen because of the lack of contact with the atmosphere, and it forms the oxygen minimum layer between the oxygen-rich intermediate and bottom waters down to the latitude of 40°S.

Ivanenkov and Gubin estimated the biological oxygen consumption (BOC) in different areas of the Indian Ocean. The Antarctic shelf area in wintertime is an ideal place for such an estimation because it is completely covered with ice which cuts off the oxygen supply and because there is no rise of deep waters poor in oxygen. Data on the Antarctic shelf area in the Indian Ocean gave the average BOC of some 0.37 ml/liter for 10 months in the upper 410 m. The annual BOC in the equatorial region in depths of 100–300 m, in the center of the North Indian Deep Water in depths of 600–1200 m, and in the North Indian Bottom Water in depths below 2000 m is estimated to be 1.5, 1.5–2.0 and 0.04 ml/liter, respectively.

The pH distribution on the same section as oxygen is shown in Fig. 32. The characteristic feature of the surface water in the Antarctic region is its very low pH with the average of 7.93–7.98 in the upper 100-m layer. This is due to the cessation of photosynthesis in the early winter (May). In the subsurface and intermediate layers, the pH depends on the rate of oxidation and the supply of waters enriched with carbon dioxide. Subtropical Subsurface Water (Central Water) between 40 and 16°S is distinguished by its high pH of 8.0–8.1 and the uniformity of its values with depths. The Equatorial Water between 6 and 10°S has a core of minimum pH (7.81–7.86) in depths of 120–300 m. The Antarctic Intermediate Water has pH values constant at the same isopycnal surfaces. The pH of deep waters is considerably affected by the dissolution of carbonates in addition to oxidation. The pH minimum agrees well with the oxygen minimum in the North Indian Deep Water due to the oxidation of organic matter. But the dissolution of carbonates causes some differences in the vertical gradients above the minimum layer in distributions of oxygen and pH.

The phosphates of the surface water varies from 1.5–1.9 mg at/m^3 in the upper layer south of the Antarctic Convergence to 0.8–0.15 mg at/m^3 in the Subtropical Water and to 0.2–0.1 mg at/m^3 in the Equatorial Water. They increase gradually with depth in the Subtropical Water to about 1.0 mg at/m^3 in the depth of 700 m, but they increase sharply in the Equatorial Water to about 1.2 mg at/m^3 in the depth of 100 m due to general upwelling there. The phosphates in the Antarctic Intermediate Water gradually increase with depth from 1.2–1.3 on the upper boundary to 1.8–1.9 mg at/m^3 on the lower boundary. The phosphates in deep water masses generally show the greatest values at each station. Those in the Circumpolar Water are 1.8–2.2 mg at/m^3 and rather uniform with depth. The largest amount is found in the North Indian Deep Water with 2.6–3.1 mg at/m^3, while these maximum values in the deep water to the south are 2.2–2.3 mg at/m^3. The large amount of phosphates in the former deep water is due to the effect of the Red Sea Surface Water. This water rich in phyto-plankton sinks to the intermediate depths and mixes with the North Indian Deep Water. The phosphates of the Antarctic Bottom Water decrease by about 0.1–0.2 mg

at/m^3 from the overlying deep water and also increase slightly northward.

The silicates in the surface waters show maximum in the Antarctic zone (35–70 mg at/m^3) in spite of the fact that diatoms, main consumers of silicates, predominate in phytoplanktons. This is due to strong mixing with deep waters there. The surface waters to the north of Subtropical Convergence uniformly show poor silicates of 5–10 mg at/m^3 due to stable stratification preventing mixing with deep waters. The increase of silicates with depth is very gradual in these areas, reaching 10 mg at/m^3 at about 800 m in the Central Water and 25–30 mg at/m^3 at 300–500 m in the Equatorial Water. The silicates in the Antarctic Intermediate Water increase from 15 mg at/m^3 at the upper limit via 25–45 mg at/m^3 in the core of 67–70 mg at/m^3 at the lower limit. The deep waters have silicates from 70–120 mg at/m^3. The silicates of the Antarctic Bottom Water have maximum values of 110–190 mg at/m^3 in the entire Indian Ocean. These values decrease slightly to 100–110 mg at/m^3 in the bottom water of the equatorial region.

Nitrites are only found in surface water masses. They are present only in summer in the Antarctic Zone in the layer from 0–25 m and not in the pycnocline. The intense decomposition of unstable organic matter, which is the main source of nitrites, occurs only in the upper 25-m layer. The nitrite maximum in the Subantarctic Zone was 8–10 mg/m^3 in the upper layer of the Subtropical Convergence. There is no nitrite in the surface water north of the Subtropical Convergence during the southern winter. There are no nitrites in the layer of 0–60 m in the North Equatorial Water, but in the pycnocline they are present in large amounts of 10.0–10.5 mg/m^3.

The maximum amount of nitrates in the surface water, 110–220 mg/m^3 is found in the Antarctic and Subantarctic Zones. There are no nitrates to the north of the Subtropical Convergence. The maximum amount of nitrates in the western part of the Indian Ocean is found in the North Indian Deep water with 320 mg/m^3 at about 12°S. In the Circumpolar Current, the water of the North Atlantic origin is detected by the least amount of nitrates, 200–210 mg/m^3.

Rochford (1963) studied distribution of organic phosphorus in the southeast Indian Ocean. On the meridional section along 112–114°E, the organic phosphorus averaged in the upper 200-m layer showed maxima (0.20–0.30 mg at/liter) on the southern boundary of the South Equatorial Current, on the Equatorial Divergence and the boundary between the Countercurrent and the North Equatorial Current. The pronounced maximum found in the vertical profiles at around 1000 m seems to correspond to the salinity minimum of the Antarctic Intermediate Water.

Tides. In Fig. 33 the cotidal lines of the M$_2$ (semidiurnal) tides are shown. It is a special feature of the

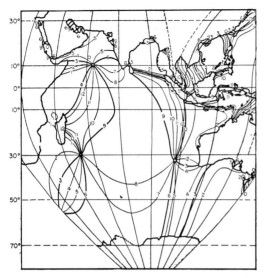

Fig. 33. The cotidal lines of the M_2 tides (Defant, 1961). (By permission of Pergamon Press, N.Y.)

Indian Ocean that variation in phase is very small when the disturbances due to the shelf are neglected. Five regions can be divided according to the tidal characteristics: (1) Western Region—the entire African Coast from the South Atlantic Ocean via Cape of Good Hope up north of Ras Hafun in Somaliland, including the west coast of Madagascar, the Comoro Islands, Amirante Island and the Seychelles. The phases lie near 0° (the equator). (2) Eastern Region—the west coast of Australia north of Freemouth across the entrance of the Timor Sea to central Java. The phases are about 45°. (3) Central Region—a wide band between the eastern and western regions from near the southern Maldive Island in the north, via Chagos, Rodriguez, St. Paul, Kerguelen Island to the Antarctic (the *Gauss* Station phase 229°). The phases are near 240° and opposite to the eastern and western sections. Also, amplitudes are high everywhere. (4) Northeastern Region—from the Gulf of Aden to the coast of Baluchistan and then to the 12°N on the southwest coast of India. The phases increases from 227° at Karachi to 332° at Bombay and Cochin. (5) Northwestern Region—the entire inner part of the Bay of Bengal including the Andaman Sea. The phases are between 30° and 130°.

The M_2 tides have three amphidromic points. Those in the Arabian Sea rotate clockwise, and the amplitudes increase from west to east. In the Bay of Bengal there is a uniform oscillation with a phase opposite to that of the open Indian Ocean to the south. The presence of the nodal line from the east coast of Ceylon to the northern point of Sumatra is recognized from the crowded cotidal lines and from small amplitudes at both sides (13 cm and 4 cm in the western and eastern side, respectively).

Cotidal lines of the K_1 tides are shown in Fig. 34 as representative of the diurnal tides. There are two major amphidromic points near the Chagos Archipelago in the north and at 55°S 30°E in the south. The northern amphidrome causes minimum amplitudes of 5–10 cm at the Chagos and on both sides of crowded cotidal lines, from northwest Sumatra to southern Ceylon to the west and southern Madagascar to the east. The northwestern part becomes antinodal and tidal ranges exceed 20 cm on the Seychelles and Laccadives and more than 40 cm on the south coast of Arabia. There is a small clockwise amphidrome at the southern entrance of the Mozambique Channel.

The actual tides are mainly composite of semidiurnal and diurnal tides. They are semidiurnal along the East African coast, but they are of a mixed type on the coasts of Arabia, Iran and India. The mixed and diurnal tides occur on the coasts of the East Indian Archipelago and of the Southeast Asian countries. The areas of the pure diurnal tides are the Bangka, Gaspar and Karimatu Straits, the southwest coast of Australia, the southern part of the South China Sea and the Java Sea.

The mean ranges of spring tides along the northern coast of the Arabian Sea are from 2.5 m at Aden to 5.7 m at Bombay, and they decrease again to 1.1 m at Cochin. The west coast of the Bay of Bengal including the coast of Ceylon has mean spring ranges of about 1 m, but those along the north and west coasts are 4.2–5.2 m due to shallow depths there. At Rangoon the spring tides exceed 7 m. The mean spring tides along the coast of South Africa are 1.7–1.9 m, and they increase in the Mozambique Channel with 3–4 m. Those along the northern coast of Australia are medium and 2.5 m

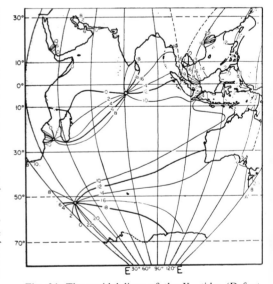

Fig. 34. The cotidal lines of the K_1 tides (Defant, 1961). (By permission of Pergamon Press, N.Y.)

in the Torres Straits, but those on the northwest coast of Australia exceed 6 m, with 8 m at Port Darwin and 10–12 m in Collier Bay. The values decrease again along the west coast, then to the southwest coast where those near Fremantle are about 0.5 m with the pure diurnal tides. The values increase again to about 1–2 m on the south coast.

Air-sea Interface Phenomena*

Heat Exchange between the Ocean and the Atmosphere. The net amount of heat received by the ocean from the atmosphere can be determined from the equation $W = S - V - L$, where S is the net radiation received by the ocean, V is the latent heat given to the air by evaporation and L is the heat flux from the sea surface to the air by Austausch. Further, $S = R - B$, where R is the radiation absorbed by the sea from the sun and the sky, and B is the back radiation from the sea to the sky. R is a function of the altitude of the sun and the total cloud amount, and one formula for it was given by Angstrom. Albrecht (1958) revised this formula by including the ratio of the total cloud amount to the amount of lower clouds and applied it to the Indian Ocean. B is obtained by Stefan-Boltzman law and equals bT_w^4, where T_w is the absolute temperature of the sea surface and b is a coefficient dependent on cloud amounts and humidity.

Albrecht determined bimonthly distributions of W for each 5° quadrangle over the Indian Ocean by use of the climatological charts of McDonald (1938), supplemented by charts (Schott, 1935) of surface water and air temperatures in four seasons. The isolines of W for every two months are expressed by full lines for negative values (heat given from the ocean to the atmosphere) and by broken lines for positive values (heat received by the ocean) with absolute values in kilocalories per square centimeter per month in Fig. 35. The annual cycle may be explained by starting from December when the sun's altitude is the highest in the southern hemisphere. In this month, heat is received by the ocean in most parts except the northern part. The maximum amount of heat gain in the zone around 40°S reaches 12 kcal/cm² month. This maximum value decreases sharply to the north and even diminishes to zero in the central part at about 18°S in the South Equatorial Current between Madagascar and Java, where evaporation is the strongest. From there, W increases again and reaches the second maximal zone with 4 kcal/cm² month at about 5°S. North of the 4°N it becomes negative and reaches the maximum heat loss (to the air) of 6 kcal/cm² month at about 20°N.

The decrease of heat gain due to evaporation caused by the Southeast Monsoon blowing over the South Equatorial Current becomes more conspicuous in February, and the area of the negative

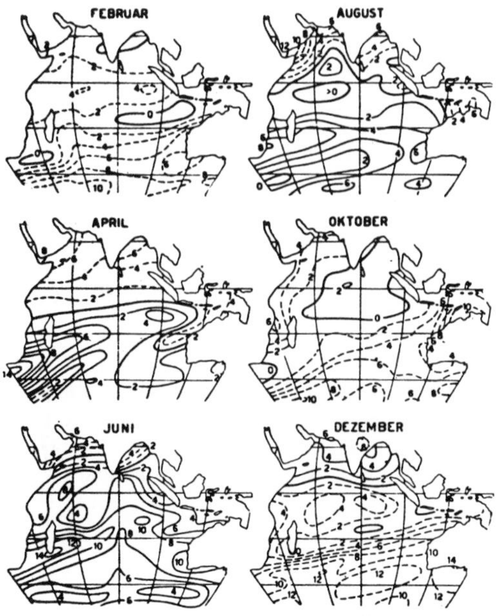

* Takashi Ichiye.

Fig. 35. Bimonthly charts of heat exchange at the sea surface (kcal 1 cm² month). Full lines = heat loss to the air. Broken lines = heat gains of the ocean.

W increases its extent in the western part of Madagascar-Java zone. The maximum zone of heat gain shifts from 40°S by about 4° latitudes, and its value decreases from December. This shift is due to the occurrence of maximum sea surface temperature with lag to the maximum of the sun's latitude. The heat loss area in the north diminishes to a small sector of the northern part of the Bay of Bengal.

In April the heat loss to the air becomes stronger over the South Equatorial Current and reaches maximum over the Agulhas Current south of Africa. The heat is received by the ocean all over north of the line between north Madagascar and south Sumatra. In June the heat gain of the ocean is limited to small areas in the northern parts of the Arabian Sea and the Bay of Bengal. The maximum heat loss belt runs again between Madagascar and Java with maximum values 12–14 kcal/cm² month over the Agulhas Current, the values decreasing northeastward. The minimum heat loss zone lies south of 40°S where the maximum heat gain occurs in February.

In August the heat gain areas to the north of the equator increase their extent. The area of larger heat loss southwest of India is a remnant of the area of the second maximum heat loss in June. The belt of maximum August heat loss in the southern hemisphere occurs at about 22°S, and does not reach Java. Also, there is a second maximum of heat loss appearing at about 45°S. The October chart shows signs of return of the southern summer. The region south of 40°S has heat gain reaching 8–10 kcal/cm² month. Also, the vast area of small heat loss appears over the South Equatorial Current where the evaporation is strong and over the Bay of Bengal where the radiation effect diminishes.

In Fig. 36, the total heat exchange per year is shown in the same way as the bimonthly charts. This chart again shows the strongest heat loss areas over the Agulhas Current south of Africa and over the South Equatorial Current between Madagascar and Java. The zone of the maximum heat gain around 45°S is recognized in this chart. A zone of weak heat gain lies between Tanganyika and Sumatra. The southern parts of the Bay of Bengal and the Arabian Sea show weak heat loss while the northern parts have strong heat gain. The regional differences in the annual heat balance may be compensated by horizontal heat transport by the ocean currents.

The bimonthly surface temperature and the heat gain of the ocean averaged over the entire Indian Ocean north of 35°S are shown in the following table.

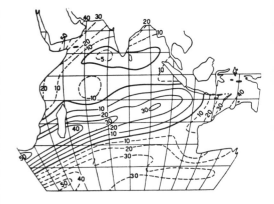

Fig. 36. The yearly sum of heat exchange (kcal 1 cm^2 year) (Albrecht, 1958).

Month	Feb.	April	June	Aug.	Oct.	Dec.
Mean temperature, °C	25.20	25.31	24.08	22.60	23.19	24.61
Mean W, kcal/cm^2 month	2.61	−0.52	−6.25	−1.62	1.78	3.95

This table shows that the effect of heat flux appears in the surface temperature about two months later. If it is assumed that the range of the mean surface temperature (2.71°C) is caused solely by the annual increase of heat flux (33.4 kcal/cm^2) determined from this table, the depth of the upper layer heated by this flux becomes about 123 m. This is plausible since the average thermocline of this area is about 200 m, below which the seasonal change of temperature almost vanishes.

Wind Waves and Swells. According to the characteristics of seas, the Indian Ocean can be divided into three regions: the region of the Westerlies in the south, the region of the Southeast Trades between Madagascar and Australia, and the region of the monsoons. The percentage frequencies of waves for different heights in different regions are as shown in the following table:

This table illustrates the large annual fluctuations in the seas in the northern region. In winter the Northeast Monsoon causes mostly small waves below 1 m. In summer, particularly from June to August, the Southwest Monsoon which often blows with forces above 7 Beaufort scale generates waves higher than 2.1 m for frequencies of 45%. The region of the trade wind has waves of small and medium heights with 80% frequency, but the Southern Westerlies cause strong waves with 50% frequency.

Stereophotographic measurements have recorded waves of 15-m height and 250-m wavelength near the Kerguelen Islands. Visual observations have recorded waves of 10–11-m height and 400-m wavelength off the east coast of Australia and swells of 7.5-m height and 341.7-m length and periods of 14.5 seconds in the southeast part.

Region	Wave Heights (m)					
	0–0.9	0.9–1.2	1.2–2.1	2.1–3.7	3.7–6.1	>6.1
(1) The Northern Region for Northeast Monsoon	55	25	10	5	5	0
(2) The Northern Region for Southwest Monsoon	15	15	25	20	15	10
(3) The Region of the Southeast Trades	35	25	20	10	5	5
(4) The Region of the Westerlies	10	20	20	20	15	5

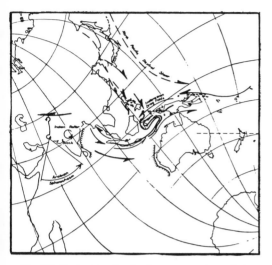

Fig. 37. Dextral torsion in the geotectonic evolution the northern Indian Ocean (Carey, 1958).

Structure of Indian Ocean*

The Indian Ocean is the perfect example of a "young" ocean area, the surrounding continental crustal areas (Africa, India, Australia, Antarctica) all being of rather similar character and apparently united in a single continent or clusters of closely related sub-continental nuclei at about the close of Precambrian time (Stille, 1948; Fairbridge, 1948, 1955)—the celebrated "Gondwanaland" of Suess (see appropriate articles in another volume).

* Rhodes W. Fairbridge.

The paleogeographic history of these marginal areas shows that in early Paleozoic, a geosynclinal trough developed down the west coast of Australia, and in the Permian, a similar geosyncline opened up along the western margin ("Malgash Trough"). At the time of the Permo-Carboniferous ice age, all the continental units appear to have been in very close juxtaposition. Up until now, paleomagnetic data have not been sufficiently numerous or precise to establish the exact relations of those continents, but there seems little doubt that since the Permian, a major breakup has occurred, with Australia moving to the east, Antarctica to the south and India to the north (Fairbridge, 1965, p. 120). It is not without interest that one of the earliest discussions of such a breakup was published on the island of Réunion (by Mantovani, 1889–90). The nature of the separation process is still highly controversial (see Fairbridge, 1964); whether it occurs by the expansion of the mantle, with continental stretching, or by some form of drift is not known. Certainly a dextral torsion seems to be involved (Fig. 37). However, any theory which involves fixed poles and fixed continents runs head on into the problem of the Permian glaciation of Gondwanaland and other stratigraphic questions.

The geophysical studies of the Indian Ocean floor confirmed what had been suspected from the geological data. The Mid-Indian Ridge separates two distinct crustal regions and is thus different from the symmetrical role which the Mid-Atlantic Ridge plays. West of the Mid-Indian Ridge is a quasi-cratonic region of former continental fragments, now partly submerged as mid-oceanic plateaus with continental late Precambrian or early Cambrian

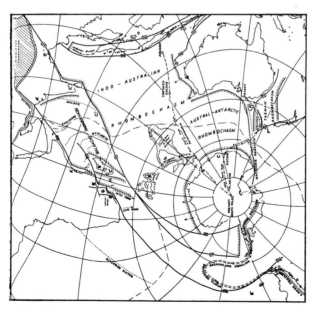

Fig. 38. Tectonic features of the Indian Ocean Polychasin, as interpreted by a theory of continental spreading (Carey, 1958).

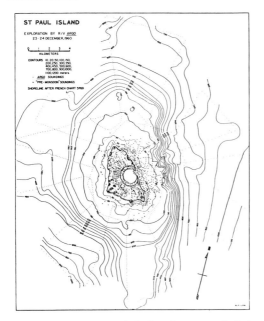

Fig. 39. St. Paul Island, Indian Ocean; a relatively youthful volcano on a fracture zone intersecting the Mid-Indian Ridge. The east side of the volcano has been lost due to a giant landslide (note outward bulge of 600 m contour; S.I.O. 1964).

granites (as in the Seychelles; see Davies and Francis, 1964) or with atoll evidence of subsidence (as in the Chagos-Laccadive Ridge, etc.). The continental-type fragments alternate with narrow zones of oceanic-type crust. As in the other oceans, the *mid-oceanic ridge* (q.v.) appears to be a belt of newly developed oceanic crustal differentiate. Basalt fragments dredged from it are of quite youthful origin and are typically oceanic.

As shown already by Gaskell's work, the northeastern Indian Ocean has a typically ocean crust, and this has been confirmed by several International Indian Ocean Expedition crossings. The Ninetyeast Ridge (of Heezen *et al.*) bisects this area in a north-south direction in one of the most remarkable rectilinear structural lines on the globe; it can only be explained as a major fracture zone complex. This entire region is completely devoid of submarine plateaus, and even seamounts are scarce until one approaches the borders of the Java Trench (inexplicably called "Indonesian Trench" by some workers although "Java" has priority of several decades).

In the eastern part of the ocean, in a triangular-shaped area abutting the West Australian mainland and pointing westward towards St. Paul (Fig. 39) and Amsterdam, there is another extensive area of plateaus and oceanic rises. A continental type

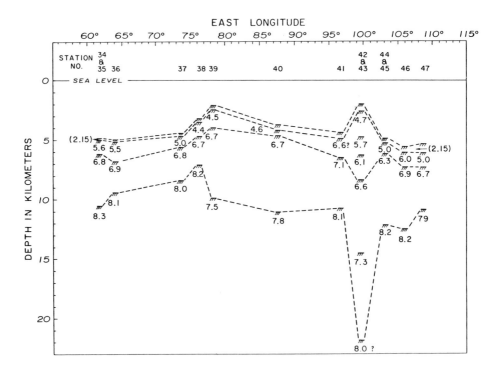

Fig. 40. Composite seismic refraction traverse from Mauritius through St. Paul and Broken Ridge to Fremantle (S.I.O. 1964).

gravity anomaly over the Exmouth Plateau was recorded by Vening Meinesz in his submarine traverse with the *K-xviii* in 1935. It is bounded to the south by the Diamantina Fracture Zone, across

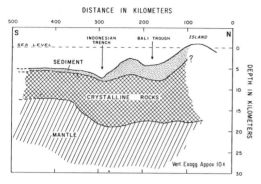

Fig. 41. Profile through the Indonesian Arc, Bali Trough, and Java Trench, based on gravity and seismic surveys (S.I.O. 1964).

which extraordinary topographic irregularities have been recognized since a trench was first discovered here by H.M.A.S. *Diamantina*; another rift in the same trend was identified somewhat to the west of this area by the Soviet vessel *Ob* and recognized as the *Ob Trench*. Oceanic crust appears abruptly along the south coast of Australia (Hawkins *et al.*, 1965).

Not far from 30°S, 65°E, near the center of the Indian Ocean, the mid-oceanic ridge splits in two, one part going southwestward to join the sector known as the Atlantic-Antarctic Rise and the other southeastward through Amsterdam and St. Paul to form the Australian-Antarctic Rise. Almost symmetrically placed again, to the south there is a triangular-shaped area of deep oceanic crust surmounted on the east by the *Kerguelen Plateau* (Aubert de la Rue, 1932). On the islands, rocks back to early Tertiary are known, and from the topographic appearance of the plateau it would seem to be "microcontinental," but precise information

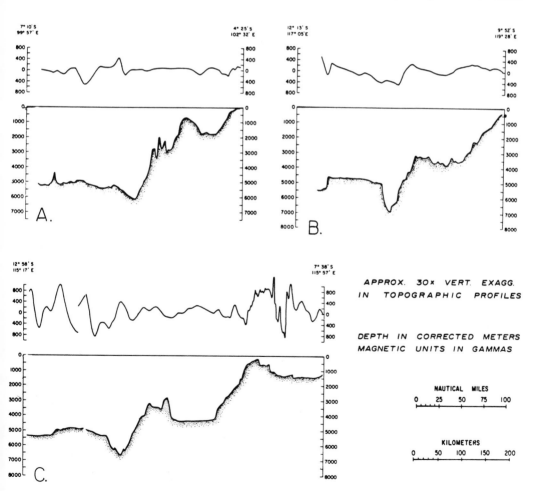

Fig. 42. Topographic and magnetic profiles through the Indonesian Arc, Bali Trough and Java Trench (S.I.O. 1964). (A) Southwest of Bangkahula (Sumatra); (B) Southwest of Sumba; (C) South of Lombok Strait.

is lacking as yet. The idea of Von Drygalski of a continuous "Kerguelen-Gaussberg Rise" was not quite correct, for the plateau is interrupted by two east-west depressions.

A composite east-west crustal section by seismic refraction across the middle part of the Indian Ocean was obtained by the Scripps R.V. *Argo* ("Preliminary results of S.I.O. Investigations in the Indian Ocean . . . 1960–63," S.I.O. Ref. 1964, **19**). Crossing the Mid-Indian Ridge from Mauritius to St. Paul, after a short section of typical oceanic crust, these investigations found that the ridge showed marked contrasts with the Mohorovicic Discontinuity varying from 7–11 km below sea level. Between St. Paul and Fremantle, the expedition crossed the edge of one of the suspected "microcontinental" blocks with a depth of a little over 2000 m, finding the "moho" at approximately 22 km below sea level. It is interesting that immediately after crossing this plateau, the investigations noted that crustal thicknesses returned to the normal oceanic pattern (Fig. 40).

Seismicity in the Indian Ocean region is concentrated in two distinctive belts: (a) along the mid-oceanic ridge (q.v.), as might be expected from its worldwide seismic character, and (b) along the Mediterranean-Himalayan-Indonesian ("Tethyan") orogenic belt to the north. The latter is subdivided into two segments of *island-arc* character. The first is a very short sector in the Arabian Sea, the Makran coast and trough where not only is seismicity felt but tsunamis also occur and small new offshore islands appear periodically (Anon., 1945). The second is the long arc from the Arakan Yoma coast of Burma, encircling the East Indian Archipelago (the "Indonesian Arc" of Heezen), to the Banda Arc ("Loop") just west of New Guinea (Figs. 41 and 42). Again, not only do seismicity and impressive vulcanicity mark this belt, but many other indicators of current orogenic activity appear also: e.g. mud volcanoes (as at Foul Island off Burma) to the famous examples in Timor. On Timor itself, young coral reefs rise from sea level to over 1000 m, showing numerous undegraded Quaternary faults, as do the young coastal sediments in Makran. It is sometimes stated that such "island arc" features are exclusively found in the Pacific and Antilles, but they are equally characteristic of all young orogenic belts.

RHODES W. FAIRBRIDGE
BRUCE C. HEEZEN
TAKASHI ICHIYE
MARIE THARP

References

Agassiz, A., 1903, "The Coral Reefs of the Maldives," *Mem. Mus. Comp. Zoo.*, **29**, 1–25, 1–168.

Albrecht, F. H. W., 1958, "Untersuchungenüber den Wärmeumsatz an der Meeresoberfläche und die Meeresströmungen im Indischen Ozean," *Geofis. Pura Appl.*, **39**, 194–215.

Andrews, C. W., 1900, "A Monograph of Christmas Island (Indian Ocean)," *Brit. Mus. Publ.*

Anon., 1945, "Earthquakes in the Arabian Sea," *Nature*, **156**, 712–713.

Anon., 1964, "Progress of the International Indian Ocean Expedition," *Intern. Geophys. Bull. No. 83*, in *Trans. Am. Geophys. Union*, **45**, 383–391.

Aubert de la Rue, E., 1932, "Étude géologique et géographique de l'Archipel de Kerguelen," *Rev. Géogr. Phys. et Geol. Dyn.*, **5**, 1–232.

Bezrukov, P. L., 1961, "Research in the Indian Ocean by the Survey Vessel *Vityaz* on its Thirty-third voyage," *Okeanologia*, **1**(4), 745–753 (translated in *Deep-Sea Res.*, **10**, 59–66.

Bezrukov, P. L., and Kanaev, V. F., 1963, "Principal features of the structure of the bottom of the northeastern part of the Indian Ocean," JPRS: 24186 TT–64–31075, *Trans. Akad. Nauk SSSR*, **153**, 926–929 (English translation).

Biewald, D., 1964, "Die Ansatstiefe der Rezenten Korallenriffe im Indischen Ozean," *Z. Geomorphol.*, **8**(3), 351–361.

Bourne, G. C., 1888, "The Atoll of Diego Garcia and the coral formations of the Indian Ocean," *Proc. Roy. Soc. London*, **43**, 440–461.

Bruns, E., 1958, "Ozeanologie," Bd. 1, Berlin, VEB Deutscher Verlag der Wissenschaften, 420pp.

Davies, D., and Francis, T. J. G., 1964, "The crustal structure of the Seychelles Bank," *Deep-Sea Res.*, **11**, 921–928.

Defant, A., 1961, "Physical Oceanography," Vol. 2, Pergamon Press, New York, London, 598pp.

Dietrich, G., 1957, "Allegemeine Meereskunde," Berlin, Gebrüder Borntraeger.

Drygalski, E. von, 1925, "Der Kerguelen-Gaussberg-Rucken, eine submarine vulkanische Hohen zone im Indisch-Antarktischen Gebiet," *Sitzer. Bayer. Akad. Wiss., Math-Naturw. Kl.*, 157–164.

Fairbridge, R. W., 1948, "The juvenility of the Indian Ocean," *Scope (W. Australia, Univ. Sci. Union J.*, **1**(3), 29–35.

Fairbridge, R. W., 1955a, "Report on the limits of the Indian Ocean," *Proc. Pan-Indian Ocean Sci. Assoc.* (Perth Meeting, 1954).

Fairbridge, R. W., 1955b, "Some Bathymetric and Geotectonic features of the eastern part of the Indian Ocean," *Deep-Sea Res.*, **2**, 161–171.

Fairbridge, R. W., 1964, "Thoughts About an Expanding Globe." In: *Advancing Frontiers in Geology and Geophysics*, 59–88.

Fairbridge, R. W., 1965, "The Indian Ocean and the status of Gondwanaland," *Progress in Oceanography*, **3**, 83–136.

Fryer, J. C. F., 1911, "The structure and formation of Aldabra and neighboring islands," *Trans. Linnean Soc. London, Ser. 2 (Zoo.)*, **14**, 397–442.

Gardiner, J. S., 1903–6, "The Fauna and Geography of Maldive and Laccadive Archipelagoes," Cambridge, 2 vols.

Gardiner, J. S., 1936, "The reefs of the Western Indian Ocean. I: Chagos Archipelago; II: The Mascarene Region," *Trans. Linnean Soc. London, Ser. 2 (Zoo.)*, **19**, 393–436.

Gardiner, J. S., and Cooper, C. F., 1907, "Description

of the expedition," *Trans. Linnean Soc. London, Ser. 2 (Zoo.),* **12**, 1–56, 111–175.

Gorbunova, Z. N., 1962, "Clay and associated minerals of the Indian Ocean sediments," *Tr. Inst. Okeanol. Akad. Nauk S.S.S.R.,* **61**, 93–103.

Hawkins, L. V., Hennion, J. F., Nafe, J. E., and Doyle, H. A., 1965, "Marine seismic refraction studies of the continental margin to the south of Australia," *Deep-Sea Res.,* **12**(4), 479–495.

Heezen, Bruce C., and Tharp, Marie, 1964, "Physiographic diagram of the Indian Ocean, the Red Sea, the South China Sea, the Sulu Sea and the Celebes Sea," *Geol. Soc. Am.*

Heezen, B. C., and Tharp, M., 1965, "Physiography of the Indian Ocean," *Phil. Trans. Roy. Soc. London, Ser. A* (in press).

Herman, Y., 1963, "Cretaceous, Paleocene, and Pleistocene sediments from the Indian Ocean," *Science,* **140**, 1316–1317.

Ivanenkov, V. N., and Gubin, F. A., 1960, "Water masses and hydrochemistry of the western and southern parts of the Indian Ocean," *Akad. Nauk S.S.S.R.,* **22**, 27–29.

Ivanenkov, V. N., and Gubin, F. A., 1961, "Water masses and hydrochemistry of the western and southern parts of the Indian Ocean," *Trudy Morskovo Gidrofiz. Inst.,* **12** *(Trans. of Marine Hydrophys. Inst.,* translated by A.G.U.).

Knauss, J. A., and Taft, B. A., 1964, "Equatorial undercurrent of the Indian Ocean," *Science,* **143**(3604), 354–356.

Kovylin, V. M., "New data on the thickness of bottom deposits in the Indian Ocean," *Dokl. Oceanology Akad. Nauk S.S.S.R.,* **136–141**, 7–9.

Lacroix, A., 1925, "Succession des éruptions et bibliographie du volcan actif de la Réunion," *Bull. Volcanol.,* (3–4), 20–56.

Lambeth, A. J., 1950, "Heard Island, geography and glaciation," *Proc. Roy. Soc., N.S.W.,* **84**, 92–98.

Lisitzin, A. P., 1964, "Distribution and chemical composition of suspended matter in the waters of the Indian Ocean," (in Russian, English abstract), *Result. Issled. Prog. Mezhd. Geofiz. Goda, Mezd. Geofiz. Komit. Presid. Akad. Nauk, SSSR, Okeanol.,* No. 10, 135pp.

Lisitzin, A. P., and Zhivago, A. V., 1960, "Marine geological work of the Soviet Antarctic Expedition, 1955–1957," *Deep-Sea Res.,* **6**, 77–87.

Mantovani, R., 1889–90, "Les fractures de l'ecorce terrestre et la theorie de Laplace," *Bull. Soc. Sci. Arts, Réunion.*

McDonald, W. F., 1938, "Atlas of Climatic Charts of the Oceans," U.S. Weather Bureau, Washington D.C.

Murray, J., and Philippi, E., 1908, "Die Grundproben der Deutschen Tiefsee Expedition," *Wiss. Ergebn. Deutschen Tiefsee Exped. "Valdivia" 1898–1899 (Jena),* **10**, 79–206.

Murray, J., and Renard, A. F., 1891, "Deep-sea deposits," *Rept. on the Voyage of H.M.S. Challenger 1873–1876,* 525pp.

Ovchinnikov, I. M., 1961, "Circulation of waters in the northern Indian Ocean during the winter monsoon," *Oceanol. Res. Articles, IGY Program (Oceanol.) Akad. Nauk USSR, Moscow,* 4, 18–24.

Pan-Indian Ocean Science Congress, 4th, Karachi, 1960, *Proc. (Sect. C Karachi: Pan-Indian Ocean Sci. Assoc.),* Secretariat, 182pp.

Pollak, M. L., 1958, "Frequency distribution of potential temperatures and salinities in the Indian Ocean," *Deep-Sea Res.,* **5**, 128–133.

Rochford, D. J., 1961, 1962, 1964, "Hydrography of the Indian Ocean, I, II, III. *Australian J. Marine Freshwater Res.,* **12**(2), 129–149; **13**(3), 226–251; **15**(1), 25–55.

Rochford, D. J., 1963, "Mixing trajectories of intermediate depth waters of the South-East Indian Ocean as determined by a salinity frequency method," *Australian J. Marine Freshwater Res.,* **14**, 1–23.

Rochford, D. J., 1963, "Some features of organic phosphorous distribution in the South-East Indian and South-West Pacific Oceans," *Australian J. Marine Freshwater Res.,* **14**(2), 119–138.

Rochford, D. J., 1964, "Salinity maxima in the upper 1000 meters of the North Indian Ocean," *Australian J. Marine Freshwater Res.,* **15**(1), 1–24.

Samuel, P., 1965, "Bibliography of physical oceanography of the Indian Ocean," Nat. Oceanog. Data Center, Washington, D.C. Special Bibliographies on Oceanog., No. 2, 122pp.

Schott, G., 1935, "Geographie des Indischen und Stillen Oceans," Hamburg, Boysen, 413pp.

Schott, W., 1939, "Deep-sea Sediments of the Indian Ocean," in "Recent Marine Sediments," pp. 396–408, Tulsa, American Association of Petroleum Geologists.

Sewell, R. B. Seymour, 1935, "Geographic and oceanographic research in Indian Waters: Pt. I. The geography of the Andaman Sea basin," *Mem. Roy. Asiatic Soc. Bengal,* **9**.

Sewell, R. B. Seymour, 1936, "An account of Horsburgh or Goifurfehendu Atoll," *John Murray Exped. 1933–34. Brit. Mus. N.H.,* **1**(5), 109–125.

Sewell, R. B. Seymour, 1936, "An account of Addu Atoll," *John Murray Exped. 1933–34. Brit. Mus. N.H.,* **1**(3), 63–93.

Shand, S. J., 1933, "The Lavas of Mauritius," *Quart. J. Geol. Soc.,* **89**, 1–13.

Starik, I. Ye, and Zharkov, A. P., 1961, "Rate of sedimentation in the Indian Ocean according to radiocarbon date," *Dokl. Oceanology, Akad. Nauk SSSR,* **136–141**, 1–3.

Stille, H., 1948, "Ur-und Neuozeane," *Abhandl. Deut. Akad. Wiss., Berlin,* **6**, 68pp.

Sverdrup, H. U., Johnson, M. W., and Fleming, R. H., 1942, *"The Oceans,"* Englewood Cliffs, N.J., Prentice-Hall, 1087pp.

Thomsen, H., 1933, "The circulation of the Indian Ocean," *J. Conseil, Conseil. Perm. Intern. Exploration Mer.,* **8**, 73.

Varadachari, V. V. R., and Sharma, G. S., 1964, "On the vergence field in the North Indian Ocean," *Bull. Natl. Geophys. Res. Inst., New Delhi,* **2910**, 1–14.

Villain, C., 1951, "Lignes Cotidale de l'Ocean Indien," *Bull. Inform., Com. Cent. Oceanogr. et Cotes,* **3**, 370–389.

Voeltzkow, A., 1901, "Uber Coccolithen und Rhabdolithen, nebst Bemerkungen über den Aufbau und die Entstehung der Aldabrainseln," *Abh. Senckenberg. Naturfossch. Ges.,* **26**, 467–537.

Voeltzkow, A., 1903–06, "Berichte uber eine Reise nach Ost-Afrika zur Untersuchung der Bildung und des Aufbaues der Riffe und Inseln des westlichen indischen Ozeans," *Z. Ges. f. Erdk. Berlin,* 1903, 560–591 (Witu, Pemba); 1904, 274–301 (Mafia, Zanzibar,

Cormoro); 1904, 426–451 (Europa atoll); 1905, 89–119, 184–211, 285–296 (Madagascar); 1906, 102–113 (Réunion, Mauritius); 1906, 179–189 (Ceylon).

Wiseman, J. H. D., and Riedel, W. R., 1960, "Tertiary sediments from the floor of the Indian Ocean," *Deep-Sea Res.*, **7**, 215–217.

Wiseman, J. D. H., and Sewell, R. B. S., 1937, "The floor of the Arabian Sea," *Geol. Mag.*, **74**, 219–230.

Wood-Jones, F., 1910, "Coral Reefs and Atolls," London, 392pp.

Wüst, G., 1934, "Anzeichen von Beziehungen zwischen Bodenstrom und Relief in der Tiefsee des Indischen Ozeans," *Naturwissenschaften*, **16**, 241–244.

Zaklinskii, G. B., 1963, "Deep circulation of water in the Indian Ocean," *Okeanologia*, **3**(4), 591–598 (translated *Deep-Sea Res.*, **11**, 286–293).

INSTRUMENTATION—*See*
OCEANOGRAPHIC INSTRUMENTATION

INTERNAL WAVES

Internal waves are subsurface waves found between layers of different density or within layers where vertical density gradients are present. They can exist in any stratified fluid and can be caused by flow over an irregular bottom, atmospheric disturbances, tidal forces, and shear flow. In deep water, the height of internal waves may be several hundred feet; however, in the main thermocline they are normally 20–50 feet high. They have an amplitude at all depths except at the bottom, where it is zero, and at the free surface, where it is negligibly small. The distribution of amplitude over depth is influenced by the density distribution, since less energy is required to displace a weak density boundary than a strong one. Because of the large vertical and horizontal displacement of particles, internal waves are important factors in water mixing and transport (La Fond and Cox, 1962; Lee and Batzler, 1964).

Theory

Theoretically, free internal waves exist only between the inertial and Väisälä frequencies (Eckart, 1960). The lower limit is a function of latitude, and the upper limit, the Väisälä or stability frequency N, is a function of depth (z),

$$N^2 = -\frac{g}{\rho}\frac{d\rho}{dz} - \frac{g^2}{c^2}$$

where ρ is density of the medium, c is wave speed in the medium, and g is gravitational acceleration.

The theory of the existence of internal plane waves, as opposed to origin or destruction, implies the perfect coherence of plane waves over space. This would mean that an internal wave would travel undistorted across an ocean. In reality, internal waves which occur naturally in the sea are not nearly this coherent. In addition, the ocean may contain an infinite number of propagating sources, the waves from which may combine randomly, sometimes reinforcing and sometimes canceling each other (Fig. 1).

In deep water, an infinite number of modes are mathematically possible for any one frequency of excitation, but physically an upper limit must exist because of the inherent shear. Each higher mode at a given frequency has a higher wave number and travels at a slower phase speed.

In general, the observed spectra of internal displacement decrease with increasing frequency. Minor peaks often appear in the spectra at tidal frequencies and near the stability frequency, but a stationary condition is not established.

Measurements

Direct. The most valuable information on internal waves is obtained by measuring vertical changes in density. A few internal waves have been measured directly by tracing their vertical oscillations. For example, a large buoyant container was floated on a given density boundary, and a recording manometer on a drum successfully furnished its depth (Kullenberg, 1935). In deeper water, it has been possible to float Swallow-type buoys on

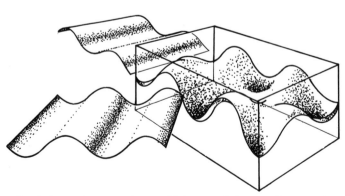

Fig. 1. Internal wave trains combining to reinforce and/or cancel out individual waves.

SEA SURFACE

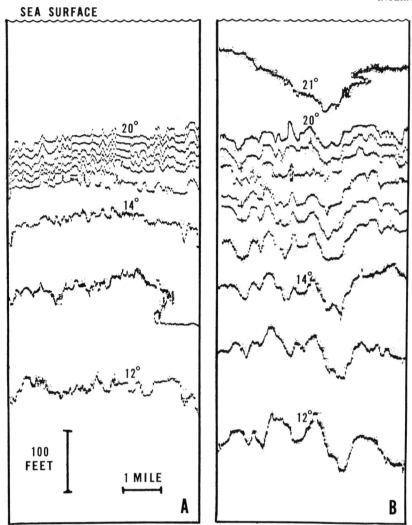

Fig. 2. Example of (A) short-wavelength internal waves in a strong thermocline and (B) long-wavelength internal waves in a weak thermocline. Isotherms in degrees Celsius.

deep density layers and have their depth transmitted acoustically to a mother ship (Pochapsky, 1963).

Internal waves can also be measured directly by use of a number of suspended or fixed current meters. However, these have been employed to only a limited extent because of the difficulties involved.

Indirect. Because the vertical density gradient may be caused by either temperature or salinity, or both, either scalar may be used to measure these values, provided no gains or losses of that scalar occur and diffusion is neglected. In the open sea, major changes in density are controlled by temperature. Also, because of their ease of accomplishment, temperature measurements have been the most commonly used indirect method of identifying internal waves.

Various instruments have been employed to measure the vertical oscillation of temperature (sometimes simultaneously with salinity). For long-period waves, reversing thermometers and water bottles have been used. Repeated bathythermograph lowerings and, more recently, vertically suspended and towed strings of fast responding thermistor beads have been utilized to establish the size and shape of all internal waves (Fig. 2).

Vertical Strings of Thermistor Beads. To determine the internal wave modes, information on complete surface-to-bottom conditions is needed. To acquire data on the speed and direction of internal waves, it is necessary to use more than one vertical string of thermistor beads. If the temperature at each thermistor is not recorded continuously, the thermistor is encapsulated in thermally insulating material in order to avoid the phenomenon of aliasing, in which high-frequency oscillations of temperature will be recorded as lower-frequency oscillations, should the sampling frequency be lower than the frequency of thermal oscillation. To avoid this uncorrectable error, a thermal lag which has a time response compatible with the sampling frequency is built around the sensor. The thermistor is usually so insulated that the time response is twice as long as the shortest period of the oscillation that is being examined. There is also the problem of the Doppler shift, due to the movement of the towed sensors. If the direction of progress and mode of the internal waves is known, it is possible to correct for this shift in frequency.

Isotherm Followers. One of the best ways to study progressive internal waves is with isotherm followers mounted on a fixed platform. These instruments follow a given temperature and thus describe the internal wave as it passes the measurement site. With three or more isotherm followers, it is possible to determine the direction and speed of internal waves in shallow water.

Data

Little information has been acquired from the deep open sea which would fully determine the nature of thermal waves throughout the water column (Lee and Cox, 1966). However, in shallow water off Mission Beach, California, a comprehensive study of internal waves employing a variety of instruments and techniques, has been conducted from a fixed platform.*

Wave Height. Time series observations in one location throughout the water column are sufficient to measure internal wave heights. The depth of a single isotherm in the thermocline was observed to fluctuate widely in water only 60 feet deep. Generally, the magnitude of the shorter-period vertical fluctuations is inversely proportional to the gradients in which they are found, and smaller fluctuations are nearly always present. A distribution of measured wave heights in this shallow water is shown in Fig. 3.

Wave Period. If a small amount of water is adiabatically displaced from its zero-order position and allowed to move freely, it will oscillate at the Väisälä frequency, provided entropy remains constant. This responds to a balance between buoyant and inertial forces. Higher-frequency internal waves are limited to regions near the maximum of N, but lower frequencies are not excluded. Superimposed on the longer-period seasonal cycles are $4\frac{1}{2}$-day cycles and diurnal cycles caused by similar wind periods. One of the main forces causing movement in the sea is that which generates tide;

*The U.S. Navy Electronics Laboratory Oceanographic Research Tower.

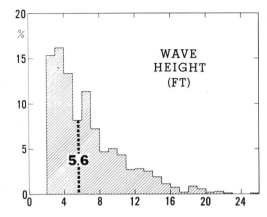

Fig. 3. Frequency distribution of internal wave heights in 60 feet of water off Mission Beach, California (for waves > 2 feet).

thus, many phenomena, including subsurface waves, have periods equal to the semidiurnal and diurnal tide. This applies to both deep- and shallow-water regions and represents the phenomenon referred to as *internal tide*. Thus, a wide spectrum of internal waves exists in the sea.

Since density in the ocean increases continuously with depth, an infinite number of modes can occur simultaneously; it is the mode that reveals how the density surfaces are displaced vertically. In first-mode waves, density surfaces are displaced in one direction only. Second-mode waves displace density surfaces upward within a certain depth interval and then downward throughout the remainder of the water depth. Third-mode waves displace from upward to downward and then upward again; this continues similarly for higher-mode waves. For each frequency of excitation, internal waves have a different wavelength for each mode; therefore, the phase velocity for each frequency is different for every mode. Only the first mode is present in the simplest case where two layers of constant (but different) density occur. The maximum amplitude of vertical displacement occurs at the boundary between two superimposed layers, and the amplitude decreases toward the upper free surface and toward the bottom boundary, becoming zero at the sea floor and insignificant at the sea surface. An example of multiple modes is shown in Fig. 4 (Lee, 1965).

In the shallow-water area off Mission Beach, the measured frequency distribution of over 1000 internal waves has been recorded (Fig. 5). Waves with periods of less than 2 minutes were excluded. Fifty per cent of all waves longer than 2 minutes had periods greater than 7.3 minutes.

Speed. For a two-layer system of long waves, in which the wavelength is great compared to the depth and the small displacement at the sea surface

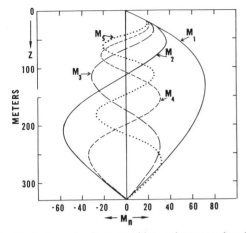

Fig. 4. Example of computed internal wave modes off Southern California (M_1 is first mode, M_2 second, etc.). The abscissa (M_n) is the relative amplitude of vertical displacement.

is disregarded, the velocity of the progressive internal wave (c) is

$$c^2 = \frac{g/k(\rho - \rho')}{\rho' \text{ ctnh } kh' + \rho \text{ ctnh } kh}$$

where h and ρ are the height and the density of the deeper layer and h' and ρ' are for the surface layer, $k = 2\pi/L$, and L is the wavelength. For short waves:

$$c^2 = \frac{g}{k} \frac{\rho - \rho'}{\rho + \rho'}$$

In shallow water, the speed of internal waves was determined by measuring vertical oscillations simultaneously in three locations, as well as observing the movement of their associated sea surface slicks. The measurements showed that off Mission Beach, internal waves moved toward shore

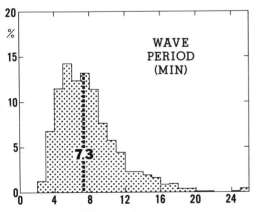

Fig. 5. Frequency distribution of internal wave frequencies in 60 feet of water off Mission Beach, California (for waves >2 minutes).

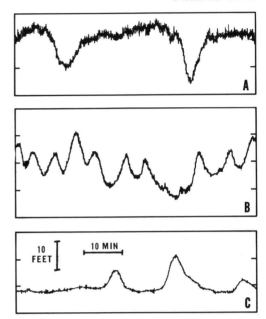

Fig. 6. Recorded shape of internal waves (A) near sea surface; (B) at intermediate depth; and (C) near sea floor.

at speeds of 0.11–0.60 knot, with an average speed of 0.31 knot in 60 feet of water. It was also determined that the depth of the thermocline had a bearing on the shape of the internal waves. The crests grew flat as they approached the sea surface. Conversely, the troughs flattened as they converged with the sea floor (Fig. 6). In addition, the face of the wave is generally steeper than the receding slope. There is some evidence that they break, as shown by occasional temerature inversions.

Propagation. Little is known about the direction of progress of internal waves in deep water. Multiple ship observations have found the internal tide progressing toward the Southern California coast (Summers and Emery, 1963). Others find internal tides moving parallel to surface tides in the eastern North Pacific (Krauss, 1965). In shallow water, the direction of propagation is almost directly toward shore.

Wave Motion

The water motions associated with internal waves have been examined by direct measurement and by analysis of their influence on sea surface features. Thus, in the sea, internal waves appear to take the form of progressive waves. In lakes and partially closed bodies of water, standing waves are found. The nature of progressive waves between two liquids of different densities is described by Lamb (1945). The theoretical water motions associated with this simple progressive wave are shown in Fig. 8.

In addition to the vertical oscillations, other evidence of this circulation in the ocean has been discovered. (1) The study of lateral shear motion has established that vertical dye streaks in the water become distorted by the shear at the thermocline. (2) Surface currents and other surface phenomena (La Fond, 1959) in the Bay of Bengal showed long streaks of alternately rough and smooth water. The ripples were 6–8 inches high and the rough water bands were 2–10 in number, some extending to the horizon. In the Andaman Sea, the bands were even more pronounced. Here bands of small, breaking whitecaps emitted a low roar as they passed a drifting ship on a calm sea. Similar phenomena of rough and smooth surfaces have been observed off southern California. By determining the thermal structure, it was found that the internal wave crest occurred directly under the roughest zone. Thus, from the surface currents, and from the thermal structure and its progressive motion, it was determined that a shallow internal wave was causing the phenomenon.

The vertical displacement (η) at the interface of a two-layer density system, ρ and ρ' is given by

$$\eta = a \cos (kx - \sigma t)$$

and the horizontal velocity of flow, u', in the upper layer is

$$u' = - (a/h') \, c \cos (kx - \sigma t)$$

where h' is the average thickness of the upper layer, a is the amplitude of the wave at the interface, and c is the wave velocity at the interface (Lamb, 1945).

If there is no appreciable flow in the y direction (normal to propagation), and no appreciable transport of surface water in the direction of propagation, the same volume of water per unit width must pass over the trough. The speed of flow in a horizontal direction must be inversely proportional to the instantaneous thickness of the upper layer z'. The value of z' becomes very small over the crests of large-amplitude internal waves near the sea surface.

In shallow internal waves, the motion over the crest is strong. The water formerly passing over the trough becomes funneled through this constriction. If the crests are very near the surface, the speed of flow is increased. The funneling of water over the crest and the reduced speed just beyond are responsible for the turbulence and ripples at the surface.

When an internal wave thermal boundary is near the sea floor, a similar action exists. The maximum turbulence will be under the trough, but the maximum speed will be in the opposite direction of wave propagation. In shallow water, the internal wave direction is shoreward; thus, the maximum speed near the bottom will be offshore. The funneling of water through the constriction created by the trough and bottom, always in an offshore direction, is undoubtedly a contributor to the offshore movement of sediment. Even in deep water, internal waves near the bottom can move sediment and form ripple marks (La Fond, 1961).

Relation to Slicks. Sea surface slicks, which are often visible evidence of internal wave flow, are seen as streaks or patches of relatively calm surface water surrounded by rippled water. The absence of wavelets in a slick gives it a glassy appearance in contrast to the adjacent rippled water.

From most angles, a slick in daytime appears brighter than its peripheral area because a smooth surface reflects the sky more than a rougher one. At night, when ambient light may exist, slicks contrast with, and appear darker than, adjacent, rippled water because their unruffled surface is less susceptible to surrounding reflection.

Slicks frequently assume the shape of broad, web-like connecting bands, and they occasionally appear as isolated patches. In the shallow ocean

CONVERGENCE UNDER SLICK   INTERNAL WAVE CREST UNDER MAXIMUM RIPPLES

Fig. 7. The appearance of sea surface slicks and rough sea surface related to internal waves.

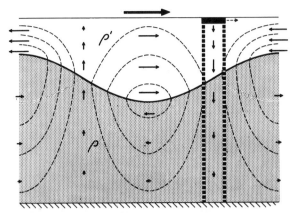

Fig. 8. Circulations associated with progressive internal waves and their relationship to sea surface slicks (η dashes are streamlines).

over a continental shelf, slicks are often contoured as long bands, more or less parallel with the coast (Fig. 7).

The occurrence of visible slicks is contingent upon wind, lighting, sufficient organic matter on the water, and the nature of internal waves. The concentration of surface film depends on the inter-relation of an internal wave height, depth and length. The average depth of an internal wave and its relation to water depth also influence the type of circulation, and thus have a bearing on the formation of slicks.

Surface slicks are sometimes observed over the trough of the depression in the thermocline. However, the slick is nearly always found on the descending thermocline, somewhere between the crest and the following trough. Although the maximum expansion of the surface layer is over the trough, the slicks are normally found at the active surface convergence zone. The significant motion is a surface convergence that creates slicks over the

trailing slope of the internal wave. This is the result of water circulation created by internal waves (Fig. 8). As the internal waves propagate shoreward, the slicks retain the same relative position to the wave, i.e., just behind the crest. Thus, by noting the position and motion of sea surface slicks, the position of internal waves and their motion can be ascertained.

Relation to Topography. Variations in the depth of water over which an internal wave propagates may modify the speed, shape and direcuon of the wave. In addition, the flow of water over an irregular bottom may create turbulence and internal waves. Features of the sea floor topography, including bottom slope, shoals, seamounts, ridges, islands, and land projections into the current, modify the water flow and thus also the thermal structure. The simplest example is where coastal wind or tidal-induced currents impinge upon the open shore. Onshore surface flow lowers the thermocline, which usually oscillates in a diurnal

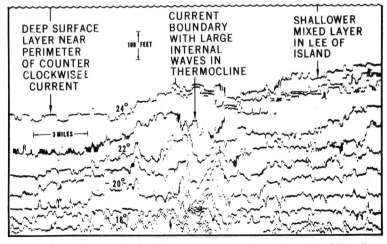

Fig. 9. Internal waves developed by current flow at the southern tip of Hawaii.

cycle; the tide influence on thermocline oscillation is generally semidiurnal. The wavelengths of internal waves decrease as they progress up a slope. Another example is flow over a shoal or seamount, which deflects the thermocline upward. The wavelengths of the internal waves become shorter and large-scale turbulence is created (Fig. 9). Flow over a ridge also causes a rise in thermocline downstream and a deflection to the right.

Islands increase the depth of the thermocline on the up-current side; turbulence develops along the sides of the island and in the island wake. The different direction of the orbital motion creates irregular temperature structures. Land projections into the current deflect the shallower, nearshore water into the main stream and cause turbulence near the point of land. In the lee of the point of land on the west coast of the United States and Mexico, there is a counterclockwise current with colder upwelled water. Thus the topographic features which cause vertical displacement in the thermocline create or modify internal waves.

EUGENE C. LA FOND

References

Eckart, C., 1960, "Hydrodynamics of Oceans and Atmospheres," London, Pergamon Press, 290pp.

Krauss, W., 1965, "The Internal Tides Off Southern California as Obtained from the USNEL Thermistor Chain Records," USNEL Report No. 1290.

Kullenberg, B., 1935, "Internal waves in the Kattegat," *Svenska Hydrogaf. Biol. Komm. Skrifter, Ny Ser. Hydrog.*, **12**.

LaFond, E. C., 1959, "Sea surface features and internal waves in the sea," *Indian J. Met. Geophys.*, **10**, 415–419.

LaFond, E. C., 1961, "Internal Wave Motion and its Geological Significance," pp. 61–77, Mahadevan Volume, A Collection of Geological Papers, Osmania University Press, Hyderabad.

LaFond, E. C., and Cox, C. S., 1962, "Internal Waves," in "The Sea," Vol. 1, pp. 731–763, New York, Interscience Publishers.

Lamb, H., 1945, "Hydrodynamics," sixth ed., New York, Dover.

Lee, O. S., 1965, "Summary of Published Information on Internal Waves in the Sea with Notes on Application to Naval Operations," USNEL Report No. 1289.

Lee, O. S., and Batzler, W. F., 1964, "Internal Waves and Sound Pressure Level Changes," in Naval Oceanographic Office, 1st U.S. Navy Symposium on Military Oceanography, pp. 47–67, 17–18 June 1964.

Lee, W. H. K., and Cox, C. S., 1966, "Time variation of ocean temperatures and its relation to internal waves and oceanic heat flow measurements," *Jour. Geophys. Res.*, **71**, 2102–2112.

Pochapsky, T. E., 1963, "Measurements of small-scale oceanic motions with neutrally buoyant floats," *Tellus*, **4**, 352–362.

Summers, H., and Emery, K. O., 1963, "Internal waves of tidal period off southern California," *J. Geophys. Res.*, **68**, No. 3, 827–839.

IRISH SEA AND CELTIC SEA

Definitions*

The Irish Sea is taken to extend from the Mull of Galloway to a line from St. David's Head to Carnsore Point. The Celtic Sea is the name given by oceanographers to the body of water over the continental shelf between the south coast of Ireland and Brittany. It is arbitrarily divided from the English Channel by a line from Land's End to Ushant, and Southern Celtic Sea is synonymous with the Western Approaches to the Channel. Lundy Island marks an arbitrary limit between the Celtic Sea and the Bristol Channel.

Relief

A series of depressions forms an axial trough extending for the whole length of the Irish Sea from north to south, showing a rough parallelism to the Irish coast and lying 20–30 miles from it. The trough contains a number of closed basins. The northernmost and deepest lies in the North Channel off the Rhinns of Galloway. Its greatest depth is 149 fathoms, at least 70 fathoms below its sill. The next greatest depths are about 80 fathoms between the Isle of Man and County Down and between Anglesey and Dublin. In general, the basins have not been surveyed on large enough scales for their contours to be known in detail. Some of them, at least, appear to have steep sides.

Celtic Sea: The axial depression of the Irish Sea continues through St. George's Channel and can be traced southward to about 51°N. The main feature of Celtic Sea relief is a number of ridges lying NE-SW. They are discussed below under the heading of Superficial Sediments.

Geology

The Irish Sea is flanked entirely by Paleozoic rocks except on the northern part of its eastern shore where Triassic rocks underlie much of the coast. There is no evidence from samples of the rocks beneath the Irish Sea. Geophysical evidence suggests that much of the Irish Sea consists of sedimentary basins of more recent date than the surrounding lands. Gravity studies by Bott (1963) indicate that the northern half of the sea is underlain by basins up to 8000 feet deep containing, probably, Carboniferous to Triassic rocks. The Isle of Man is interpreted as a horst-like uplift between these basins. To the east, the Trias is doubtless continuous with the outcrops on land. In the southern part of the sea, seismic work by Hill (1956) showed that high-velocity rocks, interpreted as Paleozoic, lay about 5900 feet below sea level in the center of Cardigan Bay and about 3300 feet below sea level further west at 52° 32′N, 5° 18′W, overlain by medium-velocity rocks interpreted as Triassic. Low-velocity rocks are present up to a maximum proved thickness of 1100

* D. T. Donovan.

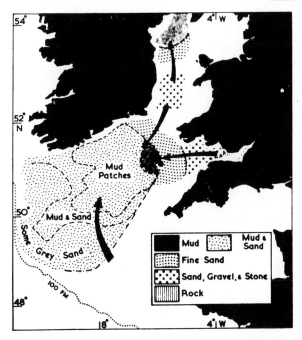

Fig. 1. Map of superficial sediments in the Irish Sea and Celtic Sea, after Stride (1963, Fig. 9). The arrows show the directions of decrease in grain size [*Quart. J. Geol. Soc. London*, **119**, 187 (1963), Fig. 9, left-hand half only].

feet. They have not been identified. It is likely from this evidence that the Irish Sea is underlain by Triassic basins of the same order of size and depth as those east and west of the Pennines (Kent, 1949).

The Bristol Channel, flanked largely by Upper Paleozoic rocks, is a syncline preserving New Red Sandstone and Jurassic up to and including Kimmeridge Clay (Lloyd, 1963). The axis of the syncline lies WNW–ESE.

The northern part of the Celtic Sea is little known. A single sample of Chalk was published by Day (1958) at 50° 20′N, 7° 09′W. Analogy with neighboring seas suggests that much of the Celtic Sea is underlain by Mesozoic and/or Tertiary rocks.

Superficial Sediments

The available information has been summarized by Stride (1963) whose map is reproduced here (Fig. 1). The coarsest deposits in the Irish Sea lie between 52° and 53°N where "stones" are recorded in numerous places, as well as sand, mud and shells. To the north and south lie areas in which fine sand is dominant, although coarser material is also recorded, and further north and south still, in areas west and southwest of the Isle of Man and south of Carnsore Point around 51° 10′N, 6° 15′W, mud only is recorded. Stride infers that sediment transport is occurring from the area of coarse

sediment toward the areas of finer-grained sediment, and this direction of transport is the same as that suggested by the orientation of sand waves. Presumably finer-grained sediment is being removed from the central area of the Irish Sea leaving sand and stones, the latter possibly derived from glacial till. Acoustic reflection work shows that bedrock in some parts of the Irish Sea floor is covered by unconsolidated sediments up to a thickness of 100 feet or more, and it is generally assumed that little or no rock is exposed. This assumption has not been tested. A study of Holocene sedimentation in the western part of the Irish Sea has recently been made by Belderson (1964).

Sediments on the floor of the Celtic Sea are known chiefly from the careful notations on British Admiralty charts 1123 and 1598. There is the same wide range of grain size which characterizes other British seas. First, there are areas of mud and muddy sand which Stride (1963) interprets as the sites of present-day sedimentation. The rest of the floor is mainly fine sand, though there are scattered records of "stones" and "gravel." A number of ridges, trending between SW–NE and WSW–ENE, occur: Jones Bank, Labadie Bank, Great Sole Bank, Cockburn Bank and others unnamed. They are up to 40 miles long and 30 fathoms high, their summits lying 34–60 fathoms below the sea surface. Their internal structure has been found by seismic profiler to be stratified, the

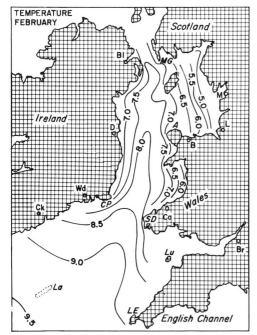

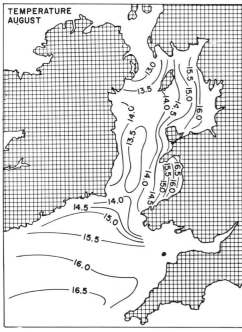

Fig. 2. Surface temperatures in February and August [Ministry of Agriculture, Fisheries and Food (U.K.), *Fishery Investigations,* **1955**, Series II, **18**, No. 8, pp. 11 and 13, Figs. 3(b) and 3(d)].

Mull of Galloway (MG), St. David's Head (SD), Carnsore Point (CP), Land's End (LE), Lundy Island (LU), Bristol (Br), Belfast (Bl), Anglesey (A), Dublin (D), Cardigan (Ca), Labadie Bank (La), English Channel, Morecambe (M), Liverpool (L), Avonmouth (AV), Cork (Ck), Waterford (Wd), Menai Bridge (MB) (N.B.: B for Bangor is slightly misplaced.)

beds being parallel to the southern slopes of the banks (Stride, 1963a). Stride believes that these ridges are sand banks, but that they lie too deep to be forming at present. Accordingly, he supposes that they were formed during low sea levels of Pleistocene or early Recent time.

Temperature*

The surface temperature in the Irish and Northern Celtic Sea in February and August is shown in Fig. 2. For the Irish Sea, vertical mixing due to the strong tides maintains the water column homogeneous right through the year so that for most of the area, the August surface temperatures represent the whole water column. Along the center line of the Celtic Sea, the annual range of temperature is about 6°C, but this becomes greater toward the coasts; near northwestern England, the range reaches 12°C. Only northwest of the Isle of Man does the surface water in summer become warmer than the bottom water, and even there no thermocline is developed comparable with that in the Celtic Sea and western English Channel. In the Northern Celtic Sea in summer, a marked thermocline develops, the bottom waters warming up only slightly. There the warmest bottom water is formed after the autumn overturn. During this century, at least until 1950, widespread warming-up of the sea has occurred (Matthews, 1914; Bowden, 1953, 1955; Cooper, 1961b).

Salinity

In the winter months, salinity is practically uniform from surface to bottom over the whole area and increases from under 32‰ off northwest England to 34.8‰ at the boundary between the Irish and Celtic Seas and to at least 35.3‰ in the Central Celtic Sea (Fig. 3). The annual cycle in the Southern Celtic Sea and the gradation of properties at the break of slope have not been studied. Such evidence as we have suggests that a rather sharp gradation in all properties may occur at the break of slope where Biscayan surface water may have salinities as high as 35.7–36.0‰. In the Celtic Sea when the summer thermocline forms, water of lower salinity overlies more saline water. In August at the boundary line between the Celtic and Irish Seas, a salinity maximum develops due to a northward extension of the Northeastern Celtic Sea eddy associated with a change in the distribution of mass due to warming of the coastal water off southwest Wales.

Tides

The vertical range of the tide is greater on the eastern than on the western side of the Irish Sea. The smallest ranges, less than 4 feet, occur on the southeastern and northeastern coasts of Ireland, whereas the largest ranges, averaging about 20

* L. H. N. Cooper.

feet, occur in Morecambe and Liverpool Bays (Bowden, 1953, 1955). In the Bristol Channel, due to its shape, the range increases eastward to Avonmouth where there is a large difference between the range at equinoctial springs (over 40 feet) and at neaps (21 feet). In the northern Celtic Sea between the longitudes of Cork and Waterford, tides are weak (0.6–0.8 knot at springs), facilitating deposition of mud. Wind-driven currents may overpower the tidal stream, but to the south, tidal currents are much stronger (1.4 knots at springs) and rotary (British Admiralty charts 1123 and 1598).

Non-tidal Currents

Knowledge of these is fragmentary. In the Celtic Sea away from the coasts, the currents or drifts are wind driven and are as variable as the wind (Cooper 1961a), but since there are prevailing winds, there are also prevailing drift currents. The prevailing and strongest winds are from west and southwest so that, allowing for the effect of the earth's rotation on the direction of wind-induced currents, Atlantic water must often enter the Celtic Sea from northwest and west to escape as a north-bound transport through the Irish Sea or as an eastbound transport through the English Channel and Straits of Dover. These outlets are narrow and cannot pass all the water pressed toward them from the Celtic Sea; eddies may form and the cyclonic eddy between Cornwall and southeastern Ireland seems reasonably persistent. This eddy is a statistical affair with marked variation in chemical properties in its different parts. The evidence based on salinity (Bowden, 1955) for the north-flowing transport through the Irish Sea · receives strong support from studies of the distribution of plankton (Williamson, 1956). The main current flows east of the Isle of Man, more easterly in spring than in autumn, and seems to drive a clockwise eddy so that along the coast of North Wales, including northern Anglesey, water tends to move westward.

Around promonotories such as Ushant, Land's End (Cooper, 1960), St. David's Head, and Carnsore Point, there is a strong tendency for narrow currents to flow with the land on the right. They are favored by neap tides in warm or wet weather and may be suppressed by dry or cold weather or by spring tides. They may have considerable biological and climatological importance. As has been stated, it seems that in summer, new water is recruited to the Irish Sea not as in winter, directly from the Celtic Sea, but around St. David's Head from the coastal water of South Wales. Such currents around headlands may enable much water to be exchanged between embayments such as the Bay of Biscay, English Channel, Bristol Channel and Irish Sea, against the main pattern of drift resulting from the prevailing winds.

Chemistry

Pioneer work of high quality for the time (Moore, Prideaux and Herdman, 1914) on the hydrogen ion concentration near the Isle of Man first established

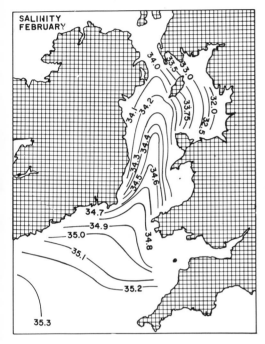

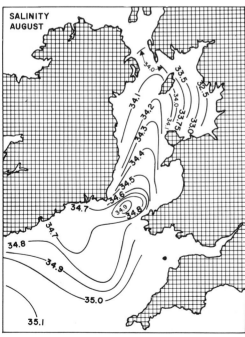

Fig. 3. Surface salinities in February and August [*Fishery Investigations,* **1955**, Series II, **18**, No. 8, pp. 31 and 33, Figs. 8(b) and 8(d)].

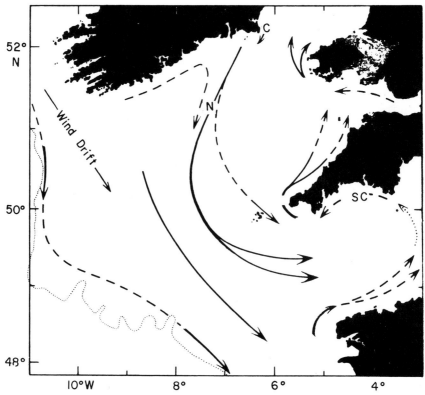

Fig. 4. Drift or current pattern of Celtic Sea when prevailing winds blow. Does not apply in June–September (*J. Marine Biol. Assoc.,* **41**, 266, Fig. 18).

the now well-known seasonal rhythm in temperate latitudes due to removal by plants in spring of carbon dioxide from the water. The cycles of phosphorus and oxygen have been established by Slinn (1957, 1958) as very similar to those in the English Channel except that the physical conditions tend to maintain vertical homogenity throughout the summer. The winter maximum for phosphate (0.7 μg-atom/liter) was about 0.2 μg-atom/liter higher than in the western English Channel in the same year. In the Celtic Sea, no seasonal studies have been made (Cooper, 1961).

Biology

Many biological publications of geological interest on the waters around the Isle of Man have appeared from the Port Erin Laboratory (University of Liverpool) and more recently from that at Menai Bridge (University College of North Wales, Bangor) but are too diverse to summarize.

D. T. DONOVAN

L. H. N. COOPER

References

Belderson, R. H., 1964, "Holocene sedimentation in the western half of the Irish Sea," *Marine Geol.,* **2**, 147–163.

Bott, M. H. P., 1963/4, "Gravity measurements in the north-eastern part of the Irish Sea," *Quart. J. Geol. Soc. Lond.,* **120**, 369–396.

Bowden, K. F., 1953, "Physical Oceanography of the Irish Sea. A Scientific Survey of Merseyside," pp. 69–80, Publ. for Brit. Assoc., Univ. Liverpool Press.

Bowden, K. F., 1955, "Physical oceanography of the Irish Sea," *Fish. Inv. (Lond.),* **18**, No. 8, 1–67.

Cooper, L. H. N., 1960, "Exchanges of water between the English and Bristol Channel around Land's End," *J. Marine Biol. Assoc. U.K.,* **39**, 637–65.

Cooper, L. H. N., 1961a, "The oceanography of the Celtic Sea. I. Wind drift," *J. Marine Biol. Assoc. U.K.,* **40**, 223–233.

Cooper, L. H. N., 1961b, "The oceanography of the Celtic Sea. II. In the spring of 1950," *J. Marine Biol. Assoc. U.K.,* **40**, 235–270.

Day, A. A., 1958, "The pre-Tertiary geology of the Western Approaches to the English Channel," *Geol. Mag.,* **95**, 137–148.

Hill, M. N., 1956, In discussion, *Quart. J. Geol. Soc. London,* **111**, 393.

Kent, P. E., 1949, "A structure contour map of the surface of the buried pre-Permian rocks of England and Wales," *Proc. Geologists Assoc. Engl.,* **60**, 87–104.

Lloyd, A. J., 1963, "Upper Jurassic rocks beneath the Bristol Channel," *Nature, London,* **198**, 375–376.

Matthews, D. J., 1914, "The salinity and temperature of the Irish Channel and the waters South of Ireland," *Sci. Invest. Fish. Br. Ire.,* **1913**, IV, 1–26.

Mitchell, G. F., 1963, "Morainic ridges on the floor of the Irish Sea," *Irish Geogr.*, **4**(5), 335–44.

Moore, B., Prideaux, E. B. R., and Herdman, G. A., 1914, "Studies of certain photo-synthetic phenomena in sea water," *Lancs. Sea-fish. Lab. Reports*, **23**, 171.

Slinn, D. J., 1957, 1958, "Phosphate and oxygen in sea water off Port Erin during the years 1955, 1956 and 1957," *Rept. Marine Biol. Sta. Port Erin*, **69**, 29–33; **70**, 27–30.

Stride, A. H., 1963, "Current-swept sea floors near the southern half of Great Britain," *Quart. J. Geol. Soc. London*, **119**, 175–199.

Stride, A. H., 1963a, "North-east trending ridges of the Celtic Sea," *Proc. Ussher Soc.*, Part 2, 62–63.

Williamson, D. I., 1956, "The plankton in the Irish Sea 1951 and 1952," *Bull. Marine Ecol.*, **4**, No. 31, 87–114.

IRMINGER CURRENT

The Danish Admiral C. Irminger started hydrographic studies of the Atlantic waters east of the southern Greenland in 1854. He described how at the surface two branches of warm Atlantic water flowed westward and northward, respectively south and west of Iceland. In 1884 E. V. Nordenskiöld named this current the *Irminger Current*. The sea south of the Greenland–Iceland Ridge and north of about 60°N is also called the Irminger Sea (q.v.).

Since then many oceanographic studies of the current were made, mainly by Scandinavian and German oceanographers, because the area is one of the important fishing grounds of the northern North Atlantic. M. Knudsen found from the data of the *Ingolf* cruise in 1895–96 that the Irminger Current separates into two branches west of Iceland: one branch flows around the northwest coast and eastward north of Iceland and the other branch meets the cold East Greenland Current and flows southward. T. Braarud and Norwegian oceanographers distinguished three water masses in the Denmark Straits from the data of the *Øst* cruise in 1929. The Danish ship *Dana* made three summer cruises in 1931–33. A. Defant, G. Böhnecke and other German oceanographers studied the deep water mass and the polar front of the Irminger Sea based on the data of the *Meteor* cruises in 1929–35. In recent years, the *Dana* has made a zonal section on 62°N between the Faeroes and East Greenland in summer almost every year since 1947. G. Dietrich made extensive studies on the hydrography of the Irminger Sea from the data of the *Anton Dohrn* cruise in 1955. In 1958, the *Gauss* and the *Anton Dohrn* made winter and summer cruises of the area.

The water of the Irminger Sea consists of four prototype water masses and their mixture. (1) Northeast Atlantic Water (NA) is warm (9.5°C), saline (35.35‰) and comes from the Gulf Stream System. (2) Irminger Sea Water (IS) is cold (4.0°C), moderately saline (34.9‰) and is formed in the Irminger Sea by convection in winter. (3) Arctic Deep Water (AD) is very cold (−0.6°C), moderately saline (34.90‰) and is formed in the European North Sea during the winter. (4) East Greenland Water (EG) is very cold (−1.8°C) and is formed below the pack ice of east Greenland coast. The salinity is less than 34.50‰ and has a wide range due to melting ice.

In the mid-depths below 100 m, the IS Water spreads northeastward from east off Cape Farewell between 40–30°W and splits into two branches west of the Icelandic Shelf. The northern branch forms a sharp front with the EG Water which is present on the East Greenland Shelf. The southern branch reaches 30°W. The area south of Iceland between 30 and 20°W is a mixing zone of the IS water and the NA water which is present extensively south of Iceland. The AD water outflows southward off northwest and east of Iceland below 400 m along the deep trench and over Faeroe Ridge, respectively.

The Irminger Current flows northward with speed of 5–10 cm/sec at the surface east of Cape Farewell between 38 and 20°W as an extention of the North Atlantic Current, turns northeastward and eastward and splits into two branches at about 62°N. The one branch flows northward between 30 and 28°W to the latitude of 65°N, northwest of Iceland, encounters the East Greenland Current and flows to the southwest. The other branch flows eastward south of Iceland with speeds of 5–15 cm/sec and meets the North Atlantic Current again. Then a part of this branch flows westward south of Iceland. Below the depth of 800 m (zero-layer), the current is less than 5 cm/sec and southerly. The volume transport (in million cubic meters per second) on the 60°N latitude is 2.8 and southward between Cape Farewell and 38°W, but it is 5.4 and northward between 38°W and the mid-Atlantic Ridge (28°W) above the zero-layer. The transport below the zero-layer is southward all through this section with a value of 9.4×10^6 m^3/sec.

Takashi Ichiye

References

Dietrich, G., 1957, "Schichtung und Zirkulation der Irminger-See im Juni 1955," *Berichte Dtsch. Wiss. Komm. Meeresforsch.*, **14**(4), 255–312.

Sverdrup, H. V., Johnson, M. W., and Fleming, R. H., 1945, "The Oceans," Englewood Cliffs, N.J., Prentice-Hall, 1086pp.

IRMINGER SEA

According to Bruns (1958, p. 208), the Irminger Sea (named after the Danish admiral who explored it in 1854) may be defined loosely as situated east of Greenland and extending into "part of the Atlantic Ocean." In the southwest, it is bordered by the Labrador Sea which is defined by a line from Cape Farewell to Cape St. Francis (eastern tip of Newfoundland). In the northeast, it borders on the Greenland Sea in Denmark Strait defined by a line from Cape Nansen in east Greenland to the north-eastern tip of Iceland. The International Hydrographic Bureau does not recognize the Irminger Sea as an autonomous water body, but on grounds of physical and chemical oceanography it is a useful designation, being particularly characterized by the *Irminger Current* (q.v.), which diverges from the North Atlantic Drift to the south of Iceland (Defant, 1936); it swings west in latitudes 60–62° to set southwesterly into the Labrador Sea; it is limited in the south by an ill-defined sinuous convergence that extends in a line from southwest of Iceland to northeast of Newfoundland. A well-defined sinuous convergence divides the Irminger Current from the East Greenland Current in the north.

Bathymetry

The deepest part of the Irminger Sea corresponds to part of the Labrador Basin, which is an almost closed depression defined by the 4000-m contour, situated south of Greenland and east of Labrador (Smith *et al.,* 1937); it extends northwest into the Labrador Sea area and northeast into a broad trough between southern Greenland and Iceland with depths of 2000–3000 m, disclosed mainly by surveys of the U.S. Coast Guard vessels *Marion* and *General Greene* between 1928 and 1935 (see Smith *et al.,* 1937). Marking its maximal depths, Heezen has postulated a complex system of graded submarine channels to form the "headwaters" of the "mid-ocean canyon" system that eventually carries turbidity deposits along the bottom to the Sohm Abyssal Plain (Heezen, Tharp and Ewing, 1959). However, surveys by the German vessel *Gauss* in 1957 found that in the Irminger Sea no such channels could be defined (Dietrich, 1959), and it would seem likely that the currents that cut the channel east of Newfoundland must be discontinuous and only operative at specific (melting) stages of the Quaternary.

The eastern border of the Labrador Basin is the Reykjanes Ridge, a sector of the Mid-Atlantic Ridge (see *Mid-Ocean Ridge*) which extends southwest from Iceland to about 53°N, 35°W where it swings sharply to the southeast for about 1000 km, in the region of the *Telegraph Plateau,* and then turns south again toward the Azores, a displacement probably corresponding to a series of major strike-slip or transform faults such as occur in the equatorial latitudes.

Sediments

Most of the southern part of the Irminger Sea is marked by globigerina ooze which reaches to the latitude of Cape Farewell. In the deeper parts of the Labrador Sea, it is largely masked by turbidites which are brought down by strong turbidity-operated bottom currents from the southern continental slopes of Greenland. Dredgings show extensive areas of glacial marine till in the north, and ice-rafted glacial boulders are found everywhere. Volcanic ash, palagonite and lava are found toward Iceland and the Mid-Atlantic Ridge. The rift commonly found at the crest of the latter is absent between 53°N and Iceland (Dietrich, 1959) in spite of some forty crossings by the *Gauss,* equipped with a high-precision depth recorder; possibly it is completely obscured by volcanic deposits southwest of Iceland.

Oceanography

The Irminger Sea essentially coincides with the effective area of the *Irminger Current* (q.v.) and related water masses. The oceanography will therefore be referred to under that entry (see also *East Greenland Current*).

Tides

Semidiurnal tide oscillations dominate the whole area with two almost similar tides daily. There is an important amphidromic node near 50°N, 35°W, which sets up two tidal "waves," diverging from about Angmagsalik and, after three hours, reaching Denmark Strait in the northeast and Cape Farewell in the southwest. Mean spring tidal range at the former is 97 cm and at the latter 251 cm. Wind surge brings up the recorded figures to 3–3.5 m.

Wave Action

The mean latitude of the passage of the powerful westerly storm tracks varies considerably from year to year, sometimes north and sometimes south of Cape Farewell (60°N); about the year 1000 A.D., when southern Greenland was much warmer than today and represented a flourishing Norse colony, from which Lief Ericson and others made the voyage across the Irminger Sea to Newfoundland, the main westerly storm tracks ran much farther north (65–70°N). Accordingly the annual intensity and character of wave action are highly variable. Nearshore, particularly in autumn, powerful katabatic winds flow down from the 3000-m ice plateau to set up sudden land wind squalls (Petersen; see Bruns, 1958).

Wave characteristics in the open sea have been recorded from Weather Ship "A" (at 62°N, 33°W), half-way between Iceland and Cape Farewell, observing a wind force of 10, a mean wave height of 9.1 m and wavelength of 146 m. Maximum observed wave height was 14.0 m (Roll; see Bruns, 1958).

RHODES W. FAIRBRIDGE

References

Bruns, E., 1958, "Ozeanologie," Berlin, Deutscher Verlag d. Wiss., 2 vols.

Defant, A., 1936, "Bericht über die ozeanogr. Untersuchungen des "Meteors" in der Dänemarkstrasse und in der Irmingersee," III, *Ber. S.B. Preuss. Akad. Wiss. Phys.-Math. Kl., Berlin,* 232.

Dietrich, G., 1959, "Small-scale topographic Features on the Bottom of the Northern Atlantic Ocean," *Int. Oceanogr. Congr., A.A.A.S. Preprints,* 17–18, (in full in *Deut. Hydrograph. Z.,* 1959).

Smith, E. H., Soule, F. M., and Mosby, O., 1937, "*Marion* and *General Greene* expeditions to Davis Strait and Labrador Sea under the direction of the U.S. Coast Guard, 1928–1931–1933–1934–1935," *U.S. Coast Guard Bull.,* **19**, 1–259.

ISENTROPIC ANALYSIS—*See* ENTROPY, ISENTROPIC FLOW—Vol. II

"ISO" TERMS—*See* Vol. II

ISOTOPE FRACTIONATION IN THE OCEAN

The element carbon has two stable isotopes, C^{12} and C^{13}. They differ only in the number of neutrons in their nucleus and hence in their atomic weights. The reaction

$$C^{12}O_2 + H_2C^{13}O_3 = C^{13}O_2 + H_2C^{12}O_3$$

has an equilibrium constant, K, such that

$$K = \frac{[C^{13}O_2][H_2C^{12}O_3]}{[C^{12}O_2][H_2C^{13}O_3]}$$

If $K = 1$, there is no isotope fractionation in this reaction. But if K is not 1, there will be an uneven distribution of isotopes with C^{13} predominating in CO_2 if K is > 1 and in H_2CO_3 if $K < 1$. The equilibrium constant depends on the free energies of the species involved and on temperature:

$$\ln K = -\Delta F^\circ / RT$$

where ΔF° is the Gibbs free energy change for the reaction, R is the gas constant, and T is the absolute temperature.

The fundamental frequencies of vibration of atoms are mass-dependent; therefore, isotopes of the same element will have slightly different free energies, and thus the equilibrium constant for an isotope exchange reaction will not be exactly unity.

The kinetics of a reaction also control isotope fractionation. A molecule of a lighter gas moves faster than a molecule of a heavier one in a ratio inversely proportional to the ratio of the square roots of the masses involved. Therefore, a light molecule has a higher probability of striking a surface more often than does a heavier one. To evaluate the relative importance of equilibrium and kinetic fractionation, the rate-controlling processes must be well understood. Biological influences often make the system even more complex as organisms are notorious fractionators.

The earliest work in the chemical differences of isotopes was done in 1939 by H. C. Urey; however, it was not until 1950, when A. O. Nier

developed a very precise mass spectrometer, that the differences in nature could be easily observed.

Because of the difficulty of measuring absolute isotopic abundances, isotope ratios relative to a standard are usually reported. This practice also allows interlaboratory calibration as the standards are widely circulated. Most measurements are reported as parts-per-thousand difference from the standard in the form:

$$\delta C^{13} = \frac{(C^{13}/C^{12})_{sample} - (C^{13}/C^{12})_{standard}}{(C^{13}/C^{12})_{standard}} \times 1000$$

Thus a positive value of δ indicates that the sample is enriched in the heavier isotope.

The stable isotopes of carbon have been selected in this discussion as an example; any other isotope pair might have been used, including radioactive ones. Of course, most of the differences in nature due to fractionation are observed in the lighter elements as the percentage difference between species is much greater here.

A major concern of marine geology is the determination of the environment of deposition of deep-sea sediments. In 1952, Craig recognized a difference in carbon isotope composition in organisms from marine and fresh-water environments. Marine forms tend to be enriched in carbon 13 relative to those from fresh water. Thus, from a study of the carbon isotope composition, it is possible to generalize as to the source of certain sediments. For example, turbidites, sediments thought to originate near land, have a lighter isotopic composition than do strictly marine deposits. This difference in carbon isotopes is also used to trace shore-line advance and retreat.

Oxygen isotopes are also used to study the environment of deposition of sediments. Since fractionation is temperature dependent, planktonic Foraminifera reflect in their oxygen isotope composition the temperature of the environment in which they grew. An analysis of the O^{18}/O^{16} ratio of these Foraminifera through cores gives a record of the climatic history of the surface water overlying the sediment. Emiliani has constructed Pleistocene temperature scales using this method. The reworking of the sediment subsequent to deposition and the possible migration of the Foraminifera within the water column during their lifetimes may complicate or invalidate this method in certain cases.

A major application of isotopic fractionation to oceanography involves a study of the hydrogen and oxygen isotopes in the water molecule itself. The vapor pressure of water molecules composed of $H^1O^{16}O^{16}$ is greater than if one of the heavier isotopes (H^2, O^{17}, or O^{18}) were substituted into the molecule. Therefore, in a mixture of $H^1O^{16}O^{16}$, $H^2O^{16}O^{16}$, and $H^1O^{18}O^{16}$, the vapor tends to become enriched in $H^1O^{16}O^{16}$, with the heavier molecules remaining in the liquid phase. This is analogous to a fractional distillation of the lighter species. Since fractionation is inversely proportional to temperature, there will be a smaller difference in isotopic composition in water evaporating in warmer regions, e.g., from the equator, than from colder areas, e.g., polar seas. In the same manner, the lighter molecules will tend to remain in the vapor phase while the heavier ones condense and fall as precipitation. Thus, water vapor from the equator will first produce a rain that is quite heavy in isotopic composition, but as the remaining vapor moves to higher latitudes, the condensate becomes lighter. Since there is greater fractionation in water evaporating from polar seas, there is little replenishment of heavier isotopes here. The net effect produces precipitation of very light isotopic composition in the polar regions relative to equatorial areas. This difference is strongly reflected in surface ocean water.

Once an isotopic difference is established in the surface ocean, mixing processes between water masses may be studied in detail. Craig has constructed δO^{18}-salinity diagrams (in contrast to the usual temperature-salinity plots) to determine differences between water masses and to give clues to their origin. His conclusion from the oxygen isotope data is that the bulk of all deep water in the ocean is formed from North Atlantic deep water through mixing processes in the Antarctic region. Pacific bottom water is composed of about 80% North Atlantic deep water and 20% Antarctic surface water. Redfield, using hydrogen isotope data, arrived at similar conclusions.

WILLARD MOORE

References

Craig, Harmon, 1953, "The geochemistry of the stable carbon isotopes," *Geochim. Cosmochim. Acta*, **3**, 53.

Craig, Harmon, 1961, "Isotopic variations in meteoric waters," *Science*, **133**, 1702.

Emiliani, Cesare, 1955, "Pleistocene temperatures," *J. Geol.*, **63**, 538.

Epstein, Samuel, 1959, "The Variations of the O^{18}/O^{16} Ratio in Nature and Some Geologic Implications," in (Abelson, Philip, editor) "Researches in Geochemistry," p. 217, New York, John Wiley & Sons.

Urey, Harold C., 1947, "The thermodynamic properties of isotopic substances," *J. Chem. Soc.*, **1947**, 562.

J

JAPAN SEA

General Features

The Japan Sea is a marginal sea of the western Pacific Ocean bounded by Japan, U.S.S.R. and Korea. The water of the Japan Sea is in communication with the East China and Yellow Seas to the south through the Korea Strait, with the main Pacific Ocean to the east through the Tsugaru Strait, and with the Sea of Okhotsk to the north through Soya and Tartar Straits. It has an area 1.008×10^6 km^2 and an average depth 1361 m. [Zenkevitch (1963) gives these data respectively, as 978,000 km^2 and 1752 m; he gives the volume as 1,713,000 km^3.] The International Hydrographic Bureau (*Sp. Paper* 23, 1953), puts the northern limit at 51° 45′N (Cape Tuik to Cape Sushcheva). The southern limit runs from Kyushu to Goto-Retto to Saisyu To (Quelpart I.) and north to Korea.

The Japan Sea has an approximately elliptical shape with its major axis directed from southwest to northeast. There are several islands or island groups within the area, but only near the margins; they are, namely, the Iki and Tsushima at the middle of Korea Strait between Korea and Kyushu, Ullung Island, and Takeshima off the east coast of Korea, Oki and Sado Islands off the coast of western Honshu, and Tobishima close to the northern Honshu.

Bottom Configuration (Bathymetry)

The straits connecting the Japan Sea to the marginal seas and the main Pacific Ocean all have very shallow sill depths, only the Korea Strait having depths exceeding 100 m. The bottom of the Japan Sea may be divided approximately into two different parts by the 40°N parallel. The northern half is comparatively flat and shelves slowly and smoothly on all sides, the deepest spot, 4049 m, being located at 43° 00′N, 137° 39′E. The bathymetry of the southern half is rather complicated. In addition to the shallow regions surrounding the Iki, Tsushima, Oki, Takeshima and Ullung Islands, there are two conspicuous isolated banks separated by deep troughs in between. They are the Yamato Bank discovered in 1924 at approximately 39°N and 135°E, and the Syunpu Bank (discovered in 1930, commonly called North

Yamato Bank) to the northwest of the former (at approximately 40°N, 134°E). The shallowest parts over these banks are 285 and 435 m, respectively. Between the Yamato Bank and Honshu, is found a trench with depth exceeding 3000 m.

Water Masses and Variation of Temperature and Salinity

The Japan Sea is divided, following the origin of the water masses, into a warmer sector on the Japanese side and a colder sector on the Korean and Siberian side. The boundary is marked by the "polar front," approximately running along the parallels of 38°–40°N or at nearly the same latitudes of the polar front in the Pacific Ocean east of Japan.

The water of the Japan Sea can be classified into the Surface Water, Middle Water and Deep Water. The Surface Water is seen from the surface to about 25 m and separated in summer by a distinct thermocline from the water below. In the warmer sector of the Japan Sea, there is a mixture of the Surface Water of high temperature and low salinity originating in the East China Sea and the coastal water from the Japanese Islands. On the other hand, the Surface Water of the colder sector is formed there by the melting of ice from early summer to the autumn, influenced by the Siberian coastal water.

The temperature and salinity fluctuate most vigorously in the Surface Water, depending on the seasons and areas. In the Korea Strait, the salinity exceeds 35.0‰ in April and May, a value more haline than the water below, and falls to 32.5‰ in August and September, whereas it varies only between 33.7 and 34.1‰ off the coast of Hokkaido. The temperature is 25°C in summer, but in winter it varies from 15°C in the Korea Strait to 5°C off Hokkaido. On the Siberian and Korean sides, the variation of salinity is not large (33.7–34.0‰).

The Middle Water is the water mass of high temperature and high salinity seen distinctly below the Surface Water in the warmer sector of the Japan Sea. It originates from the water in the intermediate layers of the Kuroshio origin off the west of Kyushu and enters into the Japan Sea during the period from the winter to early summer. However, Middle Water can be also defined in the colder sector from the distribution of dissolved oxygen. In the warmer sector, this water has the core at approximately the 50-m layer with a salinity of about 34.5‰.

The Middle Water has a rather strong vertical decrease in temperature, the average temperature of the entire Japan Sea falling from 17°C in 25 m to 2°C in 200 m. Its thickness decreases from the warmer to the colder sector, the vertical temperature gradient being much steeper in the latter. The salinity is 34.5–34.8‰ in warmer sector and about 34.1‰ in the colder. It is the largest value of salinity in all depths from the surface down to the bottom.

The Deep Water, usually called the Japan Sea Proper Water, is of extremely uniform character, with temperature 0–0.5°C and salinity 34.0–34.1‰. A closer investigation by K. Nishida shows, however, that the water temperature below 1500 m increases slightly downward due to the adiabatic heating, while the oxygen minimum is also located at this level. For these reasons, it may be more reasonable for us to designate the water above and below the 1500-m level as the Deep Water and Bottom Water, respectively. Compared with the water of other seas at the same depths, the oxygen content is extremely high (5.8–6.0 cc/liter), showing

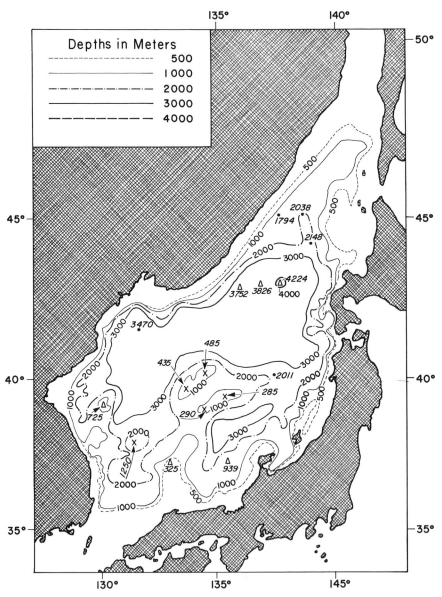

Fig. 1. Bottom configuration of the Japan Sea.

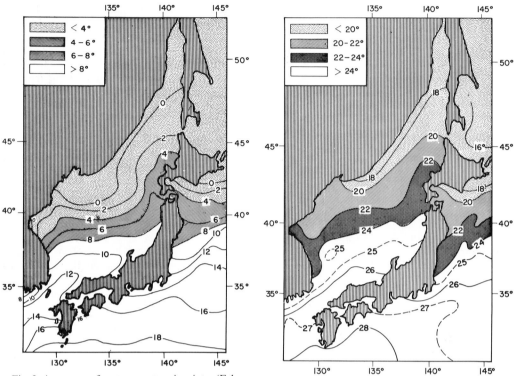

Fig. 2. Average surface temperature in winter (February), in degrees centigrade.

Fig. 3. Average surface temperature in summer (August).

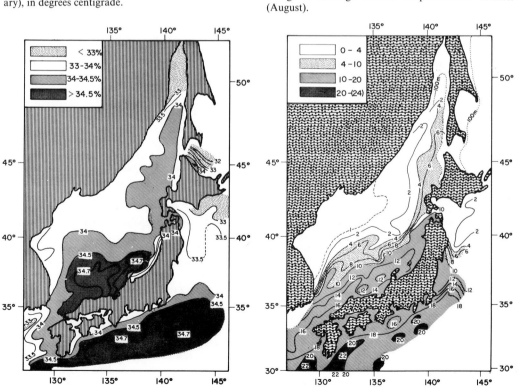

Fig. 4. Surface salinity.

Fig. 5. Water temperature in June (100-m layer) in degrees centigrade.

that renewal of the water in deep layers of the Japan Sea is active.

According to Michitaka Uda, the Deep Water of the Japan Sea is fed mostly in February and March by the surface water sinking down to deeper layers in the northern part of Japan Sea, after it gains a salinity around 34.0‰ due to horizontal diffusion and subsequently cooling in winter followed by convection.

Besides these water masses, water of low salinity in the surface layer of colder sector (1–4°C, 33.9‰) sometimes dives at the polar front and creeps southward below the Middle Water of the warmer sector. This phenomenon is similar to the penetration of the Subarctic Intermediate Water under the warm water of the Kuroshio in the Pacific off northern Japan.

In spring and summer, the warm water from the East China Sea and the cold water off the east coast of Korea both lose salinity due to the rainfall and melting of ice. These less haline waters are mixed with the surrounding water, and the salinity of the entire surface water of the Japan Sea decreases. In addition to this, they are also heated gradually during warmer months. The resulting decrease in water density leads to the formation of a distinct Upper Thermocline separating the Upper Water from the Middle Water below. This Upper Thermocline is located between the surface and the 25-m layer in warmer seasons. In the fall, the heat is lost into space from the sea surface. The surface temperature goes down and the salinity increases due to the mixing with the water masses in deeper water. The resulting intense convection increases the depth of the Upper Thermocline to 25–50 m in September, and to 50–100 m in November.

In the warmer sector, the Middle Water loses its salinity in the fall due to the inflow by the Tsushima Current of less haline water which has occupied the Korea Strait in the preceding summer. The convection in the Surface Water is intensified simultaneously, thus resulting in a decrease in the thickness of the Middle Water. In November, the Upper Thermocline vanishes at last due to the mixing between the water above and below. For this reason, we have in the fall and winter only the upper homogeneous water and cold water mass below, separated by this Lower Thermocline. The latter is seen from the 200–250 m layers in the major part of the warmer sector, but its depth decreases northward, being only about 100 m off the coast of Hokkaido.

The Lower Thermocline (and halocline) exists all the year round between the Middle Water and Deep Water, obviously depending almost entirely on the difference in the flow pattern.

In the western half of the colder sector, the depth of the Upper Thermocline still increases around December. Due to the cooling of surface water, the temperature difference vanishes between the water above and below the Upper Thermocline. Then the water becomes uniform from the surface down to 150–200 m layer in winter. This suggests that the convection is confined to the upper 200-m layer off northern Korea, the sunken water being often found as an intermediate cold water in the next spring. On the other hand, the convection seems to extend to much deeper levels off the Siberian coast and at the middle portion of the Japan Sea.

In the warmer sector, the surface temperature reaches a maximum in middle August, although the occurrence of a maximum is delayed northward and downward. Minimum temperature occurs in February or March.

On the other hand, maximum surface temperature occurs in August off the Korean coast. However, due to the strong development of the Upper Thermocline, only a very thin surface layer is influenced by the external heating. Thus, the water temperature variation at the 50–100 m layers is almost entirely controlled by advection.

According to Michio Miyazaki, the net transport of heat from the sea to the air shows, similar to other parts of the oceans, a maximum from late autumn to winter. Moreover, heat is transported from the warmer to the colder sector. In winter, the heat lost from the entire surface of Japan Sea averages 500 g cal cm^2/day—a quantity enough to freeze the seawater in the northern portion of Japan Sea, to increase the salinity of cold water below the ice, and to produce an intense convection to form the Deep and Bottom Waters. Because of the cold temperature in the major part and most depths of the Japan Sea, the water of the Tsushima Current is strongly cooled off as it flows northward.

Dissolved Oxygen

The water in the Japan Sea is extraordinarily rich in dissolved oxygen (in part because of the rich phytoplankton). The O_2 content is about 6 cc/liter or more at almost all depths, and particularly higher in the Surface and Middle Waters, showing a maximum at the 200-m layer (8 cc/liter). These figures are much higher than those in the same and deeper levels of the main Pacific Ocean and Okhotsk Sea (1–2 cc/liter). This fact suggests a more adequate aeration in the Japan Sea water than any other area.

The Surface and Middle Water are saturated with oxygen in most cases. The saturation percentage is 100% or slightly less in warmer sector, whereas the water on the Siberian and Korean sides is mostly supersaturated because of the low water temperature there. Specifically, it is 110% or even higher off the coast of northern Korea. In the Deep Water, the oxygen content is very high down to the bottom. According to K. Nishida the average values of the O_2 content and the saturation percentage are 6.04 cc/liter and 75% at 500 meters,

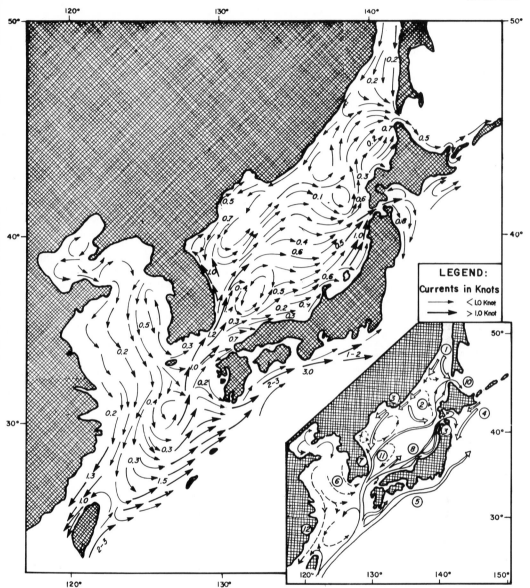

Fig. 6. Currents and currents systems in the upper layer of the Japan Sea and its adjacent waters (after M. Uda).

Key to inset:
1. Liman Current. 2. Maritime Province Cold Current. 3. North Korea Cold Current. 4. Oyashio. 5. Kuroshio. 6. Water of Low Salinity Originating in the Yellow Sea. 7. East Korea Warm Current. 8. Tsushima Current. 9. Tsugaru Warm Current. 10. Soya Warm Current. 11. South Japan Sea Gyre. 12. East China Sea Monsoon Current (Winter).

and 5.83 cc/liter and 72% at 3000 m.

Color of the Sea and Transparency

According to M. Uda, the index on the Forel's scale shows the color of the Japan Sea to be more bluish in the warmer than in the colder sector, being less than 3 and reaching as low as 2 in the area 36–38°N, 133–136°E. In the colder sector, it is mostly 4–6, while it is over 3 in the area off Vladivostok. It is particularly greenish in the northern half of this sea. Transparency amounts to more than 25 m in the area of the Tsushima Current. In the colder sector, it sometimes falls below 10 m.

Ocean Currents

The major current in the Japan Sea is the *Tsushima Current* originating in the East China Sea and mostly fed by the branch of the Kuroshio coming southwest of Kyushu Island and partly by the coastal water from China proper. The water of the Tsushima Current consists of the Surface Water and Middle Water. This current enters the Japan Sea through the Korea Strait touching the northwestern coast of Japan. On entering the Japan Sea, this current issues a branch called the East Korea Warm Current to the north, which flows up the Korean coast as far north as the area off the Yongil Bay and Ullung Island, and again turns southeast, thus joining the main flow. This current, which is about 200 km wide, washes the coasts of northern side of Japan and flows at a speed varying from 0.5–1.0 knot further northeast. It then divides into two branches, the *Tsugaru Warm Current* and *Soya Warm Current* to the Pacific Ocean and the Okhotsk Sea through the Tsugaru Strait and Soya Strait, respectively. Both of these currents are deflected to the right on leaving the straits, thus following close to the eastern coast of Honshu and the northern coast of Hokkaido, respectively.

In respect to the cold currents, there is the *Liman Current* slowly flowing southwestward in the area off the northern Maritime Province, the *North Korea Cold Current* flowing southward in the area off the Vladivostok to the east of Korea, the *Maritime Province Cold Current* or the *Mid-Japan Sea Cold Current* which originates off the Russian Tartary coast and flows toward the central portion of Japan Sea, particularly toward the entrance of the Tsugaru Strait. These three cold currents all form separated counterclockwise eddies and consist of the Surface Water and Middle Water on the colder sector of the Japan Sea. Between these warm and cold regions, a distinct boundary or the polar front is noticed.

Since the Tsushima Current belongs to the Upper and Middle Waters which is about 200 m thick and separated from the cold Deep Water below, its thickness is usually of this order. Its speed is nearly constant down to 25 m and decreases with depth from this level to less than $\frac{1}{5}$ of the surface value at 75 m. Thus, the transport of Tsushima Current is less than $\frac{1}{20}$ of that of the Kuroshio.

The speed of cold currents mentioned above is about 0.3 knot for the Liman Current and less than 0.3 knot for the Maritime Province Current. The North Korea Cold Current which is the strongest one, has a speed of 0.5 knot. It has a width of about 100 km and a thickness of 50 m. The cold currents in the Japan Sea are generally much weaker than the warm currents.

According to K. Hidaka, the average velocity of the Tsushima Current flowing through the channel between Tsushima Island and Korea is smaller in winter and increases in summer, amounting to 1.5 knot in August. There are also secular variations, and a marked period of 7 years is noticed.

The inflow of water into the Japan Sea takes place mostly through the Korea Strait, since the inflow through the Tartar Strait is negligible. The water flows out of the Japan Sea through two of the other straits.

Tides and Tidal Streams

Tidal phenomena of the Japan Sea were studied by Dr. S. Ogura who found that the Japan Sea is characterized by tides of an extremely small range. While the range off the Pacific coast is 1–2 m, it is only 0.2 m in the Japan Sea. It is a little larger along the Russian coast, amounting to 0.4–0.5 m. It increases in the Korea Strait and the Gulf of Tartary, amounting to more than 2 m at some places.

Figure 7 shows the cotidal lines for the semidiurnal component M_2 where the Roman numerals mean the time in hours elapsed after the moon crosses the meridian of 135°E and before the high water occurs. Tide waves propagate at right angles to these cotidal lines. Two amphidromic points exist off the west coast of Sakhalin and near the Korea Strait. A similar cotidal chart can be drawn for the lunisolar diurnal tide K_1. In this case, an amphidromic point exists in the Korea Strait.

Since the cross sections of Soya and Tsugaru Straits are both only $\frac{1}{8}$ of that of the Korea Strait in the west, and the sectional area of the Tartar Strait is negligible, the tidal waves enter primarily through the Tsushima Strait from the East China Sea. The amplitude of forced oscillations of the bulk

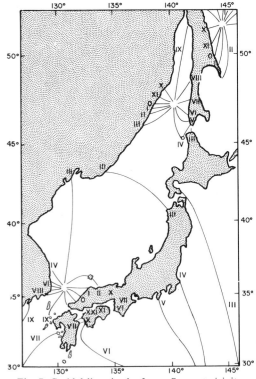

Fig. 7. Cotidal lines in the Japan Sea and vicinity.

of the water in the Japan Sea can practically be neglected.

The resultant consisting of the tidal streams and east-flowing Tsushima Current sometimes amounts to 2.8 knots. Diurnal tidal current predominates in the Tsugaru Strait, while the tidal range is larger in the semidiurnal component. Diurnal inequality is conspicuous for the tidal streams. The tidal stream in the Soya Strait is dominated by the difference of sea level between Okhotsk and Japan Seas. Diurnal inequality for tidal currents is also remarkable. Since the eastward stream is expected in the Soya Strait, the general flow is often eastward, its speed sometimes exceeding 3.5 knots.

Sea Ice

The freezing of seawater in the Japan Sea starts at the middle of November in the Tartar Strait and in early December at the head of the Gulf of Peter the Great. In the middle of December, the areas off the northern part of the Maritime Province and in the Gulf of Peter the Great are frozen. Ice is formed in mid-December in the coastal region off the Maritime Province. In January, the frozen area extends to farther off the coast. The formation of ice of course makes the navigation in these waters difficult or impossible. The freezing of seawater in the northern part of the Japan Sea is somewhat delayed, starting in early February to middle February.

The melting of ice begins in the areas farthest from the coasts. In the later half of March, no sea ice is seen except close to the coast. Along the coast of the northern Japan Sea, the ice generally melts in the middle of April, when Vladivostok also resumes its activities as a harbor. The last sea ice is seen in the Tartar Strait in the earlier and middle part of May.

The duration of ice amounts to 120 days along the coast of the Maritime Province, and even to 201 days at the Dekastri Harbor on the Tartar Strait. No severe formation of sea ice is noticed along the coast of northern Korea. On the west coast of Sakhalin, only Kholmsk is free from the ice since this part is washed by a postrunner of the Tsushima Current. Along the remaining parts on this coast, the water is frozen almost 3 months during which time navigation is suspended.

Geology

On the slopes surrounding the Japan Sea basin, there are found a number of submarine canyons. On the continental slope, these canyons end at depths of more than 2000 m, while those on the side of Japanese Islands end at a depth of only 800 m.

The continental shelves around the Japan Sea are poorly developed, the depth at their shelf-breaks being 140 m on the continental side, while it is more than 200 m along the Japanese coast west of 137°E.

According to H. Tsuya (1932), Y. Fujita (1962) and others, the Yamato Bank and other banks are composed of a number of basement rocks consisting of Precambrian granite and other Paleozoic rocks, and of the Neogene igneous and sedimentary rocks distributed overlying them. I. B. Andreeva and G. B. Udentsev (1958) indicate that the crust under the flat bottom of the northern half of this sea is of an oceanic type free from granite.

As to the formation of the Japan Sea, there have been several discussions by Japanese and Soviet scientists. As the paleogeographic studies advance, it emerges that the southern half of the present Japan Sea must have been land during the Paleozoic and Mesozoic periods and during most of the Paleogene. Thus it is definite that the Japan Sea as it stands now was formed during the Neogene and the early Quaternary periods. According to V. V. Beloussov and E. M. Ruditch's recent theory (1961), the absence of granite in the bottom of the northern half of the Japan Sea suggests the transformation of granitic layer into the basaltic by the basification accompanying the subsidence of the earth crust. Continental stretching, following a general earth expansion (*Egyed's theory*, pr. Vol. V), could account for *new* oceanic crust here.

Thus, it should be easily concluded that the northern half of the Japan Sea was once an area of land. Some Soviet geologists, such as I. V. Sysoev (1960) and others, have opinions differing from those of Beloussov *et al*. According to Sysoev, the bottom of the northern Japan Sea is a part of the old oceanic crust which was the extension of the Pacific basin, separated from it by the formation and elevation of the Japanese Islands. On the other hand, the Japanese geologist Y. Fujita considers that the bottom of the northern Japan Sea consisting of rocks having a P-wave velocity of 6.1–6.4 km/sec, is not a basaltic layer but contains some Precambrian granite. The existence at the present of such a big mass of continental material at the sea bottom more than 3000 m deep, would suggest a subsidence of the land of 2000–3000 m occurring since the Pleistocene age. M. Hoshino (1962) has pointed out a large-scale relative change of level since the late Miocene.

The Japan Sea now has communication with the Pacific Ocean and surrounding marginal seas through the Korea, Tsugaru, Soya and Tartar Straits. However, the formation of these four straits took place only in very recent geological periods. The oldest one is the Tsugaru Strait; it has been a strait since the Wisconsin Ice Age, although it may have been frequently covered with ice and available for the migration of land animals. The Korea Strait was a land bridge in the late Tertiary and permitted the migration of elephants of southern types into the Japanese Islands. This strait was only opened in the early Wisconsin Ice Age. The Soya Strait is the newest one, the fossils of mammoths excavated in Hokkaido Island indicating the existence of a Soya land bridge until the end of the Wisconsin Ice Age.

Historical

In the seventeenth century, the existence of Hokkaido and Sakhalin was not known in Europe, and the Japan Sea seems to have been understood as a gulf between Honshu, the Maritime Province and Korea. On the map of Asia published by W. J. Bleau in 1635, the area around the Japan Sea and the Okhotsk Sea was called the *Oceanus Occidentalis*. On a map of northeastern Asia published by F. de Wit in 1660, Hokkaido is indicated and the outlines of the Japan Sea are given fairly correctly except in the Sakhalin area, though no name was given to this sea.

In a map of Asia published by J. B. Homann in 1720, the area bears the name of *Mare iaponicum occidentale*, though he did not distinctly separate it from the Okhotsk Sea. It had been called by various other names such as the *Sea of Tartary* or the *Gulf of Korea*. The Russian navigator A. J. de Krusenstern first designated this sea as *Japanisches Meer* in his epoch-making world atlas published in 1815, and this name has been used ever since. In 1873, a Russian geographer, L. N. Schrenck described the Tsushima Warm Current and the Liman Cold Current in one of his papers. A Japanese explorer T. Mogami described the Kuriles and Sakhalin in 1786. Another Japanese explorer R. Mamiya in 1808 discovered the Mamiya Strait (Tartar Strait) which was thought to be a gulf before that time. In 1886–1889, S. Makaroff made an extensive survey of the Pacific Ocean and alluded to the hydrography of the Japan Sea. In 1913–1917, Yuji Wada set a great number of bottles adrift in the seas adjacent to Japan and obtained a general idea on the current systems.

In 1928–1931, the Imperial Marine Observatory in Kobe sent out a series of expeditions every summer with the Research Ship *Syunpu Maru*, and the results were published under the supervision of K. Suda and K. Hidaka. In the summer of 1932 and 1933, extensive surveys of the Japan Sea were carried out by the Japan Fisheries Agency with 34 research vessels each year. The result of these surveys was analysed by Michitaka Uda and his colleagues. These surveys for the first time gave the general outlines of the oceanography of Japan Sea.

Another multiple ship survey was carried out by the Japan Fisheries Agency under the direction of M. Uda in May and June 1941, and observations were made by the Hydrographic Department of the Imperial Japanese Navy. After World War II, the Hydrographic Office (of the Maritime Safety Board), the Maizuru Marine Observatory (Mai-

zuru), and the Japan Sea Regional Fisheries Laboratory have been engaged in further studies on the Japanese side. In the 5-year period starting in 1953, the Japan Fisheries Agency carried out cooperative surveys of the Tsushima Warm Current.

Since the end of the World War II, Soviet scientists have also been very active in the scientific exploration of the Japan Sea.

Koji Hidaka

References

Beloussov, V. V., and Ruditch, E. M., 1961, "Island arcs in the development of the earth's structure (especially in the region of Japan and the Sea of Okhotsk)," *J. Geol.*, **69**, 647–658.

Manabe, S., 1958, "On the estimation of energy exchange between the Japan Sea and the atmosphere during winter based upon the energy budget of both atmosphere and sea," *J. Met. Soc. Japan, Ser. II*, **36**, 123–134.

Shepard, F. P., Emery, K. O., and Gould, H. R., 1949, "Distribution of sediments on East Asiatic Continental Shelf," *Univ. So. Calif. (A. Hancock Fd.) Occ. Paper*, **9**.

Tsuboi, C., 1956, "Earthquake epicentres, volcanoes and gravity anomalies in and near Japan," *Trav. Assoc. Seism. Phys. GL. (U.G.G.I.) Ser. A*, No. 19, 125–127.

Uda, M., 1934, "Hydrographical studies based on simultaneous oceanographical surveys made in the Japan Sea . . .," *Records Oceanogr. Works Japan*, **6**, 19–107.

Yabe, H., 1934, "Bottom relief of the seas bordering the Japanese Islands and Korean Peninsula," *Tokyo Imp. Univ., Earthquake Res. Inst. Bull.*, **12**, 539–565.

Zenkevitch, L., 1963, "Biology of the Seas of the U.S.S.R.," New York, Interscience Publishers, translated by S. Botcharskaya.

JAVA SEA

Limits and Oceanography

(a) Limits and Dimensions. The Java Sea (center: 112°E, 5°S) covers part of the largest shelf area in the world, the Sunda Shelf, which covers 1.8 millions km². The Java Sea is sometimes grouped together with the shelf sector of the South China Sea (q.v.) as the *Sunda Sea*. They are separated by latitude 3°S. The South China Sea extends much farther north beyond the Sunda Shelf edge.

In the east, the Java Sea is bounded by the Makasser Straits, Flores Sea and Bali Sea. Although the eastern limit of the Java Sea, as drawn by the International Hydrographic Bureau (*Sp. Publ. 23*, 1953), extends to the southwest tip of the Celebes (Sulawesi), it seems best for oceanographers to take the eastern limit as coinciding with the edge of the Sunda Shelf: Kangean Island to Makassar Straits and the Little Paternoster Island. The larger area

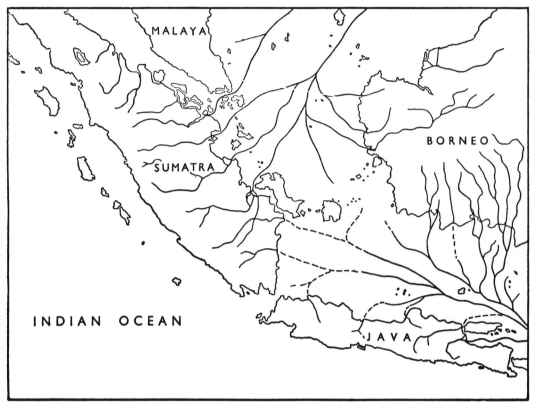

Fig. 1. Drowned river system of the South China Sea and Java Sea (North Sunda and South Sunda River: together the "Molengraaff River system") (from Umbgrove, 1949).

is given as 433,000 km², with a mean depth of 46 m and total volume of 20,000 km³. The restricted definition gives 367,000 km².

The Java Sea thus defined borders the south coasts of Kalimantan (Borneo) and closely approximates the eastern shelf edge from Makassar Straits to Bali Straits, then follows the north coast of Java, and the east coasts of Sumatra as far as Bangka. Important contributors to the knowledge of the Java Sea have been Molengraaff, Mohr, Umbgrove, Smit Sibinga (see references in Van Bemmelen, 1949), and others.

The general depth of the Java Sea is 40–50 m. The bottom of the Java Sea has an extremely low relief in which channels have been found, thanks to many early hydrographic surveys. These channels have been traced (by Molengraaff) to river mouths in East Sumatra and Malaya, west and south Kalimantan, and the north coast of Java. Two large river systems seem to have existed: the *North Sunda River* having headwaters in Sumatra and flowing northeast into the South China Sea, with its tributaries rising on Malaya and West Kalimantan; the *South Sunda River* also rising on Sumatra but flowing eastward into the present Makassar Straits receiving tributaries from South Kalimantan and Java (Fig. 1). Another interesting proof

of the former existence of the North Sunda River is shown by the occurrence of many similar species of freshwater fish in the present streams of East Sumatra and West Kalimantan, whereas no such similarity exists between the West and East Kalimantan. Dickerson (1941) proposed that the North Sunda River should be named "Molengraaff River" in honor of its discoverer. Certainly the area was continental during the late Pleistocene eustatic "lows."

Besides the channels belonging to the two Sunda rivers, many "blind" channels are located within, and at the entrances of, the major straits leading to the Java Sea and also across submarine ridges and between coral reef platforms. This type of channel is invariably deepest where the strait is narrowest, as in Bangka Strait, where the channel depth is 11 m deeper than the general depth of the Strait (10 m). These "blind" channels are the result of scouring by marine currents in the soft, unconsolidated bottom sediments.

(b) Surface Properties and Meteorology. Winds are typically monsoonal, blowing north–south near the equator, whereas in the Java Sea proper they alternate between east–southeast and north–northwest. The coral islands reflect a marked influence of the monsoons (see *Coral Reefs*, Vol. III).

TABLE 1

	Dec.–Feb.	Mar.–May	June–Aug.	Sept.–Nov.
Temperature, °C	27.5–28.8	28.0–29.1	27.0–29.0	27.8–28.3
Wind toward	ESE	Unsteady	NW	NW
(Beaufort)	1.5–3.4		1.5–4.4	0.5–2.4
Air pressure, cm	756.6–757.0	756.2–757.0	756.6–757.8	757.0–758.0
Salinity, %	31.0–32.0	29.5–32.0	31.0–33.5	32.5–33.5

Tables 1–4 showing the surface properties and meteorology of the Java Sea have been derived from a publication by the Royal Netherlands Geographical Society (1922) and also partially from recent meteorological notes.

(c) Currents and Tides. Surface currents in the Java Sea are westward for eight months, from September through May, with six months uninterrupted flow. During the remaining months the currents are reversed (Figs. 2 and 3). The influence of the predominant westward current is shown by the river mouths on the north coast of Java; many of them are deflected toward the west. The influence of the seasonal shift of the geostrophic winds on the mean sea level in the Philippines is well illustrated in Fig. 4, as compared with the Indian Ocean coast of Java. A maximum contrast in level develops about August accompanied by an important trans-

TABLE 2. SURFACE CURRENTS IN NAUTICAL MILES PER DAY IN THE JAVA SEA
(DIRECTION OF SET)

	Dec.–Feb.	Mar.–May	June–Aug.	Sept.–Nov.
Java Sea	to W	to W	to E	irregular
	5–10·	1–10	1–15	

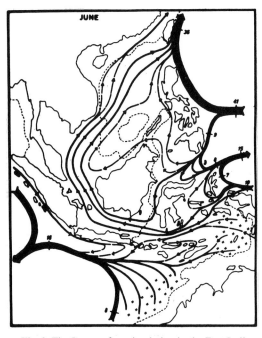

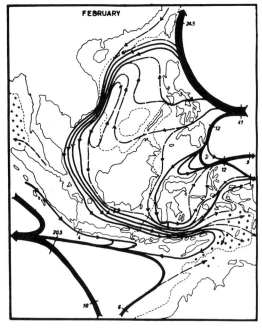

Fig. 2. The June surface circulation in the East Indies, leading to a westerly set in the Java Sea. Transports in western Pacific and northeast Indian Ocean are given in million cubic meters per second. Note upwelling (+ + +) off Sahul Shelf (from Wyrtki, 1961).

Fig. 3. The February circulation, showing easterly setting currents in the Java Sea, under the influence of the Asiatic (northwest) Monsoon. Transports are given in million cubic meters per second. Note sinking replaces upwelling along the edge of Sahul Shelf.

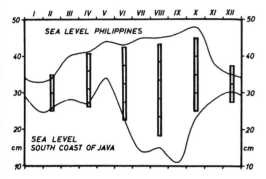

Fig. 4. Annual variation in sea level between the Philippines and the south coast of Java. Transport is shown in vertical bars, each fraction corresponding to 0.5 million m³/sec. Note how sea level is lowered along the Java coast from June to October during the southeast monsoon, but raised during the northwest monsoon. There is always a net transport from the western Pacific to the northeast Indian Ocean.

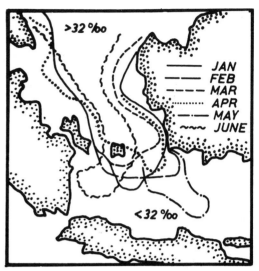

Fig. 5. Tongues of high salinity (32 ‰) enter the Java Sea during the northwest monsoon and favor coral reef growth toward the northwest.

port from north to south (over 4 million m³/sec) mainly through the South China Sea and the Java Sea.

TABLE 3. MAXIMUM TIDAL CURRENTS IN KNOTS

Toward		Java Sea
(a) Sunda Straits	2.2	N4°E and reversed
(b) West channel	1.4	N
to Surabaja	1.9	S
(c) Bangka Strait		
North entrance	1.9	S67°E and 1.0 reversed
South entrance	1.4	S45°E and 1.8 reversed

TABLE 4. TIDAL RANGE IN METERS

1.0	Average of 4 stations on Java's north coast
1.4	Sampit Bay, South Kalimantan (Borneo)

(d) Chemistry. Owing to the shallow water, mostly less than 50 m, and heavily watered marginal lands, the salinity is normally low, and less than 32‰. During the northwest monsoon, however, a tongue of high salinity enters from the South China Sea (see Fig. 5).

Bottom Sediments

The bottom sediments of the Sunda Shelf have been divided into ten sedimentary petrographic provinces by Van Baren and Kiel (1950). The characteristic features of each group shown on Fig. 6 are listed below, from youngest to oldest.

(1) Krakatau group: Hornblende, augite and abundant hypersthene still possessing glassy films.

(2) Deli group: Augite, hypersthene and 80–92 % hornblende still possessing glassy films.

(3) Bawean group: Hypersthene, hornblende and 79–98 % augite still possessing glassy films.

(4) Java group: Type I has less augite than Type II (49–90 %) but is otherwise similar in mineral composition (hornblende, augite, hypersthene) without glassy films and with ragged edges.

(5) Kalimantan group (Borneo): Andalusite; Type II is richer in epidote than Type I.

(6) Meratus-Pulau Laut group: Epidote, glaucophane, zircon and rutile.

(7) Mixture of groups 5 and 6.

(8) South China Sea group: Coarse-grained epidote and blue-green hornblende, many different mineral associations probably implying closeness to sources.

(9) Malacca group: Similar to group 8 but with more ragged hypersthene.

(10) Bangka-Billiton group: Tourmaline, zircon and rutile.

Coastal accretion on the east coast of South Sumatra and on Java's north coast, beyond the spheres of influence of large rivers, ranges between 12 and 30 m annually. Near large river mouths and particularly in deltas, coastal growth is tremendous. Recorded figures range between 75 m (Djambi, Central Sumatra) and 200 m (Bodri River, Java) annually. In spite of the high rate of sedimentation, "drowned" estuaries are common on the coasts of Sumatra and South Kalimantan. Cuspate deltas are significant on the coast of Java, while West Kalimantan has a digitate delta at the mouth of the Kapuas River, the longest river in Indonesia (1143 km).

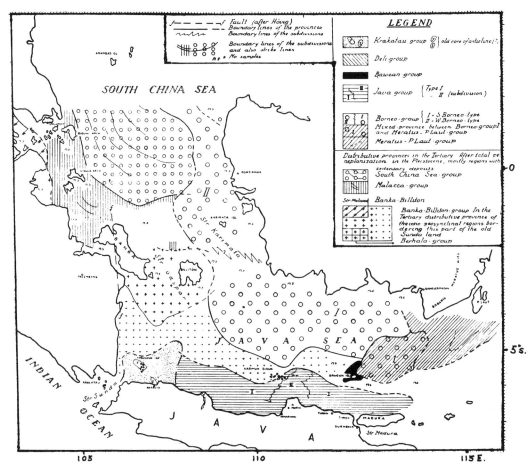

Fig. 6. Sedimentary petrology of the Java Sea (Van Baren and Kiel, 1950).

The Java Sea is largely too muddy (and in places too fresh) for corals, but rich reef growths are found in the areas of strong currents, northwest of Java, in the Thousand Islands and in the Bay of Djakarta (Batavia). Extensive studies were made by Umbgrove (1949) and Verstappen (1954).

Geophysics and Geological Structure

The Java Sea and the Sunda Shelf in general are in isostatic equilibrium with small positive gravity anomalies below 50 mgal. However, subsidence and uplift mark its periphery particularly where the shelf borders the miogeosynclines (Umbgrove's "idiogeosynclines") of East Sumatra, North Java, etc. In North Kalimantan, late Miocene peneplains have been found up to heights of about 650 m.

A profile from the Java Sea to the Indian Ocean reveals earthquake foci increasing in depth from south to north. The epicenters located below the Java Sea reach depths of 650 km. The geological interpretations of such distributions of foci in Indonesia have been discussed by Vening Meinesz,

Berlage, Gutenberg and others (see Van Bemmelen, 1949); also in the last decade by Benioff and others.

The uniform depth and the presence of former stream channels have been advanced as proofs that the Sunda Shelf bottom represents an extensive peneplain upon which the present, predominantly granitic (Triassic) islands form the monadnocks. The denudation most probably took place during several periods of progressively lower sea level during the Pliocene and Pleistocene. The lowest stage was probably during the last glaciation (Wisconsin). The extremely small gradient of the Sunda rivers indicates that the central part of the shelf has been largely stable since its submergence. During the Pleistocene glaciations, the bottom of the Sunda Shelf served as a migration route for the fauna of southeast Asia, Sumatra, Java, and Kalimantan (Borneo).

A symposium on the Java Sea, held in 1944, concluded that at the beginning of the Pleistocene, the area of the present Java Sea and parts of South Kalimantan and North Java was divided into a

North and a South Java Basin. A central land mass of low relief formed the water-shed coinciding with the east-west axis of the Java Sea.

Obdeyn suspected from historical folklore that the Sunda Straits marked by the volcano Krakatoa have only very recently been formed. Faulting and subsequent deepening by sea and tidal currents have produced the present configuration.

H. D. Tjia

References

Anon., 1922, "De zeeën van Nederlandsch Oost Indië," pp. 1–494, Leiden, Brill *(Royal Netherland Geographical Society)*.

Dickerson, R. E., 1941, "Molengraaff River," pp. 15–30, Philadelphia, *University of Pennsylvania Bicentennial Conference*.

Umbgrove, J. H. F., 1949, "Structural History of the East Indies," Cambridge, The University Press.

Van Baren, F. A., and Kiel, H., 1950, "Contribution to the sedimentary petrology of the Sunda Shelf," *J. Sediment. Petrol.*, **20**, 185–213.

Van Bemmelen, R. W., 1949, "The Geology of Indonesia; General Geology," Vol. 1A, pp. 16–31, 257–325, The Hague Martinus Nijhoff.

Verstappen, H. T., 1954, "The influence of climatic changes on the formation of coral islands," *Am. J. Sci.*, **252**, 428–435.

Wyrtki, K., 1961, "Physical oceanography of the southeastern Asian waters," *Repts. Naga Exped.*, **2**, Scripps Inst. Oceanogr., La Jolla, Calif.

K

KARA SEA

The Kara Sea (*Karskoye More*, in Russian) lies north of the West Siberian Lowland over the western parts of the Arctic continental shelf of Asia. According to the International Hydrographic Bureau (*Sp. Publ.* 23, 1953), its western limits are drawn from Vaigach Island (70°15′N, 58°25′E) across Kara Strait to the south point of Novaya Zemlya (Cape Kussov Noss); from its north point (Cape Zelaniya, or Cape Desire) to Cape Kohlsaat, the eastern limit of Franz-Josef Land; thence eastward to Cape Molotov (81°16′N, 93°43′E), being the northern limit of Severnaya Zemlya on Komosomolets Island. On the east side of this island, to southeast Cape, the eastern limit runs to Cape Voroshilov (Oktiabrskaya Revolutziya Island) to Cape Anuchin; next to Cape Unslicht on Bolshevik Island and from here to Cape Yevgenov and from Cape Pronchishchev on the mainland (USSR chart 1484). The western border is also breached,

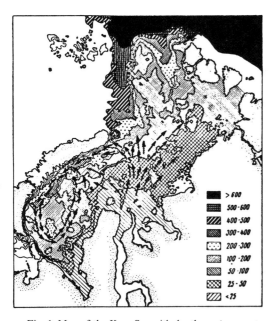

Fig. 1. Map of the Kara Sea with depths and currents (according to data of U.S.S.R. Arctic Institute; from Zenkevitch, 1963). (By permission of Interscience Publishers, N.Y.)

between the two islands of Novaya Zemlya, by the narrow Matochkin Strait. There is also a narrow strait between Vaigach Island and the mainland, Yugor Strait. The proposal (by Breitfluss, 1931) to apply Kossinna's name "Nansen Sea" (intended for the deeper region of the Arctic Basin east of the Greenwich meridian) to the northern Kara Sea has not been adopted [see *International Hydrographic Review*, 1936, **13**(25), 160].

The area of the Kara Sea is 883,000 km² with a volume of 104,000 km³. The sea is everywhere of rather shallow to medium depths, entirely on the continental shelf (*sensu lato*), although in places deeper than usual for epicontinental seas. There is a rather deep north–south rift, much broader than a submarine canyon, that forms a reentrant from the Arctic Basin into the shelf from the east of Franz-Josef Land to the northern tip of Novaya Zemlya, with depths grading down to over 600 m (maximum 620). A second reentrant rift ("trench") enters the Sea west of Severnaya Zemlya. Elsewhere the deepest spots lie in a belt east of Vaigach Island and off the eastern shores of Novaya Zemlya—the Novaya Zemlya Trough (300–400 m). The average depth is 118 m.

The floor of the Kara Sea is mainly occupied by a series of platforms or broad terraces stepping down from the southeast to north and west. Studies of the fossiliferous deposits associated with these terraces suggest the following sequence of events (Kulikov and Martinov, 1961):

Sartanian glacial (over 9000 yr)	− 100 m
Cargean Sea? (*ca.* 20,000 yr)	− 20, − 50 m
Zyrian glacial (*ca.* 50,000 yr)	− 250 m
Equivalent to Riss glacial (*ca.* 110,000 yr)	− 500 m

The limits of maximum interglacial transgression and glacial regression in the Kara Sea are illustrated in Figs. 2 and 3 by Sachs (1945, 1948).

Exploration

The area was first penetrated by ship in 1869, by Johannesen; and in 1875 it was crossed by O. Nordenskjöld, in the Swedish ship *Pröven*, again in 1876 in the *Imer* and in 1878 in the *Vega*. Early biological surveys were made by the Dutch *Varna* expedition in 1882 and the Danish *Dymphna* expedition in 1883. Nansen in the *Fram* mapped the area in 1893, followed by Toll in 1900 in the Russian

430

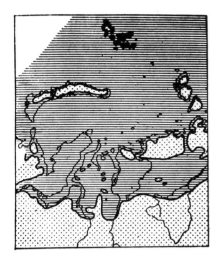

Fig. 2. Limits of greatest transgression in Quaternary Era (Sachs, 1945, 1948).

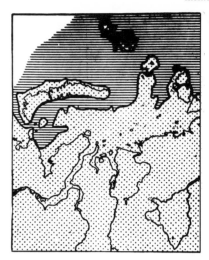

Fig. 3. Limits of the greatest regression in the Quaternary Era (Sachs, 1945, 1948).

vessel *Zarya*, by the Duke of Orleans in the *Belgica* in 1907 and by R. Amundsen in the *Maud*.

The period of energetic Russian surveys began after World War I, with the *Malygin* (for the Oceanographic Institute) and *Taimyr* (for the Hydrographic Service), beginning in 1921. Later activity by the Arctic Institute and other sponsors led to expeditions by the *Persey* (1927), *Sedov* (1929, 1930, 1934), *Lomonosov* (1931), icebreaker *Rusanov* (1931, 1932), *Knipovitch* (1932), icebreaker *Sadko* (1935, 1936, 1937), and the trawler *Maxim Gorky* (1945). The Kara Sea was explored for the first time by a United States ship in July/August 1965, by the Coast Guard icebreaker *Northwind* (Capt. K. K. Ayers) with scientists from the Columbia University Lamont Geological Observatory and Woods Hole Oceanographic Institution.

Oceanography

The Kara Sea is open to the north and northwest, but is otherwise hemmed in by islands and the mainland. Approximately 1500 km^3 of fresh river water enters the area annually, mainly from the south and southeast (Rivers Ob and Yenisei). Owing to the winter freeze, the regime shows a very marked seasonal oscillation. These fresh waters set up a northward current, diverging to the northeast along the coast of Taimyr and to the west and southwest along the coast of Novaya Zemlya, establishing a counterclockwise eddy in the southwest. The surface salinity is 7–10‰.

Atlantic waters of dense high salinity enter the sea from the north (Arctic Basin) and west (see *Barents Sea*), flowing under the less dense and less salty surface waters. In the northwest, this "Atlantic water" occurs even at the surface with 32–34‰ salinity. In the summer, the brackish surface layer is 5–8°C while the bottom water is 0 to −1.5°C.

Sea ice begins to form in September and melting starts only in June, so that the summer is short and quite cold. In the center of the sea, even in midwinter the ice is not solid or continuous. Icebergs are seen mainly in August in the area just south of the northern end of Novaya Zemlya.

Tides

As for the tides, the Kara Sea has its own amphidromic system with mean spring ranges of the semidiurnal tide $2(M_2 + S_2)$ around the southern coasts about 54–55 cm, down to 29–35 cm at the northern islands (Dietrich, 1944).

Sediments

The bottom deposits of the Kara Sea are marked by silty clay or mud (over 50% less than 0.01 mm) and terrigenous silt of glacial marine type in all the deeper areas, and are brown in color due to manganese and iron oxides (Klenova, 1936). In cores, it is seen that the brown, oxidized surface layer is replaced lower down by the reduced black manganous oxide, reflecting the activity of syndiagenetic bacteria working on the finely divided organic nutrients of the uppermost layers. The concentration or organic carbon is not overly high, however, and according to Mrs. Gorshkova (1957), is in the range of 0.27–1.99%. Large numbers of manganese ("ferromanganese") concentrations are found, which are not unusual for the Arctic continental shelves (Klenova, 1948, pp. 343, 276; also personal communication), especially where rivers drain podzol soils, although they are more characteristic of cold environments of the open ocean in abyssal depths. The counterclockwise eddy favors the accumulation of mud at quite shallow depth in the southwestern part of the basin, and further patches occur south of the north island of Navaya Zemlya,

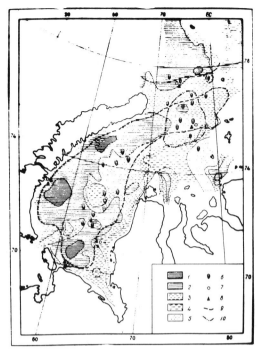

Fig. 4. Kara Sea sediments. (1) Clay and mud; (2) silt; (3) sand-mud; (4) silty sand; (5) sand; (6) no data; (7) ferromanganese concretions; (8) rock; (9) gravel; (10) limit of distribution of underlying clay (Gorshkova, 1957).

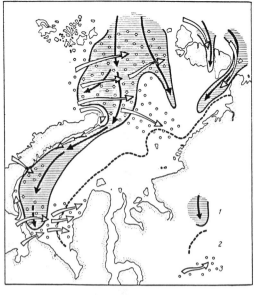

Fig. 5. Main ways of penetration into the Kara Sea of benthos of varied biogeographical nature (according to different workers; from Zenkevitch, 1963). (1) Organisms of the intermediate warm layer and of the cold deep layers; (2) northern boundary of forms brought down by the discharge from the mainland; (3) sublittoral deep-water forms and those of the Barents Sea (marked by circles). (By permission of Interscience Publishers, N.Y.)

approximately corresponding to the areas where icebergs occur in late summer.

Shallow deposits nearer the mouths of the Yenisei and Ob rivers are marked by sands and silty sands, together with the bivalves *Portlandia* and *Astarte*. Hard rock bottom is encountered in a number of areas near the margins of the submerged Pleistocene terraces. This fact corroborates the impression given by the manganese nodules and other data that the rate of sedimentation in the Kara Shelf is extremely slow and is not masked by organic oozes, since the organic productivity rates are also slow.

Fauna amd Flora

Oxygen concentration is fairly high throughout the Kara Sea waters so that this is in no way a limiting factor on organic activity. Nevertheless both pelagic and benthos life are several times poorer than in the Barents Sea (Zenkevitch, 1963), although species are numerous. Because of severe ice conditions there is no littoral fauna whatever, but the intake of Arctic water from the north brings a somewhat mixed general fauna and flora. Around the mouths of the great rivers and to 100 km seaward there are freshwater diatoms, and brackish ones extend to 200 km. In this freshwater area the phytoplanktonic biomass averages 900 mg/m³,

compared to over 1600 mg/m³ in the open northeast and only 120 mg/m³ in the restricted southwest. Zooplankton throughout are generally less than 50 mg/m³ (mostly copepods). The benthonic biomass drops from over 300 g/m³ near the shore to less than 3 g/m³ in the deeps.

RHODES W. FAIRBRIDGE

References

Dietrich, G., 1944, "Die Schwingungssysteme der halb- und eintägigen Tiden in den Ozeanen," *Veroeffentl. Inst. Meeresk. Berlin, N.F.R.A.*, **41**.

Gorshkova, T., 1957, "Deposits of the Kara Sea," (in Russian) *Tr. Vses. Gidrobiol. Obshchestva Akad. Nauk SSSR*, **8**.

Klenova, M. V., 1936, "Sediments of the Kara Sea," *Dokl. Akad. Nauk SSR*, **4**(13), No. 4 (108), 187–190.

Klenova, M. V., 1948, "Marine Geology," Moscow (in Russian).

Kulikov, N., and Martinov, V., 1961, "On the ancient shore-lines of the bottom of the Kara Sea," (in Russian). *Morskie Berega, Inst. Geol. Acad. Sci., Estonian SSR (Tallin)*, **8**, 147–154.

Zenkevitch, L., 1963, "Biology of the Seas of the U.S.S.R.," New York, Interscience Publishers, 955pp. (translation).

Cross-references: *Arctic Ocean; Barents Sea; East Siberian Sea; Laptev Sea.*

KAU BAY—*See* **HALMAHERA SEA**

KIRCHOFF'S LAW—*See* **RADIATION LAWS,** Vol. II

KURIL CURRENT—*See* **OYASHIO**

KUROSHIO CURRENT

General Features

Kuroshio is defined as a strong, belt-like, north-easterly flowing current located along the western margin of the North Pacific, running off the east coast of northern part of the Philippines and extending to the east coast of Japan. It is a continuation of the North Equatorial Current which flows in the equatorial waters and is connected to the North Pacific Current or the Kuroshio Extension, thus forming a part of the general circulation in the Pacific. The Kuroshio flows through the East China Sea near the Okinawa Islands and washes the southern Kyushu, issuing a branch which sweeps the west coast of Kyushu and flowing into the Japan Sea through the Tsushima Straits as the "Tsushima Current." The major part of the Kuroshio then sweeps the area south of Japanese Islands. After this stream leaves the region off the Honshu Island, it runs to the east in the latitudes 36–37°N. Its axis has an undulating form. Then it is split into two branches eastward and southward, the southward branch veering to southwest forming the Kuroshio Counter Current. The portion of stream in the Pacific after it leaves the Japanese Islands is called the Kuroshio Extension. The existence of the Kuroshio Extension can be traced as far east as the longitudes of about 180° and in considerable intensity to about 160°E.

The width of the current is not easy to define, but is estimated at about 80 km. The streamlines of the Kuroshio at the sea surface are represented approximately by the isotherms at the 200-m level (Fig. 4).

The depth of the Kuroshio is quite difficult to define exactly. The upper layer with strong flow of high temperature and high salinity is about 400 m thick. This can be roughly regarded as the depth of the Kuroshio, because there is the subarctic water of low temperature and salinity below.

The name "Kuroshio" means "black stream," being derived from *kuro* and *shio* meaning "black" and "stream" respectively. This current appears dark blue when seen from a great distance. Seen directly from above the sea surface, the color of the water is a beautiful ultramarine or cobalt blue.

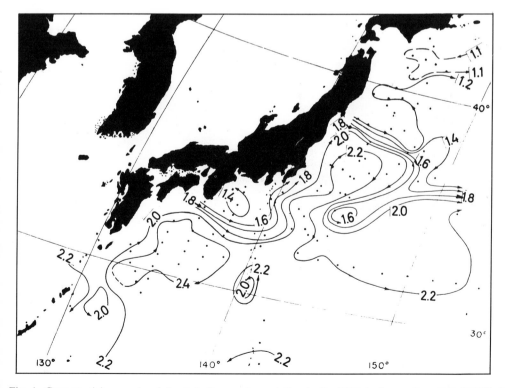

Fig. 1. Geopotential anomaly of the 0-decibar surface relative to the 1000-decibar surface (ΔD 0/1000), in dynamic meters.

On Forel's scales, the number of the Kuroshio water is 1 or 2 and occasionally 3. Secchi disk gives a transparency between 25 and 40 meters.

Origin of Kuroshio

Strictly speaking, there are series of source regions distributed along the axis of the Kuroshio. However, the primary and basic water of the Kuroshio originates from the North Pacific Central Water Masses. This water, sinking along the Subtropic Convergence between 23 and 25°N, mainly spreads southward along its isentropic surface to the core of the North Equatorial Current at depths varying from 50–100 m. Eventually its extension is found to be connected with the core of the Kuroshio. In this area, the thickness of the North Equatorial Current increases from about 200 to 400 m rather abruptly, thus showing the transition to the Kuroshio. This region which is located off the east coast of Taiwan is supposed to be the major source region of the Kuroshio. The isopycnal sections indicate that the discontinuity in the depth of density surface 24.00 approximately coincides with the Subtropic Convergence. In addition to this, the Kuroshio entrains the surrounding waters as it flows northeastward. The successive modification of this current during its flow off the coast of Taiwan, Okinawa and Japan shows the existence of these multiple supply areas.

Velocity and Transport

The Kuroshio has a velocity varying between 1 and 6 knots. It is greatest and often exceeds 5 knots off the east coast of Japan where the Kuroshio meets the Oyashio or the cold Kurile Current. Off the south coast of Japan, velocities of similar strength are seen. At the southern part of the Kuroshio, namely in the adjacent seas of Okinawa and Taiwan, the velocity is about 2 knots. Downstream, it shows an asymmetrical velocity profile with the shear zone on the left (northern) side of the current.

Near Japan, the Kuroshio transports 40–50 million m³ (approximately 40–50 million tons) of water per second. This value has been determined indirectly by various investigators using method of dynamic computation with reference levels of 800–1500 m. This value seems to be a little less than that of Gulf Stream which is about 70 million m³/sec. However, there is a large fluctuation in this figure because of the difficulty in choosing the depth of reference level and determining the width of this current. To the south, the transport seems to decrease to about 20–30 million m³/sec. Since the transport of the North Equatorial Current is estimated at about 40 million m³, about half of this transport turns to the north as the Kuroshio and the other half feeds the Equatorial Countercurrent.

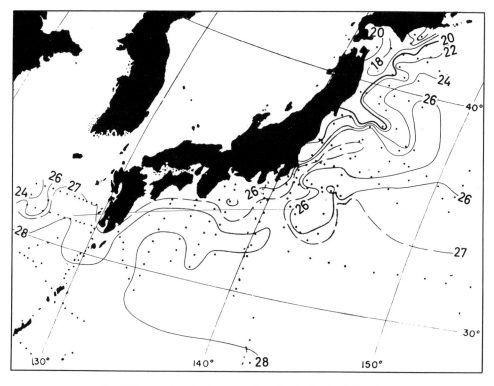

Fig. 2. Temperature in degrees centigrade at a depth of 10 meters.

Water Types of the Kuroshio

The water of the Kuroshio consists of three types, the Upper Surface Water of high temperature and high salinity (0–100 m, around 20°C. 34.5‰) overlying the high salinity Intermediate Water formed in the central Pacific between 10 and 20°N (salinity 34.9–35.1‰) and the Subarctic Intermediate Water formed in the northern Pacific by strong mixing. The last type of water is characterized by its low salinity (34.0–34.3‰), although it is doubtful if it is reasonable to include this layer in the Kuroshio, too. The Kuroshio water has a relatively low oxygen content (about 5.5 cc/liter). According to the temperature-salinity analysis, the Kuroshio water shows successive modification during its flow past the seas off Taiwan, Okinawa, southern and eastern Japan. This is due to the supply of coastal and shelf water discharged from the South China Sea, East China Sea, Yellow Sea, and from the seas adjacent to the Japanese Islands. It mixes with Subarctic Water, Subtropic Water, and upwelling deep water. Thus, the Kuroshio water is something like a mozaic of various kinds of water masses.

Variations and Meanders

In general, the speed of Kuroshio has a seasonal variation. It is strongest from spring through summer (May through August). It declines in autumn. It again strengthens in winter (January and February) and declines in early spring. Variation with a period of about 24 hours was also noticed. The Kuroshio is also accelerated by the passage of storms.

In addition to the seasonal variation, Kuroshio has secular changes. From time to time, we observe cold water masses upwelled from deeper layers. So far as is known, no conspicuous feature of an abnormal development of cold water masses beneath the Kuroshio took place before 1934. Then upwelling developed and brought the cold water mass to the surface, whose center was 200 km across during the period 1936–1940, and 5–10°C colder than the surrounding Kuroshio water at the sea surface. This water mass was identified as a mixture of Kuroshio water with the Intermediate Water and has a nature of a cyclonic eddy. The Kuroshio flows counterclockwise around this cold upwelled water.

The anomalous behavior of the Kuroshio accompanied by a cold water mass has been observed over the following periods: 1906 through 1907, 1917 through 1919, 1934 through 1947, 1954 through 1956, and 1959 through 1962. The occurrence of these cold water masses is always preceded by extreme prevalence of Oyashio Current in the north which takes place 1–5 years in advance.

Since February 1963, the water temperature

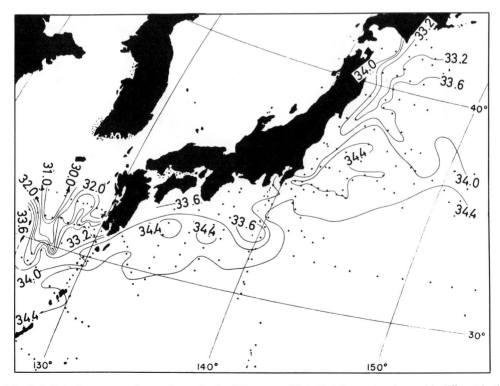

Fig. 3. Salinity in parts per thousand at a depth of 10 meters. (Note that the contour interval is different in the small area west of the Ryukyu Islands.)

along Japanese coasts has been extraordinarily low. M. Uda explains this fact by pointing out that low temperature in the western side of the Pacific is correlated with the high water temperature on the opposite side of the Pacific, namely along the west coast of North America.

In addition to these abnormalities, the Kuroshio axis fluctuates from year to year. In some years, it shows very abnormal behavior, inevitably modifying the route of the Kuroshio. Remarkable meanders are often observed in the eastern and sometimes southern seas of Japan. The undulations have amplitudes of 100–500 km and wavelengths of 300–500 km.

Immediately after leaving the coast of Japan, the Kuroshio meanders greatly in the area east of longitude 142°E. Within the latitudes 33–38°N, it shifts to the north usually at 146–147°E and 155°E, while it shifts southward at the latitudes in between.

Theories of Kuroshio

According to the theories propounded by Henry Stommel, Walter H. Munk and Koji Hidaka, the general circulation of the ocean is maintained by the stresses of the prevailing winds over the ocean. This leads to an intensification of the current close to the western boundaries. Technically, this is called the "western boundary current," and the Kuroshio corresponds to this type of current in the North Pacific. Actually this current is generated in maintaining the continuity of masses in the western Pacific between the water of the North Equatorial Current piled up in low latitudes by Northeast Trades and that driven away in higher latitudes by the prevailing westerlies. For the physical explanation of the formation of the Kuroshio, several agencies other than the stresses of winds are considered to play important roles, although wind stresses are supposed to be mainly responsible at the present.

Historical Notes

The Kuroshio in the North Pacific, which corresponds to the Gulf Stream in the North Atlantic, is well known as one of the greatest oceanic currents in the world and has been familiar to the fishermen and navigators from ancient times. G. Wüst (1936) introduced the historical development of scientific knowledge concerning the Kuroshio Current. It was first noted by B. Varenius (1750) on his geographical map. In Captain J. Cook's expedition (1776–1780), Captain J. King observed the Kuroshio and reported it in 1784. Also, Captain A. J. von Krusenstern (1804) adopted the name "Japan Current" instead of Kuroshio. In the Japanese literature, Nankei Tachibana (1800) and Bakin Takizawa (1804) described the Kuroshio Current geographically in

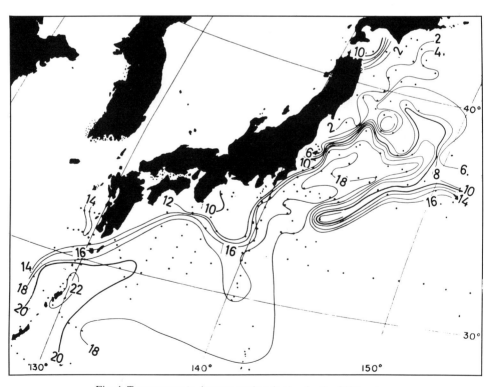

Fig. 4. Temperature in degrees centigrade at a depth of 200 meters.

detail. In 1893, Yuji Wada started the extensive investigation of the Kuroshio and the Oyashio by drift-bottle experiments. In Commodore M. C. Perry's expedition to the Orient (1852–1854), some useful contributions to the knowledge of the Kuroshio were reported. In 1913, Tasaku Kitahara started regular oceanographic observations of the Kuroshio. Since 1918 Captains R. Sigematsu, S. Kishindo and Dr. S. Ogura of the Hydrographic Department, Imperial Japanese Navy, have conducted an extensive program of offshore hydrographic observations especially in the areas including Kuroshio and extending as far down as the North Equatorial Current. During the World War II, Captain S. Kishindo carried out intensive and extensive surveys of the Kuroshio every 10 days with about 10 survey boats for support of submarine operations. Since the Kobe Marine Observatory was founded by Dr. Takematu Okada in 1920 and started oceanographic observations in Japanese waters, K. Suda, K. Hidaka and others have contributed to the knowledge of the Kuroshio. Geostrophic flows in the Kuroshio area were first computed by H. Asano (1914) of the Imperial Fisheries Institute by means of the geostrophic method. Since 1930, M. Uda has made an intensive and extensive survey of this current. In particular, he conducted a multiple ship survey of the Kuroshio area in 1932 using more than 50 research ships.

During the cooperative survey of the North Pacific Ocean north of 20°N (NorPac) carried out by Canadian, Japanese and the United States ships, Japanese oceanographers paid special attention to exploring the details of the Kuroshio. They discovered many important features of the Kuroshio, particularly its meanders after it left the Japanese Islands, by intensive operations in the area directly off the east coast of Honshu during the Inter-national Geophysical Year 1957–1958. Recent observations of Kuroshio has been mostly carried out by a number of active Japanese oceanographers such as Michitaka Uda, K. Kuenuma, Jotaro Masuzawa, Takashi Ichiye, Daitaro Syoji, Kozo Yoshida, Toshiyuki Hirano and others. On 29–31 October, 1963 the UNESCO Meeting of Marine Science Experts on the Kuroshio Region was held in Tokyo. On the first day, a symposium on the Kuroshio was held under the auspices of the Inter-Governmental Oceanographic Commission and the UNESCO Southeast Cooperation Office. On the two following days, experts from Japan, U.S.S.R., Korea, China, the Philippines, Hong Kong, Vietnam and the United States opened discussions on the Cooperative Oceanographic Survey of the Kuroshio which is to be carried out in 1965–1968 by these member countries.

KOJI HIDAKA

References

Brujewicz, S. W., 1957, "On certain chemical features of waters and sediments in north-west Pacific," *Proc. UNESCO Symp. Phys. Oceanography, Tokyo.*

Ichiye, T., 1957, "On the variation of oceanic circulation in the adjacent seas of Japan," *Proc. UNESCO Symp. Phys. Oceanography, Tokyo.*

Koenuma, K., 1939, "On the hydrography of south-western part of the North Pacific and the Kuroshio," *Mem. Imp. Mar. Obs. (Kobe),* 7, 41–114.

Shoji, D., 1957, "On the variation of daily mean sea levels and the Kuroshio from 1954 to 1955," *Proc. UNESCO Symp. Phys. Oceanography, Tokyo.*

Uda, M., 1964, "On the nature of the Kuroshio, its origins and meanders," *Studies on Oceanography,* University of Washington Press, 89–107.

Wüst, G., 1936, "Kuroshio und Golfstrom," *Veröff. lust. f. Meereskunde Berlin A,* **29**, 69pp.

Cross-references: *Ocean Currents; Pacific Ocean.*

L

LABRADOR CURRENT

The Labrador Current is a density current of secondary size which flows south along the western boundary of the Labrador Sea (see Fig. 1). It has its beginning at the Davis Strait where the south-flowing Baffin Land Current, which has followed the western boundary of Baffin Bay from the Arctic Ocean, crosses the Strait to join the last branch of the north and westward moving West Greenland Current in a ratio of volumes transported of 3 to 2. The new current is then reinforced to the south by added inflow through the Hudson Straits and the Belle Isle Straits.

It takes on a banded appearance as though these various added waters were never fully assimilated

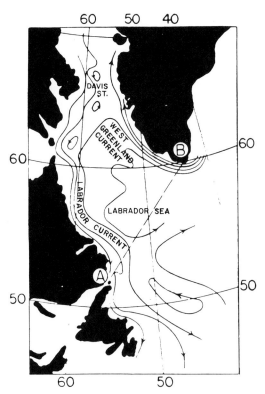

Fig. 1. Diagram of the Labrador Sea delineating the paths of the West Greenland Current and the Labrador Current nearly to its junction with the North Atlantic Current (from Smith, Soule and Mosby, 1937).

into the main water body. The two major bands appear to travel at independent speeds to the common juncture with the northeast moving branch of the Gulf Stream called the North Atlantic Current at about 42°N latitude, 50°W longitude—just southwest of the Island of New-foundland. This forms the northwest gyre of the Atlantic Ocean circulation. The Labrador Current has a counterpart in the Oyashio Current which flows southwest along the Kurile Islands to meet the Kuroshio Current on its way northeast across the North Pacific Ocean.

History of Exploration

Scientific investigations of the Labrador Sea area and into Baffin Bay were begun as early as 1867 with a report of surface temperatures by Petermann. The years 1872 and 1876 saw Bessels aboard the *Polaris* of the United States North Polar Expedition. In 1884, Hamburg made a highly accurate, comprehensive survey which was a very important contribution for its time. Dr. Martin Knudsen (famed for his work on the nature of chlorinity) was in charge of hydrographic work aboard the *Ingolf* in July 1895. He took serial samples at 15 stations across the Labrador Sea.

The United States Coast Guard began its regular ice patrols in 1914, and in 1922, it instituted regular deep oceanographic observations from the icebreakers. In 1931, it had a regular oceanographic vessel for the task of even more concentrated sampling of the entire area. There have, in addition, been other expeditions contributing to the knowledge of the area.

Hydrographic Features

At their meeting at the Davis Strait, the West Greenland Current is a relatively warm, weakly saline, wind-driven current and the Baffin Land Current is a cold, weakly saline, density or wind-driven current with its core at approximately 100 m depth. The Labrador Current comprised of these two currents continues with approximately the same characteristics as the Baffin Land Current. The core is centered at 100 m depth and only slightly distinguishable at more than 600 m. Its temperature is less than −1°C at the core, and its salinity is between 33 and 34‰. It maintains this identity over its entire course. Its path is restricted

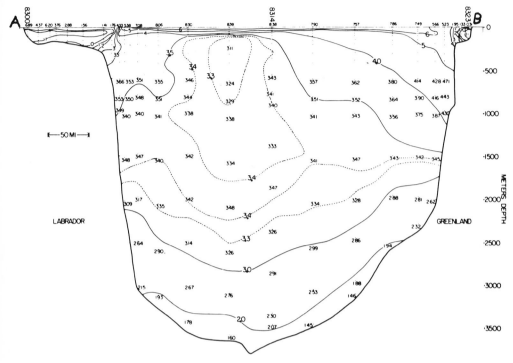

Fig. 2. Profile of the temperature structures of the Labrador Sea showing the cross section of the Labrador Current by the less than −1°C core on the left and the West Greenland Current by the core on the right (from Soule, Franceschetti, O'Hagen and Driggers, 1940).

to the shelf zone with one of two major bands well in on the shelf, while the other follows the slope contours. The velocities may attain 38 miles/day as in a 1928 Coast Guard survey. The mass transport rates vary from year to year, but an example during a year of great volume, 1933, is 5.4×10^6 m³/sec, while 1931 was a low-volume year with 3.4×10^6 m³/sec. The current also transports many icebergs south, creating hazards to navigation as far as the Grand Banks region.

Areas of upwelling formed at the front between the Labrador Current and the ocean water in the center of the Davis Strait and off the coast of West Greenland create areas of high productivity because of the concentration of nutrients (Steeman Nielsen, 1958). It has also been speculated that winter cooling may produce vertical convection currents extending from surface to bottom, which would enrich the surface waters with high concentrations of nutrients on a seasonal basis (Sverdrup, 1942).

Where the Labrador Current meets the Atlantic Current, the former sinks below the latter, thereby forming a stratified system. The area is renowned for its frequent occurrences of fog banks due to the rapid drop of surface temperature experienced by the air masses moving from a warm water area to a cold water area.

NOEL B. PLUTCHAK

References

Corwin, Nathaniel, and McGill, David A., 1963, "Nutrient distribution in the Labrador Sea and Baffin Bay," *U.S. Coast Guard Bull.*, No. 48, 79–153.

Defant, Albert, 1961, "Physical Oceanography," Vol. 1, pp. 662–669, New York, Pergamon Press.

Hill, M. N., 1963, "The Sea," Vol. 2, pp. 365, 371, New York, John Wiley & Sons.

Jacobs, W. U., 1943, "Sources of atmospheric heat and moisture over the North Pacific and North Atlantic Oceans," *Ann. N.Y. Acad. Sci.*, **44**, 19–40.

Nielsen, E. Steeman, 1958, "A survey of recent Danish measurements of the organic productivity in the sea," *Rapp. Cons. Explor. Mer.*, **144**, 92–95.

Smith, E. H., Soule, F. M., and Mosby, O., 1937, "The *Marion* and *General Greene* Expedition to Davis Strait and Labrador Sea, 1928–31–33–34–35," *U.S. Coast Guard Bull.*, No. 19, Part 2, 259pp.

Soule, F. M., Franceschetti, A. P., O'Hagan, R. M., and Driggers, V. W., 1940, *U.S. Coast Guard Bull.*, No. 48, 29–78.

Sverdrup, H. U., *et al.*, 1942, "The Oceans," Englewood Cliffs, Prentice-Hall, 1087pp.

Cross-references: *Atlantic Ocean; Ocean Currents.*

LABRADOR SEA

The Labrador Sea is bounded to the west by the coast of Labrador and the southeastern coast of Baffin Island and to the east by Greenland. The southern boundary is a line from Cape Farewell,

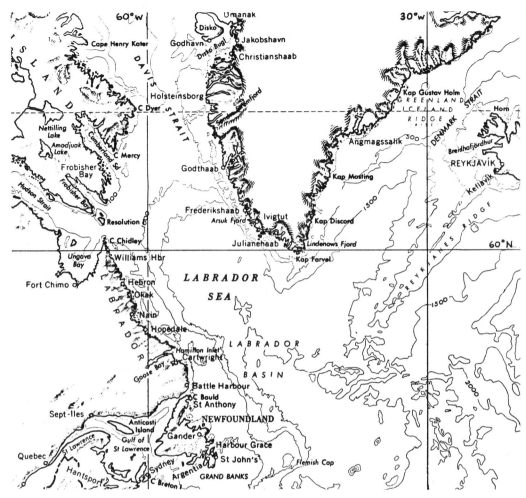

Fig. 1. Bathymetry of Labrador Sea and Irminger Sea, to the southeast and south of Greenland; from U.S. Oceanographic Office chart No. 1262A.

Greenland to Cape St. Charles at the northern side of Belle Isle Strait and the northern boundary is parallel 66°N across Davis Strait.

(1) Bathymetry and Sediments

The bottom topography shows the presence of a parallel-sided trough which is open to the southeast but bounded to the north by a submarine ridge across Davis Strait. The sill depth of this ridge is about 800 m. To the south of the ridge, the depth increases rapidly to 2000 m and then more gradually to about 3700 m in the southeastern part of the sea. In a few places the depth exceeds 4000 m. The continental shelf is very narrow off Greenland where the distance to the 200-m depth contour is about 50 km. It is wider off Labrador, with that distance being about 100 km. The central depression, the *Labrador Basin,* extends southeastward into the region of the Irminger Sea (q.v.).

The bottom sediments consist of globigerina ooze and terrigenous clays and silts. They frequently contain rock fragments and pebbles from Greenland and Baffin Island. These have been transported by floating ice and deposited when the ice melted. The organic content of the sediments is about 1% and is low compared with those in the ice-free area.

(2) Meteorology and Oceanography

The climate is of the polar and continental type almost down to 55°N on the Canadian side and is of the maritime type on the Greenland side. The annual mean air temperature is about 5–7°C higher on the Greenland side than on the Canadian side at the same latitude. The mean annual range of air temperature is larger on the Canadian side (30°C at Hopedale at 55.5°N and 37°C at Kingua-Fjord at 66.5°N) than on the Greenland side (15°C at Cape Farewell and 17°C at Godthaab at 64.2°N). The precipitation also indicates such difference between the west and east side of the sea. The annual precipitation to the south of Cape Farewell reaches about 1000 mm while it is less than 250 mm north of 55°N on the Canadian side representing the dry polar climate.

The West Greenland Current (q.v.) flows northward off the Greenland coast carrying the water of the East Greenland Current which has high salinity close to 35‰ by admixture of Atlantic water. The Labrador Current (q.v.) flows southward off Baffin Island and Labrador carrying the cold and low-salinity water from Baffin Bay and sounds of Baffin Island. Part of the East Greenland Current joins the Labrador Current to the south of Davis Strait.

The coastal water forms a narrow belt on the continental shelf off Greenland. Its salinity is low and 31–34‰. Its temperature shows a considerable annual variation from 5–6°C in summer to freezing point in winter. Beyond this water, the East Greenland Current carries the water with high salinity close to 35‰ originating from admixture of Atlantic water in the subsurface layer. This water has a temperature of about 5°C at depths below 150–200 m. The water on the Labrador continental shelf has a low salinity (30–34‰) and is colder than the Greenland coastal water with temperatures below −1°C at a depth of 100 m even in midsummer. The bulk of the waters in the Labrador Sea has a salinity around 34.9‰, the highest values 34.94‰ being found near the bottom; the temperatures are between 3.5 and 2°C, the lowest values near the bottom. The oxygen content of the waters is generally high and is between 6.0 and 6.5 ml/liter in the deep and bottom water.

The large body of water in the central part is formed by the mixing of Atlantic water and Arctic water coming partly from the East Greenland Current and partly from Baffin Bay. This mixed water is almost uniform and has salinity between 34.88 and 34.94‰. When this water is cooled in winter to temperatures between 3.5 and 2°C at the surface, it attains a high density and sinks to the depth at which the density equals the value at the surface. The high oxygen content of the deep water is an evidence of such motion. The deep and bottom water formed by sinking of the surface water flows south into the Atlantic, where it can be traced almost to the Antarctic Ocean. The average outflow of deep water from the Labrador Sea is estimated at 2 million m³/sec.

Most of the eastern one-third of the Labrador Sea is generally ice-free the year round except for a region along the coast of Southwest Greenland. This coast is open from August to December. The ice starts to form around Cape Farewell spreading to the north in December. It attains its greatest northern extent in April–May when the coast is closed from Cape Farewell to about 62°N. Between this latitude and the Arctic Circle the outer coastline is always ice free, but fjords are frozen. The Canadian side is generally ice-free until late September. From October on, the ice belt off this side increases in width from the north. By the end of December, it extends to the southern limit of the Labrador Sea. In April–May it covers the western two-thirds of the sea but in June to August it gradually disappears.

The tidal range along the Canadian side is less than 1.8 m and semidiurnal tides are predominant. The tides on the Greenland side are also regular and semidiurnal but their ranges are larger than on the Canadian side. The range is 4.12 m at Frederikshaab and decreases to the north to about 2 m on the coast of Baffin Bay.

TAKASHI ICHIYE

References

Bruns, E., 1958, "Ozeanologie," Vol. I, Berlin, VEB Deutscherverlag der Wissenschaften, 420pp.

Hood, P. J., and Godby, E. A., 1964, "Magnetic anomalies over the Mid-Labrador Sea Ridge," *Nature,* **202**, 1099.

International Hydrographic Bureau, 1937, "Limits of oceans and seas," *Special Publication No. 23,* Monaco.

Schott, G., 1942, "Geographie des Atlantischen Ozeans," Hamburg, Verlag Von C. Boysen, 428pp.

Soule, F. M., Franceschetti, A. P., O'Hagen, R. M., and Driggers, V. W., 1963, "Physical oceanography of the Grand Banks region, the Labrador Sea and Davis Strait in 1962," *U.S.C.G. Bull.,* **48**, 29–78, 95–153.

Sverdrup, H. U., 1956, "Oceanography of the Arctic," in "The Dynamic North," Book 1, No. 5, OPNAV PO 3–11, 32pp.

Cross-references: *Arctic Sea; Canadian Arctic Archipelago; East Greenland Current; Irminger Sea; Labrador Current; West Greenland Current.*

LAGOON—*See* Vol. III

LAMINAR FLOW, LAMINAR BOUNDARY LAYER

A fluid flow is laminar, a *streamline* or *sheet flow,* when each particle follows the one in front and there is no lateral mixing. It may thus be visualized in parallel layers or sheets. It is non-turbulent, i.e., in contrast to *turbulence* (q.v.) or *transitional flow.* Laminar flow occurs at low velocities, and small scale motion (low Reynold's number; see *Fluid Mechanics*). At higher Reynold's number turbulent flow takes over.

The *laminar boundary layer* is the very thin layer adjacent to a fixed boundary. The fluid (or air) velocity at the boundary itself is zero but there is a steep velocity gradient moving up or away from it, to a plane where a free air stream is possible. In this boundary layer, the molecular viscous stress is very high and greatly exceeds the Reynolds stress ("eddy shearing stress"). Appropriate to this layer (as well as for other purposes) are the *Navier-Stokes Equations,* which are the equations of motion for a

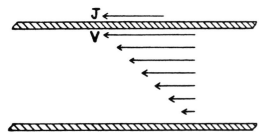

Fig. 1. Fluid shear between two parallel plates (Hess).

viscous, incompressible fluid. Where v is kinematic viscosity, p the pressure, ρ the density, F the total external force and V the fluid velocity,

$$\frac{dV}{dt} = -\frac{1}{\rho}\,\nabla p + F + v\,\nabla^2 V + \tfrac{1}{3}v\nabla(\nabla \cdot V)$$

For an incompressible fluid, the term in $\nabla \cdot V$ (divergence) disappears, and the viscosity plays a role analogous to temperature in thermal conduction and to density in simple diffusion. In atmospheric motion, *eddy viscosity* (q.v.) leads to turbulent transfer of momentum in a manner analogous to the molecular viscosity of laminar flow, but on a vastly bigger scale.

RHODES W. FAIRBRIDGE

References

Huschke, R. E. (editor), 1959, "Glossary of Meteorology," Boston, American Meteorological Society, 638pp.

Stewart, H. J., 1945, "Kinematics and Dynamics of Fluid Flow," in "Handbook of Meteorology," pp. 412–500, New York, McGraw-Hill Book Co.

Cross-references: *Streamline; Turbulence; Viscosity.*

LAPSE RATE—*See* Vol. II

LAPTEV SEA

The Laptev Sea is, for its greater part, a continental shelf sea which washes the northern shores of Asia from Mys (Cape) Chelyuskin on Taimyr peninsula to the Svyatoy Nos (Ness) in the Proliv (Strait) of Dmitriy Laptev. The western boundary of the sea stretches along the eastern coast of the archipelago of Severnaya Zemlya (North Land), and its eastern boundary stretches along the western coast of the Kotelny Island (Ostrov) and Lyakhovskiye Islands. On the north, the sea has no natural boundaries; a loxodromic curve is used instead, drawn from the Arktichesky Mys (Arctic Cape), which is the northern extremity of Severnaya Zemlya, to the point where the meridian of 139°E crosses the shelf edge (150 km north of Kotelny Island). The area of the sea within the above boundaries is 540,000 km² or 208,000 square miles. Some 64% of the whole area is less than 100 m deep.

Eastward of Taimyr peninsula the continental shelf and lowland areas occupy the Lena–Anabarsky marginal basin of Jurassic–Cretaceous age. The archipelago of Severnaya Zemlya is a continuation of Paleozoic and Mesozoic folded structures of Taimyr peninsula, and the New Siberian islands, for the most part, are a continuation of Mesozoic and Cenozoic folded structures of the Verkhoyansky Range (Gakkel, 1962; Panov, 1963).

Following a summary by Zenkevitch (1963), the Laptev Sea was first explored scientifically by Nordenskjöld on the *Vega* (1878–79). In 1893 Nansen zigzagged across the area in the *Fram*. Two early Russian expeditions were by Toll on the *Zarya* (1900–03), and Vilkitsky with the *Taimyr* and *Vaigach* (1913). After World War I, there were two more Norwegian expeditions, on the *Maud* (1918–20, and 1921–24). Soviet exploration by Khmisnikov and by Tchirikhin have used the icebreakers *Lithke* (1934) and *Sadko* (1937). The name Nordenskjöld Sea is sometimes applied to this water body, but following a decision of the Central Executive of the U.S.S.R. (reported in *International Hydrographic Review*, 1936, p. 160) the name Laptev Sea is adhered to.

Bathymetry

Bottom topography of the southern (shelf) part of the sea is highly irregular owing to numerous depressions and troughs of erosional and tectonic origin, the Pleistocene (submarine) beds of modern rivers, as well as to shallows and banks. The latter are relict forms of old islands. Ancient erosion features of bottom topography were formed as far back as the end of Pliocene and the beginning of Pleistocene when the relative sea level was 400–500 m lower than the modern one and the shoreline was in the upper part of the continental slope. Sediment was laid down in the shelf area and previously eroded valleys were partially buried under conditions of almost constantly rising sea level in the Lower and Middle Pleistocene. At the beginning of Upper Pleistocene, the regional sea level was 80–100 m higher than that of the present day but later it began to drop progressively and came close to the modern one during the Sartan mountain-valley glaciation, i.e., 20,000 years ago (Lazukov, 1964). In this respect shores of the Arctic seas, including those of the Laptev Sea, differ from all other shores of the world ocean, the level of which reached the present level only about 6000 years ago. The cause appears to be not eustatic, but geodetic, related to polar shift and other factors. The continental slope of the Laptev Sea is cut by a big trench (in some places more than 3000 m deep) which farther north passes into the Nansen geosynclinal basin (Belov and Lapina, 1961). According to Heezen and

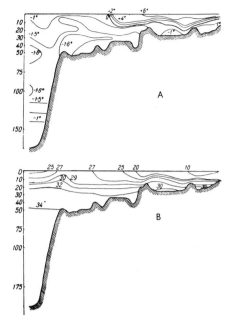

Fig. 1. Temperature (A) and salinity (B) ranges in the cross section of Laptev Sea from its southeastern part (on right of graph) to northwest (Wiese; from Zenkevitch, 1963).

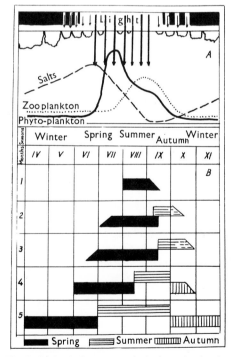

Fig. 2. Biological seasons of plankton in the Arctic Asian continental shelf seas. (A) General indices (Bogorov); (B) phytoplankton (Usachev); seasonal lengths-line (1) Arctic Ocean (circum-polar); (2) Central Kara Sea; (3) Laptev Sea; (4) Northern Barents Sea; (5) S.W. Barents Sea (from Zenkevitch, 1963).

Ewing (1963), the mid-oceanic ridge and rift may also come ashore in this area, forming the southern border of the Nansen Basin.

Sediments

At shallow depths, the sea bottom is usually composed of sand and mud, in some places including pebbles and broken boulders, while at greater depths, the bottom is formed of mud. Rivers, especially the Lena (with 11.3 million tons of suspended sediment accompanying the total annual freshwater discharge of 488 km^3) and the Yana (6.2 million tons of suspended matter per year), fundamentally affect sedimentation processes in the nearshore zone of the Laptev Sea. Due to alluviation and shore erosion the rate of sedimentation in the nearshore zone is sometimes 25 cm/yr. This is one of the causes for the formation of banks and shallows and for the progradation of shore lines in some shallow bays seaward at the rate of 1–2 m/yr (Grigoriyev, 1964).

The warming action of river waters is of considerable importance for the formation of the shore line of the low southern coast of the Laptev Sea. Almost the entire stretch of coast is composed of sandy-clay, representing permanently frozen ground, either including ice masses or having a high ice content in the upper layers.

Very often permanently frozen strata extend all over the shelf and especially in the nearshore area. Drilling carried out in this area shows that the temperature of ice-bound deposits ranges from -10 to $-1°C$. Freezing of bottom sediments in the nearshore zone also goes on at the present time, more often through the sea ice which rests on the bottom in shallow areas (see also Vol. III, article on *Permafrost*).

Coastal Geomorphology

The high ice content of quaternary strata amplifies the abrasion processes in the shore zone resulting in widespread "thermo-abrasion" and abrasion-solifluction types of shore along the southern coast of the Laptev Sea (Ionin, Kaplin and Medvedev, 1961). The rate of shore destruction in some places is sometimes 30–40 m, an average being 5 m/yr. Where Quaternary loam formations include thick ice masses, a special type of shore conditioned by thermo-abrasion process has developed. The shore in the Strait of Dmitriy Laptev is called the Mammoth coast since the Quaternary strata here are particularly replete with the remains of these extinct animals (Karelin, 1947).

The mountainous coasts of Taimyr Peninsula and of Severnaya Zemlya have precipitous cliffed shores, yet typically abrasion shores are encountered here only in short stretches. Abrasion-denudation shore lines and solely denudation types are widespread, most often due to intensive denudation processes (periglacial solifluction slopes without abrasion) and to the very short period of wave activity during a year. The numerous glaciers of Severnaya Zemlya (the total area of glaciation is 16,900 km^2) coming down to the sea along U-shaped valleys give birth to many icebergs. Many such valleys in their lower sections are fiords. The biggest fiord is confined within a graben in the Shokalsky Strait (Kaplin, 1962). The rest of the fiords are of erosional origin.

On the whole, the shoreline of the Laptev Sea is deeply indented; e.g., Khatangsky Bay, Anabarsky Bay, Oleneksky Bay, Buorkhaya Inlet, etc., cut deep inland. The shore line is rather changeable and sometimes indefinite owing to the presence of shoals and frequent on- and offshore winds.

Climate

The climate of the Laptev Sea is Arctic: the mean annual temperature is $-13°C$ and lower. A mean temperature above $0°C$ occurs only during 2–3 summer months. Maximum summer temperature on the coast is $+30°C$ (86°F), and minimum winter temperature is $-50°C$ ($-58°F$). The precipitation is not more than 100 mm (4 inches) per year.

Sea Ice and Salinity

Most of the year the sea is covered with ice which sometimes remains in the northern part over the whole summer. The ice drift direction depends on meteorologic conditions (air pressure). When there is a polar pressure maximum, an anticyclonic current circulation builds up in the Sea which favors ice drift from the Laptev Sea to the west (about 375,000 km^3). Under such conditions the surface water temperature in the western part of the sea drops from 7–8°C in the southern part to 0–1°C near the ice edge, and in the eastern part of the sea—from 10–11°C near the Lena Delta to 5–6°C in the Strait of Dmitriy Laptev and to 2°C in the Strait of Sannikov. Water salinity increases from 2–3‰ (Buorkhaya Inlet) to 30‰ near the ice edge.

When the winter Siberian anticyclone extends over the northern regions to the shelf seas, and the polar anticyclone weakens, an area of cyclonic water circulation develops. Ice drift from the Laptev Sea is weak (not more than 240,000 km^3). Cycles of 3–5 years are distinguished in the water circulation system (Sokolov, 1962). Under the existing ice regime surface, the water temperature in the warmest month (August) drops from 3–4°C (in the Lena Delta area) to 0–1°C (Belkovsky Island, Straits of Sannikov and Dmitriy Laptev). Along the Taimyr Peninsula the water temperature ranges from -0.5 to $0°C$ and only in the south does it rise to 1°C. Owing to slow ice melting, the salinity along the southern coast reaches 8–10‰, and at the Lena mouth only 5‰. To the north and northwest, near the ice edge, the salinity in the surface layer exceeds 30–31‰.

Wave Action and Tides

In the seasons when the sea is ice free, north-easterly and easterly winds prevail, but in autumn the wind direction is unstable. Mean wind velocity in this period is 5–6 m/sec, reaching a maximum of 18–25 m/sec. The most intensive wave action is observed off the western coast and in the central parts of the Laptev Sea. Waves are usually not higher than 1.5 m, but when easterly winds are blowing and a large area of seawater is free of ice, the wave height may be as great as 5–6 m.

The tidal range is not great, but due to off- and on-shore winds, sea-level fluctuations in the littoral zone may be as great as 2–3 m.

Fauna and Flora

The fauna and flora of the sea are typically Arctic. Phytoplankton is represented by marine and brackish freshwater diatom algae. The most widespread species of zooplankton are tintinnids, rotifers, copepods and amphipods. Benthic animals include foraminifera, polychaetes, isopods, bryozoa and mollusks. Fish are represented by Siberian cisco, Arctic char, omul, nelma, sturgeon, etc. (Zenkevitch, 1963).

Walrus, sea hare, seal and porpoise are representatives of the East Siberian sea mammals. Ice floes and ice islands in the open sea are inhabited by polar bears. Near the sea shore, colonies of sea gulls are abundant.

A. S. IONIN

References

(All the following are in Russian, except Heezen and Ewing, 1963, and Zenkevitch, 1963)

Belov, I. A., and Lapina, N. N., 1961, "Bottom sediments of the Arctic basin," Morskoy Transport Publishing House.

Gakkel, Y. Y., 1962, "Morphotectonic Features of the Arctic basin," in "Problems of the Arctic and the Antarctic," Morskoy Transport Publishing House, Issue 11.

Grigoriyev, N. Ph., 1964, "Peculiarities of shore formation under the polar climate conditions," Collection of Papers, "Theoretical questions of sea shore dynamics," *Scientific reports in Program XX International Geographical Congress,* Nauka Publishing House.

Heezen, B. C., and Ewing, M., 1963, "The Mid-Oceanic Ridge," in "The Sea," Vol. 3, pp. 388–410, New York, Interscience Publishers.

Ionin, A. S., Kaplin, P. A., and Medvedev, V. S., 1961, "Classification of the world sea shores," *Proc. Oceanographic Commission, Acad. Sci. USSR,* **12**.

Kaplin, P. A., 1962, "Fiord Shores of the USSR," Moscow Publishing House, Acad. Sci. USSR.

Karelin, D. B., 1947, "The Laptev Sea," Glavsevmorput Publishing House.

Lazukov, G. I., 1964, "Level fluctuations of the Polar basin in the Quaternary period," *Okeanologia,* **5**(1).

Panov, D. G., 1963, "Bottom Morphology of the World Ocean," Moscow Publishing House, Acad. Sci. USSR.

Sokolov, A. L., 1962, "Ice Drift in the Arctic basin and Changes of Ice Conditions along the Northern Sea Route," in "Problems of the Arctic and the Antarctic," Morskoy Transport Publishing House, Issue 11.

Zenkevitch, L. A., 1963, "Biology of the Seas of the USSR," New York, Interscience Publishers, 955pp. (translated by S. Bolscharskaya).

Cross-references: *Arctic Ocean; Barents Sea; Chukchi Sea; East Siberia Sea; Kara Sea.*

LATENT HEAT—*See* Vol. II

LITTORAL ZONATION—*See* LITTORAL SEDIMENTATION, Vol. III

LITTORAL ZONE (AND SEDIMENTATION FACIES)*

Introduction

The term littoral zone (from the Latin *littoralis,* of or pertaining to the shore) was originally designated by Forbes and Hanley (1853) as that area between the tide marks. Consistent with the original definition are the interpretations of Twenhofel (1926, 1950), Kuenen (1950), and Weller (1960). However, Grabau (1924), Hedgpeth (1957), and Sverdrup, Johnson, and Fleming (1942) prefer to use littoral to describe the benthic zone extending from high water on the beach to the edge of the continental shelf, using the subdivisions eulittoral and sublittoral to further delimit such a zonation. The former subdivision, eulittoral, refers to the intertidal region, whereas the latter refers to the rest of the shelf bottom facies. In accord with processes occurring in the ocean, "littoral" may refer to the region in which bottom sediments and organisms are affected by tidal phenomena, longshore currents, and the continuous or periodic motion of surge or breaking waves. This depth will exceed that of tidal variation, but the lower limit will be about 5–10 meters below low tide level, with some variation depending upon the intensity of storm waves. In addition to the aforementioned processes that both define and affect the "littoral zone," the geographic location, climatic province, and nature of substrate determine what kinds of sedimentary processes take place and what density organic populations will reach. Reef environment, rocky shores, sandy beaches and barred bays, each considered littoral as defined above, are described in the following discussion.

Reef Environment

Temperature of tropical waters permits abundant deposition of calcium carbonate by organic agents, and reefs flourish in many areas as a result. In this context, the term reef is defined as a bioherm in

* Contribution No. 684, from The Marine Laboratory, Institute of Marine Science, University of Miami.

which the most visually obvious component is hermatypic coral (Hoffmeister *et al.*, 1964). Such features often permit ready distinction of tropical littoral zones from those of other regions. However, because of the strong influence of temperature, salinity, turbidity, and water currents, death of littoral inhabitants rapidly ensues when departure from their normal station takes place or when strong fluctuations occur in the environment. Diverse reef types are found in the Atlantic Ocean, Pacific Ocean, and Gulf of Mexico; however, because of the aforementioned ecologic parameters of each environment, it is possible to characterize reef growth in general. Wells (1957) has shown that the best reef development occurs where mean annual water temperatures are approximately 23–25°C, thus restricting most reef growth to 20°N and S of the equator, except in areas such as the Gulf Stream and Kuroshio Current which are subject to the flow of meridional warm currents. Other factors of critical importance are the amount of light available for photosynthetic activities, the oxygen content of surrounding waters, and suspended sediment. The last two properties are functions of current movement in and about the reef, and thus a continuous flow of water is necessitated. In addition, currents transport nutrients to the reef colonies, in the form of planktonic organisms. However, the sediment load transported should be at a minimum, so as not to interfere with penetration of light.

Wells (1957) has listed the physiographic divisions of Indo-Pacific atolls as follows: (1) seaward slope; that area which goes down to about 15 meters and consists chiefly of rubble; (2) reef margin contains algal ridge and coralline growth; (3) reef flat—the area which undergoes diurnal tidal cycles and has large fluctuations in pH, salinity, and oxygen content; (4, 5) island and lagoon reef: where conditions permit, these features may develop; (6) lagoon slope—site of shifting sediment, which thus lacks appreciable coral growth; (7) knolls; patchy features that develop within the lagoon and are similar to micro-atolls. Seaward reefs are classified according to windward or leeward position. The chief distinction between the former and the latter are that leeward reefs tend to lack an algal ridge, steeper slopes, well-developed channels, and richer coral growth. These features are a result of protection, via their position, from the dominant storm waves, and thus organic growth is capable of being carried on without major interruption or hazard.

Coral reefs of the Gulf of Mexico and the Florida Keys–Bahama Islands groups differ from Indo-Pacific types in that they lack true inner lagoons and algal ridges (Emery, Tracey, and Ladd, 1954; Emery, 1963). In addition, reefs of the Florida Keys–Bahama Islands group tend to have their most luxuriant growth on the seaward side of the islands involved. This is attributed to the islands giving rise to unfavorable currents which carry a high suspended sediment load or consisting of higher-salinity water as a result of evaporation during the residence time of water on shallow banks.

Sediments found in the reef environment do not vary considerably in their composition, and it has been found that the primary sources are the organisms growing on the seaward sides of the reef (Emery *et al.*, 1954). Wave action is responsible for fragmenting coral growth and creating zones of rubble; this is the deepest part of the littoral zone encountered in the reef environment and is equivalent to a *mare incognitum* for many authors. Large blocks of limestone may also be found within this region and are the result of weathering and abrasion of overhanging ledges and cavernous sites (see *Biological Erosion of Limestone Coasts,* Vol. III). During times of high storm intensity, such limestone blocks may be thrown upon the reef flat and create anomalous appearances.

Fragments of coral, algae, and foraminifera (*Homotrema, Carpentaria, Calcarina spengleri, Marginopora,* and *Amphistegina*) constitute the majority of sediments found on the reef flat. On beaches of the reef environment, foraminifera make up the greater part of the sediment, their percentage increases seaward. Broken fragments of *Lithothamnion,* derived from abrasion of the algal ridge and oolites are also found on seaward beach area. In addition, along beaches, small amounts of echinoid spines, gastropod shells, and broken bryozoan tests are present. Lagoonal sediments within the reef are chiefly foraminifera, *Halimeda* debris, small coral fragments, *Inoceramus* prisms and clay component made up of abraded shell material that can account for as much as 50% of sediment.

Rocky Coasts

Rocky coasts are often the expression of relatively recent tectonic processes, such as faulting or volcanic activity. They may also represent shore lines that have managed to withstand erosion due to extreme rock durability or to insufficient wave energy. Where climatic conditions approach aridity, coastlines maintain their rocky nature because of the low intensity of chemical weathering and stream erosion. Fjord coasts also have precipitous shore lines, but are the result of glacial erosion.

Both flora and fauna of such coastlines are greatly restricted because of the requirement placed on attachment to substrate. Hard surfaces of metamorphic, igneous, or compact sedimentary rocks present the best sites. Poorly compacted sediments, such as marly limestones, chalks, or indurated sandstones, do not permit large populations to exist because of their holdfast quality.

Characters of the tidal cycle greatly influence the lives of rocky coast littoral zone inhabitants. Those species which occupy the shallowest water must contend with the problems of desiccation. Since they cannot burrow into rocks, limpets (*Patella,*

etc.) for example, modify the shape and thickness of their shell in order to adjust their osmoregulatory processes during times of exposure. In addition, the same species, and other similar types, flourish in zones of wave action because many of their competitors are not capable of securing themselves. Suspension feeders such as barnacles (*Balanus*), are the chief occupants of the most turbulent part of the rocky coast littoral zone.

Rocky coasts of the low latitudes that are subjected to exposure have very low populations because of temperature effects. Barnacles, algae, coralline growth, gastropods, and encrusting foraminifera are found below the level of tidal influence. In cooler waters, they are present with the addition of rock oysters, mussels, pholads, anemones, sea urchins and starfish. Polar waters, however, have extremely small populations on rocky coasts. The abrasive action of ice removes any species which may become temporarily present. Furthermore, melting of ice, during warm seasons, produces considerably lower-salinity water which has a detrimental effect on stenohaline marine inhabitants. Organisms capable of annual migrations or those that can live below the level of ice may be present. The latter-mentioned characteristic, however, places the animal in jeopardy of having its oxygen supply cut off. This habitat is often marked by numbers of adapted fresh-water or brackish forms (e.g., diatoms).

Sandy Shores

Sandy shores are the result of degradation of preexisting geologic units and sediment transport to a site of deposition. Such accumulations can be in the form of leeward lagoons or reef beaches, as mentioned in an above section, or they may be pocket beaches contained within rocky coastlines, coastal beaches of wide expanse, or offshore bars which themselves contain environments peculiar to the littoral zone.

Pocket beaches are embayments found between cliffed headlands, or along rocky coasts in general. Because of their indented character, they form excellent traps for sediments transported by longshore currents. Such beaches generally display well-sorted sands, although they may contain sediments ranging from silt size to that of boulders. In many cases, the composition of these sediments reflects the type of rocks immediately adjacent to the beach. For example, many Hawaiian pocket beaches have concentrations of olivine-rich sands, which are the result of the weathering of basaltic lavas. "Black sand beaches," rich in durable heavy minerals, are characteristic of very mature beaches, particularly with Precambrian hinterlands.

Many studies have shown that pocket beaches are greatly modified by seasonal changes in nearshore water characteristic. During summertime, when relatively calm conditions prevail, sands accumulate and beaches become well stratified and sorted. During winter storm periods, erosion occurs and considerable quantities of beach material are removed.

Coastal beaches are characteristic of areas in which the continental shelf is wide and areas in which a preexisting coastal plain has been well established (with preexisting, uncemented sands). Both seasonal winds and changes in nearshore water conditions affect sedimentation and erosion in such areas, but in general these sites imply relative stability of the processes mentioned. These beaches contain well-sorted sediments and are chiefly made of sand-size material.

Living populations tend to be of high density, but due to their nocturnal character they are not generally observable. Small crabs, shrimp, gastropods, and annelid worms are the dominant groups present on beaches. Offshore, beyond the surf zone, the same living species are represented; however, foraminifera become an important part of the benthic fauna, along with gastropods, pelecypods, and polychaete worms. Their presence is shown by abundant worm trails, burrows, and mounds. Vertically, such migration causes considerable disturbance of stratified sand layers and gives some sedimentary deposits an anomalous homogenous character. In other situations, benthic inhabitants may cause artificial stratification.

Where nearshore water is not quieted by protective agencies such as grasses or exposed rock formations, ripple marks become well developed. This type of sedimentary feature, in fact, can be used to some degree to measure turbulence and current action in the zone immediately offshore from the swash zone of the beach. Where marine grasses, such as *Thalassia* or *Zostera*, are present, bottom deposits will not develop rippled surfaces. Such zones are not barren of markings, as the organic features mentioned above will be more intensified because of the stillness of the water. In addition, phenomena such as "tadpole markings" will also be found, the results of a local population swimming to and fro within a restricted area. A feature marking the uppermost extent of the environment is the swash line, left by approaching waves or ebbing waters. This line consists of microdebris, such as foraminifera, small shells, seaweed, and other pieces of drifted and rafted material.

Barred Bay Environment

Many authors acknowledge the fact that environmental factors can greatly alter forms of preexisting geologic situations. Because of the extreme diversity of current phenomena, etc., within the littoral zone, there is constant reworking to form new settings. A result of this, exemplified in many areas, is the transformation of simple coastlines into the barred bay environment. Such an area generally has several shallow basins enclosed behind an extended sand bar, which may have one or more openings or channels leading into the waters behind the bar. Areas of such physiography are found along all coastlines of the United States. Sites worthy of note are the bays of Nantucket Island, Martha's Vineyard, Cape Cod Bay, Buzzards Bay, Narragansett Bay in the New England area; the sounds behind Cape Hatteras, North Carolina; St. Josephs Bay, Florida; Barataria Bay and San Antonio Bay, Texas; several bays in Baja California; and Newport Bay, California; and Yaquina Bay, Oregon. Classical overseas examples are to be seen in the southern Baltic, the Black Sea (limans), southern France, west Africa, Western Australia and southern Brazil.

In all of these, long sand spits have been built up by longshore currents and then have been partially or wholly modified by the work of wind and waves. Many workers have shown that these areas are narrow, cuspate, and in places deeply incised. It is not uncommon to find development of such features on coasts where sufficient sand is available and longshore currents or tidal gyres can cause modification. In all of the bays mentioned, tidal action or other strong currents carry out selective sorting of sediments. Little difference is caused either by narrow jetties, such as those found at Nantucket or Newport Bay, or by the wider openings of Buzzards Bay or Cape Cod Bay. Coarsest sediments are found in the inlet channels, and grain size decreases as the deeper areas of the environment are reached. It has been noted that the relationship of grain size to bathymetry is predictable, and thus by knowing one, approximations of the other can be made.

Parameters such as provenance, tectonic stage of source area, and geographic setting yield data which clearly differentiate bays, such as those mentioned above, that are outwardly similar in grain size distribution or bathymetric relationship. As stated above, geographic setting has an important control on carbonate content of littoral zone sediments. New England bays may have as little as 2% calcium carbonate, as opposed to bays in the Florida area, which in some sites may have as much as 99.9%. Obviously the proximity to the tropics has a bearing on these values. Midway up the Atlantic coast at Cape Hatteras, where the Gulf Stream is deflected offshore, carbonate content decreases, whereas quartz and feldspar percentages increase (Stetson, 1939). Further to the north, the quartz percentage approaches 90%. This increase in part reflects colder water conditions, but source area and energy are also important.

Quartz and feldspar percentages may be affected by geographic setting, but the quartz-feldspar ratio is also controlled by provenance and tectonic stage of the source area. High percentages of quartz sand should be expected where an area has had a long period of stability and also, as in the case of the New England area, where the sediments are primarily

447

derived form crystalline shield regions to the north. Krynine (1935) has shown that relief is the chief factor controlling feldspar content of a sand body. Thus, low relief of shelf areas, where there are well-developed coastal plains, permits destruction of feldspar, yielding orthoquartzitic sands. In contrast, the high feldspar-quartz ratio found in Baja and southern California is due to relatively recent tectonic activity in the source area, coupled with appreciable relief. This pattern coincides with the detrital contribution theory of Pettijohn (1957) which relates percentages of feldspar and shale to various stages of tectonics.

Littoral Deposits in the Geologic Column

Weller (1960) has stated that littoral deposits are not abundantly available for observation in ancient sediments. This concept is based upon the premise that deposits of this zone become subject to erosion as soon as sea level drops. If they are present, they are of restricted extent as in the case of narrow beach deposits or "shoestring" sands. The apparent scarcity of littoral deposits may also be due to the criteria used by many workers to define them. It has been found that more than lithologic parameters are needed, although in many cases they make an excellent basis for identification.

Foraminiferal assemblages provide a useful tool for delimiting littoral zones in both ancient and recent sediments. Common to many recent littoral regions are the *Ammonia beccarii* group, *Elphidium* spp. and various *Miliolids*. In addition, where abundant fine sediments are available, delicate hyaline tests will be found in association with arenaceous species as well as those foraminifera mentioned in the previous sections. Coarser sediments, which undergo continuous movement from current action, tend to be inhabited by porcellaneous species. Modifications of such a fauna can be expected because of the multitude of agencies which act upon the littoral environment. Such factors include the work of strong winds, which cause erosive currents to redistribute species with shells having different hydrodynamic properties. Coastal upwelling displaces deeper colder water into the nearshore environment, often causing species generally assigned a deeper habitat to be found living within the littoral zone. Water movements may also carry planktonic forms into an area totally foreign to them, especially if deep water occurs immediately offshore, as in the case of the southern California borderland. Weathering of preexisting formations may cause stratigraphic and depth assemblage anomalies. At Vera Cruz, Mexico, for example, Tertiary deep water index fossils are found inter-

mixed with living recent specimens. Furthermore, the local occurrences of highly reducing zones may produce large numbers of small forms, due to rapid mortality. Thus, size of specimens may not always be indicative of water temperature, depositional rate, or depth. In addition, abnormality of test structure may result, which can clearly be associated with drastic changes recorded within shallow waters. It can, therefore, be seen that analysis of littoral deposits necessitates including parameters such as type of coast upon which they were deposited, climatic belt, and the action of modifying agencies. When these features are considered along with lithological and paleontological evidence, interpretations of ancient littoral deposits are feasible.

Louis Lidz

References

Emery, K. O., 1962, "Coral reefs off Veracruz, Mexico," *Geofisica International*, 3(1), 11–17.

Emery, K. O., Tracey, J. I., Jr., and Ladd, H. S., 1954, "Geology of Bikini and nearby atolls: Part I, Geology," *U.S. Geol. Surv. Profess. Papers*, **260-A**, 265pp.

Forbes, E., and Hanley, S., 1853, "A History of the British Mollusca, and Their Shells," London, John Van Voorst, 4 vols.

Grabau, A. W., 1924, "Principles of Stratigraphy," Second ed., New York, A. G. Seiler, 1185pp.

Hedgpeth, J. W., 1957, "Classification of Environments," *Geol. Soc. Am. Mem.* 67, **1**, 17–27.

Hoffmeister, J. E., Jones, J. I., Milliman, J. D., Moore, D. R., and Multer, H. G., 1964, "Living and Fossil Reef Types of South Florida," Guidebook for Geological Society of America Convention, November 1964, Field trip No. 3, 28pp.

Krynine, P. D., 1935, Arkose deposits of the humid tropics, a study of sedimentation in southern Mexico," *Am. J. Sci.*, **29**, 353–363.

Kuenen, Ph., H., "Marine Geology," New York, John Wiley & Sons, 568pp.

Pettijohn, F. J., 1957, "Sedimentary Rocks," New York, Harper Bros., 718pp.

Stetson, H. C., 1939, "Conditions of the Continental Shelf," in (Trash, P. D., editor) "Recent Marine Sediments" (symposium), Am. Assoc. Petrol. Geol. Publ., Tulsa, 736pp.

Sverdrup, H. U., Johnson, M. W., and Fleming, R. H., 1942, "The Oceans, Their Physics, Chemistry and General Biology," Englewood Cliffs, N.J., Prentice Hall, 1087pp.

Twenhofel, W., 1931, "Treatise on Sedimentation," Second ed., New York, Dover Publications reprint, 2 vols.

Twenhofel, W., 1950, "Principles of Sedimentation," New York, McGraw-Hill Book Co., 673pp.

Weller, J. M., 1960, "Stratigraphic Principles and Practice," New York, Harper Bros., 725pp.

Wells, J. W., 1957, "Coral reefs," *Geol. Soc. Am. Mem.* 67, **1**, 609–631.

M

MAGNETIC SPHERULES—*See* Vol. II

MANGANESE NODULES (DEEP-SEA)

One of the most interesting discoveries made by the *Challenger* Expedition (1873–76) was that of the abundance of manganese dioxide concretions on the floors of the three major oceans (Murray and Renard, 1891). Subsequent expeditions in the Pacific Ocean have recovered manganese nodules at a surprising number of stations. Manganese nodules and crusts are a form of pelagic sedimenta-

TABLE 1. MAXIMUM, MINIMUM, AND AVERAGE WEIGHT PERCENTAGES OF 27 ELEMENTS IN MANGANESE NODULES FROM THE PACIFIC AND ATLANTIC OCEANS

Element	Weight Percentages (Dry Weight Basis)[a]					
	Pacific Ocean Statistics on 54 Samples			Atlantic Ocean Statistics on 4 Samples		
	Maximum	Minimum	Average	Maximum	Minimum	Average
B	0.06	0.007	0.029	0.05	0.009	0.03
Na	4.7	1.5	2.6	3.5	1.4	2.3
Mg	2.4	1.0	1.7	2.4	1.4	1.7
Al	6.9	0.8	2.9	5.8	1.4	3.1
Si	20.1	1.3	9.4	19.6	2.8	11.0
K	3.1	0.3	0.8	0.8	0.6	0.7
Ca	4.4	0.8	1.9	3.4	1.5	2.7
Sc	0.003	0.001	0.001	0.003	0.002	0.002
Ti	1.7	0.11	0.67	1.3	0.3	0.8
V	0.11	0.021	0.054	0.11	0.02	0.07
Cr	0.007	0.001	0.001	0.003	0.001	0.002
Mn	41.1	8.2	24.2	21.5	12.0	16.3
Fe	26.6	2.4	14.0	25.9	9.1	17.5
Co	2.3	0.014	0.35	0.68	0.06	0.31
Ni	2.0	0.16	0.99	0.54	0.31	0.42
Cu	1.6	0.028	0.53	0.41	0.05	0.20
Zn	0.08	0.04	0.047	—	—	—
Ga	0.003	0.0002	0.001	—	—	—
Sr	0.16	0.024	0.081	0.14	0.04	0.09
Y	0.045	0.016	0.033	0.024	0.008	0.018
Zr	0.12	0.009	0.063	0.064	0.044	0.054
Mo	0.15	0.01	0.052	0.056	0.013	0.035
Ag	0.0006	—	0.0003[b]	—	—	—
Ba	0.64	0.08	0.18	0.36	0.10	0.17
La	0.024	0.009	0.016	—	—	—
Yb	0.0066	0.0013	0.0031	0.007	0.002	0.004
Pb	0.36	0.02	0.09	0.14	0.08	0.10
L.O.I.[c]	39.0	15.5	25.8	30.0	17.5	23.8

[a] As determined by X-ray emission spectrography.
[b] Average of 5 samples in which Ag was detected.
[c] L.O.I. = Loss on ignition at 1100° F for 1 hr. The L.O.I. figures are based on a total weight of air-dried sample basis.

TABLE 2. CHEMICAL ANALYSES OF MANGANESE NODULES FROM THE PACIFIC OCEAN[a]

Region	Station	Longitude ° '	Latitude ° '	Depth (m)	Reduced Wt %[b]					Wt %[c]			
					Mn	Fe	Co	Ni	Cu	SiO_2	Al_2O_3	Ca	H_2O[d]
A-1	Vit 4199	W 137–53	N 35–07	5035	21.9	27.4	0.61	0.70	0.61	28.6	9.3	1.1	14.6
A-2	Vit 4370	W 153–44	N 26–12	6120	21.0	24.0	0.24	0.70	0.46	17.6	7.2	1.5	21.5
A-3	Acap-11	W 105–07	N 10–53	3275	7.6	34.5	0.07	0.08	0.17	28.5	12.5	3.0	14.0
A-4	Chal 302	W 82–11	S 42–43	2156	19.7	29.7	0.12	0.28	0.17	11.8	2.8	1.7	25.5
A-5	DWBG-37	W 143–01	S 29–09	4120	19.2	23.5	0.39	0.50	0.24	11.6	3.8	3.1	27.0
B-1	VS-78	W 113–33	N 29–03	400	52.2	1.2	0.01	0.06	0.01	8.9	3.6	1.2	13.0
B-2	Alb 4658	W 85–36	S 8–30	4330	55.0[e]	1.1[e]	0.01	0.18	0.17	6.3	2.9	1.2	13.9
B-3	DWHD-72	W 85–14	S 25–31	920	49.7[e]	2.9[e]	0.20	0.31	0.18	0.7	1.3	1.7	12.8
B-4	Japan B	E 139–05	N 34–23	260	46.3	0.8	0.11	0.06	0.01	0.9	2.3	4.0	14.2
BC-1	UNK-MS	W 113–08	N 22–30	3604	49.5	8.3	0.05	1.08	0.72	17.1	7.3	1.3	17.3
BC-2	Alb 4711	W 94–06	S 7–48	4100	50.4[e]	5.1[e]	0.07	1.52	0.79	7.9	3.4	1.7	16.2
BC-2	Alb 4676	W 81–24	S 14–29	4970	40.8[e]	13.5[e]	0.09	2.18	1.40	17.1	7.2	1.8	18.3
C-1	Vit 4191	W 135–47	N 40–20	4560	37.3	21.5	0.50	1.31	0.82	28.5	8.1	1.4	19.2
C-1	Cusp-8P	W 140–38	N 43–58	4350	36.0	19.1	0.47	1.46	0.85	25.2	7.1	1.7	18.5
C-2	Vit 4217	W 120–42	N 29–57	4017	32.4	21.7	0.29	1.44	0.87	21.6	7.9	1.3	18.9
C-2	MSN-G	W 161–08	N 14–11	5652	36.8	14.4	0.49	1.55	1.28	12.0	6.1	1.5	18.4
C-2	DWBD-2	W 130–38	N 10–26	4890	38.5[e]	12.9[e]	0.44	2.12	2.05	15.7	6.3	1.5	19.0
C-2	MSN-K	W 170–00	N 6–03	5400	44.6	8.1	0.25	2.37	2.92	11.3	6.0	1.5	17.7
C-2	MSN-S	E 171–28	S 9–00	5000	34.2	19.4	0.23	1.10	1.24	15.6	7.8	1.8	19.4
C-2	Alb 4701	W 102–24	S 19–12	4150	26.6	17.9	0.25	2.35	0.91	17.5	3.8	1.0	18.5
C-2	DWHD-47	W 102–01	S 41–59	4200	38.3[e]	15.0[e]	0.20	1.59	0.92	11.1	5.7	1.6	19.3
CD-1	Naga 15	W 148–00	N 23–54	5220	28.1	18.6	0.53	1.26	1.11	29.6	14.9	0.6	16.7
CD-1	UNK-RR	W 121–44	N 19–49	4320	38.3[e]	17.1[e]	0.65	1.95	1.36	16.8	7.1	1.3	20.3
CD-2	DWBG-17	W 135–13	S 12–51	4318	34.4	10.1	1.22	2.10	1.32	10.1	4.3	1.6	21.5
D-1	MP-43D	E 164–59	N 11–57	1900	28.7	16.9	1.54	0.62	0.16	3.6	0.9	1.6	32.0
D-1	MP-26A3	W 171–00	N 19–03	1372	33.2[e]	19.5[e]	1.39	0.88	0.22	5.7	1.9	2.2	23.9
D-2	DWBD-4	W 146–	S 17–	1700	31.7[e]	17.2[e]	2.09	0.79	0.13	1.5	0.7	3.1	24.5
D-2	DWHD-16	W 145–33	S 16–29	1270	32.8[e]	20.2[e]	1.61	0.85	0.25	2.8	1.3	2.9	27.5

[a]Chemical assays by X-ray fluorescence methods.
[b]Reduced wt %. In reducing assays to a detrital mineral free basis, SiO_2, Al_2O_3, and H_2O were considered as detrital minerals. Reduced per cents are used to allow better definition of the compositional regions.
[c]Wt % on a total weight of air-dried sample basis.
[d]H_2O determined by drying air-dried nodule samples at 200°C for two hours.
[e]Chemical analyses by wet chemical methods by the Reno Station of the U.S. Bureau of Mines through the courtesy of Mr R. B. Maurer. Director, Region II, U.S. Bureau of Mines.

tion, but because of their relatively small volume, they are of minor importance when considering the totality of oceanic sediments. From an economic standpoint, they are the most important sediment of the deep-sea floor.

Physical Forms of the Nodules

Manganese and iron peroxides are distributed on the ocean floor as grains, nodules, slabs, coatings on rocks, impregnations of porous materials, replacement fillings of coral and organic debris, and in other forms. Small manganese–iron oxide grains are an almost invariable constituent of red clays, a common constituent of the organic oozes, and a not uncommon constituent of the terrigenous sediments of the ocean floor. Com-

monly observed at the surface of pelagic sediments are the nodules which range from 0.5–25 cm, but generally average about 3 cm, in diameter. Although nodules from a particular locality often exhibit a group resemblance in size and appearance, nodules from different parts of the ocean tend to have unique physical characteristics.

Mineralogy of the Nodules

The nodules invariably show an onionskin or concentric layer structure and are frequently oolitic within individual layers; however, they have no overall crystalline structure. They consist of a number of intimately and randomly intergrown crystallites of many minerals among which are barite, rutile, anatase, goethite, and several

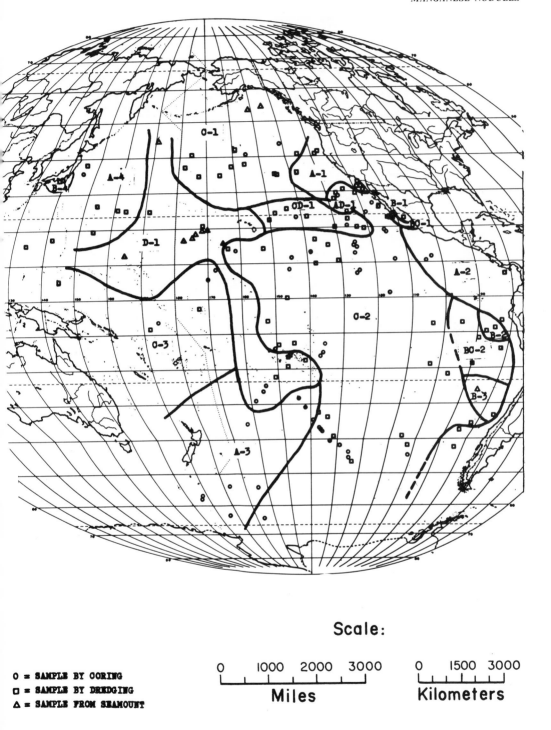

Scale:

O = SAMPLE BY CORING

□ = SAMPLE BY DREDGING

△ = SAMPLE FROM SEAMOUNT

Fig. 1. Map of the Pacific Ocean showing the compositional regions of manganese nodules in this ocean. Nodules from the A regions are high in iron; from the B regions, high in manganese; from the C regions, high in nickel and copper; and, from the D regions, high in cobalt. Also indicated on this map are sample points from which nodules have been recovered.

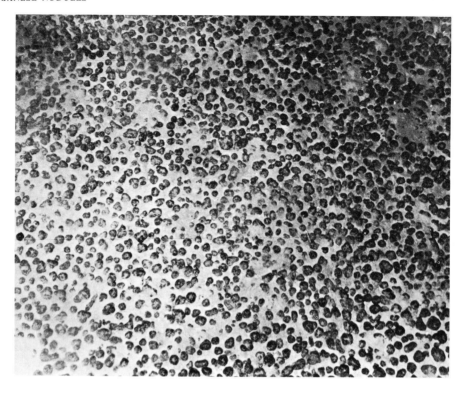

Fig. 2. A sea-floor photograph taken at S 13–53, W 150–35, 3695-meter depth and showing a concentration of manganese nodules of about 15 kg/m². The white mounds covering the nodules in a few places are sediments probably thrown up by some burrowing animal. (Photo by S. Calvert, Scripps Institution of Oceanography, U.S. Navy photo).

apparently new, and as yet unnamed, minerals of manganese (Buser and Grütter, 1956; Arrhenius, 1963). The hydrochloric acid-insoluble fraction of the nodules, which ranges from 2–40% and averages about 25% of the bulk weight of the nodules, consists principally of clay minerals together with lesser amounts of quartz, apatite, biotite, and sodium and potassium feldspars.

Chemical Composition of the Nodules

Table 1 shows the maximum, minimum, and average weight percentages of 27 elements commonly found in the manganese nodules. The samples used to compile the data of Table 1 were chosen from widely separated stations so as to yield as true a statistical average as possible. Table 2 lists a representative sampling of analyses of the nodules.

When compositional data are plotted on a map of the Pacific Ocean, definite regional variations in the composition of the nodules can be noticed. Near the continents, the nodules generally are characterized by manganese/iron ratios less than one (regions labeled A in Fig. 1). In the Gulf of California, off the southeast coast of Japan, and near the west coast of South America are zones in which the nodules show very high manganese/iron ratios, ranging from 12–62 and averaging about 30 (B regions). In the areas farthest removed from land, both continental and island, are nodules showing relatively high nickel and copper assays (regions labeled C). Centered on topographic highs in the central part of the Pacific Ocean is a region (labeled D) in which the nodules are relatively rich in cobalt. Between these primary zones appear to be transitional regions in which the nodules show compositional characteristics of the two adjacent zones.

Fig. 3. An oblique view of the ocean floor showing manganese nodules ranging in size from 2–10 cm in diameter. This photo was taken at S 21–37, W 147–40, depth of 4684 m. The nodules are about half buried in a red clay sediment and have a cap of sediment. (Photo by Carl Shipek, Official U.S. Navy photo).

Fig. 4. An oblique view of the ocean floor showing about 200 sq. ft. The nodules range from 5–10 cm in diameter. The nodules are resting on a clayey radiolarian ooze in the Clipperton Fracture Zone of the Pacific. (Photo by Carl Shipek, Official U.S. Navy photo).

Fig. 3.

Fig. 4.

Surface Concentrations of the Nodules

Manganese nodules frequently appear in photographs taken of the deep-sea floor as shown in Fig. 2. They are also recovered in core and grab samples of the sediments. Using information from these samples, measurements have been made of the weight of nodules per unit area of the ocean floor at over 100 stations in the Pacific Ocean (Mero, 1964). The average of the measurements is about 11 kg of nodules per square meter of sea floor. It is estimated that there are about 1.6×10^{12} metric tons of manganese nodules presently at the surface of the Pacific Ocean pelagic sediments. It has also been estimated that the nodules are presently forming at a rate of about 6×10^6 metric tons per year in this ocean.

The rate of formation of the associated sediments and the activity of biotic agencies which apparently work to keep the nodules at the surface of the sediments on which they lie are thought to be the prime factors affecting the concentration of the nodules at any given location in the ocean. Many other factors such as water currents, proximity of element sources, and chemical environment also play important roles in controlling both the concentration and composition of the manganese nodules.

Formation of the Nodules

Manganese, iron, and other elements are added to the ocean by rivers, volcanic eruptions, sea-floor springs, and the decomposition of submarine igneous outcrops and debris. Seawater is essentially saturated with manganese and iron in solution, and the concentrational effects of evaporation force the continual precipitation of these elements in the form of hydrated colloidal particles. These colloids apparently possess surface properties that allow them, while transiting the water column, to scavenge certain elements from solution such as nickel, cobalt, copper, molybdenum, zinc, and so forth (Goldberg, 1954). As the manganese and iron sols reach the ocean floor, they are swept along by the sea-floor water currents until they touch some solid object that is acting as a center of accretion. The mechanism by which the particles are agglomerated in the nodules is not clearly understood. At least ten different theories have been advanced ranging from the nodules being the end product in a leaching process that removes the silica, alumina, and other gangue materials, to bacterial oxidation and precipitation of the various metals. One of the latest theories involves a combination of the agglomeration of the hydrated sols and the direct precipitation of manganese ions from true solution (Goldberg and Arrhenius, 1958).

JOHN L. MERO

References

*Arrhenius, G., 1963, "Pelagic Sediments," in (Hill, M. N., editor) "The Sea," Vol. 3, pp. 655–718, New York, Interscience Publishers.

Buser, W., and Grütter, A., 1956, "Uber die Natur der Manganknollen," *Schweiz. Mineral. Petrog. Mitt.*, **36**, 49–62.

Goldberg, E. D., 1954, "Marine Geochemistry," *J. Geol.*, **62**, 249–265.

Goldberg, E. D., and Arrhenius, G., 1958, "Chemistry of Pacific pelagic sediments," *Geochim. Cosmochim. Acta*, **13**, 153–212.

*Mero, J. L., 1962, "Ocean-floor Manganese Nodules," *Econ. Geol.*, **57**, 747–767.

*Mero, J. L., 1964, "Mineral Resources of the Sea," Amsterdam, Elsevier Publishing Co., 312pp.

Murray, J., and Renard, A., 1891, "Report on Deep-Sea Deposits," *Challenger Reports*, **5**.

Nikolayev, D. S., and Yefimova, E. I., 1963, "On the age of iron-manganese concretions from the Indian and Pacific Oceans," *Geokhimiya* (in Russian), **7**, 678–688; *Geochemistry* (English translation), **7**, 703–714.

MARINE ECOLOGY

The study of interrelationships between organisms and their environment began about a hundred years ago when the fisheries biologist Karl Moebius recognized such circumstances as an oyster bed as a natural entity or *biocoenosis*. The term *ecology* in the scientific sense is attributed to Ernst Haeckel about 1866, and has since been applied to everything from molecules to man. Ecology is concerned with descriptions of natural groupings of organisms (communities), with the interrelationships of individual species to each other and to environmental factors, and with the analysis of the processes of the various interrelationships on a quantitative basis (the study of *ecosystems*). The seas of the world comprise the greatest part of the inhabitable environment of this planet (by volume about 300 times that over land), and while knowledge of marine processes is still incomplete, ecological analysis of marine life is perhaps more holistic and quantitative than that of terrestrial situations. This is a reflection of the three-dimensional nature of the marine environment and of the importance of marine fisheries. Although the sea includes representatives of several phyla not found on land, the variety of marine environments is smaller than that provided by terrestrial and fresh-water conditions, and the total number of marine species of animals is at least an order of magnitude smaller than that of the land in spite of the greater volume of living space in the oceans of the world.

(1) The Environment of the Seas. The environment of the seas is divided ecologically according to depth, distance from land and degree of light penetration and, in general, characteristic types of

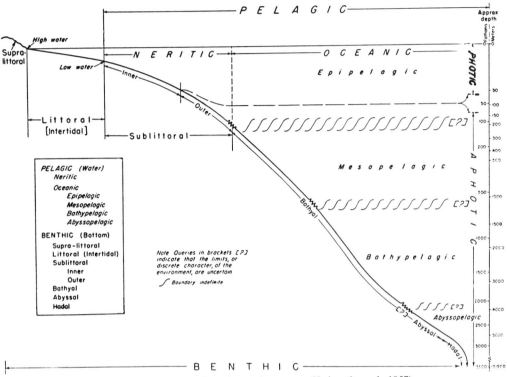

Fig. 1. Classification of marine environments (Hedgpeth *et al.*, 1957).

organisms occur in these various environmental divisions (Fig. 1).

The primary division is overlying water (pelagic) and bottom (benthic). The pelagic realm is divided into neritic, or nearshore (usually this implies that these waters have heavier phytoplankton crops, and hence are greenish, and that the nutrients from the bottom are more directly circulated), and oceanic (the blue water of the open ocean). Related to this in part is the division according to light penetration. In tropical seas removed from the influence of land, the photic zone may be as deep as 150 meters, whereas it may be only a few meters deep nearshore in temperate regions near river influences. The subdivision of the benthic zone is related also to light penetration, since the division between the two parts of the sublittoral are related to the attachment of macroscopic algae or active coral reef growth (the infralittoral or inner sublittoral) while beyond this, but still within continental influences, we recognize the circalittoral or outer sublittoral region. The classic littoral zone, however, is that between the tides (intertidal), which in tideless areas may be a very narrow vertical zone.

The pelagic regions are inhabited by floating (planktonic) or swimming (nektonic) organisms, and the benthic regions by sedentary, crawling or creeping organisms; among the animals, the benthos is further subdivided into those that live within the sediment (infauna) and those that are on the surface or attached to rocks, etc. (epifauna). Many organisms in or on the bottom, however, have larval stages which are planktonic, especially in the nearshore or neritic regions of the sea. Furthermore, many benthic organisms feed on planktonic life or detritus derived from overlying waters, and fish whose young stages live near the surface feed as adults on bottom organisms. In the deep parts of the sea (bathyal to hadal), however, there is little interchange between the upper levels, and the benthos at least is ultimately dependent upon what may descend from the surface layers, although there may be some production by autotrophic organisms in the deeps.

(2) Life in the Seas. Life along the shores, in the shallow seas and the surface layers of the oceans conforms in a general way to the temperature conditions of the seas; thus we refer to arctic, temperate or tropical floras and faunas, characteristically associated with certain temperature ranges (Fig. 2). The actual extent of these various biogeographic regions or provinces varies with season or from year to year, but the general pattern is that indicated in Fig. 3. In the deeper parts of the ocean, temperatures are uniformly cold, and many abyssal and bathypelagic animals are worldwide in distribution. Animals of the trenches (hadal), however, appear to have a higher degree of endemism. With the exception of organisms near shores, in estuaries (q.v.) and in landlocked seas of reduced salt content (see *Baltic, Black Sea,*

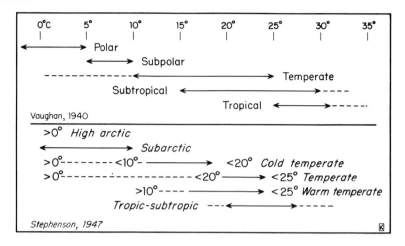

Fig. 2. Approximate temperature limits of major biogeographic regions (Hedgpeth *et al.*, 1957).

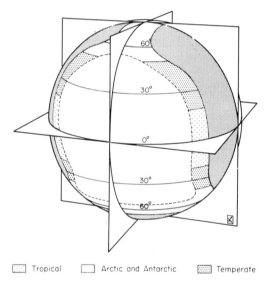

Fig. 3. Idealized symmetry of the marine realm (Hedgpeth *et al.*, 1957).

Caspian Sea), salinity is less significant than temperature in influencing the distribution of animals in the sea. Many planktonic organisms, however, are associated with specific types of water (water "masses"), with rather narrow differences of temperature and salinity, which in turn reflect the major current systems of the pelagic regions.

Temperature exerts its greatest effect on distribution during the reproductive stages of many marine organisms, which often have more precise temperature requirements for spawning and development than the adults. Accordingly, comparatively minor shifts in current patterns, bringing about changes in temperature regimes, may cause

great changes in the success or survival of such mass species as sardines and anchovies.

(3) Communities. The primary ecological unit is the *community*, a grouping of organisms characteristically occurring together, possibly dependent upon each other or at least upon common environmental requirements. Communities may be discrete and easily circumscribed, as the classic example of the oyster community (Fig. 4), or encompassing vast areas of the ocean such as the recurrent plankton groups or such complexes as the Antarctic whales and euphausiids.

In terrestrial ecology, communities are considered to succeed each other in time, resulting in the climax, the stable community associated with, but to some extent modifying, the prevailing environmental conditions over large areas. This concept, developed from the study of vegetational complexes in the northern hemisphere, appears to be less applicable to the marine environment. There is a succession of different types of organisms on newly exposed surfaces in the sea, but it is not clear that this entails a succession of dependencies or is simply the stabilization by the hydrographic regime. Communities are interrelationships of organisms that may be dependent on each other or on the common environment for food, and the interchange of organic matter is conveyed through food chains or trophic levels, beginning with the producers (phytoplankton and algae) and proceeding through various levels of herbivores and first and secondary carnivores and returned via the scavengers and detritus feeders. In general, it is estimated that about 10% of the organic material produced at one level is transferred to the next, but it may be more in some marine communities because there seems to be more complete utilization at the various trophic levels. Some marine food

Fig. 4. The oyster community or biocoenosis, at Port Isabel, Texas (original).

chains are tremendously productive, yielding millions of tons of fish or bottom invertebrates annually to the fisheries.

(4) The Ecosystem of the Sea. The ecosystem is a complex interaction of community and environmental processes (Fig. 5). The prime mover of the ecosystem is of course the sun, but of the radiant energy that reaches the surface of the sea, only about 0.2% is converted. This process, the fixation of carbon by photosynthetic or autotrophic organisms, is dependent primarily upon microscopic organisms in the sea, especially diatoms and dinoflagellates. The contribution of macroscopic algae and marine spermatophytes, even nearshore, is very small and may be disregarded for the sea as a whole, although it is significant in intertidal regions and in shallow bays. According to estimates by K. O. Emery for about 30,000 square miles of ocean off Southern California, the annual budget (in millions of tons dry weight), is as follows:

		Regeneration of nutrients	
Phytoplankton	42	From bottom	1.0
Attached plants	1.7	From the trophic levels	42.3
	43.7		43.3
Zooplankton	3.4	Organic matter in sediment	0.4
Fish	0.1	Organic matter lost	0.27
Bathypelagic organisms	2.02		
Benthos	1.5		

At the present state of our knowledge, all such estimates are admittedly approximations, and the

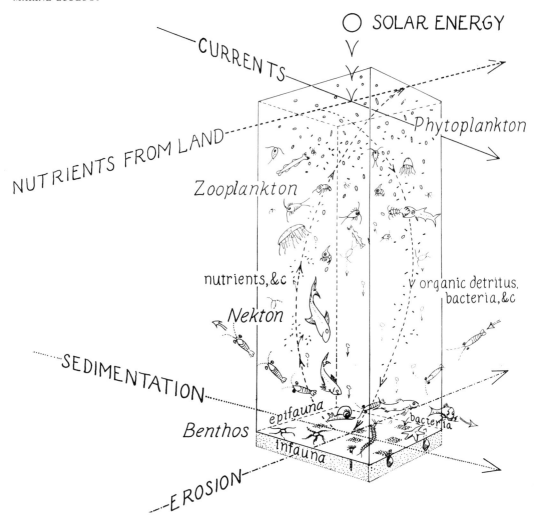

Fig. 5. The processes of the ecosystem. (*Courtesy Stanford University Press.*)

debate as to whether the sea can produce vastly greater amounts than the land or is approximately equal in total production of organic material proceeds without adequate data. A better idea of the approximate magnitude of production of some parts of the marine ecosystem is to be obtained from statistics for the heavily fished and more completely studied European seas. Pérès (1961) cites the following data:

	Average Benthic Biomass (g/m²)	Fish Catch (kg/ha)
Sea of Azov	321	80
Sea of Japan	175	28.8
North Sea	346	24.5
Baltic Sea	33	6
Barents Sea	100	4.5
White Sea	20	1.2
Mediterranean Sea	10	1.5

Because of man's ultimate dependence on still greater yields from the sea and the need for more complete understanding of the marine ecosystem to make this possible, marine ecology will become the most important aspect of oceanographic research in the future.

JOEL W. HEDGPETH

References

Bruun, A. F., 1957, "The Ecological Zonation of the Deep-Sea," *Proc. UNESCO Symp. on Physical Oceanography, Tokyo,* 1955, 160–168 (UNESCO and Japan Soc. for the Promotion of Science).

Emery, K. O., 1960, "The Sea off Southern California," pp. 139–179, New York, John Wiley & Sons.

Hardy, Alister, 1956, "The Open Sea: The World of Plankton," Boston, Houghton and Mifflin.

Hardy, Alister, 1959, "The Open Sea: Fish and Fisheries," Boston, Houghton and Mifflin, 322pp.

*Hedgpeth, Joel W. (editor), 1957, "Treatise on marine ecology and paleoecology, Vol. 1 Ecology," *Geol. Soc. Am. Mem.*, **67**, 1296pp., illus.

Pérès, J. M., 1961, "Océanographie Biologique et Biologie Marine. Tome 1. La Vie Benthique," Presses Universitaires de France, 541pp., illus.

Pérès, J. M., and Devèze, L., 1963, "Océanographie Biologique et Biologie Marine. Tome II. La Vie Pélagique." Presses Universitaires de France, 514pp., illus.

*Zenkevitch, L., 1963, "Biology of the Seas of the U.S.S.R.," New York, Interscience Publishers Inc., 955pp., illus.

MARINE GEOLOGY—TECHNIQUES AND TOOLS

Marine geology is one of the broadest fields in the modern earth sciences. As the geologic branch of oceanography, it deals with phenomena ranging in scale from the planetary to that of individual sediment particles. Most of the methods used in marine geology are essentially adaptations of the customary techniques of the normal geologist or geophysicist—sediment analyses, petrographic determinations, gravity, seismic, and magnetometer surveys—but the very specialized data-gathering methods necessary to penetrate to and under the sea floor are unique. As in all phases of geology, two primary observations must be made before any meaningful interpretation can be attempted: the geometric form and the composition of the earth's surface.

Bathymetry

In most geologic work, topographic information is taken for granted. Maps or aerial photographs can be obtained readily for any spot on the exposed face of the earth. Nautical charts, however, are intended as an aid to navigation and thus show sufficient bathymetric information for only the most general geologic interpretation. The first job of the marine geologist is the assembly of accurate, detailed topographic information to permit preliminary interpretation and to serve as a basis for planning intelligent sampling programs. Until the 1930's most soundings were made with a weighted hemp or wire line which could be lowered to the sea bottom. Obviously, detailed surveying was a time-consuming and expensive process, justified only for harbor approaches or submarine telegraph cable lines. Modification of submarine detection gear developed during World War I and II led to the development of the modern, continuously recording sonic devices. These devices, which finally came into general use in the 1950's, have permitted the accumulation of tremendous amounts of bathymetric information.

Modern sounding apparatus consists of two parts, a transducer which emits short pulses of high-frequency sound and receives their echoes from the bottom, and a continuous graphic recorder which records the precise time for the echo to return. Inasmuch as the time required for the signal to return to the surface is a function of water depth, the trace produced is a bathymetric profile of the sea floor along the ship's course. When preparing a bathymetric chart, depths are read from the trace at any convenient spacing and entered on a base map, which may then be contoured as in normal topographic work. The accuracy of the system is limited by two factors: variation in sound velocity in the water column and uncertainty as to ship's position. Sound velocity is a function of water density, so soundings can easily be corrected where hydrographic data are available. Location is a more serious problem. Close to shore, visual sights, radar, and a variety of automatic positioning systems (Loran, Shoran, Decca, and others) may be used, but farther and farther from shore greater reliance must be placed upon dead reckoning and celestial navigation, inherently approximations of location. The gyroscopic navigation systems now used in missiles and submarines promise to be extremely useful for survey work. As it now is in deep-sea work, absolute position is rarely accurate to less than several nautical miles, thus materially reducing the resolution of any survey.

In recent years, an important, strictly geologic extension of sonic sounding techniques has been developed. Low-frequency sound waves, though more rapidly attenuated in the water column than the high frequencies used for normal sounding, are able to penetrate the superficial layers of sediment and rock on the sea floor. The echoes thus may portray at least some of the geologic structure of the underlying rocks as a continuous record,

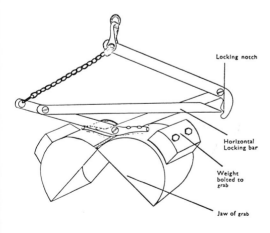

Locking notch

Horizontal
Locking bar

Weight
bolted to
grab

Jaw of grab

Fig. 1. Petersen grab, a common, effective sampler for soft bottom sediment (from Barnes, 1959).

similar to the bathymetric profiles. Gas exploders, small dynamite charges, magnetostriction devices, and electrical arcs have been used as sound sources for various types of "sub-bottom profilers." Many problems still limit the use of these devices, but in relatively shoal waters on the continental shelf they have already proved useful in petroleum exploration (see *Bathymetry, Precision Depth Recorder, Sounding,* etc.)

Geologic Mapping

Bottom sampling in the ocean has been compared unfavorably to sampling a city with a fishing line, through a fogbank, from a helicopter. Except in very shallow water, the analogy is uncomfortably appropriate. On the basis of the available topographic information, some sort of sampling device is selected and dropped to the bottom. The

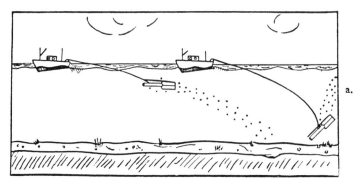

Under-way bottom sampler

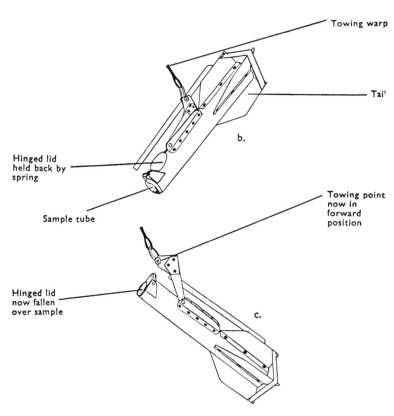

Top, going down; *bottom,* coming up

Fig. 2. Scoopfish underway sampler (from Barnes, 1959)

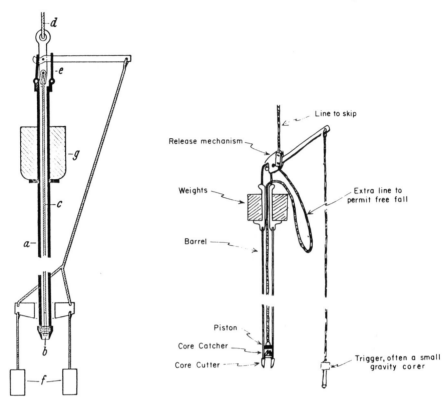

Fig. 3(A) Gravity piston corer (from Kullenberg, 1947).   Fig. 3(B). Modified Kullenberg piston corer.

sample, if successfully collected, is then assumed to be typical of a considerable area. In most cases, the assumption is justified for the rate of variation of regional trends in ocean bottom sediments and rocks appears to be low, but oversimplification is the almost inevitable result. Sampling density is severely limited by the high cost of ship time. At the present time (1964), ships adequately equipped for deep-sea geologic work cost upward of $1000/ day; thus each attempt to sample, successful or not, represents a considerable expense.

The bottom-sampling device selected for a specific problem depends upon the type of information desired, the substratum expected, and the amount of time available. If regional sediment patterns are desired, small grabs or snappers which can be operated rapidly are employed; if the occurrence and ecology of benthonic animals in relation to the sediment is of interest, then much larger grabs must be used; if the "stratigraphy" of the sediments is to be studied, a core must be taken. Large-diameter, short-barrelled cores are required for sediment structure or grain orientation studies. Where steep slopes or very irregular

bottom topography suggest the presence of consolidated rock, a dredge which can break off bits of the rock is necessary.

Sampling of unconsolidated surface sediment is usually undertaken with some type of snapper or grab. These are two- or three-part containers which are lowered open to the bottom, cocked to close on contact with the substrate, then brought to the surface. Many complex patterns of grab have been tested, but the most successful are simple, rugged boxes, completely mechanical, operated either by gravity or by a spring (Fig. 1). In areas of soft, fine-grained sediments, grabs are quite reliable, but where coarser material is found, the jaws often jam open, permitting the finer material to wash out as the sampler is drawn to the surface. Most of these devices can be operated only from a stationary ship, but the scoopfish sampler developed for the United States Navy is designed to dig its cup into the bottom, snap shut on a small sample, then rise to the surface while being towed by a moving vessel (Fig. 2). Unfortunately, the sample recovered by the scoopfish is quite small, and the device operates efficiently only in shoal water.

461

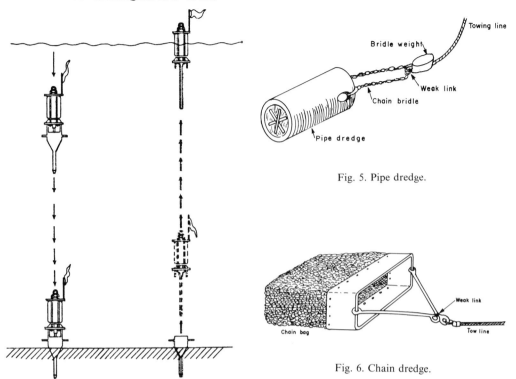

Fig. 5. Pipe dredge.

Fig. 6. Chain dredge.

Fig. 4. Stages in operation of Moore free-corer (from Moore, 1961).

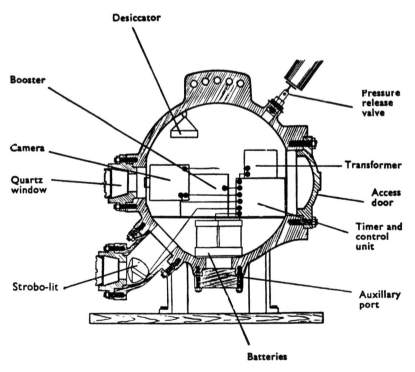

Fig. 7. Benthoscope (underwater camera; from Barnes, 1959).

Fig. 8. Thorndike camera, general assemblage with light. (Courtesy Prof. W. Thorndike.)

Fig. 9. Thorndike camera, details.

The majority of cores are taken with gravity coring devices. These consist of a metal tube, sometimes with a removable plastic lining, which is driven into the bottom sediment by weights attached to the upper end. At the bottom of the core barrel, there is a "core catcher," a contrivance with flexible brass or plastic fingers which fold down to prevent sediment from slipping out of the barrel. At the upper end of the barrel, a valve permits the escape of water displaced as the tube sinks into the sediment and also helps retain sediment while the core is returned to the ship. In all gravity coring gear, friction between the sediment and barrel prevents deep penetration and tends to cause compaction and boundary distortion in the core. The more sophisticated piston corer is equipped with a piston which is withdrawn from the coring tube at the same rate that the barrel penetrates the sediment (Fig. 3). The piston thus creates a slight vacuum in the tube, reducing boundary drag effects and eliminating compaction, though there is always the possibility that extra material may be drawn into the bottom of the barrel. Gravity cores greater than a meter or two in length are rare; piston cores have been recovered in good condition that were 25 meters long.

Coring is a time-consuming operation at sea, thus wind and current drift may move the ship appreciable distances during a single lowering. Because of this uncertainty of location, the collection of very closely spaced samples was pointless. Now, however, a gravity corer has been designed to operate free of attachment to the ship (Fig. 4). This device, the Moore free-corer, consists of two assemblies, an expendable casing and weight unit and a core tube attached to a float. The entire free-corer sinks to the bottom and into the sediment, then a delay timer releases the core and float assembly to return to the surface. A brightly colored flag and a small radar reflector permit recovery of the gear. The free-corer is heavy enough to sink directly to the bottom, uninfluenced by currents, thus closely spaced series of samples may be taken, more precisely located than any possible from a drifting vessel.

Hard rock from the sea floor is difficult to recover. The customary method is to tow a dredge, a heavy iron box or pipe, along the bottom in hope of breaking off fragments (Figs. 5 and 6). One end of the dredge is closed with chain mesh or an iron grill to trap solid fragments while permitting water and soft sediment to wash through; the other is open, attached by a chain bridle to a cable from the ship. Dredging is often a frustrating operation. Weak links are built into the towing bridles to permit the dredge to free itself if it gets caught, but these frequently malfunction and dredge and cable are lost. Even more common is the "water haul," a half-hour of dredging with nothing to show for one's efforts—either because there was no hard rock, or none could be broken off, or because the dredge was upset and the sample lost. Short, very sturdy coring tubes are sometimes used where sedimentary rocks are expected on the bottom. These are designed to punch out short cores from the rock.

Submarine Photography

Bottom photography has become a useful tool in marine geologic studies (Figs. 7, 8 and 9). Despite the obvious pressure problems with such delicate gear, both film and television cameras have been adapted for deep-sea work. Many interesting details of topography and sedimentation have been observed, including ripple marks in unconsolidated sediment, attitudes of sea-floor outcrops, and concentrations of manganese and phosphorite concretions. The film units commonly use 35 or 70 mm film and are triggered to make exposures periodically after the initial contact with the bottom. Floodlights or more often strobo-scopic flash units are necessary. Color film has been used with some success, and experiments have been made with stereophotography, which actually permits the contouring of microtopo-graphy on the sea bottom. Recent work with large grab samplers has included the installation of a camera set to photograph the substrate just before a sample is taken, so that sediment surface features and the benthonic organisms can be observed *in situ* before they are disturbed by the grab.

Manned Exploration Devices

In very shallow water, less than 60 or 80 meters, geologists can survey the bottom and collect samples directly by means of Scuba gear. Though there are many special problems involved in this work, under the impetus of continental shelf

Fig. 10. The "Vibracore" which is an effective corer of coarse sediments in shallow water.

petroleum exploration in California and elsewhere, many of the standard techniques of the field geologist have been adapted to permit operation by divers. Small submersible vehicles are now being developed to permit the examination of deeper bottoms. One such vehicle, the *Trieste*, designed by Picard and developed in Italy and France is now operated by the United States Navy; it has descended to a depth of 10,906 meters in the Marianas Trench of the Pacific. It also has been used to investigate submarine erosion and to map the deeper portions of several submarine canyons. There are plans to equip these deep diving vehicles with mechanical arms and a variety of sampling devices so that, in addition to observation, they will be able to perform useful geologic work. Underwater television systems are now becoming practical, so eventually we may have a submarine geologic robot, equipped to observe and sample under the direction of a shipboard geologist.

Contemporary equipment for marine geology used in the USSR is described by Sysoev (1959).

Hard bottom sediments, commonly found on the shallow continental shelf, consisting of sands, gravel and shells have long defied coring techniques. A recent development of the Russian vibratory drill has been adapted for submarine work and given the trade name "Vibracore." The vibrator mechanism operates from an air compressor, penetrating at about 2 m/min. Cores of 8 cm are obtained in 4 or 10 meter lengths (Fig. 10).

F. F. WRIGHT

References

Barnes, H., 1959, "Oceanography and Marine Biology," London, Allen & Unwin, 218pp.

Beckmann, W. C., Roberts, A. C., and Luskin, G., 1959, "Sub-bottom depth recorder," *Geophysics*, **24**, No. 4, 749–760.

Edgerton, H. E., 1963, "Underwater photography," in (Hill, M. N., editor) "The Sea," Vol. 3, pp. 473–479, New York, Interscience Publishers.

Ewing, M., Vine, A., and Worzel, J. L., 1946, "Photography of the ocean bottom," *J. Opt. Soc. Am.*, **36**.

Heezen, B. C., 1954, "Methods of exploring the ocean floors. A discussion," in "Oceanographic Instrumentation," *Natl. Acad. Sci. Natl. Res. Council Publ.*, **309**, 200–205.

Heezen, B. C., 1964, "Discussion of 'a note on some possible misinformation from cores obtained by piston-coring devices,'" *J. Sediment Petrol.*, **34**, 699.

Hopkins, T. L., 1964, "A survey of marine bottom samplers," in (Sears, M., editor) "Progress in Oceanography," Vol. 2, pp. 205–242, London, Pergamon Press.

Kullenberg, B., 1947, "The piston core sampler," *Svenska Hydrograf. Biol. Komm. Skrifter, Ser. hydrograf.*, **1**.

Moore, D. G., 1961, "The free-corer: sediment sampling without wire or winch," *J. Sediment. Petrol.*, **31**, 627–630.

Richards, A. F., and Keller, G. H., 1961, "A plastic-barrel sediment cover," *Deep-Sea Res.*, **8**, 306–312.

Shepard, F. P., 1963, "Submarine Geology," Second ed., New York, Harper & Row, 557pp.

Sysoev, N. N., 1959, "Soviet expedition ship *Vitiaz*," *U.S.S.R. Acad. Sci.* (*I.G.Y. series* 1957–58), *Moscow*, 31pp.

Terry, R. D., in press, "Oceanography—Its Tools, Methods, Resources and Applications," New York, The Macmillan Co.

MARINE MICROBIOLOGY

Marine microorganisms form a rather large fraction of the biomass within the seas and, therefore, are responsible for much of the chemical changes that occur in the marine environment. The marine environment is a collective term to include water, sediment, air over the water, the intertidal area, and the spray zone subject to sea salt spray.

The term marine microbiology is generally used to describe collectively the "single-celled" organisms in the seas that fall within the microscopic range. These microorganisms, sometimes classified as the *Protista*, include two functional groups; the primary producers (photo- or chemosynthetic), and the mineralizers or heterotrophic organisms. Figure 1 is an attempt to show the relationships

between the morphology of the single-celled microorganisms. Sometimes separation on a single-cell basis falls into difficulty, such as with the Volvocales, organisms that exist both singly and in colonies. However, when one looks at the basic configuration of microorganisms in the sea, it is apparent that many live in collective aggregates predicated by their growth habits and their ability to adhere to surfaces. The author prefers the single-celled criterion because such organisms do not depend upon a circulation system and have active transport between the cells and the environment; thus, they are unique with respect to their surface-to-volume ratio and their dependence on the laws of colloidal chemistry. Such a classification or grouping consequently may be based on a more functional character rather than the usual physiological criteria.

In all environments, the sum total of the processes of the living microorganisms is the production of protoplasm and the destruction of organic matter. The former is called production, and the latter, mineralization. These two processes control the major energy and carbon economy of environments. The natural balance is pictured graphically in Fig. 2. The following discussion pertains only to the marine environment as set aside from other environments by the unique properties of the salts within the water and sediments which are listed in Table 1 and their buffering capacity, the hydrostatic pressure found in the depths of the sea (average of 1 psi per two feet of depth or 1 atm per 10 meters), and the patterns of water circulation within the vast expanses of the world's oceans. The true marine microrganisms, although this may cause dispute, are those that can be isolated from the oceans and grow preferentially in seawater media. However, there are many living organisms that grow both in seawater and fresh water and have been found in the oceans and on land. Therefore, perhaps it is important not to attempt to identify a true marine organism, but to approach the subject with the idea that any microorganisms affecting the properties of seawater by their activity are considered to be marine microorganisms.

In water, microorganisms are generally considered planktonic and may either be free floating or attached to some particle or living organism. In the majority of oceans, especially deep water, the phytoplankton are more related to the free floating state because they are dependent on sunlight for energy and on dissolved inorganic ions for their nutrition, whereas the heterotrophic microorganisms, being dependent on organic matter, may not be able to absorb effectively the dilute dissolved organic materials in seawater and are more dependent on solid surfaces, either organic matter or particulate material with adsorbed organic matter on its surface. Within the sediment, the organisms may be free moving within the inter-

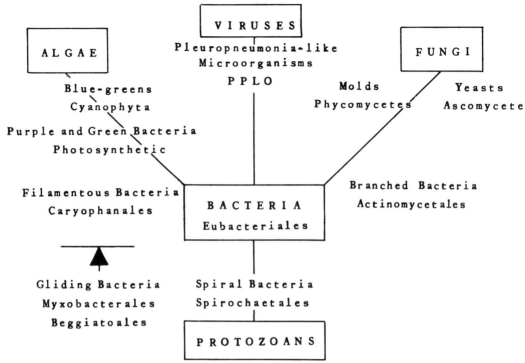

Fig. 1. Major groups of marine microorganisms and their morphological relationship.

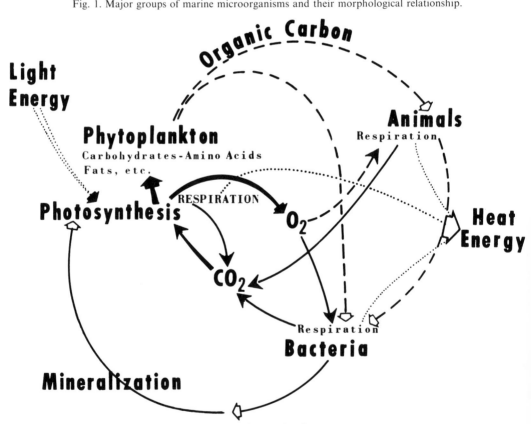

Fig. 2. Carbon cycle of nature.

TABLE 1. ABUNDANCE OF THE CHEMICAL ELEMENTS IN SEAWATERS[a]

		mg/kg	atoms/10^6 atoms Cl			mg/kg	atoms/10^6 atoms Cl
H	1	108,000.	202,000,000.	Ag	47	0.0003	0.003
He	2	0.00005	0.0004	Cd	48	0.00011	0.002
Li	3	0.2	50.	In	49	0.02	0.3
Be	4			Sn	50	0.003	0.05
B	5	4.8	830.	Sb	51	0.0005	0.008
C	6	28.	4,300.	Te	52		
N	7	0.5	70.	I	53	0.05	0.7
O	8	857,000.	100,000,000.	Xe	54		
F	9	1.3	130.	Cs	55	0.0005	0.005
Ne	10	0.0003	0.03	Ba	56	0.0062	0.008
Na	11	10,500.	850,000.	La	57	0.0003	0.004
Mg	12	1,800.	100,000.	Ce	58	0.0004	0.005
Al	13	0.01	0.7	Pr	59		
Si	14	3.	200.	Nd	60		
P	15	0.07	4.	Pm	61		
S	16	900.	52,000.	Sm	62		
Cl	17	19,000.	1,000,000.	Eu	63		
A	18			Gd	64		
K	19	380.	18,000.	Tb	65		
Ca	20	400.	19,000.	Dy	66		
Sc	21	0.00004	0.002	Ho	67		
Ti	22	0.001	0.04	Er	68		
V	23	0.002	0.08	Tm	69		
Cr	24	0.00005	0.002	Yb	70		
Mn	25	0.002	0.07	Lu	71		
Fe	26	0.01	0.3	Hg	72		
Co	27	0.0005	0.02	Ta	73		
Ni	28	0.0005	0.02	W	74	0.0001	0.001
Cu	29	0.003	0.09	Re	75		
Zn	30	0.01	0.3	Os	76		
Ga	31	0.0005	0.01	Ir	77		
Ge	32	0.0001	0.003	Pt	78		
As	33	0.003	0.07	Au	79	0.000004	0.00004
Se	34	0.004	0.1	Hg	80	0.00003	0.0003
Br	35	65.	1,500.	Tl	81	0.00001	0.00009
Kr	36			Pb	82	0.003	0.03
Rb	37	0.12	2.2	Bi	83	0.0002	0.002
Sr	38	8.	160.	Po	84		
Y	39	0.0003	0.006	At	85		
Zr	40			Rn	86	9.0×10^{-15}	8.0×10^{-14}
Nb	41			Fr	87		
Mo	42	0.01	0.2	Ra	88	3.0×10^{-11}	2.0×10^{-10}
Tc	43			Ac	89		
Ru	44			Th	90	0.0007	0.006
Rh	45			Pa	91		
Pd	46			U	92	0.003	0.02

[a] Revised from Goldberg, E. D., "Biogeochemistry of trace elements," *Geol. Soc. Am. Mem.* 67, **1**, 345–358 (1957).

stitial spaces, adsorbed to the solid sediment surfaces, or trapped in sediments of very fine particle size.

Autotrophic Microorganisms

This diverse group can be separated generally into the *photosynthetic* single-celled organisms and the *chemosynthetic* microorganisms that derive their energy from light and inorganic oxidation processes and their cell components from inorganic ions. The photosynthetic organisms are restricted to the photic zones of the water and sediment. In nearshore waters of high turbidity, this depth range may be a few centimeters or meters, whereas in the deep oceanic environment, the zone may extend down to 600 meters. Within the sediments, photosynthetic microorganisms may live to a depth of 10 mm in sand with full sunlight, either as single cells or bound together as dense algal mats. There is now considerable evidence that many of the photosynthetic microorganisms may live as heterotrophs in the absence of light, as they have been found below the euphotic zones in both water and sediment. Here they may act as mineralizers with the other heterotrophs.

The marine chemosynthetic autotrophs have generally been neglected, and very little information is available on their distribution or function in the marine environment. Inasmuch as they require reduced compounds for their energy source, they are usually associated (except for NO_2 and NH_3 commonly found in seawater) with anaerobic environments or regions of vulcanism. Except for the latter, such environments may exist in the water column as microspheres where gross metabolism during mineralization exceeds oxygen diffusion, thus producing small anaerobic zones. Other anaerobic environments are found in deep water basins or fjords or within sediments. It has been assumed generally that the anaerobic environment is restricted to a very small part of the total oceans; however, since considerable microbial activity is present in the anaerobic sediments of the continental shelves (7% of the oceanic area), it is possible that the gross result of the activities of the autotrophic chemosynthetic microorganisms is more significant than previously assumed.

In terms of productivity, the phytoplankton provide most of the primary organic matter of the sea, the other source being that of attached algae restricted to nearshore shallow water environments, and floating algae such as Sargassum. The groups of photosynthetic microorganisms represented in the sea are diatoms, blue-green algae, flagellates, and photosynthetic bacteria.

Heterotrophic Microorganisms

The heterotrophic microorganisms include those with activities that are generally considered to be mineralizing and that accomplish the stepwise degradation of protoplasm by the combined action of various species. These are adventitious unicellular organisms with numbers in proportion to the quantities of food available. In the absence of food they may be present as resistant resting cells. They are ubiquitous in the entire marine environment. Proof of their existence is the fact that very little organized organic matter accumulates in the seas at any time. The fish and larger plankton are immediately attacked by microorganisms, if they are not eaten as part of the food chain and decomposed to minerals, resistant humus such as chitin or cellulose, or ions. The organisms in the heterotrophic group include the bacteria, fungi, yeasts, protozoans and the viruses and algae.

Although the total activities of microorganisms are a product of their growth and metabolism, the results are of importance to man. As information is obtained on the independent and collective activities of the microorganisms, estimations can be made to determine the significance of each activity in the overall processes which take place in the marine environment. In more realistic terms, we would like to increase our knowledge on the potential fish or shellfish production of the entire ocean or respective parts, the destructive activities to man-made and geological structures, diagenetic changes in the present day sedimentary environment that may allow interpretation of the world's past history, information to be used in the cultivation of fish and shellfish for food purposes, pollution and methods of control, spread of diseases which may affect man, distribution of possible radioactive contaminants from fallout or from nuclear power sources, etc.

All of the above information may be obtained by a thorough knowledge of the functions of microorganisms and their role in the food chain in the oceans. Primary productivity, for example, may control the productivity of any given area. Therefore, the activities of primary productivity may be related to the mineralizing activities of microorganisms that make available certain essential nutrients, which in turn are related to circulations of the currents. The effect of microbial activity on inorganic precipitation or solution within sedimentary environments is again a function of the abundance of energy which subsequently controls the total activities of the microorganisms. In this sense, total productivity, distribution of living organisms and circulation all play an interrelated role.

With this introduction, it is now possible to treat some functions of microorganisms. An appropriate way to illustrate such functions is to divide them into processes involving chemical or related groups such as oxygen and redox potential, pH, inorganic ions, organic molecules, heat and disease, and to allow the reader to place emphasis on total activities related to pollution, destruction of man-made materials, decline and increase of populations, aquaculture, etc.

Oxygen and Redox Potential

Much of the marine environment looks essentially aerobic except for the few anaerobic basins and nearshore marine sediments. However, this aerobic appearance may be misleading because during the active states of decomposition of particulate matter or dead organisms, the inside of the organism or the particle may be anaerobic with respect to the aerobic outside. Thus many marine microorganisms, even including certain algae, must be able to grow and multiply under both aerobic and anaerobic conditions. Very little is known about the change in metabolic function during the aerobic-anaerobic transition in the sea, but *a priori* evidence indicates that some change in metabolism must be present. Essentially the chain of events is this: A diverse population of microbial species' is present normally in most environments. When food becomes available, their mineralizing and metabolic activities consume oxygen. If the particle of organic matter is large enough, the oxygen inside is consumed faster than new oxygen can diffuse into the particle, and the center becomes anaerobic. Such environmental conditions may exist either in microenvironments represented as a decomposing small or large organism, or in the stagnant basins and sediments where oxygen diffusion may be slower than consumption. In such transition zones, the state of inorganic minerals and ions may be changed and certainly the pathways of metabolism are changed, resulting in the accumulation of certain compounds such as the hydrocarbons and cellulose that are not readily oxidized in the absence of oxygen. The change in redox potential may also be reflected in a change in microbial populations; as for example, sulfate reducing organisms are active in anaerobic environments. The reduction of sulfates produces sulfides that act as scavenging agents for cations and organic materials and also hydrogen sulfide which acts as a weak acid, thus changing the pH of the environment.

pH

Even with the buffer system of seawater, microorganisms may cause relatively large fluctuations in pH. Diurnal changes may be caused by consumption and production of carbon dioxide which, in turn, change the carbonate equilibrium, producing pH changes as much as from 7.6–9.2 in seawater and surface sediments exposed to sunlight. An increase in pH is caused by production of ammonia from protein metabolism and consumption of acid compounds. A decrease in pH may be produced by organic acid production, consumption of ammonia, and reactions liberating hydrogen ion. The change in pH can affect inorganic ions through the control of direct uptake through membranes, through chelating processes by organic molecules, solubilization and precipitation, and mineralization of previously bound ions in organic matter. Organic molecules are produced as an extracellular product or intermediary product of metabolism of both autotrophic and heterotrophic microorganisms. The average dissolved organic material in seawater is about 5 ppm, ranging from 1 ppm in oceanic waters to 100 ppm in productive shallow bays. This organic matter serves as food for many other organisms; it can alter the buffering capacity of seawater and sediments, may act as a chelating substance to reduce toxicity of trace elements, forms colloids, binds other particles together both in the water and sediments, and provides a thixotrophic property to many sediments.

Disease

As decomposers, marine microorganisms may at times start on the still living organisms and thus come under the classification of disease producing. Fungi, such as *Lindra thalassiae*, attack living *Thalassia*, the common turtle grass. *Pseudomonas*, a bacterium, may attack the integument of fishes, causing tail rot, etc. Although many marine microorganisms are so-called disease producing, only one, *Erysipelothrix*, has been shown to be responsible for a human disease.

Some human pathogens and contaminants such as *Escherichia coli* may exist for a period of weeks in natural seawater but do not live or survive. Such organisms may cause disease during their period of viability.

Ion Distribution

Protoplasm produced in the marine environment contains most of the ions commonly found in seawater (Table 1). These ions, such as copper, zinc, or titanium, may be concentrated to levels several thousand times that of seawater. Many of these elements do not have known functions, while others such as copper, manganese and zinc are known to be necessary for enzyme reactions. By thus concentrating ions, liberating ions during decomposition, causing adsorption processes, changing pH and Eh, the normal microbial activities may alter the ion concentration of seawater and sediment.

Destruction and Fouling

Microorganisms are capable during their normal activities of destroying wood, corroding iron and other metals, solubilizing concrete, destroying cellulose and similar materials, degrading plasticizers, etc. By such processes, the organisms either directly or indirectly obtain energy and food substances. Microorganisms may grow on most surfaces in seawater, preparing the surface for the attachment of other living organisms that would otherwise find the surface either toxic or untenable for their attachment and growth.

CARL H. OPPENHEIMER

References

Kriss, A. E., 1959, "Marine Microbiology (Deep Sea)," Acad. Sci. U.S.S.R., Moscow, 452pp.
Oppenheimer, C. H., 1963, "Symposium on Marine Microbiology," Springfield, Ill., C. C. Thomas, 769pp.
ZoBell, C. E., 1946, "Marine Microbiology," Waltham, Mass., Chronica Botanica, 240pp.

MARINE SEDIMENTS

The first systematic classification of marine sediments was offered by Murray and Renard (1884, 1891) on the basis of their studies of the worldwide samples collected by the Challenger Expedition

TABLE 1. OCEANIC AREAS COVERED BY PELAGIC SEDIMENTS

Type of Sediment	Atlantic Ocean	Pacific Ocean	Indian Ocean	Total
	Area (10^6 km^2)	Area (10^6 km^2)	Area (10^6 km^2)	Area (10^6 km^2)
Calcareous oozes				
Globigerina	40.1	51.9	34.4	
Pteropod	1.5			
Total	41.6	51.9	34.4	127.9
Siliceous oozes				
Diatom	4.1	14.4	12.6	
Radiolarian		6.6	0.3	
Total	4.1	21.0	12.9	38.0
Red clay	15.9	70.3	16.0	102.2
Grand total	61.6	143.2	63.3	268.1

[a] H. U. Sverdrup *et al.* (1942). (By permission of Prentice-Hall, N.Y.)

(1872–76). Many of these samples are still available for study at the British Museum. Two fundamental categories were recognized: *pelagic* (pertaining to the open ocean, i.e., fine-grained material capable of being carried in suspension or fine organic debris, that fell "as a gentle rain" to the floor of the deep sea) and *terrigenous* (material of all dimensions and compositions, derived directly from continental or island sources). The following subdivisions were made:

(a) Pelagic
  (*i*) Inorganic: red clay;
  (*ii*) Organic (or Biogenic): calcareous oozes (globigerina, pteropod, coccolith oozes); siliceous oozes (radiolarian, diatom oozes).
(b) Terrigenous
  (*i*) Blue, green and red muds;
  (*ii*) Volcanic mud;
  (*iii*) Coral sand and mud.

Strictly speaking, Murray and Renard employed this mixed classification only for deep-sea deposits, and not for neritic and shallow oceanic environments. Unfortunately some of their successors assumed that it was an all-embracing system for marine sediment classification. Geikie (1903) expanded it so that the terrigenous group would take in: (A) shore deposits, and (B) infra-littoral or deeper water (shelf) deposits.

Revelle (1944) found that oxidation-state and color changes in any case rendered the terrigenous group difficult to handle and suggested that, like the pelagic, it should simply be divided into two main types: (*i*) organic muds (i.e., reef derivatives, etc.) and (*ii*) inorganic muds. Striving further toward completeness, Shepard (1948) added a *Glacial* (glacigene) *class*, and restricted the terms terrigenous and pelagic to allow red clay and the volcanic sediments to stand by themselves: (*i*) red clay, (*ii*) pelagic oozes, (*iii*) terrigenous muds, (*iv*) glacial marine sediments, and (*v*) volcanic sediments.

A different approach was made by Kuenen (1950),

TABLE 2. DISTRIBUTION IN PERCENTAGES OF AREA COVERED BY PELAGIC SEDIMENTS

	Indian Ocean (%)	Pacific Ocean (%)	Atlantic Ocean (%)
Calcareous ooze	54.3	36.2	67.5
Siliceous ooze	20.4	14.7	6.7
Red clay	25.3	49.1	25.8
Total	100.0	100.0	100.0

	Calcareous Ooze (%)	Siliceous Ooze (%)	Red Clay (%)
Indian Ocean	26.9	33.9	15.7
Pacific Ocean	40.6	55.3	68.7
Atlantic Ocean	32.5	10.8	15.6
Total	100.0	100.0	100.0

who grouped marine sediments according to location (i.e., environment) in the primary division. Thus, he considered *shelf sediments and mixed environments* (littoral, delta, lagoon and estuarine) as well as the *deep-sea group*, sometimes called *thalassic* or *thalatogenic*, in which, beside the usual *pelagic* class, he recognized a class of "*hemipelagic and terrigenous*" that included the terrigenous muds, volcanic, coral and carbonate muds. Considerable virtue is seen in the environmental approach, which is especially useful in consideration of facies. However, it might be improved by the recognition of special pigeon holes for reef environments, marine volcanic associations and the marine glacial sediments.

Genetic-geochemical Approach—The Sedimentary Cycle

In 1942, Sverdrup *et al.* offered a wholly genetic approach to marine sediments, in place of the partly descriptive, partly genetic approach of most of the above schemes. In 1964, Goldberg came back to the problem, viewing the whole sedimentary cycle as a closed (balanced) geochemical system, which, with minor modifications, can be summarized as follows:

(1) Source Materials.
(a) Meteorites (and other extraterrestrial matter);
(b) Volcanic and continental weathering products.

(2) Transport and Phase. Through the air or by water (deflation, rivers, littoral erosion, glaciers, etc.), these products are carried into the world ocean, as
(a) *Dissolved phases* (i.e., the salts, etc. of seawater);
(b) *Particulate phases* (in suspension, turbidity flow or traction).

(3) Marine Sediment Components.
(a) *Pore solutions* (connate water; that may become systematically modified and concentrated during diagenesis);
(b) *Hydrogenous components* (authigenic minerals, "halmyrolytic" or "halmeic" as Arrhenius calls them), i.e., inorganic precipitates or metasomatic products, derived entirely from seawater solution, or partially, by ion exchange or other process. Examples include ferromanganese minerals, glauconite, phosphorite, barite, phillipsite, montmorillonite and hydromagnesite.
(c) *Biogenous components* (all types of benthonic skeletal debris, coral and calcareous algal material, "biohermal" and "biostromal" assemblages, both in biocoenotic and thanatocoenotic associations. These may be massive (i.e., relatively undamaged), or detrital (wave-worked and sorted). The benthonic material is normally calcareous, but sometimes siliceous, as with sponge spicule deposits (spongolite), etc. Also the pelagic oozes—*calcareous* (globigerina, coccolith, pteropod ooze); *siliceous* (radiolaria, diatom).
(d) *Lithogenous components* (clastic debris of all grain sizes (including flocculates of extremely fine-grained colloids) derived from preexisting rocks of all sorts, siliceous, carbonate, ferruginous, etc. Included are quartz, feldspars, micas, hornblende (and other "heavy minerals"), laterite (largely as grains of hematite), clay particles (of many species), and the volcanic glasses [those unaltered by seawater, i.e., those which do not fall in class (b)]. Arrhenius (1963) believes that there are two genetic components in the deep-sea *red clay*—*chthonic* (i.e., lithogenous), and *halmeic* (i.e., hydrogenous), the former dominant in the northern hemisphere and the latter in the southern.
(e) *Cosmogenous components* (all sorts of meteoritic material, tektites, cosmic dust, magnetic spherules; these have been found in ancient sediments back to Cambrian in age, and although not bulking large, they are universally present.

Criteria for Classification

Goldberg (1964) has offered the following obser-

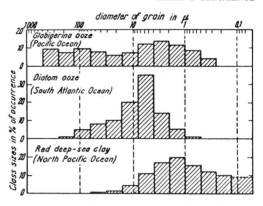

Fig. 1. Average distribution of grain sizes in the most important pelagic bottom sediments (after R. Revelle and O. Pratje, according to H. U. Sverdrup, 1942). (By permission of Prentice-Hall, N.Y.)

vation about distinguishing criteria: chemical composition of the mineral; size distribution (see Fig. 1); isotopic analyses of an element or elements; geographic occurrence; association with other minerals; and the form or habit. For any specific case, a combination of several of the cited approaches is usually necessary. As an example, the oolitic calcium carbonates, deposited inorganically in coastal waters, such as on the Great Bahama Bank, can be distinguished from organically deposited calcium carbonates by means of differences in the minor element abundances (Tatsumoto and Goldberg, 1959), the isotopic compositions of the carbon and oxygen (Lowenstam and Epstein, 1957), geographic occurrences, and mineral habits and forms in the two groups of minerals (Newell, Purdy and Imbrie, 1960). Feldspars in East Pacific Rise deposits are characterized as volcanic in origin on the basis of their size distributions as a function of distance from sources, their chemical compositions, and associations with other minerals (Peterson and Goldberg, 1962).

Although this genetic classification of sedimentary components has proved especially useful, certain ambiguities do arise. Griffin and Goldberg (1963) have indicated that in the North Pacific, ordered illites and chlorites are forming from a lithogenous montmorillonite-like clay mineral. To typify the partially converted starting substances as either lithogenous or hydrogenous is clearly inappropriate. Volcanic debris in various states of alteration is equally difficult to categorize in a clear cut way. However, the number of minerals not subject to a rigid classification is relatively small.

Transportation

(a) **River Systems.** Kuenen calculated that the total annual particulate and dissolved matter delivered by the world's rivers amounted to 12 km^3/yr. Livingston (1963) gives, for example, the figure of 5700 g/sec of dissolved minerals in the discharge of the Amazon. The location of *submarine fans or cones* (q.v.) opposite river deltas clearly correlates the latter with fluvial transport; the size of the Ganges cone is particularly impressive with 5×10^6 km^3, representing an annual transport (by eastern Himalayan rivers) of something like 0.3 km^3/yr.

(b) **Ocean Current Systems.** Dissolved phases are rapidly diffused and thus difficult to trace definitely, although certainly some more localized components can be identified, e.g., silica solutions. Biogenous particulate material is largely related to the patterns of the principal current systems and the zones of high organic productivity (related to *Planktonic Photosynthesis*, q.v., *Upwelling*, q.v.; see also Ryther, 1963). Arrhenius (1963) in particular has demonstrated the coincidence of high calcareous ooze accumulation along the belt of the intertropical convergence right across the central Pacific. Areas of low productivity and little accumulation occur in the anticyclonic gyres like the Sargasso Sea (low nutrient supply) or in the ice-covered Arctic (low nutrients, low temperature and limited light penetration). Heezen (personal communication) has pointed out that the great geostrophic currents of the world are frequently matched by deep countercurrents; at their boundary zones (sites of low energy) along the continental slope and rise, suspended sediment must settle to the bottom, leading to the curious phenomenon of thick sediments accumulating on slopes (and not necessarily, strangely enough, in trough-shaped "geosynclines").

(c) **Turbidity Current Systems.** Associated with major river sources, most submarine canyons seem to be the sources of gravitationally activated turbidity flows, the velocities of which are one or two orders of magnitude above the rates in category (b). Accordingly, lithogenous components of all sizes are transported down to the abyssal plains (q.v.). One may note that the mean direction of the initial turbidity flow may well be at 90° to the mean geostrophic current direction; the latter current is semicontinuous, while the turbidity flow is aperiodic, perhaps only once a decade or once a century.

(d) **Wind Transportation.** Charles Darwin first pointed out the probability of widespread eolian transport of desert materials to the ocean, especially in an area such as that in the eastern Atlantic, off the Sahara Desert, where the hot harmattan winds blow dusts up to 1000 miles out. Radczewski (1937) studying the *Meteor* samples found hematite-coated desert quartz grains over a broad area here; in the 5–10μ range this desert material represented up to 22% of the whole sample and in the 10–50μ range up to 39%. Goldberg (1964) suggested that fine fractions of both quartz and illite, found far out in the Pacific, away from obvious ocean current sources, could well be explained by the patterns of the upper atmospheric jet streams. Volcanic eruptions shower ash and dust over broad areas,

generally limited to about 500 km in radius (Kuenen and Neeb, 1943), but may reach further downwind. The finest dust goes up into the stratosphere and achieves almost worldwide distribution as shown also by the radioactive tracers from atomic bomb testing.

(e) **Glacial Transportation.** Ice floe and iceberg rafting are the most important transport agencies in all high latitudes; today the usual distribution range is to 55° or, in regions of strong equatorward-setting currents, as far as 45°N and S. During Pleistocene maxima these limits were generally extended to 35°, and locally to about 25° (see *Sea-ice Transportation*). Because of the large size of glacial boulders and the thin layer of postglacial sediment in many areas of the world ocean today, oceanographic rock trawls bring up the Pleistocene boulders in many regions where ice does not reach today (Lisitzin, 1960).

(f) **Biologic Transportation.** Floating vegetation is a major agency of transport, from the size of pebbles and gravel adhering to the roots of trees, carried seaward by river floods, to all sort of terrestrial organisms, from vertebrates down to gastropods, which are carried thus into highly unusual environments for fossilization (thanatocoenoses).

Sedimentation Rates

In regions of very high bottom scour such as Formosa Strait, parts of the English Channel and the Straits of Dover, and parts of Florida Straits, there is no accumulation and the chart is marked "hardground" or "rocks." In other areas near delta fronts, the sedimentation rate may exceed 1 mm/yr. In the deep sea, the rates vary from the turbidite accumulations (*abyssal plains*, q.v.) where rates may *average* 0.5 mm/yr, to regions of exclusively red clay (q.v.) with a very slow accumulation rate, below the "calcium carbonate compensation depth" (q.v.), and to regions of the carbonate oozes, at less than 4500–5000 m, where rates of sedimentation depend largely on primary productivity. Mean pelagic rates are in the range 1–10 mm per 1000 years (Menard, 1964). In iceberg melting areas, e.g., off the Newfoundland Banks, a very high dump rate is maintained over a relatively small area. (Isotopic dating results and procedures will be dealt with in another volume.) The first picture of sedimentation in depth in the deep ocean has come from the first experimental Mohole boring off Guadaloupe Island in the eastern Pacific (Murata and Erd, 1964).

Discussion

It has been remarked that seismological studies, both by explosion-refraction and reflection surveys at sea, and by long-range earthquake analyses, have shown that the sedimentary cover of the deep-sea basins is of the order of 200–500 m increasing near the margins to 1000 m and more in thickness. Distributed uniformly over the odd 4500 million years since the beginning of the earth's history, if low temperature evolution from the beginning is assumed, the 500-m thickness would call for a mean sedimentation rate of less than 1 mm per 10,000 years.

Compared with classical concepts of "normal" sedimentation rates, this figure is fantastically low. Some observers have suggested that the "Second Layer" of the seismologists (some 5 km) is in reality a very consolidated sediment, dolomite for example; there is no substantial evidence for this model. An average rate of accumulation for foraminiferal oozes in the mid-ocean, determined by carbon-14 dating for the last 20,000 years or so, is 3 cm per 1000 years. This 3 cm contains a small fraction of red clay.

In the areas where only the abyssal red clay is accumulating, an average rate of 0.04 mm per 1000 years was determined by the radium method and 0.01 mm by the ionium method. This rate is 1 cm per million years or 2800 m since the beginning of the earth, which seems to be the right order of magnitude for an average figure.

Several interpretations of these data are possible: (a) The high-rate pelagic foraminiferal sedimentation is only a phenomenon of the Cretaceous–Holocene time, prior to which no equivalent organisms existed (Kuenen, 1950). However, at 3 cm per 1000 years, this rate would build up over 200 m of sediment since the Cretaceous, leaving little room for all preexisting time. Compaction would allow only a small margin.

(b) Calcium carbonate goes slowly into solution in seawater at low temperatures with high partial pressure of CO_2. Periodic strengthening of bottom currents of polar origin might remove the carbonate fraction of the sediment, leaving only the clay fraction, a geochemical winnowing process. However, at the mean sedimentation rate for the Holocene, some 5000 m of compact lime-free clay would accumulate since the beginning of the earth (see below). Even the clays, micas and feldspars are slowly soluble so that some of these must be winnowed out too.

(c) Bearing in mind the limited data available, a third hypothesis may be postulated: that the mean sedimentation of the Holocene is not to be taken as normal for all of geological history. There is indeed a considerable weight of evidence suggesting that during the whole Quaternary period, sedimentary rates were greatly in excess of normal and varied greatly from glacial to interglacial stages. Not only were there violent climatic changes, increasing the rates of *continental erosion* (q.v., in *Geomorphology* vol. III), but there were also tectono-eustatic and glacio-eustatic reductions of basal level that accelerated stream flows and, at the same time, increased the area of the continents. It seems a reasonable deduction that the net lithogenous sedimentation during very long "quiet" geological periods was about *two orders of magnitude* below the present. This conclusion and its implications should be carried over to all our considerations of stratigraphy and historical geology, as well as to estimates of erosion in geomorphology.

(d) A fourth hypothesis is provided by the *Theory of Global Expansion*, recently developed by Carey, by Egyed and by Heezen (see Geophysics volume). It has also found favor among some Russian geologists. According to Egyed, the rate of radius expansion may be about 0.5 mm/yr. In the event of expansion of the mantle beneath oceanic areas, notably from the locus of the mid-ocean ridges, it may be reasoned that large parts of the oceanic crust are much newer than 4500 million years. It should be noted that no fossils or rocks younger than the Cretaceous have been found within the deep ocean basins. An objection to this hypothesis is that one might reasonably expect the sedimentary layer to vary, in parallel belts, growing progressively thicker (and older) as one moved away from the mid-ocean ridge and toward the continental margin. There is some evidence of this, but it might also be explained in other ways.

RHODES W. FAIRBRIDGE

References

Arrhenius, G., 1963, "Pelagic Sediments," in "The Sea," Vol. 3, pp. 655–727, New York, Interscience Publishers.

Darwin, C., 1846, "An account of the fine dust which falls on vessels in the Atlantic Ocean," *Quart. J. Geol. Soc., London,* **2**, 26.

Fairbridge, R. W., 1955, "Warm marine carbonate environments and dolomitization," *Geol. Soc. Digest,* Tulsa, **23**, 39–48.

Fairbridge, R. W., 1964, "The Importance of Limestone and its Ca/Mg Content to Palaeoclimatology," in "Problems in Palaeoclimatology," pp. 431–477, 521–530, London, Interscience Publishers.

Geikie, A., 1903, "Text Book of Geology," Fourth ed., London, Macmillan, 2 vols.

Goldberg, E. D., 1964, "The oceans as a geological system," *Trans. N.Y. Acad. Sci., Ser.* 11, **27**, 7–19.

Goldberg, E. D., and Griffin, J. J., 1964, "Sedimentation rates and mineralogy in the South Atlantic," *J. Geophys. Res.,* **69**, 4293–4309.

Griffin, J. J., and Goldberg, E. D., 1963, "Clay Mineral Distribution in the Pacific Ocean," in "The Sea," Vol. 3, pp. 728–741, New York, Interscience Publishers.

Kuenen, P. H., 1950, "Marine Geology," New York, John Wiley & Sons, 568pp.

Kuenen, P. H., and Neeb, G. A., 1943, "The Snellius Expedition (Bottom Samples)," Vol. 5, Pt. 3, Leiden, E. J. Brill.

Lisitzin, A. P., 1960, "Bottom sediments of the Eastern Antarctic and the Southern Indian Ocean," *Deep-Sea Res.,* **7**, 89–99.

Livingston, D. A., 1963, "Chemical composition of rivers and lakes," *U.S. Geol. Surv. Profess. Papers,* **440-G**, 1–64.

Lowenstam, H. A., and Epstein, S., 1957, "On the origin of sedimentary aragonite needles of the Great Bahama Bank," *J. Geol.*, **65**, 364–375.

Menard, H. W., 1964, "Marine Geology of the Pacific," New York, McGraw-Hill Book Co., 271pp.

Murata, K. J., and Erd, R. C., 1964, "Composition of sediments in cores from the experimental Mohole Project (Guadalupe site)," *J. Sediment. Petrol.*, **34**, 633–655.

Murray, J., and Renard, A. F., 1884, "On the nomenclature, origin and distribution of deep-sea deposits," *Proc. Roy. Soc. Edinburgh*, **12**, 495–529.

Murray, J., and Renard, A. F., 1891, "Deep-sea deposits," *Rept. H.M.S. Challenger* 1873–1876, 525pp.

Newell, N. D., Purdy, E. G., and Imbrie, J., 1960, "Bahamian oölitic Sand," *J. Geol.*, **68**, 481–497.

Peterson, M. N. A., and Goldberg, E. D., 1962, "Feldspar distributions in South Pacific pelagic sediments," *J. Geophys. Res.*, **67**, 3477–3492.

Radczewski, O. E., 1937, "Eolian Deposits in Marine Sediments," in (Trask, P., editor) "Recent Marine Sediments," pp. 496–502, Am. Assoc. Petrol. Geol.

Revelle, R. R., 1944, "Marine bottom samples collected in the Pacific Ocean by the *Carnegie* on its seventh cruise," *Carnegie Inst. Wash. Publ.*, **556**, Pt. 1, 180pp.

Ryther, J. H., 1963, "Geographical Variations in Productivity," in "The Sea," Vol. 2, pp. 347–380, New York, Interscience Publishers.

Sverdrup, H. W., Johnson, M. W., and Fleming, R. H., 1942, "The Oceans; Their Physics, Chemistry, and General Biology," New York, Prentice-Hall, 1087pp.

Tatsumoto, M., and Goldberg, E. D., 1959, "Some aspects of the marine geochemistry of uranium," *Geochim. Cosmochim. Acta*, **17**, 201–208.

Cross-references: *Abyssal Plain; Atlantic Ocean; Bathyal Zone; Pacific Ocean; Planktonic Photosynthesis; Turbidity Currents; Upwelling.*

MARINE SEISMIC PROFILER—*See* SEISMIC REFLECTION PROFILING

MASS MORTALITY IN THE SEA

The life of most animals is terminated by their being captured by other animals; those that die naturally are sooner or later eaten by scavengers. Bottom living invertebrates and bacteria are the chief scavengers of the sea, consuming all the soft parts and even the bones of vertebrates as these contain organic compounds. Consequently, bones are nearly absent in the sediments of the sea, though the oceans swarm with vast schools of fish. Where catastrophes occur, the situation is different. One must distinguish between limited mortalities and mass mortality. Some hundreds of fish killed by a severe storm will not leave evident traces in the sediment, but if killing attains catastrophic proportions there is a fair chance.

There are several places in the sea where killing of thousands of fish and of invertebrates repeatedly occurs. The nearly annihilated bottom fauna will repopulate the whole area only after a long interval;

in the meantime scavenging is limited. Hence, it is not only the extent of the mortality that counts, but also the interval between mortalities in the same place. The principal causes leading to catastrophes in the sea are a sudden change in temperature or salinity, red tide and lack of oxygen; such catastrophes may occur once every few years. Volcanism is often considered to be the chief cause of recent catastrophes, but this opinion is chiefly based on underestimation of other causes. In recent time, catastrophes by volcanism are rare and the intervals are great.

(1) *Temperature:* Unusually severe winters, heavy "northers" and a change in currents may bring about catastrophes.

Severe winters are normal in arctic seas, and the fauna is adapted to the prevailing conditions. In boreal areas, where winters are normally mild, widespread mortality of the shallow water fauna occurs during an abnormally severe and prolonged winter. Since these mortalities occur in abnormal winters, the interval is great.

A sudden drop in temperature often occurs in various parts of the Gulf of Mexico during heavy northers, in many years causing catastrophic killing. The shallow water fauna of the Texas coast and of the west coast of Florida are particularly subject to destruction. The rapid onset of the northers combined with the great extent of the shallow bay waters, favors the frequent occurrence of catastrophes in these areas. Every 6–10 years fish are killed in large quantities; the weight in 1947 is estimated at 16 million pounds.

Big changes in temperature occur on the boundaries of cold and warm currents. The well-known tile-fish disaster in 1882 probably was caused by a change in currents, but data concerning the temperature during the mortality are unknown. A better-studied example is the episodic mortality near Sukkertoppen (southwest Greenland) happening near the borderline of the Polar and the Irminger Currents. The temperature of the water near Sukkertoppen is chiefly dependent on the proportional strength of these two currents; catastrophes occur in years when unusual low temperatures of the water prevail.

(2) *Salinity:* In areas with regular changes in salinity, most animals are adapted, but if the change is greater or continues much longer than usual widespread mortality occurs. Animals may be killed by a decrease or by an increase in salinity. In Chesapeake Bay, heavy mortality among oysters occurs when the Susquehanna River discharges unusually large volumes of fresh water. Spectacular fish kills occur particularly in oversaline water; in the Laguna Madre, fish die in large numbers in dry and hot summers when the water becomes oversaline.

Currents may carry animals into water of lethal salinity. Freshwater plankton is killed when carried by rivers into the sea. Most fish are good swimmers, and one is inclined to think that fish might return when entering water of lethal salinity. In the Gulf of Kara Bugaz (Caspian Sea), where water of medium salinity flows through a narrow channel into the highly saline gulf, a great amount of dead fish accumulates near the entrance of the channel. In the same way dead fish are found in salt lakes near the entrance of rivers. Probably the fish enter the lakes in a layer of fresh water floating on the highly saline lake water, and they perish when this layer evaporates or is mixed with underlying water.

(3) *Red tide and lack of oxygen:* A discoloration of the water caused by a rapid multiplication of one or a few species of plankton (unicellular algae or protozoans) is called waterbloom. When those organisms die, they turn pinkish to reddish brown; "red tide" is the common name. Red tides are blooms which may or may not be lethal to aquatic organisms; many tides are harmless, others may bring about enormous destructions among invertebrates and fish; in many places killing occurs every few years. Virulent poisons were isolated from waterbloom of blue-green algae and of dinoflagellates; these poisons probably cause a major part of the catastrophes. Besides poisoning, another important factor may be lack of oxygen. Red tide occurs in waters of high production, particularly in subtropical and tropical regions (coastal waters of Florida, California, southwest Africa, India, etc.), it develops in succession after an excessive production of other organisms. The conditions are reminiscent of polluted waters where the oxygen is used up by organic decay.

The paleontological significance of mass mortality has been mentioned in connection with (a) Cuvier's theory of catastrophes; (b) the origin of bituminous shales and petroleum; (c) the origin of phosphorite.

(a) To exterminate whole species or even higher systematic units as was postulated in Cuvier's theory, the mortalities must extend over very large areas. Recent mortalities do not cover such large areas; at best, a species with a very limited distribution may be exterminated by them.

(b) Conditions leading to the formation of bituminous rocks are twofold; either the supply with oxygen to the lower water layers is scanty (stagnation) or the consumption of oxygen is high (high production areas); catastrophes by red tide and by lack of oxygen repeatedly occur in the last-mentioned case. This does not imply that the fish are the chief source material of bitumen and oil; plankton organisms are the chief contributors.

(c) Murray postulated that phosphatic concretions are formed in places where catastrophes occur, calcium phosphate being an important constituent of vertebrate bones. An argument in favor of Murray's hypothesis is the presence of numerous bones in some phosphorite deposits. Against Murray, it was argued that all decaying vertebrates float by the gases of putrefaction, and both while floating and after lodgement upon the shore they are subject to the attack of scavengers. This is not wholly correct; many fish remain on the bottom and never come to the surface. In places where catastrophes occur, a mass of carcasses has been observed on and in the sediment. Catastrophes by a sudden drop in temperature and by red tide occur near the places where phosphorite is formed. Phosphorite is precipitated in the nondepositional parts of high production areas where practically no sediment is accumulating. As phosphorus is an essential constituent of the protoplasm of living organisms, plankton will be the chief source of the phosphorite, but in some deposits the bones furnish an additional supply of calcium phosphate.

MARGARETHA BRONGERSMA-SANDERS

References

Brongersma-Sanders, Margaretha, 1957, "Mass mortality in the sea," *Geol. Soc. Am. Mem.* 67, **1**, 941–1010.

Gunter, Gordon, 1947, "Catastrophism in the sea and its paleontological significance with special reference to the Gulf of Mexico," *Am. J. Sci.*, **245**, 669–676.

Cross-references: *Kara-Bogaz Gulf* (pr Vol. VI).

MEAN SEA LEVEL

The elevation of a point on land is usually given with reference to mean sea level. For example, Mt. McKinley is 20,300 feet above sea level. Such a statement implies that sea level is fixed, and that it can be determined and defined. And this is true, to a first approximation. The surface of the water in the ocean basins is nearly perpendicular to gravity at each point; it nearly lies on an "equipotential" surface (see *Geodesy*, another volume).

To the geodesist, navigator, coastal engineer, or oceanographer, a first approximation may not be good enough. Deviations from the equipotential are found from place to place and from time to time. They amount to several meters, normally, and on rare occasions become large enough to cause severe flooding and coastal damage. Even small sea-surface slopes in the open ocean may be related to major ocean currents, and to the motion of millions of tons of water per second (see *Geostrophic Flow*). To understand and describe these motions, we need to know (1) the average elevation and shape of the sea surface, and (2) the variations with time.

At present, we have only one *direct* way of measuring the elevation of a point on the sea surface. We measure (by use of line-of-sight surveying instruments) the difference in height between a fixed object on land and the nearby sea surface. To find a reliable mean elevation, in the presence of waves, tides, etc., requires a long series of frequent observations. Such series are best collected by means of mechanical gauges; these have been used for more than a hundred years (see *Tides*).

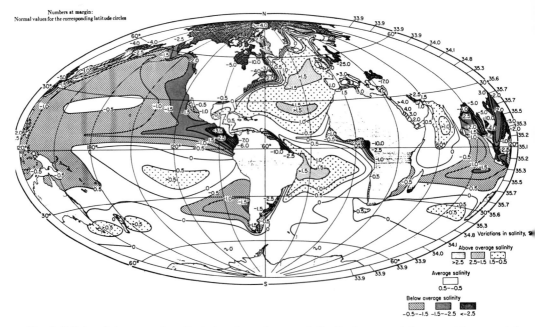

Fig. 1. Salinity of the sea surface. Deviations from the normal distribution on a globe covered by water (after G. Dietrich, 1963). (By permission of Interscience Publishers, N.Y.)

However, with land-based gauges, we can measure sea level only at the ocean's edges and at islands. Besides, we cannot compare the measurements from one place with those from another except where there is a land connection between points. For example, we cannot determine the actual difference in sea level between San Francisco and Honolulu. Measurements from space platforms (man-made satellites, the moon, etc.) offer good promise of giving us information on the actual shape of the sea surface. At present, the precision is inadequate to determine the small differences from the equipotential.

Some facts about regional differences in sea level have been inferred from data on the specific volume of the water. Cold or salty water takes up less space, per unit mass, than warm or less saline water. Specific volume can be determined from temperature and salinity measurements, and the height of a column of given mass and cross section can be computed (actually geometric height). To make the computation, we assume that there are no horizontal pressure gradients deep in the ocean. We have no pressure data, as yet, with which to test this assumption. It is consistent, however, with other oceanographic observations (small temperature gradients at depth, etc.).

The computations imply that sea level is an irregular surface (even without waves on it). There are low hills in the subtropics, gentle valleys in the subarctic and subantarctic, and east-west trending ridges and troughs near the equator. However, the relief is very low—only 1 or 2 m from hilltop to valley floor, while the distance between hill and valley is several thousand kilometers. For example, sea level is about 1 m higher southeast of Japan than it is off the Aleutian Islands.

The computations also imply that the level of the surface of the North Pacific is higher than that of the North Atlantic. The Atlantic is warmer, but the Pacific is much less saline. As a result, Pacific water has a larger specific volume, and the surface of the Pacific Ocean should stand 30–50 cm higher than that of the Atlantic (see Fig. 1). This difference in level actually exists. In fact, it was first discovered by precision leveling across the Isthmus of Panama and across the continental United States. A similar gradient may be seen down the east coast of the United States (Fig. 2).

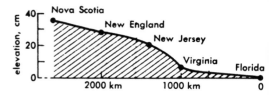

Fig. 2. Elevation of mean sea level from north to south along the eastern coast of North America. Heights refer to the elevation at Florida (based on data from Sverdrup *et al.*, 1942; McGraw-Hill Encyclopedia of Science and Technology).

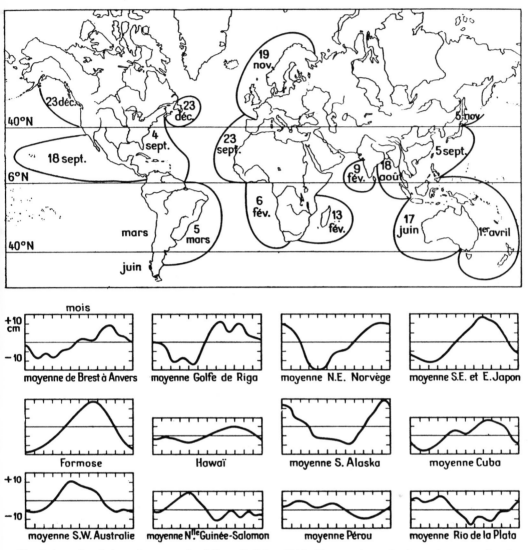

Fig. 3. Annual variations of mean sea level (from Guilcher, 1965). The map shows the times of mean maxima for groups of stations, according to Miss E. Lisitzin. The curves show annual variations in MSL (according to Pattullo et al., 1955).

The level of the surface of the real sea varies continually. The variations with time are much larger than the variations from place to place. Some typical representative features of the change with time are listed in Table 1. The first three types (waves, tsunamis, tides) are discussed elsewhere in this encyclopedia.

Storm tides are high water levels induced by on-shore winds and low air pressure. The sea acts as an inverted barometer; the surface rises approximately 1 cm for each millibar the air pressure falls. This happens along all coasts but the effects are especially large and damaging to structures on low coasts lying in the paths of storm centers. Galveston, Texas, has been inundated by hurricane-raised

TABLE 1. VARIATIONS IN SEA LEVEL

Type	Period[a]	Prevalence	Amplitude
Waves	Seconds	Virtually continuous	Up to 20 m
Tsunamis	Minutes to hours	Occasional	Up to 10 m
Tides	$12\frac{1}{2}$ hr	Daily	Up to 20 m
Storm tides	Days to years	Occasional	One to several meters
Annual tides	1 yr	Yearly	Up to 1 m
Long-period changes	Geologic time	10^2–10^7 yr	Up to 200 m

[a] Defined as the time interval between successive high waters; not all of these phenomena are strictly periodic.

storm tides. (In the northern hemisphere, storm tides are highest in the northeastern quadrant of a hurricane.) The Netherlands coastal dikes have been breached by storm tides raised by middle latitude cyclones over the North Sea.

Annual tides are usually small—20–30 cm in range. There are at least six factors involved:

(1) Changing heat content of the water with season is related to changes in specific volume and, therefore, in sea level.

(2) Changes in salinity due to rainfall or evaporation affect specific volume.

(3) Changes in the *distribution* of air pressure over the ocean induce the inverted barometer effect. (If the pressure increased everywhere over the oceans, there would be no observable effect on sea level, because seawater is nearly incompressible.)

(4) There are annual and semiannual astronomic tides.

(5) The total amount of water in the oceans varies seasonally. In March there is more water on the continents than in October, largely in the form of northern hemisphere snow.

(6) Monsoon winds and currents pile up water along coastlines.

Changing heat content (1) explains most of the observed annual variation in level between 45°N and 45°S. Changing salinity (2), while not of widespread importance, does induce (in the northern Bay of Bengal) the largest annual range in the world. Changing air pressure (3) explains most of the observed variation north of 45°N and possibly south of 45°S. Effects of (4) and (5) are both small, one or a few centimeters. The effects of winds and currents (6) are not known except in a few small areas.

Long-period changes in sea level are revealed by wave-cut benches now exposed well above high tide, and by some features that have been found now below mean sea level. The controlling factors are mainly glaciation and relief of the continental land masses. It is believed that during the earliest and warmest interglacial and preglacial condition sea level was about 100 m higher than at present. During the glacials it was at least 100 m lower than now. During the first half of the twentieth century sea level was rising slowly (about 5 cm). If the Greenland and Antarctic ice caps completely melt, sea level will rise about 75 m and will drown all of the major coastal cities of the world.

JUNE G. PATTULLO

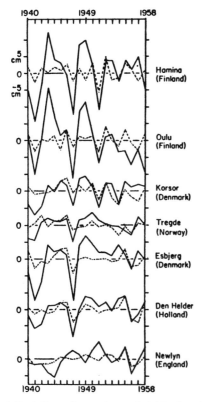

Fig. 4. Deviations of annual mean heights of sea level (Rossiter, 1963): ——— as observed, - - - - - after eliminating meteorological effects. (By permission of Interscience Publishers, N.Y.)

References

Bowden, K. F., 1960, "The effect of water density on the mean slope of the sea surface," *Bull. Géod.*, **55**, 93–96.

Dietrich, G., 1937, "Die Lage der Meeresoberfläche in Druckfeld von Ozean und Atmosphäre (mit besondere Berücksichtigung des westlichen Nordatlantischen Ozeans und des Golfs von Mexico)," *Berlin, Veroeffentl. Inst. Meereskunde, N.F., Ser. A*, **33**, 1–52.

Dietrich, G., 1963, "General Oceanography," New York, Interscience Publishers.

Donn, W. L., Pattullo, J. G., Shaw, D. M., 1964, "Sea-level Fluctuations and Long Waves," in (Hugh Odishaw, editor) "Research in Geophysics," Vol 2, pp. 243–271, Cambridge, M.I.T. Press.

Fairbridge, R. W., 1961, "Eustatic changes in sea level," *Phys. Chem. Earth*, **4**, 99–185.

Guilcher, A., 1964, "Précis d'Hydrologie, Marine et Continentale," Paris, Masson & Cie., 389pp.

Hela, I., 1947, "A study of the annual fluctuation of the heights of sea-level in the Baltic and in the North Sea," *Soc. Sci. Fennica, Commentationes Phys.-Math.*, **13**, Pt. 14.

Hela, I., 1953, "Longitudinal and transversal slope of the Florida Current," *Geophysica, Helsinki*, **5**, 3.

International Union of Geodesy and Geophysics, 1960, *Monographie*, Paris, Inst. Geogr. Nat.

Lisitzin, E., 1958, "Le Niveau Moyen de la Mer," *Bull. d'Inform. de Com. cent. d'Océanogr.*, **10**, 254–262.

Lisitzin, E., and Pattullo, J. G., 1961, "The principal factors influencing the seasonal oscillation of sea level," *J. Geophys. Res.*, **66**, 845–852.

Montgomery, R. B., 1938, "Fluctuations in monthly sea level on eastern U.S. coast as related to dynamics of western North Atlantic Ocean," *J. Marine Res.*, **1**, 165–185.

Pattullo, J., Munk, W., Revelle, R., and Strong, E., 1955, "The seasonal oscillation in sea level," *J. Marine Res.*, **14**, 88–156.

Roden, G., 1960, "On the nonseasonal variations in sea level along the west coast of North America," *J. Geophys. Res.*, **65**, 2809–2826.

Rossiter, J. R., 1963, "Long-term Variations in Sea-level," in (Hill, M. N., editor) "The Sea," Vol. 1, pp. 590–610, New York, Intterscience Publishers.

Shimizu, T., 1963, "The variation of the sea-level and the barometric pressure with Chandler's period," *Spec. Contrib., Geophys. Inst., Kyoto Univ.*, No. 3, 255–271.

Cross-reference: *Tides.*

MEAN SEA LEVEL CHANGES, LONG-TERM —EUSTATIC AND OTHER

Systematic studies of tide gauge data, climate change, and geomorphological evidence are being gradually correlated to demonstrate that the world secular rise of sea level in the period 1890–1960 was glacio-eustatic, i.e., related to melting of glaciers, in turn dependent on a rise in mean world temperatures by about 1.0°C. The local tidal data are found to be modified by steric causes (warming and expansion of water mass, etc.), by cyclic changes in mean atmospheric pressure, the related wind regimes, the Coriolis effect, and changes in the absolute height of the tide station (sediment compaction, geotectonics, and geodetic changes related to relative shift of the earth's axial dipole).

An approximate integration of these varied factors is now possible for any region of the world possessing tidal records extending over several years or more, so that a reasonable quantitative prediction of sea level change and therefore potential engineering hazards (flooding, siltation, beach erosion) is not only feasible but economically practicable.

The financial burden that nations with developed littoral areas have to bear for repairs of storm damage and coast protection shows the need for developing some method of predicting potential marine attack. It is now well-established from historical records that seasonal and periodic storm conditions can be predicted, if not to a specific, at least to a range of statistical probability. However, there are two long-term trends that tend to upset such predictions. These are (a) secular tectonic uplift or subsidence of the coast, and (b) eustatic and steric variations in mean sea level.

Effects of Relative Sea-level Change

Regardless of cause (tectonic, eustatic, etc.), a *relative* change of mean sea level, as determined on an annual or other long-term basis, has a predictable effect on the coastal sediments. In contrast to classic ideas of coast erosion, expressed for example by Douglas Johnson (1919), the effect has been reduced

to a quantitative theory by Per Bruun (1962). The early concept that sediment from an eroding beach becomes distributed evenly over the entire continental shelf down to an ultimate wave base of about −200 m is rejected. Wave base for the movement of sand is rarely more than 10 m, corresponding to the mean depth of wave break (Dietz, 1963). Thus, instead of an almost unlimited open system, the system is limited below by an effective wave base for sand of −10 m and has an upper limit at stormwave swash. In the longshore sense, the limits vary; in certain cases, the basic unit may be several hundred kilometers in length, but in others, more convenient for control studies, the beach may be isolated by headlands or deep channels to the order of 100–1000 m.

It should be stressed that although mean sea level (MSL) tends to be regarded as a fixed datum, it is in fact a variable in time. A temporary mean sea level may be established over a certain period of time, depending on a number of variables, in some regions the summer–winter periods, the monsoons, the 11- and 22-year sunspot cycles, etc. According to Bruun's formulation, with a rise of MSL, the pre-existing upper beach will be eroded to a new profile of equilibrium, with the same shape as before but displaced upward and landward.

Changes of Mean Sea Level

A pioneer study by Gutenberg (1941) of data from worldwide tide gauge records suggested that the world mean sea level was rising at about 1.1 mm/yr during the first half of the twentieth century. Further studies by Valentin (1952), Munk and Revelle (1952), Lisitzin (1958), and by Fairbridge and Krebs (1962) have confirmed this pattern, the last figure being 1.2 mm/yr (1900–50). However, this is only a mean figure, and examination of a 5-year smoothed curve shows negative oscillations (e.g., about 1907, 1920, 1945), and there are stages of very rapid rise (e.g., 1946–56 at an average rate of 5.5 mm/yr).

If one examines the world annual mean sea level curve, even more astonishing changes become apparent. In the period 1875–77 there was a total rise of 70 mm. However, it should be stressed that this figure is still "damped" by being a world average. Isolated regions and single stations show much greater figures. Such rises have been largely offset by negative swings in subsequent years, but it must be evident to the student of coastal geomorphology and engineering that if the predictable incidence of storm centers—even the "once-a-century" storm—chances to coincide with a phase of high mean sea level, very severe flooding and damage are likely to ensue.

During the last decade or so, considerably more attention has been paid to mean sea level than in the past. Initially, tide gauges were established at major ports in order to aid day-to-day shipping. After the local tidal characteristics were once established, numbers of potentially valuable stations were discontinued. This short-sighted policy is quite heartrending when one examines the records of some isolated region, and just at a critical decade one reads that the station was dismantled. Systematic records are now coordinated by the Commission on Mean Sea Level (see Doodson *et al.*, 1954) of the

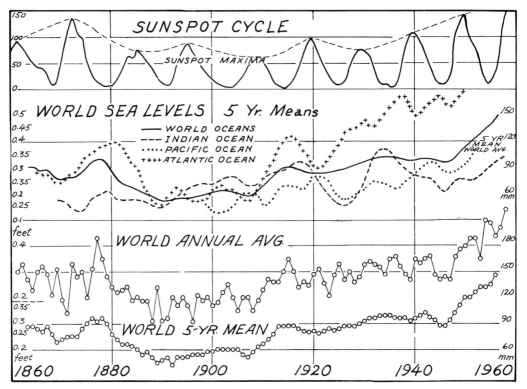

Fig. 1. Graphs of world mean sea level, for the different oceans, smoothed to 5-year means and compared with the mean sunspot maxima. It is evident that local departures occur (oceanographic and meteorologic phenomena); the mean patterns show interesting parallels (Fairbridge and Krebs, 1962).

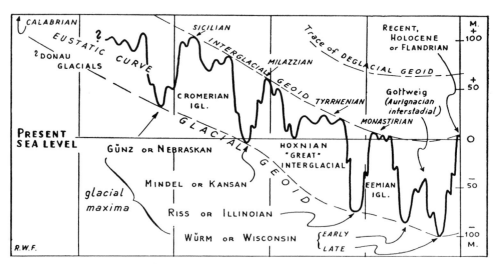

Fig. 2. Diagrammatic representation of quaternary sea-level oscillations. Absolute chronology establishes that the last major cycle is about 100,000 years, but earlier cycles cannot be dated yet, although the stratigraphic sequence is quite well established.

International Association of Physical Oceanography.

The principal purpose of this renewed interest in tide gauges is for controlling basic geodetic survey networks, but a secondary use has appeared, as a control for measurements of crustal movements. By releveling old geodetic nets, it is emerging that many parts of the earth's crust, previously considered to be tectonically "stable," are in a state of constant secular or oscillatory motion. A special study committee has been set up, the Commission on Recent Crustal Movements by the International Association of Geodesy (within the I.U.G.G.), under the chairmanship of a Russian geographer. Y. A. Mescherikov. The report and published papers of their first meeting in Leipzig, 1962, were published that same year.

With respect to the long-term coastal changes, Fig. 2 represents a tentative reconstruction; absolute dating is still very tentative. The International Association for Quaternary Research (INQUA) has a *Commission for the Study of Shorelines*. An annotated bibliography of Quaternary shore line changes on a worldwide basis was published in 1965 (Richards and Fairbridge, 1965). The INQUA has also established a *Commission on Neotectonics*.

It has long been customary for cautious geomorphologists to ascribe a coastal feature, situated today at an anomalous elevation to that expected from the genetic process, to "either change of sea level or oscillation of the earth's crust." The evidence emerging is that both factors are amply recorded as operative today in many parts of the earth.

Components of Mean Sea Level Change

Disregarding crustal change, sediment compaction, etc. (to be considered below), the components of a local mean annual sea level change can be broken down as follows:

(a) **Glacio-eustatic Change.** Worldwide effect of a hydrologic imbalance between world moisture transport to the continents (snow) and, in reverse, to the oceans (meltwater). It has been demonstrated by Ahlmann (1940) that an elevation of the mean annual temperature in the region of a small mountain glacier by 0.5°C produces an excess melting of 6×10^5 m³/km²/yr. Larger glaciers melt more slowly. A rise of world mean sea level of 1 mm would call for the melting of 0.36×10^{12} m³ of ice, or a layer 36 cm thick from ice surfaces covering 1 million km². Melting rates of this order have been widely reported by glaciological surveys during the last few years. The writer has attempted to analyze the year-to-year eustatic oscillations in the light of data on glacier retreats and advances, but without much success. There seem to be too many delaying and feedback mechanisms for an annual treatment. However, when the curves are smoothed to 5- or 10-year periods, an interesting correlation emerges between sunspots (as a measure of the UV com-

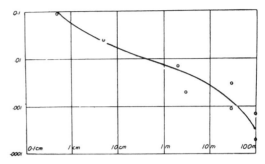

RATIO OF TEMPERATURE TO TIME

Fig. 3. The ratio of temperature (variation in degrees Celsius) to time (as the approximate period of the cycle involved), related to glacio-eustatic change (expressed in meters above or below present MSL). The scatter represents in part the difficulties of accurate observation, but in part the retardation difference between freezing and melting. Note that the water-ice volumes are limited; thus the curve is sinusoidal.

ponent of solar radiation and the resultant ozone thermal "blanket"), mean temperatures and mean sea level (Fairbridge, 1961c).

Averages of world temperature change of the last century have been prepared by Murray Mitchell (1963) showing approximately a 1°C rise for the period 1900–50. Although the temperature × time to eustatic level curve is gaussian, the middle part corresponds to a simplified formula 1°C × yr = 1 mm (eustatic change). Thus 1°C of mean world temperature change, continued over a period of 50 years, is reflected by a 50-mm change of sea level, which is so-observed (Fig. 3). For the last Ice Age a drop of 10°C over 10,000 years gave a 100-m lowering of sea level (Fairbridge, 1962, 1963).

Eustatic variation is the ultimate barometer of climatic change. The absolute range is about 200 m, corresponding in volume to 0.36×10^{12} cubic meters of water per millimeter, or 72×10^6 km³. The total volume of the world's land ice today is about 30×10^6 km³, and was about 40–45 × 10⁶ km³ greater during glacial phases. At the ice maxima, negative feedbacks would slow the glacial advance to a standstill; in other words, at about latitude 35–40° there was an equatorward limit of ice advance, along which line it would be entirely compensated by melting. At the other extreme, in a non-glacial epoch of low relief and no polar land areas, there would be no glacier ice at all. Between these two limits there is a gaussian curve of distribution. Present mean sea level is close to the midpoint on the curve. This is due to the failure of the Antarctic continent to melt more than about 10% for the time available during each interglacial phase.

The "glacio-eustatic theory" thus appears to be proved, i.e., that important and measurable sea level changes can be quantitatively related to glacial melting. Much greater precision, however, is desirable.

(b) **Other Eustatic Changes.** Apart from glacio-eustasy, two other significant factors in worldwide MSL change are recognized: *sedimento-eustatic*, those due to accumulation of sediment in ocean basins, thus a one-way, positive shift; and *tectono-eustatic*, those due to modification in the shape of ocean basins because of tectonic action, thus either positive or negative in effect. Both of these changes are related to the dimensions of the container, while glacio-eustasy relates to the volume of the contents. Studies of the rates of MSL change involved (0.01 mm/yr) have led the writer to conclude that neither is appreciable in terms of human history (Fairbridge. 1961a).

(c) **Steric Changes.** A steric phenomenon is one which involves the molecular dimensions of the material in question. In seawater, steric effects are brought about by temperature changes and by variations in salinity (and thus density). According to Munk and Macdonald (1960), if the entire sea-water column (mean depth 3800 m) were raised 1°C, the sea level surface would rise 600 mm. As noted by Fairbridge and Krebs (1962), the long-term variations of mean ocean temperature are very slow, since the physical "turnover" of ocean water is of the order of thousands of years. However, a seasonal rise and fall of shelf and estuary water temperatures may exceed something of the order of 10° over a 10-m depth range; the calculated effect would be 15.5 mm steric rise and fall. However, over a 19-year observation period in the North Sea, Rossiter (1962) failed to find any steric correlation between density and MSL. A striking temperature correlation with MSL on the other hand was shown by Gordon and Suthons (1965).

A complicating factor, furthermore, is that the temperature rise would normally be a summer effect, at which season there is generally a meteorologic effect (see below) which pushes MSL in the opposite direction. Nevertheless, studies by Patullo, Munk, Revelle, and Strong (1955) suggest that the observed MSL anomalies are generally more related to steric controls than to the atmospheric. The relative importance of each actually varies with latitude (Lisitzin and Patullo, 1961); in the tropics, temperatures are always rather stable but air pressure varies, while in the high latitudes the temperatures are seasonally very variable and exceed in effect the day-to-day pressure changes.

(d) **Meteorologic Effects.** A well-known atmospheric effect on MSL is the so-called meteorologic tide. When a low-pressure center passes over, MSL rises by as much as 1 m, and with high-pressure systems MSL is depressed. The phenomenon can be best seen on an isolated mid-Pacific coral atoll where the normal tidal range is small, perhaps only 10 cm at neaps; a high-pressure system will expose the reefs, a low-pressure center (as with a typhoon) will

so raise local MSL that ocean waves come right in across the reefs to wreak tremendous damage on the normally protected shore. It was in the tideless Gulf of Bothnia that this phenomenon was first observed in 1747 by Gissler, who concluded that sea level acts like an inverted barometer, the "*Statical Law*" (Doodson, 1924).

On an annual basis, such effects are generally smoothed out, so that MSL changes do not appear on year-to-year records. However, there are also atmospheric pressure cycles that have longer duration. Very persistent and clear is the "Southern Oscillation" (Berlage, 1957). This atmospheric pressure phenomenon affects mainly the equatorial and southern latitudes. When the western hemisphere ("Pacific Node") is high, the eastern ("Indian Ocean Node") is low, alternating in successive years.

The effect of a 1-millibar pressure anomaly is to modify MSL by approximately 10 mm. However, our studies show that, for the "Southern Oscillation" pressure anomalies of up to 1 millibar, there are sea level reactions often far in excess of 10 mm; in fact, a test comparison for Bombay showed that this only accounted for about 5% of the long-term anomalies (Fairbridge and Krebs, 1962). The longer-term pressure anomalies, such as the North Atlantic Oscillation (of 11–23 years), which has long been studied by Willett and his associates, may play an important but not as yet analyzed role.

(e) **Oceanographic Effects.** These are strictly local, or restricted to certain regions, but their net effects may totally eclipse those listed above. Generally, they are short term and tend to be associated with normal seasonal variation and storm passages. The principal components are:

(*i*) *Wind Stress Piling-up Effect.* This is characteristic of shallow shelves and gulfs. Its magnitude is inversely related to water depth. Short-term wind-stress anomalies are very considerable and may account for 30% or more of the total annual anomaly, but over long periods (5 years or so) tend to disappear. Since onshore winds often build up with lowering atmospheric pressure, it is difficult to separate the two effects (Rossiter, 1962).

A characteristic seasonal variation is the high MSL recorded in Indian stations during the summer monsoon. Variations of the mean annual sea level at Bombay through 3–11 year periods exceed 50 mm, a large fraction of this figure probably reflects the wind stress dependent upon the monsoon and the Central Asiatic pressure field.

(*ii*) *Estuary Effect.* This is noticeable where large rivers debouch. Variations in the timing and intensity of regional rainfall are closely related to the above-described pressure and wind-stress controls; however, in each of them the timing and sign may be either cumulative or opposed.

(*iii*) *Hydraulic Head Effect.* This is observed in narrow straits. In Florida Strait between Key West and Miami, there is a regular difference of MSL of 70 mm, but a secular change in the density, temperature or velocity of the Gulf Stream will modify it.

(*iv*) *Coriolis Effect*. This is to be seen in all moving bodies on a rotating globe. Since the Gulf Stream is moving northward, the Coriolis effect will tend to shift it to the right, resulting in the east side being higher (measured in the Bahamas as 590 mm higher than at Miami). Annual variations in this tilt are measured according to the velocity of the current (Fig. 4). If there were a long-term rise in effective UV solar radiation and slight reduction in the equator–pole thermal gradient, there should be a weakening of the easterly wind component off the mid-Atlantic coast, accompanied by a deceleration of the Gulf Stream and an effective rise of MSL along the coast. During the last 50 years there has been a systematic anomaly in the East Coastal tidal records, suggesting a rise in MSL of about 3 mm/yr over and above the world figure of 1.2 mm. We still lack a systematic study of the world regimes, but the MSL and temperature trends seem to bear out our reasoning that there has been a secular reduction in the velocity of the Gulf Stream.

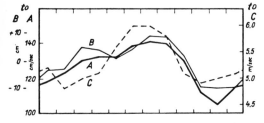

Fig. 4. Annual variation of current velocity at the sea surface A, and water level gradient B, in the Florida current, as well as the wind velocity C, of the trade winds. A (——); monthly averages of the current velocity according to ship's log observations (after F. C. Fuglister, 1951). B (——), water level difference based on an annual mean of zero between left- and right-hand side of the Florida current (Cat Key and Miami) (after H. Stommel, 1953). C (– – – –), monthly mean of the wind velocities east of the Lesser Antilles.

(*v*) *Long-term Astronomic Tidal Effects*. Effects such as the *Pole Tide* of 14 months and the 18–62-year *Nodal Tide* have been considered by Rossiter (1962), but the results are inconclusive. Still longer astronomic tides (suggested by Pettersson, 1914) should be investigated.

Tectonic Crustal Movements

Both sedimentary compaction and sedimentary collapse due to withdrawal of oil or ground water can and do cause local subsidence of the coast and lead to anomalous rise of apparent sea level and to inundation. In limited areas these foundation effects are often paramount (e.g., on the Gulf coast, in Texas; see Sheets and Weaver, 1963). Of a more long-term and widespread significance are the fundamental crustal changes.

Rossiter (1962) refers to all such changes as "changes in the distance of the tidal bench mark from the center of the earth." Thanks to the satellite tracking surveys, it is gradually emerging that quite remarkable terrestrial gravity and geodetic anomalies exist. On a regional scale further gravity anomalies are now well recognized (although mapping is still far from complete). Since the earth's anisotropy tends to be counteracted by the principle of isostasy, we may expect to find evidences of regional secular trends toward a reestablishment of equilibrium. These regions are essentially as follows:

(a) *Former glaciated regions*, where the removal of ice leads to unloading effects, notably a very rapid rise of the crust toward the middle of the former ice-covered area; thus today in central Scandinavia and central Canada, the rise may exceed 10 mm/yr. During the maximum of ice loading, the periglacial marginal areas were probably bowed up in a "marginal bulge"; the marginal bulge is now collapsing and a peripheral belt of subsidence is slowly shifting inward. In eastern North America, from New York to Newfoundland, this marginal subsidence may today amount to 1–3 mm/yr (Newman and Fairbridge, 1962).

(b) *Orogenic belts*, where certain zones are still strongly negative (subsiding) and others positive. The latter today are generally corresponding to the folded mountainous belts. Where these are cut off by the sea, jagged cliffy coasts occur and the tide gauges often show that they are still rising (at 1–3 mm/yr). In extremely seismic regions, e.g., Bay of Naples, Bay of Tokyo, southeast Alaska, southern Chile, jumps of 1 m and more are measured in single adjustments.

(c) *Sedimentary basins*, are geologically speaking to be classified as "contemporary geosynclines" of various classes. They are identified geomorphologically as a rule by their long, low, sandy coasts. These are often "coasts of submergence," disregarding Holocene eustatic oscillations, although their outlines are straight and the hinterland may display wide areas of recently emerged coastal plains. From deep bores, it is apparent that these basins have been discontinuously in subsidence for periods of the order of 10^6–10^9 years. However, the rates of subsidence are often very slow, and at less than 0.1 mm/yr.

(d) *Deltaic basins* are often located within the framework of a larger basin, but because of a locally more mobile crustal zone or negative block, very rapid subsidence occurs and the sediment pours into the depression at a phenomenal rate. The rates of subsidence in the Mississippi Delta are in the range of 1–4 mm/yr. The longest tidal record of the world

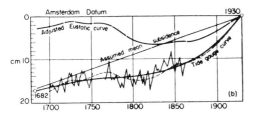

Fig. 5. Mean tide level at Amsterdam since 1682, corrected for a mean subsidence of the area (about 0.7 mm/yr); the adjusted eustatic curve approximately reflects rise and fall of mean world temperatures (Fairbridge, 1961).

(Amsterdam) suggests that this region has been subsiding at 0.7 mm/yr since 1682 (Fig. 5).

It is evident that if the world eustatic MSL has been rising at somewhat over 1 mm/yr during the last 50 years, there is a good chance that persons studying such deltas would gain the impression that the deltas were stable and so was MSL.

(e) *Broad, positive structural regions* are found in many parts of the earth, mainly near the present equatorial belt. They stand appreciably above the mean height of the continental masses and yet display rather little youthful deformation, being mainly consolidated in Precambrian time. Such high plateau-like segments are best seen in central and south Africa, Brazil, peninsular India and Western Australia.

The peripheral belts of these large areas are marked by monoclines or step-faulted terraces. Jessen (1943) called them "Randschwellen" and Bourcart (1952) described the marginal downwarp as the "Flexure continentale."

The cause of such anomalously high areas is intriguing and as yet unknown. However, the logical consequences of the new discoveries in geomagnetism should not be ignored. If it is true that the relative position of the North Pole shifted from near Alaska through about 20° of arc to its present position during the last 50×10^6 years or so, then the position of the equator relative to the continents must also have changed. Since the earth is an oblate spheroid, in which the polar radius is 22 km shorter than the equatorial, a shift in the pole will be instantly balanced by the hydrosphere, but more slowly by the lithosphere, and will leave the former equatorial bulge temporarily too high with respect to the geoid (MSL).

It is argued by the "soft earth" school that the mantle will quickly readjust to any serious deformation of the lithic crust; after all, Scandinavia and Canada have now recovered about 70% from the Pleistocene ice loading in a matter of only 10,000 years. However, there is another school, the "phase changers" or "differentiationists." These scientists point out that in an anisotropic earth, if a segment is placed under a reduced stress in the underlying

mantle there are likely to be mineral changes from high- to low-density isomorphs, and differentiation (aided by liberation of low density volatiles) will lead to lighter rock classes in general.

These *geodetic changes of sea level* do not involve water volume (as do eustatic), merely relative height. While some crustal regions are anomalously high, others are low or subsiding. The mechanisms and causes are still highly problematical, but the geological evidence seems clear enough. The geomorphological data can bring valuable evidence to bear, with data on emerged and submerged shore lines. However, until more satisfactory dating methods are developed, much of this data must remain relatively ineffectual. Although the approximate ages of the older terraces can often be determined from fossils and soils, the figures are at best very approximate. Maximum rates of differential crustal shift are of the order 0.1 mm/yr, but it should be stressed that the present coast is close to the hinge (fulcrum) of zero differential.

Finally, there is evidence of very long-term tectonic movements, possibly related to crustal subsidence in new ocean basins, that have led to a secular lowering of the deglacial geoid over the course of about one million years, of the order of 100 m (Fig. 6).

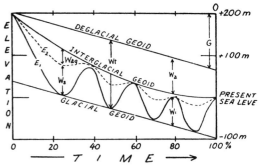

Fig. 6. Diagrammatic summation of the time/elevation relations of quaternary sea-level parameters. Actual elevation of sea level at any stage of the quaternary can be calculated by use of the formula:

$$T \times G - (Wt - Wi) = 0,$$

where T = time (expressed as a percentage from the beginning).

G = negative eustatic effect of geotectonic processes (such as downwarp of ocean basins, not locally compensated, between 200 and 50 m, suggested figure 135 m).

Wt = total water removed from ocean during glacial maxima expressed as a eustatic fall (165 m ± 20 m).

Wi = water returned to ocean in interglacials, expressed as eustatic rise (75–110 m the higher figure during warmer interglacials)

The curve E_1 (World Eustatic Curve) can be constructed by this procedure (only diagrammatic here). The broken line E_2 represents the eustatic curve restricted to Antarctica and Greenland.

It should be added that various geodetic effects, small nutations, precession and minor variations in rates of the earth's rotation, all have effects on the mean sea level over diverse regions (often latitudinally variable). The relationships have been briefly discussed by Munk and Revelle (1952) and by Munk and Macdonald (1960) but have not yet been systematically studied (Rossiter, 1962). A long-term (100 million) rotation effect has been proposed by Eardley (1964).

RHODES W. FAIRBRIDGE

References

Ahlmann, H. W., 1940, "The Styggedal Glacier in Jotunheim, Norway," *Geogr. Annaler, Stockholm,* **22,** 95–130.

Bourcart, J., 1952, "Défense de la théorie de la flexure continentale," *Compt. Rend. Congrès Geol. Intern. Alger,* Section XIII, Fasc. 14, 57–69.

Bruun, P., 1962, "Sea Level Rise as a Cause of Shore Erosion," *J. Waterways Harbors Div., Am. Soc. Civil Engrs.,* **88,** No. WW.1.

Coleman, J. M., and Smith, W. G., 1964, "Late Recent rise of sea level," *Bull. Geol. Soc. Am.,* **75,** 833–840.

Dietz, R. S., 1963, "Wave-base, marine profile of equilibrium, and wavebuilt terraces: a critical appraisal," *Bull. Geol. Soc. Am.,* **74,** 971–990.

Doodson, A. T., Egedal, J., Disney, L. P., and Rossiter, J. R., 1954, "Secular variation of sea level," *Assoc. d'Océanogr. Phys., Publ. Sci.* No. 13.

Eardley, A. J., 1964, "Polar rise and equatorial fall of sea level," *Am. Scientist,* **52,** 488–498.

Fairbridge, R. W., 1961a, "Eustatic Changes in Sea Level," in "Physics and Chemistry of the Earth," Vol. 4, pp. 99–185, London, Pergamon Press.

Fairbridge, R. W., 1961b, "Convergence of evidence on climatic change and ice ages," *Ann. N.Y. Acad. Sci.,* **95,** No. 1, 542–579.

Fairbridge, R. W., 1961c, "Radiation solaire et variations cycliques du niveau marin," *Rev. Géogr. Phys. et Géol. Dyn., Paris,* Ser. 2, **4,** 2–14.

Fairbridge, R. W., 1962, "World sea-level and climatic changes," *Quaternaria, Rome,* **6,** 180–193.

Fairbridge, R. W., 1963, "Mean sea level related to solar radiation during the last 20,000 years: *U.N.E.S.C.O./ W.M.O. Changes of Climate Symposium, Rome,* 1961, 229–242.

Fairbridge, R. W., and Krebs, O. A., Jr., 1962, "Sea level and the Southern Oscillation," *Geophys. J.,* **6,** 532–545.

Gordon, D. L., and Suthons, C. T., 1965, "Mean sea level in the British Isles," *Bull. Geodesique, Jour. Inter. Assoc. Geod.,* No. 77, 205–213.

Gutenberg, B., 1941, "Changes in sea level, postglacial uplift, and mobility of the earth's interior," *Bull. Geol. Soc. Am.,* **52,** 721–772.

Jessen, O., 1943, "Die Randschwellen der Kontinente," *Petermanns Geogr. Mitt., Erg. Heft,* 241.

Mitchell, J. M., 1963, "On the world-wide pattern of secular temperature change," U.N.E.S.C.O./W.H.O. *Changes of Climate Symposium, Rome,* 1961, 161–181.

Munk, W., and Revelle, R., 1952, "On the geophysical interpretation of irregularities in the rotation of the earth," *Monthly Notices, Roy. Astron. Soc., Geophys. Suppl.,* **6,** No. 6, 331–347.

Pattullo, J., Munk, W., Revelle, R., and Strong, E., 1955, "The seasonal oscillation in sea level," *J. Marine Res.,* **14,** 88–156.

Pettersson, O., 1914, "Climatic variations in historic and prehistoric time," *Svenska Hydrograf. Biol. Komm. Skrifter,* **5.**

Richards, H. G., and Fairbridge, R. W., 1965, "Annotated bibliography of Quaternary shorelines (1945–1964)," *Acad. Nat. Sci. Spec. Publ.* 6, 280pp.

Rossiter, J. R., 1962, "Long-term Variations in Sea-level," in (Hill, M. N., editor) "The Sea," Vol. 1, pp. 590–610, New York and London, Interscience Publishers.

Schwartz, M. L., 1965, "Laboratory study of sea level rise as a cause of shore erosion," *J. Geol.,* **73,** 528–534.

Sheets, M. M., and Weaver, P., 1963, "Faulting surface and progressive subsidence in the Texas Gulf Coast in vicinity of fluid extraction through wells," *Geol. Soc. Am., Spec. Papers,* **73** (Abstracts), 140a.

Valentin, H., 1952, "Die Küsten der Erde; Beiträge zur allgemeinen und regionalem Küstenmorphologie," *Petermanns Geogr. Mitt., Ergänzungsh.* No. 246, 118.

Cross-references: *Climatic Variation; Ice Age Theory. (Both in Vol. II; see also following article—Mediterranean Area . . .)*

MEDITERRANEAN AREA: QUATERNARY HISTORY

(1) Early Research

The concept of glacio-eustatic fluctuations of world sea level has nowhere found such enthusiastic application as in the Mediterranean Basin. L. de Lamothe noted the altimetric persistence of "raised" beaches in northern Algeria as early as 1899, suggesting a non-tectonic origin for them. In 1903, C. Depéret postulated three successive sea levels of the Pleistocene Mediterranean, and believed that they recorded interruptions of a gradual lowering of sea level during the Quaternary. The subsequent field work of M. Gignoux and A. Issel in Italy allowed Depéret to formalize a basis glacio-eustatic sequence of shore lines in 1918: +90 to 100 m (Sicilian), +55 to 60 m (Milazzian), +28 to 32 m (Tyrrhenian), +18 to 20 m (Monastirian), and +6 to 8 m (no designation).

A paleontological approach was favored by Gignoux and Issel in view of the tectonic instability of many of the Mediterranean coastlines, and this was continued by A. C. Blanc in the 1930's and 1940's (see bibliography in Howell, 1962). Blanc's particular achievement lay in the correlation of continental and estuarine deposits with the Pleistocene beaches and marine-littoral beds. His classic study of the Agro Pontino (south of Rome) and the Bassa Versilia (northwest of Pisa) showed a sequence of colder floras and faunas accompanying a marine regression to −100 m, subsequent in time to the Monastirian transgression (Tyrrhenian II) with its thermophile mollusca. In the eastern Mediterranean, Blanc's concepts were tested and applied by M. Pfannenstiel in the Bosporus–

Dardenelles area and along the coastal plain of Israel (Pfannenstiel, 1952, with earlier references).

In the following review of contemporary Pleistocene research in the Mediterranean area (see regional contributions with bibliographies in Howell, 1962) a brief discussion of the different types of sediments will be followed by an outline of stratigraphic stages and their external correlation.

(2) Characteristic Pleistocene Deposits

(a) **Marine Deposits.** Major deposits of marine Pleistocene are uncommon in the Mediterranean coastal lands. Shaley, sandy and calcareous beds of considerable thickness (up to 2000 m) are confined to a few areas, namely, the Po Valley, eastern Italy and some parts of western Morocco (Atlantic coast). All such marine series belong to the early Quaternary. Deposition can only be understood within the perspective of tectonic basins, such as the Po Valley geosyncline.

(b) **Pleistocene Beaches.** "Raised" beaches, with erosional and depositional forms, are widespread. Among these, ancient cliffs, sea caves, notches, and wave-cut platforms with veneers of marine-littoral sediments are common and can be traced at different levels along much of the western Mediterranean, northern African and Levantine coasts. The

deposits consist of shelly beach sands and conglomerates; they are often truncated and not necessarily related to erosional features. Their significance is primarily a paleontological one: distinctive "warm" or "cold" molluscan associations as well as foraminifera which may be of considerable stratigraphic value. Fossil offshore bars and lagoons also occur locally, as for example in northern Egypt.

Accurate determination of former sea levels presents a problem. In the case of former cliffed coasts, Zeuner (1961) observed that notches, sea caves or lines of holes produced by rock-boring organisms correspond closely to the former water mark in such regions as the Mediterranean where tidal amplitudes are small. In the case of bar and lagoon formations, sea-level determination can be rather difficult, but the altitude of the transition between lagoonal and terrestrial facies closely approximates former sea level (Zeuner, 1961).

In addition to accurate sea-level determinations, tectonic factors must also be considered. Many coastal sectors of France and Italy have been affected by local vertical displacements, and the oldest shore lines in most areas show evidence of warping. Areas of comparative tectonic stability do exist, however, and it may be possible to establish

TABLE 1. COASTAL STRATIGRAPHY OF THE MEDITERRANEAN AREA AND
WESTERN MOROCCO
Shore-line levels given with respect to modern sea level; continental in parentheses
(modified after Butzer, 1964, Table 2)

Climatic Oscillation	Italy	Mallorca	Morocco	Tentative Correlation
Warm	Versilian +2 m	+4, +2 m	Mellahian +2 m	Holocene
Cold	(Pontinian)	(Regression)	(Soltanian)	Würm
Warm	? Tyrrhenian III	+0.5 to 2.5 m	Ouljian + 5 m	Eem
Cold		(Regression)	Pre-Soltanian	Warthe
Warm	Tyrrhenian II +2 to 11 m	+2 to 12 m	Pre-Ouljian	Ohe?
Cold	(Nomentanan)	(Regression)	(Tensiftian)	Saale
Warm		+4 to 5 m		Transitional Holstein Saale
Warm	+16 to 20 m	+16 to 19 m	Kebibatian +15 to 20 m	Holstein
Warm	Tyrrhenian I +24 to 32 m	+23 to 34 m	Anfatian +25 to −34 m	
Cold	(Flaminian)	(Regression)	(Amirian)	Elster Complex
Cold	Later Sicilian		Regressive Maarifian (+40 to 45 m ?)	
Warm		+50, +62 m	Maarifian +55 to 60 m	Cromerian
Cold	(Cassian)		(Saletian)	
Mainly cold	Early Sicilian	+110 m	Messaoudian +90 to 100 m	Villafranchian
Warm	Emilian		(Regregian) (Moulouyian)	
Cold	Calabrian		Upper Moghrebian	

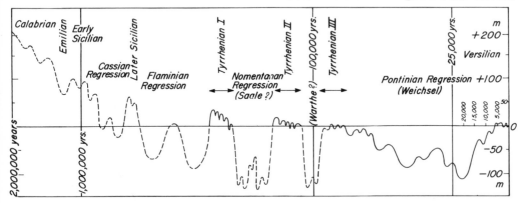

Fig. 1. Hypotheticsl Trace of Quaternary sea-level oscillations in the Mediterranean region. Time scale prior to 25.000 B.P. is logarithmic.

sound local sequences that can be traced horizontally without serious deformation. Such is the case in western Morocco, the Balearic Islands, Cyrenaica and Lebanon, for example.

(c) **Regressional Eolianites.** Some of the most common littoral facies are sand dunes blown up from the molluscan debris and beach sands exposed on the continental shelf during periods of falling sea level. Such regressional dunes or eolianites consist largely of calcite grains (locally with quartz and other insolubles up to about 50%). Deflation stops when no fresh materials are exposed so that eolianites provide invaluable stratigraphic evidence for glacial regressions (Butzer, 1963). Sands of this type are well-developed along the coasts of North Africa, the Balearic Islands, southeastern Italy, Malta, Israel and Lebanon.

(d) **Paleosols and Red Colluvial Silts.** Environmental (climatic) change on the land is partially recorded by red paleosols and by related red soil sediments. Buried and relict soils include most of the Mediterranean terra rossas, wherever they remain *in situ* on their parent materials. Analogous soils do not appear to be forming in the region today. More intensive chemical weathering, with a fairly warm and seasonally rather moist climate, seems prerequisite to soil development of this type. Hematite, the anhydrous form of ferric oxide, is responsible for the red hues and indicates persistence of a dry season. Stratigraphic evidence in Catalonia, northern Italy, the Balearic Islands and Egypt suggests several periods of red soil formation related to a humid, subtropical climate, probably during parts of the interglacial periods (Butzer, 1964, Ch. 21).

These red soils were frequently stripped by sheet flow and incorporated in colluvial silts (*limons rouges*) that mantle lower hill slopes and lowland plains in many areas (see Butzer, 1963). These heterogeneous and often detrital red colluvial beds interfinger with spring or alluvial deposits and are intercalated with littoral sediments at the coast. They record intervals of slope wash under different climatic conditions, namely torrential-type rains following seasonal droughts. Stratigraphically they date from glacio-eustatic regressions since they often extend to below modern sea level, underlying eolianites.

(e) **Alluvial Deposits.** Alluvial accumulations are commonplace in some parts of the Mediterranean region. Pleistocene fluvial silt and gravel terraces dip below modern sea level at the coasts and were clearly contemporary with glacial regressions. Laterally they may be intercalated with colluvial (slope wash) silts. The gravels are significantly better rounded than those of contemporary bed loads.

(f) **Periglacial and Glacial Features.** The glacial intervals of the Pleistocene left an unmistakeable mark on the Mediterranean uplands. Evidence of solifluction and analogous soil-frost phenomena is abundant above elevations of 1000 to 1500 m. Even in the lowlands there was conspicuous frost weathering at such times. In the higher mountains (Alps), existing cirque glaciers expanded into sizable ice streams, while new glaciers were created in now unglaciated ranges. The effect of both a moister and a colder climate during glacial-pluvial intervals (see Butzer, 1964, Ch. 19 with references) has been intensive denudation and sculpture, the impacts of which remain conspicuous today.

(3) **Pleistocene and Holocene Events**

(a) **The Calabrian and Early Sicilian Stages.** The earliest Pleistocene stage of the Mediterranean is the Calabrian, originally considered as terminal Pliocene, but now included within the Pleistocene following the recommendation of the International Geological Congress in London (1948). This stage is best represented in southern and eastern Italy where several hundred meters of deformed argillaceous beds are conformably underlain by Pliocene. The Plio-Pleistocene boundary is defined by the first appearance of boreal mollusca (such as *Cyprina islandica*) and foraminifera (such as *Anomalina baltica*). Recent oxygen isotopic temperature ana-

487

lyses showed that no major temperature change occurred at this paleontologically defined boundary (see R. Selli in Howell, 1962, with references). Rather, the amplitude of the climatic oscillations seems to have increased markedly at that point.

In western Morocco, the Calabrian is best represented by the upper, estuarine beds of the Moghrebian at Fouarat and the succeeding continental beds of the Moulouyian (G. Choubert, in Howell, 1962). The Fouarat beds contain *Elephas* (*Loxodonta*) *africanavus* and have been correlated with fossiliferous continental deposits in Algeria and Tunisia.

Since the marine Calabrian indicates a considerable depositional depth, and since the beds may be found from well below sea level to 300 m or more above it, altimetric values for this stage have little significance.

In Italy the Calabrian is conformably followed by the Emilian beds, which lack cold mollusca, and then the early Sicilian, in whose lower strata boreal species are once more abundant (see Selli in Howell, 1962). Deposits and shore line features related to the early Sicilian are widespread in many areas. An approximation of 100 m above present sea level applies to this transgression (see Fig. 1). During its terminal stages boreal mollusca are comparatively scarce.

The Calabrian and the classical, early Sicilian cannot be explained by glacio-eustatic fluctuations of sea level. They appear to be broadly contemporary with the continental Villafranchian. The data are tentatively tabulated in Table 1 below (after Butzer, 1964, p. 26ff. with references).

(b) The Later Sicilian and Tyrrhenian I Stages. In western Morocco the +100 m Messaoudian stage was followed by a marine regression contemporary with pluvial aggradation (see Fig. 1). These ferricreted conglomerates, designated as Saletian, are in turn overlain by the transgressive littoral beds of the Maarifian, which attain +55 to 60 m. The final beds of the Maarifian contain "cold" mollusca such as *Littorina littorea* and *Purpura lapillus*. This Moroccan sequence has clear parallels in the area of Rome, where a later Sicilian (+60 m) is separated from the early Sicilian by continental deposits (A. C. Blanc in Howell, 1962), or in the Bologna area, where transgressive beds overlie the classical Calabrian and Sicilian (Selli, in Howell, 1962). In both of these Italian areas, cold faunas characterize the terminal stages of the later Sicilian.

Throughout the Mediterranean, eolianites or continental deposits follow the later Sicilian. The contemporary pluvial strata of Algeria contain *Elephas* (*Palaeoloxodon*) *antiquus*. Near Rome and on Mallorca, soil frost phenomena are conspicuous. Eolianites of the Flaminian regression overlying the cool later Sicilian beds (at +50 m) of the Balearic Islands indicate a full-scale regression to below modern sea level, the exact level being undetermined.

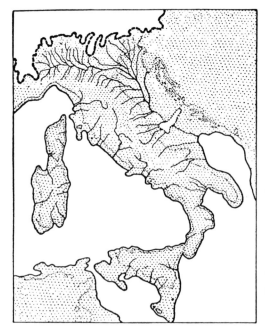

Fig. 2. Sketch-map of the central Mediterranean during a late Pleistocene low sea-level stage (Blanc, 1942).

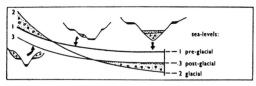

Fig. 3. Profiles controlled by changes of sea level and of climate (from G. H. Dury, 1959).

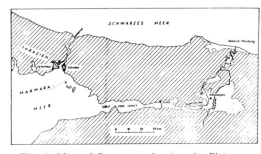

Fig. 4. Map of Bosporus, showing the Pleistocene interglacial connection with the Black Sea (Pfannenstiel, 1944).

In view of the North African mammalian faunas, this clearly glacio-eustatic regression can be broadly correlated with the Elster or Mindel glacial complex of Europe. Contemporary human traces include *Homo* (*Atlanthropus*) *erectus mauretanicus* at Ternifine, Algeria, and the early Middle Acheulian kill sites of Torralba and Ambrona in Central Spain.

The Tyrrhenian I has proved difficult to define precisely. Altimetrically the maximum transgression over the preceding littoral-continental deposits attained +34 m in tectonically stable areas. However, numerous lower substages occur as well (Butzer and Cuerda, 1962). The fauna does not seem to include thermophile species but is characterized by the first appearance of *Patella ferruginea* as well as a profusion of *Thais* (*Purpura*) *haemastoma*. Contemporary with a part of the later Tyrrhenian I was one of the most significant phases of red soil development in the Mediterranean Basin. This red paleosol may be rather useful as a stratigraphic marker. Presumably the Tyrrhenian I is the marine equivalent of the Great or Holstein Interglacial.

(c) **The Tyrrhenian II and III Stages.** The most universal beach deposits of the Mediterranean area include the thermophile Senegalian gastropod *Strombus bubonius* as well as a number of less significant associates. In the Dardanelles area and the Black Sea, *Cardium tuberculatum* has similar stratigraphic and paleo-ecological implications. The *Strombus* beaches commonly overlie a typical sequence of colluvial silts, alluvial beds and eolianites, in part showing evidence of rather cold climate suggestive of the Riss glacial complex. In Mallorca this Nomentanan regression included four substages, throughout which sea level remained well below that of today. This places the Tyrrhenian II of the *Strombus* beaches within the last major interglacial. Recent dating of contemporary mollusca by the Th^{230}/U^{239} method suggests an age of 140,000–115,000 years B.P. for the Tyrrhenian II.

The *Strombus* beaches lie in the altimetric range of +2 to 12 m in tectonically undisturbed area. On Mallorca the oldest substage is at +10.5 to 12.5 m, followed by younger oscillations at +8 to 9 m, +6 to 7.5 m and +2 to 4 m (Butzer and Cuerda, 1962). That these substages are real is shown by intermediate terrestrial deposits and minor morphological changes of certain mollusca. Possibly the classical *Strombus* beaches were preceded by an even higher stage at +15 to 20 m, converging in level with a later Tyrrhenian I beach. Unequivocal deposits seem to be absent.

The Tyrrhenian II terminates with the +2 to 4 m beach, and is separated from the Tyrrhenian III by a regression to well below modern sea level. The thermophile fauna was strongly decimated at this time, *Strombus bubonius* is either very scarce or absent, and certain of the Senegalese associates disappear. This Tyrrhenian III attains maximum elevations of +2.5 m in stable areas, and is commonly found at +1 to 2 m. In the Balearic Islands various sedimentological characteristics can be used to distinguish the convergent Tyrrhenian beaches at about +2 m: the Tyrrhenian II beds are commonly 2 m or more in thickness, consisting of fossiliferous beach sands intercalated with sterile semi-eolian beds; the Tyrrhenian III strata seldom exceed 50 to 75 cm in thickness and are dominated by continental silts and conglomerates, containing both terrestrial and marine mollusks. Th $^{230}/U^{234}$ dates from Tyrrhenian III mollusca suggest a non-glacial interval of high sea level 75,000 to 90,000 B.P., in part contemporary with the continental sedimentation that already marks the early Pontinian (Würm) regression. Possibly the preceding regression pertains to the Warthe glacial interval of the European continental stratigraphy.

(d) **The Pontinian Regression and the Question of Land Bridges.** The Tyrrhenian III was succeeded by the Pontinian regression, apparently including three major substages recorded by silt—eolianite—erosion cycles on the Balearic Islands (Butzer and Cuerda, 1962). The exact amplitude of this regression in the Rome area was at least 100 m below modern sea level and possibly a little more. No local evidence is available for the earlier regressions such as the Nomentanan.

Donn et al. (1962) have computed a theoretical world sea-level lowering of 159 m for the major Pleistocene glacial regression. Since glacio-eustatic fluctuations have been superimposed upon the gradual (tectono-eustatic) lowering of sea level evident in post-Pliocene times (Fig. 1), the major regression in the Mediterranean probably did not drop below −130 or −140 m. In other words, the regressions were insufficient to create land bridges at Gibraltar or between Tunisia, Sicily and southern Italy. The insular character of Sicily, Crete and Cyprus throughout middle and late Pleistocene times is proved on paleontological and archeological grounds (Vaufrey, 1929). The Dardanelles and Bosporus were, on the other hand, reduced to a river system draining the Black Sea at the height of the glacial regressions (threshold elevation about −45 m). Although early Acheulian hunters crossed from Morocco to Spain during the Flaminian regression, there is no evidence that the straits of Gibraltar were ever dry in post-Pliocene times.

(e) **An Evaluation of Interglacial and Glacial Age Paleoclimates.** Interglacial temperatures in the Mediterranean area may have been a little warmer than those of the present (something suggested by the isotopic temperature determinations). The presence of Senegalese faunal elements during the Tyrrhenian II and III can be better explained by a warmer Canaries Current than by substantially higher water temperatures of the Mediterranean Sea itself. In terms of moisture changes, there is nothing to suggest that the interglacials were any drier than today. On the contrary, there seem to have been wetter intervals, corresponding to formation of the red paleosols.

Glacial age temperatures were in the order of 5 to 6°C lower during the Würm, as suggested by the significance of frost weathering in the lowlands, by periglacial and glacial phenomena in the highlands and, at sea, by isotopic temperatures indicated by surface foraminifera. Temperature lowering may have been substantially greater during some of the earlier glacials. Precipitation values appear to have fluctuated considerably. Colluvial and alluvial deposits are most common early during the glacial regressions. Eolianites and ultimately semiarid soil development during the late regressional phases imply a climate a little drier than that of today. The patterns of vegetation change in parts of Italy and Spain corroborate these deductions from geomorphic evidence (see Butzer, 1964, Ch. 19). The early glacial intervals were, in effect, pluvial periods, while the later stages were semiarid.

(f) The Minor Holocene Transgressions. Although there is reliable evidence for high, post-Pleistocene (Holocene) shore lines at $+2$ and $+4$ m, such stages represent temporary oscillations only. In each well-documented example, the related beach phenomena are poorly developed, deposits are unconsolidated, while thermophile mollusca are absent and faunas are remarkably poor in species. There appears to be a prehistoric level at about $+4$ m (with some radiocarbon dates of 5000 to 6000 B.P.) and, perhaps, two further levels each at $+2$ m, one pre-Roman, the other Medieval. Sea level during the Roman period appears to have been 2 or 3 m lower than that of today.

(g) The Record of Soil Erosion in Historical Times. Modern soil erosion and accelerated runoff produce phenomena analogous to those of Pleistocene paleoclimates, and many of the larger rivers are aggrading today. As a consequence Pleistocene deposits in some parts of Italy have been either eroded away or buried under recent alluvium. Older intervals of soil stripping, in late Roman and early Medieval times, are more commonly recorded by brown colluvial silts containing abundant potsherds of Roman and later type. In northern Africa and the Balearic Islands there is reason to believe that at least some of these historical deposits reflect intervals of anomalous climate. Implied here are widespread brown silts forming low stream terraces in Morocco and Mallorca, as well as detrital wadi beds in Libya and Egypt. The historical and archeological record leaves little doubt, however, that considerable changes in land use have occurred as well. Several cycles of forest clearance, intensive cultivation and subsequent land abandonment are also recorded by pollen profiles in several parts of Spain. Such man-induced cycles inevitably brought about structural changes in the soils and at times favored soil-stripping, even on gentle slopes.

Not only do the soil erosion phenomena of the Mediterranean world comprise several generations of alluvial and colluvial deposition, they are also polygenetic in origin, reflecting natural as well as cultural changes. The effects of historical soil erosion have been grossly overestimated in the past. In many localities, Pleistocene colluvia and alluvia mantle greater areas than do historical deposits. In fact, the mountain ranges were often denuded of their soil mantles during the Pleistocene wet phases. Deforestation has accentuated their bleakness, but has not necessarily had a significant geomorphic impact.

KARL W. BUTZER

References

Butzer, K. W., 1963, "Climatic-geomorphologic interpretation of Pleistocene sediments in the Eurafrican subtropics," *Viking Fund Publ. Anthropol.*, **36**, 1–27.

Butzer, K. W., 1964, "Environment and Archeology: An Introduction to Pleistocene Geography," Aldine, Chicago, 528pp.

Butzer, K. W., and Cuerda, J., 1962, "Coastal stratigraphy of southern Mallorca," *J. Geol.*, **70**, 398–416.

Howell, F. C., editor, 1962, "Early Man and Pleistocene stratigraphy in the Circum-Mediterranean regions," *Quaternaria*, **6**, 549pp.

Pfannenstiel, M., 1952, "Die Küste Palästina-Syriens (Das Quartär der Levante I)," *Abhl. Akad. Wiss. Lit. (Mainz), Math.-Naturw. Kl.*, 333–475.

Vaufrey, R., 1929, "Les éléphants nains des iles méditeranéenes," *Arch. Inst. Paleontol. Hum., Mem. 6*, 220pp.

Zeuner, F. E., 1961, "Criteria for the determination of mean sea-level for Pleistocene shoreline features," *Quaternaria*, **5**, 143–147.

MEDITERRANEAN SEA

Introduction*

The Mediterranean Sea is located between Europe, Asia Minor, and Africa. It is completely surrounded by land except for a narrow passage to the North Atlantic through the Strait of Gibraltar and another by way of the Bosporus to the Black Sea. The Suez Canal is a man-made channel and connects the eastern Mediterranean to the Red Sea.

The Mediterranean extends over an area of 1,145,000 square miles and has an average depth of 1500 m. There are extensive areas of the sea floor below 3000 m, and the greatest depth of 5092 m occurs at the bottom of a depression in the Ionian Sea west of Peloponnesus (Hellenic Trough).

The Mediterranean can be appropriately divided into an eastern and western basin separated by a shallow sill across the Straits of Sicily, and by a restricted passage through the Strait of Messina. The two basins can be subdivided further into numerous seas with quite arbitrary boundaries. The western Mediterranean contains the Alboran Sea, the Balearic Sea, the Ligurian Sea (north of Corsica), and the Tyrrhenian Sea. In the eastern Mediterranean are found the Adriatic Sea, the Ionian Sea, the Aegean Sea, and the Sea of Marmara between the Bosporus and the Dardanelles.

* William B. F. Ryan.

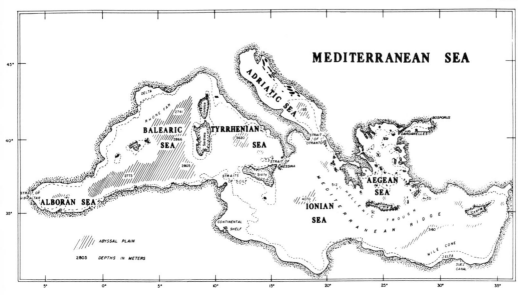

Fig. 1. Map of the Mediterranean Sea showing location of abyssal plains.

There are numerous small islands throughout the Mediterranean, particularly in the Aegean and Ionian Seas. The largest islands include Sicily, Sardinia, Cyprus, Corsica, and Crete. There are three major rivers that empty into the Mediterranean—the Rhone, the Nile, and the Po River that empties into the northern Adriatic Sea. The waters from rivers that lead into the Black Sea reach the Mediterranean by way of the Bosporus and the Dardanelles.

Bathymetry*

The Mediterranean Sea has many topographic features that are characteristic of oceanic basins. The continental shelves are moderately well developed, but they are rather narrow with widths averaging less than 25 miles. The continental slopes are generally very steep and are cut by submarine canyons. The Mediterranean canyons along the French Riviera and the west coast of Corsica are among the most thoroughly studied in the world.

In place of a continental rise, a large sedimentary cone is found off each of the two major deltas. In the western Mediterranean, this wedge, the Rhone Fan, extends seaward to the Balearic Abyssal Plain. This abyssal plain covers an area of more than 30,000 square miles and extends over the greater portion of the basin floor.

The gradients on the plain indicate that the sediment deposition by turbidity currents has been largely from the Rhone by way of channels across the fan. However, the plain is also fed to some extent from the Riviera canyons as well as from canyons along the Algerian coast.

* William B. F. Ryan.

The Tyrrhenian Sea has a central abyssal plain with a few small plains located within slope basins. A large seamount pierces the central plain and rises 2850 m above the sea floor to within 743 m of the surface. There are numerous other seamounts in this basin; several of them form islands on the continental slopes of Sicily and Calabria. Distinct ash horizons have been cored from the abyssal plain and have been correlated with historic volcanic eruptions on the Italian mainland.

The morphology of the sea floor of the eastern Mediterranean is remarkably different from that of the western Mediterranean. Despite the occurrence of a small abyssal plain in the center of the Ionian Sea, there are no major areas of flat-lying and undeformed terrigenous sediments. Instead the greater extent of the basin floor is either upwarped into a complexly fractured median ridge, or alternatively downfaulted into a series of depressions along an arc parallel to the Archipelago. The deep depressions extend from the Ionian Islands, south of Crete and Rhodes and into the Gulf of Antalya, and they form a system called the Hellenic Trough.

The greatest depth in the Mediterranean occurs in one of these depressions, where some sediment has accumulated to form a small flat pond at 5092 m. Sediments have begun to fill another depression at 4450 m south of Rhodes.

There are well-developed channels on the Nile Cone that form a large distributary system. However, these channels lead to only a very narrow abyssal plain at the base of the cone, unlike the western Mediterranean where the Rhone fan feeds the large Balearic Abyssal Plain. Presently the narrow plain at the foot of the Nile Cone is being actively deformed; parts of it have subsided over

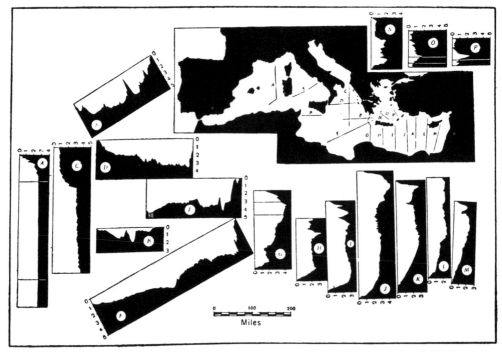

Fig. 2. Survey profiles of the bottom of the Mediterranean. The vertical exaggeration is 1:37 (after Goncharov and Mikhailov, 1964).

300 m to form graben-like structures, and parts of it have been intruded and uplifted and thus isolated from deposition by turbidity currents. This structural deformation is most likely related to the same processes that warped and fractured the median ridge and produced the Hellenic Trough. It appears that in the recent past sedimentation has not been able to keep pace with the tectonic deformation of large portions of the eastern Mediterranean.

Physical Oceanography*

The Mediterranean is surrounded by warm, dry countries, and as a consequence evaporation greatly exceeds precipitation and runoff from the rivers. In order to replenish the net loss of fresh water escaping into the atmosphere, surface water from the North Atlantic must enter into the Mediterranean through the Strait of Gibraltar. An increase in the salinity due to evaporation causes the density of the Mediterranean to also increase. The water thus sinks from the surface to fill both the eastern and western basins with a very homogeneous and relatively warm water mass. The deep and middle waters have a very narrow temperature range from 12.7–14.5°C with salinities between 38.4 and 39.0‰.

Circulation. As the surface North Atlantic water enters through the Strait of Gibraltar it generally follows the coast of North Africa and gradually spreads out over the sea surface. Some of it circu-

* William B. F. Ryan.

lates to the Ligurian Sea north of Corsica, and some of it into the Tyrrhenian Sea. There, due to the evaporation and cooling effects of dry polar air masses from the continent of Europe, the water sinks to form a definite water type of the western basins.

The North Atlantic water also flows through the Straits of Sicily into the eastern Mediterranean where part of it is deflected north into the Adriatic Sea. Again it is cooled by evaporation and sinks. It pours sporadically out over the sill of the Strait of Otranto to form a deep water mass in the eastern Mediterranean. The distribution of dissolved oxygen indicates a counterclockwise circulation of the deep water in the Ionian Sea.

The remaining North Atlantic water at the surface, now very much modified by evaporation, continues eastward to Cyprus, where during the

Fig. 3. Surface currents (solid arrows) and currents at intermediate depths (dashed arrows) in the Mediterranean Sea (after Nielsen).

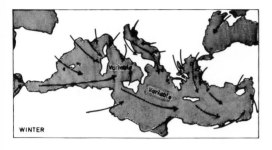

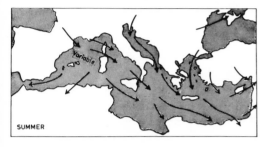

Fig. 4. Present wind system over the Mediterranean area (from Kendrew, 1953).

perature of the Mediterranean water. As a result, it pours down the continental slope until finally, at 1000 m, it reaches a level at which the deep Atlantic water is of the same density. There, the Mediterranean water leaves the bottom and spreads out north, west, and south, forming a layer that can be detected for thousands of miles in the Atlantic.

Nutrients. The Mediterranean is the most impoverished large body of water known. The nutrient content as indicated by the amount of phosphate in the water is very much lower than that of the off-lying North Atlantic. This is due initially to the fact that the water enters the Mediterranean across a shallow sill and thus is skimmed from the surface layer of the North Atlantic which is already greatly depleted. The accumulation of nutrients in the deep water is prevented by the continuous exchange of water back out through the Strait of Gibraltar. The transport of water is sufficient to ventilate the entire basin of the Mediterranean in about 75 years.

Tides. The tides of the Mediterranean are predominately semidiurnal. The eastern and western basins each have a standing wave system. The Adriatic Sea has a progressive tide with a range of

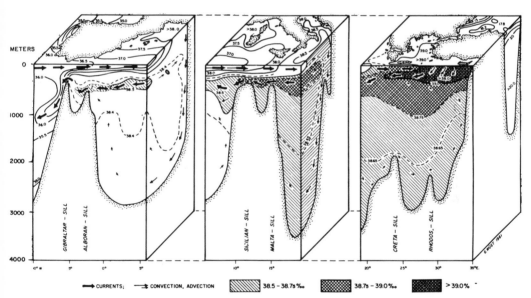

Fig. 5. Schematic block diagram of vertical circulation and distribution of salinity in the Mediterranean Sea during winter (after Wüst, 1961).

winter months it sinks to form yet another source of deep water. The influx of North Atlantic surface water carries along a large quantity of dissolved salts which must be returned to the North Atlantic since the salinity of the Mediterranean is not increasing. The return is affected by an outflowing current over the sill in the Strait of Gibraltar below the incoming current. The water that flows out at 300 m depth is considerably denser than the Atlantic water at the same level in spite of the higher tem-

about 1 m radiating around an amphidromic point near the center of the sea. The tidal range elsewhere in the Mediterranean is about 30 cm.

Sediments of Mediterranean*

Composition. The offshore deposits consist of (a) calcareous matter, chiefly coccolithophorids, but foraminifera are frequent and pteropods occur; (b)

* E. Olausson.

493

detrital matter transported by winds and currents; (c) volcanic matter, and (d) the ultimate products of weathering on land, chiefly clay minerals. The average carbonate content is about 40% in eastern Mediterranean (E.M.) cores and about 30% in western Mediterranean (W.M.) ones. The content of detrital matter changes from nil to predominating

frequencies; it is on the whole higher in W.M. cores. Sandy horizons can sometimes be recognized and cross-correlated from core to core. Volcanic ash constitutes more or less distinct layers and occurs also interspersed in non-volcanic matter. The quantities of volcanic debris are small except close to the volcanoes, e.g., near Vesuvius and Etna.

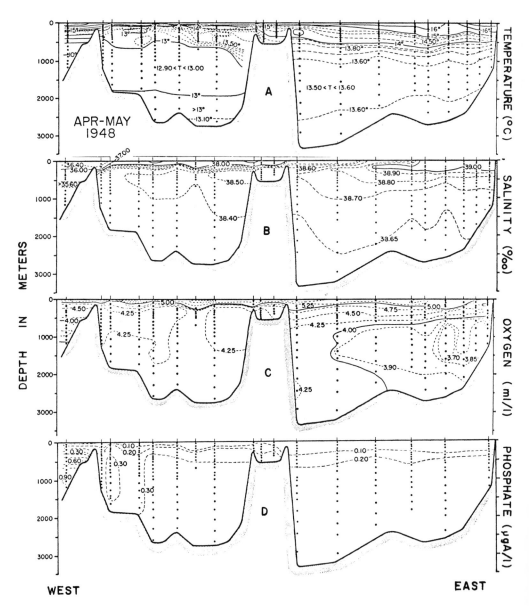

WEST   EAST

Fig. 6. Distribution of temperature, salinity, oxygen and phosphate along east–west sections. (a) The inflowing Atlantic surface water cannot be traced on the temperature profile for any great distance into the Mediterranean as the profile is north of the main current. (b) A pronounced tongue of high-salinity water is found at the extreme eastern end of the profile. It is derived from surface water in the eastern basin where evaporation greatly exceeds precipitation. (c) The lowest oxygen values occur in the deep water in the extreme eastern part of the Mediterranean. (d) This profile shows the great depletion of phosphate at depth in both Mediterranean basins (after McGill, 1961).

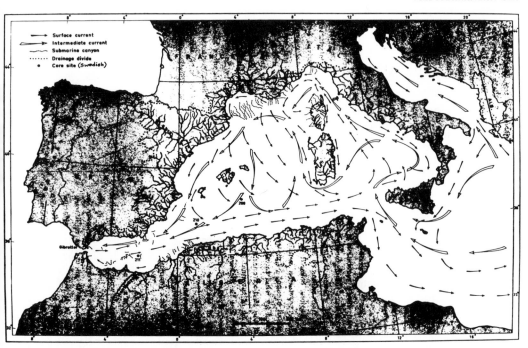

Fig. 7. The principal currents and submarine canyons in the Western Mediterranean Sea (from K. G. Eriksson).

The rate of deposition in the Levant and Ionian Sea is low and is of the same order as in the central portion of the North Atlantic, while in the western Mediterranean it is several times larger.

Eastern Mediterranean. The E.M. cores consist of alternating layers of oxidized and reduced deposits suggestive of cycles in the oxygen content at the bottom.

If there is no renewal of the deep and bottom water the oxygen there will be used up within about 1000 years. Short periods of stopped or incomplete renewal will thus not influence the life and reactions at the bottom. Longer times with decreased or stopped ventilation lead to oxygen deficiency, the oxidation of organic soft material will be incomplete, the diagenetic processes become stronger, and a H_2S zone may also develop above the sediment-water interface. In such a restricted environment, black, sapropelitic mud accumulates. The peaks of the carbon curve at Fig. 7 show the distribution of sapropelitic muds during the Upper Pleistocene. Between the sapropelitic muds and marl oozes, gray, blue and yellow muds occur. Compared with the oxidized deposits, sapropelitic muds contain 10–40 times more carbon (or 2–8 %), 10–20 times more Ba and Mo, and 2–5 times more Ni, V, Co, most or all brought down with and bound in soft organic material. Due to a constant pH (constant dissolution of minerals), their contents of P are equal.

The amount of excess inflow from the west to the eastern Mediterranean is determined by the size of evaporation minus the water supply by rivers, from precipitation, and the net inflow from the Black Sea. During a regression down to a glacial sea-level stand (− 100 m or lower), both the inflow and outflow from the Mediterranean and the eastern Mediterranean were reduced due to the fact that the straits became narrower and shallower. A larger decrease in the net inflow than in evaporation is likely, and an eventual increase in precipitation and runoff may have been insufficient to prevent a salinity increase in the eastern Mediterranean (more than in the sea). A lowered temperature of about 4°C is also likely. All these have created an increasing density of the surface water thus leading to oxidized environment. When the sea level rose, all water added to the eastern Mediterranean was poorer in salts than its own, tending to reduce the surface density. At continued transgression (above − 50 m sea-level stand) the net inflow became more important, meltwater (low density) was received from the Black Sea in large amount (the sill depth of the Bosporus is 40 m), and the temperature rose. An increased precipitation is in evidence for the Late Glacial. All these factors have lowered the density of the surface water so much that the bottom water became more or less stagnant. The stagnant or quasi-stagnant phase existed until a new equilibrium had developed in the succeeding interglacial (Postglacial).

During phases with warm winters (thermal optimum) the renewal may have been incomplete. At very high sea level, e.g., during the Holstein interglacial (about + 30 m sea level), a decrease in sur-

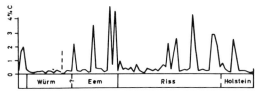

Fig. 8. The distribution of carbon in Eastern Mediterranean cores in relation to time-stratigraphic units. The carbon peaks indicate stagnant or quasis-stagnant phases of the Eastern Mediterranean. The Figure is based upon the carbon curves from the Swedish Deep-Sea Expedition cores 194 (from the top down to the broken lines) and 195, collected in the Ionian Sea.

face salinity compared with subjacent water mass was likely until a new equilibrium was established. The increased water exchanges across the straits may have been larger than an eventual increase in evaporation, thus leading to a reduced surface density. An increase of precipitation as for the onset of each glacial (or just before) can also have influenced the surface density.

Judging from Fig. 8 stagnant conditions prevailed at the very beginning of the Eem glacial and the Postglacial ($\sim$9000–5000 B.C.), the former having been the most pronounced. During deglaciation, the Black Sea received large amounts of meltwater. During Riss/Eem the surface salinity of the eastern Mediterranean water was well below that of the Atlantic water, thus reversing the currents not only in the Strait of Tunisia and Sicily but probably also in the Strait of Gibraltar. The inflowing Atlantic water may have furnished most of the western Mediterranean with oxygenated water. A core from the Tyrrhenian Sea reveals a layer rich in organic matter which may be of that age suggesting shortness of oxygen there. No younger stagnant phase are traced in cores from the western Mediterranean. No other cores from the western Mediterranean penetrate the whole Eemian stage.

The correlation between the other stagnant phases and glacial chronology and sea-level stands is only tentative which makes it difficult to decide the exact cause(s) of each stagnant or quasi-stagnant phase.

During certain stagnant phases the foraminiferal fauna developed in an abnormal way. Foraminifera that were assumed to have a shallower and a deeper habitat disappeared, while *Globigerina eggeri*, which was supposed to have a moderate depth habitat, was very abundant.

The eastern Mediterranean sediment is very poor in diatoms, which may be a consequence of the low productivity of the basin. During the stagnant phase at the Riss/Eem boundary, diatoms were interspersed in the sapropelitic muds, even constituting a thin layer of diatom mud.

Gray and blue mud dominate on the floor of the Adriatic Sea. The shelf deposits around the eastern

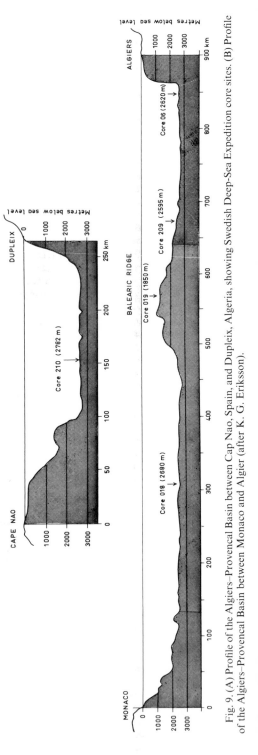

Fig. 9. (A) Profile of the Algiers–Provencal Basin between Cap Nao, Spain, and Dupleix, Algeria, showing Swedish Deep-Sea Expedition core sites. (B) Profile of the Algiers–Provencal Basin between Monaco and Algier (after K. G. Eriksson).

Mediterranean are chiefly calcareous muds and sands.

The Western Mediterranean. Gray, calcareous mud and gray marl mud are the dominating

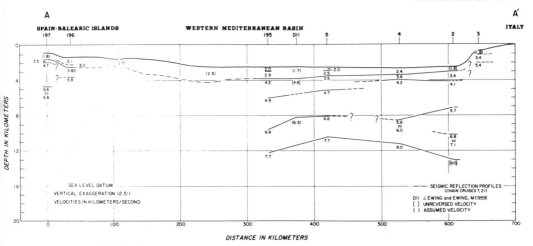

Fig. 10. Seismic structure section across the western Mediterranean (after Fahlquist, 1963).

deposits. Eolian layers are identified in cores; those of Würmian age suggest correlation with ages of loess formation. Other coarse-grained beds and laminae are probably turbidity current deposits (see *Mediterranean Sea—A Late Pleistocene Sediment Core*).

The boundary Würm/Recent appears from changes in the frequency of some foraminifera. In certain cores there is a marked drop in the phosphate content and a similar increase in the carbonate content.

The lower portion of the shelf is covered chiefly with mud, interspersed with sand grains, which continues farther down to the abyssal plain. Terrigenous or shell sands occur closer to the shore.

Crustal Structure*

Seismic refraction measurements undertaken in the western Mediterranean basins show that the crust there is of an "oceanic" nature. The depth to the Mohorovicic discontinuity is less than 12 km beneath the sea surface over the Balearic Abyssal Plain. The depth increases toward the margins of the basin and is greater than 50 km under the Maritime Alps which terminate abruptly at the French Riviera.

There is a thick section of intermediate velocity material (3.0–6.0 km/sec) underlying only 1–1.5 km of low-velocity sediments (1.7–2.5 km/sec). The low-velocity sediments are appreciably thicker in the western Mediterranean than in the eastern Mediterranean. If the intermediate-velocity layer marks the bottom of the sedimentary column, then the thickness of the sediments is surprisingly thin in view of the large drainage area of the Rhone River. There is over 6 km of sediment in the deeper part of the Gulf of Mexico.

However, if the refracting layer is consolidated sediment, or volcanic rock within the sedimentary column, the surface of this layer marks an important change in events in the history of this basin.

The magnetic field in the Mediterranean is remarkably dull, especially in the tectonically active eastern basins. There are, however, large anomalies over the seamounts in the Tyrrhenian Sea.

There is a broad band of large negative free air gravity anomalies centered over the Hellenic Trough. These anomalies are associated with the large subsidence that has occurred within the trough.

In the northern part of the western Mediterranean a 3-km downward displacement of the basin, relative to continental Europe, has been deduced from the seismic measurements. The basic cause of such large-scale vertical movements is poorly understood. The negligible free air anomalies over the western Mediterranean argue that the basin is in isostatic equilibrium. It is extremely difficult to picture how a thin "oceanic" crust that exists today could have supported the former uplift, without some sort of redistribution of density within the deep crust or upper mantle.

Structural History*

The Mediterranean is a relict sea, a remnant of a vast waterway that formerly extended from Portugal through the Alps, southeast Europe, Anatolia, Iran, the Himalayas to Southeast Asia and the Pacific. It is believed to have connected with the Maorian Geosyncline in New Zealand. This ancient seaway was called *Tethys* by Suess. Its history is very well known from Triassic times onward, but even in the Paleozoic, traces of such a connection are fairly discernible and many authors speak of a Proto- or Paleo-Tethys.

* William B. F. Ryan.

* Rhodes W. Fairbridge.

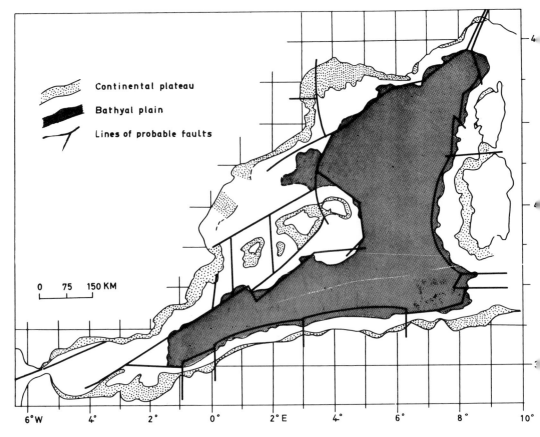

Fig. 11. The extent of the continental plateau, the "bathyal plain" (area of major sedimentation) and the location of postulated faults in the Western Mediterranean Sea area, as visualized by Bourcart (1960).

This Tethys Seaway separated the northern continents of Eurasia (and probably also the North American extension, too, Laurasia) from the southern continents formerly joined together as Gondwanaland (see recent review: Fairbridge, 1965).

Between these two great continental blocks of the primaeval "Protogaea" there seems to have been constant interaction, over the last half billion years at least. Various authors have visualized these relationships in different light. To the continental drift school (e.g., Argand, Wegener) there has been a steady approach of the two original land masses, leading to the buckling of trenches and the eventual Alpine orogenic revolution, that began in earnest in late Cretaceous times, but was revived in several phases through the Tertiary. To others (e.g., Staub, Glangeaud) there has been an "ebb and flow," sometimes compressional, sometimes tensional. The problem is by no means resolved.

WILLIAM B. F. RYAN
E. OLAUSSON
RHODES W. FAIRBRIDGE

References

Argand, E., 1922, "La tectonique de l'Asie," *Intern. Geol. Congr., 13th, Belgium, Sec.* 5, 171–322.

Aubouin, J., 1963, "La tectonique de la Méditerranée moyenne et les séismes," *Bull. Soc. Geol. France*, **5**, 1124–1129.

Aubouin, J., 1964, "Esquisse paléogeographique et structurale des chaînes alpines de la Méditerranée moyenne." *Geol. Rundschau*, **53**(2), 480–534.

Aubouin, J., 1965, "Geosynclines," Elsevier Publishing Co., Developments in Geotectonics I, 335pp.

Blanc, J. J., 1963, "Exposé sommaire sur les recherches de géologie marine et de sédimentologie en Méditerranée nore-oriental," *Rapp. Proces-Verbaux Reunions, C.I.E.S., Mer Méd., Monaco*, **17**(3), 999–1003.

Carey, S. W., 1958, "Continental Drift, a Symposium," University of Tasmania.

Defant, A., 1961, "Physical Oceanography," Vols. I and II, New York, Pergamon Press.

Emiliani, C., 1955, *Quaternaria*, **2**, 87.

Ewing, J., and Ewing, M., 1959, "Seismic-refraction measurements in the Atlantic Ocean basins, in the Mediterranean Sea, on the Mid-Atlantic Ridge, and in the Norwegian Sea," *Bull. Geol. Soc. Am.*, **70**, 291–318.

Fahlquist, D. A., 1963, "Seismic refraction studies in

the Western Mediterranean," Reference No. 63–18. Woods Hole Oceanographic Inst., 39–40.

Gennesseaux, M., 1963, "Structure et morphologie de la pente continentale de la region niçoise," *Rapp. Proces-Verbaux, Réunions, C.I.E.S., Mer. Méd., Monaco,* **17**(3), 991–998.

Glangeaud, L., 1954, "Des eruptions tertiares nord-africaines. Leurs relations avec la tectonique meditarranenne," *Intern. Geol. Congr., 19th Algiers 1952, Sec. 15,* **17**, 71–102.

Glangeaud, L., 1957, "Correlation chronologique des phenomenes geodynamiques dans les Alpes, l'Appenin et l'Atlas nord-african," *Soc. Geol. France Bull.,* **16**(7–9), 867–891.

Goncharov, V. P., and Mikhailov, O. V., 1964, "New data on the bottom relief of the Mediterranean," *Deep-Sea Res.,* **11**, 625–628.

Gregory, J. W., 1932, "A submarine trough near the Strait of Gibraltar," *Geograph. J.,* **79**, 219–220.

Guilcher, A., 1965, "Précis d'Hydrologie," Paris, Masson & Cie, 389pp.

Hofman, B. J., 1952, "The gravity field of the west Mediterranean area," *Geol. Mijnbouw, New Ser.,* **14**, 297–306.

Klemme, H. D., 1958, "Regional geology of circum-Mediterranean region," *Bull. Am. Assoc. Petrol. Geologists,* **42**(3), Pt. 1, 477–513.

Kullenberg, B., 1952, *Medd. Oceanogr. Inst. Göteberg,* No. 21.

Lacomb, H., 1963, "Eaux océaniques profondes— Portée des récentes études océanographiques en Méditerranée," *Bull. Assoc. Franc., Étude des Grandes Profondeurs Océan.,* No. 2, 1–4.

McGill, D. A., 1961, "A preliminary study of the oxygen and phosphate distribution in the Mediterranean Sea," *Deep-Sea Res.,* **8**, 259–269.

Migliorine, C. L., 1952, "Composite wedges and orogenic landslides in the Appenines," *Intern. Geol. Congr., 18th London, 1948, Sec. 13,* 186–198.

Miller, A. R., 1963, "Physical oceanography of the Mediterranean Sea: A discourse," *Rapp. Proces-Verbaux, Réunions, Comm. I.E.S., Mer Méd., Monaco,* **17**(3), 865–871.

Olausson, E., 1961, "Studies of deep-sea cores," *Repts. Swedish Deep-Sea Exped.,* 1947–48, **8**, Fasc. 4, 335–341.

Olausson, E., 1965, "Progress in Oceanography," Vol. 3, New York, Pergamon Press, 221pp.

Ortynski, H. I., Perrodon, A., and deLapparent, C., 1959, "Esquisse paleogeographique et structurale des bassins du Sahara Septentrional," *World Petrol. Congr., Proc. 5th, N. Y., Sec. 1,* 705–729.

Rept. Swedish Deep-Sea Exped., 1947–48, **8** (papers by Norin, Parker, Todd).

Saint-Guily, B., 1963, "Remarques sur le méchanisme de formation des eaux profondes en Méditerranée occidentale," *Rapp. Proces-Verbaux, Réunions, C.I.E.S., Mer Méd., Monaco,* **17**(3), 929–932.

Van Bemmelen, R. W., 1952, "Gravity field and ororgenesis in the West-Mediterranean region," *Geol. Mijnbouw,* **14**, 306–313.

Van Straaten, L. M. J. U., 1965, "Sedimentation in the north-western part of the Adriatic Sea," *Proc. Symp. Colston Res. Soc., 7th,* 143–162.

Wüst, G., 1961, "On the vertical circulation of the Mediterranean Sea," *J. Geophys. Res.,* **66**(10), 3261–3271.

MEDITERRANEAN SEA: A LATE-PLEISTOCENE SEDIMENTARY CORE

The sediment core investigated was collected from the bathyal plain in a central part of the western Mediterranean Sea at 37°26′N latitude and 01°05′E longitude. The core collected by the *Albatross* (Swedish Deep-Sea Expedition) was 9 m long; its basal bed was deposited about 30,000 years ago.

The major part of the sediment sequence consists of primary deposited material; only a minor part is redeposited sediments (turbidity current deposits). Four types have been distinguished in each of these groups.

Primary Deposited Sediments

(a) Ordinary, homogeneous sediments. The most common sediment type in the core, characterized by a low content of wind-borne material $>31\mu$ and of tests of foraminifera. Interpreted to indicate an environment with rather weak wind conditions.

(b) Ordinary, heterogeneous sediments. The contrast of the structure compared with that in the homogeneous type is principally caused by an increased supply of terrigenous minerals $>31\mu$ and of tests of foraminifera; a nearshore region was the principal source for the coarse-grained minerals. This sediment type is formed under strong wind conditions.

(c) Ordinary, shelly sediments: An extreme variety of the heterogeneous type, only found just below some erosional surfaces. The sediments consist of $>75\%$ calcareous shells or other acicular fragments of organic origin; the accumulation of shells is in part real, in part due to removal of the finer material. This kind of sediment indicates the occurrence of pronounced changes in the action of the currents.

(d) Micro-stratified sediments: Three types of such sediments have been observed. Only one type is of importance and is designated "micro-stratified wind-borne material." The most conspicuous feature of this sediment type is the thinly and regularly laminated structure, in which coarse silt alternates with silty clay, in the form of lamination, a fraction of a millimeter to a few millimeters in thickness. This alternation is repeated through sequences up to $\frac{1}{2}$ m in thickness with remarkable regularity. In one bed are found about 200 laminae within a thickness of 1 cm; in another bed between 10–100 laminae are observed. No signs of erosion are found in the beds, but the bottom usually corresponds to a surface of discontinuity. Fragments of volcanic glass, which are usually very rare in the sediments, are most frequent in these micro-stratified beds; in some such deposits, an abundance of "coaly rods" is also formed, interpreted as being the ash of burnt grass. The fact that volcanic glass and "coaly rods" are deposited together, is considered as additional evidence of their continental, wind-borne origin.

TABLE 1. PROPERTIES OF THE PRINCIPAL SEDIMENT TYPES IN CORE 210

Mean and standard error presented in percentage units

Sediment Type	Clay <2μ	Silt 2-62.5μ	Sand 62.5>μ	Sand, Decalcified >62μ	CaCO₃	Fe₂O₃	Terrigenous Minerals >31μ	Calcareous Minerals >31μ	Organic Detritus >31μ	% Benthonic Species of Total Foram. ass.
Ordinary, homogeneous sediments	56.4 ± 0.6	41.3 ± 0.6	2.2 ± 0.3	0.4 ± 0.1	36.8 ± 0.4	4.1 ± 0.1	16.8 ± 1.5	75.4 ± 2.1	3.8 ± 0.6	0.4 ± 0.1
Ordinary, heterogeneous sediments	49.4 ± 1.5	47.1 ± 1.6	3.5 ± 0.7	2.1 ± 0.9	33.0 ± 0.7	4.2 ± 0.1	17.4 ± 2.5	7.4 ± 2.6	2.9 ± 0.5	0.5 ± 0.2
Micro-stratified wind-borne sediments	28.9 ± 3.4	70.2 ± 3.3	0.9 ± 0.2	0.6 ± 0.2	40.1 ± 2.5	3.5 ± 0.2	24.7 ± 2.9	50.4 ± 6.3	10.8 ± 2.4	8.7 ± 2.9
Turbidity current deposits	19.9 ± 1.2	62.4 ± 1.7	17.8 ± 2.2	13.5 ± 4.4	49.1 ± 0.6	2.0 ± 1.4	28.3 ± 2.7	65.0 ± 3.5	4.2 ± 1.2	18.6 ± 4.5

The structure of the micro-stratified sediments is such that deposition by water currents appears unlikely. In support of this statement, it should be pointed out, that (1) the basal contact is a fairly sharp surface of discontinuity, lacking conspicuous signs of erosion; (2) the structure is one of alternating, very thin laminae, indistinctly delimited, a structure at typical of current-deposited sediments in the cores; (3) almost all elongated or flat particles are oriented parallel to the plane of sedimentation, a fact suggesting that calm water conditions existed during deposition. In view of the rather uniform grain size (cf. Table 1) and the high content of "coaly rods" and volcanic glass, such a micro-stratification structure is interpreted as resulting from a more or less rhythmic supply of wind-borne material. The mineral assemblage with its high content of microcrystalline calcite is suggestive of wind-borne material of loessic character.

Redeposited Sediments

(a) A type with a very pronounced graded bedded structure: This type is rich in tests of foraminifera and arises probably from the transportation of a great mass of sediment. Its petrographical composition is similar to the mean composition of the total core.

(b) A type with a less distinct graded bedded structure: Its grain size and mineralogical composition are very similar to that of loess. The relatively poor assemblage of foraminiferal tests has a high percentage of benthonic shallow-water species.

(c) A type (only one bed observed) with an irregularly developed graded bedded structure: It has a remarkably rich planktonic assemblage. The bed is interpreted as being derived from an unconsolidated sedimentary sequence, which after experiencing some external impulse began to flow, starting in the uppermost part of the sequence, successively lower and lower layers became involved.

(d) A type consisting almost exclusively of calcareous fragments, probably consisting of a small part of a turbidity current deposit.

General Comments

In the sediment core, 71 different beds have been distinguished, all of which differ texturally, structurally (determined microscopically in thin sections impregnated with methylmethacrylate) and/or mineralogically, and most even in color, from the adjacent sediments. The beds are separated by a sedimentation boundary, by a surface of discontinuity (mostly an erosion surface), or by a transition.

Traces of worm burrows are common in many layers. Tests of foraminifera containing hydrotroilite are present in almost all beds, indicating a reduction environment. Quartz is the most common terrigenous mineral, and grains interpreted as "desert quartz" are most common in the ordinary, heterogeneous sediments. The average content of carbonates for the total core, mainly $CaCO_3$, is 39 %; the mean content of Fe_2O_3 is 3.8 %.

The chronology of the core is based on datings by the C^{14} method using calcareous microfossils $> 44\mu$. The sediments deposited during the pre-Flandrian

regression (Table 2) are principally of the ordinary homogeneous type alternating with the ordinary, heterogeneous type, but otherwise showing only small differences in composition. This fact may indicate a fairly regular alternation in the wind

TABLE 2

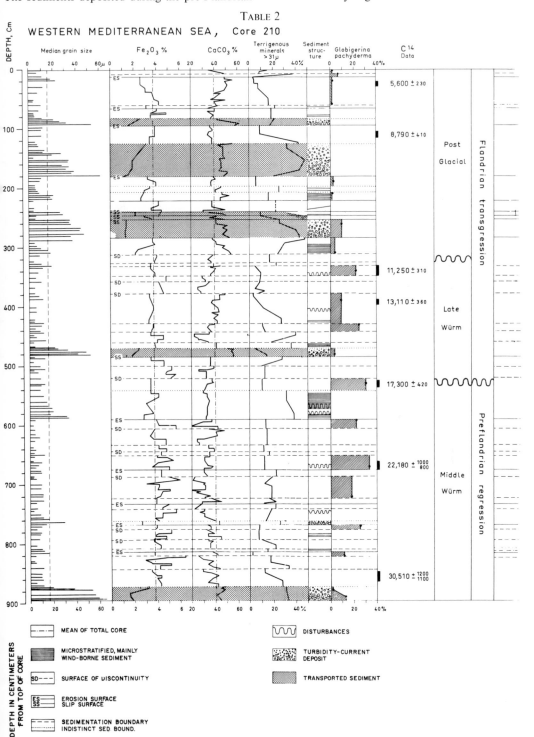

WESTERN MEDITERRANEAN SEA, Core 210

system over the western Mediterranean during most of the Würm Glacial time. Three beds of micro-stratified wind-borne material were noticed from this stage. During the Lower and Middle Flandrian transgression, the sediment composition is similar. During the transition from Late Glacial to Post-glacial, however, the climatic conditions seem to have been very irregular to judge from the abrupt changes between quite different sediment types and the relatively high frequency of beds of micro-stratified wind-borne material.

K. Gösta Eriksson

Reference

Rept. Swedish Deep-Sea Exp. 1947–1948, **8**.

MELANESIAN BASIN—*See* SOUTHWEST PACIFIC

METEORITES (ALSO AUSTRALITES)—*See* Vol. II

METEOROLOGIC-OCEAN RELATIONS—*See* OCEAN–ATMOSPHERE INTERACTION

MICROSEISMS

In its broadest sense the term microseisms, or seismic noise, designates the ground motion which is not due to earthquakes or explosions. (Some authors restrict it to mean the ground motion due to storms at sea, certainly the principal source.)

The problems of microseisms are far from solved. In 1958 Gutenberg remarked that "fifty years ago the causes and theory of microseisms were a source of extensive controversial discussions. It is still so today," while Haubrich *et al.*, in 1963 noted that "the problem is a complex one and it is not constructive to insist on a single explanation. . . ."

A theory of microseisms should not seek to explain the observations exclusively in terms of the source. Both the transmitting medium, i.e., the path of propagation, and the receiver, i.e., the seismograph, act as filters, attenuating waves of certain periods and passing others. While the effect of the former is often difficult to assess, the latter can and should always be taken into account. Optimally, thus, one would wish for synoptic observations at a seismographic station as well as at the source and along the path of propagation. Such observations are never available and their absence is a serious difficulty.

Despite these restrictions, one may classify microseisms either according to their source or according to their period. These modes of classification largely overlap. The limits given for the periods (*T*) are only indicative.

Short-period Microseisms $(0 < T < 1$ second). The largest part of these are caused by wind and human activity. The effect of wind is mostly due to its action on buildings and trees; artificial microseisms are due to traffic, trains, machinery, etc. Microseisms due to wind may occasionally have a longer period.

At a period of approximately 0.5 second, the ground displacement often shows a peak. The reason for this is unknown; it is probably due to the transmission rather than to the source. Except for this feature, the ground displacement generally decreases as the square of the frequency, i.e., the ground acceleration is roughly constant.

The difference between a noisy and a quiet site may exceed a ratio of 100/1. Sites in cities, on alluvium, near an ocean, a river, an airport, etc., are particularly noisy.

Very Long-period Microseisms $(T > 30$ seconds). Because the very long-period instruments needed for the observations have been rare, few observations are available. These microseisms are due to the displacement of air columns of unequal weight. This occurs generally during daytime. Under the slight load of these columns the ground bends, and a tilt results. This can be recorded by long-period horizontal seismographs which are very sensitive to tilt. Vertical seismographs may record this effect under particularly favorable conditions.

Pseudo-microseisms. We shall use this term to designate oscillations due to instrumental effects. Their exact cause is not always easy to ascertain. Because of the high sensitivity of modern instruments, it is imperative to prevent convection currents in the case by producing a stable thermal stratification in it. Vertical long-period seismographs either must be compensated for the Archimedian effect of barometric pressure fluctuations or must be enclosed in a rigid airtight case. Electronic seismographs may show various spurious disturbances such as those due to variation in the supply voltage.

Microseisms Due to Sea Waves. The remaining part of the spectrum $(1 < T < 30$ seconds) contains microseisms due to waves in the ocean. The most common period range is from about 5–9 seconds. Figure 1 shows a characteristic aspect. Shorter periods are observed near smaller bodies of water. Only one example of periods longer than 25 seconds has been reported to date. They are always known as "storm microseisms."

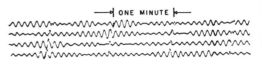

Fig. 1. Microseisms with periods of 5–6 seconds recorded by long-period Benioff seismograph at Pasadena, California (from Gutenberg, 1958).

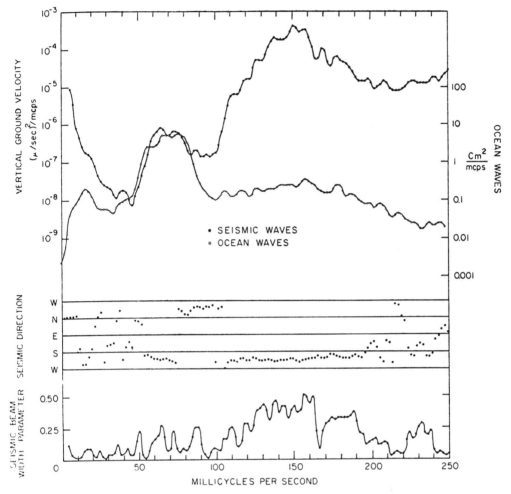

Fig. 2. *Top*: Comparative spectra of microseisms (solid points, left scale) and ocean swell (open points, right scale) in La Jolla, California. (The vertical ground velocity is thus compared to the height of the waves, not to their velocity.)

Center: Direction from which the microseisms are coming.

Bottom; Measure of the width of the beam: this parameter is 1 for a pencil beam of Rayleigh waves with no other energy present, it is 0 for isotropic radiation (from Haubrich *et al.*, 1963).

The reason for the importance of the sea in the generation of microseisms is that it offers a means of transferring the energy of the wind into the ground. A direct transfer is very inefficient due to the extreme density difference between the air and the ground.

Observations

The following facts appear to be generally true, but all are disputed to some extent:

(a) Storms (hurricanes, typhoons, etc.) in the open ocean cause microseisms and not merely the waves generated by the storm arrive near a coast (for discussion see Darbyshire, 1962).

(b) If a storm moves from the sea toward the land, the period of the microseisms decreases with time. The opposite relation holds for a storm (or a cold front) moving from land to sea.

(c) The spectrum of microseisms at a coastal station is often similar to that of the waves on a nearby shore, but the period of the microseisms is half that of the waves (see Fig. 2).

(d) There are numerous exceptions to the above rule: sometimes a 1:1 ratio holds.

(e) Progressive waves, i.e., those advancing in one direction, do not cause microseisms provided the water depth exceeds a few hundred meters.

(f) Microseisms consist mostly of Rayleigh waves, but Love waves may rarely predominate. Higher modes are present. Body waves are absent.

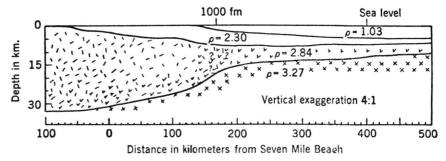

Fig. 3. Typical structure of the continental margin deduced from seismic and gravity data (from Ewing *et al.*, 1957). (By permission of McGraw–Hill Book Co., N.Y.C.)

(g) Amplitudes range from less than 0.5μ (1 inch $= 25,400\mu$) at quiet stations to well over 10μ at noisy stations during a microseismic storm.

Theory

Longuet-Higgins (1950) showed that microseisms are for the most part caused by the interference of two waves of equal wavelength traveling in opposite directions. The amplitudes of the waves may be unequal; if they are equal, standing waves (French *clapotis*) result. It is, of course, not necessary for these opposite wave trains to be conspicuous; they need merely to be present, since their effect is additive. These waves cause a compressional wave traveling vertically downward without attenuation. Since it is in phase in a horizontal plane, the pressure fluctuation on a horizontal bottom is in phase everywhere. If the interfering waves have slightly different wavelengths, the compressional wave will travel downward at an angle. The pressure wave on the bottom will now travel at a velocity determined by the relative wavelengths of the two waves.

Discussion

Some authors think that the period of the microseisms observed on land should thus be half of that of standing waves in the ocean, but this neglects the effect of the transmission: it appears that microseisms are unable to cross the boundary from the oceans to the continents due to the great difference in the structure of the crust in these regions (Fig. 3). The boundary is a "microseismic barrier."

If a storm remains distant from the continents, opposing waves may still be created up to a few tens of kilometers offshore by the interaction of the incoming and reflected swell, especially if the coast is steep. Because this offshore area is underlain by the submerged continental crust, microseisms generated there can propagate inland without difficulty.

Furthermore, the swell near the shore creates a pressure fluctuation on the bottom at its own period. The resulting ground motion is generally less than $\frac{1}{10}$ of that due to the normal microseisms. Nevertheless, in this sense, Wiechert's "surf theory" is correct.

The storm often moves closer toward the continent. As the water depth below the storm center changes from 2000 meters to less than 200 meters, the amplitude of the microseisms increases approximately tenfold (Fig. 4). This probably corresponds to the passage over the microseismic barrier. The amplitudes continue to increase until the storm reaches water a few tens of meters deep. Over still shallower water (and over land) the storm causes only microseisms of small amplitudes. The cause may be that coherent wave patterns cannot exist in shallow water. The very rapid decrease in the microseisms, despite the agitation of the sea, is due to the fact that only opposing waves can act as a source.

The gradual decrease in periods often observed in microseismic storms is due to two different reasons, depending on the circumstances.

(a) *Storm near a continent.* It appears probable that the source (opposite wave trains) is broadly distributed in frequency. However, as the water over the submerged part of the continental crust becomes shallower, the minima and maxima of the group velocity curves of Rayleigh waves shift to shorter periods. These periods tend to dominate the record because of the effect of the propagation. Thus, as the storm moves from the ocean toward the land, the periods of the microseisms will become shorter. This also explains the opposite effect observed when a storm or a cold front moves from land to sea, as near Calcutta, India, along the coast of New England and along part of the Gulf Coast. It is true that these microseisms have appreciably shorter periods to start with and that their period never becomes much greater than 5 seconds; on the other hand, microbarograms show that the air in cold fronts contains much more high-frequency energy than the normal winds. It may thus excite shorter-period waves.

(b) *Distant storm.* The periods of the ocean

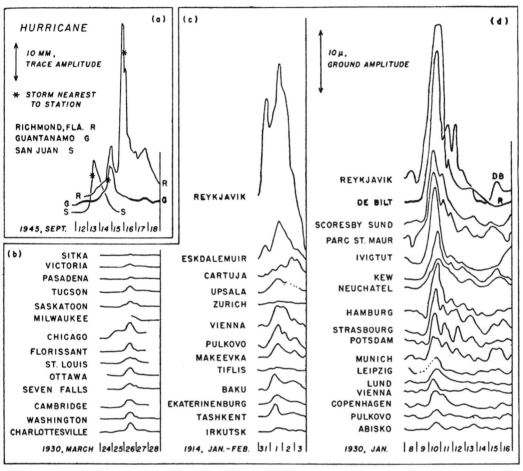

Fig. 4. Amplitudes of microseisms: (a) in the Caribbean during a hurricane (from Gilmore, 1946, p. 111); (b) in North America during a storm in eastern Canada (from Gutenberg, 1931, p. 13); (c) in Europe and Asia during a storm approaching northern Norway (from Gutenberg, 1921, p. 12); (d) in Europe and Greenland during a storm north of Scotland (from Lee, 1934b, p. 7) (all after Gutenberg, 1947).

waves arriving at a continent from a distant storm become gradually shorter due to the dispersive character of waves at sea. This spectrum, at any given time is sharply peaked. It thus excites microseisms at half its period by Longuet-Higgins' mechanism, due to the creation of opposite wave trains reflected from the shore. The effects in both cases are thus essentially the same but the cause is not.

The characteristic beats (see Fig. 1) of storm microseisms are probably due to the fact that they are generated over a fairly wide area, and cover a fairly wide band of periods.

Lakes. In addition to microseisms related to storms over the ocean, storms over smaller bodies of water also cause microseisms. Such is the case for the Great Lakes of North America, the Caspian and Black Seas and Lake Issik-Kul in the USSR, Lake Kivu in Africa, etc. The periods in these cases are much shorter (from 1–5 seconds), but the

waves on the lakes have not been measured in every case. In the Caspian Sea, though, the agreement with Longuet-Higgins' theory was excellent.

Instrumentation. For some purposes, conventional seismographs recording photographically are adequate. In most cases, though, the instruments should be long-period seismographs of high sensitivity and great dynamic range recording on magnetic tape either in analog or in digital form. Daily calibration pulses should be provided.

A station should consist of at least one such vertical and two horizontal instruments. An array of three stations is preferable but not necessary. A wave recorder located on a nearby coast is indispensable. It would be extremely desirable to install several wave recorders on a line normal to the shore and up to several kilometers or tens of kilometers away. In addition, a string of bottom pressure gauges extending offshore to large distances would also be very helpful. Finally, a few long-period seismographs solidly anchored to the bottom near the probable path of hurricanes would provide valuable information (Latham and Sutton, 1966).

Conclusions

It appears likely that more progress can be made by careful synoptic observations than by broad statistical studies. Data relating to isolated hurricanes or typhoons are likely to yield most information.

J. Cl. De Bremaecker

References

Coulomb, Jean, 1956, "L'agitation microséismique," in "Encyclopedia of Physics," Vol. 47, "Geophysics," pp. 140–152, Berlin, Springer-Verlag.

*Darbyshire, J., 1962, "Microseisms," in (Hill, M. N., editor) "The Sea," Vol. 1, "Physical Oceanography," pp. 700–719, New York, Interscience Publishers.

Donn, W. L., 1952, "Cyclonic microseisms generated in the western Atlantic Ocean," *J. Met.*, **9**. 61–71.

Ewing, W. M., Jardetzky, W. S., and Press, Frank, 1957, "Elastic Waves in Layered Media," New York, McGraw-Hill Book Co., 380pp.

*Gutenberg, Beno, 1958, "Microseisms," in (Landsberg, H. E., and Van Mieghem, J., edtitors) *Advan. Geophys.*, **5**, 53–92.

Hasselman, Kurt, 1963, "A statistical analysis of the generation of microseisms," *Rev. Geophys.*, **1**, 177–210.

Haubrich, R. A., Munk, W. H., and Snodgrass, F. E., 1963, "Comparative spectra of microseisms and swell," *Bull. Seism. Soc. Am.*, **53**, 27–37.

Latham, G. V., and Sutton, G. H., 1966, "Seismic measurements on the ocean floor, I. Bermuda Area," *J. Geophys. Res.*, **71**(10), 2545–2574.

Longuet-Higgins, M. S., 1950, "A theory of the origins of microseisms," *Phil. Trans. Roy. Soc. London, Ser. A*, **243**, 1–35.

Monakhov, F. I., 1962, "Microseisms at the bottom of the Baltic Sea and in the northern part of the Atlantic Ocean," *Izv. Akad. Nauk SSSR Ser Geofiz.* (English translation), No. 7, 573–580.

Tabulevich, V. N., 1963, "Swell, opposing winds and microseisms," *Izv. Akad. Nauk SSSR Ser. Geofiz.* (English Translation), No. 11, 1006–1010.

MID-OCEANIC RIDGE

The mid-oceanic ridge is the greatest mountain range on the earth. It is a continuous feature which extends through the Atlantic, Indian, Antarctic and South Pacific Oceans, the Norwegian Sea and the Arctic Basin for a total distance of over 35,000 miles (Figs. 1 and 2). The existence of such a world-encircling belt was sketched out by Kober (1928, Plate II). The ridge is a broad, more or less fractured swell with an elevation above the adjacent ocean-basin floor of 1–3 km and a width in most places of more than 1500 km. The lateral boundaries of the mid-oceanic ridge are defined by the first abrupt scarp, or abrupt gradient change, between the abyssal hills of the ocean basin floor and the mid-oceanic ridge (Heezen and Ewing, 1963; Heezen and Menard, 1963).

The Mid-Atlantic Ridge is that portion of the mid-oceanic ridge system which lies within the limits of the Atlantic Ocean. The Ridge consists of a broad, highly fractured median arch or swell which occupies the center third of the Atlantic Ocean. Its crest lies almost precisely on the median line of the ocean, and its lateral boundaries are formed by scarps which lie near the axes of maximum depth of the eastern and western basins. The physiographic provinces of the mid-oceanic ridge may be divided into crest provinces and flank provinces (Fig. 3). The crest provinces, which are composed of the most rugged topography, consist of the rift valley, rift mountains and high fractured plateau. The rift valley, the most striking feature on the average profile across the Mid-Atlantic Ridge, is a deep notch or cleft in the ridge crest. The floor of the valley lies about 1000 fathoms below adjacent peaks of the rift mountains and these peaks average about 1000 fathoms below the sea surface. The width of the valley between the crests of the adjacent peaks ranges between 15 and 30 miles. The rift mountains drop abruptly to the high fractured plateau, which lies in depths of 1600–1800 fathoms. On either side of the rift mountains the local relief is about 400 fathoms from peak to adjacent intermontaine valley, the distance from peak to peak ranges from 8–20 miles.

Between the outer margin of the High Fractured Plateau Provinces and the level of the ocean-basin floor lies a succession of parallel descending levels. Outward-facing scarps of varying height and intermittent length form boundaries of these levels or steps. Except for the local smooth-floored intermontaine basins in which sediments have been ponded, peaks of 200–400 fathoms form the moderately rugged relief of the flank provinces.

In the equatorial region, fracture zones which strike east-west offset the Mid-Atlantic Ridge over 2000 miles by a series of left slip faults. The magnitude of these displacements is judged by topographic discontinuities in the position of the axis of the ridge. Prominent fracture zones displace the Mid-Atlantic Ridge at 30°N, 15°N, 11°N, 1°S, and 2°S.

In the Indian Ocean, the Mid-Indian Ocean Ridge displays the same ruggedness and characteristic rift that is associated with the Mid-Atlantic Ridge. The Mid-Indian Ridge, a direct continuance of the Mid-Atlantic Ridge, continues uninterrupted from the South Atlantic to the vicinity of Rodriguez Island, at which point the ridge splits, one branch continuing toward Macquarie Island to the southeast, the other entering the Gulf of Aden where the ridge joins with the East African rift valleys (Fig. 1).

Although continuous, the mid-oceanic ridge loses some of its characteristic ruggedness and its prominent central rift valley in the eastern Pacific.

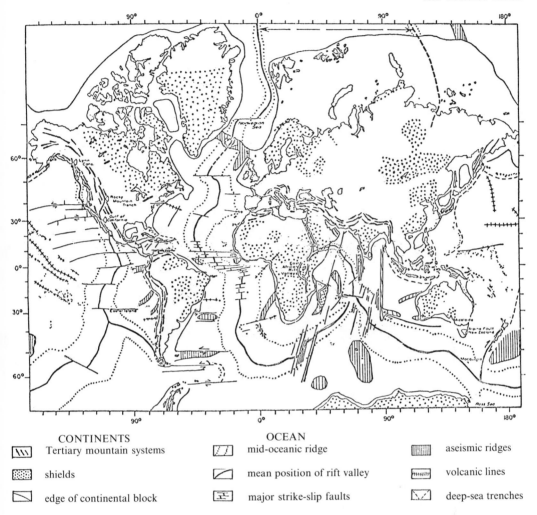

CONTINENTS

Tertiary mountain systems	
shields	
edge of continental block	

OCEAN

mid-oceanic ridge	
mean position of rift valley	
major strike-slip faults	

aseismic ridges	
volcanic lines	
deep-sea trenches	

Fig. 1. Major tectonic features of the earth. The map of the mid-oceanic rift valley is essentially a plot of the mid-oceanic earthquakes. In every area in which the bathymetry is known, the epicenter belt follows the crest of the mid-oceanic ridge. In almost every area where detailed submarine topographic studies have been carried out in the region of the epicenter belt, the median rift valley has been discovered, with the exception of certain areas of the South Pacific. Wherever the rift valley extends across continental margins, it joins either rift, graben (as in East Africa or Iceland) or great strike-slip faults (as in California or New Zealand). The axis of the mid-oceanic ridge is displaced by fracture zones in the equatorial Atlantic, Indian Ocean and in the northeast Pacific. The oceans are so poorly surveyed that it cannot be known if additional fracture zones exist. A few fracture zones are highly speculative, particularly those in the South Pacific and the Norwegian Sea. Note that the mid-oceanic ridge is a much longer and more extensive feature than the Tertiary mountain systems of the continents (after Heezen, 1962).

The East Pacific Ridge is a very broad arch which is 2–3 km high and 2000–4000 km wide (Fig. 2). The East Pacific Ridge disappears under the continent at the southern end of the Gulf of California. The relatively low relief area near the crest of the East Pacific Ridge is known as the East Pacific Rise and is composed of low, discontinuous ridges and troughs oriented parallel to the ridge axis. Step-like displacements occur on the flanks, but they appear to be randomly distributed and not continuous. Far out on the flanks bordering the central rise area, there is a continuous high-amplitude topography which is characterized by asymmetrical ridges and troughs. A few large transverse faults have been found that offset the crest of the Ridge, but more data is needed to ascertain the extent of displacement. Near Easter Island, the Chile Ridge branches off the East Pacific Ridge and runs southeast in the direction of Chile. The Chile Ridge is characterized by highly irregular relief with very deep troughs and asymmetrical ridges (Menard, 1960, 1964). (See Fig. 2; profile 8.)

507

Sediments

The sediments characteristic of the higher elevations on the ridge (less than 2500 fathoms) are predominantly of carbonate oozes consisting of the remains of planktonic (foraminifera and cocoliths) organisms. Broecker and others (1958) estimated that the rate of deposition of these sediments on the Mid-Atlantic Ridge was 2–4 cm/1000 yr. On the flanks of the mid-oceanic ridge where the depths are greater than 2500 fathoms, the carbonate fraction

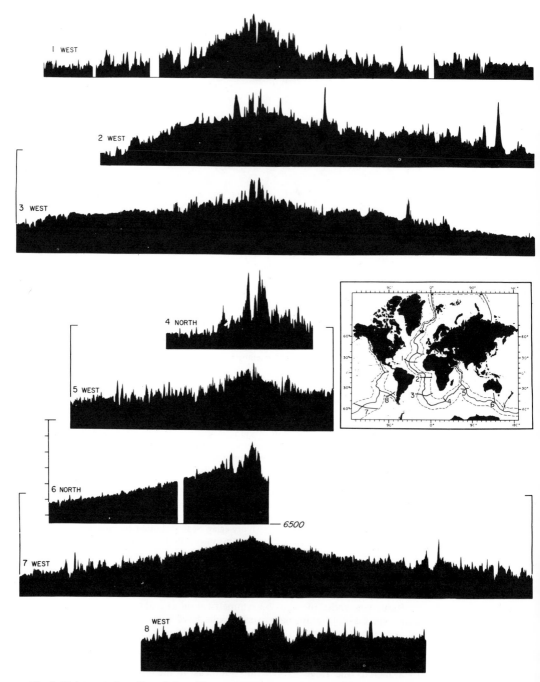

Fig. 2. Eight typical profiles of the mid-oceanic ridge in the North Atlantic, South Atlantic, Indian and South Pacific Oceans. The smooth relief across the crest of the mid-oceanic ridge in the South Pacific contrasts markedly with the rougher topography of the other oceans (after Heezen, 1962). Vertical exaggeration of profiles is 100:1.

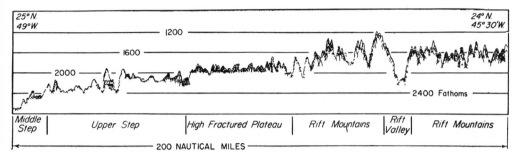

Fig. 3. Tracing of a Precision Depth Recorder record showing crest and western flank of the Mid-Atlantic Ridge (after Heezen *et al.*, 1959).

is dissolved because of the lower temperature and higher pressure. Red clay ($<2\mu$) is the major component in these deep-water deposits. The rate of deposition is more difficult to determine, but a rate of accumulation about 1 mm/1000 yr has been determined by various investigators. Other sediment types less frequently encountered on the ridge are siliceous ooze (in the Southern Ocean) composed of remains of diatoms or radiolaria and residual sand (near the crest of the ridge) composed of locally derived minerals, rock fragments and volcanic products.

Except for the questionable report of ordovician rocks on the Mid-Atlantic Ridge, the oldest sedimentary rocks dredged or cored from the Mid-Atlantic Ridge are Miocene. The few volcanic rocks taken from the ridge that have been dated have been young—<5 million years (Erickson and Kulp, 1961) and in a few cases Miocene marls have been found within pillow basalts.

All seismic reflection traverses made of the Mid-Atlantic Ridge, the Mid-Indian Ridge and the East Pacific Ridge reveal a very thin sediment veneer. In the carbonate zone (<2500 fathoms), the thickness averages less than 100 meters except in the crest province where it is usually absent (Ewing, Ewing and Talwani, 1964). The steepness of local slopes seems to control the nature of sediment accumulation. In areas where the local relief is not high, the carbonate sediments are draped over the underlying rock surface. In the crest provinces where ridges have high local relief, the slopes and peaks are sediment-free and bare rock is exposed. The sediment is ponded in adjoining flat-bottomed, sediment-filled intermontaine basins. The flat bottom strongly suggests local transport of sediment from the highs in a sufficiently fluid condition to form level surfaces. Such transport can be achieved both by intermittent turbidity currents and by deep-sea currents. Bottom photographs taken in the crest provinces have shown ripple marks and scour marks, gravel, blocks and lava pillows (Heezen and Hollister, 1964). Core analysis has revealed residual sand concentrations, graded bedding and cross-bedding (Fox and Heezen, 1965). On the flanks where depths exceeded 2500 fathoms, the red clay has an average thickness of 50 meters and is draped over the rough basement topography.

Because there is no apparent increase in sediment thickness from the crest provinces down the flanks, it does not appear that a significant volume of sediment is transported downslope off the ridge (Ewing and Ewing, 1964).

Rocks

The petrology of the mid-oceanic ridge has been inferred from petrology of island groups lying on the ridge, dredge hauls, and from residual sand. The rocks of the islands, predominantly composed of alkali basalt or its derivatives, are generally olivine bearing but sometimes olivine free (Daly, 1927; Chayes, 1963). St. Paul's Rocks, the only exception, are composed of serpentinized dunite (Tilley, 1947). Shand (1949) and Quon and Ehlers (1959) described the petrography of ten dredge hauls from the Mid-Atlantic Ridge near 30°N. The main rock types were serpentine, gabbro, and fine-grained basalt with, and occasionally without, olivine. After studying samples from the Mid-Atlantic Ridge, the Mid-Indian Ridge and the East Pacific Ridge, Engel and Engel (1961, 1964, 1965) concluded that the submerged part of the mid-oceanic ridge is composed predominantly of a low-potassium tholeiite and that only the highest parts of the ridge are composed of alkali basalts. They believe that the alkali basalt was derived by differentiation from a parent tholeiitic magma. Nicholls, Nalwalk and Hays (1964) concluded from the study of samples from three dredge hauls in the North Atlantic that the predominant rock type is high-aluminum olivine tholeiite to transitional or slightly alkali basaltic rock. Residual sands collected from 24 cores along the crest of the Mid-Atlantic Ridge between 57°S and 36°N were analyzed by Fox and Heezen (1965) and the mineral suite suggests an olivine theoleiitic source.

Recent Tectonic Activity

Even before the establishment of seismograph stations, a study of seaquakes (Rudolph, 1887) had

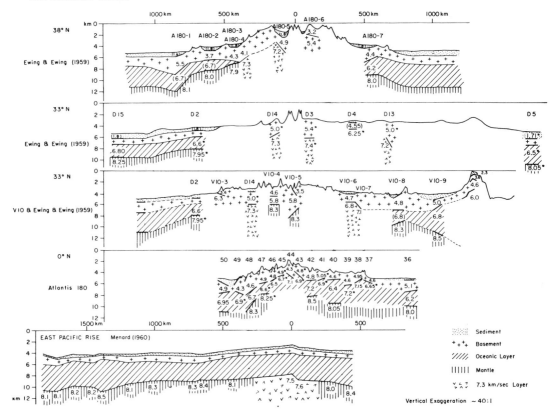

Fig. 4. Seismic cross sections of the Mid-Atlantic Ridge and the East Pacific Ridge. Note that the uplifted ocean basin crust does not thicken appreciably across the ridge crest. In the axial zone, the crustal rocks are underlain by a velocity layer which is intermediate between that of the oceanic layer and normal upper mantle velocities (after Le Pichon *et al.*, 1965).

indicated that the Mid-Atlantic Ridge is seismically active. As the world net of seismograph stations became more complete, repeated observations of mid-oceanic shallow focus earthquakes firmly established the seismicity of the Mid-Atlantic and Mid-Indian Ocean Ridges (Tams, 1931; Rothé, 1954). It was interesting to note that although the indicated width of the epicenter belt in the North Atlantic is no more than 100 miles wide, the Mid-Atlantic Ridge is 1000–1200 miles in width. A careful study of each profile across the crest of the Mid-Atlantic Ridge reveals that the axis of the epicenter belt coincides with the axis of the rift valley. Heezen and Ewing (1961) showed that the correlation of the seismicity belt and topography, in the moderately well-surveyed portions of the North Atlantic, may be extended to areas less well sounded.

In the Indian Ocean there is a clearly delineated belt of epicenters which continues uninterrupted from the South Atlantic (Rothé, 1954) to the vicinity of Rodriguez Island, at which point the seismicity belt splits, one branch continuing toward Macquarie Island, the other entering the Gulf of Aden where the

mid-oceanic ridge epicenter belt joins with the seismicity belt associated with the East African rift valleys. The connection of the mid-oceanic seismic belt with the seismic belt of the African rift valleys and the similarity of their morphologies suggest that they are structurally related and have similar origins.

The seismic belt continues along the axis of the ridge southeast from Rodriguez Island, passing near St. Paul Island, and then between Australia and Antarctica to the vicinity of Macquarie Island. Minor seismically active ridges diverge in the region toward Tasmania, New Zealand, and the Ross Sea. The great Alpine fault of New Zealand seems tectonically related to one of these ridges. From Macquarie Island to Easter Island, soundings are sparse, but a belt of earthquakes follow the axis of the ridge.

Near Easter Island, the earthquake belt splits, sending one branch southeast in the direction of Southern Chile and another north toward the Gulf of California along the axis of the East Pacific Ridge. The existence of a ridge between Easter Island and Chile, predicted on the basis of the earthquake belt (Ewing and Heezen, 1956), has been confirmed by soundings (Fisher, 1958). Along the East Pacific Ridge, epicenters appear to be more concentrated at the intersections of the transverse offsets and the crest of the ridge (Sykes, 1963).

The belt of epicenters follows the crest of the Mid-Atlantic Ridge northward through the central graben of Iceland (Rutten and Wensink, 1960) into the Norwegian Sea, where it follows the median ridge system.

The seismic belt continues north across the supposed location of the Nansen Sill between Greenland and Spitzbergen and into the Arctic Ocean. The extension of the mid-oceanic ridge system into the Arctic is based primarily on the continuous seismic belt and a few echograms from nuclear submarines (Heezen and Ewing, 1961; Sykes, 1964).

Crustal Structure

Seismic reflection results (Ewing *et al.*, 1964) revealed that the basement, which may resemble basalt, beneath the unconsolidated sediments of the Mid-Atlantic Ridge maintains its small-scale roughness from the abyssal hill province to the crest of the ridge.

In the northern Mid-Atlantic Ridge the basement thickens from $\frac{1}{2}$–1 km on the flanks to 2–3 km in the crest provinces (Fig. 4). This increase is accompanied by a seismic velocity increase from velocities of 4.5–5.0 km/sec on the flanks to velocities as

high as 5.8 km/sec in the crest zone. This seismic velocity difference is large enough to suggest a horizontal gradient in the physical properties of the basement layer. Often capping the higher-velocity basement layer is a thin layer with a velocity of 3.4 km/sec. On the basis of these low velocities and dredge hauls, it has been suggested by Hill (1960) that the low-velocity material is altered basalt. In the equatorial region, however, where the ridge is much narrower than it is to the north, the basement velocity remains low (5 km/sec) and the thickness of the basement varies negligibly across the ridge (Ewing and Ewing, 1959; Le Pichon *et al.*, 1965). Menard (1960) and Raitt (1956) have shown that like the equatorial Atlantic region, the basement thickness and velocity remain constant across the East Pacific Ridge.

Underlying the basement layer is the oceanic layer. In the northern Mid-Atlantic Ridge the flanks are characterized by thicknesses of above 5 km and velocities that range from 6.69–7.0 km/sec. The oceanic layer continuously thins toward the axis and disappears under the crest provinces. The rock underlying the basement in the crest province has a velocity of 7.2–7.6 km/sec which is intermediate between that of the oceanic layer and the normal upper mantle. This axial zone crust has not been observed in water depths greater than 3.9 km in the vicinity of the northern Mid-Atlantic Ridge. In the equatorial region of the Mid-Atlantic Ridge,

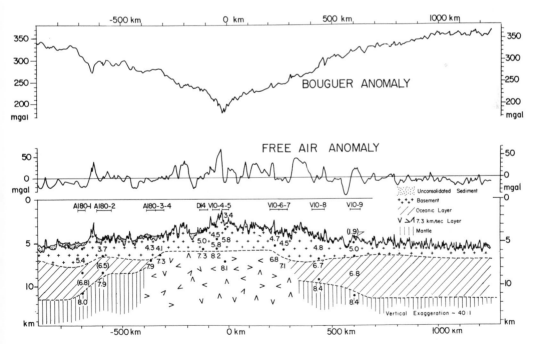

Fig. 5. Observed gravity anomalies and seismically determined structure across the north Mid-Atlantic Ridge. The fact that the free-air gravity anomaly over the entire ridge is close to zero (± 50 mgal) and that the Bouguer anomaly attains a minimum over the ridge indicates that the ridge is compensated (after Talwani *et al.*, 1965).

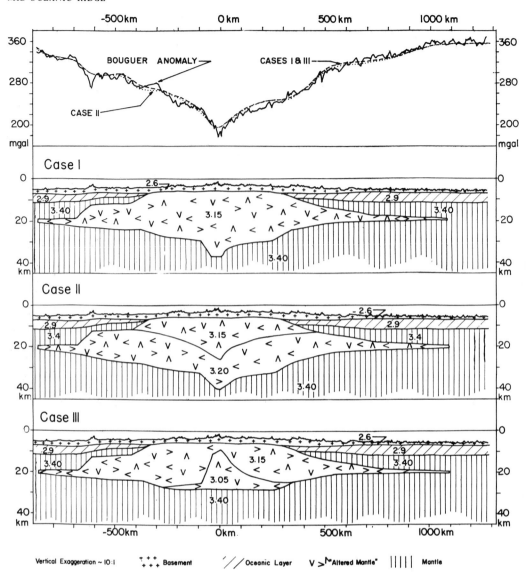

Fig. 6. Three possible crustal models across the north Mid-Atlantic Ridge which are compatible with observed gravity anomalies and seismic refraction data. The anomalous mantle was found seismically under the crest of the ridge and is assumed to underlie the normal mantle beneath the flanks of the ridge in order to provide compensation for the flanks. In case I the anomalous mantle is assumed to have a uniform density; in case II its desnity is assumed to increase downward; in case III the material constituting the anomalous mantle is assumed to be lighter near the axis of the ridge (after Talwani et al., 1965).

the oceanic crust appears to thin slightly but does not disappear, and there is some indication that the anomalous velocity material (7.2–7.6 km/sec) may lie here also beneath the ocean crust in the axial zone. Underneath the East Pacific Ridge, Menard (1960) has shown that the oceanic crust thins toward the crest of the ridge, and in the axial region the oceanic crust is also underlain by the 7.2–7.6 km/sec material.

In general, then, seismic studies have shown that the total thickness of basement and the oceanic crust under the mid-oceanic ridge is not thicker than under the ocean basins. Also, mantle velocities underneath the oceanic crust on the flanks are high (8.1–8.5 km/sec), but those underneath the axial zones are low (7.2–7.6 km/sec).

Continuous gravity measurements have been made over the Mid-Atlantic Ridge and the East Pacific Ridge (Talwani et al., 1961; Talwani et al., 1965). The free-air anomalies have small positive values over the ridge, but the values tend to become negative as the deep basins are approached (Fig. 5). Bouguer anomalies reflect the effect of the sub-bottom structure. The steep-sloped depression of the Bouguer anomaly curve over the ridge crest indicates that the ridge is compensated. The short-wavelength irregularities that are prominent on the free-air anomaly curve disappear on the Bouguer anomaly curve. This indicates that these fluctuations are due to irregularities in mass directly related to the topography.

Any structure section derived by seismic refraction methods must also be compatible with gravity measurements. In the crest region of the ridge, seismic refraction and gravity compliment each other and there is no conflict. Seismic data determine the velocity of the anomalous 7.3–km/sec velocity layer, but since no underlying layer has been found, the thickness of the anomalous layer is not known. This anomalously light mantle may be sufficient to account for the observed gravity values. On the basis of the steep gradients in the Bouguer anomaly curve, the depth to the base of the layer can be roughly estimated as 30–35 km.

The situation under the ridge flanks is more complicated. Seismic refraction data indicate that beneath the ocean crust normal mantle velocities occur. Also, seismic data show that the total thickness of the basement and oceanic crust beneath the flanks of the ridge is approximately the same as that under the ocean basins. An increase in elevation on the flanks without an increase in the thickness of low-density crustal rocks would indicate an increase in mass, which would demand the presence of a substantial positive free-air gravity anomaly. Observed free-air anomalies, however, give no indication of this. Instead, the free-air values are close to zero, which indicates isostatic equilibrium. One way to provide a compensation for the ridge flanks and also satisfy seismic data is to assume the presence of a low-velocity (7.3-km/sec) layer beneath the ridge flanks. This does not violate seismic data because a 7.3-km/sec layer would underlie a higher velocity layer and therefore would not be detected by seismic refraction studies (Fig. 6). Conclusions similar to those obtained for the Mid-Atlantic Ridge can also be derived for the East Pacific Ridge.

Although seismic refraction and gravity measurements delineate the major structural features associated with the ridge, these methods fail to reveal the fine details of the crustal structure. The magnetic anomaly pattern, however, may reveal some of the structural subtleties.

Heezen *et al.* (1953) and Ewing *et al.* (1957) noted that a large magnetic anomaly is characteristic of the rift valley. Later studies by Keen (1963) and Vine and Matthews (1963) have confirmed the results of these early studies. Bullard (1954) first recognized high heat flow values in the rift valley.

Later in the South Atlantic, Vacquier and Von Herzen (1964) found high heat flow values in the same area as the large magnetic anomalies but claimed that they are not related to the rift valley.

Profiles of total magnetic intensity anomalies from 60°N to 42°S reveal (Fig. 7) that there is a characteristic pattern to these magnetic anomalies (Ewing, Heezen and Hirshman, 1957).

A long, linear magnetic anomaly is found in all profiles over the crest zone of the ridge from 60°N–42°S. This anomaly coincides with the rift valley and the earthquake epicenter belt. The axial anomaly has two characteristic forms. North of 20°S the anomaly is a single, isolated anomaly (Fig. 7), but south of 20°S several large anomalies with amplitudes decreasing with distance from the ridge axis are characteristic. Because the anomaly is continuous over such a great distance, the body producing the anomaly must have a nearly uniform cross section and consist of material having similar magnetic properties.

The second characteristic magnetic anomaly associated with the ridge is a broad zone at least 1000 km wide which is centered on the ridge axis and is a region of relatively low-amplitude anomalies (Fig. 7). This smooth zone is interrupted along the the ridge axis by the axial anomaly which is superimposed on it. The outer limits of the axial zone are recognized by the transition to larger-amplitude and longer-wavelength anomalies which increase in amplitude toward the lower flanks of the ridge. When a trace of the magnetic anomaly is compared with a crustal cross section (Fig. 8), it is noted that the boundaries of the axial zone anomaly are defined by the low-velocity mantle and the region of high basement velocities.

The characteristic signature (steep slope, short wavelength) of the axial anomaly limits the depth of crustal models which could produce such a profile. Studies by Ewing, Heezen and Hirshman (1957) and by Heirtzler and Le Pichon (1965) indicate that the axial anomalies north of 20°S can be explained by an intrusive body lying just under the rift valley, 10–15 km wide and 5–10 km deep. The minimum susceptibility needed to produce the magnetic signature is 0.01—0.015 cgs. The uniqueness of the rift valley (magnetic signature, earthquake belt, high heat flow) suggests that the origin of this body is produced by the filling of a tensional fracture in the crust by highly magnetized volcanic material (Bullard and Mason, 1963).

This conclusion also explains the axial anomaly signature characteristic of the ridge south of 20°S. However, instead of having one singular fracture along which intrusives have migrated, there are many subsidiary fractures paralleling the main rift along which intrusion has taken place.

Vine (1963) has proposed that successive intrusions along the axis of the mid-oceanic ridge might occur when the magnetic poles are alter-

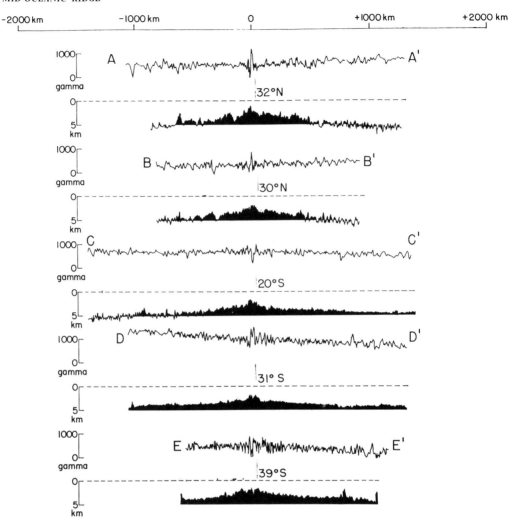

Fig. 7. Profiles of the total magnetic intensity anomaly and the basement topography for five representative crossings of the Mid-Atlantic Ridge. The magnetic records clearly illustrate the association of the large magnetic anomaly and the rift valley (after Heirtzler and Le Pichon, 1965).

nately reversed and thus the magnetic susceptibility needed in the intrusive bodies is reduced.

It is significant to note that the two characteristic magnetic axial anomalies associated with the Mid-Atlantic Ridge have been recognized on many crossings of the mid-oceanic ridge in other oceans.

The presence of high heat flow on the crest of the East Pacific Ridge was first discovered by Bullard et al. (1956). This was confirmed by Von Herzen (1959), and in 1963 Von Herzen and Uyeda found that there was evidence for two narrow belts of high heat flow along the crest of the East Pacific Ridge. This observation was substantiated somewhat by Langseth's measurements (1965). All of the studies

mentioned indicate that the broad central portion of the ridge is characterized by above-average heat flow (2–3 μcal/cm^{2}sec). The narrow zones of very high heat flow (3–8 μcal/cm^{2}sec) are superimposed on the broad high.

Studies made across the Mid-Atlantic Ridge by Bullard (1954), Bullard and Day (1961), Gerard et al. (1962), and Nason and Lee (1963) indicate that there is a single narrow peak of high (3–6 μcal/cm^2 sec) heat flow associated with the rift zone of the ridge. On the flanks of the ridge, low values predominate (1 μcal/cm^{2}sec).

Von Herzen and Langseth (1966) have found that widely scattered heat flow values for the

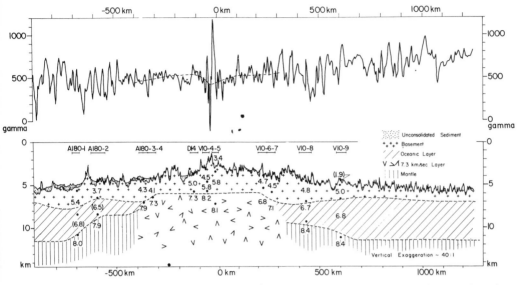

Fig. 8. Composite crustal section of the ridge from Talwani *et al.* (1965) and a magnetic profile. Note how the boundaries of the axial zone anomaly are defined by the low-velocity mantle (after Heirtzler and Le Pichon, 1965).

Mid-Indian Ocean Ridge generally agree with the trend found across the other mid-ocean ridges. Few high heat flow values have been obtained on the ridge crest (three at about 3 μcal/cm^{2}sec) and on the flanks values are not abnormally low.

The characteristic high heat flow values associated with the crest zone of the mid-ocean ridges can be best explained by the intrusion of igneous rocks along the crest zone of the ridge.

Origin

Because the mid-oceanic ridge is the longest mountain range (35,000 miles) on the earth's surface and covers an area almost equal to the area covered by the continents, its origin is of fundamental importance in consideration of the origin and deformation of the earth's crust. For this reason many theories have been proposed in an attempt to explain the origin and the structural significance of the ridge.

Any theory proposed, however, must explain the centralized earthquake activity, thin pelagic sediment blanket, high heat flow along the rift, and the rugged fractured topography. These facts lead the observer to the conclusion that most recent tectonic activity in the mid-oceanic ridge is along the axial rift. The flanks appear to be older and may have grown wider with time.

As an outgrowth of the previously mentioned facts, most workers believe that the ridge is a result of tension and that material rising from the mantle beneath the crest of the mid-oceanic ridge is adding new rock to the floor of the rift valley. Some workers have interpreted this tension in terms of continental displacement (Heezen, 1959; Dietz, 1962; Runcorn,

1962) while others, although accepting the evidence of recent tectonic activity on the mid-oceanic ridge, prefer explanations involving permanence of the continents and ocean basins (Ewing, Ewing and Talwani, 1964). Largely due to the recent and convincing paleomagnetic evidence of large continental displacements, most workers prefer explanations featuring a type of continental drift, a gradual widening of the Atlantic, Indian, and South Pacific Oceans. Many workers thus believe that as the continents moved apart, intrusions beneath the crest of the gradually widening mid-oceanic ridge created most or all of the oceanic crust (Heezen, 1959; Dietz, 1962).

The physical cause of such displacement is not understood but has been the subject of various hypotheses. The principal hypothesis employed involves thermally maintained convection currents which rise under the ridge and flow toward, and sink beneath, some indeterminate point beneath either the ocean, the continental margins, the continents, or some far-away mountain range. In any case, the low-velocity mantle under the ridge crest—if the 7.2-km/sec material is really mantle—would imply an upward flow of mantle material, although it is not at all clear if the drag of lateral flow of convection currents is a sufficient force to cause continental drift. This hypothesis requires the continuous creation of oceanic crust along the ridge crest as well as the continual destruction or disappearance of ocean crust presumably under the continental margin. An alternate hypothesis concerning the physical cause of continental displacements involves the gradual expansion of the interior of the earth, such as proposed by Egyed (see article in vol. V), without the destruction of some crust, the consequent displacement of the continents and the growth of the ocean basins by creation of crust in the mid-oceanic ridge.

BRUCE C. HEEZEN
PAUL J. FOX

References

Broecker, W. S., Turekian, K. K., and Heezen, B. C., 1958, "The relation of deep-sea sedimentation rates to variation in climate," *Am. J. Sci.,* **258**, 429–448.

Bullard, E. C., 1954, "The flow of heat through the floor of the Atlantic Ocean," *Proc. Roy. Soc. London Sci., A,* **222**, 408–429.

Bullard, E. C., and Day, A., 1961, "The flow of heat through the floor of the Atlantic Ocean," *Geophys. J.,* **4**, 282–292.

Bullard, E. C., Maxwell, A. E., and Revelle, R., 1956, "Heat flow through the deep sea flow," *Advan. Geophys.,* **3**, 155–181.

Chayes, F., 1963, "Relative abundances of intermediate members of the oceanic basalt-trachyte association," *J. Geophys. Res.,* **68**,(5), 1519–1534.

Daly, R. A., 1927, "The geology of Saint Helena Island," *Am. Acad. Arts Sci. Proc.,* **60**, 1–80.

Deitz, R. S., 1962, in (Runcorn, editor) "Ocean-basin Evolution by Sea-floor Spreading in Continental Drift," p. 338, New York, Academic Press.

Engel, A. E. J., and Engel, C. G., 1963, "Basalts dredged from the northeastern Pacific Ocean," *Science,* **140**, 1321–1324.

Engel, A. E. J., and Engel, C. G., 1964, "Composition of basalts from the Mid-Atlantic Ridge," *Science,* **144**, 1330–1333.

Engel, A. E. J., and Engel, C. G., 1965, "Igneou rocks of the Indian Ocan floor," *Science,* **150**, 605–610.

Erickson, C. P., and Kulp, J. L., 1961, "Potassium-argon dates on basaltic rocks," *Ann. N.Y. Acad. Sci.,* **91**, 321–323.

Ewing, J. I., and Ewing, M., 1959, "Seismic refraction measurements in the Atlantic Ocean basins, in the Mediterranean Sea, on the Mid-Atlantic Ridge, and in the Norwegian Sea," *Bull. Geol. Soc. Am.,* **70**, 291–318.

Ewing, M., and Ewing, J., 1964, "Distribution of Oceanic Sediments," in "Studies in Oceanography," pp. 525–537.

Ewing, M., Ewing, J., and Talwani, M., 1964, "Sediment distribution in the oceans, the Mid-Atlantic Ridge," *Bull. Geol. Soc. Am.,* **75**, 17–36.

Ewing, M., and Heezen, B., 1956, "Some problems of Antarctic submarine geology, in Antarctica in the I.G.Y.," *Am. Geophys. Union, Geology Monograph No. 1,* 75–81.

Ewing, M., Heezen, B., and Hirshman, J., 1957, "Mid-Atlantic ridge seismic belts and magnetic anomalies (abstract)," Comm. 110 bis. Assoc. Seismol. 16 ann. Gen. U.G.G.I., Toronto.

Fisher, R. L., 1958, "Preliminary report on expedition Downwind," I.G.Y. Gen. Report Series (Data Station A), No. 2

Fox, P. J., and Heezen, B. C., 1965, "Sands of the Mid-Atlantic Ridge," *Science,* **149**, 1367–1370.

Gerard, R., Langseth, M., Jr., and Ewing, M., 1962, "Thermal gradient measurements in the water and bottom sediments of the western Atlantic," *J. Geophys. Res.,* **67**, 785–803.

Heezen, B. C., 1959, Geologie sous-marine et deplacements des continents in Topographie et la Geologie des Profondus Oceaniques, Colloq. int. cent. Nat. Rech. Sci., Vol. 83, p. 295, Paris.

Heezen, B. C., 1962, "The Deep-Sea Floor," in *Continental Drift,* ed. Runcorn, Academic Press, p. 338.

Heezen, B. C., and Ewing, M., 1961, "The Mid-Oceanic Ridge and its extension through the Arctic Basin," pp. 622–642, In Raasch, G.O. (Ed.), Geology of the Arctic, Proc. First Intern. Symp. Arctic Geol., Vol. 1, Univ. Toronto Press, Toronto, 732p.

Heezen, B. C., and Ewing, M., 1963, "The Mid-Oceanic Ridge," in *The Sea,* Hill (Ed.), V. III, pp. 388–410, John Wiley & Sons, New York.

Heezen, B. C., Ewing, M., and Miller, M. T., 1953, Trans-Atlantic profile of total magnetic intensity and topography, Dakar to Barbados, *Deep-Sea Res.,* **1**(1), pp. 25–33.

Heezen, B. C., and Hollister, C., 1964, "Deep-sea current evidence from abyssal sediments," *Marine Geology,* **1**(2), 141–174.

Heezen, B. C., Tharp, M., and Ewing, M., 1959, "The floors of the oceans, 1, The North Atlantic," *Geol. Soc. Am. Spec. Paper 65.*

Heirtzler, J. R., and Le Pichon, X., 1965, "Crustal structure of the Mid-Ocean Ridges. 3, Magnetic Anomalies over the Mid-Atlantic Ridge," *Geophys. Res.,* **70**, 4013–4035.

Hill, M. N., 1960, "A median valley of the Mid-Atlantic Ridge," *Deep-Sea Res.,* **6**(3), 193–205.

Keen, M. J., 1963, "Magnetic anomalies over the Mid-Atlantic Ridge," *Nature,* **197**(4870), 888–890.

Kober, L., 1928, "Der Bau der Erde," Second ed., Berlin, Borntraeger, 499pp.

Langseth, M. G., Grim, P. J., and Ewing, M., 1965, "Heat-flow measurements in the East Pacific Ocean," *J. Geophys. Res.,* **70**(2), 367–380.

Le Pichon, X., Hautz, R. E., Drake, C. L., and Nafe, J. E., 1965, "Crustal structure of the Mid-Oceanic ridges, 1, Seismic refraction measurements," *J. Geophys. Res.,* **70**(2), 319–339.

Menard, H. W., 1960, "The East Pacific rise," *Science,* **132**, 1737–1746.

Menard, H. W., 1962, "Correlations between length and effect on very large wrench faults," *J. Geophys. Res.,* **67**(10), 4096–4098.

Menard, H. W., 1964, "Maringe Geology of the Pacific," pp. 117–152, New York, McGraw-Hill Book Co.

Muir, I. D., and Tilley, C. E., 1964, "Basalts from the northern part of the rift zone of the Mid-Atlantic Ridge," *J. Petrol.,* **5**, Part 3, 409–434.

Nanson, R. D., and Lee, W. H. K., 1962, Preliminary heat flow profile across the Atlantic, *Nature,* **196**, 975.

Nicholls, G. D., Nalwalk, N. J., and Hays, E. E., 1964, "The nature and composition of rock samples dredged from the Mid-Atlantic Ridge between 22° N and 52° N," *Marine Geol.,* **1**, 333–343.

Raitt, R. W., 1956, "Seismic refraction studies of the Pacific Ocean basin. 1. Crustal thickness of the central equatorial Pacific," *Bull. Geol. Soc. Am.,* **67**, 1623–1640.

Rothé, J. P., 1954, "La zone seismique Médiane Indo-Atlantique," *Phil. Trans. Roy. Soc. London, Ser. A,* **222**, 387–397.

Rudolph, E., 1887, "Über submarine Erdbeben und Eruptonen," Gerlands *Beit. Geophys.,* **1**, 133–373.

Runcorn, S. K., 1962, "Paleomagnetic Evidence for Continental Drift and Its Geophysical Cause," in (Runcorn, editor) "Continental Drift," p. 338, New York, Academic Press.

Rutten, M. G., and Wensink, H., 1960, "Structure of Iceland," *Intern. Geol. Congr. 18. Copenhagen,* 81–88.

Shand, S. J., 1949, "Rocks of the Mid-Atlantic Ridge," *J. Geol.,* **57**, 89–91.

Sykes, L. R., 1963, "Seismicity of the South Pacific Ocean," *J. Geophys. Res.,* **68**(21), 5999–6006.

Sykes, L. R., 1965, "The Seismicity of the Arctic," *Bull. Seismol. Soc. Am.,* **55**(2), 519–536.

Talwani, M., Heezen, B. C., Worzel, J. L., 1961, "Gravity anomalies, physiography and crustal structure of the Mid-Atlantic ridge," *Publ. Bur. Central Seismol. Intern., Sec. A, Trav. Sci.,* Fasc. 22, 81–111.

Talwani, M., Le Pichon, X., and Ewing, M., 1965, "Crustal structure of the mid-ocean ridges. 2. Computed model from gravity and seismic refraction data," *J. Geophys. Res.,* **70**(2) 341–351.

Tams, E., 1922, "Die seismischen Verhältisse des Europäischen Nordmeeres," *Centralblatt f. Mineralogie, Geologie Pal. Jahrg.,* No. 13, 385–397.

Tilley, C. E., 1947, "Mylonites of St. Paul's Rocks (Atlantic)," *Am. J. Sci.,* **245**, 485–491. (See also: *Geol. Mag.,* **103**, 120–123; 1966.)

Vacquier, V., and Von Herzen, R., 1964, "Evidence for connection between heat flow and the Mid-Atlantic Ridge magnetic anomaly," *J. Geophys. Res.,* **61**, 1093–1101.

Vine, F. J., and Matthews, D. H., 1963, "Magnetic anomalies over oceanic ridges," *Nature,* **199**(4897), 947–949.

Von Herzen, R., 1959, "Heat-flow values from the southeastern Pacific," *Nature,* **185**, 882–883.

Von Herzen, R., and Langseth, M. G., 1966, "Present status of oceanic heat-flow measurements," *Phys. and Chem. Earth* (Pergamon), **6**, 365–407.

Von Herzen, R., and Uyeda, S., 1963, "Heat flow through the eastern Pacific ocean floor," *J. Geophys. Res.,* **68**, 4219–4250.

MINERAL POTENTIAL OF THE OCEAN

As a source of minerals, the ocean has been little exploited relative to its potential. The major reasons for this default are a lack of information as to the nature of the mineral deposits of the sea, no developed technologies for extracting the many useful minerals found therein, and no pressing need for exploiting all these resources at this time. For the foreseeable future, minerals in the ocean will be exploited only if they can compete on an economic basis with those in continental deposits.

As far as mineral resources are concerned, the ocean can be divided into five regions: (1) seawater; (2) marine beaches; (3) continental shelves; (4) consolidated rocks underlying the soft surficial sediments; and (5) deep-sea floor.

Seawater

Seawater is generally considered to have dissolved in it all of the natural elements. The concentration of about 60 elements has been measured at various locations in the ocean, and Table 1 lists the concentration and total amounts of some of the elements thus far found in seawater. Covering an area of about 140 million square miles at a mean depth of about 2.5 miles, the sea holds about 330 million cubic miles of water. Seawater contains an average of 3.5% of various elements in solution, thus, each cubic mile of seawater, weighing some 4.7 billion tons, holds about 166 million tons of solids. Two elements, sodium and chlorine, constitute about 85% of the dissolved solids in seawater, while the nine most abundant elements (including Na and Cl) constitute over 99% of the total dissolved solids in seawater. Of the 60 or so elements known to be dissolved in seawater, only four have been commercially extracted in any quantity. They are sodium and chlorine in the form of common salt, magnesium and some of its compounds, and bromine. Several calcium and potassium compounds are produced as by-products in salt or magnesium extraction processes or by processing seaweeds which concentrate these elements in their cells.

The commercial extraction of any element or compound from seawater, of course, immediately makes reserves of this material unlimited, and such is the case for magnesium and bromine, the bulk of which are extracted from seawater for consumption in the United States. Bromine is almost purely a marine element; over 99% of the bromine in the earth's crust is in the ocean. There is about two cents worth of bromine per ton of seawater, so when being processed for this element, seawater is the lowest-grade ore known. Salt is commonly extracted from the ocean by means of solar evaporation. About 1.2 million tons of solar salt are produced annually in the United States, while about 6 million tons are annually produced throughout the world. Armstrong and Miall (1946) discuss the extraction of many other minerals from seawater.

Extraction Economics. In considering the economics of the extraction of minerals from seawater, one must consider not only the effort involved in recovering the element or material, but also competition from other sources of supply, distribution costs, consumption rates, and a myriad of other factors. Because of technical difficulties in operating a larger facility, a factory handling about 660 billion gallons of water per year or about 1.2 million gallons of water per minute is about as large as is practical. All this plant would be required to do is take in the seawater, perform one physical or chemical manipulation per product, recover that product in a marketable form, and dispose of the effluent in a manner so as not to dilute the incoming seawater. Such a plant would require a capital investment of about $100 million.

TABLE 1. CONCENTRATION AND AMOUNTS OF SIXTY OF THE ELEMENTS IN SEAWATER

Element	Concentration (mg/liter)*	Amount of Element in Seawater (tons/mile^3)	Total Amount in the Oceans (tons)
Chlorine	19,000.	89.5×10^6	29.3×10^{15}
Sodium	10,500.	49.5×10^6	16.3×10^{15}
Magnesium	1350.	6.4×10^6	2.1×10^{15}
Sulfur	885.	4.2×10^6	1.4×10^{15}
Calcium	400.	1.9×10^6	0.6×10^{15}
Potassium	380.	1.8×10^6	0.6×10^{15}
Bromine	65.	306,000	0.1×10^{15}
Carbon	28.	132,000	0.04×10^{15}
Strontium	8.	38,000	$12,000 \times 10^9$
Boron	4.6	23,000	7100×10^9
Silicon	3.	14,000	4700×10^9
Fluorine	1.3	6,100	2000×10^9
Argon	0.6	2,800	930×10^9
Nitrogen	0.5	2,400	780×10^9
Lithium	0.17	800	260×10^9
Rubidium	0.12	570	190×10^9
Phosphorus	0.07	330	110×10^9
Iodine	0.06	280	93×10^9
Barium	0.03	140	47×10^9
Indium	0.02	94	31×10^9
Zinc	0.01	47	16×10^9
Iron	0.01	47	16×10^9
Aluminum	0.01	47	16×10^9
Molybdenum	0.01	47	16×10^9
Selenium	0.004	19	6×10^9
Tin	0.003	14	5×10^9
Copper	0.003	14	5×10^9
Arsenic	0.003	14	5×10^9
Uranium	0.003	14	5×10^9
Nickel	0.002	9	3×10^9
Vanadium	0.002	9	3×10^9
Manganese	0.002	9	3×10^9
Titanium	0.001	5	1.5×10^9
Antimony	0.0005	2	0.8×10^9
Cobalt	0.0005	2	0.8×10^9
Cesium	0.0005	2	0.8×10^9
Cerium	0.0004	2	0.6×10^9
Yttrium	0.0003	1	5×10^8
Silver	0.0003	1	5×10^8
Lanthanum	0.0003	1	5×10^8
Krypton	0.0003	1	5×10^8
Neon	0.0001	0.5	150×10^6
Cadmium	0.0001	0.5	150×10^6
Tungsten	0.0001	0.5	150×10^6
Xenon	0.0001	0.5	150×10^6
Germanium	0.00007	0.3	110×10^6
Chromium	0.00005	0.2	78×10^6
Thorium	0.00005	0.2	78×10^6
Scandium	0.00004	0.2	62×10^6
Lead	0.00003	0.1	46×10^6
Mercury	0.00003	0.1	46×10^6
Gallium	0.00003	0.1	46×10^6
Bismuth	0.00002	0.1	31×10^6
Niobium	0.00001	0.05	15×10^6
Thallium	0.00001	0.05	15×10^6
Helium	0.000005	0.03	8×10^6
Gold	0.000004	0.02	6×10^6
Protactinium	2×10^{-9}	1×10^{-5}	3000
Radium	1×10^{-10}	5×10^{-7}	150
Radon	0.6×10^{-15}	3×10^{-12}	1×10^{-3}

* After Goldberg, 1963 (see reference in Mero, 1964).

TABLE 2. AMOUNT AND VALUE OF PRODUCTS FROM A SEAWATER FACTORY HANDLING 660 BILLION GALLONS OF WATER PER YEAR*

Material** Obtained	Factory Production (1000 Tons/yr)	Selling Price ($/ton)	Product Value ($1000/yr)	1961 U.S. Consumption (1000 Tons/yr)	Ratio of fact. production to Consumption	Estimated Land Reserves At 1961 Rates of Consumption U.S. (yr)	World† (Yr)
NaCl	76,300	10	763,000	26,100	2.9	+1000	+1000
Magnesium	45	705	31,700	45	1.0	+1000	+1000
Mg compounds	5,923	53	314,000	680	5.3	+1000	+1000
Sulfur	2,450	24	58,800	6,000	0.4	25	NA‡
$CaSO_4$	6,105	4	24,400	10,000	0.6	NA	NA
KCl	2,062	31	64,000	1,880	0.6	160	5000
Br	184	430	79,000	85	2.2	+1000	+1000
$SrSO_4$	76	66	5,000	5	15	400	NA
Borax	113	44	5,000	100	1.1	200	NA
HF	3.8	320	1,200	330	0.01	30	50
LiOH	3.4	1,080	3,240	NA	NA	NA	NA
Iodine	0.14	2,200	306	1.3	0.11	NA	NA
MoO_3	0.041	3,200	132	15	3×10^{-3}	150	100
Selenium	0.011	11,500	127	0.5	0.02	100	NA
U_3O_8	0.007	16,000	112	26	3×10^{-4}	10	30
V_2O_5	0.014	2,760	39	6.7	0.002	NA	NA
$BaSO_4$	0.24	160	38	820	2×10^{-4}	80	NA
Silver	0.0008	35,000	28	5.5	1×10^{-4}	6	20
Gold	0.00002	1×10^6	20	NA	NA	NA	NA
Tin	0.008	2,240	18	49	2×10^{-4}	NA	NA
Phosphates	0.22	70	15	6,100	3×10^{-5}	1000	1000
Aluminum	0.03	450	13	2,300	1×10^{-5}	7	120
Zinc	0.05	230	12	460	1×10^{-4}	35	30
Nickel	0.006	1,580	10	180	3×10^{-5}	3	40
Copper	0.008	620	5	1,230	1×10^{-5}	30	35
TiO_2	0.0047	540	3	570	1×10^{-5}	40	110
ThO_2	0.0002	11,000	2	0.1	2×10^{-3}	1000	NA
Cadmium	0.0004	3,600	1.5	5	8×10^{-5}	6	40
As_2O_3	0.0074	100	0.7	26	3×10^{-4}	100	NA
Cobalt	0.0002	3,040	0.6	5	4×10^{-5}	8	100
Antimony	0.0006	650	0.4	13	5×10^{-5}	3	100
MnO_2	0.005	50	0.3	1,000	5×10^{-6}	NA	35

* After McIlhenny and Ballard, 1963.
** Listed in form of dominant selling compound. Consumption statistics include other forms also.
† Assuming present level of extraction technology. +1000 indicates material extracted from sea.
‡ NA = not sufficient data available to calculate statistic.

Investment costs on this plant would be about $10 million annually.

In Table 2 are shown statistics concerning the materials that would cycle through this plant. Assuming that all the minerals listed in Table 2 could be extracted, it can be seen that only 11 minerals could be produced that would have a value of more than $1 million per year and only four more products would have a value greater than $100,000 per year. The annual gross value of all materials produced with an individual product value less than $5 million per year would be about $7 million which is some $3 million less than the investment costs. We can conclude that it would not be economic to extract from seawater any minerals or combination of minerals with a concentration in seawater less than that of boron using existing technologies. Even if these elements were to be produced as by-products of a mag-

nesium, bromine, or sulfur extraction process, it is doubtful if they could be produced profitably with present-day methods. This conclusion, of course, does not preclude the development of new processes which might be used to recover the trace elements from seawater on an economic basis; however, the nature of such processes must be fundamentally different from those with which we are now familiar.

Fresh Water. Fresh water, although not normally considered a mineral, is, potentially, one of the most important materials that can be extracted from seawater. In a few areas of the world such as Curacao Island and Kuwait, fresh water for domestic and industrial purposes is distilled from seawater. In the United States, a number of plants have been constructed and put into operation to study the various methods of extracting fresh water from the ocean. In general, the production cost of the most efficient of the processes capable of recovering fresh water on a large scale from seawater is several times the cost of obtaining it from the ground or water sheds. Under special circumstances, in coastal areas, however, the extraction of fresh water from the ocean will probably soon be economic.

Marine Beaches

Beaches are an interesting region of the ocean from a mining standpoint. Because of the crushing, grinding, and concentrating action of the ocean surf, much of the processing of minerals in the beaches has been done by nature. What mining and processing is left to do is, in general, uncomplicated and inexpensive. From marine beaches come diamonds, gold, magnetite, columbite, ilmenite, zircon, scheelite, monazite, platinum, and silica, to name the most important minerals from a commercial standpoint. Mero (1964) lists a number of beaches which are mined for minerals.

Many older beaches, now high above sea level on emerging coastlines, are being worked at present principally for zircon, magnetite, titanium, gold, or diamonds. In addition to the emerged or emerging beaches, there are a number of submerged beaches in offshore areas. These beaches were probably formed during the Pleistocene when the level of the sea fluctuated greatly and was generally much lower than it is now due to water accumulating in the continental glaciers. It can be expected that the submerged beaches in the offshore area would contain placer deposits of the same minerals that are found in the present beaches nearby. Examples of areas in which minerals were mined from the onshore beaches and are now being mined from the offshore areas are: the southwest coast of Japan where magnetite is mined; the southwest coast of Africa where diamonds are mined; and the area offshore Nome, Alaska, where gold has been found.

Because the sea stabilized for a period of time at many levels during the ice ages, there is good reason to suspect that a number of beaches would have formed in the offshore areas. Thus, the mineral production potential of the offshore areas should be much greater than the onshore potential.

Continental Shelves

The continental shelves of the world cover an area of about 10 million square miles or about 20% of the above-water continental area of the earth. As the rocks of the continental shelves are basically similar to those of the continents, it can be expected that the mineral producing potential of these rocks would be about 20% of that of the above-water continental rocks. Save for petroleum and sulfur, it may be sometime before methods can be developed to mine mineral deposits within the continental shelf rocks on an economic basis.

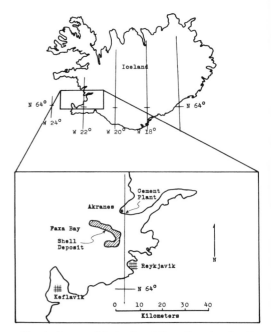

Fig. 1. A map of Iceland and Faxa Bay showing the calcareous shell deposit on the floor of this bay. This deposit is mined to provide a cement plant near Akranes with the primary raw material for the manufacture of Portland cement.

Because of their cover of water, however, the continental shelves hold other types of mineral deposits which can be exploited economically with present-day methods.

Calcareous Deposits. Calcareous shells are mined from offshore deposits in a number of locations notably in the Gulf of Mexico and offshore of Iceland. Since 1940, over 45 million tons of shells have been recovered from the area off eastern Texas for use in various chemical processes. Shell deposits in the Gulf of Mexico extend from Texas to Cape Romano, Florida, and are exploited in a number of locations. Shell deposits are mined in several other locations of the world, mainly for use as a raw material in the manufacture of portland cement.

An interesting shell deposit is mined off the southwest coast of Iceland to provide the raw material for a local cement industry in that country. Figure 1 shows the location and shape of this deposit. A shoal of rock lying west of the area of the deposit is home to a large population of various kinds of shelled animals. The winter waves break the shells free, crushing and grinding them. Tidal currents sweep the particles into Faxa Bay. The influx of shell material far exceeds the rate of extraction; thus we have a replenishing mineral deposit. This renewing feature is a common, but highly significant, feature of mineral deposits in the sea.

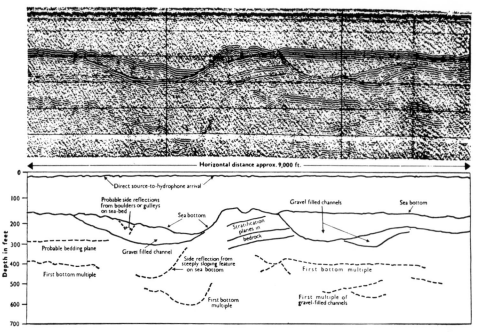

Fig. 2. An echogram of a sea-floor sonic survey illustrating the delineation of subsurface sediment interfaces and structures. Under the echogram is an interpretation of it. Sediment types can often be distinguished in the graphs.

Glauconite. Glauconite is an interesting authigenic mineral found in considerable quantity in various offshore locations. Frequently, it is found in deposits relatively uncontaminated with other materials. Containing from 4–9% of K_2O, the sea-floor glauconite might be a source of potassium for agricultural fertilizers.

Phosphorite. Of some interest at present are the phosphorite deposits found on the shelves off the coasts of many countries of the world. Thus far, phosphorite deposits have been found off Peru, Chile, Mexico, the west and east coasts of the United States, off Argentina, South Africa, Japan, and on the submerged parts of several islands around the Indian Ocean.

Off California, the sea-floor phosphorite occurs as nodules which vary in shape from flat slabs, several feet across, to oolites. The nodules are commonly found on the sea floor as a monolayer at the surface of coarse-grained sediments. The composition of the phosphorite from the southern California area is surprisingly uniform. The nodules generally assay about 30% P_2O_5 on a dry-weight basis. The mineralogy of the nodules is similar to that of the phosphorite in the Phosphoria of western United States. Emery (1960) has estimated that some 1 billion tons of phosphorite nodules can be found in the southern California offshore area.

Drowned River Valleys. In Malaysia, Thailand, and Indonesia, tin is mined from river placers onshore to the present sea level. The deposits apparently extend into the offshore areas. About ten dredges are presently operating in the Indonesian offshore area and at least one in the Thailand offshore area. Such deposits are beginning to show up with increasing frequency, mainly because of the use of new seismic prospecting methods which allow rapid delineation of these sea-floor features even though the valleys and adjacent ridges are now completely buried by sediments. Figure 2 illustrates a sea-floor sonic echogram.

Drowned river valleys may also hold substantial placer deposits of gold off Nome, of platinum off Good News Bay, Alaska, and of diamonds off the mouth of the Orange River in Southwest Africa.

Subsea-floor Consolidated Rocks

In offshore areas of England, Japan, Newfoundland, and Finland, coal and iron ore are mined from subsea-floor rocks. These deposits are generally exploited by sinking shafts in the onshore rocks and driving drifts out under the sea and into the ore veins.

Petroleum. Although oil has been produced from offshore areas since the 1890's, it is only since World War II that any extensive petroleum exploration has been done in offshore areas. At present, about 250 million barrels of oil per year are produced by offshore wells in the United States. Outside of the United States, the rate of production is also about 250 million barrels per year, about 75% of the production coming from the Persian Gulf area. The rate of production from offshore areas is rapidly rising. In 1951, W. E. Pratt (see reference in Mero, 1964) estimated that the continental shelves contained a reserve of some 1000 billion barrels of oil or an amount about equal to that estimated for the above-water continental areas.

Sulfur. Sulfur deposits are also found in the offshore areas, notably in the caps of salt domes. One such deposit was located while drilling for oil about seven miles off Grand Isle, Louisiana. This deposit is now mined by the Frasch process from the largest steel island ever built by man in the sea. Much of the sulfur of the United States is produced from salt domes in the onshore areas of the Gulf Coast region. Indications are that the concentration of salt domes offshore in this area is about the same as that onshore, and we can expect that the proportion of those domes containing minable deposits of sulfur is about the same also.

The Deep-sea Floor

In the pelagic areas of the ocean, nature is working on a truly grand scale to separate and concentrate many of the elements that enter seawater. The minerals that are formed are frequently found in high concentrations on the sea floor, since in the pelagic, or far out, areas of the ocean there is relatively little clastic material deposited to dilute the chemical precipitates. Eventually, the common igneous rocks may serve as a source of the minerals needed in any industrial society.

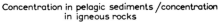
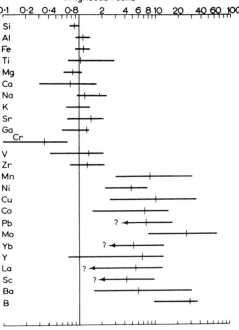

Fig. 3. Ratios of average elemental abundances in the Pacific pelagic sediments and igneous rocks. Ranges are shown by the lengths of the horizontal lines and modes by the short vertical lines (after Goldberg and Arrhenius, 1958, see reference in Mero, 1964). (By permission American Elsevier Publishing Co., N.Y.C.)

TABLE 3. STATISTICS ON AMOUNT OF AND RATE OF ACCUMULATION OF VARIOUS ELEMENTS IN RED CLAY*

Element	Abundance in Red Clay** (%)	Amount in Red Clay (trillions of tons)	Rate of Accumulation in Red Clay (millions of tons/yr)	World† Rate of Consumption (millions of tons/yr)	Ratio of Amount in Red Clay to Annual Consumption ($\times 10^6$)	Ratio of Rate of Accumulation to Rate of Consumption	World‡ Reserves in 1958 (millions of tons)	Ratio Amount in Red Clay to World Reserves ($\times 10^3$)
Al	9.2	920.	46.	4.72	200.	10	570	1620
Mn	1.25	125.	6.3	6.7	19.	1	320	390
Ti	0.73	73.	3.7	1.3	56.	3	140	520
V	0.045	4.5	0.23	0.008	550.	28	NA¶	—
Fe	6.5	650.	32.5	262.5§	2.5	0.1	1350	480
Co	0.016	1.6	0.08	0.015	110.	5	1.6	1000
Ni	0.032	3.2	0.16	0.36	8.9	0.5	13.5	220
Cu	0.074	7.4	0.37	4.6	1.6	0.1	150	50
Zr	0.018	1.8	0.09	0.002	900.	45.	NA	—
Pb	0.015	1.5	0.08	2.4	0.6	0.03	43	35
Mo	0.0045	0.45	0.023	0.040	11.	0.6	3	150

* Based on an oceanic tonnage of red clay of 10^{16} tons and a rate of accumulation of 5×10^8 tons per year. All quantities expressed in metric tons.
** After Goldberg and Arrhenius, 1958 (see reference in Mero, 1964).
† From Encyclopaedia Britannica Book of the Year, 1963.
‡ After McIlhenny and Ballard, 1963.
¶ No data available with which to calculate statistic.
§ Primary iron.

Table 4. Reserves of Metals in Manganese Nodules of the Pacific Ocean*

Element	Amount of Element in Nodules (billions of tons)**	Reserves in Nodules at Consumption Rate of 1960 (years)†	Approximate World Land Reserves of Element (years)‡	Ratio of Reserves in Nodules Reserves on Land	U.S. Rate of Consumption of Element in 1960 (millions of tons/yr) ¶	Rate of Accumulation of Element in Nodules (millions of tons/yr)	Ratio of Rate of Accumulation to Rate of U.S. Consumption	Ratio of World Consumption to U.S. Consumption
Mg	25.	600,000	L ††	—	0.04	0.18	4.5	2.5
Al	43.	20,000	100	200	2.0	0.30	0.15	2.
Ti	9.9	2,000,000	L	—	0.30	0.069	0.23	4.
V	0.8	400,000	L	—	0.002	0.0056	2.8	4.
Mn	358.	400,000	100	4000	0.8	2.5	3.0	8.
Fe	207.	2,000	500 §	4	100.	1.4	0.01	2.5
Co	5.2	200,000	40	5000	0.008	0.036	4.5	2.
Ni	14.7	150,000	100	1500	0.11	0.102	1.0	3.
Cu	7.9	6,000	40	150	1.2	0.055	0.05	4.
Zn	0.7	1,000	100	10	0.9	0.0048	0.005	3.5
Ga	0.015	150,000	—	—	0.0001	0.0001	1.0	—
Zr	0.93	+100,000	+100	1000	0.0013	0.0065	5.0	—
Mo	0.77	30,000	500	60	0.025	0.0054	0.2	2.
Ag	0.001	100	100	1	0.006	0.00003	0.005	—
Pb	1.3	1,000	40	50	1.0	0.009	0.009	2.5

* After Mero, 1964.
** All tonnages in metric units.
† Amount available in the nodules divided by the consumption rate.
‡ Calculated as the element in metric tons (from *U.S. Bur. Mines Bull.* **556**).
¶ Calculated as the element in metric tons.
§ Including deposits of iron that are at present considered marginal.
†† Present reserves so large as to be essentially unlimited at present rates of consumption.

Figure 3 illustrates one of the reasons why the sediments of the ocean will probably be used first. The pelagic sediments contain an average of about ten times as much of the industrially important metals as do the igneous rocks. These ocean-floor sediments possess other advantages when being considered as a material to mine—they are politically free and royalty-free materials, widely distributed near most markets and available to all on an equal basis. In addition, they are fine-grained, unconsolidated, and in a water atmosphere which makes the use of an automated hydraulic system for recovery practical.

Red Clay. Red clay covers about 102 million km² of the ocean floor. At an average depth of about 200 meters, there would be some 10^{16} tons of red clay on the ocean floors. At an average rate of formation variously estimated from 0.5–5 mm/1000 yr, the annual accumulation of the red clays is about $0.5–5 \times 10^8$ tons. Table 3 lists some statistics concerning the amount of various elements in the red clay presently on the ocean floor and the rate at which the elements are annually accumulating in the red clay deposits.

While from a mineral resource standpoint, the composition of the red clays is not particularly exciting, this material may have some value as a raw material to be used in the manufacture of products, or it may, in the future, serve as a source of various metals. While the average assay for

Al_2O_3 is about 15%, individual samples of red clay have assayed in excess of 25% Al_2O_3. Copper contents as high as 0.20% have been found in some red clays. Nickel, cobalt, vanadium, lead, zirconium and several of the rare earth elements show up in red clays in amounts of several hundredths of a per cent.

Calcareous Oozes. Calcareous oozes cover some 128 million km² of the ocean floor, or about 36% of its total area. The average thickness of the calcareous ooze layers has been estimated to be about 400 meters. Thus, there are about 10^{16} tons of calcareous oozes in the ocean. These oozes are estimated to be forming at an average rate of about 1 cm/1000 yr, thus, each year some 1.5 billion tons of calcareous ooze are added to the ocean floor. Limestone, for which these oozes could be substituted, is presently mined at a rate of about 0.2 billion tons/yr worldwide. If only 10% of the ocean-floor deposits proved minable, the reserves would be about 10 million years at our present rate of consumption. More interesting is that the calcareous oozes, forming at a rate of 1.5 billion tons/yr are accumulating about eight times as fast as the world is presently consuming limestone.

Siliceous Oozes. Siliceous oozes cover about 38 million km² of the ocean floor. At an assumed thickness of about 200 meters, there should be some 10^{15} tons of these oozes on the ocean floor. Normally, they could serve in most of the applications for which diatomaceous earth is used, i.e., for fire and sound insulation, in lightweight concretes, as filters, as soil conditioners and so forth.

Manganese Nodules. Probably the most interesting of the oceanic sediments, especially from an economic standpoint are the manganese nodules (see *Manganese Nodules, Deep-sea*). These small, black to brown, friable concretions were discovered to be widely distributed throughout the three major oceans of the world almost 100 years ago by the famous *Challenger* and *Albatross* expeditions.

It is estimated that there are some 1.5 trillion tons of manganese nodules on the Pacific Ocean floor and that they are forming in this ocean at an annual rate of about 10 million tons. By using the compositional data as listed in Table 1 of *Manganese Nodules, Deep-sea* (page 000), it is possible to calculate the amount of the various elements present in the nodules of the Pacific Ocean. Table 4 lists statistics concerning the amounts of various elements in the nodules and the land deposits. Even if only 10% of the nodule deposits prove economic to mine, it can be seen that there are, in general, sufficient supplies of many metals in these sea-floor deposits to last for thousands of years at our present rates of consumption.

The results of another interesting set of calculations are shown in the last three columns of Table 4. By computing the ratio of the rates at which the various metals are agglomerating in the nodules to that of the rate of consumption of those metals, it can be seen that many elements are accumulating in the manganese nodules now forming on the Pacific Ocean floor faster than they are presently being consumed, in fact, three times as fast for manganese, twice as fast for cobalt, as fast for nickel, and so on.

As is the case with many mineral deposits of the sea, the manganese nodules would be a renewable resource. The fact that many deposits of the sea are renewable resources is, of course, of academic interest only, for the reserves of the minerals contained in presently minable deposits are generally measured in terms of hundreds of thousands or millions of years.

JOHN L. MERO

References

Armstrong, E. F., and Miall, L. M., 1946, "Raw Materials from the Sea," Chemical Publishing Co., Inc., 196pp.

*Emery, K. O., 1960, "The Sea Off Southern California," New York, John Wiley & Sons, Inc., 365pp.

McIlhenny, W. F., and Ballard, D. A., 1963, "The Sea as a Source of Dissolved Chemicals," American Chemical Society Symposium on The Economic Importance of Chemicals from the Sea, April 2–4, 1963, Los Angeles, California, pp. 122–132.

*Mero, J. L., 1964, "Mineral Resources of the Sea," New York, American Elsevier Publishing Co., 312pp.

MOLUCCA SEA

(1) Limits and Oceanography

(a) **Limits and Dimensions.** The Molucca Sea (center: 127°E, 2°N) is bordered in the west as well as in the east by rows of volcanic islands, respectively the North Sulawesi (Celebes)-Sangir islands and Halmahera with surrounding islets. The northeastern limit is formed by the Snellius Ridge (submarine) separating the Molucca Sea from the Pacific Ocean, but it may be noted that the International Hydrographic Bureau (*Sp. Publ.* 23 1953) attaches the sector north of a line Sangir–Talaud Island to the Philippine Sea. The southern boundary consists of a line Obi Major to the Sula Archipelago and Tomini Gulf (Fig. 1).

The Molucca Sea is underlain by a complex series of troughs, basins, and ridges (Table 1). The area covered by this sea is approximately 200,000 km². Table 1 and others connected with the Molucca Sea have been compiled from reports of the oceanographic Snellius Expedition in 1929–30, among others by Van Riel *et al.* (1950).

The floor of the Molucca Sea may be subdivided into three north-south zones. Most western is a zone marked by the *Sangir Trough* connecting Davao Gulf in Mindanao with the Gorontalo Gulf. The central zone consists of a broad-backed ridge which is clearly outlined by the 2000 meters isobath. In the north, this ridge bears the Talaud and Miangas islands whereas in the center of the sea only two small islands are known: Maju and Tifore. The third zone is composed of a series of depressions with *Talaud* and *Morotai depressions* in the north and *Mangole–Batjan basins* in the south.

(b) **Deep-water Properties and Flow of Bottom Water.** The deep water characteristics of the temperature, oxygen content, and salinity were used by the Snellius Expedition for confirming the evidence of fresh deep-water flow replenishing the various basins in the Molucca Sea (Table 2).

The Snellius Expedition found that the Molucca Sea serves as an important passageway for the flow of deep water from the Pacific Ocean into the majority of deep-sea basins and troughs of Indonesia. The north end of the Sangir Trough is marked by a deep flow from the Pacific Ocean into the Sulawesi Sea (Fig. 2), continuing farther through the Strait of Makassar into the Flores Sea. A second flow enters the Morotai Basin and the series of depressions connected with it. A branch of this flow ventilates the Gorontalo Basin, while another branch passes through Lifamatola Strait into the Banda and Ceram seas (Fig. 1).

(c) **Surface Properties and Meteorology.** Throughout the year, the surface salinities depart at the most 0.3‰ from the average of 34.0‰. Slightly higher salinities have been recorded for the period September through November in the northern and

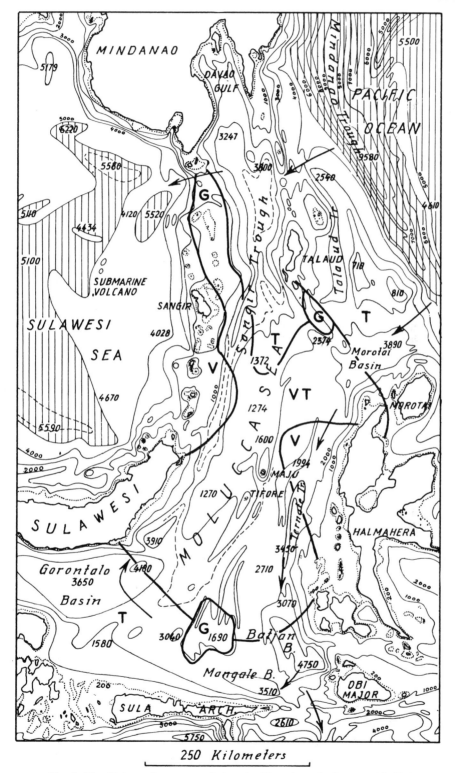

Fig. 1. The Molucca Sea, eastern Indonesia. Map shows bathymetry (shading indicates depths limited by the 5000-meter isobath), flow of bottom water (arrows) and bottom sediments. T: terrigenous mud; G: globigerina ooze; VT: volcanic and terrigenous mud; V: volcanic mud (data from the Snellius Expedition 1929–30).

TABLE 1. LIMITS AND DIMENSIONS OF DEPRESSIONS IN THE MOLUCCA SEA

Depression	Limit (m) Isobath	Area (km^2)	Sill Depth (m)	Maximum Depth (m)
Sangir Trough	3000	10,000	2050	3820
Talaud Trough	3000	2,700	3130	3450
Morotai Basin	3000	6,500	2340	3890
Ternate Trough	3000	1,000	2710	3450
Batjan Basin	3000	6,800	2550	4810
Mangole Basin	3000	1,900	2710	3510
Gorontalo Basin	3000	14,000	2700	4180

TABLE 2. DEEP-WATER PROPERTIES WITHIN THE DEPRESSIONS AND OUTSIDE THEIR RESPECTIVE SILLS

Depths of Observations at the Various Snellius Stations (m)	Temperature (°C)	Salinity (‰)	Oxygen (cc/liter)	Density
Pacific Ocean, No. 264, 1970	2.175	34.645	—	1027.695
Sangir Trough, No. 296, 3289	2.43	34.65	2.73	1027.675
Sill at No. 273, 2475	1.72	34.65	—	1027.735
Morotai Basin, No. 284, 3651	1.855	34.68	3.06	1027.745
Sill at No. 345, 2703	1.855	34.65	2.30?	1027.725
Ternate Trough, No. 347, 3011	1.855	34.66	3.04	1027.73
Sill at No. 347, 2511	1.86	34.68	3.04	1027.745
Batjan Basin, No. 80, 4586	2.21	34.66	2.63	1027.705
Sill at No. 237, 2730	2.07	34.65	2.37	1027.705
Mangole Basin, No. 227, 2934	2.08	34.65	2.85	1027.705
Sill at No. 265, 3220	1.595	34.685	3.46	1027.77
Talaud Trough, No. 285, 1916	2.27	34.62	2.60	1027.665
Sill at No. 334, 2625	2.165	34.64	2.83	1027.69
Gorontalo Basin, No. 337, 3827	2.29	34.65	—	1027.69

southern extremities of the Molucca Sea (34.6–34.8‰).

Surface temperatures are highest in June (28.3°C) and lowest in January (27.0°C).

Monsoon winds govern the area of the Molucca Sea. During the northern winter, the wind is northeast (0.5–2.4 of the Beaufort scale) and slowly swings across the equator to become a north-northwest wind (0.5–1.4) in the southern part of the sea. During the northern summer, the wind directions are reversed with strengths between 1.5–2.4. The air pressure departs only slightly from 756.5 mm throughout the year.

(d) **Currents and Tides.** During the northern summer, a surface current of 10 nautical miles per day flow southwestward along the eastern margin of the Molucca Sea. In the west half of the sea, the current direction is opposite to the earlier-mentioned current. For the latter area the currents are 10–12 nautical miles/day.

The northward flow in the west half of the Molucca Sea is maintained in the northern winter as far north as the northern tip of Sulawesi (5–20 nautical miles/day). The north half of the sea has east-southeast-directed currents (15–25 nautical miles/day), while such a direction is also found for

the current passing into the Ceram Sea at 20 nautical miles/day.

At Ternate the recorded tidal range amounts to 1.4 meters.

The Snellius Expedition also undertook current measurements down to 1500 meters deep in Lifamatola Strait between the Molucca and the Ceram seas (Fig. 3). Data from its station No. 253a in April, 1930 are reproduced below.

TABLE 3. CURRENTS IN LIFAMATOLA STRAIT

At	0 m	15 cm/sec	toward N27°E
	50 m	29 ,,	,, N56°W
	100–200 m	14 ,,	,, N63°E
	350 m	10 ,,	,, S 50°E
	500 m	8 ,,	,, S 20°W
	1200 m	3 ,,	,, N60°E
	1500 m	5 ,,	,, S 52°E

(2) Bottom Sediments

From the northern limit of the Molucca Sea to about 80 km south of the Talaud islands, the floor is composed of terrigenous mud. Locally this mud

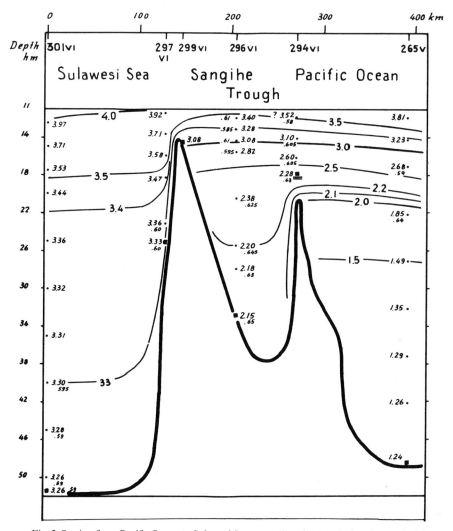

Fig. 2. Section from Pacific Ocean to Sulawesi Sea across Sangir Trough showing potential temperature and salinity (after Van Riel, 1934, Snellius Expedition).

shows a provenance of mafic igneous and alkali rocks. The central part consists of a mixture of volcanic and terrigenous muds with higher concentrations of volcanic mud near the volcanoes along the western and eastern boundaries. The floor of the southern part, i.e., the Gorontalo, Mangole, and Batjan basins, is again composed of terrigenous mud with local concentrations of actinolite. Globigerina ooze (at least 30% calcium carbonate) occurs at normal depths as in the deep oceans in patches at the southern end of the central submarine ridge of the Molucca Sea, on the submarine slopes of its western boundary, and elsewhere. Coralline mud and sand are conspicuously concentrated around the reefs and coral islands. The lowest entrances into the Molucca Sea all are marked by hard ground indicating strong currents across those thresholds.

(3) Geophysics and Geological Structure

The central ridge of the Molucca Sea coincides with a belt of negative gravity anomalies till —204 mgal. This belt continues southward across the east and southeast arms of Sulawesi (Figs. 2 and 3). The western and eastern volcanic margins are in areas of positive gravity anomalies which are generally smaller than 50 mgal but locally they may attain values slightly over 100 mgal.

Many earthquakes have been traced to possess epicenters below the Molucca Sea. In a traverse from the Pacific Ocean across the Molucca Sea toward the Asiatic Continent, it was found that earthquake foci increase in depth. Theories on the geological and geophysical implications of such distributions of foci have been discussed by Vening Meinesz, Berlage and others (see Van Bemmelen, 1949).

The volcanoes rimming the Molucca Sea are of the orogenic type with characteristically high explosive indices: 80 to over 90.

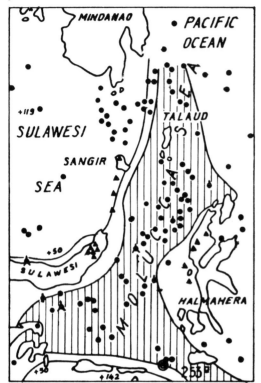

Fig. 3. The Molucca Sea, eastern Indonesia. Gravimetry (shading indicates belt of negative anomalies, with an extreme of − 204 mgal), active volcanoes (triangles) and earthquake epicenters (dots: less than 100 km deep; with one hachure; 100–199 km deep; with two hachures; 200–299 km; etc.). Double circles indicate current recording station 253a of the Snellius Expedition.

Morphological and geophysical evidence suggest that in the Molucca Sea, two series of island arcs, each composed of a volcanic and a nonvolcanic outer arc, have been fused along their outer arcs forming the central ridge in the Molucca Sea. Consequently the depressions flanking this ridge have been primarily formed by downwarping.

Many elevated Recent coral reefs (up to 50 meters) on the islands of the Molucca Sea area point to still active diastrophic movements (Kuenen, 1933). This evidence is compatible with the high seismic frequency and the large departures from isostatic equilibrium present in the area. The occurrence of shallow marine late-Tertiary sediments in many of the islands, as in the Talaud islands, Sula and Halmahera groups is conclusive proof that the deep floor and those islands are of late Tertiary or younger age. At present, the area is still subject to tectonic movements.

H. D. Tjia

References

*Kuenen, Ph. H., 1933, "The Snellius Expedition," in Geology of Coral Reefs, Vol. 5, Part 3, pp. 1–126, Utrecht, Kemink.
*Van Bemmelen, R. W., 1949, "The geology of Indonesia: General Geology," Vol. IA, pp. 257–297, The Hague, Martinus Nijhoff.
*Van Riel, P. M., Hamaker, H. C., and Van Eyck, L., 1950, "The Snellius Expedition, Tables. Serial and Bottom Observations. Temperature, Salinity and Density," Vol. 2, Part 6, pp. 1–44, Leiden, Brill.

MONSOON CURRENT—*See* **INDIAN OCEAN; SOMALI CURRENT**

MOZAMBIQUE CURRENT—*See* **AGULHAS CURRENT**

N

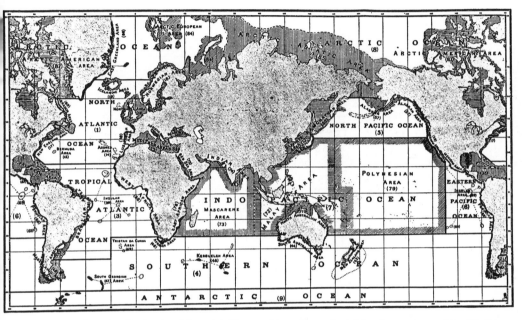

Fig. 1. Areas of marine distribution. The areas illustrated here were selected for the purposes of the Challenger Society's Bibliography of Marine Faunas, having been based on what appeared to be the natural boundaries of temperature, current, depth, etc., which affect the distribution of both floating and bottom animals (from Allen, 1928).

NATURAL REGIONS IN THE OCEANS

The geographer attempts to delineate "natural regions" on the continents in order to provide a convenient regional basis for nomenclature and integration of the *whole* landscape, rather than its description on a basis of uncoordinated detail appropriate only to the various disciplines. The same need is often felt in oceanography. Thus temperature, pressure, source, salinity, productivity, and so on, are all valid bases for cartography, but none establishes a *general characterization* of a water mass or area.

Water mass boundary, identified basically in terms of source and history, has much to commend it, but for straightforward cartographic purposes such a criterion proves difficult, for the water mass boundary is usually liable to migrate seasonally and may vary somewhat from year to year. A long-standing attempt has been made to establish the definition of the "Southern Ocean" (q.v.) in terms of the Subtropical Convergence, and numerous arbitrary limits (ranging through 30° of latitude) have been proposed for it. Almost inevitably, the desire of hydrographers for a rigid cartographic limit has led to the term being rejected altogether, except as a local description without precise limits, a decision reached long ago by Murray and Hjort (1912).

The major biogeographic boundaries, initially proposed by P. L. Sclater in 1858, apply primarily to the continents, thus *Holarctic* (roughly the northern hemisphere, above 25–35°N, *Palaearctic* being Eurasia, and *Nearctic* being North America), with *Neotropical* for South America, *Ethiopian* for Africa, *Oriental* for India (s.l.) and Southeast Asia, and *Australasian* for Australia, New Zealand, Melanesia and Polynesia. Such major divisions with many local divisions) are often applied to continental shelf biotas.

Fig. 2. Natural regions of the oceans, following the scheme of G. Schott (1936).

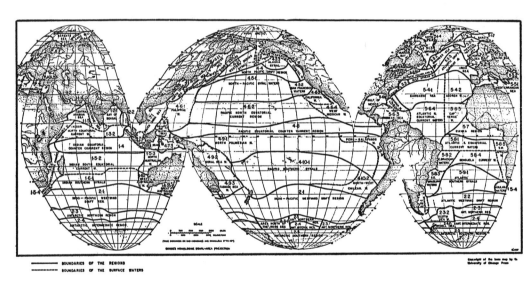

Fig. 3. Natural regions of the oceans (Hela and Laevastu, 1962).

In order to establish convenient natural regions for surface waters generally, the *Challenger Society* established a committee which drew up a scheme for worldwide oceanographic use "based on what appear to be the *natural boundaries* of temperature, current, depth, etc., which affect the distribution of both floating and bottom animals." Unfortunately, although its boundaries, largely following parallels or meridians, are easy to draw, such arbitrary generalizations inevitably cut clean across obvious unities (Fig. 1).

Another, more realistic approach has been made by G. Schott, the great marine geographer, whose basic geographies of the Atlantic and of the Indo-Pacific are still of enormous fundamental value. Schott's scheme (1936) attempted to embrace a single system that would satisfy oceanographic, climatic and biological interests. Essentially the boundaries correspond to major current systems, but others are related to biologic diffusion centers and other avowedly subjective and somewhat arbitrary preferences (Fig. 2). Schott's scheme was supported by a useful table of dimensions and percentages (for each of the three oceans); see Table 1.

TABLE 1. SCHOTT'S NATURAL REGIONS OF THE THREE WORLD OCEANS

Atlantic Ocean

Region	in 1000 km²	%
1. Northpolar Sea	11,081	10.4
2. North Atlantic Subpolar Region	3,727	3.5
3. Northwest Atlantic Marginal Sea	1,782	1.7
4. Northeast Atlantic Drift Region	8,300	7.8
5. North Sea and Baltic Sea	998	0.9
6. Gulf Stream Region	7,727	7.3
7. Sargasso Sea	6,448	6.1
8. Morocco Region	4,658	4.4
9. Mediterranean Sea and Black Sea	2,966	2.8
10. North Atlantic Trade Wind Region	8,340	7.8
11. Atlantic Equatorial Region	3,223	3.0
12. Brazil Region	8,755	8.1
13. Ascension Region	6,674	6.3
14. Southwest African Region	4,134	3.9
15. South Atlantic Mid-latitude	11,094	10.4
16. Patagonia Region	1,290	1.2
17. South Atlantic Subpolar Region	6,687	6.3
18. Atlantic Southpolar Region	8,579	8.1
	106,463	100.0

Indian Ocean

Region	in 1000 km²	%
19. Arabian Sea including Red Sea and Persian Gulf	7,456	9.6
20. Bay of Bengal	4,780	6.3
21. Indian Equatorial Region	6,956	9.0
22. Mauritius Region including Mozambique Region	16,845	21.8
23. Northwest and Southwest Australian Region	5,938	7.7
24. South Indian Mid-latitude	17,848	23.1
25. Indian Subpolar Region	11,678	14.9
26. Indian Southpolar Region	5,769	7.6
	77,270	100.0

Pacific Ocean

Region	in 1000 km²	%
27. East Asiatic Marginal Seas	9,675	5.4
28. North Pacific Mid-latitudes including Alaska Region	18,459	10.4
29. California Region	6,025	3.4
30. Mexican Region	2,089	1.2
31. North Pacific Trade Wind Region	16,593	9.3
32. Japan Region	5,526	3.1
33. Pacific Equatorial Region	15,548	8.8
34. Malaya Region (Sunda Sea)	5,875	3.3
35. South Pacific Island Region	32,040	18.0
36. Galapagos Region	17,371	9.8
37. South Pacific Mid-latitudes	32,631	18.4
38. South Pacific Subpolar Region	9,792	5.5
39. Pacific Southpolar Region	6,085	3.4
	177,709	100.0

Total World Oceans

	km²
Atlantic Ocean	106,463,000
Indian Ocean	77,270,000
Pacific Ocean	177,709,000
	361,442,000

A review and translation of Schott's ideas was given in English by James (1936).

Yet another system is one favored by the fisheries interests, this example taken from Hela and Laevastu (1961). Here again they recognize mainly currents as boundaries of the natural regions (Fig. 3). A series of code numbers were allocated (1, Indian Ocean; 2, Southern Ocean; 3, Arctic Ocean; 4, Pacific Ocean; 5, Atlantic Ocean), with secondary numerical subdivisions (e.g., Mediterranean 5.5.1; Black Sea 5.5.2; Irminger Sea 5.2.2, etc.).

The question has also been discussed by Bogorov (1962) representing a modern Russian point of view.

Finally, a system of oceanic natural regions has been most recently devised by Dietrich (1963) which may well be the closest approximation to the desired integration (Fig. 4). Basically it corresponds closely to the surface *current systems*, which are themselves components of the great water masses; it is no coincidence that this pattern also closely matches the dominant *wind systems*, though it breaks down in the regions of Dietrich's "jet stream currents," the great high-velocity geostrophic currents of the mid-latitude western margins of oceans. From the *biological* point of view, populations and communities are often limited by the thermal boundaries established along current borders, though they may well be swept along great distances from one current into another sector of the same system. *Geologically* it is frequently the current boundary itself that determines the peak zones of sedimentation, for pelagic life is likely to be most active at convergences and at upwellings, and thus leads to great accumulations of the tests from pelagic plankton; at boundaries (both at the surface and at depth on continental slopes) where eddies occur, energy is lost and terrigenous sediment in suspension is liable to fall to the bottom.

It is unfortunate that Deitrich's code letters were selected from their German equivalents, since English is the principal language of oceanography (no xenophobic tendencies implied!), but with

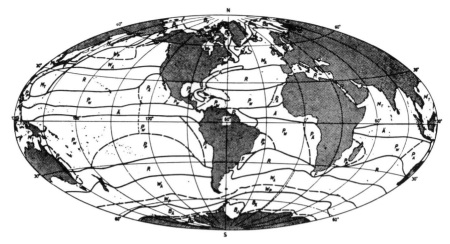

Fig. 4. Natural regions of the oceans according to G. Dietrich (1963). For abbreviations, see Table 2. (By permission of Interscience Publishers, N.Y.)

minor adjustments these could equally well provide an oceanographic "shorthand" for international use, as the modifications of the famous Koeppen system does for climates (see *Climatic Classification*, vol. II).

TABLE 2. THE DIETRICH SYSTEM OF OCEANIC NATURAL REGIONS

(Suggested modifications for international use in parentheses; R.W.F.)

P (T). *Trade Wind Ocean Regions* ("Passat" in German), persistent westerly setting currents
  $P_{\ddot{a}}$ (T_e) ditto, with 30° equatorward component
  P_w (T_w) ditto, predominantly westerly set
  P_p (T_p) ditto, with 30° poleward current
Ä (E). *Equatorial Ocean Regions* ("Äquator" in German), regions of currents directed, at times or all year to the east
M. *Monsoon Ocean Regions* ("Monsun" in German), regions of regular current reversals in spring and autumn
  M_t. Low-latitude monsoon areas of little temperature variation
  M_p. Mid to high (poleward) latitude equivalents of large temperature variations
R (H). *Horse Latitude Ocean Regions* ("Ross" in German), at times or all year marked by weak or variable currents
F. *Fast-flowing or "Jet Current" Regions* ("Freistrahl-regionen" in German), all-year, geostrophically controlled narrow current belts of mid-latitude westerly margins of oceans
W. *Westerly Drift Ocean Regions* ("Westwind" in German), marked by somewhat variable but dominantly east-setting currents all year
  WÄ(W_e), equatorward of oceanic polar front (convergence)
  W_p (W_p), poleward of oceanic polar front (convergence)
B. *Boreal Ocean Regions*, at times or throughout the year ice covered, in Arctic and Antarctic seas

RHODES W. FAIRBRIDGE

References

Allen, E. J., 1928, "Science of the Sea" (Handbook of Challenger Society), Second ed., Oxford, Clarendon Press, 502pp.
Bogorov, V. G., 1962, "Problem of the Zonality of the World Ocean," in (Gerasimov, I. P., editor) "Soviet Geography; its Accomplishments and Tasks," pp. 188–194.
Dietrich, G., 1963, "General Oceanography," New York, Interscience Publishers.
Hela, I., and Laevastu, T., 1961, "Fisheries Hydrography," Lond., Fishing News Books Ltd., 137pp.
James, P. E., 1936, "Geography of the oceans: a review of the work of Gerhard Schott." *Geogr. Rev.*, **26**, 664–669.
Murray, Sir J., and Hjort, J., 1912, "The Depths of the Ocean," London, Macmillan and Co., 821pp.
Schott, G., 1936, "Die Aufteilung der Drei Ozeane in Natürliche Regionen," *Petermanns Geogr. Mitteilungen*, No. 6, 165–170, 218–222.

Cross-references: *Oceans – Limits, Definitions, Dimensions; Vol. II, Climatic Classification,*

NAUTICAL ALMANAC—*See* **EPHEMERIS,** Vol. II

NAVIER-STOKES EQUATIONS—*See* **LAMINAR-FLOW, BOUNDARY LAYER; FLUID MECHANICS**

NAVIGATION

(1) Introduction

Navigation is the process of directing the movements of a craft or object from one point to another. It is as old as man himself, and throughout history the principles have not changed, although the means of implementation have become more sophisticated with advancing technology. Although science, engineering, and craftsmanship have left their imprint, the *art* of navigation continues as an important element of navigation in the skill needed to use the aids—both natural and man-made—and in interpreting the available information. Although techniques differ with the circumstances, navigation generally involves position, direction, distance, speed, and time.

(2) Basic Considerations

(a) Kinds of Navigation. Fundamentally, there are only two kinds of navigation: *dead reckoning* and *fixing*. The former involves determination of position by advancing or extrapolating a "known" position for estimates or measurements of distance traveled in one or more directions. Because of imperfections in determination of direction and distance, the error is cumulative. It therefore becomes desirable from time to time to determine a new position independent of the dead reckoning. This might be done by means of *piloting* or *celestial navigation*. The former establishes position or safety of the craft relative to objects or natural features external to the craft, while the latter establishes *orientation* with respect to celestial bodies too remote for position with respect to them to be significant.

(b) Position. Appropriately, a position determined by dead reckoning is called a *dead reckoning position*. One determined independently is called a *fix* or, if considered of doubtful accuracy, an *estimated position*. A *running fix* is obtained from information adjusted to a common time, except that in celestial navigation the term *fix* applies if several observations are taken within an elapsed time of several minutes. The expression *most probable position* may be applied whenever judgment is involved in interpreting the available data. Although position may sometimes be stated relative to some feature, it is generally expressed in *latitude* and *longitude*, geodetic coordinates usually being employed.

(c) Directions of Navigation. Navigators use both *rhumb lines* and *great circles*, the former being particularly useful to marine navigators for short distances because they represent constant courses and straight lines on the commonly used Mercator charts. A *course* is the intended direction of travel. *Course made good* is the direction of a point of arrival from a point of departure. *Track* is the horizontal component of the path followed or expected to be followed by a craft. The term is also used to refer to the direction or average direction of this line. *Heading* is the instantaneous or average direction in which a craft is pointed. *Bearing* is the direction of one terrestrial point from another. *Azimuth* is the horizontal direction to a point on the celestial sphere. Directions are generally expressed in whole degrees (using three digits) or degrees and tenths clockwise from a reference direction. Reference directions com-

monly used are *true north*, the northerly direction of the meridian through the observer; *magnetic north*, the direction of the horizontal component of the magnetic line of force connecting the observer with the earth's magnetic pole in the northern hemisphere; *compass north*, the northerly direction indicated by a magnetic compass; *gyro north*, the northerly direction indicated by a north-seeking gyro compass; *grid north*, the northerly direction of an arbitrary grid, used particularly in polar regions as the direction of a line parallel, on the chart, to the Greenwich meridian, with north being the northerly direction along this meridian; and *heading*, used to indicate *relative bearings*.

(d) Distance. This is commonly expressed in nautical miles (or tenths); 1 nautical mile = 1852 meters, or about 6076 feet. Shorter distance may be expressed in feet, yards, or meters. Heights are generally expressed in feet or meters, depths of water in feet, *fathoms* (of 6 feet each), or meters.

(e) Speed. This is commonly expressed in *knots*, one knot being one nautical mile per hour. For some purposes, feet, yards, or meters per second may be used.

(f) Time. This is generally expressed to the nearest minute for indicating position and to the nearest second for timing observations of celestial bodies. Either *zone time* or *Greenwich mean time* is used. Other kinds of time, discussed below under Celestial Navigation, have special uses.

(3) Charts and Publications

(a) Chart Projections. A *chart* is a map intended primarily for navigation. Except in the case of *gnomonic* charts, on which great circles appear as straight lines, charts are *conformal* or nearly so, and directions can be measured directly. The *Mercator* projection is commonly used for nautical charts and the *Lambert conformal* projection for aeronautical charts. *Transverse Mercator* and *stereographic* projections are commonly used in polar regions, with *gnomonic* and *azimuthal equidistant* finding some use there.

(b) Information Given on Charts. Standard symbols are used to depict navigational information. All charts show meridians, parallels, latitude and longitude scales, natural landmarks, man-made prominent structures, aids to navigation, magnetic variation, and hazards. Aeronautical charts show heights, airways control zones, airports, etc., and nautical charts show both depths and heights of water, chart datums, nature of the bottom, etc.

(c) Use of Charts. Charts are used both for information and for plotting of courses, dead reckoning positions, lines of position, and fixes. In deep water or away from hazards, *plotting sheets* may be used for plotting. These are blank charts showing only the graticule of meridians and parallels, usually with one or more compass roses for measurement of true directions. Printed labels are generally not shown for meridians, so that the plotting sheets can be used in any longitude.

(d) Publications. Navigational publications include *texts* and *reference books, sight reduction tables, almanacs, sailing directions* or *pilots, light lists, tide and current tables, Flight Information Manuals, Civil Air Regulations,* and various periodical publications giving information on dangers to navigation and changes in aids or regulations.

(e) Sources. Principal United States sources of charts and navigational publications are the U.S. Naval Oceanographic Office, U.S. Coast and Geodetic Survey, USAF Aeronautical Chart and Information Center, Federal Aviation Agency, U.S. Coast Guard, and the U.S. Naval Observatory.

(4) Dead Reckoning

(a) By Computation. Historically, dead reckoning has been performed by computation until modern times, when plotting became the common method. A number of methods or *sailings* have been used widely, and various tables and work forms have developed. *Plane, traverse, parallel, middle-latitude, Mercator, great-circle,* and *composite* are the names given to the sailings. Each has its use even today, both in hand calculation and in electronic computers beginning to make their appearance.

(b) By Hand Plot. Plotting or drafting directly on the chart or plotting sheet has the advantages of providing a graphical representation of the progress of the craft and often of being quicker and easier than a hand computation. It usually does not provide a convenient permanent record and may be impractical where space is limited. In aircraft, the plot is sometimes made in advance. Navigation then consists essentially of noting progress along the intended track and applying corrections from time to time to correct for departures from this line. Various plotting instruments have been developed to assist the navigator.

(c) By Mechanical Device. *Dead reckoning equipment* of various kinds and with various degrees of automation has been developed to perform the dead reckoning task. These may trace out a line on a plotting sheet or chart, or they may indicate present latitude and longitude on dials, or both. They are reset when a better position is established by fixing.

(d) Direction Measurement. Some form of compass is used to establish a reference direction. The magnetic compass used for centuries still finds many uses today, often in combination with other devices such as a gyroscope to keep it horizontal. Certain compass errors are involved. The angle between the magnetic line of force and the geographic meridian at the compass, called *variation,* is shown on the chart. Deflection of the compass card by magnetic effects associated with the craft in which the compass is mounted is called *deviation.*

This can be reduced by the process of *compass adjustment.* Residual values are determined by comparing compass and magnetic directions on various headings. These values are recorded in a *deviation table* or *deviation card* kept near the compass. The algebraic sum of variation and deviation is called *compass error.* A *gyro compass* utilizes one or more north-seeking gyroscopes to maintain the compass card in nearly a true north-south direction. A centrally located compass may be provided with *repeaters* in convenient locations throughout the craft. A directional gyro, used in aircraft, utilizes a free gyro, precessed at earth rotation rate, to maintain flight along a great circle. Other types of compasses are used for special circumstances, as in polar regions, as discussed below. A *pelorus,* or dumb compass (without a direction-seeking element), may be used for measuring bearings of aids to navigation and landmarks.

(e) Distance and Speed Measurement. Distance traveled is measured by some form of *log.* Older models were towed through the water. Modern ones are attached to the hull of the vessel. Speed may be determined by computation, using distance and time, or the log may be calibrated directly in speed. In aircraft, air speed is measured directly by *air-speed meter* or by *Mach meter.* The latter is calibrated in units of the speed of sound. Speed over the ground may be measured directly by Doppler or inertial systems, discussed below under Electronic Navigation.

(f) Height and Depth Measurement. Height of an aircraft is measured by an *altimeter.* A *barometric altimeter* measures atmospheric pressure, which decreases with height. An *absolute altimeter* measures height above the surface by means of radiant energy, usually radio waves, transmitted downward from the aircraft and reflected by the surface. Depth of water is measured aboard ship by means of a *lead* (weight) attached to a line, or more commonly by means of an *echo sounder,* similar to an absolute altimeter but using sonic or ultrasonic signals.

(5) Piloting

(a) Aids to Navigation. Piloting is used widely, natural landmarks serving as features to guide the traveler. This is particularly true on or over land. Such features have been supplemented by various man-made *aids to navigation* in the form of *lighthouses, beacons, buoys, lightships,* and various electronic aids.

(b) Informal Piloting. Piloting may be an informal procedure consisting merely of noting identifiable features as one progresses along a planned track. This is the method commonly used as one travels by automobile in familiar areas. It may also be used in the air, where it is usually called *pilotage.* It is important that this be a continuous process.

In unfamiliar territory, it may be difficult to re-establish position once it is lost. This is particularly true in flying over land with little contrast, such as Ohio farmlands or in high latitudes with numerous lakes of similar appearance. A common and effective form of piloting is known as *homing*. In its most frequently used form, this consists of heading directly toward an object. When it is reached, another object some distance ahead is selected and the process is repeated.

(c) **Fixes.** A *fix* may be established by passing directly over or alongside an identifiable object. A more common procedure is to use *lines of position*. These are lines on some point of which the craft is presumed to be located. They may be established by measuring the bearing of an identifiable object, its distance, or by noting two such objects in line. A horizontal angle between two objects may also be used. The intersection of two nonparallel lines of position establishes the *fix*. If they are obtained at different times, they are adjusted to a common time, resulting in a *running fix*, generally of reduced accuracy because of error in the estimation of the craft's velocity vector in making the adjustment. *Soundings* may also be used to fix the position of a vessel when a well-sounded bottom has distinctive features.

(6) Celestial Navigation

(a) **The Celestial Sphere.** Celestial navigation is concerned with apparent positions of celestial bodies. Such items as actual distance or physical characteristics are of passing interest to the navigator. He utilizes celestial bodies as if they were all on the inner surface of a *celestial sphere* of infinite radius concentric with the earth, and making one rotation per day with respect to the earth. Bodies that appear to move relative to the background of stars are considered to be in motion on the celestial sphere.

(b) **The Navigational Triangle.** On the celestial sphere, the spherical triangle having vertices at the celestial pole nearest the observer, at the zenith of the observer, and at the celestial body observed is known as the *navigational triangle*. Determination of a line of position by celestial navigation usually involves the solution of this triangle for an assumed position, to convert the equatorial coordinates of the body (*declination* and *hour angle*) to coordinates of the horizon systems (*altitude* and *azimuth*), and a comparison of the results with observed values.

(c) **The Celestial Line of Position.** At any given moment of time, any given altitude (elevation angle) of a celestial body defines a circle on the surface of the earth with its center at the *geographical position* of the body (the point on earth having the body in its zenith at that moment) and with radius equal to the *zenith distance* (co-altitude) of the body. Unless the computed and observed altitudes are the same, the *circles of equal altitude*

defined by these quantities have different radii. The *altitude difference*, in minutes of arc, is the normal distance, in nautical miles, from the assumed position to the observed or actual circle of equal altitude. The azimuth, or its reciprocal, indicates the direction of the normal. At the point so determined, a perpendicular to the normal is tangent to the circle of equal altitude. With the large radius usually involved, the tangent is considered to be the circle and constitutes the *celestial line of position*. The intersection of two or more such lines at the same time, or adjusted to the same time, is the *fix*.

(d) **Time.** In any form of navigation, time is involved with respect to motion of the craft. In celestial navigation, it has added significance because of the apparent motion of the celestial sphere. The geographical position moves westward at the rate of one minute of longitude (approximately one nautical mile at the equator) for each four seconds of time. Accurate time is maintained by means of *chronometers* normally kept set to *Greenwich mean time* and checked at intervals by radio time signals. It was the development of the chronometer in the eighteenth century that made practical the finding of longitude at sea. *Zone time* is normally used for indicating position. Other kinds of time have special uses in navigation. *Apparent time* relates to the actual motion of the sun uncorrected for variations of speed due to changes in the orbital speed of the earth. *Sidereal time* is based upon motions of the stars rather than the sun. The navigator customarily expresses time on the basis of a 24-hour day, not using a.m. and p.m. designations.

(e) **The Sextant.** Altitudes of celestial bodies are measured by means of a *sextant*. The mariner normally uses the visible horizon as a reference, and the aviator uses a built-in artificial horizon. Various corrections are applied to the *sextant altitude* to convert it to *observed altitude*. These corrections involve such items as atmospheric *refraction*, *semidiameter* of the sun and moon, *parallax* of a body relatively near the earth, *dip* of the visible horizon when observed from some height above the surface, and *index correction*. Some modification of the usual procedure is needed if the body is near the horizon, near the zenith, observed from the opposite horizon, or observed by a land-type artificial horizon.

(f) **Sight Reduction.** The solution of the navigational triangle usually follows observation, because the time used in the solution is that of observation, which cannot always be predicted with certainty. This may not be true in aircraft where an averaging sextant is usually used and the observation is continued over some period of time, often two minutes. Tables of logarithmic functions conveniently arranged to reduce solution time or tables of precomputed values for various values of latitude, declination, and hour angle are usually used. Where electronic computers are available, they can be programmed to relieve the navigator of this task. In the United States, most *sight reduction tables* are published by the U.S. Naval Oceanographic Office.

(g) Almanacs. Publication containing information on the equatorial coordinates of the celestial bodies commonly used by navigators are called *almanacs*, separate volumes being available for mariners and aviators. The former is geared to 0.1–mile navigation customarily used by mariners, and the latter to the 1-mile precision adequate for aviators. Almanacs also contain other useful information such as sextant altitude corrections and time of sunrise, sunset, twilight, moonrise, and moonset. In the United States, the almanacs are published by the U.S. Naval Observatory.

(h) Identification of Celestial Bodies. Navigators who make frequent use of celestial navigation learn to recognize the celestial bodies they commonly use. Certain aids are available to assist in this and to provide means of identification when bodies are observed during the brighter part of twilight or through breaks in the clouds, when star configurations may not be visible. Plastic devices called *star finders* or *star identifiers* are the most common. Computation can also be used by solving the navigational triangle in reverse. Star charts are helpful in learning to recognize star configurations.

(7) Electronic Navigation

(a) General. While electronics has been applied to navigation since the early days of radio, it has only been in recent years that this use of electricity has received widespread attention. In addition to position determination, electronics has been used for time signals, broadcast of navigational warnings, dissemination of weather and ice information, etc. Electronic computers are beginning to appear to perform various tasks for the navigator.

(b) Direction Finding. An early direct navigational use of electronics was in direction finding. In its most common form, this is accomplished by utilizing the directional properties of a loop antenna, with a vertical *sense antenna* to resolve ambiguities. Certain corrections are needed because of propagation anomalies and the influence of the craft. If the bearing determined by radio is plotted on a Mercator chart, an additional correction may be needed to convert the great circle path of the radio signal to the equivalent rhumb line. In aircraft, the indication of direction is usually automatic.

(c) Directional Transmission. The directional property of certain antenna arrays is used to establish direction from the ground transmitter. A common early example of this was the use of an Adcock antenna to establish directional beams or tracks marking the airways, each antenna array

establishing four such courses separated by approximately 90°. The airspace in the United States is now serviced by a number of omnidirectional ranges designated *VOR* or *VORTAC*, which provide a rotating pattern permitting the aircraft with suitable equipment to either (1) determine the direction of a station or (2) fly a selected course toward or away from the facility. *Consol* and *consolan* stations transmit a rotating pattern of dots and dashes permitting determination of direction by counting the number and relative order of each during a prescribed *keying cycle* and referring to a suitable chart or table. These aids are used by both ships and aircraft, mostly in ocean areas. They are particularly popular among small craft navigators who can utilize them with simple, general-purpose receiving equipment.

(d) Distance Measurement. Radar, either on the ground or aboard the craft, provides a means of measuring both direction and distance. Many of the airspace facilities are equipped with a form of secondary radar known as *distance measuring equipment* (DME). A transponder at the facility returns a signal when triggered by a signal from the aircraft.

(e) Differential Distance Measurement. Several electronic systems have been developed to establish hyperbolic lines of position. Antennas operate in pairs, one serving as *master* controlling the other, a *slave*. By measuring the difference in arrival times of synchronized pulses, or by measuring the phase difference of synchronized continuous wave signals, the navigator can determine the difference in distance from the two stations. Reference to a special chart or table, or use of an electronic computer, establishes a line of position or, if two or more such lines are available, a position. The most widely used systems of this type are *Loran A*, the more accurate cycle-matching *Loran C*, and *Decca*. A special form of the latter to permit aircraft to follow an established route over long distances such as the North Atlantic is now being developed under the name *Dectra*. A VLF system under development by the U.S. Navy is called *Omega*. Special-purpose computers, which are being developed, show promise of adding considerably to the usefulness of hyperbolic systems by providing a readout of latitude, longitude, distance and direction to one or more selected destinations, and of deviation from a selected track. Such a device would make the system suitable for use in the cockpit to provide steering information directly to the pilot.

(f) Dead Reckoning Systems. The Doppler effect is utilized in *Doppler radar* to provide a self-contained navigation system. Electromagnetic energy is transmitted in two to four narrow beams downward at an angle from an aircraft. The difference in frequency of the echo returning from the surface is proportional to speed of the aircraft.

With a good heading reference, the difference in the Doppler effect of the different beams permits determination of direction of motion. Another type of self-contained system utilizes high-grade gyroscopes to provide a stable platform and sensitive accelerometers to measure accelerations in various directions. One integration provides an indication of speed, and a second integration indicates distance traveled. A Doppler system output degrades with distance traveled, and an *inertial system* degraded with time. Because of the short flight times involved in supersonic transport flights, the inertial approach is considered particularly attractive for these aircraft.

(g) **Hybrid Systems.** Doppler and inertial systems tend to complement each other, the former being more accurate over a long time and the latter over a short time. Consequently a combined *Doppler-inertial* system has certain advantages over a system utilizing either principle alone. Inertial or Doppler-inertial systems may be combined with a celestial, hyperbolic, or other system to provide greater accuracy. Another approach is to reset the self-contained system from time to time when its accumulated error exceeds the error of an independent *fix*. Still another approach is to use the other system as a gross error check and possible back-up in case of failure. To be fully effective, a hybrid system needs a computer to provide suitable outputs, particularly if steering information is to be supplied to a pilot directly.

(8) Navigation Satellites

(a) **General.** Navigation satellites provide a new technology offering certain advantages for navigation and related functions. Since they are expensive systems to develop, implement, and maintain, their widespread use will depend upon establishment of economic justification. More than 20 techniques have been suggested. Only a few are being actively pursued.

(b) **Range Rate Technique.** If the Doppler effect of a satellite in a relatively low orbit is observed, and if the position of the satellite is known, probably by transmission of orbital parameters by the satellite itself, an observation of several minutes duration and the use of a computer permit determination of a unique position on the rotating earth.

(c) **Range Technique.** If range alone is measured from two or more satellites at suitable known positions, or from the same satellite at different times, position can be determined with somewhat simpler, less expensive equipment both in the satellite and aboard the craft. If interrogations are controlled from a ground station, and measurements and computations are made there and the results relayed by the satellite to the craft, very simple, inexpensive user equipment is needed and saturation problems are largely overcome. Addi-

tionally, other services become available, such as traffic coordination, obstacle warning, weather routing, automatic position reporting, and fleet surveillance. The user would not need to know the position of the satellite.

(d) **Angle Technique.** A satellite carrying a simple beacon might be used as an artificial celestial body. A suitable radio sextant could be used to measure altitude (elevation angle), and ordinary sight reduction tables could be used for establishing a line of position. The apparent position of the satellite would need to be known. The same radio sextant, if provided with a broad-band mode, could be used with the sun and possibly also with the moon. A highly directional, accurately stabilized antenna would be required by the user.

(e) **Hybrid Systems.** Some combination of techniques might be used to advantage, perhaps to reduce the number of satellites needed. An attractive example is a satellite provided with two orthogonal interferometers to measure two angles. If range were also measured, ground stations being used to control the operation, one satellite would be adequate to establish a position almost instantaneously.

(f) **Synchronous Satellites.** With ground-controlled systems, one or two equatorial synchronous satellites would provide continuous coverage over an area of heavy traffic such as the North Atlantic.

(9) The Practice of Navigation

(a) **General.** The principles of navigation, covered briefly above, are applicable to all types of craft. Requirements, however, differ widely. A good text or reference book should be consulted if one has problems related to his particular type of craft, mission, or geographical area.

(b) **Marine Navigation.** Marine vessels move slowly enough that time needed to obtain a fix is not critical, and relatively long intervals (several hours at sea) between fixes are generally acceptable. High accuracy is usually not a requirement except in special missions such as hydrographic surveying, geophysical exploration, or submarine cable laying or recovery. Tides and currents are important considerations, and fog is a serious handicap. Constant alertness is important, as is keeping well informed of all conditions and changes in aids. Accurate, updated charts are needed. Accurate time is essential if celestial navigation is used. It is important that all navigation equipment be kept in good condition and checked frequently. There is no substitute for judgement based upon experience and constant vigilance. In entering a harbor in reduced visibility, it is possible to anchor if entry would be unsafe.

(c) **Air Navigation.** In contrast with ships, aircraft are characterized by high speed, limited endurance, the inability to stop enroute, the availability of the third dimension, and their greater sensitivity to weather. Because of relatively high speed, the critical nature of time and limited working space, precomputation, advance planning, and greater automation are important. The ideal is to have steering information displayed to the pilot continuously in convenient form.

(d) Land Navigation. Navigation equipment for a land vehicle should be simple, rugged and reliable, and should provide direct display with minimum reliance on plotting. Land navigation may consist almost entirely of dead reckoning or piloting, depending primarily upon the availability of suitable identifiable landmarks and a reliable map, or some combination of the two. Electronic aids are generally not available, and celestial navigation is seldom used. A patrol on foot or a surveying party may have different requirements. If high accuracy is needed, survey methods may be utilized.

(e) Polar Navigation. In high latitudes, special problems are encountered. Suitable chart projections are needed because of the convergence of the meridians. Long periods of continuous daylight, semidarkness, and twilight occur. Mirages are common and excessive refraction is encountered. Aids to navigation are rare, and natural features are sometimes obscured by ice or snow. Lack of reliable surveys results in charts having little detail or questionable accuracy. Radio propagation is uncertain, and attenuation is greater under some conditions. Ice may be a problem at sea, and blowing snow on land. Both the magnetic and north-seeking gyro compasses are unreliable over relatively large areas, requiring the use of a *sun compass*, *sky compass* (using polarized sunlight during twilight), *astro compass*, or *directional gyro*. A horizon is often not available for extended periods. However, a fund of knowledge has resulted in the development of reasonably satisfactory techniques for navigation in polar regions.

(f) Navigation in Emergencies. Navigation is generally practiced under reasonably favorable conditions with adequate equipment. In case it becomes necessary to take to lifeboats or life rafts, or to return to civilization after crash of an aircraft, emergency procedures may be needed. Under such conditions, it is important to start with a reasonably accurate knowledge of present position and of the directions and distances to probable destinations. Sometimes one can salvage servicable items of standard navigation equipment. A knowledge of the fundamental principles of navigation and some ingenuity, with keen observation and alertness, will often permit return to civilization even when prospects seem unpromising. A careful analysis of the situation and good planning can pay high dividends.

(10) Space Navigation

Navigation beyond the earth's atmosphere involves the same basic principles as navigation on earth, but under unique conditions. In space, navigation is truly three-dimensional. Time has additional significance in that both the point of departure and destination are in motion, and time of arrival at a given destination in space is important. Speeds are high and variable, and long periods of weightless free-fall are likely to be encountered, as constant thrust is not needed once a spacecraft is in orbit. "Weather" is not encountered. Neither speed nor direction of motion is measured directly. Changes in speed or direction of motion are limited to small corrections because of the tremendous energy required and the need for conserving fuel. Different techniques are used for the escape, midcourse, and terminal phases. Position may be determined by measuring distance (either by ranging or by noting the apparent diameter of a nearby celestial body) and direction (relative to the celestial sphere) from the nearest body. Farther away, angles between lines of sight to bodies of the solar system and stars provide cones of position. The position of a nearby body relative to the background of stars establishes a line of position. The oldest of all forms of navigation—homing— might be used in going to another planet by first proceeding to the radial line connecting the sun and the destination planet and then staying on this moving line as one proceeds toward the destination. Techniques and equipment for this new challenge of space navigation are being developed.

(11) Conclusion

Navigation can be interesting. It is always challenging if done reliably. Science and technology have done much to provide the knowledge and tools for efficient navigation. Man, however, is still the key to safe navigation. Knowledge, skill, adequate equipment, and constant vigilance are the ingredients of successful navigation.

ALTON B. MOODY

References

Anderson, E. W., 1964, "The Principles of Navigation," Cambridge, England, W. Heffer and Sons Ltd., 400pp.

Bowditch, Nathaniel, 1962, "American Practical Navigator," U.S. Navy Hydrographic Office.

Hill, John C., II, Utegaard, Thomas F., and Riordan, Gerard, 1958, "Dutton's Navigation and Piloting," U.S. Naval Institute.

H.O. Pub. No. 216, 1955, "Air Navigation," U.S. Navy Hydrographic Office.

NEARSHORE OCEANOGRAPHY—*See* **OCEANOGRAPHY (NEARSHORE)**

NEKTON, MARINE

The nekton (Greek: *nektos*, "swimming") consists of pelagic animals such as shrimp, cephalopod mollusks and vertebrates (fish, reptiles, mammals) that are able to swim freely and are mainly independent of water and wind currents. The efficient locomotory organs and sense organs of these animals enable them to undertake active and directed movements to pursue prey organisms and to escape from predators. In some cases, they can undertake sustained long-distance migrations for reproductive or nutritional purposes. By definition, all plants are excluded from the nekton category.

Although a sharp distinction is not possible, the larger size and the stronger locomotory ability differentiate the nekton from the plankton which consists of small passively drifting organisms or larger organisms such as medusae whose movements are insignificant in comparison with the movements of the water. Many of the nektonic animals, however, have planktonic developmental stages.

The nekton forms important parts of the ecosystems of the seas and fresh water. Included in this group are a few primary consumers (herbivores), but most representatives are secondary and tertiary consumers (carnivores). Although the nekton makes up a relatively small part of the total energy pyramid of the sea and its participation in food webs is dependent, it has important feedback relationships with organisms of lower ecologic levels. Nektonic animals can directly limit populations of planktonic organisms through feeding, and their decomposition and excretory products provide raw materials for autotrophic and heterotrophic producers (Odum, 1959).

Most of the commercially important aquatic animals belong to the nekton and most of the available information relates to these. There has probably been a misinterpretation of the abundance and importance of nektonic animals due to the inadequacy of tow nets in the capture of these rapidly swimming organisms.

(1) *Composition*. Adult representatives of only three phyla, Chordata, Molluska, and Arthropoda, have become completely independent of current. Nektonic chordates include Chrondrichthyes or cartilaginous fish such as sharks and chimaeras, a vast array of Osteichthyes or bony fish, a few reptiles such as marine turtles, snakes, and crocodiles, and mammals such as seals, manatees, porpoises, and whales. Mollusks are represented by squids and a few octopods. Arthropods include only decapods such as carid shrimp, penaeid shrimp, and portunid crabs.

Of these animals, only a few viviparous sharks, porpoises, and whales are holonektonic or capable of independent navigation throughout their lives. The others are meronektonic and either possess planktonic young or benthic young or are bound themselves to a benthic or terrestrial environment during parts of their lives.

Some animals such as skates, nautiloids, cuttlefish, and some benthic and reef-inhabiting teleost fish are sometimes included in the nekton because they are capable of active swimming. These, however, are usually closely associated with benthic regions and are referred to as demersal species.

(2) *Food Relationships*. All of the nektonic animals would be classified as consumers, but an exact classification of consumer type is difficult because many of the animals show changes in diet with age or season or are constantly omnivorous.

Herbivores are sparsely represented by a few phytoplankton feeders such as menhaden and by plant grazers such as manatees. Secondary consumers are most abundant. Examples of zooplankton feeders are herring, mackerel, sprat, pilchard and some of the largest pelagic animals such as the basking and whale sharks, the manta rays, and the baleen whales. Some fish are nondiscriminating in their feeding, and the plankton sample is limited only by the size of the pores between the gill rakers. Many of the secondary consumers, however, exhibit a selection of particular plankton prey. Positive correlations between heavy concentrations of species of the copepod, *Calanus*, and abundant catches or sightings of herring, mackerel, and whale sharks and between krill (*Euphausia*) and blue and fin whales are common (Hardy, 1956). Heavy patches of phytoplankton are usually exclusive of concentrations of these zooplankton feeders.

The complicated food web of the sea is completed by nektonic scavengers such as crabs, shrimp, and some fish and by predators such as the following: tuna, bonito, many sharks and most bathypelagic and abyssopelagic fish which feed on other fish; squid and octopus which feed on fish, crustaceans, and other cephalopods; seals, sperm whales, and porpoises whose major food consists of crustaceans, squid, octopus, and fish; and killer whales that are universal carnivores. Demersal species feed mainly on benthic animals.

(3) *Distribution*. The nekton is limited by barriers of temperature, salinity, and nutrients, although these barriers are not as apparent, and have not been as completely investigated, as in the case of the benthos and the plankton (Odum, 1959). Some of the nektonic animals show a strict vertical and horizontal stratification, but many can range over considerable areas of the sea and can inhabit different pelagic provinces at various times during their lives.

Most observations show a higher rate of plankton production in high latitudes than in tropical regions, and a higher yield of nekton is correlated with this. The nekton, like the plankton, is also more abundant in neritic regions or other zones of upwelling or divergence than in open oceanic areas as a whole. Many of the mobile neritic species, however, range at times into the epipelagic oceanic zone. Recruitment of diurnal or seasonal migrants from the mesopelagic and bathypelagic zones also adds to the fauna of the epipelagic zone. Some of the adaptations of the nekton for life in coastal waters or the epipelagic zone are streamlining for more effective swimming, schooling for protection or facilitation of spawning, transparency or counter-shading and development of echo perception for location of prey.

As in the case of the benthos, the number of species and the quantity of pelagic organisms appear to be inversely proportional to depth. All organisms living in the zones below the epipelagic zone are ultimately dependent on production in the waters above. The relatively few nektonic animals of the ocean depths have remarkable adaptations for life there. Some of the adaptations reported are the following: development of black or dark-brown coloration in fish or totally red coloration in crustaceans; progressive decrease in the size of eyes with depth except in those animals that undergo diurnal or ontogenetic migrations to surface waters; formation of various angling or sensory devices such as various barbels in fish or accentuated antennae in crustaceans; development of a great variety of luminous organs particularly in the nekton of the mesopelagic zone; parasitism of males on females as in angler fish; increase in size of mouth and increased flexibility of the anterior vertebral column in many fish; development of circulatory and respiratory modifications to prevent caisson disease in vertebrate animals that show diurnal or seasonal vertical migrations or deep dives (Hardy, 1956; Bruun, in Hedgpeth, 1957).

Mass horizontal migrations for reproduction are common, but the stimuli for these migrations have not been completely ascertained. It is possible that these migrants have an internal chronometer governed by gonadal or endocrine changes. The best-studied migrations are those of the blue whale and the harp and hooded seals which move from polar seas to lower latitudes for annual breeding, the Alaska fur seal which moves south to California in the winter and returns to Bering Sea locations in the spring to breed, the catadromous American and European eels which migrate from fresh water to the Sargasso Sea to spawn, and the young elvers return to their respective continents, and the anadromous salmon which return to their natal streams to breed. It seems possible, in some cases, that the migrants may utilize a sun or starlight compass in their navigation. In the case of salmon, it has been suggested that there has been a definite olfactory conditioning by chemical characteristics of the natal stream (Brown, 1957).

(4) *Geological Significance.* The nekton contributes directly to the sediments but never to the extent that the plankton does. Total skeletal remains are relatively rare in Recent marine sediments because bones serve as food for various scavengers. On the other hand, fish scales are remarkably resistant and are very common in some

formations. Resistant structures such as teeth of sharks and fish and earbones of whales are sometimes found, notably in abyssal areas where the general sedimentation rate is low. In places where catastrophic killing occurs, accumulations of these structures may be found and they may serve as loci for deposition of manganese and iron oxides. Phosphorites are also found in regions of accumulations of vertebrate remains ("bone beds" of stratigraphy), but whether the phosphorites in general originate in masses of decaying fish or in masses of decaying plankton is an unsolved problem (Brongersma—Sanders in Hedgpeth, 1957).

The nekton is more important as an indirect contributor to sediments through decomposition and fecal materials. Benthic browsers may modify the texture of the sediments and contribute to the erosion of reefs by tearing out algae.

A study of the ecology of the nekton may lead to better interpretations of paleoecology. Morphological gradients associated with environmental gradients, as for example meristic characteristics of fish, combined with data on reproduction and migratory patterns may be of great value in evaluation of previous environmental conditions.

P. L. DUDLEY

References

*Brown, M. E., (editor), 1957, "The Physiology of Fishes," Vol. 2, "Behavior," New York, Academic Press, 526pp.

*Hardy, A. C., 1956, "The Open Sea," London, Collins, 335pp.

*Hedgpeth, J. W., (editor), 1957, "Treatise on marine ecology and paleoecology," Vol. I, "Ecology," *Geol. Soc. Am. Mem.* 67, 1,296pp.

*Odum, E. P., 1959, "Fundamentals of Ecology," Philadelphia, W. B. Saunders Co., 546pp.

NERITIC ZONE (AND SEDIMENTATION FACIES)

Neritic zone is a term used mainly by sedimentologists and stratigraphers to cover the shallow sea environment from mean low water down to 200 m (100 fathoms). Its name comes from the sea nymphs, the *Nereids* (daughters of Nereus, a sea god of Greek mythology), so-designated by the ecologist Haeckel (1890) and taken up for geologists by E. Haug (1907). It corresponds broadly to the term "shelf facies." Oceanographers and ecologists now prefer the term "littoral" for this zone (Hedgpeth, 1957), but the geologists usually apply "littoral" to both nearshore and intertidal belt.

Hedgpeth feels that "neritic" as originally defined applies to the whole shelf water mass, and "sublittoral" to the bottom environment. However, this is not very satisfactory. For some (e.g., Twenhofel, 1950) the term "littoral" is reserved strictly for the intertidal zone, but for others it is used in a loose way for the intertidal and nearshore belt (Grabau, Neaverson, and others). Most geologists prefer this last method.

Standard subdivisions occasionally used are: (a) Epineritic (0–40 m), (b) Infraneritic (40–200 m).

The water body of the neritic zone is sometimes called the *neritic realm* and is generally described as *euphotic* because in mid- and low latitudes it is penetrated by a certain amount of sunlight and is therefore the site of photosynthesis, both in planktonic and benthonic organisms. This feature distinguishes the neritic zone (rather than a fixed bathymetric figure) from the bathyal zone.

During much of Mesozoic and Paleozoic times, the neritic seas of the world were far more extensive than today (see *Expanding Earth Theory*, Vol. V, by Egyed). They have been called "*epeiric seas*" or "*epicontinental seas*" to emphasize that they are truly neritic, and not to be confused with intracontinental depressions like the Mediterranean. As such, they are marked by a considerable number of sedimentary indicators, structures and sediments pointing to wave turbulence, tidal currents, bottom crawlers and feeders, aeration, etc. (Fig. 1).

The present-day physical distribution of terrigenous sediment over the neritic zone is largely limited to wave base (q.v.), and in deeper water (infraneritic zone) sediments are pelagic or inherited from former shallow water stages (e.g., during the late Pleistocene glacio-eustatic low sea level stage).

As Twenhofel pointed out (1950, p. 127), neritic marine environments may also have been locally subjected to considerable invasions of fresh water from rivers (as today near the mouth of the Mississippi), thus modifying the local marine biota or destroying their shells (through acid reactions).

The volume of sediments in contemporary neritic basins in the world today is about 1.6×10^8 km^3 or 40 million cubic miles. The gross sediment type ratio among them is about $1:1.3:5$ for limestone: sandstone: clay (Kuenen, 1946). Fairbridge (1959) has calculated the total volume of neritic sediments in post-Proterozoic geological basins (outside of the folded belts) as 2.8×10^8 km^3 or 70 million cubic miles.

Neritic Sedimentation Types

Tercier (1940) has critically discussed the expression "neritic sedimentation" (coined by Haug), indicating that such essentially shallow, terrigenous facies are found today in many different environments, in fact that they are almost *ubiquitous*, not only on shelves, but on slopes, and even in some deep basins. He established a fundamental maxim: *Neritic sedimentation is largely dependent on the width of the shelf and on the morphology and climate of the land.* There are three main types of this neritic sedimentation:

(1) *Neritic sedimentation of paralic platforms:* For example, Sunda Shelf (Indonesia), Gulf Coast

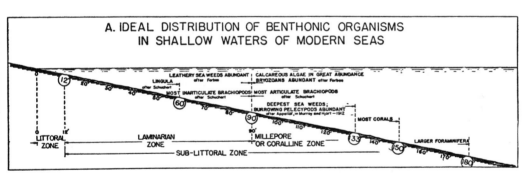

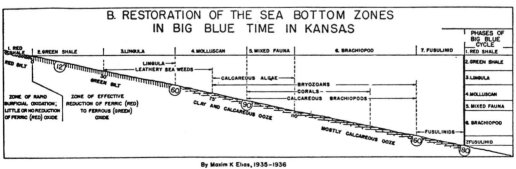

Fig. 1. Sea-bottom zones in modern and in Big Blue (Permian) seas.
(A) Ideal distribution of benthonic organisms in shallow waters of modern seas.
(B) Restoration of the sea bottom zones in Big Blue time in Kansas (Elias, 1937).

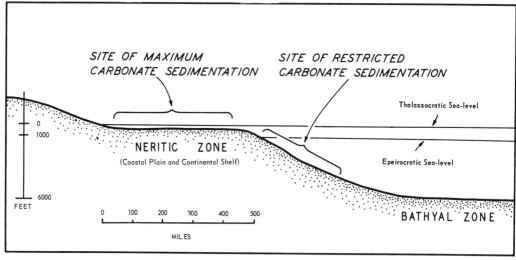

Fig. 2. Favored site for carbonate sedimentation.

(Louisiana, Texas), other great deltas (Orinoco, Amazon, Rhine, Huangho, Ganges), marked by very thick terrigenous deposits, intimately connected with estuarine and continental deposits, often accompanied by lignite or coal.

(2) *Neritic sedimentation of epicontinental platforms:* For example, Sahul Shelf (northern Australia), Yucatan, Florida, Bahama shelves, marked by calcareous sediments (locally with reefs and glauconites); very reduced terrigenous component.

The neritic setting (in mid- to low-latitudes) is particularly favorable for warming of water, biological activity and carbonate sedimentation, and since it is not infrequently superimposed on former lagoonal evaporites, it is favorably situated for eventual dolomitization by the saline flux method. In times of high sea level in the past (*thalassocratic periods*), e.g., the Ordovician or Upper Cretaceous, carbonate neritic facies were very widespread. On the other hand, in times of low sea level, such as generally followed major orogenies (*epeirocratic periods*), the continental slope was a much less favorable carbonate setting, since it dropped away rapidly into cool, dark water. Such epeirocratic conditions also favored accelerated continental erosion and the delta heads were shifted to shelf margin positions (Fig. 2). Over the course of time, sea-level oscillations, eustatic and geodetic, cause the neritic zone to seesaw across the continental shelf and coastal plain, and back again.

(3) *Neritic sedimentation of marginal platforms:* For example, insular shelves of West Indies, East Indies, Pacific coasts of North and South America, coasts of New Zealand and Japan, parts of the Mediterranean; marked by narrow shelves (backed by mountainous hinterlands) and containing an irregular mixture of facies from types 1 and 2 but dominated by coarser debris and often interfingering

sharply with the deep facies of the continental slope. However, Tercier contended that bathyal deposits are usually not so thick as thought of by Haug; neritic deposits are much thicker, because most terrigenous material is primarily deposited on the shelves.

Tercier said that, in order to reconstruct a paleogeographic environment, one requires a wide range of criteria: purely lithologic data are inadequate. One cannot, for example, say "subgraywacke lithology, therefore molasse facies, therefore paralic shelf environment." One needs data referring to the climate (lithology, paleontology), to the topography of the adjacent land (lithology, tectonics), to the dimensions and mobility of the shelf (regional geology, tectonics).

What is meant by "paralic sedimentation"? It occupies the heavily alluviated shelves, the great deltas, and is backed by broad, well-drained, but low continental land masses. This is a monotonous, uniform lithology, mostly clays, silts, and sands (orthoquartzite to subgraywacke), generally rather thick, mixed marine, estuarine, and continental; calcareous sediments usually subordinate. Petroleum accumulation is most common in paralic basins. Tercier gave as type examples the Upper Tertiary of Borneo and Sumatra, the Mississippian-Pennsylvanian of the Appalachians and western Europe, the Tertiary of the Gulf Coast, etc.

To understand the implications of "paralic," one should look to the other neritic sedimentation types envisaged by Tercier. *Epicontinental* is typified by the stable shelves of today, such as the Gulf of Carpentaria and other shelves north of Australia, the Sunda Shelf of southeast Asia, parts of Brazil and so on. In no case is there a young mountainous hinterland. According to climate and topography, they are dominated by slow accumulations of organogenic (calcareous) clastics or quartzose and other residual terrigenous sands to clays. Thus we have in the past the classical Jurassic–Cretaceous–Tertiary basins of western Europe and the calcareous and partly cyclic accumulations of the American mid-continent basins of Paleozoic age.

At the other end of the neritic scale comes Tercier's mountainous (or insular) *marginal shelves* with "geosynclinal" sedimentation. Clearly, this category includes mainly the orthogeosynclinal classes (of Stille, 1936; Kay, 1951). Great variability is the dominant characteristic of this sedimentation type, the shallows dropping away steeply to abyssal depths, as reflected in the lithology, with many coarse members reflecting a "short-run" treatment, dumped from mountain slopes into a rapidly deepening sea. However, in places there are bays, gulfs, and sections of broader shelf on these coasts today, permitting local transitions to the epicontinental or paralic types. Lithologically, we have two characteristic associations: *flysch* and the *prealpine* facies, which locally interfinger. The latter tends toward the epicontinental in character, often with much limestone, but it is generally thicker, and the terrigenous members are often coarser, while it passes more rapidly into bathyal or abyssal facies.

RHODES W. FAIRBRIDGE

References

Elias, M. K., 1937, "Depth of deposition of the Big Blue (late Paleozoic) sediments in Kansas," *Bull. Geol. Soc. Am.*, **48**, 403–432.

Fairbridge, R. W., 1959, "Statistics of non-folded basins," *Publ. Bur. Cent. Seism. Int., Ser. A*, No. 20 (Toronto Meeting), 419–440.

Haeckel, E., 1890, "Plankton-Studien," Jena (translated as "Planktonic studies," *Rept. U.S. Fish Comm.* No. 17, 1889–91, 565–641).

Haug, E., 1907, "Traité de géologie," Paris, A. Colin, 2 vols.

Hedgpeth, J. W., 1957, "Classification of marine environments," in "Treatise on marine ecology," *Geol. Soc. Am., Mem.* 67, **2**, 93–100; see also **1**, 17–27.

Kuenen, P. H., 1946, "Rate and mass of deep-sea sedimentation," *Am. J. Sci.*, **244**, 563–572.

Tercier, J., 1940, "Dépôts marins actuels et séries géologiques," *Eclog. Geol. Helv.*, **32**, 47–100.

Twenhofel, W. H., 1950, "Principles of Sedimentation," Second ed., New York, McGraw-Hill Book Co., 673pp.

Cross-references: *Littoral Zone; Marine Ecology.*

NEWTONIAN FLUID—*See* FLUID MECHANICS

NORTH SEA

The North Sea is the epicontinental sea that occupies the shelf area between the British Isles and Norway, Denmark, Germany, Holland and Belgium of continental Europe. Following the definitions of the International Hydrographic Bureau (*Sp. Publ.* 23, 1953), the southwestern boundary in the Straits of Dover runs from Leathercote Point, England (51° 10′N) to Walde Lighthouse in France (1° 55′S). In the northwest, its border is drawn from Dunnet Head in Scotland (3° 22′W) to the Orkney Islands and Shetland Islands, thence up meridian 0° 53′W to 61° 00′N, and follows this meridian east to the coast of Norway south of Sogne-Fjord. In the east, it borders against the Skagerrak, defined by a line joining Hantsholm, Denmark (57° 07′N, 8° 36′E) and the Naze (Lindesnes, Norway at 58° 7′E).

Bathymetry

According to Kossinna's statistics (slightly different boundaries from the above), the area is 575,000 km² (222,000 square miles), and assuming an average depth of 94 m (51.4 fathoms), the volume is 54,000 km³. The slope of the bottom is rather steadily down from south to north, except in the middle where the *Dogger Bank* extends east to west in a barrier that shallows to 13 m, causing turbid water and waves to break in heavy weather. South of the Dogger Bank is a broad area of irregular depths (former glacial moraine and outwash area), which includes a north–south channel (apparently a glacial spillway or scour) of 82 m (45 fathoms) known as the *Silver Pit* that leads into the Lynn Deeps and the Wash. A similar north–south slot farther east is called the *Sole Pit*. The southwestern part of the North Sea is involved in very strong tidal currents, that result in moving sandbanks and "subaqueous sand dunes" (q.v.), mainly oriented with the currents, northeast–southwest, e.g., the notorious Godwin Sands, off the coast of Kent, scene of many shipwrecks. In the extreme north is another shallow area known as the *Viking Bank*. The only important offshore island is *Heligoland*, an island fragment of the continental basement situated in the German or Heligoland Bight ("Deutsche Bucht").

A peculiar feature of the shelf is a deep channel, the *Norwegian Channel*, which encircles the southern coasts of that country from the Skagerrak to join the Norwegian Basin, with depths ranging from 250–600 m. According to some observers, it is a deep glacial scour channel (Shepard), but others (O. and H. Holtedahl) consider it to be tectonic, a rift extending from the Oslo Graben into the Scandinavian boundary fractures that are believed to separate Norway from the Norwegian Basin. Smaller clefts and rifts on the Norwegian shelf (and elsewhere) are regarded as fractures generated particularly by the repeated loading and unloading of Scandinavia by glacial ice during the Quaternary. The orientation of the clefts and channels, largely parallel to the coasts, rather than normal (like the principal glaciers), leads many observers to prefer Holtedahl's theory, although it is true that such rifts were

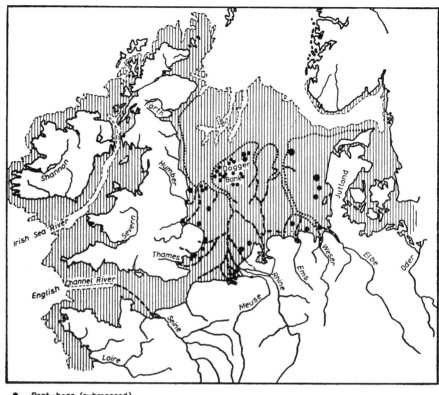

● Peat—bogs (submerged)

||||||| Areas exposed during the Wurm, today less than 160 feet deep (••••)

⌒⌒ Submerged river courses

Fig. 1. The Continental Shelf and its "river system" in the North Sea and English Channel (Termier and Termier, 1963). Old peat deposits (radiocarbon-dated to the Early Holocene) dot the area "drowned" by the Flandrian transgression.

certainly subject to secondary scouring by glacial ice.

Over the floor of the shelf there may be traced the pattern of the late-glacial rivers which were finally drowned during the rise of sea level during the last 10,000 years. Swampy areas developed peat deposits, traces of which are still found (Fig. 1). The Dogger Bank is a remnant of the last glacial moraine belt that extended from eastern England to North Germany.

Climatology

The monthly mean surface air temperature over the North Sea is minimum in February and maximum in August, having ranges of 44–58°F (6.5–14.5°C) and 41–58°F (5–14.5°C) respectively, in the north and south section. The sea is located in the southeastern section of the Iceland Low. The eastern part is a region of strong cyclogenesis except in summer. Storms often pass across the sea from west to east, with maximum frequencies in winter. The surface wind is westerly all year round, and its average Beaufort force is about 5 in winter and 3.5 in summer. Maps of pressure, temperature, fog, gales, etc., are given by Lumb (1965).

Oceanography

The monthly mean surface water temperature increases northwestward from 2°C off the Danish coast to 7.5°C in the north in February (minimum), and decreases, respectively, from 18 to 13°C in August (maximum). The monthly mean bottom temperature has a range of 3–7°C increasing northwestward in March (minimum), 16–17°C off the continental European coast in August, and 7–8°C in September to October in the central part (maximum). The annual ranges of the surface water temperature are 15.5°C off the Danish coast and 6°C in the north, and those of bottom temperature are $1.5 \sim 2$°C in the central and northern sections and 16°C along the Danish coast. The strong thermocline with temperature gradient more than 0.2°C/m appears in June southeast and south of Norway. Most of the north and central sections have the thermocline with maximum gradient of 0.7°C/m at the depth of 30–40 m in July and August.

Also, off the German shore to the Skagerrak, a second upper thermocline develops at 2.5–10 m depth. In October, the thermocline disappears except in a small portion of the central area.

The surface salinity in the central part has a range of 34.8–35.1‰, and the bottom salinity is 35.0–35.1‰. Salinity increases to the coast of Britain and to the north. The halocline is most conspicuous off the Norwegian coast and shows a vertical gradient of 0.5‰ per meter at a depth of 20–30 m.

Salinity along the German shore shows a large range from 29‰ in the summer to 32‰ in the winter. In the northern section where the North Atlantic water mass enters the North Sea, salinity of the surface and bottom water reaches more than 35.25‰ in summer.

The density distribution of the surface water in winter is from 1.02600 along the Danish coast to 1.02770 in the northern part. The surface density in summer is 1.02100–1.02650 with the same trend as in winter. The density distribution of the bottom

water in winter is almost the same as at the surface, indicating small vertical stability. The distribution in summer shows a strong picnocline at the depth of 20–30 m in the northwestern section.

The water color changes from light green along the German coast to light blue in the northern part (8–12 on the Forel scale). Transparency in the central and northern part is 15–17 m at the maximum, and a minimum of 7–8 m was observed during the winter. The data near Heligoland show the annual range of transparency of 2–5 m in winter to 7.7 m in summer.

Oxygen saturation shows maximum values of 95–116% at the surface and 83–102% at the bottom in the northern part. In some parts of the Heligoland or German Bight (Deutsche Bucht) the oxygen saturation has a minimum of 53%.

The circulation due to predominant winds and density distributions is counterclockwise in the upper layer but irregular at the bottom. The current velocity of this circulation varies locally and seasonally. The speed near the area of Shetland

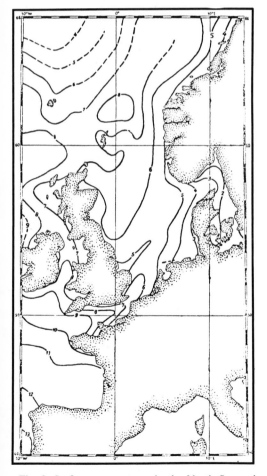

Fig. 2. Surface temperatures in the North Sea and vicinity in winter (February) in degrees C (Bruns, 1958).

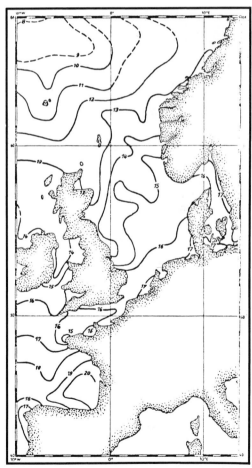

Fig. 3. Surface temperatures in the North Sea and vicinity in summer (August) in degrees C (Bruns, 1958).

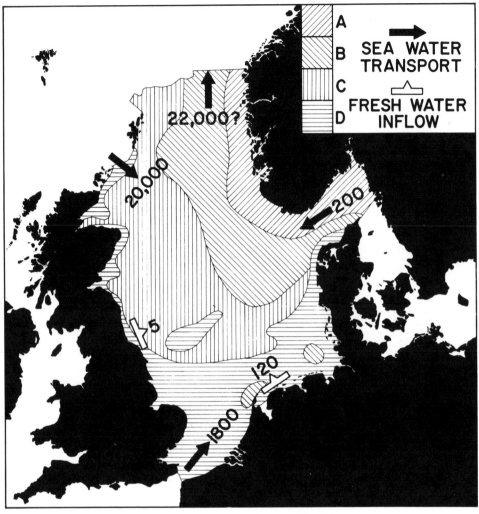

Fig. 4. Hydrographical regions of the North Sea (modified from Laevastu, 1963).

Islands changes from 0.5–0.7 knot in spring and summer to 0.25–0.35 knot in fall and winter. The speed in the central part changes 0.1–0.2 knot in summer to 0.35 knot in winter.

The North Sea can be divided in four hydrographical regions (Fig. 4) according to temperature and salinity stratification (Dietrich, 1957). Along the Norwegian coast (Region A in Fig. 4) haline stratification is present the whole year and annual salinity changes are pronounced in the upper layers. Farther out and parallel to this belt is a region (Region B) where haline stratification is still present but the annual salinity changes are irregular and less pronounced in the upper layer than in Region A. The central part (Region C) is homohaline the whole year but thermally stratified seasonally. The southern part (Region D) is homohaline and homothermal the whole year. This Figure also shows volume transport of seawater through four passages

and freshwater inflow in cubic kilometers per year. These transport values show that 90% of the inflow to the North Sea enters between the Shetland and Orkney Islands.

Wave Action

Wave observations in the North Sea have been sporadic except for systematic observations at certain lightships (Bruns, 1958, p. 218). Measurements from lightship "S2" (at 54°N, 3.5°E) on the Dogger Bank show with wind force 10, a wavelength of 82 m, and an average wave height of 3.6 m, reaching a maximum of 4.5 m. From lightship *Amrumbank* (54° 30′N, 8°E), a Beaufort wind force 7 produced 3.8-m average wave height. From lightship *Elbe I*, with winds of 23.2 m/sec (force 10), were recorded waves of period 9.8 seconds, height 4.5 m and length 120 m. On the east coast of Scotland, waves were measured with a height of 8 m and wavelength of

150 m, while maximum swell up to 10.7 m were recorded with length of 150–215 m and period 13–17 seconds.

Waves were studied by stereophotogrammetry from Heligoland; with water depths of 18 m and winds of 18–20 m/sec (Beaufort force 8–9), the wave height was 6.0 m and wavelength 157 m, producing wave heights at the cliff foot of 8–9 m. The effect of 6–7 m waves, superimposed on the storm surge of 2.6 m, coinciding with a spring tide of over 2 m in the storm of January 31, 1953, caused over 400 dike breaks in Holland, the worst Dutch dike disaster in modern history (Dietrich, 1957–63).

Tides

The tides in the North Sea are predominantly semidiurnal and ratios of diurnal to semidiurnal tides along the coast are from 0.1–0.2 except near the English Channel and Orkney Islands where they reach 0.3. The principal tide waves enter the North Sea through the northern end. A small part of the wave train passes through the Kattegrat into the Baltic. Most waves move southward, are reflected by the southern coast, and encounter a minor tidal component entering through the Straits of Dover. The cotidal lines rotate counterclockwise around two amphidromic points, at 55.8°N and 5.3°E east of Dogger Bank, and at 52.7°N and 3°E north of the Dover. The mean intervals between upper lunar transit on the Greenwich meridian and high water are 9–10 hours in the northern end, 0–3 hours in the central part and 6–7 hours between the two amphidromic points. The average spring tide ranges are 3–4.5 m along the Scotland coast, 4–7 m along the east coast of England and at the Straits of Dover, 2–3 m along the German Bight and 0–1.5 m in most

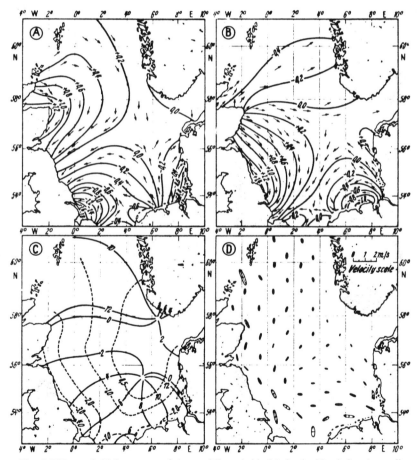

Fig. 5. Tides and tidal currents of the semidiurnal tide M_2 in the North Sea (according to W. Hansen, 1948; from Dietrich, 1963). (A) and (B) lines of equal water level (in meters); in particular, (A) at the time of the moon's passage through the Greenwich meridian, and (B) 3 hours 6 minutes later. Arrows: Tangents to the lines of equal water level derived from tidal current observations; (C) lines of equal tidal range (— — —) in meters and lines of equal time of arrival of high water (———) in hours, referred to the moon's passage through the Greenwich meridian; (D) tidal current ellipse indicating direction and length of major and minor axes.

of the open sea, in the Skagerrak and along the Norwegian coast. Tidal currents in the open sea reach 2–3 knots in general. They have higher values in some areas near the straits. For example, the speed reaches 3 knots off the Thames and 5 knots near Cuxhaven and elsewhere in the German Bight and in the Straits of Dover.

The sea level of the North Sea is very much influenced by meteorological disturbances. In recent years, two intense cyclonic disturbances, of January 8, 1949 and January 31, 1953, caused extreme storm surges. In the latter storm, the sea-level rise above the normal tide reached 2–2.6 m on the coast of Holland, 0.8–2.4 m along the coast of the German Bight, and 1.4–2.7 m on the east coast of England. Statistics show that an east–west wind is about ten times more effective than a north–south wind in producing a sea-level anomaly in the North Sea. Westerly and northerly winds produced a depression of the sea level on the English coast and a rise on the continental shore in the southeastern part of the Sea.

Ice Conditions

The western part of the North Sea is rarely frozen owing to the effect of warm and saline water of the North Atlantic Current. In the eastern and southern coasts (Denmark–Germany–Holland), the sea ice becomes general even in a mild winter due to the fresh water from rivers and from the Baltic Sea. The most extensive ice coverage occurs in February. The average ice coverage days in severe winters are about 60 days along the German coast, reaching 90–130 days at several places and about 50 days on the Danish coast. In April, the whole area becomes ice free.

Sediments and Coasts

Bottom deposits of the North Sea consist predominantly of former glacial outwash sands and gravels, some of which are reworked in postglacial drowned beaches and, in the shallows of the south and southwest, are currently subject to strong wave and current action, leading to "subaqueous sand dunes" (q.v.) and unstable sandbanks, as mentioned above. During the late glacial period and postglacial rise of sea level, temporary eustatic stillstands or withdrawals permitted coastal peat swamps to develop. These are encountered today in many places from the Dogger Bank to the Dutch coast (see Fig. 1). Former river channels can also be traced. During the early deglacial stage a meltwater channel from north Germany entered the southern North Sea and passed out through the English Channel, to join the "Channel River."

Along the southern and southeastern North Sea shores ("windward coasts"), the glacial sands have been built up into compound barrier islands and successive dune ridges, that form the protective coastal barriers of the polders of Holland and north-

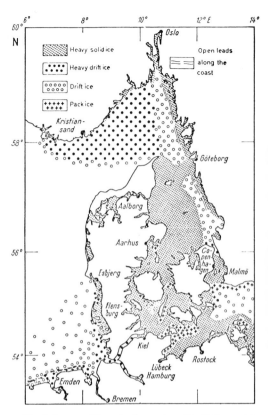

Fig. 6. Ice conditions in the eastern North Sea and in the passages to the Baltic Sea on February 22, 1947. This represents the heaviest ice conditions in the time period 1896–1955 (according to General Ice Chart of the German Hydrographic Office; from Dietrich, 1963).

west Belgium and, in a more interrupted way, the barrier islands that partially defend the mud flats of the Dutch Waddenzee, the north German Wattensee and the North Friesian "wats" that extend into western Denmark; e.g., such islands as Tessel (Texel), Vlieland, Terschelling, Ameland in Holland; Borkum, Juist, Nordeney, Langeroog and Wangeroog in northwestern Germany; Nordstrand, Pellworm, Föhr and Sylt in the German North Friesian Islands; and Rømø in Denmark. Many of these have been the sites of fundamental geological studies on the nature of shallow water and littoral sedimentation, notably by Dutch geologists from Groningen and German workers at the "Senckenberg-am-Meer" marine station (see *Wadden Sea,* pr Vol. VI).

Gravel bottom is found off the Dutch coast where the north-northeast trend swings to east-northeast, a region of maximal bottom dynamics. Scattered patches of "hardground" with gravel or glacial boulders are found also off the west coast of Denmark and off the northeast coast of England and Scotland.

Mud bottom is found in mid-depths in the southeast part of the North Sea in the "Heligoland-Grund" and "Austerngrund" (Oyster Beds), west of the west-Danish gravel bottom, as well as ex-tensively in the deeper waters north of the Dogger Bank and in the very deep Norwegian Channel (Fig. 7). Mud bottom is also recorded in many of

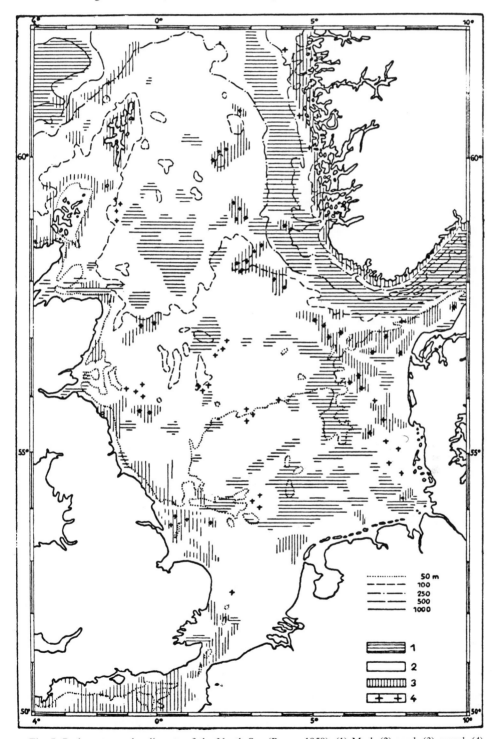

Fig. 7. Bathymetry and sediments of the North Sea (Bruns, 1958). (1) Mud, (2) sand, (3) gravel, (4) hardground (rock or boulders).

the little closed basins of the former moraine areas and off the east coast of Britain. Mud churned up by wave action along the east coast tends to be carried *into* the broad estuarine river mouths and deposited as mud flats, thus in the Wash (Evans, 1965) and around the mouth of the Thames, likewise in the formerly glaciated, partly fjord-type estuarines of Scotland, the Firth of Forth, the Firth of Tay and Moray Firth, in the south in the Friesian "wats" (wadden).

The east coast of Britain, in contrast to the accumulative character of the "windward" coasts of Denmark, Germany, and Holland, is of "lee character" (of Harmer) and marked by low cliffs for the most part and relatively little accumulation, except in an embayment like the Wash, as noted above. In those areas of soft Quaternary deposits, like the cliffs of East Anglia, the rate of cliff erosion may be fairly high, but elsewhere the resistant, mainly Paleozoic rocks maintain a stable coast.

Geological and tide gauge data suggest that the easternmost coasts of Britain, Holland and Germany are slowly subsiding (0.1–1.0 mm/yr) while Scotland, northern Denmark and Norway are rising coasts, still involved in postglacial isostatic uplift (Valentin, 1952, 1953; Vening Meinesz, 1954).

Structural History of North Sea Basin

The North Sea is strictly an epicontinental sea, underlain by thick continental crust. It fills the northern part of a shallow structural basin which surrounds the Baltic shield, partly on the site of the Lower Paleozoic Mid-European/Baltic geosyncline. It lies entirely within the geotectonic province of Paleo-Europe and abuts the Meso-Europe boundary at the Straits of Dover. The geosynclinal deposits were folded and raised into a mountain chain by the Caledonian orogeny (post-Silurian), but these were eroded away and the inner part of the range was converted to a shallow epicontinental basin during the Hercynian orogeny (post-Carboniferous), which raised a new chain of mountains across the southern end of the basin, from Wales to Bohemia (Fig. 8; Map key 9). The whole basin, as typically developed in the Mesozoic and Tertiary, is peripheral to the Baltic (Fenno-sarmatian) Shield which formerly stretched from the North Atlantic to the Urals, while its outer borders in turn were separated from the Tethys in the south and the evolving North Atlantic by a series of low semipermanent islands (Scottish-Pennine, Anglo-Belgian and Bohemian Islands), being the roots of the old Caledonian and Hercynian mountain chains.

During the late Permian, the North German Basin and the North Sea basin developed as one entity (Fig. 8; Map key 1). The Zechstein Sea which filled this basin was cut off from the Norwegian Ocean to the north by a bar or barrier; the surrounding lands were hot deserts from which alluvial fans were built out. Thus the Zechstein Sea deposited limestone and dolomite at its margins, and a thick and complex series of evaporite salts of sodium and potassium in the deeper areas. These deposits are reflected by extensive salt domes today in North Germany, Denmark and offshore areas. These conditions persisted into the lower Triassic, but in the middle Triassic, the Muschelkalk Sea reached the North Sea from the Tethys during a period of milder climate. The first appearance of the Mid-Netherlands Ridge is shown by the confining of marine Muschelkalk to the North German Basin (Fig. 8; Map key 2); elsewhere the Muschelkalk occurs in a lagoonal facies. Semiarid and emergent conditions returned in the upper Triassic, and salt was deposited in the Keuper Lake; during this period the Mid-Netherlands Ridge was further uplifted (Fig. 8; Map key 3).

In the lower Jurassic, the North Sea reverted to its typical form: there was connection with the Tethys across Lincolnshire, southern England and France. This transgression continued into the middle Jurassic, but a great regression took place in the later middle Jurassic, and the entire western part of the North Sea was covered by the deltas of Norwegian rivers. The upper Jurassic was transgressive again, and coral reefs were formed around the margins of this sea; movement continued on the mid-Netherlands Ridge, and by the end of the Jurassic period, when a total regression occurred, the southern North Sea was effectively divided into two east and west independently subsiding basins.

In the Lower Cretaceous the major openings to the south and east were closed off, the North Sea becoming a gulf of the Boreal Ocean, but they were opened up again in the earlier stages of the Cenomanian (Lower Chalk) transgression, which eventually flooded all of the area shown on the map.

After the major regression, which ended the Mesozoic (during which the connections between the North Sea and Tethys were permanetly closed off), the North German Basin became less and less important as an area of marine sedimentation (Fig. 8; Map key 4); however, it was intermittently flooded (e.g., Paleocene, Oligocene, Middle Miocene (?) for very brief periods. The Baltic Sea of today represents the last remnant of the North German basin of sedimentation. Extensions of the North Sea gradually became limited to a small part of the Paris Basin, to the London Basin, and to the West Netherlands Basin (Rhine Delta area), into which the River Rhine began to flow in the Upper Miocene.

From the Permian to the Eocene, the southern boundary of the North Sea was the northern flank of the Brabant Massif (Fig. 8; Map key 7). However, this old Anglo-Belgian island was flooded by the middle Eocene sea (Map key 4), and the Axis of Artois (Map key 8) became the new southern boundary [the Axis of Artois is the north flank of the Wealden anticline (Cretaceous to Miocene)].

The last connection with the Atlantic was made in the upper Miocene (Map key 5) around the north of the Weald; before the upper Miocene transgression, Denmark had been raised into a barrier, so that the sea extended no farther east than now, whereas during the Oligocene transgression it had extended to the Caspian.

Lower Pleistocene seas flooded small areas north of the Thames in southeast England and accumulated several hundred meters of sediment in the

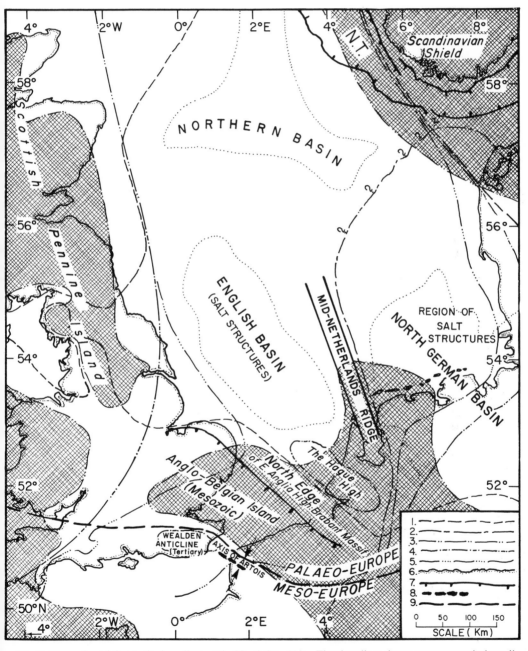

Fig. 8. Mesozoic and Cenozoic shore lines of the North Sea. *Note:* The shorelines shown represent typical conditions, rather than those of maximum transgression or regression (John Berry).

Key: (1) Upper Permian shore line (Zechstein Sea); (2) Middle Triassic shore line (Muschelkalk); (3) Upper Jurassic shore line (Corallian); (4) Middle Eocene shore line (Lutetian); (5) Upper Miocene shore line (Diestian); (6) Present shore line; (7) north edge of Brabant Massif–East Anglian high; (8) Axis of Artois; (9) southern boundary of Palaeo-Europe (northern limit of Hercynian mountain chains).

lower Rhine area, where the rate of subsidence increased during the Pleistocene, so that it now appears that the Rhine Delta is an incipient geosynclinal area. Finally, the Straits of Dover were cut by the glacially dammed waters of the rivers of Northern Europe during either the Mindel or the Riss glacial stage, forming the "Channel River" that was revived again during the Würm. The landbridge from France to England that existed during the Würm was finally cut by eustatic rise of sea level about 11,000 years ago (sill depth at Straits of Dover over 50 m). With the postglacial crustal uplift in Scandinavia and Scotland there has been complimentary downwarp along the southern North Sea, probably amplified by deep-seated geosynclinal trends.

RHODES W. FAIRBRIDGE
TAKASHI ICHIYE
JOHN BERRY

References

Bruns, E., 1958, "Ozeanologie," Vol. I, p. 420, Berlin, VEB Deutscher Verlag der Wissenschaften.

Charnock, H., 1957, "North Sea surges," *Sci. Prog. London,* **45**, 494–511.

Collette, B. J., 1960, "The Gravity Field of the North Sea," Gravity Expeditions, 1948–1958, Vol. 5, Pt. 2, Netherlands Geodetic Comm., Delft.

Defant, A., 1961, "Physical Oceanography," Vol. 2, p. 598, New York, London, Pergamon Press.

Deutsche Seewarte, 1927, "Atlas für Temperatur, Salzgehalt und Dichte der Nordsee und Ostsee," Hamburg.

Dietrich, G., and Kalle, K., 1957, "Allgemeine Meereskunde," Berlin, Gebrüder Borntraeger, 492pp. (English translation, 1963).

Evans, G., 1965, "Intertidal flat sediments and their environments of deposition in the Wash," *Quart. J. Geol. Soc. London,* **121**, 209–245.

Frazer, J. H., 1965, "Zooplankton Indicator Species in the North Sea," Robert Johnston: "The Trace Elements." *Serial Atlas of the Marine Environment,* Folio 8.

Goedecke, E., 1956, "Über das Verhalten des Oberflächensalzgehaltes in der Deutschen Bucht wahrend der Jahre 1873–1944 in Verbindung mit langjahrigen Salzgehaltsreihen der südlichen Nordsee," *Ber. Dtsch. Wiss. Komm. Meeresforsch,* **14**(2), 109–146.

Guilcher, A., 1951, "La Formation de la Mer du Nord, du Pas de Calais, et des plaines maritimes environnants," *Rév. Géogr. Lyon.,* **26**, 311–329.

Hela, I., 1947, "A study of the annual fluctuation of the heights of sea-level in the Baltic and in the North Sea," *Soc. Sci. Fennica, Commentationes Phys.-Math.,* **13**, Pt. 14.

Helland-Hansen, B., 1934, "The Sognefjord Section. Oceanographic Observations in the Northernmost Part of the North Sea and the Southern Part of the Norwegian Sea," in "James Johnstone Memorial Volume," pp. 257–274, Liverpool, University Press.

Holtedahl, H., 1958, "Some remarks on geomorphology of continental shelves off Norway, Labrador, and southeastern Alaska," *J. Geol.,* **66**, 461–471.

Holtedahl, O., 1950, "Supposed marginal fault lines in the shelf area off some high northern lands," *Bull. Geol. Soc. Am.,* **61**, 493–500.

Hull, E., 1897, "Submerged terraces and river valleys bordering the British Isles," *The Amer. Geologist,* **30**, 305–324.

Laevastu, T., 1963, "Surface Water Types of the North Sea and Their Characteristics," in "Serial Atlas of the Marine Environment," Folio 4, American Geographical Society, N.Y.

Lewis, R. G., 1935, "The orography of the North Sea Bed," *Geograph. J.,* **86**, 334–342.

Lumb, F. E., 1965, "Meteorology of the North Sea," in "Serial Atlas of the Marine Environment," Folio 9, American Geographical Society, N.Y.

Shepard, F. P., 1931, "Glacial troughs of the continental shelves," *J. Geol.,* **39**, 345–360.

Thomas, T. M., 1966, "The North Sea and its environs: Future reservoir of fuel?" *Geograph. Rev.,* **56**, No. 1, 12–39.

Tomczak, G., and Goedecke, E., 1962, "Monatskarten der Temperatur der Nordsee, dargestellt für verschiedene Tiefenhorizonte," *Deut. Hydrograph. Z.,* Reihe B (4°), Nr. 7, pp. 16 and 96 charts.

Umbgrove, J. H. F., 1945, "Periodical events in the North Sea Basin," *Geol. Mag.,* **82**, 237–244.

Valentin, H., 1952, "Die Küsten der Erde," *Petermanns Geogr. Mitt., Ergänzungsheft,* No. 246.

Valentin, H., 1953, "Present vertical movements of the British Isles," *Geograph. J.,* **119**, 299–305.

Valentin, H., 1957, "Die Grenzen der Letzten Vereisung im Nordseeraum," *Abh. Deutsch. Geographentags* (Hamburg, 1955), 359–372.

Veenstra, H. J., 1964, "Geology of the Hinder Banks, southern North Sea," *Hydrogr. Newsletter,* **1**, 72–80.

Vening Meinesz, F. A., 1954, "Earth-crust Movement in the Netherlands resulting from Fennoscandian postglacial isostatic readjustment and Alpine foreland rising," *Koninkl. Ned. Akad. Wetenschapp. Proc., Ser. B,* **57**, 142–155.

Wills, L. J., 1951, "A Palaeogeographical Atlas," Glasgow, Blackie.

Cross-references: *Baltic Sea; English Channel; Norwegian Sea.*

NORWEGIAN SEA

The Norwegian Sea is a marginal sea of the North Atlantic. According to the International Hydrographic Bureau (*Sp. Publ.* 23, 1953) it is bounded on the east by the coast of Norway, from North Cape (25° 45′E) to Bear Island and the south point of West Spitsbergen (Svalbard). The western limit extends from here to Jan Mayen Island and thence to Gerpir in Iceland (65° 05′N, 13° 30′W). The southern limit extends from here to the Faeroe Islands (Fugloe, 6° 21′S, 6° 15′W), and thence to the intersection of latitude 61° 00′N at 0° 53′W (just north of the Shetlands), following this parallel to the coast of Norway just south of Sogne-Fjord. In

Fig. 1. Bathymetric chart of Norwegian Sea (Stocks, 1950).

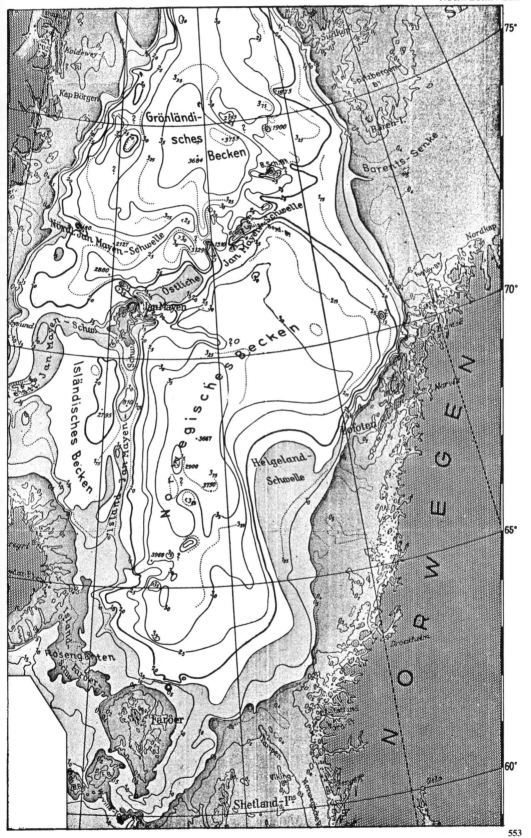

the northeast it passes into the *Barents Sea* (q.v.), in the west into the *Greenland Sea* (q.v.), in the south into the *North Sea* (q.v.), and in the southwest into the main *Atlantic Ocean* (q.v.).

In some earlier works, this sea was grouped with the Greenland Sea as the "*Greenland-Norwegian Sea.*" Kossinna classified both, along with the Arctic Sea and marginal waters in his "Arctic Mediterranean," while Stocks (1950) and others called them collectively the "European North Sea" (*Europäische Nordmeer*), a particularly unfortunate suggestion, since *Nordsee* is distinct from *Nordmeer* in German but not in other languages.

Bathymetry

The hydrographic definition approximates the *Norwegian Basin*, with two long depressions with depths over 3000 m (maximum 3960 m), a larger one to the south and a smaller one to the north. The basin is separated from the main Atlantic depression by the *Wyville Thomson Ridge* which connects Scotland and the Faeroes with the *Iceland-Faeroe Ridge* and the *Iceland Plateau*, a ridge with sill depths of about 500 m, except for a submarine channel between the Faeroes and Scotland, the *Faeroe-Shetland Channel*, over 1100 m deep, but its western end is closed by a shallow sector.

The western limit of the Norwegian Basin is part of the *mid-oceanic ridge* (q.v.) which passes through the Iceland Plateau and Jan Mayen to the north, passing just west of Spitsbergen. This feature is also called Mohns Ridge northeast of Jan Mayen. The sill depths over the ridge are of the order of 1200–1500 m. The northeastern margin is the continental shelf of the Barents Sea that runs from Norway through Bear Island to Spitsbergen. The southern edge of the Norwegian Basin is the northern border of the North Sea shelf, but a narrow tongue of deep water extends around the southern limits of Norway.

Tides

There is an amphidromic point northwest of the Shetlands, and around the margins of the Norwegian Sea the mean spring range of the semidiurnal tide is variable: in the Faeroes 32 cm, Jan Mayen 107 cm, Spitsbergen 138 cm, North Cape 232 cm, Narvik 206 cm, Trondjem 120 cm.

Meteorology

The air mass over the Norwegian Sea is Polar Maritime. In summer the Arctic frontal zone runs from Iceland to the northern part of Norway and storms frequently pass on both sides of this zone. The mean monthly surface air temperature is 15–30°F (−9 to −1°C) in February–March (minimum) and 38–52°F (3–11°C) in August (maximum). Precipitation is quite frequent all year around compared with the land areas and the Greenland Sea (q.v.) of the same latitudes. Precipitation frequency by month is 40–51% in January to March and 10–

15% in July (minimum). The predominant surface wind is north to northeast with average forces of 5–6 (Beaufort scale) in the northern part, but south of the Arctic Front (q.v.) it is south to southwest with average forces of 4–5.

The mean sea level pressure over the area is low in winter owing to development of the Icelandic Low (q.v.) over the Irminger Sea (q.v.) and high in summer owing to intensification of the Arctic High. The mean sea level isobars in January show a trough of less than 1000 millibars in the central part and they increase by 5 and 10 millibars, respectively, to the south of Spitsbergen and off Scotland. In July this central trough increases its pressure by 10 millibars.

Oceanography

The water temperature below a depth of about 100 m is not influenced by surface heating processes and is, in general, above 4°C. In the southern part it is between 8 and 9°C and decreases to about 6°C off northern Norway. Even off Spitsbergen in latitudes of 78–79°N temperatures above 5°C have been observed. Below 600 m, the temperature is about −1°C and almost uniform. Salinity of the Atlantic water entering the Norwegian Sea is 35.4‰ and decreases to the north by mixing with coastal water and water from the central parts of the sea. The salinity is about 35.1‰ off Finmark in Norway and is around 35.0‰ off West Spitsbergen. The salinity below 600 m is about 34.9‰ and almost uniform.

The water masses of the Norwegian Sea consist of the "North Atlantic Water" and the "Norwegian Deep Water." The latter is formed in winter in the western part of the sea near Jan Mayen Island. Water of salinity 34.90–34.94‰ is formed by mixture of Atlantic and Arctic water. It is cooled to a temperature of about −1.0°C and sinks to great

Fig. 2. First approximation of the surface currents in the Norwegian Sea and Greenland Sea (Helland-Hansen and Nansen, 1909).

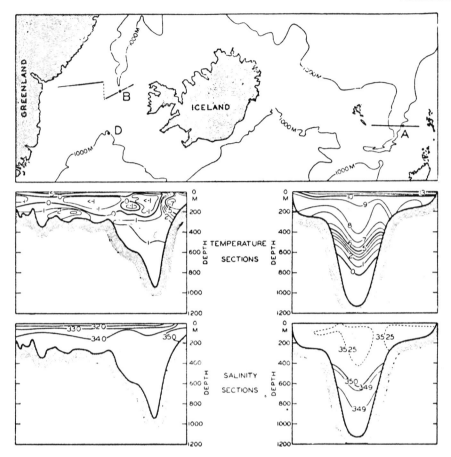

Fig. 3. Chart of the important openings between the Atlantic Ocean and the Arctic Mediterranean Sea, and vertical sections showing distribution of temperature and salinity in the Faeroe–Shetland Channel (right) and in the Denmark Strait (left). Stations A, B and D are shown, but station C lies outside of the region covered by the chart (Sverdrup, 1942).

depths. The process may vary in detail from one year to another.

Below a depth of less than 1000 m the deep water of the Norwegian Sea is cut off from the Atlantic Ocean, except for occasional southward outflows across the Faeroe-Iceland Ridge. However, this water is found in the Polar Sea down to a depth of about 1750 m.

The Norwegian Current (q.v.), a branch of the North Atlantic Current, enters the Norwegian Sea north of Scotland and flows to the northeast, off Norway, with surface velocities of about 30 cm/sec (0.5 knot). The total volume of Atlantic water entering the Norwegian Sea is 3–6 million m³/sec, and it varies considerably from year to year. As the current flows north, water is lost to the large eddies of the western section, but some water is added by outflow from the North Sea and by runoff from the Norwegian coast. Off the extreme northern coast of Norway, the current branches—one branch (the *North Cape Current*) flowing east into the Barents

Sea and the main branch flowing north along the western boundary of the Barents Sea. The latter flow continues along the west coast of Spitsbergen and mixes with the cold water of the Spitsbergen Current coming from the Barents Sea. Then, this last eddy of the Atlantic water swings east around the north of Spitsbergen and submerges under the lighter, less saline surface water of the Polar Sea. These north-setting streams encounter a sinuous Arctic Convergence south and west of Spitsbergen which marks the limit of the southward-setting polar waters. On the northwest side as far as the eastern shores of Iceland, they are cut off by a similar convergence from the south-flowing stream of the *East Greenland Current* (q.v.). The mixing with these polar waters and the associated eddy motions were first mapped approximately (see Fig. 2) by Helland-Hansen and Nansen (1909, 1920).

In the central portion of the Norwegian Sea, there is a distinctive cyclonic gyral (the Norwegian gyral) between the Norwegian current and a branch of the

Greenland current which flows southeast north of Iceland. The recent data of 1951–55 indicate that the center lies around 68°N and 13°W, considerably west of the position previously determined.

The volume transport across a section between Iceland and the Faeroe Islands is southward and varies between 4.5 and 6.2 million m³/sec. About 74% of this water is the North Atlantic water and the rest is the Norwegian Deep water. Most of the former water comes from a branch of the Irminger Current which flows eastward north of Iceland. The latter flows near the bottom of the slope off the east coast of Iceland and its speeds reach 20–30 cm/sec.

Oxygen saturation in the Norwegian Sea is high, pointing to active vertical mixing. In the southeastern section, the average saturation is 84% from the bottom to 800 m, 90% at 400 m and 100% near the surface. The minimum is about 81% between 1200 m and 1500 m and corresponds to the core of the North Atlantic water flowing to the north. The average phosphates in the southeastern section show also an almost uniform value of 78–79 mg/m³ from 600–2500 m; they show a slight decrease toward the surface. This is an important factor in the location of deep-sea fishing grounds here (Fig. 4).

Sediments

Foraminiferal and diatomaceous oozes are widespread in the deeper parts of the Norwegian Basin. In the west around Iceland and Jan Mayen there are volcanic sediments. Glacial clays, marine tills and washed erratic boulder accumulations are found in the vicinity of the continental shelves. Iceberg-rafted rocks and debris are carried over the northern and western sectors. A preliminary study of the deep-sea cores has been made by Hans Holtedahl (1959).

Structural History

The Norwegian basin is known to have offered an access for boreal waters to the North Sea and central Europe at times during the Mesozoic, and it would seem to date back to at least 200 million years. According to the reconstructions of the Early Paleozoic Caledonide mountain chains of Scotland, Norway, Bear Island, Spitsbergen, Newfoundland and Greenland, it seems very likely that these were continuous and contiguous almost throughout the Paleozoic, and that rifting and oceanic spreading began in Permian times, and continued subsequently. Prominent fault scarps along the western margins of Norway suggest that the Quaternary glaciation helped revive some old marginal fractures (O. Holtedahl, 1950). According to Stocks (1950), several graben-like troughs are identified around the borders of the Norwegian Sea: the *Norwegian channel* in the southwest, the *Faeroe-Shetland Channel*, east and south of the Faeroes, the *Barents Trough* south of Bear Island, the *Lofoton Trough* which partly separates the Helgeland Rise ("Schwelle" in German) from the mainland of Norway, and the *Jan Mayen Fracture Zone* that runs WNW–ESW across the mid-oceanic ridge, just north of Jan Mayen.

There are a large number of epicenters of shallow earthquakes along the belt of ridges running from north of Iceland, Jan Mayen to Spitsbergen (Svalbard). This belt also corresponds to a series of active volcanoes in Iceland and Jan Mayen. Epicenters are particularly numerous along the northern boundaries of the Iceland Basin and the Norwegian Basin. This suggests that the belt is a continuation of the Mid-Atlantic Ridge and is still active morphologically.

RHODES W. FAIRBRIDGE
TAKASHI ICHIYE

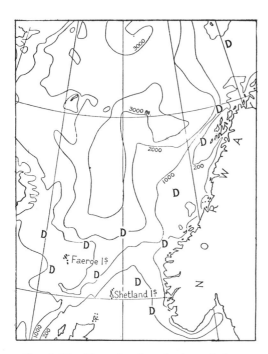

Fig. 4. The Norwegian Sea, depths and deep-sea fishing grounds (based on Hjort and Ruud, Whaling and Fishing in the North Atlantic, Fig. 2).

References

Dorsey, H. G., 1951, "Arctic Meteorology," in "Compendium of Meteorology," pp. 942–964, Boston, American Meteorological Society.

Helland-Hansen, B., and Nansen, F., 1909, "The Norwegian Sea. Its Physical Oceanography based upon the Norwegian Researches 1900–1904," *Rept. Norwegian Fishery and Mar. Invest., Bergen,* **2**(2), 390pp.

Helland-Hansen, B., and Nansen, F., 1926, "The eastern North Atlantic," *Geofys. Publikasjones Oslo,* **4**(2), 76pp.

Holtedahl, H., 1958, "Some remarks on geomorphology of continental shelves off Norway, Labrador, and southeastern Alaska," *J. Geol.*, **66**, 461–471.

Holtedahl, H., 1959, "Geology and paleontology of Norwegian sea bottom cores," *J. Sediment. Petrol.*, **29**, 16–29.

Holtedahl, O., 1950, "Supposed marginal fault lines in the shelf area off some high northern lands," *Bull. Geol. Soc. Am.*, **61**, 493–500.

Metcalf, W. G., 1960, "A note on water movement in the Greenland-Norwegian Sea," *Deep-Sea Res.*, **7**, 190–200.

Mosby, H., 1938, "Svalbard Waters," *Geofys. Publikasjones Oslo*, **12**(4), 85pp.

Saelen, O. H., 1959, "Studies in the Norwegian Atlantic Current, Part 1, The Sognefjord Section," *Geofys. Publikasjones Oslo*, **20**(13), 28pp.; "Part 2—Investigations During the Years 1954–59 in an Area West of Stad," *ibid.*, **23**(6), 82pp.

Steell, J. H., Barrett, J. R., and Worthington, L. V., 1962, "Deep currents south of Iceland," *Deep-Sea Res.*, **9**, 465–474.

Stocks, T., 1950, "Die Tiefenverhältnisse des Europäischen Nordmeers," *Deut. Hydrograph. Z.*, **3**(1/2), 93–100.

Sverdrup, H. U., 1956, "Oceanography of the Arctic," in "The Dynamic North," Book I, No. 5, OPNAV PO 3–11, 320pp.

Tait, J. B., 1957, "Hydrography of the Faroe-Shetland Channel, 1927–1952," *Marine Res.*, Scottish Home Dept., No. 2, 309pp.

U.S. Navy, Chief of Naval Operations, 1955, "Marine Climatic Atlas of the World," Vol. 1, North Atlantic Ocean, NAVAER 50-1C-528, U.S. Government Printing Office.

NUTRIENTS IN THE SEA

Besides the conservative major elements and the trace metals, there are the components in seawater in concentrations of mg atoms/m^3 that are of fundamental importance to the growth of marine phytoplankton, the base of the food chain in the sea. These components are soluble inorganic phosphate (0.1–3.5 mg atoms/m^3), nitrate (0.1–43 mg atoms/m^3), nitrite (0.1–3.5), ammonium (0.35–3.5), and hydrated silicate ions (0.1–170). These marine fertilizers are consumed only in the upper layers of the ocean where light conditions permit photosynthesis and are often limiting to growth. Inorganic phosphorus and nitrogen are regenerated primarily by bacterial decomposition of organic debris and soluble organics, and silicate is regenerated by solution of tests. The regenerated nutrients are returned to the surface by upwelling, turbulence, eddy diffusion and vertical convection.

Distribution of Nutrients in the Oceans

Nutrient concentrations (i.e., phosphate, nitrate, nitrite, ammonia and silicate) in the deep oceans are characterized by four layers: (1) a surface layer in which concentrations are low and relatively uniform with depth; (2) a layer in which concentra-tion increases rapidly with depth; (3) a layer of maximum concentration usually between 500 and 1600 meters; (4) a thick bottom layer in which there is relatively little change of phosphate and nitrate concentration with depth, although silicate may increase considerably. Figure 1 gives examples of the layers in vertical profile of nutrients in the major oceans.

Table 1 summarizes the concentration ranges of nutrients in the oceans, seas, and coastal areas, and Figs. 2, 3, and 4 show nutrient concentrations in various oceans.

The nutrient-poor surface layer is thickest in mid-latitudes in both hemispheres, and the second layer is clearly defined there. In regions of divergence at or near the equator, the surface layer is thin and the underlying gradient steep. In high latitudes, the surface layer may be absent, so that high values occur at the surface.

The differences in the nutrient content of the oceanic basins depend on the composition of the deep water masses at their origin and their subsequent modification by biological factors. Little or no deep water is formed at the northern extremities of the Pacific and Indian Oceans. The surface waters flowing south in these oceans are replaced by an influx of deep water drawn from the Southern Ocean. The deep water of the Atlantic is formed by water sinking from the surface in high northern latitudes and is replaced by surface water flowing northward. Relatively small additions are made by biological influences.

In coastal areas, estuaries and shallow seas, more information is available on the variation of nutrients and factors affecting them. Barnes (1957) and Redfield *et al.* (1963) report detailed information. The factors affecting nutrient variations here are the rate of plankton production, seasonal factors such as light, temperature, length of day, and the influx of new water masses by upwelling, river influx, and changes in currents.

Phosphorus

The phosphorus in marine organisms is in the form of orthophosphoric acid in complex, organic compounds, such as phosphoproteins, nucleo-proteins, nucleic acids, phospholipids, and other compounds. Although a rapid return of inorganic phosphate to the upper water layers may occur by chemical decomposition of simple excretory products, bacterial decomposition or organic debris and organic compounds is the predominant regeneration process. The rate of regeneration is a function of water temperature and numbers of plankton. In the laboratory, 35–55% reduction of plankton to phosphate has occurred in 17–35 days, which explains why very little organic phosphate is present below 300 meters. From a calculation involving the mean annual supply and the removal of phosphate by transport, production and decom-

TABLE 1. NUTRIENT CONCENTRATIONS IN THE OCEANS, SEAS, AND ESTUARIES

Locality	PO$_4$ (mg at./m^3)	NO$_3$ (mg at./m^3)	NO$_2$ (mg at./m^3)	NH$_3$ (mg at./m^3)	Silicate (mg at./m^3)
North Atlantic	0.0–1.25				0.5–35
Western Atlantic	0.1–2.6	0.1–27.0			
Central Atlantic	0.1–2.0	5.0–40.0			
West Coast Africa (24th parallel)	0.8–2.6				
Equatorial Atlantic	0.25–1.0				
Southeastern Atlantic	1.0–1.5				10–80
Southwestern Atlantic	1.7–2.9				
Pacific	0.5–3.9				10–170
Equatorial Pacific	0.2–2.6				5–30
Indian Ocean	0.0–3.3	0.0–36.0			10–120
Antarctic	1.0–3.0	7.1–39.3	.02–.57	3–12	4–60
North Sea	0.0–1.14	0.0–4.3			
Norwegian Sea	0.40–1.17				
Wadden Sea	0.04–0.49			.028–.102	
Black Sea	0.5–6.0				
Mediterranean	0.1–0.4				
Baltic Sea	0.15–2.0	.21–5.9		1.3–1.9	
Gulf of Finland	.19–.95	.29–5.7		1.6–2.1	
Gulf of Bothnia	.076–1.2	.50–3.5		2.6–3.3	
English Channel	.16–.65			0.4–1.2	.72–5.50
Gulf of Maine	0.0–1.8	3–15	0.0–0.35	0.0–3.8	
Long Island Sound	0.1–1.0	0.1–8.5			
Gulf of Venezuela	0.3–1.0				
Cariaco Trench	2.42				
Gulf of Panama	1.0–3.0				
Sargasso Sea	0.0–1.35	0.1–3.0			
Friday Harbor (Washington)	1.2–1.7	15–25	0.1–0.4		
Monterey Bay (California)					10–60
Puget Sound (Washington)	0.2–3.0	0.0–37.4			3.6–250
Area near Mississippi River Delta					1.5–115
Main axis of Kuroshio Current	1.0–3.0	10–36	0.1–0.3		
Upwelling area off Enou-Nada	1.0–3.0	10–20	0.1–0.4		
Kola Meridian 33° 30′E	0.65–1.14	9.15–19.2			
Gulf of Riga	0.1–.45			1.78–2.14	10.7–12.5
Sea of Azov	0.03–.58			8.5–32.1	8.9–26.7

position of all organic material in the Black Sea and the Sea of Azov, the turnover rate of phosphate was found to be 7–8 times per year.

In the Atlantic maximum phosphate (2 mg atoms/m^3) is centered around 1000 meters depth extending northward from the Antarctic. At depths greater than 1000 meters, phosphate decreases from south to north. In the Pacific, maximum phosphate concentrations (3.5 mg atoms/m^3) occur north of the equator, compared with 2.0 mg atoms/m^3 in the Antarctic. In the Pacific, there is no minimum layer of phosphate or nitrate below the maximum layer. The amounts of phosphate in the Indian Ocean (0.5–3.0 mg atoms/m^3) are intermediate to those in the Atlantic and Pacific. An intermediate maximum in the southern latitudes of the Indian corresponds to that in the Atlantic; the maximum in equatorial regions of the Indian corresponds to that of the North Pacific. See Table 1 and Fig. 3 for the distribution of

phosphorus at 2000 meters and Fig. 2 for its distribution in the Indian, Atlantic, and Pacific Oceans.

Nitrogen

The inorganic end product of oxidation of nitrogen-containing organic particles in the sea is the nitrate ion, with organic nitrogen, ammonia, and nitrite as successive intermediate stages. All inorganic forms of nitrogen are consumed by phytoplankton, sometimes to near zero concentrations in the euphotic zone. Autolysis and bacterial action are responsible for the major part of nitrogen regeneration. For some simpler substances, such as urea, chemical hydrolysis to ammonia may be important, although bacteria can also liberate ammonia from urea.

Ammonia and nitrite appear usually where plankton is decomposing in quantity. In shallow coastal waters of temperate regions, ammonia is

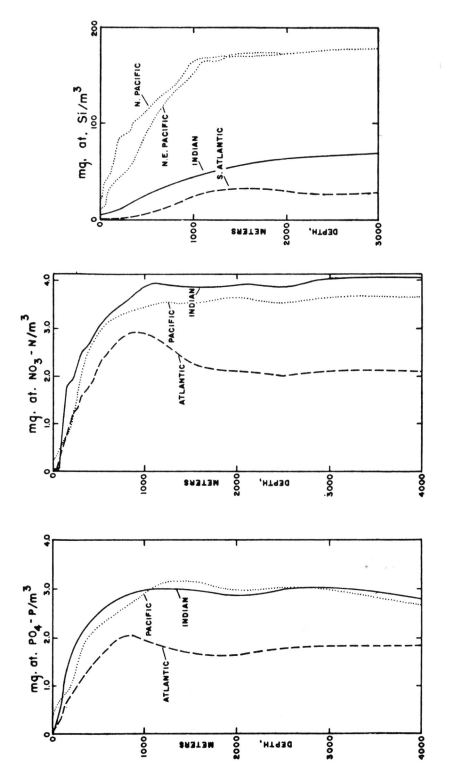

Fig. 1. Longitudinal sections in the major oceanic regions, showing distribution of nutrients (from Sverdrup, Johnson and Fleming, 1942). (By permission of Prentice-Hall. New York City.)

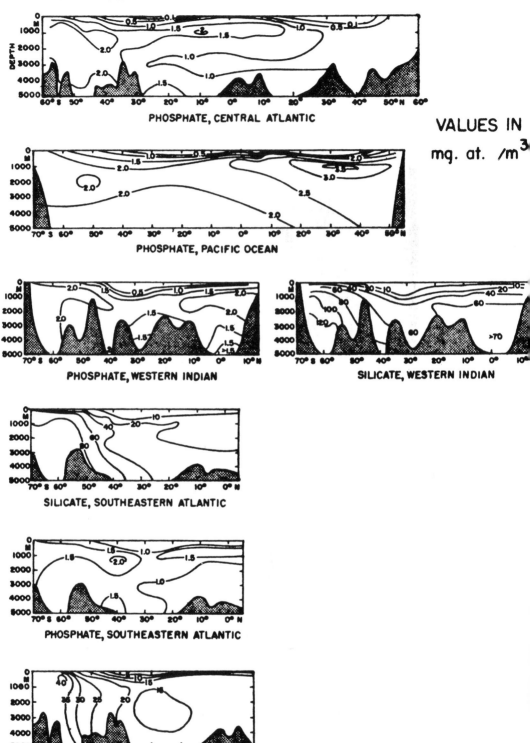

Fig. 2. Distribution of nutrients in various oceanic regions (from Sverdrup, Johnson and Fleming, 1942). (By permission of Prentice-Hall, New York City.)

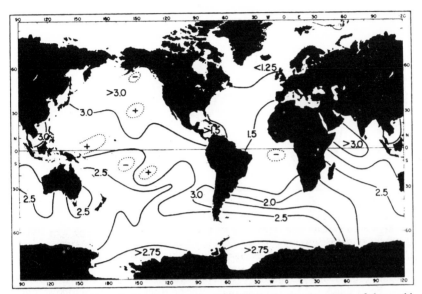

Fig. 3. Distribution of phosphorus at depth of 2000 meters in the oceans of the world. Contour interval, 0.25 mg atom/m³ (from Redfield, 1958). (*Courtesy of American Scientist*)

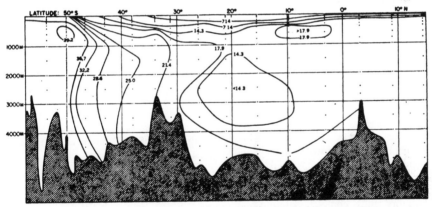

Fig. 4. Distribution of nitrate (NO₃-N) in a section from Weddell Sea northward along 30°W, across Antarctic and subtropical convergences (from Deacon, 1933; see Fig. 17).

present in very small amounts at the end of winter, but it increases in the spring and sometimes becomes the principal form in which nitrogen is available. During the fall and winter, ammonia decreases, and nitrate becomes the major inorganic nitrogen component. In the deep sea, ammonia and nitrite do not ordinarily occur in significant quantities below the euphotic zone, except in anoxic basins, such as the Cariaco Basin. The concentration of nitrite is usually lower than that of ammonia.

Nitrate occurs in higher concentrations than the other nitrogen forms and at all depths. The maximum concentration of nitrate in deep water occurs at a greater depth than that of phosphorus, suggest-

ing that the rate of regeneration of nitrate is slower than that of phosphate. In laboratory experiments, nitrate was regenerated in three or four months. However, a 50–80% decrease of plankton organic nitrogen occurred in 17–20 days (see Fig. 5).

From the data available, it is apparent that there is considerable similarity between the patterns of phosphate and nitrate distributions, although the intermediate maximum is not as clearly shown by the nitrate. The Atlantic contains much lower concentrations of nitrate than the Pacific and Indian Oceans; the concentration of nitrate in the Atlantic deep water more than doubles as it moves south to the Antarctic. The rate of increase is greater than that of phosphate, perhaps due to

561

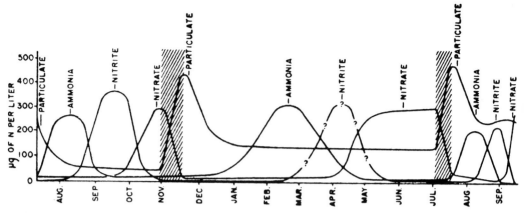

Fig. 5. Decomposition of diatoms in seawater. Shaded areas represent regeneration periods with culture exposed to light (from von Brand, Rakestraw and Renn, 1939).

slow decomposition of some of the dissolved organic nitrogen. See Table 1 and Fig. 3 for nitrate distribution.

Silicate

Silicate is required only for the formation of skeletons of diatoms and radiolaria and not for nutrition in the strictest sense. Bacteria do not appear to be involved in regeneration of silicate, but solution of falling tests is apparently the major mechanism. Diatom and radiolaria tests that have been broken up by passage through digestive tracts of marine organisms dissolve much faster than uningested tests. Rivers are continually adding silicate to seawater, but in oceanic areas near the river mouths, no increase in soluble silicate occurs. Either the silicate is rapidly used by organisms or it is precipitated in some unknown manner. Tundra drainage is believed to contribute to silicate in the oceans, and underwater volcanoes may account for some deep-water silicate.

In a laboratory study, complete solution of silicate from diatoms occurred five months after the death of diatoms. It has been computed that silicate is used up several times in one season in the English Channel, but comparable data for other regions are not available. In addition to dissolved silicate, seawater contains a material quantity of silicon in particulate matter in clay and undissolved diatom tests.

In the oceans, in general, the concentrations of silicate vary greatly in their proportion to phosphate and nitrate. In various parts of the oceans, the proportions of diatoms to other phytoplankton

not requiring silicate differ. Also, the solution of silicate from diatom tests follows a different course from the regeneration of nitrogen and phosphorus, so that silicate may be solubilized at different depths than phosphorus. In the upper water layers where silica may be used by diatoms, less than 0.5 mg atoms/m^3 silica is frequently found. The deep water of the North Atlantic contains about 35 mg atoms/m^3, while the Antarctic deep water contain 120 mg atoms/m^3. The waters of the North Pacific are very rich in silicate, containing as much as 170 mg atoms/m^3 of silica. The Indian Ocean contains in its depths as much as 120 mg atoms/m^3. In the oceans as a whole, there is no marked intermediate maximum as there is with phosphate; the concentration of silicate nearly always increases with depth. See Table 1 and Fig. 2 for silicate distribution in the oceans.

LELA M. JEFFREY

References

Barnes, H., 1957, "Nutrient elements," in (Hedgpeth, J. W., editor) "Treatise on Marine Ecology and Paleoecology," Vol. 1, pp. 297–344, G.S.A. Memoir 67, 1296pp.

Harvey, H. W., 1963, "The Chemistry and Fertility of Sea Waters," London, Cambridge University Press.

Redfield, A. C., Ketchum, B. H., and Richards, F. A., 1963, "The Influence of Organisms on the Composition of Sea Water," in (Hill, W. N., editor) "The Seas," Vol. 2, pp. 26–77, New York, Interscience Publishers, 554pp.

Sverdrup, H. U., Johnson, M. W., and Fleming, R. H., 1946, "The Oceans," New York, Prentice-Hall, Inc.

O

OCEAN-ATMOSPHERE INTERACTION (MACROPROCESSES)

(a) Steady-state Wind-driven Ocean Currents. Large-scale ocean-atmosphere interaction can best be demonstrated over the North Atlantic (Figs. 1 and 2). Analogous conditions must prevail over the other, less well-explored oceans.

The average annual wind drag on the ocean surface goes cyclonically (counterclockwise) around the low pressure centered about 60°N 30°W and anticyclonically around the high pressure centered 32°N 30°W in Fig. 1. The surface of the ocean (Fig. 2) in response forms a depression in the Baffin Sea, west of the atmospheric center of lowest pressure, and a dome on the right flank of the Gulf Stream, far west of the atmospheric center of highest pressure.

The contour lines of the topography of the ocean surface (relative to the geoid) represent the streamlines of the geostrophic part of the ocean currents. Within the uppermost ocean layer, a wind drift component of the water is superimposed. It is directed about 45° to the right of the wind at the ocean surface, turning successively to the right with depth and vanishing at about 50-meter depth. The vectorial water transport by wind drift integrated down to the bottom of the drift layer ("Ekman transport") is directed 90° to the right of the wind direction.

Due to the Ekman transport, the surface water is diverging from the atmospheric low-pressure center and converging into the center of high pressure. To keep the ocean level constant everywhere from year to year, the geostrophic part of the ocean currents must provide mass convergence

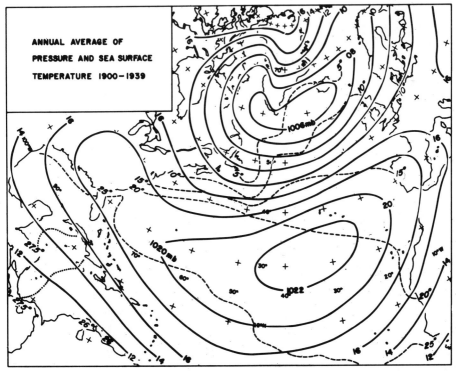

Fig. 1. Average annual pressure distribution at sea level during 1900–39. Dashed lines are average annual sea surface isotherms.

where the Ekman transport is divergent, and mass divergence where the Ekman transport is convergent. This principle was expressed by Sverdrup (1947) by the equation

$$\int_{-h}^{z_0} \rho v \, dz = \frac{r \operatorname{curl} \vec{\tau}}{2\Omega \cos \varphi}$$

where z_0 is the ocean level, $-h$ is the depth of vanishing ocean currents, ρ is the water density, v is the meridional component of geostrophic water motion, r is the radius of the earth, $\vec{\tau}$ is the wind stress vector at ocean surface, Ω is the angular rotation of the earth, and φ is the geographical latitude.

Sverdrup's equation explains the major features of the flow pattern in Fig. 2. Geostrophic flow with a poleward component provides for mass convergence and is therefore found under the northern

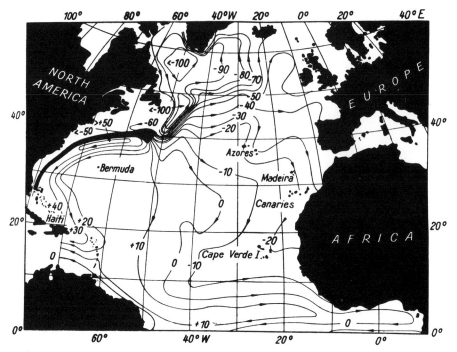

Fig. 2. Topography in dynamic centimeters of the surface of the North Atlantic Ocean (from A. Defant, 1941).

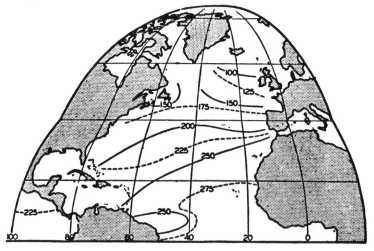

Fig. 3. Net annual surplus of radiation penetrating the water surface (g cal/cm²/day; from Sverdrup, 1942). (By permission of Prentice-Hall, Englewood Cliffs, N.J.)

system of cyclonic wind drag, while a weak southward geostrophic flow occupies most of the area under the subtropical anticyclone. To satisfy the equation of continuity, a narrow but swift Gulf Stream near North America must transport equally as much water northward as goes slowly southward over the great width between the Gulf Stream and North Africa. And the narrow south-flowing currents along the coasts of East Greenland and Labrador must compensate in analogous fashion for the mass transport in the broad and slow north-flowing branches of the Gulf Stream.

(b) Steady-state Oceanic Heat Budget. On the average during a full year, the oceans receive a surplus of radiative heat at the estimated rate mapped by W. Jacobs in Fig. 3 (based on tabulations by Kimball, 1928). In Figs. 4 and 5, the average heat flux per unit area from ocean to atmosphere is shown separately for the winter and the summer quarters. In the Tropics, about equal heat fluxes are operating summer and winter, while in middle and high latitudes, the ocean gives off very little heat in summer and much more in winter. The maximum ocean-to-atmosphere heat flux occurs where cold air from the continent flows over the warm ocean currents, the Kuroshio and the Gulf Stream. On an annual basis, the heat loss to the atmosphere from the warm ocean currents exceeds the local oceanic gain in radiative heat, as shown in Fig. 6. Such heat deficit must be counterbalanced by the "convergence of heat flux" along the warm ocean currents.

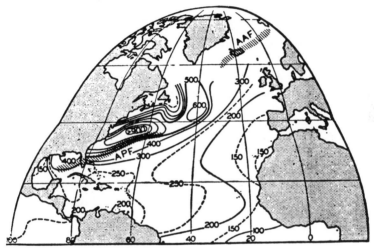

Fig. 4. Net amount of heat and latent heat transferred from oceans to atmosphere during winter half year (g cal/cm^2/day; from Sverdrup, 1942). (By permission of Prentice-Hall, Englewood Cliffs, N.J.)

Fig. 5. Net amount of heat and latent heat transferred from oceans to atmosphere during summer half year (g cal/cm^2/day; from Sverdrup, 1942). (By permission of Prentice-Hall, Englewood Cliffs, N.J.)

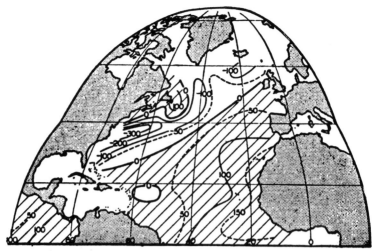

Fig. 6. Net annual heat surplus of the ocean (g cal/cm²/day). Positive surplus shaded (from Sverdrup, 1942). (By permission of Prentice-Hall, Englewood Cliffs, N.J.)

(c) Short-period Changes in the Oceanic Heat Balance. Investigations over the North Atlantic (J. Bjerknes, 1962) have shown interannual variations of as much as ±30% in the average strength of the middle latitude westerlies. The *immediate* effect of, say, an increase of the westerlies is a cooling of the ocean surface, with maximum amplitude usually found in the mid-Atlantic part of the latitude belt 50–55°N. The stronger-than-normal wind from the cold source region in the northwestern corner of the Atlantic maintains a greater-than-normal temperature deficit of the air relative to underlying water, which in turn brings about a faster-than-normal ocean-to-atmosphere transfer of heat and latent heat. Moreover, the intensified mechanical stirring of the top layer of the ocean also brings cooler water to the surface.

An interannual strengthening of the winds in the southern half of the Iceland Low must show up also in the intensification of the cyclonic curl of wind stress, and hence, after some *delay*, in an increase in volume of the north-flowing geostrophic branches of the Gulf Stream. That represents a contribution toward a warming of the ocean, especially from 50°N to the south coast of Iceland. Such a pulse of intensification of the warm north-flowing branch currents needs a sequence of strong circulation years to reverse the cooling at the ocean surface caused by the abnormally strong winds.

Years of stronger-than-normal westerlies are also characterized by strong trade winds which cool the ocean, most markedly near North Africa, but also with perceptible cooling extending westward to the Antilles. In those low latitudes, there is no restoring warming operated by geostrophic currents. The recovery from cooling by stronger-than-normal trade winds must be assured by the permanent surplus of radiative heat in low latitudes.

The waters on the cold flank of the Gulf Stream from Cape Hatteras to the Newfoundland Banks usually warm up in years of strong westerlies, because with that type of atmospheric circulation, the cold waves from North America do not penetrate in strength to the low-middle latitudes.

(d) Secular Changes in the Oceanic Heat Balance —The "Little Ice Age." The earliest maps of the average pressure distribution over the North Atlantic area, compiled by H. H. Lamb and A. I. Johnson (1959), date from the late eighteenth century and show significant differences from present conditions, especially during the winter season. Figure 7 shows the average January map for 1790–1829 compared to that for 1900–1939. The Iceland Low was less pronounced than nowadays, while more important low-pressure centers existed in the Baffin Sea and the Norwegian Sea. The oceanic response must have been: more northward branching of Gulf Stream water in the western Atlantic, under the influence of the Baffin Sea Low, and less northward branching toward Iceland. This agrees with Icelandic historical records that show persistently much longer springtime arctic pack-ice blockades from 1600 to 1900 A.D. than in our century, when the protection by warmer water from the south was reestablished. It also agrees with the earliest available temperature observations in British waters (late eighteenth century in Fig. 9) which showed the ocean to be 1–2°C colder than now.

Wintertime air temperatures in maritime locations of northwest Europe must have been lowered correspondingly. The Alps and the Scandinavian mountains had their maximum of glaciation around 1750, and the so-called Little Ice Age was

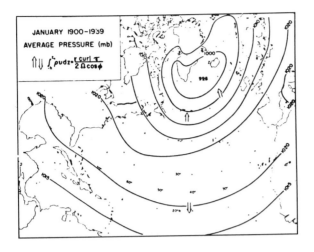

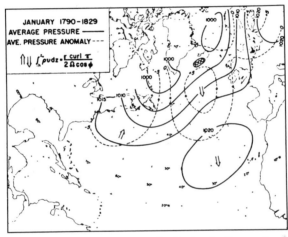

Fig. 7. *Top*: Average pressure distribution for the months of January 1900–39. ⇑ ⇓ Sense of meridional component of geostrophic water motion. *Bottom*: Same for January 1790–1829 (solid) and difference from 1900–39 (dashed). ⇑ ⇓ Sense of anomaly of meridional water motion referred to 1900–39 normal (from Lamb and Johnson, 1959).

still well entrenched during the period 1790–1829 referred to in Fig. 7. The high degree of glaciation can be understood to have resulted from the lowering of the freezing isotherm in the air masses of Atlantic origin, which provide the greater part of the snowfall on European mountains.

A further inquiry into the causes of the recent changes of climate can be made with the aid of Fig. 8, which shows the steady-state mechanism of our present climate. Figure 8 refers to the decade 1950–1959 and shows for the months of January and July the pressure distribution at sea level and the topography of the 500-millibar surface over the northern hemisphere. The 500-millibar maps show the simple background of circumpolar westerlies, which are a necessary consequence of the fundamental fact that the equatorial belt is being heated more than the poles. In addition, the maps show superimposed, geographically fixed, long waves in the upper westerlies. The map of each individual day would, in addition, show a great variety of moving disturbances of shorter wavelength, which cancel out on maps of decadal averaging over 310 days. The moving cyclonic disturbances show a statistical tendency to intensify in the geographical longitude of a trough of the upper stationary long waves and also, at times, to stagnate after reaching peak intensity. The most active formation of new cyclonic centers takes place on the polar front along the east coasts of Asia and North America, where heat and moisture are supplied, respectively, by the Kuroshio and the Gulf Stream waters. While traveling northeastward, these cyclones contribute importantly to the

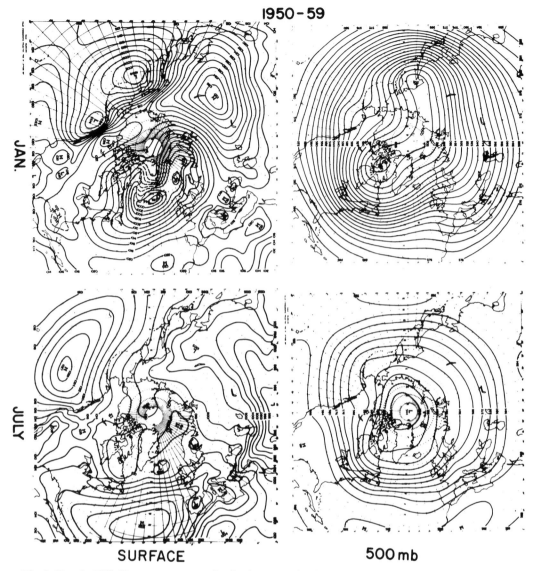

Fig. 8. Decade 1950–59 average pressure distribution at sea level, and average topography of the 500-millibar surface, in January and July (from W. R. Gommel, 1963).

rainfall maximum just east of the longitude of the stationary upper troughs.

The troughs near the east coasts of Asia and North America are the most prominent ones on the 500-millibar maps in Fig. 8, and their maximum intensity is observed in winter when frequent injections of new storm energy from polar front cyclones take place. The corresponding 500-millibar trough in July over eastern North America is just barely visible, because the polar front disturbances in summer have less energy and less of a tendency to congregate just at the eastern coastline.

Following the 500-millibar contours eastward across the Atlantic, one finds the next downwind

trough near the British Isles in July and over eastern Europe in January. In other words, there is a longer wavelength from trough to trough in winter than in summer. The theory of the dynamics of stationary upper waves calls for this seasonal change in wavelength to take place as a function of the seasonal change in the strength of the upper westerlies.

The well-established relationship between the strength of the upper westerlies and the length of the superimposed stationary waves did of course also apply during the Little Ice Age. The upper westerlies over the Atlantic sector were then weaker than at present, just as were the mid-Atlantic

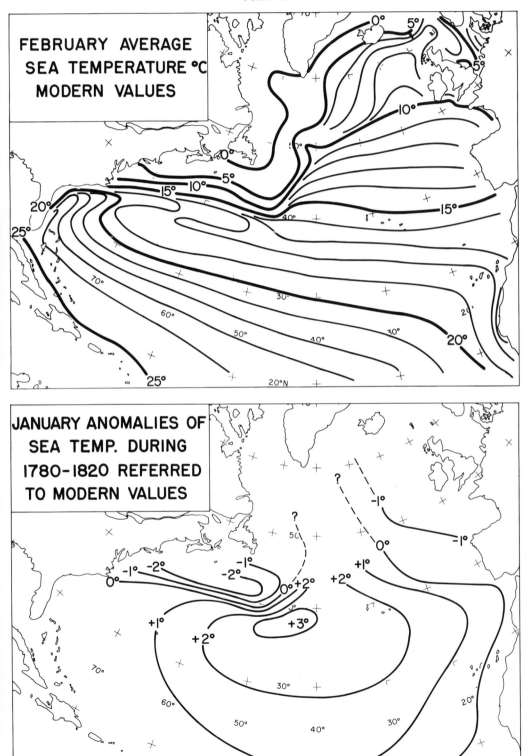

Fig. 9. *Top*: Normal February sea temperature in the twentieth century. *Bottom*: January 1780–1820 anomaly of sea temperatures referred to modern normals (from Lamb and Johnson, 1959).

surface westerlies in Fig. 7. Then also, the super-imposed stationary wave must have been shorter, thus bringing the upper trough, nowadays normally observed over Russia, to a farther west position during the Little Ice Age. That upper trough probably ran north-south along 5° or 10°E of Greenwich. It was thus shifted from the cold northern Russian plains to the warmer Norwegian Sea, where a deep surface low could be main-tained. The southern end of the same trough must have maintained semistagnant lows over the western Mediterranean. The Scandinavian moun-tains, the Alps, and the Pyrenées thus were exposed to intensified wintertime precipitation, while con-comitantly the negative temperature anomaly of East Atlantic waters kept the snow line lower than at present. In that way, the glacial anomaly, called the Little Ice Age, came into being as far as Europe was concerned.

The Little Ice Age in the Canadian Rocky Mountains can probably be explained in similar terms. Periods of weak westerlies are known to have a split North Pacific low on the surface map with the eastern center located over the Gulf of Alaska. That center of low and the corresponding upper trough, are just barely in existence on the January maps in Fig. 8. During the Little Ice Age, when the upper waves were a little shorter, the center over the Gulf of Alaska must have been located a little farther west, thus leaving room for an abundant supply of moist air to the Canadian and South Alaskan coast. The resulting positive anomaly of wintertime precipitation was probably not associated with a negative sea temperature anomaly, such as in the northeastern Atlantic, and the snow line may not have lowered. But all glaciers with high-level supply areas, of which there are many along the Pacific coast, would nevertheless record a Little Ice Age maximum.

The fundamental role of the oceans in stabilizing a Little Ice Age climate for a couple of centuries can be seen on the earliest available maps of Atlan-tic temperature anomalies. In Fig. 9 the average January sea temperature anomalies (referred to modern normals) are shown for the period 1780–1820 overlapping the period of the earliest climato-logical map in Fig. 7.

In addition to the already mentioned negative sea temperature anomaly in Icelandic and British waters, negative anomalies are also shown along the American coast from Cape Hatteras to the Grand Banks. But over the Sargasso Sea, positive anomalies prevail with a maximum of $+3°C$ on the warm side of the Gulf Stream discontinuity southeast of Newfoundland. The meteorological map (Fig. 7) justifies the negative sea temperature anomalies near the American coast by stronger- and colder-than-normal winds from the continent, whereas the positive sea temperature anomaly in the western Sargasso Sea must have come by

geostrophic water advection from the south where, at present, the opposite flow prevails. The primary meteorological cause must have been the cyclonic wind stress over the western Sargasso Sea around 1800 A.D. versus a weak anticyclonic one in modern times (Fig. 7).

A tongue of positive sea temperature anomaly may have extended northward toward the south tip of Greenland if the northward branching from the Gulf Stream actually started farther west than at present under the dual influence of an abnormally weak Iceland low and an abnormally strong Baffin Sea low. But no old sea temperature observations exist for the testing of that assumption.

What can be said with fair certainty about the oceanic feedback on the Little Ice Age climate is as follows:

(1) Polar front cyclones did find favorable condi-tions for formation and growth between the abnormally warm Sargasso Sea and the abnormally cold North American coastal waters. An uncom-monly large number of these cyclones would curve northward into the Baffin Sea, as they are known to do also nowadays in situations with a poorly developed Iceland low. The small Labrador and Baffin Land glaciers, which are at present starving for lack of wintertime precipitation, could under such conditions grow and stage a Little Ice Age simultaneous to the ones observed in Europe and in the mountains from western Canada to southern Alaska.

(2) The strengthened upper trough, tied geo-graphically to the Baffin longitude, would by atmospheric teleconnection weaken the Iceland low (half a stationary wavelength downwind) and strengthen the low in the Norwegian Sea (a full wavelength downwind).

(3) The weakening of the Iceland low meant a weakening, or even an intermittent elimination, of the Gulf Stream branch from west of the British Isles to Iceland and to the Norwegian Sea. This also made the arctic ice less exposed to melting.

(4) The lowered temperature of the Norwegian Sea together with strong cyclone activity promoted the Scandinavian glaciation.

(5) The lowered temperature of the British waters left England with less-than-normal Atlantic warming and made winters 1–2°C colder than nowdays.

(6) The cooler-than-normal Atlantic wintertime air promoted glaciation also in the Alps and the Pyrenées supported by the circumstance that the European upper pressure trough was west of its present normal wintertime position.

The question of how the Little Ice Age climate was initiated around 1600 A.D. has not been answered by the above discussion and may never be fully understood. However, further combined research in oceanography, meteorology, and glaciology in both hemispheres can probably clarify how the rather recent end phases of the Little Ice Age operated and how the new climatic trends are now being set.

It is likely that the beginning of a Great Pleistocene Ice Age after an Interglacial always was rather similar to the conditions we are able to reconstruct for the Little Ice Age. The essential difference lies in the duration of the climatic anomaly that made the glaciers grow. In the relatively brief growth period of the Little Ice Age, the influence of the ice field accretion on the planetary albedo remained an insignificant climatic effect. Not so, of course, in the Great Ice Ages, when a considerable deficit of the planetary heat budget arose from the big ice accretion. Moreover, the lowering of the ocean level during any major Pleistocene ice age strongly curtailed the exchange of water across the submarine ridges, connecting Shetland with the Faroes and Iceland, whereby the temperature of the Norwegian Sea dropped and the snow line in Scandinavia went much lower than during the Little Ice Age.

J. BJERKNES

References

Bjerknes, J., 1962, "Synoptic survey of the interaction of sea and atmosphere in the North Atlantic," *Geophysica Norvegica*, **24**, Nol 3, 115–145.

Defant, A., 1941, "Die absolute Topographie des physikalischen Meeresniveaus und der Druckflächen, sowie die Wasserbewegungen im Atlantischen Ozean. Deutsche Atlantische Expedition 'Meteor,' 1925–1927," *Wiss. Ergeb.*, **6**, 191–260.

Ekman, V. W., 1905, "On the influence of the earth's rotation on ocean currents," *Arkiv Matematik, Astron. Fysik*, **2** (11), 1–52.

Gommel, W. R., 1963, "Mean distribution of 500 mb topography and sea-level pressure in middle and high latitudes of the northern hemisphere during the 1950–1959 decade, January and July," *J. Appl. Meteorol.*, **2**, No. 1, 105–113.

Jacobs, W. C., 1942, "On the energy exchange between sea and atmosphere," *J. Marine Res.*, **5**, 37–66.

Kimball, H. H., 1928, "Amount of solar radiation that reaches the surface of the earth on the land and on the sea," *Monthly Weather Rev.*, **56**, 393–399.

Lamb, H. H., and Johnson, A. I., 1959 and 1961, "Climatic variation and the observed changes in the general circulation," *Geografiska Ann.* (*Stockholm*), **41**, No. 2–3, 94–134; and **43**, No. 3–4, 363–400.

Sverdrup, H. U., 1942, "Oceanography for Meteorologists," New York, Prentice Hall.

Sverdrup, H. U., 1947, "Wind-driven currents in a baroclinic ocean; with application to the equatorial currents in the eastern Pacific," *Proc. Natl. Acad. Sci.*, **33**, 318–326.

OCEAN-ATMOSPHERE INTERACTION (MICROPROCESSES)

Although the *importance* of the air-sea interaction is mostly expressed in terms of the macroprocesses, in the long run an *understanding* can only be achieved by a study of the microprocesses. By the microprocesses we mean the detailed mechanisms by which such entities as momentum, water vapor, heat, energy, gases and salt nuclei pass across the air-sea interface. The microprocesses are usually taken to include not only processes right at the immediate interface but also in the adjacent few tens of meters of the atmosphere and the ocean. Horizontal variations in the macroprocesses are of prime importance in the origin of ocean currents and to the major sources of energy in the troposphere. Temporal variations contribute to the variability of both oceanic and atmospheric motions. In general, study of the variability of a phenomenon requires much deeper insight than does study of the average, and it is unlikely that these variations can be understood until our knowledge of the microprocesses is greatly increased.

Until very recently, direct measurements of microprocesses have been impossible, so that indirect approximations have been used. However, new techniques have recently become available, and others are being developed, to measure the processes directly. Since attempts are being made to do this, it is necessary to review critically the more important methods used in the past. Future applications will be increasingly concerned with the synoptic scale, rather than with the climatological scale to which attention has been directed in the past, and crude methods which give reasonable results over a climatological mean may be totally misleading when applied to finer-scale phenomena.

Transfer Processes

The study of the microprocesses in the air-sea interaction is a study of the transfer across horizontal planes of such entities as the ones mentioned above. Of these, only energy can be radiated across horizontal planes by remote acting influences. All other entities must be transferred either by being bodily transported with the fluid at a rate w, the vertical component of local velocity, or else by molecular processes. Except within about 1 mm of the actual interface, the latter are of negligible importance. Since on the average the water surface is horizontal and since on the microscale we make the assumption of average horizontal homogeneity, the value of w averaged over a reasonably large area must be zero. The transfer is therefore effected by the *fluctuating* vertical velocity. If, for example, a property F tends to be more concentrated when w is positive than when it is negative, there will be a net flux of F upward. Analytically, the local instantaneous rate of transport of F upward per unit surface area is given by $\rho f w$, where f is the amount of F per unit mass and ρ is the fluid density (mass volume^{-1}). The average* value, written $\overline{\rho f w}$, is in general nonzero even though the average value of w is zero. It should be noted that although w is a fluctuating quantity, we have not said that it is a turbulent quantity, and indeed any kind of fluctuation, including many wave-like motions which would not ordinarily be called turbulence, can effect certain kinds of transport.

Usually (although not always) the direction of transport is such that the quantity F is transported down its mean gradient, i.e., $\overline{\rho f w}$ has the *opposite* sign to the vertical component of ∇f. We can express this idea by the equation

$$\overline{fw} = -K_F \frac{d\bar{f}}{dz}$$

This equation is analogous to:

$$\text{Flux} = -\kappa \frac{d\bar{f}}{dz}$$

caused by molecular diffusion, κ being the molecular diffusivity of the quantity. By analogy, then, K_F is called the "turbulent diffusivity" or "eddy diffusivity" of the quantity F. Unlike κ, K_F is not a constant; it is a function not only of z but also of the nature of the fluctuating fields of velocity and of F. This definition of K_F provides no insight into the physics of the transfer processes. It is merely a convenient label in terms of which one can discuss the efficiency of these processes.

Momentum Transfer

Perhaps the most important to the oceanographer of all the transfer processes is that of momentum. It is of less, although not negligible, important to the meteorologist. By momentum transfer we imply that F is horizontal momentum and that f is U, the momentum per unit mass, or the horizontal velocity component. The flux of momentum then is given by $\overline{\rho Uw}$, but variations in ρ are too small to be important in this transfer, so it can be written $\rho \overline{Uw}$. The velocity U can be broken down into an average velocity $\bar{U}$ plus a fluctuating velocity u. Since the average value of w is zero, $\bar{U}w$ also averages zero, and therefore $\overline{Uw} = \overline{uw}$; i.e., the upward rate of transfer of horizontal momentum across horizontal planes is given by the density multiplied by the covariance of the vertical and the horizontal fluctuating velocity components.

The rate of addition of momentum is *force*. Rate of transfer of momentum per unit area, then, is force per unit area which is a *stress* and $\tau = -\rho\overline{uw}$

---

is the stress exerted by fluid above a plane on that below. Stresses of this nature are called Reynolds stresses after Osborne Reynolds who first discussed them.

Direct measurements of $\overline{uw}$ over a water surface are just becoming possible with new equipment. Very few such measurements presently exist, and almost all data on the transfer of momentum between the atmosphere and the ocean have been obtained by *inference* from indirect measurements. Of the two most commonly used indirect methods, one, applicable only to measurement over water, involves measuring the surface slope produced by water piling up against the downwind bank; using certain assumptions, it is then possible to calculate the wind stress. Ursell (1956) showed that this technique is subject to difficulties involving the bottom topography, while recent theoretical and observational work indicates that it is also seriously affected by transfer of momentum in surface waves. Measurements of the wind stress by the surface slope method should now be viewed with a certain amount of skepticism.

In the other technique, borrowed from micrometeorology, it is assumed that we may extrapolate arguments and results applicable to the wind profile over a solid surface to that over waves. It can be shown that in a steady wind, if the density structure is neutral, the stress is virtually constant in the bottom 10–100 meters of the atmosphere, depending upon circumstances. Then, it is possible to argue that the turbulence will have a similarity structure which is fully determined by only two parameters: the height z above the surface, which determines the scale of the turbulence, and the (constant) value of stress τ, which determines its intensity. Turbulence theory is usually carried out in terms of kinematic units, i.e., properties are measured per unit mass rather than per unit volume. Kinematically then, stress is determined simply by $-\overline{uw} = u_*^2$, where u_* is called the *friction velocity*. The eddy diffusivity representation is $-\overline{uw} = K_m \, dU/dz$ where K_m is the formally defined eddy diffusion coefficient associated with momentum, and is called the "eddy viscosity." If K_m is determined by z and u_* only, then dimensionally it must be of the form $K_m = Ku_* z_0$ where the dimensionless constant K is called von Karman's constant, empirically determined to be about 0.40.

The conventional representation of stress is then, $u_*^2 = 0.4 \, u_* z \, d\bar{U}/dz$. This may be integrated to yield $\bar{U} = 2.5 \, u_* \ln z/z_0$ where z_0 is a constant of integration which is a characteristic of the surface called the "roughness parameter." Empirically, it is about one-tenth of the physical vertical scale of roughness elements on a solid surface.

The usual procedure is to plot measured values of $\bar{U}$ against log z and so infer u_* and z_0. Direct comparisons of u_*^2, so determined over solid surfaces, with measurements made with balances which detect the actual surface force, give consistent and satisfactory results. The technique is also being used over water, notably by Sheppard and by Fleagle. However, over water several difficulties arise, the most fundamental of which is that it is now much more difficult to support the assumption that the turbulence is determined by only the two parameters z_0 and u_*. For the water surface, more parameters are needed for a description. Among these are a length characteristic of the wavelength of the waves and either the acceleration due to gravity, g, or some other parameter which describes the propagation of the waves. In addition, there is difficulty not only in deciding what should be the origin of z but also in deciding what should be the origin of U. Not only does the presence of the wind cause a mean surface drift, but the waves have particle motions which also cause a mean transport of surface water. There is, furthermore, a large velocity in the forward direction at the wave crests where the water will be expected to interact most strongly with the wind; this orbital velocity is very far from negligible. In a "fully developed sea," the most common and noticeable waves propagate at nearly the wind speed and have orbital velocities at their crests which are nearly the phase velocity, thus nearly the mean wind speed; so the question of the origin of U is not a trivial one. Unfortunately, very few measurements have been taken of wind stress over fully developed seas. Where measurements have been made, mostly at short fetches, the origin of U is not a great problem, but for just this reason, it may not be possible to extrapolate the results to apply to the fully or nearly fully developed seas typical of the ocean. It may mean that our observations do not have too much relevance to what actually happens over the major part of the deep oceans. Evidently there is a great need for the more direct measurements of $\overline{uw}$, if only to give more confidence in the inferential methods.

Except by very elaborate observational arrangements, carefully controlled and expertly maintained, it is not possible to measure the wind velocity gradient over water with enough precision to determine the stress. Observational data, then, must be expressed in some form from which it is possible to compute the wind stress from such information as is likely to be available; usually only the mean wind measured at some level is known. Thus, in oceanography the representation

$$\tau = \rho_{air} \, C_D \, \overline{U}^2$$

is used. Since U is a function of z, the nondimensional "drag coefficient" C_D will depend to some extent on the level at which U is measured. Conventionally this is chosen to be 10 meters. For a long time the value $C_D = 0.0026$, based mainly on measuring water tilts, was used. More recent observations suggest that C_D is an increasing function of $\overline{U}$. Sheppard obtained $C_D = 8 \times 10^{-5} + 1.14 \times 10^{-6} \, \overline{U}$ (U in centimeters per second) from observations on wind profiles over a lake, Lough Neagh. These observations were at comparatively short fetches where, at least for the higher wind speeds, the waves were certainly not fully developed. Extrapolation to longer fetches is as yet uncertain.

Some authors have been more sanguine than are the present writers about the probability of determining a simple relationship between the wind field and the stress on the water surface. Ellison (1956) and independently Charnock (see reference in Ellison, 1956) argue that the nature of the water surface, that is the wave structure, is itself a function of the wind speed and, therefore, the value of z_0 is not an independent parameter but can be determined as a function of u_*. They propose an expression of the form

$$z_0 \propto u_*{}^2/g$$

which results in an increase in C_D with $\overline{U}$, qualitatively in agreement with Sheppard's results. Kitaigarodski has also argued, from the fairly common opinion that the wind stress is largely effected by the very small waves which quickly come into equilibrium with the local instantaneous wind, that very few parameters are required to describe the wind stress. However, these points of view are hard to maintain if the situation is examined closely. Let us for the moment ignore the difficulties of determining the origins of z and of U, and take it that the problem is to determine z_0 as a function of as few parameters as possible. If z_0 and the relevant origins are known, the drag coefficient is determinable from the expression

$$C_D = \left(2.5 \ln \frac{10}{z_0}\right)^{-2}{}^*$$

where z_0 is measured in meters. It seems only reasonable to suppose that z_0 and so also C_D and u_*, are functions of the nature of the waves on the surface of the water, the most elementary description of which is in terms of spectrum. The spatial energy spectrum of gravity waves is limited, at low values of the scalar wave number k, by a cutoff which depends on wind speed, fetch and duration of the wind. Dimensional analysis leads to the conclusion that at moderately high wave numbers, the spectrum drops off as k^{-3}, a result fairly well supported by observations. At the highest wave numbers, it is limited by effects involving capillarity and viscosity which both become much more

---

*This expression can be obtained by combining the expression for the drag coefficient with the logarithmic profile expression.

important for short waves. Now let us suppose that z_0 depends upon some moment

$$\int_0^\infty k^n S(k) \, dk$$

of the surface spectrum $S(k)$. If it depends directly on the energy spectrum ($n = 0$), then it is critically dependent upon the low wave-number cutoff, and thus not only on wind speed but also on fetch and duration of the wind. At the other extreme, we might propose that z_0 depends upon the curvature ($n = 4$) of the water surface. Then the integral clearly depends upon the high wave-number cutoff which means that z_0 depends upon temperature and upon the presence of surface contaminants. If z_0 depends upon the wave *slope* ($n = 2$), the value is critically dependent upon both cutoffs. It, therefore, seems that it will be almost impossible to determine z_0 without considering one or other of these cutoffs. It may be necessary to consider both. Unfortunately, existing observational data do not cover a wide enough range of the variables and have not on the whole been made with sufficient precision to give much insight into the possible dependency. Because the apparatus is delicate and difficult to maintain, all observations so far on the so-called logarithmic profile, have been made either in light winds or at short fetches and nothing is known of the effects of fetch and duration. At high wind speeds, without exception, observations have been made either at short fetches or at short wind durations. These difficulties are quite independent of those referred to earlier concerning the choice of origins for $\overline{U}$ and z_0, and so of the fundamental reliability of this technique over water.

The great need for directly measuring stress, by measuring the covariance of u and w, is once more evident. Furthermore, it becomes clear from the following argument that the co-spectra and quadrature-spectra of quantities such as u, w, pressure p_s at the surface, and the surface elevation are also important.

If molecular viscosity can be ignored, then the only process transferring horizontal momentum at the instantaneous water surface is the horizontal component of the force produced by the pressure p_s acting normally to the surface. It follows that the momentum flux is the covariance of p_s and $\delta\eta/\delta x$, which is the local slope of the (wavy) water surface. The entire flux, then, is associated with the mechanisms of wave generation. Drift currents arise because of the advection of momentum from upwind regions where it is produced by transfer of momentum from waves to a mean flow via the action of turbulence and other wave dissipation mechanisms. In order to be effective, surface wind pressure fluctuations of a given size must on the average travel along the surface at the phase velocity of waves of similar size, and there must be a suitable average phase difference between them. For this to happen, momentum must be fed down to the surface, via the $\overline{uw}$ mechanism, by eddies of the same size from a level, now known as the Miles' critical height, at which they are effectively transported by the wind at the wave phase velocity. Phillips (see reference in Miles, 1960) essentially proposed a mechanism of this type in which the eddies are typical of turbulence, but the pressure field associated with these is too small and insufficiently related to the waves to produce real waves at the observed rate. Miles (1960) assumed that there is a feedback from waves to eddies of the same size; then the process can be efficient in causing wave growth. Clearly in this latter process, wind fluctuations in the region below the Miles' critical level must be much more organized than ordinary turbulence, but they must here have some of the characteristics of a wave motion. This is in accord with our intuition which insists that the wind field near the surface must conform with the pattern of waves beneath. Somewhat above the critical level, the eddies will possess the characteristics of ordinary turbulence, and the degree of association with waves beneath will be small. In both regions, the downward momentum flux is effected by the covariance $\overline{uw}$.

It is evident now that the covariance of the amplitudes of those parts within a small bandwidth of wave number or frequency of a pair of u, w, p_s, $\delta\eta/\delta x$, etc., and the average phase difference between them, will describe both the structure and actions of eddies of given sizes participating in the momentum flux. The co- and quadrature-spectra provide this information, and therefore their measurement is essential in understanding the whole process of momentum flux, which is the drag of wind on the surface.

The Fluxes of Heat and Water Vapor

The flux of water vapor E is of major importance to the meteorologist since its latent heat L is the major source of energy for tropospheric motions. Evaporation at the ocean surface reduces the temperature and increases the salinity of the water; the resulting increase of density in the surface layer provides the driving force for the deep oceanic circulation. The flux per unit area of latent heat is given by putting $f = Lq$ in the general transport relation, where q is the mass of water vapor per unit mass of air, so that

$$LE = L\rho\overline{qw}$$

To calculate the actual heat transport, we consider a vertical column of air of unit areal cross section reaching down to the water surface. In conditions of average horizontal homogeneity, the net flux through the sides must be zero. Thus, in the absence of local absorption of radiated energy or of release of latent heat by condensation, the first law of thermodynamics enables us to equate the average heat flux across the water surface to the flux of internal energy, $\overline{c_v T w}$ at the top plus the mean rate of working $\overline{p w}$, at the top of the column, where $p = \rho r T$ is air pressure and r is the specific gas constant. This sum is the upward total heat flux, $\overline{\rho c_p T w}$. In these relations, c_v and c_p are the specific heats at constant volume and constant pressure. T is absolute temperature, but since only its fluctuating part is of interest, T may be expressed in degrees Celsius.

It is only now that techniques are becoming available to obtain satisfactory direct estimates of water vapor transports; such determinations have been made over land but not as yet over water. In their absence, once again, oceanographers have resorted to approximate techniques.

For latent heat transport, the representation analogous to diffusion is

$$LE = -\rho L K_w \frac{d\bar{q}}{dz}$$

where K_w is the coefficient of eddy diffusivity for water vapor.

To represent the flux of sensible heat, it must first be noted that the relevant property of the fluid is not the specific internal energy $c_v T$, but the total heat (enthalpy) $c_v T + p/\rho = c_p T$. The increment of this entity, per unit increment of vertical displacement, is reduced by the potential energy gained, which is g. The quantity conserved during vertical motion of a fluid mass is, therefore,

$$c_p T - gz$$

If this quantity is independent of z, we have the so-called adiabatic lapse rate Γ, where

$$\Gamma = g/c_p = -\frac{dT}{dz} \quad ad$$

Turbulent heat transport is expected to occur only if the temperature gradient differs from $-\Gamma$, so the upward heat flux per unit area is represented by

$$H = -c_p K_H \left(\frac{d\bar{T}}{dz} + \Gamma \right)$$

Close to the surface, $d\bar{T}/dz$ is usually large compared with Γ, which is $10^{-2}°\text{C/m}$.

In practice, the fluxes must again be related to commonly available information; this is usually confined to $\bar{U}$, $\bar{T}$, and less often $\bar{q}$, measured at deck height, and the temperature (T_s) and salinity of surface water from which the vapor pressure just over the surface, e_s, can be calculated. The similarity of form of the diffusivity expressions for E and momentum flux τ suggests that if K_w/K_m is constant, the profiles of $\bar{U}$ and $\bar{q}$ will be similar. Then

$$E/\tau = \frac{\bar{q}_2 - \bar{q}_1}{\bar{U}_2 - \bar{U}_1} \frac{K_w}{K_m},$$

where the subscripts refer to two levels z_1 and z_2.

Two recent comparisons of this formula for fluxes over land, with E and τ estimated in one case directly from eddy fluxes $(\overline{\rho f w})$ and in the other case from evaporation from small pots and drag plate measurements, showed that $K_w \approx 1.1\ K_m$ in conditions of moderate instability and moderate winds. For situations over water, if we further assume that $K_w = K_m$ and also that the mechanisms of transfer across the surface are similar and that $U_1 = 0$ at the surface, substituting for τ we find

$$E = \frac{\rho_a C_D}{1.6 \rho_a} (e_s - \bar{e}_a) U_a,$$

where the subscripts s and a refer, respectively, to the surface and to a reference level in the air, usually in the neighborhood of 6–10 meters and $e_a = 1.6\ p_a q_a$ is the vapor pressure at this reference level. The equivalent expression $E = J(\bar{e}_s - \bar{e}_a)\ \bar{U}$ has often been used to estimate the rate of evaporation from the ocean surface. The most reliable estimate of J was made by Jacobs using climatological data from four selected oceanic regions, and comparing these with the latent heat fluxes LE estimated from the corresponding climatological heat balances.

In the heat budget technique, it is assumed that the long-term absorption of heat is zero, and the study is made of whole oceans or of regions from which net heat losses by horizontal bodily transports are either unimportant, or can be reasonably accurately estimated. Then averaging over the region,

$$LE + H = I_r + T$$

where I_r is the difference in flux intensity of incoming solar and outgoing back radiation, estimated from climatological data, and T is the net heat transport into the region. This is usually written

$$LE(1 + R) = I_r + T$$

where $R = H/LE$ is called Bowen's ratio. By assuming that $K_w = K_H$ and, as in deriving the relation E/τ, that the transfer processes for heat and water vapor across the surface are similar, we find the relation

$$R = \frac{1.6\ c_p p_a}{L} \frac{\bar{T}_s - \bar{T}_a}{\bar{e}_s - \bar{e}_a}$$

where subscript s refers to the surface. Sverdrup concluded from Jacobs' data that R varies from about 0.1 in the tropics to about 0.5 at high northern latitudes. Jacobs found a value of J equivalent to 1.65×10^{-12} if all entities are expressed in cgs units; the corresponding value of C_D is 2×10^{-3}, which conforms with earlier values used. Wüst had earlier estimated J by comparison with surface evaporation estimated from that in exposed pans on ship's decks. His value for J is about 40% less than Jacobs'. Both techniques are well discussed in the articles by Jacobs (1951) and by Sverdrup (1951) listed in the references.

Wüst's technique is subject to several obvious objections, while Jacobs' technique refers solely to, and appears to give reasonable results for, climatological data; however, it is clearly unwise to extrapolate his result to apply to short-term averages. Moreover, the J-formula itself is subject to question. The formula for E/τ, only recently partially tested over land, is extrapolated to apply to air over water, then the lower level is extrapolated to the surface and again the question of the origin for $\bar{U}$ crops up. Even so, if in spite of these objections J *is* proportional to C_D, then Sheppard's results indicate that it is far from being a constant. However, perhaps the most serious objection rises from the first assumption made, that the profiles of $\bar{U}$ and $\bar{q}$ must be similar; the same assumption is made for $\bar{q}$ and $\bar{T}$, sometimes implicitly, in deriving the expression for R. In any case, if $K_w = K_H = K_m$, then the discussion of the section on momentum transfer may largely be carried over to apply not only to K_m but also to K_w and K_H. Clearly, the only way around the present uncertainties is to attempt direct measurements of the actual transport $\overline{\rho f w}$, simultaneously with measurements of profiles and waves at both short and long fetches over the ocean, in order to find the simplest parameterization possible. This will be necessary for a full development of techniques of oceanographic and meteorological forecasting on a synoptic scale. Measurements designed to fill this gap are now being made at several places.

Other Transports

The transports of entities other than momentum, heat and water vapor have been less studied and are even less understood. For gases it is usually assumed that the surface water is in equilibrium with the lower levels of the atmosphere. The problem then becomes that of the transports within the upper layer of the ocean. Of the details of the nature of motion in this layer, almost nothing is known.

Observations of salt nuclei in the atmosphere make it evident that the ocean surface is an abundant source of such particles. It seems that salt reaching the land surface from this source largely accounts for the sodium chloride found in rivers. The mechanism seems to be evaporation of spray and of droplets produced when bubbles burst, but the details are still known very uncertainly.

Blanchard has shown that bubble bursting leads to a charge separation between the resulting droplets and the surface which may be of importance in maintaining the earth's static electric field. There may well be many such, as yet unanticipated, phenomena associated with the air-sea interface.

RONALD W. BURLING
ROBERT W. STEWART

References

Batchelor, G. K., and Davis, R. M., (editors), 1956, "Surveys in Mechanics," Cambridge, The University Press.

Ellison, T. H., "Atmospheric Turbulence," pp. 400–430.

Ursell, F., "Wave Generation by Wind," pp. 216–249.

Lighthill, M. J., 1962, "Theory of wave generation by wind," *J. Fluid Mech.*, **14**, 385–398.

Malone, T. F., (editor), 1951, "Compendium of Meteorology," Waverly Press.

Jacobs, W. C., "Large-scale Aspects of Energy Transformation over the Ocean," pp. 1057–1071.

Sverdrup, H. U., "Evaporation from the Oceans," pp. 1071–1082.

Miles, J. W., 1960, "On the generation of surface waves by turbulent shear flows," *J. Fluid Mech.*, **9**, 1469–1478.

Priestley, C. H. B., 1959, "Turbulent Transfer in the Lower Atmosphere," Chicago, University of Chicago Press, 130pp. (for a comprehensive account of fluxes and a fairly complete bibliography).

OCEAN BOTTOM CURRENTS

Until very recently, oceanographers considered the deep sea to be devoid of strong currents. Thus geologists inferred that fossil ripple marks were an infallible criterion of shallow-water deposition. Wüst (1933), through an analysis of potential temperature, inferred relatively strong bottom currents in the South Atlantic. Later, through dynamic calculations, Wüst (1955, 1957) determined maximum velocities of 10–15 cm/sec. These revolutionary results, dependent on several computational assumptions and not supported by direct current measurements, were treated at first with some reservation.

Since the development of multiple exposure deep-sea cameras in the late 1940's, ripple marks and scour marks have been frequently observed in abyssal depths (Heezen and Hollister, 1964). Nevertheless, the vast majority of bottom photographs from the deep ocean show abundant tracks and trails of benthic organisms, worm tubes, fecal pellets, burrows and mounds of sediment and sessile and vagrant organisms. In the past few years, direct current measurements by neutrally buoyant floats, moored current meters and bottom current meters have indicated the presence of relatively strong and variable currents (4–40 cm/sec) at great depths. The highest velocities measured (Table 1) are competent to transport all the particle sizes found on the deep-sea floor. It seems reasonable, therefore, to expect evidence of ancient currents preserved in deep-sea sediment cores.

Bottom currents produce several characteristic types of features recognizable in bottom photographs. The effect of currents on bottom sediments can be seen as ripple marks (Figs. 1 and 2), scour

TABLE 1. RECENT NEAR-BOTTOM, DEEP-SEA, DIRECT CURRENT MEASUREMENTS AND MAXIMUM SIZE OF PARTICLES THAT COULD BE ERODED AND TRANSPORTED BY THESE CURRENTS (SEE REFERENCE IN HEEZEN AND HOLLISTER, 1964)

Source	Location	Water Depth (m)	Depth of Measurement (m)	Current Velocity (cm/sec)	Measurement Instrument	Maximum Size of Particles that Could Be		
						Eroded (mm)		Transported (mm)
						Mavis *et al.* (1935); Nevin (1946)	Hjulstrom (1935)	Rubey (1933)
Swallow and Worthington (1961)	Continental slope (33° 07'N 75° 42'W)	3230	3230	11.5 ± 1.5	Photographic bottom-current meter	0.30 (medium sand)	None	0.60 (coarse sand)
	(33° 08'N 75° 41'W)	3300 (approx.)	2800	6.1	Drogue	0.07 (very fine sand)	None	0.35 (medium sand)
McAllister (1962)	Bermuda—Plantagenet Bank	3760	3755	6.7	Savonius rotor current meter	0.10 (very fine sand)	None	0.40 (medium sand)
Swallow (personal communication, 1963)	200 miles west of Bermuda	4600	4000	42	Neutrally buoyant float	2.5–6 (medium gravel)	2 (medium gravel)	6.00 (medium gravel)
	Southwest of Cape Farewell (59°N)	2750	2245	10	Neutrally buoyant float	0.25 (fine sand)	None	0.55 (coarse sand)
	Northeast of Newfoundland (51.5°N)	2800	2700	9 (approx.)	Neutrally buoyant float	0.18 (fine sand)	None	0.51 (coarse sand)
Thorndike (1963)	Northeast of Newfoundland (51.5°N)	2500	2300	9 (approx.)	Neutrally buoyant float	0.18 (fine sand)	None	0.51 (coarse sand)
	50 miles south of Bermuda	4400	4400	7.6	Suspended drop current meter	0.15 (fine sand)	None	0.43 (medium sand)
Dill (personal communication, 1964)	North wall Puerto Rico Trench	6600	6599	14	Direct observation from *Archemede*	0.49 (medium sand)	None	0.88 (coarse sand)
Shonting and Cook (1964)	*Thresher* search area (42°N–65°W)	2300	2300	15	Drogue	0.57 (medium sand)	None	0.91 (coarse sand)

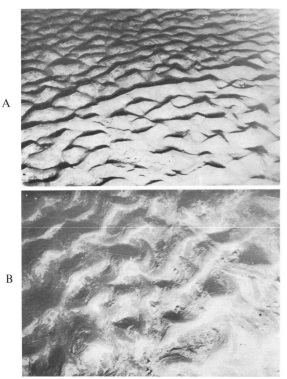

A

B

marks, current lineations (Fig. 3), and indirect evidence such as bare rock and coarse residual debris. The ripple marks observed are asymmetrical, symmetrical, longitudinal, linguoid and lunate; wavelengths generally range from 10 cm (Fig. 1) to several meters (Fig. 2), and amplitudes generally vary from barely perceptible up to 20 cm; however, amplitudes in excess of 20 cm are not uncommon. Scour marks around nodules, rocks or other solid objects are distinctive, and in regions of very high velocities, rocks occur in depressions and are sometimes concentrated in "rock nests."

The presence of bare outcrops of rock and deposits of coarse gravel constitute indirect evidence of currents since the fine sediments have been swept away. Frequently, tracks and trails cut across the ripple marks (Fig. 1), indicating the transient nature of currents that produced the ripples.

Of the thousands of photographs taken on the

Fig. 1. Ripples, Scotia Sea. Well-developed, short-crested ripples are typical of the eight camera stations taken in the northern part of the Drake Passage in water depths of approximately 4000 m. Note the crenulate track in B (left). 4010 m, 56° 18′S, 62° 51′W; Floor of Scotia Sea, southwest of Tierra del Fuego in the northern part of Drake Passage.

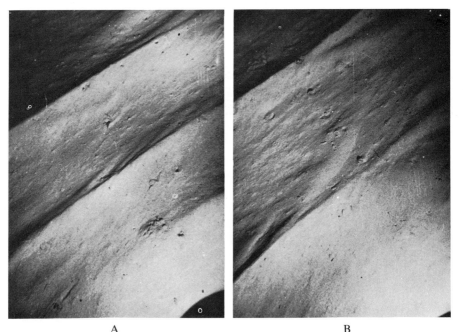

A   B

Fig. 2. Ripples, Southwest Indian Ocean. These ripples photographed 40 m above and a few miles east of the Mozambique Abyssal Plain are clearly longitudinal. The current lineations nearly parallel to the ripple crests indicate a current from lower left to upper right. One other station on the Abyssal Plain, 60 miles to the southwest, showed similar large-crested ripples in 4982 m. 4845 m, 29°21′S, 40°08′E; eastern edge of Mozambique Abyssal Plains, Southwest Indian Ocean.

Fig. 3. Current Lineations; Indian Ocean. These well-developed current lineations appear to be formed by the preferential deposition of material in the lee of solid objects. However, they also resemble deflation patterns observed on modern beaches and deserts. 4909 m, 23° 06'S, 56° 43'E; flat-floored trough south of Reunion Island, western Indian Ocean.

tops and flanks of seamounts, over three-quarters show dramatic current evidence consisting of one or more of the criteria mentioned above. Striking and rapid horizontal changes in bottom character frequently occur. Most commonly, successive photographs show rippled sand and rock outcrops. Another frequent sequence progresses from undisturbed mud to rippled sand to undisturbed mud, suggesting very local current effects. Current action has been observed on seamounts to depths exceeding 5000 m. Uncommonly, muddy unscoured bottom occurs on seamounts, in some cases even on summits (cf. Dacia Seamount). A similar distribution of current evidence is seen in the photographs from the flanks of islands.

Photographs taken from near the crests of major ridges exhibit current evidence similar to that observed on seamounts.

Several deep fracture zones which cut across the Mid-Oceanic Ridge in the equatorial Atlantic provide deep sills for water circulation. Photographs in Vema Fracture Zone at 5100 m and in Romanche Fracture Zone at 7498 m showed scattered rocks and rock outcrops. These fracture zones provide

the controlling sills (Wüst, 1936) for the circulation of bottom water from the western to the eastern basins of the Atlantic, and thus the photographic current evidence is not surprising despite the great depths.

Photographic current evidence is relatively rare on the ocean basin floor. As depth increases and globigerina ooze gives way to abyssal red clay, a significant change in bottom is seen. Less life is observed. The finer texture of the bottom sediment affects the forms produced by tracks and burrows.

Manganese nodules commonly seen in photographs from the deepest areas of the ocean generally show scour marks. Seven photograph stations in the axis of the Antarctic bottom water southeast of Bermuda show scour marks around manganese nodules in depths exceeding 4500 m. Nodules form primarily in areas of weak or moderate currents.

Very well-developed current lineations are seen in one station (Fig. 3) on a flat-floored (4900 m) trough approximately 100 miles south of Reunion Island in the Indian Ocean. These lineations appear to be formed by the preferential deposition of material in the lee of solid objects. Transverse asymmetrical ripple marks are also present on photographs from the same location, supporting the current origin for the lineations.

Very well-developed longitudinal ripples (Fig. 2) have been seen in several photograph stations in depth over 4800 m from the Mozambique Abyssal Plain. The scour marks and current lineations indicate a northerly current parallel to the axis of the ripples. Immediately before stopping for this station, the echogram recorded hyperbolic echoes tangential to the normal smooth sea floor.

Rock outcrops and scoured bottom have been observed on the steep walls of the Puerto Rico Trench and the Tonga and Kermadec Trenches.

Current evidence on the continental margin below 200 m appears to be less common at a given depth than on seamounts and other major elevations. The majority of photographs on the continental slope show a muddy bottom with an abundance of sessile and vagrant benthos. Photographs of the continental slope have revealed scour, outcrops of ancient sediments (Northrop and Heezen, 1951; Jordan, 1951), current ripples, and other current lineations.

Marginal plateaus often show ripples and scour marks. Much of the Blake Plateau east of southeastern United States is scoured free of sediment.

Current evidence is extremely rare on the continental rise, and thus those exceptional areas affected by bottom currents assume a greater importance. The vast majority of camera stations on the continental rise is typified by burrows, mounds, tracks, and trails. Attached organisms are less abundant here than on the continental slope, but burrows and vagrant life are common.

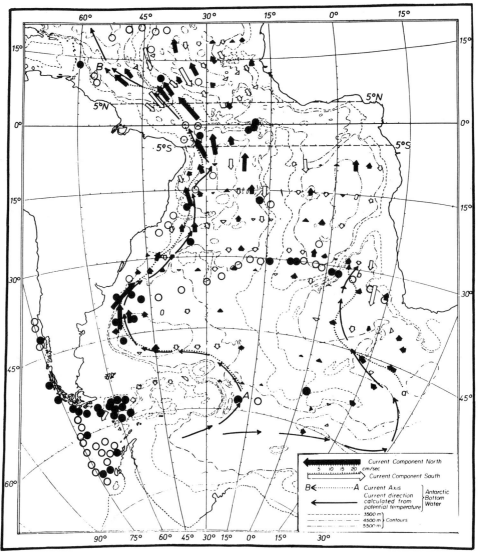

Fig. 4. Bottom Water Velocities and Bottom Photographs (modified from Wüst, 1957). Open circles indicate camera stations showing *no* current effects. Solid dots indicate photographs of scour, current lineations and ripple marks. Photographs on continental shelfs and seamounts are not shown. The Eltanin photographs concentrated in Drake Passage indicate a bottom current not shown by the arrows.

The bottom currents of the South Atlantic, as deduced by Wüst, are shown together with the distribution of bottom photographs in Fig. 4. Photographs showing bottom current evidence have been taken in the vicinity of the Antarctic bottom current. This current reaches velocities exceeding 15 cm/sec along the continental margin of Brazil and Argentina. These values based on dynamic calculations probably tend to be minimal due to the relatively large spacing of the stations. However, as Wüst (1958) has pointed out, tidal velocities of the order of 5–10 cm/sec are probably superimposed upon the calculated current velocities. Therefore, in the region of the Antarctic

bottom current, velocities may reach 20–25 cm/sec. The photographs show current lineations and ripples and current scour behind rocks that are compatible with the velocities computed by Wüst. All five of the photograph stations on the continental rise of Argentina show either current lineations or scour marks around rock outcrops. At one station on the continental rise of Brazil, crests of large ripples or dunes of undeterminable wavelength were photographed. The echogram made prior to the station indicated a generally smooth bottom with gentle undulations of 20 m amplitude and 1-km wavelength.

The outer ridge off southwestern United States

is a peculiar feature which appears to be constructed entirely of sediment. The normal ocean floor basement passes directly beneath the feature without showing any structural effect. It is probable that the ridge was constructed in its entirety by sediment transported along the sea floor by bottom currents. The scour marks, south pointing current lineations and occasional symmetrical and asymmetrical ripples found on the crest and east flank of the ridge, as well as the longer sand waves seen in echograms recorded near the crest of the ridge, indicate that the ridge is still being built by sediment transported from north to south by the deep western boundary current.

Strong currents are associated with oceanic circulation through passages between islands and continents. Photographs from the floor and sides of Florida Strait, the Strait of Gibraltar, Drake Passage (Fig. 1), and the major passages of the Lesser Antilles and the Kurile Islands typically reveal evidence of very strong currents, such as short-crested asymmetrical ripples, scour marks, current lineations, rock nests and bare rock.

Photographs on the continental slope west of Gibraltar show linguoid ripples at a depth of 1100 meters. The outflowing Mediterranean water which reaches a velocity in excess of 100 cm/sec in the strait can be identified as a distinct layer throughout the eastern North Atlantic at 1000–1250 m. The ripples photographed are associated with the outflow of Mediterranean water.

Well-developed, short-crested asymmetrical ripples were photographed in the Florida Strait at 860 m. The southward flowing bottom currents were estimated to have velocities between 10 and 60 cm/sec.

Camera stations in the northern portion of Drake Passage show evidence of strong easterly currents. Photographs typically show short-crested, linguoid and lunate ripples (Fig. 1) and occasional rock nests. Photographs in the central part of the Drake Passage generally show burrows, mounds and relative abundance of benthic life but no current effects. Water transport through the Drake Passage must be substantial. The photographs prove that high velocities occur very near the bottom, a view not generally held by earlier investigators.

On the continental rise of Antarctica west of the Antarctic Peninsula, current evidence in the form of "crag and tail" lineations and weak scour surrounding rocks has been observed in photographic stations in depths exceeding 4000 m.

Deep-sea Sands

Deep-sea sands and silts fall into three easily differentiated groups (Fig. 5): turbidite, accretionary, and residual.

The catastrophically deposited bottom-transported turbidites are characteristically graded, moderately sorted, and have well-developed primary structures. Turbidites are found downslope from potential sediment sources, on parts of the continental rise (particularly near submarine canyons), and everywhere on the abyssal plains. Turbidites may suffer erosion by deep-sea currents after deposition.

Accretionary sands consist of the tests of pelagic

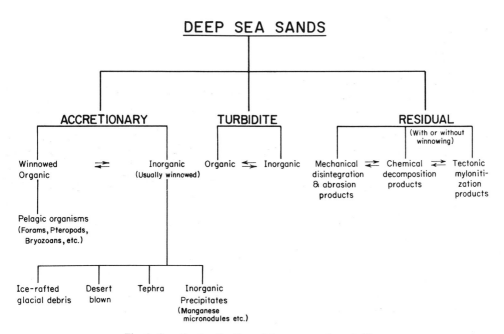

Fig. 5. Genetic classification of deep-sea sands and silts.

SUSPENSION AND TRACTION CURVES
FROM EXPERIMENTAL AND THEORETICAL DATA

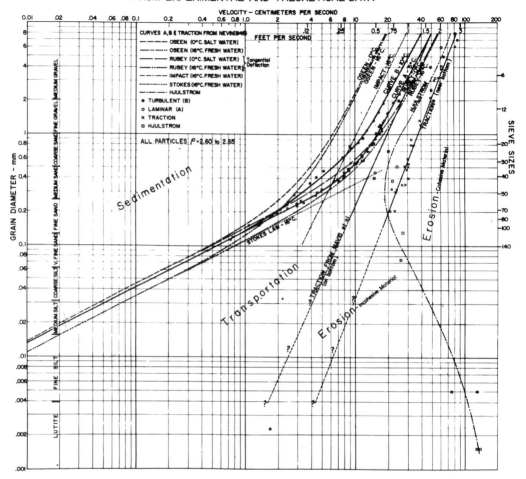

Fig. 6. Current velocities required for erosion transportation and deposition of stream-bed materials. The traction (near bottom) curve was determined by Nevin (1946) and extrapolated to bed conditions by applying a factor of 0.5. The resulting curve coincides with that of Mavis *et al.* (1935). Considerable uncertainty exists for sizes smaller than .2 mm (see references in Heezen and Hollister, 1964).

organisms, pyroclastic, eolian, and ice-rafted debris which has been winnowed by currents during and after particle-by-particle deposition. In high latitudes, ice-rafted material predominates; in low latitudes, organic debris. These sands have either sharp or gradational bedding contacts. The foraminiferal sands and in most cases the glacial sands, early reported from the crests of ridges from deep straits, seamounts, and other large topographic features, are almost entirely attributable to this class.

In certain areas of the ocean, thick tephra falls have been preserved without appreciable disturbance by bottom organisms. One such extensive fall, known as the Worzel Ash, was discovered west of Central and South America. In many cases, the bed showed no internal stratification, but in

several of the cores, the bed was several times thicker than normal and showed well-developed cross-stratification indicative of some bottom transport after deposition.

Locally derived residual sands formed without significant transportational history are the non-graded products of chemical decomposition and/or mechanical disintegration of bedrock. Residual sands are poorly sorted, usually devoid of silt and lutite. Most of the labile minerals are altered or decomposed entirely, leaving a residual deposit of the more stable minerals and alteration products characteristic of the proximal rocks. The lack of fine material in residual sand indicates appreciable bottom currents, as the weathering of rock should be expected to yield at least some fine detritus, and the deposits are in general not covered by particle-by-particle sedimentation. These deposits were early reported from the Romanche Fracture Zone. They have also been found in Vema Fracture Zone (Atlantic 11°N), and Vema Trench (Indian Ocean 9°S), and probably occur in many places on the Mid-Oceanic Ridge, on the walls of trenches, and on deep escarpments.

Current Velocities Implied by Deep-sea Sediment Structures

Current cross-stratifications in sands and silts have been observed in cores from deep ocean basins. An estimate could be made of the minimum current velocities required to form ripples, scour marks, cross-bedding, and other features observed in deep-sea photographs and cores if the critical traction transport velocities were accurately known for deep-sea sediment particles. The only studies of traction transport available were made for streams. A summary of several studies is shown in Fig. 6. These results can only serve as a first approximation, since the sea floor environment differs greatly from the average river environment. The increase in velocity required with decrease in grain size below medium sand shown by Hjulstrom's (1935) classic curve is poorly determined, and its reality has been questioned, thus leaving considerable uncertainty as to the velocities to be inferred from the various evidences of transportation of silt and lutite.

Particles of .02 mm would require a velocity of 4 cm/sec according to an extrapolation of the Mavis curve, and 60 cm/sec according to an interpolation of Hjulstrom's points. Particles of 0.2 mm would require a velocity of 10 cm/sec according to Mavis and 20 cm/sec according to Hjulstrom.

If deep-sea lutites are less cohesive than the clays used in the traction experiment cited by Hjulstrom, the velocities required to transport deep-sea silts and lutites may be closer to the extrapolated Mavis curve.

Traction experiments on deep-sea deposits must be made before the velocity significance of sediment features can be accurately evaluated. Current effects are frequently seen in globigerina ooze, a material of about 0.4-mm median grain size. Such features suggest velocities of at least 15 cm/sec. The ripples seen in many photographs of mineral sands (Fig. 1) require higher velocities. The scour and rippling of finer sediments are more difficult to interpret but may imply much higher velocities.

Although there is considerable uncertainty as to the critical traction velocity required, the minimum velocity for transport (settling velocity) is well determined. Once put into motion, particles of .02 mm would not come to rest until current velocities decreased to .03 cm/sec and particles of .2 mm would not stop until velocities fell below 2 cm/sec.

Recent oceanographic studies suggest that even in the greatest depths, velocities above those apparently required for the deposition of silt are common. Thus, the frequent occurrence of clean silt laminae in deep-sea cores may be explained by bottom current transportation.

CHARLES D. HOLLISTER
BRUCE C. HEEZEN

References

Heezen, B. C., and Hollister, C. D., 1964, "Deep-sea current evidence from abyssal sediments," *Marine Geol.*, **1**, 141–174.

Hjulstrom, F., 1935, "Studies of the morphological activities of rivers as illustrated by the River Fyris," *Bull. Geol. Inst. Univ. Upsala*, **25**, 221–527.

Jordan, G. F., 1951, "Continental slope off Apalachicola River, Florida," *Bull. Am. Assoc. Petrol. Geologists*, **35**, 1978–1993.

Northrop, J., and Heezen, B. C., 1951, "An outcrop of Eocene sediment on the continental slope," *J. Geol.*, **59**, 396–399.

Wüst, G., "Das Bodenwasser und die Gliederung der Atlantischen Tiefsee, die Statosphäre des Atlantischen Ozeans, Deut. Atlantische Expedition 'Meteor,' 1925–1927," *Wiss. Ergeb.*, **7** (1), 520pp.

Wüst, G., 1936, "Die Stratosphäre: Deutsche Atlantischene Exped. *Meteor*, 1925–1927," *Wiss. Ergeb.*, **6** (1), 109–288.

Wüst, G., 1955, "Stromgeschwindigkeiten im Tiefen- und Bodenwasser des Atlantischen Ozeans," *Deep-Sea Res.*, **3** (Suppl.), 373–397.

Wüst, G., 1957, "Quantitative Untersuchungen zur Statik und Dynamik des Atlantischen Ozeans: Stromgeschwindigkeiten und Strommungen in der Tiefen des Atlantischen Ozeans. Deut. Atlantische Expedition 'Meteor,' 1925–1927," *Wiss. Ergeb.*, **6** (2), 420pp.

Wüst, G., 1958, "Die Stromgeschwindigkeiten und Strommengen in der Atlantischen Tiefsee," *Geol. Rundschau*, **47**, 187–195.

OCEAN BOTTOM FEATURES—TERMINOLOGY AND NOMENCLATURE

Terminology of ocean bottom features is concerned with labels for *classes* of deep-sea topographical features, a series of submarine geomorphic terms. In contrast, *nomenclature* refers to the procedures of giving *specific names* to unique features.

Topographic Terms

A committee established at the Eighth International Geographical Congress (Berlin), including Alexander Supan, Otto Krümmel, Hugh Robert Mill and others, first established a basic trilingual terminology (English–French–German) summarized by Supan (1901). Since then, certain modifications have been proposed, for example, by the International Hydrographic Bureau (Niblack, 1924); by U.S. authorities (Littlehales, 1932); by the "Committee on Criteria and Nomenclature of the Major Divisions of the Ocean Bottom" of the

Association of Physical Oceanography of the U.G.G.I., established at its Edinburgh meeting, 1936; in individual proposals by Wüst (1936, 1940); by the newly constituted British National Committee of the A.P.O. (U.G.G.I.), which was reformed in 1952 with the support of the Royal Society (London) and reported on by Wiseman and Ovey (1953).

With the rapid evolution of precision depth recording, more and more detailed features can now be identified, so that gradually a more comprehensive series of terms is evolving. The following Tables are largely based on those supplied by the late Dr. Theodor Stocks, and supplemented by the writer, and a number received from Dr. Harris B. Stewart, Jr., U.S. Coast and Geodetic Survey.

Nomenclature

Most nations maintain a permanent Board of Geographic Names, as does the United States (with its headquarters in Washington); general world standards are established by the International

TABLE 1. VERTICAL CLASSIFICATION OF THE SEA FLOOR

Average Depth (m)	Bathymetric Divisions			Remarks
	English	French	German	
0–200	Continental Shelf	Plateau Continental	Schelf	Also island or insular shelf
ca. 200	Shelf, Edge, Break	Bord du Pl. C.	Schelfgrenze, Schelfrand	Also insular shelf edge
200–4000	Continental Slope passing to Continental Rise	Pente continental (Talus Contin.)	Kontinental-Abhang (a) Steilabfall (b) Fussregion	Also insular slope 200–3000 m 3000–4000 m
4000–5500	Deep Sea Floor	Mer profonde (Fond)	Tiefsee-Boden	
5500–11000	Trench	Fossé (Ravin)	Tiefsee-Gesenke (Depression)	"A long but narrow depression of the deep-sea floor having relatively steep sides" (Wiseman-Ovey)

TABLE 2. MAJOR SUBMARINE TOPOGRAPHIC FORMS

Category	Term			Definition
	English	French	German	
	(A) Elevations			
1	Ridge	Dorsale, Crête, Chaîne	Rücken	Long, narrow elevation with relatively steep sides
2	Rise, Swell	Seuil, Rameau	Schwelle	Extensive, broad elevation with relatively gentle sides, locally abrupt and/or rugged
2a	Sill	Seuil	Schwelle	Ridge or saddle forming the boundary between two basins, troughs or trenches
3	Plateau	Plateau	Plateau	Extensive flat-topped elevation of sea floor; alternatively interpreted as steep-sided (Littlehales), or gentle-sided
	(B) Depressions			
1	Basin (Ocean Basin)	Bassin (Bassin océanique)	Becken (Ozeanbecken)	More or less round or elliptical depressions of any dimension
2	Trough	Dépression (Auge)	Mulde	Long, relatively gentle-sided depression or furrow, sometimes subdivided into many smaller troughs
3	Trench	Fossé (Ravin, Sillon)	Graben	Long, narrow depression with steep sides, sometimes asymmetric in profile; major examples over 5500 m, but many minor ones of intermediate depth

TABLE 3. SECOND-ORDER SUBMARINE TOPOGRAPHIC FORMS

Category	Term			Definition
	English	French	German	
(A) Elevations				
1	Summit Height	Haut (Sommet)	Höhe, Spitze	Highest elevation of a ridge or rise
2	Crest	Crête (Ride)	Kamm	Long series of high points in a ridge
3	Dome	Dôme	Kuppe	Single elevation of over 200 m with steep sides
4	Seahigh (Hill)	(Colline)	Hügel	Elevation of up to 700 m, generally in large clusters ("abyssal hills")
5	Seamount	Montagne sous-marine (piton)	Tiefsee-Kuppe	Isolated elevation of at least 700 m
6	Guyot (Table-mount) (Oceanic Bank)	Guyot (Cone tronque)	Kuppe, Guyot	Seamount or "*tablemount*" of more or less circular form and flat top (named by Hess, after Arnold Guyot)
7	Seapeak	(Cône sous-marin)	—	Seamount with sharp, pointed top
8	Seaknoll	Colline sous-marine isolée	—	Minor elevation of sea floor in otherwise flat floor
9	Seamount Range	Chaine de montagne sous marine	—	A series of seamounts aligned along a ridge or rise
10	Seamount Chain	Ligne de montagne sous marine	—	A series of seamounts in a line, rising independently from relative flat, deep-sea floor
11	Seamount Group	Groupe de montange sous-marine	Kuppenregion	A group or cluster of seamounts without definite alignment
(B) Depressions				
1	Submarine Canyon	Canyon Sous-marin	Schelffurche	Several types may possibly be distinguished: glacially or fluvially eroded (*shelf canyons*), drowned by submergence, and those eroded by turbidity currents (*slope canyons*)
2	Gully	Chenal	Rinne	Long, narrow extension of a trough or basin
3	Gap	Couloir	Rinne	Passage with relatively steep sides cutting through a ridge or separating any two submarine elevations
4	Valley	Vallée	Tal	Submarine valley that is the extension of a continental valley
5	Caldron	Gouffre	Kessel	More or less steep-sided, round, pot-shaped depression
6	Furrow	Sillon	Furche, Schelffurche	Valley or canal-like incision in the shelf-edge, more or less normal to the latter
7	Deep-sea Channel	(Chenal Sous-marin)	(Tiefseefurche)	Valley in the deep-sea floor
8	Hole	Trou	Loch	Vertical chimney or sinkhole structure in the continental shelf floor

Committee on Geographic Names. These organizations have jurisdiction over geographic names bestowed on features of the ocean floor.

Guidelines for the selection of these oceanographic names were summarized by Wiseman and Ovey (1955). For nearly a century there have been two contrasting schools of thought about nomenclature: the personal name school and the existing name school. The former favored the bestowing of names by the discoverer, using such convenient names as his own, those of his wife, his ship, his sponsor, or anything his fancy suggested. The second category has accepted the first procedure only if no existing local name was available which could in some way be adapted. The second school has now become generally accepted, but in marine nomenclature the maps still carry many of the "personal name" suggestions; actually many of these can in fact be utilized, but only for second-order features or sounding points.

The personal name school of deep-sea topographic nomenclature was adopted by Petermann (1877), the great German geographer, by Sir John Murray of *Challenger* fame, by Alexander Agassiz and other well-known scientists. In contrast, the geographic school was supported by Neumayer, Supan, Wüst and others.

The conventions as now established require that all major topographic features receive geographic names, i.e., names that are derived from existing islands, reefs, provinces, features and so on. Several authors have proposed extremely awkward names, and a warning should be given against such procedures. Thus a ridge extending from one island to another should just receive one name—not two hyphenated. One should not use compass coordinates, because it confuses later localization of points within the feature. Thus Pandora Basin is preferred over North Fiji Basin, because the latter can be confused with the north part of the (main or south) Fiji Basin.

Accordingly all major features, such as a trench, must receive a geographic name, while a minor feature within it, say the site of a particular deep

TABLE 4. GENETIC AND GENERAL FORMS

Category	Term			Definition
	English	French	German	
			(A) Elevations	
1	Bank	Banc	Bank	Elevation of either the shelf or the deep-sea to depths of less than 200 m, often of sand (may or may not be "drowned" coral reef)
2	Seascarp (Escarpment)	Escarpement (Marche d'escalier)	(Stufe, Treppe)	Relatively long and high, rectilinear submarine cliff or wall, generally rather steep or even vertical; usually genetically part of a *fracture zone*
3	Shoal	Haut fond	Untiefe, Sand- (grund)	Potentially dangerous bank or reef for ships, conventionally taken as 11 m or less at mean low water springs
4	Reef	Récif (Ecueil)	Riff	Rocky eminence of the sea floor, generally potentially dangerous and causing waves to break and may even appear above MSL; may be coral reef or other rock
5	Pinnacle	Aiguille	Klippe (Spitze)	Sharp-pointed row of rocky points or reefs in shallow water
6	Spur	Eperon	—	Submarine projection of a mountainous ridge
7	Deep-sea Terrace	Terrasse profonde	—	Platform or step-like sector of the deep-sea floor
8	Shelf Terrace	Terrasse sur le pl. cont.	—	Similar step or series of step-like segments of the continental shelf
9	Province	Province	—	General term for a region of the ocean floor, united by some common feature
10	Deep Sea Fan or Cone	Cone profond	Tief-See Kegel	Radial feature of continental rise and/or slope, produced by clastic sedimentation, situated seaward of a major sediment source (river delta, etc.), often at terminus of submarine canyon, or cut by one
11	Archipelagic Apron	Piédestal archipél-agique	—	Similar feature of isolated ocean island or volcanic ridge
12	Levee	Levée de rive sous-marin	Tief-See Deich	An embankment bordering a deep-sea channel or shallow submarine valley, the result of "bank-flood" currents within the valley
			(B) Depressions	
1	Depth	Profondeur	Tiefe (die),	Deepest point in a trench, basin or trough
2	Deep	Fosse (la)	Tief (das)	Deep-sea plain well-differentiated within a large basin
3	Sill Depth	Profondeur de seuil	Schwellen (Sattel-Tiefe)	Lowest point on a ridge or saddle between two basins
4	Strath	Sillon, auge glaciaire	Glazial-trog	A long depression of the continental shelf, generally with greatest depths inshore and thus probably of glacial origin
5	Moat	Depression annulaire	Ringtiefe	An annual depression around the foot of sea-mount or volcanic ridges
6	Abyssal Plain	Plaine abyssale	Abyssische Tiefebene	A genetically distinguished part of a basin trench or trough that is filled with soft sediment flows, and distinguished by its almost horizontal gradient

sounding, appropriately receives the ship name. When several "depths" have been recorded by different expeditions within the same trench, it would be natural to use only the deepest in any small area. However, the accuracy of the instruments used by various ships is not as precise as might be wished; thus, although claims are often made for discoveries to the nearest meter, errors up to about 50 m in a 10,000-m sounding have been noted. This, added to navigational errors of 5–10 km, make much of this competition for recording maximum depths sound rather childish.

RHODES W. FAIRBRIDGE

References

Baulig, H., 1956, "Vocabulaire Franco–Anglo–Allemand de Geomorphologie," *Paris Publ. Fac. Lettres Univ. Strasbourg*, No. 130, 230pp.

Bourcart, J., 1944, "Geographie du fond des mers; etude du relief des oceans," Paris.

Bourcart, J., 1954, "Le Fond des Oceans," Paris.

Fairbridge, R. W., 1962, "Basis for submarine nomenclature in the South-West Pacific Ocean," *Deut. Hydrograph. Z.* **15**(1), 1–15.

International Geographical Congress, Berlin, 1901, Verh. 2, 1899, p. 370 (H. Wagner), p. 379 (O. Krümmel), p. 387 (H. R. Mill).

Littlehales, S. W., 1932, "The configuration of the oceanic basins," *Bull. Natl. Res. Council*, **85**, 13.

Niblack, A. P., 1924, "Terminology of submarine relief," *The Intern. Hydrograph. Rev.*, Monaco, **5**(2), 1.

Petermann, A., 1877, "Die Bodengestaltung des Grossen Ozeans," Gotha, *Petermann's Mitt.*, **23**, 125, Pl. 7.

Stocks, T., 1959, "Untermeerische Bodenformen," *Geogr. Taschenbuch*, Verl. Steiner, Wiesbaden.

U.G.G.I., Association d'Oceanographie physique, 1940, Publication Scientifique Nr. 8, Report of the Comm. on the Criteria and Nomenclature of the major Divisions of the Ocean Bottom, Liverpool

Wiseman, J. D. H., and Ovey, C. D., 1953, "Definitions of features on the deep-sea floor," *Deep-Sea Res.*, **1**, 11.

Wiseman, J. D. H., and Ovey, C. D., 1955, "Proposed names of features on the deep-sea floor. 2. General principles," *Deep-Sea Res.*, **2**, 261.

Wüst, G., 1936, "Die Gliederung des Weltmeeres," *Petermann's Mitt.*, No. 2, 33 (also in English translation: *Hydrograph. Rev.*, **13**(2), 46).

Wüst, G., 1940, "Zur Nomenklatur der Grossformen der Ozeanböden." *Publ. Sci. Assoc. Oceanogr. Phys.*

Cross-references: *Atlantic Ocean; Bathymetry; Natural Regions in the Oceans; Pacific Ocean.*

OCEAN BOTTOM RELIEF—*See* BATHYMETRY

OCEAN CURRENTS, INTRODUCTION

Examination of discussions on currents (Sverdrup *et al.*, 1942; Wiegel and Johnson, 1960) indicates that ocean currents can be divided into several groups: (1) currents that are related to the distribution of density in the sea, (2) currents that are caused directly by the stress of wind on the sea surface, (3) tidal currents and currents associated with internal waves, (4) currents and transport induced by surface gravity waves, and (5) local currents induced by fresh water entering the ocean at river mouths.

(1) Currents Related to Density Distribution. To this class of current belong the large-scale currents of the oceans such as the Gulf Stream (q.v.), the Kuroshio (q.v.), the Equatorial currents (q.v.), etc. These currents transport huge volumes of water— e.g., the Kuroshio current is estimated to transport 40–70 million m^3/sec. The general courses of these large-scale currents at the surface have been determined from ships' observations. At subsurface depths, the current speed and direction have been determined by the use of current meters operated from anchored ships. A discussion of the hydrodynamic theory of the large-scale ocean currents is beyond the scope of this entry and the reader is referred to the work of Sverdrup *et al.* (1942) and to other entries (*Oceanic Circulation, Dynamics*).

(2) Currents Related to Wind Stress. Wind blowing over the ocean exerts a stress on the water surface which causes a shallow wind drift. This transport of water tends to alter the density distribution and leads to corresponding currents.

Ekman (1902) examined theoretically the problem of wind drift in deep water, considering only frictional forces and the Coriolis forces (q.v.), and assuming the eddy viscosity to be constant; he concluded that in the northern hemisphere the wind drift at the surface is directed at 45° to the right of the wind. For positions below the surface, the current speed decreases with the distance below the surface and also varies in direction with the end points of the vectors going on a logarithmic spiral, commonly called the "Ekman Spiral" (q.v.; *Dynamics of Ocean Currents*). Experiments have shown that the speed of the surface wind drift was of the order of $\frac{1}{20}-\frac{1}{30}$ of the wind speed and that the direction of the drift varied considerably, with very large-scale eddies probably playing an important part in this variation; however, usually the direction of the wind drift was to the right of the wind direction by an angle varying between 30 and 60°.

In the northern hemisphere, the total transport due to wind drift is directed at right angles to the wind. Near coasts, however, certain modifications occur, and the secondary effect of the wind becomes important. For example, consider a wind in the northern hemisphere which is blowing approximately parallel to a coast with the coast on the right-hand side of an observer facing in the direction in which the wind blows. Assuming that the density of the seawater increases with depth, the direct effect of the wind causes a transport of light and warm surface water toward the coast. Because the coast represents an obstruction to this

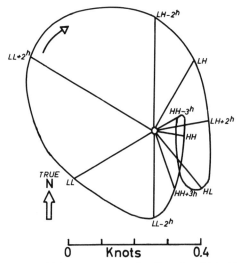

Fig. 1. Tidal current curve at San Francisco Lightship, referred to predicted time of tide at Golden Gate (U.S.C.G.S. "Coastal Tidal Currents").

flow, the light and warm water piles up against the coast, and at some distance from the coast, a denser and colder subsurface water must rise to replace that which has been carried toward the coast. The distribution of density consequently is altered, and as a secondary effect, a current develops which flows in the direction of the wind or parallel to the coast.

If the coast lies to the left of the wind direction, the light and warm surface water is transported away from the coast and is replaced by denser and colder subsurface water. This process is known as "upwelling" and also leads to an altered distribution of density and gives rise to a current flowing in the direction of the wind.

(3) **Tidal Currents.** The astronomical forces of the moon and sun cause tides in the ocean which in turn create currents. These tidal forces, combined with topographical features, give rise to three types of tidal currents: (a) the rotary type, illustrated by currents in the open ocean and along the sea coast (Fig. 1); (b) the rectilinear or reversing type, illustrated by currents in most inland bodies of water, such as in parts of San Francisco Bay (Fig. 2); and (c) the so-called hydraulic type, illustrated by the currents in straits connecting two independent tidal bodies of water, such as the Cape Cod Canal in Massachusetts, or Deception Pass in Washington. Since these three types of currents are of tidal origin, they are periodic. The tidal currents vary from locality to locality, depending upon the character of the tide, the water depth, and the configuration of the coast, but in any given locality, they repeat themselves as regularly as the tides to which they are related. In the open ocean, the tidal currents usually are rotating due to the effect of the

Coriolis force; i.e., from hour to hour the currents change in both direction and speed.

In recent years, the problem of circulation in estuaries has been studied extensively. One system classifies estuaries into four types, each with a distinct density stratification and circulation pattern, and concludes that an estuary tends to shift from type A (highly stratified) through type B (moderately stratified) to type C or D (vertically homogeneous) as a result of such factors as decreasing river flow, increasing tidal velocities, increasing width, or decreasing depth. The Mississippi River, for example, is typical of the type A estuary; whereas San Francisco Bay is typical of type D. Another system gives three types of estuarine circulations which are classified more as to the geometry of the estuary. These are (a) a narrow estuary with complete vertical mixing normal to the axis, (b) a deep estuary with vertical stratification, and (c) a wide estuary with asymmetrical circulation due to the earth's rotation.

(4) **Wave-induced Currents.** When wind blows over a water surface, energy is transmitted from the wind to the water. This energy in the water appears as surface gravity waves of a height and length which are governed by the velocity and duration of the wind and the area over which the wind blows. Associated with these waves is the orbital motion of the water particles.

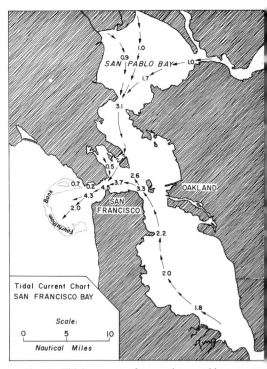

Fig. 2. Tidal currents for maximum ebb current, leaving San Francisco Bay. Velocity in knots. Note deltaic shaped sediment fan of Fourfathom Bank.

TABLE 1. RELATIVE MAGNITUDE OF OCEANIC AND ESTUARINE CURRENTS*

Type of Current	Magnitude (knots)	Authority
Large-scale mass movements		
California Current, off Monterey January 1958	0.3–0.6	Jennings and Schwartzlove (1958)
Off Southern California, 1937	0.13–0.4	Tibby (1939)
Currents caused by wind stress		
Amrum Bank Lightship	0.06–0.2†	Mandelbaum (1955)
San Francisco Lightship	0.06	Disney and Overshine (1925)
Inertial currents	Very small	Stommel (1934)
Tidal currents		
Rotary		
San Francisco Lightship	0.05	Disney and Overshine (1925)
Reversing		
San Francisco Bay, Golden Gate		
Maximum flood	3.3	U.S.C. and G.S. Tidal
Maximum ebb	4.5	Current Charts (1947)
Hydraulic		
Cape Cod Canal (maximum)	4.5	Wilcox (1958)
Wave-induced currents	Small	See Fig. 3

*From Wiegel and Johnson (1960). See references in that source.
†Depends on wind speed.

A secondary effect of the existence of surface waves is the net drift of the water mass in the direction of wave advance. Theory, which has been confirmed by experiment, shows that the water particles do not traverse a closed curve, but instead follow an open orbit. This orbital motion results in a net translation of water in the direction of wave movement with the passage of each wave and is termed "wave drift."

Longuet-Higgins (1953) developed a theory for null net transport of water for a fluid of small viscosity. An equation was derived which had viscous ("conduction") and inertia ("convection") terms. The viscous terms were those that described the diffusion of the vorticity from the bottom and surface boundary layers into the body of the fluid by the viscous action of the fluid. The inertia terms were those that described the movement of the vorticity by the mass transport current into the body of the fluid from the boundaries, e.g., the wave generator and the beach in a laboratory tank or the wave generating area and the beach, reef, or cliff, in nature. There are two outstanding features of this theory and its experimental verification. One is the fact that the transport near the bottom in shallow depths is always in the direction of wave advance. The second is the fact that for relatively shallow water, the transport is in the opposite direction to the direction of wave advance. Although the argument necessary to the solution of the

equations of a viscous fluid, mentioned above, requires that the wave amplitude be very much smaller than the boundary layer thickness, which is small, laboratory measurements show it to be useful for waves of appreciable amplitude.

The orbital motion of water particles of wind waves is modified due to the tractive force of the wind on the water surface dragging some of the water particles along in the direction of the wind so that a surface water particle may move forward in the direction of wave travel at a much higher velocity than the wave drift predicts. The dragging action of the wind acts to transport surface waters downwind at fairly high velocities, compared to the mass transport velocity; however, it should be recognized that the high degree of turbulence accompanying such wind action also tends to increase the rate of diffusion in the near-surface waters.

When waves break along a shore, a hydraulic head is established, and the water must return seaward, often first as an alongshore current inside the breaker zone, and then as a high-velocity flow seaward in a relatively narrow zone which is known as a "rip-current" (q.v., Vol. III).

Waves approaching a shore line at an angle not only undergo the changes in velocity, height, and length, but they also are bent, or refracted, because the inshore portion of the wave front travels at a lower velocity than does the portion in deeper water. Consequently, the waves "swing around" and tend to conform to the bottom contours. The characteristics of the bottom topography, the wave period and the wave direction in deep water determine the pattern of the wave crests in shallow water. The result of refraction is a change in height and direction of the waves. With very irregular bottom conditions, the heights may differ greatly between closely adjacent points along a coast.

One result of waves breaking at an angle with the coast is the generation of a littoral current. One of the important effects of littoral currents is movement of sediments along a coast as "littoral drift" (see *Sediment Transport,* Vol. III).

In addition to the general alongshore movement of sand, there is also the onshore and offshore movement of sand which occurs as a result of the changing wave conditions with the seasons. For example, along the California Coast, sand is generally moved onshore from offshore areas during the summer months when the waves are usually relatively low in height and long in period. During the winter months, however, when high short-period storm waves occur, sand is removed from the beaches and carried into offshore areas. These cyclic changes have been studied both in the laboratory and in the field.

(5) **Local or boundary currents**. In some instances, currents result in the nearshore area where water from rivers and nearly enclosed bays is discharged into the ocean with considerable momentum. The effect of such currents generally is not large relative to the major currents discussed above; however, rather large local effects may sometimes occur, such as the refraction of waves by currents and the consequent change in the wave-induced currents.

Relative Magnitude of Currents. Not only does the magnitude of the different currents vary between classes, but the magnitude of any particular class will vary from location to location and also with time at a given location. Typical examples of the magnitude and range of value of these currents are presented in Table 1.

J. W. Johnson

References

Ekman, V. W., 1902, "Om Jordrotationens inverkan pa vindstrommar i nafvet," *Nyt Magazin for Naturvidenskaberne,* **40**, No. 1, 37–63.
Longuet-Higgins, M. S., 1953, "Mass transport in water waves," *Phil. Trans. Roy. Soc. London, Ser. A,* **245**, No. 903, 535–581.
Sverdrup, H. U., Johnson, M. W., and Fleming, R. H.. 1942, "The Oceans," New York, Prentice-Hall.
Wiegel, R. L., and Johnson, J. W., 1960, "Ocean Currents, Measurement of Currents and Analysis of Data," in "Waste Disposal in the Marine Environment," pp. 175–245, New York, Pergamon Press.

OCEAN (PRIMARY PRODUCTION)—*See* **ORGANIC GEOCHEMISTRY OF THE OCEAN, NUTRIENTS AND PLANKTONIC PHOTOSYNTHESIS**

OCEANIC CIRCULATION, HEAT BY—*See* **HEAT TRANSPORT BY OCEAN CURRENTS**

OCEANIC CIRCULATION

Ocean currents are the predominantly horizontal motions of water in the sea, including the general ocean circulation, periodic, flows, and sporadic displacements of water masses. Specific examples of ocean currents are the Gulf Stream, tidal currents, and suspension flows.

General circulation may be pictured very crudely as two coupled modes of motion: systems of horizontal circulation gyres with intense flow concentrated toward the sea surface, linked to slow, generally meridional circulations of deep water in which opposed flows occur at different levels and are joined by vertical motions. Whereas portions of the flow in the horizontal gyres are sufficiently strong and distinct to be named specific currents, the latter flows are more a sluggish spreading of water and are not usually described as "currents."

Permanent anticyclonic gyres occupy the subtropical regions of the North and South Atlantic, North and South Pacific, and South Indian Oceans—water flows westward near the equator, poleward along the western sides of the oceans, eastward in mid-latitudes, and then equatorward. The northern hemisphere gyres, however, are separated from those of the southern by eastward countercurrents. In each gyre, the flow is most narrow and intense on the western side of the ocean, and rather weak and diffuse in the eastern regions. Furthermore, both northern gyres transport considerably more water, at much higher speeds, than those of the southern hemisphere. A large-scale gyre also exists in the North Indian Ocean, but its circulation reverses direction semiannually in accord with the periodic change in monsoon winds. One or more weak cyclonic gyres are found in the subpolar North Atlantic and Pacific; they contribute to the general eastward flow at mid-latitudes. No comparable subpolar gyres occur in the southern hemisphere, probably because mid-latitude zonal flow is not totally obstructed by continental barriers as in the northern hemisphere. Instead the broad, massive Antarctic Circumpolar Current flows around Antarctica, and the eastward movements of the subtropical gyres blend into it. Fig. 1 gives a rough impression of the prevailing surface currents and the pattern of these horizontal gyres (note that winter conditions are shown in the North Indian Ocean).

These large-scale circulations are quasi-geostrophic, i.e., the dominant horizontal forces are the cross-stream pressure gradient and the Coriolis force due to the earth's rotation (see *Geostrophic Motion*). Flow is directed approximately along lines of constant pressure in level surfaces, with relatively high pressure inside the subtropical gyres, low pressure inside the subpolar ones. Furthermore, the subpolar gyres enclose regions of relatively dense water; the subtropical gyres, regions of light water. Consequently, the currents are associated with large cross-stream density gradients, which, because of the geostrophic condition, require pronounced vertical shear of horizontal velocity. In fact, these currents are most intense at the sea surface, and their velocities diminish rapidly with depth, becoming small, or perhaps even vanishing, at a depth of 1 km.

The southern portion of the North Atlantic subtropical gyre is the North Equatorial Current, which flows westward between latitudes 10 and 20°N. Near South America, it is joined by a branch of the South Equatorial Current, and part of the combined flow enters the Caribbean Sea, rounds Cuba, and passes into the Straits of Florida as the Florida Current. Its continuation, the Gulf Stream (q.v.), flows along North America as a narrow intense jet: it is about 100 km wide and has maximum surface velocities of 200–300 cm/sec. It turns eastward, passes the Grand Banks of Newfoundland at about latitude 40°N, and becomes part of the complex set of generally eastward flowing currents called the North Atlantic Current or North Atlantic Drift. A portion of the latter turns south as the very weak, poorly defined Canary Current, which contributes to the North Equatorial Current. As the Gulf Stream flows northward, it increases severalfold in volume transport through lateral influxes, and becomes the greatest of the permanent ocean currents; off New England, it probably reaches to the ocean bottom (about 5 km deep) with perceptible bottom velocities and attains a volume transport well in excess of 100×10^6 m^3/sec (more than one hundred times the outflow of all the rivers of the world combined). Most of this vast flow must be confined

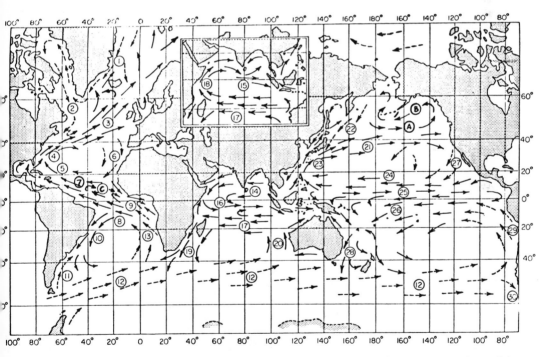

Fig. 1. Prevailing surface ocean currents in northern hemisphere winter. The top figure represents the condition during the northern summer in the Indian Ocean. (1) East Greenland Current, (2) Labrador Current, (3) North Atlantic Current, (4) Gulf Stream, (5) Antilles Current, (6) Canaries Current, (7) North Equatorial Current, (8) South Equatorial Current, (9) Guinea Current, (10) Brazil Current, (11) Falkland Current, (12) Circumpolar Current, (13) Benguela Current, (14) Northeast Monsoon Current, (15) Southwest Monsoon Current, (16) Equatorial Countercurrent, (17) South Equatorial Current, (18) Somali Current, (19) Agulhas Current, (20) West Australian Current, (21) North Pacific Current, (22) Oyashio Current, (23) Kuroshio Current, (24) North Equatorial Current, (25) Equatorial Countercurrent, (26) South Equatorial Current, (27) Californian Current, (28) East Australian Current, (29) Peru Current, (30) Cape Horn Current. (A) Subarctic or Aleutian Current, (B) Alaska Current. (C) Equatorial Countercurrent (Atlantic, modified after Chow, 1964).

to the western Atlantic, because the Mid-Atlantic Ridge blocks eastward motion below 1 or 2 km depth; southward motion in the eastern basin, moreover, is known to be much shallower and of much smaller volume transport than the Stream.

The near-surface circulation in the subpolar North Atlantic appears to be a cyclonic gyre of considerably less volume transport than the subtropical gyre. Portions of the North Atlantic Current flow towards the Arctic along the coast of Norway (Norwegian Current) and along the west coast of Iceland (Irminger Current). Return flow occurs beside Greenland through the East Greenland Current. Inflow and outflow from the Arctic Ocean are each estimated to be about 3×10^6 m^3/sec. The East Greenland Current, enhanced both by the Irminger Current and additional water from the North Atlantic Current, rounds Greenland and flows north along its west coast into the Labrador Sea and Baffin Bay (West Greenland Current). Correspondingly, the Labrador Current flows south by the coast of Labrador. Both the West Greenland and Labrador Currents are thought to transport about 6×10^6 m^3/sec. The Norwegian and West Greenland Currents, however, carry water of different physical properties from that in their southward flowing counterparts, the East Greenland and Labrador Currents; it would seem, therefore, that considerable mixing and cooling must occur in the far north.

The North Equatorial Current of the Pacific Ocean occupies about the same latitude belt (10–20°N) as the corresponding current in the Atlantic. It flows from east to west, increasing in volume transport through lateral influx; if it reaches to a depth of 1 km, it has a transport of the order 45×10^6 m^3/sec. It is a very broad current, however, and velocities seldom exceed 20 cm/sec. Somewhat east of the Philippines, it divides; one branch turns south along Mindanao, while the larger one flows northward close to the eastern side of the Philippines and Formosa. North of Formosa this current is called the Kuroshio (q.v.), or Japan Current. Near latitude 30°N, it passes through the Ryukyu Islands and continues near the coast of Japan until latitude 35°N, where it leaves Honshu and flows nearly due east (on average). Like the mid-latitude eastward flow in the North Atlantic, that in the North Pacific is both complicated and poorly defined; moreover, no single nomenclature is used to describe it. The continuation of the Kuroshio from Japan approximately to longitude 160°E is sometimes called the Kuroshio Extension, but often is not distinguished as a separate current segment. East of 160°E the flow is quite broad and slow, and the whole has been called the West Wind Drift; occasionally, however, it is subdivided into a northern part (the Aleutian or Subarctic Current) and a southern part (the North Pacific Current). Water from this eastward flow rejoins the North Equatorial Current both through diffuse southward motion in the central Pacific and in the broad, weak California Current adjacent to North America.

Like the Gulf Stream, the Kuroshio is very narrow (some 100 km wide) and may attain high surface velocities (200 cm/sec or more). If its vertical extent is only 1 km, its volume transport would be about 50×10^6 m^3/sec; on the other hand, should the current be found to extend in fact to the ocean bottom, as its Atlantic counterpart, the Gulf Stream, seems to do, its transport would be comparable to that of the Stream. Most of this flow must turn south in the western or central Pacific, however, because the California Current, although 500–1000 km wide, appears to transport only 10–15 $\times 10^6$ m^3/sec.

In the subpolar North Pacific, the near-surface currents flow in a cyclonic pattern. Near North America, a portion of the West Wind Drift turns north into a counterclockwise gyre in the Gulf of Alaska. This, the Alaska Current, is thought to have a volume transport of 10–20 $\times 10^6$ m^3/sec. Upon approaching the Aleutian Islands, it divides: one part returns directly to the eastward flow, but the other rounds the Aleutians, is joined by another branch of the West Wind Drift, and moves counterclockwise around the Bering Sea. The current then flows southward along Kamchatka and Japan as the Oyashio, and turns eastward just north of the Kuroshio. The Oyashio probably transports 7–10 $\times 10^6$ m^3/sec, and is the Pacific analog of the Labrador Current. The North Pacific subpolar circulation is markedly different from that of the Atlantic in that access to the Arctic Ocean is severely limited; considerably less than 1×10^6 m^3/sec passes through Bering Strait.

The subtropical gyres of the southern hemisphere are considerably weaker than those of the northern, although the South Equatorial Currents are somewhat stronger than their northern counterparts. The South Equatorial Current of the Atlantic Ocean flows westward between latitude 20°S and a few degrees north of the equator. As noted above, it divides near South America, and one branch joins the North Equatorial Current; the other flows poleward along the coast of South America as the Brazil Current, and then turns eastward in higher latitudes (around 40°S). As in the North Pacific, the eastward flows of middle-to-high latitudes in the South Atlantic, Pacific, and Indian Oceans are often called, rather vaguely, West Wind Drifts. (Usually, however, that portion of the flow—by far the greatest—which circles Antarctica and does not participate in the subtropical gyres is distinguished from the rest as the Antarctic Circumpolar Current.) In the eastern South Atlantic, the West Wind Drift feeds the Benguela Current, which flows north along the west coast of Africa, ultimately into the South Equatorial

Current. This subtropical gyre is shallower than that in the North Atlantic, probably extending only to 1 or 2 km depth; moreover, the volume transport of the Benguela Current seems to be only 15×10^6 m³/sec, and that of the Brazil Current, $10-20 \times 10^6$ m³/sec. Nevertheless, this gyre shows the pronounced asymmetry characteristic of the northern subtropical circulations in that the Brazil Current is about 100 km wide, but the Benguela Current, roughly 500 km.

The South Equatorial Current of the Pacific Ocean occupies about the same latitude belt as that in the Atlantic, although the flow in the southern part of the zone is sometimes called the Trade Drift to distinguish it from the more intense equatorial flow. This is the source of the East Australian Current, which flows southward adjacent to Australia and subsequently enters the West Wind Drift in the latitudes of New Zealand (near 40°S). On the other side of the Pacific, the Peru Current (or Humboldt Current) flows northward along the west coast of South America between the West Wind Drift and the South Equatorial Current. In its gross characteristics, this gyre resembles that in the South Atlantic: the East Australian Current is roughly 100 km wide and its volume transport is estimated at $10-25 \times 10^6$ m³/sec, while the Peru Current is nearly 1000 km wide and apparently transports $15-20 \times 10^6$ m³/sec. This gyre too is probably limited to the upper 1 or 2 km of the ocean.

A similar circulation prevails in the upper water of the South Indian Ocean. North of latitude 20°S, a third South Equatorial Current flows to the west; it bends south upon approaching Africa and becomes the Agulhas Current, which flows between Madagascar and the continent, is about 100 km wide, and transports something like 20×10^6 m³/sec. Near latitude 40°S it turns abruptly eastward into the West Wind Drift. Very little is known of the northward return flow.

The circulation of the North Indian Ocean, i.e. north of latitude 10°S, is quite unlike that of the Atlantic and Pacific for it varies with the monsoon winds, and its northward extent is severely limited by the Asiatic land mass. During the northern summer, when the prevailing wind blows from the ocean onto Asia, the strong, narrow Somali Current flows northeastward along the African coast and is analogous to the Gulf Stream and the Kuroshio. The Somali Current is fed by part of the South Equatorial Current and turns eastward somewhere between latitudes 5–10°N to form the rather broad Monsoon Current. During the northern winter, however, when the wind blows off Asia onto the ocean, the Monsoon Current is replaced by a westward flowing North Equatorial Current, and the Somali Current disappears, giving way to fairly broad, weak, southwestward flow. The latter flow feeds into an eastward moving Equatorial Countercurrent which lies between the North and South Equatorial Currents.

Subpolar gyres such as exist in the North Atlantic and Pacific are not present in the southern hemisphere. Instead, the mid-latitude eastward flows blend into the great, nearly zonal Antarctic Circumpolar Current, which the lack of major continental obstruction allows to encircle Antarctica. This current seems to extend to great depths, with a volume transport of the order of 100×10^6 m³/sec; thus, it is comparable in magnitude to the Gulf Stream and Kuroshio. On the other hand, it is from several hundred to 1000 km wide, and its maximum surface velocities are only about 20 cm/sec, a tenth of those in the other two currents. It may be significant that the disposition of channels and island arcs in the Southern Ocean prevents the Current from being strictly zonal: it has a small southward component over most of its extent, but just after passing Cape Horn, much of it is deflected abruptly northward some 10° of latitude. This narrow northward flow, the Falkland Current, may prove analogous to the intense western boundary currents mentioned above and indicates a greater similarity than is immediately apparent between the Circumpolar Current and the subtropical gyres.

In the Atlantic, Pacific and Indian Oceans, two major eastward flowing currents are embedded in the system of North and South Equatorial Currents. In both the Atlantic and Pacific, an Equatorial Countercurrent, 300–500 km wide, flows within the latitude belt 2–10°N; it shifts with the seasons, lying in the southern part of this belt during the northern winter, and in the northern part during the summer. The flow is concentrated toward the sea surface, with maximum velocities of 50 cm/sec, but it is highly variable both in time and longitude: volume transport estimates for the Pacific current range from $1-60 \times 10^6$ m³/sec. (Except for the reversing circulation of the North Indian Ocean, this transport variation far exceeds any reported for other major currents.) As mentioned above, the Countercurrent in the Indian Ocean occurs only during the northern winter, and unlike its Atlantic and Pacific counterparts, lies in the southern hemisphere. All three Countercurrents both feed and are fed by the North and South Equatorial Currents which flank them.

The Equatorial Undercurrent—or Cromwell Current—also flows from west to east, but it is centered precisely on the equator and is therefore enveloped by the South Equatorial Current (except in the Indian Ocean). It differs markedly from all other near-surface currents in that it is essentially a subsurface flow; its velocity maximum occurs at a depth of about 100 m, and the surface motion above the swift core is usually westward. It is roughly 300 km wide, and although only 200 m deep, it is a major ocean current because its high

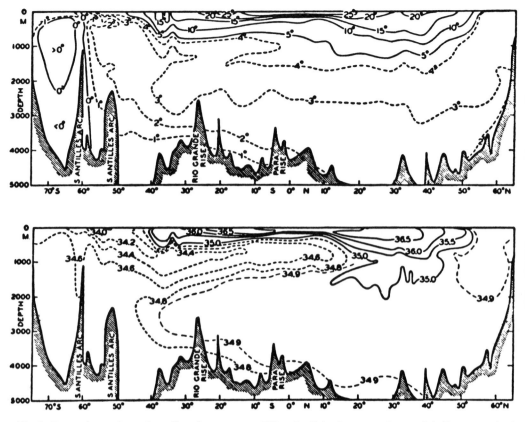

Fig. 2. Composite north-south profiles of temperature (°C) and salinity (parts per thousand) in the western basin of the Atlantic Ocean. Depths are in meters (after Wüst).

speed (maximum velocities of 100–150 cm/sec in the Atlantic and Pacific) gives it a large volume transport—about 40×10^6 m³/sec in the Pacific, and a comparable figure indicated in the Atlantic. In the Indian Ocean, the Undercurrent seems only about half as strong as in the Atlantic and the Pacific, and more markedly developed in the eastern part of the ocean than in the western. Its flow also appears to vary considerably over periods of months, but whether such variation is related to the phases of the monsoon is not clear. The relations between the Undercurrents and their surrounding waters are not yet understood, nor has the significance of their flow along the equator yet been fully perceived—flow which must, in part, be significantly non-geostrophic.

Coupled to this predominantly near-surface system of horizontal gyres and zonal flows is a deep-water convective circulation in which air-sea interaction processes produce relatively dense water at the sea surface in high latitudes; this water sinks, fills the central ocean basins, and is replaced by poleward moving water which rises from intermediate depths. The deep and bottom water of most of the world ocean (excluding

marginal seas) appears to have been formed this way in just two small areas: the Irminger Sea, between Iceland and Greenland—possibly also the adjacent Labrador Sea—and the region immediately around Antarctica, especially the Weddell Sea. From the latter source, Antarctic Bottom Water sinks into the Circumpolar Current and spreads across it toward the equator; its traces have been identified in the central Atlantic as far north as latitude 35°N, but in the Pacific and Indian Oceans, only to about latitude 20°S. This water can be recognized in Figs. 2 and 3 as the cold fresh tongue extending north from Antarctica near the ocean bottom.

North Atlantic Deep Water sinks near Greenland and moves south across the equator, overlying the Antarctic Bottom Water; it is indicated in Fig. 2 by the large southward intrusion of relatively warm, saline water. It enters the circumpolar flow, becoming considerably diluted through mixing with bottom water below and intermediate water above; the mixture is then carried eastward and becomes the deep water of the Indian and Pacific Oceans. That of the Pacific is so greatly diluted, however, that its Atlantic component is barely perceptible.

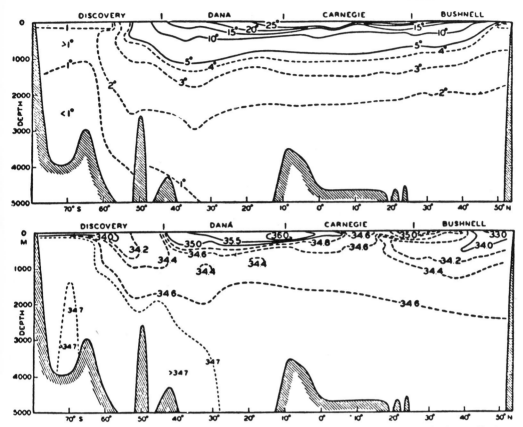

Fig. 3. Composite meridional profiles of temperature (°C) and salinity (parts per thousand) in the Pacific Ocean approximately along longitude 170°W. Depths are in meters (after Sverdrup).

(Since it is filled from this single source, the deep Pacific is much more homogeneous than the deep Atlantic.)

Surface water also sinks in a zone which encircles Antarctica roughly between latitudes 50–60°S (the Antarctic Convergence). This becomes the Antarctic Intermediate Water, which spreads northward as a relatively cold, fresh tongue at a depth of about 1 km (cf., Figs. 2 and 3). In the Atlantic, its traces are carried to latitude 35°N by the Gulf Stream, but like the Bottom Water, it can be detected in the Indian and Pacific Oceans only as far as latitude 20°S.

The distributions of temperature and salinity suggest therefore that in the Atlantic Ocean, the Antarctic Intermediate and Bottom Waters spread northward, mix into the deep water between them and return as such to near-surface regions of the Southern Ocean. This circulation pattern reaches well into the northern hemisphere, where a characteristic Deep Water is actually formed in high latitudes and contributes to the circulation. It is not clear, however, to what extent the sinking North Atlantic Deep Water derives from surface water imported over considerable distance to the

Irminger Sea and Labrador Seas, or is simply recirculated from great depths. Intermediate Water also moves northward in the Indian and Pacific Oceans, but apparently more slowly than in the Atlantic. The deep-water movements of these two oceans, however, are far less clear than those of the Atlantic: although the temperature and salinity fields definitely show northward movement from the Southern Ocean in the lower deep water, they are rather ambiguous as to its penetration into the northern hemisphere and fail to indicate the route of compensating southward motion. It has usually been supposed that since no deep water is formed in the Pacific, its deep flow is considerably more sluggish than that of the Atlantic.

The abyssal circulation is certainly much slower than any involving major surface currents: radiocarbon concentrations in the Pacific suggest speeds of the order of hundredths of a centimeter per second as typical of deep northward motion, and in the Atlantic speeds up to several centimeters per second have been estimated from the density field for deep water adjacent to South America. It is very difficult, however, to affix transport estimates to these flows, especially since they may be intermittent and not at all steady. Massive sinking in high latitudes, for instance, presumably occurs chiefly in late winter when surface water attains its minimum temperature and maximum density. Furthermore, it may well be that deep circulations of the sort sketched above are not taking place at all at the present time, but occur only during extreme climatic fluctuations; the characteristic tongues of Figs. 2 and 3 would then be simply a residue left by water movements long ceased.

Both the North Atlantic and North Indian Oceans are linked by secondary circulations to marginal seas. Evaporation over the Mediterranean and Red Seas is so intense that high-salinity surface water sinks and flows out into the Atlantic and Indian Oceans respectively on the bottom of the Straits of Gibraltar and Bab el Mandeb; it is replaced by corresponding surface inflow. The saline outflow sinks to a depth of about 1 km and, the Mediterranean water especially, spreads over very considerable regions. The Red Sea outflow is probably intermittent, but that from the Mediterranean has been estimated at 2×10^6 m³/sec. In addition, deep water from the Norwegian Sea occasionally spills into the Atlantic over the ridge between Iceland and the British Isles. Such overflows are sporadic, but when they occur, they may include transports of the order 1×10^6 m³/sec of Norwegian Sea water.

Considerable effort has been put into attempts to understand the dynamics of this general oceanic circulation. The problem is so formidable, however, that success to date has been largely rudimentary and qualitative. In particular, the characteristic east-west asymmetry in horizontal circulation patterns has been found to be a result of the meridional variation in Coriolis parameter. (For a description of the essential mechanisms, see *Gulf Stream*.) The full circulation theories invoke surface wind stress and high-latitude cooling as driving agents of the permanent ocean currents, but a discussion of them seems beyond the scope of the present article; the reader is referred to the review articles by Stommel (1957) and Fofonoff (1962), and the collection of papers edited by Robinson (1963).

Although a description of the general circulation may give an impression of uniformity and evenness, the current motions actually occurring in the sea fluctuate rapidly. Two periodicities are especially pronounced, one a forced oscillation, the other free. The tidal motions induced in the earth's fluid envelope by the gravitational attraction of the moon and sun are essentially long waves, in the sense that wavelength greatly exceeds ocean depth; consequently water particles undergo semidiurnal and diurnal horizontal displacements of several kilometers. The speeds of these *tidal currents* are of the order 10 cm/sec in the open ocean but may be very much greater in narrow

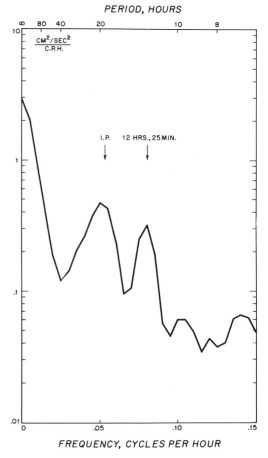

Fig. 4. Power spectrum of current speeds based on hourly readings of a 1046-hour record from a current meter moored at a depth of 500 m near 39° 30′N, 69° 30′W. Arrows indicate the exact semidiurnal tidal period and local inertial period (I.P.). (Courtesy of T. F. Webster).

bays; e.g., in the Skjerstadt Fjord, Norway, velocities have been measured up to 800 cm/sec, considerably higher than any in the permanent ocean currents. In the open ocean, these currents are generally rotary, such that water particles describe roughly elliptical trajectories, but near coasts the bottom topography restricts them to alternating motions along the shore lines.

In a rotating fluid such as the ocean, a free, horizontal oscillation may be excited in which water particles move in circular orbits. Such *inertial motion* involves balance between local particle acceleration and the Coriolis force due to the rotation of the system from which the motion is observed. On the earth, the period of this motion (inertial period) is the *half-pendulum day*, equal to twelve hours divided by the sine of the local latitude. The motions may be of comparable scale and magnitude to the tidal currents. Figure

4 is a power spectrum of current speeds obtained from a current meter moored at a depth of 500 m in the open ocean, at 39° 30′N, 69° 30′W: it shows the distribution of kinetic energy among the component oscillations of the motion as indicated by period. The pronounced, fairly sharp peaks which occur at the local inertial period and the semi-diurnal tidal period indicate that both these oscillatory currents constituted important parts of the observed motion.

By far the greatest speeds of oceanic motion occur in a type of bottom current on continental slopes and rises. If enough sediment can be stirred into suspension in the overlying water, the resulting dilute mud may become sufficiently dense to flow down a slope under the force of gravity as a *turbidity current* or *suspension flow*. A spectacular example occurred in 1929 when an earthquake under the continental slope off the Grand Banks of Newfoundland caused mud to slump, mix into the seawater, and flow down the slope over an area 1000 km long and several hundred kilometers wide. Timed by its successive breaks of telegraph cables, the current achieved enormous speeds, up to 3000 cm/sec. It is generally thought that most of the numerous submarine canyons at the edges of continental shelves were cut by such sporadic flows (see *Geostrophic Motion, Gulf Stream, Kuroshio, Physical Oceanography*).

BRUCE WARREN

References

Dietrich, G., 1963, "General Oceanography," Ch. 10, New York, London, John Wiley & Sons.

Fofonoff, N. P., 1962, "Dynamics of Ocean Currents," in (Hill, M. N., editor) "The Sea," Vol. I, Ch. 3, New York, London, John Wiley & Sons.

Hill, M. N., (editor), 1963, "The Sea," Vol. II, New York, London, John Wiley & Sons.

Robinson, A. R., (editor), 1963, "Wind-Driven Ocean Circulation," New York, Toronto, London, Random House.

Stommel, H., 1957, "A Survey of Ocean Current Theory," *Deep-Sea Res.*, **4**, 149–184.

Sverdrup, H. U., Johnson, M. W., and Fleming, R. H., 1942, "The Oceans," Ch. 15, New York, Prentice-Hall.

OCEANIC CURRENT AND WAVE RECORDING—INSTRUMENTATION

Problems of Measuring Motions in the Sea

Waves and currents may be considered as certain defined parts of the wide variety of motions which are present nearly everywhere in the sea. Waves (q.v.) are periodical motions with vertical displacement of the surface, their period spectrum ranging from 10^{-2} second (capillary waves) and 10^1 (gravity waves) to 10^4 (long-period tidal waves) and even 10^6–10^8 second fluctuations. Currents, on the contrary, may be defined as more or less turbulent horizontal motions with noticeable mass transports which can be periodical (tidal currents) or non-periodical (wind drift, density currents).

The measurement of motions of both kinds in the open oceans suffers from the lack of real fixed reference points. However, a lot of difficulties are also encountered with nearshore current measurements because it is impossible to design an ideal instrument for either waves or current recording which would be able to record the whole spectrum of motions or give answers to all questions.

Records of longer duration, instead of single observations or short records, have become more and more usual, but with this trend new problems have arisen regarding the development of evaluation techniques by which the records can be analyzed automatically to obtain the desired results.

Wave Recording

(1) Measurable Parameters. The most important qualities of waves are height and period (or frequency); other qualities such as traveling velocity and direction, wavelength, and wave energy (especially shock energy at structures) are also important.

(2) Classification according to Reference Level. (a) The first group of instruments includes those which have a really fixed reference base, i.e., instruments mounted on coastal structures such as piers, dams, piles, etc., or on underwater structures on the sea bottom.

(b) The second group comprises all methods which work without a fixed connection to the earth or to the sea bottom. Shipborne and buoy instruments belong to this group as do airborne instruments. With these methods, an artificial reference level must be created. This is generally achieved by accelerometers on stabilized platforms, the records of which are integrated twice in order to get the zero level.

(3) Types of Instruments. The various instruments can be classified also according to the utilized physical principles.

(a) The least difficulties are given where it is possible to measure height directly, e.g., by reading or photographing a lath-scale or by using a tide-gauge type with a surface float in a tube or well and taut wire transmission. An instrument with electrical step contacts actuated by rising or falling water also belongs to this group.

(b) For indirect measurements of wave heights several different methods have been used. The most frequent is to measure the pressure of the water column above the instrument. Corrections have to be applied because of density changes of the water and temperature changes within the instrument, and also because the pressure variations due to surface waves are damped with increasing depth, depending on their period.

The double-wire principle, in which the electrical

resistance between two uninsulated wires is recorded, is only suitable for surface measurements. Another similar principle makes use of the fact that the capacity of a single insulated wire against the water depends on the immersion depth.

The acoustical echo principle may be used in a twofold manner: measuring the echo time in the air from a point above sea level, or measuring in the water with an inverted echo-sounder lying on the bottom.

With two synchronized cameras mounted at a distance on shore or on board a vessel, it is possible to make stereophotographic, single, or motion pictures. Since the evaluation of these pictures is very troublesome, this has not often been done.

Airborne methods comprise photographic as well as radar or echo-sounding techniques.

For all these techniques, various difficulties must be considered and various errors corrected.

(c) Measurements of shock or impact or of the wave orbital velocity require instruments of very sturdy construction and very short response time. These qualities are given with wave force meters of the strain gauge type by which electrical resistance changes are recorded. By suitable arrangements, it is possible to record simultaneously in several depths in order to get vertical energy distribution profiles.

(d) Special instruments have been designed for different purposes, e.g., tsunami recorders with tuned hydraulic filters which suppress waves of shorter periods or tidal waves. For measuring wave front directions, the use of a triangle system has been attempted. From the recorded phase differences caused by the same wave crest at the three measuring points, the direction can be derived. However, too many errors are possible with this method, thus air photographs should be recommended instead.

(4) Analyzing Methods. Analyzing of wave records is normally done by calculating statistics of height, period and energy distribution. Electrical methods have been developed using tuned resonance filters. By playing back the record with changing speeds, the energies for different resonant frequencies which correspond to defined wave periods can be determined.

Current Recording

(1) Parameters. Normally the measuring of current velocity and direction (= current vector) is sufficient. The mean deviations are sometimes of interest as a measure of turbulence.

(2) Basic Methods. (a) Flow measurements at really fixed points are the first fundamental method. Nearshore measurements at solid constructions and near-bottom measurements with tripods or similar mounts are representative for this method. Results may be transmitted by cable to a shore station or recorded in the instrument itself.

(b) Flow measurements with moored systems which may be vessels, buoys or instruments with self-buoyancy suffer often from errors due to irregular stray motions of the mooring system (see Paquette, 1963). The results are transmitted by cables to the ship or, with buoys, sometimes by radio signals to a remote ship or shore station. Other instruments are self-recording on strip charts, films, wax paper, magnetic tapes, etc.

(c) The path method is characterized by following the path of a water particle within the current or at least, if a continuous observation is not possible, by determining the current vector, as the difference between start and end point of the path. This is done, e.g., with differences between ships' calculated and true positions or with drift bottles, drift cards or other surface floats which are recovered after some time. For deep currents, large parachutes suspended with thin wires from small surface floats have been used. Recently, subsurface floats with acoustical transmitters ("pingers") which can be adjusted to be neutrally buoyant within a certain depth layer have been constructed. The ship follows the drifting float with the aid of hydrophones.

Radioactive or dye tracers may also be used instead of solid floats; they indicate not only currents but turbulence, too.

Positioning in nearshore work can be done by optical or electrical ranging methods. In deep water work, it has been greatly improved by modern radio navigation systems and radar techniques.

(3) Flow Measuring Techniques. (a) *Velocity*. Most instruments have rotating parts like propellers, screws, paddle wheels or S-shaped rotors, whose revolutions are counted or otherwise converted into readable signals. Other types measure the hydraulic pressure against gravity, as by a pendulum, or against springs, or with a Pilot tube manometer. Besides these two groups, several other physical effects have been employed: the acoustic Doppler effect, electromagnetic induction in natural or artificial fields, the hot-wire cooling effect, etc.

(b) *Direction*. Those instruments which are used in sufficient distances from iron ships or structures usually have magnetic compasses of various designs and transmitting methods (e.g., electrical or optical). For measurements in the vicinity of ships, the bifilar suspension method is preferred. Here, the instrument measures the difference angle between current direction and bifilar-suspended frame, the latter being practically parallel to the ship's axis. With methods or instruments which give only one component of the current, measurements in a second direction are necessary for computing the true current vector.

(c) *Analyzing Methods.* The analyzing method usually depends on the problem in question. For example, for tidal currents harmonic analysis is a suitable means; for wind drift currents the dependence on the different wind directions will be of interest. Recently, automatic data processing by computers has been made possible, either by transfer of otherwise read data into punch cards or tapes, or by using a binary coded recording system (on film or magnetic tape) which can be automatically read out by a special device.

Hartwig Weidemann

References

*Böhnecke, G., 1955, "The principles of measuring currents," *Publ. Scient.*, No.14, I.A.P.O., 28pp.

*Johnson, J. W., and Wiegel, R. L., 1959, "Investigation of current measurement in estuarine and coastal waters," State Water Poll. Contr. Bd., Publ. No. 19, Sacramento, Calif., 233pp.

Paquette, R. G., 1963, "Practical problems in the direct measurement of ocean currents," Marine Sc. Instrumentation, Vol. 2, pp. 135–146, Instr. Soc. of Am., Pittsburgh.

Sinha, E. Z., and Kuehn, C. L., 1963, "Bibliography of oceanographic instruments," I., *Met. and geoastrophys.*, Vol. 14, pp. 1242–1298.

Snodgrass, F. E., 1952, "Wave measurements," Ocean. Instrumentation, Nat. Res. Counc. Publ. 309, pp. 139–165, Nat. Ac. of Sciences.

Wiegel, R. L. (editor), 1956, "Proceedings of the first Conference on Coastal Engineering Instruments," Chapters 1–13 and 16–24. Conc. Wave Res., the Eng. Found.

Wright, F. F., 1965. "Wave observation by shipboard radar," *Ocean Sci. & Ocean Engr.*—1965 (Trans. Mar. Tech. Soc.—Am. Soc. Limnol. & Oceanog. Meeting, 14–17 June 1965, Wash., D.C.), 506–14.

Cross-references: *Ocean Current; Wave Theory.*

OCEANICITY—*See* **MARITIME CLIMATE,** Vol. II

OCEANIC NATURAL REGIONS—*See* NATURAL REGIONS IN THE OCEAN

OCEANIC RISE

The bathymetric definition of an oceanic rise, as generally accepted, is "a long and broad elevation of the deep-sea floor which rises gently and smoothly" (Wiseman and Ovey, 1953). Experience has shown that this version is not quite adequate and, following Heezen *et al.* (1959), it is better described as "a large area (measured in hundreds of miles), not connected to or included in a mid-oceanic ridge or connected to a continental rise, which rises a few hundred fathoms above the surrounding abyssal floor. The topography of an oceanic rise ranges from gentle to extremely rugged." In earlier literature, the term *swell* was often applied to such features, but this term has been dropped in deference to certain oceanographers who confused it with a water wave condition (but how, it is hard to imagine).

In the Atlantic, features of this category include the *Bermuda Rise, Corner Rise, Rockall Rise, Rio Grande Rise*; in the Indian Ocean there are the

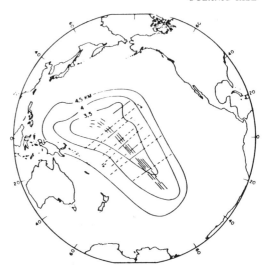

Fig. 1. Former topography of the "Darwin Rise," a hypothetical swell of mesozoic age in the central Pacific (from Menard, 1964). (By permission of McGraw-Hill Book Co., N.Y.)

Crozet Rise, Mascarene Rise, Madingley Rise, Cocos Rise, Christmas Rise, etc.; in the Pacific, the *Lord Howe Rise, Chatham Rise*, the *Marcus-Necker Rise*; and in the Arctic, the *Alpha Rise* and *Mendeleyev* or *Central Arctic Rise*. Some of these features have been described as "ridges" or "plateaus," because no firm international terminology has yet been agreed upon, and many of the features are as yet imperfectly mapped.

The term "rise" is often applied to the mid-oceanic ridge system and Menard (1964) prefers to reserve the term exclusively for it, thus Mid-Atlantic Rise, Mid-Indian Rise, East Pacific Rise (including Galapagos Rise, formerly Albatross Plateau; Easter Island Rise, etc.). Furthermore Menard postulates the existence of a *former* (Mesozoic) mid-ocean elevation in the mid-Pacific, which he calls the *Darwin Rise* (Figs. 1 and 2); since this is a geological concept, with very reduced topographic expression today, it might be wise to reintroduce that well-tried geological term *swell* for such features, which has an interpretive and genetic connotation.

For the independent oceanic rise (excluding the mid-oceanic ridge system, q.v.) perhaps the best known is the *Bermuda Rise*; it is an oval symmetrical arch, 500 by 1000 km, considerably rougher in microtopography than the continental rise, but smoother than the mid-oceanic ridge. In the west it passes gently under the abyssal plain, but in the east it is marked by scarps (almost certainly faulted) 500–1700 m high. It is partially capped by a broad plateau from which rise a number of volcanic cones, seamounts, the largest of which is Bermuda itself, which is called the *Bermuda Pedestal*, and surrounding which is a 60-km-wide sedimentary apron (see

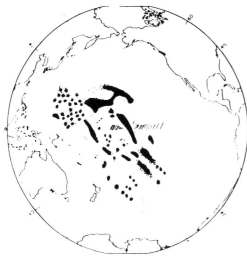

Fig. 2. Site of hypothetical "Darwin Rise" today, punctuated by submerged seamounts (guyots and atolls), following Menard (1964). (By permission of McGraw-Hill Book Co., N.Y.)

Archipelagic Apron). The rise is known to be "seismically transparent" to a depth of 2 km; i.e., it is a sedimentary accumulation. Its position close to the edge of the important oceanographic current gyre that circles the North Atlantic suggests that this accumulation of sediments here may be related to the geostrophic, Sargasso Sea affect. The same explanation cannot be offered for all rises, although geophysical data suggest that most are sedimentary in nature; others may be down-faulted fragments of former continental areas (cf. Rockall Rise, Mascarene Rise). Those closest to the continental borders are classified as "continental borderlands" (q.v.) or "submarine plateaus" (q.v.).

Finally it may be noted that "rise" is also used for minor positive undulations on the great continental shelves (Carrigy and Fairbridge, 1954). No confusion with these will result, when the context does not make it clearly evident, if one writes "shelf rise."

RHODES W. FAIRBRIDGE

References

Carrigy, M. A., and Fairbridge, R. W., 1954, "Recent sedimentation, physiography and structure of the continental shelves of Western Australia," *J. Roy. Soc. W. Australia*, **38**, 65–95.

Cloos, H., 1939, "Zur Tektonik der Azoren," *Abh. Preuss. Akad. Wiss.*, Berlin, Phys.-Math. Kl., **5**.

Engelen, G. B., 1964, "A hypothesis on the origin of the Bermuda Rise," *Tectonophysics*, **1**(1), 85–93.

Heezen, B. C., Ewing, M., Tharp, M., 1959, "The Floors of the Oceans: I. The North Atlantic," *Geol. Soc. Am., Spec. Papers*, **65**, 113pp.

Katz, S., and Ewing, M., 1956, "Seismic-refraction measurements in the Atlantic Ocean. Part VII: Atlantic Ocean Basin, West of Bermuda," *Bull. Geol. Soc. Am.*, **67**, 475–510.

Menard, H. W., 1964, "Marine Geology of the Pacific," New York, McGraw-Hill Book Co., 271pp.

Officer, C. B., Ewing, M., and Wuenschel, P. C., 1952, "Seismic-refraction measurements in the Atlantic Ocean. Part IV: Bermuda, Bermuda Rise and Nares Basin," *Bull. Geol. Soc. Am.*, **63**, 777–808.

Pirsson, L. V., 1914, "Geology of Bermuda Island; the igneous platform," *Am. J. Sci., Ser.* 4, **38**, 189–206.

Van Bemmelen, R. W., 1964, "Appendix to the contribution by G. B. Engelen on the origin of the Bermuda Rise," *Tectonophysics*, **1**(1), 95–100.

Wiseman, J. D. H., and Overy, C. D., 1953, "Definitions of features on the deep-sea floor," *Deep-Sea Res.*, **1**, 11–16.

Cross-references: *Bathymetry*.

OCEANIC VOLCANIC ROCKS—*See* pr Vol. V

OCEANOGRAPHIC SHIPS, PAST AND PRESENT

(1) Design

The research ship serves as the oceanographer's working platform. Its function is to carry scientists and instruments to sea for the purpose of conducting research. It is the oceanographer's most important and most expensive research tool. The basic measure of a ship's efficiency is the amount of effective scientific work which can be performed under the varying conditions of the open ocean far from any land base. These vessels must therefore incorporate seaworthiness, reliability, maneuverability, reasonable speed, and of course economy of operation and low initial cost. The task of designing ships for the sole purpose of conducting research is one to which naval architects have been giving considerable attention in recent years. Rosenblatt (1960) gives a comprehensive discussion of this problem. Ships used for research involving many disciplines require considerable flexibility in the equipment they carry and their use of space. Larger ships may engage in multi-discipline research on a single cruise while smaller vessels are severely limited in this respect.

Special-purpose research vessels such as research submarines, manned buoys, fisheries research ships, special ships to tend and carry deep submergence vehicles, drilling ships, and routine survey ships are often limited by the special requirements of their primary task from being economically suitable for multi-discipline operation in the more classical research investigations. As oceanography turns from the descriptive survey to a more detailed and continuous study of observed phenomena, programs are being developed in classical research which require the efficient utilization of all new techniques and specialized instruments. In the last decade, it has become important to design research vessels with a flexible arrangement which will permit utilization of even the largest instrument systems and vehicles of which helicopters, deep submergence vehicles, large buoy systems, and deep drilling rigs are examples.

Although the research ship should never limit the frontiers of science, this requirement sets an almost unattainable goal for the designer. Past experience has shown that the requirements of oceanographers are apt to advance more rapidly than the pace of research ship design, funding and construction.

(2) History

Modern oceanography is considered to have begun with the unprecedented round-the-world cruise of the British research ship H.M.S. *Challenger* from 1872–76. There had been notable cruises prior to this, such as the voyage of the H.M.S. *Endeavour* under the leadership of Captain Cook and the scientific direction of Sir Joseph Banks in 1768–71 and the voyage of H.M.S. *Beagle* from 1831–36 under Darwin, but no scientific cruise prior to that of the *Challenger* attempted to examine systematically the depth and breadth of the world's ocean in terms of its chemical, physical, and biological aspects. The H.M.S. *Challenger* was a spar-deck corvette of 2305-ton displacement and auxiliary engines of 1234 hp. In three and one-half years, she traveled 69,000 miles in the Atlantic, Indian and Pacific Oceans and penetrated as far south as the Antarctic ice barrier (Herdman, 1923). The voyage of the *Challenger* opened the era of exploratory oceanographic cruises, which in a certain sense is now coming to an end, 90 years later, as continuous work of a more detailed nature is undertaken.

In 1877 the U.S. Coast Survey steamer *Blake*, operated under the scientific direction of Alexander Agassiz, substituted steel wire rope for hemp in dredging operations in the North Atlantic and the Gulf of Mexico.

Starting in 1885, Albert I, Prince of Monaco, made extensive studies of the Mediterranean and the North Atlantic with his successive royal yachts: *Hirondelle*, *Princess Alice*, *Hirondelle II*, and *Princess Alice II*.

In 1886 Markoroff undertook a three-year round-the-world expedition on the Russian steamer *Vitiaz* to observe temperature and specific gravity of water particularly in the North Pacific, and in 1893 Nansen's drift across North Polar Sea in the *Fram* provided dramatic proof of the movement of the Arctic ice cap. In 1905 the Carnegie Institute of Washington began a comprehensive worldwide study of the magnetic, electric, and chemical properties of the oceans with the nonmagnetic ship *Galilee* and later from 1909–29 with the *Carnegie*.

The expedition of the German research vessel *Meteor* in the North and South Atlantic from 1925–27 established the basic knowledge of the general circulation in the Atlantic. The *Meteor* was an auxiliary steamer of 1200-ton displacement and carried a total compliment of 114 (Vaughan, 1927). Together with other famous ships, such as the *Discovery*, *Discovery II*, *Dana*, *Explorer*, and *William Scoresby*, she was a part of the grand era of oceanic exploration when oceanic expeditions were fitted out by governments, sent on long cruises, and dismantled upon their return, whereupon the scientist's attention was given over to working up the scientific results of the trip.

Since World War II, in addition to the round-the-world cruises of the *Albatross* of Sweden, *Galathea* of Denmark, *Discovery II* of Britain, and *Vema*, operated by Lamont Geological Observatory of Columbia University, there have been major efforts devoted to Antarctic waters (I.G.Y. and later) and to the Indian Ocean Expedition, as well as shorter individual cruises of a continuing nature and for particular scientific purposes that have become more common in oceanography.

(3) Recent Vessels

Much new construction in the past few years has tended to emphasize replacement of obsolete vessels. In the United Kingdom the (new) 2800-ton *Discovery* has replaced the 1736-ton steamer *Discovery II* of 1929. The Federal Republic of Germany, in 1964, launched the new *Meteor*.

In the United States several important new ships have been built since 1960. Of special interest is the new 2300-ton *Atlantis II* which has been added to the fleet for which the original 350-ton ketch *Atlantis* was built in 1930. The *Atlantis II* can accommodate 25 scientists with a permanent crew of 30 and has 3200 square feet of enclosed scientific laboratory space. The original *Atlantis* accommodated 9 scientists with a permanent crew of 20 and had 430 square feet of laboratory area. The new vessel is powered by twin screw direct drive uniflow steam engines and all other machinery is isolated or acoustically mounted to permit acoustical observations. Particular attention was paid in the design of the *Atlantis II* to provide flexibility for future requirements. Among these are the ability to tend and carry intermediate-sized (15-ton) deep research vehicles and to perform shallow water drilling operations through the centerwell. An interesting comparison between the *Atlantis II* of 1963 and the *Challenger* of 1872 shows that their displacements and power are approximately equal. In the first year of operation the *Atlantis II* travelled 41,800 miles or two-thirds of the total for the three-year voyage of the *Challenger*.

A comprehensive listing of oceanographic vessels of the world is available (U.S. Navy Oceanographic Office, 1963).

(4) Future Trends

The key to a successful research ship design is its ability to foster new developments in research techniques. For example, in France and the United States particularly, the development of deep submergence vehicles will require that research vessels be capable of lifting such vehicles from the water even in high seas states for servicing. The ability to safely lift vehicles of up to 100 tons in heavy seas should be possible with multipurpose but generally conventional research ships, since it is neither desirable nor economically feasible to devote a ship to this single purpose. Rather the submersible should be considered to a large extent as another research instrument to be used when and as the situation permits and the problem requires.

The utilization of submarines as primary research ships will be given attention. Manned ocean stations similar to large buoys are presently in service in Monaco and California. Small hydrofoil vessels will be efficient in high-speed survey and reconnaissance operations using continuous measurement equipment.

Conventional research ships and some special vessels with precise maneuvering control will be called upon to handle a variety of heavy equipment for buoys of greater durability, for coring and drilling devices, benthic living experiments, bottom supported instruments, and to handle towed instruments of great weight at depths of 20,000 feet or more. They also require ability to carry and operate large automated data gathering and recording installations with computers for data analysis.

A recent development sponsored by the U.S. Navy is to use commercial vessels as ships of opportunity to carry self-contained laboratories on their usual runs. This scheme will certainly be useful where scientific purpose and instrumentation are compatible with the primary purposes of cargo and passenger vessels.

R. S. EDWARDS

References

Herdman, Sir William A., 1923, "The Founders of Oceanography and Their World," London, Edward Arnold and Co.

Rosenblatt, Lester, 1960, "The design of modern oceanographic research ships," *SNAME Trans.*, **68**.

U.S. Navy Oceanographic Office, 1963, "Oceanographic Vessels of The World," I.G.Y. World Data Center for Oceanography and the National Oceanographic Data Center, U.S. Navy Oceanographic Office, Washington, D.C.

Vaughan, Thomas Wayland, *et al.*, 1927, "International Aspects of Oceanography," National Academy of Science, Washington, D.C.

OCEANOGRAPHIC SURVEYS

The beginning of systematic collection and correlation of marine observations owes much to the efforts of Matthew Fontaine Maury, who in 1853 proposed a system for international exchange of nautical information. His plan, based on standard reporting of observations in the log books of merchant marine ships, became the basis upon which hydrographic offices operate. These and similar efforts devoted to improving the safety of navigation led to the compilation of much data on temperatures, currents, tides, and meteorological conditions. However, the task of studying surface phenomena in the remote parts of the oceans and phenomena in the depths of the oceans remained for the later oceanographic expeditions.

The first of these was the great deep-sea expedition of the British Corvette H.M.S. *Challenger*, which carried out a comprehensive oceanographic survey through the Atlantic, Pacific and Indian Oceans between 1872 and 1876. This expedition was under the scientific leadership of Sir Wyville Thomson; the results, edited by Thomson and John Murray and published in fifty volumes, form the foundation of our knowledge of physical, chemical, bathymetric, geological and biological conditions in the deep oceans.

Wüst (1964) has recently summarized the major deep-sea expeditions (Table 1) along the following lines. This first epic of oceanographic research, initiated by the *Challenger*, has been termed "the era of exploration." The expedition reports resulting from these early surveys produced the first picture of the bathymetry, stratification and circulation of water masses and the conditions for life in the oceans.

The unsung heroes of this time were the crews of the various Navy hydrographic office survey ships, outstandingly those of the Royal Navy, who systematically mapped the floors of the world oceans, the continental shelves, coasts and reefs, to render all such areas safe for navigation. So accurate was their work, even though very sparse in some areas, that even today, with modern electronic equipment, the basic statistics of the ocean volumes worked out in the early part of this century are virtually unchanged (see *Oceans—Limits, Definitions, Dimensions*). Many of these vessels (as did many merchant vessels too) carried out routine meteorologic observations, water temperatures and so on. Samples of the bottom, collected by adherence to tallow in the hollow sounding lead, were marked on the Admiralty Charts, and numbers of these specimens are still retained at the British Museum.

It is common to record oceanographic expeditions and title their reports under the name of the ship on which work was done. During this early era of oceanographic surveys, the German expeditions of the ships *Gazelle, National, Valdivia, Gauss, Planet*, and *Deutschland* contributed greatly to our general knowledge of the oceans. During the same period the American expeditions of the U.S.S. *Blake* and the U.S.S. *Albatross* in the Atlantic, the Caribbean, and the North Pacific are also remembered. From 1886–89 the Russian steamer *Vitiaz* undertook a round-the-world voyage which contributed valuable physical observations. From 1884–1922

TABLE 1. REPRESENTATIVE VESSELS IN OCEANOGRAPHIC DEEP-SEA RESEARCH (1873–1960)—SLIGHTLY MODIFIED AFTER WÜST (1964) (BY PERMISSION OF PERGAMON PRESS, N.Y.)

Name of Vessel	Nationality	Commissioned	Tonnage	Ocean	Main Studies
(Ia) Era of Exploration (1873–1914)					
Challenger[a]	British	1873–1876	2306	Atlantic, Indian, Pacific	Biology, Physics, Geology
Gazelle[a]	German	1874–1876	1900	Atlantic, Indian, Pacific	Physics
Blake[a]	U.S.A.	1877–1886	400	Atlantic (Gulf Stream system)	Physics, Currents
Albatross	U.S.A.	1887–1888		North Atlantic	Biology, Physics
National[a]	German	1889	854 (gross)	North Atlantic	Plankton
Fram[a]	Norwegian	1893–1896	530	North Polar Sea	Physics
Valdivia[a]	German	1898–1899	2176 (gross)	Atlantic, Indian	Biology of great depths
Princesse Alice I and *II*[a] *Hirondelle I* and *II*[a]	Monaco	1888–1922	—	North Atlantic	Biology
Gauss[a]	German	1901–1903	1332	Atlantic, Indian, Antarctic	Physics, Geography
Planet[a]	German	1906–1907	650	Atlantic, Indian, West Pacific	Physics
Deutschland[a]	German	1911–1912	598 (gross)	Atlantic, Antarctic	Physics
(Ib) Transition to Systematic Research (1904–1924)					
Michael Sars[a]	Norwegian	1904–1913	226	Norwegian Sea, North Atlantic	Physics
Armauer Hansen[a]	Norwegian	Since 1913	53	Norwegian Sea, North Atlantic	Physics
(II) Era of National Systematic Surveys (1925–1940)					
Meteor[a]	German	1925–1927	1178	German Atlantic Exp. 65°S–20°N	Phys., Chem., Met., Geol., Biol.
Manshu	Japan	1925–1938	900	Pacific	Phys., Chem.
Meteor	German	1929–1938	1178	Iceland–Greenland waters	Physics, Chemistry Biology
Shympu Maru	Japan	1927–1930	125	Japan Sea	Phys., Chem., Biol.
Dana I[a] and *II*[a]	Denmark	1921–1935	*Dana II* 360	Atlantic, Indian, Pacific	Biology, Physics
Carnegie[a]	U.S.A.	1928–1929	568	Pacific	Physics, Biology, Sediments
Willebrord Snellus[a]	Dutch	1929–1930	1055	Indonesian Seas	Geology, Physics, Chemistry
Discovery[a] and *Discovery II*[a]	British	1930 ff	*(Discovery II)* 2100	Antarctic	Physics, Biology
Atlantis	U.S.A.	1931 ff	460	North Atlantic	Physics, Chemistry
Ryofu Maru	Japanese	1937 ff	1206	Pacific	Physics
E. W. Scripps	U.S.A.	1938 ff	140	Pacific	Physics, Chemistry Geology
Altair	German	1938	4000	Gulf Stream	Physics, Currents
Sedov	Russian	1938–1939	1538	North Polar Sea	Physics
(IIIa) Period of New Geological, Geophysical, Biological and Oceanographical Methods (1947–1956)					
Albatross[a]	Sweden	1947–1948	1450	Atlantic, Indian	Geology, Physics
Galathea[a]	Denmark	1950–1952	1600	Pacific	Biology of abyssal depths
Atlantis[a]	U.S.A.	1947 ff	460	Atlantic	Physics, Geophysics
Vema	U.S.A.	1953 ff	734	Atlantic, Indian, Pacific	Geophysics, Geology
Anton Dohrn	German	1955–1956	999	North Atlantic	Biology, Physics
Spencer F. Baird	U.S.A.	1950 ff	900	Pacific	Geophysics, Geology
Horizon	U.S.A.	1950 ff	900	Pacific	Geology, Biology

TABLE 1—*Continued*

Name of Vessel	Nationality	Commissioned	Tonnage	Ocean	Main Studies
		(IIIb) Transition to Synoptic Research in Smaller Areas (1950)			
Atlantis and other vessels	U.S.A.	1950, (1956)	—	Gulf Stream	Physics, Dynamics (Operation Cabot and second survey)
		(IV) Era of International Research Cooperation since 1957			
Crawford	U.S.A.	1957–1959	350	Atlantic IGY	Physics, Chemistry
Atlantis	U.S.A.	1957–1959	460	Atlantic IGY	Physics, Chemistry
Discovery II	British	1957–1959	2100	Atlantic IGY	Physics, Chemistry
Capitan Canepa	Argentina	1957–1960	1000	Atlantic IGY	Physics
Gauss	W. Germany	1957–1960	800	North Atlantic Polar Front and Overflow Program	Physics
Anton Dohrn	W. Germany	1957–1960	1000	North Atlantic Polar Front and Overflow Programs	Biology, Physics
Explorer and other vessels	Scottish	1957–1960	200 ft.	North Atlantic Polar Front and Overflow Programs	Biology, Physics
Vitiaz	U.S.S.R.	1957–1960	5700	All Seas (IGY Program)	Physics, Chemistry Biology, and Geology Trenches
Numerous research vessels	Japan, U.S.A., Canada	1955–1960	—	Pacific (Norpac Program)	Physics, Biology
Mikhail Lomonosov	U.S.S.R.	1957–1960	6000	All Seas (IGY Program)	Physics, Chemistry Biology
Ob	U.S.S.R.	1957–1960	12,600 (gross)	Southern Seas (IGY Program)	Physics, Chemistry Biology
Chain	U.S.A.	1958–1960	2100	Atlantic, Indian	Geophysics, Physics
Argo	U.S.A.	1959–1960	2079	Pacific, Indian	Geophysics, Physics
Shokalski	U.S.S.R.	1960	3600	All Seas	Physics, Meteorology
Woeikof	U.S.S.R.	1959	3600	All Seas	Physics, Meteorology
Pole	U.S.S.R.	1959	5000	—	Physics, etc.
Lena	U.S.S.R.	1958	12,600	Polar Seas	Physics, Meteorology
Severyanka	U.S.S.R.	1958	1050	All Seas	Submarine for oceanographic research
Numerous research vessels[b]	International	Since 1958	—	Indian Ocean Expedition Program	Physics, Geophysics, Biology, Chemistry, Geology, Meteorology

[a]Complete analysis of data published in extensive expedition reports.

[b]Countries, ships and cruises participating 1958–62 in this Indian Ocean Program are published in a chart (H.O. No. 17138B) by the U.S. Navy Hydrographic Office (Sept. 1962). The International Indian Ocean Program actually started in 1958 with the cruise of *Vema*, and in 1959 and 1960 with cruises of *Diamantina* (Australia), *Commandant Robert Giraud* (France), *Vitiaz* (U.S.S.R.), *Argo* (U.S.A.), *Requisite* (U.S.A.), and *Umitaka-Maru* (Japan).

Prince Albert I of Monaco made systematic biological studies in the North Atlantic with the *Princesse Alice I* and *II* and established his institute at Monaco to continue the work. Knudsen and others, working in Copenhagen, established the basic chlorinity, salinity, density relationships in tables which are still in use. About 1900 the Permanent International Council for the Exploration of the Sea was founded by nations surrounding the North Sea and the Baltic for the purposes of establishing a scientific basis for commercial fisheries. Toward the end of this early era of deep-sea expeditions, a center of oceanographic activity developed in Bergen, Norway. Expeditions under the direction of Fridtjof Nansen and Bjorn Helland-Hansen emphasized the importance of greater accuracy in the measurements of temperature and salinity, from which J. Sandstrom and Helland-Hansen applied the atmospheric circulation theorem of V. Bjerknes to the ocean in a simplified form. Thus, the permanent deep geostrophic terms could be calculated from the baroclinic field of mass, and a transition

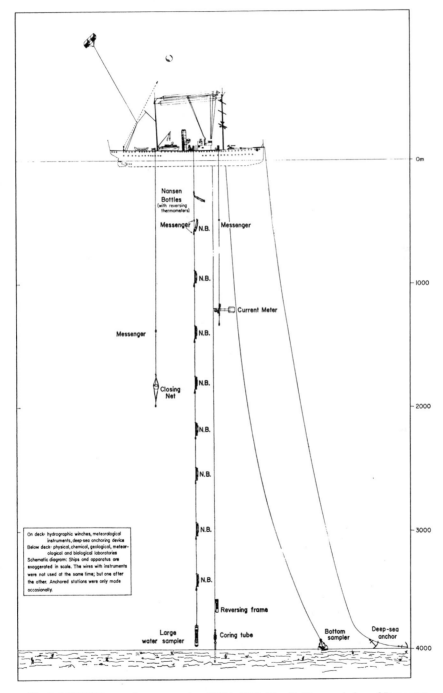

Fig. 1. METEOR on a deep-sea station (Wüst, 1964, Fig. 4). (By permission of Pergamon Press, N.Y.)

from oceanography as a descriptive and statistical branch of geography was able to develop into a *bona fide* branch of geophysics.

An era of national systematic and dynamic ocean surveys characterizes the period from 1925–40. During this period the German Atlantic expedition of the R/V *Meteor* made intensive studies on the stratification and circulation of the water masses in the Central and South Altantic between 1925 and 1927. On this expedition, closely spaced hydrographic stations with temperature, salinity, and other chemical measurements taken at standard depth intervals were made to the greatest depths. These data were combined with meteorological observations, measurements of direct currents, and echo-sounding measurements of ocean depth to provide a basis for what may be called the modern hydrographic survey. Figure 1 illustrates the composite work of a deep-sea station during this expedition. During this period many famous expeditions contributed to our basic knowledge of the oceans. These are listed for the period 1925–40 in Table 1, together with the main scientific studies which were accomplished.

The period following World War II has been termed "the period of new marine geological, geophysical, biological, and physical methods." Additional stress was placed on collecting samples and taking measurements in the greatest abyssal depths. The taking of long piston cores up to 20 m in length in the ocean-bottom sediment became standard procedure on many oceanographic surveys, and the use of improved electronic precision depth recorders became widespread. The geophysical methods and instruments were vastly improved during this period, employing both reflection and refraction explosive seismology techniques to investigate the sub-bottom layers of the ocean basins.

The most recent period of oceanographic surveys has been termed "the era of international research cooperation." Beginning with the International Geophysical Year 1957–59, the trend from more or less independent research expeditions to systematic multi-ship enterprises, often involving international participants, has been in progress. The International Cooperative Investigations of the Tropical Atlantic (ICITA) organized the first Equalant synoptic survey of the Tropical Atlantic in 1962. The International Indian Ocean Expedition (IIOE), with about fourteen participating nations, was organized about the same time.

Deacon (1962) has discussed the growth and progress of oceanographic activities from the earliest time to the present.

The task of oceanographic surveys has been to determine the shape of the sea bottom and the physical and chemical conditions of the ocean waters. These aims have expanded along with technological advances and now include determination of the history of the ocean basins and the nature of

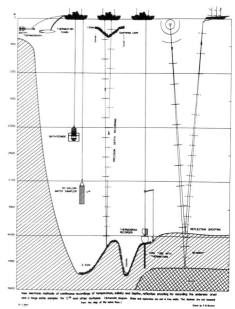

Fig. 2. New electronic methods of continuous recordings of temperature, salinity and depths, reflection shooting for recording the undersea crust, and large water sampler for C^{14} and other isotopes (Wüst, 1964, Fig. 9). (By permission of Pergamon Press, N.Y.)

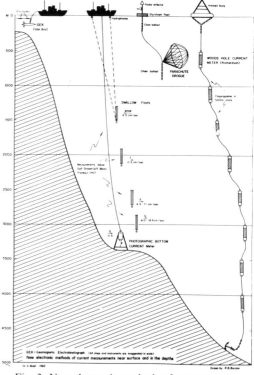

Fig. 3. New electronic methods of current measurements near surface and in the depths (Wüst, 1964, Fig. 10). (By permission of Pergamon Press, N.Y.)

the oceanic crust. The horizontal and vertical distributions of temperature, salinity and dissolved gases are studied to relate the ocean structure to the ocean circulation.

Oceanographic Survey Techniques

In the early days, oceanographic surveys were hampered by a lack of existing knowledge of ocean conditions and the primitive nature of the instruments. Today, while some of the instruments remain essentially the same, a whole new suite of tools and methods has become available to deep-sea research since World War II. The following discussion covers the activities, instruments and objectives of chief concern in a modern deep-sea oceanographic survey, exclusive of biological and meteorological studies. This does not pretend to be all inclusive, nor does it imply that all of these measurements are made on a single expedition. Figures 2 and 3 illustrate schematically the use of certain of the new techniques and devices which are discussed. In Hill (1963) can be found further discussion of modern oceanographic methods and progress by various authors.

Navigation. Navigation at sea is of primary importance to all survey work and oceanographic sampling. The standard methods of celestial navigation remain the mainstay of navigation, helped in recent years by shortwave radio transmission of time signals from various national bureaus of standards.

Since about 1950 an increasing number of shore-based electronic navigation systems have become available. Chief among these are the Loran-A and C networks and the Decca navigation system. The use of these electronic navigation aids generally increases the accuracy and frequency of survey vessel navigation fixes, but at the present time there remain vast areas of the world's surface where these networks do not exist.

In the early 1960's, the use of the transit satellite navigation system was begun; its use is increasing among ocean survey vessels. Where a suitable shipboard computer is available to process the Doppler frequency measurements of the satellite signals, positions may be quickly determined with a very high order of accuracy.

Marine radars with ranges greater than 25 miles have been in common use since the 1950's and provide valuable navigation control when used in coastal regions or from anchored-buoy radar targets in the open seas. The use of the SOFAR system for triangulation from shore-based stations to a suitable sound source has been mainly experimental.

Ocean Bottom Investigations. (1) *Echo Sounding.* In the opening era of deep-sea research, soundings were made with lead lines and after 1878 with Kelvin's sounding machine, using fine wire. Not until 1922 were automatic echo-sounding machines available, but these lacked precision timing and

adequate scale of presentation for use in the deep sea until the advent of the precision depth recorder in 1954.

This type of echo sounder, in general use today, is accurate to ± 1 fathom in 3000 fathoms. Depths are read from the echo-sounder records and written down on a plotting-sheet chart at closely spaced time intervals along a correct ship's track. A profile can then be drawn. Where a sufficient density of tracks with echo-sounding observations exists, topographic contour charts of the ocean bottom, using standard procedures, may be constructed.

(2) *Sub-bottom Refraction and Reflection Studies.* Seismic refraction techniques have been used to study the thickness and structure of submarine strata for several decades. Sonic energy from explosives is received at varying distances from the sound source by geophones or hydrophones and recorded on an oscillograph recorder having an accurate time scale. The character of the oscillogram is studied and measurement made of the time of arrival of sound waves through known paths between explosion and detector. The speed of propagation is computed from this knowledge of travel time and sound path. Two techniques are used: recording of a line of shots at a fixed receiving position or a single shot along a line of receiving positions. In each case a relationship of travel time versus distance is established and information on the number and thickness of subsurface strata and the speed of sound in each is determined. Knowledge of the speed of sound characteristic of a layer permits estimation of its composition. If the composition of a layer is known through sampling in one area, its continuation into other areas may be inferred by seismic refraction measurements.

Sub-bottom echo sounding, or seismic reflection profiling, has been practiced in recent years on many oceanographic expeditions. The principles are much the same as for regular echo sounding, but the sound source, whether electrical, mechanical, or explosive, is of lower frequency and is capable of much higher acoustical energy output, which is reflected not only from the ocean bottom, but from reflecting layers of sediment and rock beneath the bottom. Profiling tracks are normally made at cruising speeds between 4 and 10 knots, depending on the capability of the acoustical receiving equipment to minimize sea and ship noises. The signals received are filtered to further eliminate "noise" and are displayed graphically. Recording is also made on magnetic tape for later display and analysis. Using these techniques, good sub-bottom records have been obtained in typical ocean basin depths with penetrations through sediment of several thousand meters. These data are studied together with seismic refraction records, magnetic and gravity data, sediment studies, and other geological studies in order to interpret the structure and history of the ocean basins.

(3) *Bottom Core Sampling.* In the period following World War II, the piston-coring tube developed by Kullenberg and modified by Ewing made it possible to collect relatively undisturbed cores of ocean-bottom sediment 30 m in length. The apparatus, consisting of steel tubing weighted at the top, is lowered on a steel wire rope. A trigger hanging beside and about 3–10 m below the core tube, senses bottom contact and releases the corer, which free-falls this distance to the ocean bottom. The momentum of the fall drives the tubing into the sediment, while a piston inside is held motionless at the level of the ocean bottom, thereby reducing the resistance of the sediment entering the corer.

These samples are routinely taken by many oceanographic vessels for studies of the sedimentation and history of the ocean basins. Mechanical analyses are made of the size frequency distribution of the sediments; chemical and radiochemical analyses are made of the material; the content of macro- and microorganisms is carefully separated and studied for evidence of present and past sedimentary environments. Samples are taken at suitable levels in the long cores in order to perform geologic dating, using radiochemical and index fossil methods for time correlation purposes and for studies of sedimentation rates.

Core-drilling techniques and equipment developed for oil exploration have already been used for deep-ocean sampling with penetrations greater than 300 m, and increased application of these methods is expected in the future.

(4) *Dredging and Other Bottom Sampling.* Rock dredging from the ocean floor is a technique that has remained essentially unchanged since the earliest days of oceanography, using techniques and equipment borrowed from the fishing industry. In addition to simple dredges, numerous samplers are in use which obtain undisturbed large-volume (0.05 cubic meter) samples from the ocean floor. These geological and biological samples are examined for structures, chemical composition, layering, and correlation with regional and local geologic formations.

(5) *Underwater Photography.* Since World War II, underwater photography has become an important part of deep-sea research. Remote-operating cameras, housed in pressure-proof containers, are lowered to or near the ocean floor, using a hydrographic winch and wire. Below depths of 100 m, an electronic flash is used for illumination. Both single-frame and cine-camera photography are practiced, employing both black and white and color film. Stereophotography is also used. As many as several hundred single frames may be taken at a single camera station, and up to 200 feet of cine-film exposure may be obtained. Ocean bottom photographs are used to examine the biological activity at the ocean bottom, the nature of the sediment and rock outcrops on the sea floor, and their relation to bottom currents and transport processes. Stereophotography is used to measure microrelief features of the ocean bottom, i.e., ripple marks.

(6) *Gravity and Magnetic Measurements.* The oceanographic survey ship will normally take continuous gravity and magnetic measurements while engaged in bathymetric surveys. Not only are these three measurements conveniently taken together, but their results are most usefully studied together for a fuller understanding of ocean bottom and sub-bottom structures and processes.

Gravity measurements were first made at sea using the Vening Meinesz pendulum apparatus in submerged submarines. More recently, continuous underway measurements have become possible from the larger surface research vessels, using the spring-type gravity meter. Measurement is made of the variation in the acceleration due to gravity at the sea-level surface. This variation, caused by changes in the distribution of mass beneath the ship, the shape of the earth, and the centrifugal acceleration of the earth, is corrected for ocean depth. The variations in the corrected gravity anomaly are interpreted in terms of density variations beneath the ocean bottom.

Shipboard measurements of all three components of the magnetic field are seldom made, as they require a specially constructed nonmagnetic ship. Since the 1950's, the simpler measurement of total magnetic force has become an important oceanographic survey technique, using an instrument towed behind the ship at a sufficient distance to avoid the disturbance caused by the ship itself. Measurements of the total field include a local or anomalous component arising from magnetic rocks and minerals in the earth's crust down to the depth where temperatures reach the Curie point (30–40 km under the oceans). To reveal details of the geologic pattern, magnetic survey lines in a given area must be closely spaced with high navigational accuracy. Such detailed surveys have shown major structural trends and strong lineations not simply related to surface topography.

(7) *Heat Flow Measurements.* Measurements of the rate of flow of heat through the floor of the ocean have been made on oceanographic vessels since 1954. Heat flow is calculated from the temperature gradient measured between two or more points along a probe forced into the bottom sediment and from the thermal conductivity of the sediment measured on samples brought up by a coring tube. Values of heat flow may be used to infer temperatures and heat sources in the crust and mantle These values are considered on a regional basis and are correlated with other geological and geophysical measurements to study sedimentary and structural problems of ocean basins.

Measurements in the Water. (1) *Hydrographic Cast.* Of prime importance in a hydrographic survey is the measurement of temperature and salinity at standard depths in the ocean for computation of density and later analysis of water movement. The method of obtaining temperatures and seawater samples at the typical hydrographic station has remained essentially unchanged for half a century, although both thermometers and methods for salinity measurement have been improved from the earlier time. Serial measurements of temperature and samples for salinity and other water analysis are obtained by attaching water-sampling containers (approximately 1.5-liter capacity), fitted with thermometers, to a hydrographic wire at suitable intervals and lowering this assembly into the ocean until the water samplers have been placed at the depths where measurements are required. When the array is in place, and after a sufficient period of time for the thermometers to reach thermal equilibrium, a messenger or split cylindrical weight with a center hole is dropped down the wire, causing the uppermost sampler to close valves at both ends of the open-ended chamber, thereby securing a water sample. At the same time, the reversing thermometers are turned through 180° to record the temperature and another messenger is released downward to actuate the next sampler below.

Until about 1900, thermometers used in deep-sea research were of maximum-minimum type and of questionable accuracy. About this time, the reversing thermometer principle became practical and in 1925 was modified to the present design, having an accuracy of ±0.01°C under ideal usage.

Salinity determinations made between 1900 and 1960 have used the chlorinity titration method of Knudsen. The accuracy of good titration determinations is ±0.01‰ in salinity. Since 1960, increasing use has been made of electrical conductivity salinometers, considered to be accurate to ±0.005‰ in salinity. The need for the highest order of accuracy in determination of salinity and temperature stems from the requirement for determination of density to ±0.00001 in order to calculate geostrophic currents within a few centimeters per second.

The geostrophic method provides a means for computing the field of relative motion in a fluid from a knowledge of the internal distribution of pressure. Dynamic computations of permanent deep geostrophic currents in the ocean are made in this way from hydrographic station data. Hydrographic data may also be used in a descriptive manner to study the spreading and mixing of particular water masses by tracing an identifying parameter such as a maximum in salinity. This treatment corresponds to what has been called "the core method."

The hydrographic cast is also used for the collection of water samples for other chemical determinations of seawater, including nutrients, dissolved gases, trace elements, etc. (see *Chemistry of Seawater*).

Continuous *in situ* measurement of salinity, temperature, and pressure, taken with electrical sensors down to 5000 meters, is now becoming routine on many survey vessels. These continuous records, while still of lesser precision than the standard measurements, reveal a wealth of fine structure not possible by discrete measurements at standard depths.

(2) *Radiochemical Sampling.* The collection and measurement of seawater samples for radiochemical studies is an important new oceanographic-survey technique. Both naturally produced and man-made radioactive isotopes have been collected, generally in large-volume samples (200 liters and greater). The distribution of radioisotopes in the sea has revealed information on patterns and rates of large-scale circulation, based on their known radioactive decay and residence time within the ocean. Carbon 14, strontium 90, cesium 137, tritium, radium 226, and silicon 32 are among the isotopes which have been used in these studies.

(3) *Direct Current Measurements.* Direct measurements of currents in the sea cover the range of frequencies from wave motions of a few seconds to cycles on the order of one year. The method of measurement and the method of treating the data will depend upon which of these frequencies is being investigated.

Most of the surface-current information on published charts is derived from the summation of masses of ships' navigation data, prepared in a statistical manner. Direct measurements of ocean currents made in survey and oceanographic work may be classed in two categories: Eulerian methods, where the velocity of flow past a fixed point is measured as a function of depth and time; and Lagrangian methods, where the trajectories of tagged water particles or drifting objects are plotted with respect to time. Among the earliest subsurface measurements were those taken from an anchored ship by lowering a propellor-type current meter from the ship's deck to various depths in the sea. This type of measurement is still taken, but in recent years the trend has been toward longer-period recording, using arrays of current meters suspended at points along an anchor line and supported by a surface or near-surface buoy. These current meters are capable of recording internally for periods up to several months or of telemetering their information to a surface-buoy transmitter, which communicates the data by radio to a ship or shore station.

Many data on surface currents have been obtained using surface drift bottles, and this method is still in use. Lagrangian subsurface measurements have been taken in recent years using neutrally buoyant floats, whose density is adjusted so that they will move at a predetermined subsurface level along with water of a comparable density. The floats send out acoustical signals, which enable the surface vessel to track their path. Surface floats connected to a subsurface drogue by a fine wire have also been used to plot subsurface water trajectories. Dye tracers too have been used to follow the movement and mixing processes in near-surface waters.

ROBERT GERARD

References

Deacon, G. E. R., 1962, "Seas, Maps and Men," Garden City, N.Y., Doubleday & Co., 295pp.

Hill, M. N., 1963, "The Sea," Vols. 1, 2 and 3, New York, Interscience Publishers.

Wüst, Georg, 1964, "The Major Deep-sea Expeditions and Research Vessels 1873–1960," in "Progress in Oceanography," Vol. 2, pp. 1–52, New York, Pergamon Press.

Romanovsky, V., Claude Francis-Boeuf and J. Bourcart, 1953, "La Mer," Paris, Librairie Larousse, 503pp.

Cross-references: *Marine Geology; Oceanographic Ships, Oceanic Current and Wave Recording Instrumentation; Oceanography.* Pr Vol. V, *Geophysical Exploration at Sea.*

OCEANOGRAPHY

Oceanography is the unlimited science of the sea. It incorporates all of the scientific disciplines man uses to investigate nature. Basic studies in oceanography include investigations of marine life; the analyses of ocean water; examination of the ocean floor; investigation and measurement of currents, waves, and tides; and analyses of the interaction of atmosphere and sea. Oceanographic studies can be grouped by their primary scientific interest into studies of the physical, biological, geological, geophysical, or chemical aspects of the sea. However, all of these endeavors are interrelated and dependent on one another. Thus, it is necessary to study all of these phases in order to comprehend the field of oceanography.

The agencies which have financially supported the National Oceanographic Program in the United States are: Department of Defense, Department of Commerce, National Science Foundation, Department of Interior, Department of Treasury, Smithsonian Institution, Atomic Energy Commission, and Department of Health, Education and Welfare. The national oceanographic budget in 1963, for example, allowed for research, ship construction, surveys, facilities, instrumentation, a data center, and the International Indian Ocean Expedition.

In Stockholm, Sweden, the *International Council for the Exploration of the Sea* held its first meeting in 1899. Since then some 43 committees on oceanography have been organized, stressing mainly the biological aspects. The *International Association of Physical Oceanography* is associated with the I.U.G.G. (International Union of Geodesy and Geophysics), with which it holds regular joint international congresses. The first independent *International Oceanographic Congress* was held in New York in 1959; the second, in Moscow in 1966.

History

Man's first motivation to venture across the sea probably came with his desire for a new or more congenial environment. Riches from distant lands encouraged navigators to sail into unknown waters. The sea became a challenge and adventure as well as a means of travel.

About 1000 B.C., the world was thought to be a flat disk with two bodies of water, the oceans, and a large land mass (Fig. 1). On the boundary of the disk was the river "Oceanus" which circled the oceans and land. This concept of a flat world existed (outside of classical Greece) up to the time of Columbus.

According to the writings of Herodotus, Phoenician sailors circumnavigated Africa in the seventh century B.C. Reports of this expedition, ordered by King Necho of Egypt, were not accepted as credible by the scholars of that time; therefore, Africa was not yet recognized as a separate continent. Hanno, a Carthaginian, was thought to have sailed as far as Cape Palmas (Liberia) on his expedition down the west coast of Africa in about 500 B.C. By 500 B.C., Hecateus' new map of the world differed slightly from the world map of 1000 B.C. (Fig. 2). Seas to the east of the Mediterranean began to be explored and defined.

From Alexander the Great's expedition to India (329 B.C. to 325 B.C.), the Caspian Sea, Persian Gulf and Arabian Sea were related to the already known Red Sea and Mediterranean.

Pytheas, in the fourth century B.C., astronomically determined latitude. Without the knowledge of the principles of gravitation, he also described the spring tides and neap tides and related them to the phases of the moon. Diodorus wrote of an expedition that circumnavigated Britain led by Pytheas, who was one of the few Greeks to venture beyond the Mediterranean.

Aristotle's theory that the earth was a sphere was followed by constructive evidence from Hipparchus, an astronomer, Dicaearchus of Messina, and Eratosthenes of Alexandria, a writer. Dicaearchus used parallels of latitude for the first time while Eratosthenes computed the radius and circumference of the earth. Hipparchus introduced the concept of map projection so that any position on the earth could be precisely marked on a map. Navigators were then able to record their voyages through unknown waters.

In A.D. 20 Strabo wrote his book of geography containing the results of the Greek geographers. In A.D. 150, Ptolemy made the first major contribution to the world map since 250 B.C. by mapping the Indian Ocean with Africa and China as its two boundaries (Fig. 3).

It is believed that about A.D. 1000 the Vikings crossed the Atlantic from Greenland to America. Because they kept no records of their travels, little is known of these accomplishments, except for

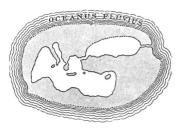

Fig. 1. Stages in the Oceanographic knowledge of the ancients (from Herdman, 1923): As known in the time of Homer—1000 B.C.

Fig. 2. Stages in the Oceanographic knowledge of the ancients (from Herdman, 1923): As known in the time of Hecataeus—500 B.C.

Fig. 3. Stages in the Oceanographic knowledge of the ancients (from Herdman, 1923): As known in the time of C. Ptolemy, an Alexandrian astronomer, 150 A.D.

radiocarbon-dated archeological traces in Newfoundland and New England.

While the Greeks did little exploring outside the Mediterranean, their great intellectual foresight and written records added to man's knowledge. The Romans traveled extensively in the Mediterranean and northwestern Europe for trading and military purposes, but they contributed very little to the exploration of the seas. With the fall of the Roman Empire, many of the records of the classical world were lost. Those records, available today, were kept by Arabian and Persian scholars through the Dark Ages. Not until the fifteenth century did marine exploration again become significant.

In the fifteenth century, Prince Henry of Portugal established a school of navigation and aroused interest in exploration. In 1497 Vasco da Gama set sail down the west coast of Africa to reach India. For the first time, European sailors had circumnavigated Africa.

Christopher Columbus believed that the world was round and had hopes of finding a new and shorter route to India when he discovered the new world. With the knowledge of another body of land, the Americas, it logically followed that another body of water must lie beyond this new continent. A Spaniard, Vasco Nunez de Balboa, was the first to view the Pacific from the new world, a hilltop in Panama.

It took nearly three years for Ferdinand Magellan's expedition to carry out the first circumnavigation of the world. Under the orders of Charles V of Spain, Magellan set out on September 20, 1519 to find the shortest route to the Spice Islands in the South Seas. Magellan believed that the Atlantic and Pacific were linked together so that he could sail around the world. The expedition set out with five ships, 268 men, and enough provisions for two years. After discovering a passage, now known as the Strait of Magellan, the expedition sailed north along the west coast of South America and across the Pacific. Magellan reached the Philippine Islands only to be killed on the island of Mactan after entering into a local quarrel among the natives. The one remaining ship *Victoria*, under the command of Sebastian del Cano, sailed into Seville in September, 1522, after crossing the South Indian Ocean and rounding the Cape of Good Hope.

Although Magellan's men had sailed around the world, it was Sir Francis Drake who discovered the water lying between South America and the Antarctic. The gap now known as Drake Passage was not discovered until sixty years after Magellan's expedition.

In the eighteenth century, James Cook revolutionized navigation and added thousands of charted miles to the world maps. Cook, on his first voyage around the world, circumnavigated New Zealand and sailed up the coast of eastern Australia. His second voyage sent him farther south, about 60°S, to circumnavigate the globe in this lower region. His ship was the first to cross the Antarctic Circle, but the expedition had to retreat because of ice. His record of reaching 71°10′S stood for nearly half a century.

In his voyages, Cook outlined much of the northwest coast of North America and located numerous Pacific Islands. Cook was killed in Hawaii while returning from an unsuccessful expedition to find the Northwest Passage. Four more attempts by the British government to discover a Northwest Passage in the early seventeenth century failed.

Under the orders of Peter the Great of Russia, Vitus Bering in 1728 had discovered the strait that separates North America from Asia. James Cook, while trying to find a Northwest Passage, added to Bering's charts. Cook had sailed as far north as 70°44′N before he was stopped by ice.

Before the nineteenth century, few sea voyages were made in the interest of oceanic study. After 1825 the science of oceanography began to materialize.

In December of 1831, the British ship *Beagle* set sail for a five-year voyage to survey the southern coast of South America and make a series of chronometrical measurements. Charles Darwin, the expedition's naturalist, was able to develop his ideas about organic evolution from observations taken while accompanying the expedition. On the *Beagle* expedition, he also made the first systematic study of the structure of oceanic islands and the origin of coral reefs. This voyage laid the foundations for many later scientific expeditions sent out by the Royal Navy, and others, notably the U.S.N. Exploring Expedition with J. D. Dana on board.

By 1839, James Clark Ross had charted 500 miles of new coastline around the north and eastern part of Baffin Islands. After having lived four winters in the Arctic, he returned to England with a large number of biological specimens. He discovered not only the northern extremity of the North American continent, but also the position of the North Magnetic Pole.

After Karl Friedrich Gauss theoretically calculated the location of the South Magnetic Pole, the British government sent Ross south to make observations of the magnetic pole and to determine its position. Ross, in the *Erebus* and *Terror*, almost the last of the sailing vessels, opened the way to the Antarctic continent by his discoveries in South Victoria Land (1840–43) as far as McMurdo Sound, less than 800 miles from the South Pole.

In the middle of the nineteenth century, Edward Forbes worked on dredging techniques in the Aegean Sea. He was really the first who studied the faunas and their relationship to physical conditions and thus was one of the founders of *marine ecology* (q.v.). His investigations of marine biology were carried out at new depths, but he erroneously concluded that living matter did not exist below 300 fathoms.

The first American to make a major contribution to oceanography was Matthew Fontaine Maury in 1855. Maury was one of the first individuals to observe that the ocean was a circulating system, with an interaction between wind and water. His publication on the interaction of wind and currents is still a basic text for physical oceanography. In 1905, V. W. Ekman gave physical significance to Maury's work.

From the cruises of the *Lightning* (1868) and the *Porcupine* (1869–70), it was observed that the water temperatures were the same at different depths in various locations in the ocean. It was concluded that the ocean contained an active circulation, and

biological dredging revealed life at unexpected depths. These results caused a fundamental revision of ideas and showed a need for more data and study.

Shortly afterward, the *Challenger* voyage (1872–76) opened up the ocean to the first complete scientific investigation from top to bottom. Under the direction of Sir Charles Wyville Thomson, professor of natural philosophy at Edinburgh, and assisted by Sir John Murray, the expedition mapped 140 million square miles of ocean floor. A total of 4417 new species of living matter and 715 new genera were discovered. Scientists aboard the *Challenger* introduced the use of oceanographic equipment at sea and analyzed as much data at sea as possible; 362 hydrographic stations were established over the 68,890 nautical miles sailed. Wire soundings were made in all depths, and the sediment samples obtained permitted the first world map of marine sediment distribution to be drawn up. The *Challenger* expedition contributed to the knowledge of the physical, biological, chemical, and geological aspects of the ocean in a way that has laid the foundation for all the oceanographic work of today.

In 1893, Fridtjof Nansen allowed his *Fram* to be frozen in the waters of the Arctic Ocean and drift across the top of the world. Nansen returned with invaluable meteorological, astronomical, and oceanographic data. The *Fram* reached a latitude of 85°57′N; only the nuclear powered submarine *Nautilus* and sister ships have traveled farther north under the ice.

From April 1925 to July 1927, scientists aboard the German research vessel *Meteor* (Speiss, Wüst, Pratje, Wattenberg, *et al.*) collected temperature data, water samples and deep-sea sediments, in addition to more than 70,000 soundings, while crossing the South Atlantic 14 times in the first systematic analysis of any ocean, prior to the Indian Ocean Expedition of 1960–65. During the post-World War I period, the British ships *Discovery I* and *Discovery II* made extensive surveys, mainly in the Southern Ocean (under the Falkland Islands Dependency program, "Discovery Committee") while taking soundings with marine biological work and making physical and chemical observations. These ships, along with other ships of their type, have opened the field of descriptive oceanography. In Britain, this work is carried on by the National Institute of Oceanography (Godalming).

On August 3, 1958, the United States nuclear powered submarine *Nautilus*, commanded by William R. Anderson, U.S.N., passed beneath the ice at the North Geographic Pole. The shortest route from Japan to Europe was now attained. The *Nautilus* had traveled 1830 miles under the ice and had taken 96 hours to complete the mission. Another new era in oceanography was opened.

In 1892 on the West Coast of the United States, investigations in marine life were begun by the

Department of Zoology of the University of California. This nucleus was eventually to become Scripps Institution of Oceanography at La Jolla. In 1930, the famous Woods Hole Oceanographic Institution was established on the East Coast of the United States, and subsequently the research ship *Atlantis* was built in 1931; this was one of the first ships built especially for oceanographic purposes; most other ships were converted older vessels.

In 1942, H. U. Sverdrup of the University of Oslo, M. W. Johnson of Scripps Institution of Oceanography, and R. H. Fleming of the University of Washington published "The Oceans, Their Physics, Chemistry, and General Biology." Although earlier handbooks of oceanography had been published in German (e.g., Krümmel), this book was the first in the English language to organize and provide factual information on all the various fields of oceanography.

Oceanographic Vessels

According to the 1961 and 1963 National Oceanographic Data Center's publication on the Oceanographic Vessels of the World, there are some 342 oceanographic vessels in operation in the world. These range from small inland boats to vessels over 200 feet in length. In the United States alone, there are more than 160 vessels of all types, but only 116 vessels are considered large enough to be equipped with oceanographic instruments. Educational institutions operate 33 of the vessels, while governmental agencies such as the U.S. Coast and Geodetic Survey, U.S. Navy, etc., operate the other 83 vessels. The United Kingdom and the Soviet Union list 22 vessels each, while Japan, Canada, and Norway list 24, 19, and 14 vessels, respectively. Three or more vessels are listed by Union of South Africa, Brazil, France, Federal Republic of Germany, India, Italy, Netherlands, Yugoslavia, Argentina, Denmark, and Pakistan.

In the 1950's, the notable bathyscaph *Trieste* was constructed under the direction of Auguste Piccard. The vessel was invented by Piccard for probing the ocean's depth without any physical contact with a parent ship. *Trieste* has traveled down to a depth of 35,800 feet in the Marianas Trench off Guam.

In 1962, Scripps Institution of Oceanography launched an ocean buoy known as FLIP (Floating Instrument Platform). The 355-foot buoy can be towed horizontally into location and placed into a vertical position so that 300 feet of the narrow buoy are below water. The ocean buoy was originally built so that oceanographers could perform acoustic experiments at sea. It should also be effective for studying currents, waves, and other properties of seawater.

Institutions of Higher Education and Research

There are relatively few institutions of higher education which offer degrees in oceanography. In the United States, degrees are offered by University of Alaska, Florida State University, Humboldt State College, University of Michigan, New York University, Agricultural and Mechanical College of Texas, Columbia University, University of Hawaii, Johns Hopkins University, Massachusetts Institute of Technology, University of Miami, U.S. Naval Postgraduate School, State University of New York Maritime College, Oregon State University, University of Rhode Island, Scripps Institution of Oceanography (University of California), University of Washington, and University of Wisconsin.

A selection of well-known oceanographic teaching and research institutions outside the United States include:

Australia: C.S.I.R.O. Fisheries Division, Cronulla, N.S.W.

Brazil: Institute of Oceanography, University of Sao Paulo, Brazil; University of Recife, Brazil.

Canada: Bedford Institute of Oceanography, Dartmouth, N.S.; Institute of Oceanography, Dalhousie University, N.S.; Institute of Oceanography, University of B.C., Vancouver; Defence Research Board, Pacific Naval Lab., Esquimalt, B.C.

England: National Institution of Oceanography, Godalming, England; Marine Biological Association of the United Kingdom, Plymouth, England; The University of Liverpool, England.

Finland: Institute of Marine Research, Helsinki.

France: Lab. de'Océanographie, Muséum d'Histoire Naturelle, Rue Cuvier, Paris; Institute of Oceanography, 195 Rue St. Jacques, Paris; Station Marine d'Endoume, Marseille; Lab. Arago, Banyuls-sur-Mer.

Germany: Institut für Meereskunde, Berlin; Deutsches Hydrographical Institution, Hamburg.

Hong Kong: Fisheries Research Unit, University of Hong Kong.

Japan: Geophys. Inst. and Dept. of Fisheries, Tokyo Univ., Tokyo; Geophys. Inst. Kyoto Univ., Kyoto; Tokyo Univ. of Fisheries, Tokyo; Geophys. Inst. and College of Fisheries, Hokkaido Univ., Sapporo and Hakodate; Tokai Fish. Res. Inst., Tokyo; Meteorol. Res. Inst., Tokyo; Hydrographic Office, Tokyo.

Monaco: Museum of Oceanography, Monaco.

Netherlands: Neth. Instituut v. Onderzoek der Zee, Den Helder; Hydrobiological Institution, Department Delta-Research, Yerseke; Rijkswaterstaat, Ijmuiden.

New Zealand: The New Zealand Oceanographic Institute, Wellington.

Norway: University of Oslo, Norway; Geophysical Institute, University of Bergen, Bergen.

South Africa: University of the Witwatersrand, Johannesburg, Transvaal; University of Cape Town, Rondebosch, Cape; Oceanographic Research Institute, Durban, Natal.

U.S.S.R.: The Institute of Oceanology, Academy of Sciences, Moscow; All-Union Research Institute of Marine Fisheries and Oceanography, Moscow; Arctic and Antarctic Research Institute, Leningrad; Hydrochemical Institute, Novocherkassk, Russia.

Yugoslavia: Institute of Oceanography, Split, Yugoslavia.

WAYNE V. BURT
S. A. KULM

References

*Carrington, Richard, 1960, "A Biography of the Sea," New York, Basic Books, Inc.

Coker, R. E., 1947, "This Great and Wide Sea," An Introduction to Oceanography and Marine Biology, New York, Harper and Brothers.

Cromie, William J., 1962, "Exploring the Secrets of the Sea," Englewood Cliffs, N.J., Prentice-Hall.

Daughterty, Charles M., 1961, "Searchers of the Sea: Pioneers in Oceanography," New York, The Viking Press.

Deacon, G. E. R. (editor), 1962, "Seas, Maps, and Men," Garden City, N.Y., Doubleday and Company.

Hearings before the Subcommittee on Oceanography of the Committee on Merchant Marine and Fisheries, House of Representatives Eighty-Ninth Congress, 1965, First Session, August 3, 4, 5, 10, 11, 12, 13, 17, 18 and 19, 1965, National Oceanographic Program—1965, Serial No. 89–13, Washington, D.C., U.S. Government Printing Office.

Herdman, Sir William A., 1923, "Founders of Oceanography and Their Work; An Introduction to the Science of the Sea," London, Edward Arnold and Company.

IGY World Data Center A for Oceanography and National Oceanography, 1961, "Oceanographic Vessels of the World, Washington, D.C., U.S. Naval Oceanographic Office (also Vol. II, 1963).

*Von Arx, William S., 1962, "An Introduction to Physical Oceanography," Reading, Mass. and London, Addison-Wesley Publishing Company.

OCEANOGRAPHY, NEARSHORE

Nearshore oceanography may be taken to include the study of all aspects of the area lying between the backshore zone and the outer edge of the continental shelf. This shallow-water area adjacent to the coast is affected by processes related both to the land and to the ocean; it is the interaction of the land and its loose sediments with the sea that gives this zone its great interest and importance. From the structural point of view, the continental shelf is part of the continent, but water from the deep oceans spreads over it. The processes which operate in the nearshore zone are many and complex, thus the interrelation between the different factors is very involved, each factor affecting and being affected by many of the others.

(a) The Solid Rocks—Cliffs, Wave-cut Platform and Shelf

Rocks outcrop in some areas on parts of the shelf and at the coast, where cliffs and wave-cut platforms are eroded. In many such areas, the relief inland is greater than that offshore, suggesting that there is a tendency for uplift and rejuvenation inland, while subsidence takes place slowly offshore, along a hinge line close to the coast. The processes at work on the shelf and platform have, on the whole, a smoothing effect, with the excep-

tion of those which erode submarine canyons. In the shallowest water, close inshore waves are probably the most effective agents of erosion, but they cannot effectively erode the bottom in depths greater than 30–40 feet (9–12 meters). In shallower water, they are responsible for eroding gently sloping wave-cut platforms beneath the cliffs; these can only be formed where the rock is not protected by a layer of loose sediment in the form of a beach, which absorbs the wave energy. Platforms are only well developed in soft rocks or places where sea level has remained relatively constant for a considerable period. A very extensive wave-cut platform can only form where the sea is transgressional. Such wave-trimmed surfaces are found beneath some marine transgressional strata, for example beneath the Upper Cretaceous sediments in Europe.

No such restrictions are imposed on processes dependent on the tide. The capacity of the tide to move material and to erode in the deeper water over the continental shelf has perhaps been underestimated. Tidal currents are likely to be strong just in those areas where waves would be less effective, for example, in narrow straits and sheltered seas with a large tidal range, such as the English Channel and North Sea. There is also a much greater depth limit to tidal scouring since tidal waves are very long compared with the depth over the shelf and the entire area can thus be affected. Tidal scouring can continue even if downwarping occurs in the shelf area to compensate the upwarping noted inland. Such deepening would tend to restrict the action of the waves on the bottom as the depth increases beyond their reach. Tidal action is much less influenced by variations of sea level than is wave scouring.

The structural process of continental flexure or cymatogenic arching, by causing downwarping of the continental shelf structurally, would help to account for the nature of the shelf. It would also allow a longer period for tidal scouring to produce the relative flatness characteristic of many shallow sea areas when compared to the adjacent land.

(b) The Sediments—Beach Deposits, Tidal Banks and Shelf Sediments

Although a considerable proportion of the shelf and coast is formed of solid rock, elsewhere there is a thick mantle of loose sediment resting on the shelf or filling basins within it, and forming beaches, dunes or marshland along the coast. Again, the major processes at work within the area depend partly on the depth of water; in the shallowest water, the waves play a dominant part in shaping the beaches and other coastal forms, such as barriers and spits. Waves are not the only force to be considered even here; tidal currents play their part and wind is effective, particularly where sand is available for dune formation.

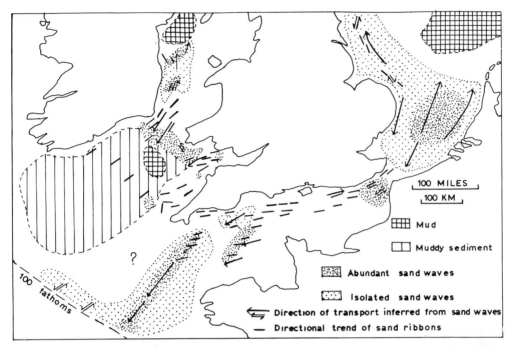

Fig. 1. Submarine features off Southern Britain, showing the significance of tidal action in this extensive shallow offshore zone (based on Stride, 1963).

Coastal vegetation also plays an important part in the formation of coastal dunes and salt marshes, and in some tropical seas, corals build fringing reefs or atolls.

The bottom relief, which is dependent on many factors, is important in determining the orientation of sandy constructional features on the coast. It exerts a strong influence on the refraction of long swells, which are the dominant waves on sandy coasts and which determine the form of coastal features, such as barriers and some forelands. Sand is the most common beach material on a world scale; hence, the long, constructive swells, which are much affected by refraction, are of great importance. Where shingle is available, however, the storm waves, which are usually generated nearer the shore by local onshore winds and are short and high, play the most important part. They build up storm ridges, such as Chesil beach in Dorset, which reaches a height of 43 feet above high tide level, well above the reach of normal waves.

In the slightly deeper water offshore, particularly where sandy sediment is abundant and the tidal currents are rectilinear, elongated interdigitating offshore banks of sand or fine shingle are often found. These banks are formed by tidal currents. Evidence of sand waves on the banks and elsewhere in the shelf zone gives valuable information concerning the directions of movements of material offshore by tidal currents. These currents can move material and form sand waves in depths up to 540 feet, e.g., at the entrance to the English Channel. In this channel and the southern North Sea, sand ribbons and sand waves indicate the direction of sediment transport, which depends on the direction of the strongest tidal streams, which are approximately reversing (see Fig. 1).

Where conditions are suitable, the greater density of sediment-laden water promotes the formation of turbidity currents, thus allowing submarine erosion to be concentrated into the head and upper part of submarine canyons within the shelf zone. Elsewhere on the shelf, where the tidal and other currents are weak or basins occur, areas of quiet sedimentation may allow fine material to accumulate; e.g., in parts of the western Irish Sea and Celtic sea, muddy sediment is now accumulating.

(c) The Water of the Nearshore Zone

The water over the continental shelf is also influenced by the proximity of land. The amount of material in suspension within it is considerably greater than in the open sea, and its temperature and salinity are also modified, particularly in those areas where large rivers discharge into the sea. In areas partially cut off from the main ocean, the local conditions of evaporation, runoff and precipitation may produce exceptional temperature or salinity or both. Thus the Baltic is much fresher than the adjacent ocean, owing to excessive runoff and precipitation in relation to evaporation, while

615

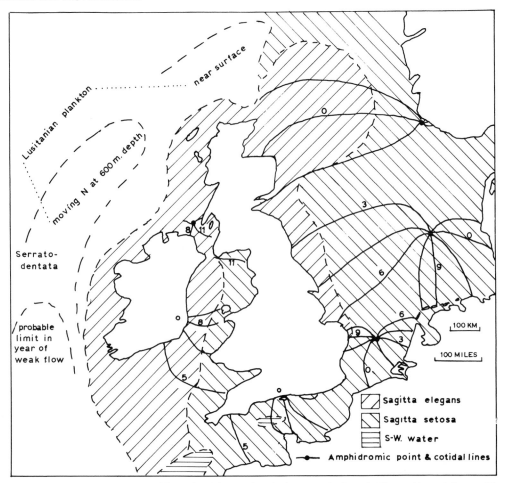

Fig. 2. Surface water types as differentiated by planktonic fauna are indicated. The position of the amphidromic points in the seas around Britain are shown, and the cotidal lines, giving the hour of high water, are included. The open circles inland indicate degenerate amphidromic points (based on Hardy, A. and Doodson and Warburg, Admiralty Manual of Tides, H.M.S.O.).

the Mediterranean and Red Sea are more saline and warmer, owing to excessive evaporation and high temperatures.

Some coastal waters, such as the southern North Sea, are considerably higher in nutrient chemicals than open seawater, resulting in their high biological productivity. Greater stirring in coastal waters by waves and tides enhances the availability of oxygen as well as nutrients. Seasonal changes in temperature tend to be rather greater and differ in character in coastal waters in areas not influenced directly by the main ocean currents.

At times, coastal water can be differentiated from oceanic water by its color, which is caused by the different plankton which flourish in it. The green water of the North Sea and English Channel can be differentiated from the deep blue of the Atlantic by the characteristic arrow worm in each type; *Sagitta elegans* occurs in the Atlantic water

and *Sagitta setosa* in the coastal water. Thus, water character is linked with oceanic life. (See Fig. 2.)

(d) The Movement of the Water—Currents and Coastal Upwelling

Some coastal waters enter into the main ocean currents, while in other areas the waters over the continental shelf move independently of the major ocean streams. An example of the latter type is the shelf current which flows southeast along the east coast of the United States in the opposite direction to the Gulf Stream system, which flows northeast along the continental slope some distance offshore. The shelf current is associated with the slope of sea level, which rises from zero in Florida upward toward the northeast to 35 cm higher at Halifax, Nova Scotia, 2600 km away.

The major ocean currents influence the coastal

zone most where they flow closely along the shore in areas where the winds blow along the coast in a specific direction, or from the land. Such areas occur on the west side of continental masses, off California, Chile and Peru, northwest Australia, west Africa (north of the Equator), and southwest Africa. A wind blowing nearly parallel to a coast on its left in the northern hemisphere will deflect the coastal water offshore and cause upwelling; this will happen in the southern hemisphere where the coast lies to the right of the wind direction. A well-known example is the Peru or Humboldt Current off western South America, where there are occasionally serious consequences in abnormal years when the process fails. Here, as a rule, the longshore north winds cause cooler water to upwell from below the surface; this water comes from relatively shallow depths, averaging about 133 meters in latitudes 3–33°S. At times, the cool water is replaced by much warmer water, extending down from the north, or warming up *in situ* when upwelling ceases. This incursion of warm water occurs roughly every seven years and causes the numerous anchovies to die or migrate offshore, with serious consequences (see: *El Niño*).

These examples show again the close link between the physical and biological character of the coastal zone and the major currents which wash its shores; some areas are abnormally cold as a result of the presence of cold currents, while other areas, of which northwest Europe is the most familiar example, are unusually warm for their latitude because of the warming influence of the ocean currents.

(e) The Fauna and Flora of the Shallow Water

The nearshore zone has a greater variety of fauna and flora than any other part of the ocean for several reasons. There is a great range of conditions present—from the surf on the rocky shores and the muddy estuaries to the variable bottom conditions on the shelf and the enriched waters close offshore in some areas. Life can flourish throughout practically all the nearshore areas. Lack of sufficient light, due to matter suspended in the water, does, however, limit growth in some areas. It has been established that primary production is much greater in coastal waters on a basis of volume. In shallow water, 10–100 mg carbon/m^3/ day is fixed, while the comparable figures for the open ocean are 1–10 mg. However, the total production may be similar in the two environments because of the restriction of depth of production in the most fertile coastal waters due to the small limit of light penetration, light being essential for photosynthesis. It has also been shown that in some temperate areas, the time of the spring flowering of plankton is earlier in the coastal waters and becomes progressively later offshore.

The coastal wave and tidal currents also help to keep some parts of the shallow zone stirred during the summer, precluding the formation of a thermocline, and allowing plant production to continue throughout the season. In the open ocean, a thermocline lowers the summer production by preventing renewal of nutrients from below. The fact that phytoplankton production is concentrated into a relatively smaller volume of water in the shallow seas is advantageous to the higher organisms that feed on the plankton.

The benthic community, both floral and faunal, whose life is passed mainly in contact with the sea-bed, is much more important in shallow water. Benthic plants are the most prolific, e.g., the large kelps off parts of California, which take advantage of the rich, cool, upwelling waters. It has been suggested that although such plants occupy only 0.1 % of the ocean area, their production is at least $\frac{1}{10}$ that of the whole phytoplankton production. Bottom fauna and demersal fish also play a very important part in the biological processes of the oceans, providing much of the food obtained from the sea, either directly or indirectly, for even some of the free-swimming pelagic fish, such as herring, spawn on the sea bed in shallow water.

(f) Waves

Waves may be generated in the open ocean, but they travel from their source toward the shallow water and many eventually break against the land; in so doing, they help to bring into being the wide variety of coastal land forms. There are various views concerning the generation of waves, but it has been shown that the depth of water does influence the size of the waves formed. Observations have shown that, in general, waves in the open ocean are shorter, but higher, than those recorded in exposed coastal stations. This is probably due to the attenuation of the shorter waves before they reach the coast, where the long swells are dominant. In enclosed coastal waters, such as the Irish Sea, the wave periods are generally much shorter, 5 seconds was found to be the most common, and heights are lower than in the open ocean.

The long swells which approach coastal waters are considerably modified as they enter water which is less than half their length in depth. Their period is the only property which remains constant, their length and velocity decrease, and their height at first decreases slightly and then increases markedly, causing a great increase in steepness before they break. Their form changes from almost sinusoidal to long, flat troughs and sharp, steep crests. The orbits also change from open circles to open ellipses, gradually increasing in size while the time which particles have to complete the orbit remains constant. When the orbital velocity exceeds the wave velocity, the wave breaks.

Mass transport is also modified in shallow water to produce a forward thrust on the bottom, which, in the absence of a compensating current due to an onshore wind, produces landward transport of sediment in a long, low swell wave. This effect is not marked in steeper waves, generated by onshore winds close to the shore. Thus constructive swells may be differentiated from destructive steep, storm waves in their effect on beach material near the coast. Where much water is carried landward by the mass transport velocity of the waves, there are sometimes compensating seaward currents concentrated into narrow bands through the breakers, forming rip currents.

The refraction of waves as they approach the shore is important in connection with coastal geomorphology; it is related to their response to the decreasing depth. Waves in deeper water travel faster than those in shallow water. Thus a wave crest is bent by refraction to become more nearly parallel to the bottom contours. As the wave crests bend, they stretch in some places and contract in others; in this way, the energy becomes dissipated along parts of the crest, usually opposite bays and over submarine valleys, while in other parts it is concentrated, e.g., on headlands and over submarine ridges. Wave refraction plays an important part in the shaping of the coastline, particularly where this is dependent on the constructive action of long swells. Thus the offshore relief, which influences the wave refraction helps to shape the shore forms in these areas. Shorter waves are less refracted and, if they approach the coast at an angle, they are responsible for longshore currents and the resulting movement of material alongshore. This is a process which is very important in explaining the incidence of coast erosion and accretion.

Where the coast is steep, waves may not break, but they will be reflected or diffracted, the latter particularly around the end of artificial harbor works or breakwaters. The power of waves to set up shock pressures when breaking against rocks or sea walls is an important process in the erosion of solid rocks by the sea to form cliffs.

(g) Tides and Internal Waves

The part played by the tide in the nearshore zone has already been commented upon in some respects; waves play the most important part on the coastline of most areas, but offshore, the tide is probably more important in shaping the relief of the shelf zone. It is responsible both for the erosion of the solid rock and for the formation of depositional offshore banks where conditions are suitable.

The tide may also be responsible for the formation of large internal waves, some of which have the same period as the tide. The effect of these internal waves is still not fully known, but they may very likely be a powerful influence in the relatively shallow water over the shelf, and may possibly extend their activity to greater depths, where ripples have been found.

Apart from the effect of tidal currents on the seabed, the rise and fall of the tide is of great importance in the coastal zone and in harbors, estuaries and some rivers, where phenomena such as tidal bores may be generated, e.g., the Petit-codiac in America and the Severn in England. The regular rise and fall of the tide is vital to the formation of tidal salt marshes, where mud is deposited as each covering tide drains off, while the flushing action of the tide keeps many estuaries open.

The nature of the tide in coastal areas depends in part also on the shape of the water body and its depth, which determines its natural period of oscillation, T, according to the relationship $T = 2L/\sqrt{gd}$, where L is the length of the water body and d is its depth. If this period approximates one of the periods of the tidal forces, the water body will respond to the tidal force and a large range will result. Owing to the effect of the rotation of the earth on a standing oscillation, the tide oscillates round a nodal point, known as the amphidromic point, whose position may be further modified by friction in shallow water, as in the North Sea (see Fig. 2). Thus the type of tide and its amplitude are dependent on the offshore form of the sea bed in part.

(h) Surges

Occasional unusually high water levels may cause great damage on low-lying coasts, such as the exceptional storm surge of 1953 in the North Sea. Such abnormal conditions are the result of peculiar meteorological conditions which generate a surge in particular physical settings. In the North Sea, the surge travels round the sea in the same anticlockwise direction as the tide. Relatively enclosed waters are particularly liable to such disturbances, which are caused by the sudden veer of wind accompanying a deep depression, moving across the northern North Sea.

Another type of meteorologically induced surge is that associated with coasts liable to be affected by tropical hurricanes. Such surges are best developed where wide shallow shelves occur, as on the Atlantic and Gulf coasts of the United States. The main surge often lasts $2\frac{1}{2}$–5 hours with a rise in level of 3–4 meters, which is comparable to the height of the largest North Sea surges.

(j) Natural Resources—Minerals and Food Supply

The nearshore zone, with its wide variety of type and deposits, and its abundant benthic, demersal and other forms of life, is naturally a rich zone for exploitation. It is probable that much of the petroleum was originally formed in the shallow water environment, and the shelf zone is now being exploited in some areas for this mineral, while phosphates, sulfur and other minerals occur in this zone also. The shallow shelf seas provide a large proportion of the food extracted from the oceans; the wide shelves off northwest Europe, Iceland and North America form the richest fishing grounds for demersal fish, while the prolific pelagic fish, found off coasts where active upwelling enriches the water, are being increasingly exploited. Peru in 1962 was second of the countries of the world in the weight of fish landed.

The richness of the nearshore zone has led to problems of a political nature, particularly in defining the limits of territorial waters, for both fishing rights and mineral extraction.

Conclusion

The many facets of nearshore oceanography are so closely interwoven that they are difficult to separate. The shelf is structurally part of the neighboring land, which provides most of the sediment that is deposited at the coast and on the shelf. The life of the nearshore zone reflects the character of the bottom and is also directly dependent on the character of the water and its movements, such as upwelling, which in turn depend on the character of the wind. The waves are also generated by the wind, and they in their turn determine in part the character of the coastal land forms, while the bottom configuration affects and is affected by both waves and tides. Thus in this shallow water zone, sea, land and air all play their part in developing its special characteristics.

CUCHLAINE A. M. KING

References

Bourcart, J., 1950, "La theorie de la flexure continentale," *C.R. Cong. Int. Geog., Lisbon* 1949, **2**, 167–190.
Emery, K. O., 1960, "The Sea off Southern California," New York, John Wiley & Sons, Inc., 366pp.
Guilcher, A., 1958, "Coastal and Submarine Morphology," London, Methuen, 274pp.
Hardy, A., 1959, "Fish and Fisheries," "The Open Sea," London, Collins, 322pp.
Hill, M. N. (editor), 1962, "The Sea," Vol. I, Chs. 15–23, New York, John Wiley & Sons, Inc.
Hill, M. N. (editor), 1963, "The Sea," Vol. II, Chs. 7, 11, 15, 17, 18, New York, John Wiley & Sons, Inc.
Hill, M. N. (editor), 1963, "The Sea," Vol. III, Chs. 13, 15, 21–24, New York, John Wiley & Sons, Inc.
King, C. A. M., 1959, "Beaches and Coasts," London, Arnold, 403pp.
King, C. A. M., 1963, "An Introduction to Oceanography," New York, McGraw-Hill Book Co., 337pp.
Lewis, W. V., 1938, "Evolution of shoreline curves," *Proc. Geol. Assoc.*, **49**, 107–127.
Lewis, W. V., and Balchin, W. G. V., 1940, "Past sea levels at Dungeness," *Geog. J.*, **106**, 258–285.
Moore, H. B., 1958, "Marine Ecology," New York, John Wiley & Sons, 493pp.
Russell, R. C. H., and Macmillan, D. H., 1952, "Waves and Tides," London, Hutchinson.
Shepard, F. P., 1963, "Submarine Geology," 2nd ed., New York, Harper and Row, 557pp.
Stride, A. H., 1963, "Current-swept sea floors near the southern half of Britain, *Quart. J. Geol. Soc.*, **119**, No. 2, 175–199.
Sverdrup, H. U., Johnson, M. W., and Fleming, R. H., 1942, "The Oceans: Their Physics, Chemistry and General Biology," Englewood Cliffs, N.J., Prentice-Hall, Inc., 1087pp.
Von Arx, W. S., 1962, "An Introduction to Physical Oceanography," Reading, Mass., Addison-Wesley, 422pp.

OCEANOGRAPHY, OPTICAL

Optical oceanography is a branch of physical oceanography which embraces the study of the optical properties of seawater and the underwater field of natural light from sun and sky. It is obvious that the optical behavior of seawater is largely determined by the properties of the water itself; on the other hand, optically active substances in dissolved or particulate form exert a most significant influence on light in the sea.

Optical measurements are an effective tool in studying problems in oceanography such as diffusion, mixing and characterization of water masses, as well as in marine biology, particularly in productivity investigations. Practical applications of optics take proper shape in underwater visibility, photography and television.

Inherent Properties of Seawater

Attenuation of Radiant Energy. The interaction of light with materials in general effects two major processes—absorption and scattering. A parallel beam of light propagating in seawater is attenuated through the combined action of absorption and scattering. Absorption is simply defined as conversion of radiant energy to other forms of energy and scattering as deviation of the beam from rectilinear propagation. The quantities involved—usually given in per cent per meter—are according to the recommendations of the Committee on Radiant Energy in the Sea (International Association of Physical Oceanography)

Attenuance = Absorptance + Scatterance

The components responsible for light attenuation in seawater are surveyed in Table 1 which shows the characteristic features in the attenuation process, in particular its wavelength dependence.

Attenuation by Pure Seawater. The attenuance of pure seawater may be considered as invariant even if it has a slight temperature effect. Experimental data in Table 2 show that pure seawater is most transparent to the blue and that the red light is strongly absorbed (the infrared is even more absorbed). Principally it acts as a monochromator selecting a narrow range of blue light at 465 mμ. The Raleigh scatter produced by the water mole-

TABLE 1. ATTENUATION OF A BEAM OF LIGHT IN SEAWATER,
WAVELENGTH = λ

	Absorptance	λ Dependence of Absorptance	Scatterance	λ Dependence of Scatterance
Water	Constant	Strong	Constant	Strong $(1/\lambda^4)$
Sea salts	Negligible	—	—	—
Yellow substance	Variable	Strong	—	—
Particles	Variable	Strong	Variable	Small

TABLE 2. LIGHT ATTENUANCE IN PURE SEAWATER

Wavelength $(m\mu)$	Attenuance (observed) $(\%/m)$	Scatterance (theoretical) $(\%/m)$	Absorptance (computed) $(\%/m)$
375	4.4	0.7	3.7
400	4.2	0.5	3.7
425	3.2	0.4	2.8
450	1.9	0.3	1.6
475	1.8	0.2	1.6
500	3.5	0.2	3.3
525	4.0	0.2	3.8
550	6.7	0.1	6.6
575	8.7	0.1	8.6
600	16.7	0.1	16.6
625	20.4	0.1	20.3
650	25.0	0.1	24.9
675	30.7	0.1	30.6
700	39.3	0.0	39.3

volume scattering function, and it illustrates the dominance of scattering through small angles, i.e., the forward scattering is very pronounced. Experimental results bear evidence of the shape of the curve in Fig. 1 being almost the same for widely different surface waters and even for lake water. This is a remarkable fact in view of the different nature of the scattering objects; a considerable part. of the material responsible for scattering, however, is made up of organic detritus such as remnants of disintegrated phytoplankton cells and of exoskeletons of zooplankton.

The theoretical function for pure water (Raleigh scatter), which is symmetrical around 90°, is also inserted in Fig. 1. The strong divergence, at small angles, of this curve and the experimental one illustrates the extreme difficulty of preparing optically pure water. In the backscattering (angle >

cules is inversely proportional to λ^4 (λ = wavelength) and is comparable to the absorptance only in the shortwave part of the spectrum. The contribution of the dissolved sea salts to the light absorptance may be neglected for all practical purposes.

Absorption by Yellow Substance. Yellow substance is distinguished from other dissolved organic matter through its light absorption which starts in the yellow and rapidly grows toward shorter wavelengths. Yellow substance is mainly carbohydrate-humic acids. It is formed by decomposition of organic matter and thus is found everywhere in the ocean; it is especially abundant in northern coastal waters where rivers bring in large quantities.

Absorption and Scattering by Particles. The particles in seawater are responsible for absorption as well as scattering. The absorption of particulate matter taken as a collective group is always stronger at the shortwave end than at the longwave end of the visible region. The scattering, on the other hand, is virtually independent of the wavelength.

A closer study of the scattering mechanism involves irradiating a constant volume of seawater and measuring the light scattered through different directions. Figure 1 shows the angular dependence of scattering for clear ocean water, or the so-called

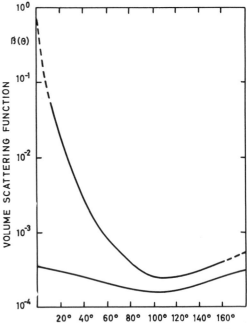

Fig. 1. Angular dependence of scattering or volume scattering function for clear ocean water (upper curve), and the theoretical function for pure water (lower curve).

Sun altitude, degrees	90	60	50	40	30	20	10	5
Reflectance, %	3	3	3	4	6	12	27	42

90°) produced by seawater, on the other hand, the molecular scattering by the water itself plays an important part.

Underwater Light

Reflection. The natural sunlight falling on the sea surface undergoes reflection defined by Fresnel's laws. With a clear sky and horizontal water surface, the true reflectance—not including light upwelling from the water—is essentially a function of the altitude of the sun (Table 3). With a low overcast cloud cover, a dependence on sun altitude also exists, and complete diffusion of light, which corresponds to a theoretical reflectance of 17%, is only attained at very low altitudes. Wave action tends to increase the reflectance at high altitudes and vice versa.

Refraction. The non-reflected light penetrates into the sea by refraction. This process is described by Snell's law; the refraction index for seawater is about 1.33. The dispersion at the surface is small and of little significance. With the angle of incidence equal to 90°, the angle of refraction will be 48.6°. Consequently, the skylight passing the horizontal water surface is compressed, by refraction, within a cone of apex angle 2 × 48.6° (Fig. 2).

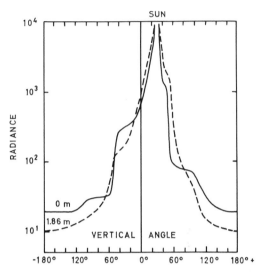

Fig. 3. Angular distribution of radiance for green light in the plane of the sun on a clear day in turbid surface water.

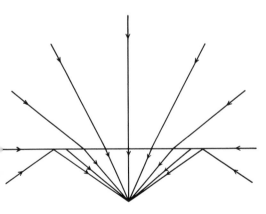

Fig. 2. Light refraction at the sea surface.

Radiance. Radiance is a basic concept in the study of the underwater light. It is defined as the energy per second received by a surface from a certain direction (flux per surface per solid angle).

The production of scattered light introduces—besides sunlight and skylight—a new component in the underwater light field. Close to the surface,

where reflection and refraction take place, the radiance distribution is rather complex. The distributions at the surface and at 1.9 m depicted in Fig. 3 concern fairly turbid water. The following principal features are distinguished. Maximum radiance occurs in the direction of the refracted sunbeam. The edge of the skylight cone of 2 × 48.6° is quite distinct. At the vertical angles +90° and −90°, peaks are present identified as upward scattered light which is totally reflected from below against the surface. A comparison between the radiance distribution at the surface and at 1.9 m reveals the somewhat paradoxical fact that the radiance in most of the angle interval between +70° and −70° increases with depth. This is attributed to the behavior of the scattered light which for most directions increases down to a maximum formed at a certain depth.

With increasing depth, the fine details in the radiance distribution disappear; the directed character gradually becomes less marked through the combined action of absorption and scattering and there is an approach of maximum radiance toward the zenith (Fig. 4). A transformation thus takes place to an asymptotic distribution which is irrespective of the surface lighting conditions and of the state of the sea surface. This distribution is symmetrical round the vertical, and its shape is

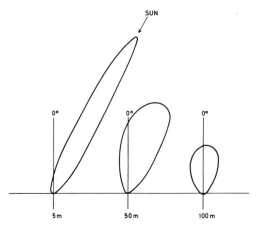

Fig. 4. Angular distribution of radiance in the plane of the sun on a clear day and its approach to the asymptotic state which is almost reached at 100 m. The three distributions are not comparable in size.

determined solely by the inherent properties of the water. It is likely to be encountered at 300–400 m in the clear ocean.

Irradiance. The routine investigation of natural underwater light is usually limited to measuring the penetration of the downward irradiance (flux per horizontal surface facing upward).The fundamental attentuation process in clear ocean water and for high sun altitudes is illustrated in Fig. 5. It is noted that with increasing depth the spectral distribution becomes peaked in the blue at about 470 mμ and that a slight asymmetry is developed since violet light is less attenuated than is green light. Another representation of these data shows the percentage of surface irradiance for different wavelengths as a function of the depth (Fig. 6). These logarithmic curves show for the most penetrant wavelengths a typical curvature which is a consequence of the aforementioned distribution of scattered light displaying a maximum at depth.

High transparency of the water is indicative of a low particle content and also of a low rate of organic production. The clearest water is en-

countered in the Sargasso Sea and in the eastern Mediterranean, whereas in upwelling regions the penetration of light is much less effective. No traces of light can be perceived by the adapted human eye at 700 m depth, even in the clearest waters.

Irradiance data for ocean water of different transparency lend themselves to a classification in terms of spectral transmittance of irradiance in the uppermost 10 m. The three types named I, II and III and shown in Fig. 7 have been derived from the available experimental material which does not, however, include measurements at high latitudes. Some types for northern coastal waters (1, 3, 5, 7, 9) are also presented even if these show less regular features.

The significant transmittance change within this family of curves is more conspicuous in the shortwave than in the longwave part. This effect is due to wavelength-selective absorption by particles and yellow substance. In oceanic areas, the selectivity is chiefly produced by particulate matter, whereas in northern coastal waters, the effect of yellow substance dominates. Overall reduced transmittance is clearly associated with a shift of maximum transmittance from blue in the clear water over green to brown in the most turbid waters.

Color. The oceanographic concept of color should strictly be defined as the color *in situ* which is irrespective of reflection conditions at the surface. The spectral distribution of transmittance affords sufficient explanation for the blue color of the ocean. It has been found in the clearest waters

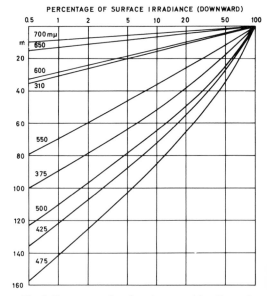

Fig. 6. Percentage of surface downward irradiance for different wavelengths as a function of depth in clearest ocean water.

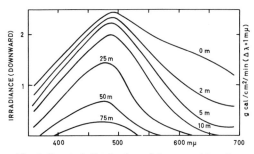

Fig. 5. Spectral distribution of downward irradiance at different depths in clearest ocean water for high sun altitudes.

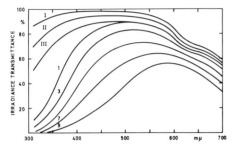

Fig. 7. Spectral transmittance of downward irradiance for the oceanic types I, II and III and for the northern coastal types 1, 3, 5, 7 and 9.

that the spectral distribution of upwelling light is peaked at 450 mμ compared with 470 mμ for the downwelling light. This is an effect of molecular scattering by the water, and it lends a typical brilliance to the blue color. It follows from the discussion in connection with Fig. 7 that reduced transmittance leads to a change of color toward longer wavelengths.

Polarization. It has been found that underwater light is partly linearly polarized well down toward the limit of the photic zone. Most of this polarization arises from the scattering of the sunbeam by particles in the sea; skylight polarization is also involved in the refraction cone $2 \times 48.6°$. The polarization is maximum in sights perpendicular to the beam, and the polarization pattern thus is dependent on the sun's position in the sky. Polarization is favored by a high directional character of the underwater light, i.e., with a clear sky at shallow depths in the clearest water and for the wavelength of least penetration.

Optical Meters. The inherent properties of seawater are determined by a beam transmittance meter. In principle this consists of a lamp unit producing a parallel beam of light which after passing one or two meters of water impinges on a detector. Comparative measurements in the red and in the ultra violet make it possible to distinguish the absorption due to particles and that due to yellow substance.

In scatterance meters, the particle content is directly measured. A volume of seawater is irradiated by a parallel beam, and the light is recorded through a fixed angle, 45 or 90°. Other meters are free angle types which aim at determining the volume scattering function.

The essential parts of natural light meters are a collector and a detector. In irradiance meters, the collector is usually an opal glass; in radiance meters, it is a Gershun tube. Photovoltaic cells or photomultiplier tubes serve as detectors. The use of interference filters affords almost monochromatic measurements. An advanced type of irradiance meter employs a telerecording system with logarithmic response.

The *in situ* meters are preferably provided with a depth sensing unit so that the optical parameters can be obtained as a function of depth by means of an *x-y* recorder.

N. G. Jerlov

References

Duntley, S. Q., 1963, "Light in the sea," *J. Opt. Soc. Am.*, **53**, 214.
Jerlov, N. G., 1963, "Optical oceanography," *Oceanogr. Mar. Biol., Ann. Rev.*, **1**, 89.
Joseph, J., 1955, "Extinction measurements to indicate distribution and transport of watermasses," *Proc. UNESCO Symp. Phys. Oceanogr., Tokyo*, 59.
Kozlyaninov, M. V., 1957, "New instrument for measuring the optical properties of sea water," *Tr. Inst. Okeanol. Akad. Nauk SSSR*, **25**, 134.
Le Grand, Y., Lenoble, Jacqueline, and Ivanoff, A., 1958, *Res. Sci. Camp. Calypso*, **9**.
Tyler, J. E., and Preisendorfer, R. W., 1962, "Light," in (Hill, editor) "The Sea," Vol. 1, p. 397.
Waterman, T. H., 1958, "Polarized Light and Plankton Navigation," in (Buzzati-Traverso, A. A., editor) "Perspectives in Marine Biology," p. 429, La Jolla.

OCEANOGRAPHY, PHYSICAL

Physical oceanography is that science which is concerned with describing the physical state of the sea, including its variations in both space and time; with formulating the physical processes which occur in the ocean and determine its state; and with predicting aspects of the system's behavior. Physical oceanography is partly a branch of physical geography, in that it describes the distribution of water masses, the conditions which form them, and the great current systems which disperse and mix them; but in addition to geography, it treats all scales of motion in the sea, their generation, energetics, and interactions, and the diverse forms of oceanic energy propagation and transport. Physical oceanography is a division of general oceanography and one of the several earth sciences, but it cannot be wholly set apart from these fields, for to varying degrees they interact and blend together. While to chemical and biological oceanography it provides data pertinent to chemical equilibria and marine ecology, at the same time, the distributions of chemical substances and marine organisms help to define water masses and delineate currents. The relief of the ocean bottom, the focus of submarine geology, is modified by currents—particularly spectacular is the cutting of submarine canyons by turbidity currents (q.v.)—and topographic features may in turn very markedly affect the paths of major currents. The relations between meteorology and physical oceanography are numerous and profound: e.g., it is largely the energy released in the condensation of water vapor obtained from the sea which drives the atmospheric circulation, while the resulting winds contribute significantly to the ocean current systems. Like the other earth sciences, physical oceanography is the study of a given, complex natural system involving many phenomena, which only with approximate success can be isolated from one another. It necessarily possesses a descriptive nomenclature peculiar to itself but it must explain the properties of its system in terms of conceptual structures derived from such more basic sciences as physics and chemistry.

The accumulation of oceanographic observations began mainly as a by-product of maritime commerce, and until recent times involved hardly more than charting coastlines and noting surface currents. Information so gained was slow to be disseminated because little was written down, most of it being transmitted orally among sailors; also, much was kept secret among small groups for security reasons. Thus, although the Carthaginian Phoenicians developed an extensive trade in the Atlantic during the first millenium B.C. (principally with Britain), knowledge of their trade routes and explorations largely vanished with their empire. Similarly, Spanish mariners of the early sixteenth century quickly learned to use the North Equatorial Current and the Gulf Stream in their passages to and from the New World, but to protect their rich cargoes, they refrained from publicizing their findings. The little material recorded during antiquity and medieval times which might be called oceanographic is contained in primitive universal geographies (principally Greek, e.g., the "Geography" of Strabo, *ca.* 20 A.D.), reports left by individual travelers, and practical manuals. A notable example of the latter is the "Periplus (pilot book) of the Erythraean Sea" (Arabian Sea), a description of trading routes, customs, and politics along the coasts of East Africa, Arabia, and India. It appeared around 60 A.D., and was probably written by an Egyptian Greek for the benefit of sailors engaged in the lucrative Indian Ocean commerce. This same traffic, nearly a millenium later, was described by the Arab traveler, El Mas'udi, in "Meadows of Gold and Mines of Gems" (947 A.D.), in part an account of his many personal voyages on trading ships in the Indian Ocean.

Such knowledge was fragmentary, disorderly, and not widespread, so that despite Norse crossings of the Atlantic in the eleventh to fourteenth centuries, and possible Chinese landings on the west coast of North America in the fifth century, a realistic conception of the shape and dimensions of the world ocean had to await the great European voyages of discovery which began at the end of the fifteenth century. Prominent among the Atlantic explorers were Diaz, Columbus, Vespucci, the Cabots, and Cabral; while the voyages of Magellan, Tasman, Bering, and Cook were of particular importance in charting the Pacific. On the other hand, although the Portuguese, led by Da Gama, opened the Indian Ocean to Western Europe, they could not add much to what the Arabs and Chinese already knew of it.

From these early explorations on, mariners observed and recorded sets and drifts due to the major surface currents. Columbus, for instance, noted the North Equatorial Current in both the Atlantic and the Caribbean Sea, while Ponce de Leon found the Florida Current, and the Cabots, the Labrador Current. Little attempt was made to map the currents accurately until Benjamin Franklin, in consultation with a Nantucket whaling captain, prepared a chart of the Gulf Stream for the use of mail packets (*Trans. Philadelphia Phil. Soc.*, 1786). Further codification of current data to aid navigators was much advanced by M. F. Maury, who, as superintendent of the U.S. Naval Observatory at the middle of the last century, organized worldwide collections of ship observations. By that time, enough voyages had been made to reveal most of the major ocean currents. In 1853 A. G. Findlay published a remarkably good chart of surface currents in the Atlantic and Pacific Oceans, which differs qualitatively from modern ones only in minor features (*J. Roy. Geogr. Soc.*). The Equatorial Undercurrents, however, were not described until 1954, because, as subsurface flows, they escaped mariners' notice.

With improvement in techniques, marine explorers began to make additional physical observations of the sea. While successful soundings at depths greater than 4000 m were not taken until 1840 (on the Antarctic voyage of James Ross), surface temperatures had often been measured in the eighteenth century by such men as Captain Cook and Benjamin Franklin, and the first serial observations on record of temperature *vs.* depth were made in the Arctic by John Ross in 1818. Among early cruises expressly for the scientific study of the ocean (as opposed to commerce, fishing, exploitation, and general-purpose discovery) was the notable Gulf Stream survey carried out in the years 1844–1860 by A. D. Bache, superintendent of the U.S. Coast and Geodetic Survey. The beginning of modern oceanography, however, is usually considered to be the voyage of H.M.S. *Challenger* (1872–1876), under the leadership of Wyville Thomson. This was the first expedition to attempt (*inter alia*) a mapping of the world-ocean floor and a systematic, global description of the vertical and horizontal distributions of temperature and dissolved constituents. Of the many oceanographic expeditions which have followed that of the *Challenger*, especially noteworthy are the German study of the South Atlantic in the *Meteor* (1925–1927), and the British investigations of the Southern Ocean with the *Discovery I*, *Discovery II*, and *William Scoresby* (1925–1939, 1950–1951). During the International Geophysical

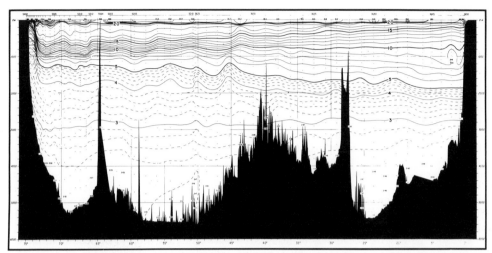

Fig. 1. Profile of temperature (°C) from Chesapeake Bay to Bermuda, then along latitude 32°N to Morocco. *Atlantis* stations 5292–5312 occupied June 1955; 5564, April 1957; 5203–5210, November 1954; *Discovery II* stations 3625–3650, November–December 1957. Depths are in meters, and longitudes are indicated at the base of the profile. (Courtesy F. C. Fuglister)

Year (1957–1958), ships of many nations performed intensive studies of both the Atlantic and Pacific. The geographical shift in Western attention since the fifteenth century, however, is exemplified by the paradox that although in classical times the Indian Ocean was the one most familiar (by virtue of its rich trade), no extensive scientific examination was made of it until the International Indian Ocean Expedition of 1960–1965.

Essential to all oceanographic surveys are methods of determining position at sea; while such data by themselves may be relatively uninteresting, few additional measurements are of much use without them. The determination of latitude by meridian altitude of sun, moon, or stars is not difficult, but not until 1785 were marine chronometers generally available which were suited to determining longitude. Celestial navigation is limited to positions once or twice a day, and is, of course, impossible in bad weather, but it is still the only technique available over most of the ocean. For limited areas, however, radio-navigation systems have been developed which permit frequent position determinations of high accuracy. With the Loran System used off the east coast of North America, one measures the difference in arrival time of pulse signals sent from two synchronized shore stations and thus locates himself on one branch of a hyperbola. By then finding an intersecting hyperbola from a second pair of stations, positions can be obtained with accuracy up to a quarter of a mile (see *Navigation*).

To determine the full detailed shape of the ocean basins, it was necessary to develop deep-sea sounding techniques. Early methods involved lowering hemp ropes and, later, piano wires weighted by a sounding lead, to the bottom, but these have been replaced by modern echo sounding, in which one measures the travel time of an acoustic signal emitted at the sea surface and reflected back from the ocean bottom. The mean depth of the world ocean has now been determined as 3790 m or, excluding marginal seas, 4100 m. In particular, the mean depths of the Atlantic, Indian, and Pacific Oceans are 3870 m, 3960 m, and 4280 m. The greatest known depth (10,863 m) is in the Mariana Trench of the Pacific Ocean (see *Bathymetry, Sounding*).

Temperatures in the ocean are measured principally by mercurial thermometer, though recently thermistors and other devices have come into limited use. Serial observations were made by the *Challenger* with maximum-minimum thermometers, but these have been supplanted by the reversing thermometer: its mercury column breaks when the thermometer is inverted, and thus gives a reading of temperature at the depth of inversion, accurate with certain instruments to 0.002°C. The inversion depth is measured by pairing one thermometer protected against water pressure with another thermometer exposed to the sea, whose reading therefore reflects not only temperature *in situ* but also pressure (hence depth). These observations are usually performed on the classical oceanographic (or hydrographic) station: single or paired reversing thermometers are mounted on open water-sampling bottles, which are themselves attached in series to a wire rope lowered into the sea. Then, when a metal "messenger" is sent down the wire, it strikes a bottle and releases a catch, causing the bottle to tip over (with thermometers), close, and secure a water sample for analysis. The messenger then strikes another catch and releases a second messenger, preattached to the wire, which trips the next bottle in series. Most of our knowledge of the ocean structure has been obtained through this slow, demanding, but highly effective method.

As long as it was thought that salt water, like fresh water, achieved its maximum density at 4°C, it was also thought that the deep ocean could be no colder than 4°C. In fact, however, 76% of the total ocean volume has a lower temperature, as suggested in Fig. 1, a profile in the North Atlantic running from Chesapeake Bay to Bermuda, then along latitude 32°N to Africa. It shows the general distribution of temperature with depth and longitude in northern temperate regions. For the meridional variation in temperature structure, see Figs. 2 and 3 of *Oceanic Circulation*.

In a very crude way the ocean may be regarded as a three-layer system: a thin, warm, surface layer, homogeneous during late winter, which may attain a thickness of up to 500 m in the western Sargasso Sea; the *main thermocline*, a transition layer some 500–1000 m thick, in which the temperature drops abruptly from about 17 to 5°C; and cold, nearly homogeneous deep water, several kilometers in extent, in which temperature decreases very slowly to the bottom. The main thermocline rises to the surface in mid-latitudes, and the polar and subpolar oceans are almost uniformly cold from surface to bottom; it rises again in the tropics, though not to the sea surface. The steep slope in isotherms on the western side of the Atlantic is associated with the Gulf Stream, and a similar one occurs in the Pacific, corresponding to the Kuroshio. Such pronounced western-boundary features are absent in the southern hemisphere where the circulations are much weaker, but the thermocline does rise somewhat toward the eastern and western coasts. Seasonal warming produces a *seasonal thermocline* in the near-surface water, which may involve temperature differences of up to 10°C by late summer; afterwards it wanes, and in late winter the upper layer is again isothermal. Little seasonal effect penetrates below 200 m. The range of temperature observed in the ocean is from the freezing point, $-1.9°C$ (certain polar surface water in winter), to above 30°C (summertime tropical surface water).

Salinity

It is useful for describing ocean structure, and essential for calculating density, to have, in addition to temperature, a parameter related to the ionic content of seawater. Convention has established it as *salinity*, the total concentration of dissolved salts, expressed in parts per thousand by weight. Since it is impractical to determine for each water sample the individual concentrations of even the major salt constituents, and quite inaccurate to evaporate the sample and weigh the solid residue, some quantity related to salinity is usually measured instead. Analysis of *Challenger* samples revealed that the major constituents exist in virtually constant proportion; hence water samples have traditionally been titrated for *chlorinity* with results accurate to about 0.02‰ in salinity units. More recently, on account of greater accuracy and ease of analysis, the electrical conductivity of seawater has replaced chlorinity as a measure of salinity; carefully performed shipboard conductivity measurements are usually accurate to 0.005‰ in salinity equivalent.

In general, the distribution of salinity in the ocean resembles that of temperature (see *Oceanic Circulation*, Figs. 2 and 3). A nearly isohaline surface layer overlies the *halocline*, a zone of rapid decrease in salinity corresponding to the main thermocline, and in the deep water beneath it, the vertical gradients of salinity are very small. In some areas, however, e.g., the Southern Ocean, pronounced salinity minima occur at mid-depths while pronounced maxima just at the top of the halocline are common to many regions. The physical boundaries and undulations of the halocline so closely match those of the main thermocline that as terms describing geographical regions, the two are virtually identical and are often used synonymously. The saltiest of the oceans is the Atlantic, which has a mean salinity of 34.92‰, in contrast to 34.62‰ for the Pacific, and 34.76‰ for the Indian Ocean. The salinity at the sea surface depends principally on the local difference between evaporation and precipitation; thus in the arid belt which includes the Sahara and Arabia, surface salinities may be as large as 37.5‰. In the open ocean, salinities usually fall in the range 33.5–37.5‰, but they approach zero near river mouths, and rise above 40‰ in the Red Sea. The most saline body of water on earth is the Kara-Bogaz-Gol, an exceptionally shallow bay (only a few meters deep) of the Caspian Sea; in effect it is a natural evaporating pan, and its gradually increasing salinity now exceeds 300‰ (see *Salinity*; also pr Vol. VI).

To a far more remarkable extent than is apparent in the figures cited, observations of temperature in a given region of the ocean correlate with those of salinity. When plotted together on a diagram having temperature and salinity as coordinates, they define a *T–S curve* characteristic of the given region. Although the scatter of points about a mean T–S curve is very great for near-surface observations, it becomes small in the thermocline, and extremely slight in the deep water. The salinity fluctuations in a group of some thousand pairs of observations made over the western North Atlantic at temperatures less than 3°C had a standard deviation within the precision of conductivity measurements. Consequently, T–S curves serve to define particular *water masses*, and single points on T–S diagrams specify *water types*. Water mass

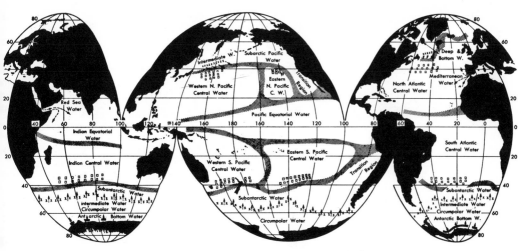

Fig. 2. Approximate boundaries of the upper water masses of the ocean. Squares indicate the regions in which the Central Water masses are formed; crosses indicate the lines along which Antarctic and Arctic Intermediate Waters sink; solid markings indicate the sources of deep and bottom water. [Courtesy W. S. von Arx (1962), after Sverdrup, Johnson, and Fleming (1942). By permission of Prentice-Hall, Englewood Cliffs, N.J.]

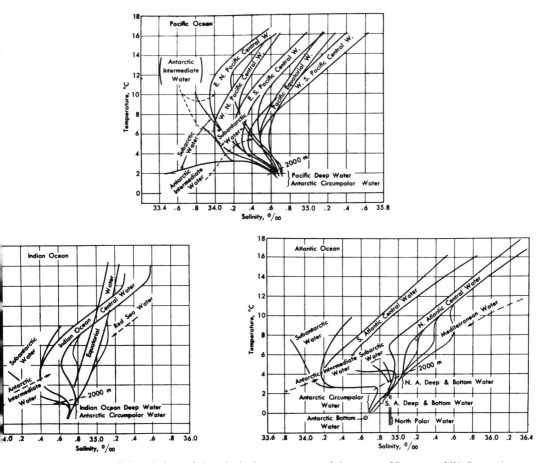

Fig. 3. Temperature-salinity relations of the principal water masses of the oceans. [Courtesy of W. S. von Arx (1962), as modified from Sverdrup, Johnson, and Fleming (1942).]

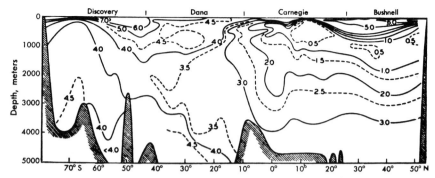

Fig. 4. Composite meridional profile of dissolved oxygen in the Pacific Ocean, approximately along longitude 170°W. Units are milliliters dissolved oxygen (measured at atmospheric pressure and 0°C) per liter of seawater. Depths are in meters (after Sverdrup).

analysis has become an important technique for investigating and describing the physical structure of the ocean.

Water Masses

Figure 2 shows a rough division of the upper world ocean into its component water masses, and Fig. 3 illustrates their temperature-salinity characteristics according to the bands they occupy on the T–S diagram. (The approximate 2000-m depth in the various water masses is suggested by labeled dashed lines.) Water masses are formed when surface water becomes sufficiently dense to sink and spread over large areas at levels appropriate to its density. The surface sources of the several kinds of Central Water are indicated on Fig. 2 by clumps of squares in mid-latitudes. Intermediate Water extends equatorward at mid-depths, principally from a zone around Antarctica, and to a much less extent from small regions in the northern hemisphere; these locations are shown by crosses and short arrows. Solid markings adjacent to Antarctica and Greenland define the sources of Deep and Bottom Water. (The movements of intermediate, deep, and bottom water are described in more detail under *Oceanic Circulation*). With decreasing temperature, most T–S curves converge toward one point, the Antarctic Bottom Water, because this single water type spreads into all three oceans as their coldest bottom water. The characteristics of a water mass may be markedly affected by secondary circulations. Intense evaporation over the Mediterranean and Red Seas, for instance, drives relatively saline outflows into the Atlantic and Indian Oceans, which are reflected in the high salinity of North Atlantic Central Water and Indian Equatorial Water (Fig. 3).

Of great importance to studies of the ocean circulation is the *age* of a water mass, defined as the time elapsed since that water was "formed" at the sea surface. For this reason, considerable attention has been given in physical oceanography to the distribution of dissolved oxygen in the sea:

water at the sea surface is presumed saturated in atmospheric gases, but after it sinks below the surface, it gradually loses oxygen through biological consumption. Unfortunately, neither the magnitude of the consumption rate nor its vertical and horizontal variation is well known. Consequently, the use of oxygen data is largely qualitative: Fig. 4, a vertical profile of dissolved oxygen along longitude 170°W in the Pacific Ocean (corresponding to the temperature and salinity profiles shown as Fig. 3 under *Oceanic Circulation*), suggests that Deep Water in the North Pacific is "older" than that in the South Pacific, but it does not tell by how much.

Another approach to age measurement has been the analysis of radiocarbon concentrations in the dissolved bicarbonate of seawater. Since oceanic radiocarbon is derived from the atmosphere, the longer a water parcel is removed from its "source," the greater is the decay of its radiocarbon, and hence the greater the difference between source and in-situ ratios of C^{14} to C^{12} concentrations. Such differences confirm that Deep Water in the North Pacific is older than that in the South Pacific, and they indicate an age difference of some three hundred years. The interpretation of C^{14}/C^{12} ratios in terms of absolute water-mass ages is rendered somewhat ambiguous, however, by uncertainties in the exact source-water ratios, the extent of mixing with other water masses, and the degree of steadiness in the general circulation. Nevertheless, on a rough overall basis, the data imply ages between a few hundred and a thousand years as appropriate to the deep water masses.

Observations of temperature, salinity, and pressure permit computation of the field of density, which is useful in studying the vertical stability of water columns, and in calculating geostrophic currents (discussed below). The effect of pressure on density is by far the greatest for the normal range of variation in these parameters, but it is only of small dynamical significance; therefore one usually takes account only of temperature and

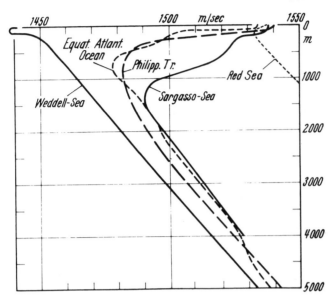

Fig. 5. Examples of the vertical variation of sound speed (in meters per second) in different parts of the ocean. Depths in meters. [Courtesy of G. Dietrich (1963).]

salinity effects, by computing densities at zero pressure. Although density increases with salinity and decreases with temperature, the vertical temperature changes in the ocean are sufficient to ensure that it increase with depth. Thus, in the main thermocline, the effect on density of the temperature decrease is about twice as great as that of the salinity decrease, and the thermocline is itself a zone of high gradient in density as well as in temperature and salinity. The usual range of zero-pressure density is 1.023–1.028 g/cm^3.

In contrast, the speed of sound depends strongly on pressure as well as temperature (increasing with both), but it is affected only slightly by existing salinity changes. Some examples of the vertical variation in sound speed are shown in Fig. 5. Temperature decreases so abruptly through the main thermocline that the temperature effect dominates over that of pressure, and sound speed at first decreases with depth; below the thermocline, however, pressure change dominates and sound speed increases. Thus, in such regions as the Sargasso Sea and Equatorial Atlantic, there exists a minimum in sound speed at mid-depths, but not in areas like the Weddell Sea which lacks a strong thermocline. Since sound rays are refracted away from regions of increased speed, this layer of minimum speed is a "sound channel," in the sense that very little acoustic energy which is released in the layer can leave it. Such energy confinement was dramatically demonstrated when an explosion in the Atlantic sound channel of only 2.7 kg of TNT was heard by geophones 5700 km away. Similar effects in the upper layers of the ocean have con-

siderable bearing on the techniques of submarine warfare and are therefore of vital concern to the major navies of the world.

Motions in the sea of current scale have been determined mainly by four methods: observations of drifting objects, tracing of water-mass properties, use of current meters, and dynamic computations. Reports of ship set and drift were the basis for Findlay's excellent chart of surface currents, while the best measurements yet made of deep motions were performed by tracking free, neutrally buoyant floats pre-ballasted to remain at a given level. Present ideas concerning the global pattern of the deep circulation, however, have been derived mainly by inference from the arrangement of water masses and the penetration of characteristic cores on charts of property distributions. Unfortunately, it is very difficult in general to construct current meters of adequate reliability and accuracy, but they have been used with much success to obtain velocity profiles across the Equatorial Undercurrents in the Pacific and Indian Oceans. Most estimates of the volume transport of currents have been made by the method of *dynamic computations*, devised in 1902 by J. W. Sandström and B. Helland-Hansen (*Rep. Norweg. Fish. Invest.*). It is based on application of the geostrophic approximation (see *Geostrophic Motion*[*]): since the vertical shear of geostrophic velocity is proportional to the horizontal density gradient, a velocity profile may be calculated by assuming or directly measuring a velocity at some one level, then vertically integrating measured horizontal density gradients. Except for the Equatorial

*See Vol. II.

Undercurrents, all major ocean currents seem to be accompanied by large gradients (note the Gulf Stream in Fig. 1) and to have velocities at depth which, if not zero, are at least much less than their surface velocities. Consequently, even if one has no actual velocity measurement, he can still achieve a fair approximation to a velocity profile and its associated volume transport from the density field alone, simply by assuming that velocity vanishes at some deep level. For a chart showing the pattern of average surface currents and a description of the general ocean circulation, see *Oceanic Circulation*.

A variety of small-scale circulations takes place in *estuaries*, coastal embayments in which river outflow meets and mixes with salt water. The character of an estuarine circulation depends on the degree of mixing, for entrainment of salt water into a fresh surface outflow requires a proportionate inflow of seawater along the bottom of the estuary; and if the mixing is so vigorous that vertical homogeneity results, the outflow and inflow may occur not at different levels but on opposite sides of the estuary instead (see *Estuary*).

In addition to the quasi-steady currents, there are also important wave motions in the sea. Those most greatly studied are probably the tides, which are long waves (wavelength much greater than ocean depth) induced by the differential gravitational attraction of the sun and moon on the ocean mass. The tides of the English Channel were noted as long ago as the fourth century B.C., by the Greek voyager Pytheas, who correctly supposed that they were related to the moon, but the first automatically registering tide gauge was not installed until 1831 (in England). The theory of tidal motion has received far more attention than that of any other kind in physical oceanography and has been investigated during the last two centuries by many eminent fluid dynamicists, including D. Bernoulli (1740), Laplace (1775), Kelvin (1867), and G. H. Darwin (1879). Since the tidal force depends on the relative orientation of sun, moon, and earth, its time-dependence is composed of a great many periodicities. Some of the important ones are the lunar and solar semidiurnal and diurnal periods, the lunar fortnightly, lunar monthly, and solar semiannual periods. These are therefore all present in observed tidal motions. The response of the ocean is also determined, however, by the earth's rotation, and the depth and shape of the ocean basins. The resulting problem is so formidable that no general hydrodynamical deduction of the tide has been achieved, and coastal predictions are based instead on harmonic analysis of tide-gauge records. As long waves, the horizontal tidal motions have no vertical shear, except as caused by friction, but they are modified by the earth's rotation in such a manner that the diurnal and semidiurnal tidal constituents tend to advance around ocean basins in a rotary fashion (the Kelvin wave): counterclockwise in the northern hemisphere, clockwise in the southern. The tidal range in sea-surface elevation is small in the deep ocean, but it increases considerably in shallow water, occasionally exceeding 15 m in the Bay of Fundy (see *Tides*).

A spectacular type of long wave is the *tsunami*, a progressive solitary wave, or small group of waves, which is generated by submarine vulcanism or earthquakes. These waves travel at enormous speeds over the open ocean—in the vicinity of 200 m/sec—and cause disastrous coastal flooding because they amplify in shallow water, like the tides, and may reach heights above 30 m (see *Tsunamis*).

The wind-induced surface oscillations are *short* waves (wavelength much less than ocean depth) and, unlike long waves, are essentially confined to the sea surface: the motion at a depth of one wavelength is less than 1% of that at the surface. Despite intensive research, the actual mechanism by which winds impart energy to waves is not clear; emphasis has variously been placed either on the direct tangential stress exerted by the wind on the sea surface or on the difference in wind pressure on the windward and leeward sides of a wave. In any case, the resulting configuration of the sea surface is usually a complex, irregular superposition of waves having a broad range of frequencies, amplitudes and propagation directions, and it has proved more fruitful to describe it statistically than in terms of individual wave components. It is usually convenient to distinguish the *sea*, or locally generated, short-period wave motion, from the *swell*, the longer, higher-period (order of ten seconds) waves caused by winds and storms some distance away. The characteristic height and period of a swell at a particular location depend on wind speed and duration at the generating area and on the distance from it. Figure 6 shows such dependence for fully developed motion, with an assumed relation between speed and duration of the generating wind, and it includes as well the time of travel of the swell to the point of observation. These results were calculated by H. U. Sverdrup and W. H. Munk, who devised empirical, statistical methods for making useful wave forecasts during the Second World War (*U.S. Navy Hydrographic Office Publ.*, **601**, 1947). In fact, since their pioneering work, prediction has become more feasible in this than in any other area of physical oceanography except for tides, and it now seems practical to predict from wind speed the distribution of energy among component frequencies of motion (power spectrum) for fully developed seas in storm areas.

Surface waves propagate by virtue of pressure gradients associated with the difference in density between water and air; consequently one should

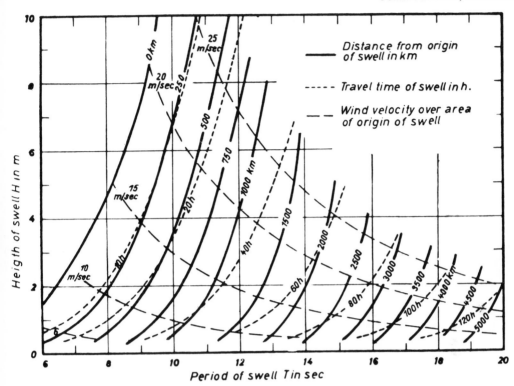

Fig. 6. Dependence of height (meters) and period (seconds) of swell on wind speed (meters per second) at the generating area and distance (kilometers) from it; for a fully developed sea at the generating area and an assumed relation between the speed and duration of the wind. Also shown is the time of travel of the swell to the point of observation (in hours). [Courtesy of G. Dietrich (1963) after Sverdrup and Munk.]

also expect to find waves along a discontinuity or sharp vertical gradient of density within the ocean itself. Such *internal waves* are well known, and have been observed over a wide range of frequencies, including those of tidal motion. As with surface waves, short internal waves are closely confined to the density interface. Because density differences within the ocean are only about one-thousandth of that between water and air, however, internal waves propagate much more slowly than surface waves of the same frequency and may attain much greater amplitudes (commonly, several tens of meters). Submarines have occasionally experienced strong vertical accelerations presumably associated with internal waves, and ships moving through a thin layer of light surface water—overlying dense water below—have encountered the phenomenon of "dead water," in which energy applied to propulsion of the ship becomes directed instead toward generating internal waves, with the result that the ship makes little or no headway.

With the development of marine meteorology, it has become less an academic matter and far more a practical one to regard the ocean and atmosphere for certain purposes as a single system. This point of view is especially pertinent to general considerations of energetics in both physical oceanography and dynamical meteorology.

The ultimate source of all oceanic and atmospheric motion is solar radiation, which is absorbed by the ocean in a very thin layer at the sea surface (thickness of the order of 10 m); part is immediately lost as back-radiation, part given off to the atmosphere by turbulent conduction, part mixed downward by turbulent motions into a layer 100–200 m thick (as in the development of seasonal thermoclines), and part is used for evaporation at the surface. The water vapor is carried up into the atmosphere and, through later condensation (mainly on salt particles thrown up from sea spray) and release of latent heat, becomes the principal energy source for the atmospheric circulation. The winds so generated then act on the sea to produce both surface waves and ocean currents. Thus thermal energy enters the atmosphere from the ocean in latent form, where 1 or 2% of it is converted to kinetic energy, and a small fraction of that is then transferred to oceanic motion.

In addition, various processes at the sea surface make gravitational potential energy available for conversion into kinetic energy of current motions: the intense, low-latitude evaporation which provides latent heat to the atmosphere at the same time increases the density of surface water by raising its salinity, while seasonal and sporadic cooling also make surface water denser, both by thermal contraction and through salinity increases following the formation of ice. With sufficient rise in density, convective motions ensue. Ultimately, the kinetic energy of the whole system returns to thermal energy by frictional dissipation.

The circulations so maintained combine to keep nearly steady the annual mean temperature distribution of the earth by transporting enough internal, mechanical, and latent energy poleward to balance the net loss of radiation in high latitudes against the net gain in low latitudes. The total energy transport across latitude circles is of the order of 10^{15} cal/sec, to which the ocean contributes roughly as much as the atmosphere in low latitudes and about 10–20% as much in high latitudes. Thus the basic energetic processes of the ocean and atmosphere couple, connect, and overlap to such a degree that scientific progress not only clarifies the peculiarly oceanic and atmospheric phenomena, but emphasizes more clearly the profound and far-reaching interpenetrations of meteorology and physical oceanography themselves.

BRUCE WARREN

References

Defant, A., 1961, "Physical Oceanography," New York, Oxford, London, Paris, Pergamon Press.

Dietrich, G., 1963, "General Oceanography," New York, London, John Wiley & Sons, Inc.

Hill, M. N. (editor), 1962, 1963, "The Sea," Vol. I; Vol. II, Section III; Vol. III, Section II, New York and London, John Wiley & Sons, Inc.

Sverdrup, H. U., Johnson, M. W., and Fleming, R. H., 1942, "The Oceans," New York, Prentice-Hall.

von Arx, W. S., 1962, "An Introduction to Physical Oceanography," Reading, Mass., London, Addison-Wesley.

Cross-references: *Bathymetry; Chemical Oceanography; Estuary; Navigation; Oceanic Circulation; Oceanography; Oceans; Salinity; Sounding; Tides; Tsunamis.*

OCEANS: LIMITS, DEFINITIONS, DIMENSIONS

(1) Limits

The division of the waters which cover approximately 71% of the surface of the earth into various oceans has differed from one period to another and with the authors of various oceanographic treatises, beginning with Claret de Fleurieu (1798–1800).

For a long time it was accepted that they were divided into five oceans: Atlantic, Pacific, Indian,

Arctic and Antarctic, following the recommendation of a committee of the Royal Geographical Society of London, under the chairmanship of Sir Roderick I. Murchison (in 1845, but only published in 1893). No natural boundary separated the Antarctic Ocean from the first three and it has been variously given at $67\frac{1}{2}°$S, 60°S, 55°S, etc. A distinctive "Southern Ocean" (q.v.) is often recognized as an informal regional unit. As for the Arctic Ocean, it communicated with the Atlantic over a long distance between Europe and Greenland and also through the Canadian passages, and the Murchison Committee put an arbitrary boundary at the Arctic Circle ($67\frac{1}{2}°$N).

Following the publication of Krümmel's paper (1879) and his classic "Handbuch der Oceanographie" (1897), it became common practice to recognize only three oceans: Atlantic, Pacific and Indian. They extended southward between arbitrary limits as far as the Antarctic continent, and all waters north of Europe, Asia, America and the Bering Strait were thought of as part of the Atlantic Ocean.

Over the past few years there has again been a trend to class separately the waters around the North Pole by reason of their distinctive characteristics, and to think in terms of four principal divisions: Atlantic Ocean, Pacific Ocean, Indian Ocean and Arctic Ocean (or Sea), which are defined as follows (Bruns, 1958):

To the west, the limit of the *Pacific Ocean* follows the length of the coasts of Asia as far as the Malay Peninsula, then the length of the northern part of the Malacca Strait and the western and southern coasts of the East Indian Archipelago. South of New Guinea it crosses the Torres Strait to the east coast of Australia, then crosses the west of Bass Strait to Tasmania, and finally follows the meridian 147°E to the Antarctic continent, the northern coast of which forms the southern boundary of this ocean. To the east, the boundary is the coasts of North and South America. To the north the limit cuts across the Bering Strait between Cape Dezhneva and Cape Prince of Wales.

The *Atlantic Ocean* is limited to the west by the eastern coasts of North and South America, from the mouth of Hudson Bay in the north to Cape Horn in the south. Beyond that, the limit follows this meridian as far as the northern coast of the Antarctic continent which forms the southern boundary of the ocean. To the east, the meridian of the Cape of Good Hope (20°E) forms the boundary, which then follows the coasts of Africa and Europe. To the north, it is separated from the Arctic Ocean by a line drawn through the northernmost point of Norway, the southernmost point of West Spitsbergen, the Denmark Strait and Greenland.

The *Arctic Ocean* (or Sea) is separated from the Atlantic Ocean and Pacific Ocean as stated above.

and is bounded by the northern coasts of Europe, Asia, North America and Greenland.

The *Indian Ocean* is bounded to the north by the southern coast of Asia, to the west by the coast of Africa and the meridian of the Cape of Good Hope, to the south by the Antarctic continent and to the east by the limits of the Pacific Ocean.

(2) Divisions

According to most authors, the oceans include seas or basins and their limits are determined on the basis of various characteristics. Istochin (in Bruns, 1958) bases the division of water on the following considerations in order of importance:

(a) Coastal contours of continents and islands;

(b) Ocean bottom features;

(c) Degree of independence of current and tidal systems;

(d) Degree of independence of atmospheric circulation;

(e) Horizontal and vertical distribution of water temperature and salinity;

(f) Other occasional factors.

Krümmel was the first to give a rigid definition of an ocean, a mediterranean sea and a marginal sea (1879, 1897). Basing his conclusions for the most part on the first two of the above considerations, morphology and hydrography, he established limits for the oceans and the principal seas. After him other authors, such as Schott (1926, 1935) and particularly Kossinna (1921), have laid down limits of seas following approximately the same principles. In addition they adopted arbitrary limits to enclose marginal seas, which are more open than mediterranean seas, a process which is of course inevitable but which may lead to differences of opinion.

Seas can hardly extend far beyond continents since their limits are based chiefly on the contours (bays, peninsulas, straits, archipelagoes, etc.) or the lie of the land which is either a continent or close to one. Thus a very extensive part of ocean waters cannot be divided according to the principles for seas. Division can, however, be based on undersea features, knowledge of which is increasing constantly since developments in the science of oceanography have made it possible to carry out extensive and exact sounding of great depths. So, in 1936 Wüst suggested using 4000-meter depth contours to mark the limits of the different parts of the oceans (see also Sverdrup *et al.*, 1942). On this basis the authors of the latter work supplied a list of 45 basins: 19 in the Atlantic Ocean (these include the Arctic Basin), 14 in the Pacific Ocean, and 12 in the Indian Ocean.

(3) Definitions

(a) Being faced with such diversity in the choice of limits, the hydrographers who took part in the First International Hydrographic Conference in London in 1919 when bringing into being the International Hydrographic Bureau thought of including among its future responsibilities that of laying down boundaries for oceans and seas for adoption by the national hydrographic offices in order to standardize the classification of hydrographic information and the arrangement of their publications (Sailing Directions, Lists of Lights, Notices to Mariners, etc.). This task was, in fact, assigned to the I.H. Bureau at the following Hydrographic Conference in 1926.

The result was *IHB Special Publication No. 23.* This work, published first in 1928, has been revised several times. A second edition and a provisional edition were published in 1937 and 1950, respectively. The current edition is entitled: "International Hydrographic Bureau—Limits of Oceans and Seas" (*Special Publication No. 23*), Third ed., 1953.

(b) This latest edition has taken into account: the criticisms or proposals offered by various hydrographic offices, particularly during international hydrographic conferences; suggestions made by certain scientific organizations; the report (1940) of the Committee nominated by the Association of Physical Oceanography during the General Assembly of the International Union of Geodesy and Geophysics in 1936 at Edinburgh to study "the criteria and nomenclature of the principal divisions of the ocean bottom"; and opinions expressed by various oceanographers.

(c) In this publication the names of the four oceans (Atlantic, Pacific, Indian, Arctic) have been retained, but they are used to designate only water not included in seas. The Atlantic and Pacific Oceans are divided into two parts, North and South, separated by the equator. Since it is generally accepted that the northern limits of Antarctic waters due to their seasonal variations, are too difficult to define in a way which would permit drawing limits for an Antarctic Ocean, the three oceans, Atlantic, Pacific and Indian, have been extended as far as the Antarctic continent and are separated by the meridians through the three southernmost points of Africa, America and Tasmania.

The straits which connect two seas are not divided but have been included in one or the other of them (in compliance with a resolution of the First International Hydrographic Conference in London in 1919).

Generally speaking, the limits have been determined to meet the specific needs of hydrography, and although they were laid down as far as possible according to oceanographic and geographic data, they are not necessarily based on the latter. They have no political significance whatsoever.

For arbitrary limits loxodromes have been adopted, since these are represented by straight lines on a Mercator projection and are in current

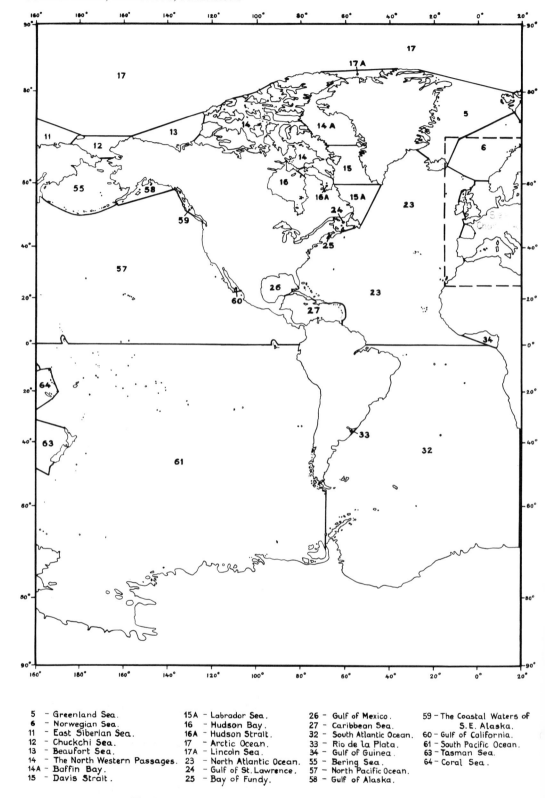

5 – Greenland Sea.	15A – Labrador Sea.	26 – Gulf of Mexico.	59 – The Coastal Waters of
6 – Norwegian Sea.	16 – Hudson Bay.	27 – Caribbean Sea.	S.E. Alaska.
11 – East Siberian Sea.	16A – Hudson Strait.	32 – South Atlantic Ocean.	60 – Gulf of California.
12 – Chuckchi Sea.	17 – Arctic Ocean.	33 – Rio de la Plata.	61 – South Pacific Ocean.
13 – Beaufort Sea.	17A – Lincoln Sea.	34 – Gulf of Guinea.	63 – Tasman Sea.
14 – The North Western Passages.	23 – North Atlantic Ocean.	55 – Bering Sea.	64 – Coral Sea.
14A – Baffin Bay.	24 – Gulf of St. Lawrence.	57 – North Pacific Ocean.	
15 – Davis Strait.	25 – Bay of Fundy.	58 – Gulf of Alaska.	

Fig. 1. Boundaries of oceans and seas in the western hemisphere.

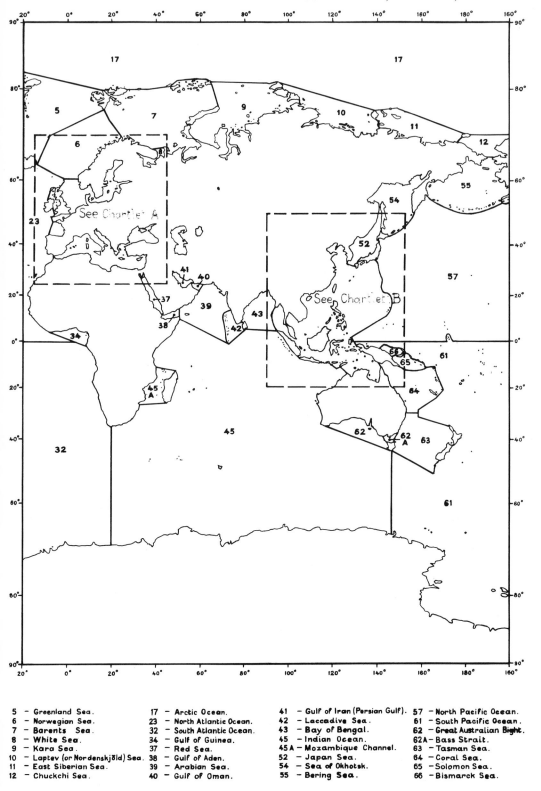

5 – Greenland Sea.	17 – Arctic Ocean.	41 – Gulf of Iran (Persian Gulf).	57 – North Pacific Ocean.
6 – Norwegian Sea.	23 – North Atlantic Ocean.	42 – Laccadive Sea.	61 – South Pacific Ocean.
7 – Barents Sea.	32 – South Atlantic Ocean.	43 – Bay of Bengal.	62 – Great Australian Bight.
8 – White Sea.	34 – Gulf of Guinea.	45 – Indian Ocean.	62A – Bass Strait.
9 – Kara Sea.	37 – Red Sea.	45A – Mozambique Channel.	63 – Tasman Sea.
10 – Laptev (or Nordenskjöld) Sea.	38 – Gulf of Aden.	52 – Japan Sea.	64 – Coral Sea.
11 – East Siberian Sea.	39 – Arabian Sea.	54 – Sea of Okhotsk.	65 – Solomon Sea.
12 – Chuckchi Sea.	40 – Gulf of Oman.	55 – Bering Sea.	66 – Bismarck Sea.

Fig. 2. Boundaries of oceans and seas in the eastern hemisphere.

use in navigation, and as far as possible, meridians and parallels have been selected since they may easily be drawn in any system of cartographic projection to allow rapid distinction between what lies to one side or the other.

The text of *I H B Special Publication No.* 23 defines in detail the limits of seas and oceans using topographic features, known geographic names and points with given geographic coordinates. Charts on which the limits are traced and the names of oceans and seas printed are provided with it.

The division of the waters of the globe, as adopted by the International Hydrographic Bureau, is shown on the four figures herewith, along with the list of oceans and seas. Ocean boundaries are as follows:

Arctic Ocean.* Between Greenland and West Spitsbergen—the northern limit of Greenland Sea (5).

Between West Spitsbergen and North East Land—the parallel of latitude 80°N.

From Cape Leigh Smith to Cape Kohlsaat—the northern limit of Barents Sea (7).

From Cape Kohlsaat to Cape Molotov—the northern limit of Kara Sea (9).

From Cape Molotov to the northern extremity of Kotel'nyy Island—the northern limit of Laptev Sea (10).

From the northern extremity of Kotel'nyy Island to the northern point of Wrangel Island—the northern limit of East Siberian Sea (11).

From the northern point of Wrangel Island to Point Barrow—the northern limit of Chuckchi Sea (12).

From Point Barrow to Cape Lands End on Prince Patrick Island—the northern limit of Beaufort Sea (13), through the northwest coast of Prince Patrick Island to Cape Leopold McClintock, thence to Cape Murray (Brock Island) and along the northwest coast to the extreme northerly point; to Cape Mackay (Borden Island); through the northwesterly coast of Borden Island to Cape Malloch, to Cape Isachsen (Ellef Ringnes Island); to the northwest point of Meighen Island to Cape Stallworthy (Axel Heiberg Island) to Cape Colgate the extreme west point of Ellesmere Island; through the north shore of Ellesmere Island to Cape Columbia thence a line to Cape Morris Jesup (Greenland).

North Atlantic Ocean. *On the West.* The eastern limits of the Caribbean Sea (27), the southeastern limits of the Gulf of Mexico (26) from the north coast of Cuba to Key West, the southwestern limit of the Bay of Fundy (25) and the southeastern and northeastern limits of the Gulf of St. Lawrence (24).

On the North. The southern limit of Davis Strait

(15) from the coast of Labrador to Greenland and the southwestern limit of the Greenland Sea (5) and Norwegian Sea (6) from Greenland to the Shetland Islands.

On the East. The northwestern limit of the North Sea (4), the northern and western limits of the Scottish Sea (18), the southern limit of the Irish Sea (19), the western limits of the Bristol (20) and English (21) Channels, of the Bay of Biscay (22) and of the Mediterranean Sea (28).

On the South. The equator, from the coast of Brazil to the southwestern limit of the Gulf of Guinea (34).

South Atlantic Ocean. *On the Southwest.* The meridian of Cape Horn (67° 16′W) from Tierra del Fuego to the Antarctic continent; a line from Cape Virgins to Cape Espiritu Santo, Tierra del Fuego, the eastern entrance to Magellan Strait.**

On the West. The limit of the Rio de la Plata (33).

On the North. The southern limit of the North Atlantic Ocean (23).

On the Northeast. The limit of the Gulf of Guinea (34).

On the Southeast. From Cape Agulhas along the meridian of 20°E to the Antarctic continent.

On the South. The Antarctic continent.

North Pacific Ocean. *On the Southwest.* The northeastern limit of the East Indian Archipelago (48) from the equator to Luzon Island.

On the West and Northwest. The eastern limits of the Philippine Sea (56) and Japan Sea (52) and the southeastern limit of the Sea of Okhotsk (54).

On the North. The southern limits of the Bering Sea (55) and the Gulf of Alaska (58).

On the East. The western limit of coastal waters of southeast Alaska and British Columbia (59), and the southern limit of the Gulf of California (60).

On the South. The equator, but excluding those islands of the Gilbert and Galàpagos Groups which lie to the north thereof.

South Pacific Ocean. *On the West.* From South East Cape, the southern point of Tasmania, down the meridian of 146° 53′E to the Antarctic continent.

On the Southwest and Northwest. The southern, eastern and northeastern limits of the Tasman Sea (63), the southeastern and northeastern limits of the Coral Sea (64), the eastern and northern limits of the Solomon (65) and Bismarck (66) Seas, and the northeastern limit of the East Indian Archipelago (48) from New Guinea to the equator.

On the North. The equator, but including those islands of the Gilbert and Galàpagos Groups which lie to the north thereof.

On the East. The meridian of Cape Horn (67° 16′W) from Tierra del Fuego to the Antarctic continent; a line from Cape Virgins to Cape

---

* The numbers in parentheses which follow refer to the numbers on the maps (Figs. 1–4).

** Chile is not in agreement with these limits.

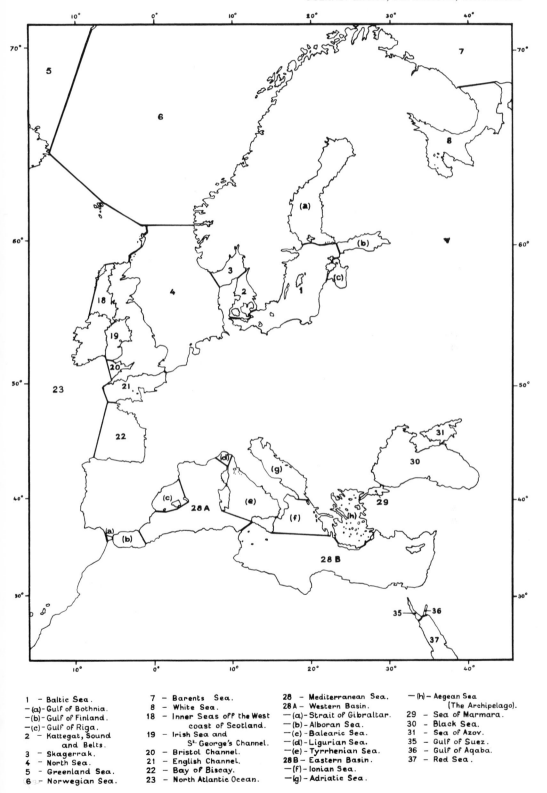

1 – Baltic Sea.	7 – Barents Sea.	28 – Mediterranean Sea.
–(a)– Gulf of Bothnia.	8 – White Sea.	28A – Western Basin.
–(b)– Gulf of Finland.	18 – Inner Seas off the West	–(a)– Strait of Gibraltar.
–(c)– Gulf of Riga.	coast of Scotland.	–(b)– Alboran Sea.
2 – Kattegat, Sound	19 – Irish Sea and	–(c)– Balearic Sea.
and Belts.	St George's Channel.	–(d)– Ligurian Sea.
3 – Skagerrak.	20 – Bristol Channel.	–(e)– Tyrrhenian Sea.
4 – North Sea.	21 – English Channel.	28B – Eastern Basin.
5 – Greenland Sea.	22 – Bay of Biscay.	–(f)– Ionian Sea.
6 – Norwegian Sea.	23 – North Atlantic Ocean.	–(g)– Adriatic Sea.

–(h)– Aegean Sea
(The Archipelago).
29 – Sea of Marmara.
30 – Black Sea.
31 – Sea of Azov.
35 – Gulf of Suez.
36 – Gulf of Aqaba.
37 – Red Sea.

Fig. 3. Boundaries of the European seas.

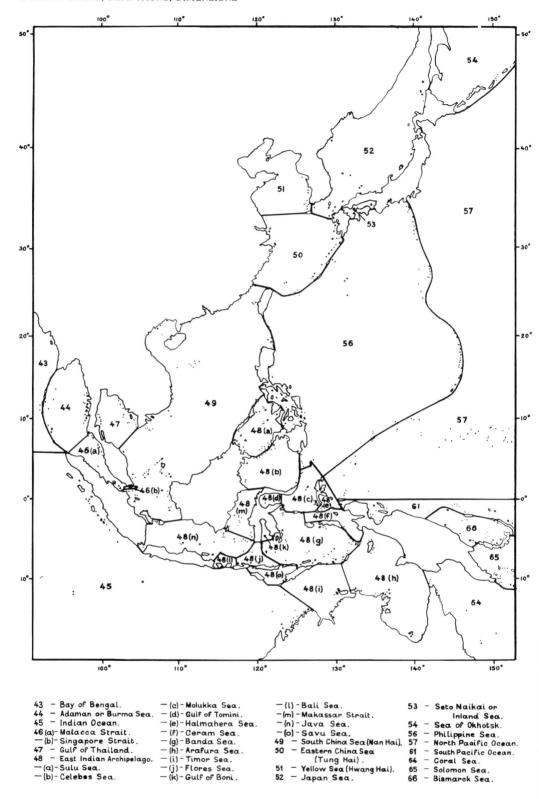

43 – Bay of Bengal.	– (c) – Molukka Sea.	– (l) – Bali Sea.	53 – Seto Naikai or
44 – Adaman or Burma Sea.	– (d) – Gulf of Tomini.	– (m) – Makassar Strait.	Inland Sea.
45 – Indian Ocean.	– (e) – Halmahera Sea.	– (n) – Java Sea.	54 – Sea of Okhotsk.
46 (a) – Malacca Strait.	– (f) – Ceram Sea.	– (o) – Savu Sea.	56 – Philippine Sea.
– (b) – Singapore Strait.	– (g) – Banda Sea.	49 – South China Sea (Nan Hai).	57 – North Pacific Ocean.
47 – Gulf of Thailand.	– (h) – Arafura Sea.	50 – Eastern China Sea	61 – South Pacific Ocean.
48 – East Indian Archipelago.	– (i) – Timor Sea.	(Tung Hai) .	64 – Coral Sea.
– (a) – Sulu Sea.	– (j) – Flores Sea.	51 – Yellow Sea (Hwang Hai).	65 – Solomon Sea.
– (b) – Celebes Sea.	– (k) – Gulf of Boni .	52 – Japan Sea.	66 – Bismarck Sea.

Fig. 4. Boundaries of the Far Eastern seas.

TABLE 1. AREA, VOLUME, AND MEAN DEPTH OF OCEANS AND SEAS (KOSSINNA, 1921)

Body	Area (10^6 km^2)	Volume (10^6 km^3)	Mean Depth (m)
Atlantic Ocean ⎫	82.441	323.613	3926
Pacific Ocean ⎬ excluding adjacent seas	165.246	707.555	4282
Indian Ocean ⎭	73.443	291.030	3963
All oceans (excluding adjacent seas)	321.130	1322.198	4117
Arctic "Mediterranean" (Ocean)	14.090	16.980	1205
American "Mediterranean" (Caribbean, Gulf of Mexico)	4.319	9.573	2216
Mediterranean Sea and Black Sea	2.966	4.238	1429
Asiatic "Mediterranean" (East Indian Arch.)	8.143	9.873	1212
Large "mediterranean" seas	29.518	40.664	1378
Baltic Sea	0.422	0.023	55
Hudson Bay	1.232	0.158	128
Red Sea	0.438	0.215	491
Persian Gulf	0.239	0.006	25
Small "mediterranean" seas	2.331	0.402	172
All "mediterranean" seas	31.849	41.066	1289
North Sea	0.575	0.054	94
English Channel	0.075	0.004	54
Irish Sea	0.103	0.006	60
Gulf of St. Lawrence	0.238	0.030	127
Andaman Sea	0.798	0.694	870
Bering Sea	2.268	3.259	1437
Okhotsk Sea	1.528	1.279	838
Japan Sea	1.008	1.361	1350
East China Sea	1.249	0.235	188
Gulf of California	0.162	0.132	813
Bass Strait	0.075	0.005	70
Marginal seas	8.079	7.059	874
All adjacent seas	39.928	48.125	1205
Atlantic Ocean ⎫	106.463	354.679	3332
Pacific Ocean ⎬ including adjacent seas	179.679	723.699	4028
Indian Ocean ⎭	74.917	291.945	3897
	361.059	1370.323	3795

NOTE: For additional statistics, see *Continents and Oceans*, Vol.III.

Espiritu Santo, Tierra del Fuego, the eastern entrance to Magellan Strait.**

On the South. The Antarctic continent.

Indian Ocean. *On the North.* The southern limits of the Arabian Sea (39) and the Laccadive Sea (42), the southern limit of the Bay of Bengal (43), the southern limits of the East Indian Archipelago (48), and the southern limit of the Great Australian Bight (62).

On the West. From Cape Agulhas in 20° longitude East, southward along this meridian to the Antarctic continent.

**Chile is not in agreement with these limits.

On the East. From South East Cape, the southern point of Tasmania down the meridian 146° 53′E to the Antarctic continent.

On the South. The Antarctic continent.

It may shortly become necessary to bring the work up to date to include the seas bordering the Antarctic continent which have been named following explorations in recent years.

(4) Dimensions

The dimensions of oceans and seas have been evaluated by various authors according to the boundaries they used. In computing area based on data which are known with a high degree of exactitude, the shape of the earth and geographic dry-land contours, results may be obtained which are very nearly exact. The determination of volume carries a much higher degree of uncertainty since full details of ocean bottom features are not yet sufficiently precise and the value of mean depth can only be approximate.

Kossinna carried out a complete set of calculations which were published in 1921 (see Table 1), but care should be taken to allow for somewhat different boundaries than here adopted. The results of this fundamental work have served as a basis for other scientists who have since put forward their own values for sea dimensions; notably Littlehales in 1932 and Stocks in 1938.

Additional statistical data on the oceans are as follows: Mean temperature $= 3.90°C$. Mean specific gravity $= 1.045$. Total mass 143×10^{16} metric tons. Mean salinity $34.75\%_{00}$, or 3.475% by weight. Thus there are 138×10^{16} tons of H_2O and 4.87×10^{16} tons of salts in the sea.

ALFREDO VIGLIERI

References

Bruns, E., 1958, "Ozeanologie," Vol. 1, VEB, Berlin, Deutscher Verlag der Wissenschaften.

Fleurieu, C. P., Claret de, 1798–1800, "Observations sur la division hydrographique du globe, et changements proposés dans la nomenclature générale et particulière de l'hydrographie," in Marchand, E., "Voyage autour du Monde," Vol. 4, pp. 1–74, Paris, Imprimerie de la République, An VIII.

International Association of Physical Oceanography (International Union of Geodesy and Geophysics), 1940, Report of the Committee on the criteria and nomenclature of the major divisions of the ocean bottom, Liverpool, Secretariat of the Association.

Kossinna, E., 1921, "Die Tiefen des Weltmeeres," Berlin, E. S. Mittler und Sohn, (*Veröffentl. Inst. Meereskunde*, N.F., No. 9).

Krümmel, O., 1879, "Versuch einer vergleichenden Morphologie der Meeresräume," Leipzig.

Krümmel, O., 1897, "Handbuch der Ozeanographie," Stuttgart, 2 vols. (Second ed., 1907).

Murchison, R. I., 1893, "Nomenclature of the oceans," *Geograph. J.*, **1**, 535–536.

Schott, G., 1926, "Geographie des Atlantischen Ozeans," Hamburg, Verlag von C. Boysen.

Schott, G., 1935, "Geographie des Indischen und Stillen Ozeans," Hamburg, Verlag von C. Boysen.

Sverdrup, H. U., Johnson, M. W., and Fleming, R. H., 1942, "The Oceans," Englewood Cliffs, N.J., Prentice-Hall, Inc.

Wüst, G., 1936, "Die Gliederung des Weltmeeres," *Petermanns Mitt.* (also *Hydr. Rev.*, **13**, 46).

OCEAN WAVES

Waves in the ocean are generated by a wide variety of forces. The different types of waves and their characteristics will be mentioned in relation to the generating agents. The most obvious and ubiquitous ocean waves are those caused by the wind blowing over the water surface, but in specific areas, special weather conditions can produce longer-period surges. Tsunamis are the result of submarine earth movements, while variations of water character can produce internal waves, and finally, the regular movement of the earth, moon and sun produces very long waves, which result in the rise and fall of the tides.

(1) Waves Caused by the Wind

(a) Sea. Wind waves in the open ocean are formed by the transfer of energy from the air to the water, so that the dimensions of the resulting waves depend on the velocity and duration of the wind. Another important factor is the length of open water available, known as the fetch. There is still some difference of opinion concerning the relationship between these variables and the height and length of the waves, although it is certain that the wave dimensions increase with increasing wind velocity and duration up to a definite maximum value. In the region where waves are being actively generated by the wind, they are called "sea," and an important aspect of this area is the very complex pattern of the sea surface. This complexity can be expressed in terms of the individual waves composing it; thus the waves can be described as a spectrum, including wave trains of a great variety of amplitudes and periods, moving in various directions. Normally, however, most of the wave energy is concentrated in a relatively narrow frequency band; this means that one wave period will be dominant in the spectrum and waves of this period will tend to be highest, because of the concentration of energy in this band. Neumann suggests that for a 20-knot wind the peak period will be 8.1 seconds, while for a 40-knot wind the 16-second period will dominate. Observations made with a ship-borne wave recorder indicate that waves in the open sea are higher but shorter than those recorded in an exposed coastal situation; in the open North Atlantic, records show that a force 4 wind produces waves of 6-second period and 2 feet height; force 6 produces 7-second and 5-foot waves, increasing to 11 seconds and nearly 20 feet for force 8 winds. Waves of 60 feet in height have been recorded by this weather ship at 61°N, 15° 20′W.

The precise method by which energy is transferred from air to water is still not quite clear, but it is related to two mechanisms. (1) The wind is deflected as it blows over the wave profile and dynamic pressure differences can feed energy into the waves. (2) When the wind is turbulent, a system of moving pressure fluctuations can react with the water by resonance to form waves, without the waves affecting the wind. Once formed, this complex spectrum of waves moves out from

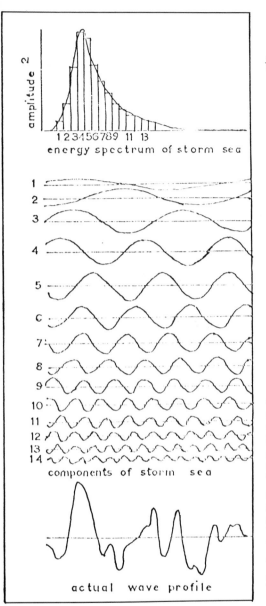

Fig. 1. Diagram to show the addition of fourteen different components of a wave spectrum to form the actual wave profile. The proportion of energy in the different parts of the spectrum is indicated in the upper part of the diagram (after Deacon, from King, 1959).

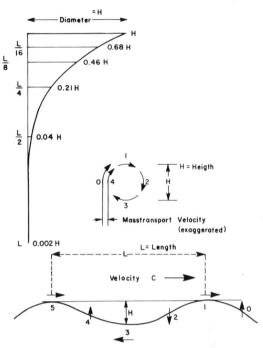

Fig. 2. Orbital motion in waves.

the generating area to become modified into "swell."

(b) Swell. High, long waves can travel immense distances before they lose their identity, because of their great energy, which is a function of their height and period. As they travel away from the generating area, they lose height slowly, mainly by spreading their energy over a widening area of ocean, but they maintain their length, traveling as a wave train at half the velocity of the individual waves making up the train. Wave heights tend to be halved after traveling 1000 miles from the generating area, but thereafter, the rate of attenuation is reduced steadily with increasing distance. Thus, it has been possible to record waves on the coast of California, which were originally generated about 7000 miles away in the South Pacific; these swell waves arrived with a period of 12–18 seconds. Waves generated by a hurricane off the eastern United States have been recorded on the coast of Cornwall, 3000 nautical miles away, arriving with gradually decreasing periods about 4–5 days after the storm.

As the waves move away from the generating area, they gradually approximate more closely the ideal sinusoidal waves in deep water, originally described mathematically by Airy and Stokes. The velocity of these waves in deep water, where $d/L > 0.5$, is entirely dependent on the wavelength. Although the wave form moves fast, the water particles travel much more slowly, their velocity depending on the period and wave height. Each water particle completes an almost circular orbit with the passage of each wave, advancing slightly in the direction of wave movement at a rate proportional to the square of the wave steepness at the surface; this is known as the mass transport velocity. The penetration of wind waves downward is very limited, however; the orbits are halved for

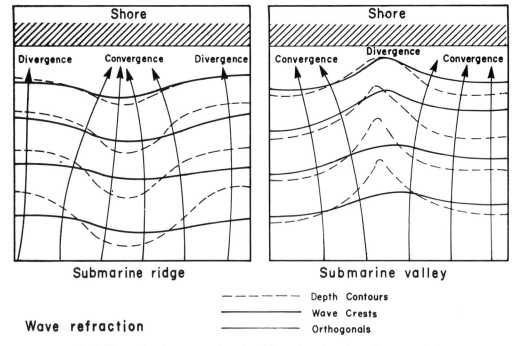

Fig. 3. Wave refraction over a submarine ridge and a submarine valley, respectively.

every $\frac{1}{9}$ of the wavelength in depth, and at a depth of 1.5 times the wavelength they are only 1/12,400 of their surface size.

(c) **Wind Waves in Shallow Water.** All the characteristics of the waves alter as they enter shallow water except the wave period; the relationship between deep water and shallow water wave dimensions is conveniently summarized in Fig. 4 of the article on *Wave Theory* by R. L. Wiegel. Another important effect of wave entry into shallow water is the refraction of the waves, a process dependent on the wavelength, the direction of deep water approach and the underwater relief. This is significant in causing concentration of wave energy on specific coastal sectors in areas where the normal waves are long and the offshore relief is complex. When the water depth is approximately 4/3 the wave height, the wave will break, forming a plunging or spilling breaker according to its steepness and the beach gradient. Where spilling breakers are common, often where the offshore gradient is slight, a wide surf zone results, and it is in this zone that most of the movement of bottom material by waves and wave erosion takes place.

(d) **Surf Beat.** A longer-period wave was recognized by Munk and Tucker from wave records taken in shallow water, the wave period being about 10 times that of the normal wind waves. These low-frequency waves travel shoreward and as yet there is no satisfactory explanation of their presence, although they seem to be related in some

way to the interaction of normal wind waves and low-frequency waves.

(e) **Ripples.** At the other end of the scale of wavelengths are the small ripples, whose length is small enough to be controlled by the ratio of surface tension to water density. The presence of ripples on the sea surface is important in its control of the roughness of the sea surface, which affects the friction of the wind over the water. The formation of longer wind waves is probably facilitated by the presence of ripples on the water surface, giving the wind a better grip on the water surface.

(2) Waves Due Primarily to Unusual Weather Conditions

Waves due to unusual weather conditions can be of considerable importance in some areas. An interesting type of wave in this category is the microseism; this could perhaps be used to give advance warning of approaching storms.

(a) **Microseisms.** A close correlation has been found between the period of ocean waves and microseismic waves, recorded on seismographs. The period of the microseism is half that of the storm wave, both having a spectrum of waves. At first it was difficult to understand how ocean waves, which are surface phenomena, could affect the bottom to generate microseisms, but Longuet-Higgins has shown that when two wave trains of equal period but unequal height meet head-on, they interact to cause pressure disturbances on the

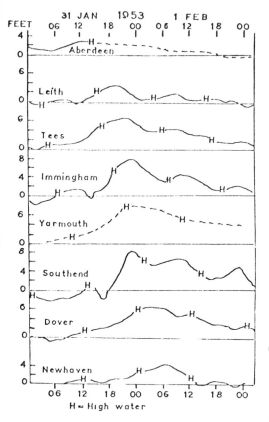

Fig. 4. The surge of 31 January to 1 February 1953, showing the residual values observed after deduction from the predicted tide curves on the North Sea coast of Britain. H = higher water (after Robinson, from King, 1959).

when a deep depression moves southeast across the sea from northern Scotland to southern Denmark at a critical speed. The surge forms a wave traveling anticlockwise around the sea at about the same speed as the normal tidal wave; it can raise the water levels 3 m above the predicted tide heights, but fortunately such high surges, for some unexplained reason, do not appear to coincide with normal high water. Nevertheless, surges can have disastrous results on the low coasts of the North Sea, as was clearly apparent after the very severe surge of 1953, when the whole level of the North Sea was raised by an average of 2 feet for a period of about 12 hours.

(3) Waves Resulting from the Characteristics of the Water—Internal Waves

Less conspicuous, but of considerable significance, are the internal waves that form at the boundary between two distinct types of water of differing density. They usually have a slower speed

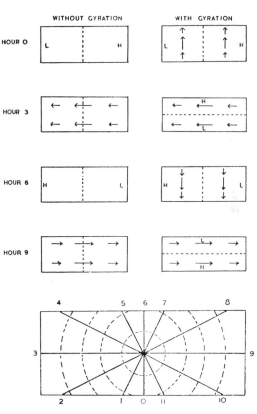

Fig. 5. (*Top*) Effects of gyration on standing oscillation in rectangular basin. (The components of the streams are drawn at their maximum rates; the broken lines join points at mean level.) (*Bottom*) Amphidromic system in small seas, directly due to lunar semidiurnal tide-generating forces, in the northern hemisphere (from Dodson and Warburg).

bottom, which initiate the microseisms. Two wave trains can meet head-on if a set of waves is reflected from a steep coast or if there is a sudden veer of wind direction in a small, intense depression, which is moving rapidly. The microseisms travel more rapidly in the earth's crust than the waves on the sea surface and can, therefore, be recorded sooner.

(b) Surges. The nature of surges can be identified by considering the curve left after the predicted tide has been subtracted from the observed tidal curve. In certain circumstances, the residual is very large and can be explained by the generation of a surge. One meteorological state giving rise to a marked surge occurs when an intense hurricane moves across a wide, shallow shelf area, e.g., along the Gulf and Atlantic coast of the United States. Such surges produce a slow gradual rise of water level in the forerunner stage, a sharp rise of 3 or 4 m characterizes the hurricane stage, lasting $2\frac{1}{2}$–5 hours, followed by resurgences after the passage of the hurricane. Surges also affect the North Sea, owing to its shallow, enclosed character,

than surface waves, but they may have a greater amplitude. These internal waves can be caused by various processes, which result in water of contrasting types being brought into juxtaposition. For example, internal waves can be created by outflow of fresh water over salt water, variations of atmospheric pressure and strong winds can initiate internal waves where there are two distinct water types, and some internal waves are probably caused by tidal movements, as the internal waves have the same period as the tide. Internal waves can be recognized by rhythmic changes of temperature at depth. Such movement of the thermocline can take place in depths up to about 60 feet, e.g., off Mission Beach, California, where the median wave height was 5.6 feet and the median period 7.3 minutes. A surface phenomenon related to internal waves is the "slick," forming a narrow linear feature of less rippled water; this normally occurs above the descending thermocline and is connected with the water circulation set up by the presence of an internal wave.

(4) Waves Caused by Submarine Earth Movements—Tsunamis

Submarine slumping or earth movements set up long-period waves in the ocean that can travel for very great distances. Such waves are long relative to the depth of the ocean and, as a result, travel at a speed dependent on the water depth. Their length may be up to 100 miles, and their velocity, in a depth of 2500 fathoms (a reasonable mean value for the ocean), would be 472 mph. Waves of this type, caused by an earthquake off southern Chile, traveled right across the Pacific and did considerable damage in Japan, New Guinea and at Sydney. These waves are refracted in the same way as ordinary wind waves, and this may account for the varying effect of the waves at different places along a coast.

(5) Waves Due to Planetary Motions—The Tide

The most regular and predictable of ocean waves are those caused by the movement of the earth, moon and sun. Like tsunamis, the length of tidal waves is so great that their velocity depends only on the depth of water, according to $C^2 = gd$, because there would be ideally only two crests and troughs around the circumference of the earth. However, the land masses prevent the formation of the ideal pattern and the actual tides are generated by the gravitational tractive force of the moon and sun on the earth. Where the ocean is of suitable dimensions to have a natural period of oscillation similar to that of the tide-producing forces, a state of resonance can be set up, and that part of the ocean will respond to the force applied. Thus a series of standing oscillations are set up; these are modified by the rotation of the earth to become amphidromic systems. In these, the tide

appears to move around the amphidromic point in an anticlockwise direction in the northern hemisphere and clockwise in the southern. Such a tidal wave has many of the characteristics of a progressive wave, having a maximum stream in the direction of propagation at high water and the reverse at low water. The fact that the different oceans can respond to the different periods of the tide-producing forces allows the variety of tidal types to be developed; thus in the Atlantic semi-diurnal tides are most common, but in parts of the Pacific the response to the diurnal forces allows mixed and diurnal tides to predominate.

(6) Conclusions

Waves have been described according to their method of formation, but they could also have been defined according to their length. The shortest waves, with periods up to $\frac{1}{2}$ minute, include ripples and wind waves and are very common. The waves of intermediate length, from $\frac{1}{2}$ minute to several hours, are relatively rare; these include tsunamis, surges and surf beat. However, the longest waves of 12-hour and 1-day periods are again worldwide and permanent; these are the regular tides. Thus the ocean surface and sub-surface waters are disturbed by many different types of wave phenomena.

C. A. M. KING

References

Hill, M. N., (editor), 1962, "The Sea," Vol. 1, "Physical Oceanography," Sec. 5, pp. 567–801, New York, John Wiley & Sons.
King, C. A. M., 1959, "Beaches and Coasts," Ch. 3, pp. 54–120, London, Edward Arnold.
Russell, R. C. H., and Macmillan, D. H., 1952, "Waves and Tides," London, Hutchinson.

Cross-references: *Fetch; Tides; Tsunami; Waves as Energy Sources; Wave Refraction; Wave Theory.*

OKHOTSK SEA (SEA OF OKHOTSK)

Introduction

The Sea of Okhotsk is one of the marginal seas of the Pacific Ocean, situated in the northwestern part of the ocean, off the coasts of Asia, and is separated from the ocean by the Kurile Islands chain and the peninsula of Kamchatka, both of which are elements of the single Kurile-Kamchatka tectonic arc. The extreme points characterizing the geographical position of the Okhotsk Sea are: the head of the Penjinskaya Guba (bay) (63°N, 164°E) in the north; Proliv (the strait) of Izmeny (Notsuke) (44°N, 145°E) in the south; the head of the Udskaya Guba (bay) (55°N, 135°E) in the west; and the mouth of the Penjina River (63°N, 165°E) in the east. The greatest stretch of the sea (SW–NE) is 1330 miles (2463 km). In the transverse, northwest direction, the width is about 800 miles (1482 km). The Kurile Straits connect the Okhotsk Sea with the Pacific Ocean, and the shallow-water Nevelsky (Tatarsky) and LaPérouse (Soya) straits with the Japan Sea.

The Okhotsk Sea is surrounded on almost all the sides by mountainous structures. To the east, west and south run the Cenozoic fold ridges of Kamchatka, Sakhalin and Hokkaido. In the northwest, the Eastern Transbaikal-Amur region of Mesozoic folds adjoins the sea. The mountain structures either come close to the coast (as in the north, northwest, south) or are separated from the latter by extensive lowlands (as in Kamchatka, the northern part of Sakhalin, and near the mouths of the Amur and other rivers). The height of the mountain chains is 1–2.5 km on an average, increasing to 3.5 km in Kamchatka.

The shore line of the Sea of Okhotsk stretches for approximately 5648 miles (10,460 km) and is notable for its considerable complexity, particularly in the west and northeast where there are a number of rather large open bays. The largest is the Gulf of Shelikhov (Zaliv Shelikhova) with the Gizhiginskaya Guba and Penzhinskaya Guba (bays) in the northeastern part of the sea. In the west, there are the bays of Aniva and Terpeniya (in South Sakhalin), the Gulf (Zaliv) of Sakhalin with the Amur estuary, the bays of Alexandra, Ulbansky, Akademii and Tugursky, the Taromskaya and Udskaya gubas (bays). In the north, there are the bays of Ushki, Shelting, Zabiyaka, Babushkin, Kekurny and the Tauyskaya Guba (bay). Along the rest of the Okhotsk Sea, coastline bays are either very small in size or absent altogether.

Islands in the Sea of Okhotsk proper are comparatively scarce in number. They are mainly nearshore islands including the Shantar Archipelago in the west, Tyuleny Island near Sakhalin, the Spaphariev and Zaviyalov Islands in the Tauyskaya Guba (bay), the Yamskiye Islands in the bay of Shelikhov and the Ptichiy Islands off Kamchatka. Only one small island of Iona is in the open sea.

The Kurile Archipelago, of about 640 miles (1185 km) in length, numbers 28 relatively big islands as well as many small islands and rocks. These islands form the Great Kurile Ridge stretching from Hokkaido to Kamchatka and the Minoz Kurile Ridge extending along the outer (oceanic) side of the Great Kurile Ridge.

The area of the Okhotsk Sea with islands is 1,583,000 km^2 and that without islands—1,579,900 km^2. The maximum depth is 3374 m, the average depth being 777 m. The volume of the Okhotsk Sea depression computed as per its average depth comes to 1,227,700 km^3 (Udintzev, 1957).

The total area of the water-collecting basin of the Okhotsk Sea is 2,666,000 km^2, and the total annual river discharge is 586 km^3. Most of the discharge (371 km^3) comes through the Amur River. The rivers of the northwestern coast (Togur, Uda, Uliya, etc.) bring in about 57.2 km^3 of water; those of the northern coast (Okhota, Kukhtuy, Ulbeya, Inya, Tauy, Yama, Gizhiga, Penzhina, etc.) carry in some 82.1 km^3; the rivers of Kamchatka, 52.3 km^3; those of the Kurile Islands and Hokkaido, 6.8 km^3; those of Sakhalin, 16.6 km^3, etc. (Bezrukov, 1960).

Bathymetry

The Sea of Okhotsk lies within the transition zone from the continent to the floor of the Pacific Ocean proper. The main features of the ocean bottom topography may be explained by this intermediate position marked as it is by youthful mountain ranges, rises and basins (Udintzev, 1957). Analyzing the bottom topography, there are three main categories: (a) continental and island shelves, (b) the bottom of the central part of the sea and (c) the bottom of the southern deep-water basin. The continental shelf occupies more than 40% of the sea area. Its width in the vicinity of the LaPérouse Strait is 120 miles; off the eastern coast of Sakhalin, 30–40 miles; in the north, 60–220 miles; in the Bay of Shelikhov, 90 miles; the southern coast of Kamchatka, 30 miles. The depth of the outer margin of the continental shelf ranges from 150–275 m in the southwest to 170–350 m in the north and 100–175 m in the east. The steepness of the continental slope toward the basins in the south, west and east ranges from a few degrees to 15–20°, while in the north it does not exceed 2°.

The floor of the central part of the sea represents a system of several elevations and troughs with sharply changing depths. The largest elevations are the rises of Akademii Nauk (named for the Science Academy) and Instituta Okeanologii (named for the Oceanologic Institute) with minimum depths of 894 and 940 m, respectively. The slopes of these rises, separated by the Makarov Trough, 1354 m deep, have preserved some traces of ancient subaerial topography partly hidden under younger sediments. Not far from South Kamchatka is found another small elevation, the Lebed Rise, about 200 m deep. East of Sakhalin is situated the extensive Deryugin Basin (1744 m maximum depth), and west of Kamchatka, there is the TINRO Basin (993 m maximum depth). Besides these, there is a small and not very deep basin (445 m maximum depth) in the Gulf of Shelikhov. This latter basin is connected by a trough (about 369 m deep) with the TINRO Basin which, in turn, is connected by the Lebed Trough (about 539 m deep) with the central part of the sea. The Deryugin Basin is connected with the southern deep-water (Kurile) basin by the Makarov Trough and Petr Shmidt Trough (about 1315 m deep). The floors

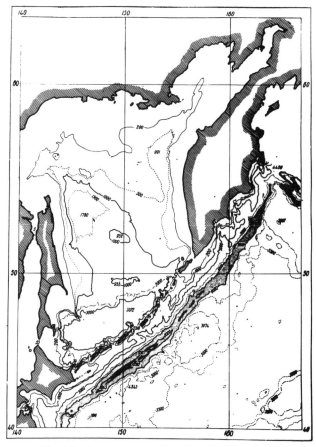

Fig. 1. Bathymetry of the Sea of Okhotsk (Udintzev).

of the basins and troughs in the central part of the sea are very rough, particularly that of the TINRO Basin.

The Kurile Basin stretching along the inner side of the Kurile Archipelago is a region of the greatest depths (over 3000 m). Here is the maximum depth of the Sea of Okhotsk (3374 m) obtained by R/V "Vityaz." On all the sides the basin is surrounded by steep (15–20°) slopes. Its floor is an abyssal plain.

Geological History

The general depression of the Sea of Okhotsk is a quasi-cratonic area that was formerly continental, or largely so, but has recently subsidied (Beloussov and Ruditch, 1960). According to Bezrukov and Udintzev (1953): "The northern shallow-water areas and the central part of the Sea of Okhotsk are a relatively stable platform which was not involved in the Tertiary folding and has experienced recent subsidence. The basins of Deryugin and TINRO have also been formed comparatively recently; they may be regarded as marginal depressions with respect to folded structures of Sakhalin

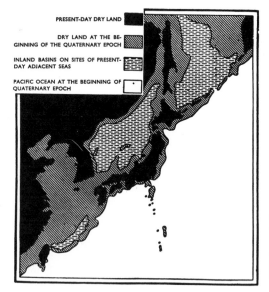

Fig. 2. Theory of H. Yabe (1929) about the origin of the Sea of Okhotsk, Japan Sea and Yellow Sea. Beginning as inland seas they appear to have gradually subsided.

and Kamchatka. They have been formed by the collapse of Tertiary fold belts and are probably still subsiding in the central part of the sea.

The southern deep-water basin is the most ancient depression zone of the Sea of Okhotsk; its development is still going on at present. The Kurile arc is a large double geanticline, the inner ridge of which is crowned by a chain of active volcanoes connected with a great deep-seated fracture. The outer ridge has, apparently, a somewhat more ancient age (Tertiary); evidences of modern volcanism on it are absent."

". . . The southern deep-water basin together with the Kurile Islands Ridge and the adjoining Kurile-Kamchatka oceanic trench are included into the zone of still-active Cenozoic folding, i.e., they are part of a modern geosynclinal system . . ." (Bezrukov, 1960, p. 24).

The former is usually classified with the exogeosynclinal class, and the latter as orthogeosynclinal.

The most intense volcanic and seismic activities are concentrated here. The strongest volcanic activity occurs in the Kurile Islands where 30 surface and a number of active submarine volcanoes are found. It is less important on Hokkaido with its 5 active volcanoes. The strongest earthquakes are also concentrated in the Kurile Islands area with shocks up to force 9. Weaker earthquakes are observed on Sakhalin (force up to 7–8) and on the northern coast (force up to 5–7). The minimum seismicity is found in the northwestern part of the sea.

According to the data of Bezrukov and Udintzev (1953), marine conditions in the southern part of the sea existed in the late Tertiary. Quaternary glaciation affected the shallow northern part which was land at that time (eustatically exposed). The postglacial transgression flooded the northern shallow-water area and the region of median rises where roughness of original terrestrial topography has still remained.

Sediments

The nearshore floor of the Sea of Okhotsk is covered with bouldery and pebbly gravel, pebbly gravel and sandy sediments (Bezrukov, 1960). The bouldery and pebbly gravel sediments (size range of over 10 cm, down to 1 mm) are encountered in some limited areas down to depths of several meters. The pebbly gravels (size range 10 cm to 1 mm) occupy broad areas not only near the shore but also in the open sea; they are also found on the summits and slopes of submarine rises. Most often, these sediments are encountered at depths of 50–250 m, but in some places they are found as deep as 1200–2500 m. In the zones of pebbly gravels, there are often small patches of pebbly shell sands or pebbly bryozoan sediments. Sands (1–0.1 mm particles) cover large areas

within continental and island shelves. They are distributed off the coasts or seaward of the belts of pebbly gravels, most often at 30–300 m depths. In the vicinity of the Kurile Islands, they are also

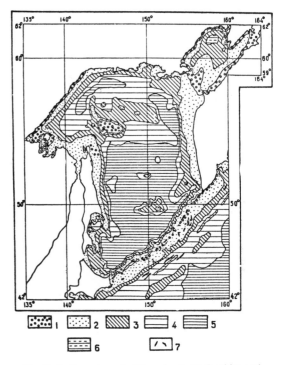

Fig. 3. Bottom deposits (Bezrukov): (1) Boulder and shingle gravels, (2) sands, (3) silts ("aleurites"), (4) silty clays with diatoms, (5) diatomaceous oozes, (6) silty clays without silica, (7) hard ground (rock floor).

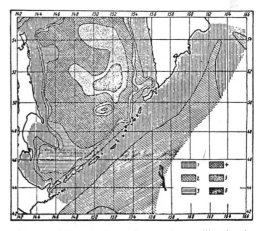

Fig. 4. Concentration of amorphous silica in the surface sediments (Bezrukov):

1. Less than 10%	2. 10–20%
3. 20–30%	4. 30–40%
5. 40–50%	6. Over 50%

found as deep as 1500–2500 m. Foraminiferal sands are also found here in some places.

In the deeper parts of the sea, there are silts ("aleurites"), aleuritic argillaceous (silty clay) and argillaceous sediments. The silts or "aleuritic" sediments (0.1–0.01 mm particles) are found mostly near the marginal regions of shelves and on slopes as well as on the submarine rises in the central part. They occupy depths down to 1000 m, dropping to 2800–3000 m in the vicinity of the Kurile Islands. Silty clay sediments (containing 50–70%

of less than 0.01 mm particles) and argillaceous sediments (with over 70% of particles less than 0.01 mm) are distributed right down to the maximum depths of the Sea of Okhotsk. They usually contain from 20 to more than 50% of amorphous silica, mainly in the form of diatom shells, so that they may be classified as siliceous or diatomaceous oozes.

Bottom sediments in the area of the Kurile Islands, as a rule, have a great admixture of pyroclastic material, and in many places they pass into strictly tuffaceous sediments of different granulometric types.

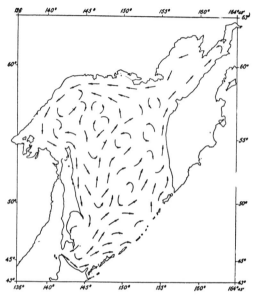

Fig. 5. Surface currents in the Sea of Okhotsk (Zenkevitch). (By permission Interscience Publishers, New York.)

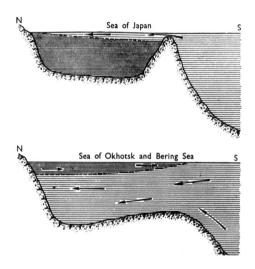

Fig. 6. Comparison between the water exchange of the Sea of Okhotsk and the Sea of Japan. While the latter is almost land-locked, the former is opened by several deep straits in the Kuril Chain (Zenkevitch, 1963).

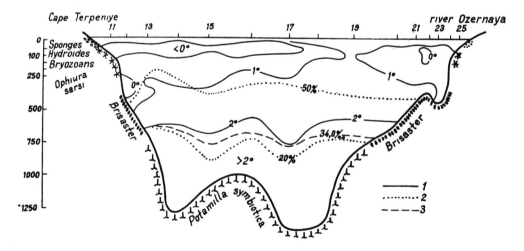

Fig. 7. Profile through the Sea of Okhotsk showing the vertical distribution of water masses and benthos (after Ushakov). *Key*: (1) temperature, (2) oxygen, (3) salinity.

The study of diatom remains, as well as of spores and pollen in the cores of bottom sediments up to 34 m long from the Sea of Okhotsk (Zhuze, Koreneva, 1959), has permitted the distinction of three warm horizons corresponding to the post-glacial (Holocene) and the last two interglacial stages (transgressive) and two horizons synchronous with the last two stages of the Quaternary glaciation (regressive).

Climate

According to Leonov (1960, p. 203): The east-facing geographical position of the Sea of Okhotsk is similar to that of China in the monsoon climate zone of the moderate latitudes. However, due to its 45–60° latitude and the fact that considerable part of it runs deep into the Asiatic continent with its extremely cold and long winter, its climate, especially that of winter in the northern part, differs little from the climate of the polar seas. From October to April, the winter monsoon affects the Sea of Okhotsk mainly with fresh north and northwest winds (75%), often reaching storm force. The summer monsoon with prevailing south-east winds alternating rather often with calms (30%) begins in May and lasts until September. Mean annual temperatures in the northern part of the Sea of Okhotsk are −6 to −6.9°C, and in the southern part, about +5°C. In January the lowest mean temperature (at the town of Okhotsk) is −25.2°C and the highest one (Cape Soya) is −6.4°C. In summer, maximum and minimum mean temperatures are approximately 18° and 11°, respectively. The annual precipitation in the north is 230–300 mm, while in the south it is 800–1000 mm, due to the influence of dry continental air in

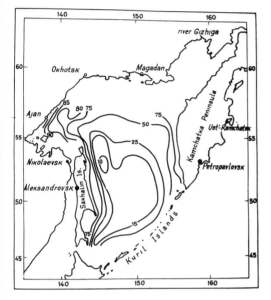

Fig. 8. Map of oxygen concentration in the bottom water, Sea of Okhotsk, in per cent saturation (Ushakov).

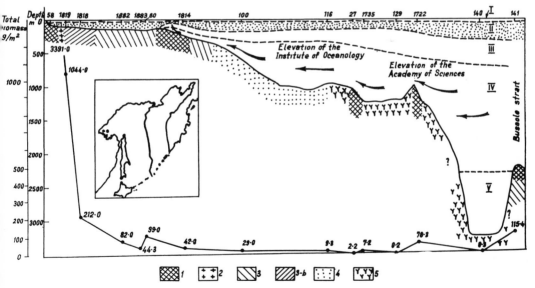

Fig. 9. A north–south profile in the Sea of Okhotsk, showing relationship of benthos to topography and water masses (Savilov).
(I) Surface water (local origin, warmed in summer. (II) Cold intermediate layer. (III) Intermediate Water Mass. (IV) Deep Pacific Water Mass. (V) Deep Water Mass of Southern Trough.
(1) Sessile sestonophages on hard floor. (2) Same, on soft floor. (3) Detritus feeders (3b. mollusca). (4) Mud eaters. (5) Same as (2).

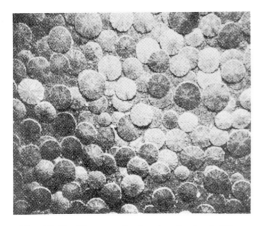

Fig. 10. To illustrate the benthos in the LaPérouse (Soya) Strait. Closely crowded echinoid community on bottom, subject to strong current action. (Photo: Zenkevitch.)

the northwest and wet maritime air in the south.

During 6–7 months each year, the Sea of Okhotsk has an ice cover. Drift ice covers three-quarters of its surface, and two-thirds of the surface for 7 months each year.

Oceanography

Wave action in the Sea of Okhotsk may reach great strength, especially during the period of autumn-winter storms and typhoons. During such periods, wave heights in the open sea may be 8–10 m and over, and wavelengths 100–130 m.

The amount of water entering the Sea of Okhotsk from the Japan Sea (through the LaPérouse or Soya Strait) amounts to approximately 15,000 km^3, that in the form of continental discharge is about 600 km^3, and from atmospheric precipitation about 900 km^3 per year (Leonov, 1960). The bulk of the Okhotsk Sea water is of the Pacific origin and enters the ocean through the various straits between the Kurile Islands. The width of the straits varies and so does their role in the water exchange between the Pacific Ocean and the Okhotsk Sea. Using Udintsev's data (1957), 43.3% of the total sum of the cross sections of the straits is accounted for by Bussol Strait or Boussole (2318 m sill depth), 24.4% by Kruzenshtern Strait (1920 m sill depth), 9.2% by Friza Strait, and 8.1% by the Fourth Kurile Strait and so on.

The surface waters of the Sea of Okhotsk are characterized by a temperature of −1.8 to +2° in winter and of about 10–18°C in summer and a salinity up to 33–34‰. Summer heating reaches down to depths of 30–75 m. It does not embrace the whole column of water cooled down in winter, and consequently, there is a cold intermediate layer with negative temperatures (to −1.6°C) at depths of about 150 m. Below this layer, the basin

is filled with warmer Pacific waters of the highest temperatures (2–2.5°C) at depths of 750–1500 m. Bottom waters in the region of maximum depths have a temperature of about 1.8°C and salinity of approximately 34.5‰.

The characteristic feature of the circulation embracing the whole body of water is the predominance of a cyclonic current system connected with cyclonic circulation of the atmosphere above the Sea of Okhotsk and the adjacent part of the Pacific Ocean (Moroshkin, 1964). Besides extensive cyclonic circulation in the central part of the sea (2–10 cm/sec velocities) and east and northeast of Sakhalin, three stationary anticyclonic eddies are observed: west of the southern extremity of Kamchatka, above the TINRO basin, and in the area of the southern basin (11–20 cm/sec velocities).

The narrow band of nearshore counterclockwise currents extends almost all along the shore line. In the southeast of the sea, this band begins in the region of the northernmost Kurile straits through which the surface waters of the Pacific enter the sea; then it spreads out along Kamchatka coast to the north. A rather strong Soya Current caused by the entry of water from the Japan Sea through the LaPérouse (Soya) Strait is a component of the nearshore current belt in the southwest. The nearshore current velocities range from 11–20 cm/sec off Kamchatka coasts, to 50–90 cm/sec in the Soya Current area.

An interesting feature of the abyssal circulation is the existence in the Sea of Okhotsk of a warm (about 2.5°) deep current entering the sea from the Pacific through a break in the outer submarine elevation of the Kurile tectonic arc near Kruzenshtern Strait. This current flows at depths of 750–1250 m and branches in two—one branch flowing northward and the other to Sakhalin and along the inner slope of the islands to the south.

The hydrodynamics of the Sea of Okhotsk is greatly affected by tidal phenomena accompanied by strong currents. The tides are mainly related to the entry of the Pacific tidal wave and have a mixed character with the diurnal component prevailing. The greatest tide amplitude (about 13 m) is characteristic of the Penzhinskaya Guba (bay). In other places, it varies from 0.8–0.9 m to almost 7 m (Leonov, 1960).

The upper layers of the water column are well aerated (about 103% of oxygenation). The oxygen minimum (to 1 ml O_2/liter) is found in the warmest deep waters (750–1500 m) which is near the bottom in the Deryugin Trough. In the southern basin, the bottom water oxygenation increases to 2.0–2.2 ml O_2/liter (20–28% of oxygenation). The Okhotsk Sea waters are rich in biogenic elements, the concentration of which increases with depth. The maximum contents of silicon and phosphorous at depth are equal to 4000 mg/liter and 90 mg/liter, respectively (Bruevich, 1956).

Biology

The water chemistry of the Sea of Okhotsk favors a magnificent development of phytoplankton, the chief components of which are peridinea (58 species) and diatom algae (290 species). The latter comprise 70–100% of the phytoplankton biomass; its content may be as large as 20 g/m³ of water (Zenkevich, 1963). *Thalassiosira nordenskioldii, Th. gravida, Chaetoceros furcellatus, Ch. constrictus*, etc., are the principal species of diatoms. Zooplankton whose biomass may in some places reach 1–3 g/m³, are represented mainly by *Metridia* sp., *Calanus finmarchinus, C. tonsus, C. cristatus, Themisto libellula*, etc.

The littoral flora of the Sea of Okhotsk includes about 300 species of algae among which *Laminaria, Thalassiphyllum, Fucus*, etc., predominate. Following Zenkevich (1963, p. 617): The average benthonic biomass of the entire Sea of Okhotsk is about 150 g/m², and the total biomass of the bottom fauna amounts to about 200 million tons. Among the various groups of animals, the first place should be assigned to the mollusks (about 30%), the second place to echinoderms (about 25%), and the third one to polychaetes (about 12%). Of great commercial value among the bottom fauna are the Kamchatka crabs (*Paralithodes camchatica*) and blue crabs (*P. platypus*) as well as some mollusks.

The ichthyofauna of the Sea of Okhotsk numbers about 300 species and subspecies of fish, 30 species of which are of commercial importance. The most important of them are salmon (*Oncorhynchus keta, O. gorbusha, O. kisutch, O. nerka*), herring (*Clupea pallasi*), cod (*Gadus macrocephalus*), dab (*Limanda aspera, L. punctatissima*), etc.

A number of marine mammals inhabit the Okhotsk Sea. Of commercial value among them are the cachalot and some seals.

V. P. Petelin

References

Beloussov, V. V., and Ruditch, E. M., 1961, "Island arcs and the development of the earth's structure (especially in region of Japan and Sea of Okhotsk," J. Geol., **69**, 647–659.

Bezrukov, P. L., 1960, "Bottom sediments of the Okhotsk Sea," *Tr. Inst. Okeanol., Akad. Nauk SSSR*, **32** (in Russian).

Bezrukov, P. L., and Udintsev, G. B., 1953, "New data on the geological structure of the Far-Eastern seas," *Dokl. Akad. Nauk SSSR*, **91**, No. 2 (in Russian).

Bruevich, S. V., 1956, "On the chemistry of bottom sediments of the Okhotsk Sea," *Tr. Inst. Okeanol. Akad. Nauk SSSR*, **17** (in Russian).

Leonov, A. K., 1960, "Regional Oceanography," Part I, Hydrometeoizdat, Moscow (in Russian).

Moroshkin, K. V., 1964, "New scheme of surface currents of the Okhotsk Sea," *Okeanologiya*, **4**, No. 4 (in Russian).

Udintzev, G. B., 1957, "Bottom topography of the Okhotsk Sea," *Tr. Inst. Okeanol., Akad. Nauk SSSR*, **22** (in Russian).

Yabe, H., 1929, "The latest land connection of the Japanese Islands to the Asiatic continent," *Proc. Imp. Acad. Tokyo*, **5** (4).

Zenkevich, L. A., 1963, "Biology of the seas of the USSR," *Izd. Akad. Nauk SSSR*. (English translation by S. Botcharskaya; New York, J. Wiley—Interscience, 955pp.)

Zhuze, A. P., and Koreneva, E. V., 1959, "Diatom and spore-pollen analysis of bottom sediments of the Far-Eastern Seas," *Izv. Akad. Nauk SSSR, Ser. Geograph.*, No. 2 (in Russian).

OYASHIO CURRENT (KURIL CURRENT)

(1) Outline

The Oyashio Current is a western boundary flow in the subpolar gyre of the North Pacific Ocean, corresponding to the Labrador Current and the Falkland Current in the North and South Atlantic, respectively. The current originates in the Bering Sea and flows southwest off Kamchatka Peninsula and the Kuril Islands, entraining the water from Okhotsk Sea. It meets the Kuroshio east of northern Japan at latitudes between 37 and 40°N. A part of the water transported by the current sinks below the warm Kuroshio water and spreads further south as an intermediate water of low salinity (Sverdrup *et al.*, 1945). The major portion turns to the east along the northern rim of the Kuroshio, forming an oceanic polar front, where the Oyashio water again diffuses southward and forms the intermediate water as far east as 170°W (Ichiye, 1962).

The Oyashio water consists of a subarctic water mass which is characterized as low temperature and low salinity. Some 4–5°C temperatures are measured in the depths between 200 and 500 meters at latitudes of about 42–45°N compared with 12–18°C of the Kuroshio water in the same depths; salinity is found to be 33.7–34.0‰ in the same depths and latitudes as above compared with 34.5 to 35.0‰ of the Kuroshio water (Sverdrup *et al.*, 1945). The water in the upper few hundred meters is abundant in nutrient salts and plankton; thus its water color is rather brownish in contrast with the deep aquamarine color of the poor nutrient water of the Kuroshio Current. The name of Oyashio in Japanese indicates that the current is productive (*Oya* meaning parent and *shio* meaning current).

(2) Dynamic Structure of the Oyashio Current

Mass transports from the surface to 1500-meter depth computed from hydrographic data obtained in 1934–37 by the Japanese Hydrographic Office vessels are schematically shown in Fig. 1. This Figure indicates that the maximum transport of Oyashio Current near the southern Kuril Islands reaches 15 million tons/sec or nearly a quarter of the total mass transport of the Kuroshio Current. One-third of this transport comes from the Bering

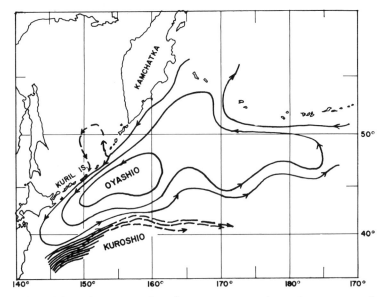

Fig. 1. Schematic representation of mass transport in the northwestern part of the North Pacific Ocean. One thick line indicates transport of 5 million tons/sec. Broken lines indicate an alternate path (in the Oyashio) or variable courses (in the Kuroshio).

Sea, another third from south of the Aleutian Islands, and the rest from a cyclonic gyre east of the southern Kuril Islands. On some occasions, a part of the water of the Oyashio Current south of Kamchatka Peninsula enters into the Okhotsk Sea and returns again to the current through straits among the Kuril Islands. However, such an exchange of water between the Oyashio Current and the Okhotsk Sea does not seem to be a permanent feature.

To the east of Japan between 37 and 42°N when the Oyashio Current contacts the Kuroshio Current, there are a number of eddies in diameters of a few hundred kilometers. Anticyclonic eddies are warmer, more saline than the cutoff of the Kuroshio Current, while cyclonic eddies are colder, less saline than the cutoff of the Oyashio Current (Ichiye, 1956; Defant, 1961). These eddies seem to have a lifetime of a few months to almost a year, particularly when they are large in size and anticyclonic (Ichiye, 1956). These eddies and meanderings of the Kuroshio Current make the circulation in this region complicated and variable with time. Hydrographic data obtained since 1947 east of northern Japan suggest rather vague seasonal shifts of the frontal zone moving to the north and south in summer and winter, respectively.

Although the Oyashio Current is a western boundary current of the subpolar gyre, the geostrophic velocities are between 0.1 and 1 knot and much less than those of the Kuroshio Current. This is due to the fact that the northern portion of the North Pacific Ocean is much smaller in its extent than the central section occupied by the counterclockwise Pacific gyre and also because the total wind stress curl is much smaller over the northern portion than over the central portion.

T. ICHIYE

References

Defant, A., 1962, "Physical Oceanography," Vol. 1, p. 729, New York–Oxford–London–Paris, Pergamon Press.

Ichiye, T., 1956, "Hydrography of the polar front region I–IV," *Oceanographical Magazine Tokyo,* **7,** 115–132, **8,** 29–63.

Ichiye, T., 1962, "On formation of the intermediate water in the Northern Pacific Ocean," *Geofis. Pura Appl.,* **51,** 108–119.

Sverdrup, H. U., Johnson, M. W., and Fleming, R. H., 1943, "The Oceans," p. 1060, Englewood Cliffs, N.J., Prentice-Hall, Inc.

Cross-references: *Kuroshio; Oceanic Circulation; Ocean Currents.*

P

PACIFIC OCEAN

Introduction*

This is the largest of the world's oceans and has the greatest average, as well as the greatest observed, depth. Its marginal seas include the *Bering, Okhotsk, Japan, Yellow, East China, Philippine, South China, Coral,* and *Tasman* Seas, as well as the smaller seas of the East Indies (Indonesian Archipelago), the *Bismarck* and *Solomon* Seas (each of these seas is described separately, q.v.). In this Encyclopedia, the Arafura Sea and Timor Sea (regarded by some as

"Pacific") are included with the Indian Ocean, and the Scotia Sea (also sometimes placed in the Pacific) can be found with the Atlantic Ocean. The Fiji Sea is included in the general description of the *Southwest Pacific* (q.v.).

In the International Hydrographic Bureau listings, the *North Pacific* is separated from the *South Pacific* by the equator, except that all of the Galápagos Islands and Gilbert Islands, which straddle the line, are placed in the South Pacific. On the other hand, Wüst (1936) proposed a series of "natural regions" with "sea" designations: Central and South Pacific, North Pacific, Guatemala, Peru, South Chile and Pacific Antarctic Seas. Apart from

* Rhodes W. Fairbridge.

Fig. 1. The Pacific scene: The lagoon of the great Aitutaki Atoll in the Cook Islands, with three generations of transport. (Photo: Teal Airways)

Fig. 2. The Pacific scene: The deeply eroded central volcanic plug of Moorea, in the Tahiti chain, a typical mature island with deep inlets and a barrier reef. (Photo: T. W. Collins, Auckland, N.Z.)

all the marginal seas, the I.H.B. also recognizes as special marginal waters: *Gulf of Alaska* (1,533,000 km²), *Queen Charlotte Sound and related Coastal Waters, Gulf of California* (160,000 km²), and *Bass Strait* (70,000 km²).

The Pacific measures 15,500 km (8350 nautical miles) from Bering Strait to Cape Adare and 17,200 km (9300 nautical miles) from Panama to Mindanao (P.I.), or 24,000 km (10,500 nautical miles), if one extends it to the Gulf of Thailand. The area (with marginal seas) is 179.7×10^6 km², and with a mean depth of 4028 m, its volume is 723.7×10^6 km³. Excluding marginal seas, these figures respectively are 165.2×10^6 km², 4282 m, and 707.5×10^6 km³; in turn one may divide these figures again into North Pacific 70.8×10^6 km², 4753 m, 336.7×10^6 km³, and South Pacific 94.4×10^6 km², 3928 m, and 370.8×10^6 km³, respectively.

According to Murray, the land area draining into the Pacific is 19,400,000 km², which is little more than 25% of that draining into the Atlantic, which itself occupies an area 45% less than that of the Pacific. The oceanographic effects of this disparity are profound, leading to a constant water surplus in the Atlantic area (q.v.), and transports toward the Pacific, both by currents via the Southern Ocean or by water vapor via the Panama Isthmus.

The boundaries of the great oceans and their marginal seas have been discussed for at least two centuries, and the boundaries employed today re-flect the immediate needs and convenience of the various disciplines rather than a co-ordinated logical approach. Only three great oceanic divisions were recommended by de Fleurieu (1798–1800), an important French hydrographer in his day, and this lead has been widely followed, e.g., by Krümmel (1897) in his "Handbuch der Ozeanographie," and by Sverdrup *et al.* in "The Oceans" (1942).

A committee of the Royal Geographical Society (London) under the chairmanship of Sir Roderick I. Murchison was formed in 1845, recommending that five oceanic divisions be recognized, thus adding Arctic and Antarctic Oceans, to be bounded by the polar circles ($67\frac{1}{2}°$N and S), and further that the Pacific be subdivided into northern, southern and intertropical sectors. Unhappily, their report, although circulated, was not printed until 1893, and in the meantime, other schemes appeared.

For the southern boundary of the Pacific (and northern border of the Antarctic or Southern Ocean), various lines were proposed from time to time. Petermann (1850; all these early references are listed in Fairbridge, 1955) proposed latitude 60°S, which is roughly the pack-ice limit. Von Boguslawski (1884) chose latitude 55°S, that of Cape Horn. Vallaux (1933) brought it up to 35°S. Sir John Herschel (1875) preferred great circle lines joining the southernmost capes of the continents; Supan's (1903) method was similar but used loxodrome (rhumb) lines. Sir John Murray (1888) after the

Challenger Expedition selected 40° for his "Southern Ocean," since it approximates the northern limit of circumpolar "West Wind Drift." Later, Murray and Hjort (1912) reverted to the three-ocean system, but continued to use the Southern Ocean as a local, informal designation (usually at approximately the Subtropical Convergence, q.v., even though it migrates seasonally), a procedure still followed by many oceanographers. This writer suggested (Fairbridge, 1955) that one might conveniently use the phrase the "Southern Ocean *sector* of the Pacific Ocean, etc."

The question may appear academic to some oceanographers, but the moment that mass-energy questions are introduced, exact volumes and areas are needed, for which precision measurements and calculations must be undertaken. Murray (1888) made a first approximation, but the figures now almost universally employed are those worked out by Kossinna (1921) and reissued with further details (1933). These figures appear elsewhere in this Encyclopedia (see *Oceans—Limits, Definitions, Dimensions*; further details, with some newer tables appear in *Continents and Oceans*, Vol. III). Kossinna's system analyzed in detail, not only the great oceans, but also all their marginal seas.

For hydrographic and navigational purposes, it is of considerable importance to establish precise boundaries with easily identified geographic coordinates. Accordingly the International Hydrographic Bureau in Monaco issues from time to time a standard list and charts indicating the lines agreed to by the hydrographic offices of the principal member governments (the latest is *Sp. Publ. 23*, 1953; a summary of this information and the maps is given in: *Oceans—Limits, Definitions, Dimensions*).

Unfortunately the arbitrary lines of the hydrographers do not always find favor with physical oceanographers and marine geologists, who prefer structural boundaries of the sea floor, which usually deflect ocean currents, so that they are often easily recognized by experts either from *p/t* data or from precision echo sounding. Accordingly, Supan (1899, 1903), Schott (1935) and Wüst (1936) have proposed boundaries that differ in some important details from the I.H.B. boundaries. These different approaches must therefore be noted in defining the Pacific borders. Here we shall include all marginal seas within the Pacific Ocean (*sensu lato*), but it should be noted that each of the marginal seas is dealt with separately in detail in this Encyclopedia.

Western Limits. In Malacca Strait, the limits are the meridian of Singapore to Sumatra (Kossinna); an alternatively east-west line from Singapore (I.H.B.); or again obliquely from Pedro Pt. to N.W. (Murchison); then by a line connecting Sumatra-Java-Roti-Timor (most authorities). From here there is a great contrast of opinion, based on whether or not the Timor Sea, Arafura Sea and Gulf of Carpentaria should be classed as Indian Ocean or

Pacific. The I.H.B. includes these with the Indonesian Archipelago and thus the Pacific; I.H.B., Vallaux, and Kossinna draw varied borders to the western Timor Sea. The Murchison Committee put the Timor Sea in the Indian Ocean and the Arafura Sea in the Pacific, and the Fisheries Division of the Australian C.S.I.R.O. follows this procedure. The shortest boundary route is across Torres Straits and from New Guinea (Vlakke Pt.) to Aru and Timor (putting Arafura Sea in the Indian Ocean); this is generally favored by geologists and recommended by Schott (1935) in his definitive work on the geography of the Indian and Pacific Oceans.

South of Australia, most authorities agree with Krümmel and Kossinna in placing the boundary at the west end of Bass Strait, but Schott put it at the east end. South of Tasmania, the Murchison Committee and the I.H.B. selected the meridian 147°E. Schott and most scientists prefer the submarine ridge that runs along the Mill Rise, then through Macquarie Island and the Balleny Islands to Cape Adare.

Eastern Limit. All authorities agree that Cape Horn is the turning point, but while many follow the Murchison Committee and I.H.B. in drawing a meridian (68°04′W) to the Antarctic Peninsula, others prefer Schott's structural line drawn around the entire Scotia Arc.

Northern Limit. While the Murchison Committee and the I.H.B. designate the boundary in Bering Straits as the Arctic Circle ($62\frac{1}{2}$°N), the shortest distance route is preferred by most scientists (see *Chukchi Sea*).

History*

The northern and eastern Pacific margins were first explored by migrants from eastern Asia, partly by land but probably also in part by canoe; judging from the archeological data now available, these migrations may have begun as long as 30,000 years ago, with successive voyages during the postglacial era. At about the same time, other migrants moved through the Lesser Sunda Islands and New Guinea into Australia and later into Melanesia.

True trans-Pacific voyages began with the Polynesians about 2000 years ago, and some relations appear to have been established between the South Pacific islanders and the earlier migrants in South America. Stick maps prepared by the Polynesians and still preserved, testify to their considerable appreciation of geography. Some enigmatic material, which suggests that much more remains to be learned of these voyages, includes the Mohenjodaro-type inscriptions at Easter Island, the miniature Easter Island-type stone heads from the south coast of Mexico, and undated inscriptions in Fiji. Interesting notes, reports and discussions of these problems

* Rhodes W. Fairbridge.

may be found in Stefansson (1947), Herrmann (1954) and Heyerdahl (1958).

Since there was a pharaonic boat canal from the Nile to the Red Sea (see summary in Herrmann, 1954), it is not surprising that Phoenician and later Arab navigators traded around the coasts of Arabia and then India, there to overlap with Chinese traders in the first millennium A.D. An Arab voyager, Soleyman, reached Canton about A.D. 850; and Al-Masudi, a Baghdad trader is known to have been to China about A.D. 956 (helpful maps of most early voyages may be found in Debenham, 1960). Thus Marco Polo was able to return home by sea from China and the western Pacific via the Malacca Straits in 1295; soon afterward, the Roman Catholic missionaries, Friar John of Monte Corvino, and later Friar Odoric, also visited Peking by way of the South China Sea. About 1325–49 the celebrated Moroccan traveller Ibn Batutu used the same route to visit Peking and return. When Vasco da Gama reached the Indian Ocean in 1497, he was able to hire an Indian pilot at Malindi (near Mombasa), and around 1502–10 the Italian traveler Ludovici de Varthema voyaged in the East Indies.

The first trans-Pacific voyage from Europe came with Magellan's great voyage; he had first come with Sequira and Serrano, in 1509, by way of the Indian Ocean to the East Indies as far as Ternate, the spice trading center. Then in 1519–21 via South America, discovering the Straits of Magellan, he crossed the mid-Pacific, only to be killed in the Philippines, the expedition around the world via the Cape being completed by Del Cano in 1521–22 in the *Victoria.*

Visits to the western coasts of the Americas soon followed the first sighting by Balboa and Pizarro from the Isthmus of Panama in 1513. Cortez reached the west coast of Mexico in 1521, and he returned to sail into the Gulf of California in 1535–36. Pizarro also came back and sailed down the coast to Peru in 1531. Alvaro de Saavedra about 1527–28 was sent by Cortez on an equatorial crossing of the Pacific from Mexico to New Guinea, but he died before the expedition returned. In 1539 Francisco proved that Lower California was not an island, as previously indicated.

There was a return of interest to the China coast when in 1540–52 Francis Xavier sailed for the East Indies via the Cape and went on to Kwantung and Japan. In 1540–46 Fernando Mendez Pinto visited the mouth of the Mekong (Vietnam) and Hainan, and went on to Japan where he met Xavier. The mid-Pacific was initially explored for the west by Alvaro de Mendaña starting from Peru and visiting the Ellice, Solomon, and Marshall Islands in 1567–68; in 1595 he returned, exploring the Marquesas and Santa Cruz, where, after his death, his chief pilot, Pedro Fernandez de Quirós, took over.

After following the footsteps of Balboa in sighting the Pacific from the Panama isthmus (in 1569), Sir Francis Drake was inspired to return in 1577–80,

sailing up the entire west coast from the Straits of Magellan as far as Vancouver Island in 1578; in 1579, he sailed from San Francisco Bay to the Philippines, and home via the Cape, the second great global circumnavigation. After the Mendaña expedition, Quirós returned and in 1605 set forth again from Callao in company with Don Diego de Prado y Tovar and Luis Vaez de Torres, discovering the Tuamotus and the New Hebrides; after they were accidentally separated here, Quirós went on to Santa Cruz and then back to Acapulco, while de Prado and de Torres proceeded westward probably to sight the middle part of Australia's Great Barrier Reefs, sailed north to Papua and then westward to discover the Torres Straits between Cape York and New Guinea, and returned by way of Manila.

The first of the great Dutch voyages to the Pacific was that of William Schouten and Jacques Le Maire in 1616, who discovered, on rounding South America (Cape Horn), that Tierra de Fuego was not attached to the Antarctic continent; previous voyagers had used the Straits of Magellan. They visited Cocos Island, Fiji and named the Schouten Islands off the coast of New Guinea. Next came Abel Janszoon Tasman, with the *Heemskerck* and *Zeehaen,* sailing from Batavia to Mauritius and then eastward, south of Tasmania (at first named Van Diemen's Land out of respect for the Governor of the Dutch East Indies) to New Zealand, Three Kings Islands, Tonga, Fiji and northern New Guinea, and back to Java. The third Dutch explorer was Jacob Roggeveen who sailed in the vessels *Arend, Thienhoven* and *The African Galley* via Cape Horn to discover Easter Island and its celebrated monuments. Later he passed through Tuamotu (Low) Islands, Apataki (Palliser) Islands, Society Islands, Samoa and New Britain to Batavia.

A rather engaging explorer was the Englishman William Dampier, really a scientist who financed his explorations with piracy (or was it that he justified his piracy with science?); in any case his journals are extraordinarily interesting. His two best known vessels were the *Batchelor's Delight* and the *Roebuck.* Between 1679–91 he circumnavigated the globe via Cape Horn, Easter Island, Baja California, the Philippines, Indo-China and northern Australia. In 1699–1700 he returned via the Cape, northern Australia and northern New Guinea.

The northernmost Pacific first became known to the west through the voyages of Vitus Bering, a Danish navigator in the service of Russia (1724–30). He crossed the Sea of Okhotsk and then came up the Kamchatka coast to discover the Strait, named after him, which proved the separation of the Americas from Asia. In 1740–41, together with Captain Chirikov in the *St. Peter* and the *St. Paul,* he explored the Aleutians and Gulf of Alaska, sighting Mt. St. Elias.

The greatest of all Pacific voyagers was probably Captain James Cook, who led a series of Royal Navy expeditions for the definite purpose of exploration and cartography. In his 1768–69 voyage, in company with Sir Joseph Banks and several other scientists, he came by way of Cape Horn and visited Tahiti to observe the transit of Venus; he then went to New Zealand, discovering Cook Strait between the two islands, and on to the east coast of Australia, which he followed up to the Endeavour River (named after his ship) and on through Torres Straits. On his second voyage in the *Resolution* (1772–74) via the Cape, he sighted the Antarctic continent on his way to New Zealand and made further explorations around New Zealand and Tahiti before returning via the Horn and Cape Town. On his third voyage with the *Resolution* and *Discovery* (1776), he again sailed via the Cape to New Zealand, thence to Tahiti, Hawaii (then called Sandwich Islands), and on to Vancouver Island, skirting the Gulf of Alaska and passing through the Bering Strait into the Chukchi Sea, returning after being stopped by the ice pack. He was tragically killed in Hawaii on the return voyage. Of great importance for Australian history were the coastal voyages of another British naval officer, Matthew Flinders, partly in company with Bass, discovering Bass Strait in 1798, and exploring much of the Great Barrier Reef lagoon and the Gulf of Carpentaria in 1803.

On the opposite shores of the Pacific in 1801–03, that giant of German science the Baron Alexander von Humboldt was exploring along the coasts of central America as far south as Peru, discovering the Humboldt Current, now known as the Peru Current (geographic names are now preferred to personal ones for major oceanographic features).

It was next the turn of the French, who dispatched the Count Jean-François La Pérouse with the ships *La Boussole* and *L'Astrolabe* to the Pacific via Cape Horn in 1785. He visited Easter Island, Hawaii, the Gulf of Alaska, Vancouver Island, then crossed to the China coast, exploring this up to Korea, the Japan Sea to discover La Perouse Strait, and on to Kamchatka; officially he was to look for the "northwest passage," but in the face of winter he turned south again to Port Jackson (Sydney); setting forth once more toward the Solomons, he was not heard of again, but in 1826 Capt. Peter Dillon found the wreckage of his ships on the reefs of Vanikoro in the north of New Hebrides.

A second French expedition to Australia was in 1800 under Captain Baudin in the *Naturaliste* and *Géographe*, with excellent scientists and navigators aboard, including François Peron and Louis Claude de Freycinet. On a second scientific expedition (1817–20), de Freycinet, in *L'Uranie* and *La Physicienne* with Arago on board, after visiting Rio de Janeiro, explored many of the Pacific islands, including Hawaii, the Mariannas and Australia, making large collections. The most indefatigable of the French explorers was certainly Jean Dumont d'Urville who carried out three major voyages

(1822–40) and circled Australia some four times, passing once through Bass Strait, once through Torres Strait, and explored New Caledonia, the New Hebrides, the Moluccas; he also crossed the south Pacific twice and made one voyage to the Antarctic continent, discovering Adélie Land.

Other great navigators began to explore the Antarctic shores of the Pacific about this time. They included Fabian von Bellingshausen, a Baltic German from Estonia, in the service of Russia, who, together with M. Lazarev in the *Vostok* and *Mirny*, after exploring the South Sandwich Islands (Scotia Arc), discovered Alexander I Island, off the coast of the Antarctic Peninsula, and the Bellingshausen Sea. Sir James Ross in 1840–43 in the *Erebus* and *Terror* made two voyages to discover the Ross Sea and map its shores. In 1839–41 Charles Wilkes led the U.S. Navy Exploring Expedition (in the *Porpoise, Vincennes, Peacock* and *Flying Fish*) around the world with the celebrated geologist C. D. Dana on board, discovering Wilkes Land in East Antarctica and carrying out valuable surveys in the Tuamotus, Tahiti, Samoa, Australia, New Zealand and Hawaii.

In the first decades of the nineteenth century there were several Pacific voyages by various Russian ships, mainly to service and survey their new Far Eastern colonies (including Alaska): I. Krusenstern, I. Lisiansky, O. von Kotzebue and Hörner (in the *Neva* and *Nadeshda*, 1803–06); L. Hagemeister (in the *Neva*, 1806–07 and in the *Kamchatka*, 1817–18); W. Golovnin (in the *Diana*, 1807–09); M. Lazarev (in the *Suvorov*, 1813–16); S. Ponafidin (in the *Suvorov*, 1816–18, and in the *Borodino*, 1819–21), and several others.

Of particular interest was the voyage of the Russian vessel *Rurik* (1815–18) under O. von Kotzebue, with A. von Chamisso, the latter a celebrated German botanist and poet whose *Tagebuch* (diary) of the voyage was published in 1821 and contained some of the first critical descriptions of coral atolls. After discovering the Romanzov, Rurik and Krusenstern islands in the Scotia arc, they made for Kamchatka, discovering Kotzebue Sound and Cape Krusenstern. On a third voyage, von Kotezbue (with E. Lenz and the famous scientist Eschholz, in the vessel *Predpriyatye*, 1823, 1826) sailed via Cape Horn, the Radak and Society Islands to Petropavlovsk (Kamchatka), visiting the Navigator Islands, Mariannes, Philippines, New Caledonia and Hawaii. (English translations of both of von Kotzebue's narratives were published in 1821 and 1830.) Original contributions to the coral reef problem were also made by Eschholz.

Other British expeditions of this early period in the Pacific included those of the *Blossom* (under Beechey, 1825–28); *Eliza Scott* and *Sabrina* (Balleny); *Discovery* and *Research* (under Ross, 1839–43); *Samarang* (under Belcher, 1843–46); *Herold* (Kelett, 1845–51); *Rattlesnake* (Stanley and Dayman, 1846–50).

In 1831 the voyage of H.M.S. *Beagle* (Capt. Fitzroy), began with Charles Darwin aboard as "naturalist," an event which ranks in natural science with the discovery of the telescope by Galileo, because it provided the vehicle for observations that led to the discovery of logic and evolution in biology, the latter having probably the most profound intellectual impact on philosophical thought in the history of mankind. In the field of geology Darwin made the first deductions of eustasy and observed that many of the shores of the Pacific were marked by tremendous uplifts of coastal terraces, while much of the Pacific Basin showed evidence of submergence, or locally, ridges of uplift paralleled by belts of downwarp, e.g., the volcanic isles of the Tahitian chain paralleled by the obviously submerged belt of atolls in the Tuamotu Group (formerly called Paumotu). For the scientific philosopher it may be mentioned that in preparation for the Pacific work, Darwin studied the Admiralty charts in the captain's cabin on the *Beagle* on the voyage out from England to Brazil and from Pernambuco sent home by mail a first draft of his coral reef theory, long before he actually set eyes on a reef; this may point up the value of preparing a good working hypothesis before adventuring into a new field.

In 1854–60 another great naturalist Alfred Russel Wallace was exploring the East Indies and New Guinea, and it was he who, independently of Darwin, worked out some of the basic principles of evolution. Of great importance for geology was his discovery of what has been called the *Wallace Line*, a remarkable boundary which he established dividing the East Indies in two, passing between Bali and Lombok, and between Borneo and Celebes (Sulawesi). He observed that west of the line the biota was largely from Southeast Asia, while east of it the organisms had mainly Australasian affinities. This has become the basis for a fundamental cornerstone in the science of biogeography. While it is still not fully understood, we seem to have here an ancient suture between two intra-migrational areas now brought (by geotectonic events) into juxtaposition; it establishes the fact that a population is not governed simply by environment, but by evolutionary distribution factors.

Next one comes to the real foundation of oceanography as a science in the Pacific, the voyage of H.M.S. *Challenger* under the command of Sir George S. Nares, with Wyville Thomson and John Murray aboard as leading scientists (1872–76). They entered the Pacific through Bass Strait and, after visiting New Zealand, passed through Torres Straits and the Moluccas to Japan, thence to Hawaii, Tahiti, Chile and the Straits of Magellan. For the first time in the Pacific, systematic deep wire sounding, sediment sampling, hydrologic measurements (temperature and salinity) and deep-sea biologic trawls were carried out. As a result of this single expedition, the following facts were established: (a) the fundamental hypsometric difference between continents and oceans; (b) the standard composition of seawater; (c) the world distribution and nature of pelagic sediments; and (d) the nature of the deep-sea fauna.

Space does not permit mentioning all vessels active in oceanographic explorations, but the following did particularly outstanding work (they are divided into national groups and with some important dates):

Austria: *Novara* (von Müllerstorf-Urbair, 1857–66), *Isbjörn* (Weyprecht, Wilczek, von Sterneck, 1871–72).

Britain: *Enterprise* (1848), *Investigator* (1849), *Nassau* (1872), *Peake* (1901), *Discovery* (1901–04), *Terra Nova* (Captain Scott), *William Scoresby, Discovery* (1926–39), *Challenger II* (1950–52), *Discovery II* (1951), etc.

Denmark: *Dana* (1928–30), *Galathea* (1950–52).

France: *Le Français* (Charcot, 1903–05), *Pourquoi Pas?* (Charcot, 1908–10), *Commandant Charcot* (P. Tschernia, 1948–51).

Germany: *Gazelle* (von Schleinitz, 1874–76), *Bismarck* (Deinhardt, 1879), *Prinz Adalbert* (Lean, 1880).

Holland: *Siboga* (W. Weber, 1899–1900), *Willebrord Snellius* (von Riel, 1929–30).

Sweden: *Albatross* (Petterson, 1950–52).

United States: *Vincennes* (1855), *Tuscarora* (Belknap, 1873–76), *Rush* (1879), *Jeanette* (De Long, 1879–82), *Albatross* (A. Agassiz, 1880–1920), *Alaska* (Belknap, 1881), *Enterprise* (1883–85), *Thetis, Nero, Carnegie* (Flemming, Ault, 1909–31), *Catalyst* (1932–36), *Hannibal* (1933–36), *Oglala* (1935), *E. W. Scripps* (1937–40), *Horizon* and *Baird* (1951–).

U.S.S.R.: *Aurora* (1953–54), *Vityaz* (Nasimov, Miklucho-Miklai, Makarov, 1870–89), *Vityaz* (N. Sisoev, 1949–55).

Meteorology*

The Pacific shows the most stable zonal development of all the oceans in the northern winter, with an almost symmetrical distribution of the principal pressure cells in the two hemispheres. On either side of the Interpropical Convergence Zone and with its broad belt of equatorial calms or doldrums (q.v.), there are the two semipermanent anticyclones, the *North Pacific* (or *Hawaii*) *High* and the *South Pacific* (or *Easter Island*) *High*, each of which strengthens during the northern summer, at a mean latitude respectively of 40°N and 30°S. In the northern winter season the North Pacific High weakens and shifts a little to south and east, but in the southern winter season the South Pacific High does not weaken or shift.

Owing to the very cold water of the Peru (Humboldt) Current in the east and the monsoonal warming of the Australia-Solomons area in the west, there is an eastward displacement of the South Pacific High, in contrast to the more centrally placed North Pacific High.

The trade winds extend as far as 25°N and S, but

* Joseph L. Reid, Jr.

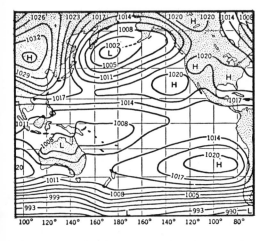

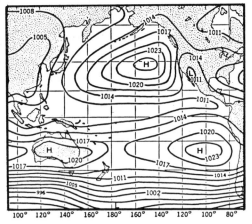

Fig. 3. Atmospheric pressure over the Pacific; above, in northern winter (January); below, in northern summer (July).

While over much of the eastern Pacific there is merely a slight seasonal shift of the trade wind limits, in the western Pacific there is a 180° seasonal wind reversal. This is all the more marked in the Northwest Pacific because in winter the Siberian High develops, leading to a very strong outflow of extremely cold, dry northwesterly winds, giving northeast China a climate somewhat like the northeastern United States, only more extreme because the Canadian High is only occasionally as strong as the Siberian High; likewise in summer the quasi-monsoonal conditions of eastern United States are not permanent as in China.

In the high latitudes of the North Pacific, the semipermanent Aleutian Low (stronger in winter) is associated with the Polar Front that often extends from Japan to Alaska, and the westerlies are strengthened and cooled by the strong winter outflow from Siberia. In summer, this is reversed by a low over Siberia and the Aleutian Low moves north and is much weaker.

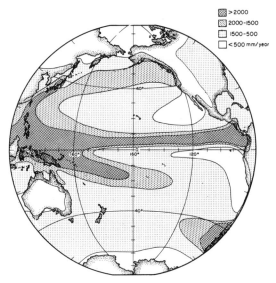

Fig. 4. Rate of rainfall over the Pacific Ocean and adjacent areas, demonstrating the control of eolian tropospheric dust transport exerted by co-precipitation with rain. The rate of rainfall over open oceanic areas is uncertain and largely extrapolated from qualitative observations at sea and from measurements on islands and continental stations.

the Southeast Trades reach north of the equator in the southern summer and there is a slight northward displacement of the thermal equator. The trades are somewhat less persistent and generally a little weaker than in the other oceans. In the eastern parts of the ocean, the trades are stronger and more reliable. The thermal equator lies about 5°N, and this belt is also marked by the heaviest rains (Fig. 4).

Monsoon (q.v.) conditions are important in both the Northwest Pacific and the Southwest Pacific. In the former, in the northern summer, the *Southwest Monsoon* affects the whole of Southeast Asia, much of China and marginal seas as far as 145°E (the Marianas) and even south of the equator, where the same airstream is amplified by the Southeast Trade Winds and the Australian High to become the *Southeast Monsoon* of the East Indies. The Southwest Pacific is affected by a Northwest Monsoon in the southern summer, influencing New Guinea, northern Australia, the Solomons, New Caledonia and to a lesser extent Fiji.

Features of particular interest are the coincidences of low precipitation with transport zones of trophospheric dust, extending downwind from the Sonoran, Atacama and Australian Deserts. Furthermore, it is interesting to note the existence of a meridional zone of high rainfall off the Asiatic coast in the middle northern latitudes. Precipitation in this zone is probably responsible for the removal from the atmosphere of the large amounts of tropospheric dust which are transported from the Asiatic continent by strong westerly winds in a zone at approximately 40°N (modified from Schott, 1935; from Arrhenius).

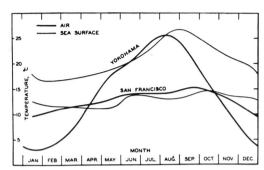

Fig. 5. Annual variation of air- and sea-surface temperatures at Yokohama and San Francisco.

In the equivalent latitudes of the South Pacific, the Australian High in winter does not block the westerly disturbances as a rule because the Polar Fronts are passing largely over the Southern Ocean, while Southeastern Australia and the islands of New Zealand receive heavy winter rains. Between the latter and the coast of southern Chile in the main belt of the westerlies, there is not one single island for a distance of 8000 km.

Physical Oceanography*

Currents. (a) The surface currents of the Pacific are driven by the trade winds and the westerlies, and surface flow is predominantly westward in low latitudes and eastward in high latitudes (Fig. 6). At the continents, the zonal flows are diverted both

* Joseph L. Reid, Jr.

north and south to form currents at the eastern and western boundaries, and a system of cyclonic and anticyclonic gyres is established as well as some up-wind return flow near the equator.

With certain limitations, Fig. 7 illustrates the flow at the sea surface. Since only the geostrophic flow (relative to the 1000-decibar surface) is represented, the field is incomplete, and one must imagine enough cross-contour flow to avoid overrunning the continents and to balance the apparent convergence at the equator.

The dominant features in middle latitudes are the huge subtropical anticyclonic circulations, i.e. the western boundary currents (the Kuroshio in the north, East Australia Current in the south), parts of the west wind drift, the eastern boundary currents, (California Current in the north, Peru or Humboldt in the south), and the westward-flowing North and South Equatorial currents a few degrees north and south of the equator.

At higher latitudes are the Antarctic Circumpolar Current (that which flows cyclonically around Antarctica) and the subarctic gyre consisting of the Alaska Current, the Oyashio Current (flowing southwestward past Kamchatka and the Kuril Islands) and part of the west wind drift.

At the equator, the flow is westward with the North and South Equatorial countercurrents flowing eastward just north and south of the equator. The South Equatorial Countercurrent is better developed in the west.

The greatest sustained speeds (more than 150 cm/sec) are found in the Kuroshio Current. Speeds as great as 50 cm/sec occur in the westward flow near

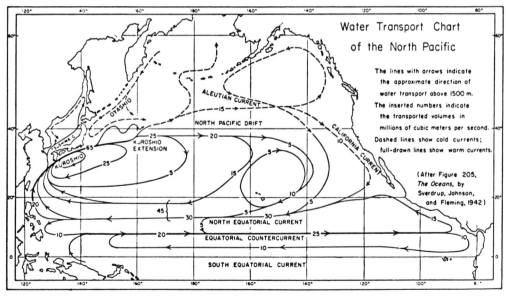

Fig. 6. Water transport and currents of the North and equatorial Pacific (from Sverdrup, Johnson and Fleming, 1942). (By permission of Prentice-Hall, N.Y.)

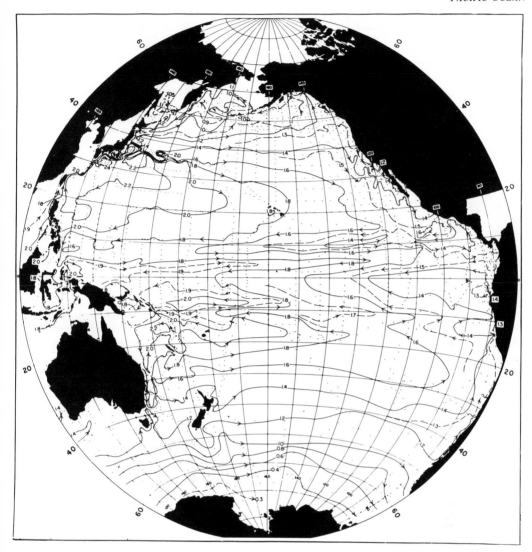

Fig. 7. Currents at the surface of the Pacific Ocean (geopotential anomaly at the sea surface with respect to the 1000-decibar surface, in dynamic meters).

the equator and in the Antarctic Circumpolar Current. Speeds of 10–40 cm/sec are found in the eastern boundary (California and Peru) currents.

(b) Subsurface countercurrents are found beneath the eastern boundary currents and along the equator.

Beneath the California and Peru currents, there are poleward currents from 50–150 km wide and extending from about 150 m beneath the surface at least several hundred meters down. In the California Current system, a countercurrent appears at the surface also in the winter months.

The Equatorial Undercurrent (see *Equatorial Currents*) is a narrow (300 km wide), swift (up to 150 cm/sec) current flowing eastward at the equator beneath the westward-flowing surface current, It has

been found between about 50 and 100 m depth, extending from at least as far west as 160°E to the Galápagos Islands (90°W).

(c) The transport of various currents has been estimated as follows:

	Transport (m³/sec)
Kuroshio	65×10^6
North Pacific Current (west wind drift)	35×10^6
California Current	15×10^6
North Equatorial Current	45×10^6
North Equatorial Countercurrent	25×10^6
Antarctic Circumpolar Current	100×10^6
Peru Current	18×10^6
Equatorial Undercurrent	40×10^6

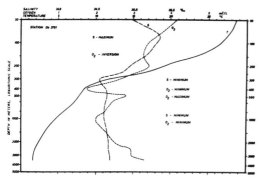

Fig. 8. Vertical distribution of temperature, salinity and oxygen content at Dana station 3751, typical for the western equatorial Pacific Ocean. Depth scale logarithmic.

Distribution of Properties at the Surface. (a) The surface temperature ranges from the freezing point at high latitudes in winter to more than 28°C in low latitudes. The isotherms do not extend east-west everywhere since some of the boundary currents (Kuroshio, East Australia, Alaska) carry warmer water poleward and others (California, Peru, Oyashio) carry cooler water equatorward. Furthermore, upwelling of cooler water from below in the eastern boundary currents and at the equator also affects the distribution of heat.

(b) The salinity at the sea surface is highest in middle latitudes, where evaporation exceeds precipitation. The highest values are a little more than 35.5‰ and a little more than 36.5‰ in the northern and southern subtropical anticyclones, respectively. Much lower values are found in the high and low latitudes where precipitation exceeds evaporation. Open-ocean values as low as 32.5‰ occur in the far north and as low as 33.8‰ in the south, near Antarctica. Near the equator, the lowest values (less than 33.5‰) are found in the east.

These distributions are also affected by the circulation. The California and Peru currents carry lower-salinity water equatorward from high latitudes, and the Kuroshio carries some lower-salinity water poleward from the equatorial region: the subtropical gyres appear as great lenses of highly saline water surrounded by lower salinity.

(c) The oxygen concentration near the sea surface is always very near the saturation concentration,

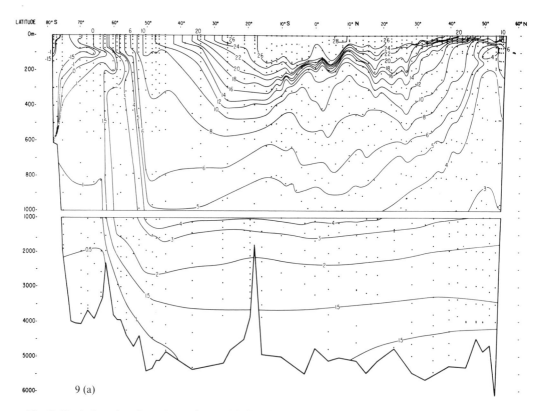

9 (a)

Fig. 9. Vertical section from Antarctica to Alaska along about 160°W longitude. Dots indicate location of observations. Depth is in meters. Vertical exaggeration is 5550 to 1 in the upper 1000 m, 1110 to 1 below 1000 m: (a) temperature in degrees Celsius; (b) salinity in parts per thousand; (c) dissolved oxygen concentration in milliliters per liter.

662

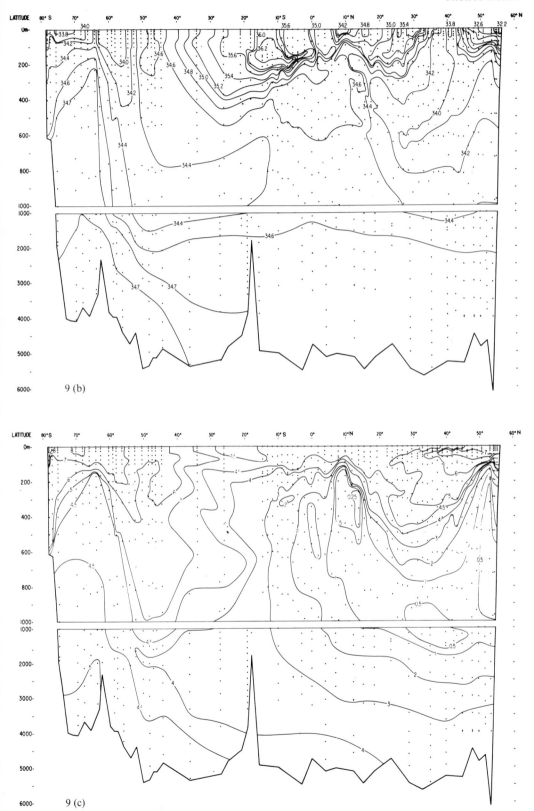

9 (b)

9 (c)

since the upper layers are in contact with the atmosphere. The saturation value depends upon both temperature and salinity, but the effect of temperature is much more important and the general distribution of oxygen at the surface markedly resembles the distribution of temperature. Oxygen concentration is high in the cold water of high latitudes, low in the warm equatorial waters (Fig. 8). At greater depths, processes of decay and consumption reduce the oxygen concentration as the water flows, and the degree of saturation with oxygen has been used as a rough indication of the "age" of the water, i.e., how long since it was in contact with the atmosphere.

Deep Flow and the Distribution of Properties beneath the Surface. The circulation of the upper water is wind driven and partly balanced geostrophically. The adjustment of the density field toward geostrophic equilibrium and the wind driven convergences and divergences cause the deeper distributions to be quite different from those at the surface. At greater depths, where the circulation is principally thermohaline, still greater differences occur [Figs. 9(a)–9(c)].

Convergence and Divergence. Within the wind driven subtropical anticyclones, there is convergence of the surface waters, and the accumulation of waters causes the mixed layer to be thick (as great as 300 m in the western area in winter). Similarly the divergence of surface waters in the high-latitude cyclones causes the deeper waters to rise toward the surface and spread out. Along the coasts of North and South America in middle latitudes, the equatorward winds cause the surface waters to move offshore, and upwelling of the deeper waters occurs. At the equator, the westward-blowing winds and the earth's rotation cause the surface waters to move away from the equator both north and south, and upwelling also occurs.

Geostrophic Adjustment. Geostrophic balance of the velocity by horizontal pressure gradients is accomplished by adjustments of the density structure: if one faces downstream the less dense water is on the right in the northern hemisphere, on the left in the south. The anticyclones are thus great basins of less dense water: dense water lies nearest the surface in the cyclonic eddies.

Penetration of Properties. Under the influence of the wind driven convergence and geostrophic balance, and the heating and evaporation at the surface, the subtropical anticyclones are great basins of warm, saline water [Figs. 9(a)–9(b)] extending more than 500 m below the surface in the central North Pacific and central South Pacific. Conversely, under the influence of the wind driven divergence, the geostrophic adjustment, and the cooling and precipitation at the surface the high-latitude cyclones are regions where cold, less saline water extends to the surface. These features are repeated in the systems of zonal flows near the equator, but

in a much reduced form: since the Coriolis force is much reduced near the equator, geostrophic balance is achieved with much smaller horizontal pressure gradients.

Deeper Circulation and Distribution of Properties. The distribution and character of the Pacific water masses are illustrated in Figs. 10 and 11. In the North Pacific high latitudes, the surface waters are quite low in salinity and even cooling them to the freezing point does not make the surface water dense enough to overturn deeper than about 200 m. The deeper water in the North Pacific must originate elsewhere and flow in through the South Pacific (since the connection with the Arctic Ocean, through Bering Strait, is too narrow to be of consequence).

These deeper waters which have been formed in the Weddell Sea and the North Atlantic, where the combination of temperature and salinity produces

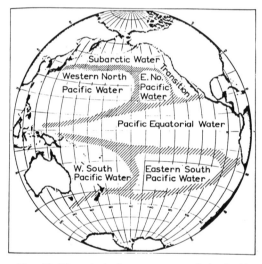

Fig. 10. The principal water masses of the Pacific, after Sverdrup, Johnson and Fleming (1942). Temperature-salinity characteristics of the water masses are given in a later section, "Horizontal Zonation." (By permission of Prentice-Hall, N.Y.)

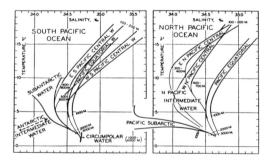

Fig. 11. Temperature-salinity relations of the principal water masses of the Pacific (Sverdrup *et al.*, 1942). (By permission of Prentice-Hall, N.Y.)

very dense water at the surface, are constantly replenished. Rising of the deeper waters of the North Pacific was first recognized about a hundred years ago, and the Pacific Ocean has been described sometimes as a huge estuary, with outflow from the North Pacific of low-salinity water at the surface (flowing back, eventually to the areas of sinking in the Atlantic) mixing with some of the deeper, more saline water flowing in at depth through the South Pacific.

Oxygen is supplied to the ocean at its surface by the atmosphere. The waters that sink in the Weddell Sea and North Atlantic are high in oxygen concentration also and tend to replenish the oxygen in the deep Pacific as they flow northward. Between the high values at the surface and at the bottom, the values of oxygen are much lower, and in parts of the subtropical North Pacific the oxygen is nearly exhausted [Fig. 9(c)].

The distribution of various nutrients in the ocean is affected by this system of deep circulation. Nutrients such as inorganic phosphate-phosphorus are consumed by plant growth at the surface and are regenerated at greater depths as the plants die, sink and decay. As a result, the nutrients are generally in greater concentration at depths of 1 or 2 km than at the surface. Inflow of the deeper water into the Pacific brings in water that is high in phosphate compared to the average concentration in the Atlantic: outflow is mostly of surface water that is somewhat lower in phosphate than the average in the Pacific. As a result, phosphate has accumulated in the Pacific and the average concentration is about twice that of the Atlantic: the phosphate brought in by the richer part of the Atlantic water is balanced by the outflow of some of the poorer water from the generally richer Pacific.

Sediments*

Introduction. The famous voyage of H.M.S. *Challenger*, 1872–76, initiated modern study of samples from the deep oceans; the description of these samples by Murray and Renard (1891) is still a classic reference. Work by Agassiz (1906, *Albatross*) and by Revelle (1944, *Carnegie*) added appreciably to the body of knowledge about sediments of the oceans. In addition, the works of Revelle *et al.* (1955), Bramlette (1961), Arrhenius (1963), and Goldberg and Arrhenius (1958) are referenced in Menard (1964). The data of Shepard (1963), Riedel and Funnell (1964), Landergren (1964), and Griffin and Goldberg (1964) are also available.

General. Our knowledge of the sediments at the bottom of the ocean is based on a rather small number of samples; over much of the Pacific Ocean the sample density is comparable to about one sample per state in the United States. Except near islands and continents, or near structurally complex

* Eric Olaussen and M. N. A. Peterson.

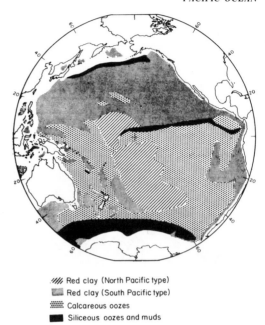

//// Red clay (North Pacific type)
▨ Red clay (South Pacific type)
▒ Calcareous oozes
■ Siliceous oozes and muds

Fig. 12. Sediments of the Pacific Ocean.

areas such as fracture zones, the depositional patterns are commonly very broad and of a scale that would suggest that they have been dominated by large-scale phenomena such as atmospheric and oceanic circulations, volcanic provinces, and the disposition of continents, or by major biological factors such as temperature, availability of nutrients, and intensity of light in the surface waters.

The longest cores now being taken are close to 30 m, but for the most part, samples are limited to the upper several meters. Recent drilling experiments in deep water have greatly increased this depth of penetration in two sites near San Diego, California, and near Guadulupe Island.

The total thickness of sediments in the Pacific Ocean is not known; however, geophysical methods indicate that there is generally a layer of perhaps unconsolidated sediments that is about 300 m thick. Beneath this is a second layer about 1 km thick that may be more consolidated sediment and volcanic rock, but actual knowledge concerning both these layers must await deeper drilling. In the Mohole test drilling off Lower California, basalt was encountered beneath 200 m of sediment.

Based on echo soundings, slopes on the surface of the sediment are, in large scale, very gentle, rarely exceeding several degrees. In small detail, however, little is known, and slopes of high angle may well be present locally.

Sedimentary Components. The components of oceanic sediments have diverse origins. Some minerals have been weathered from pre-existing rocks, largely on the continents, and have been transported

665

to oceanic realms by streams and wind. Quartz, micaceous clay minerals, chlorite, kaolinite, microcline and lesser amounts of certain metamorphic minerals are typical of this group. Some components, such as volcanic glass, high-temperature alkali and plagioclase feldspars, augite, hornblende, biotite and magnetite, have been introduced more or less directly by volcanic activity, either from within the ocean basin or from its perimeter. In some instances it is not possible to determine the origin of certain minerals from the minerals themselves, although inferences based on aerial distribution and grain or crystal size can be made. Other sedimentary material is from the hard parts of organisms that

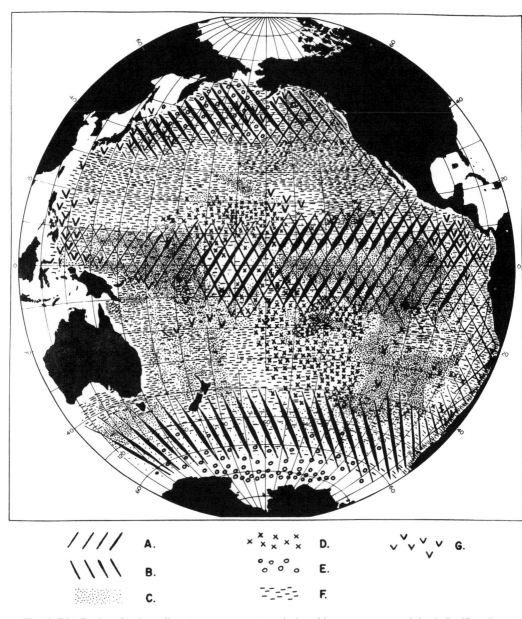

Fig. 13. Distribution of major sedimentary components, exclusive of ferromanganese nodules, in Pacific sediments. Density of pattern shows relative abundance of each component. The sediments are the sum of the components: (A) radiolaria; (B) diatoms; (C) calcium carbonate, mainly foraminifera and nannoplankton; (D) zeolite, mainly phillipsite; (E) ice-rafted debris; (F) fine-grained silicates, other than zeolites, mainly clay minerals (see Fig.14), quartz, and feldspar; (G) fresh, relatively unaltered volcanic material. Information summarized from publications and unpublished data on Scripps cores.

have lived in surface waters and have sunk after death. Calcite from Foraminifera and nanno-plankton, opal from radiolaria and diatoms, and apatite from hard parts of fish are the most important. Apatite may be present also as nodules; aragonite and calcite may also be derived from coral reefs. During and after burial, yet another important group of minerals forms, the products of crystallization from, and reaction with, sea or pore waters. Most important in this group are montmorillonite, a clay mineral, and phillipsite, a zeolite. These form most abundantly from the alteration of volcanic debris in the oceans, mortmorillonite appearing to form more readily than phillipsite. Clinoptilolite, another zeolite, also is found in some regions. Minor amounts of dolomite occur in some deep-sea deposits. Celestobarite is commonly present as small crystals. In areas that are well oxygenated at the bottom, very poorly crystallized hydrated oxides and hydroxides of ferric iron coat and impregnate other mineral crystals and grains. In anaerobic dark sediments, which are very uncommon in the Pacific, iron sulfide would be present either as tetragonal FeS or as pyrite. Over much of the surface of the ocean bottom, ferromanganese minerals form encrustations or impregnations or nodules.

The pore solutions in the sediments are sea (connate) water in various degrees of change by chemical reaction with minerals. Relative to seawater, these solutions are commonly enriched somewhat in sodium and potassium, especially in solutions taken from zeolitic sediments. Organic material is most abundant in the anaerobic sediments, but there is a small amount even in the highly oxidized sediments.

A minor, but interesting component of the deep-sea deposits is the cosmic debris (see *Cosmic Dust*; *Magnetic Spherules*). It it usually present as small spherules of nickel-iron having a mantle of oxides, but these metallic spherules must represent only that portion of the cosmic contribution that is low in silicate minerals.

More difficult to assess, but surely present, are introductions of material to the deep-sea depositional environment from below, such as solutions from compacting sediments, extrusions of liquefied sediment, and emanations from magmatic events at depth or even directly from the mantle. Erosion and redeposition can be demonstrated to occur.

The major sedimentary components combine to form a limited number of dominant sediments. A common distinction is made between *Pelagic* sediments, those having formed in the open ocean far from land by the settling of particles from or through the mass of ocean water, or by reaction with or precipitation from the seawater, and *Terrigenous* sediments, those having a considerable proportion of silt and sand-sized material that is definitely and directly derived from land.

Pelagic Clays (Mostly "Red Clay"). In the Pacific Ocean, pelagic clays are brown to reddish-brown and are found at depths generally greater than 4500 m. The most important factor that distinguishes the pelagic clays from the deposits in more shallow water is the lack of biologically derived calcite. Calcium carbonate is dissolved in the deeper water, leaving only the least soluble silicates, apatite, metallic extraterrestrial debris, and the hydrated oxides and hydroxides of ferric iron and manganese oxide to accumulate as pelagic clay. Even opaline skeletal debris appears to have dissolved in some sediments. In addition, organisms and chemical precipitates such as iron oxides and hydroxides serve as chemical scavengers which collect and transport to the sea bottom trace elements that are dispersed in the ocean water. These elements may then be concentrated in the sediments.

Gradations exist between pelagic clays composed largely of fine-grained material, such as quartz, micaceous clays and other minerals that have settled out from the overlying mass of ocean water after having been derived from the land, and those composed of authigenic material that has crystallized or largely altered at the site of sedimentation. These authigenic minerals are largely phillipsite and montmorillonite, and are mostly from the alteration of volcanic material.

Pelagic clays are very fine-grained, commonly having median diameters of less than 1μ, but an appreciable amount of coarser material is not uncommon, especially in sediments containing volcanic debris or authigenic zeolites. Crystals or phenocrysts from volcanic debris may remain as coarse grains or fragments even after the fine-

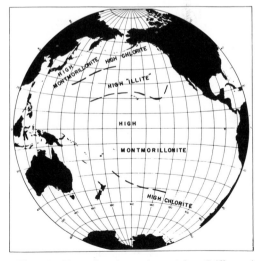

Fig. 14. Clay mineral provinces (after Griffin and Goldberg, 1964), expressed in terms of the generally most important clay mineral in the suite. (By permission of Interscience Pub. Co., N.Y.)

grained or glassy matrix has been completely altered. Shards and chips of glass partially retain their shape even when largely altered.

Carbonate Oozes. Calcium carbonate deposits are accumulated over more than one-third of the Pacific floor, and the predominant portion is south of 10°N. The carbonate ooze is distributed over relatively shallow bottom where the rate of dissolution is probably low and below the equatorial zone of the East Pacific where the dissolution locally can be higher but is counterweighted more or less by a high organic production. Most of the North Pacific is below depths of 4000 m, and the productivity of calcareous plankton is relatively low over large areas which may explain the low carbonate content there. The lack of both recent and Upper Tertiary carbonate deposits just north of the North Equatorial Divergence (about 8°N) is not fully understood.

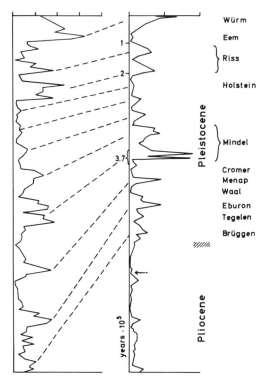

Fig. 15. This graph shows the content of entire forams per weight unit in two East Pacific cores (the Swedish cores 62 and 58). The curves reflect the rate of carbonate accumulation which is supposed to be a function of the rate of carbonate transport from the Atlantic. The ages given are Pa^{231}/Th^{230} datings of equivalent horizons of North Atlantic cores made by Rosholt *et al.*, and a K/A dating of tuff by Lippolt, the tuff considered as Uppermost Cromerian or Lower Mindelian in age. The correlation with the continental stratigraphy is tentative. The arrow indicates the horizon above which discoasters are absent.

A sharp decrease in $CaCO_3$ occurs within a range of about 500 m, and the "compensation depth" is generally somewhere between 4500–5000 m with both regional and local variations.

The concentration of calcium carbonate in the East Equatorial Pacific is highest below the Equatorial Divergence (about 75%) and decreases to the north and south due to decreased productivity. In core sequences, collected with the Kullenberg piston corer, the carbonate content changes in a regular way. It has been shown that the carbonate maxima were formed during ice ages while carbonate minima accumulated during intervening interglacials. The carbonate minima represent ages when a large portion of the calcareous matter (foraminifera) was fragmented or dissolved and only thick-walled foraminifera, as members of *Globorotalia menardii-tumida*-group and *Pulleniatina*, were preserved, while during glacials the dissolution and fragmentation of foraminifera and other calcareous matter were less intense. Foraminifera of the *Globigerina* family dissolve more easily than the foraminifera mentioned above. The large numerical and percentage increase of Globigerinas in glacial stages are therefore supposed to reflect the decreased dissolving capacity of the bottom water. The increased carbonate transport from other places (see *Atlantic Ocean*) has made possible a larger accumulation of carbonate below the East Equatorial Pacific.

The cyclic distribution of carbonates is recognized between about 8°N and 10°S in the East Pacific. In cores from the East Pacific Rise (13–15°S) or in cores from the Central Equatorial Pacific, the distribution of carbonate seems to be independent of climatic changes. However, in the latter region, changes in the dissolving capacity of the bottom water are, for example, recorded in the frequency of *Globigerina* or in the amount of entire forams per volume unit in the same way as in cores from the East Equatorial Pacific (Fig. 15).

The calcareous oozes from the South Pacific Ridge and from the Southwestern Pacific generally have a very high content of carbonate (up to 90% $CaCO_3$). The high concentration is due not to a high productivity but to a low degree of dilution. The carbonate content can thus be higher in oligotrophic regions than in more productive areas owing to scarcity of siliceous fossil remains and their generally large distance to sources of terrigenous matter. The accumulation in anticyclonic regions is, however, very slow.

The area covered by carbonate ooze was larger during the Tertiary, particularly up to the Miocene. Sediment cores passing from carbonates into radiolarian ooze or red clay have been collected, the former facies shift occurring in productive areas as below the divergences, the latter facies change noticed in oligotrophic regions. The Tertiary carbonate ooze has a comparatively larger content of coccolithophorids, particularly in cores below the present anticyclonal eddies. Pure coccolith ooze, Lower Miocene in age, is cored from the western part of the Central Pacific where Tertiary deposits often outcrop—especially on elevations. In the lower portions of the two cores at Fig. 15, collected in the East Equatorial Pacific, discoasters are frequent. Above a certain horizon they are absent. Foraminifera are more frequent in Pleistocene deposits than in Tertiary ones.

Siliceous Oozes. Along the border of the North Equatorial Divergence, radiolarian ooze is accumulated. Here, the calcareous matter is dissolved, leading to an increased proportion of siliceous organic remains compared with other constituents. The northern boundary of radiolarian ooze accumulation is determined by the decrease in productivity toward the north. Pre-Quaternary radiolarian ooze also outcrops locally.

Diatom ooze and mud are deposited south of the Antarctic Convergence where the organic production is large and the deposition of carbonate is low. North of the convergence, the organic production decreases, temperature increases and carbonate ooze accumulates. The southern boundary of the diatom mud is determined by masking with glacial detritus.

Diatomaceous deposits correspond to the upwelling zones off the coast of Peru and in the Gulf of California. Diatoms are also frequent in the sediments below the eastern portion of the Equatorial Divergence.

Below the subarctic water mass in the North Pacific, diatomaceous mud is formed which contains a large portion of glacial detritus. The boundaries are determined by the same factors as for the South Pacific diatom ooze. The relative portion of diatoms is larger in the latter area due to a higher degree of dilution with terrigenous matter in the North Pacific diatom mud.

Arrhenius has made an analysis of the size distribution of frustules of the diatom *Coscinodiscus nodulifer*. The frequency of large frustules was found to be much higher in glacial stages than in interglacial ones. This trend is, however, less conspicious in pre-Holsteinian stages.

Terrigenous Sediments. At the edges of most of the continents, the sediments differ from the pelagic sediments of the open ocean in having a considerable proportion of minerals in the coarse silt and sand-size range that are directly derived from land. Where the influx of material from land is sufficiently rapid, the organic skeletal debris typical of areas of slower detrital sedimentation is greatly diluted. In addition, authigenic phases do not have time to form near the surface.

In some instances the influx of material to the site of sedimentation must take place rapidly and episodically as a flow of a suspension of grains in water. The sediments in and associated with submarine canyons that are cut into the continental

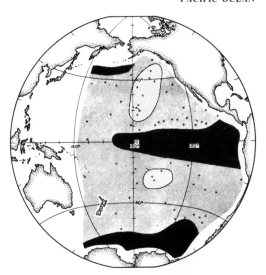

Fig. 16. Present-day organic productivity in the Pacific Ocean surface waters as indicated. by the concentration of opaline silica (mainly from diatoms and to some extent from radiolaria) in the surface layer of the bottom deposit (from Bonatti and Arrhenius).

Explanation: fine dotted, <20%; close dotted, 20–50%; black, >50%.

slopes contain beds and pockets of sand very likely transported in this manner. Submarine fans (q.v.), such as are found off the coast of central California, are notable examples of continentally derived material being introduced by water transport to the deep ocean sediments. It is not entirely clear how dense such turbid flows must be in order to transport sediment. Rather dilute suspensions may be capable of moving long distances. Moreover, some sediment from such flows must be mixed with surrounding water masses and get transported to its final depositional site by the regular movements of the seawater and gravitative settling; such sediment would, in this sense, be pelagic. In areas where trenches closely border the margins of continents, sediment transported along the bottom is trapped by the trenches, and virtually no grains larger than about 10μ are distributed from the continents to the floor of the ocean beyond the trench. Glacial marine sediments, formed by the transport of debris by floating ice, which melts and drops its load of sedimentary material, is a special and important case of the transport of land-derived material.

Terrigenous deposits are commonly grey-blue to grey-green, as distinct from the pelagic clays, which are characteristically brown-red. The blue and green hues are from the colored mineral constituents such as micaceous and chloritic minerals, amphiboles, and minor amounts of iron sulfides; water in the sediments also influences their color by helping transmit the light from the dark grains through the

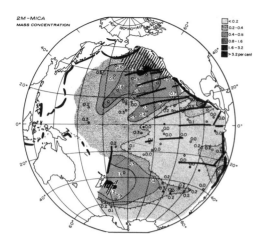

Fig. 17. Concentration distribution of mica at the present sediment surface of the Pacific Ocean floor. Features of particular interest are the zones of wind-transported mica from the Australian continent and from the Atacama Desert, and the apparent absence of a similar transport from the Asiatic continent in intermediate northern latitudes. Similar distributions are found for other detrital minerals like quartz and plagioclase. The distribution of mica and associated minerals off the North American continent is complex; south of the Murray Fracture Zone eolian transport prevails. North of that area turbidite transport appears to be responsible for much of the sediment distribution. Such geomorphological features, which are effective in protecting the oceanic basins against inflow of turbidites (fracture zones, trenches and troughs) are indicated in the map; also shown by white striping are the flat bottom areas in the northeast Pacific and off New Zealand, indicating extensive accumulation of turbidites. (Bonatti and Arrhenius.)

aggregate and through the colorless grains. Rapid rates of sedimentation, depths of sedimentation corresponding to water masses that are relatively depleted in oxygen compared to bottom water of the open ocean, and increased organic productivity because of upwelling near the edges of continents combine to increase the organic content and produce the mildly reducing conditions commonly present in sediments near continents. The reddish-brown color oxygenated sediments is caused by coatings and impregnations by hydrated oxides and hydroxides of ferric iron on mineral grains and crystals. A thin surface layer of brown sediment commonly overlies mildly reducing sediment.

Ferromanganese Nodules. Ferromanganese minerals form nodules and black coatings on objects such as volcanic rocks, pumice, bone and lumps of slightly consolidated sediment. Micronodules, about $50-100\mu$ in diameter, are common, particularly in pelagic clays that have volcanic affinity and that are dominated by authigenic minerals such as phillipsite. Large nodules, commonly from 5–20 cm in diameter, are concentrated at the surface of the sediment, in some areas, such that the bottom of the sea is virtually paved with them. Beds of comparable concentration may have been buried; individual nodules are found at depth in cores. Nodules are particularly abundant in areas of slow deposition, such as on tops of sea-mounts and in other areas where the influx of biological and detrital material is slow. Nodules most commonly range in diameter from 1–25 cm, but larger ones exist, and from bottom photographs it is clear that manganese coatings exist on rocks attached to the bottom. The nodular growth generally has a laminated structure and entrains minerals characteristic of the local sediment. From bottom photographs, it can commonly be seen that the nodules are uniformly spaced in relation to each other, suggesting that the growth of a nodule influences the growth of others near it. In addition to the dominant oxides of manganese and iron, smaller but probably valuable amounts of copper, nickel, cobalt, molybdenum, and zinc are found in the nodules. Growth of the nodular coatings appears to be very slow.

Volcanic Sediments. In some areas of the Pacific, volcanic debris that is largely or relatively unaltered forms almost pure layers. Such material can be distributed over large areas if the eruptions are into the atmosphere; distribution is much more limited if the eruptions are submarine. Submarine alteration and mixing with other sediments produce gradations with other sediment types. Lava types contributing to this kind of sediment are largely andesitic to rhyolitic, because of the explosive eruptions and relative resistance to alteration; sediments in the areas around Indonesia, the Gulf of Alaska and off Central America contain important amounts of this type of material. Basaltic volcanic sediments tend to be generally local (a good example is found near the Austral Islands) and also to change to authigenic minerals relatively rapidly compared to acidic material. The alteration of glassy debris appears to be the most important group of reactions involving the aluminosilicates that takes place in near-surface sediments of the oceans.

Coral Reefs. Coral reefs are wave-resistant ecologic units composed largely of hermatypic corals and calcareous algae, which fringe continents and islands in the Pacific where the temperature is suitable, generally a minimum of about 18°C. Lagoons within the reefs contain coral heads and debris, Foraminifera, and fine carbonate mud. Reef debris is spread down the flanks of oceanic islands to abyssal depths, where it is subject to the same dissolution effects as calcium carbonate from planktonic Foraminifera. Dolomite is found at depth in some coral islands. It is also found in abyssal sediments near such islands and is probably derived from them, the calcium carbonate having dissolved in the deep water. In areas of low rainfall, coral rock is altered to phosphate rock composed of apatite, by reaction with phosphate from guano. Reaction of calcium carbonate with the phosphate from seawater also takes place; phosphatized lower Eocene fauna has been found on Sylvania Guyot.

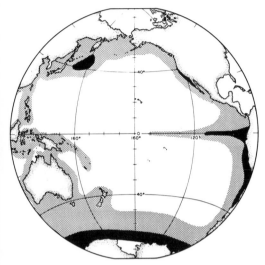

Fig. 18. Productivity of Pacific Ocean surface waters, estimated from observations of living planktonic organisms (from Sverdrup, 1954).

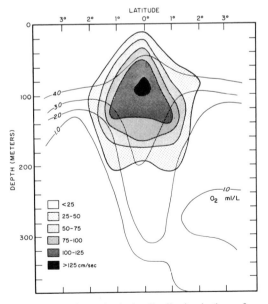

Fig. 19. Horizontal velocity distribution in the surface layer of the East Equatorial Pacific, showing velocity contours of the Equatorial Undercurrent. The figure also shows the distribution of dissolved oxygen, indirectly indicating the vertical circulation rate (from Knauss, 1960).

Sediment Distribution and Surficial Stratigraphy. At any place in the oceans the composition of the sediment is the sum of the individual sedimentary components, the distributions of which are determined by generally independent processes. Figure 13 portrays a generalized statement of the sediments of the Pacific Ocean in the upper meter to several meters. At the scale of this map it is not possible to show the ways in which the components might be distributed or mixed within the sediments; however, the broad patterns of distribution are evident. The map should be examined in conjunction with bathymetry and nutrient distribution. The clay minerals have been secondarily illustrated in terms of the generally dominant clay mineral in the suite of sheet structure silicates that are present in the sediments (Fig. 14).

The biologically productive Subarctic Current, Equatorial Current System and the West Wind Drift have beneath them highly fossiliferous sediments, ranging in composition from almost pure calcium carbonate to almost pure opaline silica, which accumulate at a relatively rapid rate. The high organic productivity results from upwelling and vertical mixing in the vicinity of the currents, bringing water rich in nutrients to the surface, where solar energy is available. In regions of lower productivity, such as that part of the East Pacific Rise from 15–40°S and the islands and seamounts of the south-central and north-central Pacific, those areas that stand above the depths at which calcium carbonate is destroyed are covered with calcareous oozes. The exact means by which the calcium carbonate is removed from sediments in deep water are not understood, but they may be related to the overlying water mass, ascending interstitial solutions, organic activity at the bottom, or some combination of these factors, varying in importance from place to place. The nature of the boundary between areas of carbonate and no carbonate has not been explored in local detail. In water deeper than the level of carbonate preservation, pelagic clays are characteristic of areas of low productivity, and sediments containing abundant opaline skeletal debris are characteristic of areas of higher organic productivity.

A broad belt of pelagic ("red") clays extends almost across the entire ocean, roughly between latitudes 20 and 40°N, interrupted mainly by carbonate-covered volcanic seamounts and islands of the North Pacific. Except within several hundred miles from the Hawaiian Islands, minerals derived from land, largely quartz and "illite," are particularly abundant in this belt. A similar but much smaller area of quartz-rich sediments is found east of Australia. Atmospheric transport, from the steppes of Asia in the northern hemisphere and from the arid interior of Australia in the southern hemisphere, has been responsible for the delivery of much of this continentally derived material to the deep oceans. In addition, near-bottom transport from North

671

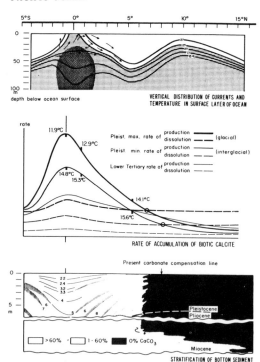

Fig. 20. The upper graph shows the thermal stratification and the vertical and horizontal circulation in the surface layer of the East Equatorial Pacific. The equatorial undercurrent is indicated by dark shading. The lower graph indicates the stratification of the bottom deposits below the equatorial zone, and the middle-diagram shows an interpretation in terms of rate of biological production represented by the rate of accumulation of calcium carbonate (from Arrhenius, 1963). (By permission of Interscience Pub. Co., N.Y.)

America seems likely in the northeastern Pacific, where there exists the main window in the otherwise almost continuous belt of trenches bounding the continents around the Pacific, and where there also exists an almost continuous downward slope from the edge of the continent well into the central Pacific. In the North Pacific, much of this belt of largely continental material is in deep enough water to contain little carbonate; however, in the lee of Australia, some areas contain abundant carbonate.

Volcanic debris from sources within the basin does not disperse far, relative to the total size of the basin. Basalt is the most abundant magma type, but locally, intermediate to acidic types are found. Small amounts of soda-rhyolite debris are present on the southern East Pacific Rise. Commonly there is evidence of recent basaltic activity along the very crest of the East Pacific Rise; in other places along the crest there is enrichment of Fe in the sediments that may be a surface manifestation of a magmatic event at depth. Heat flow is also high along the Rise.

Volcanic debris is also found distributed from volcanism around the perimeter of the Pacific, having been able to pass across the deep-sea trenches commonly bordering the ocean near volcanically active areas.

The clay mineral distribution exhibits a consistent, broad pattern. "Illite," chlorite and montmorillonite are the three main clay minerals. The distribution of "illite" is from largely continental sources. Chlorite, important in sediments of the far North and South Pacific, is from the largely mechanical weathering of rocks in cold climates, and also from the availability of abundant chlorite-bearing rocks to this type of weathering. Montmorillonite is the dominant clay mineral over the remainder of the basin. Montmorillonite occurs in three distinctly different modes: (1) as an erosional contribution from the continents, such as off southern California; (2) as a direct and apparently early-formed alteration product mainly from basic volcanic debris, in such areas as near Hawaii, parts of the very crest of the East Pacific Rise, and in a border along the volcanic fringes of the Pacific; and (3) in the presence of phillipsite.

The distribution of phillipsite is clearly related to rates of deposition, such that slow deposition, or

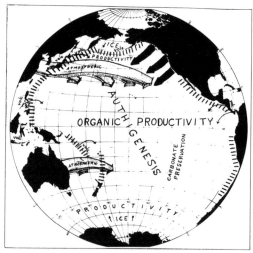

Fig. 21. Major sedimentary processes active in the Pacific Ocean. Organic productivity is high in the Equatorial Current System and in the Sub-Arctic Current and West-Wind Drift. Authigenic minerals can form prior to final burial in areas, such as the Central Pacific, where sedimentation rates are low because of slow influx from continents and where volcanic debris is in relatively greater proportion. Topographic highs retain calcium carbonate, even in areas of low productivity. Transport near bottom is inhibited by trench systems, shown by picket fence, through most of the perimeter of the basin, except off North America. Windblown dust (large, clear arrows) and volcanic debris (small, curved arrows) can cross trenches. Ice rafting is, and was, common in polar and subpolar regions.

even erosion, favors more abundant phillipsite at or near the surface. It is most abundant in areas that can be interpreted as windows in the sedimentation patterns of the other materials. The large central portion of the ocean, farthest from land, but south of 20°N latitude, is an area of slow accumulation of continentally derived material. Across this area lies the equatorial belt of high productivity. Bounding the east side is the carbonate preservation on the East Pacific Rise; bounding the west side is the complex sedimentation associated with proximity to Australia. The phillipsite is found abundantly within this area and also buried beneath sediment in some places near the edges of this area, for example, southeast of Hawaii. It is also found east of the East Pacific Rise, where the sedimentation is shielded from material from South America by both the wind and trench systems. Rates of formation of phillipsite are not known; however, it appears that the mineral forms more slowly than does montmorillonite, from the alteration of basaltic volcanic debris, under sediment-surface conditions. Surely much of the phillipsite found in the sediments is Tertiary in age. The slowness of contribution of continentally derived and biologically produced material allows an increased proportion of fine-grained volcanic debris to be accumulated, which also favors formation of phillipsite. It may also be that the Tertiary was a time of more widespread volcanism in the Pacific basin. Slowness of deposition favors reworking by organisms and currents, and in this sense the phillipsite crystals can be thought of as detrital. Microfossils are also reworked and redeposited.

Stratigraphic information is being obtained by geophysical methods, such as by continuous profile sub-bottom echo sounders, by micropaleontologic studies of cores, and by the study of various schemes of radioactive decay, one of the most promising of which may be potassium-argon dating of volcanic and diagenetic minerals. Determination of rates of sedimentation is obscured by reworking of both mineral grains and fossils and by chemical reorganization of the sediment. It is not always clear whether the ages obtained, either from paleontologic or from radiometric evidence, apply to the material forming the sediment or to the sedimentation itself. At the present time, different methods do not yield the same results; however, it does not seem probable that rates of from 0.5–10.0 mm/1000 yr for pelagic sediments would be greatly in error. Some areas show zero deposition or even erosion. Structural complexity appears commonly to increase with depth, indicating a continuous smoothing effect by sedimentation.

In biologically productive equatorial areas, the fossiliferous sediments accumulate rapidly enough so that the normal Quaternary strata of calcareous-siliceous ooze is more than 10 m thick. Nearby, in areas where deposition is less rapid, but where sediments are sufficiently fossiliferous for biostrati-graphic study, cores of Tertiary sediment are commonly taken. Cores of early Tertiary sediments appear to be largely a matter of chance, but their occurrence surely implies erosion, slumping or non-deposition in the areas in which they are taken. Tentative interpretations have been made regarding the distributions of water masses during the Tertiary, largely involving displacement of the northern boundary of the equatorial current system during the Oligocene and even greater displacement during the Eocene. It is not uncommon to find, beneath the several-meter thick mantle of quartz-rich sediment in the North Pacific, sediment types characteristic of the surface in the South Pacific, suggesting that conditions in the North Pacific during the Tertiary were similar to conditions in the South Pacific during the Quaternary. The smaller amounts of quartz in the Tertiary of the North Pacific could have been caused by tectonic or climatic changes in areas surrounding the basin.

Pyroclastics and manganese nodules are less frequent than in the South Pacific and detrital grains more common, indicating a higher rate of deposition. The accumulation rate of the red clay in the North Pacific is also higher and may be due to its closer proximity to land sources; the red clay area of the South Pacific is separated from the South American Continent by trenches and ridges which shield from influx of turbidity currents while such can spread out material from the North American shelf contributing to the pelagic deposits there. The red clay of the North Pacific can be supposed to resemble that of the Atlantic.

The manganese nodules of the North Pacific seem to be more ferruginous and contain less Mn than those from the South Pacific.

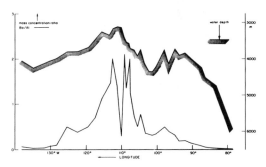

Fig. 22. Distribution of barium in a profile across the East Pacific Rise at latitude 12°S. The graph illustrates the high abundance of barium in relation to aluminum on the Rise. Both elements were determined by X-ray spectroscopy.

The elemental distribution of barium shown in this Figure parallels that of crystalline barite ($BaSO_4$) determined by X-ray diffraction. Although a minor fraction of the barium occurs in the form of the barium zeolite harmotome, the major amount of the element is present as barite (from Boström *et al.*)

It has been observed that there is a discontinuity below the North Pacific red clay, occurring at a depth of some few meters. The clay below the discontinuity resembles the red clay of the present South Pacific. The older red clay is assumed to be Tertiary in age. This observation suggests that the supply of terrigenous matter to the North Pacific has increased up from the Tertiary.

Ice-borne deposits are accumulated around the Antarctic and in the northernmost Pacific. Modern icebergs do not penetrate south of the Aleutian Islands. Pleistocene icebergs deposited matter in the Gulf of Alaska at least as far south as Vancouver-Hokkaido. Also in the South Pacific, Pleistocene icebergs reached lower latitudes than today, perhaps 10° as average and more in the southeastern Pacific.

Phosphoritic nodules are dredged at many locations in the Atlantic and the Pacific in nondepositional environments on the continental shelves. Extensive phosphate deposits occur off the coast of southern California. Barite is another interesting authigenic mineral (see Fig. 22).

Structural Pattern and History of the Pacific*

Structural History. For a century or more the structural history of the Pacific has posed one of the great enigmas of geology. Its size, structure and palaeogeographic history render it completely different from the other oceans.

It is sometimes said that the Pacific is the birth place of the moon (proposed by G. H. Darwin, 1879, and supported by Osmond Fisher, 1889; opposed by Umbgrove, 1947, and Jeffreys, 1952). It is certainly the world's greatest ocean, and its floor is studded with more volcanoes, seamounts and atolls than all the other oceans put together. Its borders are fringed with the longest continuous belts of fold mountains, embellished with more volcanoes than known anywhere else, and agitated by more earthquakes than found in all the rest of the world. The transmission of certain seismic waves appears to pass beneath the Pacific at shallower depth and higher rate than for parts of the other oceans. The floor of the mid-Pacific is covered by a thinner layer of sediment than is usual in other oceans, so we can observe structural features of the underlying crust with greater clarity. This is enough to justify a general belief among geologists and geophysicists of the solid earth that the Pacific is something special and unique in the world of geotectonics.

Geotectonic Divisions. One may distinguish within the entire Pacific region, as broadly defined above, two quite distinctive topographic provinces: (a) the "Main" or Central Pacific Basin; and (b) the marginal seas, with their numerous secondary ridges and basins (Wüst, 1936).

The Main Pacific Basin. The general floor is a

---

* Rhodes W. Fairbridge.

gently undulating abyssal plain, parts of which are extremely smooth, for tens, even hundreds of kilometers, with average depths about 5000 m. It is

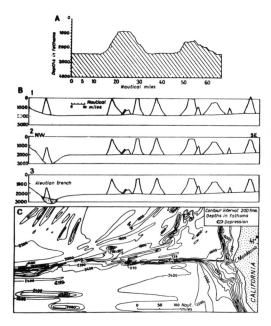

Fig. 23. Structural features of the northeast Pacific floor (Guilcher): (A) profile of a guyot and a less well-defined seamount; (B) suggested evolution of Gulf of Alaska seamount provinces (Menard and Dietz, 1961); (C) eastern third of the Mendocino escarpment (Menard and Dietz, 1952).

Fig. 24. Principal fault slip pattern of the circum-Pacific margins (Benioff, 1958).

interrupted by numbers of submarine mountains or volcanic ridges and areas punctuated by immense numbers of minor eminences, ranging from small hills to rather massive (conical) seamounts. These are disposed broadly in regions:

(a) The East Pacific Rise (Menard, 1960, 1964): A continuation of the mid-oceanic ridge (q.v.) which extends in a broad sweep from north of the Antarctic continent to the south of New Zealand, embracing the Pacific-Antarctic Ridge, the Easter Island Rise, the Galapagos Rise, to reach the American continent in the Gulf of California. Topographically it is similar to the other "mid-ocean ridges" of the Atlantic and Indian Oceans (Heezen, 1960), but it is oddly asymmetric in swinging toward the American side of the ocean. Its detailed features are similar. The crest is marked by a narrow rift, or series of graben structures, and most of the slopes (extending out gradually for 1000 km or so) appear to be disposed in irregular platforms, minor ridges and troughs, parallel to the main trend. Its average relief rises 2000–3000 m above the floor of the Main Pacific Basin, added to which are the local accumulations of volcanic islets and seamounts. A small extension of the ridge seems to exist in the Juan de Fuca Ridge off Vancouver Island (Wilson, 1965).

(b) Submarine Fans (q.v.) and Abyssal Plains (q.v.): Following much of the northeastern margin of the ocean are a series of submarine fans of considerable size, passing in places into abyssal plains. The latter are, however, rather scarce in the Pacific because usually the trenches play the role of sediment traps and prevent further passage of turbidity currents.

(c) The Archipelagic Aprons (q.v.) of the Western and Central Pacific with Volcanic Islands, Seamounts, Atolls (Menard, 1956, 1964): This region is marked by rectilinear subparallel belts of volcanic islands, seamounts and atolls. Fanning out from the foot of these submarine ridges are what appear to be overlapping sediment fans; in any case, they form smooth slopes, tilted gently to pass gradually down to the regional oceanic floor (ca. 5000–6000 m). An interesting feature of the major submarine ridges, such as that from which the Hawaiian Islands rise, is the presence of a shallow depression more or less all around the foot of the insular slopes (Dietz and Menard, 1953). The archipelagic aprons of the Main Pacific cover 13.7% of the area (Menard, 1959). Some of the belts are high (e.g., Tahiti Chain) while a parallel belt (e.g., the Tuamotus) is submerged and represented only by atolls.

(d) General Plain of Low Relief: This covers most of the floor of the Pacific at 5000–6000 m depth. It is extremely flat, but does not show the gentle uniform directional slopes of the "abyssal plains." Rather it is an undulating relief, showing slight ridges and depressions of the order of 300 m in a distance of 200 km. In some areas the maximum relief does not exceed 60 m, and in others it may

reach 500 m or more. Here and there occasional seamounts occur, but generally they are not common except in definite island belts or in specific provinces such as the Gulf of Alaska.

(e) Fracture Zones (q.v.) (Linear Escarpments): These zones of great dimensions (ca. 2000 km long) have been identified crossing the Low Relief Plains of the northeast sector and East Pacific Rise (Menard and Dietz, 1952; Menard, 1955, 1960). The principal members in the northeast are named (from north to south): the Mendocino, Murray, Clarion and Clipperton. Generally there is a small change in the general level of the plain at the escarpment, perhaps 100–300 m; but the actual escarpment may be 500 m or more because the slopes diverge above and below the escarpment.

The Peripheral Zone of Archs and Trenches. The borders of the main Pacific basin are generally well marked by a zone of deep trenches, to the continent side of which there is a folded cordillera or arcs of islands associated with one or more submarine ridges (Hobbs, 1922; Umbgrove, 1947).

On the western side of the Pacific these island arcs and trenches are isolated and separated from the continent by intermediate basins. As a result there is relatively little supply of sediment and the trenches are mostly open depressions, and certainly not choked by sediment. The floors of these western trenches are extremely narrow, but flat, owing to the inflow of a small amount of sediment. The sides are utterly precipitous, dropping at slopes of 25–45°.

Along the eastern margin, the coastal cordillera are breached by great rivers which carry large quantities of sediment into the depressions, in many places completely obscuring them. The island arcs themselves are generally disposed on a double ridge, the outer islands being non-volcanic or at least not active, while the inner belt is marked by numerous active or recently active volcanoes. This is the well-known Pacific "Girdle of Fire."

The Marginal or Intermediate Seas. Separating the island arcs from the continent on the western side only of the Pacific, is a series of large secondary seas, "inland seas," that are generally about 500–1000 km wide and equally long, if not longer. The floors of such seas are extremely variable in topography and, like the main Pacific Basin, appear to reflect structural history and the available sources of sediment supply (Dietz, 1954; Fairbridge, 1961).

Principal topographic types can be recognized from echo-sounding traverses:

(a) Volcanic Hills: A fantastically jumbled topography of steep-sided hills, reminiscent of volcanic cones, which completely cover the floor of the more remote basins, e.g., Pandora Basin (Fairbridge and Stewart, 1960).

(b) Abyssal Plains: Smooth, flat, or evenly sloping plains, which seem to be covered by sediment distributed by rapid bottom streams, such as turbidity currents. It is hard to visualize the smooth surface developed by other means, and one may notice that this surface is always a little higher (50–100 m) on the side or site where the continental sediments would seem to debouch. Thus the Tasman Basin is a little shallower in the northwest, opposite Sydney and the Hawkesbury and Hunter Rivers, which debouch there (Standard, 1961). Likewise the Fiji Basin is shallower in the northeast part where the Rewa (a large tropical stream) debouches from the heavily watered Fiji Islands. The largest of these basins is approaching 5000 m in depth, but the smaller ones are progressively shallower (2000–4000 m).

(c) "Microcontinental Block" Regions: These regions occur in many areas and consist of alternate high and low quasi-cratonic blocks, sometimes just a few kilometers apart, though often hundreds of kilometers in length. The Melanesian Border Plateau is a complex of this sort (Fairbridge, 1959).

(d) Submarine Plateaus: These plateaus are widespread, occupying shallow or intermediate depths, and isolated more or less from continents of major island masses. Typical exampes are the Coral Sea Plateau, Bellona Plateau of the Southwest Pacific. The normal depths are 500–2000 m, but their surfaces are punctuated by numerous coral atolls.

(e) Intermediate Ridges and Rises: The entire region is intersected by positive linear features, either broad hump-backed rises, or narrower, often high fragmented ridges. These features are punctuated by small volcanoes, seamounts and sometimes atolls. The principal lines are more or less continuous, and subparallel to the main peripheral belt of island-arcs and trenches. They are culminating here and there in major island units, e.g., Japan, Philippines, New Guinea, New Caledonia, New Zealand, Etc.

(f) Intermediate Troughs and Trenches: These are often associated with the above-mentioned positive features. They tend to occur in pairs, i.e., a considerable elevation is matched by an equally large parallel depression. It is interesting that the trench or trough is mostly found on the continent side of the ridge, within the intermediate, marginal sea areas, i.e., just the opposite to their orientation in the main Pacific peripheral belt.

Special Features of Pacific Structure. The Pacific Ocean is unique in many ways. It has given its name to three highly illustrative aspects: the "Pacific" coast lines, "Pacific" volcanism and "Pacific" crustal type.

"Pacific" Coastlines. Suess (that great master of the "world view") believed that coastal types reflected a characteristic geotectonic history. The "Atlantic" coastal type exposed the truncated ends of incomplete mountain ranges; they represent faulting, subsidence and generally speaking an interruption in formerly continuous or harmonious patterns. In contrast, the "Pacific" coastal type reflected the continuous linear trends of the circum-

Pacific fold mountain systems, the festoons of island-arcs and the near continuity of the adjacent foredeep trenches. Suess regarded the Pacific as playing the role of a submerged foreland against which the peripheral foldbelts were constantly being thrust. The keynote of the "Pacific" type is parallelism; mountains, coasts, beaches, reefs and trenches tend to be linear and parallel, and peripheral to the main Pacific basin.

Objections were raised against this oversimplified picture by J. W. Gregory (1912). He suggested that a subdivision should be made into a "Primary Pacific" coast type (following Suess' definition), and a "Secondary Pacific" or "Sub-Pacific" type, in which "the structure of the land had no definite relation to the trend of the coast." He noted a number of sectors, particularly in eastern Australia and in the Victoria Land sector of Antarctica, where the trend of the mountain belts is cut off by the sea as abruptly as anywhere in the Atlantic. We may note, however, that these "indefinite" or "Secondary Pacific" coasts do not face the main Pacific basin, but the marginal seas.

Along the "Primary Pacific" shore lines there are multiple old littoral terraces, the heights of which oscillate, sometimes varying through more than 1000 m within a few kilometers. The general tendency is positive (Valentin, 1952). The "Secondary Pacific" terraces are less active, but they too are unstable and one may observe the Pliocene terraces of Southeast Australia warped to 2000-m elevation in southern New South Wales. However, the majority of the "Secondary" coasts are faulted and more negative than positive.

"Pacific" Volcanism. The concept of regional petrographic suites was established half a century ago by Becke (1903) and generalized by Harker, by the names "Atlantic" and "Pacific" suites; a "Mediterranean" type was added by Paul Niggli (1923). The *"Pacific"* type was characterized by calc-alkali lavas and typical of belts of mountain building and uplift ("Anapeirean" of Jensen, 1908). Strictly speaking the "Pacific" lavas are associated mainly with the belts of circum-Pacific folding, and not with the central Pacific. The typical rocks are andesites, rhyolites and olivine basalts.

The *"Atlantic"* type was characterized by alkaline lavas and was regionally associated with zones of tension or collapse "katepeirean" of Jensen, 1908). The common rocks are olivine-free basalts, with felspathoids; an immense variety are known. Such suites are typical of mid-oceanic regions ("thalassocratons") and equally with the old continental blocks ("epeirocratons").

"Pacific" Crust. The strictly geophysical approach to the earth's crust has, over the last few decades, suggested a certain uniqueness of character for the Pacific, although some parts of other ocean floors have similar features.

(a) Gravimetric Surveys at Sea: Some forty years

ago the courageous world surveys by Vening Meinesz in dangerous, leaky old World War I submarines fired the imagination. Meinesz demonstrated a slightly positive gravity anomaly over most of the inner Pacific, as well as certain parts of the other oceans. Over the peripheral arcs he encountered the most remarkable oscillation of gravity readings, suggesting an uncompensated mass deficiency along the trenches and a mass excess beneath the island arcs. For the mid-ocean ridges there was also evidence of lighter material in thicker "roots."

(b) Seismology: Both earthquake seismology and ship-borne refraction work show that below a water layer of 5–6 km, there is, in the main Pacific Basin, a sediment layer 0.5–1.0 km thick, a "Second Layer" (marked by a compressional wave velocity of 4–6 km/sec, and thus possibly a hydrated igneous rock, like serpentine, though some geologists see it as a consolidated sediment); the Second Layer rests at the Mohorovicic Discontinuity on the mantle (velocity 8.1 km/sec). Reflection profiling in the last few years shows distinct stratification in the sediment layers, but elsewhere it may be seismically "transparent," i.e., without any good reflectors.

(c) Magnetic Characteristics: Systematic close surveys with a ship-towed magnetometer in the northeastern Pacific have disclosed a pattern of closely spaced high and low magnetic rocks of north-south orientation, which appear to be laterally displaced by the great east-west fractures (Mason, Vacquier *et al.*). It has been claimed (not without criticism) that the Mendocino Fault has a 1200-km lateral shift, the Pioneer 150 km and Murray 150 km.

(d) Heat Flow: The heat probe for use at sea developed by Bullard has shown that the usual Pacific heat flow measurement averages 1.1 microcalorie/cm²/sec, while parts of the East Pacific Rise (the central rift area) show 2–8 times this figure. On the other hand, the outer slopes of the ridge show abnormally low readings (0.14–0.97).

Intermediate Crust of the Western Pacific. One of the features of the Pacific that is perhaps most peculiar is the broad zone of marginal or intermediate seas that extend along the western borders from the Bering Sea and the Sea of Okhotsk down to the Coral Sea and the Tasman Sea. There are certain marginal seas associated with other oceans, but nowhere are they so large, numerous or widespread. Nor are they arranged specifically along the western margin.

There is not the slightest doubt that the general geology of these western Pacific intermediate seas is totally different from the main Pacific. The latest line of disturbances marks the boundary, inside which the lavas of the circum-Pacific fold-belts are characterized by the calc-alkaline suite. The line which separates these two provinces in the western Pacific, also separates two great topographic regions, the main Pacific basin and the western marginal basins. Marshall, the New Zealand geolo-

gist named this boundary the "Andesite Line" (1911). Axel Born (1933) modified it a little and so did Bryan (1944) who wanted to call it the "Marshall Line."

It has often been claimed that these marginal seas are ancient subsided parts of continents, but long-wavelength earthquake records do not disclose evidence of massive submerged continental crust here (Oliver, Ewing and Press, 1955; Officer, 1955). However, this geophysical method would not show thin or fragmentary sections of crust. Shorter-wavelength observations from Brisbane of earthquakes in the Tonga Trench do suggest a modified crust in the Coral Sea (de Jersey, 1946) although there is no evidence of it in the Tasman Sea region between Australia and New Zealand (Eiby, 1958).

Much more illuminating are the results of seismic refraction shooting, the first surveys being made in 1952 on the Scripps Expedition *Capricorn* (with the writer participating). The sedimentary layer was found to vary sharply from place to place, reaching 5–6 km under the ridges. The Second Layer of intermediate velocities thickens rapidly beneath the trenches bordering the western inner Pacific to become 10–15 km thick in Melanesia (Raitt, Fisher and Mason, 1955).

A gravity traverse of this area seemed desirable, and the writer was able to propose a joint operation involving the Australian Academy of Science, the assistance of a Royal Navy submarine H.M.S. *Telemachus,* a gravity meter from Vening Meinesz and personnel from Columbia University (Talwani, Worzel and Ewing, 1961). The traverse, from Australia-New Zealand-Tonga-Fiji and back, confirmed that there must be strong alternations in crustal thickness, as predicted. Van Bemmelen (1931) called this type of crustal region "semi-cratonic," while Stille (1940) called it "quasi-cratonic"; this second name has been the more widely adopted, the implication being of a crustal type intermediate between continental (30–40 km) "epeirocratonic," and oceanic (5 km) "thalassocratonic."

Deep-sea Trenches and Island Arcs. Another fundamental characteristic of the main Pacific Basin is the presence of a semicontinuous belt of trenches or troughs, generally on the ocean side of festoon-like chains of island arcs or littoral cordillera. Such features exist, locally, in the other oceans, but not in a peripheral belt. These belts coincide with strong negative gravity anomalies (often in excess of −100 mgal). A parallel belt of positive anomalies follows them on the continental side. Similar anomaly belts are not unique to the Pacific but are much more widespread here than elsewhere.

There are several important points about the distribution of Pacific island arcs:

(a) Island arcs occur only in the western Pacific, being replaced by littoral cordillera along the eastern margin. The two are thus geotectonically analogous, but not identical, since there are the intermediate basins in the west, lying between the island arcs and the true continent. They also occur in the Antilles and Scotia Arcs, as some sort of quasi-Pacific structures projecting into the Atlantic.

(b) Island Arcs occur generally in double lines of islands with an outer belt of entirely non-volcanic nature and an inner belt mainly of volcanoes; the outer belt may include folded and thrust sediments back to Mesozoic age. The two belts are generally 50–150 km apart. In some instances there is only a single arc of volcanoes. The "Girdle of Fire" around the Pacific is a very interrupted belt.

(c) Island Arcs are generally arcuate, as one might guess. The radius of the arc varies from about 200–2000 km. However, in some cases, e.g., the Tonga and Kermadec belts, the two rows of islands are absolutely rectilinear, despite the fact that certain authors wilfully draw curves through them.

(d) Deep-sea trenches and arcs are associated invariably with a complex seismic zone, indeed one of the most intense seismic belts in the world. Gutenberg and Richter (1950) recognize three seismic categories—shallow, intermediate and deep-focus—extending from the shallow type in the vicinity of the trench to the deep-focus shocks some 200–400 km toward the continent. Benioff (1955) interpreted this as a rising shear (at about 45°) along the ocean margin of the semi-cratonic crust. Krishnan (1961) went so far as to suggest that the entire Asia-Australia cratonic crust was being thrust forward as a shallow plate, a recent adaptation of the old Wegenerian hypothesis.

The trace of the so-called rising shear, in general, is a uniform distribution of earthquake centers along a simple plane, but the epicenters, as Gutenberg and Richter classified them, do not reflect distinct levels of earthquake shocks. Secondly, there is the interpretation of the strike movement of faults through earthquake shocks (Byerly, 1955), and many of the great western Pacific trench zones have now been correlated with strike-slip faults. This is particularly well documented in the case of the Tonga-Kermadec Line (McIntyre and Christie, 1958), which has the advantage that in the south it emerges and travels through the entire length of New Zealand as the "Great Alpine Fault," a well-known strike-slip feature (Wellman, 1956). Its total length is over 5000 km, with a right lateral (dextral) slip, and several hundred kilometers displacement. Pierre St. Amand (1959) has suggested that the entire Pacific margin is involved in analogous strike-slip faults, including the famous San Andreas Fault of California, which would appear to rotate the Pacific Basin in a counterclockwise direction by some hundreds of kilometers.

The Permanence of the Pacific. The question of the permanence of continents and oceans has so maintained itself in philosophic discussions of geology that after more than a century it is still a live issue.

The arguments range themselves into three principal categories:

(1) Biogeographical,
(2) Geochemical and geophysical,
(3) Geotectonic.

Each of these points needs thorough and *independent* testing.

Biogeographical Trans-ocean Links. As regards the biogeographical reasoning, great care must be exercised by geologists, because some biologists have been extraordinarily willing to construct entire continents, dig canals of giant proportions and change temperatures to suit their slightest whims, undertaken in order to arrange the transportation, say, of a peculiar spider from South America to Australia.

At a Pacific Science Congress held as recently as 1961 in Honolulu, an appreciable number of biogeographers (van Steenis, Skottsberg, Ronald Good and others) still clung stubbornly to the idea of a Polynesian continent, or at least to broad land connections for the now rather isolated islands.

The case for an ancient continent in the Pacific has been well presented by Haug (1900, 1909), and by Gregory (1930). The biogeographic arguments specifically called for land connections to permit the migration of high-altitude (mountain) faunas and floras in such major island masses as Hawaii, Galápagos and Fiji. From his extensive studies of Pacific island terrestrial mollusca, Pilsbury (1900) submitted that the entire area was once continental, progressively breaking up, Hawaii being the first to separate. An interesting aspect of the deep-drilling into the central Pacific atolls (Bikini, Eniwetok, etc.) has been the discovery of typical land snails at various levels down to the Miocene at least (e.g., at 251 and 552 m, see Ladd and Tracey, 1957); the former presence of far more island "stepping stones" than occur today would undoubtedly have greatly assisted the early island-to-island migrations. It seems therefore that Pilsbury's argument was well taken, but that a massive continent was not needed, because the snails (or their eggs) could be equally well transported on floating vegetation. However, some study of the bathymetry is worthwhile. The Galápagos rise at an intersection of the East Pacific Rise and short secondary ridges leading to Central and South America. Baur (1897) studied the biota with care, but then urged a "continent" to support it. It seems to be another example of using a hammer to kill a fly.

From his lifelong work, examining the flora of all Pacific islands, Skottsberg (of the Göteborg Botanical Gardens, Sweden) came to the conclusion that there was once a "*Eu-Pacific Flora,*" indigenous, continental and independent of North America and other neighboring continents. With such groups as the Philippines, New Guinea, New Zealand and Fiji, there is good evidence for former continental connections (note the shallow submarine ridges and platforms) and there is excellent geological justification (Stille, 1945, 1948). But Skottsberg (1929) included totally isolated islands as Juan Fernandez (the "Robinson Crusoe island," 500 km west of Chile), Easter Island (Rapa Nui), and so on, for which there are powerful negative arguments against massive land connections.

The question of marginal land areas along the eastern Pacific shores has long concerned paleogeographers in both North and South America, but sedimentary and structural studies (see below) show that quite small-scale marginal island ridges are all that can be justified.

The land-bridge or isthmian-link school adequately provided for marginal migrations around the entire periphery of the Pacific, trans-Aleutian and Bering, trans-Antillian, and trans-Antarctic from South America to Australia and New Zealand. With most of these connections, there is no geotectonic problem whatever. But with the last, trans-Antarctic migration, there are two serious questions:

(a) The Ross Sea-New Zealand Gap: The tectonic trends of South America, continuing through the Scotia Arc, connect with the Mesozoic folds of West Antarctica but terminate abruptly at the Ross Sea. There is no submarine ridge from here to New Zealand or to Australia. A definite crustal separation seems to be involved.

(b) The Climatic Question: Any migration along this route for the higher animals or almost any type of flora seems to be out of the question with the present climate. However, the climatic history of Antarctica (except for a brief glacial interlude in the Permian) seems to have been almost entirely nonglacial (Fairbridge, 1952). The paleoecology of most organisms found as fossils here in the early Tertiary and Mesozoic calls for warm or temperate climates (von Ihering, 1931). It has been suggested that southern hemisphere marsupials and certain conifers such as the *Araucaria* ("Norfolk Island Pine") found their way across the Pacific in warm periods via Antarctica. For the paleobotanists, an Antarctic migration route from South America to New Zealand and Australia is particularly needed since there seems to be a definite dispersal trend that way, which would not be favored by the normal wind and current methods of oceanic (i.e., floating) distribution. Hooker, Darwin, Ruetimayer, Hutton, Hedley and others have all favored continental links in or around the South Pacific.

Geotectonic Case for a Permanent Pacific. In his original suggestion of a subsiding Pacific Basin, Charles Darwin (1842) appears to have considered only a moderate "drowning," to explain the upgrowth of atoll-building corals; there was no mention of a "drowned continent." In his classical review of Pacific features, J. D. Dana (1863), who was geologist to Wilkes' American Exploring Expedition, identified fifteen subparallel ridges of volcanic islands (mainly trending WNW–ESE), but he seems to have regarded the basin as permanent. A new point of view came with Suess (1900); he called these ridges the "Oceanides," by implication, if not explicitly, suggesting the compressive, folded character of "Alpides," "Hercynides," "Caledonides," etc. He seems to have felt that they were embryonic orogenic belts, but nevertheless held that the ocean was mainly of a permanently depressed character. Indeed it offered the strong, shield-like (cratonic) foreland to the imagined pressure of the encircling island arcs.

The truth is that no continental land traces have been found anywhere within the main Pacific basin. Inclusions in volcanic necks generally contain some fragments of peridotite from the mantle, but no samples of Paleozoic or Mesozoic epicontinental rocks. No geotectonic structural trends are cut off by the Pacific (as they are in the Atlantic and Indian Ocean).

The absence of deep-sea sediment samples, older than late Mesozoic, poses a further problem. Is the Pacific crust newly developed? According to some new expanding-globe hypotheses, there would have been no Pacific depression in Paleozoic and so all of the floor must be new oceanic crust.

The marginal seas with their small basins of "new" oceanic crust and strong evidence for subsidence of submarine platforms suggest indeed a history of stretching and foundering. The thinning of former continental crust beneath them has been called "oceanization," "basification" or "basaltification" (Belousov and others); but the petrologic-geochemical nature of these processes has not been satisfactorily explained. Stille spoke of the "regeneration" of quasi-cratonic crust but refrained from postulating a mechanism. The "lost continents" of the marginal areas have received much attention and to geologists are so real that they have well-established names for them: *Tasmantis* (in the Tasman Sea region), *Archaeo Fijia* (in the Fiji Sea), the *Melanesian Continent* (generally in the Coral Sea, etc.), *Aequinoctia* (an equatorial land mass in the East Indies and New Guinea); Schuchert had a *Cascadia* (in the northeast), and von Huene had a land mass off South America; for these last two, we lack the same justification as there is for the western margin.

The orogenic belts of circum-Pacific folding, ever since Paleozoic time have been essentially parallel to the borders, and there is some evidence of growth toward the Pacific, as well as a "fretting away" by block faulting, etc., along the inner margins (eastern Australia, Greater Sunda archipelago, South China Sea, and eastern Asiatic mainland). For the Precambrian, we lack almost any trace of evidence in the marginal sea areas.

RHODES W. FAIRBRIDGE
JOSEPH L. REID, JR.
ERIC OLAUSSEN
M. N. A. PETERSON

References

Arrhenius, G., 1952, "Sediment cores from the East Pacific," *Reports of the Swedish Deep Sea Expedition*, 5.

Arrhenius, G., 1959, "Climatic Records on the Ocean Floor," Rossby Memorial Volume, New York, Rockefeller Institute Press.

Arrhenius, G., 1963, "Pelagic Sediments," in (Hill, M. N., editor) "The Sea," Vol. 3, p. 655, New York. Interscience Publishers.

Arrhenius, G., and Bonatti, E., 1964, "Neptunism and Vulcanism in the Ocean," in (Sears, M. N., editor) "Progress in Oceanography," New York, Pergamon Press.

Bader, F., 1960, "Die südhemisphärischen Coniferen als genetisches, geographisches und ökologisches Florenelement," *Erdkunde, Bonn*, 14, 303–308.

Benioff, V. H., 1958, "Circum-Pacific tectonics," *Dominion Obs., Publ.*, 20, *Ottawa*, (The mechanics of faulting), 395–402.

Benson, W. N., 1924, "The structural features of the margin of Australia," *Trans. New Zealand Inst.*, 55 (for 1923), 99–137.

Bien, G., Rakestraw, N., and Suess, H., 1960, "Radiocarbon concentration in Pacific Ocean water," *Tellus*, 12, 436–443.

Bonatti, E., and Arrhenius, G., 1965, "Colian sedimentation in the Pacific off Mexico," *Marine Geology, 3* (5), 337–348.

Born, A., 1933, "Der geologische Aufbau der Erde," *Handb. Geophys., Berlin*, 2, 565–867.

Boström, K., Bonatti, B., Holm, B., and Arrhenius, G., 1965, "Oceanic Baryte," (in press).

Bramlette, M. N., 1961, "Pelagic sediments," *Proc. Intern. Oceanogr. Congr.*, 1959, AAAS, Washington D.C.

Bryan, W. H., 1944, "The relationship of the Australian continent to the Pacific Ocean now and in the past," *J. Proc. Roy. Soc. N.S. Wales*, 78, 42–62.

Bullard, E. C., Maxwell, A. E., and Revelle, R., 1956, "Heat flow through the deep-sea floor," in (Landsberg, N., editor) *Advan. Geophys.*, 153–181.

Cromwell, T., Montgomery, R., and Stroup, E., 1954, "Equatorial undercurrent in Pacific Ocean, revealed by new methods," *Science*, 119, 648–649.

Dietz, R. S., 1954, "Marine geology of the N.W. Pacific. Japanese bathymetric chart 6901," *Bull. Soc. Geol. Am.*, 65, 1199–1224.

Dietz, R. S., and Menard, H. W., 1953, "Hawaiian swell, deep and arch," *J. Geol.*, 61, 99–113.

Dietz, R. S., Menard, H. W., and Hamilton, E. L., 1954, "Echograms of the Mid-Pacific Expedition," *Deep-Sea Res.*, 1, 258–272.

Escher, B. G., 1949, "Origin of the asymmetrical shape of the earth's surface and its consequence upon volcanism on earth and moon," *Bull. Geol. Soc. Am.*, 60, 353–362.

Fairbridge, R. W., 1961, "The Melanesian Border Plateau, a zone of crustal shearing in the S.W. Pacific," *Publ. Bur. Cent. Séismolog. Internat.*, 22, 137–149.

Fairbridge, R. W., 1962, "Basis for submarine nomenclature in the South-West Pacific Ocean," *Deut. Hydrograph. Z.*, 15.

Fairbridge, R. W., 1966, "Bathymetric features of the Melanesian region," *Deut. Hydrograph. Z.* (in press).

Fairbridge, R. W., and Stewart, H. B., Jr., 1960, "Alexa Bank, a drowned atoll on the Melanesian Border Plateau," *Deep-Sea Res.*, 7, 100–116.

Fisher, O., 1889, "Physics of the Earth's Crust," second ed., London.

Fisher, R. L., 1954, "On the sounding of trenches," *Deep-Sea Res.*, 2, 48–58.

Fleming, J. A., Sverdrup, H. U., Ennis, C. C., Seaton, S. L., and Hendrix, W. C., 1945, "Observations and results in physical oceanography, graphical and tabular summaries," *Carnegie Inst. Wash. Publ.*, 545, Scientific results of cruise VII of the *Carnegie* during 1928–1929 under command of Captain J. P. Ault, Oceanography, I–B, 315pp.

Goldberg, E. D., and Arrhenius, G., 1958, "Chemistry of Pacific pelagic sediments," *Geochm. Cosmochin. Acta*, 13, 153–212.

Griffin, J. J., and Goldberg, E. D., 1963, "Clay Mineral Distributions in Oceanic Areas," in "The Seas, Ideas and Observations," vol. 3, New York, Interscience Publishers.

Gutenberg, B., and Richter, C. F., 1950, "Seismicity of the Earth," Princeton, N.J., Princeton University Press, 273pp.

Harker, A., 1896, "The natural history of igneous rocks: I. Their geographical and chronological distribution," *Sci. Prog.*, 6, 12–33.

Hess, H. H., 1937, "Island arcs, gravity anomalies and serpentinite intrusions," *Rept. Intern. Geol. Congr.*, 17th, *Moscow*, 2, 263–283.

Hess, H. H., 1946, "Drowned ancient islands of the Pacific Basin," *Am. J. Sci.*, 244, 772–791.

Hess, H. H., 1948, "Major structural features of the western North Pacific," *Bull. Geol. Soc. Am.*, 59, 417–446.

Hobb, W. H., 1944, "Mountain growth, a study of the Southwestern Pacific region," *Proc. Am. Philos. Soc.*, 88, 221–268.

Jensen, H. I., 1908, "The distribution, origin and relationships of alkaline rocks," *Proc. Linnean Soc. N.S. Wales*, 33, 491–588.

Jersey, N. J. de, 1946, "Seismological evidence bearing on crustal thickness in the S.W. Pacific," *Univ. Queensland Papers, n.s.*, 3, 1–18.

Jousé, A., 1960, "Les diatomées des dépôts de fond de la partie nordouest de l'Océan Pacifique," *Deep-Sea Res.*, 6, 187–192.

Knauss, J., 1960, "Measurements of the Cromwell Current," *Deep-Sea Res.*, 6, 265–286.

Kuenen, P. H., 1935, "Geological interpretation of the bathymetrical results," *The Snellins Expedition*, 5, Pt. 1, 124pp.

Kuenen, R. N., 1950, "Marine Geology," New York, John Wiley and Sons, 568pp.

Lacroix, A., 1941, "Composition minéralogique et chimique des laves volcans des îles de l'Océan Pacifique situées entre l'Equateur et le Tropique du Capricorne, le 175 de longitude ouest et le 165 de longitude est," *Mém. Ac. Sc. France*, 63, 97pp.

Lake, P., 1931, "Mountains and island arcs," *Geol. Mag.*, 68, 34–39.

Landergren, S., 1964, "Geochemistry of Deep-Sea Sediments," *Reports of the Swedish Deep-Sea Expedition* 1947–48, 10.

Lisitzin, A. P., 1960, "Bottom sediments of the eastern Antarctic and southern Indian Ocean," *Deep-Sea Res.*, 7, 89–99.

Mackintosh, N. A., 1964, "Distribution of the plankton in relation to the Antarctic Convergence," *Proc. Roy. Soc., London Ser. A*, 281, 21–38.

Marshall, P., 1912, "Oceania," *Handb. der Regionale Geologie, Heidelberg,* **7,** No. 5, Sect. 1, 36pp.

Mason, R. G., 1958, "A magnetic survey off the west coast of the United States between latitudes 32° and 36°N and longitudes 121° and 128°W," *Geophys. J.,* **1,** 320–329.

Mason, R. G., and Raff, A. D., 1961, "Magnetic survey off the west coast of North America, 32°N latitude to 42°N latitude," *Bull. Geol. Soc. Am.,* **72,** 1259–1266.

McIntyre, D. B., and Christie, J. M., 1958, "The kinematics of faulting from seismic data," *Publ. Dominion Obs. Ottawa,* **20,** 385–393.

Menard, H. W., 1955, "Deformation of the northeastern Pacific basin and the west coast of North America," *Bull. Geol. Soc. Am.,* **66,** 1149–1198.

Menard, H. W., 1956, "Archipelagic aprons," *Bull. Am. Assoc. Petrol. Geologists,* **40,** 2195–2210.

Menard, H. W., 1964, "Marine Geology of the Pacific," New York, McGraw-Hill Book Co., 271pp.

Murray, J., 1888, "On the height of the land and the depth of the ocean," *Scott. Geogr. Mag.,* **4,** 1–41.

Murray, J., and Lee, G. W., 1909, "The depth and marine deposits of the Pacific," *Mem. Mus. Comp. Zoo. Harvard,* **38,** No. 1, 169pp.

Murray, J., and Renard, A. F., 1891, "Deep-sea deposits," *Report on the voyage of H.M.S. Challenger* 1873–1876, 525pp.

NORPAC Committee, 1960, "Oceanic Observations of the Pacific: 1955, the NORPAC Atlas," Berkeley and Tokyo, University of California Press and University of Tokyo Press, 123 plates.

NORPAC Committee, 1960, "Oceanic Observations of the Pacific: 1955, the NORPAC Data," Berkeley and Tokyo, University of California Press and University of Tokyo Press, 532pp.

Officer, C. B., 1955, "Southwest Pacific crustal structures," *Trans. Am. Geophys. Union,* **36,** 449–459.

Oliver, J. E., Ewing, M., and Press, F., 1955, "Atlantic and Pacific ocean basins," *Bull. Geol. Soc. Am.,* **66,** 913–946.

Raff, A. D., and Mason, R. G., 1961, "Magnetic survey off the west coast of North America, 40°N latitude to 52°N latitude," *Bull. Geol. Soc. Am.,* **72,** 1267–1270.

Raitt, W. R., 1956, "Seismic-refraction studies of the Pacific Ocean basin. Pt. I: Crustal thickness of the central equatorial Pacific," *Bull. Geol. Soc. Am.,* **67,** 1623–1640.

Raitt, W. R., Fisher, R. L., and Mason, R. G., 1955, "Tonga Trench," *Geol. Soc. Am. Spec. Papers,* **62,** 237–254.

Reid, J. L., Jr., 1961, "On the geostrophic flow at the surface of the Pacific Ocean with respect to the 1000-decibar surface," *Tellus,* **13,** 489–502.

Reid, J. L., Jr., 1962, "On the circulation, phosphate-phosphorus content and zooplankton volumes in the upper part of the Pacific Ocean," *Limnol. Oceanogr.,* **7,** 287–306.

Revelle, R. E., 1944, "Marine bottom samples collected in the Pacific Ocean by the *Carnegie* on its seventh cruise," *Carnegie Inst. Wash. Publ.,* **556,** Pt. 1, 180pp.

Revelle, R., *et al.,* 1955, "Pelagic sediments of the Pacific," *Geol. Soc. Am. Spec. Papers,* **62,** 221–236.

Riedel, W. R., and Funnell, B. M., 1964, "Tertiary sediment cores and microfossils from the Pacific Ocean floor," *Quart. J. Geol. Soc. London,* **120,** 305–368.

Schott, G., 1935, "Geographie des Indischen und Stillen Ozeans," Hamburg, Boysen.

Shepard, F. P., 1964, "Marine Geology," Second ed., Harper and Row, New York, 557pp.

Stille, H., 1944, "Geotektonische Probleme des pazifischen Erdraumes," *Preuss. Akad. Wiss., Math. Nat. Kl.,* 100pp.

*Sverdrup, H. U., Johnson, M. W., and Fleming, R. H., 1942, "The Oceans: Their Physics, Chemistry, and General Biology," New York, Prentice-Hall, 1087pp., 7 charts.

Talwani, M., Worzel, J. L., and Ewing, W. M., 1961, "Gravity anomalies and crustal section across the Tonga Trench," *J. Geophys. Res.,* **66,** 1265–1278.

Vacquier, V., Raff, A. D., and Warren, R. E., 1961, "Horizontal displacements on the floor of the northeastern Pacific Ocean," *Bull. Geol. Soc. Am.,* **72,** 1251–1258.

Valentin, H., 1952, "Die Küsten der Erde," *Peterm. Geogr. Mitt.,* **246.**

Vening-Meinesz, F. A., Umbgrove, J. H. F., and Kuenen, P. H., 1934, "Gravity expeditions at sea, 1923–1932," Vol. 2, *Publ. Netherlands Geodetic Commission, Delft,* **2.**

Von Herzen, R., and S. Uyeda, 1963, "Heat flow through the eastern Pacific Ocean floor," *J. Geophvs. Res.,* **68,** 4219–4250.

Wooster, W., and Volkman, G., 1960, "Indications of deep Pacific circulation from the distribution of properties at five kilometers," *J. Geophys. Res.,* **65,** 1239–1249.

A fundamental and continuing source of information about the Pacific is the Pacific Science Association (secretariat, Bishop Museum, Honolulu 17, Hawaii). Series of congresses have been held over the last half century, the 10th congress being held in Honolulu in 1961, and the 11th congress in Tokyo, 1966; many of the congress proceedings are still in print.

Cross-references: *Aleutian Current; California Current: East Australian Current; Equatorial Current; Kuroshio Current; Peru Current; Southern Ocean* (see also under all Marginal Seas).

PACK ICE—*See* SEA ICE

PELAGIC BIOGEOCHEMISTRY

The word pelagos implies "of the open ocean," i.e., that part of the world oceans far removed from the influence of the continents. The sediments which cover the floor of the open ocean are referred to as pelagic deposits in contrast to the terrigenous deposits characteristic of the coastal areas and primarily made of the clays, silt, and sands carried by rivers into the sea. Pelagic deposits cover some 70% of the floor of the ocean or about 50% of the earth's surface. Nearly all of the material which constitutes the pelagic sediments settles from the overlying water, although contributions by underwater volcanic activities and from surrounding topographic features by sliding,

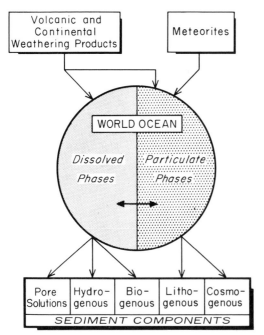

Fig. 1. Sources of material received by the world ocean and its eventual sedimentologic products (from Goldberg, 1964).

slumping and turbidity currents introduce local factors of considerable importance.

The material settling from the water column has its origin in the continental land masses, extraterrestrial (planetary) sources, the atmosphere, or the water medium proper and its biological population (Fig. 1). Constituents of pelagic sediments which come from land (lithosphere) and are transported to the open ocean by currents and water motion are known as *lithogenous* components, while particles transported or originating in the atmosphere are called *atmogenous* components. Meteoritic material has its birth in extraterrestrial planetary bodies and is constantly being received by the planet earth. Micrometeorites are also known as meteoritic dust or cosmic showers. They reach the sea surface and settle to the bottom contributing the *cosmogenous* components of deep-sea sediments.

In the water medium, chemical reactions take place between the ions and molecules in solution giving rise to insoluble compounds such as the hydrated oxides of iron and manganese, calcium carbonate, and calcium and iron phosphates which also accumulate on the bottom and constitute what oceanographers refer to as the *hydrogenous* fraction of the deep-sea sediments. The hydrogenous precipitation of iron, manganese, calcium, and other elements is controlled by the solubility product of the compounds, and the mechanism is a chemical one.

The world oceans receive large quantities of calcium from river runoff, indeed sufficient to double the calcium budget of the ocean waters in about one million years if the element were not removed from seawater. Revelle and Fairbridge (1957) calculated that this would give rise to 0.66 gram of carbonate per square centimeter per thousand years for the entire ocean floor. Calcium carbonate can be removed inorganically from seawater by the interaction of the dissolved calcium and carbonate ions forming the hydrogenous component of deep-sea sediments. Another important mechanism for the removal of calcium carbonate from seawater is a biological one and involves marine organisms which concentrate calcium in the form of calcareous shells or skeletons protecting their soft protoplasm. On death, sinking, and decay, the soft organic material decomposes, and the hard shells and skeletal remains accumulate on the bottom as the *biogenous* component of the sediments.

The removal, concentration, and transformations of chemical elements and their compounds from seawater and the corresponding energy changes brought about by marine organisms are the subjects of biogeochemistry. In this area of investigation, mention should be made of the physical-chemical changes caused by marine organisms and the microbial population of the deposits themselves. In Table 1 is illustrated the ability of marine organisms to remove and concentrate chemical elements from seawater.

Several of the elements whose existence in seawater has not been experimentally observed can be verified from analysis of the marine organisms and their skeletal remains.

Surface adsorption is another mechanism by which marine organisms remove and concentrate elements from seawater. In this case, elements are adsorbed on the surface of the organism or on their metabolic products and on the naturally occurring particulate matter which is filtered by the biosphere.

In the process of uptake, organisms are selective and exhibit a high degree of specificity for the physical-chemical and oxidation states of elements. Seawater in which trace metals exist in the presence of high concentrations of ligands (complexing agents), such as the chloride ion which constitutes 55% of dissolved solids, fluorides, phosphates and sulfates, is a favorable medium for the formation of complex compounds. The formation of complexes tend to stabilize elements in solution and increase their concentration above that controlled by the solubility product. Organic compounds from the metabolic activities of marine organisms are also effective complexing agents. Goldberg (1952) demonstrated that a marine diatom, *Asterionella Japonica*, utilizes only particulate and/or colloidal iron as a nutrient, whereas iron

TABLE 1. ENRICHMENT FACTORS OF SELECTED ELEMENTS IN MARINE ORGANISMS OVER SEAWATER; DRY WEIGHTS OF ORGANISMS ARE USED (FROM NODDACK AND NODDACK, 1939)

Vanadium	280,000
Iron	86,000
Manganese	41,000
Nickel	41,000
Silver	22,000
Cobalt	21,000
Titanium	10,000
Copper	7,500
Molybdenum	6,000
Chromium	1,400
Gold	1,400

in the ferric state present as complex ions with citrate, ascorbate, or artificial humate is not taken up by the diatom.

The bulk of particulate matter in the sea is in the form of charged colloidal particles which are effective scavengers of the oppositely charged ions in solution. From a study of the chemical composition of manganese nodules and associated pelagic clays, Goldberg (1957) postulated that titanium and zirconium should exist as anions in seawater since they are enriched in the positively charged hydrated oxides of iron.

High concentrations of quartz particles about $3-30\mu$ in diameter have been observed in pelagic sediments of the open ocean. The quartz particles are believed to have originated on land and been transported to the open sea from deserts by wind. Quartz particles may take a few years to settle through a water column a few miles deep before reaching the bottom. Such particles should, therefore, be detectable in the water proper, and one should be able to filter the water and extract them. El Wardani (1957) and, more recently, Ewing and Thorndike (1965) and Groot and Ewing (1963) did not find mineral particles in surface waters from the open ocean. However, on filtering deep waters from about 4000 meters, Groot and Ewing found surprisingly large quantities of mineral particles apart from some organisms. Ewing and Thorndike, using an optical nephelometer, detected turbid layers in the deep waters 2000–4500 meters off the East Coast of the United States. On sampling the layers, which they gave the name "nepheloid layers," they found them to be a suspension of lutite (clay-sized mineral particles).

The question arises as to how and by what mechanisms surface waters become impoverished, and also how the deep waters, well above the influence of the bottom, become enriched with mineral particles. El Wardani (1957), from a study of the body contents of planktonic microscopic filter feeders such as copepods and salps, postulated

that the biosphere of filter feeders is responsible for sweeping the surface waters clean of the mineral particles. A filter feeder with a nucleus 1 mm or more in diameter may ingest many particles of $1-10\mu$ in diameter. It is possible that the organisms utilize the organic slime adhered to the surface of the mineral particles and, because of the high rate of filtration, the time such particles spend in the water is small compared to that spent in the organism. On death and sinking, however, the organisms decay and their load of mineral particles, along with skeletal remains of the ingested diatoms, dinoflagellates, and colloidal particulate matter, are released to the water at great depths where the decaying of the organism is completed. Marine organisms, especially filter feeders, are, therefore, powerful biogeochemical agents for concentrating mineral particles from the surface waters and transporting the particles to the deeper water where they may become concentrated in layers and reach equilibrium with the fraction settling out to the bottom.

Our knowledge of the biogeochemical cycle of elements and matter in the sea is inadequate and at best only qualitative. The physical-chemical state and complex formation of elements in seawater, the chemical composition of marine organisms, the mechanisms of biological uptake of elements from the environment, chemical changes brought about by marine organisms, interbiological interactions, postdepositional changes, the geographical and density distribution of filter

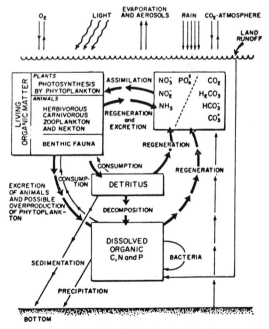

Fig. 2. A biogeochemical cycle for phosphorus and other nutrients in the sea (after Dursma).

feeders and their pumping rates, are but some of the areas in which research efforts and quantitative information are needed to better understand the problems of pelagic biogeochemistry. It is also evident from the foregoing material that biogeochemical processes in the sea are of considerable significance if we are to predict the fate and environmental history of radioactivity associated with nuclear waste, should the latter find its way accidentally or intentionally to the sea.

S. A. EL WARDANI

References

Dursma, E. K., 1961, "Dissolved organic carbon, nitrogen, and phosphorus in the sea," *Netherlands J. Sea Res.*, **1**, 1–147.

El Wardani, S. A., 1957, "On the biogeochemistry of igneous detritus," *J. Deep-Sea Res.*, **4**, 219–220.

Ewing, M., and Thorndike, 1965, "Suspended matter in deep ocean water," *Science*, **147**, 1291–1294.

Goldberg, E. D., 1952, "Iron assimilation by marine diatoms," *Biol. Bull.*, **102**, 243–248.

Goldberg, E. D., 1957, "Biogeochemistry of trace metals," *Geol. Soc. Am. Mem. No.* 67, **1**, 345.

Goldberg, E. D., 1964, "The oceans as a geological system," *Trans. N.Y. Acad. Sci., Ser.* 2, **27**, 7–19.

Groot, J. J., and Ewing, M., 1963, "Suspended clay in a water sample from the deep ocean," *Science*, **142**, 579–580.

Noddack, I., and Noddack, W., 1939, "Die Haufigkeiten Der Schwermetalle in Meerestieren," *Arkiv Zool.*, **32A**, 1–35.

Revelle, R., and Fairbridge, R., 1957, "Carbonates and carbon dioxide," *Geol. Soc. Am. Mem. No.* 67, **1**, 244.

PELAGIC DISTRIBUTION

(I) Pelagic

The oceans can be divided for study into the benthic realm, or sea bottom, and the pelagic realm, or open seawater. Pelagic organisms float or swim freely in the water; benthic organisms rest on, are attached to, or burrow into the sea bottom. With depths exceeding 10,000 meters, and an average depth of 3800 meters (nearly $2\frac{1}{2}$ miles), there is more "living room" in the pelagial realm than in any other earth environment. Pelagic distribution refers to the location, concentration, and arrangement of life in the ocean waters. (For discussions of the structure and physical-chemical nature of the pelagic realm, see *Bathymetry, Chemical Oceanography, Equatorial Currents, Ocean Currents, Oceanic Circulation Patterns, Temperature Structure in the Sea* and *Water Masses.*)

All pelagic life is divided into three somewhat artificial categories—phytoplankton, zooplankton, and nekton.

(a) Phytoplankton. This term includes the free-floating and drifting plants of the sea (such as Sargassum weed, a brown alga), the more abundant

and important microscopic diatoms, dinoflagellates, some blue-green algae, many groups of smaller photosynthetic flagellates, coccolithophores and photosynthetic bacteria. The heterotrophic bacteria, viruses, and fungi are not included in this common classification (see Oppenheimer, 1963).

(b) Zooplankton. This includes all animals unable to swim effectively against the horizontal currents of the oceans. Although usually small, size is *not* the distinctive feature of zooplankton. There are giant jellyfish that are weak swimmers and thus are members of the zooplankton. Chains of the lesser known pelagic tunicates *Salpa* may reach lengths of more than 5 meters, with single individuals almost 25 cm long. The luminescent colonial tunicate, *Pyrosoma,* may grow larger than a large watermelon. The Portuguese man-o-war, *Physalia,* may approach the size of a football.

The most abundant members of the zooplankton are the largely herbivorous crustacean copepods and euphausiids, and the carnivorous chaetognaths. Other animal groups such as the Foraminifera, Tunicata, Amphipoda, Mollusca, Coelenterata, Ctenophora, Pteropoda, and Radiolaria may sporadically become locally dominant but generally make up less than 50% of the total zooplankton biomass. In neritic waters (from the shore out to depths of 200 meters), the meroplankton (temporary plankton), composed of the eggs and larval stages of benthic and nektonic organisms, usually forms a large part of the zooplankton.

(c) Nekton. Nekton includes all animals able to swim effectively against the horizontal ocean currents for prolonged periods of time and thus able to make long migrations. Examples are fur seals which migrate from the Pribilof Islands to Southern California, whales and dolphins, tunas, swordfish, sharks and other fish including such small fish as herring which are known to migrate from Iceland to Norway (see *Nekton* for more detail). It is probably in the area of the migration of nekton that the study of pelagic distribution has its greatest economic application. The bluefin tuna of the Atlantic can migrate from the Bahamas to Norway, a distance of at least 4500 miles. The smaller Pacific albacore tuna migrates from the North Central Pacific to both Japan and California. In such cases, regulation of only one of the fishing fleets may not be effective and proper management of such populations becomes a matter of international negotiation.

(II) Factors Involved

(a) Biotic Factors. The distribution of any species is determined by biotic and physical-chemical factors. The chief biotic factors are: behaviour, reproduction, predation, and food supply. Behaviour includes the extensive migrations of the nekton, to facilitate feeding and/or reproduction. The California Grey Whale, for example,

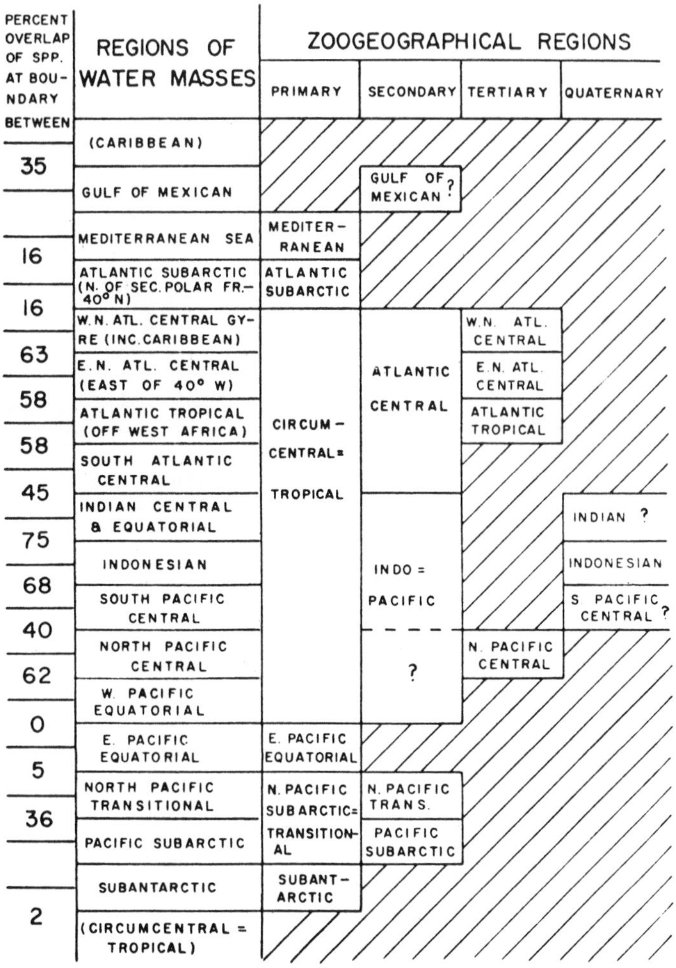

PERCENT OVERLAP OF SPP. AT BOUNDARY BETWEEN	REGIONS OF WATER MASSES	ZOOGEOGRAPHICAL REGIONS			
		PRIMARY	SECONDARY	TERTIARY	QUATERNARY
	(CARIBBEAN)				
35	GULF OF MEXICAN		GULF OF MEXICAN ?		
16	MEDITERRANEAN SEA	MEDITERRANEAN			
16	ATLANTIC SUBARCTIC (N. OF SEC. POLAR FR.—40° N)	ATLANTIC SUBARCTIC			
63	W.N. ATL. CENTRAL GYRE (INC. CARIBBEAN)		ATLANTIC CENTRAL	W.N. ATL. CENTRAL	
58	E.N. ATL. CENTRAL (EAST OF 40° W)			E.N. ATL. CENTRAL	
58	ATLANTIC TROPICAL (OFF WEST AFRICA)	CIRCUM-CENTRAL = TROPICAL		ATLANTIC TROPICAL	
45	SOUTH ATLANTIC CENTRAL				
75	INDIAN CENTRAL & EQUATORIAL				INDIAN ?
68	INDONESIAN		INDO = PACIFIC		INDONESIAN
40	SOUTH PACIFIC CENTRAL				S PACIFIC CENTRAL ?
62	NORTH PACIFIC CENTRAL		?	N. PACIFIC CENTRAL	
0	W. PACIFIC EQUATORIAL				
5	E. PACIFIC EQUATORIAL	E. PACIFIC EQUATORIAL			
36	NORTH PACIFIC TRANSITIONAL	N. PACIFIC SUBARCTIC = TRANSITIONAL	N. PACIFIC TRANS.		
	PACIFIC SUBARCTIC		PACIFIC SUBARCTIC		
2	SUBANTARCTIC	SUBANTARCTIC			
	(CIRCUMCENTRAL = TROPICAL)				

Fig. 1. Faunal boundaries, regions, and sub-regions associated with water masses and based on distributions of 135 species of bathypelagic fishes representing 18 genera (Ebeling, 1962). (This plate contains some minor errors, e.g., "Gulf of Mexican" should read "Gulf of Mexico.")

feeds on zooplankton in the Bering Sea in the summer and migrates in winter to the bays of Lower California (a distance of some 2000 miles) to bear young and to mate. In spring, the adults and young return to the Bering Sea to feed. Thus, in many nektonic species only a small part of the total possible range is occupied at any one time. The behaviour of nekton leads to very uneven or patchy distribution.

Zooplankton may also congregate for feeding or reproduction, usually in the upper 30–50 meters of the sea. Although more easily distributed by currents, many zooplankton groups can control their horizontal distribution either by vertical migration into different ocean currents or by reproductive cycles or both.

Phytoplankton are almost completely dependent on the currents for distribution; however, repro-

ductive cycles with resting stages on the bottom or in deeper water allows some control of distribution.

Ignoring patchiness, the average abundance of a pelagic species in a given area within its range is largely determined by available food, which is ultimately dependent on the supply of mineral nutrients to the phytoplankton. Thus the highest reported concentrations of nekton and zooplankton are in regions of upwelling of mineral nutrients along the eastern temperate sides of the oceans, in regions of marked seasonal overturn of water as in the subarctic and subantarctic, or in areas of nutrient replenishment from the land, especially in bays and estuaries. Special circulation features of the equatorial regions lead to mineral replacement there with resulting standing crops larger at all levels of the food web than in the central water masses to the north or south. The lowest standing crops of

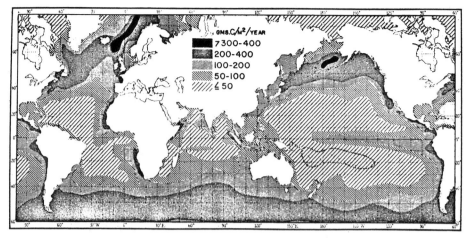

Fig. 2. Estimation of the organic production in the oceans, adapted from Fleming and Laevastu (1956). The contours are in grams of carbon biologically fixed under each square meter of sea surface per year. The area delineated by a dotted line in the central South Pacific—an area of many island chains—is probably more highly productive than indicated by the hatching.

phytoplankton, zooplankton and nekton are found in the warm central water masses (Figs. 1 and 2).

(b) Physical-chemical Factors and Horizontal Distribution. The study of pelagic distribution in early years focused largely on physical-chemical factors limiting the range of species. Temperature received the most attention, but there is still little agreement on what physical factors limit either horizontal or vertical ranges in the sea. Most workers agree with Giesbrech's division of the pelagic realm into three great provinces, *northern* and *southern cold water provinces* separated by a *warm water belt*. On the western sides of the oceans, this warm water belt extends to 45–50°N and S latitude. On the eastern margins it is much narrower, extending only to about 18–20°N and S latitude (Fig. 1; also see illustration in *Water Masses*). No agreement has been reached on finer subdivisions of the warm water belt, although recent work in the Pacific has emphasized the close relationship between species limits and the limits of water masses with their characteristic temperature-salinity-circulation patterns (see illustration in *Water Masses*). In the Pacific there appear to be unique faunas and probably floras in each water mass as well as in the transition regions between water masses. Thus it is possible to distinguish a Western North Pacific Central Fauna, an Eastern North Pacific Central Fauna, a California Current Fauna, an Equatorial Fauna that extends into the Indian Ocean, a Northern Transition Fauna, and a Subarctic Fauna (see Bieri, 1959; Bradshaw, 1959; Brinton, 1962; Ebeling, 1962; references in Brinton, 1962; Banse, 1964).

(III) Vertical Distribution and Migration

Vertical zonation of pelagic organisms is indi-

cated in the classification of marine environments discussed in *Marine Ecology*. There is as yet little agreement on the degree and nature of the zonation because of insufficient work below the 200–meter epipelagic region; complications due to seasonal, ontogenetic and daily migrations obscure zonation if it exists. Also, the depths of the water masses vary in different parts of the oceans leading to different results in different areas. There is considerable evidence that many mesopelagic (approximately 200–700 meters) and even bathypelagic (approximately 700–4000 meters) species have horizontal range limits that correspond closely to the upper (0–500 meters) water masses. This is due to the fact that the larvae and young of many of these species live in relatively narrow depth ranges near the surface (see Ebeling, 1962).

Bruun (in Hedgpeth, 1957) has vertically divided pelagic life of the warm water belt into the epipelagic zone where there is sufficient light for phytoplankton production of organic matter and the dimly lit mesopelagic zone extending below to the 10°C isotherm. Below this is the bathypelagic zone reaching to the 4°C isotherm and below this isotherm the abyssopelagic zone extending to depths of 6000 meters. In the Atlantic Ocean, his boundary of 4°C between the bathypelagic and abyssopelagic zones occurs at about 2000 meters, while in the Indian and Pacific Oceans it would be as high as 1500–1000 meters.

Vertical migration is a common phenomenon in many nekton and zooplankton species. Daily migrations from depths of 500 meters and greater are known for lantern fishes and euphausiids in the deep scattering layer (see *Deep Scattering Layer*). Seasonal migrations from the upper 100 meters to depths of 1000 meters and greater are known for

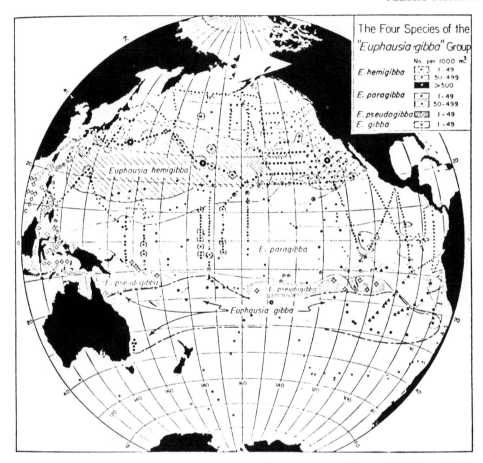

Fig. 3. Geographical distribution of the four species of the "*Euphausia gibba* group" (Brinton, 1962).

many copepods and some chaetognaths in the sub-polar and polar regions. Ontogenetic migrations to depths of 1000 meters have been demonstrated in many species of fish and invertebrates. See Cassie (1963) and Banse (1964) for comprehensive reviews of vertical distribution.

(IV) Dispersive Forces

The dispersive forces of currents and eddy diffusion tend to distribute pelagic populations throughout the world oceans. Extremes of temperature, salinity, oxygen, and mineral and organic nutrients may limit this dispersal. But in addition to these limiting factors, there are concentrating forces that tend to prevent completely random dispersal. Although the study of these concentrating forces is just beginning, four, perhaps five, fundamental concentrating mechanisms are known.

(V) Concentrating Mechanisms

A *vertical circulation cell* of pelagic organisms can be maintained by diurnal or seasonal vertical migration into currents going in opposite directions.

For example, M. W. Johnson (1949; see references of J. W. Wells, in Hedgpeth, 1957) showed that the zooplankton in Bikini lagoon is 4–5 times as concentrated as in the open ocean outside. The concentration is due largely to the vertical migration of the zooplankton during the day into a near-bottom countercurrent that prevents its being swept out of the lagoon into the open ocean. The retention of the zooplankton and its subsequent decay leads to an enrichment of the lagoon waters.

The *horizontal circulation cell* may be local and temporary as in short-lived eddies or oceanic in scale and permanent, lasting for thousands of years. Biori (1959; reference in Banse, 1964) and Brinton (1962) have shown that some species of chaetognaths and euphausiids live only within the huge circulating cells of the North and South Pacific Central Waters (Fig. 3).

A *toroidal circulation cell,* a combination of horizontal and vertical circulation cells, has been postulated by Boden (1952) and Boden and Kampa (1953) as a conserving mechanism for the mero-plankton around Bermuda (see references of J. W.

Wells, in Hedgpeth, 1957). Lagoon water, made more dense in summer by evaporation and in winter by cooling, spreads out from the island and mixes with oceanic water. This produces locally more dense water that sinks to moderate depth and may return larval forms to the vicinity of the island.

Line concentrating forces may be local or oceanic in scale. Best known are the equatorial convergences which may concentrate phytoplankton, zooplankton and nekton over distances of hundreds of miles as the result of the coming together of two nearly parallel ocean currents. On a smaller scale, Langmuir circulation cells are often seen at sea with long rows of debris concentrated in the zones of convergence. Fronts between cold and warm water may develop temporarily and concentrate pelagic life into lines.

Eddy diffusion, generally thought of as a dispersive force, may permit some zooplankton species to exist in local areas where the horizontal currents are weak. M. W. Johnson in 1960 suggested this in the case of the larvae of the spiny lobster, *Panulirus interruptus.* Such a mechanism may account for the existence of some neritic species of zooplankton, especially on the eastern sides of the oceans where currents are more sluggish.

(VI) Methods of Study

Although descriptive, experimental, and theoretical methods are available for the study of pelagic distribution, the latter two methods have been largely ignored. The massive size of the oceans and the continued difficulty of working at sea would indicate that much more attention should be paid to these latter two approaches. Even with the concerted use of all three methods, it will be many years before we reach a reasonably good understanding of pelagic distribution.

(VII) Relationship to Geology

Pelagic distribution is closely related to many paleoecologic studies. Pleistocene changes in the location of the major cold-warm-cold division have already been shown in studies of pelagic foraminifera from deepsea cores. Neritic waters should be distinguishable by their high content of larval forms of benthic invertebrates. Nektonic forms should be more patchy in distribution than zooplankton, and because they seldom occupy their total possible range at any one time, their remains may be more difficult to interpret. At present, most investigators relate the limits of ranges of pelagic species to patterns of temperature, salinity, and circulation.

ROBERT BIERI

References

*Banse, K., 1964, "On the vertical distribution of zooplankton in the sea," *Progress in Oceanography,* **2**, 53–125.

Brinton, E., 1962, "The distribution of Pacific Euphausiids," *Bull. Scripps Inst. Oceanogr.,* **8**(2), 51–270.

*Cassie, R. M., 1963, "Microdistribution of plankton," *Oceanogr. Mar. Biol. Ann. Rev.,* **1**, 223–252.

Ebeling, A. W., 1962, "Melamphaidae I," Copenhagen, *Dana Report,* **58**.

Fleming, R. H., and Laevastu, T., 1956, "The influence of hydrographic conditions on the behaviour of fish," *FAO Fisheries Bull.,* **9**(4), 181–196.

*Hedgpeth, J. W. (editor), 1957, "Treatise on Marine Ecology and Paleoecology," Vol. I, "Ecology," *Geol. Soc. Am. Mem.* 67, 1296pp.

*Oppenheimer, C. H. (editor), 1963, "Symposium on Marine Microbiology," Springfield, Ill., C. C. Thomas, 769pp.

PELAGIC LIFE

Pelagic life (Greek: *pelagios,* of the sea), a widely inclusive term, encompasses all living organisms which either swim or drift passively in the ocean. Explicitly excluded are the *benthos* (Greek: *benthos,* depth of the sea), forms of life attached or creeping on the ocean floor. Pelagic organisms are classified according to their ability to move themselves through the water. Actively swimming animals are termed *nekton* (Greek: *nektos,* swimming) and include most of the cartilaginous elasmobranchs and bony fishes, squid, some crustacea, and all marine mammals such as porpoises and whales. The term "epi-pelagic" is applied to those open-sea organisms found far from the coast and near the surface, i.e., under 100 m or so ("photic zone"), "meso-pelagic" 100–1000 m, "bathy-pelagic" 1000–4000 m, and "abysso-pelagic" 4000–10,000 m (Hedgpeth, 1957).

More diverse assemblages of pelagic life are included among those organisms which drift passively in the water, the *plankton* (Greek: *planktos,* wandering). Among planktonic organisms of the sea are animals, the *zooplankton* (Greek: *zoon,* animal), and plants, the *phytoplankton* (Greek: *phyton,* plant).

The zooplankton include, at some time during their life history, representatives of virtually every invertebrate phylum. Members of the zooplankton differ widely in size and complexity, from the large siphonophores, such as the Portuguese man-of-war found in the Gulf Stream, to the minute Radiolaria and Foraminifera, protozoa which are distributed throughout much of the oceans of the world. The temporary plankton or meroplankton, consisting of the eggs and larvae of the benthos and nekton, may at certain times of the year make up a large fraction of the zooplankton of inshore regions.

The phytoplankton include mostly minute single-celled forms of plants, diatoms and dino-flagellates, and certain species of blue-green algae. Larger drifting plants such as Sargassum may also be considered phytoplankton.

The phytoplankton are the primary producers of organic matter in the sea. Production is accomplished by photosynthesis, a process which utilizes energy derived from sunlight and inorganic materials obtained from seawater. A large proportion of the zooplankton are herbivores, particularly the microcrustaceans. Those zooplankton organisms which are herbivores serve as a link between primary producers and many of the larger carnivorous nektonic organisms.

Because of their light requirement, the phytoplankton are restricted to approximately the upper 100 m. Nekton and zooplankton are distributed throughout all known regions and depths of the ocean from the neritic waters over the continental shelves to the oceanic regions of the open sea and from the surface epipelagic zone to the abyssal depths of the ocean.

RUDOLF S. SCHELTEMA

References

Hardy, A. C., 1956, "The Open Sea—Its Natural History: "The World of Plankton," Boston, Houghton Mifflin Co., 335pp.

Hardy, A. C., 1959, "The Open Sea—Its Natural History," Part II, "Fish and Fisheries" with chapters on whales, turtles and animals on the sea floor, London, Collins, 322pp.

Hedgpeth, J. W., 1957, "Classification of marine environments," *Geol. Soc. Am., Mem.* 67, **1**, 17–28.

PELAGIC SEDIMENTS—*See* MARINE SEDIMENTS

PERSIAN GULF

The region of the Persian Gulf is one of great interest to mankind. The Mesopotamian plains in the northwest were the site of some of the earliest civilizations of human history. Today, because of the vast oil resources, the area is potentially one of the richest regions of the earth's crust. Considerable work has been done on the geology of the land areas surrounding the Persian Gulf. Compilations of the results and useful reviews have been given in Lees and Richardson (1940), Henson (1951), and Lees (1953). Some marine biological work was done by Melville, Staden and Blegvad, and some early oceanographic work by Schott and Schulz. The oceanography and marine geology, however, was not studied in detail until quite recently when Emery, Houbolt, Sugden and others studied the region (see references in Emery, 1956; Houbolt, 1957; Evans, 1965).

Dimensions and Bathymetry

This arm of the Indian Ocean has an area of 92,500 square miles (239,000 km²). Its water volume is only 6000 km³. Its length is 615 miles and it varies in width from a maximum of 210 to a minimum of 35 miles in the Straits of Hormuz. Its mean depth is 14 fathoms. It is rarely deeper than 50 fathoms (Fig. 1), although deeper water is found, greater than 60 fathoms, at its entrance. Some greater depths, up to 93 fathoms, are found at various localities within the Gulf. The deepest water is found near the Persian shore and is separated into an eastern and western area connected, through a narrow depression, by a shoal region about seventy miles inside the Straits of Hormuz. Whereas the deeper water is separated from the Persian coast by a narrow shoal area, a broad area, less than 20 fathoms in depth, occupies the southwestern side of the Gulf, being best developed in the south and narrowing toward the head of the Gulf.

Numerous islands and shoals are present, some representing crests of folds or salt plugs and others merely depositional features composed of unconsolidated and partially consolidated Quaternary deposits.

Climate

Temperatures are high, but winters are quite cool particularly at the head of the Gulf (see Table 1). The rainfall is small and is slightly higher in the northeast. It falls mainly as a few brief downpours from November to April. The relative humidity is high. Cloud cover is small but greater in winter than summer. Thunderstorms and fogs are rare in the region. Dust storms and haze occur frequently in summer time. The most common and strongest wind is the *shamal*, which blows from between north-northwest and west-northwest. This wind seldom reaches a strength of Beaufort force 6 and rarely Beaufort force 8. Squalls with waterspouts are common, particularly in autumn. The wind has been recorded to attain speeds of 95 mph in five minutes.

Oceanography

The data are sparse and result mainly from the work of Emery (1956), Sugden (1963) and others. The Gulf has a small freshwater inflow from the Tigris-Euphrates and Karun rivers at its head and also from intermittent streams on the Persian coast. The water temperature is high varying from 75–90°F in the entrance and from 60–90°F in the extreme northwest, with higher values in the shallow waters along the coasts. High salinities result from small freshwater inflow, high temperatures and evaporation in excess of the freshwater ingress. Salinities range from 37–38‰ in the entrance of the Gulf to 38–41‰ in the extreme northwest, depending in the latter upon river flow. Even greater salinities 42–60‰ are recorded from the coastal areas around the southwestern shore. It appears that water moves into the Persian Gulf, increases in salinity, sinks and passes out through

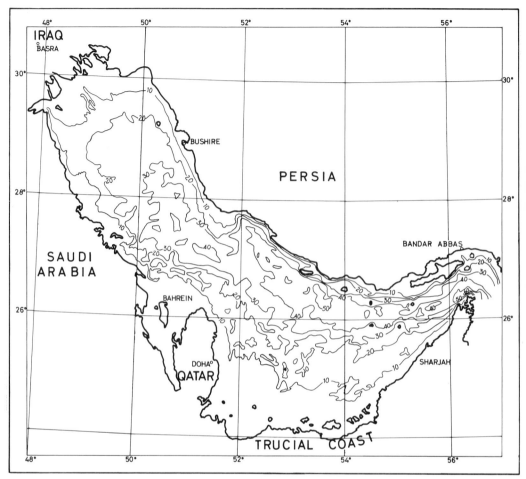

Fig. 1. A Bathymetric chart of the Persian Gulf (from Iranian Oil Co. Map, 1957). Depths in fathoms.

TABLE 1

	DAILY MAX.	TEMPERATURE °F RANGE	DAILY MIN.	RANGE	RELATIVE HUMIDITY	RAINFALL
BANDAR ABBAS	89	74–101	71	56–85	67%	6·1"
BUSHIRE	82	64–97	69	51–84	74%	10·8"
SHARJAH	89	74–103	68	54–82	67·5%	4·2"
BAHREIN	85	69–99	74	59–88	67%	2·9"
BASRA	87	64–105	64	45–81	68%	7·3"

the Straits of Hormuz, being replaced by lighter seawater flowing in over it.

Tides show marked diurnal inequality in the Persian Gulf. It is greatest in the area just east of the Qatar peninsula where the tide is even sometimes diurnal. The diurnal inequality decreases away to the northeast and southwest of this point. The tidal range is low 4.0–5.4 feet around Qatar, increasing to 10.5–11.1 feet at the head of the Gulf and to 9.2–10.5 feet at its entrance. Strong onshore winds sometimes raise the level of coastal waters to produce extensive flooding on the low shore line. Strong tidal currents (up to 4 knots) are found on the southern side of the Straits of Hormuz. Elsewhere in the Gulf tidal currents are not strong, usually $1-1\frac{1}{2}$ knots, but they may attain high velocities in the entrances to lagoons, estuaries and in narrow straits. Surface drift due to wind is sometimes so great that tidal streams when opposed to it fail to overcome it and the resultant stream continues in one direction merely changing its rate.

Waves are usually small in the Gulf. The effects of the Indian Ocean swell are only felt in the entrance. Here also, winds may oppose the tide and create very turbulent conditions. Generally, waves within the Gulf are small and are steep. Waves developed by the shamal are the most important in the southern Gulf. Large waves have been reported, but they are rarely greater than 10 feet in amplitude.

Geology

The geological framework is reasonably well known (see summaries in Lees and Richardson, 1940; Henson, 1951; Lees, 1953). The Persian Gulf is bounded on the west by the Arabian Precambrian shield covered by gently, northeasterly dipping, Paleozoic, Mesozoic and Cenozoic sediments. They are gently warped along north-south axes. The Oman mountains are the only strongly folded structure in the Arabian peninsula. On the other side of the Gulf are the northwest-southeast aligned foothills and the folded and thrust ranges of the Zagros mountains. Huge anticlines expose mostly Mesozoic rocks in the mountains but these are covered by Cenozoic sediments in the foothills. The fold zone contains some great fault slices in the northeast, exposing Paleozoic and later rocks. The fold mountains and fault slices are separated from the complex mass of the central Persian plateau by a zone of overthrusting, exposing a great variety of rock types, in the northeast extremities of the Zagros. Superimposed on this broad pattern are extensive salt plugs particularly well developed in the southwest of Persia and the southern Gulf. They appear to have had long histories but were most active in upper Tertiary times. Although movement started in Cretaceous times and even earlier in some places, the main

structure of the mountains and the broad physiography of the Persian Gulf is almost all due to Mio-Pliocene folding with subsequent warping (see Lees, 1953). The effects of an earlier Pre-Miocene block-faulted framework probably had some effect on the superimposed Tertiary folds (Henson, 1951). The area is still active today, and numerous raised beaches and uplifted planated surfaces attest to Quaternary movement.

The geological framework has emerged by the folding of a thick series of deposits which have accumulated in a northwest-southeast trough that became well defined in the Mesozoic (Lees and Richardson, 1940). The Cambrian consists of clastics, salts and thin carbonates. The Ordovician–Carboniferous is thin and mainly clastics. The Permian to Miocene was a period of mainly calcareous sedimentation with occasional incursions of clastic deposits. These calcareous deposits consist of marly sediments deposited in deeper water and often containing considerable organic matter, passing into shoal water deposits including skeletal, oolitic, reefal and dolomitic limestones. These shoal water deposits are noticeably developed to the southwest of the trough. In places, evaporites accumulated particularly on the Arabian shore and were sometimes widespread. This pattern of sedimentation closed with the deposition of a thick series of continental deposits during and succeeding the main Tertiary folding.

During the development of this thick sedimentary sequence (more than 40,000 feet of sediment having accumulated in the Persian mountain belt), conditions from time to time were favorable for the accumulations of organic matter which ultimately gave rise to the vast oil reserves of the area. The oil is exploited today from large anticlinal structures into which it has migrated. The reservoir rocks vary from Jurassic limestones and dolomites in Arabia, to Cretaceous sands and limestones in the area to the northeast, and to Tertiary limestones which are often reefal in the foothills of Persia.

Geomorphology, Marine Geology and Sedimentology

The Persian Gulf and adjoining areas show a striking modern sediment pattern (see Emery, 1956; Houbolt, 1957; Evans, 1965) (Fig. 2). On the northeast, Persia is a region of extensive continental sedimentation. Large interior basins such as the Dasht-i-Khavir, Dasht-i-Lut and Gavkhuni consisting of extensive outwash fans, dune sand areas and saline flats and swamps, are the repositories of much of the products of erosion.

The mountains reach the coast in some places to form cliffs. However, elsewhere sediment escaping to the coast builds up a complex coastal plain consisting of alluvial, estuarine, deltaic intertidal mud flat and beach ridge environments. There is a narrow coastal shelf. No modern work has been

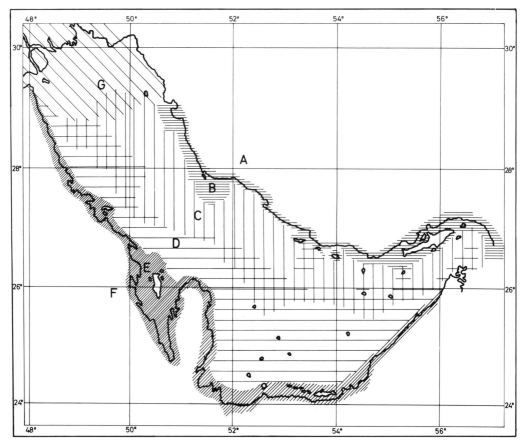

Fig. 2. The modern facies of the Persian Gulf (data from Emery, 1956; Houbolt, 1957; Evans, 1965). (A) Persian Continental Facies, (B) Persian coastal complex and shelf facies, (C) Persian Gulf trough facies, (D) Arabian shelf facies, (E) Arabian coastal complex facies, (F) Arabian continental facies, (G) Mesopotamian deltaic facies.

done on this Persian coastal plain and shelf facies.

Seaward of this zone, the deeper parts of the Persian Gulf are floored by silty clays and clayey silts with a high content of carbonate (20% CO_2). They contain $0.83-1.51\%$ organic carbon and $0.14-0.23\%$ organic nitrogen, with carbon-nitrogen ratios varying from 6.9–9.2, usually being less than ten. The carbonate fraction consists of low-magnesium calcite and dolomite with some aragonite, the dolomite probably being windblown. The coarse fractions of these sediments contain whole and fragmentary small molluskan shells, lamellibranchs, gastropods, scaphopods and some pteropods; echinoid spines and plates, Foraminifera, with planktonic forms abundant near the entrance to the Gulf; ostracods, polyzoa, serpulid worms and crab fragments; pellets, composite grains, quartz and other insolubles. Pyrite is found infilling some of the Foraminifera and molluskan shells. These marls are thought to be thin since, in some places, sediments containing oolites and having other shoal water characteristics are some-

times found exposed with only a small admixture of marl. Similarly, further to the north, frosted quartz grains are prominent. These are unlikely to reach their position under present conditions. Both oolites and the deposits containing frosted quartz grains are thought to be nearshore or coastal deposits which have been subsequently drowned. Prominent sub-bottom reflections are found in the deeper trough from depths up to 8 fathoms beneath the sediment surface. These die out as areas of coarser sediments are approached. These marly sediments are thought to have originated through mixing of material produced by breakdown of skeletal material, windblown material and also mud from the Persian coast and delta. Some of the fine-grained carbonate is probably derived from the shelf to the southwest. These sediments pass through a series of sediments of intermediate character into the sediments of the Arabian Shelf to the southwest (Houbolt, 1957).

The broad shallow shelf, generally less than 20 fathoms in depth, has a complex topography with numerous banks and shoals. There are some small islands, which are salt plugs, surrounded by reefs and rims of sediment extending southeast away from the dominant northwest wind and wave attack. Some of the shoals are capped with coral reefs and small sand cays. The bottom sediments consist dominantly of skeletal sands with variable amounts of coarser shell debris, calcilutite and some insolubles. There is a good macrofauna of mollusks and echinoids with subsidiary corals and crabs. Although there are flourishing bottom communities, there are suggestions that the high temperatures and salinities encountered in the Gulf, particularly in inshore and coastal waters, restrict the number of species of organisms living in the area (Sugden, 1963).

The carbonate fraction consists mainly of aragonite mixed with varying amounts of low- and high-magnesium calcite. These usually contain less than 0.5% organic carbon and less than 0.05% organic nitrogen. The carbon-nitrogen ratio varies from 5.0–14.2 and is usually greater than 10. The sediment consists of molluskan debris, lamellibranchs, gastropods and some scaphopods; echinoid plates and spines; Foraminifera, ostracods, crab fragments, polyzoa and serpulid worm tubes often coating shells; and, rarely, sponge spicules. Coral and algal fragments, the latter sometimes forming concretionary growths, are found in some shoal areas. Composite grains, including derived rock fragments and fecal pellets, are also found with varying amounts of quartz and other non-calcareous material. Some of the grains, particularly some species of Foraminifera, have a shiny black coating (Emery, 1956; Houbolt, 1957; Evans, 1965). The sediments seem to have formed mainly by breakdown of locally produced skeletal material by bottom scavengers, boring algae and wave and current action. They appear to show evidence of reworking and mixing of sediment of various ages. Mixed with this material is some windblown material from the bordering land masses. The calcilutite is produced by breakdown of skeletal material and precipitation of aragonite because of local spontaneous plankton blooms (Wells and Illing, 1964, see reference in Evans, 1965). The local differences in topography control sediment characteristics producing a distribution of calcarenite with small patches of calcilutite in the depressions and sheltered locations on the shelf. The latter areas may be more common off the Saudi Arabian coast where the topography appears to be more broken and complicated. The sediments are thin and, in places, barely cover the underlying rock. Sedimentation is slow and has hardly started to bury the inherited topography.

The southwest shore of the Gulf is the site of intensive rapid deposition of carbonate sediments in a complex of shoal water environments (see references in Evans, 1965). On the Trucial coast,

near Abu Dhabi, a series of islands, composed mainly of recent unconsolidated sediments with cores of Quaternary limestone of eolian and shallow water origin, encloses a series of tidal embayments and lagoons. Waters attain high temperatures and salinities in these lagoons. Strong tidal currents draining the embayments produce large tidal deltas where the waters debouch into the Southern Gulf from between the islands. These deltas are the site of extensive oolite formation. Fringing and barrier reefs are sometimes found between the tidal deltas fronting the islands. Some coral reefs are also found in the outer parts of the lagoon. The islands have sandy frontal beaches and dunes composed mainly of oolitic and skeletal sands. The sediments of the frontal barrier are composed mainly of aragonite with low percentages of low- and high-magnesium calcite with higher percentages of high-magnesium calcite in the reefal sediments. The importance of offshore supply and onshore sand transport by the waves, and subsequent building into dunes by the wind, both of which are dominantly onshore here, is well illustrated on this coast. Where the deltas front the coast and sand production is rapid, dunes are high; in the intervening areas, where there is only a slow production of skeletal sand (on the shelf to seaward) and where the nearshore profile is steeper, dunes are low.

Inside the lagoons and embayments, the islands are fringed by narrow beaches and dunes; broad intertidal flats inhabited by crabs and gastropods; and algal flats and mangrove swamps where calcilutite, heavily burrowed by crabs, accumulates. The tidal channels die out inland. They are floored by pelletal and skeletal calcarenites and calcirudites with oolites near the deltas. The shoal areas in the outer lagoon are floored by pelletal and skeletal calcarenites. Local beach ridges enclosing the intertidal flats and swamps are almost pure pelletal sand and skeletal sands. The inner parts of the lagoons are much muddier, and pelletal and skeletal calcilutites predominate. The sediments of the lagoons are dominantly aragonitic with low percentages of low- and high-magnesium calcite.

Broad intertidal flats fringe the inner shore lines, and here pelletal and skeletal calcilutites are common. Extensive algal flats develop which are often more than a mile wide. The waters enclosed under the algal mats are highly saline, and mushes of gypsum crystals occur particularly in the higher parts of the flats.

The algal flats and intertidal flats pass landward either directly or across low beach ridges composed almost entirely of gastropod shells into a low coastal plain. This salt encrusted plain, the so-called *sabkha*, shows many old strandline features such as old beach ridges and infilled tidal creeks. It has originated by the progradation of the inner coastline by extensive intertidal flat deposition over a distance of approximately 15 miles. The *sabkha* is sandy with many beach ridges where the coast is more exposed and muddier with channels and few ridges where it is better protected.

The highly saline waters of the lagoons percolate into the subsurface of this coastal plain and are drawn up to the surface by capillary action (Shearman, 1963, see references in Evans, 1965). As they move inland, they become more concentrated and differentiated, and a complex reaction occurs between them and the earlier deposited intertidal and coastal plain carbonate sediments. The result is that an interesting suite of evaporite minerals is found forming in the *sabkha* and the upper parts of the intertidal flats. Gypsum occurs at various levels and appears to be of several generations and origins. Anhydrite is found developing above the groundwater table at slightly higher levels. It occurs as courses of nodules and beds up to two feet thick with remarkable contortions and sedimentary structures seen so often in the ancient evaporites. Dolomite is found, and it appears that penecontemporaneous dolomitization of earlier calcareous sediments is taking place. Other rarer evaporitic minerals are also present. Celestite is found, particularly under the older algal mats in the sabkha, and it is probably formed as a by-product of dolomitization. Halite is also common in the sediments. The *sabkha* "evaporite" plain is bounded by the low bluffs of Tertiary rocks, which pass under the dunes of the desert inland.

The Arabian peninsula is fringed by a highland rim. Large outwash plains slope down from this rim to the interior lowlands. Much of Arabia is covered by large deserts, inside the outwash plains, such as the Great Nafud, Dahna and the Rub al Khali. The sands are mainly composed of quartz, but they are being diluted near the coast by the inland migrating carbonate sands of the Trucial Coast. As the present cycle progresses, there is the possibility of a large sheet of carbonate sands transgressing inland over continental quartz sand. This is taking place purely by eolian action and not by marine transgression. Occasionally, because of the different relationship between wind and coastal trend, some of the quartz sands reach the coast to become entrained in the sediments of the Arabian coastal complex facies. Arabia appears to be a large sediment trap losing some and gaining small amounts of sediment along its shores.

Finally in the northwest end of the Persian Gulf are the vast alluvial plains and swamps of the Mesopotamian plains, produced by the Tigris-Euphrates and Karun rivers. The history of the deltaic complex is complicated by recent tectonic movements. It appears that subsidence is taking place and accommodating the incoming river-borne sediment. The delta does not appear to be extending appreciably seaward at present (see references in Emery, 1956). However, recent marine deposits overlain by alluvium have been described from boreholes far inland from the present coast. The sediments in the vicinity of the delta contain considerable non-calcaerous material but still have fairly high carbonate contents (15–20% CO_2). They seem generally to have lower carbonate, organic carbon and organic nitrogen values than sediments of equivalent grade elsewhere in the Gulf. They contain molluskan shell debris with some corals, Foraminifera, echinoid fragments and spines, ostracods serpulid worm tubes and crab fragments. Exactly how much sediment escapes seaward to the Persian Gulf and how far the delta's influence extends is not known. However, the presence of some apparently relict sediments near the delta suggest that the rate of seaward escape of sediment is not great, unless these might have been covered.

The modern facies pattern is in many ways similar to that of the past although the modern sediments appear poorer in organic matter. The marls of the earlier troughs are equivalent to the modern trough deposits. The shelf and coastal complex have many analogous situations in the Mesozoic and Cenozoic when lagoonal and reefal and evaporitic sediments were common on the southwest of the trough (Lees and Richardson, 1940; Henson, 1951). Because of the narrow shoal area, approximtely 70 miles inside the Gulf, a drop in sea level could convert a large part of the Persian Gulf into a shoal area separated from the open sea by a very narrow inlet. Such a situation could be an ideal one for the development of extensive evaporites. Perhaps similar barriers might have been responsible for the development of the extensive Mesozoic and Tertiary evaporitic sediments (Richardson, 1940; Sugden, 1963).

It appears that the modern Persian Gulf with its striking facies pattern is an excellent model for the interpretation and understanding of the older deposits of the Middle East and elsewhere on the earth's surface.

GRAHAM EVANS

References

Emery, K. O., 1956, "Sediments and water of Persian Gulf," *Bull. Am. Assoc. Petrol. Geologists*, **40**, No. 10, 2354–2383.

Evans, G., 1966, "The Recent Sedimentary Facies of the Persian Gulf Region," *Phil. Trans. Roy. Soc.*, **A, 259**, 291–298.

Henson, F. R. S., 1951, "Observations on the geology and petroleum occurrences of the Middle East," *World Petrol. Congr. Proc. 3rd, The Hague*, Section 1, 118–140.

Houbolt, I. I. H. C., 1957, "Surface Sediments in the Persian Gulf near the Qatar Peninsula," Thesis, University of Utrecht, The Hague, Mouton, 113pp.

Lee, G. M., 1953, "Persia," *Sci. of Petrol.*, **6**, No. 1, 78–82.

Lees, G. M., and Richardson, F. D. S., 1940, "The

geology of the oil-field belt of S.W. Iran and Iraq," *Geol. Mag.*, **78**, 227–252.

Sugden, W., 1963, "The hydrology of the Persian Gulf in respect to evaporite deposition," *Am. J. Sci.*, **261**, 741–755.

Sugden, W., 1963, "Some aspects of sedimentation in the Persian Gulf," *J. Sediment. Petrol.*, **33**, 355–64.

PERU (HUMBOLDT) CURRENT

The term Peru Current, sometimes known as Humboldt Current, is applied to a system of relatively shallow currents flowing generally equatorward along the west coast of South America. The system forms the eastern limb of the counterclockwise (anticyclonic) circulation of the South Pacific, and is one of a family of current systems known as *eastern boundary currents* (others include the California Current of the North Pacific and the Canary and Benguela Currents of the Atlantic).

The Peru Current, like other eastern boundary currents, has the following general characteristics:

(1) Near surface temperatures are lower than those at comparable latitudes farther west.

(2) The speed of motion is relatively slow, and the currents are broad and shallow, with relatively small transport.

(3) Vertical motion, known as upwelling, occurs along the coastal boundary.

(4) Near surface concentrations of nutrient elements are high.

(5) Biological production is high.

Historical

The first Europeans who visited Peru, at the time of the Spanish conquest (starting in 1532), observed the prevalence of the southeast trade winds, a constant northward current, the coolness of the sea even at very low latitudes, and the abundance of marine life. Measurements of sea temperatures were not made until the eighteenth century, and in 1802 Humboldt determined that water temperatures were cooler than those of the air, and increased with increasing distance offshore. From these observations, he formulated the theory of a coastal current of Antarctic origin. Subsequently, Bougainville, de Tessan, Dinklage, Witte and others noted that the coastal temperatures did not increase steadily towards the equator, and the low temperatures were attributed to upwelling of subsurface waters caused by the offshore drag of the trade winds.

The first comprehensive study of the hydrography of the region, published by Schott (1931) was based largely on the casual observations of merchant and naval vessels. The first extensive oceanographic investigation was carried out by Carnegie in 1928–1929, followed in 1931 by that of William Scoresby. The report of the latter (Gunther, 1936) is basic to any consideration of

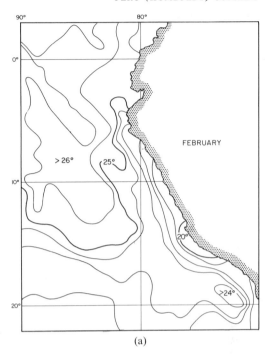

(a)

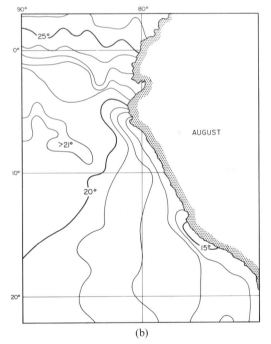

(b)

Fig. 1. Average sea surface temperature (°C) (a) in February (from Wyrtki, unpublished). (b) Same, in August.

the region. More than twenty years elapsed before a large-scale field program, the Shellback Expedition in 1952, was conducted in this part of the Pacific. Since then, scientific information has

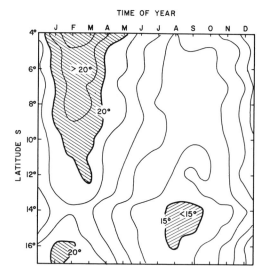

accumulated rapidly with the visits of expeditions, particularly from the U.S. and Japan, and with the establishment of active marine research programs in Ecuador, Peru and Chile.

Climatology and Surface Temperature

Prevailing winds off the coasts of northern Chile, Peru and Ecuador blow principally from the southeast and south, the so-called southeast trade winds. It is characteristic of these winds that they blow steadily from more or less the same direction throughout the year, and with somewhat greater strength during the southern winter. Surface isotherms tend to parallel the coast, with lowest

Fig. 2. Average sea surface temperature (°C) by one-degree squares and by month, along the Peruvian coast (from Wooster, 1961).

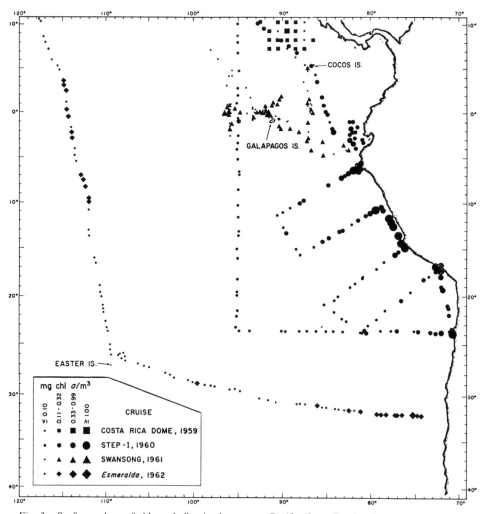

Fig. 3a. Surface values of chlorophyll *a* in the eastern Pacific (from Forsbergh and Joseph, 1964).

temperatures close inshore. Because of this, skies are usually overcast near the coast, except in southern summer, and celestial navigation is difficult (climatological information for the region is presented in Meteorological Office, 1956).

Low surface temperatures along the coast appear to result from the upwelling of subsurface water from depths of a few hundred meters. This upwelling is attributed to the combined effects of the drag of the surface winds and the rotation of the earth, causing an offshore transport of surface water which is replaced by underlying water. The intensity of upwelling is related to the intensity of wind stress. Since the trades are strongest during southern winter, when temperatures would otherwise be lower, the effect of winter upwelling is to exaggerate the annual range of temperature. During southern summer, surface winds are weaker, coastal upwelling is less intense, and the highest surface temperatures are observed (Figs. 1a and 1b show average surface temperatures in February and August, Fig. 2 the annual march of surface temperature along the Peruvian Coast).

Circulation

Between the latitudes of approximately 45°S (off the coast of Chile) and 4°S (off northern Peru), the prevailing surface currents are northward parallel to the coast inshore, with increasing westward motion farther offshore. It is not yet known whether northward flow is continuous along this stretch of coast or whether the Chile and Peru currents are separate systems, with the dividing zone somewhere near 20°S. Although the surface currents are not believed to penetrate to depths of more than a few hundred meters, few measurements of subsurface currents have been made. A southward flowing undercurrent along the coast between

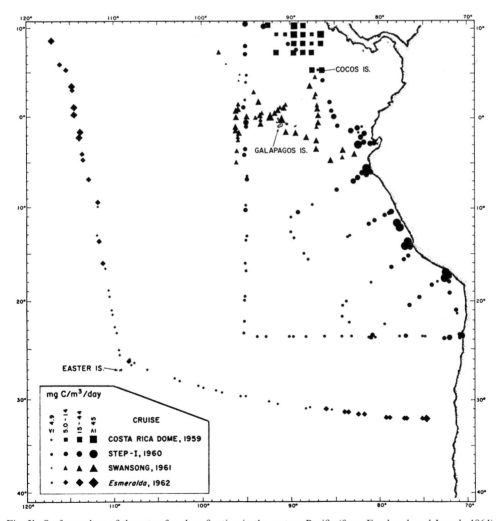

Fig. 3b. Surface values of the rate of carbon fixation in the eastern Pacific (from Forsbergh and Joseph, 1964).

6 and 23°S has recently been studied by means of parachute drogues.

Average speeds in the Peru Current are of the order of half a knot or less, and the transport of water is of the order of 15–20×10^6 m^3/sec. Some authors distinguish between a coastal current and an oceanic current, and recent observations suggest a southward counter current between these two northward components of the system.

The Peru Current leaves the coast at about 4°S turning west to merge with the South Equatorial Current. To the north of the cold, relatively salty (34.5‰ or greater) waters of the Peru Current lie warmer and relatively fresh tropical waters. The zone of transition lies south of the equator near the Peruvian coast and crosses the equator somewhere east of the Galápagos Islands. Across the transition zone, large changes of temperature, salinity and velocity have been observed.

Biological Effects

One effect of the upwelling process is to bring to the surface water which has properties characteristic of its original depth. Off the Peruvian coast, dissolved oxygen decreases below the thermocline to very low values (less than 0.25 ml/liter) and in regions of intense upwelling, surface values may be significantly undersaturated. Concentrations of elements required for plant nutrition (such as P, N, Si) increase through the thermocline and below, and upwelling leads to high values of these nutrients along the coast. The ample supply of nutrient elements is associated with high standing crops of phytoplankton and high rates of primary production (see Fig. 3). As a result, the coastal waters of the Peru Current are very rich in biological activity, supporting one of the world's greatest fisheries, that for the anchovy *Engraulis ringens*, as well as an important tuna fishery and the collection of significant quantities of guano fertilizer from sea birds.

El Niño

Each year, during southern summer, the trade winds blow with less strength, upwelling is less intense along the coast, and the transition zone between the tropical waters and the Peru current moves southward to 5 or 6°S. During occasional years, the decrease in strength of the trades is much greater than usual, southward penetration of tropical waters is more pronounced, and along central and southern Peru a thin layer of warm oceanic water of high salinity extends to within ten miles or so of the coast. This phenomenon has been called *El Niño* (i.e., The Child) because it usually begins at Christmas time; notable occurrences were in 1891, 1925, 1941, 1953, 1957–1958.

During an *El Niño*, primary production is reduced, and the anchovy appears to avoid the warm surface layer. Presumably because of their difficulty in feeding, sea birds die in large numbers, or emigrate, abandoning their young: guano production is sharply reduced as a consequence. However, there is no convincing evidence of large-scale mortality of fish, and in recent years the anchovy fishery has not been adversely affected. Often destructive rainfalls occur along the normally arid coast.

WARREN S. WOOSTER

References

Bjerknes, J., 1961, "El Niño study based on analysis of ocean surface temperatures 1935–1957," *Bull. Inter-Amer. Trop. Tuna Comm.*, **5**, 219–303.

Forsbergh, E. D., and Joseph, J., 1964, "Biological production in the eastern Pacific Ocean," *Bull. Inter-Amer. trop. Tuna Comm.*, **8**, 479–527.

*Gunther, E. R., 1936, "A report on oceanographical investigations in the Peru Coastal Current," *Discovery Rep.*, **13**, 107–276.

Meteorological Office, 1956, "Monthly Meteorological Charts of the Eastern Pacific Ocean," London, H.M.S.O., M.O. 518, 122pp.

Schott, G., 1931, "Der Peru-Strom und seine nördlichen Nachbargebiete in normaler und anormaler Ausbildung," *An. Hydrogr. u. Marit. Met.*, **59**, 161–169, 200–213, 240–252.

*Wooster, W. S., and Reid, J. L., Jr., 1963, "Eastern Boundary Currents," in "The Sea: Ideas and Observations," Vol. 2, pp. 253–280.

Wyrtki, K., 1963, "The horizontal and vertical field of motion in the Peru Current," *Bull. Scripps Inst. Oceanog.*, **8**, 313–346.

Cross-references: *El Niño; Ekman Spiral; Ocean Currents.*

pH AND Eh OF MARINE SEDIMENTS

Sediments in the marine environment consist of a mixture of many materials depending on (1) coastal effects such as tidal flats, (2) runoff erosion from land, (3) deltaic regions and river effects, (4) biological activities precipitating or accumulating calcium carbonates, (5) remains of living organisms and air-carried particles falling onto the sea surface, (6) volcanic activity, (7) the precipitation of salts from the water, and (8) the scavenging effects of particulate matter as it falls through the water column (Fig. 1). The pH of the final sediment type is dependent on the balance and buffering activity of acid-base components of the interstitial water. Most sediments, with the exception of highly productive nearshore environments, are generally in the oxygenated or positive Eh state. Rainwater usually has a pH of about 6.5 and an oxidation-reduction potential of $+400$ to $+500$ mV. As rainwater falls to the earth and slowly dissolves the rock surfaces, it brings ions and small rock particles to the oceans. These contained ions and molecules in the water control the pH and Eh of the system. Thus marine sediments are built

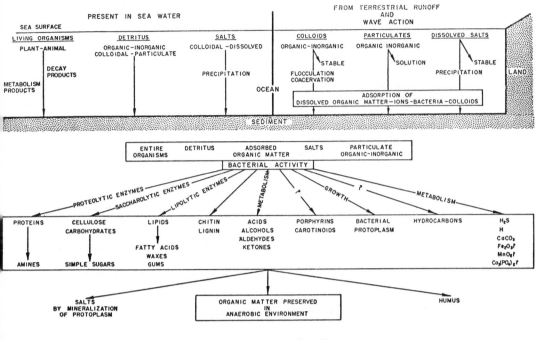

Fig. 1. Bacterial activities in sediments.

up with time from terrestrial runoff and air-carried dust.

Solubility effects and ion movement during sediment consolidation, water migration and temperature changes are relatively minor, and sediments would generally change only slowly if the environment were sterile and all activities of living organisms were absent. However, this is not the case for sediments from the Cambrian to the present where the activities of both macro- and microorganisms from the shallow water environments to the deepest areas in the sea have been a rather constant feature. Biological activities in shallow water include mechanical effects and both the photosynthetic and the metabolic activities of organisms, whereas in the aphotic zones of the seas only mechanical and metabolic activities are present.

The more stable deep-sea sediments have slow rates of accumulation, whereas the shallow water environments constantly undergo the forces of currents, tides and waves. The stability of any sedimentary environment is hard to define as even the deep water environments are subject to disturbances due to turbidity and other currents. Perhaps stability may be defined as that layer of sediments which is no longer influenced by waves and currents. In some environments, this layer may be directly at the surface; in others, it may be buried deep at a point where physical forces can no longer penetrate.

At the surface of most sediments is a layer of ooze consisting of a colloidal mass of hydrated fine particles and organic matter. This is also considered as part of the sediment. This fine ooze is in a relatively mobile state and is easily transported into the water column by waves and currents. Microscope inspection reveals that this layer consists of innumerable small particles with living organisms that are degrading organic material as a source of nutrients and, in so doing, destroy colloidal aspects and aid in the consolidation of the sediment particles.

Through the use of modern equipment it is quite easy to measure, with a reasonable degree of accuracy, the pH and Eh of marine waters and sediments. The interpretation of the data, however, is not quite so easy because of the diversity of conditions present due to the interaction of the various environmental parameters that may exist. Thus it is virtually impossible to write a reaction for any given process that may change the pH or Eh in nature because the net measurements of electrons or protons are the result of a balance between diverse properties of the sampling environment.

pH or hydrogen ion concentration is a function of the acid or base balance of materials and is measured as a function of the free hydrogen ions or protons. The classical equation for hydrogen ion concentration is the logarithmic function: $pH = -\log (H^+)$. pH may be measured colorimetrically by approximation with the use of indicators that are sensitive to hydrogen ion or by exacting electrical methods which measure the hydrogen ion concentration directly.

Oxidation-reduction is a term used to indicate the state of electrons in a system or the degree of oxidation or reduction as measured colorimetrically or as emf through electrical methods in which $Eh = E_0 + 0.03 \log [(OX)/(Red)]$ where Eh is measured in volts and E_0 is a constant.

Several instruments are available that will measure both pH and Eh operated either by line voltage or battery. Essentially these instruments are potentiometers in which emf is measured as a function of the response of specific electrodes. The pH is measured by a glass electrode and a saturated calomel half-cell. The glass electrode is sensitive to hydrogen ions or protons that change the standard emf imposed by the calomel half-cell. The instrument is calibrated to a solution of known pH on a scale between 1 and 14, where 7 is neutral (with acid below and basic above). Redox emf is measured directly between a platinum (gold may also be used) electrode and a saturated calomel half-cell. The Eh scale ranges from oxidizing $+500$ to reducing -500 mV, where 0 indicates the transition between the absence and presence of dissolved molecular oxygen and an equal balance between oxidizing and reducing materials.

The sensing tip (hemisphere) of the commercial glass pH electrode is made of specially prepared glass, is very thin and fragile, and is easily scratched by quartz and other sediment grains. Once the glass hemisphere is scratched it is no longer accurate and will give misleading results. Extreme care must be taken therefore during *in situ* measurements, and the electrodes must be standardized after each few measurements. The calomel electrode is quite resistant and can be treated rather roughly. The electrodes may be used at some distance apart as long as there is an aqueous bridge (the author often uses a separation of several feet) leaving the calomel electrode in one spot, realizing that the active electrode is the glass electrode. A shielded leakproof electrode is necessary for *in situ* measurements.

The redox electrodes are less fragile; however, care must be taken to insure that the platinum electrode is not polarized by oxygen or other polarizing substances by carefully cleaning it after each two or three measurements. The normal method of cleaning is to abrade the platinum with a cleaning powder containing diatomaceous earth. The combination of scouring powder and detergent effectively depolarizes the platinum surface. The platinum leakproof electrode does not need to be shielded, and the sensing electrode can be used at a distance of several feet from the calomel half-cell.

The emf measured must be corrected for the half-cell potential which, in turn, is influenced by temperature. The correction values of the calomel half-cell to be added to the observed values are given as follows.

Temperature	15°C	20°C	25°C	30°C	37°C
Potential, V	0.252	0.249	0.246	0.242	0.236

Because of the influence of pH on many chemical equilibria, the Eh is related to pH changes. Normally the Eh becomes more negative by about 0.06 volt for each unit increase in pH; therefore, the Eh must be corrected for pH in situations in which very accurate correlations are necessary. A standard Eh solution with a value of $+0.430$ volt at 25°C may be prepared by mixing equal quantities of $M/300$ $K_3Fe(Cn)_6$ and $M/300$ $K_4Fe(Cn)_6$ in $M/10$ KCl.

The capacity of any environment to withstand changes in pH and Eh is called, respectively, buffering and poising capacity. The buffering capacity is the ability to withstand changes in pH, and the poising capacity to withstand changes in Eh. In both systems, the capacity is a function of weakly dissociated materials that act, by dissociation, to overcome changes in hydrogen ion concentration or oxidizing and reducing substances. A weak acid and its salt are an example of a buffer, and an example of a poising substance is hydrogen or iron sulfide that slowly dissociates in the presence of an oxidizing material such as oxygen.

The pH of standard seawater is normally considered 8.2, but deviations in nature do occur as attributed to many causes. The standard pH is normally a function of the primary buffering reaction as shown by the following:

$$\begin{matrix} CO_2 \\ \| \\ H_2CO_3 \end{matrix} = HCO_3^- = CO_3^=$$

There are other organic and inorganic buffering systems prevalent in the sedimentary environment induced by biological activities. The activities of organisms within the sediment may produce an increase in pH through the production of ammonia, uptake of carbon dioxide, consumption of organic acids, production of intermediate products, and the production of acid-binding organic molecules such as certain amino acids. The reverse of these reactions may decrease the pH. Therefore, depending on environmental effects, the pH in seawater can vary from about 5.8–9.2 maximum.

The Eh may range in seawater from $+500$ to -400 mV. However, such values may be misleading because no definition of Eh is given that describes the number of oxygen molecules or electrons present. Thus a zero Eh describes a situation in which small amounts of molecular oxygen may be present that are masked by the balance of electrons within the system.

SEDIMENT PROFILE

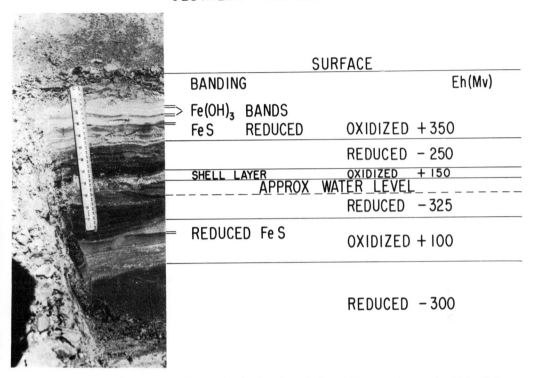

Fig. 2. A profile of a new shore sediment showing layering of pH and Eh zones due to microbial activity.

Limitations in the Accurate Measurement of pH and Eh

The sedimentary environment may appear uniform, but a close inspection shows this is not true except for a very few places. The accumulation of sediment is not a uniform vertical or lateral process, and layering produces discrete changes shown in the typical sediment profile exemplified in Fig. 2. Frequent sedimentary discontinuities occur in geologic time caused by currents, storms, and activities of burrowing organisms. The electrode probes normally used are of such a finite size that it is often impossible to detect practically the discrete changes found within vertical layering or adjacent to burrowing activities.

The pH and Eh of most sediments, except the oxidized deep-sea sediments and some other stable environments, can change rapidly when brought to the surface. The Eh of samples is also altered by atmospheric conditions, especially when the sediments are in the reduced state or at the transition state between oxidized and reduced. These changes are primarily due to the loss of CO_2 and H_2S and oxidation due to oxygen. With this in mind, one must be very careful of the manner in which sediments are collected for analyses. In general the usual apparatus used for pH and Eh measurements is accurate to 0.01 unit, which fact may be misleading because of the state of the sample, and generally it is difficult to obtain two readings that coincide, especially for reduced sediments.

Methods of Sampling

The pH and Eh must be measured as quickly as possible and with the least physical changes to the sample. The best measurements are made *in situ*. Samples taken in plastic cores may be held for an hour after retrieval but should be measured immediately. The electrodes should be inserted into the center of the extruded cores. Care should be taken not to alter or to allow oxidation to occur. Within the same moist sediment it is possible to leave the reference electrode stationary and just move the glass or platinum electrodes; such measurements may be taken at distances of 20 feet with good accuracy. Electrodes with long leads may be obtained from the manufacturer. Some advocate the practice of placing the sediment material in an enclosed glass vessel containing electrodes. This may be appropriate for well-oxidized deep-sea cores but will not suffice for layered sediments or those in which active surface diagenesis is taking place. One needs, for the glass bottle exercise, rather large uniform samples (50

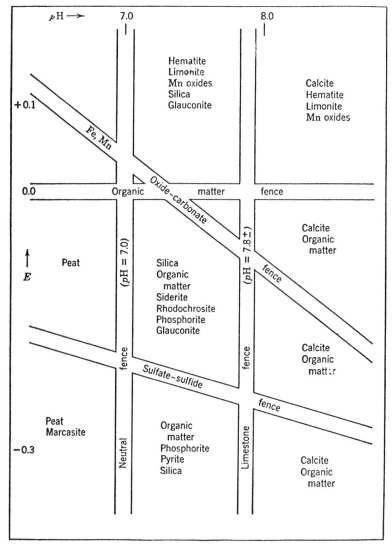

Fig. 3. Sedimentary associations in relation to environmental limitations imposed by oxidation potential and pH [after Krumbein and Garrels, *J. Geol.,* **60**, 26, (1952)].

grams), and the transfer of such samples to the bottle may produce large changes.

The best samples are those taken *in situ* and even those are inaccurate because of the limitation of the electrode size to detect the discontinuities present within the layers of most sediments.

Distribution of Eh and pH in Some Sediments

With the preceding in mind, we can approach the marine environment and its classification of pH and Eh by potentiometer, realizing that measurements must be interpreted with respect to the description of living populations within the area and chemical properties. The environmental aspects that affect the pH and Eh of marine sediments are (1) activities of living organisms, both physical and chemical, and (2) water movement during compaction, percolation, capillary effects, turbidity and density currents.

A comparison between the transition of minerals and the activities of microorganisms is given in Figs. 3 and 4. Figure 3 illustrates the relation between pH and Eh and the equilibrium of minerals. In contrast to this geological fence, Fig. 4 illustrates the pH and Eh limitations of various microorganisms in the marine environment. These microorganisms can, by having the proper nutrient sources and physical conditions, change the environment through several parts of the geological fence shown in Fig. 3. This suggests transitions that may be taking place through seasons or years at the sediment interface or particle interfaces in seawater.

The final state of consolidated sediments after sufficient deposition or lithification may thus be a function of the microbial and other biological activities within that particular sediment. Even after consolidation occurs, a violent storm, turbidity, current or the burrowing activities of larger living organisms may produce changes within discrete or fairly large areas in the sediment.

Organisms and Sediments

One of the primary modifying forces acting on the pH and Eh of sediments are living organisms.

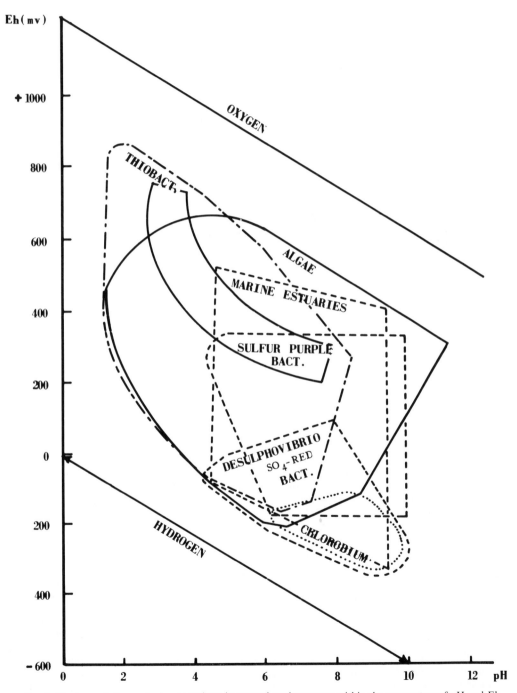

Fig. 4. The interrelations of microorganisms in natural environments within the parameters of pH and Eh.

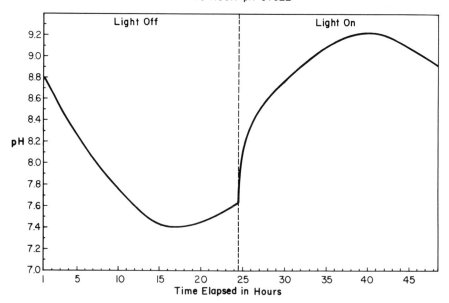

Fig. 5. The effect of photosynthesis and respiration on the pH of surface sediments containing a mixed microbial population.

Burrowing activities, even in the deep seas, will effectively plow up the surface, producing changes both physically and chemically. In such environments, the sediments that eventually become consolidated are the results of much physical movement. The greatest biological change in pH and Eh is produced during the activities of the living organisms, (1) as they consume and produce oxygen by photosynthesis and respiration, (2) by altering the carbonate buffer system by both consuming and producing carbon dioxide, and (3) during the production and consumption of acids and bases, and reduced and oxidized molecules or ions.

The two notable examples of diagenetic changes in minerals during pH and Eh are those involving carbonate systems and the iron-sulfur cycle. A typical example is found at the shoal-water sediment interface in which sunlight penetrates, thus producing a diurnal pH curve as shown in Fig. 5 in which the production of CO_2 during the night shifts the carbonate system to the left, producing a decrease in pH and vice versa during the day. The maximum amplitude in seawater is from about pH 5.6–9.5. The curve shown is typical of the combined activities of phytoplankton and bacteria in an enclosed aquarium with alternate periods of light and dark and in the presence of quartz and mg-calcite sediment. During the pH transition, quartz dissolved at the high pH and carbonate dissolved and precipitated, respectively, during the increase and decrease in pH. During the transition mg-

calcite was dissolved and a small amount of dolomite produced.

Some sedimentary changes in which pH-Eh and iron-sulfur cycles are involved are shown in Fig. 2. Within the sediment of many nearshore areas and marine lagoons, there are innumerable layers as a result of sedimentation processes. Organic matter layered with the sediment provides an energy source for microorganisms. As a result of microbial activity, oxygen is consumed and anaerobic conditions are produced, hydrogen sulfide and carbon dioxide are produced and the pH and Eh are changed accordingly. The sulfate-reducing bacteria, strict anerobes, produce sulfide that combines with ferrous iron to produce black hydrotroilite (FeS). Dark brown layers represent the reverse of the reaction where microbial activity has decreased, oxygen has diffused into the layers, and the hydrotroilite has oxidized to ferric hydroxide. In seawater at pH 7.5–8.2, iron is in the colloidal particulate state and is usually dispersed uniformly within the sediments. However, when the Eh is reduced to -200, the $Fe(OH)_3$ is reduced to $Fe(OH)_2$ in which the divalent iron is in the ion state and free to move by diffusion as it is taken up by the sulfide. Both H_2S and the CO_2 of respiration dissociate to weak acids and therefore will lower the pH. If hydrogen sulfide is oxidized or the CO_2 is removed, the reverse of the reaction takes place with a rise in pH. At this time the carbonate equilibrium will shift and carbonate precipitates. Certain fossil fish molds are thus produced in which the center of the fish is anaerobic and the surface is oxidizing. The carbon dioxide produced during such decomposition is free to migrate to the redox interface where carbonate is precipitated.

One function of microorganisms that produce a gross change in pH is the situation called a Sulfureta. In the cycle of a Sulfureta, sulfate-reducing bacteria produce sulfides from insoluble materials such as gypsum. The sulfides are oxidized by the sulfur bacteria to sulfates, producing sulfuric acid, and in some situations on land, a pH as low as 1.5 will occur.

Pure cultures of sulfate-reducing bacteria, by the process of production of sulfide and protoplasm, have also been shown to concentrate most of the heavy metal cations either by direct precipitation or through adsorption.

CARL H. OPPENHEIMER

References

Baas Becking, L. G. M., 1959, "Geology and microbiology," Contr. Marine Microbiol. N.Z. (Dept. Sci. & Ind. Res., Inf. Ser. No. 22); *N.Z. Oceanog. Inst. Mem.*, **3**, 48–64.

Baas Becking, L. G. M., Kaplan, I. R., and Moore, D., 1960, "Limits of the Natural Environment in Terms of pH and Oxidation Reduction Potentials," *J. Geol.*, **68**, 243–284.

Garrels, R. M., 1960, "Mineral Equilibria," New York, Harper Bros., 254pp.

Oppenheimer, C. H., and Kornicker, L., 1958, "Effect of microbial production of hydrogen sulfide and carbon dioxide on the pH of recent sediments," *Publ. Inst. Marine Sci. Univ. Texas*, **5**, 5–15.

ZoBell, C. E., 1946, "Studies on redox potential of marine sediments," *Bull. Am. Assoc. Petrol. Geol.*, **30**, 477–513.

PHILIPPINE SEA AND THE WATERS SOUTH OF JAPAN

Definition and Topography

According to Schott (1935), the Philippine Sea Basin covers 3.1% of the whole Pacific area. It is defined as the region lying to the east of the marginal seas of Far-East Asia and to the south of the Japanese Islands, extending to the islands of Idu, Ogasawara, Mariana, Yap, Palau, Halmahera, Mindanao, Luzon, Taiwan, Ryukyu and Kyusyu (see Fig. 1). According to Dietz (1954), the Philippine Sea Basin includes the arcuate ridges extending from Japan to Palau, in this broad sense having an area of nearly 400,000 square miles (1 million km²). It is bounded on the west by the southern half of Japan, the Ryukyu Islands and the Philippines, and on the east by the arcuate submarine ridge from Japan to Palau Islands. This deep basin is divided into an east and a west abyssal basin by the Kyusyu–Palau Ridge. These two basins (i.e., the Northwest Pacific Basin and

the West Philippine Basin) have the unusually great depth of about 6000 m (see Fig. 1).

From a regional oceanographic point of view, the waters south of Japan may be distinguished by the line of demarcation of the Subtropical Convergence running east-west about 20–23°N; the Philippine Sea in its narrow meaning lies only to the south of this line. We adopt the broad meaning (*Intern. Hydrographic Bureau Sp. Publ.* 23, 1953) in this article.

Bottom Configuration and Marine Geology

According to Dietz (1954), large-scale undulations are the dominant structure in this area and belts of seamounts are striking features. The seamounts are considered to be volcanoes, many of which are capped with coral. Tayama (1952) classified South Sea Islands on the basis of their geomorphology and genesis into a Western Group (including Mariana, Yap-Palau and Tobi Groups) and Eastern Group (including Caroline, Marshall and Central Groups) with various subgroups. Only the Western Group fall within the Philippines Sea. Corals inhabit much of this area mostly associated with a water temperature generally above 20°C and always above 15°C. A large number of seamounts have deeply submerged flat-topped summits and, thus, are classified as guyots or tablemounts.

The Basin is bounded by the Asiatic continental block on the west and by several great geanticlinal ridges, extending from Japan to Palau, on the east. Trenches, presumably marking great gashes in the earth's crust, lie eastward of these ridges. These geanticlinal ridges are active tectonic belts surmounted by volcanoes and a string of raised islands (see Fig. 2). The Kyusyu–Palau Ridge, another large geanticlinal ridge, cuts off the basin in the south. The Daito Ridge, midway between the Kyusyu–Palau Ridge and the Ryukyu Trench is intermediate, and also shows uplift.

The east basin is somewhat shallower, and it rises gently toward the Honsyu–Mariana Ridge. The west basin is unusually deep.

The Philippine Sea Basin differs from the Pacific Basin Proper in the absence of very large seamounts. The Daito Ridge is a region of rugged topography which is complex and different from that of the mountainous ridges in the Pacific Basin proper; it is well sounded, drilled and studied (Hanzawa, 1940; Ladd *et al.*, 1953).

The Andesite Line is drawn along the trench axes of the easternmost trenches and marks the true boundary of Asia. That region inside of the line was formerly continental; thus the Andesite Line represents the limit of the Pacific Basin proper. Gutenberg and Richter (1949) state that a "continental structure" is indicated for the Philippine Sea judging by the velocity of shallow earthquake waves which cross it.

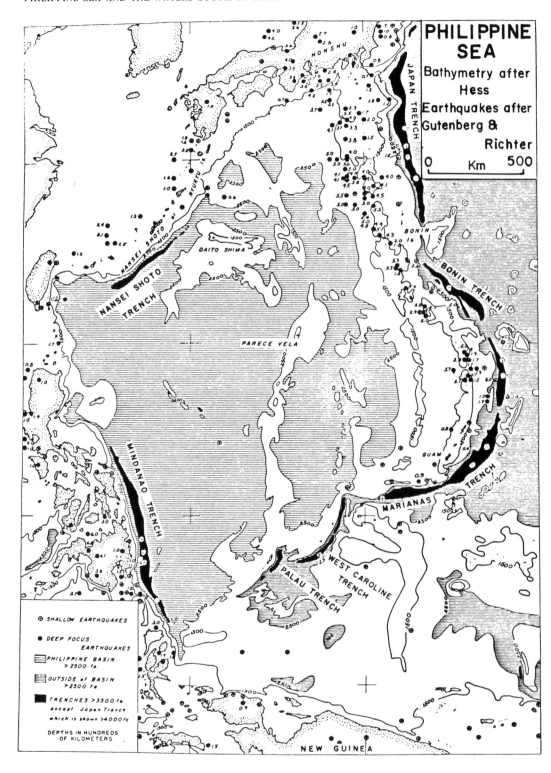

Fig. 1. Bathymetry and structure of Philippine Sea; bathymetry after Hess (1948); earthquakes after Gutenberg and Richter. (By permission of Princeton University Press, Princeton, N.J.)

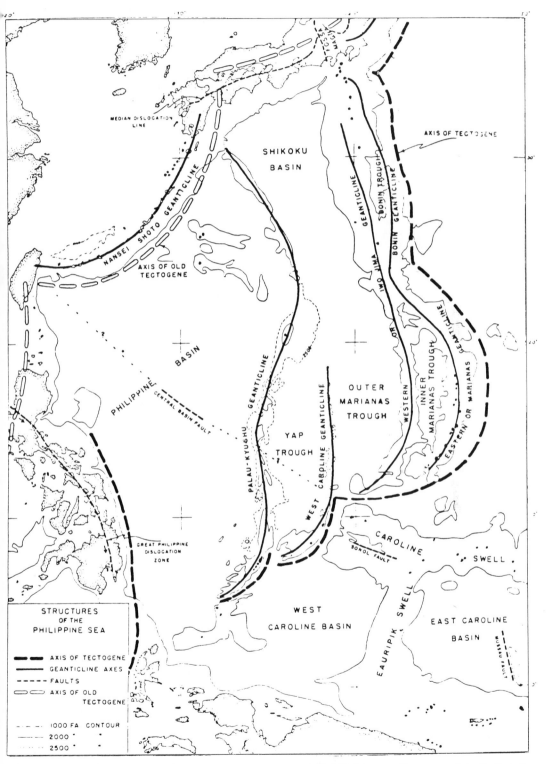

Fig. 2. Geotectonic sketch map of Philippine Sea (from Hess, 1948). The "tectogene" corresponds to the line of deep-sea trenches. "Old tectogene" represents site of earlier belt of trenches (orthogeosyncline).

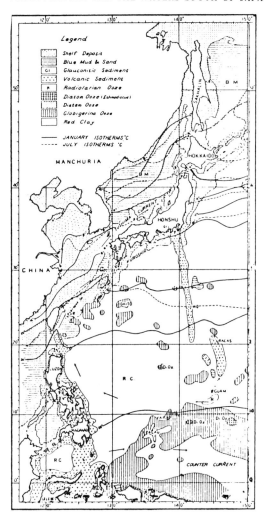

Fig. 3. Bottom deposits and isotherms of the Philippine Sea (adapted from Dietz, 1954).

MEAN WIND STRESS

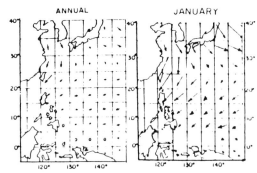

Fig. 4. (a) Mean annual wind stress over the Philippine Sea. (b) Mean wind stress in January [adapted from Malkus, 1962; after *Scripps Inst. Oceanog., Ocean. Rept.*, **14**, (1948)].

Concerning sediments, as can be seen in Fig. 3, the volcanic ones occur along the two volcanic ranges (Kyusyu–Taiwan–Luzon–Mindanao, and Idu–Ogasawara–Iwo Jima–Mariana); blue mud and sand occur along the continental shelf of the Asiatic continent and the Japanese Islands. Patches of globigerina ooze are scattered in some parts of the basin, particularly in the southern equatorial part. The major part of the basin is occupied by red clay (Hanzawa, 1928, 1935).

Climate

The major part of the Philippine Sea and the waters south of Japan is covered in summer by the western North Pacific High (anticyclone) which is called the "Ogasawara High" by the Japanese; in winter it is swept mostly by the northwesterly monsoon (cold and dry) starting from the Siberian

High of the Asiatic continent, reaching down to about 30°N or further south near the Subtropical Convergence. According to Jacobs (1942, 1951), the greatest evaporation over the entire Pacific Ocean in winter occurs in the Kuroshio Warm Current area with a rate more than 120 cm/yr, and with a second maximum in the north part of the Northeast Trade Wind zone. The greatest moisture and heat supply come from the above areas, particularly in winter (December, January, February).

In the tropical Pacific region, air temperature does not much change from winter to summer, the boundary moving to and fro between 20 and 30°C. In the mid-latitudes between the tropical zone and Japan, air temperature varies considerably from winter (about 10–15°C) to summer (25–30°C). In winter, the air temperature over the region adjacent to the Asiatic continent is lower than that over the mid-ocean in the same latitude.

Generally, in the tropics, the air is humid and hot, but coming into the Northeast Trade Wind zone, it becomes relatively cooler and fresh, due to the sunken dry air transported from the North Pacific High. However, in the Equatorial Zone, frequent calms make the climate more humid and uncomfortable.

Sea fogs are rare over the whole region, except in the northeastern part in winter or early spring. The precipitation is high in the northern part of the sea, especially over and near the Kuroshio Warm Current area. Rainfall is less in the zone of mid-latitudes (20–30°N). As shown in Fig. 4 (Malkus, 1962, after *SIO Oceanogr. Rept. No. 14*, 1948), the wind in the mid-latitude high is weaker compared to the surrounding monsoon and trade

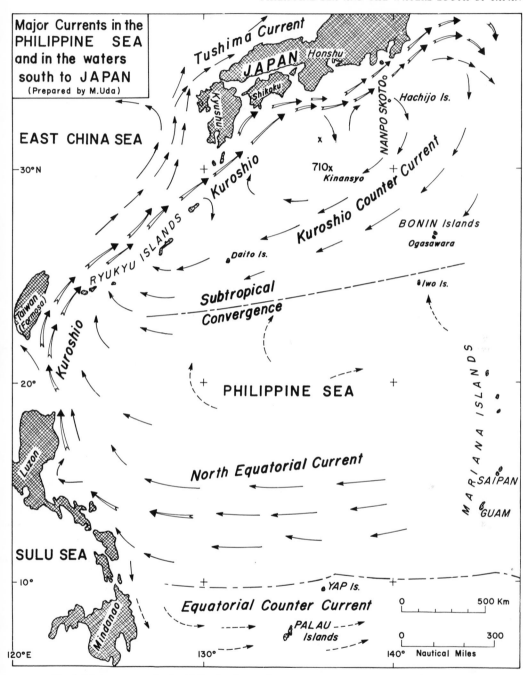

Fig. 5. Major currents in the Philippine Sea and waters south to Japan. (Prepared by M. Uda)

wind areas. In winter, the wind force attains 6 or 7 (Beaufort scale) in monsoon area and 3–5 in the trades.

Tropical cyclones (including hurricanes or typhoons) occur frequently in summer and autumn, particularly in September for severe typhoons. Typhoons generally follow a parabolic course having their turning point about 25–30°N. Ty-

phoons are normally generated in the region of tropical seas of the Marshall and Caroline Islands. In such regions, squalls occur frequently and develop sometimes into midget typhoons. The breeding area of typhoons is located within the Intertropical Convergence between the airmass brought by Northeast Trade Wind and the air mass brought by southwesterly wind over the

709

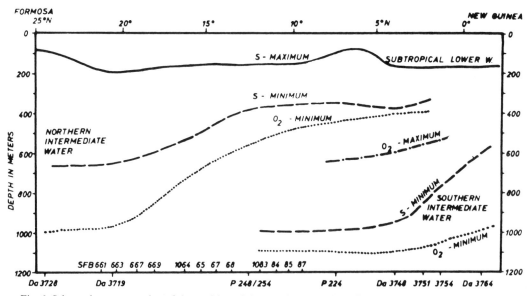

Fig. 6. Schematic representation of the position of the core layers of the different water masses in the Philippine Sea in a section from Taiwan (Formosa) to New Guinea (from Wyrtki, 1961; based largely on *Dana* Expedition data).

equator and generally in the area where the water temperature is higher than 26–27°C.

Currents and Water Masses (including Water Temperature and Salinity)

In the southern part of Phillippine Sea, the North Equatorial Current flows from east to west between 10 and 20°N with a velocity of about 0.5–2.0 knots driven by the semipermanent Northeast Trade Wind, and in lower latitudes (3–10°N) the Equatorial Countercurrent sets from west to east with a velocity of 1–2 knots. The Kuroshio Current originating from the seas east of Taiwan (Formosa) and Luzon flows in a northward direction with a velocity of 2 knots (100 cm/sec) or more and a volume transport of 40–70 million m³/sec. It turns in an easterly direction in the region south of Honshu (Japan proper) with a more accelerated velocity of 2–4 knots (Fig. 5). The name "Kuroshio" is derived from the color of the sea which is blackish, ultramarine to cobalt blue, usually, in Forel's scale, number 1 to 2 (sometimes 3), and from the transparency of the seawater measured by Secchi Disc at 25–40 m. The Kuroshio Current, a westerly intensification of the geostrophic flow, runs along the western and northern frontal zones of the North Pacific Central Water Mass (subtropic water mass) which rotates clockwise in a great gyre, corresponding to the surface highly saline water mass (of salinity 34.8–35.2‰). The water is warmer than 15°C in the upper layer above the 200-m depth throughout the whole year. The Kuroshio behaves sometimes in a peculiar meandering pattern in company with an abnormal cold water mass of cyclonic eddy

(M. Uda, 1964). According to Sverdrup (1942), Uda (1956), and Wyrtki (1961), the western North Pacific Intermediate Water has a thickness of 200–300 m, with its core depth from 200 m down to 800 m and the core salinity (34.0–34.5‰) and temperature (5°–10°C) which is dominant over the Philippine Sea (Figs. 6 and 7).

The Subtropical Convergence is located in the middle latitudes (20–28°N) in which the density in the upper layers increases rapidly poleward and is recognized by the sinking of the heavy water along it, especially in winter. The Subtropical Convergence corresponds to the southern limit for the winter fishing grounds of albacore tuna and whaling.

The pattern of the Kuroshio Counter Current by means of drift bottle experiments was first demonstrated by Y. Wada (1922) and afterwards by M. Uda (1938). It flows south of the Kuroshio to the SW–WSW through the eastern part of the Philippine Sea to its western boundary with the average velocity of 0.6–0.7 knot. The drift of current bottles onto the coasts of Miyako and Yaeyama Islands, south of Okinawa, is practically limited to the period of winter monsoon, from November to April or May. Accordingly, the Kuroshio Countercurrent in the waters south of the Kuroshio appears to flow in a southerly direction more strongly with the stronger winter monsoon. Kuroshio east off Taiwan is most strong in spring (Fig. 8).

The transparency of the seawater and its color indicate a sharp boundary at about 25°N latitude near the Subtropical Convergence in the season from January to April. The relatively cold water

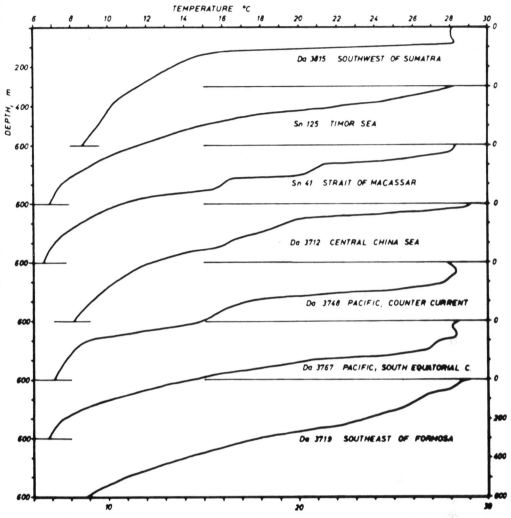

Fig. 7. (Philippine Sea) Typical curves of vertical distribution of temperature down to 600 m in South-east Asian waters. Notice that in contrast to nearly identical surface temperature, the gradient in the lowest curve (Philippine Sea) contrasts strikingly with the more equatorial profiles (from Wyrtki, 1961; based on *Dana* and *Snellius* data).

(more turbid and lower salinity) of the Kuroshio Countercurrent meets the warmer Central Pacific Water (more transparent and saline) in the North-west Pacific Ocean at the northern border of the North Equatorial Current near the Subtropical Convergence (M. Uda, 1955).

Several eddies are formed along the undulating line of the Subtropical Convergence, of which a conspicuous cyclonic eddy in the region adjacent to Ogasawara (Bonin) Islands appears in winter and spring (from February to May) corresponding to the traditional whaling ground (in the rectangle of 26–27°N, 143–144°E).

According to Sverdrup (1942), the Pacific Equatorial Water mass in the south is characterized by a straight line in the T-S correlation diagram between $T - 15°C$, $S - 35.15\%_0$ and $T - 8°C$, $S - 34.6\%_0$. A

mosaic of water masses in this region has been analyzed by K. Koenuma (1939).

Marine Biology and Fisheries

Most of the Philippine Sea and water south of Japan are poor in nutrients compared to the Oyashio Cold Current area and the coastal waters, except in the areas around or near banks, reefs, guyots and ridges, e.g., Kinan-Syo Bank, Koho-Tai Bank, Ogasawara (Bonin) Ridge, etc. Newly discovered elevations by echo sounder in this region can be exploited as tuna or skipjack fishing grounds.

The cyclonic vortices encountered along oceanic fronts or associated with the cold upwelling areas are concentrated fishing localities with high productivity, e.g., coastal fronts, Kuroshio Front,

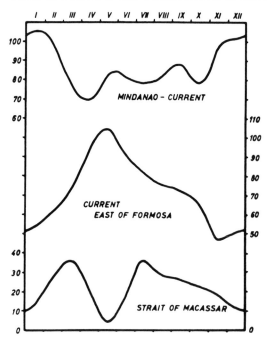

Fig. 8. Annual variation of the velocity of the current (in centimeters per second) off the east coast of Taiwan (Formosa), compared with the Mindanao Current (off the Philippines) and that in the Strait of Macassar (Wyrtki, 1961).

Subtropical Convergence and Equatorial Front, cold water mass off Kumano Nada and Enshu Nada, etc. The Kuroshio Current and its branch currents are related to the northward feeding migration of warm water fishes. The Kuroshio Countercurrent is marked by the returning migration (for skipjack, bluefin tuna, albacore tuna, etc.). The spawning grounds of the Japanese eel, pacific saury, whales and tuna are presumed to be in this area. The Idu–Ogasawara Ridge and Kyusyu–Okinawa–Taiwan Ridge constitute major migration routes for species including flying fish, sea turtles, etc.

MICHITAKA UDA

References

Biq, Chingchang, 1959, "The shape of the Philippine Basin and the relative movement between Asia and the western Pacific," *Intern. Oceanogr. Congr.* (Washington, Am. Assoc. Adv. Sci.), *Preprints,* 15.

De Terra, H., 1943, "Pleistocene geology and early Man in Java," *Trans. Am. Phil. Soc.,* 32, (3)(437–64.

Von Koeningswald, G. H. R., 1939, "Neue Menschenaffen und Vormenschenfunde," *Natur wissenschaften,* 27, 617–622.

Dietz, R. S., 1954, "Marine geology of northwestern Pacific," *Bull. Geol. Soc. Am.,* 65, 1199–1224.

Gutenberg, B., and Richter, C. F., 1949, "Seismicity of the Earth," Princeton, N.J., Princeton University Press, 273pp.

Hanzawa, S., 1928, "Preliminary report on marine deposits from the southwestern North Pacific," *Rec. Ocean. Works. Japan,* 1; 1935, *Rec. Ocean. Works. Japan,* 7, 1–7.

Hanzawa, S., 1940, "Micropalaeontological studies of drill cores from a deep well in Kita-Daito-Zima (North Borodino Island)," Jubilee publication for Prof. H. Yabe's 60th Birthday, 2, 755–802.

Jacobs, W. C., 1951, "Large scale aspects of energy transformation over the oceans," *Compendium Meteorol.*

Koenuma, K., 1939, "On the hydrography of southwestern part of North Pacific and Kuroshio," *Imp. Mar. Obs. Mem.,* 7.

Hess, H. H., 1948, "Major structural features of the Western North Pacific: an interpretation of H.O. 5485 Bathymetric chart, Korea to New Guinea," *Bull. Geol. Soc. Am.,* 59, 417–446.

Ladd, H. S., *et al.,* 1953, "Drilling on Eniwetok Atoll," *Bull. Am. Assoc. Petrol. Geologists,* 37, 2257–2280.

Malkus, J. S., 1962, "Large Scale Interactions," in "The Sea," Vol. 1, New York, Interscience Publishers.

Schott, G., 1935, "Geographie des Indischen und Stillen Ozeans," Hamburg, Boysen.

Sverdrup, H. U., *et al.,* 1942, "The Oceans," New York, Prentice Hall.

Tayama, R., 1952, "Coral Reefs in the South Seas," *Bull. Hydr. Office,* 11.

Uda, M., 1938, *Japan Imp. Fish. Expt. Sta. J.,* No. 9.

Uda, M., 1955, "On the Subtropical Convergence and the currents in the Northwestern Pacific," *Rec. Ocean. Works. Japan,* 2.

Uda, M., 1956, Proc. 8th Pac. Sc. Cong., Vol. III.

Uda, M., 1964, "On the nature of Kuroshio, its origin and meanders," *Studies of Oceanogr. Prof. Hidaka's Memor. Vol.*

Wada, Y., 1922, "Nihon Kankai Kairyu Tyosa Gyoseki," Maniti Press.

Wyrtki, K., 1961, "Physical oceanography of the southeast Asian waters," *Scripps Inst. Oceanogr., Rept. Naga Exped.,* 2.

PHYTOPLANKTON

The marine phytoplankton (Gr. plant wanderers) are unicellular, microscopic plant cells ranging in size from about 1μ to 1 mm, and include representatives of many algal groups: diatoms (Bacillariophyta), dinoflagellates (Pyrrophyta), coccolithophorids (Chrysophyta), silicoflagellates (Silicoflagellata), cryptomonads (Cryptophyta), chrysomonads (Chrysophyta), green algae (Chlorophyta), and blue-green algae (Cyanophyta). Of these, the first three groups usually predominate in marine communities, although the blue-green algal genus *Trichodesmium* frequently becomes very abundant in tropical, oceanic waters. The Red Sea is purported to have received its name from the reddish discoloration caused by the presence of *Trichodesmium*. Phytoplankton also occur in fresh water.

The diatoms possess a geological record which goes back to the Triassic. They occupy an interesting place in the plant kingdom because of their manufacture of a fairly thick (about 0.1μ), transparent, hydrated amorphous silica ($SiO_2 . nH_2O$) cell wall (frustule) which is similar to opal and which comprises from 19–77% of the dry weight. The rigid frustule consists of two equal halves (valves), one of which overlaps the other in a manner similar to that of a pill box. The frustule contains numerous perforations (areolae) of variable size and arrangement which permit the diffusion of gases and nutrients into the cell. Many species also have gelatinous threads, spines, setae, silica rods, or other protuberances, which link individual cells of the same species into chains; others are enclosed in a gelatinous envelope forming pseudo-colonies, and still others remain solitary. Cell division occurs through an asexual binary fission in which the two halves of the frustule pull apart and each daughter cell forms a new inner valve. The consequence of this mode of reproduction is that one daughter cell remains the same size as the parent cell, whereas the other is slightly smaller. Accordingly, a successive diminution in cell size occurs until a lower limit, which varies from species to species, is reached. At that time an auxospore stage occurs in which the cells become sexually differentiated into male and female cells. Fusion of gametes then occurs, followed by an exudation of the protoplasmic contents from the fertilized cell which enlarges to the adult size normal to the species, silicifies and then commences vegetative cellular division, as described. There are about 10,000 diatom species placed into two major subgroups— the centric diatoms (Centrales) which are radially symmetrical and float within the water column, and the pennate diatoms (Pennales) which are bilaterally symmetrical and predominate on the sea floor (benthic environment). Many pennate diatoms undergo jerky, propulsive movements of up to 20μ/sec, attributable to cytoplasmic streaming in a suture (raphe) exposed to the environment. Some pennate diatoms undertake diurnal vertical migrations in the upper few centimeters of the sea floor which frequently discolors tidal flats. Diatoms tend to predominate in cold waters rich in nutrients, but will thrive in tropical waters provided adequate nutrient supplies are available.

They are an extremely heterogeneous group morphologically and physiologically, and include forms which bridge the plant and animal kingdoms. There are two main subgroups: the armored forms (Peridiniales) which possess a cellulose cell wall subdivided into platelets, and the naked forms (Gymnodiniales) enclosed by a thin, structureless pellicle. One flagellum usually encircles the cell equatorially and acts as a rotator, while the second flagellum is directed backward and propels. The dinoflagellates reproduce by binary fission in which the cells divide transversely without the concomitant reduction in the cell size characteristic of the diatoms; sexual reproduction has not been demonstrated. The dinoflagellates are known for their bioluminescence, a phenomenon which has given the world-famous embayment, Bahía Fosforescente (Puerto Rico), its name, where they occur in prodigious numbers year round. Members of the dinoflagellates are also important fish parasites, while others (zooxanthellae) are symbiotic in corals and sea anemones, as well as in radiolarians and other forms. Dinoflagellates are represented by a diversity of forms in all water types, and seem to be the most varied in ecological character of the phytoplanktonic groups.

The geological record of the coccolithophorids extends back to the Cambrian, and therefore they appear to predate the diatoms and dinoflagellates. The coccolithophorids are biflagellated organisms covered with a variable number and type of minute ($1–35\mu$ in diameter) calcareous plates (coccoliths) which are usually calcitic. However, under certain nutrient and temperature conditions, vaterite or aragonite may comprise 50% or more of the coccolith structure. The coccolithophorids reproduce by binary fission, with evidence that sexual reproduction can also occur. These diminutive forms require the use of electron microscopy for an adequate description of their coccoliths, the basis of their taxonomy. Essential details of their morphology, life history, physiology and ecology are still lacking. They are mainly tropical in character, suggestive of a preference for high temperatures and low nutrient concentrations.

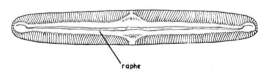

Fig. 1. A naviculoid diatom, *Pinnularia*, showing raphe, × 1200 diameters.

The dinoflagellates are motile organisms possessing two flagella, and capable of extensive diurnal vertical migrations in response to light. Their geological record extends back to the Cretaceous.

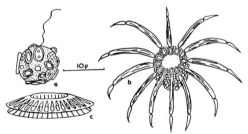

Fig. 2. Coccolithophores. (*a*) *Coccolithus* (*Pontosphaera*) *huxleyi*, (*b*) *Michaelsarsia aranea*, (*c*) a single coccolith from (*a*) as reconstructed from photographs by an electron microscope. As reproduced here it represents a magnification of 17,000 diameters.

The silicoflagellates possess a siliceous exo-skeleton of various patterns ranging in size from $10–150\mu$. Little is known about their biology, attributable in part to their relatively modest importance in the ocean. Their fossil record suggests that they were more important in geological time, a number of genera having been described from siliceous sedimentary rocks ranging in age from the Upper Cretaceous to the Recent.

The planktonic members of the blue-green algae appear to be important primarily in nutrient-impoverished tropical, oceanic environments, and in brackish waters. Members of the genus *Trichodesmium* appear capable of fixing elemental nitrogen.

The remaining groups included in the phytoplankton are primarily microflagellates whose importance, biology and phylogenetic relationships remain largely unknown.

The marine phytoplankton are of considerable interest because of their ubiquity and fundamental importance in the biological economy and geochemistry of the seas.

They consist of representatives possessing an autotrophic (photosynthetic), heterotrophic (utilize dissolved organic substances) or phagotrophic (feed on particulate matter) mode of nutrition. The autotrophic representatives, which have chlorophyll, frequently predominate and are important primary producers of organic matter (frequently expressed as carbon) by photosynthesis in which carbon dioxide, water and inorganic nutrients are elaborated into organic matter photochemically, a process in which oxygen is liberated. The oceans, which cover about 75% of the earth's surface, are inhabited by phytoplankton in the upper illuminated layers (euphotic zone) where photosynthesis takes place. In contrast, the higher algae (seaweeds), which require a substrate, occupy only the $1–2\%$ of the vast oceanic area suitably illuminated to permit their growth. A consequence of this is that the phytoplankton are responsible for the major part of the primary organic production (photosynthesis) occurring in the sea. In fact, the annual rate of net organic production by phytoplankton ($1.2–1.5 \times 10^{10}$ tons of carbon per year) is comparable to that occurring on land, and possibly even exceeds terrestrial primary production by twofold. Therefore, the ultimate source of food in the sea results from phytoplankton growth, their role being analogous to that of grasses and cereals on land in providing sustenance for herbivores (primarily zooplankton), i.e., phytoplankton are at the base of the marine food chain.

There are vertical, seasonal and regional variations in phytoplankton abundance and, hence, in primary production. The vertical distribution is influenced primarily by the depth of the euphotic zone in which photosynthesis can occur. This depth may range from less than a meter in turbid inshore areas to about 100 meters in oceanic waters. Wherever adequate light and other environmental conditions occur, including on the underside of ice, phytoplanktonic representatives are encountered. There is increasing evidence, however, that phytoplankton are not restricted to the euphotic zone. Significant populations of viable cells have been encountered in the abyssal depths down to 5000 meters and appear to be living heterotrophically.

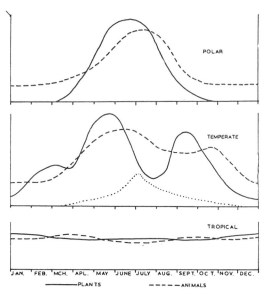

Fig. 3. The seasonal variations of plant and animal plankton in polar, temperate and tropical zones. Note that the increase in plants takes place first, when food is available the animals increase and graze down the plants. The dotted line in the temperate zone represents the abundance of dinoflagellates.

Seasonal oscillations in phytoplankton abundance, species composition and production occur in consequence of a complex interaction of light, temperature, mixing rate of the watermass, plant nutrients (N, P, Si, Fe, Mn, Mo, among other elements), and herbivore abundance. The number of phytoplankton cells may vary from less than 10^3 to more than 10^8 cells per liter of water, while the number of species may vary from less than 10 to greater than 250 per liter of water. The phytoplankton are characterized by fairly rapid growth rates of up to three cell divisions per day for diatoms, and six or more divisions per day for some of the flagellates. This permits them to exploit rapidly suitable growth conditions and contributes to seasonal pulses in abundance and production. Among the most frequent limiting factors preventing intense phytoplankton growth are inadequate illumination associated with seasonal variations in light intensity and/or insufficient retention within the euphotic zone due to excessive vertical mixing of the watermass. Nutrient limitation is another important factor. Marine phytoplankton have a protoplasmic composition of C:N:P of about 100:15:1, by atoms. During growth (photosynthesis), these elements are removed from the water at approximately these ratios, along with the simultaneous removal of other vital nutrients such as Si and Fe. Uptake of these nutrients may continue to the point where one or more may be reduced to levels incapable of supporting the existing population or sustaining further growth. Under such conditions, the population will decline until the limiting nutrients increase again to favorable concentrations. Nutrients are replenished by bacterial degradation of phytoplankton-derived dissolved and particulate organic compounds to inorganic moieties (regeneration) and/or are excreted by zooplankton or are introduced in runoff waters. Under certain conditions excessive grazing by predators leads to a decline in phytoplankton abundance, while the converse situation of a relaxation in predation at times leads to an increase providing other growth conditions are favorable.

Regional variations in phytoplankton abundance, species distribution and production are also a consequence of those environmental conditions causing seasonal variations. In those areas where two water masses diverge, as in the equatorial Pacific and Norwegian Sea, or where an upwelling of cool, nutrient-rich water ascends to the surface to replace nutrient-impoverished water displaced offshore by winds (west coasts of Africa, Central and South America), or when nutrient-rich deep water is periodically mixed with surface water (as in the Sargasso Sea), luxuriant phytoplankton growth occurs. Phytoplankton growth in the Polar regions is closely related to the seasonal variations in light intensity and is negligible in those regions which are permanently ice covered. In general, the most productive regions tend to lie in nontropical coastal regions, and in tropical coastal areas where upwelling occurs.

Prodigious blooms of phytoplankton frequently occur leading to water-mass discoloration when the population approaches 10^8 cells/liter. Periodically the coastal waters off Norway become a chalky or milky-green color due to enormous populations of the coccolithophorid *Coccolithus huxleyi*. Similarly, dinoflagellate blooms may discolor the water a rusty red ("red tide"), a condition which may be accompanied by the liberation of a potent toxin. For example, red tide blooms of *Gymnodinium brevis* in the Gulf of Mexico are frequently accompanied by a mass mortality of fishes and other animals. Similar kills have been reported from Walvis Bay, South Africa. The development of red tide blooms of the dinoflagellate genus, *Gonyaulax*, is especially insidious. A strong neurotoxin is produced which accumulates in mussels and clams ("paralytic shellfish poison") and often leads to a violent death upon their consumption by humans. Among the many recorded deaths, 150 people died from toxic shellfish consumption during 1799 near Sitka, Alaska.

Phytoplankton are rich in proteins (40–50%) and fats (20–27%) which has led to their consideration as sources of human nutriment and raw materials for industrial uses. Members of the freshwater phytoplankton, particularly the green algal genus *Chlorella*, are being grown in Japan, for example, in large outdoor troughs in pilot studies designed to assess their possible use as a food supplement. The artificial cultivation of certain marine mollusks and shrimps has become possible through the use of a diet of certain phytoplankton species which can be cultured. Mass cultures of diatoms were grown by German scientists during World War II in an unsuccessful attempt to obtain a fat supply for the munitions industry. The photosynthetic nature of the phytoplankton is also being exploited in other ways. Certain freshwater phytoplankton species are being grown in sewage waste treatment pools in which they lower pollution loads indirectly by providing oxygen for the bacterial oxidation of organic pollutants, and directly by depleting the nitrogenous and phosphorus compounds. Important byproducts of such photosynthetic waste treatment are the reclamation of water and the harvesting of the algal growth for use as feed supplements for domestic animals. Phytoplankters, principally of the genus *Chlorella*, are also being tested for possible use in life support systems for astronauts and submariners. The principle of this application is that artificially illuminated cultures are supplied with human gaseous (CO_2), liquid and particulate wastes as a nutrient source leading to continuous phytoplankton growth (photosynthesis) and oxygen liberation for human consumption.

The growth of phytoplankton is dependent upon adequate retention (flotation) within the euphotic zone. However, ultimately all phytoplankton sink to the sea floor upon death, senescence, or within fecal pellets excreted by herbivores, etc., an aspect of phytoplankton growth having important geochemical and paleoecological consequences. The origin of petroleum is possibly dependent, in part, upon settling of phytoplankton whose organic products serve as precursors. For example, phytoplankton chlorophyll degrades to phaeophytin, a substance found in sediments and petroleum. Also, hydrocarbon-like lipids occur in phytoplankton in which the $C^{13}:C^{12}$ ratios are similar to those in hydrocarbon fractions found in sediments and petroleum. The settling of large amounts of organic matter onto the sea floor following toxic red tide blooms has also been considered to represent a possible source of petroleum resulting from the bacterial reduction of organic matter to hydrocarbons.

The siliceous diatom frustules and the calcareous coccoliths of the coccolithophorids are quite resistant to dissolution and have formed extensive deposits of diatomaceous and calcareous ooze on the sea floor. This has also resulted in significant fossil deposits of diatomaceous earth which go back to the Cretaceous, and presently support an important industry. Similarly, coccolithophorids have contributed significantly to many limestone and chalk deposits from the Jurassic to the Recent.

During growth, as well as upon decomposition, phytoplankton liberate dissolved organic substances into seawater which appear to be important to geochemical processes. Recent work has shown that these substances may be removed from solution by adsorption onto the surface of air bubbles. This leads to the formation of thin, semitransparent organic aggregates usually ranging in size from about 5μ to several millimeters in diameter. Sheet-like aggregates up to about 2 meters in length have been observed occasionally. Organic aggregates, which contain about 30% organic matter, have been shown to contain from 2–10% $CaCO_3$, and to adsorb inorganic and organic phosphorus, manganese and other minor and trace elements. Aside from their utilization and decomposition by marine organisms, the sedimentation of organic aggregates, estimated at a rate of 2 meters/day, is thought to be possibly an important mechanism leading to the deposition and accumulation of certain elements in marine sediments. In addition, the trace metal chemistry of seawater appears to be influenced by aggregate formation and, through chelation, by dissolved organic substances emanating from phytoplankton growth.

THEODORE J. SMAYDA

References

*Fogg, G. E., 1965, "Algal Cultures and Phytoplankton Ecology," Madison, Wisc., University of Wisconsin Press. 126pp.

Fraser, J., 1962, "Nature Adrift, The Story of Marine Plankton." G. T. Foulis & Co. Ltd. London. 178pp.

*Lewin, R. A. (editor), 1962, "Physiology and Biochemistry of Algae," New York, Academic Press, 929pp.

Mattoni, R. H. T., Keller, E. C., and Myrick, H. N., 1965, "Industrial photosynthesis," *Bio-Science*, **15**, No. 6, 403–407.

Ryther, J. H., 1959, "Potential productivity of the sea," *Science*, **130**, 602–608.

Wangersky, P. J., 1965, "The organic chemistry of sea water," *Am. Scientist*, **53**, No. 3, 358–374.

*Wood, E. J. F., 1965, "Marine Microbial Ecology," New York, Reinhold Publishing Corp., 243pp.

PLANKTONIC PHOTOSYNTHESIS

As practiced today, this study principally considers the relationship of physical and chemical factors of the planktonic environment on photosynthesis of phytoplankton. In the case of the oceans, a lion's share of the carbon production in that body and hence the world is by marine phytoplankton, and in large lakes where water depth eliminates attached aquatics, the photosynthetic production by phytoplankton is also the largest source of carbon.

Some research workers in this field treat the entire phytoplankton populations as a photosynthetic unit with frequent use of mathematical models and biochemical elements. Other workers may isolate a single species of phytoplankton for study. The principle organisms of phytoplankton are diatoms and dinoflagellates. Fresh waters appear to have greater diversity of species than the oceans. The open oceans have more diversity than nearshore areas. Coccolithophores and blue-green algae are at times abundant in the open oceans; however, a predominant group found in fresh waters, the desmids, is missing.

All of the most common photosynthetic pigments can be observed in the phytoplankton. In the open oceans, chlorophylls a and c are the principle

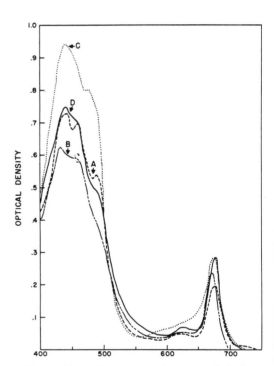

Fig. 1. Absorption spectra of extracts of plankton algae: (A) a diatom, *Cyclotella sp.*; (B) a dinoflagellate, *Amphidinium sp.*; (C) a green flagellate, *Chlamydomonas*; (D) a natural population sampled from Woods Hole waters (from Yentsch, 1960).

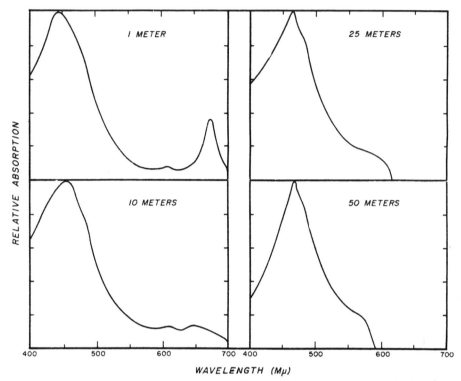

Fig. 2. Relative absorption by phytoplankton of light available at different depths in clear water (from Yentsch, 1962).

chlorophylls along with a whole host of carotenoids specific to diatoms and dinoflagellates. Chlorophyll b is at times abundant in fresh waters and polluted estuaries. Pycobilin pigments occur in both fresh and salt water, being associated with "blooms" of mostly blue-green algae.

Most research workers define phytoplankton photosynthesis by the conventional relationship,

$$CO_2 + HOH \xrightarrow[\text{chlorophyll}]{h\nu} CHOH + O_2$$

In most experiments either oxygen or carbon dioxide is measured. In recent years the adaptation of the carbon-14 technique has provided a sensitive method for measurement of photosynthetic carbon production.

The depth to which photosynthesis can be detected in a body of water depends principally upon the amount of light incident at the surface and the water transparency. The deepest euphotic zones are slightly over 100 meters in depth while the shallowest may be less than 1 meter. The water, by absorption, tends to select out specific wavelengths; thus phytoplankton living near the surface photosynthesize in "white light," while plants living at depth photosyntheses in light varying from blue light in transparent waters to yellow brown in turbid waters.

In phytoplankton the photosynthetic response to light intensity is roughly linear from zero to $\frac{1}{10}$ of full sunlight. Further increases in light intensity produce only a slight increase in photosynthetic rate and at times high intensities may inhibit the photosynthetic rate. Phytoplankton can adapt to low light intensities, and in these circumstances, which generally occur near the bottom of the euphotic zone, the intensity which "saturates" the photosynthetic rate may be 50% lower than in so called sun-adapted phytoplankton.

The principal nutrient that appears to limit phytoplankton photosynthesis is nitrogen; however, carbon dioxide may become limiting in fresh waters. In many cases, direct correlations between

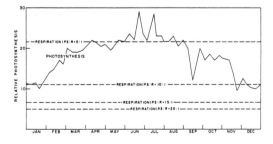

Fig. 3. Relative photosynthesis throughout a year. Different PS: R (photosynthesis: respiration ratio) values at light saturation indicated, for phytoplankton from Newport, Rhode Island (from Ryther, 1956).

photosynthetic rate and vertical turbulence have been observed. This is because the vertical mixing brings up nutrient rich bottom water into the euphotic zone. There is a delicate growth balance between nutrient enrichment by vertical mixing and light limitation. The annual cycle is interesting. For optimum photosynthesis, the depth of mixing should not be more than 2–3 times the euphotic zone. It is disastrous for the photosynthetic cell to sink out of the euphotic zone, and many organisms have morphological features and biochemical mechanisms to retard sinking.

CHARLES S. YENTSCH

References

Doty, M. S., and Oguri, M., 1957, "Evidence for a photosynthetic daily periodicity," *Limnol. Oceanog.*, **2**, 37–40.

Holmes, R. W., 1957, "Solar radiation, submarine daylight, and photosynthesis," in (Hedgpeth, J. W., editor) "Treatise on marine ecology and paleoecology," *Geol. Soc. Am. Mem. No. 67*, **1**, 109–128.

Ketchum, B. H., Ryther, J. H., Yentsch, C. S., and Corwin, N., 1958, "Productivity in relation to nutrients," *J. Conseil, Conseil Perm. Intern. Exploration Mer, Rappt. et Proc. Verb.*, **144**, 132–140.

Munk, W. H., and Riley, G. A., 1952, "Absorption of nutrients by aquatic plants," *J. Marine Res.*, **11**, 215.

Ryther, J. H., 1954, "The ratio of photosynthesis to respiration in marine plankton algae and its effect upon the measurement of productivity," *Deep-Sea Res.*, **2**, 134.

Ryther, J. H., 1956, "Photosynthesis in the ocean as a function of light intensity," *Limnol. Oceanog.*, **1**, 61.

Steemann Nielsen, E., and Hansen, V. K., 1959, "Light adaptation in marine phytoplankton populations and its interrelation with temperature," *Physiol. Plantarum*, **12**, 370.

Yentsch, C. S., 1960, "The influence of phytoplankton pigments on the color of sea water," *Deep-Sea Res.*, **7**, 1–9.

Yentsch, C. S., 1962, "Marine Plankton," in (Lewin, R. A., editor) "Physiology and Biochemistry of Algae," pp. 771–797, New York, Academic Press.

PLANKTON—*See* **PELAGIC LIFE and PHYTO-PLANKTON**

POISSON'S EQUATION—*See* Vol. II

PRANDTL NUMBERS—*See* **THERMAL INSTABILITY**

PRECISION DEPTH RECORDERS

Precision depth recorders perform the timing and recording in high-resolution echo-sounding systems by precisely recording acoustic echo time versus ship's time on permanent graphic profiles called *echograms*.

History

Marti is credited with placing the first known graphic depth recorder into use in 1922, a few years after construction and operation of the first echo sounders. By 1940, graphic recorders were widely employed in shallow-water navigation and surveying. None, however, recorded in depths greater than 1000 fathoms. The first sounders and recorders capable of sounding all ocean depths were developed for the United States Navy during World War II. Following the war these sounders were installed on oceanographic research vessels. Although good results were obtained at all depths, accuracy was limited by inability to precisely control the timing mechanism. Precision depth recorders attaining timing accuracy better than 1 part in 3000 were developed in the United States in 1953 and 1954 (Luskin *et al.*, 1954; Knott and Hersey, 1956). Subsequently British and German designs with similar high resolution and accuracy have been developed. Improvement and refinement of these and other similar instruments has steadily taken place over the last decade.

Operation

A precision depth recorder records short, discrete sound pulses sent out from a transducer and the resulting reflected echoes. Precision in timing is obtained by use of a tuning fork which serves as a constant frequency source independent of the ship's power supply. Special recording paper from continuous rolls is fed at a constant rate through the machine. Marking styli mounted on a cycling belt pass across the width of the paper at constant speed. The electrical impulses from picked up sound cause the styli to mark either by burning through the upper white layer of paper, exposing the black lower layer, or by chemical reaction with wet paper, depending on the type of machine. An outgoing sound pulse, or *ping*, is emitted from the transducer each time a stylus passes a certain point. The time interval between successive outgoing signals exactly corresponds to the time required for one stylus to traverse the working width of the paper. Thus the styli register every outgoing pulse at exactly the same distance below the top of the paper, forming the *zero line* (Fig. 1). Incoming echoes are recorded at a distance below the zero line which depends on the relationship between total echo time and the interval between outgoing signals. For example, with an interval between pings of 1 second, travel times of $\frac{1}{2}$, $1\frac{1}{2}$, and $2\frac{1}{2}$ seconds, etc., would be recorded about halfway down from the zero line. Echo times of $\frac{7}{8}$, $1\frac{7}{8}$, and $2\frac{7}{8}$ seconds, etc., would be recorded near the bottom.

Echo-sounding Units

Echo soundings are time measurements and are commonly expressed in units of $\frac{1}{400}$ second total travel time. These units are variously referred to as

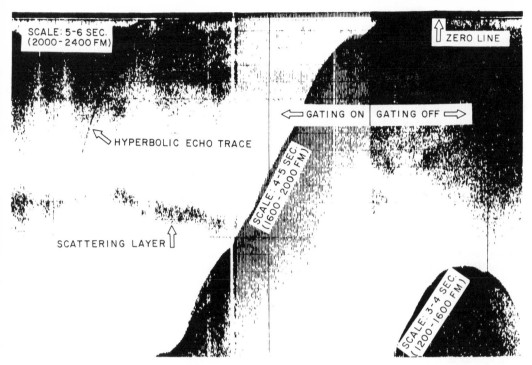

Fig. 1. Section of PDR record. Dashed horizontal lines are spaced vertically at 20/400 second (20 uncorrected fathoms), horizontally at 3 minutes ship's time. Heavy vertical lines are marked at intervals of 30 minutes.

standard units, or nominal fathoms. Currently there is a movement to convert to $\frac{1}{100}$ or $\frac{1}{1000}$ of a second. However, with current echo-sounding techniques it is difficult if not impossible to measure echo time to $\frac{1}{1000}$ of a second, and present instruments can do much better than $\frac{1}{100}$, so in the meantime the standard unit of $\frac{1}{400}$ second will likely remain in use. Units of $\frac{1}{750}$, $\frac{1}{725}$, and $\frac{1}{420}$ second are employed by certain workers, but are obviously less convenient and are not in general use.

Scales

With the 1-second ping interval, the depth scale would obviously be 0–400 units or some multiple thereof (Fig. 1). This is called a *sweep* of 400. On certain recording units several other sweeps are available. Depth range can usually be determined by switching momentarily to a slower sweep, or by sending a long ping and counting sweep intervals between departure and return. Vertical exaggeration varies with ship's speed. In a typical case, with a ship's speed of 10 knots, a paper speed of 24 in./hr, and a sweep of 400 (18 inches), the vertical exaggeration would be approximately 19:1.

Determination of Absolute Depth

Charts employing standard echo time units are used in most geological studies when the absolute depth is unimportant. However, in certain oceanographic and in most gravimetric studies absolute graphic studies absolute

depth must be determined with a high degree of precision. Inaccuracies in recorded echo distance fall into several categories: (1) those inherent in the sounding and recording instruments, (2) those due to pitch, roll, and forward motion of the ship, (3) those due to unrecorded changes in the depth of transmitter and receiver below the water line, and (4) those arising from refraction of sound rays by vertical changes in sound velocity within a water column. These errors rarely amount to more than 5–10 units.

Sound Velocity. Velocities of sound in seawater commonly range between 1450 and 1550 m/sec, but values higher than 1600 m/sec and lower than 1400 m/sec do occur. Velocities vary with temperature,

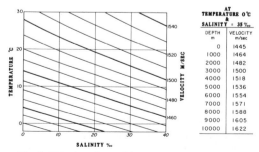

AT TEMPERATURE 0°C & SALINITY = 35‰	
DEPTH m	VELOCITY m/sec
0	1445
1000	1464
2000	1482
3000	1500
4000	1518
5000	1536
6000	1554
7000	1571
8000	1588
9000	1605
10000	1622

Fig. 2. Velocity of sound in water versus temperature, salinity and depth (after Dietrich, 1963, p. 68). (By permission of John Wiley & Sons, N.Y.)

719

salinity, and pressure (Fig. 2). Tables (Matthews, 1939) which account for geographical variations in the temperature–salinity–depth profile (for each of 52 separate oceanic regions) can be used to convert echo times to true distance (fathoms or meters).

Slope Interpretation. Sound is propagated downward from the ship's hull in an irregular conical pattern. Echoes can return from any reflecting surface normal to the direction of propagation within the effective cone of sound. Total angular width of this cone is 40–60° in most sounders, although instruments with much narrower effective beam have been developed. Echo travel paths deviate from the vertical by an amount equal to the slope of the bottom surface from which reflection occurs [Fig. 3(a)]. Where bottom slopes are so steep that no interface within the cone of sound is normal, weak reflections (side echoes) may return from the surface most nearly corresponding to the normal, or no reflection is recorded [Fig. 3(b)]. Discrete steep-sided summits reflect from any position within the effective cone of sound, giving rise to hyperbolic echoes as the ship passes over [Fig. 4(a)]. From Fig. 4(a) the relationship

$$(XO)^2 = (XZ)^2 + (OZ)^2$$

can be rewritten

$$\frac{(XO)^2}{(OZ)^2} - \frac{(XZ)^2}{(OZ)^2} = 1$$

a form of the equation of the hyperbola (Hoffman, 1957). Steep-sided ridges and valleys also cause hyperbolic echoes [Fig. 4(b)]. In areas of rugged but fine-textured topography, several bottom surfaces within the cone of sound often reflect simultaneously to give multiple echo traces.

One graphical method of slope correction is to plot a profile from the echogram at no vertical exaggeration and swing arcs with a beam compass to empirically construct an envelope representing the actual bottom. Slope corrections can be taken directly from this profile. Over a bottom surface of relatively uniform slope, equations relating recorded slope (φ) to true bottom slope (θ),

$$\sin \theta = \tan \varphi$$

echo distance (d) to true depth below the ship (D)

$$d = D/\cos \theta$$

and echo distance to horizontal distance between the ship and a line extending vertically through the echo point (x)

$$d = x/\sin \theta$$

may be useful in slope correction. Some of the three-dimensional aspects can be resolved by multiple crossings of the same area or by simultaneous use of wide-beam and narrow-beam sounding systems.

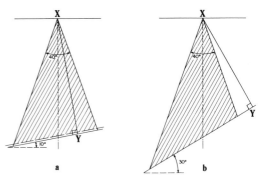

Fig. 3. Echo travel paths from slopes of 10° (a) and 30° (b). X represents position of ship. Shaded area represents cone of sound having a total angular width of 40°. XY shows approximate path along which echoes recorded at ship would travel. In (a) echo time along XY would be recorded as if its travel path extended vertically below the ship. Dashed line just above bottom would represent approximate position of recorded trace. In (b) echoes would be weak or not recorded at all.

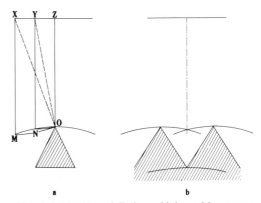

Fig. 4. (a) X, Y, and Z show ship's position over a steep-sided summit. XO, YO, and ZO represent echo travel paths at these positions. Arcs swung to M and N show how hyperbolic trace is developed. (b) Shows how hyperbolic traces might appear over steep-sided ridges and valleys.

Multiple and Other Reflections

Many echoes other than single reflections from the ocean bottom are recorded. Echoes from two or more bottom "bounces" of the sound are commonly picked up at shallow depths. These are easily distinguished because they are weaker and occur as multiples of the actual depth. Fish and other marine organisms may occur in abundance at certain levels and constitute reflecting horizons, often termed *scattering layers* (Fig. 1). Marine life near the surface reflects in a random pattern, often blackening the upper part of echograms. Where this or the outgoing ping obscures the bottom reflections, *gating* is employed, whereby transmitter and receiver operate alternately so that bottom echoes are recorded without near-surface interference (Fig. 1).

With 10–12 kc sound source, reflecting interfaces between layers of sediment at depth ranges on the order of tens of fathoms below the bottom may give rise to *sub-bottom reflections.* With lower frequency and high-energy sound sources, sub-bottom sounding can be extended to 1–2 km beneath the bottom (see *Seismic Reflection Profiling*). Sub-bottom reflections are of particular interest to geologists since they often yield information concerning attitude of strata, relative rates of deposition, and recent tectonic movements. Correlation between cores may be possible in conjunction with sub-bottom echoes.

TROY L. HOLCOMBE

References

Dietrich, G., 1963, "General Oceanography," New York, John Wiley & Sons.

Hoffman, J., 1957, "Hyperbolic curves applied to echo sounding," *International Hydrographical Review*, **34**, No. 2, 45–55.

Knott, S. T., and Hersey, J. B., 1956, "Interpretation of high-resolution echo-sounding techniques and their use in bathymetry, marine geophysics, and biology," *Deep-Sea Res.*, **4**, 36–44.

Krause, D. C., 1962, "Interpretation of echo sounding profiles," *International Hydrographic Review*, **39**, No. 1, pp. 65–123.

Luskin, B., Heezen, B. C., Ewing, M., and Landisman, M., 1954, "Precision measurement of ocean depth," *Deep-Sea Res.*, **1**, 131–140.

PRESSURE GRADIENT

In mathematics, the gradient of a quantity is defined as a vector which is directed to the maximum rate of increment of the quantity with a distance. The magnitude of this vector equals that rate. However, in meteorology and oceanography, the pressure gradient usually indicates the horizontal component of this vector, i.e., a vector having a direction of the maximum increment of the pressure in a horizontal plane and a magnitude of that rate. This is because horizontal motions in the atmosphere and the ocean are mainly caused by (horizontal) pressure gradient. In the vertical direction, the gravitational force dominates and the pressure difference only balances this force (hydrostatic equilibrium). Therefore, vertical motions in large scales are generally 100–10^5 times smaller than the horizontal motions (with larger vertical motions in the atmosphere than in the ocean), though the vertical gradient of pressure is about 10^4 times larger than the horizontal gradient both in the atmosphere and the ocean.

In the atmosphere, the pressure difference in a horizontal plane (or pressure gradient) is mainly caused by the difference of vertically averaged density of the air column above that plane. The difference of the averaged density is due to the difference of the air temperature (and to a lesser degree the humidity) in the troposphere and also to the difference of the height of tropopause. In the ocean, the pressure gradient is caused by the difference of vertically averaged density which is dependent on water temperature and salinity, by the slope of the sea surface and by the difference of the atmospheric pressure at the sea surface.

When the pressure gradient force balances with the Coriolis force only, the resultant motion is a geostrophic current (or wind). In the northern hemisphere it flows to the right of the pressure gradient force (see Fig. 1) along the

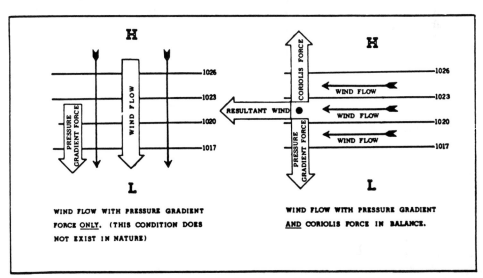

Fig. 1. If the deflective (Coriolis) force resulting from the rotation of the earth did not exist, wind would flow across isobars to lower pressure (left). Because deflective force is always at right angles to the wind, however, the wind actually flows parallel to the isobars (right).

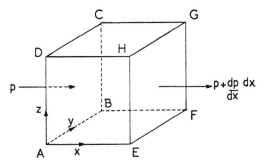

Fig. 2. The pressure gradient force (Gordon, 1962).

isobars. Its speed equals $(\rho f)^{-1}\,\Delta p/\Delta L$, where ρ is the density of the fluid, f is the Coriolis parameter, Δp is the pressure difference of two neighboring isobars, and ΔL is the distance between the isobars. The pressure gradient of 1 millibar (100 km) causes geostrophic winds of 17, 9 and 6 m/sec at latitudes 20°, 40° and 60°, respectively, at sea level with air temperature of 20°C. In the ocean, the pressure gradient of 1 decibar (100 millibars) per 100 km causes geostrophic currents of 2.0, 1.1 and 0.7 m/sec at latitudes of 20°, 40° and 60°, respectively. The slope of the sea surface of 1 m/100 km almost equals the pressure gradient of 1 decibar/100 km in the oceans. On the other hand, the effect of the atmospheric pressure gradient at the sea level on currents in the ocean is generally negligible except in severe hurricanes and cyclones.

TAKASHI ICHIYE

References

Gordon, A. H., 1962, "Elements of Dynamic Meteorology," Princeton, N.J., 217pp.

Petterssen, S., 1958, "Introduction to Meteorology," New York, McGraw-Hill Book Co., 327pp.

Sverdrup, H. U., Johnson, M. W., and Fleming, R. H., 1945, "The Oceans," Englewood Cliffs, N.J., Prentice-Hall.

Von Arx, W. S., 1962, "An Introduction to Physical Oceanography," Reading. Mass., Addison-Wesley, 422pp.

Cross-references: *Gradient Wind; Oceanic Circulation; Pressure* (Vol. II.)

PRIMARY PRODUCTION

Introduction

The study of primary production in ocean waters is concerned with the initial formation of living matter from more stable inorganic fractions. As far as known, this reaction occurs principally within a group known as phytoplankton algae which are capable of photosynthesis. This group is principally composed of microscopic diatoms, dinoflagellates, and coccolithphores (see articles on each in Vol. VII).

Because of everyday familiarity with terrestrial plants and seashore seaweeds, it is surprising to realize that the planktonic algae of the open ocean account for at least 75% of the photosynthetic production on the earth. Because of the nature of the distribution of light in seawater, photosynthetic production is confined to only the upper 100 meters in clear ocean waters which is known as the Euphotic Zone.

Light in the Euphotic Zone

From the surface of the oceans to the base of the Euphotic Zone, light intensity decreases logarithmically to about 1% of the surface intensity. Below this depth, light energy is too low for photosynthetic production to occur.

The amount of light in the Euphotic Zone depends on geography, season, time of day, the surface and the transparency characteristics of the seawater. If the ocean surface is roughened by wind action, the amount of light penetrating the surface is reduced. Likewise, the transparency of the water is reduced by suspended inorganic and organic materials, or colored solutions.

The water itself greatly modifies the wavelengths which penetrate it. The long and the very short wavelengths are quickly attenuated in the first 10–20 meters. Photosynthetic production below this depends upon the phytoplankton absorbing the wavelengths in the blue-green region of the visible spectrum.

Methods of Estimating Primary Production

Estimates of the amount of primary production in an ocean area are generally made by the measurement of the rate of carbon fixation throughout the entire Euphotic Zone. This is accomplished by addition of radioactive carbon 14 to water samples taken at specific depths throughout the Euphotic Zone. Generally, samples are taken at the surface and at depths to which 50, 25, 10, and 1% of the surface radiation penetrates. Water samples are collected in nontoxic closing bottles and are transferred to transparent glass bottles. The carbon 14 is added to the bottles which are then resuspended on a wire or rope within the Euphotic Zone for 4–6 hours during a midday period. The samples are then recovered and filtered through a membrane filter, and the radioactivity in the particulate matter on the filter is counted and can be expressed as a quantity of carbon fixed during the period of time of exposure. Quite often the vertical profile of carbon fixed by a given volume of seawater is integrated graphically, and the results are expressed as the amount of carbon fixed under a square area of sea surface.

Factors Affecting Primary Production

The primary production of the oceans varies daily, seasonally, and geographically as a function of changes in light intensity. There are, however, great variations which are the result of factors other than light intensity, which occur for the following reasons: In the photosynthetic process the phytoplankton take in from the seawater solution the essential nutrients for the formation of particulate organic material. The particulate material, which is more dense than seawater, sinks and then is subjected to bacterial attack, autolysis and grazing by marine herbivores. The net result of this process is a downward flux of plant nutrients from the Euphotic Zone, and without regeneration or mixing processes, the Euphotic Zone would become impoverished. Nutrients may be added or retained within the Euphotic Zone by bacteria or animal regeneration, i.e., biochemical recycling or by a mixing of deep nutrient-rich waters with the surface waters. Throughout the temperate oceans of the world, this vertical mixing or so-called wind mixing ("upwelling") is the process principally responsible for nutrient enrichment.

Since the planktonic plants depend on light for their growth, intense or deep vertical mixing (say, to 3–5 times the depth of the Euphotic Zone) may eventually limit the population growth. This situation occurs during winter months in temperate oceans when the incoming solar radiation is low, the density gradient in the water column is slight, and surface wind velocities are high. In temperate oceans, a "spring bloom" or flowering of phytoplankton coincides with the increase of solar radiation, the formation of a density gradient in the water column called a thermocline, and a decrease in wind velocity across the surface of the oceans.

With increasing radiation of the summer months, the surface waters are heated and may become 2–3 times less dense than the deeper underlying waters. As a result, mixing within the Euphotic Zone is almost impossible and nutrient concentrations in the Euphotic Zone are quite low. Phytoplankton populations within the zone become capable of only a slight amount of growth principally due to the limitation of nutrients.

Because of their well-known role in plant nutrition, nitrogen and phosphorus compounds have been considered as limiting nutrients to the phytoplankton. The cycling of these nutrients is very poorly understood; however, it is evident that population numbers and productive potential are low when these nutrient compounds are in very low concentration in the surface waters. Some emphasis has also been placed on the role of trace elements and vitamins as limiting factors.

The end of the phytoplankton bloom is characterized by an abrupt decline in numbers of phytoplankton cells and also their productive potential. The principal reasons for the abrupt disappearance are:

(1) The plants may sink out of the Euphotic Zone.

(2) Plants are removed from the water by grazing herbivores.

With regard to the rapid sinking of cells from the Euphotic Zone, it has been demonstrated that cells deficient in certain nutrients, mainly nitrogen and phosphorus, sink more rapidly than healthy cells. Hence, at the end of the growing season when nutrient concentrations are low, sinking of the phytoplankton plants is rapid. At all times, the numbers of phytoplankton is the result of a balance between the productive rate of the plants and the removal rate by sinking and grazing. As previously mentioned, nutrient deficiency tends to increase sinking rate. Nutrient deficiency also retards the productive rate of the planktonic plants, tilting the balance toward phytoplankton removal.

Tropical areas of the oceans are generally less productive than temperate. This is because in the tropics, the water column in the Euphotic Zone is not vertically mixed seasonally, hence nutrient concentrations are always quite low. Areas of high production of planktonic plants occur as a result of the upwelling of deep water near the coast.

Transfer of Energy from the Primary Producer to the Secondary

One of the most poorly known subjects in all biological oceanography is the transfer of energy between the primary producer and the primary consumer. In the open ocean, a great majority of the phytoplankton are consumed by herbivorous zooplankton, and only a small fraction, 1–10% of the surface production, reaches the ocean bottom to serve as a food source for the bottom-dwelling animals. The principal organisms grazing on the phytoplankton are small crustaceans known as copepods. These organisms form a great bulk of the food required for larger organisms such as the fishes.

The efficiency of food transfer is said to be high when the steps in the food chain are few. For example, the largest vertebrate in the world, the sulfur-bottom whale, feeds mostly on a crustacean known as a euphausid which in turn feeds on diatoms or small copepods. This places the whale about 3–4 steps down on the food chain sequence whereas some larger fishes may have many steps between themselves and the phytoplankton at the beginning of the food chain. This decreasing efficiency with increasing steps in the food chain is largely due to the fact that there is only a small transfer of energy between the steps, and a lion's share of the energy goes to the maintenance of the organism at each step.

Accurate estimates of the transfer of energy from phytoplankton to other organisms have been hampered because of a whole host of experimental problems. Moreover, some feel that the phytoplankton production is not sufficient to satisfy the food requirement of the secondary herbivores.

TABLE 1. GROSS AND NET ORGANIC PRODUCTION OF VARIOUS NATURAL
AND CULTIVATED SYSTEMS IN GRAMS DRY WEIGHT PRODUCED PER
SQUARE METER PER DAY
(from Ryther, 1959; for data sources see original publication)

		Gross	Net
A.	Theoretical potential		
	Average radiation (200–400 g cal/cm^2/day)	23–32	8–19
	Maximum radiation (750 g cal/cm^2/day)	38	27
B.	Mass outdoor *Chlorella* culture		
	Mean		12.4
	Maximum		28.0
C.	Land (maxima for entire growing seasons)		
	Sugar		18.4
	Rice		9.1
	Wheat		4.6
	Spartina marsh		9.0
	Pine forest (best growing years)		6.0
	Tall prairie		3.0
	Short prairie		0.5
	Desert		0.2
D.	Marine (maxima for single days)		
	Coral reef	24	(9.6)
	Turtle grass flat	20.5	(11.3)
	Polluted estuary	11.0	(8.0)
	Grand Banks (April)	10.8	(6.5)
	Walvis Bay	7.6	
	Continental shelf (May)	66.1	(3.7)
	Sargasso Sea (April)	4.0	(2.8)
E.	Marine (annual average)		
	Long Island Sound	2.1	0.9
	Continental shelf	0.74	(0.40)
	Sargasso Sea	0.74	0.35

This inbalance has led some workers to postulate physical-chemical mechanisms by which particulate matter is formed from dissolved organic fractions.

Comparison between Productivity of Ocean Communities and Those on Land

In coastal waters, the production of carbon may exceed 3.0 g/m^2/day. In offshore waters, carbon values range between 0.2–1.0 g/m^2/day. In the open ocean, the average production of carbon under a square meter is 0.3 g/day and probably never exceeds 0.8 g/day. The average annual production of carbon ranges between 25 and 100 g/m^2 of sea surface.

Table 1 compares the productivity of marine communities to land communities and cultivated systems. Deserts and most open ocean areas have comparable productivity. Also comparable are marine communities such as turtle grass, coral reefs, seaweed beds, and cultivated and cultured plants.

It is interesting to note that for most productive systems, maximum productivity is comparable; however, in the case of oceanic plankton communities, this maximum may only occur during an extremely short interval, whereas, cultivated and cultured systems may maintain this maximum for much longer periods.

Another interesting point is that the highly productive coral reefs are in ocean areas which are very poor in nutrients such as nitrogen and phosphorus. In this case, the maintenance of high productivity is principally due to the fact that new water is continually passing over the reef. Even though the amounts of nutrients are low in any one particle of water, the supply is virtually unlimited.

In conclusion, one can say that compared to fertile areas of land, most of the ocean is a desert; however, for what it lacks in production for a given area, it makes up in total size. With this consideration, the production of the oceans is 2–3 times that of the land surfaces.

CHARLES S. YENTSCH

References

Information concerning primary production can be found in the following journals:
Deep Sea Research
Limnology and Oceanography
Journal of Marine Research
Ecology

Raymont, J. E. G., 1963, "Plankton and productivity in oceans," New York, Pergamon, 672pp.

Ryther, J. H., 1959, *Science*, **130**, 602–608.

Ryther, J. H., 1963, in (Goldberg, E., editor), "The Seas," New York, Pergamon Press.

Strickland, J. D. H., 1960, *Bull. Fish. Res. Board Can.*, **122**, 1–172.

Yentsch, C. S., 1962, in (Lewin, R. A., editor) "Bio-chemistry and Physiology of Marine Algae," pp. 771–795.

Yentsch, C. S., 1963, *Oceanogr. Marine Biol. Ann Rev.*, **1**, 157–175.

PRODUCTIVITY—*See* **FERTILITY OF THE OCEAN** and **PLANKTONIC PHOTOSYN-THESIS**

R

RADIOACTIVE WASTE IN THE OCEAN

(1) Introduction

Radioactive wastes, resulting from the development and use of atomic energy, are likely to become more common as contaminants of the oceans. Their disposal from industrial sites is subject to strict regulation so that the safety of associated populations is not endangered, but all surface waters, and large volumes of deeper water, of the oceans are already contaminated by radioactivity originating from the atomic weapons which have been tested at various points on or above the earth. These wastes, aside from their hazardous natures, are useful to oceanographers as tracers of hydrographical and biological events in the seas. Mauchline and Templeton (1964) have reviewed the subject of natural and artificial radioactivity in the oceans and quote over 600 references.

(2) Sources of Radioactive Wastes

Present-day sources of radioactive wastes are:
(a) Nuclear power reactors used in generating electricity;
(b) Extraction plants processing spent fuel from nuclear reactors;
(c) Nuclear-powered ships;
(d) Weapons testing;
(e) Radioisotopes used as "tracers."
Nuclear power stations, when refueling, store the spent fuel elements (units in the core of a solid fuel reactor) in "cooling ponds," large tanks of water which permit the short-lived fission products to decay. Corrosion of the fuel elements causes the pond water to become radioactive, but the levels of radioactivity in the water are low and the water can usually be discharged directly to a large river or the sea without causing any hazard. Wastes from extraction plants processing these fuel elements are very different and present a disposal problem. Only the most dilute wastes can be dis-

charged to the natural environment, and the highly active concentrated wastes have to be stored on land in special containers. Windscale Works of the United Kingdom Atomic Energy Authority is a chemical processing plant and discharges about 90,000 curies of radioactivity per year down a pipeline which extends about 2 miles out into the Irish Sea. The reactors at Hanford General Electric Company in the state of Washington give rise to even greater quantities of wastes, some 350,000 curies of radioactivity per year passing down the Columbia River to the Pacific Ocean. But Hanford and Windscale are the only two sites where such large quantities of wastes are disposed of. Nuclear-powered ships give rise to small quantities of waste material, but they may become an important source of such material in future years. The major source of radioactive contamination of the oceans at present is the exploding of nuclear weapons which have been tested at places as far apart in the earth's surface as the Pacific and South Atlantic Oceans, the Sahara Desert, and Novaya Zemlya. The radioactive particles, which fall back to the earth's surface as "fallout," are formed when the vaporized metals and radioisotopes resulting from nuclear fission are swept up from the center of the explosion and condense as the cloud cools. These particles become dispersed throughout the lower and upper atmospheres and may return to earth many thousands of miles away from the site of the explosion. They land on the surface of the sea and, if of sufficient density, sink rapidly, but if less dense, they may remain in suspension in the water for a considerable time. The remaining source of radioactive wastes arises from the use of radioactive isotopes as "tracers." As mentioned previously, these isotopes can be used in hydrographical investigations, and sand and pebbles labeled with radioactive isotopes have been used successfully to trace movement of material of beaches and in river mouths. Isotopes are also used in laboratories to aid in studies of nutritional biochemistry and medical diagnoses; thus traces of radioactivity may enter civil sewage systems, but these can be discounted as a major source of radioactive wastes in the oceans.

(3) Composition of Wastes

The different wastes contain different radioiso-

TABLE 1. RADIOISOTOPES ORIGINATING FROM WEAPONS TESTING AND INDUSTRIAL WASTES, WHICH HAVE BEEN IDENTIFIED IN THE MARINE ENVIRONMENT. RADIOACTIVE HALF-LIFE IS DENOTED IN YEARS (y), DAYS (d), HOURS (h), OR MINUTES (m)

Isotope	Half-life	Type of Radiation Emitted	Originating from		Occurring Naturally
			Weapons	Other Wastes	
H^3	12.26y	β	+		+
C^{14}	5568y	β	+		+
P^{32}	14.22d	β	+		
Sc^{46}	83.9d	β, γ		+	
Cr^{51}	27.8d	γ		+	
Mn^{54}	291d	γ	+	+	
Fe^{55}	2.60y	γ	+	+	
Fe^{59}	45.1d	β, γ	+	+	
Co^{57}	270d	γ	+		
Co^{58}	71.3d	γ	+		
Co^{60}	5.24y	β, γ	+	+	
Zn^{65}	245d	β, γ	+	+	
As^{76}	26.4h	β, γ		+	
K^{85}	10.3y	β, γ	+		
Sr^{89}	50.5d	β	+	+	
Sr^{90}	27.7y	β	+	+	
Y^{90}	64.2h	β, γ	+	+	
Y^{91}	57.5d	β, γ	+		
Zr^{95}	65d	β, γ	+	+	
Nb^{95}	35d	β, γ	+	+	
Mo^{99}	66h	β, γ	+		
Ru^{103}	39.8d	β, γ	+	+	
Ru^{106}	1.00y	β	+	+	
Rh^{106}	130m	β, γ	+	+	
Cd^{113m}	5.1y	β, γ	+		
Cd^{115m}	43d	β, γ	+		
Sb^{125}	2y	β, γ		+	
Te^{132}	77.7h	β, γ	+		
I^{131}	8.08d	β, γ	+	+	
Cs^{137}	26.6y	β, γ	+	+	
Ba^{140}	12.80d	β, γ	+		
La^{140}	40.22h	β, γ	+		
Ce^{141}	33.1d	β, γ	+	+	
Ce^{144}	285d	β, γ	+	+	
W^{185}	75.8d	β	+		
Bi^{207}	8.0y	γ	+		
Po^{210}	138.4d	a, γ		+	
U^{234}	2.48×10^5y	a, γ	+	+	+
U^{235}	7.1×10^8y	a, γ	+	+	+
U^{238}	4.51×10^9y	a, γ	+	+	+
Np^{239}	2.35d	β, γ	+		
Pu^{239}	24,360y	a, γ	+	+	

topes. The dilute effluent from nuclear power stations comprise small quantities of such neutron-induced radioisotopes as:

$$P^{32}, Sc^{46}, Cr^{51}, Mn^{54}, Fe^{55}, Fe^{59}, Co^{60}, Zn^{65}, As^{76}, Sb^{125}, I^{131}$$

There may also be traces of radioisotopes resulting from nuclear fission:

$$Sr^{89}, Sr^{90}, Y^{90}, Zr^{95}, Nb^{95}, Ru^{103}, Ru^{106}, Rh^{106}, Ce^{144}, Cs^{137}, Po^{210}, Pu^{239}, U^{234}, U^{235}, U^{238}$$

Chemical plants processing the fuel elements produce fission products as the main constituents of the wastes, but traces of neutron-induced radioisotopes may also be present. Nuclear-powered ships produce small quantities of predominantly neutron-induced radioisotopes, and it is these isotopes which are also used in "tracer" studies.

All the radioisotopes known to be introduced to the oceans of the world by weapons testing and industrial wastes are shown in Table 1; the radioactive half-lives, i.e., the time required for the number of atoms of the radioisotope to decay to one-half of its present value, are indicated. Forty-two radioisotopes, representing 32 elements, have been detected in water and organisms of the seas and, of these, only 5 occur naturally in the environment. They are tritium (H^3) and C^{14}, which are formed in the upper atmosphere by the action of cosmic rays and reach the earth's surface by the same processes of "fallout" which return bomb debris to the earth, and the three radioisotopes of uranium which are intrinsic components of the earth's rocks and waters.

(4) Treatment and Disposal of Wastes

Collins (1960) has reviewed the methods of treatment and disposal of radioactive wastes to the marine environment, and an extensive bibliography on this subject can be found in Anonymous (1962).

The treatment of wastes prior to discharge will of course depend on the nature of the wastes and the environment receiving them. The wastes may be retained temporarily in "holding tanks," to allow short-lived radioisotopes to decay, thus decreasing the radioactivity of the final effluent, or they may require neutralization if previously subject to acid reactions. Filtration of highly radioactive particles is often effected through "sludge blankets," layers of preformed sludge kept in suspension and through which the effluent, with its fine precipitate particles, is made to pass.

The treated effluent, which usually has a low level of radioactivity and a large volume, is then pumped out into the river or down a pipeline to the sea. Wastes from nuclear-powered ships are associated with ion exchange resins which are discharged periodically from the ships during voyages and sink to the sea bed. There is also carefully controlled dumping of packaged wastes of low radioactivity content on the edges of the continental shelves, for examples by the United Kingdom in the Hurd Deep and Atlantic Shelf, and by the United States on the Pacific Shelf.

(5) Maximum Permissible Concentrations— M.P.C.'s

The level of radioactivity of the sea and its organisms has to be kept below levels which will endanger the health of people eating seafood, bathing, or using fishing gear which may become contaminated. Each site of discharge has to be examined to discover the factors which will limit the quantity of effluent discharged. For example, at Windscale Works in England, the amount of effluent discharged is restricted by the levels of radioactivity accumulated by a seaweed, *Porphyra umbilicalis*, which is collected and made into a delicacy known as laver bread. If the amount of effluent discharged were increased, it would be dangerous to eat the seaweed but not dangerous to eat the fish from the same area because the weed accumulates much more radioactivity, in this case Ru^{106}, than do fish. The "safe levels" or Maximum Permissible Concentrations (shortened to M.P.C.'s) are calculated from values given by the Inter-

national Commission on Radiological Protection (Anonymous, 1959), and the figures in this publication form the basis for estimating all M.P.C.'s of contamination by radioactivity of the food and drink of man.

(6) Monitoring

Monitoring procedures are peculiar to any one site of discharge of radioactive wastes because of the varying composition of the wastes and limiting factors of the environment. Detailed information on procedures used can be found in references quoted by Anonymous (1962) and Mauchline and Templeton (1964). Basically, the levels of gross radioactivity or of named radioisotopes in the environment are assayed regularly at time intervals of days rather than weeks or months, and the results are related to M.P.C.'s. This means that the amount of radioactivity discharged by an industrial site into the natural environment is continuously under review and is changed if necessary.

(7) Dispersion and Accumulation of Wastes in the Sea

The chemical behavior of a waste, whether "fallout" material or an industrial effluent, when it enters the sea depends to some extent on its chemical form at the time of introduction. Many different factors of the environment affect the fate of the waste, some causing dispersion and thus dilution, others concentration and thus possible retention in a restricted sea area.

Mauchline and Templeton (1964) have reviewed this subject in considerable detail.

(a) **Effects of the Inorganic Environment.** A radioactive waste usually contains several, if not many, radioisotopes of different chemical elements, and some of the radioisotopes behave differently from others. Many tend to be insoluble in seawater and are therefore present in the form of fine particles, e.g.,

$$Mn^{54}, Fe^{55}, Fe^{59}, Co^{57}, Co^{58}, Co^{60}, Y^{90},$$
$$Zr^{95}, Nb^{95}, Mo^{99}, Ru^{103}, Ru^{106}, Rh^{106},$$
$$Ce^{141}, Ce^{144}, Pr^{144}, Pm^{147}, Bi^{207}, Pu^{239}$$

Others are soluble in seawater and therefore tend to be present as ions, e.g.,

$$P^{32}, Cr^{51}, Sr^{89}, Sr^{90}, Sb^{125}, I^{131}, Cs^{137}$$

The processes which affect the radioisotopes when they enter the sea are shown in Fig. 1. Advection and turbulent diffusion disperse them, usually to a greater extent in the horizontal plane than the vertical, and so cause dilution. The sea or ocean currents carry the wastes away from the site of introduction, thus aiding dispersion. On the other hand, the physical-chemical processes of adsorption, coprecipitation, and ion exchange tend to cause flocculation and sedimentation of the

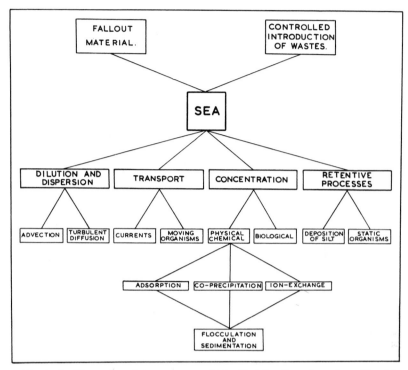

Fig. 1. An illustration of the processes which effect the dispersion of an effluent in the marine environment (after Waldichuk, from Mauchline and Templeton, 1964).

TABLE 2. CONCENTRATION FACTORS FOR RADIOISOTOPES BY TISSUES OF MARINE ORGANISMS
(AFTER MAUCHLINE AND TEMPLETON, 1964)

Isotope	Algae	Invertebrates		Vertebrates		Plankton
		Soft Parts	Skeletal	Soft Parts	Skeletal	
P^{32}	10,000	10,000	10,000	40,000	2×10^6	
Sc^{46}	1500–2600					
Cr^{51}	300–100,000	70–1000		2000		
Mn^{54}	6500	10,000		1000	2000	750
Fe^{55}, Fe^{59}	20,000–35,000	10,000	100,000	30–1000	5000	2000–140,000
Co^{57}, Co^{58}, Co^{60}	450	whole 500–3000		160	1500	
Zn^{65}		whole 5000–40,000		1000	300–3000	1000
As^{76}	200–6000	whole 20,000				
Sr^{89}, Sr^{90}	1–40	1–25	180–1000	0.1–2.0	100–200	9
Y^{90}, Y^{91}	100–1000	20–100	300	5		
Zr^{95}	350–1000					1500–3000
Nb^{95}	450–1000	whole 200,000				
Mo^{99}	10–100	100		20		
Ru^{103}, Ru^{106}, Rh^{106}	15–2000	2000		3		600–3000
Sb^{125}		100(?)		100(?)		50
I^{131}	3000–10,000	50–100	50	7–10		
Cs^{137}	1–100	10–100	0	10–100		0–5
Ce^{141}, Ce^{144}	300–900	300–2000	45	12		7500
Bi^{209}		500		50		
U^{234}, U^{235}, U^{238}	10		400	<20		
Pu^{239}				13		

radioisotopes; it is through these processes that sand, silt, and clays become contaminated, and in coastal regions, deposition of radioactive silt or clay in restricted areas of comparatively still water may, if the radioisotopes are long-lived, be dangerous for the marine organisms of the areas and the people harvesting these organisms. This is a retentive process and hinders dispersion.

(b) Biological Accumulation. The degree of accumulation of a radioisotope by an organism or a tissue of an organism is measured by the "accumulation factor" which is the number of times the concentration of the radioisotope in the organism or tissue exceeds that in an equal weight of environmental water. This factor is determined when the concentration of the radioisotope in the organism or tissue is in a steady-state condition relative to the concentration in the medium. Since for the majority of chemical elements (exceptions are quoted by Mauchline and Templeton, 1964), radioactive isotopes are accumulated by organisms to the same degree as the stable isotopes of the element, accumulation factors for radioisotopes are the same as those for stable elements. Thus many of the accumulation factors quoted in Table 2 are those of the stable isotopes.

The most important radioisotopes from the point of view of contamination of organisms are those which are accumulated to a high degree, are retained for a long time, and have long half-lives. The length of time a radioisotope is retained by an organism is measured by the "biological half-life"; this is the length of time which it takes the organism or tissue to eliminate, through metabolic processes one-half of the quantity of the radioisotope which it has accumulated. Many of the isotopes which have large accumulation factors in organisms— P^{32}, Cr^{51}, Fe^{59}, As^{76}, Nb^{95}, I^{131} —have relatively short radioactive half-lives as well as short biological half-lives. Consequently, unless the initial concentrations in the seawater are high or there is a continuous addition of these isotopes, the contamination of the organism decreases rapidly through elimination from the tissues and radioactive decay. The most dangerous radioisotopes which are found in present-day wastes are Sr^{90} and Cs^{137} which have radioactive half-lives greater than 25 years. Unlike Cs^{137}, which has a relatively short biological half-life, Sr^{90} is accumulated and retained in skeletal structures of marine organisms. Strontium behaves chemically like calcium, although the great majority of organisms discriminate against strontium in favour of calcium (Mauchline and Templeton, 1964). Most of the skeletal material formed by marine organisms in the last few years (since about 1955) is labeled with Sr^{90}, and this isotope may be useful in studying some aspects of sedimentation, etc., in future years. The majority of radioisotopes contained in radioactive wastes, however, are of little potential use in geo-

chemical studies. Cesium 137, having a radioactive half-life of over 33 years, is not accumulated by organisms to any extent and will be less liable to extraction from the water, followed by sedimentation. Consequently, it will persist in the water and may, along with C^{14} and Sr^{90}, be of use in helping to determine the mixing characteristics of the surface and deeper layers of the oceans.

Further reading in this field can be found in Anonymous (1962) and Mauchline and Templeton (1964).

J. Mauchline

References

Anonymous, 1959, "Recommendations of the International Commission on Radiological Protection," Report of Committee II on Permissible Dose of Internal Radiation (1959), London, Pergamon Press, 233pp.

*Anonymous, 1962, "Bibliographical Series No. 5. Disposal of Radioactive Wastes into Marine and Fresh Waters," International Atomic Energy Agency, Vienna, 365pp.

Collins, J. C. (editor), 1960, "Radioactive Wastes; Their Treatment and Disposal," Vol. XXI, London, E. and F. N. Spon Ltd., 239pp.

*Mauchline, J., and Templeton, W. L., 1964, "Artificial and Natural Radioisotopes in the Marine Environment," in (Barnes, H., editor) "Oceanography and Marine Biology; An Annual Review," Vol. 2, pp. 229–279, London, George Allen and Unwin Ltd.

RADIONUCLIDES IN OCEANS AND SEDIMENTS*

(1) Introduction

The radioactive nuclides found in the oceans and sediments have three distinctly different origins: (a) primordial nuclear synthesis, (b) cosmic-ray and solar proton interactions with the atmosphere and interplanetary dust, and (c) nuclear fusion and fission processes controlled by man. In addition, a number of radionuclides produced in these three ways decay to radioactive daughters. Primordial nuclides are those that were produced by nuclear genesis at the time of the creation of the elements; thus, only those radionuclides with half-lives of approximately a billion years or greater will have persisted to this day in significant amounts. The primordial radionuclides found in the oceans and sediments are initially derived from the continents. The weathering of rocks and minerals yields material that is then carried away by land runoff to rivers or by winds. In this manner, large quanti-

* Contribution No. 663 from The Marine Laboratory, Institute of Marine Science, University of Miami. Acknowledgement of support for research represented herein is accorded the U.S. Atomic Energy Commission, the Office of Naval Research, and the National Science Foundation.

ties of radioelements eventually reach the oceans, being transported either as dissolved species or in particulate form. Three primordial nuclides, U^{235}, U^{238}, and Th^{232}, decay to radioactive daughters of shorter half-life; these daughters comprise a significant portion of the radioactivity found in the ocean.

In contrast to the single-event production of primordial radioactive nuclides, there is a significant and relatively steady-state production of radionuclides through the interaction of cosmic rays (high-energy protons) with the constituents of the atmosphere, primarily with nitrogen, oxygen, and argon. These radionuclides are washed out by rain or adsorbed on particles which, in turn, settle out or are carried down by rain. Eventually, a large fraction of this material is deposited in the oceans.

With the advent of the nuclear age, a new source of radioactive material has come into existence. Initially, this "artificial" radioactivity was produced in significant quantities only in nuclear weapons tests; however, with the ever-increasing use of nuclear power, the waste products from nuclear reactors are becoming important sources of radionuclides. To date, the contribution of radioactivity from weapons testing greatly exceeds that from other man-made sources. The effect of fallout and nuclear waste on the distribution of radionuclides in nature varies with the nuclide under consideration. In the majority of cases, material that was not previously present on earth is injected in significant quantities. However, in some cases, the radionuclides produced had previously existed in nature and the net effect of the new source is to alter, sometimes considerably, the inventory and distribution.

Radioactive nuclides have come to play an important role in oceanography since their distribution in the oceans and the deep-sea sediments permits conclusions to be drawn regarding the past geological history of the earth and the dynamic processes taking place in the oceans. Radionuclides have been used in the study of diffusion processes in ocean water and in the sediments. They are also used for the tagging of bodies of water; in this way, the path of various water masses can be followed over long distances (see *Radionuclides: Their Application in Oceanography*). Similar techniques permit the description of circulation and mixing patterns in the oceans and the determination of the time element involved in the turnover of ocean water. The members of the naturally occurring radioactive uranium and thorium series have relative concentrations in the oceans that differ from those in the sediments or on the continents; a study of these differences in distribution can yield considerable information about the geochemical processes taking place in all three phases. Furthermore, knowledge of the rela-

tive distributions of the members of these series in the oceans and in the sediments enables the age of sediment layers to be determined, thus establishing an absolute time scale for geological events.

Another impetus to the study of radioactive elements in the oceans stems from the growing use of radioactive tracers and nuclear power. Increasingly large quantities of highly radioactive waste products must be disposed of, and it has been proposed that the oceans be used for this purpose. The behavior of these materials in the ocean must be more fully explored before this solution can be accepted with impunity.

In this article, the distribution of radioactive material in the oceans and sediments will be discussed with emphasis on naturally produced radionuclides. (The subject of radioactive waste in the ocean is covered by Mauchline in an article in this volume.) In discussing the behavior of elements and radionuclides in the oceans, it is convenient to specify a residence time for the material in question; the residence time R is defined as being equal to the quantity c of an element, or radionuclide, present in the ocean, divided by the input (or deposition) per unit time a:

$$R = c/a \qquad (1)$$

The calculation of residence times in this manner assumes that a steady-state situation exists, with the rate of input being equal to the deposition rate.

The residence times will vary considerably from one radionuclide to another, depending on their chemistry in the ocean and their influx or production rates. On the other hand, the concentration of many radionuclides in the sediments is generally a function of the water depth and the sedimentation rate. The components of sediments are commonly grouped according to origin: terrigenic (material derived from land), biogenic (the remains of marine organisms, principally carbonates and silicates) and authigenic (material precipitated directly from solution). The variability in sedimentation rates is chiefly due to fluctuations in the deposition rate of the terrigenic and biogenic components. As a result, the composition of the sediment and the deposition rate will be dependent on the nearness to land and the rate of production of organic material in the ocean area under consideration. For example, in the South Pacific, an area far removed from land and having a relatively low productivity, the sedimentation rate is quite low, approximately 1 mm or less per thousand years, and consists primarily of red clay. In contrast, the sedimentation rate in the Caribbean, an area of high productivity, is greater than 1 cm per thousand years and consists mostly of calcium carbonate. Although there are many qualifying factors, in general, when considered on an equal water-depth basis, the concentration of radionuclides in a low sedimentation rate area will be higher than in an

TABLE 1. DISTRIBUTIONS OF RADIONUCLIDES IN THE MARINE ENVIRONMENT[a]

Nuclide	Half-life (yr)	Concentration in Oceans (g/liter)	(dpm/liter)	Concentration in Sediments (g/kg dry sediment)	(dpm/kg dry sediment)
H^3	12.26	$(6.7–33.3) \times 10^{-16b}$	$14.4–71.9^b$		
Be^{10}	2.5×10^6	1.4×10^{-13}	4.4×10^{-3}	$(0.3–3.0) \times 10^{-10}$	$1–10$
C^{14}	5570	$(2–3) \times 10^{-14b}$	$0.2–0.3^b$	$(0.1–1.0) \times 10^{-10}$	$(1–10) \times 10^2$
Al^{26}	7.4×10^5	—	—	$(0.15–1.5) \times 10^{-12c}$	$(0.6–6) \times 10^{-2d}$
Si^{32}	500	5×10^{-19}	2.7×10^{-5}		
K^{40}	1.3×10^9	4.7×10^{-5}	720	$(0.44–11.9) \times 10^{-3}$	$(0.7–18) \times 10^4$
Rb^{87}	4.7×10^{10}	3.4×10^{-5}	6.2	$(2.3–5.7) \times 10^{-3}$	$(0.4–1.1) \times 10^3$
Sr^{90}	28	$(0.63–9.5) \times 10^{-16b}$	$0.02–0.3^b$		
Cs^{137}	30	$(0.52–2.6) \times 10^{-1}$	$0.1–0.5^b$		
Ra^{226}	1620	$(3–16) \times 10^{-14}$	$(6.6–35) \times 10^{-2}$	$(0.3–40) \times 10^{-9}$	$(0.65–87) \times 10^3$
Th^{228}	1.91	1×10^{-18}	0.2×10^{-3}		
Th^{230}	75,200	9×10^{-15}	0.4×10^{-3}	$(1–30) \times 10^{-7}$	$(0.45–136) \times 10^3$
Th^{232}	1.41×10^{10}	$(0.36–4.5) \times 10^{-9}$	$(0.87–10.9) \times 10^{-4}$	$(2–12) \times 10^{-3}$	$(0.48–2.9) \times 10^3$
Pa^{231}	32,480	2×10^{-15}	0.2×10^{-3}	$(5–150) \times 10^{-9}$	$(0.53–16) \times 10^3$
U^{234}	2.48×10^5	$(1.6–2.1) \times 10^{-10}$	$2.3–2.9$	$(0.024–4.9) \times 10^{-6}$	$(0.34–67) \times 10^3$
U^{235}	7.13×10^8	$(1.9–2.5) \times 10^{-8}$	$0.092–0.17$	$(0.028–5.8) \times 10^{-4}$	$(0.13–27) \times 10^2$
U^{238}	4.51×10^9	$(2.7–3.4) \times 10^{-6}$	$2.0–2.5$	$(0.4–80) \times 10^{-3}$	$(0.30–59) \times 10^3$

[a] Concentrations of the more important radionuclides found in the oceans and deep-sea sediments. The values given for sediments are those measured in surface sediments.
[b] Surface water only.
[c] Uranium isotope concentrations calculated from the measured total uranium content; the activity ratio U^{234}/U^{238} is taken to be 1.14 in both the water and sediment phases.
[d] Estimated.

TABLE 2. DECAY CHARACTERISTICS OF RADIONUCLIDES FOUND IN THE MARINE ENVIRONMENT[a]

Nuclide	Half-life (yr)[b]	Modes of Decay	Particle Energies (MeV)	Particle Intensities (%)	Gamma-ray Energies (MeV)	Gamma-ray Intensities
H^3	12.26	β^-	0.0181	100	None	
Be^7	53.6 days	EC	None		0.4773	10.32
Be^{10}	2.5×10^6	β^-	0.56	100	None	
C^{14}	5570	β^-	0.156	100	None	
Al^{26}	7.4×10^5	β^+ EC	β^+ 1.16 EC	85 15	1.11 1.83 2.95 Ann. Rad.	3.7 99.3 0.3

TABLE 2—*continued*

Nuclide	Half-life (yr)[b]	Modes of Decay	Particle Energies (MeV)	Particle Intensities (%)	Gamma-ray Energies (MeV)	Gamma-ray Intensities
Si^{32}	500	β^-	0.1	100	None	
K^{40}	1.3×10^9	β^- EC	β^- 1.32 EC	89 11	1.46	11
Rb^{87}	4.7×10^{10}	β^-	0.27	100	None	
Sr^{90}	28	β^-	0.54	100	None	
Cs^{137}	30	β^-	0.52 1.18	92 8	0.662	92
Ra^{226}	1620	α	4.78 4.59	95 4	0.187 0.260	4 0.001
Ra^{228}	5.7	β^-	0.055	100	0.03	Very weak
Th^{228}	1.91	α	5.421 5.338	71 28	0.085 0.214	1.6 0.27
Th^{230}	75,200	α	4.682 4.615	76 24	0.0677 0.144	0.59 0.77
Th^{232}	1.41×10^{10}	α	4.007	76	0.059	24
Pa^{231}	32,480	α	5.001 5.017 5.046 4.938	24 23 10 22	0.29 > 10 γ's 0.027–0.356	All weak
U^{234}	2.48×10^5	α	4.768 4.717	72 28	0.053 0.118	All weak
U^{235}	7.13×10^8	α	4.559 4.370 4.354 4.333 4.318 4.117	6.7 25 35 14 8 5.8	0.094 0.1096 0.144 0.165 0.185	9 5 12 >4 55
U^{238}	4.51×10^9	α	4.195 4.14	77 23	0.048	23

[a] The decay characteristics of the more important radionuclides found in the oceans and deep-sea sediments. Alpha, beta and electron capture decay are denoted by α, β and EC, respectively. Particle and gamma-ray intensities are given as the % of decays which result in the observed radiation. Only the more abundant modes of decay and transitions are noted. The presence of annihilation radiation (511-keV photons) is indicated by the abbreviation Ann. Rad.
[b] Units in years unless otherwise indicated.

area of high deposition rate. The concentrations of the more important radionuclides found in the marine environment are presented in Table 1; the decay characteristics of these nuclides are summarized in Table 2.

Of necessity, this article will be rather limited in scope and depth of coverage. For those interested in more extensive works, there is a very comprehensive review of natural and artificial radio-nuclides in the marine environment by Mauchline and Templeton (1964) with over 600 references being cited. The subject of cosmic-ray produced activity is covered in an article by Lal and Peters (1965). An extensive review of the applications of radioactivity in oceanography is presented by Koczy and Rosholt (1962). In addition, Mauchline has an article of interest in this volume. (See *Radioactive Waste in the Ocean*; also pr Vol. IV.)

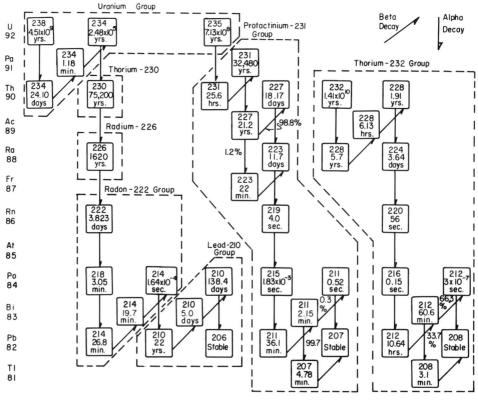

Fig. 1. The U^{235}, U^{238} and Th^{232} decay series. Vertical lines denote alpha decay; slanted lines, beta decay. Each series is subdivided into groups containing nuclides which might be expected to have similar histories in the oceans and sediments; because of the time scales involved in mixing and transport processes, the distributions of short-lived nuclides will be determined to a considerable extent by the chemical properties of the long-lived parent radionuclide and they are grouped accordingly. The grouping of nuclides in this fashion is a matter of conceptual convenience; their actual behavior in nature is much more complex.

(2) Primordial Radionuclides

The principal radioisotopes of this origin found in the oceans are K^{40}, Rb^{87}, U^{235}, U^{238}, and Th^{232}. Both K^{40} and Rb^{87} decay directly to stable daughter products. U^{235}, U^{238}, and Th^{232} decay to a series of radioactive daughters, each series being terminated by a stable lead isotope; the decay sequence for these nuclides is depicted in Fig. 1.

Under certain idealized situations, a condition known as secular equilibrium is established between the various members of a decay series such as in the uranium and thorium families; in these cases, for every decay of a parent nucleus there is a decay of a daughter nucleus. Thus, the ratio of activities of any two members in a series will be equal to 1. Secular equilibrium will be realized when U^{235}, U^{238}, or Th^{232} is isolated in a closed system for a period of time equal to several half-lives of the longest-lived daughter (e.g., in a mineral which has undergone no alteration

since the time of formation). While this situation in the strictest sense seldom occurs in nature, secular equilibrium is often approached in certain geological systems. As will be shown, the existence of, or degree of departure from secular equilibrium can yield a great deal of information concerning chemical and physical processes taking place in the system under consideration.

In discussing radionuclides in sediments, it is important to distinguish them according to mode of deposition. As previously indicated, some nuclides are transported to the oceans either in solution as dissolved species or contained in detrital particulate matter; in many cases, a nuclide will be present in seawater in both states. In addition, many radionuclides are produced in the ocean through the decay of their parents as in the uranium- and thorium-decay series. Eventually, this dissolved or suspended material will be deposited on the ocean floor to become part of the sediment. That portion of the radionuclide content

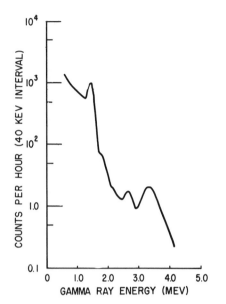

COUNTS PER HOUR (40 KEV INTERVAL)

GAMMA RAY ENERGY (MEV)

Fig. 2. The gamma-ray spectrum of seawater. The peak at 1·46 MeV is the gamma ray obtained from the electron capture decay branch of K^{40}; a large portion of the distribution at lower energies is a result of the partial energy loss of many of the 1·46-MeV gamma rays in passing through the water (from Riel *et al.*, 1960).

of the sediment that has been precipitated from solution is commonly specified as being *authigenic*, while that contained in land-derived (detrital) particles is termed *terrigenic* (terrigenous).

(a) Potassium 40. The concentration of potassium in seawater is 0.035% or approximately 1×10^{-2} moles/liter; its concentration varies very little with location. Since the abundance of K^{40} ($t_{1/2} = 1.3 \times 10^9$ years) is 0.0118% of the total potassium, the K^{40} activity of seawater is then 3.3×10^{-13} curie/ml or about 0.7 disintegration/min/ml (dpm/ml). K^{40} constitutes by far the largest single source of radioactivity present in the ocean. The gamma-ray spectrum of seawater as shown in Fig. 2 is dominated by the K^{40} 1.46-MeV gamma ray which is emitted in 11% of the decays. This spectrum was recorded in the Gulf Stream, using a large NaI (Tl) scintillation spectrometer (Riel *et al.*, 1960). The peaks between 2 and 4 MeV are believed to be chiefly associated with uranium and thorium series contamination within the detection unit itself, principally the phototube.

Pelagic sediments have a fairly uniform concentration of potassium, from 1–3% of the carbonate-free fraction; the K^{40} activity of the total sediment ranges from 7–182 dpm/kg of dry sediment. Essentially all the potassium is believed to be contained in land-derived particles of minerals and rocks which have been transported

to the oceans by rivers and wind. There is no evidence for the formation of any authigenic potassium minerals in significant quantities (see *Radionuclides: Their Application in Oceanography*—section on Dating of Ocean Sediments).

(b) Uranium. Although K^{40} is the most abundant radionuclide in seawater, the presence of uranium and thorium, albeit in considerably smaller concentrations, is of greater significance since they are of much greater utility to oceanographers. The concentration of uranium in ocean water is believed to be fairly uniform with values in the general range of 2.7–3.4×10^{-6} g/liter; the average for the Atlantic and Pacific Oceans was measured to be 3.3×10^{-6} g/liter.

The principal source of uranium in the seas is land runoff. The uranium content of rivers has been found to vary considerably with rivers draining carbonate-rich soil areas having a higher uranium content than rivers emanating from igneous-rock regions. The former have uranium contents which average as high as 2×10^{-6} g/liter, whereas the latter have an average of 0.3–0.6×10^{-6} g/liter. The average content for all river water is approximately 1×10^{-6} g/liter. This variation in uranium content of rivers is a result of the chemical behavior of uranium which tends to form soluble carbonate complexes. Uranium is believed to exist in seawater primarily as bicarbonate, carbonate, and mixed complexes of UO_2^{+2}; these complexes should be rather stable except in oxygen-poor water having an oxygen content less than 1 ml/liter. Thus, deviations from the average uranium concentration specified above might be expected in chemically reducing environments and in enclosed basins.

On the basis of the concentration of uranium in rivers, the river influx to the oceans and the concentration of uranium in the ocean, the residence time of uranium is calculated to be more than 10^5 years. Because of the long residence time, it may be assumed that the concentration of uranium in the oceans has been fairly constant for periods of time of the order of the residence time. However, there are mechanisms by which the uranium concentration might be rapidly changed. Variations may occur in the rate of supply from land or the rate of removal by trapping in nearshore reducing environments and by direct sedimentation near the mouths of rivers. In addition, uranium is enriched in some shelf sediments; at maximum glaciation, the decreased water level will expose large shelf areas and uranium in the shelf sediments may be oxidized and eventually transported in solution to the ocean. As a result, the concentration of uranium in the sea may vary in a complex fashion, perhaps by as much as a factor of two over a period of several hundred thousand years. Although the possibility of such changes exists, there is no absolute evidence that it has indeed occurred.

The activity ratio in seawater of the two primordial isotopes of uranium, U^{238}/U^{235}, is 21.8, the same as that in terrestrial material, the isotopic composition being 99.27% U^{238} and 0.72% U^{235}. Until recently, it was assumed that U^{234}, a daughter of U^{238} (see Fig. 1), was in secular equilibrium with U^{238}, in which case the decay rate of U^{234} would be equal to that of U^{238}. However, it has been found that secular equilibrium does not exist between U^{234} and U^{238} in many minerals and rocks (V. V. Cherdyntsev et al., see references in Koide and Goldberg, 1965). This discovery suggested that a similar disequilibrium might also exist in the oceans. Recently, Koide and Goldberg (1965) analyzed 21 water samples obtained from various oceans and seas; the average ratio of U^{234}/U^{238} was determined to be 1.14 ± 0.014. The values ranged from 1.13–1.17, with most falling in the range 1.13–1.15. The fractionation of these two isotopes is attributed to the changes in the chemical bonding of U^{234} produced by radioactive decay; as a result, U^{234} is preferentially complexed and leached in the weathering of rocks and minerals. This phenomenon, fractionation brought about through the increased reactivity of radioactive decay products, is a familiar one and forms the basis of a branch of chemistry known as "hot atom" chemistry.

Uranium in sediments is derived partly by precipitation from solution in ocean water and partly as detritus carried in suspension by rivers and as dust carried by wind. The concentration in recent sediments varies from 0.4–80 ppm. Uranium is taken up during the growth of marine carbonates and has been found in aragonites such as oolites and corals. The uranium content of these materials is generally about 1–4 ppm (Broecker and Thurber, 1965, and references therein). In contrast to these materials, the uranium content of the calcium carbonate fossil shells of Foraminifera (a populous marine protozoan) taken from recent pelagic sediments is approximately two orders of magnitude lower (Ku, 1965). The incorporation of uranium in corals and oolites permits the date of formation to be determined in some cases (see *Radionuclides: Their Application in Oceanography*—section on Dating of Ocean Sediments).

(c) Thorium. There is but one primordial thorium isotope, Th^{232} ($t_{1/2} = 1.41 \times 10^{10}$ years). The concentration of thorium in seawater is so low that measurements are rather difficult to make; for some years only an upper limit, 2×10^{-8} g/liter, could be estimated. Recently, several large-volume (130–190 liters) seawater samples from the North Atlantic and Caribbean have been analyzed for a number of nuclides of the uranium and thorium series (Moore and Sackett, 1964). Surface and intermediate water samples yielded concentrations of 0.36–0.64×10^{-9} g/liter; a single deep sample, taken at 4500 m, had a considerably higher con-

centration of 4.5×10^{-9} g/liter. As an indication of the experimental difficulties involved in these measurements, the Th^{232} sources would typically yield a net of 15 counts for a 5000–8000 minute counting period; as a result, the uncertainty of these measurements is rather considerable on the basis of counting statistics alone.

The Th^{232} content of sediments varies over approximately the same range in all three major oceans, both for red clay and globigerina ooze; most values fall in the range of 2–12 ppm for recent sediments (Moore and Sackett, 1964). A major portion of the thorium present in sediments is detrital in origin, only a small fraction being precipitated from solution in seawater.

Thorium is also found in marine carbonates; however, because of the low concentration of thorium in seawater, it would be expected that the thorium content of corals and oolite should be correspondingly low with respect to uranium (i.e., approximately 10 ppb). While this is often found to be true, many samples have considerably higher values; these high concentrations are interpreted as evidence of secondary addition from sediments during recrystallization (Broecker and Thurber, 1965) (see *Radionuclides: Their Application in Oceanography*—section on Dating of Ocean Sediments).

(d) Thorium^{228}, Thorium^{230}, and Protactinium^{231}. Th^{230}, commonly called ionium, and Pa^{231} are members of the U^{238} and U^{235} decay series respectively, while Th^{228} is a daughter of Th^{232} (see Fig. 1). Since Th^{228}, Th^{230}, and Pa^{231} are produced as bare ions through radioactive decay, they should rapidly become hydrated and adsorbed on particulate matter which settles to the ocean floor in a relatively short time. Accordingly, the concentrations of these nuclides in seawater should be extremely small and, as a result, very difficult to measure.

The analysis of large-volume water samples yields concentrations (per thousand liters) of approximately 1×10^{-9} μg Th^{228}, 9×10^{-6} μg Th^{230}, and 2×10^{-6} μg Pa^{231}. Expressed in terms of activity, these concentrations are equivalent to 0.2 dpm Th^{228}, 0.4 dpm Th^{230}, and 0.2 dpm Pa^{231}—all per 1000 liters. Since the average uranium concentration in seawater is about 3.3 μg/liters, this means that of the equilibrium activities of Th^{230} and Pa^{231}, less than 0.05% of the Th^{230} and less than 0.02% of the Pa^{231} produced from the decay of uranium remains in solution; the calculated residence time for ionium is less than 50 years while that of Pa^{231} is less than 100 years (Moore and Sackett, 1964).

There are two sources for the Pa^{231} and Th^{230} found in the sediments: that which is precipitated from solution in seawater and that which is produced by the decay of uranium present in the sediment. Precipitation is by far the most important source of these nuclides for recent sediments; the uranium-supported portion of Th^{230} and Pa^{231} in sediments (i.e., the amount of Th^{230} and Pa^{231} which would be derived from uranium, assuming the existence of secular equilibrium) is generally less than 10% of the total for ages less than several hundred thousand years. Concentrations found in recent sediments range from 1×10^{-10} to 3×10^{-9} gram Th^{230} per gram of sediment. On the basis of the uranium production ratio, the concentration of Pa^{231} should be approximately 5% of the Th^{230} content. The lowest concentrations of these nuclides are found in the Indian Ocean and the highest in the Pacific, these areas having, respectively, the highest and lowest sedimentation rates of the major oceans. Little data are available on the distribution of Th^{228} in sediments.

(e) **Radium**^{226}. Ra^{226}, a member of the U^{238} radioactive series, decays with a half-life of 1620 years. Its parent nuclide is Th^{230} which, in turn, is produced by the decay of U^{234}. As previously stated, the concentration of Th^{230} in seawater is at most only 1/10 of 1% of the equilibrium value calculated from the known U^{234} content of seawater. *A priori*, we would expect Ra^{226} to show the same distribution in seawater and sediments as Th^{230}. However, the average Ra^{226} content of seawater has been shown by Koczy to be approximately 1×10^{-13} g/liter; this concentration is more than 16 times the equilibrium value which could be supported by the Th^{230} content of seawater. The excess radium could not be supplied by the river discharge of land-derived radium; calculations based on an average radium concentration in river water of 2×10^{-14} g/liter indicate that this source could not increase the theoretical Th^{230}-supported radium content by more than 1% in the mixed surface layer (assumed to be a uniform 100 m deep). If we consider the effect of river influx on the radium content of the entire ocean, which has a mean depth of 4000 m, the total river inflow of Ra^{226} amounts to less than 1/40 of 1%.

The only possible major source of radium is the Th^{230} present in the sea sediments; the Ra^{226} produced by decay must then diffuse or migrate through the sediments and into the overlying water layer. The diffused radium should subsequently be affected by the existing mixing and transport processes and its distribution in the ocean should vary accordingly. This view is supported by vertical radium content profiles determined by Koczy in the oceans and in some enclosed basins. The radium concentration in the oceans shows a general increase with depth; the increase is rather rapid with an inflection point at a depth of 750–1750 m, depending on the location and the particular ocean. The increase in radium concentration toward the bottom is not uniform, and occasionally the surface layers show a higher value than layers at a few hundred meters depth. The surface values

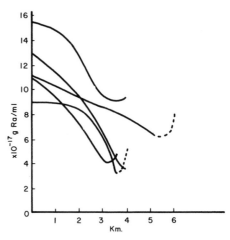

Fig. 3. The radium content of seawater from various water masses as a function of depth as measured from the ocean floor.

are found to range from $3–10 \times 10^{-14}$ g/liter while maxima occur in the range of $7–16 \times 10^{-14}$ g/liter. Some typical distributions are shown in Fig. 3.

If radium is really diffusing from the sediments, the migration should be reflected in the Ra^{226} distribution in the cores. Without diffusion, and assuming a constant sedimentation rate of Th^{230}, the concentration of radium would decrease as a function of time (and thus, depth) with a half-life characteristic of its parent nuclide, Th^{230}, with which Ra^{226} is assumed to be in secular equilibrium. The effects of diffusion would be superimposed on this exponential decay. The resulting depth-versus-concentration curve would show a pronounced rise followed by a continuous decrease with increasing depth in the core. Such a distribution has been found in a number of sediment cores analyzed for radium. These distributions can be fitted to curves computed by assuming various diffusion rates for radium. On this basis, the diffusion constant for radium is found to be about 10^{-9} cm^2/sec (Koczy, 1963).

(3) Cosmic-ray Produced Nuclides

A large number of cosmic-ray produced radionuclides have been detected in nature, particularly in rainwater. The half-lives of the more abundantly produced nuclides range from several days to millions of years. Several of these are present in concentrations sufficiently large to be readily detected and measured in seawater and ocean sediments: H^3, Be^7, Be^{10}, C^{14}, Si^{32}. These nuclides are of interest to oceanographers since they can be used as tracers to establish a time scale for such processes as circulation and diffusion in the ocean and the rates of sedimentation. The modes and rates of production of these nuclides and their concentrations in the hydrosphere are discussed in various articles referred to in Lal and Peters (1965) and in an article by Lal in pr Vol. IV: *Radionuclides, Cosmic-ray Produced.* Only cursory coverage of the more important nuclides will be presented here.

Another source of radionuclides which may be placed in this general category is that of interplanetary dust. This material consists of small particles (with radii up to 300μ) which are in more or less circular orbits around the sun. A large quantity of this matter is swept out by the earth, recent estimates of the accretion rate being of the order of 10,000 metric tons/day. Because of the very large flux of solar protons with energies in the range of 5–30 MeV, appreciable quantities of radioactivity may be produced in the dust particles during their lifetime. However, the importance of this source is yet to be determined since even such basic information as the origin and composition of the dust is still lacking. Although the quantity of radioactivity accreted in this way will most likely be quite small, it may provide us with vital information. A comprehensive review of this subject is presented by Wasson (1963).

(a) Tritium. Tritium (H^3 or T) is produced in nature by the interaction of cosmic rays with the atmosphere, principally in spallation (nuclear disintegration) reactions with oxygen and nitrogen. The average global natural production rate is estimated to be 0.25 atom/cm^2 sec. The H^3 so produced rapidly combines with hydrogen and oxygen to form HTO molecules which then enter the water cycle. Tritium has a half-life of 12.26 years and decays by beta-minus emission; the beta decay energy is only 0.0181 MeV, which makes the detection and measurement of tritium very difficult.

The natural distribution of H^3 in nature has been greatly affected by the tritium produced in nuclear weapons tests and nuclear reactor waste. The amount of tritium contributed by these two sources may exceed that previously present in nature by as much as two orders of magnitude. Indeed, the pre-nuclear age distribution and inventory is not known with certainty and can only be estimated.

The concentration of tritium is commonly specified in tritium units (TU) where one tritium unit is equivalent to a T/H atom ratio of 10^{-18}. A range of 2–10 TU is believed to be representative of the concentration of tritium in surface waters in the Equatorial Atlantic and the Pacific with the average value for the latter being 7 TU. The concentration in deep waters is considerably lower, much less than 0.1 TU; this is a consequence of the mean residence time of water above the thermocline being approximately equal to the half-life of tritium and because of the large volume of the deep water reservoir. The present detection limit of tritium counters is about 5 TU for a 16-hour count. Thus, seawater samples can be counted with

precision only after considerable isotopic enrichment; this is done by electrolyzing the water sample to a volume which is 1/10–1/100 of the starting volume, the resulting enrichment factors for H^3 being approximately 7.5 and 75, respectively.

(b) Beryllium^{10}. Be^{10}, produced by cosmic-ray spallation reactions with oxygen and nitrogen in the atmosphere, decays by beta decay with a half-life of 2.5×10^6 years. Its residence time in the atmosphere is of the order of several weeks and that in the ocean about 500 years. Thus, most of the Be^{10} inventory should be in the sediments. Because of its low production rate (a global average of 4.5×10^{-2} atom/cm^2 sec) and long half-life, measurement is difficult. Several core samples from the Pacific have been analyzed, and the activities obtained were generally in the range of 1–10 dpm/kg of sediment. Thus, large samples are required for counting. Although the absolute activity of Be^{10} is low, the *specific activity* (activity of isotope per unit weight of element) is fairly high since the concentration of beryllium in these sediments is only a few parts per million.

(c) Carbon^{14}. The interaction of cosmic rays with the atmosphere produces large numbers of high-energy neutrons which are rapidly reduced to thermal energies through repeated collisions with atmospheric gases. Essentially all the neutrons produced are captured by N^{14} in the reaction:

$$N^{14} + n^1 \rightarrow C^{14} + H^1$$

The production rate of C^{14} in the atmosphere is 1.8 atoms/cm^2 sec. Radiocarbon decays by beta-minus emission to the ground state of N^{14}, the half-life being 5570 years. The C^{14} produced in the atmosphere rapidly combines with oxygen, mixes with ordinary CO_2, and is distributed in the lower atmosphere by eddy diffusion.

The CO_2 in the atmosphere is then utilized in various life cycles and exchanges with the CO_2 in the ocean where it enters the carbon dioxide–carbonate system. Natural carbon consists of 98.8% C^{12} and 1.11% C^{13}. While alive, plants and organisms have a C^{14}/natural carbon ratio (and thus, a specific activity) essentially equal to that of the atmospheric carbon exchange reservoir; in the case of "modern" pre-nuclear age wood, the specific activity is approximately dpm C^{14}/g C, which is equivalent to about 10^{-10} gram C^{14} per gram carbon. After "death," C^{14} is no longer taken up and the ratio C^{14}/C in the material decreases exponentially with time (i.e., by 50% every 5570 years). Thus the measurement of the specific activity of carbonaceous material permits the calculation of the time which has elapsed since the object ceased to be in equilibrium with its environment.

Most of the C^{14} inventory is located in the oceans; considering the total worldwide carbon exchange reservoir, Lal estimates that approximately 94% of the radiocarbon is in the oceans, 0.4% in the sediments, and 6% in the atmosphere and biosphere. The C^{14} in the ocean sediments is present as the calcareous remains of marine organisms which, after death, settled to the ocean floor; the C^{14} content of this material can be used to determine the age of the sediment layer in which it is found and also the bulk sedimentation rate (see *Radionuclides: Their Application in Oceanography*—section on Dating of Ocean Sediments). In addition, radiocarbon is extremely useful as an ocean water tracer (see above article—section on Radio Tracer Studies of Large-scale Mixing in the Oceans).

In using C^{14} for these purposes, it is assumed that the ratio of C^{14}/C^{12} in the atmosphere has remained relatively constant over the time period of interest (several thousand years for water tracing and 50 thousand years for dating purposes). This, in turn, implies that the cosmic-ray energy spectrum and flux and the composition of the atmosphere have remained constant. All these assumptions are supported to a degree by the results of the analysis of tree rings and archeological artifacts of known age; indications are that the C^{14}/C^{12} ratio has remained constant to within $\pm 2\%$ for the past 2500 years, excluding the past 100 years, with a pronounced peak occurring 500 years ago. There is some evidence that the ratio was larger than at present for a long period of time, perhaps increasing as much as 8% some 4000 years ago (Olsson and Eriksson, 1965). However, there is some basis for assuming that the ratio C^{14}/C^{12} in the atmosphere has not changed radically for at least several tens of thousands of years although appreciable variations may have taken place.

In recent times, the ratio in the atmosphere has been altered in two different ways: the burning of fossil fuels, which adds C^{12} to the atmosphere, and the production of C^{12} in nuclear weapons tests. The increased utilization of fossil fuels in the past hundred years has resulted in the gradual reduction of the C^{14}/C^{12} ratio in the atmosphere; the ratio is estimated to have decreased by about $2.5 \pm 1.0\%$ in the period 1855–1955. This phenomenon is known as the Suess effect. The C^{14} added by nuclear weapons has sharply altered the ratio in the opposite direction; the radiocarbon from this source has doubled the activity in the atmosphere as of the autumn of 1963.

(d) Aluminum[26]. Because of its large mass relative to that of oxygen and nitrogen, Al^{26} can only be produced by cosmic-ray spallation reactions with the heavier components of the atmosphere, in particular, with argon which constitutes approximately 1% of the atmosphere. The residence time of Al^{26} in the atmosphere should be similar to that of Be^{10}, while that in the oceans is estimated to be about 100 years. As a result, most of the world inventory of Al^{26} is concentrated in the sediments. However, because of its long half-life, 7.4×10^5 years, and its very small production rate (global average estimated by Lal to be 1.4×10^{-4} atom/cm^2 sec or 0.44×10^4 atoms/cm^2 yr) the detection of this radionuclide should be very difficult even under the most favorable conditions. The highest specific activity would be obtained in areas of lowest sedimentation rate such as the South Pacific; here, the deposition rate is about 0.1 cm or 0.13 gram dry sediment per thousand years. The Al^{26} activity in recent sediments would then be about 0.06 dpm/kg (or 85 disintegrations/day/kg) of dry sediment; since the sediments are about 9% Al, the weight of aluminum in the sample would be some 90 grams. Fortunately, in its decay, Al^{26} emits rather characteristic radiations which considerably facilitate measurement; 84.6% of the decays are accompanied by the emission of a 1.83-MeV gamma ray in coincidence with two 511-keV annihilation photons.

A more important source of Al^{26} may be extraterrestrial dust; it is estimated that Al^{26} is produced in significant quantities by the interaction of solar protons with this material, principally through the Al^{27} (*p, pn*) and Mg^{26} (*p, n*) reactions. The amount of activity accreted by the earth from this source may be several times greater than that produced in the atmosphere by cosmic rays (Wasson, 1963). This view appears to be substantiated by recent measurements of Al^{26} in some Pacific sediments as carried out by Amin, Kharkar and Lal (see Lal and Peters, 1965); they obtained an average activity of 0.46 dpm/kg of dry sediment, a value which is an order of magnitude higher than that expected from cosmic-ray production in the atmosphere alone. However, because of the extremely low activities, the long counting times, and the possibility of contamination, these measurements are somewhat uncertain. The error due to counting statistics alone is approximately $\pm 50\%$. In contrast to this positive result an attempt to measure Al^{26} in matter filtered from water samples obtained from the Greenland ice sheet proved unsuccessful even though the detection sensitivity was considerably less than that required for the detection of the estimated influx rate of Al^{26} in dust. Previous attempts to measure Al^{26} in ocean sediments have also been unsuccessful.

The detection of such "large" amounts of Al^{26} from cosmic dust would be quite significant since it would permit estimates to be made of various astrophysical quantities such as the accretion rate of cosmic dust, the solar proton flux, and the orbital shrinkage times of dust particles; in addition, time-dependent variations of these values might be discernible through the variations of the Al^{26} content of cores with depth.

J. M. PROSPERO
F. F. KOCZY

References

Broecker, W. S., and Thurber, D. L., 1965, "Uranium-series dating of corals and oolites from Bahaman and Florida Key limestones," *Science*, **149**, 58–60.

Koczy, F. F., 1963, "Age determination in sediments by natural radioactivity," in (Hill, M. N., editor), "The Sea," Vol. 3, pp. 816–831, New York, Interscience Publishers.

Koczy, F. F., and Rosholt, J. N., 1962, "Radioactivity in Oceanography," in (Israel, H., and Krebs, A., editors), "Nuclear Radiation in Geophysics," pp. 18–46, Berlin, Springer-Verlag.

Koide, M., and Goldberg, E. D., 1965, "Uranium^{234}/Uranium^{238} Ratios in Sea Water," in (Sears, Mary, editor), "Progress in Oceanography," Vol. 3, pp. 173–177, London, Pergamon Press.

Ku, T., 1965, "An evaluation of the U^{234}/U^{238} method as a tool for dating pelagic sediments," *J. Geophys. Res.*, **70**, 3457–3474.

Lal, D., and Peters, B., 1965, "Changes in Terrestrial Isotope Abundances Produced by Cosmic Rays," in "Handbuch der Physik," Berlin-Heidelberg, Springer-Verlag (in press).

Mauchline, J., and Templeton, W. L., 1964, "Artificial and natural radioisotopes in the marine environment," in (Barnes, H., editor), "Oceanography and Marine Biology, an Annual Review," Vol, 2, pp. 229–279, New York, Hafner Publishing Company.

Moore, W. S., and Sackett, W. M., 1964, "Uranium and Thorium series inequilibrium in Sea water," *J. Geophys. Res.*, **69** (24), 5401–5405.

Olsson, I. U., and Eriksson, K. G., 1965, "Remarks on C^{14} dating of shell material in sea sediments," in (Sears, Mary, editor) "Progress in Oceanography," Vol. 3, pp. 253–266, London, Pergamon Press.

Riel, G. K., Dolfis, J. P., and Simons, D. G., 1960, "Spectrum of radiation background under water," *Nature*, **188** (4747), 266–268.

Wasson, J. T., 1963, "Radioactivity in interplanetary dust," *Icarus*, **2**, 54–87.

RADIONUCLIDES: THEIR APPLICATIONS IN OCEANOGRAPHY

(1) Introduction

Radioactive nuclides, naturally occurring and man-made, have come to play an important role in oceanography since their distribution in the oceans and the deep-sea sediments permits conclusions to be drawn regarding the past geological history of the earth and the dynamic processes taking place in the oceans. Radionuclides have been used in the study of diffusion processes both in ocean water and in sediments. They are used also for the tagging of bodies of water; in this way, the path of various water masses can be followed over long distances. Similar techniques permit the description of circulation and mixing patterns in the oceans and the determination of the time element involved in the turnover of ocean water. The members of the naturally occurring radioactive uranium and thorium series have relative concentrations in the oceans that differ from those in the

sediments or on the continents; a study of these differences in distribution can lead to a better understanding of the geochemical processes taking place in all three phases. Furthermore, measurement of the relative distributions of the members of these series in the oceans and in the sediments enables the age of sediment layers to be determined, thus establishing an absolute time scale for geological events.

These various applications of radionuclides to problems in oceanography are discussed in this article. Readers are referred to the article *Radionuclides in Oceans and Sediments*, for introductory material on the concentrations of the more important radionuclides in the marine environment and for an analysis of the factors influencing their distribution; data on the decay characteristics of these nuclides are also presented.

(2) Radiotracer Studies of Large-scale Mixing in the Oceans

A knowledge of the distribution and concentrations of various radionuclides in the oceans can yield a considerable amount of information regarding circulation patterns and mixing rates. To illustrate the basic principle, consider the following analogy. If a dye which has the property of having its color intensity decrease exponentially with time is added uniformly and at a constant rate to the surface of a body of water, the vertical distribution of color will vary depending on the mixing rate of the water and the decay rate of the dye. In the event that the mixing rate is very fast compared to the "half-life" of the dye, the color distribution will be uniform throughout the body. If the mixing rate is not rapid, the dye will decay to a significant degree as it is mixed downward and, as a result, the vertical distribution will not be uniform. In the case where the vertical mixing rates differ in various parts of the body of water, the surface concentrations will vary, being lowest where the mixing is greatest.

Radionuclides can be used as tracers in the same sense as the dye in the above analogy. To be suitable for such a purpose, the tracer should possess the following characteristics: (1) it should have a half-life of the same order of magnitude as the time constants of the process under study, (2) the mode and rate of injection should be known as a function of time and space, (3) the tracer should be soluble, and (4) it should be present in readily measurable quantities. However, since oceanic circulation is quite complex, a knowledge of the radionuclide distribution alone is not sufficient to determine mixing rates and patterns. This information must be correlated with the results of classical oceanographic research before it can become meaningful.

At the present time, only three naturally occurring radionuclides appear suitable for circulation studies: H^3, C^{14}, and Ra^{226}; a number of other cosmic ray produced nuclides such as Si^{28} and Be^7 may eventually be applicable (see *Radionuclides: Cosmic Ray Produced*, pr. Vol. IV). Several fallout radionuclides may also be useful. A general review of the use of radiotracers for mixing studies is presented by Broecker (1963); an extensive analysis of the various ocean mixing models is included.

(a) **Tritium.** Tritium, with its half-life of 12.26 years, would be an excellent tracer for short time scale events. On the basis of chemistry alone, tritium would be most ideal as a water tracer. However, its concentration in deep water is exceedingly small. In addition, the rates of addition and the degree of variation in the sea surface are subject to much uncertainty. Once these effects are better understood, tritium will be a useful tracer for mixing studies of surface water, since its half-life is commensurate with the mixing time of water above the thermocline. Studies with this end in mind are presently in progress.

(b) **Carbon 14.** Natural radiocarbon is the most important of the oceanic water tracers and it has been utilized for this purpose to a considerable extent, particularly by Broecker and Suess. Natural radiocarbon concentrations in seawater are expressed as differences in the C^{14}/C^{12} ratio (expressed in parts per thousand) relative to that of nineteenth century wood. However, a secondary reference standard of oxalic acid is generally used for the calibration of counters. The per mil difference δ is calculated from the expression:

$$\delta_{C14} = \frac{A_{sample} - 0.950A_{standard}}{0.950A_{standard}} \times 1000 \quad (1)$$

where A_{sample} is the net C^{14} activity of the sample; the factor 0.950 is chosen to adjust the activity of the secondary standard to the value of the nineteenth century wood.

The activity of samples must be corrected for the isotope fractionation which takes place in the chemical processes which led to the formation of the matter to be analyzed and in the chemical processing of the sample itself. This is done by measuring mass-spectrometrically the ratio C^{13}/C^{12}; the degree of C^{14}/C^{12} fractionation should then be twice that of C^{13}/C^{12}. The extent of fractionation is found to vary considerably in nature. An extreme example is the difference between marine limestone and recent wood; the former has an average C^{13}/C^{12} ratio which is some 2.6% higher than that of the latter. The degree of fractionation in the sample relative to the standard is expressed by:

$$\delta_{C13} = \frac{R_{sample} - R_{standard}}{R_{standard}} \times 1000 \quad (2)$$

where R represents the respective isotope ratios. The final C^{14} per mil deviation Δ of the unknown relative to the standard is given by:

$$\Delta = \delta_{C14} - (2\delta_{C13} + 50)\left(1 + \frac{\delta_{C14}}{1000}\right) \quad (3)$$

The concentration of C^{14} in seawater will depend on the age of the body of water in question and the degree of mixing with masses of water with differing C^{14} values. A representative study is that of Bien, Rakestraw, and Suess (1963) who studied the distributions of C^{14} as a function of latitude and depth in the Pacific and Indian oceans. Surface values of Δ were found to range from about -100 per mil to -10 per mil. The deep water range was from -180 per mil to -230 per mil. The lower activity of deep water indicates that, as would be expected, this water is considerably older than the surface water. In addition, the activity of the surface water was observed to decrease from north to south. The deep water, on the other hand, showed the opposite trend, the activity decreasing from south to north; the decreasing activity of the deep water reflects the aging of the water as it moves north. This circulation pattern is a consequence of the Antarctic Ocean being the only major source of cold water for the Pacific. This cold, more dense water sinks, and in doing so, moves north. On the basis of these measurements, it is concluded that the average northward component of the rate of water movement in the deep Pacific is 0.05 cm/sec.

The distribution of radiocarbon can be used to calculate mean residence times for the various water masses. In order to make such calculations, one must make certain assumptions about the exchange of C^{14} between the oceans and atmosphere and mixing in the oceans. This is typically done by devising box models of an ocean-atmosphere system consisting of a series of independent, well-mixed reservoirs (Broecker, 1963). In these models, carbon dioxide, having a C^{14}/C^{12} ratio typical of the entire reservoir, is exchanged with adjacent reservoirs. If it is assumed that the C^{14}/C^{12} ratio for each reservoir is constant, then the exchange rates required to maintain this distribution can be computed. For the model to be valid, the computed exchange rates must be in reasonable agreement with classical oceanographic observations.

A number of different models of varying complexity have been used. The simplest, a two-box model, divides the entire ocean system into a surface layer and the deep ocean. More elaborate models involve six boxes. While the residence times obtained vary with the model used, there is considerable agreement. It is generally concluded that the residence time of deep Pacific water is about 1000–1600 years while that of the Atlantic is approximately half that value. The residence time of surface water is quite short, 10–20 years.

The use of C^{14} as a water tracer is complicated by the Suess effect and weapons testing. Both of these sources have noticeably affected the concentration of C^{14} in surface waters; however, because of the mixing time of surface water and the large size of the deep reservoir, the effect on the concentration in deep water has been negligible in most cases.

(c) Radium 226. If it can be assumed that Ra^{226} is released from the ocean floor at a constant rate as evidence suggests, the residence time of water masses in open oceans can be determined. In order to make such a calculation, a knowledge of long-range advective processes is required as well as the radium concentration in the incoming and outgoing water. With this information, the residence time of the deep water in the Indian Ocean has been estimated by Koczy to be 500 years while that of the Pacific Ocean has been found to be 1000–3000 years. These estimates are in agreement with residence times determined by C^{14}. The measurement of shorter residence times will require the collection of considerably larger water samples since the differences in radium content of the incoming and outgoing water will be small.

It is of particular significance that radium is not exchanged with the atmosphere as is the case with C^{14}. At present, it is the only tracer which has its principal source at the ocean-sediment interface rather than at the ocean surface. Assuming that diffusion is the only factor responsible for the observed radium distribution, the vertical gradient can be used to calculate values for the rate of eddy diffusion in the ocean.

(d) Fallout Tracers. A number of radionuclides produced in nuclear weapons tests may be suitable for tracer studies. Of particular interest are C^{14}, H^3, Sr^{90}, and Cs^{137}. Sr^{90} ($t_{1/2} = 28$ years) and Cs^{137} ($t_{1/2} = 30$ years) have the advantage of not being present in the oceans prior to the bomb tests. Therefore, there is no need for a background correction. A number of measurements of Cs^{137} and Sr^{90} in the oceans have been made. The results obtained by various investigators are in considerable disagreement, with several finding very high concentrations in deep water; this latter distribution indicates much higher turnover rates than those calculated from C^{14} and Ra^{226} (see Rocco and Broecker, 1963, and references therein).

There are a number of possible explanations for these conflicting results. The most probable explanations are: (1) the vertical transport of Cs^{137} and Sr^{90} is the result of the settling of particulate matter rather than the movement of water containing the radionuclides in solution, and (2) the measurements of the nuclide concentrations are in error. The latter possibility is not too unlikely since measurements are rather difficult, involving the chemical processing of 200-liter water samples and the counting of very low levels of radioactivity (fractions of counts per minute per 100 liters for deep water samples). Considerably more experimental work is required before these questions can be satisfactorily resolved.

(3) The Dating of Ocean Sediments

The age of minerals or sediment layers can often be calculated from the quantities of radionuclides and their decay products contained in the material.

There are four basically different methods of age determinations; however, each is derived from the fundamental equation for radioactive decay which states that the number of atoms decaying per unit time (i.e., the activity) is proportional to the existing number of atoms:

$$dN/dt = \lambda N \tag{4}$$

where N is the number of atoms present and λ is a proportionality constant known as the decay constant. Integrating, we obtain:

$$N = N_0 e^{-\lambda t} \tag{5}$$

where N_0 is the number of atoms initially present and N the number present after a time t has elapsed. For λ we have:

$$\lambda = \frac{\ln 2}{t_{\frac{1}{2}}} = \frac{0.693}{t_{\frac{1}{2}}} \tag{6}$$

where $t_{\frac{1}{2}}$ is the half-life of the radionuclide in question, the time required for the number of atoms present to decrease by one-half. The decrease in the ratio N/N_0 as a function of λt is depicted in Fig. 1.

In the discussion of the various dating methods we generally assume that the following conditions prevail: (1) the sediment is deposited in a period of time which is short compared to the half-life of the radionuclide, and (2) once deposited, the sediment layer under consideration forms a closed system with no loss or gain of parent or daughter. Although these conditions are seldom encountered in nature, they are often sufficiently approximated to make dating feasible.

A discussion of the general subject of geochronology is presented by Wilson *et al.* (1956); rigorous derivations of the various types of dating equations are included. The dating of sediments is emphasized by Koczy (1963, 1965) and in references therein.

(a) Type I. If the specific activity of a sample at the time of formation is known, the sample can be dated by measuring the specific activity at the present time. This follows from Eq. (5) which, when rearranged, yields:

$$t = \frac{1}{\lambda} \ln \frac{N_0}{N} \tag{7}$$

(i) Carbon 14. The best example of this method is radiocarbon dating. The assumption is made that the ratio C^{14}/C^{12} in the carbon exchange reservoir has been constant over the dating period of interest. The age of a carbonaceous material can then be determined by measuring its specific activity and comparing it to a standard sample of "modern" carbon, since for equal weights of carbon:

$$\frac{A_{\text{standard}}}{A_{\text{sample}}} = \frac{\lambda_{C^{14}} N_{C^{14},\text{ standard}}}{\lambda_{C^{14}} N_{C^{14},\text{ sample}}} = \frac{N_{C^{14},\text{ standard}}}{N_{C^{14},\text{ sample}}} \tag{8}$$

Thus the specific activity ratio $A_{\text{standard}}/A_{\text{sample}}$ can be substituted for N_0/N in Eq. (7) to yield the age of the material. Since the discovery of C^{14} in nature by Libby (see *Radionuclides: Cosmic Ray Produced*, pr. Vol. IV), radiocarbon has proved to be extremely useful for the dating of archeological material and is now regarded as a common tool in this area.

Radiocarbon has also been used to establish the ages of suitable carbonate components in pelagic sediments in the same manner as above. However, the measured activity must be corrected for isotopic fractionation which takes place in the CO_2–HCO_3^-–$CO_3^=$ system in seawater as previously discussed. Radiocarbon dates can be readily obtained for samples up to 30,000–40,000 years old. The time scale has been extended in a few cases to 70,000 years by making use of isotopic enrichment using thermal diffusion. However, the problem of contamination with "younger" carbon becomes quite severe when analyzing old samples. For example, an infinitely old sample contaminated with 0.5% recent carbon would yield an apparent age of 41,500 years. To avoid this difficulty, shell samples must be thoroughly cleaned and carefully chosen to avoid material which shows evidence of recrystallization since this might lead to the inclusion of "younger" carbon.

The C^{14} method is the most reliable and most frequently used method for dating pelagic sediment cores. Sedimentation rates for oceans and basins are obtained by dating the core at closely spaced intervals and determining the mass deposited per unit time. The time resolution is limited by the effect of the reworking of sediment material by bottom-dwelling organisms which often churn the surface sediment to a depth of several centimeters, thereby mixing recent sediments with the deeper and older material. In areas such as in the South Pacific where sedimentation rates are of the order of 1 mm or less per thousand years, this effect can be quite significant. Another problem is presented by older sediments which are transported from adjacent areas, either by turbidity currents or slumping, and deposited on fresh sediment surfaces. A core taken from such an area will obviously yield anomalous dates for the disturbed sections. For this reason cores must be taken from areas relatively free of such occurrences. Unfortunately, the one major shortcoming of C^{14} for sediment dating is its limited time scale; 30,000 years is a short period of time, geologically speaking.

(*ii*) *Thorium 230 (Ionium).* Ionium, a daughter of U^{238}, has a very short residence time in the ocean, the Th^{230} produced from decay being rapidly hydrated and adsorbed on particulate matter which settles to the ocean floor. The concentration of Th^{230} in modern sediments is a function of the amount produced in the water column above and its dilution with detrital material and with the carbonate and silicate remains of marine organisms.

The age of a sediment layer can be determined from the ionium content per unit weight of dry sediment (the freshly deposited surface layer yielding the value for N_0) if the following assumptions are valid: (1) the concentration of uranium in the oceans has not varied significantly for the period of time of interest, (2) the sedimentation rate has also been constant for at least as long a time, (3) the Th^{230} precipitated from solution can be distinguished from that derived from other sources, and (4) ionium does not migrate in the sediments.

The validity of the assumption of the constancy of the uranium concentration is subject to debate; although the concentration appears to have been constant, trapping in reducing environments and the reworking of shelf sediments may have affected the concentration in an unpredictable fashion. In addition, sedimentation rates, particularly of the non-carbonate fraction, appear to be variable; C^{14} dating of cores indicates that this variability is associated with the effects of glaciations. Thus, sedimentation rates during the Pleistocene would not be constant.

The authigenic Th^{230} present in sediments is determined by completely dissolving the sediment sample and measuring the Th^{230} and U^{238} concentrations; assuming that U^{238} is in equilibrium with its daughters, the uranium-supported Th^{230} is calculated and subtracted from the total ionium content. The assumption of equilibrium is not valid for all types of sediments as will be shown; however, it is the best approximation that can be made under the circumstances. This correction becomes more critical with higher sedimentation rates and older core samples. For areas with very low sedimentation, the dating span extends to 500,000–700,000 years.

While the general validity of ionium dating is questionable, the specific activity of Th^{230} in sediments seems to provide an excellent measure of recent sedimentation rates. The principal assumption of the ionium sedimentation rate method is that the concentration of uranium in the oceans has not changed in the past 10,000 years (i.e., since the last glaciation), a fairly safe assumption for this short interval of time. Knowing the U^{234} concentration in seawater and the water depth in the area of interest, the amount of Th^{230} deposited per unit time per square centimeter of the ocean floor can be calculated. If the average uranium content of ocean water is assumed to be 3.3×10^{-9} g/ml, the activity ratio U^{234}/U^{238} to be 1.14, and the average ocean depth to be 4 km, the average deposition rate of Io per thousand years is calculated as 2.21×10^{-9} g Io/cm^2 per 1000 years. The sedimentation rate S is then determined by the equation:

$$S = \frac{2.21 \times 10^{-9}}{C_{Io}} \qquad (9)$$

(grams of sediment per square centimeter per thousand years) where C_{Io} is the concentration of ionium in the sediment.

If the surface sediment layer containing material less than 5000–10,000 years old is analyzed, no correction for decay need be considered since the error would amount to only a few per cent. As before, the authigenic ionium is determined by subtracting the uranium-supported equivalent assuming that the uranium present in the sediment is in equilibrium with its daughters, a situation which does not always obtain as will later be shown.

The analysis of data from 54 well-characterized sediment cores dated by various methods shows that the sedimentation rates obtained by the ionium method are much more consistent than those obtained by other means. Rates calculated for adjacent cores by this procedure are often quite similar even in cases where other methods yield inconsistent or even meaningless results; the small variability of sedimentation rates measured in this fashion indicates that single determinations are significant and representative of sedimentation over a large area.

The average recent sedimentation rate obtained from 54 cores was 0.63 gram of dry sediment per square centimeter per thousand years; converted to a volume rate, this is 0.67 cm of wet sediment per thousand years, a value very similar to the reported mean global accumulation rate during the late Pleistocene, 0.68 cm. If a density of 2.7 g/cc is assumed for dry compacted sediment, the global average rate of 0.63 g/cm^2 corresponds to 0.23 cm per thousand years or 4.5 km of sediment cover in the 2×10^9 years since the Archeozoic.

(b) Type II. In contrast to Type I dating which assumes a constant rate of supply or production, Type II assumes that a correction can be made for the effects of such variations. For example, if the concentration of a radionuclide in the ocean is constant relative to that of some reference element or nuclide, it may possibly be used as a dating tool even though the absolute concentrations of these materials in seawater may have changed. The activity of the nuclide normalized to the concentration of the reference element (or nuclide) at the fresh sediment surface serves to establish the ratio at time zero; the activity per gram of reference element should then decrease exponentially with depth in the core according to the half-life. That is:

$$\frac{N}{R} = \frac{N_0}{R} e^{-\lambda t} \tag{10}$$

where R represents the number of grams (or atoms) of reference element and the other symbols are as previously defined; N_0/R is the ratio at the sediment surface and N/R is the ratio in the layer to be dated. The ratio N/N_0 should vary as a function of time as depicted in Fig. 1.

Unfortunately, there are a number of difficulties with this method. In order to be applicable, the radionuclide and the reference element must have similar chemistries and origins. If not, variations in climate and weathering, the effects of glaciations, and the reworking of shelf sediments during periods of low sea level may all serve to alter the ratio. In addition, if the chemistries are different, we may expect the elements to have different histories in the sediment; for example, one may diffuse more rapidly than the other which would again alter their ratio as a function of time and depth within the core. Despite these difficulties, a number of procedures are based on this method.

(i) Thorium 230–Thorium 232. The method based on the thorium radioisotopes is assumed to be valid if: (1) the Th^{230}/Th^{232} ratio has remained constant in the ocean area under consideration, (2) the chemical speciation of Th^{230} and Th^{232} in seawater is similar, and (3) detrital components containing significant amounts of Th^{230} and Th^{232} are unattacked in the chemical treatment of the sediment sample. If these criteria are met, the ratio Th^{230}/Th^{232} should decrease exponentially with depth in the core.

However, the validity of these assumptions is questionable. The Th^{230}/Th^{232} ratio in the ocean may be rather variable because of the great difference between the chemistry of Th^{232} and that of the parents of Th^{230} (U^{234} and U^{238}). In addition, the chemical speciation of ionium and Th^{232} should be quite different. Ionium is produced as an ion through recoil in the radioactive decay of U^{234} which is present in solution; on the other hand, only a small fraction of the Th^{232} in the oceans ever enters solution, most of it being contained in terrigenic material (Koczy, 1963).

A considerable amount of dating work has been done in the past several years using this procedure, particularly by Goldberg and Koide (see references in Koczy, 1965). Their procedure requires that the sediment sample be leached with $6N$ HCl; supposedly, the leaching process removes the Th^{230} and Th^{232} precipitated from solution in seawater, leaving the detrital Th^{232} untouched. This assumption is crucial since the major portion of the Th^{232} in the sediments is detrital in origin. The leaching of detrital thorium would lower the Th^{230}/Th^{232} ratio, thus yielding ages which are older than the true ages.

In the many cores analyzed by this method, the Io–Th distribution in the cores has been found to be rather variable with depth. In some cases an exponential decrease of the ratio is observed, as would be hoped; however, an appreciable number of cores have been analyzed which show considerable deviations from such a decrease. In some of these, the ratio was observed to actually increase with depth. This effect has been explained as being due to the reworking of surface sediments by

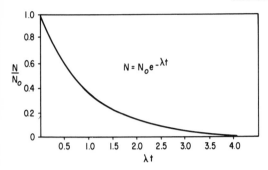

Fig. 1. The ratio N/N^0 as a function of λt in the general equation for radioactive decay.

organisms or bottom currents or both; however, this explanation is not sufficient to account entirely for the results obtained. Of greater importance may be the variable leaching of uranium minerals present in the sediments; the leaching of this material will result in the extraction of Th^{230}, daughter of U^{238}, thus increasing the Th^{230}/Th^{232} ratio and yielding an age younger than the true age. This source of error may be appreciable in areas where the uranium content of sediments is variable; in particular, the presence of volcanic matter would increase the uranium content significantly and in an erratic fashion. However, in general, the Io/Th procedure yields ages which are often several times older than those obtained by other methods; this is attributed to the leaching of detrital Th^{232} thus lowering the Th^{230}/Th^{232} ratio and yielding ages older than the true ages.

(*ii*) *Uranium 234–Uranium 238 and Thorium 230–Uranium 234.* In principle, the excess of U^{234} with respect to the concentration of its parent U^{238} in seawater could be used for the dating of pelagic sediments; the U^{234}/U^{238} activity ratio of freshly precipitated uranium should be equal to that of uranium in the overlying water, an average of 1.14. The U^{234}/U^{238} ratio of authigenic uranium in the core should decrease exponentially with the half-life of U^{234}, eventually attaining the equilibrium value of 1.0; the relationship between sediment age and the uranium activity ratio in this hypothetical situation is depicted in Fig. 2. To obtain valid ages, any dating procedure based on this method must selectively separate the authigenic uranium in the core from the detrital component since the latter will have a U^{234}/U^{238} activity ratio equal to or less than one.

A recent study of the applicability of the uranium isotope ratio method to the dating of sediments indicates that the difficulties associated with the separation of authigenic and terrigenic uranium make this method impractical (Ku, 1965). Attempts were made to separate authigenic uranium by using only the shells of pelagic foraminifera, the assump-

tion being that these organisms would only utilize uranium present in solution in seawater. However, the concentration of uranium was found to be too low in the carbonate fraction (in the order of 0.0X ppm) to be useful; hundreds of grams of carbonate material would be required in order to obtain a uranium sample sufficiently large for the precise spectrometric analysis essential for dating. Such large samples could not be readily obtained using conventional coring devices. In addition, the analysis of very old sections of cores by total dissolution gave consistently low uranium ratios in the range of 0.95 to 0.80; this is attributed to the upward migration of U^{234} in sediments, a behavior similar to that observed for Ra^{226}. Thus, this method has very little promise as a dating tool for sediments.

The excess U^{234} may prove to be useful for the dating of marine carbonates such as corals; recent carbonates have been found to contain several parts per million of U^{238} and essentially no Th^{230}, a daughter product. Thus, the ratio of U^{234}/U^{238} should decrease while the ratio Th^{230}/U^{234} should increase as a function of time. If it can be assumed that no Th^{230} is present at the time of formation of the carbonate and that the ratio of U^{234}/U^{238} has been constant for the past million years or so and, furthermore, that the system has been closed from the time of growth, then the age of the carbonate can be calculated; theoretically, the ages obtained by the Th^{230}/U^{234} and the U^{234}/U^{238} methods should agree. The Th^{230}/U^{234} method would be capable of covering a time span of about 250,000 years, while the U^{234}/U^{238} method would be applicable for ages up to 1.5 million years. The relationship between these nuclide activity ratios and sample age is depicted in Fig. 2 (Thurber *et al.*, 1965).

The results obtained by this method are somewhat erratic and often inconsistent. The principal

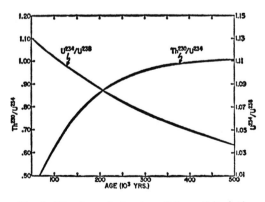

Fig. 2. The theoretical value of the activity ratios U^{234}/U^{238} and Th^{230}/U^{234} as a function of time. The initial value of the uranium ratio is assumed to be 1.15 while that of Th^{230}/U^{234} is taken as zero (figure from Thurber *et al.*, 1965).

difficulty seems to be attributable to the effects of recrystallization. Thurber *et al.* (1965) have established seven criteria which can be used to evaluate the relative validity of results obtained from samples of unknown age. These criteria were used in the analysis of coral and oolites with varying degrees of success. Their results indicate that the Th^{230}/U^{234} method can yield relatively consistent ages only in carefully selected cases; however, the uranium ratio method yields very erratic results even in these samples and its usefulness remains to be demonstrated.

(c) **Type III.** This method of radioactive dating makes use of the relationship between the radioparent and its daughter. In the cases of interest, $K^{40}-Ar^{40}$ and $Rb^{87}-Sr^{87}$, the daughter nucleus is a stable nuclide. We assume that at the time of formation, the material to be dated contains no daughter product or, if some is initially present, a mechanism is available to estimate a correction.

(*i*) *Potassium 40–Argon 40 and Rubidium 87– Strontium 87.* K^{40} and Rb^{87} have been used for the determination of ages of minerals and rocks on the continents (Wilson *et al.*, 1956). In the case of K–Ar dating, all of the daughter argon, being an inert gas, can be safely assumed to have been swept away prior to the solidification of the molten material from which the mineral is formed. As the mineral ages, the concentration of Ar^{40} increases in a predictable fashion. The one major difficulty with K–Ar dating is the loss of argon either by diffusion or by alteration of the mineral at a later time after formation; such loss would yield an age younger than the true age. In general, K–Ar ages have been found to be younger than the ages determined by other methods, thus indicating that argon loss is common.

The different chemical properties of Rb and Sr also serve to effectively fractionate these two parent–daughter elements; in any event, a correction can be made for any residual Sr^{87} present at the time of formation by analyzing the isotope ratios of the natural Rb present in the mineral. These two radioisotope systems permit the dating of minerals over almost the entire life span of the earth and they have been extensively used with considerable success.

Unfortunately, there do not seem to be any significant quantities of authigenic potassium minerals formed in the ocean or the sediments. The analysis of the mineral components of relatively recent pelagic sediments from the North Atlantic and Caribbean yields K–Ar age values in the general range of 200–400 million years, indicating that the minerals are derived from the land masses. The ages were found to vary with depth in the cores; this may be attributed to a variation in origin with time or to changes in direction of ocean circulation or wind patterns. Rubidium would not seem to be applicable for dating for the same reasons (Hurley *et al.*, 1963).

It may be possible to use the K–Ar method for the dating of sediment cores in instances where well-defined volcanic ash layers are found. Since the ash is deposited shortly after being cooled from the molten state, it can be considered to be argon free. However, argon diffusion may present a serious problem in the sediment environment. In the K–Ar analysis of detrital material in the cores cited above, the ages obtained were 10–20% younger than the land masses from which they were believed to be derived; one possible explanation for this observation would be the loss of argon from the finely divided particulate matter.

(d) **Type IV.** If two different radionuclides are produced in, or supplied to, the ocean in a constant ratio, the ratio of the activities in the sediments may be used as an age index. Ideally, the half-lives of the nuclides should differ significantly so that the change in the activity ratio as a function of time will be readily measurable. However, the difference should not be too great since the rapid disappearance of the shorter-lived nuclide relative to its companion nuclide would limit the use of the method to a short time span. Nuclides with half-lives differing by a factor of about two or three are convenient. In order to be suitable for the dating of pelagic sediments, the nuclides should have similar chemistries, their residence times in the ocean should be short with respect to their half-lives, and once incorporated into the sediment, they should form a closed system with no leaching or migration taking place.

(*i*) *Protactinium 231–Thorium 230.* Th^{230} and Pa^{231} are daughters of U^{238} and U^{235}, respectively. In many respects, these radionuclides are ideally suited for dating purposes (Koczy, 1965). Their parents are naturally occurring isotopes whose relative concentrations can be safely assumed to have been constant over the time period of interest, several hundred thousand years; thus the production ratio of the daughters should be constant even though the concentration of uranium in seawater may have changed appreciably. In addition, both Pa^{231} and Th^{230} (Io) have similar chemistries and very short residence times, several hundred years or less.

The ratio of the activities of Pa and Io in a sediment layer at a depth D is given by:

$$\left(\frac{A_{Pa}}{A_{Io}}\right)_D = 0.0938 \frac{e^{-\lambda_{Pa}t}}{e^{-\lambda_{Io}t}} = 0.0938 \, e^{-(\lambda_{Pa} - \lambda_{Io})t} \quad (11)$$

where A and λ are, respectively, the activities and decay constants of the nuclides indicated, 0.0938 is the activity ratio A_{Pa}/A_{Io} at the time of deposition (i.e., at the sediment surface) and t is the time elapsed since the deposition of the sediment layer being dated. Note that the activity ratio decreases exponentially just as in the case depicted for N/N_0 in Fig. 1. The decay of the individual nuclides and their ratio is shown plotted logarithmically in Fig. 3; the activities are given in arbitrary units so that

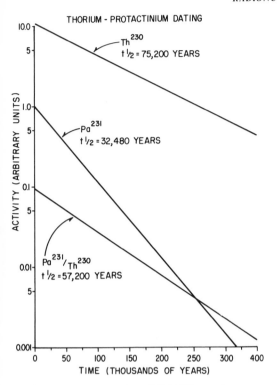

Fig. 3. The activity ratio Pa^{231}/Th^{230} in sediments as a function of time. The initial activity ratio is taken to be 0.0938, the value expected for freshly deposited ocean sediments. The decay of the individual nuclides is also shown.

the ratio A_{Pa}/A_{Io} is equal to 0.0938 at time zero as would be expected for freshly deposited sediments. The activity ratio is seen to decrease with an apparent half-life of 57,200 years.

The Pa and Io referred to in this equation are those which are precipitated from solution, the authigenic portion. This is determined by dissolving the entire sample and measuring the total Pa^{231} and Th^{230} content as well as the concentration of uranium; assuming secular equilibrium, the uranium-supported equivalents of Pa and Io are subtracted from the measured total. Because of the very low concentrations of Pa in the sediments and the uncertainty of the Io determination, the method can only be applied to the dating of materials of ages up to 150,000–200,000 years old.

The Pa–Io method has been used for the dating of pelagic sediments with some degree of success; at present, it is believed to yield the most accurate ages, with the exception of C^{14}. However, there are difficulties which stem from the assumptions made in the calculation of the uranium-supported Pa and Th in the sediments. It is tacitly assumed in making this calculation that the uranium in the sediments is in equilibrium with its daughters. This has been shown not to be true in all cases. As previously

stated, the sediments, considered on the basis of origin and composition, are comprised of three different components: carbonates and silicates which are formed in and precipitated from seawater and detrital material transported from land. The U^{234}/U^{238} activity ratio of the latter material should be less than one because of leaching. The situation with recent carbonate (and possibly silicate) sediments is somewhat different; foraminifera shells, a major component of carbonate oozes, contain uranium in concentrations of the order of $0.0X$ ppm but apparently very little Pa and Io, considerably less than equilibrium quantities. Furthermore, the ratio of U^{234}/U^{238} in this material should be approximately the same as that of seawater, 1.14.

Thus a high-carbonate surface sediment sample from an area with a sedimentation rate of 1 cm or more per thousand years may contain a significant amount of uranium which is not in equilibrium with its daughters. The net effect of this situation is to alter the Pa-Io ratio when the correction is made for uranium support. On the other hand, sediments which are primarily detrital in origin should have the opposite effect on the corrected Pa/Io ratio. The ages obtained by the Pa/Io method will be least affected in areas of low sedimentation; as sedimentation rates increase, the error in age determination will be dependent on the amounts of carbonate and silicate relative to the detrital component with the latter generally having the greatest effect on the age because of its usually higher uranium content.

Another possible problem is that of the migration of uranium or its daughter products in the sediments. Indications are that the diffusion of Pa and Io in sediments should not be significant except perhaps in areas with very low sedimentation rates; the displacement of thorium in sediments has been calculated to be about 2 cm/100,000 years compared to 20 cm/100,000 years for radium. However, the diffusion of U^{234} may be appreciable, as previously indicated; the diffusion coefficient for U^{234} in sediments is comparable to that obtained for radium (Ku, 1965). Considerably more work is required before the relative importance of these effects can be ascertained.

(ii) Aluminum 26–Beryllium 10. The dating methods discussed thus far are limited to a time span of several hundred thousand years or less, with the exception of K–Ar; the latter, if and when applicable, would permit the dating of sediments older than several million years. Thus a dating procedure is needed for the range of about 0.5–5 million years. A possible solution lies in the use of the cosmic ray produced nuclides Be^{10} and Al^{26} if the production rate can be assumed to be constant. Ideally, one would like to use the specific activities Be^{10}/Be and Al^{26}/Al as in the Type II dating method. However, because the residence times of these elements, 500 years or less, are shorter than the mixing times of the oceans, their deposition

rates are expected to vary from place to place since significant precipitation will take place before the elements have had the opportunity to mix uniformly with the water masses. In addition, there will be fluctuations in the deposition rate as a function of time due to variation in the influx rate particularly over glacial cycles. While the deposition rates of all elements are subject to such effects, the variations generally become more severe with decreasing residence times.

However, if the relative production rates of Al^{26} and Be^{10} are constant, the ratio of the activities can be used to date sediments (Lal and Peters, 1965). The age, t, of a sediment sample would then be given by:

$$\left(\frac{A_{Al^{26}}}{A_{Be^{10}}}\right)_D = \left(\frac{A_{Al^{26}}}{A_{Be^{10}}}\right)_0 e^{-(\lambda_A{^{26}} - \lambda_{Be}{^{10}})t} \qquad (12)$$

where A denotes the activity of the indicated nuclides; the subscripts 0 and D denote the activity ratios of samples taken from the top of the core and at a depth D, respectively. The activity ratio should decrease by approximately a factor of two every million years. If the principal source of production of Al^{26} and Be^{10} is through cosmic ray interactions with the atmosphere and if Lal's calculated production rates are correct, then the activity ratio of Al^{26}/Be^{10} in surface sediments should be about 10^{-2}.

The problems associated with the detection and measurement of these radionuclides were previously discussed. The major difficulty is the distressingly low level of activity of Al^{26} in sediments; of equal concern is the question of the principal mode and the constancy of production of this nuclide. If Al^{26} and Be^{10} are produced primarily by cosmic ray interactions with the atmosphere, then the assumption that the production ratio is constant is relatively safe. There is little doubt that at least 98% of the Be^{10} found in sediments has this origin. However, indications are that the major source of Al^{26} is cosmic dust; if this is so, then the ratio method cannot be used as an age index unless the accretion rate of Al^{26} can be shown to have been constant relative to Be^{10} Because so many of the parameters concerned with the production of radionuclides in cosmic dust are so poorly characterized and understood, a considerable amount of research will be required. However, these studies are extremely important in themselves and Al^{26} may prove to be much more important in this respect than as an age index (Wasson, 1963).

J. M. Prospero
F. F. Koczy

References

Bien, G. S., Rakestraw, N. W., and Suess, H. E., 1963, "Radiocarbon dating of deep water of the Pacific and Indian Oceans," *Bull. Inst. Oceanogr. Monaco,* **61**, No. 1278, 1–16.

Broecker, W. S., 1963, "Radioisotopes and Large Scale Oceanic Mixing," in (Hill, M. N., editor) "The Sea," Vol. 2, pp. 88–108, New York, Interscience Publishers.

Hurley, P. M., Heezen, B. C., Pinson, W. H., and Fairbairn, H. W., 1963, K–Ar age values in pelagic sediments of the North Atlantic," *Geochim. Cosmochim. Acta,* **27**, No. 4, 393–399.

Koczy, F. F., 1963, "Age Determination in Sediments by Natural Radioactivity," in (Hill, M. N., editor) "The Sea," Vol. 3, pp. 816–831, New York, Interscience Publishers.

Koczy, F. F., 1965, "Remarks on Age Determination in Deep-sea Sediments," in (Sears, M., editor) "Progress in Oceanography," Vol. 3, pp. 155–171, London, Pergamon Press.

Ku, T., 1965, "An evaluation of the U^{234}/U^{238} method as a tool for dating pelagic sediments," *J. Geophys. Res.,* **70**, 3457–3474.

Lal, D., and Peters, B., 1965, "Changes in Terrestrial Isotope Abundances Produced by Cosmic Rays," in "Handbuch der Physik," Berlin–Heidelberg, Springer-Verlag, in press.

Thurber, D. L., Broecker, W. S., Blanchard, R. L., and Potratz, H. A., 1965, "Uranium-series ages of Pacific atoll coral," *Science,* **149**, 55–58.

Wasson, J. T., 1963, "Radioactivity in interplanetary dust," *Icarus,* **2**, 54–87.

Wilson, J. T., Russell, R. D., and Farquhar, R. M., 1956, "Radioactivity and Age of Minerals," in (Flügge, S., editor) "Handbuch der Physik," Vol. XLVII, Geophysics I, pp. 288–362, Berlin, Springer-Verlag.

RADIUM—*See* **RADIONUCLIDES**

RADIUM IN OCEANS—*See* pr Vol. IV

RAYLEIGH NUMBER—*See* **THERMAL INSTABILITY**

RED SEA

From the narrow Straits of Bab-el-Mandeb in the south, the Red Sea extends northwestwards for 1932 km, separating the African continent from Arabia by a long narrow seaway which is only 306 km wide at its maximum breadth in the southern sector. At Ras Benas, two-thirds of the way from the southern straits to the northern Gulfs of Aqaba and Suez, the sea is only 145 km wide. South of this point, the shores are bordered by broad, reef-studded shelves which are less than 50 meters deep. These drop off abruptly to shelves about 500 meters deep which flank a deep, narrow, central trough in which depths frequently exceed 1500 or even 2000 meters. The greatest depths in the Red Sea, so far recorded, are over 2300 meters and are found in the narrow median trough in the central sector. North of Ras Benas, the shelves are narrower and the central trough broadens to a shallower irregular surface where depths seldom exceed 2000 meters. The Sinai Peninsula divides the northern extremity into the shallow Gulf of Suez on the west and the deep, narrow, high-silled Gulf of Aqaba (Eilat) on the east. The gulf is only 16 km wide but its faulted sides slope steeply downward to depths in excess of 1800 meters. Soundings in the Red Sea are scattered, and at present the details of its bathymetry are inadequately known.

Geological History and Structure

The Red Sea basin is the result of a complex system of rifts which divide the Precambrian shield plates of Africa and Arabia. The rift system is a continuation of the East African system which extends through the Red Sea into the Gulf of Aqaba and on to the Dead Sea region to the northeast.

The geophysical character of the northern Red Sea differs from that of the central and southern sectors, suggesting that the structure is more complex than a simple down-dropped segment of the earth's crust bordered by high-angle normal faults. This may be the case in the extreme northern sector where negative gravity anomalies and no appreciable magnetic anomalies suggest that the Gulfs of Suez and Aqaba, like the East African rift valleys, are simple grabens. In contrast, the central and southern sectors of the Red Sea basin exhibit positive gravity anomalies and extreme magnetic irregularity over the deep central trough. Seismic data from this region suggest that the bordering shelves are of continental type (5.9 km/sec), but the deep central region exhibits higher velocities (7.1 km/sec) beneath a sediment thickness which varies from 2–6 km. The interpretation is that the central trough in the south represents a complex rift structure in which deep basic intrusives have risen and engulfed continental remnants which have been pulled apart by tensional forces associated with the separation of the African and Arabian blocks.

Paleomagnetic evidence from the Aden volcanics suggests that a 7° counterclockwise rotation of the Arabian block has occurred since Upper Tertiary time. Geologic field studies of the areas surrounding the Red Sea indicate that the rift movement began at least as early as the Mid-Mesozoic and continued intermittently throughout the Tertiary. Faulting in the area of the Straits of Bab-el-Mandeb suggests that the Red Sea was opened to the Indian Ocean during Miocene or even Pliocene times. Marine Mesozoic and Tertiary sediments along the Gulf of Suez show that the northern end was open only to the Mediterranean until early Quaternary times.

Oceanography

The main system of circulation of Red Sea waters is at present controlled by evaporation, winds and a shallow sill in the south. This sill is 125 meters deep and is located near Great Hanish Island within the Straits of Bab-el-Mandeb. There are four major elements in the circulation system.

(1) A body of nearly isothermal, isohaline water lies below 200 meters. This water is 21.7°C with a salinity of 40.6‰. The density varies little between 28.5 and 28.6 sigma t units (i.e., 1.0285–1.0286 g/cc). It is formed in the northern sector during the winter when cooling and evaporation are at a maximum. Replenishment at the surface and subsequent mixing maintain dissolved oxygen values of 2–3 ml/liter in the deepest portions of this huge mass of water below sill depth.

(2) An inflow of Gulf of Aden waters persists at the surface throughout much of the year. No rivers flow into the Red Sea, and rainfall for the entire area is very scant. Little or no water enters via the Suez Canal. Therefore, the evaporative losses, which amount to as much as 210 cm/yr, must be met by an influx of waters through the Straits of Bab-el-Mandeb. This inflow is at the surface throughout the winter when winds from the south-southeast affect the southern sector. The surface inflow maintains itself for an undetermined period after the winds over this sector have returned to north-northwest in April or May.

(3) During the middle or late summer, the surface inflow yields to the contrary winds, and a thin wind-driven surface outflow develops on top of the inflow which continues at lower levels.

(4) During the winter and early summer, waters from the Gulf of Aden stream into the Red Sea along the surface. These are concentrated by evaporation and are cooled as they travel northward, with the result that surfaces of equal density (isopycnals) slope downward toward the sill in the south. Along these sloping surfaces of the upper 200 meters, a return flow is initiated. This culminates at the sill in a density-induced outflow which takes place under the surface inflow. The outflow of warm, dense saline water sinks rapidly in the Gulf of Aden and can be traced well into the Indian Ocean. It probably continues throughout the year, fed during certain periods by the back-flow of entering surface waters and at other seasons by the escape of bottom waters from sub-sill depths or by a combination of these effects. This relationship has not been thoroughly investigated to date. There is some indication that waters below sill depth do not contribute to the outflow during the early summer.

Dangerous cross currents of considerable magnitude have been reported in the Red Sea by many ships. The origin of the easterly or westerly sets is not known. It has even been suggested that they might be a result of errors in celestial navigation caused by atmospheric refraction.

Tides within the Red Sea are of a local, semi-diurnal type. The oscillation is such that high tide at the southern end is accompanied by low tide at the northern end, and vice versa. The spring range in the north is about 2 feet while that at the south reaches 3 feet, receiving some reinforcement from Indian Ocean tides of the Gulf of Aden through the Straits of Bab-el-Mandeb. Jidda and Suakin in the central sector are near the nodal point of this oscillation and receive no appreciable semidiurnal tide. A diurnal tide of very small amplitude has been detected in certain areas. Barometric pressure, wind and fluctuations in rate of evaporation and inflow also cause measurable seasonal and local variation in sea level. Measured seasonal differences do not exceed 1 foot, however.

Sediments within the Red Sea appear to be largely biogenic clastic calcium carbonate derived from the surrounding reefs and from the shells of pelagic organisms. Land-derived material usually makes up a small fraction of the sediment. It is brought in by wind or by intermittent runoff. In the northern sector the normally dry "wadis" very occasionally fill and run for a few hours to introduce silt-laden waters at certain scattered points. The irregular bottom topography provides isolated basins for sediment entrapment, and it is to be expected that sediment composition might vary considerably from basin to basin. Organic matter is low throughout, reaching a maximum at intermediate depths where it is associated with fine-grained carbonate material. Carbonate content decreases with depth, which may be a result of either solution or limited supply. It is interesting to note that the fine portion of the deeper sediments is reported to be calcite, in contrast to aragonite in the shallows. Aragonite should be the dominant mineral if the major contribution is from reef and shallow-water sources. It may be interpreted that the fine-grained aragonite is selectively dissolved in the deeper regions or that reef-derived products do not reach the deeper basins which may receive only the calcitic tests of pelagic Foraminifera and coccolithophorids.

On the basis of a few measurements of the concentration of chlorophyll in Red Sea waters, it appears that primary productivity is in general low. Chlorophyll values of 19 mg/m^3 compare with such areas of low productivity as the Sargasso Sea. Higher values have been obtained in sporadic blooms of discolored water. It is believed that the occasional blooming of the blue-green alga *Trichodesmium erythraeum* has given the Red Sea its name. This alga is blue-green when flourishing but turns reddish-brown when dying.

At present there is little economic exploitation of the area. Red Sea fisheries resources have been little explored. A plan has been proposed to dam the Straits of Bab-el-Mandeb in order to generate hydroelectric power. If the straits were closed it is estimated that evaporation would drop sea level within the Red Sea at a rate of 8–12 ft/yr. The main economic value of the Red Sea lies in its strategic location as it is an important, heavily traveled shipping route.

A development of considerable scientific importance has been the discovery of hot, salty brine filling the bottom few hundred meters of two deep isolated basins in the central Red Sea sector. Bottom water with anomalously high temperature and salinity and low oxygen content was first observed in this region by the Swedish Deep Sea Expedition in 1948. The values were only slightly higher than those of normal Red Sea bottom water, the anomalous water was considered to have formed by evaporation in bordering lagoons and traveled to the deep basin as a density flow along the bottom. In 1964, Swallow and Crease on the British research vessel *Discovery* found that the bottom 200 meters of the 2200-meter basin were filled with an extremely dense brine, the salinity of which exceeded 270‰ with a temperature of more than 44°C. The chemical composition of the brines departs markedly from that of normal seawater and suggests a connate origin; i.e., it has been leached out of a sedimentary formation exposed by faulting in the wall of the trough (a thick evaporite section is known from the pre-Quaternary sequence).

The chemistry of these Red Sea brines is similar to that of known connate brines from oil wells in several parts of the world. The research vessel *Atlantis II* of the Woods Hole Oceanographic Institution has further sampled the brines as well as the underlying sediment. Brine temperatures measured up to 56°C, or 133°F. The chemical analyses support the proposed connate origin, showing high concentrations of iron, zinc, copper and manganese in both the sediments and the overlying brines. The bottom sediments largely consist of amorphous iron oxide with lesser amounts of montmorillonite, sphalerite and amorphous silica, plus traces of anhydrite and dolomite. These anomalous sediments are interpreted to be precipitates from the overlying brines. This is a most important finding for economic geology because it may mean that the geochemical processes going on in these small isolated brine-containing basins in the Red Sea may be analogous to some of those that produced ore deposits in the past.

A. Conrad Neumann

References

Allan, T. D., 1964, "A preliminary magnetic survey in the Red Sea and Gulf of Aden," *Boll. Geofis. Teor. Applic.*, **6**, 199–214.

Brewer, P. G., Riley, J. P., and Culkin, F., 1965, "The chemical composition of the hot salty water from the bottom of the Red Sea," *Deep-Sea Res.*, **12**, 497–503.

Drake, C. L., and Girdler, R. W., 1964, "A geophysical study of the Red Sea," *Geophys. Jour.* **8**, 473–495.

Emery, K. O., 1964, "Sediments of Gulf of Aqaba (Eilat)," *Pap. Mar. Geol.* (Shepherd Vol.), 257–273.

Girdler, R. W., 1958, "The relation of the Red Sea to the East African rift system," *Quart. J. Geol. Soc. London*, **114**, 79–105.

Miller, A. R., Densmore, C. D., Degens, E. T., Hathaway, J. C., Manheim, F. T., McFarlin, P. F., Pocklington, R., Jokela, A., 1966, "Hot brines and recent iron deposits in deeps of the Red Sea," *Geochim. Cosmochim. Acta*, **30**(3), 341–359.

Mohamed, A. F., 1940, "The Egyptian exploration of the Red Sea," *Proc. Roy. Soc. London, Ser. B*, **128**, 306–316.

Nesteroff, W. D., 1955, "Les récifs coralliens du Banc Farsan Nord (Mer Rouge), resultats scientifiques des Campagnes de la 'Calypso': I, Campagne en Mer Rouge," *Ann. Inst. Oceanog.* (*Monaco*).

Neumann, A. C., and Chave, K. E., 1965, "Connate origin proposed for hot salty bottom water from a Red Sea basin," *Nature*, **206**, 1346–1347.

Neumann, A. C., and McGill, D. A., 1962, "Circulation of the Red Sea in early summer," *Deep-Sea Res.*, **8**, 223–235.

Said, Rushi, 1951, "Organic origin of some calcareous sediments from the Red Sea," *Science*, **113**, 517–518.

Sestini, J., 1965, "Cenozoic stratigraphy and depositional history, Red Sea coast, Sudan," *Bull. Am. Assoc. Petrol. Geologists*, **49**, 1453–1472.

Shukri, N. M., and Higazy, R. A., 1944, "Mechanical analysis of some bottom deposits of the northern Red Sea," *J. Sediment. Petrol.*, **14** (2), 43–69; **14** (2), 70–85.

Swallow, J. C., and Crease, J., 1965, "Hot salty water from bottom of Red Sea," *Nature*, **205**, 165–166.

Swartz, D. H., and Arden, D. D., Jr., 1960, "Geologic history of the Red Sea area," *Am. Assoc. Petrol. Geol.*, **44** (10), 1621–1637.

Thompson, E. F., 1939, "The general hydrography of the Red Sea: The John Murray Expedition, 1933–1934," *Sci. Rept.*, **2** (3), 83–103.

REYNOLDS, FROUDE NUMBERS—*See* Vol. II

RIPPLES—*See* **SLICKS, RIPPLES AND WIND-ROWS**

ROSS SEA

(1) Introduction

The Ross Embayment, that portion of West Antarctica included between the lines of 70–85°S latitude and 165°E–155°W longitude, is a vast 600-mile-wide shelf sea projecting some 700 miles into the Pacific sector of the Antarctic continent. Geographically, the Ross Sea can be said to occupy that part of the Ross Embayment situated north of about 77°S latitude; the Ross Ice Shelf occupies the area south of the same line.

Although exploration of this area has been underway longer and has been more extensive than for most other regions of the Antarctic, much information of a detailed nature is still not available. A general review of the relation of the Ross Sea Sector to the rest of the Antarctic continent is given by Fairbridge (1952).

(2) Oceanography

(a) Physical Oceanography. Water temperatures in the Ross Sea range from −2 to 0°C with little horizontal or vertical change evident. Similarly, only relatively minor horizontal variations in salinity have been recorded, although considerable density stratification (vertical variations) is reported, as would be expected with salinity and density ranges of 33.50–34.70‰ and 1.0267–1.0291, respectively. A small diurnal tidal variation of approximately 1 meter has been known to occur in the Ross Sea Sector, although this is based on limited data.

The general direction of surface currents and circulation along the front of the Ross Ice Shelf is from east to west at a rate of 1.0–3.0 knots with a sharp right-angled turn to the north along the western side of the Ross Sea. Current velocities near 70°S latitude decrease to approximately 0.5 knots. The areal circulation pattern is considered to be a part of the East Wind Drift, the only major current system tentatively identified in the area. A distinctive feature of the Ross Sea, compared to other coastal areas of Antarctica, is the extent of open water present—most of the area is open during February and March, broken ice coverage exists in November, December and January and relatively complete ice coverage from April through October.

(b) Submarine Geomorphology. Bathymetric data from all the area surrounding Antarctica, when compared to the relatively abundant information known from other continental areas, is quite sparse, and modifications in detail will be made with future work; however, the general outline of the major features is clear.

The continental shelf is both wide and deep in the Ross Sea Sector; the outer shelf break occurs at depths between 200–300 fathoms with an average depth of 255 fathoms. The great depth of the outer shelf has been attributed to isostatic depression by the adjacent continental ice sheet during both Pleistocene and more Recent Quaternary glaciation. Toward the outer edge, the continental shelf rises locally to form a series of elevated mounds and banks of quite irregular topography known as the Pennell Bank. These drowned banks are considered to be the submerged remnants of a large Late Pleistocene moraine. Sediment material collected from it suggest that this was probably the northernmost terminus of the Ross Ice Shelf during the last major glacial episode in the area.

Morphologically, the continental shelf of the Ross Sea can be classified into four main categories: (1) outer shelf—the deep lying terrace of the continental shelf; (2) shelf depressions—great troughs or trenches within the confines of the continental shelf; (3) inner shelf—the narrow, relatively shallow terrace bordering the landmass shoreward of the shelf depressions; and (4)

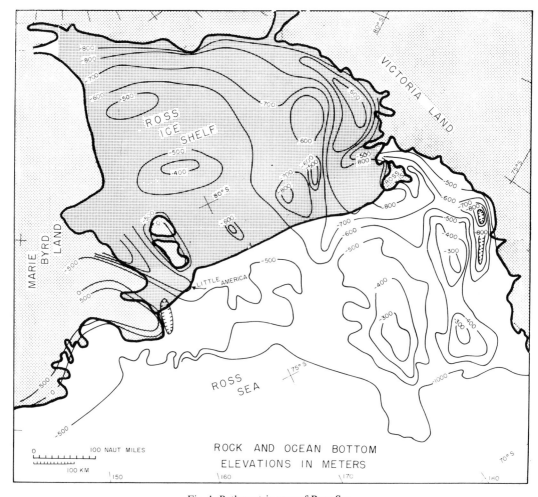

Fig. 1. Bathymetric map of Ross Sea.

morainal-like ridges (e.g., Pennell Bank) on the shelf.

Shelf depressions extending south under the Ross Ice Barrier and parallel to and bordering the Ross Embayment are found adjacent to both the western and eastern coasts of the Ross Sea. Depths as great as 600–800 fathoms have been reported in these depressions. Considerable speculation surrounds their origin.

A series of submarine ridges are found on the continental shelf of the Ross Sea area and can be divided into two types, those transverse to and those parallel to the general trend of the shore line. Soundings on these ridges as shallow as 40 fathoms have been reported. That transverse ridge situated in front of the present Ross Ice barrier and perpendicular to the shelf depressions on either end is composed of sand and clay and is clearly related to the present position of the Ross Ice Shelf.

A median ridge running north-south from 65–75°S latitude along the 180° meridian comes to the surface at Scott Island (67° 20′S). This ridge essentially separates the northern portion of Ross Sea into two separate parts.

(3) Structural Geology

The Ross Sea occupies the area of a large depression or graben that is bordered on the west by a horst or upthrown mountain range, the Transantarctic mountains, which include the mountains bordering the Ross Embayment on the west and south. Bouguer gravity data suggests that the crustal thickness along the western margin, including the mountains, is 10 km thicker than the section (28–30 km) in the Ross Embayment; the change in thickness at the eastern border of the Embayment is abrupt. A major fault is postulated to extend along the west coast of the Ross Sea along which significant horizontal displacement has occurred. Associated with the major fault are several smaller transverse faults scattered irregularly on a north–south line along Victoria Land coast. Extensive Tertiary–Quaternary volcanism has occurred along this major regional break. The volcanism, in contrast to that east of the embayment is of the "Atlantic" igneous type. Throughout the mountain system bordering this same general region (Victoria Land), other north–south and associated east–west faults are common. The eastern, southern, and western borders of the Embayment are bounded by a series of moat-like troughs, most of which appear, but are not proved, to be fault controlled.

The submarine surface of the Ross Embayment is quite deep when compared to similar areas in other parts of the world; as noted, a depth 200–300 fathoms is commonly found at the break in the slope which marks the edge of the continental shelf. Several hypotheses have been advanced to explain the shelf depression, but none is completely satisfactory. The most widely accepted hypothesis is the one which explains the depression of the shelf as being caused by isostatic adjustment owing to the weight of the continental ice cap.

(4) Sediments

(a) **General.** Sedimentation data in the Antarctic are extremely limited and only a generalized portrayal of the sediment types is possible. Immediately adjacent to and encircling the continental margin of the Antarctic is a zone of terrigenous sedimentary material of unique characteristics commonly referred to as glacial marine sediment. The outer limit of this sediment type is correlated with maximum extent of pack ice. The Ross Sea itself lies entirely within this inner zone of glacial marine sediments.

(b) **Sediment Description.** Sediments of this type are characterized by terrestrial material which has been transported either from the land or shallow water areas by ice rafting and has settled to the bottom as the ice melted. Characteristically, it is poorly sorted with particle sizes ranging from clay (0.004μ in diameter) to gravel (2000μ in size). The finer fraction is composed mainly of silt rather than the clay material common in deep ocean sediment, also it is extremely low in carbonate and organic content. As a rule, the sediments are unlaminated with the appearance of a glacial till Of the various organic remains present, diatom frustules and foraminifera tests predominate.

The sediments generally range in color from olive gray to yellowish brown, have a low-to-medium sphericity and normally are angular to subrounded in shape. In certain regions, notably in McMurdo Sound and near Cape Adare, volcanic material is prevalent, and locally within these areas becomes the dominant material present. The sediments are apparently being laid down in the same condition in which they are being released from melted ice. Distance from the Ross Ice Shelf and depth of water appear to have only a minor

effect on texture; percentages of clay and colloid run unusually high. To the north, the terrigenous material (more properly glacial marine sediment) grades gradually into a zone of diatom ooze with no sharp contact evident. The dominant minerals in the sediments are feldspar and quartz; the latter has attained its highest concentration off the southern portion of Victoria Land. A wide variety of rock and mineral species present in the sediments are of secondary importance.

Among the heavy minerals, those of the ferromagnesian group are unusually prevalent. Chemically, all of the heavy minerals are relatively unaltered, owing undoubtedly to their glacial origin. The highest heavy mineral percentage is found near Cape Adare in the Central Ross Sea area. Sediments along the front of the present Ross Ice Shelf are composed mainly of sand, gravel and small rock fragments. The central portion of the northern Ross Sea has a large area of mixed glacial marine sediment and diatom ooze. Scattered randomly over the continental shelf of the Ross Sea are smaller areas (of varying size) composed of clay, sand, mixed sand and rock fragments and hard rock bottom devoid of sediment. There appears to be no correlation with any of the common textural parameters except in the broadest sense; e.g., the mean grain size decreases slightly with depth and distance from shore. Marine currents seem to have little or no effect on the sorting of the sediment.

The type of sediment immediately surrounding the Antarctic continent and to which the term glacial marine sediment has been appended is unique among marine deposits. Early work on this subject was done by Phillippi, Pirie, Stetson and Upson, and others (see references in Hough, 1956; Thomas, 1959; Lisitzin, 1962). A good general summary with maps is provided in publication H.O. 705 of U.S. Navy Hydrographic Office.

ERNEST E. ANGINO
L. K. LEPLEY

References

*Anonymous, 1957, "Oceanographic Atlas of the Polar Seas," H.O. 705, Part I, "Antarctica," U.S. Naval Hydrographic Office.

Fairbridge, R., 1952, "The Geology of the Antarctic," in (Simpson, F. A., editor) "Antarctica Today," pp. 56–101, Wellington, New Zealand Antarctic Society.

*Hough, J., 1956, "Sediment distribution in the Southern Oceans around Antarctica," *J. Sediment. Petrol.*, **26**, 301–306.

Lisitzin, A. P., 1962, "Bottom sediments of Antarctic," in (Wexler, H., Rubin, M., and Caskey, J., Jr., editors) "Antarctic research," *Geophys. Monograph*, **7**, NAS-NRD-1036, 81–88.

Thomas, C. W., 1959, "Lithology and zoology of an Antarctic Ocean bottom core," *Deep Sea Res.*, **6**, 5–15.

ROSSBY NUMBER

This is a non-dimensional number (Ro) that defines the ratio of the inertial force to the Coriolis force (q.v.) for a given flow in a rotating fluid. With U as a characteristic velocity, f the Coriolis parameter, and L a characteristic length,

$$\text{Ro} = \frac{U}{fL}$$

In experiments of the "dishpan" type (see *Rossby Wave*, Vol. II) system which is cylindrical rather than spherical, the Rossby Number will still be a basic relationship, provided that the Coriolis parameter is replaced by a cylindrical value which is simply twice the rotation rate of the system.

An analogous but distinctive non-dimensional number is the *Thermal Rossby Number* (Ro_T), which is the inertial force due to the thermal wind (U_T) and the Coriolis force (f) in the flow of a fluid heated at the center and cooled at the rim. With L as a characteristic length,

$$\text{Ro}_T = \frac{U_T}{fL}$$

The thermal wind (U_T) is given by

$$U_T = g_\varepsilon \frac{(\Delta r\, \Theta)\delta}{f\, \Delta r}$$

where g is the acceleration of gravity, ε the coefficient of thermal expansion, $\Delta_r\, \Theta/\Delta_r$ a characteristic radial temperature gradient, and δ the depth of the fluid.

Rhodes W. Fairbridge

References

Eliassen, A., and Kleinschmidt, E., Jr., 1957, "Dynamic Meteorology," in "Handbuch der Physik, ("Encyclopedia of Physics"), Vol. 48(2), pp. 1–154, Berlin, Springer Verlag.

Fultz, D., 1951, "Experimental Analogies to Atmospheric Motions," in "Compendium of Meteorology," pp. 1235–1248, Boston, American Meteorological Society.

Huschke, R. E. (editor), 1959, "Glossary of Meteorology," Boston, American Meteorological Society. 638pp.

Rossby, C. G., 1939, "Relation between variations in the intensity of the zonal circulation of the atmosphere and the displacements of the semi-permanent centers of action," *J. Marine Res.*, **2**, 38.

Cross-references: *Coriolis Force; Thermal Instability.*
Vol. II *Atmospheric Circulation; Rossby Wave.*

ROSSBY WAVES—*See* Vol. II

S

SAHUL SHELF

As early as 1845, the existence of a vast continental shelf north of Australia was known, the "Great Australian Bank" of Earl, which he recognized seemed to "match" a "Great Asiatic Bank" (Sunda Shelf, q.v.) off Malaya.

The Sahul Shelf, named by Molengraaff and Weber (1919; see also Molengraaff, 1921), is sometimes taken to run from the North-West Cape of Western Australia to the Arafura Sea and the Gulf of Carpentaria to the Torres Straits (Fig. 1). However, apparently unknown to Molengraaff, the northeast part had been designated as *Arafura Shelf* by Krümmel (in 1897) and it seems best to retain this title. The central and southwestern parts were called *Northwest Shelf* by Krümmel, but this is an overly large designation, and since there is a

natural constriction in it, a rise at N45°W from Cape Leveque, (Fairbridge 1953) proposed that the central part be designated Sahul Shelf and the southwestern part the *Rowley Shelf* after the Rowley Shoals, three atoll reefs which form a conspicuous feature of it. The Rowley Shelf and Sahul Shelf, so designated, both have areas of about 300,000 km², while the area of the Arafura Shelf is 930,000 km². The Arafura Shelf coincides with the shallow part of Arafura Sea (q.v.) and Gulf of Carpentaria (q.v.), the Sahul Shelf with the shallow part of the Timor Sea (q.v.), and the Rowley Shelf with part of the northwestern Indian Ocean proper.

The geological history of these shelves is of profound interest. Gravity surveys by Vening Meinesz have proved that the shelf is strictly continental in character, and there is a trace of continental granitic arkose in the Aru Islands, which confirms this

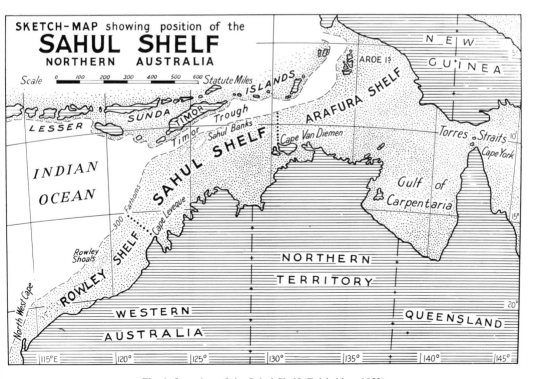

Fig. 1. Location of the Sahul Shelf (Fairbridge, 1953).

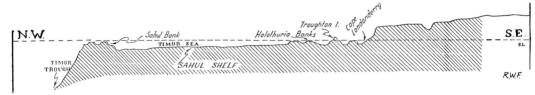

Fig. 2. Profile across the Sahul Shelf, a multiple erosion surface, here about 300 miles wide (from Fairbridge, 1950).

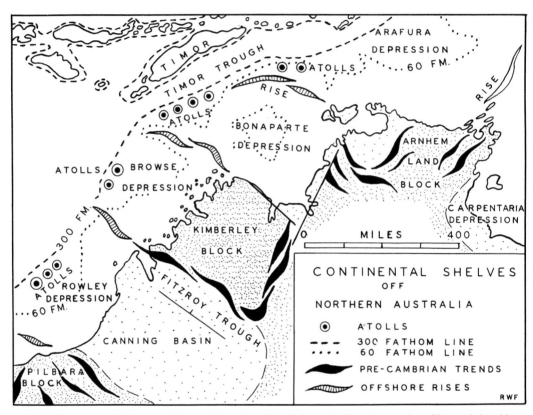

Fig. 3. The topographic features of the northern Australian shelves, showing the extension of Precambrian ridges, with intracratonic or paralic basins between.

interpretation. The shelf appears to be a complex erosion surface of considerable antiquity (Fig. 2). A close study of the shelf topography shows that it is subdivided into a series of ridges and depressions that bear a striking relationship to Precambrian structural trends of the mainland (Fig. 3). These depressions have been named Rowley, Browse, Bonaparte and Arafura Depressions in sequence. Each is marked by a row of scattered atolls near its western edge (Teichert and Fairbridge, 1948). The shelf break itself is indistinct, rounded off at about 200–300 fathoms (400–600 meters) which is quite remarkable outside of polar latitudes. Kuenen (1935) suggested that the tectonic downwarp of the Timor Trough and adjacent sea floors was respon-

sible. It is important to realize that these coral reefs are shelf atolls, i.e., they do not possess any trace of volcanic foundations like oceanic atolls, but must have grown up *in situ* during slow subsidence of the shelf margin. One may note, equally well, that there are no atolls situated on the intervening ridges or rises between the shelf depressions.

In the case of the Bonaparte depression, recent surveys have enabled Van Andel and Veevers (1965) to prepare detailed topographic and sedimentologic maps (see *Timor Sea*) which confirm that this is essentially a *closed basin* which can only be explained by rather recent tectonic subsidence. As observed by Fairbridge (1953) and confirmed by these authors, there is a complex network of Pleistocene

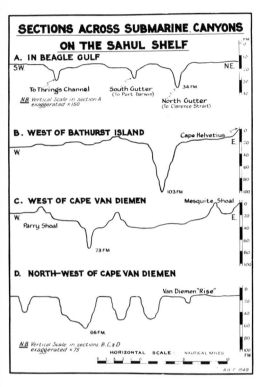

drainage channels crossing the Van Diemen Rise to reach the Timor Trough. These valleys find analogs in the Arafura Shelf and in the Sunda Shelf (long ago discovered by Molengraaff), but they are topographically distinctive in that they are in the form of subaerial canyons and "arroyos" up to 600 feet deep (Fig. 4). They have gently graded or undulating floors, so that they are not to be compared with the well-known continental slope submarine canyons; turbidity flows could have nothing to do with their origin and only a subaerial fluvial origin of glacial times can be entertained as an explanation. As an indication of the recent nature of the tectonics, there is a superposed structural pattern, which was noted already in the development of the Aru Island "sungei" channels (see *Arafura Sea*).

It is interesting that this revived tectonic activity in the structural framework of the Sahul Shelf (see gravity profiles, Fig. 5) and its neighboring shelves is affecting very largely Precambrian rocks some of which date back over one billion years during

Fig. 4. Sections across the submarine canyons (drowned subaerial drainage system) of the Sahul Shelf. Some of the channels seem to have been overdeepened by current scour (from Fairbridge, 1953).

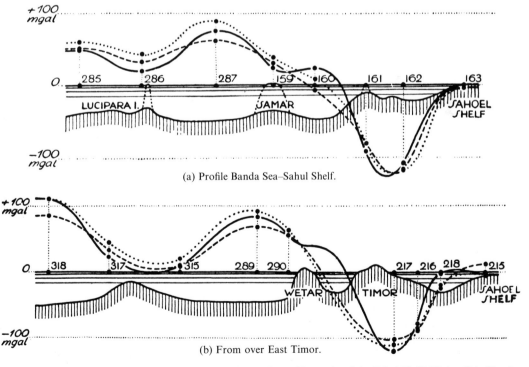

(a) Profile Banda Sea–Sahul Shelf.

(b) From over East Timor.

Fig. 5. Two gravity profiles illustrating the typical "continental" margin of the Sahul Shelf ("Sahoel" in Dutch orthography; from Vening Meinesz, 1934). (a) From the Banda Sea, (b) from East Timor. Dots=Hayford-Bowie, broken line=Heiskanen, solid line=regional anomalies.

which time there have been repeated small-scale upwarpings into ridges and, conversely, into basin developments. The latter are marked by marine transgressions of Cambrian, Ordovician, Devonian, Carboniferous, Permian, Triassic, Jurassic, Cretaceous and Tertiary ages, almost always in quite shallow neritic facies, though in the Fitzroy Trough, aided by some contemporary faulting, the mid-Paleozoic sequence was probably laid down in part in somewhat deeper seas.

One may note the remarkable structural similarities between the Sunda and Sahul Shelves today, yet also observe their distinctive histories, and distinctive climatic and sedimentational characters at the present time.

RHODES W. FAIRBRIDGE

References

Earl, G. W., 1845, "On the physical structure and arrangement of the islands of the Indian Archipelago," *J. Roy. Geogr. Soc. London*, **15**, 358–365 (author given in error as Earle, W.).

Fairbridge, R. W., 1953, "The Sahul Shelf, Northern Australia: its structure and geological relationships," *J. Roy. Soc. W. Australia*, **37**, 1–33.

Krümmel, O., 1897, "Handbuch der Ozeanographie," Stuttgart, 2 vols.

Kuenen, P. H., 1935, "Geological interpretation of the bathymetrical results," *The Snellius Expedition*, **5** (Geological Results), Pt. 1, 124pp.

Molengraaff, G. A. F., 1921, "Modern deep-sea research in the East Indian Archipelago," *Geograph. J.*, **52**, No. 2, 95–121.

Molengraaff, G. A. F., and Weber, M., 1919, "On the relation between the Pleistocene glacial period and the origin of the Sunda Sea," *Koninkl. Ned. Akad. Wetenschapp. Proc.*, **23**, 396–439.

Teichert, C., and Fairbridge, R. W., 1948, "Some coral reefs of the Sahul Shelf," *Geograph. Rev.*, **38**, 222–249.

Van Andel, Tj. H., and Veevers, J. J., 1965, "Submarine morphology of the Sahul Shelf, northwestern Australia," *Bull. Geol. Soc. Am.*, **76**, 695–700.

Vening Meinesz, F. A., *et al.*, 1934, "Gravity expeditions at sea 1923–1932," *Publ. Neth. Geod. Comm.*, **2**, 208pp.

SALINITY IN THE OCEAN

The dissolved components of seawater are transported from place to place by advective processes and move from water parcels of greater concentration to those of lesser concentration by diffusion processes. These agencies act equally on all dissolved constituents, and their effects can be traced by measuring the concentrations of any one of them. A distinction is made, however, between conservative and nonconservative properties when using the dissolved constituents as tracers in studies of the circulation. The former are the inactive solutes whose distribution is related to purely physical processes, while the latter are the biologically and chemically active constituents which, due to fractionation, may be distributed differently from the water itself.

The most useful conservative property of seawater in circulation studies is salinity. It is defined as the total amount of solid material in grams contained in 1 kg of seawater when all the bromine and iodine have been replaced by the equivalent amount of chlorine, all the carbonate has been converted to oxide, and all the organic matter has been completely oxidized.

One of the foundations of chemical and physical oceanography is the hypothesis that so far as the major dissolved constituents are concerned, seawater has constant relative composition. This hypothesis, based on the determinations of Dittmar on seawater samples collected on the famous *Challenger* Expedition (1873–1876) has not been substantially altered to the present time. Considering, then, that seawater is an aqueous solution of some dozen inorganic constituents (Table 1), the determination of any single major element can be used as a measure of other elements and of salinity. Since chloride ions make up more than 50% of the dissolved solids, this determination by titration with silver nitrate became the standard method of analysis through procedures established by The International Council for the Study of the Sea (Knudsen, 1901).

The chlorinity in grams per kilogram of seawater sample is identical with the number giving the mass in grams of atomic weight of silver just necessary to precipitate the halogens in 0.3285233 kg of seawater sample. The empirical relation between salinity S, and chlorinity, Cl, is:

$$S = 0.03 + 1.805 \, Cl$$

The accuracy of good titration determinations is $\pm 0.01\%_0$ in salinity. At the present time, most salinity determinations are made from measurement of electrical conductivity. The conductivity-salinity relationship is known, and the measurements are controlled by frequent comparison with a prepared standard water of known chlorinity. Conductivity instruments are considered to provide results accurate to $\pm 0.005\%_0$ in salinity.

Horizontal Distribution of Salinity

Extremes of salinity occur in coastal regions and certain partially enclosed seas. In the Gulf of Bothnia salinity may be as low as $5.0\%_0$, while in the Red Sea it may exceed $40.0\%_0$. The range in the open ocean is normally between 33.0 and $37.0\%_0$. The value of $35.0\%_0$ is often given for the average ocean salinity. The large-scale distribution of surface ocean salinity follows a zonal pattern, the general nature of which is shown in Fig. 1. The lowest values are in the polar regions with a secondary minimum in a narrow equatorial zone.

Maxima occur in the subtropical zones, roughly centered along 30°N and 20–30°S latitude. These maxima are highest in the Atlantic, both north and south, exceeding 37.0‰ salinity. Table 2 lists 10-degree zonal averages of surface salinity for all oceans and the world zonal averages. This table brings out the fact that the highest values occur in the northern hemisphere, its average being 35.45‰ as compared to the world average of 34.73‰.

These zonal differences are the result of physical processes related to the water budget of the oceans. Freezing of ice and evaporation tend to increase salinity, whereas precipitation, continental runoff and melting of sea ice reduce salinity. Finally,

TABLE 1. THE MAJOR CONSTITUENTS OF SEAWATER (FROM SVERDRUP *et al.*, 1942)

(Values in grams per kilogram, ‰)

Ion	Dittmar's Original Values		Recalculated, 1940 Atomic Weights		1940 Values	
	Cl = 19‰	%	Cl = 19‰	%	Cl = 19‰	%
Cl^-	18.971	55.29	18.971	55.26	18.980	55.04
Br^-	0.065	0.19	0.065	0.19	0.065	0.19
SO_4^-	2.639	7.69	2.635	7.68	2.649	7.68
CO_3^-	0.071	0.21	0.071	0.21	—	—
HCO_3^-	—	—	—	—	0.140	0.41
F^-	—	—	—	—	0.001	0.00
H_3BO_3	—	—	—	—	0.026	0.07
Mg^{++}	1.278	3.72	1.292	3.76	1.272	3.69
Ca^{++}	0.411	1.20	0.411	1.20	0.400	1.16
Sr^{++}					0.013	0.04
K^+	0.379	1.10	0.385	1.12	0.380	1.10
Na^+	10.497	30.59	10.498	30.58	10.556	30.61
Total	34.311		34.328		34.482	

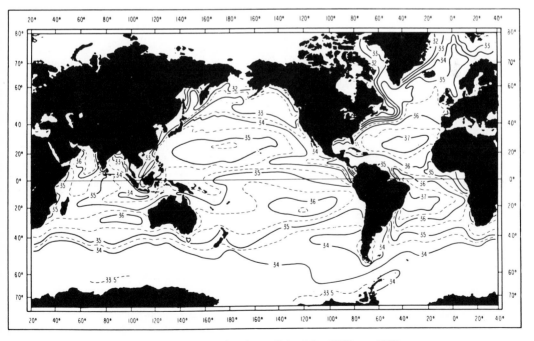

Fig. 1. Distribution of surface salinity (after Williams, 1962).

ocean currents and mixing processes decrease salinity contrasts both at the surface and throughout the ocean. Table 3 lists the processes which may increase or decrease ocean salinity. Freezing and melting do not affect salinity on a large scale, and in any event, the two effects offset one another in alternate seasons. Runoff is important only in coastal regions. One must, therefore, look to the processes of evaporation and precipitation, together with mixing, as chief agents responsible for the surface salinity distribution.

Wüst (1936) has shown that if the surface waters of salinity, S, are mixed with water of constant salinity, denoted by S_0, the change due to mixing will be proportional to $S_0 - S$. The change of salinity due to processes of evaporation and precipitation must be proportional to $E - P$. Since the surface salinity distribution remains relatively constant, the change of salinity with time must be considered zero, i.e.,

$$\frac{\partial s}{\partial t} = 0 = a(S_0 - S) + b(E - P)$$
$$S = S_0 + k(E - P)$$

This formula has been empirically tested, leading to an average value for S_0 of 34.7‰. This corresponds closely to the average value of the intermediate salinity minimum at a 400–600 meter depth and shows the importance of vertical mixing in surface salinity distribution. The average surface salinity is then expressed by:

$$S = 34.7 + 0.0137 \, (E - P)$$

The standard value of the salinity differs for the different oceans, but the general form of the equation applies if the constants S_0 and k are determined empirically for each area. The neglect of surface currents in these considerations indicates that they have only a minor role so far as the zonal salinity distribution is concerned. The processes of evaporation and precipitation are shown to be of prime importance in the surface salinity pattern, indicating extensive control by the character of the atmospheric circulation (Sverdrup et al., 1942). Figure 2 shows the distribution of surface salinity for all oceans with evaporation minus precipitation both plotted against latitude.

It is apparent from the distribution of surface salinity shown in Fig. 1 that the salinity of the Atlantic, particularly the North Atlantic, is higher than that of the Pacific Ocean. Among the reasons for this, according to Dietrich (1963), may be listed the following:

(1) The North Atlantic trade-wind belt extends into the Pacific Ocean across the Isthmus of Panama and contributes high precipitation (over 700 cm/yr) in the Gulf of Panama region.

(2) The west winds from the Pacific Ocean release their water vapor in the form of orographic precipitation while passing over the Cordilleras, returning this moisture to the Pacific. No comparable mountain barriers exist in Europe and Africa, and consequently the influences of water

TABLE 2. AVERAGE VALUES OF SURFACE SALINITY IN 10-DEGREE ZONES OF THE OCEANS (IN ‰) (AFTER WÜST, UNPUBLISHED MATERIAL)

Latitude (degrees)		Atlantic Ocean	Indian Ocean	Pacific Ocean	World Ocean
N	90–80	30.5*	—	—	30.5*
	80–70	31.7	—	—	31.7
	70–60	33.03	—	31.0*	32.90
	60–50	33.73	—	32.50	33.03
	50–40	34.85	—	33.25	33.91
	40–30	36.69	—	34.24	35.31
	30–20	36.75	(38.24)	34.92	35.71
	20–10	36.06	35.24	34.40	34.95
	10–0	35.09*	35.10	34.29*	34.58*
S	0–10	35.85	34.92	35.16	31.16
	10–20	36.66	34.77*	35.55	35.52
	20–30	36.16	35.46	35.66	35.71
	30–40	35.25	35.62	34.95	35.25
	40–50	34.24	34.37	34.37	34.34
	50–60	33.86	33.0	34.07	33.92
	60–70	33.9	34.0	33.9	33.95
	70–80	33.9*	33.9*	33.9*	33.95
70°N–0		35.45	35.38	34.17*	34.71
0–60°S		35.31	34.84*	35.03	35.03
90°N–80°S		34.87	34.87	34.58*	34.73

* = minimum.
Maximum is underlined.

TABLE 3. PROCESSES INVOLVED IN SALINITY INCREASE AND DECREASE (AFTER WÜST, 1961)

Processes of Salinity Increase	Processes of Salinity Decrease
E = evaporation	P = precipitation
F = freezing of sea water	M = melting of sea ice
C+ = advection of salty water by currents	C— = advection of less saline water by currents
V+ = vertical mixing with saltier deep water (by turbulence and dynamic convection)	V— = vertical mixing with less saline deep water (by turbulent convection)
So = solution of solid salt layers at the bottom (Suez Canal, Gulf of Aden)	R = runoff from the continents (by rivers, glaciers, and ground water)

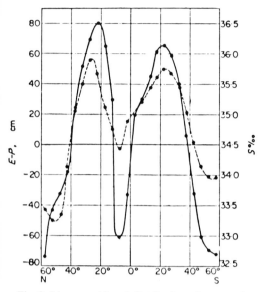

Fig. 2. Mean meridional distribution of evaporation — precipitation (E — P) and surface salinity for the entire ocean (after Defant, 1961).

vapor of Atlantic Ocean origin are much more widespread than those of Pacific origin. Therefore, a different equilibrium between the effects of oceanic circulation, mixing, and the ocean-atmosphere water exchange $(E - P)$ must be maintained for each ocean, resulting in the observed salinity distribution.

(3) The North Pacific lacks the enclosed seas, such as the Mediterranean and the Caribbean, which contribute highly saline waters at intermediate depths to the Atlantic.

The Vertical Salinity Distribution

In the three major oceans an intermediate salinity minimum exists at approximately 700–800 meters. The source region for this Subantarctic Intermediate Water can be found at the surface in the region south of 45°S latitude. Here water masses of low salinity and low temperature sink along the Atlantic Polar Front (Antarctic Convergence). The salinity minimum due to this subantarctic water extends over the entire breadth of the Atlantic Ocean between 45°S and 20°N and over the Pacific and Indian Oceans between 45°S and the equator. This tongue of low-salinity water is shown in the block diagram in Fig. 3. The Pacific Ocean has a comparable intermediate salinity minimum in the northern region due to the influence of Subarctic Intermediate Water, which is formed in the Bering Sea and the Sea of Okhotsk. The subsurface salinity distribution for the Pacific is shown in Fig. 4.

Below the intermediate salinity minimum in most ocean regions, the salinity increases with depth, forming a salinity maximum between 1500 and 4000 meters. This water mass is identified as "deep water." In the Atlantic, the upper portion of this water mass is strongly influenced by the subsurface Mediterranean outflow, which contributes water of relatively high salinity into the Atlantic system. Figure 5 shows this outflow together with the vertical salinity distribution in the Mediterranean Sea for the winter season.

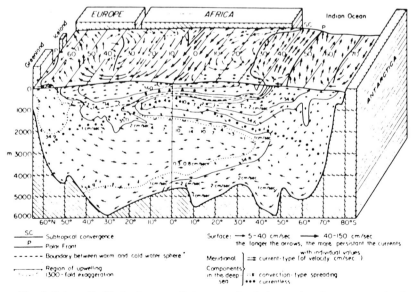

Fig. 3. Schematic block diagram of deep-sea circulation and surface currents in the Atlantic Ocean (after Dietrich, 1963).

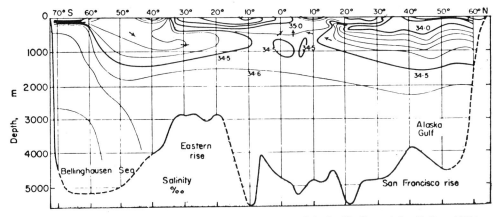

Fig. 4. Longitudinal salinity section through the central part of the Pacific Ocean (after Defant, 1961).

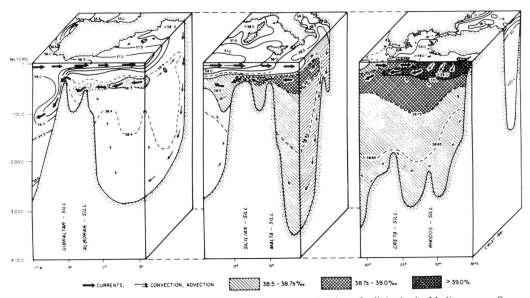

Fig. 5. Schematic block diagram of vertical circulation and distribution of salinity in the Mediterranean Sea during winter (after Wüst, 1961).

Below the depth of 4000 meters in the Atlantic, Pacific, and Indian Oceans, a water mass of Antarctic origin, having slightly lower salinity than the deep water, can be traced. This water type, called Antarctic Bottom Water, is best seen in the Atlantic cross section (Fig. 3) and is, in fact, characterized more by low temperature than low salinity.

Time Variations of Salinity

Variations of salinity in the open ocean are small. A few measurements of diurnal variations at the surface have been made (Defant, 1961), indicating that regular daily changes amount to approximately 0.10‰ salinity. The annual change

in the open ocean depends mainly on the variations of $E - P$; a maximum range for the region 18–42°N in the North Atlantic Ocean amounts to 0.11‰. In this region, the monthly variations are irregular, but in general, the maximum surface salinity for the North Atlantic is in March. In depths greater than 1000 meters, the annual range in salinity is so small (0.02–0.04‰) that variations lie very close to the observational limits of error.

In subpolar regions, annual variations in surface salinity can be relatively large, the maximum being reached just before the summer melting processes begin. In monsoonal areas the seasonal change in wind direction and consequent reversal of ocean currents, together with the abrupt change in the pattern of precipitation, may contribute towards large variations in the annual surface salinity. In the Bay of Bengal annual variations may amount to 1.0–3.0‰.

Changes in the salinity distribution related to long-term changes in climate are poorly known in that neither the climatic, nor the oceanographic, records are extensive enough to permit a correlation.

ROBERT GERARD

References

*Defant, Albert, 1961, "Physical Oceanography," Vol. 1, New York, Pergamon Press, 729pp.
*Dietrich, Günter, 1963, "General Oceanography," New York, John Wiley & Sons, 588pp.
Knudsen, M., 1901, "Hydrographical Tables," Copenhagen.
Sillén, L. G., 1963, "How has sea water got its present composition ", *Svensk Kemisk Tidskrift*, **75** (4), 161–177.
*Sverdrup, H. U., Johnson, M. W., and Fleming, R. H., 1942, "The Oceans," Englewood Cliffs, N.J., Prentice-Hall, Inc., 1087pp.
Williams, Jerome, 1962, "Oceanography: An Introduction to the Marine Sciences", Boston, Little, Brown.
Wüst, Georg, 1936, "Oberflächensalzgehalt, Verdunstung und Niederschlag auf dem Weltmeere," Festschrift Norbert Krebs (Länderkundliche Forschung), pp. 347–59, Stuttgart.
Wüst, Georg, 1961, On the vertical circulation of the Mediterranean Sea: *Journ. Geophys. Res.*, **66**, (10).
Wüst, Georg, 1961, Lectures on problems of physical oceanography; unpublished manuscripts.

SALT NUCLEI—*See* Vol. II

SAND FLOWS AND SAND FALLS

In 1959, a group of diving biologists unexpectedly observed spectacular examples of flowing sand spilling over the upper rock lip of San Lucas submarine canyon (Fig. 1) during a Scripps Institution of Oceanography expedition to the submarine canyons of Baja California, Mexico. The first observers, Conrad Limbaugh, Wheeler North, and James Stewart, were so impressed that they named these large-scale flows "rivers-of-sand" and "sand falls." The "sand falls" occurred where flowing sand spilled over abrupt drop-offs in the axis of side tributaries cut in the upper lip of the main channel of the canyon. The pictures obtained during this expedition have been widely published (North, 1960; Shepard, 1961, 1963 and 1964).

The possibility that such flows could erode the granitic bedrock of the region prompted the writer to investigate the canyons of Baja California in the spring of 1961. Subsequently, seven expeditions were made to the tip of Baja California to study the physical properties of sand flows and the

erosional features uniquely associated with flowing sand. Although small-scale sand flows have been observed in other submarine canyons (Dill, 1964a), most of the work on the physical properties and conditions leading up to a sand flow has been concentrated in the canyons of Baja California, Mexico (Dill, 1964b; Shepard and Dill, 1966).

San Lucas canyon cuts through a highly faulted and jointed granite that has many weak zones filled with broken granitic fault-breccia (Fig. 2). The trend of the main channel of the canyon runs at right angles to the regional trend of faulting. Sand flows have eroded away the weak and broken granitic blocks in the fault zones forming a series of structurally controlled tributaries along the south side of the east-west trending head of the canyon.

The first observations in 1959 occurred during a period when exceptionally large storm swells were sweeping across a tombolo which connects the mainland of Cape San Lucas to a group of large offshore granitic stacks. As water surged across the tombolo, it cut away the large body of medium grain-sized arkosic sand deposited during periods of normal wave activity. It also removed a large part of the base camp of the diving scientists. The same swell that cut the tombolo when refracted around the tip of the cape (see Fig. 1) set up strong bottom currents that moved the rapidly accumulating tombolo sands into the heads of several large side tributaries to the main channel of the canyon.

During two of the seven expeditions made to San Lucas canyon by the writer, swell from offshore tropical storms has generated similar bottom currents. These in turn cut back the beach and set into motion the sands that had accumulated in shallow water sand bars and around the heads of the canyon tributaries during periods of quiescence. This material was then carried along the bottom until it was intercepted by the heads of nearshore tributaries. The rapid addition of sand from the beaches and sand bars overloaded the marginally stable sands which had built up in the bottom of the tributaries at an angle of repose of approximately 30°.

The sand carried into the tributary heads slowly flows (Fig. 3) down the steep slopes as a series of semicontinuous progressive slumps. The flow velocity depends on the volume and rate that material is added at the head of the canyon. The velocity of flow increases at constrictions in the channel width and decreases in areas where widening occurs. Velocity is increased around objects interfering with normal flow. Flow velocities are not constant, varying from an almost imperceptible creep of individual grains, to flows with velocities between 0.10 to 0.16 knot (5–8 cm/sec) when the sediment slope increases to 37° during periods of rapid addition of sand. The sands normally found in the

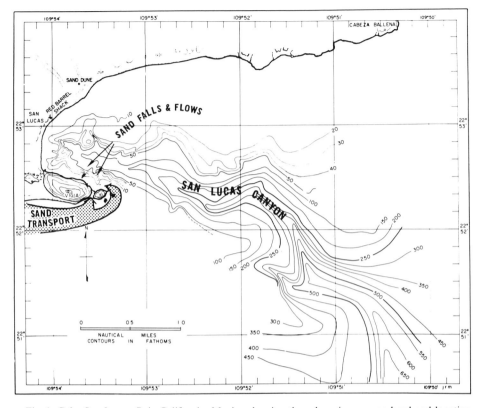

Fig. 1. Cabo San Lucas, Baja California, Mexico showing the submarine canyon head and location of side tributaries where sand flows have been observed (from Shepard and Dill, 1966).

Fig. 2. Fault breccia in the axis of a side tributary of the main channel often subjected to sand falls. The left side of the channel above the diver has been eroded by falling sand. Depth 150 feet.

Fig. 3. Sand flow (arrow) in part of the sand fill of a tributary. Highest velocities are near rock wall. Dark sands on the right are not in motion. Note how gorgonian coral is oriented perpendicular to the direction of flow. Depth 120 feet.

Fig. 4. Sand fall during May 1963 when swell from a tropical storm was dumping large amounts of sand into the head of the canyon. This fall at a depth of 135 feet was active for three days. At the base of the drop-off (165 feet) a bottom slope of 31° was reestablished and spilling sands slowed to a velocity of 0·2 knot.

tributary, at rest, can be artificially set in motion by digging away part of the fill. Sand movement will continue until a slope of approximately 30° is again reestablished by headward slumping and flow.

In areas of confinement, the flowing sand with the highest velocity has been observed to meander from one side of the channel to the other. Streaks of dark sand are developed where reduced sediment is brought to the surface by turbulence within the flowing sand. Rocks up to 6 inches (15 cm) in diameter have been observed being transported by flowing sand. The writer has followed sand flows by scuba to depths of 250 feet (76 meters) from where the flow could be seen to continue on to depths of at least 350 feet (110 meters).

Spectacular "sand falls" (Fig. 4) develop in areas where sharp drop-offs in the canyon's axial profile occur. Here the pulsation of the sand movement is readily apparent and can be correlated with the variability of swell-induced bottom currents.

During May 1963, sand flows were obsrved to have undermined and eroded the broken granite over which they flowed, and fresh granite surfaces were exposed where rock was broken away by the force of the falling sand (see Fig. 2). Pieces of eroded granite up to 8 inches (20 cm) long and 6 inches (15 cm) wide were found deeper in the canyon, and these could be fitted back into their place of origin. The removal and transportation of such rock fragments is truly an example of contemporary submarine erosion.

ROBERT F. DILL

References

Dill, R. F., 1964a, "Contemporary submarine erosion in Scripps Submarine Canyon," published Ph.D. dissertation of University of California at San Diego (Scripps Institution of Oceanography); University Microfilms Inc., Ann Arbor, Michigan, p. 269.

Dill, R. F., 1964b, "Features in the Heads of Submarine Canyons," Narrative of underwater film in (van Straaten, L. M. S. U., editor) "Developments in Sedimentation," Vol. 1, Deltaic and Shallow Marine Deposits, pp. 101–104, Amsterdam, Elsevier Publishing Co.

North, W. H., 1960, "Fabulous Cape San Lucas," *Skin Diver Magazine*, May issue, 24–26, 52.

Shepard, F. P., 1961, "Submarine canyons of the Gulf of California," *Report 21st International Geologic Congress Copenhagen Denmark*, Part 26, pp. 11–23.

Shepard, F. P., 1963, "Submarine Geology," second ed., New York, Harper and Row.

Shepard, F. P., 1964, "Sea-floor valleys of the Gulf of California," in "Marine Geology of the Gulf of California—A Symposium," *Am. Assoc. Petrol. Geologists Mem.*, **3**, 157–192.

Shepard, F. P., and Dill, R. F. (1966), "Submarine Canyons and Other Valleys of the Ocean Floor," New York, Rand McNally.

SARGASSO SEA

The Sargasso Sea is the calm center of the asymmetrical anticyclonic gyre in the North Atlantic. The asymmetry is typical of subtropical circulation; a westward shift of its center results in an intense western boundary current, the Gulf Stream, and a broad current on the eastern flank, the Canary Current. The northward arm of this gyre

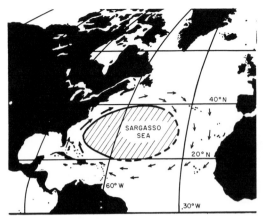

Fig. 1. Mean position of the Sargasso Sea.

is the North Atlantic Drift, and to the south, the North Equatorial Current (see Fig. 1). The western and the northern boundaries of the Sargasso Sea are well defined (solid line) owing to the high velocity gradients, but the eastern boundary, and to a certain extent the southern boundary, is weakly defined (dashed line).

The Sargasso Sea is hydrodynamically a store of potential energy. Stommel (1958) has calculated that the Sargasso Sea stores 3×10^9 ergs/cm^2 and that this is sufficient to maintain the North Atlantic clockwise gyre for 1700 days in the absence of the driving force of the wind. This potential energy is built up by action of the wind which piles the light surface water into a "hill" which floats hydrostatically on the colder water beneath. It floats slightly less than a meter higher than the sea level along the east coast of the United States (Von Arx, 1962).

The mass of warm saline water making up the Sargasso Sea is fairly thick. This can be seen from the 1936 chart of Iselin giving the depth of the 10°C isotherm surface. While it is found at only a few hundred meters to the west of the Gulf Stream, it dips down to 800–1000 meters in the Sargasso Sea. A large volume of the seawater in this floating lens has a temperature of 18°C (Worthington, 1959). The salinity is for the most part above 36.5‰, with values greater than 37‰ in the eastern margins of the Sea.

The arid atmospheric conditions over the latitudinal belts (Horse Latitudes) containing the Sargasso Sea, with the predominance of evaporation over precipitation, produce a water type characterized by high salinity which spreads away from the Sargasso Sea and covers large areas of the tropic Atlantic. This water mass is called the Subtropical Underwater (Defant, 1936). It is found between 50 and 200 meters.

The biological productivity of the Sargasso Sea is very low, due in part to the permanent thermo-cline between 400 to 500 meters which blocks the upward diffusion of nutrients. The seasonal thermocline at 100 meters causes extremely low productivity during the summer, but when this breaks up in the winter and early spring, productivity increases to values many times that of the summer. During particularly cold winters, the seasonal thermocline vanishes completely and higher than average productivity results. This occurred during the winter of 1957–1958 (Ryther, 1963).

The most characteristic plant life in the Sargasso Sea is a floating brown seaweed from which the sea gains its name, Sargassum. A. E. Parr (1939) estimates that there are 4–11 million tons of this weed floating in the sea and its environs. Occasionally it is seen that the weed is aligned, which may represent lines of convergences due to vertical thermal convection or the action of the wind. The Sargassum weed has small floats which keep it at the sea surface. These floats give the weed its name, from the Portuguese word for grape, *sargaço*.

The Sargasso Sea is a dynamical and biological oceanographic province. Similar conditions exist in other oceans though they are not as pronounced.

ARNOLD GORDON

References

Ryther, J. H., 1963, "Geographic Variations in Productivity," in "The Sea," Vol. II, pp. 347–380, New York, Interscience Publishers.

Stommel, H., 1958, "The Gulf Stream," University of California Press.

Von Arx, W., 1962, "An Introduction to Physical Oceanography," Addison-Wesley Publishing Company.

Voorhis, A. D., and Hersey, J. B., 1964, "Oceanic thermal fronts in the Sargasso Sea," *J. Geophys. Res.*, **69**, 3809–3814.

SAVU SEA

The Savu Sea ("Sawoe" in Dutch orthography) is situated between the inner and outer Banda island arcs of Indonesia—between Sumbawa–Flores–Solor–Lomblen–Pantar–Alor on the north (the volcanic row), and Sumba–Savu–Roti–Timor on the south (the non-volcanic row). According to the boundaries of the International Hydrographic Bureau (*Sp. Publ.* 23, 1953), the western limit is a line from Tanjong Karosso (the western tip of Sumba) to Toro Doro (8° 53′S, 118° 30′E) on the south coast of Sumbawa. The southern boundary runs from the east end of Sumba through Pulu Dana to Roti, and thus completely to the south of Savu itself. The eastern limit is the meridian 125° from the east end of Alor to the north coast of Timor. The surface area is about 105,000 km^2, the mean depth 1701 m, and the volume 178×10^{12} m^3.

According to the *Snellius* Expedition work (Van Riel, 1934), the central and eastern parts of the sea are the deepest, the part outlined by the 3000 m contour being designated the Savu Basin, enclosing about 30,000 km². No steep escarpments or trenches have been discovered. The maximum depth is 3470 m, south of Pantar Strait. A second small depression occurs in Ombai Strait with a depth of 3390 m. Most of the floor is an abyssal plain, apparently tilted slightly down on the north side to a depth of about 3380 m.

To the south, the Savu and Dao Straits connect

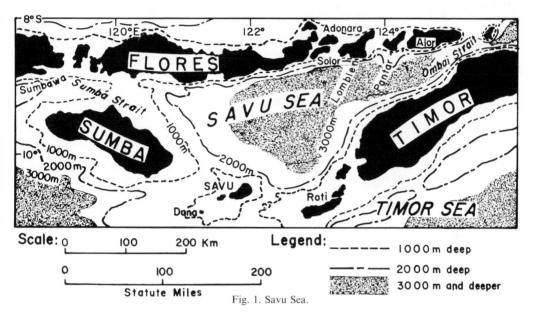

Scale: 0 ___ 100 ___ 200 Km

0 ___ 100 ___ 200

Statute Miles

Legend: — — — — 1000m deep

————— 2000m deep

3000m and deeper

Fig. 1. Savu Sea.

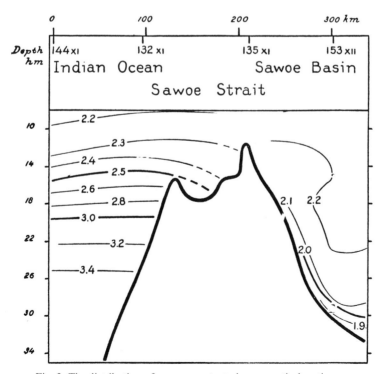

Fig. 2. The distribution of oxygen content along a vertical section across Savu Strait (Van Riel, 1943).

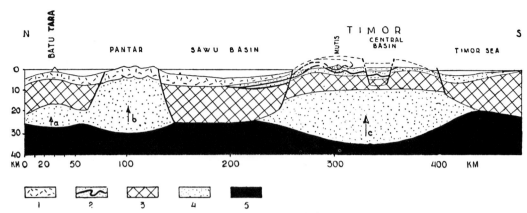

Fig. 3. Schematic section across the present Savu (Sawu) Basin and Timor Orogen (Van Bemmelen, 1949, p. 541).
Legend:
(1) Sedimentary epidermis of the inner arc, preponderantly of a volcanic facies.
(2) Sedimentary epidermis of the outer arc, preponderantly of a marine facies and with overthrust structures.
(3) Sialic crust, consisting of pre-Permian crystalline schists and consolidated plutonic intrusions of Mesozoic and Tertiary age.
(4) Active asthenoliths with their migmatite fronts, which are corroding the overlying crust.
   (a) The asthenolith under the submarine Batu Tara ridge is of a relatively small size.
   (b) The asthenolith under the inner arc is rather large. This asthenolith has been pressed up several times; it has now attained a more or less floating equilibrium. Therefore, it lacks isostatic gravity anomalies.
   (c) The asthenolith beneath Timor is the largest one. It is rising for the first time since the Permian, and has not yet attained equilibrium. It causes strong negative isostatic anomalies.
(5) Salsima layer. Intermediate parental magma.

with the Indian Ocean, with sill depths of about 1160 and 1140 m, respectively. The deepest sill connecting with the Banda Sea to the north is 1260 m between Alor and Kambing. Other northern straits such as Pantar Strait are only about 600 m. Flores and Boleng Straits are less than 200 m. The western sill, in Sumba Strait is about 900 m, and the eastern, in Ombai Strait into the Wetar Basin and thence to the Weber Deep of the eastern Banda Sea, appears to be about 1815 m. Probably the Ombai Strait is most important for renewal of bottom water.

Some early measurements of temperature and salinity were made in the Savu Sea by the German oceanographic vessel *Gazelle* in 1875 and later ones by the *Snellius* in 1929. Minimal reliable bottom (potential) temperature recorded was 3.1°C, salinity 34.49‰, oxygen 1.67 cc/liter (all at over 3200 m). The pH of deep water is 7.8 rising to 7.9 or 8.0 near the bottom, i.e., matching the sharp drop in oxygen (Van Riel, 1943).

According to Van Bemmelen (1949), the Savu Basin is one of recent subsidence. It was an uplifted area when the orthogeosynclinal depression lay over Timor; major gravitational sliding, with "pebbly mudstones," sedimentary klippes ("fatus") slipped down from this uplift into the Timor geosyncline. In late Tertiary, the relief was reversed and the Savu basin subsided. Kuenen (1935) classified the Savu Basin with his "second type, 3d

group," i.e., orthogeosynclinal (in particular, medial troughs of eugeosynclines).

Bottom sediments, reported by Kuenen and Neeb (1943), from samples collected by the *Snellius* Expedition, are largely terrigenous muds in the center and southeast (to the Timor coast and around Alor). In the abyssal plain these are mainly derived from acid igneous rocks and from metamorphic rocks supplying epidote. Calc-alkali igneous derivatives occur off Sumba, Savu and Roti. Along the south coasts of Flores, Solor and Lomblen, there are volcanic and terrigenous muds, especially dominated by volcanic material within 50–100 km of the active volcanoes of Flores and Lomblen. Globigerina ooze occurs around Sumba and Savu and Roti, coral muds off Timor and Savu. The straits have mostly hard grounds.

RHODES W. FAIRBRIDGE

References

Kuenen, P. H., 1935, "The Snellius Expedition. Geological Interpretation of the Bathymetrical Results," Vol. 5, Pt. 1, pp. 1–124, Utrecht, Kemink.

Kuenen, P. H., and Neeb, G. A., 1943, "The Snellius Expedition. Bottom Samples," Vol. 5, Pt. 3, Leiden, E. J. Brill.

Van Bemmelen, R. W., 1949, "The Geology of Indonesia. General Geology," Vol. IA, The Hague, Martinus Nijhoff.

Van Riel, P. M., 1934, "The Snellius Expedition. The

Bottom Configuration," Vol. 2, Pt. 2, Ch. 2, Utrecht, Kemink en Zoon.

Van Riel, P. M., 1943, "The Snellius Expedition. Introductory Remarks and Oxygen Content," Vol. 2, Pt. 5, Ch. 1, Leiden, E. J. Brill.

Van Riel, P. M., Hamaker, H. C., and Van Eyck, L., 1950, "The Snellius Expedition. Tables. Serial and Bottom Observations. Temperature, Salinity and Density," Vol. 2, Pt. 6, pp. 1–44, Leiden, E. J. Brill.

Cross-references: *Banda Sea; Flores Sea; Timor Sea.*

SCATTERING—*See* Vol. II

SCATTERING LAYER—*See* DEEP SCATTERING LAYER

SCOTIA SEA AND DRAKE PASSAGE

Geography

The Drake Passage is the narrowest part of the Southern Ocean that lies between the southernmost tip of South America and the Antarctic Peninsula. It is about 1000 km (430 nautical miles) wide, and its mean depth is 3400 m; its deepest spot is about 4750 m. It constitutes a bottleneck to the broad westerly flow in the continuous Southern Ocean. The sea to the east, bounded by South Georgia, the Falkland, South Sandwich, South Orkney, and South Shetland Islands, is the *Scotia Sea.*

Topography

The Scotia Sea–Drake Passage area is dominated by the Scotia Ridge, which connects Tierra del Fuego with the Antarctic Peninsula in a 4344-km

eastward lying loop, which encloses the Scotia Sea (Fig. 1). Along most of this arc, the ridge rises to within 1830 m of the surface. The Scotia Sea is equally divided into two basinal areas, the East and West Scotia Basins, by a slight rise which roughly connects South Georgia with the South Orkney Islands. On the concave eastward side of the Scotia Ridge occurs the South Sandwich Trench—the greatest depth in the Southern Ocean—8270 m.

The Scotia Ridge has three "saddles" on it where water depths of 2745 m or more occur. The first of these, east of the Burdwood Bank and west of South Georgia, is the shallowest and longest. The second saddle in the ridge is found between South Georgia and South Sandwich Islands. The axis of that portion of the ridge, of which South Georgia is emergent, points almost directly into the East Scotia Basin behind the South Sandwich Islands. Due east of South Georgia, is a wide submarine valley deepening eastward into the deepest part of the trench. The third saddle in the Scotia Ridge exists between the South Orkney Islands and the westward extension of South Sandwich Island arc. It is about 160 km wide and separates the Weddell Sea to the south from the Scotia Sea to the north.

The most recent bathymetric chart is No. 2592, issued by the U.S. Hydrographic Office in 1958. A useful relief chart can be found in the Oceanographic Atlas of the Polar Seas, Part I, Antarctica (H.O. Pub. No. 705, 1957).

Exploration

On December 13, 1577, Sir Francis Drake set out from Plymouth (England) southward, and after sighting the South American coast to the north of the River Plate, he set sail for the Strait of

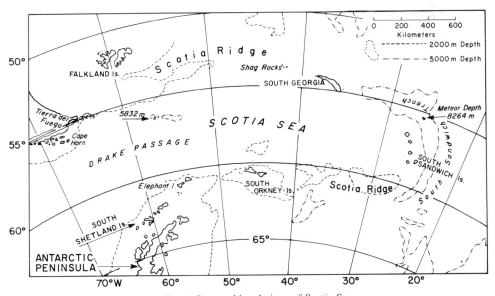

Fig. 1. Geographic relations of Scotia Sea.

Magellan with three fighting ships. After he passed through the strait on September 6, 1578, he reached the Pacific Ocean on September 16, 1578, and turned northwestward. However, a violent gale, which continued for over a month, drove Drake's ship southward to latitude 57°S. Being separated from the other two ships, Drake was forced to wait nearly another month among the islands to the south of Tierra del Fuego during which he discovered what was probably Cape Horn.

In recent times, the investigations made by the German Atlantic Expedition, the *Meteor* Expedition (Wüst, 1932), the Norwegian Antarctic Expedition (Mosby, 1934), the *Discovery* Expedition (Deacon, 1937), and many others have contributed largely to our knowledge of this part of the

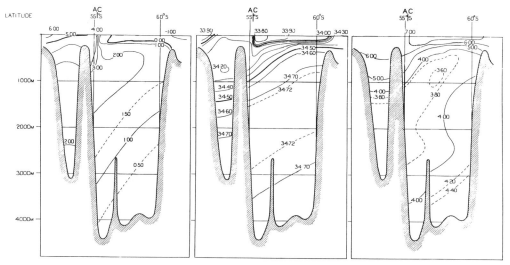

Fig. 2. The distribution of temperature, salinity and oxygen content along section I, from Elephant Island to the Falkland Islands, November 1932 (Deacon, 1937).

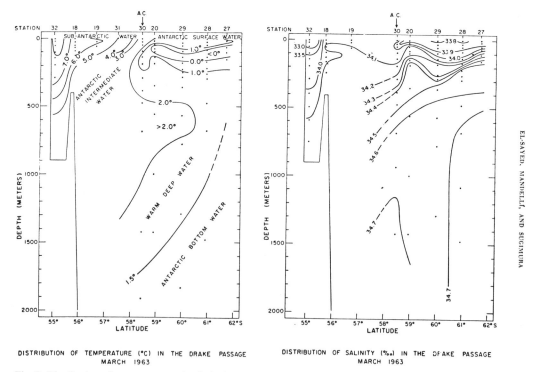

DISTRIBUTION OF TEMPERATURE (°C) IN THE DRAKE PASSAGE MARCH 1963

DISTRIBUTION OF SALINITY (‰) IN THE DRAKE PASSAGE MARCH 1963

Fig. 3. Distribution of temperature and salinity in a transect across the Drake Passage (from El-Sayed, *et al.*, 1964).

Southern Ocean. Their reports include excellent references on the meteorological, physical, chemical and biological observations of that region.

Oceanography and Meteorology

Very intense meteorological depressions move across the Drake Passage, and it is common to find differences in atmospheric pressure of 12 millibars between both ends of the Passage. These fast-moving atmospheric disturbances can induce transient currents due to the inverted barometer effect.

In latitudes between 40 and 60°S, the prevailing wind is westerly and gives rise to a drift current and a consequent surface water transport to the north. According to meteorological observations, the strongest surface wind occurs between 50 and 60°S. The water transport to the north is thus greatest between 60 and 50°S, and north of 50°S, it is comparatively smaller. This gives rise to the formation of a convergence line.

The Antarctic Convergence (or the Southern Hemisphere Polar Front) is a boundary surface which separates the heavier, colder Antarctic water to the south from the lighter but more saline water to the north. It passes through the middle of the Drake Passage at about 60°S latitude and varies with the seasons (Figs. 2 and 3). The boundary of the Antarctic Convergence is maintained because the cold Antarctic water is denser than the sub-Antarctic water and sinks sharply below the latter, without much mixing, to continue its northward flow as the Antarctic Intermediate Current.

According to the data of the *Discovery Reports*, the temperature range of the Antarctic surface water at the Convergence is approximately 0.5–3.0°C in the winter, and 3.0–5.5°C in summer.

The ice pack line is considered by some to be a truer boundary between the sub-Antarctic and the Antarctic. This definition is still controversial. The northward limit of the floating ice pack may at times coincide with the convergence but of course varies from season to season, and in the late summer may be absent all the way to the coast of the continent itself. At the close of the winter season, the frozen sea surface may extend from the continent edge northward into about 25% of the Drake Passage. In the Antarctic summer, the ice pack does not reach into the Drake Passage. The northern limit of the drift ice reaches across the Drake Passage to the tip of South America.

The principal current of Antarctic surface water in the Drake Passage flows out of the Bellingshausen Sea. This current is turned toward the north by the west coast of the Antarctic Peninsula and then flows toward the northeast through the Drake Passage. The distribution of temperature in vertical sections across the Drake Passage shows that the current is strongest at the edge of the continental shelf, for it is there, off the South Shetland Islands, that the lowest temperatures are found.

In the western half of the Scotia Sea, the direction of the current is largely influenced by the shape of the bottom. Through a topographic gap between east of the Burdwood Bank and west of South Georgia, the majority of the South Pacific–West Atlantic Ocean water pours following the general clockwise circulation of the Southern Ocean. At the gap it turns northward, and then westward into the deep trough north of the ridge as well as eastward across the Atlantic Ocean. The changes in direction of the surface currents are reflected in the shape of the Antarctic Convergence in the neighborhood of 50°W.

A generalized picture of the physical circulation in the Drake Passage and Scotia Sea can be presented as follows. Surface water around the Antarctic Continent spreads northward to about 50° where, at the Antarctic Convergence the water mass sinks below the sub-Antarctic surface water. At first, the water sinks immediately down to 400 m and then spreads almost horizontally to the latitude of the subtropical convergence region where it sinks again rapidly to 800 m or more. Here, at the subtropical convergence, the mixed water sinks and moves northward as the Antarctic Intermediate Water. There is also sinking of cold, saline and poorly oxygenated water in locations near the Antarctic Continent, forming Antarctic Bottom Water which also moves to the north. The loss of water from these two sources is compensated by the southerly flow of water from intermediate depths (2000–3000 m) which rises to the surface near the edge of the continent and thence spreads northward as the above-mentioned surface drift. Water from such great depths is extremely rich in nutrients. As we shall see later, the high fertility of the Southern Ocean lies in an explanation of its physical circulation.

Sverdrup calculated the total west-to-east water transport between Antarctica and South America (the Drake Passage). His values for total water transport in a layer from the surface to a depth of 3000 m for this area was 90 million m³/sec. This value for the Drake Passage is more than 400 times the volume of water carried by the Amazon, the World's largest river. However, according to the observations made by Kort during the Soviet Marine Antarctic Expedition, the water transport across the Drake Passage is estimated to be 150 million m³/sec.

Direct measurement of the currents in the Drake Passage made recently by the Argentine Hydrographic Service showed that surface current varied between 2 knots toward the north and 0.7 knot toward the east-northeast. Current measurements made at 56° 42′S and 66° 07′W at depths of 7, 500 and 1000 m gave the following velocities: 25, 20 and 17 cm/sec, respectively.

Bottom Deposits and Sediments

A comprehensive summary of the bottom sediments is presented in the Oceanographic Atlas of the Polar Seas, Part I, Antarctic (H.P. Pub. No. 705, 1957); also see Goodell and Osmond (1964).

On the basis of texture and genesis, five types of sediments are found in the Scotia Sea–Drake Passage area:

(1) Sand, clayey, gravelly: Most of the sand-sized grains are rock fragments. These fragments are dominated by extrusive igneous types and appear to be exclusively so along the South Sandwich Ridge. The colors of the sand are black to gray depending upon the color of the rock fragments and the amount of organic material.

(2) Silt, sandy: The sand sizes are predominantly rock fragments with foraminifera tests second in importance. The silt sizes are heterogeneous mixtures of glacial rock flour, splintered foraminiferal tests, radiolarian and diatom tests and frustules, glass and micro-manganese nodules (?). Along the Scotia Ridge and Drake Passage, the sediment colors range from yellowish gray to pale olive to pale grayish brown.

(3) Silt, clayey: A majority of the silt is probably rock flour. Occasionally diatom and radiolaria particles become numerous enough to be called diatomaceous. Glass and micro-manganese nodules often are found. The sediment colors range from yellowish gray to light olive gray over most of the Scotia Sea–Drake Passage and to light brown, more typical of "red clay," on the Pacific side of the Drake Passage.

(4) Ooze, foraminiferal (calcareous): The sediment is comprised of more than about 30% of foraminifera tests.

(5) Ooze, diatom (siliceous): The sediment comprises about 30% or more siliceous diatom and radiolarian tests and frustules and usually has a felted or matted appearance.

The coarsest sediments are found peripheral to South America, South Georgia Island, the South Sandwich Islands and the Antarctic Peninsula.

South and southeast of Tierra del Fuego the coarse sediment band widens. One reason for this disposition lies in the currents of the area that are strong enough at 4000 m to generate ripple marks 15–30 cm in length. These coarse sediments continue eastward around the Horn and compose the sea floor over the Burdwood Bank and around the Falkland Island. The amount of gravel appears to increase over the Bank, and a large portion of this material is glacial marine. In places, a large amount of mollusk and brachiopod shell is present.

A halo of coarse sediment surrounds South Georgia Island on the sea floor to a water depth of at least 2745 m except on the east where sand and gravel may be found to depths of at least 3600 m. Coarse sediments may be moving down the submarine valley east of South Georgia and into the northwestern part of the South Sandwich Trench. However, cores taken at the bottom of this part of the trench reveal only clayey silt.

The final area of coarse sediments occurs peripheral to the Antarctic Peninsula, extending north and east of the South Orkneys, and hooking south into the Weddell Sea; almost all of these sediments are glacial marines. They extend westward to about the 900-m line (the edge of the continental shelf), although occasional slumping must deliver material down the slope.

Cores taken in traverse across the zone of ooze reveal it to be a lens-shaped deposit about 40 cm thick in the center to 1–4 cm at the edges. It was found that the depositional rate for these sediments is 3–4 cm/1000 yr. This means that the upper lens is about 10,000 years old. Admixed with these sediments are terrestrially derived sands and gravel that increase in importance to the north. The surface of the sea floor throughout much of the zone of calcareous ooze is covered with manganese nodules.

Chemistry—Biology

Through the intensive work of the *Discovery* Expedition around Antarctica, the Scotia Sea–Drake Passage area came to be one of the best chemically and biologically known oceanic areas in the world (see Clowes, 1938; Hart, 1934, 1942).

The amount of nutrient salts (i.e., nitrate and silicate) in the Antarctic surface water rarely falls below the winter maximum of temperate regions. The surface water of the sub-Antarctic zone has less nutrients, but at a deeper level, between the northward movement in the Antarctic Intermediate Layer and the southward movement in the more saline deep water, phosphate and nitrate appear to be regenerated, possibly because of a large mortality of sinking phytoplankton as indicated by abundant deposits of diatom ooze below this region. The decomposition enriches the south-going deep water and, in the Antarctic zone, the highest phosphate and nitrate concentrations are found in the warm deep water. Silicates are most abundant in the bottom water, as though most of it were regenerated from the solution of the skeletons of diatoms near the bottom.

The distribution of the nutrient elements across the Drake Passage showed a substantial increase in the silicates as the convergence was crossed from north to south (from 5.3 μg at./liter to 15.2 μg at./liter. South of the convergence the silicates content continued to increase, reaching a high value of 47.8 μg at./liter near the South Shetland Islands. Surface phosphates and nitrates showed slightly higher values to the south of the convergence than to the north, with discernible increases at the convergence.

Mean phosphate (1.92 μg at./liter, nitrate (15.7 μg at./liter and silicate (18.02 μg at./liter values were reported in March 1963 from the Drake Passage (El-Sayed *et al.*, 1964) (see Fig. 4).

The concentration of plant pigments (mainly chlorophyll *a*) and the uptake of carbon 14 (as a measure of primary organic production) in the

Drake Passage decreased between Tierra del Fuego and the Antarctic Convergence; south of the convergence, they gradually increased reaching their highest values north of the South Shetland Islands. Average surface values of chlorophyll *a*

PRIMARY ORGANIC PRODUCTION

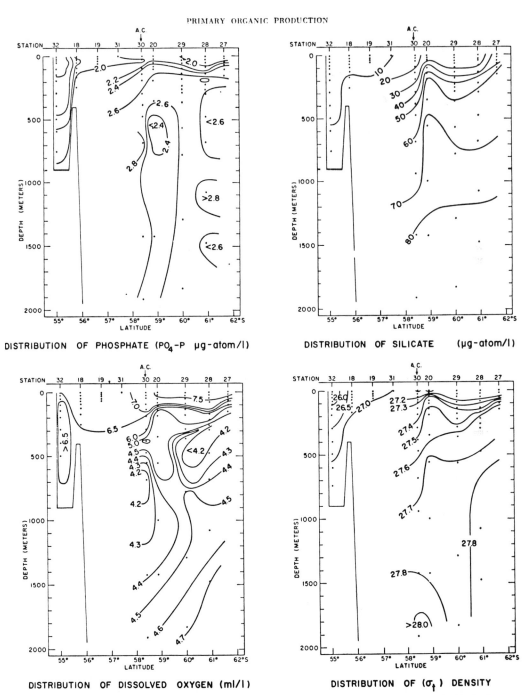

Fig. 4. Distribution of phosphates, silicates, dissolved oxygen, and density in a transect across the Drake Passage (from El-Sayed *et al.*, 1964).

and carbon-14 uptake in the Passage are: 2.4 mg/m^3 and 8.2 mg C/hr/m^3 respectively. In productivity terms, the Drake Passage exceeds those of the Arctic waters.

It was found that the Antarctic Convergence has a profound influence on the distribution and abundance of the flora and fauna in the Drake Passage. Investigators have found not only that the quantity of plankton has increased considerably south of the convergence but also that a floral and faunal change in composition took place at the convergence. Thus species of the krill (*Euphausia*), which constitutes an important part of the diet of the blue whales in Antarctica, were used by marine biologists to delineate boundaries between Antarctic and sub-Antarctic waters. Thus in the neighborhood of the convergence, if *Euphausia vallentini* or *E. longirostris* is taken in the plankton net, this is a good indication of their presence in sub-Antarctic water. On the other hand, if *E. frigida* and not *vallentini* nor *longirostris* is taken, this indicates that the convergence was crossed.

SAYED Z. EL-SAYED

References

Clowes, A. J., 1938, "Phosphate and silicate in the Southern Ocean," *Discovery Reports*, **19**, 1–120.

*Deacon, G. E. R., 1937, "The hydrology of the Southern Ocean," *Discovery Reports*, **15**, 1–124.

El-Sayed, S. Z., Mandelli, E. F., and Sugimura, Y., 1964, "Primary Organic Production in the Drake Passage and Bransfield Strait," *Antarctic Research Series*, **1**, 1–11.

Goodell, H. G., 1964, "Marine geology of the Drake Passage, Scotia Sea and South Sandwich Trench," *USNS Eltanin Mar. Geol. Cruises*, 1–8, Florida State Univ., Sediment Lab., 1–263.

Goodell, H. G., and Osmond, J. K., 1964, "Marine geology aboard USNS *Eltanin*," *Bull. U.S. Ant. Proj. Officer*, **5** (10), 87–93.

Hart, T. J., 1934, "On the phytoplankton of the South-West Atlantic and the Bellingshausen Sea," *Discovery Reports*, **8**, 1–268.

*Hart, T. J., 1942, "Phytoplankton periodicity in Antarctic surface waters," *Discovery Reports*, **21**, 261–356.

Mosby, H., 1934, "The waters of the Atlantic Antarctic Ocean," *Sci. Res. Norweg. Antarct. Exped. 1927–1928*, **1** (11), 1–131.

Wüst, G., 1932, "Das ozeanographische Beobachtungsmaterial," *Serienmessung.*, *Wiss. Ergebn. Deut. Atlant. Exped. "Meteor", 1925–1927*, **4**, 1–290.

SCUBA AS A SCIENTIFIC TOOL

Scuba (self contained underwater breathing apparatus) permits the formerly land- or deck-bound scientist to personally enter the kingdom of the sea.

For centuries, man has waded the tidal pools and shallows. He has sailed the surface. He has probed into the water—raking, scratching, netting, and dredging up samples of underwater life and bottom. More recently he has invaded this domain in diving bells, suit and helmet rigs and underwater vehicles. None of these have permitted man to comfortably study the underwater ecology with an appreciable degree of ease or continuity.

The advent of workable scuba has changed this picture. Instead of trudging on the bottom, or hanging suspended, man has almost attained the freedom of a fish. From the shore line out to an arbitrary depth of 150 feet lies an area called the "scuba zone." This is the zone accessible to the diver wearing standard scuba. That the scuba zone is a fertile area for scientific exploration is becoming ever more apparent. Scientists are constantly encountering unfamiliar flora and fauna in the scuba zone.

Studies of the interrelation of currents, salinity, temperatures, subsurface topography, sedimentary deposits, fossils, and animal life are enhanced by *personal* underwater study. It may be not too far fetched to suggest that by actually insinuating oneself into this environment a better sympathy with these factors can be achieved. This could be likened to the entomologist observing insects in their natural habitat.

Scientists of the future will be swimming with impunity in waters far deeper than 150 feet. Recent experiments such as Hans Keller's 1000-foot scuba dive, deep scuba diving from the U.S. Navy's Sea Lab II (1965), Costeau's Conshelf, Link's experiments and the Westinghouse Electric Corporation's work with the Krasberg scuba and life support equipment indicate that man may someday be able to use scuba for hours at depths of over 1000 feet. Experiments conducted by the General Electric Company using a permselective membrane may some day permit man to breathe oxygen derived from ambient seawater.

At the present time, however, most scientists will find the type of scuba perfected by Costeau and Gagnon (named "Aqualung") best suited to their needs. This is the same kind of scuba used by sport divers all over the world. It has partially replaced the "hard hat" (standard "deep-sea" diving rig) for certain kinds of commercial diving.

There are two main classifications of scuba: closed-circuit and open-circuit.

Closed-circuit Scuba

Note that there are two kinds of closed-circuit scuba. One uses oxygen as the breathing medium and is strictly limited to less than 30-foot depths. The other uses a mixed gas and is intended for extremely deep diving. In the oxygen type, the diver breathes pure oxygen. Exhalations are reconstituted by a chemical filter and rebreathed. Oxygen is manually valved into the rig, as the diver descends, in order to equalize the breathing gas pressure inside the diver and recirculator, to the ambient pressure.

Very little bubble trace can be discerned on the surface. This is one reason why underwater demoli-

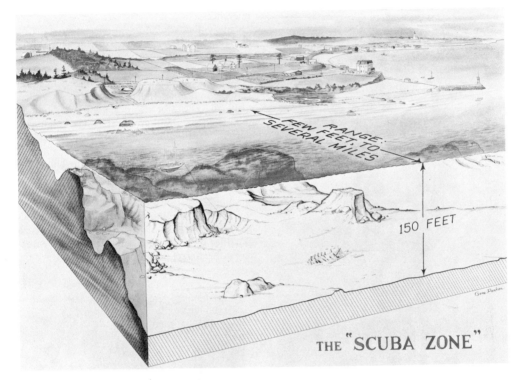

Fig. 1. The "Scuba Zone." (Sketch by Gene Parker.)

tion teams use this closed-circuit scuba. The other reason is that several hours of immersion may be achieved on one unit.

Amateur use of oxygen closed-circuit scuba is strongly discouraged. The equipment requires specialized training and facilities not available to the average diver. Depth is limited to 25 feet. Prolonged swimming at 2 atm absolute pressure (33 feet in seawater) can result in fatal oxygen poisoning.

The use of oxygen closed-circuit scuba in scientific diving is unnecessary since there is no need to extend submerged time or conceal bubbles.

The Krasberg closed-circuit mixed-gas unit also requires specialized training and facilities. With this scuba, depths of over a thousand feet are anticipated.

Open-circuit Scuba

Open-circuit scuba is recommended for scientific diving. The diver wears a high-pressure air cylinder on his back. An automatic demand regulator mounted on the valve of the tank provides air through a hose to the mouthpiece or to the mask. The diver breathes air at ambient pressure. The exhaled air bubbles out into the water, hence the name open-circuit scuba.

About an hour of submerged time is achieved with the most common size of scuba tank. This varies with depth and with the individual's respiratory rate.

Due to physiological factors, open-circuit scuba can be considered to be limited to a depth of 150 feet. A lot of research can be done in less than 30 feet of water, where the diver may remain for hours. As he descends deeper, his "bottom time" becomes progressively limited until at 150 feet he may stay only 5 minutes. It is possible for an expert to use open-circuit compressed air scuba to over 250-foot depths. However, he must remain an appreciable time at decompression stops before emerging from the water. These physiological aspects are explained more fully in the books mentioned in the references.

In addition to scuba, the diver may also need a foam neoprene ("wet") suit to protect him from cold, a weight belt, knife, compass, depth gauge, watch, and an inflatable flotation device. He might tow a surface float in which samples or tools can be carried. A diver's flag should be flown over the dive site to warn off boat traffic.

Many new pieces of accessory equipment are now available: metal detectors, underwater prospecting and mining equipment, underwater lights, self-powered sleds and towing devices, small salvage equipment, underwater cameras, communication devices, diver sonar, and a number of other items.

Scuba diving has to be experienced to be properly understood. The diver can hover almost effortlessly over most underwater locations while making continuous observations. He can rapidly change van-

highly trained experts. Details can be found in the references.

Scuba offers several advantages over some other contemporary observation or sampling media in shallow water. It must be admitted that there is no completely satisfactory artificial environment such as an aquarium in which to reproduce actual underwater conditions. Indeed, to make an authentic artificial reef of (for instance) underwater biological life would require that we reproduce conditions of current, depth, animal interdependence, and many other factors.

A sampling medium such as trawling or dredging may bring up some undamaged marine specimens. This method gives scant information regarding the specimen's relationship to its environment. Attempting to dredge or grab specimens from rocky regions is obviously even more unsatisfactory. This is compounded by the fact that marine environments vary according to reef, shoal, or bottom type. It is difficult

Fig. 2. The scuba diver. (Photo by Gene Parker.)

Fig. 3. Equipment used by scuba diver. (Photo by Gene Parker.)

tage points, pursue specimens, and handle objects. It is even possible to make notes or sketches, using special materials, underwater.

Another variation to scuba is the "Hookah." This consists of an air compressor on the surface supplying air to the diver through a long hose. The hose is plugged into the scuba regulator. The compressor and hose takes the place of the diver's scuba tank. Tethered by the hose to his surface air supply, the diver can stay submerged for hours. He does not have to surface to exchange a full tank for a depleted one. Hookah is popular for *in situ* work on underwater archeological, or other scientific, study sites.

Another type of scuba is the semi-closed-circuit scuba. This unit is designed for deep diving. It is an advanced and specialized kind of equipment for

Fig. 4. "Hard hat" diver (comparison with scuba diver). (Sketch by Gene Parker.)

to correlate marine fauna or flora with geological structures when blindly groping the bottom from the surface (e.g. by echo-sounding and dredging).

Naturally, it is not valid to state that scuba is a substitute for plankton nets, underway samplers, or some electronic devices. However, a surprising number of conventional oceanographic equipments can be used by a scuba diver. Among these are small sampling equipments like slurp guns, water bottles, traps, some samplers, some corers, small electronic gear, and of course still, movie and TV cameras.

Scuba diving is not the sole province of the young, healthy athlete. There are many divers over 60 years of age. A sound circulatory and respiratory system, the ability to swim, and an affinity for water are the prime requisites for skin diving. A good instruction course in skin diving is essential. A fully outfitted scuba diver may use from a hundred dollars to three or four hundred dollars worth of gear. Special equipment such as propulsion devices, cameras, etc., can raise the cost to four figures. Scuba diving is safer than skiing or driving an automobile, but like these avocations can be as dangerous as you make it.

EUGENE K. PARKER

References

Dill, R. F., and Shumway, G., 1954, "Geologic use of self-contained diving apparatus," *Bull. Am. Assoc. Petrol. Geologists*, **38**, 148–157.

Menard, H. W., Dill, R. F., Hamilton, E. L., Moore, D. G., Shumway, G., Silverman, M., and Stewart, H. B., 1954, "Underwater mapping by diving geologists," *Bull. Am. Assoc. Petrol. Geologists*, **38**, 129–147.

Parker, E. K., 1961, "Scuba as a Tool for Scientists," Paper for Marine Science Conference at Woods Hole Oceanographic Institution; also published by Plenum Press, 1962.

Parker, E. K., 1965, "Complete Handbook of Skin Diving," New York, Avon Books.

U.S. Navy Diving Manual, NAVSHIPS 250–538, U.S. Government Printing Office.

Cross-references: *Marine Geology; Underwater Photography.*

SEA BREEZE—*See* Vol. II

SEA ICE

Sea ice is here defined as ice formed by the freezing of seawater (it excludes icebergs and other forms of land ice). Normal seawater of 35‰ salinity (*S*, grams of salt per 1000 grams of seawater) freezes at a temperature of $-1.9°C$. Unlike fresh water which reaches its maximum density at $+4°C$, the temperature of *maximum density* of seawater depends on its salinity. For $S > 24.7‰$ (which is normally the case), the temperature of maximum density lies *below the freezing point.*

Therefore, vertical convection induced by cooling at the surface may reach considerable depth (depending on the preexisting density stratification) and continues while the ice is growing.

From an initial stage of "frazil" crystals and sludge, composed of *floating needles and platelets*, sea ice grows to a compact aggregate of roughly columnar, lamellated (0.05–0.1 cm width) crystals whose optical axes (*c*-axes) are predominantly horizontal. The extremely low solubility of salts in ice causes segregation at the interface; however, discreet *pockets of brine* become entrapped between the growing lamellae. Since the thermal conductivity of ice is about 4 times that of brine, crystals with their *c*-axes horizontal (lamellae vertical) can conduct more heat and hence grow more rapidly. This has been proposed as a possible mechanism causing the observed *grain orientation*. Another mechanism may be the preferred growth of ice in the direction of the basal plane (for reasons of molecular kinetics) which leads to a wedging out of unfavorably oriented crystals.

The composition of the brine does not change during its entrapment. Its *concentration* (normally in phase equilibrium with the surrounding pure ice) is a *function of temperature* alone. Hence, the percentage brine volume of sea ice is a function of ice salinity, usually given in grams of salt per 1000 grams of ice, and temperature (see Table 1).

The initial salinity of naturally frozen ice varies between 20‰ and 2‰; the more rapid the freezing, the saltier is the ice. Most sea ice has a salinity of 2–4‰. Immediately after sea ice has formed the process of *desalination* begins. The salinity at the surface of perennial ice is usually <0.5‰. Gravity drainage, flushing by fresh water from snow melt and, to a small extent, the migration toward the warmer surface of brine pockets as a result of a brine concentration gradient within them (Kingery, 1963) remove salt. The physical details of natural desalination are still not clearly understood.

The variable brine content makes all *physical properties* of sea ice dependent on temperature, particularly near 0°C where the brine volume varies most rapidly (see Table 1).

The *growth rate* of sea ice depends primarily on surface temperature, depth of snow cover, and turbulent heat flux in the underlying water. A semiempirical formula for the regional conditions of the central Arctic (Zubov, 1943) is $h = -25 + \sqrt{(25 + h_0)^2 + 8\Delta F}$ where h_0 is the initial ice thickness, h is the final ice thickness (both in cm), and ΔF is the number of freezing degree days of the time interval considered. In the central Arctic ($\Delta F = 7000$–8000 per year), the seasonal ice cover ($h_0 = 0$ at the end of August) is about 2 meters. Surface *ablation* occurs from June to August and averages 30–50 cm of ice (plus about 40 cm of snow with a density of ~ 0.35 g/cm^3). Bottom ablation occurs when the upward turbulent heat

TABLE 1. SOME PHYSICAL PROPERTIES OF SEA WATER AND SEA ICE (from various sources)

SEA WATER

Freezing point: $T_f(°C) = -0.055 \, S_w$ (S_w in g salt/1000 g water)
Thermal conductivity: 0.00139 cal/cm sec °C (at 0°C and 35‰ salinity)
Diffusivity for NaCl: 0.0000068 cm²/sec (at 0°C and 35‰ salinity)
Initial solid precipitation of $Na_2SO_4 \cdot 10H_2O$ at $-$ 8.2°C
                     $NaCl \cdot 2H_2O$ $-22.9°C$
                     $MgCl_2 \cdot 12H_2O$ $-36.0°C$

SEA ICE

Density: in nature mostly between 0.89 and 0.93 g/cm³, depending on temperature (T, °C), salinity (S_i, g salt/1000 g ice), and air content (v_a, cm³ air/1000 cm³ ice),

$$\rho_i(g/cm^3) = (1 - \frac{v_a}{1000}) \, (1 - \frac{0.00456 S_i}{T})0.917$$

Brine volume: $v_b \approx -55 \, S_i/T$ (v_b and S_i in ‰, T in °C)

Thermal conductivity: k (cal/cm sec °C) $\approx 0.00486 + \dfrac{0.00025 \, S_i}{T}$ (S_i in ‰, T in °C)

Specific heat: c_i (cal/g °C) $\approx 0.5 + \dfrac{4.1 S_i}{T^2}$ (S_i in ‰, T in °C)

Tensile strength: $1-1.7 \times 10^7$ dynes/cm² between -8 and $-25°C$ and $S_i < 10$‰. The strength approaches zero close to 0°C because of the rapid increase of brine volume (see above)
Shear strength: somewhat smaller than tensile strength
Crushing strength: order of magnitude 10^8 dynes/cm²
Young's modulus: E (dynes/cm²) $= (9.75 - 0.242 \, S_i) \times 10^{10}$ at $-20°C$ (S_i in ‰)
Poisson ratio: ~ 0.35
Longitudinal bulk wave velocity: 2800 m/sec at $-2°C$, 3500 m/sec at $-15°C$
Shear wave velocity: 1550 m/sec at $-2°C$, 1850 m/sec at $-15°C$
Electrical resistivity: greatly variable, no exact relationships established, changes from 25 to 25,000 ohm-meters between -1 and $-30°C$
Infrared emissivity: 0.99
Reflectivity (albedo) for visible light:

sludge	0.2
bare ice 5–10 cm thick	0.3–0.4
bare ice thicker than 50 cm	0.5–0.6
meltwater puddle	0.2–0.3
overall summer (bare and puddles)	0·5
overall winter (snow-covered)	0.85

        coefficient for visible light: 0.05–0.015 cm^{-1}
Hydrodynamic roughness parameter:

upper surface	0.02 cm
lower surface	2. cm

flux in the ocean is greater than the upward heat conduction in the ice. This is normally the case from August to October and ablates 10–20 cm at the bottom. When the ice has grown to a thickness where the annual increase equals ablation, it has reached its *equilibrium thickness* (in the Arctic about 3–4 meters in 5–8 years).

In the Antarctic, perennial sea ice is found only in the Weddell Sea and a narrow strip around the continent. Most of the antarctic sea ice is seasonal and reaches a thickness of about 150 cm in October/November.

The average minimum and maximum (autumn and spring) *extent of the sea ice cover* in the Arctic and the Antarctic are shown in Fig. 1. Arrows indicate the main features of the mean annual drift pattern. Owing to the given arrangement of land and sea, the meridional exchange of heat both in the atmosphere and in the ocean is more vigorous in the Antarctic. This is also reflected in the annual variation of the total amount of sea ice (Table 2).

Compared to the volume of the Antarctic and Greenland ice caps, the volume of sea ice on earth is insignificant. But the drastic change of reflectivity which occurs when the ocean freezes over (from 0.05–0.1 to 0.8) makes sea ice an important factor influencing the heat exchange between ocean and atmosphere. The boundaries of the sea ice toward lower latitudes are highly variable. In the Norwegian and Greenland Seas, year-to-year deviations of 300 km north or south of the average position are not uncommon.

Fig. 1. Average boundaries of sea ice (coverage at least 5–8 tenths) in autumn and spring in the Arctic and Antarctic. Arrows indicate the general drift pattern. The southward discharge of ice through the gap between Greenland and Spitsbergen has been estimated to be 3000 km³/yr.

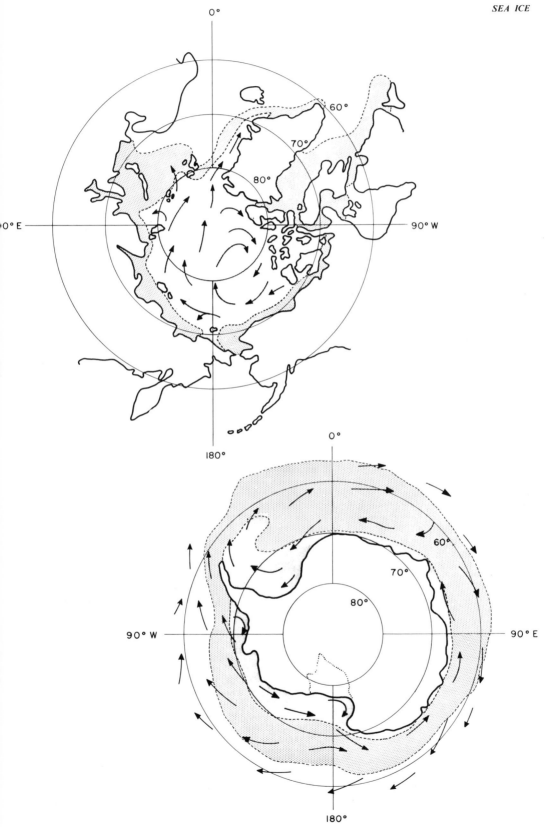

TABLE 2. ESTIMATED MASS BUDGET OF ARCTIC AND ANTARCTIC
SEA ICE

	Mean • Thickness (m)	Area at End of Summer (km²)	Area at End of Winter (km²)	Annual Variation of Volume (km³)
Arctic	3–4	9×10^6	12×10^6	9×10^3
Antarctic	1	4×10^6	20×10^6	23×10^3

Mean total mass of sea ice on earth: 4–5×10^4 km³

Total amount freezing (and melting) each year: 3×10^4 km³

The *temperature of sea ice* is controlled by the freezing point of seawater, by the thickness and the thermal properties of the ice, and by the exchange of heat with the atmosphere at the upper surface. For the central Arctic, sufficient field data are available to establish the mean annual temperature field of ice of equilibrium thickness, as shown in Fig. 2.

Natural fields of sea ice are in almost *constant motion*, forming cracks, leads, hummocks, and pressure ridges (see Glossary of Ice Terminology, 1952). The general pattern of motion, indicated in Fig. 1, is caused primarily by the tangential stress of the wind on the ice surface and, to a lesser extent, by the stress of ocean currents. If p and h denote ice density and thickness, and v the velocity of ice drift, the general equation of motion can be written

$$ph \, dv/dt = \tau_a + \tau_w + D + R + G$$

where τ_a and τ_w are the stresses exerted by air and water, D is the Coriolis force, R is the internal stress with which the ice resists its deformation, and G is the pressure gradient force due to the tilting of the sea surface on which the ice floats.

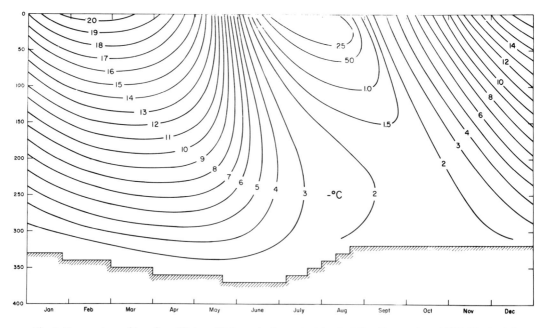

Fig. 2. Temperature of ice of equilibrium thickness in the central Arctic (after Untersteiner, 1964). The ice is bare from mid-June to the end of August. Between September and May, about 40 cm of snow accumulate on the ice surface. Since the coordinate system is fixed in the surface, all thickness changes appear at the bottom. The thinning in July and August actually occurs at the surface.

Even the steady-state case

$$0 = \tau_a + \tau_w + D + R + G$$

is a complex problem (Campbell, 1964). As a rule of thumb, the velocity of ice drift is about $\frac{1}{50}$ of the wind velocity near the ground (2 meters), at an angle of about 45° to the right of the wind vector (to the left in the southern hemisphere), or approximately parallel to the geostrophic wind.

N. UNTERSTEINER

References

Campbell, W. J., 1964, "On the steady-state flow of sea ice," Dept. of Atmospheric Sciences, University of Washington, Scientific Report.

Hunkins, K., 1960, "Seismic studies of sea ice," *J. Geophys. Res.*, **65**, 3459–3472.

Kingery, W. D., and Goodnow, W. H., 1963, "Brine Migration on salt ice," in "Ice and Snow," p. 237, Cambridge, Mass., Massachusetts Institute of Technology.

Pounder, E. R., 1962, "The Physics of Sea Ice," in "The Sea," Vol. 1, p. 826, New York, Interscience Publishers.

Schwerdtfeger, P., 1963, "The thermal properties of sea ice," *J. Glaciol.*, **4**, 789–807.

Understeiner, N., 1964, "Calculations of temperature regime and heat budget of sea ice in the central Arctic," *J. Geophys. Res.*, **69**, 4755–4766.

U.S. Navy H.O. 609, 1952, "A Functional Glossary of Ice Terminology."

Zubov, N. N., 1943, "Arctic ice," *Izdatel'stvo Glasev-morputi*, 360pp., Moscow (translated for AFCRC by USN Oceanographic Office and American Meteorological Society).

SEA ICE CLIMATIC CYCLES—*See* Vol. II

SEA ICE TRANSPORTATION

Sea ice plays an important role in distributing sediment and rock fragments of terrigenous origin to areas far from their source. As recognized over a century ago by Charles Darwin when visiting Tierra del Fuego in H.M.S. *Beagle*, there is transportation both by icebergs and by floe ice. The latter forms along the shore, freezes-in the littoral deposits and is then distributed by tides and currents. River deposits may be introduced in the sea by the same process (Kindle, 1924; Twenhofel, 1932). Certain "passengers," e.g., polar bears in the Arctic, penguins in the Antarctic, are carried widely from their original habitats.

Bottom freezing of ice shelves and ablation at the top means that gradually the material frozen into the base migrates upward. In the Ross shelf, all sorts of fresh bottom sediments and benthonic organisms, including the evaporite mineral mirabi-

lite (only stable at subzero temperatures), are now found at various heights above sea level (Debenham, 1919). As remarked by Sverdrup (1931): "Very extensive ice floes will every winter ground up in the shallow water along the coast, and during the winter mud, clay, shells, and stones become fast to the underside of these floes. . . ." After a process of successive annual meltings at the top, and freezings at the base of the floes, the debris works up to the surface, when of course it increases the rate of melting, and will in due course "sink to the bottom and be deposited at very great distances from the place where they were originally frozen fast to the ice." Littoral shells and beach sediments are often pushed high above sea level in pressure ridges that form especially when there are on-shore winds.

Pleistocene floating ice in the southern hemisphere brought rafted boulders, rather generally, as far north as 35°S and fossil penguin bones are found up to 30°S. In the northern hemisphere, the limit is closer to 40°N except where strong geostrophic currents on the east sides of the oceans set southward (the California and Canaries Currents), carrying boulders respectively to 35°N and 20°N.

The quantity of material so transported by ice floes or bergs may be judged by the thickness of postglacial sediment in many areas which may exceed 100 cm, while ice-rafted boulders appear in almost every photo of high-latitude sea floors. Massive banks of boulders off South Africa were reported by Needham (1962). Some 7500 icebergs are transported annually today by the Labrador Current, most of which run ashore and melt before reaching 55°N, some 400 reaching the Newfoundland Banks, but only 50 passing south of here (Fig. 1).

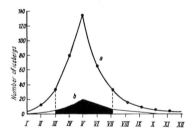

Fig. 1. Average number of icebergs per month. (a) Northwest Atlantic Ocean, south of 47°N; (b) south of the Grand Banks. Black, under surveillance by the International Ice Patrol Service (according to E. H. Smith, 1931; from Dietrich, 1963). Numbers along abscissa indicate months of the year. (By permission of Interscience Publishers, N.Y.)

In floating ice islands, it is often possible to identify several sorts of ice, including former shore ice, by the burden it carries (Fig. 2). Current systems, in relation to source areas of glaciers or littoral shore ice, dictate where various ice-borne debris is carried. Particularly favorable areas for rapid freez-

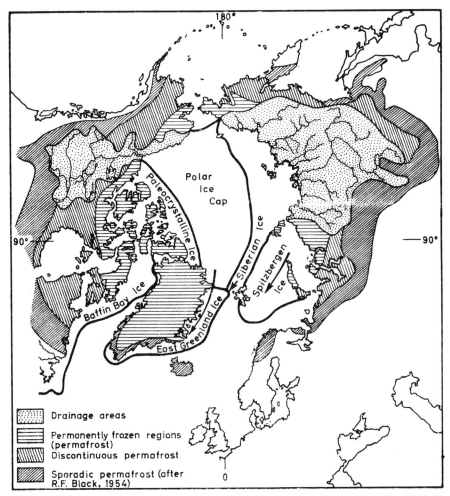

Fig. 2. The distribution of glaciers in the Arctic region (from Termier and Termier, 1963).

ing of nearshore ice are in the vicinity of the great rivers debouching into the Arctic Ocean, e.g., Mackenzie, the Ob, Yenisei and Lena (Koch, 1945).

RHODES W. FAIRBRIDGE

References

Debenham, F., 1919, "A new mode of transportation by ice, etc.," *Quart. J. Geol. Soc.,* **75,** 51–76.

Dietrich, G., 1963, "General Oceanography," New York, Interscience Publishers.

Kindle, E. M., 1924, "Observations on ice-borne sediments by the Canadian and other Arctic expeditions," *Am. J. Sci.,* **7,** 251–286.

Koch, L., 1945, "The East Greenland Ice," *Medd. Groenland,* **130**(3).

Needham, H. D., 1962, "Ice-rafted rocks from the Atlantic Ocean off the coast of the Cape of Good Hope," *Deep-Sea Res.,* **9,** 475–486.

Smith, D. D., 1964, "Ice lithologies and structure of ice island Arlis II," *J. Glaciol.,* **5**(37), 17–38.

Sverdrup, H. U., 1929, "The waters on the North Siberian Shelf," *The Scientific Results of the Norwegian North Polar Expedition with the "Maud," 1918–1925,* **4**(2) (Bergen).

Sverdrup, H. U., 1931, "The transport of material by pack-ice," *Geograph. J.,* **77,** 399–400.

Twenhofel, W. H., 1932, "Treatise on Sedimentation," Second ed., New York, Dover Publ. Reprint (1961), 460pp.

Cross-references: pr Vol. VI: *Glacial Marine Sedimentation.*

SEAMOUNTS (INCLUDING GUYOTS)

In 1952, the International Committee on Nomenclature of Ocean Bottom Features met in Monaco to define terms to be applied to submarine features. The definitions include the following descriptions of several features of major positive relief:

Seamount—An isolated or comparatively isolated elevation of the deep sea floor of approximately 1000 meters or more. A seapeak is a seamount with a pointed summit.

Guyot (syn. Tablemount)—A seamount, generally deeper than 200 meters, the top of which is a comparatively smooth platform. If the depth of the platform is less than 200 meters, the term *Oceanic Bank* is appropriate. The term was originally established by H. H. Hess in 1946 for the flat-topped seamounts he observed while conducting extensive sounding operations in the Pacific Ocean. Hess applied the term *guyot* (pronounced gee-yo) to these features in honor of Arnold Guyot, the nineteenth century Swiss-American geologist.

Seamounts vary in size from relatively small, conical peaks to massive structures such as Great Meteor Seamount in the northeast Atlantic Ocean. This seamount has a basal diameter to 110 km

and an elevation of 4000 meters above the sea floor (Pratt, 1963). The area of its flat summit platform, more than 2000 km^2, nearly equals that of the state of Rhode Island.

The flanks of small seamounts may form slopes as steep as 35°, but those of larger seamounts and guyots seldom exceed 12–14° (Emery, Tracey and Ladd, 1954). The few detailed studies of seamounts indicate that most are elliptical in plan, rather than circular.

Seamounts have been discovered in all major ocean basins. H. W. Menard has listed over 1400 for the Pacific Basin (Fig. 1), and has suggested that this represents about 10% of the true number in the Pacific Basin alone, 90% being as yet undiscovered. B. C. Heezen and others have located scores in the Atlantic Basin (Heezen, Tharp and Ewing, 1959), and the recent international explora-

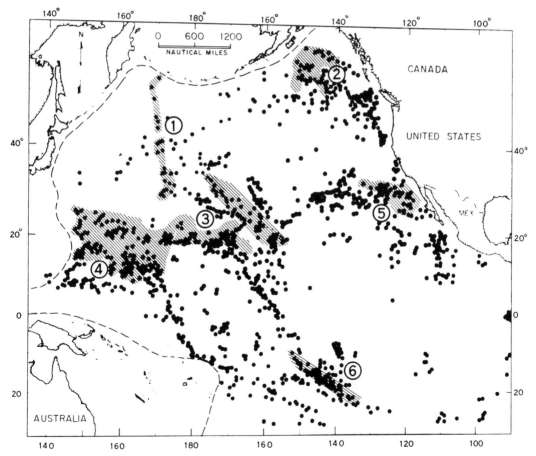

Fig. 1. The distribution of Pacific Islands and Seamounts with specific groups of seamounts numbered. Other alignments are apparent and are associated with large fracture systems and ridges on the basin floor. The dashed line marks the trace of the theoretical "andesite line" thought by some to be a lithologic boundary between continental and oceanic rock types: (1) Emperor Seamount Chain, (2) Gulf of Alaska Seamount Province, (3) Marcus-Necker Ridge and Hawaiian Swell—together these form the Mid-Pacific Mountains, (4) Caroline and Marshall Platforms, (5) Baja Seamount Province, (6) Austral Seamount Chain. Figure based on data prepared by H. W. Menard (1959) and others.

tory effort in the Indian Ocean has disclosed many unreported seamounts. The increased interest in the Arctic Ocean Basin has furnished R. S. Dietz and G. Shumway (1961) with bathymetric evidence of an extensive seamount province in the Polar Basin north of Spitsbergen.

Although seamounts are, by definition, isolated features, regional relationships indicate many occur in large chains or provinces. Several regional groups in the Pacific Basin are listed in Fig. 1. In the Atlantic Basin, the Bermuda–New England Seamount Arc is formed of two intersecting chains of seamounts, many of which have flat summit platforms. Other extensive Atlantic groups lie south of the Azores Plateau and west of the Straits of Gibraltar.

The time required to conduct detailed studies of seamounts, plus their generally remote nature, has limited the number of investigations of these features. However, a sufficient number of geographically scattered studies exist, and these will permit a general discussion regarding the lithology, structure and origin of seamounts.

The majority of samples recovered from seamounts are basic, extrusive igneous rocks of the basalt family. The few exotic lithologies reported are generally attributed to rafting, although a few samples of limestone and sandstone (similar to reef-rock or beach-rock) have been interpreted as being indigenous to the seamount. Most of the extrusive materials are extensively altered and weathered, but they are usually recognizable as

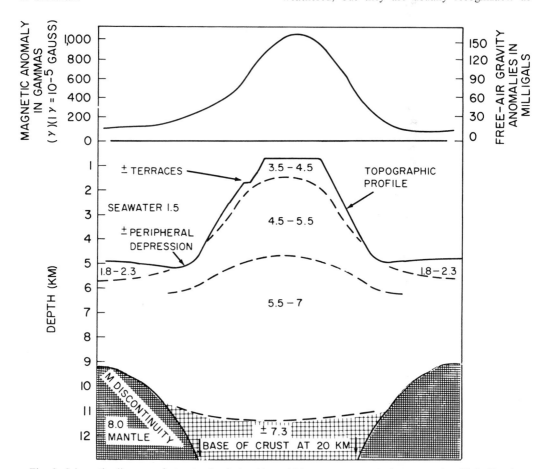

Fig. 2. Schematic diagram of structural relationships within a guyot—vertical exaggeration 20:1. Numbers indicate commonly observed seismic (compressional) velocities in kilometers per second.

Velocity (km/sec)	Material
1.8–2.3	Deep sea sediments
3.5–4.5	Mixed sediment and extrusive volcanic rubble
4.5–5.5	Extrusive volcanic rock
5.5–7.0	Dense crustal (gabbroic?) rock
± 7.3	Intermediate velocity layer recorded in some areas, assumed to be a mixture of mantle and gabbroic rock
8.0$^+$	Mantle material

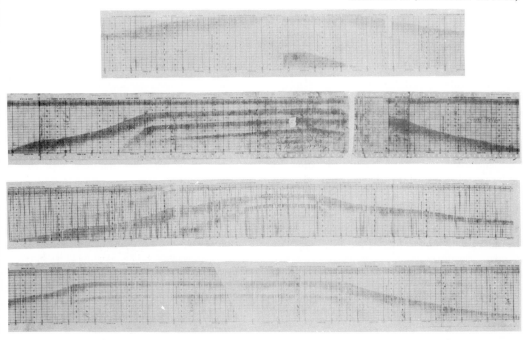

Fig. 3. Profiles across four flat topped seamounts (guyots) in the Gulf of Alaska. These records were taken in 1946 by the U.S.C. and G.S. Vessel *Surveyor* using an NMC Fathometer. The depth range represented in each profile is 2000 fathoms. (Courtesy of H. W. Menard)

porphyritic and vesicular basalts which often display flow banding or pillow structures. The microcrystalline nature of the groundmass and the structure and texture of many samples suggests most dredged materials are from the surficial parts of lava flows (Engel and Engel, 1963). Glassy palagonitic tuff is also common and may represent the chilled rind of subaqueous flows.

Photographs and dredge hauls on seamounts usually indicate that the summits and flanks are partially covered by a thin, or discontinuous, veneer of sediment.

The structural correlation between seamounts and ocean basins is less well understood than the lithological associations, but the few geophysical studies undertaken permit consideration of gross relationships. The elongate plan of many seamounts and their frequent distribution in linear chains suggest that they are caused by fissure eruptions related to patterns of stress within the oceanic crust. Seismic reflection and refraction studies show a definite internal structure within seamounts (Fig. 2). Large, positive, free-air gravity anomalies usually found over seamounts indicate a crust of greater than normal thickness and density (Woollard and Strange, 1962). Isostatic anomalies are also positive, and thus suggest that the crust beneath some seamounts may be responding to the added load imposed by the volcanic mass. Magnetic anomalies are less consistent, but they generally show highly positive values. These anomalies are

generally thought to be caused by the relatively high percentage of magnetic minerals in the volcanics and the degree of their alignment with regard to the present magnetic field.

The volcanic origin of seamounts is now acknowledged by geologists, and the original hypothesis of supposed subsidence of atoll foundations proposed by Charles Darwin more than a century ago is still favored by most researchers. In his classic treatise on coral reefs, Darwin suggested that existing and drowned atolls were merely organic caps established upon subsiding volcanic foundations (see *Coral Reefs* and *Darwin, Charles*). Although evidence for wave truncation and subsidence of the flat-topped guyots such as those shown in Fig. 3 is not indisputable, a shallow marine or subaerial phase for these features is strongly suggested by:

(1) Deep-sea photographs and dredged samples of highly rounded and obviously abraded volcanic debris.

(2) The recovery of scoriaceous material of probable pyroclastic origin.

(3) Gently sloping terraces, considered by many to be erosional, on the upper flanks of many guyots.

(4) The sheer volume of material missing from some volcanic cones which requires a rigorous erosional agent such as surf-zone activity.

(5) Several samples of Cretaceous reef-coral rudistid fauna, having a maximum depth tolerance

of 150 meters, recovered by E. L. Hamilton from the summit platforms of mid-Pacific guyots now at a depth of 1400 meters. Hamilton (1956) has also shown that the flat summit platform of several guyots is not caused by a coralline blanket deposit (an atoll with a filled lagoon), but that it is a primary surface of eroded rubble with few reef forming organisms.

Thus, the evidence suggests the flat summits of guyots are ancient abrasional platforms rather than deeply drowned atoll structures, and that submergence and the slow rate of deep-sea sedimentation has preserved the original form of these surfaces. Alternative hypotheses accounting for relative subsidence by invoking gross changes in sea level, either through Pleistocene eustatic fluctuations or volumetric increase, have generally lost favor with investigators. However, a long-term geodetic rise in sea level accompanying the suggested 20° post-Cretaceous migration of the polar axes (Fairbridge, 1961) might well account for deep guyots which otherwise require crustal subsidence of abnormal magnitude. Seapeaks, and seamounts with multiple, irregular peaks, may represent either failure of the lava pile to attain the depth of wave base or partial truncation by phreatic explosive eruptions.

Although the sequence of events in the history of a seamount is fairly clear, the process and mechanics of submergence remains a controversial problem. That part of subsidence may be localized is suggested by the observation of shallow moats about the bases of some seamounts. The presence of inclined, or tipped, summit platforms is also indicative of local preferential subsidence. Elsewhere, large areas of the oceanic crust appear to have been elastically depressed due to the increased load imposed by the extruded volcanic material. In addition, the plastic extrusion of sediments from beneath the growing lava pile must occur, and contribute to the overall amount of subsidence (Hamilton, 1957).

The history of a particular seamount may be proposed by determining the age and depth ranges of fossil fauna recovered from its surface. To date, paleontological evidence has shown no seamounts to be older than Late Cretaceous, and Pleistocene faunas indicate a water depth similar to existing conditions. Thus, some of the seamounts investigated appear to have been at, or near, sea level in Late Cretaceous time, and to have attained their present depth prior to the Pleistocene.

A highly significant result in the studies of cores obtained from deep drilling operations on several Pacific atolls was the determination of occasional emergence of atolls founded upon large seamounts (Emery, Tracey and Ladd, 1954; Schlanger, 1963). Solution unconformities, plus mineralogical and paleoecological successions show that either overall subsidence was punctuated by periodic uplift, or

fluctuations in sea level permitted temporary emergence of the atolls. The complex history of these particular atoll pedestals is clear evidence that there is more than simple subsidence involved in seamount chronology.

In the near future, isotopic dating of seamount materials may provide a greater insight into oceanic volcanism, and hence a clarification of ocean basin tectonics. Seamounts are major features of the ocean basins and are thus significant factors in the concepts of sea floor spreading, continental drift and subcrustal oceanic processes.

HAROLD D. PALMER

References

Dietz, R. S., and Shumway, G., 1961, "Arctic Basin geomorphology," *Bull. Geol. Soc. Am.*, **72**, 1319–1330.

Emery, K. O., Tracey, J. I., Jr., and Ladd, H. S., 1954, "Geology of Bikini and nearby Atolls, Pt. 1, Geology," *U.S. Geol. Surv. Profess. Papers*, **260-A**, 265pp.

Engel, C. G., and Engel, A. E. J., 1963, "Basalts dredged from the northeastern Pacific Ocean," *Science*, **140**, 1321–1324.

Fairbridge, R. W., 1961, "Eustatic Changes in Sea Level," in "Physics and Chemistry of the Earth," Vol. 4, pp. 99–185, London, Pergamon Press, 317pp.

Hamilton, E. L., 1956, "Sunken islands of the Mid-Pacific Mountains," *Geol. Soc. Mem.*, **64**, 97pp.

Hamilton, E. L., 1957, "Marine geology of the southern Hawaiian ridge," *Geol. Soc. Am. Bull.*, **68**, 1011–1026.

Heezen, B. C., Tharp, M., and Ewing, M., 1959, "The floors of the ocean, I, North Atlantic," *Geol. Soc. Am. Spec. Papers*, **65**, 122pp.

Menard, H. W., 1959, "Geology of the Pacific sea floor," *Experientia*, **15**, 205–213.

Pratt, R. M., 1963, "Great Meteor Seamount," *Deep-Sea Res.*, **10**, 17–25.

Schlanger, S. O., 1963, "Subsurface geology of Eniwetok Atoll," in *U.S. Geol. Surv. Profess. Papers*, **260-BB**, 991–1038.

Woollard, G. P., and Strange, W. E., 1962, "Gravity anomalies and the crust of the earth in the Pacific Basin," in "The crust of the Pacific Basin," *Geophys. Mono.*, **6**, 60–80, 195pp.

SEA STATE

Sea state (also "state of the sea," or simply "sea") is an old mariner's term used to signify the condition (i.e., degree of roughness) of the sea (ocean) surface. The expression may have originated in ships' logs during the sailing era. By the time the first international "meteorological" conference* met at Brussels in 1853 to discuss the question of a universal system of observations at

* This conference, called by the United States, was largely due to the efforts of Lieutenant Matthew F. Maury, Chief U.S. Delegate, and head of the Navy Depot of Charts and Instruments, which developed into the Navy Hydrographic Office.

sea, "state of sea" was included in a list of observations to be made and recorded in a "weather register" aboard ship. As is characteristic in linguistic usage, an ambiguity in meaning of sea state evolved, abetted by the practice of differentiating ocean waves into sea and swell waves.

State of the sea in a loose sense relates to the whole appearance of the ocean surface and, therefore, includes sea and swell, which are usually present together. The convention of distinguishing

sea (fresh waves being generated by local winds[**]) from swell (decaying waves originally generated by distant winds), though useful to the mariner and scientist, is rather artificial and arbitrary. A spectrum of each type wave frequently exists that is little less complex than the combined spectra of waves.

[**] Wind waves is sometimes used to denote sea waves in contradistinction to swell waves.

TABLE 1A. DOUGLAS SEA AND SWELL SCALE (COMBINED)[a]

		Swell								
		Low		Moderate			Heavy			
Sea	No swell	Short or Average	Long	Short	Average	Long	Short	Average	Long	Confused
	0	1	2	3	4	5	6	7	8	9
0 Calm	00	01	02	03	04	05	06	07	08	09
1 Smooth	10	11	12	13	14	15	16	17	18	19
2 Slight	20	21	22	23	24	25	26	27	28	29
3 Moderate	30	31	32	33	34	35	36	37	38	39
4 Rough	40	41	42	43	44	45	46	47	48	49
5 Very rough	50	51	52	53	54	55	56	57	58	59
6 High	60	61	62	63	64	65	66	67	68	69
7 Very high	70	71	72	73	74	75	76	77	78	79
8 Precipitous	80	81	82	83	84	85	86	87	88	89
9 Confused	90	91	92	93	94	95	96	97	98	99

TABLE 1B. DOUGLAS SEA AND SWELL SCALES (SEPARATE)

State of Sea

Scale No.	Description
0	Calm
1	Smooth
2	Slight
3	Moderate
4	Rough
5	Very rough
6	High
7	Very high
8	Precipitous
9	Confused

Swell

Scale No.	Description
0	No swell
1	Low swell, short or average length
2	Low swell, long
3	Moderate swell, short
4	Moderate swell, average length
5	Moderate swell, long
6	Heavy swell, short
7	Heavy swell, average length
8	Heavy swell, long
9	Confused swell

[a] From Great Britain Meteorological Office (1936).

FORCE 0 — FORCE 1 — FORCE 2 — FORCE 3 — FORCE 5 — FORCE 7 — FORCE 10 — FORCE 12

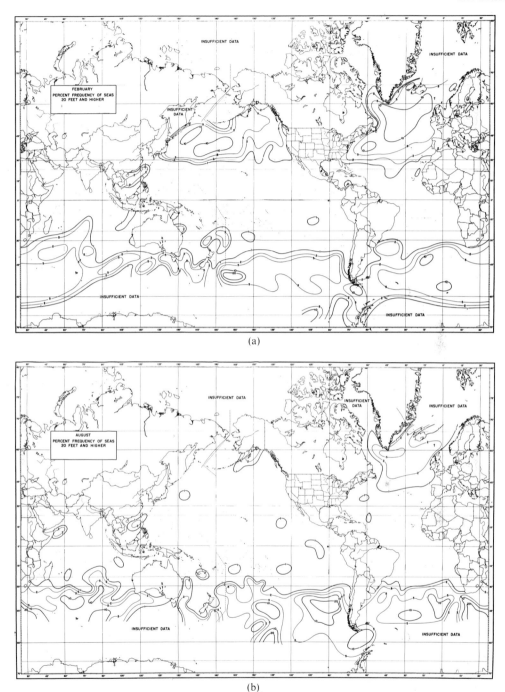

(a)

(b)

Fig. 2. Positive photo prints (large—about 15 × 20 inches) in files of sea and swell section.

Sea state in a strict sense pertains to sea waves only, a meaning that derives in part from the

Fig. 1. Selected examples of sea state from 0 to 12 on the Beaufort scale, being photographs taken from the bridges of ships at sea. (Crown Copyright, by permission; photos by A. B. Neish, R. R. Baxter, J. Hodkinson.)

development of separate scales (codes) for recording sea and swell. The Douglas scales, shown in Table 1, are an important example of various scales which mariners of different nations tended to evolve for logging sea and swell. They were devised in 1921 by Captain (later Admiral) H. P.

TABLE 2. BEAUFORT SCALE WITH CORRESPONDING SEA STATE CODES[a] [b]

Beaufort No.	Wind Speed				Seaman's Term	U.S. Weather Bureau Term	Effects Observed at Sea	Effects Observed on Land	Douglas Sea Scale	
	(knots)	(mph)	(m/sec)	(km/hr)					Term and Height of Waves (ft)	Code
0	Under 1	Under 1	0.0-0.2	Under 1	Calm		Sea like mirror	Calm; smoke rises vertically	Calm, 0	0
1	1-3	1-3	0.3-1.5	1-5	Light air	Light	Ripples with appearance of scales; no foam crests	Smoke drift indicates wind direction; vanes do not move	Smooth, less than 1	1
2	4-6	4-7	1.6-3.3	6-11	Light breeze		Small wavelets; crests of glassy appearance, not breaking	Wind felt on face; leaves rustle; vanes begin to move	Slight, 1-3	2
3	7-10	8-12	3.4-5.4	12-19	Gentle breeze	Gentle	Large wavelets; crests begin to break; scattered whitecaps	Leaves, small twigs in constant motion; light flags extended	Moderate, 3-5	3
4	11-16	13-18	5.5-7.9	20-28	Moderate breeze	Moderate	Small waves, becoming longer; numerous whitecaps	Dust, leaves, and loose paper raised up; small branches move		
5	17-21	19-24	8.0-10.7	29-38	Fresh breeze	Fresh	Moderate waves, taking longer form; many whitecaps; some spray	Small trees in leaf begin to sway	Rough, 5-8	4
6	22-27	25-31	10.8-13.8	39-49	Strong breeze	Strong	Larger waves forming; whitecaps everywhere; more spray	Larger branches of trees in motion; whistling heard in wires		
7	28-33	32-38	13.9-17.1	50-61	Moderate gale	Strong	Sea heaps up; white foam from breaking waves begins to be blown in streaks	Whole trees in motion; resistance felt in walking against wind		
8	34-40	39-46	17.2-20.7	62-74	Fresh gale	Gale	Moderately high waves of greater length; edges of crests begin to break into spindrift; foam is blown in well-marked streaks	Twigs and small branches broken off trees; progress generally impeded	Very rough, 8-12	5
9	41-47	47-54	20.8-24.4	75-88	Strong gale	Gale	High waves; sea begins to roll; dense streaks of foam; spray may reduce visibility	Slight structural damage occurs; slate blown from roofs	High, 12-20	6

Force[a]	Wind speed (knots)	Wind speed (knots)	Wind speed (mph)	Wind speed (m/s)	Description	Sea criteria	Sea state	Sea state description	Effects observed on land
10	48–55	55–63	89–102	24.5–28.4	Whole gale	Very high waves with overhanging crests; sea takes white appearance as foam is blown in very dense streaks; rolling is heavy and visibility reduced	7	Very high, 20–40	Seldom experienced on land; trees broken or uprooted; considerable structural damage occurs
11	56–63	64–72	103–117	28.5–32.6	Storm	Exceptionally high waves; sea covered with white foam patches; visibility still more reduced	8	Mountainous, 40 and higher	
12	64–71	73–82	118–133	32.7–36.9		Air filled with foam: sea completely white with driving spray; visibility greatly reduced	9	Confused	Very rarely experienced on land; usually accompanied by widespread damage
13	72–80	83–92	134–149	37.0–41.4					
14	81–89	93–103	150–166	41.5–46.1	Hurricane				
15	90–99	104–114	167–183	46.2–50.9	Hurricane				
16	100–108	115–125	184–201	51.0–56.0					
17	109–118	126–136	202–220	56.1–61.2					

[a] Since January 1, 1955, weather map symbols have been based upon wind speed in knots, at 5-knot intervals, rather than upon Beaufort number.

[b] From U.S. Navy Hydrographic Office (1958).

Douglas of the Royal Navy in analogy with the Beaufort wind force scale* and were recommended for international use at the 1929 International Meteorological Conference in Copenhagen. From day-to-day reporting of sea waves, no doubt often neglecting the observation of swell that is easily obscured when low, it would be natural for an expression such as "Sea State 5" (a very rough sea) to gain precedence among seamen, much as they might use "Beaufort 7" winds to denote a moderate gale.

Since sea waves are intimately related to the wind generating them, estimates of wind force, which are difficult to make aboard a moving ship, were generally inferred from the appearance of the sea surface. General acceptance of this practice was formally recognized at the 1939 International Meteorological Conference in Berlin when the Petersen scale,** containing specifications for the visible effects of wind force on the sea corresponding to Beaufort wind forces, was provisionally adopted. These criteria, easily aligned to the Douglas code, were a means of relating the Beaufort and Douglas scales (see Table 2).

Final refinement of the Douglas scales was achieved when sufficient observational data had been accumulated to append sea and swell height ranges to the various categories and, ultimately, photographic examples of sea states (Fig. 1). By then, however, the International Meteorological Organization (now the World Meteorological Organization) at its 1947 Washington conference adopted a single ocean wave code for observing and recording waves only. Provision for reporting more than one wave train or system is now made only if a second system differs significantly in period (time between wave crests) or direction. A "state of sea" code is retained only to be included in a marine forecast (MAFOR) issued to shipping.

Observations of sea and swell (or waves) from ship weather reports generate, when collected in repositories such as the National Weather Records Center in Asheville, North Carolina, historical (statistical) data that have many uses for the military, scientific, industrial, and shipping communities. Climatologists and oceanographers are particularly concerned with these data and have designed analyses and presentations that frequently serve the interests of the other communities.

Atlas-type presentations, for example, may give the percentage frequency of occurrence of specified sea or swell heights in the oceans of the world. Figures 2(a) and 2(b), showing isoline analyses of seas ≥ 20 feet in February and August, were were prepared at the U.S. Naval Oceanographic

* This scale was also designed by an Englishman, Admiral Sir Francis Beaufort, in 1805.
** Captain Petersen, a German sailing ship master, devised this scale.

Office. Maximum frequencies of "very high" seas (sea state 7 and greater) occur in the stormiest parts of the oceans (middle latitudes) in winter, where traveling atmospheric depressions tend to converge, stagnate, and deepen (barometric pressure decreasing). Examples of such areas are the "Icelandic" and "Aleutian lows," in the vicinities of their namesakes, that meteorologists call quasi-stationary low-pressure centers. Such very high seas, although more frequent in the middle-latitude "westerlies," can occur almost anywhere in the oceans. Low-latitude storms, called "hurricanes" in the North Atlantic, generate extremely high seas at infrequent intervals, generally in western portions of oceans.

JOHN J. SCHULE, JR.

References

Brooke Smith, L. A., Capt., R.N.R., 1936, "The observation of wind force at sea," Great Britain, Meteorological Office, *The Marine Observer*, **13**, No. 122, 54.

Great Britain, Meteorological Office, 1936, 1963, "The Marine Observer's Handbook," Sixth and Eighth eds., London, H.M. Stationery Office.

Parkhurst, P. G., 1955, "Ocean meteorology, a century of scientific progress, Part I," Great Britain, Meteorological Office, *The Marine Observer*, **25**, No. 167, 16–21, H.M. Stationery Office, London.

U.S. Navy Hydrographic Office, 1958, "American Practical Navigator," *H.O. Publ. No.* 9, Revised ed., Government Printing Office, Washington, D.C.

U.S. Navy Hydrographic Office, 1960, "Glossary of Oceanographic Terms," SP-35, First ed., Washington, D.C.

World Meteorological Organization, 1961, "Guide to Meteorological Instrument and Observing Practices" (WMO-No. 8. TP 3), Second ed., Secretariat of the World Meteorological Organization, Geneva, Switzerland.

World Meteorological Organization, 1964, "Weather Reports" (WMO-No. 9, TP. 4), Vol. B, "Codes," ed. 1954, revised 1963, Secretariat of the World Meteorological Organization, Geneva, Switzerland.

Cross-reference: *Ocean Waves.*

SEAWATER: CHEMISTRY

Seawater is a remarkable homogeneous substance consisting of about 96.5% water, 3.5% salt, small amounts of particulate matter, dissolved gases, and organic compounds. Some 98% of the hydrosphere is seawater. The dissolved salts, or salinity of surface water ranges between 33.99‰ at 50°S to 35.79‰ at 25°N. The average salinity for all ocean water is about 35‰. High salinities (up to 55‰) are observed in subtropical oceans and their landlocked extensions (e.g., Red Sea), while low salinities are found where seawater is diluted by continental rivers and melting ice. In Polar seas, the freezing of flow ice or freezing beneath ice shelves may lead to quite a strong brine in places. In some smaller landlocked embayments (i.e., Laguna Madre in the Gulf of Mexico), salinities as high as 130‰ have been observed.

It was not until the Scottish chemist Professor William Dittmar aboard the British ship H.M.S. *Challenger* in 1872–1876 made a detailed analysis of the now famous "seventy samples" taken from most of the world's oceans that the true composition of the major ionic components of seawater was established. Not only did the results of these analyses fix the concentration of the major ionic components, but they demonstrated conclusively that within narrow limits, the ratios of these components are the same for all oceanic waters. Hence, seawater can be physically described by only three parameters: temperature, pressure and a single number which will establish the concentrations of all the major components.

Considerable difficulty was encountered in obtaining a single number interpretable as the total salt composition, largely due to analytical difficulties, which led an International Commission composed of three Scandinavian oceanographers, Forch, Knudsen and Sorensen, in 1902 to standardize on a technique yielding reproducible results which does not represent the true quantity of total solids but does represent a quantity slightly less, that is closely related, and by definition is called salinity of the water. *Salinity is defined as the total amount of solid material in grams contained in 1 kg of seawater when all the carbonate has been converted to oxide, the bromine and iodine replaced by chlorine, and all organic matter completely oxidized.* Using this definition, the concept of constancy of composition and the fact that accurate analysis of chloride can reflect the quantities of the other elements led the International Commission to establish the empirical relation:

$$\text{Salinity} = 0.03 + 1.805 \times \text{Chlorinity}$$

to evaluate salinity. The chlorinity in this equation, also a defined term, is the number in grams per kilogram of a seawater sample which is identical with the number giving the mass in grams of "atomic weight silver" just necessary to precipitate the halogens in 0.3285233 kg of the seawater sample. Chlorinity is usually determined by titration with silver nitrate using a colorimetric or potentiometric end point.

To provide a primary standard for determination of salinity usable by all laboratories, the so-called Normal Water prepared by the Hydrographical Laboratories in Copenhagen, Denmark is used. Such water has been found to have a chlorinity of 19.381‰ according to the above definition. This water or a substandard referred to it is also used in standardizing physical measurements used in determining salinity.

In recent years most analyses for total salt content have been made by instrumental methods in which a property of ionic solutions such as their conductivity or refractive index is assessed. Data obtained by the conductivity methods give both greater sensitivity and accuracy ($\pm 0.005\%$ against $\pm 0.02\%$ for titration) than the older volumetric procedures and allow for strong arguments for eliminating the salinity concept in favor of a physically defined parameter. However, equally strong arguments have prevailed to convert the instrumental values to salinity in order to make easy comparison between new and old oceanographic data possible.

The constancy of composition concept used in estimating the major salt components present in seawater does not apply to a large number of the elements, the dissolved gases, organic compounds, and particulate matter present in trace quantities not greatly affecting the physical properties of the water but yet having great biological and geochemical importance. Because of the variability of these components in ocean water and the difficult chemistries involved, most of the effort in marine chemistry has recently focused in these areas. Understanding is yet incomplete concerning many problems, yet discussion will be made in light of the knowledge now available.

Composition of Seawater

Major Components. Eight ions and largely undissociated boric acid contribute 99.95% of the total salt found in seawater. Values for these components are presented in Table 1.

Values for H_3BO_3 are probably the least reliable of those presented. Boric acid does not show a constant ratio to chlorinity with depth since variable amounts (0–10%) are found complexed to organic matter. Inorganic B/Cl ratios are, however, constant except at the oxygen minimum zone where the complexed boron reaches minimum values.

Changes in the ion ratios and thereby an error in salinity measurements may be brought about by land drainage, variation in nutrients and organic matter, changes in alkalinity and pH and sedimentation processes. Careful studies have indicated that a salinity effect of only 0.023‰ occurs in the extremes between water mass differences in the Pacific Ocean. Statistical evaluation of available data show the probability of a single salinity value falling within $\pm 0.024\%$ is 0.99; ± 0.017 is 0.95; and ± 0.015 is 0.90. However, the variability in dissolved gas composition, the isotope variations and the variability in organic content makes a single element-to-salinity relation in the ± 0.005 accuracy range impossible.

Minor Components. Into this group fall essentially all the elements in the periodic table other than those listed above. These elements may be

TABLE 1. MAJOR SALT CONSTITUENTS OF SEAWATER*

Component	Concentration (‰)	% of Total Salt
Cl^-	18.980	55.04
Na^+	10.543	30.61
SO_4^{--}	2.465	7.68
Mg^{++}	1.272	3.69
Ca^{++}	0.400	1.16
K^+	0.380	1.10
HCO_3^-**	0.140	0.41
Br^-†	0.065	0.19
H_3BO_3	0.024	0.07
Total	34.455	99.95

* Values in grams per kilogram (‰) based on chlorinity of 19‰.
** Varies to give equivalent CO_3^{--} depending on pH. Value given is essentially true for pH 7.50 at 20°C.
† Corresponds to a salinity of 34.325‰.

TABLE 2. ELEMENTS OF INTERMEDIATE CONCENTRATION IN SEAWATER

Component	Concentration	Probable Species
Sr	8.0	Sr^{++}; $SrSO_4$
O	4.6–7.5 (surface)	O_2 (gas)
Si	3.0	$Si(OH)_4$
F	1.3	F^- and metal complexes
N	0.5	N_2, NH_4^+, NO_2^-, NO_3^- and organic compounds
A	0.5	A (gas)
Li	0.17	Li^+
P	0.07	HPO_4^{--}, $H_2PO_4^-$ and organic compounds
I	0.06	I^-, IO_3^-, organic compounds

arbitrarily subdivided into those of intermediate concentration (1×10^{-4} to $1 \times 10^{-6}M$) and those present in trace or microquantities (less than $1 \times 10^{-6}M$). While the composition of the major ions is considered conservative in seawater, the components included in these groups, particularly the latter, vary widely and in many cases, the quantity may be independent of the salt content. Individual analysis must be made for each species, and under widely varying oceanic environments, to gain an understanding of the distribution and the many factors controlling the observed distribution. Except in a very few cases, information in this area is incomplete and therefore subject to change as more, and perhaps better, data become available.

Intermediate Group. The intermediate group is composed of nine elements, including the three gases N_2, O_2 and argon and the three important nutrients, nitrogen, silicon and phosphorus compounds. The concentrations of this group of

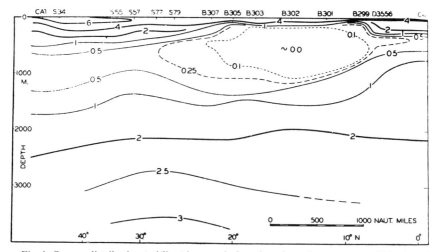

Fig. 1. Oxygen distribution (ml/liter) in a vertical section along the west coast of North and Central America at a distance of a few hundred miles from the coast (mainly based on observations of E. W. Scripps and Bushnell).

elements and their probable contributing species are given in Table 2.

Lithium has no known biological function, is not active geochemically (residence time in the ocean of 2.0×10^7 years) and tends to be conservative in distribution.

Nitrogen is present in multiple forms in the sea. Nitrogen gas, except under anaerobic conditions, is unreactive and shows only minor variations from saturation at *in situ* temperature and atmospheric pressure. The biologically important fixed nitrogen compounds vary widely in concentration with location, depth and season. Nitrate is the end product of the biological cycle and is the predominant form at depths below 150 meters in most seas. Organic nitrogen compounds have been found in all waters so far examined, but nitrite and ammonia are found in maximum concentrations at intermediate depths in middle latitudes during the spring and autumn. Nitrite concentration varies from none in many waters to as much as 50 μg/liter in regions of high biological production. Ammonia is distributed similarly and varies between 0 and 75 μg/liter. These are intermediates in the oxidative cycle of nitrogen, and their distribution and quantity mark the place and intensity of biological degradation. Nitrate concentration in the ocean varies between 1 μg/liter in some surface waters to as much as 600 μg/liter in deep Indian Ocean water.

Oxygen, while present in water and several anions, is most significant to the chemistry of seawater as the dissolved gas. Oxygen enrichment occurs only at the sea surface in exchange with the atmosphere or in the photic zone by photosynthesis. Depletion results primarily from biological activity, including the degradation of organic debris. In the photic zone, the oxygen content may increase above that found at the surface and has been found to reach values of 130% of saturation at *in situ* temperature and atmospheric pressure. At depths down to the compensation point (point at which respiration exceeds photosynthesis), oxygen production exceeds utilization but below this depth, a loss of oxygen is realized. The production of oxygen in the ocean ranges between 0.82×10^3 ml/m^2/yr in Helsingör Sound to 1.86×10^6 ml/m^2/yr in Long Island Sound with open ocean values being intermediate. Consumption of oxygen in the Atlantic has been found to be 0.21 ml/liter/yr near the surface and 1.3×10^{-3} ml/liter/yr at 2500 meters. The oxygen content of the bottom water of the eastern Atlantic does not fall below 60% saturation at *in situ* temperature and atmospheric pressure with a concentration of 4.9 ml/liter at 50°S increasing gradually to 6.4 ml/liter at 50°N. The western section is of the same general pattern with about 0.2 ml/liter less throughout. In the Pacific, subsurface waters are generally lower in oxygen concentration than the Atlantic. A typical vertical section showing the oxygen concentration along the west coast of North and Central America is shown in Fig. 1 (Sverdrup *et al.*, 1942). Similar distribution is found along the coast of South America to at least 40°S. In these areas an intensely deoxygenated zone extends from about 100–1000 meters deep. Going eastward there is a distinct increase in the oxygen content of the water column, but only at great depths (4000 meters) does the water contain as much as 4 ml/liter.

The widespread occurrence of the oxygen minimum zone at intermediate depths is a very striking characteristic of oxygen distribution. Several theories and much experimental evidence have been presented to explain this unusual feature. There is some support for each of the three most often proposed models: the minima dynamically conditioned by circulatory processes, often referred to as the resting boundary theory; the minima biochemically conditioned and represents the depth at which the specific gravity relationships between seawater and sinking detritus are such that detritus accumulates, resulting in excessive consumption; and the minima circulation conditioned by sinking of a layer of water containing maximal amounts of organic material in high latitudes. The water density is such that it moves at intermediate depths, and oxidation of the organic matter results in a lower oxygen value than the waters above or below.

Silicon occurs in seawater as the monomeric silicic acid in concentrations between 0.02 and 3 ppm at the surface to 5–10 ppm in deep water. This is well below saturation equilibrium with any of the silica bearing minerals, including quartz (7–14 ppm). Since rivers are continually adding water with silica concentrations many times these values (30–35 ppm), a very effective, but yet unknown, removal process must be functional. The silica cycle in the sea is not well understood. Diatoms and other silica-secreting organisms form opaline tests that are very resistant to solution as attested by the abundance of frustules found in the sediment, yet convincing evidence has been presented showing a rapid regeneration of silica in surface waters during high organic production. It is apparent that a portion of the tests are decomposed at the surface by the action of bacteria and digestive enzymes of plankton-feeding animals. Fluctuation of silica concentration in surface waters usually exceeds that of nitrate and phosphate, probably because regeneration depends on the activity of grazers whose population is known to be patchy.

Phosphorus in seawater having a normal pH of between 7.8 and 8.2 is present largely as a mixture of the monobasic and dibasic ions $H_2PO_4^-$ and HPO_4^{--}. In surface waters, a large portion of the total may be present as unregenerated organic phosphorus (0.0–15 μg/liter dissolved and 0–35 μg/liter particulate), and lipids containing organic phosphorus have been found in deep water of the Gulf of Mexico, Antarctic and Pacific Oceans. While other factors appear to exist, the phytoplankton productivity in the oceans is most often limited by compounds of phosphorus, nitrogen, and silicon. Large regions of the surface water of the oceans become almost completely exhausted of these nutrients. The phosphorus concentration increases with depth and generally shows a maximum in the oxygen minimum zone. The phosphorus content of the Indian and Pacific Ocean deep water (60–110 μg/liter) is about twice as high

as that found in the Atlantic (35–45 μg/liter). The differences in the two oceans are related to the nature of the deep water circulation. Phosphorites ($Ca_{10}(PO_4, CO_3)_6F_{2-3}$) occur in extensive deposits in water 100–1000 feet deep along the California coast, which is thought to occur from supersaturation of calcium phosphate under low pH and oxygen tension conditions. More detailed discussion of the nutrient elements may be found in *Nutrients of the Sea.*

Argon, the most abundant of the inert gases, is found nearly saturated in seawater at *in situ* temperatures and atmospheric pressure. Small fluctuations that do occur are thought to be caused by barometric pressure differences at the surface and slight production from K^{40} decay and temperature changes in the water after sinking to the ocean depths. It is useful to use the ratio of this gas to other gases in valuating their stability in the ocean. Such studies with N_2 show a ratio of N_2/A of 37–39 to persist, indicating the conservative nature of N_2 gas.

Strontium may be considered a conservative element but has received much recent attention because of the Sr^{90} pollution problem resulting from nuclear fission reactions. Because of the high concentration factor of strontium in the bones of many animals over that in seawater (50), the long half-life (28 years) and the energy of the beta emission (1.46 MeV), this element is considered one of the most critical as an index of radioactive contamination. The ratio of Ca/Sr in the shells of organisms is proportional to the concentration in the water in which the organisms grew. The atomic size of the strontium ion (1.27Å) is such that strontium is usually found in the crystal lattice of deposited aragonite but not in calcite.

Iodine, based on thermodynamic considerations, should be present in seawater as the IO_3^- ion; however, I^- is the predominant species. This anomaly may be caused by plant and animal utilization of iodine in the reduced forms in compounds such as thyroxine and iodotyrosine and thus inhibit the thermodynamic equilibrium.

Micro-components. Although the importance of the micro-components to the biogeochemistry of seawater has long been established, the concentration and chemical forms of these components are often in doubt. The concentration of many elements has been based on a single analysis, and where more analyses have been made, results may vary by several orders of magnitude. Most of the problem arises from the difficulty of analysis in the less than $10^{-6}M$ region, both because the analytical methods are usually at the lower limit of detectability and random contamination is difficult to control. Improvement in analytical techniques by innovation of X-ray fluorimetry, activation analysis, flame and atomic absorption spectrophotometry, improved polarography and new methods

TABLE 3. COMPONENTS OF MICRO-CONCENTRATION IN SEAWATER (FROM GOLDBERG, 1963 AND HOOD, 1963)

Component	Concentration (μ/liter)	Probable Species
	(π/liter)	
He	0.005	He (gas)
Be	0.0005	
C	560 (g); 200–3000[3]	CO_2 (gas),* diss. organic compounds†
Ne	0.1	Ne (gas)
Al	1.0–10.0	
Sc	0.04	
Ti	0.02	
V	2.0	$VO_2(OH)_3^{--}$
Cr	0.13–0.25	
Mn	0.1–8.0	Mn^{++}, $MnSO_4$**
Fe	1.7–150	$Fe_2O_3 \cdot 3H_2O$**
Co	0.2–0.7	CO^{++}, $CoSO_4$
Ni	2.0	Ni^{++}, $NiSO_4$
Cu	0.5–3.5	Cu^{++}, $CuSO_4$**
Zn	1.5–10.0	Zn^{++}, $ZnSO_4$**
Ga	0.007–0.03	
Ge	0.07	$Ge(OH)_4$; $Ge(OH)_3O^-$
As	3.0	$HAsO^{--}$; $H_2AsO_4^-$; AsO_4^{---}; H_3AsO_3
Se	4.0–6.0	SeO_4^{--}
Kr	0.3	Kr (gas)
Rb	120	Rb^+
Y	0.3	
Nb	0.01–0.02	
Mo	4.0–12.0	MoO_4^{--}
Ag	0.145	$AgCl_2^-$; $AgCl_3^{--}$
Cd	0.11	Cd^{++}
Sn	0.3	
Sb	0.5	
Xe	0.1	Xe (gas)
Cs	0.5	Cs^+
Ba	10–63	Ba^{++}; $BaSO_4$
La	0.3	
Ce	0.4	
W	0.12	WO_4^{--}
Au	0.015–0.4	$AuCl_4^{--}$
Hg	0.15–0.27	$HgCl_3^-$; $HgCl_4^{--}$
Pb	0.6–1.5	Pb^{++}; $PbSO_4$
Bi	0.02	
Rn	$0.6 (10^{-12})$	Rn (gas)
Ra	$1.0 (10^{-7})$	Ra^{++}; $RaSO_4$
Th	0.05	
Pa	$2.0 (10^{-6})$	
U	3.0	$UO_2(CO_3)^{----}$

* In presence of other CO_2 compounds.
** Evidence exists for organic complexed metal.
† Consisting of several hundred organic compounds.

in colorimetric analysis and better sampling and laboratory conditions have much improved the situation in recent years.

The concentrations and probable contributing species of the micro-components that have been determined in seawater are presented in Table 3.

Aluminium data in the literature give values ranging between 1 μg to 1 mg/liter. Recent data for deep stations in the Pacific Ocean, Weddell Sea and in nearshore water along the California coast gave dissolved aluminum values of between 1 and 2 μg/liter. Particulate aluminum was variable, the concentration depending on location and depth, but values of over 3 μg/liter were not found except in nearshore water where higher values reflect land drainage.

Manganese occurs in seawater largely as the divalent ion, part of which appears to be complexed with organic matter. Particulate manganese is not found except in surface waters, and no evi-

TABLE 4. DISTRIBUTION WITH DEPTH OF COPPER AND ZINC IN THE
GULF OF MEXICO (95° 53'W; 24° 27'N)

Depth (m)	Extractable* (μg/liter)		Non-dialyzable** (μg/liter)		Particulate† (μg/liter)		Total (μg/liter)	
	Cu	Zn	Cu	Zn	Cu	Zn	Cu	Zn
10	2.3	8.8	0.5	2.1	0.8	1.3	3.5	10.5
310	0.5	2.7	0.1	1.1	0.2	0.7	1.6	3.5
900	1.9	7.3	0.9	5.3	0.1	0.6	2.8	9.7
1200	0.5	4.7	0.2	4.1	0.6	2.3	1.4	5.0
2250	0.3	3.5	0.1	1.1	0.4	1.2	0.3	3.6
3400	0.3	3.5	0.1	1.1	0.1	0.5	0.6	1.6

* That fraction forming a solvent-soluble chelate with diethyldithiocarbamate, probably divalent.
** Fraction passing through 0.45μ millipore filter but not passing through cellulose acetate dialysis membrane (2 mμ average pore size).
† Material not passing through 0.45μ millipore filter.

dence for the colloidal MnO_2 has been found in the water column, yet it occurs widely in ferro-manganese minerals of the pelagic sediments. Whether chemical or biological oxidative processes are primarily responsible for this oxidation is still open to question.

Iron is present in seawater in the oxidized state in multiple physical forms. Very little is present in true solution because of the instability of the ferrous ion and the insolubility of the ferric hydroxides, yet stable colloids of hydrated ferric oxide occur at all depths of the ocean. The active surfaces of this colloid undoubtedly play an important role in geochemical and sedimentary processes of other microelements. The wide range of concentrations observed may partly result from the random distribution of the floccular iron colloids.

Copper and zinc have been investigated in seawater by many different analysts and analytical techniques. A wide disparity in values has resulted, but more recent work considering various physical and chemical states of the elements has provided more consistent data. Table 4 shows data for these elements for a typical station in the Gulf of Mexico. Similar distribution, but generally lower concentrations were found in the Antarctic and South Pacific Oceans. At intermediate depths, 20–80% of these elements is held in the non-dialyzable fraction with lesser amounts in the shallower and deeper waters. The significance of this apparently organic complexed portion to the chemistry of the sea has not yet been determined.

Barium is present in surface waters in the range of 10 μg/liter and steadily increases to as much as 65 μg/liter in deep ocean water. Barite is found in ocean sediments and deep seawater may be in a state of supersaturation with respect to barium sulfate.

Radium shows a similar distribution to that of barium, but the concentration of Ra^{226}, which has a radiogenic origin, is about sixfold greater than can be supported by its parent Th^{230}. It is apparent that radium diffuses into the seawater subsequent to its origin from ionium in the sediments. This, coupled with biological incorporation at the surface and subsequent release at depth during decomposition processes, may explain the radium distribution found.

Other trace elements do not lend themselves to detailed considerations, especially vertical, since in most cases relatively few samples, largely from the surface, have been analyzed.

Organic Constituents. Our knowledge of the kinds, distribution and significance of organic compounds in seawater is currently in a rapid stage of development. Organic matter in seawater is divided into particulate and dissolved on the basis of filtering through 0.45μ millipore filters with the soluble portion passing through the paper and the particulate remaining on the filter.

The quantity of dissolved organic carbon exceeds that of particulate organic carbon by a factor of 7–8 in waters rich in phytoplankton and in deep water by a factor of 1000. The amount of total organic carbon in the open ocean varies generally from 0.2–2.7 mg/liter. Higher values are found in landlocked areas; 3.3 mg/liter of carbon in the Black Sea, 4.6 in the Baltic, 6.0 in the Sea of Azov, and 8.0 in the landlocked coastal area of the Dutch Wadden Sea. Organic solute distribution is not homogeneous either horizontally or vertically, but there is a minimum of organic carbon in the oxygen minimum zone. The highest organic carbon concentrations are in waters of high phytoplankton productivity or recent productivity. Further details of the kind, amount and distribution of specific organic compounds, as presently understood are given in *Organic Geochemistry of Seawater* in this encyclopedia series.

TABLE 5. VERTICAL DISTRIBUTION OF CO_2 COMPONENTS AT A SOUTH PACIFIC STATION ($21°$ $75'S$; $72°$ $44'W$)

Depth (m)	Cl (‰)	Temperature (°C)	pH	Alkalinity (eq./liter $\times 10^{-3}$)	pCO_2 ($A \times 10^{-4}$)	HCO_3^- (Moles/liter $\times 10^{-3}$)	CO_3^{--} (Moles/liter $\times 10^{-4}$)
0	19.33	17.66	8.21	2.36	2.79	1.74	2.64
31	19.30	17.47	8.21	2.36	2.82	1.74	2.61
88	19.12	12.56	7.76	2.34	9.05	2.11	0.99
176	19.22	11.63	7.60	2.35	13.63	2.19	0.69
356	19.19	9.27	7.57	2.35	14.00	2.20	0.62
632	19.08	5.92	7.71	2.34	9.54	2.16	0.75
1562	19.15	2.78	7.70	2.39	9.74	2.23	0.68
4535	19.20	1.73	7.36	2.37	21.91	2.30	0.30

Physical Chemistry of Seawater

Thermodynamics. Most of the dissolved constituents of seawater have had many thousands of years to reach equilibrium, yet thermodynamically unstable species apparently persist. Can this be attributed to lack of reaction sites, as is often suggested, or lack of knowledge concerning the complex interaction between these apparently unstable components and other components of seawater? While many efforts have been made to approach the problem theoretically, little can be gained by such an exercise until an exact knowledge of contributing forms is known. In the case of trace components in the concentration range less than 10^{-7} or $10^{-8} M$, quite enough organic material exists in seawater to form compounds requiring different thermodynamic consideration than for the inorganic ions alone. Our knowledge of the organic components is yet too limited to make this a worthwhile consideration. Except for the major ions, members of the carbon dioxide system, and perhaps some others, few experimental data exist that permit computation of the activity coefficients or reaction equilibrium constants for the components present. For the major ions, the problem is more easily approached.

By extension of the Lewis and Randall concept of activities of ions in dilute solution to seawater (ionic strength 0.7), remarkably good agreement between calculated and measured values has resulted. Using this and other methods for activity coefficient measurements, Garrels and Thompson (1963) have produced activity data for the free ions of the major components of seawater. These are: $A_{Na^+} = 0.356$; $A_{Mg^{++}} = 0.0169$; $A_{Ca^{++}} = 0.00264$; $A_{K^+} = 0.0063$; $A_{SO_4^-} = 1.79$ (10^{-3}); $A_{HCO_3^-} = 9.74$ (10^{-4}); $A_{CO_3^-} = 4.7$ (10^{-6}). From this work the picture that emerges is that the major cations exist chiefly as uncomplexed species. Calcium and magnesium are only 10–15% complexed, and magnesium is the most active in complexing anions. The anions, except for chloride, are strongly paired with cations (most of carbonate, one-third of bicarbonate and nearly half of sulfate).

Solubility relations, closely allied with the above, are uncertain in seawater. It is, however, clear that the concentrations of the tabulated metal ions, including the alkaline earths, cannot be controlled by the solubility equilibria but by other more complicated processes.

pH. The pH is affected in seawater by temperature and salinity changes, photosynthesis and respiration, deposition of ions of the buffer system, mainly carbonate, and gaseous exchange with the atmosphere. The pH observed is usually between 7.8 and 8.3 in surface waters (being highest in the subtropica), the range depending on the combined effect of the above, but it is usually controlled to these limits by the natural buffer systems present. However, in estuaries, values as high as 9.0 have been observed at times of high photosynthesis. pH measurements may be used as a powerful tool in the interpretation of the above processes, but because of the buffer action of the carbonic (2.4 $\times$ $10^{-3} M$) and boric (4.3 $\times 10^{-4} M$) acid systems, small differences in pH must be accurately detected if this parameter is to be used to its fullest potential. Devices are now available to detect voltage changes between a glass and calomel electrode to give a sensitivity to 0.0025 pH unit. In practice, however, better than ± 0.02 pH unit is seldom achieved. The difficulty usually arises from poor sampling and electrode effects, largely caused by use of freshwater buffer systems for calibrating the instruments for seawater measurements. Recent work has been done to help resolve both these problems.

Harvey (1957) has summarized the many measurements made of the pH values of seawater. The distribution of pH with depth at a South Pacific station is shown in Table 5 and Fig. 2. In middle and lower latitudes, as in this station, the pH of surface waters down to the thermocline is uniformly higher than in deeper water. It then undergoes a sharp decrease in the decomposition zone and rises slowly to values of 7.2–7.9 in the bottom water. The variation of pH in deep water suggests the use of this parameter in water mass studies.

Oxidation Potential. Oxidation potential in the ocean is controlled by the oxygen half-cell reaction, and deviation from 0.43 volt occurs only in anaerobic conditions in some static basins, severe

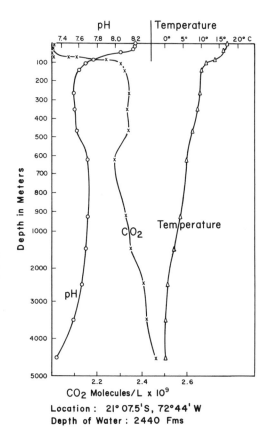

Fig. 2. The distribution of pH and temperature with depth. Measured in South Pacific.

oxygen-depleted intermediate depths, and at or below the sediment interface.

Carbon Dioxide System. Understanding the complex dynamic relationships of carbon dioxide in the air, sea and sediments is probably the most difficult problem in marine chemistry. Many of the difficulties arise from the nonequilibrium status of many of the reactions in the system and of incomplete information on many of the others.

Studies on the rate of exchange between the air and the sea have shown that equilibrium is seldom reached. In general, most of the ocean surface contains a lower concentration of gaseous carbon dioxide than the overlying atmosphere. Exceptions to this occur under conditions of local cooling and in regions of upwelling. The causes of this non-equilibrium are not clear, but it appears to be closely associated with the reaction between gaseous carbon dioxide and water: $H_2O + CO_2 \rightarrow H_2CO_3$. Only recently the forward reaction rates for this reaction were measured in seawater and found to be 3.3×10^{-2}/sec. The ionic components of the system may be calculated by use of equations summarized by Harvey (1957). Based on these

calculations, data obtained from a representative station in the South Pacific (Table 5) show that the pCO_2 concentration increases rapidly below the thermocline, and the carbonate ion concentration goes through a corresponding decrease. The alkalinity remains essentially constant with depth, showing small deviations from chlorinity. Details of this relation are discussed more fully in *Alkalinity of Seawater*.

The solubility relations of $CaCO_3$ in seawater point to the surface waters of the ocean being almost universally supersaturated with respect to all the crystal forms of calcium carbonate. Yet only in limited local areas (e.g., Bahama Banks) is evidence for chemical precipitation existent. Deeper waters are in some cases undersaturated, and in these, tests of calcareous organisms are dissolved while settling toward the bottom leaving a sediment devoid of calcium carbonate. Except in limited areas, the deep waters also are nearly saturated. Supersaturation appears to exist because of the slow rate of formation of carbonate crystals in regions of relatively high dissolved organic content and where crystal sites are lacking.

The system is heavily influenced by biological factors which impose relatively short-term stresses (often diurnal) that are reflected in a nonequilibrium status for many of the components under wide environmental situations.

Donald W. Hood

References

Garrels, R. M., and Thompson, M. E., 1962, *Am. J. Sci.,* **260**, 57–66.

Goldberg, E. D., 1963, in (Hill, W. N., editor) "The Seas," Vol. 2, New York, Interscience Publishers, 554pp.

Harvey, H. W., 1957, "Chemistry and Fertility of Sea Waters," Cambridge, Cambridge University Press, 243pp.

Hood, D. W., 1963, "Chemical Oceanography," *Oceanogr. Marine Biol. Ann. Rev.,* **1**, 129–155.

Revelle, R., and Fairbridge, R., 1957, in (Hedgpeth, J. W., editor) "Treatise on Marine Ecology and Paleocology," Vol. 1, *Geol. Soc. Am. Mem.,* **67**, 1296pp.

Sverdrup, H. V., Johnson, M. V., and Fleming, R. H., 1946, "The Oceans," New York, Prentice-Hall, Inc., 10–77.

SEAWATER: ITS HISTORY

The chemical composition of seawater was first studied on a world wide base by the *Challenger* expedition of 1877. Since that time, no systematic changes have been observed. Speculation about the history of seawater must, therefore, be based entirely on clues derived from the geologic record combined with calculations of the relevant chemical equilibria. Since Late Precambrian time (approximately 600 million years), the chemical composition

TABLE 1. EXCESS VOLATILE CONTENTS IN UNITS OF 10^{20} g (FROM WEDEPOHL, 1963)

Volatile	Igneous Rocks, i	Sediments, s	Oceans, o	Atmosphere, a	Excess, $e = s + o + a - i$	Excess (%) $\dfrac{i}{s + o + a} \times 100$
H_2O	62	260	14,000	0.06	14,200	0.42
C (includes CO_2)	3.3	620	1.5	0.023	618	1.9
Cl	1.7	38	280	—	316	0.6
S	3.4	45	14	—	56	5.8
N	0.2	5.2	0.3	38.6	44	0.5
B	0.1	1.4	0.1	—	1.4	6.6

of seawater is at least in part recorded in the extensive sequences of chemical and biochemical sediments of the stratigraphic column, and limits can be set for the possible variations of a number of important constituents. Sedimentary records of the seas of earlier times are more difficult to interpret.

Post-Precambrian History

Salt deposits and limestones are the sediments which most directly reflect the composition of the seawater from which they were deposited. Salt deposits are known from every period of the geologic column ever since Cambrian times. No systematic differences in mineralogy and chemistry between deposits of different ages seem to exist, indicating that the relative abundance of cations and anions in seawater must have remained fairly constant. Furthermore, since Late Precambrian time, the ratio of marine limestones to all other marine sediments deposited during a particular time interval has remained nearly constant. Rubey (1951) has discussed CO_2 equilibria in seawater and the effects of changes in P_{CO_2}. Because of the precipitation of $CaCO_3$, P_{CO_2} of seawater is well buffered with respect to large additions of CO_2. This buffering capacity must have existed ever since limestones have been deposited. Loss of CO_2 from seawater would lead to high pH values which cannot be tolerated by most forms of life. For these reasons it is likely that P_{CO_2} of the atmosphere-ocean system has not changed very greatly since Late Precambrian time.

However, if the addition of CO_2 to the oceans through weathering processes is compared with the loss caused by the biochemical and chemical precipitation of carbonates, a deficit exists which has been estimated by Rubey (1951) to be as large as 10^{14} grams of CO_2 per year. This deficit can be balanced only by assuming a slow and continuous degassing of the earth's interior.

A number of other volatile constituents require the existence of the same source to balance similar deficits. All such volatiles are called "excess" volatiles. Some, like argon (see Damon and Kulp,

1958), probably were degassed rapidly at an early stage of the earth's history, while others, like H_2O, were retained in melts and solids and might have appeared at the earth's surface more gradually.

Excess Volatiles

The amounts of excess volatiles present in the hydrosphere and atmosphere have been calculated by a number of workers, using the geochemical balance approach suggested by V. M. Goldschmidt. Goldschmidt assumed that the early crust consisted of igneous rocks similar in composition to igneous rocks exposed today. Erosion of a certain amount of this crust yielded the sediments and the solutes in the oceans. Balances are usually established on the basis of sodium and potassium. Barth (1960) has criticized this approach, because it does not take into account the recycling of elements (erosion of older sediments) and the storage in interstitial brines. Nevertheless, useful comparisons can be obtained in this way. Wedepohl (1963) has assembled recent values for the six most important volatiles (Table 1). For each of these volatiles, weathering of igneous rocks accounts for less than 10%, and in some cases less than 1%, of the amount present in sediments, hydrosphere and atmosphere. Degassing of the earth's core and mantle is assumed to be the source for the remaining amounts. Channels for this degassing can be volcanic exhalations or hot springs. Comparisons of the composition of the "excess" volatiles with that of volcanic gases are not meaningful, because such gases are largely contaminated with surface materials and the "excess" volatiles themselves during their passage through the crust. Isotopic analyses have shown that primary H_2O formed by degassing of the mantle constitutes certainly less than, and probably much less than, 5% of the H_2O of volcanic gases and hot springs.

Early History of the Atmosphere and Hydrosphere

Much less specific information is available with respect to the early history of seawater (Early Precambrian). The early hydrosphere may have formed in part by condensation from the early atmosphere, and speculations about the early history of seawater, therefore, center around the history of the early atmosphere. Urey compared terrestrial with cosmic abundances and came to the conclusion that on the earth H, O, N, C and S are enriched greatly over Ne, Ar, Kr and Xe with respect to the universe. He argues that these volatiles could not have been retained by the earth's gravitational field if the earth formed at a high temperature and concludes that the earth must have formed by agglomeration of cosmic dust at low temperature. Radioactive heat subsequently raised the average temperature and made the separation of core, mantle and crust possible. The early atmosphere was probably very reducing and consisted either predominantly of CH_4, H_2 and NH_3 or of H_2, H_2O and CO (Holland, 1962). This assumption is attractive because of the much greater cosmic abundance of hydrogen, because of the CH_4–NH_3 atmosphere of the outer planets (Kuiper, 1952, reference in Holland, 1962) and because a reducing environment is more favorable to the formation of the complex organic molecules necessary for the origin of life. The abundance of the individual gas species in the early atmosphere depends primarily upon the temperature at which this gas mixture was equilibrated with the earth's crust. The presence of metallic iron in the undifferentiated earth makes it likely that some of the carbon was present as graphite. If a gas phase of the system H–C–O is equilibrated with graphite, its composition can be calculated for a given temperature, provided that P_{O_2} is known. For an early crust, two mineral assemblages defining an upper and a lower limit with respect to P_{O_2} can be postulated: fayalite (Fe_2SiO_4) + magnetite (Fe_3O_4) + quartz (SiO_2) for high P_{O_2} and iron + magnetite (Fe_3O_4) below 560°C and iron + wüstite (FeO) above 560°C for the lower P_{O_2} limit. The gas pressure at which equilibration between solids and gas took place also influences the composition (though to a much lesser degree than temperature does). For reasons of reaction kinetics, a pressure of 100 bars has been assumed in the calculations. Such a pressure can exist a few hundred yards below the surface.

Figure 1 shows two sets of curves, one for low P_{O_2} and the other for high P_{O_2}. According to this model, an early cool atmosphere consisted essentially of CH_4 and NH_3. As heating of the earth proceeded, primarily through radioactive decay of K^{40} to Ar^{40}, the composition of gases escaping from deeper levels of the earth, and with it the composition of the atmosphere, changed gradually to CO_2, CO and N_2. This model gives water vapor pressures at 25°C between 10^{-9} atm (low P_{O_2}) and 10^{-4} atm (high P_{O_2}). Therefore, liquid water could not condense during this period (P_{H_2O} at 25°C must be 3×10^{-2} atm).

A second step in the development of the atmosphere was initiated by the photodissociation of H_2O to H_2 and O_2 in the upper atmosphere. Loss of hydrogen by escape from the gravitational field was responsible for a slow, but steady, increase in the P_{O_2} at the earth's surface. Assuming a gas pressure of 1 atm, a temperature of 25°C and graphite still present, P_{O_2} would have to rise only a very small amount above that of a fayalite + magnetite + quartz assemblage (from 10^{-78} to 10^{-73} atm) for P_{H_2O} to reach a value of 3×10^{-2} atm and for liquid water to form.

Early condensates were probably accumulated in a number of isolated, closed basins. Because of the large amount of CO_2 present in the atmosphere at that time, these proto-oceans must have been quite acid. Exposed rocks would weather quickly and a large amount of solutes would be carried into the basins in a short time. Early anions were probably predominantly CO_3^- and HCO_3^- rather than Cl^-. $CaCO_3$ can precipitate from such waters but, because of the high P_{CO_2}, only at high values of Ca^{++}. Some of the oldest limestones have been formed earlier than 2560 million years ago (see Goldich, 1961) and might have precipitated in evaporating basins isolated from such oceans.

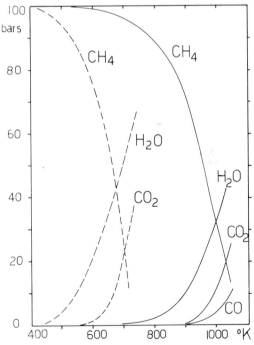

Fig. 1. Temperature (in degrees Kelvin)-pressure (in bars) diagram of a gas phase in the system C-H-O at a total gas pressure of 100 bars. Solid curves are for a gas phase equilibrated with the assemblage iron + magnetite + graphite (below 830°K) or iron + wustite + graphite (above 830°K). Dashed curves are for a gas phase equilibrated with the assemblage fayalite + magnetite + quartz + graphite.

Intense evaporation must have been widespread, and salt deposits must have formed very frequently. Continuing evaporation would probably have yielded dolomite, anhydrite, Mg sulfates and finally nahcolite ($NaHCO_3$), rather than the sequences of younger salt deposits, in which halite (NaCl) is an important constituent. Because of the complex subsequent history, none of these early salt deposits can be expected to have been preserved.

During the period just discussed, P_{O_2} was still too low for hematite to be stable. Holland (1962), from the occurrence of sedimentary uraninite deposits 1800 million years old, has concluded that P_{O_2} of the atmosphere at that time was still very low.

The very gradual increase in P_{O_2} was in part due to the fact that a large amount of the oxygen produced by photodissociation of H_2O was consumed in the oxidation of CH_4, NH_3, graphite and iron or ferrous ions. However, in the time span between 2500 and 1000 million years ago, P_{O_2} must have risen sufficiently for life to begin. As biological activity expanded, CO_2 was consumed and O_2 was produced at a much more rapid rate. Today's production of oxygen by photosynthesis far outstrips that produced by photodissociation.)

Throughout this time, H_2O continued to condense and the proto-oceans merged into oceans. As P_{CO_2} decreased, the pH of seawater rose to near its present level. Saturation with respect to $CaCO_3$ was reached at much lower concentrations of Ca^{++} and large-scale precipitation of limestones was initiated, much of it probably aided by biological processes. From this time on (perhaps 1000 million years ago), a considerable portion of the Precambrian sediments consist of carbonate rocks. Partially as a consequence of this development, chlorine became the dominant anion and seawater had probably reached a composition very near that of today's seawater.

H. P. EUGSTER

References

Barth, T. F. W., 1960, "Abundance of elements, areal averages and geochemical cycles," Geochim. Cosmochin. Acta, 23, 1–8.

Damon, P. E., and Kulp, J. L., 1958, "Inert gases and the evolution of the atmosphere: Geochim. et Cosmochim.," Acta, v. 13, 280–292.

Derpgol'ts, V. F., "The principal planetary source of natural waters," International Geol. Rev., Aug. 1964, v. 6, 1433–1444.

Goldich, S. S., et al., 1961, "The Precambrian geology and geochronology of Minnesota," Minn. Geol. Surv. Bull., 41, 154.

Goldschmidt, V. M., 1938, "Geochemische Verteilungsgesetze der Elemente IX. Die Mengenverhältnisse der Elemente und der Atom-Arten," Skrifter Norske Videnskaps-Akad. Oslo, I, Mat. Natur. Klasse 1937 No. 4, 1–148.

Goldschmidt, V. M., 1954, "Geochemistry," (ed. Alex Muir), Oxford, Clarendon Press, 730pp.

*Holland, H. D., 1962, "Model for the evolution of the earth's atmosphere," Buddington Volume, Geol. Soc. Am., 447–477.

*Rubey, W. W., 1951, "Geologic history of sea water," Bull. Geol. Soc. Am., 62, 1111–1148.

Sillén, L. G., 1963, "How has seawater gotten its present composition?" Svensk Kemisk Tidskrift, 75(4), 161–177.

Urey, H. C., 1952, "The Planets, their origin and development," New Haven, Yale Univ. Press, 245pp.

Weber, J. N., "Chloride ion concentration in liquid inclusions of carbonate rocks as a possible environmental indicator," Journal of Sed. Pet., Sept. 1964, v. 34, 677–680.

Wedepohl, K. H., 1963, "Einige Überlegungen zur Geschichte des Meerwassers," Fortschr. Geol. Rheinland Westfalen, 10, 129–150.

SEDIMENT CORING—UNCONSOLIDATED MATERIALS

The problem of sediment coring is to collect, with as little disturbance as possible, a sample or series of samples that will provide a complete section through a sedimentary deposit. Such samples can be examined chemically, mechanically and microscopically to yield information about the present nature of the sediment and, by inference, about the environment in which it was deposited.

Most sediments suitable for coring were deposited in the ocean, in a lake, or in some kind of swamp or bog. Though they pose different technical problems, all three kinds of sediment are commonly cohesive, consisting of organic matter, silt and clay. It is much easier to take cores successfully from such sediments than it is from incohesive sands and gravels. Although a beginning has been made in the vibratory sampling of incohesive sediments and although some kind of discontinuous core can usually be taken by the standard methods of well drilling, it is not generally possible to raise satisfactory cores from clean sand or other material of very low unconfined shear strength.

Cohesive soils, on the other hand, can be sampled satisfactorily in a number of ways. If the deposit is not overlain by a great depth of water, the sampler may be operated with light drill rods and forced into the sediment by hand. Standard drill rods are unnecessarily heavy, and it is customary to use specially constructed rods with easily detachable joints, or light pipe such as aluminum alloy electrical conduit. The easiest drill rods to use are the Lichtwardt type, with interlocking joints held together by a sliding sleeve and spring pin. They are solid, however, so that neither water nor drilling fluid can be pumped through them, and they are not cheap to manufacture. Standard pipe is hollow and much cheaper, but tedious to couple and may come apart if it is twisted in operation.

One of the oldest and best of the rod-operated

samplers is the Hiller device, a side-intake sampler useful in shallow lakes and without peer for raw bog peat. It consists of a hollow tube closed at both ends, about 4 cm in diameter and half a meter long. A 90° slot is cut into the tube on one side along its entire length, and a larger tube, also with a slot, encloses this tube and is free to rotate through 120° about it. The rotating tube usually has a flange extending the entire length of one side of the slot. To take a sample, the outer sleeve is rotated counterclockwise as far as it will go, which closes the inner slot, and is forced into the sediment with a little counterclockwise rotation to keep the slot closed. When the sampling depth is reached, the sampler is rotated clockwise, which brings the two slots opposite each other and affords a free passage into the chamber. A few additional turns cause the flange to scoop a sample of sediment into the chamber, and the instrument is then closed by counterclockwise rotation and withdrawn.

To assist in penetrating stiff layers in the sediment, the Hiller sampler is usually equipped with a short screw at the lower end. Less often, it is provided with removable aluminum liners which can be used to carry the entire sample back to the laboratory for examination. Otherwise, subsamples are collected in glass vials. The Hiller sample is always so disturbed as to be worthless for strength tests, and there is some risk of contamination from plastic sediment forced into the empty chamber during descent.

Unless the sediment contains large unhumified fragments of plants, a more satisfactory core can be taken with less effort by a piston corer. This is a thin-walled tube, usually about 4 cm in diameter and a meter long. The tube is fitted with a tight piston, which can be fastened at the lower end of the tube until the sampling depth is reached, and then held at that level by a cable while the sample tube is pushed down around it. This arrangement will take samples of one meter in length with very little disturbance in soft organic sediment. In resistant sediments, where the sampler is driven with a suitable hammer, the core must be taken in shorter lengths if serious disturbance is to be avoided. The piston in such a corer removes the combined atmospheric and hydrostatic pressure from the upper surface of the sediment being sampled, and so decreases the resistance to entry of the sediment. An open tube without a piston will take only a short, disturbed core even in soft mud. After a plug of sediment enters the tube it acts like a solid rod; the sampler may be pushed in farther, but it will collect nothing more. This will happen even with a piston sampler if the sediment is so stiff that the total frictional force between the entering sample and the inside of the sample tube exceeds the combined force of atmospheric and hydrostatic pressure on the cross-sectional area of the piston.

Cores taken carefully with a piston sampler have been used for mechanical tests although they are probably always slightly disturbed. For chemical and microfossil analysis they are quite satisfactory, and permit very fine stratigraphic work. If there is annual bedding in the sediment, for example, it will not be damaged by piston sampling, particularly if the samples are carried back to the laboratory in their tubes. The tubes make sturdy and convenient shipping containers, and if they are carefully stoppered the samples will remain moist and reduced in them for years.

A ship-carpenter's auger fitted for attachment to extension rods is a convenient tool for penetrating stiff layers, but it takes a sample that is even more disturbed and subject to contamination than the Hiller sampler. For drilling in permafrost, it is convenient to have a short hollow cutting head, with sharp hardened-steel teeth and spiral flutes on the outside to carry away the chips. Various other hand samplers have been used in the past (some of them, such as the Davis sampler, quite extensively), but they do not have any advantages over the types mentioned here.

Strong winter ice provides a very stable drilling platform on lakes or the ocean. Without it, the operation must be undertaken from a boat, or more conveniently, from a platform supported by two boats. The platform must be anchored carefully with a three-way mooring, using plenty of scope, and a casing pipe should extend from the platform to the mud surface unless the water is very shallow. The casing requires only tensile strength, so it need not be rigid. Standard aluminum alloy pipe works very well, but much lighter tubing is quite adequate.

Rod-sampling methods can be used in principle in any depth of water. They are commonly employed in offshore oil work and are being used in preliminary attempts to drill through the sea floor to the Mohorovicic discontinuity. In practice, rod drilling becomes very expensive as the water depth increases, so that raising a core from an ocean basin by this method is not undertaken lightly by even a large and wealthy nation. For this reason, sediment cores from the ocean and from deep lakes are usually raised with cable-operated corers.

Short cores may be taken with a gravity coring tube which is simply dropped into the bottom and then retrieved by its cable. The tube is weighted for greater penetration and equipped with fins to keep it upright as it falls through the water. Usually there is a check valve at the top of the sample tube and a core retainer at the bottom to prevent loss of the sample as the corer is being hauled up. Such samplers come in many sizes, from the old Naumann Rohrlot (conveniently used by hand from a skiff) to the Phleger corer, which is standard oceanographic equipment and used from a hydrographic winch. Even larger simple gravity tubes have been used in the past, but they are now superseded for long coring by the Kullenberg piston sampler.

The Kullenberg sampler, a modification of which is illustrated by Heezen (1952), is essentially the same as the rod-operated piston sampler, except that it is lowered at the end of a steel cable and is forced into the bottom by its own weight, which may be as much as 1000 kg. The sampler has a trigger which is tripped as it approaches the bottom, letting it fall freely for a few meters. The Kullenberg sampler is the standard instrument for raising cores from deep water and is limited in usefulness only by the depth to which it will penetrate, usually less than 20 meters. Scaling up the instrument to achieve greater penetration can be done only to a limited extent and at great expense. The penetration resistance of lake and sea sediment commonly increases linearly with depth, and there is a strong tendency for a long coring tube to bend and break instead of penetrating the sediment to its full length. This is a common accident with the present length of core tube, and the properties of slender columns are such that it is very difficult to design a coring tube of greater length that would be stiff enough, unless one were to use tungsten or some other expensive rigid metal. Finally, as the weight of the sampler increases, so must the weight of the cable and winch used to haul it, and even a Kullenberg sampler of standard size places severe demands on the winch and cable capacity of an oceanographic vessel.

In shallower water, of the order of a 100-meter depth, cores can be taken quickly and conveniently with the Mackereth sampler, a piston sampler operated by air hoses instead of rods or a cable. The power is provided by standard tanks of compressed air, which are used to anchor a remote drilling platform to the bottom, drive the sample tube into the sediment, and then float the apparatus to the surface. The sampler can be operated from a single skiff. For many sorts of stratigraphic work, such as paleomagnetic studies, its monolithic 6-meter core is a great advantage.

Probably the closest approach to undisturbed sampling is made by the Swedish foil sampler. This is a piston sampler in which the piston is attached to a number of thin steel foils held in a magazine in the sampling head. The foils unroll from the magazine as the sampler is forced into the ground around the piston, so that there is no sliding and hence no friction between the sample and the inside of the sampler. This instrument is very well suited for taking samples in varved clay deposits. In its present form, it is rather heavy and expensive for taking cores from shallow lakes, but there seems to be no reason why the basic principle should not be used in a lighter instrument—perhaps one powered by compressed air like the Mackereth sampler.

It is also possible to take cores from unconsolidated deposits by rotary drilling, wash boring and a great variety of methods that are commonly used in commercial well drilling and hard-rock coring. These are discussed in the paper by Hvorslev listed in the references.

D. A. LIVINGSTONE

References

Gumenskii, B. M., and Komarov, N. S., 1961, "Soil Drilling by Vibrations," New York, Consultants Bureau, 80pp. (translated from Russian).

Heezen, B. C., 1952, "Discussion of methods of exploring the ocean floor by R. S. Dietz," pp. 200–205, in (Isaacs, J. D., and Iselin, C. O'D., editors) "Symposium on oceanographic instrumentation" (U.S. Office of Naval Research, *Natl. Acad. Sci.—Natl. Res. Council Publ.*, **309**, 233pp.

Horton, E. E., 1961, "Preliminary drilling phase of Mohole project. I. Summary of drilling operations (La Jolla and Guadalupe sites)," *Bull. Am. Assoc. Petrol. Geologists*, **45**, 1789–1792.

Hvorslev, M. J., 1949, "Subsurface exploration and sampling of soils for civil engineering purposes," Amer. Soc. Civ. Eng., Comm. Sampling and Testing, Vicksburg, Mississippi, Waterways Expt. Sta., 521pp.

Kjellman, W., Kallstenius, T., and Wagner, O., 1950, "Soil sampler with metal foils: device for taking undisturbed samples of very great length," *Royal Swedish Geotechnical Institute, Proc.*, No. 1, 75pp.

Kullenberg, Borje, 1955, "Deep-sea coring," *Rept. Swedish Deep-Sea Exped.*, **4**, No. 2, 35–96.

Lichtwardt, R. W., 1952, "A new light-weight shaft for peat samplers," *Paleobotanist*, **1**, 317–318.

Wright, H. E., Livingstone, D. A., and Cushing, E. J., 1965, "Coring Devices for Lake Sediments," in (Kummel, Bernhard, and David Raup, editors) "Handbook of Paleontological Techniques," W. H. Freeman, San Francisco, pp. 494–520.

Cross-reference: *Marine Geology.*

SEICHE

(1) Introduction

Any system in nature that can invoke a built-in restoring force for reestablishing its equilibrium position, once it has been displaced from it, will perform *free oscillations*, provided the disturbing forces responsible for the initial displacement are not sustained. The resulting oscillations are characteristic of the system only and independent of the exciting force, except of course as to initial magnitude, and must eventually die out under the effects of friction, as the system returns to rest. Such a free oscillation in the case of a fluid in an enclosed or semienclosed basin is called a *seiche*. Where water is the medium, the oscillating system is typified by the shape of the containing basin and the depth of water within it, while the necessary restoring force is provided by the action of gravity tending always to the maintenance of a horizontal surface of the water.

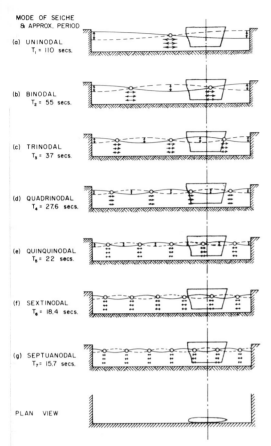

MODE OF SEICHE
& APPROX. PERIOD

(a) UNINODAL
$T_1 = 110$ secs.

(b) BINODAL
$T_2 = 55$ secs.

(c) TRINODAL
$T_3 = 37$ secs.

(d) QUADRINODAL
$T_4 = 27.6$ secs.

(e) QUINQUINODAL
$T_5 = 22$ secs.

(f) SEXTINODAL
$T_6 = 18.4$ secs.

(g) SEPTUANODAL
$T_7 = 15.7$ secs.

PLAN VIEW

Fig. 1. Seven harmonic modes of oscillation of the water body in a rectangular basin of uniform depth ($L = 2100$ feet; $h = 45$ feet; from Wilson, 1961).

The term *seiche*, supposedly derived from *siccus* (Latin), meaning *dry*, hence *exposed*, has had centuries of usage for describing the occasional rise and fall of water at the narrow end of Lake Geneva. The rhythmic nature of this movement was apparently first recorded by de Duillier (1730), though there is mention of a similar phenomenon on Lake Constance (Switzerland) in a chronicle by Schulthaiss (1549); Vaucher (1803), nevertheless, appears to have been first to note that it was a feature of many lakes and that it was in some way associated with atmospheric conditions. The essential nature and origins of the phenomenon in lakes, however, were really established by F. A. Forel (1869–1895) in a classic series of memoirs, which inspired numerous observational and hydrodynamical studies throughout the world at the turn of the century from such investigators as Plantamour, Sarasin, von Cholnoky, Delebecque, du Boys, Lauriol, Gautier and Endros (in Europe), Perkins, Denison, Bell, Dawson, Henry, Hayford and Wheeler (in America), and Airy, Chrystal, Murray, White, Watson and Wedderburn (in Britain) (see

Chrystal, 1904–1905). To Chrystal, perhaps more than anyone else, belongs the credit for having evolved the main elements of the hydrodynamical theory of seiches, though important contributions have been added subsequently by Rollin Harris, Proudman, Doodson, Sterneck, Defant, Goldsbrough, Lamb, Hidaka, Ertel, Goldberg, Caloi and others (see Defant, 1960).

(2) Features of Seiches in Fully Enclosed Basins and Lakes

(a) Nodes and Antinodes. Forel recognized that the seiche phenomenon in its most elementary form was due, in effect, to two very long waves, each of a length between crests of exactly twice the length of a lake, traveling simultaneously in opposite directions through each other. The resultant of two such waves is a "standing" wave which is characterized, in the case of the primary free oscillation of pure form, by an up-and-down movement of water at each end of the lake, such that while the water ebbs at one end it floods at the other. Between these extremes (ventral loops or *antinodes*), the lake level remains unaltered throughout complete cycles of the oscillations. The line or vertcal section across the width of the lake at which no vertical movement of the surface takes place is called a *node*, and the seiche is *uninodal* when having but one node in the length of the lake. At the node, the water motion is entirely horizontal and continuity requires that enough water must flow through the nodal section to account for the volume loss at one end of the lake in favor of the volume gain at the other. Figure 1(a) is a schematic illustration of a uninodal seiche in a simple rectangular basin of uniform depth.

(b) Merian's Formula for the Period of a Seiche. J. R. Merian (1828) had evolved the theory of the free oscillation of water in a rectangular basin of length L and depth h and shown that the period T of the motion was given by

$$T = \frac{2L}{\sqrt{gh}} \qquad (1)$$

where g is the acceleration due to gravity. Forel appears to have been the first to apply Merian's formula to the explanation of seiches in lakes by using a mean value of the depth h to overcome the difficulty of the nonuniformity of depth of most lakes. Agreement between calculated and observed periods was often surprisingly good, considering the crude approximations made in this way.

Since Lagrange (1781) had shown the velocity c of a long wave in water of uniform depth h to be

$$c = \sqrt{gh} \qquad (2)$$

it follows from Eqs. (1) and (2) that $T = 2L/c$, and therefore that the wavelength λ of the inherent wave system in the seiche is $\lambda = 2L$, as recognized by Forel.

A seiche then may be thought of as the resultant of repeated reflections of a long free gravity wave, whose length in the fundamental mode is an exact multiple (2) of the length of the lake, while traveling longitudinally from end to end. The exact over-lapping of reflections would accumulate energy, and therefore amplitude, indefinitely were it not for the fact that bottom friction and viscous turbulence limit this tendency. Since energy loss through friction is often small, seiches, once established by some initial disturbance, can be quite persistent before they die away.

TABLE 1. MODES OF FREE OSCILLATION IN BASINS OF SIMPLE GEOMETRICAL SHAPE (CONSTANT WIDTH)

BASIN TYPE		PROFILE EQUATION	PERIODS OF FREE OSCILLATION					
Description	Dimensions		Fundamental T_1^*	Mode Ratios T_n/T_1				
					$n = 1$	2	3	4
Rectangular		$h(x) = h_o$	$\dfrac{2L}{\sqrt{gh_o}}$		1.000	0.500	0.333	0.250
Triangular (Isosceles)		$h(x) = h_o\left(1 - \dfrac{2x}{L}\right)$	$1.305\ \dfrac{2L}{\sqrt{gh_o}}$		1.000	0.628	0.436	0.343
Parabolic		$h(x) = h_o\left(1 - \dfrac{4x^2}{L^2}\right)$	$1.110\ \dfrac{2L}{\sqrt{gh_o}}$		1.000	0.577	0.408	0.316
Quartic		$h(x) = h_o\left(1 - \dfrac{4x^2}{L^2}\right)^2$	$1.242\ \dfrac{2L}{\sqrt{gh_o}}$		1.000	0.686	0.500	0.388
Triangular (Right-angled)		$h(x) = \dfrac{h_1\,x}{L}$	$1.640\ \dfrac{2L}{\sqrt{gh_1}}$		1.000	0.546	0.377	0.288
Trapezoidal		$h(x) = h_o + mx$ $m = \dfrac{(h_1 - h_o)}{L}$			1.000	0.546	0.377	0.288
Coupled, Rectangular		$h(x) = h_1\ (x < o)$ $h(x) = h_2\ (x > o)$ $\left(\dfrac{h_1}{h_2} = \dfrac{1}{4}\right)$	$\dfrac{L_1}{L_2} = \dfrac{1}{2}$	$\dfrac{4L_2}{\sqrt{gh_2}}$	1.000	0.500	0.250	0.125
			$\dfrac{L_1}{L_2} = \dfrac{1}{3}$	$\dfrac{3.13\,L_2}{\sqrt{gh_2}}$	1.000	0.559	0.344	0.217
			$\dfrac{L_1}{L_2} = \dfrac{1}{4}$	$\dfrac{2.73\,L_2}{\sqrt{gh_2}}$	1.000	0.579	0.367	0.252
			$\dfrac{L_1}{L_2} = \dfrac{1}{8}$	$\dfrac{2.31\,L_2}{\sqrt{gh_2}}$	1.000	0.525	0.371	0.279

* Formulae have not been given when too involved to state simply

TABLE 2. SEICHES IN TYPICAL LAKES; OBSERVED MODES OF OSCILLATION

Name of Lake	Country	Fundamental, T_1 (min)	Observed Periods of Oscillation				
			Mode Ratios, T_n/T_1				
			$n = 2$	3	4	5	6
Geneva	Switzerland	74.0	0.480				
Constance	German–Swiss Border	55.8	0.700	0.503			
Garda	Italy	42.9	0.666	0.507	0.348	0.281	0.230
Loch Earn	Scotland	14.5	0.557	0.414	0.275	0.244	0.198
Loch Treig	Scotland	9.2	0.560				
Loch Neagh	Ireland	96.0	0.718	0.468			
Ontario	U.S.A.	289.0					
Erie	U.S.A.	858.0	0.632	0.409	0.292		
Michigan–Huron	U.S.A.	2700.0					
Michigan	U.S.A.	543.0	0.535				
Superior	U.S.A.	480.0					
Tanganyika	Africa	4.5	0.511	0.378			
Chiemsee	S. Bavaria, Germany	41.0					
Königsee	Germany	10.6					
Vättern	Sweden	179.0	0.542				
Yamanaka	Japan	15.6	0.677	0.350			
Chiuzenji	Japan	7.7					
Baikal	U.S.S.R.	278.2					
Sea of Aral	U.S.S.R.	1368.0					
Sea of Azov	U.S.S.R.	1470.0	0.603	0.522			
George	Australia	131.0					
Baltic Sea–Gulf of Fin.		1636.0					

(c) **Modes of Oscillation.** Forel discovered that binodal, trinodal and other multinodal seiches in lakes were often coexistent with the fundamental. These several modes of oscillation can be regarded as higher harmonics of the fundamental seiche, the binodal seiche, for instance, being the second harmonic, characterized by two nodes. In a simple rectangular basin of uniform depth the series of harmonic modes (up to the seventh) are related to the fundamental (first harmonic or uninodal) mode in the general manner illustrated in Figs. 1(b) to 1(g). It is apparent in this case that the period T_n of the nth harmonic (where n is an integer) is given by the generalization of Merian's formula:

$$T_n = \frac{2L}{n\sqrt{gh}} \qquad (3)$$

In general, however, the periods of free oscillation for a basin or lake of nonuniform depth and breadth are not proportional to the simple harmonic series 1, 1/2, 1/3, 1/4, ... 1/n as implied by Eq. (3), which is strictly correct only for a uniformly deep, rectangular basin. Neither the use of a mean depth h for a lake, as employed by Forel, nor the use by du Boys of the improved approximation

$$T_n = \frac{2}{n}\int_0^L \frac{dx}{\sqrt{gh(x)}} \qquad (4)$$

which takes account of the dependency of depth h on the distance x from one end of the lake to the other along a valley route ("talweg") of greatest depths, removes the difficulty of the generally observed *nonconformance* of the harmonic modal periods to the sequence 1, 1/2, 1/3, 1/4, ... 1/n.

(d) **Symmetrical Basins of Simple Depth Profile.** The difficulty was overcome by Chrystal (1904) by a proper investigation of the hydrodynamics of seiches. Chrystal studied not only the effects of various bottom profiles of mathematically tractable shape (e.g., parabolic, quartic curves) but demonstrated how the oscillating characteristics of lakes of any arbitrary shape and depth could be determined. The results showed that the quartic-profile formulas (see Table 1) provide close approximation to the oscillating behavior of a great many lakes. Since the ratio of the period T_n of the nth mode of oscillation to the fundamental period T_1 in a lake of quartic profile is

$$\frac{T_n}{T_1} = \sqrt{\frac{1+\varepsilon}{n^2+\varepsilon}} \qquad (5)$$

where ε is a dimensionless quantity depending on the quartic configuration, it is evident that if $n = 2$ and T_2/T_1 is known from observation, then Eq. (5) provides a means of calculating ε for the lake and hence of computing the higher modal periods $T_n (n > 2)$. This is a

807

particularly useful method of estimating modal periods, since the fundamental- and second-mode oscillations have a habit of prevailing together in records of lake level; their combination, in fact, was noted by Forel and Chrystal and referred to as a *dichrote* and there is generally not too much difficulty in identifying the periods T_1 and T_2 of the superposed oscillation forming the dichrote.

It is worthy of note (see Table 1) that the period of the *third* harmonic mode of oscillation in a quartic lake is exactly half that of the fundamental period, emphasizing the departure from simple harmonic sequence (1, 1/2, 1/3, . . .) given by Eq. (3). The observed periods of the first three modes of oscillation (T_1, T_2, T_3) for Lake Constance (Swiss-German border), are in the ratio 1:0.701: 0.504 which are very closely in agreement with the ratios 1:0.686:0.500 for a lake of quartic profile (cf. Table 1).

The fundamental periods and ratios of the periods of the important higher modes to that of the fundamental are given in Table 1 for a number of basins of simple depth profiles (and constant width), as derived from hydrodynamical theory. In Table 2, for comparison, the corresponding information is derived from observational data, for a number of representative lakes in different parts of the world.

(e) Basins of Variable Plan-form. If proper account be taken of the two-dimensional (plan) form of an enclosed basin, it is possible to define longitudinal and transverse coupled modes of oscillation. This is most conveniently illustrated in the case of a rectangular basin of length L and breadth B, for which the depth h is uniform. The generalization of Merian's formula, Eq. (3), now undergoes some change (cf. Lamb, 1932, p. 284) to the form:

$$\text{(i)} \quad T_{mn} = \frac{2L}{\sqrt{gh}} [\alpha^2 m^2 + n^2]^{-1/2}$$

$$\text{(ii)} \quad \alpha = \frac{L}{B} \tag{6}$$

where m and $n(= 0, 1, 2, 3, \ldots)$ are integers defining the coexisting harmonic modes or number of nodes in the transverse and longitudinal directions. Equation (3) is really a special case of Eq. (6) when $m = 0$. Alternatively if $n = 0$, the uncoupled transverse oscillations for the rectangular basin are obtained from Eq. (6) as

$$T_m = \frac{2B}{m\sqrt{gh}} \tag{7}$$

which of course is the same as Eq. (3) with B and m replacing L and n. When neither m nor n is zero, Eq. (6) gives the period of the coupled oscillation.

An interesting example of this is afforded in Fig. 2 which shows in contoured form the instan-taneous levels of the water surface at 1/12 period intervals in a cycle of oscillation in the almost perfect rectangular, and nearly completely enclosed, Duncan Basin of Table Bay Harbor, Cape Town, South Africa. These measurements were made in model experiments (Wilson, 1959) to simulate a surge problem in that harbor. The particular wave period chosen to stimulate the seiche was one (1.65 minutes) found to cause a prominent trans-verse seiche in the model basin. Figure 2 reveals that the compound oscillation within the basin was effectively one having two nodes longitudinally and one transversely. For this mode ($m = 1$, $n = 2$), Eq. (6) yields $T_{1,2} = 1.59$ minutes for the basin dimensions $L = 6500$ feet, $\alpha = 3.28$, $h = 40$ feet. A correction for model distortion, affecting the time scale, makes the period $T_{1,2} = 1.64$ minutes, in close agreement with that input into the model. Some departure from the mathematical require-ments of the nodal positions (long dash lines) in the basin is evident and may be attributed to the nonregularity of the southeast end of the basin and of the stimulation deriving from the northwest end.

For basins of variable cross section and non-uniform width and depth such as those of actual lakes (Table 2), various procedures have been evolved for calculating the free modes of oscillation. That of Chrystal (1904) can be made to yield very good results for complicated lake profiles, but other methods, notably those of Defant (1918), Proudman (1914), Hidaka (1932, 1936) and Goldberg (1949), avoid the necessity for matching the longitudinal lake profile with mathematically tractable forms. An excellent account of most of these computational methods is given by Defant (1960), and a good example of their adaptability to modern high-speed digital calculation is afforded by Platzman and Rao (1964) in their examination of the free oscillations of Lake Erie.

(f) Causes of Seiches in Lakes. The principal causes of seiches in lakes were fairly exhaustively investigated by Forel and Chrystal, among others. It was recognized that the disturbances could be triggered by a number of possible forms of excitation such as:

(a) release of pent-up water at a leeward shore through lapse of strong onshore winds;

(b) heavy rain, snow or hail over a portion of a lake;

(c) rapid change of air pressure through passage of a squall;

(d) flood discharge from rivers at one end of a lake;

(e) impacts of wind gusts on the water surface, associated with variations in wind velocity and pressure;

(f) passage of small barometric fluctuations, sometimes identifiable with air waves of a period approximately matching the seiche periods;

(g) molar disturbances of the lake beds resulting

from toroidal and spheroidal oscillations of the whole earth during major earthquakes.

Chrystal (1908), in an excellent summary of his own and other antecedent studies, showed that cause (f) was a frequent and obvious stimulant of lake seiches. The possibility of the seismic cause (g) being responsible for lake seiches in areas of the world remote from an earthquake source has only been recognized comparatively recently, although the phenomenon had been noted as long ago as 1755. In that year, the great earthquake of Lisbon caused remarkable seiches in many of the Scottish lochs and produced similar extraordinary effects in rivers and ponds throughout Europe, Scandinavia and England. The most recent example of a similar nature was associated with the great Alaskan earthquake of March 27, 1964. In lakes, ponds and rivers, bays and coastal regions of the Texas and Louisiana Gulf of Mexico coastline, waves and seiches arose suddenly within minutes

of the earthquake and caused effects remarkably similar to those reported in 1755 at the time of the Lisbon earthquake. In general, however, a seismic cause for seiches in lakes must be considered rare, and meteorological disturbances remain unquestionably the principal form of excitation.

(3) Seiches in Partially Enclosed Basins

Thus far the main discussion has been on seiches in completely enclosed bodies of water, but this article would not be complete without mention of two other important forms of seiches. These are (1) seiches occurring in semi-enclosed basins which open on seas or oceans and (2) internal seiches within lakes and inland seas, where temperature changes in the depth of water result in stratification of water masses of differing density. We shall deal with the former first.

(a) The Analogy of Sea Oscillations to Lake Seiches. Airy (1878) and Forel (1879) anticipated

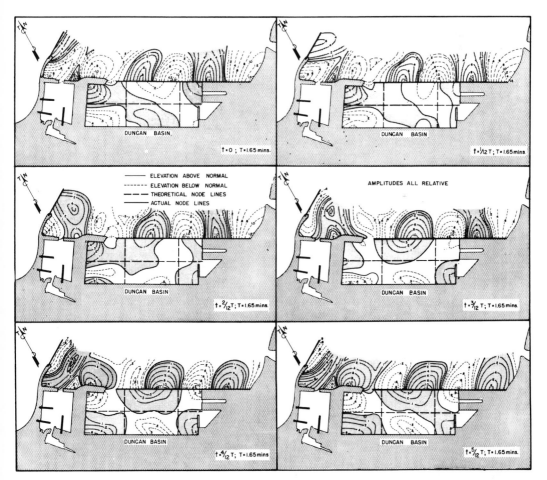

Fig. 2. Instantaneous surface levels at 1/12 cycle intervals ($T \dots 1.65$ minutes) in a model of Table Bay Harbor, Cape Town, South Africa, showing evidence of the coupled mode of oscillation ($m = 1$; $n = 2$) in the Duncan Basin (from Wilson in Permanent International Association of Navigation Congresses, 1957).

a correspondence between lake seiches and coastal oscillations of the sea, such as occur particularly in inlets, bays and gulfs. This sea phenomenon began to receive the attention of such tidal mathematicians as Rollin Harris (1908) in America, Honda, Terada *et al.* (1908) in Japan, G. H. Darwin (1910), Proudman (1914), Doodson (1920), Goldsbrough (1930), Lamb (1932) in Britain, Sterneck (1916) and Defant (1917) in Europe, but it was not until the exigencies of World War II and the postwar period arose that coastal engineers and oceanographers were led to an intensive study of the subject (Proudman, 1952; Defant, 1960). It has been found, indeed, that a close parallel exists with the lake phenomenon, but that coastal seiches possess a much more extended range of causation.

(b) **Modified Merian-type Formula for the Period of a Bay Seiche.** Hydrodynamical theory had long indicated that semienclosed bodies of water opening on larger expanses of water, such as seas, subject to a rhythmic tidal rise and fall, would respond in ways peculiar to the shape and depth of the quasi basin. In the case of a rectangular canal of length L and uniform depth h, closed at one end but open to the sea at the other, it is readily shown (cf. Lamb, 1932, p. 267) that a periodic vertical displacement of sea level will resonate within the canal if the period of the excitation is in agreement with

$$T_s = \frac{4L}{s\sqrt{gh}} \qquad (8)$$

where s is an integer of successive values 1,3,5, . . . The slowest mode of resonant oscillation ($s = 1$), in contradistinction to that occurring in an enclosed basin [Eq. (3)], now takes place about a node which lies across the mouth of the canal. The fundamental oscillation therefore consists of just one-half of the ventral loop of a standing wave [Fig. 1(a)] and has the anti-node at the head of the canal. The second mode has two nodes one of which lies at the mouth and comprises $1\frac{1}{2}$ ventral loops [equivalent to one-half of Fig. 1(c)]. The periods of all possible modes have ratios T_s/T_1 in the harmonic series 1, 1/3, 1/5, . . . and the number of nodal lines is $n = (s+1)/2$. of which one is always at the entrance.

(c) **The Mouth Correction and Influence of Bay Topography.** Table 3 shows this periodic sequence for the case cited and for a number of other forms of partially enclosed basins. The fundamental periods T_1 have been expressed in terms of Merian's formula [Eq. (1)] by the use of appropriate factors. Comparison of Tables 1 and 3 shows at once that the fundamental period for a rectangular embayment with horizontal bed is just twice that of a fully enclosed rectangular basin of equal length and depth. This statement, however, is not strictly correct owing to the need for a

mouth correction, dependent on the aspect ratio b_1/L, relating the width of the canal (at the mouth) to its length. The effect of this correction is to increase the effective length of the canal; it becomes most significant when the aspect ratio b_1/L approaches unity, as had been shown by Rayleigh (1904) in an acoustical study of resonance in rectangular organ pipes.

The fractional amount of the correction to Eq. (8), for $s = 1$, as obtained by Rayleigh and subsequently by Honda, Terada *et al.* (1908) and Neumann (1948), applied to water waves, is:

$$\beta = \frac{b_1}{\pi L}\left[\frac{3}{2} - \gamma - \ln\frac{\pi b_1}{4L}\right] \qquad (9)$$

wherein $\gamma(= 0.5772 . . .)$ is Euler's constant. Table 3, which is based on results presented by Lamb (1932) and Goldsbrough (1930), does not reflect any mouth corrections that might be applicable to the basin types shown (Lamb, 1932).

Table 3 is specifically intended to show the influence of different bay configurations and bottom profiles of simple geometrical shape on resonant periods of oscillation. The results for a semi-elliptical bay are derived from the work of Goldsbrough (1930) and are the primary modes of the unsymmetrical type for one half of a fully enclosed elliptical basin. The second mode (for $n = 2$) has a node across the mouth of the bay and a node at right angles thereto along the axis Ox (Table 3). The third mode ($n = 3$) has a node across the mouth of the bay and a nodal hyperbola within the bay. The fourth mode ($n = 4$) comprises a node at the mouth and a semi-elliptic node concentric with the boundary ellipse. The same general patterns follow for the modes of oscillation in the semi-circular embayment, which is a particular case of the semi-ellipse for the aspect ratio $b_1/L = 2$.

(d) **Influence of Aspect, Aperture Ratios and Damping.** It will not be possible here to go very fully into all the intricacies that are inherent in the oscillating characteristics of semi-enclosed basins. Besides the mouth correction effect, dependent on the aspect ratio b_1/L, there is also an influence of the aperture ratio b/b_1 (in which b is the actual width of the entrance channel) and of the length l. These influences have been investigated by Neumann (1948) and are very completely reviewed by Defant (1960). Newmann showed in particular how the oscillating characteristics of coupled basins could be determined.

Recently Miles and Munk (1961) investigated the influence of dimensional aspects on the internal response of rectangular basins to external wave stimulation. They introduced the important concept of the Q of a semi-enclosed basin, this symbol being used to define the resonant amplitude magnification on the analogy that an open basin responds like a linear damped oscillating system.

TABLE 3. MODES OF FREE OSCILLATION IN SEMI-ENCLOSED BASINS OF SIMPLE GEOMETRICAL SHAPE [based on Lamb (1932), and Goldsbrough (1930)][a]

BASIN TYPE		PROFILE EQUATION	PERIODS OF FREE OSCILLATION				
Plan Form	Depth Profile		Fundamental T_1	Mode Ratios $T_s/T_1 \left(n = \frac{s+1}{2} \right)$			
				$n = 1$	2	3	4
Rectangular	Rectangular	$h(x) = h_1$	$2.000 \dfrac{2L}{\sqrt{gh_1}}$	1.000	0.333	0.200	0.143
Rectangular	Triangular	$h(x) = \dfrac{h_1 x}{L}$	$2.618 \dfrac{2L}{\sqrt{gh_1}}$	1.000	0.435	0.278	0.203
Rectangular	Semi-parabolic	$h(x) = h_1\left(1 - \dfrac{x^2}{L^2}\right)$	$2.220 \dfrac{2L}{\sqrt{gh_1}}$	1.000	0.409	0.259	0.189
Triangular	Rectangular	$b(x) = \dfrac{b_1 x}{L}$ $h(x) = h_1$	$1.308 \dfrac{2L}{\sqrt{gh_1}}$	1.000	0.435	0.278	0.203
Triangular	Triangular	$b(x) = \dfrac{b_1 x}{L}$ $h(x) = \dfrac{h_1 x}{L}$	$1.653 \dfrac{2L}{\sqrt{gh_1}}$	1.000	0.541	0.374	0.283
Semi-elliptic	Semi-paraboloidal	$b_1/L = 2$			0.707	0.578	0.378
		$b_1/L = 4/3$	$2.220 \dfrac{2L}{\sqrt{gh_1}}$	1.000	0.554	0.493	0.323
		$b_1/L = 1$			0.447	0.468	0.264
		$b_1/L = 2/3$			0.317	0.455	0.185
Semi-circular	Semi-paraboloidal	$h(x) = h_1\left(1 - \dfrac{r^2}{L^2}\right)$	$2.220 \dfrac{2L}{\sqrt{gh_1}}$	1.000	0.707	0.578	0.378

[a] By permission of the University Press, Cambridge, Mass.

The reciprocal $1/Q$ is a measure of the damping coefficient for the basin and Q can also be thought of as a ratio of the rate at which total energy is maintained in the oscillation to the rate at which it is dissipated. A paradoxical result of their investigation was the theoretical finding that the Q of a harbor apparently tends to increase as the mouth is constricted, a result also found previously by Biesel and LeMehaute (1954) and confirmed subsequently by Ippen and Raichlen (1962) and Ippen and Goda (1963). LeMehaute (1962), Wilson (1962) and Ippen et al. (1963), however, showed that the paradox is resolved as basin closure is approached by frictional and nonlinear effects, not accounted for in the theory, and that in practice the Q of the basin does in fact decline with reduction of the entrance width.

In Table 4 examples are given of the observed oscillating characteristics of typical bays and gulfs in different parts of the world. No attempt is made to define the interrelationship of periodicities observed in any particular embayment; it is probable, however, that they will tend to accord with Table 3 if there is any resemblance of bay topography to the geometrical forms listed in Table 3.

(e) Origins of Coastal Seiches—Air Water Coupling. Coastal seiches may originate in almost all the ways (a) to (g) already listed for lake seiches. The dominant source of excitation is meteorological, but insofar as the meteorological effects of wind and pressure cause disturbances in the sea or ocean of which the coastline is a boundary, the coastal seiche phenomenon is in many cases a forced resonant or near-resonant oscillation. It is important to recognize that coastal seiches may be both free and forced. So long as long-period wave energy is impressed on the mouth of a bay or the entrance of a harbor basin, the oscillation will be forced. When this energy is withdrawn, the seiche will be free and will be sustained as long as some

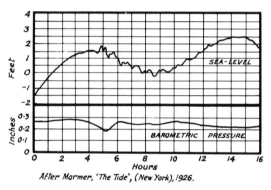

After Marmer, 'The Tide', (New York), 1926.

Fig. 3. Seiches in San Francisco Bay developing from a barometric pressure flucturation, Nov. 21, 1910; mean velocity of wind 5 mph, maximum 10 mph (from Marmer, 1926, in Permanent International Association of Navigation Congresses, 1957, Wilson, 1959, 1960).

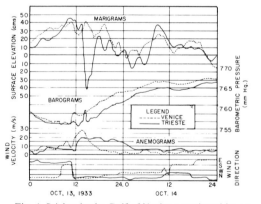

Fig. 4. Seiches in the Gulf of Venice occasioned by an atmospheric pressure front crossing the Adriatic Sea from west to east (adapted from Greco *et al.*, in Permanent International Association of Navigation Congresses, 1957).

energy remains conserved within the basin against the dissipative tendencies of bottom friction and internal viscosity effects and of radiative loss and turbulence of flushing at the basin mouth.

A frequent cause of prominent coastal seiches in bays is a direct air-water coupling of atmospheric disturbances—inherently the same phenomenon cited by Chrystal for the case of lakes. Evidence of this is displayed in Figs. 3, 4, and 5(b) all of which show that barometric oscillations occurring immediately over a coastal area can often stimulate seiches in a bay. Figure 4 is particularly interesting in showing the extraordinary effect of a pressure front moving eastward across the northern extremity of the Adriatic Sea. At Venice, it acted like a plunger in depressing the water level, and when it had reached Trieste, on the opposite side of the head of the Adriatic, its plunger action there was in perfect timing to energize a transverse seiche between Venice and Trieste. This is akin to saying that the speed of the front, V, was closely equal to the speed, c, at which a long free gravity wave in water would propagate between Venice and Trieste. Lamb (1932) and Proudman (Lamb, 1932), showed that a dynamic magnification of the water surface elevation (or depression) η, above (or below) mean level over the values η_0, which it would have if a pressure disturbance were stationary, results from the motion of the disturbance, namely

$$\frac{\eta}{\eta_0} = \frac{c^2}{c^2 - V^2} \qquad (10)$$

In the absence of damping (which, of course, is really present), this factor becomes infinitely great when $V = c$ and implies a state of resonance. Resonant air-water coupling was thus the mechanism for the Venice-Trieste seiche. Greco, Calci and Visioli (see Permanent International Association of Navigation Congresses, 1957) have shown that occurrences of this kind are by no means unique. Proudman (1929) was probably the first to explain peculiar wave phenomena off the English coast on July 20, 1929, as being the result of resonant air-water coupling from a squall line, but other unique cases of similar nature have now been accounted for along the same lines (Burns *et al.*, 1953; Ewing *et al.*, 1954; Lee Harris, 1955; Donn *et al.*, 1956; Donn, 1959; Cartwright, 1960; Inman *et al.*, 1962)—see Munk, 1962; Permanent International Association of Navigation Congresses, 1957).

Figures 3 and 5(b) are examples of bay seiches having been caused by barometric fluctuations in the absence of any strong wind or obvious front. In the case of Fig. 5(b), the seiches in Table Bay, Cape Town, South Africa, developed in clear, almost calm weather. Approximate harmonic analysis of the barogram suggests the existence of

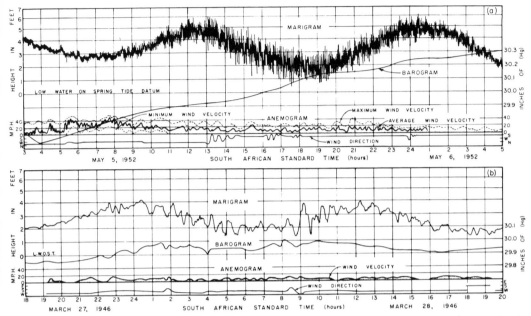

Fig. 5. Evidence of seiches in open-mouth basins and their relationship to weather disturbance: (a) combined longitudinal and transverse oscillations in the rectangular Duncan Basin of Table Bay Harbor, Cape Town; (b) seiches of Table Bay recorded in the Duncan Basin (from Wilson, in Permanent International Association of Navigation Congresses, 1957).

a composite atmospheric wavetrain comprising periodicities of 130, 82, 66, 36 and 15 minutes. Significantly, wind velocity and direction also fluctuate in a periodic manner and a 36-minute periodicity is very obvious in the anemogram. It will also be seen from Table 4 that the observed periods of oscillation of the water body in Table Bay have at least three modes which closely accord with the barometric oscillations. Again, therefore, the phenomenon must be attributed to resonant air-water coupling. Numerous examples of this phenomenon were given by Wilson (1953) who indicated the probability that the phenomenon was related to the coalescence of fast-moving and antecedent semistationary fronts of cyclonic weather systems in the South Atlantic (see Permanent International Association of Navigation Congresses, 1957; Wilson, 1959, 1960). Recently Cartwright (1960) and Donn and his co-workers (1960, 1964) have reported the same type of air-water coupling effects at Lerwick in the Shetland Islands; off the New York coast; and at St. George's Harbor, Bermuda (Tucker, 1953).

(f) **Origin of Coastal Seiches—Long-period waves.** Apart from local air-water coupling, the other obvious source by which coastal seiches may be energized is, of course, the ingress of long-period waves from the open ocean. In this case, the continental shelf, bay or inlet acts as a sounding box for selecting those frequencies in the spectrum of ocean waves to which it is most attuned.

Ocean waves of long period may be generated in essentially three ways: (i) by wind stress and atmospheric pressure fluctuations, (ii) by a near-shore phenomenon of "surf beats," and (iii) by seismic disturbances of the ocean bed, which may be considered inclusive of underwater explosions, both volcanic and man-made.

(i) *Continental Shelf Oscillations.* Not very much is really known about long-period wave generation of the first kind. Theoretically, the problem has been solved by Lamb (1932, Section 195 *et seq.*) and others, and it would seem inevitable that large cyclonic disturbances over the open ocean would entrain long waves as well as purely wind-generated waves. Discounting the well-known storm-tide effect of hurricanes, the identification of these waves in the energy spectra for localities close to shore is difficult because of the confusion provided by concomitant surf beats and coastal seiches. Munk and his collaborators (Munk *et al.*, 1959; Snodgrass *et al.*, 1962; Miller *et al.*, 1962; Munk, 1962; Tucker, 1963—see Munk, 1962; Tucker, 1963) have made significant advances in attempting to differentiate between what they term "trapped" and "leaky" modes of long wave activity. *Trapped* modes are essentially long edge-waves which, because of the obliquity of their incidence on a coast, reflect their energy alongshore without loss to the open sea (cf. Isaacs *et al.*, 1951, Munk *et al.*, 1956, and Tucker, 1963). *Leaky* modes on the other hand, at angles of incidence greater than the

TABLE 4. COASTAL SEICHES IN TYPICAL GULFS, BAYS AND HARBORS; OBSERVED MODES OF OSCILLATION

Name of Gulf, Bay or Harbor	Country	Observed Periods of Oscillation (approximate) (min)					
St. Johns Harbor	Bay of Fundy, Canada	74	42				
Narragansett Bay	Rhode Island, U.S.A.	44	46				
Vermillion Bay	Louisiana, U.S.A.	180	120				
Galveston Bay	Texas, U.S.A.	75					
San Pedro Bay	Los Angeles, California, U.S.A.	55–60	27–30	15	9–11	2–5	
San Francisco Bay	California, U.S.A.	116	47	34–41	24–27	17–19	
Monterey Bay	California, U.S.A.	60–66	36–38	28–32	22–24	16–20	10–15
Hilo Bay	Hawaii, U.S.A.	20–25	10	7			
Guanica	Puerto Rico, Caribbean	45					
Lerwick	Scotland	28–30					
Port of Leixoes	Near Porto, Portugal	20–25	13–15	3–5			
Bay of Naples	Italy	48	17–18				
Gulf of Venice–Gulf of Trieste	North Adriatic Sea	210–240	60	40	10	5	
Euripus (Gulf of Talanta)	Greece, between Is. Euboe and mainland	105	60				
Algiers	Algeria, North Africa	20–26					
Casablanca	Morocco, North Africa	35–40	18–20				
Table Bay, Capetown	South Africa	58–62	38–43	25–30	18–21	14–17	10–11
Algoa Bay, Port Elizabeth	South Africa	69–75	57	42–52	35	20–25	16–17
Tamatave	Madagascar	15	8–10	1–2			
Tuticorin, Gulf of Mannar	India–Ceylon	180					
Bay of Hakodate	Hokkaido, Japan	45–57	21–24				
Bay of Aomori	Honshu, Japan	295	103	23–26			
Bay of Ofunato	Honshu, Japan	41–44	36–39	12–17	5–6		
Bay of Nagasaki	Kyushu, Japan	69–72	54	44–45	40	32–38	22–25
Wellington	New Zealand	28	?	?			
Lyttleton	New Zealand	156	?	?			

critical "Brewster's Angle," are shelf oscillations in which some of the reflected energy is returned and lost to the open ocean. It would appear that there is evidence for both these forms of continental shelf oscillations.

(ii) *Surf Beats and Harbor Seiches.* The phenomenon of "surf beats," first recognized and named by Munk (1949), refers to a mechanism of long-wave generation which is coupled to the beats of high and low waves that are a regular feature of wind-generated waves and swells incident on a coast. Tucker (1950) confirmed a correlation between observations of swell and long-period waves and Longuet-Higgins and Stewart (1962) and Lundgren (1963) have now explained the main features of the phenomenon as the effect of "radiation stress" or "wave thrust" (Tucker, 1963). Surf beats tend to have periods of 1–5 minutes, but it is still not clear whether they are entirely responsible for the shorter-period coastal and harbor seiches that tend to result from storms that blow home to a port and also from some that do not (Wilson, 1959, 1960).

An example of such seiches is given in Fig. 5(a) which shows marigram and simultaneous baro-gram and anemogram for a station near the southwest corner of the Duncan Basin, Table Bay Harbor, Cape Town (see Fig. 2). The dense embroidery of the marigram is brought about by transverse oscillations of the type of Fig. 2, associated with uninodal longitudinal oscillations for the dock of 5.6-minute period. The obvious difference between the bay seiches [Fig. 5(b)] and the harbor seiches [Fig. 5(a)] is at once apparent. Figure 6 provides more details of typical harbor seiches in the Duncan Basin. The traces A and E are similar but out of phase by 180° in the oscillation of about 1.8 minutes, which conforms to the $(m = 1, n = 0)$ fundamental transverse mode of Eq. (6). The trace C shows strong evidence of the $(m = 0, n = 1)$ fundamental longitudinal oscillation for the basin with a period of 5.6 minutes.

(iii) *Seismic Sea Waves or Tsunamis.* The third type of long-period wave evolves from submarine earthquakes. These seismic sea waves, now familiarly known as "tsunami," may have periods covering an extensive range from minutes to hours. As a rule, however, the period range may be thought of as extending from about 5–60 minutes. Tsunami waves are impulsively generated disper-

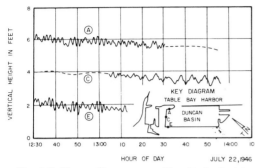

Fig. 6. Evidence of transverse and longitudinal seiches actually measured at locations A, C and E in the rectangular Duncan Basin of Table Bay Harbor, Cape Town (from Wilson, in Permanent International Association of Navigation Congresses, 1957).

sive waves which normally encompass a wide spectrum of frequencies. The waves take form as an interference effect of multiple frequencies and are subject to some wavelength and period change as they propagate over large distance (Munk, 1947; Van Dorn, 1961; Wilson, 1964, Munk, 1962; and Tucker, 1963).

The great Krakatoa eruption of 1883 is still unique for having created tsunami waves that raced across all the oceans of the world. In such far-flung places as San Francisco, Honolulu and Cape Town, to mention only a few, the waves triggered responsive seiches with widely different periods. A good example of the selective tuning that particular areas, even of a single bay, may have for waves of seismic origin, is afforded by Fig. 7, which shows the responses at four points in San Pedro Bay, California, to the Aleutian tsunami of April 1, 1946. Tsunami waves, of course, usually assail a coastline as impulsive waves of solitary or pseudo-solitary type and may wreak great damage by inundation before their effects are apparent as seiches. In the example of Fig. 7, San Pedro Bay was well sheltered from the full effects of the 1946 tsunami by its southern outlook and the west coast islands, and the scattered energy was therefore largely dissipated in seiches.

(4) Troublesome Features of Seiches

Seiches in bays and harbors, whether in lakes or along the continental and island coastlines, are troublesome in two respects (Wilson, 1950, 1953, 1957, 1959, 1961—see Permanent International

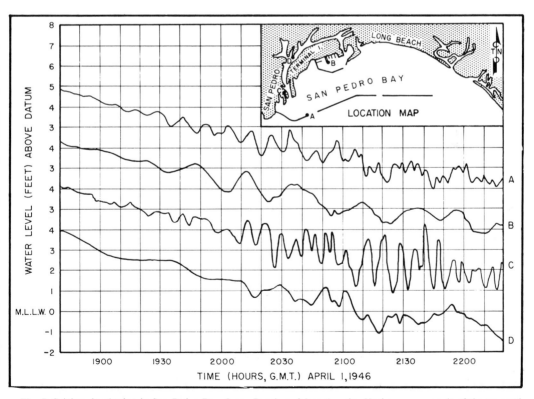

Fig. 7. Seiches developing in San Pedro Bay, Long Beach and Los Angeles Harbors, as a result of the tsunami generated by the Aleutian Trench earthquake of April 1, 1946 (from Wilson, in Permanent International Association of Navigation Congresses, 1957).

Association of Navigation Congresses, 1957. First, the longer-period bay seiches of the type of Figs. 3, 4 and 5(b) tend to cause strong reversible currents in the entrances of harbor basins which are dangerous to the navigation of large ships entering or leaving port. Secondly, the shorter-period harbor seiches of the type of Fig. 5(a) adversely affect moored shipping by inducing motion of ships as oscillators under the non-linear elastic restraint of their mooring ropes. Figure 1 suggests how this comes about in the case of a ship as berthed in the plan-view. Figure 1(b) shows that the center of the ship is close to the location of one of the nodes of the binodal oscillation between the end walls of the dock. The ship is thus subject to the strong horizontal surge of water that occurs across the node. A similar condition tends to prevail for the quinquinodal seiche of Fig. 1(c) and, somewhat less favorably, for the sextinodal seiche, Fig. 1(f). A valid conclusion therefore would be that the ship would be prone to surging under the stimulus of the second, fifth (and sixth) modes of the possible multinodal oscillations that could occur. The fundamental mode [Fig. 1(a)] would also obviously tend to affect the ship. Under severe seiche conditions, ships have been known to break all their mooring ropes, collide with each other, damage dock structures, buckle their hull plating and splinter floating fenders and dock walings; in some ports ships have been compelled to forsake their berths for safety in the roadstead. Primarily responsible for these effects are seiches in the period band between 20 seconds and 2 minutes (Wilson, 1959, 1960).

(5) Internal Seiches or "Temperature Seiches"

The phenomenon of internal seiches, first observed by Murray (1888) and by Thoulet (1894) and interpreted by Watson (1904) in the Scottish lochs, should be dealt with briefly. The phenomenon derives from the fact that thermal gradients tend to be established in lakes and seas—hence, density gradients which are quite sharp at the thermoclines or interfaces of stratified layers of water of different density. When wind blows for long periods over a lake surface, it will displace surface water to the leeward end, thereby depressing the thermocline below its equilibrium level and raising it at the windward end. The tilt of the thermocline is maintained so long as wind stress is imposed on the free surface of the lake. Withdrawal of the wind results in an internal seiche in which the thermocline oscillates about its equilibrium level.

Wedderburn (1905–1912) made detailed measurements of this phenomenon and with Young (1915) correlated it with theory. Much earlier, Stokes (1847) had evolved the theory of internal waves at the interface between fluid layers and had indicated

the period dependency on the depths and densities of the layers. For a rectangular lake of length L and depth h with upper and lower layers of depth and density respectively h_1, ρ_1, and h_2, ρ_2, the period of any nth mode of oscillation is given approximately by

$$T_n = \frac{2L}{n\sqrt{gh_2}}\left[\frac{\rho_2}{\rho_2 - \rho_1}\frac{h}{h_1}\right]^{\frac{1}{2}} \quad (11)$$

which is the result arrived at by Watson (1904) and Schmidt (1908). It is obvious that this formula yields a period of oscillation very much greater than that of the free surface [Eq. (3)]. Along with the period, the amplitude of the internal seiche is also greatly increased over that of a free surface seiche; Lake Baikal, for instance, has internal seiches up to 75 meters (250 feet) in amplitude with a period approximating 38 days.

Mortimer (1952) has extended the study of internal seiches to multilayered stratification in a beautiful series of model experiments and field observations supported by the theory of Longuet-Higgins (1952). The behavior of a three-layered system is illustrated in Fig. 8. Under a moderate wind, the bottom layer may not be sensibly disturbed by the tilting of the upper thermocline, but with increase of wind strength the lower interface is also subject to displacement as shown in Fig. 8(b). Cessation of the wind results in two internal seiches within the lake as well as a surface seiche, all with vastly different periods of oscillation.

(a) Beneficial Effects of Internal Seiches. It is manifest that the current systems that prevail in a lake which is subject to both surface seiches and internal seiches tend to be rather complex. Herein, however, is the great importance of internal seiches to the ecology of lakes and inland seas, for they generate turbulence and mixing, and disperse

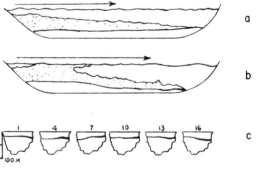

Fig. 8. Internal seiches in a stratified lake: (a) displacement of a three-layered system by a moderate wind (arrows), (b) displacement by a strong wind, (c) three-hourly observations of the position of the layer bounded by 11 and 90°C isotherms in Loch Earn, Scotland, from observations of Wedderburn (from Mortimer, 1952).

and transport heat, dissolved oxygen and plant nutrients which sustain life throughout the lake waters.

It was shown by O. Pettersson (1909) that internal waves of tidal character prevailed in the Skagerrak and that their pulsing conformed to and varied as the tidal cycle of 14 days. Wedderburn (1909) was able to show that this was the natural period for an internal bay seiche for the whole Skagerrak basin (Defant, 1960). The phenomenon is therefore a resonant forced internal seiche with amplitudes of about 25 meters (80 feet). Through the mechanism of diffusion already mentioned, these internal seiches would inevitably be of great importance for the life cycles of the Baltic Sea. Internal standing waves or seiches may otherwise occur generally in deep gulfs, bays and fjords, as shown by Sverdrup (1939) and Munk (1941), and would no doubt promote mixing and upwelling in such local areas that might otherwise escape the sweep and turnover of the great oceanic circulations.

(6) Influence of the Earth's Rotation upon Seiches

In very large lakes, seas and oceans, the essential mechanism discussed in preceding sections comes under the influence of the earth's rotation which manifests itself through the fact that the *geostrophic acceleration* (always operative on water particles as a result of the earth's rotation) becomes large enough to be significant in comparison with other accelerations disturbing the water particles. The horizontal components of this geostrophic acceleration were first taken into account by Laplace (1775) in connection with the tides, but the effect is now commonly linked with the name of Coriolis (1835). Large bodies of water in oscillation, then, are subject to the deflecting effects of Coriolis force, which varies with latitude from zero at the equator to a maximum at the poles. The general effect of Coriolis deflecting force, when it becomes sensible, is to vitiate the development of fixed nodal lines and atrophy them into nodal points or *amphidromic centers* (see *Tide*). The oscillation then rotates about the amphidromic center as a *Kelvin* wave with amplitudes increasing from zero at the center to a maximum at the boundary of the basin or sea, the rotation being anticlockwise in the northern hemisphere and clockwise in the southern. Generally speaking Coriolis effect is unimportant for seiches in all but the very largest lakes and bays normally encountered. It is, however, an important feature of the tides in seas and oceans (see *Tide*).

BASIL W. WILSON

References

Chrystal, G., 1906, "On the hydrodynamical theory of seiches" (with bibliography on seiches), *Trans. Roy. Soc. Edinburgh*, **41** (III), 599–649.

Defant, A., 1960, "Physical Oceanography," Vol. II, Chs. 6 and 16, Oxford, Pergamon Press.

Lamb, H., 1932, "Hydrodynamics," Cambridge, The University Press.

Mortimer, C. H., 1952, "Water movement in lakes during summer stratification" (Appendix by M. S. Longuet-Higgins), *Phil. Trans. Roy. Soc. London, Ser. B*, **236**, 355–404.

Munk, W. H., 1962, "The Sea," Vol. 1, Ch. 18, New York, Interscience Publishers.

Permanent International Association of Navigation Congresses, 1957, "Origin and effects of long period waves in ports," *Proc. Intern. Navig. Congr., London*, 10 papers, 227pp.

Proudman, J., 1952, "Dynamical Oceanography," Chs. 11 and 12, New York, John Wiley & Sons, Inc.

Tucker, M. J., 1963, "Long waves in the sea," *Sci. Progr. (London)*, **51** (203), 413–424.

Wilson, B. W., 1959, 1960, "Research and model studies on surge action in Table Bay Harbor, Cape Town," *Trans. S. African Inst. C.E. (Johannesburg)*, **1** (6, 7); **2** (5).

SEISMIC REFLECTION PROFILING AT SEA

Principles

The same principles of seismic reflection on land (see *Seismology* and *Geophysical Exploration at Sea* in pr. Vol. V) are applied to reflection profiling at sea. A sound pulse is reflected from interfaces between layers of different acoustical impedance. The reflection profiling technique is analogous to that of an echo sounder. Both use rapid repetition of small sound pulses which are reflected and recorded graphically in cross sectional form. The echo sounder records mainly the water-bottom interface, but the profiler traces the sub-bottom structures as well (Fig. 1).

Equipment and Operation

The equipment consists basically of a sound source, a receiving hydrophone and a recorder.

Commonly used sound sources include explosives, direct electrical discharge (sparker), plates activated by electrical or air sources (boomer and pneumatic plate gun), direct discharge of compressed air or exploding gas directly into the water (air gun and gas gun), and electromagnetic sources. Explosives generate a great amount of energy, but they do not possess the rapid fire ability of the other devices. After the initial pulse, all sources emit a series of distinct pulses called "bubble pulses" which are caused by the oscillation of a gas bubble generated by the release of energy. No bubble pulse was recorded on the profile in Fig. 1 because the explosive source was floated near the surface and the gas bubble was released to the air destroying most of the oscillation.

The hydrophone used in reflection profiling may be of the crystal, magnetostrictive or variable reluctance type. Noise from the motion of the

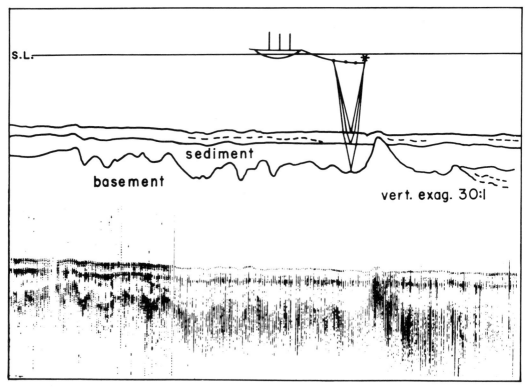

Fig. 1. Diagrammatic sketch with actual profile record below illustrating the principle of reflection profiling at sea. The profile is approximately 100 nautical miles (185 km) long. The average sediment thickness is approximately 500 m.

hydrophone in the water and from the moving ship must be kept at a minimum during recording. The slacking technique, which has proved very successful in reducing the noise level, consists of drawing in the hydrophone line between shots and slacking it during the recording. An alternate system, appropriately called an "eel," which eliminates the necessity of slacking, involves towing an array of hydrophones in a neutrally buoyant liquid-filled tube. The hydrophones are spaced in such a way that the towing noises tend to cancel, but the reflected signals are reinforced. Because the eel does not have to be slacked for each shot, it is especially suited for use with a rapidly repeating sound source.

Many types of recorders have been used, but all produce essentially the same type of record based on variable density. The record shown in Fig. 1 was recorded on a drum recorder. As the drum rotates, a stylus describes a vertical line with reflectors appearing as intense intervals. A series of reflectors laterally displaced on the record by time translation of the stylus, can be integrated by the eye to form a graphical representation of sub-bottom structures in a cross-sectional form. As the stylus advances at a constant rate and the drum rotation is constant during each recording, the

vertical exaggeration is controlled by the ship's speed. An increase in the pulse rate will result in improved resolution of features on the record.

Lower-frequency pulses penetrate sediments to greater depths, but higher frequencies are more useful in recording shallow structures in detail. Some profilers are fitted with multiple filters, amplifiers and recorders in order to record simultaneously with more than one combination of frequency and gain.

Performance

Reflectors have been recorded to depths of 5 km below the bottom and profilers have been operated successfully in 8 km of water where 1.7-second sub-bottom reflection time was recorded.

Rapid firing pulse sources with inherently quiet receiving arrays, such as eels, produce good records at speeds up to 12 knots. The data are graphically recorded and do not need lengthy reduction, correction or evaluation as is necessary in seismic refraction methods. As a result, hundreds of thousands of miles of reflection profiles have been recorded between 1961 and 1965. These profiles have contributed greatly to the rapid progress in understanding the nature of the ocean floors.

The investigations described here were supported by the United States Office of Naval Research and Bureau of Ships.

J. Ewing
T. Edgar

References

*Ewing, J. I., and Tirey, G. B., 1961, "Seismic profiler," *J. Geophys. Res.*, **66**, 2917–2927.
*Hersey, J. B., 1963, "Continuous Reflection Profiling," in (Hill, M. N., editor) "The Seas," Vol. 3, pp. 47–72, New York, Interscience Publishers.

SHEAR, WIND SHEAR—*See* Vol. II

SHEET FLOW—*See* LAMINAR FLOW, BOUNDARY LAYER

SHELF—*See* ATLANTIC COASTAL SHELF, GEOPHYSICS OF (*see* pr Vol. V)

SIBERIAN SEAS—*See* KARA, LAPTEV AND E. SIBERIAN SEA

SLICKS, RIPPLES AND WINDROWS (Surface Oceanographic Phenomena)

Slicks are smooth glassy patches or streaks on the rippled surface of oceans and are commonly seen in coastal waters, bays and lakes. When the wind is a slight breeze, the slicks are in patches. At wind speeds greater than about 7 knots, the slicks break up into windrows which have narrower bands spaced much closer together and much shorter with their long axes always oriented nearly along the wind direction. In any case the slicks are distinguished by the smooth oily appearance of wavelets and the lack of ripples.

Some people considered that the slicks are generated by the eddy structure of winds which show patches of calm areas. However, this idea is not valid in most cases, since the slicks movement is usually much slower than winds and its direction is irrelevant with wind directions. The absence of capillary crispations in the slicks indicate that the water surfaces of the slicks are contaminated by surface-active compounds of organic material which forms monomolecular layers and their surface tension is reduced appreciably. (For example, the ripples of wavelengths of about 2 cm decrease their amplitudes to 1/2.3 within 0.8 second.) The organic material comes from man-made waste near the coast and from plankton and other animals and plants in the open ocean.

It is considered that the film of organic material is formed in patches or in rows by two causes.

When the wind is low, the internal waves are the major cause for accumulation of organic material. When the wind exceeds 7 knots (Beaufort Scale 3), the cellular circulation in the upper layer seems to be the major cause.

The simplest model of the internal waves is the Stokes' type wave which is assumed to occur in a fluid with an upper layer of finite depth and uniform density lying over a heavier layer of infinite depth and uniform density. This type of model represents fairly well the actual internal waves which are pertinent to slicks. The theoretical model indicates that the convergence of the horizontal component of particle velocity on the surface lies over the trough of the interface in standing waves but over the ascending interface between the trough and the crest in progressing waves. The observations by G. Ewing (1950) with bathythermographs in the water of 15-m depth near San Diego, indicated that the slicks were arranged regularly over the troughs of the thermocline which was located at about 7 m and undulated with average wavelengths of about 300 m. However, the more elaborate measurements of La Fond (1962) with thermistor chains off Southern California showed that the slicks were on the descending thermocline somewhere between the crest and the following trough in 85 out of 105 cases.

The first systematic study of windrows in the surface layer of oceans and fresh waters was made by Langmuir (Von Arx, 1963) who observed that leaves and foams in Lake George, New York and long lines of pelagic *Sargassum* in the North Atlantic Ocean were oriented in the direction of the wind and changed their directions following the wind directions. He concluded from experimental data that the windrows are caused by the circulation with alternate left- and right-helical vortices which have their axes in the direction of the wind. Such water motion is often called Langmuir circulation. The slicks, leaves, foams and *Sargassum* are considered to be gathered on the convergence line of the surface current due to this circulation. Woodcock showed that the helical vortices are asymmetrical and are of special biological significance for pelagic organisms such as *Sargassum* and Physalia (Portuguese man-of-war).

Langmuir discovered that the row spacings in Lake George are approximately proportional to the depth of thermocline and are 5–10 m for a shallow thermocline in May and June and 15–20 m for a deep thermocline in October and November. Faller and Woodcock found from the data of *Sargassum* in the North Atlantic that the spacings are proportional to wind speeds, varying from 20 m for wind of 4 m/sec to 50 m for 12 m/sec. Welander and Ichiye independently proposed a dynamic theory that the cellular circulation is produced by differential surface wind stresses due to the variations in the roughness of the sea surface. Faller (1964) considered that the main cause of cellular motions during the strong wind is the shear-flow instability in the upper layer of the wind-drift in the ocean.

TAKASHI ICHIYE

References

Ewing, G., 1950, "Slicks, surface films and internal waves," *J. Marine Res.*, **9**(3), 161–187.

Faller, A., 1964, "The angle of windrows in the ocean," *Tellus*, **16**(3), 363–37.

La Fond, E., 1962, "Internal Waves," in (Hill, M. N., editor) "The Sea," Vol. 1, pp. 731–751, New York, Interscience Publishers.

Von Arx, W., 1963, "Introduction to Physical Oceanography," Reading, Mass., Addison-Wesley Publishing Co.

SOLOMON SEA

The Solomon Sea (sometimes given as "Solomons Sea") is a "marginal sea" of the southwestern Pacific, situated south of the Solomon Islands and New Britain and east of New Guinea. According to the International Hydrographic Bureau (*Sp. Publ. No. 23*, 1953) the southern boundary extends from Gado-Gadea Island off the southeast tip of New Guinea (10°38'S, 150°34'E) around the southern edge of the Louisiade Archipelago, along the 100-fathom line, south of Uluma (Suckling) Reef and Lawik Reef off Tagula Island, thence to the south point of Rennell Island, and so to Cape Surville (eastern tip of San Cristobal Island). The northeastern border, in the Solomons, connects the shortest distances between Bougainville, Choiseul, Santa Isabel, Malaita and San Cristobal, so that New Georgia and Guadalcanal are completely within its limits. To the south it adjoins the Coral Sea (q.v.), to the northwest the Bismarck Sea and to the northeast the main Pacific. Its limiting co-ordinates are approximately 152–162°E and $4\frac{1}{2}$–12°S, covering about 720,000 km², with a volume of approximately 1.4×10^6 km³. (Some writers, e.g., Bruns, 1958, have included the Solomons Sea within the Coral Sea, but it is structurally quite distinct.)

The earliest voyagers in this region included the Polynesians and others from southeast Asia, probably including Chinese and Arab navigators. The Spanish explorer Alvaro Mendaña crossed the Solomons Sea in 1567 after discovering San Cristobal, Guadalcanal and Santa Isabel (Ysabel). He named the group Isles de Salomon in anticipation of riches which proved rather slow to materialize. In 1768 Louis de Bougainville, voyaging north from Australia, discovered Buka, Bougainville and Choiseul.

The earliest oceanographic work in the Solomon Sea was done in the last century by the German naval vessel *Gazelle* and in the first years of the present century by other vessels of the German navy. (Germany, at that time, occupied colonies in northwestern New Guinea, New Britain and the western islands of the Solomons.) The deepest soundings were obtained in 1910 by the cruiser S.M.S. *Planet* (Capt. Dominik) the name of which is honored by the "Planet Deep." In the post-World War II period, useful traverses have been made by the Danish vessel *Galathea* (1951) and the British *Challenger* (1951).

Bathymetry

The area may be divided into two large basins, each with deeper rifts, as follows:

(a) New Britain Basin. This basin is mainly over 4000 m, with marginal depressions.

(*i*) *New Britain-Bougainville Trench*. (This has also been called "Solomons Trench" on Groll's (1912) bathymetric map of the Pacific, and "Bougainville-New Britain Trench" by Schott, 1935.) It is a "dog-leg" trench, 500 km long and everywhere below 5000 m running south of New Britain and south of Bougainville. For convenience, the west sector of the "dog-leg" is generally called New Britain Trench and the east sector the Bougainville Trench. Within the latter is situated the deepest sounding, the "Planet Deep," with 9140 m (29,988 feet), which is deeper than Mt. Everest is high.

(*ii*) *Kiriwina Trough*. This is a complementary but shallower rift along the south side of the basin, north of Kiriwina and Woodlark Islands. Its deepest sounding is 5419 m.

(b) Solomon Basin. This is situated southeast of the Woodlark Ridge and north of the Rennell Ridge. It is separated by a low sill from the San Cristobal Trench which (with several interuptions) extends the New Britain Trench south of the Solomons. It is locally over 7000 m but often less than 5000 m.

There is a third depression, a long narrow rift, the *Santa Isabel Trough* in a region popularly known as "The Slot" which separates the outer belt of the Solomons Islands from the inner row (Bougainville-New Georgia-Guadalcanal-San Cristobal). It is about 600 km long and only 50 km wide. The deepest sounding is 4340 m.

Oceanography and Climate

Surface isotherms over the Solomon Sea are always above 80°F (27°C) in a mean annual basis. It is 2°C above normal for a land-free globe according to Dietrich, (1950). Mean annual rainfall is over 75 inches (about 2000 mm) with two pronounced wet seasons about the equinoxes (doldrums). Cloud cover exists six-tenths of the time. The evaporation/precipitation ratio is therefore low and the surface salinity is thus somewhat reduced (34.5‰). In the southern hemisphere summer (January–March), the northeast Trades swing round to join with the northwest Monsoon

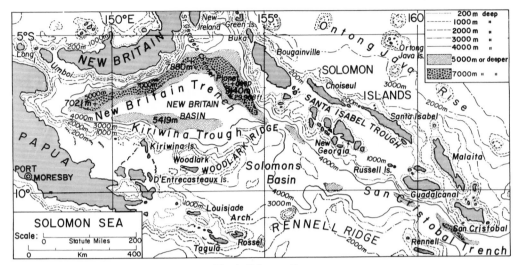

Fig. 1. Solomon Sea.

into northern Australia, with northerly winds in the Solomons. In the winter (July–September) they are replaced by the Southeast Trades. Hurricanes tend to be generated in the southern part of the Solomon Sea and move southward into the Coral Sea. This is the zone of the tropical front in March (10–15°S).

A branch of the South Equatorial Current in winter enters the Solomon Sea at the north end with divergent streams to the southwest and southeast, mostly with rates of less than $\frac{1}{2}$ knot; in the southern summer it reaches the Solomon Sea from the southeast, passing out to the north. Spring tidal ranges are about 120 cm. The entire area is dominated by a pattern of one single tide per day (Dietrich, 1944).

Sediments

Deep-sea deposits (Murray, 1906) are dominated by *globigerina ooze* in the southeast and by terrigenous deposits near the coasts. The surrounding islands are nearly all high continental islands, deeply weathered by tropical rainfall with extensive lateritic soils (providing kaolinite). There are several vigorously active volcanoes in the north (near Rabaul and on Bougainville), so that volcanic ash and tuff is widespread, distribution being favored by both the Northwest Monsoon and the prevailing surface currents. Abyssal red clay occurs in the New Britain Basin and in parts of the Sar Cristobal Trench. Coral reefs abound especially along the southern shores and in parts of the Solomons, so that most shallow water deposits are dominated by calcareous reef muds and sands. The Solomons are also highly seismic, and earthquakes tend to trigger submarine landslides and turbidity current flows into the deep trenches, so that flat-bottom, abyssal plain topography develops.

Structural History

The Solomon Sea has not been studied very thoroughly from a geophysical viewpoint, but its northern borders are marked by youthful orthogeosynclinal belts (Stille, 1945) and the New Britain-San Cristobal Trench seems to be a modern equivalent. It may be noted that this belt lies on the *interior* side of a youthful island arc, *not facing* the Pacific like those to the northwest or the Tonga-Kermadec Trenches in the south. Its essential rectilinearity and near-continuity with the Melanesian Border faults (Fairbridge, 1961) suggest that the Bougainville-San Cristobal sector of the trench system is related to strike-slip faults. The transcurrent couple is sinistral.

The northern border of the sea was termed the *Solomon Islands Plateau* by Sir John Murray (1895, 1906), but it is more like a multiple ridge. The submarine rift that separates the inner and outer row of the Solomon Islands also seems to be a major strike-slip fault, the *Santa Isabel Fault,* being responsible for the narrow Santa Isabel Trough and, to the northwest, forming a long escarpment along the Pacific side of New Ireland. The line is marked by many shallow-focus earthquakes. Intermediate-focus shocks are located 50–100 km to the southwest, i.e., coinciding with the Bougainville-San Cristobal Trench (Gutenberg and Richter, 1949–54). This reversal of the usual position of the deeper shocks in relationship to a trench is most curious: compared with the Pacific border, they are in a normal position, but the trench position is reversed. Such a relationship is compatible with a tension-shear explanation of the trench, but not with a compressional theory (Fairbridge, 1964).

A third major strike-slip line is proposed by Krause (1965), an east-west line, named the

Papua-Solomon Shear Zone, corresponding to our Kiriwina Trough. A class "a" seismic shock has occurred at its western end. Krause suggested that it is matched by another east–west line, south of the Louisiades. Between the two, he indicated a sinistral transcurrent couple.

The Rennell Ridge that marks the southern border of the Sea has been described as the *Rennell Island Arc* by Glaessner (1950).

Like the rest of the western Pacific marginal seas the Solomon basins appear to have subsided during the period late-Tertiary to Quaternary. Emerged terraces are observed up to several hundred meters on many of the islands, suggesting a differential movement in most cases. On New Georgia there is a remarkable elevated barrier reef some 50 m above sea level (see literature review by Davis, 1928). Seamounts and atolls are largely absent except along the principal ridges. Rennell Island is an uplifted atoll with a small lake as a relic of the former lagoon (Christiansen, 1964). An important barrier reef complex surrounds the Louisiade Archipelago (Tagula Barrier Reef) with large atolls along the Rennell Ridge. Another barrier complex also extends out to Kiriwina Island.

RHODES W. FAIRBRIDGE

References

Bruns, E., 1958, "Ozeanologie," *Deutscher Verlag d., Wiss., Berlin*, 2 vols.

Christiansen, Sofus, 1964, "On Lake Tegano, Rennell Island," *Geografisk Tidsskrift*, **63**, 99–111.

Davis, W. M., 1928, "The Coral Reef Problem," *Amer. Geogr. Soc. Special Publ. 9.*

Dietrich, G., 1944, "Die Schwingungssysteme der halbund eintägigen Tiden in den Ozeanen," *Veroeffentl. Inst. Meeresforsch. Berlin*, N.F.R.A., **41**.

Dietrich, G., 1950, "Über systematische Fehler in den beobachteten Wasser und Luft temperaturen auf dem Meere," *Deut. Hydrograph. Z.*, **3**.

Fairbridge, R. W., 1961, "The Melanesian Border Plateau, a zone of crustal shearing in the S.W. Pacific," *Publ. Bur. Cent. Seism.*, Ser. A, **22** (Helsinki, 1960), 137–149.

Fairbridge, R. W., 1962, "Basis for submarine nomenclature in the Southwest Pacific Ocean," *Deut. Hydrograph.*, **15**, 1–15.

Fairbridge, R. W., 1964, "Thoughts about an Expanding Globe," in "Advancing Frontiers in Geology and Geophysics," Krishnan Vol., pp. 59–88, Hyderabad, India.

Gutenberg, B., and Richter, C. F., 1949, "Seismicity of the Earth and Associated Phenomena," Princeton, Princeton University Press, 273pp. (Second ed., 1954).

Krause, D. C., 1965, "Submarine geology north of New Guinea," *Bull. Geol. Soc. Am.*, **76**, 27–42.

Krause, D. C. (in press), "Bathymetry and submarine geology of the Northern Tasman Sea-Coral Sea-Southern Solomon Sea region of the south-western Pacific Ocean," *N.Z. Oceanographic Inst.*

Stille. H., 1945, "Die tektonische Entwicklung der neoaustralischen Inselwelt," Berlin, *Geotektonische Forschungen*, Heft 7/8, 210–260.

SOMALI CURRENT

The Somali Current is an extension of the South Equatorial Current of the Indian Ocean. In the northern summer with the southwest monsoon it flows northeastward for a distance of about 1500 km along the coast of Somaliland (East Africa, to the "Horn of Africa"). Around about 6–10°N it turns into the *Monsoon Current* which continues roughly eastward. The northeast current starts in April at the time the monsoon changes from northeast to southwest. In July and August, the maximum surface current reaches 4, locally 7, knots within a width of about 150 km between 4°S and 4°N.

In September, when the monsoon starts to change, the northeastward flow is still strong near the coast, but it is weakened offshore. In November, the southwest current occurs as often as the northeast current. In January and February, the current in general flows southwestward but with surface speeds less than 2 knots. In March, the current near the coast flows northeastward again while the current offshore is to the northwest. The Somali Current is a western boundary current in the same manner as the Gulf Stream, but it disappears in the northern winter.

The surface water of the Somali Current in its principal (northeastward) stage shows a banded zone of relatively low temperature and salinity about 100–200 km off the coast. This zone turns abruptly eastward at about 6–8°N following the current. The warm and saline waters from the Gulf of Aden and the Arabian Sea move to the south and west and limit the water of the Somali Current. At the Somali coast of about 9°N the surface temperature drops to about 13 or 14°C during the southwest monsoon due to an intense upwelling. In the subsurface layers the saline waters from the Persian Gulf (with salinity 35.3–35.5‰) and from the Gulf of Aden (with salinity 35.2–35.8‰) flow southeastward off Somaliland in the depths of 200–250 m and of 600–700 m, respectively. Below 2500 m the water is of the Antarctic Circumpolar Water origin and the zone of about 100 km width of less saline water flows northeastward just off the continental shelf between the equator and 10°N, where it turns eastward.

TAKASHI ICHIYE

References

Bruns, E., 1958, "Ozeanologie," Vol. 1, Berlin, VEB Deutscher Verlag der Wissenschaften, 430pp.

Foxton, P., 1965, "A mass fish mortality on the Somali Coast," *Deep-Sea Res.*, **12**, No. 1, 17–19.

Rochford, D. J., 1964, "Salinity maxima in the upper 1000 meters of the North Indian Ocean," *Australian J. Marine Freshwater Res.*, **15**(1), 1–24.

Stommel, H., and Wooster, W. S., 1965, "Reconnaissance of the Somali Current during the southwest monsoon," *Proc. Natl. Acad. Sci.—Natl. Res. Council*, **54**(1), 8–13.

Warren, B., 1965, "The Somali Current," *Oceanus* (*Woods Hole*), **12**(1), 8–13.

SOUND PROPAGATION—*See* ACOUSTICS (UNDERWATER)

SOUNDING

(1) *Sounding*, in nautical terminology, is the procedure by which the depth of a body of water is determined.

(2) *An individual sounding* is the vertical distance from the surface of a water body to its floor or some other point beneath.

Sounding may be as simple as holding a surveyors rod (sounding pole) on the bottom of a shallow pond while floating in a skiff, or it may involve complicated measurements with sophisticated electronic equipment which times the reflection of a sound pulse from the floor of the deep ocean. Sounding the sea floor for making bathymetric charts is analogous to surveying the land surface for constructing topographic maps.

The origin of the word "sounding" is not certain, but it is thought to have come from the old French word *sonder* and the Anglo-Saxon word *sundgyrd* meaning "sounding rod."

Purpose

Sounding is accomplished first and most important, for *ship safety and navigation*; second, for *scientific investigation* because sounding is presently the basic means of determining form, and this, in turn, may be a manifestation of the earth's inner structure or of geologic processes; and third, for *engineering or economic purposes*, e.g., the best routes for transoceanic telephone cables or for offshore oil exploration.

Means of Accomplishment

Sounding is accomplished either (1) by *direct physical measurement* employing a lead line or (2) *indirectly* by measuring the time it takes for a pulse of sound, generated at the surface, to reflect from the bottom and return to the surface as an echo.

Direct Measurement. A now obsolete technique in the deep sea, this requires the use of a lead line, sometimes called a sounding line, which is dropped to the bottom. Customarily this line has a heavy weight on the end (sounding lead) and is marked at intervals with scraps of colored cloth, cord, leather, or other means to designate distance. The weight is usually hollow and filled with tallow to which bottom sediment adheres. A lead line is usually lowered by hand to depths near 20 fathoms (120 feet); at greater depths, a powered reel or drum is normally used. Deep-sea soundings with hemp rope or piano wire utilized steam or electrically driven winches. The word "fathom" pervades all literature dealing with sounding. It derives from the Anglo-Saxon word *faethm* meaning "the embracing arms"—the measure of length to which a man can extend his arms—six feet. International oceanographic practice nowadays calls for the use of the metric system.

Indirect Measurement or Echo Sounding. This exploits the fact that water is an excellent conductor of sound energy and that a sound pulse, once generated, will bounce off a reflecting surface and return to its source as an echo. If the speed of sound in the water is known, the time lapse between the initiation of the sound pulse and the return of the echo can be converted into distance, or depth, if the reflecting surface is the bottom.

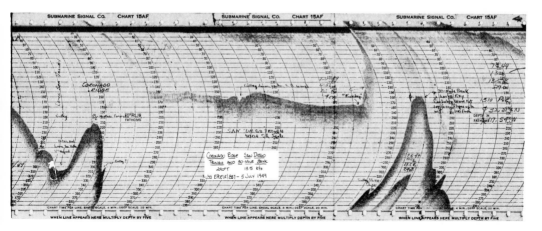

Fig. 1. Echo-sounding profile across the San Diego Trough just west of San Diego, California. The early-type recorder on the echo sounder produced a curvilinear trace giving a rather "slanted" aspect to the peaks and ridges. Not a change in scale, merely recording from 400–800 fms vice 0–400.

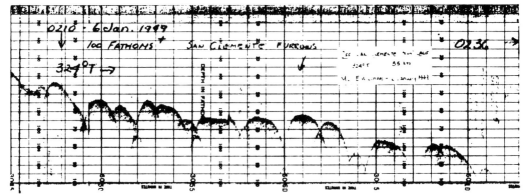

Fig. 2. Seagullies off the coast of southern California.

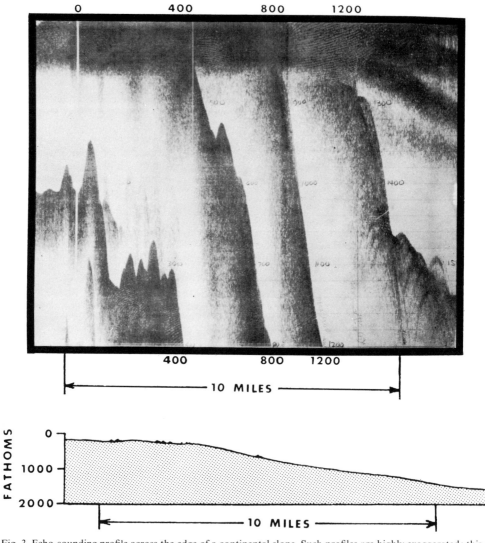

Fig. 3. Echo-sounding profile across the edge of a continental slope. Such profiles are highly exaggerated; this can be seen by comparing it with the sketch drawn at natural scale below. (*Courtesy of H. W. Menard*)

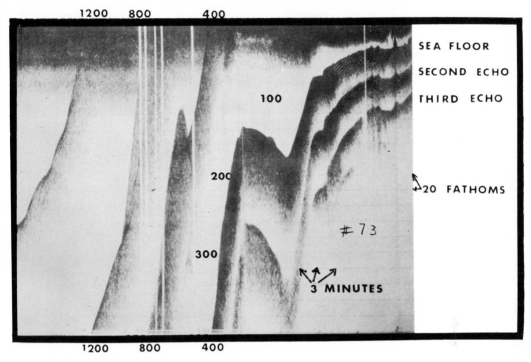

Fig. 4. Echo-sounding profile of the continental slope recorded on a Precision Depth Recorder. The instrument is constructed to show the entire slope in 400-fathom increments. (*Courtesy of H. W. Menard*)

Historical

Egyptians used sounding lines as early as 2000 B.C. as depicted by a twelfth dynasty artist. The ancient Phoenicians, who lived on the coast of Syria and colonized the north coast of Africa, were noted for their ability to navigate, and even today, hand sounding lines are sometimes jocularly referred to as "Phoenician Fathometers." Aristotle and Plutarch both wrote of their interest in ocean depths, but there is no record of any soundings by them. Columbus is reported to have used a 400 fathom sounding line in an unsuccessful attempt to sound the deep Atlantic during his voyage of 1492. Magellan, apparently using the same type of line in his 1521 circumnavigation of the globe, thought he had discovered the deepest ocean when this line failed to touch bottom in the South Pacific. In 1773, an Englishman, Captain Phipps, sounded to 1250 meters west of Norway, bringing up blue clay from the bottom; in 1818 Sir John Ross sounded to 1920 meters in Baffin Bay, and somewhat later his nephew, Sir James Clark Ross, sounded to 4435 and 4895 meters west of the Cape of Good Hope. During this period seafarers and explorers from all the maritime nations, especially the Dutch, Germans, French, and British, secured occasional deep-sea soundings and incrementally added to knowledge of the depths of the sea floor. In 1854 Mathew Fontaine Maury published a

bathymetric chart of the Atlantic with contours to 4000 fathoms, based on the limited soundings then available. The paucity of these deep-sea soundings is better understood when one considers that a single sounding could require hours of hard work and valuable ship time. Furthermore, the reliability of the measurement was frequently in serious doubt because of the drift of the ship which caused angular deviation of the sounding line and the inability to determine when the sounding lead touched bottom. Up to, and including, the famous British *Challenger* Expedition (1873–1876), deep-sea soundings were made primarily with hemp rope and a heavy weight. About 1873, single-strand piano-wire line sounding was introduced with calibrated, registering, sheaves and fast sounding reels. These were utilized with detachable sound leads invented by Midshipman J. M. Brooke of the U.S. Navy. Although these constituted a significant improvement in speed and accuracy, still by 1895 there existed only 7000 soundings deeper than 2000 meters and only 550 of these were deeper than 5500 meters. Even these numbers might have been less had it not been for the stimulus provided by the laying of transatlantic telegraph cables.

The fact that sound could be used to measure distance or depth in water was probably discovered by Dominique Francois Jean Arago, a French physicist, in 1807. Although Mathew Fontaine

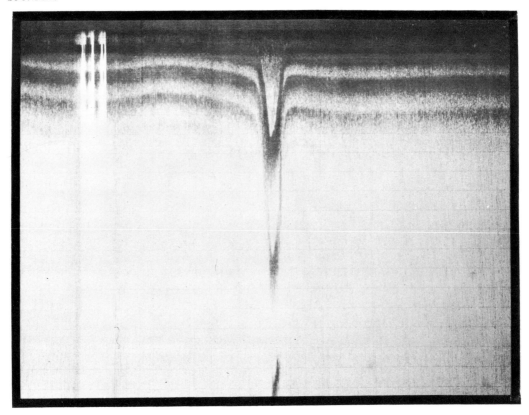

Fig. 5. Echo-sounding profile across a narrow submarine canyon on the continental shelf off Mexico just north of Acapulco. The echogram represents a depth range from the surface to 400 fathoms. Second and third "bounce" echos can be seen also. This record was secured by Spencer F. Baird at latitude 170°52′N, longitude 102°30′W. (*Courtesy of T. E. Chase*)

Maury attempted to obtain echo soundings with gunpowder as early as 1854, it was about 50 years later (1907) that the first patent on an echo-sounding apparatus was issued to an American named A. F. Eells. In 1911 Alexander Behm of Germany accomplished echo sounding to 150 meters employing rifle bullets as a sound source and photographically recording the time of arrival of the echos. Additional research on echo sounding was stimulated by the *Titanic* disaster, and in 1914, R. A. Fessenden of the United States, conducted a series of experiments off the Grand Banks which were aimed at developing a means for detecting the nearness of icebergs. These eventually culminated in the echo-sounding equipment called the Fathometer. This term is a registered trademark, but it is often used in a loose generic sense. By 1918, the United States was operating a Sonic Depth Finder using a triangulation scheme for shallow water and the Fessenden oscillator for deep water. In 1922, the U.S.S. *Stewart* echo sounded continuously with this equipment as it crossed the Atlantic at speeds of 15 knots and at depths from 9–3200 fathoms. In the same year, the

French echo sounded across the Mediterranean to depths of 3000 meters. Late in 1922, the United States conducted the first deep-sea survey off the west coast of the United States with 5000 soundings providing the basis for a bathymetric chart, and in 1923, the first graphic recorder was employed. By 1924 most of the problems basic to echo sounding, even as practiced today, were identified and understood, although they were far from solved. In 1926, the French developed a sonic system with a continuously recording graphic display using smoked paper. In 1932, the British utilized continuous recorders with electropneumatic percussive sound sources, and in 1933, a recording echo sounder called the Echograph was reported by the Germans. By the start of World War II, a variety of echo-sounding systems had the capability of recording continuously, but only to limited depths. Since the end of World War II, echo-sounding techniques and systems for recording have been continually improved and refined so that today (1964) one can obtain detailed profiles almost anywhere on the sea floor.

Techniques. Sound propagates in water as it does

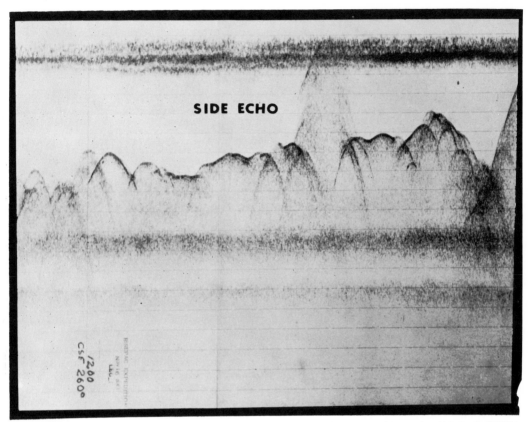

SIDE ECHO

Fig. 6. Abyssal hills on the sea floor near the crest of the East Pacific Rise. The location is latitude 5°36′N, longitude 101°45′W and the record was taken by Spencer F. Baird on the Risepac Expedition. The 400-fathom span of the PDR record is between 1600 and 2000 fathoms. (*Courtesy of T. E. Chase*.) Note the "side echo" from a submarine Hill not directly beneath the vessel.

in air, vibrating parallel to the direction of propagation by rarefaction and condensation of the elastic medium. Its speed is about $4\frac{1}{2}$ times that in air however, and, although varying considerably, averages about 1500 m/sec in salt water.

Sound Sources. (1) Explosives—Sound pulses can be generated by detonating explosives in water. The type of explosive can sometimes be selected to give a variety of spectra of frequencies. This high-energy technique is now employed largely to obtain sub-bottom profiles from horizons in and beneath the sedimentary layer of the ocean floor.

(2) Simple percussion—Sound pulses can result from imparting a physical blow to the hull of a ship floating in the water. Many systems were devised with elaborate means for doing this which incorporated pneumatic hammers, electromagnetic cocking, etc., but all are now obsolete.

(3) Electric arcs—An electrode trailed in the water can be caused to spark or arc if a high-voltage current is suddenly applied. This spark acts much as an explosive. Such systems are used effectively for sub-bottom reflection profiling.

(4) Transducers—Modern transducers may ex-

ploit the piezoelectric or magnetostrictive properties of certain materials, for example quartz, tourmaline, Rochelle salts, barium titanate, nickel and some nickel alloys. These materials have the unique characteristic of producing mechanical energy in response to an electric or magnetic stimulus with the reverse effects being possible also. Conducting coils in a magnetic field likewise transform electrical into mechanical energy and conversely. Properly coupled to the water, all these can excite acoustic waves and also signal the arrival of a pulse.

(6) Pneumatic sources—The sudden release of highly compressed air is employed in one of the most successful contemporary methods of sub-bottom reflection profiling.

(5) Gas exploders—Detonation or explosion of gas mixtures has also been used primarily to provide the acoustical energy for sub-bottom profilers.

Echo-sounding Systems. A complete echo-sounding system comprises the following elements:

(1) Sound transmitter or transducer;

(2) Sound receiver or hydrophone (in some cases this may also function as the transducer);

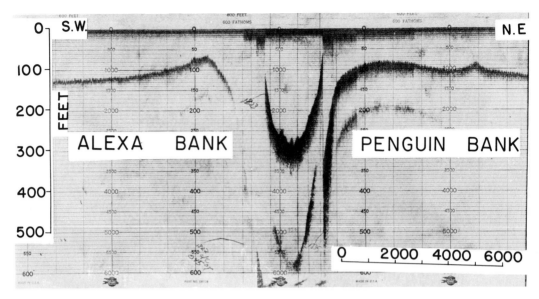

Fig. 7. Profile between two coral reef banks (Alexa and Penguin, North of Fiji, Southwest Pacific). Note change of scale from 0–600 feet on the two sides, to 0–600 fathoms in the middle. Horizontal scale in feet. (*Courtesy of Rhodes W. Fairbridge.*)

(3) Necessary electronics to perform the various timing and amplification functions;

(4) Indicator or graphic recorder.

The separation is made functionally for all the elements which are actually highly interdependent. A visual indicator, usually a flashing light which gives the depth as a function of position on the perimeter of a circular scale, is often used for monitoring depths particularly in shoal areas. Graphic recorders are of various types, but almost all modern ones automatically and continuously provide a rectilinear profile of the bottom showing depth as a function of time.

Limitations of Echo Sounding. (1) Sound speed— In the United States, most graphic recorders and indicators are set for speeds of 800 fathoms (or 4800 feet) per second, while in Europe recorders are frequently adjusted to an assumed speed of 1500 m/sec (4921 ft/sec). Because speeds may vary from 4560–5100 ft/sec, corrections are necessary if the true depth is required. Vertical sound speed is a function of pressure (depth) and the distribution of density (temperature and salinity).

(2) Directivity—In most transducers the sound is not projected as a narrow, pencil-like beam, but as a teardrop-shaped lobe with an angle of 30° or more at the apex and multiple smaller side lobes. The first echo will return from the nearest reflecting surface within the pattern, and this may not be the bottom directly under the ship. If a ship is moving across a point reflector such as a conical hill, a hyperbolic echo is recorded. In areas of high relief, corrections must be made if true depths and slopes are required.

(3) Attenuation and bottom reflectivity loss— Sound is attenuated in seawater, and much of its energy may be lost by absorption as it reflects off the bottom. Thus, in great depths, the sound pulse put in the water must be strong enough to insure that the echo can be recognized. These factors reduce range but have no effect on accuracy, at least theoretically.

Modern Advances in Echo Sounding. (1) Precision recorders—Graphic recorders which control and time the sound pulse and echo return to 1 part in 3000 are now being produced commercially. In addition, many of these recorders have a "gating" capability which permits spurious or obscuring echoes from mid-depths to be selectively precluded from the record. These instruments may permit the recording of bottom profiles on a variety of scales by controlling stylus and paper speed.

(2) Narrow-beam transducers—The advantages of echo sounding with a narrow, pencil-like beam of sound have been, until recently, outweighed by the bulk and expense of transducers required, and by the angular sweep of the beam as the ship rolled. Now a steady, narrow beam can be obtained:

(a) by utilizing gyroscopically controlled gimbal mounts which keep the transducer trained in a vertical position, or

(b) by employing crossed arrays of small transducers and hydrophones which are electronically stabilized and linked to a command gyroscope. The result is a 2° beam which points directly at the bottom even under heavy weather conditions, and records only the features which lie directly below the ship.

(3) Towed transducers—These tend to eliminate noise produced by hull mounting, and to permit greater resolution of topographic detail when towed deep and close to the bottom. They are sometimes of the "narrow-beam" type. Nor do they need always to be towed by ships or small boats. In remote or otherwise inaccessible areas, a slow and low flying aircraft, especially a helicopter, may lower a transducer into the water and take echo-sounding profiles. The advantages of such an arrangement are manifest with the limitations being primarily in the weight-carrying ability of the aircraft versus its ability to fly slowly.

(4) Compact transceivers—These have solid-state components and perform the same function as bulkier original models. They are being increasingly used in ships where space and reliability are at a premium.

(5) Inverted echo sounding—Submerged transits of nuclear submarines across the Arctic Ocean require detailed and instant knowledge of the clearance between the submarine and the overlying ice, and the thickness of the ice. To accomplish this, echo-sounding systems have been adapted so that the sound beam is directed upward or obliquely from the submarine and reflected downward from the undersurface of the ice or from the air-water interface.

(6) Complete chart-making systems—Not currently in widespread use because of expense, but under development, is digital plotting equipment which is linked to ships' automatic navigation systems and echo sounders. The soundings are accurately and automatically plotted.

Navigation

A ship is navigated primarily to insure its safe and economic transit With control by dead reckoning and careful celestial fixes, about a 1-mile accuracy is considered excellent. Even this level of accuracy could not be routinely guaranteed in oceanographic sounding, except near to coastal areas, and soundings on charts, no matter how carefully made or corrected were subject to error because of position. Such position errors, and also errors caused by transposition of numbers, confusion of geographical coordinates with soundings, and inadvertent inclusion of draftsmen's notations, persist annoyingly from one edition of a nautical chart to another. Anomalous notations of shoals are usually left because of a tendency to err on the side of safety; others may remain because of the difficulty in communicating new information to the chart makers.

Present bathymetric charts in coastal waters are almost all made from ships utilizing electronic positioning systems. With reference to pre-established shore stations, they are able to fix their position by intersecting two ranges (circular system) or by using schemes based on phase comparison (hyperbolic system). In either case, accuracy may be measured in feet or yards. Farther from shore (over 60 miles or so), long-range electronic and inertial systems may provide the control. In the latter case, the expense of procurement is high and the need for chart accuracy must justify the installation. For the future, navigation by satellite, which is, in principle, a refinement of celestial navigation, and by compact and more economic inertial systems, extends great promise for high-precision positioning anywhere on the oceans of the world.

EDWIN C. BUFFINGTON

References

Adams, K. T., 1942, "Hydrogrographic manual," Washington," *U.S.C.G.S., Sp. Publ.* 143.

Becken, B. A., 1964, "Sonar," *Advances in Hydroscience,* **1**, 1–93.

Murray, J., 1928, "The Sea Floor," in (Fowler, G. H., and Allen, E. J., editors) "Science of the Sea," pp. 241–269, Oxford, Clarendon Press.

Thomson, C. W., 1874, "The Depths of the Sea," London, Macmillan, 527pp.

Wilson, W. D., 1960, "Speed of sound in sea water as a function of temperature, pressure, and salinity," *J. Acoust. Soc. Am.,* **32**, 641–644.

SOUTH ATLANTIC CURRENT—*See* **BRAZIL CURRENT**

SOUTH CHINA SEA

Location

The South China Sea, sometimes known as the China Sea or Nan Hai, is that part of the Pacific Ocean bordered on the west by the Asian mainland, the southern limit of the Gulf of Thailand, and the east coast of the Malay Peninsula, and on the east by Formosa, the Philippines, and Borneo. Following the International Hydrographic Bureau (*Sp. Publ.* 23, 1953), the northern boundary is from the north point of Formosa to the coast of Fukien; the southern boundary is a rise between Sumatra and Borneo (about 3° 00′S) (Fig. 1). It embraces an area of about 3.4×10^6 km².

Topography

Deep Basin. The major topographic feature of the South China Sea is a deep basin of rhomboid shape; large reef-studded shoal areas occur within the basin to the south (Reed, Tizard, Nanshan Banks) and northwest (Paracel Island, Macclesfield Banks). The north central part is a deep sea basin called the China Sea Basin, with a maximum depth of 5016 meters. The central part is an abyssal plain with a mean depth of 4300 meters. Although not well sounded, some seamounts and numerous irregular topographic rises, both in the basin and along its border, are known to exist. Near Palawan and Luzon, the continental slope is rather steep, with the deepest sounding off the latter island. This feature is closed off in the south by the submarine plateau capped by Reed Bank, etc., to form the Palawan Trough which has a maximum depth of 3475 meters.

Mainland Shelf. Along the northwest side of the basin a shelf extends about 150 miles offshore and includes the Formosa Strait and the Gulf of Tonkin. The islands of Hainan and Formosa are situated on this shelf. The Gulf of Tonkin gradually deepens toward the center, but the maximum

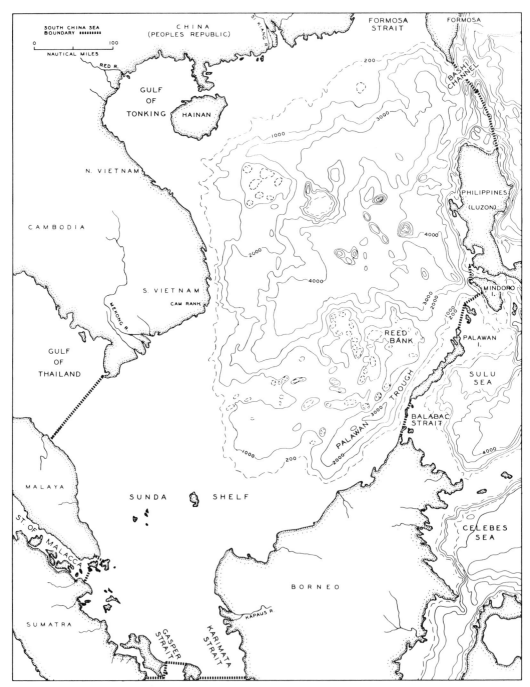

Fig. 1. General topography and boundary features of South China Sea (contours in meters) (after Udintsev).

depth is only 70 meters. In the shallow Formosa Strait, there are a number of reefs and banks. To the south off South Vietnam, the shelf narrows and connects with the Sunda Shelf.

Sunda Shelf. The Sunda Shelf covers the area between the three large islands of Sumatra, Borneo, and Java and the mainland of Asia, including the southern parts of the South China Sea, the Gulf of Thailand, and the Java Sea, as well as the shallow parts of the Straits of Malacca. Formerly called the South-East Asiatic Shelf, it is one of the largest shelves in the world. This southern part of the South China Sea is essentially a broad shallow trough, about 40 meters deep at its periphery and up to 100 meters deep in its central part. The adjoining Gulf of Thailand is about 70 meters deep in its center. To the south, between Sumatra and Borneo, the Sunda Shelf becomes shallower and the southern limits are less than 40 meters in depth.

On the bottom of the Shelf, there are a number of submerged river valleys (the so-called Molengraaff River system, named after its discoverer, by Dickerson (1941), which converge into the Sunda Depression and then into the China Sea Basin (Fig. 2). Echo profiles show that these submerged valleys and tributaries vary in width up to 3 miles. At the edge of the continental slope, near the submerged mouth of the Shelf, there is a deep valley.

Large bars are formed off the mouths of the various rivers. These rivers drain the wet tropical lands around the Sunda Shelf, and transport enormous masses of sediments.

In the South China Sea, especially the eastern part, there are a large number of peaks, which emerge as coral reefs, atolls or banks. The different reefs and islands appear to stand on a comparatively deep and level plateau which, though not adequately sounded, varies between 1700 and 2500 meters.

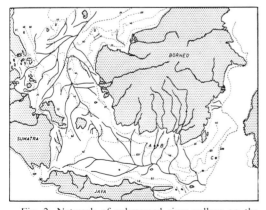

Fig. 2. Network of submerged river valleys on the Sunda Shelf (after Kuenen). The northerly group has been called the "Molengraaff River" system (Dickerson, 1941). (By permission of John Wiley & Sons, N.Y.)

Connecting Channels. The South China Sea has connecting channels ("sills" or "lintels") on several sides.

North: Besides the Formosa Strait to the north, which is about 100 miles wide with a sill depth of around 70 meters, the main entrance to the South China Sea from the Pacific Ocean is the deep Bashi Channel, the strait between the Philippines and Formosa through which an interchange of most of the surface water and some of the bottom water takes place. The sill has a threshold of about 2600 meters. Another somewhat higher sill with a depth of around 1800 meters exists just south of Formosa.

South: The main connection between the southern part of the China Sea and the Java Sea is by way of the Karimata and Gasper Straits. Almost the whole water exchange occurs through these Straits, the sill depth of which is the same as in the surrounding areas.

West: In the west the Malacca Strait, in its narrowest part, is about 30 meters deep and 17 miles wide. The depth increases gradually to about 100 meters before the continental slope to the Andaman Sea begins. On the bottom of the strait, in which strong tidal currents occur, large uniform sand ripples are formed, with crests normal to the direction of the tidal currents. The height of the ripples is between 4 and 7 meters, and their wavelength varies between 250 and 450 meters. In addition to these ripples, which are at right angles to the direction of the tidal currents, there are other large, long ridges running parallel with the direction of the tidal currents. Although this Strait is outside the prescribed boundary of the South China Sea, and the water exchange through it is weak, it is still the main, direct connection with the Indian Ocean.

East: On the east, Mindoro Channel, running along the western side of Mindoro Island, is the deepest connection between the South China Basin and the Sulu Sea, with a sill depth of about 450 meters.

The Balabac Strait just north of Borneo contains numerous coral reefs with sill depths of only 100 meters. Relatively little water is transported through this passage.

Sediments

An inner zone of mud is characteristic of the continental shelf near the Mekong and Red River deltas. Off southeast Vietnam, in the vicinity of Camranh Bay, sand, rock, and coral are commonly found except where streams are building deltas. On the eastern side of the South China Sea, many coral islands contribute to the sediments. The Sunda Shelf is covered with littoral sediments, and the submerged valleys contribute great quantities of littoral sediments throughout the Shelf. Some volcanic ash is found in the southern parts.

The sediment of the deeper parts of the South

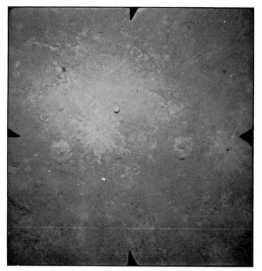

Fig. 3. Smooth clay sea floor in deep water off Luzon. Area 4 feet square. (USNEL photo by Shipek)

China Sea are mainly composed of clay with some globigerina ooze. A characteristic part of the sediments in both deep and shallow water is volcanic ash. This is found in layers having been derived from large volcanic eruptions in the East Indies, notably the enormous eruption of Krakatoa in 1883, and the ash transported throughout the entire area by both wind and currents (Fig. 3).

Geotectonics

The South China Sea is one of the largest "marginal seas" of the western Pacific (of a series extending from the Bering Sea to the Tasman Sea) that are classified by Stille as *quasicratonic* regions, i.e., basins that were formerly, at least in part, continental areas, that have rifted and collapsed during Tertiary and even Quaternary times. There is now systematic evidence that all of these basins are partly "regenerated" oceanic areas, the cause being still unknown; Beloussov speaks of "basification" of the former continental crust, leading to collapse (see his discussion in article on *Japan Sea*); Carey and others favor continental splitting and drift, during a general earth expansion (see *Expansion Theory*, in pr Vol. V).

The geotectonic evidence is clear. The China Sea Basin, covering about 1.5×10^6 km², appears to have dropped about 4 km, leaving residual submarine plateaus, the Paracel (Hsi-Sha) Islands and Macclesfield Banks in the northwest, and the great Reed-Nanshan-Tizard block (of about 250,000 km²) in the south. These plateaus are punctuated by vast numbers of coral reefs, islets and banks (described by Moore, 1889; Bassett-Smith, 1890, 1894, and others). The southern plateau is still marked on all charts as "Dangerous

Area (unsurveyed)." Many of these "banks" are drowned atolls (e.g., Rifleman, Ardasier, Gre Feza, Investigator, Owen, Spratley). Wharton, in 1890, commented on these characteristics; he recorded an offshore slope off Macclesfield Banks of 51° for 4200 feet.

Saurin (1955), in discussing the Paracels, believed that the bulk of the movement was Quaternary. Most members of this group rise to 5 meters above MSL, showing cores of phosphatized limestone (evidently pre-Wisconsin), bordered by Holocene shingle ramparts or beach ridges, and modern reefs; phosphate reserves are small (Clerget, 1932). Drowned karst features are common (Kuo, 1948). The atolls are not as a rule associated with volcanic foundations, and thus are not the oceanic type, but are drowned shelf atolls, characteristic of non-volcanic quasicratonic plateaus and ridges (Heezen's "aseismic ridges"), as seen in the Melanesian Borderland (described by Fairbridge and Stewart in 1961), in the Coral Sea Plateau, in the Paternosters and Tijger Islands of the Flores Sea, in the Maldives and Laccadives of the Indian Ocean. Atolls of this sort, with their foundations thousands of feet below hermatypic coral growth limits, conclusively prove crustal subsidence.

The foundations of the South China Sea appear to consist, partly at least, of an extension of the Indo-Sinian Shield of the mainland, which was stabilized mainly by widespread granitization and metamorphism during the Paleozoic up till Triassic. Later Mesozoic and Tertiary orogenic belts form the southern and eastern borders of the sea, in Borneo and the Philippines. Sediments in those geosynclines would appear to have been eroded (at least in part) from the land mass that has now subsided in the China Sea Basin.

Oceanography

Climate. The atmosphere-ocean energy exchange is the basis for the monsoons that characterize the climate of Southeast Asia. The main principle involved in this exchange is the difference between the heating of the land and the heating of the sea. In summer, the Asian land mass is much warmer than the sea; in the winter, the Asian land mass, particularly the Tibetan Plateau, is much colder than the sea. The summer heating of the air masses over Asia builds areas of low pressure and creates the monsoonal wind systems. In winter, the situation is reversed.

Winds. In summer (May to September), the warm air over the land is associated with a low-pressure area around which the winds circulate

Fig. 4. Surface currents in February of Southeast Asian Waters. Wind direction in upper right.

Fig. 5. Surface currents in August of Southeast Asian Waters. Wind direction in upper right (after Wyrtki).

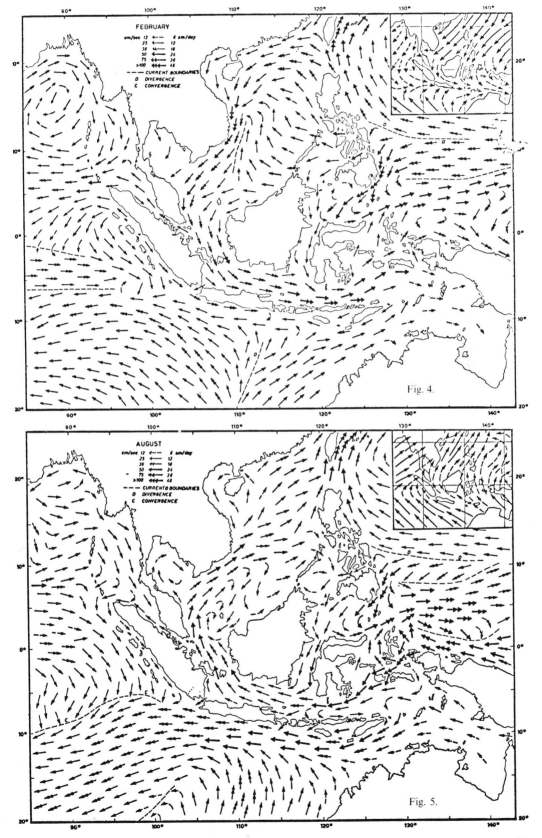

Fig. 4.

Fig. 5.

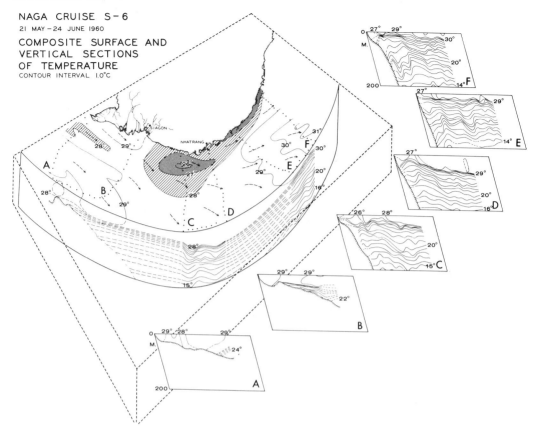

NAGA CRUISE S-6
21 MAY - 24 JUNE 1960
COMPOSITE SURFACE AND
VERTICAL SECTIONS
OF TEMPERATURE
CONTOUR INTERVAL 1.0°C

Fig. 6. Temperature structure of the surface layers of the western South China Sea.

counterclockwise. Off Vietnam, in the South China Sea, the counterclockwise circulation is demonstrated by winds having a southwesterly component.

In winter (November to March), the cold air over the land is associated with a high-pressure area around which the winds circulate clockwise. Off Vietnam, the clockwise circulation is demonstrated by winds having a northeasterly component.

Currents. The monsoon winds control the surface currents flowing into the South China Sea. In February, the flow from the north is through the Formosa Strait and Bashi Channel, and from the east through Balabac Strait (Fig. 4). The flow is generally south.

Weak countercurrents exist in the central and eastern sides of the South China Sea. These feed into the general southward component along the coast. The strongest flow is along the bulging east central part of Vietnam in January, with speeds of 3 knots. The outgoing flow is mainly through the south into the Java Sea through the Karimata and Gasper Straits and a little to the west through the Malacca Straits. Early spring is the transition period for these currents.

In August, the surface flow into the South China Sea is from the south through the Karimata and Gasper Straits, but the general trend is northeasterly (Fig. 5). The maximum flow, with current speeds of about 2 knots, is to the northeast near the South Vietnam coast. There is a weak countercurrent on the eastern side of the Sea.

Temperature Structure. The temperature structure of the upper 200 meters of the sea changes seasonally and reflects the processes taking place.

Comprehensive vertical and horizontal thermal data were obtained by the Naga Expedition on five cruises that were spaced throughout the year.

Winter: The temperature structure reflects the change from southwest to northeast winds that takes place in the fall. During the winter the northeast winds blow the surface water down the coast and deflect it against the Vietnamese shore line.

The layer above the sharp thermocline becomes deeper near the coast and reaches a depth of 150 meters. Thus the water over the western part of the Sunda Shelf is isothermal to the bottom. The runoff of northern rivers, during winter, flows south along the coast and develops vertical density gradients.

Summer: The changeover period occurs in spring. In early summer, colder water is still flowing down the North Vietnam coast and maintaining a band of less than 27°C along the coast. The changeover flow to the north takes place first along the South Vietnam coast. The summer monsoon winds develop stronger southerly currents that extend all along the coast and throughout the South China Sea. These cause the surface water to be moved away from the central or bulging part of the coast. The thermocline rises, and pronounced upwelling takes place near the coast, with water of less than 26°C at the surface (Fig. 6). The removal of surface water and shoaling of the thermocline is felt several hundred miles to the northeast. However, the maximum upwelling occurs off the central South Vietnam coast in midsummer. At this season there is even stratified water over the Banda Shelf, with a strong thermocline at the outer parts of the temperature sections.

River Runoff. Almost every feature of the oceanographic environment of the South China Sea is conditioned by the monsoon, which in-

creases during the wet summer season. This is especially noticeable in the runoff volumes of the Red River at Haiphong and the Mekong River near Saigon. During the summer the Mekong triples its annual average (4000 cu ft/sec) runoff, and the relative change is even greater for the Red River (600 cu ft/sec). This increase of runoff emphasizes the existence of the rainy monsoon, whose winds create a northerly surface current. The decrease of runoff occurs during the dry winter season when winds cause a southerly flow.

Chemistry. *Salinity.* The surface salinity of the South China Sea is dominated in winter by the inflow of higher salinity (34.5‰) water, from the open Pacific, through the Bashi Channel and Formosa Strait (Fig. 7). Because of the reduced runoff from the coastal rivers, a tongue of higher salinity water extends down the coast, but decreases in value with distance to the southern boundary of the sea. Here it is about 32.0‰. Countercurrent flow is evidenced by the lower salinity values on the eastern side of the sea.

In summer, the salinity over the South China Sea is lower because of the admixture of lower-salinity water from the Mekong River, and that

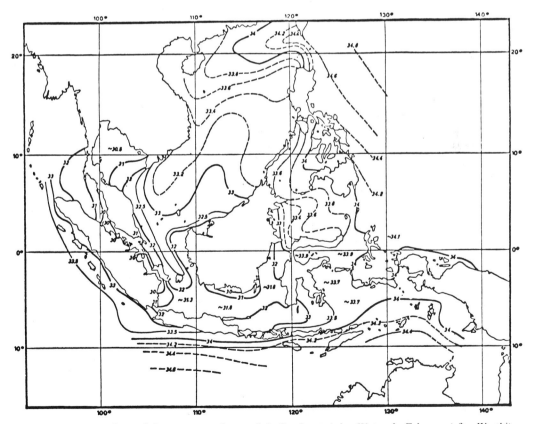

Fig. 7. Average surface salinity (parts per thousand) in Southeast Asian Waters in February (after Wyrtki).

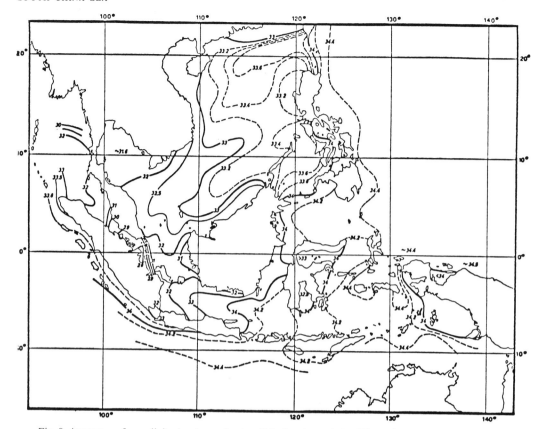

Fig. 8. Average surface salinity (parts per thousand) in Southeast Asian Waters in August (after Wyrtki).

transported northward by the strong coastal current on the western part of the Sea. The salinity of the eastern part remains high because of the weak southerly flow (Fig. 8).

The seasonal interchange of surface water is relatively thin. The deeper layers are less variable. In the northern part of the South China Sea, there is a distinct salinity maximum (about 34.7‰) between 100–200 meters and a second broad minimum layer around 500 meters. These layers, as well as those of temperature, undergo a seasonal vertical change because of the deeper intrusion from the Pacific Ocean in the north during winter (Fig. 9).

Oxygen: The surface oxygen content of 4.0 ml/liter shows saturation, but the subsurface layers show variations. At the salinity maximum, the higher oxygen saturation values occur in the north, decreasing toward the south. This decrease in oxygen from about 2.2–1.5 ml/¹liter closely corresponds with the deeper salinity minimum.

The water on the western sides of the South China Sea at depths between 200 and 3000 meters is of the same character as that of the adjacent parts of the West Pacific. Below 3000 meters, basin

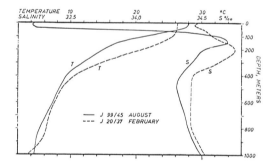

Fig. 9. Vertical temperature and salinity structures in the northern entrance of the South China Sea in February and August (after Wyrtki).

conditions exist, the temperature increases toward the bottom, and the salinity remains constant. The increase in the temperature is not large enough to cause instability since the potential temperature decreases slightly. The oxygen content is nearly constant below 3000 meters, whereas in the open ocean it increases below that depth.

E. C. LaFond

References

Dickerson, R. E., 1941, "Molengraaff River: A drowned Pleistocene stream . . ." in "Shiftings of sea floors and coastlines," *Univ. Penn. Bicentennial Conf.* 1940, 13–30.

Kuenen, P. H., 1950, "Marine Geology," New York, John Wiley & Sons, 568pp.

Kuo, L. C., 1948, "Geomorphology of the Tizard Bank and Reefs, Nan-Sha Islands, China," *Acta. Geol. Taiwan.*, **2**, 45–55.

LaFond, E. C., 1963, "Physical oceanography and its relation to the marine organic production in the South China Sea, in Ecology of the Gulf of Thailand and the South China Sea," in "A report of the results of the NAGA Expedition," *Scripps Inst. Oceanogr. Contrib.*, 63–66, 5–33.

Shepard, F. P., Emery, K. O., and Gould, H. R., 1949, "Distribution of sediments of East Asistic continental shelf," *Univ. So. Calif. (A. Hancock Fd. Publ.) Occ. Paper*, **9**.

Udintsev, G. B., *et al.*, 1963, "A new bathymetric map of the Pacific Ocean," *Acad. Sci. U.S.S.R., Soviet Geophysical Committee. Section X of the IGY Program. Oceanological Researches: Articles*, No. 9, 60–101.

VanBaren, F. A., and Kiel, H., 1950, "Contribution to the sedimentary petrology of the Sunda Shelf," *J. Sediment. Petrol.*, **20**, 185–213.

Wyrtki, Klaus, 1961, "Physical oceanography in Southeast Asian waters," *Naga Report, Scientific Results of Marine Investigations of the South China Sea and the Gulf of Thailand* 1959–1961, **2**.

SOUTHERN OCEAN

The Southern Ocean, sometimes called the *Antarctic Ocean*, or *Mer Austral* by the French, comprises the seas encircling the Antarctic continent and is thus, in one sense, a part of three other oceans. Seasonal changes render it difficult to define a rigid boundary to this ocean, but an approximate limit may be regarded as the line of the Antarctic Convergence (q.v.), the northern limit of the Antarctic surface water. This is a natural boundary and is almost continuous around Antarctica. In this consideration of the Ocean, an arbitrary limit of approximately 52°S latitude has been assumed (Herdman, Wiseman and Ovey, 1956). Statistics available for a Southern Ocean, defined by Boguslawski at 55°S (1884) give an area of 32×10^6 km^2 and a volume of 120×10^{15} m^3, but this figure could be 10% larger with the broader definition.

The term Southern Ocean is not generally used by hydrographic authorities (see International Hydrographic Bureau, 1953) but for the oceanographer, it serves conveniently to name a virtually distinct body of water with its own physical characteristics (Herdman, 1937), which supports a common fauna. To meteorologists the term connotes an area where strong westerly winds prevail, thus influencing markedly the weather over and around Antarctica. The term enables the morphologist to consider the features in the southern seas as a whole, rather than distribute them among the Atlantic, Indian and Pacific Oceans. One may conveniently refer to the "Southern Ocean sector" of each of the great oceans.

Bathymetry

The major features of the floor of the Southern Ocean are well established (Herdman *et al.*, 1956). Many thousands of individual echo soundings and continuous echograms have been taken over a number of the more interesting features in the last thirty years. The general shape of the major features is thus known to consist of three large basins separated by ridges (Fig. 2). No very detailed surveys of specific areas, however, have yet been made.

The three major basins referred to above are:

(a) *the Atlantic-Indian-Antarctic Basin* (also referred to as the *African-Antarctic Basin* or *Valdivia Basin*), bounded on the north by the South Orkney-Sandwich Ridge, the Atlantic-

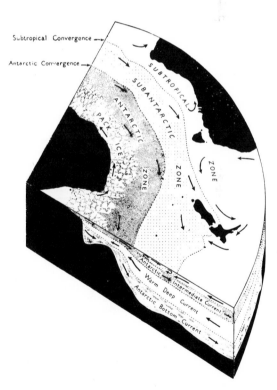

Fig. 1. Typical segment of the Southern Ocean, situated south of Australia and New Zealand. The arbitrarily established boundary of the Southern Ocean, 52°S, here corresponds roughly to the position of Antarctic Convergence. Its special relationship to the Antarctic Intermediate, deep and bottom currents, and to the Subtropical Convergence, is indicated (from Fleming, 1962).

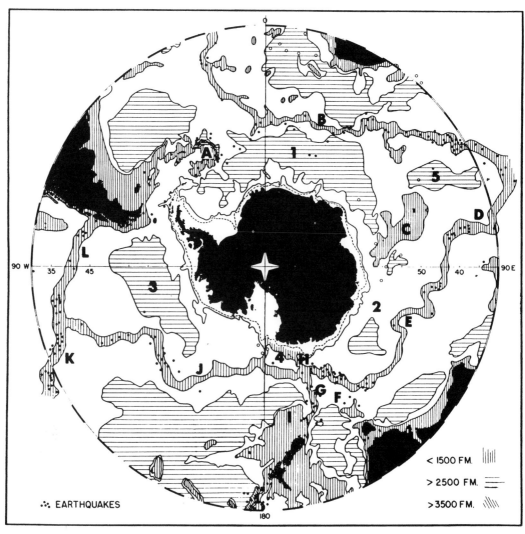

Fig. 2. Bathymetry of the Southern Ocean and adjacent oceanic regions, showing location of the Mid-Ocean Ridge, transverse ridges and basins (from Ewing and Heezen, 1956). Numerals and letters indicate respectively basins and ridge nomenclature after various authorities.

(1) *Atlantic–Indian–Antarctic Basin* (of Wüst, 1936) (alternatively *Atlantic–Antarctic Basin* of Mackintosh; *African–Antarctic Basin* or *Valdivia Basin*). (2) *Eastern Indian Antarctic Basin* (alternatively *Australian–Antarctic Basin* or *Knox Basin*). (3) *Pacific Antarctic Basin* (alternatively *Bellingshausen Basin*). (4) *Balleny Basin*. (5) *East Crozet Basin* (alternatively *S.W. Indian Basin*, or *Kerguelen Basin*, almost entirely outside of Southern Ocean).

(A) *Scotia Ridge* and *South Sandwich Trench*. (B) The *Atlantic–Indian Ridge* (*Bouvet Ridge, Prince Edward–Crozet Ridge*). (C) *Kerguelen–Gaussberg Ridge*. (D) *Amsterdam–St. Paul Plateau*. (E) *Indian–Antarctic Ridge* (*Australian–Antarctic Ridge*; or *S.E. Indian Ridge*). (F) *Mill Rise*. (G) *Macquarie Ridge*. (H) *Balleny Ridge*. (I) *Campbell Plateau*. (J) *Pacific–Antarctic Ridge*. (K) *East Pacific Rise*. (L) *South Chile Ridge*.

Antarctic Ridge, and the Prince Edward-Crozet Ridge, and on the east by the Kerguelen-Gaussberg Ridge. Its greatest depth is 5872 m, at 58° 40′S, 29° 30′E.

(b) *The Eastern Indian-Antarctic Basin* (also referred to as the *Australian-Antarctic Basin* or *Knox Basin*), lying to the east of the Kerguelen-Gaussberg Ridge, bounded on the north by the Amsterdam-St. Paul Plateau and on the south by

the Indian Antarctic Ridge. Its greatest depth is 5455 m, at 54° 32′S, 123° 05′ 00″E.

(c) *The Pacific-Antarctic Basin* (or *Bellingshausen Basin*), with a greatest depth of 6414 m at 66° 58′S, 176° 14′W. It is bounded on the west and north by the Pacific-Antarctic Ridge and the South-Eastern Pacific Plateau. A minor basin, almost an appendage to the above, is the *Balleny Basin*, situated just east of the Balleny Island.

There is a single deep-sea trench in the Southern Ocean on the east of the South Sandwich Islands and adjoining the Scotia Ridge. This is the *South Sandwich Trench*, which extends for 600 miles between 55°S 32°W and 61°S 27°W. It is roughly defined by the 3000-fathom (5486 m) contour and reaches a maximum depth of 8260 m (the *Meteor* Depth) at 55° 7.3′S 26° 46.5′W. The existence of this feature was forecast by Suess (1909), and its presence was confirmed by the *Meteor* in 1926, which crossed it, near the northern end. Between 1930 and 1938, the *Discovery II* crossed it eleven times from 54° 45′S to 60° 45′S.

The most important ridge is the *Scotia Ridge*, or Arc, or "Southern Antilles," by which the Andes are joined to the Antarctic Peninsula (Graham Land). The first mention of a possible connection around the Scotia Ridge appears to have been made by Bellingshausen early in the nineteenth century. Later, others put forward similar theories based largely on geological evidence, but it was not until the advent of echo sounding that proof of an underwater connection along the generally accepted line became available (Herdman, 1932). The earlier echo soundings, admittedly, were sparse in some areas, but there could be little doubt that an arcuate connection existed between the Andes and the Antarctic Peninsula via Staten Island, the Burdwood Bank, the Shag Rocks, South Georgia (the inclusion of which in the suggested Arc had long been a matter of controversy among geologists), the Clerke Rocks, the South Sandwich Islands, the South Orkneys, Clarence and Elephant Islands, and the Antarctic Peninsula (Graham Land). By 1939 (Herdman, 1948), many more soundings had been taken by the *Discovery II*; these, together with more geological specimens (Tyrrell, 1945) were final proof of the arcuate connection.

[Editorial note: The *Antarctic Peninsula* is the newly agreed upon name—according to the U.S. Board on Geographic Names (Dept. of the Interior, March 1964)—for the region first named "Graham Land," following its recognition and publication on nautical charts by the British Admiralty. Research a century later (by W. H. Hobbs) in old whaling logs (previously kept secret) disclosed that the area had been sighted within a few months of Capt. Bransfield's voyage (1820) by a Capt. Palmer, a whaler out of Nantucket. The name "Palmer Peninsula" was adopted for U.S. charts. Actually, the Russians under Bellingshausen may have sighted this land first. As now resolved, the northern half will be called Graham Land and the southern (below 70°S) will be called Palmer Land. R.W.F.]

The *Kerguelen-Gaussberg Ridge* separates the Atlantic-Indian-Antarctic Basin from the Eastern Indian-Antarctic Basin and exerts a profound influence on the movement of the water masses

here; it was the subject of a partial survey by the B.A.N.Z.A.R. Expedition in 1929–1931. Two shallow areas, which may be seamounts, were located, with a minimum depth of 642 m. The ridge was also crossed on various occasions by the *Discovery II*. In a traverse, 1937, the echogram showed that the bottom was extremely irregular at depths greater than 1100 fathoms (2012 m). Of the other ridges, little is known other than the broad outline, except, possibly, the Macquarie-Balleny Ridge, on which a fair number of soundings have been taken.

Charts and Maps. The U.S.H.O. Chart of Antarctica No. 2562 (1956) represents the pre-IGY status and was then the most up-to-date bathymetric chart of the Southern Ocean on a reasonably large scale. A complete revision is now overdue. A small-scale map of the bottom relief was published as an inset on the American Geographical Society's map of Antarctica (1962). Although this inset is small, the relief is well shown, but the nomenclature does not always agree with present usage. There is also a Russian bathymetric chart (1961), covering roughly the same area as Chart No. 2562, on which the bottom relief appears very similar to that shown on other maps or charts. The Russian geomorphic and sedimentological maps of the Southern Ocean, issued respectively by Zhivago (1962) and Lisitzin (1962), offer the best general coverage in these fields. The southern parts of the South Atlantic and Indian Ocean geomorphic maps of the Heezen and Tharp series are the best available in those sectors.

Geology

For many years, little was known about the geological structure of the various underwater features of the Southern Ocean, with the exception of the Scotia Ridge, and much was inferred from soundings. Dredging the sea floor for rock was not easy, even in the temperate zone; in one of the stormiest oceans, it was almost impossible.

[The following notes on the Southern Ocean geology have been contributed by the Editor:

With the advent of the International Geophysical Year (1958/1959) and the continuing exploratory efforts in the Antarctic continent, the coordinated expeditions to the Indian Ocean since then, and the general step-up in oceanographic and geophysical research, a great deal has recently been learned about the Southern Ocean region.

The existence of a worldwide Mid-Ocean Ridge (q.v.) which swings round from the South Atlantic into the Indian Ocean and again south of Australia into the Pacific was clearly indicated on a large folding map by L. Kober in 1928. Although his data were quite sparse in many places, the existence of this ridge has now been completely justified by vast numbers of echo-sounding traverses. It roughly approximates the arbitrary northern boundary of the Southern Ocean (52°S) from longitude 10°W in the Atlantic-Indian Ridge section. It then swings north-eastward in the Southwest Indian Ridge to join the Mid-Indian Ridge at 30°S in longitude 70°E. A branch of the ridge is then traced to the southeast through the Amsterdam-St. Paul Plateau to make a sinuous pattern south of Australia (the Indian-Antarctic Ridge or Australian-Antarctic Ridge), to join the Pacific-Antarctic Ridge continuing in the East Pacific (Easter Island) Rise. A branch then runs southeastward to touch land in the south of Chile, the South Chile Ridge.

Thus, the Mid-Ocean Ridge is by far the largest submarine geological structure in the Southern Ocean. With its sinuosities it is over 10,000 miles (16,000 km) long in this region. Its role in geology is still disputed, but its presence and certain attributes have been firmly established by Ewing and Heezen (1956). It is marked by a central rift zone that is characterized by abnormally high heat flow (an order of magnitude higher than normal), by very high seismicity (the vast majority of mid-ocean shocks occur in this belt), by very youthful topography (fault scarps), by rapidly alternating gravity anomalies, by basic volcanic rocks of very youthful origin (isotopic dates often indicate 5 million years and less), by a very thin sedimentary veneer if any at all, and by seismic refraction evidence that there is a "root" of modified mantle material (less dense than normal). The meaning of all this is a serious challenge, but is widely taken to imply a youthful "suture'" on the earth's surface, which may mark the site of recent expansion of the mantle (see discussion in *Mid-Ocean Ridges*).

The transverse ridges of the Southern Ocean, connecting the various sectors of the Mid-Ocean Ridge with the Antarctic Continent or with the adjacent continents, are of varied geological character.

The *Scotia Ridge* is evidently an orogenic belt that contains elements of Andean and West Antarctica rocks. There are geosynclinal sediments and volcanics (of the "Pacific Suite") ranging from older Paleozoic up to Holocene (Fairbridge, 1952).

The Scotia Ridge impinges in the north on an east-west gash, 600 miles long (the Malvines Trench), separating it from the Falklands Plateau, which has the character of an aseismic ridge (q.v.) or microcontinent in Heezen's terminology. Its geology is exposed in the Falkland Islands and discloses middle Paleozoic sedimentary rocks, clearly intermediate in character between those of the Argentine and South Africa. The rise appears to be a partly foundered or split segment of continental origin and of considerable antiquity.

The next transverse ridge to the east is the *Kerguelen-Gaussberg Ridge* that was first suggested by the German South-Polar Expedition of 1901–1903. The Gaussberg is a youthful volcano (of leucite-basalt) near the coast of Enderby Land, and the Kerguelen Islands are a large cluster of mature (Tertiary) volcanic islands rising from a broad swell, rather like that of the Azores. Although there are intermediate high points along the Kerguelen-Gaussberg Ridge like Heard Island and the BANZARE and Gribb seamounts, recent surveys have disclosed that this "ridge" is much less continuous than it appeared on the earlier maps (Zhivago, 1962). It appears to be an ill-defined structure of mainly volcanic character.

South of Australia, from Tasmania through the Mill Bank, Macquarie Island and the Balleny Islands to Cape Adare on the Antarctic mainland, there is another poorly defined elevation that appears to be of mixed origin. In the north (Mawson's Mill Rise; also referred to as South Tasmania Ridge), there may be an aseismic, continental type ridge. From Macquarie Island (a block-faulted and tilted volcanic feature) to the Balleny Islands, there is what Schott called the *Macquarie Swell*; to the north-northeast it seems to connect with New Zealand in a highly seismic zone, but bathymetrically it is cut off by a trough south of the Campbell (New Zealand) Plateau. Finally through the Balleny Islands (all basaltic volcanoes) there appears to be a volcanic ridge, Herdman's Macquarie-Balleny Ridge, about 160°E which is incompletely connected with the Tertiary basaltic volcanics at Cape Adare on the Antarctic mainland. According to Ewing and Heezen (1956), the midsection that connects the Mill Rise with the Macquarie-Balleny Ridge is part of the Mid-Ocean Ridge.

Finally, from the region of Easter Island to the southern part of Chile, there is the South Chile Ridge (see map by Menard, 1964, p. 25). It is paralleled on the north by a long narrow trough that suggests important strike-slip faulting that matches similar displacements of the East Pacific Rise. Its general character suggests a branch of the Mid-Ocean Ridge system.

Ewing and Heezen (1956) reported that many seamounts were being disclosed by the new echo sounding; many are apparently flat-topped, which geologically suggests regional subsidence of ridges and basin floors as well as some local isostatic compensation.

The three deep basins peripheral to the Antarctic continent have been sampled for sediments (see below), and recent seismic reflection profiling has disclosed a moderately thick cover of flat-lying sediments that may go back to Mesozoic times. Seismic refraction shows that such basins are underlain by thin oceanic crust. R.W.F.]

Bottom Deposits

The sediment immediately north of the Antarctic Convergence consists almost wholly of globigerina ooze, occurring in a virtually continuous belt

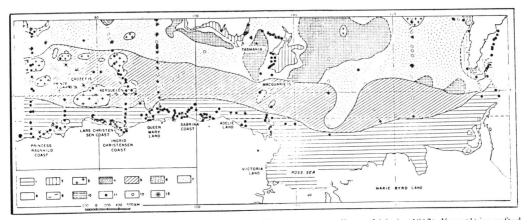

Fig. 3. Southern Ocean bottom deposits (Indian to Pacific sectors) according to Lisitzin (1962). Key: (1) ice-rafted sediments, (2) non-glacial terrigenous, (3) volcanic sediments, (4) diatom shelf clay, (5) oceanic diatom sediments, (6) sponge spicules (spongolite), (7) globigerina ooze, (8) bryozoa and coquina, (9) phosphorite and glauconite sediments, (10) red clay, (11) cores, (12) bottom samples, (13) cores plus bottom samples.

around the Southern Ocean (see Fig. 3). South of the Antarctic Convergence, where lower surface temperatures prevail, diatom ooze is found in a wide belt. There are small patches of siliceous sponge spicule ooze (spongolite) especially about 66°S, 40°E (Lisitzin, 1962). Close around the Antarctic continent, the bottom deposit is almost entirely terrigenous, unique for its marine till (moraine), with glacial mud prevailing (Neaverson, 1934). Dredgings have provided rich assortments of Antarctic glacial boulders (Stewart, 1963). During the cold periods of the Pleistocene, floating ice reached 30–40°N (Lisitzin and Zhivago, 1960) and large deposits of boulders from grounded icebergs have been found off South Africa (Needham, 1962). Some red clay is found south and southeast of Australia, on the northern fringe of the Southern Ocean in the Pacific Sector, south and west of South America, and in a small area in the Atlantic Sector centered on 40°W longitude; there is a correlation between red clay and the cold, CO_2-rich bottom waters that selectively remove any carbonate ooze (Wüst, 1934; see *Calcium Carbonate Compensation Depth*).

The areas north and south of the Antarctic Convergence yield valuable information about past temperature changes in the upper layer of the Southern Ocean, thanks to long cores from the sediment in these localities (already noted by Schott, 1939). Conditions adverse to coring, however, prevail in this area of gales and bad weather and, so far, only a few have been obtained. The layering in these cores shows that the Antarctic Convergence has both advanced and retreated several times during the Quaternary period.

That the type of sediment has a marked effect on the clarity of the echo is well known in echo sounding. Rock and red clay return good echoes, and reasonably sharp ones are returned from

radiolarian and globigerina oozes. For many years, especially on or just south of the Convergence, echo sounding with the sonic equipment then available was difficult, the echoes being either "woolly" or nonexistent. At first it was assumed that as the transmitter was working well, the microphone was defective, but echoes again became normal as the ship passed out of the region. It was not until some years later, when repeated lines of observation were made across the Antarctic Convergence in a fixed longitude that the real reason was found. Water samples taken near the bottom were found to contain such a high percentage of dead and moribund diatoms that the water resembled pea soup, inhibiting not only the outgoing sound waves, but also the returning echoes.

Nutrients

The Southern Ocean is exceptionally rich in nutrients, especially in the region of the convergences. The amounts of phosphate, nitrate and silica in the surface waters rarely drop below the winter maxima in temperate latitudes (Clowes, 1938). The surface water of the sub-Antarctic zone is less rich. Nevertheless, the entire region is "richer in life than any other comparable oceanic area" (Murphy, 1962).

Oceanic Circulation

The general principles of the circulation of the water masses of the Southern Ocean were outlined by Deacon (1936 and 1939). Over the greater part of the Ocean strong westerly winds prevail, with a consequent easterly trend in the currents (Wyrtki, 1960; Maksimov and Vorobyer, 1965). They do not flow due east, since other factors, including the topography of the bottom, deflect them north and south, and near the Antarctic coast there are movements east and north in the surface and

Fig. 4. Water transport in the Antarctic Water Ring. The water transport (3000-decibar reference surface) between two lines amounts to approximately 20 million m³/sec. (SB) South Antillean Arc; (AR) Atlantic Ridge; (KG) Kerguelen–Gaussberg Ridge; (MS) Macquarie Ridge; (SR) South Pacific Ridge (according to Sverdrup, 1942.) (By permission of Prentice-Hall, Inc. N.Y.)

bottom layers (Fig. 4). Sverdrup (1942) calculated on the basis of rather poor data that the total east-to-west transport of water through the Drake Passage constriction was 90×10^6 m³/sec, about 400 times the discharge of the Amazon, the world's largest river. Some 150×10^6 m³/sec is a more modern figure obtained by the Russian workers (Kort, 1962). About 180×10^6 m³/sec passes south of Australia, and the surplus must swing north into the Pacific. Some 190×10^6 m³/sec passes south of Africa also with some eddy loss.

The surface current near the continent is shallow, cold and of low salt content, and as it flows to the north, the loss is replaced by fresh water from melting ice, snow, rain and highly saline water from the deep southward-moving warm layer. The northward movement is due partly to the combined effect of the earth's rotation and the strong westerly wind, and partly to convection. This Antarctic water, being much heavier than the warmer surface waters farther north, tends to sink but is restricted to a shallow layer by the highly saline water of the deep current. Farther north, in the latitude where warm deep current climbs steeply over the cold bottom current, it soon sinks to a lower level as the Antarctic intermediate current. North of this latitude, although there is still a northward movement at the surface, there is room above the sinking intermediate current for a southward movement in the subsurface layer, and this current, mixing with the descending cold surface water,

gives rise to a warmer type of surface water known as subantarctic water. At the surface, the Antarctic and subantarctic currents generally meet at a sharp boundary, known as the *Antarctic Convergence* (q.v.), the position of which is determined by the latitude in which the deep water climbs steeply over the bottom water; since these two currents suffer only minor variations, the convergence is a rather fixed feature although there is minor seasonal migration (Figs. 5 and 6).

Farther north, and in part outside the arbitrary northern limit set for the Southern Ocean, there is another boundary, between the subantarctic and subtropical currents, known as the *Subtropical Convergence* (q.v.). Since both currents here are subject to considerable variations, its position may, in certain localities, vary seasonally as much as 300 miles.

Near the Antarctic continent is the narrow zone in which easterly winds prevail. Here the surface water flows westward and, in the Atlantic Sector, the movement extends into the deep layer. When the *East Wind Drift*, as this surface current is called ("Western Coast Current" according to Kort, 1962), reaches the east coast of the Antarctic Peninsula, it is deflected northward by the Scotia Ridge to flow eastward across the Atlantic in about 50°S latitude. Its presence can be determined as far east as 20°E longitude, and it is a determining factor in the distribution of the pack ice in this sector.

The Weddell Sea (q.v.), one of the seas comprising the Southern Ocean, is extremely interesting because, apart from influencing the surface current, it is the main source of Antarctic bottom water. In the southwest corner of the Sea, freezing is very intense in winter, and the deep current is impoverished by mixing. Salinity of the surface layer is raised in winter mainly by the salt left behind in the water when sea ice is formed, until it is nearly as great as that of the deep layer. The two waters then mix and sink to the bottom. This bottom water then spreads eastward around the Southern Ocean and northward in the Atlantic, Indian and Pacific Oceans. As it spreads, it mixes with more of the deep water overlaying it, particularly near the Antarctic continental slope where the deep water is most cooled by shelf water. The bottom temperature and the salinities in the great depths increase continuously toward the east, with a decrease in the oxygen content. These facts show that there is no other region around Antarctica where the cold shelf water sinks to the ocean bed. Very highly saline and very cold bottom water does form in the Ross Sea but is prevented from reaching the open ocean by the presence of a submarine ridge across the mouth of the sea. Proof that the very cold oceanic bottom water has its origin in the Weddell Sea is found when the bottom waters east and west of the Antarctic

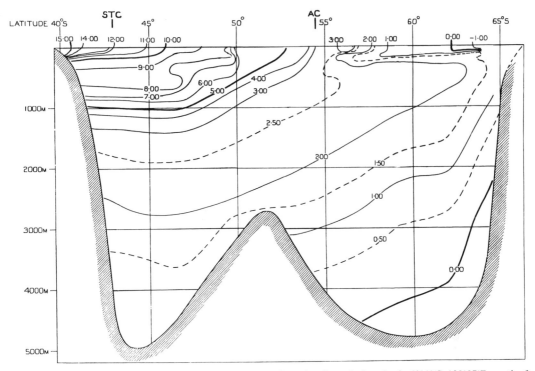

Fig. 5a. The distribution of temperature along north–south section from the ice edge in 63°41′S, 130°07′E, south of Australia, to Melbourne, Victoria; May–June 1932 (Deacon, 1937).

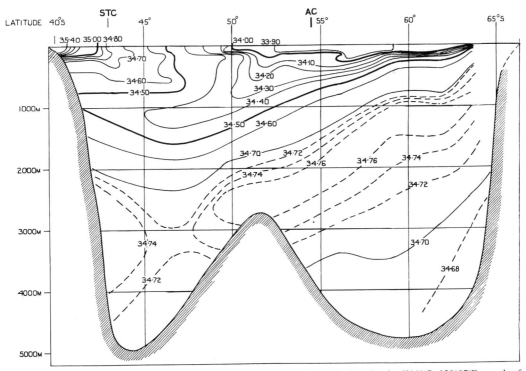

Fig. 5b. The distribution of salinity along north–south section from the ice edge in 63°41′S, 130°07′E, south of Australia, to Melbourne, Victoria; May–June 1932 (Deacon, 1937).

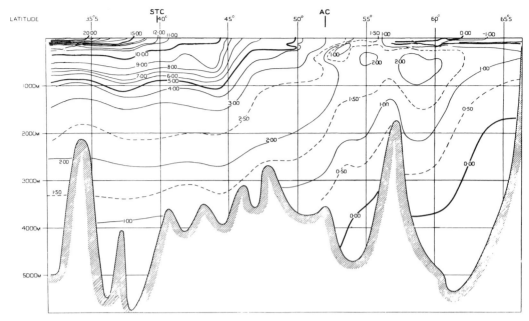

Fig. 6. The distribution of temperature along a diagonal traverse across South Indian Ocean sector from Enderby Land to Fremantle, Western Australia; April–May 1932 (Deacon, 1937).

Peninsula are compared: to the east, the water is newly formed with low temperature and salinity and a high oxygen content, whereas, to the west, salinity and temperature are much higher and oxygen content is less, because the current has traveled around the whole continent.

Ice

Ice, as icebergs (q.v.) or pack ice, constitutes one of the major hazards to navigation in the Southern Ocean (Fig. 7; see also U.S. Hydrographic Office, 1960). Little has been published on the subject of Antarctic icebergs except for charts showing the limits within which they are likely to be met, and a brief account of the icebergs and pack ice encountered by Captain James Cook, R.N., during his circumnavigation of Antarctica in 1772–1775 (Herdman, 1959). More is known about the pack ice, especially with regard to its distribution, both in summer and in winter (Mackintosh and Herdman, 1940) and Herdman (1953).

Icebergs found in the Southern Ocean originate mainly from the Filchner ice shelf in the Weddell Sea, the Ross ice shelf in the Ross Sea and the Shackleton ice shelf, in 95–100°E. Few bergs appear to be derived from the ice shelf in the Pacific Sector; those from the Ross Sea travel north and then northwest with the prevailing current, but if the ice shelf farther west does break away, the bergs cannot get clear of the stagnant body of pack ice found along the coasts between the Ross Sea and the Antarctic Peninsula. Icebergs which originate in shelf ice are tabular or flat-

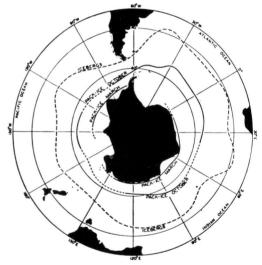

Fig. 7. Average northern limits of pack ice around the Antarctic Continent in March and October (after Mackintosh and Herdman) and average northern limit of icebergs according to British Admiralty Chart No. 1241.

topped when they break off and, so long as they stay south of the Antarctic Convergence, usually remain so. Once in warmer water, they melt quickly below the water line and thus lose stability. Normally, they then cant to expose a much worn outline, but sometimes the whole iceberg overturns before finally breaking up. The size of newly-formed bergs varies in length from a few feet to many miles (a tabular berg, over 90 miles in length, was reported in 1927 by a whaler, near Clarence Island and another "as large as the State of Connecticut" was reported during the IGY). Lengths up to 5 miles are not unusual. Height above water varies, according to the region of origin, between 90 and 140 feet; below water some must reach over 1000 feet.

The life of a normal-sized tabular berg may be quite short, especially if it gets some distance away from the coast before the winter freeze-up of the sea occurs. The following summer will see the berg well on its way to the north and east, and once across the Antarctic Convergence, it is unlikely to survive for long. If, on the other hand, an iceberg is trapped in the pack ice over a further summer, then it may well remain there for years, particularly in those regions where the surface current is negligible. The large tabular berg near Clarence Island mentioned above was still in the Southern Ocean some years later. By 1931 it had moved north and east to a position near South Georgia, where it was reported with a length of 60 miles. It was last seen some months later farther north and east, but further reduced in size.

The Antarctic pack ice, generally being more of a hindrance to navigation than individual icebergs, has been the subject of more research, especially in relation to its distribution (Mackintosh and Herdman, 1940; Herdman, 1948 and 1953). The pack ice around Antarctica generally has a well-defined northern boundary and extends north in late winter and spring, its edge lying approximately in the same position from July to October. Local conditions, such as gales, may cause a temporary displacement of the boundary, but with the return of more stable conditions, the ice edge will revert to its average position during these months.

During winter, in the Atlantic Sector of the Southern Ocean, the pack may stretch out some 900–1000 miles from the coast of Antarctica, covering the area of the very cold surface current flowing away from the Weddell Sea. Further east, where the continent lies north of the Antarctic Circle, the belt narrows considerably until the Ross Sea is reached, where the ice may once more extend 800 miles north of the shelf ice. Eastward, the belt narrows again toward the Antarctic Peninsula.

In the late summer, the pack ice melts and begins to break up, the ice edge gradually retreating toward the continent. The southern limit is reached usually in February or even March, although parts of the coasts of Antarctica, especially in the Indian Sector where the land lies north of the Antarctic Circle, may be free of ice as early as January. With the exception of the Pacific Sector, and probably the east coast of Graham Land, it is likely that nearly all parts of the fixed shelf ice or continental coast are free from pack ice from time to time

during the late summer. In the Pacific Sector, at least between the meridians of 75 and 140°W, the ice seems heavier and more stagnant. This is almost certainly due to the absence of an appreciable surface current, since the East Wind Drift has been turned north and east on leaving the Weddell Sea, and does not form again over the great part of the Pacific Sector.

The formation and distribution of pack ice have a close relationship with the distribution of surface temperature. Examination of the surface isotherms shows that in early April a wide belt of cold surface water, with a temperature of less than −1°C, surrounds the Antarctic continent. With still conditions and a low air temperature, rapid freezing of the sea begins and if still conditions continue to prevail, the ice crystals quickly become a thin sheet of ice. In the open ocean, quiet conditions seldom persist for any appreciable time, and since there is often an underlying swell, the newly formed ice is broken up, forming pancake ice. In the low temperatures of autumn, these pancakes grow rapidly to a fair size under the influence of wind, sea and snow. As winter comes on, bringing more precipitation, the pancakes grow into large floes. Further evidence of a relationship with surface temperature is the tremendous expanse of pack ice in winter, north and south of the Weddell Sea, which, in part, prevails as a tongue of ice floes stretching out far to the northeast in the very cold Weddell Sea surface current, long after the remainder of the pack ice in the area has dispersed. That this is a permanent feature of the distribution of the pack ice is borne out by the fact that its presence in late December 1772 was reported by Captain James Cook, R.N.

HENRY F. P. HERDMAN

References

American Geographical Society, 1962, Map of Antarctica, New York.

Clowes, A. J., 1938, "Phosphate and silicate in the Southern Ocean," *Discovery Rept.*, **19**, 1–120.

Deacon, G. E. R., 1937, "The hydrology of the Southern Ocean," *Discovery Rept.*, **15**, 1–124.

Deacon, G. E. R., 1939, "The Antarctic voyages of R.R.S. *Discovery II* and R.R.S. *William Scoresby*, 1935–1937," *Geogr. J.*, **93**, No. 3, 185–209.

Ewing, M., and Heezen, B. C., 1956, "Some problems of Antarctic submarine geology," in "Antarctica in the I.G.Y.," *Geophys. Mono.*, No. 1.

Fairbridge, R. W., 1952, "The Geology of the Antarctic," in "The Antarctic Today," pp. 56–101, Wellington, N.Z.

Fleming, C. A., 1952, "The Seas Between," in "The Antarctic Today," pp. 102–126, Wellington, N.Z.

Herdman, H. F. P., 1932, "Report on Soundings taken during the *Discovery* Investigations, 1926–1932," *Discovery Rept.*, **6**, 205–236, Pl. XLV–XLVII.

Herdman, H. F. P., 1948, "Soundings taken during the *Discovery* Invetigations, 1932–1939," *Discovery Rept.*, **25**, 39–106. Pl. XXIII–XXXI.

Herdman, H. F. P., 1948, "The Antarctic pack ice," *J. Glaciol.*, **1**, No. 4, 156–166, 172–173.

Herdman, H. F. P., 1953, "The Antarctic pack ice in winter," *J. Glaciol.*, **2**, No. 13, 184–193.

Herdman, H. F. P., 1959, "Early Discoverers—XII— Some notes on sea ice observed by Captain James Cook, R.N., during his circumnavigation of Antarctica, 1772–1775," *J. Glaciol.*, **3**, No. 26, 534–541.

Herdman, H. F. P., Wiseman, J. D. H., and Ovey, C. D., 1956, "Proposed name of features on the deep-sea floor," *Deep Sea Res.*, **3**, 253–261.

International Hydrographic Bureau, 1953, "The limits of oceans and sea," *Special Publication No. 23*, Third ed., Monaco.

Kort, V. G., 1962, "The Antarctic Ocean," *Sci. Am.*, **207**, 113–128.

Lisitzin, A. P., 1962, "Bottom sediments of the Antarctic," in "Antarctic research," *A.G.U. Monogr. 7*, 81–88.

Lisitzin, A. P., and Zhivago, A. V., 1960, "Marine geological work of the Soviet Antarctic Expedition 1955–1957," *Deep-Sea Res.*, **6**, 77–87.

Mackintosh, N. A., and Herdman, H. F. P., 1940, "Distribution of pack ice in the Southern Ocean," *Discovery Rept.*, **19**, 285–296, Pl. LXIX–XCV.

Maksimov, I. V., and Vorobyev, V. N., 1965, "Study of deep currents in the Antarctic Ocean," *Soviet Antarctic Exped. Inf. Bull.* (A.G.U. Washington, translation), **4**, No. 31.

Menard, H. W., 1964, "Marine Geology in the Pacific," New York, McGraw-Hill Book Co., 271pp.

Murphy, R. C., 1962, "The oceanic life of the Antarctic," *Sci. Am.*, **207**, 186–210.

Neaverson, E., 1934, "Sea-floor deposits. I. General character and distribution," *Discovery Rept.*, **9**, 295–350.

Needham, H. D., 1962, "Ice-rafted rocks from the Atlantic Ocean off the coast of the Cape of Good Hope," *Deep-Sea Res.*, **9**, 475–486.

Schott, W., 1939, "Deep-sea Sediments of the Indian Ocean," in "Recent Marine Sediments," pp. 396–408, Tulsa, American Association of Petroleum Geologists.

Stewart, D., 1963, "Petrography of some dredgings collected by operation Deep Freeze IV," *Proc. Am. Phil. Soc.*, **107**, 431–442.

Suess, E., 1909, "The Face of the Earth," Vol. 4, pp. 488–489, Oxford, Clarendon Press.

Sverdrup, H. U., Johnson, M. W., and Fleming, R. H., 1942, "The Oceans," Englewood Cliffs, N.J., Prentice-Hall, Inc., 1087pp.

Tyrrell, G. W., 1945, "Report on rocks from West Antarctica and the Scotia Arc," *Discovery Rept.*, **23**, 37–102.

U.S. Hydrographic Office, 1956, Chart No. 2562 (Antarctica), Washington, D.C.

U.S. Hydrographic Office, 1960, Sailing Directions: Antarctica, Second ed., Washington, D.C.

Wüst, G., 1934, "Anzeichungen von Beziehungen zwischen Bodenstrom und Relief in der Tiefsee des indischen Ozeans," *Naturwissenschaften*, **22**, 241–244.

Wyrtki, K., 1960, "The Antarctic circumpolar current and the Antarctic polar front," *Deut. Hydrograph. Z.*, **13**, 153–174.

Zhivago, A. V., 1962, "Outlines of Southern Ocean geomorphology," in "Antarctic research," *A.G.U. Monogr. 7*, 74–80.

SOUTHWEST PACIFIC OCEAN

Introduction

Physiography. The Southwest Pacific Ocean is generally recognized as extending from the equator through the Cook Islands and south to the region of the Subtropical Convergence in latitude 45°S. It includes part of the Southwestern Pacific Basin, the New Zealand region, and the Tasman and Coral Seas, together with the eastern Melanesian islands to the north. According to Wüst (1936), the last-named region, extending from the Melanesian Borderland to New Zealand and eastward to the Tonga–Kermadec line, should be called *Fiji Sea*.

The major physiographic elements are as follows: The whole of the easternmost part of the Southwest Pacific Ocean is occupied by the Southwestern Pacific Basin in depths of 3000 fathoms (5500 m). From the Basin arise numerous individual islands and seamounts together with dominantly linear chains of islands such as the Southern Cook group. The western margin of the Southwest Pacific Basin is formed from north to south by the Tonga and Kermadec Ridges and by the Subantarctic Slope east of New Zealand.

The central portion of the Southwest Pacific Ocean is occupied by the New Zealand Plateau, and by the three major ridges—Lord Howe Rise, Norfolk Ridge and Tonga–Kermadec Ridge—extending north and west from New Zealand, collectively known as the Melanesian complex. (One may note, however, that the ethnic boundary separating Melanesia from Polynesia passes between Fiji–New Caledonia on the one hand and Tonga–New Zealand on the other.) In the western part of the ocean, several major basins—Tasman, Coral Sea, South Fiji and North Fiji—lie with their floors in depths ranging from 2000–2700 fathoms (3650–4900 m).

One of the most striking deep-sea trench systems—the Tonga–Kermadec Trench, borders the Southwestern Pacific Basin. It is markedly linear and reaches a maximum depth of over 5500 fathoms (10,000 m).

History. The Southwest Pacific has been explored by Spanish, Portuguese, Dutch and British navigators since the sixteenth century. A substantial increase in our knowledge of both its geography and ocean depths came with the closing years of the nineteenth century. Both scientific expeditions, such as those of the *Challenger*, *Dana* and *Gazelle* as well as the hydrographic and cable surveys made by *Egeria* and *Penguin* have provided much useful data (see map of approximate courses: Fairbridge, 1962).

Physical Oceanography

The major surface current systems of the Southwest Pacific Ocean are principally derived from the west-flowing South Equatorial Current and Trade Wind Drift. The South Equatorial Current enters

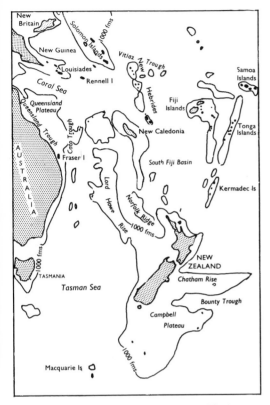

Fig. 1. Physiography of the Southwest Pacific Ocean.

the area from the east and is deflected southward through the Melanesian island groups into the Coral Sea to the northern Tasman Sea and the South Fiji Basin (Wyrtki, 1960).

The southern limit of the Ocean can be taken as the Subtropical Convergence (q.v.). This is the northern limit of subantarctic surface water that is moving north and west under the influence of prevailing westerly winds. Most of the Southwest Pacific is underlain at depths between 500 and 1500 m by the Antarctic Intermediate Layer. This cold, low-salinity water has spread north from the Antarctic Convergence, passing beneath the dominantly superficial Subtropical Convergence to become the most widely distributed hydrological feature of the Southwest Pacific. Underlying the Antarctic Intermediate Water is deep water of northern origin.

Sediments

A wide variety of sediment types is encountered on the Southwest Pacific Ocean floor (Murray, 1906). However by far the dominant sediment is calcareous ooze made up of foraminiferal tests. Below 2500 fathoms (4500 m) calcite dissolves and the bottom sediment in deeper water is a residual or wind-borne red clay (see *Calcium Carbonate Compensation Depth*).

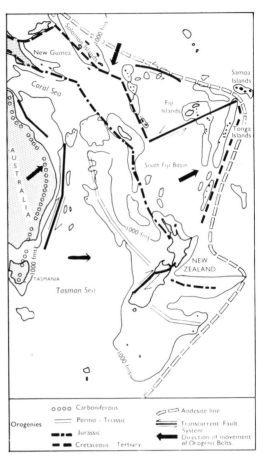

Fig. 2. Structural evolution of the Southwest Pacific (W.J.M.v.d.L.)

In volcanic areas, activity may be sufficient to produce ash and pumice which locally may dominate the sediment. The pumice may float thousands of miles and regularly reaches the beaches of eastern Australia from the New Hebrides. In most areas, some volcanic products, often minute glass shards, can be found in the surface sediment. Submarine volcanoes are surrounded by flows, products of violent eruption, and erosion of the cones themselves. In the north, the numerous coral reefs and islands are surrounded by aprons of coral debris.

In specific areas, e.g., on Chatham Rise, the occurrence of some areas of authigenic glauconite has been reported. The presence of phosphorite and manganese nodules has been noted in a few southern localities.

Terrigenous debris dominates out to about 500 fathoms around the New Zealand Plateau. In the south, glacial erratics dropped from icebergs in Pleistocene time have been found on Campbell Plateau and Chatham Rise at the present site of the Subtropical Convergence.

Structural Units

Geographically the area belongs to the Pacific, but geologically it does not. This is because of its position on the continental side of Marshall's Andesite line, which is the true boundary between the ancient oceanic and continental crusts. This boundary passes around the northern side of New Guinea, the Solomons, the Melanesian Border Plateau and the Tonga–Kermadec Ridge to New Zealand. However, a crust of continental thickness underlies only restricted parts of the area, and oceanic and intermediate quasi-cratonic crustal thicknesses are quite common.

Based on crustal thickness, Australia, Tasmania and New Guinea are continental. The Tasman Basin, the South Fiji Basin and the Coral Sea are oceanic. The other structural units in the region have an intermediate crustal thickness.

New Zealand is, like Japan, somewhat difficult to place in such a classification. A crustal thickness of 30–35 km for the New Zealand land mass seems sufficient to group it among the continents. As it is a structural part of the much wider New Zealand Plateau (Brodie, 1964) ranging in crustal thickness from 10–30 km, it seems preferable to classify New Zealand as intermediate.

The following is a summary of structural features in the Southwest Pacific:

"*Great Dividing Range*." The coastal ranges of east Australia and Tasmania (the "Great Dividing Range") mark the western structural boundary. The system was folded and partly metamorphosed during the Carboniferous and Permian. It was uplifted and block-faulted in late Tertiary and early Quaternary time.

East Australian Borderland. This comprises continental shelf, continental slope and the Coral Sea (or Queensland) Plateau. The continental shelf south of Fraser Island is fairly narrow, only 8–10 miles. North of Fraser Island, it increases to approximately 45 miles. The continental slope south of Fraser Island, averaging 6°, is much steeper than normal.

Separated from the continent by the Queensland Trough is a subcontinental region, the Coral Sea (or Queensland) Plateau which slopes gently toward the northwest. A continental slope facing the Coral Sea Basin marks its margin (Krause, in press).

Tasman Basin. This is a wedge-shaped abyssal plain between Australia, the Lord Howe Rise and the South Island of New Zealand. The Indian–Antarctic Ridge and Macquarie Ridge form the southern boundaries. The floor of the Tasman Sea, at an average depth of 2650 fathoms, slopes gently southward. Isolated seamounts, some capped with coral reefs, rise steeply from the deeper part of the basin and also from the lower western flank of the Lord Howe Rise. They are positioned along two north–south trending lines.

New Zealand Plateau. This subcontinental mass, centering on New Zealand includes the Chatham Rise, Campbell Plateau and the southwestern parts of Lord Howe Rise and Norfolk Ridge. Brodie (1959, 1964) grouped the structural features of the Plateau into three provinces.

(1) The Northwestern Province, which includes the northwest region of New Zealand, Lord Howe Rise and Norfolk Ridge, has a dominant northwest–southeast trend.

(2) The Chatham Province, with dominant east–west trends, comprises the Chatham Rise, Bounty Trough and Campbell Plateau.

(3) The Kermadec Province has a NNE–SSW trend, which is the direction of the Alpine Fault. At a slight angle, this trend can be traced northward in the New Zealand Sub-crustal Rift (Eiby, 1958, 1964) and in the Tonga–Kermadec ridge and trench system.

Remainder of the Southwest Pacific. The major features in the rest of the area are ridges, island arcs, elongated basins and trenches showing a remarkable structural interrelation (Hess and Maxwell, 1953). Two series of arcs can be distinguished, a third is possible, as recognized by Suess 80 years ago (and later reviewed by Glaessner, 1950):

(1) The Outer Melanesian Zone: Northern New Guinea—New Britain—the Solomons—the New Hebrides and the Tonga–Kermadec Islands.

This belt is of late Cretaceous–Tertiary origin, and is still active as shown by recent earthquakes and volcanic activity. On the convex side of the island arcs are deep trenches, which have provided the deepest soundings in the southern hemisphere. The northern part of the arc system, with convex sides facing Australia, is offset along the Fiji Fault by more than 1000 miles from the Tonga–Kermadec arcs with concave sides facing Australia. Between the offset ends lies a sinistral transcurrent fault which can be traced north of the South Fiji Basin. The Vitiaz Trough and a series of smaller troughs along the Melanesian Border Plateau (Fig. 2) are suspected to be the expression of another fault or shear zone bordering the Outer Melanesian arc (Fairbridge, 1961).

(2) The Inner Melanesian Zone: The Papua Peninsula, the Louisiades, Rennell Island, New Caledonia. This belt can be extended toward the westward margin of the South Island, New Zealand and the Chatham Rise, farther to the east. It is believed to be mainly late Jurassic in origin. The convex sides of the arcs are facing Australia, thus opposite in direction to most of the circum-Pacific arcs.

The two belts of island arcs are separated in the northeast by the wedge-shaped South Fiji Basin. The crustal thickness of the basin floor according to Officer (1955) is 15 km (Brodie, 1964: 10–15 km) which is considerably more than the 5-km values for the Tasman Basin and the South Pacific Basin. (3) Carey's (1958) geographic reconstruction for the early Mesozoic shows a structural trend connecting Lord Howe Rise and the Indonesian Archipelago. The Lord Howe Rise thus may have been part of a third line of island arcs, probably Permo-Triassic in age. The northern end of Lord Howe Rise is separated from the Australian continent by a deep depression, the Cato Trough. From north to south, the Queensland Trough, the Cato Trough

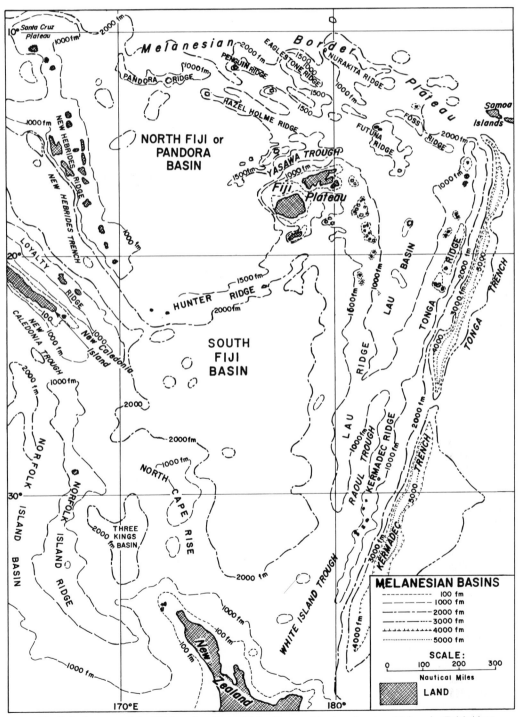

Fig. 3. Bathymetry of the Fiji Sea, showing multiple ridges and basins of eastern Melanesia (Fairbridge).
Note: a 1500 fm contour has been added in the north-east.

and the steep Australian continental slope south of Fraser Island may well be the surface expressions of yet another major transcurrent fault zone.

Synthesis

An attempt is made here to combine concepts and hypotheses on regional structural evolution into a geotectonic history of the entire southwest Pacific.

General. First of all, there is the concept of continental spreading or drift. This process disrupted the Paleozoic Gondwanaland which itself was split from the primeval Pangea. Because of later modifications to the separate blocks, reconstruction of the old continents from today's configuration is by no means as easy as solving a jigsaw puzzle. Paleontological, geotectonic and paleomagnetic interpretations permit a variety of outlines to the primeval land masses. However different the reconstructions may be, it seems certain that at one time, Australia, New Zealand and Antartctica, were part of the same continental mass. Since the Paleozoic, continental spreading, geotectonic and geochemical processes have been accelerated and are responsible for today's configuration of structural units within the Andesite line.

Secondly, the intermediate crustal thicknesses of a great many features in the southwest Pacific suggest geochemical reactions; sialization of ocean crust and the reverse simatization (oceanization) of continental crust. These processes, active respectively in zones of upheaval and subsidence, increase or decrease the thickness of an original oceanic or continental crust.

The forces activating continental spreading and the geochemistry of the earth may be convection currents in the mantle (Vening Meinesz), they may be the result of an expanding earth (Mantovani, Egyed, Carey), or they may be generated by magma differentiation resulting in upheaval and lateral spreading of megaundations (van Bemmelen). They all allow for considerable horizontal displacements of crustal material—oceanic or continental.

The horizontal movements of separate blocks can be traced along transcurrent faults. Left and right lateral transcurrent faults in the region have horizontal displacements over several hundred miles.

Other directions of movement can be derived from the curvature of island arcs and trenches which belong together genetically. However, there are strongly differing interpretations: in both unilateral and bilateral concepts of their origin, oceanic crust moves from the island arc toward and down the trench (Fisher and Hess, 1963), alternatively as it underrides the island arc along a descending shear (Benioff, 1955), or again as it tears apart, leaving the trench as an open tension gash (Heezen and others).

Regional Development. (Fig. 2) Hess and Maxwell (1953) postulated an outward migration of orogenic belts away from the Australian continent. Those of importance in the southwest Pacific are the Great Dividing Range of eastern Australia and the two or possibly three series of island arcs. Officer (1955) concludes from geophysical evidence that they have been built up one after the other on an oceanic crust and that they are not part of an extensive continent. This would mean that the Tasman Basin was pre-late Jurassic or even pre-Permo-Triassic. Gill (1952) is one who has favored the existence of an ancient "Tasmantis"-Melanesian continent from Australia to the South Pacific Basin. For the lower Devonian, for example, the existence of such a land would be needed to allow for the migration of shallow marine faunas. Carey (1958) satisfies Gill's conditions by assuming a close pre-spreading connection between New Zealand, Australia and Tasmania. To satisfy both Gill and Officer, the formation of the Tasman Basin, the opening of Carey's "East Australian Rhombochasm," must have taken place between lower Devonian and presumably Permian. The two north–south trending ranges of seamounts in the Tasman Basin might well be positioned on tensional features, reflecting the eastward movement of New Zealand away from Australia.

The curvature of island arcs with convex sides predominantly facing southwest might suggest horizontal motion of the oceanic crust in a southwest direction. This would conflict with Hess and Maxwell's concept. However, a possible solution might be found in the subsiding and lateral-spreading Darwin Rise (Menard, 1964) north and northwest of the Melanesian arc system. The lateral spreading must have resulted in southwest-directed crustal movements for the Southwest Pacific region. Possibly, the outer mobile belts of the area originated under the influence of two opposing crustal movements. This would be in agreement with the concept of Fisher and Hess on the origin of trenches. The movements seem to have been partly contemporaneous and partly succeeding. Whichever of the two movements was the dominant and/or later one would be reflected in the curvature of the arcs.

Brodie (1952) shows the structural relationship between his Northwestern and Chatham provinces. He assumes that both Chatham Rise and Campbell Plateau at one time formed the southeastern extensions of the Norfolk Ridge and Chatham Rise, respectively. The arcuate structures with concave sides facing northeast indicate a southwest-directed horizontal thrust. Starting in early Cretaceous, the eastern end of the system yielded to shearing and was consequently displaced over 300–400 miles along a right lateral transcurrent fault system (Alpine Fault and Kermadec Trench).

Menard (1964) suggests the possibility that the system of island arcs, ridges, depressions and trenches of the Southwest Pacific represents a disrupted Melanesian Rise. This is in sharp contrast with Hess and Maxwell's ideas.

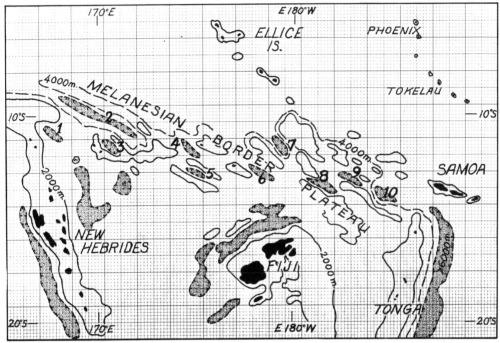

Fig. 4. Ten small troughs in the Melanesian Border Plateau (Fairbridge, 1961).

Key to troughs: 1. Vanikoro; 2. Vitiaz; 3. Strathmore; 4. Alexa; 5. Hazel Holme; 6. Rotuma; 7. Bayonnaise; 8. Horne; 9. Combe; 10. Wallis.

Strong gravity anomalies over the Tonga Trench (Talwani *et al.*, 1961) are characteristic of continental margins and confirm the seismic data of Raitt *et al.* (1955). It is curious that although the Tonga–Kermadec Trench appears to be continuous with the right lateral Alpine Fault of New Zealand and from a rectilinear border to the Melanesian complex, the northern border, the Melanesian Border Plateau (Fig. 3), is cut up into innumerable small trenches, troughs and ridges, en echelon to each other, suggesting the overlapping shears of a left lateral transcurrent lineament in the underlying basement (Fairbridge, 1961). It extends into the Solomons (see *Solomon Sea*).

Conclusion

One cannot escape the impression that the forces starting the northeastward drift of the ancient Australian continent away from Gondwana have been active ever since.

Chronologically the processes might have evolved as follows:

Paleozoic: Inception of northeast movement of the ancient Australian continent.

Late Paleozoic: Opening of the Tasman Basin.

Permian-Triassic: Inception of the Lord Howe–Campbell mobile belt possibly in connection with the Indonesian archipelago.

Triassic-Jurassic: Inception of the Papua–New Caledonia–Norfolk Ridge–New Zealand (eugeosyncline) and Chatham Rise mobile belt.

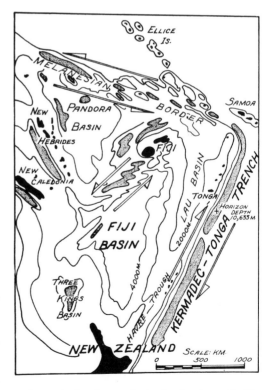

Fig. 5. Strike-slip trends in the Southwest Pacific (Fairbridge, 1961).

Cretaceous: Disruption of Chatham–Campbell province and displacement over 300–400 miles along a right lateral transcurrent fault.

Late Cretaceous–Tertiary: Inception of the Melanesian—Tonga—Kermadec mobile belt.

Tertiary and Quaternary: Disruption of the outer mobile belt and formation of the South Fiji Basin as a "rhombochasm."

W. J. M. van der Linden

References

Brodie, J. W., 1959, "Structural significance of sea floor features around New Zealand," *Geol. Rundschau.*, **47**(2), 662–667.

Brodie, J. W., 1964, "Bathymetry of the New Zealand Region," *New Zealand Oceanographic Inst. Mem.* 11.

Bryan, W. H., 1944, "The relationship of the Australian continent to the Pacific Ocean, now and in the past," *J. Proc. Roy. Soc. N.S. Wales*, **78**, 42–62.

Carey, S. W., 1958, "A tectonic approach to continental drift," *Continental Drift* (Symposium: Univ. Tasmania), 177–355.

Eiby, G. A., 1958, "The structure of New Zealand from seismic evidence," *Geol. Rundschau.*, **47**, 647–662.

Fairbridge, R. W., 1962, "Basis for submarine nomenclature in the South-west Pacific Ocean," *Deut. Hydrograph. Z.*, **15**(1), 1–15.

Gill, E. D., 1952, "Palaeogeography of the Australian–New Zealand Region in the lower Devonian time," *Trans. Roy. Soc. New Zealand*, **80**(2), 171–185.

Glaessner, M. F., 1950, "Geotectonic position of New Guinea," *Bull. Am. Assoc. Petrol. Geologists*, **34**, 856–881.

Hess, H. H., and Maxwell, J. C., 1953, "Major structural features of the South-west Pacific—A preliminary interpretation of HO 5484, bathymetric chart, New Guinea to New Zealand," *Proc. Pacific Sci. Congr. Pacific Sci. Assoc. 7th*, 1949, **2**, 14–17.

Krebs, B. N., 1964, "A bibliography of the oceanography of the Tasman and Coral Seas, 1960–1960," *New Zealand Oceanographic Inst. Mem.* 24.

Menard, H. W., 1964, "Marine Geology of the Pacific," New York, McGraw-Hill Book Co., 271pp.

Murray, J., 1906, "On the depth temperature of the ocean waters, and marine deposits of the Southwest Pacific Ocean," *Queensland Geogr. Jour.*, *N.S.*, **21**, 71.

Officer, C. B., 1955, "Southwest Pacific crustal structures," *Trans. Am. Geophys. Union*, **36**, 449–459.

Raitt, R. W., Fisher, R. L., and Mason, R. G., 1955, "Tonga Trench," *Geol. Soc. Am. Spec. Papers* 62, 237–254.

Rotschi, H., 1961, "Oxygene, Phosphate et Gaz Carbonique en Mer de Corail," *Deep-Sea Res.*, **8**(3/4), 181–195.

Rotschi, H., 1965, "Le pH et l'alcalinité des eaux profondes de la fosse des Hebrides et du bassin des Fidji," in "Progress in Oceanography," Vol. 3, pp. 301–310, New York, Pergamon Press.

Talwani, M., Worzel, J. L., and Ewing, W. M., 1961, "Gravity anomalies and crustal section across the Tonga Trench," *J. Geophys. Res.*, **66**.

Van Bemmelen, R. W., 1933, "Versuch einer geotektonische Analyse Australiens und des Südwestpazifik

nach der Undationstheorie," *Koninkl. Ned. Akad. Wetenschap Proc.*, **36**, 740–749.

Wüst, G., 1936, "Die Gliederung des Weltmeeres," *Petermanns Mitt.*, **2**, 33–38 (translated in *Hydrographic Rev.*, **13**(2), 46–55.

Wyrtki, K., 1960, "The surface circulation in the Coral and Tasman Seas," *C.S.I.R.O. Aust. Div. Fish. Oceanogr. Tech. Pap.* 8.

Wyrtki, K., 1961, "The flow of water into the deep basins of the Western South Pacific Ocean," *Australian Marine Freshwater Res.*, **13**.

Wyrtki, K., 1962, "Geopotential topographies and associated circulation in the Western South Pacific Ocean," *Australian ibid.*, **13**.

Wyrtki, K., 1962, "The subsurface water masses in the Western South Pacific Ocean," *ibid.*, **13**.

Cross-references: *Coral Sea; Pacific Ocean; Southern Ocean; Tasman Sea.* Vol. 5: *Andesite Line.*

STABILITY—*See* Vol. II

STANDING CROP—*See* FERTILITY OF THE OCEAN

STANDING WAVE—*See* MOAZAGOTL, Vol. II

STATIC INSTABILITY—*See* THERMAL INSTABILITY

CONTINENTS AND OCEANS, STATISTICS OF—*See* Vol. III

STEREOSCOPY—*See* pr Vol. VI

STORM, STORMINESS

Storm in meteorology denotes disturbed weather conditions, on various scales, that lead to high winds, heavy precipitation and related phenomena. In telecommunications an electrical storm may be related to a meteorologic event or to an extraterrestrial event such as a solar flare. In weather forecast and warning, storms are closely related to meteorologic events, but they carry specific definitions: "storms" are marked by winds of 21.9–24.8 m/sec, average 45 knots (Beaufort, force 10); "violent storms" have winds of 24.9–28.2 m/sec, average 52 knots (force 9); "hurricanes" have over 28.2 m/sec, or more than 55 knots (force 10: for full Beaufort wind force table, see *Wind*). In hydrology a "rainstorm" refers to the distribution of a specific precipitation event in time and space.

Local storms are often described in terms of their special characteristics: dust storm, sandstorm, rainstorm, snow storm, ice storm, hailstorm, wind storm. Special types, e.g., *blizzard, squall*, are treated separately (Vol. II). In many cases the local storm is merely an aspect of a major cyclonic dis-

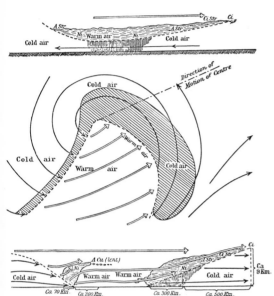

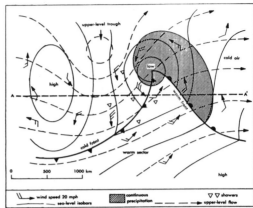

Fig. 2. Schematic diagram of sea-level fronts and isobars in a wave cyclone, with lines of flow in upper troposphere superimposed (mainly after Bjerknes and Palmén; from McGraw-Hill Encyclopedia, "Storm").

Fig. 1. The typical polar front depression (Bjerknes and Solberg, 1921). Abbreviations refer to cloud types (see Vol. II).

turbance (see below), but in others, it is an aspect of *local winds* (q.v., for example Mistral, Sirocco).

Cyclonic Storms

Several categories of cyclonic storms are recognized as products of regular synoptic situations along semipermanent frontal zones.

(a) Extratropical Cyclones. These are characteristic of the Arctic and Polar Fronts in each hemisphere (thus about 30–75° latitude). They are baroclinic zones primarily tilted poleward, marked usually by warmer air on the equator sides and colder poleward. Since there is both an equatorial/pole pressure and temperature gradient and angular velocity drop from the equator to the pole, a shear with wave-like eddies develops in the mid-latitudes. The wave in the pressure field is followed by a similar wave in the temperature pattern, lagging half a wavelength behind. Large-scale eddies evolve, sweeping up parcels of warm air, as cold air drives beneath, along a "cold front" marked by high winds, heavy clouds and rain. This lifting of warm air leads to convergence beneath, an inflow, which owing to the earth's motion (Coriolis force) develops an anticlockwise spin in the northern hemisphere and a clockwise rotation in the southern (in order to conserve angular momentum). As the air pressure drops the rate of spin increases, developing winds that may reach 100 knots in extreme cases. As the warm air rises higher, a "warm front" develops with stronger circulation aloft and further heavy precipitation, but with weaker winds below; a temporary balanced condition may develop in the late stage when a cold front

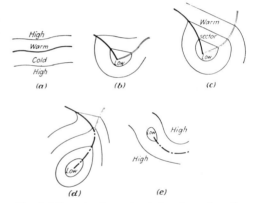

Fig. 3. Life cycle of extratropical cyclone of southern hemisphere (from Byers, 1959). (By permission of McGraw-Hill Book Co., N.Y.)

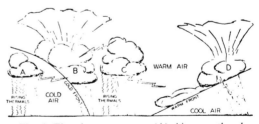

Fig. 4. Thunderstorm types. (A) Air-mass thunderstorm due to convective instability and overrunning by cold air aloft. (B and D) Frontal thunderstorms due to lifting of moist air along a frontal surface. (C) Air-mass thunderstorm due to heating and instability (Barber, 1943).

overtakes a warm front and a quasi-stationary "occluded front" forms (details, see *Cyclogenesis* and *Fronts and Frontogenesis*).

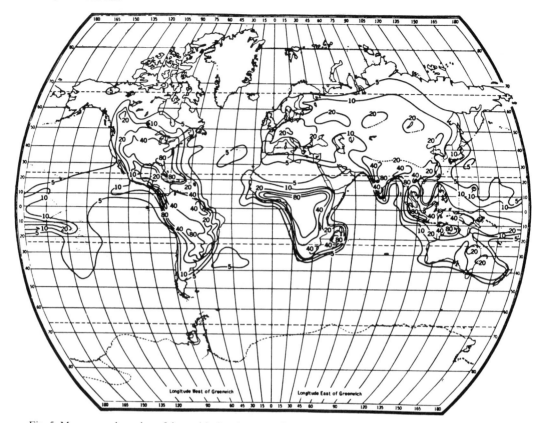

Fig. 5. Mean annual number of days with thunderstorms in the world (after Berry, Bollay and Beers, "Handbook of Meteorology"). (*Van der Grinten projection, courtesy A. J. Nystrom & Co., Chicago.*)

(b) Tropical Cyclones. These do not properly develop in the equatorial belt but only about the times when the ITC (Intertropical Convergence) lies considerably north or south of the equator, as at the summer solstices or soon after. In the northern hemisphere they are most common around August and September and in the southern hemisphere in January and February. This is because the Coriolis effect is absent at the equator and the strongest cyclonic twist develops as the storm approaches mid-latitudes. The twist is counterclockwise in the northern hemisphere, but the whole storm system tends to move initially to the west, under the effect of the tropical easterlies (the trade winds) and gradually swings to north and northeast, another Coriolis effect. These motions are, of course, opposite in the southern hemisphere. The storms are initiated about latitude 10–15° and may reach 40–50°. Wind velocities in the cyclone (also known as *hurricane, typhoon*, etc.) may exceed 200 knots, while forward motion may be 10–50 knots.

(c) Convectional Storms. These are special conditions that may develop in association with the major fronts or independently. A very high incidence of such thunderstorms may be noted in the continental

interiors (Americas, Africa, India; see Fig. 5 and Table 1). *Tornadoes* (q.v.), a special example, develop on all continents but especially in the

TABLE 1. WORLD DISTRIBUTION OF THUNDERSTORMS
(after C. E. P. Brooks)

Average number of thunderstorms per weather station

Latitude	—April–September— Conti-nents	Oceans	Total	—October–March— Conti-nents	Oceans	Total
70–60°N	3.5	—	3.5	0.1	—	0.1
60–50°N	9.5	1.7	8.0	0.2	0.1	0.2
50–40°N	13.5	2.7	9.9	1.3	0.8	1.1
40–30°N	13.9	5.3	10.3	4.0	3.2	3.7
30–20°N	15.9	5.9	12.6	4.1	4.1	4.1
20–10°N	23.1	10.8	16.9	7.3	6.3	6.8
10–0°	26.6	11.2	18.5	23.0	9.9	16.1
0–10°S	22.9	6.4	12.8	37.8	9.0	20.2
10–20°S	8.1	4.0	5.3	38.2	7.4	17.6
20–30°S	7.8	3.6	5.3	18.5	6.9	11.1
30–40°S	6.0	5.8	5.9	10.3	7.9	8.5
40–50°S	2.0	3.3	3.1	4.4	4.6	4.6
50–60°S	0.5	0.5	0.5	2.0	1.0	1.1

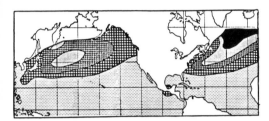

Fig. 6. Storminess on the northern oceans in December, January and February. In black area, gales (Beaufort Force 8 or higher) prevail more than 20% of the time; dark stipple, 15–20%; small hatching, 10–15%; large hatching, 5–10%; light stipple, less than 5%; areas in white, data not shown (Tannehill, 1943). (By permission of Princeton University Press, N.J.)

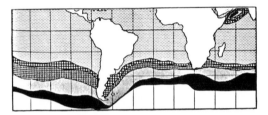

Fig. 7. Storminess in the southern oceans in June, July and August. In black areas, gales (Beaufort Force 8 or higher) prevail more than 20% of the time; dark stipple, 15–20%; small hatching, 10–15%; large hatching, 5–10%; light stipple, less than 5%; areas in white, data not shown (Tannehill, 1943). (By permission of Princeton University Press, N.J.)

United States and in Australia around latitude 30–40° as summer heating of the ground causes intense thermodynamic instability and develops a "twister" of rising air, in one of two conditions, either as a parasite to a thunderstorm, a *convectional tornado*, or in response to the advance of a strong cold front, a *cyclonic tornado*. *Waterspouts* (q.v.) develop under similar conditions, but over water especially in connection with the ITC (Intertropical Convergence). Convectional storms are also particularly prevalent during the advance of the monsoons (see Vol. II) in India, China, in northern Australia and in Africa. Orographic convection leads to mountain *thunderstorms* (q.v.) during the summer seasons in low and mid-latitudes. Finally, in relatively flat areas, especially of the subtropics, the summer *thermal lows* develop in a more or less stationary manner and instability leads to electric storms even if no precipitation occurs.

Storm Track

Storm track refers to the path followed by a center of low atmospheric pressure, principally the Westerly zonal systems, but also of tropical hurricanes.

Storm Warning

This is a weather forecast, more particularly for mariners. The U.S. Weather Bureau recognizes four degrees of storm warning (effective January 1, 1958): *small-craft warning, gale warning, whole-gale warning, hurricane warning* (see Beaufort forces in article *Wind*).

Storm Surge or Tide

This refers to any unusual rise of sea level related to storms. Three main components are recognized—the "meteorologic tide" (sea level acts as an "inverted barometer" and rises as atmospheric pressure drops, 1 cm/1 millibar), the wind-generated pile-up effect (see *Mean Sea Level*), and the true surge or seiche effect (see *Seiche* and *Storm Surges*).

Storminess

Storminess is a climatologic statistic of storm expectancy. On Figs. 6 and 7 note the relative skewness in the northern oceans and relative uniformity throughout the Southern Ocean (q.v.), the "Roaring Forties" and the "Howling Fifties." Note small patches in the Arabian Sea (q.v.), a monsoon condition, and near the Isthmus of Tehuantepec (see *Winds—Local*).

RHODES W. FAIRBRIDGE

References

Bjerknes, J., and Solberg, H., 1921, *Geofys. Publikasjoner, Oslo, II*(3), and *III*(1).

Brooks, C. E. P., 1925, "The distribution of thunderstorms over the globe," *Geophys. Mem.,* **3**, No. 24.

Byers, H. R., 1959, "General Meteorology," Third ed., New York, McGraw-Hill Book Co., 540pp.

Donn, W. L., 1965, "Meteorology," Third ed., New York, McGraw-Hill Book Co., 484pp.

Huschke, R. E. (ed.), 1959, "Glossary of Meteorology," Boston, American Meteorological Society, 638pp.

Laughton, C., and Heddon, V., 1927, "Great Storms," London, P. Allan and Co.

Ligda, M. G. H., 1951, "Radar Storm Observation," in "Compendium of Meteorology," pp. 1265–1282, Boston, American Meteorological Society.

Munk, W. H., 1951, "Ocean Waves as a Meteorological Tool," in "Compendium of Meteorology," pp. 1090–1100, Boston, American Meteorological Society.

Palmer, C. E., 1951, "Tropical Meteorology," in "Compendium of Meteorology," pp. 859–880, Boston, American Meteorological Society.

Riehl, H., 1954, "Tropical Meteorology," New York, McGraw-Hill Book Co., 392pp.

Tannehill, I. R., 1943, "Weather Around the World," Princeton, N.J., Princeton University Press, 200pp.

Trewartha, G. T., 1954, "An Introduction to Climate," Third ed., New York, McGraw-Hill Book Co., 402pp.

Cross-references: *Sea State; Seiche; Storm Surge; Wind* (partly in Vol. II). Vol. II: *Cyclogenesis; Fronts and Frontogenesis; Hail; Intertropical Convergence; Thermal Low; Tropical Cyclones; Waterspout.*

STORM SURGE

(I) Introduction

Storm surge is of atmospheric origin. The total tide includes the coupling of the storm surge and the astronomical tides caused by the gravitational forces between the earth and the sun or moon. Storm tide can be steady-state or transient when no astronomical tide is present, and both become influenced by the periodicity of any coincidence with the astronomical tide. For a steady-state wind system or storm off the coast, the storm surge, neglecting second-order effects caused by the coupling effect of the astronomical tides, is essentially steady state, and the total tide is diurnal or semidiurnal, as the case may be. The storm surge caused by a moving hurricane usually lasts through only one or two tide cycles. These are called transient surges, and Redfield and Miller (1957) consider three successive stages: the forerunner, hurricane surge, and resurgences. The forerunner is a slow gradual change in water level beginning several hours before the arrival of the storm. The hurricane surge is a sharp rise in water level that occurs approximately when the hurricane center passes near the port, and the duration of the high rise is only several hours. The resurgences are oscillations occurring after passage of the hurricane and the hurricane surge.

In addition to what is normally called storm surge, there is an additional rise in tide on the beach due to wave set-up. The problem of wave set-up is discussed by Longuet-Higgins (1963), Saville (1961), Fairchild (1958) and Dorrestein (1962). Harris (1963) gives additional evidence of wave set-up as well as high-water elevations due to wave run-up.

The wave set-up occurs between the zone of wave-break and the beach, and it can be as much as 10–20% of the incident wave height. It is because of wave set-up that the tides are always observed higher on the beach than recorded on a tide gauge at the end of a pier.

When the wave reaches the coast, it will run up the beach to higher elevations than the wave set-up. The wave set-up itself does not increase the wave run-up since wave set-up is included in wave run-up. High-water marks generally occur beyond the beach at elevations higher than wave set-up and are a consequence of wave run-up.

In practice there are three physical zones for special application of storm surge theory: (1) the open coast, (2) the entrances to bays and estuaries and over barrier islands, and (3) enclosed lakes with modifications for bays and estuaries coupled with the open coast.

(II) General

The hydrodynamical theory of surges starts with the equations of motion, of which the horizontal acceleration components are:

$$\frac{dU_x}{dt} = fU_y - \frac{1}{\rho}\frac{\delta p}{\delta x} - \frac{\delta q}{\delta x} + \frac{\delta \tau_{xy}}{\delta x} + \frac{\delta \tau_{yx}}{\delta y} + \frac{\delta \tau_{zx}}{\delta z} \tag{1}$$

$$\frac{dU_y}{dt} = -fU_x - \frac{1}{\rho}\frac{\delta p}{\delta y} - \frac{\delta q}{\delta y} + \frac{\delta \tau_{xy}}{\delta x} + \frac{\delta \tau_{yy}}{\delta y} + \frac{\delta \tau_{zy}}{\delta z} \tag{2}$$

where

$$\frac{dU_x}{dt} = \frac{\delta U_x}{\delta t} + U_x\frac{\delta U_x}{\delta x} + U_y\frac{\delta U_x}{\delta y} + U_z\frac{\delta U_x}{\delta z} \tag{3}$$

and

$$\frac{dU_y}{dt} = \frac{\delta U_y}{\delta t} + U_x\frac{\delta U_y}{\delta x} + U_y\frac{\delta U_y}{\delta y} + U_z\frac{\delta U_y}{\delta z} \tag{4}$$

where $f = 2\omega \sin \varphi =$ Coriolis parameter; q is the potential of astronomical tide forces; ρ is the density of water. The cartesian coordinate system is x and y in the horizontal and z in the vertical; t is time. The τ–values are components of turbulent stress tensor.

The above equations are usually solved when certain assumptions are introduced. The boundary conditions must be satisfied at the free surface. First approximation solutions are obtained by linearization. Higher-order approximations can be obtained in one of three ways: (1) direct integration by the method of characteristics (see Schonfeld, 1951; Freeman, 1954, 1957); (2) numerical integration by approximating the differential equations by suitable difference equations (see Doodson, 1956); and (3) linearization of the equations and setting up an iterative process by which the nonlinear equations are solved by successive approximations (see Groen and Groves, 1962).

For details of the above procedures, the reader should seek the above references. The following material introduces the practical applications of the theoretical concepts. Under various situations and assumptions, the equations are simplified and become quite adaptable for calculation purposes. A number of such situations are considered in the following sections.

(III) The Open-coast Problem

The bathystrophic storm-tide theory, originally presented by J. C. Freeman, Jr., L. Baer, and G. H. Jung (1957), explains the phenomenon of storm-tide rise along the coast caused by winds blowing parallel to the coast. Essentially this is the component of the tide arising as a result of Coriolis force which deflects a flow to the right in the northern hemisphere. Hence, northeast winds along the Texas Gulf coast or the east coast of the United States will cause a rise in the mean water level along the coast.

Based on the work of Freeman *et al.*, the following equations can be determined:

$$\frac{dS}{dX} = \frac{kUU_x}{g(h+S)} + \frac{fF_y}{g(h+S)} \tag{5}$$

where U is absolute value of wind speed; U_x is the component perpendicular to the bottom contours; f is the Coriolis parameter $= 2\omega \sin \varphi$ where ω is earth's angular velocity and φ is the latitude; k is the wind stress parameter; g is the acceleration of gravity; and h is the water depth. F_y is the flux parallel to the depth contours and is given by

$$F_y = \int_0^{(h+S)} v\, dz \tag{6}$$

where v is the water speed parallel to depth contours.

The equation for F_y is time-dependent and is given by

$$\frac{\Delta F_y}{\Delta t} = \frac{kUU_y}{g} - \frac{K}{(h+S)^{7/3}}F_y^2 \tag{7}$$

where U_y is the component of wind speed parallel to bottom contours.

Based on the Lake Okeechobee studies by the U.S. Army Corps of Engineers (1955), $k = 3.0 \times 10^{-6}$. No exact value of K has been established to date, but it is on the order of 10^{-3} or 10^{-4}. A more accurate value of K might be established by calculation using the data from Hurricane Carla of 1961 in the Gulf of Mexico and the Ash Wednesday Storm of March 1962 along the east coast of the United States.

(1) Bottom of Constant Depth, Wind Perpendicular to the Coast. If this condition exists, $U = U_x$ and $F_y = 0$, and the solution of Eq. (5) becomes

$$\Delta S = h\sqrt{\frac{2kU^2\Delta X}{gh^2} + 1} - 1 \tag{8}$$

(2) Bottom of Constant Slope. The case of wind set-up using a triangular wind stress distribution perpendicular to the coast is discussed by Reid (1957). The dynamic storm surge for a hurricane moving perpendicular to the coast with a triangular stress distribution is also discussed by Reid (1956) in which is given the useful formula

$$S_{max} = k\frac{T}{C_1}\left[\frac{h_1}{h_0}\right]^{1/4} W_m^2 Z \tag{9}$$

where $k = 3.0 \times 10^{-6}$ as before; h_1 = depth at the edge of the continental shelf; h_0 = depth near the

coast where S_{max} applies; $C_1^2 = gh_1$; $C_0^2 = gh_0$; $\bar{C} = 1/2\ (C_1 + C_0)$; $T = L/C$; L = length of continental shelf, W_m = maximum wind speed; and Z is the response factor. The response factor is a function of the ratio of the relative speed of the storm to that of the free wave, $C = \sqrt{gh}$, and the ratio of the relative size of the storm to the width of the continental shelf.

For a bottom of constant slope for a stationary storm of constant wind speed perpendicular to the coast, Bretschneider (1958) derived the following equation:

$$S = \frac{kU^2X}{g(h_1 - h - S)}\ln\frac{h_1}{h+S} \tag{10}$$

where ln is the natural logarithm to base e.

The numerical formula of Eq. (8) can be used when the traverse is taken perpendicular to the coastline. The traverse is segmented into increments, each having a constant depth equal to the mean of the depth at the beginning and end of each section. The variable wind-stress diagram is superimposed on the traverse, and computations are made for various positions of the stress diagram until the optimum position resulting in maximum surge elevation at the coast is located. This method, as well as the others mentioned above, assumes steady-state water level and no lateral flow. The effective added head due to atmospheric pressure reduction from normal is added to the component due to wind stress, that is, the rise in water level due to atmospheric pressure reduction from normal, and from Bernoulli's equation one obtains:

$$H = 1.14\Delta P \tag{11}$$

where H is in feet of water rise above normal (in absence of all other contributing factors), and ΔP is in inches of mercury fall from normal atmospheric pressure.

(3) Slightly Irregular Bottom Profile. Many such cases exist along the continental shelf of the Gulf of Mexico and the eastern Atlantic coast of the United States as well as other parts of the world. As a good approximation, one can utilize a bottom of constant slope or a series of bottoms of constant slope and solve the problem along the lines mentioned above.

(4) Irregular Bottom Profile. This is a difficult problem to consider, even with the numerical formula given by Eq. (8). Several profiles may be taken and a mean of these used. However, this tends to smooth out some of the anomalies. Whenever wind and tide data are available for past hurricanes, the numerical formula is calibrated prior to use for the design or project hurricane. In some cases, the design or project hurricane may be very similar in size, intensity, forward speed, and direction of approach to some past hurricane. If wind and tide data are available under these conditions, the calibration becomes refined and the design elevation perhaps quite accurately predicted. Statistical methods are usually not satisfactory for prediction because of lack of sufficient high-water data.

(IV) Entrances to Bays and Estuaries and Flow Over Barrier Islands

This aspect of storm surge is one of hydraulics, further complicated by wind effect. A classification of open bays and estuaries is presented by Caldwell (1955), together with a discussion by Baines (1955). The computation of tides and tidal currents as applicable to bays and estuaries is quite involved, and no single mathematical concept can be applied to all classes. The work of Einstein (1955), Dronkers and Shonfeld (1955), and Baines (1958), should be referred to. The U.S. Army Corps of Engineers Committee on Tidal Hydraulics presented an "Evaluation of Present State of Knowledge on Factors Affecting Tidal Hydraulics and Related Phenomena" (1950).

As the surge rises on the open coast, water enters the bay through the open channel, and when the water elevation on the open coast increases sufficiently, additional flow may enter over the barriers. River discharge may also be an important factor in raising the mean water level within the bay. In addition, a tilt in the bay water surface may be introduced by cross winds. The surge traveling up the bay or estuaries will be modified by refraction, shoaling, and bottom friction. The peak of the surge reaches the upper end of the bay sometime after the peak at the entrance. If the bay is sufficiently long, the flow of water is reversed at the entrance many hours before the peak surge arrives at the upper end of the bay. This is a typical condition associated with the Chesapeake Bay. Such a problem necessitates the prediction of a hydrograph on the outside entrance to the bay as well as hydrographs for various stations within the bay. The discharge through the entrance is obtained as a function of time from

$$Q = C_2 A \sqrt{2g \, |(h_0 - h_1)|} \qquad (12)$$

and

$$v = \int Q \, dt \qquad (13)$$

The cross-sectional area A depends on elevation h_0 as a function of time. The symbols h_0 and h_1 are corresponding elevations of the outside and inside hydrographs, respectively. Positive Q represents inflow when $h_0 - h_1 > 0$, and negative Q represents outflow when $h_0 - h_1 < 0$; v is the volume of flow as a function of time; C_2 is coefficient of discharge and must be determined from past conditions or assumed to be $C_2 = 0.6$.

The volume v then is a function of time and must

be accounted for by increase in stage in the bay and is obtained from

$$v = \sum_{i=1}^{i=M} h_i A_i \qquad (14)$$

where M represents the number of sections for which a hydrograph must be determined; h_i is the elevation of hydrograph of the ith section and is a function of time; A_i is surface area of the ith section and is a function of elevation h_i, and hence is a function of time.

The most general formulation for routing surges is by use of Manning's equation. The use of this method has been illustrated by Bretschneider and Collins (1962).

(V) Enclosed Lakes and Reservoirs (with Application to Open Bays)

For wind of constant speed and direction along the axis of a rectangular channel of constant depth and under steady-state conditions, the equations for wind set-up are given by Hellstrom (1941), Langhaar (1951) and Keulegan (1952), among others.

$$\frac{dS}{dX} = \frac{\gamma k U^2}{g(h+S)} \qquad \text{(slope of water surface)} \quad (15)$$

$$\int_0^L (h+S) \, dX = Lh \quad \text{(conservation of volume} \quad (16)$$
$$\text{for nonexposed bottom)}$$

$$\int_{X_0}^L (h+S) \, dX = Lh \quad \text{(conservation of volume} \quad (17)$$
$$\text{for exposed bottom)}$$

where S is wind set-up; X is horizontal distance; k is wind-stress parameter; g is acceleration of gravity; h is water depth; L is length of channel; X_0 is length of exposed bottom (when applicable); and $\gamma = 1 + \tau_b/\tau_s$ where τ_b is bottom stress and τ_s is the surface wind stress related to k, and U is the wind speed.

In the case of nonexposed bottom, $X_0 = 0$ and Eq. (16) is used to evaluate the constant of integration in the solution of Eq. (15). For exposed bottom, the constant of integration is equal to X_0 and the set-up between $X = 0$ and $X = X_0$ is $S = -h$.

The nodal point $(X = X_n, S = 0)$ for finite values of U, h, and L is given by:

$$\frac{X_n}{L} = 1 - \frac{S_{max}^2 + 2S_{max}h}{2kU^2 \, L} \qquad (18)$$

where $S = S_{max}$ at $X = L$

If the lake becomes an open bay, the same procedures can be used and modified such that the overall problem couples the open-coast storm surge via entrances, estuaries, and over barrier islands.

(VI) Use of Laboratory Studies

(1) Wind Set-up in Laboratory Flumes. Laboratory studies on wind set-up have been made at the University of California by Sibul (1955a and b),

and Tichner (1957); and at the Bureau of Standards by Keulegan (1951). The work of Van Dorn (1953) on a small pond falls between laboratory and field studies. Other recent studies by various authors in regard to relationship between wind speed and stress parameter may also be found in the literature. One difficulty with model studies is a possible scale effect. However, the studies by Tichner show important relative effects due to certain type bottom roughnesses which might occur when investigating wind set-up and water transport over grassy areas.

(2) **Mechanically Generated Surge.** A model of Narragansett Bay was constructed at the Waterways Experiment Station, U.S. Army Corps of Engineers, for the purpose of studying the behavior of a hurricane surge entering the bay from the open ocean. This gives valuable information on shoaling and refraction, provided the bottom friction can be simulated. In regard to this problem, calibration for bottom friction is made under known conditions such as in the exact reproduction of astronomical tides. Once the model is adjusted for proper bottom friction, the simulated hurricane surge is generated at the mouth of the model. This is done for past hurricane conditions. A verification of surge within the model may not be possible since in the model one cannot take into account the contribution due to the wind over the bay. Hence a correction ratio is determined. Then the design surge is applied at the mouth of the bay. The surge within the model is then adjusted in terms of the previously determined ratio to take into account the wind effect. In this manner, the design surge within the bay is considered as accurate as that which might be predicted at the mouth.

(3) **Numerical Model.** Along with the hydraulic model one may develop a numerical model which can be calibrated with the results of the hydraulic model as well as with data from past hurricanes. The advantage of the numerical model is that one may take into account the wind stress as well as bottom friction. This is a long tedious problem and must be performed on a high-speed computer. The details of the numerical model of Narragansett Bay and computations of surge have been made by the Department of Oceanography and Meteorology, Texas A and M College.

(VII) Summary

It can now be seen that when a storm or a hurricane is off the east coast or Gulf coast of the United States, there are three main problems to consider: (1) surge on the open coast; (2) hydraulic flow of water of the surge on the open coast through inlets and over barrier islands into the bays and estuaries; and (3) wind set-up within the bays. These three problems are time-dependent so that the rise in tide is coupled with the rise in tide at the inlet entrances to a bay due to the surge on the open coast.

CHARLES L. BRETSCHNEIDER

References

Baines, Douglas W., 1958, "Tidal currents in constricted inlets," *Proc., Conf. Coastal Engineering, 6th,* Ch. 31.

Bretschneider, C. L., 1958, "Engineering aspects of hurricane surge," *Proc. Tech. Conf. Hurricanes.* American Meteorological Society, Miami Beach, Florida.

Caldwell, Joseph M., 1955, "Tidal currents at inlets in the United States," *Proc. Am. Soc. Civil Engrs.,* **31,** No. 716.

Corps of Engineers, U.S. Army, 1950, "Evaluation of Present State of Knowledge of Factors Affecting Tidal Hydraulics and Related Phenomena," Committee on Tidal Hydraulics, Report No. 1.

Corps of Engineers, U.S. Army, 1955, Civil Works Investigations, Proj. CW167, "Summary Report, Waves and Wind Tides in Shallow Lakes and Reservoirs," Jacksonville District Office.

Doodson, A. T., 1956, "Tides and storm surges in a long uniform gulf," *Proc. Roy. Soc., London, Ser. A,* **237,** 325–343.

Dorrestein, R., 1962, "Wave set-up on a beach," *Proc., Tech. Conf. Hurricanes, 2nd, Nat. Hurricane Research Report No. 50,* 230–241.

Dronkers, J. J., and Shonfeld, J. C., 1955, "Tidal computations in shallow water," *Proc. Am. Soc. Civil Engrs.,* **81,** No. 714.

Einstein, H. A., 1955, "Computations of tides and tidal currents—United States practice," *Proc. Am. Soc. Civil Engrs.,* **81,** No. 715.

Fairchild, J. S., 1958, "Model study of wave set-up induced by hurricane waves at Narragansett Pier, Rhode Island," *Bull. Beach Erosion Board,* **12,** 9–20.

Freeman, J. C., Jr., 1954, "Two-dimensional storm tides in shallow water," *Proc. Assoc. International Oceanographic Phys.,* **6,** 208–208.

Freeman, J. C., Jr., Baer, Ledolph, and Jung, Glenn H., 1957, "The bathystrophic storm tide," *J. Marine Res.,* **16,** No. 1.

Groen, P., and Groves, G. W., 1962, "Storm Surges," in "The Sea," Vol. 1, Ch. 17, New York, Interscience Publishers.

Harris, D. Lee, 1963, "Coastal Flooding by the Storm of March 5–7, 1962," Manuscript of U.S. Weather Bureau presented at American Meteorological Society, Annual Meeting, 1963 (unpublished).

Hellstrom, B., 1941, "Wind Effect on Lakes and Rivers," Ingeniors Vetenshaps Akademiens, Handlingar, Nr. 158, Stockholm.

Keulegan, G. H., 1951, "Wind tides in small closed channels," *Natl. Bur. Std. Res. Papers* 2207, **46,** No. 5.

Langhaar, H. L., 1951, "Wind tides in inland waters," *Proc., No. 4, First Midwestern Conference in Fluid Mechanics.*

Longuet-Higgins, M. S., and Stewart, R. W., 1963, "A note on wave set-up," *J. Marine Res.,* **21,** No. 1, 4–10.

Redfield, A. C., and Miller, A. R., 1957, "Water levels accompanying Atlantic coast hurricanes," *Meteorol. Monographs,* **2,** No. 10, 1–23.

Reid, R. O., 1956, "Approximate Response of Water Level on a Sloping Shelf to a Wind Fetch which Moves Toward Shore," Beach Erosion Board, U.S. Army Corps of Engineers, T.M. No. 83.

Reid, R. O., 1957, "On the classification of hurricanes by storm tide and wave energy indices," *Meteorol. Monographs*, **2**, No. 10.

Saville, Thorndike, Jr., 1961, "Experimental determination of wave set-up," *Proc., Second Tech. Conference on Hurricanes, Natl. Hurricane Research Project Report No. 50*, 242–252.

Shonfield, J. C., 1951, "Propagation of Tides and Similar Waves," Thesis, Staatsdrukkerij Den Haag.

Sibul, O., 1955, "Laboratory Studies of Wind Tides in Shallow Water," Beach Erosion Board, U.S. Army Corps of Engineers, T.M. No. 61.

Tichner, E. G., 1957, "Effect of Bottom Roughness and Wind Tides in Shallow Water," Beach Erosion Board, U.S. Army Corps of Engineers, T.M. No. 95.

Van Dorn, W. G., 1953, "Wind stress on an artificial pond," *J. Marine Res.*, **12**, No. 3.

STREAMLINES AND STREAMLINE ANALYSIS

(1) Streamlines

Streamlines are used to describe the direction of motion of a fluid over a given area or through a given volume, at a particular moment in time. A streamline is defined as a line whose direction—that of its tangent in the case of a curve—at each point is the same as the direction of motion of the fluid at that point. The whole field of motion is described by an infinite set of streamlines, but in practical applications the number of streamlines necessarily depends on the scale of the motion being considered.

In meteorology, streamlines are gradient flow lines which can be drawn for any instant on a synoptic chart, thus representing winds blowing parallel to the horizontal isobars and normal to the gradient pressure. The flow is normally variable from moment to moment, but if it maintains the same pattern it is called a *steady flow* or *steady-state flow*.

Only when the field of motion is unchanging with time, so that the streamlines do not change, does a particle continue to move along a particular streamline. In general, the *path* or form of a *particle trajectory* is different from that of the streamlines to which it is tangent moment by moment. A path can be plotted indicating the progress of a particle through a given period of time. Where flow is steady, the streamline and path coincide. With changing velocities, as is normal, streamlines and paths develop different patterns. Such velocities change rather slowly; in the absence of friction, accelerating particles trend slightly across the isobars toward the lower pressure, while decelerating currents tend toward the higher pressure. The net effect of such variable flow is to approximate the same pattern as the isobars.

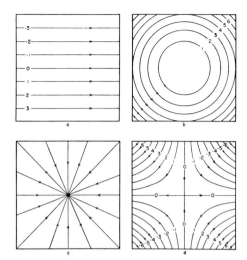

Fig. 1. Streamlines of pure constant (a) translation, (b) vorticity, (c) divergence, and (d) deformation (Hess, 1959).

If dx and dy are components of increment along a streamline, $dy/dx = v/u$, u and v being given as functions of x and y. Four basic linear velocity fields can be constructed (a) pure translation where $dy/dx = v_0/u_0$; (b) pure vorticity where $dy/dx = -x/y$, a family of circles of different radii; (c) pure divergence or convergence (depending on direction), $dy/dx = y/x$, a family of straight lines passing through the origin; (d) pure deformation, $dy/dx = -y/x$, a family of hyperboles (Hess, 1959).

Where dr is an element of the streamline and v is the velocity vector, one may write $dr \times v = 0$, or in three-dimensions, in Cartesian coordinates,

$$d\frac{x}{u} = \frac{dy}{v} = \frac{dz}{w}$$

where u, v and w are the fluid velocities, respectively, along the x, y and z axes. The relationship between path and streamline at any given point may be established by taking ψ_H as the angle in the horizontal plane measured counterclockwise from the east at that point to the projection of the wind direction. The horizontal curvature of the streamline is written

$$K_{HS}, \text{ then } K_{HS} = \frac{\partial \psi_H}{\partial S}, \text{ or } K_S = \frac{\partial \psi}{\partial s}.$$

The particle velocity is given as $v = ds/dt = ds_H/dt$.

Then $K_H = K_{HS} + \dfrac{1}{v}\dfrac{\partial \psi_H}{\partial t}$, the expression $\partial \psi_H/\partial t$ being the *local turning of the wind*.

(2) Streamline Analysis

In the middle and high latitudes, the air motion is approximately geostrophic and thus along the *isobars* (see Vol. II) although, at the surface, there is usually a component across the isobars toward lower pressure. The pattern of isobars therefore represents an approximate streamline field. For this reason, the use of streamline analysis in describing middle-latitude weather systems is mainly restricted to research studies. In the tropics, however, the decreasing value of the Coriolis parameter renders the geostrophic assumption less valid. The wind and isobars are no longer closely related as in the mid-latitudes, so that to obtain the wind in equatorial synoptic charting the streamlines are plotted rather than isobars. In this analysis, the streamline is only a direction, not a velocity. The velocity pattern can only be obtained from observations. *Isogons* or lines of equal wind direction can be plotted. Short segments drawn normal to the isogons may then be smoothed and constitute streamlines. Regions of inflow and outflow emerge from the study of such charts. Observations of velocities can be added and lines of equal value constructed to give *isotachs*. Vorticity can be determined from the isotachs and the curvature and shear of the streamlines.

Critical Speed in Sinusoidal Waves. If the earth were flat and latitude circles straight lines, a sinusoidal streamline could be drawn between latitudes φ and φ'. At time $t = 0$ the streamline cuts the mid-latitude (Y) thus:

$$Y = A_s \sin k(x - ct)$$

where A_s is amplitude and c is wave velocity. The *wave number* is designated by $k = 2\pi/L_s$ where L_s is wavelength and 2π is the linear interval of 2π length units. If the latitudinal amplitude of the streamline is σ_s, then the *Linear amplitude* (A_s) on the horizontal plane is $A_s = a \tan \sigma_s$, and the *linear wavelength* (L_s) is expressed by the angular wavelength of longitude λ_s thus:

$$L_s = \lambda_s a \cos \overline{\varphi}$$

The total number of waves around the earth's circumference is expressed as an *angular wave number* $n = 2\pi/\lambda_s$. In a sinusoidal flow pattern, a critical speed exists that is a function of latitude and angular wave number.

RHODES W. FAIRBRIDGE

References

Byers, H. R., 1959, "General Meteorology," Third ed., New York, McGraw-Hill Book Co., 540pp.
Gordon, A. H., 1962, "Elements of Dynamic Meteorology," Princeton, N.J., D. Van Nostrand Co., 217pp.
Hess, S. L., 1959, "Introduction to Theoretical Meteorology," New York, Holt and Co., 362pp.
Holmboe, J., Forsythe, G. E., and Gustin, W., 1945, "Dynamic Meteorology," New York, John Wiley & Sons, 378pp.
Huschke, R. E. (editor), 1959, "Glossary of Meteorology," Boston, American Meteorological Society, 638pp.

Palmer, C. E., 1951, "Tropical Meteorology," in "Compendium of Meteorology," pp. 859–880, Boston, American Meteorological Society.
Petterssen, S., 1956, "Weather Analysis and Forecasting," Second ed., New York, McGraw-Hill Book Co.
Riehl, H., 1954, "Tropical Meteorology," New York, McGraw-Hill Book Co., 392pp.

Cross-references: Vol. II, *Geostrophic Wind; Rossby Wave; Wind*.

SUBAQUEOUS SAND DUNES

Subaqueous sand dunes are large-scaled submarine mega-ripples and bar systems. They have been reported in the waters around Great Britain, on the Atlantic continental shelf of the United States, on the Bahama Banks, in the Malacca Straits and in the Persian Gulf. Laboratory studies have added further knowledge on their nature. Essential features are: gentle fore slope with steep lee slope, movement of whole structure by transport of sand grains from fore slope to lee slope, formation where surface current velocities are little more than one knot, direction of movement accompanying set of strongest tidal current, barchan or linear form determined by sand supply, and dimensions usually of large magnitudes.

Geologists are well aware of the eolian sand formations, described by Bagnold and Strahler as transverse, longitudinal, and crescentric dunes. Their subaqueous counterparts, however, are still relatively unfamiliar structures.

In current literature, subaqueous forms of the eolian transverse and crescentric dunes are known as *sand waves* and *submarine sand dunes* respectively. They have been reported in rivers (Lane and Eden) and estuaries (Ballade), on tidal flats (Van Straaten, Hulseman), on and between offshore sand banks (Cloet, Robinson), between islands (Guilcher), on the continental shelf generally (Van Veen, Emery and Schlee), and on calcareous banks such as the Bahamas (Rich, Newell, Illing). Longitudinal forms have been cited by Jordan (1962).

Historical Review

Large ripples with wavelengths measured in many meters rather than centimeters were described early in the nineteenth century (1838) from the Upper Ordivician of the Cincinatti Anticline by Locke, and their modern counterparts were observed off the French coast by Sial in 1841. Suter reported in 1875 that modern ripples of similar dimensions, but more pronounced asymmetrically, had been mapped in detail by engineers of the Mississippi River Survey (see also J. B. Johnson, in 1879). Four years earlier, Partiot had written of subaqueous dunes with a gentle slope upstream and a lee side declivity of forty-five degrees. In 1882, Hider referred to symmetrical ripples of gigantic proportions which developed in

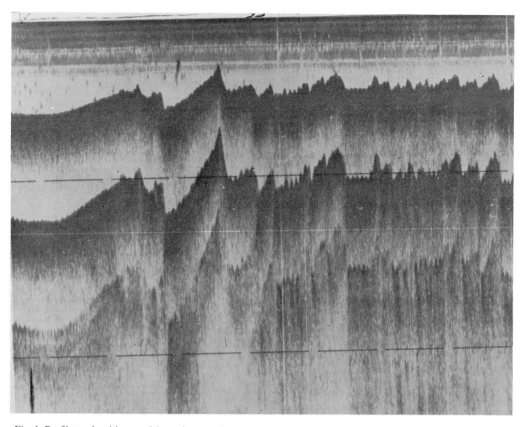

Fig. 1. Profile made with a precision echo sounder across sand waves on the continental shelf near Cape Cod (after Emery and Schlee, 1963; by permission). Note: upper trace is first echo, all others are multiples.

rivers carrying a considerable bed load as "sand waves"; he reported that a reduction in current velocity led to "large asymmetrical ripples."

G. H. Darwin, in 1883 appears to have made the first use of models for this subject. Reynolds in 1887 observed the formation of sand ripples while experimenting with artificial tidal currents in a model estuary. He assumed from the ratio of the model to nature that real tidal currents should give rise to gigantic ripples with a wavelength of about 30 meters. The first adequate description of actual tidal ripples comes from a comprehensive study in 1901 by Cornish of huge asymmetric sand waves formed by ebb tides in estuaries and by strong tidal currents on the sea floor off the coasts of Britain.

Models were again employed when Gilbert observed the formation and travel of subaqueous dunes during his classic study on the transportation of detritus by running water. Shortly afterwards, Pierce noted dune-like movement along sandy-bottomed streams at low water stage in the American southwest.

The terminology was clarified in 1919 when Bucher referred to the symmetrical flow pheno-

mena as *sand waves* and the asymmetric forms as *meta-ripples*. Later, Kindle, and Kindle and Bucher, used the following terms for the larger forms allied to ordinary ripple marks: *tidal sand waves, tidal sand ridges, meta-ripples,* and *large ripples*. Regressive sand waves, or anti-dunes, which were symmetrical and moved upstream were described by Langbein under the title of sand waves. Subsequent literature follows the convention of using the term sand wave in referring to linear subaqueous sand dunes.

Survey Methods

Recent advances in echo sounding have greatly aided the study of submarine sand features. Also, viewed from the air, formations on the bottom of moderately shallow waters can be clearly seen (Rich, 1948). A precision depth recorder is being used in the study of the Atlantic continental shelf (Fig. 1), now being carried on jointly by the Woods Hole Institution and the U.S. Geological Survey (Emery and Schlee, 1963).

In surveys of the waters around Great Britain from 1952 to 1961 aboard the R.R.S. *Discovery,* Stride and others employed both echo-sounding

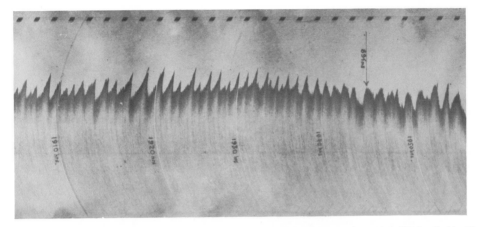

Fig. 2. Echo-sounder record (7 miles) showing sand waves near the edge of the continental shelf (after Stride, 1963; by permission). Depth: 89 fm (163 m); mean sand wave height: 5–10 m.

(Fig. 2) and echo-ranging apparatus. Echo sounding gives a profile of the floor beneath the ship with a maximum discrimination of about one meter, while echo ranging gives an oblique view of sea-floor roughness from the side of the ship out to a maximum slant range of 800 meters. During 1961 the echo range equipment aboard the *Discovery* was described in detail by Tucker and Stubbs, and its operation was described by Donovan and Stride.

Sediments

The origin of the sands which comprise modern day subaqueous sand dunes varies according to the location. Each site is indicative of its recent geological history.

The sand on the floor of the North Sea, Irish Sea, Bristol Channel, and Celtic Sea is derived mainly from Pleistocene glacial outwash deposits (Stride, 1963). All of these areas were glaciated at the same time, and today, local sand banks, headlands, beaches, and moraines furnish much of the sediments being transported along the sea floor. An important example is the Dogger Bank (Stride, 1959), a relic moraine in the central North Sea, where the fines are being winnowed out by the tidal currents. Baak noted that fluvial sediments from the Rhine also contributed to the North Sea sands during glacial periods of low sea level.

A third source of sand in this region is autochthonous fragmental calcareous material (Stride, 1963), the hard parts of marine animals living under present day conditions. Shelly deposits are important in bays on Britain's south coast according to Holme, and along the French coast as in the Bay of Mont-Saint-Michel as stated by Bourcart and Boillot. Berthois reports that to the west of this area (Brittany), sedimentary material consist almost entirely of calcareous fragmentals.

The major part of the Bahama Banks is covered

with a mantle of calcareous sands and silts (Newell, 1951; Illing, 1954). These rest on a lithified basement of similar nature. Along the edges of the Banks, the sand consists of debris of neritic organic skeletons, while elsewhere nonskeletal grains of cryptocrystalline or oolitic aragonite comprise most of the material.

Forms and Currents

As in eolian formations, whether subaqueous forms take the shape of sand waves or submarine sand dunes (barchans) seems to depend essentially upon the quantity of sediment available. Their other characteristics are similar in most respects: the asymmetric profile (Keunen, 1950; King, 1963; Stride, 1963) and the steep side indicating the direction of advance, which takes place by erosion of the gently sloping face and deposition on the steep lee side. Underwater photographs of asymmetric sand waves were taken in 1962 by Whittard.

The direction of dune advance is determined by the direction of set of the strongest tidal currents. Stride observes that a difference of 0.1 knot between peak velocities of ebb and flood tidal currents is sufficient to drive the ridges forward. The tidal currents may be increased by wind-induced currents, reaching their greatest peak when storms augment spring tides. At such times, they may move unusually large quantities of sediment.

Dimensions of submarine sand dunes and sand waves vary considerably. Kindle observed tidal sand waves rising up to $2\frac{1}{2}$ meters above the troughs at the mouth of the Avon River (Bay of Fundy), while upriver meta-ripples rarely rose more than 1 meter; Hjulström noted asymmetric, transverse sand waves moving downstream in the deep parts of large rivers with amplitudes of 0.07–5.58 meters and wavelengths of 0.6–229 meters. Cloet has reported sand waves on the northern part of Brake Bank in the North Sea that have

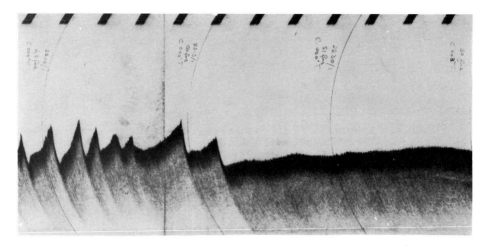

Fig. 3. Echo-sounder record (7½ miles) showing sand waves southwest of the Isle of Man (after Stride. 1963; by permission). Mean sand wave height: 2–18 m.

been measured as ½–2 meters in height and 30–150 meters in length. These were perpendicular to the trend of the bank, their steeper slopes facing north, this being the set of a current reaching 3.2 knots.

Rich (1948) observed giant submarine bars and ripples while flying over the Bahama Banks, and many geologists have confirmed these. He estimated those on Hurricane Flats to be aligned east and west, in 6–7 meters of water, and about 200–250 meters across. Southeast of Hurricane Flats, he described a rippled pattern of much finer texture, in 7–9 meters of water, as resembling a "mackerel sky." Rich noted their similarity to certain gas-bearing lenticular Paleozoic sands in Ohio.

On the rim of the banks, at depths of 2–4 meters, there are patterns suggestive of a combination of wave action and current. These are also referred to by Newell (1951) as systems of parallel, underwater oolitic "dunes" extending obliquely across the bank margin. He associated these with the strong ebb tidal currents.

In the channels between cays in the Exuma arc, Illing (1954) observed underwater crescentic dunes that were 30–70 meters from tip to tip, with their convex side toward the ocean. These submarine "barchan" dunes were formed by 2–3 knot currents flowing onto the banks. As they were not reversed at each tide, he presumed the flow tide to be the more powerful.

Where the edge of the banks had no protecting line of cays Illing observed giant ripples of shifting sand on major sand spreads or bores a mile or two in from the edge. These were in 3–7 meters of water, approximately 5–16 meters apart, and had formed at right angles to the current with their steep slopes facing out. There is a distinctly zonal grouping east of the Tongue of the Ocean. Here, sub-

marine barchan dunes were concentrated in the middle of large sand spreads, while towards the edges, they merged into linear dunes. Since the tidal currents are weakest on the sand spread and strongest in the deeper channels, Illing attributed the control of form to the consistency and regular direction of the tidal stream and the amount of sand available. It would appear that an adequate sand supply is the prime factor.

Rich (1948) noted that the water over the whole area is so shallow that storm waves continually agitate the bottom so that any patterns now visible must be considered as products of contemporary processes. The features cannot be inherited because the region was subaerial during the Wisconsin.

In waters around Britain, Stride (1963) has recorded heights up to 20 meters, wavelengths up to 1000 meters, and crest lengths as great as 40 times their separation. The largest dunes occur near the edge of the continental shelf. Off the East Anglian coast, they are commonly found with 5-meter amplitudes and 150-meter wavelengths. Where sand is abundant, heights of adjacent sand waves are similar, but where there is a paucity of sand, adjacent crests vary in height, i.e., 3–16 meters in the English Channel.

Their form, with steep lee side in the direction of movement, is adequately illustrated by the echo-sounding traces reproduced in Figs. 2 and 3. There is considerable variation in the straightness of the sand wave crests. Straight crests are associated with tidal currents which reach peak velocities in opposite directions, while sinuous crests are associated with tidal currents that have near maximum velocities occurring over a wide arc. In the northern sector of the Irish Sea and in the Bristol Channel, crests are almost straight. Sinuous

Fig. 4. Present-day transport paths on the sea floor and large regions of accumulation of sediments (shaded). Scale 1 inch to 125 miles (after Stride, 1963).

crests are found in the western sector of the English Channel and in the southern portion of the Celtic Sea (Stride, 1963).

Stride estimates that the dunes are limited to ground swept by currents which at the surface are greater than one knot. There are large areas where the tidal currents around Great Britain reach 1–2 knots and smaller areas of 3–4 knots according to Sager. Surface tides with velocities over 1 knot are found in the whole southern bight of the North Sea, in a belt over 100 km wide along the east coast of England and west coast of Germany, English Channel, Irish Sea, Bristol Channel, and in the southern Celtic Sea. The strongest bottom currents are estimated by Stride (1963) for the English Channel at depths of 100, 140 and 180 meters at 2, 1.5 and 1 knot, respectively. Pratje showed that in the English Channel, there was a simple geographical correspondence between the grade of the uppermost sediments and the peak velocity of the tidal currents over them; thus gravel was associated with currents stronger than 2.5 knots, sand with those of more than 1.5 knots, and mud with currents of less than 1 knot.

In general, the amount of material transported is a steeply increasing nonlinear function of the strength of the current. Stride and Cartwright (1958) estimate that in the southern bight of the North Sea a current of 1.5–2 knots, with ebb and flood tides differing by 0.1 knot, transports four million cubic meters of sand per year over a 70-km front.

To determine the rate of subaqueous sand dune movement, Reid placed radioactive glass, ground to the size of the local sand, on the bottom off the East Anglian coast. During a three-month period in the summer of 1957, he found a net transport of 1.75 km (thus 200 m/day) in the direction of a tidal current which reached 2 knots at springs, with ebb and flood tide differences of 1 knot. Greater transport velocity would be expected in the winter, when larger sea waves enhance the current. These rates are probably ten times those found on the outer continental shelf (Stride, 1963), for the same current peak speeds on the shelf are accompanied by ebb and flood tide differences of only 0.1 knot.

The general direction of subaqueous sand dune transport in the region of Great Britain is illustrated in Fig. 4.

Echo soundings reported by Stride and Bowers have revealed masses of recent sands which are 30 meters thick in the Irish Sea and 120 meters thick in the Celtic Sea. Cartwright and Stride (1958) have observed places in which subaqueous sand dune transport of a few meters would be sufficient to lose sand down the continental slope, which, south of 49°N, is marked by numerous submarine canyons as cited by Day, and Berthois and Brenot.

Yet another example of giant ripples in a confined strait is shown in Fig. 5, which formed at 35–40 m. in the Malacca Strait.

Summary

Subaqueous sand dunes are analogous to eolian dunes in some respects and different in others. Their features may be summarized as:

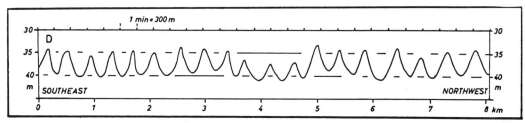

Fig. 5. Tracing of echo-sounding profile of "Sand Waves" in the Malacca Strait near One Fathom Bank (Malaya; from Wyrtki, *Naga* Report, Vol. 2, 1961, S.I.O., La Jolla).

(1) They have a gentle fore slope with a steep lee slope equal to the angle of repose of the sediment.

(2) The movement of the dunes is by erosion of material on fore slope and deposition on lee slope.

(3) They are formed where tidal surface currents are between 1 and 2 knots.

(4) The direction of movement is determined by the set of strongest tidal current, a difference of 0.1 knot being sufficient to affect the course.

(5) The pattern of individual crescentic submarine dunes (barchans) or linear sand waves (the shape) is a function of the available sand supply.

(6) Amplitudes, wavelengths, and crest lengths may vary greatly, up to 20 meters × 1 km × 40 km.

(7) The rate of transport, linearity of crests, and amplitude relationships are dependent upon the local tidal current conditions.

MAURICE L. SCHWARTZ

References

Cartwright, D. E., and Stride, A. H., 1958, "Large sand waves near the edge of the continental shelf," *Nature*, **181**, 41.

Emery, K. O., and Schlee, J. S., 1963, "The Atlantic continental shelf and slope, a program for study," *U.S. Geol. Surv. Circ.*, **481**, 11pp.

Illing, L. V., 1954, "Bahaman calcareous sands," *Bull. Am. Assoc. Petrol. Geol.*, **38**, 1–95.

Jordan, G. F., 1962, "Large submarine sand waves," *Science*, **136**, 839–848.

King, C. A. M., 1963, "An Introduction to Oceanography," New York, McGraw-Hill Book Co., 337pp.

Kuenen, P. H., 1950, "Marine Geology," New York, John Wiley & Sons, 568pp.

Newell, N. D., 1951, "Organic reefs and submarine dunes of öolite sand around Tongue of the Ocean, Bahamas," *Bull. Geol. Soc. Am.*, **66**, 1466.

Rich, J. L., 1948, "Submarine sedimentary features on Bahama Banks and their bearing on distribution patterns of lenticular oil sands," *Bull. Am. Assoc. Petrol. Geol.*, **32**, 767–779.

Stride, A. H., 1959, "On the origin of the Dogger Bank, in the North Sea," *Geol. Mag.*, **96**, 33–44.

Stride, A. H., 1963, "Current-swept sea floors near the southern half of Great Britain," *Quart. J. Geol. Soc. London*, **119**, 175–199.

Stride, A. H., and Cartwright, D. E., 1958, "Sand transport at southern end of the North Sea," *Dock Harb. Author.*, **38**, 323–324.

SUBARCTIC CURRENT—*See* **ALEUTIAN CURRENT**

SUBMARINE CANYONS AND OTHER SEA VALLEYS

The high slopes of the ocean floor are cut by numerous valleys. Many of these have steep walls, a V-shaped profile, and slope outward continuously. Thus, they resemble the canyons on land and are called submarine canyons. Some of the sea valleys have U-shaped profiles with broad flat floors. Some of the latter compare with land fault valleys, and still others show no relation to land valleys. Another type of submarine valley has small relief, natural levees on the side, and extends in a winding course across large submarine fans. Finally, there are relatively shallow ravines cutting depositional slopes such as the fronts of deltas. In considering the origin of submarine valleys, it is important to consider these types separately, rather than to attempt to apply a simple explanation that will encompass them all. Some description of these types and their origin will be given with special emphasis on the impressive submarine canyons.

Submarine Canyons

Geologists have been particularly concerned with the large canyons that have been found on the marine slopes off many portions of the continents. These great rock gorges which have walls as high or higher than those of the Grand Canyon are in the following localities: the Bahamas, Monterey Bay, California (Fig. 1), off eastern Ceylon, off western France, off northern Spain, off western Portugal, and the Bering Sea. The greatest of these, in the Bahamas, has walls almost three miles high.

Virtually all of the submarine canyons slope outward as continuously as do land river valleys. Rock found on the canyon walls ranges widely in geological age and includes such diverse types as granite, quartzite, limestone, sandstone, and soft shale. Where detailed maps of the canyons are available, they are seen to have numerous tributaries, the canyon floors are generally narrow and winding, and the walls are usually steep and

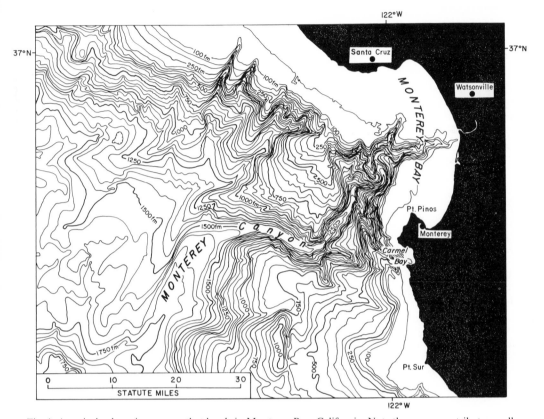

Fig. 1. A typical submarine canyon that heads in Monterey Bay, California. Note the numerous tributary valleys and the winding course (modified after Shepard and Emery, 1941).

locally include vertical and overhanging cliffs (as seen from Cousteau's diving saucer).

Repeated observations made in the shallow canyon heads close to shore have shown that they tend to fill rapidly with sediment, but that the sediment is not stable and periodically moves out along the length of the floor as slides, flows, and probably as turbidity currents (q.v.). The sediment moves through the length of the canyon and builds up great fans at the canyon mouths. Creeping of the sediment along the canyon floors is also well demonstrated, and erosion is probably produced that is somewhat comparable to that of a glacier moving down a land valley.

An interesting aspect of submarine canyons is the relation which they have to river valleys on land. Where the canyon heads occur relatively nearshore, most of them are located off river valleys or at a point where a river formerly entered the coast and has been recently diverted. Although this relationship might be thought to indicate that these submarine canyons are drowned river valleys, the case is far from clear because the character of the submarine valley is usually different from that of a river valley. Only on the west side of Corsica is there a close resemblance between the two.

The *origin* of submarine canyons is far from a settled problem. It is quite clear that erosion is taking place along the canyons and that sediment moves in large quantities along their length. On the other hand, the pattern of the canyons is very similar to that of stream canyons cut into mountain slopes. Also, there is much evidence of downwarping along the margins of the continents that would have carried old land canyons down into great depths. Perhaps the sea canyons are the combined results of drowning of old land canyons and extensive modification by marine processes. In whatever way they were formed, it is quite clear that they are not a recent product, but have been in existence for millions of years in order to allow the development of the great fans at their mouths. It is possible to estimate both the volume of these fans and the rate at which they are growing.

Fan-Valleys of the Sea Floor

Beyond the mouths of submarine canyons, the large fans referred to previously are found to have channels winding down their slopes towards the deep ocean floor (Fig. 2). These channels, called fan-valleys, have relatively low walls and are usually bordered by a raised rim that is comparable

867

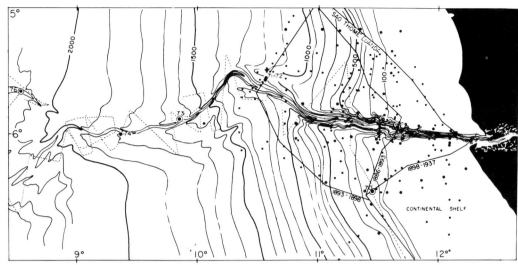

Fig. 2. Congo Canyon and the lengthy fan-valley that extends down the submarine fan west of the sharp bend in the channel. Note the natural levees and the distributaries along the lower slope (from Heezen *et a* ., 1964, *Am. Assoc. Petrol. Geol.*, p. 1131).

to the levees along the sides of river channels that cross deltas. During dives in the bathyscaph, the channels have been observed to be flat floored and covered with sand over which there is often a thin overlying layer of mud. Mud is found on the walls and levees, although cores from the levees often show thin sand layers below the mud. Walls of fan-valleys are known to be steep on the outside of the curves, and terraces are often found on the inside. These terraces are not continuous and are rather suggestive of landslide blocks that have settled on the side of the channel where there is least erosion. Outside the Congo Submarine Canyon and in the Bay of Bengal, the fan valleys extend seaward for many hundreds of miles. In some places, the levees on the sides of fan valleys rise as ridges for several hundred feet above the channel bottoms and the adjacent fan surfaces. In this respect, they are quite different from the low levees on the sides of rivers.

The origin of fan-valleys is not entirely established, but it seems likely that they are a product of turbidity currents or of some other type of flow that moves down the submarine canyons and out onto the fans beyond. It seems likely that the channels shift in position and that old channels become filled while new are excavated. This again is comparable to the shifting of channels in deltas. Distributaries are found in some fan channels, but not as commonly as in deltas.

Flat-floored Valleys of the Sea Floor

The submarine valleys with broad flat floors are very different from submarine canyons. They include several types. The simplest type is a rectilinear gash, one that is found in areas with abundant earthquakes and other indications of crustal instability. These valleys differ from submarine canyons in having few entering tributaries, relatively straight trends, and basin depressions along their lengths. They are quite clearly fault valleys akin to the fault valleys on land, such as Death Valley.

The continental shelves are crossed by many flat-floored valleys apparently of glacial origin. Such valleys are not found in unglaciated areas, but they are present on virtually all shelves where the adjacent lands have been glaciated. These troughs are usually deepest nearshore and do not continue down the slopes of the continental shelf, although submarine canyons occur in the prolongation of a few of them. This type of trough seems to be a product of glaciation, and the shelf valleys are often a continuation of the glacially excavated fiords found inland.

A third type of trough also crosses the continental shelves, but unlike the glacial trough, it slopes continuously outward. Such troughs occur uniquely off large river deltas. They have few, if any, tributaries and have relatively straight walls. The best known example is found off the Ganges Delta, and a very similar trough is located near the Indus Delta. Along one side of the Mississippi Delta, there is a trough that, unlike others of this type, appears to start more than halfway across the shelf. However, borings and sonic profiles have shown that there is a buried valley extending from the trough toward the coast. Exploration of these troughs has shown that the sediments on their floors contain sand layers, and there are indications that these sands have been transported along the valley axes. Some form of sediment flow coming

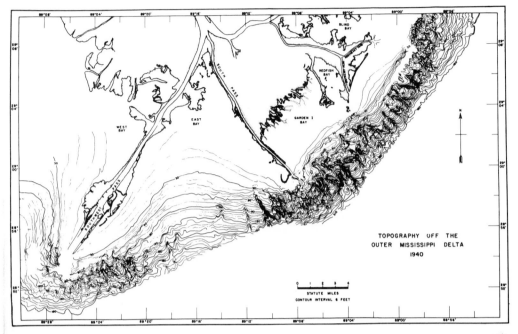

Fig. 3. Gullies in the foreset slope off the advancing Mississippi Delta. These discontinuous valleys apparently are due to slumping.

from the large rivers apparently moves along these troughs, carrying large quantities of sediment out to the deep sea. Presumably this movement is a type of turbidity current.

Ravines on Sediment Slopes

Ordinarily, where slopes have been built seaward, they are creased by a series of small ravines (Fig. 3). These are usually not more than a few feet deep, with exceptional depths up to 100 feet. They are slightly curving in trend but have few tributaries. They are discontinuous, starting at any point on the advancing slope and stopping part way down the slope. Small mounds are frequently found near their outer terminations. Samples taken on the floor of the ravines reveal muddy sediments with occasional thin partings of coarse silt. Samples from intervening ridges show the same type of sediment.

The origin of the ravines appears to be submarine slumping. The rapidly deposited delta-front sediments are metastable and subject to spontaneous liquification, starting occasional slumping action. Turbidity currents possibly may also play some part in forming the gullies. However, the fact that gullies continue only part way down the slopes and lack any concentration of coarse sediments along their floors argues against turbidity currents as an origin.

Francis P. Shepard

References

Buffington, E. C., and Moore, D. G., 1963, "Geophysical evidence on the origin of gullied submarine slopes, San Clemente, California," *J. Geol.*, **71**, 356–371.

Daly, R. A., 1936, "Origin of submarine canyons," *Am. J. Sci.*, Ser. 5, **31**, 401–420.

Heezen, B. C., 1956, "The origin of submarine canyons," *Sci. Am.* (August 1956).

Heezen, B. C., *et al.*, 1964, "Congo Submarine Canyon," *Bull. Am. Assoc. Petrol. Geologists*, **48**, pp. 1126–1150.

Kuenen, Ph. H., 1953, "Origin and classification of submarine canyons," *Bull. Geol. Soc. Am.*, **64**, 1295–1314.

Shepard, F. P., 1951, "Mass movements in submarine canyon heads," *Trans. Am. Geophys. Union*, **32**, 405–418.

Shepard, F. P., 1963a, "Submarine geology," Second ed., New York, Harper & Row (with chapters by D. L. Inman and E. D. Goldberg), 557pp.

Shepard, F. P., 1963b, "Submarine canyons," in (Hill, M. N., editor) "The Sea," New York, Interscience Publishers.

Shepard, F. P., 1965, "Types of submarine valleys," *Bull. Am. Assoc. Petrol. Geologists*, **49**, 304–310.

Shepard, F. P., and Emery, K. O., 1941, "Submarine topography off the California Coast," *Geol. Soc. Am. Spec. Paper*, **31**, 171pp.

Veatch, A. C., and Smith, P. A., 1939, "Atlantic submarine valleys of the United States and Congo submarine valley," *Geol. Soc. Am. Spec. Paper*, **7**, 101pp.

SUBMARINE CONES OR FANS

Cone or fan-shaped submarine geomorphic features that have proved to be accumulations of terrigenous sediment have been discovered offshore from most of the world's great rivers, extending down to abyssal depths. They have received a variety of names: *abyssal cones, submarine fans, deep-sea fans, subsea aprons, submarine deltas,* etc.

As stated by Heezen and Laughton (1963, p. 337): "Whatever the mechanism by which submarine canyons may have been cut into the edge of the continental shelf, it is well established that periodic turbidity currents flush sediment through them and build up depositional fans where the canyon reaches the lower gradients of the ocean basin. These deep-sea fans have been found at the bases of nearly all submarine canyons, notably the Hudson Canyon (Ericson, Ewing and Heezen, 1951), La Jolla Canyon (Menard and Ludwick, 1951), the Monterey Canyon (Dill, Dietz and Stewart, 1954), and many others off the California coast (Menard, 1955; Gorsline and Emery, 1959). A comparison of the volume of deep-sea fans off southern California has led Menard (1960) to date the fans as pre-Pleistocene. Recent surveys of the seaward extensions of

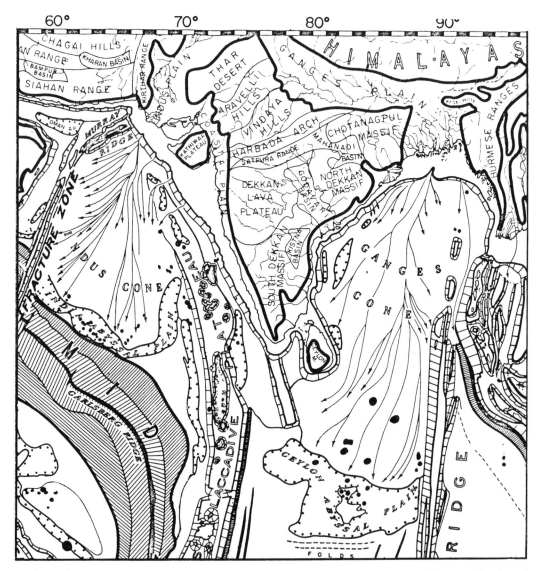

Fig. 1. The Ganges Cone (reaching the Ceylon Abyssal Plain) and the Indus Cone (reaching the India Abyssal Plain), together representing the bulk of the erosion of the Himalayas (from a segment of the Indian Ocean Physiographic Province map of Heezen and Tharp, 1965).

other submarine canyons throughout the world have also revealed the existence of deep-sea fans or families of deep-sea fans, which are collectively referred to as abyssal cones" (Heezen, Ewing, Menzies and Granelli, 1957). Heavy minerals in the sediments of adjacent fans may be quite distinct, so that it is evident that submarine fans drain specific hinterland areas in exactly the same way as do alluvial fans on land.

In their physiographic diagrams of the South Atlantic and of the Indian Ocean, Heezen and Tharp (1961, 1965) have illustrated very striking examples of such cones associated with the deltas or submarine canyons of the Amazon, Congo, and Niger (in the Atlantic), the Magdalena (Caribbean), the Ganges and the Indus (Indian Ocean).

The submarine cone of the Ganges is by far the largest in the world (2500 km, or 1400 nautical miles in length). It terminates in the Ceylon Abyssal Plain at a depth of rather over 5000 m, the mean slope down from the Sundabunds being 1:500. It should be stressed that this mean grade distinguishes this kind of feature distinctly from the *abyssal plain* (q.v.) which is by definition always marked by slopes of less than 1:1000. Given in round figures,

the area of this giant cone is over 2 million km^2 and its volume is about 5 million km^3. Considering that this represents the drainage of about 70% of the Himalayas (about 10% the volume of detritus was left in the Gangetic fluvial plain and 20% went to Indus), the figure is not so surprising; if the Himalayas began to be seriously eroded about 20 million years ago, this would account for about 0.25 km^3/yr of insoluble residue of erosion. Adding the soluble components, the erosion total might be estimated at 0.3 km^3/yr or 6 cm/century over the Indo-Tibetan Himalayas (approximately 500,000 km^2). Recent measurements in the Himalayas indicate erosion in local areas up to 10 cm/century. The mean sedimentation rate over the Ganges cone would come to 250×10^6 m$_3$/yr, or 0.1 mm/yr, or 1 cm/century.

Off the Pacific coast of North America, Menard has demonstrated the existence of a large number of smaller fans, striking examples being the Monterey Fan and Delgada Fan (see physiographic diagram in Menard, 1964), which are up to 300 km in length and up to 50,000 km^3 in volume. The complex basement tectonics of this coast are at least

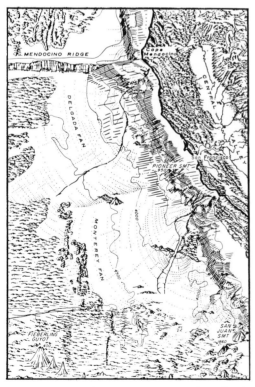

Fig. 2. The Delgada and Monterey fans, in the northeast Pacific Ocean (segment of the physiographic map by H. W. Menard, 1964). (By permission of McGraw-Hill Book Co. N.Y.

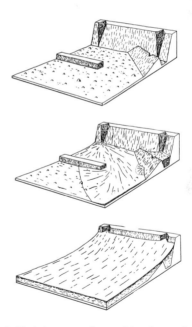

Fig. 3. Varied topography resulting from submarine fan sedimentation. Relief about 2 miles, vertical exaggeration 100 magnification. (1) Continental slope with submarine canyons (origin not relevant), and irregular deep-sea floor of abyssal hills without sedimentary cover. (2) Deposition of sedimentary blanket which thins outward. Sediment from one canyon is ponded by tilted fault block, and comparatively thick deposit is formed. Sediment from other canyon flows around low fault block. (3) More mature stage of deposition in which initial topography is completely covered. Deep-sea fans have coalesced (Menard, 1955).

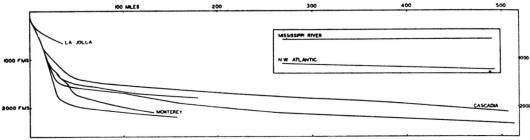

Fig. 4. Longitudinal profiles of submarine canyons and associated deep-sea channels across fans in northeastern Pacific Ocean, showing general similarities and compared with Mississippi River and Mid-Ocean Channel of northwest Atlantic (Menard, 1955).

partially "drowned" by the fans. Menard (1964, p. 220) has calculated that an average of one turbidity flow of 1×10^6 m^3/yr would be appropriate for building these fans, distributed generally and extending over the period of the late Cenozoic ($1-4 \times 10^7$ yr), with corresponding rates of erosion of the hinterland of the order of 1–3 cm/century. The contrast between this figure and that for the Himalayas reflects in the latter the much larger effective relief, the higher (monsoon) precipitation and the lack of vegetative protection in the upper third of the mountains.

Most, if not all, submarine cones or fans are marked by one or more *deep-sea channels* which are usually the distal extensions of submarine canyons cutting the upper part of the continental slope. However, as the gradient flattens on the continental rise or on the submarine fan, the canyon shallows to a "submarine valley" (in Shepard's terminology) eventually to a "superficial channel" with levees (Buffington, 1952) in the manner of a great river valley in its "old-age" course. In the case of the great Indian Ocean fans of the Ganges and Indus, the fans reach up almost to the shelf break, but there are only short canyons, respectively the "Swatch of No Ground" and "The Swatch," which extend from 100 km or so (Hayter, 1960), before reverting distally to superficial channels (such as recognized by Dietz, 1953).

An interesting feature of the American West Coast fans is the tendency for their deep-sea channels to hook sharply to the left. Menard (1955) noted not less than twelve left hooks in fifteen examples, attributing the hook to a "secondary effect of the action of the Coriolis force," which in the northern hemisphere would tend to tilt the surface of each flow up to the right, building the right bank higher and higher, forcing the flow gradually to swing left.

RHODES W. FAIRBRIDGE

References

Buffington, E. C., 1952, "Submarine natural levees," *J. Geol., 60*, 473–479.

Dill, R. F., Dietz, R. S., and Stewart, H., 1954, "Deep-sea channels and delta of the Monterey Submarine Canyon," *Bull. Geol. Soc. Am., 65*, 191–195.

Ericson, D. B., Ewing, M., and Heezen, B. C., 1951, "Deep-sea sands and submarine canyons," *Bull. Geol. Soc. Am., 62*, 961–965.

Ericson, D. B., Ewing, M., and Heezen, B. C., 1952, "Turbidity currents and sediments in the North Atlantic," *Bull. Am. Assoc. Petrol. Geologists, 36*, 489–512.

Gorsline, D. S., and Emery, K. O., 1959, "Turbidity current deposits in San Pedro and Santa Monica Basins off Southern California," *Bull. Geol. Soc. Am., 70*, 279–290.

Hayter, P. J. D., 1960, "The Ganges and Indus Submarine Canyons," *Deep-Sea Res., 6*, 184–186.

Heezen, B. C., Ewing, M., Menzies, R. J., and Granelli, N.C., 1957, "Extending the limits of the Congo Submarine Canyon," *Bull. Geol. Soc. Am., 68*, 1743–1744.

Heezen, B. C., and Laughton, A. S., 1963, "Abyssal Plains," in "The Sea," Vol. 3, pp. 312–364, New York, Interscience Publishers.

Menard, H. W., 1955, "Deep-sea channels, topography, and sedimentation," *Bull. Am. Assoc. Petrol. Geologists, 39*, 236–255.

Menard, H. W., 1960, "Possible pre-Pleistocene deep-sea fans off Central California," *Bull. Geol. Soc. Am., 71*, 1271–1278.

Menard, H. W., 1964, "Marine Geology of the Pacific," New York, McGraw-Hill Book Co., 271pp.

Menard, H. W., and Ludwick, J. C., 1951, "Applications of hydraulics to the study of marine turbidity currents," *Soc. Econ. Paleontologists Mineralogists Spec. Publ., 2*, 1–13.

Cross-references: *Submarine Canyons.* Vol. III: *Continental Erosion.*

SUBMARINE PLATEAUS

Definition*

In all the somewhat confused terminology of undersea topographic terminology, *plateau* is a happy example of a word that is used in an identical sense in the principal western languages, and its

---

* Rhodes W. Fairbridge.

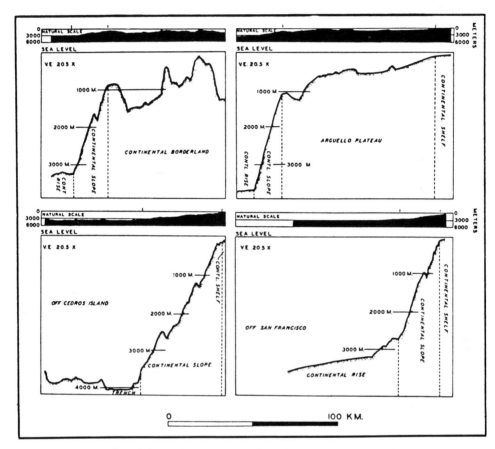

Fig. 1. Typical profiles of the continental margin off California and Mexico, showing irregular border-land compared with smooth marginal plateau (Uchupi and Emery, 1963).

definition is clear: "a comparatively flat-topped elevation of the sea floor . . . of considerable width across the summit . . . and usually rising at least 200 m from the surrounding regions" (Supan, 1903). The spelling of the plural suffix −x is acceptable, but not considered good practice in anglicized terminology, although the term is certainly of French origin.

There is some minor disagreement about the sides of plateaus; some authors wish them to be described as rising imperceptibly from the deep sea floor—others say rising abruptly. Also some writers say that the plateau must drop off on *all* sides, but numerous examples along continental borders are asymmetric and drop off on only one or two sides. These two alternatives should be written into the definition, for both varieties are well established and are used here as a basis for classification. We recognize therefore:

(a) *Marginal Plateaus*. These are closely related to *continental borderlands* (q.v.), but while the latter is defined as lying seaward of the normal continental shelf, its surface is highly irregular (e.g., the border-land off Southern California). In contrast, the

marginal plateau has an essentially flat top. As Heezen *et al.* (1959) have indicated, it is like a broad step between the upper continental rise (or slope) and the lower continental rise. They have been called *deep shelves* by Menard (1964) and appear to be down-warped equivalents of normal shelves. A useful comparison between continental borderland (southern California) and marginal plateau (Ar-guello Plateau), either of which type may have its outer slope passing down into a continental rise or trench (as with the Cedros Trench), is given by Uchupi and Emery (1963; see Fig. 1). In other instances the upper continental rise may be replaced by a trench.

(b) *Mid-ocean Plateaus*. Numerous *oceanic rises* (q.v.) have been referred to in the literature as plateaus, and here the definition needs to be tightened up somewhat. Thus the "*Telegraph Plateau*" of the North Atlantic and the "*Albatross Plateau*" of the eastern Pacific are unquestionably parts of the mid-oceanic ridge system, and their surfaces are not in the least smooth or plateau-like; they were originally called plateaus on the basis of a few scattered wire soundings, and it was not

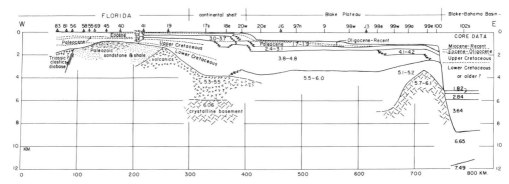

Fig. 2. East–west structure section across the Blake Plateau and the Florida Platform between latitudes 29° 00′N and 30° 00′N (after Sheridan *et al.*, 1966).

realized at first that their topography was marked by extreme irregularities, characteristic of the mid-oceanic ridge. Apart from features of that sort, in the mid-ocean there have been identified (1) *aseismic ridges* (q.v.) which appear to consist of basic igneous oceanic crust with some lower-density volcanics, but no formerly continental components; (2) *oceanic rises* (q.v.), the broad sea floor elevation, generally taken to be less precipitous and rugged than a *ridge*; where the structure is known, it seems to be largely of basic igneous crust, punctuated by seamounts or volcanic islands, e.g., Bermuda Rise, Cape Verde Rise (preferably not "plateau" since it is dome-like), Icelandic Rise, etc.; (3) true *mid-ocean plateaus*, to which Heezen has applied the genetic connotation "microcontinent."

The topographic requirement of the definition as simply a smooth, flattish surface, dropping abruptly away at the margins, can hardly have any other geophysical explanation, but that of a former land area close to sea level (to give it the flat top) and a nucleus of formerly continental material to give it a lighter specific gravity that will keep it standing high above the surrounding deep ocean floor. In numbers of cases (see below), an originally higher elevation (sea level or above) can be proved geologically.

To sum up these remarks about definition: both marginal and mid-ocean plateaus are relatively flat-topped subsea topographic features, sometimes distinctly tilted, dropping sharply away on one or more sides; geophysically they are further characterized by a basement or core of continental-type crust (but usually thinner than average for the true continent), and overlain or abutted by more or less flat-lying sediments.

Structure of Marginal Plateaus*

Structurally these features appear to differ from the normal continental shelves only in depth and are apparently the down-warped equivalents of the

---

* Robert E. Sheridan.

normal shelves. The depths of marginal plateaus range from 200–3000 m. Good representative examples are the Blake Plateau east of Florida and the Campbell Plateau east of New Zealand. Other marginal plateaus are found, e.g., in the Porcupine Bank west of Ireland, to the east of the Falkland Islands, east of Pernambuco Province, Brazil, off Vietnam (Heezen's "Saigon Bench") in the South China Sea, and several off Western Australia, including Exmouth Plateau (Fairbridge, 1955).

(a) Blake Plateau. The Blake Plateau is a broad, flat feature extending several hundred kilometers east of the narrow continental shelf bordering Florida. The shelf-like surface of this feature covers an area of nearly 130,000 km^2 at depths of 700–1000 m. Between Cape Hatteras and the Bahama Banks, the continental margin is dominated by the plateau, which is bordered on the east by the steep Blake Escarpment.

An east–west structure section based on deep borings and seismic-refraction data (Fig. 2) illustrates the correlation of the subsurface geology of the Blake Plateau and the Florida Platform. This was supplemented by several deep offshore drill holes obtained by the JOIDES (1965) operation. Considerations of the velocities measured in wells on Florida and the seaward extension of information from the JOIDES (1965) drilling to Paleocene horizons help to establish the age correlation of the offshore seismic layers. Of great stratigraphic interest is the fact that while nearshore the Eocene is extremely thick, on the plateau it thins out, but the Oligocene thickens (Fig. 3).

Since the physical (seismic velocity) boundaries do not correspond in detail to stratigraphic boundaries, only gross correlations are possible. On the Blake Plateau the Mesozoic–Tertiary boundary is within the 2.4–3.1 km/sec layer. The 3.8–4.8 and 4.1–4.2 km/sec velocities represent carbonates of Upper Cretaceous age, while the 5.1–5.2 and 5.5–6.0 km/sec horizon is at or near the top of Lower Cretaceous carbonates.

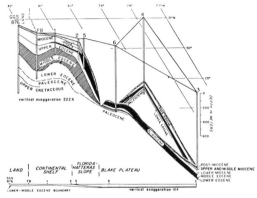

Fig. 3. Isometric fence diagram showing the stratigraphy of the continental margin off the east coast of Florida and the Blake Plateau. Note the less exaggerated form of the diagram at the bottom (JOIDES, 1965). (Courtesy T. Saito.)

Basement, observed as the 5.7–6.1 km/sec horizon, is found only on the east near the Blake Escarpment. The basement appears to form a north–south trending barrier ridge to a deep sediment-filled trough under the Blake Plateau. This trough–ridge structure is similar to the continental shelf off New Jersey.

During the Cretaceous, the steep Blake Escarpment formed by the upgrowth of coral reefs on the basement ridge. Behind this barrier reef thick carbonates were deposited in the sediment filled trough, giving a slight westward dip to the strata. Evidence of erosion in the thin Tertiary section on the Blake Plateau (JOIDES, 1965) suggests that strong currents then swept the area and prevented further deposition.

From this structure section (Fig. 2), the Blake Plateau appears to be a block of ancient continental shelf which continually subsided since Cretaceous, but which lacks a thick sequence of Tertiary sediments. The similarity of the plateau to the continental shelf farther north includes a basement of granitic character which probably consists of rocks as old as Precambrian. Indeed, the true edge of the Precambrian continental mass may be along the steep Blake Escarpment.

The relationship of the Bahama Banks to the Blake Plateau is one of superimposed slabs of thick Tertiary limestones. The magnetic anomalies over the banks indicate that the crystalline basement of Florida is not at the same depth under the Bahamas, but the anomalies are broader, suggesting that the basement becomes deeper in the area of the banks (Drake *et al.*, 1963). Talwani (1960) has interpreted the gravity anomalies of the Bahamas and concluded that the underlying crust is of continental character and about 30 km thick. On Andros Island of the Bahamas, a well which has penetrated greater than 4.4 km of pure carbonates was bottomed in

Lower Cretaceous limestone without reaching basement. This thick accumulation of limestone suggests deposition in shallow water with continued subsidence during the late Mesozoic and Cenozoic. Newell (1955) has suggested that the Bahama Banks owe their origin to upgrowth by the accumulation of coral reefs, a giant barrier reef, and such an origin would not conflict with subsidence in this area. The present relief of the banks may be localized where it is because of the warm waters, the convergence of favorable currents, and the possible discontinuance of coral growth on the Blake Plateau at the end of the Mesozoic. Apparently, the Tertiary orientations of the strong Florida Current and the Gulf Stream favored the development of coral reef banks in their present location, but not on the Blake Plateau. The Bahama Banks may also be appropriately classified as a marginal plateau.

(b) **Campbell Plateau.** The Campbell Plateau east of New Zealand is part of a broad, relatively shallow area including the Chatham Rise and Bounty Trough (Brodie, 1964). These features cover an area greater than that of New Zealand and lie at depths of 500–1000 m. Over most of the surface of this region the bottom is smooth, but on the Chatham Rise there are a few areas of rough topography. According to Cullen (1965), early Paleozoic metamorphic schists and late Tertiary sedimentary rocks are dredged from these areas of rough topography. Menard (1964) feels that the presence of truncated outcrops of late Tertiary rocks on the nearly level surface of the Chatham Rise can only be explained by erosion at a shallow depth and subsequent subsidence due to faulting. However, as on the Blake Plateau, the effects of submarine erosion by deep currents can be important in depths similar to the Chatham Rise.

That the Campbell Plateau is part of the New Zealand continental mass is evident from its crustal thickness of 20 km. This is based on investigations of the dispersion of surface waves caused by earthquakes (Adams, 1962).

Although less is known about the Campbell Plateau, there are similarities in its sedimentary structures and its relationship to the adjacent continental mass that can be compared to the Blake Plateau.

(c) **East of Falkland Islands.** This marginal plateau making up a large part of the Falkland Rise covers an area of the order of 350,000 km² and lies at depths of 2000–3000 m. The surface topography is irregular in profile, and the plateau is generally bordered by steep escarpments that separate it from the deeper ocean basins.

Preliminary interpretations of the seismic-refraction profiles of the area (Ewing and Ewing, 1959) indicate that the plateau is underlain by about 2–3 km of sediments above a basement of velocity 6.0 km/sec. This basement of continental character may

875

be related to the pre-Devonian gneisses and shists of the Falkland Islands. The geology of the Falkland Islands also includes sequences of Devonian and Permo-Triassic sedimentary rocks (Wilson, 1963). It seems probable that the continental mass, including geology of this type, extends beneath the marginal plateau east of the Falkland Islands.

(d) **East of Pernambuco Province, Brazil.** The marginal plateau here is characterized by irregular surface topography at consistent depths of 2000–3000 m and is separated from the deeper ocean basins by steep escarpments. This feature makes up the western part of the Rio Grande Rise and covers an area of about 120,000 km^2. Its boundaries do not parallel the continental margin, but the plateau protrudes from the continental slope as a prominent feature.

Preliminary interpretations of the seismic-refraction measurements of the area show that the plateau is underlain by 3.5 km of semiconsolidated and consolidated sediments above a basement of 5.9 km/sec velocity. This basement of a continental character is continuous with the Precambrian granitic basement forming the major part of the Brazilian Coastal Shield west of the Plateau. Below the 5.9 km/sec layer there appears to be a high-velocity 7.5 km/sec sub-basement layer at 10–12 km depths. This layer may be related to the oceanic crust, but the transition between the plateau and the oceanic basin is still uncertain. The structure section beneath this plateau appears to be more like that of the continental slopes than that of the ocean basins, although this type of structure may be called intermediate. If this marginal plateau is a subsiding block of ancient continental shelf, as is the Blake Plateau, the eventual evolution of the process may be that the basement crust of these features becomes intermediate in character.

Structure of Mid-ocean Plateaus*

As indicated in the definition discussion, certain areas described as "plateaus" from the mid-oceanic regions are preferably defined as "rises," etc., since precision depth recording shows that their surfaces are markedly irregular. Genetically, it is believed that smooth, essentially flat-topped platforms must have a continental origin, although the mechanism of their subsidence (continental stretching, drifting, "basification," "oceanization," or whatever) is still a matter for study and discussion (Beloussov and Ruditch, 1961; Konayev, 1963; Hsu, 1965). Kuenen (1950) stressed the importance of this question: "The problem of the subsided ancient borderlands and the disappearance of former terraces is one of the most weighty and urgent questions in the field of geology and geophysics. Until it has been solved we can never understand the fundamental features of the earth's crust. It is closely bound up with the

* Rhodes W. Fairbridge.

origin of oceans and continents, with the formation of the continental shelf and slope, with isostasy and geosynclinal evolution. In the meantime, the sweeping statement that continents cannot possibly have sunk away to form ocean beds should be avoided."

(a) **Coral Sea Plateau and Bellona Plateau.** These are two large examples in the Coral Sea (q.v.) between Australia and New Caledonia (Fairbridge, 1950). The mean plateau level is 1000 m, but in the first there seems to be a northerly tilt and the second a southerly tilt. Both are studded with enormous coral atolls and are the complex or compound shelf type, i.e., they do not have volcanic foundations but have grown up from the slowly subsiding floor of a continental shelf. The presence of such reefs is of great structural interest, because the reef-building corals are "drowned" by rapid subsidence. A reasonable mean rate of subsidence would be 1–10 mm/yr, and no catastrophic down-faulting would be possible.

(b) **Melanesian Border Plateau.** Extending from east of the Vera Cruz Islands to the banks north of Fiji, and thence nearly to the north end of the Tonga–Kermadec Ridge, there is a plateau region that is considerably cut up into small horsts and grabens, in the same manner as the continental borderland off southern California (Fairbridge, 1961), except that in this case the often postulated "Melanesian Lost Continent" or "Archaeo-Fijia" is probably of Mesozoic age and today is represented only by a few isolated island areas (New Caledonia, Fiji, etc.; see discussion in *Southwest Pacific*). Crustal thicknesses are mostly of intermediate, quasi-cratonic type. Numerous coral banks mark the higher parts of the border plateau, but a number of them are in fact "drowned" and do not reach the surface today (e.g., Alexa Bank, see Fairbridge and Stewart, 1960). Scattered volcanic centers are known, but these do not seem to be associated with atolls.

(c) **South China Sea Plateaus.** Several quite isolated submarine plateaus occur in the South China Sea, from the Paracel Islands block in the northwest to the Nanshan–Spratly–Investigator reefs in the south. Like the atolls of the Coral Sea, these reefs rise from plateaus of 500–1000 m and are largely devoid of volcanic foundations. The South China Sea basin is especially suggestive of a stretched and subsided "microcontinental" block since it is almost entirely surrounded by continental areas, such as the Southeast Asia mainland, Borneo, the Philippines and Taiwan.

(d) **Flores Sea Plateaus.** Similarly, quite surrounded by mature continental islands, in the Flores Sea (q.v.) there are numerous plateaus crowned by immense coral reefs and atolls, without associated volcanoes, thus notably in Paternoster Island and the Tijger Islands (Kuenen, 1933). No explanation except a subsidence of a former continental area is acceptable.

Fig. 4. Two contrasting areas of submarine plateaus (stippled). To the north, the isolated mid-oceanic, atoll-crowned plateaus of the South China Sea; to the south the marginal Exmouth Plateau of Western Australia, with several isolated examples (Wallaby Plateaus), from Physiographic Diagram by Heezen and Tharp (1965).

(e) Chagos-Laccadive Plateau. Here in the Indian Ocean (q.v.) there is the "type area" of classical compound atolls that grow up from foundations down to 1000 m. Gravity and seismic traverses have shown those foundations to be of continental type. This is one of the longest of such structures in the world, extending over 37° of arc (over 4000 km).

(f) Mascarene Plateau. This feature extends from the Seychelles to the Saya de Malha Bank, Nazareth

Bank, Cargados Carajos, and Mauritius. The southern part is volcanic. The Seychelles part has long attracted attention because of the presence of a large number of continental granite outcrops that have now been isotopically dated as late Precambrian or early Cambrian. Since the last century it was recognized that these indications, together with the topographic links, provided proof of a former land connection between the Indian Peninsula, Madagascar (the Malgasy Massif) and East Africa, all units in the former "Gondwanaland" continent of Suess (see *Indian Ocean*; also *Gondwanaland* in another volume).

ROBERT E. SHERIDAN
RHODES W. FAIRBRIDGE

References

Adams, R. D., 1962, "Thickness of the earth's crust beneath the Campbell plateau," *New Zealand J. Geol. Geophys.*, **5**, 74–85.

Beloussov, V. V., and Ruditch, E. M., 1961, "Island arcs in the development of the earth's structure (especially in the region of Japan and the Sea of Okhotsk)," *J. Geol.*, **69**, 647–658.

Brodie, J. W., 1964, "Bathymetry of the New Zealand Region," *New Zealand Oceanographic Inst., Mem.* 11.

Cullen, D. J., 1965, "Autochthonous rocks from the Chatham Rise, east of New Zealand," *New Zealand J. Geol. Geophys.*, **8**(3), 465–474.

Drake, C. L., Heirtzler, J., and Hirshman, J., 1963, "Magnetic anomalies off eastern North America," *J. Geophys. Res.*, **68**, 5259–5275.

Ewing, J., and Ewing, M., 1959, "Seismic refraction measurements in the Scotia Sea and South Sandwich Island Arc," *Intern. Oceanographic Congr., Preprints* (Amer. Assoc. Adv. Sci.), 22–23.

Fairbridge, R. W., 1950, "Recent and Pleistocene coral reefs of Australia," *J. Geol.*, **58**, 330–401.

Fairbridge, R. W., 1955, "Some bathymetric and geotectonic features of the eastern part of the Indian Ocean," *Deep-Sea Res.*, **2**, 161–171.

Fairbridge, R. W., 1961, "The Melanesian Border Plateau, a zone of crustal shearing in the S.W. Pacific," *Publ. Bur. Cent. Seism., Ser. A*, **22**, 137–149.

Fairbridge, R. W., 1965, "The Indian Ocean and the Status of Gondwanaland," in "Progress in Oceanography," Vol. 3, pp. 83–136, New York, Pergamon Press.

Fairbridge, R. W., and Stewart, H. B., Jr., 1960, "Alexa Bank, a drowned atoll on the Melanesian Border Plateau," *Deep-Sea Res.*, **7**, 100–116.

Heezen, B. C., and Tharp, M., 1965, "Physiography of the Indian Ocean," *Phil. Trans. Roy. Soc. London, Ser. A* (in press).

Heezen, B. C., Tharp, M., and Ewing, M., 1959, "The Floors of the Oceans: Pt. I, The North Atlantic," *Geol. Soc. Am. Spec. Papers*, **65**, 122pp.

Hsu, K. J., 1965, "Isostasy, crustal thinning, mantle changes, and the disappearance of ancient land masses," *Am. J. Sci.*, **263**, 97–109.

Joides (Joint Oceanographic Inst. Deep Earth Sampling Program), 1965, "Ocean drilling on the continental margin," *Science*, **150**(3697), 709–716.

Kanayev, V. F., 1963, "Recent vertical movements on the Far Eastern sea floors," *Okeanologiya*, **3**(4), 669–673.

Kuenen, P. H., 1933, "Geology of coral reefs," *Snellius Exped.*, **5**, Pt. 2, 125pp.

Kuenen, P. H., 1950, "Marine Geology," New York, John Wiley & Sons, 568pp.

Menard, H. W., 1964, "Marine Geology of the Pacific," New York, McGraw-Hill Book Co., 271pp.

Newell, N. D., 1955, "Bahaman Platforms," in (Poldervaart, A., editor) "Crust of the Earth," *Geol. Soc. Am. Spec. Papers*, **62**, 762pp.

Sheridan, R. E., Drake, C. L., Nafe, J. E., and Hennion, J., 1966, "Seismic-refraction study of continental margin east of Florida," *Bull. Amer. Assoc. Petrol. Geol.* (in press).

Supan, A., 1903, "Terminologie der wichtigsten unterseeschen Bodenformen," *Petermanns Mitt.* (*Gotha*), **49**, 151–152.

Talwani, M. K., 1960, "Gravity Anomalies in the Bahamas and their Interpretation," Columbia University, Unpublished Ph.D. Thesis, 89pp.

Uchupi, E., and Emery, K. O., 1963, "The continental slope between San Francisco, California and Cedros Island, Mexico," *Deep-Sea Res.*, **10**(4), 397–447.

Wilson, J. T., 1963, "A Resume of the Geology of Islands in the Main Ocean Basins; Vol. I, Atlantic and Indian Oceans," University of Toronto, Inst. Earth Sci., 175pp.

Cross-references: *Aseismic Ridges; Atlantic Ocean; Continental Borderland; Coral Sea; Flores Sea; Indian Ocean; Oceanic Rises; South China Sea; Southwest Pacific.*

SUBMARINE SPRINGS

Pausanius (8:VII) states:

"Not only here in Argolis [Greece], but also by Cheimerium in Thresprotis, is there unmistakably fresh water rising up in the sea. . . . In front of Dicaearchia also, in the land of the Etruscans [western Italy], there is water boiling in the sea, and an artificial island has been made through it, so that this water is not 'untilled' but serves for hot baths."

Since before the time of Christ, springs in the sea have fascinated philosophers, geographers, and world travelers. Concerning the island city of Aradus (2.5 miles offshore from Latakia, Syria) and now known as Arvad, Strabo the Roman geographer (B.C. 63–21 A.D.) wrote:

"It consists of a rock washed all around by the sea and is full of dwellings. . . . In war-times they get water from the channel at a short distance in front of the city. This channel has an abundant spring; and into this spring the people let down from the water-fetching boat an inverted, widemouthed funnel made of lead, the upper part of which contracts into a stem with a moderate-sized hole through it; and round this stem they fasten a leathern tube (unless I should call it bellows), which receives the water that is forced up from the spring through the funnel. Now the first water that is forced up is seawater, but the boatmen wait for the flow of pure and potable water and catch all

that is needed in vessels prepared for the purpose and carry it to the city."

In 1963, the Ralph M. Parsons Co., in cooperation with the United Nations Ground Water Project investigated the submarine springs near Chekka, Lebanon to find methods for salvaging the wasting water. The photograph of the water-sampling equipment used by the Parsons' investigators (Fig. 1) indicates that other than the substitution of plastic hose for leather, the technique for capturing water from submarine springs has changed little since the time of Strabo.

Definition

A spring is an issue of water from the earth. A submarine spring is merely an exotic form of the commonplace spring and may be defined as an issue of water from the earth beneath the sea. Thus, classifications of springs related to morphology of the conduit (fracture, fissure, fault, etc.), temperature, mineral content, gravity versus artesian, as devised by Meinzer (1923) and Kirk Bryan (1919), apply also to submarine springs.

Recognition

A submarine spring appears at the surface of the sea as a boil of water or, in a choppy sea, as a slick or smooth area in the otherwise rough water. Figure 2 is an oblique aerial photo of the submarine spring 2.5 miles offshore from the town of Crescent Beach on the northeast coast of Florida. The ocean floor adjacent to the spring is about 55 feet (17 meters) below sea level and the water issues from a sink-like crater about 50 feet (15 meters) in diameter at a depth of about 126 feet (38 meters) below sea level. The discharge was estimated at 1500 cfs (cubic feet per second) (42m³/sec) by H. K. Brooks (1961). Comparison of the chloride concentrations at the bottom and top of the water column suggested that only 1/40 of the total upwelling water at the surface was spring water. The remainder was seawater that had been sucked in and mixed convectively during the ascent of the spring water to the surface (Fig. 3). This indicates that if the discharge is weak or if it takes place at great depth (deeper than about 600 feet), the dispersion and mixing with seawater will obliterate surface evidence of the submarine discharge.

Geographic Occurrence

Less than ten scientific investigations of submarine springs have been uncovered as of this writing. The worldwide occurrence unquestionably is greater than that given in the subsequent paragraphs. Additions to the list are solicited and a letter giving particulars can be sent in care of the editor of the encyclopedia. Submarine springs have been reported at Bahrain in the Persian Gulf; off the coasts of Israel, Lebanon, Syria, Greece, Italy, France, and

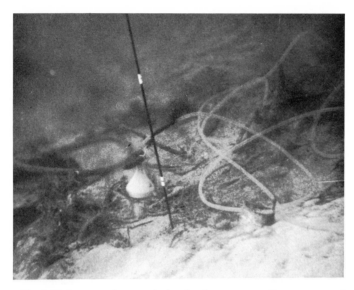

Fig. 1. Underwater photograph showing the water-sampling arrangement used by the Ralph M. Parsons Co. investigators at a submarine spring near Chekka, Lebanon. (Photo by F. J. Lampietti, Ocean Science and Engineering, Inc.)

Spain in the Mediterranean; Florida and California: the Bahama Islands and Jamaica in the West Indies; Matanzas Province in Cuba, Yucatan Peninsula in Mexico, Hawaiian Islands, American Samoa, Guam, and Japan. Possibly the most famous submarine springs are those of Bahrain in the Persian Gulf. Water vendors formerly collected drinking water by diving to the bottom of the sea with a collapsed goatskin or, alternatively, by inserting reed pipes in the springs so that the fresh water bubbled several inches above the sea surface (Williams, 1946). The source of the artesian water is reported to be the Tuwaiq Mountains in Arabia 250 miles to the west.

Submarine springs are numerous along the north and east coast of the Mediterranean. Calvino and Stefanon report on those near the French–Italian border and Curruti identifies 32 springs by name in the Gulf of Taranto, Italy. Burdon (1964) describes several springs off the coast of Greece as "drowned springs, overwhelmed when sea level rose again in postglacial/pluvial times." The spring called Anavalos of Astros, located 400 meters (1300 feet) from shore in the Gulf of Argos (Greece) was sampled with a plastic tube set in the throat of the spring fissure at 72 meters (236 feet) below sea level. The chloride content averaged about 21,600 ppm and ranged from 92–97% of the chlorinity of the surface water of the Bay of Argos, far from all contamination. Thus, the water of a submarine spring is not always fresh. Recently, hot brine (155,000 ppm Cl, 112°F, 44.4°C, Brewer *et al.*, 1965) was discovered in a trench 200 meters (650 feet) deep at the bottom of the Red Sea. Iron in the brine precipitates

Fig. 2. Oblique aerial photograph of the submarine spring located 2.5 miles offshore from the town of Crescent Beach on the northeast coast of Florida. Arrow points to spring located to the left of the 48-foot trawler. Dinghies carrying investigators are located just beyond spring and below trawler. A U-shaped line of whitecaps opens to the left as the spring water is carried in that direction by the drift current. (Photo by F. A. Kohout, U.S. Geological Survey).

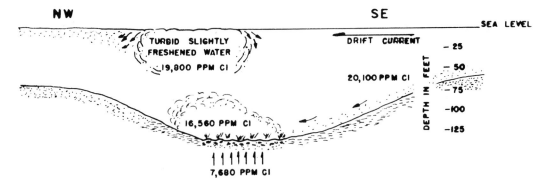

Fig. 3. Diagram of the Crescent Beach submarine spring drawn northwest to southeast across the crater showing size, slopes, and hydrographic conditions observed on June 16, 1960 (adopted from Brooks, 1961).

on contact with normal Red Sea water, and extensive iron deposits on the surrounding ocean floor (Manheim *et al.*, 1965) indicate that this brine is continuously issuing from the trench. Therefore, this oil-field-like brine may be properly considered as a submarine spring probably resulting from geothermal heating.

Numerous submarine springs occur on both the east and the west coasts of Florida where the discharge, generally brackish, occurs through round sink-like holes on the continental shelf in water depths of about 50 feet.

On the Bahama Banks platform "ocean holes," "boiling holes," or "blue holes" occur by the hundreds and were probably formed by the collapse of limestone caverns during low stands of Pleistocene sea level (Newell and Rigby, 1957, p. 28). The term blue hole comes from the relative color produced by the depth of the hole in contrast to the yellowish sand and grass of the shallow Banks. Water about 10°C cooler than the shallow water of the Banks is reported to upwell from these drowned holes during the rising tide; the water is not sucked in or "swallowed" during the falling tide. Coral growth usually surrounds the holes in a ring pattern (Newell and Rigby, 1957, Pl. II, Fig. 1), and the surface waters directly above the blue holes are reported to support a prolific fish population. These observations suggest that cold, nutrient-rich water below the thermocline in the deep ocean trenches adjacent to the Bahama Banks may be upwelling through the holes. A localized phytoplankton bloom would develop in the upwelling nutrient-rich water and this would form the base of a food chain, finally culminating in the ring-like coral growth and the observed fish population. Although no proper evidence is yet known, the blue holes are here hypothesized as relatively cool, seawater springs that flow convectively because of geothermal warming of cold seawater.

Hot and cool submarine springs are reported in Hawaii, Japan, and other Pacific volcanic islands. The temperature depends on the source of the water

(in the mountains or in the sea) and on the proximity of the water flow path to volcanic heat (Mink, 1964; Visher and Mink, 1964; Schneider, 1965). The springs of these islands are developed in lava and limestone.

Hydrologic Factors of Occurrence

The outcropping of a homogeneous aquifer in the sea bottom produces evenly distributed discharge which tends to be quickly dispersed in the large volume of overlying seawater. The occurrence of a recognizable submarine spring implies the existence of a large permeability contrast in the aquifer or in the low-permeability beds that overlie and confine the aquifer water under artesian pressure. Thus, submarine springs are reported most frequently from regions of cavernous limestone or lava flows, both of which are notoriously heterogeneous rock types. Karst topography near the sea is frequently associated with solitary submarine springs that claim great attention.

Groundwater discharge from unconsolidated non-artesian aquifers can be recognized as a slow, dispersed seepage on the exposed intertidal flat at low tide, but also, the discharge percolates upward through the sea bottom for considerable distances offshore beneath the sea (Kohout and Kolipinski, in press). Moderately higher permeability at certain points produces discrete concentrations of seepage which are properly classified as submarine springs. The aggregate discharge from these small obscure springs probably is greater than the aggregate discharge from the spectacular, solitary springs on which this article dwells.

Principles of Occurrence

The water that discharges from a submarine spring may range in salinity from fresh water to brine and the temperature may range from cooler than the ambient temperature of the surrounding ocean to very hot.

Thermal Drive. Offshore from Hawaii, Fischer *et al.* (in press), using airborne infrared scanning

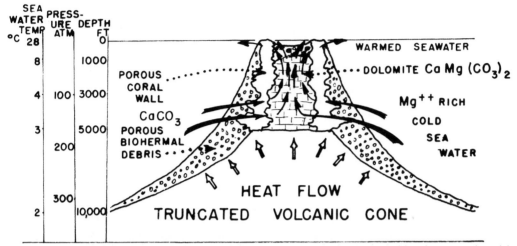

Fig. 4. Idealized diagram of a coral atoll (modified from Fairbridge, 1957, Fig. 8) showing that magnesium-rich seawater can be expected to circulate through an atoll by thermal convection resulting from upward volcanic heat flow. The conditions for conversion of permeable limestone, $CaCO_3$, to dolomite, $CaMg(CO_3)_2$, should exist somewhere within the internal core of the atoll. [Note: Fairbridge himself feels that the circulation pattern should be the reverse; dense water forms in the lagoon, and sinks through the atoll—the old volcanic cone being no longer a heat source.]

radiometers, show the existence of both warm and cool submarine springs by their differential thermal contrast compared with adjacent ocean waters. Photographic prints of the recorded electronic impulses show the differences in apparent temperature as light (warm) and dark (cool) shades of gray relative to the shade of the general sea surface.

The implications of thermally motivated groundwater circulations reach far beyond present conceptions of the definition of groundwater which tend to (incorrectly) focus attention almost entirely on the relatively fresh groundwater underlying land areas. It must be fully appreciated that there is no hydraulic discontinuity between the underground waters beneath land areas and the underground waters beneath ocean areas. This fact becomes immediately apparent when seawater intrudes into coastal fresh groundwater aquifers, as a result of pumping by municipal and private water-supply systems.

The hypothesized circulation of salty groundwater beneath an idealized atoll (Fig. 4) demonstrates that thermal submarine seawater springs should occur in the lagoons and outer reef tract of coral atolls. The intense heat flow from underlying hot volcanic rock would generate a continuous convective groundwater circulation, provided only that the rock is permeable (see Lee, 1965). The initially high permeability of coral-reef deposits is well recognized but diagenetic changes can occur so that the pore spaces of the rock may be plugged or expanded depending on the nature of the chemical alteration. Using Funifuti Atoll in the Gilbert Islands, Pacific as a model, Fairbridge (1957, p. 148) indicates that the internal core of the atoll has been changed from limestone $CaCO_3$ to dolomite

$CaMg(CO_3)_2$. Figure 4 suggests that cold magnesium-rich seawater flows into the atoll at depth and after becoming heated and losing density, it flows upward to discharge as submarine springs or seeps in the lagoon or outer reef tract. The occurrence of such salt-water springs could be determined only by careful chemical analyses of the water in various parts of the atoll. The proper physicochemical framework as outlined by Fairbridge is almost certain to exist somewhere within the atoll core so that contemporaneous, continuous dolomitization would occur.

Dolomite is not confined to the core of atolls but occurs in many parts of the geologic column throughout the world. Caverns as large as 90 feet from floor to roof have been encountered by oil exploratory wells in dolomite at depths of about 2700 feet (823 meters) in southern Florida (Kohout, 1965). Also, the carbonate sedimentation platform of the Bahama Banks is underlaid by dolomitized and cavernous rock. The possibility that the blue holes of the Bahama Banks are submarine seawater springs has been hypothesized previously. Because no volcanism exists at shallow depth, convective seawater circulation depends on the general terrestrial heat flow from the interior of the earth. That the water reported as discharging from the blue holes is cooler than the ambient temperature of the very warm water of the Banks does not bar temperature and density change as the motivating force. The obvious thermal drive of active volcanism (Fig. 4) would be modified to a more gentle circulation because of the smaller geothermal heat flow in the thick sediments underlying the Banks. Thus, cold seawater in the adjacent ocean trenches would be warmed only moderately

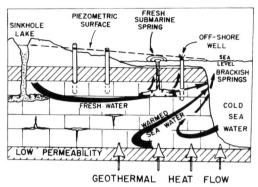

Fig. 5. Idealized diagram depicting the hydrologic conditions involved in the occurrence of submarine springs in a thick artesian aquifer far away from active volcanism.

Fig. 6. Photograph of well J-1A, 27 miles offshore from Jacksonville, Fla. showing flow above the deck of the Caldrill drilling vessel. The top of the pipe protrudes through the drilling hole in the center of the vessel to about 15 feet above sea level. The bottom of the pipe was set at 820 feet below sea level at the time of the photograph. The perspective of the photograph can be recognized from the position of the water-sky line opposite the peak of hair on the forehead of the closest man and from the wave-covered ocean surface to the left of the leg of the farthest man. (Photo by R. L. Wait, U.S. Geological Survey).

during the convective upwelling and would arrive at the discharge point cooler than the ambient temperature of shallow seawater on the platform. The verification of these hypothesized circulations must await collection of adequate temperature, water-movement, and chemical data.

Freshwater Drive. Submarine springs occur at the last exit as fresh groundwater moves from inland points of high hydraulic head to the point of lowest hydraulic head—the sea. The idealized diagram in Fig. 5 is modeled after the circumstances that exist in the Florida peninsula. Rain water is recharged into the aquifer through sinkhole lakes in the karst region of central Florida. The highest freshwater head is about 120 feet (36 meters) above sea level. a head which theoretically is capable of driving sea-water out of the aquifer to a depth of 4800 feet (1460 meters) below sea level according to the theory of hydrostatic balance between freshwater and more dense seawater (Brown, 1925). The fresh-water flows seaward through permeable limestone and dolomite beds that underlie clay and marl confining beds. As the water percolates through the rock, a hydraulic head loss occurs as shown by the slope of the piezometric surface (Fig. 5). If the two landlocked wells of Fig. 5 were cut off at land surface they would flow vigorously. The freshwater submarine spring discharges at the sea floor through a natural breach in the confining bed. As sediments are rarely, if ever, completely impermeable, water in the offshore parts of the aquifer leaks slowly upward through the confining bed and discharges into the sea so imperceptibly as to be unrecognizable. Thus, only where the confining bed has been rup-tured by solution and collapse of an underlying cavern, or by faulting, does a submarine spring discharge sufficient water to form a boil or slick.

Fresh water discharges into the sea by the easiest possible path. If the confining bed has low per-meability, the water may be forced far offshore to points where the bed terminates or is truncated by an ocean trench or strait. At this point submarine springs should issue along the continental slope. However, the water may have become salty by this time because of an admixture of seawater that has flowed into the aquifer at depth. The cold seawater loses density from being heated by terrestrial heat flow and rises to mix with the seaward-flowing freshwater. This mixing further decreases the density, and the diluted seawater flows back to the sea through the upper part of the aquifer. The process creates a continuous cyclic flow of seawater. The cyclic circulation of seawater caused by the dispersion of salt has been well established both mathematically and in the field by Cooper *et al.* (1964). The geothermal circulation must occur to some extent even in non-volcanic areas.

Figure 5 shows an offshore flowing well to indicate that the only difference between a sub-marine spring and an offshore well is that the spring discharges through a naturally occurring hole in the confining bed whereas the well discharges through a man-made hole with a pipe in it. In 1965, the JOIDES (Joint Oceanographic Institutes Deep Earth Sampling) project drilled a line of geologic exploratory wells across the continental shelf to the Blake Plateau east of Jacksonville, Florida. Figure 6 is a photograph of well J-1A, 27 miles (43 km) offshore, taken from the deck of the Caldrill offshore drilling vessel. The well discharged water of about 700 ppm chloride from a depth of 820 feet (250 meters) below sea level. The hydrostatic head was measured at 30 feet (9 meters) above sea level in spite of the fact that water was also flowing out through the annular space between the casing and the hole at the ocean floor. Manheim (personal communication) found that the interstitial water in cores of well J-2, 62 miles (100 km) offshore, contained water with a chloride content of less than 2000 ppm. Because of drilling circumstances no flow was recognized from well J-2 at the derrick floor of the Caldrill vessel.

Prevention of Waste

Little has been done to prevent the waste of or to utilize the freshwater discharged by submarine springs. The most successful, unplanned attempts at reducing this discharge have been made in large population centers where municipal and industrial pumping has reversed the hydraulic gradient to the extent that the springs have stopped flowing. However, the cessation of discharge from submarine springs usually signifies that the spring conduits have become the pathways by which seawater is intruding into municipal and industrial well fields.

F. A. KOHOUT

References

Brewer, P. G., Riley, J. P., and Culkin, F., 1965, "Chemical composition of the hot salty water at the bottom of the Red Sea," *Nature,* **206,** No. 4991, 1345–46.

Brooks, H. K., 1961, "The submarine spring off Crescent Beach, Florida," *Quart. J. Florida Acad. Sciences,* **24,** No. 2, 122–134.

*Brown, J. S., 1925, "A study of coastal ground water, with special reference to Connecticut," *U.S. Geol. Surv. Water Supply Papers,* **537.**

*Bryan, Kirk, 1919, "Classification of springs," *J. Geol.,* **27,** No. 7, 522–561.

Burdon, David J., and others, 1964, "Karst groundwater investigations, Greece," Food and Agric. Org. United Nations, FAO/SF: 2/Gre., 99pp.

*Calvino, F., and Stefanon, A., 1963, "Osservazioni geologiche sulla polla Rovereto e le altre sorgenti sottomarine della Mortola (Riviera di Ponente)," *Atti Ist. Geol. Univ. Genova,* **1,** Fasc. 1, 200–238.

Cerruti, A., 1948, "Ulteriori notizie sulle sorgenti sottomarine (citri) del Mar Grande e del Mar Piccolo di Taranto e sulla loro eventuale utilizzazione," *Boll. Pesca. Pisciocolt. Idriobiol.,* XXIV, **3,** Fasc. 1, 57–72.

*Cooper, H. H., Jr., Kohout, F. A., Henry, H. R., and Glover, R. E., 1964, "Sea water in coastal aquifers," *U.S. Geol. Surv. Water Supply Papers,* **1613-C.**

*Fairbridge, R. W., 1957, "The dolomite question," *Soc. Econ. Paleontologists Mineralogists Spec. Publ.,* **5,** 125–178.

Fischer, W. A., Davis, D. A., and Sousa, T. M., in press, "Fresh-water springs of Hawaii from infrared images," *U.S. Geol. Surv., Hydrologic Atlas,* **HA-218.**

Kohout, F. A., 1965, "A hypothesis concerning cyclic flow of salt water related to geothermal heating in the Floridan aquifer," *Trans. N.Y. Acad. Sci.,* 28, No. 2.

Kohout, F. A., and Kolipinski, M. C., in press, "Biological zonation related to ground-water discharge along the shore of Biscayne Bay, Miami, Florida," Am. Assoc. Advancement of Science symposium volume "Estuaries."

*Lee, William H. K. (editor), 1965, "Terrestrial heat flow," *Am. Geophys. Union, Geophys. Monograph Series No. 8,* 276pp.

Manheim, F. T., Hathaway, J. C., Degens, E. T., McFarlin, P. F., and Jokela, A., 1965, "Geochemistry of recent iron deposits in the Red Sea," *Bull. Geol. Soc. Am. Prog. 1965 Ann. Meetings.*

Meinzer, O. E., 1923, "Outline of ground-water hydrology, with definitions," *U.S. Geol. Surv. Water-Supply Papers,* **494.**

Miller, A. R., *et al.,* 1966, "Hot brines and recent iron deposits in deeps of the Red Sea," *Geochim. Cosmochim. Acta.*

Mink, J. F., 1964, "Groundwater temperatures in a tropical island environment," *J. Geophys. Res.,* **69,** No. 24, 5225–5230.

Neumann, A. C., and Chave, K. E., 1965, "Conate origin proposed for hot salty bottom water from a Red Sea basin," *Nature,* **206,** No. 4991, 1346–47.

*Newell, N. D., and Rigby, J. K., 1957, "Geological studies on the Great Bahama Bank," *Soc. Econ. Paleontologists Mineralogists Spec. Publ.,* **5,** 15–72.

Parsons Company, The Ralph M., 1963, "Submarine springs investigation, Lebanon," Unpublished report, Job. No. 3911, Los Angeles, Calif.

Pausanius, "Description of Greece," 1918 (translation by Jones, W. H. S., Cambridge, Mass., Harvard University Press, 4 vols.).

Schneider, Robert, 1965, "Discussion of Paper by J. F. Mink, 'Groundwater temperatures in a tropical island environment,' " *J. Geophys. Res.,* **70,** No. 16, 4073–74.

Strabo, "The Geography of Strabo," 1917 (translation by Jones, H. L., New York, G. P. Putnam's Sons, 8 vols.).

Stringfield, V. T., and Cooper, H. H., Jr., 1951, "Geologic and hydrologic features of an artesian submarine spring east of Florida," *Florida Geol. Surv. Rept. Invest.,* **7,** Pt. 2, 57–72.

Visher, F. N., and Mink, J. F., 1964, "Ground-water resources in southern Oahu, Hawaii," *U.S. Geol. Surv. Water Supply Papers,* **1778.**

Williams, M. O., 1946, "Bahrein: Port of Pearls and Petroleum," *National Geographic,* **89,** No. 2. 194–210.

SUBMARINE TOPOGRAPHY—*See* **BATHYMETRY**

SUBPOLAR CONVERGENCE—*See* **CONVERGENCE, ANTARCTIC**

SUBTROPICAL CONVERGENCE

The boundary between subantarctic and subtropical water masses which is generally found some 10° or more north of the Antarctic Con-

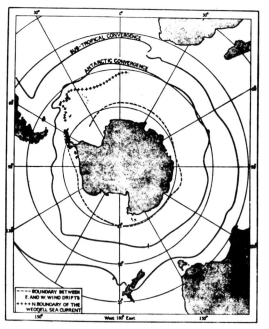

Fig. 1. The Antarctic and Subtropical Convergences (after Deacon).

vergence is often much sharper than that between Antarctic and subantarctic waters. From south to north, the temperature rises from about 10–14°C in winter and from 14–18°C in summer. The German research vessel *Meteor*, crossing the boundary in 41°S 22°E, found that it was visible from a distance as a line of current disturbance at the surface. The temperature rose by 5.6°C in 1 mile and 9.1°C in 5 miles. The accompanying increase in salinity of the surface water is about 0.5‰. Details of the water circulation are not really known, but the sharp changes seem to be caused by convergence between northward movements in the subantarctic zone with southward movements of subtropical water. It is now generally referred to as the Subtropical Convergence. Wüst used this name in 1928 for the line of convergence between currents with southward and northward components as far as it could be distinguished on charts of surface current based on ships' observations. The current boundary based on such information does not agree with the boundary of the water masses, though these can be expected to show the overall effect of the currents. The approximate position of the convergence is shown in Fig. 1.

It is pushed farthest south on the western sides of the oceans, south of the Brazil, Agulhas and East Australian Currents, and it recedes to the north on the eastern sides of the oceans. Its position, unlike that of the Antarctic Convergence, seems to depend almost entirely on surface winds

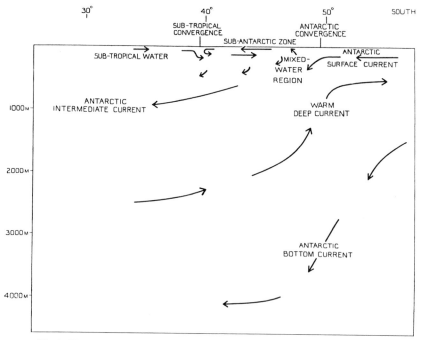

Fig. 2. The vertical circulation of water in the South Atlantic Ocean (Deacon).

and currents, and in no obvious way on events in the deep ocean (see Fig. 2). While the Antarctic Convergence is closely analagous to the atmospheric polar front, the Subtropical Convergence closely resembles the meteorological conception of an intertropical front, a relatively shallow convergence between surface winds which is liable to move discontinuously, appearing to jump from one position to another. South of the Brazil, Agulhas and East Australian Currents, continuous observations of surface temperature and salinity generally reveals sharp fluctuations which suggest irregularities in the boundary between the subtropical and subantarctic waters, and give some indication that patches of the warmer water, and perhaps patches of the colder water, become separated from their main regions. In spite of such irregularities, the position of the overall boundary between the two types of water in these western marginal regions, where the southward currents are strongest, the convergence is farthest south, and the contrast between the two types of water is greatest, seems not to vary by more than 100 miles or so from a mean position. On the eastern sides of the ocean, the convergence is farther north and the relatively few continuous records suggested that its position is more variable, like that of an atmospheric intertropical front. An examination of mean monthly temperatures of 1-degree squares by Böhnecke (1938) suggests that its variations in position are on the contrary rather small, of the same order as those of the Antarctic Convergence.

We do not know very much about the water movements in the convergence region, but vertical sections of the temperature and salinity distribution indicate that the subantarctic water sinks from the surface, where it meets subtropical water and, after considerable mixing, turns southward in the subsurface layer. Apart from the deep current, which climbs to within 200 meters or so of the surface at the Antarctic Convergence, it seems to be the only movement of relatively warm water toward the Antarctic.

G. E. R. DEACON

References

Böhnecke, G., 1938, "Temperatur, Salzgehalt und Dichte an der Oberfläche des Atlantischen Ozeans," in "Deutsche Atlantische Exped. 'Meteor' 1925–1927," *Wiss. Ergebn.*, **5**(2).

Deacon, G. E. R., 1937, "The hydrology of the Southern Ocean," *Discovery Rept.*, **15**, 1–124.

Kort, V. G., 1964, "Antarctic Oceanography," in "Research in Geophysics," Vol. 2, pp. 309–333, Cambridge, Mass., M.I.T. Press.

Rossby, C. G., 1959, "The Atmosphere and Sea in Motion," Rossby Memorial Volume, p. 27, New York, Rockefeller Institute Press.

Wüst, G., 1928, "Der Ursprung der Atlantischen Tiefenwässer," *Z. Ges. Erdkunde*, 506–534.

Cross reference: *Convergence, Antarctic.*

SULAWESI (CELEBES) SEA

(1) Limits and Oceanography

(a) Dimensions and Limits. The Sulawesi (Celebes) Sea is situated between Borneo and the southern Philippines (center: 122°E, 3°N). Steep sides, an almost equidimensional plan, and a deep and rather flat bottom characterize the basin. It is bounded on the north by the Sulu Archipelago and the southwest coast of Mindanao; on the east, it is cut off by the row of islands which connects the Philippines with Sulawesi (Celebes), a line of active orogenic volcanism in its southern part (Rittmann's explosivity index is more than 80). In the south, there is the partially volcanic north arm of Sulawesi (also of orogenic type), the northern entrance of Makassar Strait; and finally in the west, there is North Kalimantan or Borneo (Fig. 1). The Sulawesi Sea covers 280,000 km². The deepest part is located southwest of Mindanao (−6220 meters). A submarine, active volcano rises from a depth of 4000 meters at about 124°E, 4°N.

(b) Deep-water Properties and Flow of Bottom Water. The bottom water of the Sulawesi Basin is replenished by deep water from the Pacific Ocean which crosses a threshold of −1400 meters immediately south of Mindanao. From this basin, the flow proceeds through Makassar Strait to the Flores Sea in the south. This flow of deep water has been analyzed by study of the basin configuration and by comparing certain properties of the water within the basin with those of the water at sill depth outside the basin (see Table 1).

(c) Surface Properties and Meteorology. Sea surface temperatures in the Sulawesi Sea range between 28°C in April and 27°C in February. Surface salinities throughout the year are:

December–February	31–34‰ from SW to NE
March–May	32.8–33.9‰ from SW to NE
June–August	34‰ with slightly lower values in the center
September–November	33.5–34.1‰ from NW to SE

The meteorology of the Sulawesi Sea is entirely governed by the monsoons. During the northern winter, the wind blows from north and north northeast at 0.5–2.4 (Beaufort scale), and during the northern summer, it comes from the opposite directions and is weaker (0.5–1.4). For the same periods, air pressures are around 757 and 756 mm, respectively.

(d) Currents and Tides. In the northern summer, surface currents in the Sulawesi Sea are mainly directed from Mindanao toward Makassar Strait at rates up to 15 nautical miles per day (n mi/day). Exchange currents of 5–15 n mi/day exist across the ridge bearing the Sulu Archipelago. During the northern winter the south and southwestward current systems (5–20 n mi/day) are still maintained for the larger part of the sea. Next to them,

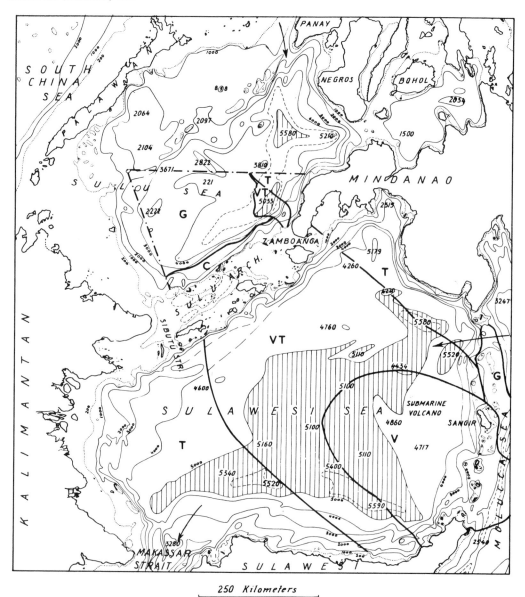

Fig. 1. The Sulawesi (Celebes) and Sulu seas, eastern Indonesia. Map shows bathymetry (shading indicates depths of more than 5000 meters), flow of bottom water (arrows) and bottom sediments. T: terrigenous mud; G: globigerina ooze; C: coralline mud and sand; VT: volcanic and terrigenous mud; V: volcanic mud (data from the Snellius Expedition, 1929–30).

westward currents of 15–25 n mi/day are found along North Sulawesi and across the Sangir Ridge. The tidal range in Menado (Sulawesi) is 2.2 meters.

The Snellius Expedition measured currents at its station 308a (see Fig. 2) from June 29 through July 1, 1930, and found:

0 meters 64 cm/sec toward N 8° W
10–100 meters 67 cm/sec toward N 28° W
150 meters 50 cm/sec toward N 88° W
250–400 meters 38 cm/sec toward S 65° W

(2) Bottom Sediments

The bottom sediments in the Sulawesi Sea change progressively from Mindanao toward the north entrance of Makassar Strait. A traverse in this direction shows first a zone of terrigenous mud about 70 km wide, followed by a broad area extending across the center of the sea composed of terrigenous and volcanic mud. Near the volcanoes in the eastern half of this region, however, volcanic mud predominates. The remaining one-third of the

Sulawesi Basin Limit: 4000 meters isobath, area: 260,000 km²		
	Properties of Water at −5138 meters (Snellius Station 301) within Basin	Properties of Water at −1440 meters (Snellius Station 296) outside Basin near Sill
Temperature, °C	3.815	3.185
Salinity, ‰	34.59	34.61
Oxygen cc/liter	2.14	2.31
pH	7.78	7.81
Density	1027.50	1027.58

* From Van Riel *et al.* (1950) and other Snellius Expedition Reports.

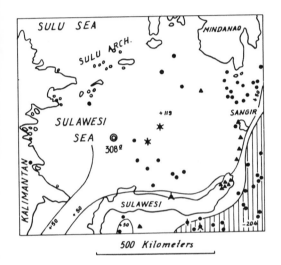

Sulawesi Sea is underlain by terrigenous mud with local concentrations of quartz sands. Globigerina ooze (30% or more of calcium carbonate) is only found above the 2000-meter isobath on the north part of the ridge which separates the Sulawesi Sea from the Molucca Sea. The absence of Globigerina ooze in other suitable localities in the Sulawesi Sea may be ascribed to the very high rate of sedimentation of terrigenous material (the basin being enclosed by submarine ridges, islands and active volcanoes) and probably also to submarine slump-

Fig. 2. The Sulawesi (Celebes) Sea, eastern Indonesia. Gravimetry, active volcanoes (triangles) and eathquake foci (dots: less than 100 km deep; with one hachure; 100–199 km; with two hachures; 200–299 km; etc.). Double circles indicate current recording station 308a of the Snellius Expedition.

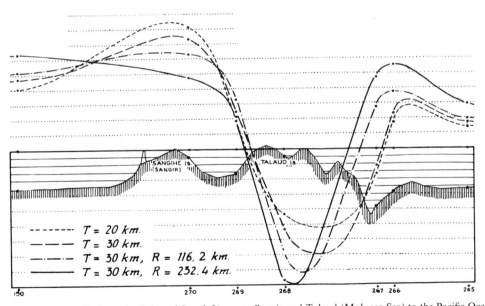

Fig. 3. Gravity profile from the Sulawesi Sea (left) across Sangir and Talaud (Molucca Sea) to the Pacific Ocean. Horizontal scale 1:5,000,000; vertical scale 10 times larger. Vertical subdivisions in oceans; 1000 meters; 10 mgal; elsewhere 2000 meters: 20 mgal (after Vening Meinesz).

ing of this material from the predominantly steep slopes of the boundaries. Neeb (1943) determined a mean rate of sedimentation of 65 cm/1000 yr for terrigenous muds in the basins and troughs of eastern Indonesia.

In the open Pacific Ocean, deep-sea red clay is found to accumulate between 4000 and 6000 meters. The notable absence of such deposits in the deeper parts of the Sulawesi Basin is primarily due to the lack of oxygen which would oxidize the blue and green terrigenous muds during their accumulation.

(3) Geophysics and Geological Structure

The basin is marked by positive gravity anomalies ranging between 50 and 100 mgal with slightly higher values in its northeastern quarter. Foci of weak to strong earthquakes are located along the limits (particularly south of Mindanao and north of Sulawesi), and some are also found within the basin. The depth of foci increases systematically from the Pacific Ocean toward the center of the Sulawesi Basin, i.e., from shallow foci in the east to 620-km depth in the central part. The theoretical implications of this evidence have been discussed by Vening Meinesz, Berlage and others (see Van Bemmelen, 1949).

The straight boundaries, the predominantly steep sides, the rather uniform depth of the floor, and the isolated nature of many minor irregularities along the western limit indicate a block-faulted origin for the Sulawesi Basin (Kuenen, 1935).

The subsidence of the basin began only in the Plio-Pleistocene. This assumption is based on the structural history of northeast Kalimantan (Borneo) where uplifting occurred during the same period (see Van Bemmelen, 1949, p. 355). Seismicity and gravity anomalies in the area support the idea of youthful origin.

H. D. Tjia

References

*Kuenen, Ph. H., 1935, "The Snellius Expedition. Geological Interpretation of the Bathymetrical Results," Vol. 5, Part 1, pp. 1–124, Utrecht, Kemink.
*Neeb, G. A., 1943, "The Snellius Expedition. The Composition and Distribution of the Samples," Vol. 5, Part 2, Section 3, pp. 55–268, Leiden, Brill.
*Van Bemmelen, R. W., 1949, "The Geology of Indonesia. General Geology," Vol. 1A, pp. 257–297, The Hague, Martinus Nijhoff.
*Van Riel, P. M., Hamaker, H. C., and Van Eyck, L., 1950, "The Snellius Expedition. Tables. Serial and Bottom Observations. Temperature, Salinity and Density," Vol. 2, Part 6, pp. 1–44, Leiden, Brill.

SULU SEA

(1) Limits and Oceanography

(a) Dimensions and Limits. Almost rhombic in plan, the Sulu Sea has its center about 121°E. 8°N

and is bounded by the north coast of Kalimantan (Borneo), the long Palawan Island, Mindoro, Panay, Negros, Mindanao Islands of the Philippines, and the straight ridge bearing the Sulu Archipelago (Fig. 1). It covers an area of about 260,000 km². Wide shelf areas are found off North Kalimantan and along the northwest boundary. A row of banks with minimum depths of less than 200 m extends across the sea parallel to Palawan Island and the Sulu island group and subdivides the Sulu Sea into a northwestern and a southeastern part. The southeastern (depth of 5580 m) Sulu Basin is outlined by the 4000 m isobath with an area of 46,000 km² and is marked by straight and steep sides. There is an intermediate terrace in the south, from 3000–5000 m depth. The boundaries of the northwestern basin (depth of 2141 m) are more irregular and gentler in slope.

(b) Deep-water Properties and Flow of Bottom Water. Van Riel et al. (1950) and other reports of the Dutch oceanographic Snellius Expedition in 1929–30 furnish the following data about water properties in the Sulu Basin at its station No. 64 (observation depth at 4268 m):

Temperature, °C	10.47
Salinity, ‰	34.47
Oxygen, cc/liter	0.57
Density, g/m²	1026.475

Because of the different properties between the deep water in the Sulu Sea and that outside the sill (depth of -270 m) leading into the Sulawesi Sea, it has been concluded that no flow of bottom water crosses this sill into the Sulu Sea. Figure 2 shows the discontinuity of the salinity conditions upon entering the Sulu Sea from the Sulawesi Sea across the sill (Sibutu Strait). However, the deep-water properties of the Sulu Sea agree well with the assumption of a 400 m deep threshold in the northwest, thus forming the connection with the deeper regions of the South China Sea.

(c) Surface Properties and Meteorology. The sea surface temperature in the Sulu Sea attains its maximum in May (28.9°C) and is lowest in February (26.9°C). Available salinity measurements show the following values:

March–May	34.2‰
June–August	33.7‰ (average)
September–November	33.5‰ (average)

From December to February, the wind blows from the northeast with strengths ranging between 1.5 and 3.4 (Beaufort scale); from June to August, it blows from the south and southeast at 0.5–1.4. The air pressures for the same periods are 757 and 755.5 mm, respectively.

(d) Currents. During the northern summer, surface currents in the Sulu Sea are generally southward at rates up to 15 knots. In the northern winter, a counterclockwise current system exists in

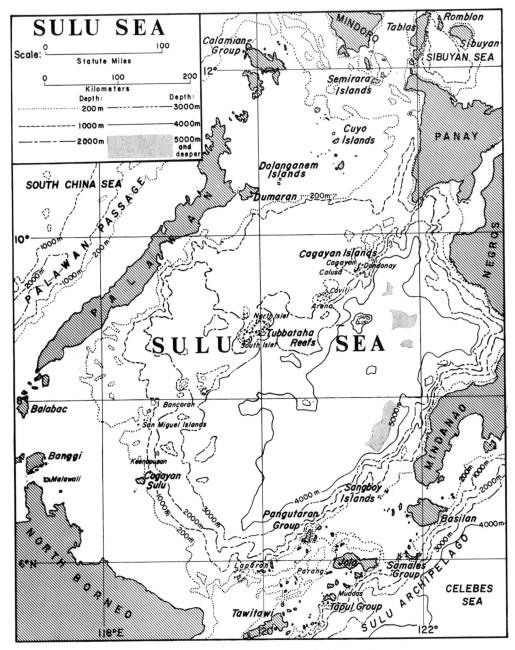

Fig. 1. Bathymetry of Sulu Sea (depths in meters).

the Sea with speeds of 10–15 knots in the north but much slower in the south.

(2) Bottom Sediments

Bottom samples were collected for a portion of the southeastern Sulu Basin by the *Snellius* Expedition, and further samples were collected by the *Recorder* (Krause, 1965). The largest part of the sampled area is covered by globigerina ooze (calcium carbonate content 30% or more), which extends to depths exceeding 4500 m. In the other basins globigerina ooze is limited to depths not exceeding 2000 m. The anomalous occurrence of this sediment in the deep Sulu Sea is attributed to the extremely low oxygen content (0.57 cc/liter) in the basin. The latter must be ascribed to the low sill (−400 m) which bars the oxygenated deeper waters of the open South China Sea from entering. Organisms in the Sulu Sea have also contributed to the decrease of the oxygen in the already

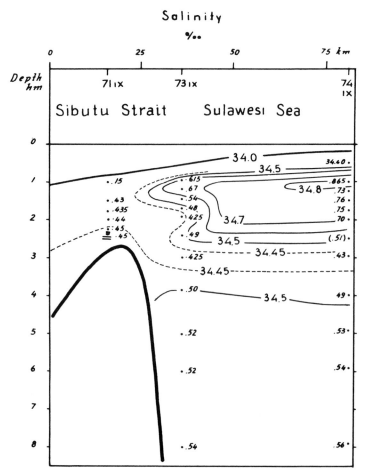

Fig. 2. Salinity distribution at the entrance of the deepest passage leading from Sulawesi (Celebes) Sea to Sulu Sea (after Van Riel, *Snellius* Expedition). Depths in hundreds of meters (hm).

oxygen-poorer higher water from the South China Sea which reaches the basin. The lack of oxygen prevents decalcification of the calcareous matter settling in the Sulu Sea. The basin floor is an abyssal plain, but nevertheless complicated by secondary structures.

A zone of coral mud and sand closely follows the Sulu chain of islands. Only a small proportion of the investigated area is covered by volcanic and terrigenous muds, i.e., off the coast of Mindanao (Fig. 1).

(3) Geological Structure

The steep and generally rectilinear sides of the southeastern Sulu Basin have led Kuenen (1935) to ascribe its origin to block faulting. The northwestern basin is more oblong in plan, with more gentle sides. It is probably the result of flexuring as well as faulting. From geological considerations in North Kalimantan, the age of subsidence of the Sulu basins has been inferred to be Pleistocene

(Reinhard and Wenk, see Van Bemmelen, 1949). The crust would be classified therefore as quasi-cratonic in Stille's terminology; the basin type is probably zeugogeosynclinal.

No gravity measurements have been carried out in the Sulu Sea. However, through its analogous structure with the Sulawesi Basin immediately next to it, the Sulu Basin should also be underlain by positive anomalies of gravity in the order of 50–100 mgal.

H. D. TJIA

References

*Krause, Dale C., 1965, "Tectonics, marine geology and bathymetry of the Celebes Sea—Sulu Sea region," *Bull. Geol. Soc. Am.*, **76** (in press).

*Kuenen, Ph.h., 1935, "The Snellius Expedition. Geological Interpretation of the Bathymetrical Results," Vol. 5, Part 1, pp. 1–124, Utrecht, Kemink.

*Van Bemmelen, R. W., 1949, "The Geology of Indonesia. General Geology," Vol. IA, pp. 356–357, The Hague. Martinus Nijhoff.

*Van Riel, P. M., Hamaker, H. C., and Van Eyck, L., 1950, "The Snellius Expedition. Tables. Serial and Bottom Observations. Temperature, Salinity and Density," Vol. 2, Part 6, pp. 1–44, Leiden, Brill.

SUNDA SEA—*See* **JAVA SEA; SOUTH CHINA SEA; SUNDA SHELF**

SUNDA SHELF

One of the largest continental shelves in the world, covering some 1.8×10^6 km^2, the Sunda Shelf (center: 108°E, 2°N), was first recognized in 1845 by Earl as the "Great Asiatic Bank." It occupies the region of the Java Sea (q.v.), the southern parts of the South China Sea (q.v.), and the Gulf of Thailand (q.v.).

Structurally, the Sunda Shelf is an integral part of the Asiatic continent contiguous to Malaya, Thailand and Vietnam. It connects (within the 100-meters contour) with Sumatra, Java and Borneo (Kalimantan). The tectonic basement seems to have been consolidated very largely by the end of the Triassic orogeny, crystalline rocks of which are seen in Borneo, Malaya and elsewhere in southeast Asia.

Van Bemmelen (1949) suggested that there has been a long-term, positive character for the center

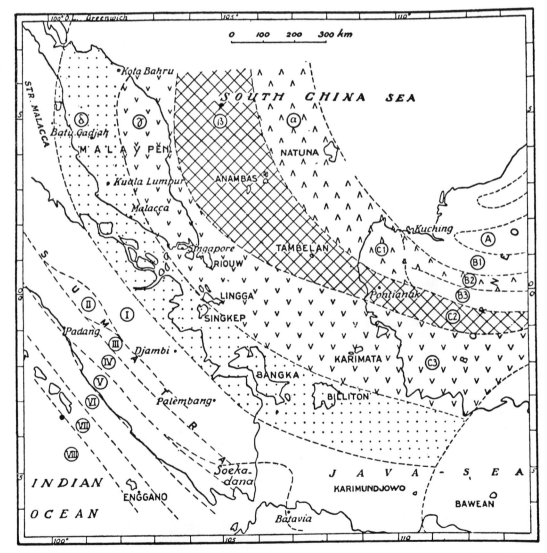

Fig. 1. Structural belts in the Sunda area (Van Bemmelen, 1949). Anambas Mountain System: (α) Natuna Zone, (β) Anambas Zone, (γ) Karimata Zone, (δ) Tin-Belt, (ε) Karimundjawa Zone. A, B and C in West Borneo have local designations. I–VIII belong to the Sumatra (Tertiary) orogenic belt.

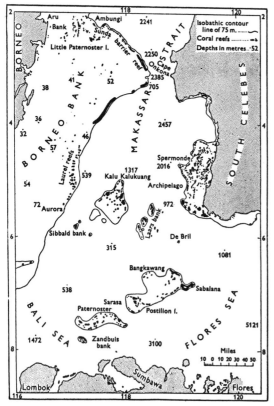

Fig. 2. Barrier reefs and atolls in Makassar Straits, including the Sunda Barrier Reef (left) (after G. A. Molengraaff).

of this great area, his "Anambas Mountain System" or "Nucleus" (from the Anambas Island, midway between Malaya and Sarawak). Around the margins of that nucleus there developed Mesozoic geosynclinal belts that were revived and displaced somewhat in the early and late Tertiary. The troughs may be traced through Sumatra, Java, the Java Sea and southeast Borneo.

To the northeast of the Sunda Shelf, in the South China Sea, there were no such sedimentary belts, but a former extension of the shelf. In late Tertiary and Quaternary, a quasi-cratonic phase was initiated, and where there was formerly a stable, positive continental block, there is now a region of general subsidence. Certain remnants subsiding more slowly than the rest are marked by platform-type (shelf) atolls; these do not have volcanic foundations, but have grown up *in situ* during slow settling of the former shelf (by 1000 meters or more).

The Sunda Shelf is marked by few coral reefs today, mostly on or around the small islands far from the muddy coasts, e.g., Anambas Is., Natuna Is., Tambelan Is., Bawean Is. and Kangean Is. In the area of strong currents at the northeast end of the Sunda Straits (between Sumatra and Java) there are many small reefs in the Thousand Is. and the Bay of Djakarta (Batavia). Along the eastern limit of the Sunda Shelf there is a rim of reefs, the southeast Borneo (Kalimantan) or Sunda Barrier Reef (Fig. 2). Sediments elsewhere are largely muddy, with sandy fractions brought in during Pleistocene exposure (see summary in *Java Sea*, based on Van Baren and Kiel, 1950).

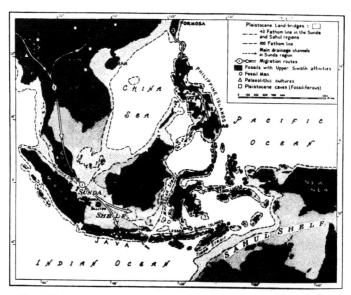

Fig. 3. Pleistocene land connections in the East Indian Archipelago during the glacial periods of low sea level and the suggested routes of migration (de Terra, 1943).

As originally studied by Molengraaff, the floor of the Sunda Shelf was exposed to subaerial erosion during the Quaternary eustatic lows that corresponded to the great glaciations. As indicated by Fairbridge (1961), there was a worldwide tectonic eustatic trend, superimposed upon the glacial/interglacial oscillations, that introduced a secular lowering of about 100 meters or so during the overall period. This phenomenon is correlated with the lowering of quasi-cratonic crustal blocks like those of the South China Sea, western Pacific basins, Mediterranean and Caribbean. For this reason, glacially lowered sea levels would not have been below the present MSL in the early Quaternary, and only the last two glaciations exposed large areas of the present shelf.

The late Quaternary exposure of the Sunda Shelf led to rivers extending their courses over the shelf surface. Two systems were recognized: the North Sunda system flowing from about the equatorial line, northward into the South China Sea basin, and the South Sunda system flowing eastward into the Flores Trough. A smaller stream system flowed out through the Sunda Straits. The name "Molengraaff River" system for this complex was proposed by Dickerson (1941) to honor its discoverer. Important economic deposits, e.g., of placer tin (cassiterite) etc., can be dredged from the drowned river gravels.

The exposure of the Sunda Shelf in the late Quaternary played a major role in permitting the immigration into the Greater Sunda Islands (Sumatra, Java, Borneo) of the larger mammals, *Elephas, Rhinoceros,* etc. At the same time, according to Weber, freshwater fish were able to migrate from streams in Malaya to those in Sumatra and West Borneo; the East Borneo rivers, however, were cut off by deep water and there the fish species are quite different. It is significant that the *Wallace Line* (q.v., pr Vol. VII), the deep channel of the Makassar Straits, Lombok Straight, etc., prevented further eastward migration, and the entry of major mammals into Celebes (Sulawasi) was only possible by means of an extensive "land bridge" (Fig. 3) via Taiwan and the Philippines, that collapsed tectonically during the Quaternary according to the deductions of the vertebrate paleontologists (de Terra, 1943; Hooijer, 1962).

RHODES W. FAIRBRIDGE

References

De Terra, H., 1943, "Pleistocene geology and early Man in Java," *Trans. Am. Phil. Soc., 32*, III, 437–464.

Dickerson, R. E., 1941, "Molengraaff River: a drowned Pleistocene stream and other Asian evidences bearing upon the lowering of sea level during the Ice Age," Philadelphia, Univ. Penna. Bicentennial Conf., pp. 13–30.

Earl, G. W., 1845, "On the physical structure and arrangment of the islands of the Indian Archipelago," *J.*

Roy. Geogr. Soc. (*London*), **15**, 358–365 (author erroneously printed as Earle, W.).

Fairbridge, R. W., 1961, "Eustatic changes in sea level," in "Physics and Chemistry of the Earth," Vol. 4, pp. 99–185, London, Pergamon Press.

Hooijer, D. A., 1962, "Paleontology of hominid deposits in Asia," *Advan. Sci.,* **18**, 485–489.

Molengraaff, G. A. F., 1921, "Modern deep-sea research in the East Indian Archipelago," *Geogr. J.,* **52**, 95–121.

Molengraaff, G. A. F., 1929, "The coral reefs of the East Archipelago," *Proc. Pacific Sci Congr. Pacific Sci. Indian Assoc. 4th Java,* **IIB**, 989–1021.

Smit Sibinga, G. L., 1948, "Pleistocene eustasy and glacial chronology in Java and Sumatra," *Verh. Ned. Geol. Mijnb. Gen. Geol.,* **15**, 1–31.

Van Baren, F. A., and Kiel, H., 1950, "Contributions to the sedimentary petrography of the Sunda Shelf," *J. Sediment. Petrol.,* **20**, 185–213.

Van Bemmelen, R. W., 1949, "The Geology of Indonesia," The Hague, M. Nijhoff, 2 vols.

Von Koenigswald, G. H. R., 1939, "Neue Menschenaffen- und Vormenschenfunde," *Naturwissenschaften,* **27**, 617–622.

Cross-references: *Continental Shelf; Eustasy; Java Sea; Sahul Shelf; South China Sea.*

SUNSPOTS AND SEDIMENTATION

Rhythm is one of the oldest of man's conscious notions. The recurrence of the seasons has ruled his existence from the beginning. Early in the last century Cuvier, animated by a scientific spirit in the modern sense of the word, drew our attention to the cyclic character of geological phenomena. But it is chiefly during the last two decades, thanks to absolute dating, there has been established a relationship between certain phenomena that we can observe directly and the motions of the solar system.

This periodicity is not only concerned with present events. Causes which are constantly renewed, are themselves prolonged in time, and the objective study of events which take place at the present time helps to explain the patterns which are a legacy of the past. Some are external (exogenic), others internal (endogenic). The former are related to celestial mechanics, predominantly by the sun and the moon, while the latter are linked to the evolution of the material of our planet.

Our purpose specifically is to examine the influence which sunspots may have on sedimentation. To begin with, let us give a brief summary of the nature of sunspots:

Sunspots (q.v.): Dark areas on the sun's surface were known to the ancient Chinese and were described by Galileo. They appear for one or more days and are rarely alone. They may be in pairs or make two big spots accompanied by several small ones. These arrangements vary endlessly. Their appearance is fibrous and liable to be modified within a few minutes. The remaining surface of the sun appears to be made of varied sparkling spots which can be several hundred kilometers in diameter. This is about the same as the diameter of the smaller spots. The latter can cover hundreds of thousands of square kilometers. The largest one was observed in 1947, extending over 15×10^{12} km^2 and consequently would have been able to cover ten planets as large as the earth.

The magnetic fields of these spots are very strong while those of the granular parts are ten or even a hundred times weaker.

The surface of the sun is a site of constant activity which consists of an uninterrupted rising of incandescent gas and a descending of gas cooled by radiation. These movements are regarded as convection currents and are partly upset by magnetic fields. This explains the formation of comparatively cool zones which look like spots when seen from the earth. In 1843, Schwabe and Dessau pointed out the cyclic character in the appearance and the number of these spots. They might have been forecast as early as 1776 by R. Wolf who collected rather accurate data from 1745–1776, and they could have been forecast with less certitude from as far back as 1610. The lapse of time between the minimum and the maximum (5.2 years) generally seems to be shorter than between the maximum and the minimum (6 years), the full cycle having a mean value of 11.2 years, but this varies considerably.

At the beginning of the 11-year cycle, most of the spots are situated between 20 and 30° solar latitude. Then they slide down with a curving motion, the incandescent material turning faster nearer equator, since there is an eastward equatorial acceleration in the sun's rotation. R. Wolf established an equation which allowed him to calculate the number of spots and set up chronological tables indicating their average dimensions.

In 1908, owing to the Zeeman effect, Heil revealed the existence of magnetic fields. Spectral observations make it possible to outline distribution maps of these fields, whatever the zone of spots may be. Since 1917, Mount Wilson Observatory has continued to publish material on the magnetic characteristics of these spots. The intensity of the largest spots may reach 3000 gauss.

In addition, the whole solar system has its own magnetic field, though comparatively weak and clearly measurable only at high altitudes. Polarity in the sun, measured in 1955, was negative for its northern hemisphere and positive for its southern hemisphere, thus opposite to what is observed on our own planet. Intensity was constantly decreasing during 1955–1956, and in 1957 the sign of the southern pole changed. At the beginning of 1958, the sun had a similar polarity in both hemispheres. The northern pole became positive in Autumn 1958—this change occurring three years after the minimum intensity of the sunspots and a little before the following maximum intensity of the sunspots.

Over the last century or two, there emerges a 22-year cycle in the magnetic properties of sunspots in the migration of the solar polarity from the northern to the southern solar hemisphere and back, each corresponding to two of the 11-year cycles.

Examples of Contemporary Exogenic Phenomena

In *biology* there is a noticeable influence of sunspots on plant evolution. As is well known, the magnitude of the annual growth of trees is indicated by the relative thickness of the growth rings which are displayed after the trunk has been cut across. A. E. Douglas after performing research on the subject in England, Sweden, Germany and Austria (1830 to 1910) estimated that the maximum thickness of growth rings of trees occur when sunspots reach their maximum. Between these two main peaks there are smaller peaks, due to various causes, for example, atmospheric precipitation, the curves of which show a periodicity of 2–3 years and another of 5.5 years.

In *climatology*, a majority of specialists believe that sunspots influence weather. Although there is no general theory at present, the evidence of 11–22 year periods is seen in oscillations of lake levels, also in anomalies of atmospheric pressure and in certain rainfall figures. Careful work carried out along the River Nile and on Lake Victoria seemed at first to show once again that the highest water level is related with the peak phases of sunspots. Köppen showed that it is in tropical areas where the temperature is at maximum that the best correlation exists. However, after 1923, Köppen's impressive curve broke up into secondary oscillations that require further analysis (Brooks, 1949).

Statistical methods have been used more and more to analyze the productivity of consumer goods; among other things, they have shown a correlation between sunspots and the price of wheat. The wheat crop was less abdunant during minimum periods and therefore more expensive (at least for the period 1800–1850).

There exists equally a close relationship with magnetic storms and the "aurora borealis" (see Vol. II). The birth rate, the death rate, frequency of sudden deaths, the great epidemics, even migrations or men's quarrelsome temper have sometimes been related to sunspots.

Erosion and Sedimentation. The cyclic character of many geological phenomena is well known, particularly those of erosion and sedimentation. Our information on this matter does not always have the desirable precision, for it concerns a new speciality and a good number of hypotheses are still open to question.

The principle of rhythm nevertheless remains undeniable. At the beginning of the century,

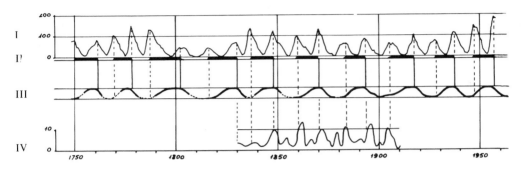

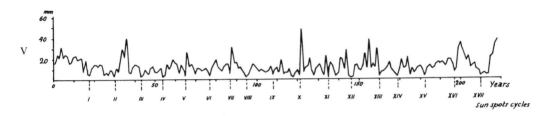

Fig. 1. (I) Ordinate—Wolf number. (II, III, IV) Abscissa—years (1750–1960). (V) Ordinate—thickness of sediments; abscissa—number of years.

(I) Periodicity of the maxima of the sunspots.

(II) Magnetic polarity of the sun and the earth in black: concordant polarities.

(III) Periodicity. Silting curve (sedimentation) and unsilting (erosion), observed on the Cayenne Beach (French Guiana), between the level of the high tide and that of the low tide.

(IV) Growth curve of the living trees in England, Norway, Sweden, Germany, Austria—maxima corresponding to median of the strong precipitations (cycles of ±5 and ±11 years) (after A. E. Douglas, in Menzel, 1959). (By permission of Harvard Univ. Press, Cambridge, Mass.)

(V) Paleoclimatic curve from a sedimentary sequence in Siberia. Rhythmic sedimentation of the alluvial and eolian complexes of the Lena (right bank, opposite the Arbine Island). Besides the 11-year cycles, periodicities of 3, 5 and 30 years may be distinguished (after Lungershausen, 1963).

Chakalsky had already established the seasonal character of the deposits of the Black Sea. Scandinavian geologists were the first to prove the cyclic character of glacial deposits (notably varves). But it is only during the last few years that geologists have been able to prove the regularity of the period of complementary erosional and sedimentational phenomena.

Recently, detailed observations have been made along the coast of French Guiana where physical and geographical conditions are particularly favorable. The coastline of the Guiana Shield is about 2000 km in length between the delta of the Amazon and the mouth of the Orinoco River. The south equatorial current from southeast to northwest moulds the coastline, carrying along the deposits of the Amazon in suspension. The trade winds which blow all the year from the northeast and from east bring the material on to the shore.

In 1901, Zuber thought that in the mouth of the Orinoco, there was a contemporary sedimentation

analogous to flysch. Between this river and the Amazon, several smaller rivers from the three Guianas (French, English, and Dutch) help to increase the volume of mud in suspension. Viewed from the air, these deposits form a ribbon about 25 km wide along the coastline, which keeps on prograding due to the mangrove which traps and stabilizes a fair amount of the mud. This phenomenon is marked by a certain periodicity: silting succeeded by scouring, sedimentation alternating with erosion. The periods are not synchronized along the coastline. The mud carried away in some places is transported toward the west by marine currents, but here and there it is held up by natural obstacles such as the estuaries of coastal streams.

Cayenne Island, the only rocky promontory of any importance between British Guiana and Brazil, is in fact a peninsula lying between two rivers and offers particularly favorable conditions for study of the phenomenon. The Precambrian headland deflects the current of the Mahury River eastward and keeps the harbor of Cayenne from much accumulation of alluvial deposits. The Cayenne River, on the west side, has an insignificant flow and its alluvial sediments for the most part do not reach the sea. Within a distance of 50 km, between Cayenne and Kourou, there is nothing to disturb the normal siltation.

In the course of seventeen years of direct observations, there have been recorded two scourings (maximum erosion), and a continuous period of silting which took place from 1946–1957. The archives of Guiana (a former colony which has become a French "Department") have publications and reports from various civil and military services which provide data on the continuity of this process as far back as 1750 and on some points as far back as 1676. The results of these researches have been indicated in curve III of Fig. 1.

The rocky beach which forms the coast comes down gently toward the sea. Progressive silting is indicated by the deposits which are exposed when the tide is low, thus during neap tides and sometimes during low spring tides, when the range is more than three meters.

At the time of the maximum silting, the sediments became overgrown by mangrove which the Municipal Council of Cayenne has had to cut down several times for reasons of health (owing to proliferation of insects). After each inversion of the silting tendency, the sea removes bit by bit the mud that had been deposited. It disappears more quickly than it accumulates; hence the curve is somewhat asymmetric.

The coincidence is perfect between the periodicity of sunspots and the maxima and minima of silting. The positive maximum (sedimentation) and the negative ones (erosion) are in correlation, the former when the earth and the sun have conflicting magnetic polarities, the latter when those polarities are concordant (negative in the northern hemisphere and positive in the southern hemisphere). This system of silting and unsilting lasts 22 years and corresponds to the complete 22-year cycle of the magnetic properties of sunspots.

It is reasonable to ask if the demonstration of such a correlation between a complex natural phenomenon and the activity of sunspots is in fact irrefutable. In the example of coastal sedimentation of the Guianas, the 22-year cycle determines the complete phenomenon, but it is the 11-year cycle which matches the growth of trees and the development of pathogenic germs: the first process is linked to magnetism and the other to the cosmic rays which penetrate the terrestrial atmosphere, leading therefore to numerous disturbances (ionospheric storms).

It would be interesting to know how far one can match the observations from Guiana with other known facts of marine sedimentation.

Examples of Exogenous Phenomena of the Past: Quaternary. The sedimentology of glacial lakes and the formation of flood plains during the Quaternary have for a long time attracted the attention of scientists because of the regularity with which the alternation of the seasonal layers has been recorded: the varved clays are particularly outstanding.

These features have been the object of numerous studies, leading among which are those of de Geer (1940) through the whole of Scandinavia. Similar research has been made in the United States (e.g., New Jersey and Connecticut), in Patagonia (Argentina and Chile), in Siberia (alluvial deposits of lower Lena), in Central Asia (Altaï, Tchouiskaia Steppe, etc.): by Sostakovitch (1939–1941), Lungerhausen (1940–1950), Nalivkin (1955), etc.

All these deposits show the superposition of numerous rhythms; from 2–3 years, 5 years, 9–13 years, 20–25 years, 30–35, 60–70 and even 100–200 years. The first two refer to the variations of climate; those of 9–13 years, and 20–25 years reveal the periodicity of sunspots. The longest alternations have been connected with the variations of effective solar radiation due to celestial mechanics (Milankowitch, 1938: periodicities of several thousand years).

On the whole, the sunspot rhythms are easily recognizable, but it is worthy to notice that the intensity of the latter is linked not to the maximum thickness but to the minimum thickness of the deposits (Lena, Central Asia). The maximum layers correspond to climatic cycles of 3–5 years (Curve V).

Although periodicity is clearly shown when dealing with continental sediments (lakes, rivers), it is not so easy with marine sediments where the deciphering is much more complicated, as one may realize from the contemporary phenomena in the Guianas where disturbances upset the pattern along the coast. On the other hand, floating timber and the growth of now fossilized shells, show a similar periodicity.

Pre-Quaternary Examples. Other examples of rhythms may be noted as far back as the Precambrian. The most constant are those of 2–3 years, 11, and 30–35 years. Their detailed study may become more precise thanks to absolute dating. Research has been made on a series consisting of an alternation of detrital and carbonate rocks of the Upper Precambrian (e.g., on the Upper Lena of Siberia) and again in coal fields with an alternation of detrital sediments and clays with coal seams, interfingering with carbonate and shaley marine sediments (Carboniferous Donetz coal field).

For a long time, geologists have been seeking to understand the nature of rhythms such as those of the flysch of different ages (mainly Upper Cretaceous and Tertiary). It appears more and more that the early tectonic interpretation of orogenic pulsation is, if it exists at all, insufficient to explain such an alternation. The study of such rocks has been undertaken in several countries (for the United States, see Bradley, 1919). The main difficulty lies in the precise definition of the main annual or seasonal cycle.

Some common mineral species frequently display regular concentric or finely stratified patterns: agate or opal, which form the filling in of the lava vesicles (Eastern Siberia), suggest rhythms of 5, 10, 20 and 25 years. Ferruginous patterns in carbonate rocks show an identical periodicity (Volga, etc.).

The travertines linked to thermal springs (Tarbagataï, Central Asia) show the same periodicity in their growth layers. It is the same with the stalactites of the Kirghiz caves whose dark corroded layers are repeated in a rhythm of 11 years.

One must conclude that a periodicity linked to sunspots cannot be doubted. Its existence is clearly proved by diverse natural phenomena on the surface of our own planet in the course of recent human history. In the Quaternary too, its traces are evident. The difficulties of deciphering are greater when dealing with marine deposits, but the observations carried on in Guiana also demonstrate its reality. The more ancient the deposits are, the more serious are the diagenetic, tectonic, and metamorphic effects that hinder the deciphering of these periods that are so short when compared to geological time.

BORIS CHOUBERT

References

Anderson, R. V., and Kirkland, D. W., 1960, "Origins of varves and cycles in Jurassic Todilto formation (New Mexico)," *Bull. Am. Assoc. Petrol. Geologists*, **44**.

Bradley, W. H., 1929, "The varves and climate of the Green River Epoch," *U.S. Geol. Surv. Profess. Papers*, **158E**.

Brooks, C. E. P., 1949, "Climate through the Ages," Second ed., London.

Choubert, B., and Boyé, M., 1959, "Envasements et dévasements du littoral en Guyane française," *C.R. Acad. Sci., Paris*, **249**.

Geer, G. de, 1940, "Geochronologia Suecia, Principles," *Kgl. Svenska Vetenskapsakad. Mdl.*, **18**(6).

Köppen, W., and Wegener, A., 1924, "Die Klimate der Geologischen Vorzeit," Berlin.

Lungershausen, G. F., 1963, "On the periodicity of geological phenomena and climatic changes," *Gos. Geol. Tech. Izd., Moscow* (in Russian).

Menzel, D. H., 1959, "Our Sun," Cambridge, Mass., Harvard University Press.

Richter-Bernburg, G., 1941, "Paläeogeographische und tektonische Stellung des Rechelsdorfer Gebirges im Hessischen Raum," *Jahrb. Reichs Anstalt*, **61**.

Schwarzbach, M., 1961, "Das Klima der Vorzeit," Ferd. Enke Verl., Stuttgart (English translation "Climates of the Past," Princeton, N.J., D. Van Nostrand Co.

Zeuner, F. E., 1961, "Dating the Past" (an Introduction to Geochronology), London.

SURFACE TENSION—*See* CAPILLARITY; CAPILLARY WAVE

SURF BEATS—*See* SEICHE

T

TASMAN SEA

(I) Introduction

The Tasman Sea is a "marginal sea" in that part of the southwest Pacific Ocean which lies between Australia and New Zealand. It is bounded in the north by the Great Barrier Reef, Coral Sea Plateau and Bellona Plateau. According to the convention of the International Hydrographic Bureau (*Sp. Publ. 23*, 1953), the northern border follows parallel 30°S from the Australian coast to 159° 18′E, then south to South East Rock (near Lord Howe Island), thence to the north point of Three Kings Islands, and the North Cape of New Zealand. Oceanographers, however, often take the border farther north to about 22°S, an ill-defined line approximately through Cato Reef to the Ile des Pins south of New Caledonia.

In the Bass Strait the I.H.B. boundary runs from Gabo Island, near Cape Howe (37° 30′S) to the

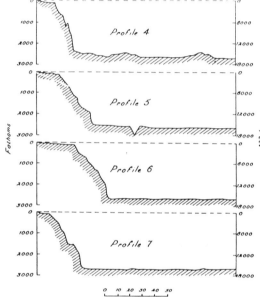

Fig. 2. Profiles of the continental shelf and slope of southeastern Australia (Standard, 1961).

Flinders Group and Eddystone Pt., Tasmania (41 S). However, oceanographers generally prefer to include Bass Strait in the Pacific realm (*sensu lato*) and the Indian Ocean border is taken at the line from Cape Otway through King Island to Cape Grim, the northwest point of Tasmania. From the Southeast Cape of Tasmania the southern boundary runs to Auckland Island (50° 55′S, 166°E) and then north to the Snares, Stewart Island and Waipapapa Point (168° 33′E) on the South Island of New Zealand.

Since marine geologists and physical oceanographers generally prefer structural boundaries, the I.H.B.'s rhumb line from Tasmania to Auckland Island is not very satisfactory, and they generally take the southern boundary farther south, following the crest of the South Tasmania Ridge (Mill Rise) to the Macquarie Ridge.

The Tasman Sea was named after the Dutch mariner Abel Tasman, who first circumnavigated the Australian continent and crossed this sea in 1642. Its shores were later explored by Captain

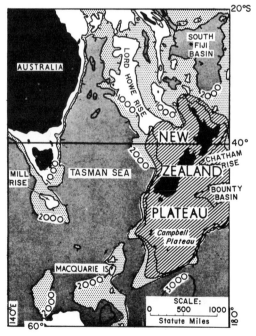

Fig. 1. General bathymetric map of Tasman Sea (after Brodie).

Cook (1768–80), Matthew Flinders (1798) and others. The bathymetry was learned in broad lines from the wire soundings of H.M.S. *Challenger* (1874–75) and a number of other traverses (*Novara*, 1857–59; *Tuscarora*, 1873–76; *Gazelle*, 1874–76; *Enterprise*, 1883–85; *Egeria*, 1887; *Penguin*, 1891–1903: *Dana,* 1928–30: *Discovery II,* 1932–33). Echo sounding work has been done in the last decade by the Royal Australian Navy survey vessels, H.M.A.S. *Barcoo* and others, by the C.S.I.R.O. Fisheries vessel *Derwent Hunter* and by New Zealand vessels H.M.N.Z.S. *Tutira, Pukaki, Taupo, Lachlan, Bellona,* and *Kiwi,* by the British research vessel R.R.S. *Discovery II,* the Danish research vessel *Galathea* and numbers of commercial ships.

(II) Bathymetry

The Tasman Sea correlates roughly with a deep basin now generally known as the *Tasman Basin,* outlined by the 4000-m contour. It was so named by Schott (1935) but was referred to variously in early works as the *Thomson Deep* named after Sir C. Wyville Thomson, of the *Challenger* Expedition, by Petermann (1877), also *Thomson Basin* (Murray, 1895), Thomson Trough (Marshall, 1910), *East Australian Basin* (Supan, 1899; Wüst, 1940; Macpherson, 1946). This basin is a natural structural and oceanographic unit, extending as far south as the Macquarie Island–Mill Rise–Tasmania Ridge (sill depth about 4500 m) and Campbell Plateau in the southeast. The floor of the basin is marked by

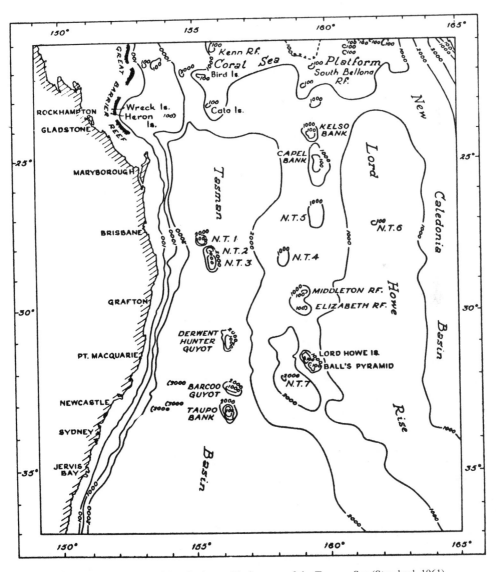

Fig. 3. Location map of the physiographic features of the Tasman Sea (Standard, 1961).

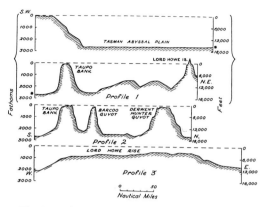

Fig. 4. Profile from southeastern Australian coast to Lord Howe Island; north–south profiles of guyots and east–west profile of Lord Howe Rise (Standard, 1961).

numbers of seamounts. The eastern parts of the basin bordering the New South Wales coast are marked by a number of small narrow rifts (first recognized as such by Standard, 1961), but not to be interpreted as a trough or trench, once called the Ulladulla Trench. Toward the north end of the basin there are several major seamounts: Derwent Hunter Guyot, Barcoo Guyot, and Taupo Bank; they recur in a north-south row parallel to and 350 km west of the north-south row that runs through Ball's Pyramid, Lord Howe Island, Elizabeth Reef and Middleton Reef (atolls).

In the north, the Tasman basin extends into the southern part of the Coral Sea. As defined by the Hydrographic Bureau, the Tasman Sea also takes in the southern parts of the *Lord Howe Rise*, the *New Caledonia Trough* and *Norfolk Ridge* (for details of these see *Coral Sea*).

The eastern borders of the Tasman Basin are marked by the *New Zealand Plateau*, the broad platform bounded by the 1000-m isobath, occupied by New Zealand and its continental foreland areas, the *Campbell Plateau*, *Chatham Rise* (both of Fleming and Reed, 1951), etc. The term was first applied by Murray (1895), but to the Lord Howe Rise, and transferred more appropriately to the New Zealand area by Marshall (1910).

The *Lord Howe Rise* is the principal ridge, forming the northeastern boundary of the Tasman Basin. It was named variously by Farquhar (1907), Marshall (1910), Fleming (1951) and others, as well as various combinations with the name New Zealand, plateau, rise, ridge, etc. It is a 1000–2000 m rise extending from the border of the New Zealand Plateau at about 40°S, northwestward to Lord Howe Island and northward into the Coral Sea area (q.v.). It has rather smooth topography, with scattered small seamounts (less than 500-m depths). Its slope to the Tasman Basin is abrupt with many small vertical scarps, and some slope reversals (antithetic steps). A gap along the rise about

36° 45′S, 166° 30′E of 820 fathoms (1500 m) has been named *Bellona Gap* by Brodie (1964).

(III) Physical Oceanography

Tides. The tidal oscillation of the Tasman Sea is predominantly lunar semidiurnal in character and appears to be due to a wave from the Pacific Ocean which passes through the Coral Sea and progresses southward between Australia and New Zealand to link with the east-going tidal oscillation of the Southern Ocean.

Surface Circulation. Both the South Equatorial Current and Trade Wind Drift passing through the Coral Sea feed the East Australian Current which flows southward over the East Australian continental slope from about 20°. This current reaches maximum velocity between 25 and 30°S (in the vicinity of Cape Byron). Seasonal maximum velocities (up to 1.5 knots on average current charts, perhaps 2–3 knots synoptically) occur in February. Lower velocities occur in winter when southerly winds are more frequent. The East Australian Current is estimated to have about 30 million m^3/sec volume transport, thus rather less than its northern hemisphere analogs, the Gulf Stream or the Kuroshio. About the latitude of Sydney the main stream of the East Australian Current is turned eastward to flow out from the Tasman Sea to the north of New Zealand. Between the latitudes of Sydney and Tasmania a series of large anti-cyclonic eddies appears to be carried southward from the deflected East Australian Current. On average current charts these appear to form a southward continuation of the East Australian Current with a north-going countercurrent to the east.

In the southern and central Tasman, the surface currents appear to be relatively weak and are generally directed northeastward, driven by the prevailing westerly winds.

Watermasses. In the Tasman Sea, water properties at the surface are derived mainly from the circulation of the East Australian Current system. This, in turn, is composed of warm, moderately saline equatorial water and of cooler, more saline subtropical water. In the south Tasman the influence of colder, less saline conditions is felt, as sub-antarctic water from the Southern Ocean converges with the Tasman circulation.

Over much of the Tasman Sea, a layer of high-salinity water is found at a depth of 100–200 m below the surface. This *subtropical lower water* can be traced back to its origin at the surface in the subtropical anticyclone in the vicinity of Easter Island, and one branch enters the Tasman Sea north of New Zealand.

Below the salinity maximum (about 35.9‰) at the core of the subtropical lower water, salinity decreases steadily to reach a minimum (about 34.5‰) at a depth of some 1000 m below the surface

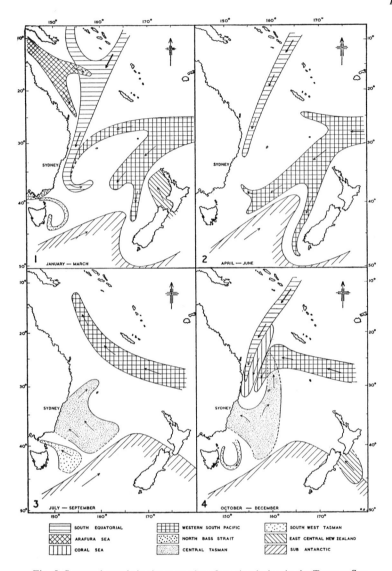

Fig. 5. Seasonal trends in the general surface circulation in the Tasman Sea (Rochford, 1959).

where the temperature is around 5°C. This minimum locates the core of the *Antarctic Intermediate Water*. This can be traced back to the surface of the Southern Ocean in the vicinity of the Antarctic Convergence. Like the Coral Sea Basin the bottom water in the northern part of the Tasman Basin is part of the Deep Water whose ultimate origin was in North Atlantic Deep Water (see *Atlantic Ocean*).

(IV) Chemical Oceanography

The P/O ratio in the water mass below the euphotic zone and above the deeper waters, above which the influence of intermediate Antarctic waters is dominant, is very close to the ratio in other oceans.

In contrast, the deeper waters, where the con-

sumption is apparently less than at the surface, are richer in oxygen, whereas for the surface waters a higher P content is found.

This confirms the Antarctic origin of the intermediate water mass, whereas the P in the surface waters show a closer relation with Pacific rather than Atlantic waters.

(V) Sediments

The slopes of the margins of the Tasman Sea are furrowed with submarine canyons down which terrigenous sediments have been transported to occupy the sea floor. Terrigenous sediments are masked in the 500–2500 fathom (approximately 1000–4500 m) zone by an abundant deposition of calcareous organic sediment principally foraminifera and coccoliths. In the deepest portions of the Tasman Sea floor the sediments are principally residual or wind-borne red and brown clays.

The volcanic seamounts of the mid-Tasman area and Lord Howe Rise have contributed a proportion of volcanic ash to the sediments.

The present rate of sedimentation from terrigenous sources is low, and although the sea floor is relatively flat it is not a true abyssal plain.

Along the ridge tops the sediments are notably coarser, and volcanic rock and pebbles occur. In the north the seamounts that approach the surface are capped with coral reefs. The southern limit of reef-building corals here corresponds approximately with the latitude of Lord Howe Island (32°S).

(VI) Structure

The Tasman Sea is underlain by a crust of oceanic thickness. The probable origin of the basin lies in the building of new crust and the stretching or drifting apart of the bordering continental masses. The disruption may have started as early as the end of the Paleozoic. On some views, major disruption did not occur until the Miocene. The central Tasmantid seamounts may well be located along a tensional rift feature.

The Lord Howe Rise is one of a series of near-parallel orogenic belts, built up on oceanic crust, that lie east of the Tasman Basin. There is little detailed geophysical data, but it can be assumed that the structural history of such a large submarine ridge as Lord Howe Rise has been complex. There is some evidence for anticlinorium type folding. On the ridge flanks and summit, basaltic volcanoes such as Lord Howe Island and isolated seamounts occur. On the adjoining Challenger Plateau abutting the New Zealand slope, near-horizontal surfaces have been cut in volcanic agglomerates, demonstrating submergence.

The Tasman Sea depression is often interpreted as a subsided subcontinent, named "Tasmantis" by Süssmilch and David (1919), in a fancied resemblance to Atlantis. Paleogeographic evidence, particularly from continental Triassic basins in eastern Australia and the Mesozoic marine troughs of New Zealand, suggests indeed that some land source area lay here. Reconstruction of the area by bringing the Lord Howe Rise close to eastern Australia and New Zealand close to the South Tasmania Ridge would perhaps meet such needs, leaving the main Tasman Basin strictly oceanic crust, as pointed out by Standard (1961).

RHODES W. FAIRBRIDGE
W. J. M. VAN DER LINDEN

References

Bogdhunov, K. T., 1962, "Tides of the Pacific Ocean," *Proc. Inst. Oceanol., Moscow,* **60**.

Brodie, J. W., 1952, "Features of the sea floor west of New Zealand," *New Zealand J. Sci. Technol. B,* **33**, 373–384.

Krause, P. C., 1966, "Bathymetry and geologic structure of the Northwestern Tasman Sea–Coral Sea–South Solomon Sea," *New Zealand Oceanogr. Inst. Mem.*

Neyman, V. G., 1960, "Quelques resultats de Observations Hydrologiques a bord de l' 'Ob' dans la mer de Tasman," *Rech. Oc. URSS.* No. 2, 96–99 (in Russian).

Murray, J., 1906, "On the depth temperature of the ocean waters, and marine deposits of the Southwest Pacific Ocean," *Queensland Geogr. J., N.S.,* **21**, 71.

Rochford, D. J., 1958, "The seasonal circulation of the surface water masses of the Tasman and Coral Seas," *C.S.I.R.O. Aust. Div. Fish. Oceanogr., Rep. 16.*

Rochford, D. J., 1958, "Total phosphorus as a means of identifying East Australian water masses," *Deep-Sea Res.,* **5**, 89–110.

Standard, J. C., 1961, "Submarine geology of the Tasman Sea," *Bull. Geol. Soc. Am.,* **72**, 1777–88.

Süssmilch, C. A., and David, T. W. E., 1919, "Sequence, glaciation and correlation of the carboniferous rocks of the Hunter River District, New South Wales," *J. and Proc. Roy. Soc. N.S. Wales,* **53**, 246–338.

Wyrtki, K., 1960, "The surface circulation in the Coral and Tasman Seas," *C.S.I.R.O. Aust. Div. Fish. Oceanogr. Tech. Pap. 8.*

Wyrtki, K., 1962, "Geopotential topographies and associated circulation in the Western South Pacific Ocean," *Australian J. Marine Freshwater Res.,* **13**.

Cross-references: *Atlantic Ocean; Coral Sea; East Australian Current; Indian Ocean; Pacific Ocean; Southern Ocean; Southwest Pacific Ocean.*

TEMPERATURE STRUCTURE IN THE SEA

Seawater temperature has long been the most commonly measured oceanographic variable (1) because it is more easily measured than are other oceanographic variables, such as water motion, density, salinity, biological populations, and (2) because of its obvious influence on marine life and on the chemical composition and the physical properties of seawater. Increasing application of its importance has made the general temperature structure of the ocean, including its variations with time and space, a major oceanographic study.

Measurement of Temperature

Sea temperatures are measured in a number of ways, with a variety of instruments, and to varying degrees of accuracy. Temperatures at the surface are taken with bucket thermometers, by ships from the injection water drawn from just below the surface, by towed surface sensors, and by planes using infrared sensors. Deep-water temperatures have been measured for nearly a century by means of reversing thermometers, which are still standard instruments for deep-water survey. The classic equipment for studying the upper layers of the sea has been the bathythermograph which enables one to map the temperature structure. More recently, fast-responding thermistor beads have been uti-

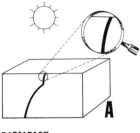 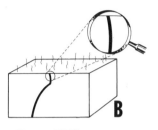

RADIATION
CONVECTION (TO)
CONDENSATION

BACK RADIATION
CONVECTION (FROM)
EVAPORATION

Fig. 1. Effect of heat transfer at the sea surface on the thermal (temperature-depth) structure of the near surface layer of the sea. (A) Factors adding heat to the sea. (B) Factors removing heat from the sea.

lized. Strings of many thermistor beads suspended vertically in the water from floating or fixed platforms can record simultaneously with reference to time and/or place. They are especially useful in studying thermal oscillations caused by internal waves passing the measurement site. Similar strings oriented in a more or less vertical line down to 800 feet may also be towed, and the sensors can be scanned and the data processed electronically, allowing a direct printout of isotherms.

Factors Controlling Sea Temperatures

Sea temperature and its variation with time and place are influenced by many environmental factors, especially in the surface layers. The two chief causes of changes in temperature, and of production or elimination of vertical temperature gradients, are: (1) energy transfer processes at the sea surface; and (2) advective transfer processes below the sea surface.

Surface Heat Transfer. The energy transfer processes that produce heating of the sea surface are: (1) the absorption of radiation from sun and sky; (2) convection of sensible heat from the atmosphere; and (3) condensation of water vapor. Conversely, cooling of the sea surface is caused by (1) back radiation from the sea surface; (2) convection of sensible heat to the atmosphere; and (3) evaporation (Fig. 1).

Because of its selective absorption by the seawater, solar radiation will tend to concentrate the highest temperatures near the surface, resulting in negative temperature gradients. By contrast, the removal of heat from the sea tends to produce positive gradients with slightly higher temperatures below the surface.

Water Motion. The advective processes that affect the sea temperature are the movements of water from one place to another without transfer of heat to or from the atmosphere. The motion is caused by external and internal forces, such as tide, current, and wind. If the temperature of the advected water in its new environment differs from

that of the adjacent water, a corresponding change will be produced in the vertical or horizontal gradients. Geographical and density boundaries influence the path of the transported water and change the gradients accordingly. The magnitude of the heating or cooling depends on difference of temperature of the two water masses and duration of flow.

As an example of the effects of advective processes, when surface water in a localized area sinks, the temperature-depth curve at the convergence becomes characterized by a thick, mixed layer over a sharp thermocline.* As another example, when the wind blows the water seaward, the subsurface water upwells; in the upwelling zone, the water is colder and the gradients weaker than in the water farther offshore.**

An important influence in creating temperature gradients is the interaction of two water masses. At the boundaries, or fronts, the intermingling of water of different temperatures creates irregular and changing gradients.

Strong winds also have a major effect. They mix the upper layers, forming an isothermal layer with a sharp underlying thermocline; the stronger the wind, the deeper is the mixed layer (Fig. 2).

Time Cycles in Temperature

Many of the factors which influence the temperature of the sea operate simultaneously, and it is difficult to establish quantitatively the effect of any single one. All can combine to cause the sea temperature to undergo time cycles.

Seasonal Cycle. The most obvious time cycle in the temperature structure is that related to the seasons of the year and to the latitude.

In the Arctic Ocean north of the Bering Strait, the sea is covered with ice in the winter, and the loss of heat from the sea surface results in virtually no vertical gradients. The spring and summer

* See pp. 907 and 911 for a definition of thermocline.
** See *Upwelling*.

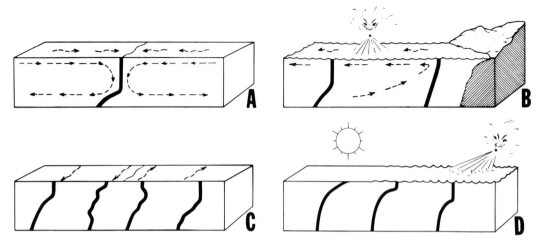

Fig. 2. Effect of some external and internal environmental factors on the thermal structure of the upper layer of the sea: (A) convergence, (B) upwelling, (C) fronts, (D) wind mixing.

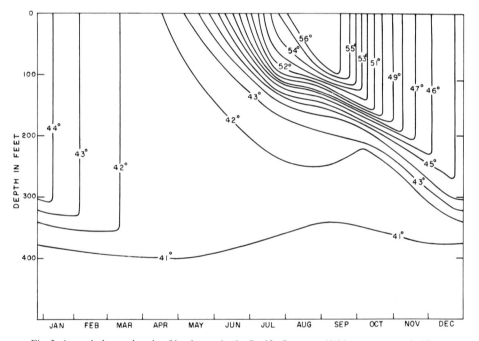

Fig. 3. Annual observed cycle of isotherms in the Pacific Ocean at 49°N (temperature in °F).

melting of this ice produces only minor gradients because the solar radiation is not strong. To the warmer south however, the greater heating season causes the development of a characteristic mixed layer, a thermocline, and gradually decreasing temperature below.

The greatest seasonal cycle in temperature gradients occurs in the temperate latitudes. Here, the winter shows a deep mixed layer with a weak thermal gradient below. With spring heating, weak gradients gradually develop at varying depths, shallowing as the season progresses. Finally, by summer, a strong shallow gradient develops. As cooling starts in the fall, the surface temperature decreases, the surface layer becomes mixed and progressively deeper, and the thermocline again becomes sharp (Fig. 3).

Diurnal Cycle. The same factors that influence

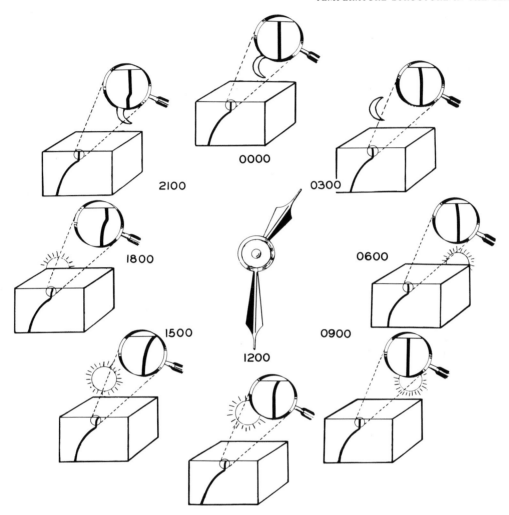

Fig. 4. Schematic representation of the diurnal cycle of temperature structure in the upper layers of the sea.

the seasonal cycle of temperatures operate during the diurnal cycle; however, the effects are not as great because the duration of the heating and cooling is relatively short. The most pronounced diurnal heating occurs at central latitudes during the summer.

A diurnal temperature-depth cycle in which no residual heat is added to, or subtracted from, the water in the 24-hour period is shown in Fig. 4. Since diurnal heating and cooling are primarily confined to the upper 30 feet, enlargements of this area are shown in the Figure.

Because of night cooling, the water is frequently isothermal near the surface at 0000 (midnight); the gradients become slightly positive by 0300 and, with continued cooling, reach a maximum by 0600. By 0900, heating has returned the water to an isothermal condition; with continued solar heating, negative temperature gradients appear by noon;

and by 1500 the surface heating reaches a maximum. The subsurface temperature maximum is reached a few hours after the surface maximum. After 1500 the surface begins to cool, producing an isothermal layer over a weak negative gradient. Cooling continues until by midnight the upper layer is again isothermal. Variations of this generalized diurnal cycle depend on the area, wind, air temperature, and many other factors.

Tidal Cycle. Tidal force is responsible for important temperature changes in the sea by causing advection of water of a different temperature, or by producing vertical oscillations. When subsurface temperatures at any one place are plotted with reference to time, considerable fluctuations are always apparent with cycles corresponding to tidal periods usually discernible. Figure 5 is an example from the mid-Pacific area in which temperatures at 100-foot intervals, from 400–900

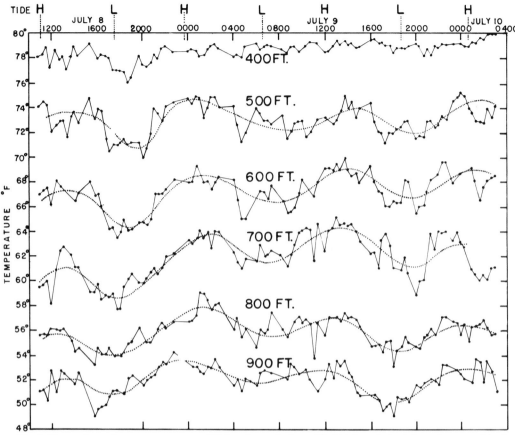

Fig. 5. Fluctuations of sea temperatures at 100-foot intervals from 400–900 feet, derived through repeated bathy-thermograph observations over a period of 40 hours near Bikini Atoll showing the thermal oscillations related to tidal cycles (H = high tide, L = low tide).

feet, are plotted with reference to time and tide. Smoothed lines drawn through the data clearly establish the tidal influence on the temperature structure, particularly around 600 and 700 feet where the temperature gradient is maximum. Many other vertical oscillations with tidal periods, called *internal tides*, have been demonstrated in various waters around the world.

Short-period Fluctuations. Significant thermal fluctuations caused by short-period internal waves occur in the 2-minute to 2-hour wave period range. They consist of rapid temperature changes with time, caused largely by the vertical motion in the thermocline. Although data relative to the world distribution, origin, height, period, or direction of travel of these internal waves are limited, it is safe to assume that such waves are universal. (See Internal Waves).

A good example of these short-period internal waves was obtained by use of a vertical string of thermistor beads at a shallow-water site off Mission Beach, California (Fig. 6). The automatically recorded temperature structure shows

numerous small waves as they pass the measurement station toward shallow water. Their period is about 10 minutes, though larger oscillations are occasionally interspersed. This example also points up the general lowering of all the isotherms by the diurnal wind cycle which alternately displaces the surface water towards and away from the shore. The lowered thermocline reaches a maximum depth at 1800 and then rises to a minimum depth at around 0800 hours.

Two-dimensional Temperature Structure

A two-dimensional vertical and horizontal temperature structure can be obtained by lowering a vertical string of sensors into the sea to a specific depth, then towing the string horizontally through the water (Fig. 7). The U.S. Navy Electronics Laboratory Sea Temperature Profiler has been successful in providing two-dimensional graphs of temperature distribution for the upper 800 feet of the sea by this technique.

General Structure. The measured thermal structures presented in Figs. 8–11 are termed "structures

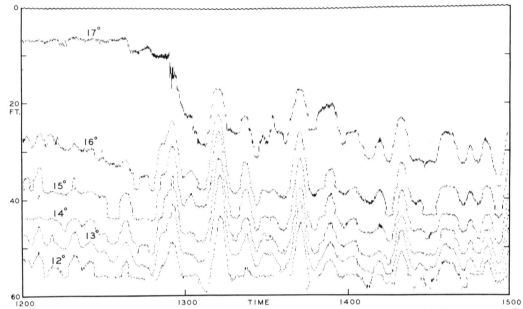

Fig. 6. Recording of short-period changes in thermal structure caused by internal waves in shallow water at U.S. Navy Electronics Laboratory's Oceanographic Research Tower off Mission Beach, California.

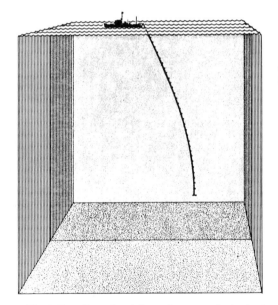

Fig. 7. Two-dimensional thermal structure is obtained by suspended sensor towed through the sea by a surface ship.

of encounter." (Since such structures are rather new and present detailed thermal pictures, we shall discuss Figs. 8–11 somewhat fully.) The vertical scale in these Figures shows depth, while the horizontal scale may be considered to reflect either time or distance. The amplitude of the vertical fluctuations is correct in either context, though some

changes will have occurred at the beginning of the section by the time (4 hours later) that the end of the section is recorded.

A thermal structure of encounter typical of the ocean is shown in Fig. 8. (The vertical scale of Fig. 8 is magnified 100 times compared with the horizontal scale, so that the isotherms appear much steeper than they were in reality; the median slope of the isotherms was actually about 0° 16′.) There is an upper layer (A) which is nearly isothermal. Occasionally there is a slight near-surface gradient caused by midday surface heating (B). The *thermocline* is defined as that area where the temperature changes most rapidly with depth or, in this recording, where the isotherms are closest together (C). The thermocline changes in strength with both distance and time. Sometimes the upper isotherm of the thermocline oscillates upward into the nearly mixed layer (D). A weaker thermocline where the isotherms are more widely spaced (E) is usually found below the main one.

The most striking feature of Fig. 8 is the roughness of the isotherms. The 20°, 13°, and 12° isotherms make vertical excursions of about 100 feet within a distance of 6–8 miles. These probably correspond to long-period internal waves. Other vertical oscillations show a variety of wavelengths, the most conspicuous having a wavelength of $\frac{1}{4}$–$\frac{1}{2}$ mile. Such oscillations appear on nearly all the isotherms and are generally in phase with each other through the thermocline, but they may be out of phase at a distance from the main thermocline. The internal waves are related to the Väisälä frequency of any given density gradient.

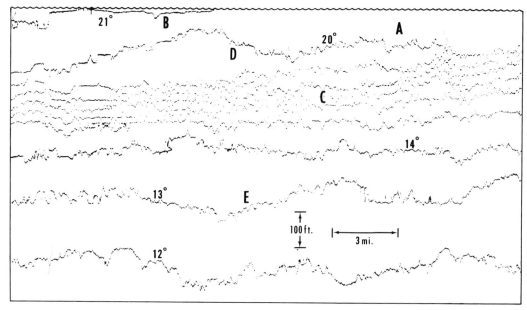

Fig. 8. Example of two-dimensional thermal structure made by towing suspended sensors at a speed of 6 knots. (A) Mixed layer; (B) near-surface heating; (C) main thermocline; (D) upper thermocline oscillation; (E) weak thermocline (temperature in whole degree Centigrade isotherms; vertical scale equals 100 times horizontal).

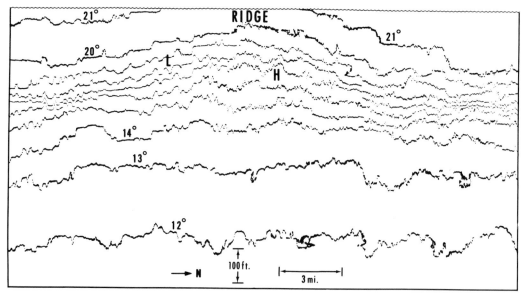

Fig. 9. Example of two-dimensional thermal structure through a *thermal ridge or dome*: L, low-frequency waves; H, high-frequency waves (temperature in whole degree Centigrade isotherms; vertical scale equals 100 times horizontal).

Thermal Ridge. The example depicted in Fig. 9, recorded during a tow made in a northerly direction in the open sea off Baja California, Mexico, is characterized by a general rise in the main thermocline, which may be called a *ridge* or *dome*.

Colder water exists at the point where the isotherms intersect the surface. Maximum bowing of these isotherms occurs on the ridge, but some bowing extends to a depth of 500 feet. The upper isotherms have a crest height of some 150 feet. This structure results from upwelling.

From the nature of the rise and the frequency of the smaller internal waves on both sides of it, some deductions regarding the circulation can be made.

For example, the isotherms on the southern (left) side of this section, are more regular and feature lower frequency internal waves (L) than do the isotherms in the northern (right) part (H). This means that in the earlier or southern part of the tow, the ship was moving in the direction of the internal-wave propagation, creating a Doppler effect. In the latter or northern part of the tow, the direction was counter to the wave propagation.

Front. Figure 10 is a vertical section observed 100 miles southeast of Baja California. It shows a boundary between two water masses and displays a thermal front, with colder surface water in the northern (left) part and warmer water in the southern (right) part. At the boundary there is a 2°C change in surface temperature. More spectacular is the nearly vertical shift in the depth of the isotherms; the displacement is detectable to 400

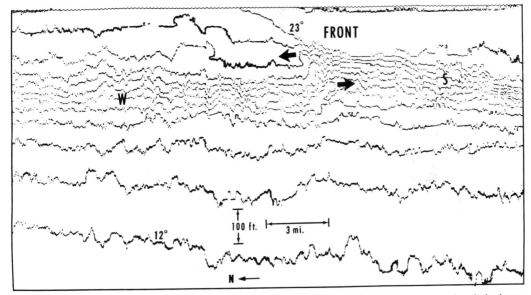

Fig. 10. Example of two-dimensional thermal structure through a *thermal front* (temperature in whole degree Centigrade isotherms; vertical scale equals 100 times horizontal).

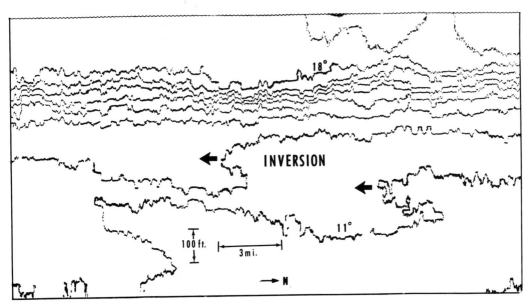

Fig. 11. Example of two-dimensional thermal structure through *temperature inversions* (temperature in whole degree Centigrade isotherms; vertical scale equals 100 times horizontal).

feet. There is also a "buckled," or S-shaped, thermocline at 150 feet, which implies that the warm southern water is overriding the cold. At 70 feet, however, the structure is reversed, making a Z-pattern, and indicating a mid-depth intrusion. In this example, the small-scale, high-frequency waves on both sides of the front are nearly the same. The vertical gradients in the thermocline, however, are weak (W) to the north and strong (S) to the south

Inversions. Figure 11 was also recorded off the coast of Baja California. Here the upper water column is colder, and the deeper isotherms show a radically different pattern from the previous examples. In the southern (left) part, the surface layer is mixed to a depth of 150 feet; in the northern (right) part, there is a weak gradient containing one isotherm above the main thermocline.

An unusual feature of this example is the temperature inversion below the main thermocline. Since the surface current and surface layer are moving south, i.e., from right to left, some of the water in the thermocline is also moving southerly and overriding the deeper water. This effect creates the weak shear, or temperature inversion, shown by the S-shape of the 11 and 12° isotherms. The inversions are weak (about 1°C) and are from 150–200 feet in height. This feature is believed to be transient in nature.

The main thermocline, which occurs between 150 and 300 feet, contains, as do all thermoclines, the smaller internal waves. This thermocline is not a sharp one that weakens with depth. It is uniform, then changes abruptly into the large inversions. This type of thermocline is typical of shear boundaries.

Power Spectra

The vertical oscillations noted in two-dimensional sea temperature isotherms vary widely with location, time, and direction of tow through the water. The spectrum of their wavelengths is broad. Some waves are 200 or 300 yards in length, others are nearly a mile, but most of them average 2–3 complete cycles per mile. One method of presenting this variation is by means of a power spectrum designed to emphasize the dominant frequencies. For such an analysis, longer data sampling sequences are desirable. One 10-hour sequence of half-minute depth readings of the 20° isotherm, in the form of a computed power spectrum, is shown in Fig. 12. This section was taken in an easterly tow about 100 miles south of Baja California.

In this example, the greatest power is concentrated in the long-period fluctuations which occur at the beginning of the spectrum where the curve runs off the diagram. These fluctuations are caused by tidal and other long-period changes, as well as by large spatial changes.

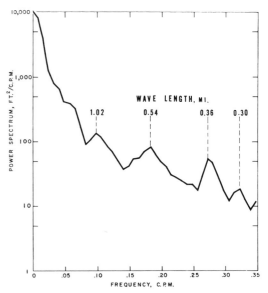

Fig. 12. Power spectrum of the depth of 20 C isotherm in a 24-mile section off Baja California.

For a towing speed of 6 knots, the peaks in this curve lie at 0.098, 0.184, 0.277, and 0.328 cycle/min; the corresponding wavelengths of encounter are 1.02, 0.54, 0.36, and 0.30 mile.

As can be seen from Figs. 8–11, the choice of isotherm or location of the section can change the distribution of power spectrum peaks exhibited. Different geographic areas exhibit characteristic spectrum peaks which are useful for frequency analysis. From the power spectrum peaks and the detailed two-dimensional thermal structures, it is possible to establish the dynamic processes taking place in the sea.

E. C. LaFond

References

LaFond, E. C., 1962, "Temperature Structure of the Upper Layer of the Sea and Its Variation with Time," in American Institute of Physics, "Temperature, Its Measurement and Control in Science and Industry," Vol. 3, Part 1, pp. 751–767, New York, Reinhold Publishing Corp.

LaFond, E. C., 1963, "Detailed temperature structures of the sea off lower California," *Limnol. Oceanog.*, **8**, No. 4, 417–426.

THERMAL INSTABILITY

A fluid heated at a lower boundary surface may develop a type of instability called *thermal instability* resulting in convection. A characteristic product of heating from below is the ideal *Bénard cell* (q.v.), but other convection cell forms are possible, all determined by a critical value of the *Rayleigh number*; the latter (Ra) is the non-dimensional ratio between the product of buoyancy forces and heat advection and the product of viscous forces and heat conduction in a fluid, thus:

$$\text{Ra} = \frac{g|\Delta_z T|\alpha d^3}{vk}$$

where g is the acceleration of gravity $\Delta_z T$ a characteristic vertical temperature difference in the characteristic depth d, the coefficient of expansion is α, kinematic viscosity is v and thermometric conductivity is k. The Rayleigh number is equal to the product of the *Grashof* and *Prandtl numbers.* The onset of instability convection occurs when the Rayleigh number exceeds a certain critical number. For instance, in a layer of fluid between two solid planes at constant temperatures this value is 1710. If the upper surface is free, this becomes 1100.

Thermal instability is involved both in the gross circulation of the atmosphere and in cumulus convection. In the ocean cooling of the upper layer is sometimes caused by this process. It is distinct from *hydrostatic instability,* which occurs when the environmental lapse rate of temperature or of density (for the water) is greater than the adiabatic lapse rate (dry adiabatic rate for dry air and wet adiabatic rate for moist air but in this process, heat conduction and viscosity are not taken into account). When the environmental rate is less than the adiabatic rate, the state of the air or water is called hydrostatic stability, vertical or convectional stability. In this state a particle of air or water makes vertical oscillations about the original location when it is displaced upwards or downwards. When the two rates are equal the air or water is in *hydrostatic equilibrium.* A particle displaced from its original position remains at the new position.

RHODES W. FAIRBRIDGE

References

Byers, H. R., 1959, "General Meteorology," Third ed., New York, McGraw-Hill Book Co., 540pp.

Huschke, R. E. (editor), 1959, "Glossary of Meteorology," Boston, American Meteorological Society, 638pp.

Kuo, H. L., 1955, "Convective instability of a rotating fluid with a horizontal temperature contrast," *J. Marine Res.,* **14**, 14–32.

Stommel, H., 1947, "The theory of convection cells," *Ann. N.Y. Acad. Sci.,* **48**, 715–726.

THERMOCLINE

A thermocline is a layer of water with a more intensive vertical gradient in temperature than that found in the layers above or below it. The term was originally proposed for a lacustrine environment, by Birge in 1897 (see Reid, 1961). In the oceans, the boundaries of this high-gradient layer usually form the division of the surface water and the intermediate and deep water below. These layers are of varying depths, thickness, areal extent, and permanence. The ultimate determinate of existence of any thermocline is the addition or loss of heat at the surface, coupled with mixing processes which transmit the temperature change to the depths (Fig. 1).

Thermoclines can be affected by practically all physical processes occurring in lakes and in the oceans (i.e., waves, currents) and by meteorological processes above the surface (i.e., wind, radiation, etc.). Thermoclines, in turn, affect various properties, such as the transmission of sound or the transparency.

Permanent Thermoclines

This is generally the deepest thermocline to be found in the sea with its upper surface residing from 100–700 meters below the surface. The term, permanent, is used because its changes do not appear to be related to seasonal or shorter periods. It tends to be symmetrical about the equator, being shallow, moderately thick and quite strong near the equator; becoming thicker, deeper and less intense in the mid-latitudes; and ending at the surface in an intense gradient in the vicinity of 50–60°N and S latitude (Fig. 2). It is generally thought to be developed by the equatorward flow of deep cold water from the poles and the poleward flow of warm surface water from the equator.

Seasonal Thermocline

This is so named because of its variation with the season. It develops in spring, becoming stronger with the summer and disappearing in the fall and winter. It is found nearer the surface than the permanent thermocline and in those areas where the seasons show noticeable differences from summer to winter. Mid-latitude oceans and lakes, in particular, demonstrate a well-developed seasonal thermocline. In spring, the water is nearly isothermal. As the weather warms, the water surface receives more heat than it loses to the air and becomes warmer. The wind then acts to cause mixing of this surface water to a slightly greater depth. As more heat is received and the wind continues to mix it deeper, the thermocline layer will be found farther below the surface. The maximum depths and intensity of the thermocline will depend on the strength and duration of the wind and the amount of radiation received.

Diurnal Thermocline

Thermoclines can develop on smaller scales. The diurnal is perhaps the smallest detectable thermocline, and this forms very near the surface during the day and disappears at night. The intensity can be affected by such things as the degree of cloudiness and the temperature difference between the sea and the air.

In recent years, more attention has been given to the thermocline and its effect upon the ocean characteristics. It causes many changes in the sound waves attempting to pass through it vertically (see also articles on *Acoustics—Underwater Sound* and *Sounding*). It appears to be the locale for transmission of waves which move along the boundaries between two layers (see *Internal Waves*).

Robinson, Stommel, and Welander have worked out two possible models of the thermohaline circulation in which a relationship between the circulation and the thermocline appears. Though the exact process of mixing is not understood in the first model, it would seem to show that hori-

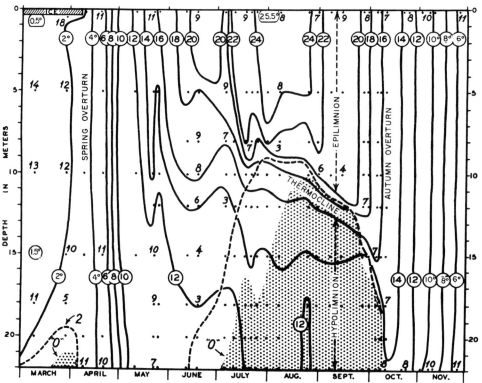

Fig. 1. A lacustrine thermocline, from the type locality. A seasonal cycle of temperature conditions in Lake Mendota (Wisconsin), a small cool latitude lake, is displayed by the solid lines. The sloping figures indicate oxygen conditions. An anaerobic condition (indicated by dots) develops below the thermocline in summer (from C. H. Mortimer in "E. A. Birge," by G. C. Sellery 1956, Univ. of Wisconsin Press, Wisconsin).

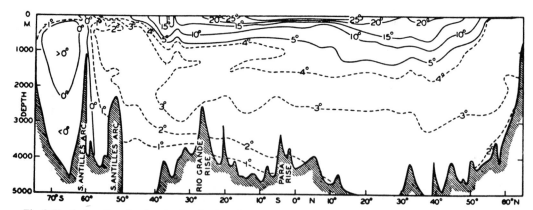

Fig. 2. Vertical section showing the distribution of temperature in the Western Atlantic Ocean. The best developed thermocline can be seen in the 15–25° isolines between 15°N and 15°S (after Wüst; taken from Sverdrup, Johnson, and Fleming, 1942).

zontal advection will have a negligible effect on the development of the thermocline; that a vertical current will form at the bottom of the thermocline; and that the thermocline is indeed restricted to subtropical areas in the ocean. The second model along slightly different lines shows typical east-west currents developing in addition to the development of the thermocline.

NOEL PLUTCHAK

References

Defant, Albert, 1961, "Physical Oceanography," Vol. 1, pp. 119–122, New York, Pergamon Press.

Reid, G. K., 1961, "Ecology of Inland Waters and Estuaries," New York, Reinhold Publishing Corp.

Robinson, Allan, and Stommel, Henry, 1959, "The Oceanic thermocline and the associated thermocline circulation," *Tellus*, **11**, No. 3, 295.

Robinson, Allan, and Welander, Pierre, 1963, "Thermal circulation on a rotating sphere with application to the oceanic thermocline," *J. Marine Res.*, **21**, No. 1, 25–38.

Stommel, Henry, and Arons, A. B., 1960, "On the abyssal circulation of the world ocean. II. An idealized model of the circulation pattern and amplitude in oceanic basins," *Deep Sea Res.*, **6**, 217–233.

TIDAL POWER—*See* pr Vol. VI

TIDES

The rhythmic diurnal or semidiurnal rise and fall of sea level is called the tide. Wherever the range in height, or the tidal flow, has been appreciable along a coast, the *rhythmic* nature of the change has fascinated human observers. Terms and phrases including the word "tide" are sprinkled throughout the poetry and folklore of many maritime lands. Also, explanation and prediction of tides was one of the earliest of man's scientific accomplishments; Leonardo da Vinci made one of the first attempts.

Only a few events in nature are really cyclic, i.e., repeat with enough regularity to be predictable months or years in advance. Every morning, day replaces night; the moon goes regularly through phases from dark to full and back again to dark; summer and winter alternate. These events cause other nearly cyclic happenings (see *Cycles and Periodicities*): roses are more likely to bloom in summer than winter; snow is more likely to fall in winter. But we cannot predict just which day will bring roses or snow, one year or ten years from now. We *can* predict the tides; we can predict how high they will be and what time of day the water level will be high and low.

This remarkable predictability is because the tides are controlled by the same circumstances that give us our measurements of time (day, month, year). Tides are caused by the physics of the solar

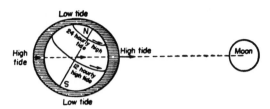

Fig. 1. Cause of the tides. The oceans facing away from the moon are less attracted by it than is the solid body of the earth; those facing the moon are more attracted than the terrestrial body. Thus, two tidal crests are formed, and between them a zone of low tide. In polar regions, high tide occurs ideally every 24 hours, at the equator every 12 hours (from Strumpf, 1959).

system, in particular the sun–earth–moon system (Fig. 1; see also *Celestial Mechanics*, Vol. II).

The Nature of Tides

Tides are waves; the typical period is 12 hours and 25 minutes (43,000 seconds) and the wavelength is half the circumference of the earth (ideally about 12,600 miles). Tides are recorded as changes in water level and are associated with water motions that are called *tidal currents*.

Tidal Heights and Ranges. The total change in sea level may be only a few feet during the day, as it is along the Mediterranean coast and at many tropical Pacific Islands. Along continental shores exposed to the major oceans, the daily tidal range (maximum height minus minimum height) is usually 4–10 feet. Some regions are famous for exceptionally large ranges: the Bay of Fundy, between Nova Scotia and the Canadian mainland, exhibits ranges up to 60 feet. Twenty-foot ranges are common on the south shore of the North Sea, along the Pacific-continental coast of Alaska, and in northwestern Australia.

There may be one high and one low tide per day (diurnal tides) or double this (semidiurnal). The two highs and two lows each day may not be identical in height. Along the Atlantic coast of the United States, two nearly equal highs and two nearly equal lows occur each day. But, along the Pacific coast, successive highs (and lows) are usually not equal, and some days, in fact, only one high and one low can be observed. On the west coast, then, the diurnal *inequality* (difference in height of successive highs) is large.

Both the *times* and *heights* of high and low tides change every day. On the average, because high tide occurs every 12 hours and 25 minutes, the high tide is observed about 50 minutes later every day.

The range of the tide changes every day, too. High tide keeps rising a little higher, and low tide drops a little lower, for about a week, and then the range decreases again. Maximum ranges occur about every 14 days. When the range is large we call it a "spring tide"; when the range is small it is called "neap tide."

The range of the tide varies markedly with season, especially at localities with large diurnal inequality. Maximum ranges, usually associated with both highest highs and lowest lows, occur near the time of the solstices—in June and December. This is also the time of maximum diurnal inequality. During spring and fall, near the times of the equinoxes, the diurnal inequality is a minimum and ranges are close to average for the year. Typical tidal cycles around 34°N on the west and east coasts of the United States are shown in Fig. 4.

A "stage" of tide, such as high tide, does not appear simultaneously at all points of a coastline.

Along the Pacific Coast, each stage seems to "flow" northward along the coast; high tide is 6–8 hours later at Port Townsend, Washington, than it is at San Diego, California. This time lag suggests that the tide may be moving like a progressive wave, with a northward component of speed of 150 mph. (The water is not moving with this speed, only the wave form; see *Waves*.)

Whether or not the tide really behaves like a progressive wave or like a standing wave cannot be determined from existing observational material. Neither tidal heights nor tidal currents have been measured in the open ocean. The difficulty is that

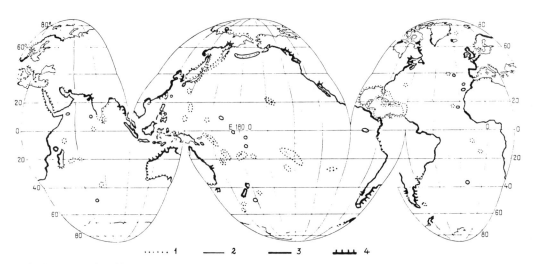

Fig. 2. Mean spring tidal ranges of the world (mainly after Rouch, in Guilcher, 1965). Explanation: (1) 0.10–1 m; (2) 1–2 m; (3) 2–4 m; (4) over 4 m.

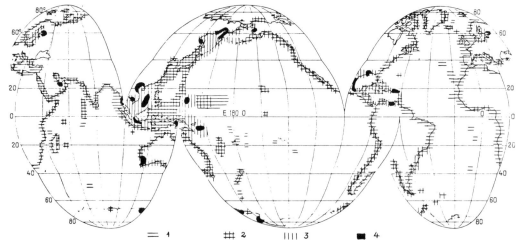

Fig. 3. Tidal types around the world (mainly after Dietrich, from Guilcher, 1965). Explanation: (1) Semidiurnal tide $\dfrac{K_1 + O_1}{M_2 + S_2}$ ratio 0–25 m; (2) mixed tide, semidiurnal preponderant 0.25–1.5 m; (3) mixed tide, diurnal preponderant 1.5–3.0; (4) Diurnal tide, over 3 m.

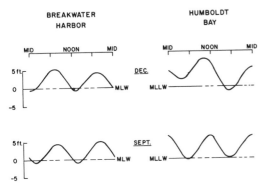

Fig. 4. Daily tidal heights at representative mid-latitude ports in the United States. Breakwater Harbor is on the east coast; Humboldt Bay is on the west coast. Note the greater diurnal inequality at Humboldt Bay, especially during the time of solstice (December). MLW indicates mean low water; MLLW indicates mean lower low water.

all present methods for measuring either heights or currents require a platform fixed with respect to the solid earth.

Tidal Currents. Tidal currents are generally weak except in shallow waters near the continents, and their direction of flow changes continuously throughout the day. When the tide is highest off San Francisco, the current offshore flows east, then it flows south, west, north and east again, actually making two (unequal) clockwise rotations in a day. The maximum speed is about half a knot; it occurs when the flow is toward the northwest (see illustration in *Ocean Currents*).

In river estuaries, the sides and bottom of the embayment restrict the water flow. Direction of flow is principally up and down the channel. Under some circumstances, high rates (faster than 5 or even 10 knots) occur. If the river flow is approximately as large in volume as the tidal flow, the estuary will become stratified, or layered, with fresh water lying on top of salty water that has flowed in from the ocean (the "salt-water wedge"). In this case, the *ebb* or outward flow of water is faster near the surface than at the bottom. The *flood* or inward flow of water is nearly uniform from top to bottom. This asymmetrical flow may have important effects on sedimentation in the estuary. River sediments tend to remain suspended and carried up and down (and periodically out of) the estuary on the ebb tide. Oceanic sediments tend to move in on the flood tide and accumulate in the estuary, since the near-bottom ebb currents are weaker than the flood currents. In estuaries with very little river flow, ebb and flood currents are nearly alike and nearly constant from top to bottom. Tidal flushing is more effective and the estuary is less of a sediment trap. In open wedge-shaped estuaries the tidal amplitude tends to rise to the head area; in long narrow

estuaries friction tends to damp out the tidal effect. In the latter a common (and quite dangerous) feature of the rising tide is an abrupt solitary wave, the *tidal bore*. The most famous is that on the River Severn, in England. A bore can be over 10 feet high and travel at 10–15 knots.

Large, broad estuaries sometimes have rotating tidal currents and wave-like tides that move progressively around the edges of the basin. This is because of the deflecting force of the earth's rotation, the Coriolis force (q.v.). Consider such an estuary in the northern hemisphere. As the flood current moves into the basin the water is deflected to the right of the direction of flow and water piles up at the shore. When the current reverses direction the water moves to the opposite side of the basin. Therefore, the Coriolis effect always produces counterclockwise rotation of the tidal crest in a bay in the northern hemisphere; in the southern hemisphere such rotation is clockwise.

Observations and Predictions. Measurements of the sea level are regularly made at several hundred seacoast locations throughout the world. The standard instrument, or "tide gauge" is a simple mechanical device. A clock drives a roll of recorder paper at a constant rate under a pen or pencil. The pen is moved by a set of gears connected to a float resting on the sea surface in a perforated tube (which damps out short-period wave action). As the float rises and falls, the pen moves back and forth across the paper. The first such device that we know of was used in London around 1850. Previously, visual observations on a "tide staff" were made. Tide gauges are being developed now to record directly in a form that can be used by modern computing machines.

The mathematician Fourier proved that series of events that repeat exactly, time after time, can be represented by a series of sinusoidal curves. Tides, as pointed out earlier, are nearly perfectly repeating. Therefore, it is possible to predict future tides, from observational data on past tides, without any understanding of tidal theory at all. And, in fact, predictions for important harbors were being made and used long before the mathematicians, astronomers, and physicists came to some agreement as to how tides are caused.

To be sure, the early predictions were empirical. The early tide predictors worked out their own individual techniques, and kept them secret, handing them down to chosen sons or other heirs.

We are not in a position to be critical of their methods; our predictions are largely empirical today. The ocean basins are very irregular structures. Movement of water from one place to another is restricted by the continents, by undersea mountains, by straits and channels. The only way we can accurately predict future tides for a particular coastal city, is to *measure* tides at that spot, preferably for at least one year. A 29-day period of

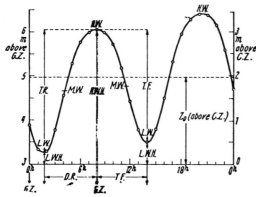

Fig. 5. Some important expressions used in connection with tides: HW = high water, LW = low water, HWH = height of high water, LWH = height of low water, TR = tide rise, TF = tide fall, DR = duration of rise, DF = duration of fall, MW = mean water, Z_0 = height of mean water, CZ = chart zero, GZ = gauge zero = NZ — 5.00 m, NZ = normal zero (Dietrich, 1963). (By permission of Interscience Publishers, N.Y.)

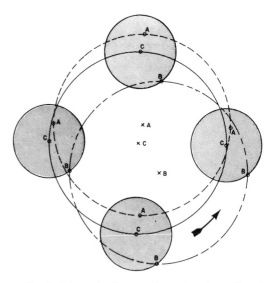

Fig. 6. Schematic diagram illustrating the orbits of three points on earth, A, B, and C. The x's indicate the centers of the orbits.

measurement is often adequate for determination of the major terms.

However, as theory has provided an understanding of tidal forces, it has also simplified and regularized the predictions. The orbits of the celestial bodies that induce the tides are known. From these, the *periods* and *frequencies* of the sine waves needed to represent the tides can be determined. (The period of the wave is the time elapsed between the appearances of successive crests at a particular spot.) Tide records for a harbor can be analyzed to determine the amplitude (half the height) that is associated with each of the indicated periods, and also to determine the phase, or time of occurrence, of the maximum (see Fig. 5).

The sine wave periods are not all simple fractions of a year and a month because the geometry of the system is more complex than simple circular orbits on a single plane. The parameters for many such sine waves, or "constituents," are determined from the records. The future occurrence of each is then predicted, and the effects of all constituents summed, to predict the actual changes in sea level.

The summation is done at national centers. The Tidal Institute in Liverpool, England, once provided for much of the world's needs. In the United States, it is the Coast and Geodetic Survey that carries out this work. In the past, these calculations have necessitated the use of large analog computers which summed up to 55 constituents mechanically. Future use of faster, more efficient, digital methods is certain.

Not all of the constituents used in the detailed work are inherent in the astronomical periodicities. Shoaling of the tidal waves as they approach shore changes the shape of the wave. This distortion is included by computing "shallow water constituents."

The Cause of the Tide

Tides are caused by the fact that the gravitational attractions of the sun and moon vary from place to place on earth. The atmosphere, the ocean and the solid earth all experience these forces but only the oceanic tides are easily perceived by the human eye. The point on earth closest to the sun is most strongly attracted; on an idealized water-covered sphere a mound of water would be formed there. The point on earth farthest from the sun is least strongly attracted; the rest of the earth is pulled away leaving a mound of water bulging out at this point also. The moon has a similar effect. When all three bodies (earth, moon, sun) lie on a line, "in conjunction," the tides are highest.

The Tide-producing Forces. Let us consider first the tidal force due to the attraction of the sun. The total gravitational attraction between the sun and the earth acts as a kind of stretchable "string" linking the centers of the two bodies. This attraction causes the earth to follow a curved path and to stay in its orbit. Now, *every bit* of mass in or on the earth moves in an orbit identical to the one traced by the center of the earth. (Neglect daily rotation, for a moment; it does not affect the argument about tidal forces.) That is, the earth moves around the sun, *not* like a toy airplane on a guide line, but more like a gyroscope on a pivot.

The occurrence of seasons is proof that the earth revolves around the sun in this way. If the earth's motion were *not* gyroscopic, one hemisphere would be perpetually hot, the other perpetually cold.

The earth's orbital motion is illustrated schematically in Fig. 6. Points A and B describe orbits identical in size and shape to the orbit described by point C. The only difference is that each orbit is displaced from every other, in exactly the same way as A, B and C are displaced from one another. The x's mark the center of the three orbits illustrated.

Since the orbits are identical, the centripetal acceleration required to keep each small portion of the earth following its orbit is the same everywhere on earth. This acceleration is supplied by the gravitational attraction of the sun. The gravitational attraction, however, is not the same from place to place on earth. The earth is not a point in space, but has size as well as mass. During northern hemisphere summer, for example, the North Pole is closer to the sun than is the South Pole, so the gravitational attraction is stronger at the North Pole.

The average gravitational attraction per unit mass must equal the average centripetal acceleration, or the earth's orbit would change. But from point to point in and on the earth, the two will not be equal. One is constant (the centripetal acceleration); the other varies with position (the gravitational attraction). This local difference causes the tide-producing force. The *centripetal acceleration* is proportional to the *average* gravitational acceleration (attraction per unit mass), and is directed toward the sun:

Centripetal Acceleration = Average Gravitational

$$\text{Acceleration} = \frac{GM_s}{r^2}$$

where

G = the universal constant of gravitation
M_s = the mass of the sun
r = the distance between the centers of the earth and sun.

Consider a point on earth directly under the sun. At this point, the gravitational acceleration is stronger than average:

$$\text{Gravitational Acceleration} = \frac{GM_s}{(r-a)^2}$$

where a is the radius of the earth.

The difference between the average and local gravitational acceleration is the tide-producing force, F_t, per unit mass:

F_t = Local Gravitational Acceleration − Average

$$\text{Gravitational Acceleration} = GM_s\left[\frac{1}{(r-a)^2} - \frac{1}{r^2}\right]$$

By neglecting small terms we find the approximation:

$$F_t = GM_s\frac{2a}{r^3}$$

The reader can convince himself that on the opposite side of the earth the difference has very nearly the

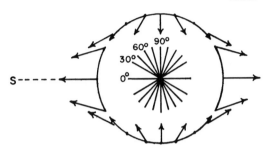

Fig. 7. Schematic diagram of the tide-producing force for one astronomic body (marked S).

same magnitude but opposite sign. At that point the distance to the sun is $r + a$; the resulting force is directed away from the sun. At all other localities, the net force is smaller than at these extreme points. Also, since the centripetal and gravitational accelerations generally do not lie on the same line, their difference must be found by vector subtraction. The distribution of the tide-producing force is illustrated in Fig. 7.

The magnitude of the tide-producing force is negligible in comparison to the earth's gravity. However, note that at most places on earth the tide producing force is partly parallel to the earth's surface. This horizontal part of the tidal force is not counteracted by any other force, so, small though it is, it causes the waters to move.

All of the preceding discussion describes tidal forces induced by one astronomic body, the sun. The earth is similarly influenced by the moon. The moon has much less mass than the sun, but it is much closer to the earth. As a result, the tide-producing force of the moon is more than twice as large as that of the sun.

Harmonic Development. From the tide-producing force can be calculated an ideal tide for a theoretical ocean devoid of continents, a concept that goes back to Newton in 1687. It would have a football (prolate spheroid) shape, with its major axis coincident with the earth–moon axis. Since not only the earth rotates but the moon swings around the earth and on a different orbit, this deformation can be calculated for any time, latitude and longitude, as the "*equilibrium tide*." Evidently it is the sum of a number of terms which vary in time harmonically and are therefore subject to rather straightforward mathematical analysis, especially in these days of electronic computers.

Since the equilibrium tide is the sum of both lunar and solar tides, calculated respectively at 55 and 24 cm, a rough approximation can be obtained by observing the relative positions of these celestial bodies with respect to the earth at any time. When they are almost in line (new moon) or opposite in the sky (full moon) the two tides will reinforce one another and lead to *spring tides*; when out of phase, at "quadrature," the two force fields tend to cancel

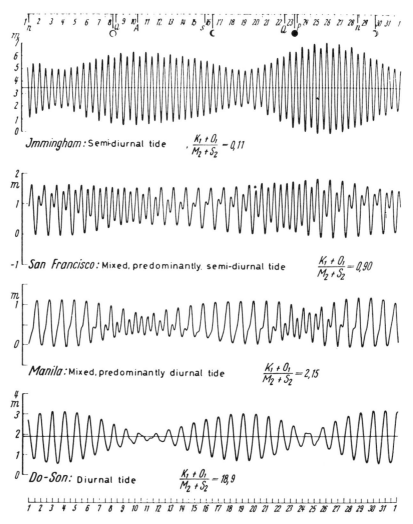

Fig. 8. Tidal curves for the month of March, 1936, referred to the corresponding chart zero. Phases of the moon: *n*,.largest northern; *s*, largest southern declination of the moon; *Q*, passage of the moon through the equator; *A*, Apogee; *P*, Perigee of the moon (Immingham is in England, Do-Son in Vietnam; from Dietrich, 1963). (By permission of Interscience Publishers, N.Y.)

one another, at least the solar cancels some of the stronger lunar effect, and we have a *neap tide*. (There is a common tendency among beginners to think of spring tides as occurring in the spring: this is completely false, for the term comes from the concept to spring or jump higher.) A secondary modification occurs when the moon is closest to the earth, giving the maximum "*perigee spring tides*" and when farthest away the minimal or *apogee* condition.

In the equilibrium tide, for both the lunar and solar forces, there are three "species of constituents": long-period, diurnal and semidiurnal. The *long-period tide* is a partial tide, symmetrical about the earth's axis, independent of longitude. It varies with the slow change of the lunar declination and

distance from the earth (information available for any period in the Nautical Almanac or Ephemeris).

Secondly, there is the *diurnal tide*, called a partial tide because it has two maxima, respectively, at 45°N and S on opposite sides of the earth, with symmetrical minima. It appears to rotate westward with respect to the earth (which is turning toward the east), in any one spot oscillating once per lunar day. Because of its symmetry, the diurnal tide becomes zero at the time when the moon's orbit curves over the equator; its value is also always zero at the poles and the equator.

Thirdly, the *semidiurnal tide* must be noted. Likewise a partial tide, it has at any time two maxima antipodally on the equator, with two intermediate equatorial minima. It also revolves westward with the lunar day, but any one spot experiences two cycles per day.

The first "almost" harmonic tidal analysis was developed by George Darwin in 1882, who allocated a series of symbols for each tidal component, with a subscript 0, 1 or 2 to indicate whether it was long-period, diurnal or semidiurnal. Because of the 12 hour/24 hour relationship, the lunar semidiurnal constituent develops a beat frequency, modulating the other cycles, leading to the spring-neap relationship; other constituents also develop similar modulations.

Tides in the Ocean. While the equilibrium tide concept spells out an ideal condition, the actual observed tides in the ocean vary considerably from the ideal. First of all, oceanic basins develop free oscillations characteristic of their respective shapes. Ordinary gravity *seiches* (q.v.) have periods up to large fractions of the day, while others, *planetary modes* have periods of several days. Furthermore, to complicate the picture, there are "meteorologic tides," rises and falls of sea level that reflect the passage of high- and low-pressure systems unrelated to celestial mechanics; since these may have amplitudes sometimes exceeding the planetary tides, in areas of low tidal range, the meteorologic effect may often mask or reduce the predicted tide. Since atmospheric pressure tends to be higher at night, on some mid-oceanic coral islands, it may contribute to the planetary tide, thus normally a low tide at night or in the early morning and a high tide after midday.

In different parts of the globe, as indicated on Fig. 3 the semidiurnal tide is dominant (e.g., Immingham, Fig. 8). In certain areas the diurnal tide is almost exclusively represented (e.g., Do-Son, Fig. 8). Elsewhere, the tides are *mixed*, with one or the other components predominant (e.g., San Francisco and Manila).

Worldwide charts of tidal conditions are constructed for each component as well as for the sum of the components. Often only the M_2 (the principal lunar semidiurnal tide) is given. Two types of chart are often combined: the *cotidal* chart, giving the *time* of maximum of each tidal wave, lines being marked 0–12 (often in Roman figures), and 0 being set at the time of the moon's passage through Greenwich; secondly there is the co-range chart, which joins points of equal vertical range. It is found that at certain points, *amphidromic points* (q.v.), the range is zero and the cotidal lines swing around these points, as might be predicted from a consideration of the earth's rotation and the Coriolis force (q.v.).

In the open ocean positions, measured at isolated island stations, the range most closely approximates the theoretical equilibrium tide, but in the narrow seas, in estuaries and within broad continental shelves considerable amplification of the range may

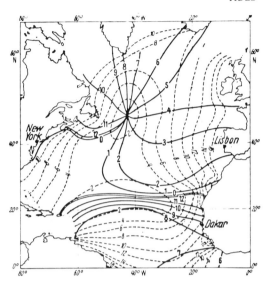

Fig. 9. Co-tidal lines and lines of equal tidal range of the principal lunar tide M_2 in the North Atlantic Ocean (according to W. Hansen, 1952; from Dietrich, 1963). Solid lines: time differences of high waters from the moon's passage through the meridian of Greenwich, in hours. Broken lines: tidal range of the M_2 tide in decimeters. (By permission of Interscience Publishers, N.Y.)

be expected. This is for two reasons: (a) as the tidal wave enters shallow water or funnel-shaped channels, the range rises approximately inversely to the fourth root of the water depth and square root of the width; (b) as the free period of the water mass approaches the period of the tide, resonance occurs. World ranges therefore vary by amounts up to two orders of magnitude (20 cm–20 m). (Details of local station ranges may be found in many of the Encyclopedia entries devoted to specific oceans and seas.)

Tidal Friction. It has been calculated by Sir Harold Jeffreys that some half of the total tidal energy is dissipated each day, mainly by friction along the bottom of shallow seas, such as the shallow part of the Bering Sea. Theoretically this friction should gradually slow the earth's rotation, but to conserve angular momentum of the earth–moon pair, the moon should slowly recede and accelerate over the course of geological time. There is some evidence (from coral daily growth rings) that 400 million years ago the days of the year numbered over 400; there is also some astronomical evidence pointing in the same direction.

Other Tidal Effects. Tides in the upper atmosphere are now recognized (in the order of 1 km and more) and are treated elsewhere (in Vol. II). Tides of the solid earth (body tides) are also subject to modern studies, although mostly limited to a few centimeters (see *Geophysics* volume).

TABLE 1. STATIONS WITH SEMIDIURNAL TIDES (from Bauer, 1933: Am. Geogr. Soc.)

Type Index and Mean Spring Range (in feet)

Station and Region	Latitude	Longitude	Index	Range
Teplitz Bay, Franz Josef Land	81 47 N	57 59 E	0.22	1.6
Virgo Bay, Spitsbergen	79 43 N	10 52 E	0.08	3.5
Melville Island, Canadian Arctic	74 47 N	111 00 W	0.17	3.8
Kingua Fiord, Baffin Island	66 36 N	67 20 W	0.04	20.4
Godthaab, Davis Strait	64 12 N	51 44 W	0.17	12.5
Nottingham Island, Hudson Strait	63 12 N	77 28 W	0.07	13.5
Ashe Inlet, Hudson Strait	62 33 N	70 35 W	0.05	30.0
Kem, White Sea	64 59 N	34 50 E	0.05	5.0
Vardö, Norway	70 22 N	31 07 E	0.11	9.0
Discovery Harbor, Robeson Channel	81 04 N	64 44 W	0.13	
Jay Mayen Island, Greenland Sea	71 00 N	8 28 W	0.17	3.6
Port Burwell, Ungava Bay	60 25 N	64 46 W	0.07	36.0
Frederikshaab, Greenland	61 59 N	49 44 W	0.22	9.0
Bergen, Norway	60 24 N	5 18 E	0.11	4.1
Quebec, Canada	46 49 N	71 11 W	0.19	14.6
St. Johns, Newfoundland	47 34 N	52 41 W	0.21	3.3
Halifax, Nova Scotia	44 39 N	63 35 W	0.20	5.2
St. John, New Brunswick	45 16 N	66 03 W	0.08	23.9
Boston, Mass.	42 21 N	71 03 W	0.16	11.0
Sandy Hook, N.J.	40 27 N	74 00 W	0.16	5.6
Philadelphia, Pa.	39 56 N	75 09 W	0.22	6.2
Savannah, Ga.	32 05 N	81 02 W	0.15	7.6
Fernandina, Fla.	30 41 N	81 28 W	0.18	6.9
Cayenne, French Guiana	4 56 N	52 20 W	0.16	6.0
Georgetown, British Guiana	6 49 N	58 10 W	0.17	7.8
Ceará, Brazil	3 41 S	38 34 W	0.07	8.2
Pernambuco, Brazil	8 04 S	34 53 W	0.09	7.0
Puerto Madryn, Argentina	42 46 S	65 01 W	0.08	13.2
Comodoro Rivadavia, Argentina	45 52 S	67 29 W	0.12	16.4
Puerto San Julian, Argentina	49 15 S	67 41 W	0.13	29.4
Puerto Gallegos, Argentina	51 37 S	69 00 W	0.10	45.6
Cape Town, South Africa	33 54 S	18 25 E	0.10	4.6
Pointe Noire, Congo (Braz.)	4 55 S	11 50 E	0.08	4.8
Duala, Cameroon	4 03 N	9 40 E	0.18	6.5
Carabane, Senegal	12 33 N	16 40 W	0.07	3.9
Dakar, Senegal	14 40 N	17 25 W	0.16	4.6
Port Étienne, Mauritania	20 55 N	17 02 W	0.07	5.5
Casablanca, Morocco	33 36 N	7 37 W	0.10	9.2
Lisbon, Portugal	38 41 N	9 06 W	0.07	12.0
Fort Socoa, France	43 24 N	1 40 W	0.07	12.2
Brest, France	48 23 N	4 29 W	0.05	19.5
Cherbourg, France	49 39 N	1 37 W	0.06	17.0
Dover, England	51 07 N	1 19 E	0.04	18.0
Liverpool, England	53 24 N	3 00 W	0.06	29.0
Hull, England	53 44 N	0 20 W	0.10	21.0
Heligoland, Germany	54 11 N	7 53 E	0.12	8.0
Roter Sand, Weser, Germany	53 51 N	8 05 E	0.10	13.0
Suez, Red Sea	29 56 N	32 33 E	0.09	7.0
False Point, India	20 25 N	86 47 E	0.18	6.8
Dublat, Hooghly River, India	21 38 N	88 6 E	0.10	11.2
Akyab, Burma	20 8 N	92 54 E	0.17	7.6
Rangoon, Burma	16 46 N	96 10 E	0.13	19.0
Mergui, Burma	12 26 N	98 36 E	0.09	18.0
Port Blair, Andaman Island	11 41 N	92 45 E	0.19	6.3
Comoro Islands, Indian Ocean	12 47 S	45 17 E	0.16	10.8
Majunga, Madagascar	15 50 S	46 21 E	0.11	10.9
Tamatave, Madagascar	18 08 S	49 26 E	0.16	7.3
Durban, Natal	29 53 S	31 04 E	0.17	5.6
Betsy Cove, Kerguelen Island	49 09 S	70 12 E	0.16	4.6
Port Chalmers, New Zealand	45 50 S	170 42 E	0.06	5.8
Westport, New Zealand	41 46 S	171 37 E	0.04	9.5

TABLE 1—*continued*

Station and Region	Latitude	Longitude	Index	Range
Port Russell, New Zealand	35 16 S	174 18 E	0.08	9.0
Wellington, New Zealand	41 17 S	174 47 E	0.11	3.6
Port Hedland, Western Australia	20 22 S	118 36 E	0.15	17.0
Apia, Samoa	13 46 S	171 44 E	0.11	3.1
Gambier Island, Tuamotu Archipelago	23 07 S	134 57 W	0.09	2.4
Pingyang, Korea	38 38 N	125 36 E	0.25	16.0
Jinsen, Korea	37 29 N	126 37 E	0.11	28.8
Panama (Naos Island), Panama	8 55 N	79 32 W	0.08	16.0
Amoy, China	24 23 N	118 10 E	0.20	15.5

TABLE 2. STATIONS WITH DIURNAL TIDES (from Bauer, 1933: Am. Geogr. Soc.)

Type Index and Mean Spring Range (in feet)

Station and Region	Latitude	Longitude	Index	Range
Pensacola, Fla.	30 21 N	87 16 W	9.11	1.5
Mobile Point (Fort Morgan), Ala.	30 14 N	88 01 W	6.82	2.1
Cat Island, Miss.	30 14 N	89 10 W	5.26	1.7
Galveston, Tex.	29 19 N	94 48 W	2.62	1.5
Tampico, Mexico	22 16 N	97 49 W	5.9	1.3
Campeche, Mexico	19 50 N	90 32 W	1.55	2.1
Vera Cruz, Mexico	19 12 N	96 08 W	4.5	2.4
Cristobal, Panama Canal	9 21 N	79 55 W	1.9	1.1
St. Thomas, Virgin Islands	18 20 N	64 56 W	3.6	1.2
Ponce, Puerto Rico	17 59 N	66 40 W	8.4	1.0
Manila, Philippine Islands	14 36 N	120 57 E	2.7	4.6
Do-Son, North Vietnam	20 42 N	106 46 E	2.0	7.6
Quin Hone, South Vietnam	13 45 N	109 15 E	2.5	4.8
Koh Hlack, Siam (Thailand)	11 48 N	99 49 E	13.3	5.6
Haifong, North Vietnam	20 52 N	106 39 E	17.5	4.3
Tandjong Buton, Linga Island	0 12 S	104 36 E	3.4	7.0
Tandjong Kalean, Banka Strait	2 00 S	105 06 E	4.0	8.8
Pontianak, Borneo	0 00	109 18 E	3.4	3.8
Soekadana, Borneo	1 14 S	109 58 E	4.9	6.4
Pulo Begar, Banka Strait	2 54 S	106 07 E	3.5	7.1
Ondiepwater Island, Billiton I.	3 18 S	107 11 E	5.4	5.5
Thousand Island (Duizend I.)	5 36 S	106 20 E	5.5	2.5
Edam Island, Java Sea	6 00 S	106 48 E	3.0	2.2
Tandjong Priok, Java Sea	6 06 S	106 54 E	3.7	2.6
Karimondjawa Island, Java Sea	5 54 S	110 24 E	3.8	1.8
Samarang, Java	7 00 S	110 24 E	2.8	4.0
Bawean Island, Java Sea	5 52 S	112 39 E	8.1	5.2
Sembilangan, Soerabaya Strait	7 05 S	112 42 E	2.1	3.0
Macassar, Celebes	5 08 S	119 25 E	2.3	3.9
Wakanai, Japan	45 25 N	141 40 E	2.5	0.8
Suttsu, Japan	42 47 N	140 16 E	1.41	0.6
Fukaura, Japan	40 41 N	139 59 E	1.32	1.2
Kamo, Japan	38 48 N	139 48 E	1.48	1.2
Maizuru, Japan	35 27 N	135 19 E	1.27	0.8
Toko, Taiwan	22 28 N	120 27 E	1.4	4.0
Finsch Harbor, New Guinea	6 35 S	147 50 E	1.9	5.0
Fremantle, Western Australia	32 03 S	115 45 E	3.36	2.1
King George Sound, Western Australia	35 08 S	118 00 E	2.48	2.6
Port Dalrymple, Tasmania	41 03 S	146 47 E	. . . .	9.0
Langr Island, Gulf of Amur	53 19 N	141 26 E	2.2	6.0
Unalga Bay, Alaska	54 00 N	166 12 W	2.5	2.9
St. Michael, Alaska	63 29 N	162 02 W	3.47	4.5
Seymour Narrows, British Columbia	50 08 N	125 23 W	1.3	8.0
Victoria, British Columbia	48 25 N	123 24 W	2.1	5.7
Rio Grande do Sul, Brazil	32 07 S	52 04 W	1.77	1.8
Ratan, Gulf of Bothnia	64 00 N	20 55 E	6.0	1.0
Suakin, Red Sea	19 07 N	37 19 E	. . . .	1.7

TABLE 3. STATIONS WITH MIXED TIDES (from Bauer, 1933: Am. Geogr. Soc.)

Type Index and Mean Spring Range (in feet)

Station and Region	Latitude	Longitude	Index	Range
Baltimore, Md. (Ft. McHenry)	39 16 N	76 35 W	0.42	1.4
Wilmington, N.C.	34 14 N	77 57 W	0.33	3.0
Nassau, Bahama Islands	25 05 N	77 21 W	0.34	4.0
Rio de Janeiro, Brazil	22 54 S	43 10 W	0.40	4.2
Montevideo, Uruguay	34 53 S	56 12 W	0.3	3.5
Buenos Aires, Argentina	34 36 S	58 22 W	0.71	2.1
Mar del Plata, Argentina	38 05 S	57 32 W	0.7	4.0
Port Louis, Falkland Islands	51 29 S	58 00 W	0.4	4.3
Hermite Island, Cape Horn	55 51 S	67 33 W	0.43	4.8
Valparaiso, Chile	33 02 S	71 38 W	0.44	3.9
Mazatlan, Mexico	23 11 N	106 27 W	0.6	3.8
Magdalena Bay, Mexico	24 38 N	112 09 W	0.52	5.5
Dan Diego, Cal.	32 42 N	117 14 W	0.41	5.1
Sausalito, Cal.	37 50 N	122 29 W	1.0	6.0
Astoria, Ore.	46 11 N	123 50 W	0.56	7.8
Clayoquot, Vancouver Island	49 09 N	125 55 W	0.51	8.5
Seattle, Wash.	47 37 N	122 20 W	0.96	9.2
Sitka, Alaska	57 03 N	135 20 W	0.51	9.9
Granite Cove, Alaska	58 12 N	136 24 W	0.44	10.8
Kokinhenic Island, Alaska	60 18 N	145 03 W	0.53	5.0
Kodiak Island, Alaska	57 47 N	152 24 W	0.52	9.0
Sanak-Peterson, Alaska	54 24 N	162 38 W	0.8	5.7
Point Barrow, Alaska	71 18 N	156 40 W	0.47	0.6
Flaxman Island, Alaska	70 11 N	145 50 W	0.7	1.0
Port Clarence, Alaska	65 13 N	166 24 W	0.74	1.1
Taraku Sima, Japan	43 38 N	146 20 E	0.94	2.5
Atsukeshi, Japan	43 02 N	144 51 E	0.9	2.7
Ohatake, Japan	41 25 N	141 10 E	0.85	2.6
Hirataka, Japan	36 51 N	140 48 E	0.88	3.0
Yokohama, Japan	35 27 N	139 38 E	1.09	4.9
Shimoda, Japan	34 40 N	138 57 E	0.76	3.6
Hamashima, Japan	34 18 N	136 45 E	0.54	4.8
Susaki, Japan	33 23 N	133 17 E	0.52	5.0
Yamakawa, Japan	31 12 N	130 38 E	0.43	9.5
Nagasaki, Japan	32 44 N	129 51 E	0.35	8.4
Tamsui, Taiwan	25 11 N	121 24 E	0.3	8.8
Naka, Okinawa I.	26 23 N	127 40 E	0.43	4.0
So-o, Taiwan	24 35 N	121 52 E	0.54	5.8
Miyakoshima, Ryukyu Archipelago	24 48 N	125 18 E	0.45	4.9
Taketomishima, Ryukyu Archipelago	24 09 N	124 05 E	0.56	4.6
Tsushima Sound, Chosen	34 17 N	129 21 E	0.32	6.7
Weihaiwei, China	37 29 N	122 13 E	0.51	9.0
Taku, China	38 58 N	117 43 E	0.57	4.5
Hongkong, China	22 18 N	114 10 E	1.0	5.1
Padang, Sumatra (Emma Haven)	1 00 S	100 18 E	0.41	5.5
Soerabaya, Java	7 06 S	112 42 E	1.05	4.9
Bajoewangi, Bali Strait	8 11 S	114 25 E	0.5	7.8
Tjilatjap, Java	7 42 S	109 00 E	0.42	5.0
Koepang, Timor Island	10 12 S	123 35 E	0.58	4.9
Swatow, China	23 23 N	116 39 E	1.0	7.5
Singapore, Malaya	1 17 N	103 51 E	0.52	8.0
Madras, India	13 05 N	80 17 E	0.3	3.1
Trincomali, Ceylon	8 33 N	81 13 E	0.35	2.0
Colombo, Ceylon	6 56 N	79 51 E	0.32	2.0
Cochin, India	9 58 N	76 15 E	0.91	2.1
Minikoy, Laccadive I.	8 17 N	73 18 E	0.85	2.5
Goa, India	15 25 N	73 48 E	0.63	5.2
Bombay, India	18 57 N	72 50 E	0.36	12.0
Karachi, Pakistan	24 47 N	66 58 E	0.56	7.3
Masqat, Arabia	23 37 N	58 35 E	0.67	6.0
Abu Shar, Persian Gulf	28 59 N	50 51 E	1.14	2.6

TABLE 3—*continued*

Station and Region	Latitude	Longitude	Index	Range
Aden, Arabia	12 47 N	44 59 E	0.86	4.9
Djibuti, French Somaliland	11 35 N	43 08 E	0.8	5.5
Port Louis, Mauritius Island	20 08 S	57 29 E	0.5	1.6
Reunion Island, Indian Ocean	21 16 S	55 35 E	0.37	3.5
Port Darwin, North Australia	12 23 S	130 37 E	0.31	16.8
Brisbane, Queensland	27 20 S	153 10 E	0.33	6.4
Sydney, New South Wales	33 52 S	151 12 E	0.37	4.2
Melbourne, Victoria	37 52 S	144 54 E	0.39	2.8
Port Adelaide, South Australia	34 51 S	138 30 E	0.39	6.3
Honolulu, Hawaii	21 18 N	157 52 W	1.09	1.5
Thorshavn, Faeroes I.	62 02 N	6 43 W	0.73	4.6
Beechy Island, Barrow Strait	74 43 N	92 00 W	0.52	5.8
Scoresby Sound, East Greenland	71 30 N	24 30 W	0.35	3.5
Tigil, Okhotsk Sea	58 00 N	158 12 E	....	7.3

State of the Art: Some Questions to be Answered

Continents, mid-ocean ridges, undersea mountain ranges and fault scarps produce a variety of partially connected ocean basins. Theoretical models that can accommodate these features are currently under development. The difficulty has been that the computing time has been prohibitive, if one wished to evaluate a dynamic model for realistic conditions. The computing machines afford some relief from this limitation. Also, some measurements of tidal elevations in the open ocean have now been made off San Diego and in the North Sea. As the severe technical difficulties of making these measurements are gradually overcome, we may hope to discover what tidal "waves" really look like and how the water moves relative to the sea floor beneath. These discoveries in turn may make it possible to evaluate the effects of friction. Not until then will we be able to speculate intelligently about tides in the future, or tides in the quite-different seas of the earth's past.

JUNE G. PATTULLO

References

Bascom, W., 1964, "Waves and Beaches," New York, Doubleday, Anshore, 267pp.

Bauer, H. A., 1933, "World map of tides," *Geogr. Rev.*, **23**, 259–270.

Defant, A., 1958, "Ebb and Flow," Ann Arbor, University of Michigan Press (semi-popular) (translated by A. J. Pomerans).

Defant, A., 1961, "Physical Oceanography," Vols. 1 and 2, New York, Pergamon Press.

Dietrich, G., 1963, "General Oceanography," New York, Interscience Publishers.

Doodson, A. T., and Warburg, H. D., 1941, "Admiralty Manual of Tides," London, H.M. Stationery Office.

Guilcher, A., 1965, "Précis d'Hydrologie Marine et Continentale," Paris, Masson & Cie, 389pp.

Hansen, W., 1962, "Tides," in (Hill, M. N., editor) "The Sea," Vol. I, No. 23, pp. 764–801 (many references), New York, Interscience Publishers.

Macdonald, G. J. F., 1964, "Tidal friction," *Rev. Geophys.*, **2**(3), 467–541.

Schureman, P., 1941, "A manual of harmonic analysis and prediction of tides," *U.S. Coast and Geodetic Survey*, *Sp. Publ.* 98.

Snodgrass, F. E., 1964, "Precision digital tide gauge," *Science*, **146**, 198–208.

Cross-references: *Amphidromic Point; Coriolis Force; Mean Sea Level; Ocean Currents; Waves.* Vol. II: *Celestial Mechanics; Climatic Variation; Cycles and Periodicities; Oscillation; Sunspot Cycle.*

TIMOR SEA

(1) Limits and Morphology

The Timor Sea covers approximately 450,000 km² between the island of Timor and the northwest coast of Australia, between Cape Don, at 131° 46′E longitude, and Cape Londonderry. According to the International Hydrographic Bureau (Sp. Publ. 23, 1953), the Timor Sea borders on the Arafura Sea in the east (a line joining Selaru I. and Cape Don), and on the Indian Ocean in the west (a line joining Roti I. and Cape Londonderry). Two morphological provinces can be distinguished: the Timor Trough in the northwest and the Sahul Shelf in the southeast (Fig. 1).

The *Timor Trough* is an elongate basin with an area of approximately 30,000 km² and a maximum depth of 3200 meters. The trough is closed at the southwestern end by a sill at approximately 1800 meters and is separated from the Aru depression to the east by a sill at 1400 meters. The trough, which forms part of van Bemmelen's (1949) Sunda Foredeep, is structurally complex. It consists of several basins along the axis that are separated by low sills and a number of fairly large perched basins on the northern slope. The southeastern slope up to the edge of the Sahul Shelf is gentle, even, and apparently depositional; the northwestern slope is steep, rocky, and highly irregular (Fig. 2).

The topography of the *Sahul Shelf* differs markedly from the flat, gently seaward-sloping

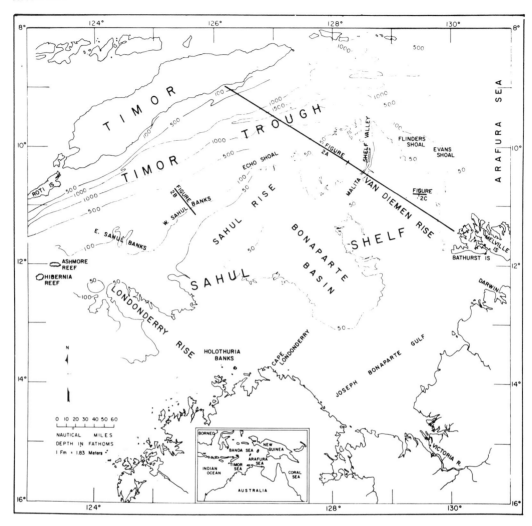

Fig. 1. The Timor Sea including the Sahul Shelf. General morphology and place names.

plain that characterizes most continental shelves. The Sahul Shelf contains a large central depression, the Bonaparte Basin, which has a maximum depth of 140 meters and is surrounded by broad rises with crests at 20–50 meters (Fairbridge, 1953). A long, narrow valley, with a maximum depth of 200 meters, connects the basin with the Timor Trough. Superimposed on this regional relief is a complex system of flat-topped banks, terraces, and deep, narrow channels. This bank and channel relief is strikingly similar to the system of subaerial erosion plains developed on the adjacent land since the late Cretaceous (Wright, 1963). Van Andel (1965) has concluded that the entire Sahul Shelf was above water and shared the erosional history of northwestern Australia until relatively late in the Pleistocene, and that little marine sedimentation has taken place on the shelf since that time.

The northwestern edge of the Sahul Shelf consists of a gradual change in slope at 110–130 meters, generally marked by a low cliff. Just beyond the shelf edge, numerous steep-sided banks rise on the upper continental slope from depths of 200–350 meters (Fig. 2). All of the banks have flat tops ranging from 20–25 meters. Beyond this string of banks, the continental shelf is generally smooth. Along the western margin there is no clearly defined shallow shelf edge; the outer shelf slopes gently seaward to a maximum depth of probably about 600 meters. Numerous banks and some atolls rise from this outer shelf (Fairbridge, 1953).

(2) Climate and Oceanography

The Timor Sea lies in the area of the shifting boundary between the southeast trade winds and the monsoon. The monsoon blows from the south-

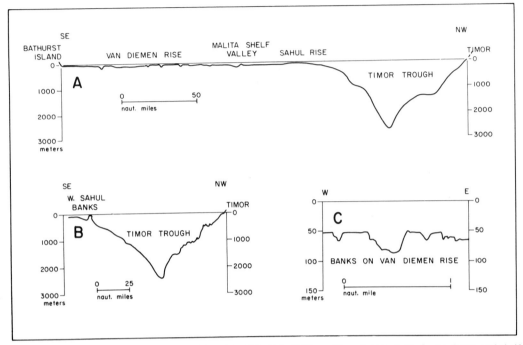

Fig. 2. The Timor Sea. Topographic profiles of the Sahul Shelf–Timor Trough (A), shelf edge bank (B), and shelf banks and channels (C). Locations on Fig. 1.

east from April to November and from the northwest from December to March. From April to November, monsoon and trade winds augment each other. Variable winds due to interaction between the trade and monsoon occur during a rainy season from December to March. From December to April, tropical cyclones are not uncommon.

Most of the present knowledge of the oceanography of the Timor Sea is based on scattered observations made since the early 1800's. Only a few oceanographic expeditions have touched the area, the most important of which was the Snellius Expedition (van Riel, 1950). The latest summary has been presented by Wyrtki (1961).

Surface Currents. A southwestward current (Timor current) of generally low velocity (0.5–1.0 knot) prevails throughout the year. The axis of the current runs close to the coast of Timor. From April to September, this current reaches close to the Australian coast, although at reduced velocity. From October to March, southwesterly winds create a weak current toward the northeast off the Australian coast. The Timor current is supplied by water from the Arafura and Banda Seas only during the time of full development of the southeast monsoon. The current transports westward between 1.0 and 1.5×10^6 m³/sec of water all year.

Temperature and Salinity. Temperature and salinity vary little throughout the year. Highest temperatures observed in April 1961 were 31.3°C

in the Bonaparte Gulf and 28.7°C near the southeast coast of Timor. The minimum mean monthly temperature for August in the Bonaparte Gulf is 23°C; the maximum exceeds 29°C from November to February. Surface salinities range from 34.7–34.5‰.

Structure. Over much of the Sahul Shelf, the water is well mixed down to the bottom, but in the deeper portions a colder water mass, which is lower in oxygen, is found below 40 meters. Deep Indian Ocean water enters the Timor Trough from the southwest over the sill. The temperature minimum in the trough lies only a little below that of the sill depth, and the oxygen content is relatively high. An oxygen minimum of approximately 2 ml/liter occurs from approximately 500–1200 meters. Below the sill depth, the water is isothermal and constant in oxygen content.

Tides. The semidiurnal tides of the Indian Ocean prevail in the Timor Sea. The tidal amplitude reaches more than 200 cm over large parts of the shelf and a maximum of 900 cm in Queens Channel. The range at Darwin is 600 cm. Strong currents are generated by these tides in the estuaries (up to 7 knots in Victoria River estuary). Tidal wave refraction over the shelf causes generally northwesterly, southeasterly currents, respectively.

(3) Sediments

Sediments of the Timor Sea, particularly those of the Sahul Shelf, are highly calcareous. In a general way, there is an inverse relation between grain size and carbonate. The sands and coarser deposits are almost entirely composed of carbonate particles except for patches of quartz sand near the Australian coast, whereas the clays and silty clays are fairly low in carbonate.

On the Sahul Shelf, fine-grained deposits, containing 25–50% of carbonate mostly in the form of skeletal debris, are restricted to the deeper portions of the Bonaparte Basin and to the numerous estuaries. The rises, the outer shelf, the banks, and the littoral zone are covered with coarser deposits ranging in size from sand upward. These deposits predominantly consist of Foraminifera, calcareous algae, coral and shell debris, and an abundance of Bryozoa. The latter distinguish the Sahul Shelf sediments from most other calcareous shelf sediments of the world. Characteristic sediments rich in the coralline alga Halimeda are found on the shelf edge banks, and coarse deposits largely composed of large Foraminifera and biscuits of calcareous algae cover the shallower bank tops on the rises. Nonskeletal carbonates such as oolites and grapestone, so characteristic of the deposits of the Bahamas, are conspicuously absent. Glauconite is widespread in the coarser shelf deposits in depths not exceeding 100 meters, and much of the skeletal material is partially glauconitized. Many of these sediments probably are relicts from lower Pleistocene sea level sands.

The Timor Trough sediments are generally silty clays, occasionally interbedded with calcareous sands consisting mainly of planktonic Foraminifera. The carbonate content of the silty clays decreases from more than 50% near the edge of the Sahul Shelf to less than 25% near the coast of Timor.

Over most of the Sahul Shelf the thickness of the marine sediments probably is small. Recent sediments in excess of 15 meters have been demonstrated only in the deeper parts of the Bonaparte Basin. Thick modern deposits also may occur in the Joseph Bonaparte Gulf. On the other hand, the Timor Trough, especially the southeastern slope, probably has been a major zone of sedimentation for a very long time.

(4) Geophysics and Structural Geology

The Timor Trough lies in the marginal zone of the belt of important negative gravity anomaly discovered by Vening Meinesz across Timor, the outer Banda Arc, Ceram, and Buru (Fig. 3). Below the Timor Sea proper, only shallow earthquakes are known. Faulting is clearly indicated along the northwestern slope of the Timor Trough; along the Sahul Shelf slope, thick sediments cover the underlying structure, but locally stronger relief indicates fault scarps. A wide zone of positive gravity anomaly over the outer Sahul Shelf and southeastern continental slope suggests a shallow base-

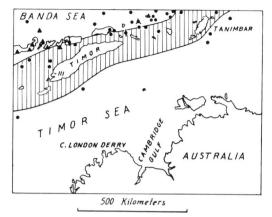

Fig. 3. The Timor Sea. Gravimetry (shaded areas indicate the belt of negative anomalies), earthquake foci (dots: less than 100 km focal depth; triangles: more than 100 km).

ment, deepening steeply toward the axis of the Timor Trough and much more gradually toward the Australian coast.

The shelf edge banks along the Sahul Shelf margin have been explained as a fringe of marginal reefs forming in shallow water and slowly growing up as the Timor Trough; later the Sahul Shelf itself subsided (Fairbridge, 1953).

Kuenen (1950), on the basis of the gravity anomaly and the position in the Indonesian orthogeosynclinal system, has classified the Timor Trough as a marginal deep. Its age is uncertain but probably no more than late Tertiary; the tectonic movements responsible for its existence probably are still active. Evidence for this young age consists of: (1) the parallelism of the trough with the late-Tertiary geanticlinal Banda arcs; (2) parallelism with the present belt of negative gravity anomalies; (3) the presence of raised Plio-Pleistocene coral reefs, which on Timor attain heights of 1283 meters; and (4) the morphological and coral atoll evidence for a recent submergence of the Sahul Shelf after a long history of continental erosion.

Tj. H. van Andel
H. D. Tjia

References

Fairbridge, R. W., 1953, "The Sahul Shelf, Northern Australia: its structure and geological relationships," *J. Roy. Soc. W. Australia*, v. 37, p. 1–33.

Kuenen, Ph. H., 1950, "Marine Geology," Ch. 3, pp. 175–209, New York, John Wiley & Sons, Inc.

Van Andel, Tj. H., Veevers, J. J., 1965, "Submarine morphology of the Sahul Shelf; Northwestern Australia," *Bull. Geol. Soc. Am.*, **76**, pp. 695–700.

Van Bemmelen, R. W., 1949, "The Geology of Indonesia," Vol. Ia, pp. 472–479, 510–530, Govt. Printing Off., The Hague.

Van Riel, P. M., Hamaker, H. C., and Van Eyck, L., 1950, "The Snellius Expedition," Tables, serial and bottom observations, Vol. 2, Pt. 6, pp. 1–44, Leiden, Brill.

Wright, R. L., 1963, "Deep Weathering and Erosion Surfaces in the Daly River Basin, Northern Territory," *J. Geol. Soc. Australia*, **10**(1), 151–163.

Wyrtki, K., 1961, "Physical Oceanography of the Southeast Asian waters," *Reports Naga Expedition*, **2**, Scripps Institution of Oceanography, La Jolla, Cal.

Cross-references: *Arafura Sea; Banda Sea; Sahul Shelf.*

TRANSPARENCY

Transparency is a general term—without strict definition—used to indicate the optical purity of seawater (see *Optical Oceanography*). Transparency is dependent on the amount of suspended matter and dissolved light-absorbing substances, in particular, yellow substance.

Transparency is roughly measured by means of a *Secchi disk*, which is a circular white disk, 43–237 cm in diameter. The disk is lowered in the water, and the depth at which it disappears from sight is observed. A crude determination of color is obtained by comparing the apparent color of the water observed against the white disk with prepared solutions according to the Forel-Ule scale (Table 1) which comprises 22 different colors. The comparison should be made in shadow without disturbing reflections.

The use of the disk method was first introduced by Secchi on the 1865 cruise of the *Immacolata Concezione* in the Mediterranean (Cialdi, 1866). Secchi disk readings are generally made in pairs, with an average taken of the two readings (usually in centimeters or meters). There is relatively little difference in the readings according to the size of

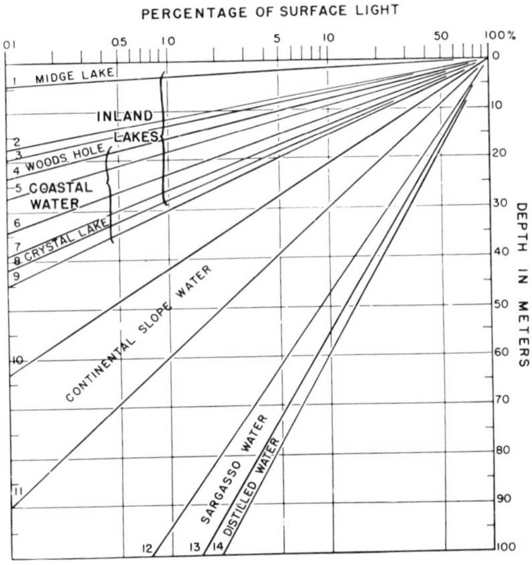

Fig. 1. Light penetration in different water types.

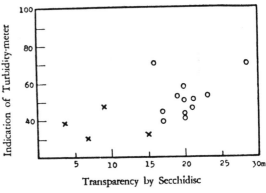

Tsugaru Strait, 0   Ishikari Bay ×

Fig. 2. Relationship between the transparency observed by Secchi disk and the indication of turbidity meter (Inoue *et al.*, 1957).

TABLE 1. THE FOREL-ULE COLOR SCALE

Solution[a]	I	II	III	IV	V	VI	VII	VIII	IX	X
1	100	98	95	91	86	80	73	65	56	46
2	0	2	5	9	14	20	27	35	44	54
3	0	0	0	0	0	0	0	0	0	0
	Blue		Greenish blue		Bluish green			Green		

Solution[a]	XI	XII	XIII	XIV	XV	XVI	XVII	XVIII	XIX	XX	XXI	XXII
1	35	35	35	35	35	35	35	35	35	35	35	35
2	65	60	55	50	45	40	35	30	25	20	15	10
3	0	5	10	15	20	25	30	35	40	45	50	55
Color	Greenish yellow					Yellow				Brown		

[a] Solution 1 = 0.5 g $CuSO_4 \cdot 5H_2O$ + 5 ml strong NH_4OH + to 100 ml H_2O.
2 = 0.5 g $K_2CrO_4 \cdot 5H_2O$ + 5 ml strong NH_4OH + to 100 ml H_2O.
3 = 0.5 g $CoSO_4 \cdot 7H_2O$ + 5 ml strong NH_4OH + to 100 ml H_2O.

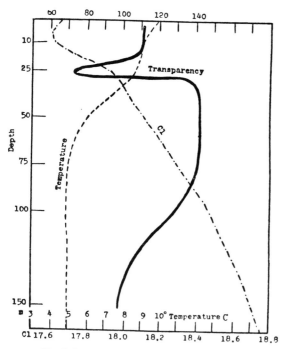

Fig. 3. Vertical distribution of transparency observed in the North Pacific (53–40°N, 163–31°W). (Inoue *et al.*, 1957.)

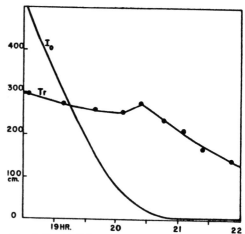

Fig. 4. Secchi disk transparency, *Tr*, at various times during the late afternoon and evening, Lake Straken, Sweden, July 27, 1936. The light intensity, I_0, at the surface is plotted on an arbitrary scale, but at 21.31 hours is 11×10^{-5} of the value at 18.45 hours (after Åberg and Rodhe).

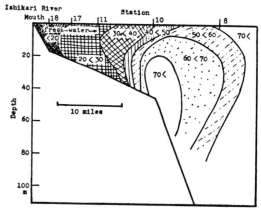

Fig. 5(a) Vertical distribution of transparency at Ishikari Bay (Inoue *et al.*, 1957).

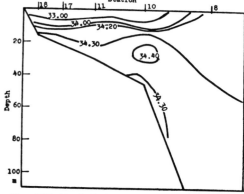

Fig. 5(b) Vertical distribution of the salinity at Ishikawa Bay (Inoue *et al.*, 1957).

the disk, within the dimensions noted above, but Juday and Birge (1933) regularly used a 10-cm disk with satisfactory results. Åberg and Rodhe (1942) have found that a disk painted in black and white quadrants gives a rather sharper reading. Turbidity meters and transparency meters of various sorts give appreciably greater readings and to far greater depths. Of great interest in Fig. 3 is the return to high transparency beyond the layer of maximum plankton. In Dietrich (1963), Fig. 63 shows by simultaneous echo sounding that this planktonic horizon is in fact a *deep scattering layer* (q.v.). A review of transparency instruments was given by Jerlov (1965). (For one described by Inoue *et al.*, 1957, see Figs. 2 and 3.)

In shallow water, light reflected from the bottom may introduce some error, since one is actually comparing the disk brightness against the brightness of the surrounding water. Corrections can be made (see Sauberer, 1939; Hutchinson, 1959). Evening operations, with diminishing incident light, show a steady drop of visibility over the twilight hours, as may be expected (see Fig. 4).

Causes of lack of transparency, apart from reduction of incident light, are manifold. Mud in suspension and plankton are the principal causes. Figures 5(a) and 5(b) show partial correlation between transparency and salinity (Inoue *et al.*, 1957), the latter probably controlling the flocculation and fallout of suspended clay as well as reflecting the inflow of open-seawater into a freshwater-fed bay.

For more sophisticated measurement techniques and discussion, see *Optical Oceanography*.

C. D. AHLQUIST
R. W. FAIRBRIDGE
G. KULLENBERG

References

Cialdi, A., 1866, "Sul Moto Ondoso del Mare," Second ed., Rome, 693pp.

Collet, L. W., 1925, "Les Lacs. Leur Mode de Formation, leurs Eaux, leur Destin," Paris, Gaston Doin, 320pp.

Dietrich, G., 1963, "General Oceanography," New York, Interscience Publishers.

Forel, F. A., 1895, "Le Léman: monographie limnologique," Vol. 2, Lausanne, F. Rouge, 651pp.

Forel, F. A., 1901, "Handbuch der Seenkunde: allgemeine Limnologie," Stuttgart, 249pp.

Hutchinson, G. E., 1957, "A Treatise on Limnology," Vol. 1, New York, John Wiley & Sons, 1015pp.

Inoue, N., Nishizawa, S., and Fukuda, M., 1957, "The perfection of a turbidity meter and the photographic study of suspended matter and plankton in the sea using an undersea observation chamber," *Proc. UNESCO Symposium on Physical Oceanography, Tokyo*, 1955, 53–58.

Jerlov, N., 1965, "The Evolution of the Instrumental Technique in Underwater Optics," in (Sears, M., editor) "Progress in Oceanography," Vol. 3, pp. 149–153, New York, Pergamon Press.

Joseph, J., 1957, "Extinction measurements to indicate distribution and transport of watermasses," *Proc. UNESCO Symposium on Physical Oceanography, Tokyo*, 1955, 59–75.

Juday, C., and Birge, E. A., 1933, "The transparency, the color and the specific conductance of the lake waters of Northeastern Wisconsin," *Trans. Wisconsin Acad. Sci.,* **28**, 205–259.

Sverdrup, H. U., Johnson, M. W., and Fleming, R. H., 1942, "The Oceans: Their Physics, Chemistry and General Biology," Englewood Cliffs, N.J., Prentice-Hall, 1087pp.

Tyler, J. E., and Preisendorfer, R. W., 1962, "Light," in (Hill, M. N., editor) "The Sea," Vol. 1, pp. 397–451, New York, Interscience Publishers.

Ule, W., 1894, "Beitrag zur Instrumentenkunde auf dem Gebiet der Seenforschung," *Petermanns Mitteilungen,* **70**.

Cross-reference: *Optical Oceanography*.

TRENCHES AND RELATED DEEP SEA TROUGHS

Definition

The morphologic definition of "trench" accepted by the Sixth International Geographical Congress (see *Geograph. J.,* 1903, **22**, p. 193; International Association of Physical Oceanography: Vaughan *et al.* 1940) is "a long and narrow depression (of the

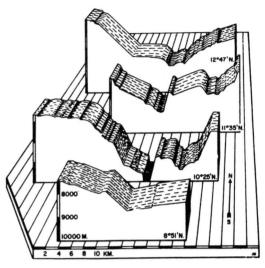

Fig. 1. Four sections of the Philippine Trench. Base line of all sections at 10,000 m; distance between each section is a little more than 100 km (from Kiilerich, 1953).

ocean floor) with relatively steep sides". The I.G.C. definition stressed its asymmetric profile and ocean-margin position, but this was dropped in later usage. The equivalent in French is *fossé* and in German *Graben*.

A clearly defined subsector of any marine depression may be designated as a *deep* (French, *fosse*, with no accent; German, *Tief*), sometimes limited by convention to below the 6000-m contour, but most workers feel that the critical contour to be selected should be merely that most clearly outlining each individual feature (regardless of absolute depth). The term *depth* in conjunction with a ship or captain's name indicates a specific sounding of greatest depth. The other terms (trench, deep) are used in conjunction with geographic names (as of adjacent islands or provinces), following the recommendations of the IAPO Committee on the Terminology of Ocean Bottom Features (Wiseman and Ovey, 1955).

The term *trough* is applied to elongate depressions of more gentle contours than trenches. From the structural and historical point of view, many trenches that have become partially filled with sediments and assumed the form of physiographic troughs might better be classified in the general category of trenches. However, not all marine troughs have had this origin.

Topography of Trenches

Because of the vertical exaggeration of precision depth recording traces and most published cross sections (often 20:1–40:1), the observer may gain the impression that the average trench is a nearly vertical-walled rift. Menard (1964) illustrates several good examples. Fisher and Hess (1963, p. 420) discuss the various slopes, which are gentle at first (4–8°), but steepen downward (10–16°). Sections of the Tonga Trench slopes reach 45°. The only comparable slopes elsewhere in the ocean are those off some atolls and barrier reefs or fault scarps such as that at the edge of the Blake Plateau off the southeastern United States.

The cross sections of trenches are generally V-shaped, but abruptly reach the floor which is almost invariably flat, varying in width from a few hundred meters to several kilometers, and often several hundred kilometers long.

Echo problems render the correct sounding of narrow, steep-sided trenches extremely difficult. Fisher (1954) has explained methods for correcting for some of the factors.

Numerous trenches are found to have an intermediate bench or series of steps or terraces on one slope or the other. Such a bench was discovered by H. W. Murray in the Aleutian Trench at about 4000

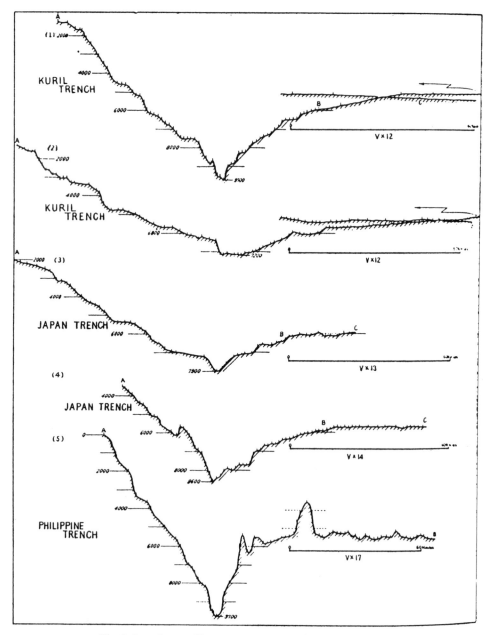

Fig. 2. Sounding profiles across western Pacific trenches (Dietz).

m; the most important one is now found to be 20–40 km wide and extends for 1500 km (Menard, 1964). Others are to be seen in the Kurile Trench, Mariana

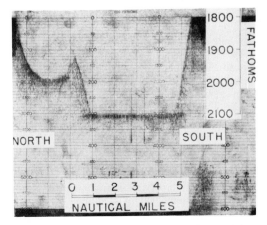

Fig. 3. Section of the flat floor of the Alexa trough at 3840 m (2100 fathoms). The lower slopes of the trough exhibit a gradient of 1:25 (22°) (from Fairbridge and Stewart, 1960).

Trench, Philippine Trench (Udintsev, 1955), Tonga Trench, Middle America Trench, and others. These steps are sometimes interpreted as the scarps of giant gravitationally slumped sectors (really tectonic units, like nappes), partly trapping and obscured by a veneer of younger sediments.

Distribution

Trenches are located in the three major oceans, but they lie predominantly around the periphery of the Pacific; they also occur along the northern borders of the Indian Ocean and follow the outer loops of the Caribbean and Scotia Arcs in the Atlantic. Additional trenches (and trench-like troughs) are located here and there within the "mediterranean" or marginal seas (Caribbean, Mediterranean, Indonesian and Melanesian basins). All of the above-mentioned examples are closely related to continental coasts or island arcs. Exceptionally certain physiographic trenches are found far from any land (e.g., *Romanche Trench* in mid-Atlantic, and the *Vema* and *Diamantina* trenches in the Indian Ocean). Some trenches are arcuate in plan, others rectilinear, and others again are "dog-legged" with a sharp 90° change in trend. Menard (1964) has

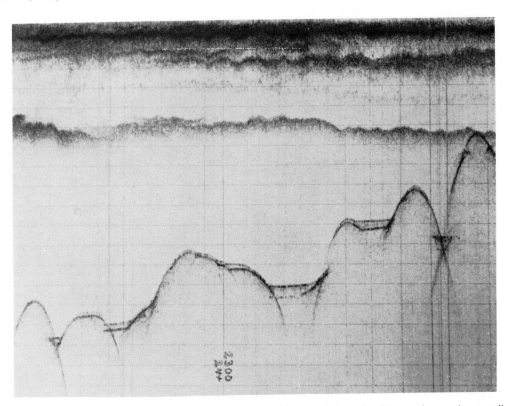

Fig. 4. Echo-sounding profile of a trench slope made on a Precision Depth Recorder. The sound energy has actually penetrated to the extent that ponded sediments can be seen in the small basins. The dark reflections at the top of the record are biological in origin and are referred to as the "Deep Scattering Layer." Profile taken by Spencer F. Baird on the seaward flank of the Peru-Chile Trench just north of Lima at latitude 9°06′S, longitude 81°20′W. The depth range is 2400–2800 fathoms. (*Courtesy of T. E. Chase*)

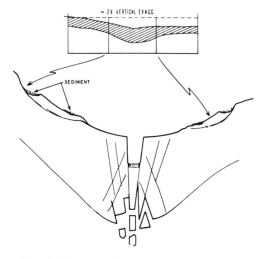

Fig. 5. Diagrammatic cross section of structural benches and central trough of a trench. Note sediment accumulation on benches produced by slumping (Menard, 1964).

noted that there is often a right-angle turn or loop at the end of a trench.

Classification

It is evident from the data of Table 1 that a simple classification of trenches and related troughs can be offered, based essentially upon distribution, structure, and morphology:

Type A—Peripheral Type. These are situated around the peripheries of the great oceans, widespread in the Pacific, limited in the Indian Ocean and even more localized in the Atlantic and Mediterranean. They are generally parallel to island arcs or young coastal cordillera. In section, the topography is highly asymmetric, with typical deep ocean floor on the "outside" (ca. 5500 m' and steep islands or sometimes even high mountains on the "inside." The contrast in elevation from maximum depths (over 10,000 m) to maximum heights in the islands or cordillera (up to 7000 m) is thus over 17 km. We correlate this type of trench always with *thalassocratonic* margins.

Type B—Marginal Sea (Reversed) Type. These

TABLE 1. TRENCHES AND RELATED TROUGHS: LOCATIONS AND DEPTHS (IN PART AFTER FISHER AND HESS, 1963; HEEZEN AND THARP, 1965; FAIRBRIDGE, 1966)

	Depth (m)	Length (km)	Mean Width (km)	Areal Extent (km²)	Volume (km³)
TYPE A (facing thalassocraton)					
Western Pacific:					
Kurile-Kamchatka Trench	10,542	2200	120	264,000	1,320,000
Japan Trench	8,412	800	100	80,000	336,000
Idzu-Bonin Trench (including Ramapo Deep)	9,810	800	90	72,000	352,800
Marianas Trench (including Challenger Deep)	11,022	2550	70	17,850	98,200
Yap (West Caroline) Trench	8,527	700	40	28,000	72,500
Palau Trench	8,054	400	40	16,000	64,000
New Guinea Trough	5,311	440	60	26,400	70,300
West Melanesian Trench	6,534	1100	60	66,000	216,000
Southwest Pacific:					
Tonga Trench	10,800–10,882	1400	55	77,000	415,800
Kermadec Trench	10,047	1500	60	90,000	450,000
Hikurangi Trough	3,590	700	40	28,000	48,400
Eastern Pacific:					
Aleutian Trench	7,679	3700	50	185,000	673,000
Cedros Trough	6,225	400	40	16,000	49,600
Middle America Trench (including Acapulco Deep)	6,662	2800	40	96,000	316,800
Peru-Chile Trench	8,055	5900	100	590,000	2,360,000
Cape Horn Trough	4,395	1050	50	52,500	115,500
Indian Ocean:					
Aru Trough	3,652	900	25	22,500	42,500
Timor Trough	3,276	800	40	32,000	51,200
Java (Indonesian) Trench	7,450	4500	80	180,000	666,000
Makran Trough	3,500	400	100	40,000	70,000
Atlantic Ocean:					
Puerto Rico Trench	8,385	1550	120	186,000	779,000
Cayman Trench	7,093	1450	70	101,500	360,000
Dominican Trench	ca. 6,200	700	30	21,000	65,000
South Sandwich Trench	8,428	1450	90	130,500	558,000
Birdwood Trough	4,758	980	40	38,200	90,800

TABLE 1—*continued*

	Depth (m)	Length (km)	Mean Width (km)	Areal Extent (km²)	Volume (km³)
TYPE B (quasi-cratonic)					
Western Pacific:					
Ryukyu (Nansei Shoto) Trench	7,507	2250	60	135,000	506,000
Philippine Trench (Cape Johnson Deep)	10,030–10,497	1400	60	84,000	420,000
Luzon Trough	4,510	600	50	30,000	67,500
Manila Trough	5,245	350	40	14,000	36,400
Moru Trough	5,842	270	50	13,500	39,400
Sangir Trough	2,867	700	70	49,000	68,600
Minahassa Trough	5,520	550	60	33,000	92,000
Flores Trough	5,123	540	40	21,600	56,160
Southwest Pacific:					
New Britain Trench	8,320	750	40	30,000	124,800
Bougainville (North Solomons) Trench	8,310	500	50	25,000	103,800
Kiriwina Trough	5,200	700	35	24,500	63,700
San Cristobal (South Solomons) Trench	8,310	950	40	38,000	159,700
Torres (North Hebrides) Trench	9,162	750	60	45,000	206,000
New Hebrides Trench	9,165	1200	70	84,000	385,000
Papuan Trough	2,300	750	80	60,000	69,000
New Caledonia Trough	3,932	600	70	42,000	84,000
Atlantic and Mediterranean:					
Malvines Trough	3,520	1250	80	100,000	175,600
Hellenic (Crete) Trough	5,121	1500	40	60,000	153,000
Indian Ocean:					
Amirante Trench	9,074	680	30	21,400	95,000
TYPE C (transverse)					
Western Pacific:					
East Caroline (Mussau) Trough	6,920	400	30	12,000	41,400
Southwest Pacific:					
Vitiaz Trench	6,150	550	60	33,000	105,600
Yasawa Trough	4,810	480	20	9,600	23,000
Also: Vanikoro, Strathmore, Alexa, Hazel Holme, Rotuma, Bayonnaise, Horne and Wallis Troughs: all small examples in the Melanesian Border Plateau					
Macquarie Trough	5,851	600	60	36,000	105,000
Atlantic Ocean:					
Romanche Trench	7,856	300	20	6,000	21,900
Indian Ocean:					
Chagos Trench	5,408	2450	70	101,500	264,000
Vema Trench	6,402	700	25	17,500	56,000
Mauritius Trench	5,564	1080	30	32,400	95,400
Diamantina Trench	8,230	2160	30	64,800	265,700
Ob Trench	5,714	550	30	16,500	45,400
TYPE D (parallel, intermediate)					
Indonesia:					
Bali Trough	4,251	2300	90	207,000	434,700
Savu Trough	3,370	270	50	13,500	29,950
Banda (Weber) Trough	7,440	650	80	52,000	192,400
And many smaller troughs					

are situated within the marginal seas, bordering the Pacific, and are also parallel to island arcs, with a notable asymmetric profile, but they face the opposite direction, i.e., away from the Pacific. This type is only found in the *quasi-cratonic* regions.

Type C—Transverse or Oblique Type. These are found crossing oceanic ridges, plateaus, or conti-

nental structures; their orientation may be transverse, oblique or en échelon. They generally lack any special continuous "facing," but are essentially symmetric in section and rectilinear in plan. The geotectonic correlation is with faulting across mid-ocean ridges, crossing quasi-cratonic regions, or entering epeirocratonic regions.

Type D—Parallel Intermediate Troughs. These occur parallel to the principal Type A and B trenches wherever there are *double* island arcs or submerged ridges (see discussion below). The intermediate trough lies between the inner (volcanic) arc and the outer (non-volcanic) arc. The trough is never as deep as the adjacent trench.

Association

The origin and nature of trenches must be partly connected with the geological and geophysical features with which they are associated. Principally these are:

(a) **Volcanic and Orogenic Arcs.** Some forty years ago, H. A. Brouwer pointed out that island arcs sometimes consisted of single belts, but often displayed two ridges, which were almost invariably arranged with an inner belt of volcanoes ("inner volcanic arc") paralleled by a trough about 50–100 km wide, in front of which came a ridge or belt of islands with strong orogenic deformation ("outer non-volcanic arc"), which in turn is paralleled by the trench, another 50–100 km oceanward. In some places, (e.g., south of Java and the Sunda Arc) the outer ridge is so depressed that the inner trough (Bali Trough) and the trench (Java Trench) are almost merged. The outer trench is sometimes paralleled by a third (very reduced) elevation, a low oceanic rise, e.g., the Christmas Rise—Roo Rise, etc., south of the Java Trench.

The volcanic belt is characterized by mainly andesitic lavas (or basalts of the calc-alkaline class, Harker's "Pacific Suite"), and hence the peripheral zone of trenches around the Pacific has become known as the Andesite Line, or occasionally as the "Marshall Line" (see references and discussion in Fairbridge, 1961).

(b) **Gravity Anomalies.** Since the time of Becker, who measured gravity in the island arcs with a primitive apparatus half a century ago, it has been known that remarkable anomalies were associated with trenches and island arcs. When Vening Meinesz developed his submarine-borne pendulum systems, a new era of observations began and numerous traverses were made over the trenches (published by the Netherlands Geodetic Commission, the last in 1948). These were extended to the

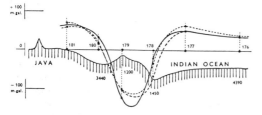

Fig. 6. Comparison between gravity anomalies and submarine relief over Java, the Bali Trough and the Java Trench to the Indian Ocean (Vening Meinesz).

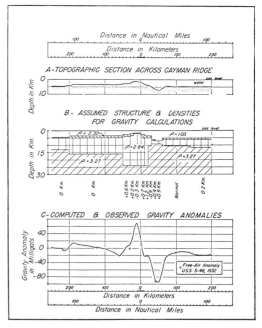

Fig. 7. Gravity observations across the Cayman Ridge and Cayman Trench from the Yucatan Basin to near Jamaica. North is on the left (gravity calculations by G. L. Shurbet).

Caribbean by Ewing (1937) and Hess (1938), to the Japan Trench by Matuyama (1936), to the Tonga Trench (Talwani *et al.*, 1961), and many other areas in recent years in considerably more detail, especially in the Puerto Rico Trench (Talwani *et al.*, 1959). Development of the surface vessel gravimeter has permitted continuous measurements to be made (Bunce and Fahlquist, 1962) so that the shape of the anomaly can be determined with great accuracy.

The trenches are marked by strongly negative gravity anomalies, both free air and isostatic, with the minimum usually centered somewhat shoreward from the trench axis.

(c) **Geomagnetic Characteristics.** Towed and air-borne magnetometer traverses have been carried out over numerous trench sectors (Tonga, Aleutian, Kurile-Kamchatka, Puerto Rico, etc.), but in general, no unusual anomalies have emerged (Bullard and Mason, 1963).

(d) **Heat Flow Measurements.** Geothermal probes have been run in the Middle America Trench, the Aleutian Trench, Peru-Chile Trench, Puerto Rico Trench, and elsewhere. Values both lower and higher than normal have been obtained, but the average is very close to the world average. This may be partly due to variations in sediment accumulation in the trenches measured (Bullard, 1963).

(e) **Seismic Refraction Surveys.** Ship-operated refraction seismology studies were first carried out by Hersey (1949) in the Puerto Rico Trench, then by

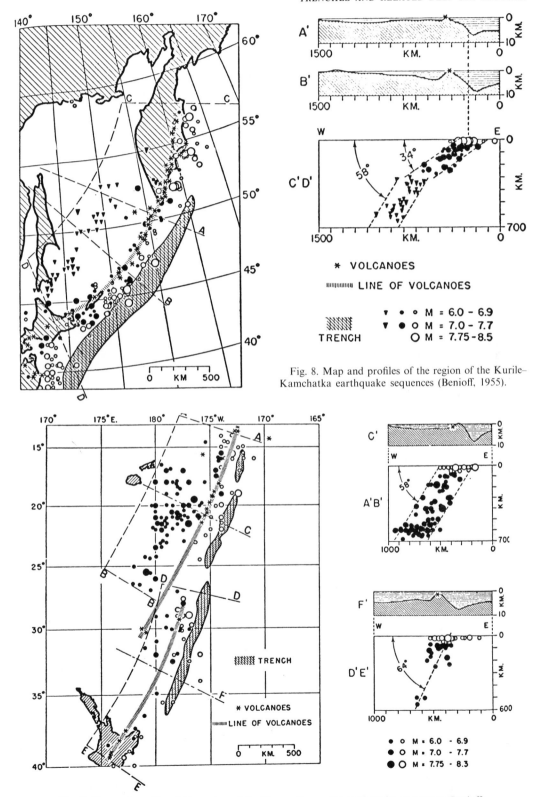

Fig. 8. Map and profiles of the region of the Kurile–Kamchatka earthquake sequences (Benioff, 1955).

Fig. 9. Map and profiles of the region of the Tonga–Kermadec earthquake sequences (Benioff).

Ewing, Sutton, Worzel and others during the next few years, and subsequently surveys have been carried out over most of the other trenches. It is found that the peripheral-type trenches mark the boundary between oceanic-type crust (about 5 km thick) and intermediate or continental crust (10–30 km thick). However, traces of the Mohorovičić discontinuity generally seem to disappear just under the trench itself (Raitt, 1956; Shor and Fisher, 1961; Bunce and Fahlquist, 1962; Shor, 1962).

(f) **Shallow and Deep Focus Earthquake Belts.** Parallel to all the peripheral and marginal (reversed) type trenches there is an important zone of earthquake epicenters (Gutenberg and Richter, 1954). The plane of earthquake foci appears to extend from near the surface on the land side of the trench down to nearly 700 km depth for some 400 km behind the trench axis. As shown first by Coulomb (1945), a giant plane appears to be dipping at 40–50° landward around the Pacific border (type "A"), but in the reversed examples (type "B" in Melanesia) the plane dips toward the Pacific. No deep focus earthquakes correlate with the transverse type trenches (type "C"). It is curious that although there are trenches and deep focus earthquakes paralleling the Pacific Coast of South America, there are no equivalents off North America, except in the Aleutians (Fig. 10).

(g) **Fault-plane Seismologic Studies.** Benioff (1949, 1954) suggested that the shallow to deep focus earthquake planes represented reverse or thrust faults, gigantic shears that far exceeded the dimensions of any known elsewhere in geology. Details of the focus locations suggest, however, that the

"planes" are simply zones where irregular failures occur. Fault-plane analyses by Hodgson (1957) suggest that the planes are sites of strike-slip motion rather than overthrusts. Apparent extension of such zones into land areas (as in California and New Zealand) suggests that they are indeed related to great strike-slip or transcurrent faults (Hess and Maxwell, 1953). This postulate is rejected by Fisher and Hess (1963).

Sediments

In those trenches farthest from continental sediment sources, there is extremely little sedimentary filling in the trenches. Many coring attempts by Scripps Expedition *Capricorn* in the Tonga Trench, for example, failed owing to encounter with hard rock flanks. Only the narrow median deeps, often but a few hundred meters across, are filled. The steep sides generally prevent any important stable accumulation on the slopes so that most of the filling is pelagic and transported by means of slumping and turbidity currents. Since such flows have a "soup"-like density, the bottom accumulation will be essentially flat, and a narrow flat floor is observed in all trenches.

In contrast to the isolated trenches, those off or near continental coasts (e.g., the Middle America, Aleutian, Hikurangi, Java, and Puerto Rico trenches) are partially filled with sediments. The Aleutian Trench is especially instructive, since it can be followed from the state of a typical, deep, empty rift in the western Aleutians (where the islands are small and sparse) to the Gulf of Alaska where its topographic entity disappears completely owing to syste-

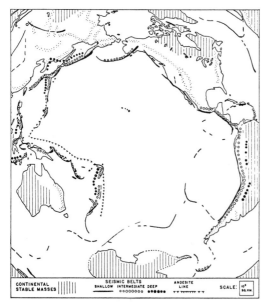

Fig. 10. Pacific Ocean with peripheral seismic belt; note Andesite line in the west (Gutenberg and Richter, 1954).

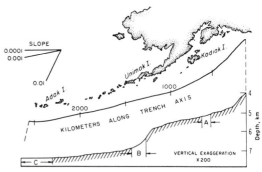

Fig. 11. Diagram of Aleutian Trench, illustrating transition from a deep open trench at C tp B, into a partly filled geosyncline at A (Menard, 1964).

matic filling by terrigenous sediments (Shor, 1962). Similarly, the Hikurangi Trench is filling from New Zealand (Menard, 1964), the Antillean Trench is filled near Barbados, and other examples in the Scotia Arc, etc., are mentioned by Ewing and Landisman (1961).

In character, the trench sediments are principally an alternation of turbidites (of mixed terrigenous origin) and pelagic deposits, mainly clays, volcanic ash, and siliceous oozes (diatoms or radiolaria). Exceptionally, as in the Peru Trench, some carbonates and possibly primary dolomites occur (E'an Zen, 1960). Observers from the bathyscaph *Trieste* in the pioneering descent into the Marianas Trench (in 1960) reported setting up a thick fog of soft gray mud as it encountered the bottom sediment. It has been suggested that the coarse clastic (sandy) debris found in the isolated Romanche Trench is nothing but finely cataclastic fault gouge or mylonite (Mellis, 1958). It has long been thought that gravitational sliding or slumping would play an important part in the filling-up of trenches. Evidence for this phenomenon is suggested by the topography of the structural benches and locally jumbled relief on many trench slopes. Massive segments with displaced facies were already noted thirty years ago in the East Indies by Kuenen. Carbonates are found buried below the maximum limit (about 5000 m), below which solution normally occurs. Benthonic foraminifera of neritic or bathyal habitat are found displaced to abyssal and hadal depths. Evidently such extensive slumping is likely to be restricted to those trenches close to continental sediment sources. In some sectors, complete filling and obliteration of the trench as a physiographic feature has taken place, and in such areas the structure constitutes a mature geosyncline (q.v., pr Vol. VII).

Those trenches far from continental sediment sources, such as the Mariana and Tonga Trenches (respectively the deepest in the northern and southern hemispheres), do not appear to be ever likely to fill up completely. Menard has suggested (1964, p. 114) that the "root" will eventually rise and "it will merely produce a low bulge at the former site of the trench."

History of Trenches

Little direct information is available on the age and longevity of trenches. Some deductions may be drawn from the geological evidence of the existence and repeated motions on strike-slip faults that may be related to them as in California and New Zealand. Some of these may date from the Mesozoic.

On one side of the Aleutian Trench, there is a guyot-type (flat-topped) seamount that has been tilted several degrees off the vertical during the subsidence of the trench (see Menard, 1964). Since these guyots mainly date from early Tertiary or late Cretaceous, it would seem that subsidence in the Aleutian Trench has been active since that time.

The best-known trench is probably that of Puerto Rico, and since the geology of the adjacent islands is fairly well known, it seems likely that its origin can be traced back to the beginning of the Tertiary, at which time deep-seated acid magmas were being emplaced in Puerto Rico itself. It appears to lie in a

complex system of WSW-ENE sinistral strike-slip faults, observed also on the adjacent islands. It would seem to have been continuously open for something of the order of 70 million years. The principal motions of other fault systems (e.g., the Great Alpine Fault of New Zealand in its relation to the Hikurangi–Kermadec–Tonga trenches) may be of similar longevity.

Another illuminating relationship is seen in the Indian Ocean. The great Java Trench system passes in the northwest into the Ganges delta, and thence into the Indo-Gangetic Plain (that today seems to be a filled geosyncline); beyond the Indus delta appears another trench-type trough, that of Makran (south of Iran), less important than the Java Trench because of the high sedimentation rate. To the northwest, the Makran Trough passes into the Mesopotamian Geosyncline. Both geosynclines date back to the Mesozoic at least, and suggest that there can be little real genetic or structural difference between trenches and certain geosynclines. The essential difference seems to be one of history, i.e., the age and the circumstances of either filling or isolation.

Peculiar abyssal faunas which appear to have been long isolated are found in the trenches. The indigenous faunas are quite distinct from one trench to the next, the isolation being maintained by the pressure adaptation of the organisms and the height of sills between trenches. L. A. Zenkevitch (1961, p. 329) says: "Our present knowledge of the taxonomy and distribution of the oceanic flora and fauna . . . (suggests) the permanent character or at least the great antiquity of the oceanic trenches themselves."

Interpretation of Trenches

For nearly a century, the existence of some trenches (in conjunction with parallel island arcs) has led geologists to conclude that they were compressional downfolds of the crust; e.g., Suess spoke of the Pacific acting as a shield, a depressed foreland against the push of orogenic pressures emanating from Asia.

The discovery of strong negative gravity anomalies along the trenches stimulated Vening Meinesz to postulate a great crustal downbuckle, called a "*tectogene*" by Kuenen (1936) and Hess (1938). Griggs (1939) offered a scale model experiment where two rollers represented twin, opposed convection cells that carried down and maintained the depressed center of the tectogene.

The work of Ewing, Worzel, Shurbet, Talwani *et al.*, mainly on the Puerto Rico Trench, shattered the tectogene hypothesis, for there appears to be no depressed root. Confirmation of this lack of a "light" axial zone, deeply depressed, has come from Raitt for the Tonga Trench and elsewhere. Ewing *et al.* believe that the Puerto Rico Trench represents an extensional feature. Studying the general tectonics of the Melanesian region, Fairbridge (1961) found evidence of general tension with torsional

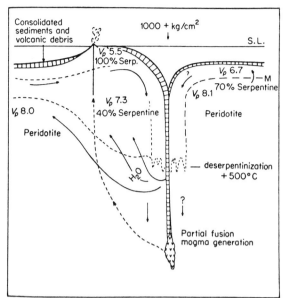

Fig. 12. Supposed structure, with typical seismic velocities (V^p in kilometers per second, for a hypothetical trench-island arc association; Fisher and Hess, 1963).

zones; such tectonics seem to have led to large-scale crustal foundering, which is hardly compatible with the idea of compressional downbuckling. Since several important Melanesian trenches face in the opposite direction to the Tonga Trench, we would have to believe in horizontal pressures in adjacent belts, simultaneously applied in opposite directions.

Hess is of the opinion that the very longevity of deep-sea trenches calls for some mechanism other than tension, since a foundered block would, if temporarily depressed, be expected to recover its former level rather rapidly by isostasy. Menard (1964) believes that some version of the Griggs-Vening Meinesz convective model (compression) could still provide the answer, while Fisher and Hess (1963) add a deserpentinized "root," that would represent a phase-controlled volume reduction, thus providing for the continued depression of the trench.

The postulated "basification" of the former crust of the marginal seas, such as those of Melanesia, advanced by Beloussov and others, calls for a still more complicated mechanism that is not at all understood. Since the geological field evidence seems to point unequivocally toward tension and general subsidence, local convective cells in the upper mantle seem to be inadequate or contradictory, and one may have to seek a broader explanation, related perhaps to earth tidal forces coupled with secular mantle expansion, such as proposed by Egyed.

It is believed by a number of geologists that the convective cell explanation of trenches runs into particularly serious difficulties if one considers all

trenches, and especially if one views them in three dimensions. Attractive as the convection cells appear in a two-dimensional diagram, it is hard to fit them into discontinuous arcuate plans. Even greater difficulties appear when one considers an area like Melanesia, where a single east-west profile passing through the northern end of the Tonga Trench (facing east and oriented NNE-SSW) would pass through the Yasawa Trench (northeast-southwest) but facing northwest, and then through the New Hebrides Trench (north-south and facing west) and then through the New Caledonia Trough (northwest-southeast and facing southwest). Small convection cells would have to boil over in all directions.

There is very strong physiographic and geologic evidence that certain trenches are parts of great transcurrent (strike-slip) faults. The Tonga–Kermadec Trenches line up directly with the Great Alpine Fault system of New Zealand which has a well-known dextral slip. Heezen and Drake (1964) report a probable dextral slip on the Vema Trench and a sinistral slip on the Romanche Trench, the latter with a 500-km displacement. The Puerto Rico Trench appears to be part of a complex North Caribbean sinistral strike-slip pattern.

If one turns to the land for analogies for deep rifts in the earth's crust, it is not difficult to point out that two of the deepest *non-marine* trenches (the Dead Sea Rift and the Salton Sea on the San Andreas Fault System) are situated in classical transcurrent faults, respectively sinistral and dextral, and with displacements of 100 km and more. In crystalline rocks in semiarid country, such rifts can remain open for long periods. There seems no reason for assuming that a deep-sea trench, far from sediment sources, cannot remain open for extended periods without calling in convection cells or some other *deus ex machina*.

To sum up, trenches are highly localized submarine gashes in the earth's crust. Their strong negative isostatic anomalies would suggest that only a brief existence was possible, yet their geological histories show that they may last 10^7 years and more. They have in the past been explained generally by some theory of compression and downbuckling. Recent geophysical surveys suggest rather a tensional history. This would be compatible with some modern theories of an expanding earth. Arcuate trenches may be explained by simple extension; rectilinear trenches by torsion (strike-slip) faults.

RHODES W. FAIRBRIDGE

References

Allen, C. R., 1962, "Circum-Pacific faulting in the Philippines-Taiwan region," *J. Geophys. Res.,* **67**(12), 4795–4812.

Benioff, H., 1949, "Seismic evidence for the fault origin of oceanic deeps," *Bull. Geol. Soc. Am.,* **60**, 1837–1856.

Benioff, H., 1962, "Movements on Major Transcurrent

Faults," Calif. Inst. Tech., Div. Geol. Sci., Contrib. 1061.

Bullard, E. C., and Mason, R. G., 1963, "The Magnetic Field Over the Oceans," in "The Sea," Vol. 3, pp. 175–217, New York, Interscience Publishers.

Fairbridge, R. W., 1961, "The Melanesian Border Plateau, a zone of crustal shearing in the S.W. Pacific," *Publ. Bur. Cent. Seism. Internat., Ser. A*, **22** (Assoc. Gen. Helsinki, 1960), 137–149.

Fisher, R. L., 1961, "Middle America Trench: topography and structure," *Bull. Geol. Soc. Am.*, **72**, 703–720.

Fisher, R. L., and Hess, H. H., 1963, "Trenches," in "The Sea," Vol. 3, pp. 411–436, New York, Interscience Publishers.

Fisher, R. L., and Raitt, R. W., 1962, "Topography and structure of the Peru-Chile Trench," *Deep-Sea Res.*, **9**, 423–443.

Fisher, R. L., and Revelle, R., 1955, "The trenches of the Pacific," *Sci. Am.*, 2–7.

Gutenberg, B., and Richter, C. F., 1954, "Seismicity of the Earth," Princeton, N.J., Princeton University Press.

Heezen, B. C., Menzies, R. J., Broecker, W. S., and Ewing, W. M., 1959, "Stagnation of the Cariaco Trench," *Intern. Oceanogr. Congr. Preprints* (Am. Assoc. Adv. Sci.), 99–102.

Heezen, B. C., and Nafe, J. E., 1964, "Vema Trench: Western Indian Ocean," *Deep-Sea Res.*, **11**, 79–84.

Horn, E., 1915, "Uber die Geologische Bedeutung der Tiefseegraben," *Geol. Rundschau*, **5**, 422–448.

Kuenen, P. H., 1936, "The negative isostatic anomalies in the East Indies (with experiments)," *Leidsche Geol. Mededeel.*, **8**, 169–214.

Lacombe, H., 1960, "Quelques traits remarquables du relief sous-marin en Mer Mediterranée et en Mer Noire," *Deep-Sea Res.*, **6**, 211–216.

Mellis, O., 1958, "Die Sedimentation in der Romanche-Tiefe (ein Beitrag zur Erklärung der Entstehung des Tiefseesands im Atlantischen Ozean)," *Geol. Rundschau*, **47**, 218–234.

Menard, H. W., 1964, "Marine Geology of the Pacific," New York, McGraw-Hill Book Co., 271pp.

Nitani, H., and Imayoshi, B., 1963, "On the analysis of the deep sea observations in the Kurile-Kamchatka Trench," *J. Oceanogr. Soc., Japan*, **19**(2), 75–81.

Officer, C. B., Ewing, J. I., Edwards, R. S., and Johnson, H. R., 1957, "Geophysical investigations in the Eastern Caribbean: Venezuelan Basin, Antilles Island Arc, and Puerto Rico Trench," *Bull. Geol. Soc. Am.*, **68**, 359–378.

Scheidegger, A. E., 1958, "Tectonophysical significance of fault plane solutions of earthquakes," *Geofis. Pura. Appl.*, **39**, 19–25.

Shor, G. G., Jr., 1962, "Seismic refraction studies off the coast of Alaska: 1956–57," *Bull. Seism. Soc. Am.*, **52**, 37–57.

Shor, G. G., Jr., and Fisher, R. L., 1961, "Middle America Trench: seismic-refraction studies," *Bull. Geol. Soc. Am.*, **72**, 721–730.

Todd, R., and Low, D., 1964, "Cenomanian (Cretaceous) foraminifera from the Puerto Rico Trench," *Deep-Sea Res.*, **11**, 395–414.

Udintsev, G. B., 1955, "Topography of the Kurile-Kamchatka Trench," *Tr. Inst. Okeanol. Akad. Naek SSSR*, **12**, 16–61 (in Russian).

Vening Meinesz, F. A., 1948, "Gravity expeditions at sea, 1923–1938," *Publ. Neth. Geod. Comm., Delft*, **4**.

Wiseman, J. D. H., and Ovey, C. D., 1955, "Proposed names of features on the deep-sea floor," *Deep-Sea Res.*, **2**, 93–106.

Zeigler, J. M., Athearn, W. D., and Small, H., 1957, "Profiles across the Peru-Chile Trench," *Deep-Sea Res.*, **4**, 238–249.

TROPOSPHERE AND STRATOSPHERE IN THE OCEAN

By analogy with the atmospheric layer classification, the ocean depths have been broadly categorized into two divisions by Defant (1928), troposphere and stratosphere. Alternatively, they are known respectively as *Warm Water Sphere* and *Cold Water Sphere*. Defant calls them "the two main oceanic subspaces." Within each there is essentially a separate circulation, though of course interaction and mixing occur.

The oceanic troposphere is restricted to the warm upper layers found in the middle and low latitudes, a region marked by strong and variable currents and atmospheric interactions. It is thus analogous in many ways to the lower atmosphere (troposphere) with its strong thermodynamic disturbances, surface friction and so on. As Defant pointed out, the most important feature of the oceanic troposphere is the strong temperature decrease and density increase with depth. The thickness of the troposphere increases poleward from about 400 m in the tropics to about 500–900 m in middle latitudes. The troposphere disappears in the subpolar zone where the oceanic polar front divides the warm water of the troposphere from the cold water of the Arctic and Antarctic, these being the sources of the stratosphere water (see *Atlantic Ocean*). Figure 1 shows the approximate tropical circulation above the thermocline.

The oceanic troposphere can be divided into three parts. The topmost part above 100 m is subject to the direct atmospheric influence (layer of surface disturbances) and the water characteristics are

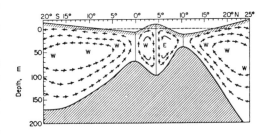

Fig. 1. Schematic representation of the zonal and meridional velocity components of the tropospheric circulation in the Atlantic Ocean (the topography of the thermocline is exaggerated in the vertical scale by about 1:1 million; that of the physical sea surface even more); W, current toward west; E, current toward east (Defant, 1961).

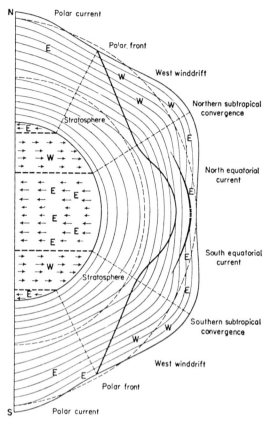

Fig. 2. Schematic representation of the hydrosphere as a circular vortex. Current zones and position of the main boundary surface and of the isobaric surfaces (with a strong exaggeration of the vertical scale; W, current toward west; E, current toward east; Defant, 1961).

homogeneous. Below this part there is a layer with maximum vertical temperature and density gradient (*thermocline*, q.v., or *discontinuity layer*) with a mean gradient of nearly 5°C/100 m. This layer acts as a barrier to vertical motion and mixing. The lowest part (below the thermocline) is the *subtroposphere*.

The *subtroposphere* is occupied by rather uniform and almost motionless water. The boundary between this layer and the oceanic stratosphere is difficult to draw because of the lack of any sharp horizon. As an approximation, the level of the intermediate oxygen minima can be used, in other words the horizon of least renewal, since Wüst (1936) showed that this was a horizon of essentially no motion, but some oceanographers had a doubt about it.

The oceanic stratosphere refers to the nearly uniform masses of cold deep water and bottom water. Temperature gradients are very weak; nevertheless, the distribution is described as *anothermic*. The gradient below 1000 m drops to 0.4°C/100 m, below 2000 m to 0.1°C/100 m and below 3000 m to 0.05°C/100m. Only in exceptional areas is there a weak temperature inversion due to powerful geostrophic currents and their eddies.

If one views (with Bjerknes) the hydrosphere as a land-free vortex about the earth's axis, the ideal water motions will be zonal (east or west) influenced by the planetary winds and the north–south differential heating. The actual physical sea surface is also influenced by the meridional components due to Ekman transports and coastal barriers so that sea level will be low at the equator, and high in the horse latitudes owing to the trade wind and westerly flows. On the other hand, the stratospheric boundary will show opposite gradients in order to compensate the pressure gradient due to

TABLE 1. LOWER LIMIT OF THE TROPOSPHERE IN THE ATLANTIC OCEAN (Defant, 1961)

Section		50°	45°	40°	35°	30°	25°	20°	15°	10°	5°	Equator
Western section	N	—	—	(1000)	850	830	820	770	550	280*	350	400
	S	—	—	400	500	550	600†	580	450	300	280*	
Central section	N	450	790	770	830	880†	870	680	470	380	330*	400
	S	—	(100)	320	500	600†	580	550	420	300*	400	
Eastern section	N	(900)	(900)	(900)	(900)†	(250)	820	680	(550)	520	400	350*
	S	—	300	470	530†	510	450	380	300*	390	400	

N. Northern Hemisphere; S. Southern Hemisphere

* Minimum values; † Maximum values.

this sea-level slope. In this way, there is no conspicuous horizontal motion in the greater depths of the ocean (see Defant, 1961, p. 576).

As pointed out by Sverdrup *et al.*, (1942) the analogy with the atmosphere implied by these terms troposphere and stratosphere is imperfect and not all of the phenomena find their counterparts. Such terms should therefore be used with caution.

RHODES W. FAIRBRIDGE

References

Defant, A., 1929, "Stabile Lagerung ozeanischer Wasser —körper und dazu gehörige Stromsysteme," *Berlin Universität, Institut f. Meereskunde, Veröff, N.F., A. Geogr.-naturwiss. Reihe*, **19**, 33pp.

Defant, A., 1936, "Die Troposphäre," *Wiss. Ergebn. Deutsche Atlantische Expedition Meteor, 1925–1927*, **6**(1), Sect. 3, 289–411.

Sverdrup, H. U., Johnson, M. W., and Fleming, R. H., 1942, "The Oceans: Their Physics, Chemistry and General Biology," Englewood Cliffs, N.J., Prentice-Hall, 1087pp.

Wüst, G., 1935, "Die Stratosphäre," *Wiss. Ergebn. Deutsche Atlantische Expedition Meteor 1925–1927*, **6**(1), Sect. 2, 288pp.

Wüst, G., 1936, "Die Tiefenzirkulation im Raum des Atlantischen Ozeans," *Naturwissenschaften*, 133.

Defant, A., 1961, "Physical Oceanography," Vol. 1, New York, Pergamon Press, 729pp.

TSUNAMI

"Tsunami" is the Japanese name for the gravity wave system formed in the sea following any large-scale short-duration disturbance of the free surface. While past tsunamis have caused great damage and loss of life along oceanic shore lines, their relative infrequency and complex local behavior has resulted in widespread misconceptions as to their true nature—even among scientists.

Tsunamis seem principally to occur following earthquakes of magnitude greater than 6.5 (Richter scale) having focal depths less than 50 km, although landslides, bottom-slumping, and volcanic eruptions have been cited as primogenitors in certain cases. Not all such earthquakes produce tsunamis, and the generation mechanism undoubtedly differs from event to event. Since the majority of them originate at great depths in the sea, their precise origins will probably remain forever obscure. Once formed, however, the wave system resembles nothing so much as that produced by tossing a stone into the middle of a large, shallow pond. In simplest aspect (more complex sources are thought to exist), the wave pattern is axi-symmetric at early times, and consists of concentric rings of crests and troughs, bounded at the outside by an intangible "front," somewhat analogous to the shock wave in a gas. The front expands everywhere outwards at the limiting velocity $c = \sqrt{gh}$ for free waves in water of depth h ($g =$ gravitational acceleration), and all other waves travel more slowly. At any instant of time, the radial separation between successive crests (wavelength) is largest near the front and becomes progressively smaller towards the center. In the absence of boundaries which produce reflections, individual waves of the system retain their identity, in contrast to the wind-generated swell, which grows and disappears before the eye in the space of a few seconds.

In general, no two waves of the system are the same size, nor does the amplitude of any wave remain the same from place to place and time to time. Within the ever-changing pattern, the energy distribution among waves is manifested by amplitude modulation of the wave train in a manner which is determined by the nature of the source, its distance from the point of observation, and the depth of water over the intervening route. Like the wave system generated in the pond by the pebble, as the tsunami spreads out over the sea surface, the amplitudes of all of the individual waves are, on the average, diminished with increasing time. This is because the wave system contains a finite and nearly constant amount of energy, which is spread thinner and thinner as the pattern expands.

Because the sea floor is not uniformly deep, but instead possesses a topographic relief which, if anything, is more differentiated than that found on land, the initial symmetry of the wave pattern soon becomes somewhat distorted. This effect, analogous to phase distortion in optics, is most marked at the outer margins of the wave pattern, and is due to the fact that the phase (wave) velocities of the longer waves asymptotically approach that of the wave front, and are more markedly influenced by the local water depth than the shorter waves farther back. As in optics, the influence of topographic irregularities which are small compared with the local wavelength is averaged out, and only features some hundreds of miles in extent can appreciably alter the symmetry.

As the waves approach the boundaries of the ocean and pass into shallow water, the individual wave amplitudes become larger, because the energy increment contained within each wave is concentrated in an increasingly smaller volume of water. Eventually, as shoaling and wave growth continue, the wave amplitudes amount to an appreciable fraction of the water depth. In this "shallow water" regime, additional modification of the wave system is brought about by amplitude distortion, which is nonlinear, has no parallel in optics, and is due to the fact that the phase speed of a free gravity wave in very shallow water is also a function of wave amplitude. Ultimately, the progress of each wave is arrested at the shore line, and its energy is divided between that fraction (about 40%) scattered back out to sea and that expended in dissipative processes along the shore.

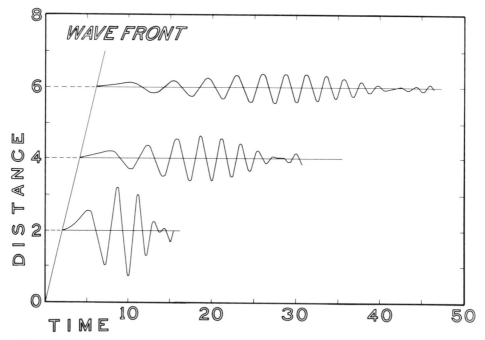

Fig. 1. Three stages of theoretical development of tsunami wave train from impulsive source in water of uniform depth. Maximum wave amplitude decays inversely as distance and time.

The situation in the immediate vicinity of the shore line is very complicated. Here, the time history of the wave motion bears little, if any, resemblance to that in deep water and, instead,

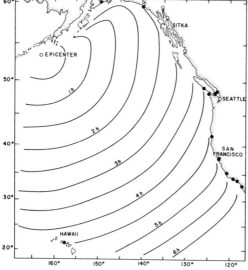

Fig. 2. Propagation of wave front across Pacific Ocean for tsunami of April 1, 1946 (Fox Islands). Solid circles show tide stations where large waves were recorded; open circles, where little or no activity occurred.

appears to be governed almost entirely by the local topography. By some as yet unexplained process, the water on the coastal shelf is set into oscillation at one or more (essentially) constant frequencies characteristic of the particular region in question. Typically, following a moderate—but abnormal—rise or recession of sea level, there are three to five major oscillations, after which there is a reduction in amplitude and gradual degeneracy to normal conditions over a period of several days. Almost all of the damage attributable to tsunamis occurs during the short interval of the large oscillations, which, in some areas, encroach upon the land to a vertical extent of some tens of feet above sea level. Such areas are relatively few, fortunately, and around most of the oceanic perimeter local oscillations rarely exceed the normal tide range.

However, even very modest, periodic variations in sea level of appropriate frequency along the coastline can excite swift currents and abnormal harmonic responses in bays and harbors, as the water level within seeks to adjust itself to that outside. These effects often cause considerable damage to ships and waterfront structures in regions relatively immune from human hazard.

W. G. Van Dorn

References

General description: Van Dorn, W. G., 1965, "Tsunamis," *Advan. Hydroscience,* **2** Acad. Press, N.Y.
Generation theory: Keller, J. B., 1961, "Tsunamis—

water waves produced by earthquakes," *Proc. Pacific Sci. Congr.* 10*th Honolulu IUGG Monograph*, **24**, 154–166.

Source mechanisms: Aki, Keiiti, 1960, "Interpretation of source functions of circum-Pacific earthquakes obtained from long-period Rayleigh waves," *J. Geophys. Res.*, **65**(8), 2405–2417.

Local effects: Shepard, F. P., MacDonald, G. A., and Cox, D. C., 1950, "The tsunami of April 1, 1946," *Bull. Scripps Inst. Oceanogr.*, 5(6), 391–528.

Tsunami decay: Munk, W. H., 1961, "Some comments regarding diffusion and absorption of tsunamis," *Proc. Pacific Sci. Congr.* 10*th Honolulu, IUGG Monograph*, **24**, 53–72.

TURBIDITY CURRENTS

Currents can be caused by horizontal differences in density within fluid or gaseous bodies. Thus, the major deep circulation of the oceans is due to differences in salinity and temperature. Turbidity currents are of the same kind, but the excess density is caused by a suspended load of sediment. The turbidity current flows downslope and spreads out on a horizontal floor. If the velocity and turbulence are sufficient to retard settling of the entrained particles, the current can flow for great distances. Gradually, the load drops out as the current slackens, until the water finally comes to rest. The deposits are called *turbidites* (q.v., pr Vol. VII). A muddy river flows irrespective of the load, and is, therefore, not a turbidity current. However, dry avalanches (*Staublawinen*) and volcanic glowing clouds (*nuées ardentes*) are turbidity currents in the atmosphere.

The concept of turbidity flow was first applied by Forel in 1885 to rivers flowing into Swiss lakes at delta fronts. But it was not till half a century later, in 1936, that Daly invoked this mechanism to explain the origin of submarine canyons. This stimulated Kuenen to study these currents experimentally in 1937, 1947, and 1950, and he was able to demonstrate the efficiency of the mechanism.

High densities in experimental flows with clay and sand produced swift currents with remarkable carrying power. Extrapolation to the size of nature indicated that high velocities must be possible. The experimental flows produced slightly muddy, graded sands, and this suggested that deep-sea sands and ancient graded sandstones might be turbidites.

In collaboration with Migliorini in 1950 and Natland in 1951, these ideas were applied to formations in Italy and Southern California. Since then countless authors have studied ancient turbidite formations. Many significant features have come to light, and the importance of the mechanism in filling geosynclinal troughs with flysch-like sediments of the alternating type (graywackesshales and graded calcarenites-marls) has been established.

In the meantime, application of the concept of turbidity flow to the present oceans by M. Ewing, Heezen, and Ericson of the Lamont Geological Observatory has met with remarkable success. Emery, Menard, Shepard, and many others have contributed important points.

Evidence for the action of turbidity currents in the oceans comes partly from topography. At the lower end of submarine canyons, low-angle fans are developed which gradually merge into abyssal plains, the slopes decreasing from 1–0.1°, but continuing to fall away from the evident source of sediment. Wherever the ocean floor is protected from the advent of turbidity currents by ridges, trenches or distances of over 2000 km, rough topography prevails. Basins like the Gulf of Mexico and most deep-sea trenches are floored by an abyssal plain. There are even a few cases known of basins with a spill-way over the lowest part of the rim that leads to a second plain at a lower level in an adjoining basin.

The origin of submarine canyons is still uncertain, although it is generally believed that they are flushed out and, to some extent, eroded by turbidity currents. But there are canyons with rocky and irregular walls that cannot be attributed to turbidity currents alone; these may be drowned river valleys.

Further evidence comes from deep-sea cores. All long samples taken on fans and abyssal plains contain layers of sand or silt—on the average of two layers per meter. But on surrounding slopes or hills rising out of the plains, such deep-sea sands are absent. This shows that the materials have been carried along the bottom, and not at a higher level. Phleger showed (1951) that the sands contain shallow-water bottom Foraminifera. Calcareous algae and large shells have also been found. The sands show graded bedding, coarse at the bottom and becoming finer toward the top, until they gradually merge into the covering pelagic sediment. Their lower surface is sharply delineated. They are partially laminated with current ripple foresetting, showing the action of a current. In successive beds, the direction remains the same and evidently points downslope. The thickness varies from barely visible to 6 meters. Individual beds have been traced by echo sounder for dozens of kilometers, because they tend to produce subsurface reflections. A few distinctive beds have been cored over areas of 5000–10,000 km².

A spectacular demonstration of the incredible scale on which the mechanism can act is provided by the aftermath of the Grand Banks earthquake of 1929. Several submarine cables on the sea floor surrounding the epicenter were broken by the shock. But, in addition, a series of delayed breaks occurred, the time lag increasing with the distance downslope from the epicenter. Ewing and Heezen in 1952 explained this by the triggering of a slide that changed to a turbidity current. It swept down the slope and out onto the adjoining abyssal plain, and abraded and snapped the cables which it crossed over lengths of 200 km. From the timing of the breaks, it followed that the velocity must have exceeded 45 knots (83 km/hr). Later, in this area, Heezen discovered a graded turbidite of about 1-meter thickness—just the amount Kuenen had deduced. It covered an area of at least 100,000 km², and was found lying on top of normal pelagic sediment. The volume of sediment must be about 100 km³, enough to load a row of tankers 20 ships wide running round the equator. This stupendous mass of sediment must have come down the slope in one great cloud, because otherwise, the deposit could not show grading. Bearing in mind that the slope is about 50 times as steep as the lower reaches of major rivers, the high velocity can be understood.

Heezen also has shown that following floods of the Magdalena and the Congo Rivers, there quite commonly occur cable breaks in the adjoining submarine canyons. Green plant remains have been found caught around the broken cables in depths of hundreds of meters.

The laboratory experiments by Kuenen showed that powerful currents of about 1 m/sec (= 2 knots) can be set up from 20 liters of suspension on a slope of 10°. Densities of 2 do not preclude swift flow, and it was found that the current velocity is proportional to the root of the slope, the density, and the hydraulic mean depth. No measurable influence of increased viscosity with high densities was found. In a trench of 30-meter length and a slope of 20 cm down over the first 2 meters, currents of 100 liters carried sand for distances of 20 meters. Sampling from the current showed that the density decreased from the bottom to the surface of the flow, and from the nose backward. Concomitantly with the density, the grain size in the suspension fell off. This shows that the coarsest sand grains were carried in suspension, for they did not lag behind the nose of the current. As the current advanced, the maximum grain size held in suspension gradually decreased.

The deposit of such a current shows excellent graded bedding both vertically and horizontally. There also occur distortions due to the unconsolidated, mobile condition of the loosely packed deposit of muddy sand.

During the experiment the deposit is seen to segregate at the bottom of the flow with waves,

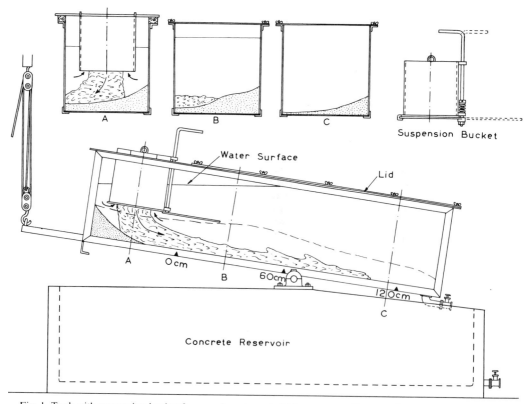

Fig. 1. Tank with suspension bucket for experiments on turbidity currents. Bottom of bucket can be turned sidewise to release suspension. (from Kuenen and Migliorini, "Turbidity Currents as a Cause of Graded Bedding," *J. Geol.*, **58**, 96, Fig. 1).

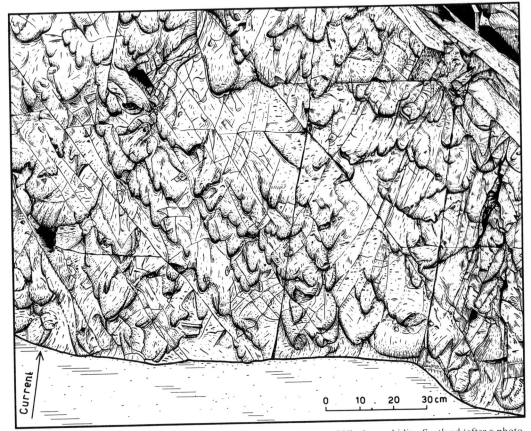

Fig. 2. Casts of flutings produced by turbidity current, visible on sole of Silurian turbidite, Scotland (after a photograph; from Kuenen, "Sole Markings of Graded Graywacke Beds, *J. Geol.*, **65**, 237, Fig. 4).

running along its surface. There is also a forward movement of the grains in the deposit that becomes slower toward the base and dies out as the layer compacts by loss of interstitial water. This moving carpet probably reduces drag along the bottom, and the gradual transition of velocity from the fast current to the stationary clear water above presumably also reduces friction. The wedge-shaped nose pushes itself under the still water, lifting it relatively slowly, thus allowing the current to attain a high velocity. The energy is provided by the vertical drop of the sediment from a shallow area to the basin floor.

Turbidity currents appear to originate in several ways. They can be triggered by a heavily charged river in spate with a density exceeding that of seawater, or by an earthquake setting off a slide. Another possibility is oversteepening of a depositional slope owing either to supply or to tectonic movement. Possibly storm waves or tsunamic waves can raise sufficient sediment to start a current. Liquefaction of loosely packed sediment has been invoked as a preliminary to sliding. A slide can change to a turbulent current by mixing

with water. But fine-grained sediment on the sea floor normally contains enough interstitial water to allow liquid flow with moderate viscosity, once turbulent movements have broken down the thixotropic cohesion of the clays.

The lowering of sea level during the Ice Age greatly stimulated the action. Large erosion valleys formed, and the excavated materials were dumped by the lengthened rivers at the shelf edge, ready to take off down the slope.

Because the deep-sea sands are undoubtedly the deposits of turbidity currents, they should resemble the ancient rocks which are claimed to be turbidites. In fact, the two are as closely alike as possible. In the ancient rocks, the grading, the lamination of the finer parts, the current ripple mark, the alternation with pelagic beds, and the difference between the fauna of the turbidites and the autochthonous fauna of the pelagic beds, are all present. There are, moreover, sole markings on the ancient graywackes produced by the turbulent scour of the muddy floor over which the current passed. They are now visible as casts filled with the sand of the turbidite. Other sole markings were developed by the drag of plants, animals, chunks of clay, and pebbles over the bottom. There are prod marks and bounce marks where an object has hit the bottom once or repeatedly. The organic hiero-glyphs are very characteristic. The great majority developed from burrows in the sea floor, the reworked sediment having been wafted away by the turbidity current during slight erosion of the mud.

Other typical properties of turbidite formations are the thick sequences, the regular bedding, and the uniform current direction shown by the sole markings. Besides these positive features, there are a number of no less typical negative characteristics. These are the absence of all shallow-water features, such as wave ripple mark, plants in situ, coral reefs, beach phenomena, large-scale cross bedding, and well-winnowed sands. Indications of emer-gence, e.g., desiccation cracks, dunes, swamps, meandering channels, etc., are likewise sought in vain.

Where a formation shows all features listed above, the conclusion is warranted that one is dealing with turbidites. But each one of these characteristics can also be encountered in other types of sediment. Thus, grading is common in river deposits, and sole markings have been found in shallow neritic formations or in the flash-flood deposits of arid climates. Hence, it is only a combination of several that can be relied upon as diagnostic.

It transpires that most turbidite formations have been classified as flysch, or at least resemble flysch from a sedimentological point of view. However, the two terms are not synonymous, for the use of flysch is restricted to post-Paleozoic rocks, and most authors require that the sediments predate the major orogeny of the geosyncline. Some flysch consists of slumped material and boulder mud-stones. On the other hand, some obvious turbidites occur in formations that are not termed flysch.

Turbidite formations have been recognized from the early Archean (e.g., the Figtree Formation of South Africa) to the Quaternary. Some of the best documented examples are the Plio-Pleistocene of the Ventura and of the Los Angeles Basins in Southern California. The species of benthonic Foraminifera in the pelagic beds still occur in the adjacent oceans. Some of these, being sensitive to temperature and pressure, are restricted to cold, deep water. On this evidence, it can be shown convincingly that deposition started in depths of 2000 meters and continued until the basins were filled up above sea level. Frequent turbidites are present all the way up to depths of a few hundred meters, as Natland and Kuenen showed in 1951. Gorsline and Emery were able to demonstrate in 1959 that the similarity between sedimentation in the present offshore basins and the oil basins just mentioned is remarkably close. The depths in which turbidites were laid down cannot be ascer-tained with any accuracy in other cases. However,

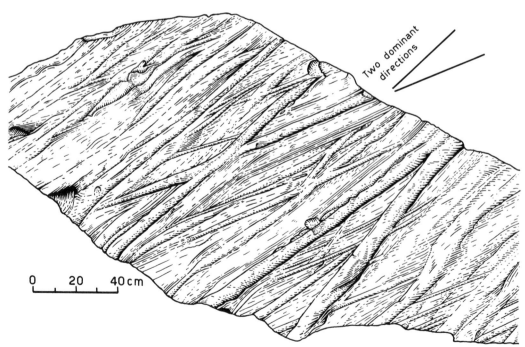

Fig. 3. Casts of grooves visible on sole of Miocene turbidite, Fiume Reno, Italy (after a photograph; *J. Geol.*, **65**, 244, Fig. 12).

Fig. 4. Casts of grooves and flutings. Note corkscrew shapes, proving turbulent current action. Miocene turbidite, Passo di Muraglione, Italy (after a photograph; *J. Geol.*, **65**, 247, Fig. 14).

faunal evidence and general considerations point to depths of deposition below the neritic zone, although the material came from shallow water.

The examination of turbidite formations has shed light on paleogeographic and structural problems. In the first place, it has become evident that many geosynclinal basins were hundreds to thousands of meters deep during part of their history. Formerly these flysch-like deposits were referred to shallow coastal environments. In the second place, determination of the current directions (by sole markings and current bedding) is a useful aid in finding the source areas for the sediment. In more than half the cases examined, the currents flowed longitudinally. Hence, the supply has not come directly from the side, as previously assumed, but either from a more distant lateral source or even from the end of the trough. The latter situation is comparable to the present supply in the Adriatic, Persian Gulf, Gulf of California, etc., where a major or even dominant source is formed by a large river entering the basin at its end.

In the French Riviera, the Oligocene flysch is found to have been partly derived from an ancient land situated in the Mediterranean. This source area, delivering great quantities of quartz sand, now lies more than 2000 meters deep. This finding confirms the conclusion drawn by Bourcart and Glangeaud that the western Mediterranean Basin is of Upper Tertiary age.

In the Apennines, Merla had found that the structure is complicated by the sliding on the argile scagliose clays of great slabs of rock, measuring many cubic kilometers. Ten Haaf's study of the turbidites in 1959 showed that the current directions in the undisturbed areas are all parallel to the axis of the geosyncline toward the southeast. In the displaced slabs, it is rotated 90° or more, clockwise in some, counterclockwise in others. This not only provides unequivocal proof of Merla's conclusion, but it adds the piquant aspect of rotational movement.

The most intricate relations so far revealed are those encountered by Polish geologists, lead by Ksiazkiewicz, in the Carpathian Mountains. Many excellent and detailed studies have been published showing that there were three parallel troughs divided by submarine ridges with islands. Laterial, oblique, and longitudinal supply occurred with transport sometimes in opposing directions in adjoining troughs.

PH. H. KUENEN

References

Hill, M. N. (editor), 1963, "The Sea," Vol. 3, "The Earth beneath the Sea, History," New York, John Wiley & Sons, 963pp.

Kuenen, Ph. H. (1964), "Deep-sea Sands and Ancient Turbidites," in "Developments in Sedimentology," Amsterdam, Elsevier, 3–33.

Kuenen, Ph. H., and Humbert, F. L. (1964), "Bibliography of Turbidity Currents and Turbidites," in "Developments in Sedimentology," Amsterdam, Elsevier, 222–246.

Potter, P. E., and Pettijohn, F. J., 1963, "Paleocurrents and Basin Analysis," Berlin, Springer, 296pp.

TURBULENCE

The Nature of Turbulent Flow

The motion of a liquid or gas is turbulent when the velocity at any point is fluctuating in magnitude and direction in a chaotic, random manner. An important criterion which distinguishes turbulence from an irregular wave motion is its diffusive action: turbulence leads to increased rates of transport of heat, momentum and other properties like salt or water vapor. Fluid particles are on the average moved further apart by turbulence.

As the velocity is increased in a flow of fixed size, a smooth or *laminar* motion will become unstable and *turbulent*, at a value of the Reynolds number $Re = \rho u d/\mu$ of a few thousand, where u is the mean velocity of flow, d is a typical dimension across the flow, ρ is the density and μ the viscosity. Geophysical flows are usually so large or fast that they must be turbulent, and turbulence is important in such varied applications as the drag exerted by the air on the ground or a river on its bed, the diffusion of heat and smoke in the atmosphere, ocean currents, and the motion of interstellar gas clouds. Stable or unstable density gradients can greatly modify turbulence and the transport produced by it, and so can special properties like compressibility (in high-speed flows) and electrical conductivity (in a magnetic field).

Early Theories

Osborne Reynolds first showed that the existence of correlated velocity fluctuations u', v' and w' in the horizontal (x and y) and vertical (z) directions must lead to increased stresses or vertical transports of horizontal momentum, of the form $\overline{\rho u' w'}$, where the bar is used to denote a time average. Such terms are called the *Reynolds stresses* and may be much larger than the viscous stress. Similar expressions can be set down for the turbulent transports of heat or salt.

Early descriptions of turbulent flows were based on analogies with molecular diffusion. The flux F_i of any property with concentration C per unit mass say, is related to the gradient dC/dz by

$$F_i = -K_i \frac{dC}{dz} \quad (i = 1, 2, \ldots)$$

i.e., the molecular diffusivities are just replaced by larger *eddy coefficients*. The transfer coefficient for momentum, corresponding to the kinematic vis-

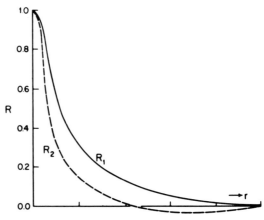

Fig. 1. Correlation functions (after Prandtl, 1952).

cosity $v = \mu/\rho$ is called the *eddy viscosity* K_M. The *mixing length* theories go further and compare turbulent "eddies" with molecules which carry their properties unchanged a distance l, then mix. L. Prandtl regarded momentum as the transported quantity, and his definition of mixing length implies $K_M = \overline{w'l}$ for vertical transport in a horizontal flow. Theories based on the transport of vorticity have also been developed. It is frequently assumed that the K_i for any other diffused property is equal to K_M, but this simplification is not always valid, especially in stable density gradients. Unlike the molecular values, the turbulent coefficients also vary with the position and direction in the flow, and with the boundary conditions. The analogy with molecules is far from perfect since it ignores the gradual interaction of fluid with its surroundings and the continuous supply of energy necessary to maintain turbulence. These semiempirical theories are still extensively used in solving practical problems, especially when only mean profiles are of interest, but they shed little light on the fundamental mechanisms of turbulent motion, and may be quite wrong in some contexts.

Statistical Properties

The more recent theories of turbulence are based on ideas introduced by G. I. Taylor. They use the statistically steady mean values which can be formed from randomly fluctuating velocity components. A basic assumption is that the laws describing a turbulent flow are independent of the exact way in which it has arisen, but depend only on the external parameters of the problem like the Reynolds number and the shape of the boundaries. Such theories deal strictly with *probability averages*, obtained by repeating an experiment many times under identical external conditions. In practice, these must be replaced by *time averages*, and this introduces special difficulties for geophysical flows, which are never completely steady or repeatable.

Even the separation into mean and fluctuating components is largely subjective and depends on the averaging interval chosen. For example, the flow near a single pressure system in the atmosphere would be a fluctuation in a monthly average of wind velocity, but it could be regarded as steady if turbulence near the ground was being studied with an averaging time of a few minutes.

Important quantities involving averages at one point are the mean velocity $\bar{u}$, the Reynolds stresses, and the mean kinetic energy per unit mass or the *intensity* of turbulence $E = \frac{1}{2}(\overline{u'^2} + \overline{v'^2} + \overline{w'^2})$. Averages may also be calculated for products of velocity components at two or more points. Typical longitudinal and transverse *correlation functions*, formed from the products of simultaneously measured velocity fluctuations u' and v' in directions parallel and perpendicular to the line joining two points a distance r apart, are shown in Fig. 1. If the turbulence is *homogeneous* in space these are

$$R_1 = \overline{u_1'u_2'}/\overline{u'^2} \quad \text{and} \quad R_2 = \overline{v_1'v_2'}/\overline{v'^2}.$$

More definite predictions about the relation between R_1 and R_2 can be made by introducing the concept of *isotropic turbulence*, that having identical statistical properties in the three component directions. This can be realized approximately in laboratory wind tunnels and sometimes in nature, and detailed verifications of many theoretical results have been made using hot-wire anemometers and electronic averaging techniques. The *autocorrelation function* may also be defined similarly in terms of the velocities at a single point, but now separated in time. At zero difference of r or t the the velocities are perfectly correlated and $R_1 = R_2 = 1$, and at large r or t these fall to zero. A natural length scale of the turbulence obtained from the correlation function is the *integral scale* $L_1 = \int_0^\infty R_1(r)\,dr$. The variation of velocity or other properties at a point may also be resolved into frequency components. The *spectrum function* is the form of the variation of kinetic energy with frequency or wave number, and it is closely related to the autocorrelation function: they are Fourier transforms of one another.

Taylor also treated the problem of diffusion using a statistical method, which provides a theoretically sounder alternative to the eddy diffusion or mixing length arguments. His theory of *diffusion by continuous movements* is based on the properties of the *Lagrangian correlation function*, which relates the turbulent velocities of a single fluid particle at different times.

Transfer of Energy and Local Isotropy of the Small Eddies

A turbulent motion is made up of a large number of components with different frequencies and length scales. When the mean flow becomes unstable,

energy is transferred first to the largest scales of turbulence, and eddies comparable with the integral scale L_1 contain most of the kinetic energy. These eddies in turn break down and lose energy to smaller scales, until eventually viscous dissipation takes place, mostly in the smallest eddies in which the velocity gradients are large. Statistically there is a flow of energy through the spectrum from the largest to the smallest scales.

The principle of *flow similarity* states that at high enough Reynolds numbers all the large-scale properties of a flow, such as the mean velocity distribution, turbulent intensities and correlation functions, do not depend directly on viscosity but only on the boundary conditions of the flow. In particular the rate per unit mass ε at which the largest eddies transfer energy to smaller scales is determined by their own structure and is approximately

$$\varepsilon = (\overline{u'^2})^{3/2} L_1^{-1}$$

where $\overline{u'^2}$ is a typical mean square turbulent velocity. ε may also be expressed exactly as the rate of working of the mean velocity gradient against the Reynolds stress, i.e., as

$$\varepsilon = -\overline{u'w'}\frac{d\bar{u}}{dz}.$$

The large separation between the scales of energy containing and dissipating eddies in flows with a high Re also has important consequences for the smaller eddies. A. N. Kolmogoroff suggested that the latter will be statistically decoupled from their energy sources, and in a state of *universal equilibrium* in which they are *locally isotropic* and steady. There is usually a substantial range of eddy sizes in the ocean or atmosphere for which this is true. Kolmogoroff's first hypothesis is that all average properties of the flow which are determined by the small-scale components (such as the *relative* motion of particles over distances small compared with L_1) should depend only on ε and $\nu = \mu/\rho$. In particular, the velocity and length scales v and η of the dissipating eddies will be of order $v = (\nu\varepsilon)^{\frac{1}{4}}$ and $\eta = (\nu^3/\varepsilon)^{\frac{1}{4}}$.

When this equilibrium range is sufficiently wide (at even higher values of Re), the larger eddies in it will be unaffected directly by viscosity. Kolmogoroff's second hypothesis is that in this *inertial subrange*, average properties of the turbulence will depend only on ε, which is the rate of transfer of energy through it. In the inertial subrange, dimensional arguments show that the dependence of the energy spectrum $E(\kappa)$ on wave number is of the form

$$E(\kappa) \propto \varepsilon^{2/3} \kappa^{-5/3}$$

The dispersion of a group of particles about its center of gravity depends on the separations y and the time t through

$$\frac{d\overline{y^2}}{dt} \propto \varepsilon^{1/3}(\overline{y^2})^{2/3}$$

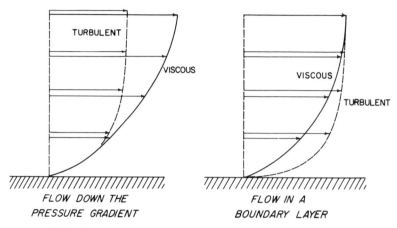

Fig. 2. Laminar and turbulent velocity profiles (after Scorer, 1958).

with certain limitations on the range of t and y. Both of these results have received good support from measurements in the ocean and the atmosphere, and there are many other simple and powerful applications. It is sometimes difficult, however, to decide when Kolmogoroff's theory can properly be applied: special care should be taken when there are energy sources at intermediate scales, e.g., cumulus clouds in the atmosphere.

Turbulence near Boundaries

Turbulent flows near a solid boundary or in a pipe are retarded by the boundary and exert a stress or drag on it, which is roughly proportional to the square of the mean velocity. Very close to a smooth surface, in the *viscous sublayer*, the stress is due to viscosity alone, but further away the Reynolds stresses are the more important. Energy fed from the mean flow to the turbulence maintains these stresses and then is mostly dissipated locally in a layer of nearly constant stress. Turbulence transfers momentum more rapidly than a purely viscous flow, so in a pipe with a given pressure gradient the velocity gradients and the mean velocity are reduced compared with the laminar case. In a *boundary layer* with a fixed velocity outside, the shear is concentrated close to the boundary and so the drag is increased in the turbulent flow.

In the turbulent part of the constant stress layer, the velocity gradient $d\bar{u}/dz$ is independent of the viscosity μ; it depends only on the density of the fluid ρ, the wall stress τ and on the distance z from the wall. Dimensional arguments show that

$$\frac{d\bar{u}}{dz} = \frac{u_*}{kz}$$

where $u_* = (\tau/\rho)^{1/2} = (\overline{u'w'})^{1/2}$ is called the friction velocity and k is von Karman's constant (experimentally, $k = 0.41$). Integrating this gives the *logarithmic velocity profile*

$$\bar{u} = \frac{u_*}{k}(\ln z + c)$$

The constant of integration c is found from the conditions at the surface; note that it does not change the shape of the profile but merely adds a constant velocity of translation to it. In *aerodynamically smooth* flows, c depends on the molecular viscosity. In *aerodynamically rough* flows, the stress is transferred directly by pressure forces to roughness elements on the surface which project above the viscous sublayer (whose thickness is of order $\mu/u_*\rho$), so viscosity does not enter explicitly and

$$\bar{u} = \frac{u_*}{k}\ln\frac{z}{z_0}$$

The length z_0 defined by this expression is called the *roughness length;* it is numerically about 1/30 of the height of physical roughness elements. Transfer of momentum to a moving surface, as in the flow of air over the sea, takes place through coupled wave motions in the air and water, and the aerodynamic roughness of the sea is much smaller than the height of the waves would suggest.

Free Turbulence

Free turbulence occurs well away from solid boundaries and is maintained by the strong shear between the moving fluid and its surroundings. Examples in nature are the jet streams, wakes of aircraft or ships, convection plumes from chimneys, and cumulus clouds. At any instant a free turbulent motion consists of a core of nearly uniform small-scale turbulence, separated by a sharp boundary from non-turbulent fluid. The edge is distorted by large eddy motions and is waving about, leading to an *intermittency* of the turbulence at any point. It is also spreading out into the surroundings, and the process of *entrainment* consists of the engulfing of fluid by the large eddies, followed by a rapid

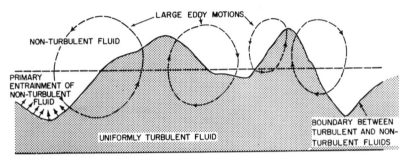

Fig. 3. Edge of a turbulent jet (Townsend, 1956). (By permission of University Press, Cambridge, Mass.)

small-scale mixing across the central part of the jet, wake or plume.

As well as being similar at all high Reynolds numbers, free flows are nearly *self-preserving*; i.e., the mean characteristics of the motion remain similar at all transverse sections of the flow as it develops and mixes. For example, because of the unsteadiness of the edge of a plume, the profiles of mean velocity or temperature at any section are close to error functions (with that for temperature slightly wider). The scales of width b_0, velocity u_0 or temperature T_0 will be functions of the distance x from the origin and the controlling physical parameters such as the flux of momentum M in a jet or of buoyancy in a plume. These functions may be determined by dimensional arguments: e.g., in a circular jet, $b_0 \propto x$ and $u_0 \propto M^{1/2} x^{-1}$. Another powerful method in the study of free flows is the use of an *entrainment constant* a. The speed u_α with which a turbulent flow moves into undisturbed fluid (or, alternatively, the external fluid is entrained across the boundary of the turbulent core) must in a self-preserving flow be proportional to the velocity scale u_0; a is the constant of proportionality $a = u_\alpha/u_0$.

The Effect of Density Differences on Turbulence

Gravitationally *unstable* distributions of density in the ocean or potential temperature in the atmosphere can produce localized turbulent motions by converting potential to kinetic energy in a fluid initially at rest: examples are turbidity currents on the sea bed, and convection elements in and below clouds. Unstable gradients can also greatly modify shear flows by causing stronger mixing. *Forced convection* is used to describe the transfer of a property like heat when the motion is dominated by the shear, and *free convection* when the unstable density gradients are more important. In the atmosphere there is often a rather sharp transition from the first near the ground to the second higher up.

Stable density gradients on the other hand tend to damp turbulence, to decrease mixing and increase velocity gradients. They are always important in the ocean, and *inversion* conditions in the atmosphere

are those in which smog forms. *Richardson's criterion* for turbulence in a stable gradient is obtained by comparing the rate of working of the shear stresses and the work done against gravity; it states that turbulence must die out if

$$R_f = \frac{K_H}{K_M} R_i = \frac{K_H}{K_M} \frac{g}{\rho} \frac{\partial \rho}{\partial z} \bigg/ \left(\frac{\partial u}{\partial z}\right)^2 > 1$$

A critical value of the *flux Richardson number* R_f (which in practice is much less than 1) is important here, not the ratio R_i originally defined by L. F. Richardson. His R_i is multiplied by the ratio of the diffusivity K_H for heat (or K_s for salt) to the eddy viscosity K_M. Differences between these are possible because of the different mechanisms of transfer—momentum can be transported vertically by pressure fluctuations associated with internal wave motion, but the turbulent transfer of heat or salt implies mixing. Turbulence may persist for large values of R_i, with K_H and K_M both larger than the molecular coefficients, provided the ratio K_H/K_M is correspondingly small. This has been confirmed by measurements in the ocean and the laboratory.

It is sometimes inconvenient to use R_f or R_i as stability parameters because they vary with height. Instead, A. S. Monin and A. M. Obukhov introduced the length $L = \overline{\rho} u_*^3/g(\overline{\rho'w'})$ which can be formed from u_* and the flux of heat or density difference. The velocity profiles and other properties of shear flows can then be put in a universal form using the non-dimensional height variable z/L. All these quantities are closely related, since $R_f = K_M/u_* L$.

J. S. TURNER

References

Batchelor, G. K., 1953, "The Theory of Homogeneous Turbulence," Cambridge, The University Press.

Prandl, L., 1952, "Essentials of Fluid Dynamics," London, Blackie.

Priestley, C. H. B., 1959, "Turbulent Transfer in the Lower Atmosphere," Chicago, University of Chicago Press.

Scorer, R. S., 1958, "Natural Aerodynamics," Oxford, Pergamon Press.

Townsend, A. A., 1956, "The Structure of Turbulent Shear Flow," Cambridge, The University Press.

Townsend, A. A., 1961, "Turbulence," in (Streeter, V. L., editor) "Handbook of Fluid Dynamics," Section 10, New York, McGraw-Hill Book Co.

TURBULENCE IN THE OCEAN

(1) Eddy Viscosity and Mixing Length

Fluid motion has two regimes: regular and steady laminar flow and irregular and unsteady turbulent flow. Laminar flow occurs when viscous force is predominant over inertia forces, while turbulent flow occurs in the opposite case. A criterion for change from laminar to turbulent motion is that a non-dimensional Reynolds' number exceeds a certain critical value. This number is equal to (characteristic velocity) × (scale length)/(viscosity), characterizing the ratio of intertia terms to viscous force (Goldstein, 1938).

Flows in the ocean are in most cases turbulent, owing to large scales, although the velocity is slow in general. Therefore, in the ordinary usage of words, flows in the ocean, like wind-driven currents, geostrophic currents and tidal currents, indicate the mean motion averaged over space and/or time. Averaged equations of fluid motion prescribe the behaviors of mean flow. These equations are different from the equations for instantaneous motion in containing additional terms called Reynolds' stresses, which arise from mean values of products of irregular components of velocity (Goldstein, 1938). Reynolds' stresses represent the effect of irregular velocity components, or turbulence, on the mean motion. In many cases of oceanic flows, turbulence seems to equalize distributions of momentum among mean flows in a similar way to irregular motions of gas molecules which generate viscous stresses proportional to space derivatives of macroscopic fluid velocities. In analogy to these viscous stresses, Reynolds' stresses are expressed as proportional to space derivatives of velocities of the mean motion, and the proportional constants are called eddy viscosity in contrast with (molecular) viscosity.

The concept of the eddy viscosity was applied to wind-driven currents by Ekman in 1905 with a certain degree of success (Defant, 1961). When only molecular viscosity of water is considered, it takes several hundreds of years for the wind of 20 m/sec to generate an ocean current of 1 m/sec to a depth of 100 m, while the same current can be generated within several days when eddy viscosity is taken into account. Eddy viscosity is much larger than molecular viscosity, since it has an order of magnitude of 100–10^{10} times the molecular viscosity, depending on scales of the mean motion. In fact, eddy viscosity is not a physical constant, but it represents characteristics of turbulence present in the motion considered.

The mixing length hypothesis is an elaboration of the eddy viscosity concept and was developed and applied to various fluid dynamic problems by Prandtl and his successors since 1925 (Goldstein, 1938). Mixing length is defined in analogy with a mean free path of gas molecules as an average distance in which eddies in a turbulent flow may travel before mixing with the ambient fluid. Then, eddy viscosity in a turbulent shear flow is expressed by (mixing length)^2 × (shear) by considering transport of momentum by eddies. Prandtl assumed further that the mixing length is proportional to the distance from a boundary and also introduced a roughness parameter which is to be added to the actual distance when the boundary surface is not smooth.

Rossby and Montgomery applied the mixing length hypothesis to derive velocity profiles of boundary flows in the ocean and the atmosphere (Defant, 1961; Ichiye, 1963). They obtained a logarithmic distribution of wind speed with height over land and sea and a power distribution of currents in a shallow sea and compared with observed data. They revised the Ekman theory of wind-driven currents by introducing a planetary boundary layer of a few hundred meters below a frictional boundary layer of a few meters near the sea surface. Mixing length increases with depth in the latter but decreases with depth in the former layer.

(2) Empirical Determination of Eddy Viscosity in the Ocean

Since eddy viscosity depends on structure of the flow, there are many studies to represent it empirically in terms of characteristic variables of the flow. Vertical eddy viscosity, due to momentum transport by eddies in the vertical direction, is related to various transport mechanisms. Dobroklonskii, Kitaigorodoskii and others expressed vertical eddy viscosity caused by wind waves in terms of their predominant amplitudes, lengths and periods (Ichiye, 1963). In the upper layer of the ocean, turbulence is generated by wind stresses. Therefore, vertical eddy viscosity, determined from observational data in this layer, is found to be proportional to the square of wind speed (Sverdrup et al., 1942). The effect of a stable density gradient is to reduce the intensity of turbulence, while shear in the mean current tends to increase its intensity. Non-dimensional Richardson number is defined as the ratio of stability to square of shear. Thus vertical eddy viscosity in a flow with density stratification decreased with increasing Richardson number, where functional relationships between them were given by Rossby and Montgomery, Munk and Anderson and Mamaev (Bowden, 1962).

Methods of determining numerical values of eddy viscosity (both horizontal and vertical. with observations are classified in two categories: from the mean velocity distribution and from the Reynolds' stresses determined by measuring fluctuating velocities. The first method was widely used before 1950 in various parts of the ocean. The vertical and horizontal eddy viscosity determined by this method ranges $0.1–10^3$ (cm²/sec) and $10^2–10^9$ (cm²/sec), respectively (Sverdrup *et al.,* 1942). The change of vertical eddy viscosity depends on water depth, stability, wind and wave effects, while that of horizontal eddy viscosity depends on the scale of motion. The largest value corresponds to the general circulation in the ocean.

The second method needs elaborate current meters, which can measure fluctuations of currents. The eddy viscosity can be determined as a ratio of the Reynolds' stress to the shear of the mean velocity. Vertical components of the Reynolds' stresses and the vertical eddy viscosity were determined in the Irish Sea by Bowden and Fairbairn in 1956 and in various seas, including the Black and Caspian Seas, the polar Sea and the Antarctic Ocean, by various Russian workers since 1958 (Bowden, 1962; Ichiye, 1963). Horitzontal components of the Reynolds' stresses were determined in the Florida Strait by Stommel with Pillsbury's drogue data, in various parts of the Gulf Stream by Webster with GEK data, and in the Kuroshio area by Ichiye with GEK data (Bowden, 1962; Ichiye, 1963). These measurements yield the horizontal eddy viscosity of $10^6–10^7$ cm²/sec. However, results of Ichiye and Webster suggest that at the coastal side of the Gulf Stream and the Kuroshio, the energy is transferred from eddies to the mean flow, contrary to ordinary turbulent flows, and thus formal derivation from Reynolds' stresses yields negative values of horizontal eddy viscosity (Ichiye, 1963).

(3) Statistical Theory of Turbulence and Its Application to the Ocean

The energy of turbulence is distributed among eddies of various sizes. Energy spectrum represents the distribution of turbulence energy among different sizes or wave numbers of eddies. Although velocities in turbulent motion are random, the energy spectrum of turbulence follows a certain rule in a statistical sense, since movement of fluid is governed by equations of motion. The shape of statistical energy spectrum (against wave numbers) was determined by many workers, including Taylor, Kolmogoroff and Batchelor, since 1935 (Lin, 1961). Particularly when eddies are isotropic, i.e., dynamic behaviors of eddies are statistically the same in all directions, analytical forms of the spectrum were obtained. Inertia terms in equations of motion indicate that eddies of larger scales break into those of smaller scales and that energy is transferred

from large eddies (small wave numbers) to small eddies (large wave numbers) except in very large-scale motion. When sizes of eddies become much smaller, energy of eddies is dissipated by viscous forces into heat. In the intermediate range of eddies, where the rate of energy transfer from larger to smaller eddies is constant, Kolmogoroff found that energy spectrum is proportional to $k^{-5/3}$, where k is the wave number.

Eddy viscosity can be defined as a product of mixing length and magnitude of turbulent velocity averaged over eddies smaller than the scale of the mean flow. Mixing length is proportional to the scale of eddies or k^{-1}, while the energy spectrum, integrated about wave number, yields the square of turbulent velocities averaged over the integration range of wave number. Therefore, when the Kolmogoroff spectrum of turbulence is used, eddy viscosity is proportional to $k^{-4/3}$ or (4/3) power of scale of the mean motion. Stommel indicated that horizontal and vertical eddy viscosities determined empirically in the ocean satisfy this law (Defant, 1961).

Energy spectrum of turbulence can be determined by measuring space or time correlations among fluctuating components of velocities. Bowden determined the turbulence energy spectrum in tidal currents of the Irish Sea from the range of k between 10^{-4} and 2×10^{-2} (cm⁻¹). His result indicated that the energy spectrum is not isotropic and horizontal components contain more energy at the lower wave number range than a vertical component. On the other hand, Grant, Moillet and Stewart measured fluctuations of tidal currents in Discovery Passage, British Columbia and determined the energy spectrum for wave numbers of 0.02–1 cm⁻¹. In this range of wave numbers larger than those studied by Bowden, the spectrum is proportional to $k^{-5/3}$, as would be expected from Kolmogoroff's theory based on isotropic assumption (Bowden, 1962; Ichiye, 1963).

T. ICHIYE

References

Bowden, K. F., 1962, "Turbulence," in (Hill, M. N., editor) "The Sea," Vol. 1, Section 6, pp. 802–825, New York and London, Interscience Publishers.

Defant, A., 1961, "Physical Oceanography," Vol. 1, p. 729, New York, Pergamon Press.

Goldstein, S., 1938, "Modern Developments in Fluid Dynamics," Vol. 1, p. 330, Oxford, Clarendon Press (reprinted in 1965 by Dover Publications).

Ichiye, T., 1963, "Oceanic Turbulence (Review)," *Technical Paper*, No. 2, p. 200 (Oceanographic Institute, Florida State University for Office of Naval Research).

Lin, C. C., 1961, "Statistical Theories of Turbulence," p. 60, Princeton, N.J., Princeton University Press.

Sverdrup, H. V., Johnson, M. W., and Fleming, R. H., 1942, "The Oceans," p. 1060, Englewood Cliffs, N.J., Prentice-Hall, Inc.

U

UNDERWATER PHOTOGRAPHY

Photography under water with hand-held cameras was pioneered by Cousteau's group of Scuba divers. It was then developed further, with fixed stands and appropriate lighting for deep-sea photography. The strength required for pressure cases, of course, rises with the increasing depth. Optical requirements, however, remain essentially constant throughout the aphotic region.

Deep-sea cameras have been pioneered by Ivanoff, Edgerton, Laughton and Shipek. A most valuable development is the combined bottom grab and camera (Menzies, Smith and Emery, 1963; Emery, Merrill and Trumbull, 1965). The photograph can depict the general character of the area, while the grab brings up a specific sample.

Underwater Photography for Divers

The underwater photographer must be a competent diver so that he can concentrate on the photographic problems without consciously thinking about the diving problems. For instance, an inexperienced diver may kick downward, stirring up clouds of sediment that will obscure the photographic subject. The underwater photographer has enough problems to contend with, such as suspended particles in the water, coloration of the water, and illumination difficulties, without having to also concentrate on how to dive.

Cameras. Most underwater cameras consist of a camera inserted in a waterproof housing. Recently cameras have been made which are waterproof and require no housing. These cameras can also be used above water. Two of the better cameras inside housing· are the Rolleiflex Camera in the Rolleimarin housing and the Hasselblad in its housing. Two cameras that need no waterproof housing are the Calypso and Nikonos cameras. The Kodak Instamatic is available in a housing. All of these cameras can utilize a flash attachment.

Lens. A wide angle lens (e.g., 35 mm) is recommended so that a large subject area can be covered from a short distance. Most underwater photographs have to be taken from close range in order to get a clear picture. In some water conditions, 3 feet from subject to camera is a maximum distance for a sharp picture. Effective camera range is about half of the distance that the human eye can see underwater. If the photographer can make out details of the subject at, say 20 feet, the camera will record much the same details at about 10 feet.

A close-up lens will often increase the choice of subject material since most marine life is very small. It will also give clearer pictures as there will be less suspended particles in the water between the subject and the camera.

The light gathering ability (speeds) of the lens is an important factor. A lens of f:3.5 or larger is preferred. A sharper image will be obtained when this lens is stopped down for example to f:5.6, than a standard camera with a f:5.6 lens wide open.

Shutter. A very fast shutter is not normally needed underwater. There is rarely need to shoot at over 1/200 of a second. Usually the ambient light is insufficient to allow high-speed pictures without sacrificing depth of field due to a widely opened lens aperture. Of course, since there is generally not much of a depth of field anyway, this is a moot point.

Light Meter. An underwater light meter is valuable since ambient light attenuates as the diver descends. As the diver nears the bottom, reflected light from the bottom can brighten the picture, particularly if the bottom is composed of white sand. Cameras that contain an automatic light meter take out the guesswork. Some plastic housings have room enough inside to insert a light meter next to the camera. A simple expedient is to seal a meter in a glass jar. Light meters in manufactured housings are available.

Contrast. There is less contrast (black against white) underwater than above water. This lack of contrast is due to suspended matter, diffusion of light underwater, and water coloration. This may result in a hazy, indistinct picture. Sunlight entering the water at an angle in the morning or later afternoon can cause shadows which give more contrast. Artificial illumination can restore contrast underwater. A high-contrast printing process can provide more contrast in the black and white print.

Film. Black and white (B & W) films generally have more latitude than color film. The shutter speed for the lens opening may be incorrect by a margin of 2 or 3 and still produce a passable picture. Modern B & W films can be "pushed" (forced) to very high ASA ratings by the use of special darkroom processes. It is possible, for instance, to shoot ASA 100 film at ASA 1000. This does away with the need for a flash in some water conditions. B & W film with an ASA rating of 100–400 ASA is adequate for most daytime (near the surface, in clear water) photography. It is best if the photographer does his own film developing and his own printing. He will be able to anticipate the corrective measures needed in the darkroom.

Color films generally require closer attention to light meter readings. High-speed Ekta (ASA 160) is good for almost all 35-mm color underwater photography. It can be processed in the home. It can be used in almost every water condition. It produces good slides and color prints. The improved high-speed Ekta can be pushed to over 500 ASA. Ekta MF offers excellent color quality and can be pushed to 250 ASA. Type S Ekta color (ASA 80) negative offers excellent color enlargements for quality pictures. Since it is a negative film it can also be used to make B & W enlargements. A commercial color laboratory may be able to compensate for lack of contrast, or for too much of one color in the print, if they are warned in advance. In some cases a film designed for artificial light can compensate for too much blue when used underwater under ambient light.

Filters. Filters will correct some of the loss of color as the diver descends in the water. Filters will also compensate for too intense a color (usually water is too blue or too green).

Flash. In very dark water an underwater flash gun is essential. The flash may be either of the flashbulb type or strobe. Unfortunately, muddy water causes the suspended particles to appear like snow in the headlights of an automobile. This may obliterate the subject. In some cases it is actually better to take the picture in turbid water, without artificial light (if there is barely sufficient ambient light), since the mud particles will not interfere as much. If the effective range of a flashbulb above water is 30 feet, it may be only about 15 feet in clear water.

A white flashbulb used with a daylight color film will have the same effect as using a red filter. This will help to subdue the blue of the water. A blue bulb should not be used underwater in color photography. The water is already blue. A No. 5 or a AG1 flash bulb are two of the most popular choices.

A strobe light has the same color characteristics as daylight. It will accentuate the blueness of the water. A red or yellow filter may be needed. Many professional underwater photographers prefer the strobe light because it gives very sharp pictures and does away with the bother of changing flashbulbs. The flashgun should be mounted a couple of feet to one side of the camera. This will reduce the "snow in the headlights effect" because most of the light is not bouncing off from the particles directly back into the lens. A flash on an extension cord may be useful to illuminate dark segments of the subject. In clear water, the flash is usually used to "fill in" shadow areas.

Shooting the Picture. Taking good underwater pictures requires a technical knowledge of photography, imagination, diving skill and patience. The secret of successful underwater shots is to move close to the subject, especially in muddy water. Since underwater exposure settings are difficult to judge, it is best to "bracket the shots." Bracketing consists of taking a picture at a correct setting and also at a greater and a lesser setting to make sure that one of the pictures will be close to the correct exposure.

EUGENE PARKER
RHODES FAIRBRIDGE

References

Baker, A. de C., 1957, "Underwater photographs in the study of oceanic squid," *Deep-Sea Res.,* **4**, 126–129.

Bunton, W. J., 1966, "Problems of Deep Underwater Photography," in "Man's Extension into the Sea," American Geophysical Union, Washington.

Cross, E. R., 1955, "Underwater Photography and TV," Exposition.

Dangeard, L., and Giresse, P., 1965, "Photographie Sous-marine et Geologie," *Cahiers Oceanographiques,* **XVII**, 4.

Emery, K. O., Merrill, A. S., and Trumbull, J. V. A., 1965, "Geology and biology of the sea floor as deduced from simultaneous photographs and samples," *Limnol. Oceanog.,* **10**(1), 1–21.

Ewing, M., Vine, A., and Worzel, J. L., 1946, "Photography of the ocean bottom," *J. Opt. Soc. Am.,* **36**, 307–321.

Hopkins, R. E., and Edgerton, H. E., 1961, "Lenses for underwater photography," *Deep-Sea Res.,* **8**(3/4), 312–317.

Laban, A., Peres, J. M., and Picard, J., 1963, "La Photographie Sous-marine Profonde et son Exploitation Scientifique," *Bull. Inst. Océanog.,* **60**(1258), 32pp.

Laughton, A. S., 1957, "A New deep-sea underwater camera," *Deep-Sea Res.,* **4**, 120–125.

Laughton, A. S., 1959, "Photography of the ocean floor," *Endeavour,* **18**, 178–185.

Laughton, A. S., 1963, "Microtopography," in (Hill, M.N., editor) "The Sea," Vol. 3, pp. 437–472, New York, Interscience Publishers.

Menzies, R. J., Smith, L., and Emery, K. O., 1963, "A combined underwater camera and bottom grab: A new tool for investigation of deep-sea benthos," *Int. Revue Ges. Hydrobiol.,* **48**, 529–545.

Parker, G., 1965, "Complete Handbook on Skin Diving," New York, Avon Books, 382pp.

Ribicoff, D., and Cherney, P., 1965, "A Guide to Underwater Photography," Greenberg, Chilton.

Schenk, H., Jr., and Kendall, H., (editors), "Underwater Photography," Second ed., Cambridge, Md., Cornell Maritime Press.

Shipek, C. J., 1960, "Photographic study of some deep sea floor environments in the Eastern Pacific," *Bull. Geol. Soc. Am.,* **71**, 1067–1074.

Smith, L. O., 1964, "Deep sea grab-photography for oceanographic sampling," *Undersea Technol.,* **5**(2), 24–26.

Thorndike, E. M., 1959, "Deep-sea cameras of the Lamont Observatory," *Deep-Sea Res.,* **5**, 234–237.

UNDERWATER SOUND—*See* **ACOUSTICS**

UNDERWATER TELEVISION

Television (TV) unlike photography, permits the viewing of underwater events as they take place. Compared to photography, a TV system can be expected to be more expensive initially, it will give poorer quality pictures, and it will be more difficult to maintain. Also, if artificial lighting is required, the power consumption may be many times that required to operate a film camera with flash illumination. The advantages of immediate and continuous observation, however, often outweigh these relative drawbacks.

The simplest TV system consists of a TV camera, a monitor unit and the interconnecting cable. Some TV systems include a camera control unit. Common accessories are artificial lights and remotely controlled positioning devices (so-called pan and tilt units).

The heart of every TV camera is its image tube. The type of image tube largely determines the sensitivity, size and complexity of the camera. Only two types of image tube are commonly used in standard TV equipment, even though there are many types available for selection for specialized applications (Kingslake, 1965). The two common types are the vidicon and the image orthicon. The vidicon offers moderate sensitivity, is compact (approximately 1 inch in diameter and 6 inches long), is well suited to unattended operation, and is the less expensive of the two. The image orthicon offers high sensitivity (several orders of magnitude greater than the vidicon), but it is much larger (approximately 3 inches in diameter and 15 inches long), requires more complex circuitry and frequently more attention to adjustments, and is more expensive. Furthermore, as the discussion of lighting (below) will show, the higher sensitivity of the image orthicon does not necessarily mean that it is capable of seeing farther under water than the vidicon. Very brief descriptions of the vidicon and image orthicon follow.

In terms of its functions, a vidicon (Kingslake, 1965) consists of two essentials: a photoconductive target supported by the faceplate (window) at one end of the tube, and an electron gun at the other. The electron gun produces a beam of electrons which scans the target surface.

The TV camera lens images the scene to be televised through the faceplate onto the target. The optical image at the front surface of the photoconductive layer (the front surface is in contact with a transparent conducting film on the faceplate, which is the signal connection to the tube) is constantly being reproduced as an "image" of positive charge on the rear surface of the photoconductive layer. The greater the illumination of a picture element, the greater is the positive charge which forms at that position on the rear surface. The scanning electron beam discharges each picture element in turn, and the greater the positive charge on an element, the larger is the number of electrons that must be removed from the beam to discharge that element. These discharging electrons flow in the load resistor circuit and there produce the output video signal.

Standard vidicons have usable sensitivities in air of about 10^{-2} foot-candles (faceplate illumination). In underwater applications, it appears that 10^{-1} foot-candle will give good pictures.

In highly simplified terms, an image orthicon (Zworykin, 1954; Kingslake, 1965) consists of three essentially independent sections. In the image section, the scene is imaged by the TV camera lens onto a photoemissive surface deposited on the rear of the glass window which forms the end of the tube. Electrons from this photoemissive surface are imaged (whence the name, image orthicon) onto the storage target where, through the process of secondary emission, they form a positive charge replica of the optical image.

The gun section of the image orthicon generates a scanning beam of electrons which slow to zero velocity as they approach the rear of the target, reverse direction and accelerate back past the electron gun to the electron multiplier section. As the beam approaches the target, a picture element with a large positive charge attracts and traps a large number of electrons from the beam. An element with a smaller positive charge (corresponding to less illumination) traps a smaller number of electrons from the beam. The beam which returns to the electron multiplier is thus modulated with videa information corresponding to the positive charge pattern previously stored at the target.

Standard image orthicons have, in air, usable sensitivities of 10^{-5}–10^{-6} foot-candles (faceplate illumination). For underwater applications at conventional TV scanning rates, faceplace illumination of 10^{-3}–10^{-4} foot-candles seems reasonable. Great caution must be exercised in comparing sensitivity figures, since the integration time, resolution, signal-to-noise ratio, and spectral response are all interrelated with the illumination. For example, in striving for higher sensitivity for a particular application, one might choose a type for its sensitivity only to find out that the integration time was incompatible with the intended application.

In applications of underwater television, the water introduces three optical effects which are normally not considered in above-surface applications. These are: (1) refractive effects, such as considerable reduction in the viewing angle when the TV camera is immersed in water, (2) absorption effects which make the wavelength of the lighting important, and (3) scattering effects (Duntley, 1963).

The refractive effects can be illustrated by an example. A TV camera lens designed to have a total horizontal viewing angle of 60° in air, will cover only 45° when placed behind a flat window immersed in water. A simple calculation based on Snell's Law will suffice. Dispersion at the interface (color fringing) is a much smaller effect and is not generally troublesome, although it should not be ignored entirely.

Water absorbs light of all wavelengths to some extent, but the region around 500μ represents the wavelength of least attenuation (Mutschlecner, 1963). If a 20–30 foot range is considered typical for TV observation, light making a round-trip path length of 40–60 feet in water is going to be strongly filtered. The spectral characteristics of the light source as well as the TV image tube should be considered.

The scattering of light by the water itself, and also by vegetable and mineral matter suspended in the water, is frequently the limiting factor on the range of underwater TV or photography. When artificial light is used, the backscatter (light scattered back toward the camera and source) causes a loss of contrast which limits the range, rather than inverse square law reduction of illumination with distance or absorption in the water. When the water is turbid to the point where the TV range is limited by backscatter, neither increasing the intensity of the light source nor increasing the camera sensitivity will yield improvement. The most practical approaches to improving the visibility under such conditions are: (a) to attempt to place the light source as near to the object under observation as possible, and (b) failing in that, to move the light source as far away from the TV camera as possible. If the water is clear and turbidity is no problem, then a more sensitive camera may offer an advantage, such as the ability to work at greater depths under natural illumination or to reduce the amount of artificial illumination required.

In arranging lighting for underwater TV, the wavelength filtering effect of the water makes it desirable to match the sensitivity curve of the image tube, the output light spectrum of the source, and the wavelength of minimum attenuation in water as closely as possible. The mercury vapor arc lamp produces a spectrum giving lower attenuation per unit length of water traversed than does an incandescent lamp. It has recently been found that the addition of thallium iodide to the mercury vapor lamp greatly increases both its luminous efficiency and the percentage of the total radiant energy which appears in the water in low-attenuation wavelength region (Larsen *et al.* 1962).

HENRY L. COX, JR.

References

Duntley, S. A., 1963, *J. Opt. Soc. Am.,* **53**, 214.
Kingslake, R. (editor), 1965, "Applied Optics and Optical Engineering," Vol. II, Ch. 6, New York, Academic Press.
Larson, D. A., Fraser, H. D., Cushing, W. V., and Unglert, M. C., 1962, "High efficiency light source through use of additives to mercury discharge," *Preprint No. 29 National Technical Conference of the Illuminating Engineering Society, Dallas.*
McGraw-Hill Book Co., 1960, "Encyclopedia of Science and Technology," Vol. 13, p. 465, New York.
Mutschlecner, J. P., Burge, D. K., and Regelson, E., 1963, *Appl. Opt.,* **2**, 1202.
Zworykin, V. K., and Norton, G. A., 1954, "Television," Second ed., Secs. 10.7, 10.8, New York, John Wiley and Sons.

UPWELLING

Upwelling is a process of vertical water motion in the sea whereby subsurface water moves toward the surface. Conversely, a downward displacement is called *downwelling* or *sinking.*

The *upwelling area* is the geographic location where the vertical motion occurs, but upwelled water and its effects on oceanographic conditions may extend for hundreds of miles. Upwelling may take place anywhere, but it is most common along the western coasts of continents.

Upwelling may be caused by wind displacing surface water away from the coast or by currents impinging on each other or on land masses. Under certain conditions in northern hemispheric regions, if persistent winds blow nearly parallel with the coast, the surface water will be deflected offshore, causing the subsurface water to upwell. Diverging currents also cause upwelling. Where the adjacent surface waters flow away from each other, the deeper water must rise. Large and small cyclonic gyrals can force upward displacements and produce upwelling. The amount or magnitude of wind-created upwelling depends on the characteristics of the wind, namely, speed, duration, fetch, and direction; consequently, it varies with the seasons (Fig. 1).

Upwelling, though an important process in the sea, is slow in its action. Off the California coast, the vertical upwelling velocity has been computed to be 20 m/month. In this particular area, the water reaching the surface comes from a relatively shallow depth, usually less than 200 meters.

The most pronounced coastal upwellings are found off the western United States, Peru, Morocco, South Africa, and Western Australia. Some coastal upwelling is created by seasonal monsoon winds, as in southeast Asia (see Bay of Bengal). In that region, the winds blow from the southwest during the summer, then reverse and come from the northeast during the winter. The persistence of the monsoon, especially from the southwest, and the orientation of the coasts cause upwelling to occur along coastal stretches of the east coast of India, Thailand, and South Vietnam. The most extensive

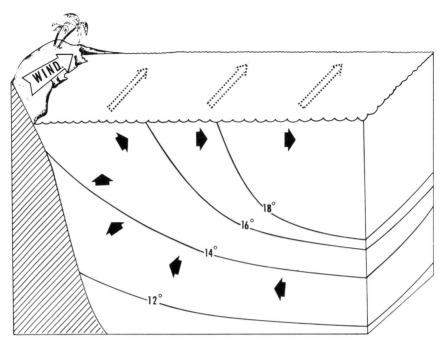

Fig. 1. Schematic representation of the water circulations and associated wind direction in coastal upwelling.

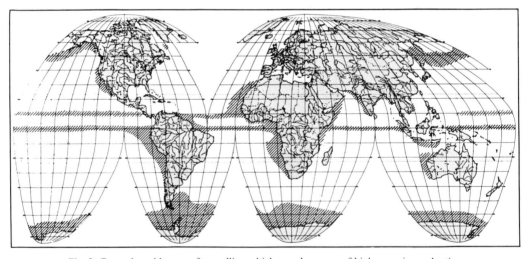

Fig. 2. General world areas of upwelling which are also areas of high organic production.

upwelling occurs off the coasts of Somaliland Arabia (see *Arabian Sea*). Ascending circulation has also been noted around the Antarctic continent, along the Aleutian chain, along the equator, and at the northern boundary of the equatorial countercurrent (Fig. 2).

Localized upwelling develops in: (1) the lees of islands; (2) the lees of major land promonotories projecting into a current; (3) over shoals or sea mounts; (4) in counterclockwise eddies in the northern hemisphere; (5) at water mass boundaries; and (6) in thermal domes or ridges in the open sea.

The importance of upwelling lies in the fact that deep water having properties different from those of the surface water is brought up to, or near, the sea surface. The most distinguishing feature of the upwelled water is that it is colder and denser than the adjacent surface water. During intense summer upwelling, surface temperatures in upwelling areas

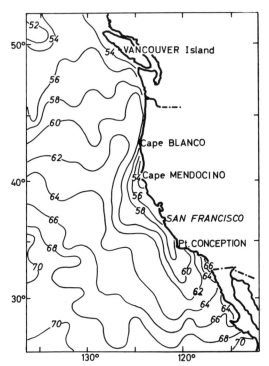

Fig. 3. Average surface temperature off the west coast of United States in July 1964 showing the colder upwelled water near the coast (temperature in degrees fahrenheit; (from Monthly Summary, U.S. Bureau of commercial Fisheries, San Diego).

can be even lower than they are in the winter. Because of the cold surface water, vertical temperature gradients are weaker during upwelling, and a subsurface isothermal layer develops at the level of the shoreward circulation.

In coastal regions, upwelled denser water creates a horizontal density gradient (Fig. 1) which, together with wind stress on the surface water, develops a geostrophic current along the coast.

Upwelled water exerts a significant influence on the meteorological conditions off a coast. If the upwelled subsurface water is colder than the air, it may cool the air and develop a situation conducive to fog, and also have other effects. Such climatic influences are especially noticeable off the central west coast of United States (Fig. 3).

Upwelled water can introduce large quantities of nutrients (phosphates, nitrates, etc.) to the euphotic or light zone; thus, upwelling is conducive to high organic production. For example, especially extensive fishing areas and kelp beds are found off the African and North and South American continents. In addition, considerable bird populations, whose guano is of economic importance, occur off Peru. Again, near the Antarctic Convergence, particularly in the Atlantic, the abundance of nutrients supports an unusually large standing crop of diatoms and flagellates which, in turn, ultimately support krill, the main food of the whale.

Upwelling also influences the benthonic forms and even the organic composition of sea floor sediments. One speculation is that if the organic matter produced is greater than can be dissolved or carried away by currents, it may accumulate on the sea floor and, over a period of time, be converted into petroleum. Favorable locations for the accumulation of organic material would be quiet, deep waters in basins and the base of the continental shelf, where turbulence sweeps the organic matter off the shelf. For petroleum formation, such depositions and accumulation would need to be covered by inorganic sediments possibly transported to the site by turbidity currents. If these speculations are correct, oil deposits are indicative of former upwelling zones, and the present upwelling zones will be future oil bearing areas.

Upwelling also introduces an abnormal rise in the calcium carbonate compensation depth (q.v.), because the cold water (also with higher pCO_2) has a greater solvent capacity of carbonate sediments than observed elsewhere.

Thus, upwelling, through its influence on thermal, chemical, biological, and geological properties, has a profound effect on the economy of the sea.

E. C. LaFond

References

Emery, K. O., 1963, "Oceanographic factors in accumulation of petroleum," *World Petrol. Congr. Proc. Sixth*, Section 1.

LaFond, E. C., 1963, "Physical Oceanography and Its Relations to the Marine Organic Production in the South China Sea," in "Ecology of the Gulf of Thailand and the South China Sea—A Report of the NAGA Expedition, 1959–1961," pp. 5–33, University of California, Scripps Institution of Oceanography, La Jolla, California, SIO Reference No. 63–6.

Sverdrup, H. U., Johnson, M. W., and Fleming, R. H., 1942, "The Oceans," p. 1087, Englewood Cliffs, N.J., Prentice Hall.

U.S. Bureau of Commercial Fisheries, 1964, "California Fisheries Market News Monthly Summary—July," Part II, Supplement 2.

V

VECTOR ANALYSIS

(1) Definition

A quantity with magnitude and direction is called a vector. Displacements, velocities, accelerations, momenta and forces are vectors. On the other hand, quantities only with magnitudes, such as, mass, length, time, volume, etc., are called scalars in order to emphasize their non-directedness. Vectors are denoted by boldface type here, although they can be denoted by an arrow above the letters. The magnitude of the Vector $\mathbf{V}$ is denoted by $|\mathbf{V}|$. For practical purposes, a vector is represented by an arrow showing its direction. The length of the arrow is the magnitude of the vector.

(2) Vector Algebra and Geometry

The addition and subtraction of the vectors are defined graphically, as shown in Fig. 1. This Figure may be interpreted as representing vectors of three dimensions. The vector $a\mathbf{V} = \mathbf{V}a$ (a is a scalar) is defined as a vector having a direction parallel to $\mathbf{V}$ and a magnitude of $a|\mathbf{V}|$. The vector with magnitude zero is called zero vector. These definitions yield equations: $\mathbf{V} + \mathbf{W} = \mathbf{W} + \mathbf{V}$, $\mathbf{U} + (\mathbf{V} + \mathbf{W}) = (\mathbf{U} + \mathbf{V}) + \mathbf{W}$, $\mathbf{V} + (-1)\mathbf{V} = 0$, $\mathbf{V} + 0 = \mathbf{V}$, $a\mathbf{V} + b\mathbf{V} = (a + b)\mathbf{V}$, $a(\mathbf{V} + \mathbf{W}) = a\mathbf{V} + a\mathbf{W}$.

Since a vector is represented with a line segment with its direction in three-dimensional space, it can be expressed with coordinates of a rectangular Cartesian system. When the initial point of a vector is taken at the origin of a Cartesian system, the vector is represented with the coordinates x, y and z of the end point. Such a vector $\mathbf{R}$ is called a position vector and denoted by $\mathbf{R}(x, y, z)$ or by $x\mathbf{i} + y\mathbf{j} + z\mathbf{k}$, where $\mathbf{i}$, $\mathbf{j}$ and $\mathbf{k}$ are the position vectors of unit magnitude (unit vectors) in the x-, y- and z-axes, respectively. The numbers x, y and z are called the components of the vector $\mathbf{R}$. The magnitude $|\mathbf{R}|$ equals $(x^2 + y^2 + z^2)^{1/2}$.

Two kinds of products of two vectors $\mathbf{U}$ and $\mathbf{V}$ are defined. One is the scalar product denoted by $\mathbf{U} \cdot \mathbf{V}$ which is a number equal to $|\mathbf{U}|\,|\mathbf{V}| \cos\theta$ where θ is the angle between $\mathbf{U}$ and $\mathbf{V}$. Then $\mathbf{U} \cdot \mathbf{V} = \mathbf{V} \cdot \mathbf{U}$. When $\mathbf{U}$ and $\mathbf{V}$ are perpendicular, $\mathbf{U} \cdot \mathbf{V} = 0$. When $\mathbf{U}$ and $\mathbf{V}$ are parallel, $\mathbf{U} \cdot \mathbf{V} = \pm|\mathbf{U}| \cdot |\mathbf{V}|$. Also, $\mathbf{U} \cdot \mathbf{U} = |\mathbf{U}|^2$ is denoted by $\mathbf{U}^2$. Then for unit vectors, $\mathbf{i}^2 = \mathbf{j}^2 = \mathbf{k}^2 = 1, \mathbf{i} \cdot \mathbf{j} = \mathbf{j} \cdot \mathbf{k} = \mathbf{k} \cdot \mathbf{i} = 0$. The distribution law $\mathbf{U} \cdot (\mathbf{V} + \mathbf{W}) = \mathbf{U} \cdot \mathbf{V} + \mathbf{U} \cdot \mathbf{W}$ is valid. By use of the distribution law and the scalar products among unit vectors, the scalar product of vectors $\mathbf{U}(x_1, y_1, z_1)$ and $\mathbf{V}(x_2, y_2, z_2)$ can be expressed in terms of the vector components as $\mathbf{U} \cdot \mathbf{V} = x_1 x_2 + y_1 y_2 + z_1 z_2$.

The other product of vectors $\mathbf{U}$ and $\mathbf{V}$ is the vector product denoted by $\mathbf{U} \times \mathbf{V}$ which is another vector having properties: (1) it is perpendicular to $\mathbf{U}$ and to $\mathbf{V}$; (2) it points to the direction a right-threaded screw advances when its head is rotated from $\mathbf{U}$ to $\mathbf{V}$; (3) $|\mathbf{U} \times \mathbf{V}| = |\mathbf{U}|\,|\mathbf{V}| \sin\theta$ where θ is the angle between $\mathbf{U}$ and $\mathbf{V}$. Thus, its magnitude is the area of the parallelogram with $\mathbf{U}$ and $\mathbf{V}$ as adjacent sides. When $\mathbf{U}$ and $\mathbf{V}$ are parallel, $\mathbf{U} \times \mathbf{V} = 0$. Also, from definitions $\mathbf{U} \times \mathbf{V} = -\mathbf{V} \times \mathbf{U}; \mathbf{U} \times (\mathbf{V} + \mathbf{W}) = \mathbf{U} \times \mathbf{V} + \mathbf{U} \times \mathbf{W}$. The definitions (1) to (3) yield the following rules for the unit vectors: $\mathbf{i} \times \mathbf{j} = \mathbf{k} = -\mathbf{j} \times \mathbf{i}; \mathbf{j} \times \mathbf{k} = \mathbf{i} = -\mathbf{k} \times \mathbf{j}; \mathbf{k} \times \mathbf{i} = \mathbf{j} = -\mathbf{i} \times \mathbf{k}$. By use of these rules, the vector product of $\mathbf{U}(x_1, y_1, z_1)$ and $\mathbf{V}(x_2, y_2, z_2)$ is expressed by $\mathbf{U} \times \mathbf{V} = (y_1 z_2 - z_1 y_2)\mathbf{i} + (z_1 x_2 - x_1 z_2)\mathbf{j} + (x_1 y_2 - x_2 y_1)\mathbf{k}$ or by a determinant with rows of $(\mathbf{i}, \mathbf{j}, \mathbf{k})$, $(x_1\ y_1\ z_1)$ and $(x_2\ y_2\ z_2)$.

The scalar triple produce $\mathbf{U} \cdot \mathbf{V} \times \mathbf{W}$, meaning $\mathbf{U} \cdot (\mathbf{V} \times \mathbf{W})$ is scalar and has the magnitude equaling the volume of the parallelepiped with $\mathbf{U}, \mathbf{V}, \mathbf{W}$ as co-initial edges. When $\mathbf{U}, \mathbf{V}$ and $\mathbf{W}$ are so oriented as form a right- or left-hand system, the sign of the triple scalar product is positive or negative, respectively. $\mathbf{U}, \mathbf{V}$ and $\mathbf{W}$ are coplanar if and only if $\mathbf{U} \cdot \mathbf{V} \times \mathbf{W} = 0$. Dot and cross may be interchanged: $\mathbf{U} \cdot \mathbf{V} \times \mathbf{W} = \mathbf{U} \times \mathbf{V} \cdot \mathbf{W}$, etc.

The definition yields the following rules:

$$\mathbf{U} \cdot \mathbf{V} \times \mathbf{W} = \mathbf{V} \cdot \mathbf{W} \times \mathbf{U} = \mathbf{W} \cdot \mathbf{U} \times \mathbf{V} = -\mathbf{V} \cdot \mathbf{U} \times \mathbf{W} = -\mathbf{U} \cdot \mathbf{W} \times \mathbf{V} = -\mathbf{W} \cdot \mathbf{V} \times \mathbf{U}$$

Also, $\mathbf{U} \cdot \mathbf{V} \times \mathbf{W} = \text{Det}\,|x_i\ y_i\ z_i|, (i = 1, 2, 3)$ where $\mathbf{U} = (x_1\ y_1\ z_1)$, $\mathbf{V} = (x_2\ y_2\ z_2)$, $\mathbf{W} = (x_3\ y_3\ z_3)$ and "Det" means a determinant with rows $(x_i\ y_i\ z_i)$.

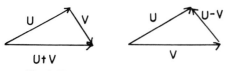

Fig. 1. Vector addition and subtraction.

(3) Vector Functions of a Single Variable

When the components x, y, z of a vector $\mathbf{R}$ are functions of t, the derivative of $\mathbf{R}$ is defined as a vector having components dx/dt, dy/dt, dz/dt. When a prime denotes the differentiation with t, the definition yields the following formulas:

$$(\mathbf{U} + \mathbf{V})' = \mathbf{U}' + \mathbf{V}', \quad [f(t)\ \mathbf{U}]' = f'\mathbf{U} + f\mathbf{U}'$$
$$(\mathbf{U} \cdot \mathbf{V})' = \mathbf{U}' \cdot \mathbf{V} + \mathbf{U} \cdot \mathbf{V}'$$
$$(\mathbf{U} \times \mathbf{V})' = \mathbf{U}' \times \mathbf{V} + \mathbf{U} \times \mathbf{V}'$$
$$(\mathbf{U} \cdot \mathbf{V} \times \mathbf{W})' = \mathbf{U}' \cdot \mathbf{V} \times \mathbf{W} + \mathbf{U} \cdot \mathbf{V}' \times \mathbf{W}$$
$$+ \mathbf{U} \cdot \mathbf{V} \times \mathbf{W}'$$

$\mathbf{U} \cdot \mathbf{U}' = |\mathbf{U}|\ |\mathbf{U}'|$. If $|\mathbf{U}|$ is constant $\mathbf{U} \cdot \mathbf{U}' = 0$ and if $\mathbf{U}$ has constant direction $\mathbf{U} \times \mathbf{U}' = 0$.

(4) Vector Fields

(a) Gradient, Divergence and Circulation. If a vector $\mathbf{V} = \mathbf{V}(x, y, z) = \mathbf{V}(\mathbf{R})$ is defined at each point $\mathbf{R} = x\mathbf{i} + y\mathbf{j} + z\mathbf{k}$ of the three-dimensional space, the family of these vectors forms a vector field. If $\varphi(x, y, z) = \varphi(\mathbf{R})$ is a function of x, y, z, then $\varphi_x \mathbf{i} + \varphi_y \mathbf{j} + \varphi_z \mathbf{k}$, where $\varphi_x = \partial\varphi/\partial x$, etc., is a vector field called the gradient of φ and written grad φ or $\nabla\varphi$ (del φ). The direction of $\nabla\varphi$ is the direction in which φ increases most rapidly (**n** is the unit vector of this direction) and $\nabla\varphi$ equals the rate of increases in that direction ($\delta\varphi/\delta n$). The gradient of φ can be written $(\delta\varphi/\delta n)\mathbf{n}$. When $\mathbf{V} = -\nabla\varphi$, φ is called the scalar potential of $\mathbf{V}$.

The divergence of a vector field $\mathbf{V} = (v_1, v_2, v_3)$ is defined by div $\mathbf{V} = \partial v_1/\partial x + \partial v_2/\partial y + \partial v_3/\partial z = v_{1x} + v_{2y} + v_{3z} = \nabla \cdot \mathbf{V}$ The last notation (del dot $\mathbf{V}$) indicates that the divergence is a scalar product of $\mathbf{V}$ and ∇ which has components $\partial/\partial x$, $\partial/\partial y$, $\partial/\partial z$.

The circulation (rotation) or curl of a vector field $\mathbf{V}$ is defined by curl $\mathbf{V} = \operatorname{rot} \mathbf{V} = (v_{3y} - v_{2z})\mathbf{i} + (v_{1z} - v_{3x})\mathbf{j} + (v_{2x} - v_{1y})\mathbf{k} = \nabla \times \mathbf{V}$ where the last notation indicates again that ∇ can be treated as a vector.

The divergence of $\nabla\varphi$ or $\nabla \cdot \nabla\varphi = \nabla^2\varphi = \varphi_{xx} + \varphi_{yy} + \varphi_{zz}$ is called Laplacian. Other formulas about the second derivatives with ∇ are as follows:

$$\nabla \times \nabla\varphi = 0, \quad \nabla \cdot \nabla \times \mathbf{V} = 0,$$
$$\nabla\nabla \cdot \mathbf{V} = \nabla \times \nabla \times \mathbf{V} + \nabla^2\mathbf{V},$$
$$\nabla \times \nabla \times \mathbf{V} = \nabla\nabla \cdot \mathbf{V} - \nabla^2\mathbf{V}$$

Expansion formulas about ∇ are

$$\nabla(\varphi\psi) = \psi\nabla\varphi + \varphi\nabla\psi \quad \nabla \cdot (\varphi\mathbf{V}) = \nabla\varphi \cdot \mathbf{V} + \varphi\nabla \cdot \mathbf{V}$$
$$\nabla \cdot (\mathbf{U} \times \mathbf{V}) = \mathbf{V} \cdot \nabla \times \mathbf{U} - \mathbf{U} \cdot \nabla \times \mathbf{V}$$
$$\nabla \times (\varphi\mathbf{V}) = \nabla\varphi \times \mathbf{V} + \varphi\nabla \times \mathbf{V}$$
$$\nabla \times (\mathbf{U} \times \mathbf{V}) = \mathbf{V} \cdot \nabla\mathbf{U} - \mathbf{U} \cdot \nabla\mathbf{V} + \mathbf{U}\nabla \cdot \mathbf{V} - \nabla\mathbf{V} \cdot \mathbf{U}$$

(b) The Line and Surface Integrals. The line integral of the function φ along the curve L is evaluated by multiplying φ at the point (x, y, z) on L by the length element ds of the curve and by integrating the product from point A along the curve to point B along the curve and is denoted by $\int_A^B \varphi(x, y, z)ds$. If $d\mathbf{r}$ denoted a vector representing an element of a curve and $\mathbf{V}$ is a vector field, the scalar product $\mathbf{V} \cdot d\mathbf{r} =$ $(v_x\dot{x} + v_y\dot{y} + v_z\dot{z})ds$, where $\dot{x} = dx/ds$ etc. The line integral of the vector $\mathbf{V}$ is denoted by $\int_A^B \mathbf{V} \cdot d\mathbf{r}$, which is the line integral of the function $\mathbf{V} \cdot \mathbf{t}$ where $\mathbf{t}$ is a vector $(\dot{x}, \dot{y}, \dot{z})$.

Take rectangular coordinates, center at $\mathbf{R}(x, y, z)$ on the plane perpendicular to the x-axis. The y and z coordinates of its four apexes are $(y - b, z - c)$, $(y + b, z - c)$ $(y + b, z + c)$ and $(y - b, z + c)$. The limit of the ratio of the line integral of $\mathbf{V}$ counterclockwise along the perimeter $\int\mathbf{V} \cdot d\mathbf{r}$ to the area $4bc$ equals $v_{3y} - v_{2z}$ as the area is diminished to zero. This limit is the x-component of the curl $\mathbf{V}$ or $\nabla \times \mathbf{V}$. When $\mathbf{V}$ represents the velocity of a rotating body with angular velocity ω about the x-axis, the components of $\mathbf{V}$ are $(0, -\omega z, \omega y)$. Therefore, in this case the limit becomes 2ω which is called x-component of the vorticity if the rotating body is fluid. Similar results are obtained for the y- and z-components of the curl $\mathbf{V}$. Therefore, the curl of the vector $\mathbf{V}$ becomes the vorticity if $\mathbf{V}$ is considered to represent the velocity of fluid motion.

The surface integral $\int_S \varphi(x, y, z)\ dS$ can be evaluated by integrating the function $\varphi(x, y, z)$ multiplied by the area element dS over the surface S. The area element vector $d\mathbf{S}$ is defined as a vector with magnitude equaling the area of the element and with a direction normal to the plane of the area. In the case of closed surfaces, the direction toward the outside is chosen. The integral of the scalar product of $\mathbf{V}$ and $d\mathbf{S}$ is called the surface integral of $\mathbf{V}$ and is denoted by $\int\mathbf{V} \cdot d\mathbf{S}$. When the surface integral of $\mathbf{V}$ is taken over the whole surface of a rectangular parallelogram bounded by the planes $X = x \pm a$, $Y = y \pm b$, $Z = z \pm c$, the limit of the ratio of the surface integral to the volume of the parallelogram $8abc$ becomes $v_{1x} + v_{2y} + v_{3z}$ as the volume is diminished to zero. This limit becomes the divergence of the vector $\mathbf{V}$. It is independent of the shape of the surface as long as the surface is closed.

(c) Stokes' and Green's Theorems. Consider any smooth closed curve L spanned by a smooth simple surface S, which is divided into infinitesimal areas dS_1, dS_2—with perimeters L_1, L_2. Then the sum of the line integrals of a vector $\mathbf{V}$ around L_1, L_2 all in the same sense is the line integral around L, since all the other parts of the integrals cancel one another (Fig. 2). From the above definition of curl, for the L_k we have $\operatorname{curl}_n \mathbf{V} = \int_{Lk} \mathbf{V} \cdot d\mathbf{r}/dS_k + \varepsilon_k$ where ε_k tends to zero with decreasing dS_k and $\operatorname{curl}_n \mathbf{V}$ is the normal component of curl $\mathbf{V}$ in the area dS_k. This equation becomes $\int_{Lk} \mathbf{V} \cdot d\mathbf{r} = (\nabla \times \mathbf{V}) \cdot d\mathbf{S}_k - \varepsilon_k dS_k$ where $d\mathbf{S}_k$ is the area element vector. Summation of these integrals yields

$$\int_L \mathbf{V} \cdot d\mathbf{r} = \int_S (\nabla \times \mathbf{V}) \cdot d\mathbf{S}$$

which is called Stokes' theorem.

In the same manner, let S be any smooth closed surface containing a volume v which can be divided into infinitesimal volumes dv_1, dv_2, with surfaces S_1, S_2, ... The sum of the surface integrals of $\mathbf{V}$

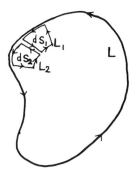

Fig. 2. Line integrals around perimeter of cells.

over S_1, S_2, ... becomes the surface integral over S. For any point inside S_k,

$$\nabla \cdot \mathbf{V} = \int_{Sk} \mathbf{V} \cdot d\mathbf{S}/\Delta v_k + \varepsilon_k$$

where ε_k is an infinitesimal. As before, summation of these integrals yields

$$\int_v (\nabla \cdot \mathbf{V}) dv = \int_S \mathbf{V} \cdot d\mathbf{S}$$

which is called Green's theorem.

When V is taken as $\varphi\mathbf{i}$, $\varphi\mathbf{j}$ and $\varphi\mathbf{k}$, the above theorem yields $\int \varphi\mathbf{i} \cdot d\mathbf{S} = \int (\partial\varphi/\partial x)dv$, etc., where $\mathbf{i}$, $\mathbf{j}$ and $\mathbf{k}$ are unit vectors on the x-, y- and z-axis, respectively. On the surface of S, $\mathbf{i} \cdot d\mathbf{S} = n_x dS$, where n_x is the x-component of the unit vector $\mathbf{n}$ normal to the surface element. Therefore,

$$\int \varphi\mathbf{n} \cdot d\mathbf{S} = \int \varphi dS = \int \nabla \varphi dv$$

(5) Applications

(a) Mechanics. A moving particle is located by its position vector $\mathbf{r} = x\mathbf{i} - y\mathbf{j} + z\mathbf{k}$ referred to a specific origin O. The velocity $\mathbf{v}$ and acceleration $\mathbf{a}$ of the particle are expressed by $\mathbf{v} = \dot{\mathbf{r}} = \dot{x}\mathbf{i} + \dot{y}\mathbf{j} + \dot{z}\mathbf{k}$ and $\mathbf{a} = \dot{\mathbf{v}} = \ddot{\mathbf{r}} = \ddot{x}\mathbf{i} + \ddot{y}\mathbf{j} + \ddot{z}\mathbf{k}$, respectively, where dots are the derivative with respect to time t. The Newtonian equation of motion is written as $m\mathbf{a} = \mathbf{F}$, where m is a mass and $\mathbf{F}$ is force.

Consider that a point with the position vector $\mathbf{r}$ rotates counterclockwise through an infinitesimal angle $d\theta$ about an axis through the origin specified by the unit vector $\mathbf{e}$ (Fig. 3). When the new position vector is denoted by $\mathbf{r} + d\mathbf{r}$, the vector $d\mathbf{r}$ is perpendicular to $\mathbf{e}$ and $\mathbf{r}$ and its magnitude equals $r \sin a \, d\theta$, where a is the angle between $\mathbf{e}$ and $\mathbf{r}$. Therefore, $d\mathbf{r} = d\theta \cdot \mathbf{e} \times \mathbf{r}$. The rotation divided by a time interval dt yields the velocity vector of the particle which is expressed by $\dot{\mathbf{r}} = \dot{\theta}\mathbf{e} \times \mathbf{r} = \boldsymbol{\omega} \times \mathbf{r}$. The vector $\boldsymbol{\omega} = \dot{\theta}\mathbf{e}$ is called angular velocity and is used to represent rotating motion. Since the angular velocity is a vector, it can be resolved into components. For example, the earth's angular velocity can be conveniently resolved into vertical and horizontal components $\Omega \sin \varphi$ and $\Omega \cos \varphi$, respectively, at any point on the earth's surface, where Ω is the magnitude of the angular velocity and φ is the latitude of the point (Fig. 4).

In order to treat motion of the atmosphere or the ocean, it is most convenient to express the motion with respect to a coordinate system fixed to the earth. Therefore, the rate of change of a vector with time will be derived for the fixed and rotating coordinate system, the latter of which has an angular velocity $\boldsymbol{\omega}$. The origin of the two systems is taken on the axis of rotation of the rotating system. Suppose a point P moves to the point P' in time dt. (Fig. 5). Let $\mathbf{r}$ be the position vector with respect to the common origin of the two systems. Then $\overrightarrow{PP'} = d\mathbf{r}$ is the displacement observed in the fixed system. Now in time dt the point P would have shifted to the point Q when observed in the rotating system, where $\overrightarrow{PQ} = \boldsymbol{\omega} \, dt \times d\mathbf{r}$. The apparent displacement $d\mathbf{r}$ as observed in the rotating system is thus $\overrightarrow{QP'}$. Therefore, $d\mathbf{r} = d\mathbf{r}_a + \boldsymbol{\omega} dt \times \mathbf{r}$. Then $\dot{\mathbf{r}} = \dot{\mathbf{r}}_a + \boldsymbol{\omega} \times \mathbf{r}$, where the suffix a refers to the rotating system. This result holds for any vector $\mathbf{U}$ as well as for the position vector $\mathbf{r}$, for which $\dot{\mathbf{r}} (= \mathbf{q})$ and $\dot{\mathbf{r}}_a (= \mathbf{v})$ are the absolute velocity and the velocity relative to the rotating system, respectively. The

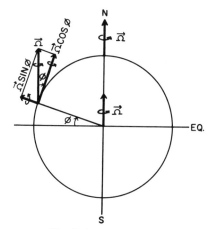

Fig. 3. Angular velocity.

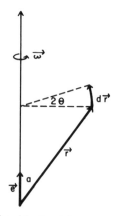

Fig. 4. Vertical and horizontal components of earth's angular velocity.

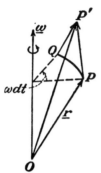

Fig. 5. Movement of a point P in the fixed and rotating coordinate systems (from Stewart, 1945). (By permission of McGraw Hill Book Co., N.Y.)

absolute acceleration is given by $\dot{\mathbf{q}} = \dot{\mathbf{v}} + \dot{\boldsymbol{\omega}} \times \mathbf{r} + \boldsymbol{\omega} \times \dot{\mathbf{r}}$. Substituting $\dot{\mathbf{v}} = \dot{\mathbf{v}}_a + \boldsymbol{\omega} \times \mathbf{v}$ and $\dot{\mathbf{r}} = \mathbf{q} = \mathbf{v} + \boldsymbol{\omega} \times \mathbf{r}$, we have $\dot{\mathbf{q}} = \dot{\mathbf{v}}_a + \dot{\boldsymbol{\omega}} \times \mathbf{r} + 2\boldsymbol{\omega} \times \mathbf{v} + \boldsymbol{\omega} \times \boldsymbol{\omega} \times \mathbf{r}$, where $\dot{\mathbf{v}}_a$ is the acceleration relative to the rotating system. Newton's principle leads to the equation of motion $m\dot{\mathbf{q}} = \mathbf{F}$, where $\mathbf{F}$ is force referred to the fixed coordinate. Therefore, the three terms other than $m\dot{\mathbf{v}}$, on the right-hand side of the above equation (multiplied by m) are considered as apparent forces which will occur only in the rotating system. The third term is called Coriolis force and the fourth term is centrifugal force. For the motion on the earth, the second term vanishes due to constancy of $\boldsymbol{\omega}$ and the centrifugal force is incorporated into gravity together with attractive force of the earth. Therefore, for the atmospheric and oceanic motion, only the Coriolis force becomes important.

(b) Fluid Dynamics. Consider a fluid particle with vector $\mathbf{r}$ at time t is moving with velocity $\mathbf{v}$. Let $\varphi(x, y, z, t)$ be any property of the particle. When the particle moves to $\mathbf{r} + d\mathbf{r}$ at time $t + dt$, the change of the property $d\varphi$ at the new position and time is due partly to the change in location and partly to the development with time. Therefore, $d\varphi = (\partial\varphi/\partial t)dt + \nabla\varphi \cdot d\mathbf{r}$. The rate of change of φ following the motion of the fluid is called the particle derivative and is denoted by $D\varphi/Dt$. Since $d\mathbf{r}/dt = \mathbf{v}$, we have

$$D\varphi/Dt = \partial\varphi/\partial t + \mathbf{v} \cdot \nabla\varphi$$

For instance, Dp/Dt denotes the rate of change of the density of ρ of a fluid particle, but $\partial\rho/\partial t$ denotes the rate of change of ρ at a particular point in space. The particle derivative of the velocity is the acceleration of the fluid particle.

Consider a surface S enclosing volume V within a fluid. The mass of fluid flowing out of S per unit time is given by $\int_S \rho\mathbf{v} \cdot d\mathbf{S}$ which equals $\int \nabla \cdot (\rho\mathbf{v}) \, dV$ from Green's theorem. This mass may be accounted for in two ways: a decrease in the density of the fluid within S, $\int(-\partial\rho/\partial t)dV$ and a source C within S, $\int\rho C \, dV$. By making V infinitesimal, we have $\partial\rho/\partial t + \nabla \cdot (\rho\mathbf{v}) = C\rho$ which is called the equation

of continuity. This can be written

$$D\rho/Dt + \rho\nabla \cdot \mathbf{v} = C\rho$$

For an incompressible fluid in the absence of sources we have $\nabla \cdot \mathbf{v} = 0$.

The forces operating on the mass of fluid enclosed by S are divided into two classes: (1) body forces which act on each particle and have intensities proportional to the mass m and (2) surface forces which act on the surface S and have intensities proportional to the area S. A fluid is ideal or viscous according to whether or not all surface forces do or do not act normal to dS. For an ideal fluid, this surface force is called pressure and is denoted by φ. The total force exerted by the pressure is $\int_S p \, d\mathbf{S}$ which equals $\int \nabla p \, dV$ by the corollary of Green's theorem. Denoted by $\mathbf{F}$ the body forces per unit mass, we have the equation of motion

$$m \, D\mathbf{v}/Dt = m\mathbf{F} - \int \nabla p \, dV$$

The volume can be taken infinitesimal and $m/V = \rho$. Thus

$$D\mathbf{v}/Dt = \partial\mathbf{v}/\partial t + \mathbf{v} \, ' \nabla\mathbf{v} = \mathbf{F} - a\nabla p$$

where a is specific volume. Introducing vorticity $\boldsymbol{\omega} = \nabla \times \mathbf{v}$, we can transform the above equation into

$$\partial\mathbf{v}/\partial t - \mathbf{v} \times \boldsymbol{\omega} = \mathbf{F} - a\nabla p - 1/2)\nabla v^2$$

A streamline is a curve, the tangent to which gives the velocity of a fluid particle there at any instant. In a steady state $(\partial\mathbf{v}/\partial t = 0)$ flow of an isentropic fluid $(a\nabla p = \nabla W)$ under conservative forces $(\mathbf{F} = -\nabla\Phi)$, we form the scalar product of the above equation with the unit vector $(\mathbf{s})$ tangent to the streamlines at each point. Since the projection of the gradient on any direction is the derivative in that direction, $\mathbf{s} \, ' \nabla = \partial/\partial s$. Since $\mathbf{s}$ and $\mathbf{v}$ have the same directions, $\mathbf{s} \, ' \mathbf{v} \times \boldsymbol{\omega} = 0$. Therefore, we have $\partial(\tfrac{1}{2}v^2 + W + \Phi) \, \partial s = 0$ or $\tfrac{1}{2}v^2 + W + \Phi =$ constant. In general, the constant takes different values on different streamlines. This is Bernoulli's equation. (q.v.).

The particle derivative of the circulation (Γ) along a closed contour is given by

$$\frac{D}{Dt}\Gamma = \frac{D}{Dt}\oint\mathbf{v} \cdot d\mathbf{r} = \oint\frac{D\mathbf{v}}{Dt} \cdot d\mathbf{r} + \oint\mathbf{v} \cdot \frac{D \, d\mathbf{r}}{Dt}$$

since not only the velocity but also the contour itself changes during movements of particles. Since $\mathbf{v}$ is the particle derivative of the position vector $\mathbf{r}$, we have $\mathbf{v} \cdot D(d\mathbf{r})/Dt = \mathbf{v} \cdot d(D\mathbf{r}/Dt) = \mathbf{v} \cdot d\mathbf{r} = d(\tfrac{1}{2}v^2)$. Therefore, the second integral vanishes since the integral of a total differential along a closed contour is zero. If $\mathbf{F} = \nabla\Phi$ (conservative force) and $a \nabla p = \nabla W$ (isentropic fluid), $D\mathbf{v}/Dt = -\nabla(\Phi + W)$. Using Stokes' formula we have

$$\int(D\mathbf{v}/Dt) \cdot d\mathbf{r} = \int\nabla \times (D\mathbf{v}/Dt) \cdot d\mathbf{S} = 0$$

because $\nabla \times \nabla(\Phi + W) = 0$. Therefore, $D\Gamma/Dt = 0$ or the circulation Γ is conserved when the contour moves with the fluid. This is called Kelvin's or Helmholtz's theorem.

In the case of atmospheric or oceanic motion, a rotating coordinate system fixed at a point on the surface of the earth is more convenient. Then the acceleration relative to the rotating system has Coriolis term $2\mathbf{\Omega} \times \mathbf{v}$, where $\mathbf{\Omega}$ is the angular velocity of the earth. Also, the body force $\mathbf{F}$ is conservative and gravity ($\mathbf{G}$) only. When the z-axis is taken vertically upward, $\mathbf{G}$ is expressed by $-g\mathbf{k}$. The equation of motion becomes

$$D\mathbf{v}/Dt + 2\mathbf{\Omega} \times \mathbf{v} = \mathbf{G} - a\,\nabla p$$

Kelvin's circulation theorem should be modified due to Coriolis term and non-isentropicity of the atmosphere and ocean. The latter effect yields the non-vanishing line integral $\oint \alpha \nabla p \cdot d\mathbf{r} = \oint \alpha\,dp$. In order to transform the line integral of the Coriolis term, the vector area of a surface capping the contour is denoted by $\mathbf{A} = \frac{1}{2}\oint \mathbf{r} \times d\mathbf{r}$, where $\mathbf{r}$ is the position vector from some origin. Then

$$D\mathbf{A}/Dt = \frac{1}{2}\oint \mathbf{v} \times d\mathbf{r} + \frac{1}{2}\oint \mathbf{r} \times d\mathbf{v} = \oint \mathbf{v} \times d\mathbf{r}$$

where the last integral is obtained by integrating the second term in the middle portion by parts. Then $2\mathbf{\Omega} \cdot D\mathbf{A}/Dt = D(2\mathbf{\Omega} \cdot \mathbf{A})/Dt = 2\mathbf{\Omega} \cdot \oint \mathbf{v} \times d\mathbf{r} = \oint 2\mathbf{\Omega} \times \mathbf{v} \cdot d\mathbf{r}$

Finally, the circulation theorem in this case becomes

$$D(\Gamma + 2\mathbf{\Omega} \cdot \mathbf{A})/Dt = -\oint a\,dp$$

The term $2\mathbf{\Omega} \cdot \mathbf{A}$ can be expressed as $2\Omega A'$, where Ω is the magnitude of earth's angular velocity and A' is the area enclosed by the projection of the contour on the equatorial plane. The above equation with this substitution is called Bjerknes' circulation theorem. The right-hand side is called the solenoid term. If $\rho = \rho(p)$, this term vanishes and the quantity $\Gamma + 2\mathbf{\Omega} \cdot \mathbf{A}$ is conserved.

When a fluid is viscous, the surface forces are not normal to the surface and are expressed by stress tensors. In an incompressible fluid, the viscous force due to the stress tensors is expressed by $\eta \nabla^2 \mathbf{v}$, where η is the viscosity coefficient.

TAKASHI ICHIYE

References

Eckart, C., 1960, "Hydrodynamics of Oceans and Atmosphere," Oxford and New York, Pergamon Press, 290pp.

Ficken, F. A., 1945, "Meteorological Mathematics and Calculations," in (Berry, F. A., *et al.,* editor) "Handbook of Meteorology," pp. 123–240, New York, McGraw-Hill Book Co.

Landau, L. D., and Lifshitz, E. M., 1954, "Fluid Mechanics," Reading, Mass., Addison-Wesley Publishing Company, 536pp.

Rutherford, D. E., 1957, "Vector Methods," Interscience Publishers, New York, 135pp.

Stewart, H. J., 1945, "Kinematics and Dynamics of Fluid Flow," in (Berry, F. A., *et al.,* editor), "Handbook

of Meteorology," pp. 411–500, New York, McGraw-Hill Book Company.

Cross-references: *Angular Momentum and Velocity; Bernoulli's Theorem; Coriolis Force; Density; Dynamics of Ocean Currents; Gravity and Geopotential; Pressure Gradient; Vorticity.* Vol. II: *Atmospheric Circulation; Centrifugal Force; Geostrophic Motion; Viscosity.*

VOLCANIC RIDGES

In the Pacific Ocean there are numbers of submarine or insular ridges, in places crowned by atolls, that lack any comparable counterpart in other oceans. Typical examples are the Hawaiian, Caroline, Marquesas, Tuamotu, Society, Tubuai, Cook, Austral and Gilbert Islands. Rows of analogous but submerged seamounts were first detected in the Gulf of Alaska by G. W. Murray (1941). The Emperor Seamount Ridge is probably the largest group of this submerged category that has been discovered so far.

There are certainly some rows of volcanic seamounts in every ocean but on nothing like the scale of the Pacific lineaments. Submarine ridges and rises in other oceans, and in the Pacific marginal seas, often have foundations of "microcontinental" blocks (Heezen's term for isolated submerged fragments of former continental crust), just as do the *continental borderlands* (q.v.) and *submarine plateaus* (q.v.), but the Pacific volcanic ridges show no trace of continental nuclei.

The orientation of these volcanic ridges is almost invariably rectilinear. Consideration of the petrology of the lavas extruded shows that in the youthful undifferentiated examples, the magma is of very deep-seated origin, from 50 km depth or more in the Mantle. The suite is Harker's "Atlantic" category, characteristic of deep fracture zones and quite distinct from the orogenic or island arc "Pacific" calc-alkaline series. Nephelene, a characteristic mantle mineral is widely present. Structural geology shows that a rectilinear fracture trend develops only as a result of strike-slip displacement. Extension or dilatation tends to produce zigzag, "normal" faults, while compression leads to overthrusting and wavy patterns. On the continents, all long, straight faults have demonstrable strike-slip displacements of the order of 50–500 km lateral shift. As long ago as 1942, Betz and Hess attributed these Pacific volcanic ridges to giant transcurrent faults.

A paradox appears, however, when one considers the great *fracture zones* (q.v.) of the ocean floors. The latter are hardly ever associated with rows of volcanoes; they are simply single vertical planes or sheaves of fractures displacing the suboceanic crust for distances comparable to (or more than) the continental transcurrent lines, sometimes with vertical components as well. Why then are there apparently similar lines of structural weakness studded with volcanoes? It may be a matter of *stage of*

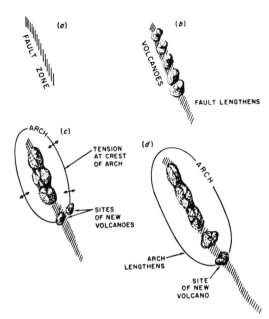

Fig. 1. Possible origin of linear development and spacing of Pacific volcanoes (Menard, 1964).

development. Another thing: they belong to a different family of trends.

A long-recognized (and often overstressed) principle of geotectonics states that the similar orientation of structural lines, folds, faults, joints, etc., is strongly suggestive of *contemporaneity*, or of *posthumous revival* in younger rocks. Associated with such trends are often intimately related conjugate patterns. In contrast, in any broad region there are often series of completely independent trends that have a demonstrably different time of origin. Thus, for example in North America, the most striking trend of the Precambrian Shield of central Canada is the northeast-southwest system; it is picked up in the subsurface of the Midwest (Nemaha axis), and marked by posthumous axes in Paleozoic and younger rocks; the entire Appalachian structural system parallels the same trend. But at the Rocky Mt. front a north-south Laramide trend becomes evident, so that even in the Precambrian nuclei of the Middle Rocky Mts. the northeast-southwest trends are cut across by these younger trends. In northwestern Europe, the northwest-southeast trends are Caledonian (older Paleozoic, as in the ancestral Applachians), but in late Paleozoic times the Hercynian trend appears with its northwest-southeast to east-west lines (picked up on the American side in the Ouachitas).

The structural trend principle is a useful one, so long as it is not overstated. It is certainly not a universal "law" but may provide an approach to the Pacific geotectonic problem. Suess (1904–24) applied names to help designate characteristic trends on the continents, and Stille (1944) added others. Principal trends so-recognized are:

(1) *Oceanide Trend* (WNW-ESE, varying to NW-SE), characteristic of the principal volcanic ridges of the mid-Pacific, from the Hawaiian to the Samoan and includes sectors on the ocean margins, in California, Mexico, Melanesian Border Plateau, New Guinea, etc. (Fairbridge, 1961a).

(2) *Andean Trend* (NNE-SSW), seen outstandingly in the northern and southern Andes (not the mid-section in Peru), in New Zealand and the Kermadec-Tonga zone.

(3) *Nippon Trend* (ENE-WSW), characteristic of the main trends of Japan, Korea and east-central China, to be picked up here and there in the Pacific floor with such features as the Marcus-Necker Seamounts (west of Hawaii).

It has often been observed by vulcanologists that volcanoes tend to coincide not merely with linear fractures, but with *intersections* of fracture lines. Studies of volcano-studded plateaus such as the Azores and Iceland seem to bear out the principle. Numerous cross-faults are recognized in Hawaii, the most mature of the Pacific volcanic ridges.

These principles may now provide a clue for dating the Pacific fractures and volcanic ridges. It is proposed that the volcano-less fracture zones are those without significant cross-fractures or conjugate patterns, and are of a different age from the various families of volcanic ridges, which do demonstrate associated cross-fractures.

Within any one particular volcanic ridge, one may observe an interesting evolutionary sequence (Chubb, 1957). In several of the major examples, the Hawaiian Ridge, for example, the latest and largest volcano lies in the southeast, while progressively older, more dissected and more subsided examples occur toward the northwest, and eventually the line is only represented by atolls and totally submerged seamounts. The newest traces of submarine volcanic activity are observed out in the ocean, southeast of Hawaii's "Big Island." As the volcanic ridge evolves, subcrustal differentiation goes on and isostatic processes begin to operate, thanks to mass transfers by magma evacuation, lava flowage, erosion and sediment accumulation. Thus a peripheral *arch* eventually evolves with peripheral swale between it and the parent ridge (Dietz and Menard, 1953; Hamilton, 1957). The isostatic adjustment is evidently sequential; well logs on Oahu already show a 400-m submergence, greatly exceeding any eustatic factor (Stearns, 1961).

The "orderly pattern" of this evolution was repeatedly pointed out by Chubb as characteristic of the "Oceanide" group of ridges, what he called the "Nephelene-bearing Zone." He believed the other groups could also be classified into petrographic subprovinces.

The marked change of structural trend from time to time suggests a planetary cause, rather than a local one, in view of the broadly isotropic nature of the thin crust of the main Pacific basin. As pointed out earlier (Fairbridge, 1961b), systematic changes of mass distribution at or near the earth's surface through time must lead to aperiodic shifts of the axis of rotation with respect to the crust, in order to reestablish the closest approximation to the theoretical spheroid. With each such polar readjustment, vertical anomalies in the crust must be compensated for by both vertical and horizontal motions (the latter due to the rotation of the globe, and at least partially confirmed by Pierre St. Armand's observation of the circum-Pacific dextral shear, 1959). It would seem likely that the Pacific fractures reflect the stress vectors of these aperiodic events through about the last 100 million years or so. Paleomagnetic tracings of the polar shifts (each being irregular in time, direction and amplitude) show a mean trajectory over this period of approximately 30° along the meridian 180°. This would leave much of the mid-Pacific with a negative anomaly with respect to the geoid. The occurrence of numerous guyots and atolls along the volcanic ridges of this region reflects regional drowning, which may be in part geodetic, following polar shifts, and only partially a result of isostatic compensation.

RHODES W. FAIRBRIDGE

References

Betz, F., and Hess, H. H., 1942, "The floor of the North Pacific Ocean," *Geograph. Rev.*, **32**, 99–116.

Chubb, L. J., 1957, "The pattern of some Pacific Island Chains," *Geol. Mag.*, **94**, 221–228.

Dietz, R. S., and Menard, H. W., 1953, "Hawaiian swell, deep and arch, and subsidence of the Hawaiian Islands," *J. Geol.*, **61**, 99–113.

Fairbridge, R. W., 1961a, "The Melanesian Border Plateau, a Zone of Crustal Shearing in the S.W. Pacific," *Publ. Bur. Cent. Seism., Ser. A.,* Fasc. 22 (Helsinki, 1960), 137–149.

Fairbridge, R. W., 1961b, "Eustatic Changes in Sea Level," in "Physics and Chemistry of the Earth," Vol. 4, pp. 99–185, London, Pergamon Press.

Fairbridge, R. W., 1965, "The Indian Ocean and the Status of Gondwanaland," in "Progress in Oceanography," Vol. 3, pp. 83–136.

Hamilton, E. L., 1957, "Marine geology of the Southern Hawaiian Ridge," *Bull. Geol. Soc. Am.*, **68**, 1011–1026.

Hess, H. H., 1946, "Drowned ancient islands of the Pacific Basin," *Am. J. Sci.*, **244**, 772–791.

Kushiro, I., and Kuno, H., 1963, "Origin of primary basalt magmas and classification of basaltic rocks," *J. Petrol.*, **4**, Pt. 1, 75–89.

Menard, H. W., 1964, "Marine Geology of the Pacific," New York, McGraw-Hill Book Co., 271pp.

Murray, H. W., 1941, "Submarine mountains in the Gulf of Alaska," *Bull. Geol. Soc. Am.*, **52**, 333–362.

St. Amand, P., 1959, "Circum-Pacific orogeny," *Ottawa, Dominion Obs. Publ.*, **20**, 403–411.

Stearns, H. T., 1961, "Pacific Island Chains," *Geol. Mag.*, **96**, 170–172.

Stille, H., 1944, "Geotektonische Probleme des Pazifischen Erdraumes," *Abhandl. Preuss. Akad. Wiss. Math.-Natur. Kl.,* No. 11, 77pp.

Suess, E., 1904–24, "The Face of the Earth," Oxford, 5 vols., (translated by Sollas).

Cross-references: *Archipelagic Aprons*; *Fracture Zones*; *Pacific Ocean*.

VORTEX TRAIL

A blunt object, towed through the water, or attached firmly in a flowing stream, sets up a turbulent wake in the down-current direction. This wake consists of several parts. A central strip, extending from the object for a distance of several diameters, is marked by a general tendency for the water to rise toward the surface and to move toward the object (i.e., counter to the direction of general flow).

On each side of the central strip is a chain of vortices. An observer standing on the object, facing downstream, would note that vortex motion in the right-hand chain is counter clockwise, whereas in the left-hand chain it is clockwise. The vortices in the two chains are staggered, so that no single vortex, in one chain, is directly opposite a vortex in the other chain. Each vortex forms behind one edge of the blunt object, peels off, and then passes downstream. Vortices take turns separating from the two trailing edges. The point of separation is the point where the *boundary layer* (q.v.) is detached from the solid surface. Space between the detached boundary layer and the object, rather than developing a vacuum, is typically filled with one or more vortices.

The obvious wake is composed of the central strip flanked by two vortex trails. Outside of the wake, however, a spiral wave may also develop. This wave forms on each side, so that there are five strips all told, with the two outermost strips meeting upstream from the blunt object. In the spiral wave, motion is down on the outside, adjacent to free flow, and up on the inside, adjacent to the vortex trail. Spiral waves appear only at higher Froude numbers, whereas the development of vortices occurs only at higher Reynolds numbers (q.v.).

A single vortex trail may form along a stream bank, downstream from that point where the boundary layer is separated from the channel wall. Sharp changes in channel width or depth, or the presence of attached roughness elements along the bed or side, may account for single vortex trails. Double vortex trails occur downstream from single objects. A triple vortex trail may develop behind rising, or falling, objects. The most common example is probably a single grain falling through water. A less common example is a *tektite* (q.v.) falling through the air at velocities sufficient to melt a thin surface layer, which then flows enough

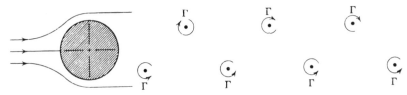

FIG. 1. Karman vortex trail (from Pao, 1961, Fig. 9-14, p. 404).

to preserve a pattern due to the presence of three vortex centers.

Detachment of individual vortices from the upper surface of the falling particle imparts to the latter a spinning and spiralling motion. A pronounced example of this can be seen when a leaf falls through the air; it reverses its swing each time a vortex peels off.

The presence of a single vortex trail downstream from a subaqueous ripple mark means that individual sand grains will be carried up into the water at the point where boundary layer separation occurs. This may be the most important mechanism, other than *shooting flow* (see Reynolds and Froude numbers), in the picking up of sand grains under flowing water. In the presence of wave action, the plunge of breaking waves, and boundary layer separation under ordinary wave bottom orbits, probably account for the scour of most sand grains which are put into motion.

Water issuing from small springs on the sea floor may develop a tripartite vortex trail. If the water bubbles up through soft clay-mud, and the spring pipe is later filled with sediment (such as sand), a scalloped cone may be preserved in the clay. Any fluid jet, such as a stream flowing into standing water (lake or sea), may develop two more-or-less permanent eddies outside the mouth, with the senses of rotation reversed from those stated in the second paragraph.

W. F. TANNER

References

Pao, R. H. F., 1961, "Fluid Mechanics," pp. 399–410; New York, John Wiley & Sons, Inc.

Schlichting, H., 1963, "Three-dimensional boundary layer flow," *Proceedings, Ninth Convention, Intern. Assoc. for Hydraulic Research*, Dubrovnik, Yugoslavia, **1961**, 1262–1290.

Tanner, W. F., 1963, "Scaled-up model in studies of sediment transport," *Bull. Am. Assoc. Petrol. Geologists*, **47**, 372.

Tanner, W. F., 1964, "Origin and maintenance of ripple marks," *Sedimentology*, **2**, 307–311.

VORTICITY

Vorticity corresponds to the angular velocity in a tiny part of a fluid, involved in curved motion or spin. It is a vector and its component in any axis is given by a ratio of the circulation around the axis to the area spanned by the contour as the latter diminishes to zero. It is defined as positive in a cyclonic sense (bearing left) and negative in an anticyclonic sense (bearing right), in the northern hemisphere. Mathematically, vorticity is the *curl* of the velocity (curl = $\nabla\times$) or $\nabla \times V$ where ∇ is the del operator, $\times$ signifies the cross product (or vector product) and V the vector of velocity.

Kelvin showed that in an ideal fluid the vorticity is conserved, i.e., there is no creation or dissipation of the vorticity. Modern numerical weather prediction is largely based on conservation of absolute vorticity, referred to the absolute (non-rotating) frame.

Circulation may be defined as the measure of mean flow of a fluid around a given closed curve, expressed as the line integral $\oint V \cdot ds$, the vector scalar (dot) product of the velocity of flow and a small distance element ds along a closed curve in the flow.

In polar coordinates it is given as $C = \oint V \cos \alpha \, ds$ where α is the angle between the direction of flow and the tangent to the curve at that point, or in cartesian coordinates

$$C = \oint (u dx + v dy + w dz)$$

where u, v, and w are the velocities of flow in the x, y, and z directions, x and y are horizontal coordinates, usually taken as east and north, while z is vertical, positive upward (see Fig. 1).

Fig. 1. Circulation (Gordon, 1962). V is the velocity of flow and α is the angle between the direction of flow and the tangent to the distance element ds at that point along the path around the closed curve in the field of motion.

Circulation about a plane curve, according to *Stokes's Theorem*, is equal to the total vorticity of the liquid multiplied by the area enclosed by the curve. Circulation per unit area equals vorticity.

In meteorology it is usual to use only the vertical component of the vorticity, which can be defined as the circulation per unit area (in practice, the limit as

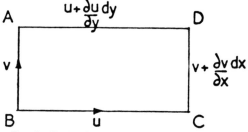

Fig. 2. Derivation of vorticity in Cartesian coordinates (Gordon, 1962).

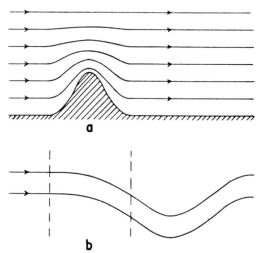

Fig. 3. Derivation of vorticity in polar coordinates (Gordon, 1962).

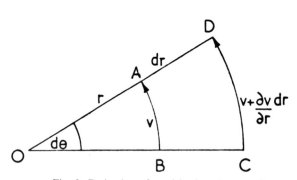

a

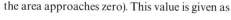
the area approaches zero). This value is given as

$$\zeta = \frac{\partial v}{\partial x} - \frac{\partial u}{\partial y}$$

where ζ is the relative vorticity, u and v are velocity components to the east and north, x and y are the distance coordinates east and north on a system of Cartesian coordinates (fixed with reference to the earth's surface). Alternatively, polar coordinates may be used.

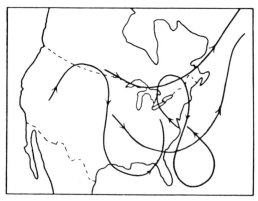

Fig. 5. Examples of constant absolute vorticity trajectories (Hess, 1959).

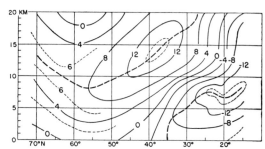

Fig. 6. Mean meridional distribution of the vorticity of the zonal wind (10^{-6} sec^{-1}) in winter (Petterssen, 1956).

b

Fig. 4. (a) Vertical cross section and (b) plan view of streamlines of an initially zonal current crossing a mountain range in the northern hemisphere, without shear (Hess, 1959). Until the air reaches the mountain there are no changes in depth or latitude to cause it to curve. When it begins to ascend the windward side of the barrier, the depth begins to decrease, generating negative vorticity which causes anticyclonic curvature. During the descent on the leeward side, the depth gradually increases causing positive vorticity and the deflection returns to zero. Absolute vorticity is conserved.

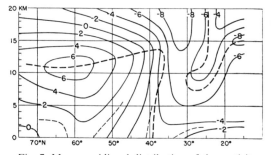

Fig. 7. Mean meridional distribution of the vorticity of the zonal wind (10^{-6} sec^{-1}) in summer (Petterssen, 1956).

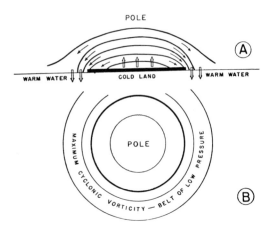

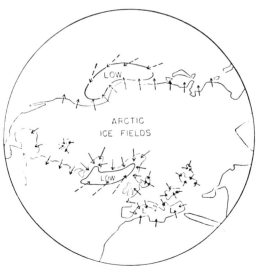

Fig. 8. (A) Diagrammatic representation of surfaces of constant potential temperature (θ surfaces) over a cold continent. Single-shafted arrows indicate the vorticity export. Double-shafted arrows indicate transfer of vorticity to and from the earth's surface. (B) The resulting pressure field at sea level, showing the Polar High (Petterssen, 1956).

Fig. 9. Diagrammatic representation of the vorticity export from cold land to warmer water. Broken arrows indicate northward drift of cyclones (Petterssen, 1956).

Since the earth's rotation also imparts a spin or vorticity to the fluid atmosphere or ocean, the Coriolis force is also included. Therefore the *absolute vorticity* is given by

$$\eta = \zeta + f$$

where η is the absolute vorticity, ζ is the relative vorticity and f is the Coriolis parameter. Positive vorticity is associated with convergence, rising air, instability, cloudiness and precipitation. Negative vorticity is associated with subsidence, fair weather, divergence and stability. This may be illustrated in the passage of air over a topographic barrier (Fig. 4).

Rossby has shown that the absolute vorticity of a moving parcel is conserved. Therefore *constant absolute vorticity* trajectories are sometimes constructed in meteorological forecasting procedures (Fig. 5).

In the zonal circulation in the troposphere it is found that relative vorticity increases in the mid-latitude toward the Jet Stream core. On Figs. 6 and 7 it may be seen that this vorticity rises from about $7 \times 10^{-6}\ \mathrm{sec}^{-1}$ in summer to about $15 \times 10^{-6}\ \mathrm{sec}^{-1}$ in winter, shifting from about latitude 40° to 60°N.

The polar land areas in winter lose heat through upward radiative transfer (with high pressure), and since these areas are (ideally) surrounded by regions of warmer water (with a belt of low pressure) there will be a horizontal pressure gradient toward the pole, increasing with elevation. Since the pressure force is to be essentially balanced by the Coriolis force both relative and absolute vorticity must increase with elevation, providing a ring-shaped belt around the ice cap of cyclonic vorticity (Fig. 8). Owing to topographic complexity in the northern hemisphere this simple model is complicated, but the main patterns tend to develop in winter for each land area.

RICHARD J. ROMMER

References

Byers, H. R., 1959, "General Meteorology," New York, McGraw-Hill Cook Co., 3rd ed., 540pp.

Defant, A., 1961, "Physical Oceanography," Vols. I and II, New York, Pergamon Press.

Hess, S. L., 1959, "Introduction to Theoretical Meteorology," New York, Holt & Co., 362pp.

Panofsky, F., 1956, "Introduction to Dynamic Meteorology," Penn. State Univ. Press.

Petterssen, S., 1956, "Weather Analysis and Forecasting," New York, McGraw-Hill Book Co., 2 vols. (2nd ed.; 1st ed. 1940).

Von Arx, W. S., 1962, "An Introduction to Physical Oceanography," Reading, Mass., Addison-Wesley, 432pp.

Cross-references: *Convergence and Divergence; Coriolis Force; Dynamics of Ocean Currents; Vector Analysis. Vol. II: Jet Stream; Solenoid; Stability.*

W

WADDEN SEA—*See* pr Vol. VI

WARM WATER SPHERES—*See* **TROPO-SPHERE AND STRATOSPHERE IN THE OCEAN**

WATER MASSES AND THE CORE METHOD

The water making up the world oceans can be categorized into divisions which are defined by specific values of the properties or by a certain relationship between the various independent parameters of seawater. Each of these divisions is given a name which describes in a qualitative manner its location and its place of origin, as the Antarctic Bottom Water which forms in various regions around the Antarctic Continent and is found at the bottom of the water column over large sections of the ocean. These water divisions

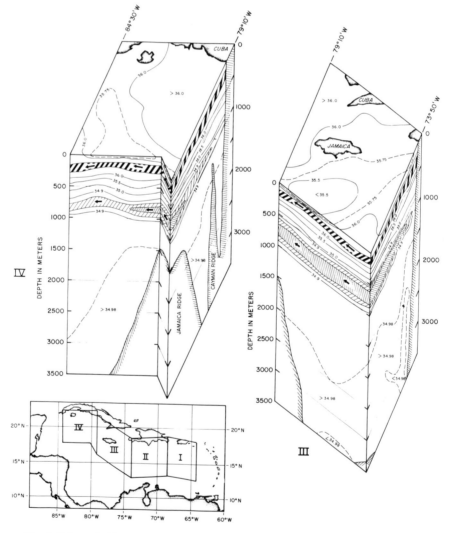

Fig. 1. Schematic block diagram of the distribution of salinity in the Caribbean Sea.

are known as *water masses*, while their place of origin is usually termed the source area. The water masses are produced in these areas by two methods, either by thermohaline alteration through sea-air interchange of material or by mixing of two or more bodies of water. After the formation, the water mass spreads at a level determined by its density relative to the vertical density column of the surrounding water, and gradually, through mixing or interaction with the atmosphere (if it spreads at the surface or near surface levels), it loses the characteristic trait, or traits, which it gained at the source area. There must be a continuous or periodical production of the water mass to prevent complete homogeneity of the oceans due to the process of mixing and diffusion.

The water masses are defined by a characteristic property or relation of the properties, usually pertaining to the temperature (or potential temperature), salinity or oxygen content. It is, therefore, possible to represent a water mass by a graphic plot of the data with two of these parameters as the coordinates. In most cases, the temperature-salinity (T-S) diagram, as developed by Helland-Hansen is sufficient for the identification of a water mass. The water mass may appear as a curve or as an area on the T-S diagram, but in cases of exceptionally homogeneous water, a single point would suffice for identification. It is more accurate to call this last case a water type and to consider the first two cases as mixtures of two or more water types; the shape of the curve or area depends upon the initial positions on a T-S diagram of the water types. However, they all are water masses in that they represent a large volume of seawater which can be recognized as being of common origin.

The deep water masses are more homogeneous than the surface water masses and are, therefore, represented by smaller segments on the T-S plot, while the latter require large areas; this can be seen on the T-S diagrams of Fig. 5. In reality, all the curves have a width of at least the accuracy of the temperature and salinity measurements, and probably wider due to secondary variations in the structure of the water mass. Thus, all the data taken in a particular water mass would fall inside of an "envelope" on the T-S diagram. This envelope is constructed to include most (90–95%) of the previous data taken in the area.

The world's major water masses are produced by thermohaline alteration. Such water masses

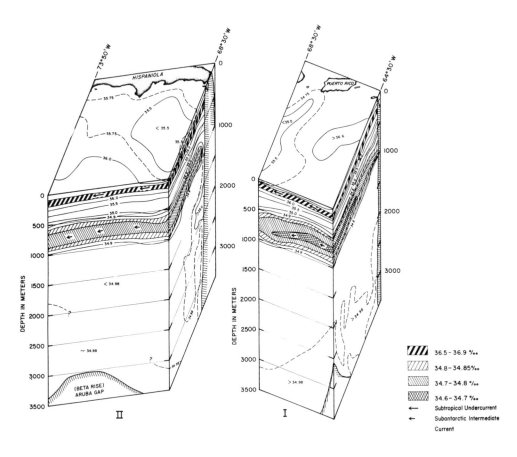

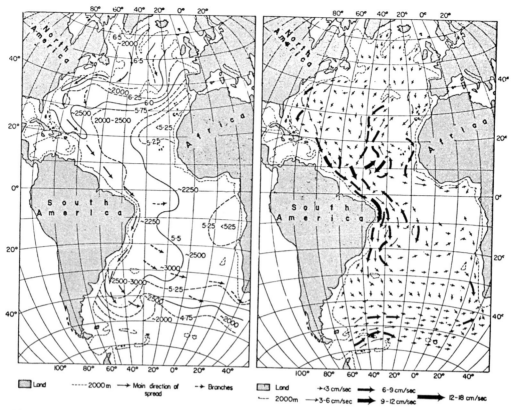

Fig. 2. Picture to the left: spreading of the core masses of the mean North Atlantic Deep Water (O₂ content in the layer of the intermediate oxygen maximum in a depth of about 2000–3000 m; the figures more than 100 indicate the depth of this maximum (according to Wüst, 1936). Picture to the right: current field in a depth of 2000 m (computed from the absolute topography of the 2000-decibar surface (according to Defant, 1941).

possess an extrema in one or more parameters. The layer in which this characteristic water flows (the depth of which is determined by its density) is called the core layer. This layer can be found by inspection of the vertical distribution of the parameters for the properties typical of the water mass. This procedure, called the core method, developed by G. Wüst in 1936, traces the spreading of water masses from their place of origin to the areas in which they can no longer be distinguished. It has successfully been applied by Wüst to the Atlantic Ocean, the Mediterranean Sea and, most recently, the Caribbean Sea. It includes the assumption of the steady-state circulation, in that all the data are treated synoptically.

In a core method study, all the oceanographic data taken in the area of interest are collected and subjected to rigorous quality control. Each extremum which is common to most of the stations is plotted on an areal map where isolines can be drawn and the main axis of spreading located. Vertical profiles, parallel and transverse to this main axis, are prepared. There is usually more than one core layer in the vertical column, and an areal

map must be prepared for each. Figure 1 is a block diagram of the salinity structure in the Caribbean Sea. The positions of the blocks are shown by the small map of the Caribbean. The southern edge of the block is constructed to be parallel to the main axis of spreading in the Sea (see *Caribbean Sea*); the meridional walls are perpendicular to this main axis. The shaded regions are the two salinity extrema layers, or core layers, the Subtropical Undercurrent (upper layer) and the Subantarctic Intermediate Water. Areal views of these layers must be prepared in a core study.

The vertical and horizontal diagrams are not confined to flat walls or surfaces of constant depth, but they follow the surfaces of the core layer itself; thus, each diagram represents the actual spreading of the water masses. If the core layer can be identified as having formed at a particular source area, points along the main axis of spreading can be plotted on a T-S diagram and the percentage of the original water remaining can be found as a function of the distance from the source area. Figure 2 shows the core map of the Middle North Atlantic Deep Water from oxygen values, and the

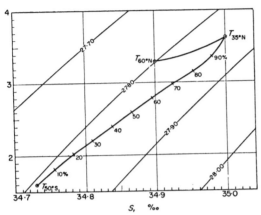

Fig. 3. Standard curve of the TS-relation in the core-layer of the mean North Atlantic Deep Water (Defant, 1961).

geostrophic currents found in this layer from the density field. Figure 3 is the T-S diagram of points along the main axis of spreading. The percentage marks are based on a 100% value for the deep water at 35°N.

Table 1 gives the parameters used to identify the main core layers in the cold water sphere of the Atlantic Ocean (according to Wüst).

There are many different water masses in the oceans, but they can be divided into general groupings. These are: the surface or near-surface masses (upper 300 meters), intermediate water masses (500–1000 meters) deep masses (1200–4000 meters), and the bottom water masses.

The largest division of the surface and near-surface group are the "central water masses" which are found in the temperate climatic zone of both hemispheres. These are characterized by high salinity and fairly warm temperatures. They may be broken down into subdivisions such as west or east central water. It is these water masses which are the source for the shallow salinity maximum core layer (subtropical undercurrent) formed by sinking at the subtropical convergences (35–40°N and S) which occur in most tropical ocean regions. Between the central water masses of the northern and southern hemisphere is the Equatorial water. This water mass is well developed in the Pacific

TABLE 1

Core Layer	Source	Parameter
Arctic and Antarctic Bottom Water	Polar regions (Weddel Sea)	Potential bottom temperature minimum
Middle and Lower North Atlantic Deep Water	Area near Greenland	Intermediate maximum of oxygen
Upper North Atlantic Deep Water	Mediterranean Sea	Intermediate maximum of salinity
Subantarctic Intermediate Water	Antarctic Polar Front	Intermediate minimum of salinity

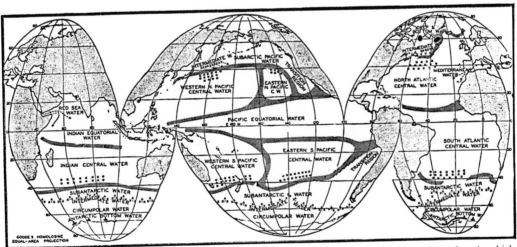

Fig. 4. Approximate boundaries of the upper water masses of the ocean. Squares indicate the regions in which the central water masses are formed; crosses indicate the lines along which the antarctic and arctic intermediate waters sink (Sverdrup, Johnson and Fleming, 1942).

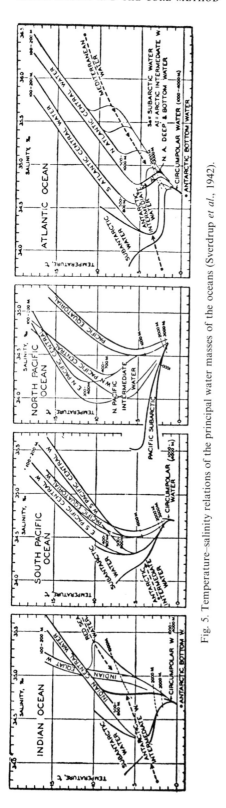

Fig. 5. Temperature–salinity relations of the principal water masses of the oceans (Sverdrup *et al.*, 1942).

and Indian Oceans, but is nonexistent in the Atlantic Ocean.

Poleward of the central waters are the cold surface waters whose source for the most part is the melting of the sea ice and thermal contact with the atmosphere. There is a transition zone between these polar surface water masses and the central waters; these are termed Subantractic or Subarctic surface waters. On the poleward edges of this zone, sinking occurs along a line of convergence. This line or Polar Front can be considered as the source area of the intermediate water masses of the world ocean. They are cold and of low salinity, and they mark the dividing surface between the upper warm water sphere and the lower cold water sphere. In the Atlantic Ocean, the best-developed intermediate water mass is that derived from the south Polar Front (Subantarctic Intermediate Water); it can be traced by the core method to 20°N. North of this latitude, there is no well-developed salinity minimum core layer; however, Arctic intermediate water does occur further north, but it is much more weakly developed and it is not as widespread as the Subantarctic Intermediate Water. The North Pacific Ocean is restricted in its circulation with the Arctic Ocean by the shallow Bering Straits; therefore, there is little Arctic Intermediate Water. However, there is sinking and production of an intermediate water, very similar to the Arctic variety, along the coast of U.S.S.R. Since this water is not of Arctic origin, it is called North Pacific Intermediate Water, but the term Subarctic Intermediate Water is used.

Deep and bottom water is produced in the Polar region, the most active being around the Antarctic continent and the region surrounding southern Greenland. The influence of the Arctic Ocean on the deep circulation of the world oceans is slight due to the isolation of the Arctic basins by submarine ridges. The bottom water production along the Antarctic continent is concentrated in various regions, the most active being the Weddell Sea, in the Atlantic Ocean sector. Therefore, it is seen that the source of most of the world's deep and bottom water is in the Atlantic Ocean. This results in a strong deep circulation, with the influence of the Atlantic Ocean reaching most of the world's oceanic regions. The Pacific Ocean is devoid of strong sources of deep water, and thus the flow below 2000 meters is probably sluggish. The Indian Ocean has a complicated deep water system which is dependent upon mixing of many other water masses rather than upon production of water types by thermohaline alteration.

Figure 4 shows the surface water masses and the positions of sinking or source areas for the intermediate, deep and bottom waters. Figure 5 displays the T-S diagrams for the principal water masses of the ocean.

ARNOLD GORDON

References

Defant, A., 1961, "Physical Oceanography," Vol. 1, New York, Pergamon Press.

Sverdrup, Johnson and Fleming, 1942, "The Oceans." Chapter 15, Englewood Cliffs, N.J., Prentice-Hall.

Wüst, G., 1936, "Schichtung und Zirkulation des Atlantischen Ozeans, Die Stratosphäre," *Wiss Erg. D. Atl. Exp. METEOR*, **6**(1), with Atlas.

WATER SPOUTS—*See* Vol. II

WATTEN MEER—*See* pr Vol. VI **WADDEN SEA**

WAVE AND CURRENT RECORDINGS—*See* **OCEAN CURRENT AND WAVE RECORDING INSTRUMENTATION**

WAVE BASE—*See* Vol. III

WAVE REFRACTION

Waves generated in the storm centers of the world pass out from the downwind ends and sides of the fetches. They then proceed to propagate across the oceans in great circles (Silvester, 1959). In so doing they spread out in ever-increasing circles, much as the ripples do on a pond when a wave is initiated by the impact of a stone. The path of any particular section of this enlarging wave crest (a great circle) can be traced with reasonable accuracy by a straight line on a number of map projections, including the gnomonic and conical types. For purposes of ascertaining the angle of approach of these waves to a point on the coast, a line can be drawn from it to the center of the storm area, as illustrated elsewhere (Silvester, 1963).

The above procedure traces the wave to the boundary between deep and shallow water for that particular wave train, at a depth equal to half the wavelength in deep water (i.e., $L_0/2 = \frac{1}{2}(C_0 T)$) where C_0 is the deep-water wave velocity and T is the wave period in seconds. From this point shoreward, the wave velocity is reduced with decreasing depth. Should a wave approach a coast obliquely to the ocean bed contours, one section of wave crest will be travelling more slowly than the other which is in deeper water. This differential in velocity will cause the crest to become twisted or refracted. While the slope of the sea bed is mild, refracted crests will be curved, but where steep features exist, abrupt changes in velocity and direction can occur.

With knowledge of the wave celerity in any given water depth, it is possible to draw the changing pattern of a wave crest as it traverses a given area of ocean (Anonymous, 1961). Such wave refraction diagrams require the underwater contour to be known throughout the area of wave travel. On hydrographic charts with depths detailed, a template can be prepared which assists in the drawing of angular changes between consecutive contours. In this process, it is convenient to trace the path of a given section of crest, which is termed the orthogonal to the wave, it being normal to the wave crest at all times.

The velocity of a wave in deep water is given by

$$C_0 = \frac{gT}{2\pi}$$

where g is the acceleration due to gravity, in appropriate units for any measuring system.

The velocity at any shallower depth d is given by

$$C_d = \frac{gT}{2\pi} \tanh \frac{2\pi d}{L_d}$$

where L_d is the wavelength in depth d. The refraction of the wave is given by

$$\frac{C_d}{C_0} = \frac{\sin \varphi_d}{\sin \varphi_0}$$

in which φ is the angle of the orthogonal with the normal to the bed contour; subscripts d and 0 refer to depths d and deep-water conditions, respectively. Thus,

$$\frac{\sin \varphi_d}{\sin \varphi_0} = \tanh \frac{2\pi d}{L_d}$$

Now, $\tanh 2\pi d/L_d$ is a function of d/L_0 (Anonymous, 1961), so that a relation exists between d/L_0, C_d/C_0, φ_0 and φ_d. This is graphed in Fig. 1 which can be used in the construction of wave refraction diagrams or for the computation of angles at any given depth in the following manner: The depth d, at which the angle is desired, is divided by the deep-water wavelength L_0 [as available elsewhere (Wiegel, 1964) for any given wave period]. From Fig. 1, C_d/C_0 is determined and traced directly down to the curves of φ_0, the approach angle to the contour at depth $L_0/2$. From this intersection, values of φ_d can be read, as illustrated in the Figure.

For cases where the underwater contours are not parallel (see Fig. 2) the procedure is modified slightly as follows: The orthogonal approaching the deep water contour ($d = L_0/2$), where the velocity is C_0, is continued midway to the first shallow-water contour C_1 angled at α to it. Its approach angle to this contour is $\varphi_0 - \alpha$ (see Fig. 2) but its angle of intersection is φ_1, given by

$$\frac{\sin \varphi_1}{\sin (\varphi_0 - \alpha)} = \frac{C_1}{C_0}$$

or by Fig. 1, if φ_0 represents the combined angle $\varphi_0 - \alpha$. Likewise for contour C_2

$$\frac{\sin \varphi_2}{\sin (\varphi_1 + \beta)} = \frac{C_2/C_0}{C_1/C_0}$$

here C_2/C_0 and C_1/C_0 are obtained from Fig. 1 for their respective d/L_0 values and the ratio used to find φ_2 when $\varphi_0 = \varphi_1 + \beta$.

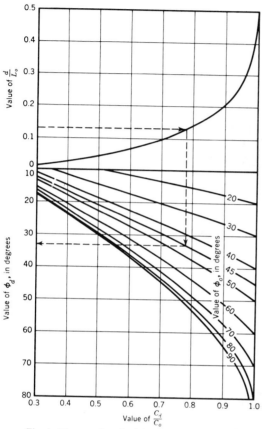

Fig. 1. Diagram for obtaining angle of refraction.

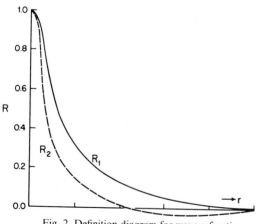

Fig. 2. Definition diagram for wave refraction.

In the case of curved contours, a tangent or mean line at the point of orthogonal intersection is used. Should the approach angle φ_0 exceed 80°, the appropriate section of Fig. 1 can be extended and enlarged to relate it to C_d/C_0 and φ_d.

Where wave orthogonals converge, as for waves traversing an underwater shoal, energy per unit length of wave crest is increased, resulting in higher waves near the shore. For waves refracting away from a location, as in the head of a submarine canyon or embayment, wave heights are reduced. These occurrences are important in the design of marine structures and in the navigability of small coastal craft.

Waves which are more locally generated produce a complex undulation on the sea surface, characterized by the multidirectional nature of their movement and the shortness of the crests due to the interference pattern set up. Refraction of such wave systems tends to lengthen the crests and produce new oscillations within this complex motion (Longuet-Higgins, 1956).

RICHARD SILVESTER

References

Anonymous, 1961, "Shore protection planning and design," *Beach Erosion Board Tech. Rep. No. 4*, U.S. Dept. of Army.
Longuet-Higgins, M. S., 1956, "The refraction of sea waves in shallow water," *J. Fluid Mech.*, **1**, 163–176.
Silvester, R., 1959, "Engineering aspects of coastal sediment movement," *J. Waterways Harbors Div.*, **85**, WW3, 11–39.
Silvester, R., 1963, "Design waves for littoral drift models," *J. Waterways Harbors Div.*, **89**, WW3, 37–47.
Wiegel, R. L., 1964, Oceanographical Engineering, *Englewood Cliffs*, Prentice-Hall, 700pp.

WAVES—*See* **OCEAN WAVES**

WAVES AS ENERGY SOURCES

It is well-known that the hydraulic energy that may be developed during storms, on a resistant shore or man-made structure such as a breakwater, is tremendous. Very great peak pressures are developed, and blocks of stone or concrete in excess of 50 tons are occasionally moved. Small pebbles have been flung to heights of 300 feet or more to shatter lighthouse windows.

From the engineering point of view, the potential harnessing of such peak energy surges is economically of little use, since for most purposes a more continuous energy potential is desirable. Long-period oceanic swells with periods of the order of 10 seconds and amplitudes of 2–5 meters in some parts of the world are sustained for extended periods. Where there is a broad shelving coast, much of this energy may be dissipated against the bottom (friction). On a steep-to coast, there are possibilities of employing the hydraulic potential for useful work.

In offshore situations, the varying pressure developed on the shelf floor may possibly be exploited some day, but at present the devices using wave energy mostly employ the pendulum principle and the wave action that results in rolling and pitching. The simplest of such devices is the navigational bell which, located in a floating buoy, would be struck by a hammer at irregular intervals depending upon the sea state. It has been reported that pendulum-system models have been worked out with a set of gears to operate a small electric generator and thus a light buoy. Alternatively, a model employing the up-and-down motion of the waves to operate an air pump, is sufficient to blow a fog horn; better still, the air pump operates a small air turbine, generating electricity to spare in heavy weather, being stored in batteries for calm days, thus creating an all-weather beacon.

RHODES W. FAIRBRIDGE

Cross-references: *Waves.* In pr Vol. VI, *Tidal Power.*

WAVE THEORY

Introduction

Waves may be generated by winds, ships, explosions, rocks thrown into the water, submarines, underwater earthquakes, moving or varying stationary pressure systems, etc. The restoring force may be primarily gravity (for waves longer than 2 cm) or surface tension (for waves shorter than about 2 cm). Damping due to viscosity or eddy viscosity may or may not be important, depending upon the wavelength compared with the distance the wave is to travel. Waves may break along one type of coast, dissipating most of their energy, or they may reflect; what they do depends largely upon the ratio of their length and steepness to a characteristic length and slope of the coast. Very long waves, such as tsunamis (q.v.), seiches (q.v.) and tides seldom break; wind-generated waves nearly always break. Thus, there must be, and there are, many wave theories, some of which consider forced waves, some free waves, some irrotational waves, some rotational waves, some uniform periodic waves of infinite extent, some wave packets.

Initial Elevation or Impulse

Suppose the water level is increased over a small area and restrained by some means, and then this restraint is removed. What would happen? Waves would propagate from the source, and the characteristics of these waves would depend upon the extent, shape, and height (or depression) of the initial elevation relative to the depth of water. If

the extent and height of the initial elevation is small compared to the water depth, waves form which can be described by linear theory. If the initial elevation is quite large relative to water depth, a bore forms first, and energy is dissipated by this bore as it travels until the energy being transmitted is small enough to be carried by a regular wave or wave system. For initial elevations of intermediate size, the resulting waves may be of a periodic (or almost periodic) nonlinear type, a solitary (nonlinear) wave, or a series of waves of superelevations (nonlinear). If the water is depressed initially, rather than elevated, the resulting waves are always of the type that can be described as linear. These statements are true provided the waves are long enough so that gravity is of much greater importance than surface tension. If surface tension is the predominant restoring force, negative solitary waves can exist.

Figure 1(a) shows a setup of the type described above, looking at one-half of a two-dimensional case. The types of waves that are generated are shown in Figs. 1(b) and (c). As λ increases and d decreases, for positive values of h, the waves become nonlinear, with a bore actually formed as the extreme case. For negative values of h (an initial depression of the water surface), the waves are always of the dispersive type, and essentially linear. The conditions for which the various types of waves form, for positive values of h, are shown in Fig. 2.

Unoki and Nakano (1953a) developed a theory for the two-dimensional case of waves of infinitesimal amplitude in water infinitely deep. The water surface elevation, y_s, for the initial conditions of $y_s = h$ over the region $-\lambda < x < \lambda$ and $y_s = 0$ for $x > \lambda$ is given by the following equation for $x >> \lambda$

$$y_s = \frac{4h}{t} \sqrt{\frac{x}{\pi g}} \sin\left(\frac{gt^2}{4x} \cdot \frac{\lambda}{x}\right) \cos\left(\frac{gt^2}{4x} - \frac{\pi}{4}\right) \quad (1)$$

y_s is the vertical coordinate of the water surface, measured as positive upward from the water surface prior to the disturbance, g is the gravitational acceleration, t is time, and x, h and λ are as defined in Fig. 1(a). The cosine term of this equation describes individual waves with the phase period, length and speed given by

$$T = \frac{4\pi x}{gt}, \quad L = \frac{8\pi x^2}{gt^2}, \quad C = \sqrt{\frac{gL}{2\pi}} = \frac{2x}{t} \quad (2)$$

which occur in groups described by the slowly varying sine term, with the following characteristics

$$T_g = \frac{4\pi x}{gt} \cdot \frac{x}{\lambda}, \quad L_g = \frac{8\pi x^2}{gt^2} \cdot \frac{x}{2\lambda}, \quad C_g = \frac{x}{t} = \text{constant} \quad (3)$$

It can be seen from Eqs. (2) and (3) that the group

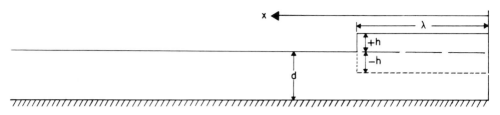

a. Initial Conditions

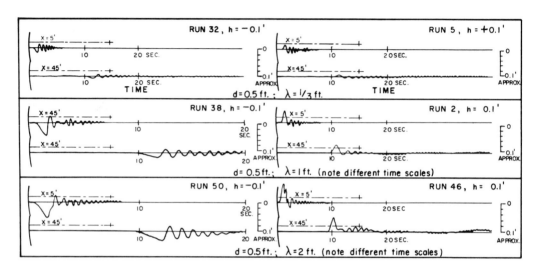

b. Effect Of λ On Waves For Both Positive And Negative Initial Elevation, h.

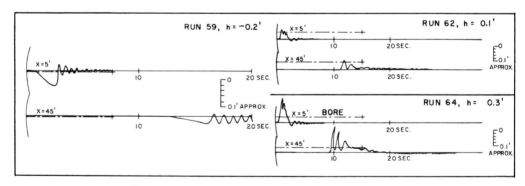

c. Extreme Case, λ = 2 ft., h = 0.35 ft. (note different time scales)

Fig. 1. Waves generated by initial elevation of water surface over limited two-dimensional area (from Prins, 1958).

travels at one-half the phase speed. The system is dispersive, i.e., it spreads as it moves from the source, and the rate at which it spreads depends upon the component phase periods, T. The phase periods, lengths and speeds are independent of the dimension of the initial elevation, being functions only of x and t. The speed of the groups, C_g also depends only upon x and t, but the period and length of the groups (T_g and L_g) depend upon the length of the initial disturbance, λ, and the amplitude depends upon the elevation of the initial disturbance, h, as well as x and t. In practice, no water is infinitely deep, and the maximum speed that a linear disturbance can travel at is $\sqrt{gd}$. It can be seen in Fig. 3 that the leading edge of the disturbance travels at a speed equal to $\sqrt{gd}$. In

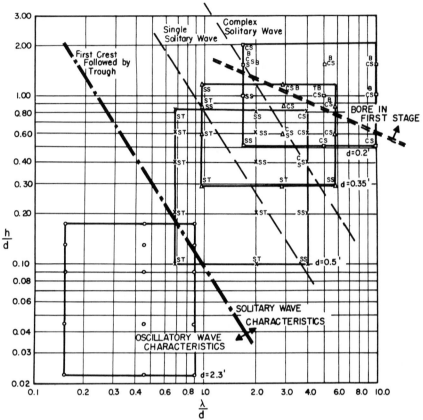

O   Oscillatory wave, part of a dispersive wave system.

ST Leading wave with solitary wave characteristics; followed by a
    trough which in turn is followed by a dispersive wave system.

SS Leading wave a single wave of solitary wave characteristics,
    separated by a more or less flat section from a small dispersive
    tail.

CS Leading part being of a complicated nonlinear system which
    separates into several humps as the system moves.

TB A bore at the start at the crest of the wave.

B   A bore.

Fig. 2. Relation between λ/d, h/d and the characteristics of the leading wave in the case of elevation from Prins, 1958).

Fig. 3 the time of arrival of phase zero points given by

$$t = \sqrt{(4\pi x/g)\,(n - 1)}, \text{ for } n = 1, 2, 3, \ldots \quad (4)$$

are also shown. In general, for small values of $+h$, and even for substantial values of $-h$, and deep water in the tank, the agreement was good. For small water depths and large values of $+h$ agreement was not good; however, there would be no reason to expect good agreement. The amplitudes predicted by the theory were almost always higher than measured values.

Ursell (1958) developed a theory for waves in water of any depth, which is useful for calculating amplitudes and lengths of the leading few waves, which is of particular importance in the study of tsunamis. The equation for the water surface elevation is

$$y_s = \frac{2h}{\pi} \int_0^\infty \cos kx \; \text{cox} \; (t\sqrt{gk \tanh kd})$$

$$\frac{\sin k\lambda}{k} \, dk \quad (5)$$

where k is the wave number, $2\pi/L$. For the region

in the vicinity of $x = t\sqrt{gd}$, for $x < t\sqrt{gd}$, an asymptotic solution to Eq. (5) is

$$y_s \approx hf(\beta)\, Ai\left[-\left(\frac{t}{\sqrt{g/d}}\right)^{2/3} f_2(\beta)\right] \qquad (6)$$

where Ai is the Airy integral and β is defined by

$$\frac{x}{t\sqrt{gd}} = \frac{1}{2}\left[1 + (2\beta/\sinh 2\beta)\right]\sqrt{\tanh \beta/\beta} \qquad (7)$$

and

$$f_1(\beta) = \frac{\sin(\beta\lambda/d)}{\beta}$$

$$\frac{(2\beta/\sinh \beta)^{1/3}\left[(\sinh 2\beta - 2\beta)/(4\beta^6/3)\right]^{1/6}}{\left[(1/\cosh^2\beta) + \left(\dfrac{\sinh 2\beta - 2\beta}{2\beta}\right)^2\right]^{1/2}} \qquad (8)$$

$$f_2(\beta) = (\beta/\sinh 2\beta)^{2/3}\,(\tanh \beta/\beta)^{1/3}$$

$$(\sinh 2\beta - 2\beta)/(4\beta^3/3)^{\,2/3}\,\beta^2 \qquad (9)$$

Unoki and Nakano (1953b) derived a theory similar to their two-dimensional theory for the three-dimensional case. The surface elevation at some distance r from the center of the initial elevation of radius R is

$$y_s = \frac{\sqrt{2}\,hR}{r}J_1(gt^2R/4r^2)\cos(gt^2/4r) \qquad (10)$$

Here, the groups are described by the slowly varying Bessel function J_1.

Theories for the three-dimensional case in water of any depth have been developed by Kranzer and Keller (1955), together with a theory for waves generated by an initial impulse. Impulsively generated waves have also been studied by Unoki and Nakano (1953a and b), as well as by other investigators. These are all linearized theories and do not describe the type of waves generated by a source which is large compared with the water depth.

Waves of Infinite Extent (Linear)

The simplest type of wave is one belonging to a train of infinite extent; these are uniform, periodic and of infinite crest length. For progressive waves, the water surface elevation is given by

$$y_s = \alpha \cos(kx - \sigma t) \qquad (11)$$

where α is half the wave height, H, and σ is the circular frequency, $2\pi/T$. The speed at which the wave progresses is

$$C = \sigma/k = (gT/2\pi)\tanh(2\pi d/L) = \qquad (12)$$
$$(gL/2\pi)\tanh(2\pi d/L)$$

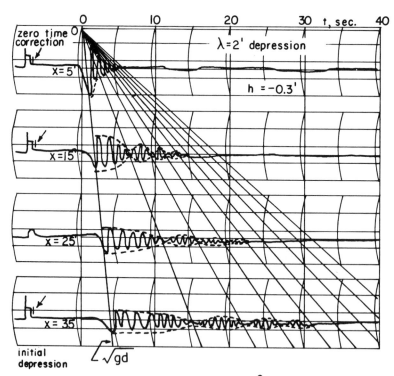

Fig. 3. Amplitude envelope zero points, $d = 2.3'$ (from Prins, 1958).

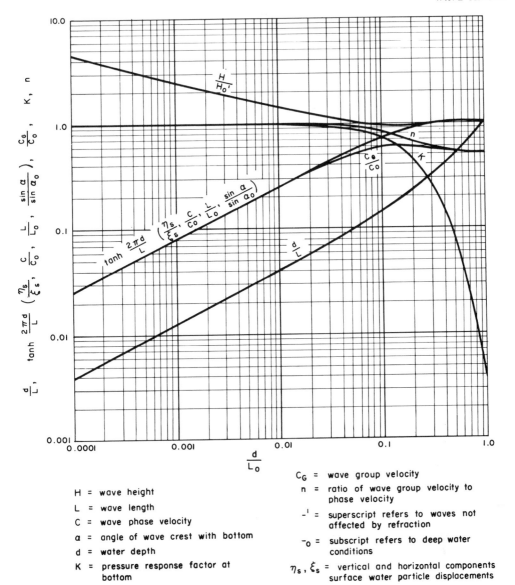

Fig. 4. Progressive wave characteristics in transitional and shallow water relative to deep water—linear theory.

C_G = wave group velocity

n = ratio of wave group velocity to phase velocity

$-'$ = superscript refers to waves not affected by refraction

$-_0$ = subscript refers to deep water conditions

η_s, ξ_s = vertical and horizontal components surface water particle displacements

H = wave height

L = wave length

C = wave phase velocity

α = angle of wave crest with bottom

d = water depth

K = pressure response factor at bottom

and, as for periodic waves

$$L = CT \tag{13}$$

the wavelength is

$$L = (gT^2/2\pi) \tanh (2\pi d/L) \tag{14}$$

In deep water ($d/L > 1/2$ for most practical purposes) $\tanh 2\pi d/L \to 1$, so the wave speed and wavelength in deep water are

$$C_0 \to gT/2\pi$$
$$L_0 \to gT^2/2\pi \tag{15}$$

In shallow water ($d/L < 1/25$ for most practical purposes), $\tanh 2\pi d/L \to 2\pi d/L$, so

$$C \to \sqrt{gd}$$
$$L \to T\sqrt{gd} \tag{16}$$

The ratios C/C_0, L/L_0 and d/L_0 are of considerable practical value. These are

$$C/C_0 = L/L_0 = \tanh 2\pi d/L \tag{17}$$

and as

$$\frac{d}{L} \tanh 2\pi d/L = \frac{d}{L_0} \tag{18}$$

Equation (17) can be plotted as a function of d/L_0 (Fig. 4). These functions, together with some other useful functions have been tabulated for easy use (Wiegel, 1954).

The water particles do not move with the phase speed, C. They move in circles in deep water and ellipses in transitional and shallow water. The horizontal and vertical components of water particle velocity, u and v, respectively, are

$$u = \frac{\pi H}{T} \frac{\cosh 2\pi (y + d)/L}{\sinh 2\pi d/L} \cos (kx - \sigma t)$$

$$v = \frac{\pi H}{T} \frac{\sinh 2\pi (y + d)/L}{\sinh 2\pi d/L} \sin (kx - \sigma t)$$

(19)

where y is the vertical coordinate measured negatively downward from the still water level.

The horizontal and vertical components of water particle displacements, ξ and η, from their mean positions x_0, y_0 are

$$\xi = -\frac{H}{2} \frac{\cosh 2\pi(y_0 + d)/L}{\sinh 2\pi d/L} \sin (kx_0 - \sigma t)$$

$$\eta = \frac{H}{2} \frac{\sinh 2\pi(y_0 + d)/L}{\sinh 2\pi d/L} \cos (kx_0 - \sigma t)$$

(20)

In deep water the velocities and motions decrease exponentially with distance beneath the surface, while in relatively shallow water the horizontal velocity and motion decrease very slowly (Fig. 5).

The pressure beneath the water surface is

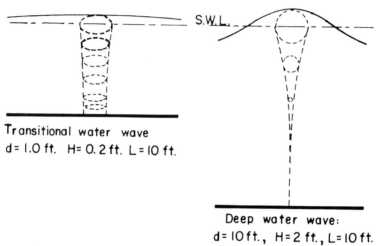

Transitional water wave
d = 1.0 ft. H = 0.2 ft. L = 10 ft.

Deep water wave:
d = 10 ft., H = 2 ft., L = 10 ft.

Fig. 5. Water particle orbits.

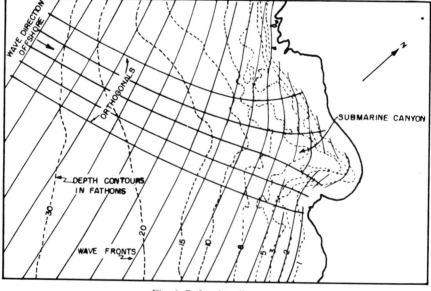

Fig. 6. Refraction diagram.

$$p = -\rho g y + \rho g a \frac{\cosh 2\pi(y+d)/L}{\cosh 2\pi d/L}$$

$$\cos (kx - \sigma t) \qquad (21)$$

where ρ is the mass density of the water and a is the wave amplitude ($H = 2a$). The average power transmitted is

$$P = \frac{1}{T} \int_0^T \int_0^{-d} (p + \rho g y) u \, dt \, dy = \qquad (22)$$

$$\frac{\rho g H^2}{8} C \cdot \frac{1}{2} \left(1 + \frac{2kd}{\sinh 2hd} \right)$$

As $\rho g H^2/8$ is the energy per unit surface area (energy density), the average power transmitted by a wave train is the product of the energy density, the wave speed and $\frac{1}{2}[1 + (2kd)/\sinh 2kd]$. As the power is the product of the energy density and the speed at which it is transmitted, the term $C \cdot \frac{1}{2}[1 + (2kd)/\sinh 2kd]$ must be the speed at which energy is transmitted by a wave system. This term is given by the symbol C_g and is called the group velocity. It is the same C_g that showed up in Eq. (3). In deep water the term in brackets in Eq. (22) approaches unity and $C_g \to \frac{1}{2}C$, while in shallow water the term approaches 2, and $C_g \to C$. The ratio C_g/C is given the symbol n and is shown in Fig. 4. This characteristic of water waves explains many observations. For example, in deep water a ship leaves a trail of ship waves although an observer sees that the wave being formed by the ship is always stationary relative to the ship; this is because the component of wave phase speed in the direction of the ship advance is the same as the ship speed, while the energy transmitted by the waves can only be transmitted at half this speed so that a system of waves forms behind the ship, with the number of waves continually increasing. In shallow water, the phase and group speeds are the same so that the power being transferred from ship to wave does not disperse in a wave train; instead the ship wave keeps increasing in height, so that at some point the linear theory fails to predict the results correctly.

If a wave system moving in water of varying depth can be considered to be neither reflecting nor losing energy, then by equating the power transmitted by the wave system per foot of wave crest in one depth with the same power in another depth, Eqs. (12) and (22) can be combined to give

$$\frac{H}{H_0} = \sqrt{(C_{g_2}/C_g)}(\sqrt{b_0/b}) \qquad (23)$$

where the subscripts 0 refer to deep water conditions and b is the distance between orthogonals (orthogonals being curves everywhere normal to the direction of wave advance). If we consider only the case in which $b_0 = b$, the wave height H is different water depths. This condition is shown as H/H_0' in Fig. 4. As a wave moves from deep water into shallow water, it at first decreases in height and then starts to increase. When the height increases to too great a value, the linear theory is no longer valid. In reality, the wave eventually becomes so steep it breaks.

Consider a wave moving over parallel bottom contours at an angle to the contours. The phase speed depends upon the water depth for a given wave period [Eq. (12)]—with the less the water depth, the lower is the wave speed—so that different parts of the wave move at different speeds, and the wave bends. This phenomenon is known as wave refraction. In nature, contours are usually not parallel, but graphical techniques have been developed to permit the drawing of refraction diagrams over irregular shoal water (Johnson, O'Brien and Isaacs, 1948) as in Fig. 6. If orthogonals are constructed on top of the wave fronts on the refraction drawings, the spreading or contraction of the orthogonals is represented by the terms b_0 and b in Eq. (23). If the distance between orthogonals in deep water is b_0, and the distance between orthogonals in water of some other depth is b, then the effect of the refraction on the change in wave height is given by $H/H_0 = \sqrt{b_0/b}$.

Consider a wave passing an impermeable breakwater. The portion of the wave incident to the breakwater is reflected, while the other portion of the wave continues on. It is not possible for an unrestrained vertical wall of water to exist so the "ends" of the reflected and transmitted waves act as sources of waves. This process, known as diffraction, is responsible for the waves in the lee of a breakwater. The expressions for wave amplitudes in the lee of a breakwater can be expressed in terms of Mathieu functions for a breakwater gap (Carr and Stelzriede, 1952) and in terms of Fresnal integrals for a semi-infinite breakwater (Blue and Johnson, 1949; Penny and Price, 1952; Wiegel, 1962).

Linear Superposition

Irregular wave systems can be handled by means of linear superposition. This has already been done in the section on waves generated by an initial elevation or impulse, in which a Fourier integral representation of an energy spectrum was used to represent a given initial elevation or impulse. Similar representations are used to describe waves generated by winds, but the phase relationships are discarded under the assumption (probably justified) that the phases have a gaussian distribution. Much work is being done at the present time to develop theories to predict the energy spectra and to measure the energy spectra of wind-generated waves in the ocean. Little work has been done on the directional spectra; however, the theory assumes the superposition of waves of infinitely long crests, whereas the waves cannot be generated with such crests, and diffraction must play an important role.

Nonlinear Wave Phenomenon

When a wave approaches an impervious break-water at an angle of less than 45°, reflection does not occur in a simple manner, rather the wave bends, becoming normal to the breakwater at the point of contact. The equivalent of the Mach reflection of blast phenomena occurs (Perroud, 1957; Sigurdsson and Wiegel, 1962). For smaller angles, the phenomenon becomes even more pro-nounced. This results in an increase in the wave amplitude along a breakwater which is particularly pronounced for a wall that has a concave plan.

When waves become fairly steep, the linear theory no longer predicts their shape, or other charac-teristics, correctly. To the third order, the Stokes' (Stokes, 1880) wave profile is given by

$$-\frac{y_s}{L} = A_1 \cos (kx - \sigma t) + A_2 \cos 2(kx - \sigma t) + \quad (24)$$
$$A_3 \cos 3(kx - \sigma t)$$

where the coefficients A_1, A_2 and A_3 are related to the wave height by

$$H/d = (L/d)[2A_1 + 2\pi^2 A_1{}^3 \cdot f_3(d/L)] \quad (25)$$

where

$$A_2 = \pi A_1{}^2 \cdot f_2(d/L), \ A_3 = \pi^2 A_1{}^3 \cdot f_3(d/L) \quad (26)$$

$$f_2(d/L) = \frac{(2 + \cosh 4\pi d/L) \cosh 2\pi d/L}{2 \sinh^3 2\pi d/L} \quad (27)$$

The waves have steeper crests and flatter troughs than linear waves. The formulation presented above is after Skjelbreia (1959) since calculations using third-order theory can be made using tables of functions published by him.

The higher-order theories for Stokes' waves predicts a phenomenon that the linear theory does not. For example, the horizontal component of water particle velocity in addition to having a second harmonic has a non-periodic term which shows a steady progression of the particles in the direction of wave advance. This term, called the mass transport velocity, is

$$\overline{U} = \frac{1}{2} \frac{\pi H}{T} \frac{\pi H}{L} \frac{\cosh 4\pi (y_0 + d)/L}{\sinh^2 2\pi d/L} \quad (29)$$

When looking at second-order terms, it is necessary to examine other types of second-order effects, e.g., the effect of viscosity. This has been done for the mass transport term (Longuet-Higgins, 1953) for the case of null mass transport. This is the case of waves moving in a tank, breaking on the beach, with the same amount of water returning seaward as is moved shoreward by the mass transport. The

result is

$$\overline{U}_{nv} = \frac{1}{4} \frac{(\pi H/T)(\pi H/L)}{\sinh^2 2\pi d/L} \Big\{ 3 + 2 \cosh 4\pi(y + d)/L$$
$$+ (2\pi d/L) \left(3\frac{y^2}{d^2} + 4\frac{y}{d} + 1 \right) \sinh 4\pi d/L$$
$$+ 3 \left(\frac{\sinh 4\pi d/L}{4\pi d/L} + \frac{3}{2} \right) \left(\frac{y^2}{d^2} - 1 \right) \Big\} \quad (30)$$

This equation shows the mass transport very near the bottom always to be in the direction of wave advance, in the opposite direction in the center, and in the direction of wave advance at the surface for $2\pi d/L$ greater than about 0.75, but in the opposite direction for water more shallow than this. Experiments (Russell and Orsorio, 1958) have verified the essential features of this theory.

Equation (21) shows that the pressure due to progressive water waves attenuates rapidly with distance beneath the surface in deep water. For standing waves this is also the case, but when the second-order theory is examined it is found that there is one second harmonic term which shows no attenuation with distance beneath the surface and is of considerable importance from the stand-point of some problems, such as the generation of microseisms. This term is

$$[(\pi H^2/4L) \tanh 2\pi d/L] \cos 4\pi t/T \quad (31)$$

The problem of the maximum steepness of waves has been the subject of many papers. Miche (1944) found that the maximum steepness of pro-gressive waves in water of any depth is given by

$$H/L = 0.142 \tanh 2\pi d/L \quad (32)$$

This has been verified by laboratory tests (Danel, 1952) as being the upper limit.

When the wavelength becomes quite long com-pared with the water depth, about $L/d > 10$ (the value depending upon H/d as well), the cnoidal wave theory is a better approximation than is the theory of Stokes waves. This theory was originally dervied by Korteweg and de Vries (1895). To the first approximation the wave profile is given by y_s, measured above the bottom

$$y_s = y_t + H cn^2 [2K(k) (x/L, t/T), k] \quad (33)$$

where cn is the "cnoidal" Jacobian elliptical function and $K(k)$ is the complete elliptic integral of the first kind of modulus k, y' is the elevation of the wave trough above the bottom, and is given by

$$\frac{y_t}{H} - \frac{d}{H} + 1 = \frac{16}{3L^2} \frac{d^3}{H} \Big\{ K(k) \Big[K(k) - E(k) \Big\} (34)$$

where H is the wave height and $E(k)$ is the complete

elliptic integral of the second kind of modulus k. The wavelength is

$$L = \sqrt{16d^3/3H} \; k \, K(k) \qquad (35)$$

and the period is related to the modulus k through

$$T\sqrt{\frac{g}{d}} = \sqrt{\frac{16d}{3H}} \left\{ \frac{kK(k)}{\sqrt{1+\dfrac{H}{d}-1+\dfrac{1}{k}\;2-3\dfrac{E(k)}{K(k)}}} \right\} \qquad (36)$$

The equations for water particle velocities and acceleration and graphs which permit the use of the cnoidal wave theory have been developed by Wiegel (1960; see Masch and Wiegel, 1961 for tables of functions).

It is interesting to note that when $k \to 0$, $cn \to$ cosine and $K(k) \to \pi/2$, and the period of the cn function $4K(k)$ is 2π. Thus, at one limit, the cnoidal wave becomes the simple wave of linear theory. At the other extreme, when $k \to 1$, $cn \to$ sech, $K(k) \to \infty$ and we have the nonlinear solitary wave

$$y_s = d + H \, \text{sech}^2 \left[\sqrt{3H/4d^3} \, (x - Ct) \right] \qquad (37)$$

where

$$C = \sqrt{gd} \, (1 + H/2d) \qquad (38)$$

This equation for the speed of the solitary wave is nearly the same as the first approximation of Laitone (1960) and is almost equal, numerically, to the equation determined empirically by Russell (1844) and theoretically by Boussinesq (1872), Rayleigh (1876) and McCowan (1891).

Forced Waves

The theories presented above were for free waves. Other waves, which are forced have not been covered due to space limitations. These include the theories of wave generation by wind and ships, harbor oscillations, and storm surges (see Wiegel, 1964).

R. L. WIEGEL

References

Blue, F. L., Jr., and Johnson, J. W., 1949, "Diffraction of water waves passing through a breakwater gap," *Trans. Am. Geophys. Union*, **30**, No. 5, 705–718.

Boussinesq, J., 1872, "Theorie des onde et de remous qui se propagent le long d'un canal ractangulaire horizontal, en communiquant au liquide contemn dans ce canal des vitesses sensiblement parielles de la surface au fond," *J. Math. Pures Appliquees*, Ser. 2, **17**, 55–108.

Carr, J. H., and Stelzriede, M. E., 1952, "Diffraction of water waves by breakwaters," in "Gravity Waves," *Nat. Bur. Std. Circ.*, **521**, 109–125.

Danel, Pierre, 1952, "On the limiting clapotis," in "Gravity Waves," *Nat. Bur. Std. Circ.*, **521**, 35–38.

Johnson, J. W., O'Brien, M. P., and Isaacs, J. D., 1948, "Graphical construction of wave refraction diagrams," *U.S. Navy Hydrographic Office Publ. No.* 605.

Korteweg, D. J., and de Vries, G., 1895, "On the change of form of long waves advancing in a rectangular canal, and on a new type of long stationary waves," *Phil. Mag.*, (5), **39**, 422–443.

Kranzer, H. C., and Keller, J. B., 1955, "Water Waves Produced by Explosions," New York University, Institute of Mathematical Sciences, IMM-NYU 222.

Laitone, E. V., 1960, "The second approximation to cnoidal and solitary waves," *J. Fluid Mech.*, **9**, Part 3, 430–444.

Longuet-Higgins, M. S., 1953, "Mass transport in water waves," *Phil. Trans. Roy. Soc. London, Ser. A*, **245**, No. 903, 535–581.

Masch, Frank D., and Wiegel, R. L., 1961, "Cnoidal Waves: Tables of Functions," Council on Wave Research, The Engineering Foundation, Berkeley, California.

McCowan, J., "On the solitary wave," *Phil. Mag.*, **32**, No. 5, 45–58.

Miche, Robert, 1944, "Mouvements ondulatoires des mer en profondeur constante au décroissante," *Annales des Ponts et Chaussees*, 25–78, 131–164, 270–292, and 369–406.

Penny, W. G., and Price, A. T., 1952, "The diffraction theory of sea waves by breakwaters, and the shelter afforded by breakwaters," *Phil. Trans. Roy. Soc. London, Ser. A*, **244**, 236–253.

Perroud, P. H., 1957, "The Solitary Wave Reflection Along a Straight Vertical Wall of Oblique Incidence," Tech. Rept. No. 99–3, Inst. of Eng. Res., Univ. of Calif., Berkeley, Calif.

Prins, J. E., 1958, "Water waves due to a local disturbance," *Proc. Sixth Conf. Coastal Engineering*, Council of Wave Research, The Engineering Foundation, Berkeley, Calif., 147–162.

Rayleigh, Lord, 1876, "On waves," *Phil. Mag.*, **1**, No. 4, 257–279.

Russell, R. C. H., and Orsorio, J. D. C., 1958, "An experimental investigation of drift profiles in a closed channel," *Proc. Sixth Conf. Coastal Engineering*, Council on Wave Research, The Engineering Foundation, Berkeley, Calif., 171–183.

Sigurdsson, Gunnar, and Wiegel, R. L., 1962, "Solitary wave behavior at concave barriers," *The Port Engineer*, 4–8.

Skjelbreia, Lars, 1959, "Gravity Waves, Stokes' Third Order Approximation; Tables of Functions," Council on Wave Research, The Engineering Foundation, Berkeley, Calif., 1959.

Stokes, G. G., 1880, "On the Theory of Oscillatory Waves," in "Mathematical and Physical Papers," Vol. 1, Cambridge, Cambridge University Press.

Unoki, S., and Nakano, M., 1953a, "On the Cauchy-Poisson waves caused by the eruption of a submarine volcano (1st paper)," *Oceanographical Magazine*, **4**, No. 4, 119–141.

Unoki, S., and Nakano, M., 1953b, "On the Cauchy-Poisson waves caused by the eruption of a submarine volcano (2nd paper)," *Oceanographical Magazine*, **5**, No. 1, 1–13.

Ursell, F., 1958, "On the Waves Generated by a Local Surface Disturbance," University of California, Berkeley, California, unpublished memorandum.

Wiegel, R. L., 1954, "Gravity Waves, Tables of Functions," Council on Wave Research, The Engineering

Foundation, Berkeley, California.

Wiegel, R. L., 1960, "A presentation of cnoidal wave theory for practical application," *J. Fluid Mech.*, **7**, Part 2, 273–286.

Wiegel, R. L., 1962, "Diffraction of waves by semi-infinite breakwater," *J. Hydraul. Div., Am. Soc. Civil Engrs.*, **88**, No. HY1, 27–44.

Wiegel, R. L., 1964, "Oceanographical Engineering," Englewood Cliffs, N.J., Prentice-Hall, Inc., 700pp.

WEDDELL SEA

(1) Geography

The Weddell Sea is located to the extreme south of the Atlantic Ocean, bounded to the west by the Antarctic Peninsula, to the south by the Filchner Ice Shelf and to the east by Coats Land. With the exception of the Ross Sea, the Weddell Sea forms the largest indentation in the otherwise roughly circular coastline of the Antarctic Continent. To the north, its basin is partially blocked by a loop of the submerged Scotia Ridge, a continuation of the Andes Mountains of South America which emerges in Antarctica as the Antarctic Peninsula. The Ridge breaks the surface as the South Shetland, South Orkney and South Sandwich Islands. The southern portion of the sea is covered by the Filchner Ice Shelf, an area of 260,000 km^2 and 230–490 m thick, which is grounded near its center by ice-covered Berkner Island.

(2) Exploration

The Weddell Sea was first successfully explored in February 1823 when James Weddell, British navigator, sailing through an ice-free sea, attained the latitude 74° 15′S and longitude 34° 17′W. The extraordinarily favorable conditions met by Weddell have not been encountered by subsequent explorers. Thus in 1840, when the French explorer Dumont D'Urville attempted to follow Weddell's route, the impenetrable ice stopped him in 64°S; three years later the British explorer James C. Ross had no better fortune. In 1893, heavy ice stopped C. A. Larsen along the eastern coast of the Antarctic Peninsula.

In 1901–1902, the Swedish Expedition's *Antarctic* under Otto Nordenskjold established a winter station on the east coast of the Antarctic Peninsula at Snow Hills Island (64° 22′S) where meteorological and magnetic work was carried on until November 1903. Early in 1903, the Scottish National Antarctic Expedition entered the Weddell Sea aboard the *Scotia*, and in March 1904 the Weddell Barrier was sighted at longitude 22°W; the area was named "Coats Land."

In December 1911, Wilhelm Filchner aboard the *Deutschland* was the first to reach the head of the Weddell Sea by an approach from the eastern side. After sighting the Weddell Barrier in latitude 76° 41′S, longitude 30° 25′W, the ship proceeded southwest and reached latitude 77° 44′S, longitude 34° 38′W.

In December 1914, Sir Ernest Shackleton aboard the *Endurance* (1914–1915) entered into the Weddell Sea, and after sailing parallel to Coats Land, his ship was frozen in and began to drift northward, until it finally was crushed and sank near 69°S, 52°W. The remarkable story of Shackleton's effort to lead his entire party to safety during the next 14 months is unparalleled in the history of exploration.

In December 1949, a major expedition to the Weddell Sea took place when Norway, Great Britain and Sweden sent the vessel *Norsel* which reached Cape Norvegia in February 1950.

During the International Geophysical Year (1957–1958), the Weddell Sea was the focus of investigations conducted at scientific stations set up in Coats Land and on the Filchner Ice Shelf by the United States, Argentina and the United Kingdom.

(3) Submarine Geomorphology

The Weddell Sea is a very deep bight, its general depth, except near the land, is between 4500 and 4700 m. In the north the Weddell Sea averages 4880 m in depth, with a maximum of 8268 m in the South Sandwich trench. Relatively shallow water is found between the South Sandwich group and the South Orkneys, while close to Coats Land, soundings of 243 and 294 m were obtained. One of the largest abyssal plains discovered to date forms the floor of the Weddell Basin. The Weddell Abyssal Plain, which has been traced as far east as 20°E longitude and 20°W longitude, is over 300 km wide from north to south. The western extremities of the Weddell Basin have not been well explored.

The continental shelf off Coats Land and Antarctic Peninsula are wider and deeper than is normal. On the east coast of the Peninsula, the shelf is at least 150 km broad, whereas off Coats Land it is comparatively narrow. This shelf is transversely breached beneath the Filchner Ice Shelf by the Crary Trough about 1060 m deep and was probably glacially cut during lower stages of sea level. From the shelf and from the mountain glaciers that face directly on the sea, great icebergs sometimes as large as the state of Connecticut, break loose to drift on the circumpolar ocean. In recent years, large tubular icebergs well over 150 km in length have been calving in large numbers from the Filchner Ice Shelf, thus causing profound geographical changes in this great embayment of the Antarctic Continent.

(4) Oceanography

Almost the entire Weddell Sea is covered with pack ice. The tide is both diurnal and semidiurnal, with a double amplitude ranging between 0.6–3.2

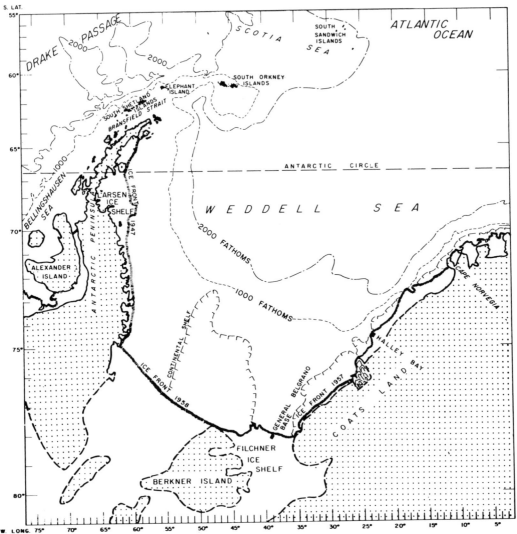

Fig. 1. Bathymetric map of Weddell Sea.

m. The mean annual surface water temperature at the South Orkneys is −1.0°C. A mean maximum (1°C) occurs here in February and minimum −1.0°C in August. In January and February the surface temperature of the sea is slightly lower than that of the air; in all other months it is higher. In the southern Weddell Sea, at Halley Bay, the peak of mean surface air temperature (1957, 1958) was in December and January (−5.5°C); the coldest months were May and August (−30.1°C and −32.3°C, respectively). Easterly winds predominated throughout the year with an annual mean speed of 6.9 m/sec. In 1957, precipitation was at a maximum in spring and fall, but in 1958 the three mid winter months provided a net accumulation of 42 cm equivalent to over half the year's net accumulation.

The winds off the Antarctic coasts are in general southeasterly. This results in a well-defined clockwise circulation within the Weddell Sea. At the eastern entrance of the Weddell Sea a current, with a speed of less than one knot, is set towards the southwest and flows approximately parallel to Coats Land. The current sweeps into the southern boundary of the Sea at 77°S before turning northward parallel to the Antarctic Peninsula coast, finally issuing from the northwestern corner of the sea. From the tip of the Peninsula the main body of the current continues in a northeasterly direction, passing south of Elephant Island, but north of the South Orkneys, where it merges with water from the Bellingshausen Sea (Hart, 1934).

Further, as a result of the southeasterly wind, the eastern borders of the Weddell Sea are free from ice while pack ice moves toward the west. The physical obstruction of the Antarctic Peninsula, together with the low average wind velocity in the Weddell Sea, is the cause of the unusual congestion of ice which generally prevails in the western Weddell Sea.

Hydrographic data taken aboard the Argentine icebreaker *San Martin* in January 1959 showed that the eastern part of the Weddell Sea had an average temperature of $-1.35°C$ and average salinity of 33.92‰. Along the coast of Coats Land from Cape Norvegia to the Argentine Base General Belgrano, the average values were $-1.07°C$ and 34.13‰ respectively. At a depth of 200 m, higher-salinity water (34.7‰) is particularly well developed in the Weddell Sea.

Vertical distribution of temperature and density in the eastern parts of the Weddell Sea, close to the Antarctic Continent, show that the bottom water is largely mixed with water of Atlantic origin as indicated by its higher temperature and density when compared with the water filling the greater depths of the western portion of this sea. Salinity observations of the Weddell Sea bottom water reveal water with salinities as high as 34.60–34.75‰. All available data so far indicate that the Weddell Sea is by far the greatest source of Antarctic bottom water, and they suggest that its bottom water is an essential constituent of the mixtures which spread northward in the Pacific and Indian Oceans as well as in the Atlantic Ocean. It has been estimated that the flow from the Weddell Sea must be at least as great as that of the highly saline water from the North Atlantic Ocean. There is some evidence from the behavior of sounding lines and dredges, from the movements of plankton and the hardness of the sea floor that the bottom current is unusually strong (see Deacon, 1963).

Very few biological investigations were carried out in the Weddell Sea. Those made by the R.R.S. *Discovery* in the northern part have revealed a great abundance of plankton in the area located between the South Georgia, South Orkney and South Sandwich Islands. Recent investigations by the writer aboard the *San Martin* showed high standing crop of phytoplankton (chlorophyll *a* up to 4.30 mg/m^3) and primary production (up to 10 mgC/m^3/hr) south of the South Sandwich Islands, while the eastern and southern parts of the Weddell Sea were relatively poor.

(5) Structural Geology

The Weddell Sea is an extension of a large depression, graben or "senkungsfeld" which lies between the eastern and western sectors of the Antarctic. This depression, which extends from the Weddell Sea to the Ross Sea, is bordered on its west side by a horst or upthrown mountain range which has been broken up by a complex system of block faults. Structurally, the Weddell Sea occupies the zone between the largely Precambrian (capped by flat-lying Beacon Sandstone and dolerites) of East Antarctica and the Paleo-Mesozoic-Cenozoic fold belts of West Antarctica (see Fairbridge, 1952).

(6) Bottom Deposits and Sediments

Sediments of the Weddell Sea consist primarily of glacial marine sediment composed mainly of material which has been transported from the land or shallow water by ice-rafting, and then dropped to the bottom when the ice melted. In the vicinity of the islands of the South Georgia–South Sandwich groups, the shallow water sediments are also partly terrigenous.

In general, the distribution of the glacial marine sediment roughly coincides with the area of pack ice. Further to the north, diatom ooze extends northward to the position of the Antarctic Convergence (Lisitzin, 1962).

Organic remains of Cambrian age were contained in limestone dredged in the Weddell Sea from a depth of 3231 m in latitude 62° 10′S, longitude 41° 20′W. These consisted of plants and animal fragments and skeletons. The plants are calcareous algae and belong to the genus *Epiphyton*. The animal remains are spicules, probably from sponges, complete and fragmentary cups of *Archaeocyathinae* and sections of the carapace of trilobites. The sponge spicules belong to the orders Tetractinellida, Hexactinellida and Heteractinellida (see Gordon, 1920).

The organic remains taken in the Weddell Sea were found to be similar to those from the Beardmore Glacier on the opposite side of Antarctica. This has led to the suggestion that the limestone formation may have been rather extensive during the Cambrian.

In a study of the Weddell Sea sediments, Pirie (1913) found clay to lie farther from the continent than mud. Sand or grit were present, but never in large quantities except off Coats Land. The proportion of rock fragments, mainly small pebbles, was highest along the Coats Land coast.

Of the erratic rock specimens obtained directly off Coats Land, granite with white feldspar was the most common igneous rock; basalt and dolerite were less abundant. A grey grit was the most common sedimentary rock; a purple sandstone was less common. In other locations, grit (both red and green), shale, and pebbles of hard mud were obtained. The shales were generally marked with glacial striae. In all these samples, the glacial mud which formed the bulk of the sample was extremely sandy. Some of the sediments resembled the Beacon Sandstone of Victoria Land in general appearance. Farther out from land other sediment types among the rafted erratics included oolitic limestone, white and dark-grey quartzite, arkose, banded shale, spotted shale and chert. Metamorphic rocks were represented by gneiss, garnetiferous gneiss, and mica-schist.

SAYED Z. EL-SAYED

References

Deacon, G. E. R., 1963, "The Southern Ocean," in (Hill, M. N., edtior) "The Sea, Ideas and Observations on Progress in the Study of the Seas," pp. 281–296.
Fairbridge, R., 1952, "The Geology of the Antarctic," in (Simpson, F. A., editor) "The Antarctic Today," pp. 56–101.
Gordon, W. T., 1920, "Scottish National Antarctic Expedition, 1902–1904: Cambrian organic remains from a dredging in the Weddell Sea," *Trans. Roy. Soc. Edinburgh*, **52**, 681–714.
Hart, T. J., 1934, "On the phytoplankton of the southwest Atlantic and the Bellingshausen Sea, 1929–31," *Discovery Reports*, **8**, 1–268.
Lisitzin, A. P., 1962, "Bottom sediments of the Antarctic," in (Wexler, H., Rubin, M. J., and Caskey, J. E., editors) "Antarctic research," *Geophys. Mono. No. 7*, NAS-NRD, No. 1036, 81–88.
Pirie, J. H. H., 1913, "Scottish National Antarctic Expedition, 1902–1904: Deep sea deposits," *Trans. Roy. Soc. Edinburgh*, **49**, Pt. 3, 645–687.

WEST AUSTRALIAN CURRENT

A part of the west wind drift of the Indian Ocean turns to the north along the Western Australian coast and becomes the West Australian Current. The current is strongly influenced by wind circulation. It is steady and strong at the surface in the southern summer, reaching the maximum velocity of 0.4–0.7 knot north of 30°S. In the southern winter, the current is weakened and separated by several branches of the southward current.

Movement of the subsurface water is geostrophic. The core of the Antarctic Intermediate water of low salinity (34.4–34.6‰) and low temperature (3–7°C) flows northward from about 34°S and 107°E to 13°S and 112°E, decreasing its depth from 1000 to 600m. The core of the Banda Intermediate water of relatively low salinity (34.6–34.7‰) and low temperature (3–4°C) spreads southwestward down to 25°S 400 km off the northwest coast of Australia at a depth of about 1400 m. To the south of this water, the core of the Northwest Indian Intermediate water of high salinity (34.7–34.9‰) and high temperature (5–8°C) flows southeastward at a depth of 1350 m. During the southeast monsoon (May to September), there is an upwelling in the upper layers of water close to the northwest coast of Australia.

TAKASHI ICHIYE

References

Bruns, E., 1958, "Ozeanologie," Vol. 1, Berlin, VEB Deutscher Verlag der Wissenschaften, 420pp.

Rochford, D. J., 1961, 1962, 1964, "Hydrography of the Indian Ocean, I, II and III," *Australian J. Marine Freshwater Res.*, **12**(2), 129–149; **13**(3), 226–251; **15**(1), 25–55.
Wyrtki, K., 1961, "The physical oceanography of Southeast Asian waters," *Naga Report 2*, Univ. of California Press.

WEST GREENLAND CURRENT

The West Greenland Current is a continuation of the East Greenland Current and flows northward along the west coast of Greenland into Davis Strait. Surface currents reach 25 cm/sec near the southern tip of Greenland but become slower northward.

The current consists of two water masses. Close to the Greenland Coast is water of low salinity (31.0–34.0‰) and of low temperature (2°C in summer), the same water as of the East Greenland Current. Beyond the slope is entrained a body of North Atlantic water of high salinity (34.95–35.00‰) and high temperature (4–6°C). This water keeps the west coast of Greenland relatively ice free. Part of the current turns around when approaching Davis Strait and joins the Labrador Current (q.v.). However, part consisting mostly of the warm and saline water continues into Baffin Bay, where it rapidly loses its character as the North Atlantic water by cooling and by mixture with the Arctic water.

TAKASHI ICHIYE
RHODES W. FAIRBRIDGE

References

Dietrich, G., 1957, "Allgemeine Meereskunde", Gebrüder Borntraeger, Berlin, 492pp.
Sverdrup, H. U., Johnson, M. W., and Fleming, R. H., 1942, "The Oceans," Englewood Cliffs, N.J., Prentice-Hall, 1087pp.

WHITE SEA—*See* BARENTS SEA

WIND—PRINCIPLES

Wind is a stream of air flowing relative to the earth's surface, usually more or less parallel to the ground. (For essentially *vertical* flow, see *Convection*.) It is caused by a *pressure gradient*, i.e., a difference in atmospheric pressure between two points, lines or surfaces. If pressure were the only factor, such wind, called *Eulerian* wind, would flow directly from areas of high pressure to those of low pressure. In the free atmosphere (except immediately above the equator), the wind is deflected by the *Coriolis effect* (q.v.) and tends to flow more *along* the isobars than across them. The closer the isobars, the

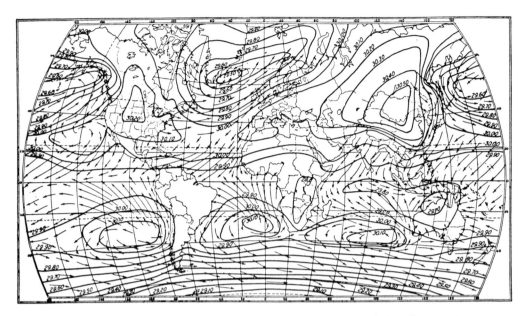

Fig. 1. Isobaric lines and winds for January (Trewartha). (Isobars in inches of mercury.)

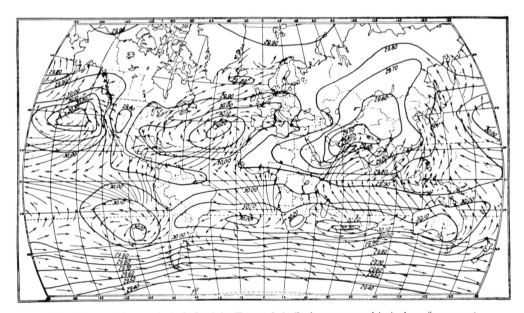

Fig. 2. Isobaric lines and winds for July (Trewartha). (Isobars expressed in inches of mercury.)

stronger is the wind. Near to the ground (below 1600–1200 meters), wind is affected by *friction* as well and is gradually slowed down and deflected inwards toward centers of low pressure or outward from centers of high pressure. The greater the friction, i.e., closer to the ground, the more effective is the deflection, which may cause the wind to make an angle of 40 or 50° from the isobars.

Toward the end of the eighteenth century H. W. Brandes had noticed that if one stood with his back to the wind, the high pressure was to the right and

a little behind, and the low pressure was to the left and a little ahead. In 1857, C. H. D. Buys Ballot formulated this observation as a rule or "law" and gave it wide publicity, especially among sailors, thereby saving many lives.

With the terminology introduced by Shaw, a *geostrophic* wind is a wind affected equally by the pressure gradient across straight isobars and by the Coriolis effect (q.v.). Its speed is inversely proportional to the spacing of the isobars and can therefore be calculated if enough isobaric data are available. The geostrophic wind may be considered the top (nonfrictional) level of the Ekman spiral. *Ageostrophic wind* is the vector difference between the actual wind and the geostrophic wind.

At lower altitudes, friction acts as a brake on the wind, and gradually deflects it, at the same time curving the isobars. The wind is then termed a *gradient* wind. Compared with the geostrophic wind for the same isobaric gradient, it is slower in cyclonic (centripetal) situations and faster in anticyclonic (centrifugal) situations.

In extremely strong recurving winds, such as tropical hurricanes (q.v.), the centrifugal force is stronger than the Coriolis effect. Shaw termed these winds *cyclostrophic.*

Jeffreys named *antitriptic* winds those in which friction predominates, e.g., mountain and valley breezes.

Periodic winds are winds which recur fairly regularly with a set periodicity as *daily* periodic winds (land and sea breezes, mountain and valley breezes) and *seasonal* periodic winds (see *Monsoons* and *Winds—Local*).

The *direction* of the wind near the surface is shown by wind vanes and wind hoses and also by smoke plumes, aloft by "pibal" (pilot balloon) or "rawin" (radiosonde). Some eight "octants" (N, NE, E, etc.) are recognized, but preferably 32 directions (N, NNE, NE, ENE, E, etc.) or 36 if every 10° angle is taken as a distinct direction. The wind is distinguished according to the direction from which it blows. A clockwise shift is called *veering*; an anticlockwise one, *backing*. In the northern hemisphere, a wind backs when a cyclone passes to the south; it also backs with increasing height. In the southern hemisphere, the directions would be reversed.

The *speed* of the wind is measured with anemometers or anemographs, graduated in meters per second, kilometers per hour, or miles per hour or, since 1949, in knots (nautical miles per hour):

$1 \, \text{m/sec} = 3.6 \, \text{km/hr} = 2.237 \, \text{miles/hr} = 1.944 \, \text{knots}$

TABLE 1. THE BEAUFORT SCALE

On Land	At Sea	Beaufort Number	Description	Speed (m/sec)	(miles/hr)
Still; smoke rises vertically	Surface mirror-like	0	Calm	0–0.2	0–1
Smoke drifts but vanes remain still	Only ripples form	1	Light air	0.3–1.5	1–3
Wind felt on face, leaves rustle, vane moves	Small, short wavelets, distinct but not breaking	2	Light breeze	1.6–3.3	4–7
Leaves and small twigs move constantly, streamer or pennant extended	Larger wavelets beginning to break, glassy foam, perhaps scattered white horses	3	Gentle breeze	3.4–5.4	8–12
Raises dust and loose paper, moves twigs and thin branches	Small waves still but longer, fairly frequent white horses	4	Moderate breeze	5.5–7.9	13–18
Small trees in leaf begin to sway	Moderate waves, distinctly elongated, many white horses, perhaps isolated spray	5	Fresh breeze	8.0–10.7	19–24
Large branches move, telegraph wires whistle, umbrellas hard to control	Large waves begin with extensive white foam crests breaking; spray probable	6	Strong wind	10.8–13.8	25–31
Whole trees move; offers some resistance to walkers	Sea heaps up, lines of white foam begin to be blown downwind	7	Stiff wind or moderate gale	13.9–17.1	32–38
Breaks twigs off trees; impedes progress	Moderately high waves with crests of considerable length; foam blown in well-marked streaks; spray blown from crests	8	Stormy wind or fresh gale	17.2–20.7	39–46
Blows off roof tiles and chimney pots	High waves, rolling sea, dense streaks of foam; spray may already reduce visibility	9	Storm or strong gale	20.8–24.4	47–54
Trees uprooted, much structural damage	Heavy rolling sea, white with great foam patches and dense streaks, very high waves with overhanging crests; much spray reduces visibility	10	Heavy storm or whole gale	24.5–28.4	55–63
Widespread damage (very rare inland)	Extraordinarily high waves, spray impedes visibility	11	Hurricane-like storm	28.5–32.6	64–72
	Air full of foam and spray, sea entirely white	12	Hurricane	32.7–36.9	73–82

Fig. 3. If we imagine the high-pressure belts as ridges and the low-pressure belts as depressions then the smooth curved line is an idealized cross section of pressure and meridional wind along a north–south profile from pole to pole. The names of the several pressure belts are given below the cross section. These belts shift north and south with the sun during the course of a year.

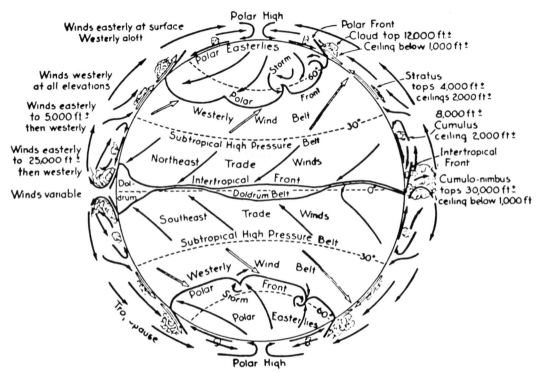

Fig. 4. Relation of the polar front to the ideal atmospheric circulation.

One distinguishes between the speed of the wind at any given moment, especially important when maximum wind *gusts* are measured, and the *mean speed*, which is usually obtained by dividing the total flow of air recorded during a period by the number of hours in that period.

The *constancy* (or *regularity*) of the wind is obtained by taking the frequency of observed wind from each direction as a percentage of total wind observations. Thus, the *prevailing* wind may be taken as the most frequent wind, irrespective of speed. It may refer to a day, month, season, year, etc.

The main components of the wind (E, W, N, S) are obtained by combining vectorially the wind direction and speed of each respective quadrant. The cumulative vector is the *resultant* wind.

Calms (i.e., absence of measurable wind) are given direction and speed 0. On the weather map, a circle denotes calm, an arrow wind. Arrows fly with the wind, and have half feathers for every 5 knots and full feathers for every 10 knots.

The *Beaufort Scale* of wind force was devised in the early eighteenth century by Admiral Beaufort for sailing purposes; it was repeatedly modified to adapt it to modern navigation and to inland observations, the latest change being the addition of grades 13–17 to include extreme hurricane (q.v.) winds, for which however, no qualitative description has been found adequate (see Table 1).

Classification of Winds

Winds may be classified in several ways, according to characteristics (e.g., force in the Beaufort Scale), origin, direction of flow, magnitude of area affected. On the basis of the magnitude of the circulation, three orders of wind systems are recognized.

(a) Primary or Planetary Winds. Winds which owe their origin to the characteristics of the earth as a planet (i.e., near-sphericity, inclination of the axis, revolution and rotation) are called *planetary*: they are the tropical easterlies or northeast and southeast trade winds (q.v.), the westerlies, the polar easterlies. To these may be added the controversial equatorial winds.

(b) Secondary Circulations. To these belong the cyclonic and anticyclonic winds, particularly associated with fronts (q.v.). In this class are the tropical cyclones, hurricanes and typhoons. Also *monsoons* (q.v.) may not be classified as planetary winds, even though they occur on a gigantic scale in Asia, because they are due to the relative location of continental and oceanic surfaces, a telluric factor. For this reason, they rightly belong to the secondary category, as *telluric* winds. To this category also belong the monsoonal and quasi-monsoonal winds of other continents.

(c) Tertiary Circulations. These are strictly *regional* winds which affect smaller areas. To these belong the etesian winds (q.v.) of the Aegean Sea, the mistral (q.v.) of southeastern France, the chinook (q.v.) of North America.

True *local winds* (see *Winds—Local*) are made distinct by local topography, e.g., the "Santa Ana" of southern California, or the "bora" (q.v.) of the Adriatic. The effect of topographic features on the wind is quite varied, and more will be said below. Many so-called local winds, however, do not belong to this class at all; they are winds, or part of wind systems, of much more extensive occurrence, to which a distinctive local name is merely given, as happens to the "Fremantle Doctor" which is the sea breeze of Perth, Western Australia, or to the so-called brisa (= breeze) of northeast Brazil and Venezuela, which in fact is the trade wind.

The term *gravity wind* is used to denote all those winds, many of them local, which are primarily due to the flow of air made relatively heavier by thermal differentials, e.g., land and sea breezes, mountain and valley breezes, glacier breeze, forest breeze.

With regard to the gradient of the land surface, local winds may be classified as *anabatic* (upslope, e.g., valley breeze) or *katabatic* (downslope, e.g., mountain breeze, glacier breeze).

Topographic features may give local or even regional winds their main characteristic, e.g., *adiabatic warming* of an airstream on the lee side of a high mountain produces the rise in temperature and desiccation characteristic of foehn chinook and zonda winds. Similarly, mountain ranges may dam up a considerable amount of air which can only pour over cols and passes (*mountain-gap* winds, in some case *strait winds*). Cold wind pouring downslope may be considerably accelerated by gravity (*fall winds*, e.g., the bora, q.v.). Wind forced through a narrow channel increases in speed through a *jet effect*, e.g., the mistral in the Rhône Valley, the Wasatch winds of Utah.

Periodicity of Winds

As to periodicity, winds may be *seasonal* (e.g., the monsoon in India, Africa, etc., but also the westerlies in Portugal or southern California), *diurnal* (e.g., land and sea breezes), *sporadic* (e.g., winds in tropical hurricanes, such as the "cordonazo" (q.v.) of western Mexico).

Some winds are *amphidromic*; i.e., they alternate their direction of flow (e.g., land and sea breezes). Most of the true monsoonal flow is not amphidromic, because the so-called winter monsoon is the trade wind, altogether different and part of the planetary circulation.

JOSEPH GENTILLI

References

Defant, F., 1951, "Local Winds," in (Malone, T. F., editor) "Compendium of Meteorology," Boston, American Meteorological Society.
Huschke, R. E., (editor), 1959, "Glossary of Meteorology," Boston, American Meteorological Society.
Keil, K., (editor), 1950, "Handwörterbuch der Meteorologie," Frankfurt.
Schamp, H., 1962, "Regelmässige, periodische und lokale Winde," *Geogr. Taschenbuch,* **1962–63**, 266–276.
Schamp, H., 1964, "Die Winde der Erde und ihre Namen," Erdk. Wiss. 8, Wiesbaden, Franz Steiner Verlag.

WINDROWS—*See* **SLICKS, RIPPLES AND WINDROWS**

Y

YELLOW SEA

The Yellow Sea (Hwang Hai) is one of the marginal seas of the western Pacific lying north of, and adjacent to, the East China Sea (Tung Hai). The boundary between the Yellow Sea and the East China Sea is not definite, but arbitrarily it is taken as the line running from Saishu Island (off Korea) to the mouth of the Yangtze River near Shanghai (China), following the practice of the International Hydrographic Bureau. It measures about 1000 km (N-S) by 700 km (E-W). The entire sea is underlain by part of the vast East Asian continental shelf and lies at less than 100 m depth (see Fig. 1). The innermost Gulf north of the Yellow Sea, limited by the line between Liao-Tung Peninsula and San-Tung Peninsula, is called the Gulf of Po Hai or Pwok Hai. The areas, volumes, mean depths and maximum depths of the Yellow Sea proper and the Gulf of Pwok Hai are shown in Table 1 (Anon., 1936; Yoshimura, 1940).

Topography

The Yellow Sea proper and Pwok Hai form a partly enclosed, wide, flat and shallow marine embayment which is encircled by the mainland of northern China, the Shan-Tung Peninsula and the Peninsula of Korea. The Yellow Sea proper is somewhat deeper than the Pwok Hai, with an oval-shaped basin, having depths about 60–80 m, elongated from north to south, and with sides sloping gently up to the coasts of Korea and China, where there are numerous submerged sand ridges, running perpendicular to the coastal lines. Strong

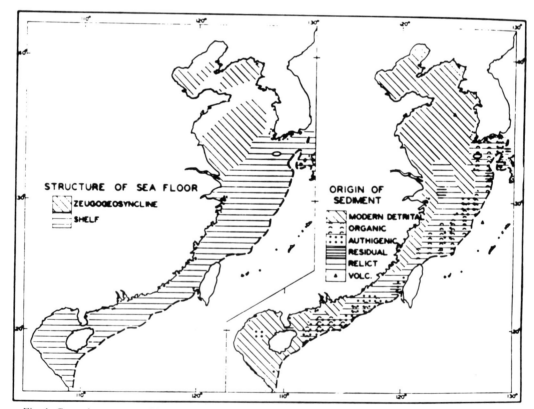

Fig. 1. General structure and bottom sediment according to origin, in the East China Sea and the Yellow Sea (after Niino and Emery, 1961).

TABLE 1.

Depth (m)	Yellow Sea Proper		Pwok Hai	
	Area (km²)	Volume (km³)	Area (km²)	Volume (km³)
0–20	93,600	7,140	42,900	1320
20–40	101,900	5,190	36,700	430
40–60	78,200	3,390	2,100	40
60–80	90,500	1,700	1,000	10
>80	39,800	200	—	—
Total	404,000	17,620	82,700	1710
Mean depth, m	44		21	
Maximum depth, m	103		72	

tidal currents flow through the narrow channels. The Ta-Shang or Great Yangtze Sand Bank lies in the south toward the boundary of the Yellow Sea and the East China Sea, and extends from west to east off the mouth of the Yangtze River (showing a nearly flat bottom over an extent of about 300-km radius with a depth of about 30 m as submerged delta, covered by gray or fine, black-spotted sand).

Sediments (Niino and Emery, 1961)

Generally, the east and west coastal regions of the Yellow Sea show a sandy bottom due to the sorting by strong tidal currents. However, the bottom of the central basin of the Yellow Sea is muddy silt due to the weaker currents. Bottom sediments of the eastern side of the Pwok Hai and the northern part of the Yellow Sea are sandy. However, on the mainland side (of China), the bottom sediment is more muddy due to the yellow mud (especially from the loess of central China) in the water discharged from the great rivers such as the Yellow River (Hwang Ho), the Liao River, the White River, the Yangtze River and the Yalu River, etc. The devastating floods carry especially large volumes of fine, yellowish mud. Along the coasts of South Korea, many small inlets represent a drowned portion of the mainland coast. Erosion in the Strait of Pwok Hai (Pe-Chih-Li) off Port Arthur was evidently caused by the scouring action of tidal current. There are also many small islets, some of which are rocky extensions of the granitic massif of Shan-Tung. The drowned western shores of the Yellow Sea and Pwok Hai surrounding the old rocky, mountainous Shan-Tung Peninsula and also the Liao-Tung Peninsula form Rias-type bays and are utilized as good anchorages and harbors (e.g., Port Arthur, Tsing Tao, Cheefoo, etc.). Rocky bottom occurs in the straits, on submarine hills, off rocky points and islands, and near the shelf-breaks; at these places, strong wave and/or current action prevents deposition of fine-grained sediments. Gravel is commonly associated with rock bottom. Rock is also common on the broad areas of the continental shelf bordering the Yellow Sea. Mud, at the other extreme, is common bottom in the middle areas of the Pwok Hai and the Yellow Sea.

Geological History

Tertiary marine sedimentary rocks occur in the South Korea, Saisyu Island, Kyushu, Taiwan and the Ryukyu Chain, whereas Tertiary non-marine strata are widespread in China and Korea. At the beginning of the Quaternary, the Yellow Sea area became land again, and afterward it returned to the present shallow sea. In short, the modern Yellow Sea was formed in the postglacial epoch. The underlying structure of the sea floor is considered to be zeugogeosynclinal which has received very significant amounts of detrital sediment. Today, the basin appears more like a paraliageosyncline.

Climate (Yoshimura, 1940; Niino and Emery, 1961)

In the Gulf of Pwok Hai and the northern Yellow Sea, the climate is Köppen's Dwa-type: a very cold, dry winter and a wet, warm summer.

During the winter season, from late November to March, a strong northerly (NNE-NW) monsoon prevails, corresponding to the steep pressure gradient between the Siberian High and the Aleutian Low (depression). In winter in the region of the Pwok Hai, the northwesterly winds are sometimes accompanied by severe blizzards. In April, at the alternating season of the monsoons, the wind is variable or indeterminate. In May, the southwest monsoon begins to operate corresponding to the changed pressure system. During the summer, the wind blows onshore with low velocities in response to the seasonal low-pressure area over China developed by solar heating and the North Pacific High Pressure area southeast of Japan. Typhoons are most frequent in the summer season from June to September; in early summer (June–July), they move landward into the continent in the direction of prevailing wind, and in late

TABLE 2. EASTERN YELLOW SEA, 60 NAUTICAL MILES OFF
ZYUN'I ISLAND (1931–1934 AVERAGE)

Depth (m)	Water Temperature (°C)		Salinity (‰)	
	February	August	February	August
0	6.2	26.2	32.3	31.5
10	6.3	24.7	32.4	31.6
25	6.3	14.4	32.4	32.2
50	6.4	7.9	32.4	32.4
83	6.6	7.9	32.4	32.3

summer (August–September), they move north-ward. In winter, typhoons do not occur in the Yellow Sea and adjacent lands. Extratropical cyclones occur in the colder season dominantly across the East China Sea and the Yellow Sea. Cyclogenesis is frequent near the oceanic front north of Taiwan in winter and spring.

Air temperature ranges between 28 and −6°C (seldom −10°C in the Pwok Hai) as the typical continental climate. The annual rainfall ranges from 500 mm in the north to 2000 mm in the south. Most of the rainfall occurs in summer (June–September) and causes river floods. Sea fog is frequent in winter, spring and early summer along the China mainland coast and in Korea, particularly in the area of cold upwelling water near the archipelago, islands and promontories from March to July. In June and July, dense advection fogs prevail along the west and south coasts of Korea.

Yellow dust-falls often occur in spring, which are sometimes dense enough to stop the traffic of boats at sea. In winter and early spring, dangerous gusty squalls are a menace to fishing boats, as they attack suddenly with the passage of a cold front.

Oceanography (Marukawa, 1918; Uda, 1930–1941; Anon., 1963)

(i) **Color of the Sea and Transparency of Sea-water.** The name of the Yellow Sea originated from the yellowish color due to the water of turbid nature mingled with the yellow (loess) soil from the Chinese mainland which is discharged through the great rivers—Yellow River, Yangtze River, etc. The muddy water color extends from the mouth of the Yangtze River to the east for more than 100 km, as far as 123°E and sometimes to 124°E. The amount of mud measures 0.2–0.6 g/liter, on the average, and at most 1.8 g/liter.

Forel's number of water color ranges from III–IV in the middle sea basin and from VI–VIII near the coasts of Korea and China (from blue color to yellowish green).

Transparency measured by Secchi disc in the southern Yellow Sea attains a value of about 15 m (comparatively transparent). However, that in the coastal waters drops to 3–5 m, which shows more turbidity than Tokyo Bay. The transparency in Pwok Hai is affected markedly by the discharged waters of the turbid Yellow River and other rivers, and it becomes less than 2 m.

(ii) **Surface Temperature.** The minimum temperature in winter (February) ranges from freezing conditions, with less than 0°C in the innermost Gulf of Pwok Hai, to 2–8°C in the Yellow Sea proper. Port Arthur does not entirely freeze in winter because the temperature minimum is 1°C higher than the freezing level. In summer (August), the shallower portions of Pwok Hai and the Yellow Sea are warmed considerably, up to 22–28°C. Accordingly, the annual range is very large, 20–28°C, a good indicator of continentality.

(iii) **Water Temperature in the Lower Layers (Uda, 1930–1941).** In winter, the temperature and the salinity in the Yellow Sea and Pwok Hai are homogeneous from surface to bottom, since complete convectional mixing prevails throughout the whole water column (see Table 2). In spring and summer, the upper layer is warmed and diluted by the fresh water from rivers. Consequently, the density in the upper layer decreases remarkably compared with the deeper heavy water which maintains the cooler temperature and higher salinity produced in winter. In the intermediate layer (10–30 m depths), sharp thermoclines, haloclines and pycnoclines are established. (The temperature drops as much as 10°C/15 m.) Figure 2 indicates the profiles of temperature and salinity in the northern part of the Yellow Sea.

The cold bottom water mass stagnates in the deeper basin of the Yellow Sea and moves slowly to the south in the summer, contrary to the north-ward movement of the warm upper water (Yellow Sea Warm Current), being compensationally subjected to the southwest monsoon.

(iv) **Salinity.** The surface salinity in the Gulf of Pwok Hai and the Yellow Sea is markedly reduced by the runoff from great rivers and is subject to large annual variation, just as with temperature. In the Pwok Hai, the dominant salinity is about 30–31‰, but approaching the entrance of the Yellow River, it sometimes falls to 22‰. In the Yellow Sea proper, salinity ranges from 31–33‰, and is mostly 31–32‰. On the basis of the regular

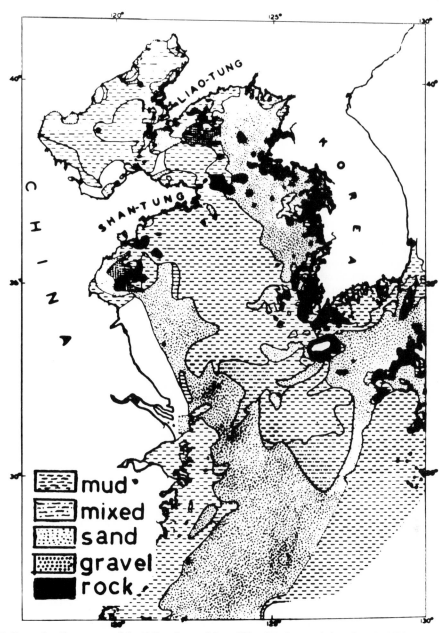

Fig. 2. General sediment map of the Yellow Sea and East China Sea. Pattern is based on 45,000 bottom notations of navigation charts (partly from Shepard, Emery and Gould, 1949; after Niino and Emery, 1961).

shipline survey between Nagasaki and Shanghai, we find that the surface salinity at about 123° 5′E drops in July from a normal of 32‰ to 20‰, and at 125°E, in July and August it drops to 19‰. Thus, in the southwest monsoon season, the increased runoff from rivers, due to the increased rainfall, causes a very low salinity in early summer. This low-salinity water spreads in two ways: the main part flows in the Tushima Warm Current and northward to Hokkaido in autumn; the other part

joins the Kuroshio Current and flows northeastward along the southeast coast of Japan.

(v) Sea Ice. The innermost Gulf of Pwok Hai freezes in winter under the effect of the severe cold of the Asian continent. The discharged river ice turns to drift ice in the shallow Pwok Hai waters. This drift ice and the frozen ice fields hinder the navigation of boats in the interior of the Gulf.

(vi) Tides and Tidal Currents (Ogura, 1934, 1936). The tidal wave enters from the south,

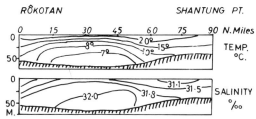

Fig. 3. Profiles of salinity from Rokotan to Shantung Pt. across the northern part of the Yellow Sea (after Uda).

moving northward into the Yellow Sea and Pwok Hai as a long wave. (The "establishment" is 7 hours near Okinawa and about 12 hours near the southern boundary of the Yellow Sea.) The tidal range is very large along the west coast of Korea. Its maximum spring tide range attains 8.2 m.

Generally, in the Yellow Sea, a semidiurnal tide prevails; however, in the innermost Gulf of Pwok Hai, a diurnal tide occurs. The tidal range amounts to 4–8 m along the west coast of Korea and to 1–3 m along the coasts of China facing the Yellow Sea and Pwok Hai (except in the innermost Pwok Hai where the range is more than 3 m). Generally, the tidal system in the Yellow Sea and Pwok Hai rotates in a counterclockwise direction with the circulation around several amphidromic points (Fig. 3).

The speed of the tidal current is less than 1 knot in the middle part of the sea; however, near the coasts and in the straits or passages, stronger currents of more than 2 knots are observed. The maximum speed observed in Meiyo-To Passage at the southwest tip of the Korean peninsula is 9.5 knots. The maximum tidal current in the Pwok Hai Channel reaches more than 3 knots. The tidal current along the China mainland coast is often more than 2–3 knots.

(vii) Oceanic Currents. The so-called Yellow Sea Warm Current is one part of the Tushima Warm Current which branches off near western Kyushu, southwest of Saishu Island, and flows northward into the middle of the Yellow Sea. Its speed is very low, being less than 0.5 knot; it develops in spring and summer, and decays in autumn and winter. This warm current is modified by the low-salinity water of coastal origin and almost loses the characteristic properties of the Kuroshio (q.v.), although it still maintains its higher salinity compared to the coastal waters in the Yellow Sea.

On the other hand, along the coast of the mainland of China, a southward-flowing coastal current exists which strengthens most remarkably in winter, accelerated by the strong, persistent winter monsoon ("northers"), with cold, turbid and low-salinity water as its characteristics. Its velocity is considered to be less than half a knot. Along the west coast of Korea, there is another cool coastal current with a velocity of less than 0.3 knot.

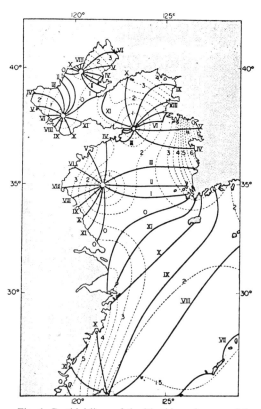

Fig. 4. Co-tidal lines of the M_2 tide and range of the semidiurnal tide in the Yellow Sea and East China Sea. Phases referred to the 135°E longitude meridian and corange $2(M_2 + S_2)$ in meters (after Ogura; from Defant, 1961).

Upwelling around promontories and islands brings cool and fertile waters, which are closely related to the sea fogs and the valuable fisheries.

M. UDA

References

Anon., 1936, "Oceanographic Manual of Korean Waters," Tyosen Govt. Fish. Expt. Station.
Anon., 1963, "Ten Years Average Oceanographic Charts," Nagasaki Marine Observatory.
Marukawa, H., 1918, "Oceanographic Investigations of the Yellow Sea," Gyogyo-Kihon-Tyosa-Hokoku.
Niino, H., and Emery, K. O., 1961, "Sediments of shallow portions of East China Sea and South China Sea," *Bull. Geol. Soc. Am.*, **72**, 731–762.
Ogura, S., 1934, "Tides," Tide Tables, Japan Hydr. Office (in Japanese).
Ogura, S., 1936, "The tides in the northern part of Hwang Hai," *Japan. J. Astr. Geophys.*, **14**, 27–55.
Uda, M., 1930, 1931, 1934, 1935, 1941, "Reports of hydrography on China Sea, Yellow Sea and Japan Sea," *J. Imp. Fisheries Inst. Japan*, Nos. 1, 2, 5, 7, 11.
Yoshimura, S., 1940, "Hydrography of the East China Sea," China Geogr. Series (in Japanese).

Z

ZOOPLANKTON

The zooplankton (Greek: *zoon*, animal; *plank-tos*, wandering) are all those animals which drift passively in the ocean. The term includes a remark-ably diverse group of creatures differing very widely in size, structure, and taxonomic position. Every important animal phylum is represented, if not throughout its entire life history, then at least for varying lengths of time as larvae. The zooplankton may be divided into two categories: (1) the holo-plankton or permanent zooplankton, which are organisms that spend their entire existence adrift; and (2) the meroplankton or temporary zoo-plankton, which are larval forms drifting passively during early life. Both the nekton and benthos contribute to the temporary plankton. The earliest recorded work on zooplankton is that of J. Vaughn Thomson, 1828, and Johannes Müller, 1844. The term *plankton* was first used by Victor Hansen, who in 1889 directed the German *Plankton Expedition*.

Types of Organisms

(a) Permanent Plankton. Phyla which contribute significantly to the holoplankton are the Protozoa, Coelenterata, Ctenophora, Chaetognatha, Anne-lida, Mollusca, Chordata, and particularly the Arthropoda. The most widespread protozoan forms are the shelled Foraminifera, Radiolaria, and Tintinnidae. Planktonic coelenterates include the small and exquisite hydromedusae (*Sarsia, Gonionemus*, <1 cm), the marvelously complex colonial siphonophores (*Physalia*, the Portuguese man-of-war; *Vellela*; *Physophora*), and the large (up to 1 meter in diameter), vividly colored, scyphozoan medusae (*Cyanea, Chrysaora, Rhizo-stoma*). The exclusively marine phyla, the Cteno-phora (*Beröe*, 10 cm; *Pleurobrachia*, 1 cm) and Chaetognatha (*Sagitta*, about 0.5 cm) are voracious carnivores on smaller zooplankton organisms. The Annelida are represented by certain Polychaeta (*Tomopteris* and certain Syllidae) especially adapted for pelagic life. Mollusca contributing to the holo-

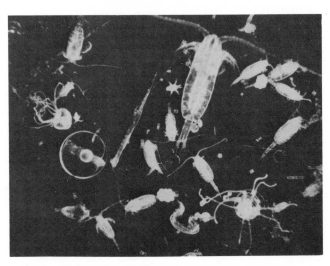

Fig. 1. Living animals of the plankton (zooplankton). The copepods *Calanus finmarchicus* (largest animal) and' *Pseudocalanus elongatus* (similar in shape, but much smaller than *Calanus*, and one with cluster of eggs); two small anthomedusae with long tentacles; a fish egg (circular object); a young arrow-worm *Sagitta* (to right of fish egg); small nauplius (larval stage) of copepod (close to left side of Calanus) and the planktonic tunicate *Oikopleura* (curly objects top right and middle bottom). Photo by electronic flash, but organisms partially narcotised (Douglas Wilson; from A. C. Hardy, 1956, p. 33). (By permission of Houghton Mifflin, Mass.)

plankton are the Gastropoda. Examples are Pteropoda (*Limacina, Clio, Diacria,* <1 cm) and specialized prosobranchs such as Heteropoda and members of the genus *Ianthina.* The frequently abundant salps, belonging to the subphylum Urochordata (Tunicata), are extensive grazers of phytoplankton.

Numerically, and through their ecological role in the food web of the ocean, the Crustacea are unquestionably the most important single element of the zooplankton. Copepods (*Calanus, Acartia, Temora,* 1–5 mm) are the most abundant crustacean organisms in the ocean, and their distribution, ecology, and physiology are the object of continuing research (Marshall and Orr, 1955; Conover, R. J., in Riley *et al.,* 1956). Numerically less abundant but yet common are Cladocera (*Evadne, Podon, Penilia,* 2 mm), Ostracoda (*Cypridina,* 5 mm), Mysidacea, hyperid Amphipoda, and certain decapod Crustacea (*Penaeus, Sergestes, Lucifer,* 1–10 cm). The Euphausiacea (*Meganyctiphanes,* 1–2 cm), or "krill," are an abundant group of Crustacea extensively fed upon by the Blue-fin, Humpback, and other baleen whales.

(b) Temporary Plankton. The meroplankton makes up a very important fraction of the zooplankton during certain months of the year. Larvae from "fouling" and bottom-dwelling invertebrate organisms may sometimes be 75% of the total zooplankton present in neritic waters (Johnston, Scott and Chadwick, 1924; see Hardy, 1956, p. 71). The floating eggs and early larvae of fish are also a conspicuous part of the meroplankton. Benthonic-invertebrate larvae originating from shallow coastal waters of the continental shelf and slope invertebrate larvae originating from shallow coastal waters of the continental shelf and slope include those of Sipunculida, Brachiopoda, Polychaeta, Stomatopoda, decapod Crustacea, cerianthids (Zoantharia), and such types as tornaria (Hemichordata), auricularia (Holothuroidea), Brachiolaria (Asteroidea), plutei (Echinoidea, Ophiuroidea), and the veligers of Gastropoda and Lamellibranchia. These larvae are frequently carried offshore but do not make up a numerically significant fraction of the epipelagic zooplankton of the open sea. Thorson (1950) has shown that in tropical waters, 70–80% of all benthonic invertebrate organisms have planktonic larvae, while in the Arctic the pelagic stage is usually suppressed.

More detailed descriptions of the many forms which constitute the zooplankton are to be found in the very readable account of Sir Alister Hardy (1956).

Abundance

Some understanding of the abundance of the zooplankton may be had from estimates made in restricted regions of the ocean. The zooplankton displacement volume, a crude measure of standing crop, has been found to be approximately the same in order of magnitude throughout the neritic waters of northeastern United States and Europe. The values range from 0.3–0.95 cc/m^3 (Bigelow and Sears, 1939; Redfield, 1941; Riley and Bumpus, 1946; Deevey, 1952; Wiborg, 1954; see Riley *et al.,* 1956, p. 150). Similar values for the open ocean are usually about one-tenth of this amount. Harvey (1950; see Hedgpeth, 1957, p. 38) has estimated 1.5 grams dry weight of zooplankton per square meter of sea surface off Plymouth, where the average depth was 70 meters. Reduced to more generally understandable figures, the average standing crop for the whole Gulf of Maine was calculated by Redfield on the basis of water-free volumes of plankton samples to be 4 × 10^6 tons. There was a net gain of 8 × 10^6 tons of zooplankton between May and September, at which time most of the production for the year occurred. The maximum figure for total standing crop determined by Harvey in 1925 for the English channel was about equal to the average value for the Gulf of Maine (Sverdrup *et al.,* 1942, p. 935).

Distribution

(a) Horizontal. Distributed throughout all known regions and depths of the sea, from estuaries and neritic regions bordering continents to the open waters of the ocean, the zooplankton serve as the link between primary producers, the phytoplankton, and the larger nektonic organisms (i.e., those harvested as food by man). Zooplankton are, however, by no means homogeneously dispersed; horizontally, the distribution is very uneven and frequently has been described as "patchy" (Hardy, 1936). In this regard, of special interest is one explanation offered by Baylor and Sutcliffe, who have shown that certain planktonic Crustacea may be markedly concentrated along windrows and slicks. Such distribution is the result of Langmuir circulation and the behavior of the organisms in response to light scatter. The scatter they attribute to the presence of particulate food material, which is formed from dissolved organic substances in seawater by the bursting of bubbles at the ocean surface (Baylor and Sutcliffe, 1963; Sutcliffe, Baylor and Menzel, 1963; see also Riley *et al.,* 1965).

(b) Vertical. The vertical distribution of zooplankton in the sea has been the subject of a recent review by Banse (1964). The abundance of zooplankton organisms decreases significantly with depth; in the abyssopelagic zone the concentration is about 1% of the surface water. Grice and Hulsemann (in press) have shown that the total volume of zooplankton by displacement was 0.055 cc/m^3 at the surface and approximately 0.0005 cc/m^3 at depths of 4000–5000 meters in the eastern Atlantic between 29 and 60°N latitude. Vino-

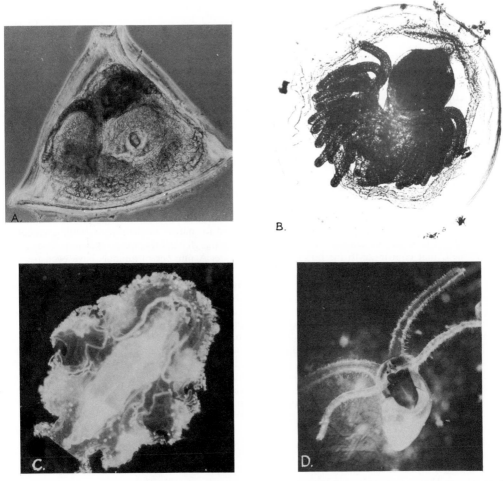

Fig. 2. Meroplankton from the open waters of the North Atlantic. A (*upper left*). Cyphonautes larva, probably that of *Membranipora tuberculata*, taken from plankton samples in the Sargasso sea. This species is commonly found encrusting fronds of Sargassum weed. Approximate size, 0.3 mm on longest side. B (*upper right*). Larva of an inarticulate brachiopod belonging to the family Lingulidae and probably referable to the Caribbean species, *Glottidia pyramidata*. These larvae can be taken throughout the Gulf Stream and the North Atlantic drift. Approximate size from the hinge to the free edge of the valve is 1 mm. C (*lower left*). Auriculaia larva of a holothuroidea found in plankton samples from the Sargasso sea. This form has the designation, *Auricularia nudibranchiata* (Chun). Its approximate length is 5 mm. D (*lower right*). Veliger larva of the semitropical gastropod, *Cymatium parthenopeum* (von Salis) which may be taken in plankton tows throughout the North Atlantic. Approximate length of shell at this stage is 4 mm.

gradov (1961; see Banse, 1964, p. 82) estimates a biomass of 10–70 mg/m³ at the surface and 0.08–0.11 mg/m³ at 4000 meters depth in the tropical Pacific. The estimates of Grice in terms of numbers of adult Calanoid copepods are about 22/m³ at the surface to 0.1/m³ at between 3000 and 4000 meters depth.

Indicator Species

The presence of exotic animals may be used as direct or corroborative evidence for the source of a water mass (Johnson and Brinton, in Hill, 1963). Plankton organisms characteristic of a particular water are known as *indicator species* since they indicate both its origin and movement. Some examples may be cited: Water from the North Sea passing southward through the English Channel can readily be distinguished from that of the ocean moving northward by the particular species of chaetognaths present; *Sagitta setosa* predominates in the former while *Sagitta elegans* is present in the latter (Russell, 1939; see Hardy, 1956, p. 30). This distinction between channel and ocean water is further confirmed in a remarkable way by the difference in growth and survival of echinoderm larvae in these two water types (Wilson, D. P.,

1952; see Hardy, 1956, p. 65). The so-called Lusitanian fauna, which frequently is found on the west coast of Ireland, originates from an admixture of water flowing out of the Mediterranean and the water of the Bay of Biscay and the Azores. It is characterized by warm-water species otherwise foreign to this latitude. The tropical and subtropical copepod *Eucalanus elongatus* is carried northward with the Gulf Stream, but only the later stages are able to tolerate the gradually cooling water at higher latitudes. Sverdrup *et al.* (1942) have suggested the prerequisites necessary in order that a form be reliably used as an indicator species. Fager and McGowan (1963) have expanded the concept of the indicator species to include natural associations of several species (or communities).

Role in the Formation of Deep-sea Sediment. There are among the zooplankton several groups of organisms which have calcareous or siliceous tests or shells that contribute to the bottom sediments of the ocean floor. The most important of these are certain Protozoa, namely several forms of Radiolaria, Foraminifera of the genus *Globigerina*, and flagellates known as coccolithophores. Among pelagic gastropods are the Pteropoda and Heteropoda. The calcified or silicified skeletal remains of these forms characterize bottom deposits generally referred to as radiolarian, globigerina, and pteropod oozes. The calcareous oozes originating from the Foraminifera, coccolithophores and Pteropoda occupy 128 million km², or about 35% of the ocean bottom. The siliceous oozes, principally from radiolarians and diatoms (the latter from the phytoplankton, q.v.), cover about 38 million km², or about 10.5% of the ocean floor (Johnson, M. V., p. 450, and Bruun, A., p. 645, in Hedgpeth, 1957). The limited thickness of bottom deposits is evidently determined by their rate of dissolution relative to that of deposition from the overlying water. Calcareous oozes, particularly those of globigerina, are uncommon at depths exceeding 4000 meters, because the $CaCO_3$ of the tests goes into solution in seawater under great pressure (Harvey, 1957).

Vertical Migration and Deep Scattering Layer

Vertical migrations of great magnitude are accomplished by some of the zooplankton, particularly certain Crustacea such as copepods and euphausids. That such relatively small animals should expend large amounts of energy to move daily up and down through the water column is indeed an enigma. The migrations may extend to depths of several hundred meters and in some instances to 1000 meters; the organisms tend to rise to the surface at sundown and descend to deeper water at sunrise. The vertical position of such zooplankton organisms has in some cases been related approximately to light intensity, but the complete explanation is probably much more

complex (Clarke and Backus, 1956). The study of vertical migration has in recent years been given further impetus by the investigation of the deep scattering layer (q.v.); there is evidence that some of the sound scattering may be caused by zooplankton organisms such as euphausids (Johnson, in Hedgpeth, 1957) or siphonophores (Barham, 1963), but Hersey and Backus (1962, in Hill, 1962, p. 534) recently concluded that the principal constituents of the deep scattering layer are probably fishes with gas-filled swim bladders.

Elements abstracted from Seawater

The zooplankton form part of the biogeochemical cycle. Animals with calcareous shells must extract calcium from the surrounding water; silicates from the sea are used by most radiolarians in the formation of their tests, while members of the genus *Acantharia* possess skeletons of strontium sulfate. A number of animals have been found to be rich in one or more elements which occur at great dilutions in seawater (Noddack and Noddack, 1940; see Harvey, 1957). Body fluids of many crustaceans contain copper as hemocyanin, while the scyphomedusan *Cyanea* has been found to contain 1.5 grams of zinc per kilogram dry weight. Indeed, certain elements such as cadmium, chromium, cobalt, tin, titanium, germanium and bismuth are present in seawater in such low concentrations that their occurrence was first inferred from the ash of marine organisms (Sverdrup *et al.*, 1942, p. 175). Phosphorous and nitrogen (as $-PO_4$ and $-NO_3$) are the most important nonconservative elements in seawater, but their concentrations in the ocean are largely the result of phytoplankton activity (Redfield, Ketchum and Richards, in Hill, 1963).

Larval Transport and Geographical Distribution of Benthonic Species

The geographical distribution of temperate and tropical benthonic invertebrate species is sometimes the result of larval dispersal by ocean currents (Eckman, 1953). For example, some species range throughout the West Indies, Bermuda, and the south Atlantic coast of the United States; likewise a number of species are common to northwest Africa and the Madeiras, Canary and Cape Verde Islands. A number of shoal water invertebrate species extend to both the eastern and the western Atlantic, and in many such instances it must be assumed that larvae have been transported across the sea. Larval transport by oceanic currents has most recently been reviewed by Thorson (1961) and by Johnson and Brinton (in Hill, 1963) who conclude that for most forms for which the life histories are known, the larval period is too short for transoceanic dispersal. Direct evidence for regular transport of larvae across the sea comes from recent data on the tropical gastropods

(Cymatiidae), certain sipunculids, and a number of other inshore tropical bottom invertebrate species (Scheltema, in press). The consequence of the long-distance transport of invertebrate larvae is that populations of bottom organisms seemingly isolated by vast areas of ocean can no longer be considered *a priori* systematically different or genetically isolated. These facts have obvious zoogeographic and evolutionary significance.

Evidence for transport of larvae from benthonic invertebrate organisms in the Pacific is scanty, and biogeographical data are very incomplete. Ostergaard (1950) has shown that 97.5% of all gastropod species on Hawaii have pelagic larvae, and he suggests that all these species probably originated from other areas in the Pacific (Micronesia). Long-distance transport of larvae from nektonic organisms is known from the interesting case of the European eel, *Anguilla vulgaris*, investigated by Johannes Schmidt (1925, see Hardy, 1956). This eel is a catadromous species which breeds in the Sargasso Sea to the southeast of Bermuda. The larvae are transported to the European coast by the Gulf Stream and the North Atlantic drift.

R. S. SCHELTEMA

References

*Banse, K., 1964, "On the vertical distribution of zooplankton in the sea," *Prog. Oceanogr.*, **2**, 53–125.

Baylor, E. R., and Sutcliffe, W. H., 1963, "Dissolved organic matter in seawater as a source of particulate food," *Limnol. Oceanogr.*, **8**, 369–371.

Clarke, G. L., and Backus, R. H., 1956, "Measurements of light penetration in relation to vertical migration and records of luminescence of deep-sea animals," *Deep-Sea Res.*, **4**, 1–14.

*Ekman, S., 1953, *Zoogeography of the Sea*, London, Sidgewick & Jackson, 417pp.

Fager, E. W., and McGowan, J. A., 1963, "Zooplankton species groups in the North Pacific," *Science*, **140**, 453–460.

Grice, G., and Hulsemann, K. (1965), "Abundance, vertical distribution, and taxonomy of Calanoid copepods at selected stations in the northeast Atlantic," *J. Zool.*, **146**, 213–262.

Hardy, A. C., 1936, "Plankton ecology and the hypothesis of animal exclusion," *Proc. Linnean Soc. London*, **148**, 64–70.

*Hardy, A. C., 1956, *The Open Sea—Its Natural History; The World of Plankton*, Boston, Houghton Mifflin, 335pp.

*Harvey, H. W., 1957, *The Chemistry and Fertility of Sea Waters*, Cambridge, Cambridge University Press, 234pp.

*Hedgpeth, J. W., 1957, "Treatise on marine ecology and paleoecology," *Geol. Soc. Am. Mem.*, **67**(1), 1296pp.

*Hill, M. N. (editor), 1962, *The Sea—Ideas and Observations on progress in the Seas. I. Physical Oceanography*, New York, Interscience Publishers.

*Hill, M. N. (editor), 1963, *Ibid, II. The Composition of Sea-water, Comparative and Descriptive Oceanography*, New York, Interscience Publishers, 554pp.

*Marshall, S. M., and Orr, A. P., 1955, *The Biology of a Marine Copepod* Calanus finmarchicus (*Gunnerus*), Edinburgh, Oliver & Boyd, 188pp.

Ostergaard, J. M., 1950, "Spawning and development of some Hawaiian marine gastropods," *Pacific Sci.*, **4**, 75–115.

*Riley, G. A., Conover, S. A. M., Deevey, G. B., Conover, R. J., Wheatland, S. B., Harris, E., and Sanders, H. L., 1956, "Oceanography of Long Island sound, 1952–1954," *Bull. Bingham Oceanogr. Coll.*, **15**, 414pp.

Riley, G. A., Van Hemert, D., and Wangersky, P. J., 1965, "Organic aggregates in surface and deep waters of the Sargasso Sea," *Limnol. Oceanogr.*, **10**, 354–363.

Scheltema, R. S., (1966), "Evidence for trans-Atlantic transport of gastropod larvae belonging to the genus *Cymatium*," *Deep-Sea Res.*, **13**, 83–95.

Sutcliffe, W. H., Baylor, E. R., and Menzel, D. W., 1963, "Sea surface chemistry and Langmuir circulation," *Deep-Sea Res.*, **10**, 233–243.

*Sverdrup, H. V., Johnson, M. W., and Fleming, R. H., 1942, *The Oceans—Their Physics, Chemistry, and General Biology*, New York, Prentice Hall, 1087pp.

*Thorson, G., 1950, "Reproductive and larval ecology of marine bottom invertebrates," *Biol. Rev.*, **25**, 1–45.

Thorson, G., 1961, "Length of pelagic larval life in marine bottom invertebrates as related to larval transport by ocean currents," in (Sears, Mary, editor) "Oceanography," *Publ. 67, A.A.A.S.*, 455–474.

INDEX*

* Words listed in small capital letters represent titles of articles; italicized numbers refer to pages on which articles begin.

transform, 297
wrench, 297
Faunas
cold, 486
warm, 486
Felder, 295
FERREL'S LAW AND BUYS BALLOT'S LAW, *266*
Ferromanganese nodules, 667, 670
FERTILITY OF THE OCEANS, *268*
FETCH, *272, 573,* 957
Fiji Sea, 653. *See also* Southwest Pacific Ocean
Filchner Ice Shelf, 986
Fix (navigation), 533, 535
FIXED PLATFORMS, *273*
Flaminian Stage, 488
Fletcher's Ice Island, 232
"Flexure continentale," 484
Flip, 275, 613
Floating ice platforms. *See* Drifting ice stations
Flood current, 915
FLORES SEA, *278*
Flores Sea Plateaus, 876
Flores Trough, 278
FLORIDA BAY, *282*
Florida Current, 175, 330, 335
Florida Platform, 874
Flow, 290. *See also* Fluid Mechanics
Flow measuring, 598
Flow, net, 293
Fluid, 288
FLUID MECHANICS, *288*
Fluid, Newtonian and non-Newtonian, 288
Flumes in storm surge studies, 858
Flux, 294
FLUX DENSITY, *294*
Flysch, 543, 943, 946
controversy over origin, 103
Foams, 819
Fondothem facies, 207
Foraminifera, 446, 1002
Force, 572
Forel's number. *See* Transparency
Forel-Ule Scale, 927
Fosse, 929
Fourier's equation, 196
Fourier integral, 983
Fourier series, 915
Foxe Basin, 357, 358, 359
Foxe Channel, 359
Fracture systems, oceanic, 295
FRACTURE ZONES, *294*
Fram (vessel), 603, 612
Fram Deep, 52
Frederick Basin, 221
Free oscillations. *See* Seiche; *also* Seismology, pr Vol. V
Frequency curve, 364
Fresh water extraction, 519, 520
Friction, 990
Froude Number, 234, 235, 290, 966
Fundy, Bay of. *See* Bay of Fundy
Furrow, submarine, 585

Galapagos Rise, 675
Ganges Canyon, 113
Ganges submarine cone, 871

Gap, submarine, 585
Gas, 288
Gas exchange (air/ocean), 188
Gas exploders, 827
Gaspé Current, 331
Gating, 720
Gazelle (vessel), 768, 820
GEK, 953
Generation of waves. *See* Waves
Geochemical circulations, 189, 190
Geochemistry, general. *See* pr Vol IV
Geofractures, 295
Geographic names (submarine), 584, 585
Geologic mapping (ocean), 461
Geophysical exploration at sea. *See* pr Vol. V
Geopotential, 306. *See also* Gravity and Geopotential
Geostrophic acceleration, 817
Geostrophic equilibrium, 664
Geostrophic method, 609
Geostrophic motion, 721. *See also* Vol. II
Geostrophic wind, 267, 990
Geosutures, 295
Geosynclinal sediment, prime source, 103. *See also* Slope deposition
Geosynclines. *See* pr Vol. VII
contemporary, 483, 937
Geothermal heat, 880
German Basin, North, 550
Glacial boulders in Southern Ocean, 841
Glacial (glacigene) class, 470
Glacial detritus, 669
Glacial marine sediment, 988. *See also* "Marine till"
Glacier melting, 481
Glacio-eustasy, 481
Glaciology. *See* pr Vol. VI
Glauconite, 520, 521, 926
Global warming, question of, 255
Globigerina oozes, 222, 470, 527, 840, 887, 889
Gondwanaland, 850, 876
Gonionemus, 999
Gorontalo Basin, 524, 527
Graben, 927
Graded bedding, 943
Gradient, 961
flow, 860
wind, 961
Graham Land, 839
Grand Banks earthquake (1929), 597, 943
GRAND BANKS AND THE EASTERN SEABOARD OF CANADA, *299*
Graphic recorders, sound velocity of, 828
Grashof number, 911
Gravitational acceleration, 917
Gravity anomalies of trenches, 35, 676, 888, 926, 934
Gravity, apparent, 305
GRAVITY AND GEOPOTENTIAL, *305,* 608
Gravity wave. *See* Tsunami
Gravity wind, 993
Graywackes, 943
Great Alpine Fault, 678, 937
Great Asiatic Bank, 755. *See also* Sunda Shelf
Great Australian Bank. *See* Sahul Shelf
Great Dividing Range, 848